Sixth Form

820 OXF

OXFORD COMPANION TO ENGLISH LITERATURE

THE OXFORD COMPANION TO
ENGLISH LITERATURE

SIXTH EDITION
REVISED

EDITED BY
MARGARET DRABBLE

OXFORD
UNIVERSITY PRESS

OXFORD
UNIVERSITY PRESS

Great Clarendon Street, Oxford OX2 6DP

Oxford University Press is a department of the University of Oxford.
It furthers the University's objective of excellence in research, scholarship,
and education by publishing worldwide in

Oxford New York

Auckland Cape Town Dar es Salaam Hong Kong Karachi
Kuala Lumpur Madrid Melbourne Mexico City Nairobi
New Delhi Shanghai Taipei Toronto

With offices in

Argentina Austria Brazil Chile Czech Republic France Greece
Guatemala Hungary Italy Japan Poland Portugal Singapore
South Korea Switzerland Thailand Turkey Ukraine Vietnam

Oxford is a registered trade mark of Oxford University Press
in the UK and in certain other countries

Published in the United States
by Oxford University Press Inc., New York

First edition 1932
Second edition 1937
Third edition 1946
Fourth edition 1967
Fifth edition 1985
Sixth edition 2000, revised 2006

British Library Cataloging in Publication Data

Data available

Library of Congress Cataloging in Publication Data

Data available

Typeset in Severin by SPI Publisher Services, Pondicherry, India
Printed in Italy
on acid-free paper by
Legoprint S.p.A.

ISBN 0–19–861453–5   978–0–19–861453–1

1 3 5 7 9 10 8 6 4 2

Contents

PREFACE

THIS volume is an updating of the Fifth Edition of *The Oxford Companion to English Literature* which was first published in 1985, and reprinted several times with corrections and revisions. It incorporates much of the material from the 1985 edition, but there have been very substantial additions and some deletions, and some different guidelines have been introduced. The most significant of these is the decision not to maintain the principle of an age barrier. In the previous volume, no writers born after 1939 were included. In this one, we have not had recourse to a cut-off birth date. It seemed important at this stage to try to be inclusive rather than exclusive. Inevitably the names of younger writers will prove more controversial, but I hope the selection here, which aims to be illustrative rather than encyclopaedic, will give a broad sense of what was being written at the turn of the millennium. I have been much helped here by younger advisers, who see a different map of literature from the one with which my generation is familiar. But I hope the solid outline of the old one remains clearly visible.

We have maintained the practice of using unsigned entries, though advisers and contributors are acknowledged on page ix. We have also stood by the principle of including foreign authors, most of whom have been treated not as they might have been in their own countries, but in the context of English literature, and I mean English literature, not literature in English, which is another matter altogether. The inclusion of foreign-language authors, as well as post-colonial and American writers in English, has made for some very difficult decisions. It would have been simpler and easier to exclude them all, but the resulting volume would, I believe, have been far less useful and less interesting.

This book remains a companion for the general reader, although it will also, I hope, be of use to the student, the scholar, and the journalist. There are fewer 'general knowledge' entries, but we have more entries on critical theory, all expressed in plain language and accessible to the non-specialist. Other growth areas of subject matter are also very striking. We have, notably, more women writers and more post-colonial writers, though inevitably we will not have included enough to satisfy experts in these fields. Space has been saved by compressing some of the entries on artists and musicians, who were very generously represented in the last edition, and by a judicious and tactful pruning of the entries for the many works of Sir Walter Scott. We have kept many but not all of the character references, and have reduced the number of cross-references. There are no hard and fast rules for finding characters: common sense is the guide, and thus Zuleika Dobson and Zeal-of-the-land Busy still appear under Z (always an underrepresented letter of the alphabet), where I guess most would expect to find them. But if you do not find your character (or your title) where you first seek for it, please try again under the most obvious alternative. We cannot cover all possibilities, and consistency, although admirable, can also be misleading.

I have had a long association with this enterprise, which has over the years generated a great deal of correspondence. Those who have written to me and to the Oxford University Press have given me a good sense of what readers want from a volume like this, and what they have missed in it. I have done my best to respond to suggestions. I recognize that the role of the work of reference is changing rapidly. It is impossible to satisfy all demands in a one-volume book.

Nevertheless, I believe that this edition has a unique value. Its contributors include some of the finest writers and scholars of our time, whose entries combine accuracy and authority with wit and independence. It is not a bland compilation, a mere list of dates and titles. We have aimed to be descriptive rather than prescriptive or judgemental, but we have not always been warily neutral. Behind the anonymity of the articles there is a good deal of personality and style.

It remains for me to thank those who have helped me through the labour of preparation, a labour which has been made simultaneously harder and easier by the new technology. The 1985 edition was compiled without benefit of word processor or electronic text. This edition has relied on the new technology, which creates some problems for an editor, while resolving others. I am very grateful to all who worked so hard to present their contributions in an editor-friendly manner.

I would like to repeat my thanks to all those who helped me at the initiation of this project in 1979, some of whom have continued to offer advice and support. I must also add my thanks to those who have helped in major and minor ways with contacts, suggestions, answers to queries, books, technological advice, and much needed moral support. These include Vivien Allen, Antonia Byatt, A. S. Byatt, Tony Callaghan, Edward Chaney, William Chislett, Jonathan Delamont, Jane Edwardes, Magdalen Fergusson, Harold Landry, Helen Langdon, Mark Le Fanu, David Lodge, Colin Lucas, Alan Myers, Lavinia Orton, Ursula Owen, Michael Sissons, Fiona Stafford, Oliver Taplin, and Tim Waterstone, as well as many readers who have written in with corrections and ideas for new entries. I would also like to thank the public libraries of the Royal Borough of Kensington and Chelsea, and their helpful librarians.

The members of my family have, as ever, been more than helpful. Several of them appear in the list of contributors, but my use of them in this capacity can hardly be construed as nepotism, for the financial rewards of writing for this volume are not great. My husband Michael Holroyd has been unfailingly patient with me in all my anxieties. I owe a great debt to my daughter Rebecca Swift, who has truly been the *Companion*'s companion, and whose advice has been immensely valuable. It was she who introduced me to my assistant Daniel Hahn, without whom I might well have been working for another millennium. I could not have completed this task without his help and the benefit of his many skills.

                                                                                                            M. D.

July 1999

ADVISERS AND CONTRIBUTORS

Isobel Armstrong (19th-century poetry), Rosemary Ashton (German), Christopher Baldick (Critical Theory), Jacques Berthoud, with Stephen Minta and Jack Donovan (French), Michael Billington (20th-century drama), R. R. Bolgar (Classics), Gordon Campbell (17th century), John Carey (Metaphysicals), Jonathan Coe (20th-century fiction), Tony Curtis (Welsh literature), Stevie Davies (17th century), Katherine Duncan-Jones (16th century), Barbara Garvin (Italian), Julian Graffy (Russian), Harriet Harvey Wood (Walter Scott), Helen Langdon (Art), Ceridwen Lloyd-Morgan (Welsh literature), Bernard O'Donoghue (Old and Middle English), Robin Robertson (20th-century poetry), Michael Rose (Music), Harvey Sachs (Music), M. A. Stewart (18th-century philosophy), Michael F. Suarez, S. J. (18th century), Sheila Sullivan (18th–19th-century topics), John Sutherland (19th-century fiction), Jason Wilson (Latin American literature), H. R. Woudhuysen (16th century).

Dawn Ades, Brian Aldiss, Carole Angier, Lisa Appignanesi, Gillian Avery, Robert Barnard, Jonathan Barnes, John Batchelor, D. Berman, Paul Binding, J. W. Binns, V. Blain, A. Bold, C. Bryce, F. Burns, Ian Buruma, Marilyn Butler, H. Carpenter, Helen Carr, Vincent Carretta, Ciaran Carson, Glen Cavaliero, Graham Caveney, Kate Clanchy, Susannah Clapp, Jeanne Clegg, Michael Coveney, Michael Cox, Patricia Craig, Ursula Creagh, David Dabydeen, Hilary Dickinson, Charles Drazin, Dorothy Driver, Tony Durham, P. Edwards, A. C. Elias, G. Engle, Michael Erben, Lukas Erne, Magdalen Fergusson, Penelope Fitzgerald, Kate Flint, R. A. Foakes, Mark Ford, Margaret Forster, Ian Gibson, Stuart Gillespie, Nicholas Gleghorn, Gill Gregory, John Gribbin, V. Grosvenor Myer, P. S. Guptara, Daniel Hahn, Alethea Hayter, Andrew Hedgecock, L. Heyworth, Lesley Higgins, Michael Hofmann, R. V. Holdsworth, P. Holland, Richard Holmes, Michael Holroyd, Ted Honderich, Michael Horovitz, J. D. Hunt, F. L. Huntley, Simon James, Jeri Johnson, Hester Jones, P. Jones, Daniel Karlin, J. P. Kenyon, Paulina Kewes, Tom Keymer, Lynn Knight, Mary Lago, Sarah Lawson, John Levitt, Paul Levy, Andrew McAllister, Peter McDonald, Helen McNeil, P. Merchant, J. Milton, Julian Mitchell, R. T. Mole, J. Moore, Sheridan Morley, Brian Morris, R. Musgrave, W. Myers, Ira Nadel, Benedict Nightingale, Sean O'Brien, Leonard Orr, Fintan O'Toole, Judith Palmer, Catherine Peters, Ralph Pite, Kate Pool, Roy Porter, Lois Potter, Jocelyn Powell, Richard Price, Tore Rem, Matthew Reynolds, R. Robbins, David Rodgers, Nicholas Royle, Salman Rushdie, M. Secrest, Roger Sharrock, Ned Sherrin, Jan Lo Shinebourne, Tom Shippey, Melanie Silgardo, Helen Small, R. D. Smith, Colin Smythe, Jane Spencer, Hilary Spurling, David Stafford, Meic Stephens, Anthony Storr, Matthew Sweet, Adam Swift, Clive Swift, Rebecca Swift, Helen Thomson, Anthony Thwaite, Antonia Till, E. M. Trahern, Jeremy Treglown, Jenny Turner, John Tydeman, Sue Vice, Brian Vickers, Stephen Wall, C. Webster, Duncan Webster, Stanley Wells, John Wilders, David Womersley, P. Wood, Gregory Woods.

The editor and publisher would like to extend particular thanks to Dr Michael Suarez and Professor Gordon Campbell for reading the entire text of the previous edition for errors, revisions, and omissions in addition to their contributions as period advisers on the sixth edition, and to Professor Henry Woudhuysen, who read and advised on the entire text of the sixth edition.

ABBREVIATIONS

a.	*ante*, before	*OED*	*Oxford English Dictionary*
ad fin.	*ad finem*, near the end	OM	Order of Merit
ASPR	Anglo-Saxon Poetic Records	*op. cit.*	*opus citatum*, work quoted
b.	born	OS	Old Style dating, or calendar
BCP	Book of Common Prayer	OT	Old Testament
BM Cat.	British Museum Catalogue	p., pp.	page, pages
Bk	Book	*PEL*	*Periods of European Literature*
c.	*circa*, about	PMLA	Publications of the Modern Lan-
cent.	century		guage Association of America
cf.	*confer*, compare	pron.	pronounced
CH	Companion of Honour	Pt	Part
ch.	chapter	*RES*	*Review of English Studies*
CHAL	Cambridge History of Ancient Lit-	*sc.*	*scilicet*, name
	erature	STS	Scottish Text Society
CHEL	Cambridge History of English Lit-	s.v.	*sub verbo*, under the word
	erature	*TLS*	*Times Literary Supplement*
CT	*The Canterbury Tales*	trans.	translation, or translated by
d.	died	vol.	volume
DNB	*Dictionary of National Biography*		
EB	*Encyclopaedia Britannica*		
ed.	editor, or edited by		
edn	edition		
EETS	Early English Text Society		
OS	Original Series		
ES	Extra Series		
SS	Supplementary Series		
	If no series is specified, the		
	volume referred to is in the		
	Original Series		
EML	English Men of Letters		
ff.	and following		
fl.	*floruit*, flourished		
Fr.	French		
Gk.	Greek		
Lat.	Latin		
l., ll.,	line, lines		
LXX	Septuagint		
ME	Middle English		
MLR	*Modern Language Review*		
N & Q	*Notes and Queries*		
NT	New Testament		
OE	Old English (Anglo-Saxon)		

Note to the Reader

Names in bold capital letters are those of real people; the headwords of all other entries are in bold upper and lower case: italics for the titles of novels, plays, and other full-length works; roman in quotation marks for individual short stories, poems, essays; ordinary roman type for fictional characters, terms, places, and so on. Entries are in simple letter-by-letter alphabetical order, with spaces, hyphens, and the definite or indefinite article ignored. This applies in all languages; but where a work written in English has a title in a foreign language, the article conditions its alphabetical ordering: 'L'Allegro' and 'La Belle Dame Sans Merci' are both listed under L, while *L'Avare* appears under *Avare, L'*. Names beginning with Mc or M' are ordered as though they were spelled Mac, St as though it were Saint, Dr as though it were Doctor; but Mr and Mrs are ordered as they are spelled. An asterisk before a name, term, or title indicates that there is a separate entry for that subject, but it has been deemed unnecessary to place an asterisk before every occurrence of the name of Shakespeare. Where a person having his or her own entry is mentioned under another heading, the surname only is given unless there are entries for more than one person of the same name, when the initial or title is shown (*Auden, F. *Bacon, Dr *Johnson): the full name appears only where this is unavoidable in the interests of clarity (Richard *Graves, Robert *Graves). Where an author and a work are mentioned together, and each has an entry, only the title of the work carries an asterisk (Pope's *Dunciad*, Fielding's *Amelia*). Old Spelling has been preferred, for both titles of works and quotations, except where its use might lead to confusion. For references to the works of Shakespeare the Alexander text has been used throughout.

A

Aaron's Rod, a novel by D. H. *Lawrence, published 1922.

The biblical Aaron was the brother of Moses, appointed priest by Jehovah, whose blossoming rod (Num. 17: 4–8) was a miraculous symbol of authority. In the novel Aaron Sisson, amateur flautist, forsakes his wife and his job as checkweighman at a colliery for a life of flute playing, quest, and adventure in bohemian and upper-class society. His flute is symbolically broken in the penultimate chapter as a result of a bomb explosion in Florence during political riots.

Aaron the Moor, a character in Shakespeare's *Titus Andronicus*, lover and accomplice of Tamora.

Abbey Theatre, Dublin, opened on 27 Dec. 1904 with a double bill of one-act plays, W. B. *Yeats's *On Baile's Strand* and a comedy *Spreading the News* by Lady *Gregory. The theatre rapidly became a focus of the *Irish Revival. In 1903 Miss A. E. *Horniman, a friend of Yeats from his London days, had been introduced by him to the Irish National Theatre Society, an amateur company led by F. J. and W. G. Fay, which had already produced several plays by contemporary Irish writers, including Yeats's *Cathleen* and G. *Russell's (Æ's) *Deirdre*. She decided to provide a permanent Dublin home for the Society (which had Yeats for its president) and took over the disused theatre of the Mechanics' Institute in Abbey Street (built on the site of a previous Theatre Royal), together with the old city morgue next door, and converted them into the Abbey Theatre, with Lady Gregory as holder of the patent. The company, led by the Fays, with Sarah Allgood as principal actress, turned professional in 1906, with Yeats, Lady Gregory, and J. M. *Synge as directors, and in 1907 successfully survived the riots provoked by Synge's *The Playboy of the Western World*. The Fays, who had become increasingly at loggerheads with Horniman, Yeats, and the leading players, left in 1908. In 1909 Lady Gregory, as patentee, withstood strong pressure from the lord-lieutenant to withdraw *The Shewing-up of Blanco Posnet*, by G. B. *Shaw, before production; but the company staged it, almost uncut, knowing they might lose their patent. It was a great success and there was no more trouble with censorship.

Meanwhile Miss Horniman had become increasingly disenchanted with the company, and in 1910 did not renew her subsidy; however she offered the purchase of the theatre on generous terms, and Yeats and Lady Gregory became principal shareholders and managers. Over the years the early poetic dramas had been gradually replaced by more natur-

alistic prose works, written by *Colum, *Ervine, L. *Robinson, *O'Casey, and others. Robinson took over the management from Yeats in 1910 and with a short break continued until he became director in 1923. There were contentious but highly successful tours of Ireland, England, and the USA.

After the First World War the Abbey's finances became perilous, although O'Casey's *Shadow of a Gunman* (1923), *Juno and the Paycock* (1924), and *The Plough and the Stars* (1926) brought some respite. In 1925 the Abbey received a grant from the new government of Eire, thus becoming the first state-subsidized theatre in the English-speaking world.

From the late 1930s more plays were performed in Gaelic, and actors were required to be bilingual. In 1951 the theatre was burned down, and the company played in the Queen's Theatre until the new Abbey opened in 1966, where the tradition of new writing by B. *Friel, Tom *Murphy, and others continues to flourish.

ABBO OF FLEURY (?945–1004), a French theologian, author of the *Epitome de Vitis Romanorum Pontificum* and of lives of the saints. He was invited to England by *Oswald (bishop of Worcester and archbishop of York) to teach in his monastery of Ramsey; it was at the request of the monks of Ramsey, he tells us, that Abbo wrote his 'Life of St Edmund' which was the source for *Ælfric's famous sermon. Abbo became abbot of Fleury where he died; during his abbacy *Aristotle's *Categories* was commented on and his *Analytics* copied in Fleury.

Abbot, The, a novel by Sir W. *Scott, published 1820, a sequel to *The Monastery*. This novel, set around the escape of *Mary Queen of Scots from Loch Leven, largely redeemed the failure of *The Monastery*. It is much better constructed, but is remembered now mainly for the portrait of Mary herself, for attracting tourist trade to Loch Leven, and for being the first sequel novel in English, thus influencing the work of *Balzac, *Trollope, and many other 19th-cent. novelists.

Abbotsford, the name of Sir W. *Scott's property near Melrose on the Tweed, purchased in 1811, which gave its name to the Abbotsford Club, founded in 1834 in memory of Sir W. Scott, for the purpose of publishing materials bearing on the history or literature of any country dealt with in Scott's writings. It ceased its publications in 1865.

À BECKETT, Gilbert Abbott (1811–56), educated at Westminster School and called to the bar at Gray's Inn.

He was the editor of *Figaro in London* and on the original staff of **Punch*. He was for many years a leader writer on **The Times* and the **Morning Herald*, and was appointed a Metropolitan police magistrate in 1849. He wrote many plays and humorous works, including a *Comic History of England* (1847–8), a *Comic History of Rome* (1852), and a *Comic Blackstone* (1846).

À BECKETT, Gilbert Arthur (1837–91), son of Gilbert Abbott *à Beckett, educated at Westminster School and Christ Church, Oxford. He was, from 1879, like his father, a regular member of the staff of **Punch*. He wrote, in collaboration with W. S. **Gilbert, the successful comedy *The Happy Land* (1873).

ABELARD, Peter (1079–1142), a native of Brittany, a brilliant disputant and lecturer at the schools of Ste Geneviève and Notre-Dame in Paris, where **John of Salisbury was among his pupils. He was an advocate of rational theological enquiry, and his *Sic et Non* could be regarded as the first text in scholastic theology (see SCHOLASTICISM). He was primarily a dialectician rather than a theologian, though his theological views were declared heretical by the Council of Sens (1142) where he was vigorously opposed by St **Bernard. He was a student of Roscelin, who is noted as the first **Nominalist and against whose views Abelard reacted. The preeminence of the University of Paris in the 12th cent. owes much to Abelard's popularity as a teacher. He fell in love with Héloïse, the niece of Fulbert, a canon of Notre-Dame in whose house he lodged; she was a woman of learning and Abelard's pupil. Their love ended in a tragic separation and a famous correspondence. Héloïse died in 1163 and was buried in Abelard's tomb. Pope's poem **'Eloisa to Abelard' was published in 1717. See J. G. Sikes, *Peter Abailard* (1932).

ABERCROMBIE, Lascelles (1881–1938). He began as a literary journalist in Liverpool, and became successively lecturer in poetry at Liverpool University (1919–22), professor of poetry at Leeds (1922–9), and reader in English at Oxford. His first volume of verse, *Interludes and Poems*, appeared in 1908 and further volumes followed, including his collected *Poems* (1930) and the verse play *The Sale of St Thomas* (1931). Abercrombie contributed to **Georgian Poetry* and several of his verse plays appeared in *New Numbers* (1914).

Abessa, in Spenser's **Faerie Queene*, I. iii, the 'daughter of *Corceca* slow' (blindness of heart), and the personification of superstition.

Abigail, in 1 Sam. 25, the wife of Nabal and subsequently of David. The name came to signify a waiting-woman, from the name of the 'waiting gentlewoman' in *The Scornful Lady* by **Beaumont and Fletcher, so called possibly in allusion to the expression 'thine handmaid', so frequently applied to herself by the biblical Abigail.

ABLEMAN, Paul (1927–   ), novelist, playwright, and screenwriter, born in Leeds. His experimental novel, *I*

Hear Voices, was published in 1958 by the **Olympia Press, and his plays include *Green Julia* (perf. 1965, pub. 1966), a witty two-hander in which two young men discuss an absent mistress, and *Tests* (1966), which collects surreal playlets written for Peter **Brook's Theatre of **Cruelty.

Abora, Mt, in Coleridge's **'Kubla Khan', is perhaps to be identified with Milton's Mt **Amara. See J. L. **Lowes, *The Road to Xanadu* (1927), 374–5.

Absalom and Achitophel, an allegorical poem by **Dryden, published 1681.

A **mock-biblical satire based on 2 Sam. 13–19, it deals with certain aspects of the Exclusion crisis, notably the intrigues of the earl of Shaftesbury and the ambition of the duke of Monmouth to replace James duke of York as Charles II's heir. Various public figures are represented under biblical names, notably Monmouth (Absalom), **Shaftesbury (Achitophel), the duke of **Buckingham (Zimri), Charles II (David), **Oates (Corah), and Slingsby Bethel, sheriff of London (Shimei). The poem concludes with a long speech by David vigorously but paradoxically affirming Royalist principles, and asserting his determination to govern ruthlessly if he cannot do so mercifully.

In 1682 a second part appeared, mainly written by N. **Tate. However, it contains 200 lines by Dryden, in which he attacks two literary and political enemies, **Shadwell as Og and **Settle as Doeg.

ABSE, Dannie (Daniel) (1923–   ), doctor and poet, born in Cardiff of a Welsh–Jewish family. His first volume of poetry, *After Every Green Thing* (1948), was followed by many others, including *Tenants of the House: Poems 1951–1956* (1957) and *Collected Poems 1948–1976* (1977); in a foreword to the latter he notes that his poems are increasingly 'rooted in actual experience', both domestic and professional, and many display a reconciliation between Jewish and Welsh themes and traditions. Other volumes include *Ask the Bloody Horse* (1986), *White Coat, Purple Coat: Collected Poems 1948–88* (1989), *Remembrance of Crimes Past* (1990), and *On the Evening Road* (1994). His novels include *Ash on a Young Man's Sleeve* (1954), an account of Welsh boyhood and adolescence, and *O. Jones, O. Jones* (1970), about a Welsh medical student in London. *A Poet in the Family* (1974) is a volume of autobiography.

Absentee, The, a novel by M. **Edgeworth, first published 1812 in *Tales of Fashionable Life*.

This novel of (largely) Irish life was first written as a play, refused by **Sheridan, then turned into a novel. A swift, vivacious story, the greater part of which is in conversation, it begins with the extravagant London life of the absentee Irish landlord Lord Clonbrony and his ambitious, worldly wife. The author shows Lady Clonbrony's attempts to buy her way into high society, her contempt for her Irish origins, and her treatment of her son Lord Colambre, who refuses to marry the heiress she provides for him. A sensible and distinguished young man, he gradually finds himself falling in love with his cousin Grace, and becomes increasingly appalled at his father's debts. He travels incognito to Ireland to visit the family estates and to see if his mother's dislike of Irish life is justified. Calling himself Evans, he visits the first of his father's estates, where he witnesses the dismissal, through a letter from Clonbrony, of the humane and honest agent Burke, who has been in much trouble with his master for not extorting sufficient income from the tenants and the land. The next estate is managed by the brothers Garraghty. Here the castle and church are half ruined, the roads are rutted, the land is ill-farmed, and the tenants are treated with callous indifference; but Lord Clonbrony is satisfied because (in spite of the Garraghtys' embezzlement) money is forthcoming. Colambre discovers that both his mother and his cousin Grace are remembered with affection by the people of the estates. He returns to London and tells his father that he will himself pay off the debts, on condition that the Garraghtys are dismissed and the Clonbrony family returns to live on its Irish estates. After the sorting out of various troubles, he and Grace become engaged, his mother resigns herself to her return, and the family leave London to live in Ireland.

Absolute, Sir Anthony, and his son Captain Absolute, characters in Sheridan's *The Rivals*.

Absurd, Theatre of the, a term used to characterize the work of a number of European and American dramatists of the 1950s and early 1960s. As the term suggests, the function of such theatre is to give dramatic expression to the philosophical notion of the 'absurd', a notion that had received widespread diffusion following the publication of *Camus's essay *Le Mythe de Sisyphe* in 1942. To define the world as absurd is to recognize its fundamentally mysterious and indecipherable nature, and this recognition is frequently associated with feelings of loss, purposelessness, and bewilderment. To such feelings, the Theatre of the Absurd gives ample expression, often leaving the observer baffled in the face of disjointed, meaningless, or repetitive dialogues, incomprehensible behaviour, and plots which deny all notion of logical or 'realistic' development. But the recognition of the absurd nature of human existence also provided dramatists with a rich source of comedy, well illustrated in two early absurd plays, Ionesco's *La Cantatrice chauve*, written in 1948 (*The Bald Prima Donna*, 1958), and *Beckett's *En attendant Godot* (1952; trans. by the author, *Waiting for Godot*, 1954, subtitled 'A Tragicomedy in Two Acts'). The Theatre of the Absurd drew significantly on popular traditions of entertainment, on mime, acrobatics, and circus clowning, and, by seeking to redefine the legitimate concerns of 'serious' theatre, played an important role in extending the range of post-war drama. Amongst the dramatists associated with the Theatre of the Absurd are Arthur Adamov (1908–70), *Albee, Beckett, Camus, *Genet, Eugène Ionesco (1912–94), Alfred Jarry (1873–1907), *Pinter, and Boris Vian (1920–59). See also CRUELTY, THEATRE OF.

Académie française, a French literary academy, established by *Richelieu in 1634 to regulate and maintain the standards of the French language. One of its functions is the compilation and revision of a French dictionary, the first edition of which appeared in 1694 and the eighth in 1932–5. The Académie has, throughout its history, exercised a considerable influence on the course of French intellectual life.

Academy, a periodical founded in 1869 as 'a monthly record of literature, learning, science, and art' by a young Oxford don, Charles Edward Cutts Birch Appleton (1841–79), who edited it until his death, converting it in 1871 into a fortnightly and in 1874 into a weekly review. It included M. *Arnold, T. H. *Huxley, M. *Pattison, and the classical scholar John Conington (1825–69) among its early contributors. In 1896 it came under the control of Pearl Craigie ('J. O. *Hobbes'); she employed as editor C. Lewis Hind, who gave it a more popular colouring. After various vicissitudes and changes of title the *Academy* disappeared in the 1920s.

ACHEBE, Chinua (1930–), author, born and educated in Nigeria, where his father taught in a school under the Church Missionary Society. He studied at University College, Ibadan, 1948–53, then worked for the Nigerian Broadcasting Service in Lagos. One of the most highly regarded of African writers in English, Achebe's reputation was founded on his first four novels, which can be seen as a sequence recreating Africa's journey from tradition to modernity. *Things Fall Apart* (1958) seems to derive from W. B. *Yeats its vision of history as well as its title; it was followed by *No Longer at Ease* (1960); *Arrow of God* (1964), a portrayal of traditional society at the time of its first confrontation with European society (a traditional society recreated in Achebe's novels by the use of Ibo legend and proverb); and *A Man of the People* (1966), which breaks new ground. Bitterness and disillusion lie just beneath the sparkling satiric surface, and the novel provides further evidence of Achebe's mastery of a wide range of language, from the English of Ibo-speakers and pidgin, to various levels of formal English. *Anthills of the Savannah* (1987), a novel told in several narrative voices, pursues Achebe's bold, pessimistic, and sardonic analysis of West African politics and corruption in its portrayal of the fate of two friends, one minister of information in the fictitious state of Kangan, the other a poet and radical editor: their resistance to the regime of the country's Sandhust-educated dictator ends in death. Other works include *Beware, Soul Brother and Other Poems* (1971), *The Trouble with Nigeria* (1983), and *Hopes and Impediments* (essays, 1988). He has been emeritus professor at the University of Nigeria, Nsukka, since 1985, but now lives in the US. See also POST-COLONIAL LITERATURE.

Achitophel, name for the earl of *Shaftesbury in Dryden's *Absalom and Achitophel*.

ACKER, Kathy (1947–97), novelist, poet, and performance artist, born in New York. On leaving university she worked as stripper and pornographic film actor, these experiences providing material for her first self-published short stories. Her style and subject matter were established in early novels like *The Childlike Life of the Black Tarantula* (1975). Influenced by W. *Burroughs, the poetry of the *Black Mountain school, and the erotic writings of Georges Bataille, she rejected plot and character in favour of fragments of autobiography, plagiarized material, and disconnected dreamlike sequences of explicit sexuality and violence. In the mid-1980s she settled in London, where the UK publication of *Blood and Guts in High School* (1984) brought her a wide audience, and was followed by *Don Quixote* (1986), *Empire of the Senseless* (1988), and *In Memoriam to Identity* (1990). She returned to the USA to make performance tours of her work. Books from this period include *My Mother: Demonology* (1995), *Pussy, King of the Pirates* (1995, also recorded as a CD with punk band the Mekons), *Bodies of Work* (1997, essays on art, culture, and sexuality), and *Eurydice in the Underworld* (1997).

ACKERLEY, J(oseph) R(andolph) (1896–1967), author, and for many years (1935–59) literary editor of the *Listener*, to which he attracted work from such distinguished contributors as E. M. *Forster and *Isherwood. *Hindoo Holiday* (1932) is based on his experiences as private secretary to an Indian maharaja; *My Dog Tulip* (1956) and his novel *We Think the World of You* (1960) both describe his intense relationship with his Alsatian dog. *My Father and Myself* (1968) is an account of his discovery of his apparently respectable father's extraordinary double life, the other side of which was described by Ackerley's half-sister Diana Petre in *The Secret Garden of Roger Ackerley* (1975); see also *My Sister and Myself: The Diaries of J. R. Ackerley*, ed. F. *King (1982). The Ackerley prize for autobiography was established in 1982: the first winner was children's writer, autobiographer, and broadcaster Edward Blishen.

ACKERMANN, Rudolph (1764–1834), German lithographer who settled in London and opened a print shop in the Strand in 1795. He played a major role in establishing lithography as a fine art, and published many handsome coloured-plate books with lithographs, hand-coloured aquatints, etc., in association with Prout, A. C. Pugin, *Rowlandson, and other artists. His publications include the *Repository of Arts, Literature, Fashions*, etc. (1809–28); *The Microcosm of London* (3 vols, 1808–11), an antiquarian and topographical work by W. *Combe; and the gift-book annual *Forget-Me-Not*, of which the first issue appeared

in 1825. Combe's *The Tour of Dr Syntax in Search of the Picturesque* first appeared as 'The Schoolmaster's Tour' in Ackermann's *Poetical Magazine* (1809–11).

ACKLAND, Rodney (1908–91), playwright, greatly admired but considered insufficiently frivolous by West End managements in the 1930s; he has been described as 'the English Chekhov', the only playwright of his generation to see how *Chekhov's revolutionary dramatic technique might be joined to the robust native tradition of mixing tragedy with comedy. His best early plays—*Strange Orchestra* (1931), *After October* (1936)—inhabit a world which recalls the seedy bohemian gentility of the novels of J. *Rhys. *Birthday* (1934) is a study of hypocrisy and repression at work inside a comfortably respectable middle-class family. *The Dark River* (1941) is a grander and more sombre portrait of England in the shadow of the Second World War. *The Pink Room* (1952), a tragi-comedy set in the summer of 1945 in a seedy London club (based on the French Club in Soho), was reviewed savagely on its opening but successfully revived at the *National Theatre in 1995 under the title of *Absolute Hell*, with Judi Dench in the principal role.

ACKROYD, Peter (1949–   ), novelist, biographer, poet, and reviewer. He had a Catholic upbringing in west London and was educated at St Benedict's School, Ealing, Clare College, Cambridge, and Yale. From 1973 to 1982 he was on the staff of the *Spectator, joining *The Times as its chief book reviewer in 1986. His first published work was a volume of poems, *London Lickpenny* (1973), republished with another collection, *Country Life* (1982), in *The Diversions of Purley* (1987). He has also published two pieces of cultural criticism, *Notes for a New Culture* (an essay on *Modernism, 1976) and a study of transvestism (*Dressing Up*, 1979). He has written lives of Ezra *Pound (1980), T.S. *Eliot (1984), *Dickens (1990, with unorthodox authorial interventions), Sir T. *More (1998) and *Shakespeare (2005), and a 'biography' of London (2000), but he is perhaps better known as a novelist preoccupied with the circular nature of time. All his novels explore, in their various ways, active relationships between the present and the historical past through narratives that subvert the distinction between invention and authenticity. In his first novel, *The Great Fire of London* (1982), the relationship focuses on a plan to film Dickens's *Little Dorrit*. London has continued to loom large in Ackroyd's fiction, both as a physical location (especially its more sinister side) and as a metaphor. His gift for historical reconstruction was demonstrated in *The Last Testament of Oscar Wilde* (1983), in which *Wilde looks back on his life from his last years of poverty and exile in Paris. *Hawksmoor* (1985) has Detective Nicholas Hawksmoor (namesake of the 18th-cent. architect *Hawksmoor) investigating a series of murders in London churches that become linked to the rebuilding of the city after the Great Fire of 1666. In *Chatterton* (1987) a similar historical dynamic is set up, with modern events being related back to the death of the poet Thomas *Chatterton and the marriage of the Victorian writer George *Meredith, while in *First Light* (1989) an archaeological discovery provides the link between past and present. Ackroyd's blending of genres continued in the visionary auto-biography *English Music* (1992), a series of lyrical dialogues on English culture, and in *The House of Dr Dee* (1993), in which the central character, Matthew Palmer, inherits an old house in Clerkenwell formerly the residence of the 16th-cent. magician John *Dee. *Dan Leno and the Limehouse Golem* (1994), set in 1880 and centring on a series of grisly murders in the East End of London, brings together the music-hall per-former Dan Leno, Charles Babbage (inventor of the Analytical Engine, a proto-computer), and the novelist George *Gissing in a characteristic commingling of genres and narrative voices. *Milton in America* (1996) is a historical fantasy that transports *Milton to the New World in 1660 in anticipation of the Restoration.

Acmeism, a school of Russian poetry, led by *Gumilev and Sergei Gorodetsky, and including among its members *Akhmatova and *Mandelstam. They gathered in a group called the Poets' Guild, organized by Gumilev in Oct. 1911. Their major concerns were the depiction of the concrete world of everyday reality with brevity and clarity and the precise and logical use of the poetic word. They declared themselves opposed to symbolist mysticism and vagueness, and announced their forerunners as Shakespeare, *Villon, *Rabelais, and *Gautier.

Acrasia, in Spenser's *Faerie Queene*, II. xii, typifies Intemperance. She is captured and bound by Sir *Guyon, and her *Bower of Bliss destroyed.

Acres, Bob, a character in Sheridan's *The Rivals*.

Actes and Monuments *of These Latter and Perillous Dayes, Touching Matters of the Church*, popularly known as the *Book of Martyrs*, by *Foxe, first published in Latin at Basle 1559, printed in English 1563, with woodcut illustrations.

This enormous work, said to be twice the length of Gibbon's *Decline and Fall*, is a history of the Christian Church from the earliest times, with special reference to the sufferings of the Christian martyrs of all ages, but more particularly of the Protestant martyrs of Mary's reign. The book is, in fact, a violent indictment of 'the persecutors of God's truth, commonly called papists'. The author is credulous in his acceptance of stories of martyrdom and partisan in their selection. The work is written in a simple, homely style and enlivened by vivid dialogues between the persecutors and their victims.

Action française, l', an extreme right-wing political group which flourished in France between 1900 and 1940, monarchist, anti-Semitic, and Roman Catholic. The newspaper *L'Action française*, its organ, was founded and edited by two literary journalists and polemical writers, Charles Maurras (1868–1952) and Léon Daudet (1867–1942), a son of Alphonse *Daudet.

ACTON, Sir Harold Mario Mitchell (1904–94), writer and aesthete, educated at Eton and Christ Church, Oxford. He spent some years in the 1930s in Peking, and wrote several works on Chinese theatre and poetry. He later returned to settle at his family home at La Pietra, near Florence. He published several volumes of poems, including *Aquarium* (1923) and *This Chaos* (1930); fiction, which includes a novel set in Peking, *Peonies and Ponies* (1941), and *Tit for Tat and Other Tales* (1972, short stories); and historical studies, which include *The Last Medici* (1932) and *The Bourbons of Naples* (1956). He also published two volumes of autobiography, *Memoirs of an Aesthete* (1948) and *More Memoirs* (1970).

ACTON, Sir John Emerich Edward Dalberg, first Baron Acton (1834–1902), born at Naples, the son of a Roman Catholic English father and a German aristocrat mother: he was brought up in a well-connected cosmopolitan world and was educated at Paris, Oscott, Edinburgh, and Munich, where he studied under the distinguished German church historian Döllinger. In the *Rambler* (converted under his direction to the *Home and Foreign Review*) he advocated Döllinger's proposed reunion of Christendom, but stopped the *Review* on the threat of a papal veto. He opposed the definition by the Catholic Church of the dogma of papal infallibility, and published his views in his *Letters from Rome on the Council* (1870). In 1874, in letters to *The Times*, he criticized *Gladstone's pamph-let on 'The Vatican Decrees'. His literary activity was great, and took the form of contributions to the *North British Review*, the *Quarterly Review*, and the *English Historical Review* (which he helped to found), besides lectures and addresses. Lord Acton was appointed Regius professor of modern history at Cambridge in 1895. One of his principal works was the planning of the *Cambridge Modern History* (1899–1912) for the *Cambridge University Press.

Adam, in Shakespeare's *As You Like It*, the faithful old servant who accompanies Orlando in exile.

Adam, the name given to a 12th-cent. Anglo-Norman play (also called the *Jeu d'Adam* and the *Mystère d'Adam*) in octosyllabics, surviving in one 13th-cent. manuscript from Tours. There are three scenes: the Fall and expulsion of Adam and Eve from paradise; Cain and Abel; and a Prophets' Play (*Ordo Prophetarum*). It is generally thought that it was written in England *c.*1140 (though Bédier doubted it), and it is regarded as important for the evolution of the medieval *mystery plays in England. Although it contains Latin as well as the vernacular, and is enacted with rudimentary staging at the church door, the play is not good evidence for the evolution from liturgical to profane staging, displaying as it does a theatrical sophistication far beyond most of the later mystery plays. There is an English edition, ed. Paul Studer (1918); see also M. D. Legge, *Anglo-Norman Literature and Its Background* (1963), 311–21.

Adamastor, (1) in *Os Lusíadas* (v. li) of *Camões, the spirit of the Cape of Storms (the Cape of Good Hope), who appears to Vasco da Gama and threatens all who dare venture into his seas; (2) the title of a poem by R. *Campbell.

Adam Bede, a novel by G. *Eliot, published 1859.

The plot was suggested by a story told to George Eliot by her Methodist aunt Elizabeth Evans of a confession of child-murder made to her by a girl in prison. The action takes place at the close of the 18th cent. Hetty Sorrel, pretty, vain, and self-centred, is the niece of the genial farmer Martin Poyser of Hall Farm. She is loved by Adam Bede, the village carpenter, a young man of dignity and character, but is deluded by the attentions of the young squire, Arthur Donnithorne, and is seduced by him, in spite of Adam's efforts to save her. Arthur breaks off relations with her, and Hetty, broken-hearted, agrees to marry Adam. But before the marriage she discovers she is pregnant, flies from home to seek Arthur, fails to find him, is arrested and convicted of infanticide, and saved from the gallows at the last moment, her sentence commuted to transportation through Arthur's intervention. In prison she is comforted by her cousin Dinah Morris, a Methodist preacher, whose strong, serious, and calm nature is contrasted with hers throughout the novel. In the last chapters, Adam discovers that Dinah loves him; his brother Seth, who had long and hopelessly loved Dinah, resigns her to him with a fine unselfishness.

The novel was immediately acclaimed for its realism, for its picturesque portrayal of rural life, and for its humour; Mrs Poyser was greeted as a comic creation on the level of *Dickens's Sam Weller and Mrs Gamp. Some critics objected to its insistence on the 'startling horrors of rustic reality' (*Saturday Review*) and its 'obstetric' details. H. *James in 1866 found Hetty Sorrel 'the most successful' of George Eliot's female figures.

Adam Bell, Clym of the Clough (or Cleugh), and William of Cloudesley, three noted outlaws, as famous for their skill in archery in northern England as *Robin Hood and his fellows in the Midlands. They lived in the forest of Engelwood, not far from Carlisle, and are supposed to have been contemporary with Robin Hood's father. Clym of the Clough is mentioned in Jonson's *The Alchemist*, I. ii; and in D'Avenant's *The Wits*, II. i. There are ballads on the three outlaws in Percy's *Reliques (Adam Bell)* and in *Child's collection. In these, William of Cloudesley, after having been captured by treachery, is rescued by his comrades. They surrender themselves to the king and are pardoned on William's shooting an apple placed on his little son's head.

Adam International Review, an irregular periodical of literature and the arts edited by Miron Grindea (1909–95), published originally in Bucharest, and in England since 1941 (No. 152). Contributors have included *Auden, T. S. *Eliot, E. *Sitwell, R. *Graves, and many major European figures. Nos 387–400 (1977) were devoted to a celebration of the *London Library.

ADAMOV, Arthur, see ABSURD, THEATRE OF THE.

Adams, Parson Abraham, a character in Fielding's *Joseph Andrews*.

ADAMS, Francis (1862–93), novelist, poet, and journalist, born in Malta, and educated at Shrewsbury School and in Paris. He travelled to Australia in 1884 for health reasons (he was tubercular) and worked there successfully as a journalist, while publishing a collection of poems, *Songs of the Army of the Night* (1888). *The Melbournians* (1892) is a novella describing social and political life in Australia and the emerging sense of national identity; *The Australians* (1893) collects articles and essays on similar themes. Adams returned to England in 1890, where he was to commit suicide. His novel, *A Child of the Age*, was published posthumously in 1894 by John *Lane in the Keynotes Series. It vividly describes the schooldays (at 'Glastonbury') and poverty-stricken struggles of would-be poet and scholar, young orphan Bertram Leicester, and is understandably suffused with a *fin-de-siècle* melancholy.

ADAMS, Henry Brooks (1838–1918), American man of letters, and grandson and great-grandson of presidents of the United States. He was born and brought up in Boston and educated at Harvard, and during the Civil War was in England, where his father Charles Francis Adams (1807–86) was a minister. On his return he taught history at Harvard, edited the *North American Review*, and, after moving to Washington, published two novels, *Democracy* (1880, anonymously) and *Esther* (1884, as 'Frances Snow Compton'). His ambitious *History of the United States during the Administrations of Thomas Jefferson and James Madison* appeared in nine volumes, 1889–91. He subsequently travelled widely in Europe; his *Mont-Saint-Michel and Chartres* (1904) is an interpretation of the spiritual unity of the 13th-cent. mind, which led to his autobiography, *The Education of Henry Adams* (1907), which describes the multiplicity of the 20th-cent. mind. In his preface, he invokes the names of *Rousseau and *Franklin as predecessors in the field of autobiography, and proceeds (speaking of himself in the third person) to analyse the failures of his formal education (which he describes as not only useless but harmful), the complexity of the 'multiverse' we now inhabit, and the predicament of modern man in an increasingly technological world. In chapter XXV, 'The Dynamo and the Virgin', he contrasts the spiritual force that built Chartres with the dynamo—'He began to feel the forty-foot dynamos as a moral force, much as the early Christians had felt the Cross . . .'—and proceeds, in the final chapters, to define his own 'Dynamic Theory of History' and the acceleration of scientific progress. There are also interesting accounts of his residence in England, and of his 'diplomatic education' in the circle of Palmerston, Lord John Russell, and *Gladstone; and a lively description of an encounter (through his friend *Milnes) with *Swinburne, whom he likened to 'a tropical bird, high-crested, long-beaked, quick-moving . . . a crimson macaw among owls'.

ADAMS, Richard (1920–   ), children's writer and novelist, born in Berkshire. He is most widely known for his highly successful fantasy *Watership Down* (1972), an anthropomorphic account of rabbit society, and has also written other works including *Shardik* (1974) and *Plague Dogs* (1977).

ADAMS, Sarah Flower (1805–48), poet, born in Essex, the daughter of a radical journalist, Benjamin Flower, and brought up as a Unitarian: after her father's death in 1829 she lived for some years in the family circle of W. J. *Fox, to whose *Monthly Repository* she contributed. She wrote a historical verse drama about martyrdom, *Vivia Perpetua* (1841), but is remembered as a writer of *hymns, which include 'Nearer, my God, to Thee' (c.1834).

adaptation, stage, film, and TV. It was the development of the cinema that made adaptation a commonplace. The early pioneers of film simply trained their cameras on the stage, producing drastically condensed versions or highlights of classic plays. The first film stars were the leading theatrical performers of the day. Shakespeare was a favourite. In 1899 Beerbohm *Tree made a short film of *King John*, and the following year Sarah *Bernhardt starred in a three-minute *Hamlet.

Most of the acknowledged landmarks in the early cinema had literary origins. Edwin S. Porter's *The Great Train Robbery* (1903) was based on a stage melodrama that had been performed in New York in 1896. D. W. Griffith's *The Birth of a Nation* (1915) was adapted from *The Clansman* (1905), a stage play (originally a novel) by Thomas Dixon, in which Griffith had appeared as an actor in 1906. Griffith was credited with creating the language of cinema, but cited the 19th-cent. novel—in particular *Dickens—as his major influence.

With the coming of sound, plays and novels could be reproduced with greater fidelity, but for the best filmmakers were less vehicles of adaptation than points of departure. 'What I do is to read a story once,' commented Alfred Hitchcock, 'and, if I like the basic idea, I just forget all about the book and start to create cinema.'

The tension between literature and film was at its most acute in the adaptations of the classics. In a review of William Wyler's 1939 version of *Wuthering Heights* the critic Dilys Powell regretted a cinema 'still beset by people who bring the book with them'. Wyler

achieved a polished piece of Hollywood film-making within the constraints of the two-hour feature, but was still criticized for omitting half of the Brontë original.

The advent of television, with the extra scope provided by weekly episodes, offered a more natural medium for faithful adaptation. From *The Forsyte Saga* (1967) to such lavish productions as *Middlemarch*, *Pride and Prejudice*, and *Vanity Fair* in the 1990s, Britain's strong literary tradition produced in the classic serial an enduring commodity.

As the appeal of adaptation lay in the commercial value of exploiting an established property, it was perhaps inevitable that, by the end of the 20th cent., the theatre should have turned back to the cinema. Long-running musicals were based on the films *Sunset Boulevard* (1950; Billy Wilder) and *Whistle down the Wind* (1961). A theatrical version of the classic Ealing comedy *Kind Hearts and Coronets* (1949; adapted from Roy Horniman's novel *Israel Rank*, pub. 1907) toured Britain to good notices in 1998. Even the French cinema classic *Les Enfants du paradis* (1944) would be brought—albeit unsuccessfully—to the London stage. The adaptation has come full circle.

ADCOCK, (Kareen) Fleur (1934–   ), poet and translator, born in New Zealand, and educated partly in England, where she settled in 1963. Her volumes of poetry include *The Eye of the Hurricane* (1964), *High Tide in the Garden* (1971), *The Inner Harbour* (1979), *Selected Poems* (1983, reissued 1991), a translated selection of medieval Latin poems, *The Virgin and the Nightingale* (1983), *The Incident Book* (1986), *Time-Zones* (1991, with elegies for her father who died in 1987), and *Looking Back* (1997). Predominantly ironic and domestic in tone, her work suggests wider horizons through her evocations of travel and of varied landscapes, and in recent years she has written about public events (e.g. the fall of communism in Romania) and environmental issues. She edited the *Oxford Book of Contemporary New Zealand Poetry* (1983) and her translations from the Latin of two *Goliardic poets, *Hugh Primas and the Arch Poet*, appeared in 1994.

ADDISON, Joseph (1672–1719), the son of a dean of Lichfield, educated at Charterhouse with *Steele and at The Queen's College, Oxford, and Magdalen, of which he became a fellow. He was a distinguished classical scholar and attracted the attention of *Dryden by his Latin poems. He travelled on the Continent from 1699 to 1703, and his *Dialogues upon the Usefulness of Ancient Medals* (published posthumously) were probably written about this time. In 1705 he published *The Campaign*, a poem in heroic couplets in celebration of the victory of *Blenheim. He was appointed undersecretary of state in 1706, and was MP from 1708 till his death. In 1709 he went to Ireland as chief secretary to Lord Wharton, the lord-lieutenant. He formed a close friendship with *Swift, Steele, and other writers and was a prominent member of the *Kit-Kat Club. Addison lost office on the fall of the Whigs in

1711. Between 1709 and 1711 he contributed a number of papers to Steele's *Tatler* and joined with him in the production of the *Spectator* in 1711–12. His 18 *Spectator* essays (5 Jan.–3 May 1712) on *Paradise Lost* are an important landmark in literary criticism. His *neo-classical tragedy *Cato* was produced with much success in 1713, and during the same year he contributed to Steele's periodical the *Guardian* and during 1714 to the revived *Spectator*. His prose comedy *The Drummer* (1715) proved a failure. On the return of the Whigs to power, Addison was again appointed chief secretary for Ireland, and started his political newspaper the *Freeholder* (1715–16). In 1716 he became a lord commissioner of trade, and married the countess of Warwick; the marriage was rumoured to be unsuccessful. In 1718 he retired from office with a pension of £1,500. His last year was marked by increasing tension in his friendship with Steele, as several of his papers in the *Old Whig* bear witness. Addison was buried in Westminster Abbey, and lamented in an elegy by *Tickell. He was satirized by Pope in the character of *'Atticus'.

Addison's prose was acclaimed by Dr *Johnson in his *Life* (1781) as 'the model of the middle style; on grave subjects not formal, on light occasions not groveling', and Addison himself said, 'I shall be ambitious to have it said of me, that I have brought philosophy out of closets and libraries, schools and colleges, to dwell in clubs and assemblies, at tea-tables and coffee-houses.' He admired *Locke and did much to popularize his ideas. He attacked the coarseness of *Restoration literature, and introduced new, essentially middle-class, standards of taste and judgement; Bonamy Dobrée described him as 'The First Victorian'. One of his most original and influential contributions to the history of literary taste was his reassessment of the popular ballad, previously neglected as a form, in essays in the *Spectator* on *Chevy Chase* and *The Children in the Wood*.

P. A. Smithers, *Life of Joseph Addison* (1968) and W. Graham, *Letters of Joseph Addison* (1941) are standard biographical resources. In addition to editions of the *Tatler, Spectator*, and *Guardian*, see *The Freeholder*, ed. J. Lehney (1979).

Addison of the North, the, see MACKENZIE, H.

Adelphi, started in 1923 as a monthly journal under the editorship of J. M. *Murry, intended as a mouthpiece for D. H. *Lawrence and himself. On the verge of folding in 1927, it was resumed (with financial aid from readers) as the *New Adelphi*, but as a quarterly. Murry's editorship ended with a D. H. Lawrence memorial number in 1930, and the periodical was taken over by Max Plowman and Richard Rees, under the name the *Adelphi*, incorporating the *New Adelphi*, which ran until 1955. Contributors to the three series include W. B. *Yeats, T. S. *Eliot, A. *Bennett, H. G. *Wells, *Day-Lewis, *Orwell, and *Auden.

ADOMNAN, St (*c.*625–704), abbot of Iona from 679, who *Bede says was the author of a work on 'The Holy Places' (*Ecclesiastical History*, V. 15, 21), and who is also credited with writing an extant life of St *Columba.

Adonais, an elegy on the death of *Keats, by P. B. *Shelley, written at Pisa, published 1821.

Composed in 55 Spenserian stanzas, the poem was inspired partly by the Greek elegies of *Bion and *Moschus (both of which Shelley had translated) and partly by Milton's *Lycidas*. Keats is lamented under the name of Adonais, the Greek god of beauty and fertility, together with other poets who had died young, such as *Chatterton, *Sidney, and *Lucan. His deathbed is attended by various figures, both allegorical and contemporary, including *Byron 'the Pilgrim of Eternity' (st. 30). Shelley, the atheist, accepts the physical facts of death, but insists on some form of Neoplatonic resurrection in the eternal Beauty of the universe, 'a portion of the loveliness | Which once he made more lovely' (st. 43). The style is deliberately grand and marmoreal—'a highly wrought *piece of art*'—and lacks intimacy. Yet Shelley strongly identified himself with Keats's sufferings, and in his preface he attacks the Tory reviewers with a pen 'dipped in consuming fire'. The poem ends with astonishing clairvoyance: 'my spirit's bark is driven | Far from the shore . . .'

ADONIS, pen-name of Ali Ahmad Sa'id (1930–   ), poet and scholar, born in Syria, and educated at Damascus University; in 1956 he settled in Lebanon, where in 1968 he founded the influential magazine *Mawaqif*. Many of his poems, which explore classical themes as well as the tragedy of Beirut in the 1980s, have been translated into English, and he has himself translated into Arabic works by *Racine and *Saint-John Perse.

Adriana, in Shakespeare's *The Comedy of Errors*, the jealous wife of Antipholus of Ephesus.

Adriano de Armado, see ARMADO.

Advancement of Learning, The, a treatise by F. *Bacon, published 1605, systematizing his ideas for the reform and renewal of knowledge. Book I has a dual task: to defend knowledge in general from all its enemies, ecclesiastical and secular, and to argue for its dignity and value. Surveying the discredits that learning has brought upon itself, Bacon writes brilliantly satirical accounts of medieval Scholasticism, which restricted intellectual enquiry to the text of *Aristotle, and Renaissance Ciceronianism, with its slavish imitation of *Cicero's style. These and other 'diseases' have deflected knowledge from its true goal, 'the benefit and use of man'.

Book II then undertakes a 'general and faithful perambulation of learning', identifying 'what parts thereof lie fresh and waste', not properly developed. Bacon surveys the whole of knowledge, human and divine (that is, theology), under three headings, history, poetry, and philosophy, corresponding to the three faculties of memory, imagination, and reason. The result is a tour de force, showing a remarkably wide grasp of many subjects and a penetrating insight into the kind of research needed to develop them, including original analyses of rhetoric, psychology, ethics, and politics. Bacon's 'small globe of the intellectual world', as he called it, has important links with his essays.

Adventurer, see HAWKESWORTH.

Adventures of Master F.J., The, by G. *Gascoigne, see F.J.

Adventures of Philip on *His Way Through the World, Showing Who Robbed Him, Who Helped Him, and Who Passed Him by, The,* the last complete novel of *Thackeray, serialized in the *Cornhill Magazine Jan. 1861–Aug. 1862, with illustrations by the author and Fred Walker.

The story is told by Arthur Pendennis, now a middle-aged married man. His young friend Philip is the son of a fashionable doctor, George Firmin, who, as 'George Brandon', had appeared as the seducer of Caroline Gann in 'A Shabby Genteel Story', an unfinished tale published in 1840 in *Fraser's Magazine. Firmin had abandoned Caroline, having tricked her into a false marriage, and then run away with an heiress, Philip's mother, now dead. Firmin is being blackmailed by the disreputable parson Tufton Hunt, who performed the mock marriage ceremony with Caroline Gann and threatens to prove that the marriage was in fact valid. Caroline, calling herself Mrs Brandon, and known affectionately as 'the little Sister', is a nurse who has tended Philip through an attack of fever, and now looks on him as her own son. She refuses to give the evidence which will disinherit him. However, Dr Firmin, having lost his own money and Philip's fortune, absconds to America, and Philip's cousin Agnes, daughter of a pretentious toady, Talbot Twysden, breaks off her engagement to Philip. While visiting Pendennis and his family in Boulogne, Philip comes across General Baynes, co-trustee with Dr Firmin of Philip's inheritance. Knowing that Baynes will be ruined by any financial claim on him, Philip does not pursue his legal rights. He falls in love with Baynes's daughter Charlotte, and marries her in spite of her mother's fierce opposition, Thackeray's prejudices against mothers-in-law being here prominently displayed. Philip is struggling to make a living as a journalist, in a manner that recalls Thackeray's own early struggles. A happy ending is achieved through the device of a suddenly rediscovered will, made by Lord Ringwood, Philip's great-uncle. Philip, the only one of the old man's haughty and capricious relatives never to toady to him, has been left a large legacy.

Æ, see RUSSELL, G. W.

Aeglamour, (1) the *'Sad Shepherd' in Jonson's drama of that name; (2) a character in Shakespeare's *The Two Gentlemen of Verona.

aeglogue, see ECLOGUE.

ÆLFRIC (*c*.955–*c*.1010) was a monk of Winchester (where he was a pupil of *Æthelwold), Cerne Abbas, and Eynsham near Oxford where he was abbot. His chief works are the *Catholic Homilies* (990–2), largely drawn from the church Fathers, and the *Lives of the Saints* (993–8), a series of sermons also mostly translated from Latin, employing skilfully the idiom of English and the alliteration and metrical organization of Old English poetry. Several other English works of his survive, all with an educational purpose; these include his Latin *Grammar* (his most popular work in the Middle Ages, judging by the number of manuscripts and by his being called 'Grammaticus' in the 17th and 18th cents); his *Colloquy* between a teacher and pupil on one side and various representatives of walks of life on the other: a ploughman, a shepherd, a hunter, and so on; and a translation of the *Heptateuch*, the first seven books of the Bible. Ælfric is the most prominent known figure in Old English literature and the greatest prose writer of his time; he is celebrated not only for his stylistic excellence but also for his educational principles and the breadth of his learning as a product of the 10th-cent. Benedictine Revival in England.

Catholic Homilies, First Series (Text), ed. P. Clemoes (EETS SS 17, 1995); *Homilies of Ælfric: A Supplementary Collection*, ed. J. C. Pope (EETS OS 259 and 260, 1967 and 1968); *Ælfric's Catholic Homilies, Series 2. Text*, ed. M. Godden (EETS SS 5, 1979).

ÆLFTHRYTH (Elfrida) (*c*.945–*c*.1000), the daughter of Ordgar, ealdorman of Devon, the second wife of King Edgar and the mother of Ethelred the Unready. She was said to have caused the death of her stepson Edward the Martyr, according to a story that first circulated in the late 11th cent. but for which there seems little evidence.

Ælla, an interlude or tragedy by *Chatterton, written in the winter of 1768–9, published 1777. Ælla, Chatterton's major fictitious character (with no historical basis) was introduced first in 'Songe toe Ella'; in *Ælla* he appears as Saxon 'warde' of Bristol Castle, newly married to Birtha, whose wedding celebrations are interrupted by news that the Danes have landed, and who is driven to a tragic death by the plotting of Celmonde, his rival in love. The piece is composed mainly in ten-lined stanzas, handled with considerable assurance and virtuosity, and contains one of Chatterton's most admired passages, the song of the minstrels beginning 'O! synge untoe mie roundelaie, | O! droppe the brynie teare wythe mee' (ll. 961 ff.).

AENEAS SILVIUS PICCOLOMINI, see PICCOLOMINI.

Aeneid, The, see VIRGIL.

AESCHYLUS (525–456 BC), the earliest of the three great Athenian tragic poets. He has some claim to be regarded as an inventor of the genre, since, where there had previously been the chorus and only one actor, he introduced a second actor and subordinated choral song to the dialogue. He is noted for the scope and grandeur of his conceptions and style, but only seven of his many plays have survived, three of which form the famous trilogy the *Oresteia (Agamemnon, Choephoroe, Eumenides), which describes the murder of Agamemnon by his wife and his son's subsequent vengeance. Aeschylus was hardly known in England before T. *Stanley's edition of the plays in 1663. Milton gave some Aeschylean traits to *Samson Agonistes (1671) and in the next century the primitivists John Brown (1725) and William Duff (1770) praised Aeschylus's 'irregular greatness, wildness and enthusiasm'; but his true popularity dates from the 19th cent. and centres initially on the play Prometheus Bound. *Byron's 'Prometheus' (1816) was followed by Shelley's *Prometheus Unbound (1820), S. T. *Coleridge's essay On the Prometheus of Aeschylus (1825), and a translation of the play (1833) by Elizabeth Barrett (*Browning). Interest in the great cosmic rebel was a feature of the *Romantic movement, but in the second half of the century there was only R. *Browning's outline of the legend in 'With Gerard de Lairesse' (1887) and *Bridges's Prometheus the Firegiver (1883). From *Landor on attention shifted rather to the Oresteia and has stayed there in the 20th cent., resulting in *O'Neill's Mourning Becomes Electra (1930), a recasting of the Oresteia in terms suggested by Freudian psychology, and, less obviously, T. S. *Eliot's The Family Reunion (1939). See also Browning's *The Agamemnon of Aeschylus. There have been notable translations by Louis *MacNeice (Agamemnon, 1936) and T. *Harrison (the Oresteia, 1981).

AESOP (6th cent. BC), to whom tradition attributes the authorship of the whole stock of Greek fables, is probably a legendary figure. The fables were orally transmitted for the most part, but some were put into verse by Babrius (3rd cent. AD), while some were translated into Latin by Phaedrus (1st cent. AD) and Avianus (?4th cent. AD). They became known to the West in the Renaissance through the 14th-cent. prose version compiled by the Byzantine scholar Maximus Planudes. *Erasmus produced a Latin edition in 1513 which was then widely used in schools. They were widely imitated and adapted throughout the 18th cent. Richard *Bentley's attack on the antiquity of the 'Aesopian' fables in his Dissertations (1697, 1699) was one of the notable contributions to the controversy satirized in Swift's *The Battle of the Books.

Aesthetic movement, a movement which blossomed during the 1880s, heavily influenced by the *Pre-Raphaelites, *Ruskin, and *Pater, in which the adoption of sentimental archaism as the ideal of beauty was carried to extravagant lengths and often accompanied by affectation of speech and manner and eccentricity of dress. It and its followers (e.g. *Wilde) were much ridiculed in *Punch, in *Gilbert and Sullivan's Patience (1881), etc. See also ART FOR ART'S SAKE and GROSVENOR GALLERY.

ÆTHELWOLD, St (?908–84), born at Winchester. He entered the monastery of Glastonbury, of which *Dunstan was abbot, and became dean there. He subsequently re-established a monastic house at Abingdon, introducing the strict Benedictine Rule from Fleury, and he was appointed bishop of Winchester (963) after Edgar became king of England and Dunstan archbishop of Canterbury (960). He co-operated with Dunstan and *Oswald in the Benedictine Reforms of his century, expelling the secular clergy from Winchester, Chertsey, Milton, and Ely, and replacing them with monks. He rebuilt the church at Peterborough and built a new cathedral at Winchester. He was an important figure too in the revival of learning, as his pupil *Ælfric testifies; most significantly, he translated the Rule of St Benedict (c.960), and wrote the Regularis Concordia, the code of the new English rule in the 10th-cent. Revival.

Aethiopica, a Greek romance by the 3rd-cent. AD Syrian Heliodorus of Emesa, displays the common characteristics of the genre: the lovers are parted, and there is the usual emphasis on travel through strange lands as they seek each other and on the maintenance of chastity in the face of temptations and dangers. As often happens the intercalated stories have a 'realistic' character depicting Greek middle-class life, in sharp contrast to the romantic adventures that dominate the main narrative. The Aethiopica was printed in 1534 and became widely known through *Amyot's French translation (1547) and *Underdowne's English version (1569), and its influence on the romantic novels of the next half-century was considerable: Sidney's *Arcadia, *Barclay's Argenis, *d'Urfé's L'Astrée are all indebted to it.

Affectionate Shepheard, The, see BARNFIELD.

Agamemnon of Aeschylus, The, a translation by R. *Browning, published 1877. It aroused controversy because of its uncompromising literalness, which Browning defended strongly in his preface, along with his spelling of Greek names ('Olumpos' for 'Olympus', etc.). The translation (or 'transcription', as Browning termed it) may be taken as an attack on the Hellenism of, e.g., M. *Arnold; by making his own version 'literally' unreadable, Browning countered Arnold's claim that the Greeks were masters of the 'grand style'.

Agape, in Spenser's *Faerie Queene, IV. ii. 41, the Fay, mother of Priamond, Diamond, and Triamond, who, seeking to obtain for her children from the Fates

Long life, thereby did more prolong their paine.

The word in Greek means affection, charity.

AGARD, John, see BLACK BRITISH LITERATURE and PERFORMANCE POETRY.

Aga saga, a journalistic term that was coined (1992, in Publishing News, by Terence Blacker) to describe a kind of fiction which dwells on middle-class country or village life: the Aga (a stove of Swedish provenance) indicating traditional British rural values. The name of Joanna Trollope (1943–   ) is often associated with the genre, though by no means all of her work fits with the generally comforting implications of the label. See also ROMANTIC FICTION.

AGATE, James Evershed (1877–1947), dramatic critic, born in Lancashire, the son of a cotton manufacturer's agent; he was educated at Manchester Grammar School, then worked in his father's business for some years. He began to write for the *Manchester Guardian* in 1907, and later settled in London, where he wrote *theatre criticism for the *Sunday Times.* Agate also published novels and, more memorably, a nine-part autobiography, *Ego* (1935–48), in the form of a diary, recording his life in literary and theatrical London and describing the personalities of the day.

AGEE, James (1909–55), American novelist, poet, writer on *film, and screenwriter, also known for his semi-autobiographical novel *A Death in the Family* (1957), a moving account of a family in Tennessee shattered by the father's death in a car accident.

Agenda, a literary periodical of poetry, criticism, and translations, founded in 1959 and edited by William Cookson (1939–2003) and Peter Dale. It has published work by D. *Jones, *MacDiarmid, and *Pound, as well as special issues devoted to their work, and has also championed W. *Lewis. Other contributors have included C. *Tomlinson, C. H. *Sisson, W. C. *Williams, M. *Hamburger, and B. *Bunting.

agents, literary. The role of literary agent—that is, of middleman between author and publisher—began to develop towards the end of the 19th cent., with A(lexander) P(ollock) Watt (1834–1914) frequently cited as the founder of the profession. Newspaper agencies and dramatic and lecture agents had existed earlier in the 19th cent., and the *Society of Authors had recently been founded to protect the rights of authors, but Watt appears to have been the first reputable literary agent, whose clients included *Hardy, *Kipling, and *Haggard. Other major figures in the early years were James Brand Pinker (1863–1922), who represented *Conrad and Arnold *Bennett and encouraged new authors, and American-born Curtis Brown (1866–1945). The influence of the agent was not universally acceptable; the *Society of Authors was at first sceptical, as were some authors (including G. B. *Shaw) and many publishers, notably William Heinemann (1863–1920), who argued that an agent interfered with the natural relationship between author and publisher. But others spoke up well for the profession, including Bennett, who wrote in a letter to the *Author* (July 1913) that 'every author of large and varied output ought to put the whole of his affairs into the hands of a good agent', and by the end of the 1930s animosity had largely evaporated, all parties agreeing

that agents could provide an indispensable service in terms of placing work, agreeing on contracts, sieving manuscripts, intervening in disputes, etc. See J. Hepburn, *The Author's Empty Purse and the Rise of the Literary Agent* (1968). In the 1980s and 1990s, the power of the literary agent continued to grow, as publishing became more commercial and more competitive: agents found themselves able to command very high advances for their more valuable (and not always their more literary) clients. Few agents have appeared in works of fiction and drama: an exception is the theatrical agent Peggy Ramsay (1908–91), who was portrayed on film by Vanessa Redgrave in *Prick up Your Ears* (1987, from the life of Joe *Orton by John Lahr) and on stage in A. *Plater's *Peggy for You* (1999).

Age of Innocence, The, see WHARTON.

Age of Reason, The, by *Paine, published as a whole 1795; the first part appeared in 1793, but no copies are extant. The work was written in Paris at the height of the Terror, the second part during Paine's imprisonment when his own life was at risk. In it he states, 'I believe in one God, and no more', and proceeds to attack Christianity and the Bible: the Old Testament consists of 'obscene stories and voluptuous debaucheries', whereas the New is inconsistent, and the account of the Virgin Birth, for example (a passage that was found particularly shocking), merely 'hearsay upon hearsay'. He concludes with a plea for religious tolerance. The work was widely attacked as blasphemous and scurrilous, occasionally praised as blunt and plain; its apparent flippancy was certainly intended to be provocative, and long remained so.

Agnes Grey, a one-volume novel by A. *Brontë, published 1847.
It is the story of a rector's daughter, the narrator, who takes service as a governess, first with the Bloomfield family, whose undisciplined children are described as 'tigers' cubs', and then with the Murrays, where the conduct of her eldest charge, Rosalie, a heartless coquette, is contrasted with her own dignified, stoical, and gentle behaviour. Rosalie marries ambitiously and unhappily, but Agnes is happily united with Mr Weston, the curate, the only one to have shown kindness in her days of servitude. The novel is lightened by passages showing Agnes's warm response to the natural world and in particular her feeling for the sea, which forms the background for her final reunion with Mr Weston.

Agramant, in *Orlando innamorato* and *Orlando furioso,* the emperor of Africa, supreme ruler of the infidels and a descendant of Alexander the Great, who leads his hosts against Charlemagne.

Agravain, Sir, in the Arthurian legends the second son of King Lot of Orkney and Arthur's sister Morgawse, the brother of *Gawain, *Gareth, and *Gaheris. He conspires against Launcelot and discloses to Arthur

Launcelot's love for Guinevere, and Launcelot kills him for this at Guinevere's door. He is called 'Agravayn a la Dure Mayn' (of the hard hand) in *Sir *Gawain and the Green Knight* (l. 110) and *Chrétien's *Perceval* (ll. 8139–40), and in the German *Parzifal* (dating from c.1205).

Agrican, in *Orlando innamorato*, the king of Tartary to whom the hand of *Angelica has been promised. He besieges her in Albracca and is slain by Orlando.

AGRIPPA, Henricus Cornelius, of Cologne (1486–1535), a scholar and writer on the occult sciences. He wrote *De Occulta Philosophia Libri Tres* (1533) and *De Incertitudine & Vanitate Scientiarum* (1530), and argued against the persecution of witches. Jack Wilton and the earl of Surrey meet him in the course of their travels (Nashe, *The Unfortunate Traveller*). He is said to be the astrologer Herr Trippa of *Rabelais's Third Book.

Aguecheek, Sir Andrew, in Shakespeare's *Twelfth Night*, a foolish knight whose name suggests that he is very thin. Touches of pathos include his best-known line 'I was adored once too' (ii. iii. 170).

Ahab, (1) in the OT, 1 Kgs 16–22, a king of Israel who married Jezebel: in Jer. 29: 21–2, a lying prophet; (2) a character in Melville's *Moby-Dick*.

Ahasuerus, see WANDERING JEW.

AICKMANN, Robert, see GHOST STORIES and HORROR.

Aids to Reflection, a religious and philosophical treatise by S. T. *Coleridge, published 1825.

As a result of his 'Thursday classes' at Highgate, Coleridge compiled this unsystematic collection of commentaries and aphorisms on selected passages from the 17th-cent. Anglican divine Archbishop Leighton. Intended primarily as a religious guide to young men and a work of biblical scholarship, it stresses the importance of Christianity as a 'personal revelation'. Another 'main object' was to develop further his famous distinction between Reason and Understanding, originally drawn from *Kant, as the source respectively of 'Moral' and 'Prudential' action. The massive and frequently chaotic footnotes contain much fascinating literary material, such as discussions of symbolism and metaphor.

AIKEN, Conrad Potter (1889–1973), American author born in Georgia, brought up in Massachusetts, and educated at Harvard, where he was in the class of 1911 with T. S. *Eliot. He made the first of many journeys to Europe in 1911, and lived in England for extended periods in the early 1920s and mid-1930s, writing at one time as London correspondent for the *New Yorker* as 'Samuel Jeake, Jr'. His first volume of poetry, *Earth Triumphant* (1914), was followed by many others, including *The Jig of Forslin* (1916); *Senlin: A Biography* (1918); *John Deth* (1930); and *Preludes for Memnon* (1931). His long poems, which he described as 'symphonies', show the somewhat diffused and diffuse influence of his *Modernist contemporaries and friends. He also published several novels, which show a debt to *Joyce and *Freud, and his own desire to explore 'the fragmented ego'; these include *Blue Voyage* (1927) and *A Heart for the Gods of Mexico* (1939), both concerned with actual and metaphorical journeys. *Ushant* (1952) is a psychological autobiography, with portraits of *Lowry and of Eliot, who appears as 'Tsetse', an illustration of Aiken's fondness for pun and verbal invention. His short stories were collected in 1960, and his criticism, *A Reviewer's ABC*, in 1958. His *Selected Letters* were published in 1978.

His daughter Joan Delano Aiken (1924–2004) is a well-known British novelist and writer of children's books, and has written several entertaining sequels to the novels of J. *Austen.

AIKIN, Anna Laetitia, see BARBAULD.

AIKIN, John (1747–1822), physician, author, and Dissenter, and brother of Anna Laetitia *Barbauld, with whom he wrote *Evenings at Home* (6 vols, 1792–6), for children; he also wrote and collaborated with others in several volumes of memoirs and biography. The last decades of his life were spent in the radical and Dissenting stronghold of Stoke Newington, and he was until 1806 literary editor of the *Monthly Magazine*.

Aimwell, a character in Farquhar's *The Beaux' Stratagem*.

AINGER, Alfred (1837–1904), a popular lecturer and preacher who was canon of Bristol (1887–1903), master of the Temple (1894–1904), author of a life of C. *Lamb (1882) and a life of *Crabbe (1903), and editor of Lamb's works (1883–1900).

AINSWORTH, William Harrison (1805–82). He published his first novel, *Sir John Chiverton* (written with J. P. Aston), anonymously in 1826: this was followed by *Rookwood* (1834, also anon.), romanticizing the career of Dick Turpin, and *Jack Sheppard* (1839), exalting the life of another highwayman. These *'Newgate' novels were satirized by Thackeray in 1839–40 in *Catherine*. Meanwhile in 1837 Ainsworth had published *Crichton*, the story of a swashbuckling Scot in France. From 1840 to 1842 he edited *Bentley's Miscellany*, then from 1842 to 1853 *Ainsworth's Magazine*, and finally the *New Monthly Magazine*. He wrote 39 novels, chiefly historical; the Lancashire group, beginning with *The Lancashire Witches* (1848) and ending with *Mervyn Clithero* (1857), cover 400 years of northern history. Among the most successful of the novels are *Jack Sheppard*, *Guy Fawkes* (1841), *Old St Paul's* (1841), *Windsor Castle* (1843), and *The Lancashire Witches*. His swift narrative and vivid scene-setting made him extremely popular with enormous sales in the mid-century, but his reputation has not been sustained.

AKENSIDE, Mark (1721–70), poet and physician, the son of a butcher of Newcastle upon Tyne. He studied at Edinburgh and Leiden, where he met his friend and patron Jeremiah Dyson. His *Pleasures of Imagination (1744)* was republished in a new version in 1757. He also wrote a number of odes and minor poems, many of them alluding to 'the banks of Tyne' where he composed them. His 'Hymn to the Naiads', written in 1746 and published in *Dodsley's Collection of Poems* (1758), is a dazzling display of classical erudition, and other poems reveal his keen interest in the scientific theories of the *Enlightenment. His haughty and pedantic manner is said to have been satirized by Smollett in *Peregrine Pickle*.

AKHMATOVA, Anna, pseudonym of Anna Andreyevna Gorenko (1889–1966), Russian poet. She spent her childhood in Tsarskoe Selo, outside St Petersburg. In 1903 she met the poet *Gumilev, whom she married in 1910 and with whom she visited Paris, where she was drawn by Modigliani. Her first poetry was published in 1907. In 1911 she joined the Guild of Poets, the founders of Russian *Acmeism, along with Gumilev and *Mandelstam. She was divorced from Gumilev in 1918. Her collections of poetry *Evening* (1912), *Rosary* (1914), *White Flock* (1917), *Plantain* (1921), *Anno Domini MCMXXI* (1921), bringing Acmeist clarity to the delineation of personal feeling, won her enormous renown. No books of her poetry were published between 1923 and 1940, and she was increasingly attacked as 'out of step with the new age'. The arrest of her son Lev Gumilev in 1934 led her to write the first poem in her devastating cycle on the Stalinist terror, *Requiem 1935–1940* (first published in Munich in 1963). In 1940 the ban on her publication was lifted and *From Six Books* appeared. From 1940 until 1962 she worked on *Poem without a Hero*, a complex analysis of her age and her relationship with it, including her significant meeting with *Berlin in 1945. In August 1946 she was picked out for attack by the Party during the post-war cultural freeze (Stalin's cultural henchman, Andrei Zhdanov, notoriously called her poetic persona 'half-nun, half-whore'), and expelled from the Union of Writers. After Khrushchev's 'secret speech' of February 1956 the literary rehabilitation of Akhmatova began. In 1962 she had a meeting in Leningrad with *Frost, and in 1965 she visited Oxford to be awarded an honorary D.Litt. Major translations of Akhmatova's work include *Poems of Akhmatova* (trans. Stanley Kunitz and Max Hayward, 1973) and *Requiem and Poem without a Hero* (trans. D. M. *Thomas, 1976). *The Complete Poems of Anna Akhmatova*, trans. J. Hemschemeyer and ed. R. Reeder, appeared in 1992. See *Anna of all the Russias*, by E. *Feinstein (2005).

AKSAKOV, Sergei Timofeyevich (1791–1859), Russian author, who in his autobiographical trilogy *A Family Chronicle* (1856), *Recollections* (1856), and *The Childhood Years of Bagrov Grandson* (1858, the second in the chronological scheme) depicted family life in a rural community, showing a passionate sympathy with nature. They remain extremely popular in Russia, and were translated by J. D. Duff as *A Russian Gentle-*

man (1915), *A Russian Schoolboy* (1917), and *Years of Childhood* (1915). Aksakov was a lifelong friend of *Gogol, whom he recalled in *A History of My Acquaintance with Gogol* (1855).

ALABASTER, William (1568–1640), an Elizabethan divine and Latin poet, educated at Westminster and Trinity College, Cambridge. Between 1588 and 1592 he produced two notable works in Latin; an unfinished epic on Queen Elizabeth, which has been preserved in manuscript, and of which Spenser said, 'Who lives that can match that heroick song?' (*Colin Clouts Come Home Againe*); and the tragedy *Roxana*, which Dr *Johnson thought contained the best Latin verse written in England before *Milton. In 1596 Alabaster became chaplain to Robert Devereux, earl of *Essex, and sailed with him to Cadiz. In 1597 he became a Roman Catholic (influenced by the same priest who temporarily converted *Jonson) and was arrested and deprived of Anglican orders. His sonnets (first published in 1959) were probably written about this time. Often written in the dramatic Petrarchan form, they are among the earliest *metaphysical poems of devotion and seem to have been composed during the course of a profound religious experience. It was, however, as a theologian that Alabaster was chiefly known in his own day. His first major essay in mystical theology, *Apparatus in Revelationem Iesu Christi*, was written in exile in the Low Countries and declared heretical by the Holy Office. He revolted from the Roman Church and by 1613–14 was again a Protestant, later becoming a doctor of divinity at Cambridge and chaplain to the king. In 1618 he married Katherine Fludd, a widow, and was linked by marriage to the celebrated physician and alchemist Robert *Fludd. After 20 years of vicissitudes his life now became settled and he devoted his later years to theological studies: *De Bestia Apocalyptica* (Delft, 1621), *Ecce Sponsus Venit* (1633), *Spiraculum Tubarum* (1633). In 1635 he published a scholarly abridgement of Schindler's Hebrew lexicon.

ALAIN-FOURNIER (1886–1914), French novelist, the author of *Le Grand Meaulnes* (1913; trans. as *The Wanderer*, 1928; *The Lost Domain*, 1959). This is a semi-autobiographical story of a schoolmaster's teenage son and his memories of an idealized friendship with the charismatic but irresponsible Augustin Meaulnes, who opens up his world to new possibilities and introduces him to the beautiful but elusive Yvonne de Galais. Born Henri Alban Fournier, he first published under the pseudonym 'Alain-Fournier' when he discovered that he shared his name with a prominent admiral and a celebrated racing driver. He was an ardent admirer of the works of T. *Hardy, which had a powerful influence upon him. Although he had begun *Le Grand Meaulnes* as early as 1905, soon after meeting Yvonne de Quiévrecourt (with whom he fell in love, and who became the Yvonne of the novel), it was not completed until 1913, when he was back in Paris having completed his National Service. After five years of civilian life, during which he worked as a literary columnist and gave private French lessons (to a young T. S. *Eliot, among others), he was called up to fight in the First World War. He was killed in action on the Meuse in 1914. *Les Miracles*, a collection of stories and poems, was published in 1924.

A la recherche du temps perdu, a novel by M. *Proust, published in seven sections between 1913 and 1927. The English translation by C. K. Scott Moncrieff, *Remembrance of Things Past*, appeared between 1922 and 1931; a fully revised version of this translation by Terence Kilmartin was published in 1981, and further revisions suggested in part by the second Pléiade edition of 1987–9, ed. Jean-Yves Tadié, were made by D. J. *Enright, 1992, after Kilmartin's death. The seven sections of the novel are: *Du Côté de chez Swann* (1913, *Swann's Way*), *A l'ombre des jeunes filles en fleurs* (1919, *Within a Budding Grove*), *Le Côté de Guermantes* (1920–1, *The Guermantes Way*), *Sodome et Gomorrhe* (1921–2, *Cities of the Plain*), *La Prisonnière* (1923, *The Captive*), *Albertine disparue*, now renamed *La Fugitive* (1925, *The Sweet Cheat Gone*), and *Le Temps retrouvé* (1927, *Time Regained*).

A la recherche is a novel of circular construction: it ends with the narrator Marcel's discovery of his artistic vocation, a discovery which will lead him to the writing of the book the reader has just experienced. The dominant tone of the work is one of loss, of despair at the apparent irrecoverability of past experience and regret at the vanity of human relationships and of human endeavour seen in the perspective of the destructive power of time. The search proclaimed in the novel's title is, however, vindicated by the narrator's discovery that the past is, in fact, eternally alive in the unconscious, and that it may be rescued from oblivion, either through the chance operation of sensory perception (the power of 'involuntary' memory) or through the agency of the work of art. But if the novel is thus fundamentally an account of an artistic vocation, the narrator's progress is characterized by a sustained analysis of a wide range of subjects: the psychology of family relationships and of sexual relations, both homosexual and heterosexual; the aesthetics of the novel, of music, and of painting; and the fluidity of contemporary French society, satirized through the rise of the rich and vulgar Madame Verdurin into the ranks of the declining Guermantes aristocracy.

Alastor, a visionary poem by P. B. *Shelley, largely written in Windsor Great Park in the late summer of 1815, published 1816. 'Alastor' is a transliteration from the Greek, meaning the 'evil spirit or demon of solitude', who pursues the Poet to his death because he will not be satisfied by domestic affections and 'human sympathy'. Composed in Miltonic blank verse, laboured but sometimes translucently descriptive, the poem reflects Shelley's early wanderings: it tells how the Poet left his 'alienated home', abandoned an 'Arab maiden', and vainly pursued his vision of ideal love 'through Arabie | And Persia, and the wild Carmanian waste' until he reached a remote river in the Indian Caucasus, where he died alone, exhausted, and unfulfilled. This *rite de passage* includes the dream of a 'veilèd maid' who dances with shimmering erotic intensity (ll. 129–222). The work is closely associated with Shelley's prose essays 'On Love' and 'On Life'.

Alban, St (d. ?304), the first British martyr, who is said to have been put to death under the edicts of Diocletian. While still a pagan, the story goes, he had sheltered in his house a Christian cleric by whom he was converted. Immediately after his conversion he was executed, accompanied by miracles, on a hill overlooking the Roman town of Verulamium, now St Albans.

Albany, duke of, in Shakespeare's *King Lear*. He maintains his integrity in spite of marriage to the wicked *Goneril; in the quarto text (1608) he speaks the closing lines of the play. Albany, according to *Holinshed, was the northern part of Britain, from the Humber to Caithness.

Albany, Albainn, Albin, Albania, ancient poetic names of Gaelic origin for the northern part of Britain.

ALBEE, Edward Franklin (1928–), American playwright, associated with the Theatre of the *Absurd, whose later explorations of sexual fantasy, frustration, and domestic anguish also recall the plays of T. *Williams. His works include the macabre one-act satiric comedy *The American Dream* (1961); the more naturalistic marital tragi-comedy of academe *Who's Afraid of Virginia Woolf?* (1962); *Tiny Alice* (1965), a fantasy of wealth and corruption; and *A Delicate Balance* (1966), a tragi-comedy set in a hard-drinking domestic environment. Later plays include *The Lady from Dubuque* (1980), *Marriage Play* (1986), *Three Tall Women* (perf. Vienna 1992, NY 1994, of which the leading character is based on his adoptive mother), and *The Goat, or Who is Sylvia?* (2002), a domestic tragicomedy.

ALBERTI, Leon Battista (1404–72), Italian architect, scholar, and theorist, whose treatises on painting and sculpture (*Della pittura*) and on architecture (*De Re Aedificatoria*; English trans. G. Leoni, 1726) had a profound influence on Renaissance and subsequent architecture.

ALBERTUS MAGNUS (1193 or 1206–80), St Albert of Cologne, a Dominican friar who was a native of Swabia and a great *Scholastic philosopher. He was an interpreter of Aristotle, whose doctrines he expounded at Cologne and Paris; he was the first Western thinker to outline the complete philosophy of Aristotle. *Aquinas was among his pupils. His wide learning earned for him the title 'Doctor Universalis', and his total *œuvre*, printed at Lyons in 1651, extends to 21 folio volumes of which six are commentaries on Aristotle. He also wrote an influential *Summa Theologiae*.

Albion, an ancient poetical name for Britain, perhaps derived from its white (Latin *albus*) cliffs, visible from the coast of Gaul. *Blake frequently uses Albion as a personification of England, in such works as *Visions of the Daughters of Albion* (1793), *The Four Zoas*, and *Jerusalem*, where he adapted the traditional presentation of England as a giant to his own mythological purposes. M. *Horovitz's Penguin anthology *Children of Albion: Poetry of the 'Underground' in Britain* (1969) and its successor *Grandchildren of Albion* (1992, pub. by New Departures) are a conscious tribute to Blake, as is A. *Henri's poem 'Mrs Albion You've Got a Lovely Daughter', which portrays Liverpool as 'Albion's most lovely daughter'.

Albions England, see WARNER, W.

Album Amicorum, an 'album of friends', the predecessor of the modern autograph album, popular from the 16th cent. with travelling students and scholars. Typically an entry would contain a biblical or classical motto, a personal device or coat of arms, a dedication, and an autograph. There are many examples in the British Library.

Albumazar, see TOMKIS.

alcaics, a lyric metre named after the Greek poet Alcaeus, born *c*.620 BC. The form was favoured by *Horace, and imitated in English by *Swinburne, *Tennyson ('Milton: Experiments in Quantity') and other poets.

Alchemist, The, a comedy by *Jonson, performed by the King's Men 1610, printed 1612, by many considered the greatest of his plays.

Lovewit, during an epidemic of the plague, leaves his house in Blackfriars in London in charge of his servant Face. The latter, with Subtle, a fake alchemist and astrologer, and Dol Common, his consort, use the house as a place for fleecing a variety of victims. To Sir Epicure Mammon, a voluptuous knight, and Ananias and Tribulation Wholesome, fanatical Puritans, they promise the philosopher's stone, by which all metals may be turned to gold; to Dapper, a lawyer's clerk, a charm to win at gambling, bestowed by his aunt, the Queen of Fairy; to Drugger, a tobacconist, a magical way of designing his shop to improve trade; to Kastril, a country bumpkin who wants to learn the language of quarrelling, a rich marriage for his widowed sister Dame Pliant. Surly, a gamester, sees through the fraud and attempts to expose it by presenting himself disguised as a Spaniard, but the dupes refuse to listen and drive him away. Lovewit's unexpected return puts Subtle and Dol to flight, and Face makes peace with his master by resourcefully marrying him to Dame Pliant.

Alcina, in *Orlando innamorato* and *Orlando furioso*, a witch who was mistress of an enchanted garden, and changed her lovers into beasts, stones, or trees. *Astolfo and *Rogero were among her prisoners.

Alcmena, see AMPHITRYON.

ALCOTT, Louisa M(ay) (1832–88), American author, born in Pennsylvania, the daughter of educationalist and Transcendentalist Bronson Alcott (1799–1888), friend of *Emerson and *Thoreau. From an early age she published sketches, stories, etc., to help support her impractical father and family, and achieved fame and financial security with *Little Women* (1868–9), which was followed by several other works in the same vein. She also wrote sensational novels and straight adult novels, and was involved in various reform movements, including women's suffrage.

ALCUIN (Albinus: English name Ealhwine) (735–804), theologian, man of letters, and the principal figure in the literary and educational programme of *Charlemagne in the 'Carolingian Renaissance'. He was born at York and educated in the cloister school there under Archbishop Egbert. He met Charlemagne at Parma in 780, and settled on the Continent, becoming abbot of Tours in 796. He wrote liturgical, grammatical, hagiographical, and philosophical works, as well as numerous letters and poems in Latin, including an elegy on the destruction of Lindisfarne by the Danes. He was primarily an educationalist rather than an original thinker. He adapted *Tertullian's 'What has Athens to do with Jerusalem?' to ask his famous question about the inappropriateness of heroic writing in monasteries, 'Quid Hinieldus cum Christo?' (Ingeld being a character in *Beowulf*). But his enduring legacy was the Carolingian educational curricula and the Carolingian minuscule script developed in his writing school. (See also ANGLO-LATIN LITERATURE.)

See M. L. Laistner, *Thought and Letters in Western Europe, AD 500–900* (1957); E. S. Duckett, *Alcuin, Friend of Charlemagne* (1951).

Alcyon, in Spenser's *Daphnaïda* and *Colin Clouts Come Home Againe*, is Sir A. *Gorges, on whose wife's death the *Daphnaïda* is an elegy.

Aldhelm, St (*c*.639–709), the first bishop of Sherborne (705). He was educated under *Theodore at Canterbury (671) and was a major figure in the intellectual movement led by him. He was the author of a number of Latin works which reveal a wide knowledge of classical and Christian authors. His ornate and difficult vocabulary—his *verborum garrulitas*—shows the influence of Irish models. He was abbot of Malmesbury and built churches at Malmesbury, Bruton, and Wareham and monasteries at Frome and Bradford. His most important work is *De Septenario, the Letter to Acircius* (i.e. Aldfrith, king of Northumbria) which contains his own Latin riddles, the *Aenigmata*. Alfred says he was a popular vernacular poet but, as far as we know, none of this work survives. (See also ANGLO-LATIN LITERATURE.)
Aldhelmi Opera, ed. R. Ehwald (1919).

ALDINGTON, Richard (Edward Godfree) (1892–1962), educated at University College London, which he left without taking a degree. Early in his literary career he made the acquaintance of *Pound, who introduced him to Hilda *Doolittle (H.D.), whom he married in 1913, and of F. M. *Ford, for whom he worked briefly as secretary. He and H.D. both worked as editors on the Imagist periodical the *Egoist* and in 1915 Aldington's first volume of poetry, *Images 1910–1915*, was published by the Poetry Bookshop. (See IMAGISM.) Subsequent volumes include *Images of War* (1919) and *A Fool i' the Forest* (1925), which shows perhaps an excessive debt to *The Waste Land*. Aldington achieved popular success with his first novel, *Death of a Hero* (1929, abridged; Paris, 1930, unexpurgated), based on his own war experiences. It relates the life and death of George Winterbourne, killed in action in 1918; the first two parts dwell on his youth and 'advanced' marriage, satirizing the complacency and frivolity of pre-war middle-class and bohemian England, and Part III is a horrifying description of life at the front in France. His later novels (*The Colonel's Daughter*, 1931; *All Men Are Enemies*, 1933) made less impact. From 1928 Aldington lived mainly abroad, in France and the United States. Of his later works the best known are his biographies, which include *Portrait of a Genius, But . . .* (1950), a controversial life of D. H. *Lawrence, who had at one time been a close friend, and his even more controversial life of T. E. *Lawrence, *Lawrence of Arabia: A Biographical Enquiry* (1955), which caused a furore by its attack on Lawrence as an 'impudent mythomaniac'. This, in the view of Aldington's admirers, was the cause of his diminishing reputation and the decreasing availability of his works, which include many translations, an autobiography (*Life for Life's Sake*, 1941), and critical essays. His correspondence with *Durrell, *Literary Lifelines*, ed. I. S. MacNiven and H. T. Moore, was published in 1981.

ALDISS, Brian Wilson (1925–   ), novelist, short story writer, and critic, born in Norfolk, best known for his works of *science fiction and his involvement with the cause of science fiction as a literary genre; he has edited many collections and anthologies and has written a history of the subject, *Billion Year Spree* (1973 revised, with David Wingrove, as *Trillion Year Spree*, 1986). His many works which employ classic devices—lost spaceships, threatened utopias, time-warps, etc.—include *Non-Stop* (1958), *Greybeard* (1964), and *Enemies of the System* (1978); his sense of the tradition is manifested in *Frankenstein Unbound* (1973), which pays tribute to his view of M. *Shelley's work as 'the first novel of the Scientific Revolution', 'a meeting with the Romantic and scientific', and which describes a meeting between an American from AD 2020 with the Shelleys, *Byron, and Frankenstein himself. Similarly, *Moreau's Other Island* (1980) picks up the theme of H. G. Wells's *The Island of Dr Moreau* (1896). *Helliconia Spring* (1982),

Helliconia Summer (1983), and *Helliconia Winter* (1985) form an epic trilogy describing the evolution of a whole planetary system, in which each season lasts for centuries. More recent works include . . . *And the Lurid Glare of the Comet* (1986), *Craken at Critical* (1987), *Ruins* (1987), *Forgotten Life* (1988), *Dracula Unbound* (1991), and *Remembrance Day* (1993), a philosophical novel about an American academic investigating the deaths of four people in an IRA bombing in an attempt to prove that their fate was preordained. His short stories have been collected in *Best Science Fiction Stories of Brian W. Aldiss* (1988) and *A Romance of the Equator: Best Fantasy Stories of Brian W. Aldiss* (1989). *Bury My Heart at W. H. Smith's* (1990) and *The Twinkling of an Eye* (1998) are volumes of autobiography.

ALDRIDGE, James (1918–   ), Australian-born journalist, prolific novelist, and children's writer, resident for many years in England, whose strong left-wing convictions and Marxist interpretations of historical events led to an enthusiastic reception of his work in the Soviet Union. His early novels (*Signed with Their Honour*, 1942; *The Sea Eagle*, 1944; and *Of Many Men*, 1946) record the Second World War in a plain, strong narrative style: later works return to this theme, but also deal with crises of capitalism past and present, and the death of the British Empire.

ALDUS MANUTIUS (1449–1515), Venetian scholar, printer, and publisher. In 1493 he published his own Latin grammar, and in 1495 he opened his own press, which initially specialized in Greek texts, including a monumental edition of *Aristotle in five volumes. His roman and italic type, which was cut by Francesco da Bologna, and his Greek types greatly influenced the design of printers' letters. He introduced the publication of Latin texts in octavo formats, and these inexpensive alternatives to scholarly folios were sold in large numbers. His edition of *Erasmus' *Adages* in 1508 became a best-seller all over Europe.

ALEXANDER VI, see BORGIA, R.

ALEXANDER, Sir William, earl of Stirling (?1567–1640), Scottish poet, courtier, and friend of *Drummond of Hawthornden, secretary of state for Scotland from 1626 until his death. His chief poetical works are a collection of songs and sonnets, *Aurora* (1604), a long poem on *Doomsday* (1614) in eight-line stanzas, and four tragedies on Darius, Croesus, Alexander, and Caesar, which are the source of some of the most striking lines in Webster's *The White Devil* and *The Duchess of Malfi*.

ALEXANDER THE GREAT (356–323 BC), son of Philip II of Macedon and Olympias, born at Pella, and educated by *Aristotle, became king of Macedon in 336 BC upon the murder of his father. He caused the Greek states to nominate him to conduct the war against Persia and in 334 crossed the Hellespont. He captured the family of

Darius and extended his conquests to Egypt, where he founded Alexandria; and, after completely defeating the Persians at the battle of Arbela in 331, to India. He married Roxana, the captive daughter of Oxyartes, a Bactrian prince, and a second wife, Barsine, daughter of Darius and Statira. He is said to have destroyed Persepolis, the capital of the Persian empire, at the instance of the courtesan Thaïs (331). He died of fever at Babylon when only 32 years old. His horse was named Bucephalus.

Alexander was made the centre of a cluster of medieval legends, comparable to the cycles concerning *Charlemagne and King *Arthur. The chief of the romances concerning him are the great French *Roman d'Alexandre* of the 12th cent., of some 20,000 alexandrines, and the English *King Alisaunder* of the early 14th cent., 8,000 octosyllabic verses. The story of the rivalry of his two wives forms the subject of Lee's tragedy *The Rival Queens*.

ALEXANDER OF HALES (1170/80–1245), a native of Gloucestershire, studied at Paris and taught theology there. For a short time he held various ecclesiastical appointments in England and he became archdeacon of Coventry. Returning to Paris he entered the Franciscan order and continued to teach theology, becoming the first member of this new order to hold the chair of theology there. He wrote glosses on the *Sententiae* of *Peter Lombard. According to R. *Bacon the *Summa Theologica* which goes under his name was not by him but put together by other Franciscan theologians, partly drawing on his teachings. It influenced the Italian-born theologian Bonaventura (1217–74), who refers to it in 1250, and Alexander is important as evidencing a distinct Augustinian–Franciscan philosophical tradition in the first half of the 13th cent. In the later Middle Ages he was called the 'Doctor Irrefragabilis'.

Alexander and Campaspe, see CAMPASPE.

Alexander's Feast, see DRYDEN.

Alexandrian Library, the, formed at Alexandria by the Ptolemaic rulers of the 3rd cent. BC. It was the largest library in the ancient world, and variously said to contain between 100,000 and 700,000 manuscripts. According to *Plutarch, there was a serious fire at the library when Julius Caesar was besieged in Alexandria; later legends expanded the fire into total destruction of the library.

Alexandria Quartet, see DURRELL.

alexandrine, an iambic line of six feet, which is the French heroic verse, and in English is used, for example, as the last line of the Spenserian stanza or as a variant in a poem of heroic couplets, rarely in a whole work. The name is derived from the fact that certain 12th- and 13th-cent. French poems on *Alexander the Great were written in this metre. (see also METRE.)

ALFIERI, Vittorio (1749–1803), Italian tragedian and poet. He gave up his own estates and, in his treatise *Della tirannide* (*On Tyranny*, 1789, written 1777), advocated the revolutionary overthrow of all tyrannies. In another, *Del principe e delle lettere* (*On the Prince and on Letters*, 1785–6), he argued for the independence of writers from court patronage. Between 1777 and 1789 he wrote 19 austerely concise tragedies on historical themes, of which the finest, *Saul* (1782), turns the king into a figure that may be compared with *Sturm und Drang* heroes. He hailed the French Revolution in the ode 'Parigi sbastigliata' ('Paris Unbastilled', 1789), but satirized its excesses in *Il misogallo* (*The Anti-Gaul*, 1793–9). His autobiography (*Vita*, 1803) is pre-Romantic both in its melancholy and in its strong-willed hatred of oppression. He was the devoted lover of the countess of Albany, wife of the Young Pretender.

ALFRED (the Great) (848–99), king of the West Saxons from 871 to his death, important in the history of literature for the revival of letters that he effected in his southern kingdom and as the beginner of a tradition of English prose translation (though there were some Northumbrian translations of Latin before him). He translated (before 896) the *Cura Pastoralis* of *Gregory with a view to the spiritual education of the clergy, and a copy of this was sent to each bishop. The preface to this translation refers to the decay of learning in England and indicates Alfred's resolve to restore it. He then translated (or had translated) the *Historia Adversus Paganos* of *Orosius, inserting the latest geographical information at his disposal, notably accounts of the celebrated voyages of the Norwegian Ohthere to the White Sea and of *Wulfstan in the Baltic, both of which are full of interesting detail. He had a translation made of *Bede's *Ecclesiastical History* with some omissions, but giving a West Saxon version of the Hymn of *Cædmon, and translated the *De Consolatione Philosophiae* of *Boethius, with some additions drawn from exegetes such as Remigius of Auxerre. The loose West Saxon version of *Augustine's *Soliloquia* is also probably the work of Alfred. He composed a code of laws, drawing on the Mosaic and earlier English codes. The *Anglo-Saxon Chronicle*, the systematic compilation of which began about 890, may represent in part his work or inspiration. The characteristic virtue of Alfred's style lies in his principle of idiomatic translation, 'sometimes sense for sense', which gives vividness to his English versions. The absence of this distinctive quality from the translation of Bede has led to the questioning of its authenticity as an Alfredian text. See Asser's *Life of Alfred*, in *Alfred the Great*, ed. S. Keynes and M. Lapidge (1983); E. S. Duckett, *Alfred the Great and His England* (1961).

Alfred, *a Masque*, containing 'Rule, Britannia', see THOMSON, J. (1700–48).

Algarsyf, one of the two sons of King Cambuscan, in *Chaucer's 'Squire's Tale' (see CANTERBURY TALES, 11).

Algrind, in Spenser's *Shepheardes Calender*, Edmund Grindal, archbishop of Canterbury, 1576–83.

ALI, Tariq (1943–   ), polemicist, activist, film-maker, novelist, and playwright, born in Lahore, educated in Pakistan and at Exeter College, Oxford, where he became president of the Oxford Union. In the 1960s and 1970s he was known as a political activist, founding the Vietnam Solidarity Campaign and editing the underground publications *Black Dwarf* and *Red Mole*. His histories of the period give an international perspective on a time of rapid social and political change: *Streetfighting Years: An Autobiography of the Sixties* (1970, 1987); *1968 and after: Inside the Revolution* (1978); and *1968: Marching in the Streets* (with Susan Watkins, 1998). His role as activist continued through membership of the editorial board of *New Left Review* and his work as a producer of cultural and political documentary films for Channel Four. Ali's plays with Howard *Brenton blend historical analysis, farcical satire, tragedy, and song: *Iranian Nights* (1989) is an ironic treatment of the *fatwa* on Salman *Rushdie, while *Moscow Gold* (1990) charts the rise of Mikhail Gorbachev. His 'Islam Quintet' so far comprises *Shadows of the Pomegranate Tree* (1992), set during the collapse of the Muslim civilization in Andalusia; *The Book of Saladin* (1998), a fictional memoir of the 12th-cent. Kurdish liberator of Jerusalem; *The Stone Woman* (2001), set in the late 19th-cent. Ottoman empire; and *A Sultan in Palermo* (2005), set in medieval Palermo.

Alice's Adventures in Wonderland, a story for children by Lewis Carroll (see DODGSON), published 1865.

   Originally entitled *Alice's Adventures under Ground*, and written for his young friend Alice Liddell, it tells how Alice dreams she pursues a White Rabbit down a rabbit-hole to a world where she encounters such celebrated characters as the Duchess and the Cheshire Cat, the Mad Hatter and the March Hare, the King and Queen of Hearts, and the Mock Turtle. It contains the poems 'You are old, Father William', 'Beautiful Soup', and others, and Carroll's typographical experiment 'Fury and the Mouse', in the shape of a mouse's tail: it proved a lasting success and has been translated into many languages. See also THROUGH THE LOOKING-GLASS.

alienation effect, a term used to describe attempts by author or director to prevent the reader or audience from identifying with, trusting, or taking for granted what is happening in the text or on stage: such devices can include narrative interventions, disruptions of mood and sequence, and introduction of non-realistic effects. *Brecht was the most celebrated exponent of the technique but it has been very widely adopted. (From the German *Verfremdungseffekt*.)

Alifanfaron, in medieval romance, the pagan emperor of Taprobane, in love with the daughter of Pentapolin, the Christian king of the Garamantes. *Don Quixote takes two flocks of sheep for their opposing armies and attacks what he supposes to be Alifanfaron's forces.

Alisaunder, see KING ALISAUNDER.

ALISON, Archibald (1757–1839), Scots episcopalian, father of Sir A. Alison (below). He wrote *Essays on the Nature and Principles of Taste* (1790), a study of the role of the imagination and of the association of ideas in aesthetic perception. Alison claims that poetry and drama are distinctive in their capacity to present a 'unity of character or expression' not found either in daily life or narrative writing, and finds the appeal to mixed emotions in tragi-comedy 'utterly indefensible'. He thus thinks *Corneille a sounder dramatist than Shakespeare. The work went into six lifetime editions and influenced *Jeffrey. Alison's wife Dorothea Gregory grew up in the household of Mrs E. *Montagu.

ALISON, Sir Archibald (1792–1867), son of A. Alison (above), educated at Edinburgh University and called to the Scottish bar. He was a frequent contributor to *Blackwood's Magazine* and author of various historical works, including a *History of Europe during the French Revolution* (1833–42), and various legal works, including *Principles of the Criminal Law in Scotland* (1832) and *Practice of the Criminal Law* in Scotland (1833); he also wrote an autobiography, edited by his daughter and published in 1883.

Allan-a-Dale, one of the companions of *Robin Hood, and the subject of a song in the fourth canto of Scott's *Rokeby*.

allegory, a figurative narrative or description, conveying a veiled moral meaning; an extended metaphor. As C. S. *Lewis argues in *The Allegory of Love*, the medieval mind tended to think naturally in allegorical terms, and *Auerbach suggested that towards the end of the Middle Ages 'every kind of serious realism was in danger of being choked to death by the vines of allegory' (*Mimesis*, ch. 10). Nevertheless allegorical works of great vitality continued to be produced, ranging from Spenser's *Faerie Queene* and Bunyan's *Pilgrim's Progress*, both of which use personifications of abstract qualities, to Dryden's political allegory *Absalom and Achitophel*, which conceals real identities; and there are strongly allegorical elements in many more recent works, such as Hawthorne's *The Marble Faun* and V. Woolf's *Between the Acts*.

'Allegro, L'', see 'L'ALLEGRO'.

Allen, Benjamin and Arabella, characters in Dickens's *Pickwick Papers*.

Allen, (Charles) Grant (Blairfindie) (1848–99), born in Canada, educated in America, France, and at Merton College, Oxford. He was a schoolmaster for several years and went to Jamaica, as professor of mental and moral philosophy, where he formulated his evolutionary system of philosophy based on the works of H.

*Spencer. On his return to England he published *Physiological Aesthetics* (1877), which introduced his name to the leaders of thought in London, and he was soon contributing articles on popular scientific and other subjects to the **Cornhill* and other journals. Next came *The Colour-Sense* (1879), which won praise from A. R. **Wallace, C. *Darwin, and T. H. *Huxley. He began writing fiction, at first with stories for **Belgravia*, later collected as *Strange Stories* (1884). His first novel, *Philista* (1884), was followed by nearly 30 books of fiction including his best-selling *The Woman Who Did* (1895), intended as a protest against the subjection of women. It is the tale of a woman of advanced views who believes that marriage is a barbarous institution, incompatible with the emancipation of women; she lives with the man she loves, bears his child, but is left alone, when he inconveniently dies, to endure the consequent social ostracism. Mrs Fawcett and other feminists condemned the novel and its author as 'not a friend but an enemy' of the movement.

ALLEN, Ralph (1694–1764), a man of humble origins who rose to considerable eminence and prosperity in Bath (where he was known as the 'Man of Bath'), and was generally beloved for his unobtrusive generosity, both public and private. Most notably (in the field of literature) he assisted the struggling *Fielding, who later portrayed him as Squire Allworthy in **Tom Jones* and dedicated **Amelia* to him. After the novelist's death, Allen provided for the education and support of his children. S. *Richardson, *Pitt the elder, W. *Warburton, and Mrs *Delany were among his friends. Pope praised him in the *Epilogue to the Satires* as one who 'did good by stealth'. See B. Boyce, *The Benevolent Man* (1967).

ALLEN, Walter Ernest (1911–95), writer, scholar, and critic, born in Birmingham, and at one time part of a 'Birmingham Group' of writers which included John Hampson (author of *Saturday Night at the Greyhound*, 1931), Walter Brierley, Peter Chamberlain, and Leslie Halward. His works include his popular and influential study *The English Novel* (1954), *Rogue Elephant* (1946), *All in a Lifetime* (1959, fiction, based in part on his father's life), and a memoir, *As I Walked down New Grub Street* (1981).

ALLEN, William (1532–94), cardinal. Educated at Oriel College, he left Oxford in 1561 and was instrumental in the founding of seminaries for the training of Roman Catholic missionaries at Douai, Rome (where life at the English College is vividly described by A. *Munday in *The English Romayne Lyfe*, 1582), and Valladolid. As well as his own controversial writings he inspired and was involved in the translation of the Douai–Rheims Bible (1582–1609/10), for long the traditional Roman Catholic version of the Scriptures in the vernacular.

ALLENDE, Isabel (1942–), Chilean writer born in Lima who has lived in exile in Venezuela and in California. Her first novel, *La casa de los espíritus*

(1982; *The House of the Spirits*, 1985), explores three generations of women as a family saga ending in the 1973 coup in a style that moves from magical exaggerations to documentary. In the same vein she wrote *De amor y de sombra* (1984; *Of Love and Shadows*, 1987), *Eva Luna* (1987; 1988), whose stories become the tropical and erotic *Cuentos de Eva Luna* (1990; *The Stories of Eva Luna*, 1990) and *El plan infinito* (1991; *The Infinite Plan*, 1993). Allende wrote movingly about the death of her daughter (*Paula*, 1994; 1995) and about love and recipes in *Afrodita: cuentos, recetas y otras afrodisiacas* (1997; *Aphrodite: A Memoir of the Senses*).

ALLESTREE, Richard (*fl.* 1617–43), see [ALMANACS].

ALLESTREE, Richard (1619–81), see WHOLE DUTY OF MAN, THE.

ALLEYN, Edward (1566–1626), an actor (R. *Burbage's chief rival) and partner of *Henslowe, with whom he built the Fortune Theatre, Cripplegate. There he acted at the head of the Lord Admiral's Company, playing among other parts the leading roles in Marlowe's **Tamburlaine*, **The Jew of Malta*, and **Dr Faustus*. He acquired great wealth, bought the manor of Dulwich, and built and endowed Dulwich College. His first wife was Henslowe's stepdaughter, his second the daughter of *Donne. He was a patron of *Dekker, John *Taylor (the 'water poet'), and other writers.

All for Love, or *The World Well Lost*, a tragedy by *Dryden produced and published 1678.

Written in blank verse in acknowledged imitation of Shakespeare's **Antony and Cleopatra*, it is Dryden's most performed and his best-known play. It concentrates on the last hours in the lives of its hero and heroine. In contrast to Shakespeare's play, it is an exemplary neo-classical tragedy, notable for its elaborately formal presentation of character, action, and theme. (See NEO-CLASSICISM.)

ALLIBONE, S. A., see CRITICAL DICTIONARY OF ENGLISH LITERATURE, A.

ALLINGHAM, Margery Louise (1904–66), crime novelist, educated at the Perse School, Cambridge, which she left at the age of 15. She began to write for periodicals when young, and introduced her deceptively vacuous detective-hero Albert Campion in *The Crime at Black Dudley* (1929). He reappeared in many of her best-known works, along with his manservant Lugg and Charles Luke of the CID: these include *Flowers for the Judge* (1936), *More Work for the Undertaker* (1949), and *The Beckoning Lady* (1955). Atmospheric, intelligent, and observant, her works have maintained their popularity although they have a strong period flavour. (See DETECTIVE FICTION.)

ALLINGHAM, William (1824–89), born in Co. Donegal. He worked as a customs officer, first in Ireland, then in England, where he settled in 1863. His friends in the literary world included *Patmore, *Carlyle, D. G.

*Rossetti, and notably *Tennyson; his diary, published in 1907, covers four decades and has many vivid portraits of his contemporaries. His first volume, *Poems*, appeared in 1850, and contains his best-known work 'The Fairies' ('Up the airy mountain'); it was followed by several others, including the long poem *Laurence Bloomfield in Ireland* (1864) and various collections and anthologies of verse for children, some with illustrations by Rossetti, *Millais, K. *Greenaway, and his wife Helen Paterson.

alliteration, the commencement of two or more words in close connection with the same sound, as in e.g. G. M. *Hopkins's 'The Windhover':

> I caught this morning morning's minion, kingdom of daylight's dauphin, dapple-dawn-drawn Falcon . . .

It was used to excess by many late 19th-cent. poets, notably *Swinburne, whose 'lilies and languors of virtue' and 'raptures and roses of vice' are characteristic examples from *'Dolores'. (See also ALLITERATIVE VERSE.)

alliterative prose, a tradition of Old and Middle English prose elevated in style by the employment of some of the techniques of *alliterative verse. Its most distinguished exponents are *Ælfric and *Wulfstan in Old English, and the writers of the *'Katherine Group' in Middle English. R. W. *Chambers, in his essay 'On the Continuity of English Prose from Alfred to More' (1932), saw this alliterative thread as a common factor in English writing from Old English to the Renaissance.

Alliterative Revival, a collective term for the group of alliterative poems written in the second half of the 14th cent. in which alliteration, which had been the formal basis of Old English poetry, was again used in poetry of the first importance (such as *Piers Plowman* and *Sir *Gawain and the Green Knight*) as a serious alternative to the continental form, syllabic rhyming verse. Three views have been advanced to account for its emergence: (1) that it was a conscious return to traditional forms as politics became again more English than French, a nationalist movement like the attempted modern linguistic revivals in Wales or Ireland; (2) that it was merely a resurfacing of literature which had continued throughout the period since the Conquest but had not been officially published; (3) that it was a straightforward development of the loose alliterative poetry of the previous century which the new movement only enhanced. The last view, argued by Thorlac Turville-Petre (*The Alliterative Revival*, 1977), is now thought the most persuasive. As well as their common formal elements, many of the poems are linked by a serious interest in contemporary politics and ethics (*Wynnere and Wastoure, Death and Liffe, The Parlement of the Three Ages, Piers Plowman*).

alliterative verse, the native Germanic tradition of English poetry and the standard form in Old English up to the 11th cent., recurring in Middle English as a formal alternative to the syllable-counting, rhymed verse borrowed from French (see ALLITERATIVE REVIVAL). The Old English line was (normally) unrhymed, and made up of two distinct half-lines each of which contained two stressed syllables. The alliteration was always on the first stress of the second half-line, which alliterated with either, or both, of the stresses in the first half-line; e.g.

x   x   x
Nāp nihtscūa,   norþan snīwde (*Seafarer, 31)
(The shade of night grew dark, it snowed from the north).

In Middle English, even among the poets of the Revival, the alliterative rules were much less strict, although the alliteration was often very dense:

> 'I have lyved in londe', quod I, 'My name is Longe Wille'   (*Piers Plowman B XV. 152).

Nothing after Middle English could categorically be said to be 'alliterative verse', despite its recurrent use as a device throughout English poetry, except perhaps for the rather self-conscious revival of the form in the 20th cent. by such poets as *Auden and *Day-Lewis.

All Quiet on the Western Front, see REMARQUE.

All's Lost by Lust, a tragedy by W. *Rowley, acted by the Prince's Men c.1619, printed 1633. The story, taken from a legendary episode in Spanish history, concerns Roderick, king of Spain, his general Julianus, and Julianus' daughter Jacinta, who is raped by Roderick and later mutilated and murdered, along with her father, by Roderick's Moorish successor. The play remained popular throughout the 17th cent., and was twice adapted during the Restoration. The story is also the subject of *Landor's *Count Julian* (1812) and *Southey's *Roderick* (1814).

All's Well that Ends Well, a comedy by *Shakespeare, first printed in the First *Folio of 1623. It used to be thought to be the play referred to by *Meres as *Loue Labours Wonne*, which would mean that it was written before 1598; but its close affinity to *Measure for Measure* suggests a date around 1604–5. Both plays are generally classified as 'tragi-comedies' or 'problem comedies'.

Its chief source is Boccaccio's *Decameron* (Day 3, Tale 9), which Shakespeare may have read either in the translation by *Painter, or in the French version by Antoine le Maçon. Bertram, the young count of Rousillon, on the death of his father is summoned to the court of the king of France, leaving his mother and with her Helena, daughter of the famous physician Gerard de Narbon. The king is sick of a disease said to be incurable. Helena, who loves Bertram, goes to Paris and effects his cure by means of a prescription left by her father. As a reward she is allowed to choose her husband and names Bertram, who unwillingly obeys the king's order to wed her. But under the influence of the worthless braggart *Parolles, he at once takes service with the duke of Florence, writing to Helena that until she can get the ring from his finger 'which never shall come off', and is with child by him, she may not call him husband. Helena, passing through Florence on a pilgrimage, finds Bertram courting Diana, the daughter of her hostess there. Disclosing herself as his wife to them, she obtains permission to replace Diana at a midnight assignation with Bertram, having that day caused him to be informed that Helena is dead. Thereby she obtains from Bertram his ring, and gives him one that the king had given her. Bertram returns to his mother's house, where the king is on a visit. The latter sees on Bertram's finger the ring that he had given Helena, suspects Bertram of having destroyed her, and demands an explanation on pain of death. Helena herself now appears, explains what has passed, and claims that the conditions named in Bertram's letter have been fulfilled. Bertram, filled with remorse, accepts her as his wife. The sub-plot, concerning the braggart Parolles, has been felt by some readers, including Charles I, to dominate the play, and in performance it has often done so.

All the Year Round, see HOUSEHOLD WORDS.

Allworthy, Squire, and his sister Bridget, characters in Fielding's *Tom Jones*. The character of Squire Allworthy was based on Fielding's friends and benefactors R. *Allen and G. *Lyttelton.

Alma (in Italian meaning 'soul', 'spirit'), in Spenser's *Faerie Queene*, II. ix, xi, represents the virgin soul. She is the Lady of the House of Temperance, where she is visited by Prince *Arthur and Sir *Guyon, and defended against her enemies by the former.

almanacs were, technically, tables of astronomical and astrological events of the coming year, and as such had existed since antiquity; with the advent of printing they proliferated, and by the 17th cent. in England were the most popular literary form, containing a wide range of material, from feast days, farming notes, tables of interest, to scurrilous verses and wild and colourful prophecies. They flourished particularly strongly from 1640 to 1700, when they engaged in political, social, and religious controversy, playing an active part in the ferment of the times. Well-known publishers and compilers of almanacs included Richard Allestree (active between 1617 and 1643, Derby and Coventry); the most famous of all, *Lilly; John Gadbury (1627–1704), astrologer and physician; John Partridge (1644–1715), who published almanacs from 1678; and Francis Moore, father of *Old Moore. In the 18th cent. growing scepticism and a declining interest in astrology led to a loss of vitality in the form, although Old Moore continued to be bought by the less educated classes in vast quantities, and still sells well today, as does the more prosaic reference book *Whitaker's Almanack* (see WHITAKER). See Bernard Capp, *Astrology and the Popular Press: English Almanacs 1500–*

1800 (1979), and Keith Thomas, *Religion and the Decline of Magic* (1971).

Almeria, the heroine of Congreve's *The Mourning Bride*.

Almeyda, a character in Dryden's *Don Sebastian*.

Almoran and Hamet, see HAWKESWORTH.

Alonso, the king of Naples in Shakespeare's *The Tempest* who helped Antonio depose Prospero. It is on the return from his daughter's wedding in Tunis that his ship is wrecked and that his son Ferdinand finds a bride in Miranda.

Alonzo the Brave and the Fair Imogine, a ballad by M. G. Lewis, which appears in *The Monk*.

Alph, in Coleridge's *'Kubla Khan', the sacred river in Xanadu. For its connection with the river Alpheus and with the Nile, see J. L. *Lowes, *The Road to Xanadu* (1927).

Alton Locke, Tailor and Poet: An Autobiography, a novel by C. *Kingsley, published 1850.

The eponymous narrator, son of a small London tradesman and educated by a widowed Baptist mother, is apprenticed to a sweating tailor in whose workshop he experiences at first hand the miseries of the working classes and becomes imbued with the ideas of *Chartism; the material used in this section was first used by Kingsley in a stirring pamphlet, *Cheap Clothes and Nasty*, published earlier the same year. Locke's gift for poetry gains him the friendship first of an old Scottish bookseller, Saunders Mackaye, and then of a benevolent dean, his daughter Lillian (with whom he falls in love), and her cousin Eleanor. Under their influence he momentarily consents to the emasculation of his revolutionary poems before publication, a weakness he bitterly regrets. Roused by the taunts of his Chartist comrades, he undertakes a mission that involves him in a riot and is jailed for three years. On emerging, he learns that Lillian is engaged to his prosperous time-serving cousin; he falls ill (and during his fever undergoes an interesting evolutionary dream, seeing himself transformed from a group of polyps through higher forms of life to man), is nursed by Eleanor and by her converted from Chartism to Christian Socialism. He emigrates to America and dies on the voyage. The novel, despite its weaknesses, is a powerful social document, and had an impact similar to that of Disraeli's *Sybil* and Mrs Gaskell's *Mary Barton*, the latter of which Kingsley much admired.

ALVAREZ, Al(fred) (1929–   ), poet, broadcaster, and critic, born in London, and educated at Oundle and Corpus Christi, Oxford. His works include *The Shaping Spirit* (1958), a critical study of modern poetry, and *The Savage God: A Study of Suicide* (1971), which opens with an account of the death of *Plath, whom he knew, and whose work he published when he was poetry editor of the *Observer*. He edited an influential anthology of verse, *The New Poetry* (1962, with work by *Hughes, *Gunn, *Larkin, and others), and has also written on subjects as diverse as poker playing (*The Biggest Game in Town*, 1983), mountain climbing, and oil rigs.

Amadis of Gaul (*Amadís de Gaula*), a Spanish or Portuguese romance, written in the form in which we have it by Garcia de Montalvo in the second half of the 15th and printed early in the 16th cent., but taken from 'ancient originals' now lost, perhaps by Joham de Lobeira (1261–1325) or by Vasco de Lobeira (d. 1403), the materials of the story being of French source. Many continuations were written relating to the son and nephew of Amadis, Esplandian and Florisando.

Perion, king of Gaul (?Wales), falls in love with Elisena, daughter of Garinter, king of Lesser Britain; their child Amadis is cast away in a box on a river, and later washed ashore and reared by Gandales of Scotland. Until his identity is revealed he is known as 'The Child of the Sea'. He becomes the flower of chivalry and achieves wonderful feats of arms. He loves Oriana, daughter of Lisuarte, king of Great Britain, who is sought in marriage by the emperor of Rome and granted to him by her father, but rescued by Amadis, whence arises a great conflict. The emperor arrives with his fleet, but is defeated and killed. Amadis then comes to the succour of Lisuarte, reconciliation follows, and all ends happily.

The romance was translated into French by Herberay des Essarts in 1540, into English by *Munday (?1590), and an abridged version by *Southey appeared in 1803. *Amadis of Gaul* and **Palmerin of England* were two of the works specially excepted from the holocaust of romances of chivalry carried out by the curate and barber in **Don Quixote*.

Amadis of Greece, a Spanish continuation of the seventh book of **Amadis of Gaul*, of which Lisuarte of Greece, the grandson of Amadis, is the hero. The work is probably by Feliano de Silva (16th cent.).

Amara, Mt, a place in Abyssinia, where the kings of that country secluded their sons, to protect themselves from sedition (**Paradise Lost*, IV. 281). It figures as 'Amhara' in Johnson's **Rasselas*.

Amaryllis, the name given to a shepherdess by *Theocritus, *Virgil, and *Ovid. Spenser, in **Colin Clouts Come Home Againe*, uses the name to signify Alice, one of the daughters of Sir John Spencer of Althorp. She became the countess of Derby for whom Milton wrote his **'Arcades'.

Amaurote, or 'shadow city', the capital of More's **Utopia*. *Rabelais (II. xxiii) uses the name 'Amaurotes' for an imaginary people invaded by the Dipsodes.

Amazing Marriage, The, a novel by G. *Meredith, published 1895. This novel, written in Meredith's oblique, opaque late manner, is an extreme exploration of the battle between the sexes, conducted on a very

public stage amidst much gossip (Dame Gossip being one of the narrators). The marriage in question is that of the wild, courageous, and headstrong Carinthia, brought up in the Austrian mountains and left almost destitute on the death of her legendary father, the 'Old Buccaneer': she marries Lord Fleetwood, wealthy and arrogant, who proposes to her impulsively at a dance and is held to his promise. He dramatically abandons her on the wedding night, and the novel pursues their struggle for dominion within the marriage and her eventual triumph. Gower Woodseer, who is a friend to both parties and serves as go-between, is based on R. L. *Stevenson.

Ambassadors, The, a novel by H. *James, published 1903.

This is one of the novels in which, with much humour and delicacy of perception, the author depicts the reaction of different American types to the European environment. Chadwick Newsome, a young man of independent fortune, the son of Mrs Newsome of Woolett, Massachusetts, a widow of overpowering virtue and perfection, has been living in Paris and is reported to have got entangled with a wicked woman. Mrs Newsome has decided to send out an ambassador to rescue Chad and bring him home. This ambassador is the elderly, amiable, guileless Strether, dependent on Mrs Newsome, for whom he entertains prodigious respect and to whom he has allowed himself to become engaged. The story describes Strether's evolution in the congenial atmosphere of Paris, his desertion to the side of Chad and the bewitching comtesse de Vionnet (he is convinced that the relation between them is virtuous), and his own mild flirtation with the pleasant cosmopolitan Maria Gostrey. Meanwhile his attitude and the disquieting report of Waymarsh, Strether's stolid and conscientious American friend, have caused dismay at Woolett, and Mrs Newsome sends out a fresh ambassador in the person of her daughter, the coldly glittering Sarah Pocock. The attempts to bamboozle Sarah utterly fail, and she presents her ultimatum— immediate return to America—to the delinquents Chad and Strether. Chad, exhorted by Strether, refuses to abandon the lady; and Strether is accordingly notified that all is over between him and Mrs Newsome. Then, and then only, an accident throws Strether unexpectedly into the company of Chad and Mme de Vionnet in circumstances which leave no doubt as to the nature of their real relations. Sadly disillusioned, but still insisting on the necessity of Chad's loyalty to Mme de Vionnet, Strether from a sense of duty turns his back on Paris.

ambiguity, see SEVEN TYPES OF AMBIGUITY.

Ambit, a literary and artistic quarterly founded in 1959 by Dr Martin Bax, who edited it in association with J. G. *Ballard, Edwin Brock, E. A. *Markham, and others. Contributors have included P. *Porter, E. *Morgan, F.

*Adcock, Jeff Nuttall, G. *Ewart, D. M. *Thomas, Ruth *Fainlight, and many others.

AMBLER, Eric (1909–98), writer of thrillers, *spy fiction, and screenplays. His many works of fiction include *The Dark Frontier* (1936), *Uncommon Danger* (1937), *Epitaph for a Spy* (1938), *Cause for Alarm* (1938), *The Mask of Dimitrios* (1939), *Journey into Fear* (1940), *The October Man* (1948), *Judgement on Deltcher* (1951), *The Schirmer Inheritance* (1953), *Passage of Arms* (1959), *Dr Frigo* (1974), *Send No More Roses* (1977), and *The Care of Time* (1981). An edited volume, *To Catch a Spy: An Anthology of Favourite Spy Stories*, was published in 1964. *Here Lies: An Autobiography* appeared in 1985. *The Story So Far*, a collection of stories previously unpublished in book form together with reminiscences, was published in 1993.

Ambree, Mary, a legendary English heroine, supposed to have taken part in the siege of Ghent in 1584, when that town was held by the Spaniards. A ballad about her is included in Percy's *Reliques*, and she is referred to by *Jonson (*Epicene*, IV. ii; *Tale of a Tub*, I. iv; and *Fortunate Isles*) and other Elizabethan dramatists.

Ambrose, St (c.340–97), born at Trèves, a celebrated bishop of Milan (elected against his will by the people when still a catechumen), one of the Four Doctors of the Church, and a vigorous opponent of the *Arian heresy. He developed the use of music in church services, restoring the ancient melodies and founding what is known as the Ambrosian chant (as opposed to the Gregorian chant, introduced two centuries later under *Gregory the Great). He composed several hymns, among which an old tradition includes the 'Te Deum', and he was a voluminous writer, though a great part of his output is no more than a translation of Greek Fathers such as *Origen. He baptized St *Augustine and demonstrated the power of the Church by excluding the Emperor Theodosius from the cathedral at Milan until he repented and did penance for the massacre at Thessalonica (390).

Letters, trans. M. M. Beyenka (1954); F. H. Dudden, *St Ambrose: His Life and Times* (2 vols, 1935).

Ambrose's Tavern, the scene of the *Noctes Ambrosianae*, is loosely based on a real Edinburgh tavern of the same name, first described by *Lockhart in *Peter's Letters to His Kinsfolk*.

Amelia, a novel by H. *Fielding, published 1752 (for 1751).

Joseph Andrews and *Tom Jones* end with the heroes and heroines about to embark on married life; in *Amelia* Captain and Mrs Booth have already enjoyed some happy years together, and the book is much concerned with married tenderness and family happiness. The character of Amelia, loving, forgiving, yet strong and spirited, is known to be a portrait of Fielding's wife Charlotte, who died in 1744, and the character of Captain Billy Booth clearly contains some elements of Fielding's own, although it altogether lacks his determination and industry. Certain incidents, such as that of Amelia's broken nose, are thought to refer to episodes in their life together. However, the novel is by no means an autobiography. Set in and against a London of almost unrelieved squalor, corruption, and violence, it opens in the court of the 'trading Justice', Justice Thrasher, who has the innocent, penniless Booth thrown into Newgate because he cannot bribe his way out of trouble. The filth and brutality of the prison, filled with sick, dying, and often innocent people, provides a sombre background against which Amelia's virtue shines. In prison Booth meets an old acquaintance, Miss Matthews, a courtesan who has the means to buy a clean cell and who invites Booth to share it with her. Although filled with remorse, he does so, and they exchange their stories. Booth describes his runaway marriage (in which he was assisted by the good parson Dr Harrison), his happiness with Amelia, their lives in the country, his soldiering, and Amelia's arrival in France when he was ill. There they had lived with the huge, pugnacious Colonel Bath and his sister, who had since married a Colonel James. James now bails out Booth, and takes Miss Matthews as his mistress. Booth begins a life of gambling, as he hangs about the haunts of the great and wealthy angling for a commission: Amelia's life is one of poverty and distress, but even when Booth fails to return from his gambling for her frugal but lovingly prepared meal of hashed mutton she does not upbraid him. And always hovering in the background is the kindly Dr Harrison, who protects and helps them as he can. 'My Lord', a flamboyant and menacing character who is never given a name, begins, with Colonel James, to lay plans to ensnare Amelia. The Booths' friendly landlady, Mrs Ellison (who is, unknown to Amelia, not only a cousin of My Lord's but also his procuress), arranges for Amelia to be attended at an oratorio by My Lord in disguise, and then introduces him as her cousin. My Lord becomes extremely agreeable, offers to acquire a command for Booth, and showers presents on Amelia's adored children. She then receives an invitation to a masquerade, but is sharply warned by a fellow lodger, the learned widow Mrs Bennet, and she does not go. She learns that Mrs Bennet was once herself seduced by My Lord, after an invitation to a masquerade. After various other dangers and complications, during one of which Mrs Bennet, to Amelia's fury, succeeds in obtaining Booth's commission for her own new husband, the good Dr Harrison arrives, eventually pays off Booth's debts, and arranges for him to return to the farming life he loved. Amelia discovers that she is heiress to her mother's fortune, and the Booths retire to a happy and prosperous country life.

The book sold extremely well, but was attacked by many, led by *Richardson and *Smollett, and Fielding made alterations in later editions. It was his own favourite among all his books.

American Democrat, The, or Hints on the Social and Civic Relation of the United States of America, by J. F. *Cooper, published 1838. In this vigorous work Cooper examined and set forth, to the offence of his countrymen, the defects and dangers of democracy as it flourished in America.

American Senator, The, a novel by A. *Trollope, published 1877.

Elias Gotobed, senator for the fictional state of Mickewa, comes to England on a fact-finding tour, and finds 'irrational and salutary' English manners and customs more than he can understand. In this quiet exposition of country life in and around the town of Dillsborough, two love stories are highlighted. The first is a conventional Trollopean love-triangle, in which Mary Masters prefers her childhood sweetheart Reginald Morton to a neighbouring gentleman-farmer, Larry Twentyman. The second deals with Arabella Trefoil's pursuit of the wealthy Lord Rufford, despite a prior engagement to Reginald's cousin John.

American Taxation, On, a speech by E. *Burke, made in 1774 on a motion for the repeal of the American Tea Duty.

After dealing with the narrower arguments regarding the expediency of the proposal, Burke turns to a broad historical view of the subject, going back to the Navigation Act and explaining the course of British policy. He shows that the Tea Duty is at variance with the declarations of ministers and an 'exhaustless source of jealousy and animosity' without practical benefit. He exhorts the government to abandon it. 'Do not burden the Americans with taxes. You were not used to do so from the beginning. Let this be your reason for not taxing. These are the arguments of states and kingdoms. Leave the rest to the schools.'

AMHURST, Nicholas ('Caleb D'Anvers') (1697–1742), poet and polemicist, who satirized Oxford University in his periodical Terrae Filius (1721) and conducted, during its most effective period, the chief opposition journal of his day, the *Craftsman (1726–50).

Amiatinus Codex, the best extant manuscript of the Vulgate, so called from the abbey of Monte Amiata, to which it was presented. It was discovered in the 19th cent. to have been written in England, early in the 8th cent., at Wearmouth or Jarrow. It was probably copied from an Italian original. It is now in the Laurentian Library in Florence.

AMIEL, Henri-Frédéric (1821–81), Swiss author. His remarkable diary was published first in part in 1883 (Fragments d'un journal intime, 2 vols) and translated by Mrs H. *Ward in 1885. It has since been re-edited and augmented.

Aminta, see TASSO.

Amintor, the hero of Beaumont and Fletcher's *The Maid's Tragedy.

AMIS, Sir Kingsley (1922–95), novelist and poet, born in south London and educated at the City of London School and St John's College, Oxford. He lectured in Swansea, then at Cambridge (1949–63). He published volumes of poetry, Bright November (1947) and A Frame of Mind (1953), but achieved popular success with his first novel, Lucky Jim (1954), whose hero, lower-middle-class radical lecturer Jim Dixon, with his subversive attitudes (anti-establishment, anti-pretension, anti-arts-and-crafts) was hailed as an *'Angry Young Man'. Its setting in a provincial university was also indicative of a new development in fiction (see COOPER, W., LARKIN, BRAINE), a movement that Amis confirmed in That Uncertain Feeling (1955) and Take a Girl Like You (1960). I Like It Here (1958), a xenophobic and slight novel set in Portugal, displays Amis's deliberate cultivation, for comic effect, of a prejudiced and philistine pose which was to harden into an increasingly conservative and hostile view of contemporary life and manners. His subsequent work is marked by much versatility; although best known for satiric comedy (One Fat Englishman, 1963, set in America; Ending up, 1974, a savage study of old age; and Jake's Thing, 1978, a dissertation on middle-aged impotence and its causes), he has also successfully attempted many other genres. The Anti-Death League (1966), while in some respects offering the satisfaction of a conventional spy story, is a serious protest against God's inhumanity to man, and a tribute to 'the unaided and self-constituted human spirit, the final proof of the non-existence of God'. The Green Man (1969) is a novel of the supernatural, The Riverside Villas Murder (1973) an imitation of a classic detective story. Amis's enthusiasm for I. *Fleming's work expressed itself in The James Bond Dossier (1965) and Colonel Sun (1968), published under the pseudonym of Robert Markham. Russian Hide-and-Seek (1980), a 'melodrama', is set in the 21st cent. when England is being ruled by the Russians. Stanley and the Women (1984) was followed by The Old Devils (1986), which won the *Booker Prize. Set in Wales, it tells the story of a group of retired friends and their wives, whose lives revolve round social drinking, and the effect on them of the reappearance of Alun Weaver, a professionally Welsh literary pundit. In Difficulties with Girls (1988), Patrick Standish and Jenny Bunn, from Take a Girl Like You, reappear as a married couple. You Can't Do Both (1994) is a semi-autobiographical story, set between the wars, about the progress of Robin Davies from south London suburbia, through Oxford, and on to a lectureship in a provincial university. The Amis Collection: Selected Non-fiction 1954–1990 (1990) was followed by the publication of Amis's Memoirs (1991). A collection of short stories, Mr Barrett's Secret, appeared in 1993. His Collected Poems 1944–1979 appeared in 1979. (See also MOVEMENT, THE.)

AMIS, Martin Louis (1949–   ), novelist and journalist, the son of Sir Kingsley *Amis. Educated at Exeter

College, Oxford, he was an editorial assistant on the *Times Literary Supplement* 1972–5, and later assistant editor; from 1977 to 1979 he was literary editor of the *New Statesman*. Stylistically flamboyant, his novels depict, often in disturbing and explicit detail, the violence and moral ambiguities of late 20th-cent. urban society. His first novel, *The Rachel Papers* (1973), is the story of Charles Highway, a sexually precocious teenager who plans the seduction of an older woman. Sex is treated both graphically and satirically in *Dead Babies* (1975). This was followed by *Success* (1978) and a metaphysical thriller, *Other People* (1981). *Money* (1984), subtitled *A Suicide Note*, centres on the aptly named John Self, a film producer who becomes overwhelmed by a series of catastrophes. The novel is memorable for its linguistic dexterity and inventiveness. In 1987 Amis published *Einstein's Monsters*, a collection of five short stories with an introductory essay, which reflect a preoccupation with the threat of nuclear annihilation. *London Fields* (1989), part thriller, part surrealist fable, balances violent action with the comic potential of the central character, Keith Talent ('a very bad guy'). *Time's Arrow* (1991), Amis's most ambitiously structured novel, the story of a Nazi war criminal in which the normal chronological sequence of events is reversed, was followed by *The Information* (1995), which uses the rivalry of two writers to speculate on the growing insignificance of both people and books in the newly revealed dimensions of time and space, and *Night Train* (1997), a typically Amisian variation on the American detective story. Amis has also published two volumes of essays and journalism: *The Moronic Inferno and Other Visits to America* (1986) and *Visiting Mrs Nabokov and Other Excursions* (1993). *Experience* (2000), is a volume of memoir, and *Yellow Dog* (2003) a novel satirizing the monarchy and the pornography industry.

Amis and Amiloun, a late 13th-cent. romance of 2,508 lines, adapted from an Anglo-Norman lay, about the virtue of friendship. Amis and Amiloun are two noble foster-brothers, bound in close friendship. Amiloun takes the place of Amis in a trial by combat and is punished for this deception with leprosy. Amis is told by an angel that only a bath made from the blood of his two children will cure the leprosy, and he provides this for his friend. At the end the children are brought back to life. *Morris and *Pater (in *Studies in the History of the Renaissance*) both tell the story as *Amis and Amile*. It was traditionally thought that the romance, while it was interesting and popular, was badly constructed, but criticism in the 1960s and 1970s has argued its virtues. The standard edition is by MacEdward Leach (EETS os 203, 1937).

Amoret, in Spenser's *Faerie Queene*, iii. vi, xii and iv. vii, daughter of the nymph Chrysogone and twin sister of *Belphoebe. She is 'Of grace and beautie noble Paragone', and has been married to Sir *Scudamour,

but carried off immediately after by the enchanter *Busirane and imprisoned by him until released by *Britomart. *Timias loves her, but being reproved by Belphoebe leaves her. This incident refers to the displeasure of Queen Elizabeth at the relations of *Ralegh with Elizabeth Throckmorton.

Amoretti, a series of 89 sonnets by *Spenser, which have been thought to illustrate the course of his wooing of Elizabeth Boyle. (Sonnets 35 and 83 are identical.) His marriage to her was celebrated in *Epithalamion, which was printed with the *Amoretti* in 1595.

AMORY, Thomas (?1691–1788), born in Ireland and educated in Dublin. He had some medical training, then spent the rest of his life as a leisured gentleman in Dublin and London. He worked for many years, by his own account, on a vast work on *The Ancient and Present State of Great Britain*, but the manuscript was accidentally burned. From his memory of it he assembled a rambling miscellany of travel and discourse, on his Unitarian beliefs, antiquities, medicine, landscape, and nature. This was to appear as a series, *Memoirs Containing the Lives of Several Ladies of Great Britain*, but the first volume, published in 1755 and intermittently centred on Mrs Marinda Benlow, was the only one to appear. In it a visit to the Hebrides is followed by a lavish description of Green Island, to the west of St Kilda, which is inhabited by a society of learned and accomplished ladies, in a luxuriant setting of statuary and tropical vegetation. In 1756 and 1766 Amory published *The Life and Opinions of *John Buncle, Esq.*, in which the slim narrative of a journey through tremendous landscapes is filled out with impassioned discourse and marital adventure.

Amos Barton, *The Sad Fortunes of the Rev.*, see SCENES OF CLERICAL LIFE.

Amphialus, a character in Sidney's *Arcadia* who has the bad luck always to injure those he loves.

amphibrach, a foot consisting of a long between two short syllables.

Amphitryon, a comedy by *Dryden, produced and published 1690.

Adapted from the comedies of *Plautus and *Molière on the same subject, it represents the story of Jupiter's seduction of Alcmena in the guise of her husband Amphitryon. In this he is aided by Mercury, who is disguised as Amphitryon's slave Sosia. The cruel abuse of mortal love by the gods is in striking contrast to the play's uninhibited eroticism. The same story was adapted by *Giraudoux in his *Amphitryon 38* (1929).

Amurath (Murad), the name of several Turkish sultans. Amurath III in 1574 murdered his brothers on succeeding to the throne, and his successor in 1596 did the same. Shakespeare in 2 *Henry IV* makes the newly acceded Henry V reassure his brothers with the words

'Not Amurath an Amurath succeeds, | But Harry Harry' (v. ii. 48).

Amyntas, in Spenser's *Colin Clouts Come Home Againe*, may represent Ferdinando Stanley, earl of Derby.

AMYOT, Jacques (1513–93), a French writer, whose version of *Plutarch was translated into English by Sir T. *North.

anachrony, the narration of events outside their logical sequence, normally in retrospective 'flashback' (analepsis), less commonly by anticipatory 'flashforward' (prolepsis).

anacoluthon (Greek, 'wanting sequence'), a sentence in which a fresh construction is adopted before the former is complete.

ANACREON (6th cent. BC), a Greek lyric poet who is supposed to have written extensively on love and wine, but only a handful of his genuine poems survive. A large collection of 'anacreontic' verse, of unknown origin, was printed for the first time in Paris in 1554; these verses were immediately imitated by the poets of the *Pléiade who popularized the genre. *Drayton, *Jonson, *Herrick, *Lovelace, *Cowley, all owed a debt to 'Anacreon'. In 1800 T. *Moore published a translation of the *Odes of Anacreon* in English verse.

anacrusis (Greek, 'striking up'), an additional syllable at the beginning of a line before the normal rhythm, e.g. the 'and' in the second of the following lines:

> Till danger's troubled night depart
> And the star of peace return.
> (T. *Campbell, 'Ye Mariners of England')

Analytical Review (1788–99), an important literary and radical periodical, published by J. *Johnson, which was an early influence in encouraging the growth of *Romanticism. *Gilpin's theories on the *picturesque, and some of *Wordsworth's early poems, were given sympathetic attention; the work of *Bowles, *Southey, *Lamb, and other young writers was published. The *Review* attempted to comment, often fully, on every book published.

ANAND, Mulk Raj (1905–), Indian novelist, writing in English, who was born in Peshawar and educated at the universities of Punjab and London. After the war he settled in Bombay, having published early work in *Criterion, *New Writing, and other English periodicals. Anand made his name with the novel *Untouchable* (1935), which recounts a day in the life of a street sweeper, roused to hopes of a classless and casteless society by Gandhi (who advised Anand on the manuscript of the work). This was followed by other novels describing the lives of the poor, including *Coolie* (1936) and a trilogy (*The Village*, 1939; *Across the Black Waters*, 1940; *The Sword and the Sickle*, 1942) which describes the life of a rebellious and independent young Sikh peasant from the Punjab who fights for the British army in the First World War. The best known of Anand's later works is *Private Life of an Indian Prince* (1953).

Ananias, the fanatical Anabaptist in Jonson's *The Alchemist*.

anapaest (Greek, 'reversed'), a reversed dactyl, a metrical foot composed of two short followed by a long syllable.

anaphora (Greek, 'carrying back'), the repetition of the same word or phrase in several successive clauses; for instance, 'Awake up, my glory; awake, lute and harp; I myself will awake right early' (Ps. 57: 9)

Anarchy, The Mask of, see MASK OF ANARCHY, THE.

Anastasius, see HOPE, T.

anastrophe (Greek, 'to turn upside-down'), a figure of speech in which the normal syntactic order of words is inverted, typically for the sake of emphasis or rhyme, as in 'Matter too soft a lasting mark to bear' (A. *Pope).

Anatomie of Abuses, The, see STUBBES.

Anatomy of Melancholy, The, by Robert *Burton, first published 1621, enlarged in successive editions between then and 1651.

In appearance the *Anatomy* is a medical work, in effect an affectionate satire on the inefficacy of human learning and endeavour. Burton finds melancholy to be universally present in mankind, 'an inbred malady in every one of us', to avoid which we are advised: 'Be not solitary, be not idle.' The book is made up of a lengthy introduction and three 'partitions', the first on the nature, causes, and symptoms of melancholy, the second on its cure, and the third on two special forms—love-melancholy and religious melancholy. Burton was a learned man, and quotes and paraphrases an extraordinary range of authors, making his book a storehouse of anecdote and maxim. Its tone suits Burton's choice of pseudonym, 'Democritus Junior': *Democritus was 'the laughing philosopher'. The *Anatomy* made its author's reputation in his own lifetime, was admired by Dr *Johnson, and gave Keats the story for *'Lamia'.

Ancient Mariner, *The Rime of the*, a poem by S. T. *Coleridge, published 1798 in *Lyrical Ballads.

An ancient mariner meets three gallants on their way to a marriage feast, and detains one of them in order to recount his story. He tells how his ship was drawn towards the South Pole by a storm. When the ship is surrounded by ice an albatross flies through the fog and is received with joy by the crew. The ice splits and the bird moves on with the ship; then inexplicably the mariner shoots it. For this act of cruelty a curse falls on the ship. She is driven north to the equator and is becalmed under burning sun in a rotting sea. The albatross is hung round the neck of the hated mariner. A skeleton ship approaches, on which Death and Life-in-Death are playing dice, and when it vanishes all the crew die except the mariner. Suddenly, watching the beauty of the watersnakes in the moonlight, he blesses them—and the albatross falls from his neck. The ship sails home and the mariner is saved, but for a penance he is condemned to travel from land to land and to teach by his example love and reverence for all God's creatures. The activities of a parallel spirit world are described in marginal notes to the poem.

J. L. *Lowes, in *The Road to Xanadu* (1927), traces the sources of Coleridge's story and imagery. The poem was derided when it first appeared, but has since come to be regarded as one of the great poems of *Romanticism. R. P. *Warren reinterprets the symbolism of the poem, based on an opposition between Sun and Moon, in *Selected Essays* (1964).

Ancients and Moderns, *Quarrel of the*, see BATTLE OF THE BOOKS, THE.

Ancrene Wisse (often called *Ancrene Riwle*), a book of devotional advice, written for three sisters by a chaplain in about 1230. Seventeen manuscripts, whole or partial, survive: 11 in English (the language of the original), four in Latin, and two in French. It is admired as a work of great charm and expressiveness and regarded as the greatest prose work of the Early Middle English period. It has important linguistic and thematic connections with the group of texts known (from the subject of one of them) as the *'Katherine Group'. The book is divided into eight sections, each dealing in an accessible way with one division of the religious rule. E. J. Dobson (see below) believes that the work was written after 1215 and evolved in a series of revisions in the 1220s, and argues from an internal semi-acrostic on the name 'Brian of Lingen' that the author may have been an Augustinian priest connected with Wigmore Abbey in north-west Herefordshire, probably for the nuns of Limebrook (or Lingbrook).

MS of Corpus Christi College, Cambridge, ed. J. R. R. *Tolkien (EETS 249, 1962); selections (Parts 6 and 7: on Penance, and on Love) ed. G. Shepherd (1959); trans. M. B. Salu (1956); E. J. Dobson, *The Origins of Ancrene Wisse* (1976).

ANDERSEN, Hans Christian (1805–75), Danish writer, born in Odense, the son of a cobbler and a washer-woman. His earliest ambitions were theatrical, and he trained as a singer and actor before achieving success as a playwright and novelist. From 1831 onwards he travelled widely in Europe, and remained a passionate traveller all his life, making his first visit to England in 1847. By this time he had already gained an international reputation for his fairy stories, which first appeared in Danish from 1835 onwards, and in English in 1846 in three separate translations, by Charles Boner, Mary Howitt, and Caroline Peachey. These stories, which include such haunting tales as 'The Little Mermaid', 'The Snow Queen', 'The Ugly Duckling', 'The Red Shoes', and 'The Emperor's New Clothes',

were deeply rooted in Danish folklore, but were also shaped by Andersen's own psychological experiences and his at times morbidly acute sensitivity, and many of his narratives were wholly original. They were much admired by *Dickens, to whom Andersen dedicated *A Poet's Day Dreams* (1853) and with whom he stayed at Gad's Hill in 1857. Andersen's other works were also read and admired in England: E. B. *Browning wrote warmly to her future husband of his novel *The Improvisatore* (1845), and her last poem was written for him in 1861 shortly before her death. See also CHILDREN'S LITERATURE.

ANDERSON, Sherwood (1876–1941), American writer, born in Ohio, who made his name as a leading naturalistic writer with his third book, *Winesburg, Ohio* (1919), a collection of short stories illustrating life in a small town. He published other collections, including *The Triumph of the Egg* (1921) and *Death in the Woods* (1933), in which he continued to illustrate the frustrations of contemporary life, a theme also explored in his novels, which include *Poor White* (1920), *Dark Laughter* (1925), and the semi-autobiographical *Tar: A Midwest Childhood* (1926). His *Memoirs* (1942) and *Letters* (1953) were posthumously published.

Andreas, an Old English poem of 1,722 lines divided into 15 fits, in the *Vercelli Book, based on a Latin version of the Greek Apocryphal *Acts of Andrew and Matthew amongst the Anthropophagi*. It was previously believed to be by *Cynewulf or by one of his followers influenced by *Beowulf, but it is now thought probable that *Andreas* is later than Cynewulf, towards the end of the 9th cent. See *Andreas and the Fates of the Apostles*, ed. K. R. Brooks (1961).

ANDREAS CAPELLANUS (fl. 1180s), is usually believed to have been a chaplain to *Marie de Champagne, though there is no historical evidence for him. His book *De Arte Honeste Amandi* (also entitled *De Amore*) is a handbook of procedure in love in three sections: Book I, concerned with the nature of love and procedure in it; Book II, on how love can be retained; and Book III, on the rejection of love. Andreas's work corresponds very closely to the writings of *Ovid on whom he often draws explicitly; especially influential are the *Ars Amatoria* and the *Remedia Amoris*. The whole work has a sceptical, Ovidian tone, and it has been very authoritative in the definitions of *courtly love from Gaston Paris to the present day. Its excessive authority in English discussion is attributable principally to the prominence given to it by C. S. *Lewis in *The Allegory of Love* (1936). It has been edited (in the original Latin) by P. G. Walsh (1982) and translated (with an excellent introduction) by J. J. Parry as *The Art of Courtly Love* (1941).

ANDREEV, Leonid Nikolaevich (1871–1919), Russian prose writer and dramatist who achieved great popularity in the early 20th cent. His first collection of stories (1901) was an enormous success. Among his most important stories are 'The Abyss' and 'In the Fog' (1902), which treat sexual themes with a new frankness, 'The Red Laugh' (1904), a response to the 'madness' of the Russo-Japanese War, and 'The Story of the Seven Who Were Hanged' (1908), which examines political terrorism. His major plays are *The Life of a Man* (1906) and *He Who Gets Slapped* (1915). Andreev opposed the October Revolution and died in exile in Finland.

ANDREW OF WYNTOUN, see Wyntoun, Andrew of.

ANDREWES, Lancelot (1555–1626), educated at Merchant Taylors' School and Pembroke Hall, Cambridge, bishop successively of Chichester, Ely, and Winchester. He was renowned for his patristic learning and was one of the divines appointed to translate the Authorized Version of the *Bible. He was a major influence in forming a distinctively Anglican theology, reasonable in tone and based on sound scholarship: his friends included *Camden, *Selden, G. *Herbert, and *Casaubon. He was a highly popular preacher, and as a writer is remembered for his sermons, which in T. S. *Eliot's view 'rank with the finest English prose of their time' (*For Lancelot Andrewes*, 1928). The opening of Eliot's 'Journey of the Magi' ('A cold coming we had of it') is drawn from Andrewes's *Sermon 15: Of the Nativitie*. The sermons are in the *metaphysical style that preceded the plainer preaching of the Puritans and *Tillotson; they combine minute textual analysis, classical quotations, and verbal play with homely imagery and passages of powerful simplicity. His *Works* (11 vols, ed. Wilson and Bliss) appeared 1841–54 and a selection by G. M. Story in 1967.

Androcles and the Lion; the story used by G. B. *Shaw in the play of that name appears first in *Gellius, 5. 14.

Anecdotes of Painting in England, a work by Horace *Walpole, based on some 40 manuscript notebooks which he bought from the widow of the celebrated engraver *Vertue in 1758. The first two volumes appeared in 1762–3 and the third, with his *Catalogue of Engravers*, in 1765. The work surveys English art from medieval times to Walpole's own, and is at once a valuable and scholarly record and a reflection of Walpole's developing aesthetic taste.

Aneirin, The Book of, the name given to a 13th-cent. Welsh manuscript which contains the poem *Y Gododdin*, attributed to the bard Aneirin (or, incorrectly, Aneurin) who lived in the second half of the 6th cent. The poem commemorates a British defeat at Catraeth (Catterick, Yorkshire). See *Canu Aneirin*, ed. Sir Ifor Williams (1938), and *The Gododdin* by K. H. Jackson (1969).

Anelida and Arcite, an incomplete poem by *Chaucer in 357 lines. It is set, like 'The Knight's Tale' (*Canterbury Tales*, I), in Theseus's Thebes and draws more on *Boccaccio's *Teseida* than on the sources it acknowledges, Statius and Corinna. The simple story tells of the faithlessness of Arcite to Queen Anelida in 210 lines of rhyme-royal, as a preface to the elaborate *Compleynt* of Anelida in 140 lines of varying and accomplished metrical patterns.

Angelica, (1) in *Orlando innamorato* and *Orlando furioso*, the daughter of *Galafron, king of Cathay, the object of Orlando's love and the cause of his madness. For the story see under the above-named poems. Wordsworth in *The Prelude* (Bk. IX) refers to her 'thundering through the woods upon her palfrey'. See also *Paradise Regained*, III. 341; (2) the heroine of Congreve's *Love for Love*; (3) the heroine of Thackeray's *The Rose and the Ring*.

Angel in the House, The, a sequence of poems by C. *Patmore. The first and second parts, *The Betrothal* and *The Espousals*, both in octosyllabic quatrains, were published 1854 and 1856 respectively; the third and fourth parts, *Faithful for Ever* (1860) and *The Victories of Love* (1861), both in octosyllabic couplets, were published as *The Victories of Love* in 1863.

The work is a celebration of married love, with lyrical and reflective passages linked by a narrative in which Felix courts and weds Honoria, a dean's daughter; in the last two parts Frederick, a rival for Honoria's hand, marries Jane and learns to love her before her early death. It was immensely popular with the Victorian public, though its mixture of high-flown sentiment and banal details about middle-class life made it the object of much mockery from more sophisticated authors like *Swinburne, and *Gosse referred to Patmore as 'this laureate of the tea-table, with his humdrum stories of girls that smell of bread and butter' (*Athenaeum*, June 1886). V. *Woolf, in a lecture on 'Professions for Women' (1931), spoke of the need for women writers to 'kill the Angel in the House'.

Angelo, the seemingly puritanical deputy to the duke in Shakespeare's *Measure for Measure*.

ANGELOU, Maya (1928–), African-American autobiographer and poet, born in St Louis, Missouri. Rooted in a rich folk tradition of rural black culture, *I Know Why the Caged Bird Sings* (1970), the most famous of her five volumes of autobiography, charts her harrowing childhood in Arkansas, her segregation in Southern schools, and the beginning of her enduring relationship to literature. The other volumes, *Gather Together in My Name* (1974), *Singin' and Swingin' and Gettin' Merry like Christmas* (1976), *The Heart of a Woman* (1981), and *All God's Children Need Traveling Shoes* (1986), record her flamboyant career as a singer and dancer, her years in the Harlem Writers' Guild, and her role within the civil rights movement. An exuberant and technically assured poet with a commitment to the politics of race and gender, Angelou's works of poetry include *Just Give Me a Cool Drink of Water 'fore I Diiie* (1971), *And Still I Rise* (1978), and *I Shall Not Be Moved* (1990).

Anglo-Indian literature. Present-day India boasts an English-language literature of energy and diversity, and has spawned a striking literary diaspora. Some writers of Indian descent (V. S. *Naipaul, Bharati Mukherjee) now reject the ethnic label of 'Indian writers'. Mukherjee sees herself as American, while Naipaul would perhaps prefer to be read as an artist from nowhere and everywhere. For some Indian critics, English-language Indian writing is a post-colonial anomaly; its continuing use of the old colonial tongue is seen as a fatal flaw and renders it inauthentic. However, others have argued that English became a naturalized subcontinental language long ago. And it is part of the achievement of English-language Indian writers to have found literary voices as distinctively Indian, but also suitable for all purposes of art, as those other languages forged in Ireland, Africa, the West Indies, and the United States.

The first Indian novel in English was *Rajmohan's Wife* (1864), a poor melodramatic thing. The writer, Bankimchandra Chatterjee, reverted to Bengali and immediately achieved great renown. For 70 years there was no English-language fiction of quality. It was the generation of Independence which provided the true architects of the new tradition. Nehru's niece Nayantara Sahgal (1927–), whose early memoir *Prison and Chocolate Cake* (1954) contains perhaps the finest evocation of the heady time of Independence, became a major novelist. Mulk Raj *Anand was influenced by both *Joyce and *Marx, but most of all, perhaps, by the teachings of Mahatma Gandhi. Raja *Rao, a scholarly Sanskritist, wrote determinedly of the need to make an Indian English for himself, and his *Kanthapura* (1938) has been much praised. The centenarian autobiographer Nirad C. Chaudhuri (1897–1999) was an erudite and mischievous presence. His view, to summarize it, was that India has no culture of its own, that Indian culture was brought in from outside by successive waves of conquerors. That he always swam so strongly against the current has not prevented *The Autobiography of an Unknown Indian* (1951) from being recognized as a masterpiece.

The most significant writers of this first generation are opposites: R. K. *Narayan and G. V. *Desani. Narayan's books fill a good-sized shelf; Desani is the author of a single work of fiction. Narayan offers a gently comic realism leavened by touches of legend; Desani, a rowdy, linguistically pyrotechnic comedy, like that of an Indian *Sterne. Ved *Mehta is best known for his volumes of autobiography, including *Vedi*, a dispassionate, affecting memoir of a blind boyhood. (More recently, Firdaus Kanga (1959–), in his autobiographical fiction *Trying to Grow* (1990), has also transcended physical affliction with high style and comic brio.

Ruth Prawer *Jhabvala is the author of *Booker Prize winner *Heat and Dust*, a fine short story writer, and successful screenwriter with Merchant–Ivory; Anita *Desai is a novelist of Austen-like subtlety

and bite. Though V. S. Naipaul approaches India as an outsider, his engagement with it has been intense, and his three non-fiction books on India, *An Area of Darkness* (1964), *A Wounded Civilization* (1977), and *India: A Million Mutinies Now* (1990), are key texts, and not only because of the hackles they have raised. Many Indian critics have taken issue with the harshness of his responses. Some have fair-mindedly conceded that he attacks things worth attacking.

In the 1980s and 1990s, a second literary generation established itself, the best-known and perhaps the most influential member being Salman *Rushdie, who gave Indian writing a much wider currency. Bapsi Sidhwa is technically Pakistani, but her novel *Ice-Candy-Man: Cracking India* (1989) is one of the finest responses to the horror of the division of the subcontinent. Gita Mehta's *A River Sutra* (1993) is a serious attempt by a thoroughly modern Indian to make her reckoning with the Hindu culture from which she emerged. Padma Perera, Anjana Appachana, and Githa Hariharan confirm the quality of contemporary writing by Indian women.

A number of different manners are evolving: the Stendhalian realism of Rohinton *Mistry, the lighter, more readily charming prose of Vikram *Seth, the elegant social observation of Upamanyu Chatterjee (1959–) (*English August*, 1988), the more flamboyant manner of Vikram Chandra (1961–) (*Love and Longing in Bombay*, 1997). Amitav Ghosh (1956–) has written novels as well as non-fiction (*In an Antique Land*, 1992). Sara Suleri's memoir of Pakistan, *Meatless Days* (1990), is a work of originality and grace, and Amit *Chaudhuri's languorous, elliptical prose is impressively impossible to place in any category at all.

A third generation is now emerging. The Keralan writer Arundhati Roy's first novel *The God of Small Things* (1997) is ambitious and written in a highly wrought style. Ardashir Vakil's *Beach Boy* (1997) is a tale of growing up in Bombay, sharp, funny, and fast. Kiran Desai's lively *Hullabaloo in the Guava Orchard* (1998) is a stylish Calvino-esque fable.

See *The Vintage Book of Indian Writing 1947–1997*, ed. Salman Rushdie and Elizabeth West (1997).

Anglo-Latin literature to 1847. From the 7th to the mid-19th cents, some thousands of English writers produced Latin writings in great quantity, both in prose and in verse, addressed to a Latin-reading public in continental Europe as well as in England. *Bede, *Aldhelm, and *Alcuin are prominent authors of significant and much-read works in the period before the Norman Conquest. From the 12th cent. onwards many Anglo-Latin writers were dominant and achieved European renown. *Geoffrey of Monmouth's *Historia Regum Britanniae* (History of the Kings of Britain) (c.1138) was a principal source which disseminated the Arthurian legends, and is extant in almost 300 manuscripts. Chroniclers such as *William of Malmesbury and *Henry of Huntingdon were historians also renowned for their literary qualities. Virtually every literary genre is found, including hymns, letters, saints' lives, and poetry of all kinds in both quantitative and stressed metres. Epic is represented by Joseph of Exeter's *De Bello Troiano* (On the Trojan War, *c*.1185), satire against the religious orders by Nigel *Wireker's *Speculum Stultorum* (The Mirror of Fools, *c*.1180), lyric and occasional poetry by Peter of Blois. Gervase of Tilbury and the Anglo-Welshman Walter *Map shared a taste for folklore narratives, for stories, and for wonders. Among works of literary criticism are *Geoffrey de Vinsauf's *Poetria Nova* (New Poetics) (*c*.1210) and John of Garland's *Parisiana Poetria* (Parisian Poetics) (*c*.1235). A great deal of Latin continues to be written in the 13th and 14th cents, culminating in John *Gower's 10,000-line *Vox Clamantis* (The Voice of One who Cries out) (*c*.1385), of which the first book is on the Peasant's Revolt. The 15th cent. represents a low point for the Latinate tradition, but it revives in the 16th cent. under the impact of humanism and the regeneration of the universities. Thomas *More wrote Latin epigrams and other poems, as well as the classic *Utopia* (1516). Queen Elizabeth's tutor Roger *Ascham produced the most elegant Latin letter-book to appear from 16th-cent. England. The Latin poetic tradition in particular was regenerated. Thomas *Campion's love elegies, first published in 1595, exceed in sensuous frankness his English poems, and many major English poets of the 16th and 17th cents such as *Milton, *Herbert, *Crashaw, *Marvell, and *Cowley also wrote much Latin poetry. The much-admired and reprinted *Parthenicon* (Writings of a Maid) (Prague, *c*.1606) of Elizabeth Jane Weston was the first substantial volume of collected poetry by a female British writer to appear under her own name. In the 18th cent. Dr *Johnson, *Addison, and T. *Gray all wrote Latin verses. After 1750 the Latin tradition declines into literary trifling, except for the voluminous productions of Walter Savage *Landor, the last significant English poet to write in Latin. The publication of his extensive *Poemata et Inscriptiones* (Poems and Inscriptions) of 1847 may be said to bring the Anglo-Latin tradition to a close. See Michael Lapidge, *Anglo-Latin Literature, 600–899* (1996); id., *Anglo-Latin Literature, 900–1066* (1993); A. G. Rigg, *A History of Anglo-Latin Literature 1066–1422* (1992); J. W. Binns, *Intellectual Culture in Elizabethan and Jacobean England: The Latin Writings of the Age* (1990); L. Bradner, *Musae Anglicanae: A History of Anglo-Latin Poetry 1500–1925* (1940).

Anglo-Norman, or **Anglo-French,** designates the French language as spoken and written in the British Isles from the Norman Conquest until the 14th cent. It was a western type of French which, transplanted to Britain, developed characteristics of its own at an increasing rate. The earliest Anglo-Norman work of real literary merit, *The Voyage of St Brendan*, composed in the first half of the 12th cent., shows relatively few insular traits, whereas the French of the *Contes*

moralisés of Nicole Bozon (early 14th cent.) illustrates the disintegration of later Anglo-Norman. The French of *Gower in his *Mirour de l'omme* is continental French, which was studied in its own right by Englishmen of the later medieval period. Anglo-Norman has many works of a moralizing nature as well as chronicles and practical works drawn from Latin sources. The *Mystère d'Adam* (see ADAM), the first French dramatic work of any moment, was almost certainly written in England. An Anglo-Norman type of French continued to be used for official documents and in English courts of law long after it had ceased to be spoken. See M. D. Legge, *Anglo-Norman Literature and Its Background* (1963).

Anglo-Saxon. The Latin form of the word (*Anglo-Saxonicus*) applies originally to the people and language of the Saxon race who colonized the southern parts of Britain (as distinct from the northern parts colonized by the Angles), to distinguish them from continental Saxons; hence, the 'Anglo' element is adverbial and the word does not mean, as was erroneously supposed, the combination of Angles and Saxons: i.e. the people and language of the whole of England. For the latter the term 'Old English' is more correct. The word became applied in the erroneous way very early; *Ælfric (*c*.1000) refers to the West Saxon he spoke as 'English'. So the 'correct' distinction, made by the *OED* and enforced by modern scholars (especially at Oxford), between 'Old English' and 'Anglo-Saxon' is a somewhat pedantic one (the term 'Anglo-Saxon' is still used at Cambridge, as in the 1941 book by the Chadwicks, *The Study of Anglo-Saxon*); since the revival of such studies in the 16th cent., 'Anglo-Saxon' has been used as the general term, without a sense of geographical distinction.

Anglo-Saxon Chronicle, The, an early record in English of events in England from the beginning of the Christian era to 1154, surviving in seven manuscripts in which Plummer (see below) descried four groups: the Parker Chronicle, named from Archbishop Parker (1504–75); the Abingdon Chronicles; the Worcester Chronicle; and the Laud Chronicle, named from Archbishop *Laud (1573–1645), of which the most famous version is the *Peterborough Chronicle*. The most important and fullest are the Parker and Laud chronicles. It is believed to have developed from the brief annalistic entries in Easter tables, and the entries up to 449 are as brief as the single-sentence Latin annals in those tables. The entries after 449 are sporadically more lengthy, and the most celebrated are those for 449 itself (the arrival of *Hengist and Horsa), for 755 (the story of *Cynewulf and Cyneheard), for 893 to 897 (Alfred's last series of Danish wars), and for the disastrous years of Stephen's reign at the end of the Peterborough Chronicle. Most celebrated of all is the occurrence of the poem on the battle of *Brunanburh (937); other lyrical passages or poetry or semi-poetry occur in the entries for 942, 959, 973 (in praise of King Edgar, ending in verse with his death in 975), 1011 (the martyrdom of Archbishop Ælfheah), and 1040 (the death of Prince Alfred). The organization of the Chronicle's records in a more orderly way is attributed to *Alfred in the course of his literary ventures in the 890s. Editors and commentators have tended to look upon the Chronicle in too narrowly stylistic a spirit and to dismiss much of it as dry or cursory; but its importance in historical, linguistic, and literary terms is enormous.

C. Plummer, *Two of the Saxon Chronicles Parallel* (2 vols, 1892); G. N. Garmonsway (trans.), *The Anglo-Saxon Chronicle* (1953); D. Whitelock, D. C. Douglas, and S. I. Tucker (trans., 1961); A. Gransden, *Historical Writing in England c.550–c.1307* (1974), 32–41.

Angria and **Gondal,** imaginary kingdoms invented by the *Brontë children, as a further development of games and stories inspired by a box of wooden soldiers brought home by their father in 1826. Early games created the Glass Town Confederacy on the west coast of Africa; the capital city, Glass Town or Verdopolis, owed much in its architecture to the engravings of J. *Martin. Later Emily and Anne broke away and invented the kingdom of Gondal, which was to provide the setting for many of Emily's poems, including some of her finest; the initials and names attached to them (A.G.A., J. Brenzaida, R. Alcona, etc.) represent characters in the Gondal epic, of which no prose fragments remain. Charlotte and Branwell, in 1834, jointly created the kingdom of Angria, of which the principal characters were Alexander Percy, the earl of Northangerland, and Arthur Wellesley, marquis of Douro, later known as duke of Zamorna. Charlotte wrote many Angrian tales, most of them tragic and Byronic tales of passion; the tales of 1837–9 ('Julia', 'Mina Laury', 'Caroline Vernon', and 'Henry Hastings') foreshadow many of the themes of her mature novels. See F. E. Ratchford, *The Brontës' Web of Childhood* (1944).

Angry Young Men, a journalistic catchphrase loosely applied to a number of British playwrights and novelists from the mid-1950s, including K. *Amis, J. *Osborne, *Sillitoe, and C. *Wilson, whose political views were radical or anarchic, and who described various forms of social alienation. It is sometimes said to derive from the title of a work by the Irish writer Leslie Paul, *Angry Young Man* (1951).

Animal Farm, a novel by G. *Orwell, published 1945.
It is a satire in fable form on revolutionary and post-revolutionary Russia, and, by extension, on all revolutions. The animals of Mr Jones's farm revolt against their human masters and drive them out, the pigs becoming the leaders. Eventually the pigs, dominated by Napoleon, their chief, become corrupted by power and a new tyranny replaces the old. The ultimate slogan runs 'All animals are equal but some animals are more equal than others.' Napoleon, ruthless and cynical, represents Stalin, and Snowball, the idealist

whom he drives out, Trotsky. Boxer, the noble cart-horse, stands for the strength, simplicity, and good nature of the common man.

Anima Poetae, see NOTEBOOKS, by S. T. *Coleridge.

'Annabel Lee', a poem by E. A. *Poe.

ANNA COMNENA (1083–?1148), historian, was the daughter of the Byzantine Emperor Alexius I, Comnenus. She tried in vain to usurp the succession from her brother to her husband, whose death in 1137 brought an end to her worldly ambitions. She retired to a monastery, where she wrote the *Alexiad*, a history in 15 books, and in the main part a panegyric about her father's life. She figures in Scott's *Count Robert of Paris*, and is the subject of a poem by *Cavafy.

Annales Cambriae, a 10th-cent. series of Welsh annals, of interest for the information they offer about *Gildas and about some aspects of the *Arthur story, such as the battle of Badon, which they place in 518, and the battle of Camlan in 539 in which, they say, Arthur and Modred fell.

Annals of the Parish, a novel by J. *Galt, published 1821.
In it the Revd Michael Balwhidder, a self-important old minister, chronicles with self-revealing irony the events, great and small, that affect the homely lives of the parishioners of Dalmailing in Ayrshire during the period 1760–1810. His solemn juxtaposition of national and domestic events is used with ludicrous effect. The book covers in some detail the social and economic changes affecting the people of the town, and is the source of the term 'utilitarian' adopted by J. S. *Mill.

Anne of Geierstein, or *The Maiden of the Mist*, a novel by Sir W. *Scott, published 1829. It is set in 15th-cent. Switzerland. For his material on the Vehmgericht (one of its most interesting parts), Scott returned to an early favourite, *Goethe's *Götz von Berlichingen*, which he had translated in 1799. Written in the aftermath of Scott's bankruptcy, he found it a laborious task. To his surprise, it enjoyed considerable success.

Annual Register, The, an annual review of events of the past year, founded by *Dodsley and *Burke in 1758, which still survives. The first volume appeared on 15 May 1759, and was highly successful; *Prior described it as 'the best and most comprehensive of all the periodical works, without any admixture of their trash, or any tediousness of detail'. It also published poetry, literary articles, etc. Burke edited it anonymously for several years.

Annus Mirabilis, a poem in quatrains by *Dryden, published 1667.
Its subjects are the Dutch War (1665–6) and the Fire of London. Prefaced by 'Verses to her Highness and Dutchess' [of York], it indicates that even in the 1660s Dryden's optimism about the monarchy, mercantilism,

and the *Royal Society (of which he was a fellow) did not preclude the oblique expression of an ironic vision of history. Queen Elizabeth II, to the bewilderment of some journalists, drew on Dryden's poem in a speech (24 Nov. 1992) referring to the fire of Windsor in that year, using the words 'Annus Horribilis'.

ANOUILH, Jean (1910–87), French dramatist, author of over 50 dramatic works, and, from the mid-1930s, one of the most popular playwrights in France. Among his works are *Le Bal des voleurs* (1938; *Thieves' Carnival*, 1952), *Antigone* (1944; 1946), *L'Invitation au château* (1947; *Ring round the Moon*, 1950), *La Valse des toréadors* (1952; *The Waltz of the Toreadors*, 1956), and a number of plays dealing with historical figures, including *L'Alouette* (1953; *The Lark*, 1955), on *Joan of Arc, *Pauvre Bitos* (1956; *Poor Bitos*, 1964), on Robespierre, and *Becket ou l'honneur de Dieu* (1959; *Becket; or, The Honour of God*, 1960), on *Becket.

ANSELM, St (1033–1109), a native of Aosta in northern Italy and a pupil of *Lanfranc at the abbey of Bec in Normandy, where he succeeded Lanfranc as prior. While he held this office he visited England, where William Rufus appointed him to the see of Canterbury, which had been vacant, in 1093, again in succession to Lanfranc. Anselm accepted the office with reluctance, and when the king again began to tyrannize over it he withdrew to Rome (1097), to return to England at the accession of Henry I (1100). He wrote many theological and philosophical works, the most famous of which are the *Monologion, Proslogion*, and *Cur Deus Homo*. He was the cornerstone of the Augustinian tradition in the Middle Ages with its emphasis on Faith in search of Reason; the original title of his *Proslogion* was *Fides Quaerens Intellectum*. In this book is propounded the famous 'Ontological Argument': if God is defined as a Being than which no greater can be conceived of, then he must exist in reality since otherwise a Being of identical attributes with the further conceivable attribute of existence in reality would be greater. This argument has presented logical problems for philosophers ever since, including B. *Russell at one stage of his career.

Anselm of Canterbury: Works, trans. J. Hopkins and H. Richardson (vol. i, 1974, contains *Monologion and Proslogion*); R. W. Southern, *St Anselm and his Biographer* (1963).

ANSON, George, Baron Anson (1697–1762). He made his famous voyage round the world in 1740–4; an account of it compiled, according to the title-page, by his chaplain Richard Walter appeared in 1748. It is the source of Cowper's poem *'The Castaway', which describes the fate of a seaman washed overboard while manning the shrouds.

ANSTEY, Christopher (1724–1805), remembered as the author of the highly successful *New Bath Guide* (1766), later illustrated by *Cruikshank (1830), which consists of a series of letters in colloquial verse to and from several people, retailing the adventures of Squire Blunderhead and his family in Bath. The manners of the fashionable town and its visitors are described with good humour.

ANSTEY, F., the pseudonym of Thomas Anstey Guthrie (1856–1934), author of many novels of fantasy and humour and of innumerable comic sketches and stories. The great success of *Vice Versa* (1882), in which Mr Bultitude is magically transformed into his son, and vice versa, enabled Anstey to leave the bar in order to write. His long association with *Punch, beginning in 1886, encouraged his skill in parody and burlesque; his series of *Voces Populi, Mr Punch's Pocket Ibsen*, and many others became very popular. His many novels of magic, besides *Vice Versa*, include *Tourmalin's Time Cheques* (1891), *The Brass Bottle* (1900), and *In Brief Authority* (1915).

Anthology, *The Greek*, a collection of some 3,700 epigrams (mostly short poems in elegiac couplets) by more than 300 writers, arranged in subjects in 15 books; the subjects include Christian poems, sculpture, morality, homosexual love, and riddles. The anthology was prepared in *c.* AD 980 by a Byzantine scholar (or scholars) who augmented a collection of ancient epigrams assembled in the previous century with a large number of uncollected poems. The manuscript of the anthology was first discovered by *Salmasius in the Palatine Library at Heidelberg in 1606. Modern editions of the *Anthology* contain a 16th book, which was assembled by the Byzantine monk Planudes in 1299; the Planudean anthology was published in 1494 and was widely read and imitated during the Renaissance.

Antigonus, a Sicilian lord in Shakespeare's *The Winter's Tale*, husband of *Paulina, and notable for his manner of death indicated by the stage direction '*Exit, pursued by a bear*' (III. iii. 58). Shakespeare took the name from *Plutarch; it was also used by Beaumont and Fletcher in *The Humorous Lieutenant.

Anti-Jacobin (1797–8), a short-lived but remarkable journal founded by *Canning and a group of brilliant, high-spirited friends, including G. *Ellis and *Frere, to combat the radical views supported by the *Monthly Magazine, Coleridge's *Watchman, and other *Jacobin influences, and to deride their supporters. Edited by *Gifford, it was a political miscellany of strongly Tory outlook, which included much pungent parody and satire; 'The Needy Knife-Grinder', a parody of *Southey; 'The Loves of the Triangles', a parody of E. Darwin's *The Loves of the Plants; 'The Rovers', a burlesque on the romantic solemnities of German drama; and 'The New Morality', directed against French propaganda, are well-known examples. The *Anti-Jacobin* came to an end in 1798, when many of its chief contributors moved on to the Tory *Quarterly Review*, but its crusade was continued briefly in enfeebled form by the *Anti-Jacobin Review and Magazine*.

antinomian, one who maintains that the moral law is not binding upon Christians, under the 'law of grace'. A sect appeared in Germany in 1535 which was alleged to hold this opinion. (See HUTCHINSONIANS.)

Antipholus, the name of the twin brothers, sons of Egeon, in Shakespeare's *The Comedy of Errors*.

Antiquary, The, a novel by Sir W. *Scott, published 1816.

A gallant young officer, known as Major Neville, believed to be illegitimate, falls in love in England with Isabella Wardour who, deferring to the prejudices of her father Sir Arthur Wardour, repulses him. Assuming the name of Lovel, he follows her to Scotland, meeting on the way Jonathan Oldbuck, laird of Monkbarns, a learned and garrulous antiquary and a neighbour of Sir Arthur. Lovel saves the lives of Sir Arthur and his daughter at the peril of his own and rescues Sir Arthur from the financial ruin that the deceptions of the German charlatan Dousterswivel have brought on him. Finally he turns out to be the son and heir of the earl of Glenallan and marries Isabella. The characters of the young lovers are without interest or colour and their predicament is unconvincing. The charm of the book, Scott's 'chief favourite among all his novels', lies in the character of Oldbuck, based, according to Scott, on a friend of his boyhood, George Constable, but a recognizable portrait of Scott himself, and in the minor characters: the Mucklebackit family, the gossips in the village post office, the shrewd and kindly Edie Ochiltree, the king's bedesman. The ironic deflation of the various antiquarian and heroic pretensions of the sub-plot are in effective contrast to the overblown Gothic background to the main plot.

antistrophe ('turning about'), in a Greek chorus, the response to the strophe, recited as the chorus proceeded in the opposite direction to that followed in the strophe. See ODE.

antithesis, a figure of speech in which sharply contrasted ideas are juxtaposed in a balanced or parallel phrase or grammatical structure, as in 'Hee for God only, shee for God in him' (J. *Milton).

Antonio, (1) the title character in Shakespeare's *The Merchant of Venice*, who opens the play with the words 'In sooth, I know not why I am so sad', and puts his wealth at the disposal of his friend *Bassanio; (2) the sea-captain who devotedly rescues the shipwrecked Sebastian in *Twelfth Night*; (3) the brother of Leonato in *Much Ado about Nothing*; (4) the father of *Proteus in *The Two Gentlemen of Verona*; (5) the usurping brother of *Prospero in *The Tempest*.

Antonio and Mellida, a two-part play by J. *Marston, printed 1602, probably acted two years earlier; it provided Jonson with materials for his ridicule of Marston in *The Poetaster*.

In Part I of the play Antonio, son of Andrugio, duke of Genoa, is in love with Mellida, daughter of Piero, duke of Venice. The two states are at war and Genoa has been defeated, and a price set in Venice on the heads of Antonio and Andrugio. Antonio, disguised as an Amazon, comes to Piero's court to see Mellida. Mellida flees with Antonio but is captured. Andrugio offers himself as a victim to Piero, who appears to relent and assents to the marriage of Antonio and Mellida, and the first part closes joyfully.

In Part II Piero reveals his true character. He kills Andrugio, contrives the dishonour of Mellida in order to prevent the match, plots the death of Antonio, and gains the hand of Andrugio's widow. Mellida dies broken-hearted. Antonio, urged by the ghost of his father, assumes the disguise of a fool and kills Piero.

Antony and Cleopatra, a tragedy by *Shakespeare probably written 1606–7, not printed until the First *Folio of 1623. Its chief source is the *Life of Antony* by *Plutarch, as translated by Sir T. *North, which Shakespeare followed extremely closely in places, as in Enobarbus's famous speech beginning: 'The barge she sat in, like a burnish'd throne, | Burn'd on the water' (II. ii. 195–6). Minor sources include the plays by the countess of *Pembroke and S. *Daniel.

The play presents Mark Antony, the great soldier and noble prince, at Alexandria, enthralled by the beauty of the Egyptian queen Cleopatra. Recalled by the death of his wife Fulvia and political developments, he tears himself from Cleopatra and returns to Rome, where the estrangement between him and Octavius Caesar is terminated by his marriage to Octavia, Caesar's sister, an event which provokes the intense jealousy of Cleopatra. But the reconciliation is short-lived, and Antony leaves Octavia and returns to Egypt. At the battle of Actium, the flight of the Egyptian squadron is followed by the retreat of Antony, pursued to Alexandria by Caesar. There, after a momentary success, Antony is finally defeated. On the false report of Cleopatra's death, he falls upon his sword. He is borne to the monument where Cleopatra has taken refuge and dies in her arms. Cleopatra, fallen into Caesar's power but determined not to grace his triumph, takes her own life by the bite of an asp. See also ALL FOR LOVE.

APELLES (fl. 330–320 BC), a Greek painter, famous in antiquity. The names and in some cases descriptions of 30 of his pictures are known, but as no ancient copies or imitations of them survive, the quality of his work remains unknown. Born on the island of Cos, he won the favour of *Alexander the Great, who would not allow anyone else to paint his portrait and who is reputed to have given Apelles his mistress, Pancaspe (the *Campaspe of English literature), when the artist fell in love with her while painting her in the nude. After Alexander's death Apelles went to the court of Ptolemy I of Egypt, where he produced the 'Calumny' which *Botticelli tried to recreate on the basis of *Lucian's account. He was the inventor of the self-portrait, and some of the conventions he established—

representing his sitters full or three-quarter face and, with more crowded compositions, stringing out his figures in a line—were widely copied during the Renaissance.

Apemantus, the 'churlish philosopher' in Shakespeare's *Timon of Athens*.

aphorism, a term transferred from the 'Aphorisms of Hippocrates' to other sententious statements of the principles of physical science, and later (e.g. in Coleridge's *Aids to Reflection*, which are divided into 'Aphorisms' and 'Comments') to statements of principles generally. Thence it has come to mean any short pithy statement into which much thought or observation is compressed. J. S. *Mill wrote a fragment on aphorisms, and J. *Morley a short discourse on the same subject. See *The Oxford Book of Aphorisms* (1983), compiled by John Gross.

Apocalypse, the, from a Greek verb meaning 'to disclose', a 'revelation' or an 'unveiling', and the title given to the book of Revelation in the NT. The term 'apocalyptic literature' is used in a broader sense to describe prophetic writings generally, of a range which includes many of the works of *Blake, of *Yeats (e.g. 'The Second Coming'), D. *Lessing's *The Four-Gated City*, the 'disaster' novels of J. G. *Ballard, and other *science fiction writers, etc. D. *Lodge has described *Mailer's *The Armies of the Night* and *Barth's *Giles Goat-Boy* as 'products of the apocalyptic imagination' (*The Novelist at the Crossroads*, 1971), a mode of imagination which many have seen as peculiarly strong in the 20th cent. when, in Mailer's words, 'reality is no longer realistic'. See also F. *Kermode, *The Sense of an Ending* (1967), which discusses the implications for fictional narrative of the Judaeo-Christian view of history as linear, i.e. as possessing a beginning, a middle in which narrator and reader exist, and a necessarily different ending.

Apocrypha, the, in its special sense, those books included in the Septuagint and Vulgate versions of the OT which were not written in Hebrew and not counted genuine by the Jews, and which at the Reformation were excluded from the Sacred Canon by the Protestant party, as having no well-grounded claims to inspired authorship. They are 1 and 2 Esdras, Tobit, Judith, the Rest of Esther, the Wisdom of Solomon, Ecclesiasticus, Baruch (with the Epistle of Jeremiah), the Song of the Three Holy Children, the History of Susanna, Bel and the Dragon, the Prayer of Manasses, 1 and 2 Maccabees.

The texts of the Apocryphal Gospels, Acts, Epistles, and Apocalypses are printed in *The Apocryphal New Testament*, trans. M. R. *James (1924).

APOLLINAIRE, Guillaume (1880–1918), French poet, prose writer, and art critic. He was a prominent figure in the avant-garde in Paris during the early years of the 20th cent., and an ardent supporter of contemporary developments both in poetry and in painting (*Méditations esthétiques: les peintres cubistes*, 1913; English trans., 1944). His principal volumes of poetry are *Alcools* (1913, English trans., 1964), and *Calligrammes* (1918).

APOLLODORUS (2nd cent. BC), Athenian grammarian. He was known to have written about the gods, and an extant treatise on mythology, the *Bibliotheca*, was attributed to him. First printed in 1555, this work was widely used in the second half of the 16th cent. and, directly or indirectly, provided *Johnson and *Milton with some of their mythological material.

APOLLONIUS RHODIUS (of Rhodes) (fl. end 3rd cent. BC), Alexandrian poet. He chose for his epic a conventionally heroic legend, 'The Voyage of the Argo', but he treated his subject with psychological insight, emphasized its romantic features, and left his readers keenly aware of his own presence as authoritative narrator. In short, he introduced into the genre many elements that were not found in *Homer. Apollonius had an important disciple in *Virgil. There are echoes of his verse in *Paradise Lost*, and he was naturally W. *Morris's main source for *The Life and Death of Jason*.

Apollyon, 'The Destroyer', the angel of the bottomless pit (Rev. 9: 2). He figures in Bunyan's *Pilgrim's Progress*.

Apologia pro Vita Sua, see NEWMAN, J. H.

Apology for Poetry, An, see DEFENCE OF POETRY, A.

Apology for Smectymnuus, see SMECTYMNUUS.

aposiopesis, a rhetorical artifice in which the speaker comes to a sudden halt in the middle of a sentence, as if unable or unwilling to proceed. See *Sterne's definition and illustration in *Tristram Shandy*, ii. 6.

Apostles, the, an exclusive intellectual society (officially 'the Cambridge Conversazione Society') formed in Cambridge in 1820, for the purpose of friendship and formal discussion. During the 19th cent. members included A. *Hallam, *Tennyson, *Milnes, and R. C. *Trench, and the 20th cent. saw a new age of brilliance, largely inspired by the influence of G. E. *Moore, with members such as *Keynes, *Strachey, B. *Russell, L. *Woolf, and E. M. *Forster. Members are elected for life.

apostrophe (Greek, 'to turn away'), a figure of speech in which the writer rhetorically addresses a dead or absent person or abstraction, e.g. 'Milton! thou shouldst be living at this hour' (*Wordsworth, 'London, 1802').

Appius and Virginia, (1) a tragedy traditionally attributed to *Webster, but by some authorities to *Heywood, in whole or part. R. *Brooke first seriously questioned the Webster attribution in 1913, and suggested Heywood; F. L. *Lucas in his 1927 edition of Webster argues for a distribution of scenes between the two playwrights; and A. M. Clark concludes in 'The Authorship of *Appius and Virginia*' (*MLR* Jan. 1921) that Webster revised the play, but 'the bulk of the play is Heywood's alone'. The date of production is uncertain (?1603–34) and it appears not to have been printed until 1654. The plot is taken from the classical legend (see VIRGINIA) which forms one of the stories in Painter's *Palace of Pleasure*; (2) a tragedy by J. *Dennis.

Apprentice's Vade Mecum, The, a handbook by S. *Richardson.

APULEIUS (*c.* AD 123–after 170), North African Roman poet, philosopher, and rhetorician, whose best-known work, *Metamorphoses* or *The Golden Ass*, was popular from the 14th cent. onwards and became a quarry for the novella, for which its intercalated stories served as a model. *Boccaccio borrowed three and others appeared in the 15th-cent. *Cent Nouvelles nouvelles*, both of which were translated into English. Generally, the adventures of the ass stand at the beginning of that *picaresque tradition which eventually produced *Tom Jones*. Special mention must be made of one story, *Cupid and Psyche*.

AQUINAS, St Thomas (*c.*1225–74), an Italian philosopher and Dominican friar from Aquino in southern Italy, the greatest of the medieval Scholastic theologians. He represents in his writings, especially in the *Summa Theologica*, the culmination of Scholastic philosophy, the harmony of faith and reason, and in particular the reconciliation of Christian theology with Aristotelian philosophy (see SCHOLASTICISM). The *Summa*, which is unfinished, is a vast synthesis of the moral and political sciences, brought within a theological and metaphysical framework. He was called the 'Doctor Angelicus', and by his school companions 'the Dumb Ox'. His followers are called Thomists, and they are still an active school in contemporary philosophy, especially in France. He is a very important influence on *Dante's *Divina commedia* whose philosophical framework is based on Aquinas (see *Paradiso*, x–xiii). His other major works are the *Summa Contra Gentiles* and a series of commentaries on *Aristotle. He promoted and used the translation of the works of Aristotle from Greek into Latin by William of Moerbeke. See F. C. Copleston, *Aquinas* (1955); *Summa*, trans. in 20 vols (1911–25), by Fathers of the Dominican Province.

Arabia Deserta, see DOUGHTY.

Arabian Nights Entertainments, or *The Thousand and One Nights*, is a collection written in Arabic which was made known in Europe through the French translation (from a Syrian manuscript) of Antoine Galland (1646–1715), whose version appeared between 1704 and 1717. An anonymous 'Grub Street' version appeared in English *c.*1708, and E. W. *Lane's bowdlerized version appeared in 1838–40. The first claim to a complete English translation was by John Payne (1842–1916), which appeared in a limited edition, published by the Villon Society, 1882–4. This was followed by the most celebrated version, by Sir Richard *Burton (1885–8), also published through a subscription society to avoid prosecution for obscenity: despite its dependence on Payne, its audacity, and its eccentric and archaic vocabulary, this was a critical and financial success, though all of these rival versions had their defenders. A later French version (1899–1904) by J. C. Mardrus (1868–1949), though not now considered of high scholarship, was much admired for its literary and erotic qualities by *Gide and *Proust, and at one point T. E. *Lawrence contemplated translating it into English.

The tales derive from Persian, Arabic, and, it has been argued, Indian sources, and most are set in Baghdad, Cairo, and Damascus. The framework (the story of the king who killed his wives successively on the morning of the consummation of their marriage, until he married the clever *Scheherazade, who saved her life by the stories she told him) is taken from a lost book of Persian fairy tales, called *Hazar Afsanah* (A Thousand Tales) which was translated into Arabic *c.* AD 850; it is mentioned by the Arabic encyclopaedist al-Mas'udi (*d.* AD 956). Other stories of different origins were added to this at various dates by professional storytellers, and a standardized collection by an unknown Egyptian editor appeared towards the end of the 18th cent. Dating of the stories is difficult: Burton believed that the Sindbad tales, which were added to the cycle in the early modern period, dated back to the 8th cent., and the latest came from the 16th cent. An attempt to establish the archetypal manuscript of the *Nights* has been made by Muhsin Mahdi (*Alf Layla wa-Layla*, 1984).

The stories, dismissed by most Arab scholars as merely popular and no true part of the classical Arabic literature, captivated the European imagination, and contributed greatly to the vogue for Oriental tales in the 18th and early 19th cents. Their influence continued through the 20th cent., and may be seen in the work of writers as varied as *Barth, *Borges, *Byatt, A. *Carter, *Pasolini, and *Rushdie. See *The Arabian Nights: A Companion* by R. Irwin (1994).

ARAGON, Louis (1897–1982), French poet, novelist, essayist, journalist, and political activist. He began his career under the influence of *Dada, and later became one of the leading exponents of *Surrealism. In 1919, with *Breton and Soupault, he founded the review *Littérature*, and in 1924, with Breton, *La Révolution surréaliste*. His first collections of poetry were *Feu de joie* (1920) and *Le Mouvement perpétuel* (1926). In 1927 he joined the Communist Party, and finally broke with the surrealist movement in 1932. During the Second World War he became one of the most popular of French Resistance poets, with *Le Crève-cœur* (1941), *Les Yeux d'Elsa* (1942), *Le Musée Grévin* (1943), and *La*

Diane française (1945). His novels include *Le Paysan de Paris* (1926), *La Chasse au Snark* (1929), *Les Cloches de Bâle* (1934; *The Bells of Basel*, 1936), *Les Beaux Quartiers* (1936; *Residential Quarter*, 1938), and *La Semaine Sainte* (1958; *Holy Week*, 1961).

Araygnement of Paris, The, a pastoral play in verse by G. *Peele, published 1584.

It was written for and played before Queen Elizabeth, whose beauty and virtue are duly celebrated. Paris is tending his flocks on Ida, with Oenone his wife, when he is called on to decide to which of the three goddesses, Juno, Pallas, or Venus, the golden apple shall be awarded. He decides in favour of Venus, who carries away Paris, leaving Oenone disconsolate. Juno and Pallas arraign Paris before the gods of partiality in his judgement. The case is referred to Diana. She evades the delicate choice by awarding the apple to the nymph Eliza, 'our Zabeta fayre', i.e. Queen Elizabeth.

ARBER, Edward (1836–1912). He began his career as an admiralty clerk, 1854–78, but studied English literature at King's College, London, and in 1881 became professor of English at Mason College, Birmingham. He produced *English Reprints* (1868–71), *A Transcript of the Registers of the Company of Stationers of London, 1554–1640* (1875–94), and *Term Catalogues, 1668–1709* (1903–6).

ARBLAY, Madame d', see BURNEY, F.

ARBUCKLE, James (d. 1742), Irish poet, educated at Glasgow, where he clashed with the Calvinist authorities for his active part in politics and student dramatics. He espoused the philosophy of the third earl of *Shaftesbury. In association with *Hutcheson he wrote moral and aesthetic essays which were serialized in the *Dublin Weekly Journal* (1725–7) and later reissued as *Hibernicus's Letters* (1729), and he attempted a short-lived Dublin periodical, the *Tribune*, in 1729. His student poetry was published in broadsheets or in *The Edinburgh Miscellany* (1720). He was at one time befriended by *Swift and in 1730 published the parody 'A Panegyric on the Reverend D—n S——t' formerly ascribed to Swift himself. Some classical translations and other manuscript poetry are now in the National Library of Wales.

ARBUTHNOT, John (1667–1735), MD of St Andrews and from 1705 physician to Queen Anne, whose death was a blow to his prosperity. In 1711 he formed a close friendship with *Swift, and he was acquainted with most of the literary men of his day including *Pope, who in 1735 was to address to him one of his finest satirical epistles, generally known as *Prologue to the Satires*. Arbuthnot's *History of *John Bull*, a collection of pamphlets issued anonymously in 1712 advocating the termination of the war with France, was included in Pope and Swift's *Miscellanies* of 1727. In 1712 he also published a satiric pamphlet, *The Art of Political Lying*. He was a member of the *Scriblerus Club and

principal author of the *Memoirs of *Martinus Scriblerus*, which were published with Pope's *Works* in 1741. He and Pope assisted *Gay in writing the unsuccessful comedy *Three Hours after Marriage* (1717). Many anonymous works were attributed to him, and he also wrote on mathematics and on medical matters; his *An Essay Concerning the Nature of Ailments* (1731) is a farsighted account of the importance of diet, though ironically he himself died of illnesses associated with overeating. He published one poem, *ΓΝΩΘΙ ΣΕΑΥΤΟΝ* (*Know Thyself*, 1734, anon.). He was a much loved figure, witty, kind-hearted, and absentminded, and his satires are plain, clear, homely, and predominantly good-natured. Dr *Johnson described him as 'the most universal genius' (*Life and Works*, ed. G. A. Aitken, 1892).

'Arcades, Part of an Entertainment Presented to the Countess Dowager of Darby at Harefield, by som Noble Persons of Her Family', by *Milton, written ?1630–?3 possibly at the suggestion of his friend Henry *Lawes, published 1645.

This short piece consists of a song by nymphs and shepherds as they approach the seat of state of the countess, an address to them by the Genius of the Wood, and two further songs. The particular event which occasioned this celebration is not known. See *Milton's Aristocratic Entertainments* (1985) by Cedric C. Brown.

Arcadia, a bleak and mountainous district in the central Peloponnese which became, thanks to references in *Virgil's *Eclogues*, the traditional and incongruous location of the idealized world of the *pastoral. Virgil himself was keenly aware of the clash between the realistic and idealizing purposes of the genre, and his use of the term may have reflected this awareness. But the writers who revived the pastoral in the Renaissance knew nothing about the real Arcadia and the idealized landscape reigns supreme in their work.

Arcadia, a series of verse eclogues connected by prose narrative, published 1504 by *Sannazar, occupied with the loves, laments, and other doings of various shepherds in Arcadia. The work, which was immensely popular, was a link between the *pastorals of *Theocritus and *Virgil and those of *Montemayor, *Sidney, *Spenser, and later writers.

Arcadia, The, a prose romance by Sir P. *Sidney, including poems and pastoral eclogues in a wide variety of verse forms. It exists in two versions: the first, completed by 1581, and much of it written at *Wilton, is known as the *Old Arcadia*. Its survival as an independent work was discovered by Bertram Dobell in 1906–7. The second version, now known as the *New Arcadia*, was Sidney's radical revision, made about 1583–4 but never completed. It breaks down in the third of the original five books, having already run to twice the length of the original. It was this revised version which was first printed, on its own in 1590, with chapter divisions and summaries 'not of Sir *Philip Sidneis* dooing', and then in 1593 and thereafter with books iii–v of the *Old Arcadia* added to make a complete-seeming but hybrid work. It was the hybrid *Arcadia* only that was available to readers until the 20th cent.

The *Old Arcadia* is in five 'Books or Acts', sometimes quasi-dramatic in use of dialogue, interspersed with a large number of poems and songs. The first four books are followed by pastoral eclogues on themes linked or contrasted with the main narrative. The story is of the attempts of Arcadia's ruler, the foolish old duke Basilius, to prevent the fulfilment of an oracle by withdrawing to two rustic 'lodges' with his wife Gynecia and their daughters Pamela and Philoclea. Two young princes, Musidorus and Pyrocles, gain access to the retired court by disguising themselves as, respectively, a shepherd and an Amazon. A complicated series of intrigues ensues, with Basilius and Gynecia both falling in love with the disguised Pyrocles; Musidorus meanwhile becomes enmeshed with the family of Dametas, an ill-bred herdsman who has been made Pamela's guardian, his shrewish wife Miso, and foolish daughter Mopsa. Pyrocles succeeds in seducing Philoclea and Musidorus attempts to elope with Pamela, but their schemes go awry when Basilius appears to die of a potion believed by his wife to be an aphrodisiac, and Pyrocles and Philoclea are discovered in bed by Dametas. The climax of the narrative is a trial presided over by Euarchus, the just ruler of Macedon, who sentences Gynecia to be buried alive and Pyrocles and Musidorus to be executed. Their disguises and assumed names prevent Euarchus from recognizing the young men as his own son and nephew, but even when their identities are revealed he asserts that 'If rightly I have judged, then rightly have I judged mine own children.' The day is saved by Basilius' awakening from what turns out to have been only a sleeping potion. Among the minor characters Philisides, a melancholy gentleman-poet, is a version of Sidney himself. Strephon and Klaius, two shepherds in love with the mysterious Urania, recite two of the most elaborate love-complaints in the romance, the first being the double sestina 'Ye goat-herd gods, that love the grassy mountains'. Other memorable poems include the anatomical praise of Philoclea's beauties 'What tongue can her perfections tell', the echo poem in hexameters 'Fair rocks, goodly rivers, sweet woods, when shall I see peace?', the asclepiadics 'O sweet woods, the delight of solitariness', the beast-fable on tyranny 'As I my little flock on Ister bank', and the sonnet 'My true love hath my heart, and I have his'.

No new poems were added in the *New Arcadia*, but the method of narration was made far more complex, both stylistically and thematically. Major new characters include Basilius' wicked sister-in-law Cecropia and her well-meaning but unfortunate son Amphialus, who is in love with Philoclea. The first two books are

enlarged by the addition of tournaments and courtly spectacles and by detailed accounts of the exploits of Pyrocles and Musidorus before they reached Arcadia. In the third revised book mock battles give way to real ones, after the two Arcadian princesses and the disguised Pyrocles have been taken captive by Cecropia; their sufferings in prison are powerfully described, in particular those of the patient and dignified Pamela, whose prayer in prison was later to be allegedly used by Charles I:

> Let calamity be the exercise, but not the overthrow of my virtue: let their power prevail, but prevail not to destruction: let my greatness be their prey: let my pain be the sweetnes of their revenge: let them (if so it seem good unto thee) vex me with more and more punishment—but, ô Lord, let never their wickedness have such a hand, but that I may carry a pure mind in a pure bodye. (Bk III, ch. 6)

*Milton in *Eikonoklastes* attacked the monarch for his use of a prayer from a 'vain amatorious Poem'. The *New Arcadia* breaks off in mid-sentence just as rescue seems to be at hand for the imprisoned and besieged princesses.

The composite *Arcadia*, as printed from 1593 onwards, was attacked by *Hazlitt as 'one of the greatest monuments of the abuse of intellectual power upon record', mainly because of its prose style. T. S. *Eliot, more damningly still, called it 'a monument of dulness'. It was, however, a highly popular book throughout the 17th cent., and its plot material was frequently plundered by dramatists. Shakespeare based the Gloucester plot of *King Lear* on Sidney's story of 'the *Paphlagonian* unkinde king', and *Richardson took the name of his first heroine, Pamela, from Sidney's romance. The later 20th cent. showed signs that it was beginning to be appreciated again. C. S. *Lewis said that 'What a man thinks of it, far more than what he thinks of Shakespeare or Spenser or Donne, tests the depth of his sympathy with the sixteenth century.' Jean Robertson edited the *Old Arcadia* in 1973. *The New Arcadia*, ed. Victor Skretkowicz, was published in 1987.

Archer, (1) a character in Farquhar's *The Beaux' Stratagem*; (2) Isabel, the heroine of H. James's *The Portrait of a Lady*.

ARCHER, William (1856–1924). He was born in Scotland, educated in Edinburgh, and spent large parts of his boyhood in Norway, where he became acquainted with the works of *Ibsen. He became a drama critic in London in 1879 (see THEATRE CRITICISM) and worked thereafter for various papers, exercising much influence. The establishment of Ibsen and of G. B. *Shaw owed much to his encouragement. He translated Ibsen's *Pillars of Society*, which became in 1880 the first Ibsen play to be produced in London, where it made little impression. Archer published *English Dramatists of Today* in 1882, a study of *Henry Irving*

(1883), and *Masks or Faces?* (1888). In 1889 his translation of *A Doll's House* was produced, and gave rise to much antagonism, which increased with the production of *Ghosts* and *Hedda Gabler* in 1891. In 1890 Archer published a study of *Macready and then in 1891 his five-volume edition of Ibsen's prose dramas in translation (some with collaboration). He and his brother produced a translation of *Peer Gynt* in 1892 and Archer's own collected criticism, *A Theatre World*, appeared in 1897. The collected works of Ibsen appeared in 1906–7, and in the latter year Archer's detailed proposals, with *Granville-Barker, for a *National Theatre. In 1919 he assisted with the establishment of the New Shakespeare Company at Stratford-upon-Avon. In *The Old Drama and the New* (1923) he pressed the merits of Ibsen, Shaw, and *Galsworthy, among others; and in the same year his own play, *The Green Goddess*, was produced with great success in the USA and later in London. A biography by P. Whitebrook was published in 1993.

archetype, a primary symbol, action, setting, or character-type that is found repeatedly in myth, folklore, and literature. Religious mystics have at various times proposed that there is a universal symbolic language of dreams and visions; and in the 20th cent. this notion was encouraged by the speculative anthropology of J. G. *Frazer and the psychology of *Jung, who claimed that human beings shared a 'collective unconscious' for which archetypal images, whether in dreams or in imaginative literature, provided evidence. Archetypal criticism (see also MYTH CRITICISM) under Jung's influence has sought to trace the recurrence of such symbols and types as the Earth Mother, the Quest, the Paradisal Garden, and the Trickster. Maud Bodkin's *Archetypal Patterns in Poetry* (1934) was an early example. The wider significance of archetypes in literature was explored by N. *Frye.

Archgallo, see ARTEGAL.

Archimago, or **Archimage,** in Spenser's *Faerie Queene*, is the great enchanter, symbolizing Hypocrisy, who deceives *Una by assuming the appearance of the *Redcrosse Knight (I. i). His deceits are exposed and Archimago is 'layd full low in dungeon deepe' (I. xii. 36). From this he emerges in Bk II to seek vengeance on Sir *Guyon for what he has suffered at the hands of the Redcrosse Knight, and employs *Braggadochio for the purpose.

Arch-poet, the, the name given to the anonymous German writer of *Goliardic Latin poetry whose patron was Rainald of Dassel, archchancellor of Frederick Barbarossa and archbishop of Cologne. His best-known poem is the 'Confession' (see F. J. E. Raby, *The Oxford Book of Medieval Latin Verse*, 1959 etc., No. 18, 263–6). The term was used by *Pope and *Fielding as equivalent to *poet laureate.

Arcite, see PALAMON AND ARCITE.

Arden, (1) a large forest in Warwickshire often referred to in romance literature. In Drayton's *Poly-Olbion* it extends from the Severn to the Trent (XIII. 16); (2) the forest which is the setting for the pastoral parts of Shakespeare's *As You Like It*, often assumed to be identical with (1) and perhaps so intended by Shakespeare, but also suggesting the forest of Arden northeast of Bordeaux and (more traditionally) the forest of Ardennes in what is now Belgium; (3) the surname of Shakespeare's mother Mary; (4), based on (1) and (2), the distinguishing name of a series of scholarly editions of Shakespeare's plays initiated by W. J. Craig and R. H. Case in 1899, and revised under the general editorship of Una Ellis-Fermor, H. F. Brooks, H. Jenkins, and Brian Morris (1946–82); a third series under the general editorship of Richard Proudfoot, Ann Thompson, and David Scott Kastan was begun in 1995.

ARDEN, John (1930–   ), playwright, born in Barnsley, Yorkshire, and educated at the universities of Cambridge and Edinburgh, where he studied architecture. In 1957 (the year in which he married Margaretta D'Arcy) he had his first professional production, at the *Royal Court, of *The Waters of Babylon*, a grotesque, satirical, sprawling play about a corrupt municipal lottery organized by a slum landlord. This was followed by *Live Like Pigs* (1958), dealing with social conflict and violence on a housing estate. *Serjeant Musgrave's Dance* (1959), set in a colliery town in the north of England in 1860–80, shows Musgrave, a deserter from the British army, attempting to exact revenge for the death of a colleague, but finding that violence breeds violence: as his co-deserter concludes, 'You can't cure the pox by further whoring.' Arden here mixes a rich, idiosyncratic, semi-historical prose with ballad and verse, as he does in *Armstrong's Last Goodnight* (1964), another fable about violence, set in the Border country in the 1530s, and figuring Sir D. *Lindsay as principal opponent of the freebooter John Armstrong of Gilnockie, whose hanging ends the play; Arden in a preface says he has composed a 'Babylonish dialect' based on the Scots of *Dunbar, *Henryson, and *MacDiarmid, inspired by A. *Miller's method in *The Crucible*. In a preface to *The Workhouse Donkey* (1963), a play about municipal corruption, Arden claims that 'the theatre must be catholic' and celebrate the Dionysian attributes of 'noise, disorder, drunkenness, lasciviousness, nudity, generosity, corruption, fertility and ease'. Widely praised as one of the most innovatory dramatists of the 1960s, his later plays (written with M. D'Arcy) have been less exuberant and ambiguous, and more deliberately socialist and doctrinaire. His first novel, *Silence among the Weapons*, a rambling, picaresque work set in the 1st cent. BC, appeared in 1982.

Arden of Feversham, *The Tragedy of Mr,* a play published 1592, author unknown. It has been attributed to Shakespeare, and its latest editor, M. L. Wine

(1973), claims that internal stylistic evidence qualifies it for a place in the 'Shakespeare apocrypha'.

The play deals with the persistent and eventually successful attempts of Mistress Arden and her paramour Mosby to murder Arden: they hire two murderers, Black Will and Shakebag. The crime is discovered, and Mosby and Mrs Arden executed. The play's source is an account in *Holinshed of an actual murder committed in Feb. 1551. *Lillo wrote a play on the same subject.

ARDIZZONE, Edward Jeffrey Irving (1900–79), painter, watercolourist, and printmaker, and one of the best known of 20th-cent. illustrators, of both adult and children's books.

ARENDT, Hannah (1906–75), historian, philosopher, and social scientist, born in Hanover, educated at the universities of Marburg and Freiburg and in Heidelberg, where she studied under Karl Jaspers (some of whose works she edited). She left Germany in 1933, worked in France for the immigration of Jewish refugee children to Palestine, then moved to the United States (1941) where she later became a citizen. Her works include *On Revolution* (1963) and an influential analysis of the trial in 1961 of the Nazi leader Adolf Eichmann, *Eichmann in Jerusalem: A Report on the Banality of Evil* (1963, and subsequently revised), which proved an important contribution to the literature of the *Holocaust. She was a friend of Mary *McCarthy, and their correspondence was published as *Between Friends*, ed. C. Brightman (1995).

Areopagitica: *A Speech of Mr John Milton for the Liberty of the Unlicenc'd Printing, to the Parliament of England,* by *Milton, published in 1644. The title imitates the *Areopagiticus* of the Athenian orator Isocrates, which was addressed to the Council that met on the Areopagus in Athens. This discourse, one of Milton's most impassioned prose works, was an unlicensed and unregistered publication. It attempted to persuade Parliament to repeal the licensing order of 14 June 1643, which effectively reinstated the Stuart machinery of press censorship. Milton opens with a selective history of licensing, identifying it with the Papal Inquisition, which he satirizes. He sanctions the reader's freedom to judge for himself between good and bad books, since good and evil are inseparable in the fallen world ('from out the rind of one apple tasted . . . two twins cleaving together') and the condition of virtue is the recognition of evil and the power to resist it: 'I cannot praise a fugitive and cloistered virtue.' Milton goes on to argue that the regulation of reading is in practice ineffective, ironically suggesting that it logically entails the censorship of all 'recreations and pastimes'. Finally, he analyses Truth as complex and many-angled, scattered in the fallen world, to be recovered by sifting and debate. He quotes the case of *Galileo, whom he recalls meeting under house arrest, 'grown old, a prisoner to the Inquisition'. Milton builds

his rhetoric to a magnificent exhortation to the 'Lords and Commons of England' to consider 'what Nation it is whereof ye are . . . A Nation not slow and dull, but of a quick, ingenious and piercing spirit . . . methinks I see in my mind a noble and puissant nation rousing herself like a strong man after sleep, and shaking her invincible locks. Methinks I see her as an eagle mewing her mighty youth.' But this optimistic vision is burdened with anxiety lest the fragile concord of political and religious interests break down: Milton insists on limits to tolerance, which he does not extend to Roman Catholics, regarded as the enemy of Truth and of the Protestant state.

Arethusa, (1) a legendary fountain in Ortygia, named after a nymph with whom the river-god Alpheus fell in love: she fled from him to Ortygia, where Artemis transformed her into a fountain, but Alpheus, flowing beneath the sea, was united with her; (2) a character in Beaumont and Fletcher's *Philaster.*

ARETINO, Pietro, or the Aretine (1492–1556), born at Arezzo in Italy, whence his name. He was author of five comedies and a tragedy, and also of satires and other works of a scandalous or licentious character. He is frequently mentioned in English works of the Elizabethan and later periods and differently appreciated, in comments ranging from 'It was one of the wittiest knaves that ever God made' of Nashe (*The Unfortunate Traveller*) to 'that notorious ribald of Arezzo' of Milton (*Areopagitica*).

Argalia, in Boiardo's *Orlando innamorato*, the brother of *Angelica.

Argante, (1) in the *Brut* of *Laʒamon, *Morgan le Fay, of whose name it may be a corruption. She is the fairy queen to whom Arthur, after the last battle, is borne to be healed of his wounds in Avalon; (2) in Spenser's *Faerie Queene* (III. vii), a mighty and licentious giantess, typifying lust, daughter of Typhoeus the Titan.

Argantes, in Tasso's *Jerusalem Delivered*, a fierce Circassian, a champion on the pagan side, finally killed by Tancred.

Argosy (1) *A Magazine of Tales, Travels, Essays and Poems*, a periodical owned and edited 1865–87 by Mrs H. *Wood, who was herself a major contributor: it published work by many leading writers, including A. *Trollope, C. *Kingsley, and C. *Reade, and it survived until 1901; (2) *The World's Best Stories* (1926–40; as *The Argosy of Complete Stories*, 1940–74), consisted largely of reprints of work by established writers, including *Conrad, H. E. *Bates, *Maugham, *Sansom, and many others.

ARGYLE, Archibald Campbell, eighth earl, first marquess of (1598–1661), who took a prominent part in the events in Scotland that contributed to the downfall of Charles I. He figures in Scott's *A Legend of Montrose*, where his character is contrasted with that of his great rival, the earl of *Montrose. He was beheaded.

ARGYLE, John Campbell, second duke of (1678–1743), a prime agent in bringing about the union of England and Scotland and a distinguished military commander (he suppressed Mar's rising of 1715). He figures in Scott's *The Heart of Midlothian*.

Arian heresy, named after its promulgator Arius, a Libyan priest born about the middle of the 3rd cent. and parish priest near Alexandria *c.*310, declared that God the Son, because begotten by the Father, must have an origin in time and therefore is not 'consubstantial' with the Father. This breach of the doctrine of the Trinity was condemned at the Council of Nicaea, summoned by Constantine in 325, which produced the Nicene Creed as the official declaration of the Church. Most of the 'barbarian' tribes who overran the Western Roman Empire (except the Franks, Angles, and Saxons) were converted by Arian preachers, so the heretical doctrine remained active up to the 6th cent. in the beliefs of such leaders as Alaric.

Ariel, (1) an airy spirit in Shakespeare's *The Tempest*, whom Prospero has released from bondage under the 'damn'd witch Sycorax' and employs as executor of his magical schemes; (2) a rebel angel in Milton's *Paradise Lost* (VI. 371); (3) in Pope's *Rape of the Lock* (II. 53 ff.) the chief of the sylphs whose 'humbler Province is to tend the Fair'.

Shakespeare's character (1) has inspired many later writers to identify the name 'Ariel' with poetic imagination. T. S. *Eliot called five Christmas poems (1927–54) 'Ariel poems', for instance, the first *Penguin paperback was *Maurois's life of *Shelley called *Ariel* (1935), and there have been several literary journals with 'Ariel' as title. See also PLATH.

ARIOSTO, Ludovico (1474–1533), born at Reggio. He spent the greater part of his life at Ferrara and for many years was in the service, first of Cardinal Ippolito, and then of Duke Alfonso I, of Este. This family he exalted in his poem *Orlando furioso*, published in its final form in 1532, the greatest of Italian romantic epics. He also wrote Italian and Latin lyrics, satires (known to *Wyatt), and four comedies, of which one, *I suppositi* (1509), came through to Shakespeare's *The Taming of the Shrew* via Gascoigne's *Supposes*.

ARISTOPHANES (*c.*448–380 BC), Athenian comic dramatist whose satirical plays, the only surviving representatives of the Old Comedy, attacked individuals rather than types. Because of the difficulties of his language and the obscurity of his contemporary references, Aristophanes did not receive much attention in England until the 19th cent., which produced translations by B. H. Kennedy (*The Birds*, 1804), Thomas Mitchell, and *Frere. These were followed by versions by B. B. Rogers (1904 onwards), which were ingenious but failed to find favour with scholars; by G.

*Murray; and by Dudley Fitts, whose version of *Lysistrata* was performed with considerable success in 1957 at the *Royal Court. Other recent translations include A. H. Sommerstein's *Three Plays* (1973).

The extant works of Aristophanes are *The Acharnians*; *The Knights*; *The Clouds*; *The Peace*; *The Wasps*; *The Birds*; *The Frogs* (of which the best-known lines are the onomatopoeic chorus, 'Co-ax, co-ax, co-ax, Brekekekek co-ax'); *Plutus*; *Lysistrata* and *Ecclesiazusae*, both dealing with government by women; and *Thesmophoriazusae*, which presents the trial and conviction of *Euripides at the female festival of the Thesmophoria.

Aristophanes' Apology, Including a Transcript from Euripides: Being the Last Adventure of Balaustion, a long poem in blank verse by R. *Browning, published 1875 as a sequel to *Balaustion's Adventure*.

The core of the poem is a protracted argument between Balaustion and *Aristophanes as to the moral, social, and metaphysical value of the different aesthetics they espouse; Balaustion defending the visionary humanism of *Euripides, Aristophanes his own coarse realism. Part of Balaustion's argument consists in reading Euripides' play *Herakles* (whose plot, the madness of Herakles and his destruction of his family, constitutes the thematic focus of the poem). The poem is by no means the straightforward defence of Euripides by Browning that it has been taken to be: Balaustion, not Browning, is the speaker. The structure—a monologue containing the narrative of a dialogue and the reading of a play—is arguably Browning's profoundest exploration of the relation of poetic discourse to absolute values such as 'truth' or 'reality'. The poem also contains the remarkable fragment 'Thamuris marching', which reworks some of the material of '*Childe Roland to the Dark Tower Came'.

ARISTOTLE (384–322 BC), born at Stagira, in Macedon, where his father was physician to the king Amyntas II. Sent to Athens in 367, he studied under *Plato for 20 years. Then after a period of travel he was appointed by Philip of Macedon to be tutor to the future *Alexander the Great in 342 and seven years later returned to Athens where he opened a school in the Lyceum, a grove outside the city. His extant works are believed to have been the notes he used for his lectures. They cover logic, ethics, metaphysics, physics, zoology, politics, rhetoric, and poetics. Transmitted through translations, they shaped the development of medieval thought first in the Arab world, then in the Latin West, where Aristotle came to be regarded as the source of all knowledge. His logical treatises won a central place in the curriculum during the 12th cent. Then after a brief struggle his ethical, metaphysical, and scientific works were harmonized with Christianity and constituted the subject matter of higher education from the 13th to the 17th cent. They shaped the thinking of Englishmen writing in Latin from

*Grosseteste to *Herbert of Cherbury, and their influence can be traced in *Spenser, *Donne, and occasionally in Sir T. *Browne. By the end of the 17th cent., however, the Aristotelian world-view had fallen out of favour except for the *Poetics. This treatise, virtually unknown during the Middle Ages, came into prominence in the middle of the 16th cent. and contributed to the rise of *neo-classicism. It has left its mark on the critical writings of *Sidney, *Dryden, and even Dr *Johnson.

ARLEN, Michael (1895–1956), novelist, born Dikran Kuyumjian in Bulgaria of Armenian descent and educated at Malvern College and Edinburgh. He wrote many ornate and mannered novels of fashionable London life, but is chiefly remembered for his best-seller *The Green Hat* (1924), which narrates the short life and violent death of *femme fatale* and dashing widow Iris Storm, owner of the hat of the title and a yellow Hispano Suiza. In 1928 Arlen married and settled in the South of France, returning to London to offer his services during the war, where he was injured in a bombing raid. He eventually settled and died in New York.

Armadale, a novel by Wilkie *Collins, published in 1866. This is an intricately plotted *sensation novel, with two heroes, one fair, prosperous, and cheerful, the other penniless, dark, and disturbed. Both are named Allan Armadale, and both are infatuated with a compelling red-haired villainess, Lydia Gwilt. The complications stem from the previous generation, when the father of the dark Armadale murdered the father of the other. The dark Armadale, after a miserable childhood, adopts the name Ozias Midwinter, and meets the fair Armadale by chance. They become friends, but Armadale has a prophetic dream which convinces Midwinter that he is doomed to harm his friend. Lydia Gwilt, privy to the mystery surrounding them, marries Midwinter under his real name, becoming Mrs Armadale; her plan to murder Armadale and produce the marriage certificate in order to inherit his money is frustrated by Midwinter, and Lydia dies herself.

Armado, Don Adriano de, a 'braggart' 'fantastical' Spaniard in Shakespeare's *Love's Labour's Lost.* His name is connected with the Spanish Armada of 1588.

Armida, in Tasso's *Jerusalem Delivered,* the niece of Hidraotes, king of Damascus, a powerful magician. She offered her services to the defenders of Jerusalem when it was besieged by the Christians under Godfrey of Bouillon, and going to the Christian camp lured away by her beauty many of the principal knights. She inveigled them by magic power into a delicious garden, where they were overcome by indolence. Among her captives were *Rinaldo of Este and *Tancred.

Arminianism, the doctrine of James Arminius or Marmensen (d. 1609), a Dutch Protestant theologian, who put forth views opposed to those of *Calvin, especially on predestination, refusing to hold God responsible for evil. In 1618–19 his doctrines were condemned by the synod of Dort; but they spread rapidly and were embraced, in whole or in part, by large sections of the Reformed Churches.

ARMITAGE, Simon (1963–   ), poet, born in west Yorkshire, where he still lives. His first collection, *Zoom!* (1989), drew on his work as a probation officer and on the rhythms of the Yorkshire vernacular, as well as on *Lowell and Frank O'Hara. Its immediacy, wit, and originality brought him huge critical acclaim and popularity. Both its success and its themes were continued in *Kid* and *Xanadu,* a poem-film (both 1992). *A Book of Matches* (1993) introduced an element of introspection, which was developed in the wintry *Dead Sea Poems* (1995) and came to dominate in *CloudCuckooLand* (1997), where the stars are viewed as a paradigm of his emotions.

ARMSTRONG, John (1709–79), Scottish poet and physician, and friend of *Thomson (who portrayed him in *The Castle of Indolence*), *Smollett, and *Fuseli, with whom he made a continental tour in 1771. He is principally remembered for his didactic poem in blank verse *The Art of Preserving Health* (1744) and for a satirical epistle of literary criticism in heroic couplets, *Taste* (1753). He quarrelled with his friend *Wilkes over the latter's attacks on the Scots in the *North Briton.

ARMSTRONG, William, known as Kinmont Willie (fl. 1596), a Border moss-trooper, whose nickname is taken from his castle of Kinmont in Canonby, Dumfriesshire. He was captured in 1587 but escaped; he was imprisoned in 1596 at Carlisle, but was rescued by the Scottish warden. His fate is unknown. He is the hero of the ballad 'Kinmont Willie', included in Scott's *Minstrelsy of the Scottish Border.

ARNE, Thomas Augustine (1710–78), composer, and the leading musical figure of mid-18th-cent. London theatre, who produced operas, *masques, and incidental music for plays. His *Artaxerxes* was probably the most popular full-length English opera before the 20th cent.; the masque of *Alfred* (1740) added 'Rule Britannia' to the canon of English song; and his many celebrated Shakespeare settings include 'Where the bee sucks', 'When daisies pied', and 'Fear no more the heat of the sun'. He collaborated with *Garrick for the Shakespeare Jubilee in an 'Ode upon Dedicating a Building to Shakespeare'.

ARNOLD, Sir Edwin (1832–1904). He won the *Newdigate Prize at Oxford in 1852, and was principal of the Poona College, Bombay Presidency, 1856–61. He then joined the staff of the *Daily Telegraph,* of which he became editor in 1873. He published several volumes of poems and translations, some from the Sanskrit, and was remembered for his *The Light of Asia, or The Great Renunciation* (1879), a poem of eight books in blank verse, in which, in his own words, he attempted 'by the medium of an imaginary Buddhist votary to depict the life and character and indicate the philosophy of that noble hero and reformer, Prince Gautama of India, founder of Buddhism'.

ARNOLD, Matthew (1822–88), eldest son of Thomas *Arnold, educated at Rugby, Winchester, and at Balliol College, Oxford, where he formed a close friendship with *Clough, and won the *Newdigate Prize with a poem on Cromwell. He became a fellow of Oriel College, then in 1847 secretary to Lord Lansdowne. In 1851 he became an inspector of schools, in which capacity he served for 35 years, travelling extensively throughout England, and observing at first hand the social conditions that prompted much of his later critical work. His first volume of poems, *The Strayed Reveller, and Other Poems* (by 'A', 1849), contains 'The Forsaken Merman', 'The Sick King in Bokhara', and sonnets written at Balliol, including 'Shakespeare'. In 1851 he married Fanny Lucy Wightman, who was to bear six children, three of whom predeceased him. Part of 'Dover Beach' (1867) dates from his honeymoon, which continued on the Continent, and also inspired his 'Stanzas from the Grande Chartreuse' (1855). *Empedocles on Etna, and Other Poems* appeared, also anonymously, in 1852; it contained *'Tristram and Iseult' and some of the 'Marguerite' poems, including 'Yes! in the sea of life enisled', now thought to have been addressed to Mary Calude of Ambleside, whom he had met while staying at the Arnold holiday home at Fox How. In 1853 appeared a volume of poems containing extracts from the earlier books, and *'Sohrab and Rustum', *'The Scholar-Gipsy', 'Memorial Verses to Wordsworth' (who had been a personal friend of the Arnolds), and 'Stanzas in Memory of the Author of "Obermann"', which show how profoundly Arnold had been affected by *Senancour's novel and by the *mal du siècle* expressed by other European writers. His preface discusses the problems of writing poetry in an 'age wanting in moral grandeur'. *Poems, Second Series*, including 'Balder Dead', appeared in 1855; *Merope, a Tragedy* in 1858; and *New Poems*, including *'Thyrsis', 'Rugby Chapel', and 'Heine's Grave', in 1867.

In his maturity Arnold turned increasingly to prose, writing essays on literary, educational, and social topics that established him as the leading critic of the day and which greatly influenced writers as diverse as Max Weber, T. S. *Eliot, F. R. *Leavis, and R. *Williams. His lectures on translating *Homer, with his definition of 'the grand style' (delivered in 1860, while he was professor of poetry at Oxford), were published in 1861 (see TRANSLATION, THEORY AND ART OF); *Essays in Criticism (First Series)* in 1865 (*Second Series*, 1888); *On the Study of Celtic Literature* (which caused Oxford to establish a chair of Celtic studies) in

1867; *Culture and Anarchy* in 1869; *Friendship's Garland* in 1871; *Literature and Dogma*, a study of the interpretation of the Bible, in 1873. In these and other works, Arnold sharply criticized the provincialism, *philistinism, sectarianism, and utilitarian materialism of English life and culture, and argued that England needed more intellectual curiosity, more ideas, and a more comparative, European outlook. The critic, he said, should be flexible, tactful, free of prejudice; his endeavour should be 'to see the object as in itself it really is'. His fame as a critic grew steadily, and in 1883 he delivered a series of lectures in America (undertaken partly to finance his feckless son Richard, who had inherited some of his father's early extravagances). He died in Liverpool, where he was awaiting the arrival of his daughter Lucy, who had married an American.

Special reference is due to Arnold's attempts to secure the improvement of education, particularly secondary education, in England. In 1859 and 1865 he visited the Continent to study educational systems, and produced reports (*The Popular Education of France*, 1861; *A French Eton*, 1864; *Schools and Universities on the Continent*, 1868), arguing that England badly needed more educational organization and could learn much from European models.

There is a biography by Park Honan (1981). *Poetical Works*, ed. C. B. Tinker and H. F. Lowry (1950); *Poems*, ed. and annotated K. Allott (1965); *The Complete Prose Works of Matthew Arnold*, ed. R. H. Super (1960–77).

ARNOLD, Thomas (1795–1842), educated at Winchester and Oxford, remembered principally as the headmaster (1828–42) of Rugby, which, through various reforms, he raised from a state of decline to the rank of a great public school. His concept of the public school had a profound and lasting influence, and he was held in great personal veneration by his pupils, who included his son Matthew *Arnold, *Clough, A. P. *Stanley, and T. *Hughes, author of *Tom Brown's Schooldays*. A Broad Churchman, he wrote in favour of church reform and Catholic emancipation, and attacked the Tractarians of the *Oxford movement. He was the author of several works on Roman history, influenced by *Niebuhr, and was appointed Regius professor of modern history in 1841. The standard life is by A. P. Stanley, 1844.

Art and Letters, an illustrated quarterly edited by Frank Rutter, 1917–20; from 1919 to 1920 with O. *Sitwell. It published T. S. *Eliot, W. *Lewis, A. *John, and Edward Wadsworth.

ARTAUD, Antonin (1896–1948), French actor, director, and dramatic theorist. In a series of manifestos, collected in *Le Théâtre et son double* (1938; *The Theatre and Its Double*, 1958), he called for a return to the primitive and the ritualistic in drama (enshrined in the frequently misunderstood notion of a 'Theatre of

*Cruelty'), in opposition to the realistic theatre of a dominant rationalist culture.

Artegal ('Archgallo' in Geoffrey), legendary king of Britain, son of the savage Morvidus and brother of Gorbonian whom he succeeds (described in *Geoffrey of Monmouth's *Historia Regum Britanniae*, iii. 17). He was deposed for his crimes and replaced by his brother Elidurus the Dutiful; when he returned from exile Elidurus restored him to the throne. The story is the subject of *Wordsworth's poem 'Artegal and Elidure'.

Artegall, Sir, in Spenser's *Faerie Queene*, V, the champion of Justice. *Britomart, to whom his image has been revealed by a magic mirror, is in love with him, and her quest of him ends in their union. Representing Lord Grey de Wilton, he undertakes the rescue of Irena (Ireland) from the tyrant Grantorto. Jointly with Prince *Arthur he slays the *soldan (Philip II of Spain). His name perhaps signifies 'equal to Arthur'.

Arte of English Poesie, see PUTTENHAM.

Arte of Rhetorique, see WILSON, T.

art for art's sake, a phrase associated with the aesthetic doctrine that art is self-sufficient and need serve no moral or political purpose. The phrase *l'art pour l'art* became current in France in the first half of the 19th cent. and *Gautier's formulation in his preface to *Mademoiselle de Maupin* (1835), which denied that art could or should be in any way useful, was admired by *Pater, one of the leading influences on the English *'Aesthetic' movement of the 1880s. (See WILDE, DOWSON, JOHNSON, L., SYMONS, A.) Pater in his conclusion to *The Renaissance* (1873) spoke of 'the desire of beauty, the love of art for art's sake'.

Artful Dodger, the, a member of Fagin's gang in Dickens's *Oliver Twist*.

Arthour and of Merlin, Of, a later 13th-cent. non-alliterative romance in 9,938 lines of short rhyming couplets, preserved in the Auchinleck manuscript (four other manuscripts contain a lesser, variant version). It has been suggested that it may be by the same writer as *King Alisaunder* and *Richard Cœur de Lion*. It probably comes from Kent, and it seems to derive from a French source related to the Vulgate *Merlin* cycle. The last two-thirds of the poem is taken up with a repetitive series of combats and minor battles. It has been edited by O. D. Macrae-Gibson, *Of Arthour and of Merlin* (EETS OS 268, 1973).

Arthur, King. The romantic figure of King Arthur has probably some historical basis, and there is reason to think that, as *Nennius states, he was a chieftain or general (*dux bellorum*) in the 5th or 6th cent. The *Annales Cambriae* place the battle of Mt Badon, 'in which Arthur carried the cross of our Lord Jesus Christ on his shoulders', in 518, and the 'battle of Camlan, in which Arthur and Medraut fell' in 539. The contem-porary chronicler *Gildas makes no mention of Arthur (though he refers to the battle of Badon), nor do some of the principal Welsh bards of the 6th and 7th cents. But there is mention of him in certain ancient poems contained in the *Black Book of Carmarthen* and more especially in the ancient Welsh romance *Culhwch and Olwen*, where he figures with Kay, Bedevere, and *Gawain (Gwalchmei). According to the *Arthur* of the marquis of Bath's manuscript (1428: ed. F. J. Furnivall, EETS OS 2, 1864), he died in 542 after a reign of 22 years. He was said to be the father of *Modred by his half-sister Morgawse; his sister was Anna. Guinevere was the daughter of Arthur's ally Leodegan. According to *Malory, the Grail was accomplished 454 years after the passing of Christ (i.e. in 487). The legend of the return of Arthur to rule Britain again is told by *Malory and in the stanzaic Le *Morte Arthur*. According to the alliterative *Morte Arthure*, he definitely died.

The Arthur of the cycle of legends first appears at length in the *Historia Regum Britanniae* of *Geoffrey of Monmouth. According to this, Arthur is the son of *Uther Pendragon and Ygaerne (Igraine), wife of Gorlois of Cornwall, whom Uther wins through Merlin's magic. At the age of 15 he becomes king and, with his sword Caliburn (Excalibur), slays Childric, defeats the heathen, and conquers Scotland, Ireland, Iceland, and Orkney. He marries Guanhamara, a noble Roman lady, and holds his court at Caerleon on the Usk. He is summoned to pay tribute to the Emperor Lucius of Rome, resists, and declares war. Guanhamara and the kingdom are left in the charge of Modred, his nephew. On his way to Rome he slays the giant of St Michael's Mount; his ambassador Walwain (Gawain) defies the emperor and fights him bravely. When Arthur is about to enter Rome he is warned that Modred has seized Guanhamara and the kingdom. He returns with Walwain, who is slain on landing; Modred retreats to Cornwall where, with all his knights, he is slain in a final battle. Arthur is mortally wounded and is borne to the island of *Avalon for the healing of his wounds, and Guanhamara becomes a nun. This version of Geoffrey's was developed by the 12th-cent. Norman writer *Wace; the Round Table is first mentioned by him as a device for the settlement of disputes over precedence; and Wace says that the wounded king is expected to return to rule the Britons again. Wace was the principal source of *Laȝamon's *Brut*, the first English version of the story which adds to both the magical and martial aspects. In Laȝamon, Arthur is borne off after the last battle at Camelford to *Argante (Morgan le Fay) in Avalon in a magic boat. The story was very significantly developed in the French *'Matter of Britain', by such writers as *Marie de France, *Chrétien de Troyes, and the authors of the 13th-cent. Vulgate prose cycles, and it became the centre of a mass of legends in several languages, most importantly German. Other characters—Merlin, Launcelot, and Tristram—gradually became associated with Arthur, and he himself is the central character only in the narratives describing his early years and his final battle and death; in the intervening tales his court is merely the starting point for the adventures of various knights. Through the history of the legends Arthur himself is exceeded in excellence by first *Gawain and then *Launcelot. The story of Arthur as given here is the basis of Malory's *Morte D'Arthur which was the most authoritative version of the legend in the English tradition. Malory's version gives great prominence to the exploits of the knights of the Round Table, the quest of the Holy Grail, the love of Launcelot and Guinevere and the love of Tristram and Isoud. For other Arthurian writings, see TENNYSON, A., WILLIAM OF MALMESBURY, GLASTONBURY. See J. D. Bruce, *The Evolution of Arthurian Romance from the Beginnings down to the Year 1300* (2 vols, 1923); R. W. Ackerman, *An Index of the Arthurian Names in Middle English* (1952); R. S. Loomis (ed.), *Arthurian Literature in the Middle Ages* (1959); R. Barber, *King Arthur in Legend and History* (1973); C. E. Pickford, *The Arthurian Bibliography* (1981–).

Arthur, Prince, in Spenser's *Faerie Queene*. He symbolizes 'Magnificence' (?Magnanimity), in the Aristotelian sense of the perfection of all the virtues. He enters into the adventures of the several knights and brings them to a fortunate conclusion. His chief adventures are the slaying of the three-bodied monster *Geryoneo and the rescue from him of Belge (the Netherlands) (v. x, xi); and, jointly with *Artegall, the slaying of the *soldan (Philip II) in his 'charret hye' (the Armada) (V. viii).

art nouveau, a decorative style that flourished throughout Europe and America from the 1880s to c.1914, characterized by asymmetry, sinuous lines, and a flame-like patterning of the surface; its motifs—the willowy, elongated, female figure with flowing locks and the fantastic curves of stylized flowers—are romantic and touched by *fin-de-siècle* decadence. In England art nouveau follows the Arts and Crafts movement and looks back to *Blake; the style tends to be sparser and more geometric than on the Continent. The first British works of art nouveau are a chair of 1881 and a title page to *Wren's City Churches* (1883) both by A. H. Mackmurdo (1851–1942). The 1890s were a brilliant period for the art nouveau book. Art-oriented literary periodicals played an important role; Mackmurdo's *Century Guild Hobby Horse* (1884) was followed by the *Dial* (1889–97), the *Yellow Book* (1894–7), and the *Savoy* (1896–8). The most distinguished illustrators were *Beardsley, *Ricketts, L. *Housman, Charles Conder (1868–1909), and T. S. *Moore. In the 1900s the more geometric style of the Glasgow school—of whom Jessie M. King (1876–1949) was the most brilliant illustrator—dominated. The style lingered on in the 20th cent., in the decadent works of 'Alastair' (Hans Henning Voight, c.1889–1933) and in the fairy-tale illustrations of *Rackham and Edmund Dulac (1882–1953).

Art of English Poesie, Observations in the, an attack on the use of rhyme in English poetry by T. *Campion, to which S. Daniel replied in his *Defence of Ryme*.

Arts Council of Great Britain, the, was incorporated by royal charter in 1946 for the purpose of developing greater knowledge, understanding, and practice of the fine arts and to increase their accessibility to the public. It grew out of the wartime Council for the Encouragement of Music and the Arts, which began in 1940 with a grant of £25,000 from the Pilgrim Trust. The first chairman was Lord Macmillan; the vice-chairman and prime mover Dr Thomas Jones, CH. M. *Keynes was chairman from 1942 to 1945. See also under PATRONAGE.

Arveragus, the husband of Dorigen in Chaucer's 'Franklin's Tale'. See CANTERBURY TALES, 12.

Arviragus, the younger son of *Cymbeline, in Shakespeare's play of that name. He appears under the name of Cadwal. In Spenser's *Faerie Queene* (II. x. 51), Arviragus is Cymbeline's brother.

Asaph, in the second part of *Absalom and Achitophel* written chiefly by *Tate, is *Dryden, and refers to the Asaph of 1 Chr. 16: 4–7 and 25: 1, and the hereditary choir, the 'Sons of Asaph', who conducted the musical services of the Temple.

ASAPH, St (d. c.600), a pupil of St *Kentigern in his monastery at Llanelwy, and his successor as its prior. He was the first bishop of that see which took his name.

Ascent of F6, The, a play by W. H. *Auden and C. *Isherwood, published 1936, first performed 1937.

The central character, Michael Ransom, 'scholar and man of action', succumbs to his mother's persuasions and leads a mountaineering expedition up F6, a mysterious and haunted peak on the borders of disputed colonial territory; all his men die en route and he himself dies as he achieves his mission, destroyed by his own self-knowledge, having rejected (in conversation with a mystic abbot, strongly reminiscent of *Hilton's *Lost Horizon*) the possibility of evasion and the contemplative life. A chorus of suburban Everyman, Mr A and Mrs A, comments in verse on his heroic exploits and their own dull lives. The Establishment figures are presented satirically, the figures of the mother and the comrades with more ambiguity; Ransom himself was in part modelled on T. E. *Lawrence, the Truly Strong Weak Man. The play is a parable about the nature of power and will and leadership, with both political and Freudian implications, and may be seen to reflect the growing apprehension of and attraction towards the 'strong man' at this period of the 1930s.

ASCHAM, Roger (1515/16–68), educated at St John's College, Cambridge, where he distinguished himself in classics, becoming college reader in Greek in 1540. In 1545 he published *Toxophilus*, a treatise on archery.

This delightful book, set in the form of a dialogue between Toxophilus (lover of shooting) and Philologus (lover of books), was immediately popular, gaining Ascham a royal pension of £10 a year. It provided the model for many later treatises in dialogue form, including *The Compleat Angler*. He succeeded Grindal as tutor to Princess Elizabeth in 1548, holding this post for less than two years. His brief encounter with Lady Jane Grey (then aged 13) in 1550 has inspired numerous paintings, plays, and other works, such as Landor's *'Imaginary Conversation'* between them. In 1550–3 he travelled on the Continent as secretary to Sir Richard Morison, English ambassador to Charles V, and on his return wrote his interesting *Report of Germany*. In 1554 he became Latin secretary to Queen Mary, being tacitly permitted to continue in his Protestantism, and he was renewed in this office under Elizabeth. He was afflicted by poverty in the last decade of his life; this was probably not caused, as *Camden claimed, by his addiction to dicing and cock-fighting, but by his responsibility for a large family which included his mother-in-law and her younger children. *The Scholemaster* was published posthumously by his widow in 1570. Its three most distinctive features are: Ascham's dislike of corporal punishment; the Ciceronian technique of double translation, from Latin into English and back again; and his attitude to Italy. While placing a high value on Italian language and culture, Ascham felt that it was a most dangerously corrupting country for English travellers: 'I was once in Italie my selfe: but I thanke God, my abode there, was but ix. Dayes: And yet I sawe in that litle tyme, in one Citie, more libertie to sinne, than ever I hard tell of in our noble Citie of London in ix. yeare.' *The Scholemaster* was an immediate influence on Sidney's *Defence of Poetry*, as well as an important landmark in later educational theory. Ascham's English works are notable for their relaxed, personal style and for considerable economy of expression. Dr *Johnson wrote an anonymous *Life of Ascham* to accompany James Bennet's edition of 1761. There has been no complete edition of Ascham's *Works* since J. A. Giles's in 1864–5, but Lawrence V. Ryan has edited *The Schoolmaster* (1967) and has written a detailed study of Ascham (1963).

asclepiads, a metre used by *Sappho and other Greek poets, and named after Asclepiades of Samos (fl. 290 BC), who revived it. It was used in English by P. Sidney in his *Arcadia*.

ASHBERY, John (1927–   ), American poet, born in New York. He graduated from Harvard in 1949, by which time he had already composed the title poem of his first volume, *Song Trees*, which was published in the Yale Younger Poets series edited by W. H. *Auden in 1956. Ashbery spent most of the following decade in Paris, where his work grew more experimental and disjunctive. His second collection, *The Tennis Court Oath* (1962), is his most radical, and has proved an important influence on the development of the American school of the 1970s which became known as 'Language Poetry'. Ashbery did not achieve canonical status until the publication of his sixth volume, *Self-Portrait in a Convex Mirror* (1975). He was the first of the so-called 'New York School'—normally seen as comprising Frank O'Hara, Kenneth Koch, and James Schuyler—to achieve wide recognition. His poetry is characterized by its openness to the vagaries of consciousness, its wry, beguiling lyricism, and its innovative use of forms such as the pantoum and the sestina. Ashbery's most vociferous advocate has been Harold *Bloom, who has frequently declared him the most significant poet since Wallace *Stevens.

Ashendene Press, see PRIVATE PRESSES.

ASHFORD, Daisy (Mrs James Devlin) (1881–1972). She wrote *The Young Visiters*, a small comic masterpiece, while still a young child in Lewes. It was found in a drawer in 1919 and sent to Chatto and Windus, who published it in the same year with an introduction by J. M. *Barrie, who had first insisted on meeting the author in order to check that she was genuine. The book, a sparkling, misspelt, and unpunctuated view of High Life and the adventures of Ethel Monticue and her admirer Mr Salteena, has proved very popular.

ASHMOLE, Elias (1617–92), antiquary and astrologer. He studied at Brasenose College, Oxford, and, as a Royalist, held several government appointments. His chief work was *The Institution, Laws and Ceremonies of the Order of the Garter* (1672), but he also edited work by Dr *Dee and was associated with *Lilly, whose autobiography appeared with Ashmole's *Memoirs* in the 1774 edition. In 1682 he presented his collection of curiosities, bequeathed to him by *Tradescant, to Oxford University, thus founding the Ashmolean Museum. A five-volume edition of his autobiographical and historical notes, correspondence, etc., edited by C. H. Josten, appeared in 1966.

'Ash Wednesday', a poem by T. S. *Eliot.

ASIMOV, Isaac, see SCIENCE FICTION.

Asolando, the last volume of poems by R. *Browning, published 1889. The title derives from a fanciful verb 'asolare', 'to disport in the open air, to amuse oneself at random', attributed to *Bembo at the time of his residence in Asolo, in northern Italy. Asolo had played an important part in Browning's life and work (see PIPPA PASSES).

The poems fall into three main groups: an opening series of love lyrics; a group of anecdotal poems and longer narratives; and a concluding group of meditative or reminiscent dramatic monologues. The 'Epilogue' to the volume, containing the famous self-description 'One who never turned his back but marched breast forward' etc., stands as a traditional proof of Browning's optimism; the 'Prologue' is better verse and a better guide. But the finest poem in the volume is undoubtedly 'Beatrice Signorini', the last of Browning's great poems about Italian painters.

Asseneth, in a variant of the story of Joseph and Potiphar's wife, is Potiphar's daughter, whom Joseph consents to marry if she will renounce her gods, which she does. An angel signifies approval and Pharaoh gives a feast to celebrate the nuptials. The story, perhaps of early Christian invention, was made the subject of a French prose romance, early in the 14th cent., by Jean de Vignai.

ASSER (d. 910), a monk of St David's, Pembrokeshire, who entered the household of King *Alfred (c.885) and studied with him for six months of each year. He received the monasteries of Amesbury and Banwell, and later a grant of Exeter and its district; he was bishop of Sherborne (892–910). In 893 he wrote a Latin life of Alfred and a Chronicle of English History for the years 849 to 887. Since the only Alfredian translation he mentions is Waerferth's version of *Gregory's *Dialogues*, it is assumed that all other translations are later than 893, the date of Asser's *Life*. The authenticity of the *Life* has been questioned, some scholars believing the work to be an 11th-cent. forgery. But there seems to be no conclusive evidence that it does not belong to the 890s. There is an edition by W. H. Stevenson (1904).

assonance, the correspondence or rhyming of one word with another in the accented and following vowels, but not in the consonants, as, e.g. in Old French versification. The term is now more broadly used to cover a wide range of vowel correspondences, from the deliberate reverberation of the last line of *Yeats's 'Byzantium'—'That dolphin-torn, that gong-tormented sea'—to the subtle echoes and repetitions of Keats in *'To Autumn': 'Then in a wailful choir the small gnats mourn | Among the river sallows, borne aloft | Or sinking as the light wind lives or dies.'

Astarte, the Phoenician goddess of love. This is the name which Byron gives to his half-sister Augusta *Leigh in his drama *Manfred.

ASTELL, Mary (1666–1731), born in Newcastle upon Tyne. Often referred to as 'the first English feminist', she published a number of essays and tracts about the status and plight of women and the relation between the sexes. Her publications include *Some Reflections on Marriage* (1700) and, perhaps her best-known work, *A Serious Proposal to the Ladies for the Advancement of Their True and Greatest Interest* (1694), written by 'a lover of her sex'. The *Serious Proposal* seeks to enhance women's situation and self-esteem, hence earning Astell a reputation for feminist thinking, but it also endorses some degree of female subordination within marriage.

Astolat ('Ascolet' in the stanzaic Le *Morte Arthur*), the place where Launcelot meets Elaine Le Blank, is, according to Malory's *Morte D'Arthur*, Guildford in Surrey. Elaine is 'the Fair Maid of Astolat' and Tennyson's *'Lady of Shalott'.

Astolfo, in *Orlando innamorato* and *Orlando furioso*, a courteous and graceful English knight, one of the suitors of *Angelica and at one time a prisoner of *Alcina. He receives from *Logistilla a magic horn, the blast of which fills its hearers with panic, and a book that tells him all he wishes to know. He gets possession of the hippogriff of *Rogero, and, with an Englishman's partiality for travel, flies about the world, relieves Prester John in Nubia of his troubles with harpies, visits paradise, whence St John carries him in a chariot to the moon. There, in a valley, are collected all the things that are lost on earth, lost kingdoms, lost reputations, lost time, and in the heap he finds the lost wits of Orlando, which he restores to the crazy hero. As regards his description as an English knight, it appears that in the earlier French chanson he figures as *Estout de Langres*, or *Lengrois*, corrupted into *Lenglois* and *L'Englois* (F. J. Snell, in *PEL*, 'The Fourteenth Century').

Astraea, a name adopted by Afra *Behn under which she is ridiculed by *Pope.

Astraea Redux, see DRYDEN.

'Astrophel', a pastoral elegy, written by *Spenser in ?1591–5 on the death of Sir P. *Sidney, who was mortally wounded in 1586 at Zutphen. Spenser had previously lamented him in *'The Ruines of Time'. *Swinburne used the title for a volume of his poems in 1894.

Astrophel and Stella, a sequence of 108 sonnets and 11 songs by Sir P. *Sidney, written about 1582. They plot the unhappy love of Astrophel ('lover of a star') for Stella ('star'). As several sonnets make clear, e.g. 37, referring to one that 'Hath no misfortune, but that Rich she is', Stella is to be identified with Penelope *Rich; but the exact nature of Sidney's real, rather than poetic, relationship with her can never be known. Apart from snatching a kiss while she is asleep, Astrophel in the sequence achieves nothing, and the story breaks off—'That therewith my song is broken'—rather than being resolved. Poetically, however, the sonnets are an outstanding achievement, being written throughout in versions of the exacting Italian sonnet form, and displaying a striking range of tone, imagery, and metaphor. The best known is 31, 'With how sad steps, ô Moone, thou climb'st the skies'. There were two editions of *Astrophel and Stella* in 1591 which began a craze for sonnet sequences; from 1598 onwards it was included in editions of *The Arcadia.

asyndeton, the omission of conjunctions for rhetorical effect, either between clauses, as in 'I came, I saw, I conquered', or between nouns: 'The courtier's, soldier's, scholar's eye, tongue, sword' (*Hamlet*, III. i. 60); this second type is sometimes called brachylogia.

As You Like It, a comedy by *Shakespeare, registered 1600 and probably written 1599–1600. It was first printed in the *Folio of 1623. Firm evidence that it was performed before James I at Wilton has never been found. Shakespeare's chief source was Lodge's *Rosalynde, but some notable characters, such as *Jaques and *Touchstone, have no original there.

Frederick has usurped the dominions of the duke his brother, who is living with his faithful followers in the forest of *Arden. Celia, Frederick's daughter, and Rosalind, the duke's daughter, living at Frederick's court, witness a wrestling match in which Orlando, son of Sir Rowland de Boys, defeats a powerful adversary, and Rosalind falls in love with Orlando and he with her. Orlando, who at his father's death has been left in the charge of his elder brother Oliver, has been driven from home by Oliver's cruelty. Frederick, learning that Orlando is the son of Sir Rowland, who was a friend of the exiled duke, has his anger against the latter revived, and banishes Rosalind from his court, and Celia accompanies her. Rosalind assumes a countryman's dress and takes the name Ganymede; Celia passes as Aliena his sister. They live in the forest of Arden, and fall in with Orlando, who has joined the banished duke. Ganymede encourages Orlando to pay suit to her as though she were his Rosalind. Oliver comes to the forest to kill Orlando, but is saved by him from a lioness, and is filled with remorse for his cruelty. He falls in love with Aliena, and their wedding is arranged for the next day. Ganymede undertakes to Orlando that she will by magic produce Rosalind at the same time to be married to him. When all are assembled in presence of the banished duke to celebrate the double nuptials, Celia and Rosalind put off their disguise and appear in their own characters. News is brought that Frederick the usurper, setting out to seize and destroy his brother and his followers, has been converted from his intention by 'an old religious man' and has made restitution of the dukedom.

Conversation rather than plot dominates this play, however, much of it provided by the reflections of Jaques and Touchstone, and by the large number of songs, more than in any of Shakespeare's other plays, including such lyrics as 'Under the greenwood tree' (which *Hardy used as the title for a novel) and 'Blow, blow, thou winter wind' (in II. v and II. vii respectively).

Atalanta in Calydon, a poetic drama by *Swinburne, published 1865. It tells the story of the hunting of the wild boar sent by Artemis to ravage Calydon in revenge for its neglect of her: Meleager slays the boar, presents the spoils to the virgin athlete and huntress Atalanta, and then himself dies through the intervention of his mother Althaea. The work brought Swinburne fame, and was highly praised for its successful imitation of Greek models (though the subject had not been treated by any Greek dramatist); some critics pointed out its 'anti-theism', and W. M. *Rossetti compared it to Shelley's *Prometheus Unbound. It is now chiefly remembered for the 'chorus' beginning 'When the hounds of spring are on winter's traces . . .'

Atalantis, The New, see MANLEY, MRS.

Atellan fables were sketches depicting scenes from rustic life, presented on a crude stage with stock characters (the foolish old man, the rogue, the clown), and seem to have been the earliest form of drama to flourish in ancient Rome. It was imported from Campania where Oscan, a language akin to Latin, was spoken. The genre may have originated from the town of Atella as its name suggests, but the so-called Atellan fables seem to have been similar to the Phlyax farces which were popular at the time in the Greek-speaking world.

ATHANASIUS, St (c.296–373), bishop of Alexandria in the reign of the Emperor Constantine and persecuted by him and by his successor Constantius II whose autocratic religious policies Athanasius strongly opposed. He was an uncompromising opponent of Arianism (see ARIAN HERESY) and defended the decisions of the Council of Nicaea (325), which he attended. His works include the influential *De Incarnatione* and a life of St Antony of Egypt. The Athanasian Creed, which begins with the words 'Quicunque vult', has been attributed to him.

Atheism, The Necessity of, a prose pamphlet by P. B. *Shelley and his friend T. J. *Hogg, published anonymously at Oxford, 1811. Using the sceptical arguments of *Hume and *Locke, the authors—then both undergraduates—smartly demolish the grounds for a rational belief in the Deity. The pamphlet ends with a flourishing 'Q.E.D.', as in a schoolboy's exercise, which caused great offence, as did its title. They were both expelled from the university for circulating the work to heads of colleges and to bishops, and 'contumacy' in refusing to answer questions about it. It is probably the first published statement of atheism in Britain.

Atheist's Tragedy, The, a tragedy by *Tourneur, printed 1611.

D'Amville, the 'atheist', desiring to increase the wealth of his family, wishes to marry his son to Castabella; she is betrothed to Charlemont, the son of his brother Montferrers, and D'Amville arranges that Charlemont shall go abroad on military service. During his absence D'Amville and Belforest, Castabella's father, achieve their purpose, aided by the lecherous Levidulcia, Belforest's second wife, and Castabella is married to the sickly and impotent Rousard; Charlemont, in one of the best-known speeches of the play, is falsely reported to have died at the siege of Ostend. ('Walking next day upon the fatal shore . . .', II. i. 78 ff.) D'Amville then murders Montferrers. Charlemont, exhorted by his father's ghost to 'leave revenge unto the king of kings', now returns. D'Amville endeavours to procure his murder, but vengeance comes upon him in the death of his two sons, and he himself accidentally dashes out his own brains when raising the axe to execute Charlemont, held on a murder charge; he confesses his sins and dies and Charlemont and Castabella are united, Charlemont expressing the 'anti-revenge' sentiment: 'Now I see | That patience is the honest man's revenge.' (See also REVENGE TRAGEDY.)

Athelston, a highly unhistorical but lively verse romance from about 1350, in 811 lines, whose only connection with the historical Athelstan (Alfred's grandson) is his being succeeded by a virtuous Edmund. The romance tells of the chance meeting in a forest of four messengers, one of whom, Athelston, becomes king of England, and the subsequent relations between the four. One becomes archbishop of Canterbury; one becomes earl of Dover, plots against the king, and is executed; and the fourth becomes earl of Stane and the father of Athelston's chosen successor Edmund. The poem is in the dialect of the north-east Midlands, but Trounce in his edition derives it from an Anglo-Norman metrical original.

See edition by A. M. Trounce (EETS 224, 1933; rev. 1951); *Medieval English Romances*, Part I, ed. A. V. C. Schmidt and N. Jacobs (1980).

Athenaeum (1828–1921), J. S. *Buckingham's literary review, followed a general monthly magazine of this name (1807–9). The founder wished the journal to become a true 'Athenaeum', the resort of thinkers, poets, orators, and other writers, and he attacked the *Quarterly Review* for the political bias of its literary criticism. Co-proprietors included at various times J. H. *Reynolds, T. *Hood, and A. *Cunningham. Dilke was editor 1830–46, and the list of contributors in the 19th cent. included *Lamb, *Darley, *Hogg, Hood, *Landor, *Carlyle, R. *Browning, *Lang, and *Pater. The scope of the review was enlarged in the 20th cent., but its contributors were no less eminent; they included *Hardy, K. *Mansfield, T. S. *Eliot, R. *Graves, *Blunden, V. *Woolf, and J. M. *Murry, who became editor in 1919. Its reputation and authority altered little during its long history. In 1921 it merged with *Nation*, ran for ten years as *Nation and Athenaeum*, and in 1931 was purchased by the *New Statesman*. See L. A. Marchand, *The Athenaeum* (1941).

Athenian Gazette, later the *Athenian Mercury*, a periodical published by *Dunton, a question-and-answer paper designed to resolve 'the nice and curious questions proposed by the Ingenious', and thus a precursor of *Notes and Queries*. It first appeared in Mar. 1691, and flourished until 1697, with Samuel Wesley (1662–1735), father of John *Wesley, as partner. The queries ranged over a vast area, from the theological to the matrimonial, from the scientific to the literary, and it was praised and read by authors as diverse as *Halifax, *Swift, *Defoe, and *Temple.

ATKINSON, Kate (1951–   ), novelist and short story writer, born in York and educated at Dundee Univer-

sity. Her first novel, *Behind the Scenes at the Museum* (1995), is a sharp family drama of sibling rivalry and suppressed memory set largely in York of the 1950s, some of it in Ruby Lennox's home above a pet shop: it mixes social comedy with poignant elements of ancestral time travel and flashback. *Human Croquet* (1997), also set in the north of England, centres on the narration of Isobel Fairfax and again employs a complex time pattern, this time intercutting the recent and at times very distant past.

Atlantic Monthly, an American, and more particularly a New England, magazine of literature, the arts, and politics, founded in 1857. J. R. *Lowell was its first editor (1857–61) and O. W. *Holmes's contribution of *The Autocrat at the Breakfast-Table* added greatly to its early success. Lowell's distinguished successors included W. D. *Howells (1871–81) and T. B. Aldrich (1881–90). It maintains its traditions, and continues to include many leading American men and women of letters among its contributors.

Atlantis, *The New*, see NEW ATLANTIS, THE.

Atom, *The History and Adventures of an*, an anonymous satire by T. *Smollett, published 1769.

The attribution to Smollett is on 18th-cent. rumour and internal evidence only. No references to it occur in his letters, in his wife's, or in those of his many correspondents, yet much of it seems to reflect what is known of Smollett's thoughts and feelings at the time. Strongly influenced by *Rabelais, the work is a violent political satire, largely couched in crude physiological terms, many of them scatological. The Atom, which in its various transmigrations has lived in the body of a Japanese in Japan, relates his experiences and observations to Nathaniel Peacock. Japan is a thin fiction for England, and the various Japanese politicians and figures of power represent Englishmen of the day; among many others, the demagogue Taycho is *Pitt, Fika-Kaka is Newcastle, and Yak-Strot the hated Bute. The 'mob' is characterized as sheeplike, malevolent, and stupid.

Atossa, the wife of Darius and mother of Xerxes, appears in *The Persians* of *Aeschylus. See also MORAL ESSAYS.

ATTERBURY, Francis (1662–1732). He became bishop of Rochester in 1713 after holding various important preferments. He engaged in the *Phalaris controversy and in the theological and political disputes of the day, and was imprisoned in 1720 for alleged complicity in a Jacobite plot. He subsequently left the country and died in exile. He was a close friend of *Pope, *Swift, and other literary figures, and was one of the most noted preachers of his day; his *A Discourse Occasioned by the Death of Lady Cutts* (1698) was delivered as the funeral sermon of the second wife of Baron Cutts (1661–1707); she died aged 18. His *Miscellaneous Works*, ed. J. Nichols, were published in 1789–98.

Attic, a form of Greek spoken in Athens during its period of literary pre-eminence, became later the basis of the common speech (κοινή) of the Greek-speaking East. Attic style was the product of a reaction against the turgid and aphoristic diction fashionable in the 1st cent. BC. Moulded on the great Athenian orators, it aimed at a dry, grammatically correct lucidity and was imitated in Rome where Brutus shone as its exponent.

Atticus, the character under which *Pope satirized *Addison in lines written in 1715, first printed in the *St James's Journal* (15 Dec. 1722) and finally in an altered version in Pope's *Epistle to Dr Arbuthnot* (1735), ll. 193–214. The original Atticus (109–32 BC), so called from his long residence in Athens, was a friend of Cicero.

ATWOOD, Margaret (1939–), Canadian poet and novelist, born in Ottawa, who spent much of her early life in the northern Ontario and Quebec bush country. Her first volume of poetry, *The Circle Game*, appeared in 1966, to be followed by several others. Her first novel, *The Edible Woman* (1969), was followed by *Surfacing* (1972), *Lady Oracle* (1976), and *Life before Man* (1979), all novels, and a controversial study of themes in Canadian literature, *Survival* (1972). She also compiled *The New Oxford Book of Canadian Verse in English* (1983). More recent works include *Murder in the Dark* (1983), a collection of short prose pieces; *Bluebeard's Egg and Other Stories* (1983), and *Unearthing Suite* (stories, 1983). *The Handmaid's Tale* (1985) is a futuristic fable, set in the imaginary Republic of Gilead, about a woman whose only function is to breed. *Cat's Eye* (1988) presents the memories of a painter, Elaine Risley, haunted by a childhood tormentor who was also her best friend. Later novels include *The Robber Bride* (1994), the story of three friends in Toronto whose lives are disrupted by a *femme fatale*; *The Blind Assassin* (2000), winner of the *Booker Prize; and the dystopian *Oryx and Crake* (2003).

aubade (Provençal *alba*; German *Tagelied*), a dawn song, usually describing the regret of two lovers at their imminent separation. The form (which has no strict metrical pattern) flourished with the conventions of *courtly love (see the lament of Troilus, *Troilus and Criseyde*, III. 1450, 'O cruel day') and survives in such modern examples as *Empson's 'Aubade' (1940), with its refrain 'The heart of standing is you cannot fly'.

AUBIN, Penelope (1679–1731), novelist, translator, and dramatist, born in London, who became a prolific professional writer in the 1720s, probably during widowhood. Her seven popular novels, from *The Strange Adventures of the Count de Vinevil* (1721) to *The Life and Adventures of the Young Count Albertus* (1728), combined travel adventure, seduction narrative, and Christian precepts. She produced four translations from French and edited two works on morality by Sieur de Gomberville. Her play *The Humours of the Masqueraders* had a short run in 1730. Possibly a Catholic, Aubin preached near Charing Cross in the late 1720s.

AUBREY, John (1626–97), antiquary and biographer, born near Malmesbury, Wiltshire, the oldest surviving son of a well-to-do Herefordshire family. A lonely early childhood gave him delight in society, and he became familiar with many of the distinguished men of his time, including *Hobbes, whom he first met while still a boy in 1634. His education at Trinity College, Oxford, was interrupted by the Civil War. In 1648 he was the first to discover the ruins of Avebury, and devoted much time to archaeological research, keenly deploring the neglect of antiquities; in 1662 he was nominated one of the original fellows of the *Royal Society. His *Miscellanies* (1696), a book of stories and folklore, was the only work completed and published in his lifetime. His 'Perambulation of Surrey', based on a tour in 1673, was included in Rawlinson's *Natural History and Antiquities of Surrey* (1719), and his *Natural History of Wiltshire* appeared (ed. J. Britton) in 1847, but he is chiefly remembered for his *Lives* of eminent people, much used (and in his view somewhat abused) by A. *Wood. He collected these over a period of years, constantly adding to his notes, deploring his own lack of method ('I now set things down tumultuarily, as if tumbled out of a Sack'), and depositing his manuscripts in the Ashmolean Museum in 1693. Early editions (1813, 1898) were bowdlerized. The *Lives* are a lively and heterogeneous mixture of anecdote, first-hand observation, folklore, and erudition, a valuable, open-minded, entertaining (if at times inaccurate) portrait of an age. (See BIOGRAPHY.)

Auburn, see DESERTED VILLAGE, THE.

Aucassin and Nicolette, a 13th-cent. courtly story in northern French, composed in alternating prose and heptasyllabic verse, now believed to be a loving pastiche of the excesses of courtly love romances. The writer was probably a northern *jongleur* in the early part of the century, unfamiliar with the Provençal setting of the story. It is discussed or translated by *Swinburne, *Pater, and *Lang. The story tells of how Aucassin, the son of Count Garins of Beaucaire, loves Nicolette, a Saracen captive. Garins opposes their love and imprisons them both; but they escape and, after a series of adventures, they are married and become lord and lady of Beaucaire. There is an edition by M. Roques (1921); see also *Aucassin and Nicolette, and Other Tales*, ed. and trans. Pauline Matarasso (1971).

AUCHINLECK, see BOSWELL.

AUDEN, W(ystan) H(ugh) (1907–73), the youngest son of a doctor, brought up in Birmingham and educated at Gresham's School, Holt. He began to be taken seriously as a poet while still at Christ Church, Oxford, where he was much influenced by Anglo-Saxon and Middle English poetry, but also began to explore the means of preserving 'private spheres' (through poetry) in 'public chaos'. Among his contemporaries, who were to share some of his left-wing near-Marxist response to the public chaos of the 1930s, were *MacNeice, *Day-

Lewis, and *Spender, with whom his name is often linked. (See PYLON SCHOOL.) After Oxford, Auden lived for a time in Berlin; he returned to England in 1929 to work as a schoolteacher, but continued to visit Germany regularly, staying with his friend and future collaborator *Isherwood. His first volume, *Poems* (including some previously published in a private edition, 1928), was accepted for publication by T. S. *Eliot at Faber and Faber and appeared in 1930; it was well received and established him as the most talented voice of his generation. *The Orators* followed in 1932, and *Look Stranger!* in 1936. In 1932 he became associated with Rupert Doone's Group Theatre, which produced several of his plays (*The Dance of Death*, 1933; and, with Isherwood, *The Dog beneath the Skin*, 1935; *The Ascent of F6*, 1936; *On the Frontier*, 1938); these owe something to the early plays of *Brecht. (See also EXPRESSIONISM.) Working from 1935 with the GPO Film Unit he became friendly with *Britten, who set many of his poems to music and later used Auden's text for his opera *Paul Bunyan*. In 1935 he married Erika Mann to provide her with a British passport to escape from Nazi Germany. A visit to Iceland with MacNeice in 1936 produced their joint *Letters from Iceland* (1937); *Journey to a War* (1939, with Isherwood) records a journey to China. Meanwhile in 1937 he had visited Spain for two months, to support the Republicans, but his resulting poem 'Spain' (1937) is less partisan and more detached in tone than might have been expected, and in January 1939 he and Isherwood left Europe for America (he became a US citizen in 1946) where he met Chester Kallman, who became his lifelong friend and companion. *Another Time* (1940), containing many of his most famous poems (including 'September 1939' and 'Lullaby'), was followed in 1941 by *The Double Man* (1941, published in London as *New Year Letter*), a long transitional verse epistle describing the 'baffling crime' of 'two decades of hypocrisy', rejecting political simplifications, accepting man's essential solitude, and ending with a prayer for refuge and illumination for the 'muddled heart'. From this time Auden's poetry became increasingly Christian in tone (to such an extent that he even altered some of his earlier work to bring it in line and disowned some of his political pieces; this was perhaps not unconnected with the death in 1941 of his devout Anglo-Catholic mother, to whom he dedicated *For the Time Being: A Christmas Oratorio* (1944). This was published with *The Sea and the Mirror*, a series of dramatic monologues inspired by *The Tempest. The Age of Anxiety: A Baroque Eclogue* (1948) is a long dramatic poem, reflecting man's isolation, which opens in a New York bar at night, and ends with dawn on the streets.

Auden's absence during the war led to a poor reception of his works in England at that period, but the high quality of his later work reinstated him as an unquestionably major poet; in 1956 he was elected professor of poetry at Oxford, and in 1962 he became a student (i.e. fellow) of Christ Church. His major later collections include *Nones* (1951, NY; 1952, London), *The Shield of Achilles* (1955), which includes 'Horae Canonicae' and 'Bucolics', and is considered by many his best single volume; and *Homage to Clio* (1960), which includes a high proportion of light verse. Auden had edited *The Oxford Book of Light Verse* in 1938, and subsequently many other anthologies, collections, etc.; his own prose criticism includes *The Enchafèd Flood* (1950, NY; 1951, London), *The Dyer's Hand* (1962, NY; 1963, London), and *Secondary Worlds* (1968, T. S. Eliot Memorial Lectures). He also wrote several librettos, notably for *Stravinsky's *The Rake's Progress* (1951, with Kallman). *About the House* (1965, NY; 1966, London), one of his last volumes of verse, contains a tender evocation of his life with Kallman at their summer home in Austria. Auden spent much of the last years of his life in Oxford, and died suddenly in Vienna. His *Collected Poems*, edited by Edward Mendleson, were published in 1991. A volume of *Juvenilia*, edited by Katherine Bucknell, appeared in 1994.

Auden's influence on a succeeding generation of poets was incalculable, comparable only with that, a generation earlier, of *Yeats (to whom Auden himself pays homage in 'In Memory of W. B. Yeats', 1939). His progress from the engaged, didactic, satiric poems of his youth to the complexity of his later work offered a wide variety of models—the urbane, the pastoral, the lyrical, the erudite, the public, and the introspective mingle with great fluency. He was a master of verse form, and accommodated traditional patterns to a fresh, easy, and contemporary language. A life by Humphrey Carpenter was published in 1981. See also *The Auden Generation* by S. Hynes (1976).

Audrey, in Shakespeare's *As You Like It*, the country wench wooed and won by Touchstone.

AUDUBON, John James (1785–1851), an American ornithologist of French descent, noted for his remarkable pictures of birds. The colour prints of his *The Birds of America* were issued serially in London in 1827–38, and the accompanying text, 'Ornithological Biography', in which he was assisted, in 1831–9. He also published, again with assistance, *Viviparous Quadrupeds of North America* (plates 1842–5; text 1846–54). His important *Journal* appeared in 1929.

AUERBACH, Erich (1892–1957), born in Berlin, professor of Romance philology at Marburg from 1929 to 1935. Dismissed by the Nazis, he went to Istanbul, where he taught at the Turkish State University from 1936 to 1947; he then moved to the United States, and from 1950 was professor of French and Romance philology at Yale. He published several books on medieval literature, Christian symbolism, and methods of historical criticism; his best-known work is *Mimesis: The Representation of Reality in Western Literature*, first published in German in 1946 (trans. 1953), a wide-ranging discussion taking texts from *Homer, through *Dante, Shakespeare, *Cervantes, etc., and ending with V. *Woolf, to explore the classical doctrine of levels of representation. He concludes that 'it was the story of Christ, with its ruthless mixture of everyday reality and the highest and most sublime tragedy, which conquered the classical rule of styles' in the Middle Ages, and contrasts this with the achievements of modern *realism.

Aufidius, general of the Volscians, first enemy and then ally of *Coriolanus in Shakespeare's play of that name.

Augusta, the name used for London in Thomson's *The Seasons.

Augusta Leigh, *Byron's half-sister: see LEIGH.

Augustan age, a term derived from the period of literary eminence under the Roman Emperor Augustus (27 BC–AD 14) during which *Virgil, *Horace, and *Ovid flourished. In English literature it is generally taken to refer to the early and mid-18th cent., though the earliest usages date back to the reign of Charles II. Augustan writers (such as *Pope, *Addison, *Swift, and *Steele) greatly admired their Roman counterparts, imitated their works, and themselves frequently drew parallels between the two ages. *Goldsmith, in *The Bee*, in an 'Account of the Augustan Age of England' (1759), identifies it with the reign of Queen Anne, and the era of *Congreve, *Prior, and *Bolingbroke. See also NEO-CLASSICISM. See H. Weinbrot, *Augustus Caesar in 'Augustan' England* (1978).

AUGUSTINE, St (d. 26 May, between 604 and 609), first archbishop of Canterbury. He was prior of Pope *Gregory's monastery of St Andrew in Rome and in 596 was sent by that pope with some 40 monks to preach the gospel in England, arriving there in 597. He was favourably received by King Æthelbert of Kent, who was afterwards converted and gave Augustine a see at Canterbury. Augustine was consecrated 'Bishop of the English' at Arles. He founded the monastery of Christ Church at Canterbury, and a number of other churches, none of which still survives. See M. Deanesly, *Augustine of Canterbury* (1964).

AUGUSTINE, St, of Hippo (354–430), born at Tagaste in North Africa, his mother being Monica, already a devout Christian. He was trained as a rhetorician and abandoned the Christianity in which he had been brought up (though not baptized). He had an illegitimate son, Adeodatus. He was a Manichaean for some time, but was converted (387) after hearing the sermons of *Ambrose, bishop of Milan, where Augustine taught rhetoric. The scene of his conversion is vividly described in his *Confessions* (c.400), which contains a celebrated account of his early life. He became bishop of Hippo (396) and was engaged in constant theological controversy, combating Manichaeans, Donatists, and Pelagians. The most important of his numerous works is *De Civitate Dei* (The City of God, 413–27), a treatise in

vindication of Christianity. His principal tenet was the immediate efficacy of grace, and his theology (which contains a significant *Neoplatonic element, probably from *Plotinus) remained an influence of profound importance on Franciscans, Cistercians, and others in the Middle Ages, when it was often characterized as being an alternative orthodoxy to the Dominican system of *Aquinas. His views on literature became standard in the Middle Ages, particularly as they are expressed in *De Doctrina Christiana*, and they have often been cited as an authority by 20th-cent. 'exegetical' critics of medieval literature such as D. W. Robertson who are sometimes called 'Augustinian critics'.

De Doctrina Christiana, trans. D. W. Robertson (1958); *The City of God*, trans. R. H. Barrow (1950); *Confessions*, trans. F. J. Sheed (1943); Peter R. L. Brown, *Augustine of Hippo: A Biography* (1967).

'Auld Lang Syne', a song whose words were contributed by *Burns to the fifth volume of James Johnson's *Scots Musical Museum* (1787–1803). It was not entirely of Burns's composition, but was taken down by him, he wrote, 'from an old man's singing'.

In fact the refrain, at least, had long been in print, and the first line and title appear in a poem by A. *Ramsay. Sir Robert Aytoun (1570–1638) has also been credited with the original version.

Aureng-Zebe, a tragedy by *Dryden, produced 1675, published 1676.

The plot is remotely based on the contemporary events by which the Mogul Aureng-Zebe wrested the empire of India from his father and his brothers. The hero is a figure of exemplary rationality, virtue, and patience, whose stepmother lusts after him and whose father pursues the woman with whom Aureng-Zebe is himself in love. Apparently highly schematic in its organization, this last of Dryden's rhymed heroic plays evinces a deeply disturbing awareness of the anarchy and impotence which threaten every aspect of human life, emotional, moral, and political.

Aurora Leigh, described by its author E. B. *Browning as a 'novel in verse', published 1857, is the 11,000-line life-story of a woman writer. Her rejection of, and final reunion with, her philanthropist suitor Romney Leigh (and a melodramatic sub-plot in which a seamstress is trapped into a brothel) are less important than the poem's forceful and often witty speculations on the poet's mission, on social responsibilities, and on the position of women, its vivid impressionistic sketches of crowds and social groups, and its glimpses of dewy English countryside and luminous Italian landscapes.

AUSTEN, Jane (1775–1817), novelist, born in the rectory at Steventon, Hampshire, the sixth child in a family of seven. Her father, the Revd George Austen, was a cultivated man, comfortably prosperous, who taught Jane and encouraged her both in her reading and in her writing. As a child and young woman she read widely, including, among novelists, *Fielding, *Sterne, *Richardson, and F. *Burney; and among poets, Sir W. *Scott, *Cowper, and her particular favourite, *Crabbe. Her life is notable for its lack of events; she did not marry, although she had several suitors, one of whom she accepted one evening, only to withdraw her acceptance the following morning. She lived in the midst of a lively and affectionate family, with occasional visits to Bath, London, Lyme, and her brothers' houses. Any references there may have been to private intimacies or griefs were excised from Jane's letters by her sister Cassandra, after Jane's death, but the letters retain flashes of sharp wit and occasional coarseness that have startled some of her admirers. The letters cover the period 1796–1817, and her correspondents include Cassandra, her friend Martha Lloyd, and her nieces and nephews, to whom she confided her views on the novel (to Anna Austen, 9 Sept. 1814), '3 or 4 families in a Country Village is the very thing to work on'; (to J. Edward Austen, 16 Dec. 1816) 'the little bit (two Inches wide) of Ivory on which I work with so fine a brush, as produces little effect after much labour'. In 1801 the family moved to Bath, in 1806, after Mr Austen's death, to Southampton, and in 1809 to Chawton, again in Hampshire; for a few weeks before her death Jane lodged in Winchester, where she died of Addison's disease. The novels were written between the activities of family life, and the last three (*Mansfield Park, *Emma, and *Persuasion) are known to have been written in the busy family parlour at Chawton.

The Juvenilia, written in her early and mid-teens, are already incisive and elegantly expressed; Love and Friendship was written when she was 14, A History of England ('by a partial, ignorant and prejudiced historian') at 15; at 16 A Collection of Letters; and sometime during those same years, Lesley Castle. *Lady Susan is also an early work, written probably in 1793–4. Of the major novels, *Sense and Sensibility was published in 1811, *Pride and Prejudice in 1813, Mansfield Park in 1814, Emma in 1816, *Northanger Abbey and Persuasion posthumously in 1818. They were, however, begun or completed in a different order. The youthful sketch Elinor and Marianne (1795–6) was followed in 1797 by First Impressions, which was refused without reading by the publisher Cadell; Elinor and Marianne was rewritten in 1797–8 as Sense and Sensibility. Northanger Abbey followed in 1798–9 and was in 1803 sold to the publishers Crosby and Sons who paid the author £10 but did not publish. In 1809 Sense and Sensibility was again revised for publication, and First Impressions was recreated and renamed Pride and Prejudice.

Between the writing of Northanger Abbey and the revision of Sense and Sensibility she wrote an unfinished novel, *The Watsons, probably begun in 1804 and abandoned in 1805, on her father's death—an event which may account for her comparatively long silence at this period. Mansfield Park was begun at Chawton in 1811, Emma in 1814, Persuasion in 1815; and in 1817,

the year of her death, the unfinished *Sanditon. It is likely that although Northanger Abbey was, together with Persuasion, the last of the novels to be published, it was the earliest of the completed works as we now have them.

The novels were generally well received from publication onwards; the prince regent (whose librarian urged Austen to write 'an historical romance, illustrative of the history of the august house of Coburg') kept a set of novels in each of his residences, and Sir W. *Scott praised her work in the *Quarterly Review in 1815; he later wrote of 'that exquisite touch which renders ordinary commonplace things and characters interesting'. There were, however, dissentient voices; C. *Brontë and E. B. *Browning found her limited, and it was not until the publication of J. E. Austen Leigh's Memoir in 1870 that a Jane Austen cult began to develop. Since then her reputation has remained consistently high, though with significant shifts of emphasis, some of them springing from D. W. Harding's seminal essay, 'Regulated Hatred: An Aspect of the Work of Jane Austen' (*Scrutiny, 1940), which presents her as a satirist more astringent than delicate, a social critic in search of 'unobtrusive spiritual survival' through her works. See Jane Austen: The Critical Heritage, ed. B. C. Southam (1968). The standard text of the novels (6 vols, 1923–54) is by R. W. Chapman, who also edited the letters (new edn 1995 by D. Le Faye). There are biographies by C. *Tomalin and David Nokes, both 1997.

AUSTER, Paul (1947–   ), American novelist, screenwriter, poet, and playwright, born in Newark, New Jersey, and educated at Columbia University. He began to write while earning his living as a translator, caretaker, switchboard operator, editor, and cook on an oil tanker. His earliest one-act plays were influenced by *Pinter and *Beckett, and his first novel, Squeeze Play, was a *Chandleresque thriller published under the pseudonym 'Paul Benjamin'. He gained critical recognition with his New York Trilogy (City of Glass, 1985; Ghosts, 1986; and The Locked Room, 1987), which uses the conventions of the detective novel to investigate urban isolation, identity, and the link between language and meaning. Further examination of the possibilities and limitations of fictional genres followed with the dystopian fable In the Country of Last Things (1987), and Moon Palace (1989), which links a *picaresque plot to developments in American history. The Music of Chance (1991), an allegory of two men forced to build a wall, was filmed in 1993 by Philip Haas. In the early 1990s Auster worked on an adaptation of his own short tale, Auggie Wren's Christmas Story, with the director Wayne Wang. This collaboration produced two films, both released in 1995: Smoke (with a script by Auster) and Blue in the Face (directed by Wang and Auster and improvised around their loose sketches) are uncharacteristically optimistic stories of urban life.

AUSTIN, Alfred (1835–1913), of a Roman Catholic family, educated at Stonyhurst and Oscott College; he shortly abandoned his faith. Upon inheriting a fortune from his uncle, he gave up a career as a barrister for literature. An ardent imperialist and follower of *Disraeli, he became in 1883 joint editor with W. J. *Courthope of the newly founded *National Review*, and was its sole editor for eight years from 1887. Between 1871 and 1908 he published 20 volumes of verse, of little merit. A prose work, *The Garden that I Love* (1894), proved popular, and in 1896, to widespread mockery, Austin was made *poet laureate, shortly afterwards publishing in *The Times* an unfortunate ode celebrating the Jameson Raid. Himself a waspish critic of his contemporaries, he was much derided and parodied as a poet. His *Autobiography* appeared in 1911. See N. B. Crowell, *Alfred Austin*, Victorian (1953).

autobiography in its modern form may be taken as writing that purposefully and self-consciously provides an account of the author's life and incorporates feeling and introspection as well as empirical detail. In this sense autobiographies are infrequent in English much before 1800. Although there are examples of autobiography in a quasi-modern sense earlier than this (e.g. Bunyan's conversion narrative *Grace Abounding*, 1666, and Margaret *Cavendish's 'A True Relation', 1655–6) it is not until the early 19th cent. that the genre becomes established in English writing: *Gibbon's *Memoirs* (1796) are a notable exception.

From 1800 onwards the introspective Protestantism of an earlier period and the Romantic movement's displeasure with the fact/feeling distinction of the Enlightenment provided for personal narratives of a largely new kind. They were characterized by a self-scrutiny and vivid sentiment that produced what is now referred to, following Robert *Southey (1809), as *autobiography*. Early in the 19th cent. William Wordsworth gives in *The Prelude* (1805) a sustained reflection upon the circumstances of he himself being the subject of his own work; and in the second half of the century John Henry *Newman in his *Apologia pro Vita Sua* (1864) publicly and originally reveals a personal spiritual journey. This latter with its public disclosure of the private domain had a dramatic and far-reaching influence upon the intelligentsia of late Victorian society. With its discussion of private experience, autobiography in the 20th cent. became increasingly valued not so much as an empirical record of historical events (although this has remained important) but as providing an epitome of personal sensibility among the intricate vicissitudes of cultural change. Vera *Brittain achieved a seriousness of observation and affect to provide in *Testament of Youth* (1933) a major work on the conduct of the First World War. In the area of more domestic, but no less social concerns J. R. *Ackerley in his *My Father and Myself* (1968) constructed an autobiography of painful frankness in a disquisition upon his unusual family relations, his affection for his dog, and the tribulations of his homosexuality. More recently in a continuing vein of contemporary commentary Tim Lott in *The Scent of Dead Roses* (1996) discussed the suicide of his mother and amalgamated autobiography, family history, and social analysis in a virtuoso performance of control and pathos. Useful works on English autobiography are Wayne Shumaker, *English Autobiography* (1954), and James Olney, *Metaphors of Self* (1972). The standard source for examples of autobiographies in Britain before 1951 is William Matthew's *British Autobiographies* (1955). The most comprehensive survey of premodern autobiographical writings is by Georg Misch (1878–1965) in his *Geschichte der Autobiographie* (4 vols, 1949–69, History of Autobiography). The importance of autobiography for hermeneutical analysis within the human sciences was adumbrated by Misch's father-in-law Wilhelm Dilthey (1833–1911) in his *Einleitung in die Geisteswissenschaften* (1883, Introduction to Human Sciences). The truthfulness or not of autobiography is essentially a matter that must be left to biographers and philosophers. The plausibility of an autobiography however must find its authentication by the degree to which it can correspond to some approximation of its context. Autobiographies are increasingly used in the social sciences to discuss the diffuse space between sociality and ego.

Autolycus, (1) in Greek mythology, a son of Hermes celebrated for his craft as a thief, who stole the flocks of his neighbours and mingled them with his own; (2) the roguish but charming pedlar in Shakespeare's *The Winter's Tale*, so named because he is 'a snapper-up of unconsidered trifles'.

Avalon, in the Arthurian legends, one of the Celtic 'Isles of the Blest' (comparable to the classical 'Fortunate Isles'), to which Arthur is carried after his death. The name is variously explained as the island of apples (by *Geoffrey of Monmouth, among others) and as the island of Avalloc who ruled it with his daughters, including Morgan. *Glastonbury has also been identified as the burial-place of Arthur and hence with Avalon. For discussion, see R. S. Loomis in R. S. Loomis (ed.), *Arthurian Literature in the Middle Ages* (1959), 65–8.

AVELLANEDA, Alonso Fernández de, the name assumed by the author of the false Part II of *Don Quixote*, issued in 1614. Cervantes's own Part II appeared in 1615.

AVERROËS (Abū a'l-Walīd Muhammad bin Ahmad bin Rushd) (1126–98), a Muslim physician born at Córdoba in Spain (Chaucer's Physician knows of him: *Canterbury Tales*, General Prologue, 433), and a philosopher, the author of a famous commentary on *Aristotle. He is placed in the Limbo of the Philosophers with *Avicenna by *Dante (*Inferno*, iv. 144). He is the inspiration for 'Latin Averroism' (1230 and afterwards), associated with Siger of Brabant, which regarded Aristotle as absolute in philosophy even when his view of things was not reconcilable with the absolute truth of Faith, a view which was repeatedly opposed (as by *Aquinas) and condemned (as by Tempier, 1277) until *Ockham in the 14th cent., when it became the unofficial norm. He is of immense importance as the conveyor of Aristotle back into the Western tradition, and he attracted a great deal of attention. His view that the active intellect was separable and distinct from the passive was opposed by Aquinas in *De Unitate Intellectus*.

AVICENNA (Abū-a'Ali al-Husayn bin Sīna) (980–1037), a Persian physician (a capacity in which he was known to Chaucer's Physician—*Canterbury Tales*, General Prologue, 432—and Pardoner—VI. 889) and philosopher, a voluminous writer who made commentaries on *Aristotle and *Galen. His views of love have been said to be influential on the ideas of *courtly love, by A. J. Denomy in *The Heresy of Courtly Love* (1947), and he was a major influence on the development of 13th-cent. *Scholasticism in his reordering of *Neoplatonism on an Aristotelian basis. *Dante places him with *Averroës in the limbo of the philosophers (*Inferno*, iv. 143).

Avon, the Sweet Swan of, *Shakespeare, born at Stratford-upon-Avon, first so called by Ben *Jonson in his commemorative poem in the First *Folio, 1623, 'To the memory of my beloved, The AUTHOR MR. WILLIAM SHAKESPEARE: AND what he hath left us'.

Awkward Age, The, a novel by H. *James.

Awntyrs of Arthure at the Terne Wathelyne, The (The Adventures of Arthur at the Tarn Wadling, in Cumberland), an alliterative poem in 715 lines probably from the last quarter of the 14th cent. from the region of Cumberland or the Scottish Lowlands, surviving in five 15th-cent. manuscripts. It seems to have borrowed from the alliterative *Morte Arthure and from Sir *Gawain and the Green Knight. The romance is in two parts: in the first, while out hunting, Gawain and Gaynor (Guinevere) are visited by an apparition, from the lake, of Gaynor's mother who asks for 30 masses to be said for the relief of her suffering soul (a motif derived from the legend of the trental of St *Gregory); the ghostly figure attacks the vices of Gawain, Arthur, and the court. This criticism links the first to the second part of the poem set at Arthur's court in which a knight, Sir Galeron of Galway (Galloway), demands the return of lands which Arthur had confiscated and given to Gawain. Honour is satisfied: the knight's lands are returned, and Gaynor has the masses said for her mother. The poem (in complex 13-line stanzas) is impressively written and is one of the most admired alliterative poems.

It has been edited by R. Hanna (1974); see also J. Speirs, *Medieval English Poetry* (1957), 252–62 (first part of poem).

Ayala's Angel, a novel by A. *Trollope, published 1881.

Egbert Dormer fails to provide for his daughters, and on his death Lucy and Ayala are farmed out to relations. The romantic Ayala has a high ideal of the man she wishes to marry, but must choose from the vulgar Captain Batsby, her callow cousin Tom Tringle, and ugly Jonathan Stubbs. Stubbs's persistence and good sense overcome all Ayala's objections, and he ends the novel transfigured into her 'Angel of Light'. Meanwhile the practical Lucy has attached herself to a penniless but deserving sculptor. Incidental interest derives from the matrimonial tribulations of the daughters of the wealthy Sir Thomas Tringle.

AYCKBOURN, Sir Alan (1939–), playwright, born in London, whose first plays were produced at Scarborough, where he has since 1971 been artistic director of the Theatre-in-the-Round. His first London success, *Relatively Speaking* (1967, pub. 1968), was followed by many others, including *Absurd Person Singular* (1973, pub. 1974); *The Norman Conquests* (1974, pub. 1975; a trilogy with elaborately overlapping action covering the same period of time and the same events from different points of view); *Absent Friends* (1975, pub. 1975); and *Joking Apart* (1979, pub. 1979). The plays are comedies of suburban and middle-class life, showing a keen sense of social nuance and of domestic misery and insensitivity, and displaying the virtuosity of Ayckbourn's stagecraft; Benedict Nightingale (*An Introduction to Fifty Modern British Plays*, 1982) comments that they succeed as comedies despite 'an intricacy of plot better fitted to farce, and themes sometimes more suited to tragedy', and detects, in common with other critics, an increasingly sombre note in his work. Later plays include *Sisterly Feelings* (1980), *A Chorus of Disapproval* (1986), *Women in Mind* (1986), *A Small Family Business* (1987), *A Man of the Moment* (1990), *Invisible Friends* (1991), and *Wildest Dreams* (1993).

Ayenbite of Inwit, a devotional manual translated in 1340 by Dan Michel of Northgate, Canterbury, into English prose from the French moral treatise *Les Somme des vices et des vertues*, also known as *Le Somme le roi* because it was composed for Philip III of France in 1279 by its author, the Dominican Frère Loren of Orléans. The French original may have been one of the sources for Chaucer's 'Parson's Tale' (see *CANTERBURY TALES, 24), and it is possible that the English version too was known to Chaucer. The manuscript claims to be in the author's hand, and it is full of elementary translating errors. The text has very little literary interest and is of note only as a specimen of the Kentish dialect in the 14th cent. It has been edited by R. Morris (EETS OS 23, 1866), rev. P. O. Gradon (1965).

AYER, Sir A(lfred) J(ules) (1910–89), educated at Eton and Christ Church, Oxford, Grote professor of minds and logic at University College London (1946–59), Wykeham professor of logic at Oxford University

(1959–78). He was the author of *Language, Truth and Logic* (1936), which was the first exposition of logical positivism in the English language, *The Foundations of Empirical Knowledge* (1940), and *The Problem of Knowledge* (1956), as well as volumes of philosophical essays and histories of modern philosophy. In these volumes, he carried further the traditions of British empiricism. He also published two volumes of autobiography, *Part of My Life* (1977) and *More of My Life* (1984).

Ayesha, (1) a novel by *Morier; (2) a novel by Sir H. R. *Haggard.

Aymon, *The Four Sons of,* a medieval French romance telling of Charlemagne's struggle with these four noblemen, the eldest and most important of whom was *Rinaldo. The English prose version of the romance is founded on *Caxton's printed version (1489–91), there being no surviving manuscript. It has been edited by O. Richardson, EETS ES 44 (1884, repr. Kraus 1973).

Ayrshire Legatees, The, a novel by J. *Galt, published 1821.

   The book largely takes the form of letters recording the adventures of a worthy Scottish minister, Dr Zachariah Pringle, and his family, in the course of a visit which they pay to London in order to take possession of a legacy. Their naïve comments on their experiences, and the comments of their friends in Scotland on the letters themselves, produce what is in effect a social satire, on travellers, on London society, and on the 'douce folk' at home.

AYRTON, Michael (1921–75), artist and writer, whose varied output of sculptures, illustrations, poems, and stories reveals an obsession with flight, myths, mirrors, and mazes. As a young man he worked for a while with Wyndham *Lewis, and an exhibition, *Word and Image* (National Book League, 1971), explored their literary and artistic connections. His writings include *The Testament of Daedalus* (1962, poetry), *Fabrications* (1972, short stories), and *The Maze Maker* (1967) and *The Midas Consequence* (1974), both novels.

AYTOUN, William Edmonstoune (1813–65), a descendant of the poet Sir Robert Aytoun (1570–1638), the reputed author of the lines on which Burns based *'Auld Lang Syne'. Educated at Edinburgh University, he divided his life between law and literature, becoming professor of belles-lettres at Edinburgh in 1845, and sheriff of Orkney in 1852. He is remembered for his share of the *Bon Gaultier ballads (1845), and for his *Lays of the Scottish Cavaliers*. The first of the lays appeared in *Blackwood's Magazine* in Apr. 1843, and the volume was published in 1849. Modelled on Sir W. *Scott and *Macaulay, these patriotic ballad-romances, based on stories of *Montrose, Dundee, and other Scottish heroes, were extremely popular. Aytoun also wrote *Firmilian, or The Student of Badajoz* (1854), a mock-tragedy in which he parodied the poems of the *Spasmodic school; it played a decisive role in ending the vogue for such works.

B

Bab Ballads, a collection of humorous ballads by W. S. *Gilbert (who was called 'Bab' as a child by his parents), first published in *Fun*, 1866–71. They appeared in volume form as *Bab Ballads* (1869); *More Bab Ballads* (1873); *Fifty Bab Ballads* (1877).

Babbitt, a novel by S. *Lewis.

BABBITT, Irving (1865–1933), American critic and professor at Harvard, born in Ohio. He was, with Paul Elmer More (1864–1937), a leader of the New Humanism, a philosophical and critical movement of the 1920s which fiercely criticized *Romanticism, stressing the value of reason and restraint. His works include *The New Laokoon* (1910), *Rousseau and Romanticism* (1919), and *Democracy and Leadership* (1924). T. S. *Eliot, who described himself as having once been a disciple, grew to find Babbitt's concept of humanism inadequate as an alternative to religion, and described it (in an essay published in 1928 in *Forum*) as 'a product—a by-product—of Protestant theology in its last agonies'.

BABEL, Isaak Emmanuilovich (1894–?1941), Russian Jewish writer born in Odessa, the son of a shopkeeper. After an Orthodox Jewish upbringing, he arrived in Petrograd in 1915. *Gorky published Babel's first story in 1916. From 1917 Babel served as soldier and war correspondent, taking part in the Polish campaign with the First Cavalry in 1920. From this came his masterpiece, the collection of stories *Red Cavalry* (1923–5), which describes with harsh vigour the savagery of war and its paradoxical fascination for the intellectual Jewish narrator Lyutov. Many of Babel's other stories are loosely autobiographical ('The Story of My Dovecot', 'First Love'), but he also wrote a cycle of stories about a very different Jewish life, that of the Odessan gangster Benya Krik ('The King', 'How It Was Done in Odessa', and others). Neither his ornamentalist style nor his themes found favour with the Soviet authorities, and in the late 1920s he came under increasing pressure. This led to almost total artistic silence, but he was again attacked at the First Congress of the Union of Soviet Writers. He was arrested in 1939 and disappeared into the Soviet penal system: the date of his death is tentative. Like other writers, Babel was posthumously rehabilitated, and editions of his work appeared in the Soviet Union in the 1950s and 1960s, though his Jewishness would seem to be the reason for a tacit new ban on publication of his work. In the rest of the world his reputation as a master of the short story continues to grow. *Red Cavalry* was trans-lated by J. Harland in 1929, and the *Complete Works* (2002) by Peter Constantine.

Babylon, an old ballad, the plot of which is known 'to all branches of the Scandinavian race', of three sisters, to each of whom in turn an outlaw proposes the alternative of becoming a 'rank robber's wife' or death. The first two chose death and are killed by the outlaw. The third threatens the vengeance of her brother 'Baby Lon'. This is the outlaw himself, who thus discovers that he has unwittingly murdered his own sisters, and thereupon takes his own life. The ballad is in *Child's collection (1883–98).

BACH, German family of musicians, of which Johann Sebastian (1685–1750) has become a central figure in British musical appreciation since a revival of interest in the early 19th cent. led by Samuel Wesley (1766–1837, son of C. *Wesley) and *Mendelssohn. His youngest son, Johann Christian (1735–82), settled in London in 1762 and became known as the 'English Bach': he became music-master to the family of George III, and though his operas for London were in the prevailing Italian fashion he also wrote various arias in English and some settings of folk songs. He was painted by his friend *Gainsborough and is buried in St Pancras churchyard.

Back to Methuselah: *A Metabiological Pentateuch* (1918–20) is an infrequently performed cycle of five plays by Bernard *Shaw, beginning in the Garden of Eden and reaching the year ad 31,920, which examines the metaphysical implications of longevity. Shaw revised the text and its preface, and added a postscript, in the mid-1940s when choosing *Back to Methuselah* to represent his work in the Oxford University Press *World's Classics series.

Backbite, Sir Benjamin, one of the scandal-mongers in Sheridan's *The School for Scandal*.

Bacon, Friar, see FRIER BACON, AND FRIER BONGAY.

BACON, Francis, first Baron Verulam and Viscount St Albans (1561–1626), the fifth son of Sir Nicholas Bacon, lord keeper to Queen Elizabeth 1558–79, by his second marriage, to Lady Anne Cooke. Bacon's mother was the daughter of Sir Anthony Cooke, tutor to King Edward VI, and was an exceptionally gifted scholar and translator in her own right. One of her sisters married the queen's chief minister, *Burleigh. Bacon was born in London, at York House in the Strand, and with his brother Antony went up to Trinity College, Cambridge, between 1573 and 1575; they were tutored by the master, John Whitgift, subsequently archbishop of Canterbury. As part of his grooming for high public office he spent from 1576 to 1579 with the queen's ambassador to France, Sir Amias Paulet, studying statecraft and performing diplomatic duties. Bacon's public career suffered two serious setbacks. His father died suddenly, in Feb. 1579, having settled estates on his first four sons, and in the process of doing so for his youngest. Deprived of an inheritance, Bacon returned to England to become a lawyer, entering Gray's Inn in 1579, graduating in 1582. His abilities were soon recognized, and he was appointed a lecturer in law and invited to sit on government legal committees while still in his twenties. In 1581 he became an MP (for Bossiney, Cornwall) and served in every parliament until 1621, first in the Commons, then in the Lords. He achieved recognition as a parliamentary speaker, but his boldness in the 1593 session in opposing the unusually heavy taxes that the queen wanted led to his being expelled from royal favour, promotion to higher legal office going to his rival, *Coke. The queen continued to employ Bacon in various legal offices, severely testing his loyalty to the Crown by appointing him one of the prosecutors of his former patron the earl of *Essex, whose increasingly headstrong behaviour led him eventually to the scaffold. Under King James, Bacon achieved the public offices for which he had so long been preparing. Knighted in 1603, he became king's counsel in 1604, solicitor-general in 1607, attorney-general in 1613, a privy counsellor in 1616, lord keeper in 1617, and lord chancellor in 1618. Having more than emulated his father in public office, he excelled him in rank, being elevated to the House of Lords as Baron Verulam in 1618, and created Viscount St Albans in 1621. Although remarkable, the promotion was well deserved, for Bacon impressed everybody with his forensic skills, intellectual penetration, and ability to present complex issues clearly. But the higher reaches of state office carried their own dangers, and Bacon increasingly found that his carefully worked out advice and counsel were ignored both by James and by the court favourite, the first earl of *Buckingham. In the absence of a proper salary structure, government officials under James depended for their livelihood on gifts from suitors and on selling their office, leading to a high degree of corruption from which many (particularly Buckingham) profited. In 1621 a parliamentary group bent on reform, led by Coke and Sir Lionel Cranfield, attacked the system of monopolies, where lucrative patents were allocated by nepotism (Buckingham's two brothers benefited richly) and enforced by illegal means. While attempting to censure Bacon, who as head of the Court of Chancery had issued licences to patentees at the king's request, they heard of two aggrieved suitors who had followed the custom of giving presents to Bacon as presiding judge, but had not won their case. The government's enemies succeeded in having him impeached in the House of Lords on charges of bribery, even though (unlike other venial judges) he had never allowed such presents to sway his judgement, and at this point both James and Buckingham abandoned him as scapegoat for their own unpopular policies. Bacon's career was ruined: he was given a huge fine, imprisoned in the Tower, and forbidden to come within 10 miles of the court. But the fine was never collected; the imprisonment lasted three days, the whole affair being cynically intended to placate the reform party, while the real abuses continued. Deprived of power, Bacon was vulnerable to Buckingham's greed, and was made to sell York House in the Strand. Out of office, he devoted himself fully to writing, producing in quick succession *A History of the Life and Reign of King *Henry VII* (1622), the *De Dignitate & Augmentis Scientiarum* (1623, a Latin expansion of *The Advancement of Learning*), the *Essays* (1625), and the posthumously published *New Atlantis* (1627). Until his downfall, Bacon's writings were the product of the vacations or other leisure time in a busy public career. Simultaneously a Protestant or moderate Calvinist (as his *Confession of Faith* shows) and a humanist, sharing that movement's emphasis on the individual's duty to take part in a *vita activa* for the common good, all Bacon's intellectual activities were directed towards practical ends, from which the whole of society would benefit. He outlined many schemes for reforming the laws, making them easier to understand and more coherent; he wanted the universities to widen their curriculum from the three traditional professions (theology, law, medicine) to take in the 'arts and sciences at large'; and he was ahead of his time in realizing that a continuous growth of knowledge was possible. Bacon's plan to reform the whole of natural philosophy (or science), outlined in the fragmentary *Instauratio Magna* (1620), of which the *Novum Organum* was the only more or less complete part, aimed to effect a new union between 'the mind and the universe', from which would spring a range of inventions to 'overcome the necessities and miseries of humanity'. (See also BACONIAN THEORY.)

Bacon's writings inspired the founding of the *Royal Society in 1662, and had a considerable influence on *Hobbes, *Boyle, *Locke, *Defoe, and many others. The fullest edition of his works was prepared by James Spedding (14 vols, 1857–74); see also *Francis Bacon*, ed. Brian Vickers (1996).

BACON, Roger (1210/14–after 1292), the 'Doctor Mirabilis', a philosopher who studied at Oxford and Paris where he probably became Doctor before returning to England c.1250, at which time, probably, he joined the Franciscan order. It is likely that he remained at Oxford until c.1257 when he incurred the suspicions of the Franciscans and was sent under surveillance to Paris where he remained in confinement for ten years. He produced at the request of his friend Pope Clement IV (1265–8) Latin treatises on the sciences (grammar, logic, mathematics, physics, and modern philosophy); his great work is the *Opus Maius*, and he also completed an *Opus Minus* and an *Opus Tertium*. He was again in confinement for his heretical propositions, *c.*1278–92, and is said to have died and been buried at Oxford. He has been described as the founder of English philosophy. A conservative in theology, which he regarded as incomparably supreme among the arts, he advocated support for it from an appeal to experience rather than from the Scholastic method of argument employed in the *Summa* of *Albertus Magnus and *Alexander of Hales. He begins by stating the chief causes of error to be ignorance of languages, especially Greek, bad Latin translations, and lack of knowledge of the natural sciences, especially mathematics. At the same time, his outlook remained partly mystical. His attack on the Scholastic method was taken up again and developed by William of *Ockham in the next century. He was a man of immense learning, with a wide knowledge of the sciences and of languages: Greek, Hebrew, and Aramaic. He was also a practical scientist; he invented spectacles and indicated the method by which a telescope might be constructed. He was vulgarly regarded as a necromancer in the Middle Ages because of his interest in the new sciences, especially chemistry and alchemy.

Bacon and Bungay, (1) the rival publishers in Thackeray's *Pendennis*; (2) see FRIER BACON, AND FRIER BONGAY.

Baconian theory, the theory that F. *Bacon wrote the plays attributed to *Shakespeare. It was started in print in the mid-19th cent., and is based partly on (supposed) internal evidence in Shakespeare's plays (the knowledge displayed and the vocabulary), and partly on external circumstances (the obscurity of Shakespeare's own biography, and the assumption that the son of a Warwickshire husbandman was unlikely to be capable of such skilful creations). Some holders of the theory have found in the plays cryptograms in support of it, e.g. in the word 'honorificabilitudinitatibus' in *Love's Labour's Lost* (v. i), which has been rendered in Latin as 'These plays, F. Bacon's offspring, are preserved for the World'; the word, however, is found elsewhere as early as 1460. The best recent treatment of the topic is to be found in S. *Schoenbaum, *Shakespeare's Lives* (1970).

Badman, *The Life and Death of Mr*, an allegory by *Bunyan, published 1680.

The allegory takes the form of a dialogue, in which Mr Wiseman relates the life of Mr Badman, recently deceased, and Mr Attentive comments on it. The youthful Badman shows early signs of his vicious disposition. He beguiles a rich damsel into marriage and ruins her; sets up in trade and swindles his creditors by fraudulent bankruptcies and his customers by false weights; breaks his leg when coming home drunk; and displays a short-lived sickbed repentance. His wife dies of despair and Badman marries again, but his second wife is as wicked as he is and they part 'as poor as Howlets'. Finally Badman dies of a complication of diseases. The story is entertaining as well as edifying and has a place in the evolution of the English novel.

Badon, Mt, the scene of a battle connected with *Arthur, first mentioned by *Gildas without reference to Arthur. It was almost certainly a real battle, fought against the Saxons or Jutes by the Britons somewhere in the south of England. The *Annales Cambriae* give the date of the battle as 518, declaring that Arthur carried the cross of Christ as his standard there; but it is likely that this is merely an embellishment of Gildas. *Geoffrey of Monmouth identifies Badon as Bath; other authorities say it was Badbury near Wimborne.

BAEDEKER, Karl (1801–59), editor and publisher, of Essen, Germany. He started the issue of the famous guidebooks in Koblenz, and this was continued by his son Fritz, who transferred the business to Leipzig. The term 'Baedeker raids' was applied to the deliberate bombing in the Second World War of provincial cities of great historic and cultural importance, such as Bath, Exeter, and Norwich.

BAGE, Robert (1720–1801), Quaker, revolutionist, and a paper-maker by trade, was much influenced by *Rousseau and other French thinkers. He was the author of six novels: *Mount Henneth* (1781); *Barham Downs* (1784); *The Fair Syrian* (1787); *James Wallace* (1788); *Man as He Is* (1792); and *Hermsprong, or Man as He Is Not* (1796). His original talent was much admired by Sir W. *Scott and other discerning critics. Scott included the first, second, and fourth of the works in the 'Ballantyne Novels'. *Hermsprong*, the most remarkable of Bage's works, is the story of a 'natural' man, brought up without the 'civilized' conventions of morality or religion, among Native Americans (see PRIMITIVISM). Bage did not care to think of his works as 'novels', but rather as illustrations of certain views and attitudes.

BAGEHOT, Walter (1826–77), born in Langport, Somerset, educated at Bristol and University College London. He was called to the bar and then joined the shipping and banking business of his father. He contributed articles on economic, political, historical, and literary subjects to various periodicals, became joint editor with R. H. *Hutton of the *National Review* from 1855, and editor of *The Economist* from 1860 until his death. He was author of *The English Constitution* (1867; ed. R. H. S. Crossman, 1963), which takes the form of a philosophical discussion appraising the actual values of the elements of the constitution and has remained a classic introduction to the study of English politics, in spite of historical change. His *Physics and Politics* (1872) is 'an attempt to apply the principles of natural selection and inheritance to political society'. *Lombard Street* (1873) is a lively analysis of the money market of his day. Among his other works are *Biographical Studies* (1881) and *Lit-*

erary Studies (1879–95), which includes critical essays on Shakespeare, *Sterne, and the notable 'Wordsworth, Tennyson, and Browning, or Pure, Ornate, and Grotesque Art in English Poetry'. See *Collected Works*, ed. N. A. F. St John-Stevas (8 vols, 1965–74) and *Life* by N. A. F. St John-Stevas (1959).

Bagford Ballads, The, illustrating the last years of the Stuarts' rule and the last years of the 17th cent. They were published by the Ballad Society in 1878. They were assembled by John Bagford (1651–1716), originally a shoemaker, a book-collector who made for Robert Harley, first earl of Oxford, the collection of ballads that was subsequently acquired by the duke of *Roxburghe, and at the same time made a private collection for himself.

Bagnet, Mr and Mrs, characters in Dickens's *Bleak House*.

BAGNOLD, Enid Algerine (Lady Jones) (1889–1981), novelist and playwright, who spent much of her early childhood in the West Indies, returning to England to Prior's Field, an intellectually progressive school run by the mother of A. *Huxley. She worked as nurse and ambulance driver during the First World War (see her *Diary without Dates*, 1917) and married in 1920, but continued to write and move in artistic and bohemian circles, writing several novels, of which the best known and commercially most successful was *National Velvet* (1935, filmed 1944 with Elizabeth Taylor as the girl who wins the Grand National). Of her plays, the most successful was *The Chalk Garden* (1955). Her *Autobiography* was published in 1969.

Bagstock, Major Joe, a character in Dickens's *Dombey and Son*.

BAILEY, Nathan or Nathaniel (d. *c*.1742), author of the *Universal Etymological Dictionary* (1721), a forerunner of Dr *Johnson's, and very popular. Johnson used Bailey's *Dictionarium Britannicum* (1730), embracing the 1721 volume, while compiling his own work.

BAILEY, Paul (1937–   ), London-born actor turned novelist, who studied at the Central School of Speech and Drama. His first novel, *At the Jerusalem* (1967), was a pioneering example of what was to become the 'old-people's-home' genre. Other works include *Trespasses* (1970, whose hero attempts to survive his wife's suicide); *A Distant Likeness* (1973, the story of a policeman unnerved by his own violent impulses); *Peter Smart's Confessions* (1977); and *Old Soldiers* (1980), which describes the interwoven London odysseys of two very different old men. *Gabriel's Lament* (1986) is the story of Gabriel Harvey and his vexed relationship with his elderly, priapic, coarse, racist, and opinionated father Oswald and his vanished young mother, who abandons him as a child: the plot followed Gabriel's migrations through various vividly evoked and eccentrically populated London neighbourhoods, and includes a return to the one-time workhouse, the

Jerusalem, where Gabriel works as a skivvy before becoming a successful writer. The novel ends with an epiphany in the academic Midwest. Gabriel reappears in *Sugar Cane* (1993) as joint confessor (with venereologist Esther Potocki) to the tales of a youth, Stephen, caught up in a Dickensian underworld of rent boys in the pay of 'the Bishop', a late 20th-cent. version of Fagin. Bailey also published a biography of a brothel keeper, *An English Madam: The Life and Work of Cynthia Payne* (1982), and a volume of memoirs, *An Immaculate Mistake* (1990), recording his working-class childhood and his intense relationship with his dominating mother.

BAILEY, Philip James (1816–1902). After embarking on a career as a barrister, he retired in 1836 to his father's house at Old Basset, near Nottingham, where he wrote *Festus*, published in 1839. A second edition appeared in 1845, and the final edition of 1889, which exceeded 40,000 lines, incorporated the greater part of three volumes of poetry that had appeared in the interval (*The Angel World*, 1850; *The Mystic*, 1855; *Universal Hymn*, 1867). *Festus* is Bailey's own version of the legend of Goethe's *Faust*; it was also strongly influenced by *Paradise Lost*. At one time it was immensely popular, admired for its 'fire of imagination' (E. B. *Browning), but, like the other works of the *Spasmodic school of which Bailey was considered the father, it is now little read.

Bailiff's Daughter of Islington, The, an old ballad included in Percy's *Reliques*. A squire's son loves the bailiff's daughter of Islington (probably the place of that name in Norfolk), but his friends send him to London bound as an apprentice. After seven years the lovers meet again and are united.

BAILLIE, Joanna (1762–1851), Scottish dramatist and poet, brought up in Lanarkshire, but later settling in London. She published a book of verse (*Poems; Wherein It Is Attempted to Describe Certain Views of Nature and of Rustic Manners*) in 1790, but achieved success in 1798 with her first volume of *Plays on the Passions*, in which each verse drama displays the effect of one particular passion. *Basil*, on the subject of love, and *De Montfort*, on hatred, were the most successful; *De Montfort* was produced by *Kemble and Mrs *Siddons in 1800. The volume brought her the friendship of Sir W. *Scott, who called her 'the immortal Joanna', but her dramas were strongly criticized by *Jeffrey in the *Edinburgh Review*. A second volume of the *Passions* appeared in 1802, *Miscellaneous Plays* in 1804, and a third *Passions* volume in 1812. Her tragedy *Constantine Paleologus; or The Last of the Caesars* (1804) was considered by J. S. *Mill to be 'one of the best dramas of the last two centuries'. Her most successful play, *The Family Legend*, based on a bitter Scottish feud, was produced in 1810 with a prologue by Scott and an epilogue by *Mackenzie. Scott described it as a 'complete and decided triumph' and it established

Miss Baillie as a literary and social success. Her house in Hampstead became a meeting place for many of the literary figures of her time.

BAILLIE, Robert (1599–1662), Scottish Presbyterian divine, who was with the Covenanters' army in 1639 and in 1640 went to London to draw up accusations against *Laud. An opponent of religious toleration, he attacked the Independents in *Anabaptism* (1647) as anarchists and sexual deviants. His *Letters and Journals*, ed. D. Laing (1842), are valuable records of the Civil War.

Bailly, Harry, in Chaucer's *Canterbury Tales* the host of the Tabard Inn where the pilgrims meet in the General Prologue. We learn his name ('Herry Bailly') from the Cook's Prologue (l. 4358) and he has been tentatively identified with an ostler of that name in the Subsidy Rolls for Southwark 1380/1 and perhaps with the member of Parliament for Southwark 1376/7 and 1378/9. See account in Riverside edition, note on l. 751, p. 825. He initiates the storytelling competition which forms the basis of the work, and acts as master of ceremonies along the way.

BAIN, Alexander (1818–1903), son of a weaver, born in Aberdeen. He left school when 11 years old to work in his father's trade, but continued his studies and obtained at 18 a bursary at Marischal College. He visited London and made the acquaintance of *Mill and *Carlyle. In 1860 he was appointed professor of logic in Aberdeen. His two principal philosophical works were *The Senses and the Intellect* (1855) and *The Emotions and the Will* (1859). His autobiography was published in 1904.

BAINBRIDGE, Beryl (1934–   ), novelist, born in Liverpool, and educated at the Merchant Taylors' School, Liverpool. She began her career as an actress, and her first novels (A *Weekend with Claude*, 1967; *Another Part of the Wood*, 1968) were little noticed, but in the 1970s a series of original and idiosyncratic works established her reputation. These include *The Dressmaker* (1973), *The Bottle Factory Outing* (1974), *Young Adolf* (1978), and *Winter Garden* (1980). Short, laconic, and rich in black comedy, they deal with the lives of characters at once deeply ordinary and highly eccentric, in a world where violence and the absurd lurk beneath the daily routine of urban domesticity, evoked in carefully observed detail: in *Injury Time* (1977), for example, a quietly illicit dinner party becomes headline news when invaded by a gang of criminals on the run who take its guests hostage. The juxtaposition of the banal and the bizarre is also a feature of the dialogue, which shows a fine ear for the oddities of contemporary speech. Other novels include *Harriet Said* (1972), *Watson's Apology* (1984, a reconstruction of a Victorian murder), *Filthy Lucre* (1986), *An Awfully Big Adventure*

(1989), and *Birthday Boys* (1991, based on R. F. *Scott's Arctic expedition). A selection of her short stories, *Mum and Mr Armitage*, was published in 1985, and a collected edition in 1994. *Every Man for Himself* (1996) is a recreation of the fatal four days' voyage of the Titanic, narrated by Morgan, the nephew of the owner of the shipping line. *Master Georgie* (1998) is set during the Crimean War, and *According to Queeney* (2001) is written from the viewpoint of the daughter of Dr *Johnson's friend, Mrs *Thrale.

BAJAZET, or **BAJAYET,** ruler of the Ottomans (1389–1402), overran the provinces of the Eastern empire and besieged Constantinople, but was interrupted by the approach of Timour (Tamerlane), and was defeated and taken prisoner by him. He figures in Marlowe's *Tamburlaine the Great* and Rowe's *Tamerlane.

BAKER, Sir Samuel White (1821–93), traveller and big game hunter. He explored Ceylon, where he established an agricultural settlement in Nuwara Eliya, superintended the construction of a railway across the Dobrudja, and in 1861 undertook the exploration of the Nile tributaries, during which he discovered and named Lake Albert Nyanza (Lake Albert). His adventures are vividly described in his works, which include *The Rifle and Hound in Ceylon* (1854), *The Nile Tributaries of Abyssinia* (1867), and *Ismailia* (1874).

BAKHTIN, Mikhail Mikhailovich (1895–1975), Russian critic, who studied classics at Petrograd University. While developing his original theoretical approach in the 1920s and 1930s with a circle of collaborators including the Marxist scholars V. Voloshinov and P. Medvedev, he suffered periods of unemployment and internal exile during Stalin's purges, eventually securing a teaching position in Saransk. During a severe paper shortage, Bakhtin tore up his own manuscripts to roll cigarettes. Apart from *Problems of Dostoevsky's Poetics* (1929), he could publish little until the post-Stalin cultural thaw of the 1960s, when his book *Rabelais and His World* (1965) appeared, followed in the 1970s by a number of essays written at earlier times; some of these were translated as *The Dialogic Imagination* (1981). Confusingly, works by Voloshinov and Medvedev also came to be attributed to Bakhtin. In Western academic criticism since the late 1970s Bakhtin's influence has been widespread, partly because of his attractive notion of the *carnivalesque in his study of Rabelais, but more for his concept of 'dialogism', in which language (and truth) are viewed as an open field of interactive utterances, and literature—especially the novel—is valued for keeping in play a variety of voices and languages.

Balaam, Sir, the subject of satire in Pope's *Moral Essays* (Ep. iii. 339–402), a religious 'Dissenter' and frugal citizen who, tempted by wealth, becomes a corrupt courtier. He has been tentatively identified as Thomas Pitt (1653–1726), grandfather of William *Pitt the elder.

BALAKIREV, Mily Alexeyevich (1837–1910), Russian composer. Early in his career, between 1858 and 1861, he wrote an overture and incidental music to *King Lear, which he revised in 1902–5: there seems to have been no stage production in mind, but the piece is satisfying both as an interpretation and as a musical whole. He was an aggressive and obstinate character, and the acknowledged leader of the Russian nationalist school of composers: it was he who pressed upon *Tchaikovsky the plan for a symphonic work based on *Romeo and Juliet, and who later bullied the composer into writing his *Manfred symphony.

Balan, see BALYN.

Balaustion's Adventure: *Including a Transcript from Euripides,* by R. *Browning, published 1871.

The story, suggested by a passage in *Plutarch's *Life of Nicias,* is set just after the defeat of the Athenian expedition against Sicily in 413 BC. A group of pro-Athenians from Rhodes, inspired by the young girl Balaustion, is intercepted on its voyage to Athens by a pirate ship and is forced to seek shelter in the harbour of Syracuse, where it is refused entry until it is discovered that Balaustion can recite a play by *Euripides, who was greatly admired in Sicily although neglected in his native Athens. The play is *Alcestis,* a performance of which Balaustion narrates, mingling with the text her own comments and descriptions. Browning is thus able to represent Euripides' play in his own interpretation, within the framework of another speaker's consciousness, a marriage of conventional drama with dramatic monologue which continues the experiment with form begun with *The Ring and the Book. The plot of the *Alcestis,* with its concentration on a woman's love for her husband and her rescue from Death by a heroic figure, also links the poem to *The Ring and the Book,* and the character of Balaustion has, like that of Pompilia, been thought to be modelled on Elizabeth Barrett (to whom there is a direct allusion at ll. 2668–71). Balaustion reappears in *Aristophanes' Apology.

BALBOA, Vasco Núñez de (1475–1517), one of the companions of *Cortés, the conqueror of Mexico. He is said to have joined the expedition of 1510 to Darien as a stowaway. It was he who first, in 1513, discovered the Pacific Ocean, not Cortés, as *Keats supposed when he wrote:

> Or like stout Cortez when with eagle eyes
> He stared at the Pacific.

(Nor was Balboa silent on this occasion, as Keats makes Cortés. He exclaimed 'Hombre!') Balboa was beheaded by Pedrarias, governor of Darien, on a charge of treason.

'Balder Dead', a poem by M. *Arnold.

BALDWIN, James (1924–87), black American novelist, born in Harlem, the son of a preacher. His first novel, *Go Tell It on the Mountain* (1953), set in Harlem, was followed by several on a more international scale, dealing with both homosexuality and the situation of American blacks; they include *Giovanni's Room* (1956), *Another Country* (1962), and *Just above My Head* (1979). He also wrote short stories, political and autobiographical essays, and plays, including *Blues for Mister Charley* (1964).

BALDWIN, William, see MIRROR FOR MAGISTRATES, A.

BALE, John (1495–1563), bishop of Ossory, author of several religious plays, a history of English writers, and numerous polemical works in favour of the cause of the Reformation. He is notable in the history of the drama as having written *King John,* the first English historical play, or at least a bridge between the *morality and the historical play proper.

BALESTIER, Charles Wolcott (1861–91), American author and publisher, who visited England in 1888 to secure English manuscripts for Lovell, the publishing company which had issued his novel *A Fair Device* (1886). He became a director of Heinemann and Balestier, a firm which published English and American books on the Continent. He is remembered for his collaboration with *Kipling (who married his sister in 1892): he wrote the American chapters for *The Naulahka* (1892) and Kipling dedicated his *Barrack-Room Ballads* to him in the same year.

BALFOUR, Arthur James, first earl of Balfour (1848–1930), philosopher and distinguished statesman, educated at Eton and Trinity College, Cambridge, notable in a literary connection as the author of philosophic and other works, some of which attracted wide attention. These include *A Defence of Philosophic Doubt* (1879), *The Foundation of Belief* (1895), *Questionings on Criticism and Beauty* (Romanes Lecture, 1909), *Decadence* (Henry *Sidgwick Memorial Lecture, 1908), *Theism and Humanism* (Gifford Lectures, 1915), and *Theism and Thought* (Gifford Lectures, 1923). *Chapters of Autobiography* (1930, ed. Mrs Dugdale) is a fragment of autobiography. In 1893 he was president of the *Society for Psychical Research.

Balfour, David, a character in R. L. Stevenson's *Kidnapped and *Catriona.

Balin, see BALYN.

'Balin and Balan', one of Tennyson's *Idylls of the King, first published 1885. It is the story of two brothers who kill each other unwittingly, Balan mistaking for a demon the impassioned Balin, who is driven to frenzy by a conviction of Guinevere's adultery. (See BALYN.)

BALIOL, John de (d. 1269), father of John de Baliol, king of Scotland (1292–6). He founded Balliol College,

Oxford, about 1263, as an act of penance imposed for having 'vexed and damnified' the churches of Tynemouth and Durham.

BALL, John, the leader of the Peasants' Revolt of 1381. He is the subject of W. Morris's *A Dream of John Ball*.

ballad, originally a song intended as an accompaniment to a dance; hence a light, simple song of any kind, or a popular song, often one attacking persons or institutions. Broadside ballads, such as those hawked by Autolycus in *The Winter's Tale*, were printed on one side of a single sheet (a *'broadside'* or 'broadsheet') and sold in the streets or at fairs. In the relatively recent sense, now most widely used, a ballad is taken to be a single, spirited poem in short stanzas, in which some popular story is graphically narrated (e.g. *Sir Patrick Spens*), and in this sense of the word the oral tradition is an essential element, though there has been much discussion as to the origin and composition of the old English ballads. In the great collection of F. J. *Child, *English and Scottish Popular Ballads* (5 vols, 1882–98), the oldest ballad is *Judas* (c.1300), with an uncharacteristically religious theme; ballads more traditionally deal with the pagan supernatural (e.g. *Tam Lin*), with tragic love (e.g. *Barbara Allan*), or with historical or semi-historical events, e.g. the Border ballads, or the *Robin Hood ballads. There was a notable awakening of interest in the form in Britain in the 18th cent., which led to the researches and collections of *Percy (*Reliques*, 1765) and *Ritson, to the forgeries of *Chatterton and the adaptations of *Burns, and to the deliberate antiquarian imitations of *Tickell (*Lucy and Colin*), Percy himself (*The Hermit of Warkworth*), Mallet (*'William and Margaret'), Goldsmith (*'The Hermit'), and others. Scott's *Minstrelsy of the Scottish Border* is a mixture of traditional ballads, adaptations, and imitations, whereas the *Lyrical Ballads* of *Wordsworth and *Coleridge manifests, in poems like 'The Idiot Boy' and the *Ancient Mariner*, their own interpretation and development of the term. The form has continued to inspire poets, from *Keats (*'La Belle Dame sans Merci') to W. *Morris, *Hardy, *Yeats, and *Causley, and flourishes in a popular folk form as well as in a more literary guise. The ingredients of ballads, both ancient and modern, vary, but frequently include the use of a refrain (sometimes altered slightly at the end of each stanza, to advance the story), stock descriptive phrases, and simple, terse dialogue. See G. H. Gerould, *The Ballad of Tradition* (1932) and M. J. C. Hodgart, *The Ballads* (1950). (For 'ballad stanza' see METRE.)

ballade, strictly a poem consisting of one or more triplets of seven- or (afterwards) eight-line stanzas, each ending with the same line as refrain, and usually an envoy addressed to a prince or his substitute; e.g. *Chaucer's *Compleynt of Venus*. It was a dominant form in 14th- and 15th-cent. French poetry, and one of its great masters was *Villon. The form enjoyed a

minor English revival in the late 19th cent. in the work of *Swinburne, *Henley, and *Dobson.

ballad opera, a theatrical and musical form, popular in the 18th cent., in which the action of the play (usually comic) is carried in spoken prose, interspersed with songs set to traditional or currently fashionable melodies. The first ballad opera, *The Beggar's Opera* (1728) by Gay, with music arranged by J. C. Pepusch, is also the most famous. Its success touched off a series of imitations, and the ballad opera became the main weapon of the English faction in its battle with the Italian operatic invaders, *Handel at their head. But its vogue was short-lived and began to decline at the end of the next decade, though it left an heir in the English comic opera of the later 18th cent.: works like *Arne and *Bickerstaffe's *Thomas and Sally* (1760) or *Love in a Village* (1762) or Linley and Sheridan's *The Duenna* (1775) are very close to the ballad opera.

BALLANTYNE, James (1772–1833), brother of John *Ballantyne, at first a solicitor, then a printer in Kelso. He printed Scott's *Minstrelsy of the Scottish Border* in 1802, and continued to print Scott's works. He transferred his press from Kelso to Edinburgh in 1802 and Scott became a partner in 1805. In 1809 he took a quarter share in the publishing and bookselling business of John Ballantyne and Co., started by his brother and Scott. Although his printing business was highly successful, he was bankrupted by the crash of Constable and Co. in 1826.

BALLANTYNE, John (1774–1821), brother of James *Ballantyne. He became in 1809 manager of the publishing firm started by himself and Sir W. *Scott. While his brother's printing business flourished, the publishing and bookselling firm did not, and was allowed to run down. Scott planned *Ballantyne's Novelist's Library* (1821–4) solely for Ballantyne's financial benefit, but only one volume was published before Ballantyne's death.

BALLANTYNE, R(obert) M(ichael) (1825–94), a nephew of the Ballantyne brothers (above). He began his career in the Hudson's Bay Company, and in 1848 published his diary, *Hudson's Bay*. He then returned and worked for *Constable's printing firm, and in 1856 published his first adventure story, *Snowflakes and Sunbeams; or The Young Fur Traders* (soon known only by its subtitle). After the success of *The Coral Island* in 1857 he became an extremely successful professional writer of stories for boys. In search of authentic background he travelled widely, visiting Norway, Canada, Algeria, and elsewhere, and working at various occupations, including fireman and miner. He wrote over 80 novels; his narrative skill, the interest of his settings, and the manly virtues of his heroes ensured their popularity well into this century. Among his best-known works are *The Gorilla Hunters* (1862) and *Black Ivory* (1873).

BALLARD, J(ames) G(raham) (1930–   ), English novelist and short story writer, born in Shanghai and educated at Cambridge. He became known in the 1960s as the most prominent of the 'New Wave' *science fiction writers. His first short story was published in 1956 in *New Worlds*, a periodical to which he continued to contribute during the influential editorship of *Moorcock. His first novel, *The Drowned World* (1962), a 'catastrophe' novel in which the world turns into a vast swamp, was followed by *The Drought* (1965), in which he imagined post-apocalyptic landscapes and populated them with realistically observed, ultra-obsessive characters. *Crash* (1973) was an outstanding, outrageous work, years ahead of its time, if there could ever be a time when the eroticism of car accidents would be an acceptable subject for a novel. His collections of short stories include *The Terminal Beach* (1964), *The Disaster Area* (1967), and *Vermilion Sands* (1971). In *Empire of the Sun* (1984, filmed 1988) he turned away from science fiction to draw on his own wartime experiences in a Japanese prison camp in China. Other novels include *The Venus Hunters* (1986), *The Day of Creation* (1987), *Running Wild* (1988), *War Fever* (1990), *The Kindness of Women* (1991), and *Rushing to Paradise* (1994), a disturbing contemporary fable about eco-fanaticism. *Cocaine Nights* (1996), set in a high-security leisure-oriented Mediterranean resort complex, represents Ballard at a new peak in his considerable storytelling powers. Ballard has been viewed increasingly as an important figure in the literary mainstream.

Balnibarbi, in *Gulliver's Travels*, the country, subject to the king of Laputa, of which Lagado is the capital, where in every town there is an academy of 'projectors', engaged on inventions for increasing the welfare of mankind, none of which come to perfection.

Balor, the chief of the *Fomors of Gaelic mythology. One of his eyes had the power of destroying whatever it looked on. The eye was put out and Balor himself slain by Lugh, the sun-god, at the great battle of Moytura.

Balthazar ('possessor of treasure'), (1) one of the three Magi, represented as king of Chaldea; (2) the name assumed by Portia as a lawyer in Shakespeare's *The Merchant of Venice*, also that of one of her servants.

Balyn (Balin Le Savage) and Balan are the subjects of the second Book in Malory's *Morte D'Arthur* (the second part of the first of Malory's *Works* in Vinaver's edition, headed 'The Knight with the Two Swords' which refers to Balyn). The two are brothers who kill each other unknowingly after a series of linked adventures; Balyn is the more prominent, though the two are sometimes confused in Malory. Balyn deals King Pellam the *Dolorous Stroke which causes the Waste Land, a disaster which is redeemed by the Grail Quest. He also kills the *Lady of the Lake when she seeks his head as reward for giving Arthur *Excalibur.

BALZAC, Honoré de (1799–1850), French novelist, author of the great series of co-ordinated and interconnected novels and stories known collectively as the *Comédie humaine*. The 91 separate completed works—137 were planned—that make up the whole were written between 1827 and 1847. The preface (1842) to the first collected edition (1842–8) of Balzac's works, which first applies the general title to them, sets out his grand design to give an authentic and comprehensive fictional representation of French society in the latter years of the 18th cent. and the first half of the 19th. Critical analysis was an essential part of his aim, and by bold analogies between the novelist's art and that of the natural scientist and the historian he claimed for his 'studies' the orderly method, seriousness of purpose, and intellectual scope of these disciplines. The novels were classified under three main heads: (1) *Études de mœurs* (by far the largest category, subdivided into those dealing with private, provincial, and country life, Paris, military matters, and politics); (2) *Études philosophiques*; (3) *Études analytiques*. The cast of the *Comédie humaine* comprises more than 2,000 characters, some of them, like the master-criminal Vautrin or the moneylender Gobseck, appearing at different stages of their careers in several novels. Characteristically, Balzac interests himself in the supernatural and the mysterious (especially in the *Études philosophiques*), in the operation of the passions, in the role of money in shaping personal and social relations, in the determining effect of environment on the individual, and, conversely, in the various courses taken by energy and ambition in pursuit of social fulfilment. A list of the masterpieces of the *Comédie humaine* would include: *La Peau de chagrin* (1831), *Illusions perdues* (1837–43), *Le Médecin de campagne* (1833), *La Rabouilleuse* (1840), *La Cousine Bette* (1846), and *Le Cousin Pons* (1847). His influence on later fiction has been immense, and his work is an essential reference point in the history of the European novel.

BAMFORD, Samuel (1788–1872), weaver and poet, born in Middleton, Lancashire. He became a *Chartist activist, and in his *Passages in the Life of a Radical* (1840–4) gives a vivid first-hand description of the Peterloo massacre (1819) which both he and his wife witnessed: he was subsequently arrested and imprisoned for a year. He wrote a quantity of popular verse: his *Homely Rhymes, Poems and Reminiscences* (1843) collects some political poems, some pastoral, and a few written in dialect, many of them displaying considerable verve and energy. *Early Days*, an account of his childhood and of old Lancashire customs, was published 1848–9.

Ban, in the Arthurian legends, king of Benwick in Brittany, brother of Bors, and the father of *Launcelot.

Bananas, a literary periodical which ran from 1975 to 1981, edited by E. *Tennant (1975–9) then by Abigail Mozley (1979–81), with contributions from Ted

*Hughes, J. G. *Ballard, A. *Sillitoe, E. *Feinstein, Heathcote *Williams, and others.

BANDELLO, Matteo (1485–1561), a Lombard who fled to France and was made bishop of Agen by Francis I; he was the best writer of Italian short stories in the 16th cent. Many of his tales were translated by Belleforest into French (1564–82) and 13 of these French versions were rendered into English by Geoffrey Fenton in his *Certaine Tragicall Discourses* (1567). Painter's *Palace of Pleasure* includes 25 of Bandello's tales, nine translated from the Italian and 16 from Belleforest. Bandello is the source of plots for many English plays, including *Much Ado about Nothing*, *Twelfth Night*, and *The Duchess of Malfi*.

Bangorian Controversy, a church controversy of the early years of George I, which followed a sermon by B. *Hoadly. The Anglican Church, committed to the hereditary principle of monarchy, found itself in difficulties on the death of Queen Anne and the succession of the Hanoverians; strict churchmen refused to take the oath of allegiance and became 'nonjurors'. Hoadly's sermon, preached before the king (and said to have been suggested by him) in 1717 and immediately published, was called 'The Nature of the Kingdom or Church of Christ' and its text was 'My kingdom is not of this world.' It attacked church authority, establishing conscience and sincerity as guide and judge in religious matters. It provoked over 200 incensed replies, notably from *Law and T. *Sherlock.

BANIM, John (1798–1842), Irish novelist, dramatist, and poet, chiefly remembered for his faithful drawing of Irish life and character contained in the highly successful *Tales by the O'Hara Family*, partly written with his brother Michael and published in 1825, 1826, and 1827. Several of the novels later published separately first appeared in the *Tales*. Novels chiefly written by John include *The Nowlans* (1833), *The Boyne Water* (1836), and *John Doe* (1842). His *Damon and Pythias*, a tragedy successfully performed in London in 1821, was followed by other successful dramas.

Michael Banim (1796–1874) claimed after his brother's death that he was himself responsible for 13 of their joint 24 works; according to his claim, his own books include *The Croppy* (1828), a sombre tale of the uprising of 1798, *The Mayor of Windgap* (1835), and *The Town of the Cascades* (1864).

BANKS, Iain Menzies (1954–), Scottish novelist and science fiction writer, born in Dunfermline. He came to controversial prominence with his first novel, *The Wasp Factory* (1984), a macabre tale of teenage fantasies of death and destruction, narrated by 16-year-old Frank Cauldhame, who lives with his 'scientist' father on the east coast of Scotland: it was condemned by some for its graphic violence but praised by others for its targeting of macho values. Succeeding novels, such as *Walking on Glass* (1985), *The Bridge* (1986), *Espedair Street* (1987), *Complicity* (1993, about a journalist investigating a series of bizarre deaths), and *A Song of Stone* (1997, a post-apocalyptic story set around an ancestral castle in the aftermath of a civil war), more than fulfilled his early promise. Under the name Iain M. Banks he has also written several science fiction novels, including *Consider Phlebas* (1987), *Feersum Endjinn* (1993), *Excession* (1996), and *Inversions* (1998). *The State of the Art* is a collection of short fiction, both science fiction and mainstream, also published under the name of Iain M. Banks.

BANKS, Sir Joseph (1743–1820), eminent explorer and naturalist, who studied the flora of Newfoundland in 1766, accompanied *Cook round the world, and subsequently visited the Hebrides and Iceland. He became a member of Dr Johnson's literary *Club, and was president of the *Royal Society 1778–1820.

BANKS, Lynne Reid (1929–), novelist and children's writer, born in London. Her first novel, *The L-Shaped Room* (1960), about Jane, a young girl, pregnant with an illegitimate child and living in a London bedsit, was a great success (film, 1962). This was followed by a number of other novels for adults, including *An End to Running* (1962); *Children at the Gate* (1968); *The Backward Shadow* (1970) and *Two is Lonely* (1974), sequels to *The L-Shaped Room*; *The Warning Bell* (1984); and *Casualties* (1986). From the 1970s she became better known as a writer for children and adolescents with books such as *One More River* (1973), set during the Six Day War of 1967, and *The Adventures of King Midas* (1976).

Bannatyne Club, the, founded in 1823, with Sir W. *Scott as president, for the publication of old Scottish documents (see Lockhart's *Scott*, lviii). The club was dissolved in 1861. George Bannatyne (1545–1608), in whose honour it was named, was the compiler in 1568 of a large collection of Scottish poems.

Bannockburn, near Stirling, the scene of the great battle in 1314 when Robert Bruce utterly routed the English under Edward II, and all Scotland was thereby lost to the latter. The battle is described in Scott's *Lord of the Isles*, vi.

Banquo, Scottish general and companion of *Macbeth in Shakespeare's play of that name, to whom the witches prophesy that his issue will be kings. According to *Holinshed he was the founder of the House of Stuart, and so an ancestor of James I and VI.

Bantam, Angelo Cyrus, in Dickens's *Pickwick Papers*, grand master of the ceremonies at Bath.

BANVILLE, John (1945–), novelist and journalist, born in Wexford, literary editor of the *Irish Times* since 1989. His fiction is characterized by a densely referential and ironic style and by a preoccupation with the act of writing itself. *Long Lankin* (1970), his first book, was a collection of episodic short stories and a concluding novella, 'The Possessed', which was drawn on for his first novel, *Nightspawn* (1971), in which the narrator becomes a character in his own plot. *Birchwood* (1973), a novel with an Irish country-house setting, was followed by a trilogy of fictional biographies of figures from the history of science—*Doctor Copernicus* (1976), *Kepler* (1981), and *The Newton Letter: An Interlude* (1982)—in which the scientific search for certainty mirrors an exploration of the relationship between fiction and reality. The central figure of *Mefisto* (1986) is Gabriel Swan, a man obsessed by numbers. *The Book of Evidence* (1989) was followed by two loosely connected sequels: *Ghosts* (1993), whose protagonist, a scientist previously convicted of murder, goes with two companions to an almost deserted island, and *Athena* (1994), in which the same narrator becomes ensnared in a criminal conspiracy involving stolen works of art. *The Untouchable* (1997) is a deft transmutation of a spy novel, with a character based on Anthony Blunt. *The Sea* (2005, *Booker Prize) is a novel of grief, recollection and loss.

Barabas, the *'Jew of Malta', in Marlowe's play of that name.

BARAKA, Amiri, see PERFORMANCE POETRY.

Barbara Allan, a Scottish *ballad included in Percy's *Reliques*, on the subject of the death of Sir John Grehme for unrequited love of Barbara Allan, and her subsequent remorse. *Barbara Allen's Cruelty*, another ballad on the same theme, is also in the *Reliques*.

barbarian, see PHILISTINE.

BARBAULD, Mrs Anna Laetitia, née Aikin (1743–1825). She published several popular volumes of prose for children with her brother John *Aikin, and edited William *Collins (1794), *Akenside (1794), and S. *Richardson's correspondence (6 vols, 1804). After the suicide in 1808 of her mentally unstable husband, the Revd Rochemont Barbauld, she threw herself into increased literary activity, editing *The British Novelists* in 50 volumes (1810). She was a friend of Mrs H. *More, Mrs *Montagu, and a circle of Dissenting radical intellectuals, and supported radical causes (*Corsica: An Ode*, 1768; *Epistle to Wilberforce*, 1791). Her poem beginning 'Life, I know not what thou art' was much admired by *Wordsworth, but a more interesting production is her poem in heroic couplets *Eighteen Hundred and Eleven* (1811), which foretells the decline of Britain's 'Midas dream' of wealth, and the rise of prosperity and culture in America, whose tourists will come to visit with nostalgia 'the gray ruin and the mouldering stone' of England.

BARBELLION, see CUMMINGS, B. F.

BARBEY-D'AUREVILLY, Jules-Amédée (1808–89), French novelist and critic. He earned his living by literary journalism, and his collected articles—at once brilliant, prejudiced, and prophetic—fill several volumes. His major novels, *L'Ensorcelée* (1854) and *Le Chevalier des Touches* (1864), and his short stories, *Les Diaboliques* (1874), excel in their evocation of the desolate Cotentin landscapes of his childhood and its ancient Catholic and royalist traditions; and in their creation of proud, flamboyant, and tormented characters often susceptible to supernatural powers. His style combines spontaneity and elegance.

BARBOUR, John (c.1320–95), a Scottish poet, archdeacon of Aberdeen in 1357 and one of the auditors of the exchequer in 1372, 1382, and 1384. He probably studied and taught at Oxford and Paris. The only poem ascribed to him with certainty is *The Bruce* (*The Actes and Life of the Most Victorious Conquerour, Robert Bruce King of Scotland*), in over 13,000 lines, which dates from 1376; even if it is his, it has been argued that the poem was tampered with by John Ramsay, the writer of both the manuscripts in which the poem survives (from 1487 and 1489). The poem is a verse chronicle of the deeds of Bruce and his follower James Douglas, and it contains a celebrated, graphic account of *Bannockburn. Of the three other works sometimes attributed to him, *The Troy Book* has been denied him on linguistic grounds; *The Lives of the Saints* (50 legends, certainly from Barbour's period and area of origin) is disputed; and *The Buik of Alexander*, a translation of two French romances, may be his.

The Bruce, ed. W. W. Skeat in 4 vols (EETS es 11, 21, 29, 55, 1870–89); *The Bruce: A Selection*, ed. A. Kinghorn (1960); *The Bruce: A Selection*, ed. A. N. Douglas (1964); *The Buik of Alexander*, ed. R. L. G. Ritchie (Saltire Society Classics, 4 vols, 1920–8).

Barchester Towers, a novel by A. *Trollope, published 1857, the second in the *'Barsetshire' series.

Archdeacon Grantly's hopes of succeeding his father as bishop of Barchester are dashed when an ineffectual evangelical, Dr Proudie, is set over him by a new Whig government. The novel is a record of the struggle for control of the diocese. Mrs Proudie, the bishop's overbearing wife, shows her strength when she selects Mr Quiverful as the future warden of Hiram's Hospital. Despite the efforts of Mr Slope, the bishop's oily chaplain, and Grantly to push the claims of Mr Harding, Quiverful gains the appointment. When the old dean dies, Slope, anxious to take his place, persuades a national newspaper to advertise his own merits, and the conflict with Mrs Proudie intensifies. Slope's marital ambitions, however, start to get in his way. His designs on the fortune of Mrs Bold, Harding's widowed daughter, are handicapped by his flirtation with the fascinating but penniless Signora Vesey-Neroni, and the scandal is his undoing. The Puseyite Dr Arabin succeeds to the deanery and marries Mrs Bold, while Mrs Proudie sees to it that Slope is dismissed from his chaplaincy.

BARCLAY, Alexander (?1475–1552), poet, scholar, and

divine, probably of Scottish birth. He was successively a priest in the college of Ottery St Mary, Devonshire, a Benedictine monk at Ely, a Franciscan at Canterbury, and rector of All Hallows, Lombard Street, London. He translated Brant's *Narrenschiff* into English verse as *The Ship of Fools* (1509) and wrote his *Eclogues* at Ely (*c*.1513–14). He also translated a life of St George from *Mantuan and *Sallust's *Bellum Jugurthinum* (*c*.1520).

BARCLAY, John (1582–1621), a Scot born at Pont-à-Mousson in France, author of the extremely popular Latin romance *Argenis* (1621), which refers to real historical events and personages under a veil of allegory. He also wrote *Euphormionis Satyricon* (?1603–7), a satire on the Jesuits in the form of a *picaresque novel, also in Latin.

BARCLAY, Robert (1648–90), Scottish Quaker whose *Apology for the True Christian Divinity* (1678) is a reasoned defence of Quakerism. His collected works, *Truth Triumphant*, with a preface by W. *Penn, were published in 1692.

Bard, The, a Pindaric *ode by *Gray, published 1757, based on a tradition that Edward I ordered the violent suppression of the Welsh bards.

It opens with the surviving bard's cursing of the conqueror as he and his army return from Snowdon in 1283; he laments his slaughtered comrades, whose ghosts prophesy the fate of the Plantagenets. The bard then foretells the return of the house of Tudor and commits triumphant suicide. Johnson's dismissal of the poem (*Lives of the English Poets*, 1781) outraged its many admirers, who regarded it as a fine example of the *sublime, and it exerted a considerable influence on the imagination of both poets and painters (e.g. *Blake and J. *Martin).

Bardell, Mrs, in Dickens's *Pickwick Papers*, Mr Pickwick's landlady, who sues him for breach of promise.

Bardolph, a red-nosed rogue who is a soldierly companion of *Falstaff in Shakespeare's *1 and 2 *Henry IV*; and in *Henry V* is hanged for robbing a French church shortly before the battle of Agincourt. In *The Merry Wives of Windsor* Falstaff finds him a post as tapster at the Garter Inn.

BARETTI, Giuseppe Marc'Antonio (1719–89), born at Turin. He came to London in 1751 and, among other pursuits, taught Italian. One of his pupils was C. *Lennox, who introduced him to Dr *Johnson. The two became friends, and Baretti's standard work, *A Dictionary of the English and Italian Languages* (1760), was clearly influenced by Johnson's dictionary. In 1768 he published *An Account of the Manners and Customs of Italy*, a riposte to the *Letters from Italy*, by Samuel Sharp, which he considered a grossly unfair portrayal of his native land. In 1769 he was tried for stabbing a man in the street in self-defence; his acquittal was received with relief by his many eminent friends, who

included *Reynolds, *Burke, and *Garrick. His *A Journey from London to Genoa* was published in 1770. In these and other works he stimulated interest in and understanding of Italian literature and culture. His *Easy Phraseology for the Use of Young Ladies* (1775) sprang from lessons in conversation with one of the daughters of Mrs *Thrale, and was published with a preface by Johnson. An irascible man, Baretti finally quarrelled with Johnson over a game of chess.

BARHAM, R(ichard) H(arris) (1788–1845). He held various preferments, including that of a minor canon of St Paul's. His *The Ingoldsby Legends; or Mirth and Marvels, by Thomas Ingoldsby Esquire* were first published from 1837 in *Bentley's Miscellany and the *New Monthly Magazine*, and first collected in 1840. Their lively rhythms and inventive rhymes, their comic and grotesque treatment of medieval legend, and their quaint narratives made them immensely popular. One of the best known is the story of the Jackdaw of Rheims, who stole the archbishop's ring, was cursed, fell ill, but recovered when the curse was lifted, and became devout.

BARING, Maurice (1874–1945), educated at Eton and Trinity College, Cambridge. Versatile, prolific, and successful, he produced articles, plays, biography, criticism, poetry, translations, stories and novels, and works on painting and music, amounting to some 50 volumes. A gift for languages led him to the foreign office, and later as a reporter to the Russo-Japanese War. He is credited with having discovered *Chekhov's work in Moscow and helping to introduce it to the West. His *Landmarks in Russian Literature* appeared in 1910, *An Outline of Russian Literature* in 1914, and *The Oxford Book of Russian Verse* in 1924. Of his various novels *C* (1924), *Cat's Cradle* (1925), *Daphne Adeane* (1926), and *The Coat without Seam* (1929), all set in his own high social world, were very successful, and are still well regarded for their acute, intimate portrait of the time. Baring's conversion to the Roman faith is reflected in two historical novels of Tudor times, *Robert Peckham* (1930) and *In My End Is My Beginning* (1931). His novella *The Lonely Lady of Dulwich* (1934) is often held to be the best of his works.

BARING-GOULD, Sabine (1834–1924). He travelled much on the Continent with his parents during his boyhood, then was educated at Clare College, Cambridge. In 1867 he married a mill girl, an experience described in his first novel *Through Fire and Flame* (1868): they produced a large family of 14 children. From 1881 until his death he was both squire and rector of Lew Trenchard in Devon. An extremely prolific writer and an enthusiastic if unscholarly antiquary, he wrote dozens of works on travel, religion, folklore, local legend, and folk song, composed various hymns (including 'Onward Christian Soldiers'), and published some 30 novels, of which the most celebrated, *Mehalah* (1880), was compared by *Swinburne to *Wuthering Heights. He also wrote a life of R. S. *Hawker, The Vicar of Morwenstow (1876).

BARKER, George Granville (1913–91), poet, born in Essex of an English father and Irish mother, and educated (briefly) at the Regent Street Polytechnic. His first publication was Thirty Preliminary Poems (1933), which was followed by Poems (1935), Calamiterror (1937, a semi-political poem inspired by the Spanish Civil War), and Lament and Triumph (1940). In 1939 he taught in a Japanese university, then lived in America and Canada from 1940 and 1943; he then returned to England, though living for further periods in America and Italy. His relationship with E. *Smart at this period is recorded in her prose poem By Grand Central Station I Sat Down and Wept (1945). His subsequent volumes include Eros in Dogma (1944), The True Confession of George Barker (1950, augmented 1965) and Collected Poems 1930–1965 (1965). Barker's earlier work is characteristically rhetorical, Dionysiac, and surreal, though some critics have suggested that he achieves disorder more by accident than intent; a neo-Romantic and a self-styled 'Augustinian anarchist', he has a marked penchant for puns, distortion, and abrupt changes of tone. His True Confession, written as he reached the age of 35, presents the poet as irreverent, defiant, offhand, Rabelaisian, and guilt-ridden at once ('this rather dreary | Joke of an autobiography'); its later stanzas, and works such as Villa Stellar (1978) and the long title poem of Anno Domini (1983), have a more sombre, reflective, questioning tone, although they too have moments of exuberance.

BARKER, Harley Granville-, see GRANVILLE-BARKER, H.

BARKER Howard (1946–   ), British dramatist born in London and educated at Sussex University. He came to prominence with a series of scathing dramas about the injustices of society: these included Stripwell (1975), Fair Slaughter (1977), The Loud Boy's Life (1980), No End of Blame (1981), Scenes from an Execution (1984), and two plays set in a nightmarish Britain of the future, That Good between Us (1977) and The Hang of the Gaol (1978). His work, never wholly realistic, gradually became more darkly comic in tone, more exotic in language and form, and less direct in its attack on Establishment targets: as witness The Castle (1985), Seven Lears (1989), and Ten Dilemmas (1992). Despite its complexities, Barker's work has acquired a cult following, reflected in the formation in 1989 of the Wrestling School, a theatre company specializing in the production of his plays that was still active in 1999. He has also written for television and adapted Middleton's *Women Beware Women (1986) for the stage.

BARKER, Jane (1652–1732), poet and novelist, from Wiltsthorpe, Lincolnshire, who practised as a healer in London, and converted to Catholicism. *Jacobite convictions inform her writing. Her verse was published as Poetical Recreations (1688) or preserved in manuscript volumes transcribed in France, where she lived after the 1688 Revolution. Virtually blind from the 1690s, she returned to England in 1704. Her prose fictions, some centring on Galesia, her self-portrait, are Love Intrigues (1713), the innovative story of a spinster and author, the romance Exilius (1715), and collections of stories, A Patch-Work Screen (1723) and The Lining to the Patch-Work Screen (1726).

BARKER, Pat(ricia) (1943–   ), novelist, born in Thornaby-on-Tees, north Yorkshire. She studied at the London School of Economics in the 1960s, then had a brief teaching career before making her notable debut as a novelist with Union Street (1982). This episodic account of the lives of seven working-class neighbours partly recalled the northern realist novels of *Barstow and *Sillitoe, with one crucial difference: Barker's main characters were women. Leavening the occasional brutalism of her narratives with generosity and flashes of humour, Barker gave the novel a unique texture which Hollywood tried to replicate, with comically disastrous results, in the movie adaptation Stanley and Iris (1989). Her next two novels were Blow Your House down (1984), in which a group of prostitutes attempt to eke out their livelihood in fear of a marauding serial killer, and The Century's Daughter (1986), an ambitious alternative history of the 20th cent. as told by the elderly Liza Jarrett Wright to her sympathetic social worker. In The Man Who Wasn't There (1989), Barker achieved a feat of sustained empathy with its hero, a daydreaming, fatherless teenager growing up in the 1950s, but her real breakthrough came with the First World War novel Regeneration in 1991. Based on an encounter between *Sassoon and the psychologist and anthropologist William Rivers (1864–1922) at Craiglockhart War Hospital in 1917, it was followed by The Eye in the Door (1993) and The Ghost Road (1995, winner of the *Booker Prize), which concentrate on the fortunes of bisexual soldier Billy Prior. The trilogy has a tragic grandeur and rigorous lack of sentimentality quite unlike other fictional accounts of this period. Despite its contemporary setting, the First World War also haunts Another World (1998), the powerful story of a Newcastle family collapsing under the guilty weight of history.

Barkis, in Dickens's *David Copperfield, the carrier, who sent a message by David to Clara Peggotty that 'Barkis is willin''.

Barlaam and Josaphat, a late 12th-cent. Anglo-Norman romance, interesting as a Christianized version of the legend of Buddha. It appears first in the works of John of Damascus (8th cent.). In the story Josaphat, the son of an Indian king, Abenner, is converted by the Christian hermit Barlaam. Abenner, after first being hostile to Christianity, is converted too before his death, whereupon Josaphat abdicates to become a hermit. See edition by J. Koch, Altfranzösische Bibliothek, i (1879).

BARLOW, Joel (1754–1812), American poet and diplomat, born in Connecticut, who is remembered as the author of *The Columbiad* (1787, originally published as *The Vision of Columbus* and revised and renamed in 1807), a lengthy patriotic epic in heroic couplets, and of the more enjoyable mock epic *The Hasty-Pudding* (1796). Barlow was one of the 'Hartford Wits', and was, like most of them, a graduate of Yale.

Barnaby Rudge, a novel by *Dickens published in 1841 as part of *Master Humphrey's Clock*. The earlier of Dickens's two historical novels, it is set at the period of the Gordon anti-popery riots of 1780, and Lord George Gordon himself appears as a character. Like the later *A Tale of Two Cities*, it contains powerful evocations of mob violence, culminating in the sack of Newgate: Dickens wrote, 'my object has been to convey an idea of multitudes, violence and fury; and even to lose my own dramatis personae in the throng'.

Reuben Haredale, a country gentleman, has been murdered, and the murderer never discovered. His brother Geoffrey Haredale, a Roman Catholic, and the smooth villain Sir John Chester (who models himself on Lord *Chesterfield) are enemies; Chester's son Edward is in love with Haredale's niece Emma, and the elders combine, despite their hatred, to thwart the match. The Gordon riots, secretly fomented by Chester, supervene. Haredale's house is burned and Emma carried off. Edward saves the lives of Haredale and Emma and wins Haredale's consent to his marriage with the latter. Haredale discovers the murderer of his brother, the steward Rudge, father of the half-witted Barnaby and the blackmailer of Barnaby's devoted mother Mrs Rudge. Rudge is hanged, Barnaby (who had been swept along as unwitting participant in the riots) is reprieved from the gallows at the last moment, and Chester is killed by Haredale in a duel.

The vivid description of the riots forms the principal interest of the book, which also displays Dickens's concern with the demoralizing effect of capital punishment in the character of Dennis the Hangman and Hugh, the savage ostler who turns out to be Chester's son. Other characters involved in the plot include the upright locksmith Gabriel Varden, with his peevish wife and their coquettish daughter Dolly; Simon Tappertit, his aspiring and anarchic apprentice, and Miggs, his mean and treacherous servant; John Willett, host of the Maypole Inn, and Joe, his gallant son, who finally wins Dolly; and Grip, Barnaby's raven.

Barnacles, the, in Dickens's *Little Dorrit*, types of government officials in the 'Circumlocution Office'.

BARNARD, Lady Anne, see LINDSAY, A.

Barnardine, in Shakespeare's *Measure for Measure*, a prisoner 'that apprehends death no more dreadfully but as a drunken sleep; careless, reckless, and fearless of what's past, present, or to come'.

Barnavelt, Sir John van Olden, a historical tragedy, probably by J. *Fletcher and *Massinger, acted in 1619, within months of the execution of its real-life protagonist. This remarkable play was discovered by A. H. Bullen among the manuscripts of the British Museum, and printed in his *Old English Plays* (1883, vol. ii). An edition by W. P. Frijlinck was published in 1922.

The play deals with contemporary events in Holland. Barnavelt, the great advocate, disturbed by the growing power of the prince of Orange and the army, under cloak of religious movement conspires against him and raises companies of burghers in the towns to resist the army. The plot is discovered, the companies disarmed, and Barnavelt's principal associates are captured. One of these, Leidenberch, confesses. Barnavelt, who by virtue of his great position is still left at liberty though suspect, upbraids him and tells him that death is the only honourable course left to him. Leidenberch, in remorse, takes his own life. The prince of Orange, who had hitherto counselled moderation, now convinced of the gravity of the conspiracy, advises severe measures. Barnavelt is arrested, tried, and executed. An edition by T. H. Howard-Hill was published by the Malone Society in 1980.

BARNES, Barnabe (1571–1609), son of the bishop of Durham, educated at Brasenose College, Oxford. Early in 1598 he attempted to kill the recorder of Berwick with poisoned claret, but he successfully evaded sentence, living mainly in Durham. His sonnet sequence *Parthenophil and Parthenophe: Sonnettes, Madrigals, Elegies and Odes* had been published in 1593, and *A Divine Centurie of Spirituall Sonnets* in 1595. He published *Foure Bookes of Offices* in 1606, and in 1607 a vigorous Machiavellian drama, *The Divils Charter: A Tragaedie Conteining the Life and Death of Pope Alexander the Sixt*, said to have been performed before the king. It includes such melodramatic scenes as the murder of Lucrezia *Borgia with poisoned face wash. Though *Courthope described Barnes's poetry as 'a mixture of nonsense and nastiness', it is actually remarkable for its vigour and technical range. *Parthenophil and Parthenophe* was edited by V. A. Doyno in 1971.

BARNES, Djuna Chappell (1892–1982), American novelist, illustrator, short story writer, and playwright, born in Cornwall-on-Hudson; she studied art in New York, leading a bohemian life in Greenwich Village, then moved to Paris. Her publications include *A Book* (1923), a volume of plays, poems, and stories; *Ryder* (1928), a novel dealing with a man, his mother, and his mistress; *Ladies Almanack* (1928, privately printed in Paris), an erotic 18th-cent. pastiche of lesbian life; *The Antiphon* (1958), a verse drama. She is best remembered for *Nightwood* (1936), a novel which T. S. *Eliot described in his preface as one that would 'appeal primarily to readers of poetry . . .' and possessing 'a quality of horror and doom very nearly related to that of Elizabethan tragedy'. It evokes, in highly wrought, high-coloured prose, a nightmare cosmopolitan world (chiefly located in Paris and New York) peopled by tormented and mutually tormenting characters, linked by the enigmatic doctor, priest of the secret brotherhood of the City of Darkness; it mingles elements of *fin-de-siècle* decadence with premonitions of the neo-Gothic. Her *Selected Works* appeared in 1962.

BARNES, Julian Patrick (1946–   ), novelist, educated at the City of London School and Magdalen College, Oxford. He worked as a lexicographer on the *OED* supplement (1962–72) and as a reviewer for the *New Statesman*, the *Sunday Times*, and the *Observer*. His novels embrace an unusual blend of domestic realism and metaphysical speculation, sometimes combining them in one work. *Metroland* (1980) moves from a London schoolboy's suburbia to student Paris in 1968, and back again to marriage and mortgage in 1977. *Before She Met Me* (1982) deals with a recurrent theme of sexual jealousy, which resurfaces in *Talking It over* (1991), in which a rejected husband creates chaos by insisting on attending his ex-wife's second marriage to his ex-best friend. *Flaubert's Parrot* (1984), which won the Prix Médicis, is set in *Flaubert's Rouen and Croisset; it is a mixture of biographical detection, literary commentary, and fictional self-analysis, told in the person of Geoffrey Braithwaite, a retired doctor. *Staring at the Sun* (1986), which opens in the 1930s and ends in the 21st cent., deals with fear of death and the ageing process through its female protagonist Jean and her son Gregory. *A History of the World in 10½ Chapters* (1989) is a series of essays or stories linked by the theme of shipwreck and survival. *The Porcupine* (1992) is a satirical novella inspired by a visit to post-communist Bulgaria. *England, England* (1998) is a satire set in the near future, in which a tycoon with infantile delusions gathers a team of experts to transport or recreate every well-known aspect of English life, past and present, on the Isle of Wight. *Letters from London 1990–1995* (1995) reprints selections from Barnes's *New Yorker* column. *Cross Channel* (1996) and *The Lemon Table* (2004) are volumes of short stories, and *Arthur and George* (2005) is a historical novel based on a *cause célèbre* adopted by Conan *Doyle. He has also published several thrillers under the pseudonym Dan Kavanagh.

BARNES, William (1801–86), born near Sturminster Newton, of a farming family. He began work at the age of 14 for a solicitor, then moved to Dorchester where he contributed poems to the local paper. He learned Greek, Latin, and music, taught himself wood-engraving, and in 1823 became a schoolmaster at Mere. He married in 1827 and in 1835 moved his flourishing school to Dorchester. He was deeply interested in grammar and language, studied French, Italian, Welsh, Hebrew, Hindustani, and other languages, and waged a lifelong campaign to rid English of classical and foreign influences, suggesting many 'Saxonized' alternatives, such as 'sun-print' for photograph and 'fall-time' for autumn. He registered as a 'Ten-Year' man at St John's, Cambridge, in 1838, to study for a BD degree (which he acquired in 1851), was ordained in 1848, and took up the living of Whitcombe, moving to Cambe in 1862. *Orra, a Lapland Tale* appeared in 1822 and his *Poems of Rural Life in the Dorset Dialect* in 1844; *Hwomely Rhymes* followed in 1859 and *Poems of Rural Life*, written in standard English, in 1868. His collected dialect poems appeared as *Poems of Rural Life in the Dorset Dialect* in 1879.

As well as his volumes of poetry, Barnes also contributed articles on archaeology and etymology to the *Gentleman's Magazine* and, from 1852, to the *Retrospective Review*. He wrote textbooks, a primer of Old English (*Se Gefylsta*, 1849), *Philological Grammar* (1854), a *Grammar . . . of the Dorset Dialect* (1863), and other works reflecting his interest in philology and local history. He was one of the founders of the Dorchester Museum and as an old man became famed as a repository of old sentiments, customs, and manners.

According to his many admirers, who included *Tennyson, G. M. *Hopkins, *Hardy, and *Gosse, Barnes was a lyric poet of the first rank, but the difficulties presented by the Dorset dialect have greatly restricted his audience and contributed to the image of a quaint provincial versifier. His poems evoke the Dorset landscape, country customs (as in 'Harvest Hwome' and 'Woodcom' Feast'), and happy childhood, although his few poems of grief, such as 'Woak Hill' and 'The Wind at the Door', written after the death of his wife, are among his best. He was greatly interested in versification, prosody, and the techniques of verse (particularly in alliteration), and the wide variety of his forms much intrigued Hardy; his noun-combinations ('heart-heaven', 'sun-sweep', and 'mind-sight') foreshadow Hopkins. The dialect poems for which he is best remembered were written largely between 1834 and 1867; his standard English poems, written before and after those dates, were preferred by his publisher, Macmillan, and by Hardy. Hardy wrote an affectionate portrait in the *Athenaeum* on his death, and a poem, 'The Last Signal'. There is a life by W. T. Levy (1960).

Barney, in Dickens's *Oliver Twist*, a Jew, associate of Fagin.

BARNFIELD, Richard (1574–1620), educated at Brasenose College, Oxford. He published *The Affectionate Shepheard* in 1594, *Cynthia: With Certaine Sonnets* in 1595, and *The Encomion of Lady Pecunia* (the praise of money) in 1598. Two of his *Poems, in Divers Humors* (1598) appeared also in *The Passionate Pilgrim* (1599) and were once attributed to Shakespeare, the better known being the ode 'As it fell upon a day | In the merry month of May'. *The Affectionate Shepheard* is a pastoral (based on *Virgil's second eclogue) describing the love of Daphnis for Ganymede, and includes a rather surprising digression on the 'indecencie of mens long haire'. The 20 sonnets in *Cynthia* are also to Ganymede. Barnfield has the distinction of being the only Elizabethan poet other than Shakespeare known to have addressed love sonnets to a man.

baroque (from Portuguese *barroco*, Spanish *barrueco*, a rough or imperfect pearl), originally a term of abuse applied to 17th-cent. Italian art and that of other countries, especially Germany, influenced by Italy. It is characterized by the unclassical use of classical forms, and by the interpenetration of architecture, sculpture, and painting to produce grandiose and emotional effects.

In a literary context the word baroque is loosely used to describe highly ornamented verse or prose, abounding in extravagant conceits; it is rarely used of English writers (with the exception of the Italianate *Crashaw), but frequently applied to *Marino, whose name became synonymous with Marinism, and to Góngora, whose name supplied the term *Gongorism.

Barrack-Room Ballads, see KIPLING.

BARRÈS, Maurice (1862–1923), French novelist and essayist, deputy for Nancy (1889–93) and Paris (1906–23). Active in politics, Barrès was a committed nationalist–Boulangiste, anti-Dreyfusard, and militant of the Ligue de la patrie française. His reputation as a novelist rests largely upon his attempt to chronicle his times in three didactic trilogies. *Le Culte du moi* (*Sous l'œil des barbares*, 1888; *Un homme libre*, 1889; *Le Jardin de Bérénice*, 1891) locates a source of moral energy in a sense of self that is at once disciplined and liberated. The spiritual benefits of a living relationship with one's regional patrimony of family, native environment, and inherited tradition become the focus of attention in *Le Roman de l'énergie nationale* (*Les Déracinés*, 1897; *L'Appel au soldat*, 1900; *Leurs Figures*, 1902), which follows the fortunes of seven young men who leave Lorraine, Barrès's own province, to pursue their careers in Paris. *Les Bastions de l'Est* (*Au service de l'Allemagne*, 1905; *Colette Baudoche*, 1909; *Le Génie du Rhin*, 1921) explores the meeting of the French and German national characters in the eastern provinces of Alsace and Lorraine. *La Colline inspirée* (1913) presents the conflict between the Roman Catholic Church and a religious community rooted in regional consciousness.

BARRETT, Elizabeth, see BROWNING, E. B.

BARRIE, Sir J(ames) M(atthew) (1860–1937), born in Kirriemuir in Scotland, the son of a handloom weaver, educated at Dumfries and Edinburgh University. He began work with the *Nottinghamshire Journal*, an experience described in *When a Man's Single* (1888). In the same year he began his series of *'Kailyard school' stories and novels (for which he drew considerably on his mother's memories) based on the life of 'Thrums', his home town of Kirriemuir. These included *Auld Licht Idylls* (1888), *A Window in Thrums* (1889), and his highly successful *The Little Minister* (1891), a work which Barrie came to dislike. His first play, *Richard Savage*, was performed in London in the same year. In 1894 he married the actress Mary Ansell, divorce following in 1909. In 1896 he published his frankly adoring portrait of his mother,

Margaret Ogilvy, and the first of his two most revealing books, *Sentimental Tommy*, followed in 1900 by *Tommy and Grizel*, which contains hints of *Peter Pan*. Meanwhile came his sentimental comedy *Quality Street*, performed in 1901, and in 1902 the enduring successful play *The Admirable Crichton* (see CRICHTON). *Peter Pan* was first performed in 1904 and was followed by a story, *Peter Pan in Kensington Gardens*, in 1906 and by the play in book form in 1911. Meanwhile a highly successful play with a political background, *What Every Woman Knows*, was performed in 1906. *Dear Brutus* (1917) and *Mary Rose* (1920) were the last of his successful dramas, *The Boy David* (1936) failing to capture attention. Several one-act plays, including *The Old Lady Shows Her Medals* (1917) and *Shall We Join the Ladies?* (1921), were well received.

He was made a baronet, awarded the OM, and received several honorary degrees. His fame and success were considerable for the first half of the 20th cent., but his unfashionable whimsicality has come to obscure the best of his work: *Peter Pan*, however, remains popular. See *J. M. Barrie and the Lost Boys* (1979) by Andrew Birkin. (See CHILDRENS'S LITERATURE.)

BARRINGTON, Daines (1727–1800), lawyer, antiquary, and naturalist and friend of G. *White, whose *Natural History of Selborne* takes the form of letters of Barrington and *Pennant.

BARRY, Elizabeth (1658–1713), a celebrated actress who owed her entrance to the stage to the patronage of the earl of *Rochester. She created more than 100 roles, including Monimia in Otway's *The Orphan*, Belvidera in *Venice Preserv'd*, and Zara in *The Mourning Bride*. *Otway was passionately devoted to her, but she did not return his affection.

BARRY, Sebastian (1955–), Irish playwright, poet, and novelist, born in Dublin and educated at Trinity College, Dublin. After an early career as a poet, Barry successfully brought poetry back to the stage. His plays use dense, lyrical, but utterly lucid language to replace dramatic conflict, conjuring the spirits of people forgotten by Irish history. In *Boss Grady's Boys* (1988), the central characters are lonely old bachelors in rural Ireland. In *Prayers of Sherkin* (1990), they are biblical utopians waiting for the apocalypse on a remote island. *White Woman Street* (1992) has an Irish outlaw about to rob a train in the Wild West. *The Steward of Christendom* (1995) centres on the Lear-like former head of the loyalist police in Dublin ending his days in an asylum. His novels are *The Whereabouts of Eneas McNulty* (1998), *Annie Dunne* (2000), and *A Long Long Way* (2005).

Barry Lyndon, see LUCK OF BARRY LYNDON, THE.

Barsetshire Novels, the, of A. *Trollope are the following: *The Warden, *Barchester Towers, *Doctor

Thorne, *Framley Parsonage, *The Small House at Allington, and *The Last Chronicle of Barset.

BARSTOW, Stan(ley) (1928–   ), novelist, born in Yorkshire, the son of a miner and educated at Ossett Grammar School. His first novel, A Kind of Loving (1960), is the first-person, present-tense narration of office-worker Vic Brown, trapped into marriage by his infatuation for small-minded Ingrid and harassed by his mother-in-law; it was followed by other vivid portrayals of Yorkshire life, including Ask Me Tomorrow (1962) and Joby (1964), which contributed to the development of the regional novel associated with *Sillitoe, *Waterhouse (who adapted A Kind of Loving for the screen), *Braine, and others. Later novels include Just You Wait and See (1986), Give Us This Day (1989), and Next of Kin (1991).

BARTH, John Simmons (1930–   ), American novelist, whose essay 'The Literature of Exhaustion' argued that fiction was unable to keep up with the rapidly changing face of the post-war world. Consequently his own work has tended towards metafiction (Giles Goat-Boy, 1966), historical pastiche (The Sot-Weed Factor, 1960), and academic parody (Sabbatical, 1992). His playful brand of postmodernism—intrusive narrators, self-reflexive stories—suggests a body of work that is constantly turning in on itself, a project whose appeal is watching it implode. His conceit has won him more critical acclaim than it has readers.

BARTHES, Roland (1915–80), French literary critic, essayist, and cultural theorist, who was born in Cherbourg. His early life was marred by ill health, and he worked intermittently as a teacher and journalist until in 1960 he became a director of studies at the École Pratique des Hautes Études in Paris. His early book Le Degré zéro de l'écriture (Writing Degree Zero, 1953) is a notable response to *Sartre on questions of literary style and political commitment. His witty articles on the workings of modern bourgeois ideology in cinema, wrestling, and popular magazines were collected in Mythologies (1957), together with a more theoretical essay on the analysis of myths that is derived from *Saussure. His commitment to *structuralism continued in Éléments de sémiologie (Elements of Semiology, 1965), in his analysis of fashion magazines in Système de la mode (The Fashion System, 1967), and in essays proclaiming the *'death of the author'. As the scientific pretensions of structuralism came under assault from *Derrida and others, Barthes moved into a new phase of more personal and essayistic reflection in his book on Japan, L'Empire des signes (Empire of Signs, 1970), and in his influential study of *Balzac's writing, S/Z (1970). In these and later works of his 'post-structuralist' period, he emphasizes the multiple, open meanings of texts, and the jouissance (sexual bliss) of reading, notably in Le Plaisir du texte (The Pleasure of the Text, 1973). The wistful and fragmentary late works Roland Barthes par Roland Barthes (1975), Fragments d'un discours amoureux (A Lover's Discourse, 1977), and La Chambre claire (Camera Lucida, 1980) mix autobiography and aphorism in a manner remote from the certainties of the 1960s. He was killed by a laundry-van while crossing the road near the Collège de France, where he had been a professor since 1976. His influence has been widespread, especially in his defence, partly inspired by *Brecht, of *Modernist experiment against the traditions of *realism.

BARTHOLOMAEUS ANGLICUS (fl. 1230–50), also known as Bartholomew de Glanville, though the addition 'de Glanville' is most uncertain; a Minorite friar, professor of theology at Paris, and author of De Proprietatibus Rerum, an encyclopaedia of the Middle Ages first printed c.1470. A 14th-cent. English version by John of *Trevisa was issued by Wynkyn de *Worde, c.1495.

Bartholomew, massacre of St, the massacre of Huguenots throughout France ordered by Charles IX at the instigation of his mother Cathérine de Médicis, and begun on the morning of the festival, 24 Aug. 1572.

Bartholomew Fair, a comedy by *Jonson, performed by the Lady Elizabeth's Men 1614, printed 1631.

The play is set at the fair which took place at Smithfield on 24 Aug., St Bartholomew's day, and follows the fortunes of various visitors to it: Littlewit, a proctor, his wife Win-the-fight, his mother-in-law Dame Purecraft, and her mentor the ranting Puritan Zeal-of-the-land Busy, who come to eat roast pig; the rich simpleton Bartholomew Cokes, Wasp, his angry servant, and Grace Wellborn, who is unwillingly betrothed to Cokes; Justice Adam Overdo, who attends the fair in disguise in order to discover its 'enormities'; and two gallants, Quarlous and Winwife, who intend to jeer at the fair-people. Many mishaps and misunderstandings ensue, which result in Busy, Wasp, and Overdo being placed in the stocks, Cokes being robbed of all his possessions, including his future wife, who is won by Winwife, and Quarlous marrying Dame Purecraft. The play ends with the performance of a puppet-play written by Littlewit, in imitation of Marlowe's *Hero and Leander. Zeal-of-the-land Busy is defeated in a debate with one of the puppets about the morality of play-acting, and Overdo, reminded that he is 'but Adam, flesh and blood', agrees to renounce his censoriousness and invites everyone home to supper.

'Bartleby the Scrivener' (1856), a short story by H. *Melville. When the narrator, a New York lawyer, asks his scrivener (copier of legal documents) to help him, Bartleby replies, 'I would prefer not to', and with Bartleby's reiterated declaration what began as a humorous anecdote turns into a fable of existential refusal unto death.

BARTRAM, William (1739–1823), American Quaker naturalist and traveller, author of Travels through

North and South Carolina, Georgia, East and West Florida, the Cherokee Country, the Extensive Territories of the Moscogulges, or the Creek Confederacy, and the Country of the Chactaws (1791), a travel book much admired by *Coleridge and *Wordsworth, both of whom drew on its descriptions of the natural wonders of the new world: for an account of echoes in the *Ancient Mariner, *'Kubla Khan', 'Ruth', and other poems, see J. L. *Lowes, *The Road to Xanadu* (1927).

Bas Bleu, see MORE, H.

BASHKIRTSEFF, Marie (Mariya Konstantinovna Bashkirtseva) (1859–84), Russian artist and diarist whose *Journal de Marie Bashkirtseff*, written in French and posthumously published in 1887, attained a great vogue by its morbid introspection and literary quality, and was translated into several languages (English trans. 1890, by Mathilde *Blind).

Basic English, see RICHARDS, I. A.

Basil (1852), the second novel of Wilkie *Collins, and an early example of the *sensation genre: a sombre exploration of sexual obsession. Basil, a serious young man of good family, becomes infatuated with a veiled woman he sees on an omnibus, Margaret Sherwin, the young daughter of a linen draper. They marry, but the marriage is kept secret and unconsummated for a year. When Margaret goes to a party with Robert Mannion, her father's confidential clerk, who has a sinister power over her, Basil follows. He sees them leave together and go to a dubious hotel. Listening through a partition wall, he realizes they are lovers. When Mannion leaves, Basil attacks him, leaving him horribly disfigured and blinded in one eye. Basil collapses in delirium, but later recovers. Mannion reveals that his father was hanged for forgery, and that Basil's father refused to help him. Margaret, visiting Mannion in hospital, contracts typhus and dies. Basil flees London; Mannion pursues him to Cornwall. In a clifftop confrontation Mannion falls to his death.

Basilikon Doron, see JAMES I AND VI.

Basilius, (1) the foolish old duke in Sidney's *Arcadia; (2) in *Don Quixote, the rival of Camacho.

BASKERVILLE, John (1706–75), English printer, first a writing-master in Birmingham. By 1754 he had established a printing office and type-foundry in Birmingham. His books are notable for the quality of presswork, type, and paper. His first book was a Latin *Virgil, 1757, followed by a *Milton in 1758. He was the first to use 'wove' (extra smooth) paper, and gave his pages a gloss by hot-pressing them after printing. In order to print the *Book of *Common Prayer* (3 edns, 1760–2) and the Bible (1763), Baskerville bought a nomination as supernumerary printer to the University of Cambridge. His books are among the masterpieces of English printing; but they did not sell, and after his death his types were sold to *Beaumarchais

for his great edition of *Voltaire (1784–9): they are still in existence, and some are in the possession of the *Cambridge University Press. See *The Survival of Baskerville's Punches* (1949) by J. G. Dreyfus. Baskerville gave his name to the roman typefaces based on his designs in current usage.

BASKETT, John (d. 1742), king's printer. He was printer to the University of Oxford, 1711–42. He printed editions of the *Book of *Common Prayer*, and the 'Vinegar Bible' in two volumes (1716–17), of which it was said that it was 'a basketful of errors'.

BASSANI, Giorgio (1916–2000), Italian novelist and short story writer. His main theme was the onset of anti-Semitism in a provincial town. His best-known works are *Storie ferraresi* (1956; five of which are translated as *A Prospect of Ferrara*, 1962), and *Il giardino dei Finzi Contini* (*The Garden of the Finzi-Contini*, 1962).

Bassanio, in Shakespeare's *The Merchant of Venice, an impoverished young man who is the lover of Portia.

'Bastard, The', see SAVAGE.

Bastard, Philip the, son of Sir Robert Falconbridge in Shakespeare's *King John. He is a lively commentator on events, and speaks the play's last lines:

> Come the three corners of the world in arms,
> And we shall shock them. Nought shall make us rue,
> If England to itself do rest but true.

Bates, Charley, in Dickens's *Oliver Twist, one of the pickpockets in Fagin's gang.

BATES, Henry Walter (1825–92), naturalist, who visited Pará with A. R. *Wallace in 1848 and the Amazons in 1851–9. His researches revealed over 8,000 species new to science. He published *The Naturalist on the Amazons* in 1863.

BATES, H(erbert) E(rnest) (1905–74), novelist and short story writer, born in Northamptonshire. With the encouragement of E. *Garnett (of whom he wrote a study, 1950) he published his first novel, *The Two Sisters* (1926), which launched him on a prolific career. His works include volumes of stories, *The Woman Who Had Imagination* (1934), *The Flying Goat* (1939), and *The Beauty of the Dead* (1940), and novels, *The Fallow Land* (1932), *Love for Lydia* (1952), and *The Darling Buds of May* (1958). Many of them were successfully televised. He also published three volumes of autobiography, *The Vanished World* (1969), *The Blossoming World* (1971), and *The World in Ripeness* (1972).

Bates, Miss and Mrs, characters in Jane Austen's *Emma.

BATESON, F(rederick Noel) W(ilse) (1901–78), critic, scholar, and editor, educated at Charterhouse and Trinity College, Oxford. He edited the *Cambridge Bibliography of English Literature* (1940) and founded *Essays in Criticism*, which he edited from 1951 to 1974. His critical works include *Wordsworth: A Re-

interpretation (1954) and *Essays in Critical Dissent* (1972).

Bath, in Somerset, is the site of a Roman spa, Aquae Sulis, probably built in the 1st and 2nd cents AD. The legendary prince Bladud was said to have discovered the hot springs. Much of the extensive Roman baths has been excavated, and fragments of a temple, as well as tombs, altars, etc., have been found. The King's Bath was built in 1597 and during the 17th cent. it was used for medicinal purposes.

In the 18th cent. Bath was transformed into a social resort by Richard ('Beau') *Nash, who became master of ceremonies, Ralph *Allen, who promoted the development of the city, and John Wood, father and son, who designed the Palladian public buildings and houses. It is the subject of very frequent literary allusion, having been visited among many others by Smollett, Fielding, Sheridan, F. Burney, Goldsmith, Southey, Landor, J. Austen, Wordsworth, Cowper, Scott, T. Moore, and Dickens. Its ruins seem to be the subject of the OE poem *'The Ruin'. It was once a cloth-making centre, and is mentioned in this connection by Chaucer (*Canterbury Tales*, General Prologue, 447, concerning the 'Wife of Bath').

Bath, Wife of, see CANTERBURY TALES, 6.

Bath Guide, The New, see ANSTEY, C.

bathos (Greek, 'depth'). The current usage for 'descent from the sublime to the ridiculous' originates from *Pope's satire *Peri Bathous, or The Art of Sinking in Poetry* (1727). The title was a travesty of *Longinus' essay *On the Sublime*.

Bathsheba Everdene, a character in Hardy's *Far from the Madding Crowd*.

Batrachomyomachia, or the *Battle of the Frogs and Mice*, a burlesque Greek epic which used at one time to be attributed to *Homer. It describes in *mock-heroic Homeric style a battle between mice and frogs in which Zeus and Athena join. T. *Parnell's version of the *Batrachomyomachia* attacking *Dennis and *Theobald appeared in 1717, which was relatively late in the history of the genre.

Battle, Sarah, the subject of one of Lamb's *Essays of Elia*, 'Mrs Battle's Opinions on Whist'; a character drawn from Mrs Burney, wife of Admiral Burney and sister-in-law of F. *Burney.

Battle Abbey Roll, the, probably compiled about the 14th cent., purporting to show the names of families that came over to England with William the Conqueror. The roll itself is not extant: the 16th-cent. versions by *Leland, *Holinshed, and Duchesne are all said to be imperfect and to contain names which have obviously no right there.

Battle of Alcazar, The, a play in verse by *Peele, published 1594.

It deals with the war between Sebastian, king of Portugal, and Abdelmelec, king of Morocco, who had recovered his kingdom from a usurper, Muly Mahamet. The latter invokes the assistance of Sebastian, offering to give up the kingdom of Morocco to him and to become his tributary. Sebastian sails with his fleet to Morocco and at the battle of Alcazar is killed, as are also Abdelmelec and Muly Mahamet, the latter being drowned while fleeing from the field. Sebastian is assisted in his expedition by the adventurer *Stukeley, who is likewise killed at the battle (which was fought in 1578). There survives an interesting contemporary 'plot', or playhouse summary, of this play which has been edited by W. W. *Greg. Though A. H. Bullen called the play 'tiresome windy stuff', it contains some remarkable passages, such as the description of the 'princely ospraie'.

'Battle of Hohenlinden, The', a poem by T. *Campbell, describing a battle in Bavaria in 1800, in which the French defeated the Austrians.

Battle of Maldon, see MALDON, BATTLE OF.

Battle of Otterbourne, see OTTERBOURNE, THE BATTLE OF.

Battle of the Books, The (*A Full and True Account of the Battel Fought Last Friday, between the Antient and the Modern Books in St James's Library*), a prose satire by *Swift, written 1697, when Swift was residing with Sir W. *Temple, published 1704.

Temple had written an essay on the comparative merits of 'Ancient and Modern Learning' (the subject at that time of an animated controversy in Paris), in which by his uncritical praise of the spurious *Epistles of *Phalaris he had drawn on himself the censure of William Wotton and *Bentley. Swift, in his *Battle of the Books*, treats the whole question with satirical humour. The 'Battle' originates from a request by the moderns that the ancients shall evacuate the higher of the two peaks of Parnassus which they have hitherto occupied. The books that are advocates of the moderns take up the matter; but before the actual encounter a dispute arises between a spider living in the corner of the library and a bee that has got entangled in the spider's web. Aesop sums up the dispute: the spider is like the moderns who spin their scholastic lore out of their own entrails; the bee is like the ancients who go to nature for their honey. (The phrase 'Sweetness and Light' which Aesop uses to describe the contribution of the ancients, in contrast with the 'Dirt and Poison' of the moderns, was adopted by Arnold in *Culture and Anarchy*.) Aesop's commentary rouses the books to fury, and they join battle. The ancients, under the patronage of Pallas, are led by Homer, Pindar, Euclid, Aristotle, and Plato, with Sir W. Temple commanding the allies; the moderns by Milton, Dryden, Descartes, Hobbes, Scotus, and others, with the support of Momus and the malignant deity Criticism. The fight is conducted with great spirit. Aristotle aims an arrow at Bacon but hits

Descartes. Homer overthrows Gondibert. Virgil encounters his translator Dryden, in a helmet nine times too big. Boyle transfixes Bentley and Wotton. On the whole the ancients have the advantage, but a parley ensues and the tale leaves the issue undecided.

Battle of the Frogs and Mice, see BATRACHOMYOMACHIA.

Baucis and Philemon, a poem by *Swift, published 1709; Baucis and Philemon were the aged couple who entertained the gods unawares, and whose cottage was transformed by Zeus into a temple. In Swift's version, the couple entertain two hermits; their cottage becomes a church and Philemon the parson, an elevation described with some irony.

BAUDELAIRE, Charles (1821–67), French poet. His *Les Fleurs du mal* (1857), a series of 101 exquisitely crafted lyrics in a variety of metres, including many sonnets, is one of the great collections of French verse. It represents a determined attempt to create order and beauty, notably by the discovery of hidden relations or 'correspondences', in a world which is largely perceived as ugly and oppressive. In musical language and evocative images, the poet explores his own sense of isolation, exile, and sin, his boredom and melancholy, the transporting power of love, the attractions of evil and vice, the fascination and the degradation of Paris life. On publication of *Les Fleurs du mal* Baudelaire was fined and six of the poems were banned from subsequent editions as offensive to public morals; these were accordingly omitted from the second (1861) and the third, posthumous, edition (1868), by which time some 50 new poems had been added. Baudelaire's prose works include *Petits Poèmes en prose* (*Le Spleen de Paris*) (1869) and translations of *Poe's tales: *Histoires extraordinaires* (1856) and *Nouvelles Histoires extraordinaires* (1857). He gave a detailed account of the effects of opium and hashish in *Les Paradis artificiels* (1860), which contains a commentary on the translated extracts from De Quincey's *Confessions of an English Opium Eater*. His reputation as a critic, which has increased steadily since his death, is now firmly established. Most of his critical writing, including essays on the Paris salons of 1845, 1846, and 1859, on Delacroix, on such contemporary writers as *Gautier and *Flaubert, and on *Wagner, were collected in the posthumous volumes *Curiosités esthétiques* and *L'Art romantique* (1868). His *Journaux intimes* were published in 1887.

BAWDEN, Nina Mary, née Mabey (1925–), novelist and children's writer, born in London, educated at Ilford County High School and Somerville College, Oxford. Her many well-crafted and closely observed novels of middle-class life, in which the turmoil that often exists beneath the surface of outwardly ordered lives is deftly uncovered, include *Who Calls the Tune* (1953), *Change Here for Babylon* (1955), *Just Like a Lady* (1960), *A Woman of My Age* (1967), *The Birds on the Trees* (1970), *Anna Apparent* (1972), *Afternoon of a Good Woman* (1976), *Walking Naked* (1981), *The Ice House* (1983), *Circles of Deceit* (1987), *Family Money* (1991), and *A Nice Change* (1997). She has also written extensively for children, notably *Carrie's War* (1973), the story of children evacuated to Wales during the Second World War, and *The Peppermint Pig* (1976), about an Edwardian family suddenly reduced to poverty. A memoir *In My Own Time* (1994) was followed by *Dear Austen* (2005), addressed to her husband Austen Kark who died in the Potters Bar rail crash (2002), which features in David *Hare's play, *The Permanent Way*.

BAX, Sir Arnold (1883–1953), English composer and writer. Though he was of English ancestry an early encounter with the poetry of *Yeats brought out a strong Celtic strain in Bax, and he spent much time in Ireland. Under the pseudonym 'Dermot O'Byrne' he published novels, stories, and poetry, and in his early days in Dublin was considered as much a writer as a composer. His greatest achievement as a composer was in symphonic and instrumental music, but he was prolific in all forms, from the early *Celtic Song Cycle* (1904, words by Fiona Macleod—W. *Sharp) onwards. He made many settings, both for solo voice and vocal ensembles, of texts from all periods, from medieval poetry to *Hardy, *Housman, and *Colum. His autobiographical sketch *Farewell My Youth* (1943) is one of the best books of its kind by a musician.

BAXTER, James K(eir) (1926–72), New Zealand poet, educated episodically at the University of Otago, and in Christchurch and Wellington, after spending nearly two years as a boy with his parents in Europe. He wrote prolifically, surviving a period of alcoholism, and in 1961 became a Roman Catholic, devoting his last years to social work with the drunks, homeless, and drug addicts of Wellington and Auckland. His early volumes (*Beyond the Palisade*, 1944; *Blow, Wind of Fruitfulness*, 1948; *The Fallen House*, 1953) dealt with themes of nature, place, nationality, and guilt, sometimes using the ballad form to satiric effect: in later work he moved on to express himself in a colloquial yet spiritual style, describing his own mission amongst the poor, and drawing on Christian imagery, small daily events, and the Maori language to create an intensely personal voice. Volumes include *Pig Island Letters* (1966), *Jerusalem Sonnets* (1970), and *Autumn Testament* (1972).

BAXTER, Richard (1615–91), a Presbyterian divine who sided with Parliament and was a military chaplain during the Civil War. He was author of *The Saint's Everlasting Rest* (1650; the book that Mrs Glegg in *The Mill on the Floss* used to favour in a domestic crisis) and of *Call to the Unconverted* (1657), both of which played an important part in the evangelical tradition in England and America. Fined, imprisoned, and persecuted after the Act of Uniformity under both Charles II and James II for his Nonconformist preaching, he shared his sufferings with his young wife 'who cheerfully went with me into prison'. In her memory he wrote his moving *Breviate of the Life of Margaret Charlton* (1681). He was fined by Judge Jeffreys on the charge of libelling the Church in his *Paraphrase of the New Testament* (1685). His numerous writings include a lengthy autobiography, *Reliquiae Baxterianae* (1696), which gives a vivid portrait of the strife of the Interregnum and the Restoration, and several well-known hymns (e.g. 'Ye holy angels bright'). See N. H. Keeble, *Richard Baxter: Puritan Man of Letters* (1982).

Bayard, or **Baiardo,** the magic horse given by Charlemagne to Renaud, son of Aymon, or *Rinaldo, which figures in *The Four Sons of *Aymon, *Orlando innamorato*, and *Orlando furioso*. Bayard was formerly used as a mock-heroic allusive name for any horse, and also as a type of blind recklessness [OED].

Bayes, the name under which *Dryden is ridiculed in Buckingham's *The Rehearsal*.

BAYLE, Pierre (1647–1706), French Protestant scholar and philosopher, who lived in Rotterdam from 1681, where his major work, the *Dictionnaire historique et critique*, was published (2 vols, 1695, 1697; 2nd, rev. and enl., edn. 1702). Most of the entries in the *Dictionnaire* were biographical articles on important personages of biblical, classical, and modern history, in the course of which, especially in the discursive footnotes, many theological and philosophical questions, some of them contentious, were subjected to rigorous critical analysis. Bayle's method rested on the systematic comparison of sources and scientific consideration of evidence. He deployed the erudition that made his work a source-book of historical and religious criticism in a humane and enquiring spirit, impatient of credulity, superstition, and intolerance. There were English translations of the *Dictionnaire* in 1710, 1734–8 (rev.), and 1734–41 (much enlarged, as *A General Dictionary, Historical and Critical*).

BAYLEY, John (1925–), novelist and critic, and from 1975 to 1992 Warton professor of English literature in Oxford. He married Iris *Murdoch in 1956, and described their relationship and her suffering from Alzheimer's in *Elegy for Iris* (1998), *Iris and the Friends* (1999), and *Widower's House* (2001). His critical works range from *The Characters of Love* (1960) to *The Poetry of A. E. Housman* (1990), and his novels include *In Another Country* (1986), a comic work about British Intelligence during the First World War, and *Alice* (1994), a social comedy exploring sexual *mores*.

BAYLY, Nathaniel Thomas Haynes (1797–1839), the author of many well-known and much ridiculed verses, including 'I'd be a butterfly' and 'She wore a wreath of roses'. He also wrote at great speed many pieces for the stage, including *Perfection* (1836), a successful farce.

Bayona, see NAMANCOS.

Bazzard, Mr, in Dickens's *Edwin Drood*, Mr Grewgious's clerk.

BBC, the British Broadcasting Corporation (initially, from 1922, the British Broadcasting Company Ltd), was established by royal charter as a publicly owned broadcasting authority supported by licence fee in 1927: its first and highly influential manager was John, later Lord, Reith (1889–1971). Its remit was to inform, educate, and entertain. By 1998 it maintained two national TV networks, five national radio networks, regional and local broadcasting, as well as a world service transmitting in English and many foreign languages. It is the world's largest commissioner of creative work in terms of classical music, drama, and the short story. Chiefly in radio it has established itself as a commissioner of new translations from leading writers; amongst which might be included Nevill Coghill's version of *Chaucer's *Canterbury Tales* broadcast by the Third Programme in 1946/7 (pub., 1951). In 1924 the BBC commissioned and broadcast the first play written for radio, *Danger*, by R. *Hughes, set underground at the scene of a mining disaster. The radio play became an art form in its own right and attracted novelists and poets as well as dramatists. D. L. *Sayers wrote a 12-part serial on the life of Christ, *The Man Born to Be King*, which caused a sensation when broadcast during the war years (1941–2), and A. *Christie's long-running thriller *The Mouse Trap* began its life as a radio play entitled *Three Blind Mice* (1947). S. *Hill, A. *Carter, and R. *Tremain have written profusely for radio.

Novelist P. H. *Newby was on the staff for many years, becoming controller of Radio Three and then managing director of radio. G. *Orwell (Eric Blair) was on the staff and encouraged by Douglas Cleverdon (1903–87) wrote some of *1984* in Broadcasting House, which it is said served as a model for the Ministry of Truth. A number of poets were BBC employees, including Terence Tiller, G. *MacBeth, A. *Thwaite, Roy *Campbell, Derek *Mahon, Patric Dickinson, and P. *Muldoon. Most notable was Louis *MacNeice, who wrote many poetic dramas for radio, chief among them *Christopher Columbus* (with music by W. *Walton) and *The Dark Tower*, broadcast in 1946. Cleverdon, features producer and bibliophile, gave encouragement and employment to D. *Thomas: his reward was *Under Milk Wood*, which remains the best known of all radio plays. Also encouraged by Cleverdon was Henry *Reed, who wrote a number of poetic dramas but is best remembered for the seven social satires about the 'composeress' Hilda Tablet transmitted in the mid-1950s.

In the 1950s and 1960s, untrammelled by the *censorship of the lord chamberlain which restricted theatrical presentation, many new writers turned to radio, which with the growth of television had become a minority medium and could risk experiment at low cost. Encouraged by editors and producers such as

Donald McWhinnie, Barbara Bray, Michael Bakewell, Richard Imison, Martin Esslin, and John Tydeman, new, often first plays were forthcoming from S. *Beckett, Caryl *Churchill, J. *Orton, H. *Pinter, J. *Mortimer, R. *Bolt, Giles Cooper, T. *Stoppard, Bill Naughton, John *Arden, D. *Rudkin, Alun *Owen, James Saunders, and Alan *Plater. This tradition of discovering and encouraging new dramatists continues. Anthony Minghella, Martin Crimp, Louise Page, Hanif *Kureishi, and Howard *Barker all wrote early plays for radio. Many plays were developed into successful stage plays, e.g. Mortimer's *A Voyage round My Father*, Naughton's *Alfie*, Bolt's *A Man for All Seasons*, and Stoppard's *Indian Ink*. *A Hitch Hiker's Guide to the Galaxy*, by Douglas Adams (1952–2001), was a cult success which began in 1978 on radio, as did *The Secret Life of Adrian Mole* (1982) by Sue Townsend. (On his first appearance, Adrian was called Nigel.) Light entertainment on TV and radio have made many contributions to the art of comedy, the most notable original programmes being the *Goons* (1951 as *Crazy People*; as *The Goons* from 1955) and *Monty Python's Flying Circus* (1969). *The Archers*, a 15-minute daily soap opera about the life of country folk in the fictitious village of Ambridge, commenced national transmission on radio on 1 Jan. 1951. Television became the dominant broadcasting medium in the 1950s: major screenwriters are entered under their own names. See also ADAPTATION.

BEACH, Sylvia (1887–1962), bookshop owner and publisher, born in Baltimore, Maryland; owner from 1919 of the Shakespeare and Company bookshop and lending library on the Left Bank in Paris, meeting place for writers as diverse as *Joyce, *Hemingway, *Gide, and Sherwood *Anderson. When Joyce could find no publisher for *Ulysses* after instalments of its serialization in the *Little Review* had been found obscene, she published it under the Shakespeare and Co. imprint in 1922, funding the enterprise through subscription. See Beach, *Shakespeare and Company* (1959) and Noel Riley Fitch, *Sylvia Beach and the Lost Generation: A History of Literary Paris in the Twenties and Thirties* (1983).

'Beachcomber', the pseudonym attached to a column of fantastic and surreal humour published in the *Daily Express*: it was coined in 1919 by journalist and author (Dominic) Bevan (Wyndham) Lewis (1891–1969), who bequeathed it to his friend John Cameron Morton (1893–1975). Morton wrote under this name from 1924 to 1975, at first daily, later weekly, and many of his articles have been published with illustrations by Nicolas Bentley in various collections.

BEARDSLEY, Aubrey Vincent (1872–98), illustrator and writer, notorious in the 1890s as the outstanding artist of *fin-de-siècle* decadence. His disturbingly erotic drawings develop rapidly from the murky sensuality of *Pre-Raphaelite medievalism to rococo wit and

grace. Beardsley's most important illustrations are for *Wilde's *Salome* (1894), *Pope's *The Rape of the Lock* (1896), the *Lysistrata* of *Aristophanes (1896), and *Jonson's *Volpone* (1898). He was art editor of the *Yellow Book* in 1894; the Wilde scandal led to his dismissal in 1895; he then became art editor to the *Savoy*. Beardsley's most significant achievement as a writer is *The Story of Venus and Tannhauser*, a charmingly rococo and highly cultivated erotic romance. An expurgated version entitled *Under the Hill* was published in the *Savoy*; an unexpurgated edition was privately printed in 1907; it contains a cruel caricature of Wilde as 'Priapusa, the fat manicure and fardeuse'. In 1897 Beardsley, encouraged by J. *Gray and his friend Raffalovich, converted to Catholicism; he died of consumption. In 1916 his sister Mabel died of cancer; W. B. *Yeats, who had known them both, wrote a sequence of poems, 'Upon a Dying Lady', inspired by her.

Beat and Beat Generation. 'Beat' was a term first used by the notorious hustler and drug addict Herbert Huncke (1916–96) to describe his own state of anomic drifting and social alienation. 'Beat' was quickly picked up by *Kerouac as a triple entendre—an epithet that brought together a sense of being 'beaten' with the state of being 'beatific', as well as suggesting the pulse and 'beat' of music. The pioneers of the movement were *Ginsberg, whose book *Howl* (1956) protested that America had seen 'the best minds of my generation destroyed by madness', and Kerouac, whose *On the Road* (1957) reinvented a mythic landscape of highways, bars, and male bonding. With other writers such as Gregory Corso (1930–) and *Burroughs, the Beats developed an aesthetic based on the spontaneity of jazz, Buddhist mysticism, and the raw urgency of sex.

Although not published until the 1950s, the group met through their connections with Columbia University a decade earlier. They shared an apartment on 115th Street, New York, where they began to talk of a 'New Vision'—a reaction against what they saw as the sterile nonconformity of post-war America. When this philosophy began to appear as Beat literature, it met with censorship and outrage. *Howl* was the subject of an obscenity trial in 1956, but was eventually found by the judge to be 'a plea for holy living'. Burroughs's *Naked Lunch* (1959) was also tried for obscenity by a court in Chicago, and although the prosecution won, the novel was subsequently cleared on appeal.

The influence of Beat can be traced through to the punk poetry of Patti Smith and the lounge-lizard lyrics of musicians such as Tom Waits. The once-rebellious Beats are now a respectable area of academic enquiry, and biographers and Hollywood have confirmed their iconic status.

Beatles, the, a group of young working-class musicians from Liverpool (George Harrison, John Lennon, Paul McCartney, and 'Ringo' Starr), whose songs and lifestyle, from 1962 until their break-up in 1970, attracted a vast following, and not only from teenagers; many of their lyrics (e.g. 'Penny Lane', 'Eleanor Rigby', 'She's Leaving Home') have been highly praised, and they had a considerable influence on the success of the *Liverpool poets and the *underground poetry movement. *Larkin described their work as 'an enchanting and intoxicating hybrid of Negro rock-and-roll with their own adolescent romanticism', and 'the first advance in popular music since the War' (9 Oct. 1983).

Beatrice, (1) see DANTE; (2) heroine of Shakespeare's *Much Ado about Nothing*, who explains her sprightly temperament in the words 'there was a star danc'd, and under that was I born' (II. i. 303).

BEATTIE, James (1735–1803), professor of moral philosophy at Marischal College, Aberdeen. His *Essay on the Nature and Immutability of Truth* (1770) was an attempt to refute *Hume and *Berkeley. As a poet he is remembered for *The Minstrel*, a poem in Spenserian stanzas tracing 'the progress of a poetical Genius, born in a rude age, from the first dawning of fancy and reason'; Edwin, the son of a shepherd, a solitary and sensitive boy, finds his education in nature, in a manner that foreshadows Wordsworth's *Prelude*. Bk I appeared in 1771, Bk II in 1774, and they were many times reprinted, though the work remained unfinished.

Beau Brummell, see BRUMMELL.

Beauchamp's Career, a novel by G. *Meredith, published 1876.

In this novel of politics, much concerned with the contemporary state of Britain, Nevil Beauchamp begins his career as an idealistic young naval officer. In spite of his mildly subversive views on political and social questions, he earns the approval of his wealthy aristocratic uncle Everard Romfrey, a traditionalist who detests radicals and their like. After the Crimean War, Nevil plunges into politics, stands unsuccessfully as a Radical candidate for Parliament, and becomes the friend of Dr Shrapnel, humanitarian, republican, and freethinker, detestable to Mr Romfrey and his friends. In his rage at various rumours and misrepresentations, Romfrey horsewhips Shrapnel, incurring the fury of his nephew, who demands that his uncle apologize to his friend. This hopeless enterprise becomes an obsession with Nevil, who is also distracted by his own inconclusive love affairs, torn between his early passion for Renée de Croisnel, a spirited and intelligent young woman (now the unhappy wife of an elderly Frenchman), and his love for a soft and decorous English girl, Cecilia Halkett. Gallantry and indecision lose him Renée, who has fled from her husband; and he also loses Cecilia, who is married by her father to Nevil's dull second cousin. Harassed and unhappy, Nevil falls desperately ill, near to death. His danger moves his proud uncle to present himself at Shrapnel's cottage, where Nevil lies, and to offer his apology at last.

Nevil recovers and marries Shrapnel's ward Jenny Denham, a genial and sympathetic girl. But after a few months of happiness he is drowned trying to rescue an unknown child from the sea. Renée was Meredith's favourite among all his women characters.

Beau Geste, see WREN, P. C.

Beaumains ('Fair hands'), the nickname given contemptuously by Sir Kay, the steward, to Gareth, the brother of Gawain, when as a probationer knight of the Round Table he is sent to work in the kitchens. See GARETH AND LYNETTE.

BEAUMARCHAIS, Pierre-Augustin Caron de (1732–99), French dramatist. He is remembered for two comedies of intrigue, *Le Barbier de Séville* (1775; English trans., *The Barber of Seville*, 1776), and *Le Mariage de Figaro* (1784; *The Marriage of Figaro*, 1785). The scheming and resourceful valet Figaro, hero of both plays, is presented with evident class-conscious sympathy, while the later play is quite openly anti-aristocratic in its implications. The plays respectively inspired operas by *Rossini (1816) and *Mozart (1786).

BEAUMONT, Francis (1584–1616), born at Grace-Dieu in Leicestershire, of an ancient family, and the third son of a justice of common pleas. He was educated at Broadgates Hall, Oxford, but took no degree, and was entered at the Inner Temple in 1600. The anonymous Ovidian poem *Salmacis and Hermaphroditus* (1602) has been attributed to him. He collaborated with John Fletcher in dramatic works from about 1606 to 1613 (for a list of their plays, see under FLETCHER, J.). His earliest known play, *The Woman Hater*, a Jonsonian comedy of humours, was probably performed 1605, published 1607: recent linguistic analysis assigns some scenes in this to Fletcher, whereas *The Knight of the Burning Pestle* (?1607) is now generally considered to be Beaumont's alone. Beaumont retired c.1613, when he married profitably and moved to Kent. He was buried in Westminster Abbey.

Dryden, in *Of Dramatick Poesy* (1668), pays tribute to the success of the Beaumont and Fletcher plays on the Restoration stage, and comments that both writers had 'great natural gifts improved by study; Beaumont especially being so accurate a judge of plays that Ben Jonson, while he lived, submitted all his writings to his censure, and, 'tis thought, used his judgement in correcting, if not contriving, all his plots.' Beaumont and *Jonson wrote one another commendatory verses, but Jonson's comment to *Drummond of Hawthornden (that Beaumont 'loved too much himself and his own verses') was less flattering. In the 17th cent. opinion tended to ascribe the tragic scenes in the collaborative effort to Beaumont, the comic to Fletcher, but modern critics reject this neat division, and are themselves divided about attribution. (See under FLETCHER, J. for further details.)

BEAUMONT, Sir George Howland (1753–1827), patron

of art and friend and benefactor of *Wordsworth, who frequently visited him at Coleorton Hall; in his dedication to Sir George of his 1815 volume, Wordsworth wrote, 'some of the best pieces were composed under the shade of your own groves, upon the classic ground of Coleorton.' Sir W. *Scott described Beaumont as 'the man in the world most void of affectation', and said he 'understood Wordsworth's poetry, which is a rare thing' (*Journal*, 14 Feb. 1827). Beaumont also encouraged and supported *Coleridge and helped to procure his pension.

Beauty and the Beast, a fairy tale of which the best-known version was adapted by Mme de Beaumont from one of the *Contes marins* (4 vols, 1740–1) of Mme de Villeneuve. A somewhat similar story is included in the *Piacevoli notti* of *Straparola.

BEAUVOIR, Simone de (1908–86), French novelist and essayist. Her novels reflect the major preoccupations of the *existentialist movement: *L'Invitée* (1943; *She Came to Stay*, 1949), *Le Sang des autres* (1944; *The Blood of Others*, 1948), *Les Mandarins* (1954; *The Mandarins*, 1956). Her highly influential feminist essay *Le Deuxième Sexe* appeared in 1949 (*The Second Sex*, 1953), and she published four volumes of autobiography, including *Mémoires d'une jeune fille rangée* (1958; *Memoirs of a Dutiful Daughter*, 1959) and *La Force de l'âge* (1960; *The Prime of Life*, 1960. *Beloved Chicago Man: Letters to Nelson Algren 1947–64* (1997) collects her correspondence with her American lover, the writer Nelson Algren (1909–81). See also FEMINIST CRITICISM and SARTRE.

Beaux' Stratagem, The, a comedy by *Farquhar, produced 1707.

Aimwell and Archer, two friends who have spent their inheritance, arrive at the inn at Lichfield, in search of the adventure that will rehabilitate their fortunes. To save money Archer pretends to be Aimwell's servant. There is much speculation as to who they are, and Boniface the landlord concludes that they are highwaymen. This curiosity is shared by Dorinda, daughter of the wealthy Lady Bountiful, who has fallen in love with Aimwell at first sight—in church—and Mrs Sullen, wife of Lady Bountiful's son, a drunken sot. Aimwell, thinking Dorinda a suitable prey, gets admission to Lady Bountiful's house on a pretext, with Archer, between whom and Mrs Sullen a mutual attraction has sprung up. An attack by rogues on the house is the occasion of the rescue of the ladies by Aimwell and Archer, and they both press the advantage thus gained. But Aimwell, who has passed himself off as his elder brother Lord Aimwell, smitten with remorse in presence of the trustfulness of Dorinda, confesses the fraud. At this moment Mrs Sullen's brother opportunely arrives, to rescue his sister from the brutality of Sullen. He brings news of the death of Aimwell's elder brother and of the accession of Aimwell to title and fortune. Sullen at the same time willingly agrees to the dissolution of his marriage, so that Mrs Sullen is free to marry Archer, and all ends happily.

BEAVERBROOK, William Maxwell ('Max') Aitken, first Baron (1879–1964), newspaper proprietor, born in Canada, the son of a Presbyterian minister; he made a fortune as a financier, then came to England in 1910, and embarked on a career in politics. In 1916 (the year in which he became Lord Beaverbrook) he bought the *Daily Express*, launched the *Sunday Express* in 1918, and in 1923 gained control of the *Evening Standard*, of which his friend Arnold *Bennett became the influential reviewer; his drive for high circulation was immensely successful, and he became the most powerful figure in popular journalism, setting the stamp of his own flamboyant personality and prejudices on the papers he owned. He enjoyed controversy, from the 'Empire Crusade' of his early years to the anti-Common Market stand of his old age. His own works include *Canada in Flanders* (2 vols, 1915–17), *Politicians and the Press* (1925), *Politicians and the War* (2 vols, 1928, 1932, which provided much of the background for Bennett's novel *Lord Raingo*, 1926), and *The Decline and Fall of Lloyd George* (1963). According to A. J. P. *Taylor (*Beaverbrook*, 1972), E. *Waugh denied that Beaverbrook was the original of Lord *Copper in *Scoop* (1938), but he appears as Lord Ottercove in the novels of *Gerhardie, and suggested some of the characteristics of Sir Bussy Woodcock in *Wells's *The Autocracy of Mr Parham* (1930). (Wells to Beaverbrook: 'I wanted a man who had made money fast and had an original mind. You seem to be the only one who answers to that description in London.')

BECCARIA, Cesare (1738–94), Italian aristocrat and jurist, whose essay *Dei delitti e delle pene* (*Of Crimes and Punishments*, 1764), a masterpiece of the Italian Enlightenment, inspired European schemes to improve prison systems, followed in England by *Bentham.

Beck, Madame, a character in *Villette* by C. Brontë.

BECKET, St Thomas (?1118–70), son of Gilbert Becket, of a Norman family of knights, educated in London and Paris; he subsequently studied canon law at Bologna and Auxerre. Henry II appointed him chancellor and made him his intimate friend and companion. In 1162 Thomas reluctantly became archbishop of Canterbury, an office which required him to become the champion of the rights of the Church which Henry was attempting to curtail. In particular he opposed the Constitutions of Clarendon (1164) which reimposed the relations between Church and state that had prevailed in the time of William I. One measure in particular, that no clerical appeal to Rome could be made without the authority of the king, was contentious. Becket was exiled on the Continent for seven years; he returned to England in 1170 after a brief reconciliation with Henry was effected, but when the old arguments were revived he was assassinated on the king's orders in the cathedral at Canterbury on 29 Dec. 1170. The king, officially at least, claimed that his orders had been misinterpreted, and harmony with the pope was only restored by his humiliation and flagellation at Avranches. Becket's shrine at Canterbury became the most famous in Christendom as a place where miracles were performed, and it was the objective of *Chaucer's pilgrims 200 years later. The story of Becket has been the subject of plays by *Tennyson, T. S. Eliot (*Murder in the Cathedral), and by *Anouilh in French. See H. *Belloc, St Thomas of Canterbury (1933). (See also ANGLO-LATIN LITERATURE.)

BECKETT, Samuel Barclay (1906–89), born at Foxrock, near Dublin, the second son of a quantity surveyor, and brought up as a Protestant by a mother whom he describes as 'profoundly religious'. He was educated at Portora Royal School, Enniskillen, and at Trinity College, Dublin, where he read English, French, and Italian. He then taught for two terms in Belfast before going to Paris as lecteur d'anglais at the École Normale Supérieure; there in 1928 he met *Joyce, with whom he formed a lasting friendship. His first published work was an essay on Joyce (1929) and he assisted with the translation into French of the 'Anna Livia Plurabelle' section of *Finnegans Wake. His first story, 'Assumption', appeared in *transition (1929) and in 1930 he returned as lecturer to Trinity College, resigning after four terms to embark on five unsettled, solitary years in Germany, France, Ireland, and London, before settling permanently in France. During this period (aided by a small annuity) he reviewed, translated, published poems in various periodicals, and wrote a study of *Proust (1931). More Pricks than Kicks (1934, stories) was followed by several full-length novels, including Murphy (1938), a grimly entertaining Irish evocation of London life, and Watt (1953), both written in English. His trilogy Molloy (1951); Malone Meurt (1951; Beckett's own English version, Malone Dies, 1958); and L'Innommable (1953; The Unnamable, 1960) were all originally written in French, and all three are interior monologues or soliloquies, desolate, terminal, obsessional, irradiated with flashes of last-ditch black humour: Malone Dies opens with the characteristic sentence 'I shall soon be quite dead at last in spite of all', and the last volume trails away with '. . . where I am, I don't know, I'll never know, in the silence you don't know, you must go on, I can't go on, I'll go on.' Beckett's highly distinctive, despairing, yet curiously exhilarating voice reached a wide audience and public acclaim with the Paris performance in 1953 of En attendant Godot (pub. 1952); the English version, *Waiting for Godot (1955), also made a great impact, and from this time Beckett became widely known as a playwright associated with the Theatre of the *Absurd, whose use of the stage and of dramatic narrative and symbolism revolutionized drama in England and deeply influenced later playwrights, including *Pinter,

*Fugard, and *Stoppard. Subsequent stage plays include Fin de partie (first performed in French at the Royal Court, 1957; English version, Endgame, pub. 1958), a one-act drama of frustration, irascibility, and senility, featuring blind Hamm and his attendant Clov, and Hamm's 'accursed progenitors', who spend the action in ashcans; Krapp's Last Tape (1958, pub. 1959), written for the Irish actor Patrick Magee, a monologue in which the shabby and aged Krapp attempts to recapture the intensity of earlier days by listening to recordings of his own younger self; Happy Days (1961, pub. 1961), which portrays Winnie buried to her waist in a mound, but still attached to the carefully itemized contents of her handbag; Come and Go (1966, pub. 1967), a stark 'dramaticule' with three female characters and a text of 121 words; the even more minimal Breath (1969), a 30-second play consisting only of a pile of rubbish, a breath, and a cry; and Not I (1973, pub. 1973), a brief, fragmented, disembodied monologue delivered by an actor of indeterminate sex of whom only the 'Mouth' is illuminated. Beckett has also written for television (Eh Joe, 1966) and, more frequently, for radio, and his Collected Poems in English and French was published in 1977. He was awarded the *Nobel Prize in 1969.

BECKFORD, William (1759–1844), son of a wealthy lord mayor of London. He was an MP, a traveller, and a man of great wealth, who spent large sums in collecting curios and paintings and in the creation and decoration of Fonthill Abbey, a Gothic extravaganza, where he lived in almost complete and scandalous seclusion from 1796 until he was obliged, because of his extravagance, to sell it in 1822. He is remembered chiefly as the author of the *Oriental tale *Vathek, but he wrote several other works, including two books of travel, Dreams, Waking Thoughts, and Incidents (1783, suppressed by the author and revised 1834) and Recollections of an Excursion to the Monasteries of Alcobaça and Batalha (1835), both of which reveal genuine powers of description and an ironic observance of customs and manners. See J. Lees-Milne, William Beckford (1976); A. B. Fothergill, Beckford of Fonthill (1979). (See also GOTHIC NOVEL; GOTHIC REVIVAL.)

Becky Sharp, see SHARP, R.

BEDDOES, Thomas Lovell (1803–49), educated at Charterhouse and Pembroke College, Oxford, the son of the physician, radical, and writer Dr Thomas Beddoes (1760–1808), who had been friend and doctor of *Coleridge, *Wordsworth, and *Southey. Thomas also studied medicine and in 1835 settled at Zurich, living thereafter mostly abroad. He published in 1821 The Improvisatore and in 1822 The Brides' Tragedy. His most important work, Death's Jest-Book, or the Fool's Tragedy, was begun in 1825 and repeatedly altered at various times, not being published until 1850, after his death by suicide at Basle. It is in blank verse, heavily influenced by Elizabethan and Jacobean tragedy, and shows Beddoes's obsession with the macabre, the supernatural, and bodily decay; these interests were to appeal strongly to *fin-de-siècle* poets such as A. *Symons who compared Beddoes to *Baudelaire and *Poe, and wrote in praise, 'there is not a page without its sad, grotesque, gay or abhorrent imagery of the tomb'. He is now best known for his shorter pieces, such as 'Dream Pedlary' ('If there were dreams to sell, | What would you buy?') and the lyrics which appear in *Death's Jest-Book* ('If thou wilt ease thine heart | Of love and all its smart'), although some of his blank verse has undeniable power and originality. His poetical works were edited by *Gosse in 1890 and 1928, and H. W. Donner's edition, *Plays and Poems* (1950), has a biographical introduction.

BEDE (Baeda, or 'The Venerable Bede') (673–735), historian and scholar, when young placed in the charge of *Benedict Biscop, the abbot of Wearmouth. From there he went in 682 to Jarrow in the care of its first abbot, Ceolfrid, and there he spent most of his life. He was a diligent teacher and scholar of Latin and Greek, and he had many pupils among the monks of Wearmouth and Jarrow. He was buried at Jarrow, but his remains were moved to Durham during the first half of the 11th cent. He was first called 'Venerabilis' during the 9th cent. His *Historia Ecclesiastica Gentis Anglorum* was finished in 731, by which time he had written nearly 40 works, mostly biblical commentaries. His early treatise *De Natura Rerum* was modelled on the *Origines* of *Isidore of Seville and contains rudimentary natural science, referring phenomena to natural causes. His other influential work of history is the *Lives of the Abbots*, which gives an account of the earlier abbots in the Northumbrian Revival such as Ceolfrid and Benedict. There is a famous description of his death in a letter of his pupil Cuthbert. See *Bede: His Life, Times and Writings*, ed. A. H. Thompson (1935). (See also ANGLO-LATIN LITERATURE.)

BEDE, Cuthbert, see BRADLEY, E.

Bedevere, Sir, one of the most celebrated knights in the Arthurian legends, called earl of Normandy by *Laʒamon who also says he died in the Roman wars. According to *Malory only he and his brother Lucan, Arthur's butler, survived with Arthur the last battle against Modred; like Arthur Lucan dies after the battle. It was Bedevere who at Arthur's bidding threw *Excalibur into the lake and carried the king to the barge which bore him away to *Avalon.

BEDFORD, Sybille (1911–), author, born in Charlottenburg, the daughter of Maximilian von Schoenbeck, and educated privately in England, Italy, and France. *The Sudden View* (1953; reissued as *A Visit to Don Otavio*, 1960), a description of travels in Mexico, was followed by her best-known novel, *The Legacy* (1956), a sophisticated account, partly through a child's eyes, of the complex matrimonial and financial affairs

of a wealthy German family in the years immediately preceding the First World War. *A Favourite of the Gods* (1962) and *A Compass Error* (1968), both novels with Jamesian echoes, were followed by a two-volume biography of A. *Huxley (1973, 1974). *Jigsaw: An Unsentimental Education* (autobiographical fiction, 1989) was followed by a volume of memoir, *Quicksands* (2005).

Bedlam, a corruption of Bethlehem, applied to the Hospital of St Mary of Bethlehem, in Bishopsgate, London, founded as a priory in 1247, with the special duty of receiving and entertaining the clergy of St Mary of Bethlehem, the mother church, as often as they might come to England. In 1330 it is mentioned as 'an hospital', and in 1402 as a hospital for lunatics. In 1346 it was received under the protection of the City of London, and on the dissolution of the monasteries it was granted to the mayor and citizens. In 1547 it was incorporated as a royal foundation for the reception of lunatics. In 1675 a new hospital was built in Moorfields, and this in turn was replaced by a building in the Lambeth Road in 1815, now the Imperial War Museum.

From Bedlam are derived such expressions as *Tom o' Bedlam and Bess o' Bedlam for wandering lunatics, or beggars posing as lunatics.

Beelzebub, the name of a demon or devil, derived from Bible translations of Greek, Hebrew, and Assyrian words denoting 'fly-lord', 'lord of the high house', but understood from NT times as 'lord of the underworld'. In Matt. 12: 24 Beelzebub is spoken of as 'prince of the devils'. He was seen in medieval and Renaissance times as Satan's second-in-command, a lurid figure in popular mythology and morality plays. He accompanies Lucifer in Marlowe's *Dr Faustus*; Milton gives the name to one of the fallen angels, next to Satan in power (*Paradise Lost*, I. 79) and Golding adopted one version of it for the title of his novel *Lord of the Flies*.

BEER, Patricia (1919–99), poet. She was born in Devon, the daughter of a railway clerk and a mother who was a member of the Plymouth Brethren; she described her background vividly in her autobiographical *Mrs Beer's House* (1968). The legends and landscapes of the West Country also form the background for many of her poems (collections include *The Loss of the Magyar*, 1959; *The Estuary*, 1971; *Driving West*, 1975; *Selected Poems*, 1980; *The Lie of the Land*, 1983), and her historical novel *Moon's Ottery* (1978) is set in Elizabethan Devon.

BEERBOHM, (Sir Henry) Max(imilian) (1872–1956), critic, essayist, and caricaturist, born in London and educated at Charterhouse and Merton College, Oxford. He did not complete a degree but drew on Oxford for his one completed novel, *Zuleika Dobson* (1911), a fantasized distillation of the Oxford atmosphere of the 1890s. His writing, like his personality, was characterized by elegance and by a light but incisive touch in applying irony and wit to society's foibles and to the idiosyncrasies of writers, artists, and politicians. His first published book and collection of essays in this vein was somewhat audaciously entitled *The Works of Max Beerbohm* (1896), followed by *More* (1899), *Yet Again* (1909), *And Even Now* (1920). *A Christmas Garland* (1912) expertly parodied the literary styles of H. *James, *Wells, *Kipling, and other leading contemporary writers. His best short stories were collected in *Seven Men* (1919). As an associate in the 1890s of *Wilde and *Beardsley, of the *Rhymers Club, the Bodley Head publishing circle, and the New English Art Club, he was well placed to observe and comment upon audant-garde tendencies of the period. As half-brother of the actor-manager Beerbohm *Tree, Max had entrée into theatrical circles and was brilliant, if not always happy, as a dramatic critic of the *Saturday Review* from 1898 to 1910; he succeeded G. B. *Shaw, whose valedictory essay in that journal dubbed him 'the incomparable Max'. His dramatic criticism is collected in *Around Theatres* (1953) and *More Theatres* (1968). His caricatures, as elegant and as individual as his literary works, complement them with delicacy of line, witty captions, and unerring selection of salient characteristics. Among the best-known collections of these are *Caricatures of Twenty-Five Gentlemen* (1896), *The Poets' Corner* (1904), and *Rossetti and His Circle* (1922). In 1910 Max married the actress Florence Kahn and settled in Italy, his permanent home for the remainder of his life except for the periods of the two World Wars. During visits to England in the 1930s he began a new career as broadcaster; his commentaries on England then and now are collected in *Mainly on the Air* (1957).

BEETHOVEN, Ludwig van (1770–1827), German composer, whose immense reputation, established during his lifetime, has never diminished. He has always had supporters in England: the Ninth Symphony was written in response to a commission from the Philharmonic Society of London, whose directors sent £100 for his relief during the last months of his life. He himself professed great admiration for the English and constantly planned visits to London, but never succeeded in making any. Between approximately 1810 and 1816, taking over a task previously performed by *Haydn, he made arrangements with accompaniment for piano trio of some 140 Scottish, Irish, Welsh, and English folk songs for the Edinburgh publisher George Thomson. Apart from these, and the rather questionable play made with the tunes of 'God Save the King' and 'Rule Britannia' in the so-called 'Battle' Symphony written to celebrate Wellington's victory at Vitoria and in sets of piano variations written 1802–3 (no opus numbers), there is no other Beethoven composition that has a direct connection with English literature, though he confessed himself moved and influenced by Shakespeare and is believed to have taken *The Tempest* as an inspiration for his Piano Sonata in D minor, Op. 311, No. 2. His *Coriolan* overture was written for a play on the theme of Coriolanus by the Viennese poet H. J. von Collin, who also began to write a libretto for *Macbeth* for which Beethoven sketched some music, probably in 1808, but the project was abandoned.

Beggar's Bush, The, a drama by J. *Fletcher and *Massinger, possibly with scenes by *Beaumont; it was probably performed 1622, published 1647.

Florez, the rightful heir of the earldom of Flanders, but ignorant of his rights and living as a rich merchant at Bruges, is in love with Bertha, who is heiress of Brabant, but has been stolen away and placed with the burgomaster of Bruges and is equally ignorant of her rights. Gerrard, father of Florez, who has been driven from Flanders, has concealed himself among the beggars near Bruges, is their king, and watches over the interests of Florez. Wolfort, the usurper, proposes to marry Bertha and restore her to her rights, thus obtaining possession of Brabant. He sends Hubert, one of his nobles, who is in love with Jacqueline, Gerrard's daughter, to effect his purpose. Hubert, however, joins the beggars, among whom Jacqueline is living, and plots with Gerrard to get Wolfort into their power. In this they are successful. The identity of Florez and Bertha is revealed and they are married.

The play has been admired for the intricacies of the plot, and for the realistic portrayal of its 'ragged regiment' of beggars, whose dialogue is enlivened by thieves' cant: *Coleridge, in his *Table Talk* (17 Feb. 1833), declared, 'I could read the *Beggar's Bush* from morning to night. How sylvan and sunshiny it is!'

Beggar's Daughter of Bednall Green, The, a ballad written in the reign of Elizabeth I and included in Percy's *Reliques*.

Bessee is the fair daughter of a blind beggar, employed at the inn at Romford and courted by four suitors, a knight, a gentleman of good birth, a merchant of London, and the innkeeper's son. They all withdraw their suit on being referred by her to her father, except the knight. The old beggar gives her as dowry £3,000, two pounds for every one the knight puts down. It now appears that the beggar is Henry, son of Simon de Montfort, who has assumed the disguise of a beggar for safety.

The story forms the basis of *Chettle and *Day's *The Blind-Beggar of Bednal-Green* (1600, printed 1659). J. S. *Knowles also wrote a comedy called *The Beggar's Daughter of Bethnal Green*; and R. *Dodsley wrote a musical play, *The Blind Beggar of Bethnal Green*.

Beggar's Opera, The, a *ballad opera by J. *Gay, produced 1728.

The play arose out of *Swift's suggestion that a Newgate pastoral 'might make an odd pretty sort of thing'. The principal characters are Peachum, a receiver of stolen goods, who also makes a living by informing against his clients; his wife and his daughter Polly; Lockit, warder of Newgate, and his daughter

Lucy; and Captain Macheath, a gallant highwayman. Polly falls in love with Macheath, who marries her. Peachum, furious at her folly, decides to place her in the 'comfortable estate of widowhood' by informing against Macheath, who is arrested and sent to Newgate. Here he makes a conquest of Lucy, and there ensues a spirited conflict between Lucy and Polly, the rival claimants of his heart. ('How happy could I be with either, | Were t'other dear charmer away!') In spite of her jealousy, Lucy procures Macheath's escape. The play, which combines burlesque of Italian opera and political satire (notably of Sir R. *Walpole) with some of Gay's most brilliant songs and scenes of genuine pathos, was an unparalleled success, and is said to have brought Gay some £800. (It was said to have made Gay rich, and *Rich—the producer—gay.) It was frequently revived in the 20th cent., and a *Brecht–Weill version was performed in 1928.

BEHAN, Brendan (1923–64), Irish playwright, born in Dublin, the son of a house-painter. He was arrested in 1939 for his involvement with the IRA, and his subsequent period of Borstal training is described in his autobiographical *Borstal Boy* (1958). His best-known works are *The Hostage* (1958), a sprawling tragi-comedy about an English soldier kidnapped and held hostage in a Dublin brothel, and *The Quare Fellow* (1959), set in an Irish prison on the eve of a hanging. Both were first directed in Britain by Joan *Littlewood.

BEHN, Mrs Afra or Aphra, probably née Johnson (1640–89). She was born in Kent and visited Surinam, then a British colony, in 1663 with members of her family. On her return to England the following year she married Behn, a city merchant probably of Dutch descent, who died within two years. She was employed in 1666 by Charles II as a spy in Antwerp in the Dutch war. Her first play, *The Forced Marriage* (1670), was followed by some 14 others, including her most popular, *The Rover* (in two parts, 1677–81), dealing with the adventures in Naples and Madrid of a band of English Cavaliers during the exile of Charles II; its hero, the libertine Willmore, was said to be based on *Rochester, though another model may have been her lover John Hoyle, lawyer and son of the regicide Thomas Hoyle. *The City Heiress* (1682) is a characteristic satiric comedy of London life and, like Otway's *Venice Preserv'd*, contains a caricature of *Shaftesbury. *The Lucky Chance* (1686) explores one of her favourite themes, the ill consequences of arranged and ill-matched marriages. Her friends included *Buckingham, *Etherege, *Dryden, and *Otway, and she was a staunch defender of the Stuart cause. She also wrote poems and novels and edited a *Miscellany* (1685). Her best-remembered work is *Oroonoko, or The History of the Royal Slave*, based on her visit to Surinam. Perhaps the earliest English philosophical novel, it deplores the slave trade and Christian hypocrisy, holding up for admiration the nobility and honour of its African hero. Despite her success she had even in her lifetime to contend with accusations of plagiarism and lewdness, attracted in her view by her sex, and as late as 1905, in an edition of her novels, Ernest Baker described her work as 'false, lurid and depraved'. V. Woolf in *A Room of One's Own* (1928) acclaims her as the first English woman to earn her living by writing, 'with all the plebeian virtues of humour, vitality and courage', and comments that she was buried 'scandalously but rather appropriately' in Westminster Abbey. See M. *Duffy, *The Passionate Shepherdess* (1977). (See RESTORATION.)

Belarius, in Shakespeare's *Cymbeline*, the banished lord who, under the name of Morgan, acts as foster-father to the king's two sons.

Belch, Sir Toby, in Shakespeare's *Twelfth Night*, a roistering humorous knight, uncle to Olivia.

Belford, John, Lovelace's principal correspondent in Richardson's *Clarissa*.

Belgravia, an illustrated monthly edited by M. E. *Braddon, which ran from 1866 to 1899, and published work by many well-known writers, including *Hardy, Wilkie *Collins, *Harte, and *Ouida. See also GHOST STORIES.

Belial, adapted from the Hebrew words beli-ya'al, means literally 'worthlessness' and 'destruction', but in Deut. 13: 13, and elsewhere, in the phrase 'sons of Belial', it is retained untranslated in the English version, as a proper name. It has thus come to mean the spirit of evil personified, and is used from early times as a name for the devil or one of the fiends, and by Milton (*Paradise Lost*, I. 490) as the name of one of the fallen angels. The phrase 'sons of Belial' was a republican term of odium for Cavaliers in the English Revolution: Milton evokes them in *Paradise Lost*, I. 501, as 'the sons | Of Belial, flown with insolence and wine'.

Believe as You List, a tragedy by *Massinger, acted 1631, not published until 1849. The original play was banned because it dealt with recent Spanish and Portuguese history. Massinger ingeniously transferred the story back to the safer days of the Roman Empire.

Antiochus, king of lower Asia, returns years after his defeat and supposed death at the hands of the Romans. In his fight for recognition he is constantly opposed by the ruthless and indefatigable Roman envoy Flaminius. The Carthaginian Senate is too frightened to back him, and Prusias, king of Bithynia, who at first shelters and encourages him, is intimidated into changing his mind. Antiochus, imprisoned and humiliated, refuses to deny his own identity, and is led out to death. The play is a fine study of the recurring conflict between nationalism and imperialism.

The manuscript of the play is one of the most interesting of those preserved from the earlier 17th cent. It is in Massinger's own hand, and has been extensively worked over by the book-keeper of the King's Men to prepare it for performance.

Belinda, (1) a character in Vanbrugh's *The Provok'd Wife*; (2) the heroine of Pope's *The Rape of the Lock*; (3) the title of a novel by M. *Edgeworth; (4) a novel by H. *Belloc.

BELINSKY, Vissarion Grigorevich (1811–48), Russian literary critic whose influence on Russian and Soviet aesthetic theory has been immense. Particularly in his final years, he used literary criticism for the discussion of moral and social issues, and was thus the first in a continuing line of 'civic' critics. His major work is contained in *Literary Reveries* (1834), in numerous annual literary surveys, and in his work on *Pushkin and *Gogol, particularly the *Letter to Gogol* (1847). Belinsky wrote a long and interesting essay on *Hamlet* (1838), and admired *Byron, Sir W. *Scott, and J. F. *Cooper. His work can be read in English in *Selected Criticism* (trans. Ralph Matlaw, 1962).

BELL, (Arthur) Clive (Heward) (1881–1964), art critic, educated at Cambridge where he came under the influence of G. E. *Moore and met members of what was to be the *Bloomsbury Group. In 1907 he married Vanessa Stephen (see BELL, V.). In 1910 he met R. *Fry, whose views contributed to his own theory of 'Significant Form', outlined in *Art* (1914), which held that form, independent of content, was the most important element in a work of art. With Fry, he was a champion of the Post-Impressionists. In *Civilization* (1928) he argued (with provocative and ironical undertones) that civilization, in itself artificial and characterized by tolerance, discrimination, reason, and humour, depended on the existence of a (not necessarily hereditary) leisured élite. His other works include *Old Friends: Personal Recollections* (1956).

BELL, Currer, Ellis, and Acton, see BRONTË, C., E., and A.

BELL, Gertrude Margaret Lowthian (1868–1926), the daughter of an ironmaster baronet, born at Washington Hall, Co. Durham, and educated at Lady Margaret Hall, Oxford, where she was the first woman ever to get a first in modern history. At 23 she became engaged to a diplomat who died a few months later, and in middle life she was passionately attached to a married man who was killed at Gallipoli. After a dozen years of world travel and mountaineering, in which she distinguished herself by redoubtable first ascents in the Alps, she began her solitary travels as a field archaeologist in Syria, Asia Minor, and Mesopotamia. Her knowledge of the desert Arabs and Middle East politics caused her recruitment to the Arab Bureau in Cairo in 1915, and later her appointment in Iraq as oriental secretary to the British high commissioner. She died in Baghdad. Apart from important specialized archaeological works and political reports, her best-known books were *Safar Nameh: Persian Pictures* (1894), *The Desert and the Sown* (1907), and *Amurath to Amurath* (1911). In these, and in her brilliant *Letters* (1927) and diaries—largely quoted in *Gertrude Bell: From Her Personal Papers*, ed. Elizabeth Burgoyne (1958 and 1961)—she vividly conveyed the landscapes and personalities of the desert, wittily recapturing in remembered dialogue the idiomatic flavour of the original; she was an accomplished linguist in Arabic and Persian, and published a translation of *Hāfiz. See H. V. F. Winstone, *Gertrude Bell* (1978).

BELL, Martin (1918–78), poet, born in Southampton, educated at the University of Southampton. He was a member of the *Group; his *Collected Poems 1937–66* (1967) celebrates fellow poets, provincial schoolmasters, the French symbolists, Groucho Marx, grand opera, and 'the shining rebels' of his pantheon, while satirizing conventional notions of patriotism and religion.

BELL, Vanessa, née Stephen (1879–1961), painter, and elder sister of V. *Woolf. She married Clive *Bell in 1907, was a central figure in the *Bloomsbury Group, and from c.1914 lived with the painter Duncan Grant (1885–1978).

Bella Wilfer, a character in Dickens's *Our Mutual Friend*.

Bellair, a character in Etherege's *The Man of Mode*.

Bellamira, a comedy by Sir C. *Sedley, produced 1687. Founded on *Terence's *Eunuchus*, it is coarse but lively. Dangerfield, a braggart and a bully, whose cowardice is exposed in an adventure similar to that of *Falstaff at Gadshill, is an amusing character.

BELLAMY, Edward (1850–98), American novelist and political theorist, born in Massachusetts, whose fame rests upon his popular *utopian romance *Looking Backward: 2000–1887* (1888). Its hero, Julian West, a young Bostonian, falls into a hypnotic sleep in 1887 and wakes in the year 2000 to find great social changes. Squalor and injustice have disappeared, private capitalism has been replaced by public, and everyone works for and is a member of the state. The moral, social, and cultural benefits of the new system are everywhere apparent. This work had an immense vogue; a Nationalist Party was formed to advocate its principles, and Bellamy lectured widely and wrote other works to further his views before dying of tuberculosis. He was widely read in Europe, and imitated by, among others, H. G. *Wells.

Bellario, (1) in Shakespeare's *The Merchant of Venice*, Portia's lawyer cousin; (2) the name assumed by the heroine of Beaumont and Fletcher's *Philaster*, when disguised as a page.

Bellaston, Lady, a character in Fielding's *Tom Jones*.

'Belle Dame sans Merci, La', see LA BELLE DAME SANS MERCI.

BELLENDEN, or **BALLANTYNE,** John (c.1500–c.1548), Scottish poet and translator into Scots of *Livy.

Bellerus, the name of a fabulous person introduced by

Milton in his *Lycidas* to account for Bellerium, or Bolerium, the Roman name of Land's End, in Cornwall.

Belle's Stratagem, The, a comedy by Mrs H. *Cowley, produced 1780.

Doricourt returns from his travels to marry Letitia Hardy, whom he has not seen since his childhood, the match having been arranged by their parents. He finds her beautiful but lacking in animation; she falls in love with him at once. Distressed by his cold reception, she determines to win him by first disgusting him through the assumption of the manners of a country hoyden, and then conquering his heart by her sprightliness at a masquerade, and this scheme she successfully accomplishes.

BELLI, Giuseppe Gioachino (1791–1863), Italian poet, whose vernacular Roman sonnets (*I sonetti*, ed. G. Vigolo, 1952) represent the outlook and customs of Roman plebeians. They were written between 1827 and 1849, but because of their blasphemous and erotic satire he kept them secret and seems to have tried to suppress them after the revolutionary threat of 1848–9. Some critics postulate an early liberal period up to this point, followed by Catholic reaction: it is more likely that Belli's intense questioning of the mysteries denotes that he was always fundamentally devout. His mask of ethnography, using sonnet form not as the trajectory of his own feeling but as a sampling device for social reality, allows him to attribute forbidden thoughts to his interlocutors. In more than 2,000 sonnets he presents a *comédie humaine* that embraces the Bible, Roman history, ancient and modern, and the daily lives of characters ranging from popes to prostitutes and ghetto Jews. For the sounds of 'Romanesque' he devised his own spelling, yet he is not a 'dialect' poet: his idiom is his own, using all the resources of literary Italian, as well as popular speech, to explore an extreme range of poetic registers. He also wrote some 45,000 verses in academic Italian, of little poetic value. First described in English by F. *Trollope, various of his works have been translated by R. *Garioch, by Harold Norse, and by A. *Burgess.

Bell Jar, The, a novel by S. *Plath, published 1963 under the pseudonym of Victoria Lucas, and under her own name in 1966.

It opens in New York in the summer of 1953 (the year of the execution of the Rosenbergs, an event which provides a recurrent motif) as the narrator, Esther Greenwood, a highly ambitious, intelligent college girl from Boston, spends time working on a trainee programme for a women's magazine with a group of other award-winning young women, and throws herself recklessly into the dangers of city life. Her story is interwoven with recollections of her boyfriend, Yale medical student Buddy Willard, who represents in part the threats of the flesh, in part the dullness of the provincial existence she fears will engulf her. She returns home, suffers a nervous breakdown, undergoes ECT, attempts suicide, is kept in psychiatric care, and in the penultimate chapter succeeds in losing her virginity to a mathematics professor. At the end of the novel, after the suicide of one of her old friends and fellow inmates, she prepares to leave the asylum and return to college. The subject matter of the novel, which is written in a taut, controlled, colloquial yet poetic prose, is highly autobiographical.

BELLOC, Hilaire (Joseph Hilary Pierre) (1870–1953), born in France, of part-French Catholic ancestry, and educated at *Newman's Oratory School and at Balliol College, Oxford. From 1906 to 1909, and again in 1910, he was Liberal MP for Salford. He became a prolific and versatile writer of poetry and verses; essays on religious, social, and political topics; biography; travel; literary criticism; and novels. His first publications were, in 1896, *A Bad Child's Book of Beasts* and *Verses and Sonnets* (which he later withdrew); other books of verse included *Cautionary Tales* (1907) and *Sonnets and Verse* (1923). His most celebrated serious lyrics are probably 'Tarantella' ('Do you remember an inn, Miranda?') and 'Ha'nacker Mill'. He was an active journalist, literary editor of the *Morning Post* from 1906 to 1910, founder of the *Eye-witness* (1911), and writer of innumerable essays and reviews. His books attacking and satirizing Edwardian society (some with G. K. *Chesterton) include *Pongo and the Bull* (1910) and *The Servile State* (1912); of his many books propounding Catholicism, *Europe and Faith* (1920) was well regarded. His many biographies include *Danton* (1899), *Marie Antoinette* (1909), *Cromwell* (1927), and *Charles II* (1940); and his histories *The French Revolution* (1911) and a substantial *History of England* (1915). *The Cruise of the Nona* (1925), the most intimate of his books, contains many of his most personal reflections. His most successful book of travel, *The Path to Rome* (1902), which was published with his own sketches and illustrations, is an account of a journey which he undertook, largely on foot, from the valley of the Moselle to Rome; it is interspersed with anecdotes, reflections, and dialogues between 'Lector' and 'Auctor' and ends with his arrival; other travel books include *Sussex* (1906) and *The Pyrenees* (1909). Of the novels *Mr Clutterbuck's Election* (1908), *The Girondin* (1911), *The Green Overcoat* (1912), and *Belinda* (1928) were among the most highly regarded. The last, the author's favourite, is a brief and highly individual love story, related with romantic feeling but much irony as well. A biography by A. N. *Wilson was published in 1984.

BELLOW, Saul (1915–2005), novelist. He was born in Canada of Russian-Jewish parents, and educated from the age of 9 in Chicago, a city evoked in many of his works, including his first short novel *Dangling Man* (1944), a first-person account of a man waiting, unemployed, for his army draft. *The Victim* (1947) deals with the relationship between Jew and Gentile.

The Adventures of Augie March (1953) opens in Chicago, 'that sombre city', and provides a lengthy, episodic, first-person account of Augie's progress from boyhood, moving to Mexico, then Paris. *Seize the Day* (1956), a novella, deals with middle-aged Wilhelm, still oppressed by his powerful father. *Henderson the Rain King* (1959), designed on a grand and mythic scale, records American millionaire Gene Henderson's quest for revelation and spiritual power in Africa, where he becomes rainmaker and heir to a kingdom. *Herzog* (1964) reveals the inner life of a Jewish intellectual, Moses Herzog, driven to the verge of breakdown by his second wife's adultery with his close friend; he writes unsent letters about himself and civilization to the living and the dead, seeking above all the intensity that drives so many of Bellow's characters. ('The soul requires intensity. At the same time virtue bores mankind.') *Mr Sammler's Planet* (1969), set in New York, reflects, through the one-eyed Polish-Jewish elderly survivor Sammler, on evolution and the future of civilization, combining metaphysical speculation with a vivid physical sense of daily city life. *Humboldt's Gift* (1974) is the story of Charlie Citrine, a successful writer and academic plagued by women, lawsuits, and mafiosi, whose present career is interwoven with memories of the early success, failing powers, and squalid death of his friend Von Humboldt Fleischer, whose poetic destiny he fears he may inherit, together with his manuscripts. *The Dean's December* (1982) is a 'tale of two cities', both seen through the eyes of Albert Corde, who visits Bucharest to see his dying mother-in-law, where he reflects on the contrasts between the violence and corruption of Chicago and the bureaucratic chill of eastern Europe; the novel has, like much of Bellow's work, a strongly apocalyptic note. Other works include *Him with His Foot in His Mouth and Other Stories* (1984) and *More Die of Heartbreak* (1987). Two novellas, *A Theft* (1989) and *The Bellarosa Connection* (1989), were included, with the title story, in *Something to Remember Me by* (1991). *The Actual* (1997), set amongst the Chicago super-rich, recounts the enduring love of ageing narrator Harry Trellman for his old school friend Amy, and his last novel, Ravelstein (2000), is based on Bellow's friendship with Chicago professor Allan Bloom (1930–92). *It All Adds Up* (1994) is a collection of non-fiction pieces. Bellow also wrote a play, *The Last Analysis* (1964). He was awarded the *Nobel Prize for literature in 1976.

Bells, The (1871), a dramatic adaptation by L. Lewis of *Le Juif polonais* by Erckmann-Chatrian, the story of a burgomaster haunted by the consciousness of an undiscovered murder that he has committed. It provided H. *Irving with one of his most successful parts.

Bells and Pomegranates, the covering title of a series of plays and collections of shorter dramatic poems by R. *Browning, published 1841–6, comprising *Pippa Passes* (1841), *King Victor and King Charles* (1842), *Dramatic Lyrics* (1842), *The Return of the Druses*

(1843), *A Blot in the 'Scutcheon* (1843), *Colombe's Birthday* (1844), *Dramatic Romances and Lyrics* (1845), and *Luria* and *A Soul's Tragedy* (1846). The title baffled the critics; Elizabeth Barrett finally persuaded Browning to explain it in the last number, which he did by saying that it indicated 'an alternation, or mixture, of music with discoursing, sound with sense, poetry with thought; which looks too ambitious, thus expressed, so the symbol was preferred'. The 'symbol' derives from Exod. 28: 33–4, where it relates to the ornamentation and embroidery of the high priest's robe. The separate numbers were bound together and sold as a single volume after 1846.

Beloved, a novel by Toni *Morrison (1987), set in 1873 in America. The narrative technique is deliberately non-linear and complex, the language richly poetic and suffused with biblical references. Sethe, a former slave, lives with her daughter Denver and the ghost of her dead baby girl. The book opens with the unexpected arrival of Paul D., one of the five men with whom Sethe had formerly been enslaved at Sweet Home, a Kentucky farm. Paul D. moves in, and as they face the past together, their tragic story unfolds. Meanwhile, an uncanny girl called Beloved comes to live with them. It emerges that Beloved is an incarnation of the daughter Sethe had murdered, in a fit of hysteria, in order to prevent their being torn apart. In three sections of poetry, the meaning of 'Beloved' is explored; the word transcends its character, and becomes a symbol for all dead and suffering slaves. The book is dedicated to 'Sixty Million and more'. See SLAVERY, LITERATURE OF.

Belphegor, the Septuagint and Vulgate form of the Moabitish 'Baal-peor' mentioned in Num. 25.

In *Machiavelli's *Novella di Belfagor* (probably written *c*.1518), the name is given to an archdevil sent by Pluto to the world to investigate the truth of the complaints made by many souls reaching hell, that they have been sent there by their wives. Belphegor has orders to take a wife, arrives in Florence well provided with money and a retinue of devils as servants, and marries. But he is unable to put up with his wife's insolence and prefers to run away from her and return to hell. There are echoes of this legend in one of the stories of B. *Rich's *Farewell to Militarie Profession* (1581), and in Jonson's *The Devil Is an Ass* (1616). J. *Wilson produced a tragi-comedy, *Belphegor; or The Marriage of the Devil*, in 1677–8.

Belphoebe, in Spenser's *Faerie Queene*, the chaste huntress, daughter of the nymph Chrysogone and twin sister of *Amoret; she partly symbolizes Queen Elizabeth. Belphoebe puts *Braggadochio to flight (II. iii), finds herbs to heal the wounded *Timias ('whether it divine *Tobacco* were, | Or *Panachaea*, or *Polygony*', III. v), and rescues Amoret from *Corflambo (IV. vii).

Belshazzar's feast, the feast made by Belshazzar the son of Nebuchadnezzar and the last king of Babylonia, at which his doom was foretold by writing on the wall, as interpreted by Daniel (Dan. 5). Belshazzar was killed in the sack of Babylon by Cyrus (538 BC). He is the subject of dramas by H. *More and *Milman, R. *Landor's *The Impious Feast*, a poem by *Byron, and an oratorio by W. *Walton.

Belton Estate, The, a novel by A. *Trollope, published 1866.

Will Belton unexpectedly becomes the heir to an entailed estate in Somerset. On his first visit to Belton Castle he falls in love with the squire's daughter, Clara Amedroz, only to find that Clara has already promised herself to a lukewarm cousin, Captain Aylmer MP. When her father dies Clara, feeling bound by her engagement, goes to live for a trial period at Aylmer Park. But the family—particularly the ferociously condescending Lady Aylmer—find neither Clara's independence of mind nor her want of fortune to their liking. This inevitably leads to a quarrel with Captain Aylmer and, when Will Belton renews his suit, Clara is only too happy to accept the man to whom she has, all along, been attracted.

Belvidera, the heroine of Otway's *Venice Preserv'd*.

BELY, Andrei (Boris Nikolaevich Bugaev) (1880–1934), Russian novelist, poet, and literary theorist, born in Moscow, who became a key figure in the Russian symbolist movement. In 1903, after an exalted correspondence, he met *Blok, with whom he was to have a long 'inimical friendship', and for whose wife he conceived a complex passion. His reputation was established with three books of poetry, *Gold in Azure* (1904), *Ashes* (1909), and *The Urn* (1909), the last of which was inspired by his love for Lyubov Bloka. In 1912 he met the anthroposophist Rudolf Steiner, and after following him around Europe he settled in Dornach in 1914. In 1916 he returned to Russia, and after the revolution he engaged in teaching both literature and anthroposophy. During this period Bely wrote *Kotik Letaev* (1915–16), a fictionalized account of his consciousness as a young child, memorably described by *Zamyatin as the only anthroposophical novel in existence. Bely's most important novel is *Petersburg* (1913–16), which is written in a rhythmical prose that at times approximates the rhythms of poetry: it is set in the revolution of 1905: against a background of hallucinatory St Petersburg, a group of radicals attempt the assassination of a senator. *Petersburg* is overwhelmingly concerned with questions of identity and consciousness, and the appearance of its definitive version the same year as *Joyce's *Ulysses* is a remarkable coincidence, for their shared interest in neologism, leitmotif, mythology, parody, and experiment has been much noted. Its reputation as an inaccessible masterpiece has at last been modified by the appearance of an excellent translation (by Robert Maguire and John Malmstad, 1978). Bely's four-part memoirs, *Diary of an Eccentric* (1921), *Reminiscences of Blok* (1923), *On the Border of Two Centuries* (1930), and *Between Two Revolutions* (1935), are widely regarded as Russia's finest autobiography.

BEMBO, Pietro (1470–1547), Italian humanist, who became bishop of Bergamo, a cardinal, and historiographer of Venice. He wrote prose and verse in Latin and Italian, his Italian being studiously modelled on Petrarchan Tuscan, as his Latin was on the Ciceronian. He was a devoted admirer of Lucrezia *Borgia, to whom he dedicated his dialogue on love, *Gl'Asolani* (1505); this work provided the title of R. *Browning's last volume of poems, *Asolando*. (Asolo is a small town north of Venice.) *Gl'Asolani*, modelled on *Plato's *Symposium*, also provided *Castiglione with the philosophical basis for his *Courtier* (in which Bembo himself figures prominently), and was useful to *Spenser in composing his *Fowre Hymnes*.

Ben Gunn, a character in Stevenson's *Treasure Island*.

BENAVENTE Y MARTÍNEZ, Jacinto (1866–1954), Spanish playwright and critic, who was awarded the *Nobel Prize in 1922. He was the author of many satirical comedies (in all he wrote some 170 plays) which include *La noche del sábado* (1903, *Saturday Night*) and *Los intereses creados* (1907, *Vested Interests*).

Bend in the River, A, a novel by V. S. *Naipaul, published 1979.

It is the first-person narration of trader and storekeeper Salim, a Muslim from the east coast of Africa, whose family, of Indian origin, had been settled there for centuries. He buys a small business in a town in a French-speaking Central African state, and sets himself up there. The novel traces his personal relationships—with his servant Metty, the son of slaves from the coast; with the handsome, self-absorbed Indian couple Mahesh and Shoba, who win the Bigburger franchise; with village trader and reputed witch Zabeth and her lycée-educated son Ferdinand, who becomes commissioner and rescues Salim from prosecution in the last chapter; with Indar, English-university-educated boyhood friend; with Nazruddin, entrepreneur from the coast who becomes a property-owner in Gloucester Road, London; with Father Huisman, whose knowledge of and veneration for African religion ends in assassination and decapitation; and with Raymond, white historian of Africa and adviser to the president, and his wife Yvette, with whom Salim has a violently sensual affair. It also charts the progress of the state itself, through revolution, counter-revolution, the nationalization of property (including Salim's), prosperity, and bloodshed, as the president attempts to combine new technology and new mythology in his image of the new Africa. Predominantly pessimistic in tone, with something of *Conrad's sense of the futility and corruptibility of human endeavour, the novel is an unsparing investigation of the cost of change and the meaning of culture.

Benedick, in Shakespeare's *_Much Ado about Nothing_, a sworn bachelor who falls in love with *Beatrice; 'Benedict' has been used subsequently to refer to a newly married erstwhile bachelor.

BENEDICT BISCOP, St (?628–89), a thegn of Oswiu, king of Northumbria, who after making two pilgrimages to Rome retired to the Isle of Lérins, where he adopted the monastic life. After two years he again went to Rome and was directed by the pope, Vitalian, to accompany Theodore of Tarsus from Rome to Canterbury. He was then appointed abbot of St Peter's, Canterbury (669), resigning the dignity two years later to visit Rome once more. During this journey he collected and brought back many volumes and relics. On his return he founded (in 674) the monastery of St Peter at the mouth of the river Wear, importing workmen to build a church of stone and to glaze the windows. Once more he went to Rome, bringing back a further store of books and relics. After this he founded the sister monastery of St Paul at Jarrow. He was buried in his church at Wearmouth, having left directions for the careful preservation of his library. He is regarded as one of the originators of the artistic and literary development of Northumbria in the next century, celebrated by *Bede in his _Lives of the Abbots_ (716–20).

BENÉT, Stephen Vincent (1898–1943), American poet, born in Pennsylvania and educated at Yale. He is best known for his narrative poem of the Civil War, _John Brown's Body_ (1928), and for some of the poems in _Ballads and Poems_ (1931), including the popular 'American Names', with its resounding last line, 'Bury my heart at Wounded Knee'. He also wrote what he called 'bread-and-butter' novels and short stories, and worked as a screenwriter in Hollywood for some time. His folk opera _The Devil and Daniel Webster_, performed in 1939, for which he wrote the libretto, was based on his own short story (1937), and presents the successful appeal of the legendary *Webster against the devil's claim to the soul of New Hampshire farmer Jabez Stone.

Ben-Hur: _A Tale of the Christ_, a historical novel, published 1880, about the early days of Christianity by Lew (Lewis) Wallace (1827–1905), an American novelist who had been a general in the Civil War. It was filmed twice by MGM, in 1925 as a silent epic, and in 1959 as an expensive spectacle.

'Benito Cereno' (1856), a short story by H. *Melville.
  A Gothic tale of white masters and implacable black revenge, it is set off the coast of Peru in 1799, where the amiable, condescendingly racist Yankee Captain Delano goes to the aid of a drifting slave-ship. Delano suspects piracy from the erratic Captain Benito Cereno and his devoted black servant Babo, when in fact the slaves have rebelled, enslaving Cereno and slaughtering their master Don Aranda, whose skeleton has been turned into a ghoulish figurehead with the slogan 'Follow Your Leader'. Cereno escapes with Delano, only to die later, and the recaptured slaves are executed, unrepentant. _Benito Cereno_ was dramatized by R. *Lowell in 1967.

BENJAMIN, Walter (1892–1940), German critic and essayist, born to a Jewish family in Berlin, and educated in Berlin, Freiburg, Munich, and Bern. He failed to gain academic employment, his thesis on German baroque drama being rejected as incomprehensible by the University of Frankfurt, and worked as a literary journalist, translator, and radio scriptwriter. Adopting the principles of Marxism, he befriended *Brecht, writing in defence of the playwright's methods. Upon Hitler's accession to power in 1933 he went into exile in Paris, where he undertook a study of *Baudelaire and the urban experience. The invasion of France in 1940 led him to seek an escape route to the USA through neutral Spain, but when he was stopped at the Spanish border he took his own life. His essays on literature, criticism, modern culture, and the philosophy of history show an unusual combination of Jewish mysticism, *Modernism, and Marxism. Posthumously selected and republished, notably in _Illuminationen_ (1961, ed. H. *Arendt) and _Versuche über Brecht_ (_Understanding Brecht_, 1966), they have been influential in the reshaping of *Marxist literary criticism and more widely in cultural studies and philosophy. Portions of his unfinished Paris project have been translated as _Charles Baudelaire: A Lyric Poet in the Era of High Capitalism_ (1973).

BENLOWES, Edward (?1602–76), poet, heir to a wealthy Catholic family, though he became a Protestant. He was a friend of *Quarles and P. *Fletcher in Oxford. His principal work was _Theophila, or Love's Sacrifice_ (1652), in 13 cantos, celebrating the epic progress of the soul in learned, obscure, and occasionally grotesque conceits and language; it was praised by *D'Avenant but ridiculed by Samuel *Butler, *Pope, and *Warburton. A critical biography by H. Jenkins appeared in 1952.

Bennet, Mr and Mrs, Jane, Elizabeth, Mary, Kitty, and Lydia, characters in J. Austen's *_Pride and Prejudice_.

BENNETT, Alan (1934–   ), dramatist and actor, born in Yorkshire and educated at Exeter College, Oxford. He made his name with the satirical review _Beyond the Fringe_ (1960, pub. 1963, with Jonathan Miller and others), and his other works, most of which are satirical comedies, include _Forty Years on_ (1968, pub. 1969), set in a public school, which has much fun at the expense of the *Bloomsbury Group, T. E. *Lawrence, and other fashionable cultural figures; _Getting on_ (1971, pub. 1972); and _Habeas Corpus_ (1973). A more sombre work, _The Old Country_ (1977, pub. 1978), deals with the theme of exile through the life of an English spy in the Soviet Union; one of his many television plays, _An Englishman Abroad_ (pub. 1982, broadcast 1983), deals with the same subject through a poignant evocation of

Guy Burgess's real-life encounter in Moscow with the actress Coral Browne. Other works include *The Insurance Man* (1986); *A Question of Attribution* (staged 1988, televised 1991), a treatment of the treachery of the art historian Sir Anthony Blunt; *The Madness of George III* (perf. 1991, pub. 1992); *The History Boys* (2004), set in a northern Grammar School; and *Talking Heads*, a series of monologues originally written for television (1987, pub. 1988). *Writing Home* (1994) is a collection of journal entries, reminiscences, and reviews, including 'The Lady in the Van', on a tramp who camped out in his garden. *Untold Stories* (2005) is a volume of autobiography, written after he was diagnosed with cancer.

BENNETT, (Enoch) Arnold (1867–1931), novelist, born in Hanley, Staffordshire, the son of a self-educated solicitor. He was destined to follow in his father's footsteps, but at the age of 21 he went to London where he worked as a clerk before establishing himself as a writer. His first stories were published in **Tit-Bits* (1890) and the **Yellow Book* (1895), and his first novel, *A Man from the North*, appeared in 1898. In 1893 he became assistant editor and subsequently editor of the periodical *Woman*, launching himself on a career of remarkable versatility. In 1902 he moved to Paris, returning to England to settle permanently in 1912 with his French wife Marguerite, from whom he later separated. In 1926 at the suggestion of his friend *Beaverbrook he began an influential weekly article on books for the *Evening Standard* which continued until his death from typhoid. He had a lifelong passion for the theatre and wrote several successful plays, notably *Milestones* (1912, with E. Knoblock, author of *Kismet*), but his fame rests chiefly on his novels and short stories, the best known of which were set in the Potteries of his youth, a region he recreated as the 'Five Towns'. *Anna of the Five Towns* (1902), the story of a miser's daughter, shows clearly the influence of the French realists whom he much admired. *The Old Wives' Tale* (1908) was followed by the Clayhanger series (*Clayhanger*, 1910; *Hilda Lessways*, 1911; *These Twain*, 1916; *The Roll Call*, 1918). The novels portray the district with an ironic but affectionate detachment, describing provincial life and culture in documentary detail, and creating many memorable characters— Darius Clayhanger, the dictatorial printer who started work aged 7 in a pot-bank, the monstrous but good-hearted Auntie Hamps, Edwin Clayhanger, frustrated architect, and Hilda Lessways, the independent and strong-willed young woman who marries Edwin. Two volumes of short stories, *The Grim Smile of the Five Towns* (1907) and *The Matador of the Five Towns* (1912), are set in the same region, as are several minor novels. Bennett shows a concern for obscure and ordinary lives which also manifests itself in the best novel of his later period, *Riceyman Steps* (1923), the story of a miserly second-hand bookseller, set in drab Clerkenwell. But he also wrote many entertaining lighter works, displaying a love of luxury and fantasy, among them *The*

Grand Babylon Hotel (1902), *The Card* (1911), and *Mr Prohack* (1922). His *Journal*, begun in 1896, modelled partly on that of the *Goncourt brothers, was published in 1932–3, and offers a striking portrait both of the period and of his own highly disciplined working life. Bennett's letters, ed. James Hepburn, were published in four volumes (1966–86); there is a biography by M. *Drabble (1974).

BENOÎT DE SAINTE-MAURE, a 12th-cent. trouvère, born probably at Sainte-Maure in Touraine and patronized by Henry II of England, for whom he composed a verse history of the dukes of Normandy. His best-known work is the *Roman de Troie*, based on the writings of *Dares Phrygius and *Dictys Cretensis. The *Roman* was translated into Latin prose by *Guido delle Colonne, and thus served as a source on which many subsequent writers drew including *Boccaccio, followed by *Chaucer, who is believed to have made considerable direct use of Benoît. His works have been edited by L. Constance (6 vols, 1904–12).

BENSON, A(rthur) C(hristopher) (1862–1925), eldest surviving son of E. W. Benson (1829–96), archbishop of Canterbury, and brother of E. F. and R. H. Benson (below). He was from 1915 master of Magdalene College, Cambridge. He published many volumes of biography, family reminiscences, reflection, criticism, etc., and had a facility for writing public odes and verses, typified by his 'Land of Hope and Glory'. From 1897 until 1925 he kept a diary, amounting to five million words; extracts were published by *Lubbock in 1926, but the papers were locked away for 50 years. David Newsome makes use of them in his biography *On the Edge of Paradise: A. C. Benson*, the Diarist (1980, a work which reveals Benson's deeply depressive tendencies) and edited *Edwardian Excursions* (1981), selections from the manuscript covering 1898–1904.

BENSON, E(dward) F(rederic) (1867–1940), brother of A. C. and R. H. *Benson, an extremely prolific and popular novelist, whose works include *Dodo* (1893, followed by other 'Dodo' novels) and *Queen Lucia* (1920, followed by other 'Lucia' novels), and various volumes of reminiscences (*As We Were*, 1930; *As We Are*, 1932; etc.) which are a rich source of anecdote. In his later years he lived at Lamb House, Rye, once the home of H. *James.

BENSON, R(obert) H(ugh) (1871–1914), younger brother of A. C. and E. F. Benson (above), and like them an extremely prolific writer. He was ordained in 1895 but became a Roman Catholic in 1903, and most of his work consists of Catholic apologia: he wrote sensational apocalyptic novels (e.g. *The Lord of the World*, 1907), melodramatic historical novels (e.g. *Come Rack! Come Rope!*, 1912), and modern novels usually involving an impossible moral conundrum (e.g. *The Average Man*, 1913), and also published sermons, poems, etc. He was, briefly, a friend and collaborator of F. W. *Rolfe.

BENTHAM, Jeremy (1748–1832), educated at Westminster and the Queen's College, Oxford. He was called to the bar at Lincoln's Inn, but found the practice of the law courts morally and intellectually distasteful; he set himself the task of working at and giving theoretical justification for a simple and equitable legal system. He published anonymously in 1776 *Fragment on Government*, in form a criticism of *Blackstone's *Commentaries*, in which he first sketched his theory of government. While in Russia, 1785–8, he wrote his *Defence of Usury* (1787) and a series of letters on a *Panopticon* (1791), a scheme for improving prison discipline. In 1789 he published *Introduction to Principles of Morals and Legislation* (which had first been printed in 1780). Besides these he produced a number of works on ethics, jurisprudence, logic, and political economy, his influence proving greatest in the first two of these spheres, but he did not care to publish; the vast mass of his papers were never properly prepared for publication. His only large work was the *Principles*; the rest were pamphlets. In the dissemination of his views Bentham was greatly assisted by his devoted disciple Étienne Dumont of Geneva, who compiled a number of treatises based on Bentham's manuscripts and published them between 1802 and 1825 in French. A considerable number of Bentham's published works are retranslations of Dumont.

It is in the *Fragment on Government* and more fully in the *Principles* that he enunciates the political and ethical theory of Utility by which he is best remembered. 'It is the greatest happiness of the greatest number that is the measure of right and wrong.' Pain and pleasure are the 'sovereign masters' governing man's conduct; 'it is for them alone to point out what we ought to do.' Pleasures and pains can be quantitatively measured according to their duration, intensity, certainty, and propinquity. When the pleasures and pains resulting from any act to all the members of the community affected have been measured by these standards, we are in a position to determine the moral quality of the act. The criterion of the goodness of a law is the principle of Utility, the measure in which it subserves the happiness to which every individual is equally entitled. The motive of an act always being self-interest, it is the business of law and education to make the sanctions sufficiently strong to induce the individual to subordinate his own happiness to that of the community. Bentham believed it possible that the quantitative value of pains and pleasures as motives of action could be minutely calculated, which would give scientific accuracy to morals and legislation.

Bentham did not share the theoretical views of the French revolutionists, and he criticized the *Declaration of the Rights of Man* in his *Anarchical Fallacies* (included in his collected works). His democratic views are expressed in his *Constitutional Code* (1830). His *Chrestomathia*, a series of papers on education, appeared in 1816. He also propounded a number of valuable reforms in the administration of

English justice, which since his time have been applied. In 1824 with the assistance of J. *Mill he founded the *Westminster Review*, the organ of the philosophical radicals, which lasted until 1914. J. S. *Mill, in his essay *Bentham* in this same review (1838), gives an interesting summary of Bentham's notorious hostility to imaginative literature, quoting the aphorisms 'Quantity of pleasure being equal, push-pin is as good as poetry', and 'All poetry is misrepresentation', and criticizing Bentham's own involuted prose. True to his own utilitarian principles, Bentham left his body to be dissected and his skeleton, dressed in his own clothes, is still to be seen at University College London.

BENTLEY, Edmund Clerihew (1875–1956), son of a civil servant, born in London and educated at St Paul's (where he became a lifelong friend of *Chesterton) and Merton College, Oxford. He was called to the bar, but made his career as a journalist on the *Daily News* and *Daily Telegraph*. In *Biography for Beginners* (1905) he invented the wittily absurd verse-form called *clerihew after his second name, and in *Trent's Last Case* (1913) he produced the prototype of the modern detective novel. See E. C. Bentley, *Those Days* (1940); introduction by B. R. Redman to *Trent's Case Book* (1953).

BENTLEY, Phyllis, see REGIONAL NOVEL.

BENTLEY, Richard (1662–1742), born at Oulton in Yorkshire, educated at St John's College, Cambridge, and appointed by *Stillingfleet tutor to his son, 1683–9. He made his reputation as a scholar with his *Letter to Mill* (1691), a critical letter in Latin on the Greek dramatists, and the following year delivered the first Boyle Lectures, printed in 1693 as *The Folly and Unreasonableness of Atheism*. He became keeper of the king's libraries in 1694, and during 1697–9 was engaged in the famous Phalaris controversy, during which he proved the *Epistles of *Phalaris* to be spurious (see BATTLE OF THE BOOKS, THE) and queried the antiquity of *Aesop's fables. In 1699 he was appointed master of Trinity College, Cambridge, which he ruled with such despotic power that his mastership was a succession of quarrels, scandals, and litigation. Among his greatest critical works were his bold revisions of the texts of *Horace and Manilius; he was the last great classical scholar before the divergence of Greek and Latin studies. He was caricatured in *The Dunciad* (IV. 201 ff.) and elsewhere; *Pope's enmity was said to be based on Bentley's dismissal of his version of *Homer. Bentley's arbitrary revision of *Paradise Lost, published in 1732 with over 800 suggested emendations, was based on the belief that Milton had been ill-served by an incompetent amanuensis and a careless editor; the quality of his proposals may be judged by his attempt at improving the last two lines of the epic:

Then hand in hand with social steps their way
Through Eden took with heav'nly comfort cheer'd.

There is a life of Bentley by *Jebb (1882).

BENTLEY, Richard (1708–82), son of R. Bentley (above). He is remembered as the friend of Horace *Walpole and *Gray, and made a considerable contribution to the Gothic fantasy of *Strawberry Hill, designing chimney-pieces, ceilings, etc. He also illustrated Gray's poems in 1753 with designs described by *Clark as 'the most graceful monument to Gothic Rococo' (*The Gothic Revival*, 1928). He was idle and improvident, and lived for a while in Jersey to escape his creditors. Walpole quarrelled with him in 1761, and Bentley struggled on in London as a playwright and pamphleteer. (See also Chute.)

BENTLEY, Richard (1794–1871). He learned the printing and publishing trades with his uncle John *Nichols, and began in business on his own in 1819. He included T. *Moore, both *Disraelis, and *Dickens among his authors. In 1830 he joined with Henry *Colburn to found the firm of Colburn and Bentley, which in 1837 established *Bentley's Miscellany*, a magazine which was immensely successful. A cheap series of 'Standard Novels', comprising 127 volumes, was also popular. Bentley was succeeded in the business by his son George Bentley (1825–95), who introduced many novelists to the public, including Wilkie *Collins and Mrs H. *Wood.

Bentley's Miscellany (1837–69), a very successful periodical consisting of essays, stories, and poems, but mainly of fiction, begun by R. Bentley (above). *Dickens was the first editor, and *Oliver Twist* appeared in its pages in 1837–8. J. H. *Reynolds, *Hook, *Maginn, *Ainsworth, and later *Thackeray and *Longfellow were among its contributors. *Cruikshank and *Leech provided lively illustrations. In its early heyday the *Miscellany* covered, with biography or critical articles, all the important writers of the early 19th cent.

Benvolio, in Shakespeare's *Romeo and Juliet*, a cousin and friend of Romeo.

Benwick, Captain, a character in J. Austen's *Persuasion*.

Beowulf, an Old English poem of 3,182 lines, surviving in a 10th-cent. manuscript. It tells of two major events in the life of the Geatish hero Beowulf: the first when, in his youth, he fights and kills first Grendel, a monster who has been attacking Heorot, the hall of the Danish king Hrothgar, and then Grendel's mother who comes the next night to avenge her son; the second, 50 years later, when Beowulf, who has for a long time been king of the Geats, fights a dragon who has attacked his people, in a combat in which both Beowulf and the dragon are mortally wounded. The historical period of the poem's events can be dated in the 6th cent. from a reference to Beowulf's King Hygelac by the historian *Gregory of Tours; but much of the material of the poem is legendary and paralleled in other Germanic historical-mythological literature in Norse, Old English, and German.

Although it has been suggested that the date of the poem may be nearer to that of its manuscript in the 10th cent., the poem is generally dated in the 8th cent., perhaps in its second quarter, at a time when England was being won over from paganism to Christianity. This date is taken to account for the strong thread of Christian commentary which runs through the poem, seemingly inappropriate to the date of its historical events. The degree of Christian morality inherent in the poem has been one of the two principal critical talking points about *Beowulf*; the second is the consistency or otherwise of the poem's construction. W. P. *Ker (in *Epic and Romance*, 1896) regarded the monster stories as insignificant and the peripheral historical allusions as weighty and important. This view was most famously opposed by *Tolkien in 'The Monsters and the Critics' (1936) where he argued that it was precisely the superhuman opposition of the heathen monsters that elevated the poem to heroic stature, and that all the other allusions were related directly to the transient grandeur of Beowulf's life and battles with the monsters.

Beowulf is much the most important poem in Old English and it is the first major poem in a European vernacular language. It is remarkable for its sustained grandeur of tone and for the brilliance of its style, both in its rather baroque diction and in the association of the elements of its plot.

Ed. F. Klaeber (1922, etc.); C. L. Wrenn (1953; rev. W. F. Bolton, 1973); trans. E. T. Donaldson (1966); G. N. Garmonsway and others in *Beowulf and Its Analogues* (1968); R. W. *Chambers, *Beowulf: An Introduction* (3rd edn with supplement by C. L. Wrenn, 1959); L. E. Nicholson (ed.), *An Anthology of Beowulf Criticism* (1963). *Heaney's new translation appeared in 1999.

Beppo: A Venetian Story, a poem in *ottava rima* by *Byron, published in 1818. This poem, in which Byron began to find the voice and style of *Don Juan*, marked a turning point in his career. Digressive, witty, and informal, it tells with great zest and style the story of a Venetian carnival, at which a lady's husband, Beppo, who has been absent for many years, returns in Turkish garb, and confronts her and her *cavalier servente*. Full reconciliation follows, in what the narrator implies is the civilized Venetian manner, over a cup of coffee. Byron's praise of Italy's climate and women is offset by his lengthy satirical asides about English rain and English misses who 'smell of bread and butter'.

BÉRANGER, Pierre-Jean de (1780–1857), French poet. He gained a great reputation in the post-Napoleonic period for his popular songs, many of which display his sympathy for the oppressed and his hostility to the restored Bourbon monarchy. He published a series of *Chansons* from 1815 onwards, and from the 1830s to the end of the century his poetry was widely translated both in Britain and the USA. *Thackeray wrote four

'Imitations of Béranger', including a version of 'Le Roi d'Yvetot', one of the best-known of Béranger's satirical poems.

Berenice, daughter of Agrippa I (grandson of Herod the Great), and wife of her uncle Herod, king of Chalcis. After his death in AD 48, she lived with her brother Agrippa II. She is the Bernice of Acts 25. Titus during his campaigns in Judaea fell in love with her and she accompanied him on his return to Rome. But the Romans disapproved of the connection and he dismissed her. The rupture of their relations is the subject of *Racine's *Bérénice* and of *Otway's *Titus and Berenice*.

BERENSON, Bernard (1865–1959), art historian and philosopher, born in Lithuania and educated in America. In 1887 he settled in Europe. In *Italian Painters of the Renaissance* (first published as separate essays, 1894–1907) he developed the theory that the 'tactile values' of a work of art, i.e. its ability to communicate a sense of form, stimulated in the spectator a state of increased awareness of 'life enhancement'. *Italian Pictures of the Renaissance* (1932) is a list of attributions and locations of all important Italian paintings of the Renaissance. He also wrote on history, aesthetics, and politics.

BERGER, John (1926–   ), novelist and art critic, born in London and educated at the Chelsea College of Art and Central School of Art. He became well known as a broadcaster and journalist holding Marxist views, and also published several novels: *A Painter of Our Time* (1958), *The Foot of Clive* (1962), *Corker's Freedom* (1964), *G* (*Booker Prize, 1972), and *To the Wedding* (1995). Works of non-fiction include *A Fortunate Man* (1967), the story of a country doctor. *Pig Earth* (1979), a study in stories, poems, and narrative of the plight of the French peasant facing the threat of migrant industrialized labour, *Once in Europa* (stories, 1989) and *Lilac and Flag* (1991) form a trilogy. Other works include *Keeping a Rendezvous* (1992), a collection of essays and poems. One of his most influential texts has been *Ways of Seeing* (1972), based on a BBC TV series, and written with colleagues, which explores painting and commercial imagery in a context of cultural capitalism: it drew on and helped to popularize the concepts of W. *Benjamin. See *Ways of Telling* (1986), a commentary by Geoff *Dyer.

BERGERAC, Cyrano de, see CYRANO DE BERGERAC.

BERGSON, Henri (1859–1941), French philosopher, professor at the Collège de France from 1900 to 1921, awarded the *Nobel Prize for literature in 1927. His major works, all of them clearly and vividly written and accessible to the non-specialist reader, are: *Essai sur les données immédiates de la conscience* (1889), *Matière et mémoire* (1896), *L'Évolution créatrice* (1907), *Les Deux Sources de la morale et de la religion* (1932). In these studies Bergson elaborated a philosophical position in broad opposition to scientific materialism and positivism. Centring his enquiry on the self and its direct intuitions, he argued for the importance to a true understanding of experience of 'real duration', in contrast to measured time, as an immediate datum of consciousness which is intuitively perceived. Consciousness itself was above all the operation of memory, not mere habitual recollection but that pure memory which retains the totality of our conscious states, to be selected by the brain when necessary in order to guide spontaneous action in relation to what is about to happen. This conviction of the primacy of creative inner experience was extended to the cosmic plane in the notion of the *élan vital*, or vital impulse, which Bergson conceived as directing the evolutionary process towards ever new forms and increasingly complex states of organization. Hence the pre-eminent value in morals and religion of what is spiritual, creative, 'open', over what is formal, fixed, 'closed'. Bergson explored the aesthetics of comedy in *Le Rire: essai sur la signification du comique* (1900), where the comic is found to arise when we perceive in human actions those automatic, repetitive, or disjointed qualities that make against the essential spontaneity of life. Laughter is regarded as society's defence against such failure of adaptive power.

Berinthia, a character in Vanbrugh's *The Relapse* and Sheridan's *A Trip to Scarborough*.

BERKELEY, George (1685–1753), philosopher, born at Dysart Castle in Co. Kilkenny, and educated at Kilkenny College and Trinity College, Dublin. He visited England in 1713 and became associated with *Steele, *Addison, *Pope, *Arbuthnot, *Swift, and others. He travelled abroad for the next seven years, and in 1728 went to America in connection with an abortive scheme for a missionary college in Bermuda. He was appointed dean of Derry in 1724 and bishop of Cloyne in 1734, remaining at Cloyne till 1752. He then retired to Oxford, where he died.

His chief philosophical works are *An Essay towards a New Theory of Vision* (1709, 1710, 1732), *A Treatise Concerning the Principles of Human Knowledge* (1710, 1734), and *Three Dialogues between Hylas and Philonous* (1713, 1725, 1734). In 1712 he published controversial sermons on 'passive obedience' and a year later contributed essays against the Whig freethinkers to the *Guardian*. His three-volume compilation *The Ladies Library* appeared in 1714. Returning to the attack on the freethinkers and the defence of his own philosophy in the 1730s, he issued his dialogue *Alciphron* (1732, 1752) and *The Theory of Vision Vindicated and Explained* (1733). In 1734 he published *The Analyst*, criticizing *Newton's theory of fluxions; and in 1735–7 *The Querist*, dealing with questions of economic and social reform. *Siris*, a miscellany on the virtues of tar-water for the body and of a more mystical philosophy than that of his earlier years for the soul, appeared in 1744. The standard critical edition of

Berkeley's works, ed. Luce and Jessop, was published in 1948–57; a defective supplement to vol. i was added by the publishers of the 1979 reprint. A new critical edition of Berkeley's philosophical notebooks (G. H. Thomas) appeared in 1976.

In his works on vision, Berkeley seeks to show the mind-dependence of the ideas derived from sight, and explains their 'arbitrary' though constant connection with the more primary ideas of touch by analogy with the way in which written words 'signify' speech. His other philosophy is partly inspired by, and partly a reaction to, the work of *Locke (see ESSAY CONCERNING HUMAN UNDERSTANDING) and of Nicolas Malebranche, who accepted variant versions of *Descartes's dualism of spirit and matter which would logically lead, in Berkeley's view, to scepticism and atheism. Only particular things exist, and since these are only a complex of sensations, if we abstract from them that of which we have perception, nothing remains. The 'support' of ideas or sensations is percipient mind. The *esse* of material things is *percipi*. Locke's distinction between the primary and secondary qualities of bodies therefore has no validity; both are exclusively mind-dependent. Spirit is the only real cause or power. Of the existence of our own percipient mind we each have knowledge from experience. The existence of other finite spirits is inferred by analogy from their effects. For the same reason we believe in the existence of God, who speaks to us in the whole system of nature, through the sense-experiences produced in our minds in a regular and uniform manner. In redefining his philosophical position against the freethinkers in *Alciphron*, Berkeley sees a fruitful parallel between the language of religion and the language of science; both use their artificial notations not as marks for non-spiritual realities, but in the formulation of general rules of practice for sentient beings.

Berkeley was a master both of English prose and of the dialogue form; he is remarkable for his lucidity, grace, and dignity of expression. Before leaving for America he wrote a set of 'Verses on the prospect of planting arts and learning in America', in which occurs the often quoted line, 'Westward the course of empire takes its way'.

BERKELEY, Sir Lennox (1903–89), English composer. Of partly French descent, he always stood a little apart from the mainstream of the English musical tradition. His earlier compositions are predominantly instrumental, and some of the best of his vocal works have texts from foreign sources, but there are several beautiful settings of English words, including two groups by *de la Mare, *5 Songs*, and *Songs of the Half-Light* (1964); *5 Poems of W. H. Auden* (1958); *Herrick Songs* with accompaniment for harp (1974); and choral settings of *Crashaw, *Donne, *Herrick, *Bridges, and G. M. *Hopkins. For the stage he wrote incidental music for *The Tempest* (1946) and *The Winter's Tale* (1960) and four operas: *Nelson* (1954), with a libretto by

Alan Pryce-Jones; *Ruth* (1956) to a text by Eric Crozier; and two one-act operas, *A Dinner Engagement* (1954) and *Castaway* (1967), both with words by Paul Dehn. His son Michael (1948–) is also a composer.

BERKENHEAD, or **BIRKENHEAD,** Sir John (1617–79), the principal editor and writer of the influential Royalist Oxford-based newsbook *Mercurius Aulicus* (1643–5), which was renowned for its cavalier insouciance and wit and condemned by its opponents as a 'Court Buffon', putting off everything with 'a jest and a jeer'. Berkenhead also wrote many pamphlets and much polite and satiric verse, including a mock-heroic piece called 'A Jolt', based on an incident when *Cromwell was thrown from his coach in Hyde Park. He is notable as one of the first writers to make a career in journalism, but he also maintained contact with the more fashionable world of letters, including among his friends K. *Philips and W. *Cartwright. A life by P. W. Thomas appeared in 1969, which describes him as 'a caricaturist of invention and exceptional acuteness' and credits him with raising journalistic standards. (See also NEWSPAPERS, ORIGINS OF.)

BERKOFF, Steven (1937–), actor, director, playwright, born of immigrant Russian Jewish parentage in the East End of London. After schooling in Hackney—like *Pinter and *Wesker—he worked as a waiter and a salesman. He trained as an actor in London and with the mime artist Jacques le Coq in Paris. He formed the London Theatre Group in 1968 and caused a sensation with his adaptation of *Kafka's *The Trial* (1969). He remained a vigorous maverick in the fringe theatre movement of the subsequent two decades, playing the leading role in his own productions of his own demotic verse plays *East* (1975), *Greek* (1979), *Decadence* (1981), and *West* (1983). His hilarious domestic fantasy *Kvetch* won the Best Comedy in the Evening Standard Awards in 1991. Success as a screen villain in Hollywood subsidizes his single-minded stage career, and a prolific writing output includes two essential volumes: *I Am Hamlet* (1989) and his memoirs *Free Association* (1996).

BERLIN, Sir Isaiah (1909–97), distinguished philosopher and historian of ideas, educated at St Paul's School and Corpus Christi College, Oxford, and later, among many other academic distinctions, Chichele professor of social and political theory (1957–67) and president of the *British Academy (1974–8). Berlin is best known as a political philosopher for his defence of liberalism and moral pluralism (see *Four Essays on Liberty*, 1969), views which, as historian of ideas, he has explored in his work on the recognition of the historical dimension of philosophical thought in, among others, *Vico and *Herder (*Vico and Herder*, 1976). His *Russian Thinkers* (1978), a collection of essays about the intelligentsia of 19th-cent. Russia, includes 'The Hedgehog and the Fox', a discussion of *Tolstoy focusing on the tension between monist and pluralist visions of the world and of history. There is a life (1998) by M. *Ignatieff.

BERLIOZ, Hector (1803–69), French composer, whose enthusiasm for English literature is manifested in many of his works. The early *Waverley, Rob Roy*, and *Roi Lear* overtures proclaim their origins clearly, though *Le Corsaire*, which seems to suggest *Byron in its final version (1852), began with a different title and later became *Le Corsaire rouge* (after J. F. *Cooper's *The Red Rover*). More specifically Byronic in inspiration is the symphony with viola solo *Harold en Italie* (1834). The *Neuf Mélodies irlandaises* (later renamed *Irlande*) are settings of poems by T. *Moore, and include a version of the *Elegy on the Death of Robert Emmet* that is one of Berlioz's most powerful songs. This appears to have been composed under the overwhelming impact of Berlioz's passion for Harriet Smithson, the Irish actress whom he had first seen as Ophelia in September 1827: five years later she became his wife. This had been his first experience of Shakespeare—'a voice of the burning bush, amid the storm clouds, the thunder and the lightning of a poetry that was new to me'. The astonishingly original *Fantaisie sur la Tempête* (1830) preceded the *Lear* overture by a year: it was later incorporated in the lyric monodrama *Lélio, ou le retour à la vie* (1832) in which the composer's Shakespearian obsession is worked out in a mixture of music and spoken monologue. Later Hamlet works include the 'Marche funèbre' (1848) and 'La Mort d'Ophélie' (1842). Meanwhile 1839 brought to fruition the huge dramatic symphony *Roméo et Juliette*, a masterpiece that contains the most deeply felt music ever written on a Shakespearian theme. For his last composition Berlioz turned *Much Ado about Nothing* into the witty and enchanting *Béatrice et Benedict* (1962). Shakespeare could not be excluded from *Les Troyens*, the vast Virgilian epic which he finished in 1858 but never heard complete: the words for the love duet in Act IV are drawn entirely from the last act of *The Merchant of Venice*. 'It is Shakespeare who is the real author of both words and music,' wrote the composer. 'Strange that he, the poet of the North, should have intervened in the masterpiece of the poet of Rome . . . What singers, these two!'

'Bermudas', see MARVELL.

BERNANOS, Georges (1888–1948), French novelist and essayist. He emigrated to Brazil in 1938, returning to France with the Liberation in 1945. His novels, notably *Sous le soleil de Satan* (1926), *Journal d'un curé de campagne* (1936), and *Nouvelle Histoire de Mouchette* (1937), dramatize through the tormented lives of priests or outcasts an intensely religious vision of the world. His polemical attacks on 20th-cent. values, especially after the emergence of Fascist Spain and Germany, are scarcely less original. He has been widely translated into English, especially by P. Morris.

BERNARD, St (1090–1153), abbot of the Cistercian foundation of Clairvaux at the age of 24 and a developer of the Augustinian contemplative theological tradition with its emphasis on Faith rather than Reason, was one of the foremost figures of the 12th-cent. monastic Reformation. He preached the Second Crusade, and opposed the dialectical theological method of *Abelard which he had condemned at Soissons and Sens. The characteristic quality of his thought was a lively and personal mysticism; he developed and preached 'the Cistercian Programme', a progression from carnal to spiritual love which, in its literary application, became one of the most important elements of medieval poetry from the *troubadours to *Dante. In his mysticism the stress is on God's grace, according to the Augustinian school, rather than on the deliberate achievement of man's contemplative efforts which was the aspect emphasized by the *Neoplatonists and their followers in the prose mysticism of the 14th cent. See B. S. James, *St Bernard of Clairvaux* (1959).

BERNARD OF MORLAIX (12th cent.), a Benedictine monk of the monastery of Cluny in Burgundy who wrote the Latin poem 'De Contemptu Mundi', *c*.1140, a powerful satire. J. M. *Neale translated several of his hymns from part of Bernard's output.

BERNARDIN DE SAINT-PIERRE, Jacques-Henri (1737–1814), French natural philosopher and novelist, a friend and follower of *Rousseau, of whom he left an account in *La Vie et les ouvrages de Jean-Jacques Rousseau* (1820). His *Études de la Nature*, a series of essays in natural history and philosophy discovering the operations of Divine Providence in the order and harmony of Nature, appeared in 1784; in the third edition of the *Études* (1788) he included the work of fiction now regarded as his masterpiece and which was to achieve phenomenal popularity, *Paul et Virginie*. This pastoral romance tells the story of the idyllic childhood of two children of French parentage, Paul and Virginie, who are brought up as brother and sister by their mothers on a tropical island, the Île de France (Mauritius). The two mothers, refugees from social disgrace in France, determine that their children shall be reared in conformity with Nature's laws, and accordingly accustom them to a simple, frugal, and hardworking existence free from social prejudice, religious superstition, or fear of authority. In these conditions Paul and Virginie grow to adolescence, healthy, humane, pious, and benevolent, actively supporting their less fortunate neighbours. But Virginie is sent to Paris at the behest of a rich maiden aunt who desires to educate her to receive her fortune. On her return, her vessel is caught in a hurricane and thrown onto the reefs within sight of shore; Virginie refuses to undress to save herself, and is drowned when the ship founders. Paul and the two mothers die soon after of shock and grief. The novel was translated by H. M. *Williams (1796).

BERNERS, Lord (Gerald Hugh Tyrwhitt-Wilson), 14th Baron Berners (1883–1950), composer, novelist, painter, and conspicuous aesthete, perhaps best remembered for his ballet music of the 1920s and 1930s, notably *The Triumph of Neptune* (1926) with scenario by S. *Sitwell; he also wrote the music and designed the settings and costumes of the choral ballet *A Wedding Bouquet* (1936, text by G. *Stein). He published several novels, including *Far from the Madding War* (1941), and two volumes of memoirs, *First Childhood* (1934) and *A Distant Prospect* (1945).

BERNERS, John Bourchier, second Baron (1467–1533), statesman and author. He was chancellor of the exchequer in 1516 and attended Henry VIII at the Field of the Cloth of Gold. He translated the *Chronicles* of *Froissart (1523–5); *Huon of Bordeaux* (probably printed c.1515); Guevara's *Il libro aureo di Marco Aurelio* (1535); and a Spanish work, the *Castell of Love* (printed in about 1548).

BERNERS, Juliana, see BOOK OF ST ALBANS, THE.

BERNHARDT, Sarah (-Marie-Henriette) (1844–1923), French actress. In a career that spanned 60 years and took her to many parts of the world, including numerous appearances in London and New York, she attained great celebrity in both tragedy and comedy. Among her famous roles were Doña Sol in *Hugo's *Hernani*, Adrienne Lecouvreur in the play of the same name by Scribe and Legouvé, Phèdre in *Racine's tragedy, Marguerite in the younger *Dumas's *La Dame aux camélias*, several parts in plays by Sardou, and Napoleon's son in *Rostand's *L'Aiglon*. From 1899 she managed her own Théâtre Sarah Bernhardt, taking the role of Hamlet there. Her memoirs, *Ma Double Vie*, were published in 1907.

BERNI, Francesco (1496/7–1535), a Tuscan poet, author of facetious, burlesque compositions, whose style was imitated by Byron in his *Don Juan* and *Beppo*. Berni also wrote a Tuscan version of Boiardo's *Orlando innamorato*, which for a long time was regarded as superior to the original.

Berowne, or **Biron,** one of the three lords attending the king of France in Shakespeare's *Love's Labour's Lost*. From scoffing at love he becomes an extravagant lover of Rosaline, but she dismisses him at the end of the play to 'jest a twelvemonth in an hospital'.

BERRY, James (1924–   ), poet, born in Jamaica, who came to London in 1948 and worked until 1977 as an overseas telegraphist. Since then he has done much work in the field of multicultural education, and edited various anthologies, including *Bluefoot Traveller: An Anthology of Westindian Poets of Britain* (1976), *Dance to a Different Drum* (1983, a Brixton Festival anthology), and *News from Babylon* (1984). His own collections include *Fractured Circles* (1979) and *Lucy's Letter and Loving* (1982). *When I Dance* (1988) is a volume of poems, songs, and 'work-sing' for children, mixing inner city subject matter with rural Caribbean motifs. *A Thief in the Village* (1987), *Anancy-Spiderman* (1989), and *The Future-Telling Lady* (1991) are collections of stories for children. (See also JAZZ POETRY.)

BERRYMAN, John (1914–72), American poet. He was born John Smith in Oklahoma but took his stepfather's name after his father's suicide. Much of his poetry is anguished and confessional, exploring personal guilts and religious doubts, but it is also learned and often witty, and technically highly organized if idiosyncratic. His work includes *Poems* (1942), *The Dispossessed* (1948), and *Homage to Mistress Bradstreet* (1956), the last a complex biographical ode inspired by the first New England poet Anne *Bradstreet. *77 Dream Songs* (1964), with their imaginary and protean protagonist Henry, were completed by *His Toy, His Dream, His Rest* (1968), and together form his major work. He committed suicide in Minneapolis.

Bertram, count of Rousillon, in Shakespeare's *All's Well that Ends Well*, the reluctant husband of *Helena.

BERTRAM, Charles (1723–65), sometimes self-styled Charles Julius, literary forger, English teacher in a school for naval cadets at Copenhagen. He produced between 1747 and 1757 an alleged transcript of a manuscript work on Roman antiquities by Richard of *Cirencester, together with a copy of an ancient itinerary of Britain, at many points supplementing and correcting the itinerary of Antoninus. He also published works of *Gildas and *Nennius, with the text of his forgery and a commentary on it, at Copenhagen, 1757, and several philological works. His imposture was finally exposed by B. B. Woodward in the *Gentleman's Magazine*, 1866–7.

Bertram, Sir Thomas and Lady, their sons Thomas and Edmund, and their daughters Julia and Maria, characters in J. Austen's *Mansfield Park*.

Bertram; or *The Castle of St Aldobrand*, a tragedy by C. R. *Maturin, produced with great success by *Kean, 1816. An overwrought drama, centred on a *Byronic hero, of love, madness, and suicide, it was the object of hostile criticism by Coleridge in his *Biographia Literaria*.

BESANT, Mrs Annie, née Wood (1847–1933). After an unhappy marriage with a brother of Sir W. *Besant, she became a secularist, a Fabian, a trade union organizer, and, in association with *Bradlaugh, an enthusiast for birth control. She then became a theosophist and pupil of Mme *Blavatsky, and an active supporter of the Indian nationalist movement.

BESANT, Sir Walter (1836–1901), educated at King's College, London, and Christ's College, Cambridge. He published *Early French Poetry* (1868) and *The French Humourists* (1873). He was secretary to the Palestine Exploration Fund (1868–86) and with W. H. Palmer wrote *Jerusalem* (1871). From 1871 to 1882 Besant collaborated with J. *Rice and together they produced several best-selling novels, including *Ready-Money Mortiboy* (1872), *The Golden Butterfly* (1876), and *The Chaplain of the Fleet* (1881). He was deeply interested in the life of the poor, especially in the East End of London, and the terrible social conditions of industrial workers, and draws attention to these in *All Sorts and Conditions of Men* (1882) and *Children of Gibeon* (1886); he stimulated the foundation of the People's Palace, Mile End (1887), for intellectual improvement and rational amusement. In 1884 he founded the *Society of Authors, and became editor of the *Author* in 1890; he defined the financial position of authors in *The Pen and the Book* (1899). His other books include the historical works *Rabelais* (1879) and *Captain Cook* (1890) and several histories of different parts of London. *A Survey of London* (1902–12) and his autobiography (1902) appeared posthumously.

BESS OF HARDWICK, Elizabeth Talbot, countess of Shrewsbury (*c*.1520–1608), daughter and co-heir of John Hardwick of Hardwick, Derbyshire. She is described as 'a woman of a masculine understanding and conduct; proud, furious, selfish, and unfeeling' (T. *Lodge). To her care and to that of her husband, the sixth earl of Shrewsbury, Mary Queen of Scots was entrusted in 1569 at Tutbury. She married her daughter to Charles Stuart, younger brother of Darnley (Arabella Stuart was the issue of the marriage), and was imprisoned in the Tower in consequence. She was herself four times married and inherited the fortunes of her four husbands, her income being estimated at £60,000. She built Chatsworth (not the present building) and Hardwick Hall.

Bessus, in Beaumont and Fletcher's *A King and No King*, a cowardly braggart.

Bessy, one of the stock characters, a man dressed as a woman, in the medieval *sword-dance and in the *mummers' play.

bestiaries, medieval treatises derived from the Greek *Physiologus*, which was a collection of about 50 fabulous anecdotes from natural (mostly animal) history, followed by a 'moralization' of the anecdotes for a Christian purpose. The Greek original dates from some time between the 2nd and 4th cents AD, and it was translated into many languages, most influentially Latin. In the 12th cent. additions began to be made to the Latin version from the popular encyclopaedia of the Middle Ages, the *Etymologiae* of *Isidore of Seville. Those written in England in the 12th and 13th cents were often richly illustrated with miniatures. The Old English poems 'The Panther' and 'The Whale' are isolated examples of the kind; the Middle English Bestiary, coming from the north-east Midlands in the second half of the 13th cent., has 802 lines in various metres. Their method of moralization was influential on the relations between story and moral in many medieval texts, as well as being a popular source for such works as Sir T. Browne's *Pseudodoxia Epidemica.

F. McCulloch, *Medieval Latin and French Bestiaries* (1960); T. H. *White, *The Book of Beasts* (1954: a translation of a 12th-cent. Latin bestiary); Middle English version ed. R. Morris in *An Old English Miscellany* (EETS OS 49, 1872; repr. 1927, 1–25).

Bethgelert, or **Beddgelert,** a village at the foot of Snowdon, where Llewelyn the Great had his abode. Gelert was a hound given by King John to Llewelyn. On one occasion this favourite hound was missing when Llewelyn went hunting. On his return he found the hound smeared with blood, his child's bed in disorder, and the child not to be seen. Thinking that the hound had devoured the child, the father killed Gelert with his sword. The child, awakened by the hound's dying yell, cried out from under a heap of coverings, and under the bed was found a great wolf which the hound had slain. The earliest published version of this story is in *Musical and Poetical Relicks of the Welsh Bards* (1784), by Edward Jones. It is also the subject of a ballad by William Robert Spencer (1769–1834, one of the many translators of Bürger's *'Lenore'), entitled 'Beth Gelert, or The Grave of the Greyhound', published in his *Poems* (1811).

BETJEMAN, Sir John (1906–84), poet, born in Highgate, the son of a manufacturer of household articles; the name is of Dutch origin. He was educated at Marlborough, which he disliked, and at Magdalen College, Oxford, where he became friendly with *Auden and *MacNeice, was encouraged by *Bowra, and adopted the pose of aesthete and bon viveur, while remaining, as he always maintained, essentially middle-class in his outlook. He left without taking a degree, worked briefly as a schoolmaster, then began to write, in 1931, for the *Architectural Review*; meanwhile he was beginning to publish poems in magazines ('Death in Leamington' appeared in the *London Mercury* in 1930), and his first collection of verse, *Mount Zion*, appeared in 1931. This was followed by other collections, including *Continual Dew: A Little Book of Bourgeois Verse* (1937), *New Bats in Old Belfries* (1945), *A Few Late Chrysanthemums* (1954), and his extremely successful *Collected Poems* (1958, expanded 1962). His blank-verse autobiography, *Summoned by Bells* (1960), which covers his boyhood and life at Oxford, was followed by two more collections, *A Nip in the Air* (1972) and *High and Low* (1976). He was appointed *poet laureate in 1972. His poetry, which has reached an unusually wide public (while numbering Auden and *Larkin amongst its advocates), is predominantly witty, urbane, satiric, and light of touch, a comedy of manners, place names, and contemporary allusions, but many have commented on the underlying melancholy, the chill of fear, the religion which dwells more on hope than faith; Larkin points to his 'heterogeneous world of farce and fury, where sports girls and old nuns jostle with town clerks and impoverished Irish peers' (*Observer*, 1983). In the preface to *Old Lights for New Chancels* (1940) Betjeman writes of his own 'topographical predilection' for 'suburbs and gaslights and Pont Street and Gothic Revival churches and mineral railways, provincial towns and garden cities', a predilection also displayed in his editing and writing of Shell Guides (some illustrated by his friend John Piper), and various works on architecture, beginning with *Ghastly Good Taste* (1933). Betjeman's popularity as a public personality and the apparent facility of his verse contributed to a neglect of his poetry in critical circles in the late 1950s and early 1960s, when it was seen as lightweight, but it has since found new admirers in a second generation of readers and poets. *Letters 1926–1951*, edited by his daughter Candida Lycett-Green, was published in 1994.

Betrothed, The, a novel by Sir W. *Scott, published 1825.

This, the first of Scott's two *Tales of the Crusaders*, was so much disliked by James *Ballantyne and *Constable that publication was suspended while he embarked on *The Talisman*. Eventually the two were published as a package, the success of *The Talisman* redeeming what Scott himself perceived as the failure of *The Betrothed*. The Crusades feature in *The Betrothed* only to explain the absence of Hugo de Lacy, to whom the heroine is betrothed, the action, which includes some fine battle descriptions, taking place entirely on the Welsh Marches.

BETTERTON, Mrs Mary (c.1637–1712), the wife of T. *Betterton, at first known on the stage as Mrs Saunderson, the first notable actress on the English stage (until 1660 female parts were taken by men or boys). Mrs Betterton was the first woman to act a series of Shakespeare's great female characters, such as Lady Macbeth, Ophelia, and Juliet.

BETTERTON, Thomas (1635–1710), the greatest actor in the Restoration. He joined *D'Avenant's company at Lincoln's Inn Fields, and was associated in the management of the Dorset Gardens Theatre from 1671. With most of his fellow actors he revolted against the harsh management of C. Rich (father of John *Rich) and established a rival company at Lincoln's Inn Fields in 1695, opening with Congreve's *Love for Love*. In 1705 his company moved into the theatre erected by *Vanbrugh in the Haymarket. His 180 roles included Hamlet, Mercutio, Sir Toby Belch, Bosola (in the *Duchess of Malfi*), and Heartwell (in Congreve's *The Old Bachelor*). His dramas include *The Roman Virgin*, acted 1669, adapted from *Webster's *Appius and Virginia*; *The Prophetess* (1690), an opera from the *Prophetess* of *Beaumont and *Fletcher; *King Henry IV* (1700, in which he played Falstaff) from Shakespeare; *The Amorous Widow* (1670), from *Molière's *George Dandin*.

BETTY, William Henry West (1791–1874), a phenomenally successful boy actor, known as 'the Young Roscius', in reference to the famous Roman actor. He made his debut in Belfast at the age of 12, playing four roles in four nights, one being that of Romeo. Proceeding to Dublin, he added Hamlet, Prince Arthur, and other parts to his repertoire. He continued his success in Scotland, and arrived in London in 1804, aged 13. At Covent Garden he played many major roles, including Richard III and Macbeth; there were riots for admission, he was presented to the royal family, and the House of Commons suspended a sitting to enable MPs to see his Hamlet. His final appearance as a boy actor was in 1808. He then went to Cambridge to study, returning to the stage in 1812. But his career as an adult actor was not a success, and he finally retired, a very rich man, in 1824.

Between the Acts, the last novel of V. *Woolf, published shortly after her death in 1941. Although much of its composition was overshadowed by the war, it has a richness of invention missing from her previous work, *The Years*, and has been seen as her final statement on art as the transforming and unifying principle of life.

The action takes place at a middle-sized country house, Poyntz Hall, the home for a mere 120 years of the Oliver family, and Woolf's central metaphor is the enacting of a village pageant, which aspires to portray nothing less than the sweep of English history, by means of songs, tableaux, parody, pastiche, etc.; it ends by presenting the audience its own mirror image, in the present, as a megaphoned voice demands how civilization could be built by 'orts, scraps and fragments like ourselves?' The pageant is directed by the sexually ambiguous Miss la Trobe, who represents the ever-dissatisfied artist ('A failure', she groans, at the end), and its scenes are interwoven with scenes in the lives of the audience; together, the illusion and the reality combine as a communal image of rural England, past and present—'a rambling capricious but somehow unified whole', as Woolf originally envisaged the novel.

Beulah, Land of, see Isa. 62: 4. Derived from the Hebrew word for 'married', Beulah was traditionally equated with the erotic garden-paradise of the biblical Song of Songs allegorized by Christians as the marriage of Christ and his Church. In Bunyan's *Pilgrim's Progress* Beulah is a pastoral paradise of birdsong and eternal flowers. Hearing the 'voice of the turtle in the land' the pilgrims learn that 'the contract between the bride and bridegroom' is renewed, and view the New Jerusalem from its borders. Beulah signifies God's bounty and the promise of the soul's eternal union with its creator. Beulah is used by *Blake to represent a state of Light (often associated with the third state of vision and sexual love): its symbol is the moon.

Beuves de Hanstone, see BEVIS OF HAMPTON.

BEVINGTON, Louisa S. (1845–95), poet and progressive thinker, born in London. She married a German artist, Ignatz Guggenberger, in 1883. She published several volumes of poetry, including *Key-Notes* (1876) and *Poems, Lyrics and Sonnets* (1882), which explore the nature of evolution, at times with a spare questioning lyricism in the vein of T. *Hardy. She also wrote and lectured on rationalism, religion, property, and evolutionary theory. Her last collection of poems, *Liberty Lyrics*, was published by James Tochatti's Liberty Press in 1895, and expresses her radical political sympathies.

Bevis: *The Story of a Boy*, a novel by R. *Jefferies, published 1882.

In this joyful evocation of a country childhood, revealing the secret world of two imaginative and adventurous boys, Bevis and Mark, Jefferies draws largely on his own boyhood in Wiltshire. The farm, the woods, the lake, become the Roman world (or any other world), the Unknown Island becomes the Hesperides, and the solemn games, adventures, and incidental terrors are played out in storm and sun, by day and under the stars, almost always out of doors.

Bevis of Hampton, a popular verse romance from the late 13th or early 14th cent. in 4,620 lines (12-line tail-rhyme 1–474 and short couplets 475–end), based on a 12th-cent. Anglo-Norman *chanson de geste* entitled *Beuves de Hanstone* and on a subject popular throughout Europe, from Ireland, to Italy, to Russia. Bevis's mother, the wife of Guy, earl of Southampton, has her husband murdered, marries the murderer, and sells Bevis into slavery in the East. The rest of the story is taken up with Bevis's conversion of and marriage to Josian, the daughter of the king of Arabia, and their adventures in Europe, England (where he kills the emperor of Germany, his father's murderer), and the East. The story is told in Drayton's *Poly-Olbion* (II. 259); Bevis's sword was called 'Morglay' and his horse 'Arundel'.

Ed. E. Kölbing (EETS ES 46, 48, 65, 1885–94; repr. 1 vol., 1973); discussion in L. A. Hibbard, *Medieval Romances in England* (2nd edn, 1960, 115–26).

BEWICK, Thomas (1753–1828), wood-engraver, son of a Northumbrian farmer. He was apprenticed to, and subsequently partner of, Ralph Beilby (1744–1817), a metal-engraver in Newcastle. He engraved blocks for *Gay's *Fables* (1779), *Select Fables* (1784), *A General History of Quadrupeds* (1790), *Fables of Aesop* (1818), the poems of *Goldsmith and T. *Parnell (1795), and other books; his most celebrated and successful work was *A History of British Birds* (1797, 1804). *Ruskin wrote of the 'flawless virtue, veracity, tenderness, the infinite humour of the man', and his vignettes of country life, as well as his close observations of animal life in its natural setting, were much admired by *Wordsworth, C. *Brontë, *Carlyle, and *Audubon, who visited him in his workshop in 1827. His *Memoir* (1862) is a vivid record of a north-country childhood and a craftsman's life.

Bhagavad-gītā, a section of the *Mahābhārata, in dialogue form, in which Krishna, an incarnation of the deity, instructs and exhorts his pupil and favourite, Arjuna, one of the five sons of the Pandavas, as they stand poised for battle. It was the first section to be translated into English by Charles Wilkins, a senior merchant in the East India Company, as *The Bhagvat-Geeta, or, Dialogues of Kreeshna and Arjoon* (1785). In an advertisement prefacing the translation, Wilkins states that he has been authorized by the court of directors of the company, at the particular desire of Warren *Hastings: Hastings responded in a letter to the chairman, 'I should not fear to place, in opposition to the best French versions of the most admired pages of the *Iliad* or the *Odyssey*, or the 1st or 6th books of our own Milton, highly as I venerate the latter, the English translation of the Mahabarat.'

BHATT, Sujata (1956–), Indian poet, born in Ahmedabad; she has lived, studied, and worked in the USA and graduated from the Writers' Workshop at the University of Iowa. Her first collection *Brunizem* (1988) won the Commonwealth Poetry Prize, and attracted attention for its juxtaposition of bilingual Gujerati and English texts within the construct of the poems, a device used to invoke the otherness and alienation of the poet from the reader. This was followed by *Monkey Shadows* (1991) and *The Stinking Rose* (1994).

Bianca, (1) sister of Katherina, the title character in Shakespeare's *The Taming of the Shrew*; (2) a Venetian courtesan, mistress of *Cassio, in his *Othello.

Biathanatos, see DONNE.

Bible, the, (1) The Old Testament. The oldest surviving Hebrew text (Codex Babylonicus Petropolitanus) is comparatively recent, dating only from AD 916. It is a Masoretic text, i.e. one prepared by the guild of scholars called Masoretes. Of much earlier date (5th cent. BC) is the Samaritan text of the Pentateuch. We have also the Targums or Aramaic paraphrases, written at various times subsequent to the date when Aramaic superseded Hebrew as the language spoken by the Jews (shortly before the Christian era). The Greek version, known as the Septuagint, of the 3rd cent. BC is of far greater importance. Other translations into Greek were made in the 2nd cent. AD and were collected in parallel columns, together with the current Hebrew text and a revised text of the Septuagint, by *Origen in his Hexapla. This has perished with the exception of the revised Septuagint, of most of which we possess an 8th-cent. copy. In addition to the above, there was an old Latin version (known as Vetus Itala) of an early Greek translation, of which fragments alone remain, and which was superseded by Jerome's Latin text, known as the *Vulgate.

(2) The New Testament. Manuscripts in Greek and manuscripts of translations from the Greek into Latin, Syriac, and Coptic are extant. The most important of

these are the Greek, of which the chief are the Codex Vaticanus and the Codex Sinaiticus, uncial manuscripts of the 4th cent.; the Codex Bezae, containing the Greek text on the left-hand page and the Latin on the right, probably earlier than the 6th cent.; and the Codex Alexandrinus, an uncial of the 5th cent. Of the Latin versions there were, before Jerome undertook their revision in the Vulgate, two main types current respectively in Africa and Europe. Several manuscripts of these survive. Of the Vulgate text there are a large number of manuscripts, of which the best are Northumbrian (based on Italian originals), Irish, and Spanish. (See in this connection AMIATINUS CODEX and LINDISFARNE GOSPELS. See also BIBLE, THE ENGLISH; POLYGLOT BIBLE; LUTHER; GUTENBERG; and ULFILAS.)

Bible, the English. Apart from paraphrases attributed to *Cædmon and the translation by *Bede of part of the Gospel of St John, the earliest attempts at translation into English of the Holy Scriptures are the 9th- and 10th-cent. glosses and versions of the Psalms, followed by the 10th-cent. glosses and versions of the Gospels (the Durham Book, or *Lindisfarne Gospels, and the West-Saxon Gospels), and *Ælfric's translation of the OT at the close of the same cent. After this little was done until the time of *Wyclif, to whom and his followers we owe the two 14th-cent. versions associated with his name, the first complete renderings into English of the Scriptures. Of these two versions taken from the Latin text, which appeared about 1382 and 1388, it is doubtful how much was Wyclif's own work. The second, or revised version, was a great improvement on the first, and is a readable and correct translation.

*Tyndale was the first to translate the NT into English from the Greek text; this he probably did in Wittenberg, the translation being printed first at Cologne, and when this was interrupted, at Worms (1525–6). In 1530 his translation of the Pentateuch was printed at Marburg, followed by a translation of the Book of Jonah. These translations were made from the Hebrew, with reference also to the *Vulgate, *Erasmus' Latin version, and *Luther's Bible. The Authorized Version (see below) is essentially the text of Tyndale. The complete English Bible that bears the name of *Coverdale was printed in 1535. It is not a translation from the original texts, but probably from Luther's version, the Zurich Bible, and the Vulgate, with assistance from Tyndale's version. A second edition was issued in 1537. The Prayer Book text of the Psalms is largely Coverdale's version.

'Matthew's Bible' was issued in 1537, under the pseudonym of Thomas Matthew, by John Rogers (?1500–55). He was a friend of Tyndale, was converted to Protestantism, and prepared and annotated his version for publication. Rogers was burnt at Smithfield in Mary's reign.

'Taverner's Bible' was a revision of Matthew's. It appeared in 1539. Richard Taverner (?1505–75) was a

religious author who was patronized by Wolsey and Cromwell, was sent to the Tower on the latter's fall, but subsequently obtained the favour of Henry VIII.

The 'Great Bible', also called 'Cranmer's Bible', was brought out in 1539 under the auspices of Henry VIII; Coverdale was placed by Cromwell in charge of its preparation. The printing of it was begun in Paris and finished in London.

Towards the end of Henry VIII's reign there were interdictions on the use of the Bible. During Mary's reign, the reformers took refuge, some in Frankfurt am Main, some in Geneva, where in 1560 appeared the Genevan or 'Breeches' Bible. It had a marginal commentary which proved agreeable to the Puritans.

In 1568 was published the 'Bishops' Bible', an edition promoted by Archbishop *Parker to counteract the popularity of the Calvinistic Genevan Bible; while Romanists made a translation, known as the Douai–Rheims version, which appeared, the NT in 1582, the OT in 1609–10. It is characterized by the frequent use of Latinisms. (See ALLEN, WILLIAM.)

The 'Authorized Version' arose out of a conference at Hampton Court, convened by James I in 1604, between the High Church and Low Church parties. The undertaking was proposed by Dr Reynolds, president of Corpus Christi College, Oxford, and was supported by the king. The revisers were 47 in number, divided into companies dealing with various sections of the Bible, and were drawn from the most eminent scholars and divines of the day. They were instructed to follow the text of the 'Bishops' Bible' wherever they could. The work of revision and retranslation occupied three years and a half, and the so-called 'Authorized Version' (it was not authorized by any official pronouncement) appeared in 1611. It is practically the version of Tyndale with some admixture from Wyclif. Two issues of it were made in 1611, known respectively as the 'He Bible' and the 'She Bible', because in the first the words in Ruth 3: 15 read 'and he went into the citie', and in the second 'and she went into the citie'. Modern bibles are based with slight variations on the 'She Bible'. Various editions of the Bible, such as the Breeches Bible and the Vinegar Bible, are named after eccentricities of wording or mistakes in the printed text.

In 1870 the Convocation of Canterbury appointed a committee to consider the question of revision of the Authorized versions. The Revised Text was published, of the NT in 1881, of the OT in 1885.

The Revised Standard Version (RSV), a translation produced in the United States and published between 1946 and 1957, stood in the tradition of the Authorized Version, but aimed to eliminate excessively archaic language. The RSV became the standard text in many churches and scholarly communities, and remained in widespread use until the early 1990s, when a further revision, the New Revised Standard Version (NRSV) was published (1990). This brought the text into more contemporary language, and adopted a gender-inclusive style; an Anglicized edition was published in 1995.

In 1947, a new translation into modern English was begun by a Joint Committee of the Churches in the United Kingdom (excepting the Roman Catholics). A team, made up largely of British scholars, worked in separate groups on the OT, Apocrypha, and the NT. The result of their work appeared as the New English Bible (NEB), the NT being published in 1961, and the OT and Apocrypha, with a limited revision of the NT, in 1970. The work of translation continued after 1970, now with the full support of the Roman Catholic Church, and a further extensive revision, the Revised English Bible (REB), was published in 1989.

From the 1960s onwards, the work of revision became a constant process, reflecting changes in language, culture, and new textual evidence, especially from the Dead Sea Scrolls found at Qumran. The USA in particular spawned numerous translations and paraphrases, each attempting to address a particular perceived need. Amongst the most popular versions were the Good News Bible or Today's English Version, the NT appearing in 1966 with a complete Bible in 1976. This translation relied heavily on the principle of dynamic equivalence, and sought to express biblical language in everyday terminology; a limited revision was published in 1994. The New International Version (NIV) (NT 1973, complete Bible 1978, Anglicized 1979) became immensely popular in the 1980s and 1990s, especially amongst British and American evangelicals, whilst the Roman Catholic Church produced the Jerusalem Bible (JB) in 1966, based largely on the work of French scholars of the 1940s; the JB was thoroughly revised as the New Jerusalem Bible (NJB) in 1985, with some books extensively retranslated to achieve a more readable and dignified style.

Bible in Spain, The, a narrative of travel by *Borrow, published 1843.

Borrow travelled in Spain as distributor of bibles for the British and Foreign Bible Society from 1835 to 1840, and this book purports to be an account of his adventures in a country racked by civil war. It is difficult to say how far the various incidents recounted actually occurred; but the vivid picture that the author gives of Spain is unquestionably realistic, and the work is one of the finest of English travel books.

Bibliographical Society, the, founded in 1892. Its *Transactions* were first published in 1893 (merged with the *Library* in 1920). The Society also published separate monographs, and in 1926 issued the invaluable *Short-Title Catalogue of English Books, 1475–1640* (work continued by *Wing). Volume ii (I–Z) of a revised and enlarged version was published in 1976; volume i (A–H) appeared in 1986.

Bickerstaff, Isaac, a fictitious person invented by *Swift. A cobbler, John Partridge, claiming to be an astrologer, had published predictions in the form of an *almanac. Swift in the beginning of 1708 produced a parody entitled *Predictions for the Ensuing Year, by Isaac Bickerstaff,* in which he foretold the death of Partridge on 29 Mar. On 30 Mar. he published a letter giving an account of Partridge's end. Partridge indignantly protested that he was still alive, but Swift retorted in a *Vindication* proving that he was really dead. Other writers took up the joke, and *Steele, when he launched the *Tatler* in 1709, adopted the name of Bickerstaff for the supposed author.

BICKERSTAFFE, Isaac (1733–?1808), an Irish playwright who arrived in London in 1755 and produced many successful comedies and opera librettos. His *Love in a Village* (1762), with music by *Arne, has a claim to be the first comic opera, and contains the well-known song about the Miller of Dee ('There was a jolly miller once'). *The Maid of the Mill* (1765, with music by Samuel Arnold and others) was also very successful; Bickerstaffe acknowledged Richardson's *Pamela* as the source of his plot. *The Padlock, with music by *Dibdin, was performed in 1768, as was *Lionel and Clarissa,* which reappeared as *The School for Fathers* in 1772. *The Hypocrite* (1768, adapted from Molière's *Tartuffe* and *Cibber's *The Non-juror*) contains the well-known character of a hypocrite, Mawworm. Bickerstaffe also wrote adaptations of *Wycherley and *Calderón, and a version of *Inkle and Yarico. In 1772 Bickerstaffe fled to France, suspected of a homosexual offence, and spent the rest of his life in obscurity. *Garrick was implicated in the scandal in a lampoon, *Love in the Suds* by W. Kenrick (?1725–79), subtitled 'the lamentations of Roscius for the loss of his Nyky'. Long after Bickerstaffe's disappearance, his ex-colleague Dibdin was defending himself from the charge of plagiarizing his songs. Nothing is known of the circumstances of his death. See *The Dramatic Cobbler* (1971), a life by Peter Tasch.

Bidpai or **Pilpay,** *The Fables of,* or *Kalilah and Dimnah,* is the title taken from the Arabic version of a lost original of the *Panchatantra,* a celebrated Sanskrit collection of fables, the source of much European folklore. 'Bidpai' is a corruption of 'bidbah', the title of the chief scholar at the court of an Indian prince.

The fables were translated into many European languages, the first English version coming via the Italian in a version by Sir T. *North as *The Morall Philosophie of Doni* (1570). See *The Ocean of Story* (1928) by Norman Penzer.

BIERCE, Ambrose (1842–?1914), American writer, born in Ohio. He served in the Civil War, 1861–5, and afterwards became a prominent journalist, living and working for a time in England (1872–6). He returned to San Francisco, and later worked as a correspondent in Washington. He published much, and collected his writings together in 12 vols (1909–12), but is best known for his short stories, realistic, sardonic, and strongly influenced by *Poe. They were published in *Tales of Soldiers and Civilians* (1891), a title which was changed to *In the Midst of Life* (1892;

rev. edn 1898). Tired of life and America, he travelled to Mexico in 1913 and mysteriously disappeared, it is thought in the fighting of the Mexican Civil War.

Big Brother, in Orwell's *Nineteen Eighty-Four*, is the head of the Party, who never appears in person, but whose dominating portrait in every public place, with the caption 'Big Brother is watching you', is inescapable.

Bildungsroman, the term applied to novels of 'education' (in the widest sense), of which many of the best examples are German. Wieland's *Agathon* (1765–6) is usually thought of as the first example of the genre, but the best and most imitated was *Goethe's Wilhelm Meisters Lehrjahre* (*Wilhelm Meister's Apprenticeship*, 1795–6), which became celebrated in England through *Carlyle's translation in 1824. Wilhelm provides the model of the innocent, inexperienced, well-meaning, but often foolish and erring, young man who sets out in life with either no aim in mind or the wrong one. By a series of false starts and mistakes and with help from well-disposed friends he makes in the course of his experiences, he finally reaches maturity and finds his proper profession. T. *Mann was Goethe's most distinguished successor with his philosophical novel *Der Zauberberg* (*The Magic Mountain*, 1924). The genre overlaps with the older type of the *picaresque novel, but is more philosophical. The German term *Bildungsroman* has been adopted in English criticism as a result of the fame during the 19th cent. of *Wilhelm Meister* and Carlyle's semi-fictional *Sartor Resartus* (1833–4).

Billickin, Mrs, in Dickens's *Edwin Drood*, a cousin of Mr Bazzard, who lets lodgings in Bloomsbury.

Billy Budd, Foretopman (written 1891, published 1924), a novella by H. *Melville, a symbolic tale built out of Melville's egalitarian meditations on the mutiny at Spithead in 1797 and a family story of how Melville's older brother presided over the court martial and execution of an insubordinate sailor.

Billy, 'the handsome sailor', wrongly accused by the satanic master-at-arms Claggart and unable to defend himself verbally because of a stammer, strikes Claggart dead. After being tried by the liberal Captain Vere, Billy is hanged, his last words being 'God bless Captain Vere!' Then, in apparently Christ-like apotheosis, 'the East was shot through with a soft glory as of the fleece of the Lamb of God', and the sailors question whether Billy has actually died. *Britten's setting of *Billy Budd* (1951) has become one of the most admired operas in the modern repertoire.

Billy Liar, see WATERHOUSE.

BINGHAM, Joseph (1668–1723), fellow of University College, Oxford. He withdrew from the university, being unjustly charged with preaching heretical doctrine, and became rector of Headbourne Worthy, near Winchester, where he wrote *Origines Ecclesiasticae, or The Antiquities of the Christian Church* (1708–22), a very learned work which long retained its authoritative character.

Bingley, Charles, and his sister Caroline, characters in J. Austen's *Pride and Prejudice*.

Binnorie, or *The Twa Sisters*, an old ballad, possibly of Scandinavian origin, in *Child's collection. Two sisters are in love with the same knight; the elder drowns the younger, whose body drifts downstream to the mill. A harper makes a harp from her breastbone, strung with her hair, and when he visits her father's hall it sings in reproach 'Woe to my sister, false Helen!'

BINYON, (Robert) Laurence (1869–1943), educated at St Paul's and Trinity College, Oxford; he entered the British Museum where in 1909 he became assistant keeper in the department of prints and drawings. He published many works on art, chiefly English and oriental, including *Painting in the Far East* (1908) and a study of oriental aesthetics, *The Flight of the Dragon* (1911). His dramas included *Attila* (1907) and *Arthur* (1923), the latter with music by T. *Elgar. His war poems include his much anthologized 'For the Fallen' ('They shall grow not old, as we that are left grow old'); two long odes, *The Sirens* (1924) and *The Idols* (1928), received much acclaim among traditionalists. The *Collected Poems* appeared in 1931. His last volume of verse, *The Burning of the Leaves*, was published posthumously in 1944, and *The Madness of Merlin*, the unfinished first part of a lengthy projected verse drama, in 1947.

Biographia Literaria, a work of philosophical autobiography and Romantic literary criticism, by S. T. *Coleridge, published 1817.

Originally conceived in 1814 as a short explanatory preface to the *Sibylline Leaves*, it rapidly expanded into a two-volume apologia for his 'literary life and opinions'. Part I is broadly autobiographical, describing Coleridge's friendship with *Southey and with the *Wordsworths at Stowey, and going on to trace his struggle with the 'dynamic philosophy' of *Kant, *Fichte, and *Schelling in Germany. The humorous narrative is gradually overwhelmed by Romantic metaphysics; ch. XIII contains his famous distinction between Fancy and Imagination. Part II is almost entirely critical, attacking Wordsworth's preface to the *Lyrical Ballads and then marvellously vindicating the poetry itself. Coleridge concentrates on the psychology of the creative process, and propounds new theories of the origins of poetic language, metre, and form, as the interpenetration of 'passion and will' (chs XV–XVIII). Other chapters discuss the poetry of Shakespeare, *Milton, *Daniel, G. *Herbert, etc., as exemplary of true 'Imagination' and the 'language of real life'. Though maddeningly unsystematic in structure, the book is a touchstone of Romantic criticism; it also gives some impression of Coleridge in full conversational flight.

biography, see overleaf.

BION (c.100 BC), a Greek pastoral poet who is reputed to have been born in Smyrna and to have died prematurely in Sicily. His best-known work is a lament for Adonis, which was imitated by *Ronsard and other continental poets and of which echoes can be found in Shakespeare's *Venus and Adonis*, in T. *Lodge, and in Abraham *Fraunce. Keats's *Hyperion* is indebted to its picture of Adonis, and it served as one of Shelley's models for *Adonais*. Later *Bridges' *Achilles in Scyros* took some of its detail from Bion's idyll.

BIRD, Isabella Lucy (1831–1904), traveller, born in Yorkshire, who spent much of her life when in Britain with her sister in Edinburgh and on the Isle of Mull. Advised to recuperate abroad after a spinal operation in 1850, she embarked on a series of travels which clearly suited her naturally restless disposition, and she wrote several vivid accounts of them, notably *A Lady's Life in the Rocky Mountains* (1879), *Unbeaten Tracks in Japan* (1880), and *The Golden Chersonese* (1883, a journey through Malaysia). She appears as a character and as a type of the intrepid Victorian woman in Caryl Churchill's *Top Girls*.

Birds of America, The, (1) an ornithological work by J. J. *Audubon; (2) the title of a novel by M. *McCarthy.

Birkin, Rupert, a character in D. H. Lawrence's *Women in Love*.

Birnam Wood, see MACBETH.

Biron, see BEROWNE.

BIRRELL, Augustine (1850–1933), chief secretary for Ireland, 1907–16. He made his name as an author with a volume of lightweight essays, *Obiter Dicta* (1884), which he followed with other essays and works on *Hazlitt (1902), *Marvell (1905), and others. His son Francis Birrell (1889–1935), journalist and dramatic critic, was associated with the *Bloomsbury Group.

BISHOP, Elizabeth (1911–79), American poet, born in Massachusetts, and brought up by her maternal grandparents in Nova Scotia after the death of her father and collapse of her mother. She was educated at Vassar, where in 1934 she met Marianne *Moore, with whose work her own has much affinity. She later travelled widely, finally settling in Brazil; the titles of some of her volumes (*North and South*, 1946; *Questions of Travel*, 1965; *Geography III*, 1976) reflect her preoccupation with place and movement, and her verse is reticent, objective, spare yet colloquial. Her *Complete Poems 1927–1979* appeared in 1983. Robert Giroux edited her *Collected Prose* (1984) and *One Art: The Selected Letters* (1994).

BISHOP, Sir Henry Rowley (1786–1855), highly regarded in his day as a prolific composer of songs and opera; but the enormous list of his stage works (which includes eight pieces based on *Scott, all served up within a year of the respective novels) does not bear inspection today, and he is chiefly remembered for the

song 'Home, Sweet Home'. The tune originally appeared as a 'Sicilian Air' in a volume of *National Airs* edited by Bishop in 1821, and was reused as the theme song of the opera *Clari* (1823) with words by the American actor and playwright John Howard Payne (1791–1852).

BISHOP, John Peale (1892–1944), American poet and story writer, educated at Princeton with E. *Wilson and F. S. *Fitzgerald. His *Collected Essays* and *Collected Poems* were published in 1948.

BLACK, William (1841–98), Scottish novelist, an early member of the *'Kailyard school', whose first triumph was *A Daughter of Heth* (1871) followed by *The Strange Adventures of a Phaeton* (1872), *A Princess of Thule* (1873), *Madcap Violet* (1876), and *Macleod of Dare* (1879). He continued to write prolifically but without his earlier success.

Blackacre, the widow, a character in Wycherley's *The Plain-Dealer*.

Black Beauty, see SEWELL; also CHILDREN'S LITERATURE.

Black Book of Carmarthen, The, a Welsh manuscript of the 12th cent., containing a collection of ancient Welsh poetry, interesting among other things for references to King *Arthur.

Black Book of the Admiralty, an ancient code of rules for the government of the navy, said to have been compiled in the reign of Edward III.

black British literature, see p.104.

Black Dwarf, The, a novel by Sir W. *Scott, in *Tales of My Landlord*, 1st series, published 1816. The first of the *Tales of My Landlord* and published anonymously, the novel's most interesting feature today is Scott's treatment of deformity. At the time of writing, he was preoccupied by the possible influence of Byron's lameness (which Scott himself shared) on his character. There are other correspondences between Scott's personal history and the situation of the Dwarf, who was superficially based on an actual dwarf, David Ritchie.

Blackfriars Theatre was built within the boundaries of the old Dominican monastery lying between Ludgate Hill and the river. The first theatre on the site was adapted for performances by Richard Farrant, master of the Children of Windsor Chapel in 1576; the second, in a different part of the old building, was bought and adapted by J. *Burbage in 1596, but was handed over to the Children of the Chapel because of local opposition. It reverted to James's son R. *Burbage in 1608. Shakespeare had a share in the new company that performed there. The building was demolished in 1655.

BLACKLOCK, Thomas (1721–91), 'the blind bard', born in Dumfriesshire, the son of a bricklayer; he lost his
(cont. on p.106)

Biography is as old as gossip, and may be as ephemeral. Yet in the last 40 years it has achieved a Golden Age, and found a favoured if controversial place in literary and intellectual life. It has risen to power as virtually a new genre, challenging the novel in its ability to depict character and explore ideas through narrative, with some 3,500 new subjects appearing each year. But it has also courted sensationalism and scandal.

The modern form is comparatively recent. The Greeks and Romans bequeathed a public tradition of life-writing to English authors through the works of *Xenophon, *Suetonius, and *Pliny, and notably through T. *North's great Tudor translation of *Plutarch's *Lives of the Noble Grecians and Romans* (1579), with its emphasis on political and military prowess. There was also a native tradition of early hagiography, as in *Ælfric's *Lives of the Saints* (993–8), in which homily and legend mingled with lurid descriptions of 'conversion' experiences. In the 17th cent. Izaak *Walton wrote pious lives of the poets *Donne (1640) and *Herbert (1670). The eccentric antiquary John *Aubrey gathered a splendid collection of donnish scurrilities and courtly tattle ('the very *pudenda* are not covered') in his *Brief Lives* (MS 1693), though these were not published until 1813.

But the true English form really became popular in the 18th cent., with numerous biographical collections such as the lives of criminals in the *Newgate Calendar* (gathered in five volumes, 1773) and Samuel *Johnson's *Lives of the English Poets* (1779–81); Johnson combined both in his *Life of Mr Richard Savage* (1744), a gripping account of the ill-starred career of a *Grub Street poet and convicted murderer, told as a black comedy of moral outrage played against a passionate apologia for his friend. The rich human appeal that Johnson saw in the new form was set out in his seminal essay 'On the Genius of Biography', in *Rambler* No. 60 (1750). 'No species of writing . . . can more certainly enchain the heart by irresistible interest, or more widely diffuse instruction to every diversity of condition . . . We are all prompted by the same motives, all deceived by the same fallacies, all animated by hope, obstructed by danger, entangled by desire, and seduced by pleasure.'

The scope for emotional intimacy was further explored by the philosopher William *Godwin in the moving biographical *Memoir* (1794) of his wife, the embattled feminist Mary *Wollstonecraft who twice tried to commit suicide as the result of an unhappy love affair in Paris at the time of the French Revolution. He depicted her memorably as 'a female Werther'.

But it was James *Boswell, in his celebrated *Life of Samuel Johnson Lld* (1791), who created the first distinctive masterpiece of English biography, using vividly dramatized scenes (worked up from his *Journals*) within a meticulous chronological narrative. Boswell gives Johnson both a sombre inner life (touched by the tragedy of his melancholia and physical disabilities) and a robust social existence in tavern and drawing room, drawn with penetrating humour.

The imaginative tension between the two selves —the private and the public Johnson—became a hallmark of what the English form could achieve, a true rival to the novel. It also clearly reflects the ethos of the European *Enlightenment (Boswell knew *Hume, *Voltaire, and *Rousseau): fearless and rational enquiry into the human condition, bringing better understanding of ourselves, and greater toleration of other natures and beliefs. This too became a touchstone of the developing genre.

The great flowering of Victorian biography that followed (virtually unmatched in Europe except for *Sainte-Beuve's essays) is still being reassessed. Though many biographers like Boswell were close friends of their subjects—*Lockhart writing of his father-in-law *Scott (1837–8), John *Forster of his confidant *Dickens (1872–4), *Carlyle of lost companion *Sterling (1851), and *Froude of his master Carlyle (1881)—the public was again demanding monuments to virtue. This affected even such a sympathetic study as Mrs *Gaskell's *Life of Charlotte Brontë* (1857), with its deliberate suppression of romantic episodes. An apotheosis was reached in Leslie *Stephen's editorship of the *Dictionary of National Biography*, a collection of more than 10,000 public life-notices launched in 26 volumes between 1885 and 1890, as much a feat of Victorian teamwork and engineering as the Forth Bridge.

Yet perhaps we still see these too much through the eyes of Lytton *Strachey. His four elegant and mocking studies (with a satiric preface) in *Eminent Victorians* (1918)—of Cardinal *Manning, Florence Nightingale, Dr T. *Arnold of Rugby, and General Gordon—refreshingly liberated the artistic form of English biography once more. But at the same time (as a contemporary of *Freud) Strachey played gleeful havoc with easy accusations of hypocrisy, debunking any notion of spiritual heroism.

Nonetheless, his work encouraged valuable experiments in the structure of biographical narrative, and a much more sophisticated approach to the contradictions of human character. These experiments have become an influential part of the modern English tradition, already pioneered by Edmund *Gosse, who followed a standard Victorian life of his father, the botanist and Christian fundamentalist P. H. Gosse (1890), with a devastating reappraisal in *Father and Son* (1907), transformed by the radical device of rewriting the story through his own eyes as a child.

Other influential experiments include Virginia *Woolf's glamorous *Orlando* (1928, a disguised life of V. *Sackville-West through four centuries and a sex change), and *Flush* (1933), a light-hearted life of the *Brownings seen through the eyes of their pet dog. A. J. A. *Symons explored biography as an ornate and labyrinthine detective story, in *The Quest for Corvo* (1934). An actual legal case, an embargo on biographical research brought by a living subject, turned Ian *Hamilton's *In Search of J. D. Salinger* (1988) into a mordant study of the ethics and psychology of life-writing itself. Julian *Barnes's *Flaubert's Parrot* (1984) was a brilliant postmodern parody of the art of biographical misinterpretation, interweaving the figure of a pedantic, fictional biographer with genuinely illuminating scholarship.

Far from undermining mainstream biography, these experiments have encouraged ever more detailed research, with finer and more stylish narrative techniques. This is especially true in literary biography, which has returned with great confidence to the large, comprehensive form of 'Life and Work' considered as a single dramatic and psychological unity. Outstanding among these are Richard *Ellmann's scholarly Irish trilogy, lives of *Yeats (1948), *Joyce (1959), and *Wilde (1987), and Michael *Holroyd's flamboyant and socially expansive portraits of Lytton Strachey (1967–8, a tragi-comic masterpiece of Bloomsbury life), Augustus *John (1974–5), and G. B. *Shaw (1988–92). New ground has also been broken with Ray Monk's limpid philosophical lives of *Wittgenstein (1990) and Bertrand *Russell (1995), Peter *Ackroyd's *Dickens* (1990, with fictional interludes), and Hermione Lee's fine thematic approach to the life of Virginia Woolf (1996). An older tradition of colonizing European subjects, initiated by G. H. *Lewes's *Goethe* (1855), has re-emerged with George Painter's *Proust* (1959), David Sweetman's *Picasso* (1973), and Graham Robb's vigorous portraits of *Balzac (1994) and *Hugo (1997).

One of the most remarkable developments is the renewed interest in lives of women, in a response to feminism. Notable work has been done here by Hilary Spurling on the life of Ivy *Compton-Burnett (1974, 1984), Victoria *Glendinning on the adventures of Vita Sackville-West (1983), and Claire *Tomalin on Mary Wollstonecraft (1974) and the 19th-cent. actress Dorothy *Jordan (1994). Tomalin's *The Invisible Woman* (1990) transforms the life of Dickens by investigating it through the eyes of his secret mistress, Nellie Ternan; and this form of 'microbiography'—concentrating on a single significant relationship or episode—may herald a movement away from the monolithic, single life.

There is also increasing interest in the lives of scientists such as Humphry *Davy and *Newton; and a number of the formative intellectual figures of modern culture—*Darwin, Freud, Einstein, *Sartre—have been the subject of revealing and controversial studies. Altogether a new kind of biographical pantheon is emerging, a sort of collective British memory—a literary equivalent of the National Portrait Gallery.

There is now a considerable body of theoretical and discursive work on biography as an artistic form. Early explorations were Woolf's lively essays on the 'New Biography' (1925), and the French biographer André *Maurois's shrewd appraisal *Aspects of Biography* (1928). Several modern practitioners have also defended the form: Robert *Gittings in his short but panoramic overview *The Nature of Biography* (1978); Richard Ellmann with mischievous wit in *Golden Codgers* (1976), which popularized Joyce's term 'biografiend'; and Leon Edel (biographer of Henry *James) in his striking meditations *Writing Lives: Principia Biographica* (1984).

These try to deal with a number of recurrent issues: the ethics of 'invading' privacy; the ambiguity of the links between art and life; the questionable objectivity of such sources as letters and diaries; the distortions involved in 'plotting' a life as a continuous narrative; the role of empathy and psychological 'transference' between author and subject; and the vexed question of the 'celebrity' life which produces endless new and competing versions (some 500 lives of Napoleon, 200 lives of *Byron, 40 lives of Marilyn Monroe, and already five lives of Sylvia *Plath).

If the form has seen a Golden Age, its future is by no means certain. It may be petrified by the growing weight of academic research; it may be liquefied by the populist demands of television documentaries, historical feature films, or simply sensationalist journalism (the life of Diana, princess of Wales, is a cautionary tale). It is difficult to tell what effect the vast increase in electronically available historical databases will eventually have. It is possible that the professional biographer, who works out of lonely passion for his subject, intent on creating a work of historical art in 'trying to bring the dead back to life again' (Richard *Holmes, *Footsteps*, 1984), will soon become a quaint, antiquarian figure, outmoded by anonymous software experts and fashionable spin-doctors. Or it is possible that the English form, which combines so wonderfully the imaginative and the critical spirit, has triumphs yet to come.

Black British literature has its origins in slave narratives of the 18th cent., the most famous of which was Olaudah Equiano's *The Interesting Narrative* (1789), which became an instant best-seller, with thousands of copies being bought by sympathizers of the Abolition movement (widely regarded by historians as the first mass philanthropic movement in Britain). The book, which went through 17 editions and reprints between 1789 and 1827, tells the story of Equiano's Ibo childhood; his kidnapping and enslavement in the Caribbean; his successful efforts to emancipate himself; and his subsequent travels in Britain and Europe as a free man. Equiano's story, packed with remarkable adventures, is a moving testimony to courage in the face of tragedy and despair; but although he did not hesitate to describe the brutalities of slavery, Equiano expressed no resentment against his masters: indeed it was the stress he placed on Christian forgiveness that engaged many of his readers. Rather than risk alienation by strident denunciations of slavery, Equiano adopted an almost self-deprecatory tone. His strategy was to persuade people of the injustices of slavery by calm reasoning and appeals to the heart. He was also aware of the need to craft his writing, to use language vividly and with deliberate artistry, in order to prove that an African was just as capable of creative expression as any white man, and should therefore be accorded the same rights.

Equiano was not the first African to publish a book in England. That distinction belongs to Ignatius *Sancho, whose *Letters* were published in 1782. Sancho was born in 1729 on board a slave ship crossing the Atlantic. His mother died soon afterwards and his father committed suicide rather than face a life of slavery. After being brought to England, Sancho was taken up by the duke of Montague, under whose patronage he acquired a classical education. During his life he wrote poetry, two stage plays, and musical works, and became friendly with a number of distinguished figures of the day, including *Gainsborough (who painted his portrait), Laurence *Sterne, and Samuel *Johnson. Sancho's letters, written somewhat in the style of Sterne, were enormously popular. The first edition attracted more than 1,200 subscribers and the book

was cited by Abolition sympathizers as evidence of the African's intellect and humanity.

Other ex-slaves living in England who also published their memoirs included Ukawsaw Gronniosaw (*A Narrative of the Most Remarkable Particulars in the Life of James Albert Ukawsaw Gronniosaw*, 1770), Ottobah Cugoano (*Thoughts and Sentiments on the Evil and Wicked Traffic of the Slavery and Commerce of the Human Species*, 1787), John Jea (*The Life, History and Unparalleled Sufferings of John Jea, African Preacher of the Gospels*, 1814), and Mary Prince (*The History of Mary Prince, a West Indian Slave*, 1831). The achievement of such writers was all the more extraordinary given the unimaginably difficult circumstances they had been forced to endure, and the fact that they were largely self-educated. Where once black people had been packed in the holds of slave ships 'like books upon a shelf' (in the words of the Revd John *Newton, an ex-slave-ship captain), by the end of the 18th cent. they had become articulate and creative, using the medium of print to establish a new strand of English literary culture.

Black people continued to publish books throughout the 19th cent., amongst them Mary Seacole, whose *Wonderful Adventures of Mary Seacole in Many Lands* (1857) provides a rare record of a black woman's experience of the male-dominated world of the British Empire. Seacole, a self-taught nurse, practised in her home country of Jamaica before travelling through Latin America, where she treated diseases such as cholera and yellow fever. She came to London in 1854 intending to volunteer for nursing duties in the Crimea, but was rejected because of her colour. Nevertheless, at her own expense, she set off for the Crimea, where she established a hospital for the care of British troops. As a result of her exceptional work she became a household name, and in 1857 a benefit festival in her honour was held in the Royal Surrey Gardens, attracting 40,000 people over four consecutive nights. 'Never', commented *The Times*, 'was hearty and kindly greeting bestowed upon a worthier object.'

British black literature in the 20th cent. continued largely in an autobiographical mode, grafting fiction on to self-confession. The post-war arrival of immigrants into Britain generated a literature preoccupied with both the perils and pleasures of exile. There was an eager British readership for accounts of the immigrants' cultural background, as well as of their struggles to integrate into British society. Black writers saw post-war Britain through West Indian eyes, giving new vigour to descriptions of familiar urban and rural scenes. The Trinidadian Sam *Selvon's Lonely Londoners (1963), for instance, revisits the grand historical sites of London (Trafalgar Square, Westminster Bridge, Piccadilly Circus) and describes them from the perspective of the naïve foreigner and small-islander. In so doing, Selvon resurrects and adapts the 18th-cent. English literary genre of fictionalized travel writing (such as James Miller's Art and Nature, 1738), in which the character of a foreigner is used to comment satirically on British life and manners. Selvon's immigrants engage not only with the day-to-day realities of racist violence and discrimination, but also with the 'grand narratives' of British history.

Selvon's novel was an early attempt to use a West Indian creolized English as a narrational mode. West Indian Creole (sometimes called 'patois', or 'nation language') evolved from the language of slaves, who were forced to learn English but who did so while retaining some of the grammatical structures of their own African languages. Although derided by many British people as 'broken English', or as worthy only of comic expression, creolized English continues to be the literary language of choice amongst many black British writers. Selvon's purpose in using such language was to give a naturalistic flavour to his account of immigrant life. Later writers, such as David *Dabydeen, Linton Kwesi *Johnson, James *Berry, Fred *D'Aguiar, Grace *Nichols, John Agard, and Amryl Johnson, use West Indian Creole or black British English self-consciously, thereby asserting self-sufficiency and spiritual independence from 'the mother country', as well as confessing alienation from the wider society. Their writings, in a dense and difficult version of standard English, deliberately resist what one writer has called 'an easy consumption' by British readers. If writers like Selvon were concerned to show the West Indian as a likeable, poignant figure, deserving of acceptance by British society, the generation that followed were keen to assert the qualities of difference, signalled by the language they used.

A crucial concern in contemporary black British literature continues to be the memorializing of slave history. Grace Nichols's I Is a Long Memoried Woman (1983), Caryl *Phillips's Cambridge (1991), David Dabydeen's Turner (1994), and Fred D'Aguiar's Feeding the Ghosts (1997) all either rework British slave narratives or reimagine the experiences of *slavery. The lives of hundreds and thousands of labourers shipped from India to work in the Caribbean plantations during the 19th cent. are also remembered in the novels of both V. S. *Naipaul (A House for Mr Biswas, 1961) and Lakshmi Persaud (Butterfly in the Wind, 1990).

Poets like Linton Kwesi Johnson see a continuum of racial violence from the era of slavery to present-day Britain. His Dread Beat and Blood (1975) is suffused with a sense of historical hurts, and explores the desire of the African to retaliate with violence, as in earlier slave revolts. Others, like Faustin Charles (Days and Nights in the Magic Forest, 1986), relish the retaliation symbolized by cricketing victories over English teams by the West Indies. The violence of bat against ball is located within the black experiences of enslavement and degradation: 'The game swells with blood,' in Charles's words. A different kind of violence concerns women writers—namely that of black male upon black female. Joan Riley's The Unbelonging (1985) echoes Alice *Walker's The Color Purple in telling of sexual abuse of a young girl by a cruel and perverse father. Andrea Levy's Small Island (2004), in contrast, attempts an even-handed generosity in its multiple point-of-view portrayal of the relationships of Jamaican RAF airman Gilbert Joseph, his educated Jamaican wife Hortense, and their white landlady Queenie in post-war London in the 1940s.

If black British literature is now largely set in degraded urban landscapes, and has as its themes loneliness, harassment, and exploitation, it is not only because black writers remain passionately conscious of their slave past; they also continue to perceive British society as being racially determined.

See: Peter Fryer, Staying Power: The History of Black People in Britain (1984); Pabhu Guptara, Black British Literature: An Annotated Bibliography (1986); David Dabydeen, A Reader's Guide to West Indian and Black British Literature (rev. edn, 1997); Black England: Life before Emancipation (1995) by Gretchen Gerzina and London Calling: How Black and Asian Writers Imagined a City (2003) by Sukhdev Sandhu.

sight when six months old. He published his first volume of poems in 1746, republished with an account by J. *Spence in 1754. He was befriended by *Hume, and in turn wrote in praise of *Burns, whom he received with kindness in Edinburgh. His poetry was, Dr *Johnson pointed out, largely derivative. There is an account of his meeting with Johnson in Boswell's *Journal of a Tour to the Hebrides. His collected poems with a life by H. *Mackenzie appeared in 1793.

BLACKMORE, Sir Richard (1654–1729), physician to Queen Anne who produced some indifferent poems of great length, heroic and epic, and *Creation: A Philosophical Poem* (1712), which was warmly praised by Dr *Johnson. He was one of the few poets added to *Lives of the English Poets* by Johnson's own choice. Pope in *The Dunciad* mocked his 'sonorous strain'.

BLACKMORE, R(ichard) D(oddridge) (1825–1900), son of a clergyman, educated at Blundell's School, Tiverton, and at Exeter College, Oxford. He was called to the bar, but his occasional epileptic fits forced him to take up a country life, first as a schoolmaster, then as a fruitgrower at Teddington, where he lived till his death. He was happily married to an Irishwoman, Lucy Maguire; they had no children. He published several volumes of poems and translations from *Theocritus and *Virgil, but his fame rests almost entirely on one of his novels, *Lorna Doone* (1869). He wrote 13 other novels, including *Cradock Nowell* (1866), *The Maid of Sker* (1872), *Alice Lorraine* (1875), and *Springhaven* (1887). These pastoral tales, stirring in incident and with a slightly grotesque humour, are often ill-constructed and prolix, and sometimes over-lush in style, but their great excellence is the intricacy of their descriptions of lovingly observed climate, wildlife, and vegetation. Blackmore was a sincere and kindly but reserved and eccentric man, absorbed in his experimental fruit-farming. See Waldo H. Dunn, *R. D. Blackmore, the Author of 'Lorna Doone'* (1956); Kenneth Budd, *The Last Victorian: R. D. Blackmore and His Novels* (1960).

Black Mountain poets, a group of poets associated with Black Mountain College, an experimental liberal arts college founded in 1933 near Asheville, North Carolina, which became in the early 1950s a centre of anti-academic poetic revolt. A leading figure was Charles Olson (1910–70), rector of the college from 1951 to 1956, whose *Projective Verse* (1950) was a form of manifesto, laying much emphasis on the dynamic energy of the spoken word and phrase and attacking the domination of syntax, rhyme, and metre. His students and followers included R. *Creeley, Robert Duncan (1919–), and Denise *Levertov. The *Black Mountain Review* (1954–7; edited by Creeley) also published work by *Ginsberg and *Kerouac, thus heralding the *Beat Generation.

BLACKMUR, R(ichard) P(almer) (1904–65), American poet and critic, associated for many years with Princeton, where he was professor from 1948 to 1965. His critical works, which include *The Expense of Greatness* (1940), *Language as Gesture* (1952), and *The Lion and the Honeycomb* (1955), link him with the *New Criticism; he was one of the early champions of the art of W. *Stevens.

Black Papers, see EDUCATION, LITERATURE OF.

Blackpool, Stephen, a character in Dickens's *Hard Times.*

Black Prince, the (1330–76), a name given (apparently by 16th-cent. chroniclers) to Edward, the eldest son of Edward III and father of Richard II. The origin of the title is unknown; it has been conjectured that it may have been because of the fear he inspired in battle (as at Poitiers in 1356) or because of his wearing black armour. His death led to a return to the domination of the English court by *John of Gaunt, opposition to whom had been led by the Black Prince. See R. Barber, *Edward, Prince of Wales and Aquitaine: A Biography of the Black Prince* (1978).

BLACKSTONE, Sir William (1723–80). He became the first Vinerian professor of English law at Oxford in 1758 and lectured there until 1766; his annual lectures became the basis of his *Commentaries on the Laws of England* (4 vols, 1765–9) which exerted a powerful influence, remained for many years the best historical account of English law, and is still regarded as a classic. It was criticized by *Bentham in his *A Fragment on Government* (1776) for its acceptance of the existing state of the law.

BLACKWOOD, Algernon (1869–1951). He led an adventurous early life and when almost starving found work in journalism in New York—a period described in *Episodes before Thirty* (1923). His work included travel, adventure, humour, and some work of a semi-mystical nature, but the stories for which he is chiefly remembered deal in the psychic and macabre. *The Empty House and Other Ghost Stories* appeared in 1906, at which time he was greatly encouraged by *Belloc. More than 30 books followed, culminating in *Tales of the Uncanny and Supernatural* (1949).

BLACKWOOD, Lady Caroline (1931–96), novelist, short story writer, reporter, born in Ulster. Her first husband was the artist Lucian Freud (1922– , grandson of S. *Freud) and her third Robert *Lowell. Her publications include *The Stepdaughter* (1976, novel), and *Good Night Sweet Ladies* (1983, stories). Non-fiction includes *On the Perimeter* (1984), an account of the pacifist anti-nuclear Women's Group encamped outside the American airbase at Greenham Common, Berkshire, and *The Last of the Duchess* (1995), a sardonic description of the last days of the duchess of Windsor. Her most remarkable work is the novella *Great Granny Webster* (1977) which describes the austere, empty life of the title character, seen through the eyes of her great granddaughter: the old woman's loveless fate is contrasted with that of suicidal socialite Aunt Lavinia, and that of the narrator's grandmother, who is in a mental institution. It also contains a notable addition to the 'decaying country house' motif in Anglo–Irish fiction.

BLACKWOOD, William (1776–1834), Scots publisher, founder of the firm of William Blackwood and Son, and of the highly successful *Blackwood's (Edinburgh) Magazine* in the conduct of which he took a decided interest. He early recognized the talent of *Galt, whose *The Ayrshire Legatees* he published, and of S. *Ferrier. In 1810 he bought the *Edinburgh Encyclopaedia*, which he saw finally completed in 1830. His sons, in turn, became editors of *Blackwood's*; his son John (1818–79) was an admirer of G. *Eliot, published much of her work, and became a friend.

Blackwood's Magazine (1817–1980), or 'the Maga', was an innovating monthly periodical begun by W. *Blackwood as a Tory rival to the Whiggish *Edinburgh Review. It began in April 1817 as the *Edinburgh Monthly Magazine* and in October that year continued as *Blackwood's Edinburgh Magazine* until Dec. 1905; from Jan. 1906 onwards it became *Blackwood's Magazine*. Although its politics were the same as those of the *Quarterly Review*, it was intended to be sharper, brighter, and less ponderous. The first editors were shortly replaced by *Lockhart, John *Wilson, and J. *Hogg, who gave the 'Maga' its forceful partisan tone. Its notoriety was early established with the publication in 1817 of the so-called *'Chaldee MS', in which many leading Edinburgh figures were pilloried; and with the beginning, also in 1817, of the long series of attacks on the *'Cockney School of Poetry', directed chiefly against Leigh *Hunt, *Keats, and *Hazlitt. Blackwood had to pay damages more than once, notably to Hazlitt, for the venom of his writers' pens, and John *Murray gave up the London agency for the magazine in protest. *Blackwood's* did however give considerable support to *Wordsworth, *Shelley, *De Quincey, *Mackenzie, *Galt, Sir W. *Scott, and others, and did much to foster an interest in German literature. Unlike the *Edinburgh* and the *Quarterly* it published short stories and serialized novels. The *Noctes Ambrosianae*, though of ephemeral interest, was a highly popular series of sketches. Soon after 1830 the magazine became a purely literary review, and continued through the 19th cent. as a prosperous and respected literary miscellany, publishing *Conrad, *Noyes, *Lang, and many others. It continued, in a diminished form, until 1980.

BLAIR, Eric, see ORWELL.

BLAIR, Hugh (1718–1800), Scottish divine and professor of rhetoric in Edinburgh, remembered for his famous sermons (5 vols, 1777–1801) and for his influential and often reprinted *Lectures on Rhetoric and Belles Lettres* (2 vols, 1784). He belonged to a distinguished literary circle which included *Hume,

*Carlyle, Adam *Smith, and W. *Robertson. He was a warm defender of *Macpherson; his *A Critical Dissertation on the Poems of Ossian* (1763) found that *Fingal* possessed 'all the essential requisites of a true and regular epic'.

BLAIR, Robert (1699–1746), educated at Edinburgh and in Holland, and ordained minister of Athelstaneford in 1731. He published in 1743 *The Grave*, a didactic poem of the *graveyard school, consisting of some 800 lines of blank verse. It celebrates the horrors of death ('In that dread moment, how the frantic soul Raves round the walls of her clay tenement'), the solitude of the tomb, the pains of bereavement, the madness of suicide, etc., ending more perfunctorily with thoughts of the Resurrection. It has passages of considerable power and, like Young's *Night Thoughts*, was illustrated by *Blake.

BLAKE, William (1757–1827), the third son of a London hosier. He did not go to school, but was apprenticed to James Basire, engraver to the Society of *Antiquaries, and then became a student at the *Royal Academy. From 1779 he was employed as an engraver by the bookseller J. *Johnson, and in 1780 met *Fuseli and *Flaxman, the latter a follower of *Swedenborg, whose mysticism deeply influenced Blake. In 1782 he married Catherine Boucher, the daughter of a market-gardener; their childless marriage was a lasting communion. Flaxman at this period introduced him to the progressive intellectual circle of the Revd A. S. Mathew and his wife (which included Mrs *Barbauld, H. *More, and Mrs E. *Montagu), and Mathew and Flaxman financed the publication of Blake's first volume, *Poetical Sketches* (1783). In 1784, with help from Mrs Mathew, he set up a print shop at 27 Broad Street, and at about the same period (although not for publication) wrote the satirical *An Island in the Moon*. He engraved and published his *Songs of Innocence* in 1789, and also *The Book of Thel*, both works which manifest the early phases of his highly distinctive mystic vision, and in which he embarks on the evolution of his personal mythology; years later (in *Jerusalem*) he was to state, through the character Los, 'I must Create a System, or be enslav'd by another Man's', words which have been taken by some to apply to his own need to escape from the fetters of 18th-cent. versification, as well as from the materialist philosophy (as he conceived it) of the *Enlightenment, and a Puritanical or repressive interpretation of Christianity. *The Book of Thel* presents the maiden Thel lamenting transience and mutability by the banks of the river of Adona; she is answered by the lily, the cloud, the worm, and the clod who assure her that 'He, who loves the lowly' cherishes even the meanest; but this relatively conventional wisdom is challenged by a final section in which Thel visits the house of Clay, sees the couches of the dead, and hears 'a voice of sorrow' breathe a characteristically Blakean protest against hypocrisy and restraint—'Why a tender curb upon the youthful, burning boy? Why a tender little curtain of flesh upon the bed of our desire?'—a message which sends Thel back 'with a shriek' to the vales of Har. The ambiguity of this much-interpreted poem heralds the increasing complexity of his other works which include *Tiriel* (written 1789, pub. 1874), introducing the theme of the blind tyrannic father, 'the king of rotten wood, and of the bones of death', which reappears in different forms in many poems; *The Marriage of Heaven and Hell* (engraved c.1790–3), his principal prose work, a book of para-doxical aphorisms; and the revolutionary works *The French Revolution* (1791); *America: A Prophecy* (1793); and *Visions of the Daughters of Albion* (1793), in which he develops his attitude of revolt against authority, combining political fervour (he had met *Paine at Johnson's) and visionary ecstasy; Urizen, the deviser of moral codes (described as 'the stony law' of the Decalogue) and *Orc, the Promethean arch-rebel, emerge as principal characters in a cosmology that some scholars have related to that of *Gnosticism. By this time Blake had already established his poetic range; the long, flowing lines and violent energy of the verse combine with phrases of terse and aphoristic clarity and moments of great lyric tenderness, and he was once more to demonstrate his command of the lyric in *Songs of Experience* (1794) which includes 'Tyger! Tyger! burning bright', 'O Rose thou art sick', and other of his more accessible pieces.

Meanwhile the Blakes had moved to Lambeth in 1790; there he continued to engrave his own works and to write, evolving his mythology further in *The Book of *Urizen* (1794); *Europe, a Prophecy* (1794); *The Song of *Los* (1795); *The Book of Ahania* (1795); *The Book of Los* (1795); and *The Four Zoas* (originally entitled *Vala*, written and revised 1797–1804), and also working for the booksellers. In 1800 he moved to Felpham, Sussex, where he lived for three years, working for his friend and patron *Hayley, and working on *Milton* (1804–8); in 1803 he was charged at Chichester with high treason for having 'uttered seditious and treasonable expres-sions, such as "D–n the King, d–n all his subjects . . ." ', but was acquitted. In the same year he returned to London, to work on *Milton* and *Jerusalem: The Em-anation of the Giant Albion* (written and etched, 1804–20). In 1805 he was commissioned by *Cromek to produce a set of drawings for R. *Blair's poem *The Grave*, but Cromek defaulted on the contract, and Blake earned neither the money nor the public esteem he had hoped for, and found his designs engraved and weakened by another hand. This was symptomatic of the disappointment of his later years, when he appears to have relinquished expectations of being widely understood, and quarrelled even with some of the circle of friends who supported him. Both his poetry and his art had failed to find a sympathetic audience, and a lifetime of hard work had not brought him riches or even much comfort. His last years were passed in obscurity, although he continued to attract the interest and admiration of younger artists, and a commission in 1821 from the painter John Linnell produced his well-known illustrations for the Book of Job, published in 1826. (It was Linnell who introduced Blake to Samuel *Palmer in 1824.) A later poem, 'The Everlasting Gospel', written about 1818, shows un-diminished power and attack; it presents Blake's own version of Jesus, in a manner that recalls the paradoxes of *The Marriage of Heaven and Hell*, attacking the conventional 'Creeping Jesus', gentle, humble, and chaste, and stressing his rebellious nature, his for-giveness of the woman taken in adultery, his reversing of the stony law of Moses, praising 'the Naked Human form divine', and sexuality as the means whereby 'the Soul Expands its wing', and elevating forgiveness above the 'Moral Virtues'.

At Blake's death, general opinion held that he had been, if gifted, insane; *Wordsworth's verdict, accord-ing to C. *Robinson, was that 'There was no doubt that this poor man was mad, but there is something in the madness of this man which interests me more than the sanity of Lord Byron and Walter Scott', a view in some measure echoed by *Ruskin, who found his manner 'diseased and wild' but his mind 'great and wise'. It was not until A. *Gilchrist's biography of 1863 (signifi-cantly describing Blake as 'Pictor Ignotus') that interest began to grow. This was followed by an appreciation by *Swinburne (1868) and by W. M. *Rossetti's edition of 1874, which added new poems to the canon and established his reputation, at least as a lyric poet; his rediscovered engravings considerably influenced the development of *art nouveau. In 1893 *Yeats, a devoted admirer, produced with E. J. Ellis a three-volume edition, with a memoir and an interpretation of the mythology, and the 20th cent. saw an enormous increase in interest. The bibliographical studies and editions of G. *Keynes, culminating in *The Complete Writings of William Blake* (1966, 2nd edn), have added greatly to knowledge both of the man and his works, revealing him not only as an apocalyptic visionary but also as a writer of ribald and witty epigrams, a critic of spirit and originality, and an independent thinker who found his own way of resisting the orthodoxies of his age, and whose hostile response to the narrow vision and materialism (as he conceived it) of his *bêtes noires* Joshua *Reynolds, *Locke, and I. *Newton was far from demented, but in part a prophetic warning of the dangers of a world perceived as mechanism, with man as a mere cog in an industrial revolution. There have been many interpretative studies, relating his work to traditional Christianity, to the *Neoplatonic and Swe-denborgian traditions, to Jungian *archetypes and to *Freudian and *Marxist theory; the Prophetic Books, once dismissed as incoherent, are now claimed by many as works of integrity as well as profundity. Recently, Blake has had a particularly marked influence on the *Beat Generation and the English poets of the *underground movement, hailed by both as liberator; *Auden earlier acclaimed him ('New Year Letter', 1941) as 'Self-educated Blake . . .' who 'Spoke to Isaiah in the

Strand I And heard inside each mortal thing I Its holy emanation sing'.

See also *Blake Books* (1977) by G. E. Bentley Jnr, including annotated catalogues of his writings and scholarly works about him; *The Complete Poetry and Prose of William Blake*, ed. D. V. Erdman (1965, 1988); *Blake's Illuminated Books*, 6 vols (1991–5), gen. ed. D. Bindman; and J. Viscomi, *Blake and the Idea of the Book* (1993), an authoritative account of Blake's graphic process; The William Blake Archive: http://jefferson. village.virginia.edu/blake (ed. M. Eaves, R. Essick, J. Viscomi). There is a life by P. *Ackroyd, (1995).

BLAMIRE, Susanna (1747–94), poet, daughter of a Cumberland farmer, whose works were published anonymously, in single sheets and magazines, or circulated among friends during her lifetime: they were collected as *The Poetical Works of Miss Susanna Blamire, The Muse of Cumberland* (pub. 1842) by Patrick Maxwell of Edinburgh with the help of Dr Henry Lonsdale of Carlisle. They range from dialect songs ('The Siller Croun'—'And ye shall walk in silk attire') to chatty, informal verse epistles and the heroic couplets of 'Stoklewath; or, The Cumbrian Village'. She gives a vivid, attractive, and practical picture of rural life and manners.

BLANCH, Lesley (1904–   ), romantic biographer, orientalist, and travel writer, best known for her memorably entitled group biography, *The Wilder Shores of Love* (1954), dedicated to her then husband, novelist Romain Gary (1914–80). It tells the lives of four women 'enthralled by the Oriental legend': these include Isabel Burton née Arundell, wife of Sir R. *Burton. *Pavilions of the Heart* (1974) is an anthology of various historic erotic venues. Blanch edited the memoirs of Harriette *Wilson as *The Game of Hearts* (1957), and in 2005 published a memoir, *Journey into the Mind's Eye*.

Blandamour, in Spenser's *Faerie Queene*, Bk IV, a 'jollie youthfull knight', 'His fickle mind full of inconstancie', who consorts with *Paridell and *Duessa.

blank verse, verse without rhyme, especially the iambic pentameter of unrhymed heroic, the regular measure of English dramatic and epic poetry, first used by *Surrey *c.*1540.

Blast, see VORTICISM.

Blatant Beast, in Spenser's *Faerie Queene*, Bk VI, a monster, the personification of the calumnious voice of the world, begotten of Envy and Detraction. Sir *Calidore pursues it, finds it despoiling monasteries and defiling the church, overcomes it, and chains it up. But finally it breaks the chain, 'So now he raungeth through the world againe.' Cf. QUESTING BEAST.

BLATCHFORD, Robert Peel Glanville (1851–1943), journalist and socialist, and son of a touring actor and actress; he wrote for the Manchester *Sunday Chronicle*, was one of the founders of the Manchester Fabian Society in 1890, and in 1891 left the *Sunday Chronicle* with four colleagues to start a socialist weekly, the *Clarion*, in which appeared his series of articles, *Merrie England*; these appeared as a book in 1893, sold enormously, and made many converts to the cause of socialism. His autobiography, *My Eighty Years*, appeared in 1931.

BLAVATSKY, Madame Helena Petrovna (1831–91), a Russian whose adventurous career took her to Mexico, Europe, India, and Tibet. She became interested in spiritualism in New York in 1873, and in 1875 founded, with Col. H. S. Olcott and W. Q. Judge, the Theosophical Society, which she and Olcott re-established in India in 1879. It aimed to promote universal brotherhood, the study of Eastern literature and religion, and research into the unfamiliar laws of nature and the latent faculties of man. Despite widespread scepticism about her powers, she had many followers, including A. *Besant, and *Yeats in an account of his visits to her in London described her as 'a great passionate nature, a sort of female Dr Johnson' (*The Trembling of the Veil*, 1926). She was in many ways a forerunner of the 20th-cent. *New Age movement. See SOCIETY FOR PSYCHICAL RESEARCH.

Bleak House, a novel by *Dickens, published in monthly parts 1852–3.

The book contains a vigorous satire on the abuses of the old court of Chancery, the delays and costs of which brought misery and ruin on its suitors. The tale centres in the fortunes of an uninteresting couple, Richard Carstone, a futile youth, and his amiable cousin Ada Clare. They are wards of the court in the case of Jarndyce and Jarndyce, concerned with the distribution of an estate, which has gone on so long as to become a subject of heartless joking as well as a source of great profit to those professionally engaged in it. The wards are taken to live with their kind elderly relative John Jarndyce. They fall in love and secretly marry. The weak Richard, incapable of sticking to any profession and lured by the will-o'-the-wisp of the fortune that is to be his when the case is settled, sinks gradually to ruin and death, and the case of Jarndyce and Jarndyce comes suddenly to an end on the discovery that the costs have absorbed the whole estate in dispute.

When Ada goes to live with John Jarndyce she is accompanied by Esther Summerson, a supposed orphan, one of Dickens's saints, and the narrative is partly supposed to be from her pen.

Sir Leicester Dedlock, a pompous old baronet, is devotedly attached to his beautiful wife. Lady Dedlock hides a dreadful secret under her haughty and indifferent exterior. Before her marriage she has loved a certain Captain Hawdon and has become the mother of a daughter, whom she believes dead. Hawdon is supposed to have perished at sea. In fact the daughter lives in the person of Esther Summerson, and Hawdon in that of a penniless scrivener. The accidental sight of his handwriting in a legal document reveals to Lady Dedlock the fact of his existence, and its effect on her alerts the cunning old lawyer Tulkinghorn to the existence of a mystery. Lady Dedlock's enquiries bring her, through the medium of a wretched crossing-sweeper, Jo, to the burial-ground where her former lover's miserable career has just ended. Jo's unguarded revelation of his singular experience with this veiled lady sets Tulkinghorn on the track, until he possesses all the facts and tells Lady Dedlock that he is going to expose her next day to her husband. That night Tulkinghorn is murdered. Bucket, the detective, presently reveals to the baronet what Tulkinghorn had discovered, and arrests a former French maid of Lady Dedlock, a violent woman, who has committed the murder. Lady Dedlock, learning that her husband knows her secret, flies from the house in despair, and is found dead near the grave of her lover, in spite of the efforts of her husband and Esther to save her.

Much of the story is occupied with Esther's devotion to John Jarndyce; her acceptance of his offer of marriage from a sense of duty and gratitude, though she loves a young doctor, Woodcourt; Jarndyce's discovery of the state of her heart; and his surrender of her to Woodcourt.

There are a host of interesting minor characters, among whom may be mentioned Harold Skimpole (drawn 'in the light externals of character' from Leigh *Hunt), who disguises his utter selfishness under an assumption of childish irresponsibility; Mrs Jellyby, who sacrifices her family to her selfish addiction to professional philanthropy; Jo, the crossing-sweeper, who is chivied by the police to his death; Chadband, the pious, eloquent humbug; Turveydrop, the model of deportment; Krook, the 'chancellor' of the rag and bone department, who dies of spontaneous combustion; Guppy, the lawyer's clerk; Guster, the poor slavey; the law-stationer Snagsby; Miss Flite, the little lunatic lady who haunts the Chancery courts; and Jarndyce's friend, the irascible and generous Boythorn (drawn from W. S. *Landor).

For many of Dickens's contemporaries, this novel marked a decline in his reputation; individual characters (notably Jo and Bucket) were praised, but it was charged with verbosity and 'absolute want of construction'. Later readers, including G. B. *Shaw, *Chesterton, *Conrad, and *Trilling, have seen it as one of the high points of his achievement, and the herald of his last great phase.

BLEASDALE, Alan (1946–   ), playwright, born and educated in Liverpool. He is the author of several stage plays, including *Having a Ball* (1981), a comedy set in a vasectomy clinic, *Are You Lonesome Tonight?* (1985), about the singer Elvis Presley, and *On the Ledge* (*National Theatre, 1993), which is dramatically staged in a tower block with rioters below. He is perhaps best known for his TV work, which includes *Boys from the Blackstuff* (1982), about a group of unemployed men in Liverpool, and *G.B.H.* (1991), a seven-part serial about corrupt left-wing local politics. His streetwise Liverpool lad Scully first emerged on *BBC Radio 4, then on TV in 1984.

Blefuscu, in Swift's *Gulliver's Travels*, an island separated from Lilliput by a narrow channel.

Blenheim, battle of (1704), at which the first duke of Marlborough defeated the French and Bavarians, was celebrated in poems by *Addison (*The Campaign*, 1705) and *Southey. Southey's version ('The Battle of Blenheim', 1798) is a sharply anti-militaristic ballad in which old Kaspar describes Marlborough's victory to his grandchildren, Peterkin and Wilhelmine; in spite of the bloodshed and carnage of the battle, it was (he repeatedly and ironically assures them) 'a famous victory'. Blenheim Palace at Woodstock was built (1705–22) for Marlborough by *Vanbrugh, with gardens by Henry Wise and Launcelot *Brown.

'Blessed Damozel, The', a poem by D. G. *Rossetti, of which the first version appeared in the *Germ* (1850); many revised versions appeared subsequently.

In this poem, heavily influenced by *Dante, Rossetti describes the blessed damozel leaning out from the ramparts of Heaven, watching the worlds below and the souls mounting to God, and praying for union with her earthly lover in the shadow of the 'living mystic tree'. One of his earliest and most influential poems, it shows the *Pre-Raphaelite interest in medieval sacramental symbolism (she has three lilies in her hand, seven stars in her hair, and a white rose in her robe) and Rossetti's concept of an ideal *platonic love, which he was to develop in later works. He also painted the same subject in later years.

BLESSINGTON, Marguerite, countess of (1789–1849), travelled on the Continent with her husband and with *D'Orsay, with whom she ultimately lived. She published *A Journal of Conversations with Lord Byron* (1832), which records in lively detail her encounters with *Byron in Italy, and is of great importance in any consideration of Byron's life abroad. She also wrote *The Idler in Italy* (1839) and *The Idler in France* (1841), as well as a number of novels.

BLICHER, Steen Steensen (1782–1848), Danish pastor, poet, and short story writer, who was born and spent most of his life in Jutland, a region which he celebrated in his work. He is best known for his *Diary of a Parish Clerk* (1824), a poignant and stoic tale of endurance and disappointment, and a masterly character study, written in the form of a journal by an unreliable narrator. He translated *Ossian and *Goldsmith, and was much influenced by *Scott.

Blifil, Master, a character in Fielding's *Tom Jones*.

Blimber, Dr, and his daughter Cornelia, characters in Dickens's *Dombey and Son*.

BLIND, Mathilde (1841–96), poet, born Mathilde

Cohen in Mannheim, Germany; she took the name of her stepfather Karl Blind (1826–1907), who came to England in 1852 as a political refugee. Her brother Ferdinand committed suicide at the age of 17 after a failed assassination attempt upon Bismarck. Her unorthodox and eventful upbringing led her to challenge religious and social orthodoxies: she translated D. F. *Strauss's *The Old Faith and the New* (1873), became involved in the women's movement, and translated the journals of Marie *Bashkirtseff from the French (1890). Her first volume of poetry was published pseudonymously in 1867: this was followed by several others, all of which show a keen sense of social concern and a positivist outlook. They include *The Heather on Fire: A Tale of the Highland Clearances* (1886), and the intellectually ambitious and challenging *The Ascent of Man* (1889), a poem in three parts and varied verse forms, which gives a vivid account of Darwinian evolution from chaos, through the 'cruel strife', 'eternal hunger', and indifference of nature, to Man—'from Man's martyrdom in slow convulsion | Will be born the infinite goodness—God'. She wrote a life of G. *Eliot (1884).

Blind Beggar of Bethnal Green, The, see BEGGAR'S DAUGHTER OF BEDNALL GREEN, THE.

Blind Harry, see HENRY THE MINSTREL.

BLISS, Sir Arthur (1891–1975), composer, who became known as an *enfant terrible* of music with works like *Madam Noy* (1918), a 'witchery' with words by E. H. W. Meyerstein, and *Rout* (1920), which uses nonsense syllables in the vocal part, but later works reverted to a more romantic idiom in the tradition of *Elgar. His first substantial setting of literary texts was the *Pastoral: Lie Strewn the White Flocks* (1928), which brings together poems by *Jonson, *Fletcher, *Poliziano, W. *Owen, R. *Nichols and *Theocritus. The choral symphony *Morning Heroes* (1930), with words by *Homer, *Whitman, Li-Tai-Po, Owen, and Nichols, provided a deeply personal expression of the composer's attitude to war. He also wrote settings for G. M. *Hopkins, *Day-Lewis, *Pope, T. S. *Eliot, and others. In 1934–5 Bliss worked in close collaboration with *Wells on music for the film *Things to Come*—the best known of several film scores he produced during the next twenty years. Works for the stage include incidental music for *The Tempest* (1921) and a full-scale opera, *The Olympians* (1949), with a libretto by J. B. *Priestley.

Blithedale Romance, The, a novel by *Hawthorne, published 1852, and based on Hawthorne's own residence in 1841 at the *Transcendental co-operative community at Brook Farm.

It is narrated by a poet, Miles Coverdale, who visits Blithedale Farm, near Boston, where he meets the exotic, wealthy, and queenly Zenobia (said to be based on Margaret *Fuller, although she is mentioned by name in the text, possibly to warn readers against the identification), the philanthropic, but self-engrossed, inhuman, and fierce, social reformer Hollingsworth, and the gentle, delicate girl Priscilla. Coverdale broods on *Fourier, *Carlyle, and *Emerson, while both the women (who turn out to be half-sisters) fall in love with Hollingsworth; Zenobia is rejected and drowns herself, Hollingsworth marries Priscilla, and Coverdale remains a sceptical, solitary observer of mankind's aspirations and its disappointments.

BLIXEN, Karen Christentze, née Dinesen (1885–1962), Danish writer, who wrote mainly in English, under the name of 'Isak Dinesen'. Born at Rungsted, Denmark, she rebelled against bourgeois Danish society, studied art in Copenhagen, Paris, and Rome, then married her cousin, Baron Bror von Blixen-Finecke, in 1914. They ran a coffee plantation in Kenya, which she continued to manage after her divorce; the story of this failed enterprise is told in *Out of Africa* (1937), written after her return to Denmark in 1931. From childhood she had interested herself in writing, working on sketches for stories, writing plays, and eventually contributing to periodicals, but her first major publication was *Seven Gothic Tales* (1934), a stylish collection exhibiting aristocratic hauteur, a neo-Gothic use of fantasy, the macabre, and the bizarre, and manifesting her admiration for *fin-de-siècle* French decadence. This was followed by several other collections, which won her a considerable international reputation. There is a life by Judith Thurman (1982).

BLOK, Aleksandr Aleksandrovich (1880–1921), Russian Symbolist poet, playwright, and critic. Born into an academic St Petersburg family, he was one of a number of young poets influenced by the philosopher Vladimir Solovyev, from whom Blok took the central theme of his early poetry ('The Verses about the Beautiful Lady', 1901–2), Sophia, the feminine personification of Divine Wisdom. In 1903 he married Lyubov Dmitrievna Mendeleeva, whom he in some degree identified with this cult, and in 1904 he met *Bely. Loss of faith in his ideal, the experience of urban life, and the disillusionment following the débâcle of the Russo-Japanese War and the failure of the 1905 Revolution are all reflected in the gloom and pessimism of his second period (1904–8). Major works of these years are the narrative poem *The Night Violet* (1906), the cycles *The City* (1904–8), *The Snow Mask* (1907), and *Faina* (1906–8), and a bitter play satirizing his former ideals, *The Puppet Show* (1906). Some of Blok's most powerful work is contained in the cycles of his third period (1907–21), the urban poetry of *The Terrible World* (1907–16), *The Italian Verses* (1909), *Carmen* (1914), resulting from his love affair with the opera singer Lyubov Aleksandrovna Delmas, and *Native Land* (1907–16), which contains his late poems on the theme of Russia. Blok greeted the Russian Revolution romantically, as an expression of cosmic upheaval, and wrote his famous poem 'The Twelve', which ends with the image of Christ leading a band of Red Guards, in Jan. 1918 (trans. C. Bechhofer,

1920). After the revolution he took part in various state literary activities, but ceased to write poetry. His *Selected Poems* (trans. Jon Stallworthy and Peter France) appeared in 1970.

BLONDEL DE NESLE, a French *trouvère who wrote in Picardy in the late 12th cent. and whose poems keep very close to the terminology and spirit of the troubadours. A famous legend makes him a friend of *Richard Cœur de Lion: Richard, on his return from the Holy Land in 1192, was imprisoned in Austria. Blondel set out to find him and, when he sat under a window of the castle where Richard was imprisoned, he sang a song in French that he and the king had composed together; half-way through he paused, and Richard took up the song and completed it. Blondel returned to England and told of the king's whereabouts.

BLOOD, Thomas (?1618–80), an adventurer who, among other exploits, headed an unsuccessful attempt to take Dublin Castle from the Royalists in 1663, and tried to steal the crown jewels from the Tower in 1671. He figures in Scott's *Peveril of the Peak.*

Bloodaxe Books, Newcastle-based independent poetry press, founded by editor Neil Astley in 1978. Since then, Bloodaxe has become a major force in poetry publishing in Britain, building up a large and diverse list of new and established English-language poets as well as European and international poetry in translation. A wide net approach to new voices has collected some of the most interesting younger poets, for example *Armitage and *Maxwell, who are published alongside such established figures as *Holub and T. *Harrison, and Nobel laureates *Tagore, *Montale and *Elytis.

Bloody Brother, The, or *Rollo, Duke of Normandy*, a play by J. *Fletcher, B. *Jonson, G. *Chapman, and P. *Massinger, performed *c*.1616, published 1639. It was very popular in the 17th cent. An edition by J. D. Jump was published in 1948, reissued 1969.

The duke of Normandy has bequeathed his dukedom to his two sons Rollo and Otto. Rollo, the elder, a resolute and violent man, in order to secure the whole heritage, kills his brother and orders the immediate execution of all who refuse to further his ends, including his old tutor Baldwin. The latter's daughter Edith pleads for his life, and her beauty captivates Rollo, but his reprieve comes too late. Edith determines to avenge her father's death, and prepares to kill Rollo when he comes to woo her. His apparent repentance shakes her determination. While she hesitates, the brother of another of Rollo's victims enters and kills the tyrant. The scene between Latorch, Rollo's favourite, and the Astrologers was probably written by Jonson, as also part of Act IV, sc. i.

It contains the lyric 'Take, O, take those lips away', which occurs with certain changes in *Measure for Measure.*

BLOOM, Harold (1930–   ), American critic, born in New York and educated at Cornell and Yale. He has spent his working life as a Yale professor, specializing in the Romantic literary tradition, as in *The Visionary Company* (1961), in opposition to T. S. *Eliot's classical critical orthodoxy. His works on individual poets include *Shelley's Myth-Making* (1959), *Yeats* (1970), and *Wallace Stevens* (1977); but he is better known for his ambitious reconsideration of poetic tradition in *The Anxiety of Influence* (1973) and *A Map of Misreading* (1975), which propose that major poets struggle against the suffocating weight of their predecessors, creating new poems by 'misreading' older ones through a complex series of rhetorical defence mechanisms. Several later works develop this thesis in more detail. A more popular work is *The Western Canon* (1994), which defends the 'great' writers against egalitarian critical trends.

Bloom, Leopold Paula, and his wife Molly, characters in Joyce's *Ulysses.*

BLOOMFIELD, Leonard (1887–1949), an American linguist whose book *Language* (1933) was a major influence on the development of 'Structural Linguistics', putting forward the idea that the analysis appropriate to a particular language must be inferred from its own structure, not brought to bear on it from general linguistic principles. The approach of the book is behaviourist and empiricist, arguing that a speech act is fully explained by the human needs that cause it to be made (though this full explanation is often not available). This approach, characterized as 'Bloomfieldian', prevailed in some circles up to the 1950s; it was opposed by *Chomsky, though the origins of his analyses of grammar lie in Bloomfield's system. See LINGUISTICS.

BLOOMFIELD, Robert (1766–1823), born in Suffolk. He worked as a farm labourer and then as a shoemaker in London, enduring extreme poverty and often unable to afford paper to write on. He is remembered chiefly as author of *The Farmer's Boy* (1800, ed. *Lofft), which was illustrated with engravings by *Bewick and which related the life of Giles, an orphan farm labourer, throughout the seasons. A vogue for tales of rustic life led to the immense sale of 26,000 copies in under three years, and translations into Italian and French. Bloomfield wrote various other tales in verse between 1802 and 1811, but died in penury.

Bloomsbury Group, the name given to a group of friends who began to meet about 1905–6; its original centre was 46 Gordon Square, Bloomsbury, which became in 1904 the home of V. *Bell and V. *Woolf (both then unmarried). It was to include, amongst others, *Keynes, *Strachey, D. *Garnett, D. Grant, E. M. *Forster, and R. *Fry. This informal association, based on friendship and interest in the arts, derived many of its attitudes from G. E. *Moore's *Principia Ethica*; 'By far the most valuable things . . . are . . . the pleasures of human intercourse and the enjoyment of beautiful objects; . . . it is they . . . that form the rational ultimate end of social progress.' Its members, many of whom were in conscious revolt against the artistic, social, and sexual restrictions of Victorian society, profoundly affected the development of the avant-garde in art and literature in Britain. Bloomsbury was attacked by *Leavis as dilettante and élitist, and its aims and achievements fell temporarily out of favour, but the late 1960s witnessed a great revival of interest and the publication of many critical and biographical studies (notably *Holroyd's two-volume life of Strachey, 1967–8) seeking to reassess Bloomsbury's influence.

Blot in the 'Scutcheon, A, a tragedy in blank verse by R. *Browning, published in 1843 as no. V of *Bells and Pomegranates. It was produced at Drury Lane in 1843, ran for three nights, and caused a final rift between Browning and *Macready, who had rejected Browning's two previous plays and expressed doubts about the success of this one. Browning's friends accused Macready of sabotaging the production, and the quarrel was instrumental in Browning's decision to write no more stage plays. (See also COLOMBE'S BIRTHDAY.)

Set in an aristocratic household of the 18th cent., the play concerns the tragic outcome of an illicit love affair between Mildred Tresham and Lord Henry Mertoun, although the central role is that of Mildred's brother and guardian, Lord Tresham.

BLOUNT, Martha (1690–1762), and her sister Teresa (b. 1688), close friends of *Pope, who met them c.1705. He corresponded with both, and visited them at their family seat of Mapledurham. They were of an old Catholic family. Later he began to address his attentions more exclusively to the less attractive Martha, who was rumoured to be his mistress. He dedicated his Epistle . . . on the Characters of Women (*Moral Essays) to Martha, and also (almost certainly) 'To a Young Lady with the Works of Voiture'; 'To the Same on her Leaving the Town after the Coronation', which describes Zephalinda banished from social delights to 'old-fashion'd halls, dull aunts, and croaking rooks' was probably addressed to Teresa.

Blouzelinda, a shepherdess in *The Shepherd's Week by J. Gay.

BLOW, Dr John (1649–1708), composer and organist, who became organist at Westminster Abbey at the age of 19, and from 1674 was master of the children of the Chapel Royal, where he exerted an important influence and was 'Master to the famous Mr H. Purcell' (then some 15 years old). He was a prolific composer of church music and anthems and his many court odes include settings of *D'Urfey, N. *Tate, *Cowley, and *Dryden. He composed what may be considered the first English opera of which the music has survived, Venus and Adonis (c.1684), which antedates *Purcell's

Dido and Aeneas, for which it was clearly an important model, by about five years. The librettist is unknown.

Blue Bird, The, see MAETERLINCK.

Blue Stocking Circle, Blue Stocking Ladies; an informal group of intelligent, learned, and sociable women, which flourished in London in the second half of the 18th cent. The origin of the name almost certainly lies with the stockings of Benjamin Stillingfleet, who was too poor to possess fine evening clothes, and who came to the circle's evening receptions in his daytime stockings of blue worsted. Someone, traditionally Admiral Boscawen, transformed Stillingfleet's stockings into the collective name of the ladies who held the receptions. The group was of considerable size, but the chief hostesses and female members were Mrs *Vesey, Mrs *Montagu, Mrs *Carter, Mrs *Chapone, Mrs *Boscawen, Mrs *Delany, and, later, H. *More. *Swift wrote to Mrs Delany in 1734, 'A pernicious error prevails . . . that it is the duty of your sex to be fools.' Mrs Vesey, who was the first to try to show the world that many women were capable of rational conversation, held her first reception for men and women of both the fashionable and literary worlds in the early 1750s. As described later by Hannah More, the sole purpose of a Blue Stocking evening was conversation. There were no cards, and no refreshment other than tea, coffee, or lemonade. Learning was to be given free expression, but not be disfigured by pedantry; politics, scandal, and swearing were not allowed. The evenings became so popular that they were held not only by the circle's most famous hostesses but in the houses of Sir Joshua *Reynolds, Mrs *Thrale, the countess of Cork and Orrery, and many others. The company was divided evenly between men and women; among the most famous of the men in regular attendance were *Garrick, Horace *Walpole, Dr *Johnson, *Boswell, Reynolds, S. *Richardson, *Lyttelton, and *Beattie. Dr Johnson, who was largely ignored by the fashionable world, was lionized at any Blue Stocking evening, with duchesses, lords, knights, and ladies, in Boswell's words of 1781, 'four if not five deep around him'. Hannah More wrote a poem, Bas Bleu (1786), describing the charm of Blue Stocking society, and characterizing the chief of her friends. The expression 'Blue Stocking' seems to have been applied in the 18th cent. both affectionately and derisively, but tends now to be used pejoratively to describe a pedantic woman.

Blumine, in Carlyle's *Sartor Resartus, the lady with whom Herr *Teufelsdröckh falls in love (probably based on a Miss Margaret Gordon, whom Carlyle knew and admired before he met Jane Welsh).

BLUNDEN, Edmund Charles (1896–1974), born in London; his family moved soon after to Kent, the countryside of which was to become one of the chief subjects of his poetry. He was educated at *Christ's Hospital and the Queen's College, Oxford. In 1914 he experienced war in the trenches and later wrote poems, such as 'Third Ypres' and 'Report on Experience', which have come to be regarded as among the best of their kind; memories of the war, and guilt at his own survival, became important themes in his later writing. In 1920 he published a small edition of manuscript poems of *Clare, whose work he rescued from obscurity. Volumes of poems largely of rural life (*The Waggoner*, 1920; *The Shepherd*, 1922; and *English Poems*, 1925), together with several slim limited editions, were followed by a spell teaching in Tokyo, and in 1928 by his best-known work, *Undertones of War*, which describes the double destruction of man and nature in Flanders. His first *Collected Poems* appeared in 1930, as did a biography of Leigh *Hunt. In 1931 he produced a collected edition of the work of W. *Owen. Further volumes of his own poems were collected as *Poems 1930–1940*; a study of *Hardy appeared in 1941, and a biography of *Shelley in 1946. After another period in Tokyo he published in 1950 a volume of poems, *After the Bombing*, more contemplative and searching than his previous work. In 1953 he was professor in Hong Kong, and in 1954 produced an edition of the poems of the almost unknown I. *Gurney. He was appointed professor of poetry at Oxford in 1966. Throughout his working life as a teacher and scholar he produced a wide variety of critical and editorial work, with an emphasis on Clare, the Romantics, and his fellow war poets. Although heralded as one of the leaders of the *Georgians, Blunden belonged to no group; his precise natural imagery is, in his best work, fused with his own moods and attitudes, and with those of the countrymen and -women who inhabit his landscapes. After many years in the making, his reputation stands high.

BLUNT, Wilfrid Scawen (1840–1922), poet, diplomat, traveller, anti-imperialist, and Arabist, who married in 1869 Annabella King-Noel, *Byron's granddaughter; his own career as amorist appears to have been modelled on that of Byron, and his first volume of poetry, *Sonnets and Songs by Proteus* (1875, subsequently revised), passionately addresses various women. It was followed by several other volumes of verse, which include love lyrics, evocations of the Sussex countryside, and adaptations from the Arabic. He also wrote and agitated in support of Egyptian, Indian, and Irish independence, thus earning the approval of G. B. *Shaw (see the preface to *John Bull's Other Island*) and a brief spell in an Irish prison which inspired his sonnet sequence *In Vinculis* (1889). His many friends in the literary and political world included Lord *Lytton, *Curzon, *Morris, Lady *Gregory, A. *Meynell, and *Wilde, and in later years he received the homage of *Yeats and *Pound. *My Diaries* appeared in two volumes, 1919–20, and there is a life by Elizabeth Longford, *A Passionate Pilgrimage* (1979).

BLYTHE, Ronald George (1922–   ), author, born in Suffolk, whose works include *The Age of Illusion*

(1963), a study of England between the wars; *Akenfield: Portrait of an English Village* (1969), a study of an East Anglian village, evoked through a series of tape recordings of conversations with its inhabitants, linked by the author's own descriptions and interpretations; *The View in Winter: Reflections on Old Age* (1979), again based on tape-recorded interviews; and various critical and topographical studies.

BLYTON, Enid, see CHILDREN'S LITERATURE.

BOADICEA, or **BONDUCA,** corrupt forms of the name Boudicca, queen of the Iceni in the east of Britain, who led a revolt against the Romans but was finally defeated by Suetonius Paulinus in AD 61 and killed herself. She is the eponymous subject of a play (*Bonduca*) by J. *Fletcher, and of an ode by W. *Cowper.

Boar's Head Inn, the celebrated in connection with *Falstaff. It was in Eastcheap, and according to H. B. Wheatley (*London, Past and Present*, 1891) was 'destroyed in the Great Fire, rebuilt immediately after, and finally demolished . . . in 1831'. It is the subject of a paper in W. *Irving's *Sketch Book*, and provides the theme of one of *Goldsmith's essays, 'A Reverie at the Boar's-head-tavern in Eastcheap' originally published in 1760 in the *British Magazine*, in which the author imagines himself dozing by the fire and transported back in time to the days of Mistress Quickly and her guests.

Bobadill, Captain, the boastful, cowardly soldier in Jonson's *Every Man in His Humour*, a part several times acted by *Dickens in the 1840s.

bob and wheel, a metrical pattern used, for example, in *Sir *Gawain and the Green Knight*, at the end of the strophes of the main narrative. The 'bob' is a short tag with one stress and the following 'wheel' is a quatrain of short lines rhyming a b a b:

> . . . And al waz holȝ in with, nobot an olde cave
> Or a crevisse of an olde cragge, he couþe hit noȝt deme
>   wiþ spelle.
> 'We! Lorde,' quoþ þe gentyle knyȝt,
> 'Wheþer þis be þe grene chapelle?
> Here myȝt aboute mydnyȝt
> þe dele his matynnes tell!'
>   (*Sir Gawain*, ll. 2,182–9)

Here the words 'with spelle' form the 'bob', leading into the 'wheel' of the quatrain.

BOCCACCIO, Giovanni (1313–75), Italian writer and humanist, born at or near Florence, the son of a Florentine merchant. His formative years, from about 1325 until 1340, were spent in Naples, where he began his literary studies and wrote some of his first works. His outlook was greatly conditioned by the aristocratic society in which he moved and especially by his contacts with the Angevin court, but the tradition that he fell in love with Maria d'Aquino, illegitimate daughter of King Robert of Naples, is now discredited. He returned to Florence in 1340, and witnessed the ravages of the Black Death in 1348, described in the introduction to the first day of *The Decameron. From 1350 onwards the municipality of Florence employed him on various diplomatic missions. His friendship with *Petrarch—whom he first met in 1350—gave a powerful impetus to his classical studies, and his house became an important centre of humanist activity. He wrote a life of *Dante and was the first to deliver a course of public lectures on the text of the *Divina commedia (1373–4). Boccaccio's chief works, apart from The Decameron, were: Filocolo, a prose romance embodying the story of *Floris and Blanchefiour; Filostrato, a poem on the story of Troilus and Cressida; Teseida, a poem on the story of Theseus, Palamon, and Arcite, which was translated by *Chaucer in the 'Knight's Tale'; Ameto, a combination of allegory and pastoral romance; the Amorosa visione, an uncompleted allegorical poem; Fiammetta, a psychological romance in prose, in which the woman herself recounts the various phases of her unhappy love; the Ninfale fiesolano, an idyll translated into English (from a French version) by an Elizabethan, John Golburne. He also wrote a number of encyclopaedic works in Latin which were widely read in England: the De Genealogia Deorum; the De Claris Mulieribus; and De Casibus Virorum Illustrium, which was a source book for references to tragedy by Chaucer, by *Lydgate in The Fall of Princes, and for stories in *A Mirror for Magistrates. (See Willard Farnham: The Medieval Heritage of Elizabethan Tragedy, 1956.)

Boccaccio is an important figure in the history of literature, particularly of narrative fiction; among the poets who found inspiration in his works were Chaucer, Shakespeare, *Dryden, *Keats, *Longfellow, and *Tennyson.

BODEL, Jean, see Matter of Britain, France, Rome.

BODLEY, Sir Thomas (1545–1613), was educated at Geneva, whither his parents had fled during the Marian persecution, and subsequently at Magdalen College, Oxford. From 1588 to 1596 he was English diplomatic representative at The Hague. He devoted the rest of his life to founding at Oxford the great Bodleian Library (see Libraries). It was opened in 1602. In 1609 Bodley endowed it with land in Berkshire and houses in London.

BOECE, see Boethius.

BOECE, or **BOËTHIUS,** Hector (?1465–1536), a native of Dundee and a student in the University of Paris, where in the College of Montaigu with *Erasmus he became a professor. In 1498 he was appointed first principal of the newly founded King's College in the University of Aberdeen. He published Latin lives of the bishops of Mortlach and Aberdeen (1522), and a Latin history of Scotland to the accession of James III (1526), the latter including many fabulous narratives, among others that of Macbeth and Duncan, which passed into *Holinshed's chronicles and thence to Shakespeare.

BOEHME, Jacob (1575–1624), a peasant shoemaker of Görlitz in Germany, a mystic. The essential features of his doctrine were that will is the original force, that all manifestation involves opposition, notably of God and nature, that existence emerges from a process of conflict between pairs of contrasted principles (light and darkness, love and anger, good and evil, and so forth) and that in this way the universe is to be seen as the revelation of God. The doctrine of Boehme strongly influenced W. *Law. English translations of Boehme's works, by various hands, appeared in 1645–62. A reprint of the works in English, ed. C. J. Barker, was published in 1910–24.

BOETHIUS, Anicius Manlius Severinus (c.475–525), born at Rome and consul in 510, in favour with the Goth Theodoric the Great who ruled over the city; but he incurred the suspicion of plotting against Gothic rule, was imprisoned, and finally cruelly executed in 525 at Pavia. In prison he wrote the De Consolatione Philosophiae, his most celebrated work and one of the most translated works in history; it was translated into English in the 890s by *Alfred and in almost every generation up to the 18th cent. notably by *Chaucer (as Boece) and by *Elizabeth I into florid, *inkhorn language. It was translated into French by Jean de Meun, and was one of the most influential books of the Middle Ages. It is now generally believed that he was a Christian, though this is rarely explicit in the Consolation, whose philosophy is broadly *Neoplatonic. Its form is 'Menippean Satire', i.e. alternating prose and verse. The verse often incorporates a story told by *Ovid or *Horace, used to illustrate the philosophy being expounded—a relationship which was itself influential on medieval moral narrative. But the influence of the book is found everywhere in the work of Chaucer and his 15th-cent. followers. Before the Middle Ages, Boethius was of most importance for his translations of and commentaries on *Aristotle which provided the main part of what was known of Aristotle before the recovery of most of his writings from Arabic scholars in the 12th cent. The works here transmitted include the Categories, De Interpretatione, the Topics, and the Prior and Posterior Analytics. See C. S. *Lewis, The Discarded Image (1964), pp. 75–90; translation by R. Green (1962); H. R. Patch, The Tradition of Boethius (1935).

Boffin, Mr and Mrs, characters in Dickens's *Our Mutual Friend.

BOHN, Henry George (1796–1884), publisher and bookseller, who amassed a valuable collection of rare books and in 1841 published his Guinea Catalogue, an important early bibliographical work. In 1846 he started his popular Standard Library (followed by the Scientific Library, Classical Library, Antiquarian Library, etc.), the whole series numbering over 600 volumes. He was an accomplished scholar and translated several volumes for his 'Foreign Classics' series, and compiled a *Dictionary of Quotations* (1867).

BOIARDO, Matteo Maria (1441–94), poet and courtier at the Este court in Ferrara. He was one of the finest lyric poets of the Quattrocento, but his reputation rests centrally on his chivalric epic, the unfinished *Orlando innamorato*, which was widely read for centuries in a version in standardized Tuscan Italian by Francesco *Berni.

BOILEAU, (-Despréaux), Nicholas (1636–1711), French critic and poet. A friend of *Molière, *La Fontaine, and *Racine, legislator and model for French *neo-classi-cism at its apogee, he achieved legendary status in his lifetime. His dozen-odd epistles and satires and his *Art Poétique* (1674), a four-canto poem of great wit and elegance, establishing canons of taste and defining principles of composition and criticism, achieved international currency. His *mock-epic *Le Lutrin* (1674, 1683) was widely influential in England. *Dry-den, *Pope, and *Addison regarded him as the supreme post-classical arbiter of literary judgement.

BOITO, Arrigo (1842–1918), Italian composer, poet, and librettist, whose chief importance in musical history is as a producer of librettos for other com-posers. His first attempt, a version of *Hamlet* (1865), showed exceptional sensitivity and ingenuity, and his two Shakespearian texts for *Verdi are among the best examples of the form ever produced. *Otello* (1887) makes some concessions to the operatic convention, particularly in the treatment of Iago, but the courage-ous decision to cut the first act cleverly tightens the dramatic structure and provides a superb operatic opening, as well as reflecting Dr *Johnson's criticism of the original play. *Falstaff* (1893), based on *The Merry Wives of Windsor*, is a still more remarkable achieve-ment: Boito was ruthless in pruning the incoherent plot and in his determination to 'squeeze all the juice out of that enormous Shakespearian orange without letting useless pips slip through into the glass' he reduced Shakespeare's scenes from 23 to 6, while filling out the figure of *Falstaff with passages lifted wholesale from both parts of *Henry IV*.

Boke of Cupide, The, see CLANVOWE.

Boke of the Duchesse, The, see BOOK OF THE DUCHESS, THE.

BOLAND, Eavan (1944–   ), Irish poet born in Dublin. She spent some of her childhood from the age of 15 in London, an experience evoked in several of her poems. She was educated at Trinity College, Dublin, where she read Latin and English. She began to write when young, and her first collection, *New Territory* (1967), was followed by *The War Horse* (1975), *In Her Own Image* (1980), *Night Feed* (1982), *The Journey* (1987), *Outside History* (1990), *In a Time of Violence* (1994), and *The Lost Land* (1998). Her *Collected Poems* was published in 1995. *Object Lessons* (1995) is a prose

work reflecting on women, poetry, and the Irish literary temperament, in which she pays tribute to the powerful early inspiration of *Plath. Her work has a wide thematic range, drawing on classical and Irish myth, on domestic life and maternal experience, informed by a strong visual sense (several of her works are evocations of works of art), bearing witness to the influence of her painter-mother. She writes evocatively and sensuously of flowers and fabrics, of colours and cosmetics, of the 'sexuality, ritual and history' of female lives, but her verse is characteris-tically spare, lyric, and condensed. She has worked in Ireland and England and has been from 1995 a professor of English at Stanford University, California, and more recently director of the Creative Writing Program there.

Bold, John, a character in Trollope's *The Warden*. Mrs Bold, his widow, figures prominently in its sequel, *Barchester Towers*, and in *The Last Chronicle of Barset*, where she is the wife of Dean Arabin.

Bold Stroke for a Wife, A, a comedy by Mrs *Centlivre, produced 1718.
   Colonel Fainall, to win the consent of Obadiah Prim, the Quaker guardian of Anne Lovely, to his marriage with the latter, impersonates Simon Pure, 'a quaking preacher'. No sooner has he obtained it than the true Quaker arrives and proves himself 'the real Simon Pure', a phrase that was long in common use.

Boldwood, Farmer, a character in Hardy's *Far from the Madding Crowd*.

Bolingbroke, Henry, duke of Hereford, son of *John of Gaunt. He deposes *Richard II in Shakespeare's play of that name, and becomes *Henry IV.

BOLINGBROKE, Henry St John, first Viscount (1678–1751), sometimes said to have been educated at Eton and Christ Church, Oxford, though there is no record of his having attended either institution. It appears instead that he received his education at Sheriffhales Academy and at other Dissenting academies, although he subsequently sponsored legislation for the sup-pression of Nonconformist schools. He was elected to the House of Commons in 1701 for the riding of Wootton Basset, Wiltshire, a constituency represented previously by his father and his grandfather. In Parliament he soon became a leading figure in the Tory party; he distinguished himself by his eloquence in defending the interests of country or landed gentlemen in opposition to the financial or monied interests associated with the Whigs. He was appointed secretary of war in 1704 and secretary of state in 1710; his efforts as minister to wage war with France were hindered, he claimed, by the lack of support given Britain by other governments, a complaint given forceful expression by his friend *Swift in *The Conduct of the Allies* (1711). St John was made Viscount Bolingbroke in 1712; he took part in negotiating the Treaty of Utrecht in 1713; and he remained a dominant figure in the Tory party until the death of Queen Anne. After the accession of George I, Bolingbroke fled to France and declared his allegiance to the Pretender, James Stuart; he was convicted of high treason and his peerage was withdrawn. Bolingbroke lived in exile in France for the next decade. In an attempt to justify his conduct in the eyes of his fellow Tories he wrote *A Letter to Sir William Wyndham* in 1717; this long letter was widely circulated, but not published until after his death, in 1753. In France, Bolingbroke read widely and wrote several philosophical essays which reflect the influence of *Locke. These writings provoked the outrage of Dr *Johnson and others when they were published, also posthumously (in 1754), because of their scepticism concerning revealed religion. It has often been supposed that Pope's *Essay on Man* (1734) was inspired by Bolingbroke's philosophical writings, but the influence appears to have been more personal than philosophical; the Renaissance Platonism which informs Pope's 'Essay' has no parallel in Bolingbroke's fragmentary philosophical works.

In 1723 Bolingbroke received a qualified pardon from the king; he was not allowed to resume his seat in the House of Lords, but he returned to England in 1725 to a life of political journalism in the company of Pope, Swift, *Gay, and *Lyttelton. In articles written for the *Craftsman* he attacked the policies and practices of the Walpole administration. He deplored, in particular, the practice of 'influence' or 'corruption' which allowed the administration to maintain power in Parliament by awarding offices, honours, and salaries to their supporters. Bolingbroke denounced this practice as a violation of the British constitution, which required the independence of Parliament from the Crown. He appealed to Walpole and others to set aside their party differences of Whig and Tory and govern in a manner consistent with the constitution. These articles were collected in two volumes as *A Dissertation upon Parties* (1735) and *Remarks on the History of England* (1743). He retired to France in 1735, disenchanted with government and opposition alike in England. From his retreat he addressed letters on the need for an active and united opposition to corruption (*A Letter on the Spirit of Patriotism*, written in 1736) and on the role of a monarch in a free government (*The Idea of a Patriot King*, written in 1738). These essays, like his earlier political writings, reflect the influence of *Machiavelli and the classical republican tradition, particularly in their insistence on the importance of cultivating the public virtues of prudence, eloquence, and the spirit of liberty. The patriotic politician is enjoined to oppose the government in power, not for the satisfaction of his own ambitions, but out of a deeper allegiance to the constitution. The patriot king, like a Machiavellian prince, must be prepared to act, when necessity requires, to bring the government back to its first principles; if corruption has attacked the constitution

itself, the king may be obliged to reconstitute the state or found it anew. This classical republican or civic humanist perspective also appears in Bolingbroke's *Letters on the Study and Use of History*, also written in 1736–8, published in 1752. In this work he denounced contemporary English historical writing as merely antiquarian; he exhorted his readers to find in history illustrations and examples which would inspire men to higher standards of public and private virtue. Like his early philosophical fragments, these writings were circulated among his friends on the understanding they would not be published. His later years, following his return to England in 1743, were filled with acrimony on this account; he found that Pope had printed an edition of *The Idea of a Patriot King* and therefore he decided to publish the two essays on patriotism and a patriot king in 1749, with an introduction in which he denounced the perfidious conduct of his then deceased friend. Pope was defended by *Warburton, who was in turn excoriated by Bolingbroke in *A Familiar Epistle to the Most Impudent Man Living* (1749).

Bolingbroke's many posthumous publications excited intense controversy in the decade which immediately followed his death. The political essays published in his lifetime had a more lasting influence: in England, in the movement for parliamentary reform in the 18th and 19th cents; and, in America, on the ideas of John Adams, Thomas Jefferson, and other publicists and statesmen of the revolutionary era. See S. W. Jackman, *Man of Mercury* (1965); I. Kramnick, *Bolingbroke and his Circle* (1968); H. T. Dickinson, *Bolingbroke* (1970).

BÖLL, Heinrich (1917–85), German author of novels and short stories, mostly on the subject of wartime and post-war Germany. He is highly acclaimed for his realistic portrayal of the social problems of a country recovering from guilt and defeat, for example in *Und sagte kein einziges Wort* (*And Never Said a Word*, 1953) and *Billard um halb zehn* (*Billiards at Half-Past Nine*, 1959). His later works, such as *Gruppenbild mit Dame* (*Group Portrait with Lady*, 1971), *Die verlorene Ehre der Katharina Blum* (*The Lost Honour of Katharine Blum*, 1974), and *Fürsorgliche Belagerung* (*The Safety Net*, 1979), show a concern for topical problems like the hounding of individuals by the gutter press (*Katharina Blum*) and the coming to terms, private and public, with terrorism (*The Safety Net*). Böll received the *Nobel Prize for literature in 1972.

BOLT, Robert Oxton (1924–95), dramatist and screenwriter, born and educated in Manchester. He worked in an insurance office and in the RAF before attending Exeter University: he then became a schoolmaster until his first West End success in 1957 with *Flowering Cherry* (pub. 1958), a Chekhovian domestic drama about an insurance salesman incapable of fulfilling his own dreams of a better life. This was followed by *The Tiger and the Horse* (1960, pub. 1961), reflecting Bolt's own involvement with the campaign for nuclear disarmament, and *A Man for All Seasons* (1960, pub. 1960), his best-known work, based on the life of Sir T. *More. *Vivat, Vivat Regina* (1970) was based on the conflict between *Elizabeth I and *Mary Queen of Scots. A recurrent theme is the conflict between private and public conscience, and although some critics have labelled his works as unadventurous and 'middle-brow', their simplicity and stagecraft have made them highly effective in performance. He worked successfully in film, writing original screenplays and adaptations: these works include *Lawrence of Arabia* (1962), based on the exploits of T. E. *Lawrence, *Ryan's Daughter* (1970), and *The Mission* (1986).

bombast, from 'cotton stuffing', a term used to describe verbose and exaggerated language.

Bombastes Furioso, a farce by W. B. *Rhodes, produced with great success in 1810 and published in the same year, and in an 1830 edition with illustrations by *Cruikshank.

Bombastus, in Butler's *Hudibras* (II. iii), refers to *Paracelsus.

BOND, (Thomas) Edward (1934–), playwright, born in north London, the son of an East Anglian labourer who had moved to London in search of work. Bond was educated at a secondary modern school, where his interest in the theatre was aroused by a performance of *Macbeth; after leaving school early and working at a series of dead-end jobs, he began to write for the theatre. *The Pope's Wedding* was given a Sunday night performance at the *Royal Court in 1962, and in 1965 his grim portrait of urban violence, *Saved, aroused much admiration as well as a ban from the Lord Chamberlain (see CENSORSHIP). Other provocative works followed, including *Early Morning* (1969); *Lear* (1971, pub. 1972), a version of Shakespeare which stresses the play's physical cruelty; *The Sea* (1973), a black country-house comedy; *The Fool* (1975, pub. 1976), based on the life of *Clare; *Restoration* (1981), a Brechtian revolutionary historical drama with songs; and *Summer* (1982), set in a post-war Eastern European state. Bond's theatre is an outspoken indictment of capitalist society; his belief that violence occurs in 'situations of injustice' and that it therefore flourishes as 'a cheap consumer commodity' under capitalism, continues to arouse extreme responses from critics and audiences. Later works include *The War Plays* (1985), about life after a nuclear holocaust, and a play for television, *Olly's Prison* (1992).

Bond, James, the debonair hero of the thrillers of I. *Fleming, and of their celluloid successors, repeatedly engaged, as '007, Licensed to Kill', in daring acts of espionage involving evil foreigners and dangerous and beautiful women, from which he invariably emerges triumphant.

Bondman, The, a tragi-comedy by *Massinger, acted 1623, published 1624.

A decadent and debauched aristocracy in Sicily has to import Timoleon to lead them into battle against the Carthaginians. Cleora, who despises the corruption of her society, is loved by Leosthenes, whose jealousy as he goes off to the wars makes her bind her eyes and swear she will not look at anyone until he returns. In the absence of the army, the oppressed slaves stage a rising under the leadership of the demagogue Marullo, but during the rising Marullo protects Cleora. When the army returns and eventually subdues the rebel slaves, Cleora rejects the suspicious, overbearing Leosthenes and to everyone's horror throws in her lot with the imprisoned leader of the slaves. Fortunately he turns out to be her former suitor Pisander.

This is one of the best of Massinger's tragi-comedies, with some well-developed characters and some fine satirical scenes. It is informed by his contempt for the arrogance of an effete aristocracy, which may well reflect Massinger's opinion of the ethics of the Jacobean court.

Bonduca, a tragedy by J. *Fletcher, probably performed 1613–14, published 1647.

The tragedy is based on the story of *Boadicea, as given by *Holinshed, but the principal character is her cousin, the wise, patriotic, chivalrous, and battle-hardened Caratach (*Caractacus), whose counsel to the vainglorious and impetuous Bonduca is disastrously ignored. After the defeat of the Britons in battle, Bonduca and her daughters defiantly commit suicide; the last act is devoted to the flight of Caratach and his young nephew Hengo, 'a brave boy', who is killed in a scene of much carefully contrived pathos (greatly admired by *Swinburne). Caratach survives, yielding to the 'brave courtesies' of the Romans, to be led off to Rome as a prisoner.

Bon Gaultier, the pseudonym (taken from *Rabelais) under which W. E. *Aytoun and T. *Martin published in 1845 *A Book of Ballads*, a collection of parodies and light poems. Among the authors parodied are *Tennyson (notably 'Locksley Hall', in 'The Lay of the Lovelorn') and E. B. *Browning (in 'The Rhyme of Sir Lancelot Bogle'). Martin also used the pseudonym in his contributions to *Tait's Magazine* and *Fraser's Magazine*.

Boniface, (1) the landlord of the inn in Farquhar's *The Beaux' Stratagem*; whence taken as the generic proper name of innkeepers; (2) in Scott's *The Monastery*, the abbot of Kennaquhair.

BONIFACE, St (680–755), 'the Apostle of Germany', whose original name is said to have been Wynfrith. He was born at Kirton or Crediton in Devon, and educated at a monastery in Exeter and at Nursling near Winchester. He went to Rome in 718 and, with authority from Pope Gregory II, proceeded to Germany, where he preached, established monasteries, and organized the Church. He was killed with his followers at Dokkum in Frisia. See C. H. Talbot (ed. and trans.), *The Anglo-Saxon Missionaries in Germany* (1954).

BONNEFOY, Yves (1923–), French poet and critic, born in Tours, and educated at the Lycée Descartes. He went to Paris in 1944, where he met A. *Breton and became involved with the *surrealist movement. His first major volume, *Du mouvement et de l'immobilité de Douve* (1953; *Of the Motion and Immobility of Douve*) made a profound impression, and was followed by other works of growing power and authority (*Hier régnant désert*, 1958; *Dans le leurre du seuil*, 1975; *Début et fin de la neige*, 1991) and several volumes of critical prose and art history. The poet of stone, snow, death, rain, and water, Bonnefoy writes with a deep, spare, majestic seriousness. He has also translated into French many of the works of Shakespeare.

Booby, Sir Thomas and Lady, and Squire Booby, characters in Fielding's *Joseph Andrews*.

Booker Prize for Fiction, a prize founded (as the Booker-McConnell Prize for Fiction) in 1969, and financed by Booker, part of the Iceland Group plc, awarded annually to the best full-length novel published in the previous 12 months; its aim is to stimulate the kind of public interest aroused in France by the Prix *Goncourt. (See Appendix 3 (*d*) for list of winners.) *Consuming Fictions: The Booker Prize and Fiction in Britain Today* (1996) by Richard Todd discusses the commercial impact of the prize.

book history, or 'the history of the book', an imprecise label used to identify an interdisciplinary field of historical study, the origins of which can conveniently be traced to the publication in France of Lucien Febvre and Henri Jean Martin's *L'Apparition du livre* (1958). The field gained wider recognition, however, with the appearance in 1979 of works by two American scholars, *The Printing Press as an Agent of Change* by Elizabeth Eisenstein and *The Business of Enlightenment: A Publishing History of the Encylopédie* by Robert Darnton; and during the 1980s with the monumental *Histoire de l'édition française*, edited by Martin and Roger Chartier. Though other French and American historians have had a significant impact on the development of the field, book history has from the start traversed many disciplinary and national boundaries, involving an international network of sociologists, anthropologists, economists, art historians, librarians, and bibliographers as well as literary critics and theorists. The influence of the historically rigorous British bibliographical tradition exemplified by such scholars as R. B. McKerrow and Philip Gaskell is particularly noteworthy. Again, though the field is commonly identified with the study of the book, its object is the history of written communication encompassing the production, publication, distribution, control, collection, conservation, reading, and uses of script and print in all media, including manuscripts, pamphlets, periodicals, newspapers, books, and the

Internet. Building on such established areas of enquiry as author–publisher relations, the history of copyright legislation and censorship, bibliography and book design, and the sociology of reading and reader response, book history has opened up new intellectual territories in a wide range of traditional disciplines, asking new questions, developing new methodologies, and identifying new sources. Among historians, it has led to a reassessment of the significance of the document conceived not simply as a source of evidence but as an agent of historical change. In literary studies, it has insisted on the importance of material considerations in textual interpretation. Here book historians share some preoccupations with British Cultural Materialists like R. *Williams and American *New Historicists like Stephen Greenblatt, but their closest allies are the revisionist bibliographers and textual critics of the 1980s, notably Jerome McGann and D. F. McKenzie. Indeed, McKenzie's 'sociology of the text', first announced in the title of his Panizzi lectures in 1985 and intended there to point towards a radical transformation of Anglo-American bibliography, is often treated as a synonym for 'book history'. These various cross-disciplinary movements shaped the emergent field, and in the process initiated a significant reappraisal of such fundamental concepts as 'author', 'reader', and 'text'. Book historians insist, for instance, on the historical importance of authors and readers, while recognizing that cultural intermediaries (printers, binders, publishers, booksellers, reviewers, etc.) have a significant role to play in the overall process of text production, transmission, and the formation of meaning. It follows from this that, for them, the history of successive versions of texts, where old works are put to new uses in new forms, offers primary evidence of cultural change. Starting from the premiss that the book, like any mode of inscription, is a complex system of signs—encompassing the publisher's imprint, typographical layout and design, paper, binding, illustrations, and the text itself—book historians have begun to rethink and rewrite social, political, and cultural history.

Book of Martyrs, see ACTES AND MONUMENTS.

Book of St Albans, The, the last work issued by the press that was set up at St Albans about 1479, soon after *Caxton had begun to print at Westminster. It contains treatises on hawking and heraldry, and one on hunting by Dame Julians Barnes, probably the wife of the holder of the manor of Julians Barnes near St Albans. (The name Juliana Berners, and her identity as abbess of Sopwell in Hertfordshire, are 18th-cent. inventions.) The book is a compilation, not all by one hand. An edition printed by Wynkyn de *Worde in 1496 also included a treatise on 'Fishing with an Angle'. There is an edition by W. Blades (1901).

Book of the Duchess, The, a dream-poem in 1,334 lines by *Chaucer, probably written in 1369, in octosyllabic couplets. It is believed, in accordance with a long-standing tradition (which was questioned in the 1950s), to be an allegorical lament on the death of Blanche of Lancaster, the first wife of *John of Gaunt, who died in Sept. 1369.

The love-lorn poet falls asleep reading the story of Ceix (Seys) and Alcyone and follows a hunting party. He meets a knight in black who laments the loss of his lady. The knight tells of her virtue and beauty and of their courtship, and in answer to the dreamer's question declares her dead. The hunting party reappears and a bell strikes twelve, awakening the poet, who finds his book still in his hand. The poem is one of Chaucer's earliest works, but it has great charm and accomplishment. It is founded on the French tradition of the dream as a vehicle for love poetry. 'A Complaynt of a Loveres Lyfe' by *Lydgate is based on it. For an account of the poem, see A. C. Spearing, *Medieval Dream-Poetry* (1976), 49–73, and B. A. Windeatt, *Chaucer's Dream-Poetry: Sources and Analogues* (1982).

Bookseller, see WHITAKER.

Book Trust, formerly known as the National Book League, an independent charitable organization founded in 1925 as the National Book Council by the Society of Bookmen (Harold Macmillan, *Galsworthy, Stanley Unwin, Maurice Marston, and others); its function is to promote books and reading by working with all branches of the book world (booksellers, publishers, authors, printers, librarians, teachers, etc.). The Council was renamed the National Book League in 1945, and moved in 1980 from its central London premises at 7 Albemarle Street to Book House, Wandsworth. It took the name of Book Trust in 1986. Its services include the Book Information Service, Young Book Trust (the children's division of Book Trust which houses a library of every children's book published in the last two years), and the administration of literary prizes, including the *Booker, the John Llewellyn *Rhys Prize for a writer under 35, and the Orange prize for fiction.

BOOTH, Charles (1840–1916), a successful shipowner, was author of a monumental inquiry into the condition and occupations of the people of London, of which the earlier part appeared as *Labour and Life of the People* in 1889, and the whole as *Life and Labour of the People of London* in 17 volumes (1891–1902). Its object was to show 'the numerical relation which poverty, misery and depravity bear to regular earnings and comparative comfort, and to describe the general conditions under which each class lives'. He was aided in the survey by his wife's cousin Beatrice *Webb, who gives an account of him and his work in *My Apprenticeship* (1926) and credits him with the introduction of the Old Age Pensions Act 1908.

BOOTH, William (1829–1912), popularly known as 'General Booth', the leader of the revivalist movement known from 1878 as the Salvation Army, which sprang from the Christian Mission which he founded in Whitechapel in 1865. Booth, the son of a failed speculative builder in Nottingham, was entirely ignorant of theology, but possessed of eloquence, fervour, and a sense of the practical and spiritual needs of the poor which made him a powerful force in social and religious life. G. B. Shaw's *Major Barbara* (perf. 1905) was based on first-hand knowledge of the Salvation Army.

Booth, William, the hero of Fielding's *Amelia*.

Boots Library, a circulating library (see LIBRARIES, CIRCULATING) established at the end of the 19th cent. by Nottingham businessman and philanthropist Jesse Boot (1850–1931). Unlike *Mudie's it catered largely for provincial and suburban subscribers, and by the mid-1930s was the largest of its kind, with over 400 branches. The stock was categorized as 'Light Romance', 'Family Stories', etc., and librarians were trained to make suggestions in line with the taste of their readers. *Betjeman in 'In Westminster Abbey' (1940) wrote

> Think of what our Nation stands for,
> Books from Boots, and country lanes . . .

See also Nicola Beauman, *A Very Great Profession; The Woman's Novel 1914–39* (1983).

Borderers, The, a verse drama by *Wordsworth, set on the borders of England and Scotland during the reign of Henry III. It was composed 1796–7, and published in its final draft in 1842. It has many echoes of Shakespeare (of *King Lear* in particular), and also of *Schiller's *The Robbers*, but it also represents an important stage in Wordsworth's mastery of the medium of blank verse, and expresses his struggles with ideas of liberty, law, and 'Man's intellectual empire' inspired by the French Revolution. Marmaduke (Mortimer in earlier texts), the leader of a band of outlaws, is falsely persuaded by Oswald (earlier named Rivers) that the old blind Baron Herbert is an impostor about to procure the seduction of his own daughter; Marmaduke hesitates to kill the old man, but is nevertheless responsible for his death upon a barren heath. Oswald, who had presented murder as a liberating act, is killed by the band of outlaws, and Marmaduke, who has too late discovered his victim's innocence, embraces a life of wandering and exile.

Border Minstrelsy, see MINSTRELSY OF THE SCOTTISH BORDER.

BORGES, Jorge Luis (1899–1986), Argentinian writer, born in Buenos Aires and educated (1914–18) in Geneva; one of his grandmothers was English and from an early age he read English literature (notably the works of *Wilde, *De Quincey, R. L. *Stevenson, and *Chesterton). After some time in Spain, where he was associated with the Spanish literary movement *ultraísmo* (a form of Spanish *Expressionism), he returned in 1921 to Argentina, where for a time he championed the ultraist cause, partly through the periodical *Proa*. His first volume of poetry, *Fervor de Buenos Aires* (1923), was followed by many other volumes of verse and essays, but he is best known for his short stories, of which the first volume, *Historia universal de la infamia* (1935; *A Universal History of Infamy*), has been acclaimed as a landmark in Latin American literature and the first work of *magic realism. Originally published in an Argentinian evening paper, the stories recount the lives of real and fictitious criminals (some ascribed also to fictitious authors), and are an early illustration of Borges's enduring preoccupation with the relationship of fiction, truth, and identity; with violence; and with the puzzles of detective fiction. (With his friend Adolfo Bioy Casares he collaborated in several tales of crime and detection.) Subsequent collections of short stories included *Ficciones* (1945) and *El Aleph* (1949); the publication of a selection entitled *Labyrinths* in Paris in 1953 established his international reputation, and it was translated into English in 1962. Many of his best-known stories deal with the cyclical nature of time; they are themselves labyrinthine in form, metaphysical in their speculations, and often dreamlike in their endlessly reflected facets of reality and arcane knowledge. Borges worked as a librarian for some years in a municipal library (1938–46) and some of his stories (e.g. 'The Library of Babel' and 'Tlön, Uqbar, Orbis Tertius') take on the quality of a bibliographer's nightmare. Borges was relieved of this post for political reasons, but with the overthrow of the Peronist regime he became in 1955 the director of the National Library of Buenos Aires. By the 1950s, however, his eyesight was failing, and in his last years he was almost totally blind; in later years he wrote more poetry than prose, but a late collection of stories, *El informe de Brodie* (*Doctor Brodie's Report*), appeared in 1971.

BORGIA, Cesare (?1475–1507), favourite son of Rodrigo *Borgia (Pope Alexander VI) and brother of Lucrezia *Borgia. Notorious for his crimes, he was at the same time a man of great military capacity and one of the early believers in the unity of Italy. His career is said to have inspired much of *Machiavelli's *Il principe*. His power came to an end after his father's death; he fled to the court of Navarre, and was killed in the service of the king.

BORGIA, Lucrezia (1480–1519), daughter of Rodrigo (below) and sister of Cesare Borgia (above). She was married when very young to Don Gasparo de Procida, but the marriage was annulled by her father and she was betrothed in 1492 to Giovanni Sforza. This engagement was also cancelled by her father for political reasons, and Lucrezia was married to Alfonso of Aragon, the illegitimate son of Alfonso II of Naples. This marriage, which eased relations between her father (Pope Alexander VI) and Naples, ended with the murder of her husband in 1500, probably on the orders of her brother. She subsequently married Alfonso

d'Este, heir to the duke of Ferrara, being at the time 22. She became duchess of Ferrara in 1505, and thereafter presided over the court, which under her patronage became a centre for artists, poets, and men of learning, such as *Ariosto, *Titian, and *Aldus Manutius.

BORGIA, Rodrigo (1431–1503), Pope Alexander VI, a Spaniard by birth, and the father of Cesare and Lucrezia *Borgia; he was elected to the pontificate in 1492. His policy was mainly directed towards the recovery of the Papal States and the unscrupulous promotion of the interests of his own family, though he was also a generous patron of the arts. The combination of ruthless dynastic ambition and a voracious sexual appetite gave him a reputation throughout Europe as the pope whose personal immorality was unprecedented even by the normal standards of the Curia. The tradition that the Borgias possessed the secret of a mysterious and deadly poison has not been substantiated by historical research, but in England it captivated the Elizabethan imagination and is mentioned many times in the literature of the period. *The Divils Charter* by B. *Barnes is a *Machiavellian drama based on 'the Life and Death of Pope Alexander the Sixt', taken from *Guicciardini.

BORON, Robert de, a 12th–13th-cent. French poet who composed a trilogy (*Joseph d'Arimathie* in 3,514 lines; *Merlin*, a fragment of 502 lines; and *Perceval*) in which he developed the early history of the Holy *Grail in Britain, linking it with the Arthurian tradition. The works are dated c.1202 by P. Le Gentil (in *Arthurian Literature in the Middle Ages*, ed. R. S. Loomis, 1959, ch. 19). See D. C. Cabeen (ed.), *Critical Bibliography of French Literature* (i, 1952, by U. T. Holmes).

Borough, The, a poem by *Crabbe published 1810, in twenty-four 'letters', describing, with much penetration and accuracy of detail, the life and characters of the church, the school, the professions, the surroundings, the workhouse, the prisons, the sea, and other aspects of the town of Aldeburgh, Suffolk. The work, which is uneven in quality, took eight years to complete. Two of the most successful tales, concerning *Peter Grimes and *Ellen Orford, were combined in *Britten's opera *Peter Grimes* (1945).

BORROW, George Henry (1803–81), educated at Edinburgh High School and at Norwich. He was articled to a solicitor, but adopted literature as a profession. During his apprenticeship he edited *Celebrated Trials, and Remarkable Cases of Criminal Jurisprudence* (1825), an impressive piece of hack-work undertaken for a London publisher, and then travelled through England, France, Germany, Russia, Spain, and in the East, studying the languages of the countries he visited (though there is some suggestion that he exaggerated both his linguistic achievements and the extent of his travels). In Russia and Spain he acted as agent for the British and Foreign Bible Society. Finally he married a well-to-do widow and settled near Oulton Broad in

Suffolk. He published a number of books based in part on his own life, experiences, and travels: *The Zincali, or An Account of the Gypsies in Spain* (1841), *The Bible in Spain* (1843), *Lavengro* (1851), *The Romany Rye* (1857), and *Wild Wales* (1862). His works have a peculiar picaresque quality, and contain vivid portraits of the extraordinary personages he encountered; his own personality also emerges with much force. Though physically robust and energetic he had suffered since his youth from bouts of manic depression that he referred to as 'the Horrors' which often temporarily frustrated him. In *Lavengro, The Romany Rye*, and *The Bible in Spain* fact is inextricably combined with fiction; and *Lavengro* he himself describes as 'a dream partly of study, partly of adventure'. The standard biography is by W. I. Knapp (2 vols, 1899); see also D. Williams, *A World of His Own* (1982).

Bors de Ganys, Sir, in *Malory, king of Gannes, brother of Lionel and Ban, and cousin of *Launcelot. He was one of the three successful knights in the Quest of the Grail, after which he became a hermit at Glastonbury. He is sometimes confused with his father, King Bors of Gaul.

BOSCÁN DE ALMOGÁVER, Juan (c.1487–1542), a Spanish poet born at Barcelona, who did much to introduce Italian verse forms into the poetry of his country. He was an intimate friend of another Spanish poet, *Garcilaso de la Vega, and the two are mentioned together by Byron in *Don Juan* (i. 95).

BOSCAWEN, Mrs Frances (1719–1805), an eminent *Blue Stocking hostess, and the wife of Admiral Boscawen, who is traditionally supposed to have transformed Benjamin Stillingfleet's blue stockings into a name for his wife's learned and literary female friends. Hannah *More greatly admired Mrs Boscawen, finding her 'polite, learned, judicious and humble'; and in her poem *Bas Bleu* (1786) she accords her, with Mrs *Vesey and Mrs *Montagu, the 'triple crown' as the most successful of the Blue Stocking hostesses.

Bosola, a character in Webster's *The Duchess of Malfi*.

BOSSUET, Jacques Bénigne (1627–1704), French preacher. His reputation as the greatest French orator rests on his sermons, pronounced chiefly in the course of his duties as bishop of Condom and bishop of Meaux, and especially on his funeral orations, celebrating many of the greatest figures at the court of Louis XIV, including Henrietta Maria, wife of Charles I, Marie Thérèse, wife of Louis XIV, and the Grand Condé. His style was usually simple, direct, and dignified, but capable of rising to grandeur when dealing with the mysteries of mortality and faith. A dogmatist on principle (he defined a heretic as 'he who has an opinion'), he was involved in a number of notorious disputes with Protestants. These had some effect on English religious controversies of the time.

Bostonians, The, a novel by H. *James, published 1886.

Basil Ransom, a young lawyer fresh from Mississippi and the humiliations of the Civil War, has come north in search of a career. In Boston he calls on his cousin Olive Chancellor and her widowed sister, the girlishly arch Mrs Luna. Olive, a wealthy chill feminist, introduces him to a reformist group (acidly portrayed by James) at the house of the selfless and well-meaning Miss Birdseye. Selah Tarrant, a charlatan faith-healer and showman, is presenting his young daughter Verena. She is an 'inspirational' speaker, and while Basil Ransom is attracted by her prettiness Olive is intensely moved by the girl's performance, and sees her as a valuable instrument for the cause. She removes Verena from her unacceptable parents and sets about her education. Out for revenge rather than equality, she attempts to instil in the girl her own distrust and loathing for men. Ransom, contemptuous of reform and reformers, opens a battle for possession of Verena. Olive, full of hatred for Ransom and now passionately attached to the girl, tries to freeze him out. But Verena is now playing a double game. Attracted by Ransom and frightened by Olive's intensity, she has begun to doubt her role. As she is about to make her first public appearance Verena, schooled to be the banner of the suffragette movement, is carried off by Ransom, a mediocre young man who believes that woman's highest achievement is to be agreeable to men.

BOSWELL, James (1740–95), the eldest son of Alexander Boswell, Lord Auchinleck (pron. Affleck), a Scottish judge who took his title from the family estate in Ayrshire. He reluctantly studied law at Edinburgh, Glasgow, and Utrecht, his ambition being directed towards literature and politics, as was manifested by numerous pamphlets and verses which he published anonymously from 1760 onwards, many of them also expressing his love of the theatre. He was in London in 1762–3, where he met Dr *Johnson on 16 May 1763; he then went to Holland (where he met and courted *Zélide) and on through Europe to Italy. His extraordinary persistence in pursuit of the great achieved meetings with *Rousseau and *Voltaire; Rousseau inspired him with zeal for the cause of Corsican liberty, and he visited Corsica in 1765, establishing a lifelong friendship with General Paoli. On his return to Scotland he 'passed advocate' and was to practise there and in England for the rest of his life. His first substantial work, *An Account of Corsica* (1768), was followed in December of the same year by a book of essays 'in favour of the brave Corsicans' which he edited; he was to remain loyal to this cause, creating a sensation by his appearance at the Shakespeare Jubilee in 1769 in Corsican dress. In this year he married his cousin Margaret Montgomerie, after a lengthy succession of attempted courtships and successful philanderings with others; she bore him several children. Although his family remained in Scotland, Boswell longed for the diversions of London, which he visited as frequently as possible, spending much time with Johnson, whose biography he already projected. They made their celebrated tour of Scotland and the Hebrides in 1773, in which year Boswell was elected a member of the *Club. From 1777 to 1783 he contributed a series of essays, as 'The Hypochondriack', to the *London Magazine, on such subjects as drinking (a constant preoccupation), diaries, memory, and hypochondria. In 1782 his father (with whom his relationship had been complex and at times unhappy) died, and Boswell inherited the estate. His last meeting with Johnson was in 1784; his *Journal of a Tour of the Hebrides* appeared in 1785 after Johnson's death. The rest of Boswell's life was devoted to an unsuccessful pursuit of a political career (he was recorder of Carlisle, 1788–90) and to the immense task of assembling materials for and composing his life of Johnson, a labour in which he was encouraged by *Malone. *The Life of Samuel *Johnson Lld* appeared in 1791. Boswell's volatility, his promiscuity, his morbid fits of depression, his ambitions, and his emotional involvement in the affairs of his clients are frankly revealed in his letters (notably to his two old university friends, William Johnson Temple and John Johnston) and in private papers and journals, many of which were discovered at Malahide Castle and Fettercairn House; they cover his continental tour as well as his London visits, and have been edited, principally by F. A. Pottle, from 1928 in various volumes.

Bothie of Tober-na-Vuolich, The, see CLOUGH.

BOTOLPH, or **BOTULF, St** (d. 680), an Englishman who studied in Germany and became a Benedictine monk. He founded a monastery at an unidentified place in East Anglia called Icanhoh (perhaps near the present town of Boston), which was destroyed by the Danes. He died, with a high reputation for sanctity, at Botolphstown (Boston). Four churches in London are dedicated to him, and he is also commemorated in Botolph's Lane and Botolph's Wharf.

Botteghe oscure (literally 'dark shops'), a review edited in Rome by Marguerite Caetani, 1949–60, which established itself as a leading international periodical. The contributors, who included Dylan *Thomas, *Auden, *Bellow, *Grass, *Camus, *Montale, etc., were published in their own language.

BOTTICELLI, Sandro (c.1445–1510), Florentine painter, whose most famous paintings, *La primavera* (c.1477–8) and *The Birth of Venus* (c.1485–90) are complex allegories that reflect the humanist and classical interests of the time. He also painted many altarpieces and portraits. His later works, perhaps in response to the teachings of *Savonarola, are wilder and more dramatic. At the time of his death Botticelli's decorative style had become old-fashioned, and he is only rarely mentioned again before the 19th cent. when his popularity soared. *Pater's essay 'Sandro Botticelli' (1870) dwells on his sense of mystery and sadness—on the brooding faces of his 'peevish-looking' Madonnas, and on the cold light and grey water of *The Birth of Venus*. Pater's descriptions opened the eyes of the English decadents to the painter's enigmatic beauty, and he became a cult figure.

Bottom, Nick, the weaver in Shakespeare's *Midsummer Night's Dream*. The name had no anatomical connotations in Shakespeare's time, but referred, here, to the clew on which thread was wound. A *'droll', *The Merry Conceited Humours of Bottom the Weaver*, adapted from Shakespeare's play, was printed in 1661.

BOTTOMLEY, Gordon (1874–1948), a bank clerk who became a prolific and successful poet and man of letters. His first volume of poems, *The Mickle Drede*, appeared in 1896, and his work was included in E. *Marsh's first volume of *Georgian Poetry* in 1912. He attempted the epic and sublime, as well as the lyric, and his *Poems of Thirty Years* (1925) show the marked influence of *Shelley. He hoped to promote a poetic revival in the theatre; of his poetic plays *King Lear's Wife* (1915) and *Gruach* (1921) were the most successful.

BOUCICAULT (originally Boursiquot), Dion(ysius Lardner) (1820–90), playwright, born in Dublin and educated at University College School, London. He began his career as an actor and achieved great success with his comedy *London Assurance* (1841), written under the pseudonym of Lee Morton. He subsequently wrote and adapted some 200 plays, including *The Corsican Brothers* (1852, from the French), *The Poor of New York* (1857), *The Colleen Bawn; or The Brides of Garryowen* (1860), *Arra-na-Pogue; or The Wicklow Wedding* (1864), and *The Shaughraun* (1874). One of the dominant figures of 19th-cent. theatre, his career was marked by spectacular successes and reverses, and he was responsible for important innovations, such as the introduction of a royalty from plays and copyright for dramatists in America. With the rise of realism and the emergence of *Ibsen and G. B. *Shaw, his work fell out of fashion, but it influenced *O'Casey, who praised his 'colour and stir', and some of his plays have been successfully revived. There is a life by R. Fawkes, 1979.

BOUDICCA, see BOADICEA.

BOUILLON, Godefroi de (Godfrey of Bouillon) (d. 1100), duke of Lower Lorraine, leader of the First Crusade and proclaimed 'Protector of the Holy Sepulchre' in 1099. He appears in Tasso's *Jerusalem Delivered* and in Scott's *Count Robert of Paris*.

Bounderby, Josiah, a character in Dickens's *Hard Times*.

Bountiful, Lady, a character in Farquhar's *The Beaux' Stratagem*.

Bounty, The Mutiny and Piratical Seizure of H.M.S., by Sir J. Barrow, published 1831.

HMS *Bounty*, which had been sent to the South Sea Islands to collect bread fruit trees, left Tahiti early in 1789 for the Cape of Good Hope and the West Indies. On 28 April of that year Fletcher Christian and others seized Lt Bligh, the commander, and placed him with 18 loyal members of the crew in an open boat, which they cast adrift. The boat eventually reached Timor. Meanwhile the *Bounty* sailed east with 25 of the crew to Tahiti, where 16 were put ashore. These men were later arrested and many of them were drowned when HMS *Pandora* sank. Fletcher Christian and eight of his companions, together with some Tahitians, went on and settled on Pitcairn Island. There they founded a colony, of which Alexander Smith (now calling himself John Adams) became the leader, and which was eventually taken under the protection of the British government. These famous events form part of Byron's poem *'The Island', and have been the subject of books and films.

boustrophedon, from the Greek words meaning 'ox turning', written alternately from right to left and left to right, like the course of the plough in successive furrows, as in various ancient inscriptions in Greek and other languages.

bouts-rimés 'The bouts-rimez were the favourites of the French nation for a whole age together . . . They were a List of Words that rhyme to one another, drawn up by another Hand, and given to a Poet, who was to make a poem to the Rhymes in the same Order that they were placed upon the list.' Addison, *Spectator*, No. 60.

BOWDLER, Thomas (1754–1825), MD of Edinburgh, who published in 1818 his *Family Shakespeare*, dedicated to the memory of Mrs *Montagu; she had published a much respected *Essay on the Writings and Genius of Shakespeare* in 1769. He may have been aided in this enterprise by his sister Henrietta Maria Bowdler (1754–1830), who also published poems and sermons, and it has been argued that she was the prime mover, but the extent of her collaboration has not been firmly established. As is shown by the prefaces, the Bowdlers' love and admiration of Shakespeare were profound; nevertheless they believed that nothing 'can afford an excuse for profaneness or obscenity; and if these could be obliterated, the transcendant genius of the poet would undoubtedly shine with more unclouded lustre'. Profanity they found only a small problem; 'God' as an expletive is always replaced by 'Heaven', and other brief passages and exclamations cut. But they confessed to enormous trouble with the endless indecency scattered throughout the plays. Their method was to cut, not to substitute; they in fact added almost nothing except prepositions and conjunctions. But the cutting is severe; for instance, Juliet's speech of longing for Romeo, 'Gallop apace . . .', is cut from 30 lines to 15, and many of her Nurse's comments have gone; in Lear's speech of

madness, 'Aye, every inch a king . . .', 22 lines of verse are cut to seven. Bowdler found *1* and *2 *Henry IV* 'the most difficult of all the histories for family reading'. Doll Tearsheet is entirely removed, but Bowdler apologizes that even with the omission of many obscenities 'perfect delicacy of sentiment' could not be achieved. **Measure for Measure* was found to contain so many indecent expressions interwoven with the text that they could do nothing better than to print, with a warning, *Kemble's version for the stage. Failure is admitted with *Othello* ('unfortunately little suited to family reading'), and it is recommended that it be transferred 'from the parlour to the cabinet'.

The work was extremely successful, and went through many editions. Similar excisions were inflicted on Gibbon's *Decline and Fall*. With the verb 'to bowdlerize', or expurgate, 'Dr Bowdler' joins the small band of those who have given their names to the language.

BOWEN, Elizabeth Dorothea Cole (1899–1973), Anglo-Irish novelist and short story writer. Born in Dublin, she spent much of her childhood at the family home in Co. Cork which she inherited in 1930 and described in *Bowen's Court* (1942). In 1923 she published her first collection of short stories, *Encounters*, and married Alan Cameron. They lived for ten years in London, vividly evoked in many of her works; her skill in describing landscape, both urban and rural, and her sensitivity to changes of light and season are distinguishing features of her prose. Her novels include *The Hotel* (1927), *The Last September* (1929), *The House in Paris* (1935), *A World of Love* (1955), and *Eva Trout* (1969). The best-known are probably *The Death of the Heart* (1938) and *The Heat of the Day* (1949). The first (which clearly demonstrates her debt to H. *James) is the story of Portia, a 16-year-old orphan whose dangerous innocence threatens the precarious, sophisticated London lives of her half-brother Thomas and his wife Anna, and who is herself threatened by her love for the glamorously despairing young Eddy, a young admirer of Anna; the second centres on the tragic wartime love affair of Stella Rodney and Robert Kelway, and their reactions to the revelation, through the sinister Harrison, that the latter is a spy. The war inspired many of Elizabeth Bowen's best short stories, including 'Mysterious Kôr' (*Penguin *New Writing*, 1944); A. *Wilson in his introduction to her *Collected Stories* (1980) praised her as one of the great writers of the blitz. Other stories (e.g. the title story of *The Cat Jumps*, 1934) reveal subtle deployment of the supernatural. She writes most confidently of the upper middle and middle classes, but within that social range her perceptions of change are acute; her works already strike the reader with a powerful sense of period, through their accurate detail and keen response to atmosphere. See V. *Glendinning, *Elizabeth Bowen: Portrait of a Writer* (1977).

BOWEN, Marjorie, the best-known pseudonym of

Gabrielle Margaret Vere Campbell (1886–1952), prolific writer of historical novels, children's stories, etc.; G. *Greene in his essay 'The Lost Childhood' (1951, included in *Collected Essays*, 1969) claims that her first novel, *The Viper of Milan* (1906), so affected his imagination that it inspired him to be a writer and supplied him 'once and for all with a subject'.

Bower of Bliss, the, in Spenser's *Faerie Queene* (II. xii), the home of *Acrasia, demolished by Sir *Guyon.

Bowge of Courte, The, an allegorical poem in seven-lined stanzas by *Skelton, satirizing court life (*c.*1498). The word 'bowge' is a corrupt form of 'bouche', meaning court rations, from the French 'avoir bouche à cour', to have free board at the king's table.

BOWLES, Caroline Anne (1786–1854), poet and prose writer, born near Lymington, Hampshire, the only child of Captain Charles Bowles (East Indian Co., retired) and his wife Anne. Educated at home, Caroline grew up among adults in a largely female household where her writing and drawing accomplishments were encouraged from an early age. Left alone and impoverished at the age of 30, she sought advice about publication from *Southey, thus beginning a correspondence (pub. 1880) and friendship lasting 20 years until their marriage in 1839 after the death of his first wife. Before this she published five volumes of verse, two of prose sketches (*Chapters on Churchyards*, 1829) and one of mixed genre (*Solitary Hours*, 1826). Her finest achievement is her blank verse autobiography, *The Birth-Day* (1836), which was much admired by the Wordsworth household, but her work also encompassed comedy, satire, and social protest. Southey acknowledged her superior poetic gift, but owing to her insistence on anonymous publication her reputation was never consolidated in her lifetime. Her *Poetical Works* appeared posthumously in 1867.

BOWLES, Jane, née Auer (1917–73), wife of Paul *Bowles, chiefly remembered as a writer for her short novel *Two Serious Ladies* (1943), an exotic, disjointed, staccato work about two contrasted lives. Her play *In the Summer House* (perf. 1953) was praised by T. *Williams as 'elusive and gripping'. Her *Collected Works* were published in 1984: *Everything is Nice* (1989) adds some previously uncollected short fiction. The story of her obsessional and self-destructive life is told in *A Little Original Sin* (1981) by Millicent Dillon.

BOWLES, Paul (1910–99), American writer, born in New York, who married Jane Auer (see above) in 1938. In 1948 they went to Tangier, where they lived intermittently for the rest of their lives, and where they became familiar landmarks in the expatriate gay community, and points of call for many literary visitors in search of the exotic. His works, most of which are set in Morocco, include *The Sheltering Sky* (1949), 'an adventure story in which the adventures take place on two planes simultaneously: in the actual desert and in the inner desert of the spirit'. *Let it Come Down* (1952) describes the disintegration of bank clerk Nelson Dyer in Tangier: *The Spider's House* (1955) is set in Fez and *Up above the World* (1966) follows a doomed American couple in central America. *Without Stopping* (1972) is an autobiography.

BOWLES, William Lisle (1762–1850), educated at Westminster and Trinity College, Oxford, vicar of Bremhill and a canon of Salisbury. He is remembered chiefly for his *Fourteen Sonnets* published in 1789. His work was greatly admired by the youthful *Coleridge (who in 1796 dedicated his *Poems* to Bowles), as well as by *Lamb, *Southey, and many others. *Byron, however, describes him as 'the maudlin prince of mournful sonneteers', and was roused to further anger by Bowles's strictures on *Pope, of whom Bowles published an edition in 1806.

Bowling, Tom, (1) a character in Smollett's *Roderick Random*; (2) see DIBDIN, C.

BOWRA, (Sir Cecil) Maurice (1898–1971), scholar and critic, from 1922 a fellow and from 1938 until 1970 warden of Wadham College, Oxford, where his wit, hospitality, and energy made him a legendary figure and earned him the gratitude and friendship of many, including *Connolly and *Betjeman; Betjeman in *Summoned by Bells* recalls the 'learning lightly worn' and 'The fusillade of phrases. "I'm a man | More dined against than dining."' Bowra published various works on and translations of Greek literature, notably *Pindar, and edited *The Oxford Book of Greek Verse in Translation* (1938) and two books of Russian verse in translation (1943, 1948): *The Heritage of Symbolism* (1943) and *The Creative Experiment* (1949) are both commentaries on modern literature.

Bowzybeus, a drunken swain, the subject of the last pastoral in *The Shepherd's Week* by J. Gay.

Box and Cox, a *farce by J. M. *Morton, adapted from two French vaudevilles, published 1847.

Box is a journeyman printer, Cox a journeyman hatter. Mrs Bouncer, a lodging-house keeper, has let the same room to both, taking advantage of the fact that Box is out all night and Cox out all day to conceal from each the existence of the other. Discovery comes when Cox unexpectedly gets a holiday. Indignation follows, and complications connected with a widow to whom both have proposed marriage; and finally a general reconciliation. It was adapted into an operetta, *Cox and Box*, by Sir Francis Cowley *Burnand.

Boy and the Mantle, The, a ballad included in Percy's *Reliques, which tells how a boy visits King Arthur's court at 'Carleile', and tests the chastity of the ladies there by means of his mantle, a boar's head, and a golden horn. Sir Cradock's (Cradoc's) wife alone successfully undergoes the ordeal.

Boy Bishop, one of the choirboys formerly elected at the annual 'Feast of Boys' in certain cathedrals, to walk in a procession of the boys to the altar of the Innocents or of the Holy Trinity, and perform the office on the eve and day of the Holy Innocents, the boys occupying the canons' stalls in the cathedral during the service. Provision for this is made in the Sarum Office (see E. K. *Chambers, *The Mediaeval Stage*, App. M). The custom dates from the 13th cent. and lasted until the Reformation. Boy Bishops were appointed also in religious houses and in schools.

BOYD, William Andrew Murray (1952–   ), novelist, born in Accra, Ghana. Educated at Gordonstoun and the universities of Nice and Glasgow and at Jesus College, Oxford. From 1980 to 1983 Boyd was a lecturer in English at St Hilda's College, Oxford. *A Good Man in Africa* (1981) is a comic tale of diplomatic life in a minor West African posting somewhat in the manner of Kingsley *Amis. A collection of short stories, *On the Yankee Station*, appeared in 1981 and was followed by *An Ice-Cream War* (1982), a serio-comic tale set in East Africa during the First World War which won the John Llewellyn *Rhys Memorial Prize. *Stars and Bars* (1984), which was also adapted for television, and *The New Confessions* (1987), the sadly comic autobiography of a self-styled genius, consolidated Boyd's reputation as an accomplished storyteller with an instinct for inventive comedy. *Brazzaville Beach* (1990) is again set in Africa, and explores the theme of the origins of human and animal violence. *The Blue Afternoon* (1993) tells the story, set in 1936, of a young female architect who meets an enigmatic stranger claiming to be her father. *Armadillo* (1998) recounts the adventures in late 20th-cent. London of a Romany-born loss adjuster and *Any Human Heart* (2002) takes the form of journals written by a fictitious 20th-cent. novelist. Boyd has written television screenplays, two of which—*Good and Bad at Games* and *Dutch Girls*—were published together as *School Ties* (1985). *The Destiny of Nathalie 'X'* (1995) is a further collection of stories.

BOYDELL, John (1719–1804), engraver and publisher, who with his nephew Josiah Boydell opened their Shakespeare Gallery in Pall Mall in 1789. Originally it contained 34 paintings of subjects from Shakespeare, by many of the most famous artists of the day, including J. *Wright of Derby (Prospero's Cell); *Fuseli (scenes from *A Midsummer Night's Dream*, *Macbeth*, and *Hamlet*) and Joshua *Reynolds (Henry VI at the deathbed of Beaufort). The collection was later expanded, and many engravings of the works were sold.

BOYER, Abel (1667–1729), a French Huguenot who settled in England in 1689. He published a yearly register of political and other occurrences, and a periodical, *The Political State of Great Britain* (1711–29). He also brought out an English–French and a French–English dictionary, a *History of William III* (3 vols, 1702–3) and a *History of the Life and Reign of Queen Ann* (1722). He translated into English the memoirs of *Gramont (1714) and *Racine's *Iphigénie*.

BOYLAN, Clare (1948–   ), Dublin-born novelist, journalist, and short story writer. Her first novel, *Holy Pictures* (1983), is a tragi-comic family story set in the 1920s seen through the eyes of young Nan Cantwell: in the same year appeared her first volume of stories, *A Nail in the Head*. Other novels include *Last Resorts* (1984), a holiday romance; *Black Baby* (1988), a satiric comedy about a child sold to a woman by nuns; *Home Rule* (1992), which traces the earlier life of Nan Cantwell's grandparents in the 1890s; and *Room for a Single Lady* (1997). Boylan's prose is lively, witty, at times lyrical, and she has a particular gift for recalling the memories of childhood and the delights and embarrassments of erotic adventure. Other volumes of stories include *Concerning Virgins* (1989), *That Bad Woman* (1995), *The Stolen Child* (1996).

BOYLE, John, fifth earl of Orrery (1707–62), son of Charles Boyle (1676–1731), and an intimate friend of *Swift, *Pope, and Dr *Johnson. His *Remarks on the Life and Writings of Dr Jonathan Swift* were written in a series of letters to his son Hamilton at Christ Church, Oxford, and published in 1751. These letters give a critical account of Swift's character, his life, his relations with Stella and Vanessa, and his friendship with Pope and others—*Gay, P. *Delany, and Dr Young, 'his intimate friends, whom he loved sincerely'. Orrery discusses Swift's work: poetry, political writings, letters, *Gulliver's Travels, *A Tale of a Tub*, etc. Although he deplores Swift's misanthropy 'which induced him peevishly to debase mankind, and even to ridicule human nature itself' (Letter VI), he says that the character at which Swift aimed and which he deserved was that of 'an enemy to tyranny and oppression in any shape whatever' (Letter XVII).

BOYLE, Robert (1627–91), 14th child of Richard Boyle, first earl of Cork, educated at Eton and privately. While touring in Switzerland as a teenager he experienced a conversion, which caused him to devote the rest of his life to science and good works. He eschewed marriage, wrote prolifically, and became the dominant figure in English science between F. *Bacon and I. *Newton. Robert Hooke was his technical assistant in experiments on air which led to the first formulation of 'Boyle's Law'. Boyle's 'corpuscularianism', a rendering of the mechanical philosophy, exercised great influence throughout Europe. Among his more popular scientific writings *The Sceptical Chymist* (1661) is the best known and *The Origin of Forms and Qualities* (1666) anticipates much of the philosophy of *Locke. Among his early writings were the romances *Seraphic Love* and *The Martyrdom of Theodora*, the latter of which was turned into an opera libretto for *Handel. These exercises in moralizing find their echoes in many of Boyle's religious and philosophical writings. Samuel *Butler and *Swift wrote parodies of his

Occasional Reflections (1665), a work which also supplied Swift with one of the central storylines in **Gulliver's Travels*.

Boyle paid for the translation of the New Testament into Irish and other languages, supported evangelical schemes abroad, and in his Will made provision for the foundation of a series of annual lectures in defence of natural and revealed religion. The first series of Boyle Lectures was delivered by Richard **Bentley in 1692. The influence of these lectures was at its peak during the first 20 years; especially important were the lectures delivered by Bentley, John Harris, S. **Clarke, William Whiston, John Woodward, and William Derham, all of whose statements of natural theology were published as substantial volumes.

BOYLE, Roger, first earl of Orrery (1621–79), author of *Parthenissa* (1654–65), the first English romance in the style of **La Calprenède and M. de **Scudéry, which deals with the prowess and vicissitudes of Artabanes, a Median prince, and his rivalry with Surena, an Arabian prince, for the love of Parthenissa. Boyle also wrote a *Treatise on the Art of War* (1677), two comedies, and some rhymed tragedies, which include *Mustapha* (1665), based on Mlle de Scudéry's *Ibrahim* and the history of **Knolles. His plays were edited in two volumes by W. S. Clark, 1937.

Boythorn, a character in Dickens's **Bleak House*.

BOZ, the pseudonym used by **Dickens in his contributions to the *Morning Chronicle* and in the **Pickwick Papers*, 'was the nickname of a pet child, a younger brother, whom I had dubbed Moses, in honour of the Vicar of Wakefield; which being facetiously pronounced...became Boz' (Dickens, preface to *Pickwick Papers*, 1847 edn).

Brabantio, in Shakespeare's **Othello*, the father of Desdemona.

BRACEGIRDLE, Anne (?1673/4–1748), a famous actress, the friend of **Congreve, to the success of whose comedies on stage she largely contributed. She also created Belinda in Vanbrugh's **The Provok'd Wife*, and played Portia, Desdemona, Ophelia, Cordelia, and Mrs Ford. She was finally eclipsed by Mrs **Oldfield in 1707 and retired from the stage. The age of 85, registered when she was buried in Westminster Abbey, is probably mistaken.

Brachiano, a character in Webster's **The White Devil*.

BRACKENBRIDGE, Hugh Henry (1748–1816), American novelist, poet, and lawyer, born in Scotland, and educated at the College of New Jersey (later Princeton). His satirical novel *Modern Chivalry*, published in instalments from 1792 to 1815, gives a good description of men and manners during the early days of the American republic, and manifests Brackenbridge's allegiance to the robust tradition of the English novel in **Smollett and **Fielding.

BRACTON, BRATTON, or **BRETTON,** Henry de (d. 1268), a judge and ecclesiastic, and author of the famous treatise *De Legibus et Consuetudinibus Angliae*, the first attempt at a complete treatise on the laws and customs of England. He also left a 'Note-book' containing some 2,000 legal cases with comments.

Bradamante, in **Orlando innamorato* and **Orlando furioso*, a maiden warrior, sister of **Rinaldo. She fights with the great **Rodomont. **Rogero comes to her assistance and falls in love with her. **Spenser owed much to Bradamante in fashioning his Britomart in **The Faerie Queene*.

BRADBROOK, Muriel Clara (1909–93), scholar, educated at Girton College, Cambridge, of which she was mistress from 1968 to 1976. Known primarily as an Elizabethan scholar, her works range from *Themes and Conventions of Elizabethan Tragedy* (1935, rev. 1980) and a study of the **School of Night (1936) to *The Rise of the Common Player* (1962), in which she examines the social implications of drama as a performing art, but she also wrote on **Conrad, M. **Lowry, V. **Woolf, T. S. **Eliot, and other 20th-cent. literary figures. Her *Collected Papers* (2 vols) appeared in 1982.

BRADBURY, Sir Malcolm Stanley (1932–2000), critic and novelist, born in Sheffield, and educated at the universities of Leicester, London, and Manchester; he held several academic appointments, and in 1970 became professor of American studies at the **University of East Anglia, where he was instrumental in setting up a creative writing course. His critical works include *Possibilities: essays on the state of the novel* (1973), *The Modern American Novel* (1983), *No, Not Bloomsbury* (essays, 1987), *Ten Great Writers* (1989), *The Novel Today* (revised edn., 1990), and *From Puritanism to Postmodernism* (1991), and studies of E. **Waugh (1992) and **Bellow (1982); his approach combines a respect for pluralism with an admiration for the experiments and fictive devices of the American novel and of British writers such as **Fowles. His first three novels are satirical **Campus novels; *Eating People is Wrong* (1959) relates the amorous and pedagogic adventures of ageing liberal humanist Professor Treece in a second-rate redbrick provincial university; *Stepping Westward* (1965) is set in the mid-west of America; and *The **History Man* (1975) is set in the new plate-glass university of Watermouth. *Rates of Exchange* (1983) takes academic linguist Dr Petworth on a British Council lecture tour to an Eastern European country where there is no British Council; the novel's imagery and plot spring from **Structuralist concepts of culture, and it is a witty and satiric commentary on cultural exchange. *Cuts: A Very Short Novel* (1987) is a satire on Thatcherite Britain. *Dr Criminale* (1992) tells the story of a journalist's search for the mysterious Dr Bazlo Criminale and *To the Hermitage* (2000) interweaves past and present journeys, invoking **Diderot's sojourn at the court of Catherine the Great.

BRADBURY, Ray Douglas (1920–   ), American **science fiction and fantasy writer and poet, born in Illinois and living from 1934 in Los Angeles, where he educated himself in the public library and began to write stories. He has published many short stories and novels, including perhaps his best-known single work, *Fahrenheit 451* (1953), set in an authoritarian future state where reading is banned: fireman Montag is employed to burn books but rebels and makes a bid for freedom. It was filmed by F. Truffaut in 1966.

BRADDON, Mary Elizabeth (1837–1915), privately educated, was an actress for three years in order to support herself and her mother. She met John Maxwell, a publisher of periodicals, in 1860, and acted as stepmother to his five children before marrying him in 1874 upon the death of his insane wife; she had six children by him. She published several works, including *Garibaldi and Other Poems* (1861), before the appearance of the sensational *Lady Audley's Secret* (1862, first serialized in *Robin Goodfellow* and the *Sixpenny Magazine*), which won her fame and fortune. The bigamous pretty blonde heroine, who deserts her child, murders her husband, and contemplates poisoning her second husband, shocked Mrs *Oliphant who credited Miss Braddon as 'the inventor of the fair-haired demon of modern fiction'. The novel has been dramatized, filmed, and translated and remained in print throughout the author's life. She published a further 74 inventive, lurid novels including the successful *Aurora Floyd* (1863), *The Doctor's Wife* (1864), *Henry Dunbar* (1864), and *Ishmael* (1884) and edited several magazines including *Belgravia* and *Temple Bar*. She was often attacked for corrupting young minds by making crime and violence attractive, but she won some notable admirers including *Bulwer-Lytton, *Hardy, *Stevenson, and *Thackeray. (See SENSATION, NOVEL OF.) See also GHOST STORIES.

BRADLAUGH, Charles (1833–91), social reformer and advocate of free thought, who, after being employed in various occupations, became a lecturer and pamphleteer on many popular causes, under the name 'Iconoclast'. His voice was to be heard on platforms throughout the country and in the *National Reformer* (of which he became proprietor) which was a chief outlet for his friend James *Thomson's poems. He was elected MP for Northampton in 1880, but was unseated having been refused the right to make affirmation of allegiance instead of taking the parliamentary oath; he was re-elected but it was not until 1886 that he took his seat, having agreed finally to take the oath. He became a popular debater in the House. He was engaged in several lawsuits to maintain freedom of the press. In association with Mrs *Besant, he republished a pamphlet, *The Fruits of Philosophy*, advocating birth control, which led to a six-month prison sentence and a £200 fine; the conviction was quashed on appeal.

BRADLEY, A(ndrew) C(ecil) (1851–1935), brother of F. H. *Bradley, professor of literature at Liverpool, then

Glasgow, and from 1901 to 1906 professor of poetry at Oxford. He is particularly remembered for his contributions to Shakespearian scholarship; his best-known works are *Shakespearean Tragedy* (1904) and *Oxford Lectures on Poetry* (1909). L. C. *Knights in his essay 'How many children had Lady Macbeth?' (1933) represented a new generation of critics in his mockery of Bradley's 'detective interest' in plot and emphasis on 'character' as a detachable object of study, but Bradley's works retain their interest and some admirers.

BRADLEY, Edward (1827–89), educated at University College, Durham (which suggested his pseudonym, 'Cuthbert Bede'), and rector of various country livings, is remembered as the author of *The Adventures of Mr Verdant Green* (1853–7), a novel which traces the Oxford career of a gullible young undergraduate, fresh from Warwickshire, from his freshman days to graduation and marriage. It was reprinted in 1982 with an introduction by A. *Powell. Bradley also contributed extensively to periodicals, illustrated his own works, and drew for *Punch*.

BRADLEY, F(rancis) H(erbert) (1846–1924), brother of A. C. *Bradley, and fellow of Merton College, Oxford. He published *Ethical Studies* in 1876, perhaps most notable for its essay on 'My Station and its Duties', and *Principles of Logic* in 1883. His *Appearance and Reality* (1893) was considered an important philosophical discussion of contemporary metaphysical thought; Bradley was greatly concerned to draw attention in England to continental philosophy, and particularly to Hegelianism. *Essay on Truth and Reality* appeared in 1914. He was admired by T. S. *Eliot, who noted that his own prose style was 'closely . . . formed on that of Bradley'. See R. Wollheim, *F. H. Bradley* (1959).

BRADLEY, Dr Henry (1845–1923), philologist, principally remembered for his work on the *Oxford English Dictionary*, with which he was associated for 40 years, from 1884. He became second editor in 1887 and succeeded James *Murray as senior editor on Murray's death in 1915. Among Bradley's works may be mentioned the successful *The Making of English* (1904, rev. 1968). A memoir of Bradley by *Bridges is prefixed to *Collected Papers of Henry Bradley* (1928).

BRADSHAW, Henry (1831–86), bibliographer, scholar, antiquary, and librarian of the University of Cambridge (1867–86) where he reformed the department of early printed books and manuscripts. He published treatises on typographical and antiquarian subjects, including some important original discoveries.

Bradshaw's Railway Guide was first published in 1839 in the form of Railway Time Tables by George Bradshaw (1801–53), a Quaker engraver and printer. These developed into *Bradshaw's Monthly Railway Guide* in 1841 and it continued to be published until May 1961.

BRADSTREET, Anne (*c.*1612–72), American poet, was born in England and emigrated with her father Thomas Dudley and husband Simon Bradstreet in 1630, settling first at Ipswich, then in North Andover, Massachusetts. She had eight children. Her poems were published in London without her knowledge in 1650, under the title *The Tenth Muse Lately Sprung up in America*, and a posthumous second edition with her own corrections and additions was published in Boston (1678). She admired and was influenced by *Quarles and Sylvester's translation of *Du Bartas, and her work was highly praised in her own time. Her later and shorter poems are now more highly regarded than her longer philosophical and historical discourses, and she has received much attention both as a woman writer and as the first poet of the New World. *Berryman pays tribute to her in his poem *Homage to Mistress Bradstreet* (1956).

BRADWARDINE, Thomas (*c.*1280–1349), Oxford theologian appointed archbishop of Canterbury immediately before his death of the plague in August 1349. His *De Causa Dei* reasserted the primacy of faith and divine grace in opposition to the rationalist sceptics (whom he characterized as New Pelagians) of the tradition of *Ockham and *Holcot. Like his direct contemporary *Fitzralph he was a member of the circle of Richard de Bury. He has been called a determinist and a preacher of predestination because of his insistence on the involvement of God's will as a primary cause in every action of the human will, the independence of which is thus reduced. The effect of this, as of the arguments of his opponents, was to destroy the 13th-cent. synthesis of Faith and Reason, but in this case giving the primacy unconditionally to Faith/Theology over Reason/Philosophy.

BRAGG, Melvyn (1939–   ), novelist, journalist, and broadcaster, brought up in Cumberland, which forms the setting of several of his works, and educated at Wadham College, Oxford. Well-known as the presenter of the television arts programme *The South Bank Show*, and *In Our Time* (BBC Radio 4), he was made a life peer in 1998. His novels include *Without a City Wall* (1968), *The Silken Net* (1971), *The Maid of Buttermere* (1978), and *A Time to Dance* (1990). *The Soldier's Return* (1999) and its sequel *A Son of War* (2001) describe soldier Sam Richardson's return to his family in a small village in post-war Cumberland.

Braggadochio, in Spenser's *Faerie Queene*, the typical braggart. His adventures and final exposure and humiliation occur in II. iii; III. viii, x; IV. iv, v, ix; V. iii. Cf. *Trompart.

BRAHMS, Caryl (1901–82), the pen-name of Doris Caroline Abrahams, and **SIMON**, S. J. (Secha Jascha Skidelsky, 1904–48, born in Harbin, Manchuria), international specialists respectively in ballet criticism and international bridge. They collaborated to write a series of comic crime novels set in the mad world of a touring Russian ballet, *A Bullet in the Ballet* (1937), *Casino for Sale* (1938), and *Six Curtains for Stroganova* (1944). They also pioneered funny anachronistic historical fiction, including *Don't Mr Disraeli* (Victorian, 1940), *No Bed for Bacon* (Elizabethan, 1941), *No Nightingales* (1944), and *Trottie True* (Edwardian, 1947). After Simon's death, Brahms completed their last book *You Were There* (1950) and published several novels herself, notably *Away Went Polly* (1953); she collaborated with Ned Sherrin on novels, plays, and musicals, and was a regular contributor to the satirical TV programme *That Was the Week that Was*.

BRAINE, John Gerard (1922–86), novelist, born and educated in Bradford, who was for many years a librarian in the north of England. His first novel, *Room at the Top* (1957), set in a small Yorkshire town, was an instant success, and its hero, Joe Lampton, was hailed as another of the provincial *'angry young men' of the 1950s. Lampton, a ruthless opportunist working at the Town Hall, seduces and marries the wealthy young Susan Browne, despite his love for an unhappily married older woman. *Life at the Top* (1962) continues the story of his success and disillusion. Braine's later novels express his increasing hostility to the radical views with which he was once identified. They include *The Crying Game* (1964), *Stay with Me till Morning* (1968), *The Queen of a Distant Country* (1972), *The Pious Agent* (1975), *Finger of Fire* (1977), *One and Last Love* (1981), and *The Two of Us* (1984).

Brainworm, the wily, high-spirited servant in Jonson's *Every Man in His Humour*.

BRAMAH, Ernest (Smith) (?1868/9–1942), born in Manchester. He failed as a farmer and turned to journalism, writing for J. K.*Jerome's *To-Day* and other publications. He is remembered for *Kai Lung's Golden Hours* (1922), a pseudo-Oriental tale, using a *Scheherazade framework, and for other Kai Lung stories (*The Wallet of Kai Lung*, 1900; *Kai Lung Unrolls His Mat*, 1928). These are written in an ornate, whimsical manner and have no authentic Chinese background: the famous account of the origins of the willow pattern design in chapter 2 of the *Golden Hours* is a sly satire on trade union practices.

Bramble, Matthew and Tabitha, characters in Smollett's *Humphry Clinker*.

Brambletye House, see SMITH, H.

Bramine's Journal, The, see ELIZA, THE JOURNAL TO.

Brandon, (1) Colonel, a character in J. Austen's *Sense and Sensibility*; (2) George, the assumed name of George Firmin in *Thackeray's *A Shabby Genteel Story*; (3) Mrs, a character in Thackeray's *The Adventures of Philip*.

Branghtons, the, in Fanny Burney's *Evelina*, the heroine's vulgar relatives.

Brangwane, Bragwaine, Bregwaine or **Brangane,** the maidservant of Isoud (Iseult); see TRISTRAM AND ISOUD.

BRANTÔME, Pierre de Bourdeilles, seigneur de (*c.*1540–1614), French memorialist. His career as an officer and courtier offered him every opportunity to observe the private conduct of the great figures of the day. His memoirs (pub. posth., 1665–6) include the notorious *Vie des dames galantes*, which repeat the scandals of court intrigues in a lively and uncensorious style.

Branwen, see MABINOGION.

Brass, (1) a character in Vanbrugh's *The Confederacy*; (2) Sampson and his sister Sally, characters in Dickens's *The Old Curiosity Shop*.

Brat Pack, a phrase coined by the media to describe a group of young novelists from New York which emerged in the mid- to late 1980s. Also known as 'The Blank Generation', they write fiction inhabiting a youth culture of fast-lane living—cocaine, nightclubs, Music Television (MTV), and hedonistic abandon. Bret Easton Ellis's *Less than Zero* (1984) and Jay McInerney's *Bright Lights, Big City* (1984) heralded this new mood of fashionable disaffection. Written in hypnotically dead-pan voices, they described lives that consisted of a cool surface bereft of substance. Tama Janowitz's collection of short stories, *Slaves of New York* (1987), was a notable addition, and critics often tended (wrongly) to equate the writers with their characters. Their obsession with celebrity and vacuity reached apocalyptic proportions with Ellis's *American Psycho* (1991), a novel in which the narrator, Patrick Bateman, blends into the persona of a serial killer. Ellis was attacked for misogyny and gratuitous violence, though others (most famously *Mailer and Fay *Weldon) defended the book as a satire on the urban consumer driven mad by dizzying excess. McInerney changed milieu in *Brightness Falls* (1992) and *The Last of the Savages* (1996), though in *Model Behaviour* (1998) he returns to familiar territory of a society saturated by celebrity.

BRATHWAITE, Edward Kamau (1930–   ), poet, born in Barbados, educated there and at Pembroke College, Cambridge. From 1955 to 1962 he taught in Ghana, then returned to the West Indies. He has written works on West Indian history and culture, and his volumes of poetry include *The Arrivants: A New World Trilogy* (1973), which consists of *Rights of Passage* (1967), *Masks* (1968), and *Islands* (1969). The poem explores the complex Caribbean heritage and search for identity, using (but not exclusively) vernacular rhythms and diction; its references range from Afro-Caribbean religious beliefs to cricket matches at the Oval. *Mother Poem* (1977), *Sun Poem* (1982), and *X-Self* (1987) form a trilogy about Barbados, 'most English of West Indian islands'.

Brave New World, a novel by A. *Huxley, published 1932.

It is a dystopian fable about a world state in the 7th cent. AF (after Ford), where social stability is based on a scientific caste system. Human beings, graded from highest intellectuals to lowest manual workers, hatched from incubators and brought up in communal nurseries, learn by methodical conditioning to accept their social destiny. The action of the story develops round Bernard Marx, an unorthodox and therefore unhappy Alpha-Plus (something had presumably gone wrong with his antenatal treatment), who visits a New Mexican Reservation and brings a Savage back to London. The Savage is at first fascinated by the new world, but finally revolted, and his argument with Mustapha Mond, World Controller, demonstrates the incompatibility of individual freedom and a scientifically trouble-free society.

In *Brave New World Revisited* (1958) Huxley reconsiders his prophecies and fears that some of these may be coming true sooner than he thought.

BRAWNE, Fanny (1800–65), the young woman with whom *Keats fell in love in 1818. To what extent she returned or understood his passion for her (expressed in many of his letters and several poems) is not clear, but some kind of engagement took place, and after his death she wore mourning for him for several years. She married in 1833. His letters to her were published in 1878 and in the collected edition of 1937; hers to his sister, also called Fanny, were published in 1937.

Bray, Madeline, a character in Dickens's *Nicholas Nickleby*.

'Bray, Vicar of ', see VICAR OF BRAY, THE.

Brazen, Captain, a character in Farquhar's *The Recruiting Officer*.

BRECHT, Bertolt (1898–1956), German dramatist and poet. After emigrating (to the United States, where he collaborated on translations and productions of his plays with Eric Bentley and Charles Laughton), he settled in 1949 in East Berlin, where he founded and directed the Berliner Ensemble. After his death his widow, the actress Helene Weigel, directed the company until she died in 1971. Brecht's early plays, e.g. *Baal* (1922) and *Trommeln in der Nacht* (*Drums in the Night*, 1922), show kinship with *Expressionism. *Mann ist Mann* (*Man is Man*, 1927) anticipates Brecht's later systematic development of his famous '*alienation effect', and *Die Dreigroschenoper* (*The Threepenny Opera*, 1928), his version of *The Beggar's Opera*, was one of the theatrical successes of Weimar Germany, not least in the bourgeois circles which were satirized in the work. His theory of 'epic theatre' rejected Aristotelian principles, regarded a play as a series of loosely connected scenes, dispensed with dramatic climaxes, and used songs to comment on the action. The theory is best illustrated in *Leben des Galilei*

(*The Life of Galileo*, 1937–9), *Der gute Mensch von Sezuan* (*The Good Woman of Setzuan*, 1938–41), *Mutter Courage* (*Mother Courage*, 1941), based on a story by *Grimmelshausen, and *Der kaukasische Kreidekreis* (*The Caucasian Chalk Circle*, 1948). All these plays call for highly stylized acting which, like his general theory of drama, expounded in its most mature form in his essay *Kleines Organon für das Theater* (*Little Treatise on the Theatre*, 1949), discards the notion that drama should seek to create the illusion of reality. Some of Brecht's plays, e.g. *Die heilige Johanna der Schlachthöfe* (*St Joan of the Stockyards*, 1929–30), have a particularly direct anti-capitalist theme, and others, e.g. *Der aufhaltsame Aufstieg des Arturo Ui* (*The Resistible Rise of Arturo Ui*, 1941), combine this with the theme of Hitlerism. The didactic plays of the period around 1930, e.g. *Der Jasager/Der Neinsager* (*He Who Said Yes/ He Who Said No*) and *Die Massnahme* (*The Measures Taken*), are closely connected with the interests of the Communist Party, with which Brecht was intimately associated from the late 1920s. He was never a member of the Party, however, and his relations with it, even in his last years in East Berlin, became rather uncertain. Brecht's plays include adaptations of Marlowe's *Edward II* (1924) and Shakespeare's *Coriolanus* (1951/2, pub. 1959). W. H. *Auden collaborated with Brecht on an adaptation of Webster's *The Duchess of Malfi* for the New York Broadway (perf. 1946). Since the first visit of the Berliner Ensemble to London in 1956, Brecht's plays have been produced frequently in Britain. British playwrights of the 1960s, particularly *Bond and *Arden and, more recently, Howard *Brenton, are clearly influenced by Brecht's radical approach, in theme and treatment, to drama. Brecht was also an outstanding lyric poet.

Breck, Alan, a character in R. L. Stevenson's *Kidnapped* and *Catriona*.

BRENAN, Gerald (Edward Fitz-Gerald Brenan) (1894–1987), author born in Malta, who lived in Spain from 1920 and wrote various works on Spanish literature, including *The Literature of the Spanish People* (1951) and a study of St *John of the Cross (1972). He was friendly with several members of the *Bloomsbury Group, as he records in his autobiography *A Life of One's Own* (1962), where he describes his meeting with Ralph Partridge in 1914 and gives an unusually vivid account of the 'exhilaration' of serving as a young soldier on the French front in the First World War. *Personal Record 1920–1972* was published in 1974. See *The Interior Castle* (1992), a life by Jonathan Gathorne-Hardy.

BRENDAN, St (?484–?577) of the monastery of Clonfert in Ireland, about whom grew up a tradition of legendary voyages as a Christianized version of the Old Irish genre *imram*, describing sea adventures; other examples are 'The Voyage of Bran' and 'The Voyage of Maeldune' of which the latter too was Christianized.

The *Navigatio Sancti Brandani* is one of the earliest substantial texts in *Anglo-Norman, but there are earlier Latin versions, none from before the 10th cent. The legends of Brendan have been revived in popularity at various times, for example by M. *Arnold. The most familiar stories are those of the meeting with Judas cooling himself on a rock on Christmas night, a privilege allowed him once a year; and of the landing on a whale, mistaking it for an island, and its being aroused by the lighting of a fire. A traditional Irish story credits Brendan with reaching America nearly a thousand years before Columbus, a theory of which the credibility was put to the test in the 1970s, with doubtful results.

See Lady *Gregory, *The Voyages of Saint Brendan the Navigator and Stories of the Saints of Ireland* (1906/7), ed. C. Smythe (1973).

BRENTON, Howard (1942–), playwright born in Portsmouth, educated at Chichester High School and Cambridge. His father was a policeman who later became a Methodist minister in Yorkshire. Coppers and clergy feature heavily in many of the short Brenton plays which powered the London fringe in the early 1970s. An avowed socialist slightly adrift since the collapse of communism, Brenton is a unique and powerful voice whose plays combine jagged writing with raw, Jacobean theatricality. His first full-scale *Royal Court play *Magnificence* (1973) was followed by a collaboration with David *Hare, *Brassneck* (1973), *The Churchill Play* (1974), in which the great leader rose from his own catafalque in a grim new Britain, and four controversial successes at the *National Theatre: *Weapons of Happiness* (1976); a new version of *Brecht's *Galileo*; *The Romans in Britain* (1980), an allegory of the British in Northern Ireland, which attracted an ill-fated private prosecution by Mrs Mary Whitehouse; and *Pravda* (1985), again with David Hare, which monitored the takeover of a supine newspaper business by a reptilian colonial magnate, Lambert Le Roux, memorably played by Anthony Hopkins. *Moscow Gold* (1990), with Tariq *Ali, and *Berlin Bertie* (1992) tackle new political realities. *Diving for Pearls* (1989) is a vivid novel, *Hot Irons* (1995) a collection of occasional pieces and production diaries.

Brer Fox and **Brer Rabbit,** the chief characters in *Uncle Remus*. See Harris, J. C.

BRETON, André (1896–1966), French poet, essayist, and critic, one of the founders of *Surrealism. He collaborated with Philippe Soupault on *Les Champs magnétiques* of 1920, an early experiment in automatic writing, and he wrote his first Surrealist Manifesto in 1924, followed by a second in 1930 and *Prolegomènes* (1942). He was instrumental in the direction of two surrealist periodicals, *La Révolution surréaliste* (1924–30) and *Le Surréalisme au service de la révolution* (1930–3). He produced a number of volumes of poetry, including *Clair de terre* (1923), *Le Revolver à cheveux* blancs (1932), and *L'Air de l'eau* (1934), as well as narrative works, *Nadja* (1928; English trans., 1960), *Les Vases communicants* (1932), and *L'Amour fou* (1937). His theoretical essays are collected in *Les Pas perdus* (1924), *Point du jour* (1934), and *La Clé des champs* (1953). He was also the author of a volume on art, *Le Surréalisme et la peinture* (1928).

BRETON, Nicholas (?1555–1626), educated at Oxford, the author of a miscellaneous collection of satirical, religious, romantic, and political writings in verse and prose. His stepfather was George *Gascoigne. From about 1576 he seems to have settled in London, and between 1575 and 1622 he published well over 50 books including: *The Wil of Wit, Wits Will, or Wils Wit* (c.1582); *The Pilgrimage to Paradise, Joyned with the Countesse of Penbrookes Love* (1592); *Wits Trenchmour* (a dialogue on angling, 1597); *The Figure of Foure, or A Handfull of sweet Flowers* (c.1597); *Pasquils Mad-Cap* (1600); *The Soules Heavenly Exercise* (1601); *Olde Mad-cappes new Gally-mawfrey* (1602); *Fantasticks: Serving for a Perpetuall Prognostication* (a collection of observations on men and nature arranged calendar-wise, c.1604); *The Honour of Valour* (1605); *The Good and the Badde, or Descriptions of the Worthies, and Unworthies of this Age* (1616); *Conceyted Letters, Newly Layde Open* (1618). His best poetry is to be found among his short lyrics in *Englands Helicon* (1600) and in his volume of pastoral poetry *The Passionate Shepheard* (1604). His works were edited by *Grosart in 1879, and poems not included by Grosart were edited, with much information about his works, by Jean Robertson in 1952.

Breton lays, in English literature of the Middle English period, are short stories in rhyme like those of *Marie de France; the English examples are by no means a clearly defined group, and they often owe their identification to the fact that they say they are Breton lays, or that the same story is told by Marie in French. See EMARÉ, ORFEO, SIR, DEGARÉ, SIR; the other English examples are *Sir Landeval, Lai le Freine, The Erle of Tolous, Sir Gowther*, Chaucer's 'The Franklin's Tale' (see CANTERBURY TALES, 12) and *Gower's 'Tale of Rosiphilee' (*Confessio Amantis*, Bk IV). See T. C. Rumble (ed.), *The Breton Lays in Middle English* (1965); M. J. Donovan, *The Breton Lay: A Guide to Varieties* (1969).

Bretton, John, a character in *Villette* by C. Brontë, introduced in the opening chapters as Graham Bretton.

Brewer's Dictionary of Phrase and Fable, by the Revd Ebenezer Cobham Brewer (1810–97), first published 1870, regularly revised. It contains explanations and origins of the familiar and unfamiliar in English phrase and fable, including colloquial and proverbial phrases, embracing archaeology, history, religion, the arts, science, mythology, fictitious characters and titles, etc.

Briana, in Spenser's *Faerie Queene (VI. i), the mistress of a castle who takes a toll of ladies' locks and knights' beards to make a mantle for her lover Crudor.

Bridehead, Sue, a character in Hardy's *Jude the Obscure.

Bride of Abydos, The, , a poem in irregular stanzas by *Byron, one of his 'Turkish tales', published in December 1813: it sold 6,000 copies within a month. The beautiful Zuleika, daughter of the Pacha Giaffir, is destined to marry the rich, elderly Bey of Carasman, whom she has never seen. She confesses her grief to her beloved brother Selim, who takes her to his grotto where he reveals himself in magnificent pirate garb and declares he is not her brother but her cousin. He begs her to share his future, but Giaffir and his soldiers arrive and Selim is killed. Zuleika dies of grief. In the first draft Zuleika and Selim were not cousins but half-brother and sister: a variation of the incest theme to which Byron was frequently drawn.

Bride of Lammermoor, The, a novel by Sir W. *Scott, published 1819 in *Tales of My Landlord, 3rd series. The darkness and fatalism of this novel, published in the third series of *Tales of My Landlord*, have traditionally been ascribed to Scott's almost mortal illness while he was writing it, as have minor confusions in the plot; but recent research shows that most of it was written earlier. The pessimistic tone of what has been described as the most pure and powerful of his tragedies remains unexplained. The dramatic possibilities of the story of Lucy Ashton's frustrated love for the Byronic Master of Ravenswood, her stabbing of the alternative bridegroom forced upon her on the wedding night, and her own insanity and death, were to be seized on by Donizetti for his opera *Lucia di Lammermoor*. The comic interest in the novel is provided by Ravenswood's henchman Caleb Balderstone, though Scott admitted that, in his creation, 'he had sprinkled too much parsley over his chicken'.

Brideshead Revisited, a novel by E. *Waugh, published 1945.

Narrated by Charles Ryder, it describes his emotional involvement with an ancient aristocratic Roman Catholic family, which grows from his meeting as an undergraduate at Oxford the handsome, whimsical younger son, Sebastian Flyte, already an incipient alcoholic. Through Sebastian Charles meets his mother, the devout Lady Marchmain, who refuses to divorce Lord Marchmain, exiled to Venice with his mistress; the heir, Lord Brideshead; and the sisters Julia and Cordelia. Lady Marchmain attempts to enlist Charles's support in preventing Sebastian's drinking, but Sebastian finally escapes to North Africa, where, after his mother's death, he becomes some kind of saintly down-and-out. Meanwhile Charles, now an unhappily married but successful artist, falls in love with Julia, also unhappily married; they both plan to divorce and begin a new life, but the power of the

Church reclaims Julia, and they part for ever. The narrative is set in a wartime framework of prologue and epilogue, in which Charles is billeted in Brideshead, the great country house which had once dominated his imagination. In a 1959 preface, Waugh (for whom this novel marked a departure from his earlier satiric style) said that his theme was 'the operation of divine grace on a group of diverse but closely connected characters', but also conceded that the book was 'infused with a kind of gluttony, for food and wine, for the splendours of the recent past, and for rhetorical and ornamental language, which now with a full stomach I find distasteful'; these aspects contributed greatly to the success of the lavish, lengthy, nostalgic television adaptation, shown in 1980.

'Bridge of Sighs, The', a poem by T. *Hood, published 1843, one of the most popular of his serious works. It is a morbid and ostensibly compassionate elegy on the suicide by drowning of a 'Fallen Woman', a favourite Victorian theme, which dwells in some detail on her youth and beauty, her penitence for her 'evil behaviour', and on the 'cold inhumanity' of the world which cast her out.

BRIDGES, Robert (1844–1930), educated at Eton and Corpus Christi College, Oxford; afterwards he studied medicine at St Bartholomew's Hospital, and he continued to practise until 1881. At Oxford he met G. M. *Hopkins, who became a close and influential friend, and whose complete poems Bridges eventually published in 1918. Bridges's first book, *Poems*, was published in 1873, and further volumes, with additional poems, followed over many years. *The Growth of Love*, a sonnet sequence, appeared in 1876 with some success, and in an enlarged form in 1890. Two long poems followed, *Prometheus the Firegiver* (1883) and *Eros and Psyche* (1885). Between 1885 and 1894 he wrote eight plays. He wrote two influential essays, *Milton's Prosody* (1893) and *John Keats* (1895); and between 1895 and 1908 wrote the words for four works by H. *Parry. He was much interested in the musical settings of words, and edited several editions of the *Yattendon Hymnal* from 1895 onwards. In 1898 appeared the first of the six volumes of his *Poetical Works* (1898–1905). His poetry appeared in one volume in 1912, and received great critical and popular acclaim. The following year he was appointed *poet laureate, and became one of the founders of the *Society for Pure English, many of whose tracts he wrote or edited. For many years he was closely connected with the *Oxford University Press, which he advised on many matters of style, phonetics, spelling, and typography. In 1916 he published a highly successful anthology of prose and verse, *The Spirit of Man*, which included six poems by Hopkins, little of whose work had yet been published. *October and Other Poems* appeared in 1920, *New Verse* in 1925, and then in 1929 *The Testament of Beauty*, a long poem, in four books, on his spiritual philosophy, which he regarded as the culmination of his work as a poet, and

which met with high acclaim and sold extremely well. His lyric verse has been much anthologized, and some of it (including 'London Snow', 'A Passer-by', 'Asian Birds', and 'A Dead Child') became widely known. His collected prose works, mostly on poets and various literary topics, were published between 1927 and 1936.

BRIDIE, James, pseudonym of Osborne Henry Mavor (1888–1951), son of a Glasgow engineer, who trained and practised as a doctor; questions of medical ethics and practice appear frequently in his plays. He began his career as a playwright with a cheerful morality, *The Sunlight Sonata*, with Tyrone Guthrie in Glasgow in 1928; *The Anatomist* (1930), a comedy on the graverobbers Burke and Hare, established his name. His plays fall roughly into four groups: those on biblical themes, such as *Tobias and the Angel* (1930), *Jonah and the Whale* (1932), and *Susannah and the Elders* (1937); those with medical themes, such as *A Sleeping Clergyman* (1933); portrait plays, including *Mr Bolfrey* (1943); and experimental, symbolist, and partly poetic plays such as *Daphne Laureola* (1949) and his last play, the dark, foreboding *The Baikie Charivari* (1952). Many of Bridie's dramas, with their bold characterization, lively debate, and humour, are reminiscent of *morality plays. Bridie assisted in the establishment of the Glasgow Citizen's Theatre in 1943, founded the first College of Drama in Scotland in 1950, and worked diligently for various artistic enterprises such as the Edinburgh Festival. His modest autobiography, *One Way of Living*, appeared in 1939.

BRIEUX, Eugène (1858–1932), French dramatist of contemporary morals, championed as 'the greatest writer France has produced since Molière' by G. B. *Shaw, whose wife translated his *Maternité* in *Three Plays by Brieux* (1913, with an introduction by Shaw). A second volume, *Woman on Her Own, False Gods and The Red Robe: Three Plays by Brieux* (1916), has translations by Mrs Shaw, J. B. Fagan, and A. B. Miall and an introduction by Brieux.

Brigadore, in Spenser's *Faerie Queene*, the horse of Sir *Guyon, stolen by *Braggadochio (v. iii. 34).

Briggs, (1) a character in Fanny Burney's *Cecilia*, drawn in some respects from the sculptor *Nollekens; (2) Miss, a character in Thackeray's *Vanity Fair*, companion first to Miss Crawley and then to Becky.

BRIGGS, Raymond Redvers (1934–   ), London-born illustrator and author of books for children, best known for his comic-strip *Father Christmas* (1973) and its sequels; for *Fungus the Bogeyman* (1977), with a lavatory attendant hero; and for *The Snowman* (1979). *When the Wind Blows* (1982) is a remarkable addition, also in comic-strip form, to the literature of the nuclear holocaust, portraying the reality of nuclear war for an ordinary couple, Jim and Hilda, as they take refuge in their hopelessly inadequate home-made fall-out shelter. *Ethel and Ernest* (1998), a memoir of his parents, is also in comic-strip form.

BRIGHOUSE, H., see HOBSON'S CHOICE.

BRIGHT, John (1811–89), born in Rochdale of Quaker stock, renowned political agitator and orator, prominent member of the Anti-Corn Law League, and with *Cobden a leading representative of the emergence of the manufacturing class in England after the 1832 *Reform Bill. He was successively MP for Durham (1843), Manchester, and Birmingham, and held various posts in *Gladstone's governments, from 1868 onwards.

Brighton Rock, a novel by G. *Greene, published 1938.
   Set in Brighton in the criminal underworld of gang warfare and protection rackets, it describes the brief and tragic career of 17-year-old Pinkie, 'The Boy', whose ambition is to run a gang to rival that of the wealthy and established Colleoni. He murders a journalist called Hale, marries a 16-year-old girl, the downtrodden Rose (like himself a Roman Catholic), to prevent her giving evidence in court against him, and is driven to further crimes and eventual death by the almost casual pursuit of Ida, a justice-seeking acquaintance of Hale. Pinkie's corruption and Rose's innocence are shown as in some way complementary, and the vigorous, fun-loving, stout-drinking, single-minded Ida is not portrayed with sympathy; the novel (originally described by Greene as 'an entertainment') foreshadows the religious complexity and ambiguities of later works, and Greene later claimed to regret the detective story element of the opening section (*Ways of Escape*, 1980, ch. 2).

BRINK, André Philippus (1935–), South African playwright, novelist, short story writer, and critic, born in Vrede, Orange Free State, and educated at Potchefstroom University and (1959–61) at the Sorbonne in Paris. Since 1991 he has been professor of English literature at the University of Cape Town. A prolific author who writes in both English and Afrikaans, he was widely snubbed during the era of apartheid by the Afrikaans literary community for his dissident views. His *Kennis van die aand* (1973), translated into English as *Looking on Darkness* (1974), was banned by the South African government and brought him to international notice. It tells the story of a coloured actor, Joseph Malan, who after training in London returns to South Africa to work against apartheid by cultural means. After a passionate affair with a white woman, whom he eventually kills, Malan is executed by the Security Police. The ban on the novel was lifted in 1982. The English versions of his novels include *An Instant in the Wind* (1976), a tale, set in the mid-18th cent., of a white woman and a black servant stranded together in the wilderness of the South African interior; *Rumours of Rain* (1978) and *A Dry White Season* (1979), both of which explore the moral ambiguities of Afrikaner nationalism; *A Chain of Voices* (1982), about a group of

slaves accused of killing a wealthy Afrikaner farmer during the early 19th cent.; *The Wall of the Plague* (1984), in which the medieval Black Death is presented as a metaphor of apartheid; *States of Emergency* (1988), a love story set within the context of national violence and embodying aspects of Brink's own personal life; *An Act of Terror* (1991), a political thriller turning on a plot to assassinate the South African president; and *On the Contrary* (1993), a picaresque biography of an 18th-cent. adventurer, Estienne Barbier. He has also written travel books, plays, and children's books. *Mapmakers*, a collection of essays on literature, politics, and culture, appeared in 1983.

Brisk, a voluble coxcomb in Congreve's *The Double Dealer*.

Brisk, Fastidious, a foppish courtier in Jonson's *Every Man out of His Humour*.

Britannia, or, according to the subtitle, *A Chorographical Description of the Most Flourishing Kingdomes of England, Scotland, and Ireland, and the Ilands Adioyning, out of the Depth of Antiquitie*, by W. *Camden, published in Latin 1586, the sixth (much enlarged) edition appearing in 1607. It was translated in 1610 by *Holland. It is in effect a guidebook of the country, county by county, replete with archaeological, historical, physical, and other information.

Britannia's Pastorals, see BROWNE, W.

British Academy, the, a society, incorporated in 1902, for the promotion of the study of the moral and political sciences, including history, philosophy, law, political economy, archaeology, and philology. It publishes Proceedings, administers endowments for a number of annual lectures, encourages archaeological and oriental research, etc. Its first secretary was Sir I. *Gollancz.

British Library, the see LIBRARIES.

British Magazine, a periodical miscellany founded in 1759 by *Newbery, which ran from Jan. 1760 to Dec. 1767. It was edited by *Smollett, and one of its principal contributors was *Goldsmith. It published a large amount of fiction (including a serialization of Smollett's *The Life and Adventures of Sir Launcelot *Greaves*, 1760–1), and also reviews, essays, etc.

British Museum, the, Bloomsbury. It occupies the site of the old Montagu House, which was acquired in 1753 to house the collection of curiosities of Sir H. *Sloane. These were from time to time enormously increased, notably by the purchase of the *Harleian manuscripts, the gift by George II and George IV of royal libraries, the purchase of the Elgin Marbles, and the acquisition of Egyptian antiquities (including the Rosetta Stone), and of the Layard Assyrian collections. The new buildings, designed by Sir Robert Smirke, were erected in 1823–47. The great Reading Room, designed by *Panizzi, the librarian, was opened in 1857; it closed in its familiar form in 1998, and the new British Library at St Pancras opened to the public on 24 Nov. 1998.

Britomart, the heroine of Bk III of Spenser's *Faerie Queene*, the daughter of King Ryence of Britain and the female knight of chastity. She has fallen in love with *Artegall, whose image she has seen in a magic mirror, and the poet recounts her adventures in her quest for him. She is the most powerful of several types of Queen Elizabeth in the poem.

Briton, a weekly periodical conducted in 1762 by *Smollett in Lord Bute's interest. Wilkes's *North Briton* was started in opposition to it.

BRITTAIN, Vera Mary (1893–1970), writer, pacifist, and feminist. The daughter of a wealthy manufacturer, she was brought up in the north of England, and educated at Somerville College, Oxford. Her education was interrupted by the First World War, during which she served as a VAD nurse, and which caused the death of her fiancé in France. Her *autobiographical *Testament of Youth* (1933) is a moving account of her girlhood and struggle for education (she came under the influence of O. *Schreiner while still at school) and of her war experiences. She returned to Oxford after the war, where she formed a close friendship with Winifred *Holtby, recorded in *Testament of Friendship* (1940). She also published various volumes of poetry, fiction, essays, etc.

BRITTEN, (Edward) Benjamin (1913–76), English composer. Skilful judgement in choice of texts and sensitivity in the setting of words have been characteristic features of his work, which was in many cases ideally served by the artistry of his friend Peter Pears (1910–86), the tenor, for whose voice much of Britten's music was designed. Early works like the *Serenade* for tenor, horn, and strings (1943) or the *Spring Symphony* (1949) brought together poems ranging from a medieval dirge through *Spenser, *Jonson and *Herrick to *Blake, *Tennyson, and *Auden. Britten's friendship with Auden resulted in a number of settings during the 1930s and 1940s as well as Britten's first opera, *Paul Bunyan* (1941). This was withdrawn and not revived until 1976, but Britten's second venture, *Peter Grimes* (1945), established him as an opera composer of importance, the first to emerge in this country since *Purcell and *Handel. The choice of *Crabbe's poem, with its 'outsider' protagonist, and Britten's concern with youthful innocence and misunderstanding, set a trend which was to be followed in later works: *Billy Budd* (1951), drawn from *Melville's story with a libretto by E. M. *Forster, or *The Turn of the Screw*, from H. *James. The latter is described as a 'chamber opera', a form to which Britten had turned for economic reasons: *The Rape of Lucretia* was a move towards simplification which was to lead to the three *Parables for Church Performance*, stylized pieces on the model of the *Nōh play, all with librettos by *Plomer (1964, 1966, 1968). Plomer also provided the text for

the ill-starred 'coronation' opera, *Gloriana* (1953): later more traditional operas included *A Midsummer Night's Dream* (1960), *Owen Wingrave* (1970), after H. James, and *Death in Venice* (1973), after T. *Mann. Britten also wrote many fine solo settings of individual poets. The *War Requiem* (1962) was written to celebrate the dedication of the new cathedral at Coventry: the Latin Mass for the Dead is punctuated by settings for solo voice of poems by W. *Owen, and the implications and ironies of the juxtapositions as well as the emotional expressiveness of the music itself create a work whose universality of appeal is comparable only to that of *Peter Grimes* in Britten's output. He was created Baron Britten of Aldeburgh in 1976, and the Aldeburgh Festival continues to celebrate his memory. There is a life by H. Carpenter (1992).

Broad Church, a popular term especially current in the latter half of the 19th cent. for those in the Church of England who sought to interpret the creeds in a broad and liberal manner, and whose theological beliefs lay between Low and High Churchmen. The expression was used by A. P. *Stanley in one of his sermons, about 1847, though the term appears to have originally been proposed by A. H. *Clough. The existence of the Broad Church school owes much to the influence of T. *Arnold and to Romantic philosophy as interpreted by *Coleridge who earned the title of 'Father of the Broad Church Movement'. Other characteristic representatives of the school were Thomas *Hughes, *Jowett, *Pattison, and most of the other writers for *Essays and Reviews*. Their successors are more commonly known as Modernists.

broadside, a sheet of paper printed on one side only, forming one large page; a term generally used of *ballads, etc., so printed.

Brobdingnag, see GULLIVER'S TRAVELS.

Broceliande, a legendary region adjoining Brittany, in the Arthurian legends, where *Merlin lies. *Wace in his *Roman de Rou* says that he made a disappointing visit there (i.e. to Brecheliant in Brittany) and found nothing (ii. 6395 ff.); there is a legendary Tomb of Merlin there still. Broceliande is made the magical forest of Calogrenant's story in *Chrétien's *Yvain*.

BROCH, Hermann (1886–1951), Austrian writer, born in Vienna to Jewish parents. After publishing his vast pessimistic trilogy *Die Schlafwandler* (*The Sleepwalkers*, 1930–2) he was imprisoned by the Nazis until his emigration to America was secured by influential friends including James *Joyce. There he wrote his best-known work, *Der Tod des Vergil* (*The Death of Vergil*, 1945), which imagines the interior monologue of the poet as he lies dying and reflects on the artistic value of the *Aeneid*. Clearly a major writer, Broch nonetheless has an unremitting heaviness of touch, which has muted his influence on world literature.

BRODSKY, Joseph (1940–96), Russian poet, born in

Leningrad. He began writing poetry at the age of 18, and was soon discovered by Anna *Akhmatova. In 1964 he was tried for 'parasitism', and spent a year and a half in exile in northern Russia, working on a state farm. He was exiled from the then Soviet Union in 1972; he lived briefly in London and Vienna, before settling in the United States, where he held a number of university posts. His first volume of poetry in English, *Joseph Brodsky: Selected Poems* (1973), shows that although his strength was a distinctive kind of dry, meditative soliloquy, he was also immensely versatile and technically accomplished in a number of forms. In *A Part of Speech* (1980) he collaborated with a range of distinguished translators including Derek *Walcott, Richard *Wilbur, and David McDuff. The award of the *Nobel Prize in 1987 coincided with the first legal publication of his poetry in Russia. The following year saw the publication of *To Urania: Selected Poems 1965–1985*, which brings together translations of his earlier work with poems composed in English during his years of exile. In many of these poems he reflects on his exile, on memory and memories, and the passage of time. He published two collections of essays in English, *Less than One: Selected Essays* (1986) and *On Grief and Reason* (1995); these are made up of critical studies (*Mandelstam, *Auden, *Hardy, *Rilke, *Frost), autobiographical sketches, and portraits of a number of his contemporaries, including Akhmatova, Nadezhda Mandelstam, Auden, and *Spender. His other prose writing includes *Watermark* (1992), an episodic account of his fascination with the character and history of Venice. He died in New York.

Broken Heart, The, a tragedy by J. *Ford, printed 1633.

The scene is Sparta. Penthea, who was betrothed to Orgilus whom she loved, has been forced by her brother Ithocles to marry the jealous and contemptible Bassanes, who makes her life so miserable that presently she goes mad and dies. Ithocles returns, a successful general, and is honourably received by the king. He falls in love with Calantha, the king's daughter, and she with him, and their marriage is sanctioned by the king. Orgilus, to avenge the fate of Penthea, of which he has been the witness, entraps Ithocles and kills him. During a feast, Calantha hears, in close succession, of the deaths of Penthea, of her father, and of Ithocles. She dances on, apparently unmoved. When the feast is done, she sentences Orgilus to death, and herself dies broken-hearted.

Spartan values (courage, endurance, self-control) dominate the action, and the characters represent abstractions rather than individuals. The grave, formal, stately language, and emblematic imagery make it Ford's finest dramatic achievement.

BROME, Alexander (1620–66), a Royalist poet and friend of I. *Walton and *Cotton, both of whom addressed verses to him. He wrote many attacks on the Rump Parliament, including a ballad entitled *Bumm-foder: or Waste-Paper Proper to Wipe the Nations Rump with* (?1660). He also translated *Horace, wrote songs, and was the author of one comedy, *The Cunning Lovers* (1654).

BROME, Richard (c.1590–1652/3), servant or perhaps secretary to *Jonson, whose friendship he afterwards enjoyed and whose influence is clear in his works, as is that of *Dekker. *The Northern Lass*, his first extant play, was printed in 1632. *The Sparagus Garden* (a place to which more or less reputable persons resorted to eat asparagus and otherwise amuse themselves), a comedy of manners, was acted in 1635. *The City Witt* was printed in 1653. *A Joviall Crew*, his best and latest play, was acted in 1641, often revived, and later turned into an operetta. Fifteen in all of his plays survive, including romantic dramas in the manner of *Fletcher and *Middleton.

BRONTË, Anne (1820–49), sister of Charlotte and Emily *Brontë. She was educated largely at home, where, as the youngest of the motherless family, she may have fallen under the Wesleyan influence of her Aunt Branwell, who is thought to have encouraged her tendency to religious melancholy. As a child she was particularly close to Emily; together they invented the imaginary world of Gondal, the setting of many of their poems. Anne accompanied Charlotte to Roe Head in 1836–7, and became governess to the Ingham family at Blake Hall in 1839; from 1840 to 1845 she was governess to the Robinson family at Thorp Green Hall, near York. Her brother Branwell joined her there as tutor in 1843, and became disastrously involved with Mrs Robinson. Anne's recollections of her experiences with the over-indulged young children and the worldly older children of these two households are vividly portrayed in *Agnes Grey* (1847). The novel appeared under the pseudonym Acton Bell, as did a selection of her poems, published with those of her sisters, in 1846. Her poems, which show the influence of *Cowper and *Wesley, explore religious doubt and confront Calvinist despair: among the most moving are 'To Cowper', 'My God (oh let me call thee mine)' and a Gondal lyric, 'Song: We know where deepest lies the snow'. Her second novel, *The Tenant of Wildfell Hall* (1848), portrays in Arthur Huntingdon a violent, infantile, but sexually attractive drunkard clearly to some extent drawn from Branwell; Charlotte, in her 'Biographical Notice' (1850), felt obliged to comment that 'the choice of subject was an entire mistake', and insists that her sister's nature was 'naturally sensitive, reserved and dejected'. The novel may be read as a scathing indictment of sexual double standards enshrined in marriage law and the educational system. Anne died at Scarborough, where she was buried. See *The Poems of Anne Brontë* (1979, ed. E. Chitham); *Anne Bronte* (1989) by E. Langland; and *A Life of Anne Brontë* (1991) by E. Chitham.

BRONTË, (Patrick) Branwell (1817–48), the brother of Charlotte, Emily, and Anne *Brontë. As a boy he was much involved with his sisters' literary efforts, and collaborated with Charlotte in creating the imaginary world of *Angria. His ambitions as a painter and writer were frustrated; he took to drink and opium, and after a brief spell as a tutor became assistant clerk to a railway company, but was dismissed in 1842 for culpable negligence. In 1843 he joined Anne at Thorp Green Hall as tutor, but became emotionally involved with his employer's wife, Mrs Robinson. The affair ended disastrously, and he returned to Haworth in 1845, where his rapid decline and death caused much suffering to his family.

BRONTË, Charlotte (1816–55), daughter of Patrick Brontë, an Irishman, perpetual curate of Haworth, Yorkshire, from 1820 until his death in 1861. Charlotte's mother died in 1821, leaving five daughters and a son to the care of their aunt, Elizabeth Branwell. Four of the daughters were sent to a Clergy Daughters' School at Cowan Bridge (which Charlotte portrayed as Lowood in *Jane Eyre), an unfortunate step which Charlotte believed to have hastened the death in 1825 of her two elder sisters and to have permanently impaired her own health. The surviving children pursued their education at home; they read widely, and became involved in a rich fantasy life that owes much to their admiration of *Byron, Sir W. *Scott, the *Arabian Nights, the Tales of the Genii, and the engravings of J. *Martin. They began to write stories, to produce microscopic magazines in imitation of their favourite *Blackwood's Magazine, and Charlotte and Branwell collaborated in the increasingly elaborate invention of the imaginary kingdom of *Angria, Emily and Anne in the invention of Gondal. (For a discussion of the juvenilia, see F. E. Ratchford, The Brontës' Web of Childhood, 1941.) In 1831–2 Charlotte was at Miss Wooler's school at Roe Head, whither she returned as a teacher in 1835–8, and where she met her two close friends, Ellen Nussey and Mary Taylor. In 1839 she was a governess with the Sidgwick family, near Skipton, and in 1841 with the White family at Rawdon. In 1842 she went with Emily to study languages at the Pensionnat Heger in Brussels; they were recalled at the end of the year by their aunt's death, and in 1843 Charlotte, whose thirst for wider experience was much greater than her sister's, returned alone for a further year. She fell deeply in love with M. Heger, who failed to respond to the letters she wrote to him after her return to Haworth; a project to establish her own school, with her sisters, also failed. In 1845 she 'discovered' (or so she alleged) the poems of Emily, and, convinced of their quality, projected a joint publication; a volume of verse entitled Poems by Currer, Ellis, and Acton Bell (the pseudonyms of Charlotte, Emily, and Anne) appeared in 1846, but did not sell and received little attention. By this time each had finished a novel; Charlotte's first, *The Professor, never found a publisher in her lifetime, but Emily's *Wuthering Heights and Anne's *Agnes

Grey were accepted by Thomas Newby in 1847 and published in 1848. Undeterred by her own rejections, Charlotte immediately began Jane Eyre (in Manchester, where her father was undergoing an operation for cataract); it was published in 1847 by Smith, Elder and achieved immediate success, arousing much speculation about its authorship. To quell the suspicion (encouraged by the unscrupulous Newby) that the Bell pseudonyms concealed but one author, Charlotte and Anne visited Smith, Elder in July 1848 and made themselves known.

She was not able to enjoy her success and the many invitations now extended to her; Branwell, whose wildness and intemperance had caused the sisters much distress, died in Sept. 1848, Emily in Dec. of the same year, and Anne the following summer. Through this tragic period she persevered with the composition of *Shirley, which appeared in 1849. The loneliness of her later years was alleviated by friendship with Mrs *Gaskell, whom she met in 1850 and who was to write her biography (1857). In the same year she prepared and published a memorial edition of Wuthering Heights and Agnes Grey, with a preface to the former, a 'Biographical Notice of Ellis and Acton Bell', and a further selection of hitherto unpublished poems. *Villette, founded on her memories of Brussels, appeared in 1853. Although her identity was by this time well known in the literary world, she continued to publish as Currer Bell. In 1854, after much persistence on his part and hesitation on hers, she married her father's curate, A. B. Nicholls, but died a few months later of an illness probably associated with pregnancy. 'Emma', a fragment, was published in 1860 in the *Cornhill Magazine with an introduction by *Thackeray, and many of her juvenile works have subsequently been published, adding to our knowledge of the intense creativity of her early years. In her lifetime, Charlotte was the most admired of the Brontë sisters, although she came in for some criticism (which deeply wounded her) on the grounds of alleged 'grossness' and emotionalism, considered particularly unbecoming in a clergyman's daughter: M. *Arnold wrote in a letter (1853) that her mind contained 'nothing but hunger, rebellion and rage', and H. *Martineau offended her by claiming that Villette dealt excessively with 'the need of being loved', and was passionately anti-Catholic. More widespread, however, was praise for her depth of feeling and her courageous realism, and her works continue to hold high popular and critical esteem. The standard biographies are E. Gaskell, The Life of Charlotte Brontë (1857), and W. Gérin, Charlotte Brontë: The Evolution of Genius (1967): see also Juliet Barker, The Brontës (1994); The Brontës: Their Lives, Friendships and Correspondence (4 vols, ed. T. J. Wise and J. A. Symington, 1932).

BRONTË, Emily Jane (1818–48), sister of Charlotte and Anne *Brontë, briefly attended the school at Cowan Bridge with Charlotte in 1824–5, and was then educated largely at home, where she was particularly close to Anne, with whom she created the imaginary world of Gondal, the setting for many of her finest narrative and lyric poems. She was at Roe Head in 1835, but suffered from homesickness and returned after a few months to Haworth; she was even more intensely attached than her sisters to the moorland scenery her work evokes so vividly. She was for a time, probably in 1838, governess at Law Hill, near Halifax, and in 1842 spent nine months in Brussels with Charlotte, studying French, German, and music: her French 'Devoirs' from this period survive, as does M. Heger's praise of her abilities in music and logic. She returned on her aunt's death at the end of the year to Haworth, where she spent the rest of her life, and continued to pursue her studies of German and music. In 1845 Charlotte 'discovered' Emily's poems, and projected a joint publication, *Poems, by Currer, Ellis and Acton Bell*, which appeared in 1846. *Wuthering Heights* was written between Oct. 1845 and June 1846, and published by T. C. Newby after some delay in Dec. 1847. Unlike Charlotte's *Jane Eyre*, it met with more incomprehension than recognition, and it was only after Emily's death (of consumption) that it became widely acknowledged as a masterpiece; in her posthumous 'Biographical Notice' (1850) Charlotte felt obliged to comment on the 'horror of great darkness' that seemed to her to brood over the work. Emily's response to her apparent lack of success, like so much in her character, remains enigmatic. Unlike Charlotte, she had no close friends, wrote few letters, and had few but strong loyalties; the vein of violence (exemplified in the story of her subduing the dog Keeper with her bare hands), of stoicism, and of mysticism in her personality have given rise to many legends but few certainties. She is now established as one of the most original poets of the century, remembered for her lyrics (e.g. 'The night is darkening round me'), for her passionate invocations from the world of Gondal ('Remembrance', 'The Prisoner'), and her apparently more personal visionary moments ('No coward soul is mine'). *Wuthering Heights*, which was at first regarded by many as excessively morbid and violent, was gradually reassessed, and by 1899 Mrs H. *Ward was praising Emily's masterly fusion of romance and realism at the expense of Charlotte's shrill didacticism. The 20th cent. produced a great deal of critical and biographical commentary: C. P. Sanger analysed her careful plotting in *The Structure of 'Wuthering Heights'* (1926); F. *Kermode proposed a variety of readings in *The Classic* (1975); Terry Eagleton proposed a Marxist reading in *Myths of Power* (1975); and J. Hillis Miller explored the complex narrative structure in *Fiction and Repetition* (1982). See also E. Chitham, *A Life* (1987); S. Davies, *Emily Brontë: Heretic* (1994); Juliet Barker, *The Brontës* (1994); See also *The Belgian Essays*, ed. S. Lonoff (1996), and *Poems*, ed. D. Roper and E. Chitham (1994).

BROOK, Peter (1925–), theatre director, educated at Magdalen College, Oxford. The most innovative director of post-war Britain and Europe, he has worked with the Royal Shakespeare Company and the *National Theatre, directing classics (memorably, *King Lear*, 1962, and *A Midsummer Night's Dream*, 1970) and modern plays, but is most celebrated internationally for his experimental work. Landmark productions include *Weiss's *Marat/Sade* (1964), *The Ik* (1975, a multicultural drama of African famine based on an anthropological premiss), the *Mahabharata* (1985; UK 1988), and *L'Homme qui* (1993), based on a work by O. *Sacks. Working with an international Paris-based company, travelling widely, and transcending conventional notions of text and theatrical space, he has been a powerful influence on 20th-cent. theatre, drawing inspiration from many sources. His travels to Iran in 1971 with Ted *Hughes resulted in Hughes's play in an invented language, *Orghast*. He published a memoir, *Threads of Time*, 1998. See also CRUELTY, THEATRE OF.

BROOKE, Emma Frances (1845–1926), radical novelist, journalist, and poet. Educated at Newnham College, Cambridge, and the LSE, she published *Millicent: A Poem* (1881) as 'E. Fairfax Byrrne', writing as Brooke after 1887, although her *New Woman novels, *A Superfluous Woman* (1894) and *Transition* (1895), appeared anonymously. She contributed widely to periodicals and newspapers, was secretary to the Karl Marx Club, and joined the Fellowship of the New Life commune, before moving in the 1880s to a radical community in Kent. An early member of the Fabian Society, her socialist commitments informed her *Tabulation of the Factory Laws of European Countries* (1898).

BROOKE, Frances (1724–89). She spent some years with her husband in Quebec, but the rest of her life as a writer in London. She conducted *The Old Maid* in 1755–6, then in 1760 published *Letters from Juliet Lady Catesby*, translated from Riccoboni, in which intricate currents of feeling are carefully traced. The highly successful *History of Lady Julia Mandeville* followed in 1763, relating the tragic story of the trusting and artless Harry and Lady Julia. It is a book of considerable pessimism, in which the virtuous do not prosper but die. *The History of Emily Montague* (1769), set in Quebec and the frozen Canadian winter, relates the tremulous love story of Emily with Edward Rivers. In 1777 came *The Excursion*, which exposes the superficial nature of 'good breeding'. Young Lord Melvile's education in correct behaviour is displayed confusingly at odds with the generous impulses of his heart. Frances Brooke wrote several works of history and translation, and various dramatic works, including the tragedies *Virginia* (1756) and the *Siege of Sinope* (1781); she enjoyed a continuing success with a musical play, *Rosina*, in 1783 onwards.

BROOKE, Henry (1703–83), educated in Dublin. He attended the Temple, and returned in 1740 to Dublin, where he then chiefly lived. While in London he became a friend of *Pope and other literary men. In 1735 he published *Universal Beauty*, a poem which was thought to have greatly influenced E. *Darwin's *The Botanic Garden*. Encouraged by *Garrick, he wrote several plays, but his tragedy *Gustavus Vasa* (1739) was prohibited on the grounds that the villain resembled Sir R. *Walpole. In 1765–70 he published his highly successful *The Fool of Quality*, and in 1774 another novel, *Juliet Grenville*, both of which are notable for their looseness of structure and for a sustained tone of high sensibility. Brooke wrote much on Irish subjects, and advocated a relaxation of the anti-Catholic laws.

BROOKE, Jocelyn (1908–66), novelist, educated at Bedales and Worcester College, Oxford, who worked at various jobs and spent some time as a regular soldier after serving during the war with the Royal Army Medical Corps. His works include the semi-autobiographical trilogy *The Military Orchid* (1948), *A Mine of Serpents* (1949), and *The Goose Cathedral* (1950), which recall his school and army days; the first uses as its central symbol his search for the vanished military orchid and the pastoral 'Land of Lost Content', and concludes that it has 'gone with scarlet and pipe-clay, with Ouida's guardsmen and Housman's lancers; gone with the concept of soldiering as a chivalric and honourable calling'. His other works include two volumes of poems, *December Spring* (1946) and *The Elements of Death* (1952), and the novel *The Image of a Drawn Sword* (1950).

Brooke, Mr, and his nieces Dorothea and Celia, characters in G. Eliot's *Middlemarch*.

BROOKE, Rupert Chawner (1887–1915), born at Rugby, where his father was a master at the school and where he was educated. A young man of remarkable beauty and charm, he won a scholarship to King's College, Cambridge, where he spent five years as a leader of the literary world. He began to publish poems in journals in 1909, the year in which he settled at Grantchester (about which he later wrote his celebrated poem) and also travelled in Germany. *Poems 1911* was well received, as was his work in the first and second volumes of *Georgian Poetry*, edited by his friend E. *Marsh. In 1913 he won a fellowship to King's; wrote a stark one-act play, *Lithuania*; and suffered a serious breakdown, which led him in 1913 to travel in the USA, Canada, and the Pacific, where, in Tahiti, he wrote 'Tiara Tahiti' and other poems, often thought to be among his best. In 1914 he joined the RNVR and took part in the Antwerp expedition. His five 'War Sonnets', which included 'The Soldier' ('If I should die'), appeared in *New Numbers* early in 1915. The ecstatic reception they received made him the nation's poet of war, a reputation further enhanced by the posthumous publication of *1914 and Other Poems* in 1915. Brooke was then dispatched to the Dardanelles, but he died of blood-poisoning on the way and was buried on Scyros. His dazzling reputation survived for many years, but he is now chiefly valued for his highly accomplished lighter verse, such as 'The Old Vicarage, Granchester' and 'Heaven'; for the Tahiti poems; for a few sonnets (other than the war sequence); and for an intriguing last fragment 'I strayed about the deck'. His work on the dramatist *Webster was published in 1916, as were his *Letters from America*; the *Collected Poems*, with a memoir by Edward Marsh, appeared in 1918, and further poems were added in the *Poetical Works* edited by G. *Keynes in 1946. A biography by C. *Hassall was published in 1964.

BROOKE-ROSE, Christine (1926–), novelist and critic, born in Geneva, brought up bilingually in Brussels, London, and Liverpool, and educated at Somerville College, Oxford, and University College, London. She was professor of English language and literature at the University of Paris from 1975 to her retirement in 1988. Her first novel, *The Languages of Love* (1957), is a cosmopolitan Bloomsbury romance, much of it centred on the Reading Room of the *British Museum. She is best known for her experimental novels, marked by bilingual neologisms, which have some affinity with the *nouveau roman*; these include *Out* (1964), *Such* (1966), *Between* (1968), and *Thru* (1975). After nearly a decade she published *Amalgamemnon* (1984), about a university teacher who is made redundant. This was followed by *Xorandor* (1986), which concerns twins who make contact with a 4,000-year-old being through computer technology, *Verbivore* (1990), and *Textermination* (1991). Her critical works include *A Rhetoric of the Unreal* (1981). *Remake* (1996) is an autobiographical novel (in which she refers to herself for much of the text as 'the old lady'): it gives a vivid, non-chronological account of her experiences as a young WAAF officer at Bletchley Park during the war (BP was 'a first training of the mind, a first university'), of her second marriage to a handsome Polish poet, Janek (the novelist Jerzy Pieterkiewicz), and of her retirement in Provence.

BROOKNER, Anita (1928–), novelist and art historian, educated at King's College London, and at the Courtauld Institute of Art. She was the first woman to occupy the Slade Chair of Art at Cambridge (1967–8) and has published several works of art history, including studies of Watteau, Greuze, and Jacques-Louis David. Her first work of fiction, *A Start in Life*, which tells the story of Dr Ruth Weiss, an authority on *Balzac, whose life has been shaped by literature, was published in 1981, since when she has produced a succession of elegantly written novels. Though restricted in theme and social context, they are finely realized, dealing often with women whose lives, through circumstances or cultural conditioning, have become something to be endured. In *Providence* (1982) the central character, Kitty Maule, is an academic working on the Romantic tradition who becomes infatuated with a professor of medieval history. *A Misalliance* (1986) is the story of Blanche Vernon, whose husband has deserted her for a younger woman. In *Brief Lives* (1990) the relationship between a former singer and her self-obsessive friend Julia is examined. *A Closed Eye* (1991) is about a woman married to a much older man who falls in love with the husband of a friend. Other novels include *Look at Me* (1983), *Latecomers* (1988), *Fraud* (1992), *Incidents in the Rue Laugier* (1995), and *Visitors* (1997). *The Next Big Thing* (2002) has, unusually in her work, a male protagonist. *Hotel du Lac* (1984), in which a romantic novelist, Edith Hope, takes refuge in a Swiss hotel out of season and meets a man whom she thinks will transform her life, won the *Booker Prize and was adapted for television by Christopher *Hampton in 1986.

BROOKS, Cleanth (1906–94), American critic, born in Kentucky, and educated at Vanderbilt and Tulane Universities, then at Oxford, before becoming a teacher at Louisiana State University and later at Yale. His college textbook *Understanding Poetry* (with R. P. *Warren, 1938) helped to establish the methods of the *New Criticism in classrooms. His major works of poetic criticism, *Modern Poetry and the Tradition* (1939) and *The Well Wrought Urn* (1947), both regard irony and paradox as the typical virtues of poetry, in lucid developments from T. S. *Eliot's critical arguments. He collaborated with W. K. Wimsatt in *Literary Criticism: A Short History* (1957), and wrote two books on W. *Faulkner. His later essays appeared in *The Hidden God* (1963) and *A Shaping Joy* (1971).

BROPHY, Brigid Antonia (1929–95), novelist, daughter of the author John Brophy (1899–1965), and wife of the art historian Michael Levey, educated at St Hugh's College, Oxford. Her novels include *Hackenfeller's Ape* (1953), *Flesh* (1962), *The Snow Ball* (1962), *In Transit* (1969), in which the narrator, waiting in an airport lounge, explores his/her own identity through a series of reflections, verbal fantasies, and typographical experiments, and *Palace without Chairs* (1978). Her non-fiction works (which, like her fiction, express her interest in opera and the visual arts) include *Black and White: A Portrait of Aubrey Beardsley* (1968) and a life of *Firbank, *Prancing Novelist* (1973). She wrote plays and short stories, and was actively involved in the campaign for *Public Lending Right.

Brothers, The, a comedy by R. *Cumberland, produced 1769.

The younger Belfield has been dispossessed of his estate by his brother, who has left his wife, Violetta, and is now courting Belfield's own sweetheart Sophia, from whom Belfield has been forcibly parted. A privateer, wrecked on the coast, turns out to have on board both the younger Belfield and Violetta. Their unexpected arrival frustrates the designs of the elder brother, and the lovers are reunited.

BROUGHAM, Henry Peter, Baron Brougham and Vaux (1778–1868). He was educated at Edinburgh High School and University, and rose to be lord chancellor. He was a man of tremendous activity. His legal career was of the highest distinction, and included the defence of Queen Caroline in 1820, but he also took an important part in the founding of London University, and vigorously promoted the Mechanics' Institute and the Society for the Diffusion of Useful Knowledge. In the history of literature he is remembered principally as one of the founders, with *Jeffrey and Sydney *Smith, of the *Edinburgh Review* in 1802. He also wrote *Observations on the Education of the People* (1825); *Historical Sketches of Statesmen in the Time of George III* (1839–43); *Demosthenes upon the Crown*, Translated (1840); and *The Life and Times of Lord Brougham*, published posthumously in 1871. He is said to have been the author of the disparaging article on *Hours of Idleness* in the *Edinburgh Review* of Jan. 1808, an article which provoked Byron into writing *English Bards and Scotch Reviewers*. Of the many squibs written on Brougham's character and activities, the most famous is the lampoon in Peacock's *Crotchet Castle*, where Brougham appears as the 'learned friend' who 'is for doing all the world's business as well as his own'.

The brougham, a one-horse closed carriage, with two or four wheels, is named after him.

'Brougham Castle, Song at the Feast of', a poem by *Wordsworth, composed in 1807. See under SHEPHERD, LORD CLIFFORD, THE.

BROUGHTON, Rhoda (1840–1920), the daughter of a clergyman, who spent many years in Oxford with her widowed sister. Her many light, witty novels of country-house and town life, with their lively and articulate heroines, gained her a reputation for audacity of which a younger and more outspoken generation deprived her—to her own private amusement. She began her career with the three- and two-decker novels that were still popular (*Not Wisely, but too Well*, 1867; *Cometh up as a Flower*, 1867; *Nancy*, 1873), but was possibly more at home with the form of her later short, sharp, observant one-volume novels, which include *Mrs Bligh* (1892), *Dear Faustina* (1897), *Lavinia* (1902, which boldly presents an anti-Boer War hero, fond of old lace), and *A Waif's Progress* (1905). G. B. *Shaw described her as 'the first to give us sincere pictures of the girls who drift from womanhood with some obsolete schooling and no training whatever . . . eventually suffering the doom of the unfit' ('Fact and Fiction').

Browdie, John, in Dickens's *Nicholas Nickleby*, a bluff, kind-hearted Yorkshireman, who befriends Nicholas and Smike.

BROWN, Charles Brockden (1771–1810), acclaimed as the first professional American author. He was born in Philadelphia, and worked briefly as a lawyer before writing the four *Gothic novels for which he is remembered, *Wieland* (1798), *Arthur Mervyn* (1799), *Ormond* (1799), and *Edgar Huntly* (1799). Although obviously indebted to *Godwin and A. *Radcliffe, these were pioneer works which gave Gothic romance an American setting, and Brown's psychological interest in obsession, seduction, madness, and cruelty made him a precursor of *Poe. He was admired in England, notably by Sir W. *Scott and *Keats, and *Shelley was so affected by him that he playfully named many of his friends after Brown's heroes and heroines; *Peacock was to write, 'nothing so blended itself with the structure of [Shelley's] interior mind as the creations of Brown.'

BROWN, Curtis, see AGENTS, LITERARY.

BROWN, George Douglas, see DOUGLAS, GEORGE.

BROWN, George Mackay (1921–96), Scottish poet, novelist, playwright, and short story writer, born and brought up in Orkney, where he remained almost the whole of his life, only once visiting England. Educated at Newbattle Abbey College, under E. *Muir, and at the University of Edinburgh. Although versatile in the variety of its literary forms, all his work springs from a deep local source and is rooted in Norse saga, island folklore, the cycles of rural life, and a deep Christian faith. His volumes of poetry include *Loaves and Fishes* (1959), *The Year of the Whale* (1969), and *Following a Lark* (1996). He also published several collections of short stories, including *A Calendar of Love* (1967) and *A Time to Keep* (1969). His first novel, *Greenvoe* (1972), was set on an imaginary northern island, Hellya, which becomes the site for a military project called Operation Black Star. The story describes the resulting destruction of the village of Greenvoe against the unchanging and self-renewing backdrop of nature. This was followed by *Magnus* (1973) and in 1994 he published *Beside the Ocean of Time*, set on another fictitious Orcadian island, Norday, which evocatively describes the imaginings of Ragnarson, a crofter's son. Other works include *An Orkney Tapestry* (1969), a medley of prose and verse, and a posthumously published *Autobiography* (1997).

BROWN, John (1800–59), commemorated in the well-known marching song 'John Brown's Body' and in *Whittier's poem 'John Brown of Osawatomie'. He migrated in 1855 from Ohio to Kansas, where he became a leader of the anti-slavery movement. On the night of 16 Oct. 1859, at the head of a small party of his followers, he seized the arsenal of Harper's Ferry, Virginia, intending to arm the slaves and start an uprising. He was quickly captured, tried by the Virginia authorities, and hanged at Charlestown.

The author of the song is unknown, but it is most frequently attributed to Thomas B. Bishop (1835–1905) of Portland; set to an old Methodist hymn-tune, it became the most popular marching song of the Federal forces.

BROWN, Dr John (1810–82), Edinburgh physician and essayist, most of whose writings are contained in his three volumes of *Horae Subsecivae* (1858–82), including *Marjorie Fleming* and the memorable dog story *Rab and His Friends*.

BROWN, Lancelot (1716–83), landscape architect, known as 'Capability' Brown because he was reputed to tell patrons that their estates had 'great capabilities'. Notable among his creations are the lake at *Blenheim and the park at Chatsworth. Although attacked by later devotees of the *picturesque, he was a key figure in its development, and his landscapes were deliberately fashioned to evoke the landscapes of *Claude.

BROWN, Thomas (1663–1704), satirist, educated at Christ Church, Oxford, where he wrote 'I do not love you, Dr Fell' (see FELL). He later settled in London as Tory pamphleteer, translator, and hack writer. See B. Boyce, *Tom Brown of Facetious Memory* (1939).

BROWN, T(homas) E(dward) (1830–97), born in the Isle of Man and educated there and at Oxford; he was second master at Clifton 1864–93. He published *Betsy Lee: A Foc's'le Yarn* (1873), *Foc's'le Yarns* (1881), and other books of verse, most of it in the Manx dialect, and dealing with Manx life. Many of his non-dialect poems display a deeply felt and freshly conveyed sense of the beauty of the West Country landscape, far superior to his most anthologized piece, 'A garden is a lovesome thing, God wot'. His collected poems were issued in 1900 and reprinted in 1952 (2 vols) with a memoir by *Quiller-Couch, originally published in 1930.

BROWNE, Charles Farrar (1834–67), American humorous moralist, born in Maine, who wrote under the pseudonym 'Artemus Ward'. He purported to describe the experiences of a travelling showman, using, like 'Josh Billings' (H. W. Shaw), his own comic phonetic spelling. He became a contributor to *Punch* and died in England.

BROWNE, Hablot Knight (1815–82). Under the pseudonym 'Phiz', he illustrated some of the works of *Dickens, *Surtees, *Smedley, etc.

BROWNE, Robert, see BROWNISTS.

BROWNE, Sir Thomas (1605–82), born in London and educated at Winchester and Pembroke College, Oxford. He toured Ireland before studying medicine at Montpellier and Padua, and received a doctorate from Leiden. After writing *Religio Medici*—first published without his consent in 1642—he settled in Norwich in about 1637 to practise medicine, remaining there for the rest of his life. In 1646 appeared his most learned and ambitious work, *Pseudodoxia Epidemica*, commonly known as *Vulgar Errors*. In the 1650s he wrote for friends the shorter tracts *Hydriotaphia* or *Urn Burial*, *The Garden of Cyrus*, and *A Letter to a Friend* (published 1690), the latter overlapping in content with *Christian Morals*, a sententious piece said by his daughter Elizabeth to be a continuation of *Religio Medici*; it was first published in 1716 and re-edited in 1756 by Dr *Johnson, who prefaced it with a substantial 'Life'. *Certain Miscellany Tracts*, on a wide range of topics in human and natural history, were also published posthumously. He was knighted in 1671 by Charles II, and lies buried in the church of St Peter Mancroft, Norwich.

BROWNE, William (?1590–1645), born in Tavistock and educated at Exeter College, Oxford. He published *Britannia's Pastorals* (Bks I and II, 1613, 1616), a narrative poem dealing with the loves and woes of Marina, Celia, etc., in couplets interspersed with lyrics; Bk III, unfinished, remained in manuscript until 1852. He contributed to *The Shepheard's Pipe* (1614) with *Wither and others. Among various epitaphs he wrote the well-known lines on the dowager countess of *Pembroke, 'Underneath this sable hearse | Lies the subject of all verse'. His poetry displays genuine love and observation of nature, and its sensuous richness influenced *Keats; he was also admired by Milton, whose *'L'Allegro' and *Lycidas* contain echoes and imitations.

BROWNING, Elizabeth Barrett (1806–61), eldest of the twelve children of Edward Moulton Barrett, whose wealth was derived from Jamaican plantations; she spent her childhood at Hope End in Herefordshire. Although largely self-educated at home, she learnt much from correspondence with her scholarly neighbours U. *Price and Hugh Stuart Boyd, became deeply versed in the classics and in prosodic theory, and later published translations from ancient and Byzantine Greek poetry. In 1832 the Barrett family moved to Sidmouth, and in 1835 to London; in 1838 Elizabeth Barrett, seriously ill as a result of a broken blood-vessel, was sent to Torquay and here, two years later, her eldest brother Edward was drowned, to her lifelong grief. She returned to London, still an invalid, in 1841. In 1845 Robert *Browning began a correspondence with her which led to their meeting and to an engagement, necessarily secret since the tyrannical Mr Barrett ruled his adult sons and daughters as though they were still children and forbade any of them to marry. In Sept. 1846 Browning and Elizabeth Barrett were secretly married and left for Italy. Casa Guidi in Florence became their base for the rest of Mrs Browning's life, though they paid long visits to Rome, Siena, Bagni di Lucca, Paris, and London. Their only child, Robert Wiedemann (known as Penini), was born in 1849. Throughout her married life Mrs Browning was passionately interested in Italian and French politics

and an ardent partisan of Italian unity. She also became fascinated by spiritualism, though this—unlike her political enthusiasms—played no part in her poetry. Her intensely happy 15 years of marriage ended with her death in Browning's arms.

Mrs Browning's juvenilia, *The Battle of Marathon* (1820), *An Essay on Mind* (1826), and a translation of *Prometheus Bound*, with other poems (1833), appeared anonymously, and the first two were privately printed at her father's expense. *The Seraphim, and Other Poems* (1838) was her first work to gain critical and public attention. Her next set of *Poems* (1844) was so highly regarded that, when *Wordsworth died in 1850, her name was widely canvassed as his most appropriate successor as poet laureate. Throughout her married life her poetic reputation stood higher than Browning's in general contemporary opinion, though her progressive social ideas and her audacious prosodic experiments—perhaps the most appealing aspects of her work to many 20th-cent. readers—were considered alarming by readers in her own day. Her *Sonnets from the Portuguese* first appeared in a collected edition of her poems in 1850; *Casa Guidi Windows*, on the theme of Italian liberation, in 1851; and her magnum opus, *Aurora Leigh*, in 1857. The stridently political *Poems before Congress* (1860) injured her popularity. *Last Poems*, issued posthumously in 1862, contained some of her best-known lyrics. Since her death many volumes of her spirited and engaging letters, including her exchange of love letters with Browning and her correspondence with such friends as M. R. *Mitford and *Haydon, have been published. The Brownings were friends with Ruskin, Carlyle, Tennyson, Thackeray, Landor, Rossetti, Hawthorne, and many other famous contemporaries, on all of whom Mrs Browning's large-mindedness, vivid intelligence, and quietly sympathetic manner made a lifelong impression. There are biographies by Dorothy Hewlett (1953), G. B. Taplin (1957), and M. *Forster (1988).

BROWNING, Oscar (1837–1923), was a pupil of W. J. *Cory at Eton, and from 1860 to 1875 was himself assistant master there. He was then a history lecturer at King's College, Cambridge, where he became a legendary figure: fat, vain, snobbish, and quarrelsome, he nevertheless commanded considerable loyalty from his favoured pupils, and enjoyed his own somewhat ridiculous reputation and the anecdotes he inspired. For accounts of his personality, see E. F. *Benson's *As We Were* (1930) and A. C. *Benson's *Memories and Friends* (1924). He published various historical and biographical works, including a life of G. *Eliot (1890), whom he had known since his Eton days. There is a life by I. Anstruther (1983).

BROWNING, Robert (1812–89), the son of Robert Browning (d. 1866), a clerk in the Bank of England, and Sarah Anna Wiedemann (d. 1849), of German-Scottish descent, brought up with his only sister Sarianna in Camberwell in south-east London, receiving his education mainly in his father's large (6,000 vols) and eclectic library. The contrasting influences of his boyhood were those of his reading (particularly of *Shelley, *Byron, and *Keats) and of his mother's strong Nonconformist piety. He wrote a volume of lyric poems, *Incondita*, at the age of 12, but subsequently destroyed them: two survive. In 1828 he enrolled at London University, but dropped out in his second term. His first published poem, *Pauline*, appeared anonymously in 1833 and attracted little notice. Browning travelled to Russia in 1834 and made his first trip to Italy in 1838. *Paracelsus* (1835) was a critical success, as a result of which Browning formed several important friendships, notably with J. *Forster and *Macready, who persuaded him to write for the stage; he also met *Carlyle, *Dickens, and *Tennyson. In 1837 his play *Strafford* was produced at Covent Garden. He next published *Sordello* (1840), whose hostile reception eclipsed his reputation for over 20 years, and the series of plays and collections of shorter poems called *Bells and Pomegranates* (1841–6). He began corresponding with Elizabeth Barrett (see BROWNING, E. B.) in Jan. 1845 when, after returning from his second trip to Italy, he read and admired her 1844 *Poems*. He met her first in 1845; their relationship had to be kept a secret from her father, and they finally married and eloped to Italy in Sept. 1846. They lived mainly in Italy (first in Pisa and then in Florence) until Elizabeth's death in 1861. They had one child, Robert Wiedemann Barrett Browning ('Pen', 1849–1913). In 1850 Browning published *Christmas-Eve and Easter-Day* and in 1855 the masterpiece of his middle period, *Men and Women*, which, together with *Dramatis Personae* (1864), began to revive his reputation; the revival was completed by the triumph of *The Ring and the Book* (1868–9), though Browning was never to achieve the commercial success of Tennyson. Meanwhile he had returned to England after the death of Elizabeth; from 1866, after his father died, he lived with his sister, generally spending the 'season' in London, and the rest of the year in the country or abroad. He formed a wide circle of acquaintances in London society, and was awarded an honorary degree by Oxford University, and an honorary fellowship by Balliol College, Oxford, whose master *Jowett was a close friend. The Browning Society was founded in 1881. Browning's publications after *The Ring and the Book* were: *Balaustion's Adventure* (1871), *Prince Hohenstiel-Schwangau* (1871), *Fifine at the Fair* (1872), *Red Cotton Night-Cap Country* (1873), *Aristophanes' Apology* (1875), *The Inn Album* (1875), *Pacchiarotto . . . with Other Poems* (1876), *The Agamemnon of Aeschylus* (1877), *La Saisiaz* and *The Two Poets of Croisic* (1878), *Dramatic Idyls* (1879), *Dramatic Idyls, Second Series* (1880), *Jocoseria* (1883), *Ferishtah's Fancies* (1884), *Parleyings with Certain People of Importance in Their Day* (1887), and *Asolando* (1889, published on 12 Dec., the day of Browning's death). Browning issued collections of his work in 1849, 1863, 1868, and 1888–9. The most recent collected edition (1981) contains Browning's fugitive pieces, of which the most notable are the fine unfinished poem known as 'Aeschylus' Soliloquy', the sonnet 'Helen's Tower', 'Gerousios Oinos', the sonnet 'Why I am a Liberal', and the sonnet 'To Edward Fitzgerald' (a savage attack after Browning read a disparaging reference to his wife in one of *Fitzgerald's posthumously published letters). Browning's only prose works of importance are two 'essays' on *Chatterton (1842) and *Shelley (1852), the first in the form of a review (of a book on another subject) and the second as the introduction to a collection of letters of Shelley (which turned out to be forgeries). His correspondence with Elizabeth Barrett has been published, along with other separate volumes of letters; a collected edition is in progress. Browning died in Venice and is buried in Westminster Abbey.

Brownists, adherents of the ecclesiastical principles of Robert Browne (?1550–?1633), who preached c.1578 denouncing the parochial system and ordination, whether by bishops or by presbytery. About 1580 he, with Robert Harrison, collected a congregation at Norwich, which they called 'the church', but which was familiarly known as 'the Brownists'. He finally submitted to the bishop of Peterborough and became for 40 years rector of Achurch in Northamptonshire. He is regarded as the founder of Congregationalism.

BROWNJOHN, Alan Charles (1931–), poet, born in London and educated at Merton College, Oxford, who taught in various schools and other institutions from 1953 to 1979, before becoming a full-time writer. An early booklet of poems, *Travellers Alone* (1954), and his first volume, *The Railings* (1961), were followed by several other volumes. *Collected Poems 1952–83* was published in 1983 and reissued in 1988 to include most of the poems published in a subsequent volume, *The Old Flea-Pit* (1987). A further collection, *The Observation Car*, was published in 1990. Brownjohn's poetry is, characteristically, good-humoured, ironic, and urbane, and, in P. *Porter's phrase, it unites 'wit and civic responsibility' in its survey of contemporary social, domestic, and literary life. He has also written for children (*Brownjohn's Beasts*, 1970) and edited several anthologies and written a critical study of P. *Larkin (1975). A novel, *The Way You Tell Them*, was published in 1990, and *The Long Shadows* in 1997.

Brownlow, Mr, a character in Dickens's *Oliver Twist*.

Bruce, The, see BARBOUR.

BRUEGEL, Pieter (c.1525/30–69), Netherlandish genre, landscape, and religious painter, and a brilliant draughtsman. He first became known for his allegorical and satirical prints and his paintings crowded with little figures that look back to the demonic imagery of Bosch. Much of his imagery is drawn from proverb and folklore. In 1565 he painted his most famous works, great cosmic landscapes representing *The Months*, and in 1566–8 his celebrated scenes of rustic genre, *The Peasant Wedding Feast*. His latest works, e.g. *The Blind Leading the Blind*, are tragic indictments of the human condition. He has been the subject of a vast amount of scholarly literature and virulent controversy, and his paintings have inspired writers, including W. C. *Williams and, notably, W. H.*Auden, in his 'Musée des Beaux Arts', on the *Fall of Icarus*.

BRUMMELL, George Bryan (1778–1840), generally called Beau Brummell, a friend of the prince regent (George IV) and leader of fashion in London. He died in poverty at Caen.

Brunanburh, a poem in Old English, included in four manuscripts of the *Anglo-Saxon Chronicle* under the year 937, dealing with the battle fought in that year at Brunanburh between the English under Athelstan, the grandson of Alfred, and the Danes under Anlaf from Dublin, supported by the Scots led by Constantine II and the Welsh. The site of the battle is unknown, but it is thought to be somewhere on the west coast of Britain between Chester and Dumfries. The poem is a triumphant celebration of the deeds of Athelstan and his brother and successor Edmund, in their defeat of the invaders. *Tennyson wrote a verse translation (*Ballads and Other Poems*, 1880). There is an edition by A. Campbell (1938).

Brunhild, see BRYNHILD.

BRUNO, Giordano (1548–1600), Italian philosopher, born near Nola, who saw God as the unity reconciling spirit and matter. He was in early life a Dominican friar, but broke from his order and left Italy to avoid prosecution for heresy. He converted to Calvinism in Geneva, but was later excommunicated. He moved to France and then to England, where his scornful view of Oxford philosophy prompted him to embody his own views in a series of Italian dialogues and poems, some of them dedicated to *Sidney, under whose auspices he visited Oxford. He left for France and then Germany, where he was excommunicated by the Lutheran Church, and returned to Italy in the mistaken belief that it would be safe to do so. He was accused of heresy, imprisoned for seven years, and finally burnt at the stake in Rome. He wrote a fine comedy, *Il candelaio* (*The Candlemaker*, 1582). See F. *Yates, *Giordano Bruno and the Hermetic Tradition* (1964). His writings were much admired by *Joyce, who mystified his friends by enigmatic references to 'the Nolan'.

Brut, or **Brutus,** legendary founder of the British race. *Geoffrey of Monmouth states that Walter, archdeacon of Oxford, gave him an ancient book in the British tongue containing an account of the kings of Britain from Brutus to Cadwallader. This Brutus was son of Sylvius, grandson of Ascanius and great-grandson of Aeneas. Having had the misfortune to kill his father, he collected a remnant of the Trojan race and brought them to England (uninhabited at the time 'except by a few giants'), landing at Totnes. He founded Troynovant or New Troy (later known as London) and was the progenitor of a line of British kings including Bladud, *Gorboduc, Ferrex and Porrex, *Lud, *Cymbeline, *Coel, *Vortigern, and *Arthur. The name 'Troynovant' is a back-formation from 'Trinovantes', the name of the powerful British tribe that lived north and east of London. Drayton, in his *Poly-Olbion* (i. 312), relates the legend, and *Selden, in his *Illustrations* to that work, discusses its probability.

His name came to be used to mean 'chronicle of the Britons', by Geoffrey of Monmouth's followers such as *Wace and *Laȝamon after Geoffrey began his history of the kings of Britain with him. No doubt the phonetic echo (cf. Romulus/Rome) led to the adoption of this eponymous progenitor for the Britons.

Brut, The Prose, a long English version, translated between 1350 and 1380, of the Anglo-Norman prose *Brut* which extends up to 1333. Over 100 copies of the English are extant. It has a strong Lancastrian bias which differentiates it from the 15th-cent. *Brut*, composed in London *c*.1461 and pro-York. See above and the discussions in A. Gransden, *Historical Writing in England II* (1982), 73–7 and 220 ff.

Brute, Sir John and Lady, characters in Vanbrugh's *The Provok'd Wife*.

Brutus. In Shakespeare's *Julius Caesar*, Decius Brutus is one of the conspirators. Marcus Brutus is the idealistic friend of Caesar who is persuaded by *Cassius to join the conspiracy. Caesar receives his wound from Brutus with the legendary words '*Et tu, Brute?*—Then fall, Caesar!' (III. i. 76). Antony's tribute to Brutus after his death as 'the noblest Roman of them all' (v. v. 68) is well known. The internal deliberations of Brutus have been seen as precursors of those of *Hamlet, hero of what was probably Shakespeare's next play.

BRYAN, Sir Francis (d. 1550), poet, soldier, and diplomatist. He was Henry VIII's permanent favourite, held various court posts, and was sent on diplomatic missions. He behaved discreditably in the matter of the execution of his cousin Anne Boleyn, and accepted a pension vacated by one of her accomplices. Thomas Cromwell, in writing of this circumstance to Gardiner and Wallop, calls him 'the vicar of hell', which became a popular nickname. It is to this, no doubt, that Milton in the *Areopagitica* refers when he writes, 'I name not him for posterities sake, whom *Harry* the 8. nam'd in merriment his Vicar of hell.' He was a friend of *Wyatt, who addressed his third satire to him. Bryan contributed to *Tottel's *Miscellany* and his poetry was highly valued in his day, but is now undiscoverable.

BRYANT, William Cullen (1794–1878), American poet, born in Massachusetts. He first practised law, but then entered journalism, and was for 50 years editor of the

145   BRYDGES | BUCKINGHAM

New York *Evening Post*. He began to make a name as a poet as early as 1817, when his Wordsworthian blank verse meditation 'Thanatopsis' was published in the *North American Review*, and confirmed his reputation with *Poems* (1821), which contains his well-known 'To a Waterfowl', 'The Yellow Violet', and 'Green River'. His next volume, *Poems* (1832), which contains 'The Death of the Flowers' and 'To the Fringed Gentian', was followed by several other collections.

BRYDGES, Sir Samuel Egerton (1762–1837). He devoted his life to literary work and considered himself to be a great writer, but he was successful only as a bibliographer. He published his valuable *Censura Literaria* in 1805–9 and 1815; *The British Bibliographer* in 1810–14; and *Restituta: or Titles, Extracts, and Characters of Old Books in English Literature Revived* in 1814–16. Of his novel *Arthur Fitz-Albini* (1798) J. *Austen mildly observed, 'there is a very little story.' His *Autobiography, Times, Opinions, Contemporaries of Sir Egerton Brydges* (1835) is a confused and opinionated narrative of little interest.

BRYHER, the pseudonym, adopted from the name of one of the Isles of Scilly, of (Annie) Winifred Ellerman (1894–1983), novelist, poet, and patron of the arts. The daughter of a wealthy shipping magnate, she lived for many years at Geneva; her friends in the literary world included the *Sitwells and, notably, H. *Doolittle, whom she met in 1918, and whom she both protected and dominated for years.

Brynhild, or **Brunhild,** one of the principal characters in the *Vǫlsunga saga* and the *Nibelungenlied*.

BUCHAN, John, first Baron Tweedsmuir (1875–1940), born in Perth, the son of a minister. He was educated at Glasgow and Brasenose College, Oxford, and while still at Oxford published a novel (*Sir Quixote of the Moors*, 1895) and essays (*Scholar Gipsies*, 1896), and contributed to the *Yellow Book*. From 1901 to 1903 he was in South Africa with the High Commission working on reconstruction after the Boer War, and later combined a literary career with a career in public life, culminating with the post of governor-general of Canada, 1935–40. He wrote many non-fiction works, including lives of *Montrose (1913) and *Scott (1932), but is remembered for his adventure stories, the first of which was *Prester John* (1910), set in Africa, in which a young Scot becomes embroiled in a plot involving a legendary necklace of rubies, a villainous Portuguese, and a doomed African visionary with a mission to restore 'Africa to the Africans'. Many of his other tales feature a recurring group of heroes (Richard Hannay, Sandy Arbuthnot, Peter Pienaar, Edward Leithen, etc.); favoured settings include Scotland, the Cotswolds, and South Africa, although the last, *Sick Heart River* (1941), prefiguring his own death, is set in the icy wastes of Canada. The stories are packed with action, often involving elaborate cross-country chases; the characterization is simple, the landscapes are lovingly

evoked. The most popular include *The Thirty-Nine Steps* (1915; filmed by Hitchcock, 1935), *Greenmantle* (1916), *Mr Standfast* (1918), and *John Macnab* (1925). There is a life by Janet Adam Smith (1965). See also SPY FICTION.

BUCHANAN, George (1506–82), born near Killearn in Stirlingshire; he studied at St Andrews and Paris, and became tutor to a natural son of James V. He satirized the Franciscans, thus provoking Cardinal Beaton, and was imprisoned at St Andrews. Escaping, he went to the Continent, became a professor at Bordeaux, where he had *Montaigne among his pupils, and in 1547 was invited to teach in the university of Coimbra, but was imprisoned by the Inquisition, 1549–51. After some years in France he returned to Scotland and professed himself a Protestant. He became a bitter enemy of *Mary Queen of Scots, in consequence of the murder of Darnley, and vouched that the compromising Casket Letters were in her handwriting. He wrote his *Detectio Maria Scotorum Regina* in 1571. He was tutor to James VI and I during 1570–8. Chief among his many writings are his Latin poem *Sphaera*, an exposition of the Ptolemaic system as against that advocated by *Copernicus, four Latin plays (including *Baptistes*, 1577), an important political treatise, *De Iure Regni apud Scotos* (1579), and Latin *Rerum Scoticarum Historia* (1582), which for long was regarded as a standard authority. His first elegy, 'Quam misera sit conditio docentium literas humaniores Lutetiae', describes the hard lot of the student at Paris. His versions of the Psalms were, from 1566, immensely popular. There is a life of him by I. D. McFarlane (1981).

BUCHANAN, Robert Williams (1841–1901), poet, essayist, novelist, and playwright, the son of a socialist and secularist tailor who owned several socialist journals in Glasgow. He came to London in 1860 and made a name for himself as a man of letters, but his many novels, poems, and plays are now forgotten, and he is remembered largely for his attacks on *Swinburne (whom he called unclean, morbid, and sensual, and satirized in a poem 'The Session of the Poets' in the *Spectator*, 1866) and on the *Pre-Raphaelites, principally D. G. *Rossetti, whom he attacked in 'The Fleshly School of Poetry' in the *Contemporary Review* (1871) under the pseudonym 'Thomas Maitland'. After Rossetti's death he recanted in an essay in *A Look round Literature* (1887), in which he declared that Rossetti 'uses amatory forms and carnal images to express ideas which are purely and remotely spiritual'.

Bucket, Inspector, the detective in Dickens's *Bleak House*.

BUCKHURST, Lord, see SACKVILLE, T. and C.

BUCKINGHAM, George Villiers, second duke of (1628–87), a prominent figure in the reign of Charles II and an influential member of the *Cabal, and the Zimri of Dryden's *Absalom and Achitophel*. He was the author of verses, satires, and the burlesque *The Rehearsal, which was much performed in the 18th cent. with topical additions and substitutions. Famed for his debauchery and amorous adventures, as well as for the vicissitudes of his public life, he died miserably at Kirby Moorside; the death of 'this lord of useless thousands' in 'the worst inn's worst room' is described by Pope in a famous passage in his *Epistle III* (*Moral Essays). He also figures in Scott's *Peveril of the Peak.

BUCKINGHAM, James Silk (1786–1855), author and traveller, and founder of the *Athenaeum.

Buckingham, duke of, in Shakespeare's *Richard III; he acts as Richard's ally in murdering Lord *Hastings and in elevating him to the throne, but defects to the support of Richmond after his master fails to reward him. The line 'Off with his head! So much for Buckingham' occurs in C. *Cibber's adaptation (1700), which was the stage version generally used until H. *Irving's production in 1877.

BUCKLE, Henry Thomas (1821–62). He received no school or college training, but inherited money from his father and devoted himself to travelling on the Continent, where he acquired several languages and became a radical freethinker. He was also among the world's strongest chess-players in the 1840s, giving up serious play in favour of writing. The first volume of his *History of Civilization in England* appeared in 1857 and the second in 1861. These were only to be introductory portions of a far larger work, which the author's premature death of typhoid at Damascus prevented him from executing. Buckle criticized the methods of previous historians and sought to establish a scientific basis, arguing that changing phenomena have unchanging laws and that the growth of civilization in various countries depended on the interrelated factors of climate, food production, population, and wealth. The work achieved great success, was much admired by C. *Darwin, and gained an international reputation; it was particularly admired in Russia. See J. M. Robertson, *Buckle and his Critics* (1895).

BUDÉ, Guillaume (1467–1540), French humanist. He did important work in Roman law and in numismatics, but was primarily celebrated for his contribution to Greek scholarship, notably the *Commentarii linguae graecae* (1529). He did much to encourage the revival of classical learning in France, was instrumental in the founding of what was to become the Collège de France, and, as royal librarian under Francis I, laid the basis for the future Bibliothèque Nationale.

BUDGELL, Eustace (1686–1737), a cousin of *Addison, a miscellaneous writer who contributed to the *Spectator and is mocked by Pope in *The Dunciad and other works. He lost money in the *South Sea Company, became involved in various lawsuits, and eventually committed suicide.

BUFFON, Georges-Louis Leclerc, comte de (1707–88), French naturalist, curator of the Jardin du Roi and author of the monumental *Histoire naturelle, générale et particulière* in 36 vols (1749–88), for which he enjoyed immense public esteem during his lifetime. The *Natural History*, which was completed after Buffon's death in eight additional vols (1788–1804) by E. de Lacépède, aimed at a comprehensive view of living creatures in their environment and included (in *Théorie de la terre*, 1749, and *Époques de la nature*, 1778) reconstructions of the geological periods of the earth. Buffon's method combines detailed observation with bold generalization and poetic vision: both his descriptions of animals and his hypothetical accounts of geological epochs are vividly and imaginatively rendered. He refused to enter into the controversy aroused by his conception of the earth's history, maintaining deistic views and the unity of all creation with man as its centre and crown. Buffon was a notable stylist. His ideals of order, harmony, and decorum are set out in his *Discours sur le style* (1753), originally his address on being received into the *Académie française, later published as a supplement to the *Natural History*; it contains the celebrated dictum: 'le style est l'homme même'.

Buffone, Carlo, in Jonson's *Every Man out of His Humour, 'a public scurrilous profane jester', from the Italian *buffone*, 'jester', the origin of the English 'buffoon'.

Bufo, a character in *Pope's *Epistle to Dr Arbuthnot* (ll. 230–48), a patron of the arts 'fed with soft Dedication all day long' who may represent some of the traits of the earl of Halifax and of *Dodington.

Bukton, the dedicatee of an 'Envoy' by *Chaucer, probably dating from 1396. It is not certain which (if either) of two claimants in modern scholarship is Chaucer's subject.

BULGAKOV, Mikhail Afanasevich (1891–1940), Russian prose writer and dramatist, born in Kiev, the son of a professor at the theological academy. He studied medicine and began his literary career by writing stories drawn from his experience as a doctor. After the revolution he worked in Moscow as a journalist and wrote satirical and humorous stories and plays. In the late 1920s he came under increasing pressure from party-oriented critics. He wrote a letter to Stalin on 28 March 1930 asking permission to emigrate. Stalin replied with the offer of a post at the Moscow Art Theatre, and in 1932 intervened again by ordering a revival of Bulgakov's play *The Days of the Turbins*. Thereafter the relationship between the writer and the state became his key subject until his early death. His major works include stories: 'The Adventures of Chichikov' (1922, evidence of his great admiration for *Gogol), 'The Fatal Eggs' (1924), 'The Heart of a Dog' (1925); novels: *The White Guard* (1925, a sympathetic portrait of a White Russian family in Kiev after the

Revolution), *The Theatrical Novel* (*Black Snow*) (1936–7); and plays: *The Days of the Turbins* (1925–6), an adaptation of *The White Guard*, *Flight* (1925–8), *A Cabal of Hypocrites* (*Molière*) (1930–6). His masterpiece, *The Master and Margarita* (1928–40, not published until 1966–7), is a Faustian tale of the devil's appearance in contemporary Moscow and his relationship with a writer and his beloved.

BULL, John (?1562–1628), English composer and keyboard player. Unusually for his period, Bull wrote no songs, no madrigals, and only a few sacred vocal compositions; his works for organ and virginals, however, are among the most important of their day. The latter seem to have included a modest *Ayre* which, the original manuscript being lost, now exists only in a 19th-cent. copy; it bears an interesting resemblance to the tune of 'God Save the King' and has often been claimed as the origin of the British *national anthem. Bull left England in 1613 to escape prosecution for adultery and fornication, and never returned.

Bull, John, see JOHN BULL.

BULLOUGH, Geoffrey (1901–82), scholar and head of the department of English at King's College, London (1946–68). His principal works were an edition of *Greville's poems and plays (1939) and his definitive account of the *Narrative and Dramatic Sources of Shakespeare* (8 vols, 1957–75).

Bulstrode, Mr, a character in G. Eliot's *Middlemarch*.

BULWER-LYTTON, Edward George Earle Lytton, first Baron Lytton (1803–73), son of General Bulwer, who added his mother's surname to his own when he inherited Knebworth in 1843. Educated at Trinity Hall, Cambridge, he embarked on a career in politics as MP for St Ives and a keen Reform member in 1831; he was subsequently MP for Lincoln and in 1858–9 secretary for the colonies. He financed his extravagant life as a man of fashion by a versatile and prolific literary output, publishing either anonymously or under the name of Bulwer Lytton. His first success, *Pelham: or The Adventures of a Gentleman* (1828), was of the *fashionable school, a lively novel set in an aristocratic social and political world, bearing some resemblance to Disraeli's recent *Vivian Grey*; it brought him considerable acclaim and established his reputation as a wit and dandy. Sir W. *Scott found it 'easy and gentleman-like' but complained of 'a slang tone of morality which is immoral'. His *'Newgate' novels were more in the 'reforming' manner of *Godwin, e.g. *Paul Clifford* (1830), about a philanthropic highwayman, and *Eugene Aram* (1832), about a repentant murderer. He also wrote novels of domestic life, such as *The Caxtons: A Family Picture* (1849); many popular *historical novels, including *The Last Days of Pompeii* (1834), in which the panoramic splendours show his admiration for J. *Martin, *Rienzi, the Last of the Roman Tribunes* (1835), and *The Last of the Barons* (1843); tales

of the occult, including *Zanoni* (1842) and *A Strange Story* (1862); and a *science fiction fantasy, *The Coming Race* (1871). Other novels include *Falkland* (1827), *The Disowned* and *Devereux* (1829), *Godolphin* (1833), *Ernest Maltravers* (1837), *Harold, the Last of the Saxons* (1848), *My Novel, or Varieties in English Life* (1853), *What Will He Do with It?* (1858), *Kenelm Chillingly* (1873), and *The Parisians* (1873, unfinished). He was also editor of the *New Monthly Magazine*, 1831–3, and the author of three plays, *The Lady of Lyons, or Love and Pride*, a romantic comedy first performed in 1838; *Richelieu, or the Conspiracy*, a historical play in blank verse performed in 1839; and *Money*, a comedy performed in 1840, all of which have been successfully revived. He published several volumes of verse, including his earliest *Byronic tale, *Ismael* (1820); *The New Timon* (1846), an anonymous satirical poem in which he attacked *Tennyson as 'School-Miss Alfred', thus aggravating previous criticisms and stinging Tennyson into a bitter response in verse, mocking Lytton as a rouged and padded fop; and an epic, *King Arthur* (1848–9). Bulwer-Lytton made many enemies in his career, which was not helped by his disastrous marriage and separation from his wife Rosina in 1836 (see below); he was the frequent butt of *Fraser's Magazine*, of *Lockhart, and of *Thackeray. Nevertheless he had powerful friends and admirers, including *Disraeli and *Dickens, and his works span many of the changes in 19th-cent. fiction and are of considerable sociological interest.

BULWER-LYTTON, Rosina, Lady (1802–82), novelist, born in Ireland, the daughter of Francis and Anna Wheeler. Her mother was a radical feminist, her father an alcoholic: they separated when Rosina was 10 and she was brought up by relatives. Moving to London in her early twenties, she made friends with Letitia *Landon and Lady Caroline *Lamb, and in 1827 married Edward Bulwer, later Bulwer-Lytton (above). Their stormy separation in 1836, after the birth of two children and his increasing unfaithfulness, permanently embittered her. Feeling acutely the powerlessness of a woman in her situation she turned to near-libellous publication, producing *Cheveley, or The Man of Honour* (1839), satirizing her husband's hypocrisy, followed by a string of equally spirited but less successful novels, as well as various public petitions and pamphlets. He retaliated by intimidating her publishers, withholding her allowance, denying her access to the children, and finally, in 1858, by having her forcibly committed to an asylum from which she was released only by public outcry. She published a memoir, *A Blighted Life*, in 1880. Her life was published in 1887 by Louisa Devey.

Bumble, the beadle in Dickens's *Oliver Twist*, a type of the consequential, domineering parish official.

Bumby, Mother, a fortune-teller frequently alluded to by the Elizabethan dramatists. *Lyly wrote a Terentian comedy, entitled *Mother Bombie* (1594), which is, says *Hazlitt, 'very much what its name would import, old, quaint, and vulgar', 'little else than a tissue of absurd mistakes, arising from the confusion of the different characters one with another, like another Comedy of Errors, and ends in their being (most of them), married . . . to the persons they particularly dislike'.

Bunbury, an imaginary character introduced by Wilde in *The Importance of Being Earnest*.

BUNBURY, Henry William (1750–1811), amateur artist and caricaturist who had many friends in the literary world, and in 1771 married Catherine Horneck, *Goldsmith's 'Little Comedy'.

Buncle Esq., John, see JOHN BUNCLE ESQ.

BUNGAY, Thomas, known as 'Friar Bungay' (fl. 1290), a Franciscan, who was divinity lecturer of his order in Oxford and Cambridge. He was vulgarly accounted a magician and is frequently referred to in that capacity. (See FRIER BACON, AND FRIER BONGAY.)

BUNIN, Ivan Alekseevich (1870–1953), Russian prose writer and poet. The son of gentry from Voronezh in central Russia, he worked as a young man as assistant editor of a provincial newspaper. His first poem was published in 1887, his first stories in the early 1890s, and his first collection of prose, *To the Edge of the World*, in 1897. In the early years of the 20th cent. he attained great popularity. Love and rural life are prominent themes, and he was a consistent opponent of *Modernism. Among his best works of the period are *The Village* (1910), *Sukhodol* (1911), and *The Gentleman from San Francisco* (1914). In these years he travelled widely in Europe, Asia, and Africa. Totally opposed to the October Revolution, he left Russia in 1918, eventually reaching France and permanent exile. *The Accursed Days* (1925) is a diary of the post-revolutionary period, *The Life of Arsenev* (1927–9) an autobiographical novel. In 1933 Bunin became the first Russian to win the *Nobel Prize for literature. His final volume of stories, *Dark Avenues*, appeared in 1946. Bunin's reputation has risen continuously since his death. He is the Russian translator of Byron's *Cain*, *Manfred*, and *Heaven and Earth*, Longfellow's *The Song of *Hiawatha*, and *Tennyson's *Lady Godiva*. There have been a number of translations of Bunin's work into English since the first, *The Gentleman from San Francisco and Other Stories*, translated by D. H. *Lawrence, S. S. Koteliansky, and L. *Woolf (1922).

Bunsby, Captain John, a character in Dickens's *Dombey and Son*, a friend of Captain Cuttle.

Bunthorne, Reginald, the principal male character in Gilbert and Sullivan's opera *Patience*, a 'fleshly poet', in whose person the *Aesthetic movement of the 1880s was caricatured.

BUNTING, Basil (1900–85), poet, born in Scotswood-on-Tyne, near Newcastle, and educated at Quaker schools (Ackworth and Leighton Park). He worked in Paris as a sub-editor on the *Transatlantic Review 1923–4, and in the 1930s followed *Pound to Italy, where he met *Yeats and the American poet Louis *Zukofsky. From 1947 to 1952 he worked in Persia, where he married Sima Alladadian, a Kurdo-Armenian. He returned in 1952 to Newcastle to work on a local paper. Although he had been published abroad (*Redimiculum Matellarum*, Milan, 1930; *Poems*, Texas, 1950; *The Spoils*, 1951, *Poetry Chicago*) and had a considerable reputation among younger American poets as an important figure in the *Modernist movement, he was virtually unknown in his own country until the appearance of his long, semi-autobiographical, and deeply Northumbrian poem *Briggflatts* (1966), which firmly established his presence: this poem was named after the Quaker hamlet of Briggflatts, now in Cumbria. His reappearance as a poet was in a large part due to the friendship and intervention of poet Tom *Pickard, who met him in 1964 and for whom he read *Briggflatts* in 1965 at the Newcastle poets' meeting place, Mordern Tower. His *Collected Poems* (1978) includes translations ('Overdrafts') from Latin and Persian. *The Complete Poems*, edited by Richard Caddel, was published in 1994.

BUNYAN, John (1628–88), born at Elstow, near Bedford, the son of a brazier. He learned to read and write at the village school and was early set to his father's trade. He was drafted into the parliamentary army and was stationed at Newport Pagnell, 1644–6, an experience perhaps reflected in *The Holy War*. In 1649 he married his first wife, who introduced him to two religious works, Dent's *Plain Man's Pathway to Heaven* and Bayly's *Practice of Piety*; these, the Bible, the Prayer Book, and Foxe's *Actes and Monuments* were his principal reading matter. In 1653 he joined a Nonconformist church in Bedford, preached there, and came into conflict with the Quakers (see under FRIENDS, SOCIETY OF), against whom he published his first writings, *Some Gospel Truths Opened* (1656) and *A Vindication* (1657). He married his second wife Elizabeth c.1659, his first having died c.1656 leaving four children. As an itinerant tinker who presented his Puritan mission as apostolic and placed the poor and simple above the mighty and learned, Bunyan was viewed by the Restoration authorities as a militant subversive. Arrested in Nov. 1660 for preaching without a licence, he was derided at his trial as 'a pestilent fellow', to which his wife riposted, 'Because he is a tinker, and a poor man, therefore he is despised and cannot have justice.' Bunyan spent most of the next 12 years in Bedford Jail. During the first half of this period he wrote nine books, including his spiritual autobiography, *Grace Abounding to the Chief of Sinners* (1666). In 1665 appeared *The Holy City, or The New Jerusalem*, inspired by a passage in the Book of Revelation. In 1672 he published *A Confession of my Faith, and a Reason of my Practice*. After his release in

1672 he was appointed pastor at the same church, but was imprisoned again for a short period in 1677 during which he probably finished the first part of *The Pilgrim's Progress*, which had partly been written during the latter years of the first imprisonment. The first part was published in 1678, and the second, together with the whole work, in 1684. His other principal works are *The Life and Death of Mr *Badman (1680) and *The Holy War* (1682). Bunyan preached in many parts, his down-to-earth, humorous, and impassioned style drawing crowds of hundreds, but was not further molested. There are recent editions of his more important works by R. Sharrock, who also wrote a biography. See also *A Turbulent, Seditious and Factious People: John Bunyan and his Church* by C. *Hill (1988).

BURBAGE, James (c.1530–97), actor, a joiner by trade. He was one of the earl of Leicester's players in 1572. He leased land in Shoreditch (1576), on which he erected, of wood, the first building in England specially intended for plays. In 1596 he acquired a house in Blackfriars, and converted it into the *Blackfriars Theatre. He lived in Halliwell Street, Shoreditch, 1576–97. The first English playhouse is mentioned in an order of council, Aug. 1577, and was known as 'The Theatre'; the fabric was removed, in Dec. 1598, to the Bankside and set up as the *Globe Theatre.

BURBAGE, Richard (?1567–1619), actor, son of James *Burbage, from whom he inherited a share in the *Blackfriars Theatre and an interest in the *Globe Theatre. He acted as a boy at The Theatre in Shoreditch and rose to be an actor of chief parts, 1595–1618, in plays by Shakespeare, *Jonson, and *Beaumont and *Fletcher. He excelled in tragedy. Burbage lived in Halliwell Street, Shoreditch, 1603–19. He is known also as a painter in oil-colours and is known to have collaborated with Shakespeare on an 'impresa', a tilting shield for the earl of Rutland, in 1613.

Burbon, Sir, in Spenser's *Faerie Queene* (v. xi), represents Henry of Navarre.

BURCKHARDT, Jacob (1818–97), Swiss historian born in Basle. He is principally known in Britain for his great work *Die Kultur der Renaissance in Italien* (1860, trans. as *The Civilization of the Renaissance in Italy*, 1929, 1951), a survey which discusses the arts, politics, philosophy, etc. of the period and propounds the view that it was at this time that man, previously conscious of himself 'only as a member of a race, people, party, family or corporation', became aware of himself as 'a spiritual *individual*'. This concept of the Italian Renaissance has been both highly influential and much attacked, as has Burckhardt's wide historical pessimism; some, however, have seen him as a precursor of *existentialism.

burden, the refrain or chorus of a song, a set of words recurring at the end of each verse, or the dominant theme of a song or poem.

BÜRGER, Gottfried August, see LENORE and WILD HUNTSMAN.

BURGESS, Anthony (John Anthony Burgess Wilson) (1917–93), novelist, born in Manchester, of a Catholic family, and educated at the University of Manchester. His original ambitions were musical, and his varied early career included some years (1954–60) as an education officer in the colonial service in Malaya and Borneo. During this period he wrote his first three novels, set in the Far East, *Time for a Tiger* (1956), *The Enemy in the Blanket* (1958), and *Beds in the East* (1959), published together as *The Malayan Trilogy* in 1972. *A Clockwork Orange* (1962), an alarming vision of violence, high technology, and authoritarianism, appeared in a film version by Stanley Kubrick in 1971. His many other works include his comic trilogy about the gross and fitfully inspired poet Enderby (*Inside Mr Enderby*, 1963, under the pseudonym 'Joseph Kell'; *Enderby Outside*, 1968; *The Clockwork Testament*, 1974), which traces the literary, amorous, and digestive misfortunes and triumphs of Enderby in England, Rome, Tangiers, and New York, and displays a fine flair for pastiche, satiric social comment, and verbal invention. *Earthly Powers* (1980) is a long and ambitious first-person novel, narrated by a successful octogenarian homosexual writer, Kenneth Toomey, in which real and fictitious characters mingle to produce an international panorama of the 20th cent. *Enderby's Dark Lady* (1984) was followed by *The Kingdom of the Wicked* (1985), about early Christianity, *The Piano-players* (1986), *Any Old Iron* (1989) and *The Devil's Mode* (stories, 1989). *A Dead Man in Deptford* (1993) is a brilliant and moving recreation of the life and death of the Elizabethan poet and playwright Christopher *Marlowe. Two volumes of 'Confessions', *Little Wilson and Big God* and *You've Had Your Time*, appeared in 1987 and 1990. *Mozart and the Wolf Gang* (1991) is a collection of imaginary conversations, with the composer as the central character. Burgess also wrote critical works, notably on *Joyce; composed many orchestral works; written screenplays and television scripts, innumerable reviews (see *Homage to QWERTYUIOP*, 1987), and a biography of Shakespeare (1970).

BURGON, John William (1813–88), appointed dean of Chichester in 1876. He is remembered as the author of the poem 'Petra' (1845), which contains the well-known line 'A rose-red city—"half as old as time"'.

BURGOYNE, Sir John (1722–92), nicknamed 'Gentleman Johnny', remembered principally as the general who was forced to capitulate to the Americans at Saratoga in 1777. He was the author of a clever and successful comedy *The Heiress* (1786), in which the vulgarity of the rich Alscrip family is contrasted with the native good breeding of Clifford, Lord Gayville, and his sister; while the temporary humiliation of the virtuous heroine Miss Alton, who is driven to take service in the Alscrip family until she is discovered to be an heiress and Clifford's sister, provides a sentimental interest. He also wrote *The Maid of the Oaks* (1774), a cheerful little comedy of country life. He figures in G. B. *Shaw's play *The Devil's Disciple* (1900).

Burgundy, duke of, the 'wat'rish' suitor of *Cordelia in Shakespeare's *King Lear*.

'Burial of Sir John Moore, The', see WOLFE, C.

BURIDAN, Jean (14th cent.), French nominalist philosopher, born in Artois c.1300, and rector of the University of Paris in 1328 and 1340. He was a leading scientist of his day, influential on *Leonardo da Vinci. There is no evidence in his works for the sophistry called 'Buridan's ass' (which will starve to death for lack of incentive when placed between two pieces of food and drink of identical attractiveness). Dante, following Aristotle, has a dog which dies in a similar dilemma.

E. Faral, 'Jean Buridan', *Histoire littéraire de la France*, xxxviii (1949), 462–605.

BURKE, Edmund (1729–97), the second son of an Irish Protestant attorney and a Catholic mother, who was educated at Trinity College, Dublin, and came to London in 1750, where he entered the Middle Temple. He was more interested in literature than the law, and was to make many lasting friendships with eminent literary and artistic figures, including Dr *Johnson (of whose *Club he was a founding member), *Goldsmith, *Reynolds, *Garrick, and the *Blue Stocking Circle. In 1756 he married Jane Nugent, and in the same year published *A Vindication of a Natural Society* and in 1757 *A Philosophical Enquiry into the *Sublime and Beautiful.* In 1759 with *Dodsley he started the *Annual Register* to which he contributed until 1788; in the same year he became private assistant to W. G. ('Single-Speech') *Hamilton, with whom he remained until 1765, when he transferred his services to the marquis of Rockingham and was elected MP for Wendover. He first spoke in the House in 1766 on the American question, and during the following years vehemently attacked the Tory government. In 1768 he purchased an estate at Beaconsfield for a considerable sum, which aroused allegations (still debated) about speculations with East India stock. He published his *Observations on a Late Publication on the *Present State of the Nation* in 1769, and his *Thoughts on the Cause of the *Present Discontents* in 1770. In 1773 he visited France, where he met Mme du *Deffand, *Diderot, and the *Encyclopaedists, and saw Marie Antoinette, a vision that was to inspire, years later, some of the best-known passages of *Reflections on the *Revolution in France* (1790). In 1774 he became MP for Bristol, and made his speeches *On *American Taxation* (1774) and *On *Conciliation with America* (11 Mar. 1775, shortly before the war with America began). His *Letter to the Sheriffs of Bristol* was written in 1777, and his powerful speech against employing Indians in the war was made in 1780. His championship of free trade with Ireland and

Catholic emancipation lost him his seat in Bristol in 1780; he became MP for Malton in 1781, in which year, in the midst of a busy political life, he found time to respond generously to *Crabbe, who appealed to him for patronage. His attacks on the conduct of the American war contributed to North's resignation in 1783. Burke became paymaster of the forces in 1782, resigned with Fox, and returned to the same office (the highest he ever held) under the coalition government. He took an active part in the investigation of the affairs of the East India Company; his famous speeches on the East India Bill and *On the Nabob of Arcot's Private Debts* were delivered in 1783 and 1785, and he opened the case for the impeachment of *Hastings in 1788. In the same year he supported *Wilberforce in advocating abolition of the slave trade. The French Revolution prompted his *Reflections* and other important works, including *An Appeal from the New to the Old Whigs* (1791), a defence against the charge of inconsistency in his attitude to the French and the Americans, and *Letters on a *Regicide Peace* (1795–7). He retired in 1794 and received a pension from the ministry, for which he was criticized, chiefly by the duke of Bedford and earl of Lauderdale; he defended himself in his *Letter to a Noble Lord* (1796), in which he alludes movingly to the death of his only son Richard in 1794.

Burke's political life was devoted to five 'great, just and honourable causes': the emancipation of the House of Commons from the control of George III and the 'King's friends'; the emancipation of the American colonies; the emancipation of Ireland; the emancipation of India from the misgovernment of the East India Company; and opposition to the atheistical Jacobinism displayed in the French Revolution. For his support of this last cause he was bitterly attacked by those who considered he had betrayed his earlier faith in political liberty (e.g. *Paine, *Godwin, *Bentham, and James *Mill), and his friend Goldsmith, a Tory, described him earlier in 1774 in a celebrated mock-epitaph as one who 'born for the universe, narrowed his mind, | And to party gave up what was meant for mankind' (*Retaliation*, 1774). Yet as writer and orator he won admiration from all sides (although, paradoxically, many of his best speeches were failures and were said to have emptied the House). *Macaulay, at one point describing his later style as 'ungracefully gorgeous' (1837), also declared him the 'greatest man since Milton'; M. *Arnold considered that he was 'so great, because, almost alone in England, he brings thought to bear upon politics, he saturates politics with thought' (1864). Wordsworth in *The Prelude* saluted him as one who 'declares the vital power of social ties | Endeared by custom', in which role he also, according to his biographer *Morley, had considerable influence on the political thought of *Coleridge.

His works were published in 16 vols, 1803–27; his correspondence in 9 vols, ed. T. W. Copeland, 1958–70; there are lives by J. Prior (1824), J. Morley (1879), and P. Magnus (1939), among others.

151   BURKE | BURNETT

BURKE, Kenneth (1897–1986), American literary theorist. He was born in Pittsburgh, and studied at Ohio State University and at Columbia University. He lived among artists in Greenwich Village, and acted as compositor for the first American printing of T. S. *Eliot's '*The Waste Land'. He worked as a music critic for New York magazines, and as a market gardener. His early writings include a novel, a book of short stories, a literary essay, *Counter-Statement* (1931), and a theoretical work on systems of interpretation, *Permanence and Change* (1935). *The Philosophy of Literary Form* (1941) collects his critical essays of the 1930s. His mature work on rhetoric and the psychology of human 'motives' embodied in language appears in *A Grammar of Motives* (1945), *A Rhetoric of Motives* (1950), and the essays collected in *Language as Symbolic Action* (1966). Written while Burke taught part-time at Bennington College, Vermont, these are complex investigations into the workings of metaphor and other 'master-tropes', and propose a scheme of analysis by which formal features of texts can be understood in larger political and psychological terms. Although sometimes grouped with the *New Critics, he worked to a much broader agenda that included constructive engagements with *psychoanalytic and *Marxist criticism.

Burke's Peerage, properly *A Genealogical and Heraldic History of the Peerage and Baronetage of the United Kingdom,* first compiled by John Burke and published in 1826. Since 1847 it has been published annually.

BURLEIGH, or **BURGHLEY,** William Cecil, Lord (1520–98), lord treasurer under Queen Elizabeth, and her chief minister. He had previously been secretary to Lord Protector Somerset; secretary of state, 1550–3; and employed in negotiations by Queen Mary. He is introduced in Sheridan's *The Critic, where, in Puff's tragedy, he comes on the stage and shakes his head, being too much occupied with cares of state to talk, whence the expression, 'Burleigh's nod'.

burlesque, from the Italian *burla,* ridicule, mockery, a literary composition or dramatic representation which aims at exciting laughter by the comical treatment of a serious subject or the caricature of the spirit of a serious work. Notable examples of burlesque in English literature are Butler's *Hudibras and Buckingham's *The Rehearsal.

BURNAND, Sir Francis Cowley (1836–1917), a regular contributor to *Punch from 1863; his series 'Happy Thoughts' (1866) was very popular. He was editor of *Punch,* 1880–1906. He wrote many burlesques and adaptations of French *farces, and his operetta *Cox and Box,* with music by *Sullivan, adapted from J. M. Morton's *Box and Cox, was performed in 1867.

BURNE-JONES, Sir Edward Coley (1833–98), painter and designer, born in Birmingham, and educated at Oxford, where he came under the influence of *Morris

and, through him, of D. G. *Rossetti, under whom he studied painting. He was much impressed by the medieval worlds of *Malory and of K. H. *Digby's *The Broad Stone of Honour* (1822), and later by the Italian Primitive painters; his best-known works (e.g. *King Cophetua and the Beggar Maid,* 1884) tend to portray women with a characteristic willowy, dreamlike beauty. He designed tapestry and stained glass for Morris and Co., and illustrations for the Kelmscott Press.

Burnell the Ass, the hero of the *Speculum Stultorum* by *Wireker. Burnell, who represents the monk who is dissatisfied with his lot, is an ass who wants a longer tail. He goes to Salerno and Paris to study, and finally loses his tail altogether. In the course of his travels he hears the tale that Chaucer alludes to in 'The Nun's Priest's Tale' (*CT* VII. 3,312–16; see CANTERBURY TALES, 20): the priest's son Gandulf breaks a cock's leg by throwing a stone at it. Later, on the morning when he is to be ordained, the cock fails to crow in time to rouse him and he loses his benefice.

BURNET, Gilbert (1643–1715), educated at Marischal College, Aberdeen, a popular preacher, a latitudinarian, and a Whig. He refused four bishoprics before he was 29, and in 1674 was dismissed from the post of king's chaplain for his outspoken criticisms of Charles II. He went to the Continent, and in 1686 to The Hague, where he became an adviser of William of Orange. He became bishop of Salisbury in 1689. His account of the deathbed repentance of *Rochester, *Some Passages in the Life and Death of the Right Honourable John Wilmot Earl of Rochester,* appeared in 1680 and his *History of the Reformation in England* in three volumes, 1679, 1681, 1715. His best-known work, *The History of My Own Times,* is a mixture of history, autobiography, and anecdote, and was published posthumously (2 vols, 1724, 1734). Other works include *Memoires of the . . . Dukes of Hamilton* (1677) and *Life of Sir Matthew Hale* (1682). The standard biography is by T. E. S. Clarke and H. C. Foxcroft (1907).

BURNET, Thomas (?1635–1715), a Yorkshire divine and master of Charterhouse. He was the author of *The Theory of the Earth* (2 vols, 1684–90), translated by himself from the Latin and edited by B. Willey, 1965. It is an imaginative and romantic cosmogony, suggested to him by a voyage across the Alps. It contains, particularly in the third book, descriptive passages that are highly sonorous and magniloquent. The work was much praised by Addison in No. 146 of the *Spectator.

BURNETT, Frances (Eliza) Hodgson (1849–1924), a prolific author, who wrote many novels and other books for adults, but is remembered for her work for children; in particular for the immensely successful (but much derided) *Little Lord Fauntleroy* (1886), whose character was based on her second son, Vivian, and whose velvet suit began an abiding fashion; and for *The Secret Garden* (1911), a widely admired children's classic about a spoilt, ill-tempered orphan, Mary, who finds an abandoned garden. While trying to revive it she encounters Colin, her sickly and hysterical cousin; as they work in the garden together he achieves health and she happiness. There is a life by Ann Thwaite (1974). (See CHILDREN'S LITERATURE.)

BURNEY, Dr Charles (1726–1814), organist, musical historian, and minor composer, the friend of *Garrick, Joshua *Reynolds, Dr *Johnson, and many members of aristocratic and literary society. He was the father of Fanny *Burney. He wrote a *History of Music*, published in four volumes, 1776–89. He also wrote accounts of the travels he made in France, Italy, Germany, and the Low Countries in order to collect material for the work. (See also under MUSIC, LITERATURE OF.)

BURNEY, Charles (1757–1817), son of Dr *Burney, famous in his time as a classical scholar. After his death the British Museum bought his library of over 13,000 volumes, which included classical books and manuscripts and the largest extant collection of early English newspapers.

BURNEY, Fanny (Frances, Mme d'Arblay) (1752–1840), daughter of Dr *Burney. She lived in her youth in the midst of that London society which included Dr *Johnson, *Burke, *Reynolds, *Garrick, the *Blue Stocking Circle, and many members of the aristocracy. In 1778 she published anonymously her first novel *Evelina* and the revelation of its authorship brought her immediate fame. She published *Cecilia* in 1782, and in 1786 was appointed second keeper of the robes to Queen Charlotte. Her health was never good, but she lived a busy family and social life, much of which is reflected in her novels. In 1793 she married General d'Arblay, a French refugee in England. In 1796 she published *Camilla*. She and her husband were interned by Napoleon and lived in France from 1802 to 1812. *The Wanderer* (1814) was not a success. In 1832 she edited the *Memoirs* of her father. She was a prodigious writer of lively letters and journals; her *Early Diary 1768–1778*, which includes attractive sketches of Johnson, Garrick, and many others, was published in 1889, and her later *Diary and Letters . . . 1778–1840*, with a vivid account of her life at court, in 1842–6. (In Sept. 1811 she endured and survived a mastectomy; her description of this appalling experience was used by P. *Fitzgerald in *The Blue Flower*.) (30 Sept., vol. vi of *Journals and Letters*.)

Her three major novels take as their theme the entry into the world of a young girl of beauty and understanding but no experience, and expose her to circumstances and events that develop her character; they display, with a satirical eye and a sharp ear for dialogue, the various social levels and the varied company in which she finds herself. Her novels were enjoyed and admired by J. *Austen, among many others. A complete edition of her letters and journals (10 vols, 1972–

81) appeared under the general editorship of Joyce Hemlow, who also wrote a life, *The History of Fanny Burney* (1958).

'Burning Babe, The', see SOUTHWELL.

BURNS, Alan (1929–), novelist, born in London, since 1975 also a lecturer in creative writing. His work is marked by a commitment to experimental narrative, with techniques encompassing surrealism and the use of 'found conversation'. *Europe after the Rain* (1965), his second novel, is a challenging narrative set in a future Europe devastated by catastrophic war. The prose is abrupt and austere, the mood one of isolation and horror. In *The Day Daddy Died* (1981), his approach is more traditional but retains a subversive edge. Currently in charge of the creative writing MA course at Lancaster University, his most recently published novel is *Revolutions of the Night* (1986).

BURNS, Christopher (1944–), novelist and short story writer, born in Egremont, Cumbria. Never parochial, he has set his novels in South America (*Snakewrist*, 1986), in the Swiss Alps (*The Condition of Ice*, 1990), along the Nile (*In the Houses of the West*, 1993), and on the Cumbrian coast (*The Flint Bed*, 1989). His fifth novel, *Dust Raising* (1996), is narrated by a sculptor whose family suffers a hammer blow by the sudden reappearance of a daughter from his first marriage. His complex male narrators tend to find redemption through self-awareness. The short fiction collected in *About the Body* (1988) is often unsettling, characters falling into traps through their own foolishness.

BURNS, Richard (1958–92), English novelist, poet, radio and TV dramatist, born and died (committed suicide) in Sheffield. Common to his five serious novels and two fantasy 'romps' is the alienation of his main characters from the worlds they inhabit. In his first published novel, *A Dance for the Moon* (1986), a poet falls mentally ill after witnessing the horrors of the First World War. In *The Panda Hunt* (1987), a Chinese-American in the 1920s joins a panda hunt in China, where he feels just as cut off from the world and society as he did in Paris and the USA.

BURNS, Robert (1759–96), one of seven children born to a cotter near Alloway in Ayrshire. His father moved his family from one unprofitable farm to another, but was determined that his sons should be well educated. At various schools Robert was given a thorough grounding in English, including classic authors from Shakespeare onwards, and a knowledge of French and mathematics. He read voraciously for himself, and began to write occasional verses when he was still at school. His spare time was fully employed on the ailing farm as labourer and ploughman. The experience of poverty and injustice as a youth no doubt increased his belief in the equality of men, which led him to become an ardent supporter of the early days of the French Revolution. After his father's death in 1784 he and his brother Gilbert continued to farm, now at Mossgiel in the parish of Mauchline, which is often mentioned in the poems he was now beginning to write in some quantity. To this period at Mossgiel belong *'The Cotter's Saturday Night', 'To a *Mouse', 'To a Mountain Daisy', *'Holy Willie's Prayer', the Epistles to Labraik, *'The Holy Fair', and many others. He was much influenced at this time by Mackenzie's novel *The Man of Feeling, a book he loved 'next to the Bible'. In 1785 he met Jean Armour, who was eventually to become his wife, but continued his long series of entanglements with women, many of whom are mentioned in his poems (for instance, Alison Begbie as 'Mary Morison', Mary Campbell in 'To Mary in Heaven').

In this and the following year he wrote prolifically, but his problems, both financial and domestic, became so acute that he thought of emigrating to Jamaica. However he sent his poems to a publisher in Kilmarnock, and when Poems, Chiefly in the Scottish Dialect appeared in 1786 it was an immediate success. Burns found himself fêted by the literary and aristocratic society of Edinburgh, not only for his poetic skills but because he appeared, in Mackenzie's words, as 'a Heaven-taught ploughman'. His attractive appearance and his gregarious temperament led him into a life of dissipation and amorous complexity. In 1787 he met Mrs M'Lehose, with whom he corresponded at length in high-flown terms, addressing her as 'Clarinda', signing himself 'Sylvander'. He was encouraged to write in the rhetorical and sentimental fashion of the day, and in this mode he wrote a great deal—'The Lament', 'Despondency', and 'Address to Edinburgh' are examples—but fortunately his own characteristic voice was not subdued. A second edition of the Poems appeared in 1786, and Burns was asked if he would help to collect old Scottish songs for *The Scots Musical Museum. He responded with an energy and enthusiasm that were to last until his death. He collected, amended, and wrote some 200 songs, which include many of his best-known lyrics, such as *'Auld Lang Syne', 'O my luve's like a red, red rose', 'Ye Banks and Braes', and the battle song in which Robert Bruce addresses his army before Bannockburn, 'Scots wha hae wi'Wallace bled'. In 1787 he travelled in the Highlands and the Borders, collecting tunes and words, and contributed in 1792 to Select Scottish Airs. For all this work he took no money, regarding it as his patriotic duty. He did, however, continue to write and publish work of his own.

In 1788 he finally married Jean Armour, and settled on a poor farm at Ellisland, near Dumfries. A year later he eventually secured a post as an Excise officer, and in 1791 relinquished his farming life with relief and moved to Dumfries. Farming had always been a source of strain and anxiety to him, and he never, in *Wordsworth's words, 'walked in glory and in joy | Following his plough along the mountainside'. Also in 1791 he

published his last major poem, *'Tam o' Shanter'. Turning against the French at last, he joined the Dumfries Volunteers in 1795, dying the following year of rheumatic heart disease.

Burns wrote with equal facility in correct 18th-cent. English and in his native Scots. In some of his songs, most notably in 'The Cotter's Saturday Night', English and Scots are both used. The Scottish poems owe much to Scottish song, to the early Scottish poets (such as *Ramsay), and to the 18th-cent. poet *Fergusson. His songs, his satires, his animal poems, and his verse letters, together with his one narrative poem 'Tam o' Shanter', contain the best of his work. His work was much admired by his contemporaries, and *Lamb declared that in his own youth 'Burns was the god of my idolatry.' His popularity with his fellow-countrymen is reflected in celebrations held all over the world on 'Burns Night', 25 Jan., his birthday. His Poems and Songs (with music) were edited in three volumes by J. Kinsley (1968); see also D. *Daiches, Robert Burns (1950, rev. 1966) and R. T. Fitzhugh, Robert Burns, the Man and the Poet (1970).

BURNSIDE, John (1955–   ), poet and novelist, born in Fife where he currently lives. Early collections, The Hoop (1988), Common Knowledge (1991), and Feast Days (1992), show a fusion of autobiographical fragments with spiritual and natural landscapes, and a recurrence of imagery from Celtic mythology and a Catholic upbringing. His preoccupation with aspects of identity, memory, and the supernatural inform The Myth of the Twin (1994), in which the 'other' or 'anima' is represented as inhabiting a parallel dimension to the self. Later volumes include Swimming in the Flood (1995) and The Asylum Dance (2000). His first novel, The Dumb House (1997) was followed by others, including The Locust Room (2001), set in 1975 during the reign of terror of a Cambridge rapist.

BURRAGE, A. M., see GHOST STORIES.

BURROUGHS, Edgar Rice (1875–1950), American novelist and writer of *science fiction, remembered principally for his adventure stories about Tarzan, who first appeared in Tarzan of the Apes (1914) and who rapidly gained popularity as hero of many sequels, films, radio programmes, and comic strips. Tarzan is the son of a British aristocrat, abandoned in the jungle as a baby and reared by apes.

BURROUGHS, William S(eward) (1914–97), American novelist, probably more famous for his life than his literature. His first novel, Junkie (1953), gave a semi-autobiographical account of his time as a drug addict. The Naked Lunch (1959) made him a cause célèbre through its graphic descriptions of sexual sadism, heroin abuse, and darkly satirical imaginings of a totalitarian state. Subsequent novels pursued these themes, with books like The Soft Machine (1961), The Wild Boys (1971), and Cities of the Red Night (1981) focusing on the nature of power and the dynamics of control. His belief that 'Language is a virus' led him to employ the 'cut-up' technique—a process whereby words or sentences would be taken from any source and reassembled in a way that would *defamiliarize them. A similar philosophy underpinned his approach to painting, in 'shot-gun art', in which a can of paint would be placed in front of a canvas, and exploded by being shot at. The random and anarchic were seen as cities of opposition to a universe that he considered to be pre-recorded. Although a homosexual, he married twice and accidentally shot his second wife Joan during the staging of a William Tell act. His enthusiasm for firearms was unaffected by this event, and his unrepentant drug-identity gave him an iconic status that would be used in such films as *Drugstore Cowboy* (1991) and by rock bands such as Nirvana and REM. See also BEAT GENERATION.

BURTON, Sir Richard Francis (1821–90), explorer, swordsman, anthropologist, and linguist, and one of the most flamboyant characters of his day. He left Oxford without graduating and in 1842 joined the Indian army. He left India in 1849, and subsequent travels took him to the forbidden city of Mecca (which he visited in disguise), to Africa on several expeditions, to the Crimea, to Salt Lake City (where he studied the Mormons), and as consul to Brazil, Damascus (1869–71), and Trieste (1871) where he died. He published over 40 volumes of travel, including his *Personal Narrative of a Pilgrimage to El-Medinah and Meccah* (1855–6) and *The Lake Regions of Central Africa* (1860); several volumes of folklore; two of poetry; and translations from Latin and Portuguese. He was a formidable linguist, speaking 25 languages and many more dialects. He is best remembered for his unexpurgated versions of the *Arabian Nights* (1885–8), *The Kama Sutra* (1883), *The Perfumed Garden* (1886, from the French), and other works of Arabian erotology. His interest in sexual behaviour and deviance (which he shared with his friends *Milnes and *Swinburne) and his detailed, frank, and valuable ethnographical notes led him to risk prosecution many times under the Obscene Publications Act of 1857, and his more erotic works were published secretly or privately. On his death his wife Isabel destroyed his papers and diaries, including the manuscript of his translation from the original Arabic of *The Perfumed Garden*, on which he had been working for 14 years.

BURTON, Robert (1577–1640), educated at Nuneaton and Sutton Coldfield schools and Brasenose College and Christ Church, Oxford, rector of Segrave, Leicestershire. He was author of *The Anatomy of Melancholy*.

BURUMA, Ian (1951–), cultural historian, critic, sinologist, born at The Hague, known for his books and essays on the Far East, including *A Japanese Mirror: Heroes and Villains in Japanese Culture* (1983), *God's Dust: A Modern Asian Journey* (1988), and *The Wages of Guilt: Memories of War in Germany and Japan* (1995). *Playing the Game* (1991) is a novel which explores national identity through a quest for the legendary Indian cricketer K. S. Ranjitsinhji.

BURY, Richard de (1281–1345), named from his birthplace, Bury St Edmunds. He was tutor to Edward III when prince of Wales, became bishop of Durham, and is celebrated as a patron of learning and a collector of books. He wrote *Philobiblon*, a Latin autobiographical sketch of a lover of letters, first printed in 1473 and edited by M. Maclagan (1960). An English translation was published in the edition by E. C. Thomas (1888, 1903).

BUSBY, Richard (1606–95), educated at Westminster and Christ Church, Oxford, a famous headmaster of Westminster School from 1638 to 1695. Among his pupils were *Dryden, *Locke, *Atterbury, and *Prior.

Bush Theatre, the, founded in 1972 by Brian McDermott above a small public house in Shepherds Bush in West London. It rapidly became famous for its passionate commitment to new writing, and the skill with which actors, writers, and directors were matched, from Richard Wilson directing Alan Rickman in Dusty Hughes's *Commitments* (1980) to Conor McPherson directing his own play *St Nicholas* with actor Brian Cox (1996). Many plays, including Liverpool-born playwright Jonathan Harvey's *Beautiful Thing* (1993), transferred to larger theatres, but the Bush's intimacy, with the audience perched on an L-shaped bank of seating, has made it a challenge in its own right.

Busie Body, The, a comedy by S. *Centlivre, produced 1709.

Sir George Airy and Miranda are in love with one another, but her guardian, Sir Francis Gripe, has the design of marrying her himself and believes that she loves him. The devices by which his intentions are defeated, and those by which Charles, Gripe's son, secures the hand of Isabinda, whom her father intends for a Spanish merchant, occupy the play. The character of Marplot, whose well-meant but misdirected interference constantly endangers the course of true love, has enriched the language with a name for the blundering busybody.

Busirane, in Spenser's *Faerie Queene* (III. xi and xii) the 'vile Enchaunter' symbolizing unlawful love. He is struck down by *Britomart in his castle and forced to release *Amoret. On the door of one of the rooms of the castle was written:

Be bold, be bold, and every where Be bold;

but on another iron door,

Be not too bold.

Bussy D'Ambois, a tragedy by *Chapman, written ?1604, published 1607. The most famous of Chapman's plays, it was very popular in its day, and was revived at the Restoration, when *Dryden savagely attacked it in terms that nevertheless suggest its dramatic power: 'when I had taken up what I supposed a fallen star, I found I had been cozened with a jelly; nothing but a cold, dull mass, which glittered no longer than it was shooting; a dwarfish thought, dressed up in gigantic words . . .' (1681).

Bussy D'Ambois (in real life, Louis de Bussy-d'Ambois), a man of insolence and fiery courage, is raised from poverty and introduced to the court of Henri III of France by Monsieur, brother of the king, his protector. He quarrels with the king's courtiers, of whom he kills three in an encounter, and even with the duc de Guise. He embarks on an affair with Tamyra, wife of Montsurry (Montsoreau); Monsieur, who also desires Tamyra, betrays Bussy to Montsurry. Montsurry by torture forces Tamyra to lure Bussy into a trap; he is overpowered and killed, dying defiantly on his feet. ('Here like a Roman statue I will stand | Till death hath made me marble.') Chapman's sequel is *The Revenge of Bussy D'Ambois.

The story is the same as that told by *Dumas *père* in *La Dame de Monsoreau* (1846); both writers make the same alteration of historical fact, which was that not Monsieur but the king, who detested Bussy, revealed Bussy's amour to Montsoreau.

BUTLER, Lady Eleanor, see LLANGOLLEN, THE LADIES OF.

BUTLER, Joseph (1692–1752), son of a Presbyterian linen-draper at Wantage, who was educated at Oriel College, Oxford. A youthful correspondence with S. *Clarke on natural theology was published in 1716. In 1736 he was brought into prominence by being appointed clerk of the closet to the queen, and in 1738 bishop of Bristol, from which he was translated to Durham in 1750.

His reputation stemmed from the publication in 1726 of *Fifteen Sermons* preached at the Rolls Chapel, in which he defines his moral philosophy, affirming an intuitional theory of virtue. While recognizing benevolence and a due degree of self-love as elements in virtuous conduct, he regards conscience as governing and limiting them by considerations, not of happiness or misery, but of right and wrong. In 1736 appeared his *Analogy of Religion*, an enormously popular defence of the Christian religion against the Deists, in which Butler argues that belief in immortality, revelation, and miracles is as reasonable as the beliefs upon which natural religion is founded. Appended to this work are two further essays: 'Of Personal Identity' contains influential criticism of *Locke and more particularly Anthony *Collins; and 'Of the Nature of Virtue' counteracts the incipient utilitarianism found in some other philosophers of the moral sense tradition. A useful collection of essays on him is *Joseph Butler's Moral and Religious Thought*, ed. C. Cunliffe (1992).

BUTLER, Samuel ('Hudibras') (1613–80), born at Strensham, a hamlet south of Worcester, the son of a farmer, and educated at the King's School, Worcester.

He is said to have served as a clerk to a local justice of the peace and later to have become secretary to the countess of Kent. By 1661 he was steward at Ludlow Castle to Richard Vaughan, earl of Carbery. The most significant event in an otherwise obscure life was the publication in 1663 of his *Hudibras, which instantly became the most popular poem of its time. It was probably as a result of its success that he became secretary to the second duke of *Buckingham. In 1677 he was awarded an annual pension of £100 by Charles II, but by then he himself appears to have given currency to the complaint that, though a loyal satirist, he had been left to endure his old age in poverty. He wrote a number of shorter satirical poems, including 'The Elephant in the Moon', an attack on the *Royal Society, and a great many prose 'Characters'. See *Hudibras*, ed. John Wilders (1967); *Characters*, ed. C. W. Daves (1970); *Prose Observations*, ed. Hugh de Quehen (1980); *Hudibras Parts I and II and Selected Other Writings*, ed. Wilders and de Quehen (1973).

BUTLER, Samuel (1835–1902), the son of a clergyman and grandson of a bishop, educated at Shrewsbury and St John's College, Cambridge. Religious doubts prevented his taking holy orders and in 1859 he went to New Zealand, where he achieved success as a sheep-farmer. *A First Year in Canterbury Settlement* (1863), compiled by his father from Samuel's letters, was published in 1863 in a New Zealand journal and became the core of *Erewhon. He returned to England in 1864 and settled in Clifford's Inn, where he began to study painting (at which he worked for ten years) and exhibited occasionally at the Royal Academy. In 1872 he published *Erewhon*, anonymously, which enjoyed a brilliant but brief success. In 1873 appeared *The Fair Haven*, an elaborate and ironic attack on the Resurrection, which brought him encouragement from C. *Darwin and L. *Stephen. A journey to Canada in 1874–5 inspired his well-known poem 'A Psalm of Montreal', first printed in the *Spectator in May 1878, in which he laments (with the refrain: 'O God! O Montreal!') the Canadian philistinism that relegated a Greek statue of a Discobolus to a room in the Natural History Museum used by a taxidermist, who explained that the statue was 'vulgar' because 'he hath neither vest nor pants to cover his lower limbs'.

Between 1877 and 1890 Butler produced a series of works of scientific controversy, many of them directed against certain aspects of Darwinism, in particular C. *Darwin's theory of natural selection: they include *Evolution, Old and New* (1879), *Unconscious Memory* (1880), and three articles on 'The Deadlock in Darwinism' (*Universal Review*, 1890). Butler's espousal of the cause of *Lamarck and creative evolution won him the praise of G. B. *Shaw in his preface to *Back to Methuselah* (1921); Shaw also praised Butler's outspoken views on religion and the 'importance of money' in his preface to *Major Barbara* (1907).

In 1881 Butler published *Alps and Sanctuaries of*

Piedmont and the Canton Ticino, the first of several animated works on art and travel. He experimented with musical composition, including a comic pastoral oratorio, *Narcissus* (1888), written in collaboration with his great friend Festing Jones. In 1896 appeared his *The Life and Letters of Dr Samuel Butler*, his revered grandfather, who had been headmaster, bishop, and geographer. A long interest in *Homer led to his theory of the feminine authorship of the *Odyssey* and its origin at Trapani in Sicily. *The Authoress of the 'Odyssey'* appeared in 1897, and translations of the *Iliad* and the *Odyssey* into vigorous colloquial prose in 1898 and 1900. A quirky study, *Shakespeare's Sonnets Reconsidered*, appeared in 1899, and *Erewhon Revisited* in 1901. Butler's most revealing work, on which he had been labouring for many years, was his semi-autobiographical novel, *The Way of All Flesh*, published posthumously in 1903. He left six large Notebooks, full of incident, self-revelation, and ideas; selections of these were published by Festing Jones in 1912.

BUTOR, Michel (1926–   ), French novelist and one of the creators of the *nouveau roman*; notable in an English context for his novel *L'Emploi du temps* (1957; English trans., *Passing Time*, 1961), a remarkable evocation of Manchester, where Butor worked for a year as an export clerk.

Buzfuz, Mr Serjeant, in Dickens's *Pickwick Papers*, counsel for the plaintiff in *Bardell* v. *Pickwick*.

BYATT, Dame A(ntonia) S(usan) (1936–   ), novelist and critic, born in Sheffield, the daughter of a barrister, and educated at the Mount School, York, and Newnham College, Cambridge. Her first novel, *Shadow of a Sun* (1964), describes the efforts of Anna to escape from the shadow of her novelist father; *The Game* (1967) also explores the influence of art on life through the relationship of two sisters, one an Oxford don, the other a popular novelist. *The Virgin in the Garden* (1978) is set largely in the coronation year of 1953; the second Elizabethan Golden Age is celebrated by a performance at a Yorkshire country house of a new verse drama by public schoolmaster Alexander Wedderburn, in which schoolgirl Frederica Potter plays the role of the Virgin Queen. Rich in complex allegorical allusions to *Spenser, *Ralegh, Shakespeare, and many others, the novel also provides a realistic and vivid portrait of the Potter family, and of provincial life in the 1950s. Frederica's story is continued in *Still Life* (1985), *Babel Tower* (1996), and *A Whistling Woman* (2002). Other works include *Sugar and Other Stories* (1987) and *Possession* (1990), which won the *Booker Prize. It concerns a group of 20th-cent. academics who reconstruct the relationship between two (fictitious) Victorian poets, Randolph Henry Ash and Christabel LaMotte. The novel is remarkable for its convincing pastiches of 19th-cent. literary style. *Angels and Insects* (1992) contains two novellas, *Morpho Eugenia* and

The Conjugal Angel, and is again set in the mid-19th cent. Other works include a three-story sequence, *The Matisse Stories* (1993); a collection of original *fairy tales, *The Djinn in the Nightingale's Eye* (1994); *The Little Black Book of Stories* (2003); and a novel, *The Biographer's Tale* (2000). Margaret *Drabble is her sister.

By-ends, Mr, in Bunyan's *Pilgrim's Progress*, 'a very arch fellow, a downright hypocrite; one that would be religious, which way ever the world went: but so cunning, that he would be sure never to lose or suffer for it'. His conversation with Money-love, Save-all, and Hold-the-world was added in the second edition.

BYRD, William (?1543–1623), English composer. Byrd was the father figure of Elizabethan music, a pupil and colleague of *Tallis (whose career stretched back into the reign of Henry VIII) and in his turn the teacher of *Morley and Tomkins, and very probably Philips, *Weelkes, and *Bull, as well. He composed prolifically in all forms: the largest section of his output is devoted to sacred music, for both Anglican and Catholic rites (he was himself a Catholic), but there is an impressive list of secular vocal works as well. In comparison with some of his later Elizabethan successors (*Wilbye, to take an extreme case) he appears a very universal genius.

Though he lived and composed well into the reign of James I, Byrd's musical character was formed essentially in the early part of Elizabeth's, and when the Italian *madrigal arrived in England in the 1580s and 1590s he treated it with circumspection. He experimented with the form in *Psalmes, Sonets, and Songs* of 1588, and again in *Songs of Sundrie Natures* in the following year, though the pieces he produced are mostly based on earlier traditions and have little of the new Italian model about them; neither these pieces, nor the later *Psalmes, Songs, and Sonnets* (1611), were called 'madrigals' by Byrd himself, the title being foisted on them by the scholars of the 19th cent. He kept all his life a preference for the poetry of his earlier days: *Sidney's name appears as an author from time to time, along with *Ralegh, *Dyer, and minor figures like Geoffry Whitney, William Hunnis, and *Churchyard, but the majority of the texts he set, as was customary at that time, were anonymous.

BYROM, John (1692–1763), born near Manchester, educated at Merchant Taylors' School and at Trinity College, Cambridge, under the reign of *Bentley, in whose defence he wrote, and to whose daughter he may have addressed *A Pastoral*, published in the *Spectator, 1714. He invented his own system of shorthand or 'tychygraphy', had many varied literary, linguistic, religious, and scientific interests, and was from 1724 a fellow of the *Royal Society; his varied acquaintance included *Hartley, the *Wesleys, J. *Butler, and, notably, *Law, of whom he left interesting accounts in his *Private Journals and Literary Remains*, published in 1854–7. Byrom had Jacobite sympathies and was, like Law, a non-juror; he was the author of the ambiguously loyal toast beginning 'God bless the King! I mean the Faith's Defender . . .' His *Miscellaneous Poems* (1773) include some curious versifications of Law's *Serious Call*, which had amused Law, and the well-known hymn 'Christians, awake! Salute the happy morn'. His *Journals* give the impression of a light-hearted and good-natured man paradoxically attracted to the mysticism of writers like *Boehme, Male-branche, Tauler, and Suso (the latter both disciples of *Eckhard).

BYRON, George Gordon, sixth baron (1788–1824), son of Captain John Byron, 'Mad Jack', who eloped with and married Lady Carmarthen, and had by her a daughter, Augusta, who was to be of great importance in Byron's life. As his second wife Captain Byron married Catherine Gordon of Gight, an impetuous Scot, who became Byron's mother. The boy was born with a club-foot, which (it is generally supposed) had a profound effect on his future temperament. Mary *Shelley was to write, 'No action of Lord Byron's life—scarce a line he has written—but was influenced by his personal defect.' Pursued by creditors, the family moved in 1789 to Aberdeen, where Byron was educated until he was 10. His father died in 1791, and the fifth baron's grandson was killed in 1794; so when the baron himself died in 1798, Byron inherited the title. He and his mother moved south, visited his future inheritance, the dilapidated Gothic Newstead Abbey, and Byron was eventually sent to Harrow School. Staying at Newstead in 1802 he probably first met his half-sister, Augusta. In 1805, an extremely handsome young man, he went up to Cambridge, where he attended intermittently to his studies between extravagant debauches there and in London. His first published collection of poems, *Hours of Idleness*, appeared in 1807, and was bitterly attacked, probably by *Brougham, in the *Edinburgh Review*. Byron avenged himself in 1809 with his satire *English Bards and Scotch Reviewers*. In 1808 he returned to Newstead, in 1809 took his seat in the House of Lords, then left for the first of his prolonged travels abroad. Between 1809 and 1811 he visited Portugal, Spain, Malta, Greece, and the Levant. In 1809 he began the poem that was to become *Childe Harold* and completed two cantos; he wrote one of his most famous lyrics, *'Maid of Athens'; he swam the Hellespont; and he became fired with the wish, which was to lead to his return and death, that Greece should be freed from the Turks.

Back in England in 1811 he again met Augusta. In that year, and in 1813, he spoke effectively on liberal themes in the House of Lords. His first great literary triumph came with the publication of the first two cantos of *Childe Harold's Pilgrimage* in March 1812. He was lionized by aristocratic and literary London, survived a hectic love affair with Lady Caroline *Lamb, and became the constant companion of Augusta. In 1813 he wrote *The Bride of Abydos* in a week, and *The Corsair* in ten days: *The Giaour* appeared in the same year. In 1814 Augusta gave birth to a daughter, who was generally supposed to be Byron's and was almost certainly so. In the same year he wrote *Lara. After a long and hesitant courtship he married in 1815 Lady Melbourne's niece Annabella Milbanke. In the same year their daughter Ada was born, and Byron published *Hebrew Melodies. But his debts were accumulating, doubts were cast upon his sanity, and public horror at the rumours of his incest was rising. Annabella left him to live with her parents, and a legal separation was eventually arranged.

Ostracized and deeply embittered, Byron left England in 1816, never to return, and travelled to Geneva, where the *Shelleys and Claire *Clairmont had rented a villa. Here Byron wrote *The Prisoner of Chillon; Claire was by now his mistress. He wrote two acts of *Manfred, Canto III of *Childe Harold*, and several shorter poems, but after four months left for Italy. His daughter by Claire, Allegra, was born in Jan. 1817 in England. While living a riotous life in Venice in the same year, he devised and published an Armenian dictionary and wrote the third act of *Manfred. While travelling to Rome he passed Tasso's cell, which inspired his *Lament of Tasso, and in Rome he began the fourth and last canto of *Childe Harold. He returned to Venice and there wrote *Beppo, his first work in the ironic, colloquial style which was to lead him to *Don Juan. Newstead Abbey was at last sold, and Byron was free of financial worries. In 1818 he wrote *Mazeppa, and began *Don Juan, the first two cantos of which were published in 1819 by John *Murray, reluctantly and anonymously, and which were denounced in *Blackwood's as 'a filthy and impious poem'. However, it was much admired by *Goethe, a fact which Byron found greatly encouraging. In this year he met Teresa, Countess Guiccioli, to whom he became deeply attached. They lived first in Venice, then he followed her and her household to Ravenna, where he wrote *The Prophecy of Dante. In 1820 he continued with Cantos III and IV of *Don Juan, wrote *Marino Faliero, and became deeply involved with the cause of the Italian patriots. Teresa left her husband for Byron in 1821, and Shelley rented houses in Pisa both for Byron and for the Gambas, Teresa's family. While at Ravenna and Pisa that year Byron became deeply interested in drama, and wrote *The Two Foscari, *Sardanapalus, *Cain, the unfinished *Heaven and Earth, and the unfinished *The Deformed Transformed. He thought well of his dramatic works and regretted they were not better received. In the same productive year he also wrote *The Vision of Judgement and continued with *Don Juan. The death in 1822 of his daughter Allegra, whom he had continually failed to visit, was a great grief to him. With the Gambas he left Pisa for Livorno, where Leigh *Hunt joined them. Hunt and Byron co-operated in the production of the *Lib-

eral magazine, the three issues of which contained successively *The Vision of Judgement, Heaven and Earth*, and a translation from *Pulci. Now in Genoa, Byron wrote *Werner*, a verse drama based on a tale by Harriet and Sophia *Lee, and was much preoccupied with *Don Juan* and with thoughts of Greece. In 1823 he wrote *The Age of Bronze*, a satirical poem on the Congress of Verona, and *The Island*, but he had come to feel that action was more important than poetry, and he told Lady *Blessington, 'I have a presentiment I shall die in Greece.' By July he was ready to sail, and Goethe sent him good wishes in verse. In Jan. 1824, after various mishaps and escapes, he arrived at Missolonghi. He formed the 'Byron Brigade' and gave large sums of money, and great inspiration, to the insurgent Greeks, but he was dismayed by their disarray. Before he saw any serious military action he died of fever in April. Memorial services were held all over Greece, but his body was refused by the deans of both Westminster and St Paul's. After his old friend *Hobhouse had arranged for the coffin to lie in state for a few days in London, it was interred in the family vault at Hucknall Torkard, near Newstead.

Byron's poetry, although widely condemned on moral grounds, and frequently attacked by critics, was immensely popular in England and even more so abroad. He noted in his Journal in 1822 that his sales were better in Germany, France, and America than at home. Much of his poetry and drama exerted great influence on *Romanticism. His legacy of inspiration in European poetry, music, the novel, opera, and painting, has been immense. B. *Russell wrote that 'As a myth his importance, especially on the continent, was enormous.'

He was an indefatigable writer of letters and journals, many of which (T. *Moore asserted) were written with an eye to publication. They provide a brilliantly vivid commentary both on his own life and on the times in which he lived. Moore's life was published in 1830 (*Letters and Journals of Lord Byron, with Notices of his Life*, 2 vols) and a three-volume biography by L. A. Marchand was published in 1958. Marchand also edited the letters (11 vols, 1973–81) and the *Complete Poetical Works* (3 vols, 1980–1) are edited by J. J. McGann. See also *Byron: The Flawed Angel* (1997) by Phillis Grosskurth and *Byron: Life and Legend* (2002) by Fiona MacCarthy.

Byron, Harriet, the heroine of Richardson's *Sir Charles *Grandison*.

BYRON, John (1723–86). As a midshipman on the *Wager*, one of the ships of *Anson's squadron in his famous voyage, he was wrecked on an island off the coast of Chile in 1741. His 'Narrative' of the shipwreck, published in 1768, was used by his grandson Lord *Byron in his description of the storm and wreck in *Don Juan*.

BYRON, Robert (1905–41), travel writer, Byzantinist, and aesthete, educated at Eton and Merton College,

Oxford. His works include *The Station* (1928, an account of a visit to Mount Athos), *The Byzantine Achievement* (1929), and *The Appreciation of Architecture* (1932), but he is chiefly remembered for his classic study *The Road to Oxiana* (1937), a record in the form of diary jottings of a journey from Venice through the Middle East and Afghanistan to India in search of the origins of Islamic architecture and culture; it contains passages that, in the opinion of travel writer Bruce *Chatwin (in a 1981 introduction), place him in 'the rank of Ruskin'. Byron died when his ship was hit by a torpedo.

Byron, *The Conspiracy and Tragedy of Charles Duke of*, a two-part play by *Chapman, published 1608.

The play deals with the intrigues of Charles Gontaut, duc de Biron, a brave soldier who had fought successfully and been nobly rewarded by Henri IV of France, but whose overweening ambition made him disloyal to the king. His plots are discovered, he asks forgiveness, and is pardoned. But his restless ambition makes him prepare a new conspiracy, which is revealed to the king. He is arrested and condemned to death. He professes his innocence and is reduced to frenzy and despair when he realizes that he is to die.

Byronic, characteristic of or resembling *Byron or his poetry; that is, contemptuous of and rebelling against conventional morality, or defying fate, or possessing the characteristics of Byron's romantic heroes, or imitating his dress and appearance; as *Meredith describes it, 'posturing statuesque pathetic'; or in the words of *Macaulay, 'a man proud, moody, cynical, with defiance on his brow, and misery in his heart, a scorner of his kind, implacable in revenge, yet capable of deep and strong affection'.

BYWATER, Ingram (1840–1914), educated at University College School and King's College School, London, and at The Queen's College, Oxford, and a fellow of Exeter College, an eminent Greek scholar. He succeeded *Jowett as Regius professor of Greek in 1893. He had acquired a European reputation by his edition (1877) of the Fragments of *Heraclitus. His monumental edition of the *Poetics* of *Aristotle appeared in 1909. He made important contributions to the *OED*, and guided the critical methods of the editors of the long series of Oxford Classical Texts.

Byzantine, the word used to designate the art, and especially the architecture, developed in the eastern division of the Roman Empire. This eastern division endured from the partition of the empire between the two sons of Theodosius in AD 395 to the capture of Constantinople, its capital, formerly known as Byzantium, by the Turks in 1453. Byzantine architecture is distinguished by its use of the round arch, cross, circle, dome, and rich mosaic ornament. St Mark's at Venice is a prominent example. Byzantium stands as an important symbol in the poems of *Yeats ('Sailing to Byzantium', 'Byzantium'), where it appears to represent the undying world of art, contrasted with the 'fury and the mire of human veins'; but the word 'byzantine' is also sometimes used (with reference to history rather than art) to convey a sinister sense of *Oriental intrigue.

C

cabal, from the Hebrew word *qabbalah*, a secret intrigue of a sinister character formed by a small body of persons; or a small body of persons engaged in such an intrigue; in British history applied specially to the five ministers of Charles II who signed the treaty of alliance with France for war against Holland in 1672; these were Clifford, Arlington, *Buckingham, Ashley (see SHAFTESBURY, first earl of), and Lauderdale, the initials of whose names thus arranged happened to form the word 'cabal' [*OED*].

Cade, Jack, Rebellion of, a popular revolt by the men of Kent in June and July 1450, Yorkist in sympathy, against the misrule of Henry VI and his council. Its intent was more to reform political administration than to create social upheaval, as the revolt of 1381 had attempted. Its leader Jack Cade, who is said to have been Irish, took the name Mortimer and marched triumphantly into London where his followers beheaded Say, the lord treasurer. After a fight on London Bridge, Cade was abandoned by his followers, whereupon he retreated into Sussex where he was killed. He appears as a character in Shakespeare's 2 *Henry VI.

Cadenus and Vanessa, a poem by *Swift, written in 1713 for Esther Vanhomrigh ('Vanessa'). It is the narrative, in mock classical form, of the author's relations with 'Vanessa' and an apology for his conduct. 'Cadenus' is an obvious anagram of 'Decanus', dean. Miss Vanhomrigh evidently took no exception to his statement of the facts, since she preserved the poem and desired it to be published. It appeared in 1726, three years after her death.

Cadwal, in Shakespeare's *Cymbeline, the name of Cymbeline's younger son *Arviragus during his childhood in Wales.

CADWALLADER, (1) the son of Cadwallon, died in 689 according to *Geoffrey of Monmouth. He is the last of the British kings of England, according to the various *Brut chronicles which conclude with him. After his day, which was characterized by plague and desolation, the British would be called Welsh (foreign) and the Saxons rule instead in England, until the time prophesied by *Merlin for the return of a British king. He joined Penda (according to Geoffrey, Cadwallader's maternal uncle) against Eadwine, the Anglian king of Northumbria; (2) a character in Smollett's *Peregrine Pickle*; (3) a Mrs Cadwallader figures in George Eliot's *Middlemarch*.

CÆDMON (fl. 670) entered the monastery of Streaneshalch (Whitby) between 658 and 680, when already an elderly man. He is said by *Bede to have been an unlearned herdsman who received suddenly, in a vision, the power of song, and later put into English verse passages translated to him from the Scriptures. The name Cædmon cannot be explained in English, and has been conjectured to be Celtic (an adaptation of the British Catumanus). In 1655 François Dujon (Franciscus Junius) published at Amsterdam from the unique Bodleian MS Junius II (*c*.1000) long scriptural poems, which he took to be those of Cædmon. These are *Genesis*, *Exodus*, *Daniel*, and *Christ and Satan*, but they cannot be the work of Cædmon. The only work which can be attributed to him is the short 'Hymn of Creation', quoted by Bede, which survives in several manuscripts of Bede in various dialects.

Caelia, in Spenser's *Faerie Queene (I. x) the Lady of the House of Holiness, mother of Fidelia, Speranza, and Charissa (Faith, Hope, and Charity).

Caerleon, see CARLIOUN.

CAESAR, Gaius Julius (102/100–44 BC), Roman politician who in his middle forties surfaced as a general of genius. Victor in the factional struggles that destroyed the republic, and eventually dictator, he prepared the ground for six centuries of imperial rule. He was also a writer of exceptional ability and has left a lucid account of his campaigns in his *Commentaries*. Since he cuts an attractive figure in the correspondence of *Cicero (the principal contemporary source for the events of his lifetime) and is praised by the biographers and historians who served his imperial successors, and since he had a love affair with Cleopatra, the most fascinating woman of his day, later ages came to look upon him as a superman. The *Commentaries on the Gallic War* were translated in part by A. *Golding (1565) and C. Edmondes (1600), but they were read in the original by every English schoolboy, and mentions of Caesar abound in English literature. *Dryden for example cites his opinions repeatedly. But the true signposts to the nature of his reputation are Shakespeare's *Julius Caesar* (*c*.1599) and *Shaw's *Caesar and Cleopatra* (1901).

Caesar and Pompey, a Roman tragedy by *Chapman, published 1631, but written between 1599 and 1607.

It deals with the contention of Caesar and Pompey, the events leading to the battle of Pharsalus (48 BC), the murder of Pompey, and the suicide of Cato of Utica. The latter is the real hero of the play, of which the motto is 'Only a just man is a free man'.

caesura, in Greek and Latin prosody, the division of a metrical foot between two words, especially in certain recognized places near the middle of the line; in English prosody, a pause about the middle of a metrical line, generally indicated by a pause in the sense.

Café Royal, a French-style café-restaurant at 68 Regent Street, which was for several decades from the 1880s onwards the haunt of artists and writers and the scene of many artistic gatherings, scandals, and celebrations. Its habitués included *Whistler, *Wilde, *Dowson, A. *Symons, *Crowley, F. *Harris, *Firbank, *Beerbohm, and G. B. *Shaw; it appeared in the novels of D. H. *Lawrence (as The Café Pompadour, in *Women in Love), of *Maugham, Arnold *Bennett, E. *Waugh, and others, and was painted and sketched by *Beardsley, Sickert, and others. Its famous Brasserie closed in 1951. See *Café Royal: Ninety Years of Bohemia* (1955) by G. Deghy and K. Waterhouse.

Cain: A Mystery, a verse drama in three acts by *Byron, published 1821. Cain, bewildered by the toil imposed upon him by another's fault, and by the mystery of the 'evil' consequences of 'good' knowledge, is confronted by Lucifer, who teaches him to question the wicked works and ways of God, the 'Omnipotent tyrant'. Byron's bold intellectual speculations on the origins of matter and life are displayed as Lucifer takes Cain on a dazzling tour of the cosmos: they visit earlier worlds peopled by pre-Adamite beings, witness the extinction of species, and contemplate the populous realm of the dead. Cain curses his parents and 'He who invented life that leads to death'. On his return to earth Cain expresses his doubts and fears to his sister-bride Adah, and is reluctant to share his favoured brother Abel's sacrifice to Jehovah. In a fit of passion, revolted by the barbaric blood-sacrifice and a God who could delight in such offerings, he strikes Abel and kills him, thus bringing into the world Death, the thought of which had empoisoned his life. Cursed by Eve, rejected by Adam, and marked on the brow by an angel of the Lord, Cain sets forth into exile with his wife and children, knowing that they will further the doom of mankind. This powerful and spirited enquiry into original sin, heredity, free will, and predestination caused intense indignation, and the publisher, John *Murray, was threatened with prosecution. Byron diplomatically denied that the views represented were his own.

CAINE, (Sir Thomas Henry) Hall (1853–1931), novelist of Manx and Cumberland parentage who worked as teacher, architect's assistant, and journalist in his early years. In 1878 he delivered a lecture at the Free Library in Liverpool on D. G. *Rossetti, which brought him into correspondence with the poet; Caine was befriended by Rossetti and spent the last few months of Rossetti's life as his housemate: see Caine's *Recollections of Dante Gabriel Rossetti* (1882). He edited an anthology, *Sonnets of Three Centuries* (1882), in which all three

Rossettis and W. B. *Scott were represented. He then turned to fiction, with sensational success, writing novels which achieved wide popularity, many set in the Isle of Man: titles include *The Manxman* (1894), *The Christian* (1897), *The Eternal City* (1901), *The Prodigal Son* (1904), and *The Woman of Knockaloe* (1923). *The Woman Thou Gavest Me* (1913) was an attack on women's position in society and a criticism of the marriage laws. See Vivien Allen, *Hall Caine: Portrait of a Victorian Romancer* (1997) which describes his career, his friendships with Bram *Stoker and G. B. *Shaw, and his marriage to child-bride Mary Chandler.

CAIRD, (Alice) Mona (1855–1932). She combined polemical feminist writing, particularly on the patriarchal institution of marriage (essays collected as *The Morality of Marriage*, 1897) with *New Woman fiction. She celebrated women's drive to determine their own lives: in *The Daughters of Danaus* (1894) the heroine leaves husband and family to study music. Other novels in which she interrogates what was considered 'proper' womanly behaviour and the stifling effect of conventionality include *The Wing of Azrael* (1889) and *The Stones of Sacrifice* (1915). Caird also campaigned extensively against vivisection: see *A Sentimental View of Vivisection* (1895) and *Beyond the Pale* (1897).

Caius, Dr, a French physician in Shakespeare's *The Merry Wives of Windsor*. Kent in *King Lear* makes a reference to 'your servant Caius' (v. iii. 283). Neither character appears to carry any allusion to the real life Dr John Caius, refounder of Gonville and Caius College, Cambridge.

Calantha, the heroine of Ford's *The Broken Heart*.

CALDERÓN DE LA BARCA, Pedro (1600–81), the great Spanish dramatist and successor of Lope de *Vega, born in Madrid and educated at Salamanca. After a turbulent early life he was ordained priest in 1651; he enjoyed royal favour, and in 1663 became chaplain of honour to the king. He wrote some 120 plays— tragedies, comedies of manners, histories, philosophical dramas—and, in later life, more than 70 highly regarded *autos sacramentales*, allegorical religious plays with subjects from mythology and the Old and New Testaments, dramatizing aspects of faith. Of his secular plays, one of the best known is *El alcalde de Zalamea* (c.1643), in which the peasant-mayor takes revenge on the captain who has seduced his daughter and is rewarded by Philip II by being made mayor for life. Other works include *La vida es sueño* (1635), a baroque philosophical romance which he also rewrote as an *auto*, and *El mágico prodigioso* (1637), a religious drama set in the reign of Diocletian. E. *FitzGerald translated eight of his plays (1853, 1865), and there are more literal translations by D. F. MacCarthy (1853–70). R. *Campbell's translation of *El médico de su honra* (1635), a play about the apparently justified murder of a falsely suspected wife, was published in 1960 as *The Surgeon of his Honour*.

Caleb Williams (*Things as They Are: or The Adventures of Caleb Williams*), a novel by W. *Godwin, published 1794. This work is remarkable as an early example of the propagandist novel, as a novel of pursuit, crime, and detection, and as a psychological study. It was designed to show 'the tyranny and perfidiousness exercised by the powerful members of the community against those who are less privileged than themselves'. A provocative preface to the original edition was withdrawn.

It is related in the first person by its eponymous hero. The first part of the book deals with the misdeeds of Tyrrel, an arrogant and tyrannical country squire, who ruins a tenant on his estate, Hawkins, for refusing to yield to one of his whims, and drives to the grave his niece Miss Melville for refusing to marry a boor of his selection. In the course of these events he comes into conflict with the idealistic and benevolent Falkland, a neighbouring squire, knocks him down in public, and is shortly after found murdered. Suspicion falls on Falkland but is diverted to Hawkins and his son, who are tried and executed. From this time Falkland becomes eccentric and solitary. Caleb Williams, the self-educated son of humble parents, is appointed his secretary, and convinces himself that Falkland is in fact Tyrrel's murderer. The remainder of the book concerns Falkland's unrelenting persecution of Williams, despite Williams's devotion to his employer and refusal to betray his secret. Williams is imprisoned on a false charge of robbing his employer, escapes, but is tracked by Falkland's agents until, in despair, he lays a charge of murder against Falkland, is confronted with him, and, although he has no proof to offer, through his generosity and sincerity wins from the murderer a confession of guilt. Godwin's original ending was radically different; in it Falkland maintains his innocence and Williams ends, nearly demented, in jail. *Hazlitt paid tribute to the power of the narrative when he wrote, 'no one ever began *Caleb Williams* that did not read it through'. Godwin reinforces his political points by documentary references in footnotes to such works as the *Newgate Calendar and John *Howard's *The State of the Prisons in England and Wales 1770–80*. The edition by David McCracken (1970) has the alternative ending printed as appendix.

calendar, the system according to which the beginning and length of the year are fixed.

The Julian Calendar is that introduced by Julius Caesar in 46 BC, in which the ordinary year has 365 days, and every fourth year is a leap year of 366 days, the months having the names, order, and length still retained. This was known as 'Old Style' when the Gregorian Calendar was introduced.

The Gregorian Calendar is the modification of the preceding, adapted to bring it into closer conformity with astronomical data and the natural course of the seasons, and to rectify the error already contracted by its use. This modification was introduced by Pope Gregory XIII in 1582, and adopted in Great Britain in 1752 (see CHESTERFIELD). It was known as 'New Style'. The error, due to the fact that the Julian year of $365\frac{1}{4}$ days (allowing for leap years) was 11 minutes 10 seconds too long, amounted in 1752 to 11 days, and in order to correct this, 2 Sept. was in that year followed by 14 Sept., while century years were to be leap years only when divisible by 400 (e.g. 1600, 2000). See also USSHER.

Calendar of Modern Letters (1925–7), a literary periodical, first a monthly, then a quarterly, edited by E. *Rickword and Douglas Garman. It published fiction by D. H. *Lawrence, *Pirandello, A. E. *Coppard, *Gerhardie, and others; in its critical articles (some in a series called 'Scrutinies') it praised Lawrence and T. F. *Powys, faintly praised S. T. *Warner and others, condemned the 'non-combatant' and uncommitted critical attitudes of *Gosse and the grossness of Arnold *Bennett, found the products of *Bloomsbury to be on the whole frivolous and sentimental, and praised the critical approach of I. A. *Richards. *Towards Standards of Criticism: Selections from the Calendar of Modern Letters* was published in 1933 with an introduction by *Leavis, and *Scrutiny* upheld many of its attitudes.

CALENIUS, Walter (d. 1151), a name used by *Bale for a writer who was archdeacon of Oxford, 1115–38. This Walter, according to *Geoffrey of Monmouth, brought from Brittany the Celtic chronicle which Geoffrey professed to translate. 'Calena' being, in the bastard Latin of the 16th cent., used for Oxford, Bale meant by 'Calenius' only Walter of Oxford. He is sometimes confused with later archdeacons of Oxford, Walter of Coutances (1183) and Walter *Map.

Caliban, in Shakespeare's *The Tempest*, is described in the *Folio 'Names of the Actors' as 'a salvage and deformed slave'. His name probably derives either from 'Carib' or 'cannibal'. Son of the witch *Sycorax and the original possessor of *Prospero's island, he is only semi-human, but has often been portrayed sympathetically in modern productions: the poetic qualities of his speeches and *post-colonial readings of the text have facilitated this.

'Caliban upon Setebos', a poem by R. Browning, included in *Dramatis Personae*.

Caliburn, see EXCALIBUR.

Calidore, Sir, the Knight of Courtesy, the hero of Bk VI of Spenser's *Faerie Queene*. He pursues and chains the *Blatant Beast. One of Keats's earliest poems, the fragment 'Young Calidore is paddling o'er the lake' (1816), was inspired by him.

Calista, the heroine of Rowe's *The Fair Penitent*, in which the 'gay Lothario' figures as her lover.

Calisto and Melibea, see CELESTINA.

CALLAGHAN, Morley (1903–90), Canadian novelist of Irish Catholic descent, born and educated in Toronto. After the publication of his first novel, *Strange Fugitive* (1928), he travelled to Paris, where in 1929 he renewed contact with *Hemingway, whom he had met while working for the *Toronto Star*; his experiences there are recorded in *That Summer in Paris* (1963), with portraits of Scott *Fitzgerald and other expatriate Americans. He published short stories and several novels, and is best remembered for the triptych of novels *Such is My Beloved* (1934), in which Father Dowling, an idealistic and innocent young priest, generously but unwisely befriends two prostitutes; *They Shall Inherit the Earth* (1935); and *More Joy in Heaven* (1937), on the theme of a bank robber turned 'prodigal son'. These works share an impressively spare and simple prose and narrative style, and a religious concern with the redemption of the ordinary.

CALLIL, Carmen Thérèse (1938–   ), publisher, of Irish-Lebanese-Australian descent, born in Australia and educated at the University of Melbourne. She came to England in 1960 and in 1972 founded the influential Virago Press, of which she was chairman 1972–95: this made an important contribution to *feminist criticism and literature, enlarging the canon by the addition of many out-of-print works, and re-establishing writers such as Antonia *White, W. *Cather, and Christina *Stead.

CALLIMACHUS (*c.*310–after 246 BC), perhaps the finest of Hellenistic poets and a scholar who worked in the library at Alexandria. Much admired by Roman poets in the 1st cent. BC—*Catullus imitated his poem on the 'Lock of Berenice'—he was admired also by the Byzantines. But many of his works were lost in the upheavals of the 13th cent., and his manuscript tradition has preserved only six hymns, 60 epigrams, and a number of fragments. A difficult author, Callimachus found few readers until the end of the 17th cent., after which a number of editions appeared including one to which Richard *Bentley contributed (1697). He was imitated by *Akenside in his 'Hymn to the Naiads'. One of his epigrams served as a model for W. J. *Cory's 'They told me Heraclitus . . .' (1845), and material of a mythological sort drawn from his hymns can be found in Tennyson's *'Tiresias' and *Bridges' *Prometheus the Firegiver* (1883).

CALVERLEY, Charles Stuart (born Blayds, assumed Calverley from 1852) (1831–84), became a barrister of the Inner Temple, but his career was hindered by the effects of a serious skating accident. He became known under the initials C.S.C. as a writer of light verse, parodies, and translations, some of which now bring to mind the works of *Betjeman. *Verses and Translations* appeared in 1862, *Fly Leaves* in 1872.

CALVIN (from Calvinus, the Latinized form of Cauvin), Jean (1509–64), French theologian and reformer. Born of a well-to-do middle-class family, he studied canon and civil law, became interested in Greek and Hebrew, and by 1533 was giving signs of commitment to the doctrines of the Reformers. In 1536 he published the first (Latin) edition of his *Institution de la religion chrétienne* in Basle, and settled in Geneva, establishing moral and political ascendancy over that city in 1541. In addition to continuous revisions of his *Institution* (the French version was published in 1541), he produced a succession of influential pamphlets, sermons, commentaries, and letters. The *Institution* was conceived as a defence of the Reformed Faith. It repudiated scholastic methods of argument in favour of deductions from biblical authority and the moral nature of man, and it advocated the doctrines of sin and grace—with the attendant doctrine of predestination derived from St Paul—at the expense of salvation by works. Calvin was an unswerving opponent of episcopacy, favouring the voice of independent congregations. The influence of his ideas in 16th- and 17th-cent. England can scarcely be exaggerated. The clarity, conciseness, energy, and austerity of his use of the vernacular mark a significant advance in the development of French prose.

CALVINO, Italo (1923–85), Italian novelist and short story writer. His first work, *Il sentiero dei nidi di ragno* (*The Path of the Nest of Spiders*, 1947), which deals with the resistance against Fascism, is one of the main novels of *neo-realism. In his later work he explored the limits of realism by delving into fantasy and myth, and by his punctilious description of minute fragments of life. He has written three allegorical novels: *Il visconte dimezzato* (*The Cloven Viscount*, 1952), *Il barone rampante* (*Baron in the Trees*, 1957), which plays with the 'reality' of *Richardson and *Fielding, and *Il cavaliere inesistente* (*The Non-existent Knight*, 1959), which plays with conventions of Renaissance chivalrous epic. His critique of neo-capitalism emerges in such novels as *La speculazione edilizia* (*Building Speculation*, 1957). His later novels move into fabulous realms—for example, *Le città invisibili* (*Invisible Cities*, 1972); but in *Palomar* (1983) he reverts to exploring the minutest details of experience. His inventive ironic fantasies are comparable to those of *Borges, and he was deeply interested in folklore and *fairy stories. (See also MAGIC REALISM.)

Cambalo, one of the two sons of King Cambuscan, in Chaucer's 'Squire's Tale': see CANTERBURY TALES, 11; see also Cambell (below) for the continuation of his story in Spenser's *Faerie Queene*.

Cambell, or Cambello, the name given by Spenser in *The Faerie Queene*, IV. iii, to *Cambalo, whose tale he borrows from 'Dan Chaucer', well of English undefyled', and completes. Cambell is brother of *Canacee, for whom there are many suitors. It is arranged that the strongest of these, three brothers, shall fight with Cambell and the lady be awarded to the victor. Two of the brothers are defeated: the contest between the third, *Triamond, and Cambell is undecided, each wounding the other. They are reconciled by Cambina, Triamond's sister; Canacee is awarded to Triamond and Cambell marries Cambina. The magic ring of Canacee in the 'Squire's Tale' reappears in the *Faerie Queene*, with the power of healing wounds.

Camber (Kamber), according to legend one of the sons of Brutus (see BRUT), the legendary first king of Britain. Camber is supposed to have given his name to Cambria (Wales), but this is in fact a Latinized derivative of *Cymry* (Welshmen). See *Geoffrey of Monmouth's *History*, ii. 1.

Cambridge Bibliography of English Literature, an invaluable reference work in four volumes, edited by F. W. *Bateson, published 1940, with a supplement, edited by George Watson, 1957. It was succeeded by the *New Cambridge Bibliography of English Literature* of which vol. i (600–1660) appeared in 1974; vol. ii (1660–1800) in 1971; vol. iii (1800–1900) in 1969, all edited by Watson. Vol. iv (1900–50), edited by I. R. Willison, appeared in 1972, and vol. v (the Index), compiled by J. D. Pickles, in 1977.

Cambridge Platonists, a group of Anglican divines who had close connections with Cambridge University and tried to promote a rational form of Christianity in the tradition of *Hooker and *Erasmus. The group included Benjamin Whichcote (1609–83), appointed provost of King's College by Parliament (1644) and dispossessed at the Restoration (1660). His writings, mostly sermons and letters, were published posthumously. Posthumous publication was the fate also of the only volume (*Select Discourses*, 1660) produced by Whichcote's pupil John Smith (1618–52): M. *Arnold said that his sermon 'On the Excellency and Nobleness of True Religion' contained all that ordinands needed to know outside of the Bible. Henry More (1614–87) remained all his life a fellow of Christ's College, refusing all preferment. His early poetry in *Psychodia Platonica* (1642) has some remarkable as well as some remarkably awkward passages. His prose works (eleven were published during his lifetime) are profound, complex, overloaded with learning, and their interpretation is made difficult by More's conflicting attitudes. He attacked superstition but had himself a keen taste for the occult; he wanted to simplify religion so that all could understand it, but was bitterly opposed to the emotional fervour that had most appeal for the uneducated; at one time he was full of praise for *Descartes, later he censured him as a materialist. Ralph Cudworth (1617–88), master successively of Clare Hall (1645) and Christ's College (1654), had a more lucid style and a more logical mind, and his major work, *The True Intellectual System of the Universe* (1678), must be regarded as the group's most detailed manifesto. Another fellow of Emmanuel College often included in the group was Nathaniel Culverwell (d.

1651), but his outlook differed from that of the rest, being more Calvinist and Aristotelian.

The aims of the group were to combat materialism, which was finding a forceful exponent in T. *Hobbes, and to reform religion by freeing it from fanaticism and controversy. Drawing inspiration from *Plato and *Plotinus, they maintained that Sense reveals only appearances, Reality consists in 'intelligible forms' which are 'not impressions printed on the soul without, but ideas vitally protended or actively exerted from within itself'. They held furthermore that Revelation, the Rational Order of the Universe, and human Reason were all in harmony, so that to search for Truth was to search for God. They rejected the Calvinist doctrine that human nature was deeply corrupt, capable of salvation only through the action of a Divine Grace granted to some and withheld from others, and saw Man as 'deiform', able to advance towards perfection through Reason and the imitation of Christ. Reason for the Cambridge Platonists was not just power of critical thought, but to function effectively had to result in virtuous behaviour. Truth and Goodness were inseparable.

These doctrines were presented in a rhetorical, quotation-laden, often verbose, late Renaissance manner which has masked their revolutionary character, but it is evident that they prepared the way for the *Deism of the 18th cent. The odd fact that Cudworth's daughter was one of *Locke's patrons was in a way symbolic.

Cambridge University Press. Books were first printed at Cambridge in 1521–2 by John Siberch (John Lair of Siegburg), a friend of *Erasmus. A charter was granted to the University by Henry VIII in 1534 authorizing the printing of books there, but not until 1583 was the first university printer, Thomas Thomas, appointed. The undertaking was opposed by the *Stationers' Company as an infringement of their privilege, but the University finally vindicated its rights. The activity of the Press was developed under the influence of R. *Bentley (1662–1742) when the present system of control by a Syndicate, or committee of senior academics, was instituted. The Press evolved from the original system under which licensed printers did some work for the University, through a partnership with a dynasty of printer-publishers (the Clays) to full control, by the Syndicate and its permanent staff, of its own large printing-house and worldwide publishing business, issuing schoolbooks, textbooks, works of learning and reference, journals, Bibles, and prayer books as part of the University's charitable function of fostering 'education, learning, religion, and research'. With a history of continuous activity since 1584, the Press claims to be the oldest printer-publisher in England, perhaps in the world. The Press has been a notable scientific publisher from I. *Newton and *Ray through Rutherford, Schrodinger, Sherrington to the present day. *Jebb's and *Housman's editions of

165

CAMBUSCAN | CAMLANN

classical authors, Ventris and Chadwick on the decipherment of Mycenean Greek, Needham on *Science and Civilisation in China*, Runciman's *History of the Crusades*, C. S. *Lewis and F. R. *Leavis on literature, indicate the range and level of publication. The most obviously 'Cambridge' publication is the great range of collaborative histories first planned by *Acton (Cambridge Ancient History, Cambridge Medieval History, Cambridge Modern History) and extended since his death.

Cambuscan, in Chaucer's 'Squire's Tale' (see CANTERBURY TALES, 11), a king of Tartary.

Cambyses, King, subject of a tragedy (1569) by T. *Preston, which illustrates the transition from the morality play to the historical tragedy. It is founded on the story of Cambyses (king of Persia) in Herodotus; its bombastic grandiloquence became proverbial and is referred to in *1 *Henry IV*, II. iv: 'I must speak in passion, and I will do it in King Cambyses' vein.' Among the characters are three comic villains, Ruff, Huff, and Snuff, who figure again in the *Martin Marprelate controversy in the course of Lyly's *Pappe with an Hatchet*.

CAMDEN, William (1551–1623), antiquary and historian, educated at *Christ's Hospital, St Paul's School, and Magdalen College, Broadgates Hall, and Christ Church, Oxford. In 1593 he was appointed headmaster of Westminster School; one of his pupils was *Jonson, who said that he owed Camden 'All that I am in arts, all that I know'. He made tours of antiquarian research up and down England, publishing his *Britannia* in 1586, of which the sixth, greatly enlarged, edition appeared in 1607. In 1615 he published *Annales . . . Regnante Elizabetha . . . ad Annum 1589*, a civic history; the second part was published posthumously in 1627. He founded a chair of ancient history in Oxford. He wrote principally in Latin, but his *Britannia* was translated into English by *Holland in 1610, and his *Annales*, by other hands, in 1625, 1630, and 1635.

Camden Society, the, founded in 1838 in honour of W. *Camden, for the purpose of publishing documents relating to the early history and literature of the British Empire. In 1897 it was amalgamated with the *Royal Historical Society.

Camelot, the seat of King Arthur's court, is said by *Malory to be Winchester. It may be Camelford in Cornwall, the name actually given it by *Laȝamon; Selden, following Drayton's *Poly-Olbion*, identifies it as South Cadbury in Somerset, and *Leland says he found traces of Arthur in Queen's Camel in Somerset which (he says) was previously called Camelot. Loomis says it is a fusion of *Avalon, the location of Arthur's last battle, and Caerleon in South Wales. Colchester has also claimed it. See R. S. Loomis, *Arthurian Tradition and Chrétien de Troyes* (1949), 480–1.

CAMERON, Julia Margaret, née Pattle (1815–79),

photographer, born in Calcutta, into an artistic and well-connected family; she had many friends in the literary world, and her portraits of *Carlyle, *Tennyson, *Jowett, Anne Thackeray *Ritchie, and many others are outstanding: one of the most celebrated is of her niece Mrs Herbert Duckworth, later the wife of L. *Stephen and mother of V. *Woolf. She lived from 1860 till 1875 at Freshwater, Isle of Wight, and many of her photographs were designed to illustrate poetic works, notably her neighbour Tennyson's; she was also fond of allegorical and symbolic subjects which she composed in a style strongly influenced by the *Pre-Raphaelites. Unconventional and striking in dress and manner, she was described by Lady Ritchie as 'a woman of noble plainness'.

CAMERON, (John) Norman (1905–53), poet, born in India of Scottish parents. He was educated in Edinburgh and at Oriel College, Oxford, worked (1929–32) as an education officer in Nigeria, then (after staying in Majorca with Robert *Graves) returned to England, where he worked for an advertising agency. During and immediately after the war (until 1947) he worked in government propaganda with the British forces in Italy and Austria. His poems were published in periodicals during the 1930s, principally in *New Verse*; his collections include *The Winter House* (1935) and *Forgive Me, Sire* (1950). His *Collected Poems* were published posthumously in 1957 with an introduction by Graves. His poems are brief, lucid, and concentrated, built usually on a single image or parable: Dylan *Thomas wrote (in an undated letter to Henry Treece), 'A poem by Cameron *needs* no more than one image; it moves around one idea, from one logical point to another, making a full circle. A poem by myself *needs* a host of images . . .'

Camilla, or a *Picture of Youth*, a novel by F. *Burney, published 1796.
The author always insisted this was not a novel but a *work*, in which characters and morals were to be put into action. It relates the stories of a group of young people, the lively and beautiful Camilla Tyrold, her sisters, and her exotic, selfish cousin Indiana Lynmere; and centres on the love affair of Camilla herself and her eligible, but cool and judicious, suitor Edgar Mandlebert. Its happy consummation is delayed over five volumes by intrigues, contretemps, and misunderstandings, many of them designed to exhibit the virtues and failings of Camilla, or to test and improve her character. The book, especially in its earlier volumes, contains humour, inventive incident, and lively characterization, especially of some of the minor characters such as the grotesque tutor Dr Orkborne, the fop Sir Sedley Clarendel, and Camilla's uncle Sir Hugh Tyrold.

Camillo, in Shakespeare's *The Winter's Tale*, a Sicilian lord.

Camlann, according to the 9th–10th-cent. *Annales

Cambriae the place of the battle in 537 in which *Arthur and Medraut (Modred) fell. It may possibly be Slaughter or Bloody Bridge on the River Camel, near Camelford in Cornwall; *Malory, a very long time after the historical sources, says the battle was near Salisbury and the sea.

CAMÕES, or **CAMOËNS,** Luís de (1524–80), a Portuguese poet of Galician stock, who led a troubled and adventurous life, losing an eye in service against the Moors, suffering imprisonment, and being shipwrecked off the coast of Cochin China, among other misfortunes. He died miserably in Lisbon. He wrote plays, sonnets, and lyrics, but is remembered outside his own country for his great epic poem *Os Lusíadas* (1572), the *Lusiads*. Its subject is the history of Portugal, and it celebrates the descendants of Lusus, the legendary founder of Lusitania, or Portugal, and more particularly the exploits of Vasco da Gama, the Portuguese navigator. In ten cantos of eight-lined stanzas, it follows the voyages of Gama, interweaving the past and present history of the nation; it contains such well-known episodes as the story of *Iñez de Castro (Canto III); the tournament of 'the Twelve of England', in which the duke of Lancaster arranges combat between English and Portuguese knights (Canto VI); and the arrival of Gama's men at the Isle of Love (possibly Zanzibar) (Canto IX), where Gama is allegorically wedded to Tethys, the sea goddess. Sir Richard *Burton, who translated much of Camões, praised this last section as 'the most charming pictures ever painted by [his] rich and amorous fancy—pictures which a Tasso might have imitated but not excel' (1881). There are other English translations by Sir Richard *Fanshawe (1655, a spirited version in stanza form); W. J. Mickle (1776, in heroic couplets); and J. J. Aubertin (1878, in stanza form).

Campaspe, a prose comedy by *Lyly, published 1584 under the title *Alexander, Campaspe and Diogenes*. Alexander the Great, enamoured of his Theban captive Campaspe, gives her freedom and engages *Apelles to paint her portrait. Apelles and Campaspe fall in love, and when the portrait is finished Apelles spoils it so as to have occasion for further sittings. Alexander suspects the truth and by a trick makes him reveal it. He surrenders Campaspe to Apelles and returns to his wars, saying 'It were a shame *Alexander* should desire to commaund the world, if he could not commaund & himselfe.' The play includes the charming lyric, '*Cupid and my Campaspe* playd | At Cardes for kisses . . .' The story of Alexander, Campaspe, and Apelles is told in *Pliny's *Natural History*, 35. 10.

CAMPBELL, Joseph (1879–1944), Irish poet, who published some of his works under the Irish version of his name, Seosamh MacCathmhaoil. He was born in Belfast, spent some years in London as secretary of the Irish National Literary Society, was later interned as a Republican in Ireland, and spent some years in America. Most of his lyrics and ballads are based on Irish legend and folklore; his collections include *The Garden of Bees* (1905), *The Gilly of Christ* (1907), and *Earth of Cualann* (1917). His *Collected Poems*, with an introduction by A. *Clarke, was published in 1963.

CAMPBELL, Ramsey (1946–   ), English *horror novelist and short story writer, born in Liverpool. His very early work, written while still in his teens, bears the stamp of H. P. Lovecraft, but Campbell soon developed his own approach characterized by a sly and subtle undermining of his characters' perceptions of reality.

CAMPBELL, (Ignatius) Roy(ston Dunnachie) (1901–57), born in Natal, came to England in 1918. In 1924 he published, to great acclaim, *The Flaming Terrapin*, an exuberant allegorical narrative of the Flood, in which the terrapin represents energy and rejuvenation. Returning to South Africa, he founded in 1926 with *Plomer a satirical literary magazine, *Voorslag* ('Whiplash', 1926–7), which he and Plomer wrote largely by themselves until joined by *van der Post; in 1928 he published *The Wayzgoose*, a satire on South African life. Now living in Provence, he published *Adamastor* (1930), and in 1931 *The Georgiad*, a long, biting attack on the *Bloomsbury Group. *Flowering Reeds* (1933), a book of gentler lyrics, was followed in 1934 by his first autobiography, *Broken Record*, a swashbuckling narrative of adventure and blatantly Fascist opinions. In 1935 he became a Roman Catholic. His next book of verse, *Mithraic Emblems*, appeared in 1936, and in 1939 a long poem, *Flowering Rifle*, a noisily pro-Fascist work which brought him much opprobrium. During the Second World War he fought in Africa, and in 1941 published *Sons of the Mistral*, a selection of his best poems. His *Collected Poems* appeared in 1950. *Light on a Dark Horse* (1951) is a second autobiography, propagating his legend. He did much translation in the course of his life, chiefly from French and Spanish, and in 1952 published an important study and translation of *García Lorca. He was killed in a car crash in Portugal. See P. Alexander, *Roy Campbell* (1982).

CAMPBELL, Thomas (1777–1844), son of a Glasgow merchant, educated at Glasgow University and closely associated with the founding of the University of London (now University College London) in the late 1820s. He published *The Pleasures of Hope* in 1799, *Gertrude of Wyoming* in 1809, *Theodric, and Other Poems* in 1824, and *The Pilgrim of Glencoe, and Other Poems* in 1842. He was immensely popular in his own day, but is now chiefly remembered for his war-songs, *'The Battle of Hohenlinden', 'The Battle of the Baltic', and 'Ye Mariners of England'; and for his ballads, such as 'The Soldier's Dream', 'Lord Ullin's Daughter', 'Lochiel's Warning', and 'Lines on Revisiting a Scene in Argyllshire'.

CAMPION, St Edmund (1540–81), fellow of St John's College, Oxford (1557), who went to Douai in 1571 and graduated there, and joined the Jesuits in 1573. He returned to England in 1580, preached privately in London, was arrested in 1581, sent to the Tower, examined under torture, and executed. He was beatified in 1886 and canonized in 1970. E. *Waugh published a life of him (1935).

CAMPION, Thomas (1567–1620), poet, musician, and doctor, educated at Cambridge and Gray's Inn; he studied medicine in middle age, receiving an MD from the University of Caen in 1605. Five songs by him were appended to the unauthorized *Astrophel and Stella* in 1591; in 1595 he published his Latin *Poemata*, collaborated with Philip *Rosseter in *A Booke of Ayres* (1601), and between about 1613 and 1617 published four *Bookes of Ayres*, with many settings composed by himself, and his *Songs of Mourning* for Prince Henry. His *Observations in the Art of English Poesie* were published in 1602, defending classical metres against 'the vulgar and unarteficiall custome of riming'. The treatise includes such beautiful illustrative poems as 'Rose-cheekt *Lawra*, come'. In the early years of James I's reign he wrote a number of court masques. His poems and the *Observations* were edited by W. R. Davis in 1967.

campus novel, a novel set on a university campus; most are written by novelists who are also (temporarily or permanently) academics, and notable English examples include K. *Amis's *Lucky Jim* (1954), D. *Lodge's *Changing Places* (1975), M. *Bradbury's *The History Man* (1975) and H. *Jacobson's *Coming from Behind* (1983).

CAMUS, Albert (1913–60), French novelist, dramatist, journalist, and essayist. He was born in Algeria, which provides the setting for many of his works. Through *L'Étranger* (1942; *The Outsider*, 1946), *La Peste* (1947; *The Plague*, 1948), both novels, and *Le Mythe de Sisyphe* (1942; *The Myth of Sisyphus*, 1955), and *L'Homme révolté* (1951; *The Rebel*, 1953), he explored the implications of the 'absurd' nature of the human condition. His novel *La Chute* appeared in 1956 (*The Fall*, 1957), and in 1957 his collection of short stories *L'Exil et le royaume* (*Exile and the Kingdom*, 1958). He wrote a number of plays, including *Caligula* (1944, trans. 1948), and several adaptations for the stage, including one from *Faulkner's *Requiem for a Nun* (1956). He was awarded the *Nobel Prize for literature in 1957. A life by Olivier Todd was published in 1997. (See also ABSURD, THEATRE OF THE.)

Canacee, the daughter of King Cambuscan in Chaucer's 'Squire's Tale' (see CANTERBURY TALES, 11) and in Spenser's *Faerie Queene*, Bk IV.

Candide, a philosophical fable by *Voltaire, published in 1759. It recounts the adventures of its innocent young hero, Candide, brought up in the home of Baron Thunder-ten-tronckh in Westphalia, where he is much influenced by the tutor *Pangloss, an apparently incurable optimist and a follower of *Leibniz. Driven from home because of his love for the baron's daughter Cunégonde, Candide is first pressed into the Bulgar army, by which Cunégonde is subsequently raped and reported killed. A series of grotesque misfortunes ensues for all the characters, providing witty and devastating satires of Church, state, philosophy, and the professions. An interlude in the rich and happy country of Eldorado in South America comes to an end because of Candide's restless quest for Cunégonde, with whom he is eventually reunited. He has lost his wealth and she her beauty, but they marry, and settle down with Pangloss and other travelling companions to run a small estate and to cultivate their garden.

Candour, Mrs, one of the scandal-mongers in Sheridan's *The School for Scandal*.

CANETTI, Elias (1905–94), born in Bulgaria of a Spanish- and German-speaking Jewish family. He was educated largely in Zurich and Frankfurt, and gained a doctorate in chemistry at the University of Vienna. In 1939 he came to London, where he settled, and became a familiar figure in Hampstead and a close friend of Iris *Muldoch. His best-known work, a novel, was published as *Die Blendung* in 1935, and in an English translation by C. V. Wedgwood as *Auto da Fé* in 1946. Inspired by the burning of the Palace of Justice in Vienna in 1927, it centres on Peter Kien, a Sinologist, who lives for his books, and finally sets fire to his own library. Canetti's sociological study of crowd behaviour *Masse und Macht* (1960) appeared as *Crowds and Power* in 1962. He also published plays, essays, and three volumes of autobiography: *Die gerettete Zunge* (1977), translated as *The Tongue Set Free* (1979); *Die Fackel im Ohr* (1980), translated as *The Torch in My Ear* (1989); and *Das Augenspiel* (1985), translated as *The Play of the Eyes* (1990). He was awarded the *Nobel Prize for literature in 1981.

CANNING, George (1770–1827), Tory statesman and author, educated at Eton and Christ Church, Oxford. He was appointed foreign secretary in 1822 and prime minister in 1827. Apart from his political speeches (published 1828), he is remembered in a literary connection as founder of and contributor to the *Anti-Jacobin, the chief object of which was to ridicule the Revolutionary party. He was also a frequent and influential contributor to the *Quarterly Review* and a witty literary parodist. His *Poems* were published in 1823.

canon, a body of approved works, comprising either (i) writings genuinely considered to be those of a given author; or (ii) writings considered to represent the best standards of a given literary tradition.

'Canon's Yeoman's Tale, The', see CANTERBURY TALES, 22.

Canterbury Tales, The, *Chaucer's most celebrated work probably designed about 1387 and extending to 17,000 lines in prose and verse of various metres (though the predominant form is the rhyming couplet). The General Prologue describes the meeting of 29 pilgrims in the Tabard Inn in Southwark (in fact they add up to 31; it has been suggested that the prioress's 'preestes three' in line 164 may be an error since only one 'Nun's Priest' is mentioned in the body of the work). Detailed pen-pictures are given of 21 of them, vividly described but perhaps corresponding to traditional lists of the orders of society, clerical and lay (see J. Mann, *Chaucer and Medieval Estates Satire*, 1973). The host (see BAILLY) proposes that the pilgrims should shorten the road by telling four stories each, two on the way to Canterbury and two on the way back; he will accompany them and award a free supper on their return to the teller of the best story. The work is incomplete; only 23 pilgrims tell stories, and there are only 24 stories told altogether (Chaucer tells two). In the scheme the stories are linked by narrative exchanges between the pilgrims and by prologues and epilogues to the tales; but this aspect of the work is also very incomplete. It is uncertain even, in what order the stories are meant to come; the evidence of the manuscripts and of geographical references is conflicting, as is the scholarly interpretation of that evidence. The order that follows is that of the Ellesmere manuscript, followed in the best complete edition of Chaucer, *The Riverside Chaucer* (ed. L. D. Benson et al., 1988).

(1) 'The Knight's Tale', a shortened version of the *Teseida* of *Boccaccio, the story of the love of Palamon and Arcite (told again in Shakespeare's *The Two Noble Kinsmen*), prisoners of Theseus king of Athens, for Emelye, sister of Hippolyta queen of the Amazons, whom Theseus has married. The rivals compete for her in a tournament. Palamon is defeated, but Arcite, the favourite of Mars, at the moment of his triumph is thrown and injured by his horse through the intervention of Venus and Saturn, and dies. Palamon and Emelye, after prolonged mourning for Arcite, are united. *Riverside* follows the Ellesmere division of the tale into four parts, but it is not so divided in all the manuscripts. An interesting interpretation of the tale as ironic is given by Terry Jones in *Chaucer's Knight* (1978).

(2) 'The Miller's Tale', a ribald story of the deception, first of a husband (a carpenter) through the prediction of a second flood, and secondly of a lover who expects to kiss the lady's lips but kisses instead her 'nether eye'. He avenges himself on her lover for this humiliation with a red-hot ploughshare. The Tale has been said to be a parody of a courtly-love story.

(3) 'The Reeve's Tale' is a *fabliau about two clerks who are robbed by a miller of some of the meal which they take to his mill to be ground, and who take their vengeance by sleeping with the miller's wife and daughter. There are two manuscript versions of a French analogue in Bryan and Dempster, *Sources and Analogues of Chaucer's Canterbury Tales* (1941), 126–47, 'Le Meunier at les II clers'. In Chaucer's context, it is an obvious rejoinder to the miller's tale of the duping of a carpenter, the reeve's profession.

(4) 'The Cook's Tale' of Perkyn Revelour only extends to 58 lines before it breaks off. It is another ribald fabliau which ends with the introduction of a prostitute, and it has been suggested that Chaucer may have decided that the occurrence of three indecent tales together was unbalanced. The tale of *Gamelyn, not by Chaucer, is introduced for the cook in some manuscripts. The cook himself, Roger (by nickname traditionally Hodge) of Ware (l. 4336), has been identified with an attested cook of that name. See *Riverside*, p. 814.

(5) 'The Man of Law's Tale' is the story of Constance, daughter of a Christian emperor of Rome, who marries the sultan of Syria on condition that he become a Christian and who is cast adrift in a boat because of the machinations of the sultan's jealous mother. It is a frequently told medieval story, paralleled by the romance *Emaré* and by *Gower's Constance story in *Confessio Amantis*, ii. 587 ff.; there is argument about the priority of Chaucer's and Gower's versions. It is certain, at least, that Chaucer's is based on a passage in the early 14th-cent. Anglo-Norman Chronicle by *Trivet. Both Trivet's and Gower's versions are in Bryan and Dempster.

(6) 'The Wife of Bath's Tale' is preceded by an 856-line prologue in which she condemns celibacy by describing her life with her five late husbands, in the course of which Chaucer draws widely on the medieval anti-feminist tradition, especially on Jean de Meun's *La Vielle* (the Duenna) in the *Roman de la rose*. After this vigorous, learned, and colourful narrative, the following tale, though appropriate, seems rather flat. It is the story of 'the loathly lady' (paralleled by Gower's 'Tale of Florent' in *Confessio Amantis*, i. 1396 ff., and by the romance *Weddynge of Sir Gawen and Dame Ragnell*, edited in D. B. Sands, *Middle English Verse Romances*, 323–47) in which a knight is asked to answer the question, 'what do women most desire?' The correct answer, 'sovereignty', is told him by a hideous old witch on condition that he marry her; when he does she is restored to youth and beauty. Since Kittredge (*Chaucer and his Poetry*, 1915, 185 ff.) it has generally been thought that this Prologue-Tale sets in motion a discussion of marriage, 'The Marriage Group', which is taken up (after interruptions) by the clerk, the merchant, and the franklin (see 9, 10, 12, below).

(7) 'The Friar's Tale' tells how a summoner meets the devil dressed as a yeoman and they agree to share out what they are given. They come upon a carter who curses his horse, commending it to the devil; the summoner asks the devil why he does not take the horse thus committed to him and the devil replies that it is because the commendation does not come from the heart. Later they visit an old woman from whom the summoner attempts to extort twelve pence, whereupon she commends *him* to the devil. The devil carries him off to hell because her curse was from the heart. The story is widely attested in popular tradition, and its motif is referred to as *ex corde*, 'from the heart'.

Chaucer's exact source is not known, but it is clear that the friar tells it to enrage the summoner on the pilgrimage, who interrupts the narrative and rejoins with a scurrilous and discreditable story about a friar.

(8) 'The Summoner's Tale' tells of a greedy friar who undertakes to divide a deathbed legacy amongst his community; he receives a fart and has to devise an ingenious stratagem to divide it with perfect justice.

(9) 'The Clerk's Tale', which the poet tells us he took from *Petrarch, was translated into Latin by the latter from the Italian version of Boccaccio in *The Decameron (Day 10, Tale 10). Boccaccio was the first writer (in 1353) to take the story from popular currency, and there are several versions of the story in Italian, Latin, and French before Chaucer's (indeed it is clear that Chaucer's version is rather more dependent on a French prose version than on Petrarch's Latin). The story tells of patient Griselda and her trials by her husband, the Marquis Walter. Chaucer's version has more hints of criticism of the relentless husband than any of his predecessors (except Boccaccio, whose narrator frowns on Gualtieri's 'strange desire' to try his wife's obedience). Apologists for 'The Marriage Group' (see 6 above) regard the tale as a response to the wife of Bath, partly because the Clerk concludes with an expression of good will towards her (IV. 1170 ff.).

(10) 'The Merchant's Tale', in which the merchant, prompted by the tale of Griselda's extreme obedience, tells his 'Tale' of January and May, the old husband with his young wife, and the problems with obedient fidelity involved in this relationship. After a lengthy review of the pros and cons of taking a young wife, January ignores the good advice of Justinus in favour of the time-serving opinion of Placebo and marries May. When he goes blind she makes love to her suitor Damyan in a pear-tree round which January wraps his arms. Pluto mischievously restores January's sight at this point, but Proserpine inspires May to explain that the restoration of his sight was brought about by her activities in the pear-tree and that this had been their purpose. Critics have argued about the relative proportions of mordancy and humour in the tale; see E. Talbot Donaldson in Speaking of Chaucer (1970), 30–45. There are parallels to the various sections of the story in French, Latin, Italian, and German (see D. S. Brewer (ed.), Medieval Comic Tales, 1973, German no. 3 and Latin, (o)).

(11) 'The Squire's Tale', of Cambuscan, king of Tartary, to whom on his birthday an envoy from the king of Arabia brings magic gifts, including a ring for the king's daughter Canacee, which enables her to understand the language of birds. A female falcon tells Canacee the story of her own desertion by a tercelet. The tale is incomplete but it seems likely that Chaucer meant to finish it, judging from the fact that there is no suggestion that it is unfinished in the laudatory words of the franklin that follow it (V. 673 ff.). The precise origin of the tale is unknown, but a number of parallels

are suggested by H. S. V. Jones in Bryan and Dempster, pp. 357–76.

(12) 'The Franklin's Tale', of Dorigen, wife of Arveragus, who to escape the attentions of her suitor, the squire Aurelius, makes her consent depend upon an impossible condition, that all the rocks on the coast of Brittany be removed. When this condition is realized by the aid of a magician, the suitor, from a generous remorse, releases her from her promise. Chaucer states that the tale is taken from a *'Breton lay', but if this is true, the original is lost. There are a number of parallels in medieval literature, of which the closest is Boccaccio's Il filocolo, Question 4. See N. R. Hayely, Chaucer's Boccaccio (1980).

(13) 'The Physician's Tale' tells of Virginia who, at her own request, is killed by her father to escape the designs of the corrupt judge Apius. The original source is *Livy's History, and this is what Chaucer cites, though his version seems to rely principally on the Roman de la rose, ll. 5589–658, by Jean de Meun.

(14) 'The Pardoner's Tale' follows a prologue in which he declares his own covetousness, and takes covetousness as its theme, relating it to other sins: drunkenness, gluttony, gambling, and swearing. Three rioters set out to find Death who has killed their companion; a mysterious old man tells them they will find him under a particular tree, but when they get there they find instead a heap of gold. By aiming to cheat each other in possessing the gold they kill each other. The character of the pardoner in the prologue here is related to Faus-Semblant (False-Seeming) in Jean de Meun's part of the Roman de la rose, ll. 11065–972 (a section corresponding to the Middle English Romaunt of the Rose, Fragment C, lines 6061 ff.: Robinson, pp. 621 ff.). There are many analogues for the tale, in Latin, Italian, and German, but Chaucer's exact source, if he had one, is not known.

(15) 'The Shipman's Tale.' There is a similar story in The Decameron (Day 8, Tale 1). The wife of a niggardly merchant asks the loan of a hundred francs from a priest to buy finery. The priest borrows the sum from the merchant and hands it to the wife, and the wife grants him her favours. On the merchant's return from a journey the priest tells him that he has repaid the sum to the wife, who cannot deny receiving it.

(16) 'The Prioress's Tale' tells of the murder of a child by Jews because he sings a Marian hymn while passing through their quarter and of the discovery of his body because of its continued singing of the hymn after death. There are a great many parallels for the story. Some critics, perhaps anachronistically, see the bland anti-Semitism of the story as a comment on the uncritical nature of the prioress.

(17) 'Chaucer's Tale of Sir Thopas' is a witty and elegant parody of the contemporary romance, both in its subject and in the unsubstantiality of its *tail-rhyme form. Its butts are no doubt general; but it can perhaps be taken to have special reference to the heroes it catalogues (VII. 898–900): Horn Child, the legend of

Ypotys, *Bevis of Hampton, *Guy of Warwick, the unidentified Pleyndamour, and *Libeaus Desconus. It is closest, it has been argued, to the last of these.

(18) When the Host interrupts the tale of Sir Thopas, Chaucer moves to the opposite extreme with a heavy prose homily, 'The Tale of Melibeus'. This story of the impetuous Melibeus and his wise wife Prudence dates from Italy in the 1240s, when the story was written in Latin prose for his third son by Albertano of Brescia. Chaucer's immediate source was the 1336 version in French prose by Renaud de Louens.

(19) 'The Monk's Tale' is composed of a number of 'tragedies' of persons fallen from high estate, taken from different authors and arranged on the model of Boccaccio's *De Casibus Virorum Illustrium*. The tale is in eight-line stanzas.

(20) 'The Nun's Priest's Tale' is related to the French cycle of Renart (see REYNARD), telling of a fox that beguiled a cock by praising his father's singing and was in turn beguiled by him into losing him by pausing to boast at his victory. The mock-heroic story is full of rhetoric and exempla, and it is one of the most admired of the Tales, regarded as the most typically 'Chaucerian' in tone and content. The fable is very familiar, but the parallels to Chaucer's treatment of it are not very close. The famous ending of the tale invites the reader to 'take the morality' of the Tale in spite of its apparent lightness of substance, on the grounds that St Paul says everything has *some* moral; this invitation has been taken with surprising solemnity by many critics.

(21) 'The Second Nun's Tale', in rhyme-royal, is perhaps translated from the life of St Cecilia in the *Golden Legend of Jacobus de Voragine. It describes the miracles and martyrdom of the noble Roman maiden Cecilia and her husband Valerian.

(22) 'The Canon's Yeoman's Tale' is told by a character who joins the pilgrims at this late stage (VIII. 554 ff.) with his master, the dubious canon whose alchemical skills the yeoman praises. The first 200 lines of the tale tell of the Alchemist's arcane practice and its futility, before proceeding to the tale proper which tells of how an alchemical canon (who is *not* his master, he protests, perhaps suggesting that it is) tricks a priest out of £40 by pretending to teach him the art of making precious metals. The dishonesty of the alchemists was much discussed and condemned in the 14th cent.; there is a close analogue to Chaucer's story in one of the *Novelle* of Sercambi (included in Bryan and Dempster, pp. 694–5). The most significant literary parallel, of course, is Jonson's *The Alchemist*.

(23) 'The Manciple's Tale' is the fable of the tell-tale crow, told by many authors from *Ovid in *Metamorphoses* (2. 531–62) onwards. Phebus (Phoebus) has a crow which is white and can speak. It reveals to Phebus the infidelity of his wife (nameless in Chaucer, but Coronis in Ovid and most of the writers who follow him) and Phebus kills her in a rage. Then, in remorse, he plucks out the crow's white feathers, deprives it of speech and throws it 'unto the devel', which is why

crows are now black. A very similar version of the story is told in Gower's *Confessio Amantis* (iii. 768–835), and there are other examples by Guillaume de *Machaut and in the *Ovide moralisé* (c.1324). As well as these, J. A. Work in Bryan and Dempster edits as analogues a story from *The Seven Sages of Rome* which does not name Phebus and which exchanges the fates of wife and bird, as well as some sententious parallels from *Boethius and Jean de Meun.

(24) 'The Parson's Tale' which concludes the work (and was, no doubt, meant to, even if the main body of the *Tales* is incomplete) is a long prose treatise, ostensibly on Penitence but dealing at most length with the *Seven Deadly Sins. The two principal sources are Raymund de Pennaforte's *Summa* (dating from the 1220s) for the sections on Penitence, and Guilielmus Peraldus's *Summa Vitiorum* (probably from the 1250s) for the Seven Deadly Sins.

Most manuscripts have 'The Parson's Tale' leading straight into Chaucer's closing 'Retracciouns' in which he takes leave of his book. He asks forgiveness of God for his 'translacions and enditynges of worldly vanities', including 'The Tales of Caunterbury, thilke that sownen into [i.e. tend towards] synne'. But this rhetorical conclusion need not be read as a revocation of his work by the poet; following St Augustine's *Retractationes*, many medieval works end by distancing the writer from the non-spiritual elements in his work: the Author's Epilogue in *The Decameron* and Chaucer's *Troilus* are other familiar examples. See N. F. Blake, *The Canterbury Tales, Edited from the Hengwrt Manuscript* (1980); H. Cooper, *The Canterbury Tales* (1989). Also an edition by V. A. Kolve and G. Olsen (1989).

canto, a subdivision of a long narrative or epic poem, employed in the works of *Dante, *Ariosto, *Tasso, and others; *Spenser was the first to employ the term in English.

CANUTE (Cnutr), a Dane who was king of England 1016–35. The old legend of his failing to repel the sea is told by Holinshed, VII. xiii, after *Henry of Huntingdon (who may have invented it) and *Gaimar.

Canute, The Song of, a famous early English poetic fragment stated to have been composed and sung by the king as he rowed past Ely, and recorded by a monk of Ely in 1166. It begins

> Merie sungen the munechis binnen Ely
> Tha Cnut ching reu ther by.

Can You Forgive Her?, a novel by A. *Trollope, published 1864–5, the first in the *'Palliser' series.

Alice Vavasor, a girl of independent spirit and means, is engaged to the 'paragon' John Grey but, seemingly distressed by his perfection, she jilts him in favour of her less reputable cousin George Vavasor. George's finances and expectations are in a parlous state, and Alice uses her means to help him to a political career. George is disinherited by his grandfather.

Ruined, and having lost his parliamentary seat, George takes ship for America, pausing only to make a murderous attempt on Mr Grey. When, after a suitable interval, John Grey proposes again to Alice, he is accepted. This part of the novel's plot derives from a play in blank verse, *The Noble Jilt*, written by Trollope in 1850.

Interwoven with this story is the account of the early married life of Alice's friend Lady Glencora. Lady Glencora has made a splendid match with Plantagenet Palliser, nephew and heir of the old duke of Omnium, but remains in love with the handsome wastrel Burgo Fitzgerald. When she meets Burgo at Lady Monk's ball, Glencora is tempted to elope with him, but is dissuaded by the timely arrival of Mr Palliser. Palliser decides to take his wife out of harm's way, and arranges an extensive foreign tour, despite the fact that his political ambitions have just been crowned with an offer of the post of chancellor of the exchequer. On the Continent Plantagenet and Glencora come to a better understanding, and the novel ends with the birth of an heir.

There is a comic sub-plot, dealing with the efforts of a rich widow, Alice's Aunt Greenow, to dispose of her heart and fortune.

Capability Brown, see BROWN, L.

ČAPEK, Karel (1890–1938), Czech novelist and dramatist, born in Bohemia, the son of a doctor, and educated at the universities of Paris, Berlin, and Prague. He and his brother, painter and stage-designer Josef Čapek (1887–1945), began to write plays together c.1910; the best known of their joint works is *The Insect Play* (1921), a satire on human society and totalitarianism. Čapek's best-known independent work was *R.U.R.* (1920, first performed in England in 1923), a play set 'on a remote island in 1950–60'. The title stands for 'Rossum's Universal Robots', and the concept of the mechanical robot (a word coined from the Czech 'robota', meaning drudgery) opened up a whole new vein of *science fiction, as well as adding a word to the English language. In Čapek's play the robots, having acquired human emotions, rebel against their servile status and destroy their masters. His other plays include *The Makropulos Affair* (1923), a play about longevity with some similarity to G. B. *Shaw's *Back to Methuselah* (which Čapek had not at the time read) in which he arrives at conclusions in his own view diametrically opposed to Shaw's. Čapek also wrote several Wellsian utopian romances, such as *The Manufacture of the Absolute* (1923) and *War with the Newts* (1936); a trilogy of more realistic novels, *Hordubal*, *The Meteor*, and *An Ordinary Life* (1933–4); and various travel books and essays, including *Letters from England* (1923).

CAPELL, Edward (1713–81), Shakespearian commentator. His edition of Shakespeare in ten volumes (1768) was the first to be based on complete and careful collations of all the old copies, and it is his arrangement of the lines that is now usually followed. His *Commentary, Notes and Various Readings to Shakespeare*, begun in 1774, was published in 3 vols in 1783. Capell was responsible for the first full scholarly discussion of Shakespeare's sources, and for the first attempt to establish the relationship between the *Folios and quartos; he supported the authenticity of the three parts of *Henry VI, *Titus Andronicus, *Love's Labour's Lost, and *The Taming of the Shrew. He was attacked by *Malone and *Steevens, but the soundness of his judgement makes his edition of lasting value.

CAPGRAVE, John (1393–1464), an Augustinian friar who spent most of his life in the friary at King's Lynn. He wrote a number of theological and historical works in Latin. In English he wrote lives of St Gilbert of Sempringham and St Catherine of Alexandria, and a small body of unremarkable poetry. His most significant English work is his *Chronicle* of English history up to AD 1417, which is marked by simplicity and lucidity of style.

Ed. P. J. Lucas, *John Capgrave's Abbreviation of Chronicles* (EETS, 1983).

CAPOTE, Truman (1924–84), American author, born in New Orleans, whose work ranges from the light-hearted story of playgirl Holly Golightly in *Breakfast at Tiffany's* (1958) to the grim investigation *In Cold Blood* (1966), a 'non-fiction novel' or work of *faction, in which Capote recreated the brutal multiple murder of a whole Kansas family by two ex-convicts, and traces the lives of the murderers to the moment of their execution.

Captain Singleton, Adventures of, see SINGLETON.

Capulets, in Shakespeare's *Romeo and Juliet*, the noble Veronese house (the Cappelletti) to which Juliet belongs, hostile to the family of the Montagues (the Montecchi).

Carabas, Marquess of, a character in (1) the fairy tale of *Puss in Boots*; (2) a song by *Béranger; (3) *Disraeli's *Vivian Grey*; (4) *Thackeray's *Book of Snobs*.

CARACTACUS, or **CARADOC,** king of the Silures in the west of Britain during the reign of Claudius. He was defeated by the Romans and fled to Cartimandua, queen of the Brigantes, who betrayed him. He was taken a prisoner to Rome in AD 51, where his noble spirit so pleased the emperor that he pardoned and released him. He figures as Caratach in Fletcher's *Bonduca. W. *Mason wrote a play *Caractacus* and he provides the theme of a cantata by *Elgar (1898).

CARADOC, see CARACTACUS.

Carbonek, see CORBENIC.

Carcanet Press, a small press established in South Hinksey, Oxford, in 1969 by poet, editor, and novelist Michael Schmidt (1947–   ): it moved to Manchester in 1971. It has published a wide and important range of new poetry in English and translation, as well as reviving neglected classics, and since 1981 has also published works of fiction.

Cardenio, a lost play by Shakespeare, probably in collaboration with *Fletcher, acted at Court in 1613. *Theobald in his play *Double Fals'hood* (1728) claimed to have made use of an old prompt copy of *Cardenio*, but this has never been seen since and Theobald's version lacks Shakespearian touches. It may be assumed, however, that Shakespeare's play, like Theobald's, was based on the story of Cardenio and Lucinda in *Don Quixote* (Part 1, chs. 24–8); Cardenio is the Ragged Knight, who, driven mad by the loss of his loved Lucinda, haunts the Sierra Morena, and is eventually reunited with her.

Cardinal, The, a tragedy by J. *Shirley, acted 1641, printed 1652.

This was the first play Shirley wrote for the King's Men, and both he and his contemporaries thought it his best work. The Duchess Rosaura, a young widow, wants to marry Alvarez, but the diabolical cardinal, chief adviser to the king, has forced her into a contract with his nephew Columbo. She tricks Columbo into releasing her from this contract, but on the night of her wedding to Alvarez a group of masquers (Columbo and his followers in disguise) kill the bridegroom during a dance. The duchess feigns madness and plots revenge. Columbo is killed in a duel by Hernando, a soldier who has been wronged by him. The final scene is a series of tricks. The vengeful cardinal attempts to rape the duchess and is stabbed by Hernando, who has been in hiding. Hernando then kills himself. The cardinal declares that he has already poisoned the duchess and offers her an antidote, drinking it himself as a sign of good faith. He then reveals that the 'antidote' was a poison, which he took in the belief that his wounds were mortal; a doctor tells him that they were not. The king sums up by wishing that rulers had more trustworthy advisers.

CARDINAL, Marie (1929–2001), French novelist, born in Algeria. Her first novel, *Écoutez la mer* (1962), was followed by several others, but she was best known internationally for her widely translated *Les Mots pour le dire* (1975; *The Words to Say It*, 1984), a remarkable and pioneering feminist autobiographical novel describing her childhood in Algeria, her difficult relationship with her mother, and the successful psychoanalysis that enabled her to become a writer.

CARDUCCI, Giosuè (1835–1907), Italian poet and classicist, winner of the *Nobel Prize (1906). His poetry celebrates Italy's classical heritage at the expense of Romanticism and the Church. His early hymn to Satan ('A Satana', 1863) is republican in spirit, but he was to become poet laureate in middle age. Some of his best poems are in *Rime nuove* (*New Rhymes*, 1861–7); *Odi barbare* (*Barbarian Odes*, 1873–89), based on

classical quantitative metre, and *Rime e ritmi* (*Rhymes and Rhythms*, 1887–9).

Carduel, see CARLIOUN.

Careless Husband, The, a comedy by C. *Cibber, performed and published 1704 (imprint 1705).

Sir Charles Easy, who neglects his wife and carries on an intrigue with her maid Edging and with Lady Graveairs, discovers that his wife is aware of his infidelities and is moved to reconciliation by her tolerance and virtue. The coquette Lady Betty Modish is led to accept the suit of the honourable Lord Morelove (contrasted with the boastful and immoral Lord Foppington) by a plot to excite her jealousy, followed by reproaches from Sir Charles. In his dedication, Cibber claims that he has set out to avoid coarseness and to imitate the conversation of the polite world, and the work was praised for its 'elegant dialogue', though harsher critics maintained that Cibber knew little of the social milieu he described.

Caretaker, The, a play by H. *Pinter, performed and published in 1960.

One of Pinter's characteristically enigmatic dramas, it is built on the interaction of three characters, the tramp Davies and the brothers Aston and Mick. Aston has rescued Davies from a brawl and brought him back to a junk-filled room, in which he offers Davies a bed and, eventually, an ill-defined post as caretaker. The characters reveal themselves in inconsequential dialogue and obsessional monologue. Davies is worried about his papers, the blacks, gas leaks, and getting to Sidcup; Aston reveals that he has suffered headaches ever since undergoing electric shock treatment for his 'complaint'; Mick, the youngest, is alternately bully, cajoler, and materialist visionary, with dreams of transforming the room into a fashionable penthouse. In the end both brothers turn on Davies and evict him. The dialogue is at once naturalistic and surreal; the litany of London place names (Finsbury Park, Shepherd's Bush, Putney) and of decorator's jargon (charcoal-grey worktops, teak veneer) serves to highlight the no-man's-land in which the characters in fact meet.

CAREW (pron. Carey), Thomas (1594/5–1640), son of a master in chancery. He was educated at Oxford and became secretary to Sir Dudley Carleton at Venice and subsequently at The Hague. He won the favour of Charles I, was appointed to an office at court, and received an estate from him. His elegy for *Donne was published with Donne's poems in 1633, his masque *Coelum Britannicum* (with settings by I. *Jones) was performed before the king in 1634, and his *Poems* appeared in 1640. He was a close friend of *Suckling and one of the best known of the *Cavalier poets; his works include many graceful, witty, and often cynical songs and lyrics, and several longer poems, including the erotic 'A Rapture', and 'To Saxham', a country-house poem in the genre of *Jonson's 'To Penshurst', by whom, with Donne, he was much influenced. The standard edition of his work is by R. Dunlap, 1949.

CAREY, Henry (?1687–1743), wrote farces, operas, and burlesques, which include *Chrononhotonthologos* (1734) and *The Dragon of Wantley* (1737). He is also remembered as the inventor of the nickname 'Namby-Pamby' for Ambrose *Philips ('Namby-pamby's little rhymes | Little jingles, little chimes, | To repeat to little miss, | Piddling ponds of pissy-piss'—1725) and as the author of the words and music of 'Sally in our Alley' (1715?).

CAREY, Peter Philip (1943–   ), Australian novelist, born at Bacchus Marsh, Victoria, educated at Geelong Grammar School and, briefly, at Monash University. After leaving university he worked for advertising agencies in Melbourne and London, moving to Sydney in 1974. Though a self-proclaimed Australian writer, Carey is a fabulist who does not write in any recognizable national tradition. His is an idiosyncratic voice, his fiction combining realism and the surreal, satire with a keen sense of the fantastic, matter-of-factness with phenomena that Carey himself has called 'not real but something parallel'. Two volumes of short stories, *The Fat Man in History* (1974), which established Carey as a new force in Australian writing, and *War Crimes* (1979), were followed by a darkly comic novel, *Bliss* (1981), in which an advertising executive dies three times and is resurrected on each occasion, and the exuberantly written *Illywhacker* (1985), the reminiscences of a 139-year-old con man. His next novel, *Oscar and Lucinda* (1988), a rich and subtle love story set in the 19th cent., won the *Booker Prize for fiction and confirmed Carey's stature as one of the most original and accomplished novelists of his generation. *The Tax Inspector* (1991), a satire of modern life in Sydney, was followed by *The Unusual Life of Tristan Smith* (1994), a picaresque but insistently disturbing fable set in the imaginary country of Efica, which once more blends realism, satire, and fantasy. *Jack Maggs* (1997) is a historical novel about a criminal returning to England from Australia; *True History of the Kelly Gang* (2001, *Booker Prize) is a narrative *tour de force* told through the voice of outlaw and folk hero Ned Kelly.

Carker, James, a character in Dickens's *Dombey and Son*.

Carleton, Memoirs of Captain, see MEMOIRS OF CAPTAIN CARLETON.

CARLETON, William (1794–1869), born in Tyrone, the son of a peasant farmer; he wrote many stories of Irish peasant life, both melancholy and humorous. *Traits and Stories of the Irish Peasantry* (1830–5) was followed by *Tales of Ireland* in 1834. His novels include *Fardorougha*, the Miser (1839), a powerful study of an Irish farmer and usurer, torn between avarice and his love for his son; and *The Black Prophet* (1847), a bleak story of the potato famine.

Carlioun (sometimes Carduel), in Malory's *Morte

D'Arthur, the city where Arthur was crowned and held his court, probably Caerleon-upon-Usk, though in places Carlisle appears to be meant.

CARLISLE, Frederick Howard, fifth earl of (1748–1825), Chancery guardian to *Byron and attacked by him in *English Bards and Scotch Reviewers*. His tragedy *The Father's Revenge* was praised by Dr *Johnson and Horace *Walpole.

CARLISLE, Richard, see ROMANTIC FICTION.

Carlos, Don, the deformed son of Philip II of Spain. The marriage of the latter with Elizabeth of France, who had been affianced to Don Carlos, forms the subject of Otway's tragedy *Don Carlos* and of *Verdi's opera.

CARLYLE, Alexander (1722–1805), nicknamed 'Jupiter', educated at Edinburgh University, Glasgow, and Leiden, a minister and leader of the Scottish 'Broad Church' party. He was author of an interesting autobiography (printed 1860) which refers to various notable events and personalities of the period.

CARLYLE, Jane Baillie Welsh (1801–66), born in Haddington, East Lothian, the daughter of a doctor. She showed considerable powers both of intellect and of character while still at school, and in 1821 was introduced by her former tutor Edward Irving to Thomas *Carlyle. Together and by correspondence she and Carlyle studied German literature, he effectively taking on the role of tutor, then of lover; they were married in 1826. Much of her energy during her married life was devoted to domestic chores and to the humouring and protection of a temperamental husband, but she is nevertheless remembered as one of the best letter-writers in the English language, witty, caustic, and observant, and as a literary hostess who impressed all who met her. Her vast circle of friends, acquaintances, and correspondents included Mazzini, R. *Browning, *Tennyson, J. *Forster, and G. *Jewsbury (who spent much time with Jane Carlyle during her husband's years of obsession with Lady Ashburton), but many of her best letters were written to her relatives in Edinburgh and Liverpool and, most notably, to Thomas himself, with whom she corresponded copiously during their temporary separations. Her kindness and generosity are as remarkable as her wit; one of her most famous letters, about the loneliness of her life at Craigenputtock, was written to cheer a dissatisfied schoolmistress in Carlisle who aspired to be a writer (Letter to Mary Smith, Jan. 1857). Her subjects include personalities, travels, books, and, notably, her servants; she commented, 'I think, talk, and write about my servants as much as Geraldine [Jewsbury] does about her lovers.' Various collections and selections of her letters have been published, including editions by J. A. *Froude (1883), Leonard Huxley (1924), and T. Scudder (1931).

CARLYLE, Thomas (1795–1881), born at Ecclefechan,

in Dumfriesshire, the son of a stonemason; his parents were serious, industrious, and devout, and belonged to a Dissenting branch of the Presbyterian Church. Carlyle, intended by them and by himself for the ministry, was educated at Annan Academy and at the University of Edinburgh, where, affected by the legacy of the *Scottish Enlightenment, he abandoned this resolve; he taught for a while at Annan and Kirkcaldy and then took to literary work, tutoring and reviewing. He studied German literature; his life of *Schiller appeared in the *London Magazine in 1823–4 and was separately published in 1825; his translations of *Goethe's Wilhelm Meister's Apprenticeship and Wilhelm Meister's Travels appeared in 1824 and 1827 respectively, the latter being included in his anthology of selections from German authors, German Romance (4 vols, 1827). In 1826 he married Jane Welsh (see above) and after two years in Edinburgh they moved for financial reasons to her farm at Craigenputtock, an isolated dwelling on the lonely moors of Nithsdale. 'Signs of the Times', an attack on *utilitarianism, appeared in 1829 in the *Edinburgh Review; *Sartor Resartus followed in *Fraser's Magazine in 1833–4, a highly idiosyncratic and personal work which showed his great debt to German philosophy and literature. In 1834 the Carlyles moved to Cheyne Row, Chelsea, where he worked on his History of the *French Revolution, which appeared in 1837; the manuscript of the first volume was accidentally used to light a fire while on loan to J. S. *Mill, but with characteristic perseverance Carlyle rewrote it. This work, somewhat to his own surprise, established Carlyle's reputation, and he from this time onward strengthened the position that made him known as 'the Sage of Chelsea'. His series of lectures, On *Heroes, Hero-Worship and the Heroic in History, delivered in 1840 and published in 1841, attracted glittering and fashionable audiences, and taught him to distrust (and indeed to abandon) his own blend of 'prophecy and play-acting'; it also brought him and his wife many new and influential friends. In Chartism (1839) and Past and Present (1843) Carlyle applied himself to what he called 'the Condition-of-England question', attacking both laissez-faire and the dangers of revolution it encouraged, castigating an economic and political climate where Cash Payment had become 'the sole nexus between man and man', and manifesting with more passion than consistency a sympathy with the industrial poor which heralded the new novels of social consciousness of the 1840s (see GASKELL and DISRAELI, B.). His evocation in Past and Present of medieval conditions at the time of Abbot Samson (see JOCELIN DE BRAKELOND) provided a new perspective on machinery and craftsmanship that was pursued by *Ruskin and W. *Morris, but Carlyle, unlike some of his followers, turned increasingly away from democracy towards the kind of feudalism which he saw expressed in the rule of the 'Strong Just Man'. His 'Occasional Discourse on the Nigger Question' (1849) and Latter-Day Pamphlets (1850) express his anti-democratic views in an exaggerated form. His admiration for *Cromwell was expressed in his edition of Oliver Cromwell's Letters and Speeches (2 vols, 1845), and for *Frederick the Great of Prussia in a lengthy biography, some 14 years in preparation, which appeared in 1858–65, 6 vols. A more modest and, to 20th-cent. tastes, more readable work, a life of his friend *Sterling (with some remarkable reminiscences of *Coleridge), appeared in 1851.

Jane Carlyle died in 1866, a blow which he said 'shattered my whole existence into immeasurable ruin', and he thereafter wrote little of importance. He gave her papers and letters in 1871, with ambiguous instructions, to his friend and disciple J. A. *Froude, who published them after Carlyle's death, in 1883; Froude also published Carlyle's Reminiscences (1881) and a four-volume biography (1882–4). These posthumous publications caused much controversy, largely by breaking the conventions of Victorian *biography (against which Carlyle had himself fulminated) to suggest marital discord and sexual inadequacy on Carlyle's part.

Carlyle's influence as social prophet and critic, and his prestige as historian, were enormous during his lifetime; G. *Eliot in the Leader (1855) wrote, 'there is hardly a superior or active mind of this generation that has not been modified by Carlyle's writings', and he was later described by *Yeats in his Autobiography as 'the chief inspirer of self-educated men in the 'eighties and early 'nineties'. In the 20th cent. his reputation waned, partly because his trust in authority and admiration of strong leaders were interpreted as foreshadowings of Fascism. His prose, which had always presented difficulties, became more obscure with the lapse of time; his violent exclamatory rhetoric, his italics and Teutonic coinages, and his eccentric archaisms and strange punctuation were already known by the late 1850s as 'Carlylese'; H. *Martineau described him as 'the greatest mannerist of the age', and *Aytoun ridiculed him, along with the *Spasmodics, for 'dislocating language'. But many of his coinages have become accepted as part of the language, and his work continues to attract scholars and biographers. Many different collections and editions of his letters have been published, and The Collected Letters of Thomas and Jane Carlyle, ed. C. R. Sanders and K. J. Fielding (7 vols, 1970–   ), is in progress.

Carmarthen, The Black Book of, see BLACK BOOK OF CARMARTHEN, THE.

Carmelide (Camylyard in *Malory), the realm of King Leodegan (Lodegraunce in Malory), the father of Guinevere. Like many other Arthurian places, it is localized both in Cornwall and in the North.

Carmina Burana, a compilation of 228 Latin and German poems, discovered in the monastery of Benediktbeuern in 1803, whence it is also known as the 'Benediktbeuern manuscript'. It was probably written c.1230, perhaps in Carinthia, and is the work of three compilers. It contains works of three kinds, corresponding to the categories of poetry written by the 12th-cent. troubadours: moral-satirical poems; love poems; and poems of camaraderie, many of them drinking-songs. It is the most important collection of *Goliardic Latin poetry in particular, and contains poems by many identified poets: Walter of Chatillon, Hugh of Orleans, the *Arch-poet, and Philip the Chancellor, for example. Carl Orff used a selection for his scenic cantata Carmina Burana (1935–6). The standard edition is by Hilka, Schumann, and Bischoff (1930–70).

CARNEGIE, Andrew (1835–1919), the son of a damask-linen weaver of Dunfermline, taken when a child to America by his parents who emigrated thither during the 'hungry forties'. At the age of 13 he began work in a cotton factory. Later, by his energy and shrewd speculative investment, he became enormously rich and one of the foremost ironmasters of the United States. In 1900 he published The Gospel of Wealth, maintaining that a 'man who dies rich dies disgraced', and set about the distribution of his surplus wealth. From a literary point of view, the most important of his many benefactions was his provision of public librar-ies in Great Britain and the United States, on condition that the local authorities provided site and mainten-ance. (See LIBRARIES, PUBLIC.)

carnivalesque, a term coined by the Russian critic M. M. *Bakhtin to describe various manifestations of popular humour and cultural resistance to the re-straints of official cultural hierarchies. The institution of carnival itself provides a model for understanding some of the more playful effects of literature, prin-cipally in the novel and dramatic literature. According to this view, some kinds of literary comedy are rooted in folk traditions of mockery directed at the Church and other authorities.

carol, a word whose etymology is obscure, and of which the earliest meaning appears to be a round dance; thence a song, originally the song of joy sung at Christmas time in celebration of the Nativity. The first known collection of Christmas carols was printed by Wynkyn de *Worde in 1521.

CAROLINE, Queen, (1) consort of George II, who figures in Scott's *The Heart of Midlothian and is prominent in the memoirs of the time; (2) consort of George IV, who figures in *Byron's poems, etc.

CARPENTER, Edward (1844–1929), educated at Cam-bridge, where he became fellow of Trinity Hall and curate to F. D. *Maurice. In 1874 he abandoned fellowship and orders and moved north, working for some years as University Extension lecturer before settling at Millthorpe, near Chesterfield, where he pursued, by precept and example, his own concept of socialism and communal fellowship, in a manner

much influenced by *Thoreau and also by *Ruskin and W. *Morris. He wrote and lectured in support of varied progressive causes (sexual reform, women's rights, clean air, anti-vivisection, industrial reorganization, etc.), and his own lifestyle and revolt against middle-class convention (expressed by sandals, vegetarianism, overt homosexuality, praise of manual labour and the working man) became an important symbol of liber-ation for many, including E. M. *Forster. Of his many writings the best remembered is probably his long poem Towards Democracy (published in 4 parts, 1883–1902), in which he expresses his millenarian sense of the cosmic consciousness and 'spiritual democracy', and of the march of humanity towards 'freedom and joy'; both manner and content are much influenced by *Whitman and the *Bhagavad-gītā. His autobiog-raphy, My Days and Dreams, was published in 1916; see also C. Tsuzuki, Edward Carpenter, Prophet of Human Fellowship (1980).

CARPENTER, John (?1370–?1441), town clerk of Lon-don, 1417–38, a generous patron and a friend of *Whittington and of *Pecock. *Hoccleve wrote a ballad to him, appealing for money. He compiled the Liber Albus, a valuable collection of records of the City of London, and he left lands for educational purposes, from which the City of London School was founded. See Liber Albus, ed. H. T. Riley (1859); T. Brewer, Memoir of the Life and Times of John Carpenter (1856).

CARR, J(ames Joseph) L(loyd) (1912–1994), novelist, children's writer, and independent publisher, born and educated in Yorkshire, and at Dudley Training College. His works include A Season in Sinji (1968, a cricket story); The Harpole Report (1972); How Steeple Sinderby Won the FA Cup (1975); and The Green Children of the Woods (1976). A Month in the Country (1980) is a short novel set in the summer of 1920: the narrator Birkin, a war survivor, is engaged in restoring a wall painting in the village church at Oxgodby, where he meets another survivor who is camping out in the next meadow while seeking to discover a 14th-cent. tomb. The Ballad of Pollock's Crossing (1985), set in the 1920s, takes a young Yorkshire schoolteacher to the American Midwest, where he challenges what was then the American orthodoxy of Indian history.

CARRACCI, Annibale (1560–1609), the greatest of a family of Bolognese painters who championed the clarity of the classical tradition and the glowing, sensuous colours of Venice. His best work is the decoration of the Farnese Gallery (1595–1604), which for the next two centuries was as famous as *Raphael's Farnesina or the Sistine chapel, both of which he emulated. Annibale was much admired in literary England in the 18th and early 19th cents; parallels have been drawn between his paintings and the poetry of *Dryden and *Pope. Fielding, in *Joseph Andrews, caricatures him as Hannibal Scratchi.

CARRINGTON, Dora de Houghton (1893–1932), painter, diarist, and letter writer, born in Hereford, educated at Bedford High School: she studied art at the Slade School in London where her work was much admired by C. R. W. Nevinson and Mark Gertler, both of whom became infatuated with her. It was not until her extraordinarily vivid diaries and charmingly illustrated letters were posthumously edited for publication by D. *Garnett (1970) that she became known to the general public. That book told the story of her mysterious and passionate love for the homosexual L. *Strachey, after whose death she committed suicide. There is a biography (1989) by Gretchen Gerzina; two books on her art, one by her brother Noel Carrington (1978), the other by Jane Hill (1994); and a film called *Carrington* (1995) by C. *Hampton.

CARROLL, Lewis, see DODGSON.

CARSON, Ciaran (1948–   ), Irish poet, educated at Queen's University, Belfast. After his first volume, *The New Estate* (1976) Carson's mature work uses complex, digressive narratives, influenced by his Irish-speaking background, to explore history, memory, and the layered maps of Belfast life from the 17th cent. to the post-1969 *Troubles (*The Irish for No*, 1987; *Belfast Confetti*, 1989). His long lines and complex sentences have now taken on rhyme and include versions of *Baudelaire and of *Rimbaud's 'Le Bateau ivre'. Richly physical and sensuous, Carson's poems reinvigorate aspects of the Symbolist imagination. See *First Language* (1993) *Opera et Cetera* (1996), and *Breaking News* (2003).

CARSON, Rachel (1907–64), American zoologist, educated at Johns Hopkins University, who is remembered as a pioneer ecologist and popularizer of scientific information. Her works include *The Sea around Us* (1951), *The Edge of the Sea* (1955), and *Silent Spring* (1963), a powerful attack on the indiscriminate use of pesticides and weed-killers.

CARTER, Angela Olive, née Stalker (1940–92), English novelist, poet, and essayist, born in Eastbourne and educated at Bristol University. Her work is imbued with a keen sense of the macabre and the wittily surreal and draws heavily on symbolism and themes derived from traditional fairy tales and folk myths. Her first two books, a volume of poetry (*Unicorn*, 1966) and a thriller (*Shadow Dance*, 1966), were followed by *The Magic Toyshop* (1967, filmed 1986), which associated her with the tradition of *magic realism and won the John Llewellyn Rhys Memorial Prize. *Several Perceptions* (1968) won the Somerset *Maugham Award. Succeeding novels developed further a characteristic neo-Gothic ambience, often underpinned by a strong, but never intrusive, feminist sensibility: *Heroes and Villains* (1969), set in the aftermath of nuclear conflict, the more conventional *Love* (1971), and *The Infernal Desire Machines of Dr Hoffman* (1972). After *Fireworks: Nine Profane Pieces* (1974) her next novel, *The Passion of New Eve* (1977), was centrally concerned with feminist issues, as was a later cultural study, *The Sadeian Woman* (1979). *Nights at the Circus* (1984), about a female Victorian circus performer called Fevvers who can fly, confirmed her as a gifted literary fabulist, while her ability to evoke and adapt the darker resonances of traditional forms of *fantasy was brilliantly deployed in *The Bloody Chamber and Other Stories* (1979), which contains one of her best-known reworkings of traditional material, 'The Company of Wolves' (based on the story of Little Red Riding Hood), filmed in 1984. Her last novel, *Wise Children* (1991), was a chronicle of two theatrical families. She translated the fairy tales of Charles *Perrault (1977) and, in collaboration with the artist Michael Forman, produced a retelling of Sleeping Beauty and other fairy tales (1982). She also compiled *The Virago Book of Fairy Tales* (1990; 2nd vol., 1992); *Black Venus* (1985) is a collection of short stories. A selection of her critical writings, *Expletives Deleted*, was published posthumously in 1992. A further posthumous collection of stories and sketches appeared in 1993 as *American Ghosts and Old World Wonders*.

CARTER, Mrs Elizabeth (1717–1806), scholar and poet, born in Deal, the daughter of the Revd Nicholas Carter, who was a friend of the publisher E. *Cave. With a persistence that was to win the praise of V. Woolf in *A Room of One's Own* she learned Latin, Greek, and Hebrew in childhood with her brothers, later acquiring French, Italian, German, Portuguese, and Arabic. Dr *Johnson thought her one of the best Greek scholars he had known. In 1738 she published her early poems, and Johnson, as a high honour, invited her to contribute to the *Rambler, for which she wrote numbers 44 and 100. She made various translations, and spent seven years on her translation of *Epictetus, which appeared with great success in 1758 and gained her a European reputation. She was not herself a hostess, and she was notably unfashionable in dress, but she was loved and revered in *Blue Stocking society.

CARTER, Martin (1927–97), poet, born in Georgetown and educated at Queen's College, Guyana. In 1975 he spent a year at Essex University as poet in residence, the longest time spent away from his homeland. With his stirring and influential volume about political oppression, *Poems of Resistance* (1954), he established an international reputation. Other volumes include *Jail Me Quickly* (1964), *Poems of Succession* (1977), and *Poems of Affinity* (1980).

CARTLAND, Barbara, see HISTORICAL FICTION.

Carton, Sydney, a character in Dickens's *A Tale of Two Cities*.

CARTWRIGHT, Jim (1958–   ), dramatist, born in Farnworth, the impoverished Lancashire town that inspired his first play, *Road* (1986), a series of brash, lively sketches evoking a turbulent night in a run-down working-class community. This was followed by *Bed* (1989), about Britain's forgotten elderly; *Two* (1989), about life in a pub; *The Rise and Fall of Little Voice* (1994), about a mother's exploitation of her reclusive daughter's talent for mimicry; and a raucously poetic portrait of sexual chaos and pain, *I Licked a Slag's Deodorant* (1996). Cartwright has also written extensively for radio and television.

CARTWRIGHT, Justin (1945–   ), novelist and screen writer, born in South Africa, and educated there, in the USA, and at Oxford. His works cast a satiric and oblique light on late 20th-cent. civilization. *Interior* (1988) is an exploration-quest novel set in a fictitious African state, where Tim Curtiz looks for his missing journalist father. *Freedom for the Wolves* (1983), also set in Africa, interweaves the historical past of *Rhodes and Rider *Haggard with the 20th-cent. present of the 1960 Sharpeville massacre, as James Thompson claims his inheritance. *Look at It This Way* (1990) reintroduces Curtiz, now a cultural columnist, in a sharp, satiric view of London life in the later 1980s, touched by scandal in the city, filtered through advertising imagery, and surreally menaced by the threat of an escaped lion. In *Masai Dreaming* (1993) Curtiz returns to Africa, this time in search of material for a screenplay about the life of a French-Jewish ethnologist who was thought to have died in Auschwitz. *In Every Face I Meet* (1995) is a tragi-comic portrait of London at the time of Nelson Mandela's release. Both *Leading the Cheers* (1998, based on a school reunion) and *The Promise of Happiness* (2004, a tense family drama) contrast cultural expectations on either side of the Atlantic, with a sharp eye for contemporary detail.

CARTWRIGHT, Thomas (1535–1603), a leading Puritan theologian educated at St John's College, Cambridge. A Marian exile, he left the country three times during Queen Elizabeth's reign and was deprived of his Lady Margaret professorship. He died before he could fully represent his Presbyterian views to James I.

CARTWRIGHT, William (1611–43), Oxford scholar, preacher, poet, and dramatist, one of the 'sons' of *Jonson. His most successful play, *The Royal Slave*, was performed before Charles I in 1636, and revived by professional players at Hampton Court at the queen's request. The 1651 edition of his works, *Comedies, Tragicomedies, with Other Poems*, was prefaced by over 50 commendatory verses from fellow Royalists.

CARVER, Raymond (1939–88), American short story writer and poet, born in Clatskanie, Oregon. His first collection of poetry, *Near Klamath*, was published in 1968. This was followed by *Winter Insomnia* (1970) and *At Night the Salmon Move* (1976).

Although he claimed that he would like to be remembered as a 'poet and short-story writer and occasional essayist—in that order', it is for his short stories that he became best known. He came to prominence with the publication in 1976 of his first collection, *Will You Please Be Quiet, Please?* This was followed by three other collections, *What*

We Talk About When We Talk About Love (1981), *Cathedral* (1983), and *Elephant* (1988). Like the stories of Richard *Ford and Tobias *Wolff, with whom he shares the label of 'Dirty Realism', his work deals powerfully with unremarkable, glamourless small-town lives, described in pared-down, simple prose.

Carver continued to write poetry through the 1980s, publishing *Where Water Comes Together with Other Water* in 1985 and *Ultramarine* the following year, as well as *Fires* (1983), a volume which combined poetry and short stories and a selection of his essays. He completed his last collection of poetry, *A New Path to the Waterfall* (1989), shortly before his death in 1988. An edition of his collected poems, *All of Us*, was published in 1996.

CARY, Elizabeth, Viscountess Falkland (1585–1639), strong-minded only child of judge Sir Thomas Tanfield. A self-taught linguist, she had mastered five languages before marriage at 15 to Henry Cary, later Lord Falkland. Secretly embracing Roman Catholicism, she separated from Falkland in 1625, was subsequently disinherited by her father, and died of consumption, in loneliness and want. She composed several verse translations and is recognized as author of the closet drama *The Tragedie of Mariam* (1613), ascribed to 'E.C.', the first known play in English by a woman. The drama raises Mariam, the 'shrew' wife of Herod, to tragic status: Mariam's outspoken intransigence and 'world amazing wit' are shown as weapons which society turns against a woman of genius. The play reflects Cary's own life, in the complex acrimony between dictatorial husband and dissident wife, and in its theme of society's destruction of women abdicating the private sphere for a public or published role. As the Chorus puts it: 'she usurps another's right, | That seeks to be by public language graced.' The play is written in verse which varies between alternately rhyming quatrains and stanzaic form, the effect being lyric rather than dramatic.

CARY, Henry Francis (1772–1844), educated at Oxford, an assistant librarian at the British Museum from 1826 to 1837. He translated Dante's *Divina commedia*, producing with his translation the first Italian text of Dante to be printed in England. The *Inferno* appeared in 1805, and together with the *Purgatorio* and the *Paradiso* in 1814. *Coleridge praised 'the severity and learned simplicity' of Cary's diction, and the work became well known. He wrote a series of appreciative articles (collected in 1846) on the early French poets, then little regarded, in the *London Magazine*.

CARY, (Arthur) Joyce (Lunel) (1888–1957), novelist, born in Londonderry. He was educated at Clifton College and Oxford, and studied art in Edinburgh and Paris. He took part in the Balkan War (1912–13), joined the Nigerian political service in 1913, and served with the Nigerian regiment in the Cameroons campaign, 1915–16. In 1920 he returned to England and devoted himself to writing. His early 'African' novels, *Aissa Saved* (1932), *An American Visitor* (1933), *The African Witch* (1936), and *Mister Johnson* (1939), show with shrewd sympathy the relations between Africans and their British administrators. His major work consists of two trilogies: *Herself Surprised* (1941), *To Be a Pilgrim* (1942), and *The Horse's Mouth* (1944), chiefly concerned with the life of the artist Gulley *Jimson; and *Prisoner of Grace* (1952), *Except the Lord* (1953), and *Not Honour More* (1955), a study of politics. The major theme of the novels, which exhibit a vast range of characters, is the necessity for individual freedom and choice. Two further novels are studies of childhood: *Charley is my Darling* (1940) and the semi-autobiographical *A House of Children* (1941). Cary also wrote political studies, such as *Power in Men* (1939) and *The Case for African Freedom* (1941); poetry, including *Marching Soldier* (1945) and *The Drunken Sailor* (1947); a study in aesthetics, *Art and Reality* (1958); short stories, such as *Spring Song and Other Stories* (1960); and an unfinished novel with a religious theme, *The Captive and the Free* (1959). A biography by J. W. Noble appeared in 1973.

CARY, Lucius, see FALKLAND, SECOND VISCOUNT.

CARY, Mary (from 1651 known as Rande) (b. *c*.1621, fl. 1653). A Londoner during the English Revolution, she was one of the most formidable intellectuals of the Fifth Monarchist movement, who constructed a systematic programme of radical social reform (including wage ceilings, postal service, and stamp tax) for the millennium, which she expected to begin in 1701. She maintained the equal right of women 'saints' to speak on public matters, and spoke for the poor and oppressed. Her most important works are *The Little Horn's Doom and Downfall* (1646), which predicts the fall of Charles I, the utopian *A New and More Exact Map* (1651), and *Twelve Proposals* (1653).

CARYLL, John (1625–1711), diplomatist and secretary to Mary of Modena. He was the author of a tragedy, *The English Princess: or The Death of Richard III* (1667), and a comedy, *Sir Salomon* (1670). His nephew, also John Caryll (?1666–1736), was a friend and correspondent of Pope, to whom he suggested the subject of *The Rape of the Lock*.

CASABIANCA, Louis (1755–98), a Corsican naval officer who perished with his little son at the battle of Aboukir. He is the subject of a well-known poem by F. *Hemans.

CASANOVA, Giacomo (1725–98), Italian autobiographer. In the course of an adventurous life throughout western Europe he wrote a number of historical works in Italian, but his reputation rests on the posthumously published *Mémoires* (12 vols, 1826–38) written in French. These are primarily an account of an extraordinary succession of sexual encounters, but they also provide an intimate portrait of the manners of the age and achieve considerable psychological consistency.

Casaubon, Mr, a leading character in G. Eliot's *Middlemarch*.

CASAUBON, Isaac (1559–1614), French classical scholar, born in Geneva of Huguenot refugee parents; professor of Greek at the Academy of Geneva, 1582–96; professor of classical letters at the University of Montpellier, 1597–9; sub-librarian at the Royal Library in Paris, 1605–10. From 1610 until his death he lived in London, receiving a pension from James I and becoming naturalized in 1611. Casaubon published critical editions and commentaries on the works of a number of ancient authors, chiefly Greek, including *Theophrastus (1592) and the Hellenistic writer of the 2nd cent. AD, Athenaeus (1597). He projected a major work of church history in the form of a criticism of the 'Annals' of the Italian Roman Catholic Baronius, but only the first volume (*De Rebus Sacris et Ecclesiasticis Exercitationes XVI ad Baronii Annales* 1614) was finished when he died. He left a diary in Latin of his daily activities, the *Ephemerides*. There is a life of Casaubon by *Pattison (1875).

Casby, Christopher and Flora, characters in Dickens's *Little Dorrit*.

Casca, one of the conspirators in Shakespeare's *Julius Caesar*, who affects a blunt and surly manner of speech.

Case is Altered, The, a comedy by *Jonson, performed *c*.1597–8, printed 1609.

Count Ferneze sees his elder son Paulo go off to the wars against Chamont, the son of the French general whose capture of Vicenza had resulted in the apparent death of Ferneze's younger son, Camillo. Paulo is taken prisoner, but on the other hand his general Maximilian brings back Chamont and his friend Gasper captive. It is agreed that Gasper shall return and effect an exchange between Paulo and Chamont, but Gasper impersonates Chamont, and Chamont himself departs. The trick is discovered, and Ferneze is on the point of executing Gasper, when Chamont returns with Paulo, and it is moreover discovered that Gasper is Ferneze's son Camillo. There is also a farcical sub-plot, involving the attempts made by the clowns Juniper, Onion, and Christophero to steal the daughter and the treasure of the supposed beggar Jacques de Prie. The play seems to have been published without Jonson's permission, for he omitted it from the folio of his works.

CASLON, William (1692–1766), the first English type-founder to make a complete range of Roman and Italic types of his own design, besides cutting Greek and exotic scripts. From 1725 onwards his types superseded those hitherto imported from abroad in English printing, and they are still in use. His foundry was carried on by his descendants until 1872.

Cassell's Weekly, a periodical founded in 1923, and at first edited by N. Flower; after 32 issues it was taken over by T. P. *O'Connor, and changed its title to *T.P.'s and Cassell's Weekly*, which ran until 1929. It published work by E. M. *Forster, Arnold *Bennett, *Wells, and others.

Cassio, Michael, in Shakespeare's *Othello*, a sophisticated Florentine who at the opening of the play has just been appointed as Othello's lieutenant.

Cassius, in Shakespeare's *Julius Caesar*, friend of *Brutus and leader of the conspiracy against Caesar.

Cassivelaunus (called 'Cassibelan' in Shakespeare's *Cymbeline* I. i. 30), according to *Geoffrey of Monmouth's *History* (iv. 1–2) the brother and successor of *Lud as king of Britain, led the resistance to Julius Caesar's second invasion (54 BC). He was defeated and sued for peace, and (according to Geoffrey) is buried at York. His successor as king was Tenvantius, duke of Cornwall, whose son and successor was Cymbeline.

'Castaway, The', a poem by *Cowper, written 1799, published 1803. It is based on an incident from *Anson's *Voyage round the World*. Cowper depicts with tragic power the suffering of a seaman swept overboard and awaiting death by drowning. Mr Ramsay in V. Woolf's *To the Lighthouse* is given to declaiming its last lines: 'We perish'd, each alone: | But I beneath a rougher sea, | And whelm'd in deeper gulphs than he.'

CASTELNUOVO-TEDESCO, Mario(1895–1968),Italian composer, whose prolific output contains an unusually high proportion of Shakespearian works, including operas and overtures, several of which had considerable success. But greater musical interest perhaps attaches to the *33 Shakespeare Songs* (1921–5) in which an original and eclectic mind produces settings which are varied and unconventional. There is a set of *28 Shakespeare Sonnets* (1944–7) and a chamber opera, *The Importance of Being Earnest* (1962), after *Wilde.

CASTELVETRO, Ludovico (1505–71), Italian scholar and critic from Modena, best known for his commentary on Aristotle's *Poetics* (1570, 1576), which included a Greek text, an Italian translation, and a critical discussion. His views on the *unities, more rigid than Aristotle's own, had considerable influence on the development of neo-classical theory.

CASTIGLIONE, Baldassare (1478–1529), Italian humanist, chiefly known for his prose dialogues *Il libro del cortegiano* (1528), translated into English as *The Courtyer* (1561) by *Hoby. In these dialogues, which take place at the court of Urbino and are presided over by the duchess, 19 men and four women (all historical characters) discuss the qualifications for the ideal courtier, who should unite ethical and intellectual virtues, military and sporting prowess, and yet display his talents with an easy grace and nonchalance. The book ends with a discussion of love by *Bembo, describing the 'ladder' whereby the lover

ascends from love of one person to love of the abstract good. The work had much influence on the literature of England, e.g. on *Surrey, *Wyatt, *Sidney, *Spenser, and Shakespeare; and later on W. B. *Yeats, whose poem 'In memory of Major Robert Gregory', for example, laments the 'soldier, scholar, horseman' as 'our Sidney and our perfect man'. See also Ruth Kelso, *The Doctrine of the English Gentleman in the Sixteenth Century* (1929).

Castle Dangerous, a novel by Sir W. *Scott, published 1831 in *Tales of My Landlord*, 4th series. Both the plotting and writing show the effects of the paralytic strokes which Scott had already suffered in 1831 and which were to kill him a year later. In spite of this, there are passages of the old brilliance in his story of the 13th-cent. Scottish War of Independence and the taking of Castle Douglas by Robert the Bruce and the Black Douglas, an episode which he had used in 1818 in his 'Essay on Chivalry'.

Castle of Indolence, The, a poem in Spenserian stanzas by J. *Thomson published 1748.

According to Patrick Murdoch, Thomson's biographer, the poem grew out of 'a few detached stanzas, in the way of raillery on himself and some of his friends' written in 1733 (*Works*, 1762). It consists of two cantos, of which the first describes the castle of the wizard Indolence, into which he entices weary pilgrims who sink into torpor amidst luxurious ease; Thomson draws sketches of various real people, including himself, his patron *Lyttelton, Patrick Murdoch, and J. *Armstrong. The inmates, becoming diseased, are thrown into a dungeon to languish. The second canto describes the conquest of the castle by the knight of Arts and Industry. *Wordsworth, amongst many others, praised its harmonious verse and pure diction.

Castle of Otranto, The; *A Gothic Story*, by Horace *Walpole, published 1764, title-page 1765.

The first of the true *'Gothic' novels, this was an immediate success, and has run to over 150 editions since its original publication. Walpole wrote of its composition, 'I gave rein to my imagination; visions and passions choked me.' The narrative is filled with ghosts, vaults, giants, living statues, mysterious appearances, and violent emotions of terror, anguish, and love. Walpole's fear of ridicule led him to publish the first edition anonymously, with an elaborate preface describing the author as 'Onuphrio Muralto', an Italian canon of Otranto, writing somewhere between the 11th and 13th cents.

Prince Manfred, the tyrant of Otranto, has a devoted wife, Hippolita; a son, Conrad; and a daughter, Matilda. At his wedding to Isabella of Vicenza, Conrad is crushed to death by a vast, black-plumed helmet, which belongs to the nearby statue of the Old Prince, Alfonso the Good. A bold young man in the crowd is accused of causing Conrad's death and imprisoned beneath the helm. Manfred, distracted by a cryptic prophecy, determines that he must have an heir to Otranto. Wildly he decrees that he will divorce Hippolita and marry Isabella, at which the portrait of his grandfather descends accusingly from the wall, beckons him away, and vanishes. Meanwhile the terrified Isabella tries to escape through a gloomy vault at night, where she is assisted by the mysterious young man who has escaped from the helm. Manfred begins a frenzied search for Isabella, only to be confronted by Friar Jerome, who has given the girl sanctuary in his nearby monastery. The young man, Theodore, now accused of being Isabella's lover, is discovered to be Jerome's son, and Jerome is revealed as the count of Falconara. The black plumes wave, and Frederic of Vicenza arrives, demanding Isabella and the resignation of Manfred. But Isabella has vanished from the monastery. Matilda secretly frees and arms Theodore, who rescues Isabella in an eerie forest cave and wounds her father, whom he mistakes for an enemy. When all are again gathered at the castle he relates the story of his destitute and wandering life, and Jerome confirms that Theodore's mother was indeed the daughter of Alfonso. Both Isabella and Matilda have now come to love Theodore. Matilda refuses as passionately to be given to Frederic as Isabella refuses to accept Manfred. Blood runs from the nose of Alfonso's statue. On hearing a rumour that Isabella is with Theodore in the churchyard, Manfred rushes thither, and stabs the woman—only to find it is his daughter, Matilda. His grief, and Hippolita's, is terrible. The walls of the castle fall, and the giant image of Alfonso rises to heaven. Manfred reveals that his grandfather poisoned Alfonso in order to gain Otranto. He and Hippolita retire to the religious life, and eventually Isabella marries Theodore, the new and rightful Prince.

Castle of Perseverance, The, a *morality play in 3,700 lines, dating from the first quarter of the 15th cent., one of the group (the others are *Mankind* and *Wisdom*) known as *Macro* plays from their 18th-cent. owner. It is the earliest surviving complete morality. A huge play, divided into four parts, it is of interest as an exhaustive compendium of such morality features as a battle between vices and virtues, a mixture of allegorical (Backbiter) and diabolical (Belyal) figures, and the enactment of Death and Judgement; but it is also highly significant in the history of English theatre, largely because of a diagrammatic representation of the Castlemound as 'Theatre in the Round' which its staging requires. There is an edition by P. Happé in *Four Morality Plays* (1979); see also R. Southern, *The Medieval Theatre in the Round* (2nd edn, 1975).

Castle Perilous, in *Malory the castle of the lady Lyonesse in which she is held captive by Ironsyde before her release by Gareth of Orkney. (See GARETH AND LYNETTE.)

Castle Rackrent, a novel by M. *Edgeworth, published 1800.

This work may be regarded as the first fully developed *historical novel and the first true *regional novel in English. Set, according to the title-page, 'Before the year 1782', the characters, the life of the country, and the speech, are unmistakably Irish. It is a brief, high-spirited work, narrated in his old age by the devoted Thady Quirk, steward to three generations of Rackrents. This racy character, for whom the Rackrents could do no wrong, was based (the author wrote) on her father's steward John Langan, who 'seemed to stand beside me and dictate'. The rattling narrative begins with the wild life of the hard-drinking Sir Patrick, 'inventor of raspberry whisky', who lived before Thady's time. He was succeeded by the litigious and debt-ridden Sir Murtagh, a skinflint who died of a fury. His brother Sir Kit, who inherits, brings to the castle his unfortunate English Jewish wife, who has 'never seen a peat-stack or a bog' and who, after many arguments over sausages, diamonds, and other matters, is shut up in the castle for seven years, until her gambling husband is killed in a duel. Meanwhile the cunning young lawyer Jason Quirk, Thady's son, is gathering more and more of the family's affairs into his hands. The next heir, Sir Condy, is an ardent, extravagant politician, who tosses a coin to decide whether to marry the rich Isabella Moneygawl or the pretty Judy M'Quirk (Thady's grandniece). He marries Isabella and, keeping lavish open house in their tumbledown castle, they finally exhaust the last resources of the Rackrents. When the bailiffs arrive Isabella flees and Jason Quirk is found to own almost everything. The castle is sold and Condy amuses himself by feigning death at his own wake. When he eventually dies Isabella contests the property, but Jason (who is hated by the countrymen but admired by his father) emerges as a 'high gentleman with estates and a fortune'.

Miss Edgeworth wrote the book without her father's knowledge, and it is one of the few he did not 'edit'. The second half, relating to Sir Condy, was not written until two years after the first.

CASTLEREAGH, Robert Stewart, Viscount Castlereagh (1769–1822), was chief secretary for Ireland 1799–1801, when he secured the passing of the Act of Union. During a long political life he discharged many high offices. As foreign secretary from 1812 to 1822 he took a leading part in the European settlement at the Congress of Vienna and after Waterloo, restraining the Allies from retaliation on France. He was greatly disliked by many of the young writers of his day, who felt that he opposed the cause of liberty. There is, for instance, a virulent attack on him in the Dedication to Byron's *Don Juan*; and Shelley, in *The Mask of Anarchy* (which was provoked by the massacre of Peterloo, 1819), wrote:

> I met Murder on the way—
> He had a mask like Castlereagh.

catachresis (Greek, 'to misuse'), a rhetorical figure, sometimes also called 'abusio', in which a word is used with seeming disregard for its ordinary denotation or grammatical function, as in *Milton's 'blind mouths' or E. E. *Cummings's 'the voice of your eyes is deeper than roses'.

Catch-22, a comic, satirical, surreal, and apocalyptic novel by J. *Heller, published in 1961, which describes the ordeals and exploits of a group of American airmen based on a small Mediterranean island during the Italian campaign of the Second World War, and in particular the reactions of Captain Yossarian, the protagonist. The title of the novel has passed into the language to describe a situation of deadlock, composed of two mutually exclusive sets of conditions: the original instance in the novel of 'Catch-22', defined in ch. 5, concerns pilot Orr, Yossarian's room-mate. According to Doc Daneeka, 'Orr was crazy and could be grounded. All he had to do was ask; and as soon as he did, he would no longer be crazy and would have to fly more missions. Orr would be crazy to fly more missions and sane if he didn't, but if he was sane he had to fly them. If he flew them he was crazy and didn't have to; but if he didn't want to he was sane and had to.' Yossarian is deeply impressed by the 'elliptical precision' of this catch, which he compares to 'good modern art'.

catharsis, a much-disputed term used by Aristotle in his *Poetics, where he speaks of the function of tragedy which should succeed in 'arousing pity and fear in such a way as to accomplish a catharsis (i.e. purgation) of such emotions'. Aristotle here seems to be responding to *Plato's view that poetic drama improperly fed the passions by a counter-suggestion that on the contrary it helped to cleanse and release them. The concept has been redefined by generations of critics, including *Castelvetro, G. E. *Lessing, *Goethe, and *Schopenhauer, and Milton gives his own interpretation in his preface to *Samson Agonistes: 'Tragedy . . . said by Aristotle to be of power by raising pity and fear, or terror, to purge the mind of those and such like passions, that is to temper and reduce them to just measure with a kind of delight, stirr'd up by reading or seeing those passions well imitated'.

CATHER, Willa Sibert (1876–1947), American novelist, born in Virginia, but brought up from the age of 8 in Nebraska, and educated at the University of Nebraska. After a period of teaching and journalism, during which she published her first book of poems, *April Twilights* (1903), and a book of short stories, *The Troll Garden* (1905), she worked on the staff, then as editor, of *McClure's Magazine* in New York from 1906 to 1912. Her first novel, *Alexander's Bridge* (1912), was followed by *O Pioneers!* (1913), about a Swedish immigrant family struggling to establish itself in the Nebraskan prairies; *The Song of the Lark* (1915), a study of the professional dedication of an opera singer, Thea

Kronberg; *My Ántonia* (1918), the story of an immigrant girl from Bohemia, settled in Nebraska, narrated by her childhood friend Jim Burden; and *One of Ours* (1922). *A Lost Lady* (1923) is a delicate, double-edged evocation of elegant, warm-hearted Marian Forrester, married to the ageing railroad builder Captain Forrester in the small and dwindling town of Sweet Water in the Midwest; she is observed by her admirer from boyhood, Niel Hebert, who watches as she becomes the mistress of Forrester's friend Ellinger, then, after the captain's death, the apparent victim of a destructive rising young business man, Ivy Peters; but, with characteristic subtlety of plot, she escapes both Sweet Water and Niel's condemnation. Cather's range and complexity are further demonstrated in *The Professor's House* (1925), a rich and suggestive work which contrasts the middle-aged disillusion of Professor St Peter with his memories of his favourite student, the brilliant explorer and inventor Tom Outland, whose haunting discovery of an ancient New Mexican cliff city is recorded in Book II of the novel; New Mexico also provides the vividly pictorial setting for another major work, *Death Comes for the Archbishop* (1927), a historical novel based on the French Catholic mission of Father Latour, and his years of work with the peasant population. Her other works include two studies of the dangers and rewards of unconventionality: *My Mortal Enemy* (1926), in which Myra Henshawe lives to regret her runaway marriage and fallen fortunes, and *Lucy Gayheart* (1935), the story of a music student caught in the tension between the values of her home town and the values of the artistic world. The dual impulse towards exploration and cultivation, towards art and domesticity, towards excitement and safety, is a constant theme in Cather's work, treated with much flexibility and a marked lack of didacticism; she was a pioneer not only in her treatment of the frontiers of the West, but also in her development of the American novel. She records her own debt to another pioneer, S. O. *Jewett, in *Not under Forty* (1936). See also E. K. Brown, *Willa Cather: A Critical Biography* (1953).

Catherine, a novel by *Thackeray, published serially in *Fraser's Magazine, 1839–40.

Thackeray took the outline of the story of the murderess Catherine Hayes from the *Newgate Calendar, and deliberately made his novel as grim and sordid as possible, in reaction against the popular 'Newgate novels' of *Bulwer-Lytton, *Ainsworth, and others. However, the lively ironic characterization of the heroine and two invented characters, her seducer Galgenstein and his companion Corporal Brock, transcend the original intention.

CATHERINE OF ARAGON, Queen, the wife of Henry VIII, whose divorce is one of the principal incidents in Shakespeare's *Henry VIII.

Catherine de Bourgh, Lady, a character in J. Austen's *Pride and Prejudice*.

Catiline, a Roman tragedy by *Jonson, performed 1611, based principally on *Sallust's *Catiline* and *Cicero's orations.

The play concerns the events of the year 63 BC, when Catiline organized a conspiracy to overthrow the existing government and to renew with the aid of Sulla's veterans the scenes of bloodshed which Rome had recently seen. Cicero and Antonius were elected consuls, and Catiline, secretly encouraged by Caesar and Crassus, prepared for a rising. Cicero, warned by Fulvia, the mistress of one of the conspirators, of the intention to assassinate him as a first step in the movement, summons the senate and accuses Catiline, who leaves Rome and joins the troops raised by his adherents at Faesulae. Cicero obtains evidence of the guilt of the conspirators through the ambassadors of the Allobroges, and submits it to the senate, which condemns them to death. Catiline falls in the decisive engagement between his troops and those of the government commanded by Petreius.

The play's first performance was a notorious failure, as Jonson noted in an angrily defensive preface to the printed text.

CATNACH, James (1792–1841), a publisher in Seven Dials, London. He issued at a very low price a large number of chapbooks, ballads, and broadsides, many of them about crimes, highwaymen, and executions, which throw much light on his period.

Cato, a tragedy by *Addison, produced 1713.

It deals with the death of Cato the republican, who commits suicide rather than submit to the dictator Caesar; love interest is added by the devotion of Juba, Cato's Numidian ally, to Cato's daughter Marcia. Dr *Johnson described it as 'rather a poem in dialogue than a drama', but it proved popular on stage and was frequently performed; it owed its success partly to the political intentions imputed to it.

Catriona, the sequel to R. L. Stevenson's *Kidnapped*.

CATULLUS, Gaius Valerius (c.84–c.54 BC), one of the most versatile of Roman poets, who wrote love poems, elegies, and satirical epigrams with equal success. He was also among the first to introduce into Latin the mannered style of the Hellenistic school. His work remained virtually unknown during the Middle Ages, but after a manuscript of his poems had come to light at Verona in the 14th cent. he exercised an extensive, if imprecise, influence. He left his mark on *Campion's *Bookes of Ayres*, on *Jonson's songs, and generally on *Herrick and *Lovelace. Leigh *Hunt translated his *Attis* (1810) and *Tennyson, visiting Sirmione where Catullus once had a house, wrote his pathetic 'Frater Ave atque Vale'. There are few direct echoes of Catullus' work, but poets all over Europe were stimulated by his freshness and simplicity.

CAUDWELL, Christopher, pseudonym of Christopher St John Sprigg (1907–37), a Marxist literary critic who joined the Communist Party in 1935 and the International Brigade in 1936; he was killed in Spain. He published poems, novels (under both real and pen-name), and many books on aircraft, but is known for his critical works *Illusion and Reality* (1937) and *Studies in a Dying Culture* (1938). These attempted to define a Marxist theory of art and called on writers of the 1930s to commit themselves to the culture of the revolutionary proletariat. (See MARXIST LITERARY CRITICISM.)

Cauline, Sir, the subject of a ballad included in Percy's *Reliques*. A young knight at the court of the king of Ireland falls in love with Christabelle, the king's daughter, is banished, returns in disguise and slays a grim 'Soldan' giant who is a suitor for the princess, but is himself mortally wounded. Christabelle dies of a broken heart.

CAUSLEY, Charles (1917–2003), poet, born in Launceston, Cornwall, where he was educated and where, after six wartime years in the Royal Navy, he himself became a teacher. He began writing in the navy. His first collection of verse, *Farewell, Aggie Weston* (1951), was followed by several others, including *Survivor's Leave* (1953), *Union Street* (1957), *Johnny Alleluia* (1961) *Underneath the Water* (1968), and *Figgie Hobbin* (1970). His interest in and understanding of children is expressed in various collections of children's stories and anthologies of verse. His poetry is marked by a powerful simplicity of diction and rhythm, and shows the influence of popular songs (when young he played the piano in a dance band) and the ballad tradition. Innocence is a recurrent theme, and his admiration for *Clare is the direct inspiration of several poems. Religious and seafaring images, often interwoven, are also characteristic. His own selection of *Collected Poems 1951–75* appeared in 1975. Later works: *The Hill of the Fairy* (1967), *The Animals' Carol* (1978), *Secret Destinations* (1984), *Early in the Morning* (1986), *Jack the Treacle Eater* (1987), *A Field of Vision* (1988), and *Collected Poems* (1992). He also published two verse plays, *The Gift of a Lamb* (1978) and *The Ballad of Aucassin and Nicolette* (1981).

CAUTE, (John) David (1936–), novelist and historian, born in Alexandria and educated at Wellington and Oxford. His first novel, *At Fever Pitch* (1959), was followed by many more, which range in theme from *The Decline of the West* (1966), an epic of post-colonial power struggle, violent conflict, and race/sex relations, set in French West Africa, to *Veronica or The Two Nations* (1989), a story spanning the post-war period of a boy's incestuous and damaging passion for his half-sister. Caute's political studies include *The Fellow-Travellers: Intellectual Friends of Communism* (1973; rev. 1988) and *Under the Skin* (1983), an account of the collapse of white Rhodesia. *Fatima's Scarf* (1998) is a carefully researched novel set in the Yorkshire town of 'Bruddersfield' (a coinage borrowed from J. B. *Priestley) which explores the complex responses of the Muslim community in Britain and beyond to the publication of *Rushdie's *Satanic Verses*, and the public debates surrounding the issue. *The Dancer Defects: The Struggle for Cultural Supremacy during the Cold War* (2003) is a major and wide-ranging study of cultural diplomacy and the arts, discussing film, the visual arts, theatre, and ballet, and analysing the roles of many writers, including *Brecht, Arthur *Miller, *Sartre, *Camus, and Tom *Stoppard.

Cautionary Tales for Children Designed for the Admonition of Children between the ages of eight and fourteen years (1907), one of the most enduring works of Hilaire *Belloc, which parodies a genre of admonitory *children's literature popular in England in the late 18th and 19th centuries: it is also indebted to Heinrich Hoffmann's *Struwwelpeter*. It contains seven macabre moral tales in verse, which include the story of Jim, who let go of his nurse's hand and was eaten by a lion; Henry King, whose chief defect was chewing little bits of string; and Matilda, who told lies and consequently was burned to death. The verses have attracted many illustrators, including Belloc's friend Lord Basil Blackwood (B.T.B.), the cartoonists Nicholas Bentley and Posy Simmonds, and the cult America author and surrealist Edward St John Gorey (1925–2000).

CAVAFY, Constantine (1863–1933), poet, born in Alexandria of Greek parents from Constantinople. His father, who died in 1870, was a partner in an export firm with branches in England and Alexandria, and Constantine was at school in England between the ages of 9 and 16. On the collapse of the family business the Cavafys returned to Alexandria, where Constantine spent the rest of his life, living quietly with his mother, then alone, and working for many years as clerk in the ministry of public works. He published two privately printed pamphlets of verse, in 1904 and 1910, and later distributed his work to friends in broadsheets; his local reputation grew, but recognition from the English-reading world was achieved largely through the influence of E. M. *Forster, who met him in Alexandria in 1917 and maintained a long friendship and correspondence. His poems, all fairly short, are both lyrical and colloquial, ranging from the personal confession to the dramatic monologue, and in subject matter treating historical themes and characters (Julian the Apostate, Mark Antony, the fall of Constantinople) with great verve and originality, homosexual themes with frankness, and contemporary Alexandrian café life with realism and a strong sense of place. There have been several translations, including versions by J. Mavrogordato (1951), Rae Dalven (1961), and E. Keeley and P. Sherrard (1975).

Cavalier, Memoirs of a, see MEMOIRS OF A CAVALIER.

Cavaliers, a name given to supporters of Charles I in the Civil War, derived from the Italian for horseman or knight and carrying overtones of courtly gallantry. 'Cavalier lyrics' is the term applied to lyrics by *Carew, *Lovelace, *Suckling, and *Herrick (the last of whom was not a courtier) and to work similar in tone and style. These poets were not a formal group, but all were influenced by *Jonson and like him paid little attention to the sonnet; their lyrics on the whole are distinguished by short lines, precise but idiomatic diction, and an urbane and graceful wit. In 'The Line of Wit' (*Revaluation*, 1936) *Leavis states that the line 'runs from Ben Jonson (and Donne) through Carew and Marvell to Pope'.

CAVE, Edward (1691–1754), who called himself 'Sylvanus Urban', the son of a Rugby cobbler. He became a London printer and publisher, chiefly remembered as the founder of the *Gentleman's Magazine*, to which his friend Dr *Johnson contributed extensively. Cave handled the *Rambler* at a loss between 1750 and 1752. On his death Johnson published a biographical sketch, *The Life of Edward Cave* (1754).

CAVENDISH, George (?1499–?1561), a gentleman of Thomas Wolsey's household, and author of a remarkable biography of the cardinal (*The Life and Death of Cardinal Wolsey*), in which with much art he contrasts the magnificence of the cardinal's life with his subsequent disgrace, and indicates 'the wonderouse mutabilitie of vayn honours ... And the tykkyll trust to worldly prynces'. It was first printed in 1641, but was previously circulated in manuscript.

CAVENDISH, Margaret, See NEWCASTLE, MARGARET CAVENDISH, DUCHESS OF

Cave of Mammon, see MAMMON, THE CAVE OF.

Cawdor, thane of, at the beginning of Shakespeare's *Macbeth*, condemned to death for treachery by *Duncan and his title bestowed on Macbeth.

CAXTON, William (c.1422–91), born in Kent, the first English printer, and a prominent merchant. After apprenticeship in London he spent 30 years in the Low Countries. From 1465 to 1469 he was governor of the English merchants at Bruges, and he successfully negotiated commercial treaties with the dukes of Burgundy. He began translating the *Recuyell of the Historyes of Troye* (printed in Bruges, 1473–4) but did not finish it until 1471 in Cologne because he became secretary to the household of Margaret of Burgundy, the sister of Edward IV, in 1469. After his return to Bruges from Cologne (where he probably worked in a printing house), he presented the book to Margaret and next printed, also in Bruges with the calligrapher Colard Mansion, *The Game and Playe of the Chesse*. He set up a press at Westminster in 1476—his first dated book printed there is *The Dictes or Sayengis of the Philosophres* (1477)—and printed about 100 books, a number of them his own translations from French. He used eight founts of type, the first of which he brought from Bruges, and he began to use woodcut illustrations *c*.1480. His translations contributed to the development of 15th-cent. prose style, though his own style is somewhat rambling and ill-constructed, manifesting the weaknesses of the elaboration of courtly writing without its virtues. It was his modified version of *Malory that appeared as Malory's work before the discovery of the Winchester manuscript by W. F. Oakeshott in 1934.

Ed. W. J. B. Crotch, *Caxton's Prologues and Epilogues* (EETS OS 176, 1927; reprinted 1957); N. F. Blake, *Caxton and His World* (1969), *Caxton's Own Prose* (1973); ed. N. F. Blake, *Selections from William Caxton* (1973). *William Caxton: A Quincentenary Biography* (1976) is a detailed and scholarly work by G. D. Painter, which discusses every known Caxton document and edition.

CD-ROM (Compact Disc Read Only Memory), a 12 cm diameter disc resembling an audio CD, used as a distribution medium for computer software, multimedia, databases, and reference works. The text of the 22-volume *Encyclopaedia Britannica* occupies one CD-ROM. The more capacious DVD (Digital Versatile Disc), developed primarily for video, will allow publishers to issue high-quality illustrated books or entire libraries of text on a single disc.

CECIL, David (Lord Edward Christian David Gascoyne) (1902–86), scholar and biographer. He was educated at Eton and Christ Church, Oxford, and was Goldsmiths' professor of English literature at Oxford, 1948–69. His many works include a study of *Cowper (1929), a life of Melbourne (2 vols, 1939, 1954), a study of *Hardy (1943), *Two Quiet Lives* (1948; studies of T. *Gray and D. *Osborne), *The Cecils of Hatfield House* (1973), *A Portrait of Jane Austen* (1978), and *A Portrait of Charles Lamb* (1983).

Cecilia, or *Memoirs of an Heiress*, a novel by F. *Burney, published 1782.

This was the second of Fanny Burney's novels, and she wished it to be 'true to life'. Cecilia Beverley has inherited a large fortune on the condition that her future husband takes her name. Until she comes of age she is required to live with one of her three guardians. The first is Harrel, a gambler, who, failing in his attempt to exploit his ward, kills himself; the second is the vulgar and avaricious Briggs; the third, the Hon. Compton Delvile, is a man of arrogant family pride. Cecilia and his son Mortimer fall deeply in love with one another; but old Delvile is furious at the idea that his son should exchange his name for Cecilia's. However, a marriage is arranged on the basis that Cecilia will renounce her fortune and Delvile keep his name. But the plan is defeated by the crafty Monckton, whom Cecilia has regarded as a friend, but who hopes to win both her and her fortune when his wife dies. Monckton's treachery is exposed; Cecilia, who has been driven

to madness and almost to death by her tribulations, marries her beloved Mortimer; and old Delvile is eventually reconciled to the match.

The novel was immensely successful; Dr *Johnson admired 'the general Power of the whole', and *Burke praised the humour, the sentiment, the moral tone, and the dialogue.

Ceix and Alceone, see GOWER, J., and BOOK OF THE DUCHESS, THE.

CELA, Camilo José (1916–2002), Spanish novelist, author of over 50 books, including novels, poetry, essays, short stories, and travel writing. Born in a small town in Corunna to a Spanish father and an English mother, he was educated at the University of Madrid and served under Franco in the Spanish Civil War. In 1942 he published his first novel, *La familia de Pascual Duarte* (*The Family of Pascual Duarte*, 1964), a compelling and sometimes brutal story told by a murderer awaiting execution. After problems with the Spanish censor, *La colmena* was first published in Argentina (1951; *The Hive*, 1953). This novel, now considered his masterpiece, is an account of three days in Madrid in the immediate aftermath of the Civil War. Cela himself described it as 'no more than a pale reflection, a humble shadow of daily, harsh, profound and painful reality'. The narrative experimentation of this and other novels have resulted in Cela's being credited with the renaissance of the Spanish novel. He was awarded the *Nobel Prize in 1989.

CELAN, Paul, the pseudonym of Paul Anschel (1920–70), poet, born in Czernowitz, Bukovina (then in Romania) of a Jewish family; both his parents died in an extermination camp, and he was interned for two years in a Romanian labour camp. He settled in Paris in 1950, and finally drowned himself in the Seine. He wrote in German, and translations into English include *Nineteen Poems* (1972, by M. *Hamburger), *Selected Poems* (1972, Hamburger and C. Middleton), and *Poems* (1980), selected, translated, and introduced by Hamburger. His work is some of the most significant to have been inspired by the *Holocaust.

Celestial City, in Bunyan's *Pilgrim's Progress*, signifying the heavenly 'new Jerusalem' of Rev. 21: 2.

Celestina, or the *Tragi-Comedy of Calisto and Melibea*, a Spanish novel in dialogue which has had several stage adaptations. The first known edition appeared about 1499, in 16 acts, and a later version, in 1502, in 21 acts. It is reasonably certain that Acts II–XVI were written by Fernando de *Rojas, although the authorship of Act I and the later additions is still disputed.

The work is essentially dramatic, and marks an important stage in the literary history of Spain and of Europe. Though, as *Mabbe, its translator, observes, 'some part of it seemeth somewhat more obscene than may suit with a civil style', it is an extremely vivid, entertaining work, one of the first to present romance in everyday life. The reader is brought into disreputable, but admirably depicted, company. The principal characters are Calisto, a young gentleman of birth and fortune; Melibea, a modest and romantic young lady; Celestina, a crafty, wise old bawd; Parmeno and Sempronio, the rascally braggart servants of Calisto; and Elicia and Areusa, two wenches. Calisto casually meeting Melibea falls violently in love with her, but is, from her modesty, sharply repulsed. On the advice of one of his servants he calls in the aid of Celestina, who deflects Melibea from the path of virtue and brings about a general catastrophe. Celestina is murdered by Parmeno and Sempronio for a share in the reward that she has received, and they are punished with death for their crime. Calisto is killed in one of his secret meetings with Melibea, and she in despair kills herself.

An excellent and racy, if exuberantly diffuse, translation into English prose, *The Spanish Bawd*, was made by Mabbe, and published in 1631. The early part of *Celestina* was translated into English verse by *Rastell, provided with a happy ending, and published, about 1525, as 'A new commodye in englysh in maner of an enterlude', better known as 'An Interlude of Calisto and Melebea'. It is one of the first English dramatic works that approach true comedy. A new translation by P. Hartnoll appeared in 1959, and one by J. M. Cohen in 1964.

Rojas's borrowings from *Petrarch are discussed in A. D. Deyemond, *The Petrarchan Sources of La Celestina* (1961).

Celia, in Shakespeare's **As You Like It*, daughter to Duke Frederick, who chooses to share *Rosalind's banishment in the Forest of *Arden, adopting the name Aliena.

CÉLINE, Louis-Ferdinand (1894–1961), pseudonym of L.-F. Destouches, French novelist. His first novel, *Voyage au bout de la nuit* (1932, English trans. John Marks, 1934), describing the experiences and opinions of an unsavoury and truculent slum doctor during and after the First World War, earned him the reputation of a right-wing misanthrope. His later novels, including *Mort à crédit* (1936), *D'un château à l'autre* (1957), and *Nord* (1960), have drawn increasingly respectful critical attention to the systematic indecorousness of his narratives, to the nightmare power of his vision, and to the profligate resourcefulness of his language.

CELLINI, Benvenuto (1500–71), a Florentine goldsmith and sculptor, and author of one of the most vivid and interesting autobiographies ever written. It was first published (dedicated to Richard Boyle) at Naples in 1730; English translations include that by T. Roscoe (1791–1871), and one by J. A. *Symonds, published 1888. Cellini combined the characters of artist and bravo; he was arrogant, passionate, conceited, and vainglorious. His autobiography gives a vivid account of the personalities and events of his time, including the Sack of Rome (1527), in which he took part; he also describes artistic techniques such as bronze casting. He went to France and worked for Francis I.

Celtic literature. There was little sense of common elements or purpose in literature in the Celtic languages (Irish, Scottish, Welsh, Cornish, and Breton) before the series of 'Celtic Revivals' which began in the 18th cent. and culminated with M. *Arnold and *Yeats in the late 19th cent. However, common themes can be seen, such as in the writings brought together by Kenneth Jackson in *A Celtic Miscellany* (1951) and in the Arthurian world which had expanded to a pan-European tradition. The postulation of a distinctively 'Celtic Note' was the not ungenerous but still stereotyping work of Arnold in *On the Study of Celtic Literature* (1866), following Ernest *Renan, and it was widely challenged in the 20th cent. See J. T. Koch and J. Carey, *The Celtic Heroic Age* (1994); A. Rees and B. Rees, *Celtic Heritage: Ancient Tradition in Ireland and Wales* (1961); S. *Deane, *Celtic Revivals*, chapters 1–2 (1985). Celtic folklore and *fairy stories were collected by John Rhŷs in *Celtic Folklore: Welsh and Manx* (1901, repr. 1980) and by William Jenkyn Thomas in *The Welsh Fairy Book* (1907).

Celtic Twilight, The, a collection of stories by *Yeats, published 1893, illustrating the mysticism of the Irish and their belief in fairies, ghosts, and spirits. It has since become a generic phrase (slightly ironical) for the whole *Irish Revival in literature.

Cenci, The, a verse tragedy by P. B. *Shelley, largely written at Livorno, in summer 1819, published 1819 and 1821.

The melodramatic plot is taken from the true story of Beatrice Cenci, who was tried and executed for the murder of her father, Count Francesco Cenci, at Rome in 1599. Shelley was attracted by the themes of incest and atheism: the play concentrates on the Iago-like evil of the count and the inner sufferings of Beatrice, whose justification men seek with 'restless and anatomizing casuistry'. Shelley claimed to have been influenced by the dramatic style of *Calderón, but in fact the play is indebted to Shakespeare for much of its construction and language: Beatrice's great speech on the prospect of death, 'So young to go | Under the obscure, cold, rotting, wormy ground!' (v. 4), is based on Claudio's in *Measure for Measure* (III. i). Surprisingly Shelley hoped for a popular theatrical success at Drury Lane or Covent Garden; the play was eventually produced in Paris in 1891.

censorship has a long and complex history, dating back to the early days of printing when proclamations against heretical and seditious books were issued under various monarchs, from 1529 under Henry VIII onwards. Protests against censorship produced some notable literary works, including the satires of *Harvey and *Nashe, and the tracts of *'Martin Marprelate', as well as Milton's defence of freedom, *Areopagitica. The spread of journalism also created new problems for the authorities. Control and licensing of the press continued under the Restoration and thereafter, a landmark case being that of John *Wilkes, the proprietor of the *North Briton, who successfully defended a libel action taken out against him for expressing views about the government of George III.

The 20th cent. has seen some changes in the nature of censorship of the arts, which has gradually been relaxed: milestones have been the successful prosecution for obscenity of Joyce's *Ulysses (1918) and the successful defence of Lawrence's *Lady Chatterley's Lover (1960). In 1964 a case was brought against the publishers of Hubert Selby Jnr.'s Last Exit to Brooklyn which was found to have contravened the 1959 Obscene Publications Act, and the defence's argument of literary merit was rejected by the jury. The verdict was reversed on appeal in 1968, which year also heralded the Theatres Act, which took control of the theatres out of the hands of the Lord Chamberlain's office for the first time in over 300 years. The only noteworthy legal action against a theatrical work after 1968 was the 1982 private prosecution taken out against Howard *Brenton's The Romans in Britain, alleging an act of gross indecency (a simulated homosexual rape) contrary to the Sexual Offences Act. The case collapsed on technical grounds. In 1988, the West Midlands Police removed a book of photographs by Robert Mapplethorpe from the library of the University of Central England on the grounds that it was material contrary to the Obscene Publications Act. The Crown Prosecution Service decided not to proceed with the case. Religious fundamentalism was responsible for the furore surrounding Salman *Rushdie's The Satanic Verses (1988).

The libel laws continue to be used to censor and in 1977 Gay News was convicted, in a case brought by Mary Whitehouse and the National Viewers and Listeners Association, of blasphemous libel for publishing a poem by James *Kirkup. The defence's argument of literary merit was ruled inadmissible. Political censorship has also been a feature of the latter part of the century. In 1987, the government obtained injunctions against the sale and syndication in Britain of Spycatcher, Peter Wright's memoirs of his time in MI5, in which he made allegations about covert government operations. The book was in fact available all over the world and in foreign newspapers on sale in Britain.

Cyberspace and the Internet are new areas where censorship battles are being fought. The view that the Internet is the last uncensored forum for debate and expression was challenged in 1999 by a libel action taken out against the Internet service provider Demon Internet. The action states that Demon was liable for libellous statements made by subscribers to its service.

CENTLIVRE, Susannah (?1669–1723), actress, dramatist, and poet, both of whose parents died when she was still a child. After an adventurous early career she married in 1707 Joseph Centlivre, cook to Queen Anne. He appears to have been her third husband. Her early plays, including her first, The Perjured Husband (1700), appeared under the name Susannah Carroll, taken from her second husband. An ardent Whig and anti-Jacobite, she was a friend of *Farquhar, *Steele, and *Rowe, and it may have been her mockery of priests and Catholicism that earned her a place in Pope's *The Dunciad. She wrote 19 plays, chiefly comedies, between 1700 and 1722, the best being comedies of intrigue and manners. The Gamester (1705, based to some extent on Regnard's Le Joueur) shows Valere torn between his love of Angelica and of gambling: in a dramatic scene she, disguised as a beau, wins from him her own picture as a stake, and thus leads him to repentance. The Wonder: A Woman Keeps a Secret (1714) provided *Garrick with one of his most successful parts, and *The Busie Body (1709) and *A Bold Stroke for a Wife (1718) were also frequently revived.

Cent Nouvelles nouvelles, Les, a collection of French tales, loosely modelled on Boccaccio's *Decameron, and written down probably between 1464 and 1467. The tales, predominantly licentious in character, were related at the court of Philip, duke of Burgundy, some by the duke himself, most by members of his household.

Certain Sonnets, 32 sonnets and poems by Sir P. *Sidney appended to editions of the *Arcadia from 1598 onwards. The last two sonnets are rejections of secular love, the second beginning:

> Leave me ô Love, which reachest but to dust,
> And thou my mind aspire to higher things:
> Grow rich in that which never taketh rust:
> What ever fades, but fading pleasure brings.

In the 19th cent. editors used, incorrectly, to append these two sonnets to *Astrophel and Stella.

CERVANTES SAAVEDRA, Miguel de (1547–1616), the great Spanish novelist and dramatist, born in Alcalá de Henares of an ancient but impoverished family, and wounded, losing for life the use of his left hand, at the battle of Lepanto (1571). He was taken by pirates in 1575, and spent the next five years as a prisoner at Algiers. The remainder of his life was, for the greater part, occupied with a struggle to earn a livelihood from literature and humble government employment. His first attempt at fiction was a pastoral novel, La Galatea (1585), which was followed by his masterpiece, *Don Quixote, of which the first part was published in 1605, the second in 1615. He also wrote a number of plays (16 of which survive), a collection of highly accomplished short stories (Novelas ejemplares, 1613), and a tale of adventure, Persiles y Sigismunda, published posthumously in 1617. J. *Fletcher drew largely on these last two for the plots of his plays.

Chabot, The Tragedy of, by *Chapman, probably

revised and added to by *Shirley, written between 1611 and 1622, published 1639.

Philip de Chabot, high admiral of France under Francis I, a loyal servant of the king, incurs the enmity of Montmorency the high constable, Poyet the chancellor, and their faction. By fearless insistence on his innocence he infuriates the king, is accused on trumped-up charges, and found guilty of high treason by the judges under pressure from the chancellor. The king pardons him and discovers the misconduct of the chancellor, who is tried and sentenced. But Chabot's heart is broken by the unjust treatment he has suffered and he dies.

Chadband, a character in Dickens's *Bleak House.*

Chaffanbrass, Mr, a character in Trollope's novels *The Three Clerks,* *Orley Farm,* and *Phineas Redux,* a celebrated Old Bailey barrister of slovenly and unprepossessing appearance, whose speciality is the successful defence of the apparently indefensible criminal.

Chainmail, Mr, a character in Peacock's *Crotchet Castle.* He believes the 12th cent. to be the best period in 'English History'.

'Chaldee MS, The: A Translation from an Ancient Chaldee Manuscript', published in *Blackwood's Magazine* 1817. The article, purporting to be an ancient manuscript and written in pseudo-biblical prose, describes the conflict between the two Edinburgh publishers *Blackwood and *Constable (owners, respectively, of *Blackwood's* and the *Edinburgh Review*), and contains many venomous descriptions of well-known Edinburgh figures. Its publication created a furore. Although anonymous, the piece was conceived by *Hogg, who later admitted he supplied 'the kernal', and was written by John *Wilson and *Lockhart, who, according to Hogg, were the 'young lions of Edinburgh' who added the 'devilry'. Blackwood had to pay damages, but the circulation of the 'Maga' rose.

CHALKHILL, John (d. 1642). He entered Trinity College, Cambridge, in 1610, and was the author of a pastoral *Thealma and Clearchus,* published 1683 with a preface by I. *Walton, and reproduced in *Saintsbury's *Caroline Poets,* vol. ii (1906), and of other verse included in *The Compleat Angler.*

CHALMERS, Thomas (1780–1847). He became professor of moral philosophy at St Andrews in 1823, and of theology at Edinburgh in 1828. From his early days as a minister in Glasgow he was known as one of the most formidable orators of the Scottish pulpit; he was a pioneer of popular education and an intellectual defender of Christianity. His chief importance lies in his leadership of the movement which led to the disruption of the Scottish Established Church and the founding of the Free Church of Scotland in 1843; he became its first moderator. His many works, mainly on natural theology and social economy, included 'The Adaptation of External Nature to the Moral and Intellectual Constitution of Man' (1833, the first of the *Bridgewater Treatises*).

CHAMBERLAYNE, Edward (1616–1703), tutor to the duke of Grafton and to Prince George of Denmark, and author of *Angliae Notitia, or the Present State of England* (1669), a handbook of social and political conditions which met with extraordinary success and was enlarged by his son John Chamberlayne.

CHAMBERLAYNE, William (1619–89), a physician at Shaftesbury in Dorset. He published a play, *Love's Victory* (1658), but is remembered for his *Pharonnida* (1659), a heroic romance in five books of rhymed couplets, recounting the adventures of the knight Argalia, his beloved Pharonnida, and the villainous Almanzor. *Saintsbury summarizes its incoherent plot, in his preface to his edition (*Caroline Poets,* vol. i, 1905). *Southey admired its 'sublimity of thought and beauty of expression'.

CHAMBERS, Sir E(dmund) K(erchever) (1866–1954), Shakespearian scholar and dramatic historian, educated at Marlborough and Corpus Christi College, Oxford, entered the education department of the civil service in 1892 where he remained until 1926. During this time he contributed articles to the *Academy and the *Athenaeum and in 1904–5 he was dramatic critic of the *Outlook* and the *Academy.* His major works of dramatic history, which began as 'a little book about Shakespeare', grew into the monumental *The Medieval Stage* (2 vols, 1903), *The Elizabethan Stage* (4 vols, 1923), and *William Shakespeare: A Study of Facts and Problems* (2 vols, 1930). His scholarly achievements are the more remarkable for being the fruits of his spare time. As well as editions of all Shakespeare's plays for the Red Letter Shakespeare and an important lecture on 'The Disintegration of Shakespeare' (1924) he published *Arthur of Britain* (1927), a synthesis and reassessment based on available evidence; biographies of *Coleridge (1938) and M. *Arnold (1947); editions of *Donne, *Milton, *Beaumont and *Fletcher, among others; and the *Oxford Book of Sixteenth Century Verse* (1932).

CHAMBERS, Ephraim (d. 1740), educated at Kendal grammar school, published his *Cyclopaedia,* the first true English encyclopaedia (which has no connection with the current *Chambers's Encyclopaedia*) in 1728. It had some influence on *Johnson's *Dictionary.* (See also ENCYCLOPÉDIE, L'.)

CHAMBERS, R(aymond) W(ilson) (1874–1942), born in Staxton, Yorkshire, graduated from University College London (1894), and afterwards librarian and (in succession to W. P. *Ker) Quain professor there (1922–41). The range of his scholarly interests extended from Old English to the Renaissance; his most celebrated works are *Widsith* (1912); *Beowulf: An Introduction to the Study of the Poem* (1921), which remained for 60 years the authoritative study of the poem's background; *On the Continuity of English Prose from Alfred to More* (1932), tracing a chronological line between his two major interests; *Thomas More* (1935); and *Man's Unconquerable Mind* (1939), a collection of essays of which the most striking are on *Langland, *More, and the philologists of UCL. He became president of the *Philological Society in 1933. He died at Swansea after evacuation to Wales in the Second World War. A memorial lecture to him was endowed at London University; the first lecture, on Chambers himself, was given in 1951 by C. J. Sisson.

CHAMBERS, Robert (1802–71). He founded with his brother the publishing firm of W. and R. Chambers, Edinburgh, and wrote and issued a number of books on Scottish history, biography, and literature. He established *Chambers's Journal* in 1832, and his firm issued *Chambers's Encyclopaedia*, which was begun in 1859, completed in 1868, and has been through many subsequent editions. He wrote and published anonymously in 1844 *Vestiges of the Natural History of Creation* in which he maintained a theory of biological evolution produced by the action of universal and progressive natural law. Though found odious by churchmen and incompetent by scientists, the *Vestiges* was immensely influential in popularizing an evolutionary view of nature.

Chambers's Journal (originally *Chambers's Edinburgh Journal*), one of the most popular of the 19th-cent. journals of literature, science, and the arts, founded by R. *Chambers in 1832. It changed its name in 1854, and survived until 1938.

CHAMISSO, Adelbert von (1781–1838), German zoologist and poet, chiefly remembered for his story *Peter Schlemihls wundersame Geschichte* (*The Strange Story of Peter Schlemihl*): see SCHLEMIHL.

Champion, which ran from 1739 to 1741, an anti-Jacobite, opposition journal written largely by H. *Fielding. In its columns Captain Hercules Vinegar, his wife, and their two sons discourse in various forms of essays, sermons, sketches, and letters on the political, social, and domestic problems of the day. The *Champion* contains some of the best of Fielding's journalistic work.

Chances, The, a play by J. *Fletcher, almost certainly his unaided work, written ?*c*.1617, printed 1647. The plot is based on one of *Cervantes's *Novelas ejemplares*; the 'chances' are the coincidences by which Constantia, who is eloping with the duke of Ferrara, and the duke himself, are brought into a number of complications, from which they are extracted by Don John and Don Frederick, two Spanish gallants, Dame Gillian their landlady at Bologna, and Peter Vecchio, a wizard. It was very popular after the Restoration, and was adapted by *Buckingham (1682), whose version was in turn successfully adapted by *Garrick.

CHANDLER, Raymond (1888–1959), American writer of thrillers and detective stories, born in Chicago but brought up from the age of 7 in England, where he was educated at Dulwich College. He returned to America in 1912 and settled in California, where he worked for an oil company before embarking on a career as a writer. Many of his early stories were published in the 1930s in *Black Mask*, a magazine founded in 1920 by *Mencken and *Nathan; his first novel, *The Big Sleep* (1939), introduced his detective narrator, cool, attractive, wise-cracking, lonely tough guy Philip Marlowe, who owes something to Chandler's admiration for *Hammett. Later works include *Farewell, My Lovely* (1940), *The High Window* (1942), *The Lady in the Lake* (1943), and *The Long Goodbye* (1953), all of which were filmed. His works have been greatly admired by British intellectuals; in an appreciation (*Harper's*, 1948) *Auden spoke for many when he wrote that Chandler's thrillers were 'serious studies of a criminal milieu, the Great Wrong Place, and his powerful but extremely depressing books should be read and judged, not as escape literature, but as works of art'.

CHANDOS, Sir John (d. 1370), English soldier, 'the flower of all chivalry' (*Froissart). He fought at the siege of Cambrai, 1337, at Crécy, 1346, and at Poitiers, 1356, where he saved the life of the *Black Prince. Edward III granted him a manor in Lincolnshire and lands in the Cotentin, and in 1360 appointed him his regent and lieutenant in France. He died of wounds in a battle near Poitiers and the French king declared that Sir John alone could have made the peace permanent between England and France.

Sir John was one of the founders of the Order of the Garter, and one of the 25 original knights.

Changeling, The, a tragedy by T. *Middleton and W. *Rowley, printed 1653, but acted as early as 1622.

Beatrice-Joanna, daughter of the governor of Alicant, is ordered by her father to marry Alonzo de Piracquo. She falls in love with Alsemero, and in order to avoid the marriage employs the ill-favoured villain De Flores, whom she detests but who cherishes a passion for her, to murder Alonzo. To the horror of Beatrice, De Flores exacts the reward he had lusted for. Beatrice is now to marry Alsemero. To escape detection she arranges that her maid Diaphanta shall take her place on the wedding night; and to remove a dangerous witness, De Flores then kills the maid. The guilt of Beatrice and De Flores is revealed to Alsemero, and they are both brought before the governor, whereupon they take their own lives. The title of the play is taken from the sub-plot, in which Antonio disguises himself as a crazy changeling in order to get access to Isabella, wife of the keeper of a madhouse. The main plot is taken from John Reynolds's *God's Revenge against Murther* (1621).

CHANNING, William Ellery (1780–1842), an American Unitarian clergyman, much involved in the Unitarian controversy, c.1815. He exercised a marked influence on American intellectual life, and is considered a forerunner of the *Transcendentalists. His *Remarks on American Literature* (1830) calls for a literary Declaration of Independence. His many pamphlets on slavery, pacifism, social questions, etc. are included in his collected *Works* (6 vols, 1841–3).

His nephew, also William Ellery Channing (1818–1901), poet and Transcendentalist, contributed frequently to the *Dial* and is remembered largely as the friend of *Emerson (who first brought his poetry to public attention) and of *Thoreau, whose biography Channing wrote. His first volume of verse, *Poems* (1843), was followed by several others. Thoreau referred to Channing's poetic style as 'sublime-slipshod'.

CHANNON, Henry 'Chips', see DIARIES.

Chanson de Roland, see ROLAND and CHANSONS DE GESTE.

chansons de geste, epic poems in Old French embodying legends which had grown up about earlier historical figures. The earliest extant versions are from the 12th cent. and use the legends to embody problems and difficulties of feudal society: either the stresses within the feudal system itself caused by conflicting loyalties, as in *Raoul de Cambrai* and *Girart de Roussillon*; or those caused by the impact of the Crusades on feudalism, as in the *Chanson de Guillaume* and, above all, in the *Chanson de Roland* (see ROLAND). These epics gradually grew into three cycles, first delineated by Bertran de Bar-sur-Aube, a writer of two such poems in the early 13th cent.: first, the *geste du roi*, those dealing with the *Charlemagne of legend and his knights; secondly, those dealing with Charlemagne's rebellious vassals, the *geste de Doon de Mayence*; and thirdly, the William of Orange cycle, the *geste de Garin de Monglane*. The genre followed the usual development of narrative literature during the Old French period: the earliest poems, the *Roland* and *Gormont and Isembart*, are heroic; the 12th-cent. poems, with William of Orange as their hero, are more realistic; the later poems have courtly and marvellous elements in them, and lose the tragic seriousness of the earlier works. Similarly, the later ones become more elaborate in style, while the early poems were written in a simple, formulaic style of great dramatic force. The only parallel English poems are those concerned with Charlemagne, such as the fragmentary Middle English *Song of Roland* (see FERUMBRAS, SIR, and OTUEL, SIR). See K. Voretsch, *Introduction to the Study of Old French Literature* (English trans., 1931).

Chanticleer, the cock in *Reynard the Fox*, and in Chaucer's 'The Nun's Priest's Tale' (see CANTERBURY TALES, 20) as Chauntecleer.

chapbook, a modern name applied by book-collectors and others to specimens of the popular literature which was formerly circulated by itinerant dealers or chapmen, consisting chiefly of small pamphlets of popular tales, ballads, tracts, etc. They were illustrated with wood-blocks, and consisted of 16 pages octavo or 24 pages duodecimo, and were sold generally at a penny to sixpence. They reproduced old romances, such as *Bevis of Hampton* and *Guy of Warwick*, or such stories as *'John Gilpin'*, *Robinson Crusoe*, or nursery rhymes and fairy tales. They were issued in great numbers throughout the 18th cent.

Chapel, Children of the, see PAUL'S, CHILDREN OF.

Chaplin, Sid, see REGIONAL NOVEL.

CHAPMAN, George (?1559–1634), born near Hitchin, in Hertfordshire. His Homeric translations suggest that he had a university education, possibly at Oxford, if A. *Wood is to be believed. Some of his young manhood was spent as a soldier in the Netherlands. After more than a decade as a professional playwright he began to pursue courtly patrons, with limited success, and turned to his major work of translating Homer, completed in 1616. Minor works of translation occupied him until his death, which seems to have been in poverty.

Chapman's earliest published works were non-dramatic poems: *The Shadow of Night* (1594), a pair of complex Neoplatonic poems on night and day; *Ovid's Banquet of Sense* (1595), an allegorical account of *Ovid's courtship of Corinna; and his completion of Marlowe's *Hero and Leander* (1598). Seven comedies are extant: *The Blind Beggar of Alexandria* (1598), *An Humorous Day's Mirth* (1599), *All Fools* (1605), *The Gentleman Usher* and *Monsieur D'Olive* (1606), *May-Day* (1611), and *The Widow's Tears* (1612). He collaborated with *Jonson and John *Marston on a further comedy, *Eastward Hoe*, in 1605, which led to a short period of imprisonment for Jonson and Chapman because of its anti-Scottish satire. The tragedies consist of two two-part plays, *Bussy D'Ambois* (1607) and *The Revenge of Bussy D'Ambois* (1613), *The Conspiracy of Charles*, Duke of *Byron and *The Tragedy of Byron* (1608), and one single play, *Caesar and Pompey* (1631). *The Tragedy of *Chabot* (1639) appears to be a Chapman tragedy revised by James *Shirley. Chapman also collaborated with *Fletcher, Jonson, and *Massinger in writing *The Bloody Brother* (c.1616, pub. 1639). The first of his Homeric translations, *Sevaen Bookes of the Iliades of Homere*, appeared in 1598 in a hasty publication devised to mark the earl of Essex's embarkation for Ireland; 12 books of the *Iliad* appeared in c.1609; the complete *Iliad* and *Odyssey* were published together in 1616 as *The Whole Works of Homer; Prince of Poetts*. Jonson praised Chapman as second only to himself as a writer of *masques, though all that survives is *The Memorable Mask* (1613), presented in the Middle Temple and Lincoln's Inn to celebrate the marriage of Princess Elizabeth.

Chapman's literary reputation has often sprung from peripheral associations rather than direct knowledge. *Keats's sonnet beginning 'Much have I travell'd in the realms of gold' has commended Chapman's Homer to generations of readers who have not themselves 'looked into' it. He was long the favourite candidate for the 'rival poet' referred to in Shakespeare's *Sonnets*. 'The proud full sail of his great verse' of Sonnet 86 was linked with the distinctive 14-syllable lines of Chapman's *Iliad*, and the 'affable familiar ghost' of the same sonnet with the spirit of Homer, by which Chapman claimed to be directly inspired. Chapman was once seen as a crucial figure in a secret society of freethinkers called the *School of Night, of which Marlowe, *Harriot, and Matthew Roydon were also members. Though there are links between Chapman and all these figures, it is not now thought that they took such a formal shape. As poet and dramatist, Chapman is most often seen as a genius manqué, whose learning and energy were never sufficiently disciplined. T. S. *Eliot called him 'potentially the greatest artist' of the Elizabethan dramatists. Perhaps the only lines of Chapman's poetry that are still well known are these from *Bussy D'Ambois*:

> Man is a torch borne in the wind; a dream
> But of a shadow, summ'd with all his substance.

His complete plays were edited by T. M. Parrott (1910, 1914), and a few individual plays have appeared in the Revels Plays series. P. Bartlett edited the *Poems* (1941) and Allardyce Nicoll the Homer (1957); editions of the comedies and the tragedies were produced under the general editorship of Allan Holady in 1970 and 1987.

CHAPMAN, Guy, see JAMESON, S.

CHAPMAN, John (1821–94), the son of a Nottingham druggist and shopkeeper; he moved to London early in life and established himself as a publisher and editor. He published G. *Eliot's translation of Strauss in 1846, and she stayed in his home and literary headquarters at 142 Strand in 1851; in the same year he purchased the *Westminster Review*, of which she became assistant editor, and for which she wrote regularly. Chapman edited the *Review* continuously for 43 years until his death. A strikingly handsome man and a notorious philanderer, married to a wife considerably older than himself, Chapman was a conspicuous figure in literary London; *Carlyle, commending him to R. *Browning in 1851, wrote that he had 'real enthusiasm (tho' a soft and slobbery) in him'. He qualified as a physician in 1857 and wrote various medical works, but appears to have been something of a quack. He died in Paris. His diaries for 1851 and 1860 survive, which, edited by G. S. Haight (*George Eliot and John Chapman, with Chapman's Diaries*), shed considerable light on both their personalities.

Chapman and Hall, a publishing company founded in 1830 at 186 Strand, London, by Edward Chapman and William Hall. It owed much of its success to its early association with *Dickens (*Pickwick Papers* having originated in a suggestion from Hall) and published

many distinguished and popular authors, including *Carlyle, *Kingsley, Mrs *Gaskell, and *Trollope. G. *Meredith was for a time literary director, and Arthur Waugh, father of Evelyn *Waugh, became chairman and managing director in 1902 and wrote a history of the firm (*A Hundred Years of Publishing*, 1930). The firm was sold to Methuen in 1938, and scientific and technical books now appear under its imprint.

CHAPONE, Mrs (Hester), née Mulso (1727–1801), born at Twywell, Northamptonshire. She educated herself despite early discouragement and wrote her earliest dated poem 'To Peace. Written during the Late Rebellion. 1745' when only 18. In London she became a member of the *Blue Stocking Circle, and knew Samuel *Johnson, who admired her poetry, particularly 'To Stella', a poem against love and in praise of the calm joys of friends. She married John Chapone in 1760, who unfortunately died in 1761; thereafter, she lived alone in London, publishing *Letter Written on the Improvement of the Mind* (1773) to much applause. *Miscellanies in Verse and Prose* followed in 1775. Dr Johnson invited her to contribute to the *Rambler, of which No. 10 is partly hers. Her works were highly regarded and went into many editions. Although 30 years younger, she was a particular friend of S. *Richardson, who called her 'little spit-fire' and with whom she discussed his female characters; Mrs *Delany asserted that Mrs Chapone was the model for one or two of Richardson's heroines. Her *Works* and *Posthumous Works* appeared in 1807.

Characteristics of Women, see JAMESON, A. B.

Characters of Shakespear's Plays, essays by W. *Hazlitt, published 1817. They comment not only upon Hamlet, Macbeth, and other fictional heroes, but also upon the distinctive qualities of each major drama, and more generally upon the 'magnanimity' of Shakespeare's imagination. Especially notable is the essay on *Coriolanus*, which considers the affinities between poetic imagination and political power. Hazlitt rebukes S. *Johnson for his unimaginative treatment of Shakespeare, and attempts a more flexibly sympathetic appreciation.

character-writing. Books of 'characters' were popular in the 17th cent., and many were based, though some loosely, on *Theophrastus translated by *Casaubon in 1592 and by Healey (printed 1616, but previously circulated). The first was published in 1608 by J. *Hall, followed by *Overbury in 1614, the *Satirical Essays, Characters and Others* of J. *Stephens in 1615, Geffray Mynshul's *Certain Characters and Essays of Prison and Prisoners* in 1618, *Earles's *Microcosmographie* (1628), Richard Brathwait's *Whimzies* (1631), and others. The 'characters' gave generalized but detailed descriptions of the behaviour and appearance of a class or type; they were on the whole short, succinct, pointed, and less discursive than the essay, also a popular literary form of the period. *La Bruyère's much admired 'Characters'

(1688) were translated into English in 1699. See B. Boyce, *The Theophrastan Character in England to 1642* (1947) and C. N. Greenough, *A Bibliography of the Theophrastan Character in English* (1947).

'Charge of the Light Brigade, The', a poem by *Tennyson, first published in the *Examiner* in 1854 only weeks after the famous charge (25 Oct. 1854) at Balaclava, near Sebastopol, during which, owing to a misunderstood order, 247 officers and men out of 637 were killed or wounded. The line 'Someone had blundered', suggested by a phrase in a report in *The Times*, was omitted from the version published in 1855 (*Maud, and Other Poems*) but later reinstated.

CHARKE, Mrs Charlotte (1713–c.1760), the youngest child of Colley *Cibber. She early displayed a fondness for masculine dress and pursuits, was widowed in 1737 after an early marriage to a violinist, and pursued a varied career as waiter, pastrycook, strolling player, etc. Her *Narrative of the Life of Mrs Charlotte Charke* (1775) vividly describes her family background and later misfortunes.

CHARLEMAGNE (742–814), king of the Franks (768) and crowned by Pope Leo III as Emperor of the West (800), the son of Pepin the Short. He and his *Paladins are the subject of numerous *chansons de geste*, of which the *Chanson de Roland* is the most famous (see ROLAND). Of the three groups of French *chansons de geste* concerned with Charlemagne, only the first, the *geste du roi*, is represented in English, in such romances as *Otuel*, *Sir *Ferumbras*, and *The Sege of Melayne*. As well as being the subject of romances, Charlemagne is of significance in English literature for the tradition of learning he established at his court (led by the Northumbrian *Alcuin) which King *Alfred copied a century later. See P. Wolff, *The Awakening of Europe* (English trans. A. Carter, 1968).

CHARLES, duc d'Orléans (1394–1465), French poet, and a member of the French royal family. He fought at the battle of Agincourt in 1415, was captured, and held prisoner in England until 1440. On his return to France he established his court at Blois, where he received many literary figures. He is often considered to be the last important poet in the French courtly tradition; he wrote numerous elegant ballades, chansons, complaintes, and rondeaux. A large number of English poems, many of which are versions of Charles's French lyrics, are also probably to be attributed to him.

CHARLES XII (1682–1718), king of Sweden, and a great military commander, who led his forces successfully against the northern coalition. He captured the capital of Poland from Augustus the elector of Saxony, and invaded Russia, defeating Peter the Great at Narva (1700) and being in turn totally defeated at Poltava in 1709, after which he retreated to Turkey. He returned in 1714 to Stralsund, which alone remained to him of his continental possessions, but was driven thence to Sweden. He was killed at Frederikshald in a war with Norway. His life was written by *Voltaire. Johnson (*The Vanity of Human Wishes*) says of him:

> He left the name at which the world grew pale,
> To point a moral or adorn a tale.

(See also MAZEPPA.)

CHARLES, Faustin, see BLACK BRITISH LITERATURE.

CHARLETON, Dr Walter (1619–1707), fellow of the *Royal Society. His *Chorea Gigantium* (1655) attempted to demonstrate that Stonehenge was a Danish coronation site and prompted one of *Dryden's finest early poems, 'To my Honour'd Friend, Dr Charleton' (1663), in which royalist, scientific, commercial, patriotic, and religious sentiments are subtly interwoven.

***Charley's Aunt*,** a highly popular *farce by (Walter) Brandon Thomas (1856–1914), produced in 1892 and still performed.

Charmian, in Shakespeare's *Antony and Cleopatra* and Dryden's *All for Love*, Cleopatra's chief waiting woman. In Shakespeare she laments her dead mistress as 'A lass unparallel'd' (v. ii. 314).

Charmond, Felice, a character in Hardy's *The Woodlanders*.

CHARTIER, Alain (c.1385–c.1435), French poet and prose writer. His most famous poem was *La Belle Dame sans mercy* (1424), a story of unrequited love in 800 octosyllabic lines; an English translation, falsely ascribed to *Chaucer, appeared c.1526. His most famous prose work, the *Quadrilogue invectif* of 1422, is a bitter attack on the divisions within French society and a passionate appeal for national unity. His Latin prose work *De Vita Curiali*, a disillusioned account of court life, was translated into English by *Caxton.

Chartist movement, a chiefly working-class political movement between 1837 and 1848, arose as a result of the *Reform Bill of 1832, which had excluded the working classes from political rights for lack of the necessary property qualification. Their six-point 'People's Charter' consisted of: Universal Suffrage, Vote by Ballot, Annually Elected Parliaments, Payment for Members of Parliament, Abolition of the Property Qualification, and Equal Electoral Districts. The movement had an enormous following but failed through poor leadership, though the points eventually became law between 1860 and 1914, except for Annually Elected Parliaments. The movement was alluded to by novelists of the mid-19th cent. who were concerned with the *Condition of England question, in particular B. Disraeli in *Sybil, and C. Kingsley in *Alton Locke; and also by *Carlyle in his essay 'Chartism'. The Chartists themselves also produced a considerable amount of literature, including the documentary accounts of S. *Bamford, and many short-lived periodicals sprang up (the *Northern Star*, the *Chartist Circular*, the *Star of Freedom*, the *Red Republican*, and others). Chartist poets and novelists, some of them writing in prison, included master bootmaker Thomas Cooper (1805–92), author of the lengthy and ambitious *The Purgatory of Suicides* (1853), a 'working man's epic' in Spenserian stanzas, who was imprisoned for 'incitement to riot'; E. *Elliott of Sheffield, the so-called 'Corn Law Rhymer'; Ernest Jones (1819–68/9?), orator and publisher, and author of an unfinished novel *De Brassier*; Thomas Martin Wheeler, author of *Sunshine and Shadow*, published in 37 parts in the *Northern Star* (1849–50); wood engraver William James Linton (1812–97); and textile worker Gerald Massey (1828–1907) whose *Original Poems and Chansons* appeared in 1847. See Martha Vicinus, *The Industrial Muse: A Study of Nineteenth Century British Working Class Literature* (1974), D. Thompson, *The Chartists* (1984), and *An Anthology of Chartist Poetry*, ed. P. Scheckner (1989).

Chaste Mayd in Cheap-side, A, by T. *Middleton, written 1613, printed 1630, now widely believed his best comedy.

The play centres on the attempt of the dissolute Sir Walter Whorehound to pass off his mistress as his niece and to marry her to the foolish pedantic son of Yellowhammer, a rich goldsmith; while Whorehound himself is to marry Yellowhammer's daughter Moll. The first part of the plot succeeds, but the second fails. For Moll and the resourceful young Touchwood are in love with one another, and their attempts to evade the parents and get married, though repeatedly foiled, are finally successful.

CHATEAUBRIAND, François-René, vicomte de (1768–1848), one of the major figures of early French Romanticism. He achieved great celebrity with *Le Génie du Christianisme* (1802), a work of Christian apologetic which accompanied and contributed to the post-revolutionary religious revival in France. It argues with great eloquence for the emotional and imaginative appeal of religion to the deepest instincts of man's nature. 'Of all the religions that have ever existed'—thus the author sums up his thesis—'the Christian religion is the most poetical, the most favourable to freedom, art and letters; the modern world owes all to it, from agriculture to the abstract sciences.' From this work Chateaubriand detached two fragments, inspired in part by his stay in America (1791), which he published separately: *Atala* (1801; trans. 1802), the tragic romance, set in Louisiana, of the Indian maiden Atala and her lover Chactas; and *René* (1805, trans. 1813), the story of a young European devoured by a secret sorrow (his temperament and early circumstances resemble the author's) who flies to the solitudes of America to find solace for profound melancholy and unsatisfied longings. *Les Martyrs* (1809, trans. 1812) is a prose epic of early Christianity. *Mémoires d'outre-tombe* (1849–50), his posthumously published autobiography, now regarded as his most accomplished

work, gives a penetrating and brilliantly written account of the author's life against the varied background of an age of political upheaval. Between 1793 and 1800 Chateaubriand lived in exile in England, mainly in London, where he published an *Essai sur les révolutions* (1797). Under Louis XVIII he returned to London in 1822 as French ambassador. He translated *Paradise Lost* as *Le Paradis perdu* (2 vols, 1936).

CHATHAM, earl of, see PITT, W.

CHATTERTON, Thomas (1752–70), the posthumous son of a Bristol lay clerk and schoolmaster, began to write verse while still at school at Colston's Hospital; one of his earliest poems is a satire, 'Apostate Will', composed in 1764. He left school aged 14 and was apprenticed to an attorney. In 1768 he published in *Felix Farley's Bristol Journey* a passage of pseudo-archaic prose, of which he claimed to have discovered the original in a chest in St Mary Redcliffe. This attracted the attention of various local antiquaries, for whom he provided fake documents, pedigrees, deeds, etc. He had by this time already written some of his 'Rowley' poems, including his 'Bristowe Tragedie'; these purported to be the work of an imaginary 15th-cent. Bristol poet, Thomas Rowley, a monk and friend of William Canynge, a historical Bristol merchant. He also fabricated prose correspondence between the two and other background documents. He offered some of the poems (without success) to *Dodsley in Dec. 1768; in 1765 Dodsley had published Percy's *Reliques*, a work which greatly encouraged the growing interest in antique and *primitive poetry. In March 1769 Chatterton sent to Horace *Walpole a short treatise on painting 'bie T. Rowleie', which Walpole temporarily accepted as authentic. In the same month he published in the *Town and Country Magazine* the first of seven Ossianic pieces in poetic prose, 'Ethelgar. A Saxon poem', though he took care in this and similar pieces to avoid using the Scottish background of *Macpherson. The only Rowleian piece published in Chatterton's life was 'Elinoure and Juga', which appeared in the same periodical in May 1769. In April 1770 he went to London, writing home at first 'in high spirits', and claiming 'great encouragement' from Dodsley and others, but within four months he committed suicide by taking arsenic, apparently reduced to despair by poverty. He wrote a good deal in these last months, including a burletta, *The Revenge* (no record of performance); the satirical 'Kew Gardens', modelled on the satires of Charles *Churchill; and one of his finest Rowleian pieces, 'An Excelente Balade of Charitie'. The Rowley poems were first published in 1777 by Thomas Tyrwhitt, and a year later Thomas *Warton publicly raised doubts of their authenticity; the controversy raged for decades, and Rowley continued to find champions until *Skeat's edition of 1871.

Chatterton's life, work, and tragic death had a powerful effect on the *Romantic imagination; *Wordsworth wrote of him as 'the marvellous Boy,

The sleepless Soul that perished in his pride', and *Keats, who dedicated *Endymion to his memory, described him in a letter as 'the purest writer in the English Language. He has no French idioms or particles, like Chaucer—'tis genuine English Idiom in English words.' In his Rowley poems, Chatterton employs a variety of verse forms, including Spenserian stanzas, rhyme-royal, and the ballad; notable among them are his Pindaric *ode, 'Songe to Ella' in which Ella (or, as often, Ælla) makes his first appearance, and 'Ælla' itself, 'a tragycal enterlude'. The famous painting of The Death of Chatterton (1856) in the Tate Gallery by Henry Wallis, much admired by *Ruskin, is not based on any authentic portrait or likeness, as none survived. The fullest life is by E. H. W. Meyerstein (1930), and there is a two-volume edition of the Complete Works, ed. D. S. Taylor and B. B. Hoover (1971).

CHATWIN, (Charles) Bruce (1940–89), travel writer and novelist, born in Sheffield. After Marlborough College, he had an impressive career at Sotheby's auction house, then studied archaeology at Edinburgh University. He travelled widely in Asia, Africa, and Europe, developing a passionate interest in nomads which was to last throughout his life, and in the early 1970s worked on the Sunday Times Magazine, where his subjects included feral children, Russian avant-garde art, and Indira Gandhi. His first book, In Patagonia (1977), an imaginative blend of history, biography, anecdote, and geography, expanded the concept of *travel writing. It mixes fact and fiction, delights in arcane data and paradox, and is written in a pungent style, with short sentences and exotic vocabulary; it contains autobiographical detail but abstains from confession. Four books followed in his lifetime. The Viceroy of Ouidah (1980) is a fictionalized account of a real-life slave-trader. On the Black Hill (1982, novel) tells the story of reclusive Welsh twin brothers. His best-selling work, The Songlines (1987), incorporates some of his early speculations about nomads in a study of Aboriginal creation myths. Utz (1988) is a study of a collector of Meissen porcelain in Prague. A selection of miscellaneous writings, selected by Chatwin before his death, was published posthumously in 1989 as What Am I Doing Here; other aspects of his work are represented in Photographs and Notebooks (1993), edited by David King and F. *Wyndham. A portrait of the author, With Chatwin, by Susannah Clapp, was published in 1997, and a life by Nicholas Shakespeare in 1999.

CHAUCER, Geoffrey (c.1343–1400), the son of John Chaucer (c.1312–68), a London vintner. The date of his birth has been much argued, all views now placing it between 1339 and 1346. In 1357 he served with Lionel, afterwards duke of Clarence. In 1359 he was in France with Edward III's invading army, was taken prisoner, and ransomed. He married, perhaps in 1366, Philippa, the daughter of Sir Paon Roet of Hainault and the sister of *John of Gaunt's third wife Katherine Swynford.

Philippa died in 1387 and Chaucer enjoyed Gaunt's patronage throughout his life. He held a number of positions at court and in the king's service, and he travelled abroad on numerous occasions on diplomatic missions; as well as missions to France, he made a journey to Genoa and Florence in 1372–3 in the course of which he could theoretically have met *Boccaccio and (slightly more plausibly) *Petrarch. He was sent on to France and Lombardy in 1378. In 1374 he was appointed controller of customs in the port of London and leased his house over Aldgate. He was knight of the shire for Kent in 1386 and probably lived in Kent for most of the rest of his life. His last official position was deputy forester in the King's Forest at Petherton in Somerset (1391–8 at least) and it is possible that he lived there for some time. He was buried in the Poets' Corner of Westminster Abbey where a monument was erected to him in 1555. The known facts of his life are well summarized in The Riverside Chaucer (ed. L. D. Benson et al., 1988), pp. xi–xxii. His writings develop through his career from a period of French influence in the late 1360s (of which the culmination was *The Book of the Duchess in about 1370), through his 'middle period' of both French and Italian influences (including *The House of Fame in the 1370s and the mature Italian-influenced works of which the most important is *Troilus and Criseyde, c.1385), to the last period of most of *The Canterbury Tales and his short lyrics; but this chronology is not very enlightening. His prose works include a translation of *Boethius (Boece) and the challenging A Treatise on the Astrolabe, written to 'little Lewis', probably the poet's son. Portraits of Chaucer occur in three places: in the Ellesmere MSS (now in the Huntington Library and the basis of most modern editions); in the manuscript of Troilus and Criseyde in Corpus Christi College, Cambridge; and in *Hoccleve's The Regement of Princes, beside lines 4,995–6 (in several manuscripts: the best is the one dating from Hoccleve's time, British Library Harley 4866, edited by Furnivall for EETS ES 72).

See D. A. Pearsall, The Life of Geoffrey Chaucer: A Critical Biography (1992); P. Boitani and J. Mann (eds.), The Cambridge Chaucer Companion (1986); J. D. North, Chaucer's Universe (1988); J. A. Burrow (ed.), Geoffrey Chaucer.

Chaucerians, Scottish, the name traditionally given to a very diverse group of 15th- and 16th-cent. Scottish writers who show some influence from *Chaucer, although the debt is now regarded as negligible or indirect in most cases. See JAMES I (of Scotland); KINGIS QUAIR, THE; HENRYSON; DUNBAR; DOUGLAS, GAWIN.

Chaucer Society, founded in 1868 by *Furnivall, for the purpose of collecting materials for the study of *Chaucer.

CHAUDHURI, Amit (1962–   ), Indian writer who was born in Bombay but grew up in Calcutta, where most of his fiction is set. Chaudhuri is a miniaturist, writing up the details of Indian middle-class life in prose of crystalline calm. *A Strange and Sublime Address* (1991) described the gradual awakening to life of a young writer-to-be in a vibrant Calcutta household. *Afternoon Raag* (1993) found its narrator studying at Oxford and remembering his earlier life in Bombay. *Freedom Song* (1998) returned to Calcutta to follow the interconnected lives of three Bengali families, observed with the contemplative humanity that is Chaudhuri's trademark. See ANGLO-INDIAN LITERATURE.

CHAUDHURI, Nirad C., see ANGLO-INDIAN LITERATURE.

Chauntecleer, see CHANTICLEER.

Cheeryble Brothers, Ned and Charles, characters in Dickens's *Nicholas Nickleby*.

CHEEVER, John (1912–82), American novelist, whose sophisticated, ironic novels and short stories (many published in the *New Yorker*) satirize affluent suburban New England life, and have gained a growing following in England. His novels include *The Wapshot Chronicle* (1957), *The Wapshot Scandal* (1964), *Bullet Park* (1969), and *Falconer* (1977). He was awarded the *Pulitzer Prize for fiction in 1979 for *The Stories of John Cheever*. His *Letters* were published in 1987, edited by his son Benjamin Cheever.

CHEKE, Sir John (1514–57), fellow of St John's College, tutor to Edward VI, and subsequently the first Regius professor of Greek at Cambridge. He was imprisoned by Queen Mary, 1553–4. He was an eminent scholar and, though he wrote little in the vernacular (but many Latin translations from the Greek), was influential in promoting a simple style of English prose. He is referred to ('O soul of *Sir John Cheek*') in *Milton's Sonnet XI, 'A Book was writ of late'.

CHEKHOV, Anton Pavlovich (1860–1904), Russian dramatist and short story writer. He studied medicine in Moscow, where he began writing short humorous stories for journals. Among the greatest of his mature stories are 'A Dreary Story' (1889), 'Ward No. Six' (1892), 'My Life' (1896), 'Ionych' and the trilogy 'The Man in a Case', 'Gooseberries', and 'About Love' (all 1898), and 'The Lady with the Little Dog' (1899). Chekhov's first successful play was *Ivanov* (1887), and he then wrote several light one-act comedies. His status as a dramatist, however, rests on his four late plays. *The Seagull* (1895) was produced at the State Theatre of St Petersburg, but its originality was badly understood by the actors and the first night was a disaster. After this Chekhov's plays were staged by the Moscow Art Theatre, founded by Konstantin Stanislavsky and Vladimir Nemirovich-Danchenko in 1898. A triumphant new production of *The Seagull* was followed by *Uncle Vanya* (1900), *Three Sisters* (1901), and *The Cherry Orchard* (1904). These productions established the Art Theatre's reputation and style. In 1901 Chekhov married the Art Theatre actress Olga Knipper. Another actor to appear in the Art Theatre's

Chekhov productions was Vsevolod Meyerhold, whose own later anti-naturalistic, anti-Stanislavskian productions of the plays were probably more true to the intentions of a playwright who had always chafed at Stanislavskian naturalism.

Chekhov's success and influence in England has been immense. Since 1903 most of his work has been translated. The first major translation is that by C. *Garnett, *The Tales of Tchehov* (1916–22) and *The Plays of Tchehov* (1923–4). The major modern translation is that by Ronald Hingley, *The Oxford Chekhov* (9 vols, 1964–80). The first English productions of his plays were George Calderon's staging of *The Seagull* in Glasgow in 1909 and the Incorporated Stage Society's 1911 London production of *The Cherry Orchard*, much admired by Arnold *Bennett. E. M. *Forster, V. *Woolf, *Gerhardie, J. M. *Murry (who placed him above *Joyce and *Proust), and especially K. *Mansfield were among early admirers. Katherine Mansfield's stories are held to be the main channel through which his work influenced England, and her letters are full of expressions of her temperamental sympathy for him. G. B. *Shaw declared that reading Chekhov's plays made him want to tear up his own, and he went on to write *Heartbreak House* as a tribute to him. He is also held to have influenced E. *Bowen, *O'Faolain, *Maugham, H. E. *Bates, *Ackland, and others. Chekhov's work is characterized by its subtle blending of naturalism and symbolism; by its sympathetic, humane, but acutely observed portraits of a threatened upper class stifled by inactivity and ennui; and above all by its unique combination of comedy, tragedy, and pathos, and the sensitivity of its movement from one mode to another.

Chemical Generation, see under WARNER, A., and WELSH, I.

CHÉNIER, André-Marie (1762–94), French poet, born in Constantinople of mixed French and Greek parentage. He played an active part as a political journalist during the French Revolution, was arrested in March 1794, and died on the guillotine. His poetry remained unpublished in his lifetime, but the example of his life and death made a considerable impression on subsequent generations; the first collected edition of his poems, in 1819, gained wide popularity, exercising an influence on the *Romantic and *Parnassian movements. His poetry reveals his affinities with the classical world, particularly with the elegiac verse of the *Greek *Anthology*, and his involvement in the social and political issues of the revolution.

Cherry and Merry, in Dickens's *Martin Chuzzlewit*, Pecksniff's daughters, Charity and Mercy.

Cherry and the Slae, The, see MONTGOMERIE.

Cheshire Cheese, the, 'an ancient eating-house in Fleet Street' where the *Rhymers Club met for some years in the 1880s and 1890s; it is described by *Yeats

195 CHESTER | CHETTLE

in his autobiography *The Trembling of the Veil* (1922): he also celebrated 'Poets with whom I learned my trade, Companions of the Cheshire Cheese' in his poem 'The Grey Rock' (*Responsibilities*, 1914).

Chester, Sir John, and Edward his son, characters in Dickens's *Barnaby Rudge*.

CHESTERFIELD, Philip Dormer Stanhope, fourth earl of (1694–1773), the son of Lady Elizabeth Savile, for whom *Halifax had written his 'Advice to a Daughter' (1688). He was a distinguished statesman and diplomatist, ambassador at The Hague 1728–32 and lord lieutenant of Ireland 1745–6. He was keenly interested in the literary world, and in his youth was a friend of *Pope, *Gay, and *Arbuthnot. He wrote political tracts, contributed to the *World*, and was responsible for securing the adoption of the New Style Gregorian *Calendar in 1751, but is chiefly remembered for his 'Letters' to his natural son Philip Stanhope (1732–68), which were written (not for publication) almost daily from 1737 onwards. These consist largely of instruction in etiquette and the worldly arts, and became after publication (by the son's widow in 1774) a handbook of good manners; it appears that the young man was shy and awkward, and his father is full of useful advice about deportment (laughter occasions 'a shocking distortion of the face' and should be avoided), conversation, approaches to women (described as 'children of larger growth'), etc. Although widely admired, the letters increasingly attracted criticism, as the century became less cynical and more sentimental; Dr *Johnson declared that they 'teach the morals of a whore and the manners of a dancing-master' and *Cowper, in his 'Progress of Error', described their author as 'Graybeard corrupter of our listening youth'. After his son's death Chesterfield turned his attention to his godson, also Philip, his letters to whom were published by Lord Carnarvon in 1890. A complete edition of all his letters by B. Dobrée appeared in 1932.

Chesterfield is also remembered in connection with Johnson's *Dictionary*. Johnson had addressed the 'Plan' of that work to Chesterfield, but it was received with neglect, probably unintentional; on publication of the *Dictionary*, Chesterfield wrote two papers in the *World* commending it. Thereupon on 7 Feb. 1755 Johnson addressed to him the famous letter in which he bitterly rejected a notice which 'had it been early, had been kind; but it has been delayed till I am indifferent, and cannot enjoy it; till I am solitary, and cannot impart it; till I am known, and do not want it'. Chesterfield received this with good nature, and would show it to visitors with admiration. Johnson's own hostility softened over the years.

Chester plays, see MYSTERY PLAYS.

CHESTERTON, G(ilbert) K(eith) (1874–1936), born on Campden Hill, London, and educated (with his friend E. C. *Bentley) at St Paul's School. He made his name in journalism (according to him 'the easiest of all pro-

fessions'), writing (with *Belloc) for the *Speaker*, in which both took a controversial, anti-imperial, pro-Boer line on the Boer war; his long and fruitful friendship with Belloc earned them both, from G. B. *Shaw, the twin nickname of 'Chesterbelloc'. His first novel, *The Napoleon of Notting Hill* (1904), a fantasy set in a future in which London is plunged into a strange mixture of medieval nostalgia and street warfare, develops his political attitudes, glorifying the little man, the colour and romance of 'Merry England', and attacking big business, technology, and the monolithic state. These themes echo through his fiction, which includes *The Man Who Was Thursday: A Nightmare* (1908), an alarming but rollicking fantasy with a surreal anarchist background which attacks *fin-de-siècle* pessimism, and his many volumes of short stories, of which the best known are those which feature Father Brown, an unassuming East Anglian Roman Catholic priest, highly successful in the detection of crime by intuitive methods, who first appears in *The Innocence of Father Brown* (1911); Chesterton himself became a Roman Catholic in 1922. He published several volumes of verse; his most characteristic poems (with some exceptions, such as 'The Donkey', from *The Wild Knight*, 1900, and 'Lepanto', from *Poems*, 1915) tend to celebrate the Englishness of England, the nation of Beef and Beer, e.g. 'The Secret People' (1915) and 'The Rolling English Road' (1914).

Chesterton also wrote literary criticism, including works on R. *Browning (1903), *Dickens (1906), and Shaw (1910), and many volumes of political, social, and religious essays, including *Heretics* (1905), *Orthodoxy* (1909), and *The Everlasting Man* (1925); also an *Autobiography* (1936). He contributed regularly to the *Eye Witness*, later the *New Witness* (1911–23), of Belloc and his brother Cecil Chesterton (1879–1918), and edited it from 1925 (when it was revived as *G.K.'s Weekly*) until his death. Much of his vast output has proved ephemeral, but Chesterton's vigour, idiosyncrasies, optimism, puns, and paradoxes celebrate the oddity of life and the diversity of people and places with a peculiar and at times exhilarating violence. Later selections of his non-fiction prose and his short stories were edited, with introductions, by, respectively, *Auden (1970) and K. *Amis (1972).

CHESTRE, Thomas, see SIR LAUNFAL.

CHETTLE, Henry (*c*.1560–?1607), the son of a London dyer, apprenticed to a printer and for a time a partner in a printing business. Upon its failure he took to writing plays, of which he is reputedly the author of about 13 and the joint author of considerably more (including *The Blind-Beggar of Bednal-Green*, with J. *Day). The only extant play attributed to him alone is *The Tragedy of Hoffman* (*c*.1603), dealing with the story of a Danish pirate who is executed and the revenge and execution of his son. He edited and was possibly the author of *Greenes Groats-Worth of Witte* in 1592, and wrote two satirical pamphlets, *Kind Harts Dreame*

(?1593) and *Piers Plainnes Seauen Years Prentiship* (1595). He also published *Englandes Mourning Garment*, an elegy on Queen Elizabeth, in 1603.

Chevy Chase, The Ballad of, one of the oldest of the English ballads, probably dates in its primitive form from the 15th cent. Its subject is the rivalry of the neighbouring families of Percy and Douglas, heightened by the national quarrel between England and Scotland. Percy, earl of Northumberland, has vowed to hunt for three days across the Scottish border 'maugre the doughty Douglas'. The two parties meet and fight, there is great slaughter on both sides, and both Percy and Douglas are killed (cf. OTTERBOURNE). The ballad is quoted and discussed by *Addison, who admired its 'majestic simplicity' and compared it to Virgil, in the *Spectator* (Nos. 70 and 74, May 1711). It is included in Percy's *Reliques*.

chiasmus, a figure of speech by which the order of the words in the first of two parallel clauses is reversed in the second, e.g. 'He saved others; himself he cannot save.'

CHICHELE, or **CHICHELEY,** Henry (?1362–1443), archbishop of Canterbury, son of a yeoman of Higham Ferrers, Northamptonshire. He was educated at Winchester and New College, Oxford, and became archbishop in 1414. He founded the Chichele chest in Oxford University for the relief of poor students, built a house for Cistercians in Oxford, and was co-founder with Henry VI of All Souls College. There is a life by A. Duck (Latin 1617; expanded in English 1699).

Chicken Soup with Barley (1958), the first of a trilogy, by A. *Wesker, which introduces the Kahn family in their east London home in 1936; Sarah, a warm-hearted communist Jewish matriarch, supports opposition to the Fascist marches, but her husband Jack is less enthusiastic. He becomes enfeebled by successive strokes, but she battles for her ideals, also manifested in her daughter Ada and her volatile son Ronnie, who returns at the end of the play from working as a cook in Paris with many of his illusions shattered. Sarah urges him to keep fighting: 'You've got to care or you'll die.' See also ROOTS.

Chickerell, Ethelberta, a character in Hardy's *The Hand of Ethelberta*.

CHILD, Francis James (1825–96), American scholar and professor of English literature at Harvard. He edited *Spenser (5 vols, 1855) and wrote a pioneering study of *Chaucer (*Observations on the Language of Chaucer*, 1863), but is most widely known for his great collection of *English and Scottish Popular Ballads* (5 vols, 1882–98). (See BALLAD.)

Childe, in 'Childe Harold', 'Childe Roland', etc., signifies a youth of gentle birth, and is used as a kind of title. In the 13th and 14th cents 'child' appears to have been applied to a young noble awaiting knighthood.

Childe Harold's Pilgrimage, a poem in Spenserian stanzas by *Byron, of which the first two cantos appeared in 1812, Canto III in 1816, and Canto IV in 1818. The poem describes the travels, experiences, and reflections of a self-styled and self-exiled pilgrim, Childe Harold, whose wanderings correspond in many ways to Byron's own, although Byron denied that he identified himself with Harold, and wrote in an addition to his preface (1813) that the pilgrim 'was never intended as an example'—rather, he was 'a modern Timon, perhaps a poetical Zeluco'. Harold, a melancholy, defiant outcast, is the first of a series of histrionic *Byronic heroes: his character reappears, with little significant development, in *The Corsair, *Manfred, and other works. The first two cantos describe how the wanderer, sated with his past life of sin and pleasure, finds distraction by travel: he journeys through Portugal, Spain, the Ionian Islands, and Albania, interspersing his evocations of the glorious scenery with diatribes against the Convention of Cintra ('Britannia sickens, Cintra! at thy name'), with an 11-stanza description of the bloody sport of bull fighting, and (Canto II) with a savage attack on Lord Elgin, the 'last dull spoiler', for his pillage of the Greek antiquities. He salutes Albania and its wild, martial, and exotically garbed people, then once more laments the lost liberty of Greece. In Canto III, written six years later, the pilgrim still 'wrung with the wounds that heal not', travels to Belgium, the Rhine, the Alps, and Jura: Stanza XXI introduces his celebrated passage on the battle of Waterloo, 'There was a sound of revelry by night . . .' Later stanzas (LXXVI–CVIII) pay tribute to 'wild Rousseau, The Apostle of affliction' and to *Gibbon, 'Sapping a solemn creed with solemn sneer; The lord of irony'. In Canto IV, dedicated to his friend and travelling companion *Hobhouse, he abandons the device of the pilgrim and speaks directly, in a long meditation on time and history, on Venice and *Petrarch, on Ferrara and *Tasso, on *Boccaccio and Florence, and on Rome—'Oh Rome! my country! city of the soul! The orphans of the heart must turn to thee . . .' The Canto concludes with a passionate invocation of 'the deep and dark blue Ocean', 'the image of eternity'. The poem enjoyed great success. After the publication of Cantos I and II in March 1812 Byron wrote, 'I woke and found myself famous.' Later, however, he claimed that he came to dislike it as 'the false exaggerated style of youth'. The author's copious notes pursue many of the themes of the poem with wit and indignation.

Childe Roland, in an old Scottish ballad, a son of King Arthur. His sister, Burd Ellen, is carried away by the fairies to the castle of the king of Elfland. Aided by the instructions of Merlin, Childe Roland makes his way into the castle and rescues his sister.

> Child Rowland to the dark tower came,
> His word was still 'Fie, foh, and fum,
> I smell the blood of a British man.'
> (Shakespeare, *King Lear*, III. iv)

*Halliwell (*Nursery Rhymes*) thinks that Shakespeare is here quoting from two different compositions, the first line from a ballad on Roland, the second and third from the story of Jack the Giant-Killer.

'Childe Roland to the Dark Tower Came', a poem by R. *Browning, published in *Men and Women*. The title derives from a snatch of song recited by Edgar in *King Lear* (see above).

A knight errant crosses a nightmare landscape in search of the Dark Tower (or has been deceived into doing so; it is not clear which); he eventually reaches the Tower and blows his horn defiantly at its foot. The poem ends with the title phrase, and there is no indication of what happened next. Because the story is told by the knight himself, the poem's form raises insoluble problems of interpretation, and the poem is both profoundly satisfying as a dream narrative and profoundly disturbing as an impenetrable allegory—of life, of art, or of both. Browning consistently refused to explain the poem, saying simply that it had come upon him as a dream. The intensity of the poem's language remained unsurpassed in Browning's work until the fragment known as 'Thamuris marching' appeared in *Aristophanes' Apology*.

CHILDERS, (Robert) Erskine (1870–1922), writer and political activist. He was from 1895 to 1910 a Clerk in the House of Commons, served in the Boer War, and then devoted himself to Irish affairs. In 1920 he settled in Ireland and in 1921 was appointed director of publicity for the Irish Republicans. In 1922 he was court-martialled and shot by firing squad. As a writer he is remembered for his novel *The Riddle of the Sands* (1903), often described as the first example of *spy fiction, a sea story about two amateur British yachtsmen sailing in the Baltic who discover German preparations for an invasion of England.

Childe Waters, one of the most beautiful of the old ballads, celebrating the constancy of Ellen to Childe Waters, her heartless lover, whom she serves as a page, receiving cruel and degrading treatment. Her child is born in a stable, where she is tending her master's horse. He hears her singing a lullaby and wishing herself dead, relents, and marries her. The ballad is in Percy's *Reliques*.

Child of the Jago, A (1896), a novel by A. *Morrison, which describes the boyhood of Dick Perrott in an East End slum off Shoreditch High Street, and gives a vivid account of the violent crime of the neighbourhood known in real life as 'The Nichol'. Dicky's good instincts are frustrated by the environment, his father is hanged for murder, and he dies aged 17 in a street fight. In an 1897 preface Morrison rejected the label of 'realist', but his work belongs to the same school as that of G. *Moore and resembles the early *Maugham.

Children in the Wood, The, popularly known as the story of the Babes in the Wood. It is the subject of an old ballad, included in *Percy's and *Ritson's collections.

A Norfolk gentleman leaves his property to his infant son and daughter and gives the children into his brother's charge; the wicked uncle plans to acquire the property by making away with them. He hires two ruffians to slay them in a wood. One of these, more tender-hearted than the other, repents and kills his fellow, then abandons the children in the wood. The children perish, and a robin covers them with leaves. The surviving ruffian confesses, and the wicked uncle dies miserably.

Children of the Chapel of Paul's, see PAUL'S, CHILDREN OF.

Children's literature, see overleaf.

Chillingworth, Roger, in Hawthorne's *The Scarlet Letter*, the name assumed by Hester Prynne's husband.

CHILLINGWORTH, William (1602–44), a scholar and fellow of Trinity College, Oxford. He embraced Romanism and went to Douai in 1630, but abjured that creed in 1634. He was one of the literary coterie that gathered round *Falkland at Great Tew, and was the author of the controversial work *The Religion of Protestants a Safe Way to Salvation* (1638).

Chillip, Dr, in Dickens's *David Copperfield*, the physician who attended Mrs Copperfield at the hero's birth.

Chimène, or Ximena, the wife of the *Cid.

Chimes, The, a Christmas book by *Dickens, published 1845.

It is the story of a nightmare or vision in which Toby Veck, porter and runner of errands, under the influence of the goblins of the church bells and a dish of tripe, witnesses awful misfortunes befalling his daughter, a vision happily dissipated at the end; together with some social satire on justices, aldermen, and the like, in the persons of Sir Joseph Bowley and Mr Chute.

Chips with Everything, see WESKER.

Chivery, Mr and 'Young John', characters in Dickens's *Little Dorrit*.

Chloe, the name under which Pope satirizes Lady Suffolk, mistress of George II (*Moral Essays*, ii. 157), although in other verses and letters he shows her much respect.

The 'Chloe' or 'Cloe' in Horace *Walpole's letters was the duke of Newcastle's French cook Clouet.

CHOMSKY, Noam (1928–   ), professor of modern languages and linguistics at Massachusetts Institute of Technology, after *Saussure the most important figure in modern *linguistics. Two of his books, in particular, proposed a radically new view of the nature and analysis of language: *Syntactic Structures* (1957) and *Aspects of the Theory of Syntax* (1965). Following on from the systems of grammatical analysis developed

(cont. on p.200)

The juvenile book trade in England had its beginnings in the desire of 17th-cent. Protestants to save the souls of children. Benjamin Harris (fl. 1673–1710), an Anabaptist and a pioneer printer of news-sheets, was one of the first to publish popular educational works. Both *War with the Devil* (1673), a verse dialogue by Benjamin Keach, and Harris's own sensational *Protestant Tutor* (1679) went into many editions. Nathaniel Crouch (?1632–1725), an associate of Harris's, recognized the profit to be derived from such works, and his versified Bible stories, *Youth's Divine Pastime* (3rd edn., 1691), includes many crudely violent, even salacious, episodes. James Janeway's *A Token for Children (1672)* was the first book to feature children only, but the longest-lived Puritan classic was Isaac *Watts's *Divine Songs for the Use of Children* (1715).

There was to be no fiction until the mid-18th century. Traditional stories like the *Robin Hood saga and *Bevis of Hampton, were abhorred by Puritans. Though translations of French fairy-tales by Mme d'Aulnoy and Charles *Perrault appeared in 1699 and 1729 respectively, these were not intended for children, nor were the *Arabian Nights tales. But in 1749 Sarah *Fielding included two fairy-tales in *The Governess, or Little Female Academy*, the first juvenile novel. As Iona and Peter *Opie have shown, nursery rhymes were first collected in 1744 when Mary Cooper, widow of a London printer, published *Tommy Thumb's Pretty Song Book, Voll. [sic] II*, apparently preceded shortly before by *Tommy Thumb's Song Book*. 1744 was also the year John *Newbery published his first book for children, *A Little Pretty Pocket Book*. Newbery was the first publisher to make a commercial success of children's books; one of his better-known titles was *The History of Little Goody Two-Shoes* (1765), featuring an enterprising female Dick *Whittington.

Newbery's boisterous jollity went out of fashion, and late Georgian children were expected to be rational and well informed. Maria *Edgeworth was one of the few writers to combine information and moral instruction with art. Catherine *Sinclair intended *Holiday House* (1839) as a corrective to the moral tale, but even this account of two turbulent children ends in a lugubrious deathbed scene.

There was to be much in this vein from evangelical writers. Mary Martha *Sherwood's *History of the Fairchild Family*, the first part of which appeared in 1818, was one of the most widely read juvenile books of the century. With the spread of Sunday schools and increasing literacy a huge market for religious fiction was created, stories of street waifs by such writers as

Hesba *Stretton being particularly popular. Charlotte *Yonge, in her pamphlet *What Books to Give and What to Lend* (1887) had separate sections for 'drawing-room books' and books for the poor.

Into the first category came works such as *Alice's Adventures in Wonderland* (1865), which had its roots in the violence and anarchy of nursery rhymes, as did Edward *Lear's nonsense poems. Edgar Taylor's 1823 translation of *Grimm's tales, and three separate translations of Hans *Andersen in 1846, indicated that fantasy was now acceptable, though it was often used for didactic ends, as in Charles *Kingsley's *The Water-Babies* (1863). George *MacDonald's finely wrought fantasies, such as *At the Back of the North Wind* (1871) and *The Princess and the Goblin* (1872), leave the reader to infer the meaning.

Other Victorian 'drawing-room' writers include Juliana Horatia *Ewing and Mary Louisa *Molesworth, whose works have not worn well. Public school stories, such as Thomas *Hughes's *Tom Brown's Schooldays* (1857) and F. W. *Farrar's *Eric, or Little by Little* (1858), an emotional but veiled account of sexual corruption, were very popular with working-class boys, and adventure writers such as R. M. *Ballantyne, G. A. *Henty, and W. H. G. *Kingston were read by both boys and girls. The greatest example of the genre is Robert Louis *Stevenson's *Treasure Island* (1883).

The turn of the century saw a great flowering. Rudyard *Kipling's work included animal stories in the two *Jungle Books* (1894–5), the amoral school world of *Stalky & Co* (1899), the nonsense of *The Just-So Stories* (1902), and the subtle historical narratives in *Puck of Pook's Hill* (1906) and *Rewards and Fairies* (1910). Edith *Nesbit created attractively high-spirited and independent children in her three stories about the Bastable family, and Beatrix *Potter, the supreme stylist, began her series of sardonically humorous animal stories with *The Tale of Peter Rabbit* (1902). Kenneth *Grahame, who had broken new ground with his realistic evocation of childhood in *The Golden Age* (1895) and *Dream Days* (1898), surprised and at first disappointed his admirers with an animal fantasy, *The Wind in the Willows* (1908), now a classic.

Perhaps roused by J. M.Barrie, whose *Peter Pan* had been enthusiastically received in 1904, Edwardian literati made a cult of childhood. Belief in fairies was sedulously cultivated: *fairy stories were used to impart religious and sex instruction, magazines were devoted to them, and writers ranging from Walter *de la Mare to Enid Blyton (1897–1968), the most prolific children's writer of the 20th cent., introduced fairies in verse and stories.

The real world had little place in pre-1950s books; middle-class parents wished to shelter their young. With *Swallows and Amazons* (1930) Arthur *Ransome began an enduring fashion for holiday adventures; school and pony stories were particularly popular with girls. There was some distinguished fantasy-writing, as in the Dr Dolittle books by Hugh Lofting (1886–1947), John *Masefield's *The Midnight Folk* (1927) and *The Box of Delights* (1935), J. R. R. *Tolkien's *The Hobbit* (1937), and T. H. *White's *The Sword in the Stone* (1938), while the characters and aphorisms from A. A. *Milne's *Winnie-the-Pooh* (1926) and *The House at Pooh Corner* (1928) have become as famous as those in *Alice*.

There was a second flowering of children's books after the Second World War. Rosemary Sutcliff (1920–92) was foremost among the writers of historical fiction, with outstanding novels about Roman and Viking Britain; in *The Owl Service* (1967) and *Red Shift* (1973) Alan Garner (1934–) wove myth with characters from the past and the present, a recurring theme also with Penelope *Lively. Joan Aiken (1924–2004) and Leon Garfield (1921–96) wrote fast-paced historical melodrama, the former fantastic and richly comic, the latter macabre. The post-war period also produced many classic works of fantasy, including C. S. *Lewis's Narnia cycle, Mary Norton's *The Borrowers* (1952) and its sequels, Philippa Pearce's *Tom's Midnight Garden* (1958), and Richard *Adams's animal epic, *Watership Down* (1972).

The 1980s were dominated by Roald *Dahl, whose anarchic tales of (typically) smart children and grotesque adults were often cruel but almost always very funny. But the years since Dahl's death in 1990 have seen a burst of activity that has put even his wild creations in the shade. Many children's authors of the 1970s and 1980s have continued to produce excellent and popular fiction — authors like Diana Wynne Jones and Susan Cooper (both writers of sophisticated fantasy) and Dick King-Smith, best known for his animal stories for younger readers. At the same time a new generation of writers has been achieving unprecedented commercial success and critical support. Pre-eminent must be J.K. Rowling's series of books about a schoolboy wizard that began in 1997 with *Harry Potter and the Philosopher's Stone*. A large adult readership contributed to the remarkable worldwide success of the books; the sixth, published in 2005, sold over two million copies in the first 24 hours on sale in the U.K., with sales estimated at over 300 million worldwide.

But Harry Potter is not alone in breaking new commercial ground for children's books; real-life (but soft-hearted) stories by Jacqueline Wilson have sold over 20 million copies in the UK, as well as making her the most borrowed author in the country's libraries; and there are countless other children's writers who now appear regularly on consolidated adult-and-child bestseller lists. The Alex Rider books by Anthony Horowitz and the Artemis Fowl books by Eoin Colfer have been particularly well-received by readers, and with Potter are among the books that have been said to have had some impact on the reading-habits of a typically reluctant audience – boys in particular.

But children's books have broken new ground in content as well as in sales figures. Writing for children has ceased to be the poor relation in the publishing family, with a recognition that the potential scope of children's books need not be less ambitious than that of those written for adults. No subject is now taboo — there are books written for young teenagers about sex and drugs and abuse and domestic violence.

In the past decade the teenage novel has come of age. Where once teen novels were few and far between (and not always of the best), now writers like the haunting David Almond, the taboo-busting Melvin Burgess and Aidan Chambers, Kevin Brooks, Geraldine McCaughrean, Gillian Cross and Jan Mark, are exploring themes and forms in books with great energy and imagination. And even those who claim to be immune to fantasy have found themselves succumbing to the mysteries of Philip Pullman's *His Dark Materials* trilogy – the third of which, *The Amber Spyglass*, in 2001 became the first children's book to be named the Whitbread Book of the Year.

Pullman's was only one of a number of so-called 'crossover' novels, novels with reach into both adult and child/teen readership (with a single book often cannily issued in two editions, identical save for a different jacket design). Mark Haddon's *The Curious Incident of the Dog in the Night-Time* (2003), narrated by a boy with Asperger's Syndrome, is one of the most remarkable of these.

Pottermania and the rise of the crossover novel have boosted public awareness of the children's novel. The year 1999 saw the inauguration of illustrator Quentin Blake (who most famously collaborated with Roald Dahl) as the first Children's Laureate, a post charged with promoting children's reading and the status of children's books. Blake was followed by the popular and critically lauded novelists Anne Fine (in 2001) and Michael Morpurgo (in 2003), with children's favourite Jacqueline Wilson named as the fourth in 2005.

by L. *Bloomfield and Chomsky's teacher Zellig Harris, Chomsky's 'generative grammar' proposes a set of 'deep structure' grammatical rules which produce a set of sentences at the 'surface structure' of language. A grammar of a language would be a set of rules which generates 'all and only the correct sentences of the language'. The significance of his emphasis is that it brings linguistic analysis closer to analyses of mental operations such as are conducted by psychologists and logicians; his approach has more in common, in some of its aspects, with 17th-cent. 'Cartesian' notions of 'Universal Grammar' than with the taxonomic endeavours of pre-Saussurean philology.

Chomsky: Selected Readings, ed. J. P. B. Allen and P. Van Buren (1971); N. Chomsky, *Reflections on Language* (1975); J. Lyons, *Chomsky* (1970).

CHOPIN, Fryderyk Franciszek (1810–49), Polish composer. Chopin, who lived in Paris from the age of 21 onwards, was one of the central figures of the musical Romantic movement. The circumstances of his life, and his notorious liaison with the novelist G. *Sand, combined with the poetry of his piano playing and the strong emotional appeal of his compositions, made him a legend in his own time; after his death he came to be seen as the archetype of the consumptive Romantic artist, and his slighter works were on the piano in many Victorian drawing rooms. His music is a great deal better than this popular image suggests, particularly in the larger works not aimed at the aristocratic salons of which he was so assiduous a frequenter, and its influence on later composers was profound. Unlike most of his contemporaries, however, he never tried to relate his music to literary, pictorial, or autobiographical themes, and his few songs are written entirely to Polish texts.

CHOPIN, Kate, née O'Flaherty (1850–1904), daughter of an Irish immigrant father and Creole mother; she was born in St Louis, Missouri, and brought up in a largely female household. She married Oscar Chopin, a Creole, and went to live in New Orleans, Louisiana, spending her summers at Grand Isle, a fashionable resort off the south coast. Her husband's business did not prosper and he returned to the family plantation in the Cane River district, where he died of swamp fever in 1882, leaving her with six children to support. After paying off his debts she returned to St Louis and began to write, using as material her memories of New Orleans and of Cane River, the latter providing material for three collections of short stories. She was originally acclaimed as a 'local colourist', but has posthumously won recognition for *The Awakening* (1899), which tells the story of Edna Pontellier, married to a successful Creole business man, and leading a life of leisure which she finds vaguely dissatisfying. She commits adultery with one young man, while believing herself in love with another, and on the last page swims naked out to sea and presumably drowns. It was considered scandalous and morbid, and, discouraged by its hostile reception from writing more full-length fiction, Chopin turned to poems, essays, and short stories until her death from a brain haemorrhage.

choriamb, a metrical foot of four syllables, the first and last long, the two others short. A choree is a trochee (see METRE).

CHRÉTIEN DE TROYES (fl. 1170–90), regarded as the greatest of the writers of courtly romances, wrote in French in the second half of the 12th cent. He is believed to have written a romance of *Tristan*, but four complete romances of his survive, all written in octosyllabic rhyming couplets: *Erec and Enide* (c.1170); *Cligés* (c.1176); *Yvain* (c.1177–81); and *Lancelot*, or *Le Chevalier de la charrette* (c.1177–81); the last 1,000 of the 7,000-odd lines of the latter were written by Godefroy de Lagny. As well as these four he left incomplete the lengthy *Perceval* or *Le Conte du Graal* (1181–90) of which 9,234 lines survive. There are also two short *trouvère* poems by him, and he lists at the beginning of *Cligés* a number of other complete, mostly Ovidian, poems. All that is known for certain of the writer is that he lived and worked for some time at the court of *Marie de Champagne. His influence on all subsequent Arthurian literature, including English, is general rather than particular, but the English romance *Iwain and Gawain* is a loose translation of his *Yvain*. The qualities required of a courtly lover were partly inferred from *Lancelot* by G. Paris in 1883 (see COURTLY LOVE).

There is an English translation of the four completed romances by W. W. Comfort (Everyman, 1914, etc.). For general discussion and reference to French editions, see 'Chrétien de Troyes' by Jean Frappier, in R. S. Loomis (ed.), *Arthurian Literature in the Middle Ages* (1959), 157–91.

'Christabel', a poem by S. T. *Coleridge, published 1816.

The poem is unfinished. The first part was written at Nether Stowey in 1797, the second (which contains Lake District local colour) at Keswick in 1800; Coleridge made plans for Part III but found himself unable to continue with it. It is a medieval romance of the supernatural, written in what is sometimes referred to as 'Christabel metre'—that is, in four-foot couplets, mostly iambic and anapaestic, used with immense variety, so that the line length varies from seven syllables to ten or eleven.

Christabel, praying at night in a wood for her betrothed lover, discovers the fair Geraldine in distress and takes her to the castle of her father, Sir Leoline. Geraldine claims to have been abducted from her home by five warriors, and to be the daughter of Sir Leoline's estranged friend Sir Roland of Vaux. She shares Christabel's chamber for the night, and bewitches her as they lie in one another's arms. In the morning she meets Sir Leoline, who vows reconciliation with her father and vengeance on the 'reptile souls' of her abductors. Christabel, who has seen Geraldine's true malignant serpent nature, is at first silenced by the spell placed upon her, but manages to implore her father to send Geraldine away, although she can offer no explanation for this plea. Sir Leoline, offended by his daughter's insult to a guest, turns from her to Geraldine, and so the poem ends. The imagery throughout is strongly sexual, and the theme would appear to be connected with the corruption and seduction of innocence. To Coleridge's disappointment, Wordsworth did not include the poem in the second edition of the *Lyrical Ballads. Coleridge's sources have been traced by A. Nethercot, *The Road to Tryermaine* (1939).

Christ and Satan, an Old English poem of 733 lines in three sections, found in the *Junius manuscript. Clubb, in his 1925 edition, dated the work (more exactly than seems justified) 790–830, and said it was of Anglian origin. Like many of the poems in the Junius manuscript, it used to be attributed to *Cædmon, but it is now said to be a mixture of his 'school' and that of *Cynewulf. The subjects of the three sections are: Satan's lament for his fall; the *Harrowing of Hell; and the temptation of Christ by Satan.

Christian and **Christiana,** the hero of Bunyan's *The Pilgrim's Progress* and his wife, who is introduced in the second part.

Christian Hero, The: *An Argument Proving that No Principles but Those of Religion Are Sufficient to Make a Great Man*, a treatise by *Steele, published 1701.

Finding, as the author tells us, military life 'exposed to much Irregularity', he wrote this little work 'with a design to fix upon his own Mind a strong Impression of Virtue and Religion, in opposition to a stronger Propensity towards unwarrantable Pleasures'. In it he stresses the value of the Bible as a moral guide and the failure of Stoic philosophy. The treatise ends with a comparison between Louis XIV and William III, and includes a significant passage recommending, in contrast with the immorality that pervaded most of the writings of the day, a chivalrous attitude towards women. The work is important as one of the first signs of a change of tone in the English literature of the period. (See also STOICISM.)

Christian Morals, see BROWNE, T.

Christian Year, The, see KEBLE.

CHRISTIE, Dame Agatha, née Miller (1890–1976), born and brought up in Torquay. She was educated at home, and in 1914 married Archibald Christie. During the First World War she worked as a hospital dispenser, which gave her a knowledge of poisons which was to be useful when she started writing detective stories. Her marriage broke up in 1926, and in 1930 she married the archaeologist Max Mallowan, whom she accompanied on his excavations of sites in Syria and Iraq. Her first detective novel, *The Mysterious Affair at Styles* (1920),

introduced Hercule Poirot, the Belgian detective who appeared in many subsequent novels (her other main detective being the elderly spinster Miss Marple). In the next 56 years she wrote 66 detective novels, among the best of which are *The Murder of Roger Ackroyd* (1926), *Murder on the Orient Express* (1934), *Death on the Nile* (1937), and *Ten Little Niggers* (1939). She also wrote six novels under the pseudonym Mary Westmacott, two self-portraits (*Come Tell Me How You Live*, 1946; *An Autobiography*, 1977), and several plays, including *The Mousetrap*, which was first performed in London in 1952 and was still running at the turn of the century, 47 years later. Her prodigious international success seems due to her matchless ingenuity in contriving plots, sustaining suspense, and misdirecting the reader, to her ear for dialogue, and brisk, unsentimental commonsense and humour. Her style is undistinguished and her characterization slight, but sufficient for the exigencies of the form. See R. Barnard, *A Talent to Deceive* (1980); C. Osborne, *The Life and Crimes of Agatha Christie* (1982).

CHRISTINE DE PISAN (*c*.1364–*c*.1430), French poet and prose writer. She produced a large number of works, including courtly ballades, rondeaux, and virelais, moral and didactic poems, a biography of Charles V, and several specifically feminist works, such as *L'Epistre au dieu d'amours* (1399), an eloquent denunciation of anti-feminist attitudes, *La Cité des dames* (1405, English trans. 1521), and *Le Livre des trois vertus* (1406). A number of English translations of her work appeared in the late 15th and early 16th cents and a new translation of *La Cité des dames* by Earle Jeffrey Richards, *The Book of the City of Ladies*, was published in 1983 with a foreword by Marina *Warner, in which she relates 'the *querelle des femmes*—the woman question in late 14th- and early 15th-cent. France' to 'today's debate about the equality of women'.

Christis Kirk on the Green, an old Scottish poem, doubtfully attributed to James I or James V of Scotland, in nine-lined stanzas with a 'bob' after the eighth line, descriptive of the rough fun, dancing, and love-making of a village festival or 'wappinshaw'. Two additional cantos were composed by *Ramsay.

Christmas Carol, A, a Christmas book by *Dickens, published 1843.

Scrooge, an old curmudgeon, receives on Christmas Eve a visit from the ghost of Marley, his late partner in business, and beholds a series of visions of the past, present, and future, including one of what his own death will be like unless he is quick to amend his ways. As a result of this he wakes up on Christmas morning an altered man. He sends a turkey to his ill-used clerk Bob Cratchit, positively enjoys subscribing to Christmas charities, and generally behaves like the genial old fellow that he has become.

Christmas-Eve and Easter-Day, a poem by R. *Browning, published 1850. The poem is in two parts, in octosyllabic metre, with an irregular rhyme-scheme. The first part, 'Christmas-Eve', in the form of a narrative combining realistic and visionary elements, accepts that denominational religion is an imperfect medium for divine truth, but emphasizes the need to choose the best method of worship according to one's lights; the second part, 'Easter-Day', in the form of an imagined dialogue, examines the difficulties of holding to the Christian faith at all, and argues that the condition of doubt is, in fact, essential to the existence of human faith. The poem, the first to appear after Browning's marriage, shows the influence of E. B. *Browning's strong intellectual and emotional engagement with religious polemic, acting on Browning's own Nonconformist upbringing.

Christ's Hospital, London, the most famous of the Blue-Coat or charity schools, was founded under a charter of Edward VI as a school for poor children, in buildings that before the dissolution had belonged to the Grey Friars. *Coleridge, *Lamb, Leigh *Hunt, and Edmund *Blunden were educated there.

Christs Teares over Jerusalem, a tract by T. *Nashe, published 1593. Nashe here figures as a religious reformer. He applies Christ's prophecy of the fall of Jerusalem as a warning to sinful London and analyses with his usual vigour the vices and abuses of contemporary society.

Christs Victorie and Triumph, see FLETCHER, GILES (the younger).

chronicle play, a type of drama popular in the 1590s and the early 17th cent., in which scenes from the life of a monarch or famous historical character were depicted. Examples are Shakespeare's *Henry V and *Henry VIII, the Sir Thomas *More play, and *Dekker and *Webster's Sir Thomas Wyat.

chronicles, see under ANGLO-SAXON CHRONICLE, THE, ANNALES CAMBRIAE, ASSER, BEDE, CAMDEN, CAPGRAVE, CIRENCESTER, EADMER, FABYAN, FLORENCE OF WORCESTER, GEOFFREY OF MONMOUTH, GILDAS, GIRALDUS CAMBRENSIS, HALL, E., HARRISON, W., HOLINSHED, HOVEDEN, JOCELIN DE BRAKELOND, NENNIUS, PETERBOROUGH CHRONICLE, THE, RICHARD THE THIRDE, ROBERT OF GLOUCESTER, SPEED, J., STOW, P. VERGIL, WACE, WILLIAM OF MALMESBURY, WILLIAM OF NEWBURGH, WYNTOUN.

Chronicles of the Canongate, The, an inclusive title for Sir W. Scott's novels *The Highland Widow, and *The Fair Maid of Perth, and a story, *'The Two Drovers', to which the author attached the fiction that they were written by Mr Chrystal Croftangry, who draws on the recollections of his old friend Mrs Bethune Baliol, a resident in the Canongate, Edinburgh. Mr Croftangry's own story, notable among Scott's shorter sketches, forms an introduction to the Chronicles.

Chrononhotonthologos, a burlesque of contemporary drama by H. *Carey, 'the Most Tragical Tragedy that

ever was Tragediz'd by any Company of Tragedians', acted 1734.

Chrononhotonthologos is king of Queerummania, and two of the characters are Aldiborontiphoscophornia and Rigdum-Funnidos, names which Sir W. *Scott gave to James and John *Ballantyne, on account of the pomposity of the one and the fun and cheerfulness of the other.

Chrysaor, in Spenser's *Faerie Queene (V. i. 9 and V. xii. 40), the sword of Justice, wielded by Sir *Artegall. The Chrysaor of Greek mythology was a son of Poseidon and Medusa.

CHRYSOSTOM, St John (c.345–407), a Greek Father of the Church, born at Antioch in Syria; he was baptized in 370 and spent ten years in the desert in ascetical study. He became bishop of Constantinople where he preached so eloquently against the vices of the city and its empress Eudoxia that he was condemned by a packed synod and banished to Nicaea. His name means 'Golden-mouth', in tribute to his eloquent preaching; in his writings he stressed the ascetical element in religion and the need for personal study of the Scriptures. Amongst his many writings the most celebrated are his Commentaries on the Gospel of St Matthew and on the Epistles to the Romans and Corinthians, all translated in A Library of the Father of the Holy Catholic Church (J. H. Parker, 1852, etc.). See also D. Attwater, St John Chrysostom (1939).

CHUDLEIGH, Mary, Lady, née Lee (1656–1710), born in Winslade, Devon. She married George Chudleigh; the couple had two sons and a daughter. She was influenced by Mary *Astell, with whom she corresponded and wrote, in answer to Astell's Some Reflections on Marriage, her poem, The Ladies Defence (1701); in it Melissa argues robustly with three prejudiced men about the need for female education and the damaging effects of male contempt. In her Poems on Several Occasions (1703) solitude looms large; the Essays upon Several Subjects in Verse and Prose followed in 1710.

Chuffey, in Dickens's *Martin Chuzzlewit, Anthony Chuzzlewit's old clerk.

CHURCHILL, Caryl (1938–), playwright, born in London and educated in Montreal and at Lady Margaret Hall, Oxford. Most of her plays, predominantly radical and feminist in tone, have been performed at the Royal Court Theatre, in association with the *English Stage Company: they include Owners (1972, pub. 1973), a satire on property and capitalism; Light Shining in Buckinghamshire (1976, pub. 1978); Cloud Nine (1979, pub. 1979), a comedy in two acts, the first exploring sexual repression in Victorian Africa, the second set in London in 1979 and exploring contemporary sexual identity; *Top Girls (1982, with an all-female cast); Softcops (1984, with an all-male cast); A Mouthful of Birds (1986); *Serious Money

(1987); *Ice Cream* (1989); *Hot Fudge* (1989); *Mad Forest* (1990); *The Skriker* (1994, about a shape-shifter); and *Blue Heart* (1997). She has also written radio and television plays.

CHURCHILL, Charles (1731–64), the son of a poor clergyman, educated at Westminster and St John's College, Cambridge. His university career was interrupted by an early marriage, and he was ordained 'through need, not choice' in 1756, succeeding his father as curate at St John's, Westminster. He was oppressed by poverty until the publication of *The Rosciad* and *The Apology* (both 1761), which brought him fame and between £750 and £1,000. He increasingly abandoned the church, leading a worldly and dissipated life, and by 1762 was a close friend of *Wilkes, writing for his paper the *North Briton* and attacking his opponents in satiric verse. *The Prophecy of Famine* (1763) is a mock-pastoral and a powerful satiric attack on Bute, J. *Home, and other Scots. Other targets were *Smollett (*The Author*, 1763); *Hogarth (*The Epistle to William Hogarth*, 1763, inspired by Hogarth's caricature of Wilkes); *The Duellist* (1764, an attack on Samuel Martin, who had wounded Wilkes in a duel); *The Candidate* (1764, directed against Lord Sandwich, 'Jemmy *Twitcher'); and *The Times* (1764), a more generalized attack on vice and homosexuality. *Gotham* (1764), which his old school friend *Cowper found a 'noble and beautiful poem', describes Churchill as Patriot King (see BOLINGBROKE) of an ideal state. Its heroic couplets mark the transition to the softer usages of the later 18th cent. Churchill died young at Boulogne on his way to visit Wilkes in France; Wilkes promised to edit his papers, but neglected to do so. His admirers included *Boswell (who defended him from Dr *Johnson's attacks, and discounted his violent prejudice against the Scots), Cowper, and *Byron, but, as Boswell predicted, his dependence on topical references has led to his neglect. His poems were edited, with a short life, by J. Laver (2 vols, 1933) and by D. Grant (1956).

Churchill, Frank, a character in J. Austen's *Emma*.

CHURCHILL, Rt. Hon. Sir Winston Leonard Spencer (1874–1965), eldest son of Lord Randolph Churchill (third son of the seventh duke of Marlborough). He entered the army in 1895 and served in Cuba, India, Egypt, and the Sudan; was present as a war correspondent at Spion Kop, Diamond Hill, etc.; and served in France as lieutenant-colonel in 1916. He was undersecretary of state for the colonies, 1906–8; president of the board of trade, 1908–10; home secretary, 1910–11; first lord of the admiralty, 1911–15; secretary of state for war, 1918–21; for the colonies, 1921–2; chancellor of the exchequer, 1924–9; prime minister, 1940–5 and 1951–5. Among his publications are: *The Story of the Malakand Field Force* (1898), *The River War* (1899), *London to Ladysmith via Pretoria* (1900), *Ian Hamilton's March* (1900), *Lord Randolph Churchill* (1906–7), *My African Journey* (1908), *Liberalism and the Social*

Problem (1909), *The World Crisis* (4 vols, 1923–9), *My Early Life* (1930), *Marlborough* (1933–8), *War Speeches 1940–5* (1946), *The Second World War* (6 vols, 1948–54), and *A History of the English-Speaking Peoples* (4 vols, 1956–8). He was awarded the *Nobel Prize for literature in 1953. Vols i and ii of the official biography, by his son Randolph Churchill (1911–68), appeared in 1966–7; Martin Gilbert succeeded as official biographer (vols iii–viii, 1971–88).

CHURCHYARD, Thomas (?1523–1604), at one time page to Henry Howard, earl of *Surrey. He lived a wandering life, partly as a soldier in Scotland, Ireland, France, and the Low Countries, partly as a hanger-on of the court and the nobility. He published, c.1552, *A Myrrour for Man*. Between 1560 and 1603 he issued a multitude of broadsheets and small volumes in verse and prose, several containing autobiographical pieces and notices of current events. His best-known works are *Shores Wife* (1563), in the *Mirror for Magistrates*, and the *Generall Rehearsall of Warres* (1579), in which he made use of his own experience as a soldier. Spenser in his *Colin Clouts Come Home Againe* refers to Churchyard as 'old *Palemon*. . . That sung so long untill quite hoarse he grew'.

CHUTE, John (1701–76), friend and correspondent of Horace *Walpole, whom he met in Florence in 1740. He remodelled his own family estate, the Vyne, in Hampshire, and contributed greatly to the creation of *Strawberry Hill. Walpole referred to him as 'my oracle in taste, the standard to whom I submitted my trifles, and the genius that presided over poor Strawberry!' (letter to *Mann, 27 May 1776). He has been credited with more fidelity to antiquity than his fellow connoisseur, the more fantastic Richard *Bentley.

CIBBER, Colley (1671–1757), son of Caius Cibber the sculptor, educated at Grantham School; he became an actor in 1690. His first play, *Love's Last Shift* (1696), of which *Congreve said that 'it has only in it a great many things that were like wit, that in reality were not wit', introduced the character of Sir Novelty Fashion, who was transformed into Lord Foppington in Vanbrugh's *The Relapse. Cibber wrote in his varied theatrical career many plays and adaptations, notably *She Would and She Would Not* (1702), *The Careless Husband* (1704), both comedies, and a successful adaptation of Shakespeare's *Richard III* (1700). *The Non-juror* (1717), a comedy based on Molière's *Tartuffe, was ridiculed by *Pope in a pamphlet, and Cibber became the hero of Pope's *Dunciad in its final edition, after becoming poet laureate in 1730. He attracted many enemies by his rudeness and vanity, and as a writer was more concerned with theatrical effect than with literary merit, but nevertheless made a significant contribution to 18th-cent. drama, particularly to the genre of *sentimental comedy; his plays were highly praised by *Smollett and *Walpole, and Samuel Derrick in 1759 described *The Careless Husband* as 'not only the best comedy in the English but in any other language'. In 1740 Cibber published his autobiography, *An Apology for the Life of Mr Colley Cibber, Comedian*, which gives a vivid picture of the theatrical life of the time, and contains striking portraits of *Betterton, Mrs *Bracegirdle, and others. His reference in this work to *Fielding as 'a broken wit' provoked the already hostile playwright-turned-novelist to yet more satire, notably in the opening chapter of *Joseph Andrews*. A biography, *Mr Cibber of Drury Lane* by R. H. Barker, was published in 1939.

Cibber, Mrs (1714–66), actress, see under CIBBER, T.

CIBBER, Theophilus (1703–58), son of Colley *Cibber, actor and hack-writer. He was born during the Great Storm and had an appropriately stormy career. His wildness and eccentricities provoked much scandal, as did his marriage in 1734 to Susanna Maria Arne (1714–66), sister of Dr *Arne. She became with his encouragement a distinguished tragic actress, but he also encouraged for mercenary reasons her relationship with a well-to-do lover, John Sloper, and all three became involved in disgrace and a notorious lawsuit in 1738. Her career recovered but his was ruined, and after struggling along in minor roles he was drowned in another storm on the way to keep an engagement at the Smock Alley Theatre in Dublin.

CICERO, Marcus Tullius (106–43 BC), referred to sometimes as Tully, the most influential of Roman prose writers. Born into a rich provincial family, he studied philosophy as well as rhetoric and law. Early success as a pleader and as a politician led to his becoming consul in 63 BC when he suppressed the conspiracy of Catiline. He supported the senatorial party against Julius *Caesar. After the assassination of Caesar he attacked Mark Antony in a series of speeches and was put to death. His influence on later ages has been remarkable for its variety. His writings left their mark on ethics, epistemology, and political thought, on men's ideals of conduct, on the development of oratory and letter writing, on literary style, the popularity of paradox, and the viability of Latin as an international language. During the Middle Ages Cicero figured primarily as a master of rhetoric. The textbook *De Inventione* remained the best known of his works and was imitated by *Alcuin. But some importance must be assigned to the *De Amicitia*, which served Aelred of Rievaulx and others as a model for disquisitions on Christian love, and also to the few erudite scholars who even at this early stage attempted to copy Cicero's style. It was enthusiasm for a more systematic form of such imitation that distinguished the Renaissance, when it had the result of popularizing for a time the Ciceronian period with writers like *Ascham and when it had the additional result of promoting that Ciceronianism deplored by G. *Harvey, which destroyed Latin as an international language by insisting on its limitation to the words and idioms that Cicero had employed. The Renaissance also paid careful attention to Cicero the thinker. His works contributed substantially to the late 16th-cent. revival of *Stoicism and Scepticism. Cicero stood behind *Hume's systematic doubt as he stood behind the half-hearted republicanism that led up to the French Revolution.

Cid, the (c.1030–99), the favourite hero of Spain in whose story history and myth are difficult to disentangle. Rodrigo Díaz de Vivar, el Cid Campeador ('el Seyd', the lord, 'Campeador', champion), of a noble Castilian family, rose to fame by his prowess in the war between Sancho of Castile and Sancho of Navarre, and in conflicts with the Moors. Having incurred the jealousy of Alphonso, king of Castile, he was banished and became a soldier of fortune, fighting at times for the Christians, at others for the Moors. His principal feat was the capture of Valencia from the Moors after a siege of nine months. He died of grief at the defeat of his force.

In myth his character has been glorified into a type of knightly and Christian virtue and patriotic zeal. His achievements are narrated in the *Poema de mio Cid* of the 12th cent. (the most important of early Spanish poems, some 3,700 irregular lines), in the Spanish Chronicle of the 14th cent., and in numerous ballads. The chronicles relating to him were translated by R. *Southey (1808). The Cid is the subject of the most famous drama of *Corneille. The Cid's horse was called Babieca, and his wife Ximena.

Cider with Rosie, see LEE, L.

Cinderella, a *fairy tale, from the French of *Perrault, translated by Robert Samber (?1729). Various operas have been based on this well-known fairy tale, including *Rossini's *La Cenerentola* (1817), and it is one of the most popular subjects for Christmas pantomimes.

CINTHIO (GIRALDI, Giambattista) (1504–73), born at Ferrara, the author of the *Hecatommithi*, or 'hundred tales', told after the manner of Boccaccio's *Decameron* by ten ladies and gentlemen sailing to Marseilles after the sack of Rome in 1527. Some of these were incorporated by Painter in his *Palace of Pleasure*, providing the plots of Shakespeare's *Othello* and *Measure for Measure*, and of plays by *Beaumont and *Fletcher and *Shirley. His nine tragedies and his treatise on tragedy had a decisive influence on the development of 16th-cent. drama in Italy; his first and most famous play, *Orbecche* (1541), showing divine retribution on the royal house of Persia, was closely modelled on *Seneca's *Thyestes*, and was full of Senecan blood and horrors. *Praz claims in *The Flaming Heart* (1958) that 'Cinthio provides the link between the Senecan tyrant and the Elizabethan villain', but P. R. Horne in *The Tragedies of Giambattista Cinthio Giraldi* (1962) questions this view.

circulating libraries, see LIBRARIES, CIRCULATING.

Circumlocution Office, the type of a government department, satirized in Dickens's *Little Dorrit.*

CIRENCESTER, Richard of (d. ?1401), a monk of St Peter's, Westminster, who compiled a *Speculum Historiale,* AD 447–1066. See BERTRAM, C.

citizen comedy, an early 17th-cent. type of play, usually set in contemporary London and dealing with the common life of the middle classes. Jonson's *Bartholomew Fair* and Middleton's *A Chaste Mayd in Cheap-side* are examples of the genre.

Citizen of the World, The, by *Goldsmith, a collection of 119 letters purporting to be written by or to an imaginary philosophic Chinaman, Lien Chi Altangi, residing in London. They first appeared as *Chinese Letters* in Newbery's *Public Ledger* between Jan. 1760 and Aug. 1761, and were republished under the above title in 1762.

They are a series of whimsical or satirical comments on English life and manners, with character sketches and episodes strung on a slender thread of narrative. The best-known character sketches are those of the 'Man in Black', a covert philanthropist, son of a good-hearted but feckless clergyman, which may contain hints of a self-portrait (Letters 26 and 27) and 'Beau' Tibbs, an affected nonentity who claims acquaintance with the great and whose wife, 'at once a slattern and a coquette', talks of countesses while she washes shirts (Letters 54 and 55).

City Heiress, The, a comedy by A. *Behn.

City Madam, The, a comedy by *Massinger, acted 1632, printed 1658.

The wife and daughters of Sir John Frugal have become proud and extravagant as a result of their wealth. When the girls drive away their suitors, Sir Maurice Lacy and Mr Plenty, by setting exorbitant conditions for marriage, Sir John decides to teach them a lesson and at the same time test the character of his brother Luke, a ruined prodigal whom he has taken into his house where he occupies a servile position, feigning virtue and humility. The merchant pretends to retire to a monastery, handing over his property and the management of his family to Luke, who then acts with great harshness to Lady Frugal and her daughters and Sir John's debtors and apprentices. Sir John returns with Lacy and Plenty disguised as Indians, and exposes Luke's hypocrisy. He is welcomed by his family, who promise to reform their ways.

City of Destruction, in Bunyan's *Pilgrim's Progress,* typifies the state of the worldly and irreligious.

'City of Dreadful Night, The', see under THOMSON, J. (1834–82).

City Witt, The, or *The Woman Wears the Breeches,* a comedy by *Brome, printed 1653, one of the best of Brome's comedies.

Crasy, a young citizen, has been ruined by his generous and easy-going disposition, and is cursed moreover with a virago for a mother-in-law, Mrs Pyannet Sneakup. From her he gets no mercy in his misfortune, and the friends whom he has helped in the past turn from him when he comes to them for assistance. His wife indulges her amorous proclivities as soon as he leaves her. He determines to show them all that his past good nature was not due to want of wit and, disguising himself in various characters, plays on their several vices to extort from them the money and jewels he has lent them or they have stolen from him. Aided by his servant Jeremy, who passes himself off as the rich widow Tryman, he contrives a marriage between the latter and his malignant brother-in-law, a drubbing for each of his wife's would-be lovers, and humiliation for his mother-in-law. The pedant Sarpego, with his comically apposite snatches of Latin, who refuses to repay him a loan of £10, does not escape his share of punishment.

'Civil Disobedience', see THOREAU.

Civil Wars between the Two Houses of Lancaster and York, The, an epic poem by S. *Daniel, of which the first four books appeared in 1595. The complete work, comprising eight books, was published 1609. It contains some 900 eight-line stanzas, of a grave and philosophic cast and marked by strong patriotism. The first book deals with the period from the Conquest to Hereford's rising against Richard II, the remaining seven with that from the Wars of the Roses to the accession of Edward IV and his marriage with Lady Elizabeth Grey.

CIXOUS, Hélène, see FEMINIST CRITICISM.

CLAIRMONT, Claire (1798–1879), daughter of Mary Clairmont, who became William *Godwin's second wife. She accompanied Mary Godwin, her stepsister, on Mary's elopement with *Shelley, and in spite of pursuit remained with them on the Continent, thus giving rise to many of the calumnies directed against Shelley. She returned to London with the Shelleys in 1816, fell in love with *Byron, and when he went to Switzerland induced the Shelleys to follow him with her. Byron's daughter Allegra was born to her in 1817. In 1818 Byron demanded the baby, offering to acknowledge and educate her. Strongly against her will, and against the advice of Shelley, Claire surrendered the child. Much to her distress, Byron in 1821 placed the child in a convent near Ravenna, where she died of a fever in 1822. Claire's subsequent life was spent in Russia, Italy, and Paris. See *The Journals of Claire Clairmont* (1968) and *The Clairmont Correspondence* (2 vols, 1995), ed. M. K. Stocking.

CLANCHY, Kate (1965–   ), poet, born in Glasgow. Her first book *Slattern* (1995) was acclaimed for its highly melodious yet taut handling of the language, and for its acute observation of men, marriages, and adolescents which often draws on her experience as a school-teacher in the East End of London. It includes a series of love poems remarkable for their lucid description of female desire and hurt. In *Samarkand* (1999) she addresses a greater range of issues, using longer, often narrative forms to explore masculine violence, national identity, fulfilment in love, grief, and, in the sequence 'The New Home Cabaret', the meaning of 'home'.

Clandestine Marriage, The, a comedy by *Colman the elder and *Garrick, performed 1766; it caused a rift between the two collaborators when Garrick refused to take the role of Lord Ogleby.

Lovewell, the clerk of Mr Sterling, a wealthy and purse-proud London merchant, has secretly married his employer's younger daughter Fanny. The father has arranged a marriage between his elder daughter and Sir John Melvil, nephew of Lord Ogleby, who accepts the alliance for mercenary reasons. Ogleby and Melvil arrive at Sterling's house to make the final arrangements, when Melvil suddenly reveals his aversion to the proposed match and his passion for the more attractive Fanny. The latter repels his advances, but hesitates to reveal her marriage. Melvil turns to Mr Sterling and induces him, for a financial consideration, to allow him to transfer his suit to Fanny. But now Mrs Heidelberg, Mr Sterling's wealthy sister (whose eccentric speech foreshadows that of Mrs *Malaprop), intervenes, resenting the affront to the family, and orders Fanny to be packed off from the house. Fanny in despair applies to the amorous old Ogleby, who, mistaking her inarticulate confession for a declaration of love for himself, announces that he himself will marry her, thereby increasing the confusion. Finally a lover is discovered in Fanny's bedroom, and the household assemble outside the door for the exposure of the villain. When he turns out to be Lovewell, Lord Ogleby good-naturedly intervenes on behalf of the guilty couple and all ends well.

CLANVOWE, Sir John (d. 1391), possibly born in Hergest, Hereford, and died near Constantinople, a diplomat and a member of the king's household. He was one of the Lollard Knights, and the author of the pacifist and puritanical work *The Two Ways*. He was a friend of *Chaucer, and he may also have been the author of *The Cuckoo and the Nightingale or The Boke of Cupide*, an elegant debate-poem in 290 lines which was included by *Skeat in his *Chaucerian and Other Pieces*. The manuscript ends *Explicit Clanvowe*, but this may just as well refer to Sir John's son Thomas (d. 1410). *Wordsworth translated it, and it was said in the 19th cent. to be 'one of the prettiest things in Medieval Literature'.

The Works of Sir John Clanvowe, ed. V. J. Scattergood (1975) (i.e. *The Two Ways* and *The Cuckoo and the Nightingale*); K. B. McFarlane, *Lancastrian Kings and Lollard Knights* (1972), 165 ff., 197 ff., 230 ff.

Clapham Sect, the name given by Sydney *Smith to a group of evangelical and anti-slave-trade philanthropists, centred on Clapham, whose members included *Wilberforce, Zachary Macaulay (father of T. B. *Macaulay), the scholar and pamphleteer Granville Sharp, and the Thornton family, ancestors of E. M. *Forster.

Clare, Angel, a character in Hardy's *Tess of the D'Urbervilles*.

CLARE, John (1793–1864), poet, the son of a labourer, born in Helpstone, Northamptonshire, a neighbourhood to which he remained deeply attached, where he worked as hedge-setter and day labourer. In 1820 he published *Poems Descriptive of Rural Life and Scenery*, and in the same year married Martha Turner, having parted from his first love, Mary Joyce, a sorrow which troubled him throughout his life. His successful first volume was followed by *The Village Minstrel* (1821), *The Shepherd's Calendar* (1827), and *The Rural Muse* (1835). In 1832 he left his native cottage for Northborough, only 4 miles away, but the move, to one so deeply attached to place, was disturbing, and reinforced the theme of loss in his work. In 1837 he was admitted as insane to an asylum in High Beach, Epping, whence he escaped in 1841, walking home to Northamptonshire in the delusion that he would there be reunited with Mary, to whom he thought himself married. He was once more certified insane, and spent the rest of his life in Northampton General Asylum, where he was allowed much freedom. The declining sales of his work may have contributed to his mental troubles, for by the 1830s the vogue for rural poetry and 'ploughman' poets such as *Burns and R. *Bloomfield was passing; and Clare's work remained little read until this century, when various new editions of his poetry, autobiographical prose, and letters made it available once more, together with much previously unpublished work. Clare is now recognized as a poet of great truth and power; his much anthologized asylum poems have perhaps tended to obscure the real nature of his gifts, and recently more attention has been paid to his highly personal evocations of landscape and place. His best poems ('Remembrances', 'The Flitting', 'Decay') demonstrate a complex sensibility and fine organization, and have been variously read as laments for lost love and talent, for the death of rural England, or for lost innocence. Unlike many poets from a similar background, he never succumbed to the taste of his patrons for artificial poetic diction (although he greatly admired James *Thomson) and insisted to his publisher John *Taylor that he would continue to write in his own language, dialect, and idiosyncratic grammar. Many poets, including E. *Blunden, G. *Grigson, and C. *Day-Lewis, have written of their admiration for his work and contributed towards his fuller recognition. His *Poems* (1935), *Prose* (1951), and *Letters* (1951) were edited by J. W. and A. Tibble; *The Shepherd's Calendar*, and his *Later Poems* (ed. E. Robinson and D. Powell, with M. Grainger) in 1984. (See *John Clare: A Biography* (2003) by Jonathan Sate.)

CLARENDON, Edward Hyde, earl of (1609–74), educated at Magdalen Hall, Oxford; he later studied law. He entered Parliament in 1640 and at first sided with the popular party, but as a strong Anglican he was from 1641 onwards one of the chief supporters and advisers of the king. He followed Prince Charles into exile to Scilly and Jersey, where he began his History. At the Restoration he returned as lord chancellor and played a leading role in reorganizing the country, but fell out of favour, partly through the ill-success of the Dutch war; he was impeached in 1667 and fled to France, where he spent his last years revising and completing his history and writing his own life. He died at Rouen. His daughter Anne Hyde had in 1660 married the future James II.

The History—*The True Historical Narrative of the Rebellion and Civil Wars in England*—was first printed from a transcript under the supervision of Clarendon's son in 1702–4, but the first true text was edited by W. D. Macray (6 vols, 1888). His autobiography, *The Life of Edward, Earl of Clarendon*, appeared in 1759. The *History of the Rebellion* (as it is frequently known) is a composite work, put together from material written at different periods and in widely differing circumstances, and is uneven in accuracy and penetration, but it remains a classic work, in part written with an eye on posterity, for publication when 'the passion, rage and fury of this time shall be forgotten'. It is also an important contribution to the art of *biography and autobiography, and memorable for its portraits of figures as varied as *Falkland, *Godolphin, *Laud, and *Strafford. Clarendon also wrote a history of the Irish rebellion, of lesser interest, published in 1721. A useful volume of *Selections from Clarendon*, ed. G. Huehns, appeared in 1955, and was reprinted with an introduction by H. Trevor-Roper in 1978.

Clarendon's works were presented to the University of Oxford by his heirs, and from the profits of the History a new printing-house, which bears his name, was built for *Oxford University Press.

Clarion, a socialist weekly which ran from 1891 to 1932, founded by R. *Blatchford, his brother Montague Blatchford, A. M. Thompson, and E. F. Fay.

Clarissa: *or The History of a Young Lady*, an *epistolary novel by S. *Richardson, published 1748 (for 1747)–1749, in eight volumes. About one-third of the work (which is in all over a million words) consists of the letters of Clarissa and Lovelace, mainly written to Anna Howe and John Belford respectively, but there are over 20 correspondents in all, displaying many points of view and variations in style.

Lovelace, a handsome, dashing rake, is courting Arabella Harlowe, the elder sister of Clarissa. The Harlowes are an acquisitive, ambitious, 'narrow-souled' family, and when Lovelace transfers his affections to Clarissa they decide he is not good enough and that Clarissa must marry the wealthy but ugly Solmes, whom she detests. When she refuses she is locked up and humiliated. Lovelace, cleverly representing himself as her deliverer, plays on her fears, convinces her that he is forwarding her reconciliation with her family, and persuades her to escape under his protection to London. There he establishes her in a superior brothel, which she at first supposes to be respectable lodgings. She unwaveringly resists his advances and he, enraged by her intransigence, is also attracted by it and finds his love and respect for her increase. Her emotions are likewise deeply confused; she is fascinated by his charm and wit, but distrusts him and refuses his eventual proposals of marriage. In his growing insistence, Lovelace overreaches himself, interfering with her letters, deceiving her over a supposed emissary from her family, violently assaulting her, and cunningly ensnaring her after her escapes. As she unhappily but stubbornly resists, he becomes more obsessive in his determination to conquer, and makes an attempt to rape her. He claims to believe her resistance is no more than prudery and that, once subdued, she will turn to him: 'Is not *this* the hour of trial—And in *her*, of the trial of the virtue of her whole Sex, so long premeditated, so long threatened?—Whether her frost be frost indeed? Whether her virtue be principle?' (vol. v, Letter 31). To Clarissa chastity represents identity, and the climax of her tragedy comes when Lovelace, abetted by the women of the house, drugs and rapes her, an event he reports in one of the shortest letters of the work: 'And now, Belford, I can go no farther. The affair is over. Clarissa lives.' (Vol. v, Letter 32.)

Slowly Clarissa loses grip of her reason, and Lovelace realizes that he has lost the very dominance he had hoped to establish. Cut off from family, friends, and even correspondence, Clarissa eventually escapes, only to find herself trapped in a debtor's prison. She is rescued by Belford, who looks after her with affectionate care. Lovelace is overwhelmed by remorse. Clarissa recovers her sanity, but almost ceases to write, and her long decline and Christian preparation for death are reported largely in letters by Belford. After her death her cousin, Colonel Morden, kills Lovelace in a duel. Because of its great length, the novel has been more admired than read, but it has always been held in high critical esteem; the characters of the protagonists are developed with great subtlety, and the irresolvable nature of their conflict takes on an emblematic and tragic quality unique for its author and its period.

CLARK, Brian (1932–), stage and television playwright, born in Bournemouth and educated at Redland College of Education, Central School of Speech and Drama, and Nottingham University. His best-known work, *Whose Life Is It Anyway?*, about a permanently paralysed man and the debates surrounding his resolution to die, was originally written as a TV play and screened in 1972; it was successfully adapted for the stage (Mermaid Theatre) in 1978. Other plays include *Can You Hear Me at the Back?* (1979), about events surrounding a new town's fifteenth anniversary, and the ten-part TV serial *Telford's Change* (1979).

CLARK, Kenneth Mackenzie, Lord (1903–83), author, art historian, and public official. The only child of wealthy and neglectful parents, he was educated at Winchester (where he aspired to be an artist) and at Oxford, where he turned to art history. His first book, *The Gothic Revival* (1928), was hailed as original and audacious; his approach, derived from *Ruskin and also from *Berenson (with whom he studied), was interpretative rather than pedantic. He was director of the National Gallery from 1934 to 1945, and held many other public posts in later life. Other publications include a study of *Leonardo da Vinci (1939), *Landscape into Art* (1949), and his major work, *The Nude: A Study of Ideal Art* (1953); also two volumes of autobiography, *Another Part of the Wood* (1974) and *The Other Half* (1977). His television series *Civilization*, published in book form in 1969, was popular with a very large audience. His son Alan Clark (1928–99), historian and parliamentarian, acquired notoriety for his frank political *diaries.

CLARKE, Arthur C(harles) (1917–), prolific and popular writer of *science fiction, whose great technical expertise in the realm of aeronautics and astronautics is manifested both in his fiction, which includes *Childhood's End* (1953), *The City and the Stars* (1956), *The Nine Billion Names of God* (1967), and *2001: A Space Odyssey* (1968), and in his many non-fiction works on space travel.

CLARKE, Austin (1896–1974), Irish poet and verse dramatist, born in Dublin, and educated at the Jesuit Belvedere College and University College, Dublin (in the footsteps of *Joyce). He worked for some 15 years in England as journalist and book reviewer, returning to Dublin in 1937. He published some 18 volumes of poetry, from his first, *The Vengeance of Fionn* (1917, a narrative poem based on the story of Diarmid and *Grainne), to his *Collected Poems* of 1974. His early work is much influenced by *Yeats and the *Celtic Twilight, but much of his later work is sharply satiric and highly critical of his own nation's attitudes; in form it is subtle and complex, with an unobtrusive technical expertise. Clarke was also greatly interested in verse drama; he founded the Dublin Verse-Speaking Society in 1938, which developed into the Lyric Theatre Company and performed many of his own plays as well as those of *Bottomley, T. S. *Eliot, and others. Clarke's plays are rooted in medieval Irish legend, but many have pantomime or farcical elements; he considered that the tradition of verse drama at

the *Abbey Theatre had suffered through too much solemnity. His *Collected Plays* were published in 1963. He also wrote three prose romances, various works on Irish literature, and two autobiographical volumes, *Twice round the Black Church* (1962) and *A Penny in the Clouds* (1968).

CLARKE, Charles Cowden- (1787–1877), the son of *Keats's enlightened schoolmaster, and a close friend of the poet. Keats's 'Epistle to Charles Cowden-Clarke' is full of affection and gratitude. Cowden-Clarke lectured frequently between 1834 and 1856 on Shakespeare and general literature, and many of his lectures were published. With his wife Mary Victoria Cowden-Clarke (below) he produced editions of Shakespeare, G. *Herbert, and other poets. Also with his wife he wrote *Recollections of Writers* (1878), a lively and valuable collection of reminiscences of their close friends Keats, *Lamb, Mary *Lamb, Leigh *Hunt, Douglas *Jerrold, and *Dickens.

CLARKE, Gillian (1937–), Welsh poet, born in Cardiff. Her first poems appeared in *Poetry Wales* in 1970. She was editor of the *Anglo-Welsh Review* from 1975 to 1984. Her three main collections of verse are *Letter from a Far Country* (1982), *Letting in the Rumour* (1989), and *The King of Britain's Daughter* (1993); her *Selected Poems* appeared in 1985 and her *Collected Poems* in 1997. Her work, which combines a lyrical intensity with keen observation of the natural world, explores the role of women in domestic situations and the complexities of Welsh myth. She is president of the Taliesin Trust, which runs Ty Newydd, the writers' centre at Llanystumdwy, near Criccieth in Gwynedd.

CLARKE, John Cooper, See PERFORMANCE POETRY.

CLARKE, Mary Victoria Cowden- (1809–98), the joint author, with her husband Charles Cowden-Clarke (above), of *Recollections of Writers*, and the author of the excellent *Complete Concordance to Shakespeare*, published in monthly parts in 1844–5.

CLARKE, Samuel (1675–1729), educated at Caius College, Cambridge, metaphysician, moralist, and a defender of rational theology; although a critic of the *Deists, he had sympathy with some of their teaching. He believed that there exists in the nature of things, an immutable agreement or harmony of certain things and circumstances, apparent to the understanding. Clarke's principal works were his *Boyle Lectures delivered in 1704 and 1705, published 1705–6, *A Demonstration of the Being and Attributes of God and A Discourse Concerning the Unchangeable Obligation of Natural Religion*.

CLARKSON, Laurence (1615–67), a pamphleteer whose spiritual autobiography *The Lost Sheep Found* (1660) charts his progress through many religious affiliations; from his Church of England boyhood in Lancashire he became Anabaptist, Seeker, Ranter, and finally *Muggletonian, suffering imprisonment for his views. His tracts, written with originality, force, and feeling, shed an interesting light on the adventurous and speculative ideas of the age: in *A Single Eye All Light, No Darkness*, he argued that all things, even sin, are from God: 'What act soever is done by thee in light and love, is light and lovely, though it be that act called adultery' (1650).

classicism, classic, are terms used in several different and at times overlapping senses. A 'literary classic' is a work considered first-rate or excellent of its kind, and therefore standard, fit to be used as a model or imitated; a series such as the *World's Classics includes work from many different genres, including poetry, fiction, autobiography, biography, letters, and history. More narrowly, 'classicism' may be taken to denote the deliberate imitation of the works of antiquity, and in this sense is often qualified as *'neo-classicism', which flourished in England in the late 17th and 18th cents. An elaboration of this concept leads to a distinction between classicism and *Romanticism; the Romantic movement, which dominated the early 19th cent., and which saw itself in part as a revolt against classicism, led in turn to a reaction at the beginning of the 20th cent. from writers such as T. S. *Eliot and T. E. *Hulme, whose concern was to stress man's limitations rather than his perfectibility and illimitable aspirations, and who emphasized the virtues of formal restraint in literature rather than the virtues of inspiration and exuberance.

The shades of meaning which the terms have acquired lead at times to apparent confusion: when one speaks of the drama of *Racine and *Corneille as 'classical', and the drama of *Shakespeare or *Hugo as 'romantic', one is not depriving Shakespeare or Hugo of classic status, nor suggesting that Shakespeare himself had any sense of such a contrast; whereas Hugo wrote as a conscious rebel against classicism. *Auden and Dylan *Thomas, near-contemporaries, are frequently described as exemplars of, respectively, the classical and the romantic in modern poetry, and both are widely considered classics of their own period and aesthetic approach. The use of the phrase 'a minor classic' raises yet more problems of definition, indicating the adaptability rather than the precision of the term.

CLAUDEL, Paul (1868–1955), French poet and dramatist. He spent 40 years abroad as a diplomat, mostly in the United States, South America, and the Far East. Converted to Catholicism in 1886, he expressed a passionate and dogmatic personality in a form of versification he made uniquely his own: the long magniloquent phrases of the so-called *verset claudélien* which he forged out of the prose of *Rimbaud's *Les Illuminations* and the Old Testament. His major plays, *L'Annonce faite à Marie* (1912; *Tidings Brought to Mary*, 1916) and *Le Soulier de satin* (1928–9; perf. 1943), and his *Cinq Grandes Odes* (1910) exerted a strong influence on the following generation of poets, notably Pierre-Jean Jouve, but left very little mark on English writing.

CLAUDE LORRAIN (1600–82), landscape painter from Lorrain, who worked mainly in Rome. He was the first artist to be inspired by the Roman Campagna and its legends. In the 18th cent. the English traveller on the *Grand Tour was deeply moved by Claude's idyllic landscapes and vision of lost splendour; many of his pictures and engravings were brought back to England where they deeply influenced the way artists and writers looked at the natural world. Poets like James *Thomson and J. *Dyer frequently invoke Claude's name to suggest a Virgilian serenity, contrasting with *Rosa's landscapes. Landscape gardeners emulated Claude's compositions, which were important to the theory of the *picturesque. Enthusiasts looked at the Lake District as though it were a sequence of pictures by Claude or Rosa, and Thomas *Gray carried a 'Claude glass', a blackened convex mirror which enabled the traveller to pick out an instant Claudian view. Romantic poets responded more intensely to the elusive beauty of Claude's later works, and the 'fairyland' beauty of *The Enchanted Castle* (London, National Gallery) moved both *Hazlitt and *Keats. Keats was directly inspired by it. Claude's reputation waned with *Ruskin, who saw him as a pallid precursor of *Turner.

CLAUDIAN (Claudius Claudianus) (fl. *c.* AD 395–404), the last great Latin poet to be a pagan, was born in Alexandria and wrote in Rome. His short epic *De Raptu Proserpinae* influenced Spenser's account of the garden of Proserpina (*Faerie Queene*, II. vii. 52) and was translated by Leonard Digges (1617). One of his shorter works, the idyll on the 'Old Man of Verona', was translated by *Cowley.

Claudio, (1) the lover of Hero in Shakespeare's *Much Ado about Nothing*; (2) the brother of Isabella and betrothed husband of Julietta in his *Measure for Measure*.

Claudius, in Shakespeare's *Hamlet*, brother of old Hamlet and husband of his widow *Gertrude. Shakespeare may have taken his name from the incestuous Roman Emperor Claudius (10 BC–AD 54), who appears as the hero-narrator of the well-known novel *I, Claudius* (1934), by R. *Graves.

CLAVELL, John (1603–42), a highwayman, condemned to death and then pardoned (1627). He published a metrical autobiography, *Recantation of an Ill Led Life* (1628), which begins 'Stand and Deliver' to your observation | Right serious thoughts', and proceeds to describe the highway law and organization of thieves. *The Soddered Citizen*, a comedy of which he was reputed author, was performed by the King's Men c.1630.

CLAVERHOUSE, Graham of, see GRAHAM OF CLAVERHOUSE.

Claverings, The, a novel by A. *Trollope, published 1867.

Harry Clavering is a gentleman-engineer who becomes engaged to his master's daughter, steady Florence Burton. Julia Brabazon, an old flame, returns to London newly widowed after marrying the dissipated Lord Ongar for money. Harry is called in to protect her from the machinations of the sycophantic Sophie Gordeloup and the scheming Count Pateroff, and Lady Ongar offers to renew their old engagement, but Harry remains true to Florence. He gets his reward when his rich relations go to their fate in a fishing accident in the North Sea, and he becomes heir to the Clavering fortunes.

Clayhanger, see BENNETT, ARNOLD.

Claypole, Noah, in Dickens's *Oliver Twist, a fellow apprentice of the hero in the establishment of Mr Sowerberry, the undertaker, and subsequently one of Fagin's gang of thieves.

Cleanness (or *Purity*), an alliterative poem in 1,812 lines from the second half of the 14th cent., the only manuscript of which is the famous Cotton Nero A. X which is also the sole manuscript of *Pearl, *Patience, and Sir *Gawain and the Green Knight. It deals with three subjects from the Scriptures and is hardly more than a vigorous paraphrase of them: the Flood, the destruction of Sodom and Gomorrah, and the fall of Belshazzar. It has some passages of great power, such as the denunciation of Sodom and the description of the destruction of Babylon. Modern critical practice usually treats the four poems in the manuscript as the work of a single author, regarding *Cleanness* as the earliest on grounds of quality (*Pearl* comes first in the manuscript). There is an edition by J. J. Anderson (1977).

CLELAND, John (1709–89). He was educated at Westminster School, became consul in Smyrna, worked in the East India Company in Bombay, and spent much time in wandering and travel. Although *Memoirs of a Woman of Pleasure* (often known as *Fanny Hill*), published 1748–9, had an enormous sale, and brought his publisher £10,000, it brought him only 20 guineas. He was summoned before the Privy Council for indecency, but discharged. In 1751 he published the *Memoirs of a Coxcomb,* and in 1764 *The Surprises of Love.* He wrote various plays, engaged in much journalistic work, and between 1766 and 1769 published three philological studies, with special references to Celtic.

CLEMENS, S. L., see TWAIN.

CLEMENT OF ALEXANDRIA (b. *c.* AD 160), a Greek Father of the Church, born in Alexandria, and the first to apply Greek culture and philosophy to the exposition of Christianity. Of his four surviving works, the *Exhortation to the Greeks* is an attempt to convert the Greeks to Christianity, influenced by the Platonist Christian exegete Philo. See R. B. Tollinton, *Clement of Alexandria: A Study in Christian Liberalism* (2 vols, 1914).

CLEMO, Jack (Reginald John) (1916–94), a poet, born at St Austell, Cornwall, the son of a clay-worker. From childhood he suffered from poor eyesight and, subsequently, deafness, eventually becoming completely blind. He came to general critical notice with his novel *Wilding Graft* (1948), which was admired by T. F. *Powys. His poetry includes *The Map of Clay* (1961), with an introduction by Charles *Causley, and *The Echoing Tip* (1971), which evoke with a kind of visionary grimness the tormented landscapes of the clay pits and express his own Calvinist faith. *Broad Autumn* (1975) was followed by *The Bouncing Hills* (1983), *The Shadowed Bed* (a novel, 1986), *A Different Drummer* (1986), *Selected Poems* (1988), and *Approach to Murano* (1992). He also wrote two volumes of autobiography, *Confessions of a Rebel* (1949) and *The Marriage of a Rebel* (1980).

Clennam, Arthur and Mrs, characters in Dickens's *Little Dorrit.

Cleon, (1) governor of Tarsus in Shakespeare's *Pericles*; (2) title of a poem by R. Browning, included in *Men and Women.

Cleopatra, a tragedy in blank verse by S. *Daniel, published 1594.

It is on the Senecan model, and deals with the story of Cleopatra after the death of Antony. Octavius Caesar endeavours to persuade her to leave the monument that she had caused to be built, in order that he may have her to grace his triumph. Feigning to yield, she asks permission first to sacrifice to the ghost of Antonius. After the performance of the rites she dines with great magnificence, and by her order a basket of figs is brought her which contains an asp. With this she does herself to death. Her son Caesarion about the same time is murdered at Rhodes and the race of the Ptolemies becomes extinct.

clerihew, an epigrammatic verse form invented by Edmund Clerihew *Bentley, consisting of two rhymed couplets, usually dealing with the character or career of a well-known person, e.g.

> Sir James Jeans
> Always says what he means;
> He is really perfectly serious
> About the Universe being Mysterious.

'Clerk's Tale, The', see CANTERBURY TALES, 9.

CLEVELAND, John (1613–58), *Cavalier poet, born at Loughborough, the son of a clergyman, and educated at Cambridge. He joined the king's camp in Oxford during the Civil War as an active Royalist; he wrote there one of his best-known satires 'The Rebel Scot', which contains the couplet commended by Dr *Johnson, 'Had Cain been Scot, God would have changed his doom | Not forced him wander, but confined him home.' Although criticized during his life as an academic and coterie poet, his works were highly popular, and 25 editions (none, apparently, with his supervision) appeared between 1647 and 1700. *Dryden's opinion of him as one 'who gives us common thoughts in abstruse words' eventually prevailed, but the 20th-cent. revival of interest in the *metaphysicals and in political satire has led to more serious consideration. An edition by B. Morris and E. Withington appeared in 1967.

CLIFFORD, Lady Anne, countess of Pembroke, Dorset, and Montgomery (1590–1676), sole surviving child of George, the third Duke of Cumberland, who excluded her as a female from his baronial titles and estates. She focused her life on resisting both her husbands, the earls of Dorset and Pembroke, and James I, to win possession of her titles and Westmorland estates, to which she triumphantly moved in 1649. She assembled a manuscript archive, with scholarly apparatus, and commissioned a magnificent dynastic triptych to substantiate her claim. Her personal diaries of the years 1603, 1616–17, and 1619 (the 'Knole diary') chronicle her marital estrangements and her implacable refusal to surrender her dynastic claim, even to being locked in a room with King James, her uncle, cousin, lords, a lord chief justice, and her husband: 'but I would never agree to it without Westmoreland. At which the king grew in a great chaff.' She also left a 'day book', an intimate record of how she lived and felt in extreme old age as matriarch, landowner, and sheriff in Westmorland. V. *Sackville-West, herself debarred inheritance of Knole by her sex, edited *The Diary of Lady Anne Clifford* (1923); see also R. T. Spence, *Lady Anne Clifford* (1997).

CLIFFORD, Lord, the Shepherd, see SHEPHERD, LORD CLIFFORD, THE.

CLIFFORD, Martin, see HAMILTON, CHARLES.

CLIVE, Mrs Caroline Archer (1801–73), who wrote chiefly under the initial 'V'. She was lame from an early age and the consequent privations of her infirmity were often reflected in her verse. Her first volume of poems, *IX Poems by V* (1840), attracted high praise, but her reputation rests on her powerful novel *Paul Ferroll* (1855); the hero murders his wife who had prevented him from marrying the woman he loved, escapes suspicion, and marries his true love, who, after 18 years of happy marriage, dies of shock when Paul Ferroll voluntarily confesses his crime in order to save innocent suspects. By substituting villain for hero, *Paul Ferroll* was a forerunner of the purely sensational novel (see SENSATION, NOVEL OF). *Why Paul Ferroll Killed his Wife* (1860) was less successful. Mrs Clive was accidentally burned to death while writing in her boudoir.

CLIVE, Kitty (Catherine) (1711–85), the celebrated comic actress, renowned for her red face and vulgar good nature. She was a close friend of Horace *Walpole, and his neighbour at *Strawberry Hill, where he gave her for life a small house called Little Strawberry Hill, later known as Cliveden.

Clockmaker, The, see HALIBURTON.

Clockwork Orange, A, a novel by A. *Burgess, published in 1962. Set in the near future, it is the first-person narration of Alex, who recounts his life from the age of 15 as leader of a gang of thugs to his emergence from State Jail 84F after a period of experimental aversion therapy which has left him unable to enjoy his former pleasures of rape, assault, and listening to Beethoven while indulging in fantasies of crime. Written in what Alex calls 'nadsat', which is a brilliantly inventive mix of neologisms and archaisms, the novel conjures up a lawless dystopian world of youth violence and institutional mind-manipulation in which Alex eventually comes to see himself as a self-pitying victim. The novel was adapted by Stanley Kubrick (1971), who later withdrew his film from distribution in England for disputed reasons, connected to allegations that it acted as an incitement to violence.

Cloddipole, one of the rustics in Gay's *The Shepherd's Week*.

Cloister and the Hearth, The, a novel by C. *Reade, published 1861.

The story is set in the 15th cent. Gerard, the son of a mercer living in Tergou in Holland, is destined to enter the Church, but falls in love with Margaret Brandt, whose father is an impoverished scholar suspected of sorcery. They become betrothed, but the burgomaster Ghysbrecht, together with Gerard's scheming brothers and his outraged father, prevent the marriage and succeed in having the young man imprisoned. He contrives to escape and finds Margaret, but he is relentlessly pursued and has to leave Holland. He travels through Germany and Burgundy to Italy, encountering many dangers and hardships and meeting all conditions of men, from bishop to beggar, in palace, monastery, road, and tavern: the richness and complexity of detail is intended to assist the sense of 'reality' sought by the author. While he is in Italy Gerard hears of Margaret's death; not realizing the news is a trick, he throws himself in despair into a world of gambling, drinking, and women. Margaret meanwhile has borne his son and lives in wretchedness at his loss. Eventually sickened by his life, Gerard renounces the world, takes his vows as a Dominican monk, and in the guise of Father Clement travels slowly back to Holland. He is overjoyed to find Margaret alive, but agonized at his predicament, for his love for her is as strong as ever. Because of his son he allows himself to return to her and becomes accepted as the vicar of Gouda. The pain of his struggles to remain true to his vows slowly subsides, and he and Margaret achieve a peace in which passion is subsumed in the love of God. However, when she is dying, both confess to each other the strength of their human love. Their son, the end of the story indicates, is the future philosopher *Erasmus.

The novel was based on Reade's short story 'A Good Fight' (published in *Once a Week* in 1859), in which the fight refers to the struggle against sexual feeling, a theme common in Reade's work. The novel arose from his discovery, in 'a musty chronicle' (the *Colloquia* and the letters of Erasmus), of the story of Erasmus's father, an obscure cleric.

Clorin, a character in *The Faithful Shepherdess* by J. Fletcher.

Clorinda, in Tasso's *Jerusalem Delivered*, a leader of the pagan forces, the daughter of the king of Ethiopia, who had been lost as a baby in the forest and suckled by a tigress. Tancred, who has fallen in love with her, wounds her fatally and unwittingly in a night attack, and she pleads for baptism before dying in his arms.

Cloten, the clownish son of the queen in Shakespeare's *Cymbeline*.

Cloud-cuckoo-land (Nephelococcygia), an imaginary city built in the air in *The Birds* of *Aristophanes.

Cloud of Unknowing, The, a mystical prose work, probably from the north-east Midlands, dating from the second half of the 14th cent., and one of the most admired products of the Middle English mystical tradition. Its popularity is indicated by its survival in 17 manuscripts; the author was presumably a priest, though no more certain identification of him has resulted from the many recent speculations about him. He also wrote *The Book of Privy Counselling*, *The Epistle of Prayer*, and *Deonise Hid Divinite*, in the opinion of most commentators; it is likely that three other works linked with the *Cloud* in the various manuscripts are by him too: *Benjamin Minor*, *The Epistle of Discretion in Stirrings*, and *Of Discerning of Spirits*. None of the other works or translations has the same life or cogency in argument of the *Cloud* itself. Ed. P. Hodgson (EETS 218, 1944; rev. 1958); trans. C. Wolters (1961).

CLOUGH, Arthur Hugh (1819–61), son of a Liverpool cotton merchant, a pupil at T. *Arnold's Rugby, and a scholar at Balliol College, Oxford. He took a second and told Dr Arnold in June 1841 'I have failed.' He became a fellow of Oriel, but resigned; he became principal of University Hall, London, then an examiner in the Education Office. His career was inconclusive, and he was tormented by doubt when the Rugby indoctrination was challenged by the religious ferment of Oxford. Yet out of religious doubt and minutely analysed uncertainties Clough wrote lasting poetry, and *Gosse called his 'the sympathetic modern accent'. He died in Florence, and M. Arnold's *'Thyrsis' was written to commemorate his death.

The Bothie of Tober-na-Vuolich (1848), originally published as *The Bothie of Toper-na-fuosich*, is a poem in hexameters about a student reading party in Scotland. Philip falls in love with Elspie, a peasant who represents 'work, mother earth, and the objects of living'. There is no place for them in English society, so 'they rounded the globe to New Zealand'. M. Arnold said the poem had 'freshness, life, naturalness . . . the true Homeric ring'.

'Amours de Voyage' (first published in the *Atlantic Monthly*, 1858) is similar in form, but *epistolary. Claude, travelling in Rome at the time of the siege, is paralysed by 'terrible notions of duty', unable to form political commitment or to respond to Rome, which he finds 'rubbishy'. (Of St Peter's, 'Alas, Bernini has filled it with sculpture.') He cannot follow his impulse to court Mary, whose mother 'grates the fastidious ear with a slightly mercantile accent'. Clough wrote in a letter, 'Poetry should deal more than at present it usually does with general wants and ordinary feelings.'

Clough is also remembered for 'Dipsychus' (published posthumously, 1865), a Faustian dialogue set in Venice in which the tempting spirit describes the protagonist as 'An o'ergrown baby, sucking at the dugs | Of instinct dry long since'. The best known of his shorter poems, sharply contrasted, are 'Say not the struggle nought availeth' and the satirical 'The Latest Decalogue', both published posthumously in *Poems, 1862*, with a Memoir by F. T. *Palgrave.

Club, the (sometimes known later as the Literary Club), an informal group founded by Dr *Johnson at the suggestion of Joshua *Reynolds in the winter of 1763–4. It met at the Turk's Head, Soho, and the nine original members included *Goldsmith and *Burke; those elected later included *Percy (elected 1765), *Garrick and *Boswell (1773), C. J. *Fox and *Steevens (1774), Adam *Smith (1775), *Banks (1778), and *Malone (1782). See COFFEE HOUSES.

Clumsy, Sir Tunbelly, a character in Vanbrugh's *The Relapse* and Sheridan's *A Trip to Scarborough*.

CLUYSENAAR, Anne (1936–   ), poet, and daughter of the painter John Cluysenaar, born in Brussels; she moved to Britain in 1939. Educated at Trinity College, Dublin, and Edinburgh University, she has published several volumes of poetry, including *Nodes* (1971), *Double Helix* (1982), and *Timeslips* (1997), which includes the haunting sequence 'The Vaughan Variations', meditations on the lives and work of Henry and Thomas *Vaughan. Her bilingual, painterly, and exilic experience has led her to a nature poetry which ponders displacement in space and in geological and historical time. She lives in Usk, Wales.

Clym of the Clough, see ADAM BELL.

CNUT, or **CNUTR,** see CANUTE.

Coart, Couwaert, or **Cuwaert,** the name of the hare in *Reynard the Fox*.

Coavinses, in Dickens's *Bleak House*, see NECKETT.

COBB, Richard Charles (1917–96), historian and author, educated at Merton College, Oxford, professor of modern history at Oxford 1973–84. Most of his works deal with French history and sociology and provide an evocative, eclectic portrayal of French life and culture; they include *Reactions to the French Revolution* (1972), *Death in Paris 1795–1801* (1978), and *Promenades* (1980). *Still Life* (1983), a memoir of his childhood in Tunbridge Wells, was followed by *A Classical Education* (1985), *People and Places* (1985), and *Something to Hold Onto* (1988).

COBBE, Frances Power (1822–1908), philanthropist and author of works mainly on religious and social questions. She was a strong theist, supporter of women's rights, a prominent anti-vivisectionist, and became associated with Mary Carpenter in her ragged school and reformatory work. Her numerous writings include *The Theory of Intuitive Morals* (1855–7), *Broken Lights* (1864), *Darwinism in Morals* (1872), and *The Duties of Women* (1881). Her travels in Italy and the East are described in *Italics* (1864) and *Cities of the Past* (1864). Her autobiography appeared in 1904.

COBBETT, William (1763–1835), the son of a farmer near Farnham, and self-educated, who enlisted as a soldier and served in New Brunswick from 1784 to 1791. He obtained his discharge, brought an accusation of peculation against some of his former officers, and in 1792 retired, first to France then to America, to avoid prosecution. There he published in 1796 *The Life and Adventures of Peter Porcupine*, a provocatively pro-British work, and in 1801 his *Works*, critical of America. He returned to England in 1800, and became an anti-radical journalist, founding and writing *Cobbett's *Political Register* from 1802. Soon, however, as a result of what he observed, his views began to change, and from about 1804 he wrote more and more positively in the radical interest, suffering two years' imprisonment for his attack on flogging in the army. He published Parliamentary Debates, afterwards taken over by *Hansard, and *State Trials*; wrote an entertaining English grammar (1817); and a number of books on economic subjects. At the same time he was farming in Hampshire and later in Surrey. From 1817 to 1819 he was again in America. The reflections assembled in 1830 as *Rural Rides* began to appear in the *Political Register* from 1821. His *History of the Protestant 'Reformation' in England and Ireland* appeared in 1824; his *Advice to Young Men* in 1829. He became MP for Oldham in 1832. Throughout his life he was an avid reader and a prolific writer. He wrote with perspicuity and vigour, in a prose style commended by *Hazlitt as 'plain, broad, downright English', and he produces without artifice (particularly in *Rural Rides*) an engaging and idiosyncratic portrait of himself. There are biographies by G. D. H. *Cole (1924) and G. Spater (1982).

COBDEN, Richard (1804–65), son of a Sussex farmer, who settled in Manchester in 1832. He was the foremost leader of the Anti-Corn Law League, and contributed powerfully to the repeal of the Corn Laws in 1846. He was an apostle of free trade and negotiated the commercial treaty with France, 1859. He was successively MP for Stockport (1841), the West Riding of Yorkshire, and Stockdale.

COCKBURN, Alison, née Rutherford (c.1712–94), Scots poet and songwriter, whose lively soirées brought together most of the literary talent of 18th-cent. Edinburgh. She was friendly with *Hume, was admired by *Burns, and was on close terms with the family of Sir W. *Scott, to whom she was distantly related. She wrote one of the well-known versions of 'The Flowers of the Forest'. (See also ELLIOT, J.)

COCKBURN, Catharine, née Trotter (1679–1749). She had her first tragedy, *Agnes de Castro*, performed at the Theatre Royal, Drury Lane, when she was 15 and published a year later. She made the acquaintance of *Congreve, and wrote four other stage works and occasional poetry. She developed an interest in philosophy and published several works in explication and defence of the writings of *Locke, both during and after Locke's life. In later life she wrote on moral philosophy and in defence of S. *Clarke.

COCKBURN, Henry Thomas, Lord Cockburn (1779–1854), educated in Edinburgh. He shared with *Jeffrey the leadership of the Scottish bar for many years. His *Memorials of His Times* (1856) gives a vivid account of literary circles in Edinburgh, and includes descriptions of *Brougham, Jeffrey, John *Wilson, Sydney *Smith, and the founding of the *Edinburgh Review*. His *Life of Jeffrey* was published in 1852.

Cocke Lorells Bote, a popular verse satire of the early 16th cent. in which types of the various tradesfolk take ship and sail through England. The captain of the 'Bote' is Cocke Lorell, a tinker and probably a historical personage. It is an interesting picture of low life.

Cock Lane Ghost, a supposed ghost to which were attributed mysterious noises heard at 33 Cock Lane, Smithfield, in 1762. They were discovered to be due to the imposture of one William Parsons and his daughter. Dr *Johnson took part in the investigation of the mystery, and wrote a brief 'Account of the Detection of the Imposture in Cock-Lane', published in the *Gentleman's Magazine* (Feb. 1762). Charles *Churchill seized the opportunity to attack him in his satire *The Ghost* (1762) for credulity, and, more woundingly, for his long delays in producing his edition of Shakespeare.

Cockney School, a term apparently first used in *Blackwood's Magazine* in Oct. 1817, when *Lockhart and his associates began a series of attacks 'On the Cockney School of Poetry'. Leigh *Hunt was the chief target, but *Hazlitt and *Keats were also objects of frequent derision. The Londoners, all of humble origin, were contrasted with the great writers, all of whom 'have been men of some rank', and Hunt was particularly singled out for his 'low birth and low habits'. The virulence of the attacks, which described the writers as 'the vilest vermin' and of 'extreme moral depravity', was sustained over several years, and included the cruel and famous passages on Keats's *Endymion* in 1818. After his death Keats was described as a man 'who had left a decent calling [i.e. pharmacy] for the melancholy trade of Cockney-poetry'.

Cocoa-Tree Club, in St James's Street, originally a chocolate house of the same name dating from the early 18th cent. After being a Tory centre and subsequently, in 1745, a resort of the *Jacobite party, it became a fashionable club where, as Horace *Walpole's letters attest, there was gambling for high stakes.

COCTEAU, Jean (1889–1963), French poet, novelist, dramatist, film director, and critic. He was prominently associated with *Modernism in literature, art, music, ballet, and the cinema, collaborating with many of the leading figures in Europe, such as Diaghilev, *Picasso, and *Stravinsky. He produced numerous volumes of poetry; novels, including *Le Grand Écart* (1923; *The Grand Écart*, 1925) and *Les Enfants terribles* (1929; English trans. 1930, and, as *Children of the Game*, 1955); several sketches for ballets, including *Parade* (1917); films, such as *La Belle et la bête* (1945); and plays, including *Orphée* (1926; English trans. 1933) and *La Machine infernale* (1934; *The Infernal Machine*, 1936), a reworking of the Oedipus myth.

codex, a manuscript volume e.g. of one of the ancient manuscripts of the Scriptures, or of the ancient classics [*OED*]. See entries under AMIATINUS CODEX and BIBLE (*Codex Bezae, Codex Vaticanus, Codex Alexandrinus,* etc.).

Codlin and Short, in Dickens's *The Old Curiosity Shop*, travel about the country with a Punch and Judy show. Thomas Codlin is a surly misanthrope, Short (real name Harris, familiarly known as 'Short Trotters') is a cheerful little man.

CODRINGTON, Christopher (1668–1710), born in Barbados, and educated at Christ Church, Oxford, became captain-general of the Leeward Islands in 1697. He spent the last years of his life in study on his Barbados estates, which he bequeathed to the Society for the Propagation of the Gospel, for the foundation of a college in Barbados. He also left his books and £10,000 to All Souls College, Oxford, a bequest out of which was founded the Codrington Library.

COE, Jonathan (1961–), novelist, short story writer, and journalist, born in Birmingham. His first two novels, *The Accidental Woman* (1987) and *A Touch of Love* (1989), are playful and experimental. *The Dwarves of Death* (1990), while less self-conscious, does not entirely eschew the experimental approach; he con-

structs the novel like a popular song, even incorporating a middle eight—a hilarious account of waiting for a bus that never comes. A touching and entertaining romp through the hand-to-mouth world of semi-professional musicians trying to make a go of it in London, *The Dwarves of Death* is as much a low-key thriller as a vicious attack on the musicals of Andrew Lloyd Webber. *What a Carve Up!* (1994) is, in every sense, a bigger book. In it a writer is commissioned to write a book about a powerful Yorkshire family, the Winshaws, for a vanity publisher. Exploiting an extraordinary cast of characters to the full, Coe dissects the body politic of Conservative Britain in the 1980s. The scope is ambitious, taking in the art world and factory farming, the depletion of the NHS and the war against Saddam, political corruption and family betrayal. *The House of Sleep* (1997), also carefully plotted, explores themes of narcolepsy, dreaming, cinema, and transsexuality. *The Rotters' Club* (2001) evokes boyhood in Birmingham in the 1970s; and *The Closed Circle* (2004) is a sequel. Coe has also written biographies of James Stewart, Humphrey Bogart, and B. S. *Johnson (*Like a Fiery Elephant*, 2004.)

Coel (King Cole of the nursery rhyme) was a duke of Colchester who, according to *Geoffrey of Monmouth's *History* (v. 6), became king of Britain for a short time. He was succeeded by the Roman Constantius, who married Coel's daughter Helen, thus transferring the kingship into Roman hands. See *Chesterton's parodies in 'Variations on an Air Composed on Having to Appear in a Pageant as Old King Cole', in *New Poems* (1932).

Coelebs in Search of a Wife, a novel by H. *More, published 1809. The book, which was immensely successful, consists of a collection of sharp social sketches and moral precepts, strung together by the hero's search for a wife, who must possess the qualities stipulated by his departed parents.

COETZEE, J(ohn) M(ichael) (1940–), South African novelist and academic, born in Cape Town, educated at the university there and at the University of Texas, where he received his doctorate. He has held academic posts in both the USA and South Africa and since 1983 has been professor of general literature at the University of Cape Town. His first book, *Ducklands* (1974), contains two linked novellas, one concerning the American involvement in Vietnam, the other about an 18th-cent. Boer settler. *In the Heart of the Country* (1977), which was filmed in 1986 as *Dust*, focuses on the meditations of a disturbed Afrikaner spinster. *Waiting for the Barbarians* (1980), a powerful allegory of oppression, was followed by the *Booker Prize-winning *The Life and Times of Michael K* (1983), in which a man takes his ailing mother back to her home in the country as South Africa is torn by civil war; *Foe* (1986); *White Writing* (1988); *Age of Iron* (1990), a compelling story of a woman dying from cancer and her relationship with a homeless alcoholic who camps outside her house; and *Doubling the Point* (1992). *The Master of Petersburg* (1994) is set in 1896, and follows an exiled Russian novelist back to St. Petersburg where he becomes entangled in a web of intrigue. *Disgrace* (1999, *Booker Prize) is the painful story of a middle-aged professor of English charged with sexual harassment who seeks refuge on his daughter's farm in the Eastern Cape, in the desolate landscape of post-apartheid South Africa. He was awarded the *Nobel Prize for literature in 2003.

coffee houses were first introduced in the time of the Commonwealth; the first recorded in England was in Oxford in 1650 (mentioned by A. *Wood), and the first in London was in 1652, in St Michael's Alley, off Cornhill, at the Sign of Pasqua Rosee. They were much frequented in the 17th and 18th cents for political and literary discussions, circulation of news, etc. Among the most celebrated coffee and chocolate houses were the Bedford (Covent Garden, a favourite with actors), Button's (Russell Street, Covent Garden, popular with *Addison and his circle), Don Saltero's (Cheyne Walk, founded by a one-time servant of Sir H. *Soane), Garraway's (Change Alley, Corn Hill, a meeting place for stockjobbers in the days of the *South Sea Company), the Grecian (Essex Street, off the Strand, frequented by members of the *Royal Society), Slaughter's (St Martin's Lane, a favourite of *Hogarth and other artists), White's (a chocolate house in St James's), and Will's (Bow Street, frequented by authors, wits, and gamblers, and particularly associated with *Dryden). Their decline during the 18th cent. has been in part attributed to the increasing popularity of clubs, such as the *Club, the *Kit-Cat Club, the *Cocoa-Tree Club, and the Brothers Club, founded in 1711 by *Bolingbroke. There is a description of coffee houses in *Macaulay's *History of England*, ch. III. See also Aytoun Ellis, *The Penny Universities* (1956) and B. Lillywhite, *London Coffee Houses* (1963).

COKE, Sir Edward (1552–1634), English jurist, called to the bar in 1578. By favour of *Burleigh, he became recorder of London in 1592 and attorney-general in 1594, in which capacity he represented the Crown at the trials of *Essex and Southampton (1600–1), *Ralegh, and the Gunpowder Plot conspirators (1605). He became chief justice of the Common Pleas in 1606 and in that capacity came into conflict with King James about the jurisdiction of the common law courts. In 1613 he became chief justice of the King's Bench and a member of the Privy Council, but conflict with the king continued, and in 1616 he was dismissed by the Council. Coke's importance as a jurist rests on his *Reports* (1600–15), the first textbook of early modern law. The first book of the *Institutes*, known as 'Coke upon Littleton' (1628), is a legal encyclopaedia; the last three books (1641) form the basis of modern British constitutional law.

Coke, Lady Mary (1726–1811), a daughter of John, duke of Argyll, the reluctant wife of Edward, Viscount Coke. An eccentric and striking woman, she was a friend of Horace *Walpole, who accompanied the second edition of his *The Castle of Otranto* with a sonnet addressed to her. Her entertaining *Letters and Journals* were privately printed (1889–96).

'Colbeck, The Dancers of', see HANDLYNG SYNNE.

COLBURN, Henry (d. 1855), a very successful publisher who founded the *New Monthly Magazine* in 1814 and the *Literary Gazette* in 1817, and who published the fashionable and profitable novels of Lady *Morgan and T. *Hook. He was the first to publish *Evelyn's *Diary*, in 1818, and *Pepys's newly deciphered *Diaries* in 1825. In 1830 he went into partnership with Richard *Bentley and together they published a successful series of Standard Novelists (1835–41). He died a very rich man.

Cold Comfort Farm (1932), the first novel of Stella Gibbons (1902–90), a witty and highly successful parody of the earthy primitive school of regional fiction popular at the beginning of the century (by e.g. Sheila *Kaye-Smith (1887–1956), M. *Webb, and D. H. *Lawrence).

Flora Poste visits her relatives the Starkadders in Sussex, and finds herself in a household of seething emotion, gloom, and rural intrigue, which she proceeds to reform. The descriptive 'purple passages' common to the genre are obligingly marked with asterisks by the author, after the method 'perfected by the late Herr *Baedeker'.

Cole, King, see COEL.

Cole, G(eorge) D(ouglas) H(oward) (1889–1959), Fabian economist. He was converted to socialism after reading W. *Morris's *News from Nowhere*. Educated at St Paul's School and Balliol College, he subsequently held important academic posts at Oxford. He became prominent immediately before the First World War as a leading exponent of guild socialism (as opposed to the bureaucratic socialism of B. and S. *Webb), and published in 1913 his first major work, *The World of Labour*. During the 1930s he was acknowledged as the most prolific writer on the intellectual history of British Socialism in articles in the *New Statesman* and in his works, which included *A History of Socialist Thought* (1953–8). He was married to Margaret Postgate (sister of Raymond Postgate), with whom he collaborated in detective fiction.

COLENSO, John William (1814–83), bishop of Natal, where he pioneered the writing of Zulu. He was denounced for his strong views on Zulu polygamy in relation to Christian conversion and for applying the Christian ethic to the problem of race relations in southern Africa. In 1861 he issued his commentary *St Paul's Epistle to the Romans*, which aroused a storm of controversy by its repudiation of much orthodox sacramental theology and its denial of everlasting punishment; further protest was aroused by his *The Pentateuch and the Book of Joshua Critically Examined* (1862–79), which challenged the historical accuracy and authorship of these books. In 1863 he was deposed by Bishop Gray of Capetown but Colenso denied his jurisdiction and, by a series of judicial decisions, secured possession of the see.

COLERIDGE, Hartley (1796–1849), the unworldly eldest son of S. T. *Coleridge, who inherited many of his father's gifts, including verbal eloquence, but achieved little, losing his Oxford fellowship for intemperance and failing as a schoolmaster. In 1833 he published *Poems, Songs and Sonnets* (the sonnets of which were much praised), and in the same year his unfinished *Biographia Borealis*, retitled *Worthies of Yorkshire and Lancashire* in 1836. He contributed to *Blackwood's Magazine*, the *London Magazine*, and other literary journals, and in 1840 published his edition, with brief biographies, of *Massinger and *Ford. His *Essays and Marginalia*, edited by his brother Derwent, were published posthumously in 1851. He spent his childhood and the latter part of his life in the Lake District, where he died. He is the subject of two important poems by his father, *'Frost at Midnight' and 'The Nightingale'.

COLERIDGE, Mary (1861–1907), the great-great-niece of S. T. *Coleridge, who published her first volume of verse, *Fancy's Following*, with the encouragement of *Bridges in 1896, and a second, *Fancy's Guerdon*, in 1897. Two sonnets, 'True to myself am I' and 'Go in the deepest, darkest dead of night', have been much anthologized. Her first novel, an original and fantastical romance, *The Seven Sleepers of Ephesus* (1893), was praised by R. L. *Stevenson but achieved little success; her second, *The King with Two Faces* (1897), a historical romance centring on Gustavus III of Sweden, was well received. She contributed extensively to various journals, such as the *Monthly Review* and the *Cornhill*. In 1900 she published *Non Sequitur*, a collection of lively and ironic essays; her unpublished remains appeared as *Gathered Leaves* in 1910.

COLERIDGE, Samuel Taylor (1772–1834), poet, critic, and philosopher of *Romanticism. Youngest son of the vicar of Ottery St Mary, Devon, he was destined for the Church. A temperamental, dreamy child, he was sent away after his father's early death to *Christ's Hospital school, London, where his precocious classical reading and powers of 'inspired' talk (which never left him) attracted a circle of young admirers, including Leigh *Hunt and the future essayist *Lamb. At Jesus College, Cambridge (1792–4), a brilliant career in classics was diverted by French revolutionary politics, heavy drinking, and an unhappy love affair, which led Coleridge to enlist in desperation in the 15th Light Dragoons under the name of Comberbache. He was bought out under an 'insanity' clause by his brother, but did not take a degree.

In the summer of 1794 an undergraduate walking-tour through Oxford brought him the passionate friendship of *Southey, and together they invented *Pantisocracy, a scheme to set up a commune in New England. Coleridge now published his first poetry in the *Morning Chronicle*, a series of sonnets to eminent radicals including *Godwin and J. *Priestley. To finance Pantisocracy, he and Southey gave political lectures in Bristol and collaborated on a verse drama, *The Fall of Robespierre* (1794); they also simultaneously courted and married two sisters, Sara and Edith Fricker. After quarrelling with Southey over money and politics, Coleridge retired with Sara to a cottage at Clevedon, where their first son Hartley (above), named after the philosopher David *Hartley, was born. Here Coleridge edited a radical Christian journal, the *Watchman*, which ran for ten issues; and published *Poems on Various Subjects* (1796), which included the 'Monody on the Death of Chatterton' and 'The Eolian Harp'. He considered entering the Unitarian ministry and preached throughout the West Country; he also took opium in periods of sickness and depression.

In June 1797 Coleridge walked to Racedown, Dorset, where he met *Wordsworth and his sister Dorothy. The intense friendship that sprang up between the three shaped their lives for the next 14 years and proved one of the most creative partnerships in English Romanticism. It was based on a mutual love of poetry, critical discussion, and hill-walking; and an impassioned response to the political and social problems of the age. Between July 1797 and Sept. 1798 they lived and worked intimately together; the Coleridges at Nether Stowey, Somerset, and the Wordsworths 2 miles away at Alfoxden, on the edge of the Quantock hills, where they were visited by Lamb, *Hazlitt, and others. Here Coleridge wrote a moving series of blank verse 'conversation' poems, addressed to his friends: 'Fears in Solitude', 'This Lime Tree Bower My Prison', 'The Nightingale', and *'Frost at Midnight'. He also composed his celebrated opium-vision *'Kubla Khan'. At Wordsworth's suggestion, Coleridge wrote 'The Rime of the *Ancient Mariner', which recounts a nightmare sea-voyage with powerful metaphysical overtones; and started three other ballads, of which the best is *'Christabel', a tale of spiritual seduction set in a medieval castle. A selection from their work appeared as the *Lyrical Ballads* (1798), intended as an 'experiment' in English poetry, which, after a poor critical reception, achieved a revolution in literary taste and sensibility.

Disenchanted with political developments ('France: An Ode'), Coleridge now turned towards Germany, where he spent ten months (1798–9), partly in the company of the Wordsworths, studying *Kant, *Schiller, and *Schelling. Returned to London, he translated Schiller's verse play *Wallenstein*, engaged in journalism for D. *Stuart of the *Morning Post*, and first began to plan a great work on metaphysics. In 1800 he moved to the Lake District with the Wordsworths, but his marriage was increasingly unhappy and he had fallen disastrously in love with Wordsworth's future sister-in-law Sara Hutchinson, as recorded in 'Love' (1799) and other 'Asra' poems. His use of opium now became a crippling addiction. Many of these difficulties are examined in the brilliant and emotional *'Dejection: An Ode' (1802). During these years he also began to compile his *Notebooks, daily meditations on his life, writing, and dreams, which have proved among his most enduring and moving works. In 1804 Coleridge went abroad alone, the first of many attempts to restore his health and remake his career: he worked for two years as secretary to the governor of wartime Malta, and later travelled through Sicily and Italy. In 1807 he separated from his wife and went to live again with the Wordsworths and Sara Hutchinson at Coleorton, Leicestershire: here Wordsworth first read him 'The Poem to Coleridge' which became *The Prelude. In 1808, though ill, Coleridge began his series of Lectures on Poetry and Drama, which he continued sporadically over the next decade to audiences including *Keats and *Byron, and which as his *Shakespearean Criticism introduced new concepts of 'organic' form and dramatic psychology. In 1809–10 he wrote and edited with Sara Hutchinson's help a second periodical, the *Friend, 'a literary, moral, and political weekly paper' that ran for 28 issues: it contains the seeds of all his mature philosophic criticism. The intellectual effort, combined with the struggle against opium, shattered his circle of friends: Sara left for Wales, Dorothy grew estranged, he quarrelled irrevocably with Wordsworth. Coleridge fled to London, where between 1811 and 1814 he was on the verge of suicide, sustained only by his friends the Morgans, who took him to live in Calne, Wiltshire. Nevertheless he continued lecturing and journalism, and his play *Remorse, a melodrama of the Spanish Inquisition, had a succès d'estime at Drury Lane (1813). After a physical and spiritual crisis at the Greyhound Inn, Bath, in the winter of 1813–14, Coleridge achieved a rebirth of his Christian beliefs, openly admitted his opium addiction, submitted himself to a series of medical régimes, and began slowly to write again. To this period belong the touching prose 'commentary' printed in the margins of the 'Mariner'; his essay 'on the Principles of Genial Criticism', adapted from Kant; and his *Biographia Literaria (1817), a major work of poetic criticism, philosophy, and humorous autobiography.

In the spring of 1816 Coleridge found permanent harbour in the household of Dr James Gillman, a young surgeon living at Highgate, London, where he remained for the rest of his life. His by now almost legendary reputation among the younger Romantics was assured by Christabel and Other Poems (1816), which included for the first time 'Kubla Khan', and 'The Pains of Sleep'; it was published partly through *Byron's influence. Sibylline Leaves, the first edition of his collected poems, was published in 1817 and expanded in 1828 and 1834; *Zapolya in 1817. He became the centre of a new circle of young disciples: *Carlyle christened him 'the Sage of Highgate', and Lamb—who dedicated the *Essays of Elia to him—described him as 'an Archangel a little damaged'.

His remaining prose works had a more openly social and religious slant: his two Lay Sermons (1816, 1817) were addressed to the 'Higher' and 'Middle' classes on questions of reform and moral responsibility. A final three-volume edition of The Friend added his 'Treatise on Method', originally written as an introduction to the Encyclopaedia Metropolitana, which makes a Baconian attempt to explain the growth of knowledge itself. His *Aids to Reflection (1825) had a fruitful influence on *Sterling, *Kingsley, and the young Christian Socialists; while his Church and State (1830), a short monograph on the concept of a national 'Culture' and the 'clerisy' responsible for it, was taken up by M. *Arnold and *Newman. Coleridge also gave lectures on general literature and philosophy, which survived in the form of notes and shorthand reports.

All these later works develop Coleridge's leading critical ideas, concerning Imagination and Fancy; Reason and Understanding; Symbolism and Allegory; Organic and Mechanical Form; Culture and Civilization. The dialectical way he expresses them is one of his clearest debts to German Romantic philosophy, and represents a decisive counter-attack against British *utilitarianism. His final position is that of a Romantic conservative and Christian radical, who strangely foreshadows much of the spiritual 'anxiety' of European *existentialism. He also wrote some haunting late poems, 'Youth and Age', 'Limbo', 'Work without Hope', and 'Constancy to an Ideal Object'. He died of heart failure at 3 The Grove, Highgate. The last echoes of his inspired conversation were captured in Table Talk (1836).

Coleridge has been variously criticized as a political turn-coat, a drug addict, a plagiarist, and a mystic humbug, whose wrecked career left nothing but a handful of magical early poems. But the shaping influence of his highly imaginative criticism is now generally accepted, and his position (with his friend Wordsworth) as one of the two great progenitors of the English Romantic spirit is assured. Nothing has re-established him as a creative artist more than the modern editions of his Letters (6 vols, 1956–71), and his Notebooks (4 vols, 1957–90). There is a religious and metaphysical dimension to all his best work, both poetry and prose, which has the inescapable glow of the authentic visionary.

Modern biographies include those by E. K. *Chambers (1938), Walter Jackson Bate (1968), Molly Lefebvre (1974), and Richard *Holmes (2 vols, 1989, 1998). Hazlitt's superb essay 'On My First Acquaintance with Poets' (1823) is indispensable.

COLERIDGE, Sara (1802–52), daughter of S. T. *Coleridge, who grew up largely without her father in the company of *Southey and his family and of the *Wordsworths. She was, in Wordsworth's words, 'remarkably clever'; she read widely and acquired six languages. She married her cousin Henry Nelson Coleridge, and after his death continued with the labour of editing and annotating her father's papers, which she performed with such skill that much of her work still stands. In 1822 she translated Dobrizhoffer's Latin *Account of the Abipones* and in 1825 the *Memoirs of the Chevalier Bayard*. *Pretty Lessons for Good Children* appeared in 1834, and in 1837 her long prose narrative 'Phantasmion', set in the Lake country of her childhood and relating in the manner of a fairy-tale the story of Phantasmion and Iarine. She was greatly esteemed in London literary society, and was the friend of *Macaulay, the *Carlyles, and *de Vere, among many others. The lively and engaging *Memoir and Letters*, published by her daughter in 1873, provides much information on the literary and personal lives of the Coleridges, the Wordsworths, and the Southeys. She appears, with Dora Wordsworth and Edith Southey, in Wordsworth's poem 'The Triad' (1828).

COLET, John (1466–1519), born in London of rich parentage, one of the principal Christian Humanists of his day in England. He studied at Oxford and in Italy, and he lectured at Oxford on the New Testament from 1496 to 1504, *Erasmus being among his audience. As dean of St Paul's (1505) he founded and endowed St *Paul's School, writing for it a latin grammar for which *Lily, the first headmaster, wrote the syntax; from this work and others is derived the grammar authorized by Henry VIII, which was known from 1758 as the Eton Latin Grammar. He was a famous preacher and lecturer, a pioneer of the Reformation in England. He first came to notice with his lectures on the Epistles of St Paul at Oxford in 1497–8 which draw on *Neoplatonism from *Plotinus to Pseudo-*Dionysius to *Pico della Mirandola. He was a vitriolic and powerful opponent of *Scholasticism, of ecclesiastical abuses, and of foreign wars. He was a friend of Erasmus and *More. See the biography by J. H. Lupton (1887), who also edited the 1497–8 *Expositions*, on St Paul to the Romans and on the First Epistle to the Corinthians.

COLETTE, (Sidonie Gabrielle) (1873–1954), French novelist. Having achieved success in the music hall of the 1890s, she established her reputation as a writer with *Chéri* (1920) and *La Fin de Chéri* (1926), narratives evoking the tragic passion of a young man and an older woman. The short, intense *récits* which she made her speciality include *La Maison de Claudine* (1922), *Le Blé en herbe* (1923), *Sido* (1929), *La Naissance du jour* (1932), *Le Képi* (1943), and *Gigi* (1943). They express a sensibility shaped by the style of the *belle époque* and informed by a sensual responsiveness to the life of nature and the world of childhood. She continues to hold attention for the vividness and precision of her insights into the crises of womanhood. She has been variously translated into English, notably by E. McLeod and R. Stenhouse.

Colin Clout, the name adopted by *Spenser in *The Shepheardes Calender* and *Colin Clouts Come Home Againe*. Colin Clout is also the name of a rustic in Gay's *The Shepherd's Week*. See also COLLYN CLOUTE.

Colin Clouts Come Home Againe, an allegorical pastoral written by *Spenser on his return to Kilcolman after his visit to London of 1589–91, published 1595. It was dedicated to *Ralegh 'in part of paiment of the infinite debt in which I acknowledge my selfe bounden unto you, for your singular favours and sundrie good turnes shewed to me at my late being in England'.

The poem describes in allegorical form how Ralegh visited Spenser in Ireland and induced him to come to England 'his *Cynthia* to see'—i.e. the queen. There is a charming description of the sea voyage; after which the poet tells of the glories of the queen and her court and the beauty of the ladies who frequent it. Then follows a bitter attack on the envies and intrigues of the court. The poem ends with a definition of true love and a tribute to Colin's proud mistress *Rosalind.

Colkitto, 'or Macdonnel, or Galasp', in Milton's first *Tetrachordon sonnet, was the lieutenant-general of the marquis of Montrose in his campaign on behalf of Charles I. He was called Alexander Macdonnel, Mac-Colkittoch, MacGillespie, that is, Alexander Macdonnel, the son of Colkittoch, the son of Gillespie (Galasp). He figures in Scott's *The Legend of Montrose*.

Colleen Bawn, The (meaning 'the fair girl'), a play adapted in 1860 by *Boucicault from a novel, *The Collegians*, by *Griffin.

Collegiate Ladies, in Jonson's *Epicene*, a coterie of domineering women 'between courtiers and country madams, who live from their husbands and give entertainment to all the wits and braveries [beaux] of the time'. Wycherley copied them for Lady Fidget and her cronies in *The Country Wife*.

COLLIER, Jane (1715–55), satirist, born near Salisbury, where she lived for 30 years. In London she became a member of S. *Richardson's circle, contributing advice on *Clarissa and collaborating with her companion S. *Fielding on an experimental dialogue-novel, *The Cry* (1754). Her other notable work is *An Essay on the Art of Ingeniously Tormenting; With Proper Rules for the Exercise of that Pleasant Art* (1753). A spoof conduct manual in the manner of *Swift's ironic *Directions to Servants*, the *Essay* gleefully outlines 'a complete system for the practice of tormenting your friends'. It was revived in three editions of 1804–6, and may have influenced J. *Austen.

COLLIER, Jeremy (1650–1726), a nonjuring clergyman who refused to swear the oath to William and Mary and was outlawed in 1696 for publicly absolving on the scaffold two of those found guilty of plotting to assassinate William III. He became a nonjuring bishop in 1713. He is chiefly remembered for his *Short View of the Immorality and Profaneness of the English Stage* (1698), in which he attacked *Dryden, *Wycherley, *Congreve, *Vanbrugh, *D'Urfey, and *Otway, complaining particularly of profanity in stage dialogue and mockery of the clergy. The work created a great impact; Congreve and D'Urfey were prosecuted, *Betterton and Mrs *Bracegirdle were fined, and several of the poets replied, though not very effectively. Although the kind of play to which Collier objected continued to flourish, notably in the work of Congreve, Vanbrugh, and *Farquhar, its days were numbered, and Collier contributed towards the climate that produced the 'reformed' drama of C. *Cibber and his successors. (See also RESTORATION.) Collier published a learned *Ecclesiastical History of Great Britain* in 1708–14.

COLLIER, John (1901–80), poetry editor of *Time and Tide* during the 1920s and 1930s, but remembered as a novelist and writer of fantastic stories combining satire with the macabre and the supernatural. His best-known novel is *His Monkey Wife* (1930), describing the marriage between a repatriated explorer and his pet chimpanzee. In 1935 he moved to the USA and made his living as a screenwriter in Hollywood. *The John Collier Reader* (1972) is an anthology of his major stories with an introduction by A. *Burgess.

COLLIER, John Payne (1789–1883), antiquary, whose achievements first received public attention with *The History of English Dramatic Poetry to the Time of Shakespeare: And Annals of the Stage to the Restoration* (1831) which contained valuable new documentary information but was contaminated with his own fabrications, the first of his insidious literary frauds. He dedicated the *History* to the duke of Devonshire (then lord chamberlain) who showed his appreciation by entrusting to him his library and making him his literary adviser. He was also given free access to Lord Ellesmere's manuscripts at Bridgewater House. In 1840 he founded the Shakespeare Society for which he published many rare works including *The Memoirs of Edward Alleyn* (1841); as director of the Society many rare documents were made available to him on which he based his researches and forgeries. But it was his falsifications of the marginal corrections of the so-called Perkins Folio (a second *Folio of Shakespeare's plays dated 1632, with a possibly forged signature of Tho. Perkins on its cover) that finally brought him discredit.

Doubt was cast on the nature and extent of Collier's frauds by D. Ganzel in a biography, *Fortune and Men's Eyes* (1982).

COLLIER, Mary (?1690–c.1762), poet. Known as 'the Washer-woman', Collier, born near Midhurst, Sussex, was, by her own account in 'Remarks of the Author's life, drawn by herself', taught to read but otherwise uneducated and earned a living 'washing, brewing and such labour'. *The Woman's Labour: An Epistle to Mr. Stephen Duck* (1739) stoutly defended the industry of independent women like herself against *Duck's criticism published in 'The Thresher's Labour'. Collier's *Poems on Several Occasions* (1762) gained a favourable reception.

COLLINGWOOD, R(obin) G(eorge) (1889–1943), philosopher and archaeologist. He was educated by his father before going to Rugby and University College, Oxford, and in 1935 became professor of metaphysical philosophy in Oxford. He combined philosophy with the history and archaeology of Roman Britain. His chief work in the latter field was *Roman Britain and the English Settlements* (with J. N. L. Myres, 1936). In his vigorous *Autobiography* (1939) and *The Idea of History* (1946) he maintained the identity of philosophy and history. Earlier books included an *Essay on Philosophical Method* (1933) and *The Principles of Art* (1938).

COLLINS, An (fl. 1640s–1650s), unknown save for her published volume of devotional lyrics, *Divine Songs and Meditacions* (1653), a sequence of confessional poems with a prose preface, which represents the author as a single woman of moderate Puritan allegiance whose chronic ill health and morbid anxiety had been vanquished by the discovery of 'sacred joy' and curative self-expression. The volume, which has been read as a diary, is a poetic conversion narrative, in a naïve version of the Puritan plain style (she calls it her 'homely dress'), with copious, though often gauche, stanzaic experimentation. In 'Another Song' Collins adapts the idea of the *hortus conclusus* of the Song of Solomon ('A garden inclosed is my sister, my spouse', 4: 12) to the single woman's marriage to Christ. *Divine Songs and Meditacions* (1961, ed. S. Stewart) reproduces half the text of the sole original copy, in the Huntingdon Library, California.

COLLINS, Anthony (1676–1729), freethinker, born at Heston, Middlesex, and educated at Eton and King's College, Cambridge. In 1703 he became intimate with *Locke. His debate on immortality with S. *Clarke— each man issuing four pamphlets (1707–8)—established his reputation as a leading freethinker. His materialistic theory of mind is satirized in the *Memoirs of *Martinus Scriblerus* (1741). The boldly insinuating *Discourse of Free-Thinking* (1713), his best-known work, drew angry replies from Richard *Bentley, *Berkeley, *Steele, Whiston, *Hoadley, and, in *Mr C . . .s Discourse . . ., Put into Plain English* (1713), from *Swift.

Collins's classic defence of determinism, *A Philosophical Inquiry*, appeared in 1717. Between 1720 and 1721 he collaborated with Trenchard and Gordon on the anticlerical periodical the *Independent Whig*. In

Grounds and Reasons of the Christian Religion (1724) he contests the Messianic prophecies. Overtly or covertly, Collins attacked nearly every part of Christian theology; T. H. *Huxley described him as 'the Goliath of Freethinking'.

COLLINS, John Churton (1848–1908), lecturer and critic, educated at Balliol College, Oxford. He was known in literary circles for his long pursuit of the academic recognition of English in the university curriculum, and for his arguments in favour of the conjunct study of English and classical literature, which drew support from M. *Arnold, T. H. *Huxley, and *Swinburne, who became a close friend and correspondent. His frequent and often controversial articles appeared in the *Quarterly Review, the *Pall Mall Gazette, and other journals. His efforts were rewarded when in 1893 a final honours school was established at Oxford, and in 1904 when he became professor of English literature at Birmingham. He edited the works of *Tourneur (1878), of R. *Greene (1905), and Lord *Herbert of Cherbury's poems (1881); his critical works included *Ephemera Critica* (1891) and *Voltaire, Montesquieu and Rousseau in England* (1908). He was found drowned at Oulton Broad.

COLLINS, (William) Wilkie (1824–89), novelist, elder son of the painter William Collins, who was born and lived for most of his life in the Marylebone district of London. Educated at private schools in London, he claimed he learned far more of significance in Italy, where he travelled with his family as a boy, 1836–8. He worked briefly for a tea-importer, and was called to the bar, but never practised. His first published book was a biography of his father (1848), followed by his only historical novel, *Antonina* (1850). His second novel, *Basil* (1852), was admired by *Dickens, who employed Collins as a writer for *Household Words*. The two writers became personal friends and occasional collaborators, and Collins's third novel, *Hide and Seek* (1854), is his most Dickensian work. With the publication of his fifth and most successful full-length novel, *The Woman in White* (1860), Collins became a popular and highly successful writer of intricately plotted stories of mystery, suspense, and crime, though his work continued to attract condemnation for sensationalism. (See SENSATION, NOVEL OF.) His portrayal of attractive but transgressive women such as Magdalen Vanstone in *No Name* and Lydia Gwilt in *Armadale*, now considered a significant feature of his work, was particularly attacked. His four novels of the 1860s, *The Woman in White, No Name* (1862), *Armadale* (1866), and *The Moonstone* (1868), are his most important works. Collins suffered from severe attacks of a rheumatic illness which caused him great pain, only relieved by the use of opium. One of his worst attacks occurred while he was writing *The Moonstone*, and he made use of the effects of opium in the plot of the novel. It used to be considered that Collins's opium habit, and the loss of Dickens's constructive criticism

after 1870, led to a disastrous decline in the quality of his writing. However his explorations of the darker side of Victorian society and his interest in abnormal physiology and psychology are now seen as innovative, and recent critical re-evaluation has found much of interest in later 'novels with a purpose' such as *Man and Wife* (1870), *The Law and the Lady* (1875), and his anti-vivisection novel *Heart and Science* (1883). Collins had a lifelong interest in the theatre, and five of his original plays were produced, as well as a number of theatrical adaptations of his novels, of which *Man and Wife* and *The New Magdalen*, both produced in 1873, were the most successful. The only play for which he is now remembered is *The Frozen Deep* (1857), written for Dickens's amateur company, with Dickens playing the lead, and his other plays have not been revived or reprinted. Collins's private life was as much a cause of scandal as his fiction. He never married, but from 1859 lived openly with Caroline Graves, a widow from a working-class background. The romantic story that she was the original 'woman in white' is unlikely to be true. In 1868 he began another liaison with Martha Rudd, the daughter of a farm labourer, who had worked as a servant. By her he had two daughters and a son. Caroline Graves left Collins in 1868, but returned to him two years later, and remained with him for the rest of his life, though his relationship with Martha Rudd (known as Mrs Dawson) also continued until his death. Recent biographies by William Clarke, *The Secret Life of Wilkie Collins* (1988), and Catherine Peters, *The King of Inventors* (1991), contain new information. See also Andrew Gasson, *Wilkie Collins: An Illustrated Guide* (1998), Sue Lonoff, *Wilkie Collins and his Victorian Readers* (1982), and Jenny Bourne Taylor, *In the Secret Theatre of Home: Wilkie Collins, Sensation Narrative, and Nineteenth Century Psychology* (1988).

COLLINS, William (1721–59), the son of a Chichester hatter. He was educated at Winchester (where he first met his friend J. *Warton) and Oxford, and published his *Persian Eclogues* (1742) while an undergraduate. He moved to London in the 1740s, where he met James *Thomson, *Armstrong, and Dr *Johnson, and embarked on many abortive literary enterprises. His *Odes on Several Descriptive and Allegoric Subjects* (1746, dated 1747) made little impression at the time, but was to have considerable influence; the volume includes his well-known 'Ode to Evening' and 'How Sleep the Brave', and odes to Pity, Fear, Simplicity, and other abstractions. (See ODE.) The last work published in his lifetime was an ode on the death of Thomson (1749), and in 1750 he presented an unfinished draft of his *Ode on the Popular Superstitions of the Highlands* (pub. 1788) to J. *Home. Thereafter he suffered increasingly from severe melancholia, and died in Chichester, where he had been living for some time. Johnson in his *Lives of the English Poets* commented on his wildness and extravagance, which produced harshness and obscurity as well as 'sublimity and splendour', but later poets responded more eagerly to his lyrical intensity and to his conception of poetry as visionary and sacred (see SUBLIME); with *Gray he was one of the dominant influences of the later 18th cent.

The first collected edition was by John *Langhorne (1765, with memoir): the standard modern edition is by R. Lonsdale (1977, with Gray and *Goldsmith), and a biography by P. L. Carver was published in 1967.

Collins, William, a character in J. Austen's *Pride and Prejudice*, a pompous, silly, and self-satisfied young clergyman, excessively obsequious to persons of high social station. The fulsome letter of thanks that he addresses to Mr Bennet (ch. xxiii, though the text is not given) after his stay with the family has led to his name being colloquially associated with such 'bread-and-butter' letters.

COLLIS, John Stewart (1900–84), the son of an Irish solicitor, who was, like his brother Maurice Stewart Collis (1889–1973), a writer of biographies and other works, but is remembered largely for *While Following the Plough* (1946) and *Down to Earth* (1947: as one volume, *The Worm Forgives the Plough*, 1973), works inspired by the years he spent working as a farm labourer in Dorset and Sussex during the Second World War. His autobiography, *Bound upon a Course* (1971), brought him belated recognition as a pioneer in the ecological movement, who wrote with imagination and authenticity of rural life.

Collyn Clout, a satirical poem by *Skelton, directed against ecclesiastical abuses, written about 1521. See also COLIN CLOUT.

COLMAN, George, the elder (1732–94), born in Florence, the son of the British envoy there, and educated at Westminster, where he was a school fellow of *Cowper and Bonnell Thornton (1724–68); with the latter he edited the *Connoisseur* (1754–6). He was called to the bar in 1757, but devoted himself increasingly to the theatre, partly through the influence of his friend *Garrick, with whom he collaborated in writing *The Clandestine Marriage* (1766), which caused a rift between them when Garrick refused to appear as Lord Ogleby. He was manager of Covent Garden, 1767–74, and of the Haymarket, 1777–89. He wrote many plays, including *Polly Honeycombe* (1760), *The Jealous Wife* (1761), and *Tit for Tat* (1786), adapted Shakespeare and *Beaumont and *Fletcher for the stage, and translated the comedies of *Terence (1765). He was elected to Dr Johnson's literary *Club in 1768. R. B. Peake's *Memoirs of the Colman Family* appeared in 1841.

COLMAN, George, the younger (1762–1836), son of the above, educated at Westminster and the universities of Oxford and Aberdeen. He made his name with the musical romantic comedy *Inkle and Yarico* in 1787, which was followed by other sentimental and humorous operettas. Among many other dramatic works, *The*

Iron Chest of 1796 is a dramatization of *Caleb Williams* by Godwin. Colman's comedy of contemporary life, *The Heir-at-Law* (1797), became famous for the character of Dr Pangloss, a greedy, pompous pedant. *John Bull* (1803) contains a sketch of the supposed British character in Job Thornberry.

Colombe's Birthday, a play in blank verse by R. *Browning, published in 1844 as no. VI of *Bells and Pomegranates*. In the aftermath of his quarrel with *Macready (see BLOT IN THE 'SCUTCHEON, A) Browning wrote the play for his rival Charles Kean, whose wife was to have taken the title role; but Kean's wish to delay the production for a year or more decided Browning to withdraw and publish it: he never wrote for the stage again. The play ran for seven nights at the Haymarket theatre in 1853 with Browning's friend Helen Faucit (see STRAFFORD) in the title role: it had a critical success. The play (whose events are unhistorical) is set in 17th-cent. Germany, on the day that Colombe is to celebrate her birthday and the first anniversary of her accession to the duchy of Juliers and Cleves.

Colonel Jack, *The History and Remarkable Life of Colonel Jacque, Commonly Call'd*, a romance of adventure by *Defoe, published 1722.

The supposed narrator, abandoned by his parents in childhood, falls into bad company and becomes a pickpocket. His profession grows distasteful to him, he enlists, and presently deserts to avoid being sent to serve in Flanders. He is kidnapped, sent to Virginia, and sold to a planter. He is promoted to be an overseer, is given his liberty, becomes himself a planter, and acquires much wealth. He returns home and has a series of unfortunate matrimonial adventures, but finally ends in prosperity and repentance.

COLONNA, Vittoria (1490–1547), Italian poet, widely praised by her contemporaries, including *Sannazar, *Castiglione, *Bembo, *Tasso, and *Michelangelo, for the sonnets of her *Rime spirituali* (1540). The first hundred sonnets mourn the premature death of her husband, the marquis of Pescara, and others treat philosophical themes in an austere style that reflected her Calvinist sympathies. Her *Canzoniere* (*Songbook*) was published in 1544.

colophon, from Gk. κολοφών, summit, 'finishing touch', the inscription or device, sometimes pictorial or emblematic, placed at the end of a book or manuscript, and containing the title, the scribe's or printer's name, the date and place of printing, etc.; now the publisher's imprint, or logotype, usually found on the title-page and often on the spine of a book.

COLUM, Padraic (1881–1972), Irish poet and playwright, born in Co. Longford, where his father was master of a workhouse, and educated at Trinity College, Dublin, where he met *Joyce, who became a close friend. Prominent amongst the younger members of the *Irish Revival, he wrote several plays for the

*Abbey Theatre, including *Thomas Muskerry* (1910), which was strongly attacked for its gloomily realistic Ibsenite portrayal of Irish life. His first collection of poems, *Wild Earth* (1907), was followed by many others (*Collected Poems*, 1953) and by works on Irish and Hawaiian folklore. He contributed a preface to Joyce's *Anna Livia Plurabelle* (1928), and he and his wife Mary wrote a memoir, *Our Friend James Joyce* (1958).

COLUMBA, or **COLUMCILLE, St** (521–97), a recluse of Glasnevin, near Dublin, and the founder of churches in Derry and other places. He went to Scotland in 563 and founded the monastery of Iona, from which the conversion of Scotland and Northumbria by the Celtic Church proceeded. The book of his miracles was written by *Adomnan of Iona. See W. D. Simpson, *The Historical St Columba* (1927).

COLVIN, Sir Sidney (1845–1927), critic of art and literature, educated at Trinity College, Cambridge, Slade professor of fine art at Cambridge 1873–85, director of the Fitzwilliam Museum in 1876, and keeper of the department of prints and drawings at the British Museum 1883–1912. Besides contributing many articles to periodicals, mainly on the history and criticism of art, he published several volumes including lives of W. S. *Landor (1881) and *Keats (1887). He was honorary secretary of the Society of Dilettanti, 1891–6, moved in artistic and literary circles, and corresponded with some of the most eminent intellectuals of his day (see E. V. *Lucas, *The Colvins and Their Friends*, 1928). He edited the Edinburgh edition of R. L. *Stevenson's works (1894–7) and *The Letters of R. L. Stevenson* (1899 and 1911) and in 1895 published the *Vailima Letters* written to him by Stevenson, 1890–4.

COMBE, William (1741–1823), educated at Eton. He published a number of metrical satires, including *The Diaboliad* (1776), directed against Lord Irnham; and many other works in prose and verse, including *The Devil upon Two Sticks in England* (1790) and *The Microcosm of London* (1808). He is particularly remembered for the verses that he wrote to accompany *Rowlandson's coloured plates and drawings of the adventures of 'Dr Syntax'. The first of these works, *The Tour of Dr Syntax in Search of the Picturesque*, a parody of the popular books of picturesque travels of the day, and particularly of the works of *Gilpin, appeared in *Ackermann's *Poetical Magazine* in 1809, and in 1812 as a book which went into many editions. Dr Syntax is the grotesque figure of a clergyman and schoolmaster, who sets out during the holidays, on his old horse Grizzle, to 'make a TOUR and WRITE IT', and meets with a series of absurd misfortunes. This was followed in 1820 by *The Second Tour of Dr Syntax in Search of Consolation* (for the loss of his wife) and in 1821 by *The Third Tour of Dr Syntax in Search of a Wife*. The three Tours were collected in 1826. Combe also wrote the letterpress for Rowlandson's *The English Dance of Death* (1815–16), *The Dance of Life* (1816), and *Johnny Quae Genus* (1822), another Syntax story.

Comédie humaine, La, see BALZAC.

comedy had its roots in a fertility ritual that in ancient Greece was an occasion for crude satire aimed at named persons. Already during the lifetime of its supreme exponent, *Aristophanes, such personal abuse became unacceptable, and an Athenian law of 414 BC forced the replacement of individuals by fictional types as targets for attack. Aristotle defined comedy as written about persons of minor importance whom their faults rendered ridiculous. This 'New Comedy', known to us through the Latin adaptations of *Plautus and *Terence, had a restricted range of characters: grumbling middle-aged men and women, young lovers, boastful soldiers, parasites, prostitutes, slaves. Superseded by *mime under the Roman Empire, classical comedy vanished from the stage during the Middle Ages when a homespun variety of farce was preferred, but was performed again in Italy at the end of the 15th cent. and soon gave rise to Italian imitations, of which *Machiavelli's *Mandragola* is the best known. The great comic playwrights of the late 16th and 17th cents, Shakespeare, Lope de *Vega, *Jonson, *Molière, drew on both the classical tradition and medieval farce, some adding a poetic dimension, others making their plays vehicles of social criticism. Writers in *Restoration England and the 18th cent. followed the pattern set by their predecessors, widening the range of characters and making use of sentiment and realism. But after the Romantic period serious comedy blended inextricably with the realist drama that explored the problems of everyday life. Only light comedy survived as a distinct genre akin to *farce. See also SENTIMENTAL COMEDY.

Comedy, The Divine, see DIVINA COMMEDIA.

Comedy of Errors, The, a comedy by *Shakespeare, acted at Gray's Inn 1594, first printed in the First *Folio (1623).

Syracuse and Ephesus being at enmity, any Syracusan found in Ephesus is put to death unless he can pay a ransom of 1,000 marks. Egeon, an old Syracusan merchant, has been arrested in Ephesus and on the duke's order explains how he came there. He and his wife Emilia had twin sons, exactly alike and each named Antipholus; the parents had purchased twin slaves, also exactly alike, each named Dromio, who attended on their sons. Having in a shipwreck been separated, with the younger son and one Dromio, from his wife and the other son and slave, Egeon had never seen them since. The younger son (Antipholus of Syracuse) on reaching manhood had gone (with his Dromio) in search of his brother and mother and had no more been heard of, though Egeon had now sought him for five years over the world, coming at last to Ephesus.

The duke, moved by this tale, gives Egeon till evening to find the ransom. Now, the elder Antipholus (Antipholus of Ephesus), with one of the Dromios, has been living in Ephesus since his rescue from shipwreck and is married. Antipholus of Syracuse and the other Dromio have arrived there that very morning. Each twin retains the same confusing resemblance to his brother as in childhood. From this the comedy of errors results. Antipholus of Syracuse is summoned home to dinner by Dromio of Ephesus; he is claimed as husband by the wife of Antipholus of Ephesus, the latter being refused admittance to his own house, because he is supposed to be already within; and Antipholus of Syracuse falls in love with Luciana, his brother's wife's sister. Finally Antipholus of Ephesus is confined as a lunatic, and Antipholus of Syracuse takes refuge from his brother's jealous wife in a convent.

Meanwhile evening has come and Egeon is led to execution. As the duke proceeds to the place of execution, Antipholus of Ephesus appeals to him for redress. Then the abbess of the convent presents Antipholus of Syracuse, also claiming redress. The simultaneous presence of the two brothers explains the numerous misunderstandings. Egeon recovers his two sons and his liberty, and the abbess turns out to be his lost wife Emilia.

COMENIUS, John Amos (Jan Komenský) (1592–1670), Moravian educational reformer, chiliast, and pansophist. He completed his studies in Heidelberg in 1614 and was ordained in 1618. He gained European fame in 1631 with the publication of *Janua Linguarum Reserata*, published in England as *The Gates of Tongues Unlocked and Opened*. In 1637 *Hartlib published *Conatuum Comenianorum praeludia* (in 1639 as *Pansophiae Prodromus* and in 1642 in English as *A Reformation of Schools*). Comenius visited London in 1641, where he wrote *Via Lucis*, then travelled in northern and middle Europe, finally settling in Amsterdam, where he wrote his last great work, *De Rerum Humanorum Emendatione Consultatio Catholica*, much of which was presumed lost until 1934 and which was published in its entirety in 1966. His *Orbis Sensualium Pictus*, with a Latin and German text, appeared in 1658, and was published in English in 1659 as *Comenius's Visible World*, the first schoolbook consistently to use pictures in the learning of languages. He believed in a system of universal wisdom, and his most lasting contribution was in the field of pedagogy.

COMESTOR, Petrus (d. 1179), from Troyes in Champagne, named 'the feeder' because of his voracity in studying books. He was the author of a *Historia Scholastica*, a collection of scriptural narratives with commentary which was very popular throughout the Middle Ages in a French translation, and was one of the first of the very many commentators on the *Sententiae* of *Peter Lombard. He became chancellor of the University of Paris in 1164. His work was familiar to *Chaucer, and *Dante places him among the Doctors of the Church in the heaven of the sun (*Paradiso*, xii. 134) as 'Pietro Mangiadore'.

Comical Revenge, The, or *Love in a Tub*, a comedy by *Etherege, acted 1664.

The serious part of the plot, in heroic couplets, deals with the rivalry of Lord Beaufort and Colonel Bruce for the hand of Graciana. A duel ensues. Bruce is defeated, tries to kill himself in despair, is cured of his wound, and consoled with Graciana's sister. The comic and farcical part, in prose, centres on the French valet Dufoy, who for his impudence is confined by his fellow servants in a tub. His master Sir Frederick Frolick, a debonair libertine, is courted by a rich widow; he cajoles her out of £200 and finally marries her. There is a foolish country knight, Sir Nicholas Cully, whom two rogues cozen out of £1,000. The knaves and the fool are exposed, and for punishment married off against their will and expectation.

comics, comic strips, flourished from the end of the 19th cent. with *Ally Sloper's Half-Holiday* (1884–1923), widely acknowledged as the publication that established the form, although comic strips had appeared earlier in papers such as *The Graphic* (1869–1932); Edwin John Brett's *The Boys of England* (1866–99, a highly successful mixture of fiction, 'sport, travel, fun and instruction'); and *Funny Folks* (1874–94; 'A Weekly Budget of Funny Pictures'). Ally Sloper was a sharp, gin-drinking, working-class anti-hero, the first regular character in the comic world. The growing boom continued with such publications as *Comic Cuts* (1890–1953) and *Chips* (1890–1953); *The Gem* (1907–39) and *The Magnet* (1908–40; see HAMILTON, CHARLES); with boys' adventure comics such as *Adventure* (1921–61), *Wizard* (1922–63), and *Hotspur* (1933–59); and with *Beano* (1938–) and *Dandy* (1937–), both still flourishing with many of their original characters. *Rainbow* (1914–56), with its hero Tiger Tim, was the first coloured comic designed exclusively for children, and described itself as 'The Children's Paper Parents Approve of', whereas *Chips* less loftily called itself 'The "Kid" 's Quietener, Father's Comfort, and Mother's Joy'. The battle between the subversively entertaining and the morally improving continued; Rupert Bear, who first appeared in the *Daily Express* on 8 Nov. 1920 (the creation of Mary Tourtel, distinguished by being written in rhyming couplets), was on the side of the angels, as was Dan Dare in *Eagle*. The founding of *Eagle* in 1950 by Lancashire vicar Marcus Morris was directly prompted by the growing infiltration of American horror comics, and it aimed to combine high moral values with the thrills of space adventure; the original series came to an end in 1969, but Dan Dare himself survives in *2000 AD*.

'Coming of Arthur, The', one of Tennyson's *Idylls of the King* published 1869. It describes the newly crowned Arthur's first meeting with Guinevere, and their marriage.

Coming Race, The, a novel by *Bulwer-Lytton, published 1871.

The narrator describes his visit to a subterranean race of superior beings that long ago took refuge, possibly from the biblical flood, in the depths of the earth. There they have evolved a highly sophisticated civilization, with the aid of a form of energy called Vril, which has great powers of destruction as well as great utility. Much of the novel is devoted to a satiric account of the narrator's own democratic society, of which he is initially proud, and to praise of the underground society, which has no war, no crime, and no inequality, and where women are stronger than men and free to choose their own mates. This involves the narrator in some embarrassing situations with his host's daughter Zee; he convinces her that he would never be happy in her world, and she returns him to the upper earth, aided by her mechanical Vril-powered wings. 'Love is swifter than Vril' is one of her more romantic statements. He is left to prophesy the death of the human race at the hands of 'our inevitable destroyers'. The sublime subterranean landscapes recall the paintings of J. *Martin, whose work Bulwer-Lytton much admired, and a memory of the novel lingers on in the trade name of the product 'Bovril', derived from 'Vril'.

commedia dell'arte, Italian popular character comedy, in which masked professional actors improvised on a traditional plot. It developed in the 16th cent., probably from the 'commedia erudita' (Renaissance learned comedy, following *Plautus and *Terence), but some critics postulate an even earlier origin in the mime of the popular Latin *Atellan fables. Its main characters came to be fixed into farcical types (e.g. Harlequin, Pulcinella, Pantaloon, Columbine). It was dying out by the 18th cent. when *Goldoni refreshed its types with a richer psychology.

COMMINES, Philippe de (c.1445–1511), French chronicler. He served in a diplomatic capacity under Charles the Bold of Burgundy, and subsequently under Louis XI and Charles VIII of France. His *Mémoires*, first published in 1524–8, are in two parts, the first dealing with the reign of Louis XI, the second with Charles VIII's Italian campaign. They were first translated into English by Thomas Danett (1596), and were the inspiration for Scott's *Quentin Durward.

Common Prayer, The Book of. This was evolved in the 16th cent. to meet the popular need for aids to devotion (not entirely satisfied by the *primers) and the demand for the use of the vernacular in church services. Its development was gradual. The Sarum breviary was reissued in 1541 and ordered to be used throughout the province of Canterbury 1542. The reading in churches of a chapter of the Bible in English, and the litany in English (probably the work of *Cranmer), were introduced in 1544, and an English communion service in 1548. About the same time the primers were revised, and the King's Primer issued in 1545 in the interest of uniformity; it included the English Litany. Cranmer and a commission each drafted a scheme for a prayer book, and these were discussed in Edward VI's reign, leading to the successive issue of the Prayer Books of 1549 and 1552. In the latter the form of the *Book of Common Prayer* was practically settled, though a revision was made under Elizabeth (1559), minor changes under James I, and the final text is that of 1662. As it stands the Prayer Book represents largely the work of Cranmer; N. *Ridley may perhaps claim some share.

Alternative forms of service in contemporary language were published in 1980 and recommended for general use in church services in preference to the 1662 Prayer Book. This gave rise to vigorous argument, inside and outside the Church of England, as to the respective merits of attempting to improve the congregation's understanding of the liturgy and of preserving its traditions and literary qualities.

Common Reader, The, the title of two collections of essays by V. *Woolf, taken from Dr Johnson's life of Gray in *Lives of the English Poets*, which concludes with a famous paragraph in praise of the *Elegy*: 'In the character of his Elegy I rejoice to concur with the common reader . . . The *Church-yard* abounds with images which find a mirror in every mind, and with sentiments to which every bosom returns an echo.'

Commonwealth of Oceana, The, a political work by J. *Harrington, published 1656 and dedicated to *Cromwell; in form it is part historical analysis, part *utopia, and part a written constitution.

Harrington analyses the events leading to the Civil War (particularly the decay of the feudal system and the new allegiances of freeholders), using both historical and fictional names; *Coke appears as himself, whereas Oceana is England, the Normans become the Neustrians, Henry VII becomes Panurgus, etc. He then proceeds to draw up a plan for an ideal republic, under the leadership of the Archon, Olphaus Megaletor, an idealized Cromwell figure. He expresses his admiration for the republics of Greece and Rome and for the Venetian republic, and frequently invokes *Machiavelli as 'the only politician of later ages'. His own proposals include the dividing of the great estates, a two-chamber system, indirect election by ballot, rotation in office, a popularly elected poet laureate, and a National Theatre: 'An equal commonwealth . . . is a government established upon an equal agrarian, arising into the superstructures or three orders, the senate debating and proposing, the people resolving, and the magistracy executing by an equal rotation through the suffrage of the people given by the ballot.' Overall, he proposes a carefully worked-out system of checks and balances, far from utopian in its concept of human nature, which *Hume was to describe as 'the only valuable model of a commonwealth that has yet been offered to the public'. Harrington's *Oceana* is an intended contrast to Hobbes's *Leviathan*, to which he frequently refers: Hobbes, says *Aubrey, 'remained silent' on the subject.

communitarianism, a diverse movement in social and political thought, developed primarily in the USA and Canada in the 1980s and 1990s, reacting to the excessive individualism taken to be characteristic of liberal perspectives in academic political philosophy and to the supposed fragmentation of modern societies. Communitarian philosophers, often consciously seeking to revive republican, *Aristotelian, or *Hegelian traditions, in various ways accuse liberal theory of neglecting the individual's dependence on community. Some, such as Michael Sandel (*Liberalism and the Limits of Justice*, 1982), a critic of *Rawls, argue that people's attachments to others may be constitutive of their identities as individuals (rather than freely chosen), while others, like Charles Taylor (*Sources of the Self*, 1990), emphasize the social and cultural preconditions of liberal individualism. The more sociological strand of communitarian thought points to increasing feelings of isolation and loss of community among members of the advanced liberal democracies (Robert Bellah et al., *Habits of the Heart*, 1985), and Amitai Etzioni, founder of the 'Communitarian movement', advocates a new balance between individual rights and social responsibilities (see esp. *The Spirit of Community*, 1993) and has had some influence on political debate in the USA and the UK.

COMNENA and **COMNENUS,** see ANNA COMNENA.

comparative literature, an academic discipline in which literary works and traditions of more than one nation or language are studied, thus permitting fuller understanding of international literary movements and affiliations. By contrast with nationally or linguistically defined disciplines such as 'English literature', comparative literature ranges freely across frontiers in search of cross-cultural influences and correspondences. The name does not imply any obligation to compare different national literary traditions—an exercise often attempted in the 19th cent. by critics such as Mme de *Staël and M. *Arnold. The discipline has been more favoured by American universities—notably Chicago and Columbia—than by British. Distinguished practitioners have included I. *Babbitt and E. *Auerbach.

complaint, a poetic form derived from the Latin *planctus*, bewailing the vicissitudes of life (as in *Hoccleve's *Complaint*) or addressed to a more particular end (such as *Chaucer's 'Complaint to his Purse'). The form is particularly common in poems up to the Renaissance; thereafter the terms *'elegy' and 'lament' were used.

Complaint, The, or *Night Thoughts on Life, Death, and Immortality*, see NIGHT THOUGHTS.

Complaint of Buckingham, The, a poem by T. *Sackville, contributed by him to *A Mirror for Magistrates*.

Henry Stafford, duke of Buckingham, after his rebellion against Richard III, takes refuge with a dependant, Humfrey Banastair. Banastair betrays him to the king and Buckingham is executed. As his corpse lies on the ground it raises its head and heaps curses on Banastair and his children.

'Complaint of Rosamund', a poem by S. *Daniel in rhyme-royal appended to *Delia*.

Complaynt to the King, see LINDSAY, D.

Compleat Angler, The, or *The Contemplative Man's Recreation*, a discourse on fishing by I. *Walton, first published 1653, the second much enlarged edition 1655, fifth edition with a continuation by *Cotton, 1676.

It takes the form of a dialogue, at first between the author Piscator (a fisherman), Auceps (a fowler), and Venator (a hunter), each commending his own recreation, in which Auceps is silenced and Venator becomes a pupil of the angle; then between Piscator and Venator alone. The author instructs his pupil in the art of catching various kinds of freshwater fish, with directions for dressing some of them for the table. The five days' fishing expedition along the river Lea also contains interludes of verse and song, angling anecdotes, moral reflections, and snatches of mythology and folklore. In Cotton's continuation Piscator and Viator (who turns out to be Venator) fish along the river Dove which divides Derbyshire and Staffordshire; there are fuller instructions for making artificial flies (Walton was not an experienced fly-fisher) and descriptions of the picturesque scenery of the district.

Walton's various sources include *The Treatise of Fishing with an Angle* (*The Book of St Albans*, 1496) and an anonymous book, *The Art of Angling* (in which Piscator and Viator both appear), published in 1577, of which the only known copy was discovered in 1954.

Complutensian Polyglot Bible, The, see XIMÉNEZ DE CISNEROS.

COMPTON-BURNETT, Dame Ivy (1884–1969), novelist, who embarked on a serious career as a writer only with *Pastors and Masters* (1925), which meant that she had in some ways less in common with the *Modernism of her contemporaries than with the post-war generation of novelists such as E. *Waugh and *Powell, whose brittle, deflationary wit, irony, and satirical exuberance are reflected especially in early works like *Brother and Sisters* (1929) or *More Women Than Men* (1933). But her highly condensed and abstracted novels, composed almost entirely in dialogue, were so unlike anyone else's that their impact was often compared to that of post-impressionism in painting. They are all dated round about the turn of the century and set in large, gloomy, generally dilapidated houses full of servants, children, and dependent relatives. Each family is ruled in almost complete isolation from the outside world by a more or less tyrannical parent or grandparent: hence the consistently high rate of domestic crime ranging from adultery, incest, and child abuse to murder and fraud. Dame Ivy held that 'nothing is so corrupting as power', and her inward-looking, self-contained, and heavily monitored high Victorian households provided her with an ideal environment in which to examine the misuse of power together with the violence and misery that follow.

Her personal life was effectively destroyed by the First World War and, when she eventually recovered from a protracted physical and emotional breakdown in the early 1920s, she found herself increasingly preoccupied with the eruption of passionate and disruptive forces smouldering beneath the smooth surface of a deceptively calm and well-ordered society. Her chief formative influences were G. *Eliot (imitated with unhappy results in *Dolores*, 1911, and afterwards crucially rejected), the Greek tragic dramatists, and S. *Butler. After 1925 she published another 18 novels, of which *A House and Its Head* (1935), *A Family and a Fortune* (1939), and *Manservant and Maidservant* (1947) are perhaps outstanding. See H. Spurling, *Ivy When Young: The Early Life of I. Compton-Burnett 1884–1919* (1974) and *Secrets of a Woman's Heart: The Later Life of I. Compton-Burnett 1920–1969* (1984).

COMTE, Auguste (1798–1857), French philosopher, in early life secretary to C. H. de *Saint-Simon, with whom he shared the conviction that throughout history the mind and political institutions had evolved in close relation, and that a new phase of mental development had been entered. Comte set himself to frame a general system of human conceptions as they had developed to their existing state: such is the plan of his *Cours de philosophie positive* (6 vols, 1830–42). The *Système de politique positive* (4 vols, 1851–4) gave a fuller treatment of political philosophy and its applications. The main departments of human knowledge, Comte argued, passed of necessity through three successive phases: the theological, the metaphysical, and the positive. This was the 'Law of the Three States' and it applied to the historical progress of the mind and to the development of the individual mind alike. The positive or scientific state, which had been attained but not brought to completion, was the 'normal' or final state of humanity. It was characterized by the abandonment of the search for absolute causes and the recognition of the 'laws of succession and relation' that govern phenomena as the true object of knowledge.

Comte's aim was to prepare the way for bringing the science of social phenomena, sociology, into its final, positive, state and so lay the foundations of a social and political system proper to the age of industry. Temporal power was to be vested in a self-perpetuating élite of industrial chiefs. A separate spiritual authority would be established in the form of a priesthood with the duty of educating and informing opinion in the general truths of the positive philosophy and their practical

corollaries, and of administering a formal religion centred on the cult of Humanity (conceived as a Great Being composed of those men and women, past, present, and to come, whose lives had been, were, or would be devoted to human progress or well-being). A preponderant place was to be given in the organization of religious and social life to the influence of women on the feelings, in order to foster altruism, the basis of the Comtean morality, expressed in the motto: 'Live for Others'.

Comte's principal English followers were F. *Harrison, E. S. Beesly, J. H. Bridges, and Richard Congreve. The *Cours de philosophie positive* was condensed, with the author's approval, in English translation by H. *Martineau (*The Positive Philosophy of Auguste Comte*, 2 vols, 1853); the *Système de politique positive* was translated by Harrison, Bridges, and others as *The System of Positive Polity* (4 vols, 1875–7). G. H. *Lewes provided an exposition of the leading ideas of the *Cours* in *Comte's Philosophy of the Sciences* (1853). J. S. *Mill gave a critical account of Comte's thought in *Auguste Comte and Positivism* (1865); *Lettres inédites de John Stuart Mill à Auguste Comte* was published in Paris in 1899.

Comus, *A Maske Presented at Ludlow Castle, 1634: on Michaelmasse Night, before the Right Honorable John Earl of Bridgewater, Lord President of Wales*, by *Milton, first printed, anonymously and untitled, 1637.

This work was written at Hammersmith at the suggestion of Milton's friend H. *Lawes; its purpose was to celebrate the earl of Bridgewater's entry on the presidency of Wales and the Marches, and the roles of the Lady and her two brothers were taken by his daughter Alice, aged 15, and her 11- and 9-year-old brothers. Although described as a 'masque', *Comus* depends little on spectacle and may be defined as a *pastoral drama. Comus himself is a pagan god invented by Milton, son of Bacchus and Circe, who waylays travellers and transforms their faces to those of wild beasts by means of a magic liquor. The Lady, benighted in a forest and separated from her brothers, comes across Comus in the guise of a shepherd; he leads her off to his cottage, offering protection. The brothers appear and are told what has happened by the Attendant Spirit Thyrsis, also disguised as a shepherd; he warns them of the magic power of Comus and gives them a root of the plant Haemony as protection. The scene changes to 'a stately Palace', where Comus with his rabble tempts the Lady to drink his magic potion, and with much eloquence urges her not to be 'cosen'd with that same vaunted name Virginity'. She defends herself and Chastity with such spirit that even Comus feels her possessed of 'some superior power'. At this point the brothers burst in and disperse the crew. Unfortunately they have not secured the wand of Comus and are unable to release the Lady from her enchanted chair, which provides an opportunity for

Thyrsis to invoke *Sabrina, goddess of the neighbouring river Severn, in the lovely song 'Sabrina Fair, | Listen where thou art sitting'. She arrives, the Lady is freed, and the Lady and her brothers are returned to Ludlow and presented to their parents. The richness and variety of the poetry, which moves from blank verse to rhymed octosyllabics to song, and the abundance and grace of the pastoral, pagan, and Christian allusions combine with an Elizabethan freshness and Spenserian charm, though the action has been justly but somewhat irrelevantly criticized as 'a dramatised debate' (E. Welsford, *The Court Masque*, 1927). See C. C. Brown, *Milton's Aristocratic Entertainments* (1985).

Conan, in the legends relating to *Finn (Fingal), 'in some respects a kind of Thersites, but brave and daring even to rashness' (author's notes to *Waverley*). Having visited the infernal regions, he received a cuff from the Arch-fiend, which he instantly returned with the words 'blow for blow'.

CONAN DOYLE, Arthur, see DOYLE, A. C.

conceit, an elaborate metaphor comparing two apparently dissimilar objects or emotions, often with an effect of shock or surprise. The *Petrarchan conceit, much imitated by Elizabethan sonneteers and both used and parodied by Shakespeare, usually evoked the qualities of the disdainful mistress and the devoted lover, often in highly exaggerated terms; the *metaphysical conceit, as used by *Donne and his followers, applied wit and ingenuity to, in the words of Dr *Johnson, 'a combination of dissimilar images, or discovery of occult resemblances in things apparently unlike', e.g. Donne's famous comparison of two lovers to a pair of compasses.

Conchubar, or **Conchobar** (pron. Conachoor), in the Ulster cycle of Irish mythology, king of Ulster, see CUCHULAIN and DEIRDRE.

Conciliation with America, On, by *Burke, speech made in the House of Commons on 22 Mar. 1775.

This, one of Burke's greatest speeches, was a last effort to find a peaceful solution of the difference with the American colonies. Burke's proposal is to restore order and repose to the empire 'by restoring the former unsuspecting confidence of the colonies in the mother country'. He rejects the use of force, as inapplicable to the 'fierce spirit of liberty' prevailing in the English colonies. He traces the 'capital sources' from which this spirit has grown up, descent, religion, remoteness of situation; and propounds three options, to change this spirit, to prosecute it as criminal, to comply with it as necessary. He shows the first two courses to be impossible or inexpedient. He dismisses American representation in Parliament as impracticable. He finds the solution in the taxation of America through grants by the local legislatures and not by imposition. His trust is in America's interest in the British constitution: 'My hold of the colonies is in the close

affection which grows from common names, from kindred blood, from similar privileges, and equal protection.' 'Magnanimity in politics is not seldom the truest wisdom; and a great empire and little minds go ill together.'

concrete poetry, a term used to describe a kind of experimental poetry developed in the 1950s and flourishing in the 1960s, which dwells primarily on the visual aspects of the poem (although two other forms of concrete poetry, the kinetic and the phonetic, have also been distinguished). An international movement was officially launched at the National Exhibition of concrete art in São Paulo in 1956; a Brazilian 'Pilot Plan' or manifesto, published in 1958, stated that 'concrete poetry begins by being aware of graphic space as structural agent'. Concrete poets experiment with typography, graphics, the 'ideogram concept', computer poems, collage, etc., and in varying degrees acknowledge influence from *Dada, Hans Arp, Schwitters, Malevich, and other visual artists. Ian Hamilton *Finlay (1925–   ), one of the leading Scottish exponents, expresses his own affinity with 17th-cent. *emblems and poems such as G. *Herbert's 'Easter Wings', which use the shape as well as the sense of a poem to convey meaning. E. *Morgan, also a Scot, has written a variety of concrete poems, which were criticized by some devotees of the form as being 'too verbal'. Mary Ellen Solt in 'A World Look at Concrete Poetry' (*Hispanic Arts*, 1/3–4, 1968) declares that 'the concrete poet seeks to relieve the poem of its centuries-old burden of ideas, symbolic reference, allusion and repetitious emotional content.' Others claim a less radical role, pointing to Herbert, *Blake, Carroll (C. L. *Dodgson), *Pound's use of Chinese characters, and E. E. *Cummings as evidence of a long tradition of typographical experiment. See *An Anthology of Concrete Poetry* (1967), ed. Emmett Williams.

CONDELL, Henry, see HEMINGES.

CONDER, Charles, see ART NOUVEAU.

CONDILLAC, Étienne, abbé de (1715–80), French philosopher. His *Essai sur l'origine des connaissances humaines* (1746, 1771) and *Traité des sensations* (1754, 1778) carry the empiricism of *Locke to a systematic extreme, deriving all subsequent operations of the mind, including the ideas of God and of the immortality of the soul, from their alleged origin in sensation. He polarized Enlightenment opinion against Cartesian metaphysics.

Condition of England, a phrase coined by T. *Carlyle in the opening words of *Past and Present* (1843) to describe the social and political inequalities in what B. *Disraeli, in *Sybil* (1845), was to term the 'Two Nations of England, the Rich and the Poor'. It formed the subject matter of social investigators and writers of government 'blue books', and of *social problem novelists, and developed the question asked by Carlyle in *Chartism* (1839): 'Is the condition of the English working people wrong; so wrong that rational working men cannot, will not, and even should not rest quiet under it?' See also CHARTIST MOVEMENT.

CONDORCET, Jean Antoine Nicolas Caritat, marquis de (1743–94), see PHILOSOPHES.

coney-catching, see ROGUE LITERATURE.

Confederacy, The, a comedy by *Vanbrugh, produced 1705, adapted from Dancourt's *Les Bourgeoises à la mode*.

Gripe and Moneytrap, two rich usurers, are niggardly husbands, and Gripe's wife Clarissa, in order to pay her debts, is obliged to pawn her necklace with Mrs Amlet. Mrs Amlet has a knave of a son, Dick, who passes himself off as a colonel, and is trying to win by fair means or foul the hand of Gripe's daughter Corinna, assisted in the plot by Brass, who acts as his footman, and by Flippanta, Clarissa's maid. Meanwhile Gripe falls in love with Moneytrap's wife and Moneytrap falls in love with Gripe's wife. This the ladies communicate to each other and contrive to turn to their mutual advantage. By their directions, Brass and Flippanta, who act as go-betweens, extract £250 apiece from the would-be lovers to relieve their ladies' immediate necessities. The two couples take tea together, each of the four pleased with the course of events, but the pawned necklace brings about a general exposure. Clarissa has told her husband that she has lost it, and he has warned the goldsmiths to look out for it. Dick has stolen it from his mother and sent Brass to try to sell it. The goldsmith to whom Brass offers it now brings it to Gripe. Dick's true character and the pawning of the necklace are thus brought to light. But all ends well, Corinna agreeing to take Dick despite all, and Mrs Amlet endowing him with £10,000.

Confessio Amantis, see GOWER, J.

confessional poetry, a term principally applied to the self-revealing style of writing and use of intimate subject matter adopted and pioneered in America by R. *Lowell (*Life Studies*, 1959): other writers in the tradition have included *Berryman, *Sexton, and *Plath. A new wave of confessional writing in prose occurred in the 1980s and 1990s when a vogue for *autobiographical material, family history, and frank memoirs coincided in Britain with a new sense of male interest in domestic and psychological matters hitherto regarded as predominantly female terrain: this resulted in 'New Man' writing by Blake *Morrison, Nick *Hornby, and others. See also LADS' LITERATURE, for a related and reactive variant of the phenomenon.

Confessions of a Justified Sinner, see PRIVATE MEMOIRS AND CONFESSIONS OF A JUSTIFIED SINNER by J. Hogg.

Confessions of an English Opium Eater, by *De Quincey, published 1822 (enlarged version 1856).

De Quincey's study of his own opium addiction and its psychological effects traces how childhood and youthful experiences are transformed, under the influence of opium, into symbolical and revealing dreams. The central experience for subsequent dream-formations was his childhood loss of his sister, duplicated by the disappearance of the 15-year-old prostitute Ann, who befriended him during his months of homeless near-starvation in London. The euphoric reveries of the early stages of his addiction and the appalling nightmares of the later stages are described in sonorous and haunting prose, and the work, first appearing in the *London Magazine* in 1821, conferred instant literary fame on De Quincey, whose first book it was. In 1856 he greatly extended the *Confessions* for a collected edition of his works, but thereby blunted its effect.

Confidence-Man: His Masquerade, The (1857), a novel by H. *Melville.

A comic allegory set on the ironically named Mississippi steamboat *Fiddle*, Melville's last novel shows a cross-section of mid-century America and, through them, humanity, being gulled by a satanic trickster who magically metamorphoses into the shape appropriate to his victim's desires. Melville's nihilist fable expresses a profound philosophical and social pessimism.

CONGREVE, William (1670–1729), born at Bardsey, near Leeds, of an ancient family. Because his father was commander of the garrison at Youghal, he was educated at Kilkenny school and Trinity College, Dublin, at both of which he was a fellow student of *Swift. He entered the Middle Temple, but soon gave up law for literature, published a novel of intrigue, *Incognita* (1691), and in 1693 suddenly achieved fame with his comedy *The Old Bachelor*. Of his other comedies, *The Double Dealer* was published in 1694 (first performed 1693), *Love for Love* in 1695, and *The Way of the World* in 1700. In these Congreve shows himself the master of *Restoration comedy, studying the social pressures on love and marriage with wit and subtlety. His one tragedy, *The Mourning Bride*, was produced in 1697. In 1698 he replied to the attack made on him in the *Short View* of Jeremy *Collier. After 1700 he wrote comparatively little for the stage; he was by then in comfortable circumstances, holding more than one government post, and enjoying general admiration and the friendship of men like Swift, *Steele, and *Pope. He was visited by *Voltaire, and had an affair with the duchess of Marlborough, who bore him a daughter. He was throughout the friend of Mrs *Bracegirdle. He was buried in Westminster Abbey.

Coningsby, a novel by B. *Disraeli, published 1844.

In the preface to the Hughenden edition of his novels in 1870 Disraeli declares that his purpose in the trilogy *Coningsby*–*Sybil*–*Tancred* was to describe the influence of the main political parties on the condition of the people, and to indicate how those conditions might be improved. His theme is that the Crown must govern justly and the Church inspire. His purpose was avowedly political, and he chose the novel as the most effective influence on public opinion. *Coningsby* celebrates the new Tories of the 'Young England' set, whose opposition to Whiggery and whose concern at the treatment of the poor and the injustice of the franchise is strongly reflected in the narrative.

The high-spirited and generous Coningsby, whose parents both die, is sent to Eton by his wealthy and powerful grandfather Lord Monmouth, who represents the old type of oppressive Tory aristocrat. There Coningsby becomes the friend, and saves the life of, Oswald Millbank, who is the son of an energetic Lancashire manufacturer, detested by Monmouth. At Cambridge and thereafter Coningsby develops political and social ideals far removed from those of his grandfather, and meanwhile falls in love with Oswald's sister Edith. His behaviour so angers Monmouth that when the old man dies Coningsby finds he has been disinherited. He has to forgo his life of affluence and set to work in the Inns of Court. Gradually Millbank, who had been opposed to Coningsby's marriage to his daughter, begins to realize the young man's worth; he helps him to stand for Parliament and sees him returned. Edith and Coningsby are married and Coningsby's fortunes are restored.

The vigorous portrait of Lord Monmouth is based on Lord Hertford, who was also the model for *Thackeray's Lord Steyne. Sidonia, the wise old Jew who appears also in *Tancred*, reflects aspects of Lord Rothschild; and Rigby, possibly the most unpleasant of all Disraeli's characters, is based on J. W. *Croker. *Coningsby* was immensely successful and came to be regarded as a manifesto for Young England.

Connoisseur, a periodical edited by G. *Colman the elder, and journalist and wit Bonnell Thornton (1724–68). It ran from Jan. 1754 to Sept. 1756, and *Cowper was among its contributors.

CONNOLLY, Cyril Vernon (1903–74), educated at Eton and Balliol College, Oxford; he became a journalist and critic, and a regular contributor to the *New Statesman*. He was literary editor of the *Observer*, 1942–3, and was for many years a weekly reviewer for the *Sunday Times*. In 1939, with *Spender, he founded *Horizon*, and edited it until it closed in 1950. His only novel, *The Rock Pool* (Paris, 1936; London, 1947), is a satiric extravaganza with echoes of *Firbank and E. *Waugh; it describes the adventures of a young literary stockbroker in Trou-sur-Mer, an artistic expatriate colony on the French Riviera. His works include *Enemies of Promise* (1938), critical essays, with an autobiographical section, 'A Georgian Boyhood', vividly recalling his schooldays (and the distinctive Etonian literary tradition of light verse, *Pre-Raphaelite-style Homer, etc.); *The Unquiet Grave* (1944), subtitled 'A Word Cycle' and published under the pseudonym of Palinurus (the drowned pilot of the *Aeneid*), which consists of aphorisms, reflections, etc.; and various collections of essays (*The Condemned Playground*, 1945, which displays his gift for parody; *Previous Convictions*, 1963; *The Evening Colonnade*, 1973, and others). Connolly's favourite themes include the dangers of early success and the hazardous lure of literary immortality, but he also celebrated the ephemeral pleasure of food, wine, and travel. A biography by Jeremy Lewis was published in 1997.

CONQUEST, (George) Robert (Acworth) (1917–), poet, historian, and critic, educated at Winchester and Magdalen College, Oxford, who edited the important and controversial anthology *New Lines (1956). His publications include *Poems* (1955), *Between Mars and Venus* (1962), *Arias from a Love Opera* (1969), and several works on the former USSR.

Conquest of Granada by the Spaniards, The, in two parts (Part I produced in Dec. 1670, Part II in Jan. 1671; both pub. 1672). Written in resounding rhyming couplets, this ten-act heroic extravaganza by *Dryden depicts the troubled but finally fortunate loves of the noble if impulsive Almanzor and the Moorish beauty Almahide. With its ample cast of characters, including the vividly drawn *femme fatale* Lyndaraxa, and its epic setting against the background of the Spanish reconquest of Granada torn by the tribal rivalry between the Abencerragos and the Zegrys, the play was an artistic success and a huge box-office hit. As such it became the main target of the duke of *Buckingham's and others' burlesque in *The Rehearsal*, in which its high-blown verse and its larger-than-life hero were savagely satirized.

CONRAD, Joseph (Józef Teodor Konrad Korzeniowski) (1857–1924), novelist and short story writer, born of Polish parents in the Russian-dominated Ukraine. His father's political sympathies caused the family to be exiled to Volagda in northern Russia, where Conrad's mother died when he was 7. After their return to Poland his father also died and Conrad was taken under the wing of his uncle, Tadeusz Bobrowski, who was to be a continuing influence on his life. From an early age he longed to go to sea and in 1874 he went to Marseilles, embarked on a French vessel, and began the career as a sailor which was to supply so much material for his writing. In 1886 he became a British subject and a master mariner and in 1894, after 20 years at sea, he settled in England and devoted himself to writing. He published his first novel at the age of 38, writing in English, his third language.

In 1895 Conrad married Jessie George, by whom he was to have two sons, and his novel *Almayer's Folly* appeared in the same year. This was followed by *An Outcast of the Islands* (1896), in which there is still evidence of his struggle with both technique and the English language; but with *The Nigger of the 'Narcissus'* (1897) and *Lord Jim* (1900) he showed himself a master of his craft. The sea continued to supply the setting for most of his novels and short stories. His narrative technique is characterized by a skilful use of breaks in time-sequence and he uses a narrator, Marlow, who provides a commentary on the action not unlike that of a Greek chorus. Conrad has been called an Impressionist and the movement of the stories, of the images and emotions, is portrayed through each character's private vision of reality. He collaborated with F. M. *Ford on *The Inheritors* (1900) and *Romance* (1903), but eventual disagreements brought their association to an end. *Typhoon* (1903) was followed by a major work, *Nostromo* (1904), an imaginative novel which again explores one of Conrad's chief preoccupations—man's vulnerability and corruptibility. In *'Heart of Darkness'* (1902), one of his best-known short stories, Conrad had carried this issue to a terrifying conclusion. *The Secret Agent* (1907) and *Under Western Eyes* (1911) are both novels with political themes, the latter set in Switzerland and Russia and centred on the tragedy of the student Razumov, caught up in the treachery and violence of revolution. Although warmly supported by E. *Garnett and the agent J. B. Pinker, and praised by Arnold *Bennett, *Galsworthy, H. *James, and other influential men of letters, Conrad's work was generally ill received by critics and public alike, and he was plagued with money problems. Some of his stories were serialized in *Blackwood's Magazine*, but it was the novel *Chance* (1913) that brought Conrad his first popular and financial success; it is the story of Flora de Barral, lonely daughter of a crooked financier, and combines the attractions of a sea background with the theme of romantic love and more female interest than is usual with Conrad. His other major works include *Youth* (1902), *The Mirror of the Sea* (1906), *Victory* (1915), *The Shadow-Line* (1917), *The Rescue* (1920), and *The Rover* (1923). Conrad's autobiography, *A Personal Record*, appeared in book form in 1912 and his unfinished novel *Suspense* was published in 1925.

By the time of his death, Conrad was well established in the literary world as one of the leading *Modernists; a decline of interest in the 1930s was followed by increasing scholarly and critical attention, pioneered in part by a study in 1941 by M. C. *Bradbrook, and by an essay in the same year by *Leavis in *Scrutiny* (later reprinted in *The Great Tradition*) in which Conrad is placed 'among the very great novelists in the language'. See J. Baines, *Joseph Conrad: A Critical Biography* (1960); F. R. Karl, *Joseph Conrad: The Three Lives* (1979); and Z. Najder, *Joseph Conrad: A Chronicle* (1983). His *Collected Letters*, ed. F. Karl and L. Davis, were published in five vols, 1983–96.

Conscious Lovers, The, the last comedy of *Steele, based on the *Andria* of *Terence, performed 1722.

Young Bevil is, at his father's desire, about to marry Lucinda, daughter of the wealthy Mr Sealand. But he loves Indiana, an orphan whom he met destitute and

friendless in a foreign town and has honourably supported. Not wishing to oppose his father openly, he makes known to Lucinda his aversion to the proposed match, the more readily as he knows his friend Myrtle loves her. In doing this he offends Myrtle, is challenged to a duel, and declines, thus exhibiting the folly of duelling, a favourite theme with Steele. Indiana turns out to be a lost daughter of Mr Sealand, who is happy to bestow her on Bevil; Myrtle gains Lucinda. The play, with its high moral tone, was a success, and considerably influenced the drift towards *sentimental comedy in England and in France.

consonance is the repetition of end or medial consonants, as in 'blank' and 'think', or 'The curfew to*lls* the kne*ll* of parting day' (*Gray's *Elegy*).

CONSTABLE, Archibald (1774–1827), a Scots publisher whom Sir W. *Scott described as 'of uncommon importance to literature'. He was an expert in antiquarian books, yet he also possessed a flair for choosing contemporary authors and he published most of Scott's early work. He established the highly successful *Edinburgh Review* in 1802, paying his contributors handsomely, and bought the *Encyclopaedia Britannica* in 1812. Yet in 1826 he went bankrupt, heavily involving Scott in his debts. He was an enthusiast for the new concept of cheap books, and in 1827 established Constable's Miscellany, a series of volumes on literature, art, and science.

CONSTABLE, Henry (1562–1613), educated at St John's College, Cambridge; he embraced Roman Catholicism, and withdrew to Paris. He published *Diana*, a volume of sonnets, in 1592; it was republished in 1594 with additions by other poets. He was sent as papal envoy to Edinburgh in 1599 and pensioned by the French king. He came to London in 1603, was imprisoned in the Tower in 1604, and released the same year. He died at Liège. Verses by him were embodied in various collections, among others in *Englands Helicon*. His poems were edited by Joan Grundy in 1960. Many of his sonnets are modelled on or translated from sonnets by Desportes.

CONSTABLE, John (1776–1837), landscape painter, born at East Bergholt, Suffolk, the son of a miller. His works develop from the tranquillity of the early exhibited landscapes (*The Haywain*, 1821, National Gallery, London) to the sombre drama of *Hadleigh Castle* (1829, Tate Gallery, London). Constable's relationship with the Romantic poets has been much discussed by scholars; he is linked to them by his feeling for the simplest facts of nature and by his sense of their moral power. Yet Constable disliked the Lake District, where he met *Wordsworth and *Coleridge in 1806, and his tastes were generally more traditional—for *Cowper and *Gray, whose *Elegy* he illustrated, and for Thomson's *The Seasons* and R. *Bloomfield's *The Farmer's Boy* (1802)—and lines from these works sometimes accompanied his pictures. Constable was a friend of Joseph Farington, of J. T. Smith, of Sir G. *Beaumont, and of Charles Leslie. (See ROMANTICISM.)

Constance, (1) a princess in a frequently told medieval story which appears in the *Canterbury Tales* (see 'The Man of Law's Tale') as well as in *Gower's *Confessio Amantis*; (2) in Shakespeare's *King John*, the mother of Arthur, the king's nephew.

CONSTANT, Benjamin (Henri-Benjamin Constant de Rebecque) (1767–1830), French novelist, political philosopher, and politician, born at Lausanne of a family of French Protestant origins, who had his university education at Oxford (briefly), in Germany, and at Edinburgh. He was intermittently in Paris after 1795 and held office under the Consulate, but went into exile in 1803. From Hanover he published the anti-Napoleonic pamphlet 'De l'esprit de conquête et de l'usurpation' (1813). His political career in the Liberal opposition begins after the Restoration. Constant is remembered for the political and religious treatises *De la religion considérée dans sa source, ses formes et ses développements* (5 vols, 1824–31), but much more for the literary masterpiece *Adolphe* (first published in London in 1816), a short novel of psychological analysis reflecting at some points his own liaison with Mme de *Staël. His *Journaux intimes*, first published in 1895, appeared in a complete edition in 1952; his *Cahier rouge*, recounting the first 20 years of his life, in 1907, and *Cécile*, the fragment of an autobiographical novel, in 1951. (See also ZÉLIDE.)

Constant Couple, The, or *A Trip to the Jubilee*, a farcical comedy by *Farquhar, produced 1699, which was very successful owing chiefly to the amusing character of Sir Harry Wildair, 'an airy gentleman, affecting humorous gaiety and freedom in his behaviour'. It had a less successful sequel in *Sir Harry Wildair* (1701).

CONSTANTINE, David (1944–   ), poet, born in Salford, fellow in German at The Queen's College, Oxford. *A Brightness to Cast Shadows* (1980) and *Watching for Dolphins* (1983) introduced a poet of rare lyric intensity. Learned but direct, Constantine offers a world lit by the supernatural, drawing freely on classical and Romantic traditions and standing at their intersection in 'Watching for Dolphins' itself, a poem of the longing for transcendence. *Selected Poems* appeared in 1991, followed by the epic *Caspar Hauser* (1994) and *The Pelt of Wasps* (1998). Constantine has also translated the *Selected Poems* of Friedrich *Hölderlin (1996).

Contarini Fleming; *A Psychological Romance*, a novel by B. *Disraeli, published 1832.

This novel, which remained Disraeli's own favourite, was the last in the group *Vivian Grey–Alroy–Fleming, although it was published before *Alroy*. In the preface to the 1845 edition of his novels, Disraeli describes how in this book he attempted to provide a complete picture of the development of a poet. In making his hero the son of both Saxon and Venetian

lineage, living in 'a northern court', Disraeli attempts to show the effects on character of North and South. Contarini is an impetuous, handsome boy, rebellious at school, from which he runs away. His kindly father sends him to a university, and then introduces him to society, where his wit and moody brilliance bring him great success. But society palls and, after various wild adventures in the northern forests, he finds his way to Venice, the home of his mother's family, where he is captivated by the beauty of the city and where he meets his cousin Alceste, whom he marries. She dies within a year and to calm his grief he again takes up his travels, before returning to an estate near Naples, where he intends to live in solitude in 'the study and creation of the beautiful'. The influence of *Goethe's *Wilhelm Meister* and of the *'Byronic' hero are evident.

Contemporary Review, founded in 1866 and edited for many years by Sir Percy Bunting. It covered religious, political, and literary subjects; in 1955 it incorporated the *Fortnightly, and now deals largely with current affairs.

Conversation, *A Complete Collection of Polite and Ingenious*, by *Swift, published 1738.

In this entertaining work Swift good-humouredly satirizes the stupidity, coarseness, and attempted wit of the conversation of fashionable people. In three dialogues he puts into the mouth of various characters, Lord Sparkish, Miss Notable, Lady Smart, Tom Neverout, etc., samples of questions and answers, proverbial sayings, and repartees, fitted, as he explains in the amusing introduction, 'to adorn every kind of discourse that an assembly of English ladies and gentlemen, met together for their mutual entertainment, can possibly want'. The work was published under the pseudonym of 'Simon Wagstaff, Esq.'

CONWAY, Anne, Viscountess (d. 1679), metaphysical writer and friend of Henry More (see CAMBRIDGE PLATONISTS). Her posthumous *Principles of the Most Ancient and Modern Philosophy* (Latin 1690, English 1692) influenced *Leibniz.

COOK, David (1940–   ), novelist, actor, and television playwright, born in Preston. He began his career as an actor after training at the Royal Academy of Dramatic Art. His first novel, *Albert's Memorial* (1972), concerns the tragi-comic friendship between widowed Mary and homosexual Paul: this was followed by *Happy Endings* (1974) about the relationship between a 12-year-old boy and a schoolteacher. *Walter* (1978) is the story of a well-intentioned and sensitive young man with severe learning difficulties trying to cope with the challenges of work, institutional life, and his mother's death: *Winter Doves* (1979) is a sequel in which Walter escapes to freedom with his friend June. Other works include *Sunrising* (1984), a historical novel set in poverty-stricken rural middle England and London in the 1830s; *Missing Persons* (1986), *Crying out Loud* (1988), and *Second Best* (1991), about a single man's attempt to adopt a 10-year-old boy. Cook's work displays a deep and humane sympathy with the disadvantaged, the sexually marginalized, and those with mental or learning problems. A TV adaptation of *Walter* with Ian McKellen in the title role was chosen to launch Channel Four in 1982.

COOK, Eliza (1818–89). Largely self-educated, she began writing verse at an early age. Her first volume, *Lays of a Wild Harp* (1835), appeared when she was 17. Encouraged by early success, she began contributing regularly to periodicals including the *Weekly Dispatch*, in which her most popular poem 'The Old Armchair' first appeared in 1837. Her poems were characterized by an unaffected domestic sentiment which appealed strictly to popular uncultured tastes. She conducted *Eliza Cook's Journal* from 1849, but her failing health caused its demise in 1854. Her complete poetical works were published in 1870.

COOK, James (1728–79), celebrated circumnavigator, left records of his three principal voyages in *An Account of a Voyage round the World 1768–71* (1773), compiled by J. Hawkesworth from the journals of Cook and his botanist *Banks (Cook's own journal of this voyage was edited by Wharton in 1893); *A Voyage towards the South Pole . . . 1772–3* (1777); *A Voyage to the Pacific Ocean . . . 1776–1780* (1784, the third volume by Capt. T. King). Passages from Cook's second volume provided sources for the story and imagery of Coleridge's *'Ancient Mariner' (see J. L. *Lowes, *The Road to Xanadu*, 1927). Cook was murdered by natives in Hawaii.

COOKSON, Catherine Anne (1906–98), novelist, born in Jarrow, most of whose many novels celebrate life in her native Tyneside. She was the illegitimate daughter of a domestic servant and tells the story of her own childhood in her memoir *Our Kate* (1969). Her novels are romantic but also realistic, featuring strong and resourceful heroines: one of her most popular characters was 'Mary Ann', who featured in a long series. Her works were outstandingly popular, as her high *Public Lending Right ratings demonstrated, and she was a generous benefactor to the arts and literary causes.

'Cook's Tale, The', see CANTERBURY TALES, 4.

Coole Park, Co. Galway, home of Lady *Gregory, famous as the headquarters of the *Irish Revival. Summer home of W. B. *Yeats for nearly 20 years, it was the subject of many of his poems, notably 'In the Seven Woods', 'Coole Park, 1929', and 'Coole Park and Ballylee, 1931'. Guests who carved their names on its famous autograph tree (a copper beech) included G. B. *Shaw, J. M. *Synge, W. B. Yeats, J. B. *Yeats, A. *John, G. W. *Russell (Æ), and D. *Hyde. The house, described by Lady Gregory in *Coole* (1931, enl. 1971), was pulled down in 1941.

COOPER, Lady Diana, née Manners (Viscountess Norwich) (1892–1986), actress and hostess, remem-

bered in a literary context as a friend of many writers and artists, as the model for characters in works by A. *Bennett, E. *Waugh, and others, and as the wife of historian and diplomat (Alfred) Duff Cooper (1890–1954). She published three volumes of memoirs, *The Rainbow Comes and Goes* (1958), *The Light of Common Day* (1959), and *Trumpets from the Steep* (1960).

COOPER, James Fenimore (1789–1851), born in New Jersey. He spent his youth partly on the family estate at Cooperstown on Otsego Lake (NY), partly in the merchant marine (after dismissal from Yale), partly in the American navy. He then settled down as a country proprietor and writer of novels. His second book *The Spy* (1821), a stirring tale of the American Revolution, brought him into prominence. *The Pioneers* (1823) was the first of his best-known group of novels, *Leather-Stocking Tales*, called after the deerskin leggings of their hero, pioneer scout Natty Bumppo (alias 'Deer-slayer', 'Pathfinder', or 'Hawkeye'); the sequels were *The Last of the Mohicans* (1826), *The Prairie* (1827), *The Pathfinder* (1840), and *The Deer-slayer* (1841). They deal with adventures of the frontier and give a vivid picture of American Indian and pioneer life; *Parkman, in an 1852 appreciation, echoes the familiar comparison with Sir W. *Scott and, despite some reservations about the loquacity of the characters, the bloodthirstiness of some of the scenes, and improbabilities of plot, finds his descriptions 'instinct with life, with the very spirit of the wilderness; they breathe the sombre poetry of solitude and danger.'

From 1826 to 1833 Cooper travelled in Europe, and on his return appeared several highly critical accounts of European society, including *England, with Sketches of Society in the Metropolis* (1837; which nevertheless contains some appreciative comments, notably of the famous breakfasts of S. *Rogers); this was violently attacked in Britain, notably by *Lockhart. Cooper was, however, also deeply critical of American democracy, and expressed his conservative opinions directly in *The American Democrat* (1838) and fictionally in *Homeward Bound* and *Home as Found* (both 1838). Among his many other works the scholarly *The History of the Navy of the United States* (1839); *Satanstoe* (1845), a historical novel of manners; and *The Crater* (1848) could be mentioned to illustrate his fertility and variety. A collection of *Letters and Journals* (6 vols, ed. J. F. Beard) appeared in 1960–8. See also two influential essays by D. H. *Lawrence, in *Studies in Classic American Literature* (1923), which provoked a continuing discussion of Cooper's role as myth-maker.

COOPER, William, pseudonym of Harry Summerfield Hoff (1910–2002), who taught physics in a Leicester school before the war, during which period he published novels under his own name. After the war he embarked on a career in government service, and the civil service features in much of his work, as it does in that of his colleague C. P. *Snow. His most influential novel, *Scenes from Provincial Life* (1950), was hailed as seminal by writers of the 1950s, who also chose provincial, anarchic but ambitious, lower-middle-class heroes, and a low-key realist tone. It was followed in 1961 by *Scenes from Married Life*, and in 1982 by *Scenes from Metropolitan Life*, originally written as the middle volume of the trilogy. In these novels Joe Lunn narrates his own story, from his schoolmaster days in a provincial city when his mistress Myrtle is trying to marry him, through the post-war years in London when he is trying to marry Myrtle, to his successful marriage to schoolmistress Elspeth. A sequel, *Scenes from Later Life*, appeared in 1983 and another, *Scenes from Early Life*, in 1990. *Immortality at Any Price* was published in 1991.

Cooper's Hill, see DENHAM.

COPE, Wendy Mary (1945–), poet, educated at Farringtons School in Chiselhurst, Kent, and at St Hilda's College, Oxford. She trained as a teacher at Westminster College, Oxford, and taught in London primary schools before becoming television columnist for the **Spectator* (1986–90). A gifted parodist, her first collection of poetry, *Making Cocoa for Kingsley Amis* (1986), was an instant success and established her as a skilfully subversive humorist able to use traditional verse forms to effective satirical purpose, especially when directed at the sexual psychology of men. A collection of rhymes for children, *Twiddling Your Thumbs* (1988), was followed by *The River Girl* (1991), also for children. Other collections include *Serious Concerns* (1992) and *If I Don't Know* (2001).

COPERNICUS, Latinized form of the surname of Nicolas Koppernik (1473–1543), astronomer, native of Torun, Poland, who propounded in his *De Revolutionibus* (1543) the theory that the planets, including the earth, move in orbits round the sun as centre, in opposition to *Ptolemy's earlier geocentric theory. Only after a century of fierce debate was the superiority of the heliocentric theory accepted in the scientific and scholarly world.

Cophetua, King, a legendary king in Africa, who cared nothing for women until he saw a beggar maid 'all in gray', with whom he fell in love. He married her and together they lived 'a quiet life during their princely reign'. The tale is told in one of the ballads included in Percy's **Reliques*, where the maid's name is given as Penelophon. Shakespeare, in **Love's Labour's Lost* (IV. i), gives it as Zenelophon. There are other references to the story in Shakespeare's **Romeo and Juliet* (II. i) and in 2 **Henry IV* (v. iii), in Jonson's **Every Man in His Humour* (III. iv), and in **Tennyson's 'The Beggar Maid'* (1842); it was the subject of a well-known painting by *Burne-Jones (1884).

COPPARD, A(lfred) E(dgar) (1878–1957), the son of a tailor, who worked through many jobs before he became a full-time writer, and supplemented his meagre earnings with money prizes won through his athletic skills. His first collection of short stories, *Adam and Eve and Pinch Me* (1921), established his name and led to much encouragement, including that of F. M. *Ford. His first book of verse, *Hips and Haws*, appeared in 1922, and thereafter he produced a book of stories or verses almost every year until the early 1950s. The first part of an autobiography, *It's Me O Lord*, was published posthumously in 1957. The deceptive simplicity of Coppard's stories conceals a widely admired technical skill; many of the most characteristic tales are set in robust country backgrounds, and display a deep sympathy for the oddity and misfit.

COPPE, Abiezer (1619–72), a *Ranter, preacher, mystic, and pamphleteer, famed for his eccentric behaviour (he preached naked in the streets of London, denouncing the rich); his two *Fiery Flying Rolls* (1649) are charged with fervour and compassion, and are written in a highly original poetic prose described by Christopher *Hill (*The World Turned upside down*, 1972) as 'unlike anything else in the seventeenth century'. In 1650 these pamphlets were burned as blasphemous, by order of Parliament. Imprisoned at Newgate, Coppe partially recanted. He practised medicine after the Restoration in Surrey, as 'Dr Higham'.

Copper, Lord, the domineering newspaper magnate in E. Waugh's **Scoop*. His foreign editor Salter was given to saying 'Definitely, Lord Copper' when he was right, and 'Up to a point, Lord Copper' when he was wrong.

copyright. The first English Copyright Act in England was the Statute of Anne (1709). Copyright is the statutory right of authors, dramatists, artists, and composers to prevent others from exploiting their work without their permission. It is a property right and, in the same way as a tangible property, copyright can be bought, inherited, willed, or leased. In addition, copyright law confers certain moral rights including the right to be identified as the creator of a work and the right not to have that work altered detrimentally. All original material qualifies for copyright protection, regardless of its artistic merit, immediately it is recorded in writing or in another form. There are no formal registration procedures. Copyright provides creators with the economic and moral control over their work which is vital to ensure that they are able to continue to create and earn from their skill and labour. Authors' attitudes to copyright can however be ambivalent: they appreciate the need for new work to be enriched by the traditions of the past and at times they may rely very directly on the work of others in the creation of new work, such as *biographies, academic works, *translations, and *adaptations. There is also a danger that, if too rigidly enforced, the existence of copyright could become a tool for censorship or a bar to the free circulation of ideas. The law aims to reconcile these opposing concerns and is thus more limited than other property rights: broadly speaking, and with many variations, copyright in Europe and the USA currently lasts until 70 years after the author's death. In addition, the law provides for works to be used without permission in a range of special circumstances, including the quoting of limited extracts for purposes of criticism, review, research, or private study, or for teaching. See *Copinger and Skone James on Copyright*, 14th edition (1999) by Kevin Garnett, Jonathan Rayner James, and Gillian Davies, which has a chapter on the history of copyright.

copyright libraries may, under the Copyright Act, 1911, claim a free copy of any book published in Britain. There are six: the British Library, London; the Bodleian, Oxford; the University Library, Cambridge; the National Library of Wales, Aberystwyth; the National Library of Scotland, Edinburgh; and Trinity College, Dublin: see under LIBRARIES.

Corah, name for Titus *Oates in Dryden's *Absalom and Achitophel*.

coranto, or current of news, the name applied to periodical news-pamphlets issued between 1621 and 1641 (their publication was interrupted 1632–8) containing foreign intelligence taken from foreign papers. They were one of the earliest forms of English journalism, and were followed by the *newsbook. See also NEWSPAPERS, ORIGINS OF.

Corbaccio, the deaf old miser in Jonson's *Volpone*.

Corbenic, the castle where the *Grail is found in the Arthurian legends. R. S. Loomis (*The Grail from Celtic Myth to Christian Symbol*, 1963) believes that the name may be a miswriting for 'Corbenoit', blessed horn, which was one of the archetypal ingredients (the horn of Bran) in the Grail story, misunderstood as *cor(s)*, body (of Christ). However this may be, there is little evidence of any awareness of this etymological archetype in any of the surviving Grail stories.

CORBETT, or **CORBET,** Richard (1582–1635), the son of Vincent Corbet, a Surrey gardener, of whom *Jonson said in an elegy, 'His mind as pure and neatly kept | As were his nourseries . . . .' Richard was educated at Westminster and Christ Church, Oxford, became chaplain to James I and, later, bishop first of Oxford, then of Norwich. He was generous, witty, and eloquent, and his poetry—*Certain Elegant Poems* (1647) and *Poetica Stromata* (1648)—ranges from the entertaining traveller's story of 'Iter Boreale' and the ironical verses on 'The Distracted Puritane' to the charming little poem 'To his son, Vincent Corbet' on his third birthday. His best-known poem is probably 'A Proper New Ballad, entitled The Fairies Farewell' which begins 'Farewell rewards and fairies'. He also addressed some amusing lines to *Coryate after the latter's return from a journey in Europe. He pronounced the funeral oration for *Bodley. An edition of his poems, edited by J. A. W. Bennett and H. R. Trevor-Roper, was published in 1955.

Corceca, in Spenser's *Faerie Queene* (I. iii. 18), 'blindness of heart', an old blind woman, mother of *Abessa (Superstition).

Cordelia, in Shakespeare's *King Lear*, the youngest of the king's three daughters.

CORELLI, Marie, pseudonym of Mary Mackay (1855–1924). She studied music and turned to fiction at the age of 30 with her first novel, *A Romance of Two Worlds* (1886), which was followed by many more romantic melodramas. She hypnotized her public with her exuberant imagination and her far-fetched theories on anything from morality to radioactive vibrations. She achieved outstanding success at the turn of the century, *Gladstone and *Wilde being among her admirers, but her popularity turned to ridicule long before her death. Her other novels include *Barabbas* (1893), *The Sorrows of Satan* (1895), *The Mighty Atom* (1896), *The Master Christian* (1900), *Temporal Power* (1902), *The Young Diana* (1918), and *The Secret Power* (1921).

Corflambo, in Spenser's *Faerie Queene* (IV. vii and viii), 'a mightie man . . . Ryding upon a Dromedare on hie, | Of stature huge, and horrible of hew', who symbolizes lust. He carries off *Amoret, who is released from him by *Timias and *Belphoebe. He is slain by Prince *Arthur.

CORIAT, Thomas, see CORYATE.

Corinthian Tom, a character in *Egan's *Life in London*.

Coriolanus, a play by *Shakespeare first printed in the *Folio (1623), in which, before the late insertion of *Troilus and Cressida*, it seems to have been placed first of the tragedies. In order of composition, however, it was probably Shakespeare's last tragedy, written about 1608. Its source is *North's version of *Plutarch's 'Life of Caius Martius Coriolanus'. The play has never been a very popular one, but in the 20th cent. its political and military themes have stimulated some interest; see for instance the two poems by T. S. *Eliot yoked by the title *Coriolan*. The opening scene, in which Menenius Agrippa tells the citizens of Rome a fable of the body's members rebelling against itself, was a popular Renaissance allegory of the state.

Caius Marcius, a proud Roman general, performs wonders of valour in a war against the Volscians, and captures the town Corioli, receiving in consequence the surname Coriolanus. On his return it is proposed to make him consul, but his arrogant and outspoken contempt of the Roman rabble makes him unpopular with the fickle crowd, and the tribunes of the people have no difficulty in securing his banishment. He goes to the Volscian general Aufidius, his enemy of long standing, is received with delight, and leads the Volscians against Rome to effect his revenge. He reaches the walls of the city, and the Romans, to save it from destruction, send emissaries, old friends of Coriolanus, to propose terms, but in vain. Finally his mother Volumnia, his meek wife Virgilia, and his son come to beseech him to spare the city and he yields to the eloquence of his mother, suspecting that by so doing he has signed his own death warrant: makes a treaty favourable to the Volscians, and returns with them to Antium, a Volscian town. Here Aufidius turns against him, accusing him of betraying the Volscian interests, and with the assistance of conspirators of his faction, publicly kills Coriolanus.

CORNEILLE, Pierre (1606–84), French dramatist. Born in a family of magistrates, he was educated at a Jesuit school, studied the law, and practised in the Rouen magistrature until 1630. Although the 33 plays that make up his *œuvre* exploited every dramatic genre available to him, he is best known as the creator of French classical tragedy. Elements of tragic form, including the observation of the *unities and the use of the alexandrine, had been evolving in the work of his predecessors, but he gave this form its appropriate content by confining the action of the play to a conflict between passion and duty at a point of moral crisis. His first great play, *Le Cid* (1637), inspired by Spanish drama (see Cid), achieved a triumph which provoked a cabal, and eventually an adverse judgement by the *Académie française. After a period of discouragement, he followed *Le Cid* with three further masterpieces: *Horace* (1640), dramatizing a conflict between domestic and patriotic imperatives; *Cinna* (1641), exploring the tensions between justice and mercy; and *Polyeucte* (1643), presenting the dilemma of a Christian martyr caught between the desire for glory and the prompting of affection. Corneille's world is a heroic one, but the heroism is grounded in psychological and social reality. The magnifications of tragedy are qualified by comic and even pastoral perspectives; and the aim of the drama remains less to exalt his audience than to show it the facts of its own nature. He exerted a powerful influence on the English dramatists of the *Restoration, particularly *Dryden. The best 17th-cent. translations are by Katherine *Philips (the 'matchless Orinda').

Cornelia, a tragedy translated by T. *Kyd from a Senecan play by Robert Garnier, published 1594. It was reissued in the following year under the title *Pompey the Great, His Faire Corneliaes Tragedie.*

It deals with the story of Cornelia, daughter of Metellus Scipio and wife of Pompey the Great. The latter, after the battle of Pharsalus, is killed on the way to Egypt. Scipio assembles new forces, but after being defeated by Caesar at Thaspus in Africa and again at sea stabs himself. The play largely consists of Cornelia's lamentations for her misfortunes.

CORNFORD, Frances (1886–1960), poet, born in Cambridge where she spent most of her life. She published several volumes of verse but is best known for her triolet 'To a Fat Lady Seen from a Train', with its curiously memorable though undistinguished lines 'O why do you walk through the fields in gloves, | Missing so much and so much? | O fat white woman whom nobody loves'. Her *Collected Poems* appeared in 1954. She was a granddaughter of C. *Darwin and mother of J. *Cornford.

CORNFORD, (Rupert) John (1915–36), poet, the son of Frances *Cornford and the distinguished scholar Francis M. Cornford. By the time he enrolled at Trinity College, Cambridge, in 1933 he had become heavily involved with radical politics and communism. In 1936 he was the first Englishman to enlist against Franco in the Spanish Civil War, and was killed in action the same year. His poems had been published in various periodicals (*New Writing*, the *Cambridge Review*, the *Student Vanguard*) and were collected with various prose pieces, mainly political, in *John Cornford: A Memoir*, ed. Pat Sloan (1938).

Cornhill Magazine (1860–1975), a literary periodical of consistently high quality which began with *Thackeray as editor and specialized in the serialization of novels. Trollope's *Framley Parsonage* was succeeded by the novels of, among others, Mrs *Gaskell, *Reade, G. *Eliot, and *Hardy; many poems of *Tennyson, R. *Browning, and *Swinburne first appeared in it, as well as work by *Ruskin, *MacDonald, and another of its editors, L. *Stephen. It continued in this century to publish the work of many major writers, both creative and critical.

Corn Law Rhymer, see Elliott.

Corno di Bassetto, the name under which G. B. *Shaw wrote his music criticism. See also under music, literature of.

CORNWALL, Barry, pseudonym of Brian Waller Procter (1787–1874). He practised as a solicitor and barrister in London, and was made a commissioner in lunacy. He began to contribute to the *Literary Gazette* in 1815 and became a friend of Leigh *Hunt, *Lamb, and later *Dickens. Under his pseudonym he enjoyed great popular success, particularly as a writer of songs and lyrics. His *Dramatic Scenes* (1819) was praised by Lamb, and his poem *Marcian Collona* (1820), a verse tale of madness and passion, was well received by the public. However, *Keats and *Shelley were disparaging about his work, and *Darley complained of Cornwall's 'eternal cud of rose-leaves'. In 1821 *Macready successfully produced Cornwall's one drama, *Mirandola*. His *English Songs* appeared in 1832, and he also wrote biographies of Lamb and *Kean.

coronach, a lament or dirge, in the Highlands of Scotland or Ireland: a 'wailing together': Sir W. *Scott made use of the form in *The Lady of the Lake*.

Corridors of Power, The, see Snow.

Corsair, The, a poem by Lord *Byron, published 1814. Conrad, a pirate chief, a *'Byronic' character of many vices but with the virtue of chivalry, receives warning that the Turkish Pacha is preparing to descend upon his island. He takes leave of his beloved Medora, arrives at the Pacha's rallying-point, and introduces himself as a dervish escaped from the pirates. However, his plans go amiss, and he is wounded and taken prisoner, but not before he has rescued Gulnare, the chief slave in the Pacha's harem, from imminent death. She falls in love with him, and finally brings him a dagger with which he may kill the Pacha in his sleep. Conrad revolts from such an act, whereupon she herself kills the Pacha and escapes with Conrad. When they arrive at the pirate island Conrad finds Medora dead from grief at the reported killing of her lover. Conrad disappears and is never heard of again: but see LARA.

CORSO, Gregory, see BEAT.

CORTÁZAR, Julio (1914–84), Argentinian novelist and short story writer, born in Brussels. He is best known for his influential experimental novel *Rayuela* (1963; *Hopscotch*, 1966), an adventure story whose flexible structure invites the reader to choose the sequence in which to read its chapters, and whether to include a number of expendable chapters. (See INTERACTIVE FICTION.) Deeply influenced by the French *surrealists and by English-language writers of the macabre (especially *Poe), Cortázar also published several collections of fantastic short stories, including *Bestiario* (1952; *Bestiary*) and *Todos los fuegos el fuego* (1966; *All Fires the Fire*, 1973). His collage-book, *La vuelta al día en ochenta mundos* (1967; *Around the Day in Eighty Worlds*, 1986), combines pieces of short fiction with studies of *Keats and Shakespeare. He translated *Robinson Crusoe* into Spanish, as well as works by Poe and *Chesterton.

cortegiano, Il, see CASTIGLIONE.

CORTÉS, Hernando (1485–1547), the conqueror of Mexico. He entered Mexico City in 1519. It was not he but *Balboa who was the first European to gaze on the Pacific (see *Keats's sonnet 'On First Looking into Chapman's Homer').

Corvino, one of Volpone's would-be heirs in Jonson's *Volpone*.

CORVO, Baron, see ROLFE.

CORY, William Johnson (1823–92), assistant master at Eton, 1845–72. On leaving he changed his name from Johnson to Cory. He published various educational works, but is best remembered for his volume of poems *Ionica* (1858), and in particular for the translation that it contains of the epigram of Heraclitus of Halicarnassus by *Callimachus, 'They told me Heraclitus, they told me you were dead.' He also wrote the 'Eton Boating Song', published 1865. His letters and journals were edited by F. Warre-Cornish (1897).

CORYATE, Thomas (?1577–1617), the son of a rector of Odcombe, whose fame as a traveller was legendary in his lifetime and long outlasted it. He travelled in 1608 through France, Italy, Switzerland, Germany, and Holland, mainly on foot. He published in 1611 a long narrative of his travels entitled *Coryats Crudities*, a much shorter sequel, and *The Odcombian Banquet*, a reprint of the verses printed with the *Crudities*. In 1612 he set out overland to India, travelling through Constantinople, Palestine, Mesopotamia, and reaching Agra in 1616. He died at Surat. A letter of his from the court of the Great Mogul is printed by *Purchas, and this and another letter from the East are included in a compilation called *Thomas Coriate Traveller for the English Wits: Greeting*. Coryate wrote in an extravagant and euphuistic style ('He is a great and bold carpenter of words', said *Jonson), and was well known as an eccentric and amusing character; there are many references to him in 17th-cent. literature. See M. Strachan, *The Life and Adventures of Thomas Coryate* (1962).

Corydon, a shepherd who figures in the *Idylls* of *Theocritus and the *Eclogues* of *Virgil, and whose name has become conventional in pastoral poetry.

Costard, a clown in Shakespeare's *Love's Labour's Lost*.

Coterie, a sophisticated avant-garde periodical, edited by Chapman Hall, of which six numbers appeared in 1919–20, and a seventh, edited by Russell Green, in 1920. It was superseded by *New Coterie* (1925–7), handsomely illustrated, with covers by William Roberts. Contributors included D. H. *Lawrence, T. S. *Eliot, A. *Huxley, E. *Sitwell, and R. *Aldington.

COTGRAVE, Randle (c.1569–1653), author of a famous French–English dictionary published 1611. He was a scholar of St John's College, Cambridge. He had a wide knowledge not only of French and French literature, but of the slang of the day and also of natural history. *Urquhart relied largely upon his dictionary for the translation of *Rabelais.

Cotswold Olimpick Games, yearly celebrations held during Whit week on the hillside above Chipping Campden in Gloucestershire. With James I's permission, they were first organized in 1612 by Robert Dover (1582–1652), of Cambridge and Gray's Inn, using traditional pastimes and customs such as horse racing, coursing, wrestling, backsword fighting, leaping, and dancing, and were commemorated in *Annalia Dubrensia* (1636), a collection of poems by 34 writers including *Drayton, *Jonson, T. *Randolph, and T. *Heywood. The frontispiece portrays Robert Dover, mounted, ceremonially dressed in the king's clothes, in front of his castle, with the games in progress. Suspended during the Civil War, the games were later continued as Dover's Meeting until 1852. The games are described in *Somervile's *Hobbinol* (1740), originally 'The Wicker Chair' (1708), and in Richard *Graves's *The Spiritual Quixote* (1773). They were again revived in 1963 and are held annually on the Friday of Spring Bank Holiday week on Dover's Hill.

'Cotter's Saturday Night, The', a poem by *Burns, published 1786. The verses describing the cotter's home, and the introduction of the daughter's young man, are in Scots, while those expounding religious and patriotic themes are in English.

COTTLE, Joseph (1770–1853), a bookseller of Bristol, who published the *Lyrical Ballads* and other work by *Wordsworth, *Coleridge, and *Southey. He was the author of a poem, 'Malvern Hills', published 1798, and edited with Southey the works of *Chatterton in 1803. His brother Amos Cottle (?1768–1800) translated, probably from Latin, the Edda of Saemund, published in 1797 under the title of *Icelandic Poetry*. The verse is limp, and *Byron wrote of him, 'Amos Cottle strikes the lyre in vain' (*English Bards and Scotch Reviewers*, l. 396).

COTTON, Charles (1630–87), of Beresford Hall, Staffordshire, the son of Charles Cotton, a close friend of *Wotton, *Donne, *Selden, and other writers; the younger Charles was himself a friend of *Lovelace and of I. *Walton. He wrote the dialogue between Piscator and Viator which forms the second part in the fifth edition of *The Compleat Angler* (1676), and published in 1664 *Scarronides*, a mock-heroic burlesque of *Virgil (which *Pepys found 'extraordinary good'), and in 1665 a burlesque of *Lucian. His translation of *Montaigne, closer but less colourful than *Florio's, appeared in 1685. His *topographical poem *The Wonders of the Peake* (1681) celebrates the beauties and curiosities of the Peak district (the seventh wonder being Chatsworth). Cotton's love of his native landscapes and particularly of 'fair Dove, princess of rivers' is also expressed in many of his *Poems on Several Occasions* (1689). *Wordsworth and *Coleridge both admired his work, making particular mention of 'Ode upon Winter' and 'The Retirement'. Cotton also wrote love poems, some addressed to his first wife Isabella, sister of Colonel Hutchinson (see HUTCHINSON, L.). His poems were edited by J. Buxton in 1958.

COTTON, Sir Robert Bruce (1571–1631), educated at Westminster School and Jesus College, Cambridge, an antiquary and collector of manuscripts and coins. He gave the free use of his library to *Bacon, *Camden, *Ralegh, *Selden, *Speed, *Ussher, and other scholars, and sent a gift of manuscripts to the Bodleian Library on its foundation. He joined the parliamentary party and published various political tracts. The Cottonian Library, largely composed of works rescued from the dissolved monasteries, was left to the nation by Sir John Cotton (1621–1701), grandson of Sir Robert; it was placed in Essex House, then in Ashburnham House, where it suffered severely from fire in 1731. It was removed to the British Museum in 1753 and is now in the British Library. It includes such treasures as the *Lindisfarne Gospels and other splendid biblical manuscripts such as the Codex Purpureus, the manuscript of *Beowulf, and the famous manuscript that includes *Pearl and Sir *Gawain and the Green Knight.

Countess Cathleen, The, a play in blank verse by *Yeats, published 1892. It is based on the story of Countess Kathleen O'Shea, told in Yeats's compilation *Fairy and Folk Tales of the Irish Peasantry* (1888). The scene is laid 'in Ireland in old times' at a period of famine. The people sell their souls to the demons for food. The countess does all she can to relieve their needs, till the demons steal her wealth. Finally she sells her own soul to the demons for a great sum, sacrificing her hope of salvation for the people. But at the end she is forgiven, for her intention was good. The play was first performed in Dublin in 1899, and marked the beginning of the *Irish Revival in the theatre.

Count Robert of Paris, a novel by Sir W. *Scott, published 1831, the year before the author's death. This was one of the *Tales of My Landlord*, 4th series, the last of the Waverley novels. It was written in ill health and betrays the decline of his powers. The novel, set in the 11th-cent. First Crusade, was almost the last worked on by Scott and was unfinished when he left for Italy in search of health. The ending was produced by *Lockhart after the departure of Scott, who never realized what had been added to it. The work is confused and rambling, but also has examples of grotesqueries unparalleled elsewhere in his work.

Country Wife, The, a comedy by *Wycherley, published and probably first performed 1675. It is now considered by many to be his finest play, a sharp satiric attack on social and sexual hypocrisy and greed and on the corruption of town manners, but even in the author's time (see his own jokes on the subject in *The Plain Dealer*) was attacked for its alleged obscenity. *Garrick's version, *The Country Girl* (1766), aimed to remove the original's 'immorality' and 'obscenity', and with them cut the character of Horner, a central figure of the plot, a witty libertine who spreads a false report that he is impotent as a result of an operation for the pox, and thus gains access to the favours of various women, each of whom believes he has sacrificed reputation for her sake.

The main plot concerns Mr Pinchwife, who comes to London for the marriage of his sister Alithea, bringing with him his artless young wife Margery; his excessive warnings against wrongdoing put ideas into her head, and she is eventually seduced by Horner, innocently protesting the while that she is merely behaving as town ladies do. Alithea's suitor Sparkish loses her to a new lover, Harcourt, through the opposite fault of excessive credulity. Pinchwife's conclusion, as he apparently accepts the excuse of Horner's impotence, is 'Cuckolds like Lovers shou'd themselves deceive.'

Courcy, Lord and Lady de, and their sons and daughters, characters in A. *Trollope's *Barsetshire series of novels, types of a worldly, self-seeking, heartless aristocracy.

Courier, an evening newspaper of high repute in the early part of the 19th cent., under the management of D. *Stuart. *Coleridge, *Wordsworth, *Lamb, and *Southey were among its occasional contributors, and *Galt was at one time its editor.

COURTELINE, Georges, see FARCE.

courtesy literature, as a distinct literary genre teaching courtiers and others good manners and morals, was imported into England through works such as *Il cortegiano* of *Castiglione (translated by *Hoby in 1561), *Il galateo* of Giovanni della Casa (translated by Robert Peterson in 1576), and Stefano Guazzo's *La civil conversatione* (Bks I–III translated by G. *Pettie in 1581, Bk IV by B. *Yonge in 1586). One of the most popular native examples of this type of writing was H. *Peacham's *The Compleat Gentleman* (1622).

COURTHOPE, William John (1842–1917), educated at Harrow and Corpus Christi and New College, Oxford. He became a civil service commissioner and professor of poetry at Oxford. His important contributions to English literature include the last five volumes of the standard edition of *Pope's works, including a life (1871–89), and a *History of English Poetry* (1895–1910). Among his other works were *Ludibria Lunae* (1869), a satirical burlesque on women's rights, *Paradise of Birds* (1870), and *The Country Town and Other Poems* (1920).

Courtier, The (*Il cortegiano*), see CASTIGLIONE.

courtly love. The term 'amour courtois' was coined by Gaston Paris in 1883 in the course of an essay on the *Lancelot* of *Chrétien de Troyes, to describe the conception of love developed by the Provençal troubadours in the 12th cent., which had become the central theme of lyric and epic poetry in France and Germany by 1200. Its relation of lover to adored lady is modelled on the dependence of feudal follower on his lord; the love itself was a religious passion, ennobling, ever unfulfilled, and ever increasing. The common (though not universal) requirement of non-fulfilment meant that the love was usually premarital or extramarital. A code of practice for courtly lovers, *De Arte Honeste Amandi* (*c.*1185), was written by *Andreas Capellanus, who may have been a chaplain at the court of *Marie de Champagne. Though the poetry of the troubadours is the first definable occurrence of the phenomenon in western Europe, many aspects of courtly love are much older and have affinities with the poetry of *Ovid and with the religious terminology of love used by Arabic writers. From its beginnings in Provence the writing of this kind of poetry had spread to northern France and to the German *minnesingers and epic by 1200; the most influential works in the 13th cent. were the *Roman de la rose* (Guillaume de Lorris, *c.*1230, and Jean de Meun, *c.*1275), and the lyric poems

of the *dolce stil nuovo* in Italy at the end of the century; Guinicelli, Cavalcanti, and *Dante's *Vita nuova*. Though the elements of courtly love are found in many places in medieval and Renaissance English literature, it is never the central theme of medieval English poetry, probably because it only reached England in the period of its decadence, after the mid-13th cent. and mostly as presented through the sceptical satire of writers such as Jean de Meun. See P. Dronke, *Medieval Latin and the Rise of the European Love-Lyric* (1968), R. Boase, *The Origin and Meaning of Courtly Love* (1977); B. O'Donoghue, *The Courtly Love Tradition* (1982).

court of love, an institution said to have existed in Provence and Languedoc in the 12th cent., principally on the authority of *Andreas Capellanus, at which a noble tribunal of lords and ladies made pronouncements on cases of love. No doubt such courts, like that of *Marie de Champagne claimed by Andreas, were largely a literary fiction or a later post-literary development.

Court of Love, The, an early 15th-cent. allegorical poem in 1,442 lines of rhyme-royal, once doubtfully attributed to *Chaucer and included by *Skeat in his *Chaucerian and Other Pieces*, published as vol. vii of his large edition of Chaucer (pp. 409–47). It is in the tradition of the *Roman de la rose*, describing the visit of the poet to the Court of Venus and the love scenes he saw portrayed there, and ending with a May Day concert of birds when they sing descants on the opening words of psalms. It claims to be the work of 'Philogenet of Cambridge, clerk'.

Covent Garden, in London, the old Convent Garden of Westminster. At the dissolution of the monasteries it passed into the hands of the Russell family, who built Bedford House north of the Strand and laid out the garden for building, with the market as the centre. I. *Jones built St Paul's Church there, and the piazza that runs along two sides of the market place. Many celebrated people lived in Covent Garden (Sir K. *Digby, *Kneller, *Lely, Zoffany (1733–1810), Lady M. W. *Montagu, among others), and the Bedford, Will's, and Button's *coffee houses were in the neighbourhood. Covent Garden is frequently mentioned in 17th- and 18th-cent. literature, generally as a centre of dissipation. It remained the principal wholesale market in London for vegetables, fruit, and flowers until the 1970s.

The first Covent Garden Theatre was opened by J. *Rich in 1732. It was burnt down in 1808, and its successor in 1856. In these, many famous actors were seen, including *Garrick, the *Kembles, Mrs *Siddons, and *Macready. The new theatre (by Barry) opened in 1858 has been the principal home in England of grand opera.

Covent-Garden Journal, a periodical issued twice a week during 1752 by H. *Fielding, containing some of the best work of his journalistic career. Under the name of Sir Alexander Drawcansir, Censor of Great Britain, Fielding attacks political abuses, scandal, hypocrisy, meanness, sexual morality, fashion, and many other targets. It contained an attack on Smollett's *Peregrine Pickle* and *Roderick Random*, to which that author replied in a slanderous pamphlet, *A Faithful Narrative of . . . *Habbakuk Hilding, Justice, Dealer, and Chapman.

COVENTRY, Francis (1725–54), from 1751 perpetual curate at Edgware. He was the author of *The History of Pompey the Little: or The Life and Adventures of a Lap-Dog* (1751), a satire in the form of the life of a dog 'born A.D. 1735 at Bologna in Italy, a Place famous for Lap-Dogs and Sausages'. He undergoes many vicissitudes, passing from one owner to another of very diverse stations; Lady M. W. *Montagu in a letter to her daughter declared it 'a real and exact representation of Life as it is now acted in London'. An edition by R. A. Day appeared in 1974.

Coventry miracle plays, or *Ludus Coventriae*, see MYSTERY PLAYS.

COVERDALE, Miles (1488–1568). He studied at Cambridge, was ordained priest in 1514, and adopted Lutheran views. He translated at Antwerp, apparently in the pay of Jacob van Meteren, the *Bible and *Apocrypha from German and Latin versions with the aid of *Tyndale's New Testament. His translation was first printed perhaps at Cologne; a modified version was issued in 1537. Coverdale also superintended the printing of the Great Bible of 1539 (see under BIBLE, THE ENGLISH). He was bishop of Exeter in 1551–3, and was allowed to leave England in 1554 after Queen Mary's accession. He was in England again in 1559, published his last book, *Letters of Saintes*, in 1564, and was rector of St Magnus, London Bridge, from 1563 to 1566. His collected works, which include translations of theological tracts and German hymns, were published in 1844–6. If he was in fact (which has been questioned) the translator of the version of the Bible attributed to him, he is entitled to the credit for much of the noble language of the Authorized Version, and in particular for the Prayer Book version of the Psalter.

Coverdale, Miles, the narrator of Hawthorne's novel *The Blithedale Romance*.

Coverley, Sir Roger de, a character described in the *Spectator*, a member of the Spectator Club, 'a gentleman of Worcestershire, of ancient descent, a baronet. His great-grandfather was inventor of that famous country-dance which is called after him. He is a gentleman that is very singular in his behaviour, but his singularities proceed from his good sense . . . It is said he keeps himself a bachelor, by reason he was crossed in love by a perverse beautiful widow of the next county to him.' (No. 2, by *Steele.) He figures in a number of *Spectator* papers by both *Addison and Steele, and is pictured at home, at church, at the assizes, in town, etc. His death is reported in No. 517, by Addison.

COWARD, Noël (1899–1973), actor, dramatist, and composer, born in Teddington, Middlesex, the son of a piano salesman and an ambitious mother who from an early age encouraged his theatrical aspirations. His first play was performed in 1917, but he achieved fame with *The Vortex* (1924), in which he himself appeared as Nicky Lancaster, a young drugaddict tormented by his mother's adulteries. More characteristic of his talent were his comedies *Fallen Angels* (1925), *Hay Fever* (1925, about the eccentric, theatrical, guest-confusing, self-regarding Bliss family), *Private Lives* (1933, about two disastrous interconnected second marriages), *Design for Living* (1933, about a successful *ménage à trois*), and *Blithe Spirit* (1941), which features the hearty medium, Madame Arcati, and Elvira, a predatory ghost. The smart sophistication, technical accomplishment, and convention-defying morality (or amorality) of these pieces captured the public of the day, but another and more sentimental side of Coward was revealed in his patriotic works (*Cavalcade*, 1931) and wartime screenplays such as *Brief Encounter* (1944) and *This Happy Breed* (1942). After the war Coward continued to write prolifically; his plays were less well received, to his own surprise, and he was outspoken about his contempt for the new *kitchen sink school of realism and for the 'pretentious symbolism' of *Beckett. He had a new lease of life as cabaret entertainer at the Café de Paris, London, and in Las Vegas; then, in 1963, a revival of *Private Lives* at Hampstead Theatre Club precipitated a new wave of interest in Coward's work and many more revivals, including prestige productions at the *National Theatre. Coward was knighted in 1970, and died in Jamaica. He also published volumes of verse, short stories, a novel (*Pomp and Circumstance*, 1960), and two volumes of autobiography. *The Noel Coward Diaries* (1982, ed. G. Payn and Sheridan Morley), which cover his life from 1941 to 1969, are an entertaining fund of theatrical gossip, criticism of fellow playwrights, and admiring comments on the royal family.

COWLEY, Abraham (1618–67), the posthumous son of a London stationer, King's scholar at Westminster, and scholar and fellow of Trinity College, Cambridge. His precocity is shown by 'Pyramus and Thisbe', a verse romance written when he was 10 years old, and 'Constantia and Philetus', written two years later (both included in *Poetical Blossomes*, 1633). *Loves Riddle*, a pastoral drama, and *Naufragium Joculare*, a Latin comedy, appeared in 1638. On the outbreak of the Civil War Cowley left Cambridge for Oxford, where he contributed to the Royalist cause by writing a satire, *The Puritan and the Papist* (1643), and a political epic, *The Civil War*. (Bk I of *The Civil War* was published in 1679; the two other books were presumed lost until recently discovered and edited.) In 1644 he left Oxford for Paris, where he was in the service of Henry Jermyn at the court of Henrietta Maria. In 1654 he returned to England, apparently as a Royalist spy, and was imprisoned briefly in 1655; however, his conduct at this time, together with various remarks in the preface to *Poems* (1656), gave rise to doubts in certain quarters about his continuing loyalty to the Royalist cause. At the Restoration he was disappointed in his expectation of a reward for his services, though the earl of St Albans and the duke of Buckingham combined to provide him with a competence. He spent the last years of his life in retirement, at Barnes and later Chertsey. On his death Charles II bestowed on him the epitaph 'That Mr Cowley had not left a better man behind him in England.' He is buried in Westminster Abbey.

His principal works, besides those mentioned above, are *The Mistress* (1647), a collection of love poems; 'Miscellanies' in *Poems* (1656); also in the same collection 'Davideis', an epic on the biblical history of David, and 'Pindarique Odes' (see ODE), in which he introduces the irregular ode imitated by *Dryden and others; *Ode, upon the Blessed Restoration* (1660); and *Verses on Several Occasions* (1663). His prose works, marked by grace and simplicity of style, include *A Proposition for the Advancement of Learning* (1661), *The Visions and Prophecies Concerning England* (1661), and some 'Essays', notably one 'Of My Self' containing interesting particulars of his early life (first published in *The Works*, 1668). His plays include *The Guardian* (1650), written to entertain the prince of Wales on his visit to Cambridge in 1642, which he later revised as *Cutter of Coleman Street* (1663).

Cowley's life was written by his friend and literary executor *Sprat and is prefixed to *The Works* (1668).

COWLEY, Hannah, née Parkhouse (1743–1809). She wrote a number of comedies and two tedious tragedies; her comedies include *The Runaway* (1776), *A Bold Stroke for a Husband* (1783), and her most successful, *The Belle's Stratagem*, performed 1780. They tend to preach the importance of marriage and the domestic virtues. She also wrote long narrative romances, and corresponded as 'Anna Matilda' in poetry in the *World with Robert Merry (see DELLA CRUSCANS), a correspondence satirized by *Gifford.

COWPER, William (1731–1800), elder son of the rector of Great Berkhamsted, Hertfordshire, whose mother died when he was 6. He was educated at a private school (where he was bullied) and at Westminster, where he was a contemporary of Charles *Churchill and W. *Hastings. He was called to the bar in 1754. Sensitive and hypochondriac by nature as a child, he began to suffer from severe depression, and when called for examination for a disputed clerkship in the House of Lords he broke down completely and attempted suicide; his illness may have been aggravated by the failure of his hope of marrying his cousin Theodora Cowper. From this time he was subject to periods of acute melancholia which took a religious form; he felt himself cast out of God's mercy, and wrote later in his moving autobiographical *Memoir* (c.1767, pub. 1816), 'conviction of sin and expectation of instant judgement never left me.' He spent some months in Dr Cotton's Collegium Insanorum at St Albans, and turned increasingly to evangelical Christianity for consolation. In 1765 he became a boarder (in his own words, 'a sort of adopted son') in the home of the Revd Morley Unwin at Huntingdon, and on Morley's death moved with Mary, his widow, to Olney.

There he came under the influence of J. *Newton, the evangelical curate, with whom he wrote *Olney Hymns* (1779); his contributions include 'God moves in a mysterious way' and 'Oh, for a closer walk with God'. He became engaged to Mrs Unwin, but suffered another period of severe depression and made another suicide attempt; he spent a year with the Newtons before returning to Mrs Unwin's home. A calmer period followed, during which at her suggestion he wrote his satires ('Table Talk', 'The Progress of Error', 'Truth', 'Expostulation', 'Hope', 'Charity', 'Conversation', and 'Retirement') which were published in 1782 with several shorter poems (including 'Verses Supposed to be Written by Alexander Selkirk'; see SELKIRK); in the same year he wrote 'John Gilpin' and in 1783–4 his best-known long poem *The Task* (1785), both subjects suggested by his new friend and neighbour Lady Austen. The volume in which these appeared also contained 'Tirocinium', a vigorous attack on public schools. In 1786 he moved with Mrs Unwin to Weston Underwood, where he wrote various poems published after his death, including the unfinished 'Yardley-Oak' (admired by *Wordsworth), the verses 'On the Loss of the Royal George' ('Toll for the brave . . .'), 'To Mary', and 'The Poplar-Field'. His translation of *Homer, published in 1791, was not successful. From 1791 Mrs Unwin suffered a series of paralytic strokes; she died in 1796, leaving Cowper in severe depression from which he never fully recovered.

He wrote *'The Castaway' shortly before his death; like many of his poems it deals with man's isolation and helplessness. Storms and shipwrecks recur in his work as images of the mysterious ways of God, and Cowper's search for a retired and quiet life of simple domestic and rural pleasures gave him little sense of permanent security. Yet his poems and his much-admired letters (published posthumously) have been highly valued for their intimate portrait of tranquillity and for their playful and delicate wit. His sympathetic feelings for nature (expressed in the lines from *The Task* admired by J. *Austen's Fanny Price, 'Ye fallen avenues! Once more I mourn, | Your fate unmerited') presage *Romanticism, and his use of blank verse links that of James *Thomson with that of *Wordsworth. He was also, like his evangelical friends, a champion of the oppressed, and wrote verses on *Wilberforce and the slave trade. Whether religion was cause or cure of his depression has been much disputed; the sense of guilt and paranoia displayed in his *Memoir* has much in common with that in Bunyan's *Grace Abounding*. A life by his friend W. *Hayley was published 1803–4; see also *The Stricken Deer* (1929) by David *Cecil and a critical biography by M. Quinlan (1953). Cowper's *Letters and Prose Writings*, ed. J. King and C. Ryskamp, appeared in 3 vols, 1979–82.

Cox and Box, see BURNAND and FARCE.

Crab, in Shakespeare's *Two Gentlemen of Verona*, Launce's dog, whose name suggests the sourness of a crab-apple.

CRABBE, George (1754–1832), born in Aldeburgh, Suffolk, where his father was a collector of salt-duties. He was apprenticed to a doctor and during that time, in 1775, he published *Inebriety*, a derivative but vigorous poem on the evils of drink. During his apprenticeship he met Sarah Elmy (the 'Mira' of his poems and journals), whom he married ten years later. He then began to practise as the parish doctor in Aldeburgh, meanwhile writing, reading, and studying botany. In 1780 he determined on a career in writing and went to London, where he became almost destitute before he was generously befriended by *Burke. On Burke's advice, and with his literary help, he published *The Library* (1781), a poem in the manner of *Pope containing the author's reflections on books and reading. Burke introduced Crabbe to influential friends, including *Fox, *Reynolds, and Dr *Johnson, and encouraged him to take orders. In 1781 he became curate at Aldeburgh, then from 1782 to 1785 was chaplain to the duke of Rutland at Belvoir, where he found stimulating company and leisure for writing. In 1783, after advice and revision from Burke and Johnson, he published *The Village*, a poem in heroic couplets which established his reputation and made plain his revulsion from the conventions of the *pastoral and the myth of the Golden Age, painting instead a grim, detailed picture of rural poverty and of a blighted, infertile landscape, described with a botanist's precision.

In the same year he married Sarah Elmy, and in 1785 published a satirical (and probably early) work, *The Newspaper*. A long interval followed, during which he published nothing of importance, although he wrote and destroyed several unpublished novels, and during which he held (1789–1814) a living at Muston, Leicestershire, from which he was absent 1792–1805, living in Suffolk. In 1807 appeared a volume containing his previous works, some new shorter poems, *'The Parish Register' (which revealed his gift as a narrative poet), and another, atypical, narrative in 55 eight-line stanzas, 'Sir Eustace Grey', set in a madhouse, in which Sir Eustace relates, to a 'Physician' and a 'Visitor', the tale of his guilt (he had killed his wife's lover in a duel) and his subsequent demented hallucinations. Alethea Hayter, in *Opium and the*

Romantic Imagination (1968), relates the peculiarly vivid dream descriptions to Crabbe's opium-taking, a habit he had adopted in 1790 on a doctor's recommendation.

In 1810 he published *The Borough, a poem in 24 'letters' in which he illustrates the life of a country town (based on Aldeburgh), and which includes the tales of *'Peter Grimes' and *'Ellen Orford'. This was followed in 1812 by *Tales in Verse. In 1813 Sarah died at Muston, after a depressive illness, and Crabbe began to visit London more frequently. In 1814 he was appointed vicar of Trowbridge, and in 1819 published *Tales of the Hall*, a series of varied stories. He visited Sir W. *Scott in Edinburgh in 1822 and became his friend. He died in Trowbridge and much unpublished work was found, some of which (for instance 'The Equal Marriage' and 'Silford Hall') was published in a collected edition in 1834; later discoveries appeared in *New Poems* (1960), ed. A. Pollard. The standard edition of the poems is by A. Ward, 3 vols (1905–7).

Throughout the upheaval represented by the *Romantic movement, Crabbe persisted in his precise, closely observed, realistic portraits of rural life and landscape, writing mainly in the heroic couplets of the *Augustan age, and attempting to

> paint the cot
> As Truth will paint it, and as Bards will not.
> (*The Village*)

*Byron called him 'Nature's sternest painter yet the best', Scott called him 'the English Juvenal', and he was the favourite poet of J. *Austen. See *The Life of George Crabbe by His Son* (1834, with the *Poetical Works*, and 1947 with an introduction by E. *Blunden) and *George Crabbe* (1977) by T. Bareham.

Crabshaw, a character in Smollett's *Sir Launcelot *Greaves*.

CRACE, Jim (1946–   ), novelist, born in Hertfordshire. In the late 1960s he worked as a teacher in Botswana and as a television producer in the Sudan; after many years as a freelance journalist, he published his first book *Continent* in 1986. Crace's own epigraph to this collection of linked stories, set in a wholly imaginary sixth continent, identified its themes as 'trade and superstition', and these are the subjects to which he returns again and again in his writing. *The Gift of Stones* (1988), ostensibly a novel about Stone Age Britain, can also be read as a bracingly modern allegory of free market economics; as indeed can *Arcadia* (1992), despite its setting in a timeless future and a nameless city where all human life seems to be confined within the precincts of a vast shopping mall. *Signals of Distress* (1994), which describes the human and economic consequences of a shipwreck off the English coast in the 19th cent., showcases his talent for historical reconstruction to the full. On the surface *Quarantine* (1997) is a typical Crace novel, a scrupulous reimagining of desert life in the 1st cent., with its arid landscape evoked in unforgiving detail. But the book's cool debunking of religious myth—one of the main characters is Christ, who in this version fails to survive his 40 days in the wilderness—also attracted a good deal of attention. *Being Dead* (1999) also explores the subject of mortality, decay, and decomposition.

CRACHERODE, Clayton Mordaunt (1730–99), scholar and book-collector. Inherited wealth enabled him to acquire a fine collection of books and prints, which he bequeathed to the British Museum. His special interest was in early editions of the classics and the Silver Age of Latin, as well as in the art of early printing.

Craftsman, a periodical started in Dec. 1726 by Nicholas *Amhurst ('Caleb D'Anvers'), to which *Bolingbroke contributed his 'Remarks upon the History of England' (Sept. 1730–May 1731) and his 'Dissertation upon Parties' (1733). William Pulteney, later earl of Bath, was another leading contributor. Its title was intended to indicate Sir R. *Walpole as a 'man of craft'; and its essence (so far as it was political) lay in its opposition to Walpole and his cabinets.

CRAIG, (Edward Henry) Gordon (1872–1966), artist, actor, wood-engraver, writer, and stage designer, the son of Edward William Godwin and Ellen *Terry; he chose his own name, Craig, from the island Ailsa Craig. He began his career as an actor, then edited the *Page* (1898–1901), a periodical in which he published his own woodcuts. After directing in London he moved to the Continent, where he developed his avant-garde, anti-realist stage and lighting designs; in 1905 in Berlin he formed a liaison with the dancer Isadora Duncan, who bore him a child. (This was only one of many similar episodes in his colourful emotional life.) In the same year he published his first book, *The Art of the Theatre*, which was further expanded as *On the Art of the Theatre* (1911); several other works on the same subject followed, including *Towards a New Theatre* (1913). In 1908 in Florence he founded a theatre magazine, *The Mask*, which he edited (with a wartime interlude) until 1929. His radical ideas on design and stagecraft had considerable influence in both Europe and America, and his wood engravings contributed to a revival of the art. His memoirs of his early years, *Index to the Story of my Days*, were published in 1957.

CRAIGIE, Sir William Alexander (1867–1957), lexicographer and philologist, co-editor of the *Oxford English Dictionary* and its first *Supplement*, co-editor (1925–44) of the *Dictionary of American English*, editor (1919–55) of the *Dictionary of the Older Scottish Tongue*, and a notable contributor to Anglo-Norman, Frisian, and Icelandic philology.

CRAIK, Mrs (Dinah Maria Mulock) (1826–87), a prolific writer of novels, poems, children's books, fairy tales, essays, and short stories. A novel, *The Ogilvies* (1846), followed by *Olive* (1850), established her name, but she wrote nine further novels before *John Halifax, Gentle-*

man (1856), the great and prolonged success for which she is chiefly remembered. Her short stories were collected under the title *Avillion* in 1853 and her *Collected Poems* appeared in 1881. She was awarded a Civil List pension in 1864, but put it aside for authors less fortunate than herself.

crambo poem, one designed to exhaust the possible rhymes with someone's name. See MOLLY MOG.

CRANE, (Harold) Hart (1899–1932), American poet, born in Ohio. He published two volumes of verse, *White Buildings* (1926) and *The Bridge* (1930), the latter an obscure but powerful work which explores the 'Myth of America', with many echoes of *Whitman; its national symbols include Brooklyn Bridge itself, invoked in its Proem, and such historical and legendary characters as Columbus, *Rip Van Winkle, *Pocahontas, who, the poet explains, is the 'mythological naturesymbol chosen to represent the physical body of the continent, or the soul'. Crane was an alcoholic, and committed suicide by jumping from a steamer in the Caribbean after spending some time in Mexico. His *Complete Poems and Selected Letters and Prose*, ed. B. Weber, appeared in 1960, and his correspondence with Y. *Winters was published in 1978.

CRANE, Stephen (1871–1900), born in New Jersey, the son of a Methodist minister. He worked as a journalist in New York before attempting to publish his first novel, *Maggie: A Girl of the Streets* (1893), which was too grim to find a readership. His next work, *The Red Badge of Courage* (1895), a study of an inexperienced soldier (Henry Fleming) and his reactions to the ordeal of battle during the American Civil War, although based on no personal experience of war was hailed as a masterpiece of psychological realism, and Crane found himself working as a war reporter in Mexico, Cuba, and Greece. He came to England (where his novel had been even more warmly greeted than in the USA) in 1897, already ill with tuberculosis; he developed a close friendship with *Conrad (to whose work his own was compared), and met many other literary figures, including H. G. *Wells, who described his short story 'The Open Boat' (1898; it was based on personal experience of shipwreck) as 'an imperishable gem'. He died in Baden-Baden, almost immediately after his arrival, having been rushed there for a cure by his common-law wife Cora Stewart. His other works include two volumes of free verse, short stories, and sketches; his *Letters* (ed. R. W. Stallman and Lillian Gilkes) were published in 1960.

CRANE, Walter (1845–1915), designer, illustrator, painter, and writer. Crane is most famous for his coloured picture books for children and for his flower books; some of these he wrote himself. He cherished ambitions as a philosophical painter and poet, and developed the themes of his allegorical pictures—*The Roll of Fate* (1882), *The Bridge of Life* (1884)—in accompanying poems. His most elaborate verse,

The Sirens Three, was published in the *English Illustrated Magazine* (1885), with his own decorations. Crane, deeply influenced by W. *Morris, played an important role in the Arts and Crafts Movement; he was convinced of the value of the crafts and of good design and discussed his belief in *The Claims of Decorative Art* (1892). In the 1880s he became a socialist, and created many designs, cartoons, and verses for the socialist cause. His lectures on art education were published as *The Bases of Design* (1898) and *Line and Form* (1900).

Cranford, a novel by Mrs *Gaskell, published serially in *Household Words*, 1851–3.

Cranford, a series of linked sketches of life among the ladies of a quiet country village in the 1830s, is based on Knutsford in Cheshire where Mrs Gaskell spent her childhood. It centres on the formidable Miss Deborah Jenkyns and her gentle sister Miss Matty, daughters of the former rector. Moments of drama are provided by the death of the genial Captain Brown, run over by a train when saving the life of a child; by the panic caused in the village by rumours of burglars; by the surprising marriage of the widowed Lady Glenmire with the vulgar Mr Hoggins, the village surgeon; by the failure of a bank which ruins Miss Matty, and her rescue by the fortunate return from India of her long-lost brother Peter. But the greatest charm of *Cranford*, which has kept it unfailingly popular, is its amused but loving portrayal of the old-fashioned customs and 'elegant economy' of a delicately observed group of middle-aged figures in a landscape.

CRANMER, Thomas (1489–1556), archbishop of Canterbury, a fellow of Jesus College, Cambridge. He propounded views in favour of the divorce of Henry VIII from Catherine of Aragon, was appointed to the archbishopric in 1533, and maintained the king's claim to be the supreme head of the Church of England. He supervised the production of the first prayer book of Edward VI, 1549; prepared the revised prayer book of 1552; and promulgated the 42 articles of religion (afterwards reduced to 39) in the same year. To meet the need for suitable sermons, he contributed to and probably edited the first book of *Homilies issued in 1547. In Queen Mary's reign he was condemned for heresy by Cardinal Pole, recently appointed archbishop of Canterbury, and degraded in 1556. He signed six documents admitting the supremacy of the pope and the truth of all Roman Catholic doctrine except transubstantiation, in vain; he was burned at the stake, repudiating these admissions, on 21 Mar. 1556 at Oxford, holding his right hand (which had written his recantation) steadily in the flames, that it might be the first burnt. He compiled a *Reformatio Legum Ecclesiasticarum* (1550), which was published in a translation by W. Haddon and J. *Cheke in 1571, and wrote on Anglican discipline and theology; but his chief title to fame is that of being the principal author of the English liturgy.

CRASHAW, Richard (1612/13–49), poet. He lost both mother and stepmother before he was 9, and his father, a noted Puritan divine, died in 1626. He was educated at Charterhouse and Pembroke Hall, Cambridge, where he came under the influence of High Church friends including *Ferrar, whom he visited at *Little Gidding. From 1635 to 1643 he was a fellow at Peterhouse. He became a Catholic convert *c*.1645 and fled to Paris, where his friend *Cowley persuaded Queen Henrietta Maria to interest herself on his behalf. Through her influence he moved to Italy, first as attendant on Cardinal Palotta, then in 1649 in a minor post at the Santa Casa of Loreto, where he died shortly after. His principal work was the *Steps to the Temple* (1646), a collection of religious poems influenced by *Marino and the Spanish mystics, which has been acclaimed as the height of baroque in English poetry. To this was attached a secular section, the *Delights of the Muses*, containing 'Music's Duel', a paraphrase of the Latin of Strada, in which nightingale and lute-player contend until the former fails and dies: also 'Wishes. To His (Supposed) Mistresse', which begins 'Who'er she be | That not impossible she'. His best-known poems are those addressed to St *Theresa, the 'Hymne' beginning 'Love, thou art absolute, sole Lord | Of life and death' and 'The Flaming Hart', the second of which was added to the second edition of 1648 and printed in an expanded version in the posthumous collection *Carmen Deo Nostro* (1652). Both celebrate the bliss of martyrdom in characteristically baroque imagery of doves, darts, hearts, and 'delicious wounds'. The extravagant conceits of 'The Weeper', addressed to Mary Magdalen, were much ridiculed in subsequent periods. *Praz (*The Flaming Heart*, 1958) describes his work as 'the literary counterpart, though a minor one, to Rubens's apotheoses, Murillo's languors and El Greco's ecstasies'. His poems were edited by L. C. Martin (2nd edn) in 1957.

Cratchit, Bob, a character in Dickens's *A Christmas Carol.

Crawford, Henry and Mary, characters in J. Austen's *Mansfield Park.

CRAWFORD, Robert (1959–   ), poet and critic, born at Bellshill, near Glasgow; he studied English at Glasgow University and teaches at the University of St Andrews. His work appeared in *New Chatto Poets 2* (1989), which was followed by his first collection, *A Scottish Assembly* (1990). In the same year appeared *Sharwaggi*, a joint collection with poet W. N. Herbert, a volume which evokes the urban landscapes of Scotland in a rich and at times fantastic variety of demotic dialects, linguistic experiments, and 'translations'. Later collections include *Talkies* (1992) and *Masculinity* (1996). Much of Crawford's good-humoured yet sharp poetry explores questions of Scottishness, of national and cultural identity, but he also celebrates the domestic and the personal with tenderness and grace.

Crawley, (1) the Revd Josiah, one of the most memorable characters in A. Trollope's 'Barsetshire' novels, figuring most prominently in *The Last Chronicle of Barset* and also in *Framley Parsonage*; (2) Sir Pitt, his sister Miss Crawley, his sons Pitt and Rawdon, characters in Thackeray's *Vanity Fair*.

Creakle, in Dickens's *David Copperfield*, the bullying headmaster of the hero's first school.

CREELEY, Robert (1926–2005), American poet and lecturer, and one of the *Black Mountain group; he edited (1954–7) the *Black Mountain Review*. His verse is plainer, more personal, less rhetorical than that of his associates; his *Collected Poems 1945–1975* was published in 1983.

CREEVEY, Thomas (1768–1838), Whig MP successively for Thetford and Appleby. *The Creevey Papers* (ed. Sir H. Maxwell), published 1903, consisting of letters to his stepdaughter Elizabeth Ord, extracts from his journal, and letters to Creevey from various important persons, are interesting for their gossip and the light they throw on the characters of prominent persons and on the society of the later Georgian era. He was in Brussels for some years from 1814 and left a classic first-hand account of the city at the time of Waterloo. In Creevey's old age, when the Whigs were in power, he held office as treasurer of ordnance and afterwards as treasurer of Greenwich Hospital. Charles Greville in the *Greville Memoirs, 20 Feb. 1838) refers to Creevey's cheerful and sociable disposition; he was at once 'perfectly happy and exceedingly poor'. See also *Creevey's Life and Times* (1934), ed. J. Gore, a further selection with commentary.

CREIGHTON, Mandell (1843–1901), educated at Merton College, Oxford, where he became fellow and tutor, devoting himself to ecclesiastical, Italian, and Byzantine history. He was ordained in 1870 and was vicar of Embleton from 1875 to 1884, when he was elected to the chair of ecclesiastical history at Cambridge. During this time he continued his important *History of the Papacy during the Period of the Reformation* (5 vols, 1882–94). He was first editor of the *English Historical Review*, from 1886, and was selected bishop of Peterborough in 1891 and of London in 1897. His other works include *The Tudors and the Reformation* (1876), *The Age of Elizabeth* (1876), and lives of Simon de Montfort (1876), Cardinal Wolsey (1888), and Queen Elizabeth (1896). His *Life and Letters* by his widow appeared in 1904.

Cresseid, see TESTAMENT OF CRESSEID, THE; **Cressida,** see TROILUS AND CRESSIDA; see also TROILUS AND CRISEYDE.

CRÈVECŒUR, Michel-Guillaume de (1735–1813), known as J. Hector St John de Crèvecœur, born at Caen in France of a good but impoverished family. He emigrated to Canada and served under Montcalm, then moved south, landing at New York in 1759 and taking American citizenship in 1765. He then settled in Orange County, New York State, where for several idyllic years he farmed, until the revolution obliged him to flee to Europe. These years were the basis of his famous work, much admired by the Romantics, *Letters from an American Farmer* (published in London 1782), which describe rural life and customs with simplicity, artistry, and vigour; the third essay is on the subject of 'What is an American?' D. H. *Lawrence commented on his role as myth-maker in *Studies in Classic American Literature* (1923), and described him as the 'emotional prototype' of the American (as distinct from *Franklin, 'the real practical prototype').

Crewler, the Revd Horace and Mrs, characters in Dickens's *David Copperfield*, the parents of Sophy, whom Traddles marries.

CRICHTON, James, 'The Admirable' (1560–82), Scots adventurer, scholar, linguist, and poet, who served in the French army, travelled in Italy, and died in a brawl in Mantua. His colourful career is recounted by *Urquhart and is the subject of a historical novel by H. *Ainsworth. *Barrie's play *The Admirable Crichton* concerns a polymath manservant cast away with his employers on a desert island.

Cricket on the Hearth, The, a Christmas book by *Dickens, published 1846.

John Peerybingle, carrier, and his much younger wife, Dot, are as happy a couple as possible, although the venomous old Tackleton, who himself is about to marry the young May Fielding, throws suspicion on Dot's sincerity. This suspicion appears to be disastrously verified when an eccentric old stranger takes up his abode with the Peerybingles and is discovered one day by John, metamorphosed into a bright young man by the removal of his wig, in intimate conversation with Dot. By the fairy influence of the Cricket on the Hearth John is brought to the decision to pardon her offence, which he attributes to the incompatibility of their ages and temperaments. But there turns out to be no occasion for forgiveness, for the bright young man is an old friend, the lover of May Fielding, believed dead, who has turned up just in time to prevent her marrying Tackleton. Among the other characters are Caleb Plummer and his blind daughter Bertha, the toymakers; and Tilly Slowboy, most loving and incompetent of nurses.

Crimsworth, William, the hero of C. Brontë's *The Professor*.

Criseyde, see TROILUS AND CRISEYDE.

Crisparkle, the Revd Septimus, a character in Dickens's *Edwin Drood*.

Crispinus, a false poet in Jonson's *Poetaster*, in part a caricature of J. *Marston.

Criterion (1922–39), an influential literary periodical launched as a quarterly and edited by T. S. *Eliot; *The

Waste Land appeared in its first issue. It became the *New Criterion* in 1926, and in 1927, briefly, the *Monthly Criterion*, but then reverted to its original title and quarterly publication. It included poems, essays, short stories, and reviews, and published work by *Pound, *Empson, *Auden, *Spender, *Grigson, etc.; it also introduced the work of *Proust, *Valéry, *Cocteau, and other European writers. Eliot disowned any particular programme, claiming that his magazine represented a 'tendency', 'toward something which, for want of a better name, we may call classicism', but later critics have detected in the *Criterion* a sympathy towards Fascist ideology. Despite this, it continued to enjoy immense literary prestige until it closed in 1939 under the pressure of what Eliot described as 'a depression of spirits' induced by 'the present state of public affairs'.

Critic, The, *or a Tragedy Rehearsed,* a comedy by R. B. *Sheridan, produced 1779.

Based on Buckingham's *The Rehearsal*, *The Critic* is an exuberant burlesque on the problems of producing a play. The work under rehearsal by its distraught producer is 'The Spanish Armada', a ludicrous parody of the modish tragic drama of the day (see, for example, CUMBERLAND, R.; COLMAN, G, THE ELDER). Mr Puff, the author of 'The Spanish Armada' and an enterprising promoter of literary wares, has invited to the rehearsal Dangle and Sneer, two savage and inept theatre critics, and Sir Fretful Plagiary (a caricature of Cumberland). His absurd historical drama, written in both the bombastic and the sentimental styles, introduces Sir Walter *Ralegh, Sir Christopher Hatton, the earl of Leicester, Lord Burleigh, and others, at the time when the armada is approaching. Meanwhile Tilburina, the daughter of the governor of Tilbury Fort, complicates the plot with her love for Don Ferolo Whiskerandos, a Spanish prisoner. The action of the main play, including the solemn discussions by the author and his guests, their confused involvement with the rehearsal, and continual interruptions by producer, actors, and stage hands, continues with undiminished vivacity to the end.

Critical Dictionary of English Literature, A, *from the Earliest Accounts . . . to the Middle of the Nineteenth Century,* by Samuel Austin Allibone (1816–89), first published in the USA in 1858 and in London in 1859. In the editor's words, 'the fruits of many years of anxious research and conscientious toil', this vast work, the first of its kind on a comprehensive scale, includes biographical entries for 30,000 authors and entries for an even greater number of books. The aim was to direct the public to 'the Best Works of the Best Authors', and each book of any note is described with generous extracts from contemporary reviews and other critical writing. The interpretation of 'English Literature' is wide, as the 'Best Books' for doctors, lawyers, merchants, farmers, etc., were also included. The work was highly successful, with a new edition in 1871, and two supplements in 1891.

Critical Quarterly, a literary review founded in 1959 and edited by C. B. Cox and A. E. Dyson. It publishes essays, reviews, and poetry, and contributors have included A. *Wilson, P. *Larkin, D. *Davie, D. J. *Enright, W. *Empson, S. *Heaney, and others.

Critical Review (1756–90), a Tory and Church journal, founded in opposition to the liberal *Monthly Review.* Much of its space was devoted to public affairs, but it also provided full and balanced reviews of a wide range of books. Dr *Johnson thought well of it and contributed many articles, as did *Goldsmith. It was edited from 1756 to 1759 by *Smollett, who proved a controversial editor.

criticism, schools of, see under DECONSTRUCTION; FEMINIST CRITICISM; MARXIST LITERARY CRITICISM; MYTH CRITICISM; NARRATOLOGY; NEW CRITICISM; NEW HISTORICISM; POSTMODERNISM; PRACTICAL CRITICISM; PSYCHOANALYTIC CRITICISM; READER-RESPONSE THEORY; SOCIALIST REALISM; STRUCTURALISM AND POST-STRUCTURALISM. See also under ARCHETYPE.

Croaker, a character in Goldsmith's *The Good-Natur'd Man.*

CROCE, Benedetto (1866–1952), Italian philosopher, historian, and critic. His aesthetics and criticism, published in his journal *La critica* from 1903 to 1944, were profoundly influential in Italy before the Second World War. His most influential work is *Estetics come scienza dell'espressione e linguistica generale* (*Aesthetics as the Science of Expression and General Linguistics*, 1902). Central to all phases of his thought is the concept of art as a 'lyrical intuition'. His best criticism is in *Poesia popolare e poesia d'arte* (*Popular Poetry and Literary Poetry*, 1933), an original interpretation of Italian literary history from the 14th to the 16th cents; in his essay on *Ariosto, Shakespeare, Corneille* (1920); and in *La poesia* (*Poetics*, 1936). His historical works include detailed analysis, as in *Storia d'Europa nel secolo XIX* (*History of Europe in the 19th Century*, 1932), as well as theory, such as *La storia come pensiero e come azione* (*History as Thought and as Action*, 1938), which asserts that history is always the history of freedom.

CROCKETT, S. R., see KAILYARD SCHOOL.

Crockford, *Crockford's Clerical Directory,* first published 1857. A book of reference for facts relating to the clergy and the Church of England.

Croft, Admiral and Mrs, characters in J. Austen's *Persuasion.*

CROKER, John Wilson (1780–1857), an MP, secretary to the admiralty, and a prominent Tory politician. He was a regular contributor to the *Quarterly Review*, in which he made very plain his Tory and Anglican stance, even in his literary reviews, and for which he acted as an important link with circles of political power. Known for his bitter opposition to most of the younger writers of his day, he became (and has remained) notorious for his criticism of Keats's *Endymion* in 1818. *Shelley (in his preface to *Adonais*) and *Byron (in his jingle 'Who killed John Keats?') established the belief, still quoted, that Croker's review hastened the death of the poet. Yet Croker's views on *Endymion*, although blinkered and ungenerous, were considerably more temperate than those of *Lockhart in *Blackwood's*, and there is some justice in his comments on Keats's diction and versification. Croker was a painstaking scholar, and an expert on the 18th cent. His books include *An Intercepted Letter from Canton* (1804), a satire on Dublin society; a reliable edition of Boswell's *Life of Samuel *Johnson*, in 1831, and in the same year *Military Events of the French Revolution of 1830*; and *Essays on the Early Period of the French Revolution* (1857). He was a much hated man, caricatured in three contemporary novels: Peacock's *Melincourt* (1817); Lady *Morgan's *Florence Macarthy* (1818); and Disraeli's *Coningsby* (1844); and was detested by his lifelong enemy *Macaulay 'more than cold boiled veal'. It appears that he was the originator of the political term 'Conservative', which first appeared in an article of his in the *Quarterly Review* in Jan. 1830. *The Croker Papers*, published 1884, cover Croker's political life 1808–32 and are of considerable historical interest.

CROKER, Thomas Crofton (1798–1854), an Irish antiquary who worked in the admiralty, and was probably the first collector to regard national and folk stories as a literary art. *Researches in the South of Ireland* appeared in 1824; *Fairy Legends and Traditions in the South of Ireland*, which delighted Sir W. *Scott and was very successful, in 1825–8; *Legends of the Lakes* in 1829; and *Popular Songs of Ireland* in 1839. These works, together with Croker's many contributions to literary and antiquarian journals, provide a rich source of information on Irish folklore.

CROLY, George (1780–1860), educated at Trinity College, Dublin, and rector of St Stephen's Walbrook. He was author of *Paris in 1815* (1817), a work which owes much to Byron's *Childe Harold*; *Catiline* (1822), a tragedy; *May Fair* (1827), a satire; and, most notably, *Salathiel* (1829), a romance of the *Wandering Jew, Rome under Nero, and the siege of Jerusalem by Titus. *Marston* followed in 1846, a romance to which the French Revolution and the Napoleonic wars provide the background. He published numerous other narrative and romantic poems, as well as religious and historical works. Byron in *Don Juan* refers to Croly as 'the Revd Rowley Powley'.

CROMEK, Robert Hartley (1720–1812), engraver, appears also to have been a shifty literary speculator who made many enemies, notably *Blake. He published *Reliques of Burns* in 1808, and in 1810 a volume of *Select Scottish Songs* by *Burns. In the same year he published *Remains of Nithsdale and Galloway Song*, much of which consisted of the poems of A. *Cunning-

ham, which the author had disguised as ancient songs. It seems probable that Cromek knew of and ignored the deception. Blake expressed his enmity in the couplet, 'A petty, sneaking knave I knew | O! Mr Cr——, how do ye do?'

CROMPTON, Richmal, see CHILDREN'S LITERATURE.

CROMWELL, Oliver (1599–1658), soldier, politician, general, and from 1653 to 1658 lord protector, the subject of innumerable contemporary pamphlets, satires, odes, and panegyrics. *Marvell's 'An Horatian Ode upon Cromwell's Return from Ireland', written in 1650, and his *The First Anniversary of the Government under his Highness the Lord Protector* (1655) are notable expressions of balanced admiration for Cromwell's 'active star'; 'If these the times, then this must be the man.' *Milton, who was Latin secretary to the newly formed Council of State from 1649, appealed to him in the sonnet 'Cromwell, our chief of men' as the defender of conscience and liberty, and *Waller (his cousin) wrote in praise of his government and foreign policy. *D'Avenant's plays *The Cruelty of the Spaniards in Peru* (1658) and *The History of Sir Francis Drake* (1659) were intended to support Cromwell's war against Spain. After his death Cromwell was variously depicted by writers and historians as honest patriot, 'frantic enthusiast' (*Hume), corrupt hypocrite, and true Englishman: *Carlyle in his lecture on the 'Hero as King' (1840) and his *Letters and Speeches of Oliver Cromwell* (1845) praised him as a Puritan hero, God-sent to save England, grappling 'like a giant, face to face, heart to heart, with the naked truth of things'.

CROMWELL, Thomas, earl of Essex (?1485–1540), secretary to Cardinal Wolsey and subsequently to Henry VIII, and his chief adviser in ecclesiastical matters. He was the principal promoter of the dissolution of the monasteries. He negotiated Henry's marriage with Anne of Cleves, and the failure of this match and of the policy that underlay it, coupled with the intense unpopularity of the minister, led to his downfall. A bill of attainder was passed and Cromwell was executed.

Cromwell, The True Chronicle Historie of the Whole Life and Death of Thomas Lord, a play published in 1602 and stated in the title to have been 'written by W.S.' It was included in the third and fourth Shakespeare Folios (1664 and 1685). The play has little merit and is certainly not by Shakespeare.

CRONIN, A(rchibald) J(oseph) (1896–1981), born in Dunbartonshire. He studied medicine in Glasgow, then practised as a doctor for some years before devoting himself to an extremely successful career as a middlebrow novelist whose works reached an even wider audience through film and television: his best-known novels (e.g. *The Stars Look down*, 1935; *The Citadel*, 1937) combine in their subject matter the appeal of medicine and of mining, reflecting his own early experiences as a doctor in south Wales.

Crosbie, Adolphus, a character in A. *Trollope's *The Small House at Allington.

'Crossing the Bar', a poem in four stanzas by Lord *Tennyson, written Oct. 1889 while crossing the Solent and published that year. It is published as the last poem in most editions of Tennyson's work, in accordance with his own wishes.

CROSSLEY-HOLLAND, Kevin (1941–), poet and translator from Old English, born in Buckinghamshire and educated at Bryanston School and St Edmund Hall, Oxford. His collections include *The Rain-Giver* (1972), *The Dream-House* (1976), *Time's Oriel* (1983), *Water-slain* (1986), the title work of which is a sequence of 25 poems vividly evoking a village and its people—the beachcomber, the wildfowler, the local historian, the publican, the children—and *The Painting-Room* (1988). His translations include *The Battle of Maldon and Other Old English Poems* (1965), *Beowulf* (1968), *Storm and Other Old English Riddles* (1970), *The Exeter Book Riddles* (1978), and *The Old English Elegies* (1988). Although he has travelled widely and his spells abroad are reflected in his subjects, the strongest pull in his work is towards the landscape and interwoven history and legend of East Anglia, to its maltings, granaries, and woodlands, but most particularly to the 'marsh, mud, creeks, shifting sand' of its coastline. His works for children, many based on East Anglian folk tales and Norse myths, include *Havelock the Dane* (1964), the haunting *The Green Children* (1966), *The Pedlar of Swaffham* (1971), and *The Wildman* (1976). He has also written librettos from his own works, notably with composer Nicola LeFanu.

Crotchet Castle, a satire by *Peacock, published 1831.
   As in most of Peacock's books, the story assembles a group of theorists at a country house, such as Mr Skionar (who resembles *Coleridge), Mr MacQuedy (a Scottish economist who suggests J. R. MacCulloch), Mr Chainmail (who wants to revive the Middle Ages, possibly based on the historian Samuel Rush Meyrick, 1783–1848), and others. The Revd Dr Folliott, though more amiable and learned than Peacock's previous clerics, is also mocked for his bigoted conservatism. The dinner-table conversations at Crotchet Castle turn on the clash between Folliott's Toryism and MacQuedy's progressivism. The guests take a journey by river and canal to Wales, reminiscent of a trip Peacock took up the Thames with *Shelley in 1815. In Lady Clarinda, Peacock supplies the most spirited and cynical of his heroines. She has a foil in the romantic Susannah Touchandgo, who retires to a simple life in Wales after her father, a banker, absconds. The book ends with an assault by the mob on Mr Chainmail's 12th-cent. castle, an ironic comment on the more visionary schemes to solve the troubles of the age of reform.

CROUCH, Nathaniel, see CHILDREN'S LITERATURE.

Crow, a volume of poetry by Ted *Hughes.

Crowdero (meaning 'fiddler', because he plays on a 'crowd' or 'fiddle'), a member of the bear-baiting mob in Butler's *Hudibras.

Crowe, Captain, a character in Smollett's *Sir Launcelot *Greaves.

CROWE, Catherine, see GHOST STORIES.

CROWE, William, see LEWESDON HILL.

CROWLEY, 'Aleister' (really Edward Alexander) (1875–1947), son of a rich brewer turned Plymouth Brother, a diabolist and a prolific poet who claimed to be the Beast from the Book of Revelation. He joined the Order of the Golden Dawn, a group of theosophists involved in Cabbalistic magic, of which *Yeats was a member, and precipitated its dissolution when it rejected his claims to ascend to a higher spiritual grade. See *The Confessions of Aleister Crowley*, ed. John Symonds and Kenneth Grant (1971).

CROWNE, John (?1640–?1703), probably the son of an emigrant to Nova Scotia, where he appears to have spent some of his youth. A prose romance, *Pandion and Amphigenia* (1665), was followed by his first comedy, *The Country Wit* (1675), containing the character of Sir Mannerly Shallow, subsequently developed into *Sir Courtly Nice in the play of that name (1685). He wrote several other comedies, a court masque, *Calisto* (1675), and eleven tragedies, including the two-part rhymed *The Destruction of Jerusalem* (1677), *Thyestes* (1681), and *Caligula* (1698). The success of the tragedies is said to have owed much to expensive and elaborate scenery. He was part author, with *Dryden and *Shadwell, of *Notes and Observations*, a satirical attack on *The Empress of Morocco* by *Settle. Although Crowne was a favourite of Charles II, *Dennis said that he had 'a mortal aversion to the court'; he himself claimed in his later years that his plays were 'successful, and yet clean'.

Croyland, or *Crowland, History, The,* a chronicle of the 14th or 15th cent., printed by Sir H. *Savile in 1596 and for long erroneously attributed to Ingulf, abbot of Croyland (d. 1109), secretary to William the Conqueror. It was shown by Sir F. *Palgrave and others to be a forgery of the 15th cent.

CRUDEN, Alexander (1701–70), born in Aberdeen. He established a bookshop in London in 1732 and in 1737 published his *Biblical Concordance*; its later editions (1761 and 1769) remain standard works of reference. His eccentricities verged on insanity, and he believed himself in later life called upon to reform the nation.

Cruelty, Theatre of, a phrase associated with French director *Artaud, and introduced to Britain during the 1960s through the work of P. *Brook and critic and director Charles Marowitz (1934–), who chose the name for their experimental theatre group in homage to Artaud: the most celebrated production of the movement was Brook's version of *Weiss's *Marat/Sade*. The emphasis of this style of theatre was as much on gesture and movement as on text.

CRUIKSHANK, George (1792–1878), illustrator and caricaturist, son of Isaac Cruikshank, also a caricaturist. His vast amount of work was largely in political caricature, but among the books he illustrated were: Burns's *'The Jolly Beggars' in 1823; *Grimm's *Popular Stories* in 1824–6; Cowper's *John Gilpin* in 1828; Rhodes's *Bombastes Furioso* in 1830; Defoe's *Robinson Crusoe* in 1831; *Sketches by Boz* in 1836, which began a long association with Dickens including the illustrations to *Oliver Twist* in 1837; Scott's *Waverley* in 1836–9; *Ainsworth's *The Tower of London* in 1840; *Thackeray's *Legend of the Rhine* in 1845; H. B. *Stowe's *Uncle Tom's Cabin* in 1853. In 1835 he became the editor of *The Comic Almanack*, a predecessor of *Punch*.

Crummles, Mr Vincent, Mrs, and Ninetta ('the infant phenomenon'), characters in Dickens's *Nicholas Nickleby*.

Cruncher, Jerry, a character in Dickens's *A Tale of Two Cities*.

Cry, the Beloved Country, a novel by Alan Paton, published 1948. Paton (1903–88) was educated at the University of Natal, and was national president of the South African Liberal Party until it was declared illegal in 1968.

The Revd Stephen Kumalo sets off from his impoverished homeland at Ndotasheni, Natal, for Johannesburg, in search of his sister Gertrude and his son Absalom. He finds Gertrude has turned to prostitution, and Absalom has murdered the son of a white farmer, James Jarvis. Absalom is convicted and condemned to death, and Kumalo returns home with Gertrude's son and Absalom's pregnant wife. The novel ends with the reconciliation of Jarvis and Kumalo, and Jarvis's determination to rise above tragedy by helping the poor black community. The book is a moving plea for racial understanding and co-operation.

C.S.C., see CALVERLEY.

Cuala Press, a *private press founded in 1902 at Dundrum, Co. Dublin, by Elizabeth and Lily Yeats, sisters of W. B. *Yeats, to stimulate local crafts and employment. It was originally called the Dun Emer Press, changing its name in 1908, and it flourished as the Cuala Press until the late 1940s, publishing work by Yeats, *Synge, *Gogarty, Lady *Gregory, etc.

Cuchulain (pron. Cuhoolin), one of the principal heroes of the Ulster cycle of Irish mythology, the nephew or ward of Conchubar, king of Ulster. He is supposed to have lived in the 1st cent. AD. His birth was miraculous, and he showed his strength and prowess at an early age. While still a child he killed the terrible watchdog of the smith Culain and compensated the owner by undertaking to guard his house in the dog's place, whence the name of Cuchulain, signifying 'Culain's hound'. Of his numerous feats of valour, which won him the love of many women, the chief was his defence of Ulster, single-handed, against Medb (pron. Maeve), queen of Connaught, who attacked it in order to carry off the Brown Bull of Cuailgne (pron. Cooley). Cuchulain was killed, aged 27, by Lugaid, son of a king of Ulster, and the daughters of Calatin the wizard, in vengeance for their fathers whom Cuchulain had slain.

A series of the legends about him have been translated by Lady *Gregory (*Cuchulain of Muirthemne*). He figures in *Macpherson's Ossianic poems as 'Cuthullin'.

Cuckoo and the Nightingale, The, see CLANVOWE.

Cuddy, a herdsman or shepherd, in *The Shepheardes Calender* of Spenser and *The Shepherd's Week* of Gay.

CUDWORTH, Ralph (1617–88), see CAMBRIDGE PLATONISTS.

Cuff, Sergeant, the detective in W. Collins's *The Moonstone*.

CUGOANO, Ottobah, see BLACK BRITISH LITERATURE.

CULPEPER, Nicholas (1616–54), apothecary, Puritan, and republican. He conducted a campaign against the monopoly of the College of Physicians, and in 1649 published an English translation of the college's *Pharmacopoeia*, thus making its contents available for the first time to the poor who could not afford doctors' fees. Both this work and his *The English Physician Enlarged, or the Herbal* (1653) sold in vast quantities, but his infringement of the monopoly made him many enemies and he was the object of much slander and abuse.

cultural appropriation, a term used to describe the taking over of creative or artistic forms, themes, or practices by one cultural group from another. It is in general used to describe Western appropriations of non-Western or non-white forms, and carries connotations of exploitation and dominance. The concept has come into literary and visual art criticism by analogy with the acquisition of artefacts (the Elgin marbles, Benin bronzes, Lakota war shirts, etc.) by Western museums. The term has emerged in the last 20 years as part of the vocabulary of the post-colonial critique of Western expansionism. One early significant discussion was by Kenneth Coutts-Smith in 'Some General Observations on the Concept of Cultural Colonialism' (1976), where he brings together the Marxist notion of 'class appropriation' (the dominant class appropriating and defining 'high culture') and what he calls 'cultural colonialism', though he himself does not combine the two in the phrase 'cultural appropriation'. The problem had been identified earlier in the century, though not in these terms, by the New Negro and Harlem Renaissance writers in the USA, who were concerned by the caricature of the African-American voice and folk traditions in minstrelsy shows and in such popular successes as J. C. *Harris's Brer Rabbit stories. On the other hand, Harlem Renaissance writers such as Alain Locke (1886–1954) welcomed the *Modernist enthusiasm for African art. In more recent discussion the Modernist engagement with what were seen as primitive art forms (see PRIMITIVISM) has been seen as highly problematic. As this suggests, how an artist or writer's use of other cultures should be judged is a matter of interpretation: what one critic might condemn as 'cultural appropriation' another would discuss more neutrally as 'influence', or even praise as 'postmodern hybridity'. One of the finest discussions of these issues, although it does not use the term 'cultural appropriation', is Michael North's *The Dialect of Modernism: Race, Language, and Twentieth-Century Literature* (1994). North is centrally concerned with what has been called 'voice appropriation', for example G. *Stein's use of an African-American voice in her short story 'Melanctha'. 'Voice appropriation' has also been debated in terms of gender, as in feminist critiques of *Joyce's representation of female consciousness in the Molly Bloom sequence.

Culture and Anarchy, a collection of essays by M. *Arnold, published 1869. This work contains many of Arnold's central critical arguments.

The first chapter is devoted to his concept of culture as 'sweetness and light', a phrase adopted from Swift's *The Battle of the Books*; Arnold presents culture as the classical ideal of human perfection, rather than 'a smattering of Greek and Latin'. Subsequent chapters set forward his definitions of Barbarians, *Philistines, and the Populace, and contrast the spirit of Hebraism (as manifested in primitive Christianity and Protestantism) with that of Hellenism, with its aim of seeing 'things as they really are'; both are important contributions to human development and should not be mutually exclusive.

CULVERWEL, Nathaniel (d. 1651), see CAMBRIDGE PLATONISTS.

CUMBERLAND, Richard (1732–1811), educated at Westminster School and Cambridge, the author of a number of highly successful *sentimental comedies, of which *The West Indian* and *The Brothers* are the most interesting. He also wrote tragedies; two novels, *Arundel* (1789) and *Henry* (1795); a translation of the *Clouds* of *Aristophanes; and an autobiography. Cumberland is caricatured by *Sheridan as Sir Fretful Plagiary in *The Critic*.

CUMBERLAND, William Augustus, duke of (1721–65), third son of George II, and in command of the English army at Culloden (1746); known as 'the Butcher' on account of the severity with which he stamped out disaffection among the Highlanders. He figures in Scott's *Waverley*.

CUMMINGS, Bruce Frederick (1889–1919), diarist and biologist, born in Barnstaple, known under his pseudonym of W. N. P. Barbellion as the author of a diary covering the years 1903–17, *The Journal of a Disappointed Man*, which was published in 1919 with an introduction by H. G. *Wells, who described it as a 'specimen, carefully displayed and labelled' of 'a recorded unhappiness'. It is largely an account of the author's struggle with an illness (diagnosed as disseminated sclerosis) that made him increasingly introspective; he alternates between moods of elation, egotism, self-disgust, and physical nausea, leading more and more of a substitute existence through his diaries, and noting that 'as I become more static and moribund, they become more active and aggressive.' He clearly intended publication, and modelled his work to some extent on the immensely successful diary of M. *Bashkirtseff ('She is impressionable, volatile, passionate—ill! So am I.'); the last entry was made on 21 Oct. 1917, after which 'Barbellion's' death was recorded, but in fact Cummings survived to see his own work published, and his *A Last Diary* (1920, ed. A. J. and H. R. Cummings) covers the last two years of his life.

CUMMINGS, E(dward) E(stlin) (1894–1962), American poet, born in Cambridge, Massachusetts, and educated at Harvard. His first book, *The Enormous Room* (1922), an account of his three-month internment in a French detention camp in 1917, won him an immediate international reputation for its brilliant prose and its iconoclastic views, with *Dos Passos, Robert *Graves, T. E. *Lawrence, and V. Larbaud among its earliest admirers. In 1923 appeared *Tulips and Chimneys*, the first of 12 volumes of poetry. Strongly influenced by the English Romantic poets, by *Swinburne, and by *Pound, and marked by *Dada and the jazz age, the early poems attracted attention more for their experimental typography and technical skill than for their considerable lyric power; the frankness of his vocabulary and the sharpness of his satire also created some scandal. In *Eimi* (1933), a typographically difficult but enthralling journal of a trip to Russia, he broke in disillusion from his earlier socialist leanings, and thenceforth his work reflected his increasingly reactionary social and political views. His later lyrics, on the other hand, achieved a greater depth and simplicity. His other works include essays, plays, and *Tom* (1935), a satirical ballet based on H. B. *Stowe's *Uncle Tom's Cabin*. Cummings opened new perspectives for an entire generation of American and British poets, including *Auden and *Spender. His *Complete Poems: 1910–1962* was published in 1980.

CUNNINGHAM, Allan (1784–1842), born in Dumfriesshire, apprenticed to his brother as a stonemason. As a boy he walked in *Burns's funeral procession. He was an avid reader, and became a friend of J. *Hogg. In 1809 *Cromek was collecting songs in Scotland, and Cunningham, when he found his own poems were not acceptable, profited from the vogue for *primitivism by disguising them as old Scottish songs, many of which Cromek then published in 1810 as *Remains of Nithsdale and Galloway Song*. Cromek persuaded him to come to London, and introduced him to Sir Francis Chantrey, whose secretary he became. He was soon a frequent contributor to the *London Magazine* and to *Blackwood's*. He published *Traditional Tales of the English and Scottish Peasantry* in 1822; *The Songs of Scotland* in 1825; various romantic tales between 1826 and 1836; *Lives of the Most Eminent British Painters, Sculptors, and Architects* in 1829–33; and in 1834 an edition of Burns. Several of his poems and ballads, such as 'A wet sheet and a flowing sea' and 'Hame, hame, hame', which were very popular in his lifetime, are still remembered.

CUNNINGHAM, John (1729–73), the son of a Dublin wine-cooper. He wrote a successful farce, *Love in a Mist* (1747), then came to England and joined a group of travelling players, though it appears he had little talent as an actor. He also wrote contemplative pastoral verse imitative of *Gray and *Shenstone (*Poems Chiefly Pastoral*, 1766). He died in Newcastle upon Tyne.

CUNNINGHAME GRAHAM, Robert Bontine (1852–1936), horseman, writer, anti-imperialist, and social reformer, the son of a Scottish laird and a half-Spanish mother. During a flamboyant and varied career he was a rancher in Argentina, an outspoken MP (he was imprisoned after Bloody Sunday, 1887), and a traveller in remote parts of the world, particularly in Spanish America, where he gained an intimate knowledge of gaucho life and of the older civilization surviving from the period of Spanish rule. His many stories, books, and articles include remarkable and exotic tales of travel. *Mogreb-el-Acksa* (1898) recounts his attempt to reach the forbidden city of Tarudant in Morocco; G. B. *Shaw in his preface to *Captain Brassbound's Conversion* claimed it as his inspiration for the play, and it was also much admired by *Conrad. Other titles include *Thirteen Stories* (1900), *Success* (1902), *Scottish Stories* (1914), and *The Horses of the Conquest* (1930); he also wrote several volumes of Latin American history. See A. F. Tschiffely, *Don Roberto* (1937), an account of Graham's life and their friendship, and Alexander Maitland, *Robert and Gabriela Cunninghame Graham* (1984).

CUNOBELIN (Cymbeline), a king of Britain in the early years of the Christian era, and father of *Caractacus. See CYMBELINE.

Cupid and Campaspe, see CAMPASPE.

Cupid and Psyche, the allegorical centrepiece of the *Golden Ass* of *Apuleius, in which the author blends a familiar folk tale depicting an enchanted suitor and his abandoned bride with a Hellenistic epyllion about the god of love which has some of the trappings of a philosophical myth. Psyche, daughter of a king, is beloved by Cupid, who visits her nightly, but remains invisible, forbidding her to attempt to see him: one night she takes a lamp and looks at him as he sleeps, and agitated by his beauty lets fall a drop of hot oil on his shoulder. He departs in wrath, leaving her solitary and remorseful. Like the hero of the novel in which her tale is set, Psyche has forfeited her happiness through misplaced curiosity, and has to regain it through painful wanderings. The irony evident in the treatment of the gods and the rich decoration of the setting of certain scenes betray an indebtedness to a Hellenistic original, while many elements of the fable—the magic palace, the enchantress (Venus) to whom the hero (Cupid) is in thrall, the tasks the heroine has to perform and the animals that aid her—belong to the world of the folk tale. Apuleius' story has been retold by W. *Browne (*Britannia's Pastorals*, Bk III), by S. *Marmion (*Cupid and Psyche*), by W. *Morris (*The Earthly Paradise*), and by *Bridges (*Eros and Psyche*). Pater's *Marius the Epicurean* provides a prose version. Milton's *Comus* (1003–11) contains a reference to Apuleius' story and *Keats's 'Ode to Psyche' owes a debt to it.

Cure for a Cuckold, A, a comedy by J. *Webster and W. *Rowley, possibly with T. *Heywood, written 1624/5, printed 1661.
    It deals with the love affairs of two couples, Bonville and Annabel, and Lessingham and Clare; and contains a notable duel scene on Calais sands.

Curious Impertinent, The (or *The Fatal Curiosity*), an episode in *Don Quixote (I. 30–5) which provided the plot for more than one English 17th-cent. drama. Anselmo, having married the beautiful Camilla, urges his friend Lothario to test her virtue. Lothario, at first reluctant, yields to the constant pressure of his friend. Camilla's lapse encourages the licentiousness of her maid Leonela, which leads to the discovery of her mistress's infidelity, the death of Anselmo and Lothario, and Camilla's retirement to a convent.

CURLL, Edmund (1683–1747), a bookseller and pamphleteer who specialized in scandalous biographies, seditious pamphlets, pirated works, and pornography; he was imprisoned in 1724 for publishing *Venus in the Cloister: or The Nun in her Smock* (a characteristic title), though he denied that it was his. He made many enemies in the literary world, including *Pope, who pilloried him in *The Dunciad*. Pope was involved in various manœuvres to encourage Curll to publish an unauthorized edition of his letters (which he did, in 1735), in order to appear himself to be pushed into publishing the authentic versions. Curll is also mentioned in *Swift's poem 'On the Death of Dr Swift'. A life by R. Straus, *The Unspeakable Curll*, appeared in 1927.

CURNOW, Allen (1911–2001), New Zealand poet and critic, born at Timaru. After a period as a journalist in New Zealand before, during, and for a time after the Second World War, he joined the English department of the University of Auckland in 1951 and taught there until 1976. From an early stage he was seen to be an important figure in the creation of a truly New Zealand poetry. His first significant book, *Not in Narrow Seas* (1939), was followed by several others in the 1940s; and his editing of *A Book of New Zealand Verse* (1945; rev. 1951) and then *The Penguin Book of New Zealand Verse* (1960) was both influential and controversial. An increasingly prolific and audacious writer, since the 1970s he was recognized not only as his country's leading poet but as a poet with an international reputation. A number of collected and selected volumes are drawn on in *Early Days Yet: New and Collected Poems 1941–1997* (1997).

Cursor Mundi, a northern poem dating from about 1300 surviving in seven manuscripts of about 24,000 short lines, supplemented in most of them by another 6,000 or so lines of devotional material. It is founded on the works of late 12th-cent. Latin writers who wrote various pseudo-histories made up of hagiographic, legendary, and biblical material. This poem covers mankind's spiritual history from the Creation to the Last Judgement, divided into Seven Ages, and is a very successful, readable piece of popular instruction. It has been edited by R. Morris (EETS OS, 7 vols, 1874–93).

CURTIS, Tony (1946–   ), Welsh poet and critic, born in Carmarthen and educated at University College, Swansea. His collections include *Album* (1974), *The Deerslayers* (1977), *Preparations* (1980), which contains several moving and intimate poems commemorating his father's death, *Letting Go* (1983), and *Selected Poems 1970–85* (1986). Much of his poetry is deeply rooted in Welsh culture and landscape, with particular reference to Pembrokeshire, and some of his best poems are inspired by animals, the natural world, and domestic life, but in later work his references become more international, his subjects widening to include historical incidents and the *Holocaust. *Wales, the Imagined Nation* (1986) is an examination of Welsh national and cultural identity, a theme on which he has written extensively.

CURZON, Robert, 14th Baron Zouche (1810–72), author of a *Visit to the Monasteries of the Levant* (1849), a record of his travels undertaken in search of manuscripts to Mount Athos, Greece, Palestine, and Egypt, *An Account of the most Celebrated Libraries of Italy* (1854), and *Armenia* (1854).

CURZON OF KEDLESTON, George Nathaniel, Marquess (1859–1925), educated at Eton and Balliol College, Oxford, MP for Southport (1886), viceroy of India (1899–1905), chancellor of Oxford University (1907), and secretary of state for foreign affairs, 1918–22. He travelled widely, and the results were embodied in the authoritative *Persia and the Persian* (1892), and in books on the Far East and Asiatic Russia. His energy, pomposity, and enjoyment of the splendour and formality of official life have made him a legendary figure.

Custom of the Country, The, a tragi-comedy by J. *Fletcher and P. *Massinger, composed between 1619 and 1622, and derived from the *Persiles y Sigismunda* of *Cervantes. Famed for its obscenity, it was described by *Dryden as containing more bawdry than any Restoration play, and *Pepys declared it 'of all the plays that ever I did see, the worst—having neither plot, language, nor anything in the earth that is acceptable' (2 Jan. 1667). The plot is set in motion when Count Clodio, an Italian governor, claims his *droit de seigneur* ('the custom of the country') from Zenocia on her marriage to Arnoldo; she, Arnoldo, and Arnoldo's brother Rutilio escape by sea, but Zenocia is captured by a Portuguese captain and placed in service in Lisbon with Hippolita, who subsequently falls in love with Arnoldo and seeks Zenocia's destruction. There is an elaborately interwoven sub-plot involving Rutilio, his adventures in a brothel, and a duel. An adaptation by Nicholas Wright, with the action set in southern Africa, was performed in 1983.

Custom of the Country, The, a witty and satiric novel by E. *Wharton in which a beautiful, energetic, destructive, and ambitious American, Undine Spragg, works her way to wealth and power through a succession of marriages—to Ralph Marvell, of the old New York aristocracy; to Marquis Raymond de Chelles, of the French aristocracy; and finally to billionaire Elmer Moffatt of Apex City, Kansas, who is revealed to have been her first husband in a secret marriage.

Cute, Alderman, a character in Dickens's *The Chimes*, said to be based on Sir Peter Laurie, the City magistrate.

CUTHBERT, St (d. 687). In his youth he kept sheep on the hills near the Lauder, a tributary of the Tweed. He entered the monastery of Melrose, of which he became prior. In course of time he was sent to fill the post of prior of Lindisfarne, on which the monastery of Melrose then depended; and after several years, feeling himself called to a life of perfect solitude, he retired to the small island of Farne. In 684, at a synod held under St Theodore, archbishop of Canterbury, he was selected for the see of Lindisfarne, and to overcome his unwillingness to accept it King Egfrith himself, accompanied by the bishop of the Picts, visited him on his island. After two years, feeling death approaching, he retired to the solitude of his island, and died in his cell on 20 Mar. (his feast day) 687. His body, which was said to have remained for many years in a state of incorruption and was carried away by the monks when they were driven by the Danes from Lindisfarne, was finally buried in Durham Cathedral.

CUTLER, Ivor, see PERFORMANCE POETRY.

Cuttle, Captain Edward, a character in Dickens's *Dombey and Son*. His favourite expression is, 'When found, make a note of.' (See NOTES AND QUERIES.)

Cymbeline, a play by *Shakespeare, first published in the Folio of 1623. It may have been written in 1609/10; *Forman saw a performance of it, perhaps at the *Globe, probably in Apr. 1611. Its sources are *Holinshed, *A Mirror for Magistrates, and perhaps Boccaccio's *Decameron (see also PHILASTER). Though included among the tragedies in the First *Folio, the play is now generally classified as a 'romance', and is more highly regarded than it was by Dr *Johnson, who said that 'To remark the folly of the fiction, the absurdity of the conduct, the confusion of the names and manners of different times, and the impossibility of the events in any system of life, were to waste criticism upon unresisting imbecility, upon faults too evident for detection, and too gross for aggravation.' The play was much loved in the 19th cent., however; *Tennyson died with a copy of it on the coverlet of his bed. G. B. *Shaw wrote an emended version of the long fifth act, published in 1938 under the title *Cymbeline Refinished*.

Imogen, daughter of Cymbeline, king of Britain, has secretly married Leonatus Posthumus, a 'poor but worthy gentleman'. The queen, Imogen's stepmother, determined that her clownish son Cloten shall marry Imogen, reveals the secret marriage to the king, who banishes Posthumus. In Rome Posthumus boasts of Imogen's virtue and makes a wager with Iachimo that if he can seduce Imogen he shall have a diamond ring that Imogen had given him. Iachimo is repulsed by Imogen, but by hiding in her bedchamber he observes details of Imogen's room and her body which persuade Posthumus of her infidelity, and he receives the ring. Posthumus writes to his servant Pisanio directing him to kill Imogen; but Pisanio instead provides her with male disguise, sending a bloody cloth to Posthumus to deceive him that the deed is done. Under the name Fidele Imogen becomes a page to Bellarius and the two lost sons of Cymbeline, Guiderius and Arviragus, living in a cave in Wales. Fidele sickens and is found as dead by the brothers, who speak the dirge 'Fear no more the heat o'th'sun'. Left alone she revives, only to discover at her side the headless corpse of Cloten which she believes, because of his borrowed garments, to be that of her husband Posthumus. A Roman army invades Britain; Imogen falls into the hands of the general Lucius and becomes his page. The Britons defeat the Romans, thanks to the superhuman valour in a narrow lane of Bellarius and his two sons aided by the disguised Posthumus. However, Posthumus, pretending to be a Roman, is subsequently taken prisoner and has a vision in jail of his family and Jupiter, who leaves a prophetic document with him. Lucius pleads with Cymbeline for the life of Fidele/Imogen: moved by something familiar in her appearance, he spares her life and grants her a favour. She asks that Iachimo be forced to tell how he came by the ring he wears. Posthumus, learning from this confession that his wife is innocent but believing her dead, is in despair till Imogen reveals herself. The king's joy at recovering his daughter is intensified when Bellarius restores to him his two lost sons, and the scene ends in a general reconciliation. Posthumus' words to Imogen on being reconciled with her, 'Hang there like fruit, my soul, | Till the tree die!' were described by Tennyson as 'the tenderest lines in Shakespeare'.

Cymochles, in Spenser's *Faerie Queene (II. v, vi, and viii), 'a man of rare redoubted might', 'given all to lust and loose living', the husband of *Acrasia and brother of *Pyrochles. He sets out to avenge on Sir *Guyon the supposed death of his brother, but *Phaedria intervenes. He is finally slain by Prince *Arthur.

Cymodoce, one of the Nereids. Cymodoce is the name of the mother of Marinell in Spenser's *Faerie Queene (IV. xii). *Swinburne's 'Garden of Cymodoce' in *Songs of the Springtides* is the island of Sark.

CYNEWULF, probably a Northumbrian or Mercian poet of the late 8th or 9th cent. At one time a great number of Old English poems were attributed to him (notably *Andreas, *Guthlac A and B, *The Phoenix, and the *Dream of the Rood), but modern scholarship restricts attribution to the four poems in the *Exeter Book and the *Vercelli Book which end with his name in runes. The poems are *Juliana*, *Elene*, *The Fates of the Apostles*, and *Christ II* (the last is a poem on the Ascension in the Exeter Book placed between poems on the Incarnation and on the Last Judgement, the three together being taken as a composite poem, *Christ*). *Elene* is the story of the finding of the Cross by St Helena, the mother of the Emperor Constantine.

Trans. C. W. Kennedy, *The Poems of Cynewulf* (1910: repr. 1949; contains the attributed as well as the signed poems); K. Sisam, 'Cynewulf and His Poetry' (*Studies in the History of Old English Literature*, 1953, ch. 1); *Juliana*, ed. R. Woolf (1955).

Cynthia, (1) a name for Artemis or Diana, from Mount Cynthus in Delos, where Artemis was born, and used poetically to denote the Moon; (2) the name given by the Roman poet *Propertius to his mistress; (3) deriving from (1), a name used by *Spenser (in *Colin Clouts Come Home Againe), *Ralegh, and others to denote Elizabeth I as virgin moon-goddess; (4) in Congreve's *The Double Dealer, the daughter of Sir Paul Plyant, affianced to Mellefont; (5) in Mrs Gaskell's *Wives and Daughters, Cynthia Kirkpatrick, stepsister of Molly Gibson.

Cynthia, *Ocean's Love to*, a poem by *Ralegh reflecting on his shifting relationship with Elizabeth I. The title plays on Ralegh's name (Walter/Water). Spenser in *Colin Clouts Come Home Againe (1595) referred to Ralegh's authorship of

a lamentable lay . . .
Of *Cynthia* the Ladie of the sea,
Which from her presence faultlesse him debard.

Ralegh may have written a longer poem or sequence of poems on this theme; what survives in Ralegh's own hand is a 522-line piece 'The 21th: and last booke of the Ocean to Scinthia' and a 22-line fragment 'the beginninge of the 22 boock, entreating of Sorrow'. Cf. Walter Oakeshott, *The Queen and the Poet* (1960).

Cynthia's Revels, an allegorical comedy by *Jonson, performed 1600, printed 1601.

The play satirizes various court vices represented by characters whose names typify their failings: Argurion, money; Asotus, prodigality; Anaides, impudence; Hedon, voluptuousness; Moria, folly; Phantaste, frivolity; Philautia, self-love; Amorphus, who has 'lost his shape' through too much travel. Having drunk of the Fountain of Self-Love (the subtitle of the play), the courtiers are emboldened to appear before Queen Cynthia in a masque devised by the wise poet Crites, in which each character is made to impersonate his complementary virtue. With the aid of Mercury, who had been sent by Jove to purge the court, Crites exposes the masquers, and as a penance they are sent on a pilgrimage to drink the waters of Mount Helicon, the fountain of truth. The song of Hesperus in Act V, 'Queen and huntress, chaste and fair', is one of Jonson's most beautiful lyrics.

Cypress, Mr, a character in Peacock's *Nightmare Abbey*, a caricature of *Byron.

Cypresse Grove, A, see DRUMMOND OF HAWTHORNDEN.

CYRANO DE BERGERAC, Savinien (1619–55), a French soldier and duellist, whom a wound in the Spanish War turned into a dramatist and novelist. He is the subject of a highly successful play by *Rostand.

D

DABYDEEN, David (1956–), Guyanese-born poet and novelist, educated at Cambridge and at University College London. Recurrent themes in Dabydeen's poetry include an exploration of the experience of slavery and indentureship, the cultural denigration and dislocation resulting from colonialism, and the power of language to redeem. *Slave Song* (1984) is notable for its innovative use of Guyanese rural Creole; the poems are accompanied by a 'translation' and commentary in Standard English highlighting the historical and cultural power relationships between the two forms of language. *Turner* (1994) uses language that approaches Standard English and exhibits a sensuous lyrical beauty in contrast to the harshness and vulgarity of language in *Slave Song*. This long poem takes the submerged African head in *Turner's painting *The Slave Ship* (1840) as its starting point and negotiates the problems of history and identity the Middle Passage represents, exploring the creative as well as dislocating aspects inherent in this experience. His first novel, *The Intended* (1991), set in multicultural south London, follows the learning experiences of a clever Guyanese schoolboy: this was followed by *Disappearance* (1993), narrated by a West Indian engineer working in a Kentish village, and *The Counting House* (1996). Dabydeen has written extensively on cultural diversity and post-colonial issues, and teaches at the University of Warwick.

DACRE, Charlotte, see ROMANTIC FICTION.

dactyl, a metrical foot consisting of one long followed by two short syllables, or of one accented followed by two unaccented (derived from the three joints of the finger, δακτύλος). See METRE.

Dada (Fr. 'hobby-horse', a name chosen at random from a dictionary), a movement in art and literature founded c.1916 in Zurich and more or less simultaneously in New York. The movement's aim was nihilistic, a denial of sense or order; it lasted until the early 1920s, with Paris as its centre from 1920. Writers connected with Dada included Tristan Tzara, who appears as a character in Stoppard's *Travesties*, which is set in Zurich during the First World War. Notable among Dada artists were Hans Arp, Marcel Duchamp, and Man Ray. *Aragon and A. *Breton went on to develop the *surrealist movement which evolved in part from Dada.

DADD, Richard (1817–86), English painter, who is best known for his fairy pictures (see FAIRY STORIES) filled with meticulous, tiny detail. They follow Joshua *Reynolds, *Fuseli, and Joseph Noel Paton in illustrating scenes from *A Midsummer Night's Dream* and *The Tempest*. Dadd went mad in 1843 and murdered his father; he spent the rest of his life in Bethlehem Hospital and in Broadmoor. His most famous work is *The Fairy Fellers Master-Stroke* (1855–64, Tate Gallery, London); a recently discovered manuscript poem (dated 1865) explains its subject in detail.

Dagon, the national deity of the ancient Philistines, represented as half man, half fish (Judg. 16: 23; 1 Sam, 5: 1–5). In Milton's *Paradise Lost*, I. 462, he appears as a fallen angel: see also *Samson Agonistes*.

D'AGUIAR, Fred (1960–), poet and novelist, born in London, and brought up as a child in Guyana: he returned to school in Britain aged 12, and went on to study at the universities of Kent and Warwick. He has written three volumes of poetry, *Mama Dot* (1985), which explores his early life in Guyana, *Airy Hall* (1989), and *British Subjects* (1993), which closely examines British and transcultural identity and contains a sequence called 'Frail Deposits', dedicated to Wilson *Harris, about a return trip to Guyana. His novels are *The Longest Memory* (1994), an intense, closely researched, lyrical, brutal evocation of the life of Whitechapel, an 18th-cent. plantation slave in Virginia; *Dear Future* (1997); and *Feeding the Ghosts* (1997), about the voyage of a slave ship returning from Africa, the captain of which throws his sick slaves overboard and is held to account by a survivor. His stage play, *A Jamaican Airman Foresees His Death*, was staged at the *Royal Court in 1995; *Bill of Rights* (1998) is a long poem on the theme of the 1978 Jonestown massacre/mass suicide in Guyana. See BLACK BRITISH LITERATURE and SLAVERY, LITERATURE OF.

DAHL, Roald (1916–90), short story writer, novelist, and children's writer, born of Norwegian parents in Llandaff, Glamorgan. His first collection of stories, *Over to You* (1946), drew on his wartime experiences as a fighter pilot. Dahl published several more collections, including *Someone Like You* (1953), *Kiss Kiss* (USA 1959, UK 1960), *Switch Bitch* (1974), and *The Wonderful Story of Henry Sugar and Six More* (1977). A number of stories were dramatized for television, and subsequently republished, as *Tales of the Unexpected*, and a collected edition of his short stories appeared in 1991. Dahl's penchant for the *conte cruel* was adapted with international success for children in *Charlie and the Chocolate Factory* (1964), *George's Marvellous Medicine* (1981), *Revolting Rhymes* (1982), and *The Witches* (1983) (See CHILDRENS' LITERATURE.)

DAICHES, David (1912–   ), scholar and author, educated at George Watson's College, Edinburgh, and Edinburgh University. He has held various academic posts and written on a wide variety of subjects: his works include studies of R. L. *Stevenson (1947), *Burns (1950), and Sir W. *Scott (1971); a *Critical History of English Literature* (4 vols, 1960); *Scotch Whisky* (1969); and two autobiographical works which vividly evoke his unusual childhood as son of a Jewish scholar and rabbi in Edinburgh (*Two Worlds*, 1957; *Was; A Pastime from Time Past*, 1975).

Daily Courant, the first English daily newspaper, started in March 1702. It contained foreign intelligence, translated from foreign newspapers. It lasted till 1735. (See NEWSPAPERS, ORIGINS OF.)

Daily Express, a daily paper founded in 1900 by Sir A. *Pearson.

Daily News was founded by *Dickens in 1845 as a Liberal rival to the *Morning Chronicle*; the first issue appeared on 21 Jan. 1846. Dickens himself edited the paper for 17 numbers only, then handed over to John *Forster. Among notable contributors and members of its staff at various times may be mentioned H. *Martineau, *Lang, G. B. *Shaw, *Wells, Arnold *Bennett, and the eminent war correspondent Archibald Forbes (1839–1900). It became the *News Chronicle* in 1930, having absorbed the *Daily Chronicle*, and survived under this title until 1960.

Daily Telegraph, founded in 1855, the first daily paper to be issued in London at a penny. Its enterprising character and rather highly coloured style proved so successful that for a time it enjoyed a larger circulation than any other English newspaper, and in its early days, with T. *Hunt as assistant editor, its political views were radical. After a period of decline in the early 20th cent., circulation recovered in the 1930s; in 1937 the *Morning Post* was at its own request amalgamated. The *Sunday Telegraph* was added in 1961. Among famous members of its staff have been G. A. *Sala, Sir E. *Arnold, and Edward Dicey (1832–1911).

Daisy Miller, one of H. *James's most popular stories, published 1879, dramatized by James 1883.

Daisy Miller travels to Europe with her wealthy, commonplace mother, and in her innocence and audacity offends convention and seems to compromise her reputation. She dies in Rome of malaria. She is one of the most notable and charming of James's portrayals of 'the American girl'.

Dale, (1) Laetitia, a character in Meredith's *The Egoist*; (2) Lily, the heroine of A. *Trollope's novel *The Small House at Allington*, and an important character in *The Last Chronicle of Barset*.

d'ALEMBERT, or **DALEMBERT,** Jean le Rond (1717–83), see PHILOSOPHES and ENCYCLOPÉDIE.

DALI, Salvador Felipe Jacinto (1904–89), Spanish painter, writer, and showman, born in Figueres, Catalonia. He was already in debt to *Surrealism before he joined the movement in 1929 after making the film *Un chien andalou* with Luis Buñuel. His most arresting paintings were produced approximately between 1925 and 1938, including *The Great Masturbator* (1929). The essay on Millet's *Angélus* (written *c.*1934) is his most original theoretical work. *The Secret Life of Salvador Dali* (1942) is an amusing if unreliable guide to his early exploits, and the novel *Hidden Faces* (1944) is a not unimpressive attempt to advertise the virtues of unconsummated love. See Ian Gibson, *The Shameful Life of Salvador Dali* (1997).

Dalila, see DELILAH.

DALRYMPLE, Sir David, Lord Hailes (1726–92), Scottish jurist, historian, and antiquary, a friend of *Boswell, Dr *Johnson, and Horace *Walpole. He published much, including his *Annals of Scotland* (1776, 1779, 1797), a valuable study of Scottish history which Johnson much admired. He was also keenly interested in ancient Scottish poems and ballads, and corresponded with *Percy on this subject.

Damoetas, (1) a shepherd in the *Idylls* of *Theocritus and the *Eclogues* of *Virgil; (2) a character in Sidney's *Arcadia*, a base herdsman who has become a royal favourite; (3) an old shepherd (representing a Cambridge academic?) in Milton's *Lycidas*.

Damon, a shepherd singer in *Virgil's eighth *Eclogue*; a name adopted by poets for a rustic swain. Cf. *Epitaphium Damonis*, *Milton's Latin elegy on his friend *Diodati.

Damon and Pithias, a rhymed play by R. *Edwards, acted probably 1564, printed 1571.

Damon and Pythias, Pythagorean Greeks, visit Syracuse, and the former is presently arrested on a baseless charge of spying and conspiring against Dionysius the tyrant of Syracuse, who orders his execution. Damon obtains a respite of two months to return home in order to settle his affairs, Pythias offering himself as security for his return. Damon is delayed and arrives when Pythias is just about to be put to death. They contend which shall be executed, each striving to save the other. Dionysius, impressed with their mutual loyalty, pardons Damon and asks to be admitted to their brotherhood.

In the original classical legend it is Phintias (of which 'Pythias' is a corruption), not Damon, who is sentenced, and Damon goes bail for him.

DAMPIER, William (1652–1715), navigator, explorer, and buccaneer, who travelled to South America, Yucatan, the Pacific, Australia, and the East Indies in the course of an adventurous career which ended in some disgrace, after accusations of brutality and drunkenness. His accounts of his travels, written in a lively and straightforward style and showing precise scientific observation, were extremely popular, and heralded an era of great interest in travel and voyage literature. (*New Voyage round the World*, 1697; *Voyages and Descriptions*, 1698; *A Voyage to New Holland*, 1703–9; edited by J. *Masefield in 2 vols, 1906.) Dampier also figures in W. *Rogers's journal of his privateering expedition during which *Selkirk was rescued from Juan Fernandez. (See also ROBINSON CRUSOE.)

DANA, Richard Henry (1815–82), son of the poet and journalist Richard Henry Dana (1787–1879), born in Massachusetts. He broke off his education at Harvard to embark as a common sailor, hoping to recover from 'a weakness of the eyes', and is remembered for his realistic and lively account of his voyage from Boston around Cape Horn to California, published anonymously in 1840 as *Two Years before the Mast*.

Dance of Death, or *danse macabre* (or *danse macabré*), gave expression to the sense especially prominent in the 15th cent. (perhaps as a consequence of the plague and the preaching of the mendicant friars) of the ubiquity of Death the leveller. The Dance appears to have first taken shape in France, as a mimed sermon in which figures typical of various orders of society were seized and haled away each by its own corpse (not, as later, by the personification of Death). The earliest known painting of the Dance, accompanied by versified dialogues between living and dead, was made in 1424 in the cemetery of the Innocents in Paris, and the German artists (including *Holbein) who later depicted it appear to have drawn inspiration from French sources. The origin of the word *macabre* or *macabré* has been the subject of many conjectures, such as that the latter is a corruption of Old French *Macabé*, to refer to a mystery play in which the Apocryphal killing of the Maccabees by Antiochus was represented.

Dandie Dinmont, in Scott's *Guy Mannering*, a sturdy hospitable Liddesdale farmer and the owner of a special breed of terriers.

DANE, Clemence, the pseudonym of Winifred Ashton (1888–1965), playwright and novelist, whose first play, *A Bill of Divorcement* (1921), had a success never quite matched by her later works (*Will Shakespeare*, 1921, a blank verse drama; *Wild Decembers*, 1932, a play about the *Brontës). Her novels include *Regiment of Women* (1917) and *Legend* (1919).

Dangerfield, a character in (1) Sedley's *Bellamira*; (2) Scott's *Peveril of the Peak*; (3) *The Ginger Man* by *Donleavy.

Daniel, an Old English poem of 764 lines found in the *Junius manuscript, paraphrasing the Old Testament Book of Daniel. See F. A. Blackburn (ed.), *Exodus and Daniel: Two Old English Poems* (1907).

DANIEL, Charles Henry Olive (1836–1919), scholar, fellow, and provost of Worcester College, Oxford, remembered for his lifelong interest in printing. He established a private press at Oxford, where he used the *Fell types and produced some fine examples of typography, including plays and poems of *Bridges.

The 'Daniel Mark', sometimes called the '*Misit Mark*', the special note of the press, represents Daniel in the lions' den with the motto: 'Misit Angelum suum' ('He sent his Angel').

See *The Daniel Press 1845–1919* (1921), a memorial volume compiled by his friends.

DANIEL, Samuel (?1562–1619), the son of a music-master. He entered Magdalen Hall, Oxford, in 1579, and after visiting Italy, where he met the pastoral poet *Guarini, he became tutor to William Herbert, third earl of Pembroke, and later to Lady Anne Clifford, daughter of the countess of Cumberland. In 1592 he published *Delia*, a collection of sonnets inspired by *Tasso and Desportes, to which was appended the 'Complaint of Rosamund'. Spenser mentioned him by name in *Colin Clouts Come Home Againe*, praising *Delia*, but predicting that

> most me seemes, they accent will excell,
> In Tragick plaints and passionate mischance.

Daniel made the transition to tragedy forthwith, his next work being *Cleopatra* (1594), a Senecan tragedy closely related to the countess of Pembroke's *Antonie*, itself translated from Garnier in 1590. *'Musophilus: Containing a Generall Defence of Learning' appeared in 1599. In 1603 he welcomed James I's accession with a *Panegyrike Congratulatorie*, and published also his verse 'Epistles' and *A Defence of Ryme*, the last being a reply to T. *Campion's *Observations in the Art of English Poesie*. His career as a court poet developed with his masques and plays, *The Vision of the 12 Goddesses* (1604), *The Queenes Arcadia* (1606), *Tethys Festival* (1610), and *Hymen's Triumph* (perf. 1614, pub. 1615). Early in 1604 he became licenser for the Children of the Queen's Revels, but he gave over this lucrative office in April 1605. This may have been because of the row caused by his second tragedy *Philotas*, performed in the autumn of 1604, which was held—perhaps justly—to allude closely and sympathetically to the rebellion of the earl of *Essex in 1600. Daniel affixed an 'Apology', claiming that any resemblance to the Essex affair was purely coincidental, when the play was published in 1605. His position at court appears to have recovered thereafter. His weightiest work was his *Civil Wars*, a verse epic on the Wars of the Roses. Four books appeared in 1595, and the complete eight books in 1609. A prose history of England from the Romans to Edward III, *The Collection of the History of England*, was his last work. *Jonson called Daniel 'a good honest Man, . . . but no poet'; other contemporaries esteemed him, such as W. *Browne, who called him 'Well-languag'd Danyel'. In later times his greatest admirers have been in the Romantic period: *Lamb, *Wordsworth, and *Coleridge were among those who read him appreciatively, the last finding his style and language as 'pure and manly' as Wordsworth's own. The bibliographical complexity of Daniel's texts, combined with a decline in admiration for his plain manner, may account for the lack of any complete edition of his works since *Grosart's of 1885–96.

Daniel Deronda, a novel by G. *Eliot, published 1876, the last of her novels.

Gwendolen Harleth, high-spirited, self-confident, and self-centred, marries Henleigh Grandcourt, an arrogant, selfish, and cold-hearted man of the world, for his money and his position, to save her mother, sisters, and herself from destitution and in spite of the fact that she knows of the existence of (and has indeed met) Lydia Glasher, who has had a long-standing affair with Grandcourt, and children by him. She rejects Mrs Glasher's appeals and threats, and suffers in consequence in terms of guilt and a sense of her husband's increasing power over her. In her misery she comes increasingly under the influence of Daniel Deronda, who becomes her spiritual adviser. He is an idealistic young man, whose own parentage is involved in mystery; it is gradually revealed that he is not, as he had assumed, an illegitimate cousin of Grandcourt's, but the son of a Jewish singer of international renown. This discovery strengthens his bonds with Mirah, a young Jewish singer whom he has saved from drowning, and her brother Mordecai, an intellectual Jewish nationalist. Gwendolen's husband is drowned at Genoa, in a manner that leaves her feeling partly guilty for his death; she confesses to Deronda, but shortly discovers to her initial despair that he is to marry Mirah and devote himself to the Jewish cause and the founding of a Jewish national home. Notable among the minor characters is Klesmer, the musician, who persuades Gwendolen that her talent as a singer, though acceptable in an amateur, would not repay training, thus unwittingly pushing her towards her disastrous marriage. One of the themes of the novel is the nature of professional and artistic dedication, explored through Gwendolen's dilettante expectations, Klesmer's seriousness and insistence on constant application, Mirah's acceptance of a hard-working but less than illustrious career, and the passionate and self-glorifying commitment of Deronda's mother, who had been obliged to sacrifice her own child to her success.

The Jewish plot has been severely handled by critics, by H. *James (*Daniel Deronda: A Conversation*, 1876) for being 'at bottom cold', and by *Leavis (*The Great Tradition*, 1948) as 'embarrassingly fervid'. Leavis also traces the debt of James in *The Portrait of a Lady*.

d'ANNUNZIO, Gabriele (1863–1938), Italian novelist, playwright, and poet. An irredentist nationalist, he effectively urged the entry of Italy into the First World War on the side of the Allies, and himself took part in spectacular exploits by sea and air. In 1919, with a small volunteer force, he occupied Fiume where he remained as dictator until 1921. One of his novels, *Il piacere* (*The Child of Pleasure*, 1890), is one of the significant texts of European Decadence. His later novels, which include *Trionfo della morte* (*Triumph of Death*, 1894) and *Il fuoco* (*The Flame of Life*, 1900), were strongly influenced by Nietzschean ideas. Some of his plays were set to music, one in French, *Le Martyre de Saint Sébastien* (1911), by *Debussy, and *Parisina* (1913) by Mascagni. His best play is *La figlia di Iorio* (*Iorio's Daughter*, 1904), set in his native Abruzzi. D'Annunzio is at his best in his lyrics in *Alcyone* and in *Maia*, part of a four-volume collection entitled *Laudi* (*Praises*, 1904). As a poet he was influenced by *Symbolism and the *Pre-Raphaelites. His prose style was admired by *Joyce.

DANTE ALIGHIERI (1265–1321) was born at Florence of a Guelf family. The circumstances of his early life are obscure, but we know that in 1277 he was formally betrothed to his future wife, Gemma Donati, and that in 1289 he took part in military operations against Arezzo and Pisa. During this early period of his life he fell in love with the girl whom he celebrates under the name of Beatrice in the *Vita nuova* and the *Divina commedia*. Her identity has been much discussed, but the generally accepted view is that she was Bice Portinari, who became the wife of Simone de' Bardi. When she died, in 1290, Dante was grief-stricken and sought consolation in the study of philosophy. In 1295 he became active in the political life of Florence. In June 1300 he was one of the municipal priors who banished the leaders of the White and Black Guelf factions, and in Oct. 1301 he was one of the three envoys sent to Rome to negotiate with Boniface VIII. He was never to set foot in Florence again, for during his absence the Blacks seized power and Dante, whose sympathies were with the Whites, became the victim of political reprisals and was for the rest of his life to lead a wandering existence. He died at Ravenna, where he had for some years found refuge.

The precise dating of Dante's works presents problems as yet unsolved. The first in order of composition (apart from his earliest lyric poems) was the *Vita nuova*, written in the period 1290–4, in which Dante brings together 31 poems, most of them relating to his love for Beatrice. A linking prose narrative tells the story of his love and interprets the poems from the standpoint of one who has come to see his beloved as the instrument of his spiritual salvation. There is a translation by D. G. *Rossetti (1861). The *Convivio*, or *Banquet*, is an unfinished philosophical work, planned as a series of 14 treatises, each in the form of a prose commentary on one of Dante's own *canzoni*. The four completed treatises, written between 1304 and 1308, draw on numerous philosophical sources, but principally on *Aristotle. The Latin treatise *De Vulgari Eloquentia*, begun shortly before the *Convivio*, is also unfinished. The completed part consists of an enquiry into the form of vernacular language most suitable for lofty poetry, followed by the beginning of a discussion of the technique of the *canzone*. It is a pioneering work in the field of linguistic history. The *Monarchia*, written in the period 1309–12, is a Latin treatise on the universal empire and the relations between emperor and pope. It is very uncertain when Dante began his masterpiece, the *Divina commedia*. (See entry under this heading for his influence on English writers.) It may have been begun as early as 1307, or possibly not until 1314 or later, and was finished just before his death.

Daphnaïda, an elegy by *Spenser closely modelled on Chaucer's *Book of the Duchess*. See ALCYON.

Daphnis and Chloe, a Greek pastoral romance written by an otherwise unknown 'Longus' sometime between the 2nd and 6th cents AD. It describes in formal style the wakening of passion in its two protagonists. *Amyot's translation into French made it a popular text, and there were two translations into English, by Angel Day (1587, from Amyot) and George Thornley (1657, from a Greek text). G.*Moore produced a modern version in 1924, and the story provided the subject of a ballet with music by Ravel and choreography by Fokine, composed for Diaghilev and first performed in 1912.

Dapper, the clerk in Jonson's *The Alchemist* who is gagged and locked in the privy for most of the play.

d'ARBLAY, Mme, see BURNEY, F.

Darcy, Fitzwilliam and his sister Georgiana, characters in J. Austen's *Pride and Prejudice*.

Dares Phrygius, a Trojan priest mentioned by *Homer (*Iliad*, 5.9). He was supposed to have been the author of an account of the fall of Troy of which a Latin prose version is extant. This work, *De Excidio Troiae*, dating probably from the 5th cent. AD, provided, together with the complementary history of *Dictys Cretensis, the only detailed account of the Trojan War available in the medieval West. Everything written about Troy before the middle of the 17th cent. was to some extent dependent, directly or indirectly, on the narratives of Dares and Dictys.

Dark as the Grave Wherein My Friend Is Laid, a novel by M. *Lowry, based on a journey to Mexico taken in 1945–6 and published posthumously in 1968. The title is taken from *Cowley's elegy 'On the Death of Mr William Harvey'.

Darkness at Noon, a novel by A. *Koestler, published 1940, translated from German.

It deals with the arrest, imprisonment, trial, and execution of N. S. Rubashov in an unnamed dictatorship over which 'No. 1' presides. Koestler describes Rubashov as 'a synthesis of the lives of a number of men who were victims of the so-called Moscow trials', and the novel did much to draw attention to the nature of Stalin's regime.

DARLEY, George (1795–1846), born in Dublin, the eldest of the seven children of a merchant, and educated at Trinity College, Dublin. He settled in London in 1821, and earned his living by writing

textbooks on mathematics and as dramatic critic for the *London Magazine* and later as art critic for the *Athenaeum*; he was a forerunner in the English rediscovery of early Italian painting. His first published poem was *The Errors of Ecstasie* (1822). *Sylvia*, a pastoral drama which was the most successful of his works in his own lifetime, followed in 1827. Many of his lyrics were published in magazines, the best known being *Syren Songs*, 'Serenade of a Loyal Martyr' (which may have influenced *Meredith's 'Love in the Valley'), and 'It is not Beauty I demand', a 17th-cent. pastiche which F. T. *Palgrave included in his *Golden Treasury* under the impression that it was a genuine Caroline poem. Darley also published two historical plays, *Thomas à Becket* and *Ethelstan*. His finest work was his unfinished *Nepenthe*, privately printed 1835, an allegory of the imagination in excesses of joy or melancholy, partly inspired by *Milton, *Shelley, and *Keats, but containing some remarkable lyrics and passages of wild fantasy and highly skilled versification.

Darley suffered all his life from a very severe stammer, which cut him off from most social activities, and he also had recurring headaches, probably some form of migraine. He never married, and his life was reclusive, but his friends—who included *Lamb, H. F. *Cary, *Clare, A. *Cunningham, *Milnes, and *Carlyle—admired him as an amiable, high-minded, and unjustly neglected poet, though he made some enemies by his virulent dramatic criticism. See C. C. Abbott, *The Life and Letters of George Darley* (1928); *Selected Poems of George Darley, with an Introduction and Notes* by Anne Ridler (1979).

Darnay, Charles, a character in Dickens's *A Tale of Two Cities*.

Dartle, Rosa, a character in Dickens's *David Copperfield*.

DARWIN, Charles Robert (1809–82), born at Shrewsbury, grandson of E. *Darwin, and educated at Edinburgh University and Christ's College, Cambridge. He embarked in 1831 with *Fitzroy as naturalist on the *Beagle*, bound for South America, returned in 1836, and published in 1839 his *Journal of Researches into the Geology and Natural History of the Various Countries Visited by H.M.S. Beagle*. His great work *On the Origin of Species by Means of Natural Selection* appeared in 1859. Darwin had received from A. R. *Wallace a manuscript containing a sketch of his theory. Building upon the Uniformitarian geology of Charles Lyell (1797–1875), which supposed a very great antiquity for the earth and slow, regular change, Darwin argued for a natural, not divine, origin of species. In the competitive struggle for existence, creatures possessing advantageous mutations would be favoured, eventually evolving into new species. In the 'survival of the fittest' (a phrase coined by H. *Spencer, but accepted by Darwin) organic descent was achieved by natural selection, by analogy with the artificial selection of the stockbreeder. An agnostic, Darwin saw no higher moral or religious ends in evolution, only chance and necessity. Other evolutionists, such as Wallace and Spencer, by contrast, identified evolution with progress. Darwin's book gave rise to intense opposition, but found distinguished supporters in T. H. *Huxley, Lyell, and Sir Joseph Hooker (1817–1911); the reverberation of his ideas can be seen throughout the literature of the second half of the 19th cent. In *The Descent of Man* (1871) Darwin discussed sexual selection, and argued that man too had evolved, from the higher primates, whereas Wallace made man a partial exception to this rule. Despite religious and humanist fears, evolutionism in general quickly won acceptance, but natural selection, Darwin's evolutionary mechanism, foundered for want of an adequate theory of inheritance until the rediscovery of Mendelian genetics, which led to the emergence of the modern evolutionary synthesis in the 1920s. A dedicated naturalist, Darwin also wrote extensively on barnacles, earthworms, and orchids, and was a pioneer observer of animal behaviour. *The Life and Letters of Darwin*, edited by his son Francis Darwin, appeared 1887–8, and several further volumes of letters have also been published. For an account of the profound impact of his work on 19th-cent. fiction, see *Darwin's Plots* (1983) by Gillian Beer.

DARWIN, Erasmus (1731–1802), educated at Cambridge. He spent part of his life as a physician at Lichfield, where he established a botanical garden. Declaring that 'the general design . . . is to enlist imagination under the banner of Science', he embodied the botanical system of *Linnaeus in his long poem *The Loves of the Plants*, published 1789. The work reappeared as Part II of *The Botanic Garden* (1791), of which Part I was 'The Economy of Vegetation'. The poem is in heroic couplets, in imitation of *Pope. The goddess of Botany, descending to earth, expounds various natural phenomena throughout the four cantos of Part I, while Part II describes 'the Ovidian metamorphosis of the flowers, with their floral harems', stamens and pistils figuring as beaux and belles. The work contains an interesting embryonic theory of evolution, similar in many ways to that developed by the poet's grandson, C. *Darwin. The poem was ridiculed by *Canning and *Frere in 'The Loves of the Triangles', published in the *Anti-Jacobin* in 1798. In his prose *Zoonomia* (in which *Wordsworth found the story of Goody Blake), published 1794–6, Darwin further describes the laws of organic life, both plant and animal, on an evolutionary principle. His heretical views on creation brought him into some disrepute. Anna *Seward published *Memoirs* of him in 1804, and his grandson Charles published a life in 1879.

DARWISH, Mahmoud (?1942–   ), Palestinian-born poet, who worked as a journalist in Haifa before moving to Cairo, Beirut, and Paris. He has published several volumes of poetry, mostly of national and political protest, sympathizing with the poor and dispossessed: a selection translated from the Arabic by Ian Wedde and Fawwaz Tuqan appeared in 1973, followed by *The Music of Human Flesh* (1980, trans. D. Johnson-Davies) and *Sand and Other Poems* (1986, trans. Rana Kabbani).

DARYUSH, Elizabeth (1887–1977), poet, daughter of R. *Bridges. Her volumes of poetry include *Verses* (1930), *Verses, Third Book* (1933), *The Last Man, and Other Poems* (1936), and *Verses, Seventh Book* (1971); her *Collected Poems*, published in 1976 with an introduction by D. *Davie, was an attempt to recover her work from what several poets (including Y. *Winters and R. *Fuller) saw as undeserved neglect. Her experiments with syllabics show an affinity with the *sprung rhythm of G. M. *Hopkins, and her poetry has also been compared to that of *Hardy.

DAS, Kamala (1934–   ), Indian poet and novelist, born in Kerala, south India, into a literary household where both her mother and her grandparents were prominent Malayali poets. Das, bilingual in English and Malayalam, writes her poetry only in English. Prominent for her intimate and outspoken exploration of sexuality and domestic oppression, she created a stir with her autobiography *My Story* (1976). Her volumes of poems include *Summer in Calcutta* (1965), *The Descendants* (1967), and *The Old Playhouse and Other Poems* (1975). In 1985 she was awarded the Asian World Prize for literature.

DASENT, Sir George Webbe (1817–96), educated at Magdalen Hall, Oxford. He spent four years in Stockholm from 1841 studying Scandinavian literature and northern mythology. In 1845 he joined the staff of *The Times* and in 1853 became professor of English literature at King's College, London. He devoted much of his life to the popularization of Scandinavian literature and the interpretation of Icelandic sagas, publishing many translations. Among his publications are *Prose, or the Younger Edda* (1842), dedicated to *Carlyle, who had encouraged him, the *Grammar of the Icelandic or Old Norse Tongue* (1843), *Popular Tales from the Norse* (1859), and *The Story of Burnt Njal* (1861).

Dashwood, Mrs, her daughters Elinor, Marianne, and Margaret, and their stepbrother John, characters in J. Austen's *Sense and Sensibility*.

Datchery, Dick, the name assumed by one of the characters in Dickens's *Edwin Drood*; his identity is not revealed when the fragment ends.

d'AUBIGNÉ, Théodore-Agrippa (1552–1630), French Huguenot leader and writer. After participating in the wars of religion and witnessing the accession of Henry IV, he withdrew to his Poitou domains in 1593 and, in order to escape further persecution, to Geneva in 1620.

Soldier, architect, administrator, scholar, and poet, he was one of the complete men of his age. His literary output is as varied as it is innovatory. His early love lyrics, *Printemps* (first pub. 1874), are passionate and 'metaphysical'; his epic poem *Les Tragiques* (1616) is a violent and visionary representation of the fate of the Huguenots in 16th-cent. France; his *Histoire universelle* (1616–20) is a personal and historical narrative of religious and political events in France between 1550 and 1601; his burlesque novels, *Adventures du baron de Faeneste* (1617) and *Confession de Sancy* (pub. 1660), satirize religious absurdity and vice; and his autobiography, *Sa vie à ses enfants*, justifies the course of a tumultuous life.

DAUDET, Alphonse (1840–97), French novelist, best known for his charming sketches of life in his native Provence (*Lettres de mon moulin*, 1869; expanded edn, 1878) and as the creator of Tartarin, the character who is the sum and epitome of those qualities supposed to make up the meridional temperament, combining the powers of self-deception and enthusiasm for adventure of Don Quixote with the timidity of Sancho Panza. His comic exploits are related in *Tartarin de Tarascon* (1872), *Tartarin sur les Alpes* (1885), *La Défense de Tarascon* (1886), and *Port-Tarascon* (1890). The novel in two parts *Le Petit Chose* (1868) is semi-autobiographical. Daudet's other novels, which make up the bulk of his output, portray the social and professional life of Paris in a broadly *naturalistic vein, e.g. *Fromont jeune et Risler aîné* (1874), *Le Nabab* (1877), *Numa Roumestan* (1881), *Sapho* (1884).

DAUMIER, Honoré (1808–79), French painter and lithographer. More than 4,000 of his political and satirical cartoons were published in *Charivari, Caricature*, and *Le Figaro*.

D'AVENANT, Sir William (1606–68), born and educated in Oxford, rumoured to be the natural son of Shakespeare. His first play, *The Tragedy of Albovine*, was printed in 1629 but probably never performed; *The Cruel Brother* was performed in 1627, printed 1630. In 1630–2 he was gravely ill with syphilis, a subject referred to in his own works and in the jests of others; his first play on his recovery was probably his comic masterpiece *The Wits*, performed 1633, printed 1636. In 1638 he succeeded to *Jonson's pension as unofficial *poet laureate, then actively supported Charles I in the Civil War and was knighted by him in 1643 at the siege of Gloucester. In 1645 he visited Paris, where he met *Hobbes, to whom he addressed his *Preface* (1650) to *Gondibert* (1651). He was imprisoned in the Tower, 1650–2, and is said to have been saved by *Milton. With *The Siege of Rhodes* (1656) he simultaneously evaded the ban on stage plays and produced one of the earliest English operas (but see also FLECKNOE), with an entertainment that combined music and instruction. After the Restoration he and T. *Killigrew the elder obtained patents from

Charles II giving them the monopoly of acting in London; his charter for the Duke's House, Lincoln's Inn, was later transferred to Covent Garden. Among the innovations of the period were movable scenery and the use of actresses. In conjunction with *Dryden D'Avenant adapted various of Shakespeare's plays to suit the taste of the day, among them *The Tempest* (1667); he is satirized with Dryden in Buckingham's *The Rehearsal*. His poems and songs (which include 'The lark now leaves his watry nest') were edited by A. M. Gibbs in 1972.

DAVID, Elizabeth, née Gwynne (1913–92), writer on *food and cookery, whose early works (*A Book of Mediterranean Food*, 1950; *French Country Cooking*, 1951; *Italian Food*, 1954) were read avidly by a generation brought up on a wartime diet; they were enjoyed for their new recipes, for their loving descriptions of continental meals, and for gastronomic quotations from H. *James, *Smollett, *Marinetti, etc. She became respected for her scholarly approach to the history of gastronomy. Her later works include *English Bread and Yeast Cooking* (1977) and *An Omelette and a Glass of Wine* (1984).

David, Song to, see SMART.

David and Fair Bethsabe, *The Love of King*, a play in blank verse by *Peele, printed 1599. Its sources are mainly scriptural, offering a highly poeticized account of King David's seduction of Bethsabe (Bathsheba) and the death of his son Absalon.

David Copperfield, a novel by *Dickens, published 1849–50. 'Of all my books,' wrote Dickens, 'I like this the best', and it has always been a favourite with a wide public. It is (in some of its details) Dickens's veiled autobiography.

David Copperfield is born at Blunderstone (of which the original is the village of Blundeston) in Suffolk, soon after the death of his father. His mother, a gentle, weak woman, marries again, and her second husband Mr Murdstone, by cruelty disguised as firmness and abetted by Miss Murdstone his sister, drives her to an early grave. Young Copperfield, who has proved recalcitrant, is sent to school, where he is bullied by the tyrannical headmaster Creakle, but makes two friends in the brilliant and fascinating Steerforth and the good-humoured plodding Traddles. Thence he is sent to menial employment in London, where he lives a life of poverty and misery, enlivened by his acquaintance with the mercurial and impecunious Mr Micawber and his family. He runs away and walks penniless to Dover to throw himself on the mercy of his aunt Betsey Trotwood, an eccentric old lady who had renounced all interest in him from his birth because, contrary to her firm expectation, he had been born a boy instead of a girl. He is kindly received and given a new home, which he shares with an amiable lunatic, Mr Dick. This poor gentleman is perpetually engaged on a memorial regarding his affairs, but is unable to complete it owing to the inevitable intrusion into it of King Charles's head. Copperfield continues his education at Canterbury, living in the house of Miss Trotwood's lawyer Mr Wickfield, whose daughter Agnes, a girl of exceptionally sweet and high-minded disposition, exercises a powerful influence on the rest of his life. He then enters Doctors' Commons, being articled to Mr Spenlow, of the firm of Spenlow and Jorkins. Meanwhile he has come again into touch with Steerforth, whom, ignorant of his true character, he introduces to the family of his old nurse Clara Peggotty, married to Barkis the carrier. The family consists of Mr Peggotty, a Yarmouth fisherman, his nephew Ham, and the latter's cousin Little Em'ly, a pretty, simple girl whom Ham is about to marry. The remaining inmate of Mr Peggotty's hospitable home is Mrs Gummidge, another dependant and a widow, whose peevish laments for her forlorn condition are patiently borne by Mr Peggotty. Steerforth induces Em'ly to run away with him, thereby producing intense misery in the Peggotty household. Mr Peggotty sets out to find her, following her through many countries, and finally recovering her after she has been cast off by Steerforth. The latter's crime also brings unhappiness to his mother and to her protégée Rosa Dartle, who has long loved Steerforth with all the suppressed violence of a passionate nature. The tragedy finds its culmination in the shipwreck and drowning of Steerforth, and the death of Ham in trying to save him.

Meanwhile Copperfield, blind to the affection of Agnes Wickfield, marries Dora Spenlow, a pretty empty-headed child, and becomes famous as an author. Dora dies after a few years of married life and Copperfield, at first disconsolate, awakens to a growing appreciation and love of Agnes. Her father has fallen into the toils of a villainous and cunning clerk, Uriah Heep, who under the cloak of fawning humility has obtained complete control over him, reduced him to the verge of imbecility, and nearly ruined him. Uriah also aspires to marry Agnes. But his misdeeds, which include forgery and theft, are exposed by Micawber, employed as his clerk, with the assistance of Traddles, now a barrister. Uriah is last seen in prison, under a life sentence. Copperfield marries Agnes. Mr Peggotty, with Em'ly and Mrs Gummidge, is found prospering in Australia, where Mr Micawber, relieved of his debts, appears finally as a much-esteemed colonial magistrate.

'Davideis', see COWLEY, A.

***David Simple,** The Adventures of, in Search of a Real Friend*, a novel by S. *Fielding, published 1744, and described by the author as 'a Moral Romance'. This was one of the earliest novels (published four years after Richardson's *Pamela*) to examine minutely what the author's brother, Henry *Fielding, described in his preface to her book as 'the Mazes, Windings, and Labyrinths' of the heart.

David discovers that his beloved younger brother,

with the aid of two trusted family servants, has defrauded him of his inheritance. Horrified by this deceit, he sets out on a quest to see if he can find a true and honest friend. Everywhere he encounters self-seeking, hypocrisy, and dishonesty; his friend Mr Orgueil is unmasked by Mr Spatter, Mr Spatter is exposed by Mr Varnish, Mr Varnish by David himself. Eventually he meets Cynthia, who has been excluded from her share of her father's fortune and is harshly treated by her mistress. He also encounters a brother and sister, Valentine and Camilla, whose scheming stepmother has alienated their father's affection from them. The four friends, all of whom have suffered because of their trusting innocence, live together in rich, happy companionship; in time David is married to Camilla and Valentine to Cynthia. David shares his fortune with them, and Valentine and Camilla are reconciled with their father.

In the sombre *Volume the Last* (1753) both couples face dire financial loss. Once again friends prove cruel and false, the terrible figure of Mrs Orgueil hovers malevolently, and the crushing of the innocent moves remorselessly on. There is no happy release, and by the end only Cynthia and one of David's children survive.

DAVIDSON, John (1857–1909), a reluctant schoolmaster in Scotland from 1872 to 1899, who settled in London in the latter year, having already published several plays. He contributed to the *Yellow Book, and his collection of verse *Fleet Street Eclogues* (1893), which showed a genuine poetic gift, was followed by several others. Between 1901 and 1908 he wrote a series of 'Testaments' expounding in blank verse a materialistic and rebellious philosophy, described very fully in the introduction to *The Theatrocrat God and Mammon*, an intended trilogy of which the first two parts were published in 1907. T. S. *Eliot expressed his debt to Davidson's use of 'dingy urban images' and colloquial idiom in a preface to a selection, edited 1961 by M. Lindsay, singling out for particular praise his best-known ballad, the defiant and satiric 'Thirty Bob a Week'.

DAVIDSON, Thomas, see FABIAN SOCIETY.

DAVIE, Donald Alfred (1922–95), poet and critic, born in Barnsley, and educated at Barnsley Holgate Grammar School and at Cambridge, where he was much influenced by the ethos of F. R. *Leavis and the Cambridge English school; he describes his ambiguous feelings towards this heritage in his memoirs, *These the Companions* (1982). His critical work *Purity of Diction in English Verse* (1952) expressed many of the anti-Romantic, anti-bohemian ideals of the *Movement and of his fellow contributors to *New Lines. His volumes of poetry include *Brides of Reason* (1955), *A Winter Talent* (1957), *Essex Poems* (1969), and *In the Stopping Train* (1977); two volumes of collected poems appeared in 1972 (1950–70) and 1983 (1971–83). His poems are philosophical, speculative, and erudite, manifesting a mind that (in his own phrase) 'moves most easily and happily among abstractions', yet they also vividly evoke the various landscapes of his travels and academic appointments, from Ireland to California, from Essex to Italy, and show a marked rejection of the English provincialism which characterized some of his friends from the Movement. Davie has also written on Sir W. *Scott (1961), *Pound (1964), *Hardy (1972), and others, and adapted the *Pan Tadeusz* of *Mickiewicz in *The Forests of Lithuania* (1959).

DAVIES, Idris (1903–53), Welsh poet, born in Rhymney, Monmouthshire, who worked as a collier before entering Loughborough College, where he trained as a teacher. His poems were published in three main collections, *Gwalia Deserta* (1938), *The Angry Summer* (1943), and *Tonypandy and Other Poems* (1945); his *Selected Poems* appeared in the year of his death. Almost all his work is passionately concerned with the plight of the industrial valleys of south Wales during the inter-war years, in particular the crisis of the General Strike of 1926 and its effects on the working class. The standard edition is *The Complete Poems of Idris Davies*, ed. Dafydd Johnston (1994).

DAVIES, John (c.1564–1618), of Hereford, poet and writing-master. He published several volumes of verse, epitaphs, and epigrams, etc., including *Microcosmos* (1603), *The Muses Sacrifice*, containing the famous 'Picture of an Happy Man' (1612), and *Wits Bedlam* (1617). Some of his epigrams, most of which are contained in *The Scourge of Folly* (1611), are valuable for their notices of *Jonson, *Fletcher, and other contemporary poets.

DAVIES, Sir John (1569–1626), a Wiltshire man of good family, educated at Winchester and at The Queen's College, Oxford; he became solicitor- and attorney-general for Ireland, and was subsequently appointed lord chief justice of the King's Bench as a reward for maintaining the legality of Charles I's forced loans. He died before taking up this office. His *Orchestra, or A Poeme of Dauncing*, published in 1596, describes the attempts of the suitor Antinous to persuade Penelope to dance with him, giving a long account of the antiquity and universality of dancing. The *Hymnes of Astraea* and *Nosce Teipsum* both appeared in 1599: the latter, written in quatrains, is a philosophical poem on the nature of man and the nature and immortality of the soul. His *Epigrammes* and *Gullinge Sonnets* reflect his keen and satirical interest in the contemporary scene. His poems were edited by Robert Krueger in 1975.

DAVIES, Thomas (?1712–85), actor and bookseller who, according to his friend Dr *Johnson, was driven from the stage by Churchill's attack in *The Rosciad*— 'he mouths a sentence as curs mouth a bone.' He introduced *Boswell to Johnson in his bookshop in Russell Street, Covent Garden, in 1763. An amiable and sociable man, he appears frequently in Boswell's *Life*, often as the recipient of help from Johnson, who encouraged him to write his lively life of *Garrick (1780), himself supplying information about Garrick's early years.

DAVIES, W(illiam) H(enry) (1871–1940), poet, born in his grandfather's house in Newport, who went as a young man to America, where he spent several years on the road, returning after a brief trip home to seek his fortune in the Klondike. On the second visit he lost a leg in an accident, an experience recounted in a few laconic paragraphs in his *The Autobiography of a Super-Tramp*, published in 1908 with a preface by G. B. *Shaw, who did much to encourage the young poet and who interested himself in Davies's first volume, *The Soul's Destroyer and Other Poems* (1905). This was followed by several other volumes, and growing praise from writers such as E. *Thomas; he made many friends in the literary and artistic world. His best-known poems record his sharp and intense response to the natural world. In 1923 he married a girl much younger than himself, and he tells the story of his extraordinary courtship in *Young Emma*, posthumously published in 1980. His *Complete Poems*, with an introduction by O. *Sitwell, appeared in 1963.

DAVIES, (William) Robertson (1913–95), Canadian novelist, playwright, and critic, born in Thamesville, Ontario (the fictional Deptford). The family later moved to Kingston, Ontario (the fictional Salterton). Davies was educated at Upper Canada College, Toronto, Queen's University, Kingston, and Balliol College, Oxford, where he took his B.Litt. degree in 1938. For a time he acted with a provincial theatre company and then taught and acted at the Old Vic in London. It was there he met Brenda Matthews, whom he married in 1940. After returning to Canada he became literary editor of *Saturday Night* in Toronto and, in 1942, joined the editorial staff of the Peterborough *Examiner*, owned by his father, becoming joint owner and editor in 1946. In 1960 he was appointed professor of English at the University of Toronto and in 1963 became the first master of the university's Massey College. Between 1943 and 1953 he had written regular columns for the *Examiner* and other papers under the pseudonym Samuel Marchbanks, and these pieces were collected as *The Diary of Samuel Marchbanks* (1947), *The Table Talk of Samuel Marchbanks* (1949), and *Samuel Marchbanks' Almanack* (1967). *A Voice from the Attic* (1960) contains, amongst other pieces, review articles published in *Saturday Night* from 1953 to 1959. Further reprinted journalism can be found in *The Enthusiasms of Robertson Davies* (1979) and *The Well-Tempered Critic* (1981), both edited by Judith Skelton Grant. Davies has been an important figure in Canadian drama, as both a playwright and critic. His Oxford thesis was published in 1939 as *Shakespeare's Boy Actors*, which formed the basis of his successful junior course-book *Shakespeare for Young Players* (1942). His topical one-act plays for

adults include *Overlaid* (1948) and *Hope Deferred* (published in 1949 in *Eros at Breakfast and Other Plays*). Amongst the best of his full-length plays are *Fortune, My Foe* (1949), *At My Heart's Core* (1950), *A Jig for the Gypsy* (1954), *Hunting Stuart* (written in 1955, pub. 1972), and *General Confession* (written 1956, pub. 1972). It is, however, as a writer of fiction that he has achieved international eminence. His principal work as a novelist is contained in three extensive trilogies: the Salterton Trilogy—*Tempest-Tost* (1951), *Leaven of Malice* (1954), and *A Mixture of Frailties* (1958), which won the Leacock Award for Humour—a sequence of urbane comedies of manners; the Deptford Trilogy, usually considered the best of the three—*Fifth Business* (1970), *The Manticore* (1972), and *World of Wonders* (1975)—which moves towards the mode of fictional autobiography; and the Cornish Trilogy—*The Rebel Angels* (1981), the *Booker shortlisted *What's Bred in the Bone* (1985), and *The Lyre of Orpheus* (1988)—which marks a further shift of focus, this time towards satirical 'anatomies'. A collection of 18 ghost stories, originally read at Massey College's Christmas celebration between 1963 and 1980, was published as *High Spirits* in 1982. *The Cunning Man* (1995) follows the consequences of the death of a priest who collapses and dies while celebrating Holy Communion.

DAVISON, Francis, see POETICAL RHAPSODY, A.

DAVY, Sir Humphry (1778–1829), professor of chemistry at the Royal Institution, who greatly advanced knowledge of chemistry and magnetism and invented the miner's safety-lamp. In early youth he assisted his friend *Cottle, Wordsworth's publisher, in correcting the proofs of *Lyrical Ballads*. His collected works, prose and verse, with a memoir by his brother, were published in 1839–40. Among these is a brief dialogue, *Salmonia, or Days of Fly-Fishing, by an Angler* (1828), reminiscent of I. *Walton's book. Davy was a friend of Sir W. *Scott and there is a pleasing account in *Lockhart's *Life of Scott* of Davy's visits to Abbotsford.

DAVYS, Mary (1674–1732), novelist and playwright, who moved after her husband's death from Dublin to York and then Cambridge, where she scraped a living writing and running a coffee shop. Her novels include the travel anecdotes of *The Fugitive* (1705, rev. by 1725 as *The Merry Wanderer*); *The Reform'd Coquet* (1724), whose hero disguises himself as the heroine's guardian; *Familiar Letters* (1725), light-hearted courtship exchanges between a Whig and a Tory; and *The Accomplish'd Rake* (1727), a satirical account of a 'modern fine gentleman'. One comedy, *The Northern Heiress* (1716), was performed; the other, *The Self-Rival*, was not staged, but published in her two-volume *Works* (1725).

Daw, Sir John, in Jonson's *Epicene*, a cowardly braggart who pretends to learning.

DAWSON, Jennifer, (1929–2000), novelist, brought up in Camberwell, south London. She graduated in history from St Anne's College, Oxford, won the Dawes–Hickes Scholarship for Philosophy, and went to University College London. After working at the Clarendon Press, Oxford, she spent a year as a social worker in a psychiatric hospital outside Worcester. Her first novel, *The Ha-Ha* (1961), relates, in a first-person account, the experiences in a mental institution of an intelligent, sensitive, and eccentric patient, Josephine, followed by her amusing and sometimes surreal return to health. The novel anticipates later shifts in attitudes to mental illness and explores the 'damp cellar of guilt' present in society. Dawson's later work includes *Fowler's Snare* (1963); *The Cold Country* (1965); *Strawberry Boy* (1976); *A Field of Scarlet Poppies* (1979); and a volume of short stories, *Hospital Wedding* (1978).

Day, Fancy, a character in Hardy's *Under the Greenwood Tree*.

DAY, DAYE, or **DAIE,** John (1522–84), the foremost English printer of the reign of Elizabeth I. He published Protestant devotional books under Edward VI and was imprisoned by Queen Mary; later he held lucrative monopolies for the Psalms in metre, the catechism, and the ABC, printed the first church music book in English (1560), and the first English edition of Foxe's *Actes and Monuments* (or *Book of Martyrs*) (1563). He was patronized by M. *Parker, at whose behest he was the first to print Old English, having type made for it.

DAY, John (c.1574–c.1640), playwright, who collaborated with *Dekker and others in a number of plays. Of his own extant works *The Isle of Gulls*, suggested by Sidney's *Arcadia*, appeared in 1606, and *Law-Trickes* and *Humour out of Breath* in 1608. His best work, *The Parliament of Bees*, appeared perhaps in 1607, although the earliest extant copy is of 1641. It is a dramatic allegory or masque, containing a series of 'characters' of different bees with their virtues and vices, and ending with Oberon's Star Chamber, where he pronounces penalties on the offenders, the wasp, the drone, and the humble bee. It is a charming and inventive piece; the lines 'When of a sudden, listening, you shall hear | A noise of horns and hunting, which shall bring | Acteon to Diana in the spring' suggested a passage of *The Waste Land* to T. S. *Eliot. Day's works were collected by A. H. Bullen (1881). The *Parnassus Plays* have been doubtfully attributed to Day.

DAY, Thomas (1748–89), an admirer of *Rousseau and a friend of R. L. Edgeworth (1744–1817, father of Maria *Edgeworth), who was keenly interested in educational theory and natural upbringing; he was the author of the celebrated children's book *The History of Sandford and Merton* (3 vols, 1783–9), which was intended to illustrate the doctrine that man may be made good by instruction and by an appeal to reason. It consists of a series of episodes in which the rich and objectionable Tommy Merton is contrasted with the upright and tender-hearted Harry Sandford, a farmer's son; eventually Tommy is reformed, partly through the intervention of their tutor, Mr Barlow. Despite its didacticism, this work was very popular, went through many editions, and was translated into several languages. Day also wrote *The History of Little Jack* (1788), the story of a young wild boy suckled by goats. He himself died from a fall from an unbroken colt.

DAY-LEWIS, Cecil (1904–72) (who wrote as C. Day Lewis), born in Ireland, the son of a Church of Ireland minister; the family moved to England in 1905 and his mother died three years later. He was educated at Sherborne and Wadham College, Oxford, where he was befriended by *Bowra and became associated with a group of young left-wing poets of which *Auden was the acknowledged leader, and with whom he edited *Oxford Poetry* (1927). (The nick-name 'MacSpaunday' was coined by R. *Campbell: see also PYLON SCHOOL.) He worked for some years as a schoolmaster and was politically active during the 1930s, writing for the *Left Review*, supporting the *Left Book Club, speaking at meetings, etc.; he joined the Communist Party in 1936 and in 1937 edited a socialist symposium, *The Mind in Chains*, with contributions from *Upward, *Madge, R. *Warner, and others. These preoccupations are not reflected in his earliest verse (e.g. *Beechen Vigil*, 1925), but become apparent in *Transitional Poem* (1929), *From Feathers to Iron* (1931), and *The Magnetic Mountain* (1933) which have a strong revolutionary flavour, prophesying a new dawn: 'We shall expect no birth-hour without blood.' The title poem of *A Time to Dance* (1935) more ambiguously celebrates in verse strongly reminiscent of G. M. *Hopkins the heroic flight of Parer and M'Intosh to Australia. The poor reception of *Noah and the Waters* (1936), a verse morality play about the class struggle, may have encouraged him to turn from political poetry to the more personal and pastoral themes of his later years. During the 1930s he also embarked, under the pseudonym of 'Nicholas Blake', on a successful career as a writer of *detective fiction; his first work in this genre, *A Question of Proof* (1935), introducing his Audenesque detective Nigel Strangeways, was followed by some twenty others. *The Friendly Tree* (1936) was the first of three largely autobiographical novels.

In 1938 he moved with his family to Musbury, Devon; his poetry of this period (*Overtures to Death*, 1938; *Poems in Wartime*, 1940) reflects obvious concerns. He also published in 1940 the first of his translations, a version of *Virgil's *Georgics*, before working for some time for the Ministry of Information. From this time (despite an emotional private life), he became an increasingly establishment figure (having already endured much mockery from *Grigson for joining the Book Society Committee in 1937); he delivered the Clark Lectures in Cambridge in 1946 (*The Poetic Image*, 1947), broadcast frequently, gave recitals, sat on committees, judged awards, etc., mean-while consolidating his literary reputation with a translation of *Valéry (1946), further translations of Virgil (*The Aeneid*, 1952; *The Eclogues*, 1963), and collections of original verse, including *An Italian Visit* (1953), recording a journey with R. *Lehmann, and incidentally describing his own generation as 'an odd lot; sceptical yet susceptible, | Dour though enthusiastic, horizon-addicts and future-fans . . .' He was professor of poetry at Oxford from 1951 to 1956, the first poet of distinction to hold the post since M. *Arnold, and in 1968 was appointed poet laureate. His autobiography *The Buried Day* (1960) is much amplified by a biography by Sean Day-Lewis, the elder son of his first marriage, published in 1980, a detailed, questioning account of his father's 'divided heart' and search for identity.

Deane, Mr and Lucy, characters in G. Eliot's *The Mill on the Floss*.

DEANE, Seamus (1940–), Irish poet, scholar, and novelist, born in Derry and educated at Queen's University, Belfast, and Cambridge. His many works of criticism include *Celtic Revivals* (1985) and *The French Revolution and Enlightenment in England 1789–1832* (1988). He is the general editor of the *Field Day Anthology of Irish Writing 550–1988* (1991). In his three collections of poetry, *Gradual Wars* (1972), *Rumours* (1977), and *History Lessons* (1983), Deane focuses often on the political and social landscape of Northern Ireland, from contemporary and historical perspectives, showing sectarian violence and enmities as forming a lethal undercurrent to the domestic world. These themes are beautifully realized in his autobiographical novel *Reading in the Dark* (1996), which recreates his native Derry of the 1940s and 1950s, a place haunted by the *Troubles and hidden tragedies.

Deans, David, and his daughters Jeanie and Effie, the principal characters in Scott's *The Heart of Midlothian*.

'Death and Dr Hornbook', a satirical poem by *Burns, published 1786. Dr Hornbook was a doctor in Burns's parish of Mauchline. In the poem the poet meets Death, who describes to him the knavery and quackery of the doctor.

death of the author, a slogan coined in 1968 by the French critic R. *Barthes in an iconoclastic essay that also called for the 'birth of the reader', into whose hands the determination of literary meanings should pass. The principle of authorial control over literary (or other) texts had been challenged before (see INTENTIONAL FALLACY), but Barthes invoked larger *structuralist principles to argue that it is in the nature of writing to erase its supposed human originators, who are in any case really the scribes of self-generating linguistic codes and systems.

Death's Jest-Book, see BEDDOES.

De BERNIÈRES, Louis (1954–), novelist, whose experiences working in a village in Colombia give colour to his trilogy *The War of Don Emmanuel's Nether Parts* (1990), *Señor Vivo and the Coca Lord* (1991), *The Troublesome Offspring of Cardinal Guzman* (1992). These inventive, eventful, and poetic works, set in a fictitious South American country, mingle elements of *magic realism, eroticism, classical myth, philosophy, and political satire, while maintaining a strong narrative line. *Captain Corelli's Mandolin* (1994) is a historical romance which takes place during the Second World War on the vividly realized Greek island of Cephallonia during the German/Italian occupation: set against the farcical brutalities of war, the love affair of Pelagia, daughter of the scholarly Greek Doctor Iannis, with a musical Italian officer mixes bizarre humour with a poignant spirit of optimism.

De Bourgh, Lady Catherine, a character in J. Austen's *Pride and Prejudice*.

DEBUSSY, (Achille-) Claude (1862–1918), French composer, two of whose Preludes for piano claim English inspiration—*La Danse de Puck* (Book 1) and *Hommage à S. Pickwick* (Book 2). The only English poet he ever set was D. G. *Rossetti, whose 'The Blessed Damozel' provided the text for an early cantata, *La Damoiselle élue* (1888): a second, a translation by Pierre Louÿs of 'Willowwood', was never finished. Debussy considered an opera from *As You Like It, but shelved it in favour of *Maeterlinck's *Pelléas et Mélisande*. He later worked intensively on a project for two short operas based on *Poe: in 1889 he had begun a symphonic work on *The Fall of the House of Usher* (now lost), a theme which preoccupied him nearly to the end of his life. Only the libretto and 21 pages of the opera score survive.

Decadence, see MODERNISM.

Decameron, The, a collection of tales from many sources by *Boccaccio, written probably over many years, but assembled in their definitive form between 1349 and 1351.

Florence being visited by the plague in 1348, seven young ladies and three young men leave the city for neighbouring villas, the beauty of which is described, and spend part of each of ten days (whence the title) in amusing one another with stories, each person telling one tale on each day, so that there are 100 tales in all. The work had much influence on English literature, notably on *Chaucer (though possibly indirectly, through a translation: Chaucer nowhere mentions Boccaccio in any of his works); many of the tales were incorporated in Painter's *Palace of Pleasure*. A credible case has been made by H. G. Wright for *Florio as the translator of the first English version of *The Decameron* (1620); see his *Boccaccio in England from Chaucer to Tennyson* (1957).

Decline and Fall, the first novel of E. *Waugh, published with great success in 1928.

It recounts the chequered career of Paul Pennyfeather, sent down from Scone College, Oxford, for 'indecent behaviour', as the innocent victim of a drunken orgy. Thus forced to abandon a career in the Church, he becomes a schoolmaster at Llanabba Castle, where he encounters headmaster Fagan and his daughters, the dubious, bigamous, and reappearing Captain Grimes, and young Beste-Chetwynde, whose glamorous mother Margot carries him off to the dangerous delight of high society. They are about to be married when Paul is arrested at the Ritz and subsequently imprisoned for Margot's activities in the white slave trade, a sentence he bears stoically on the grounds that 'anyone who has been to an English public school will always feel comparatively at home in prison'; however, Margot (now Margot Metroland) arranges his escape, and he returns incognito but under his own name ('a *very* distant cousin') to resume his theological studies at Scone.

Decline and Fall of the Roman Empire, *The History of the*, a work by *Gibbon, vol. i of the first (quarto) edition published 1776, vols ii and iii 1781, and the last three vols 1788.

This, the most celebrated historical work in English literature, falls into three divisions, as defined by the author in the preface, according to a plan that expanded during composition: from the age of Trajan and the Antonines to the subversion of the Western Empire; from the reign of Justinian in the East to the establishment of the second or German Empire of the West, under *Charlemagne; from the revival of the Western Empire to the taking of Constantinople by the Turks. It thus covers a period of about 13 centuries, and comprehends such vast subjects as the establishment of Christianity, the movements and settlements of the Teutonic tribes, the conquests of the Muslims, and the Crusades. It traces in fact the connection of the ancient world with the modern.

Gibbon's great erudition, breadth of treatment, and powerful organization render this a lasting monument, of substantial accuracy as well as elegance. His measured and dignified prose is cool, lucid, and enlivened by ironic wit, much of it aimed at the early Church and the credulity and barbarism that overwhelmed the noble Roman virtues he so much admired. J. B. Bury's editions (1896–1900, 1909–14, 1926–9) are supplemented with notes incorporating subsequent research, but most of Gibbon's scholarship remains unchallenged. There is an edition by D. Womersley, 3 vols (1994).

deconstruction, an approach to the reading of literary and philosophical texts that casts doubt upon the possibility of finding in them a definitive meaning, and that traces instead the multiplication (or 'dissemination') of possible meanings. A deconstructive reading of a poem, for instance, will conclude not with the discovery of its essential meaning, but with an impasse ('aporia') at which there are no grounds for choosing between two radically incompatible interpretations. According to deconstruction, literary texts resist any process of interpretation that would fix their meanings, appearing to 'undo' themselves as we try to tie them up. The basis for this apparently perverse approach to reading lies in a certain view of the philosophy of language, and specifically of the status of writing, as developed since 1966 by the French philosopher *Derrida, and by his American followers at Yale and elsewhere, including *de Man. On this view, derived from a critical reassessment of *Saussure, meaning can never be fully 'present' in language, but is always deferred endlessly—as when one may look up a word in a dictionary, only to be given other words, and so on *ad infinitum*. While speech gives the illusion of a fixed origin—the presence of the speaker—that can guarantee the meaning of an utterance, writing is more clearly unauthenticated and open to unlicensed interpretation. Derrida's alarmingly simplified account of the history of Western philosophy since *Plato proposes that the dominant metaphysical tradition, in its deep suspicion of writing, has repeatedly tried to erect a fixed point of reference (a 'transcendental signified' such as God, Reason, absolute truth, etc.) outside the promiscuous circulation of *signifiers, one that could hold in place a determinate system of truths and meanings. The project of deconstruction, then, is not to destroy but to unpick or dismantle such illusory systems, often by showing how their major categories are unstable or contaminated by their supposed opposites. In philosophical terms, deconstruction is a form of relativist scepticism in the tradition of *Nietzsche. Its literary implications are partly compatible with the *New Criticism's rejection of the *'intentional fallacy' or any notion of the author fixing a text's meanings (see also DEATH OF THE AUTHOR), as they are with New Critical interest in paradox as a feature of poetry; but they go further in challenging the claims of any critical system to possess 'the meaning' of a literary (or any other) work. In some forms of deconstruction, notably that of de Man, literary texts are held to be more honest than other writings, because they openly delight in the instabilities of language and meaning, through their use of figurative language for instance. The deconstructive style of literary analysis commonly emphasizes this through puns and wordplay of its own. Exemplary deconstructive readings may be found in P. de Man, *Allegories of Reading* (1979), J. Hillis Miller, *Fiction and Repetition* (1982), and B. Johnson, *The Critical Difference* (1985). See also STRUCTURALISM AND POST-STRUCTURALISM.

Dedalus, Stephen, a character in J. Joyce's *A Portrait of the Artist as a Young Man* and *Ulysses*.

Dedlock, Sir Leicester, Lady, and Volumnia, characters in Dickens's *Bleak House*.

DEE, Dr John (1527–1608), mathematician and astrologer. He was educated at St John's College, Cambridge, and travelled in Europe in 1548–51. He became a fellow of Trinity College, Cambridge, where the stage effects he introduced into a performance of the *Peace* of *Aristophanes procured him his lifelong reputation of being a magician, which was confirmed by his erudition and practice of crystallomancy and astrology. He wrote *Monas Hieroglyphica* (1564); a preface to the first English translation of Euclid (1570); and *General and Rare Memorials Pertayning to the Perfect Arte of Navigation* (1577). He was a profoundly learned scholar and hermeticist, but also a sham. Among the many who consulted him on astrological matters were Sir P. *Sidney and Sir E. *Dyer. Many books survive from his remarkable library. There is a life of him by P. J. French (1972).

DEEPING, (George) Warwick (1877–1950), prolific and successful novelist, who caught the popular imagination with *Sorrell and Son* (1925), the story of a wounded ex-officer who takes a job as under-porter in a hotel to earn money to ensure an appropriate private education for his son Christopher, where he will not be exposed to 'class hatred' or 'the sneers of the new young working-class intellectuals' in the social war that Sorrell envisages.

defamiliarization, the process by which literary works unsettle readers' habitual ways of seeing the world. According to the literary theories of S. T. *Coleridge in *Biographia Literaria* (1817), of P. B. *Shelley in *Defence of Poetry* (1840), and of several modern *formalist critics, it is a distinctive feature of literature, especially poetry, that it tears away what Shelley called the 'veil of familiarity' from the world, making us look at it afresh. The Russian theorist V. Shklovsky's concept of 'estrangement' (*ostranenie*) has influenced modern restatements of the case.

Defarge, M. and Mme, characters in Dickens's *A Tale of Two Cities*.

Defence of All Learning, see MUSOPHILUS.

Defence of Poetry, an essay by P. B. *Shelley, written at Pisa 1821, first published 1840. It was begun as a light-hearted reply to his friend Peacock's magazine article *'The Four Ages of Poetry', which humorously argued that the best minds of the future must turn to economic and social sciences, rather than poetry. In vindicating the role of poetry in a progressive society, and defending the whole notion of imaginative literature and thinking (not just 'poetry') within an industrial culture, Shelley came to write his own poetic *credo* with passionate force and conviction. Against a background of classical and European literature, he discusses in some detail the nature of poetic thought and inspiration; the problems of translation; the value of erotic writing; the connections between poetry and politics; and the essentially *moral* nature of the imagination—an emphasis he drew from *Coleridge.

Throughout, Shelley associates poetry with social freedom and love. He argues that the 'poetry of life' provides the one sure response to the destructive, isolating, alienating, 'accumulating and calculating processes' of modern civilization; 'the creative faculty to imagine that which we know'. There are superb literary evocations of the Greeks, *Dante, and *Milton.

The essay is not a regular treatise. It draws on many of Shelley's earlier prefaces and essays, notably *A Philosophical View of Reform*. Though diffuse in places, it frequently sharpens to epigrammatic point: 'the great instrument of moral good is the imagination'; 'the freedom of women produced the poetry of sexual love'; and the famous peroration, ending 'Poets are the unacknowledged legislators of the world'—which must be read in context and which echoes in part the argument of Imlac in Johnson's *Rasselas*.

Defence of Poetry, A, an essay by P. *Sidney written in 1579–80. *Gosson's *Schoole of Abuse*, dedicated to Sidney in 1579, may have helped to stimulate the composition of the *Defence*, but Sidney's chief aim was probably to write an English vindication of literature to match the many recently written on the Continent in Italian, French, and Latin. Two editions of the work appeared posthumously in 1595: one, published by Ponsonby, bore the title *The Defence of Poesie* and the other, published by Olney, *An Apologie for Poetrie*. Most modern editors have preferred the first title both because Ponsonby was the official publisher of Sidney's remains and because Sidney in the opening paragraph speaks of being moved 'to make a pitiful defence of poor poetry'.

Sidney expounds the antiquity of poetry in all cultures, 'whose milk by little and little enabled them to feed afterwards of tougher knowledges'. He demonstrates its superiority to philosophy or history as a means of teaching virtue. After defining and distinguishing the 'parts, kinds, or species' of poetry, vindicating each in turn, he digresses to England: he sees contemporary poetry as having reached a low ebb, with little to be admired since *Chaucer, but affirms with prophetic confidence that major poetry in every genre, including drama, can be written in the English language. *A Defence of Poetry* is remarkable for the lightness of Sidney's style and the catholicity of his examples, often drawn from experience:

> I never heard the old song of Percy and Douglas that I found not my heart moved more than with a trumpet; and yet is it sung but by some blind crowder, with no rougher voice than rude style.

(See CHEVY CHASE.) The poetic qualities of the essay in themselves illustrate the power of imaginative writing:

> Nature never set forth the earth in so rich tapestry as divers poets have done; neither with so pleasant rivers, fruitful trees, sweet-smelling flowers, nor whatsoever else may make the too much loved earth more lovely. Her world is brazen, the poets only deliver a golden.

Defence of Ryme, a treatise by S. *Daniel written in reply to T. *Campion's *Observations in the Art of English Poesie*.

DEFFAND, Mme du, Marie de Vichy-Chamrond (1697–1780), a French literary hostess, whose salon was frequented by *Montesquieu, *D'Alembert, and others, and who became blind in later life. Horace *Walpole was her close friend, and a large number of her letters to him survive (ed. Mrs Paget Toynbee, 1912). Walpole's letters to her were destroyed by his request.

de FILIPPO, Eduardo (1900–84), Italian playwright and actor, who draws on Naples, his native city, for his themes, characters, and language. His major plays are: *Filumena Marturano* (*Filumena*, 1946), *Le bugie hanno le gambe lunghe* (*Lies Have Long Legs*, 1947), *La grande paura (The Great Fear*, 1948), *Sabato, domenica, lunedì* (*Saturday, Sunday, Monday*, 1959).

DEFOE, Daniel (1660–1731), born in London, the son of James Foe, a butcher. He changed his name to Defoe from c.1695. He attended Morton's academy for Dissenters at Newington Green with a view to the ministry, but by the time he married Mary Tuffley in 1683/4 he was established as a hosiery merchant in Cornhill, having travelled in France, Spain, the Low Countries, and possibly Italy and Germany; he was absorbed by travel throughout his life. He took part in Monmouth's rebellion, and in 1688 joined the advancing forces of William III. His first important signed work was *An Essay upon Projects* (1697), followed by *The True-Born Englishman* (1701), an immensely popular satirical poem attacking the prejudice against a king of foreign birth and his Dutch friends. In 1702 appeared *The Shortest Way with Dissenters*, a notorious pamphlet in which Defoe, himself a Dissenter, ironically demanded the total and savage suppression of dissent; for this he was fined, imprisoned (May–Nov. 1703), and pilloried. While in prison he wrote his *Hymn to the Pillory*, a mock-Pindaric *ode which was sold in the streets to sympathetic crowds. Meanwhile various business projects (the breeding of civet cats, marine insurance, a brick works) had come to grief, and Defoe's fortunes were revived by *Harley, the Tory politician, who arranged a pardon and employed him as a secret agent; between 1703 and 1714 Defoe travelled around the country for Harley and Godolphin gathering information and testing the political climate. Defoe wrote many pamphlets for Harley, and in 1704 began the *Review*; in the same year appeared his pamphlet *Giving Alms No Charity* and in 1706 *True Relation of the Apparition of One Mrs Veal*, a vivid report of a current ghost story, probably by Defoe. Certain anti-Jacobite pamphlets in 1712–13 led to his prosecution by the Whigs and to a brief imprisonment.

He now started a new trade journal, *Mercator*, in place of the *Review*. In 1715 he was convicted of libelling Lord Annesley (by implying that he was a Jacobite); he escaped punishment through the intervention of Townshend, the Whig secretary of state.

Defoe was an extremely versatile and prolific writer, and produced some 250 books, pamphlets, and journals, many anonymously or pseudonymously, but the works for which he is best known belong to his later years. *Robinson Crusoe appeared in 1719, the Farther Adventures following a few months later. The next five years saw the appearance of his most important works of fiction: Captain *Singleton in 1720; *Moll Flanders, A Journal of the *Plague Year, and *Colonel Jack in 1722; *Roxana, the *Memoirs of a Cavalier (now considered to be certainly by Defoe), his tracts on Jack *Sheppard, and A New Voyage round the World in 1724; The Four Voyages of Capt. George Roberts in 1726. His Tour through the Whole Island of Great Britain, a guidebook in three volumes (1724–6), is a vivid first-hand account of the state of the country, gleaned from his many travels, the last of which he appears to have taken in 1722. His last principal works were The Complete English Tradesman (1726), Augusta Triumphans (1728), A Plan of the English Commerce (1728), and The Complete English Gentleman, not published until 1890. He died in his lodgings in Ropemaker's Alley, Moorfields, and was buried in what is now Bunhill Fields. Defoe's influence on the evolution of the English novel was enormous, and many regard him as the first true novelist. He was a master of plain prose and powerful narrative, with a journalist's curiosity and love of realistic detail; his peculiar gifts made him one of the greatest reporters of his time, as well as a great imaginative writer who in Robinson Crusoe created one of the most familiar and resonant myths of modern literature. Important work on the Defoe canon by P. N. Furbank and W. R. Owens includes The Canonisation of Defoe (1988), Defoe De-attributions (1994), and A Critical Bibliography of Daniel Defoe (1998).

Deformed Transformed, The, an unfinished poetic drama by *Byron, written in 1822 and published in 1824. Arnold, a hunchback, is reviled and rejected by his mother for his deformity in the opening scene: he resolves on suicide, but is prevented by a stranger, who offers to change his shape and summons up Caesar, Alcibiades, and others as models. Arnold chooses the form of Achilles, but retains his own name: the stranger takes on Arnold's form and follows him as his servant. They take part in the sack of Rome in 1527, where Arnold distinguishes himself. The fragment ends with the opening chorus of Part III, in praise of peace. This version of the Faust legend is in part a meditation on the inspirational effects of disfigurement: 'deformity is daring. | It is its essence to o'ertake mankind.'

Degaré, Sir, a metrical romance in 1,073 lines of short couplets from the early 14th cent. in a south Midland dialect, one of the Middle English Breton lays.

Degaré, the son of a princess of Brittany who has been raped by a knight, is abandoned in a forest with a purse of money, a letter of directions, and a pair of gloves which are to fit the lady that he is to marry. The poem recounts Degaré's prowess in the course of his searches for his parents. The lady that the gloves fit is, in the event, his own mother who recognizes him with joy as her son immediately after their wedding ceremony and before its consummation. Rosemary Woolf makes the interesting suggestion that the romance may be a medievalizing of Oedipus, as Sir *Orfeo is of Orpheus. The name is probably a corruption of 'l'esgaré', 'the lost one' (apparently punned on in line 214, 'almost lost it is'), and is thought to be the origin of 'Diggory'. See edns by W. H. French and C. B. Hale, Middle English Metrical Romances (1930), i. 287–320, and in Medieval English Romances, Part II, ed. A. V. C. Schmidt and N. Jacobs (1980).

DEIGHTON, Len, see SPY FICTION.

'Deil, Address to the', a satirical poem by *Burns, published 1786. In vigorous, familiar terms the poet scolds the devil for all the trouble he causes in the world.

Deirdre, the heroine of the tale of 'The Sons of Usnach' (pron. 'Usna'), one of the 'Three Sorrowful Stories of Erin'. She was the daughter of Fedlimid, harper to King Conchubar (pron. Conachoor) of Ulster, and Cathbad the Druid prophesied that her beauty would bring banishment and death to heroes. Conchubar destined her for his wife and had her brought up in solitude. But she accidentally saw and fell in love with Naoise (or Naisi; pron. 'Neesha' as in 'Portlaoise'), the son of Usnach, who with his brothers carried her off to Scotland. They were lured back by Conchubar and treacherously slain, and Deirdre took her own life. See Lady *Gregory, Cuchulain of Muirthemne, and the dramas on Deirdre by G. W. *Russell (Æ), *Synge, and *Yeats.

Deirdre of the Sorrows, see SYNGE, and under DEIRDRE.

Deism, or 'natural religion', the belief in a Supreme Being as the source of finite existence, with rejection of revelation and the supernatural doctrines of Christianity.

The Deists, who came into prominence at the end of the 17th and during the 18th cent. (the word in English dates from the 1680s), were much influenced by the views of Lord *Herbert of Cherbury, often known as 'the father of Deism'. They include Charles Blount (1654–93), *Toland (author of Christianity Not Mysterious, 1696), Matthew Tindal (1657–1733, author of Christianity as Old as the Creation, 1730), Anthony *Collins (author of A Discourse of Freethinking, 1713), Thomas Chubb (1679–1747), and the third earl of

*Shaftesbury. *Locke, who rejected the label of Deist, nevertheless contributed significantly to the movement with his *Reasonableness of Christianity* (1695). One of the most cogent refutations was by J. *Butler in his *Analogy of Religion* (1736), in which he argues that natural religion is no more credible and acceptable than revealed religion.

'Dejection: An Ode', an autobiographical poem by S. T. *Coleridge, first published in the *Morning Post*, 1802.

Originally composed as a much longer verse letter to his beloved Asra (Sara Hutchinson), it describes the loss of his poetical powers, the dulling of his response to Nature, the breakdown of his marriage, and the paralysing effect of metaphysics (or opium). Paradoxically this is achieved in verse of great emotional intensity and metrical brilliance. *Wordsworth partly answered it in his *'Intimations of Immortality' ode.

DEKKER, Thomas (?1572–1632). He was born and mainly lived in London, the manners of which his writings vividly illustrate. He suffered from poverty and was several times imprisoned for debt, briefly in 1598–9 and from 1612 for a period of nearly seven years; the six prison chapters added in 1616 to his prose work *Lanthorne and Candle-Light* (first version 1608), and *Dekker His Dreame* (1620), evoke his own experiences of imprisonment. Despite this he is held to have been of a cheerful, good-natured temperament. He was engaged by *Henslowe about 1595 to write plays (over 40 of which are now lost) in collaboration with *Drayton, *Jonson, J. *Webster, and many others.

He published *The Shoemakers' Holiday* and *Old Fortunatus*, comedies, in 1600. Having been ridiculed, jointly with J. *Marston, by Jonson in his *Poetaster*, he retorted in *Satiromastix* (presumably in collaboration with Marston), a play produced in 1601. His other principal plays are *The Honest Whore*, of which Part I, in collaboration with *Middleton, appeared in 1604 and Part II, written 1604/5, in 1630; *Patient Grissil* (1603), written in collaboration with *Chettle and Haughton; *The Witch of Edmonton*, written in collaboration with J. *Ford and W. *Rowley in 1621, first published 1658. He also collaborated with Webster in *Westward Hoe* (written 1604, pub. 1607) and *Northward Hoe* (written 1605, pub. 1607), with Middleton in *The Roaring Girle* (written 1604–10, pub. 1611), and with Massinger in *The Virgin Martyr* (written 1620, pub. 1622). His tragi-comedy *Match Mee in London*, written 1604/5, was published 1631. Dekker also wrote pageants, tracts, and pamphlets. His pamphlet *The Wonderfull Yeare* (1603) is a poignant description of London during the plague of that year; it was used by Defoe for his *Journal of the Plague Year*. *Newes from Hell* (1606) is an imitation of *Nashe; *The Guls Horne-Booke* (1609) is a satirical book of manners.

Dekker's work is noted for its realistic and vivid portrayal of daily London life, both domestic and commercial, for its sympathy with the poor and oppressed, including animals tortured for man's amusement, and for its prevailing cheerfulness, though E. D. Pendry in an introduction to a selection of prose works (1967) stresses that he could be tough and bitter as well as whimsical. His dramatic works were collected by R. H. Shepherd, 1873, and edited by F. T. Bowers in 4 vols (1953–61).

DELAFIELD, E. M., the pen-name of Edmée Elizabeth Monica Dashwood, née De La Pasture (1890–1943), novelist, journalist, magistrate, and pillar of the Women's Institute, whose many popular novels include *The Diary of a Provincial Lady* (1930), a gentle satire of a middle-class life of laundry lists, cooks, and visits from the vicar.

de la MARE, Walter (1873–1956), born in Kent of well-to-do parents. He attended St Paul's Choir School. At 16 he began to work for an oil company, where he stayed for 20 years. In his mid-twenties he began to contribute poems and stories to various magazines, and in 1902, under the name of Walter Ramal, published *Songs of Childhood*, a volume which attracted little notice. Subsequently de la Mare published many volumes of poetry for both adults and children including, for adults, *The Listeners*, his first successful book, in 1912; *The Veil* in 1921; various volumes of *Collected Poems*; *The Burning Glass* in 1945; and two long visionary poems, 'The Traveller' (1946) and 'The Winged Chariot' (1951). Among many volumes for children were *Peacock Pie* (1913), *Tom Tiddler's Ground* (1932), and *Bells and Grass* (1941). Several collections were amalgamated in *Collected Rhymes and Verses* (1970) and *Collected Poems* (1979). De la Mare's highly individual prose works include the novels *Henry Brocken* (1904), in which the hero encounters writers of the past; *The Return* (1910), an eerie story of spirit possession, and in the same year a very successful children's story, *The Three Mulla-Mulgars* (later *The Three Royal Monkeys*); 'The Almond Tree' (in *The Riddle*, 1923), in which an uncomprehending child relates the events of his parents' breaking marriage; and the celebrated *Memoirs of a Midget* (1921), describing the world of the minute Miss M. Many volumes of short stories, often arresting or bizarre, for both adults and children, include *Broomsticks* (1925), *The Lord Fish* (1933), and *The Scarecrow* (1945). De la Mare's highly successful anthologies, incorporating long prefaces and commentaries, include *Come Hither* (1923), a widely admired collection for children; *Behold This Dreamer* (1939); and *Love* (1943). Essays and critical work include studies of R. *Brooke (1919) and Lewis Carroll—C. L. *Dodgson—(1932), and an edition of C. *Rossetti in 1930.

Remembered chiefly as a poet, for both adults and children, de la Mare was fluent, highly inventive, technically skilful, and unaffected by fashion. In his favourite themes of childhood, fantasy, and the numinous, commonplace objects and events are invested with mystery, and often with an undercurrent of melancholy. He was awarded the CH in 1948, the OM in 1953, and is buried in St Paul's Cathedral.

DELANE, John Thaddeus (1817–79), educated at King's College, London, and Magdalen Hall, Oxford, the famous editor of *The Times*, 1841–77. He was caricatured by Trollope in *The Warden* as 'Tom Towers'.

DELANEY, Shelagh (1939–   ), playwright, who was born in Salford, left school at 16, and is known for *A Taste of Honey*, which she wrote when she was 17 after seeing *Rattigan's play *Variations on a Theme*. It was presented by Joan *Littlewood in 1958 and was hailed as a landmark in the new school of *'kitchen sink' realism, a movement partly inspired by reaction against the drawing-room drama of Rattigan and *Coward. Much of her subsequent work was written for the cinema and television, including *Charley Bubbles* (1968) and *Dance with a Stranger* (1985).

DELANY, Mrs Mary, née Granville (1700–88), a member of the *Blue Stocking circle, who became a friend and correspondent of *Swift, married his friend Patrick *Delany in 1743, and knew many other eminent literary figures, including *Pope, *Burke, and Horace *Walpole. She was a favourite of the royal family, and introduced Fanny *Burney to court. Her *Autobiography and Correspondence* (1861–2, 6 vols, ed. Lady Llanover) gives a spirited account of 18th-cent. court, literary, and social life.

DELANY, Patrick (?1685–1768), Irish divine, friend of *Swift, husband of Mary *Delany. He was the author of *Observations upon Lord Orrery's Remarks on the Life and Writings of Dr Jonathan Swift* (1754), a series of letters, signed 'J.R.', written in an attempt to correct what he describes as 'the very mistaken and erroneous accounts [of Swift] that have been published'. See BOYLE, J.

de la RAMÉE, Marie Louise, see OUIDA.

Delectable Mountains, in Bunyan's *Pilgrim's Progress*, 'Emmanuel's Land' (meaning 'God-with-us'), within sight of the *Celestial City. Inhabited by gentle shepherds, the mountains signify the pastoral care of a Nonconformist church community.

DELEDDA, Grazia (1871–1936), Italian novelist and winner of the *Nobel Prize (1926). She is, with *Verga, a major writer of *verismo. Her best novels, drawn from her Sardinian background, are *Elias Portolu* (*The Woman and the Priest*, 1900; English trans. 1928, introduction by D. H. *Lawrence), *Canne al vento* (*Canes in the Wind*, 1913), *Cenere* (*Ashes*, 1903), and an autobiographical novel, *Cosima* (1937).

Delia, a collection of sonnets by S. *Daniel.

Delilah (Dalila in Milton's *Samson Agonistes*), in Judg. 16, a woman of the valley of Sorek, loved by Samson; she persuaded him to tell her the secret of his strength and (by cutting off his hair) betrayed him to the Philistines. A favourite figure in Renaissance pictorial art (e.g. *Rubens, *Samson and Delilah*, 1609–10), her shearing of Samson's hair represented an archetypal symbol of man's vulnerability to female perfidy. In Milton's version she is Samson's second wife.

DeLILLO, Don (1936–   ), American novelist, born and brought up in the Bronx, New York, and educated at Fordham University. Like T. *Pynchon, he employs black comedy and the language of science to deal with themes of paranoia and consumerism. His first book, *Americana* (1971), is a road novel in which a television executive attempts to impose meaning on his experiences by filming them. This was followed by *End Zone* (1972), which mixes American football with metaphysics, and *Great Jones Street* (1973), a satirical exploration of the world of a disaffected rock star. There are echoes of *Borges and *Sterne in *Ratner's Star* (1976), a sprawling fable about scientific understanding and the nature of fiction. Subsequent works exhibit greater sophistication of subject matter and technique. *Players* (1977) deals with language, terrorism, and the sterility of affluent urban lives. *Running Dog* (1978), a spy thriller and satire of consumerism, concerns the search for a pornographic film shot in Hitler's Berlin bunker. *The Names* (1982) concerns a murderous sect, and *White Noise* (1984) is an environmental disaster story narrated by the professor of Hitler studies at a Midwestern university. His version of the Kennedy assassination, *Libra* (1988), focuses on the role of Lee Harvey Oswald in shaping the American psyche. Both *Mao II* (1991), a postmodern tale of celebrity, terrorism, and the behaviour of crowds, and *Underworld* (1997), a multilayered secret history of the Cold War, examine the significance of spectacular events and media imagery in shaping the development of memory, history, and mass psychology.

DELIUS, Frederick (1862–1934), English composer. In spite of his German descent and the fact that he spent most of his mature life in France, there is an English quality about much of Delius's music, which has always been appreciated more in England than elsewhere. His operas have librettos generally either by himself or based on foreign authors (Keller, Jacobsen), but there are several settings of English and American poets among his other vocal works. A lifelong enthusiasm for *Whitman produced the texts for *Sea Drift* (1904), regarded by many as Delius's finest achievement, and also for *Songs of Farewell* (1930) and *Idyll: Once I passed through a populous city* (1932). Two settings of *Dowson, *Songs of Sunset* (1906–7) and *Cynara* (begun in 1907, but completed in 1929), draw out the nostalgic element in his romanticism. There are early settings for *Shelley and *Tennyson and a beautiful setting of W. E. *Henley (*A Late Lark*, 1925). In later life Delius became blind and totally paralysed: the last work he completed with his own hand was the incidental music for *Flecker's *Hassan* (1920–3), after which all his works were taken down to dictation by the young Yorkshireman Eric Fenby, who has left a moving account of this labour of love.

DELL, Ethel M., see ROMANTIC FICTION.

Della Crusca, the name of a literary academy established in Florence in 1582, with the principal object of purifying the Italian language. The first edition of its dictionary appeared in 1612.

Della Cruscans, a band of poets, led by Robert Merry (1755–98), who produced affected, sentimental, and highly ornamented verse towards the end of the 18th cent. After a wandering and varied career, Merry lived in Florence from 1784 to 1787 as a member of the *Della Crusca academy. With Mrs *Piozzi and others he produced in 1785 a *Miscellany*, in which he signed his work 'Della Crusca'. 'Anna Matilda' (H. *Cowley) was another copious writer of the school, who contributed with Merry and others to the *British Album* in 1790, a volume which proved very successful until the publication in 1791 of *Gifford's *The Baviad*, a savage satire on the Della Cruscans, followed by *The Maeviad* in 1795, part of which was also directed against them.

DELONEY, Thomas (?1560–1600), a silk-weaver by trade, whose place of birth and education are unknown, though he was certainly able to translate from Latin. He wrote broadside ballads on popular subjects, including three early ones on the defeat of the Armada in 1588. He is now best known for his four works of prose fiction, originally published between 1597 and 1600: *Jack of Newberie*; *The Gentle Craft* and *The Gentle Craft. The Second Part*; and *Thomas of Reading*. His fiction celebrates the virtues and self-advancement of hard-working craftsmen, especially in the cloth trade, and has been much admired in modern times for its effective use of dialogue. *The Gentle Craft* includes the story of Simon *Eyre, the shoemaker's apprentice who became lord mayor and founder of Leadenhall, which was adapted by Dekker in *The Shoemakers' Holiday*. The scene in *Thomas of Reading* in which the host and hostess of the tavern screw their courage up before murdering Thomas Cole has been seen as an analogue to *Macbeth*.

de MAN, Paul (1919–83), American critic, born in Antwerp, and educated at the Université Libre de Bruxelles. After an unsuccessful career in publishing, he emigrated to the USA in 1948, and studied at Harvard before following an academic career at Cornell, Johns Hopkins, and Yale. His major works, *Blindness and Insight* (1971), *Allegories of Reading* (1979), and *Rhetoric of Romanticism* (posth., 1984), examine the figurative nature of literary language and the gulf between language and meaning. He transformed academic analysis of literary *Romanticism by discarding the accepted view that Romantic poetry reconciles the human mind with nature; on the contrary, he argued, it reveals and laments the impossibility of such reconciliation. The leading Ameri-

can exponent of *deconstruction, he explored with notable rigour the ways in which literary works paradoxically undermine their apparent meanings. Four years after his death, articles he had written during the German occupation of Belgium (one of them tainted by anti-Semitic remarks) were rediscovered. Opponents of deconstruction seized upon these as evidence of a supposed moral deficiency in a critical method practised 40 years later by de Man and his—mostly Jewish—associates. Posthumous works include *The Resistance to Theory* (1986).

Demetrius, (1) in Shakespeare's *Titus Andronicus*, younger son of *Tamora the Goth, one of the rapists of *Lavinia; (2) one of the young lovers in his *A Midsummer Night's Dream*; (3) Demetrius Fannius in Jonson's *Poetaster*, a satirical portrait of *Dekker; (4) lover of Celia in Fletcher's *The Humorous Lieutenant*. From classical times onwards the name seems to have had villainous associations.

DEMOCRITUS (b. *c.*460 BC), a celebrated Greek philosopher, born at Abdera. He wrote on the natural sciences, mathematics, morals, and music. He advanced (with Leucippus) the theory that the world was formed by the concourse of atoms, the theory subsequently expounded by *Lucretius and confirmed and developed by scientists of the *Enlightenment. *Juvenal speaks of him as ever laughing at the follies of mankind, and he is sometimes known as the 'laughing philosopher' in opposition to the melancholy *Heraclitus.

Demogorgon , a mysterious infernal god, was brought from obscurity by *Boccaccio in *Genealogia Deorum*, and appears in *Ariosto, in Spenser's *Faerie Queene* (I. v. 22), in Milton's *Paradise Lost* (II. 965), and in Dryden's *Spanish Fryar*. He is a prominent figure in Shelley's *Prometheus Unbound*; his name may have attracted *Shelley because it is compounded of 'Demos' (people) and 'Gorgo' (the name of some terrifying demigods) and so fitted his conception of Necessity and particularly that Historical Necessity which he thought would bring about an initially alarming but ultimately beneficial social revolution.

de MONTHERLANT, Henry, see MONTHERLANT.

de MORGAN, William Frend (1839–1917), educated at University College London. At first he devoted his attention to art and in particular to the production of stained glass and glazed pottery, working for a time in association with his friend W. *Morris; he published two treatises on the craft of pottery. He was particularly successful with decorative tiles, but ill health brought this pursuit to an end, and at the age of 67 he embarked somewhat casually on the writing of fiction, his first and best novel, *Joseph Vance* (1906), proving to his astonishment a great success. It is the rambling but entertaining tale of a drunken builder's son befriended by a middle-class family, who graduates from Oxford and becomes an engineer and inventor. This was followed by several others; the last two, *The Old Madhouse* (1919) and *The Old Man's Youth* (1921), left unfinished on his death, were skilfully completed by his widow, the artist Evelyn de Morgan. See A. M. D. W. Stirling, *William de Morgan and His Wife* (1922).

Demos, a novel by George *Gissing, published anonymously in three volumes in 1886 by Smith, Elder. The proletarian agitator Richard Mutimer unexpectedly inherits a fortune, and builds an Owenite community, New Wanley. He marries the middle-class Adela Waltham, who then finds the hidden will that dispossesses him. Mutimer's subsequent scheme to encourage saving by the working class is defrauded, and he is stoned to death by a mob. Adela marries the true heir, aristocratic Hubert, and Wanley improbably reverts to its pre-industrialized state. *Gladstone was briefly thought to be the novel's author; its poet-cum-politician Westlake is based on William *Morris.

DEMOSTHENES (*c.*383–322 BC), the greatest orator of ancient Athens. T. *Wilson, who translated his *Philippics* (1570), said that they were 'Most nedefull to be redde in these daungerous dayes of all them that loue their Countries libertie'. Sir P. *Sidney thought him most worthy to be imitated. Dr *Johnson pictured him speaking to brutes.

Dempster, Mr and Janet, characters in G. Eliot's 'Janet's Repentance' (see SCENES OF CLERICAL LIFE).

DENHAM, Sir John (1615–69), born in Dublin and educated at Trinity College, Oxford. A Royalist, he was forced to surrender Farnham Castle, of which he was governor, in 1642, fled to the Continent in 1648, and was appointed surveyor-general of works at the Restoration. His tragedy *The Sophy*, set in the Turkish court, was performed in 1641, and he also published occasional verses, satires, and a free translation from *Virgil (*The Destruction of Troy*, 1656). He is chiefly known for his *topographical poem *Cooper's Hill*, piratically published 1642, an early and influential example of what was to become a very popular genre. (See Pope's WINDSOR FOREST.) It combines descriptions of scenery with moral, historical, and political reflections, and contains the well-known address to the Thames, 'O, could I flow like thee', which was singled out for praise by Dr *Johnson for its economy of language, smoothness, and sweetness. *Dryden also praised his work highly, as 'majestic' and 'correct'. His poetry (and notably his use of the heroic couplet) played an important part in the transition from what were seen as the rugged eccentricities of the *metaphysicals to the neo-classicism of the *Augustan age. (See also WALLER.)

Denis Duval, *Thackeray's last, unfinished, novel, published in the *Cornhill Magazine* 1864.

The story begins in Rye, in the second half of the 18th cent. The narrator, Denis Duval, grows up in a colony of French Protestant refugees. A French noblewoman, Mme de Saverne, escapes from the persecution of her husband and comes to England with the help of the sinister Chevalier de la Motte, who was intended to become the villain of the novel. She takes refuge with her old nurse, Denis's mother, and Denis falls in love with her little daughter Agnes. Denis has to leave home and go to sea after he has exposed the smuggling activities of his grandfather and the treasonable behaviour of de la Motte, and the fragment ends at this point. Thackeray intended Denis to encounter a series of adventures at sea, and to return to rescue Agnes from the machinations of de la Motte.

Dennis, in Dickens's *Barnaby Rudge*, the hangman and one of the leaders of the no-Popery riots.

DENNIS, John (1657–1734), son of a saddler, educated at Harrow and Caius College, Cambridge. He was a poet and dramatist, but is best known for his criticism, which combines a respect for *neo-classical theory with a passion for the *sublime (particularly as manifested by *Milton), and with a dislike for the new *sentimental comedy. He declared that the 'Rules of *Aristotle' were 'nothing but Nature and Good Sense reduc'd to a Method', maintaining that *Paradise Lost was not so much 'against the Rules' as 'above them all'. His critical works (ed. E. N. Hooker, 2 vols, 1939–43) include *The Advancement and Reformation of Modern Poetry* (1701), *The Grounds of Criticism in Poetry* (1704), and *An Essay on the Genius and Writings of Shakespeare* (1712). His tragedies include *Appius and Virginia*, unsuccessfully produced in 1709, which was mocked by Pope in his *Essay on Criticism* ('Appius reddens at each word you speak', l. 585); this started a feud between the two writers, their interchanges including Pope's *Narrative of Dr Robert Norris . . .* (1713) and Dennis's *Remarks upon Mr Pope's Homer* (1717). Dennis also features as 'Sir Tremendous' in Pope's *Three Hours after Marriage* (1717), 'tremendous' being one of his favourite terms of praise. But Pope accepted and acted upon some of his critical comments, and shortly before Dennis's poverty-stricken death wrote a prologue for his benefit performance.

DENNIS, Nigel Forbes (1912–89), novelist, playwright, journalist, and critic, born in Surrey, but educated abroad, in Southern Rhodesia and Germany. He worked for many years in America, where his first novel, *Boys and Girls Come out to Play* (1949), is largely set. His best-known work is *Cards of Identity* (1955), a satiric fantasy set in an English country house, which comments harshly but with much incidental comedy on post-war social change and insecurity and the ease with which the human personality can be controlled. *A House in Order* (1966) is a more abstract, Kafkaesque treatment of the problem of identity in which the imprisoned narrator, confined to a greenhouse, tries to ignore the world at war outside by cultivating his own garden. Dennis also published three plays, several critical works, and was for some time co-editor of *Encounter.

DENT, J. M., see EVERYMAN'S LIBRARY.

De Nugis Curialium, see MAP; also the subtitle of the *Policraticus* of *John of Salisbury.

Deor, an Old English poem from the 9th or 10th cent. in the *Exeter Book, of 42 lines divided into seven unequal sections and containing the refrain 'that passed; so can this'. Deor seems to be a minstrel who has fallen out of favour and consoles himself by considering the past misfortunes of others such as Wayland the Smith, Theodoric, and Hermanric. It is one of the group of poems in the Exeter Book referred to as 'elegies', short poems whose theme is usually the transience and unreliability of the world, sometimes (though not in *Deor*) ending with a Christian consolation. See edition by Kemp Malon (4th edn, 1966).

De Profundis, 'Out of the depths', the first two words of the Latin version of Psalm 130. It is the title of the prose apologia of *Wilde. See Ross, R.

'Deputy', in Dickens's *Edwin Drood, the nearest thing to a name acknowledged by the imp who attends on Durdles.

De QUINCEY, Thomas (1785–1859), second son of a linen merchant, born in Manchester and educated at schools in Bath and Winkfield, ending at Manchester Grammar School, from which he ran away to the homeless wanderings in Wales and London which he was to describe in *Confessions of an English Opium Eater. He afterwards went to Worcester College, Oxford, and—having made the acquaintance of *Coleridge and *Wordsworth—settled at Grasmere in the cottage formerly occupied by the Wordsworths. In 1804, while at Oxford, he had begun to take opium, and from 1812 he became an addict. In 1817 he married Margaret Simpson, daughter of a local farmer, by whom he had eight children, and in the following year, having by then exhausted his private fortune, he started to earn a living by journalism. *Confessions of an English Opium Eater*, by which he made his name, was published in 1822. For the next 30 years he earned a precarious living, mainly in Edinburgh, by tales, articles, and reviews, mostly in *Blackwood's and Tait's*, including *Klosterheim* (1832), *Recollections of the Lake Poets* (1834–9), 'Sketches ... from the Autobiography of an English Opium Eater' (1834–41, later entitled *Autobiographic Sketches*), 'Suspiria de Profundis' (1845), and 'The English Mail Coach' (1849). A collected edition of his works, *Selections Grave and Gay*, was started under his supervision in 1853, and occupied him until his death.

Since nearly all De Quincey's work was journalism, written under pressure to support his family, it is more remarkable for brilliant tours de force such as 'On the Knocking on the Gate in "Macbeth"', 'On Murder

Considered as One of the Fine Arts', and 'The Revolt of the Tartars', than for sustained coherence. Eclectic learning, pungent black humour sometimes degenerating into facetiousness, a stately but singular style, distinguish all his writing. His impressionistic reminiscences both of his own childhood and of his literary contemporaries are memorably vivid. His greatest, though never completed, achievement was his psychological study of the faculty of dreaming in 'Suspiria de Profundis' and 'The English Mail Coach', in which he traced—25 years before Freud was born—how childhood experiences and sufferings are crystallized in dreams into symbols which can form and educate the dreamer's personality, and can also give birth to literature, either as poetry or as 'impassioned prose', as De Quincey called his own climaxes of imagery. His influence, both on other writers such as *Poe and *Baudelaire (half of whose *Paradis artificiels* is a direct translation from De Quincey) and on ordinary readers tempted to experiment with opium, has been immense and sometimes malign. See E. Sackville-West, *A Flame in Sunlight: The Life and Work of Thomas de Quincey* (1936); H. A. Eaton, *Thomas de Quincey* (1936).

DERRIDA, Jacques (1930–2004), French philosopher, born to a Jewish family in Algiers, who studied in Paris at the École Normale Supérieure, where he later taught from 1964 to 1984. He subsequently held visiting professorships at Yale and other American universities. Following publication in 1967 of *De la grammatologie* (*Of Grammatology*) and *L'Écriture et la différence* (*Writing and Difference*), he enjoyed a huge influence upon academic literary theory in the USA, as the founder of *deconstruction, a subtly and often playfully sceptical approach to the relations between language and meaning, which was adopted by *de Man and others as a valuable method for exploring problems of literary criticism. Among many later works are *La Dissémination* (*Dissemination*, 1972), *Glas* (1976), and *La Carte postale* (*The Post Card*, 1980). (See STRUCTURALISM AND POST-STRUCTURALISM.)

Derriman, Festus, a character in Hardy's *The Trumpet Major.

'Der wilde Jäger', see WILD HUNTSMAN.

DESAI, Anita (1937–), novelist and short story writer, born in India and educated in Delhi; her father was Bengali, her mother German. Her elegant and lucid novels, which vividly evoke the atmosphere, society, and landscapes of India, include *Fire on the Mountain* (1977) and *Clear Light of Day* (1980). *Games at Twilight* (1978) is a collection of short stories, and her works for children include *The Village by the Sea* (1982), a story of change in a small fishing village near Bombay. This was followed by *Clear Light of Day* (1980), *In Custody* (1984), *Baumgartner's Bombay* (1988), and *Journey to Ithaca* (1995). See also POST-COLONIAL LITERATURE.

DESANI, G. V. (?1909–   ), Indian writer, born in Nairobi, Kenya; he lived in Britain during the Second World War, where he became a regular lecturer and broadcaster. His prose poem *Hali* (1950) was published with a preface by E. M. *Forster, but he is known principally for his eccentric and inventive novel *All about H. Hatterr* (1948), in which Hatterr, son of a European merchant seaman and 'an Oriental, a Malay Peninsula-resident lady, a steady non-voyaging non-Christian human', seeks wisdom from the seven sages of India. This was revised and republished in 1972 with an introduction by A. *Burgess. His hybrid and 'dazzling, puzzling, leaping prose' has been described by *Rushdie (*Indian Writing, 1947–1977*, pub. 1997) as 'the first genuine effort to go beyond the Englishness of the English language'. A collected volume of stories was published in 1990. See ANGLO-INDIAN LITERATURE.

DESCARTES, René (1596–1650), French philosopher and mathematician. After a period of extensive travelling he went into studious retirement, first in Paris until 1629, then in Holland until 1649 when he accepted an invitation to visit Sweden, where he died. His main works are: *Discours de la méthode* (printed as an introduction to the conclusions of his scientific research in 1637), *Méditations philosophiques* (originally published in Latin in 1641), *Principia Philosophiae* (1644), and *Traité des passions de l'âme* (1649). They have exerted a unique influence on European thought. Philosophically his starting point is the problem of certainty posed by *Montaigne's radical scepticism: in other words, the necessity of a method productive of reliable propositions. Rejecting the accumulated preconceptions of the past ('systematic doubt'), he proposes to reconstruct the whole of philosophy on the basis of a few self-evident intuitions, such as the existence of the self in consciousness ('cogito ergo sum') and of elementary logical truths, such as the principle of non-contradiction. From these premisses he attempts to deduce the existence of God as guarantor of the reliability of the perceptible world, and thus of its susceptibility to scientific analysis. As a mathematician (he made major contributions to algebraic notation and coordinate geometry), he considered mathematical reasoning to be applicable to the whole of science. Although his astronomical theories were demolished by I. *Newton, his reduction of matter to the quantifiable has remained fundamental to science. In epistemology and ethics, his rigorous dualism (between mind and body) has been immensely influential, though it has come under suspicion in recent years. He is generally regarded as the founder of modern philosophy.

DESCHAMPS, Eustache (*c*.1346–*c*.1406), French poet. He was a disciple of *Guillaume de Machaut, influential in the development of the ballade, and the writer of the first treatise on poetry in French. He addressed one of his 'Balades de moralitez' to *Chaucer, whom he styled 'grant translateur, noble Geffroy Chaucier'.

Desdemona, the heroine of Shakespeare's *Othello*.

Deserted Village, The, a poem by *Goldsmith, published 1770, in which he evokes the idyllic pastoral life of Auburn, 'loveliest village of the plain', in its days of prosperous peace, now over; the poet laments the growth of trade, the demand for luxuries, and the mercantile spirit which have depopulated such villages and driven 'a bold peasantry, their country's pride' to emigration. *Boswell attributes the last four lines to Dr *Johnson. Auburn was long identified with Lissoy, where Goldsmith spent much of his childhood, but is now believed to be a composite portrait, based also on Goldsmith's observations of the declining English countryside. Goldsmith's idealized descriptions of a happy rural community provoked a protest in Crabbe's *The Village* and have also been the focus for much discussion of the Tory view of a Golden Age.

Despair, representing the most potent temptation to beset the Christian pilgrim, appears in Spenser's *Faerie Queene*, I. ix, as an aged cavern dweller whose call to suicide has a narcotic mellifluousness. Despair was understood to be the unforgivable 'sin against the Holy Ghost'. In Bunyan's *Pilgrim's Progress* he appears as Giant Despair, resident of *Doubting Castle, where he imprisons Christian and Hopeful. Great-heart kills him in Part II.

Desperate Remedies, a novel by *Hardy, published 1871.

This was the first of Hardy's published novels. Cytherea Gray, who loves and is loved by Edward Springrove, becomes lady's maid to Miss Aldclyffe. The contrivances of Miss Aldclyffe, the discovery that Edward is already engaged, and the need to support a sick brother, drive Cytherea to marry Aeneas Manston, Miss Aldclyffe's villainous and illegitimate son, whose first wife is supposed to have perished in a fire. As soon as she is married Cytherea discovers that Edward is free from his engagement and that Aeneas's wife is probably still alive. Ingenious investigations reveal that Aeneas murdered his first wife in order to gain Cytherea. He hangs himself in his cell and the lovers are united.

Destiny, a novel by S. *Ferrier, published 1831.

The earnest evangelical tone of the book almost overwhelms the sense of comedy shown in her other novels. The story relates, in a complex plot, the fortunes of the various members of the Malcolm family: Glenroy, a Highland chief, married to the London-bred Lady Elizabeth Waldegrave, who finds the conditions of Scottish life so intolerable she leaves him; Glenroy's poor but worthy cousin Captain Malcolm, and his son Ronald; another cousin, the misanthrope Inch-Orran, who disappoints Glenroy by leaving his estate to Ronald and his father; Glenroy's nephew Reginald, who becomes engaged to Edith, the chief's daughter, then jilts her to marry her half-sister; and Ronald, who disappears after a shipwreck in order to leave his father in possession of the Inch-Orran property, and returns, after years away, to marry the jilted Edith.

De TABLEY, Lord, see WARREN, J. B. L.

detective fiction, see overleaf.

Deus ex machina, 'God from the machine', an unexpected event or intervention in a play or novel, which resolves a difficult situation. When a god was introduced in the ancient Greek drama, he was brought onto the stage by some mechanical means (μηχανή). *Euripides was particularly fond of the device.

de VERE, Aubrey Thomas (1814–1902), born in Co. Limerick, the son of Sir Aubrey de Vere (1788–1846, himself a poet), educated at Trinity College, Dublin. He came early under the influence of *Wordsworth and *Coleridge and had many friends in the literary world, including *Tennyson, Sir H. *Taylor, the *Brownings, and *Ruskin; in 1851, in the footsteps of his friend *Newman, he was received into the Roman Catholic Church. His voluminous works include *The Waldenses, or the Fall of Rora, with Other Poems* (1842); *English Misrule and Irish Misdeeds* (1848), which displays Irish sympathies, as do many of his works; and *Recollections* (1897). He is the subject of a memoir (1904) by Wilfrid Ward. See also M. P. Reilly, *Aubrey de Vere: Victorian Observer* (1956).

de VERE, Edward, see OXFORD.

DEVEREUX, Robert, see ESSEX.

Devil Is an Ass, The, a comedy by *Jonson, acted by the King's Men 1616, printed 1631.

Fitzdottrel, a foolish country squire, is cheated out of his estate by Meercraft, a 'projector', who parades various fantastic schemes for making money and deludes him with the promise that he will make him duke of Drowndland through a project for land reclamation. When Fitzdottrel finds he has made over his estate to the wrong person, he pretends to be bewitched in order to have the contract declared void, but eventually confesses to the fraud. He then learns that Wittipol and Manly, who had intrigued to seduce his wife, have out of admiration for her virtue safeguarded his estate. A secondary plot concerns Pug, a minor devil who has been allowed by Satan to try his hand at iniquity on earth for a day and is taken on by Fitzdottrel as a servant. He finds himself completely outdone in wickedness by human knaves, is sent to Newgate, and returns to hell baffled.

Devils, The, a play by J. *Whiting, based on A. *Huxley's *The Devils of Loudon*.

'Devil's Thoughts, The', a satirical poem by S. T. *Coleridge and R. *Southey, published 1799, describing the Devil going walking and enjoying the sight of the vices of men. The poem was imitated by *Byron in his 'Devil's Drive', and by *Shelley in his 'Devil's Walk'.

Devil upon Two Sticks in England, The, a continuation by W. *Combe, published 1790, of *Lesage's *Le Diable boiteux*. S. *Foote also wrote a farce called *The Devil upon Two Sticks*, produced 1768.

DEWEY, John (1859–1952), American philosopher, one of the leaders of the Pragmatist school, and educationist, born in Vermont. His chief works are: *Critical Theory of Ethics* (1891), *Studies in Logical Theory* (1903), *Democracy and Education* (1916), *Human Nature and Conduct* (1922).

DEWEY, Melvil (1851–1931), American librarian, invented the Dewey decimal system of library classification.

Dewy, Dick, a character in Hardy's *Under the Greenwood Tree*.

DEXTER, Colin, see DETECTIVE FICTION.

DHONDY, Farrukh (1944–   ), writer, broadcaster, and educationalist, born in Poona, India, and educated there and at the universities of Leicester and Cambridge. He has written several books for young people, set in Britain and written in a contemporary multicultural idiom: these include *Come to Mecca* (1978), *The Siege of Babylon* (1978), and *Black Swan* (1992), which interweaves the life of schoolgirl Rose Hassan with a 16th-cent. plot involving *Marlowe and *Forman. *Poona Company* (1980) is an evocation of his own schooldays.

Dial, (1) (1840–4), the literary organ of the American Transcendental movement (see TRANSCENDENTAL CLUB), of which M. *Fuller was editor; she was succeeded by *Emerson. It contained contributions by *Thoreau. (2) (1889–97) (Nos 1–5), a literary and artistic periodical edited by *Ricketts and Charles Shannon. The 'Dial Group' also included T. S. *Moore and Lucien Pissarro (1863–1944). (3) (1880–1929), a literary monthly founded in Chicago, which moved in 1918 to New York. In its last decade it was one of the most important international periodicals, publishing work by T. S. *Eliot, *Yeats, D. H. *Lawrence, *Pound, *Cummings, *Aiken, and many others. Scofield Thayer was editor from 1925. It was expensively printed and paid well; *Connolly described it as 'the most successful of eclectic magazines, rich, discerning' with 'a distinct impression of modishness in its later numbers as the twenties entered their sleek decline' ('Little Magazines', 1964, printed in the *Evening Colonnade*, 1973).

Diall of Princes, the title of the translation by Sir T. *North of Guevara's *El relox de principes*, published 1557.

Dialogues Concerning Natural Religion, a treatise on natural theology by *Hume, written in the 1750s and published posthumously 1779. The work is modelled on *Cicero's *De Natura Deorum*. It portrays in 18th-

(cont. on p.278)

Crime has been a staple of storytelling since its beginnings, and misdirection of the reader, for example about facts (Tom *Jones's parentage), or emotions (in *Emma or *Much Ado about Nothing), has equally had its special position, leading to striking revelations at a late crisis point. The classic English detective novel marries the two elements. Its particular form owes its greatest debt to E. A. *Poe, whose three or four detective stories written in the 1840s strikingly anticipate many of the genre's main features. In particular English writers followed him in creating detectives who were remote from the common herd, creatures of pure ratiocination, emotional hermits who observed but did not participate in the hurly-burly of life around them. The fact that the steely logic of Poe's detective Dupin often leads him to conclusions that border on the absurd does not seem to have worried most readers.

Around mid-century there were other detectives, such as Charles *Dickens's Bucket (*Bleak House, 1853) and Wilkie *Collins's Sergeant Cuff (*The Moonstone, 1868), who were apparently more homely and engaging. But after the triumphant debut of Sherlock *Holmes in A Study in Scarlet (1887) it was Poe's model which won the day, and traces of the stereotype can be found in figures such as Baroness *Orczy's Old Man in the Corner, Agatha *Christie's Poirot, P. D. *James's Dalgliesh, and Colin Dexter's Inspector Morse.

Conan *Doyle was the master of the short story, packing each one with observation, conflict, and sharply dramatized character-types. His success, and the huge sums a Holmes story commanded, attracted hordes of followers and imitators, of whom Arthur *Morrison and G. K. *Chesterton were notable. The most engaging of the figures produced in reaction to Holmes's intellectuality and near-inhumanity was E. W. *Hornung's Raffles, the gentleman burglar who figures in a story series of notable quality. Holmes and Raffles, both quintessential late Victorian figures, contrast oddly: Raffles, nominally the social outcast, has for the most part perfectly conventional social attitudes, whereas Holmes, who in most cases acts for and reinforces the existing social order, is an outsider who is frequently sceptical about, if not downright contemptuous of, the people he represents.

After the First World War public taste shifted away from the short story to the novel-length tale. The so-called Golden Age is often said to have been inaugurated by Trent's Last Case (1913) by E. C. *Bentley (1875–1956) but it was led by a quartet of writers who are still widely read today: Agatha Christie, Dorothy L. *Sayers, Margery *Allingham, and Ngaio *Marsh, supported by numerous figures who have lasted less well, such as R. Austin Freeman (1862–1943) and John Dickson Carr (1906–77). They were productive, consistent, and unembarrassed by the idea they were satisfying a need for entertainment. Christie in particular gave the public for 25 years or so after The Murder of Roger Ackroyd (1926) a stream of ingenious and satisfying puzzles whose solutions habitually left her readers feeling agreeably fooled. The books of her later years, being more loosely plotted, were much less satisfying. The genre as she moulded it is a highly artificial one, elegant in form and construction if not always in style, and its elements of challenge from writer to reader proved extremely popular with between-war readers. Its social attitudes were surprisingly conventional, granted the politically volatile climate of opinion, and its dramatis personae were drawn largely from the gentry and professional classes.

The 'silly ass' detective was a phenomenon of the period, initiated by Sayers's Wimsey. It even crossed the Atlantic to take the outrageous but hardly convincing form of Philo Vance, the detective of S. S. Van Dine (1888–1939). In time, though, the echoes of Bertie *Wooster had to be softened or forgotten, since they harmed these figures' credibility as detectives: Wimsey became the ardent and persistent suitor, and Allingham's Albert Campion became so fey and self-effacing a figure that many readers would be hard put to it to name which of her books he does and which he does not appear in.

After the Second World War the artifice of the Golden Age writers, their insistence on murder as game, seemed increasingly irrelevant, though Edmund Crispin (1921–78) gained a following for his jokey books, and Christianna Brand (1907–88), in bravura performances such as Tour De Force (1955), proved there was still sap in the old branch. Most of the writers preferred to aim for greater realism, specializing in believable studies of the murderous mind or of everyday situations into which murder erupts. This generation, which included Julian *Symons and Michael Gilbert, produced many fine if unshowy novels, but never rivalled in popularity the older generation, who were mostly still producing a best-seller a year, and in the case of Allingham some of the finest novels in the English crime tradition.

It was left to two writers who emerged in the 1960s and 1970s to re-establish the English detective novel as a popular force with a new generation of readers. Both P. D. James and Ruth *Rendell wrote novels in the whodunnit tradition, though Rendell gave the impression of regarding these as the lesser part of her output, and James disguised the vital surprise element in a massive and intricate narrative plan with accretions of realistic detail. Neither would have anything to do with the Never-nevershire settings of some of the Golden Age writers, and their contemporary grasp was often superior to that of many mainstream novelists. James's Inspector Dalgliesh, though, is a traditional lonely outsider, a reputable poet, shy of emotional involvements, while Rendell could produce, in the opening pages of *Wolf to the Slaughter*, a masterpiece of reader misdirection in the Christie tradition. The realistic and contemporary feel to both writers' novels has aided their transfer to television, and the success of these series, and of Dexter's Morse, has boosted the popularity of modern crime fiction as a whole.

The whodunnit tradition may not seem the easiest to marry with a realistic surface and treatment, but several modern writers have done it successfully. Reginald Hill does so in *Under World* (1988), a study of a mining community as the industry disintegrates. His detective duo Pascoe and Dalziel, university-educated cop allied to heavy traditional cop, allows a variety of treatments, depending on which of the team is in the ascendant. *Pictures of Perfection* (1994), for example, is as delicate an entertainment as the genre is capable of. Many writers have pushed their British policemen in the direction of the tougher American police procedural, but in such novels as Ian Rankin's Inspector Rebus series the British whodunnit seems just as close as the American model. Private detectives are now the exception, and though the policemen who have taken over may be vivid individuals like Hill's thuggish Dalziel, they are more likely to be greyer, more everyday figures (Dorothy Simpson's Thanet and Catherine Aird's Sloane spring to mind) who allow the burden of each book to fall unequivocally on the murder situation and the principal suspects.

At century's end the vigour and variety of British crime writing are more impressive than ever. Studies of the mind of a criminal (going back to *Godwin and the Newgate novelists in the 1830s) are frequent, led by Ruth Rendell (*Master of the Moor*, 1982) and her alter ego Barbara Vine (*A Dark-Adapted Eye*, 1986). Margaret Yorke is mistress of low-key studies of situations in which ordinary people get entangled, with murderous consequences. Sheila Radley's *A Talent for Destruction*

(1982) is another notable work in this tradition. Comedy has not been buried with the Golden Age, and a more modern vein has been exploited by Simon Brett, Peter Lovesey (*The False Inspector Dew*, 1982), and Caroline Graham (*The Killings at Badger's Drift*, 1987). Historical crime has made a strong comeback, with the Brother Cadfael novels of Ellis Peters (1913–95), Edward Marston's Elizabethan theatre series, and, most surprising of all, Lindsey Davis's Falco novels, which transplant the atmosphere and strategies of American private-eye fiction to ancient Rome.

Regionalism too has made a strong showing in recent years, to challenge the dominance of London in the Holmes era and the geographical vagueness of the Golden Age novels. Scotland is the setting in the novels of Rankin and Peter Turnbull, Yorkshire in those of Hill and Peter Robinson, Nottingham in those of Ian Harvey, and the West Country in those of W. J. Burley and in many of Andrew Taylor's. All use their chosen milieu with a strong sense for the landscape and its moulding of people. Michael *Dibdin, more exotically, has set his novels in Venice.

The continuing popularity of the detective novel is undoubted: the returns from the *Public Lending Right system attest to this. The fact that it is a popular form that engages the mind rather than the emotions has always given it a degree of respectability: to be seen reading a Sayers or Rendell is very different from being seen reading a Barbara Cartland or an Alistair Maclean. The intricacy of the plots, the skill with which the author produces yet disguises the clues vital to the solution, give particular pleasure, so that a rereading of a Christie novel, for example, can provide delighted recognition of how an apparently flat narrative has concealed quicksands of mistaken assumptions. Though murder has been almost a *sine qua non* of detective fiction since the 1920s, the shock or *frisson* that murder might be expected to produce is almost always lacking: the body is merely the means to a detection process. Though in the last twenty or thirty years crime novels have become more realistic, delight in gore and exploitation of horror and pain are still largely absent from the British product. When hanging was abolished, the demise of the detective novel was predicted as a consequence, but this was to misunderstand its whole nature. The point of a mystery is that the culprit is revealed to general surprise, not that vengeance is exacted for his crime.

cent. terms the conflict between scientific theism and philosophical scepticism, on the question of whether the human mind is capable of inferring the nature of the source of order in the universe.

Dialogues of the Dead, Four, by *Prior, written 1721, imaginary conversations on the model set by *Lucian and perhaps directly suggested by *Fénelon's *Dialogues des morts* (1712–30). The first is between 'Charles the Emperor and Clenard the Grammarian' on the subject of greatness; the second is between 'Mr John Lock and Seigneur de Montaigne'; the third between 'The Vicar of Bray and Sir Thomas More'; and the fourth between 'Oliver Cromwell and his Porter'.
*Lyttelton also wrote *Dialogues of the Dead* (1760).

Dialogus de Scaccario, or **Dialogue of the Exchequer,** is the work of Richard Fitz-Nigel, treasurer of England from 1195 or 1196 to 1198, and bishop of London 1189–98. It takes the form of a dialogue in Latin between teacher and pupil, and is one of the principal sources of our knowledge of the Norman administration in England before Magna Carta.

Diana, a character in Shakespeare's *All's Well that Ends Well*.

Diana of the Crossways, a novel by G. *Meredith, published 1885.

Diana is based on the writer Caroline *Norton, whose husband had tried to divorce her. After the family's protests Meredith included a note that the work 'is to be read as fiction'.

The beautiful and impulsive Irish girl Diana Merion marries Mr Warwick, a man incapable of understanding the remarkable qualities of his wife. Her innocent indiscretions arouse his jealousy and he brings an action for divorce, citing Lord Dannisburgh (drawn from Melbourne), which he loses. Percy Dacier, a rising young politician, falls in love with Diana, but when she is about to live with him, openly and rashly, the dangerous illness of her friend Lady Dunstane recalls her sense of duty and propriety. Dacier perseveres, and she is once more on the point of joining him when he discovers that an important political secret which he had confided to her has been passed to a London newspaper. When she admits her indiscretion he leaves in a fury and marries a young heiress. Diana's husband dies and she eventually recovers from her heartache to wed her faithful adorer Thomas Redworth, who, without being brilliant, has the wit and understanding to appreciate her. Crossways, the name of her house, indicates the novel's emphasis on a historical moment which proved a turning point in marital and sexual politics.

DIAPER, William (1685–1717), poet, born in Somerset, who wrote *Nereides; or, Sea-Eclogues* (1712), in which the speakers are mermen and mermaids and the landscapes subaqueous: *Swift found them 'very pretty' (*Journal to Stella*, 12 March 1712) and briefly

interested himself in Diaper's career in the Church. He also wrote *Dryades* (1712) and a *topographical poem, 'Brent' (printed 1754): he was curate of Brent from 1709 and his poem gives a vivid and watery picture of the damp Somerset levels, where rabbits took to the water with ducks, and all food tasted of frog. He translated Part 1 of Oppian's *Halieuticks*, a Greek didactic poem on fish and fishing. See *Complete Works*, ed. D. Broughton (1952).

diaries, diarists. The tradition of diary-keeping in England seems to date from the 17th cent. The motives of the earlier diarists are unknown but an awareness that they were living in turbulent times may have inspired the most celebrated of diarists, *Pepys and *Evelyn. *The Diary of Ralph Josselin*, 1616–83, ed. Alan Macfarlane (1976), gives an intimate portrait of the domestic life, illnesses, and religious attitudes of a clergyman-farmer in Essex. There are many nonconformist diaries, including those of the ex-communicant Oliver Heywood (1630–1702), published in four volumes (1881–5), and the Presbyterian Peter Walkden (1684–1769): the *Journal* of the Revd John *Wesley is perhaps the finest example in this tradition. Self-awareness emerges in the licentious *London Journal* of *Boswell, written for his friend John Jonston, and unpublished until 1950, when it was edited by F. A. Pottle. By the late 18th cent. diary-keeping was commonplace, and authors frequently intended publication, as did Fanny *Burney, whose first diary (1767) was addressed to Nobody 'since to Nobody can I be wholly unreserved'. *Byron's friend Thomas *Moore instructed his executors to publish his *Journal* (1818–41) to 'afford the means of making some provision for my wife and family'. Literary and artistic circles are recorded in the journals of Dorothy *Wordsworth, and in those of the painter Benjamin Robert *Haydon, whose last entry records his suicide.

The flourishing tradition of political diaries began with the *Memoirs* (1821–60) of Charles *Greville, clerk to the Privy Council, which were criticized for indiscretion when published between 1874 and 1887. Twentieth-cent. diarists have made a virtue of indiscretion, and have also benefited from post-Freudian self-analysis. The diaries of diplomat Harold *Nicolson and the urbane parliamentarian and socialite Henry 'Chips' Channon (1897–1958), the latter edited by Robert Rhodes James from a massive 30 volumes in 1967, are as noteworthy for their colourful gossip as for their historical records. Twentieth-cent. literary diarists, with widely contrasted styles and purposes, include V. *Woolf, A. *Bennett, E. *Waugh and N. *Coward. Architectural historian James Lees-Milne (1908–97) published several highly praised sharp and anecdotal volumes principally describing upper-class and country-house life. The late 20th-cent. vogue for sexual candour is exemplified in the *Diaries* (1986, ed. John Lahr) of the homosexual playwright Joe *Orton. Recently the questionable practice of writing diaries for virtually immediate publication has become routine in both politics and the arts: notable examples are the *Diaries* (1993) of politician Alan Clark, son of Kenneth *Clark; *Peter *Hall's Diaries* (1983, ed. John Goodwin) and *The Roy Strong Diaries 1967–87* (1997), by art historian and arts administrator Sir Roy Strong (1935–). Comic fictional diaries were popular in the 1880s, the most celebrated example being the *Grossmiths' *The Diary of a Nobody* (1892), and have recently been successfully revived with *The Secret Diary of Adrian Mole, aged 13¾* by Sue Townsend *(1982: originally created for the *BBC*) and Helen Fielding's *Bridget Jones's Diary* (1996).

Diarmid, or **Diarmait O'Duibhne,** in the legends and relating to the Irish hero *Finn, the lover of *Grainne.

Diary of a Country Parson, The, see WOODFORDE.

Diary of a Nobody, The, by G. and W. *Grossmith, published 1892.

Charles Pooter's diary covers 15 months of his life in the early 1890s. His entries, describing the events of his life with his wife Carrie in Brickfield Terrace, Holloway, reveal in cumulative detail the society of anxious gentility in which he lives. Pooter emerges as worthy, deferential, and acutely sensitive to minor humiliations, such as those he suffers at the Mansion House reception or the Volunteer Ball. The wide variety of people who impinge upon him include his son, the 'fast' young Lupin, and his shocking fiancée Daisy Mutlar; the revered superior, Mr Perkup; the fashionable spiritualist, Mrs James of Sutton, who unsettles Carrie; the noisy Gowing, the fatuous Padge, cheeky errand boys, and tiresome servants. Text and illustrations reveal much precise contemporary background, including the details of clothes, the plaster antlers and splayed fans of the décor, the new fad for the bicycle, the fashion for imitations of Sir H. *Irving, and the admired slang and popular songs of the time. *Belloc's assertion that Pooter was 'an immortal achievement' is not often challenged.

DIBDIN, Charles (1745–1814), actor, dramatist, and songwriter, born at Southampton, who is best remembered for his sea songs, including 'The Lass that Loved a Sailor' and 'Tom Bowling', said to have been inspired by his brother Tom, a naval captain who died at Cape Town in 1780. He wrote many musical entertainments (including *The Waterman*, 1774) and dramatic monologues; also an autobiography, *The Professional Life of Mr Dibdin . . . with the Words of Six Hundred Songs* (4 vols, 1803), in which he describes his relations with *Garrick and others. His son Charles (1768–1833), by the actress Harriet Pitt, was also a playwright; his son Thomas John (1771–1841) composed some 2,000 songs, many attributed to his father.

DIBDIN, Michael John (1947–), crime novelist, born in Wolverhampton and brought up in Northern Ireland, educated at the University of Sussex and the University of Alberta, Canada. Before becoming a full-time writer in 1989 he earned his living through house painting, teaching English in Perugia, Italy, and drafting dictionary entries for the Oxford University Press. He is admired for taking the crime genre into areas associated with literary fiction: his novels, characterized by their wit, pessimism, and strong sense of place, explore the moral complexities of urban life, sexual behaviour, and the demands and deceptions of the world of work. *The Last Sherlock Holmes Story* (1978) and *A Rich Full Death* (1986) are pastiche thrillers with historical settings. The Inspector Aurelio Zen books (*Ratking* (1988), *Vendetta* (1990), *Cabal* (1992), *Dead Lagoon* (1994), *Così Fan Tutti* (1996), and *A Long Finish* (1998)) are set in Italy: the forensic detail of the traditional detective story is rejected in favour of an examination of corruption, bureaucracy, and the complex manœuvres of the detective's professional and personal life. *Dirty Tricks* (1991) blends suspense and black comedy, while *The Dying of the Light* (1993) reworks the conventions of the country-house mystery to produce a disturbing social satire. *Dark Spectre* (1995), the story of a murderous religious sect, combines features of the 'police procedural' story with reflections on the rootless nature of urban life, the acceptance of violence, and the complexity of group behaviour. (See also DETECTIVE FICTION.)

DIBDIN, Thomas Frognall (1776–1847), nephew of Charles *Dibdin, educated at Oxford, a renowned bibliographer and librarian to Lord Spencer at Althorp. He published his *Introduction to the Knowledge of Rare and Valuable Editions of the Greek and Latin Classics* in 1802, and in 1809 his *Bibliomania* ('a bibliographical romance'), which did much to stimulate interest in old books and rare editions. Dibdin became the first secretary of the bibliophiles' *Roxburghe Club when it was founded in 1812. *A Bibliographical, Antiquarian, and Picturesque Tour in France and Germany* was published in 1821, and his *Library Companion* in 1824. In his *Bibliophobia* (1832) he comments with surprise on the respectful manner of the publisher John *Murray to his authors, and examines the depressed state of the book trade. *Reminiscences of a Literary Life* followed in 1836, and his *Bibliographical, Antiquarian, and Picturesque Tour in the Northern Counties of England* in 1838.

Dick, Mr, the amiable lunatic in Dickens's *David Copperfield*.

DICK, Philip K., see SCIENCE FICTION.

DICKENS, Charles John Huffham (1812–70), born in Portsmouth, the son of a clerk in the navy pay office. He spent the happiest period of his boyhood in Chatham; this was followed by a period of intense misery which deeply affected him, during which his father was imprisoned for debt in the Marshalsea and he himself (aged 12) worked in a blacking warehouse. Memories of this painful period inspired much of his fiction, notably the early chapters of *David Copperfield*. He then worked as an office boy; studied shorthand; and became reporter of debates in the Commons for the *Morning Chronicle*. He contributed to the *Monthly Magazine* (1833–5), to the *Evening Chronicle* (1835), and to other periodicals the articles subsequently republished as *Sketches by 'Boz', Illustrative of Every-Day Life and Every-Day People* (1836–7); these attracted much attention and led to an approach from *Chapman and Hall which resulted in the creation of Mr Pickwick, and the publication in 20 monthly numbers (beginning April 1836) of The Posthumous Papers of the Pickwick Club, published in volume form in 1837 when Dickens was only 25 years old. (See PICKWICK PAPERS.) After a slow start the series achieved immense popularity, and Dickens, with his young wife Catherine Hogarth, embarked on a promising future, courted by publishers, admired by the public, and befriended by celebrities. On Christmas Day 1836 he met John *Forster, who became his close friend and biographer.

In 1837 (a year overshadowed by the death of his much-loved sister-in-law Mary) *Oliver Twist* began to appear in monthly numbers in *Bentley's Miscellany, a new periodical of which Dickens was the first editor. It was followed by *Nicholas Nickleby, also in monthly numbers. In 1840 a new weekly was launched, written wholly by Dickens, called *Master Humphrey's Clock; it was originally intended to carry short sketches as well as instalments of the full-length novels *The Old Curiosity Shop (1840–1) and his long-deliberated *Barnaby Rudge (1841), but the novels proved so popular that the linking by 'Master Humphrey' was dropped. In 1842 he and his wife visited America, where he was rapturously received. His first impressions were favourable, but disillusion followed and his *American Notes* (1842) caused much offence in America, as did his portrayal of American stereotypes in *Martin Chuzzlewit (1843–4). While in America he advocated international copyright and the abolition of slavery.

The sales of *Martin Chuzzlewit* were disappointing, but the demands of the public and his own growing family were met by the success of *A Christmas Carol (1843), the first of a series of Christmas books (*The Chimes, *The Cricket on the Hearth, The Battle of Life, and *The Haunted Man), works described by him as 'a whimsical sort of masque intended to awaken loving and forebearing thoughts'. In 1844 he paid a long visit to Italy, which produced 'Pictures from Italy' contributed to the *Daily News, a new radical paper founded by Dickens in 1846 and briefly edited by him. He began *Dombey and Son (1848) during a visit to Switzerland in 1846. In 1850 he started the weekly periodical *Household Words, in 1859 it was incorporated into All the Year Round, which he continued to edit until his death. In this he published much of his later writings, including the Christmas stories that replaced the Christmas books. *David Copperfield* appeared in

monthly numbers in 1849–50; *Bleak House* in 1852–3; and A Child's History of England (a work which manifests his own historical bias: his heroes were Alfred and Cromwell) appeared irregularly, 1851–3. *Hard Times appeared in 1854, *Little Dorrit in 1855–7, *A Tale of Two Cities in 1859, *Great Expectations in 1860–1, and *Our Mutual Friend in 1864–5.

During these years of intense productivity he also found time for his large family, for a vast circle of friends, and for philanthropic enterprises, at times combined with his passion for amateur theatricals; it was a fund-raising performance of Wilkie *Collins's The Frozen Deep in 1857, in aid of *Jerrold's family, that introduced him to the young actress Ellen Ternan. His admiration for her further strained his deteriorating relationship with his wife, and he and Catherine separated in 1858. He defied scandal, protested his own innocence (and that of his sister-in-law Georgina, for many years his devoted housekeeper, whose name gossip had also linked with his), and continued to appear in public, distracting himself from domestic sorrow by throwing his restless energy into public readings of his own works. These, though immensely successful, were physically and emotionally exhausting. He revisited America in 1867–8, delivered a series of readings there, and on his return continued to tour the provinces. He died suddenly in 1870, leaving unfinished his last novel, The Mystery of *Edwin Drood.

Dickens captured the popular imagination as no other novelist had done and, despite some murmurs against his sensationalism and sentimentality and his inability to portray women other than as innocents or grotesques, he was also held in high critical esteem, admired by contemporaries as varied as Queen *Victoria and *Dostoevsky. But it was not until this century that he began to attract serious academic attention; see in particular G. *Orwell, 'Charles Dickens', in Inside the Whale (1940), H. House, The Dickens World (1941), and E. *Wilson, 'Dickens: The Two Scrooges' (1941). Later criticism has tended to praise the complexity of the sombre late works at the expense of the high-spirited humour and genius for caricature traditionally labelled 'Dickensian'. Mention should also be made of the series of distinguished illustrators inseparably connected with his work, which includes H. K. *Browne ('Phiz'), *Leech, *Cruikshank, G. Cattermole, and S. L. Fildes; also of his collaboration with Wilkie Collins in various stories which appeared in Household Words.

J. Forster, The Life of Dickens (1872–4); Edgar Johnson, Charles Dickens: His Tragedy and Triumph (1952); G. H. Ford, Dickens and His Readers: Aspects of Novel Criticism since 1836 (1955); P. A. W. Collins, Dickens and Crime (1962); P. Collins (ed.), Dickens: The Critical Heritage (1971). A collected edition of Dickens's c.14,000 letters, instigated by Humphry House, was published under the general editorship of Madeline House, Graham Storey, and Kathleen Tillson, vols i–xi (1965–99), vol. xii (2001).

DICKENS, Monica Enid (1915–92), English novelist, born in London, the great-granddaughter of Charles *Dickens. Her works of fiction included the best-selling *One Pair of Hands* (1939), based on her experiences as a cook and general servant, *One Pair of Feet* (1942), reflecting her years as a wartime nurse, and *My Turn to Make the Tea* (1951), which drew on her time as a reporter on a local newspaper. She continued to incorporate first-hand experiences into her novels with *No More Meadows* (1953) and *Kate and Emma* (1964), which arose from her involvement with the National Society for the Prevention of Cruelty to Children, while her work for the Samaritans (the first American branch of which she founded in 1974) produced *The Listeners* (1970). She moved to America on her marriage to an American naval commander, but returned to England in 1985 after his death.

DICKENSON, John (fl. 1591–8), a minor Elizabethan writer and poet. His *Arisbas* (1594) is a euphuistic romance and *The Shepheardes Complaint* (?1596), written in English hexameters with connecting prose passages, is reminiscent of Sidney's *Arcadia*. His *Greene in Conceipt: New Raised from His Grave* (1598) tells the 'Tragique Historie of faire Valeria of London'.

DICKINSON, Emily Elizabeth (1830–86), American poet, born in Amherst, Massachusetts, the daughter of a successful lawyer. She was educated at Amherst Academy (1834–47) and Mount Holyoake (1847–8); during her early years she was lively, witty, and sociable, but from her mid-twenties she gradually withdrew into an inner world, eventually, in her forties, refusing to leave her home, and avoiding all contact with strangers, although she maintained intimate correspondences with people she never saw face to face. Her emotional life remains mysterious, despite much speculation about a possible disappointed love affair, for which one candidate is the Revd Charles Wadsworth, with whom she corresponded and who twice visited her; another is Samuel Bowles, editor of the *Springfield Republican*, to whom she sent and addressed many poems. She wrote poetry from girlhood onward, but only seven poems out of nearly 2,000 are known to have been published during her lifetime, and those appeared anonymously and much edited. She at one stage actively sought publication, but her contemporaries found her work bewildering, and she appears to have accepted her lot as an unrecognized writer—her 'Barefoot-Rank'. From c.1858 she assembled many of her poems in packets of 'fascicles', which were discovered after her death; a selection, arranged and edited by Mabel Loomis Todd and T. W. Higginson, appeared in 1890. Full publication was delayed by family difficulties, but eventually other editions and volumes of letters appeared, restoring her individual punctuation and presentation. At first regarded as an eccentric minor poet, she is now considered a major writer of startling originality. Her work presents recurrent themes—a mystic apprehension of the natural world, a preoccupation with poetic vocation, fame, death, and immortality—and is expressed in a rhetoric and language of her own, cryptic, elliptical, and at times self-dramatizing and hyperbolic. Her imagery reflects an intense and painful inner struggle over many years; she refers to herself as 'the queen of Calvary', and her verse is full of allusions to volcanoes, shipwrecks, funerals, storms, imprisonments, and other manifestations of natural and human violence. Her simultaneous conviction of isolation and 'election' was dramatized in her way of life, which is vividly described in R. B. Sewall's biography (2 vol., 1974).

DICKINSON, Goldsworthy Lowes (1862–1932), humanist and historian, educated at Charterhouse and at King's College, Cambridge, where he was to become a fellow and to spend much of his life as teacher and mentor. He was a member of the *Apostles, and a friend of R. *Fry and other members of the *Bloomsbury circle. He wrote on Hellenism, Plato, and the Socratic method: see *The Greek View of Life* (1896), *The Meaning of Good* (1901), *A Modern Symposium* (1905), and other works. He was also much interested in China: his *Letters from John Chinaman*, first published anonymously in the *Saturday Review* (1901), preceded his only visit to that country in 1913. He was deeply shocked by the outbreak of the First World War, and in later years, became involved in the work of the League of Nations, the concept of which he had helped to initiate, and the name of which he may have invented. A biography by E. M. *Forster (1934) celebrates his friend Goldie as 'affectionate, unselfish, intelligent, witty, charming'.

dictionary. The origins of the English dictionary are found in the late 16th cent. when people became aware of the two levels of English ('learned', 'literary', *'inkhorn', distinct from 'spoken', 'popular') to an extent that made it desirable to gloss one in the other's terms, as previously Latin or French had been glossed by English. Cawdrey's *Table Alphabeticall of Hard Wordes* (1604), containing about 3,000 words, might be called the first English dictionary; Henry Cockeram's *English Dictionarie* (1623) translates hard words to easy as well as easy to hard. The first major English dictionary was N. *Bailey's *Universal Etymological English Dictionary* (1721), which had more entries than its famous successor Dr *Johnson's Dictionary (1755). Johnson's Dictionary is one of the two great landmarks in English lexicographical history; Johnson illustrates his words in practice, and attempts to indicate the connotations of words, as well as offering their exact meaning. A number of 19th-cent. dictionaries attempted to develop these empirical tendencies in Johnson. But the second great landmark is the greatest dictionary of any modern language, *The Oxford English Dictionary* (1884–1928), edited by J. A. H. *Murray, H. *Bradley, W. A. *Craigie, and C. T. *Onions. The *OED* attempts to give a full history of the development of all English words since the 12th cent., with full illustrative quotations, ordered according to the principal distinct senses of the word. It has been updated by a series of supplements under the editorship of R. W. Burchfield. The possibility of a dictionary organized on synchronic, rather than historical, principles was brought closer when in 1984 the *OED* files began to be converted into a computerized database. The other major English language dictionary is N. *Webster's dictionary of American English (1828; *Third New International Dictionary*, 1961), the Third being controversial on its appearance for its omission of indications of inferior usage in categories such as 'slang', 'obscene', etc. See J. A. H. Murray, *The Evolution of English Lexicography* (1900); J. R. Hulbert, *Dictionaries, British and American* (1955); J. H. Sledd and G. J. Kolb, *Dr Johnson's Dictionary* (1955); T. Starnes and G. E. Noyes, *The English Dictionary from Cawdrey to Johnson* (1946); E. L. McAdam and G. Milne (eds.), *Johnson's Dictionary: A Modern Selection* (1963); H. D. Weinbrot (ed.), *New Aspects of Lexicography* (1972).

Dictionary of National Biography, The, designed and published by George *Smith, begun in 1882 with Sir L. *Stephen as editor. It included in its original form biographies of all national notabilities from earliest times to 1900. The work has been continued by the publishing of decennial supplements. Stephen was succeeded in the editorship by Sir Sidney *Lee. Their names appear jointly on the title-pages of vols xxii–xxvi (1890), and Lee's name alone from vol. xxvii till 1911. In 1917 the *DNB* was transferred to *Oxford University Press. The 1912–21 volume was edited by H. W. C. Davis and J. R. H. Weaver; 1922–30 by J. R. H. Weaver; 1931–40 by L. G. Wickham Legg; 1941–50 by L. G. Wickham Legg and E. T. Williams; 1951–60 by E. T. Williams and Helen Palmer; 1961–70 by E. T. Williams and C. S. Nicholls; 1971–80 and 1981–5 by Lord Blake and C. S. Nicholls; 1986–90 by C. S. Nicholls. A complete revision, *The Oxford Dictionary of National Biography* (*ODNB*), edited by Colin Matthew (1941–99) and Brian Harrison, appeared in 2004, in 60 volumes and in an online version.

DICTYS CRETENSIS is the supposed author of a diary of the Trojan War which we possess in Latin. In the preface, written in the 4th cent. AD, Lucius Septimius claims that he translated the work from a Greek version prepared for Nero from a Phoenician original. Dictys claims to have been present at the siege of Troy as a companion of the Cretan Idomeneus. Like the narrative of *Dares Phrygius his diary is probably a fabrication, but the two were the chief sources of medieval Trojan legends.

Diddler, Jeremy, the chief character in James Kenney's farce *Raising the Wind* (1803). Jeremy's habit of continually borrowing small sums which he does not pay back probably gave rise to the present sense of the verb 'diddle'—to cheat or deceive.

DIDEROT, Denis (1713–84), French philosopher and man of letters. The son of a prosperous artisan, he became a leading member of the *Enlightenment. He began by translating *Shaftesbury (1745), and continued to maintain his interest in English culture, publishing an influential appreciation of S. *Richardson (1761). He also wrote two mediocre sentimental dramas, *Le Fils naturel* (1757) and *Le Père de famille* (1758) which demonstrate his faith in the dramatic viability of bourgeois domestic subjects, a theory influenced by *Lillo; he also adapted E. *Moore's prose tragedy *The Gamester*, as *Est-il bon? Est-il méchant?* (which was never performed). He developed a scientific empiricism which, far from turning him into a mere experimenter, served only to stimulate the originality of his thought. His *Pensées sur l'interprétation de la nature* (1754), for example, anticipated evolutionary ideas on the nature and origin of life. In 1746 he assumed what became, in effect, a 20-year editorship of the *Encyclopédie. He closed his literary career with a number of seminal narratives, notably *Le Neveu de Rameau* (1761, later translated by *Goethe) and *Jacques le fataliste* (1773, a work influenced by *Sterne), which explore the complexities of the relations between psychology and morality. *La Religieuse* (*The Nun*, written 1760, pub. 1796, trans. 1797) is a mildly erotic romance about the sufferings of a young woman forced to become a nun. See *Diderot: A Critical Biography* (1992) by P. N. Furbank.

DIDION, Joan (1934–), American essayist and novelist, known for her uncompromising depictions of contemporary American society, in collections of essays such as *Slouching towards Bethlehem* (1968), in which the deteriorating California of the 1960s comes to represent the decline in seriousness of the USA and the world. This was followed by *The White Album* (1979) and *Sentimental Journeys* (1993; originally published as *After Henry*, 1992), where she brings her laconic prose and sense of cultural despair to scrutinize three American cities. She has published four novels which deal with the difficulties faced by women in a patriarchal society: in *Play It As It Lays* (1970) the main character has a mental breakdown, in *The Book of Common Prayer* we see the collapse of a mother–daughter relationship. Following a visit to San Salvador in 1973 she wrote *Salvador* (1983), describing the repressive political regime. This was followed by *Miami* (1987), where she traced the attempts of marginalized Hispanic communities to become integrated into society. *Joan Didion: Essays and Conversations* was published in 1984.

Dido Queene of Carthage, The Tragedie of, written by *Marlowe and *Nashe, possibly while they were at Cambridge together. It was performed at unknown dates by the Children of the Queen's Chapel, and published in 1594. It is closely based on Virgil's *Aeneid* (Bks 1, 2, and 4), depicting Dido's failure to persuade Aeneas to stay with her in Carthage and her subsequent suicide.

'Dies Irae', 'Day of wrath', the first words of one of the greatest medieval Latin hymns, authorship of which is attributed to Thomas of Celano (d. *c.*1255), the biographer of St *Francis. It is a common feature of the sung requiem mass.

Dietrich of Bern, the name given in the *Nibelungenlied* to Theodoric 'of Verona', a great king of the Ostrogoths (*c.*454–526), who invaded Italy and decisively defeated Odoacer at Verona (Bern) in 489. He was the hero of the German epics of the 13th cent. and of the Teutonic race in general, and the centre round which clustered many legends.

DIGBY, Sir Kenelm (1603–65), author, diplomatist, naval commander (who defeated the French and Venetian fleets in Scanderoon harbour (now İskenderun, Turkey), 1628), and one of the first members of the *Royal Society; he discovered the necessity of oxygen to the life of plants, but less scientifically believed in the curing of wounds by 'powder of sympathy'. In 1625 he secretly married the celebrated beauty Venetia Stanley, and gives an account, under disguised names, of his wooing in his *Private Memoirs* (published 1827); her situation is said to have provided the plot of *Shirley's *The Wedding,* and her death in 1633 was lamented by *Jonson, *Habington, and others. He published a criticism of Browne's *Religio Medici* in 1643, and wrote 'Of Bodies' and 'Of the Immortality of Man's Soul' in the same year. A life by R. T. Petersson appeared in 1956.

Digby Plays, the, three late *mystery plays from East Anglia, probably dating from the early 16th cent., bearing on them the name or initials of Myles Blomefylde (1525–1603), a collector of books from Bury St Edmunds. These long plays are outcrops from the mystery cycles, found with non-literary material in Digby MS 133. They are *Mary Magdalen, The Conversion of St Paul,* and *The Killing of the Children of Israel;* all of them, but especially *Mary Magdalen,* have considerable literary and theatrical interest. They have been edited by D. C. Baker, J. L. Murphy, and L. B. Hall Jr (EETS OS 283, 1982).

Dilettanti, Society of the, originally founded about 1732 as a dining society by some gentlemen of wealth and position who had travelled in Italy. It soon devoted itself to the patronage of the fine arts. It has chiefly encouraged the study of classical archaeology. See Lionel Cust's history of the society (1898).

DILKE, Sir Charles Wentworth (1843–1911), radical statesman, educated at Trinity Hall, Cambridge, and later called to the bar. He became member of Parliament for Chelsea in 1868 and held offices under *Gladstone. On his father's death in 1869 he inherited the baronetcy and the proprietorship of the *Athenaeum* and *Notes and Queries.* He was the author of

Greater Britain (1868), a record of his travels through English-speaking countries; *Problems of Greater Britain* (1890), an account of questions dealing with the empire; and *The Fall of Prince Florestan of Monaco* (1874), a political satire. In 1885 he married the widow of Mark *Pattison (née Emilia Francis Strong, 1840–1904, historian of French art and author of *Claude Lorrain,* 1884; *The Shrine of Death,* 1886; etc.). It has been suggested that Dilke might have succeeded Gladstone but for his connection with a divorce scandal (*Crawford* v. *Crawford and Dilke*) which led to his defeat and temporary retirement in 1886. He was returned member for the Forest of Dean in 1892. See R. Jenkins, *Sir Charles Dilke: A Victorian Tragedy* (1958).

DILLON, Wentworth, fourth earl of Roscommon (?1633–85), educated at Caen, author of a blank-verse translation of *Horace's *Ars Poetica* (1680) and an *Essay on Translated Verse* (1684). In 1685 he became the first critic publicly to praise *Paradise Lost.*

Dimmesdale, the Revd Arthur, a character in Hawthorne's *The Scarlet Letter.*

Dinmont, see DANDIE DINMONT.

DIODATI, Charles (d. 1638), schoolfellow and close friend of *Milton, and son of an Italian Protestant settled in London. Milton addressed to him two Latin elegies and an Italian sonnet, and mourned him in the pastoral *Epitaphium Damonis* (?1640).

DIODORUS SICULUS, a Greek historian of the latter half of the 1st cent. BC. The surviving portion of his history of the world was translated into Latin by Poggio, and Bks 1–5, which gave an account of Egypt, Assyria, and early Greece, were widely read in the 16th and 17th cents. *Skelton produced a translation into English, and there are references to it in D. *Lindsay, *Kirke, *Milton, and even W. *Morris.

DIONYSIUS THE AREOPAGITE, (1) a disciple of St Paul, passingly mentioned (Acts 17: 34); (2) more importantly, a 5th-cent. Neoplatonic writer (now known as Pseudo-Dionysius) claimed to be this disciple, in an attempt to give canonical authority to elements of mysticism and *Neoplatonism which he attempted to introduce, with considerable success. His works, the most important of which was *The Divine Names,* first appeared in 532. This work, and the Commentary on it by Maximus the Confessor (580–662), was very influential on *Scotus Erigena and on the whole medieval mystical tradition. The 14th-cent. mystical prose work *Deonise Hid Divinite* (EETS OS 231, 1949, ed. P. Hodgson) is founded on him, as its name suggests, and John *Colet later drew on him for his lectures in Oxford 1497–8.

Dionyza, in Shakespeare's *Pericles,* wife of Cleon, governor of Tarsus, to whom Pericles entrusts his daughter *Marina.

'Dipsychus', a poem by *Clough.

dirty realism, a phrase coined in 1983 by editor Bill Buford to describe the work of a group of American writers whom he included in *Granta 8*. These were Frederick Barthelme (b. 1943), Raymond *Carver, Bobbie Anne Mason (b. 1941), Jayne Anne Phillips (b. 1952), Richard *Ford, Elizabeth Tallent (b. 1954), and Tobias *Wolff. Buford describes them as being characterized by a flat low-key realism, and by 'unsurprised' language, pared down to the plainest of plain styles, dealing with unadorned daily life. They were neither a group nor a movement, and went their own ways, but the tag proved memorable.

discourse, a linguistic or rhetorical term with a multitude of senses, ranging from a single extended speech to the whole realm of language in practical use. In linguistics, 'discourse analysis' is a formal study of the ways in which sentences are connected into larger units of speech or writing. In modern literary and cultural analysis, especially in the post-*structuralist mode inaugurated by M. *Foucault, a particular discourse is understood to be a field of linguistic power in which certain authorities (e.g. judges or priests) define an object of expertise and a special vocabulary for discussing it, along with rules governing what is appropriate for each party to say in certain exchanges (e.g. sentencing, confession). Use of the term often indicates a desire to study specific contexts of linguistic and literary usage, rather than the abstract codes of 'language' in general.

Discourse Concerning the Original and Progress of Satire, A, by *Dryden.

The Discourse was published with *The Satires* (1693) of *Juvenal and *Persius, translated by various hands, among them Dryden's. Less impressive for its scholarship (which is not, however, negligible) than for its broad sense of the principles underlying literary and social history, it distinguishes between 'Varronian', 'Horatian', and 'Juvenalian' satire in a way that has considerably influenced criticism of Dryden's own satirical works and that of his Augustan successors.

DISKI, Jenny (1947–), novelist and critic, born in London. After a disturbed childhood, some of it spent in institutional care, she studied anthropology, a discipline which informs much of her fiction. Her bold and painful first novel, *Nothing Natural* (1986), describes an independent, socially responsible single mother in London trapped in a sadomasochistic relationship which plunges her into suicidal depression. *Rainforest* (1987) is an ecological drama about sexual obsession, chaos, and order, which moves between the tropical forests of Borneo, Surrey, and north London. Other works, which continue to investigate social and sexual roles, and extreme states of consciousness, include *Then Again* (1990, which interweaves the past and present of the divided-adopted Esther/Elizabeth in an exploration of Jewish persecu-

tion, religious obsession, historic identity, and disturbed adolescence), *Happily Ever After* (1991), and *Monkey's Uncle* (1994). *The Dream Mistress* (1996) again explores sexuality and identity, using as focus a derelict bag lady discovered on the streets of Camden Town in north London. A volume of autobiography, *Skating to Antarctica* (1997), describes her passion for oblivion symbolized by a voyage to Antarctica. The narrative, which explores an obsession with the colour white, is given dramatic contrast through scenes of recollection stimulated by her daughter's curiosity about the past and a painful family history.

DISRAELI, Benjamin (1804–81), first earl of Beaconsfield, politician, prime minister, and novelist. The oldest son of I. *D'Israeli, Benjamin attended private schools in and near London, but acquired much of his education in his father's extensive library. When he was 15 he wrote a short tale, 'A True Story', which Leigh *Hunt published in the *Indicator* in 1820. At 17 he was articled in Lincoln's Inn but was more interested in the literary world inhabited by his father. He was to attempt an ambitious variety of literary forms (including epic, verse tragedy, and satire) before he settled on the novel. In 1826, with profits from speculative ventures in the Americas, he and John *Murray established a daily paper, the *Representative*, in opposition to *The Times, and the organization was well advanced when the boom collapsed and Disraeli withdrew; the new paper survived for seven months at great loss. *Vivian Grey, his first novel, was no doubt partly written (as were some others) to pay off debts. It was published anonymously in 1826, and its success and notoriety encouraged him to provide a continuation in 1827. In the same year he published a political satire, *Popanilla*. Between 1828 and 1831 he travelled in Spain and Italy, and made much use of these, and of subsequent travels in Albania, the Levant, and Egypt, in future novels. In 1831 he published *The Young Duke*, with a dashing, reckless, Byronic young dandy hero who takes to high society, gambling, and racing before discovering true love for his guardian's daughter May. This was followed by *Contarini Fleming (1832) and *Alroy* (1833), a highly coloured *Oriental historical romance which makes much play with cabbalistic lore and with the supernatural. In 1833 appeared 'Ixion in Heaven', a burlesque published in the *New Monthly; in 1834 a light political satire, *The Infernal Marriage*, and *The Rise of Iskander*, set in warring Albania; his one long, serious, but unsuccessful attempt at poetry, *The Revolutionary Epic*, in blank verse; and an anonymous novel, written with his sister Sarah, *A Year at Hartlebury*, the authorship of which he never admitted. *A Vindication of the English Constitution* (which contained several of the ideas developed later in *Coningsby and *Sybil) appeared in 1835; the *Junius-inspired *Letters of Runnymede*, together with *The Spirit of Whiggism*, in 1836; and in those years also various stories in *Heath's Book of Beauty*. By 1834 Disraeli had established himself in the highest social and political society, which was vividly reflected in his next two novels: *Henrietta Temple* is a lyrical and occasionally melodramatic exploration of young love, begun in 1834, during Disraeli's open love affair with Lady Henrietta Sykes, then resumed in seclusion to escape arrest for debt in 1836. *Venetia*, also a love story, set in the 18th cent. but drawn partly from the lives of Shelley and Byron, is more restrained. Both were published in 1837, the year in which Disraeli entered Parliament as member for Maidstone. *Count Alarcos*, an abortive attempt at verse drama set in 13th-cent. Spain, was published in 1839, but was not performed until 1868 when Disraeli was prime minister.

Disraeli's fame as orator and wit continued to flourish, as did his parliamentary career, and for a while his political and literary interests worked together. The trilogy for which he is most renowned, *Coningsby* (1844), *Sybil* (1845), and *Tancred* (1847), was written, he declared, because it was through novels that he felt he could best influence public opinion, and they may be regarded as the first truly political (*'Condition-of-England') novels in English, which owe much to the Blue Book enquiries of the day as well as to personal observations made during a tour of the north of England in 1844. The first two, much of which are concerned with the conditions of the rural and urban poor, were particularly successful, and certain attitudes in them foreshadowed future social legislation: in them, Disraeli spoke for the 'Young England' party of which he had become a recognized leader. ('Almost everything that is great has been done by youth.') In 1852 Disraeli published *Lord George Bentinck: A Political Biography*, in tribute to his late friend and colleague, whom he had succeeded as leader of the Tory party in 1848, and who had supported him in his courageous stand for the removal of the civil and political constraints which prevented Jews from entering Parliament. He published no more novels for more than 20 years, as his political career intensified, culminating in his appointment as prime minister, briefly in 1868, and then in 1874.

Lothair appeared in 1870, and the first collected edition of the novels, with an illuminating preface by the author, was published in the same year. He became earl of Beaconsfield in 1876, the year in which he bestowed upon Queen Victoria the new title of empress of India. *Endymion* (1880), his last completed novel, for which he was offered the enormous sum of £10,000, was set in the period of his youth. He died when he had completed only nine brief chapters of the intriguing *Falconet*, which aimed at a satirical portrait of Gladstone in Joseph Falconet, a brilliant but humourless young MP from Clapham.

Disraeli declared, 'My works are my life', and that anyone wishing to know him would find him there. Many of the characters were intended as portraits of prominent men and women of the time. A combination of fascination and amused contempt for high society; a clever vein of irony; a gift for the telling epigram, shrewd observations of personal and political manœuvre; an apparently genuine sympathy for poverty and oppression; a skill in the portrayal of clever women and of tender relationships between parents and children; and a brisk readability distinguished his novels. But a deficiency of creative power, revealed in some feeble characterization and long passages of rhetorical musing, has meant that in spite of their original popularity they have never received high critical acclaim. Even in his own day *Wordsworth described them as 'trashy' and *Trollope found them 'spurious'.

Disraeli's famous comment, 'When I want to read a novel I write one', was made on the publication of *Daniel Deronda* in 1876.

D'ISRAELI, Isaac (1766–1848), the father of B. *Disraeli, was descended from a Levantine Jewish family who had settled in Italy. He had hoped to become a creative writer, but instead turned largely to literary history. In 1791 he published the first volume of *Curiosities of Literature*, the last volume of which appeared in 1834. It was the first of several discursive and entertaining collections. His most remarkable and original work was *The Literary Character* (1795), in which he attempts to identify the qualities of temperament common to creative writers. *Byron's annotations and encouragement led to an expanded version of the book. *Calamities of Authors* followed in 1813, *Quarrels of Authors* in 1814. His study in five volumes of *The Life and Reign of Charles I* appeared in 1828–30, and *Amenities of Literature* in 1840. He also published several novels and essays, and his works were much read and enjoyed, notably by Byron, who found them both amusing and instructive.

dissociation of sensibility, a phrase coined by T. S. *Eliot in his essay 'The Metaphysical Poets' (1921) to describe a separation of thought from feeling in English poetry since the mid-17th cent. Whereas *Donne and the other 'metaphysical' poets were capable of a 'direct sensuous apprehension of thought', Eliot argued, *Milton, *Dryden, and their successors, especially the Victorian poets, suffered from a general malaise of 'the mind of England' in which thought and feeling were cultivated separately. The argument was never supported in convincing detail, and the causes of the supposed dissociation—religious, scientific, or political—never clearly identified; but Eliot's conception of English poetic history as a process of psychic and linguistic disintegration was endorsed by *Pound, *Leavis, and the American *New Critics, who sometimes referred to the phrase.

dithyramb, a lyric poem in a lofty style with a flute accompaniment in the Phrygian mode. Supposedly invented by Arion (7th cent. BC) it was originally antistrophic and sung in honour of Bacchus. Later dithyrambs were monostrophic and could be addressed to other gods.

diurnalls, see NEWSBOOKS.

Divan, a collection of short lyrics by *Hāfiz.

Dives and Pauper, a lengthy prose dialogue from 1405–10, dealing with poverty and the Ten Commandments.

Divina commedia, the greatest work of *Dante, comprising the *Inferno,* the *Purgatorio,* and the *Paradiso,* in *terza rima* (lines of 11 syllables, arranged in groups of three and rhyming a b a b c b c d c).

The *Inferno* is a description of hell, conceived as a graduated conical funnel, to the successive circles of which the various categories of sinners are assigned. The *Purgatorio* is a description of Purgatory, a mountain rising in circular ledges, on which are the various groups of repentant sinners. At the top of the mountain is the earthly paradise, where Dante encounters Beatrice. In his visit to hell and purgatory, Dante has for guide the poet *Virgil, and there he sees and converses with his lost friends or former foes. The *Paradiso* is a vision of a world of beauty, light, and song, where the Poet's guide is Beatrice. The poem is not only an exposition of the future life, but a work of moral edification, replete with symbolism and allusions based on Dante's wide knowledge of philosophy, astronomy, natural science, and history.

Dante's name first occurs in English in *Chaucer, and that of Beatrice in *Sidney; Dante was read and admired in the 17th cent. by *Milton, Jeremy *Taylor, and Sir T. *Browne, among others. The first acknowledged translation was by the artist Jonathan Richardson in 1719, a blank-verse version of the famous Ugolino episode (*Inferno,* Canto xxxiii), which remained a favourite with translators, including T. *Gray; it was also the subject of one of *Blake's illustrations. However, Dante was by no means always highly regarded or even read in the 18th cent.; Horace *Walpole in a letter to *Mason (25 June 1782) referred to him as 'extravagant, absurd, disgusting, in short a Methodist parson in Bedlam'. His reputation rose in the 19th cent. with the admiration of *Byron, *Shelley, *Carlyle, and others, and with the enthusiasm of political refugees such as *Foscolo and Gabriele Rossetti. (See *Dante in English Literature from Chaucer to Cary,* by Paget Toynbee, 2 vols, 1909.) In the 20th cent. he profoundly influenced T. S. *Eliot; his essay *Dante* (1929) and the many references and quotations in his poetry brought Dante to the attention of a new readership. Eliot particularly praises his universality, his 'visual imagination', and his power to make 'the spiritual visible'.

Among well-known translations are those of H. F. *Cary (1805–14, blank verse); *Longfellow (1867, blank terzine); P. H. Wicksteed (1899, prose); H. F. Tozer (1904, prose); G. L. Bickersteth (1932–55, *terza rima*); L. *Binyon (1933–43, *terza rima*); J. D. Sinclair (1939–46, prose); D. L. *Sayers (1949–62, *terza rima*); and C. H. *Sisson (1980, unrhymed verse). For a detailed account of Dante's translators, see G. F. Cunningham, *The Divine Comedy in English* (2 vols, 1965–6).

DIXON, Ella (Nora) Hepworth (1857–1932), daughter of William Hepworth Dixon, editor of the *Athenaeum. A prolific journalist (editing the *English-Woman,* 1895–1900), she published collections of short comic pieces (*My Flirtations,* 1892) and short stories (*One Doubtful Hour,* 1904) and a notable *New Woman novel, *The Story of a Modern Woman* (1894). Dealing with women's employment and with sexual double standards, it stresses the importance of solidarity between women. Like her short story 'The World's Slow Stain', the novel satirizes the *Yellow Book circle and Oscar *Wilde (she wrote for his magazine, *Woman's World*). Dixon's autobiography, *As I Knew Them,* appeared in 1930.

DIXON, Richard Watson (1833–1900), educated at Pembroke College, Oxford, where he became the intimate friend of *Burne-Jones and W. *Morris. He was closely involved in the *Pre-Raphaelite movement before marriage and various preferments distanced him from his early life. He became a minor canon in Carlisle in 1868 and published, despite difficulties of access to libraries, an important *History of the Church of England from the Abolition of the Roman Jurisdiction* (1878–1902). His original and striking poetry found few but discriminating admirers, including *Bridges and G. M. *Hopkins; his correspondence with Hopkins (ed. C. C. Abbott, 1935), covering the years 1878–88, in which the two poets offer each other support and encouragement, is of great interest. His long narrative poem *Mano* (1883), set in the year AD 999 as the world awaits the millennium, recounts in *terza rima* the adventures of Mano, a Norman knight; but as a poet Dixon is now better remembered for his shorter pieces ('Dream', 'The Wizard's Funeral'), reprinted with a memoir by Bridges in a selection in 1909. See J. Sambrook, *A Poet Hidden* (1962).

DNB, see DICTIONARY OF NATIONAL BIOGRAPHY.

Dobbin, Colonel William, a character in Thackeray's *Vanity Fair.

DOBELL, Sydney Thompson (1824–74). He published in 1850 *The Roman,* a dramatic poem inspired by sympathy with oppressed Italy which had some success, and in 1854 *Balder,* one of the most extreme productions of the *Spasmodic school. This lengthy dramatic poem, of which only the first part was completed, describes the inner turmoil and aspirations of a young poet, who has taken his bride and baby daughter to live in 'a tower gloomy and ruinous' while he plans his great work. His search for the ultimate experience of death is rewarded by the death of his baby in mysterious circumstances; his wife Amy goes mad; and finally, unable to witness her sufferings, Balder kills her. Balder's destructive egoism so shocked readers that Dobell prefaced a second edition with an explanation, claiming that his hero was not held up for admiration, but as a warning. Balder's lines 'Ah! Ah! Ah! | Ah! Ah! Ah! Ah! Ah! Ah! Ah! Ah! Ah! Ah!' demonstrate the violent incoherence of which the school was capable, and which was so ridiculed by *Aytoun, but the poem nevertheless contains some notable lyric passages. In 1855 Dobell published (jointly with Alexander *Smith) *Sonnets on the War* and in 1856 *England in Time of War*, which contains the ballad with the refrain 'O Keith of Ravelston' ('A Nuptial Eve'), much admired by D. G. *Rossetti.

DOBSON, Henry Austin (1840–1921), educated at Beaumaris Grammar School and at Strasbourg. He entered the board of trade, where he served from 1856 to 1901, with *Gosse as close friend and colleague. He was an accomplished writer of verse of the lighter kind, with a particular fondness for French forms such as the triolet and the rondeau; many of his best-known poems evoke the courtly elegance of French society of the 18th cent. as portrayed, notably, by *Watteau. His collections include *Vignettes in Rhyme* (1873), *Proverbs in Porcelain* (1877), and *At the Sign of the Lyre* (1885). His knowledge of the 18th cent. was also displayed in prose biographies of *Hogarth (1879), *Steele (1886), *Goldsmith (1888), Horace *Walpole (1890), S. *Richardson (1902), and F. *Burney (1903). Under the title of *Four Frenchwomen* (1890) he published essays on Charlotte Corday, Mme Roland, the Princesse de Lamballe, and Mme de Genlis. He also published three series of *Eighteenth Century Vignettes* (1892/4/6), besides several volumes of collected essays. See *Austin Dobson* (1928) by Alban Dobson, with essays by Gosse and *Saintsbury.

Doctor, etc., The, a miscellany by R. *Southey, published 1834–47 (7 vols).

It consists of a series of essays and observations on a great variety of subjects, reflecting Southey's wide range of reading and interests. It differs from a commonplace book in that the articles are connected, somewhat loosely, by the story of an imaginary Dr Dove of Doncaster and his horse Nobs. It is an original and often humorous work, which was never finished, and is chiefly renowned for containing the nursery story of 'The Three Bears'.

Doctor Angelicus, *Aquinas; **Invincibilis,** *Ockham; **Irrefragabilis,** *Alexander of Hales; **Mirabilis,** Roger *Bacon; **Subtilis,** *Duns Scotus; **Universalis,** *Albertus Magnus.

Dr Faustus, *The Tragical History of,* a drama in blank verse and prose by *Marlowe, published 1604 and, in a radically different version known as the 'B-text', 1616. The earliest known performance was by the Lord Admiral's Men in 1594. It is perhaps the first dramatization of the medieval legend of a man who sold his soul to the devil, and who became identified with a Dr Faustus, a necromancer of the 16th cent. The legend appeared in the *Faustbuch,* first published at Frankfurt in 1587, and was translated into English as *The Historie of the Damnable Life, and Deserved Death of Doctor John Faustus.* Marlowe's play follows this translation in the general outline of the story, though not in the conception of the principal character, who from a mere magician becomes, under the poet's hand, a man athirst for infinite power, ambitious to be 'great Emperor of the world'.

Faustus, weary of the sciences, turns to magic and calls up Mephistopheles, with whom he makes a compact to surrender his soul to the devil in return for 24 years of life; during these Mephistopheles shall attend on him and give him whatsoever he demands. Then follow a number of scenes in which the compact is executed, notable among them the calling up of Helen of Troy, where Faustus addresses Helen in the well-known line: 'Was this the face that launched a thousand ships . . . .' The anguish of mind of Faustus as the hour for the surrender of his soul draws near is poignantly depicted. Both in its end and in the general conception of the character of Faustus, the play thus differs greatly from the *Faust* of *Goethe.

Dr Jekyll and Mr Hyde, The Strange Case of, a novel by R. L. *Stevenson, published 1886.

Dr Jekyll, a physician conscious of the duality, the mixed good and evil, in his own nature, and fascinated by the idea of the advantage that would arise if these two elements could be clothed in different personalities, discovers a drug by means of which he can create for himself a separate personality that absorbs all his evil instincts. This personality, repulsive in appearance, he assumes from time to time and calls Mr Hyde, and in it he gives rein to his evil impulses. The personality of Hyde is pure evil. It gradually gains the greater ascendancy, and Hyde commits a horrible murder. Jekyll now finds himself from time to time involuntarily transformed into Hyde, while the drug loses its efficacy in restoring his original form and character. On the point of discovery and arrest he takes his own life.

Doctor Thorne, a novel by A. *Trollope, published 1858, the third of the *'Barsetshire' series.

Dr Thorne's brother seduced the sister of a Greshambury stonemason, Roger Scatcherd, and was killed by him. Dr Thorne adopts the child of this liaison, hushes up the circumstances of her birth, and introduces her to the best local circles. There she meets and falls in love with Frank Gresham, heir to the Greshambury estate. The estate is heavily mortgaged, and the leading creditor happens to be Sir Roger Scatcherd, the former stonemason, who has now served his prison term, married, and made money as a railway contractor. It seems incumbent upon Frank to marry wealth, and release the property from embarrassment, and he halfheartedly sets about courting Miss Dunstable, whose money rests in patent medicine. Sir Roger Scatcherd dies of drink and his dissipated son Louis almost immediately follows him, leaving the Scatcherd fortunes without an heir. Thorne reveals Mary's true identity and, as Scatcherd's next of kin, she inherits. The marriage with Frank can now proceed, and Frank's maternal relatives, the de Courcys, gloss over Mary's illegitimacy. The temporizing of the grandiloquent de Courcys in the marriage-mart forms the secondary plot of the novel, a comedy heightened by the Lady Amelia's marriage to the family lawyer Mr Gazebee.

The plot of *Doctor Thorne* was suggested to the author by his brother, T. A. Trollope.

DOCTOROW, E(dgar) L(aurence) (1931–   ), American novelist who began his career as a script reader for Columbia pictures. His first novel, *Welcome to the Hard Times* (1960), reworks the western as a semi-philosophical treatise. *The Book of Daniel* (1971) is a fictionalized account of the Rosenberg trial and has much in common with R. Coover's *The Public Burning* (1977). His most commercially successful novel, *Ragtime* (1975), blends real-life figures of the early 20th cent. with a cast of emblematic Jewish and African-American characters. Subsequent work focuses on the Great Depression and its aftermath and includes *Loon Lake* (1980), *World's Fair* (1985), and *Billy Bathgate* (1989). *The Waterworks* (1994) centres on life in 19th-cent. New York.

DODD, William (1729–77), a popular preacher and the king's chaplain whose extravagance and debts led him to forge a bond in the name of his former pupil, the fifth Lord Chesterfield. Despite the efforts of Dr *Johnson and others, he was convicted and hanged. His many works include *The Beauties of Shakespeare* (1752) and *Thoughts in Prison* (1777).

DODDRIDGE, Philip (1702–51), a Nonconformist divine, a celebrated hymn-writer, and author of *The Rise and Progress of Religion in the Soul* (1745), a much-reprinted work notable for its literary as well as its devotional quality. He also published in 1747 *Some Remarkable Passages in the Life of Col. James Gardiner*, the reformed rake and colonel of dragoons (1688–1745) who became a religious enthusiast, was killed at Prestonpans, and figures in Scott's *Waverley*.

DODGSON, Charles Lutwidge (1832–98), celebrated under his pseudonym Lewis Carroll, the third in a family of eleven children of considerable literary and artistic interests; they produced family magazines which display Dodgson's love of parody, acrostics, and other word games and puzzles; he was later to invent many educational board games. He was educated at Rugby and Christ Church, Oxford, where he became a lecturer in mathematics in 1855. His most famous work, *Alice's Adventures in Wonderland* (1865), originated in a boat trip with the young daughters of H. G. *Liddell, Lorina, Alice, and Edith; it was for Alice that he expanded an impromptu

story into book form. *Through the Looking-Glass and What Alice Found There* followed in 1871: both volumes were illustrated by *Tenniel. One reviewer attributed the success of these works to the fact that, unlike most children's books of the period, they had no moral and did not teach anything. Dodgson's other works include *Phantasmagoria and Other Poems* (1869), *The Hunting of the Snark* (1876), and *Sylvie and Bruno* (1889, vol. ii, 1893, both parts expanded from a short story, 'Bruno's Revenge', published in *Aunt Judy's Magazine*, 1867). The most valuable of his various mathematical treatises is his light-hearted defence of Euclid, *Euclid and His Modern Rivals* (1879). Dodgson was also a keen amateur photographer, with a particular interest in photographing little girls, whose friendship he valued highly; he also took some striking portraits of the sons of his friend *Tennyson. His diaries were edited by R. L. Green (2 vols, 1953), his letters by M. N. Cohen with R. L. Green (2 vols, 1979), and there are lives by Anne Clark (1979) and Morton N. Cohen (1995).

DODINGTON, George Bubb (1691–1762), a time-serving politician who attained high office and a peerage (as Baron Melcombe). He was author of a Diary, published posthumously in 1784, which throws much light on the venal politics of his day. It was edited in 1965 in 2 vols by J. Carswell and L. A. Dralle as *The Political Journal of George Bubb Dodington*. His verses appeared in Dodsley's *Collection of Poems* (1755, 1758). Dodington was also a patron of the arts, and in particular of E. *Young, James *Thomson, who dedicated *Summer* to him, and H. *Fielding, who did the same with *Jonathan Wild*: in this guise he may be the *Bufo of Pope's satire. He also appears in a poem by R. *Browning (*Parleyings with Certain People*, 1887).

DODSLEY, Robert (1703–64), wrote several poems while a footman in the service of the Hon. Mrs Lowther, including *Servitude* (anon., 1729) and *The Muse in Livery; or The Footman's Miscellany* (1732). He was encouraged by his employer and other fashionable patrons, and in 1735 set up as a bookseller (with assistance from *Pope) at 'Tully's Head' in Pall Mall; his brother James (1724–97) became a partner and eventually succeeded him. He wrote several plays, including a tragedy, *Cleone* (1758), a musical afterpiece, *The Blind Beggar of Bethnal Green* (1741), and *The Toyshop, a Dramatic Satire* (1735). But he is chiefly remembered as the publisher of works by Pope, Dr *Johnson, E. *Young, *Goldsmith, T. *Gray, *Akenside, and *Shenstone and of the *Select Collection of Old Plays* (12 vols, 1744) and *A Collection of Poems, by Several Hands* (1748–58, revised and continued by Pearch, 1775). His *Collection* in particular was a classic and influential statement of mid-18th-cent. taste. In 1758 he founded, in conjunction with *Burke, *The Annual Register*. He also has the credit of having suggested the compiling of a dictionary to Dr Johnson. See R. Straus, *Dodsley: Poet, Publisher and Playwright* (1910).

Dodson and Fogg, in Dickens's *Pickwick Papers*, Mrs Bardell's attorneys.

Doeg, Dryden's name for *Settle in *The Second Part of *Absalom and Achitophel*.

Dogberry and Verges, in Shakespeare's *Much Ado about Nothing*, constables. Dogberry is a precursor of Mrs *Malaprop in his gift for misapplying words.

DOGGETT, Thomas (c.1670–1721), Dublin-born comic actor, joint manager of the Haymarket, and subsequently of Drury Lane Theatre, and friend of *Congreve and C. *Cibber.

dog-Latin, bad unidiomatic Latin; ' "Nescio quid est materia cum me", Sterne writes to one of his friends (in dog-Latin, and very sad dog-Latin too)'; *Thackeray, *The English Humorists of the Eighteenth Century*, vi.

Dolabella, a character in Shakespeare's *Antony and Cleopatra*, and in Dryden's *All for Love*.

Dol Common, one of the cheaters in Jonson's *The Alchemist*.

Doll Tearsheet, Falstaff's tavern mistress in Shakespeare's 2 *Henry IV*.

Dolly Varden, a character in Dickens's *Barnaby Rudge* who gave her name to a type of large picture hat.

Dolon, in Spenser's *Faerie Queene* (V. vi), 'A man of subtill wit and wicked minde', who tries to entrap *Britomart.

'Dolores', a poem in anapaests by *Swinburne, included in *Poems and Ballads* (1866).

One of his most notorious works, it addresses Dolores, 'Our Lady of Pain', in a profane hymn to perverse and cruel sensual delights, and contains some of his most parodied lines, e.g. 'the lilies and languors of virtue' and 'the raptures and roses of vice'. It clearly shows Swinburne's obsession with erotic pain and the image of a 'splendid and sterile' *femme fatale*, and, with other poems in the volume ('Faustine', 'Anactoria', 'Les Noyades', 'Laus Veneris', etc.), understandably provoked violent abuse. It was also much admired by many, including *Ruskin, who is said to have exclaimed during a recitation 'How beautiful! How divinely beautiful!'

Dolorous Stroke, the, the stroke dealt by *Balyn to King Pellam in Bk II of Malory's *Morte D'Arthur* (in 'The Knight with the Two Swords', the second book in the first of the *Works* in Vinaver's edition). It causes the devastation of three kingdoms and the deaths of the people in Pellam's castle, and Merlin prophesies that its disastrous effect will only be cured by the achievement of the Grail by *Galahad. Merlin links in an obscure way this slight narrative event with the whole decline of the world of Arthur, and the story is the starting point of the anthropological investigation in J. L. Weston's *From Ritual to Romance* (1920).

Dombey and Son, *Dealings with the Firm of*, a novel by *Dickens, published 1847–8.

When the story opens Mr Dombey, the rich, proud, frigid head of the shipping house of Dombey and Son, has just been presented with a son and heir, Paul, and his wife dies. The father's love and ambition are centred in the boy, an odd, delicate, prematurely old child, who is sent to Dr Blimber's school, under whose strenuous discipline he sickens and dies; the death of the little Dombey moved the nation nearly as much as the death of Little Nell in *The Old Curiosity Shop*, though later chapters were seen by many as a disappointment. Dombey neglects his devoted daughter Florence, and the estrangement is increased by the death of her brother. Walter Gay, a good-hearted youth in Dombey's employment, falls in love with her, but is sent to the West Indies by Dombey, who disapproves of their relationship. He is shipwrecked and believed drowned. Dombey marries again—a proud and penniless young widow, Edith Granger—but his arrogant treatment drives her into the arms of his villainous manager Carker, with whom she flies to France. They are pursued, Carker meets Dombey in a railway station, falls in front of a train, and is killed. (As Humphry House points out in *The Dickens World*, 1941, the effect of the railways on English life and the changing landscape is a dominant theme in the novel.) The house of Dombey fails; Dombey has lost his fortune, his son, and his wife; Florence has been driven by ill-treatment to fly from him, and has married Walter Gay, who has survived his shipwreck. Thoroughly humbled, Dombey lives in desolate solitude till Florence returns to him, and at last finds the way to his heart.

Among the other notable characters in the book are Solomon Gills, the nautical instrument-maker and uncle of Gay, and his friend Cuttle, the genial old sea-captain; Susan Nipper, Florence's devoted servant; Toots, the innocent and humble admirer of Florence; Joe Bagstock, the gouty retired major; and 'Cousin Feenix', the good-natured aristocrat.

Domesday Book, 'the Book of the day of assessment', is the name applied since the 12th cent. to the record of the great inquest or survey of the lands of England made by order of William the Conqueror in 1086. It contains a record of the ownership, area, and value of lands, and of the numbers of tenants, livestock, etc. The manuscript is in the Public Record Office in London.

DOMETT, Alfred (1811–87), remembered as a friend of R. *Browning, who lamented his departure for New Zealand in 1842 in 'Waring'. Domett remained in New Zealand until 1871, and was prime minister there for a brief period; on his return Browning encouraged the publication of his long poem about Maori life, *Ranolf and Amohia, a South-Sea Day Dream* (1872). Their correspondence was edited in 1906 by F. G. Kenyon.

DONAGHY, Michael (1954–), American poet, born to Irish parents in New York and now living in London.

His first collection, *Shibboleth* (1988), displays a rest-less imagination bringing impressive technical skills to bear on a wide-ranging subject matter, from the anecdotal to the philosophical. Themes of music and memory are central to Donaghy's work, frequently traditional music among the emigrant Irish, and in the sequence O'Ryan's Belt (*Errata*, 1993), issues of identity underlie the precarious survival of songs from forgotten musicians. *Errata* also sees Donaghy settling into longer, narrative forms to which his talent is particularly suited.

DONATUS, Aelius (4th cent. AD), a grammarian who taught at Rome and had St *Jerome among his pupils. He was the author of a Latin grammar, *Ars Grammatica*, known as the 'Donet' or 'Donat', which has served as the basis of later works. A 'Donet' is hence used for an introduction to, or the elements of, any art or science. It is mentioned in *Piers Plowman*, A V. 123, and other early English works.

Don Carlos, a tragedy by *Otway, in rhymed verse, produced 1676.

Philip II, king of Spain, having married Elizabeth of Valois, who had been affianced to his son Don Carlos, is stirred to jealousy by their mutual affection. This jealousy is inflamed by the machinations of Ruy Gomez and his wife the duchess of Eboli, till he believes in their guilty relations; he causes the queen to be poisoned and Don Carlos takes his own life, the king discovering too late their innocence.

DONIZETTI, Gaetano (1797–1848), Italian composer and one of the principal exponents of 19th-cent. Italian opera. *Scott and *Byron are both represented amongst his many opera texts: in *Parisina* (1833) the events of Byron's poem are fairly used as a framework for Felice Romani's libretto, but in *Marino Falieri* (1835) the primary source is a play by the French author Casimir Delavigne. The connection between *Il diluvio universale* (1830) and Byron's *Heaven and Earth* is even more remote, as it is with Scott in *Elisabetta, o il Castello di Kenilworth* (1829), where the novel had already been filtered through two French stage adaptations, *Hugo's *Amy Robsart* and Scribe's *Leicester*. But *Lucia di Lammermoor* (1835) remains a strong version of one of Scott's most dramatic stories, treated with passion and insight.

Don Juan, according to a Spanish story apparently first dramatized by *Tirso de Molina in *El burlador de Sevilla*, and subsequently by *Molière in *Le Festin de pierre* and in *Mozart's *Don Giovanni*, was Don Juan Tenorio, of Seville. Having attempted to ravish Doña Anna, the daughter of the commander of Seville, he is surprised by the father, whom he kills in a duel. A statue of the commander is erected over his tomb. Juan and his cowardly servant Leporello visit the tomb, when the statue is seen to move its head. Juan jestingly invites it to a banquet. The statue comes, seizes Juan, and delivers him to devils. Don Juan is the proverbial heartless and impious seducer. His injured wife is Elvira.

Don Juan is also the subject of plays by *Shadwell (*The Libertine*), *Goldoni, *Pushkin, and *Montherlant, and of a poem by *Byron (see below). For R. *Browning's Don Juan see FIFINE AT THE FAIR, and for *Shaw's see MAN AND SUPERMAN. Molière's version was translated by Christopher *Hampton (pub. 1974). *The Joker of Seville* (pub. 1978) by *Walcott is an adaptation of *El burlador de Sevilla*, based on R. *Campbell's blank verse translation.

Don Juan, an unfinished epic satire in *ottava rima* by Lord *Byron, published 1819–24.

Don Juan, a young gentleman of Seville, is sent abroad by his mother at the age of 16, in disgrace after an intrigue. His ship is wrecked and the passengers take to the long-boat. After many tribulations, in the course of which first Juan's spaniel and then his tutor are eaten by the crew, Juan is cast up on a Greek island. He is restored to life by Haidée, the daughter of a Greek pirate, and the pair fall in love. The father, who is supposed dead, returns, finds the lovers together, and captures the fighting Juan, who is put in chains on one of the pirate's ships. He is then sold as a slave in Constantinople to a sultana who has fallen in love with him. He arouses her jealousy and is threatened with death, but escapes to the Russian army, which is besieging Ismail. Because of his gallant conduct he is sent with dispatches to St Petersburg, where he attracts the favour of the Empress Catherine, who sends him on a political mission to England. The last cantos (the 'English cantos') of the unfinished work are taken up with a satirical description of social conditions in England and with the love affairs of Juan.

With *Beppo Byron had found in *ottava rima* a new form for his new voice, and he adopted it for *Don Juan*. He told his publisher, John *Murray, 'I *have* no plan . . . the Soul of such writing is its licence . . . .', but he did undoubtedly intend a longer work than the one which was cut short by his death, after 16 cantos and a fragment of a 17th. He wished the poem to be 'a little quietly facetious upon everything'. Almost every serious passage is abruptly punctured; as *Hazlitt wrote, after the 'intoxication' comes 'the splashing of the soda-water'. The outspoken wit and satire are especially directed at hypocrisy in all its forms, at social and sexual conventions, and at sentimentality. There are many attacks on the objects of Byron's scorn, among them *Southey, *Coleridge, *Wordsworth, *Wellington, Lord Londonderry, and many others. The poet told Lady *Blessington in 1823 that 'there are but two sentiments to which I am constant—a strong love of liberty, and a detestation of cant.' Both sentiments receive full expression in the poem.

Don Juan himself is a charming, handsome young man, who delights in succumbing to the beautiful women he meets, but his character is little more than the connecting thread in a long social comedy, a poetical novel, of satirical fervour and wit. The first two cantos were ill-received by the critics, who called them 'an insult and an outrage' and 'a filthy and impious poem', but the work became increasingly successful with the general public and was much admired by *Goethe, who translated a part of it.

DONLEAVY, J(ames) P(atrick) (1926–   ), novelist, born in Brooklyn of Irish parents, educated at Trinity College, Dublin, and an Irish citizen since 1967. He is best known for *The Ginger Man* (1955), a comic and bawdy account, much influenced by *Joyce, of Sebastian Dangerfield's adventures as a law student in Dublin. His other novels include *A Singular Man* (1964), *The Beastly Beatitudes of Balthazar B* (1968), *The Destinies of Darcy Dancer, Gentleman* (1977), *Schultz* (1979), *Leila* (1983), *Are You Listening Rabbi Löw* (1987), and *That Darcy, That Dancer, That Gentleman* (1990). He has also written several plays, including *Fairy Tales of New York* (1960) and various stage adaptations of his own novels. *The History of the Ginger Man*, an autobiography, was published in 1993.

DONNE, John (1572–1631), related on his mother's side to Sir T. *More, born into a Catholic family, his uncle Jasper Heywood being the leader of the Jesuit mission in England. His father, a prominent member of the London Ironmongers' Company, died when Donne was 4, and six months later his mother married a Catholic physician, Dr John Syminges. Educated at home by Catholic tutors, Donne went at the age of 11 to Hart Hall, Oxford (now Hertford College), favoured by Catholics because it had no chapel, so that recusancy attracted less notice. He may have transferred to Cambridge, but his religion (which he appears to have renounced c.1593) debarred him at this point from taking a degree in either university. In 1589–91 he may have travelled on the Continent, to Italy and Spain. He sailed as a gentleman volunteer with *Essex to sack Cadiz (1596) and with *Ralegh to hunt the Spanish treasure ships off the Azores (1597). His poems 'The Storm' and 'The Calm' commemorate these voyages. Donne became secretary to Sir Thomas Egerton, lord keeper of the great seal, and in 1601 he was elected MP for Brackley, Northamptonshire, an Egerton seat. He forfeited his chance of a civil career when late in 1601 he secretly married Ann More, Lady Egerton's niece: he was dismissed from Egerton's service and briefly imprisoned. Donne's next 14 years were marked by fruitless attempts to live down his disgrace. At first he depended on the charity of friends and of his wife's relations, living with his ever-growing family in a cottage at Mitcham. In 1612 he moved to a London house owned by his patron, Sir Robert Drury of Hawstead, Suffolk, whom he had accompanied on his continental travels. In honour of Sir Robert's dead child Elizabeth, whom Donne had never met, he wrote his extravagant *Anniversaries*. Other friends and patrons in these years were Sir Walter Chute, with whom Donne went to the Continent in 1605–6, Sir Henry

Goodyer, probably Donne's closest friend, Lucy, countess of Bedford, Magdalen Herbert (mother of G. *Herbert), and Sir Robert Ker, Viscount Rochester, to whom Donne offered his services in the Essex divorce case. Despite Ker's good offices, James I considered that Donne was unfit for confidential employment and urged him to enter the Church, which he did in 1615. James made him a chaplain-in-ordinary and forced Cambridge (which regarded him as a careerist) to grant him a DD. In the Church Donne held several livings and the divinity readership at Lincoln's Inn. His wife died in 1617 at the age of 33, after giving birth to their 12th child, and the following year Donne went as chaplain to the earl of Doncaster in his embassy to the German princes. His 'Hymn to Christ at the Author's Last Going into Germany', full of apprehension of death, was written before this journey. In 1621 Donne procured the deanery of St Paul's. One of the most celebrated preachers of his age, as well as its greatest non-dramatic poet, he died on 31 March 1631, having first, as his earliest biographer I. *Walton records, had his portrait drawn wearing his shroud and standing on a funeral urn.

Donne was celebrated by contemporaries for his abandoning of Elizabethan classicism's 'soft, melting Phrases' through an 'imperious Wit' (T. *Carew). His earliest poems, his 'Satires and Elegies', often lubricious, dazzlingly argued, and luridly self-dramatizing, belong to the 1590s. His unfinished satirical epic 'The Progress of the Soul' bears the date 1601, and some of his Holy Sonnets were probably written in 1610–11. His 'Songs and Sonnets' are, however, largely impossible to date. These love poems encompass the intimate and tender but intellectually strenuous 'Valediction: Forbidding Mourning', the dark turbulence of 'Twicknam Garden', the sombre majesty of 'A Nocturnall upon S. Lucies Day', and libertine lyrics founded on an emotionally complex misogynist casuistry.

Donne's prose works include *Pseudo-Martyr* (1610), an attack on Catholics who had died for their faith, and *Ignatius His Conclave*, an attack on the Jesuits (1611). *Biathanatos*, a defence of suicide, to which Donne confessed a 'sickely inclination', was probably written at this time, but its subject matter made it unpublishable until after his death. His *Essays in Divinity* (1651) were composed in preparation for his ordination and the *Devotions* (1624) were assembled in less than a month from notes made during a near-fatal fever. His sermons appeared after his death in three volumes, *LXXX Sermons* (1640), *Fifty Sermons* (1649), and *XXVI Sermons* (1660). These were edited by his son John and based on texts which Donne himself prepared from his rough preaching notes during two periods of rest in the country in 1625 and 1630: their memorable exhortations include the well-known 'No man is an Iland . . . never send to know for whom the bell tolls, it tolls for thee'. His poems were collected by his son John and published in 1633 (second, enlarged, edn 1635). See also METAPHYSICAL POETS.

R. C. Bald, *John Donne: A Life* (1970); J. Carey, *John Donne: Life, Mind and Art* (1981); *Elegies and Songs and Sonnets* (ed. H. *Gardner, 1965); *Divine Poems* (ed. H. Gardner, 1952; 2nd edn, 1978); *Satires, Epigrams and Verse Letters* (ed. W. Milgate, 1967); *Epithalamions, Anniversaries and Epicedes* (ed. W. Milgate, 1978); *Paradoxes and Problems* (ed. H. Peters, 1980); *Ignatius His Conclave* (ed. T. S. Healy, SJ, 1969); *Essays in Divinity* (ed. E. M. Simpson, 1952); *Devotions upon Emergent Occasions* (ed. J. Sparrow, 1923); *Sermons* (ed. G. R. Potter and E. M. Simpson, 10 vols, 1953–62). There is no collected edition of Donne's letters, the best available approach to one still being E. *Gosse, *Life and Letters* (2 vols, 1899).

Donnithorne, Arthur, a character in G. Eliot's *Adam Bede.

Don Quixote de la Mancha, a satirical romance by *Cervantes, published 1605, a second part appearing 1615. Cervantes gave to his work initially the form of a burlesque of the ballads and romances of chivalry (see AMADIS OF GAUL and PALMERIN OF ENGLAND), which were already beginning to lose their popularity. But he soon ceased to write mere burlesque, as the character of his hero developed and deepened, and his work acquired the richness and profundity that have made it one of the most popular classics ever written.

Don Quixote, a poor gentleman of La Mancha, a man of gentle and amiable disposition and otherwise sane, has had his wits disordered by inordinate devotion to the tales of chivalry, and imagines himself called upon to roam the world in search of adventures on his old horse Rosinante, and accoutred in rusty armour, accompanied by a squire in the shape of the rustic Sancho Panza, a curious mixture of shrewdness and credulity, whom he lures with the prospect of the governorship of the island of Barataria. Quixote conforms to chivalric tradition by electing a good-looking girl of a neighbouring village as the mistress of his heart, under the style of Dulcinea del Toboso, an honour of which she is entirely unaware. To the disordered imagination of the knight the most commonplace objects assume fearful or romantic forms, and he is consequently involved in the most absurd adventures, as in the famous episode (Pt I, ch. viii) when he tilts at windmills, imagining them to be giants. Finally one of his friends, the bachelor Samson Carrasco, in order to force him to return home, disguises himself as a knight, overthrows Don Quixote, and requires him to abstain for a year from chivalrous exploits. This period Don Quixote resolves to spend as a shepherd, living a pastoral life, but, falling sick on his return to his village, after a few days he dies. The plot also contains several lengthy digressions, including the story of the *Curious Impertinent, and the story of *Cardenio and Lucinda.

After the appearance of the first part of *Don Quixote* in 1605, a continuation was issued by a writer who styled himself Alonso Fernandez de Avellaneda, a forgery which stimulated Cervantes to write his own second part. The book was translated into English between 1612 and 1620 by Thomas Shelton, and in 1700–3 by *Motteux; J. M. Cohen's Penguin Classic version first appeared in 1950. *Don Quixote* supplied the plots of several 17th-cent. English plays, and inspired and continues to inspire innumerable imitations. *Unamuno described Don Quixote and Quixotism as the genius of the Spanish nation, but he has also been adopted by many other countries.

Don Sebastian, a tragi-comedy by *Dryden, produced 1689, published 1691.

The play is based on the legend that King Sebastian of Portugal survived the battle of Alcazar. He and the princess Almeyda, with whom he is in love, are captured by Muley Moloch, who spares their lives until he discovers that they have secretly married. In love with Almeyda himself, he orders Dorax, a renegade Portuguese nobleman, to execute Sebastian, but Dorax, once Sebastian's favourite, refuses to do so. Muley Moloch is killed in a revolt, but Sebastian and Almeyda then discover that their marriage is incestuous, and they renounce each other and their thrones. However, they do not renounce the memory of their love, which is subsumed in ecstatic and total submission to the decrees of an inscrutable Providence. Counterpointing this main plot is a notably erotic and earthy sub-plot. The play is Dryden's most complex dramatic treatment of a number of important political, sexual, and religious themes.

Doolittle, Eliza, the flower seller in Shaw's *Pygmalion.

DOOLITTLE, Hilda (1886–1961), who wrote as 'H.D.' She was born in Bethlehem, Pennsylvania, and in 1911 followed her friend *Pound to Europe, where both became leading members of the Imagist movement (see IMAGISM). She married *Aldington in 1913, but the marriage was not a success. Her several volumes of poetry, from her first, *Sea Garden* (1916), to her last, the quasi-epic *Helen in Egypt* (1961), show a deep involvement with classical mythology, a mysticism in part influenced by her Moravian ancestry, a sharp, spare use of natural imagery, and interesting experiments with *vers libre*. She also published several novels, including *Bid Me to Live* (1960), a *roman à clef* about her *Bloomsbury years, and *Tribute to Freud* (1965), an account of her analysis by Freud in 1933.

Doomsday Book, see DOMESDAY BOOK.

Dora Spenlow, in Dickens's *David Copperfield, the hero's 'child-wife'.

DORÉ, (Louis Auguste) Gustave (1832–83), French illustrator and caricaturist, who became well known in London both for his illustrations of the Bible (1866) and for his drawings and engravings of London life, done in 1869–71, which appeared in B. *Jerrold's *London* (1872); they show many aspects of the city, but dwell on the picturesque clutter and squalor of the poorer districts. Doré also did a series of steel engravings for Tennyson's *Idylls of the King* (1868–9), and illustrated Coleridge's *Ancient Mariner* (1875) and the works of *Dante, *Balzac, *Ariosto, *Rabelais, *Cervantes, and many others. For many years his works were on permanent exhibition at the Doré Gallery in Bond Street, which opened in 1867. The 'agreeable terror' of his illustrations appealed to generations of children. A life by Jerrold was published in 1891.

DORFMAN, Ariel (1942–), dramatist, was born in Argentina but was a Chilean citizen, until the accession to power of General Pinochet in 1973 exiled him to America, where he became research professor of history and Latin American studies at Duke University, North Carolina, in 1992. He achieved worldwide success with his English-language *Death and the Maiden* (1990), about the attempts of a Latin American torture victim to restore her self-respect and ailing marriage by punishing the doctor she believes presided over her suffering. Subsequent plays include the complex *Reader* (1995) about a censor who discovers that the subversive book he wants to ban describes his own life, and *Widows* (1996), written in collaboration with Tony Kushner, and involving the peasant mothers, wives, and daughters of men murdered by a military regime. Dorfman has also published a book of cultural criticism, *How to Read Donald Duck* (1971), novels, and collections of poems and short stories.

Doric, an adjective from Doris, a small district south of Thessaly from which the Dorians, one of the four Greek tribes, were conventionally supposed to have emigrated to the Peloponnese about the 12th cent. BC. Archaeological evidence has failed so far to support this traditional theory, but a people speaking a common dialect (Dorian) was certainly dominant in southern and western Greece in historical times. Since the Dorians were regarded as uncivilized by the Athenians, 'Doric' came to mean 'rustic' in English and was applied particularly to the language of Northumbria and the Lowlands of Scotland, and also to the simplest of the three orders in architecture.

Dorigen, the heroine of 'The Franklin's Tale' (see CANTERBURY TALES, 12.

Dorimant, a character in Etherege's *The Man of Mode* based on *Rochester.

DOROTHEA, St, a Christian martyr who suffered in the persecution under Diocletian (303). Her story forms the subject of *The Virgin Martyr* by Massinger and Dekker.

Dorothea Brooke, the heroine of G. Eliot's *Middlemarch*.

d'ORSAY, Count Alfred Guillaume Gabriel (1801–52), a Frenchman who, coming to London in 1821, soon made himself famous as wit, dandy, and artist. He was adopted by the earl and countess of Blessington. In 1823, with his benefactors, he travelled to Genoa, where he met *Byron and made a rapid pencil sketch of the poet which has survived. In 1827 he married Lady Harriet Gardiner, Lord Blessington's daughter by a former marriage, but a separation took place almost immediately. He was prominent in the society of Gore House, at which Lady *Blessington entertained literary, political, and artistic London.

DORSET, earl of, see SACKVILLE, C., and SACKVILLE, T.

DOS PASSOS, John Roderigo (1896–1970), American novelist, born in Chicago and educated at Harvard, who served in Europe during the First World War as a member of the French ambulance service. His first important novel, *Three Soldiers* (1921), which has war as its subject, was followed by many others, as well as poetry, essays, travel writings, memoirs, and plays, which include *The Garbage Man* (1925); *Airways Inc.* (1929); and *Fortune Heights* (1933), published in 1934 as *Three Plays*. He is chiefly remembered for his novels *Manhattan Transfer* (1925), a collective portrait in hundreds of fictional episodes of life in New York City, and *U.S.A.* (1938), a trilogy composed of *The 42nd Parallel* (1930), *1919* (1932), and *The Big Money* (1936). *U.S.A.* tries to capture, through a diversity of fictional techniques, the variety and multiplicity of American life in the first decades of the 20th cent.; it presents various interlocking and parallel narratives, against a panoramic collage of real-life events, snatches of newsreel and popular song, advertisements, etc., with a commentary by the author as 'The Camera Eye'.

DOSTOEVSKY, Fyodor Mikhailovich (1821–81), Russian prose writer. Born in Moscow, he studied from 1838 to 1843 at the St Petersburg Engineering Academy. His first published work, a translation of *Balzac's *Eugénie Grandet*, appeared in 1844, followed by his first original work, the short story 'Poor Folk' (1846), 'The Double' (1846), 'White Nights' (1848), and other short prose pieces. In April 1849 Dostoevsky was arrested as a member of the socialist Petrashevsky circle. After a macabre mock execution, he was sent to a Siberian penal settlement for four years, to be followed by four years as a private soldier. During his imprisonment he underwent a religious crisis, rejecting the socialism and progressive ideas of his early years, and replacing them by a belief in the Russian Orthodox Church and the Russian people. His next publication, *The Village of Stepanchikovo*, appeared only in 1859. Then came *Notes from the House of the Dead* (1860–1), based on his period of imprisonment, which, along with the novel *The Insulted and the Injured* (1861), appeared in the journal *Time*, which he founded with his brother Mikhail. In 1862 he travelled abroad, visiting England, France, Germany, and Italy. His views on western Europe are recorded in *Winter Notes on Summer Impressions* (1863). In London, which he describes as 'Baal', centre of world capitalism, he saw the Crystal Palace of the 1862 World Exhibition, an image he was to use to express the corruption of the modern scientific world in *Notes from Underground* and other works. Another impression reflected in his later work was his horror at the poverty of Whitechapel and the prostitutes of the Haymarket. In London he also visited *Herzen and Bakunin. In 1863 *Time* was suppressed. Dostoevsky made further trips abroad throughout the 1860s. The series of brilliant works which followed, *Notes from Underground* (1864), *Crime and Punishment* (1866), *The Idiot* (1868), *The Devils* (1872), *An Adolescent* (1875; also translated as *A Raw Youth*), and *The Brothers Karamazov* (1880), are those on which his reputation is based. In them Dostoevsky reveals extraordinary powers of character analysis, considers profound religious and political ideas, and shows himself to be a significant and powerful thinker. Among English writers Dostoevsky admired Shakespeare, Sir W. *Scott, *Byron, and in particular *Dickens, who had been known and translated in Russia since around 1838. In his Omsk prison Dostoevsky read *Pickwick Papers* and *David Copperfield*. His letters and notebooks are full of references to Dickens, and they share an interest in such major subjects as the city, children, crime, and the suffering of the innocent.

Notes from the House of the Dead was translated into English in 1881, and many of Dostoevsky's novels appeared in English in the 1880s. R. L. *Stevenson was an early admirer, saying in 1886 of *Crime and Punishment*, 'The greatest book I have read in ten years . . . Many find it dull: Henry James could not finish it: all I can say is, it nearly finished me. It was like having an illness.' Its influence on *Dr Jekyll and Mr Hyde* (1886) is apparent, but in general the response of late 19th-cent. England to Dostoevsky was cool. The main impact of his work in England followed the appearance of *Baring's *Landmarks in Russian Literature* (1910), *Murry's *Fyodor Dostoevsky* (1916), and above all the translations by C. *Garnett (1912–20). There are notable recent translations by David McDuff.

Dotheboys Hall, in Dickens's *Nicholas Nickleby*, the school conducted by Mr Squeers.

Double Dealer, The, a comedy by *Congreve, produced 1693, published 1694.

The entire action of the play takes place in Lord Touchwood's house in the three hours after dinner on the night before Mellefont, nephew and prospective heir of Lord Touchwood, is about to marry Cynthia, daughter of Sir Paul Plyant. Lady Touchwood, a passionate and promiscuous woman, is in love with Mellefont's friend, and because he rejects her advances, she determines to prevent the match and ruin him in Touchwood's esteem. She finds a confederate in Maskwell, the Double Dealer, who has been her lover, pretends to be Mellefont's friend, and aspires to cheat him of Cynthia and get her for himself. He leads Plyant to suspect an intrigue between Mellefont and Lady Plyant, and Touchwood an intrigue between Mellefont and Lady Touchwood; and contrives that Touchwood shall find Mellefont in the latter's chamber. Mellefont is disinherited and Cynthia is to be made over to Maskwell. Their plot, however, here goes wrong. Touchwood informs Lady Touchwood of Maskwell's intention to marry Cynthia. This awakens her jealousy. She upbraids Maskwell and is overheard by Touchwood, who now perceives Maskwell's treachery, and defeats his final attempt to carry off Cynthia.

Double Deceit, The, or *The Cure for Jealousy*, a comedy by W. *Popple.

Double Marriage, The, see MASSINGER.

Doubting Castle, in Bunyan's *Pilgrim's Progress*, the castle of Giant Despair.

DOUCE, Francis (1757–1834), antiquary and book-collector. His *Illustrations of Shakespeare* (1807) was a pioneering assemblage of sources and analogues, and he published a large number of learned articles, but his most lasting achievement was his personal collection of books, manuscripts (including the famous illuminated 'Douce Apocalypse'), and coins, which he bequeathed to the Bodleian Library, Oxford.

DOUGHTY, Charles Montagu (1843–1926), educated at Caius College, Cambridge, principally remembered for his remarkable record of *Travels in Arabia Deserta*, carried out in 1876–8, first published 1888, republished 1921 with an introduction by T. E. *Lawrence, and widely read in E. *Garnett's abridged version, *Wanderings in Arabia* (1908). It is notable for its extraordinary and eccentric style: Doughty disapproved of 'Victorian prose', and mingled his own with Chaucerian and Elizabethan English and Arabic. Attempts to revive interest in his equally eccentric poetry, by invoking comparisons with G. M. *Hopkins, have failed, and his volumes of verse, which include the epic *The Dawn in Britain* (6 vols, 1906), *Adam Cast Forth* (a sacred drama, 1908), and *Mansoul, or The Riddle of the World* (1920), are largely forgotten. A life by D. G. *Hogarth was published in 1928.

Douglas, a romantic tragedy by J. *Home, based on a Scottish ballad, and first performed in Edinburgh in 1756, where it caused violent controversy and protests from those who believed it improper for a minister of the Church to write for the stage. *Hume and Adam *Smith supported it; it was a great success, and frequently revived.

Old Norval, a shepherd, brings up the infant son of Douglas, supposed dead by his mother, now Lady Randolph. Young Norval saves Lord Randolph's life, and is reunited with his mother, only to be slain through the machinations of Randolph's heir Glenalvon; his mother in despair hurls herself (off-stage) from a cliff.

DOUGLAS, Lord Alfred Bruce (1870–1945), poet, and friend of *Wilde, whom he met in 1891, and who addressed to him his letter from prison, *De Profundis*. Douglas translated Wilde's *Salome* from French to English (1894), and published several volumes of verse which show a distinctly minor talent, although his sonnets have had their admirers. He was editor of the *Academy* from 1907 to 1910. He also wrote various defensive accounts of his relationship with Wilde, including *Oscar Wilde and Myself* (1914) and the less extreme *Oscar Wilde: A Summing up* (1940); his autobiography appeared in 1929. Douglas was much given to litigation, and in 1924 was imprisoned for a libel on W. S. *Churchill. *Bernard Shaw and Alfred Douglas: A Correspondence* (1982, ed. M. Hyde) admirably illustrates Douglas's weaknesses and *Shaw's forbearance.

DOUGLAS, the Black, (1) Sir James Douglas (?1286–1330) who, in 1319, in the days of Robert Bruce and Edward II, invaded England and plundered the towns and villages of the north. He three times destroyed an English garrison in his castle of Douglas, and it is on one of these incidents that Scott bases the story of *Castle Dangerous*. (2) Sir William Douglas, lord of Nithsdale (d. ?1392), illegitimate son of Archibald, third earl of Douglas; (3) the 'Degenerate Douglas!' addressed in a sonnet by *Wordsworth, see OLD Q.

DOUGLAS, Gawin, or Gavin (?1475–1522), Scottish poet and bishop of Dunkeld, third son of Archibald, fifth earl of Angus. He wrote an allegorical poem, *The Palice of Honour* (first published c.1535), and *King Hart*, a homiletic allegory (first printed 1786), has also been attributed to him. He was best known for his translation of the *Aeneid* (*Eneados*, with prologues, 1553), the earliest translation of the classics into English, or rather, as he commented (prologue I, ll. 117–18), into 'Scottis'. He was one of the first to draw the distinction between *Scots and 'Inglis', and unlike many of his contemporaries, he wrote only in the vernacular. Earlier versions of the *Aeneid* and *The Palice of Honour* existed but have disappeared. His works were edited by John Small of Edinburgh in 1874, and his shorter poems by P. J. Bawcutt (1967), who also wrote a critical study (1976). *Pound, among others, admired him, saying that 'he gets more out of Virgil than any other translator', and there is evidence that his version was used by *Surrey and T. *Sackville.

DOUGLAS, George, the pseudonym of George Douglas Brown (1869–1902), the son of an Ayrshire farmer, who was educated at Glasgow University and Balliol College, Oxford. He settled in London where he wrote magazine and boys' fiction. In 1901 he published *The House with the Green Shutters*, which received high critical acclaim. The work, written from a standpoint of realism in contrast with the sentimental view of Scotland depicted by the *'Kailyard school', is set in the village of Barbie and describes the rise of the tyrannical, dull-minded John Gourlay who builds his business on his feckless wife's dowry. His house, which

becomes the 'passion of his life', gives him a sense of triumph over the village, but his world finally collapses with the failure of his business and the disgrace of his son, and retribution falls. Brown died suddenly the year after the novel's publication, leaving other works unfinished.

DOUGLAS, Keith Castellain (1920–44), educated at *Christ's Hospital and Merton College, Oxford, where *Blunden was his tutor. His verses began to appear in periodicals in the 1930s, but the only volume published in his lifetime was *Selected Poems* (1943). He was killed in Normandy, and inevitably is remembered largely as a war poet, whose descriptions of wartime Cairo and desert fighting and whose contemplations of death ('Simplify me when I'm dead') show a rapidly maturing energy and simplicity of diction. His vivid experimental narrative of desert warfare, *Alamein to Zem Zem*, was published posthumously in 1946; his *Collected Poems* appeared in 1951, ed. J. Waller and G. S. Fraser. A selection with an introduction by Ted *Hughes appeared in 1964 and the *Complete Poems* in 1979, edited by Desmond Graham, who published a life in 1974.

DOUGLAS, Mary (1921–), social anthropologist, educated at a convent school and at St Anne's College, Oxford. After *The Lele of Kasai* (1963) her work has been predominantly theoretical. *Purity and Danger* (1966) considered ritual pollution, and *Natural Symbols* (1970) secular and religious ritual as a form of communication. Both used examples from contemporary Western society as well as exotic cultures and reached a wide non-academic audience. Other books include *The World of Goods: Towards an Anthropology of Consumption* (1979); *How Institutions Think* (1986); and *In the Wilderness: The Doctrine of Defilement in the Book of Numbers* (1993), which returns to ideas about pollution and the purity of the social body.

DOUGLAS, (George) Norman (1868–1952), novelist and essayist, who spent much of his life abroad, principally in Italy. He is chiefly remembered for his travel books about Capri, Tunisia, and Calabria, published as *Siren Land* (1911), *Fountains in the Sand* (1912), and *Old Calabria* (1915), and for his novel *South Wind* (1917), which celebrates the pleasures of the hedonistic life on the island of Nepenthe. In the 1920s and 1930s he was a well-known figure in the expatriate literary community of Florence, where his account of his quarrel with D. H. *Lawrence, *D. H. Lawrence and Maurice Magnus: A Plea for Better Manners*, was published in 1924. There is a life by M. Holloway (1976).

Douglas Tragedy, The, a ballad included in Sir W. Scott's *Minstrelsy of the Scottish Border*, the story of the carrying off of Lady Margaret by Lord William Douglas. They are pursued by her father and seven brothers, who fall in the ensuing fight. Douglas dies of his wounds and she does not survive him.

DOVE, Rita (1952–   ), American poet, born in Akron, Ohio. Her collections include *The Yellow House on the Corner* (1980), *Thomas and Beulah* (1986), *Grace Notes* (1989), and *Mother Love* (1995), a powerful lyrical exploration in varied 14-line stanzas of the resonance of the Demeter/Persephone myth, rich in classical allusion, personal emotion, and contemporary colouring. She has also published a novel, *Through the Ivory Gate* (1992). She was the US poet laureate 1993–5.

Dove Cottage, a short distance from the north-east shore of Grasmere, taken by *Wordsworth and his sister at the end of 1799 when they migrated to the Lakes. They occupied it till the end of 1807. It was subsequently occupied by *De Quincey.

DOVER, Captain Robert, see COTSWOLD OLIMPICK GAMES.

'Dover Beach', a poem by M. *Arnold.

Doves Press, see PRIVATE PRESSES.

DOW, Alexander (d. 1779). He joined the army in India, where he spent much of his life. In 1768 he joined the fashion for *Oriental tales with *Tales . . . of Inatulla of Delhi*, a series of flamboyant and ribald stories which met with some success. In the same year he published *The History of Hindostan*; two dramas, *Zingis* and *Sethona*, followed in 1769 and 1774.

DOWDEN, Edward (1843–1913), educated at Queen's College, Cork, and Trinity College, Dublin, where he became professor of English literature in 1867. He was a noted Shakespearian scholar and made his reputation with the publication of *Shakspere: A Critical Study of His Mind and Art* (1875) which influenced future approaches to Shakespearian biography. This was followed by *Shakspere* (1877), a primer, and editions of single plays. He wrote other volumes of criticism, a life of *Shelley (1887), short biographies of *Southey, R. *Browning, and *Montaigne, and published editions of *Spenser and other English poets.

Dowel (Dobet, Dobest), see PIERS PLOWMAN.

DOWIE, Ménie Muriel (1867–1945), novelist and travel writer. She began publishing articles, short stories and verse in the late 1880s, mostly unsigned or under pseudonyms, including 'Princess Top-Storey' and 'Judith Vermont', but made her name with her autobiographical travel book *A Girl in the Karpathians* (1891). A collection of essays, *Women Adventurers* (1893), followed, then her first novel, *Gallia* (1895). Its frank treatment of sexual relations established her as a leading *New Woman writer. She wrote two further novels: *The Crook of the Bough* (1898) and *Love and His Mask* (1901). Her short stories, originally published in the *Yellow Book* and *Chambers' Journal*, were collected as *Some Whims of Fate* (1896) and her *Country Life* column was reprinted as *Things about Our Neighbourhood* (1903). She withdrew from the literary scene after

her scandalous divorce from Henry Norman in January 1903.

DOWLAND, John (1563–1626), English composer and lutenist, generally considered the greatest of all English songwriters. On failing to receive one of the vacant posts of lutenist to Queen Elizabeth in 1594 he travelled abroad, visiting various German and Italian courts and returning to England in 1597, when he issued *The First Booke of Songes or Ayres of Fowre Partes with Tableture for the Lute*, the earliest and most popular book of its kind. Being passed over again for a court post, he went back to Germany and by 1598 was lutenist at the court of Christian IV of Denmark. *The Second Booke of Songs or Ayres* (1600) and *The Third and Last Booke of Songs* (1603) were both published during his absence from London, but by 1606 he was permanently back in England where he brought out a fourth collection of songs, *A Pilgrimes Solace*, in 1612. By now he was famous as a lute composer all over Europe, above all for the widely disseminated song 'Flow, my teares' (1600), later arranged for instruments as the *Lachrymae* pavane and several times referred to in contemporary literature under that title: he was at last appointed lutenist to James I, though he appears to have written little of importance after this date.

A few of the texts set by Dowland are known to be by courtly amateurs like Sir F. *Greville, Sir E. *Dyer, or the earls of *Essex, Cumberland, or Pembroke and there is an occasional poem by *Donne or *Peele. But many more have texts by unknown authors: in the best of them and particularly in the tragic ones like 'In darknesse let mee dwell', 'Sorrow, stay', or 'Flow, my teares', music and words are fused in a singleness of conception that is hard to parallel. There is a life by Diana Poulton (2nd edn 1982).

Dowsabel, an English form of the Latin female name Dulcibella, used generically for a sweetheart.

DOWSON, Ernest Christopher (1867–1900), born in Kent, the son of well-to-do but later impoverished parents. After erratic schooling he went in 1886 to The Queen's College, Oxford, where he read widely and made many friends, including L. P. *Johnson, but left without taking his degree. He assisted with his father's dwindling docking business, and established himself in the London society of *Beardsley, *Le Gallienne, *Wilde, and their friends. He contributed poems to the *Yellow Book*, the *Savoy*, and the anthologies published by the *Rhymers Club, and in 1891 met 'Missie', Adelaide Foltinowicz, a girl of 12, who later became an important symbol of lost love and innocence in his verse. He enjoyed a widely varied literary and social life between drawing rooms, taverns, and the *Café Royal; his feelings for the Roman Catholic Church, into which he was received in Sept. 1891, appear to have been as much aesthetic as religious. His father was now suffering from advanced tuberculosis, and died (possibly by suicide) in 1894; within months his mother

297

hanged herself. Dowson's stories *Dilemmas* appeared in 1895, and at about that time he began to move restlessly between London, France, Ireland, and back again, living an ever wilder and more intemperate life. The first of his two books of poetry, *Verses* (containing his celebrated 'Non Sum Qualis Eram', better known as 'Cynara'), appeared in 1896, and his second, *Decorations* (half of which consists of his experiments with 'prose poems'), in 1899. His one-act verse play *The Pierrot of the Minute* was published in 1897.

The poems, which display much variety in stanza and prosody, group themselves chiefly into love poetry, including 'Cynara'; devotional poems, of which 'Nuns of the Perpetual Adoration' and 'Carthusians' are perhaps the most successful; poems of the natural world, such as 'Breton Afternoon'; and above all poems of ennui and world-weariness, such as the well-known 'Vitae Summa Brevis' ('They are not long, the days of wine and roses'), 'To One in Bedlam', and several translations and adaptations of *Verlaine. See also ART FOR ART'S SAKE. See a life by M. Longaker (1944, rev. 1967); a volume of *Reminiscences* (1914) by his friend and fellow poet Victor Plarr; and his *Letters*, ed. D. Flower and H. Maas (1967).

DOYLE, Arthur Conan (1859–1930), educated at Stonyhurst and Edinburgh; he became a doctor and practised at Southsea, 1882–90. He is chiefly remembered for his widely celebrated creation of the subtle, hawk-eyed amateur detective Sherlock Holmes, whose brilliant solutions to a wide variety of crimes began in *A Study in Scarlet* (1887), continued through a long line of stories, chiefly in the *Strand Magazine*, and were collected in *The Adventures of Sherlock Holmes* (1892), *The Memoirs of Sherlock Holmes* (1894), *The Hound of the Baskervilles* (1902), and other works. His friend and foil, the stolid Dr Watson with whom he shares rooms in Baker Street, attends him throughout most of his adventures. (See DETECTIVE FICTION.) As well as his 'Holmes' stories, Doyle wrote a long series of historical and other romances. Notable among them are *Micah Clarke* (1889), *The White Company* (1891), *The Exploits of Brigadier Gerard* (1896), the first of many 'Gerard' tales, *Rodney Stone* (1896), and *The Lost World* (1912). In 1902 Doyle wrote an influential pamphlet, 'The War in South Africa', which was much translated; and later many books on public themes, including a long history of the Flanders campaign in the First World War. His one-act play *Waterloo* provided Sir H. *Irving in 1894 with one of his most successful parts. In 1926 Doyle published his *History of Spiritualism*, one of several books he wrote on the subject, in which he was greatly interested: his interest in fairies is a connection with the work of his uncle Richard *Doyle, illustrator of many *fairy stories.

DOYLE, Sir Francis Hastings Charles (1810–88), fellow of All Souls and professor of poetry at Oxford, who published several volumes of verse, which include the patriotic military ballads 'The Loss of the Birkenhead' and 'The Private of the Buffs'.

DOYLE, Richard (1824–83), illustrator, the son of the caricaturist John Doyle (1797–1868) and uncle of A. C. *Doyle. He worked for *Punch* and designed the cover (with Mr Punch, Toby, and a margin of nymphs, goblins, and satyrs) that lasted from 1849 to 1956. He illustrated chiefly *fairy stories, including *Ruskin's *The King of the Golden River* (1851) and W. *Allingham's *In Fairyland* (1870), and also some of *Dickens's Christmas Books; and published books of annotated drawings, including *The Foreign Tour of Brown, Jones and Robinson* (1854), whose comic adventures in England and on the Rhine he had depicted in *Punch*.

DOYLE, Roddy (1958–), novelist, born in Dublin, whose first three novels, *The Commitments* (1987), *The Snapper* (1990), and *The Van* (1991), describe the adventures and misadventures of the Rabbitte family in a northern suburb of Dublin: in the first, Jimmy organizes with temporary success a band to bring 'soul to the people'; in the second, his sister Sharon has an illegitimate baby; in the third, Jimmy Sr struggles to survive being made redundant and goes share in a chip van with his friend Bimbo while his wife Veronica discovers education. These were published together as the Barrytown trilogy in 1992. The dialogue is lively, contemporary, authentic, and the large Rabbitte family is portrayed with affection and sympathy. *Paddy Clarke Ha Ha Ha* (1993, *Booker Prize), set in Barrytown in 1968, vividly evokes the childhood world at school, at play, and at home of a 10-year-old boy, whose life is overshadowed by the breakdown of his parents' marriage. *The Woman Who Walked into Doors* (1997) is the powerful, tragic, tough, first-person narration of determined survivor Paula Spencer, alcoholic mother of four, widowed when her violently abusive husband is shot by the Gardai during the course of an armed robbery. Doyle has also written two plays, *Brownbread* (1987), in which a group of Barrytown youths kidnap a bishop, and *War* (1989), based on a public house quiz.

Drab, term used first by C. S. *Lewis (*English Literature in the Sixteenth Century*, introduction) to denote poetry and prose of the later medieval period until the early Renaissance: 'a period in which, for good or ill, poetry has little richness either of sound or images'. Although Lewis claimed that the term was not dyslogistic, it has generally been used, by Lewis and by later critics, to characterize works of the Tudor period which are unappealing to a modern ear. Typically, 'Drab' poets wrote in strongly rhythmical verse forms such as *poulter's measure, making use of alliteration and of poetic 'fillers' such as 'eke', and employed few Latinate words. An example from *Tottel's Miscellany* illustrates these features:

I know under the grene the serpent how he lurkes.
The hammer of the restles forge I wote eke how it
wurkes.
I know and can by roate the tale that I would tel:
But oft the wordes come furth awrie of him that
loueth wel.

Yet many so-called 'Drab' writers, such as *Wyatt, have
been much admired in modern times. The Tudor
translators of *Seneca's plays were highly regarded by
T. S. *Eliot, who edited the *Tenne Tragedies* in 1927; and
many other 'Drab' translations were of crucial importance for the later Renaissance in England, such as Sir T.
*Hoby's version of *Castiglione's *Il cortegiano* (1561)
and A. *Golding's of *Ovid's *Metamorphoses* (1567).

DRABBLE, Margaret (1939–), novelist, born in
Sheffield, and educated at the Mount School, York,
and Newnham College, Cambridge. She published her
first novel, *A Summer Birdcage*, a short first-person
account of the relationship between two young graduate sisters, in 1963. This was followed by *The Garrick
Year* (1964), with a theatrical background; *The Millstone* (1965), the story of a young, academic, unmarried
mother; *Jerusalem the Golden* (1968), about the social
ambitions of a girl who comes to London from the
north of England; *The Waterfall* (1969), the story of a
passionate and adulterous love affair; *The Needle's Eye*
(1972), which depicts an heiress who takes voluntary
poverty upon herself; *The Realms of Gold* (1975), about
a career woman who has achieved international
recognition as an archaeologist; *The Ice Age* (1977),
a condition-of-England novel that documents the
effects of the oil crisis on social attitudes; and *The
Middle Ground* (1980), which tells the story of a
journalist who comes to doubt her feminist creed.
After working on *The Oxford Companion to English
Literature* from 1979 to 1985 she published a trilogy of
novels—*The Radiant Way* (1987), *A Natural Curiosity*
(1989), and *The Gates of Ivory* (1991)—which follows
the fortunes of three women friends through the social
and political changes in Britain in the 1980s, opening
up in the last volume to a vision of war-torn Cambodia.
Her early novels deal primarily with the dilemma of
educated women caught in the conflicting claims of
maternity, sexuality, and economic independence: her
later novels have a wider canvas. These include *The
Peppered Moth* (2001), a four-generation family saga;
and *The Red Queen* (2004), a transcultural tragicomedy
set partly in 18th-cent. Korea. She has written biographies of A.*Bennett (1974) and Angus *Wilson (1995).
A. S. *Byatt is her sister and she is married to Michael
*Holroyd.

Dracula, a novel by B. *Stoker, published 1897, the
most famous of all tales of vampirism.

The story is told through the diaries of a young
solicitor, Jonathan Harker, his fiancée Mina, her friend
Lucy Westenra, and Dr John Seward, the superintendent of a large lunatic asylum at Purfleet, in Essex. It
begins with Harker's journey to Count Dracula's eerie
castle in Transylvania, in connection with the count's
purchase of Carfax, an ancient estate adjoining Dr
Seward's asylum. After various horrifying experiences
as an inmate of the castle, Jonathan makes his way to a
ruined chapel, where he finds 50 great wooden boxes
filled with earth recently dug from the graveyard of the
Draculas, in one of which the un-dead count is lying,
gorged with blood. These boxes are shipped from
Varna to Whitby and thence to Carfax. Dracula dis-
embarks at Whitby in the shape of a wolf, having
dispatched the entire ship's crew en route, and proceeds to vampirize Lucy who, despite multiple blood
transfusions and the occult precautions of Dr Seward's
old teacher Professor Van Helsing, dies drained of
blood but remains un-dead until staked through the
heart. The rest of the book tells of the attempt to save
Mina from Dracula's insidious advances and of the
search for the boxes of earth, his only refuge between
sunrise and sunset. All but one of these are neutralized
with fragments of the Host. The last, with Dracula in it,
is followed by Van Helsing and the others back to
Transylvania where, after a thrilling chase, the count is
beheaded and stabbed through the heart, at which his
body crumbles to dust.

Dracula—tall and thin, with his beaky nose, pointed
ears, cruel and sensual features, and 'peculiarly sharp
white teeth' protruding over his lips—has been the
subject of many films, the most notable being F. W.
Murnau's silent *Nosferatu* (1922) and Tod Browning's
early talkie *Dracula* (1931).

Dragon of Wantley, The, the title of a humorous ballad, probably of the 17th cent., satirizing the old verse
romances, and of a burlesque opera based upon it by H.
*Carey, performed in 1737. The story is of a Yorkshire
dragon from Wantley (Wharncliffe, near 'fair Rotherham') which devoured children and was killed by 'a
kick on the Back-side' from Moore of Moore Hall. The
ballad was included in Percy's *Reliques*, where the
dragon was identified as Sir Francis Wortley, who was
in conflict with his parishioners over tithes, and Moore
as the attorney who took their part.

DRAKE, Sir Francis (?1540–96), circumnavigator and
admiral, born near Tavistock, Devon. His early sea
career is uncertain, but he was undoubtedly engaged in
the Guinea trade with Sir John *Hawkins. He commanded the *Judith* in Hawkins's ill-fated expedition to
San Juan de Ulúa of 1567, and made three voyages to
the West Indies in 1570–2. In 1577 he set out in the
Pelican (afterwards renamed the *Golden Hind*) for the
river Plate, sailed through the Straits of Magellan,
plundered Valparaíso, rounded the Cape of Good
Hope, and completed the circumnavigation of the
world. He was knighted by Elizabeth on his return in
1581. Under a commission from Elizabeth he plundered Santiago and burnt Vigo in 1585, and took San
Domingo and Cartagena. In 1587 he destroyed a

Spanish armament in the harbour of Cadiz. Drake, as vice-admiral, commanded one of the divisions of the English fleet against the Armada. He was subsequently associated with Sir John Norris in an expedition which in 1589 plundered Corunna and destroyed much Spanish shipping. Drake died in Jan. 1596 off Portobello in the course of an unsuccessful expedition to the West Indies; Hawkins had died on the same expedition a few weeks earlier. The narratives of some of his expeditions figure in *Hakluyt and *Purchas, and he became the hero of many legends. *Newbolt assimilated Drake's achievements into the public school ideal in his popular poem 'Drake's Drum' (1895).

Dramatic Idyls, a volume of six poems, of medium length, four of them in the same metre, by R. *Browning, published 1879. After the publication of a sequel (below), the collection was called 'Dramatic Idyls, First Series'. The spelling 'Idyl' differentiated the poems from *Tennyson's 'Idylls'. The poems are among the finest of Browning's later period, particularly 'Ivàn Ivànovitch', a story based on a Russian folk-tale of a woman who threw her children to the wolves in order to save her own life. The collection has a notable unity of tone, and focuses on human behaviour in conditions of extreme stress.

Dramatic Idyls, *Second Series,* a volume of six poems by R. *Browning, published 1880 and influenced by the success of the 1879 volume (above). Although the collection does not have the unity of the first series, it demonstrates Browning's continuing interest and vitality in the dramatic monologue form, notably 'Clive'.

dramatic irony, or **tragic irony,** a figure of speech in which what is said by the characters in a play has a different and more serious meaning to the audience who are more aware than are the characters concerned of the catastrophe which is either impending or has occurred. As, for example, Duncan's speech in *Macbeth on arriving at Macbeth's castle, where his murder has already been planned, or Macbeth's 'Fail not our feast' to Banquo when he has arranged Banquo's murder for that same evening.

Dramatic Lyrics, a collection of poems by R. *Browning, published in 1842 as No. III of *Bells and Pomegranates. Browning's publisher, *Moxon, persuaded him to vary the format of the series, which had been intended to consist solely of plays. The collection included some of Browning's best-known poems such as 'My Last Duchess', 'Porphyria's Lover', and 'The Pied Piper of Hamelin'.

dramatic monologue, generally, a poem delivered as though by a single imagined person, frequently but not always to an imagined auditor: the speaker is not to be identified with the poet, but is dramatized, usually ironically, through his or her own words. The tradition of the verse epistle may be seen to have contributed to the development of the dramatic monologue, which found one of its most accomplished exponents in R. *Browning ('My Last Duchess', 1842; 'Caliban upon Setebos', 1864). The form was employed by many 19th- and 20th-cent. poets, including *Tennyson, *Hardy, *Kipling, *Frost, *Pound, and T. S. *Eliot, and several Victorian women poets found it a useful vehicle for giving voice to women's concerns and repressions.

Dramatic Romances and Lyrics, a collection of poems by R. *Browning, published 1845 as No. VII of *Bells and Pomegranates. Many of the poems were revised before publication in consultation with Elizabeth Barrett (*Browning), whom Browning was courting at the time. The collection included some of Browning's best-known poems, such as 'How They Brought the Good News from Ghent to Aix', 'The Lost Leader', and 'The Flight of the Duchess'.

Dramatis Personae, a collection of poems by R. *Browning, published 1864, of which a few had been published previously, but most were new. They were marked by Browning's grief after the death of his wife (see BROWNING, E. B.) in 1861, and by his searching examination of the relation of human to divine love, especially as it concerns the nature of belief. A striking unity of theme and structure makes the collection an intermediate stage in Browning's development between *Men and Women and *The Ring and the Book. Several of the poems are anthology favourites—notably 'Rabbi Ben Ezra' and 'Prospice'— but the heart of the collection are the long dramatic monologues such as 'A Death in the Desert', 'Caliban upon Setebos', and 'Mr Sludge, "the Medium"'.

DRAPER, Mrs Elizabeth (1744–78), the wife of Daniel Draper (an official of the East India Company), with whom *Sterne fell in love in 1767 and to whom he wrote the *Journal to *Eliza and Letters of Yorick to Eliza.

Drapier's Letters, The, a series of pamphlets published by *Swift in 1724. The word 'Drapier' = 'Draper'.

A patent had been granted to the duchess of Kendal for supplying copper coins for use in Ireland, and by her had been sold to a certain William Wood for £10,000. The profit on the patent would have been apparently some £25,000, but would have had the devastating effect of devaluing Ireland's already weak currency. In 1723 the Irish Houses of Parliament voted addresses protesting against the transaction, and Swift took up the cudgels on behalf of the Irish. Writing in the character of a Dublin draper, he published a series of four letters in which he prophesies economic ruin to the Irish if 'Wood's half-pence' were admitted into circulation, and he addressed a fifth letter of protest, also signed Drapier, to Viscount *Molesworth. The letters produced an immense effect and the government was forced to abandon the project and compensate Wood; Swift was thus established as an Irish national hero. Two more Drapier letters, written at the same period, one addressed to 'Lord Chancellor

Middleton' and the other to 'both Houses of Parliament', were published in 1735: for details, see the Clarendon edition, H. Davis (1935).

Drawcansir, a character in Buckingham's *The Rehearsal*, parodying Almanzor in *Dryden's The Conquest of Granada*; he appears briefly in the last act in a mock-heroic stage battle, and according to the stage directions, 'kills 'em all on both sides'. *Carlyle, in his history of *Frederick the Great, refers to the 'terrific Drawcansir figures' of the French Revolution, 'of enormous whiskerage, unlimited command of gunpowder . . . and even a certain heroism, stage-heroism'.

DRAWCANSIR, Sir Alexander, pseudonym of H. *Fielding, under which he contributed to the *Covent-Garden Journal*.

DRAYTON, Michael (1563–1631), born at Hartshill, in Warwickshire. His early life was probably spent in the service of Sir Henry Goodere of Polesworth. Little is known of Drayton's personal life, though dedications and epistles reveal his circle to have included such friends as *Stow, *Camden, *Jonson, and W. *Drummond. He died in comparative poverty, but was buried in Westminster Abbey, where Lady Anne Clifford, countess of Dorset, paid for his handsome monument.

He was an extremely prolific writer, producing historical, *topographical, and religious verse, as well as odes, sonnets, and satires. He revised and tinkered with his early work repeatedly, not always to good effect. His earliest work was *The Harmonie of the Church*, paraphrases from the OT and Apocrypha (1591). In 1593 he published *Idea: The Shepheards Garland*, eclogues in the Spenserian manner including praise of Queen Elizabeth (in the Third Eglog) and lament for the death of *Sidney (in the Fourth). Drayton's *Ideas Mirrour*, a sonnet sequence, was published in 1594; in its final version, entitled *Idea* (1619), it included the famous sonnet 'Since there's no help, come let us kiss and part'. His poems on legendary and historical figures began in about 1594 with *Peirs Gaveston*, followed by *Matilda* (1594), *Robert, Duke of Normandy* (1596), and *Mortimeriados* (1596), later revised as *The Barrons Wars* (1603). *Englands Heroicall Epistles* (1597) was modelled on *Ovid's *Heroides*; it consists of twelve pairs of verse letters exchanged by lovers from English history, such as Henry II and Fair Rosamond, Edward IV and Jane Shore, Lord Gilford Dudley and Lady Jane Grey. Another Ovidian poem was *Endimion and Phoebe* (1595), a minor source for Keats's *Endymion*. Among later works, *The Owle*, an obscure satire, appeared in 1604; *Odes* in 1606. This innovatory collection included 'To the Virginian Voyage' and 'To the Cambro-britans and Theyr Harp', his 'Ballad of Agincourt', which opens with the lines:

> Fayre stood the winde for *France*
> When we our sailes advaunce.

He later wrote a narrative poem on the same subject, *The Battaile of Agincourt* (1627), which Jonson professed to admire; the same volume also included *The Miseries of Queene Margarite*, *Nimphidia, The Court of Fayrie*, and the interesting epistle to Henry Reynolds 'Of Poets and Poesie'. Drayton's largest project, the great topographical poem on England, *Poly-Olbion, was completed in 1622, the first part having appeared in 1612. His *Works* have been definitively edited in six volumes by J. W. Hebel, K. Tillotson, and B. H. Newdigate (1931–41, rev. 1961).

'Dream, The', a poem by *Byron, written in 1816, describing his early love for his cousin Mary Chaworth, 'the solitary scion left | Of a time-honour'd race', whose great-uncle William Chaworth had been killed by the fifth Lord Byron. Mary married John Musters in 1805, but her marriage proved unhappy, and she became mentally disturbed—'The Lady of his love:—Oh! She was changed | As by a sickness of the soul.'

Dream of Gerontius, The, see NEWMAN, J. H.

Dream of John Ball, A, a historical socialist fantasy by W. *Morris, published in *Commonweal*, Nov. 1886–Jan. 1887, in volume form 1888. It takes the form of a dream in which the narrator is carried back to the time of the early stages of the Peasants' Revolt in 1381; he encounters the 'hedge-priest' John Ball, and in their final night-long dialogue Morris both satirizes the 19th-cent. present and offers hope for a future when men 'shall see things as they verily are' and rise in successful protest against their exploitation.

Dream of the Rood, an Old English poem of 156 lines, found in the 10th-cent. *Vercelli Book, in three parts: a description of the poet's vision of the cross and the address to him by the cross describing the Crucifixion (paralleled in part by the Northumbrian runic inscriptions on the 8th-cent. *Ruthwell Cross in Dumfriesshire); a homiletic address to the dreamer by the cross; and a declaration of faith and confidence in heaven by the dreamer himself. There has been much argument about the coherence of the poem; it seems likely that, as it stands, it was composed in one piece, drawing on an earlier cross prosopopoeia related to the tradition of riddles in Old English and Latin. The poem is greatly admired for the devotional simplicity of its first, narrative section, and for the ingenious web of imagery upon which it is constructed. There are editions by B. Dickins and A. S. C. Ross (rev. 1963) and M. Swanton (1970).

DREISER, Theodore Herman Albert (1871–1945), American novelist, born in Indiana, the son of a devout Catholic German immigrant father, and brought up in semi-poverty. He left his family at the age of 15 for Chicago, and after various jobs became a journalist, meanwhile writing his first novel, *Sister Carrie* (1900), a powerful account of a young working girl's rise to the 'tinsel and shine' of worldly success, and of the slow decline of her lover and protector Hurstwood. It was withheld from circulation by its publishers, who were apprehensive about Dreiser's frank and amoral treatment of Carrie's sexuality and ambition, and he continued work as a hack journalist until the greater success of *Jennie Gerhardt* (1911), again a novel of a working girl's betterment through liaisons. This was followed by the first parts of a trilogy about an unscrupulous business magnate, Frank Cowperwood (*The Financier*, 1912; *The Titan*, 1914; *The Stoic* was published posthumously in 1947). *The Genius* (1915) is a study of an artist, with much autobiographical material. *An American Tragedy* (1925) is the story of Clyde Griffiths, son of unworldly, evangelist parents, who escapes from them to what seems to him the vastly more exciting and colourful life of a bell-boy in a Kansas City hotel; he moves to New York State to work in a collar factory, and when his girl friend Roberta becomes pregnant he drowns her, possibly accidentally in the event, though after much anguished premeditation, and is tried and condemned to death. Dreiser's many other works include *Dreiser Looks at Russia* (1928, written after travels in Russia), *Tragic America* (1931), and *America Is Worth Saving* (1941), which express the growing faith in socialism that replaced the nihilistic naturalism and pessimism of his earlier works. Dreiser has frequently been described as a clumsy stylist, with a weak sense of structure; even his supporter and friend H. L. *Mencken thought *Sister Carrie* a poorly balanced narrative, but the power, originality, first-hand observations, and moral independence of his work has ensured him a lasting readership and a serious reputation as an artist. One of his earliest English admirers was Arnold *Bennett, whose review of *Sister Carrie* in the *Academy* was notably more favourable and enlightened than the American reviews.

'Dreme, The', see LINDSAY, D.

DREYFUS, Alfred (1859–1935), a captain in the French army, subject of a notorious judicial miscarriage. In 1894 an unsigned official letter, addressed to the German military attaché in Paris and listing a number of documents which were to be sent to him, was purloined from the German embassy and handed to the French ministry of war. The similarity of the handwriting to that of Dreyfus, a Jew who held an appointment at the ministry, led to his arrest, trial, and sentence to imprisonment for life on Devil's Island off the coast of Guiana. In 1896 Colonel Picquart of the secret service came upon evidence indicating that the true criminal was a Major Esterhazy. But opposition involving the use of forgery, intimidation, and a violent anti-Semitic press campaign was raised against a retrial. In the course of this controversy *Zola published his famous letter, entitled 'J'accuse', in the newspaper *L'Aurore* (Jan. 1898), and was condemned in consequence to a year's imprisonment. Dreyfus was pardoned by the government in 1899 after a second trial had reaffirmed his guilt. It was not until 1906 that the second verdict was quashed by the Court of Appeal, and Dreyfus reintegrated into the army. The controversy gave rise to the term *Dreyfusard*, to signify a supporter of the innocence of Dreyfus. Extracts from the papers of Colonel Schwartzkoppen, the German military attaché in Paris at the time, confirming Esterhazy's guilt, appeared in 1930.

DRINKWATER, John (1882–1937), the son of a schoolmaster, a prolific poet, dramatist, critic, and actor. His first volume of *Poems* appeared in 1903, and his work appeared in all five volumes of *Georgian Poetry*, and was collected in 1933 in *Summer Harvest*. In 1907 he founded the company which later became the Birmingham Repertory Theatre, and he wrote many plays, including *Abraham Lincoln* (1918), *Oliver Cromwell* (1921), *Mary Stuart* (1922), and a successful comedy *Bird in Hand* (1927). He also wrote stories and plays for children, and produced critical studies of (among others) W. *Morris, *Swinburne, *Byron, *Cromwell, *Pepys, and Shakespeare. Two volumes of an unfinished autobiography, *Inheritance* and *Discovery*, appeared in 1931 and 1932.

DROESHOUT, Martin (1601–c.1650), engraver of the portrait of Shakespeare on the title-page of the First *Folio (1623). *Schoenbaum says: 'How he obtained the commission we do not know—perhaps his fee was as modest as his gifts' (*William Shakespeare: A Documentary Life*, 1975, 258).

drolls, or **droll-humours,** in Commonwealth days when stage plays were forbidden, were farces or comic scenes adapted from existing plays or invented by the actors, produced generally at fairs or in taverns. A few drolls, which are supposed to have been adapted and performed by an actor named Robert Cox, were published in 1655, but most were published after the Restoration by Francis Kirkman in *The Wits, or Sport upon Sport* (two parts, 1662, 1673). 'Bottom the Weaver', which was published separately in 1661, is described on the title-page as having been 'often publickely acted by some of his majesties comedieans, and lately, privately, presented by several apprentices for their harmless recreation'. It is not known how many of the other drolls achieved performance.

Dromio, the name of the twin slaves in Shakespeare's *The Comedy of Errors*.

Drugger, Abel, the credulous tobacconist of Jonson's *The Alchemist*. The character was one of *Garrick's most famous parts, and his success prompted Francis Gentleman's *The Tobacconist* (1770), an adaptation in which Drugger becomes the hero.

Druidism, see STUKELEY, W.

DRUMMOND OF HAWTHORNDEN, William (1585–1649), born at the manor of Hawthornden near Edinburgh, and educated at Edinburgh University. He then travelled in Europe, acquiring a broad education and familiarity with the works of poets in many languages, including *Du Bartas, *Ronsard, *Tasso, and *Marino; he settled on his estate on his return, c.1610, where he had an imposing library, and eventually turned to literature himself. His works include pamphlets and verses in the Royalist cause, laments for the early death of his betrothed in 1614/15 (he did not marry until 1632), satires and hymns, and a history of Scotland 1423–1524, first published in 1655. His best-known prose work was *A Cypresse Grove* (1623), a meditation on death. He was a correspondent of *Drayton, and in the winter of 1618/19 was visited by *Jonson, an event recorded in his Conversations, with many of Jonson's often-quoted comments on his fellow poets. Drummond's poems were edited by E. *Phillips in 1656.

Drury Lane, London, was so called from the Drury family, who had a large house there from Tudor times. The Theatre Royal, Drury Lane, was originally a cockpit, converted into a theatre in the time of James I. It was rebuilt by T. *Killigrew (1612–83), to whom Charles II granted a patent in 1662, again by Sir C. *Wren in 1674, and again in 1812, when the reopening was celebrated in *Rejected Addresses. Junius Brutus Booth, *Garrick, Mrs *Siddons, J. P. *Kemble, and *Kean are among the famous actors who have appeared there. In the 19th cent. it was the great house of Christmas pantomimes, and after the Second World War many successful American musicals were staged there including *Oklahoma!* (1947) and *South Pacific* (1951), both by Rodgers and Hammerstein, and *My Fair Lady* (1958, adapted from Shaw's *Pygmalion*).

Dryasdust, Dr Jonas, a fictitious character, a prosy antiquary, to whom Sir W. *Scott addresses the prefaces of some of his novels.

DRYDEN, John (1631–1700), educated at Westminster School under *Busby and at Trinity College, Cambridge. He inherited a small estate, but supported himself mainly by his writing. His first major poem was the *Heroique Stanza's* (1658) on the death of Cromwell: he later celebrated the king's return with *Astraea Redux* and *To His Sacred Majesty*. Other poems were addressed to Sir Robert Howard, whose sister Lady Elizabeth Dryden married in 1663; the earl of *Clarendon, *Charleton, and Lady Castlemaine. He also published a long poem in quatrains, *Annus Mirabilis* (1667), but most of his early writing was for the theatre and included several rhymed heroic plays, *The Indian Queen* (1664, in collaboration with Sir Robert Howard), *The Indian Emperour* (1665, which has the Mexican ruler Montezuma as subject), *Tyrannick Love* (1669), and *The Conquest of Granada* in two parts (1670). He also wrote comedies, *The Wild Gallant* (1663), *The Rival Ladies* (1664), *Sir Martin Mar-all* (1667, in collaboration with the duke of *Newcastle), *An Evening's Love* (1668), and a radical adaptation of *The Tempest* (1667, with *D'Avenant). He was most original, however, with his tragi-comedies, *Secret Love* (1667), *Marriage-à-la-Mode* (1672), *The

Assignation* (1672), and a second Shakespeare adaptation, *Troilus and Cressida* (1679). All these plays, together with the operatic adaptation of *Paradise Lost, under the title *The State of Innocence, and Fall of Man* (unperformed, pub. 1667) and the immensely successful *Oedipus* (1678, with N. *Lee), reveal Dryden's considerable interest in philosophical and political questions. He became *poet laureate in 1668, and historiographer royal in 1670.

Dryden constantly defended his own literary practice. His first major critical work was *Of Dramatick Poesie* (1668). Subsequent essays include *A Defence of an Essay* (1668), preface to *An Evening's Love* (1671), *Of Heroick Plays* (1672), *Heads of an Answer* (to *Rymer, c. 1677, pub. 1711), and *The Grounds of Criticism in Tragedy*, prefixed to preface to *Troilus and Cressida* (1679). *Aureng-Zebe* (1675) was his best rhymed heroic play. The prologue, however, denounces rhyme in serious drama, and his next tragedy, *All for Love* (1678), was in blank verse. Much of Dryden's criticism was devoted to the assessment of his Elizabethan predecessors, Shakespeare, *Jonson, and *Fletcher. Despite his genuine respect for their achievement, Dryden was unsparing in his enumeration of what he perceived as their 'faults', although he frequently modified both his critical views and his artistic practice. This flexibility as critic and dramatist left him vulnerable to attack. He was represented as Bayes in *The Rehearsal* (1671) by *Buckingham, and physically assaulted in 1679, possibly at the instigation of *Rochester. His principal opponent was *Shadwell, whom Dryden ridiculed in *Mac Flecknoe (c.1676, pub. 1682). Other poems in which he develops his critical principles include many witty and imaginative prologues and epilogues, and poems about, or addressed to, fellow writers and artists, notably Lee, *Roscommon, *Oldham, *Congreve, and *Kneller.

The constitutional crisis of the late 1670s and early 1680s saw Dryden's emergence as a formidable Tory polemicist. His contribution to the political debate included plays, especially *The Spanish Fryar* (1680), *The Duke of Guise* (1682, written with Lee), and the operatic *Albion and Albanius* (1685); his celebrated satires *Absalom and Achitophel* (1681), *The Medall* (1682), and a number of lines for N. *Tate's *The Second Part of Absalom and Achitophel* (1682), as well as a host of partisan prologues and epilogues. His interest in religion was also heightened at this time. In *Religio Laici* (1682) he offers a defence of the Anglican *via media*. However, following the accession of James II Dryden became a Catholic and wrote *The Hind and the Panther* (1687) in support of his new co-religionists. At the death of Charles II he attempted a Pindaric *ode, *Threnodia Augustalis* (1685), the first of several poems in this form, notably *To the Pious Memory . . . of Mrs Anne Killigrew* (1686), *A Song for Saint Cecilia's Day* (1687), 'An Ode, on the Death of Mr Henry Purcell' (1696), and *Alexander's Feast* (1697), which was later incorporated into *Fables Ancient and Modern* (1700).

Dryden also wrote numerous witty elegant songs for his many plays.

In 1689 he lost both his court offices and returned to the theatre. Two of his late plays, *Don Sebastian* (1689) and *Amphitryon* (1690), are excellent; *Cleomenes* (1692) is intellectually impressive; and only *Love Triumphant* (1694) is a failure; but Dryden was tired of the theatre and turned to the politically less compromising work of translating. His immense and splendid achievements in this field include translations of small pieces from *Theocritus and *Horace, and more substantial passages from *Homer, *Lucretius, *Persius, *Juvenal, *Ovid, *Boccaccio, and *Chaucer, as well as the whole of *Virgil. His version of the *Georgics* is especially magnificent. In all these translations he made frequent but subtle allusions to his Jacobite principles. He also returned to criticism, notably in preface to the *Sylvae* (1685), *A Discourse Concerning the Original and Progress of Satire (1693), Dedication to *Examen Poeticum* (1693), and Dedication of the *Aeneis* (1697). His culminating and most impressive achievement both as critic and translator was *Fables Ancient and Modern*, which should be read as a whole, and to which 'The Secular Masque' (1700) is a wise and noble coda. He was buried in Westminster Abbey. (See also RESTORATION.)

Other works by Dryden include:
Plays: *Amboyna* (1673, a tragedy), *Mr Limberham* (1679, a sexually explicit comedy), and a dramatic opera, *King Arthur* (1691). Poems: 'Upon the Death of Lord Hastings' (1649), *Britannia Rediviva* (1688), *Eleonora* (1696). Prose works: *His Majesty's Declaration Defended* (1681), *Life of Plutarch* (1683), *Vindication of the Duke of Guise* (1683), *Character of St Evrémond* (1692), *Character of Polybius* (1693), *Life of Lucian* (1711), translations of Maimbourg's *The History of the League* (1684), Bouhours' *Life of St Francis Xavier* (1686), Du Fresnoy's *De Arte Graphica* (1695).
The standard complete edition is *The Works of John Dryden*, ed. E. N. Hooker et al. (1956–), 20 vols pub. as of 1997. Other editions include Sir W. *Scott's (18 vols, 1808, with life as vol. i, rev. edn by *Saintsbury, 18 vols, 1882–93); *Dramatic Works*, ed. M. Summers (6 vols, 1931–2); *Poems*, ed. J. Kinsley (4 vols, 1958; *The Poems of John Dryden*, ed. P. Hammond (4 vols. 1995–); *Of Dramatic Poesy, and Other Critical Essays*, ed. G. Watson (2 vols, 1962); Letters, ed. C. E. Ward (1942) See also J. A. Winn, *John Dryden and His World* (1987); J. and K. Kinsley (eds.), *Dryden: The Critical Heritage* (1971); P. Harth, *Contexts of Dryden's Thought* (1968) and *Pen for a Party* (1993).

dub, dub poetry. Dub is an instrumental version of a reggae musical recording where the music is driven by a heavy mix of drum and bass sounds with the piano and guitar sounds being filtered through compressors and echo chambers. Dub poetry is a style of poetry that is performed to a sound track of dub music. When performing without music, the performer will deliver the words using the musical rhythms of reggae music and will sometimes burst into song. This style of music is also noted for its political and social commentary.

Du BARTAS, Guillaume de Saluste, seigneur (1544–90), French poet. He published a number of moral epics, including *Judith* (1574; English trans. 1584), but his most famous work was the creation epic *La Semaine* (1578; complete English trans. by *Sylvester, *Devine Weekes and Workes*, 1605). Partly because of his Protestant convictions, he was more influential in England than in France; *Spenser, *Sidney, and *Milton were familiar with his work, either in the original or through translation: it was praised by *Daniel, *Drayton, *Lodge and *Marston, but *Dryden found it 'abominable fustian'.

du BELLAY, Joachim (1522–60), French poet. In 1549 he published *La Deffence et illustration de la langue françoyse*, the manifesto of the *Pléiade, and, in 1549–50, the first French sonnet sequence, *L'Olive*. He spent the years 1553–7 in Rome, and on his return to France published two further sequences, *Les Antiquitez de Rome* and *Les Regrets*, and also a sequence of 15 sonnets which he appended to the *Antiquitez*. *Spenser's versions (as *The Visions of Bellay*) appeared in the *Complaints* of 1591; an earlier form of the *Visions* appeared in the *Theatre for Worldlings* of 1569.

Dubliners, a volume of short stories by *Joyce, published in 1914. Focusing on life in Dublin, the stories follow a pattern of childhood, adolescence, maturity, and public life, culminating with the longest, 'The Dead', frequently described as 'the finest short story in English'. Joyce intended them to be a 'chapter of the moral history [of Ireland]', set them in Dublin 'because that city seemed to [him] the centre of paralysis', and wrote them in what he called 'a style of scrupulous meanness'. Because of Joyce's frankness and his insistence on publishing without deletion or alteration, he found himself in the first of what would be several battles with publishers who refused to print his work without excisions, as well as the focus of a brief campaign for freedom to publish (in the pages, for example, of the *Egoist).

Du BOIS, William Edward Burghardt (1868–1963), black American author, social reformer, and activist, whose many historical and sociological studies include *The Souls of the Black Folk* (1903), a collection of essays which criticizes Booker T. *Washington for being insufficiently militant about black rights. He became increasingly radical and anti-imperial during his long career, and in the year before his death moved to Ghana and became a citizen of that country.

DUBOS, Abbé Jean-Baptiste (1670–1742), diplomat, historian, critic, perpetual secretary of the *Académie française from 1722 until his death. He was a friend of *Bayle, whose philosophical scepticism he found increasingly congenial, and of *Locke, whose

*Essay, in Coste's French translation, he helped to publicize at the beginning of the century. His *Réflexions critiques sur la poésie et sur la peinture* was published in Paris in 1719 and in an English translation in 1748. For at least 50 years it was the most influential work of its kind in Europe. Among French writers who owed much to it were *Voltaire and later *Taine, while in Britain *Hume followed Dubos closely in his essay 'Of the Standard of Taste' (1757).

Dubos's confessedly eclectic work was a temperate defence of the moderns in the debate between the ancients and the moderns. He grounds his view on a discussion of six main questions: (*a*) the nature of poetic or pictorial beauty; (*b*) the relations between beauty and conformity to rules; (*c*) how the arts influence each other; (*d*) the qualities needed by great artists; (*e*) how artistic reputations are established; (*f*) why some ages seem to be more artistically fertile than others. Dubos argues that the arts are valued for the pleasure they are designed to provide; those best able to judge are not critics, scholars, or fellow artists, but the public, who rely on their inner conviction or sixth sense. The main task of reason is to justify the verdicts already delivered by sentiment, by finding out which features of a work cause pleasure. Genuine sentiment is immune to specious reasoning. Dubos also holds that taste is influenced more by physical than social factors, as can be seen by the effects of age and physiology. Later writers sought to examine Dubos's unanalysed notion of pleasure, and the respective roles of thought and feeling, or reason and sentiment, in the experience, appreciation, and judgement of art.

DUBRIC, or **DUBRICIUS, St** (d. 612), the reputed founder of the bishopric of Llandaff, said by *Geoffrey of Monmouth to have crowned *Arthur king of Britain at Silchester, and to have been archbishop of Caerleon. He is mentioned in Tennyson's *'The Coming of Arthur'.

Duchess of Malfi, The (*The Tragedy of the Dutchesse of Malfy*), by *Webster, written 1612/13, printed 1623. The story is taken from one of *Bandello's *novelle*, through Painter's *Palace of Pleasure*, and also shows the influence of Sidney's *Arcadia*.

The duchess, a high-spirited and high-minded widow, reveals her love for the honest Antonio, steward at her court, and secretly marries him, despite the warnings of her brothers, Ferdinand, duke of Calabria, and the Cardinal, and immediately after informing them that she has no intention of remarrying. Their resistance appears to be induced by consideration for their high blood, and by, as Ferdinand later asserts, a desire to inherit her property; there is also a strong suggestion of Ferdinand's repressed incestuous desire for her. The brothers place in her employment as a spy the cynical ex-galley-slave Bosola, who betrays her to them; she and Antonio fly and separate. She is captured and is subjected by Ferdinand

and Bosola to fearful mental tortures, including the sight of the feigned corpse of her husband and the attendance of a group of madmen; finally she is strangled with two of her children and Cariola, her waiting woman. Retribution overtakes the murderers: Ferdinand goes mad, imagining himself a wolf ('A very pestilent disease . . . they call licanthropia'); the Cardinal is killed by the now remorseful Bosola, and Bosola by Ferdinand. Bosola has already killed Antonio, mistaking him for the Cardinal. The humanity and tenderness of the scenes between the Duchess, Antonio, and their children; the pride and dignity of the Duchess in her suffering ('I am Duchesse of Malfy still'); and individual lines such as the celebrated 'Cover her face: Mine eyes dazell: she di'd yong' have long been admired, but until recently critics have been less happy about the overall structure, the abrupt changes in tone and the blood bath of the last act. There have been many revivals, emphasizing T. S. *Eliot's point that Webster's 'verse is essentially dramatic verse, written by a man with a very acute sense of the theatre' (1941).

DUCK, Stephen (1705–56), born in Wiltshire. He began his working life as a farm labourer. Almost entirely self-educated, he took to writing verse, and through Lord Macclesfield came to the notice of Queen Caroline, who gave him a pension and made him a yeoman of the guard in 1733. In 1746 he took holy orders but drowned himself ten years later in a fit of despondency. According to J. *Spence (in a life attached to Duck's *Poems on Several Occasions*, 1736) his early reading consisted largely of *Milton, whose lofty blank verse he feared to emulate, and of the *Spectator*. His best-known poem, *The Thresher's Labour* (in heroic couplets), is a vividly realistic portrayal of the unremitting toil of the labourer's life, but his less successful works degenerated into conventional pastoral and artificial diction. (See also PRIMITIVISM.)

DUDLEY, Robert, earl of Leicester (1532/3–88), courtier and favourite of Queen Elizabeth I. Uncle of Sir P. *Sidney, he was a notable patron of writers and poets, including *Spenser. His personal power and ambitions provoked much hatred and a tradition of literary attacks, the most famous of which is Sir W. *Scott's *Kenilworth*.

Duenna, The, a comic opera-play by R. B. *Sheridan, produced 1775. The play contains much music, a great deal of which consists of pleasant airs familiar to the audiences of the time.

Don Jerome, an irascible father, is determined his daughter Louisa shall marry a rich Jew, Isaac. Louisa, however, is in love with Antonio, who is far from rich. Jerome discovers that the duenna is acting as an intermediary between Louisa and Antonio, dismisses the duenna, and locks up Louisa. Louisa, disguised as the duenna, escapes from the house, leaving the duenna to take her place. Isaac is duped into marrying the duenna, and inadvertently into bringing Antonio and Louisa together.

Duessa, in Spenser's **Faerie Queene*, the daughter of Deceit and Shame, Falsehood in general, in Bk I signifies in particular the Roman Catholic Church, and in V. ix, Mary Queen of Scots.

DUFFY, Carol Ann (1955–   ), poet, born in Glasgow. She moved to Staffordshire as a child, and graduated in philosophy from Liverpool University in 1977. Since then she has worked as a freelance writer in London and Manchester. Her debut collection, *Standing Female Nude* (1985), announced her interest in the **dramatic monologue, frequently using the voices of outsiders—the dispossessed, the insane, and those, especially women, ignored by history. Her interest in the speaking voice led her to the demotic and to a supple, distinctive grammar with frequent use of short sentences and italics. In *Selling Manhattan* (1987) her subtle rhythms marked by assonance and internal rhymes began to be used in more personal verse and in love poems as well as monologues. The themes of nostalgia, desire, loss, and memory, the search for 'first space and the right place' begun here came to predominate in *The Other Country* (1990) and *Mean Time* (1993), which contain several already much-anthologized love poems and lyrics of Larkinesque plangency as well as Duffy's characteristic satire, politics, and narrative. Her range, craft, many awards, and gift as a public performer have made her one of Britain's most popular, respected, and influential poets.

DUFFY, Sir Charles Gavan (1816–1903), Irish nationalist and Australian statesman, born in Monaghan, Ireland, the son of a journalist. He is remembered in a literary connection as having started in 1842, with two barristers, Thomas Osborne Davis and John Dillon, a journal called the *Nation*, for which he gathered a brilliant staff of 'Young Irelanders' and in which he proclaimed the cause of national unity and emancipation. He emigrated to Australia, but returned to Europe in 1880 and settled at Nice. **Yeats, describing a return visit by Duffy as elder statesman, says that 'in all his writings, in which there is so much honesty, so little rancour, there is not one sentence ... distinguished because of its thought or music', and gives an account of the gap between the two generations of Irish nationalists (*Autobiographies*, Book 2).

DUFFY, Maureen Patricia (1933–   ), writer, educated at King's College, London. She has published plays, poetry, and non-fiction (including a life of A. **Behn, *The Passionate Shepherdess*, 1977), but is perhaps best known as a novelist. Her first novel, *That's How It Was* (1962), is a moving autobiographical account of her childhood and of her relationship with her mother, who died of tuberculosis when she was 14. It was followed by many others, some of which deal frankly with the subject of gender and homosexuality; they include *The Paradox Players* (1967), *Wounds* (1969),

Capital (1975), and *Londoners* (1983), a sardonic but poignant view of the writer's lot in the contemporary cosmopolitan bedsitter London of Earl's Court; the sex of the narrator, Al, is left intentionally ambiguous. Later novels include the disturbing *Gor Saga* (1981), which reflects her concern for animal rights and which was dramatized for television in 1988 as *First Born*, and *Illuminations* (1991), about a woman who translates the letters of an 8th-cent. nun. *Restitution* (1998) is a post-**Holocaust novel, exploring family guilt, set in England and Berlin, and *Alchemy* (2004) is a mystery interweaving lives from the 17th and the 21st centuries. Her poetry includes *The Venus Touch* (1971), *Evesong* (1975), and *Memorials of the Quick and the Dead* (1979). A volume of collected poems (1949–84) was published in 1985. She has also written a play about Virginia **Woolf, *A Nightingale in Bloomsbury Square* (1974), and a trilogy of plays based on Greek myths: *Rites* (1969), *Solo*, and *Old Tyme* (both 1970). *The Erotic World of Faery* (1972) is a Freudian study.

DUGDALE, Sir William (1605–86), Garter king-of-arms, and author of *The Antiquities of Warwickshire* (1656), a topographical history that set new standards of fullness and accuracy for the genre and inspired, amongst others, A. **Wood. His *Monasticon Anglicanum*, written in collaboration with Roger Dodsworth, an account of the English monastic houses, appeared in three volumes (1655–73). In 1658 he published his *History of St Paul's Cathedral*, and in 1662 *The History of the Imbanking and Drayning of Divers Fenns and Marshes*, which incidentally gives much information of antiquarian and historical interest. He also wrote *Origines Judicales* (1666), a history of English laws, law courts, and kindred matters, and *The Baronage of England* (1675–6).

DUHIG, Ian (1954–   ), Irish poet, born in London, educated at Leeds University, a former worker with the homeless. Duhig is a learned and witty poet, versed in Irish language (see 'According to Dineen') and history, drawn to the arcane and absurd and capable of a rococo splendour. *The Bradford Count* (1991) features monologues by David Livingstone and a depressed medieval monk. *The Mersey Goldfish* (1995) was followed by *Nominies* (1998), which includes ballads of destitution as well as the black-comic tour de force 'The Ballad of Freddie the Dolphin'. *The Lammas Hireling* appeared in 2003.

DUJARDIN, Édouard, see SYMBOLISM and STREAM OF CONSCIOUSNESS.

Duke of Milan, The, a tragedy by **Massinger, printed 1623, one of his earliest independent plays and a popular one. It is based on the story of Herod and Mariamne as told by Josephus.

Lodovico Sforza, duke of Milan, has, in the war between the Emperor Charles and the king of France, allied himself with the latter. On their defeat, he goes to surrender himself to Charles, but, fearing for his life, leaves a written instruction with his wicked favourite Francisco to put his beloved wife Marcelia to death if he himself is killed. Francisco, seeking to corrupt Marcelia in revenge for the dishonouring of his own sister Eugenia by Sforza, reveals the existence of the warrant to her, but fails to move her chastity and only incenses her against the duke, so that on his return after a reconciliation with Charles she receives him coldly. This, coupled with accusations from various quarters of his wife's intimacy with Francisco, makes the duke suspicious of her. Francisco now tells Sforza that Marcelia made amorous advances to him, which so inflames the duke with anger that he stabs her to death; dying, she reveals the truth, leaving her husband distracted with remorse. Francisco flees, then returns to court disguised as a Jewish doctor, and undertakes to restore Marcelia to life. He is discovered and tortured, but not before he succeeds in poisoning the duke.

Duke's Children, The, a novel by A. *Trollope, published 1880, the last novel in the *'Palliser' series.

The duchess of Omnium encourages Frank Tregear, a young Conservative with little fortune, in his suit to her daughter Lady Mary Palliser, but after the death of the duchess Tregear has no one to plead his cause with the Liberal duke, and the match is broken off. Meanwhile the duke shows mounting concern at the behaviour of his eldest son and heir, Lord Silverbridge. After being sent down from Oxford, Silverbridge immerses himself in London club-life, and becomes well known for his interest in the turf. He becomes part-owner, with the unsavoury Major Tifto, of a racehorse waggishly named 'The Prime Minister', and loses £70,000 betting on its performances in the Derby and St Leger. The duke pays his son's debts and hints that marriage might help him to settle down in life, whereupon Silverbridge admits his involvement with an impoverished but well-born cousin of Tregear's, Lady Mabel Grex, who is herself in love with Tregear, though she knows she can never afford to marry him. Tregear finds a seat in Parliament, finally convincing the duke of his political and personal integrity. The duke sanctions his marriage to Lady Mary, and is prepared to encourage Silverbridge's marriage to Lady Mabel, when he discovers that his son has fallen in love with the brilliant American Isabel Boncassen. Although the duke finds it hard to reconcile himself to the idea of a wedding between a future duke of Omnium and a girl whose family has risen from obscurity in two generations, even though Mr Boncassen is a respected scholar, Silverbridge's determination and Isabel's charm make him give way gracefully in the end. Lady Mabel, a character of tragic dimensions, is left to solitary disappointment.

Dulcinea del Toboso, the name given by *Don Quixote to the peasant girl Alonza Lorenzo, whom he elects to be mistress of his heart. Hence the English use of the name Dulcinea for a sweetheart.

Dumaine, in Shakespeare's *Love's Labour's Lost, one of the three lords attending the king of Navarre.

DUMAS, Alexandre (1802–70), French novelist and playwright, known as 'Dumas *père*'. One of the pioneers of the Romantic theatre in France, he achieved great popularity with a series of colourful, swiftly moving dramas mostly on historical subjects, including: *Henri III et sa cour* (1829), *Antony* (1831, dealing with contemporary social life), *La Tour de Nesle* (1832), and *Kean* (1836, in which the English tragedian is the central character of a comedy). The historical novels on which his reputation now chiefly rests began to appear serially at prodigious speed around 1840. *Les Trois Mousquetaires* (1844); *Vingt ans après* (1845), and *Le Vicomte de Bragelonne* (1848–50), set in the 17th cent., follow the adventures of d'Artagnan, who comes from Gascony to Paris in the reign of Louis XIII to join the king's musketeers, and shares the fortunes and exploits of three of them, Athos, Porthos, and Aramis, over 20 years. The action of other novels is laid against the wars of religion in 16th-cent. France (e.g. *La Reine Margot*, 1845) or the period of the late 18th cent. and the revolution (e.g. *Le Collier de la reine*, 1849–50; *La Comtesse de Charny*, 1852–5). His masterpiece of mystery and adventure, *Le Comte de Monte Cristo* (1844–5), recounts the elaborate vengeance of Edmond Dantès, falsely accused as a Bonapartiste conspirator in 1815, and imprisoned for many years in the Château d'If. Dumas's astonishing energy also found expression in numerous books of travel, 22 volumes of *Mémoires* (1852–5), several children's stories, and a *Grand Dictionnaire de cuisine* (1872, posthumous).

DUMAS, Alexandre (1824–95), known as 'Dumas *fils*', son of the above, French novelist and playwright. His first, and most remarkable, venture into the theatre was *La Dame aux camélias* (1852), a dramatization of his own novel (1848) of the same title. The story of the love, doomed by social disapproval, of the reformed courtesan Marguerite Gautier for the respectable Armand Duval, it held the stage with great success for half a century. Thereafter Dumas *fils* turned to the writing of social-problem dramas, such as *Le Demimonde* (1855), *Le Fils naturel* (1858), *Les Idées de Madame Aubray* (1867), *L'Étrangère* (1876).

du MAURIER, Dame Daphne (1907–89), novelist, born in London, the daughter of actor-manager Gerald and granddaughter of George *du Maurier. It was not until her family bought a second home in Cornwall that she escaped the social life she hated, and which had interfered with her writing. Living alone there through the winter of 1929–30 she produced her first novel, *The Loving Spirit* (1931), which was an immediate success, satisfying the inter-war longing for romantic sagas. V. *Gollancz, who published her frank memoir of her father (*Gerald*, 1934), encouraged her to develop her powerful narrative skill and evocation of atmosphere, and the result was *Jamaica Inn* (1936). Married in 1932 to Major Frederick Browning, she was obliged to go abroad with him when he was posted to Egypt, where she became desperately homesick: this unhappy period produced *Rebecca (1938), a study in jealousy based on her own feelings towards a former fiancée of her husband's. It became a worldwide and enduring best-seller. She wrote ten more novels, two plays, several collections of short stories and three biographies, but Rebecca remained her finest work, ensuring her lasting fame even though it overshadowed the rest of her work. A biography by Margaret *Forster was published in 1993.

du MAURIER, George Louis Palmella Busson (1834–96), artist and writer, born in Paris. He spent his childhood there and in London, and became between 1856 and 1860 an art student in Paris and Antwerp. He contributed to *Punch and other periodicals and illustrated editions of Mrs *Gaskell, *Meredith, *Hardy, and H. *James, among others. In 1865 he began to write humorous verse, including 'The History of the Jack Sprats', and a parody of W. *Morris's ballads, 'The Legend of Camelot', with mock *Pre-Raphaelite illustrations. In 1891 he published his first novel, Peter Ibbetson, largely based on his early childhood in Paris, and turning on two supernaturally related dreams. His next novel, *Trilby, for which he is still remembered, appeared in 1894; its vast fame and success continued for many years. The Martian, a story based on school life, appeared posthumously in 1897.

Dumbello, Lady, in A. Trollope's *Barsetshire series of novels, the married name of Griselda, daughter of Archdeacon Grantly.

dumb show, a piece of silent action or stage business, especially in the Elizabethan and Jacobean theatre, where speech is expected but not actually delivered. These shows, such as the one before the play scene in *Hamlet or Revenge's in *The Spanish Tragedy, suggest by mime and symbolism what is shortly to take place and its meaning.

DUNBAR, William (?1456–?1513), Scottish poet and priest, an MA of St Andrews (1479). He was wrecked off Zeeland while carrying out a diplomatic mission for James IV; in 1500 he was awarded a royal pension. He wrote 'The Thrissill and the Rois', his first great poem, in 1503; 'The Dance of the Sevin Deidly Synnis', part of 'Fasternis Evin in Hell', in 1507; and at about the same time 'The Goldyn Targe', the 'Lament for the Makaris', and 'The Tretis of the Tua Mariit Wemen and the Wedo', as well as numerous minor pieces. The poem which opens 'London, thou art of townes A per se' is not now thought to be Dunbar's, but he did write 'To Aberdein', celebrating Queen Margaret Tudor's entry into the town in 1511. He probably fell at the battle of *Flodden; certainly no poems indubitably by him survive from a date later than 1513.

'The Thrissill and the Rois' is a political allegory in rhyme-royal, the Rose representing Margaret Tudor, married to James IV, the Thistle. The 'Tua Mariit Wemen and the Wedo' (widow), a visionary dialogue in which the three interlocutors relate their experiences of marriage, is a satire on women reminiscent of Chaucer's wife of Bath's prologue in the *Canterbury Tales. 'The Goldyn Targe' is an allegory in which the poet, appearing in a dream before the court of Venus, is wounded by the arrows of Beauty in spite of the shield ('targe') of Reason. In 'The Dance of the Sevin Deidly Synnis' the poet in a trance sees the fiend Mahoun call a dance of unshriven outcasts, who are characterized with great vigour. The 'Lament for the Makaris' may also relate to the tradition of the *Dance of Death. It is a powerful elegy for the transitoriness of things, with its refrain 'Timor mortis conturbat me', and in particular for the deaths of Dunbar's fellow poets, including *Chaucer, *Gower, and *Henryson. Dunbar's satirical energy and Rabelaisian humour are particularly well displayed in 'The *Flyting of Dunbar and Kennedie'. See Poems, ed. J. Kinsley (1979); biography by J. W. Baxter (1952); T. Scott, Dunbar: A Critical Exposition of the Poems (1966).

Duncan, king of Scotland in Shakespeare's *Macbeth; murdered in his sleep by Macbeth.

DUNCAN, Robert, see BLACK MOUNTAIN POETS.

Dunciad, The, a *mock-heroic satire by *Pope, of which three books were published anonymously in 1728. In 1729, again anonymously, Pope published The Dunciad Variorum, which added notes and other 'scholarly material' to the poem. Pope did not openly acknowledge its authorship until 1735. The New Dunciad was published in 1742, and forms the fourth book of the complete work as it appeared in 1743. The poem had been under preparation for some years and its issue was determined by the criticisms of Pope's edition of Shakespeare contained in *Theobald's Shakespeare Restored. Theobald was made the hero of the poem in its earlier form, but in the final edition of 1743 C. *Cibber was enthroned in his stead. The satire is directed against 'Dulness' in general, and in the course of it all the authors who have earned Pope's condemnation are held up to ridicule. But the work is not confined to personal abuse, for literary vices receive their share of exposure. The argument of the poem is as follows.

Bk I. The reign of Dulness is described. Bayes (i.e. Cibber) is shown debating whether he shall betake himself to the church, or gaming, or party-writing, but is carried off by the goddess and anointed king in the place of *Eusden, the poet laureate, who has died.

Bk II. This solemnity is graced by games, in which poets, critics, and booksellers contend. There are races, with various accidents, in which booksellers pursue the phantom of a poet; exercises for the poets; and finally a test for the critics, to decide whether they can hear the works of two authors read aloud without sleeping. But presently spectators, critics, and all fall fast asleep.

Bk III. The king, slumbering with his head on the lap of the goddess, is transported to the Elysian shades, where, under the guidance of *Settle, he sees visions of the past and future triumphs of the empire of Dulness, how this shall extend to the theatres and the court, the arts and the sciences.

Bk IV. The realization of these prophecies is described, and the subjugation of the sciences and universities to Dulness, the growth of indolence, the corruption of education, and the consummation of all in the restoration of night and chaos.

Dun Cow, *Book of the*, an Irish manuscript of the 11th cent. containing mythological romances. A fragment of it survives, containing in particular many of the feats of *Cuchulain.

Dun Cow of Dunsmore, a monstrous animal slain by *Guy of Warwick.

Dun in the Mire, where 'Dun' (originally a dun horse) is a quasi-proper name for any horse, an old Christmas game (also called 'drawing Dun out of the mire'), in which the horse in the mire is represented by a heavy log, and the players compete to lift and carry it off.

> If thou art Dun, we'll draw thee from the mire.
> (Shakespeare, *Romeo and Juliet*, i. iv. 41)

DUNMORE, Helen (1952–), English poet, novelist, and children's writer. Her poetry collections include *The Sea Skater* (1986) and *The Raw Garden* (1988). Her adult novels include *Going to Egypt* (1992), *Zennor in Darkness* (1993), *Burning Bright* (1994), *A Spell of Darkness* (1995, winner of the Orange Prize), *Talking to the Dead* (1996), *Your Blue-Eyed Boy* (1998), *The Siege* (2001, set in Leningrad), and *Mourning Ruby* (2003). All are marked by richly textured writing, tangy descriptions of food and sex, and an eerie sense of place which matches their mysterious plots, often concerned with long-buried family secrets and betrayals. *Love of Fat Men* (1997) is a collection of short stories.

Dunmow Flitch, according to an ancient custom of the manor of Dunmow in Essex, a side of bacon given to any married couple who after 12 months of marriage could swear that they had maintained perfect harmony and fidelity during that time. The antiquity of the custom is shown by the reference to it in the prologue to Chaucer's 'Wife of Bath's Tale' (see CANTERBURY TALES, 6):

> The bacoun was nought fet for hem, I trowe,
> That some men fecche in Essex at Dunmowe.

The custom is said to have been instituted by Robert Fitz-Walter in 1244 and is still observed.

DUNN, Douglas Eaglesham (1942–), Scottish poet and critic, professor of English at St Andrews University since 1991. He was born at Inchinnan, Renfrewshire, and educated at Renfrew High School,

the Scottish School of Librarianship, and, from 1966 to 1969, at the University of Hull. After graduating at Hull he worked in the Brynmor Jones Library under Philip *Larkin, whose influence was apparent in Dunn's first collection, *Terry Street* (1969), closely observed and blackly humorous vignettes of a working-class Hull suburb. This was followed by *Backwaters* and *Night* (both 1971), *The Happier Life* (1972), and *Love or Nothing* (1974), which both moved away from the urban realism of his first volume, *Barbarians* (1979), and *St Kilda's Parliament* (1981). He moved back to Scotland in 1984 and the following year published the moving *Elegies*, written after the death of his wife from cancer, and a collection of short stories about rural Scotland, *Secret Villages*. A second collection of stories, *Boyfriends and Girlfriends*, was published in 1995. *Selected Poems: 1964–1983* appeared in 1986 and two further collections of verse, *Northlight*, with poems set in Scotland, Italy, Australia, and France and including an elegy for Larkin, and *Dante's Drum-Kit*, in 1988 and 1993. He is the editor of *The Faber Book of Twentieth-Century Scottish Verse* (1992) and *The Oxford Book of Scottish Short Stories* (1995). His translation of *Racine's *Andromaque* was published in 1990.

DUNN, Nell (1936–), novelist and playwright, whose early works of fiction *Up the Junction* (1963) and *Poor Cow* (1967; filmed, Ken Loach, 1968) showed a sensitive ear for working-class dialogue and an uninhibited approach to female sexuality. Her other works include *The Only Child* (1978, a tale of the rich) and *My Silver Shoes* (1996), which takes up the story of Joy from *Poor Cow*—now middle-aged, but still full of spirit, and locked into an embattled and intense relationship with her ageing but inexhaustible mother. Dunn's best-known play *Steaming* (perf. 1981) is a comedy with an all-female cast set in a Turkish bath, where a disparate group of women learn to combine to tackle the threatened closure of their refuge: other dramatic works with a darker edge include *The Little Heroine* (1988) and *Sisters* (1994).

DUNNE, J(ohn) W(illiam) (1875–1949), pioneer aircraft designer and author of the widely read *An Experiment with Time* (1927) and *The Serial Universe* (1934), in which he outlined a theory of time to account for such phenomena as precognition, previsional dreaming, etc. He quotes in support *Wells's *The Time Machine*, but Wells was to reply that Dunne had taken his concept of 'duration as a dimension of space' too seriously. Dunne's concept proved a useful dramatic device to J. B. *Priestley in his 'Time' plays, and is mentioned with interest by G. *Greene (who asks if it is possible for novelists to draw their symbols from the future as well as from the past: see *Ways of Escape*, ch. 3).

DUNSANY, Edward John Moreton Drax Plunkett, 18th Baron (1878–1957), of Anglo-Irish parentage, associated with the *Irish Revival, and a friend of *Yeats,

*Gogarty, and Lady *Gregory. His first book of (non-Celtic) mythological tales, *The Gods of Pegana* (1905), was illustrated by S. H. Sime (1867–1941), whose weird *fin-de-siècle* drawings were to accompany many subsequent fantasies, including *The Book of Wonder* (1912), *The King of Elfland's Daughter* (1924) and *The Blessing of Pan* (1927). Dunsany's first play, *The Glittering Gate*, was performed at the *Abbey Theatre in 1909; this and many later plays show the influence of *Maeterlinck's not dissimilar vein of *fantasy. His short plays were popular with the Little Theatre movement in America, and his full-length *If* (an *oriental tale) was a success in London in 1921. In more realistic vein Dunsany wrote the popular 'Jorkens' stories, beginning with *The Travel Tales of Mr Joseph Jorkens* (1931). He also wrote novels, essays, verse, and a series of autobiographies. See Mark Amory, *Lord Dunsany* (1972).

DUNS SCOTUS, John (c.1266 or 1270–1308), the 'Doctor Subtilis', a Scottish Franciscan who entered the order at Dumfries in 1278. He lectured on the *Sententiae* of *Peter Lombard at Oxford, probably 1300–4, and at Paris, probably 1304–5. He was among those expelled from Paris by Philip the Fair in 1305, and he died at Cologne, probably on 8 Nov. 1308. His principal works were his two series of commentaries on the *Sententiae*, the *Reportata Parisiensia* (?1306) and the *Opus Oxoniense* (?1297); most of the reconstruction of his thought is based on the latter. He wrote many other works in his brief lifetime, though many of those attributed to him are, at least in part, of disputed authorship (such as the *De Anima* and the important, advanced *Theoremata*); the uncertainty of the states in which the manuscripts of his work survive, combined with the extreme sophistication of his thought, make detailed understanding of his systematic beliefs very difficult. His principal significance in the history of *Scholasticism is that he drove the first wedge between theology and philosophy (a split which widened throughout the 14th cent.), with his emphasis on the separation (already noted by Thomas *Aquinas) between God as necessary Being from all contingent Beings, and (shifting away from Aquinas) the impossibility of arguing from the latter to the former. Although this emphasis, together with his associated Augustinian-Franciscan stress on faith and will rather than reason, distinguishes him from the synthesis of Aquinas, he resembles him in the employment of an emphatically *Realist metaphysics in the theory of Essences, and in his incorporation of a good deal of *Aristotle into his metaphysics. He was much influenced too by Arabic philosophers, especially *Avicenna, with their emphasis on Being as the metaphysical object. His great significance is that he straddles the dividing line between 13th-cent. system-building and 14th-cent. scepticism. The word 'dunce', first in the sense of 'a maker of impossibly ingenious distinctions', derives from him (Aqui-

nas was called 'the dumb ox'); some of his formal metaphysical distinctions were referred to by G. M. *Hopkins in his development of a poetic psychology, and it has been argued by John MacQueen that Scotus was an influence on *Langland. His works have been edited by Vives (26 vols, 1891–5).

DUNSTAN, St (c.910–88), born at Glastonbury of a noble family, and educated by Irish scholars there. He became a favourite with King Athelstan, but withdrew from the court in disfavour and stayed with his kinsman Ælfheah (Elphege) who became bishop of Winchester in 934 and who persuaded Dunstan to take monastic vows. He is also said to have practised the arts of metalworking, painting, and transcribing. He was restored to favour by King Edmund, who appointed him abbot of Glastonbury (939). He made it a famous school, restoring it spiritually and materially. He was one of the chief advisers of kings Edmund and Eadred (who succeeded in 946); but when King Eadwig succeeded Eadred, he incurred his disfavour (according to a traditional story, by rebuking the king for his lasciviousness with two 'loose women' at his coronation) and retired to Flanders in disgrace in 956. Edgar recalled him and appointed him bishop of Worcester (957), London (959), and Canterbury (960). Dunstan set about restoring and reforming English monasteries (as *Ælfric says) and making the Danes an integral part of the nation. He averted civil war by crowning Edward the Martyr in 975, and he foretold to King Ethelred the Unready the calamities which would befall the nation because of Edward's murder. In his last years the onus of the revival was carried by his successors and colleagues Æthelwold and *Oswald. See D. Knowles, *The Monastic Order in England* (1940); J. A. Robinson, *The Times of St Dunstan* (1923).

DUNTON, John (1659–1733), a publisher and bookseller who between 1691 and 1697 issued the *Athenian Gazette* (afterwards *Athenian Mercury*), dealing with philosophical and scientific matters, and incorporating a quiz in the form of questions sent in by readers. He also wrote many political pamphlets and *The Life and Errors of John Dunton* (1705).

Durandarte, a hero of Spanish legend and ballad, killed at Roncesvalles. See *Don Quixote* (II. xxiii). He is the subject of a ballad by M. G. *Lewis.

DURAS, Marguerite (1914–96), French novelist, screenwriter, playwright, and film director, born in Indo-china. She used her own experience as source material, and, while her early works were traditional, after 1950 she more or less abandoned conventional narrative, her work becoming more symbolic and employing some of the techniques of the *nouveau roman. In *L'Amant* (1984), for which she won the Prix Goncourt, she returns to the autobiographical material first explored in *Un barrage contre le Pacifique* (1950). Intensely passionate and deeply personal, it is widely seen as her most significant novel, although it may be for her screenplay for Alain Resnais's *Hiroshima mon amour* (1959) that she is more widely remembered.

D'Urberville, Alec, a character in Hardy's *Tess of the D'Urbervilles.*

DURCAN, Paul (1944–   ), Irish poet, born in Dublin, educated at University College, Cork. Prolific since *O Westport in the Light of Asia Minor* (1975), Durcan is an acclaimed performer of his poems. Powered by parallelism, refrains (indebted, perhaps, to the Catholic liturgy), and startling transitions, Durcan's monologues and fantasias are variously comic, painful, and imponderable. His most accessible poems are satires on the constriction of Irish life by ignorance, prejudice, and authority, often religious in origin ('Irish Hierarchy Bans Colour Photography'). *Daddy, Daddy* (1990) deals hilariously and poignantly with the poet's relationship with his father, a sternly Republican judge, in a series of what are in effect love poems. Durcan has also written memorably of the failure of marriage ('The Pietà's Over'), while his greatest originality lies in his utopianism—life revised by humane fantasy (as in 'The Haulier's Wife Encounters Jesus on the Road near Moone'), often with an erotic cast. See *A Snail in My Prime: New and Selected Poems* (1993) and *Christmas Day* (1996).

Durdles, the stonemason in Dickens's *Edwin Drood.*

DÜRER, Albrecht (1471–1528), German painter and engraver, the son of a Hungarian goldsmith who settled in Nuremberg. His friendship with the great humanist scholar Willibald Pirkheimer stimulated his interest in the new learning of the Renaissance and he made two journeys to Italy, introducing to the north the ideals and forms he encountered there. His most famous engravings, and those which have most fascinated literary men, are *Knight, Death and the Devil* (1513) and *Melencolia I* (1514). In 1636 Arundel, a passionate collector of Dürer, bought the Pirkheimer library with many books illuminated by the artist. The northern Renaissance aroused little enthusiasm in 18th-cent. England, but interest revived in the 19th cent. J. *Thomson's *City of Dreadful Night* contains a long description of *Melencolia*, which in turn reappears in *Kipling, and *Ruskin and G. *Eliot both admired him. See E. Panofsky, *The Life and Word of Albrecht Dürer* (1943).

d'URFÉ, Honoré (1567–1625), French author of *L'Astrée* (published in four parts, 1607–27), a prose romance in a pastoral setting celebrating the virtues of a refined life which enjoyed great popularity, influencing English playwrights under Charles I. It was praised by *La Fontaine and *Rousseau for the sensitivity of its natural descriptions.

D'URFEY, Thomas (1653–1723), a French Huguenot by descent, familiarly known as Tom Durfey, who wrote a large number of songs, tales, satires, melodramas, and farces. A friend of Charles II and James II, he was still writing in the reign of Queen Anne, and was one of the most familiar figures of the day, given to singing his own songs in public. His comedies include *Madame Fickle* (1676), *The Virtuous Wife* (1679), and the more sentimental *Love for Money* (1691). He was attacked by Jeremy *Collier and replied in a comedy, *The Campaigners* (1698), with an unrepentant prose preface. His works include many adaptations: *Bussy D'Ambois, *Cymbeline (as *The Injured Princess*), and a three-part dramatization of *Don Quixote (1694–6) with music by *Purcell. His *Wit and Mirth, or Pills to Purge Melancholy* (6 vols, 1719–20) is a collection of songs and ballads.

Durindana, or Durandal, the sword of *Roland or *Orlando, which had been that of Hector of Troy.

DURKHEIM, Émile (1858–1917), French sociologist. His significance as a major figure in modern sociology proceeds from his attempt to establish sociology as a science. His studies of criminality (*De la division du travail social*, 1893), of suicide (*Le Suicide*, 1897), and of magic (*Les Formes élémentaires de la vie religieuse*, 1912) served to mark out the sociological field and to determine the nature of the sociological fact. In 1898 he founded *L'Année sociologique*, the first sociological review.

DURRELL, Lawrence George (1912–90), poet, novelist, and travel writer, born in India; he returned to England in his late teens, and thereafter travelled widely, living in Paris in the 1930s, and then for much of his life in the eastern Mediterranean. Although he began to write and publish both verse and prose when very young (his first pamphlet of verse appeared in 1931, his first novel, *Pied Piper of Lovers*, in 1935) his work made little impact for some years. He was first recognized as a poet: his collections include *A Private Country* (1943); *Cities, Plains and People* (1946); *On Seeming to Presume* (1948); *The Tree of Idleness* (1955). His *Collected Poems* appeared in 1960. His first novel of interest, *The Black Book: An Agon*, heavily influenced by Henry *Miller, published in Paris in 1938, did not appear in Britain until 1973; it is a mildly pornographic fantasia, peopled by prostitutes and failed artists, intended by the author as 'a savage charcoal sketch of spiritual and sexual etiolation'. It was with the publication of *Justine* (1957), the first volume of his *Alexandria Quartet*, that Durrell achieved fame: *Balthazar* and *Mountolive* followed in 1958, and *Clea* in 1960. Set in Alexandria during the period just before the Second World War, the first three novels cover roughly the same period of time and the same events, while *Clea* advances the action in time; the central topic, according to Durrell, is 'an investigation of modern love'. Principal characters include the narrator L. G. Darley, his Greek mistress Melissa, the British ambassador Mountolive, the British intelligence agent Pursewarden, the artist Clea, and Justine (who is Jewish) and her wealthy Coptic husband Nessim. All are bound together in a web of political and sexual intrigue: each novel reveals different aspects of the truth. The style is ornate, lyrical, and sensual, perhaps too much so for English tastes, as the *Quartet* tends to be more highly regarded abroad than in Britain. Durrell's later novels, which include *Tunc* (1968), *Nunquam* (1970), *Monsieur* (1974), and *Constance* (1982), show even greater disregard for British respect for realism. His best-known travel books are his three 'island' books, *Prospero's Cell* (1945), based on his pre-war years in Corfu; *Reflections on a Marine Venus* (1953), based on his experiences as information officer in Rhodes, 1945–6; and *Bitter Lemons* (1957), on Cyprus.

Lawrence Durrell's brother, the zoologist Gerald Malcolm Durrell (1925–95), was also a writer, well known for his popular accounts of animal life and his own zoo on Jersey: titles include *The Overloaded Ark* (1953), *My Family and Other Animals* (1956), *Island Zoo* (1961).

DÜRRENMATT, Friedrich (1921–90), Swiss dramatist, a writer of grotesque black comedy, because he thought that after the Second World War tragedy was a form no longer applicable to our modern 'upside-down world'. His best-known plays are *Der Besuch der alten Dame* (*The Visit*, 1956) and *Die Physiker* (*The Physicists*, 1962). Both are absurdist dramas dealing with power and responsibility, the first with reference to money, the second on the theme of the criminality of atomic physics. His plays include adaptations of Shakespeare's *King John* (1968) and *Titus Andronicus* (1970). Dürrenmatt has also written many radio plays and some critical essays.

Dusty Answer, a novel by R. *Lehmann; the title is taken from Meredith's *Modern Love*.

Dutch Courtezan, The, a comedy by *Marston, printed 1605.

Young Freevill, being about to marry Beatrice, daughter of Sir Hubert Subboys, determines to break his connection with Franceschina, the Dutch courtesan. He introduces the latter to his self-righteous friend Malheureux, who becomes violently enamoured of her. She consents to gratify his passion if he will kill Freevill, and bring proof of the deed in the shape of a ring given to him by Beatrice. Freevill consents to help him; a pretended quarrel is arranged, Freevill disappears, and Malheureux takes the ring to Franceschina, who hastens to communicate the news to old Freevill and Sir Hubert Subboys. Malheureux is arrested for the murder of Freevill and sentenced to death. At the last moment young Freevill appears, and begs forgiveness for the device that he has adopted to cure his friend of his passion. Franceschina is condemned to be whipped and jailed.

DYCE, Alexander (1798–1869), scholar, who edited a large number of the works of Shakespeare and his contemporaries. His editions include the works of G. *Peele (1828 and 1829–39), T. *Middleton (1840),

*Beaumont and *Fletcher (1843–6), *Marlowe (1850), J. *Ford (1869), R. *Greene (1831, 1861), and J. *Webster (1830, 1857). As well as producing a full edition of Shakespeare's works (1857, 1864–7) he was the first editor of *Sir Thomas *More (1844). He left his valuable collection of books and manuscripts to the Victoria and Albert Museum.

DYCK, Sir Anthony Van, see VAN DYCK.

DYER, Sir Edward (1543–1607), educated either at Broadgates Hall or Balliol College, Oxford. He was introduced at court by the earl of *Leicester, and took part in the queen's entertainment at Woodstock in 1575. The most famous poem attributed to him, *'My mind to me a kingdom is', is probably not his work, but by Edward De Vere, earl of *Oxford. Few authentic poems have survived: those which do show him to be a rather old-fashioned courtly poet. One of the best of his surviving poems is 'The lowest trees have tops' which was set by *Dowland in 1603. There is an account of his life and works by R. M. Sargent (1935).

DYER, Geoff (1958–   ), writer of fiction and non-fiction, born in Cheltenham. His first, Brixton-based novel, *The Colour of Memory* (1989), was followed by *The Search* (1993), in which a man is asked to track down a woman's husband. *Paris Trance* (1998), Dyer's third novel, is set in the French capital. Dyer's enthusiasm for the subjects covered is the link between his non-fiction works: *Ways of Telling*, (1986) a critical study of the work of John *Berger, *But Beautiful: A Book about Jazz* (1991), *The Missing of the Somme* (1994), and *Out of Sheer Rage: In the Shadow of D. H. Lawrence* (1997).

DYER, George (1755–1841), educated at *Christ's Hospital and Emmanuel College, Cambridge, usher at Dedham Grammar School and later at a school in Northampton. He published his *Poems* in 1792, and various critical essays from time to time. He is remembered as a friend of *Lamb, who writes of him as a gentle and kindly eccentric. He is the subject of Lamb's essay 'Amicus Redivivus' in *The Last Essays of Elia*, which describes how Dyer, departing from Lamb's cottage in Islington, marched absent-mindedly into the nearby river and disappeared. His rescue and resuscitation are affectionately described.

DYER, John (1699–1757), Welsh poet, briefly educated at Westminster. He studied law, then painting (with Jonathan Richardson), and eventually became a clergyman. He is remembered chiefly for his *topographical poem in tetrameter couplets, *Grongar Hill* (1726), which describes the scenery of the river Towy. He also wrote *The Ruins of Rome* (1740) and *The Fleece* (1757), a poem about the wool trade, which contains fine early industrial and pastoral landscapes, as well as much practical information. Dr *Johnson and many others scorned *The Fleece* for its prosaic subject and prolix manner, but *Wordsworth admired it greatly, addressed a sonnet to Dyer ('Bard of the Fleece . . . .'), and in his notes to *The Excursion* comments 'He wrote at a time when machinery was first beginning to be introduced, and his benevolent heart prompted him to augur from it nothing but good.'

DYLAN, Bob (1941–   ), adopted name of American singer-songwriter Robert Allen Zimmerman, whose lyrics have been highly praised both by poets and by some academics.

Dynasts, The, an Epic-Drama of the War with Napoleon, in Three Parts, Nineteen Acts and One Hundred and Thirty Scenes, by T. *Hardy, published in three parts, 1904, 1906, 1908.

This vast and original work, for which Hardy had read extensively, was shaping itself in his mind for nearly 30 years before he began to publish it. It is written partly in blank verse, partly in a variety of other metres, and partly in prose. The events of history with which it deals are recounted in the descriptive passages and stage directions. The work centres on the tragic figure of Napoleon. Part I opens with the year 1805, and Napoleon's threat of invasion. It presents the House of Commons discussing the repeal of the Defence Act, Napoleon's coronation at Milan, the preparations at Boulogne for the invasion of England, the battles of Ulm and Austerlitz, Trafalgar, the death of Nelson, and the death of Pitt.

Part II covers the defeat of the Prussians at Jena, the meeting of Napoleon and Alexander at Tilsit, the battle of Wagram, the fall of Godoy and the abdication of the king of Spain, and war in Spain, the divorce of Josephine, and Napoleon's marriage with Marie Louise.

Part III presents the Russian expedition of 1812, the British victories in the Pyrenees, the battle of Leipzig, Napoleon's abdication, his return from Elba, the ball in Brussels, Quatre-Bras, and Waterloo. Accompanying the major scenes are small vignettes, seen at close quarters, showing how these great events affected English rustics in Wessex, private soldiers, camp followers, and other ordinary people. Above them all, supernatural spectators of the terrestrial action, are impersonated abstractions, or Intelligences; the Ancient Spirit of the Years, the Spirit of the Pities, the Spirits Sinister and Ironic, and the Spirit of Rumour, with their attendant choruses, the Shade of the Earth, and the Recording Angels. Above all is the Immanent Will, the force, unconscious and heedless, that moves the world. They are introduced not, as the author is careful to point out in his preface, 'as a systematized philosophy warranted to lift "the burthen of the mystery" of this unintelligible world' but to give by their comments a universal significance to the particular events recounted.

After the experience of the First World War Hardy felt that he should not have ended the work with a glimpse of hope for mankind. The drama was intended 'simply for mental performance', but scenes from it were produced in London in 1914, when Rebecca *West found it 'one of the greatest plays' that had been seen on the English stage. The cinematic nature of the work has often been noted.

Dystopia, a term coined to convey the opposite of *utopia: the dystopian mode, which projects an unpleasant or catastrophic future, is frequently used by *science fiction writers.

E

EADMER (d. ?1124), a monk of Canterbury who wrote a Latin chronicle of the events of his own time down to 1122, *Historia Novorum in Anglia*, a biography of his friend and leader *Anselm, and an early Marian work, the *Liber de Excellentia Beatae Mariae*. The *Historia* and the life of Anselm were edited together by M. Rule (Rolls Series 1881, 1884).

EAGLETON, Terry, see MARXIST LITERARY CRITICISM.

Eames, Johnny, a character in A. *Trollope's novels *The Small House at Allington* and *The Last Chronicle of Barset*.

EARLES, or **EARLE,** John (?1601–65), a member of *Falkland's circle at Great Tew, who became tutor to Prince Charles in 1641, served him as chaplain during his exile in France, and after the Restoration became bishop of Worcester, then Salisbury, in which roles he defended persecuted Nonconformists. *Microcosmographie* (1628) was a collection of character sketches, chiefly by his hand, based on the model of *Theophrastus, though some of them are responses to the harsher and more satiric 'characters' of *Overbury (e.g. his 'Good Old Man', compared with Overbury's 'Old Man'). He analyses varied social and moral types, ranging from the plain country fellow to the pot poet, with wit, sympathy, and insight. (See CHARACTER-WRITING.)

Early English Text Society, the, founded in 1864 by *Furnivall for the publication of Early and Middle English texts.

Earnshaw, Catherine, Hindley, and Hareton, characters in Emily Brontë's *Wuthering Heights*.

Earthly Paradise, The, a poem by W. *Morris, published 1868–70, consisting of a prologue and 24 tales, in Chaucerian metres.

The prologue tells how a company of Norsemen, fleeing from the pestilence, set sail in search of the fabled Earthly Paradise 'across the western sea where none grow old'. They are disappointed in their quest and return after long wanderings, 'shrivelled, bent and grey', to a 'nameless city in a distant sea' where the ancient Greek gods are still worshipped. They are hospitably received and there spend their remaining years. Twice in each month they meet their hosts at a feast and a tale is told, alternately by one of the elders of the city and one of the wanderers. The tales of the former are on classical subjects (Atalanta, Perseus, the Apples of the Hesperides, etc.), those of the latter from Norse and other medieval subjects, including 'The

Lovers of Gudrun', a version of the *Laxdaela* saga. Between the tales are interpolated lyrics describing the changing seasons, and the whole work is prefaced by an apology which contains some of Morris's best-known (and in a sense most misleading) lines, in which he describes himself as 'the idle singer of an empty day', 'born out of my due time'. Although the plan of the work owes a debt to *The Canterbury Tales*, it is almost entirely static, and its narrators undifferentiated; highly popular in its day, it has since been seen as symptomatic of the weaknesses of Victorian late Romanticism.

Earwicker, Humphrey Chimpden, a character in Joyce's *Finnegans Wake*.

Eastern, see ORIENTAL.

East Lynne, see WOOD, E.

Eastward Hoe, a comedy by G. *Chapman, *Jonson, and J. *Marston, printed 1605, having been previously performed by the Children of the Revels at the Blackfriars. A passage derogatory to the Scots (III. iii. 40–7) gave offence at court, and Chapman and Jonson were imprisoned, but released on the intercession of powerful friends. The play is particularly interesting for the light it throws on London life of the time. Like Dekker's *Shoemaker's Holiday*, it gives a sympathetic picture of a tradesman.

The plot contrasts the careers of the virtuous and idle apprentices, Golding and Quicksilver, of the goldsmith Touchstone; and the fates of his two daughters, the modest Mildred, who marries the industrious Golding, and the immodest Gertrude who, in order to ride in her own coach, marries the penniless adventurer Sir Petronel Flash. Golding soon rises to the dignity of a deputy alderman, while Sir Petronel, having sent off his lady in a coach to an imaginary castle of his and filched her dowry, sets off for Virginia, accompanied by the prodigal Quicksilver, who has robbed his master. They are wrecked on the Isle of Dogs, and brought up before Golding, the deputy alderman. After some days in prison, where their mortifications lead them to repent, they are released at Golding's intercession.

Eatanswill, the scene of the parliamentary elections in Dickens's *Pickwick Papers*.

Ecclesiastical History of Bede, see HISTORIA ECCLESIASTICA.

Ecclesiastical Politie, Of the Laws of, see LAWS OF ECCLESIASTICAL POLITIE.

Echidna, in Spenser's *Faerie Queene* (VI. vi), is the mother of the *Blatant Beast. In Greek mythology, a monster, half woman and half snake.

ECKHARD, Johannes (?1260–1327), known as 'Meister Eckhard', a German Dominican who was conferred doctor by Boniface VIII but was later summoned before the bishop of Cologne and obliged to recant some of his opinions. He is regarded as the founder of German mysticism and one of its greatest exponents. English trans. by J. M. Clark included in his *Meister Eckhart: An Introduction* (1957).

eclogue, the term for a short pastoral poem, comes from ἐκλογή (a choice), the title given in Greek to collections of elegant extracts. The Latinized form *ecloga* was used, however, for any short poem and attached itself particularly to *Virgil's pastorals which their author had called *bucolica*, a name commonly applied to the Idylls (εἰδύλλια——short descriptive poems) of *Theocritus that Virgil had imitated. The terms eclogue, bucolic, and idyll have been widely used as synonyms, except that grammarians have made an effort to confine 'eclogue' to poems in dialogue form. The alternative spelling 'aeglogue' was prompted by a mistaken derivation from the Greek αἴξ, a goat.

Eclogues, The, of A. *Barclay, written *c.*1513–14, interesting as the earliest English *pastorals, anticipating *Spenser. They are moral and satirical in character, dealing with such subjects as the evils of a court life and the happiness of the countryman's lot. They are modelled upon *Mantuan and the *Miseriae Curialium of* *Piccolomini.

ECO, Umberto (1932–), Italian semiologist. His works include: *Thema: omaggio a Joyce* (*Themes: Homage to Joyce*, 1958, tape with music by Luciano Berio), *La struttura assente* (*The Absent Structure*, 1968), *Le forme del contenuto* (*The Forms of Content*, 1971), *A Theory of Semiotics* (1975), and *Opera aperta* (*The Open Work*, 1962). His historical mystery novel *Il nome della rosa* (*The Name of the Rose*, 1981), concerning a series of murders in a medieval monastery, was an international best-seller and was subsequently filmed with Sean Connery in the role of the 'detective', Brother William of Baskerville. His second novel, *Foucault's Pendulum*, was published in 1989. *How to Travel with a Salmon and Other Essays*, a collection of miscellaneous pieces, some previously unpublished, appeared in 1994. He has influenced the development of European semiotics (see SAUSSURE).

Economist, The, a weekly financial and commercial review founded in 1843. James Wilson was its first editor. It advocated free trade and the repeal of the Corn Laws and took up a sound attitude in opposition to the reckless railway speculation of the middle of the century. Among its later editors was *Bagehot, Wilson's son-in-law.

It remains a specialist review, and was considerably modernized under the successful editorship of Alastair Burnet (1965–74). The contributions remain anonymous.

Ector, Sir, in Malory's *Morte D'Arthur*, the knight to whom the infant King Arthur was entrusted. He was father of Sir *Kay, the steward.

Ector de Marys, Sir, in *Malory, the illegitimate son of King *Ban of Benwick and half-brother of *Launcelot. It is he who, in the last section of the *Morte D'Arthur*, finds Launcelot dead and utters his great lament over him.

Edda, an Old Norse name of uncertain meaning given to a 13th-cent. poetic manual written by *Snorri Sturluson, known as the Prose, Younger, or Snorra Edda. The same name was applied in the 17th cent. to a manuscript collection of poems, the Poetic or Elder Edda. The Prose Edda is divided into a prologue and three parts: the 'Gylfaginning', or Deluding of Gylfi, a series of mythological stories in the form of a dialogue between one Gylfi and the Norse gods; the 'Skáldska-parmál', or Poetic Diction, in which Snorri illustrates the elaborate diction of *skaldic verse, retelling many myths and legends; and the 'Háttatal', or List of Metres, a long poem each strophe of which exemplifies a different Norse metre. Snorri's work is valuable for the stories it enshrines, the verses it has preserved, and Snorri's own gifts as a storyteller. The Poetic Edda was compiled in about 1270, but some of the poems in it undoubtedly belong to a much earlier age. The poems fall into two groups: heroic lays about legendary Germanic heroes such as Sigurðr and Helgi; and mythological lays, such as the Vǫlsunga saga, a history of the Norse gods from creation to apocalypse, and the Hávamál, the words of the High One, Oðinn. *Auden wrote free translations of many Eddaic lays. See *The Prose Edda of Snorri Sturluson*, trans. J. I. Young (1954); *The Poetic Edda*, i: *Heroic Poems*, ii: *Mythological Poems*, ed. U. Dronke (1969–97, parallel trans.); *Norse Poems* by W. H. *Auden and P. B. Taylor (1981); E. O. G. Turville-Petre, *Origins of Icelandic Literature* (1953).

EDDISON, E. R., see FANTASY FICTION.

EDDY, Mrs Mary Baker Glover (1821–1910), born at Bow, New Hampshire. She was the founder of Christian Science, the doctrine of which she expounded in *Science and Health with Key to the Scriptures* (1875); the Christian Science Association was formed the following year.

EDEN, Emily (1797–1869), daughter of William Eden, first Baron Auckland. She moved in prominent Whig circles and was a close friend of Melbourne. When Melbourne appointed her brother governor-general of India in 1835, she accompanied him, travelled with him, and acted as his hostess, which she continued to do after his return until his death in 1849. She published *Portraits of the People and Princes of*

India (1844) and *Up the Country* (1866); *Letters from India* appeared in 1872, and a collection of her letters edited by her great-niece Violet Dickinson in 1919. Her two novels *The Semi-detached House* (1859, anon.) and *The Semi-attached Couple* (1860, by 'E.E.'), written some 30 years earlier, both deal with fashionable society, and combine shrewd perception, wit, and good nature; their plots and characterization owe much to J. *Austen, whom she greatly admired and frequently mentions. They are a valuable record of social life, shedding a revealing light on attitudes to marriage, politics, and manners, and have been several times reprinted, most recently in 1979.

Edgar, (1) in Shakespeare's *King Lear*, the legitimate son of Gloucester, who for much of the play (II. iii–IV. i) is disguised as the Bedlam beggar 'poor Tom'; (2) the master of Ravenswood, hero of Scott's *The Bride of Lammermoor*.

EDGAR, David (1948–   ), dramatist, born in Birmingham, and educated at Oundle School. He studied drama at Manchester University, after which he worked as a journalist in Bradford and wrote political plays for a touring theatre company, the General Will. His early work included a satirical pantomime on the Conservative prime minister Edward Heath, *Tedderella* (1971), and *Dick Deterred* (1974), a pastiche melodrama about Richard Nixon and the Watergate scandal. *Destiny* (1976), a play about Fascism in British society, was produced by the Royal Shakespeare Company. He came to general prominence in 1980 with his hugely successful eight-hour adaptation of Dickens's *Nicholas Nickleby*. *Maydays* (1983), the first play by a contemporary dramatist to be staged by the RSC at the Barbican Theatre, dealt with the post-war decline of socialism. His work also includes *Entertaining Strangers* (1985), set in 19th-cent. Dorchester, on which he worked with community playwright A. *Jellicoe; *That Summer* (1987), about the British miners' strike of 1985; *The Shape of the Table* (1990), set in communist eastern Europe; and *Pentecost* (1994). He has also written for radio and television and in 1991 adapted Stevenson's *The Strange Case of* *Dr Jekyll and Mr Hyde* for the *National Theatre.

Edge-Hill, see JAGO.

EDGEWORTH, Maria (1768–1849), the eldest daughter of the first wife of Richard Lovell Edgeworth (1744–1817), a wealthy Irish landlord of a large estate in Co. Longford, who was to marry three more wives after the death of Maria's mother in 1773 and to father in all 22 children. He was an eccentric, radical, and inventive man, deeply interested in the practical applications of science and in education: his friends included E. *Darwin, Mrs *Barbauld, and T. *Day. His influence on Maria was profound; he frequently 'edited' her work (which involved cutting, correcting, and occasionally contributing passages), managed her literary career, and imparted to her many of his own enthu-

siasms. They wrote together *Practical Education* (1798), a treatise which owes much to *Rousseau, although its tone is less theoretical.

Maria spent her infancy in Ireland, received some schooling in England, and when she was 15 returned to live the rest of her life with her family in Ireland. Her first publication was *Letters to Literary Ladies* (1795), a plea for women's education. From then on she wrote prolifically for some 40 years and established a high reputation. She visited London in 1803, when she was fêted by the literary world, meeting, among others, *Byron, Sydney *Smith, Joanna *Baillie, and Crabb *Robinson. She visited Sir W. *Scott at Abbotsford in 1823, and he returned the visit in Ireland in 1825. He greatly admired her work, described her as 'the great Maria', and acknowledged his debt to her Irish novels in the preface to his 'Waverley' edition of 1829. J. *Austen sent her a copy of *Emma*, and later admirers included *Macaulay, *Thackeray, *Ruskin, and *Turgenev.

Although not generally regarded as a novelist of the first rank, Miss Edgeworth appears to have initiated, in *Castle Rackrent*, both the first fully developed *regional novel and the first true *historical novel in English, pointing the way to the historical/regional novels of Scott. Her writings fall into three groups: those based on Irish life (considered her finest), *Castle Rackrent* (1800) and *The Absentee* (first published in *Tales of Fashionable Life* in 1812) together with the lesser *Ormond* (1817); those depicting contemporary English society, such as *Belinda* (1801—commended by the heroine of *Northanger Abbey*), *Leonora* (1806), *Patronage* (1814), and *Helen* (1834); and her many popular lessons and stories for and about children, including *The Parent's Assistant* (1796–1800), *Moral Tales* (1801), *Popular Tales* (1804), and *Harry and Lucy Concluded* (1825). See M. S. Butler, *Maria Edgeworth* (1972).

Edinburgh Review (1802–1929), a quarterly periodical, established by F. *Jeffrey, Sydney *Smith, and H. *Brougham, and originally published by A. *Constable. It succeeded immediately in establishing a prestige and authority which (shared with the *Quarterly Review*) lasted for over a century. *Carlyle described it as 'a kind of Delphic oracle'. Under the influence of its first editor, Jeffrey, its politics became emphatically Whig, but although it was anxious for reform in many spheres an effort was made to hold a balanced view. Only a section of the journal was reserved for literature, but the views expressed there were highly influential and the few books selected for review were very fully considered. Although Jeffrey perceived the genius of *Keats, his veneration for 18th-cent. literature led him to notorious and scathing denouncements of *Wordsworth, *Coleridge, and *Southey as the 'Lake School'. Between Jeffrey's resignation in 1829 and the demise of the *Review* in 1929 contributions were published from almost all the major writers and critics of the 19th and early 20th cents.

Edmund, in Shakespeare's *King Lear*, the villainously self-seeking bastard son of the earl of Gloucester.

education, literature of. Before the 17th cent. educational writing sought mainly to improve the classical curriculum (*Ascham's *The Scholemaster*, 1570), but calls for change came from *Milton (*A Small Tractate on Education*, 1650) and *Locke (*Some Thoughts Concerning Education*, 1693). Richard Lovell Edgeworth and Maria *Edgeworth's *Practical Education* (1798), influenced by *Rousseau, concerned the education of both sexes from infancy onwards, and had sections on moral development as well as on grammar and arithmetic. In the late 18th and 19th cents. writing, particularly by Nonconformists, centred on the irrelevance of the classical curriculum and the need for a secular, scientific, and technological education. Such aims were expressed by Joseph *Priestley (*Essay on a Course of Liberal Education for a Civil and Active Life*, 1765); *Godwin (*Enquiry Concerning Political Justice*, 1793); *Bentham (*Chrestomathia*, 1816), J. S. *Mill, Herbert *Spencer, and T. H. *Huxley: supporters of a liberal education based on the classics included Thomas and Matthew *Arnold and J. H. *Newman (*On the Scope and Nature of University Education*, 1852). Works on women's education included those of Mary *Wollstonecraft and E. *Darwin's *Plan for the Conduct of Female Education in Boarding Schools* (1797). *Paine's *Rights of Man* (Part II, 1792) included a plan to finance the education of all up to the age of 14. Robert *Owen's *A New View of Society* (1814) and Robert Dale Owen's *An Outline of the System of Education at New Lanark* (1824) explained their theories: discussion rather than rote learning, avoidance of rewards and punishments. William Lovett's *Chartism: A New Organisation of the People* (1840) and William *Morris's *A Factory as It Might Be* (1884) had sections on education.

The progressive education movement of the early 20th cent. focused on manner rather than content. W. B. Curry (*The School and a Changing Civilization*, 1934) and A. S. Neill (*Hearts Not Heads in the School*, 1944; *Summerhill*, 1960) set out ideas for education based on mutual trust between children and adults. Curry, like Karl Mannheim (*Man and Society*, 1940; *Diagnosis of Our Time*, 1943), saw education as a way towards a free and peaceful society. A. N. *Whitehead's *The Aims of Education* (1929) emphasizes the role of activity in the acquisition of ideas. Child-centred ideas influenced state education, though these were based on Swiss psychologist Jean Piaget's ideas about child development rather than those of Neill and Curry. (See *Children and Their Primary Schools*, HMSO, 1967, known as the 'Plowden report'.) In 1969 C. B. Cox and Brian Dyson edited *Fight for Education: A Black Paper*, first in a series of 'Black Papers' (the most recent 1977,

ed. Cox and Rhodes Boyson) which alleged falling standards and blamed child-centred methods for this.

The debate focused in the 1950s and 1960s on class inequality (B. Jackson and D. Marsden, *Education and the Working Class*, 1962; A. H. Halsey et al., *Origins and Destinations*, 1980) but from the 1970s ethnicity and gender became important issues: see *How the West Indian Child Is Made Educationally Subnormal in the British School System* (B. Coard, 1971), which stimulated further research, and *Feminism, Education and Social Justice* (1993, ed. M. Arnot and K. Weiner).

Edward, an old Scottish ballad of domestic tragedy, included in Percy's *Reliques* and beginning:

> Why, does your brand sae drop wi' blude,
> Edward, Edward?

Edward II, a tragedy in blank verse by *Marlowe probably first performed 1592, published 1594.

It deals with the recall by Edward II, on his accession, of his favourite, Piers Gaveston; the revolt of the barons and the capture and execution of Gaveston; the period during which Spenser (Hugh le Despenser) succeeded Gaveston as the king's favourite; the estrangement of Queen Isabella from her husband; her rebellion, supported by her paramour Mortimer, against the king; the capture of the latter, his abdication of the crown, and his murder in Berkeley Castle. The play was an important influence on Shakespeare's *Richard II*.

Edward III, *The Raigne of King*, a historical play, published 1596, of uncertain authorship, attributed by some, at least in part, to Shakespeare.

The first two acts are concerned mainly with the dishonourable wooing of the countess of Salisbury by the king, who is finally brought to a sense of shame by her determination to kill herself if he pursues his suit. The rest is occupied with the French wars.

Edwardian, strictly, of the reign of Edward VII, but the term is commonly used (in contrast with 'Victorian') of the years 1900–14. H. G. *Wells, who stands in a symbolic relation to the Edwardian period as *Wilde stood in a symbolic relation to the 1890s, wrote that Queen Victoria sat on England like a great paperweight, and that after her death things blew all over the place. This expresses well the excitement, the new sense of freedom, and the lack of direction, in Wells himself and in Arnold *Bennett, *Galsworthy, E. M. *Forster, and other liberal writers of the period. It was an era of outstanding achievement in the theatre (with G. B. *Shaw and *Granville-Barker) and, especially, in the novel, notably in the great works of H. *James's last phase and the radical experiments of *Conrad (and his collaborator F. M. *Ford). At the same time strongly traditional themes in the writing of the period—the empire as a source of national pride, the countryside as the custodian of national values, the upper-class house party representing the whole of English life—support the still current alternative sense of the word 'Edwardian', referring to a period of sunlit prosperity and opulent confidence preceding the cataclysm of the Great War.

EDWARDS, Amelia B., see GHOST STORIES.

EDWARDS, G(erald) B(asil) (1899–1976), remembered as the author of *The Book of Ebenezer Le Page* (1981), an autobiographical first-person novel set in Guernsey, written in a variant of Guernsey English, laced with French patois. It has no regular linear narrative, but builds up a distinctive and personal portrait of life on the island from the last decade of the 19th cent. to the 1960s—its landscape, its religious communities, its trades, its old families and customs. Edwards led a somewhat rambling life, spending his last years near Weymouth: his manuscript was eventually published with the encouragement of Edward Chaney and his wife, to whom it is dedicated, with an introduction by John *Fowles.

EDWARDS, Jonathan (1703–58), born in Connecticut, the philosopher, ardent divine, and formidable preacher who provoked the religious revival in New England known as the 'Great Awakening'. In his *Treatise Concerning Religious Affections* (1746) he nicely discriminated between the state of grace and the state of worldliness; and his attempt to make this distinction a criterion of fitness to receive the Eucharist led to his dismissal from the charge of the church of Northampton, Massachusetts, in 1750. He was then for six years a missionary to the Native Americans. His principal philosophical work, *A Careful and Strict Enquiry into the Modern Prevailing Notions of . . . Freedom of Will* (1754), in which he attacked from a predestinarian standpoint the *Arminian view of liberty, occasioned *Boswell's remark that 'the only relief I had was to forget it', and Dr *Johnson's aphorism, 'All theory is against the freedom of the will; all experience for it.' (Boswell, *Life of Johnson*, ed. G. B. Hill, iii. 291, 1778.) From 1957 to 1997 14 volumes of his *Works*, gen. eds. P. Miller, J. E. Smith, and H. S. Stout, have appeared.

EDWARDS, Richard (?1523–66), of Corpus Christi College and Christ Church, Oxford, master of the children of the Chapel Royal, 1561. He composed *Palamon and Arcite* (now lost) for Queen Elizabeth's entertainment at Oxford, 1566. *The Excellent Comedie of . . . *Damon and Pithias* (printed 1571) is his only extant play. He was the compiler of the *Paradise of Dainty Devises*, published after his death (1576).

'Edwin and Angelina', see HERMIT, THE.

Edwin Drood, *The Mystery of*, an unfinished novel by *Dickens, published 1870.

The fathers of Edwin Drood and Rosa Bud, both widowers, have before their deaths betrothed their young children to one another. The orphan Rosa has been brought up in Miss Twinkleton's school at Cloisterham (Rochester), where Edwin, also an orphan, has an uncle, John Jasper, the precentor of the cathedral, to whom he is devoted and who appears to return the devotion. It is understood that the two young people are to marry as soon as Edwin comes of age, although this very understanding has been fatal to love between them. Jasper, a sinister and hypocritical character, gives Rosa music lessons and loves her passionately, but inspires her with terror and disgust. There now come upon the scene two other orphans, Neville and Helena Landless. Neville and Edwin at once become enemies, for Neville admires Rosa and is disgusted at Edwin's unappreciative treatment of her. This enmity is secretly fomented by Jasper and there is a violent quarrel between the young men. On the last of Edwin's periodical visits to Cloisterham before the time of his anticipated marriage, Rosa and he recognize that this marriage will not be for their happiness and break off the engagement. That same night Edwin disappears under circumstances pointing to foul play and suggesting that he has been murdered by Neville Landless, a theory actively supported by Jasper. But Jasper receives with uncontrollable symptoms of dismay the intelligence that the engagement of Edwin and Rosa had been broken off before Edwin's disappearance, and this betrayal of himself is noted by Mr Grewgious, Rosa's eccentric, good-hearted guardian. Neville is arrested but, as the body of Edwin is not found, is released untried. He is ostracized by public opinion and is obliged to hide himself as a student in London. The remainder of the fragment of the novel is occupied with the continued machinations of Jasper against Neville and his pursuit of Rosa, who in terror of him flies to her guardian in London; with the countermoves prepared by Mr Grewgious, assisted by the amiable minor canon Mr Crisparkle and a new ally, the retired naval officer Mr Tartar; also with the proceedings of the mysterious Mr Datchery, directed against Jasper. Of the solution or catastrophe intended by the author no hint exists, beyond those which the fragment itself contains, and the statement as to the broad lines of the plot given by J. *Forster. There have been many conjectures, turning mainly on two points: whether Edwin Drood had in fact been murdered or had miraculously survived; and who was Datchery. It has been suggested, for instance, that Datchery was Drood himself, or Tartar, or Grewgious, or Grewgious's clerk Bazzard, or Helena Landless, in disguise.

Mention should also be made of some notable characters: the fatuous Mr Sapsea, auctioneer and mayor; Mr Honeythunder, the bullying 'philanthropist'; the grim stonemason Durdles and his attendant imp 'Deputy'.

There have been several attempts at continuations, from *John Jasper's Secret* (1871–2) by H. Morford and others, to recent versions such as one by Leon Garfield (1980) and one contained in *The Decoding of Edwin Drood* (1980) by C. Forsyte. For further interpretations, see *A Reader's Guide to Charles Dickens* (1973) by P.

*Hobsbaum, *The Wound and the Bow* (1941) by E. *Wilson, and an article by W. W. Robson in the *TLS*, 11 Nov. 1983.

EGAN, Pierce, the elder (1772–1849), is remembered as the author of *Life in London; or The Day and Night Scenes of Jerry Hawthorn Esq. and Corinthian Tom*, issued in monthly numbers from 1820 (the completed book in 1821), illustrated by George and Robert *Cruikshank. The book is a description of the life of the 'man about town' of the day, interesting for the light it throws on the manners of the period and for the many slang phrases it introduces. In 1824 Egan began the issue of a weekly paper, *Pierce Egan's Life in London and Sporting Guide*, which subsequently developed into the sporting journal *Bell's Life in London*. His son, also Pierce Egan (1814–80), was associated with him in several of his works, and wrote a vast number of novels.

Egeon, in Shakespeare's *The Comedy of Errors*, the Syracusan merchant who is father of the Antipholus twins.

EGERTON, George, the pen-name of Mary Chavelita Dunne (1859–1945), short story writer, born in Australia of Irish-Welsh parentage and brought up in Ireland. Her adventurous early life included an elopement to Norway and two marriages, the first to George Egerton Clairemont, the second in 1901 to a theatrical agent, Reginald Golding Bright. Her first volume of short stories, *Keynotes* (1893), published by John *Lane with a cover by *Beardsley, created something of a sensation with its echoes of Scandinavian realism and portraits of the *New Woman; it was dedicated to *Hamsun, with whom she had fallen briefly in love and whose novel *Hunger* she later (1899) translated. Other works include *Discords* (1894) and *The Wheel of God* (1898). See T. de Vere White, *A Leaf from the Yellow Book* (1958).

EGERTON, Sir Thomas, Baron Ellesmere and Viscount Brackley (1540–1617), lord chancellor from 1603 till his death. He befriended F. *Bacon. *Donne was his secretary for four years (1597–1602) and S. *Daniel and J. *Owen addressed poems to him. He left judicial and legal treatises in manuscript. It was to his third wife that Milton's *'Arcades' was addressed.

Eglantine, or **Eglentyne,** Madame, the prioress in Chaucer's *Canterbury Tales*.

Egoist, originally the *New Freewoman: An Individualist Review*, founded by Harriet Shaw *Weaver and Dora Marsden. It published articles on modern poetry and the arts, and from being a feminist paper became, under the influence of *Pound and others, a mouthpiece for the Imagist poets (see IMAGISM). It ran from 1914 to the end of 1919, first fortnightly and then monthly, with *Aldington as assistant editor, followed by T. S. *Eliot in 1917. Marsden and Weaver succeeded each other as nominal editors and it was due to Weaver

that Joyce's *Portrait of the Artist as a Young Man* was published serially in the magazine in 1914–15.

Egoist, The, a novel by G. *Meredith, published 1879.

The central character, the Egoist himself, is Sir Willoughby Patterne, rich and handsome, with a high position in the county, but totally blind to his own arrogance and to the needs of the women he loves. Laetitia Dale, an intelligent young woman but past her first bloom, has loved him for many years, and his vanity has been flattered. But the dashing Constantia Durham is a greater prize, and she accepts his proposal. However, she soon discerns the true Sir Willoughby and elopes with Harry Oxford, an officer in the hussars, thus bringing Willoughby his first bewildering humiliation. Soon he discovers the qualities he requires in Clara Middleton, the daughter of an elderly scholar (said to be a sketch of Meredith's first father-in-law, *Peacock), whose passion for wine overwhelms even his affection for his daughter. Clara, bewitched by Willoughby's charm and surroundings, becomes engaged to him, but soon perceives his intention of directing and moulding her; her attempts to free herself from the entanglements of the engagement form the main theme of the book. Clara envies but cannot emulate Constantia, and Willoughby struggles frantically against an incredible second jilting. Clara is meanwhile seeing more and more of Vernon Whitford, a poor and earnest young scholar (based on L. *Stephen), who lives at Patterne and is tutor to young Crossjay, son of a poor relation, an officer of the marines. The spirited Crossjay is finally the means of Clara's release, for he unintentionally overhears Willoughby, seriously shaken by Clara's wish to be free, seeking a way out of his humiliation by proposing to Laetitia Dale, a proposal which she, with sad dignity, refuses. So Willoughby finds himself once more and trebly humiliated. However, in the end his persistence achieves the reluctant Laetitia, and Clara marries Vernon Whitford. The sharp compressed dialogue of the last chapters is among Meredith's most brilliant.

egotistical sublime, a phrase coined by *Keats to describe his version of *Wordsworth's distinctive genius. See under NEGATIVE CAPABILITY, and see also ROMANTICISM.

Eikon Basilike, *the Pourtraicture of His Sacred Majestie in His Solitudes and Sufferings*, a book of which Dr John Gauden (1605–62), bishop of Worcester, claimed authorship. It purported to be meditations by Charles I, and was long so regarded; it was published ten days after his execution, 30 Jan. 1649, and appealed so strongly to popular sentiment that 47 editions of it were published, and Parliament thought it necessary to issue a reply, *Milton's *Eikonoklastes* (1649). ('Eikon Basilike' means 'royal image' and 'Eikonoklastes' 'image breaker'.) *Eikonoklastes* takes the *Eikon* paragraph by paragraph in an effort to refute it: it also attacks the 'miserable, credulous and deluded' public with much vigour. Gauden's claim, which was not made known until 1690, is discussed at length in F. F. Madan's *A New Bibliography of the Eikon Basilike* (1950).

Eikonoklastes, see EIKON BASILIKE.

Eisteddfod, the. It has its origins in medieval Wales, in the formal gatherings of professional poets. The first may have been held in Cardigan in 1176. However, the structure and practices of the modern bardic establishment, the *gorsedd*, were devised in the late 18th cent. by the antiquary and opium addict Edward Williams, 'Iolo Morganwg'. The ceremony of chairing the winning poet became an integral part of the local, regional, and school eisteddfodau which are still held throughout Wales, and of the national youth eisteddfod. The National Eisteddfod, a week-long peripatetic festival held annually in August, alternately in north and south Wales, is the most important. Prose, drama, music, dance, arts and crafts, and a host of fringe and youth activities have been added to the traditional poetic contests. The introduction of a 'Welsh-only' rule in 1937 has helped to make it the most important cultural event in the calendar for Welsh speakers of all ages.

E.K., see KIRKE.

ekphrasis, a literary work which attempts to evoke, describe, or reproduce the impact of a work of art: the form is much used in 20th-cent. poetry.

Elaine (variously spelt), in Malory's *Morte D'Arthur*, is the name of several ladies whose identities sometimes overlap: (1) Elaine Le Blank, the daughter of Sir Bernard of Astolat and known as the Fair Maid of Astolat (*Tennyson's Shalott), who falls in love with Launcelot and dies for love of him (see LAUNCELOT OF THE LAKE); (2) Elayne the Fair or Sans Pere (Peerless), the daughter of King Pelles and the mother, by Launcelot, of *Galahad; (3) Elayne the sister of Morgawse and Morgan le Fay in the opening pages of Malory; (4) Elayne the wife of King *Ban and mother of Launcelot; (5) Elayne the daughter of King Pellinore.

élan vital, a phrase coined by *Bergson to describe the vital impulse which he believed directed evolutionary growth. See also under MAN AND SUPERMAN.

Elayne, see ELAINE.

Elder Brother, The, a drama by J. *Fletcher, written c.1625, probably with *Massinger, who completed it about 1635 (after Fletcher's death). The story was suggested in part by *Overbury's Theophrastan 'character' of 'An Elder Brother' (1614).

Lewis, a French lord, proposes to marry his daughter Angelina to one of the sons of Brisac, a country gentleman. Charles, the heir of Brisac, devoted to study, declines marriage; and Brisac thereupon proposes that Angelina shall marry the younger brother, Eustace, and that Charles shall be induced to surrender the bulk

of his inheritance to Eustace, who eagerly falls in with the proposal. The plan is almost executed when Charles sees Angelina and they fall in love. Eustace, a poor-spirited courtier, is routed, and after various complications the lovers are united.

ELEANOR OF AQUITAINE (1122–1204), the grand-daughter of the first troubadour whose work survives, Guilhem IX of Aquitaine, and inheritor of the kingdom of Aquitaine, married for her inheritance by Louis VII of France in 1137. She had two daughters by him before their divorce (encouraged by her enemy St *Bernard of Clairvaux who deplored the southern worldliness that she brought to the Parisian court) in 1152. She was immediately remarried to Henry Plantagenet of Anjou, the future Henry II of England, to whom she bore eight children including the future *Richard I (b. 1157) and, the youngest, the future King John (b. 1166). After the death of Henry II in 1189 she was regent of England in the absence of her son Richard until his death in 1199. She was an immensely influential patron of the arts, particularly in her patronage of the development of courtly poetry in Poitiers, a function carried on by her daughter *Marie de Champagne. Among others she brought the troubadour Bernart de Ventadorn (fl. 1170s) to Poitiers, perhaps fuelling troubadour influence on more northerly French poetry.

elegiac, (1) in prosody, the metre consisting of a dactylic *hexameter and *pentameter, as being the metre appropriate to elegies; (2) generally, of the nature of an *elegy.

elegy, from the Greek, the word has been variously used with reference to different periods of English. In Old English a group of short poems in the *Exeter Book whose subject is the transience of the world, sometimes relieved by Christian consolation, are called elegies (see WANDERER, THE; SEAFARER, THE; DEOR; RUIN, THE). From the 16th cent. onwards the term was used for a reflective poem (*Coleridge called it the kind of poetry 'natural to the reflective mind') by poets such as *Donne; later it was applied particularly to poems of mourning (from Milton's *Lycidas), and the general reflective poem, as written by Coleridge and *Yeats, sometimes called 'reverie'. The great English mourning elegies are *Lycidas* (for E. *King), Shelley's *Adonais* (for *Keats), Tennyson's *In Memoriam* (for A. H. *Hallam), M. Arnold's *Thyrsis* (for *Clough), and *Hopkins's *Wreck of the Deutschland*. T. Gray's *Elegy Written in a Country Church-Yard* is a general poem of mourning, combined with the reflective mode. (See ELEGIAC.)

'Elegy on the Death of a Mad Dog', a poem by Goldsmith, from *The Vicar of Wakefield*.

Elegy Written in a Country Church-Yard, a meditative poem in quatrains by T. *Gray, published 1751, but begun some years earlier. The churchyard is perhaps that of Stoke Poges, where Gray often visited members of his family. The poem, which contains some of the best-known lines in English literature, reflects on the obscure destinies of the villagers who lie buried ('Full many a flower is born to blush unseen') and then describes the supposed death of the melancholy and unknown author. Critics have related the closing stanzas both to Gray's fears about his own poetic destiny, and to the early death of his friend Richard *West in 1742.

Elene, see CYNEWULF.

'Elephant in the Moon, The', see BUTLER, S. (1613–80).

ELFRIDA, see ÆLFTHRYTH.

ELGAR, Sir Edward William (1857–1934), the most important figure in music in England between the death of *Handel and the First World War; he created a musical style in which romanticism and emotional sensitivity blend with an unmistakably English inspiration. The so-called *Enigma Variations* (1899) and *The Dream of Gerontius* (1900), a setting of the greater part of *Newman's poem, are recognized as a landmark in English oratorio. *The Apostles* (1903) and *The Kingdom* (1906) are based on texts which the composer (a Roman Catholic) selected from the Bible. But Elgar's greatest claim to fame is as a symphonic composer: the concert overture *Froissart* (1890) is a generalized tribute to chivalry, but the masterly symphonic study *Falstaff* (1913) has a precise and detailed programme and comes high on any list of works inspired by Shakespeare. His subject here was not the Falstaff of *The Merry Wives of Windsor*, and therefore of *Verdi's opera, but the subtler figure of *Henry IV and V. Elgar's songs for solo voice are not of great importance (apart from the early *Sea Pictures*, 1899) but there are a number of beautiful choral pieces and a curiously autobiographical setting of O'Shaughnessy's 'Ode', *The Music Makers* (1912). Works like *Fringes of the Fleet* (poems by *Kipling) and *The Spirit of England* (*Binyon) belong to the period of the First World War and, with the immense success of 'Land of Hope and Glory' (words by A. C. *Benson) and the *Pomp and Circumstance* style, have contributed to an image of Elgar far removed from the sensitive and reserved figure of fact.

Elia, see ESSAYS OF ELIA.

Elidure, see ARTEGAL.

ELIOT, George (Mary Ann, later Marian, Evans) (1819–80), the youngest surviving child of Robert Evans, agent for an estate in Warwickshire. In her girlhood she was particularly close to her brother Isaac, from whom she was later estranged. At school she became a convert to evangelicalism; she was freed from this by the influence of Charles Bray, a freethinking Coventry manufacturer (a development which temporarily alienated her father), but remained strongly influenced by religious concepts of love and duty; her works contain many affectionate portraits of Dissenters and clergymen. She pursued her education rigorously, reading widely, and devoted herself to completing a translation of *Strauss's *Life of Jesus*, which appeared without her name in 1846. In 1850 she met J. *Chapman, and became a contributor to the *Westminster Review*; she moved to 142 Strand, London, in 1851, as a paying guest in the Chapmans' home, where her emotional attachment to him proved an embarrassment. She became assistant editor to the *Westminster Review* in 1851, and in the same year met *Spencer, for whom she also developed strong feelings which were not reciprocated, though the two remained friends. In 1854 she published a translation of *Feuerbach's *Essence of Christianity*; she endorsed his view that religious belief is an imaginative necessity for man and a projection of his interest in his own species, a heterodoxy of which the readers of her novels only gradually became aware. At about the same time she joined G. H. *Lewes in a union without legal form (he was already married) that lasted until his death; they travelled to the Continent in that year and set up house together on their return. He was to be a constant support throughout her working life and their relationship, although its irregularity caused her much anxiety, was gradually accepted by their friends. 'The Sad Fortunes of the Rev. Amos Barton', the first of the *Scenes of Clerical Life*, appeared in *Blackwood's Magazine* in 1857, followed by 'Mr Gilfil's Love-Story' and 'Janet's Repentance'; these at once attracted praise for their domestic realism, pathos, and humour, and speculation about the identity of 'George Eliot', who was widely supposed to be a clergyman or possibly a clergyman's wife. She began *Adam Bede* (1859) in 1858; it was received with great enthusiasm and at once established her as a leading novelist. *The Mill on the Floss* appeared in 1860 and *Silas Marner* in 1861. In 1860 she visited Florence, where she conceived the idea of *Romola, and returned to do further research in 1861; it was published in the *Cornhill* in 1862–3. John Blackwood, son of William *Blackwood, was unable to meet her terms; by this time she was earning a considerable income from her work. *Felix Holt, the Radical* appeared in 1866. She travelled in Spain in 1867, and her dramatic poem *The Spanish Gypsy* (conceived on an earlier visit to Italy, and inspired by Tintoretto) appeared in 1868. *Middlemarch* was published in instalments in 1871–2 and *Daniel Deronda*, her last great novel, in the same way in 1874–6. She was now at the height of her fame, and widely recognized as the greatest living English novelist, admired by readers as diverse as *Turgenev, H. *James, and Queen *Victoria. In 1878 Lewes died. Her *Impressions of Theophrastus Such* appeared in 1879, and in 1880 she married the 40-year-old John Walter Cross, whom she had met in Rome in 1869 and who had become her financial adviser. The marriage distressed many of her friends, but brought the consolation of a congratulatory note from her brother Isaac, who had not communicated with her since 1857. She died seven months later.

After her death her reputation declined somewhat, and L. *Stephen indicated much of the growing reaction in an obituary notice (1881) which praised the 'charm' and autobiographical elements of the early works, but found the later novels painful and excessively reflective. V. *Woolf defended her in an essay (1919) which declared *Middlemarch* to be 'one of the few English novels written for grown-up people', but critics like David *Cecil and Oliver Elton continued to emphasize the division between her creative powers and supposedly damaging intellect. In the late 1940s a new generation of critics, led by *Leavis (*The Great Tradition*, 1948), introduced a new respect for and understanding of her mature works; Leavis praises her 'traditional moral sensibility', her 'luminous intelligence', and concludes that she 'is not as transcendently great as Tolstoy, but she *is* great, and great in the same way'.

As well as the novels for which she is remembered, she wrote various poems, including 'O may I join the choir invisible' (1867), 'Agatha' (1869), *Brother and Sister* (1869), a sonnet sequence recalling her happy childhood, 'The Legend of Jubal' (1870), and 'Armgart' (1871); also the short stories 'The Lifted Veil' (1859) and 'Brother Jacob' (1864). Her letters and journals were edited by Cross (3 vols, 1885); her complete letters were edited by G. S. Haight (9 vols, 1954–78), who also wrote a life (1968). *A Writer's Notebook 1854–1879* and *Uncollected Writings* were edited by Joseph Wiesenfarth (1981). See also *George Eliot: A Life* by Rosemary Ashton (1996).

ELIOT, T(homas) S(tearns) (1888–1965), a major figure in English literature since the 1920s. He was born at St Louis, Missouri, and educated at Harvard, the Sorbonne, and Merton College, Oxford, where he pursued a doctoral thesis on F. H. *Bradley begun at Harvard. In 1914 he met *Pound, who encouraged him to settle in England; in June 1915 he married Vivien Haigh-Wood, and in the same month his poem 'The Love Song of J. Alfred Prufrock' appeared (also with Pound's encouragement) in *Poetry*. Eliot taught briefly during the war, then in 1917 began to work for Lloyds Bank; from 1917 he was also assistant editor of the *Egoist*. His first volume of verse, *Prufrock and Other Observations* (1917), was followed by *Poems* (1919), hand-printed by L. and V. *Woolf at the *Hogarth Press; these struck a new note in modern poetry, satiric, allusive, cosmopolitan, at times lyric and elegiac. In 1922 Eliot founded a new quarterly, the *Criterion*; in the first issue appeared, with much éclat, *The Waste Land*, which established him decisively as the voice of a disillusioned generation. In 1925 he left Lloyds and became a director of Faber and Faber, where he built up a list of poets (*Auden, G. *Barker, Pound, *Spender, etc.; see also FABER BOOK OF MODERN VERSE) which

represented the mainstream of the modern movement in poetry in England: from this time he was regarded as a figure of great cultural authority, whose influence was more or less inescapable.

In 1927 he became a British subject and a member of the Anglican Church; his pilgrimage towards his own particular brand of High Anglicanism may be charted in his poetry through 'The Hollow Men' (1925), with its broken asseverations of faith, through 'The Journey of the Magi' (1927) and 'Ash-Wednesday' (1930), to its culminating vision in *Four Quartets* (1935–42). His prose also shows the same movement; for example, the title essay of *For Lancelot Andrewes* (1928) praises tradition, prayer, and liturgy, and points away from 'personality' towards hierarchy and community, and in the preface to this collection he describes himself as 'classical in literature, royalist in politics, and Anglo-Catholic in religion'. The same preoccupation with tradition continued to express itself in his critical works, and developed in part from the concept of *'dissociation of sensibility' which he had formulated in 1921. (See also here HULME, whose views influenced Eliot.)

In the 1930s Eliot began his attempt to revive poetic drama. *Sweeney Agonistes* (1932), an 'Aristophanic fragment' which gives, in syncopated rhythms, a satiric impression of the sterility of proletarian life, was followed by a pageant play, *The Rock* (1934), *Murder in the Cathedral* (1935), *The Family Reunion* (1939), and three 'comedies': *The Cocktail Party* (1950), *The Confidential Clerk* (1954), and *The Elder Statesman* (1959). These last were not wholly successful attempts to clothe profound ideas in the garb of a conventional West End play. Eliot's classic book of verse for children, *Old Possum's Book of Practical Cats* (1939), which reveals the aspect of his character that claimed the influence of *Lear, achieved a considerable stage success in a musical adaptation, *Cats*, in 1981.

Eliot was equally influential as critic and poet, and in his combination of literary and social criticism may be called the M. *Arnold of the 20th cent. Among his critical works may be mentioned: *The Sacred Wood: Essays on Poetry and Criticism* (1920) (which contains the essay on *Hamlet*, coining the phrase *'objective correlative'); *The Use of Poetry and the Use of Criticism* (1933); *Elizabethan Essays* (1934); *The Idea of a Christian Society* (1940); *Notes towards the Definition of Culture* (1948); *Poetry and Drama* (1951); *On Poetry and Poets* (1957). *Leavis, himself much influenced by Eliot, has pointed out the vital connections between Eliot's creative work and critical attitude (in, e.g., his revaluation of *Donne, *Marvell, Elizabethan and Jacobean verse drama, *Milton, *Dryden, and his praise of *Dante, *Laforgue, and the French symbolists): 'Eliot's best, his important criticism has an immediate relation to his technical problems as the poet who, at that moment in history, was faced with "altering expression"' ('T. S. Eliot's Stature as Critic', *Commentary*, Nov. 1958).

Eliot was formally separated from his first wife (whose ill health, both physical and mental, had caused him much stress and misery) in 1932–3; she died in 1947. The following year he was awarded the *Nobel Prize for literature and the OM. He married his second wife, Valerie Fletcher, in 1957. See *The Waste Land* with biographical introduction by Valerie Eliot (1971), and Helen Gardner, *The Composition of Four Quartets* (1978). See also *T. S. Eliot* by P. *Ackroyd (1984).

elision, the suppression of a vowel or syllable in pronouncing.

Elissa, (1) a name borne by Dido; (2) in Spenser's *Faerie Queene* (II. ii), one of the two 'froward sisters' of the sober *Medina.

Eliza, The Journal to, by L. *Sterne, written 1767, first published 1904.

The *Journal*, also called by Sterne the *Bramine's Journal*, was kept intermittently between mid-April and November of 1767, and describes with fulsome pathos, often in the persona of Yorick, sometimes as 'Bramin' to 'Bramine', his love for the young Mrs Elizabeth *Draper and his torment at their separation. She was the wife of an official of the East India Company, and Sterne knew her for only a few months before she returned to her husband in India. The first instalments of the *Journal*, sent abroad to Eliza, appear to have been lost, and Sterne never attempted to publish the remainder, which was not discovered until 1851. At the time of its writing Sterne was also engaged on *A Sentimental Journey*, in which Eliza is often invoked and extolled, but the lachrymose *Journal* exhibits little of the verve of *A Sentimental Journey*. The work contains puzzling passages of Sterne's self-plagiarism, including a section copied almost exactly from a love letter to his wife written 30 years before.

ELIZABETH I (1533–1603), a daughter of *Henry VIII and Anne Boleyn, and queen of England from 1558 to 1603. She was celebrated by the greatest poets of her age, including *Spenser, *Ralegh, and *Shakespeare, under such names as *Cynthia and *Gloriana (with many allusions to her semi-mythological role as Virgin Queen) and has been the subject of innumerable plays, novels, romances, and biographies. She was famed for her ready wit and for the stirring eloquence called forth in, for example, her speech at Tilbury on the approach of the Spanish Armada. She also wrote poetry, which was highly praised by her courtiers and by *Puttenham, who used one of her few undisputed works ('The doubt of future foes', on the conspiracies of *Mary Queen of Scots) as an example of rhetoric in his *Art of English Poesy*. Her verses, which include a dozen or so undisputed lyrics and epigrams, various doubtful attributions, and translations from *Boethius, *Horace, and *Plutarch, were edited by L. Bradner (1964).

Elizabethan literature, a name often applied vaguely to the literature produced in the reigns of Elizabeth I and the first Stuarts. See under DRAB and GOLDEN.

'Ellen Orford', one of the tales in Crabbe's *The Borough*. It tells the story of a courageous woman, who, after a neglected childhood, is seduced and abandoned. Her child turns out to be an idiot, her husband dies, and his death is followed by the deaths of their children. She becomes a teacher but blindness forces her to retire, and she finds consolation in her trust in God. She appears in *Britten's *Peter Grimes*.

ELLIOT, Jean or Jane (1727–1805), third daughter of Sir Gilbert Elliot of Minto, author of the most popular version of the old lament for Flodden, 'The Flowers of the Forest', beginning 'I've heard them lilting at our ewe-milking'. It was written *c.*1763, published 1769, and republished by *Herd in 1776. Another popular version was written by A. *Cockburn.

Elliot, Sir Walter, his daughters Elizabeth, Anne, and Mary, and his heir William Walter Elliot, characters in J. Austen's *Persuasion*.

ELLIOTT, Ebenezer (1781–1849). He became a master-founder in Sheffield, and is remembered as the 'Corn Law Rhymer'. In 1829 he published *The Village Patriarch*, in which Enoch Wray, an old blind mason, reflects upon rural life and the bitter poverty brought about by cruelty and injustice. *Carlyle, writing in the *Edinburgh Review* in 1832, found great interest in the poem, and 'a manful tone of reason and determination'—but nevertheless urged Elliott to abandon poetry for prose. *Corn Law Rhymes* (1830) is a collection of simple poems which employ both satire and pathos in fiercely condemning the Bread Tax. The book was immensely successful, at a time when sales of poetry were very low. Some of Elliot's poems are of genuine quality, and his themes of poverty and oppression are deeply felt. His collected works were published in 1846.

ellipsis, the leaving out from a sentence words necessary to express the sense completely.

ELLIS, A. E. (1920–2000), the pseudonym of Derek Lindsay, author of *The Rack* (1958), a remarkable novel set in a sanatorium in the French Alps, to which a group of tubercular students is sent by the International Students' Organization after the Second World War. Paul Davenant, orphaned, ex-army, ex-Cambridge, remains there for over two years, and the novel gives a harrowing and detailed yet at times tragi-comic account of the desperate fluctuations of his health and spirits, of the bizarre routine of the institution to which he gradually becomes accustomed, and of the eccentricities and manipulations of staff and fellow inmates. Paul falls in love with a fellow sufferer, a young and beautiful Belgian, Michèle Duchesne, an experience which heightens both hope and despair. The author evokes the enclosed atmosphere of the clinic, where 'finally one doesn't even seriously think in terms of leaving— it's as though one's past life were something one had once read about in a half-forgotten novel' (ch. 11), yet he also gives a sense of the vast spaces of the mountain landscape, and of the vast questions posed by Paul's sufferings on 'the rack of this tough world'.

ELLIS, Alice Thomas (Anna Haycraft) (1932–2005), born in Liverpool, educated at Bangor Grammar School and Liverpool School of Art. In 1977 she published *The Sin Eater* and in 1980 *The Birds of the Air*; both were awarded a Welsh Arts Council Award. In 1982 *The 27th Kingdom* appeared, and in the same year she produced *The Other Side of the Fire*. Set in a small Welsh rural community, *Unexplained Laughter* (1985) is characteristically witty, succinct, elegantly polished, and compelling. The novel epitomizes Ellis's distinctive blend of flamboyant comedy and understanding of suffering. Between 1987 and 1990, she published a trilogy: *The Clothes in the Wardrobe*, *The Skeleton in the Cupboard*, and *The Fly in the Ointment*, plus, also in 1990, *The Inn at the Edge of the World*. Like *Unexplained Laughter*, this ghost story is steeped in Celtic feeling and enlivened by the author's incisive wit. Further fiction includes the collection of short stories *The Evening of Adam* (1994) and *Fairy Tale* (1996). Ellis's abundant non-fiction includes *A Welsh Childhood* (1990) and her stout defence of Catholic orthodoxy, *Serpent on the Rock* (1994).

ELLIS, George (1753–1815), one of the talented group who, with *Canning and *Frere, founded and contributed to the *Anti-Jacobin* in 1797. His *Poetical Tales by Sir Gregory Gander* appeared in 1778, and his contributions to the Whig *Rolliad* in 1784, but his most important works were his translations and selections from Middle English verse: *Early English Poets* (1801) and *Specimens of Early English Romances in Metre* (1805).

ELLIS, Henry Havelock (1859–1939), born in Croydon, Surrey. He spent some early years studying and teaching in Australia. He returned to London in 1879 and eventually qualified as a physician, although much distracted by his literary pursuits. These included reviewing, translating, and editing the unexpurgated *Mermaid Series of Elizabethan dramatists (1887–9) and the Contemporary Science Series. In 1884 he met Olive *Schreiner, who became an intimate friend and who shared his interest in progressive thought, particularly in the realm of sexuality, the subject with which he is most closely identified; other friends included E. *Carpenter, Arthur *Symons, and the advocate of birth control, Margaret Sanger. His 'new marriage' to the equally progressive (and lesbian) Edith Lees (1861–1916) was not wholly successful. An energetic if not entirely fearless pioneer in the field of sexology, his works (which include *The New Spirit*, 1890; *Sexual Inversion*, 1897, with J. A. *Symons;

Affirmations, 1898; *The Dance of Life*, 1923; and his autobiographical *My Life*, 1939, as well as many other volumes on the psychology of sex, marriage, censorship, social hygiene, etc.) had a considerable and liberating influence. He had many followers, although the scientific accuracy of his investigations has been questioned, and he damaged his own reputation by indiscriminate publication and by his apparent misunderstandings of *Freud. See P. Grosskurth, *Havelock Ellis* (1980).

ELLISON, Ralph Waldo (1914–94), born in Oklahoma City, and remembered for his novel *Invisible Man* (1952), which tells the story of a New York immigrant black who lives in a coal hole, in hiding from himself and 'the Brotherhood'. This novel had to bear the burden of recognition as the first great black classic, and he found it difficult to follow, as a subsequent more militant generation accused him of appeasement as a 'white nigger', but it is still much read and admired.

ELLMANN, Mary, see FEMINIST CRITICISM.

ELLMANN, Richard (1918–87), scholar and biographer, born in Michigan and educated at Yale University and Trinity College, Dublin. In 1970 he became Goldsmiths' professor of English literature at Oxford. His publications include *Yeats: The Man and the Mask* (1948, rev. 1979) and several works on *Joyce, including notably his monumental, imaginative, and revelatory biography *James Joyce* (1959, rev. 1982), which made a highly influential contribution to the new conception of the art of *biography that developed at this period. He also edited (with Robert O'Clare) *The Norton Anthology of Modern Poetry* (1973) and the *New Oxford Book of American Verse* (1976). His *Oscar Wilde* appeared in 1987.

ELLWOOD, Thomas (1639–1713), Quaker and friend of Milton, whose chance comment on *Paradise Lost*, 'Thou hast said much of paradise lost, but what hast thou to say of paradise found?', suggested the subject of *Paradise Regained*. Ellwood's autobiography, *The History of the Life of Thomas Ellwood* (1714), is a vivid memoir of Restoration spiritual dissidence. His poetry included a five-book sacred work, the *Davideis* (1712).

'Eloisa to Abelard', a heroic epistle by *Pope, published 1717. Pope's version of the tragic love of Héloïse and *Abelard was highly popular; it portrays Héloïse, in a Gothic seclusion of 'grots and caverns', still tormented by passionate love, unable to renounce for God the memory of 'unholy joy'.

ELSTOB, Elizabeth (1683–1756), born in Newcastle upon Tyne, a pioneer in Anglo-Saxon studies, as was her brother William (1673–1715). After his death poverty obliged her to set up a school in Evesham, then to become governess to the children of the duchess of Portland. Her publications include *An English-Saxon Homily on the Birthday of St Gregory*

(1709) and *The Rudiments of Grammar for the English-Saxon Tongue, First Given in English; with an Apology for the Study of Northern Antiquities* (1715). See also HICKES.

ELTON, Ben (1959–), English playwright, novelist, and scriptwriter. As a stand-up comedian and co-writer of television comedies such as *Blackadder* and *The Young Ones* he was one of the most influential entertainers of the 1980s, pioneering a style of articulate, politically acute comedy which subsequently filtered down into the work of many young novelists. His own early novels *Stark* (1989), *Gridlock* (1991), and *This Other Eden* (1993) were commercial rather than critical successes, but *Popcorn* (1996) was widely acclaimed. A coruscating attack on Hollywood's glorification of violence, it also found an afterlife, like its successor *Blast from the Past* (1998), as a popular West End play.

Elton, the Revd Philip, a character in J. Austen's *Emma.

ÉLUARD, Paul (1895–1952), French poet, prominent exponent of *Surrealism from 1919 to 1938. He collaborated with Max Ernst on *Les Malheurs des immortels* (1922) and with *Breton on *L'Immaculée Conception* (1930). Among his volumes of surrealist poetry are *Les Dessous d'une vie ou la pyramide humaine* (1926), *Capitale de la douleur* (1926), *L'Amour, la poésie* (1929), *La Vie immédiate* (1932), *La Rose publique* (1934), and *Les Yeux fertiles* (1936). He broke with the surrealist movement in the late 1930s, and joined the Communist Party in 1942. He became one of the leading writers of the French Resistance (*Poésie et vérité*, 1942; *Au rendez-vous allemand*, 1944).

Elvira, (1) the wife of *Don Juan; (2) the heroine of *Dryden's *The Spanish Fryar*; (3) the mistress of Pizarro in *Sheridan's play *Pizarro*.

ELYOT, Kevin (1951–), playwright born in Birmingham, where he was a chorister in the cathedral. He was educated at Bristol University and worked as an actor before riding the crest of a new wave of plays about modern homosexual love, loss, and betrayal with his impressive debut *Coming Clean* (1982) at the *Bush Theatre. *My Night with Reg* (1994) at the *Royal Court was a black-laced comedy of homosexual affection composed in three short movements, each section divided by a period of time and a death. In *The Day I Stood Still* (1998) at the *National Theatre, Elyot, who writes, you feel, from direct experience, and about people he knows well, experimented further with time-shifts between the past and present in charting the unrequited passion of a music-loving loner in north London. Other work includes versions of *Ostrovsky's *Artists and Admirers* (1992) for the Royal Shakespeare Company and Wilkie *Collins's *The Moonstone* (1996) for BBC television.

ELYOT, Sir Thomas (c.1490–1546), author of the *Boke Named the Governour*, published in 1531, a treatise on education and politics which displays the influence at this time of the classics, and Plato in particular, and illustrates the evolution of English prose. To this book Elyot owed his appointment as ambassador to Charles V. He wrote a number of other works, including *The Doctrinall of Princis* (c.1533), translated from Isocrates, *The Image of Governance* (first pub. 1540), *The Castell of Helthe* (c.1537), an important manual of health, and Platonic dialogues and compilations from the Fathers. His translations did much to popularize the classics in England. His *Dictionary* (Latin and English, 1538) was the first book published in England to bear this title. There is a life by S. E. Lehmberg (1960).

ELYTIS, Odysseus (1911–96), Greek poet. Born in Heraklion, Crete, he was educated in Athens and at the Sorbonne. He became associated with the so-called 'Thirties Generation' of poets, including *Seferis, who were much influenced by *Éluard and other members of the French *surrealist movement. His most famous poem, *To Axion Esti* (1959; trans. Edmund Keeley and George Davidis, 1974), is divided into three sections: 'The Genesis' introduces an innocent first person who, in 'The Passion', is witness to the horrors of the Second World War; in 'The Gloria', despite the destruction he has witnessed, he expresses his excitement at discovering he is still able to find beauty in the world. Like much of his work, the *Axion Esti* combines a vivid sense of Greece's history and cultural heritage, sacred and secular, with a very personal perspective. Elytis's approach to the Greek language is original, and often favours flourishes of sound, rhythm, and image over meaning which is frequently opaque or elusive. He published 17 volumes of poetry, numerous translations, and two volumes of critical essays. He was awarded the *Nobel Prize in 1979. The first complete collection of his poetry in English was published in 1997.

Emaré, a mid-14th-cent. verse romance of 1,035 lines in a north-east Midland dialect, written in 12-line tail-rhyme stanzas. It is a Breton lay (on the grounds that its introduction says it is) on the model of the repeatedly told Constance story; the name 'esmaré' could be a variant of the French word for 'tried', 'troubled'. The area of origin of the only manuscript might suggest a connection with the version of the story told by Nicholas *Trivet earlier in the 14th cent.; he was the first to call the heroine Constance. Emaré, like Constance, is repeatedly cast adrift, in this case first by order of her unnatural father and later by her mother-in-law, as was traditional in the story. At the end she is reunited with her lost son and her penitent husband. It has been edited by W. H. French and C. B. Hale, in *Middle English Metrical Romances* (1930), ll. 421–55.

emblem book. In its widest sense, an emblem is a visual representation carrying a symbolic meaning: hence, *Yeats's 'tower | Emblematical of the night' ('Dialogue of Self and Soul'). Most often, however, the word refers to a genre of verbal-pictorial art which is particularly associated with the Renaissance. One source of this genre was the belief that Egyptian hieroglyphics had been symbols rather than part of a language; this view was derived from the *Hieroglyphics* of Horapollo (or Horus Apollo), a Greek manuscript discovered in 1419, which was generally thought to be the work of an Egyptian in the 2nd or 4th cent. AD. Other important sources were the *Physiologus* and the epigrams of the Greek *Anthology*.

The first emblem book, the *Emblematum Liber* of Alciati (or Alciato), was published in 1531. Each emblem consists of a motto, a symbolic picture, and an explanatory set of verses called an epigram. This format is followed by most other emblem books. All three parts of an emblem contribute to its meaning: e.g. Alciati's picture of a bee-hive in a helmet, together with the motto *Ex bello pax* and the explanatory epigram, means that the weapons of war may be turned into the works of peace. Writers often borrowed one another's pictures and wrote new verses which reinterpreted them. In *A Theatre for Worldlings* (1569) *Spenser translated verses from *Petrarch and *du Bellay which had been used for a Dutch emblem book, but the translation was printed without the original plates. The earliest English emblem book to contain illustrations as well as verses was Geoffrey Whitney's (?1548–?1601) *A Choice of Emblemes* (1586), which distinguished three categories: natural, historical, and moral. The 17th cent. produced many religious emblem books, of which the most famous English example was the *Emblemes* of Quarles (1635). The children's figures of these emblem books represent Divine Love (God) and Earthly Love (Man); they have been derived from the Cupid figures of earlier love emblems. A *Collection of Emblems*, also illustrated, was published by G. *Wither (1634–5).

The poetry of some religious poetsz of the period, such as G. *Herbert and H. *Vaughan, is sometimes described as emblematic, though their books were not illustrated. *Bunyan also wrote an emblem book without pictures (*A Book for Boys and Girls*, 1686). By then the form had already gone out of fashion; it enjoyed something of a revival in the Victorian period.

Emblemes, a book of short devotional poems by *Quarles, first published 1635 and much reprinted; it was adapted from two Jesuit *emblem books, *Typus Mundi* (1627) and Herman Hugo's *Pia Desideria*. The poems are in various metres, each based on some scriptural text, and some in the form of dialogues, e.g. between Eve and the Serpent, between Jesus and the Soul, and between the Flesh and the Spirit. The engravings are mostly by William Marshall (fl. 1617–48).

EMECHETA, (Florence Onye) Buchi (1944–), Nigerian novelist, born near Lagos, the daughter of a railway porter. She left her home country at the age of 20 with four small children and moved to London. In 1972 she enrolled for a degree in sociology at the University of London and published a series of articles in the *New Statesman* which formed the basis of her first novel, *In the Ditch* (1972), and its sequel, *Second-Class Citizen* (1974). Both were published in one volume as *Adah's Story* (1983). Succeeding novels, *The Bride Price* (1976), *The Slave Girl* (1977), and *The Joys of Motherhood* (1979), dealt with the position of women in Nigerian society. In 1980 she returned to Nigeria as a visiting professor at Calabar University, an experience which influenced her novel *Double Yoke* (1982). Also published in 1982 was *Destination Biafra*, a fictional account of the Nigerian civil wars which draws on the experiences of family and friends. *Gwendolen* (1989) focuses on the subject of child abuse and cultural isolation. She has also written children's books, including *Nowhere to Play* (1980) and *The Moonlight Bride* (1981), and plays for television. Her autobiography, *Head above Water*, was published in 1986. See also POST-COLONIAL LITERATURE.

Emelye, the lady loved by Palamon and Arcite in Chaucer's 'The Knight's Tale' (see CANTERBURY TALES, 1). She figures as Emilia in *The Two Noble Kinsmen*.

EMERSON, Ralph Waldo (1803–82), American philosopher and poet, born in Boston, the son of a Unitarian minister who died when he was 8, leaving him and four brothers (one mentally retarded) to the care of their mother and aunt, in straitened circumstances. He was educated at Harvard, studied theology, was ordained, and became a pastor in Boston, but resigned his charge (shortly after the death of his first wife) because he felt unable to believe in the sacrament of the Lord's Supper. Dejected and with uncertain prospects, he departed in 1832 for Europe, and in 1833 visited England, where he met *Coleridge and *Wordsworth, and notably *Carlyle, who after a day's intensive conversation at Craigenputtock became a lifelong friend and correspondent. On his return to America Emerson embarked on a career as lecturer, evolving the new quasi-religious concept of *Transcendentalism, which found written expression in his essay *Nature* (1836): 'Nature is the incarnation of thought. The world is the mind precipitated.' This form of mystic idealism and Wordsworthian reverence for nature ('What is a farm but a mute gospel?') was immensely influential in American life and thought, and Emerson, like his friend Carlyle, was revered as a sage. In 1835 he married and settled in Concord; his 1837 Harvard address, 'The American Scholar', urged America (as *Channing had recently done) to assert its intellectual independence: 'We have listened too long to the courtly muses of Europe.' The *Dial*, founded in 1840, was edited by Emerson from 1842 to 1844, and published many of his gnomic, rough-hewn, but frequently striking poems, including 'The Problem' and 'Woodnotes'. His first volume of essays (1841) contains 'Self-Reliance' ('Whoso would be a man, must be a nonconformist . . . A foolish consistency is the hobgoblin of little minds'); 'Compensation'; and 'The Over-Soul', which proposes a mystic Unity 'within which every man's particular being is contained and made one with all other'. His second *Essays* (1844) contains 'The Poet', in which he urges the 'incomparable materials' of America, 'our log-rolling, our stumps and their politics, our fisheries, our Negroes and Indians . . . America is a poem in our eyes; its ample geography dazzles the imagination, and it will not wait long for metres.' This challenge was to be met by one of Emerson's most devoted disciples, *Whitman, although other American writers, including *Melville and *Hawthorne, deplored what they perceived as his cloudy rhetoric and empty optimism.

In 1845 Emerson delivered the lectures later published in 1850 as *Representative Men*; these studies of *Plato, *Swedenborg, Napoleon, and others owe something to Carlyle's concept of the Hero. In 1847 he revisited England on a lecture tour, staying in London in the home of his publisher, J. *Chapman; he was greatly admired in this country and his *English Traits* (1865), a perceptive study of the English national character, won him more readers. On his return to America he was actively engaged in the anti-slavery campaign, and continued to lecture and write (including poems and prose for the *Atlantic Monthly*) until, in his last decade, he gradually lost his mental powers and became a quiet blank. Of his many later works, mention should be made of his moving tribute to his friend and follower *Thoreau (1862) in which, after a warm appreciation, he mildly deplored Thoreau's want of ambition, a comment which takes on an ironic light in view of Emerson's current neglect as a writer and Thoreau's great and continuing influence. A definitive edition of Emerson's *Collected Works*, ed. R. E. Spiller and others (vol. i, 1971) is in progress, as is a complete 16–volume edition of the *Journals* and *Notebooks* (of which 8 vols. published 1960–6).

Emilia, (1) in Shakespeare's *Othello*, the plain-spoken wife of *Iago. In Cyprus she waits on Desdemona and shares her confidence, most memorably in the 'willow-song scene' (IV. iii); (2) the lady loved by Palamon and Arcite in Chaucer's 'The Knight's Tale' (see EMELYE), who also figures in *The Two Noble Kinsmen*; (3) Peregrine's love in Smollett's *Peregrine Pickle*.

Eminent Victorians, a biographical work by L. *Strachey.

Em'ly, Little, a character in Dickens's *David Copperfield*.

Emma, a novel by J. Austen, begun 1814, published 1816.

Emma, a clever, pretty, and self-satisfied young woman, is the daughter, and mistress of the house, of Mr Woodhouse, an amiable old valetudinarian. Her former governess and companion, Anne Taylor, beloved of both father and daughter, has just left them to marry a neighbour, Mr Weston. Missing Miss Taylor's companionship, Emma takes under her wing Harriet Smith, parlour-boarder at the school in the neighbouring village of Highbury. Harriet, a pretty, pliant girl of 17, is the daughter of unknown parents. Emma's active mind sets to work on schemes for Harriet's advancement, but her interfering and injudicious attempts lead in the end to considerable mortification. She first prevents Harriet from accepting an offer of marriage from Robert Martin, an eligible young farmer, as being beneath her. This tampering greatly annoys Mr Knightley, the bachelor owner of Donwell Abbey, who is Emma's brother-in-law and one of the few people able to see that she has faults. Emma has hope of arranging a match between Harriet and Mr Elton, the young vicar, only to find that Elton despises Harriet and has the presumption to aspire to her own hand. Frank Churchill, the son of Mr Weston by a former marriage, an attractive but thoughtless young man, now comes to visit Highbury. Emma first supposes him in love with herself, but presently thinks that Harriet might attract him, and encourages her not to despair. This encouragement, however, is misunderstood by Harriet, who assumes it is directed, not at Frank Churchill, in whom she has no interest, but at the great Mr Knightley himself, with whom Emma is half unwittingly in love. Emma then suffers the double mortification of discovering, first, that Frank Churchill is already engaged to Jane Fairfax, niece of Miss Bates, who lives in the village; and second, that Harriet has hopes, which appear on the surface to have some foundation, of supplanting her in Mr Knightley's affections. However, Mr Knightley in the end proposes to the humbled and repentant Emma, and Harriet is happily consoled with Robert Martin.

The novel is generally considered Jane Austen's most accomplished work, and the one which most fully realizes her own recommendation of '3 or 4 families in a Country Village' as 'the very thing to work on'. Minor characters include the vulgar Mrs Elton, with her frequent references to her 'caro sposo' and her brother-in-law's seat at Maple Grove, and the garrulous old maid Miss Bates, who lives with her widowed mother and enjoys 'a most uncommon degree of popularity for a woman neither young, handsome, rich nor married', and who becomes the occasion of one of Emma's educational moments at the celebrated outing to Box Hill (ch. 43) when Emma is reprimanded by Mr Knightley for making a joke at Miss Bates's expense.

EMPEDOCLES (*c*.484–*c*.424 BC), a Greek scientist, philosopher, and advocate of democracy who lived in Agrigentum in Sicily. He was responsible for demonstrating the existence of air, used experimentation in medicine, and taught that the universe was in a state of unending change thanks to the contrary action of Love, which united the four elements, and Strife, which drove them apart. Legends accumulated round his name: he was supposed to work miracles, controlling the winds and raising the dead, and to have met his death plunging into the crater of Etna. The opposition of Love and Strife is mentioned by Spenser (*Faerie Queene*, IV. x). The legend of Empedocles' death is referred to in *Paradise Lost* (III. 471), by *Lamb in 'All Fools Day', and by *Meredith in *Empedocles*; but the finest work it inspired is M. Arnold's *Empedocles on Etna* (1852) which shows the conflict between sensuous emotion and disciplined thought.

Empedocles on Etna, a dramatic poem by M. *Arnold, published anonymously 1852.

Arnold portrays the philosopher *Empedocles, who committed suicide by throwing himself into the crater of Etna, on the verge of his last act: his physician friend Pausanias tries to cheer him, accompanied by songs from the unseen harp player Callicles. Empedocles expresses his intellectual doubts, dismissing the reassuring platitudes of religion and philosophy; man's yearning for joy, calm, and enlightenment is in itself no proof that these things exist or can be attained. He dismisses Pausanias, grieves over his own 'dwindling faculty of joy', concludes that he is man no more, but 'a naked, eternally restless mind', and finally, in a kind of triumph, concluding that at least he has been ever honest in his doubts, hurls himself to his death.

EMPSON, Sir William (1906–84), poet and critic, educated at Winchester and Magdalene College, Cambridge, where he studied mathematics, then English under I. A. *Richards. He taught in universities in China and Japan, and subsequently became professor of English at Sheffield. He published two volumes of verse, *Poems* (1935) and *The Gathering Storm* (1940); *Collected Poems* (revised) appeared in 1955. His criticism includes *Seven Types of Ambiguity* (1930), *Some Versions of Pastoral* (1935), *The Structure of Complex Words* (1951), and *Milton's God* (1961). Empson's poetry makes use of analytical argument and imagery drawn from modern physics and mathematics; a technical virtuoso, he offered (in his own words) 'a sort of puzzle interest', and employed metaphysical conceits and linguistic, metrical, and syntactical complexities. *Wain praised his 'passion, logic and formal beauty', which widely influenced younger writers, particularly those associated with the *Movement. *Using Biography* (1984), a posthumous collection of essays, 1958–82, constitutes a spirited attack on the *New Criticism's neglect of biographical interpretation. See *William Empson: Among the Mandarins* (2005) by John Haffenden.

enallage, a rhetorical figure in which one grammatical form is substituted for another, as in 'We was robbed!' (Joe Jacobs) or 'Thank me no thankings, nor proud me no prouds' (*Romeo and Juliet*, III. v. 153).

Encounter, a political, cultural, and literary review, founded in 1953, and originally edited by S. *Spender and Irving Kristol; subsequently by Melvin J. Lasky, F. Kermode, A. *Thwaite, N. *Dennis, and others. D. W.

Brogan, in an anthology selected from its first ten years, described it as 'a *journal de combat* ... the organ of protest against the *trahison des clercs*', and its political tone at this period reflected some of the Anglo-American anti-Soviet spirit of the Cold War. But it was also the vehicle for N. *Mitford's celebrated formulation of the 'U' and 'Non-U' concept (1955), and C. P. *Snow pursued the *Two Cultures controversy in its pages (1959–60). It has also published poetry by R. *Lowell, *Plath, *Roethke, *Auden, *Larkin, *Amis, and many others, and articles by *Koestler, *Popper, V. S. *Naipaul, etc.

Encyclopaedia Britannica. The word encyclopaedia means instruction in the whole circle of learning. Among early precursors of the *EB* may be mentioned *Le Grand Dictionnaire* (1674) of Louis Moréri (1643–80), the *Dictionnaire historique et critique* (1697) of *Bayle, the *Cyclopaedia* (1728) of Ephraim *Chambers, and the great French *Encyclopédie* of the 18th cent.

The first *Encyclopaedia Britannica* was issued by a 'Society of Gentlemen in Scotland' in numbers (1768–71), the editor being William Smellie, a printer, afterwards secretary of the Society of Scottish Antiquaries. It was a dictionary of the arts and sciences. The second edition (1777–84), in ten volumes, added history and biography. The third edition, in 15 volumes, appeared in 1788–97; and the fourth edition, in 20 volumes, in 1801–10. The undertaking was taken over by Constable in 1812, and the copyright sold after the failure of that house in 1826. After some further editions it passed to Cambridge University for the publication in 1910–11 of the 11th edition in 28 volumes [*EB*]. The 10th and 11th editions were by Hugh Chisholm. The 14th edition, under the editorship-in-chief of J. L. Garvin, was published in London and New York in 1929. Since then a system of continuous revision has replaced the making of new editions, though the arrival of the *CD-ROM has called into question the future of the work. A CD-ROM version appeared in 1998. (See also CHAMBERS'S ENCYCLOPAEDIA.)

Encyclopaedists, the collaborators in the *Encyclopédie* of *Diderot and *d'Alembert.

Encyclopédie, L', a dictionary of universal knowledge published between 1751 and 1776 in 35 volumes under the editorship of *Diderot, with (until 1758) *d'Alembert as his chief assistant, and with the leading intellectuals of the age, including *Voltaire, *Montesquieu, *Rousseau, *Buffon, and *Turgot, as contributors. It attempted nothing less than the provision of a rational explanation for all aspects of existence, and it can be regarded as the most representative monument of the *Enlightenment. Its attacks on superstition and credulity attracted the hostility of Church and state. Something of the historical significance of the work can be gauged from the fact that the original investment of one million francs produced a profit of 300 per cent.

Endimion, *the Man in the Moone*, an allegorical prose play by *Lyly, published 1591.

Endimion abandons Tellus (the earth) in consequence of a hopeless passion for Cynthia (the moon). Tellus conspires with the witch Dipsas against Endimion, who is sent to sleep for 40 years. Cynthia breaks the spell and releases Endimion with a kiss. The dramatic element is slight, the allegory perhaps relating to the rivalry between *Elizabeth I (Cynthia) and *Mary Queen of Scots (Tellus), and the favour of Elizabeth for Leicester (Endimion).

ENDŌ, Shûsaku (1923–96), Japanese novelist, who became a Roman Catholic at the age of 11. He later studied French literature in France. The gap between Christian and traditional Japanese morality became his main theme. *The Sea of Poison* (1957) explores Japanese war guilt from a Christian perspective. *Silence* (1966) is about Portuguese missionaries in 16th-cent. Japan and the slaughter of the Japanese Christians.

Endymion, a poem in four books, by *Keats, written 1817, published 1818.

The poem tells, with a wealth of epithet and invention, the story of Endymion, 'the brain-sick shepherd-prince' of Mount Latmos, who falls in love with Cynthia, the moon, and descends to the depths of the earth to find her. There he encounters a real woman, Phoebe, and giving up his pursuit of the ideal he falls in love with her. She, however, turns out to be none other than Cynthia, who, after luring him, weary and perplexed, through 'cloudy phantasms', bears him away to eternal life. With the main story are woven the legends of Venus and Adonis, of Glaucus and Scylla, and of Arethusa. The poem includes in Bk I the well-known 'Hymn to Pan', and in Bk IV the roundelay 'O sorrow'.

In his preface Keats describes the work as 'a feverish attempt, rather than a deed accomplished'. It is a work, rich in luxuriant imagery, of an immature genius, the product of sensation rather than thought. The allegory, which is sometimes obscure, appears to represent the poet pursuing ideal perfection, and distracted from his quest by human beauty. The work was violently attacked in the *Quarterly Review* and in *Blackwood's*, in which *Lockhart described the poem as one of 'calm, settled, imperturbable drivelling idiocy'.

Endymion, a novel by B. *Disraeli, published 1880.

This was the last of Disraeli's novels, set in an earlier period of his life between about 1830 and the early 1850s, and describing with vivacity the political and social scene of that time, as well as the antagonism between Whig and Tory, the power of the great political hostesses, the *Tractarians, railway mania, the *Chartists, and the story of Louis Napoleon as 'Florestan'. There are many other identifications: Lord Palmerston appears as the engaging Lord Roehampton; Lady Jersey as the relentless Zenobia; Bismarck as

Ferroll, Cardinal *Manning as Penruddock, Rothschild as Mr Neuchatel; *Cobbett and *Cobden combine in Job Thornberry, *Thackeray (in revenge for his *Codlingsby*) is satirized as St Barbe.

Endymion, a reflective, sweet-natured boy, is the twin of the fiery, ambitious Myra, and the book is much concerned with their close relationship. Their father, Pitt Ferrars, is a rising young politician, who is enabled to move in the highest social circles in the expectation of a great inheritance, and of soon achieving cabinet rank. When neither comes to him he kills himself, leaving his family almost destitute. Endymion obtains a clerkship at Somerset House, and after Myra has rejected Penruddock, because of her bond with Endymion, she obtains a place as companion to Adriana Neuchatel, the daughter of a kindly Jewish banker. Myra's beauty and wit bring her great success in society and she marries Lord Roehampton, who finds the retiring Endymion a place as secretary to a cabinet minister. The young man becomes deeply interested in the plight of the poor, and in Manchester becomes a friend of Job Thornberry, a bold young radical and political economist. Throughout the novel there are rumblings of social unrest, and reports of incendiaries. Eventually Endymion is persuaded by Myra, and by Lady Montfort (whom he loves), to enter Parliament. After the death of Lord Roehampton Myra marries the exiled monarch Florestan and, reluctantly parting from her brother, goes to live abroad. When she too is free, Endymion marries Lady Montfort. On the death of the prime minister Endymion is asked to form the next government, and Myra returns to visit him in his triumph.

Enemy, a periodical which ran to three issues, 1927–9, edited and largely written by W. *Lewis.

ENGELS, Friedrich (1820–95), German philosopher, the son of a factory owner who supervised his father's business in Manchester. He wrote influential essays on the social and political conditions in Britain in the 1840s, including *The Condition of the Working Class in England* (1845), in which he praised *Carlyle as the only British writer to take account (in *Past and Present*, 1843) of the atrocious working conditions of the urban poor. Engels collaborated with *Marx, whom he helped to support when the latter settled in London in 1849, in writing *The German Ideology* (1845–6, but not published until 1932), a critique of German philosophy as lacking in social application; the *Manifesto of the Communist Party* (1848); and their great work, *Das Kapital*, the third volume of which Engels completed after Marx's death (vols i-iii, 1867/84/94).

Much has been extrapolated about Engels's views on literary theory from two letters, both written to aspiring novelists: in the first, written to Minna Kautsky in 1885, he says he is by no means opposed to literature designed to further social or political ideas (*Tendenzpoesie*), but that he believes 'the thesis must spring forth from the situation and action itself, without being explicitly displayed'. The second, written in English to Margaret Harkness in 1888 on receipt of a copy of her proletarian novel *A City Girl*, criticizes her work for being 'not quite realistic enough . . . Realism, to my mind, implies, besides the truth of detail, the truthful reproduction of typical characters under typical circumstances . . . . In *City Girl*, the working class appears as a passive mass, incapable of helping itself . . . .': but he reiterates that 'the more the opinions of the author remain hidden, the better the work of art'. These letters have been taken both to justify and to oppose the necessity for political commitment in art. (See also MARXIST LITERARY CRITICISM.)

Englands Helicon, a miscellany of Elizabethan verse, published in 1600, with additions in 1614, edited by H. E. Rollins (1935). It is the best collection of lyrical and pastoral poetry of the Elizabethan age, and includes pieces by *Sidney, *Spenser, *Drayton, R. *Greene, T. *Lodge, *Ralegh, *Marlowe, and others.

England's Parnassus, a collection of extracts from contemporary poets, by R. Allott, published in 1600.

England, Their England, an affectionately satirical comic novel by A. G. Macdonell, published 1933, in which Donald Cameron, like its author a Scot invalided away from the Western Front, carries out research for a book on the English by consorting with journalists and minor poets, attending a country-house weekend, serving as private secretary to a member of Parliament attending the League of Nations, and, in the novel's best-known episode, playing village cricket.

English, the Germanic language spoken in England which takes its name from the Angles (who first committed their dialect to writing) and was extended to refer to all the dialects of the vernacular, Saxon and Jutish too. Old English (formerly *Anglo-Saxon) is the English language of the period ending soon after the Norman Conquest (c.1100–50); the major compositions in it are the epic poem *Beowulf* (manuscript c.1000) and a major body of lyric poetry, including the *Elegies and *The Dream of the Rood*. Middle English is used to describe the language from then to about 1500, a period during which London English gradually became the dominant dialect and in which the major writer is Chaucer. Modern English, founded on the dialect of the east Midlands in Middle English, extends from 1500 to the present day.

English Association, the, founded in 1906 to promote the teaching and advanced study of the English language and of English literature, and to unite all those who are interested in these subjects. It mounts conferences, and publishes journals, including *English*, *Use of English*, and *Essays and Studies*.

English Bards and Scotch Reviewers, a satirical poem by *Byron in heroic couplets, published 1809. Angered by *Brougham's contemptuous criticism of his *Hours of Idleness* in the *Edinburgh Review*, Byron responded

with this witty and spirited attack on *Jeffrey, *Southey, *Wordsworth, *Coleridge, and Sir W. *Scott. He also poured patrician mockery on the 'doggrel' and 'childish prattle' of many of the minor poets and poetasters (*Bowles, *Cottle, and many others) of the Romantic movement, while upholding and defending those (e.g. *Rogers, *Crabbe) who continued to sustain the classical traditions of *Dryden and *Pope. It is a fine piece of invective, filled with woundingly memorable insults.

English Comic Writers, The, by W. *Hazlitt, published 1819.
   The essays cover a wide range of humorous dramatists, poets, novelists, and essayists, from Elizabethan times to the late 18th cent., and are marked by Hazlitt's characteristic vigour and enjoyment.

Englishman's Magazine (1831–3), an original and ambitious literary monthly, edited by E. *Moxon, which published poems, criticism, and essays, as well as notes on drama, music, and art. It published the work of the unknown young *Tennyson, as well as that of *Hood, *Lamb, Leigh *Hunt, *Clare, A. H. *Hallam, and others. It vigorously supported *Wordsworth and the *'Cockney School', defending them against *Blackwood's, the *Quarterly, and similar journals. Unusually for the time, more than half the contributions were signed. The *Englishman's* seems to have been killed by John *Wilson's scathing comments in *Blackwood's* on Hallam's effusive article proclaiming the genius of Tennyson.

English Review, a periodical founded in 1908 through the inspiration of a group of writers including *Conrad, H. G. *Wells, and E. *Garnett, with the purpose, in the words of its first editor F. M. *Ford (then Hueffer), of 'giving imaginative literature a chance in England'. It was backed at first by Arthur Marwood, the 'heavy Yorkshire squire' and friend of Ford, from whom Ford drew many of the characteristics of Christopher Tietjens in *Parade's End*. The first issue, in which appeared *Hardy's poem 'A Sunday Morning Tragedy', was published in Dec. 1908. The period of Ford's editorship (until Feb. 1910) was one of great distinction: Ford published work by established writers such as Arnold *Bennett, *Galsworthy, H. *James, and Wells, and by newcomers such as D. H. *Lawrence and W. *Lewis, amongst others. He was, however, impractical by temperament, ran the *Review* into financial difficulties, and was replaced by Austin Harrison, who remained editor until 1923. It was eventually merged with the *National Review*.

English Stage Company, the, an organization founded in 1956 by George Devine (1910–66) to present modern plays and encourage new dramatists; its home was the *Royal Court Theatre, London. Its first production was A. *Wilson's *The Mulberry Bush* (2 Apr. 1956), and it subsequently produced important new work by *Osborne, *Wesker, *Arden, *Bond, *Logue, *Storey,

*Orton, *Jellicoe, N. F. *Simpson, *Beckett, Christopher *Hampton, Heathcote *Williams, David *Hare, E. A. Whitehead, Brian *Friel, *Fugard, Mustapha Matura, Caryl *Churchill, Howard *Barker, Howard *Brenton, and others. (See also KITCHEN SINK DRAMA.)

English Traveller, The, a romantic drama by T. *Heywood, written c.1624, printed 1633.

Geraldine, returning from his travels, finds that the lady he loves has been married to Wincot, an old gentleman to whom he is under obligations. He and the lady bind themselves, she that she will marry him after Wincot's death, he that he will remain single till then. A plot by his treacherous friend Delavil leads to Geraldine's discovery that Delavil has seduced Wincot's wife. Heartbroken, Geraldine decides to leave the country. Before doing so he attends a farewell feast given him by Wincot. Wincot's wife hypocritically taxes him with his desertion of her, whereupon he reveals his discovery and upbraids her as an adulteress. She, in contrition and despair, dies.

There is a humorous underplot, borrowed from the *Mostellaria* of *Plautus: the prodigal son who wastes his father's substance during the latter's absence on a voyage, the father's unexpected return, the tricks of a resourceful servant to postpone the discovery of the prodigal's doings, and the final pardon and general reconciliation.

'Enid', see IDYLLS OF THE KING, THE.

Enitharmon, in the mystical books of *Blake, the female counterpart and emanation of *Los, who represents Time, as she represents Space. She also represents Inspiration. She is the mother of the rebellious *Orc. See under URIZEN and EUROPE: A PROPHECY.

enjambment, a technical term in verse, signifying the carrying on of the sense of a line or couplet into the next.

Enlightenment, a term (originally taken from the German *Aufklärung*) generally used to describe the philosophic, scientific, and rational spirit, the freedom from superstition, the scepticism and faith in religious tolerance of much of 18th-cent. Europe. The ancestors of the movement were *Descartes, *Locke, *Shaftesbury, and *Newton. *Voltaire, *Rousseau, *Condorcet, and *Buffon were associated with the Enlightenment in the minds of English readers, as was one of its great monuments, *L'*Encyclopédie*. The *Encyclopaedia Britannica* was in part a product of the distinct and important intellectual movement sometimes described as the *Scottish Enlightenment. In England many writers and poets echo or develop the educational and political ideas of the Enlightenment, including *Godwin, *Shelley, E. *Darwin, *Akenside, and the *Edgeworths. *Blake subscribed to the politics of the Enlightenment, but not to what he saw as the 'single vision' of Newtonian materialism. *Paine was much influenced by the politics of the French Enlightenment and his *The Rights of Man* and the American Declaration of Independence were also characteristic products. On a more literary level, some have seen a connection between the philosophy of the Enlightenment, the growth of literary realism, and the rise of the novel: *Romanticism was in part a reaction.

ENNIUS, Quintus (239–169 BC), the father of Roman poetry. An Italian from Calabria, he introduced scansion by quantity, the hexameter, and many Homeric devices, so that his *Annals* have been called an epic though they do not centre on a single complete action. The 550 lines that have survived from his work show him to have achieved a rugged grandeur. *Dryden mentions him a number of times in his critical essays, stressing *Virgil's debt to him and comparing him to *Chaucer.

Enobarbus (Domitius Ahenobarbus), close companion and friend of Antony in Shakespeare's *Antony and Cleopatra*, who deserts him for Octavius Caesar after his fortunes have declined (IV. v). It is he who describes Antony's first meeting with Cleopatra in the famous 'barge' speech (II. ii).

Enoch Arden, a narrative poem by *Tennyson, published 1864; the story was suggested by his friend *Woolner.

Enoch Arden, Philip Ray, and Annie Lee are children together in a little seaport town; both boys love Annie, but Enoch wins and marries her. They live happily for some years, until Enoch is compelled through temporary adversity to go as boatswain in a merchantman. He is shipwrecked, and for more than ten years nothing is heard of him; Annie, consulting her Bible for a sign, puts her finger on the text 'Under the palm tree', which, after a dream, she interprets to mean that he is in heaven. She marries Philip, who has long watched over her. Tennyson then turns to Enoch on his desert island, which is described in a fine, clear, bright Parnassian passage, and contrasted with the 'dewy meadowy morning-breath of England' for which he yearns. He is rescued and returns home, but when he discovers that Annie has remarried does not reveal himself, resolving that she shall not know of his return until after his death. The last lines—'And when they buried him the little port | Had seldom seen a costlier funeral'—have caused much offence to some, but others have found them to echo a curiously ambiguous attitude to Providence which pervades the whole poem.

Enquiry Concerning Human Understanding, see HUME.

Enquiry into the Present State of Polite Learning, An, a treatise by *Goldsmith, published 1759.

This was Goldsmith's first considerable piece of writing, in which he examines the causes of the decline of 'polite learning' from ancient times, through the Dark Ages, to its present state in Italy, Germany, Holland, France, and England, with perfunctory references to Spain and the Scandinavian countries. He attributes the alleged decay in England to the low status of the writer, driven to hack-work for the booksellers through lack of patronage—'We keep him poor, and yet revile his poverty'; also to the 'disgusting solemnity' and lack of comic spirit among poets, the restrictive conditions of the theatre, and the carping of critics. His attack on theatrical managers and actors offended *Garrick, and (according to T. *Davies) he toned it down for the second edition of 1774.

ENRIGHT, D(ennis) J(oseph) (1920–2002), poet, born in Leamington and educated at Leamington College and Downing College, Cambridge. He taught English literature for 25 years, mainly in the East; many of his poems are set in Japan, Egypt, Singapore, and Germany, and concern cultural differences and misunderstandings, themes which he also explored in various critical essays and in his autobiographical *Memoirs of a Mendicant Professor* (1969). His first collection of verse, *The Laughing Hyena and Other Poems* (1953), was followed by several others, including *Bread rather than Blossoms* (1956), *Addictions* (1962), *Sad Ires* (1975), *A Faust Book* (1979; a sequence of poems on the *Faust legend), *Under the Circumstances* (1991), and *Old Men and Comets* (1993). His *Collected Poems*, with new poems, appeared in 1981 (new edn, 1987). He also published novels for children (*The Joke Shop*, 1976; *Wild Ghost Chase*, 1978; *Beyond Land's End*, 1979) and various other prose works, including *The World of Dew: Aspects of Living in Japan* (1955), *Insufficient Poppy* (1960, a novel), and works of criticism, including *Man Is an Onion* (1972, collected reviews and essays). His anthology *Poets of the 1950s* (1955) brought together many of the poets to appear in R. Conquest's *New Lines, and in his preface to his anthology *The Oxford Book of Contemporary Verse 1945–1980* (1980) he reasserted the claims of 'the poetry of civility, passion, and order' against those of the confessional mode, as written by R. *Lowell, *Berryman, and others. His own work was predominantly detached and ironic in tone (although by no means impersonal) and wide-ranging in its subject matter. He also edited *The Oxford Book of Death* (1983) and *The Oxford Book of the Supernatural* (1994). *Byblows: Uncollected Poems* (1996) was followed by *Collected Poems, 1948–1998* (1998).

Entail, The, a novel by J. *Galt, published 1823, a satire on the corrupting effects of greed.

Claud Walkinshaw, a successful packman, cruelly disinherits his eldest son in favour of his second, who is a half-wit. Walkinshaw is thereby enabled to recover the ancestral property of his family. The disastrous consequences of his act recoil upon himself, and on his children and grandchildren. As a study in obsession the book is powerful, and it was admired by *Byron.

envoy, or envoi (from French 'a sending' or 'missive'), an additional stanza, of half the length of the regular stanza, in a form such as the eight-line stanza *ballade or the 11-line stanza *chant royal*, incorporating a refrain if there is one. It was a very widely occurring device in European poems of the Middle Ages, extending for example to the *amhran* (song) at the end of Irish stanzaic poems, but it has had curiously little impact in English. Chaucer's 'Envoys' (to Bukton and Scogan) do end with a section headed Envoy, but they are in the same form as the main stanzas. His titles are probably using the form in the more general French sense of 'missive', i.e. letter. The form was used correctly (and rather self-consciously) by *Scott, *Southey, and *Swinburne.

ENZENSBERGER, Hans Magnus (1929–), German poet, essayist, polemicist, and commentator, born in Bavaria, and brought up in Nuremberg. His works have been widely translated. The first English selection was *poems for people who don't read poems* (1968, trans. M. *Hamburger, Jerome Rothenberg, and the author), which contained work from his early German volumes 1959–64. *Der Untergang der Titanic* (1978: trans. by the author as *The Sinking of the Titanic*, 1981) was written during and after a stay in Cuba: its 32 cantos interweave his Cuban experience with life in Berlin and with cultural, political, and historical speculation about the foundering of Western civilization. Other volumes include *Mausoleum* (1975, prose poems) and *Zukunftsmusik* (*Music of the Future*, 1991). His *Selected Poems* (trans. M. Hamburger) appeared in 1994. Enzensberger's work is remarkable for its humane engagement, its direct, powerful, and resonant language, its wide range of historical and cultural reference, and its accessibility: he has reached out to a large readership while confronting serious issues with subtlety and sympathy.

Eōthen, see KINGLAKE.

epanalepsis, a rhetorical figure in which the same word is repeated at the beginning and end of a sentence or clause, as in 'Bold was the challenge and he himself was bold' (*Spenser) or 'Common sense is not so common' (*Voltaire).

'EPHELIA', pseudonym of a female lyric poet, possibly attached to the Restoration court, inconclusively identified as Joan Philips, although it has been suggested that the author was a male or a group of male rakes. Ephelia's *Female Poems on Several Occasions* (1679) are chiefly pastoral and amatory, addressed to 'Strephon' and written with technical panache. The poet, who praises fellow female poets *Orinda and Aphra *Behn, laments male inconstancy and adapts pastoral and courtly conceits to the mortifying position of an unrequited female lover in a male world.

epic, a poem that celebrates in the form of a continuous narrative the achievements of one or more heroic personages of history or tradition. Among the great epics of the world may be mentioned the *Iliad, *Odyssey, and Aeneid of classical, and the *Mahābhārata and Rāmāyaṅa of Hindu literature; the Chanson de *Roland; the Poema del Cid (see CID, THE); Milton's *Paradise Lost; Boiardo's *Orlando innamorato; Ariosto's *Orlando furioso; Tasso's *Gerusalemme liberata; and *Camões's Lusiads.

Epicene, or The Silent Woman, a comedy by *Jonson, acted by the Children of the Queen's Revels 1609–10, printed 1616.

Morose, an egotistic old bachelor with a pathological aversion to noise, proposes to disinherit his nephew Sir Dauphine Eugenie, whom he suspects of ridiculing him, by marrying and producing children, provided he can find a silent woman. Cutbeard, his barber, has found such a one in Epicene. Immediately after the wedding Epicene proceeds to torment her husband by turning into a loquacious shrew, and his agony is increased when Dauphine and his friends Truewit and Clerimont arrive with a rowdy party of guests and musicians to celebrate the marriage. Among the guests are a henpecked bearward, Captain Otter, and his Amazonian wife, the *Collegiate Ladies, and two boastful knights, Amorous La Foole and John Daw, whose cowardice is exposed when Truewit tricks them into fighting a duel. Driven frantic by the hubbub, and having unsuccessfully sought grounds for divorce from a parson and canon lawyer (in fact impostors planted by Dauphine, who chatter interminably to no purpose), Morose accepts Dauphine's offer to rid him of Epicene for £500 a year and the reversion of his property. Whereupon Dauphine pulls off Epicene's wig and reveals that, unknown to everyone else, including the audience, she is a boy whom he had trained for the part. *Dryden thought this play the most perfectly plotted of all comedies.

epic simile, an extended simile which compares one composite action with another, often with a digressive effect; it originates in *Homer, and was imitated by *Virgil, *Dante, and, in English, notably by *Milton. It is frequently parodied by *Fielding.

EPICTETUS (c. AD 60–after 100), a *Stoic philosopher, said to have been a freedman. He wrote nothing himself; the Encheiridion, or collection of his principles, was compiled by his disciple Arrian. Epictetus held health, pleasure, possessions to be of no account. Virtue alone mattered, and that resided in the will which should direct man to abstain and endure. The Encheiridion was translated from the Greek by John Healey (1610). It influenced *Chapman and was highly valued by *Dryden and M. *Arnold.

EPICURUS (341–270 BC), the founder of the school of philosophy that bears his name. After teaching in various places he settled finally in Athens. Some fragments of his writings survive, but his ideas are perhaps best studied in the De Rerum Natura of *Lucretius. Epicurus adopted the atomic theory of *Democritus but postulated an indeterminacy in the movement of his atoms which allowed him to believe in free will. In ethics he regarded the absence of pain—ἀταραξία or peace of mind—as the greatest good. Conventional moralists tended to describe him as a contemptible pleasure-seeker, but his life had been marked by rigorous abstinence from greed, lust, and anger, a fact which made Sir T. *Browne defend his reputation (*Pseudodoxia, 7. 17). Epicureanism in a modified form, amounting perhaps to no more than a gentlemanly avoidance of over-rigid principles, was common at the end of the 17th cent. It found its high priest in the French exile *Saint-Evrémond, for whose translated essays *Dryden wrote an appreciative preface (1692).

epigram, originally an inscription, usually in verse, e.g. on a tomb; hence a short poem ending in a witty turn of thought; hence a pointed or antithetical saying.

Epigrams, The, a collection of poems by *Jonson, printed 1616, including 'Inviting a Friend to Supper', 'On My First Son', 'The Famous Voyage', and addresses to *Donne and King James.

epiphany, 'manifestation', usually used in a Christian context to refer to the festival commemorating the manifestation of Christ to the Gentiles in the persons of the Magi (celebrated on 6 Jan., or Twelfth Night); but adapted by *Joyce to describe the sudden 'revelation of the whatness of a thing', the moment in which 'the soul of the commonest object seems to us radiant'. He uses the word in this sense in Stephen Hero, an early draft of *A Portrait of the Artist as a Young Man. These 'sudden spiritual manifestations' have been detected by critics in other revelatory moments in Joyce's work, and in the work of other writers; they bear some similarity to the 'spots of time' described by Wordsworth in *The Prelude (see Bk XII, ll. 208 ff.).

Epipsychidion, an autobiographical poem by P. B. *Shelley written at Pisa in 1821, and published there anonymously in the same year.

Composed in couplets of breathless energy, the poem celebrates Shelley's lifelong search for the eternal image of Beauty, in the earthly form of his various wives, mistresses, and female friends: notably Harriet Westbrook, Mary *Shelley, Claire *Clairmont, and Emilia Viviani—to whom the work is addressed: 'In many mortal forms I rashly sought | The Shadow of that idol of my thought.' Though drawing on the courtly love and planetary imagery of *Petrarch and *Dante, the work is passionately sexual as well as platonic: it ends with an invitation to Emilia to elope to 'an isle under Ionian skies, | Beautiful as a wreck of Paradise'. There is an attack on conventional marriage, 'the dreariest and longest journey', and praise of 'Free' or 'True' Love (ll. 148–73). Yet despite its blaze of amorous rhetoric, the poem is partly also a study of the creative process itself.

The title remains a puzzle: perhaps from the *epi-psyche* the 'soul out of my soul', or beloved; or perhaps with ironic reference to the *epithalamium*, the conventional marriage song. A close biographical reading reveals much sly humour.

Epistolae Obscurorum Virorum (*Epistles of Obscure Men*), published 1515–17, an anonymous collection of letters in mock-medieval Latin purporting to be written by various bachelors and masters in theology to Ortuinus Gratius, a famous opponent of the new learning, in which they incidentally expose themselves to ridicule and to scurrilous charges. The letters are attributed principally to Ulrich von Hutten (1488–1523), soldier, humanist, and supporter of *Luther, and were written in connection with the celebrated *Reuchlin–*Pfefferkorn controversy.

epistolary novel, a story written in the form of letters, or letters with journals, and usually presented by an anonymous author masquerading as 'editor'. The first notable example in English, written entirely in epistolary form, was a translation from the French in 1678, *Letters of a Portuguese Nun.* In 1683 A. *Behn published *Love-Letters between a Nobleman and His Sister*, and many similar tales of illicit love and love manuals followed. Thus when *Richardson, the first and perhaps greatest master of the form, came to write *Pamela* (1741) he felt a duty to rescue the novel from its tainted reputation. The immediacy of the epistolary form lends itself to intense subjective analysis, but also to charges of implausible absurdity (fully exploited by Fielding in *Shamela*). Between the 1740s and about 1800, when the form chiefly flourished, it was employed not only by Richardson but by *Smollett, *Bage, J. *Moore (the elder), and F. *Burney, among many others. After 1800 both M. *Edgeworth and J. *Austen experimented with the form, as did *Swinburne, and H. *James attempted it in short stories, but it is now rarely adopted. W. *Golding's *Rites of Passage* (1980) provides an interesting variation in the form of an epistolary journal. (See also NOVEL, RISE OF THE.)

Epithalamion, a hymn by *Spenser, perhaps in celebration of his marriage with Elizabeth Boyle in 1594. The poem was printed with the *Amoretti in 1595. Its beauty of composition has always been much admired, and in 1960, Kent Hieatt (in his *Short Time's Endless Monument*) demonstrated that its 24 stanzas represent the hours of Midsummer Day.

epithalamium, or **epithalamion,** a poem or song written to celebrate a marriage. The form flourished in the Renaissance, one of the most notable examples being Spenser's *Epithalamion.

eponymous, that gives his name to anything, used for example of the mythical personages from whose names the names of places or peoples are reputed to be derived. It is now most frequently used in the phrase 'the eponymous hero/heroine' of a work: e.g. *Tom Jones or *Clarissa.

Eppie, in G. Eliot's *Silas Marner*, the daughter of Cass and adopted child of Silas.

EQUIANO, Olaudah, see BLACK BRITISH LITERATURE.

ERASMUS, Desiderius (*c*.1467–1536), great Dutch humanist, born at Rotterdam. Under pressure of his guardians he became an Augustinian monk, but thanks to the protection of the bishop of Cambrai was allowed to leave the cloister and travel extensively in Europe. He came more than once to England, where he was welcomed by the great scholars of the day, *More, *Colet, and *Grocyn, and was induced by *Fisher to lecture at Cambridge on Greek from 1511 to 1514. He was a friend and patron of *Holbein, whom he introduced to More, and by whom he was painted several times. He received from Archbishop Warham the benefice of Aldington in Kent and, on resigning it, a pension which was continued until his death. His principal works were a new edition of the Greek New Testament (1516), followed by Latin paraphrases (1517–24); *Encomium Moriae* (*The Praise of Folly*, 1511, a satire written at the suggestion of More, principally directed against theologians and church dignitaries); *Enchiridion Militis Christiani* (1503, a manual of simple piety according to the teaching of Jesus Christ, which was translated perhaps by *Tyndale into English, and also into other languages); *Institutio Christiani Principis* (*Education of a Christian Prince*); the vivid and entertaining *Colloquia* and letters furnishing autobiographical details and pictures of contemporary life, which were drawn upon by C. Reade in *The Cloister and the Hearth* and by Sir W. Scott in *Anne of Geierstein*. His *Adagia* (1500), a collection of Latin and Greek proverbs traced to their source with witty comments, one of the first works of the new learning, was much drawn upon by *Rabelais and by many English writers. His many editions and translations of the Bible, early Christian authors, and the classics revolutionized European literary culture. Erasmus prepared the way for the Reformation by his writings. With the movement itself he sympathized at first, but he refused to intervene either for or against *Luther at the time of the Diet of Worms, although invoked by both sides. He urged moderation on both and disclaimed sympathy with Luther's violence and extreme conclusions, and at a later stage (1524, in his tract on 'Free Will') entered into controversy with him. The standard edition of the letters of Erasmus (11 vols, 1906–47) was edited by P. S. and H. M. Allen.

ERCELDOUNE, Thomas of, called also the Rhymer and Learmont (fl. ?1220–?97), seer and poet, mentioned in the chartulary (1294) of the Trinity House of Soltra as having inherited lands in Erceldoune, a Berwickshire village. He is said to have predicted the death of Alexander III, king of Scotland, and the battle of Bannockburn, and is the traditional source of many (fabricated) oracles, one of which 'foretold' the accession of James VI to the English throne. He is the reputed author of a poem on the *Tristram story, which Sir W. *Scott considered genuine; it probably emanated from a French source. The romance of 'True Thomas' and the 'ladye gaye', popularly attributed to him, may be placed after 1401 (ed. J. A. H. *Murray, 1875).

ERDRICH, Louise (1954–   ), novelist and poet, born in Minnesota. She was raised in North Dakota, which has remained her fictional terrain. Of German–American and Chippewa descent (a member of the Turtle Mountain Chippewa tribe), she has dramatized the condition of Native Americans through a combination of naturalistic description of reservation life and an interest in tribal and ancestral pasts, which parallels the techniques of *magic realism. Her novels include *Love Medicine* (1984), *The Beet Queen* (1986), and *Tracks* (1988).

Erewhon (e-re-whon, an anagram of 'nowhere'), a satirical novel by S. *Butler, published anonymously 1872.

The narrator (whose name is revealed in *Erewhon Revisited* as Higgs) crosses a range of mountains and comes upon the undiscovered country of Erewhon. He is first thrown into jail, where he is helped by his beautiful girl jailer, Yram. On his release he is lodged with Mr Nosnibor (Robinson) and his family. In this society morality is equated with health and beauty, and crime with illness. The Unborn select their parents, who have to endure their selection. The Musical Banks produce a currency which is venerated but not used. The development of machinery, which had at one stage threatened to usurp human supremacy, had led to a civil war and is now forbidden. The country is ruled by so-called philosophers and prophets, whom Higgs sees to be merely faddists and fanatics. When he is threatened with prosecution for contracting measles, Higgs announces that he will visit the air-god and end the terrible drought; with Nosnibor's daughter Arowhena, he escapes in a balloon to England, where they marry. The story, which was written over a period of ten years, had its origin in Butler's article 'Darwin among the Machines', published in New Zealand in 1863.

Erewhon Revisited, a sequel to *Erewhon*, by S. *Butler, published 1901.

John, the son of Higgs and Arowhena, is the writer of this account of his father's return to Erewhon. After 20 years Higgs finds that his ascent in the balloon has become that of a god, the Sunchild, in a sun-chariot, his conversation has become the basis of sacred texts, a temple has been built to him at Sunchildiston, and that the new religion is organized by two cynical exploiters, professors Hanky and Panky. Once again Higgs's life is threatened, but again he escapes and, after further bewildered wanderings in Erewhon, returns, half unhinged, to England.

Eric, or, Little by Little, see FARRAR.

ERIGENA, see SCOTUS ERIGENA.

Erl-King, the German *Erl-könig* (alder-king), an erroneous rendering of the Danish *eller-konge*, king of the elves, a malignant goblin who, in German legend and in *Goethe's poem on the subject, haunts the Black Forest and lures people, particularly children, to destruction. Goethe's poem was the foundation of one of *Schubert's best-known songs ('Erlkönig', written 1816), and was translated by Sir W. *Scott.

ERNULF, or **ERNULPHUS** (1040–1124), bishop of Rochester, supposed compiler of the *Textus Roffensis*, a collection of laws, papal decrees, and documents relating to the church of Rochester. The comprehensive curse or excommunication of Ernulphus figures in Bk III, chs x, xi of Sterne's *Tristram Shandy.

Eros, in Shakespeare's *Antony and Cleopatra*, is the faithful attendant of Antony, and kills himself to avoid killing his master.

Erse, a term formerly used for Irish Gaelic (i.e. Irish) or occasionally (and inaccurately, since the term is the Lowland Scots word for Irish) for Scots Gaelic.

ERVINE, St John Greer (1883–1971), playwright and novelist, was born in Belfast of a long-established Ulster family. Many of his early plays (including *Mixed Marriage*, 1911; *The Magnanimous Lover*, 1912; and *John Ferguson*, 1915) were performed at the *Abbey Theatre in its realist phase, and dealt with themes of religious violence and conflict in Northern Ireland. Ervine later moved to England, where he wrote as drama critic for the *Morning Post and the *Observer, and achieved his first West End success with *The First Mrs Fraser* (1929), which was followed by many other popular comedies. He also published several novels, and studies of C. S. *Parnell (1925), General *Booth (1934), and G. B. *Shaw (1956).

ESENIN, Sergei Aleksandrovich (1895–1925), Russian poet of peasant origins who, on arriving in Moscow in 1911, gave poetry readings in his peasant's smock to admiring aristocratic audiences. He greeted the October Revolution as a revival of a Russia of peasants and joined a group of peasant poets led by Nicolai Kliuyev (1887–1937), who died in the purges. He was also associated with the Imaginists, who, though unconnected with *Pound and *Imagism, did attempt to shape the perceptions of readers through images. The second of his marriages (1922) was to dancer Isadora Duncan with whom he visited the United States. His last years were characterized by disillusionment, drunkenness, and excess, and he committed suicide in Leningrad, writing his last poem in his own blood. A selection of his poetry was translated by Geoffrey Thurley as *Confessions of a Hooligan* (1973).

Esmond, see HISTORY OF HENRY ESMOND ESQUIRE, THE.

Esmond, Beatrix, a character in Thackeray's *The History of Henry Esmond* and, as Baroness Bernstein, in *The Virginians*.

ESQUEMELING, EXQUEMELING, or **OEXMELIN,** Alexander Olivier, a Dutch physician, who lived with the buccaneers, 1668–74, and published an account of them (including Sir Henry Morgan, 1635–88, a Glamorgan-born buccaneer who later became deputy governor of Jamaica) and their doings. This was translated into Spanish, French, and English: there is a recent translation by A. Brown, *The Buccaneers of America* (1969).

ESQUIVEL, Laura (1950–   ), Mexican writer of best-selling novels. Her first novel *Como agua para chocolate* (1989, *Like Water for Chocolate*) fuses a romantic but deferred love affair that ends with death by orgasm with a family saga traced through women in the kitchen, with actual recipes, in a fluent style of exaggerations where metaphors are literal (see MAGIC REALISM). Esquivel scripted the film made by ex-husband Alfonso Arau in 1993. The well-crafted, self-conscious playfulness of Esquivel's *La ley del amor* (1995; *The Law of Love*, 1996) includes a CD and comic book sections, in a *science fiction format.

Essay Concerning Human Understanding, a philosophical treatise by *Locke, published 1690 (2nd edn, 1694; 4th, 1700; 5th, 1706; all with large additions).

The Essay is an examination of the nature of the human mind and its powers of understanding. Locke begins in Bk I by rejecting the doctrine of 'innate ideas', maintaining that all knowledge is based on experience. The objects of understanding are termed by him *ideas*, and Bk II provides an account of the origin, sorts, and extent of our ideas. The source of ideas is *experience*, the observation of external objects or of the internal operations of the mind, i.e. sensation or reflection. Sensation is always of a quality. Qualities are either primary (extension, figure, mobility, and number); or secondary, not really belonging to things but imputed to them, depending on our subjective perception, and inscrutably connected with the primary qualities, which alone really belong to things. A number of simple ideas being constantly found to go together, the mind is led to suppose a substratum for them, and this we call *substance*, but we have no other idea of its nature. We are equally ignorant of spiritual substance, the substratum of the operations of the mind: we do not even know whether material and spiritual substance are the same or different. The idea of cause or power is derived from experience, principally of the workings of the mind; this discussion of power leads Locke into a long and subtle account of the 'freedom of the will'.

In Bk III Locke discusses language. He holds that words have meaning insofar as they stand for ideas in the mind; distinguishing between 'real' and 'nominal' essence, he argues that terms for natural kinds (e.g. 'gold', 'horse') can express only nominal essences or sets of ideas; they cannot latch on to the real essences or hidden constitutions of the things themselves, which may always remain beyond our grasp.

Bk IV defines knowledge as the perception of the agreement or disagreement of ideas. It is either intuitive and direct, demonstrative (through the interposition of a third idea), or 'sensitive', i.e. based upon perception. Knowledge in matters of real existence is limited to two certainties, of our own existence, by intuition, and of the existence of God, by demonstration. We have a lesser degree of certainty of the existence of finite beings without us, for which we must rely on sensitive knowledge. If the mind perceives nothing but its own ideas, how can we know that they agree with the things themselves? Locke advances various arguments for the possibility of 'real' knowledge (i.e. knowledge about real things), but points out that even if we admit its validity, this knowledge is narrowly limited: we know only of the existence together, here and now, of collections of simple ideas; we cannot demonstrate the necessity of their coexistence. There are therefore very few general propositions, carrying with them undoubted certainty, to be made concerning substances; a perfect science of natural bodies is unattainable. Experience and history are all we can attain to, from which we may derive advantages of ease and health. Knowledge at once general and real must be, not of the relations of ideas to reality, but of ideas to each other, as, e.g., in mathematics, and also, Locke oddly thought, in ethics (though on the latter point he is more doubtful in his *Reasonableness of Christianity*). The faculty that God has given us in place of clear knowledge is judgement, whereby the mind takes a proposition to be true or false without demonstration. Locke discusses the relations of faith and reason. Unlike F. *Bacon and *Hobbes, he holds that faith is nothing but the firm assent of the mind, which should not be accorded to anything except for good reason. Revelation must be judged by reason. But the field of knowledge being so limited, it must be supplemented by faith, and this is the basis of his *Reasonableness of Christianity* (1695).

Essay on Criticism, a didactic poem in heroic couplets by *Pope, published anonymously 1711. It begins with an exposition of the rules of taste and the authority to be attributed to the ancient writers on the subject. The laws by which a critic should be guided are then discussed, and instances are given of critics who have departed from them. The work is remarkable as having been written when Pope was only 21.

Essay on Man, a philosophical poem in heroic couplets by *Pope, published 1733–4, part of a larger poem projected but not completed.

It consists of four epistles addressed to *Bolingbroke, and perhaps to some extent inspired by his fragmentary philosophical writings. Its objective is to vindicate the ways of God to man; to prove that the scheme of the universe is the best of all possible schemes, in spite of appearances of evil, and that our failure to see the perfection of the whole is due to our limited vision. 'Partial Ill' is 'universal Good', and 'self-love and social' are both directed to the same end: 'All are but parts of one stupendous whole | Whose body Nature is, and God the soul.' The epistles deal with man's relations to the universe, to himself as an individual, to society, and to happiness. D. *Stewart thought the Essay 'the noblest specimen of philosophical poetry which our language affords' (*Active and Moral Powers*, 1828), but Dr *Johnson commented, 'Never were penury of knowledge and vulgarity of sentiment so happily disguised.' Pope's attempts to prove that 'Whatever is, is right' anticipate the efforts of Pangloss in *Voltaire's *Candide*.

Essay on the Learning of Shakespeare, An, by Richard Farmer (1735–97), published 1767. This brief volume consists of a forceful presentation of Farmer's views, and a scornful refutation of his opponents', on the subject of Shakespeare's knowledge of languages, ancient and modern. Farmer's conclusion is that Shakespeare's studies were 'most demonstratively confined to Nature and his own Language'.

Essays, The, of F. *Bacon, first published in 1597, together with the 'Christian Meditations' and 'Of the Colours of Good and Evil', consisted of ten essays, in extremely bare style. The sentences are printed separately, marked with a paragraph sign, giving them the status of aphorisms, discrete observations drawn from experience, in the realm of public life. The second edition (1612) contained 38 essays, in a more varied style, and on a wider range of topics: a manuscript copy now in the British Library describes them as his 'writings . . . in Moralitie, Policie [politics] and Historie'. In this collection Bacon began to fill a lacuna he had noted in his *Advancement of Learning* (1605), the lack of concrete knowledge of the different 'natures and dispositions' of human beings, and how they were affected by psychological and social factors (such as gender, health, social standing, physical appearance). The final version, now called *Essays or Counsels, Civil and Moral* (1625), included 58 essays, filling in more of these gaps in treating both 'civil' or public life, and the *mores* or behaviour of private individuals. Bacon's approach varies greatly from essay to essay, approaching each topic from several different viewpoints, juxtaposing systematic analysis with brilliant aperçus. The styles used range from the detached and laconic to the passionately engaged, especially when expressing his moral beliefs. Dr *Johnson said that the *Essays* were 'the observations of a strong mind operating upon life; and in consequence you find what you seldom find in other books'.

Essays and Reviews, a collection of essays on religious subjects from a *Broad Church standpoint published in 1860. Among them were M. *Pattison's 'Tendencies

of Religious Thought in England 1688–1750' and *Jowett's 'On the Interpretation of Scripture'. The other essayists were the Revd H. B. Wilson (editor), Frederick Temple, Rowland Williams, Baden Powell, and C. W. Goodwin. A meeting of the bishops, urged on by Samuel Wilberforce, in 1861 denounced the book for its liberalism. Williams and Wilson were condemned to deprivation for a year, but were acquitted on appeal. The *Essays* were finally synodically condemned in 1864.

Essays in Criticism, three series of essays by M. *Arnold, published in 1865, 1888, and 1910. The title was adopted by F. W. *Bateson for a periodical founded in 1951, in which he intended to combine 'social relevance' and 'scholarly standards', and in which the influence both of Arnold himself and of *Scrutiny* may be detected.

Essays of Elia, The, miscellaneous essays by C. *Lamb, of which the first series appeared in the *London Magazine* between 1820 and 1823, in which latter year they appeared as a separate volume. *The Last Essays of Elia* was published in 1833. Lamb adopted the name Elia, which was that of a former Italian clerk at the South Sea House, ostensibly to save the embarrassment of his brother John, who worked at that same place, but also, one must suppose, for literary reasons. The essays are all cast as if written by Elia, but they are not reliably autobiographical, even when seeming so. The fanciful, old-fashioned character of the narrator is maintained throughout. He is, in Lamb's words, 'a bundle of prejudices' with a strong liking for the whimsical, the quaint, and the eccentric. The tone is never didactic or seriously philosophical, and all the more disturbing aspects of life are avoided. The style is very literary and carefully wrought, filled with archaisms and with echoes of Lamb's master *Sterne. Some of the best-known essays were: 'Some of the Old Benchers of the Inner Temple'; 'Christ's Hospital'; 'The South Sea House'; 'Mrs Battle's Opinions on Whist'; 'Dream Children'; and 'A Dissertation on Roast Pig'. The collected essays of 1823 did not sell well, to Lamb's great discouragement. A falling off in the quality of the *Last Essays* is very apparent.

ESSEX, Robert Devereux, second earl of (1566–1601), the stepson of Queen *Elizabeth's old favourite the earl of *Leicester. He was regarded as the natural successor to *Sidney, whose widow he married in 1590. A period of intense and lucrative favour in the 1590s culminated in his dispatch to Ireland in March 1599 to suppress Tyrone's rebellion. Shakespeare referred optimistically in *Henry V* (v. prologue 29–34) to the successful return of 'the General of our gracious Empress', but in fact Essex's return was sudden and ignominious. He came back without leave, having panicked at his lack of success, and after almost a year of house arrest he made an abortive attempt at rebellion in the City of London in Feb. 1601. A special performance of Shakespeare's

337

Richard II, showing a monarch willingly abdicating an unpopular rule, had been among the activities by which Essex and his friends fomented discontent. Essex was executed on 25 Feb., the episode casting a dark shadow over the last 18 months of Elizabeth's reign. He was a literary patron of some discernment, and himself wrote poems of which a small handful have survived. L. *Strachey's *Elizabeth and Essex* (1928) is a highly coloured and highly readable fictionalization; among many more recent biographies is Robert Lacey's *An Elizabethan Icarus* (1971).

Estella, a character in Dickens's *Great Expectations*.

Esther Lyon (or **Bycliffe**), the heroine of G. Eliot's *Felix Holt*.

Esther Summerson, a character in Dickens's *Bleak House*, and narrator of part of the story.

Esther Waters, a novel by G. *Moore, published 1894.
It is the story of the life of a religiously minded girl, a Plymouth Sister, driven from home into service at 17 by a drunken stepfather. She obtains a situation at Woodview, the house of the Barfields, where a racing stable is kept, and all above and below stairs (except Mrs Barfield, a Plymouth Sister like Esther) are wrapped up in gambling on races. There, in a moment of weakness, she is seduced by a fellow servant and deserted. She has to leave her place, though kindly treated by Mrs Barfield. Then follows a poignant tale of poverty, hardship, and humiliation: the lying-in hospital, service as wet-nurse, other miserable situations, even the workhouse, in the mother's brave struggle to rear her child. Her seducer re-enters her life, marries her, and makes a good husband. But he is a bookmaker and publican; exposure to weather at the races ruins his health and trouble with the authorities over betting at his public house causes the latter to be closed. He dies, and leaves his wife and son penniless. Finally Esther returns to Woodview, where she finds peace at last with Mrs Barfield, now a widow, living alone and impoverished in a corner of the old house.

ESTIENNE, in Latin Stephanus, the name of a family of French printers and scholars. Henri Estienne (d. 1520), of a Provençal family, came to Paris in 1502 and founded a printing house. His son Robert (1503–59) was printer to Francis I, and printed a number of important works and compiled the best Latin dictionary of the time, *Thesaurus Linguae Latinae* (1532). He was a Protestant, and in 1551 was exiled to Geneva. His son Henri Estienne (1531–98) spent most of his life at Geneva, where he printed for the Republic, but also visited France, Italy, Flanders, and England: an ardent Hellenist, he printed works of Greek authors and compiled a *Thesaurus Graecae Linguae* (1572).

Estrildis, a German princess captured and brought to England by King *Humber according to *Geoffrey of Monmouth's *History*, ii. 2–5. *Locrine, king of Britain, fell in love with her and they had a daughter Habren

(*Sabrina). Locrine put aside his wife Gwendolen for her, but she exacted vengeance on him by pursuing and slaying him in battle and having Estrildis and her daughter drowned in the river Severn, thereafter named from the daughter. Geoffrey says: 'It thus comes about that right down to our own times this river is called Habren in the British language, although by a corruption of speech it is called Sabrina in the other tongue' (ii. 5; Penguin trans. Lewis Thorpe, 1966, 77). In *Wace and *Laȝamon the river is called 'Auren' which Madden, in his edition of Laȝamon, identifies as the Dorset Avon. The story is treated in *Lodge's 'The Complaynt of Elstred' (1593), in Spenser's *Faerie Queene* (II. x), and in *Swinburne's drama *Locrine* (1887). See *Comus in which *Milton makes Thyrsis invoke Sabrina as the goddess of the river Severn.

ETHEREGE, or **ETHEREDGE,** Sir George (1636–91/2). He seems to have spent part of his early years in France, and was a man about town in London when his first comedy, *The Comical Revenge, or Love in a Tub*, was performed in 1664. The serious portions are in rhymed heroics, setting a fashion that was followed for some years, while the lively and realistic comic underplot, in prose, was the foundation of the English comedy of manners of *Congreve and *Goldsmith; Etherege drew his inspiration in part from *Molière's farces and from Italian mime, styles which were to have important influence on the lighter modes of English drama for the rest of the century. In 1668 *She Wou'd if she Cou'd* was performed, and in the same year Etherege travelled to Turkey as secretary to the ambassador, returning in 1671. His best play, *The Man of Mode*, was performed in 1676. He married a wealthy widow and was knighted, c.1680, and was an envoy of James II in Ratisbon (Regensburg), 1685–9; his *Letterbook* recording his stay and his nonchalant attitude to his duties was edited in 1928 by S. Rosenfeld. He died in Paris, a Jacobite exile. His polished and fashionable comedies were savagely attacked as immoral and coarse by the more genteel generation of *Steele, and the 19th cent. found them formless and plotless, but they now enjoy a high reputation.

Ettrick Shepherd, the, a name given to James *Hogg.

Eugene Aram, a novel by *Bulwer-Lytton, published 1832. It is the story of a schoolmaster, driven to crime by poverty, who is later tormented by remorse. The same subject suggested T. *Hood's poem 'The Dream of Eugene Aram'.

Eugenius, a minor character in *Tristram Shandy*, and *A Sentimental Journey*, by L. Sterne, thought to be based on Sterne's friend *Hall-Stevenson.

EULENSPIEGEL, Till, a German peasant of the early 14th cent. whose jests and practical jokes form the subject of a collection of satirical tales; one of these incidents features in Chaucer's 'Summoner's Tale' (see CANTERBURY TALES, 8). The earliest surviving printed edition, in High German, was published in Strasbourg in 1515, and there were early translations into English, Czech, Danish, Flemish, French, Latin, Polish, and Swedish. In England Till was known as Owlglass; an abridged translation into English by William Copland was published as *A Merye Jest of a Man that Was Called Howleglas* (c.1555). Several references in *Jonson and John *Taylor assume a familiarity with Owlglass as prankster.

Euphorion, in Pt II of Goethe's *Faust*, represents, at one stage of the drama, Lord *Byron, whom Goethe laments in a dirge.

Euphues, a prose romance by *Lyly, of which the first part, *Euphues: The Anatomy of Wit*, was published 1578, and the second, *Euphues and His England*, 1580. The plot of each is very slender and little but a peg on which to hang discourses, conversations, and letters, mainly on the subject of love. The work is largely based on North's *Diall of Princes*.

In the first part Euphues, a young Athenian, visits Naples, where he makes the acquaintance of Philautus, an Italian, and a friendship develops between them. Nonetheless Euphues proceeds to oust Philautus from the affections of Lucilla, to be in turn ejected by one Curio. Euphues and Philautus, after upbraiding one another, unite in holding Lucilla 'as most abhominable', and part friends, Euphues returning to Greece and leaving behind him a pamphlet of advice to lovers, which he terms 'A cooling Carde for Philautus'.

In Pt II Euphues and Philautus travel to England, where their adventures are even less entertaining than at Naples. They are largely concerned with the love affairs on which Philautus embarks, in spite of the advice of Euphues to use circumspection in his dealings with English ladies; and much space is occupied by a discussion on such questions as 'whether in love be more required secrecie or constancie'. Finally Euphues is recalled to Greece. From Athens Euphues addresses a letter to the ladies of Italy, 'Euphues' Glasse for Europe', in which he describes England, its institutions, its ladies, its gentlemen, and its queen; and a final letter of general advice from Euphues to Philautus completes the work.

Euphues is famous for its peculiar style, to which it has given the name 'euphuism'. Its principal characteristics are the excessive use of antithesis, which is pursued regardless of sense, and emphasized by alliteration and other devices; and of allusions to historical and mythological personages and to natural history drawn from such writers as *Plutarch, *Pliny, and *Erasmus. Sir W. *Scott satirized euphuism in the character of Sir Piercie Shafton in *The Monastery* and C. *Kingsley defended *Euphues* in *Westward Ho!*

Euphues Golden Legacie, see ROSALYNDE.

Euphuism, see EUPHUES.

EURIPIDES (485–406 BC), Greek tragedian of whose 92 plays only 19 survive. Ten have survived because they were used in schools c. AD 200: *Alcestis, Medea, Hippolytus, Andromache, Hecuba, The Trojan Women, The Phoenician Women, Orestes, The Bacchae,* and *Rhesus*. Nine other plays survive in a single manuscript (which also contains the other 10 plays): *Electra, Helen, The Children of Heracles, Heracles, The Suppliant Women, Iphigenia in Aulis, Iphigenia in Tauris, Ion,* and *Cyclops*. The plays of Euripides are characterized by an ambivalent attitude towards the national religious myths, which he sometimes seems to deploy purely for their dramatic potential. He is also unusually successful in his characterization of ordinary human beings.

*Petrarch ranked him next to *Homer, and G. *Buchanan took him as a model for his two Latin plays. Milton's *Samson Agonistes* was the first English tragedy to show his influence. *Dryden praised his depiction of human behaviour, and *Shelley translated his satyr play *Cyclops*. But it was at the end of the 19th cent. that Euripides truly made his mark. W. *Morris sentimentalized the *Medea* in *The Life and Death of Jason* (1867) and the *Alcestis* in *The Earthly Paradise* (1868–70). R. *Browning, commenting on the *Alcestis*, arraigned Admetus in *Balaustion's Adventure* (1871) and defended Euripides in *Aristophanes' Apology* (1875). T. S. *Moore tried his hand at the Phaedra story and G. *Murray's translations (1904–8) scored a remarkable theatrical success. More recently W. *Soyinka produced a notable version of the *Bacchae* (1993), and elements of this story have appeared in many other works, including the novels of *De Bernières: *Alcestis* is used by T. S. *Eliot in *The Cocktail Party*.

Europe: *A Prophecy*, a poem by W. *Blake, printed 1794 at Lambeth, in which Blake portrays the oppression of Albion during the 1,800-year sleep of *Enitharmon, the female principle, and the approach of the French Revolution, symbolized by her son, the terrible *Orc, spirit of revolt. The frontispiece of *Europe* portrays *Urizen as the Creator with his measuring instruments, and I. *Newton appears in the poem as an ambiguous herald of change.

EUSDEN, Laurence (1688–1730), poet laureate from 1718 until his death. He had celebrated the marriage of the duke of Newcastle, who gave him the laureateship. Pope refers to his notorious drinking habits in *The Dunciad* (I. 293):

> Know, Eusden thirsts no more for sack or praise;
> He sleeps among the dull of ancient days.

EUSEBIUS of Caesarea, in Palestine (AD 265–340), bishop of Caesarea, and a celebrated historian and theologian. His *Chronicle* in Greek (known in a Latin version by *Jerome) contains an epitome of universal history and chronological tables, the foundation of much of our knowledge of the dates of events in Greek and Roman history. He was involved in the *Arian controversy, was one of the leaders at the Council of Nicaea, and voted for the 'Nicene formula'. He was a voluminous writer and a valuable authority on the early Church, showing diligence and sincerity. His *Ecclesiastical History*, which earned him the title of 'Father of church history', was completed c.325.

Eustace, Lizzie, heroine of A. Trollope's novel *The Eustace Diamonds*.

Eustace Diamonds, The, a novel by A. *Trollope, published 1873, the third in the *'Palliser' series.

Lizzie Eustace marries for money and, when Sir Florian Eustace dies, she not only inherits the family estates at Portray, but pockets the family diamonds as well, despite the demands of the Eustace lawyers that they be returned. She looks for support to her cousin and legal adviser Frank Greystock, but when his engagement to the demure governess Lucy Morris proves too durable, she sets her cap at the stuffy Lord Fawn. Fawn proposes, but stipulates that the necklace must be returned to the Eustace estate. Lizzie retires to Portray, and assembles a curious collection of house guests, including dashing Lord George de Bruce Carruthers, who becomes her third suitor, and the fashionable preacher Mr Emilius, who becomes her fourth. When Lizzie and her entourage set off southwards, Lizzie's bedroom is robbed at Carlisle. The thieves get away with the casket but not the jewels, which Lizzie has extracted for safe keeping. The police begin to be suspicious, and when Lizzie is robbed a second time she is unable to conceal her trickery. Lord Fawn drops her immediately, Frank Greystock stops procrastinating and marries Lucy Morris, Lord George disappears, and Lizzie has no alternative but to marry Mr Emilius—without, as it will turn out, sufficiently enquiring into his shady past.

evangelical, a term applied from the 18th cent. to that school of Protestants which maintains that the essence of 'the gospel' consists in the doctrine of salvation by faith in the atoning death of Christ, lays more stress on faith than on works or on sacramental grace, and upholds the verbal inspiration of the Bible. As a distinct party designation, the term came into general use, in England, at the time of the Methodist revival; and it may be said, with substantial accuracy, to denote the school of theology which that movement represents.

Evan Harrington, a novel by G. *Meredith, published 1861.

Evans, Sir Hugh, Welsh parson in Shakespeare's *The Merry Wives of Windsor*.

EVANS, Margiad (Peggy Eileen Whistler) (1909–59), novelist, essayist, poet, and writer of short stories. She spent most of her life in the south Herefordshire countryside whose atmosphere pervades her work. With her first novel, *Country Dance* (1932), she established and defined herself as a writer of the Welsh Border, with a strong female voice. Her next three novels, *The Wooden Doctor* (1933), *Turf or Stone* (1934), and *Creed* (1936), were more experimental, but drawn from her own life in the Ross-on-Wye district, as were her short stories, collected in *The Old and the Young* (1948). *Autobiography* (1943) interweaves close observation of nature with her own inner life, whilst in *A Ray of Darkness* (1952) she explores in poetic and mystic terms the onset of epilepsy, a symptom of the brain tumour which caused her early death.

EVANS, Mary Ann, see ELIOT, G.

Evelina, or *A Young Lady's Entrance into the World*, an *epistolary novel by F. Burney, published anonymously 1778. The novel, her first, enjoyed a great success. Sir John Belmont, disappointed of the fortune he expected to receive with his wife, abandons her and their child Evelina, who is brought up in seclusion by a guardian, Mr Villars. Evelina, who has grown up a beautiful and intelligent girl, goes to visit a friend, Mrs Mirvan, in London, where she is introduced into society and falls in love with the handsome and noble Lord Orville. But she is much mortified by her vulgar grandmother Mme Duval, her ill-bred relatives, and the pursuit of her bold and persistent lover Sir Clement Willoughby. Sir John Belmont is asked to recognize Evelina as his daughter, but he insists that his daughter has been in his care since infancy. It is now discovered that Lady Belmont's nurse had passed her own child off on Sir John. Evelina is recognized as his heir, and joyfully marries Lord Orville.

The novel enjoyed huge success, numbering among its admirers Dr *Johnson (who preferred it to the work of *Fielding), *Burke, *Gibbon, *Reynolds, *Sheridan, and many others from both fashionable and literary circles. The young author's mastery of character, speech, pathos, and satire, was, and still is, much admired. The *Critical Review* wrote, 'Readers will weep . . . will laugh, and grow wiser.'

EVELYN, John (1620–1706), born at Wotton House, Surrey, and educated at Balliol College, Oxford. After his father's death in 1640 he spent much time on the Continent, settling in England with his wife in 1652. He was a member of the *Royal Society, a Royalist in sympathy, and a man of varied cultural interests, including gardening; among his friends were Jeremy *Taylor and *Pepys. He published in 1661 *Fumifugium or The Inconvenience of the Air and Smoke or London Dissipated*; in 1662 *Sculptura*, on engraving; and in 1664 his influential work *Sylva*, a book on practical arboriculture; *Navigation and Commerce* in 1674; and a number of translations from the French on architecture, gardening, etc. He is remembered principally for his *Memoirs or Diary*, first published in 1818 and in a full and authoritative edition by E. S. de Beer in 1955 (6 vols). It covers most of his life, describing his travels abroad, his contemporaries, and his public and domestic concerns, and is an invaluable record of the period. He appears not to have composed regularly day by day, but on occasion some time after the event; he also added to and began to transcribe his own work. His diary is thus less spontaneous and personal than that of Pepys, though its more sober and religious tone is due more to his character than to its method of composition. His *Life of Mrs Godolphin* was first printed in 1847, and various other minor works have been published. (See also DIARIES.)

'Evening, Ode to', see COLLINS, W.

Evening's Love, An, or *The Mock Astrologer*, a comedy by *Dryden, produced 1668, published 1671. Combining elements of Spanish intrigue comedy and fast-moving farce with sexually explicit language, it proved a commercial though not an artistic success. The plot, borrowed from M. de *Scudéry, *Corneille, Quinault, *Molière, and others, shows the exploits of two English cavaliers, Wildblood and Bellamy, in Madrid at carnival time. In the course of the play Bellamy acts the part of the eponymous astrologer, and both men gain Spanish wives while also helping their host Don Lopez to one. Most memorable are the scenes featuring Wildblood's spirited mistress Jacinta testing her lover in the guise first of a Moor and then of a Mulatta. Despite Wildblood's spectacular failure to remain faithful to her on both occasions, Jacinta forgives him and agrees to marry him. The preface to this play is among the most stimulating of Dryden's critical essays. He defends drama as entertainment, and replies to charges of plagiarism, offering his most explicit statement on literary appropriation to this date. The preface represents his views when he was least sympathetic to *Jonson and is therefore of importance in the dispute with Jonson's champion *Shadwell which culminated in *Mac Flecknoe*.

'Eve of St Agnes, The', a narrative poem in Spenserian stanzas by *Keats, written 1819, published 1820.

The poem is set in a remote period of time, in the depths of winter. Madeline has been told the legend that on St Agnes's Eve maidens may have visions of their lovers. Madeline's love, Porphyro, comes from a family hostile to her own, and she is herself surrounded by 'hyena foemen, and hot-blooded lords'. Yet he contrives to steal into the house during a ball on St Agnes's Eve, and with the aid of old Angela is secreted in Madeline's room, where he watches his love prepare for sleep. When she wakes from dreams of him, aroused by his soft singing, she finds him by her bedside. Silently they escape from the house, and fly 'away into the storm'. With its rich and vivid imagery, its heightened atmosphere of excitement and passion, the poem is generally regarded as among Keats's most successful works.

Everdene, Bathsheba, a character in Hardy's *Far from the Madding Crowd*.

Ever Green, The, see RAMSAY, A.

Evergreen Review (1957–73; briefly revived 1983–4, last issue No. 98, 1984), an avant-garde American literary periodical, edited by Barney Rosset (1922–), famed for its radical politics and uncensored writings on sex; contributors included *Beckett, W. *Burroughs, *Cummings, *Nabokov, *Kerouac, *Ginsberg, and Che Guevara.

'Everlasting Gospel, The', see BLAKE.

Everyman, the title of a popular morality play of c.1509–19, in 921 lines, almost certainly derived from its Dutch close counterpart *Elckerlijc* (see below). Everyman is summoned by death and, in the last hour of his life, he discovers that his friends Fellowship, Kindred, Cousin, and Goods will not go with him. He is dependent on the support of Good Deeds whom he has previously neglected. It is the most admired of the English *morality plays and it has had a revival of popularity in the 20th cent. The lines of Knowledge have become legendary:

> Everyman, I will go with thee and be thy guide.
> In thy most need to go by thy side.

See A. C. Cawley (ed.), *Everyman and Medieval Miracle Plays* (1956); E. R. Tigg, 'The Dutch *Elckerlijc* Is Prior to the English *Everyman*' (1981).

Everyman, a literary weekly of 'Books, Drama, Music, Travel', which ran from 1929 to 1935, becoming more political than literary in its later years; the first series (1929–32) was edited by C. B. Purdom (1883–1965). Contributors included D. H. *Lawrence, G. B. *Shaw, W. *Lewis, G. D. H. *Cole, and G. *Greene.

Every Man in His Humour, a comedy by *Jonson, performed by the Lord Chamberlain's Men 1598, with Shakespeare in the cast, printed 1601. In his folio of 1616 Jonson published an extensively revised version, with the setting changed from Florence to London and the characters given English names.

In the latter version Kitely, a merchant, is the husband of a young wife, and his 'humour' is irrational jealousy. His house is resorted to by his brother-in-law Wellbred with a crowd of riotous but harmless gallants, and these he suspects of designs both on his wife and on his sister Bridget. One of these young men is Edward Knowell, whose father's 'humour' is excessive concern for his son's morals. Bobadill, one of Jonson's greatest creations, a 'Paul's man', is a boastful cowardly soldier, who associates with the young men and is admired by Matthew, a 'town gull' and poetaster, and Edward's cousin Stephen, a 'country gull'. Out of these elements, by the aid of the devices and disguises of the mischievous Brainworm, Knowell's servant, an imbroglio is produced in which Kitely and his wife are brought face to face at the house of a water-bearer to which each thinks the other has gone for an amorous assignation; Bobadill is exposed and beaten; Edward Knowell is married to Bridget; and Matthew and Stephen are held up to ridicule. The misunderstandings are cleared up by the shrewd and kindly Justice Clement.

To the folio version Jonson added a prologue giving an exposition of his dramatic theory.

Every Man out of His Humour, a comedy by *Jonson, acted by the Lord Chamberlain's Men at the newly built Globe Theatre 1599, printed 1600.

The play parades a variety of characters dominated by particular 'humours', or obsessive quirks of disposition: Macilente, a venomous malcontent; Carlo Buffone, a cynical jester; the uxorious Deliro and his domineering wife Fallace; Fastidious Brisk, an affected courtier devoted to fashion; Sordido, a miserly farmer, and his son Fungoso, who longs to be a courtier; Sogliardo, 'an essential clown, enamoured of the name of a gentleman'; and Puntarvolo, a fantastic, vainglorious knight, who wagers that he, his dog, and his cat can travel to Constantinople and back. By means of various episodes, such as Macilente's poisoning of Puntarvolo's dog and Brisk's imprisonment for debt, each character is eventually driven 'out of his humour'. Two judicious onlookers, Mitis and Cordatus, oversee the action throughout, and provide a moral commentary. Their opening debate with their friend Asper, who represents Jonson, contains an exposition of Jonson's theory of humours.

Everyman's Library, a series of reprints of the world's masterpieces in literature founded in 1906 by publisher Joseph Malaby Dent (1849–1926) and first edited by Ernest Rhys (1859–1946); the series also includes some original works of reference.

Evidences of Christianity, see PALEY, W.

EWART, Gavin Buchanan (1916–95), poet. He contributed to G. Grigson's *New Verse* when he was 17; his first volume, *Poems and Songs*, appeared in 1939. After the war he worked for many years as an advertising copywriter before becoming, in 1971, a full-time freelance writer. His second volume, *Londoners*, followed his first after a long interval, in 1964, and after that he published several volumes of poetry, mainly of light, comic, satiric, and erotic verse which shows the influence of *Auden: these include *Pleasures of the Flesh* (1966), *Or Where a Young Penguin Lies Screaming* (1977), *All My Little Ones* (1978), *More Little Ones* (1982). *The Collected Ewart 1933–1980* (1980) was followed by *The New Ewart: Poems 1980–1982* (1982), *Capital Letters* (1983), *Late Pickings* (1987), *Selected Poems 1933–1988* (1988), *Penultimate Poems* (1989), and *Collected Poems 1980–1990* (1991). He also edited the *Penguin Book of Light Verse* (1980) and *Other People's Clerihews* (1983), and was himself a master of the *limerick, the *clerihew, and the occasional verse.

EWING, Mrs (Juliana Horatia) (1841–85), writer of children's stories, whose inventive and unsentimental tales brought her much success and admiration. Her first volume was *Melchior's Dream* (1862), and after

that most of her work first appeared in *Aunt Judy's Magazine*, edited by her mother Mrs Gatty. Of her many publications the most enduring were probably *The Land of the Lost Toys* (1869); *Jackanapes* (1879), a touching soldier-story illustrated by Randolph Caldecott; *A Flat Iron for a Farthing* (1872); and *Lob-Lie-by-the-Fire* (1873). (See CHILDREN'S LITERATURE.)

Examination of Sir William Hamilton's Philosophy, a treatise by J. S. *Mill, in which he attacks *Hamilton's epistemology and his logic, published 1865, amplified in subsequent editions.

The most important part of the work is the doctrine developed by Mill in regard to the external world (expressed in the famous phrase 'permanent possibility of sensation') and the mind or self. 'If we speak of the Mind as a series of feelings, we are obliged to complete the statement by calling it a series of feelings which is aware of itself as past and future; and we are reduced to the alternative of believing that the Mind, or Ego, is something different from any series of feelings, or possibilities of them, or of accepting the paradox, that something which *ex hypothesi* is but a series of feelings, can be aware of itself as a series.' 'I ascribe a reality to the Ego—to my own Mind—different from that real existence as a Permanent Possibility, which is the only reality I acknowledge in Matter.'

Examiner, (1) a Tory periodical started by *Bolingbroke in Aug. 1710; *Swift briefly took charge in October (Nos 14–46), and was succeeded by Mrs *Manley in 1711. It engaged in controversy with Steele's *Guardian and *Addison's *Whig Examiner*. It lasted with interruptions until 1716. (2) (1808–81), a radical weekly periodical, established by John and Leigh *Hunt. It remained independent and individual until its end, but its first 20 years were of particular interest because of Leigh Hunt's support, as editor, for the work of his friends, in particular of *Shelley, *Keats, *Lamb, and *Hazlitt, whose writing was often bitterly attacked, in particular by the *Quarterly and *Blackwood's (see also COCKNEY SCHOOL). The political section of the journal ardently supported reform, and frequently derided the prince of Wales. Both the Hunts were fined £500 and sentenced to two years' imprisonment for a libel on the prince.

Excalibur, a corrupt form of 'Caliburn' (the name used in *Geoffrey of Monmouth), was King Arthur's sword, which he drew out of a stone when no one else could move it or which was given to him by the Lady of the Lake (*Malory, Bk I). Malory says that the name means 'cut-steel', but the Welsh form in the *Mabinogion is related to the Irish *Caladbolg* (battlesword), a famous legendary sword. According to Malory, when Arthur was mortally wounded in the last battle, he ordered Sir Bedevere to throw Excalibur into the lake. A hand rose from the water, took the sword, and vanished.

Excursion, The, a poem in nine books by W. *Wordsworth, published 1814. This is the middle section of a projected three-part poem 'on man, on nature and on human life', of which this part alone was completed. The whole work was to have been entitled 'The Recluse', 'as having for its principal subject the sensations and opinions of a poet living in retirement'. It was planned in 1798, when Wordsworth was living near *Coleridge at Alfoxden. *The Prelude was originally intended to be the introduction to the first part of 'The Recluse'.

The story is very slight. The poet, travelling with the Wanderer, a philosophic pedlar, meets with the pedlar's friend, the sad and pessimistic Solitary. The source of the Solitary's despondency is found in his want of religious faith and of confidence in the virtue of man, and he is reproved with gentle and persuasive argument. The Pastor is then introduced, who illustrates the harmonizing effects of virtue and religion through narratives of people interred in his churchyard. They visit the Pastor's house, and the Wanderer draws his general and philosophic conclusions from the discussions that have passed. The last two books deal in particular with the industrial expansion of the early part of the century, and the degradation that followed in its train. The poem ends with the Pastor's prayer that man may be given grace to conquer guilt and sin, and with praise for the beauty of the world about them. Bk I contains 'The Story of Margaret' or *'The Ruined Cottage', originally written as a separate poem.

Exequy, An, see KING, H.

Exeter Book, the one of the most important manuscripts containing Old English poetry, copied about 940, given by Bishop Leofric (d. 1072) to Exeter Cathedral, where it still remains. It contains many of the most admired shorter poems, such as *The Wanderer, *The Seafarer, *Deor, *Widsith, *'The Ruin', *'Wulf and Eadwacer', *The Wife's Lament, *The Husband's Message, and Resignation, more or less all of which are grouped together as 'The Exeter Book Elegies', as well as a famous collection of Riddles (ed. C. Williamson, 1977; see also an excellent translation by K. *Crossley-Holland, 1978) and some longer poems of a religious nature, notably *Guthlac, Christ, *The Phoenix, and *Cynewulf's Juliana. Also of interest are the Physiologus and Maxims.

Anglo-Saxon Poetic Records, vol. iii (in ASPR, 6 vols, ed. G. V. Krapp and E. V. K. Dobbie, 1931–53); ed. I. Gollancz and W. S. Mackie, EETS 104 and 194 (1895, 1934).

existentialism, the name commonly given to a group of somewhat loosely associated philosophical doctrines and ideas which found expression in the work of such men as *Sartre, *Heidegger, *Marcel, *Camus, and Karl Jaspers (1883–1969). Though the theories advanced by different existentialist writers diverge widely in many important respects, so that it would be misleading to speak of a philosophical 'school' or 'movement', certain underlying themes can be singled out as characteristic. Existentialists tend, for example, to emphasize the unique and particular in human experience; they place the individual person at the centre of their pictures of the world, and are suspicious of philosophical or psychological doctrines that obscure this essential individuality by speaking as if there were some abstract 'human nature', some set of general laws or principles, to which human beings are determined or required, by their common humanity, to conform. Each person is what he or she chooses to be or become, and cannot escape responsibility for character or deeds by claiming that they are the predetermined consequence of factors beyond one's power to control or resist: nor can we justify what we do in terms of external or 'objective' standards imposed upon us from without.

Exodus, a 590-line poem in Old English, based on the biblical story, contained in the *Junius manuscript and probably dating from the early 8th cent. It used to be attributed to *Cædmon, and it contains a vigorous description of the destruction of the Egyptians in the Red Sea. The narrative departs considerably from the letter of the biblical narrative, and discussion of the poem has centred mostly on possible explanations for its allusive structure and the fact that it draws material from various parts of the Bible. It has been edited by E. B. Irving (1953).

Experience, Songs of, see SONGS OF INNOCENCE.

Expressionism, a term coined in the early 20th cent. to describe a movement in art, then in literature, the theatre, and the cinema, characterized by boldness, distortion, and forceful representation of the emotions. One of its earliest manifestations was in the group of German painters, Die Brücke ('the Bridge'), formed in Dresden in 1905 and influenced by Van Gogh and Munch: a later group was Der blaue Reiter ('the Blue Rider', from the title of a painting by Kandinsky), formed in 1911, which was more concerned with the evocative qualities of colour and pattern, unrelated to content. In the theatre the term has been associated with the works of *Toller, *Strindberg, Wedekind, and early *Brecht, and embraces a wide variety of moods—satirical, grotesque, visionary, exclamatory, violent, but always anti-naturalistic. The epitome of Expressionism in German cinema was Robert Wiene's The Cabinet of Dr Caligari (1919). Expressionism flourished principally in Germany, and took little root in Britain, though W. *Lewis and *Vorticism have some affinities with it, and traces of its influence can be found in the verse dramas of *Auden and *Isherwood, and later in the cinema (e.g. G. *Greene's The Third Man, directed by Carol Reed, 1949).

Eyeless in Gaza, a novel by A. *Huxley, published 1936. The title is a quotation from the first speech in Milton's *Samson Agonistes.

It traces the career of Anthony Beavis from the death of his mother in his early boyhood in 1902, through various emotional entanglements and intellectual quests, to his involvement with a pacifist movement in 1935; it uses a complicated but clearly demarcated system of sections in non-chronological flashback. At preparatory school Beavis is acquainted with three characters whose lives deeply affect his own: his closest friend, the sensitive intellectual Brian Foxe (modelled on Huxley's brother Trevenen) who later, like Trevenen, commits suicide; Hugh Ledwidge, pompous victim, with whose wife Helen he has an affair; and Mark Staithes, who becomes a Marxist and leads Beavis to a revolution in Mexico where he loses a leg and Beavis finds a faith. The main theatre of the novel is a sophisticated, iconoclastic, intellectual, middle-class English world. The real and the ideal, the physical and the intellectual, attraction and nausea are sharply contrasted throughout, and Beavis's search for a mystical wholeness is brought to what some have seen as a satisfactory conclusion, others a vague and wordy evasion. Much of the novel, written over a period of four years, is clearly autobiographical: the loss of his mother, the death of his brother, the father's remarriage, his involvement with the Peace Pledge Union, all fiind their fictional counterparts.

EYRE, Simon (d. 1459), according to *Stow, a draper who became mayor of London, was a generous benefactor of the city, and built Leadenhall as a public granary and market. He figures in Dekker's *The Shoemakers' Holiday.*

EZEKIEL, Nissim (1924–2004), one of India's best-known poets, born in to an Indian Jewish family, and educated in Bombay and at Birkbeck College, London. Editor, art critic, lecturer, seminarist, playwright, advocate of the controlled use of LSD, Ezekiel helped to create a significant literary climate for a whole generation of Indian poets writing in English. The discipline, precision, and critical range of his own writing set standards of excellence and remain an enduring influence. His eight volumes of poetry include *A Time to Change* (1952), *The Unfinished Man* (1960), and *The Exact Name* (1965).

F

Faber Book of Modern Verse, The, an anthology published in 1936, edited by M. *Roberts, which did much to influence taste and establish the reputations of a rising generation of poets, including *Auden, *MacNeice, *Empson, *Graves, Dylan *Thomas. In his introduction, Roberts traces the influences of *Clough, G. M. *Hopkins (himself well represented), the French *symbolists, etc. on modern poetry, defines the 'European' sensibility of such writers as T. S. *Eliot, *Pound, and *Yeats, and offers a persuasive apologia for various aspects of *Modernism which the reading public had resisted, identifying them as an apparent obscurity compounded of condensed metaphor, allusion, intricacy and difficulty of ideas, and verbal play. The poet, he declared, 'must charge each word to its maximum poetic value': 'primarily poetry is an exploration of the possibilities of language.'

FABIAN, Robert, see FABYAN.

Fabian Society, the, a society founded in 1884 consisting of socialists who advocate a 'Fabian' policy, as opposed to immediate revolutionary action, and named after Quintus Fabius Maximus, nicknamed *Cunctator* or 'the Delayer' (see below). One of its instigators was Thomas Davidson (1840–1900), the illegitimate son of a Scottish shepherd, a charismatic figure with many disciples who was also responsible for founding in 1883 the Fellowship of the New Life, a body which at first attracted some of the same membership, although its aims were mystical and philosophical rather than political. The Fabians aimed to influence government and affect policy by permeation rather than by direct power, and to provide the research and analysis to support their own views and introduce them to others. One of their methods was the publishing of tracts, or *pamphleteering: the first two Fabian tracts were *Why Are the Many Poor?* (1884) by W. L. Phillips, a house painter and one of the few working-class members, and *A Manifesto* (1884) by G. B. *Shaw. Shaw wrote many other important tracts, as did S. *Webb: *Fabian Essays in Socialism* (1889), edited by Shaw, and with contributions by Webb, Sydney Olivier, and A. *Besant sold well and attracted much attention. The Society itself continued to attract a distinguished membership of politicians, intellectuals, artists, and writers, ranging from Keir Hardie, Ramsay Macdonald, and G. D. H. *Cole to E. *Carpenter, E. *Nesbit, R. *Brooke, and W. *Crane. See Margaret Cole, *The Story of Fabian Socialism* (1961) and N. and J. Mackenzie, *The First Fabians* (1977).

FABIUS (Quintus Fabius Maximus) (d. 203 BC), nicknamed *Cunctator* (the man who delays taking action), was appointed dictator after Hannibal's crushing victory at Trasimene (217 BC). He carried on a defensive campaign, avoiding direct engagements and harassing the enemy. Hence the expression 'Fabian tactics' and the name of the *Fabian Society (1884), dedicated to the gradual introduction of socialism.

fable, a term most commonly used in the sense of a short story devised to convey some useful moral lesson, but often carrying with it associations of the marvellous or the mythical, and frequently employing animals as characters. *Aesop's fables and the *'Reynard the Fox' series were well known and imitated in Britain by *Chaucer, *Henryson, and others, and *La Fontaine, the greatest of modern fable writers, was imitated by *Gay. *Mandeville's *The Fable of the Bees*, Swift's *Gulliver's Travels*, and Orwell's *Animal Farm* may be described as satirical fables. The form enjoyed something of a vogue in the 1920s and 1930s, in works by T. F. *Powys, D. *Garnett, John *Collier, and others, and has always been popular in children's literature.

Fable of the Bees, The, see MANDEVILLE, B. DE.

Fables, Ancient and Modern, by *Dryden, published 1700.
   Verse paraphrases of tales by *Ovid, *Boccaccio, and *Chaucer are interspersed with poems of Dryden's own, and together with the preface, in itself one of the most important examples of Dryden's criticism, they compose themselves into an Ovidian and Catholic meditation on the place of nature, sex, and violence in the flux of history.

fabliau, a short tale in verse, almost invariably in octosyllabic couplets in French, dealing for the most part from a comic point of view with incidents of ordinary life. The fabliau was an important element in French poetry in the 12th–13th cents. In English, it has come to be applied loosely to tales with a sexual element, such as Chaucer's tales of the Miller, the Summoner, and the Pardoner in the *Canterbury Tales*. See J. Hines, *The Fabliau in English* (1993), and P. Nykrog, *Les Fabliaux* (1973).

FABYAN, Robert (d. 1513), chronicler, sheriff of London in 1493. He reworked various sources into *The Concordance of Chronicles*, a compilation extending from the arrival of Brutus in England (see BRUT) to the death of Richard III (first printed 1516; ed. Ellis, 1811). His chronicles are of importance with respect to the history of London, and were several times brought up to date.

Face, one of the rogues in Jonson's *The Alchemist.*

faction, a term coined *c.*1970 to describe fiction based on and mingled with fact, at first applied particularly to American works of fiction such as *In Cold Blood* (1966) by *Capote and *The Armies of the Night* (1968) by *Mailer. The genre has continued to flourish, as the *historical novel has gained a new lease of seriousness: works such as *Keneally's *Schindler's Ark*, based on documentary evidence, interviews, and research, may be classified as fiction or non-fiction. This particular example was classified as fiction in Australia and the UK, but published as non-fiction under the title *Schindler's List* in the USA.

Faerie Queene, The, the greatest work of *Spenser, of which the first three books were published 1590, and the second three 1596.

The general scheme of the work is proposed in the author's introductory letter addressed to *Ralegh. By the Faerie Queene the poet signifies Glory in the abstract and *Elizabeth I in particular (who also figures under the names of *Britomart, *Belphoebe, *Mercilla, and *Gloriana). Twelve of her knights, the 'patrons' or examples of 12 different virtues, each undertake an adventure, on the 12 successive days of the queen's annual festival, and an account of their origins was to have been given in the last of 12 books. Prince Arthur symbolizes 'magnificence', in the Aristotelian sense (says the author) of the perfection of all the other virtues (he must have meant not 'magnificence' but 'magnanimity', or 'gentlemanliness'). Arthur has a vision of the Faerie Queene and, determining to seek her out, is brought into the adventures of the several knights and carries them to a successful issue. This explanation, given in the introduction, does not appear from the poem itself, for the author starts at once with the adventures of the knights; as we have it the poem does not conform to his scheme. Of the six books Spenser published, the subjects are:

I, the adventures of the *Redcrosse Knight of Holiness (the Anglican Church), the protector of the Virgin *Una (truth, or the true religion), and the wiles of *Archimago and *Duessa;

II, the adventures of Sir *Guyon, the Knight of Temperance, his encounters with *Pyrochles and *Cymochles, his visit to the Cave of *Mammon and the House of Temperance, and his destruction of *Acrasia and her *Bower of Bliss. Canto x of this Book contains a chronicle of British rulers from *Brut to Elizabeth;

III, the legend of Chastity, exemplified by Britomart and Belphoebe;

IV, the legend of *Triamond and *Cambell, exemplifying Friendship; together with the story of *Scudamour and *Amoret;

V, the adventures of *Artegall, the Knight of Justice, in which allegorical reference is made to various historical events of the reign of Queen Elizabeth: the defeat of the Spaniards in the Netherlands, the recantation of Henry IV of France, the execution of *Mary Queen of Scots, and the administration of Ireland by Lord Grey de Wilton;

VI, the adventures of Sir *Calidore, exemplifying Courtesy.

There is also a fragment on *Mutabilitie, being the sixth and seventh cantos of the legend of Constancie, which was to have formed the seventh Book. This fragment contains a charming description of the seasons and the months.

The work as a whole, modelled to some extent on the *Orlando furioso* of Ariosto, suffers from a certain monotony, and its chief beauties lie in the particular episodes with which the allegory is varied and in descriptions, such as those of the Cave of Mammon and the temptation of Sir Guyon by the Lady of the Idle Lake, in Bk II. The meaning of many of the allusions, which must have added to the interest of the work for contemporaries, is now lost. The poem is written in the stanza invented by Spenser (and since utilized by James *Thomson, *Keats, *Shelley, and *Byron), in which a ninth line of twelve syllables is added to eight lines of ten syllables, rhyming a b a b b c b c c.

Fagin, a character in Dickens's *Oliver Twist.*

Fainall and Mrs Fainall, characters in Congreve's *The Way of the World.*

FAINLIGHT, Ruth (1931–   ), poet and translator, born in New York, but for many years resident in England. In her first collection, *Cages* (1966), her distinctively cool, ironic, yet not dispassionate voice spoke clearly: it shows some affinity with the tone of R. *Graves, whom she and her husband A. *Sillitoe knew in their early years together in Majorca. This volume was followed by several others, including *To See the Matter Clearly* (1968), *The Region's Violence* (1973), *Another Full Moon* (1976), *Sibyls and Others* (1980), *Fifteen to Infinity* (1983), *The Time of Fear* (1994), *Sugar-Paper Blue* (1997), and *Burning Wire* (2002). Her topics are domestic and global; she combines the personal and the austerely detached, and excels at the uncanny casual moment of recognition. She has also published short stories and translations from the Portuguese.

FAIRFAX, Edward (?1568–1635), Yorkshire scholar and gentleman, remembered for his translation of Tasso's *Jerusalem Delivered* as *Godfrey of Bulloigne Done into English Heroicall Verse* (1600). A new edition by K. M. Lea and T. M. Gang was published in 1981.

Fair Maid of Perth, *Saint Valentine's Day*, or The, a novel by Sir W. *Scott, published 1828, as the second of the *Chronicles of the Canongate. The novel, set at the end of the 14th cent. in Perth, where the Highlands touch the Lowlands, is chiefly remembered for its study of constitutional cowardice. It tells of the attempt to end the discord caused by the enmity of clans Chattan and Quhele by mortal combat of 30 picked champions on each side before the king. The default of one of the Clan Chattan men leaves a vacancy which is filled by the hero of the story, Henry Smith, who seeks an opportunity to face Conachar, chief of Clan Quhele, his rival for the love of the Fair Maid, Catharine Glover. Conachar, formerly apprentice to Catharine's father, combines a hot temper with cowardice. In the battle, he is protected by his foster-father, Torquil of the Oak, who, with his eight sons, stands between Conachar and danger until all are dead; left to face Henry Smith, he runs from the battlefield. The battle, and the sub-plot of the assassination of the king's heir, the duke of Rothesay, make this one of the most bloody and violent of Scott's novels.

Fair Maid of the West, The, or *A Girl Worth Gold*, a comedy of adventure by *Heywood, in two parts, Pt I *c.*1600, Pt II *c.*1630, both printed 1631.

The first part opens with a vivid scene at Plymouth, where *Essex's expedition is on the point of sailing for the Azores (1597), and gallant Master Spencer has the misfortune to kill a man while protecting Bess Bridges, 'the flower of Plymouth', from insult. He has to fly the country, but first makes provision for Bess by handing over to her the Windmill Tavern at Fowey, which she subsequently conducts with equal spirit and decorum. Meanwhile Spencer, who has sailed to the Azores, is wounded to the point of death in trying to stop a quarrel. He sends a message to Bess, bidding her adieu and making over all his property to her. Bess employs part of this to fit out a privateer, in which she sets sail to bring home his body. Instead she rescues Spencer himself, who has recovered and been captured by Spaniards. After many adventures, leading as far as Morocco, Bess is finally united to her lover. The first part makes a breezy and entertaining melodrama, but Pt II, a less effective sequel, contains more extreme coincidences and intrigues, including a 'bed-trick' and supposed deaths.

Fair Penitent, The, a tragedy in blank verse by N. *Rowe, produced 1703.

The plot of the play is that of Massinger and Field's *The Fatal Dowry*, shortened and somewhat modified at the end. Charalois becomes Altamont; Beaumelle, Calista; Rochford, Sciolto; Romont, Horatio; and Novall, Lothario. The play was extremely successful and was constantly revived until the early 19th cent. The 'haughty, gallant, gay Lothario' has become pro-verbial, and was a model on which Richardson drew Lovelace in *Clarissa*. In revivals of the play *Garrick acted Lothario, and subsequently Mrs *Siddons, Calista. Dr *Johnson said of it that 'there is scarcely any work of any poet at once so interesting by the fable, and so delightful by the language.' He observes, however, with reference to the title of the play, that Calista 'may be reasonably suspected of feeling pain from detection rather than from guilt'.

Fair Quarrel, A, a comedy by J. *Middleton and W. *Rowley, published 1617.

Captain Ager receives from a fellow officer an insult which reflects on his mother's virtue. A duel is arranged, but Ager is too conscientious to fight unless he is satisfied that his cause is a just one. He tells his mother of the accusation, which she at first indignantly denies, but presently, in order to prevent the duel, admits to be true. Ager then declines to fight, and is branded by his adversary as a coward. Having now what he considers an adequate reason, he fights and defeats his enemy. They are reconciled and all ends well.

fairy stories have existed in the oral tradition of all cultures, but entered the mainstream as a distinct literary genre at the time of the publication of the stories of *Perrault, written for a fashionable and sophisticated adult salon audience. Many earlier lit-erary works (including those of *Chaucer, *Boccaccio, *Malory, *Straparola, and the Neapolitan Giambattista Basile, author of *Il pentamerone*, published posthu-mously 1634–6), had featured fairies and tales of the supernatural, but it was in the last two decades of the 17th cent. that a new vogue for the written fairy tale was established. Perrault's cousin Marie-Jeanne l'Héri-tier de Villandon (1664–1734; *Œuvres meslés*, 1695) and her friend Henriette-Julie de Castelnau, comtesse de Murat (1670–1716), both published stories. Marie-Catherine, Baronne D'Aulnoy (d. 1705), produced well-known tales such as 'La Chatte blanche' (The White Cat), 'Le Serpentin vert' (The Green Worm), and 'L'Oiseau bleu' (The Blue Bird), and many more, featuring disguise, shape-changing, cross-dressing, and beast-husbands (*Les Contes des fées*, 1696): these were almost immediately translated into English (some appearing in 1699; 3 vols, 1721–2) and remained popular well into the 19th cent.

The translation of story collections from other cultures reinforced the popularity of the fairy story: the *Fables of *Bidpai* had reached England from the Arabic in *North's version of 1570, and were repub-lished in French in 1697. The *Arabian Nights* in French (1704) and English (c.1708) had an immense influence on the *Oriental tale and the development of the novel. During the 18th cent. fairy stories flourished, both in versions from the French, and in homegrown popular forms, despite protests from some education-alists that they were unwholesome and immoral. During the 19th cent. historians of folklore, notably the brothers *Grimm, made the fairy story a respect-able subject for academic research, and from 1823 many new tales were introduced to the British canon: at the same period T. C. *Croker was making an important collection of Irish folk tales, and H. C. *Andersen's stories were appearing in Danish. The northern and Nordic theme continued with the re-telling of Norse myths by Annie and Eliza Keary (*The Heroes of Asgard*, 1857) and Sir George *Dasent

(*Popular Tales from the Norse*, 1859). Andrew *Lang, towards the end of the century, made important collections from many sources, and produced from 1889 his own very popular Fairy Books. Sir John Rhŷs collected stories in *Celtic Folklore, Welsh and Manx* (1901, repr. 1980). A. *Rackham's illustrations of Grimm, *Barrie, and others made memorable contributions to the genre in its heyday before the First World War: Barrie's *Peter Pan* proved one of the most enduring of original stories with fairy characters.

The 20th cent. witnessed the rise of psychoanalytic and anthropological studies of legend, myth, and fairy story, by *Freud, *Jung, *Frazer, and others, and produced Bruno Bettelheim's classic work *The Uses of Enchantment: The Power and Importance of Fairy Tales* (1978), which argues that stories offer children a valuable tool for psychological growth and adjustment. Other surveys of the genre include *The Ocean of Story* (1928) by Norman Penzer; Russian structuralist and narratologist Vladimir Propp's *Morphology of the Folk Tale* (1928; trans. 1968); Maureen *Duffy, *The Erotic World of Faery* (1972); Jack Zipes, *Breaking the Magic Spell: Radical Theories of Folk and Fairy Tales* (1979). Marina *Warner's *From the Beast to the Blonde* (1994) emphasizes the subversive elements in fairy tales, and discusses the tradition of female transmission of them: she brings her study up to date with consideration of the contribution to the genre of the Walt Disney film and its images of female heroism. American poet Robert Bly offered a reading of a Grimm story in his *Iron John* (1990), which stresses the importance of the masculine principle and male ritual.

The late 20th cent. saw a revival of interest in the adult fairy tale, as authors freed themselves from the constraints of realism to explore the world through myth and fantasy: A. S. *Byatt, Angela *Carter, Italo *Calvino, Michèle *Roberts, and Salman *Rushdie have all used the genre to remarkable effect, but a familiarity with fairy story also discreetly underlies many more conventional narratives. Fairy stories for children continue to be published through the whole range of the market, from popular mass market versions of old favourites to sophisticated and handsomely illustrated adaptations by well-known authors: Victorian fairy painting also enjoyed a late 20th-cent.vogue, as witnessed by an exhibition at the Victoria and Albert Museum, 1997, which included works by *Burne-Jones, *Dadd, Richard *Doyle and his brother Charles, Joseph Noël Paton (1821–1901), A. Rackham, and Edmund Dulac (1882–1953).

Faithful, in Bunyan's *Pilgrim's Progress*, the companion of *Christian; he is put to death at *Vanity Fair.

Faithful Shepherdess, The, a pastoral tragi-comedy by J. *Fletcher, printed not later than 1610.

The action takes place at night in the woods of Thessaly, and revolves around the central figure of the faithful shepherdess herself, Clorin, who has dedicated herself to a life of chastity in memory of her dead love.

Thenot is in love with her, or rather with the image of her fidelity, for when she pretends to accept him, he spurns her. Other characters in the amorous round include Amarillis, who loves Thenot, who in turn loves Amoret; the wanton Cloe and the coy Daphnis; and the Sullen Shepherd, who intervenes by transforming Amarillis into the form of Amoret. With the aid of various magic herbs, a satyr, and the god of the river, all is happily resolved.

FALCONER, William (1732–69), son of a barber and himself a seaman, author of *The Shipwreck* (1762, rev. 1764, 1769), a poem in three cantos recounting the wreck of a ship on the coast of Greece, which had considerable vogue in its day. Falconer was drowned at sea.

Falkland, one of the principal characters in Godwin's *Caleb Williams.

FALKLAND, Lucius Cary, second Viscount (1610–43), a famous Royalist, 'a man learned and accomplished, the centre of a circle [at the village of Great Tew, near Oxford] which embraced the most liberal thinkers of his day, a keen reasoner and an able speaker, whose convictions still went with the Parliament, while his wavering and impulsive temper, his love of the Church, his passionate longings for peace, led him to struggle for a king whom he distrusted, and to die for a cause that was not his own' (J. R. *Green). He fell at Newbury. The circle at Great Tew included *Jonson, *Suckling, *Sandys, *Earles, *Godolphin, and *Chillingworth; also *Clarendon, who draws a memorable portrait of him. Falkland wrote verses and theological works (*Discourses of Infallibility* and a *Reply*, 1660).

FALKNER, J(ohn) Meade (1858–1932), novelist, antiquary, and topographical writer, who rose to a senior position with a firm of Newcastle armaments manufacturers, and later became honorary librarian to the dean and chapter of Durham. He is remembered for his three novels: *The Lost Stradivarius* (1895), a tale of the supernatural set largely in Oxford and Naples; *Moonfleet* (1898), a romance involving smuggling; and *The Nebuly Coat* (1903), an antiquarian romance dealing with a church threatened by collapse, in which Falkner was able to display his love and knowledge of ecclesiastical history and architecture, heraldry, etc. He also wrote poetry, a volume of which was published as *Poems* (*c*.1933); three of his poems appear in *Larkin's *The Oxford Book of Twentieth-Century English Verse* (1973).

Fall of Robespierre, The, a drama written in 1794 by *Coleridge, who wrote Act I, and R. *Southey, who wrote Acts II and III.

False One, The, a drama attributed to J. *Fletcher, in which *Massinger may also have had a share, performed *c*.1620, printed 1647.

The play deals with the joint occupation of the throne of Egypt by Ptolemy and his sister Cleopatra;

the treacherous murder of Ptolemy by Septimius, 'the False One'; and the entanglement of Caesar by the charms of Cleopatra.

Falstaff, Sir John, a character in Shakespeare's *1* and *2* *Henry IV* and *The Merry Wives of Windsor*. To Dr *Johnson 'unimitated, unimitable' a 'compound of sense and vice'; the subject of *Morgann's important early critical essay. His remote historical original seems to have been the Wycliffite Sir John *Oldcastle, but his more important literary foundations lie in the stock figure of the *Vice, together with some elements of the Plautine *miles gloriosus. He is fat, witty, a lover of sack and of jests, and skilful at turning jokes on him to his own advantage—'I am not only witty in myself, but the cause that wit is in other men' (*2 Henry IV*, I. ii. 8–9). In *1 Henry IV* he is shown as the drinking companion of Prince *Hal, and anticipates great advancement when Hal becomes king. Hal humours him, allowing him to give his own version of the *Gadshill encounter with the men 'in buckram', to mimic his father, Henry IV, and even to take credit for the death of *Hotspur at the battle of Shrewsbury. In *2 Henry IV* he is seen little with Hal, but is portrayed as old, ill, and unscrupulous in his financial dealings with Mistress *Quickly and with his old friend Master Justice *Shallow, from whom he borrows £1,000. His embodiment of anarchy is suggested in his confrontation with the Lord Chief Justice (I. ii). On succeeding to the throne Hal/Henry V rejects him in the speech beginning 'I know thee not, old man. Fall to thy prayers', which Falstaff throws off by assuring his friends that he will be sent for privately. In *Henry V*, however, Mistress Quickly tells us that 'the King has kill'd his heart' (II. i), and she later describes his death, in a tavern, in a speech which includes the famous line (as emended by *Theobald) 'his nose was as sharp as a pen, and 'a babbl'd of green fields'. The Falstaff of *The Merry Wives of Windsor* is a diminished figure, whose attempts to mend his fortunes by wooing two citizens' wives simultaneously end in his discomfiture in Windsor Forest. It is this Falstaff, however, who is the subject of at least nine operas, including *Verdi's *Falstaff* (1893), and *Vaughan Williams's *Sir John in Love* (1929). *Elgar's symphonic study *Falstaff* (1913) is based on the Henry plays. Falstaff is also the eponymous hero of a highly praised Rabelaisian novel (1976) by Robert Nye.

Fanny Hill, see MEMOIRS OF A WOMAN OF PLEASURE.

Fanny Price, a character in J. Austen's *Mansfield Park*.

FANSHAWE, Anne, Lady (1625–80), née Harrison, wife of Sir Richard *Fanshawe. She shared her husband's travels and her affectionate *Memoirs*, written between 1674 and 1676, were first printed in 1829: 'whatever was real happiness, God gave it me in him.'

FANSHAWE, Sir Richard (1608–66), poet, translator, diplomat, born in Hertfordshire and educated at Cambridge. He was a supporter of the Royalist cause, as was his wife Anne, whom he married in 1644 (see above). After the Restoration he served as ambassador in Portugal, then Spain, where he died. His first published work was a translation of *Guarini's *Il pastor fido* (*The Faithful Shepherd*, 1647): a reissue of this the following year contained some of his own poems, including a delightful ode urging the pleasures of country living, some accomplished *Spenserian stanzas, and sonnets from the Spanish, translated with much elegance. A selection from *Horace (1652) was followed by the *Lusiads* of *Camões (1655), which he prepared in retirement during the Civil War.

fantasy fiction, see overleaf.

FANTHORPE, U(rsula) A(skham) (1929–), poet, born in Kent, and educated at Oxford. She was a teacher in Cheltenham before receiving critical acclaim and a wide readership for her first volume, *Side Effects* (1978), which was followed by *Standing to* (1982), *Voices off* (1984), *Neck Verse* (1992), and other volumes. Her poetry is lucid and accessible; her tone is both wry and lyrical, and her subject matter ranges from the classical to the historical and the domestic.

farce, a form of popular comedy with its distant roots in the improvisations which actors introduced into the text of medieval religious dramas (the word is derived from the word *farce*, stuffing). Later forms include the *interludes performed in the 15th and 16th cents, and the classical farce of *Molière, whose works were freely adapted by British dramatists. The 19th-cent. middle-class French farce, as practised by Eugène Labiche (1815–88), Georges Feydeau (1862–1921), and Georges Courteline (1858–1929), has also proved popular in adaptation. In England, the full-length home-grown farce emerged in the 19th cent.: Morton's *Box and Cox* was a famous if isolated example, and *Pinero also wrote several, including *The Magistrate* (1885), *The Schoolmistress* (1886), and *Dandy Dick* (1887). *Gilbert and Sullivan's farcical comic operas belong to the same period. *Charley's Aunt* (1892) by Brandon Thomas (1856–1914), a comedy with an excellent opportunity for cross-dressing (an Oxford undergraduate impersonates his own rich Brazilian aunt), is still frequently performed. The term 'farce' is now generally used to cover a form of theatre which employs ridiculous situations, mistaken identities, split-second timing, and marital misadventures (hence the term 'bedroom farce'): later exponents include Ben Travers (1886–1980), whose celebrated 'Aldwych farces' included *A Cuckoo in the Nest* and *Rookery Nook*, both 1926; Ray Cooney (1932–), who wrote many plays for actor-manager Brian Rix at the Whitehall; A. *Ayckbourn, M. *Frayn, Joe *Orton, and T. *Stoppard. Dario *Fo is notable among those who have used the farce for serious political purposes. Television has produced a new genre of serial and surreal farce in the Monty Python series, and John Cleese's hotel comedy *Fawlty Towers*.

Farfrae, Donald, a character in Hardy's *The Mayor of Casterbridge.*

Far from the Madding Crowd, a novel by T. *Hardy, published 1874. The title is a quotation from Gray's *Elegy Written in a Country Church-Yard.*

The theme, which occurs in others of Hardy's novels, is the contrast of a patient and generous love with unscrupulous passion. The shepherd Gabriel Oak serves the young and spirited Bathsheba Everdene, owner of the farm, with unselfish devotion. She depends greatly on his support, but cannot regard him as a suitor. Another of her admirers is a neighbouring farmer, Boldwood. The dashing Sergeant Troy loves one of Bathsheba's servants, Fanny Robin, but after a fatal misunderstanding deserts her and she eventually dies in childbirth in the workhouse. Troy has meanwhile captivated and married Bathsheba, but soon begins to neglect and ill-treat her. When he hears of Fanny's death he leaves the farm, disappears, and is deemed to have been drowned. Farmer Boldwood, now obsessed with Bathsheba, gives a party at which he pledges Bathsheba to marry him some time in the future. Troy reappears at the party and Boldwood, driven to madness by his reappearance, shoots him. Boldwood is tried and pronounced insane. Gabriel and Bathsheba are at last married.

Hardy made a stage version of the novel, which was eventually produced by the Hardy Players in Dorchester in 1924.

FARJEON, Eleanor (1881–1965), born in London into a highly literary Hampstead family, became well known as a children's writer after the success of *Martin Pippin in the Apple-Orchard* (1921, not originally written for children); she followed it with many volumes of poems, fantasies, stories, etc., and *A Nursery in the Nineties* (1935), reminiscences of her childhood. She was a close friend of E. *Thomas: see her *Edward Thomas: The Last Four Years* (1958).

FARMER, Richard, see ESSAY ON THE LEARNING OF SHAKESPEARE, AN.

Farmer's Boy, The, see BLOOMFIELD, R.

FARNOL, (John) Jeffery (1878–1952), historical novelist, whose tales of adventure and the open road, many of them set in the Regency period (*The Broad Highway*, 1910; *The Amateur Gentleman*, 1913; and many others) were immensely popular; they show a debt both to *Borrow and to *Weyman.

FARQUHAR, George (?1677–1707), born in Londonderry, was a sizar at Trinity College, Dublin, and became an actor, but gave up the stage in consequence of accidentally wounding a fellow player. He took to writing comedies, and produced *Love and a Bottle* in 1698, *The Constant Couple, or A Trip to the Jubilee* in 1699, *Sir Harry Wildair* in 1701, *The Inconstant* and *The Twin Rivals* in 1702, *The Stage Coach* (with *Motteux)

in 1704, *The Recruiting Officer* in 1706, and *The Beaux' Stratagem* in 1707. The last two are the best of his plays and are still regularly performed; *The Recruiting Officer* was used by *Brecht as the basis of his *Pauken und Trompeten* (1955). They are marked by an atmosphere of reality and good humour, revealing the easygoing character of the author, though his satire is sometimes pungent. He is said to have been deceived by his wife, from love of him, about her fortune, but to have always treated her with tenderness and indulgence. He died in poverty. A present of 20 guineas from the actor Robert Wilks gave him the means of writing his last play, *The Beaux' Stratagem*, and he lived just long enough to hear of its success. (See RESTORATION.)

FARRAR, F(rederic) W(illiam) (1831–1903), philosopher and theologian, eventually dean of Canterbury, who, when a master at Harrow, published *Eric, or, Little by Little* (1858), an edifying story of school life, partly autobiographical, which achieved enormous success. As well as many works of theology, he also wrote *Julian Home: A Tale of College Life* (1859) and *St Winifred's, or The World of School* (1862). (See also CHILDREN'S LITERATURE.)

FARRELL, J(ames) G(ordon) (1935–79), novelist. Born in Liverpool, the son of an accountant, he was educated at Rossall School and Brasenose College, Oxford, where, in his first term, he contracted poliomyelitis. He later travelled widely in America, Europe, and the East. His first novel, *A Man from Elsewhere* (1963), was set in France, his second, *The Lung* (1965), describes the experiences of a polio victim, and *A Girl in the Head* (1967) the desultory adventures of Count Boris Slattery in an English seaside town called Maidenhair. His first substantial novel, *Troubles* (1970), is set in Ireland, in the decaying Majestic Hotel, just after the First World War, against a background of Sinn Fein violence. *The Siege of Krishnapur* (1973, *Booker Prize) deals with the events of the Indian Mutiny, in a characteristically ironic and comic vein. *The Singapore Grip* (1978) moves closer to the epic, blending real and fictitious characters and describing the fall of Singapore to the Japanese, an event which Farrell portrays as a death-blow to the British Empire. His last three novels involved considerable historical research, and all reflect a sense of the end of the empire and the stubborn, at times heroic, at times stupid, refusal of his characters to recognize the course of history. His most vivid creation is Major Brendan Archer, courteous, faithful, and chivalrous, holding fast to his own code of civilized conduct in increasingly violent circumstances: he appears in *Troubles* and again in *The Singapore Grip*. Similarly the sardonic kindly rationalist Dr McNab from *The Siege* reappears in *The Hill Station* (1981), which was left unfinished when Farrell was accidentally drowned, shortly after moving from London to Ireland.

During the second half of the 20th cent. fantasy fiction has become one of the most productive and commercially successful of literary genres in English. In one sense this is not surprising. Literature containing elements of the fantastic is as old as literature in English (or in any language), and includes such works as *Beowulf*, with its fire-spewing dragon and man-eating ogres, *Sir *Gawain and the Green Knight*, with its enchantresses and shape-shifting giant, or Sir Thomas *Malory's Le *Morte D'Arthur*, Edmund *Spenser's *The Faerie Queene*, or Shakespeare's *Midsummer Night's Dream* and *The Tempest*, with their respective complements of enchanted swords, elvish knights, fairies, and wizards. The literature of the fantastic at any date can draw on a seemingly inexhaustible reservoir of concepts and characters from the age-old, international, and pre-literary genre of the folk tale, or tale of wonder.

Literature of the fantastic should, however, be distinguished from fantasy fiction, a genre in some respects decisively modern. Readers and writers in a period dominated by science and by a rationalistic world-view face problems in entertaining such concepts as those listed above, now known or at least very generally thought to be impossible or non-existent. The problems were until recently increased by the low rating given to fantasy and the fantastic by practitioners of the realistic novel. In what one might call the post-Quixotic era (see CERVANTES), fantasy was marginalized into becoming a form for satire, for diversion, and above all for children.

Major writers within this marginal/non-adult mode include for instance George *MacDonald and Lewis Carroll (see DODGSON). Fantasy fiction, however, began to win a kind of autonomy as early 20th-cent. authors ceased to try to locate elements of the fantastic within the real world, and followed the late romances of William *Morris (1834–96) in creating frankly imaginary otherworlds as locations for their narratives. A major lead was given by the Irish writer Lord *Dunsany (1878–1957), whose volumes of short stories began with *The Gods of Pegana* (1905), but whose most influential novel, *The King of Elfland's Daughter*, did not appear until 1924. The location of Dunsany's fictions is characteristically unstated and impossible to determine. They could be set on earth in the far and forgotten past, in the far and unknown future, in some simply unknown country, or on the borders of Elfland or Faerie. All these locations have been used by later fantasy authors, as have settings on other planets, in parallel universes, or in the byways of our own 'here and now'. The essence of fantasy fiction, however, is liberation from the constraints of what is known, coupled with a plausible and persuasive inner coherence. The reader of fantasy accepts the rules set up by the fiction, and ignores, or relishes, the contrast with the rules of everyday reality, often glimpsed in fantasy as a horrific world of tedium and mediocrity.

Fantasy fiction continued to be developed by writers such as E. R. Eddison (1882–1945), whose most popular work has remained *The Worm Ourobouros* (1922), which, after a rather awkward induction locating events on an imagined Mercury, tells a tale of war between Demonland and Witchland; or Mervyn *Peake, whose Gormenghast trilogy is set for the most part within the politics and rituals of a single gigantic castle. Both these writers were, however, isolated figures. Fantasy fiction began to create a readership for itself with the appearance of collective schools of writers, aware of each other's work and supporting regular publication in (usually) monthly magazines in the USA.

The first of these was the group centred on *Weird Tales*, a magazine which began publication in May 1923, and including primarily H. P. Lovecraft, Robert E. Howard, and Clark Ashton Smith. Of these Lovecraft (1890–1937) pioneered the tale which exploits an imaginary mythology, while Smith (1893–1961) created a series of imaginary lands in far past or far future, including Atlantis, Hyperborea, and Zothique. It was the work of Robert E. Howard (1906–36), however, which had the most influence on the future, through his creation of the character Conan the Barbarian, and his image of violent prehistoric civilizations in which warriors find themselves continually pitted against wizards and magicians. The subgenre of 'sword-and-sorcery' has remained prolific ever since, the best of its practitioners including Fritz Leiber (1910–92), with his Fafhrd and Gray Mouser series begun in 1939; Jack Vance (1916–   ), whose *The Dying Earth* (1950) borrows its far future setting from Smith; John Brunner (1934–95), Larry Niven (1938–   ), and Michael Shea (1946–   ), authors respectively of *The Traveller in Black* (1971), *The Magic Goes Away* (1978), and *Nifft the Lean* (1982). Howard's Conan stories have meanwhile been continued posthumously by several writers, as have stories based on Lovecraft's Cthulhu mythology.

The other major early fantasy magazine was the short-lived *Unknown*, which lasted for only 39 issues between 1939 and 1943. In this brief period, though, *Unknown* took up the challenge of relating fantasy to the real world of logic and science, its authors typically working from the premiss that magic could have been developed into a controllable technology and used in parallel with, or totally replacing, conventional science, in some imagined parallel universe. 'Worlds where magic works' were created in *Unknown* by Robert Heinlein (1907–88), and in particular by the Incomplete Enchanter series of L. Sprague de Camp (1907–2000) and Fletcher Pratt (1897–1956), in which modern scientists find themselves able to move into the worlds of Norse, Finnish, or Irish mythology, or the romance settings of Spenser or Ariosto, and to establish themselves as magicians there by their (comically imperfect) understanding of magical law. The *Unknown* tradition has been continued since by such authors as Poul Anderson (1926–) and Randall Garrett (1927–87). It is notable that all these authors have also been prominent in science fiction. Fantasy fiction in the manner of *Unknown* is a highly rationalized and even argumentative mode.

The greatest influence within the fantasy genre, however, has been another maverick, J. R. R. *Tolkien. His first published fantasy, *The Hobbit* (1937), was written for children, but its three-volume successor *The Lord of the Rings* (1954–5) caught the attention for the first time of a mass adult readership and inspired generations of imitators. Tolkien used his expert scholarly knowledge of Old English and Old Norse to recreate the world of Germanic folk tale, with its dwarves, elves, trolls, barrow-wights, and wizards, as a consistent and coherent whole instead of a scattering of suggestive fragments. To this he added creatures of his own invention, such as hobbits, ents, and wraiths, a complete mythology, chronology, and cartography, and a compelling plot centred on the fear and rejection of power and the Ring.

Tolkien owed nothing to the American traditions mentioned above, and little to earlier authors such as Dunsany and Eddison. His work, however, inspired emulation, above all by its ambitious scope. Later authors have followed him in the urge to write nothing less than trilogies, and in recognizing the need to create otherworlds whose complexity far outruns the immediate needs of plot. Among the most significant of his followers are Stephen Donaldson (1947–), whose seven-volume *Chronicles of Thomas Covenant* sequence, begun in 1977, develops the ecological motif already strong in Tolkien; David Eddings (1931–), with the Belgariad, Malloreon, and Elenium sequences begun in 1982, 1987, and 1989 respectively; and Michael Scott Rohan (1951–), with his Winter of the World trilogy (1986–8).

Three other trends within fantasy fiction deserve brief mention. One is the continuing production of high-quality 'children's literature', or writing for young adults, as for instance in the four-volume Wizard of Earthsea sequence (1968–90) by Ursula *Le Guin. A second is the revival, often by feminist authors such as Angela *Carter, of the ancestral form of the *fairy tale. The third is the continuing ability of fantasy writers to write comically, now best exemplified by the Discworld books of Terry Pratchett (1948–). The first volume in this sequence, *The Colour of Magic* (1983), relied on overt parody of Leiber, Lovecraft, and others, with Howard and Tolkien not far away, but the series has gone on to create a world of its own.

Reasons for the popular appeal of fantasy fiction no doubt include discontent with the mundanity of everyday life in consumer societies, openly voiced in Le Guin's *The Beginning Place* (1980), and the associated yearning for more natural and colourful environments, as for instance in the Mythago Wood sequence of Robert Holdstock (1948–). Fantasy has, however, also shown itself ready to deal with questions of the utmost contemporary importance, in particular, with the nature and origins of evil. T. H. *White declared that the theme of his Arthurian fantasy *The Once and Future King*, written for the most part between 1938 and 1941, was to find 'an antidote to war', and the theme is powerful in the work of several of the authors mentioned above. Fantasy fiction has shown itself capable of dealing with topics which seem outside the range of the traditional realist novel, and speaks for and to a contemporary mass audience whose taste it has itself created.

See: Brian Attebery, *Strategies of Fantasy* (1992); Tom Shippey, *The Road to Middle-Earth* (2nd edn 1992); Tom Shippey (ed.), *The Oxford Book of Fantasy Stories* (1994); John Clute and John Grant (eds.), *The Encyclopedia of Fantasy* (1997).

FARRELL, J(ames) T(homas) (1904–79), American naturalist novelist, Chicago-born, and best known in Britain for his trilogy about Studs Lonigan, a young Chicago Catholic of Irish descent. *Young Lonigan* (1932) describes his boyhood, *The Young Manhood of Studs Lonigan* (1934) his desultory career as house painter, small time crook, etc., and *Judgement Day* (1935) his unemployment during the Depression and early death from a heart condition aggravated by poverty and poor living.

Fashion, Sir Novelty and Young, characters in Vanbrugh's *The Relapse*, who reappear in Sheridan's adaptation *A Trip to Scarborough*.

fashionable novel, or 'silver-fork school', a class of novel, popular c.1825–50, which held up for admiration the lives of the wealthy and fashionable. *Hook was one of the leaders of this highly successful school of writing. *Hazlitt, in his essay on 'The Dandy School' (*Examiner*, 1827), castigates the narrow superficiality of such novels which encourage the reader, he feels, only to 'the admiration of the folly, caprice, insolence, and affectation of a certain class'. *Bulwer-Lytton (whose own *Pelham* was a celebrated example) held that the genre was influential in the paradoxical sense that its effect was ultimately to expose 'the falsehood, the hypocrisy, the arrogant and vulgar insolence of patrician life'. M. W. Rosa, in *The Silver-Fork School* (1936), discusses the work of S. *Ferrier, T. H. *Lister, *Disraeli, P. *Ward, Mrs *Gore, and others, and argues that the school 'culminated in a single great book—*Vanity Fair*'. (See also NOVEL, RISE OF THE.)

FASTOLF, Sir John (1380–1459), a successful soldier in the French wars of Henry IV and Henry V, who contributed towards the building of philosophy schools at Cambridge and bequeathed money towards the foundation of Magdalen College, Oxford. He figures prominently in the *Paston Letters. In Shakespeare's 1 *Henry VI, however, he is presented as a coward who repeatedly betrays the heroic Talbot, is stripped of his Garter, and banished by the king. The *Folio text calls him *'Falstaff', but from *Theobald onwards it has become traditional to call him 'Fastolfe' to distinguish him from his similar but more purely fictitious namesake. To Shakespeare's audiences, however, the figures probably appeared identical, despite historical and chronological difficulties.

Fatal Curiosity, The, a tragedy in blank verse by *Lillo, first produced by *Fielding in 1736. It is based on an old story of a Cornish murder, but its plot is archetypal and appears in many literatures; Lillo's version influenced the German 'fate-drama', and *Camus used it in *Le Malentendu* (1945).

Old Wilmot, under stress of poverty and urged by his wife, murders a stranger who has deposited a casket with them, only to find the victim is his son, supposed lost in a shipwreck.

Fatal Dowry, The, a tragedy by *Massinger and *Field, acted c.1617–19, printed 1632. The play is based on one of the *controversiae* (or imaginary legal disputes) of Seneca the elder.

Charalois's father, the distinguished marshal of the duke of Burgundy, has died in debt, and his creditors refuse to allow his body to be buried. Charalois offers to go to prison if the creditors will release the body. The offer is accepted; Charalois goes to prison with his friend, the blunt soldier Romont. Rochfort, ex-president of the parliament, touched by the piety of Charalois and the honesty of Romont, procures their release, and moreover gives Charalois his daughter Beaumelle to wife. She is presently found by Romont exchanging kisses with her former suitor, the mean-spirited fop Novall. Charalois, at first incredulous, presently himself finds Beaumelle and Novall together, and forcing a duel on the latter kills him. He calls upon Rochfort to judge his daughter. The father himself condemns her, and Charalois stabs her. But the father immediately turns on Charalois and upbraids him for his lack of mercy. Charalois is tried for the murder of Novall and Beaumelle and acquitted, but is killed by a friend of Novall, who in turn is killed by Romont.

Rowe's *The Fair Penitent is founded on this play.

Fatal Marriage, The, or *The Innocent Adultery*, a tragedy by *Southerne, performed 1694.

Biron, having married Isabella against his father's wish, is sent by him to the siege of Candy and reported killed. His widow is repudiated by the father and brought to misery. During seven years she is courted by Villeroy, and finally, from gratitude for his devotion and urged by Carlos, Biron's younger brother, she marries him. Biron, who has all this time been a captive, now returns and reveals himself to Isabella. Carlos, it now appears, had known that Biron was alive, but had concealed his knowledge, wishing to oust him from the succession. For the same reason he had urged the marriage of Isabella, in order finally to ruin her and her son in his father's estimation. Carlos waylays and mortally wounds Biron. Isabella, already distracted by the situation in which she finds herself, takes her own life. The guilt of Carlos is exposed.

The play is founded on A. *Behn's novel *The Nun or The Perjur'd Beauty* but, unlike Mrs Behn's heroine, Southerne's Isabella is portrayed as a helpless victim, 'born to suffer' and condemned by fate to 'a long line of woe'. The role was originally played by Mrs *Barry with great effect, and was subsequently played by many leading actresses, including Mrs *Cibber, Mrs *Siddons, and Fanny *Kemble. The play was revived by *Garrick in 1757 as *Isabella, or The Fatal Marriage*; he cut out the comic sub-plot and made other minor alterations.

Fata Morgana, see MORGAN LE FAY.

Father and Son, see GOSSE.

Fathers of the Church, the early Christian writers, a term usually applied to those of the first five cents. Sometimes the Greek and Latin Fathers are distinguished, the former including *Clement of Alexandria, *Origen, Cyprian, *Athanasius, Basil the Great, Gregory Nazianzen, and *Chrysostom; the latter *Tertullian, *Jerome, *Ambrose, *Augustine, *Gregory (Pope Gregory I), and *Bernard.

Faulconbridge, Robert and Philip, the legitimate and illegitimate sons of Sir Robert Faulconbridge in Shakespeare's *King John.* Philip's true father is *Richard I (Cœur de Lion). See also under BASTARD.

FAULKNER (originally Falkner), William Cuthbert (1897–1962), American novelist, born in Mississippi, where his family had long been settled; he spent most of his life there, in the town of Oxford, and the history and legends of the South, and of his own family, were the material of his greater books. After a desultory education and working at various odd jobs, he met S. *Anderson while working as a journalist in New Orleans, who encouraged him to write his first novel, *Soldier's Pay* (1926). This was followed by others, including *Sartoris* (1929), the first of the series in which he describes the decline of the Compson and Sartoris families, representative of the Old South, and the rise of the crude and unscrupulous Snopes family. The principal setting of these novels is 'Jefferson'—a composite picture of several Mississippi towns—in the mythical Yoknapatawpha County. *The Sound and the Fury* (1929) is a narrative tour de force in which Faulkner views the decline of the South through several eyes, most remarkably those of Benjy Compson, a 33-year-old 'idiot'. The work is an astonishing display of technical brilliance written in a sombre and lyrical mood. *As I Lay Dying* (1930) is equally distinguished, and demonstrates Faulkner's comic as well as his tragic vision, in his account of the death of poor white Addie Bundren, and of her children's grotesque attempts to fulfil her wish to be buried in Jefferson. He made his name, however, not with these but with a more sensational work, *Sanctuary* (1931). *Light in August* (1932) and *Absalom, Absalom!* (1936) confirmed his reputation as one of the finest of modern novelists. Other important works include *The Hamlet* (1940), *Intruder in the Dust* (1948), and several volumes of short stories, collected in 1950. He was awarded the *Nobel Prize in 1949. In England he found an early champion in Arnold *Bennett, who wrote warmly of his work in the *Evening Standard*, having been introduced to it by R. *Hughes, who wrote a preface for the 1930 English edition of *Soldier's Pay.*

FAULKS, Sebastian (1953–), journalist and novelist, born in Berkshire and educated at Emmanuel College, Cambridge. His novels include *A Trick of the Light* (1984), *The Girl at the Lion d'Or* (1988, set in France during the 1930s), *A Fool's Alphabet* (1992), and *Birdsong* (1993), a novel with a double time-scale set largely in France in the trenches during the First World War and dealing in part with the underground lives of sappers: there is a vivid account of the night before the battle of the Somme. *Charlotte Gray* (1998) explores Franco-British relations and the Nazi occupation of France during the Second World War. *The Fatal Englishman: Three Short Lives* (1996) is a collection of biographical essays linked by a common theme of early death, and a self-destructive impulse: the painter Christopher Wood; pilot and author Richard *Hillary; and journalist Jeremy Wolfenden. The action of *On Green Dolphin Street* (2001) takes place during the Cold War.

Faust, the subject of the great dramas of *Marlowe and *Goethe, was a wandering conjuror, who lived in Germany about 1488–1541 (H. G. Meed, *Johann Faust*, 1930) and is mentioned in various documents of the period. (He is not to be confused with Johann *Fust or Faust, the printer.) For Marlowe's play see DR FAUSTUS. *Faust*, the drama by Goethe, was begun by him about the year 1770 and not completed till just before his death in 1832. It consists of two parts, the first published 1808, the second 1832.

It begins with a prologue in heaven, in which Mephistopheles obtains permission to try to effect the ruin of the soul of Faust, the Lord being confident that he will fail and predicting the ultimately positive conclusion at the end of Pt II. The play itself opens with a soliloquy by Faust, disillusioned with the world and despairing. Mephistopheles having presented himself, Faust enters into a compact to become his servant if Faust should exclaim, of any moment of delight procured for him, 'Stay, thou art so fair.' Then follow the attempts of Mephistopheles to satisfy Faust, culminating in the incident of Gretchen (Margaret), whom Faust, at the devil's instigation, though not without some rebellion by his better self, seduces, bringing about her miserable death. This is the end of Pt I, Faust being left remorseful and dissatisfied.

The story of Pt II is extremely complex and its symbolism obscure. It consists in the main of two portions, of which the first is the incident of Helen of Troy, originally written as a separate and complete poem. Helen, symbolizing perfect beauty as produced by Greek art, is recalled from Hades and ardently pursued by Faust, but finally reft from him. Euphorion, their son, personifying poetry and the union of the classical and the Romantic, and at the end representing Lord *Byron, vanishes in a flame. In the second portion (Acts IV and V) the purified Faust, pursuing the service of man, reclaims from the sea, with the help of Mephistopheles, a stretch of submerged land. But Care attacks and blinds him. Finally satisfied in the consciousness of good work done, he cries to the fleeting moment, 'Ah, stay, thou art so fair', and falls dead. Hell tries to seize his soul, but it is borne away by angels.

Faustus, Doctor, see DR FAUSTUS.

FAWCETT, Millicent Garrett, see WOMEN'S SUFFRAGE.

Fawn, The, see PARASITASTER, THE.

Feast of Fools, a medieval festival originally of the sub-deacons of the cathedral, held about the time of the Feast of the Circumcision (1 Jan.), in which the humbler cathedral officials burlesqued the sacred ceremonies. A lord of the feast was elected, styled bishop, cardinal, abbot, etc., according to the locality (cf. BOY BISHOP). (See also FOOL.) The Feast of Fools had its chief vogue in the French cathedrals, but there are a few English records of it, notably in Lincoln Cathedral and Beverley Minster. See E. K. *Chambers, *The Mediaeval Stage* (1903).

Feathernest, Mr, in Peacock's *Melincourt*, a caricature of *Southey.

FEAVER, Vicki (1943–), poet, born in Nottingham. *Close Relatives* (1981), a series of portraits and acute, sympathetic observations of human relationships, introduced Feaver's characteristic style: deceptively plain language enlivened by taut rhythms and suddenly enlarged by boldly imaginative metaphors. *The Handless Maiden* (1994) is more clearly, though never dogmatically, feminist in theme, and also more emphatic in its use of myth, both as metaphor and in *dramatic monologues such as 'Circe' and the celebrated 'Judith'. Feaver's craft and vigour have brought her many awards, particularly for individual poems.

Feeble, in Shakespeare's 2 *Henry IV* (III. ii), one of the recruits brought before *Falstaff, who is a 'woman's tailor', a phrase with bawdy connotations.

Feenix, Cousin, a character in Dickens's *Dombey and Son*, the nephew of Mrs Skewton, and cousin of Edith, Dombey's second wife.

FEINSTEIN, Elaine (1930–), novelist, poet, and translator, born in Bootle and educated at Newnham College, Cambridge. Her novels, which include *The Circle* (1970), *Children of the Rose* (1975), and *The Shadow Master* (1979), show a development from the experimental towards the naturalistic; *The Survivors* (1982) is a saga about a Jewish immigrant family in Liverpool. A selection of her poems, *Some Unease and Angels* (1977), contains new work and work from earlier collections, and a selection of her notable translations (pub. 1971) of the poetry of *Tsvetayeva. A further volume of poems, *Badlands*, appeared in 1987, the same year as *A Captive Lion*, her biography of Tsvetayeva. Her life of *Pushkin appeared in 1998.

Félibrige, a literary movement founded in 1854 by seven Provençal poets under the leadership of Frédéric Mistral (1830–1914) to foster a renaissance of Provençal writing. Its most memorable products are Mistral's vernacular epics *Mireio* (1859) and *Calendau* (1867). It has served as an inspiration to a number of more recent movements favouring dispossessed languages and cultures.

Felix Holt, the Radical, a novel by G. *Eliot published 1866.

Set in 1832 in Loamshire, it vividly evokes the political ferment and corrupt electioneering tactics of the times. Harold Transome arrives home after many years in the East to inherit the family estate on his elder brother's death, and startles his family by standing as a Radical candidate. Although good-natured and intelligent, his political convictions are not incompatible with 'treating' the local workers, and his character is strongly contrasted with that of Felix Holt, austere, idealistic, and passionate, who although educated has deliberately chosen the life of an artisan, and who aims to stir his fellow workers to a sense of their own worth and destiny. The heroine, Esther, who supposes herself to be the daughter of old Lyon, the Independent minister, has an innate love of refinement, and when Felix chastises her for her frivolity she gains a new consciousness, and gradually falls in love with him. A complex and somewhat implausible chain of events reveals that Esther is in fact the heir to the Transome estate; Harold woos her, from motives not entirely mercenary, and Esther is forced to choose between his worldly attractions, and poverty with Felix, who has been imprisoned for his rash but innocent involvement in a riot. She renounces her claim to the estate and chooses Felix. It is revealed to Harold at the end of the novel (the reader having known from the beginning) that he is not his father's son, but the son of the hated lawyer Jermyn; the account of the years of suffering of the proud and lonely Mrs Transome, subjected in secrecy to a man she no longer respects, ever fearful of her son's discovery, befriended only by her faithful servant Denner, forms, in the view of *Leavis, the most successful part of the book, though H. *James (who found the whole plot clumsily artificial) declared that, although intensely drawn, she was dramatically superfluous.

FELL, Dr John (1625–86), dean of Christ Church, Oxford, and bishop of Oxford, and an early promoter of the *Oxford University Press, to the development of which he greatly contributed. Fell was author of a critical edition of Cyprian (1682), and edited with many arbitrary alterations the *Historia Universitatis Oxoniensis* of A. *Wood. He is the subject of the well-known epigram beginning 'I do not love you, Dr Fell', a translation by T. *Brown of *Martial, *Epigrams*, 1. 32.

FELL, Margaret (1614–1702), an early leader of the Society of *Friends, converted by G. *Fox in 1652 during his stay at her home, Swarthmore, in Cumberland, which became the Friends' administrative centre. She was of gentry origin, a powerful character and an organizer of genius, who co-ordinated the growing movement, wrote copiously on religious and political issues, interceded personally with Charles II on behalf of persecuted Friends, and suffered grievous imprisonments in the 1660s. She became the first to enunciate the Friends' peace principles in 1660, and claimed full spiritual equality for women in *Women's Speaking Justified* (1666). After the death of her first husband, Judge Thomas Fell, she married Fox in 1669, but chiefly lived and travelled apart from him, continuing her radical activities into her eighties. See M. M. Ross, *Margaret Fell: Mother of Quakerism* (1984 edn); B. Y. Kunze, *Margaret Fell and the Rise of Quakerism* (1994); S. Davies, *Unbridled Spirits* (1998).

FELLTHAM, Owen (1623–68). He published a series of moral essays, *Resolves* (c.1620), when 18 years old, contributed to *Jonsonus Virbius* (see JONSON), famously called Charles I 'Christ the Second', and published a *Brief Character of the Low Countries* (1652).

Female Quixote, The, or *The Adventures of Arabella*, a novel by C. *Lennox, published 1752.

This vivacious and ironical work was probably the most consistent of the various attempts to reproduce the spirit of *Cervantes in English. Arabella, the daughter of a marquis, grows up in a remote castle into a beautiful young woman with a passion for reading romance and a determination to live herself in such a world. A naïve delight in her own beauty leads her to assume that all men are her slaves, and potential abductors and ravishers; so that innocent men who find themselves in her company are constantly thrown into confusion by her impassioned accusations. Nevertheless she is benevolent and virtuous, and sharply contrasted with her envious, worldly female cousin. After many ludicrous events at home, she travels, with her devoted cousin Mr Glanville and other friends, to Bath and London, where her beauty and singularity lead to dreadful confusions, a duel, illness, and expected death. But the ferment subsides, and Arabella marries the patient, sensible Mr Glanville. The novel was successful and praised by *Fielding.

female, or **feminine, rhymes,** see RHYME.

feminist criticism, a modern tradition of literary commentary and polemic devoted to the defence of women's writing or of fictional female characters against the condescensions of a predominantly male literary establishment. The beginnings of this movement are to be found in the journalism of Rebecca *West from about 1910. More influential as founding documents are the essays of V. *Woolf, notably *A Room of One's Own* (1929) and *Three Guineas* (1938), and S. de *Beauvoir's book *Le Deuxième Sexe* (1949; *The Second Sex*, 1953). In its developed form, the tradition was reborn amid the cultural ferment of the post-1968 period, especially in the United States. The misogynist or belittling attitudes of male critics and novelists were subjected to ironic scrutiny in Mary Ellmann's *Thinking about Women* (1968) and to iconoclastic rage in Kate Millett's *Sexual Politics* (1970), the latter work berating D. H. *Lawrence and N. *Mailer in particular. Many feminist academics continued the investigation into stereotyped representations of female characters,

for example in S. Cornillon (ed.), *Images of Women in Fiction* (1972). Concentration upon the offences of male writers tended to give way in the later 1970s to woman-centred literary histories seeking to trace an autonomous tradition of women's literature and to redeem neglected female authors. Influential examples of such work in America were Ellen Moers, *Literary Women* (1976), Elaine Showalter, *A Literature of Their Own* (1977), and Sandra M. Gilbert and Susan Gubar, *The Madwoman in the Attic* (1979). By the beginning of the 1980s, feminist criticism was becoming more self-critical and internally differentiated: the mainstream of American feminist criticism eschewed 'male' literary theory and saw its own purpose as the affirmation of distinctly female 'experience' as reflected in writing; but black-feminist and lesbian-feminist critics objected that their own experiences were being overlooked. Meanwhile the value of 'experience' as a clue to women's writing was doubted by feminists allied to *Marxist criticism, *psychoanalytic criticism, and post-*structuralism, especially but not exclusively in Britain and France. One such school, led by the French writers Julia Kristeva, Hélène Cixous, and Luce Irigaray, sought to define an *écriture féminine* (for which 'feminine writing' would be a misleading translation) on the basis of a psychological 'politics' of language itself: if language belongs not to women but to a masculine social order, the distinctive female literary strategy will be to subvert it with bodily, even orgasmic, pulsations. British feminist criticism, although drawing upon both American and French approaches, has usually been more historical and sociological. Feminist criticism has thus become a varied field of debate rather than an agreed position. Its substantial achievements are seen in the readmission of temporarily forgotten women authors to the literary *canon, in modern reprints and newly commissioned studies by feminist publishing houses such as Virago (1977) and the Women's Press (1978), in anthologies and academic courses.

FÉNELON, François de Salignac de la Mothe (1651–1715), French theologian and educator. Appointed archbishop of Cambrai, he wielded considerable influence at court until his political independence and his quietism—which earned the censure of *Bossuet—relegated him to his diocese. His best-known works were written for his pupil, the duc de Bourgogne, grandson of Louis XIV: *Télémaque* (1699), a didactic romance modelled on Telemachus' voyage in the *Odyssey*, teaching the skills and virtues of the enlightened monarch, and *Dialogues des morts* (1712–30), presenting the lives of the heroes and statesmen of history for the edification of the prince.

FENN, G. Manville, see HISTORICAL FICTION.

Fenton, a spendthrift young gentleman in love with Anne Page in Shakespeare's *The Merry Wives of Windsor*.

FENTON, James (1949–   ), poet, reporter, and librettist, born in Lincoln, educated at the Choristers' School, Durham, Repton, and Magdalen College, Oxford, where he won the *Newdigate Prize for poetry with a sonnet sequence called 'Our Western Furniture'. He has worked as a political and literary journalist and as a freelance correspondent in Indo-China, as theatre critic of the *Sunday Times* and, from 1984 to 1986, as chief book reviewer for *The Times*. In 1994 he was elected professor of poetry at Oxford. Though he is predominantly a satirist, the main stylistic influence on his work is W. H. *Auden. His first collection, *Terminal Moraine* (1972) displayed an imagination hungry for stimulus of all kinds, from politics to anthropology and horticulture. *The Memory of War* (1982), which reprinted several poems from the first volume and all those from his 1978 pamphlet *A Vacant Possession*, is similarly eclectic in its inspiration and exuberant in execution, although several pieces, grounded in his experiences as a reporter, display sombre authority in the contemplation of war and its aftermath. *Manila Envelope* (1989) was published from the Philippines, where he was working as a correspondent, and a collection of his reportage from Vietnam, Korea, and the Philippines, including his celebrated eyewitness account of the fall of Saigon, was also published in 1989 as *All the Wrong Places: Adrift in the Politics of Asia*. *Out of Danger* appeared in 1993 and won the Whitbread Award for poetry. He worked as librettist and translator for the 1985 musical adaptation of *Hugo's *Les Misérables*. A collection of satirical poems, *Partingtime Hall*, written in collaboration with John *Fuller, was published in 1987.

Ferdinand, (1) in Shakespeare's *Love's Labour's Lost*, the king of Navarre; (2) in his *The Tempest*, son of *Alonso, king of Naples, and lover of *Miranda; (3) in Webster's *The Duchess of Malfi*, the brother of the duchess.

Ferdinand Count Fathom, *The Adventures of*, a novel by T. *Smollett, published 1753.

In his dedication Smollett outlines his ideas on form in the novel. It should create 'a large diffused picture' dominated by a central figure to which various groups and episodes are subordinated; within this framework digression may be permitted. In these *Adventures* the figure of Count Fathom, a deliberately created monster 'from the purlieus of treachery and fraud', is starkly contrasted with the noble Count de Melvil and his son Renaldo. Fate and coincidence play a decisive part in the story, much of which is written in a *mock-heroic style. The character of the book changes considerably in the last quarter, which becomes self-consciously *'romantic', in many ways anticipating the later *Gothic novel.

Far from being a count, Ferdinand is the son of a camp-follower of Marlborough's army. While she is robbing the dead on the field of Petervarad she saves Count de Melvil, who becomes Ferdinand's benefactor and brings the boy up with his own son. At 16 Ferdinand plans to seduce Melvil's daughter, and by the time he is 18 he is established in Vienna with his friend, the evil Ratchcali, as womanizer, cheat, and social success. In London, again with Ratchcali, he conquers fashionable society with his talents and charm, organizes a swindle in fake antiques, and continues with his seductions, driving Elenor to Bedlam and Celinda to drink. After further successes in Bristol he is exposed cheating at cards, betrayed, and thrown into the debtor's prison. Freed by young Melvil, he shows his gratitude by creating bitterness between Melvil and his love Monimia, but fails in his attempt to rape her. As he cannot now return to high society, he takes up medicine, but his scandalous life and a legal action brought by a cleric ruin his repute. A rapid series of events bear down on him. In an attempt to escape he marries a wealthy widow, but he is again indicted and again imprisoned, when at last signs of remorse begin to appear. He now almost disappears from the story, the rest of which relates, with lachrymose sentiment and many *frissons* of horror (including a hint of necrophilia), the misfortunes and eventual joys of young Melvil and Monimia.

FERGUSON, Adam (1723–1816), one-time chaplain to the Black Watch, who succeeded *Hume as Advocates' Librarian in 1757, was professor in turn of natural philosophy, moral philosophy, and mathematics at Edinburgh after 1764, and was a member of the *Select Society and co-founder of the *Royal Society of Edinburgh. His writings include *The Morality of Stage-Plays Seriously Considered* (1757), written in defence of J. Home's *Douglas*, performed the previous year; *An Essay on the History of Civil Society* (1767), a pioneer work in political sociology; *The History of the Progress and Termination of the Roman Republic* (3 vols, 1783); and *Principles of Moral and Political Science* (2 vols, 1792). This last work carries further the analysis of human character begun in the *Essay*, and offers a more teleological ethic than is found in other moralists of the period. Ferguson is also more explicit in the development of the sharp contrast between questions of fact and questions of value. In the *Essay* he has a discussion 'Of the History of Literature', in which he argues that poetry is a more original and natural form of literary expression than prose, and that all literature develops better in periods and contexts of great social activity than in leisure and solitude.

FERGUSON, Sir Samuel (1810–86), an important figure in the *Irish Revival, who was educated at Trinity College, Dublin, and became the deputy keeper of the records of Ireland. Among many translations and works based on Gaelic legend, he published a widely praised elegy on Thomas Davis, a nationalist leader, in 1845; *Lays of the Western Gael* (1865); and an epic, *Congal* (1872), on the last stand of Irish paganism against Christianity. A long narrative poem, 'Conary', based on a bardic story, and a retelling of the legend of

*Deirdre both appeared in 1880. *Ogham Inscriptions in Ireland, Wales, and Scotland*, his most important antiquarian work, was published in 1887. A biography, *Ascendancy of the Heart*, by R. O'Driscoll, appeared in 1976.

FERGUSSON, Robert (1750–74). He was obliged by poverty to leave St Andrews on his father's death, and subsequently worked as a clerk in the Commissary Office. His first poems were published in Ruddiman's *Weekly Magazine* (1771), in imitation of English models, and his first *Scots poem, 'The Daft Days', appeared in 1772. A volume appeared in 1773 which was to have a profound influence on *Burns, who found himself inspired to 'emulating vigour': Fergusson's 'The Farmer's Ingle', a vernacular description of homely rustic life, is a clear foreshadowing of Burns's *'The Cotter's Saturday Night'. Fergusson vividly evokes the street life, taverns, and amusements of Edinburgh, and mocks the established literary world in satirical attacks on Dr *Johnson and *Mackenzie ('The Sow of Feeling'). In 1773 he developed manic-depressive symptoms, and died not long after being shut up in the local Bedlam. An edition of his works in two volumes with a life by M. P. McDiarmid appeared in 1954–6.

Ferishtah's Fancies, a volume of poems by R. *Browning, published 1884. The main part of the collection consists of 12 poems focused on the sayings of an imaginary Persian sage, Ferishtah, on various moral and religious topics. The device of a non-Christian speaker to suggest Christian teaching (Ferishtah with his parables recalls Jesus) had been used before by Browning, in such poems as 'Cleon' (see MEN AND WOMEN), but not in so systematic a format.

FERLINGHETTI, Lawrence (1920–   ), American *Beat poet. Although born in New York, he was the mainstay of the San Francisco Renaissance—the West Coast wing of the Beat movement. In 1953 he co-founded City Lights Books, a publishing house and bookstore that specialized in Beat poetry. He was arrested in 1956 for publishing *Ginsberg's *Howl* and wrote a full account of the trial ('Horn on Howl') for the *Evergreen Review* (1957). His own work includes poetry collections such as *Coney Island of the Mind* (1958) as well as two volumes of plays. Unlike many of his contemporaries he disapproved of the Beat's emphasis on the self and argued for a more directly political project with which they could be aligned. He was a fervent supporter of the Cuban Revolution and most famously composed the poem 'One Thousand Fearful Words for Fidel Castro' after his visit there in 1960. He also appeared in the Band's final concert, *The Last Waltz* (1978), reading his ersatz version of 'Our Father'.

FERMOR, Patrick Leigh (1915–   ), travel writer, of English and Irish descent, educated at the King's School, Canterbury. In 1933 Fermor set off on foot for Constantinople: the journey was the subject of a planned trilogy of which two volumes, *A Time of Gifts* (1977) and *Between the Woods and the Water* (1985), have been published, the first covering the Hook of Holland to Hungary, the second Transylvania to the Danube. The historical imagination, the sense of place, and the evocation of youth, expressed in prose that ranges from the lyrical to the erudite, have been much admired. After leaving Constantinople, Fermor continued to live and travel in the Balkans and Greece: during the German occupation of Crete he lived for more than two years disguised as a shepherd and captured the commander of the German forces in Crete, an episode which became the basis of a film, *Ill Met by Moonlight* (1956). After the war Fermor became director of the British Institute in Athens. His first travel book, *The Traveller's Tree* (1950), is a vivid account of a journey through the French Caribbean, where his novella, *The Violins of Saint-Jacques* (1953), is also set. His account of travels in the southern Peloponnese (*Mani*, 1958) and northern Greece (*Rommeli*, 1966) are at once erudite studies of local customs and dialect and evocations of village life. *A Time to Keep Silence* (1957) and *Three Letters from the Andes* (1991) originate in letters to his wife.

FERRAR, Nicholas (1592–1637), educated at and fellow of Clare College, Cambridge, a member of Parliament and active in the affairs of the Virginia Company. In 1625 he retired to *Little Gidding, an estate belonging to his mother, and established there with his brother, his brother-in-law John Collett, and their families a religious community based on Anglican principles. Ferrar wrote little himself, but was a close friend of G. *Herbert, who on his deathbed entrusted to him the manuscript of his poems *The Temple*, published 1633.

Ferrars, (1) Mrs, and her sons Edward and Robert, in *Sense and Sensibility* by J. Austen; (2) William, and his children Endymion and Myra, in *Endymion* by B. Disraeli.

Ferrau, or **Ferragus,** in *Orlando innamorato* and *Orlando furioso*, a Moorish knight of Spain, one of the suitors for the hand of *Angelica, and the slayer of her brother *Argalia.

FERRERS, George, see MIRROR FOR MAGISTRATES, A.

Ferrex and Porrex, see GORBODUC.

FERRIER, James Frederick (1808–64), nephew of Susan *Ferrier, educated at Edinburgh University and Magdalen College, Oxford. He studied German philosophy at Heidelberg and was successively professor of civil history at Edinburgh (1842–5) and of moral philosophy and political economy at St Andrews (1845–64).

   His idealistic philosophy, connected with that of *Berkeley, is set forth in *The Institutes of Metaphysic* (1854) and *Lectures on Greek Philosophy and Other Philosophical Remains* (mostly published in *Blackwood's, 1838–43, and in volume form 1866). The principal positions of his philosophy are two: first, that

'Along with whatever any intelligence knows, it must, as the ground or condition of its knowledge, have some cognisance of itself.' Nor can it know itself except in relation with objects. Mind and matter, *per se*, are unknowable. Secondly, that we can be ignorant only of what is capable of being known. From these positions he argues that it is necessary to 'conceive a supreme intelligence as the ground and essence of the Universal whole'. In substance, Ferrier's conclusions closely resemble those of *Hegel, though reached independently and from a different starting point; *De Quincey said that Ferrier produced 'German philosophy reflected through a Scottish medium'.

FERRIER, Susan Edmonstone (1782–1854), the daughter of an Edinburgh lawyer who was a friend of Sir W. *Scott. She was the successful author of three good novels of Scottish life: *Marriage* (1818), *The Inheritance* (1824), and *Destiny* (1831). Her object was avowedly to instruct, particularly on the subject of marriage, but her method lies in shrewd observation and comedy.

Ferumbras, or **Firumbras, Sir,** a Middle English metrical romance of 10,540 short lines related to the French Charlemagne romances *Fierabras* and the *Destruction de Rome*. It is one of the more artistic of the English romances of 'the matter of France', and more distinguished than the version known from its 19th-cent. owner as the 'Fillingham Firumbras' (ed. M. I. O'Sullivan, EETS os 198, 1935). The story tells of the capture by Ferumbras, the son of the sultan of Babylon, of Rome and the Holy Relics, of his combat and later friendship with Oliver, and of the conversion to Christianity of Ferumbras and his sister Floripas. The two become friends of Roland, Oliver, and Charlemagne, and Floripas marries Guy of Burgundy. The same story is told in *The Sowdone of Babylon*, a version from about 1400 of a lost French romance. Ed. S. J. Herrtage (EETS es 34, 1879; repr. 1966).

Feste, in Shakespeare's *Twelfth Night*, *Olivia's jester. His name, which indicates mirthfulness, occurs only once. He concludes the play with his song 'When that I was and a little tiny boy'.

Festin de pierre, Le, see DON JUAN.

festivals, literary. The first post-war literary festival took place in Cheltenham in 1949; this was a small-scale local occasion, which aimed to bring writers and readers together. A Writers' Conference in Edinburgh in 1962, attached to the well-established Edinburgh Festival of music and drama, was attended by *Spender, *Spark, *Durrell, Rebecca *West, Angus *Wilson, and others, and achieved notoriety through lively debates on drugs and homosexuality: this was a landmark in the dawn of the *performance age. Since then, scores of festivals have sprung up across the country, usually offering a week or fortnight of events, including readings, lectures, book signings, and writing workshops. Festivals range from the national (or international, as Cheltenham has now become), to the local (for example, the Lancaster LitFest, established in 1978, which seeks primarily to promote local writing) or specialist (poetry at Aldeburgh or drama at the Royal Court Young Writers Festival). Among the most popular are the Edinburgh Book Festival, established in 1983, and the Hay-on-Wye Festival, established in 1988, both annual events. Others include Ways with Words, held annually at Dartington Hall in Devon, and the thrice-annual Ilkley Festival (est. 1973). Literary festivals grew in number and prominence, especially during the 1980s when their potential as effective publicity and marketing tools became apparent. Many major book launches are now accompanied by author appearances on the festival circuit. Both Toronto and Adelaide are well known for their successful international programmes.

FET, Afanasy Afanasevich (A. A. Shenshin) (1820–92), Russian lyric poet, and a close friend of *Turgenev. His first volume of verse appeared in 1850, but by the late 1850s Fet's concern for 'pure art' and his themes from nature, which he describes with startling freshness, went out of fashion. In his last years four collections entitled *Evening Lights* were published and he found a new fame with the younger generation of Russian symbolist poets. The first selection of his poetry in English, *I Have Come to You to Greet You* (trans. James Greene), appeared in 1982.

FEUCHTWANGER, Lion (1884–1958), German Jewish novelist and playwright, best known as the author of *Die Hässliche Herzogin* (1923, *The Ugly Duchess*) and *Jud Süss* (1925, *Jew Süss*), a florid and operatic historical romance set in 18th-cent. Germany. He lived as an expatriate in France, was interned by the Vichy government, then escaped to the USA, where he settled in Hollywood. *Jew Süss*, in a translation by W. and E. *Muir (1927), was highly praised by Arnold *Bennett in his *Evening Standard* column ('a complete picture of a complex social organism'), and became a best-seller. Feuchtwanger appears as a character in Christopher *Hampton's play *Tales from Hollywood* (1983).

FEUERBACH, Ludwig (1804–72), German philosopher and critic of the Bible, a disciple of *Hegel. Feuerbach's most influential work was *Das Wesen des Christentums* (*The Essence of Christianity*, 1841), in which he asserted that Christianity is a man-created myth, satisfying man's need to imagine perfection: 'Man, by means of the imagination, involuntarily contemplates his inner nature; he represents it as out of himself. The nature of man, of the species . . . is God.' G. *Eliot, who translated the work into English in 1854, wrote that she agreed with Feuerbach's religion of humanity, and her novels show the influence not only of Feuerbach's thought but also of his application of religious terms to a secular philosophy.

Fezziwig, Mr and Mrs, characters in Dickens's *A Christmas Carol*.

Fiammetta, the name given by *Boccaccio to the lady he loved, and the title of one of his works.

FICHTE, Johann Gottlieb (1762–1814), German philosopher, a pupil of *Kant, from whose dualism he subsequently dissented. He became professor of philosophy at Jena in 1794, but was accused of atheism and dismissed. He subsequently lectured in Erlangen and Berlin. Fichte's philosophy is pure idealism. Though his philosophical system grew out of Kant's, it has the distinguishing feature that the thinking self, or *ego*, is seen as the only reality. This *ego*, in defining and limiting itself, creates the *non-ego*, the world of experience, as its opposite, the medium through which it asserts its freedom. He expounded this doctrine in his principal work, *Wissenschaftslehre* (*Doctrine of Knowledge*, 1794). Influenced by the humiliation of Prussia in 1806–7, he became increasingly interested in the idea of nationhood, and sought reality, not in the *ego* but in the notion of a divine idea lying at the base of all experience, of which the world of the senses is the manifestation. His *Reden an die deutsche Nation* (*Speeches to the German Nation*, 1814) helped to arouse the patriotism of his contemporaries under the Napoleonic occupation. His view of history as the biography of its heroes greatly influenced *Carlyle, particularly in the latter's lectures *On *Heroes and Hero-Worship* (1841), as did his idealism. See *Sartor Resartus* for Carlyle's use of Fichte's idea of the world of Appearances as a vesture under which lies the essence or Divine Idea.

FICINO, Marsilio (1433–99), Italian humanist and philosopher, and a highly influential exponent of Platonism. He translated into Latin many important works of *Plato and the *Neoplatonists (e.g. Porphyry, *Plotinus, Proclus, and *Dionysius the Areopagite), sought to establish an essential harmony between Platonism and Christianity, and under the patronage of Cosimo de'Medici was the leader of a 'Platonic Academy' at Florence. His views influenced *Reuchlin and *Colet and were an inspiration to many English poets, including *Sidney and *Milton.

Fidele, in Shakespeare's *Cymbeline*, the name assumed by *Imogen when disguised as a boy, suggesting her faithfulness.

Fidessa, in Spenser's *Faerie Queene* (I. ii), the name assumed by the fair companion of *Sansfoy, whom the *Redcrosse Knight takes under his protection after slaying that 'faithlesse Sarazin'. She turns out to be the false *Duessa.

FIELD, Eugene (1850–95), American journalist, poet, and bibliophile, born in Missouri. He wrote light verse for adults and children, and his collection *A Little Book of Western Verse* (1889), which contains 'Little Boy Blue' and 'Dutch Lullaby' (better known later as 'Wynken, Blynken and Nod'), had a considerable vogue in England.

FIELD, Michael, the pseudonym of Katharine Bradley (1846–1914) and her niece Edith Cooper (1862–1913). Bradley, born in Birmingham and educated at Newnham College, Cambridge, became deeply attached to her invalid sister's daughter Edith, and they shared their lives and studied and travelled widely together. Bradley published first under the pseudonym of Arran Leigh: together they adopted the name of Michael Field with the publication of *Callirrho, and Fair Rosamund* (1884). They produced more than 20 volumes of verse drama and poetry. Their early work draws sensuously and erotically on pagan classical themes: *Long Ago* (1889) deals with the story of Sappho. They had many acquaintances in the literary and artistic world, including G. *Meredith, *Wilde, John *Gray (who assisted their conversion to Roman Catholicism), and *Ricketts, who illustrated some of their work. A selection from their journals was edited by T. Sturge *Moore in 1933.

FIELD, Nathan (1587–1619/20), actor and dramatist, educated at St Paul's. He was impressed into the company of the Children of the Chapel, and probably succeeded to Shakespeare's place as actor and shareholder in the King's Men, c.1616. He wrote two comedies, *A Woman Is a Weathercock* (1609), which shows the influence of *Jonson and includes a parody of a speech in *The Spanish Tragedy*, and *Amends for Ladies* (1610). He later collaborated with a number of other dramatists, including *Fletcher and *Massinger, and is best known for his share of Massinger's *The Fatal Dowry*.

FIELDING, Henry (1707–54), the son of a lieutenant (who later became lieutenant-general), born at Sharpham Park, the house of his maternal grandfather in Somerset. His mother died when he was 11, and when his father remarried Henry was sent to Eton. There he was happy, enjoyed his studies, and made lifelong friends of *Lyttelton, who was to become a generous future patron, and of *Pitt the elder. At 19 he attempted to elope with a beautiful heiress, but failing in this settled in London, determined to earn his living as a dramatist. Lady M. W. *Montagu, a distant cousin, encouraged him, and in 1728 at Drury Lane his play *Love in Several Masques* was successfully performed. In the same year he became a student of letters at Leiden, where he remained about 18 months, greatly enlarging his knowledge of classical literature. On his return to London he continued his energetic but precarious life as a dramatist, and between 1729 and 1737 wrote some 25 assorted dramas, largely in the form of farce and satire, and including two adaptations of *Molière, *The Mock Doctor* and *The Miser*. In 1730 three of his plays were performed: *The Author's Farce*; *Rape upon Rape*, a savage satire on the practices of the law, embodied in Justice Squeezum;

and the most successful of all his dramas, *Tom Thumb (which was published in a revised form the following year as *The Tragedy of Tragedies, or The Life and Death of Tom Thumb the Great*), one of several extravagant burlesques modelled on Buckingham's *The Rehearsal, of the turgid fashionable tragedies of the day. *Hogarth designed the frontispiece, and a long and close friendship began. *Don Quixote*, a satire which is part a tribute to *Cervantes, appeared in 1734. In the same year Fielding married Charlotte Cradock, who became his model for Sophia in *Tom Jones and for the heroine of *Amelia*, and with whom he enjoyed ten years of great happiness until her death. His improvidence led to long periods of considerable poverty, but he was greatly assisted at various periods of his life by his close and wealthy friend R. *Allen, who became, with Lyttelton, the model for Allworthy in *Tom Jones*. In 1736 Fielding took over the management of the New Theatre, for the opening of which he wrote the highly successful satirical comedy *Pasquin*, which aimed at various religious and political targets, including electioneering abuses. But *The Historical Register for 1736* was fiercer political satire than *Walpole's government would tolerate, and the Licensing Act of 1737, introducing censorship by the lord chamberlain, brought Fielding's career in the theatre to an end.

He entered the Middle Temple and began to read for the bar. In 1739–40 he wrote most of the columns of the *Champion*, a satirical and anti-Jacobite journal. In 1740 he was called to the bar but his health began to fail and he suffered acutely from gout. In the same year Richardson's *Pamela appeared and enjoyed tremendous popular success; in 1741 Fielding expressed his contempt in his pseudonymous parody *An Apology for the Life of Mrs *Shamela Andrews*. Meanwhile, because of increasing illness, he was unable to pursue his legal career with any consistency. Instead, in 1742, he produced *The Adventures of *Joseph Andrews and His Friend, Mr Abraham Adams*, for which he received from his publisher £185 11s. In 1743 his old friend *Garrick put on Fielding's *The Wedding Day*, and in the same year Fielding published three volumes of *Miscellanies*, which included *A Journey from This World to the Next* and a ferocious satire, *The Life and Death of *Jonathan Wild the Great*. In 1744 he suffered a terrible blow in the death of his wife, and for a year or so he wrote little except a preface to his sister Sarah's novel *David Simple*, and some journalism, particularly the *True Patriot* and the *Jacobite's Journal*. In 1746 he probably began *The History of Tom Jones, a Foundling*, and in 1747 caused some scandal by marrying his wife's maid and friend Mary Daniel. With the aid of Lyttelton, he was appointed JP for Westminster in 1748 and once again joined battle, now from the inside, with legal corruption and the 'trading justices' who imposed and embezzled fines. In 1749 *Tom Jones* was enthusiastically received by the general public, if not by *Richardson, *Smollett, Dr *Johnson, and other literary figures. In the same year his legal jurisdiction was extended to the whole county of Middlesex, and he was made chairman of the quarter sessions of Westminster. From his court in Bow Street he continued his struggle against corruption and lawlessness and, with his blind half-brother and fellow magistrate Sir John Fielding, strove to establish new standards of honesty and competence on the bench. He wrote various influential legal enquiries and pamphlets, including a proposal for the abolition of public hangings. In 1751 he published *Amelia*, which sold the best of all his novels. He returned to journalism in 1752 with the *Covent-Garden Journal*, and published in 1753 a humane and exhaustive *Proposal for Making Effective Provision for the Poor*. He organized and saw successfully implemented a plan for breaking up the criminal gangs who were then flourishing in London. But his gout, asthma, and other afflictions were now so far advanced that he had to use crutches, and in 1754, in hope of improvement, he set off with his wife and one of his daughters for Portugal. *The Journal of a Voyage to Lisbon*, published posthumously in 1755, describes in unsparing detail the departure and journey. He had prepared it for the press ('a novel without a Plot') before he died in Lisbon in October.

Fielding is generally agreed to be an innovating master of the highest originality. He himself believed he was 'the founder of a new province of writing' and Sir W. *Scott commended him for his 'high notions of the dignity of an art which he may be considered as having founded'. His three acknowledged masters were *Lucian, *Swift, and Cervantes. In breaking away from the epistolary method of his contemporary Richardson, and others, he devised what he described as 'comic epics in prose', which may be characterized as the first modern novels in English, leading straight to the works of *Dickens and *Thackeray. The standard biography is M. C. Battestin, *Henry Fielding* (1989). The standard edition is the Wesleyan Edition (1967–   ) with 11 volumes printed as of 1997.

FIELDING, Sarah (1710–68), sister of H. *Fielding. For much of her life she lived quietly near London, where she became part of S. *Richardson's circle, and later near Bath. In 1744 she published her best-known work, *The Adventures of *David Simple*, a 'Moral Romance', with (in its second edition of that year) a preface by her brother Henry. The book was only moderately successful, but sold well in France. *Familiar Letters between the Principal Characters in David Simple* followed in 1747, and in 1753 the sombre *Volume the Last*, completing the story of Simple. Her *The Governess* (1749) is a literary landmark, being the first English novel written for children. With Jane *Collier she published *The Cry* (1754), a clever dialogue between Portia (the Solo) representing integrity, and an audience (the Chorus) representing malice and ignorance. The parallel of author against critic is implied throughout. There followed *The Lives of Cleopatra and Octavia* (1757), a series of dramatic monologues in which the subtle self-seeking of Cleopatra is contrasted with the honesty of Octavia. In 1759 appeared *The History of the Countess of Dellwyn*, tracing the disastrous relationship of an old husband and a young wife. The light-hearted *History of Ophelia* (1760) relates the adventures of an ingenuous young woman constantly astonished by the unquestioned conventions of society. Translations of *Xenophon's *Memorabilia* and *Apologia* appeared in 1762.

Sarah Fielding was one of the earliest of the English novelists to explore with close attention varying states of feeling and the roots of motive. Like her brother Henry, she seems to have been particularly interested in self-deception, but her gift was in following what her friend Richardson described as 'the finer springs and movements' of the heart. She was almost certainly the author of *Remarks on Clarissa* (1749).

FIENNES, Celia (1662–1741), granddaughter of the first Viscount Saye and Sele, probably born at Newton Toney near Salisbury. Nearly all that is known about her life is to be found in her Journal, of which an incomplete version was published in 1888 under the title *Through England on a Side Saddle in the Time of William and Mary*. A definitive edition, *The Journeys of Celia Fiennes*, ed. Christopher Morris, was published in 1947. Between 1685 and 1703 Celia Fiennes travelled into every county of England, and her Journal provided the first comprehensive survey of the country since *Harrison and *Camden. She recorded throughout what interested her: enclosures, mining, cloth manufacture, gardens, and domestic architecture; and while living in London she described in detail the coronations of James II, William and Mary, and Anne.

Fierabras, or **Fierebras,** see FERUMBRAS.

Fifine at the Fair, a poem in alexandrine couplets by R. *Browning, published 1872.

The speaker is Don Juan, who is strolling with his wife Elvire near Pornic in Brittany, where a fair is being held. Don Juan, attracted by the gypsy dancer Fifine, dissertates to Elvire on the nature of his feelings, contrasting the intense ephemerality of desire with the dull permanence of love, this initial theme then giving rise to a series of brilliant variations on the interconnected topics of knowledge, identity, and truth in life and art. The poem's interest in the casuistry of an overwrought self-consciousness has been attributed in part to Browning's bitterness in the aftermath of his quarrel with Lady Ashburton, which began in 1869 with a failed proposal of marriage (whether from him to her or vice versa is uncertain) and was still going on in 1871; Fifine would stand for Lady Ashburton in the interpretation, and Elvire for Elizabeth Barrett (*Browning). But this background is not essential to a reading of the poem. Browning told his friend *Domett that the poem was 'the most metaphysical and boldest he had written since Sordello, and [he] was very doubtful as to its reception by the public'. The

comparison with *Sordello* is illuminating: the poem may be regarded as Browning's mature return to the difficulty and splendour of the earlier work. The poem indeed proved baffling to the public and critics, though its modern critical standing is high.

Figaro, the barber in *Beaumarchais's *Le Barbier de Séville* and hero of his *Le Mariage de Figaro*, a witty resourceful fellow, and a rebel against the abuses of the *ancien régime*.

FIGES, Eva (1932–   ), novelist and feminist, born in Berlin. She came to England in 1939, and during the 1960s belonged to a circle of 'experimental' writers which also included B. S. *Johnson, Alan *Burns, and Ann *Quin. Her novels are poetic and fragmented, her preferred form the *interior monologue. They include *Winter Journey* (1967), *Days* (1974), *Waking* (1981), *Ghosts* (1988), and *The Tree of Knowledge* (1990), a fictionalized biography of John *Milton's wife. Her non-fiction works include *Patriarchal Attitudes* (1970), a ground-breaking work of *feminist social and literary criticism, and *Sex and Subterfuge: Women Writers to 1850* (1982).

film, literature of. In 1915 the American poet Vachel Lindsay published *The Art of the Moving Picture*. It was a controversial title for a book about a medium regarded as little more than a fairground attraction, and the seriousness of Lindsay's approach was the more remarkable for the cultural isolation in which he was writing.

The cinema established its intellectual credentials in Europe during the 1920s with the pioneering Soviet cinema of Eisenstein, Vertov, Dovzhenko, and Pudovkin; the avant-garde in France; and the Golden Age of silent cinema in Germany. Recognition of a new art led to the creation of institutions that provided the means of serious appraisal, notably the London Film Society, founded by Ivor Montagu and Hugh Miller in 1925, and the film magazine *Close-up* (1927–33).

The most significant 'school' of writing gathered around the British Documentary Film Movement, under the leadership of its founder John Grierson (1898–1972); Grierson's didactic approach required that film should be written about as well as practised. In 1929, shortly before joining Grierson's film unit, Paul Rotha wrote the hugely influential *The Film till Now*, the first history of world cinema in English. In 1932 the documentarists found an unofficial mouthpiece in the Edinburgh-based magazine *Cinema Quarterly* (1932–5), which they later renamed *World Film News* (1936–8). Chief among its contributors were Grierson, Basil Wright, Edgar Anstey, and Arthur Elton.

The realistic cinema this group argued for was at odds with the escapist fare of the 1930s commercial film industry. This gulf between what the cinema could be and what it was represented a perennial dilemma for serious writers on the medium. 'I cannot help wondering whether from this great moneyed industry anything of value to the human spirit can ever emerge,' commented Graham *Greene, who reviewed films for the *Spectator during the second half of the 1930s.

The war years ushered in a new commitment. A. R. Manvell's Pelican *Film* (1944) and the *Penguin Film Review* (1946–9) enjoyed a large general readership. Among newspaper critics, Dilys Powell of the *Sunday Times and Richard Winnington of the *News Chronicle stood out, the one as compassionate as the other was caustic. In America James *Agee contributed perceptive reviews for *Time* and the *Nation*. Like Greene, he joined the film-makers, writing several screenplays, most notably *The African Queen* and the *Night of the Hunter*.

It took a new generation of writers from outside the establishment to challenge the industry. The group of Oxford students associated with the film magazine *Sequence*, who went on to revive a moribund *Sight and Sound*, included Gavin Lambert, Lindsay Anderson, Karel Reisz, and Tony Richardson. These were of the *'Angry Young Men' generation, and (like the *Cahiers du cinéma* critics in France) they carried their philosophy into the making of film. They were chiefly responsible for the vitality of the British cinema in the 1960s.

The cinema's gain was film literature's loss. There were no voices of comparable insight to continue the *Sequence* tradition, and the link between the film-writers and the film-makers was broken. The growth of the academic study of film in the 1970s and 1980s encouraged the pedestrian and the dogmatic. Endless books on the cinema—whether they propounded auteur theory or semiotics or cultural studies—forsook the intelligent general reader for arcane interpretation. In these years the most persuasive writing on film belonged to individual voices. Basil Wright wrote the superb one-volume history *The Long View* (1974), and David Thomson the idiosyncratic and personal *Biographical Dictionary of the Cinema* (1975). The collections of Pauline Kael's writings for the *New Yorker*, which had begun in 1965 with *I Lost It at the Movies*, remained essential reading; Michael Powell contributed the baroque and brilliant *A Life in Movies* (1986) and David Sherwin, who had collaborated with Lindsay Anderson on *If...*, *O Lucky Man!*, and *Britannia Hospital*, produced his comic masterpiece *Going Mad in Hollywood* (1996). But as the cinema became increasingly conformist and formulaic in the 1990s, these landmarks came to seem as isolated as Vachel Lindsay's book had been in 1915.

FILMER, Sir Robert (c.1590–1653), a defender of the divine right of kings. His *Patriarcha, or The Natural Power of Kings*, written ?1638, published 1680, was attacked and ridiculed by *Locke in his first *Treatise of Government* (1690). He also opposed the witch-hunting mania.

Filostrato, a poem in *ottava rima* on the story of Troilus and Cressida, by *Boccaccio (1335), of special interest as the source of Chaucer's *Troilus and Criseyde*.

FINCH, Anne, see WINCHILSEA.

Fingal, an Ancient Epic Poem, in Six Books: Together with Several Other Poems, Composed by Ossian, the Son of Fingal. Translated from the Galic Language (1762), and *Temora, an Ancient Epic Poem, in Eight Books (1763).

These epics, which purported to be translated from an ancient Gaelic original, were in fact largely the work of J. *Macpherson; the first was based loosely on various old ballads and fragments, the second was entirely invented. Macpherson transforms the legendary Irish hero *Finn or Fionn into the Scottish Fingal, ignores various episodes and characters in the original Fenian and Ossianic stories (including *Grainne, Finn's faithless wife, and her lover Diarmid, who do not appear at all), and brings together Fingal and Cuthullin (the Irish *Cuchulain) who according to legend were divided by centuries. Morven, Fingal's kingdom in the north-west of Scotland, is Macpherson's invention. The original Finn MacCoul, whether historical or mythical, is usually assigned to the 3rd cent. AD; he was the son of Comhal, and father of Ossian the warrior bard; he was also leader of the Fianna or *Fenians, a semi-mythical military body said to have been raised for the defence of Ireland against the Norse. Fingal is pictured by Macpherson as fighting both the Norwegians and the Romans under Caracalla—'Caracul, King of the World'. The astonishing sway of Macpherson's version is indicated by the fact that even *Gibbon took the trouble to discuss it; he writes (though with some irony) of 'the tenderness, the elegant genius of Ossian', and contrasts the 'untutored Caledonians, glowing with the warm virtues of nature' with 'the degenerate Romans, polluted with the mean vices of wealth and slavery'. The appeal of *Fingal* lay in its *primitivism, its qualities of the *sublime, and its sentiment. H. *Blair found that it conformed to the rules of *Aristotle, and bestowed upon it such epithets as 'grand . . . pathetic . . . serious . . . grave . . . wild and romantic . . . sublime and tender'. In fact Macpherson conformed a little too closely to the rules, and the Homeric, biblical, and Miltonic echoes in his work helped to draw attention to its lack of authenticity.

FINLAY, Ian Hamilton (1925–   ), Scottish poet, graphic artist, and sculptor, born in Nassau in the Bahamas and brought up in Scotland. He became widely known in the 1960s as a leading figure in the *concrete poetry movement, and has published many handsome and innovative pamphlets and volumes of verse in association with his own Wild Hawthorn Press and other little presses. His creation of a sculpture garden at Stonypath, Little Sparta, in southern Scotland is celebrated for its combinations of nature, word, image, and artefact, and its reconciliation of the classical with the modern.

Finn, or **Fionn,** the principal hero of the southern or later cycle of Irish legends, also called the Fenian or Ossianic cycle. Finn MacCoul has been thought a historical personage by some modern authorities; others regard him as mythical. He was the son of Cumal (Comhal) and father of Ossian, and is supposed to have lived in the 3rd cent. AD, a contemporary of King Cormac. The king appointed him chief of the Fianna (pron. Fēna) or *Fenians, a military body composed of men of exceptional strength and prowess, of whose heroic or romantic deeds there are endless tales. Finn was chosen their leader not for surpassing physical qualities, but on account of his truth, wisdom, and generosity. He is said to have perished in an affray with mutinous Fenians in AD 283.

For the story of Finn, Grainne, and Diarmid see GRAINNE; see also FINGAL.

Finn, Phineas, hero of A. Trollope's novels *Phineas Finn* and *Phineas Redux*.

Finnegans Wake, a prose work by J. *Joyce, published 1939. It is written in a unique and extremely difficult style, making use of puns and portmanteau words (using at least 40 languages besides English), and a very wide range of allusion. The central theme of the work is a cyclical pattern of history, of fall and resurrection inspired by *Vico's *Scienza nuova*.

This is presented in the story of Humphrey Chimpden Earwicker, a Dublin tavern-keeper, and the book is apparently a dream-sequence representing the stream of his unconscious mind through the course of one night. Other characters are his wife Anna Livia Plurabelle, their sons Shem and Shaun, and their daughter Isabel. In the relationships of these characters all human experience, mythical and historical, is seen to be historically subsumed. In spite of its obscurity it contains passages of great lyrical beauty, and also much humour.

Finnsburh, *The Fight at* (known as 'The Finnsburh Fragment', to distinguish it from the 'Finnsburh Episode' in *Beowulf*), a 48-line fragmentary poem in Old English dealing with part of the tragic tale of Finn and Hildeburh, a later part of which is sung by the scôp in *Beowulf*, II. 1063–1159. An attempt is made to heal the long-standing feud between the Danes and the Frisians by the marriage of the Frisian king Finn to Hildeburh, the sister of Hnaef who is king of the Half-Danes. Apparently after a period of peace, the feud breaks out again in a bloody battle at Finn's court and Hnaef is killed, as is his nephew, the son of Finn and Hildeburh. The beginning of this battle is the subject of the fragment; the *Beowulf* episode seems to begin almost immediately after its end as Hildeburh laments the tragedy. After an uneasy winter truce, during which the Danes have to remain as guests of Finn, the slayer of their leader, the Danes gain vengeance by killing Finn when the spring comes. The fragment is included by F. Klaeber in his edition of *Beowulf* (1922, etc.) and in other editions such as Wrenn's; see also interpretation in Part III of R. W. *Chambers's *Beowulf: An Introduction* (rev. C. L. Wrenn, 1959, 245–89).

FIONA MACLEOD, see SHARP, W.

Fiordespina, in *Orlando furioso*, a princess who falls in love with *Bradamante, being led by her armour to take her for a man.

FIRBANK, (Arthur Annesley) Ronald (1886–1926), novelist, son of Sir Thomas Firbank, MP (1850–1910), and grandson of Joseph Firbank (1819–86), a wealthy self-made railway contractor; he derived from the latter an income which enabled him to travel extensively and to pay for the publication of most of his own work. His education was largely private until he went to Trinity Hall, Cambridge, where he took no examinations, but met R. H. *Benson, who received him in 1907 into the Roman Catholic Church. He had already published in 1905 a volume of two stories, *Odette d'Antrevernes* (revised version, 1916) and *A Study in Temperament*; this was followed by several novels: *Vainglory* (1915); *Inclinations* (1916); *Caprice* (1917, the story of the spectacularly brief and dazzling theatrical career of the daughter of a rural dean); *Valmouth* (1919, set in a watering place dominated by the erotic and manipulative black masseuse Mrs Yajñavalkya); *Santal* (1921, set in North Africa); and *The Flower beneath the Foot* (1923). A play, *The Princess Zoubaroff*, was published in 1920. The first of his novels to be financed by a publisher, not by himself, was *Prancing Nigger* (1924), which appeared under that title in America, and under his own preferred title, *Sorrow in Sunlight*, in Britain; set in the West Indies, 'with a brilliant background of sunlight, sea, and as tropical' as he could make it, it describes the social aspirations and adventures of a black family, the Mouths. (In this novel he himself appears, characteristically, as the name of an orchid, 'a dingy lilac blossom of rarity untold'.) His last finished work, *Concerning the Eccentricities of Cardinal Pirelli* (1926), appeared shortly after his death, from a disease of the lungs, in Rome; other posthumous publications include *The Artificial Princess* (1934) and *The New Rythum and Other Pieces* (1962); the latter includes a very early work, *Lady Appledore's Mésalliance*, and chapters from an unfinished novel, set in New York, on which he was working when he died.

Dandy, aesthete, exotic, homosexual, and habitué of the *Café Royal, Firbank received little encouragement as a writer during his lifetime (except from such pro-Modernists as the *Sitwells), but nevertheless succeeded in creating a distinctive 'Firbankian' style, in both life and works. His use of dialogue, his oblique narration, his highly coloured fantasies, and his intense concentration of language and image are now seen as truly innovative, and some writers have claimed that he did more to liberate the novel from 19th-cent. concepts of realism than *Joyce himself. Those who show traces of his influence include E. *Waugh, I. *Compton-Burnett, *Gerhardie, and M. *Spark. See *Ronald Firbank: A Memoir* (1930) by I. K. Fletcher, and Brigid *Brophy's appreciative critical biography *Prancing Novelist* (1973). *The Early Firbank* (1991) collects all his writings up to 1908.

Fir Bolgs, legendary early invaders of Ireland, according to tradition of an Iberian tribe, who were driven into Arran, Islay, and the Hebrides by the *Milesians.

FIRDAUSI, Abul Kasim Mansur (*c*.950–1020), Persian poet and author of the *Shahnama* (or *Shanameh*), the great epic which recounts the legendary history of the ancient kings and heroes of Persia. It is known to English readers principally through M. *Arnold's version of one of its main incidents, *'Sohrab and Rustum'.

Firumbras, Sir, see FERUMBRAS.

FISCHER, Tibor (1959–   ), novelist, born in Stockport of Hungarian parents, and educated at Cambridge. His first novel, *Under the Frog,* is a tragi-comic account of life in Hungary after the war and during the revolution of 1956, seen in part through the eyes of a travelling basketball team. This was followed by *The Thought Gang* (1994), in which a failed philosopher and a one-armed bank robber combine forces to form 'The Thought Gang', and plan the ultimate bank robbery. *The Collector Collector* (1997) is the anecdote-filled tale of a garrulous Sumerian bowl with a mischievous streak and a memory full of fantastic stories.

FISHER, St John (1469–1535), educated at Michael-house (absorbed in Trinity College, 1546), Cambridge, of which he was appointed master in 1497. He became chancellor of the university and bishop of Rochester, 1504, and was president of Queens' College, Cambridge, from 1505 to 1508. He was a patron of *Erasmus and induced him to lecture on Greek at Cambridge from 1511 to 1514. He wrote three treatises against the Lutheran Reformation and was fined for denying the validity of the divorce of Queen Catherine, 1534. He was committed to the Tower for refusing to swear to the Act of Succession, and the pope did not improve his chances of escape from death by sending him a cardinal's hat while he was in prison. Fisher was deprived, attainted, and beheaded for refusing to acknowledge *Henry VIII as supreme head of the Church. His Latin theological works were issued in 1597 (republished 1967); his English works, edited by J. E. B. Mayor, appeared in 1876. His English prose style showed a great advance, in point of rhetorical artifice and effect, on that of his predecessors. He was canonized in 1935 and is commemorated on 22 June.

Fisher, Roy, see JAZZ POETRY.

FitzBoodle, George Savage, one of *Thackeray's pseudonyms. As the narrator of the *FitzBoodle Papers,* published in *Fraser's Magazine* 1842–3, FitzBoodle, a bachelor clubman, tells the story of his own amorous misadventures.

FITZGERALD, Edward (1809–83). FitzGerald, whose parents owned estates in England and Ireland, was the third son in a family of eight and was born in Suffolk, where he spent most of his life. He was educated at the King Edward VI Grammar School, Bury St Edmunds, and Trinity College, Cambridge. He never engaged in any profession or made any extended travels, but often visited London. His quirky but engaging personality made him much beloved by many close friends, who included *Thackeray, Alfred and Frederick *Tennyson, and *Carlyle. He lived for 16 years in a cottage on his family's estate at Boulge, and for the last 23 years of his life he was based in Woodbridge. In these years he spent much time sailing with Lowestoft fishermen off the Suffolk coast. His first published book (1849) was a biography of the Quaker poet Bernard Barton, whose daughter he afterwards married; the middle-aged couple were incompatible and separated after a few months. In 1851 he published *Euphranor, a Dialogue on Youth* and later he produced translations of plays by *Calderón, *Aeschylus, and *Sophocles, a collection of aphorisms, and a selection of *Crabbe's poetry. His only celebrated work is his free translation of *The Rubáiyát of *Omar Khayyám* (1859). His other translations from Persian included Attar's *Bird Parliament* and Jami's *Salaman and Absal.* He was a prolific and delightful letter writer, whose anecdotes of his literary friends have been a gold mine to biographers. His *Collected Letters,* which had previously appeared in selected versions, was published in 1980, ed. A. M. and A. B. Terhune.

FITZGERALD, F(rancis) Scott (Key) (1896–1940), American novelist and short story writer, born in Minnesota and educated at Princeton, where, as a friend and contemporary of E. *Wilson, he aimed for stardom in the social, athletic, and literary fields. His first novel, *This Side of Paradise* (1920), made him instantly famous; shortly after its publication he married the glamorous Zelda Sayre, and together they embarked on a life of high living, big spending, and party-going, fortified by a view of themselves as representative figures of the 'Jazz Age'. He published stories in fashionable periodicals such as the *Saturday Evening Post, Vanity Fair,* and the *Smart Set,* in which he chronicled the mood and manners of the times; these were collected as *Flappers and Philosophers* (1920) and *Tales of the Jazz Age* (1922), the latter including his child's-eye fantasy of extravagance, 'The Diamond as Big as the Ritz'. *The Beautiful and Damned* (1922), a novel about a wealthy, doomed, and dissipated marriage, was followed by *The Great Gatsby* (1925), widely considered his finest work. This is the story of shady, mysterious financier Jay Gatsby's romantic and destructive passion for Daisy Buchanan, played against a backdrop of Long Island glamour and New York squalor; the story is narrated by the innocent outsider Nick Carraway, Gatsby's neighbour and Daisy's distant cousin, who observes from a distance as adultery, hard drinking, fast driving, and finally murder take their toll, as the age of 'miracles, art and excess' turns to ashes. More short stories followed (*All the Sad Young Men*, 1926; *Taps at Reveille*, 1935), but by this time Zelda was suffering from mental breakdown, Scott from the effects of their violent lives, and *Tender is the Night* (1934, but later in various revised versions) records, through the story of American psychiatrist Dick Diver and his schizophrenic wife Nicole, his own sense of impending disaster. This novel, with its Riviera setting and cast of predominantly idle, wealthy expatriates, was not well received in the America of the Depression, and Fitzgerald's own 'crack-up' accelerated, as Zelda failed to recover: he died in Hollywood, of a heart attack, after working as a screenwriter, leaving his last novel, *The Last Tycoon*, unfinished. It appeared in 1941, edited by E. Wilson, and was followed by a posthumous collection (1945), in which he records that 'ten years this side of fortynine, I suddenly realised that I had prematurely cracked', and analyses his own deterioration. See *The Far Side of Paradise* (1951, rev. 1965), a biography by A. Mizener.

FITZGERALD, Penelope Mary (1916–2000), only daughter of the essayist and humorist E. V. *Knox. She was born in Lincoln and educated at Wycombe Abbey and Somerville College, Oxford. In 1941 she married Desmond Fitzgerald (d. 1976). Her first book was a biography of the *Pre-Raphaelite painter Edward *Burne-Jones (1975), which was followed by a composite biography of her father and his three brothers (1977). In the same year she published her first novel, *The Golden Child*, a murder mystery involving an exhibition of Egyptian treasures in a London museum. *The Bookshop* (1978) describes life in a small Suffolk community, while *Offshore* (1979), which draws on the author's own experiences and which won the *Booker Prize for fiction, is about life among a group of houseboat-owners on the Thames during the 1960s. This was followed by *Human Voices* (1980), a gently comic story of the BBC during the Second World War; *At Freddie's* (1982), set in a West End stage school; *Innocence* (1986), which has an Italian setting; *The Beginnings of Spring* (1988), the story of an Englishman born and living in Moscow whose wife suddenly leaves him without explanation; and *The Gate of Angels* (1990), a love story set in Edwardian Cambridge. *The Blue Flower* (1996) recreates the life of the German Romantic poet Novalis (F. L. *Hardenberg). She also wrote a biography of the poet Charlotte *Mew and her circle, published in 1984.

Fitzpiers, Edred, a character in Hardy's *The Woodlanders*.

FITZRALPH, Richard (d. 1360), frequently referred to as 'Armachanus', chancellor of Oxford (1333) and archbishop of Armagh (1347). He was greatly admired as a preacher, attacked the friars, and was arraigned before the pope at Avignon in 1357 to defend his opinions, which he did in his *Defensio Curatorum*. He was regarded as the official spokesman of the secular clergy against the friars, and he wrote a treatise against the friars' doctrine of obligatory poverty, *De Pauperie Salvatoris*, in which he discussed 'dominion' or 'lordship', taking a view on the subject similar to that later adopted by *Wyclif. See K. Walsh, *A Fourteenth-Century Scholar and Primate: Richard Fitzralph in Oxford, Avignon and Armagh* (1981).

Fitzrovia, a term coined to describe the area north of Oxford Street, London, which centred first on the Fitzroy Tavern, 'a largish pub on the corner of Charlotte Street', and which was, in the words of A. *John (*Finishing Touches*, 1964), 'the Artist's Quarter, its only rival being Chelsea'; its focus then moved, according to Julian Maclaren-Ross (*Memoirs of the Forties*, 1965), to the Wheatsheaf. Dylan *Thomas, W. *Empson, Tambimuttu of *Poetry London*, W. *Lewis, G. *Orwell, and many of the characters observed by A. *Powell were among its habitués.

FITZROY, Vice-Admiral Robert (1805–65). He commanded the *Beagle* in the surveying expedition to Patagonia and the Straits of Magellan (1823–36), having C. *Darwin as naturalist for the last five years; like Darwin, he wrote a narrative of the voyage. He was governor of New Zealand 1843–5. He became chief of the new meteorological department of the board of trade in 1854, suggested the plan of the Fitzroy barometer, and instituted a system of storm warnings, the first British weather forecasts. He died by his own hand.

FITZSTEPHEN, William, author of a Latin life of *Becket (c.1180), which contains a valuable account of early London first printed in *Stow's *Survey of London* (1598). It was translated by H. E. Butler in F. M. Stenton, *Norman London: An Essay* (1934).

Fizkin, Horatio, in Dickens's *Pickwick Papers*, the Buff candidate in the Eatanswill election.

F.J., *The Pleasant Fable of Ferdinando Jeronimi and Leonora de Valasco*, normally referred to, from its running headline, as *The Adventures of Master F.J.*; a novella by G. *Gascoigne, supposedly translated 'out of the Italian riding tales of *Bartello*', but probably his own invention.

It concerns the love affair between F.J., a Venetian, and the lady of the house where he is staying in Lombardy. The love affair is pursued and discussed in a large number of letters and poems; after enjoying Leonora's favours for a time, F.J. is supplanted by her secretary, and returns to Venice, 'spending there the rest of his dayes in a dissolute kind of lyfe'. The novella exists in two versions: the first, printed in *A Hundreth Sundrie Flowres* in 1573, is set in the north of England, is frankly erotic, and has every appearance of being a *roman à clef*. The second, printed in *The Posies of George Gascoigne* (1575), is more fully Italianate and has been to some extent expurgated.

Flamineo, a character in Webster's *The White Devil*.

FLANAGAN, Mary (1943–), novelist and short story writer, born in America to Irish parents, resident in England since 1969. Flanagan's work thrives on the tension between her characters' often transgressive behaviour and her own immaculate, disciplined prose. Her novels *Trust* (1987) and *Rose Reason* (1991) have a Jamesian leisure and complexity; *Bad Girls* (1984) and *The Blue Woman* (1994) are punchy collections of stories; *Adèle* (1997) a disturbingly erotic novella.

Flashman, a character in *Tom Brown's Schooldays* by Thomas *Hughes, revived in a series of humorous novels by George MacDonald Fraser (see HISTORICAL FICTION).

FLATMAN, Thomas (1637–88), educated at Winchester and New College, Oxford, much esteemed as a painter of miniatures; he also wrote poetry. *Poems and Songs* (1674) contains 'A Thought of Death', 'Death, a Song', and 'The Dying Christian to his Soul', the last of which was imitated by *Pope.

FLAUBERT, Gustave (1821–80), French novelist, one of the masters of 19th-cent. fiction, born in Rouen, the second son of a physician. His first published novel, *Madame Bovary* (1857), the story of the adulteries and suicide of a doctor's wife in provincial Normandy, is notable for its rigorous psychological development, and manifests the qualities that mark all of his mature work: authenticity of detail, an impersonal narrative method, a precise and harmonious style. Certain passages in *Madame Bovary* having been judged to be offensive to public morals, Flaubert, his publisher, and his printer were tried but acquitted. Ancient Carthage is minutely recreated in his next novel, *Salammbô* (1862), for which he undertook detailed researches. *L'Éducation sentimentale* (1869), Flaubert's 'moral history of the men of my generation', charts the progress and decline of the successive amours, enthusiasms, and ambitions of Frédéric Moreau and his circle of friends, against the background of Paris in the 1840s. The unfinished and posthumously published *Bouvard et Pécuchet* (1881), relating the various projects and experiments of two retired copying clerks, was to form 'a sort of farcical critical encyclopaedia'. His three stories, *Trois Contes* (1877, 'Un cœur simple', 'La Légende de Saint-Julien l'Hospitalier', 'Hérodias') are set respectively in his own period, in the Middle Ages, and in biblical antiquity: the first (in which the simple servant Félicité, after a lifetime of pious drudgery, confuses the Holy Ghost with a stuffed parrot) is the best known. The fantastic visions of *La Tentation de Saint-Antoine* (1874) had exercised him intermittently over more than 25 years. Flaubert's *Correspondence* (1973–), which contains searching reflections on the art of fiction and the life of the novelist, has earned him the reputation of the exemplary artist.

Flavius, the faithful steward of *Timon of Athens in Shakespeare's play.

FLAXMAN, John (1755–1826), English neo-classical sculptor and draughtsman. Flaxman was steeped in the writings of *Winckelmann, and his linear style is influenced by Greek vases and classical reliefs. He designed very many funerary sculptures, of which the most famous is the monument to the earl of Mansfield (1793–1801, London, Westminster Abbey). From 1787 to 1794 he studied in Rome and here created a series of illustrations to the *Iliad* and the *Odyssey* (*Pope's translation, published 1793) which won him an immense reputation throughout Europe. His illustrations to Dante's *Divina commedia* (1793) were commissioned by T. *Hope and praised by *Goethe (1799). Flaxman maintained a lifelong friendship with *Blake; the two artists influenced one another, and Blake engraved Flaxman's illustrations to *Hesiod in 1817. He was created professor of sculpture at the Royal Academy in 1810, and his lectures were published posthumously in 1829.

Fleance, son of *Banquo in Shakespeare's *Macbeth*, who escapes (III. iii) from Macbeth's hired killers in fulfilment of the witches' prophecy that Banquo's issue will be kings.

FLECKER, James (Herman) Elroy (1884–1915), educated at Uppingham and Trinity College, Oxford, where he was influenced by the last flowering of the *Aesthetic movement. In the course of a career in the consular service (which further emphasized his love of the East), he produced several volumes of lyrical romantic verse, some of which was included in *Georgian Poetry*: his collections include *The Bridge of Fire* (1907), *Forty-Two Poems* (1911), and his best-known collection, *The Golden Journey to Samarkand* (1913). He also published *The Grecians* (1910), a dialogue on education, and an experimental, highly individual novel, *The King of Alsander* (1914). Flecker died of tuberculosis. The work for which he is best remembered, the poetic Eastern play *Hassan*, was published posthumously in 1922, and his other play, *Don Juan*, in 1925.

FLECKNOE, Richard (d. ?1678), a lay brother, said to have been a Roman Catholic priest, a writer with an interest in experimental forms, many of whose works were published privately. His *Miscellanea* (1653) includes a defence of the stage (in his 'Discourse upon Languages') and a lament for the theatres silenced under the Commonwealth. His *Ariadne* (1654) is probably the first English opera, though the music (which he composed himself) is lost; its preface, which discusses the use of recitative and the art of writing words for music, shows that he was familiar with current developments in Italy. His *Love's Dominion* (1654), a pastoral with songs, was performed privately on the Continent, and acted after the Restoration under the title *Love's Kingdom*. Its reputation for insipidity, and *Marvell's earlier satire ('Flecknoe, an English priest at Rome', ?1645), suggested to Dryden his attack on *Shadwell, *Mac Flecknoe.

Fledgeby, in Dickens's *Our Mutual Friend*, a cowardly villain, who conceals his moneylending business under the description 'Pubsey and Co.'

Fleet Prison, in the neighbourhood of the present Farringdon Street, London, alongside the Fleet river. It was built in the time of Richard I, and long afterwards served as a place of imprisonment for persons condemned by the Star Chamber. After the abolition of the latter in 1640, it served mainly as a debtors' prison, until demolished in 1848, and it figures as such in Dickens's novels, notably *Pickwick Papers*.

Fleet Street, previously the headquarters of London journalism, takes its name from the old Fleet river, which, running south from Hampstead, along the line of the Farringdon Road, flowed into the Thames at Blackfriars, passing under the Fleet Bridge at what is now Ludgate Circus. In its upper course it appears to have been known as the Hole Bourne (Holborn), or the Turnmill Brook. Boats could ascend the Fleet as far as the Holborn Bridge as late as the 16th cent. (*Stow). *Wren's plan for rebuilding London after the Great Fire proposed to canalize it as far as Holborn Bridge.

FLEMING, Ian Lancaster (1908–64), journalist and thriller writer, educated at Eton and Sandhurst; he subsequently worked for Reuters and as foreign manager of Kemsley newspapers. His first novel, *Casino Royale* (1953), introduced his handsome, tough, romantic hero James Bond, who subsequently appeared in many other adventures with exotic settings, including *Live and Let Die* (1954), *Diamonds Are Forever* (1956), *From Russia with Love* (1957), *Goldfinger* (1959), and *On Her Majesty's Secret Service* (1963). Bond also appeared in many highly popular films, which mingle sex and violence with a wit that, for some, renders them intellectually respectable: these include *Dr No* (1962), *From Russia with Love* (1963), and *Goldfinger* (1964). See also SPY FICTION.

FLEMING, (Robert) Peter (1907–71), journalist and travel writer, brother of Ian *Fleming, was educated at Eton and Christ Church, Oxford. He wrote regularly for the *Spectator* (in later years as 'Strix') and *The Times*, but is remembered largely for his travel books, which include *Brazilian Adventure* (1933), a characteristically light-hearted and debonair account of a search party in the Mato Grosso, and *News from Tartary* (1936), an account of an overland journey from Peking to Kashmir.

Fleming, (1) Rose and Agnes, characters in Dickens's *Oliver Twist*; (2) Archdeacon, in Scott's *The Heart of Midlothian*; (3) Lady Mary, in his *The Abbot*; (4) Sir Malcolm, in his *Castle Dangerous*; (5) Paul, in *Longfellow's Hyperion*; (6) Farmer, Rhoda, and Dahlia, in Meredith's *Rhoda Fleming*.

Fleshly School of Poetry, see ROSSETTI, D. G., and BUCHANAN, R.

FLETCHER, Giles, the elder (1546–1611), educated at Eton and King's College, Cambridge, of which he became a fellow, 1568; he was sent as envoy to Russia in 1588. He published *Of the Russe Common Wealth*, a pioneering account of Russian government, in 1591. His *Licia, or Poemes of Love* (1593) is notable both for being one of the first sonnet sequences to follow the publication of *Astrophel and Stella* (1591) and for having a dedication in which he sets out his belief that 'a man may write of love, and not bee in love, as well as of husbandrie, and not goe to plough.' He was the uncle of John *Fletcher and father of Giles and Phineas *Fletcher. His English works were edited by Lloyd E. Berry (1964).

FLETCHER, Giles, the younger (?1586–1623), the younger son of Giles *Fletcher the elder, educated at Trinity College, Cambridge. He was rector of Alderton, Suffolk, and a poet of the Spenserian school whose allegorical treatment of religious themes is said to have influenced *Milton. His principal work was *Christs Victorie, and Triumph in Heaven, and Earth, over, and after Death* (1610). His works and those of his brother Phineas (below) were edited by Boas in two volumes, 1908; he is generally considered the better poet.

FLETCHER, John (1579–1625), born at Rye in Sussex, where his father (subsequently chaplain at the execution of *Mary Queen of Scots and bishop of Bristol and of London) was then minister. John Fletcher was nephew of Giles *Fletcher the elder and cousin of Giles the younger and Phineas *Fletcher. He was educated at Corpus Christi College, Cambridge, and, his father dying (in debt and under royal displeasure) in 1596, he was left to make his own way in the world. Little is known of his early life; about 1606 he began to write plays in collaboration with F. *Beaumont, and, before his death of the plague, he produced some 15 plays with Beaumont, some 16 of which he was sole author, and collaborated with *Massinger, *Rowley, *Middleton, *Jonson, *Chapman, *Shakespeare and others in the writing of many other works.

The principal plays of which Fletcher was probably sole author are: *The Faithful Shepherdess* (printed not later than 1610); *Wit without Money*, a comedy, printed 1639; *Valentinian*, perf. 1610–14; *The Loyal Subject*, acted 1618; *The Mad Lover*, acted ?1616; *The Humor-

ous Lieutenant, acted 1619; *Women Pleased*, a comedy, perf. *c*.1620; **The Wilde Goose Chase*, perf. 1621; *The Pilgrim*, a comedy, perf. 1621; *The Island Princess*, a romantic comedy, perf. 1621; *Monsieur Thomas*, a comedy, perf. 1619, printed 1639; **The Woman's Prize*, written 1604–17; *A Wife for a Month*, a romantic drama, perf. 1624; **Rule a Wife and Have a Wife*, perf. 1624; **The Chances*, written *c*.1617.

Plays certainly or probably by Beaumont and Fletcher are: *Four Plays in One*, four short plays (two founded on *Boccaccio, one on *Bandello, one an allegory about false and true friends) probably acted *c*.1608 (possibly with collaboration from N. *Field); *The Scornful Lady*, perf. 1610, printed 1616; **Philaster*, written 1609; **The Maid's Tragedy*, written 1610–11; **A King and No King*, perf. 1611; *The Coxcomb*, a romantic comedy, perf. 1612; *Cupid's Revenge*, a tragedy based on material in the second book of Sidney's **Arcadia*, perf. 1612, printed 1615; *The Captain*, a comedy, perf. 1612–13; *The Honest Man's Fortune*, printed 1647; **Bonduca*, perf. 1613–14; *The Knight of Malta*, a tragi-comedy performed before March 1619, printed 1647; **Thierry King of France*, printed 1621 (with Beaumont and Massinger); *Love's Cure* (later rewritten by Massinger, printed 1647).

Probably by Fletcher and some other dramatists: *Love's Pilgrimage* and *The Double Marriage*, comedies, printed 1647; *Sir John Van Olden *Barnavelt*, perf. 1619; **The False One*, perf. *c*. 1620; *The Little French Lawyer*, **The Custom of the Country*, and *The Laws of Candy*, all printed 1647; **The Spanish Curate* and **The Beggar's Bush*, both perf. 1622. In all the above Fletcher certainly or probably collaborated with Massinger. The romantic drama **The Lover's Progress*, perf. 1623, was later revised by Massinger. *The Maid in the Mill* was written by Fletcher and Rowley (licensed 1623). **The Elder Brother*, printed 1637, is thought to have been written by Fletcher and revised by Massinger. *The Fair Maid of the Inn* was probably the result of a collaboration between Fletcher and Massinger, possibly with assistance from Jonson, *Webster, and Rowley. *The Nice Valour*, a comedy, printed 1647 (which contains the lyric 'Hence all you vain delights', which suggested **'Il Penseroso'*), was probably by Fletcher and Middleton. **The Bloody Brother, or Rollo, Duke of Normandy* (perf. *c*.1616) is by Fletcher, Jonson, Chapman, and Massinger. *The Noble Gentleman*, a comedy, acted 1626, is probably by Fletcher, possibly with Beaumont or Rowley. Fletcher also collaborated with Shakespeare in **The Two Noble Kinsmen* and **Henry VIII*.

The attribution of various plays in the Beaumont and Fletcher canon by use of versification and idiom tests was pioneered by F. G. Fleay, in 'On Metrical Tests as Applied to Dramatic Poetry' (1874), and his successors in the field include E. H. C. Oliphant (*The Plays of Beaumont and Fletcher*, 1927); C. Hoy ('The Shares of Fletcher and His Collaborators in the Beaumont and Fletcher Canon', in *Studies in Bibliography*, 1956–7, 1958–62); and B. Hensman, *The Shares of Fletcher,*

Field, and Massinger in Twelve Plays of the Beaumont and Fletcher Canon (1974). An edition of the works under the general editorship of F. Bowers is in preparation, ten volumes having appeared, 1966–96. Meanwhile the standard edition remains that of A. Glover and A. R. Waller (10 vols, 1905–12), and various works have been edited separately (see under individual entries).

FLETCHER, Phineas (1582–1650), the elder son of Giles *Fletcher the elder, educated at King's College, Cambridge, and rector of Higay, Norfolk. Like his brother Giles (above), he was a poet of the Spenserian school. His chief work, *The Purple Island* (1633), is an allegory of the human body and mind; *The Locusts, or Apollyonists* (1627) is a violently anti-Catholic piece with a conclave in hell thought by some to have influenced *Milton. *Brittain's Ida* (1628), attributed to *Spenser, appears to be his. The works of Giles and Phineas were edited in 2 vols, 1908–9, by Boas.

Flintwinch, a character in Dickens's **Little Dorrit*. His wife was known as Affery.

Flite, Miss, a character in Dickens's **Bleak House*.

Flodden, or **Floddon Field,** the battle of Flodden, in Northumberland, fought on 9 Sept. 1513, when the earl of Surrey on behalf of Henry VIII (then in France) defeated James IV of Scotland, the latter being killed on the field. It was made the subject of poems, of rejoicing or lament, on both sides of the border. *Skelton's 'Agaynst the Scottes' is a rude song of exultation of the English victory, and several English ballads appeared. On the Scottish side there is the beautiful lament 'The Flowers o' the Forest', of which the most popular version is by J. *Elliot: see also COCKBURN, A. The battle is described in the sixth canto of Scott's **Marmion: A Tale of Flodden Field*.

FLORENCE OF WORCESTER (d. 1118), a monk of Worcester, traditionally regarded as the author of the *Chronicon ex Chronicis* (based on the work of Marianus, an Irish monk, as well as on a lost version of the **Anglo-Saxon Chronicle* up to 1130) from its beginning to 1117, when it was continued by other hands to its end in 1295. A modern view regards the *Chronicon* as the work of John of Worcester, the claims of the name of Florence being on the material of the Chronicle up to 1117, not on its writing. For all matters relating to the medieval chronicles, see A. Gransden, *Historical Writing in England c.550–c.1307* (1974).

Florent, see GOWER, J., and CANTERBURY TALES, 6.

Flores and Blancheflour, see FLORIS AND BLANCHEFLOUR.

Florimell, in Spenser's **Faerie Queene*, Bks III and IV, the type of chastity and virtue in woman. She is in love with the knight Marinell, who 'sets nought' by her. She takes refuge from her pursuers in the sea and is imprisoned by Proteus. Finally the heart of Marinell is touched by her complaint, and Neptune orders Proteus to release her.

FLORIO, John (c.1553–1626), son of an Italian Protestant refugee, born in London and educated at Magdalen College, Oxford. After a spell as tutor to the earl of Southampton he was reader in Italian to Anne of Denmark, wife of James I (1603), and groom of the privy chamber from 1604. His interesting collections of Italian–English dialogues, *Firste* and *Second Frutes*, were followed in 1598 by an Italian dictionary entitled *A Worlde of Wordes*; it was revised and augmented as *Queen Anna's New World of Words* (1611). His most important work was his translation from *Montaigne: *Essayes or Morall, Politike and Millitarie Discourses* (1603, 1613). Not only did Florio make Montaigne's work available in English, but he displayed great resourcefulness and ingenuity in the process of translation. Florio's friends included *Daniel and *Jonson, and some have thought that Shakespeare ridiculed him in *Love's Labour's Lost*. Certainly Shakespeare drew on Florio's version of Montaigne, in *The Tempest* and elsewhere. Florio has also been suggested as the earliest translator of the *Decameron*. There is a book on him by F. A. *Yates (1934).

Floris and Blanchefiour, a Middle English metrical romance in 1,083 lines from the first half of the 13th cent., based on a 12th-cent. French original and surviving in four later manuscripts, all of which lack the opening lines.

Floris and Blanchefiour are brought up together: he is the son of a Saracen king and she the daughter of a Christian lady who has been captured and brought to the king's court. They fall in love and Blanchefiour is banished. Floris sets off to find her, equipped with a precious cup and a magic ring which prove instrumental in his finding her and their ultimate marriage by consent of the emir. The story, which has analogues in the *Arabian Nights* and elsewhere, is the subject of *Boccaccio's *Filocolo*. The English romance is one of the most popular and 'romantic' of its genre. See editions by A. B. Taylor (1927) and in D. B. Sands, *Middle English Verse Romances* (1966), 279–309.

Florizel, in Shakespeare's *The Winter's Tale*, the prince of Bohemia who falls in love with the rustic *Perdita. 'Florizel' was the name adopted by George IV, when prince of Wales, in his correspondence with Mary *Robinson, the actress, with whose performance as Perdita he had been captivated.

Flosky, Mr, a character in Peacock's *Nightmare Abbey*, who illustrates the transcendentalism of *Coleridge.

Floure and the Leaf, The, a 15th-cent. allegory in 595 lines of rhyme-royal, formerly attributed to *Chaucer and included by Skeat in *Chaucerian and Other Pieces*, appended as vol. vii to his edition of Chaucer. The votaries of the flower and the leaf were the two parties in the mannered, courtly debates on love in the French poetry of writers such as *Deschamps. In the English poem, the poet wandering in a grove sees the white company of knights and ladies of the leaf (Diana, goddess of chastity) and the green company of the flower (Flora), 'folk that loved idleness' and had delight 'of no businesse but for to hunt and hauke and pley in medes'. It has the rather limited charm of its tradition, and it was modernized by *Dryden in his *Fables Ancient and Modern*. There is an edition by D. A. Pearsall (1962).

'Flowers of the Forest, The', see ELLIOT, J., and COCKBURN, A.

FLUDD, Robert (1574–1637), educated at St John's College, Oxford, and on the Continent; he became a fellow of the Royal College of Physicians in 1609, and had a successful practice. He entered the debate on the authenticity of the *Rosicrucian texts with his defence, *Apologia*, in 1616, and was deeply interested in Hermeticism and Neoplatonism, which he held to be of greater authority than *Aristotle and *Galen. His views on the universe as macrocosm–microcosm attracted much controversy, but despite his own mystical views on the circulation of the blood, he was the first to defend W. *Harvey's *De Motu Cordis*. The standard biography is by J. B. Craven, 1902; see also *The English Paracelsians* (1965) by A. G. Debus and *The Rosicrucian Enlightenment* (1972) by F. A. *Yates.

Fluellen, a pedantic but courageous Welsh captain in Shakespeare's *Henry V*.

Flute, in Shakespeare's *A Midsummer Night's Dream*, a bellows-mender, who takes the part of Thisbe in the play of 'Pyramus and Thisbe'.

flyting, derived from the Old English word *flītan*, to quarrel or dispute, was a verse contest in obloquy, practised in particular by the Scottish poets of the early 16th cent. The most famous example is the 'Flyting of *Dunbar and Kennedie'.

FO, Dario (1926–), Italian playwright, actor, director, and political activist, born in Varese in northern Italy. He has written and produced many classical *farces and comedies, often in collaboration with his wife Franca Rame: many of these have been performed worldwide in various adaptations and translations. Well known among them are *Morte accidentale di un anarchico* (1970; *Accidental Death of an Anarchist*, 1979), inspired by a 1969 bomb explosion in Milan and the subsequent death in police custody of innocent suspect Pino Pinelli; *Non si paga, non si paga!* (1970; *Can't Pay, Won't Pay*); and *Clacson Trombette & Pernacchi* (1981; *Trumpets and Raspberries*, 1984), a comedy which uses a mistaken identity ploy to explore political corruption and the workings of the Fiat corporation. Fo was awarded the *Nobel Prize in 1997.

Foedera, Conventiones et Cujuscunque Generis Acta Publica, a collection of public records in 20 volumes, by *Rymer and Robert Sanderson, published 1704–35. The documents (treaties, letters, etc. between kings of England and foreign states and sovereigns) extend down to 1654, and provide for the first time a printed record of the central documents of English history.

FOGAZZARO, Antonio (1842–1911), Italian novelist and essayist. His humour and powers of characterization are at their best in *Piccolo mondo antico* (*The Little World of the Past*, 1895), set north of Lake Lugano during the last ten years of Austrian rule, and reflecting the author's Catholic preoccupations. Owing to his unorthodoxy two of his novels, *Il santo* (*The Saint*, 1905) and *Leila* (1910), were placed on the *Index Expurgatorius.

FOLENGO, Teophilo (1491–1544), an Italian monk, who under the pseudonym 'Merlin Coccai' wrote a long burlesque-heroic poem, *Opus Macaronicum*, in *macaronic Latin hexameters. Its hero is Baldus, who has for followers the giant Fracassus and the cunning Cingar. Rabelais's *Panurge is partly modelled on the latter.

folios and quartos, Shakespearian. Shakespeare's earliest published plays are referred to as folios or quartos according to the folding of the printed sheets and therefore the size of the book: folios being large, tall volumes and the quartos smaller and squarer.

Of about 750 copies of the First Folio printed between Feb. 1622 and Nov. 1623 and sold, probably for 15 shillings each unbound, by the *Jaggards, some 250 survive, 80 or so in the Folger Shakespeare Library and five, the next largest collection, in the British Library. A second Folio was issued in 1632, containing 'An Epitaph on . . . Shakespeare' by *Milton, which was his first published poem. A third Folio was issued in 1663, whose second impression of 1664 contained *Pericles* and six apocryphal plays; the fourth and last Folio was published in 1685. Except for the text of *Pericles* none of the Folios later than the first has any textual integrity.

Thirty-six plays, 18 printed for the first time, were arranged by *Heminges and Condell into sections of comedies, histories, and tragedies for F1. It was dedicated to William Herbert, earl of Pembroke, and Philip Herbert, earl of Montgomery, and contains the *Droeshout portrait and a list of 'the Principall Actors in all these Playes', together with commendatory verses by contemporaries including *Jonson.

During his lifetime 18 of Shakespeare's plays were published in quartos, and *Othello* appeared in 1622. Following A. W. *Pollard's analysis, it has generally been thought that over half of those quartos are 'bad' ones. The traditional explanation for this was that their texts are extremely corrupt as a result of their reconstruction from memory by a member, or members, of

their cast. Thus, Q1 of *The Merry Wives of Windsor* (1602) is probably based on the recollections of the actor who played the part of the Host. Some 'bad' quartos, for example *The First Part of the Contention* (1594) and *The True Tragedy of Richard Duke of York* (1595), were once thought of as source plays (for 2 and 3 *Henry VI*); similarly the quarto *The Taming of a Shrew* (1594) may be 'bad' and the Folio text, *The Taming of the Shrew*, is 'good'. In two cases, *Romeo and Juliet* (1597) and *Hamlet* (1603), 'good' second quartos were soon issued (in 1599 and 1604–5 respectively) to correct the 'bad' first quartos. The nature and number of these 'bad' quartos has been much disputed and hypotheses about their origins have included the possibility that they derive from shorthand accounts taken down by members of the theatrical company or of the audience, that they represent authorial first drafts, and that they represent shortened or altered versions of the play made for various circumstances, such as provincial touring.

Textual criticism and bibliography have largely been concerned with establishing relationships between the 'good' quartos (and in some cases the 'bad' ones as well) and their versions in the Folio, to determine on which text an editor is to base his edition. In trying to establish this relationship scholars have mainly sought to determine the nature of the copy of which the printers made use. The chief types of copy which have been distinguished are: (1) 'foul papers', that is an original authorial draft, as in Q1 of *A Midsummer Night's Dream* (1600); (2) a fair scribal copy, as in F's text of *The Tempest*; (3) a prompt copy from the theatre, as in F's text of *As You Like It*; (4) a memorial text, as discussed above; and (5) a reconstructed text, that is one based on an early quarto but where some kind of manuscript copy has also been used as in the case of F's *Richard III*. There is still much disagreement about the nature of these categories and into which ones the plays in their various quarto and folio versions belong.

The fullest accounts of F1 are W. W. *Greg's *The Shakespeare First Folio* (1955) and C. *Hinman's *The Printing and Proof-Reading of the First Folio of Shakespeare* (1963); see also his Norton Facsimile of F (1968; 2nd edn, 1996). Sixteen facsimiles of quartos were issued in the Oxford Shakespeare Quarto Facsimiles series, ed. W. W. Greg and C. Hinman (1939–75) and the series has been continued by the *Malone Society. Stanley Wells and Gary Taylor, *William Shakespeare: A Textual Companion* (1987) provides a valuable introduction to the subject.

folklore, the traditional beliefs, legends, and customs current among the common people; and the study of them. The term was first introduced by W. J. *Thoms in the *Athenaeum* (1846).

folk song, a song, origin usually unknown, that is handed down orally from generation to generation, evolving as it does so at the whim of individual performers, and often existing in different forms in different parts of the country. In England the first person to make any systematic attempt at recording the material in this field was *Percy in the middle of the 18th cent.; he was concerned only with the poetry, but interest in the music followed naturally enough. The end of the 19th and the beginning of the 20th cents saw an immense increase of activity in the collection, transcription, and publication of folk songs, before the rapidly increasing industrialization and urbanization of the whole country effectively wiped them out for ever. See also SHARP, C.; GRAINGER, P.; HOLST; VAUGHAN WILLIAMS.

Fomors, the sea-giants of Gaelic mythology. They are represented as more ancient than the gods (the *Tuatha Dé Danann), and as having been ousted by them and destroyed at the battle of Moytura (C. Squire, *Mythology of the British Islands*, 1905). See also BALOR.

Fondlewife, one of the characters in Congreve's *The Old Bachelor*.

FONTANE, Theodor (1819–98), German travel writer and novelist. His travel writing includes an account of his first summer in London (*Ein Sommer in London*, 1954) and many volumes describing travels in Germany. He is best known for the novels *Frau Jenny Treibel* (1892), an ironic criticism of middle-class hypocrisy and small-mindedness, and *Effi Briest* (1895), the story of a spoilt but charming girl who marries an older man on the advice of her parents and because she is infatuated with the idea of marriage and social status. Effi's adultery, discovered by her stiff husband several years later, is punished by his banishing her and indoctrinating their child against her. Fontane has been compared to *Flaubert and *Tolstoy in his handling of the theme of adultery.

FONTENELLE, Bernard le Bovier (1657–1757), French man of letters. The nephew of *Corneille, he was a man of wide curiosity and learning. His varied output is notable for his *Dialogues des morts* (1683), a deceptively light-hearted attack on received ideas, and for his *Entretiens sur la pluralité des mondes* (1686), a graceful introduction to contemporary astronomical ideas and speculations, which represented the first true case of scientific popularization. His demystifying influence strongly marked the early phase of the *Enlightenment.

Fonthill Abbey, see BECKFORD, W.

food, the literature of. This has a relatively short history. Guillaume Tirel, called 'Taillevant' (d. ?1395), is the only medieval cook about whose life anything is known. The first great French cookery book, Le Cuisinier françois, was published in 1651 by François Pierre de la Varenne. Menon (first name unknown) was a mid-18th-cent. chef who seems to have invented the phrase 'La nouvelle cuisine' in a book of that name in 1742; François Marin was an author-chef associated with Menon. François Massialot (1660–1773), one of

the few chef-writers whose dates are known, recorded courtly recipes, but acknowledged the culinary needs of the bourgeoisie. The ideas of Antonin Carême (1784–1833) on the architectural appearance of food dominated the 19th cent. Up to this point, it is to be doubted whether many cooks could read: the books must have been intended for other, literate members of the household. Alexis Soyer (1809–58) was a chef and social reformer who wrote recipes for all classes who could read. Georges Auguste Escoffier (1846–1935) was the first businessman-chef: his contribution was to codify thousands of recipes. Neither of these, and few of their successors, were literary writers, but compilers of practical manuals, as was Mrs Beeton (1836–65) whose name remains well known: her famous book on *Household Management* (1861) first appeared in the *Englishwoman's Domestic Magazine*, 1859–61, and was many times reprinted under various titles. The first modern non-recipe food writing is probably that of Jean Anthelme Brillat-Savarin (1755–1826), lawyer and gastronome, whose *La Physiologie du gout* (1825) contains several of the most famous aphorisms about food such as 'The destiny of nations depends on how they nourish themselves.'

Most of the canon of food literature was written in the 20th cent. In Britain there were those who were principally providers of recipes, such as E. *David and J. *Grigson, and their heirs such as Claudia Roden (1936–   ) with *A Book of Middle Eastern Food*, 1968; *The Book of Jewish Food*, 1997. But literary writing about food is more closely allied with journalism than with cookery books, and outstanding practitioners include Alan Davidson (1924–2003), author of several magnificently researched books on fish, and American-born Paul Levy (1941–   ), whose *The Official Foodie Handbook* (1984, with Ann Barr) caught the mood of the 1980s and remains an interesting social document. (Literary food writing has been more common in North America than in Britain.) Of many distinguished general books on food, mention might also be made of Dorothy Hartley's historical survey *Food in England* (1954), and Patience Gray's Mediterranean essays *Honey from a Weed* (1986).

Descriptions of food and meals have been used to delineate characters, set social background, and advance the plots of novels throughout the history of the form: *Dickens, *Trollope, V. *Woolf, and many others have written memorable food scenes. A recent genre of fiction where food is at the centre has produced works such as John Lanchester's *The Debt to Pleasure* (1996), which features a foodie serial killer, and novels by *Esquivel and *Allende have included recipes as part of the text.

fool, the, a character appearing in various forms in English drama, most notably in the works of Shakespeare and his contemporaries. The character has a variety of origins, from the medieval court jester to the licensed clown of the *Feast of Fools. He appears in numerous incarnations in Shakespeare: as the simpleton (the clown in *The Winter's Tale*), the rogue (*Autolycus) and the wise court jester (*Touchstone in *As You Like It*), licensed to speak his wisdom, however satirically and however disrespectful. He is also related to the Arlecchino of the *commedia dell'arte*.

Richard *Tarlton was the most famous comic actor of his day, known for his talent for improvised doggerel; he played the main comic parts in the Queen's Company of players until his death in 1588; he is believed to have been the inspiration for the character of *Yorick in *Hamlet*. In Shakespeare's company the part of the fool was played by William *Kemp until his retirement c.1599, when he was replaced by Robert Armin, a somewhat more subtle actor for whom Shakespeare probably wrote the more complex parts of the fool in *King Lear* and *Feste in *Twelfth Night*. In their day, these three were among the best-loved actors in their company. They were closely associated with the parts they played, and Kemp's own name often appeared in the place of the characters' in early copies of the plays.

Fool of Quality, The, a novel in five volumes by H. *Brooke, published in Dublin 1765–70 and in London 1766–70.

In this unusual and impassioned work, which was highly influential in its day, Harry Clinton, the Fool of Quality, born in the later 17th cent., is the second son of the earl of Moreland; the narrative follows his education, growth, and manhood. The most important adult in his world is not his decadent father but his merchant uncle, Mr Clinton (sometimes Fenton), whose enlightened views on Harry's education (much influenced by *Rousseau's Émile and *Locke's On Education) guide the boy's growth into a wise and generous adult. Clinton is more than a merchant, for he carries a hint of kingly or even divine power. Harry is protected from calamity largely by his innocence, but Clinton possesses an omnipotence which enables him to rescue the unfortunate, such as Hammel Clement and his family, from terrible misfortune and destitution; and a philosophy which reconciles human wretchedness with divine providence. The various episodes, which are interrupted by much literary and philosophical digression (as well as by curious discussions between the author and a 'friend' on passages in the book itself) fluctuate between extremes of the euphoric and the despairing, and the tone of the narration is held at a high level of tearful, ecstatic, or nostalgic sensibility.

The book appealed greatly to *Wesley and to *Kingsley (who found it 'more pure, sacred and eternal than anything since the *Faerie Queene*', and who drew on it for his own novel *Yeast*); both produced new editions of it. (See also SENTIMENTAL NOVEL and BILDUNGSROMAN.)

FOOTE, Samuel (1720–77), actor and dramatist, who spent three years at Oxford, where he dissipated a fortune. He then turned to the stage, and as an actor was particularly successful in comic mimicry; acting in his own plays, he caricatured his fellow actors and other well-known persons, often savagely. He wrote a number of dramatic sketches, depending for their success on topical allusions, of which *Taste* (1752) was the first. *The Minor* (1760), a satire directed against the Methodists in which Foote mimicked *Whitefield as 'Dr Squintum', was his most powerful work. Other works include *The Liar* (1762), *The Patron* (1764, depicting *Dodington), and *The Mayor of Garret* (1764). In *The Maid of Bath* (1771) Foote pilloried Squire Long, the unscrupulous sexagenarian lover of Miss Elizabeth Linley, who was to marry *Sheridan. *The Nabob* (1772) was aimed at the directors of the East India Company and *Piety in Patterns* (1773) ridiculed *sentimental comedy and Richardson's *Pamela*. Foote had a leg amputated in 1766, after falling off his horse, but this did not quell his spirit; he received as compensation a patent for a theatre and built the new Haymarket in 1767. He was known to his contemporaries as 'the English Aristophanes'. His works were collected in 4 vols (1770–86).

Fopling Flutter, Sir, a character in Etherege's *The Man of Mode*.

Foppington, Lord, a character in Vanbrugh's comedy *The Relapse* and Sheridan's *A Trip to Scarborough*; also in C. Cibber's *The Careless Husband*.

Ford, and Mrs Ford, characters in Shakespeare's *The Merry Wives of Windsor*.

FORD, Ford Madox (formerly Ford Hermann Hueffer) (1873–1939), the son of Dr Francis Hueffer, a music critic of *The Times*, and grandson of Ford Madox Brown; much of his childhood was spent in *Pre-Raphaelite circles, an inheritance which deeply affected him and towards which he expressed ambiguous feelings in both critical and fictional works. His first published works were fairy stories (*The Brown Owl*, 1892, etc.). In 1894 he eloped with and married Elsie Martindale, an act which was prelude to a turbulent emotional life. In 1898 he met *Conrad and they collaborated in various works including the novels *The Inheritors* (1901) and *Romance* (1903); for some years they worked in happy intimacy, united by their faith in 'the novel as a work of Art', although from 1901 their relationship deteriorated: Ford's own published recollections of it are revealing but not reliable. During a diverse and productive literary career Ford published over 80 books, both fiction and non-fiction, and developed his own theory of 'Impressionism' in the novel. His *Fifth Queen* trilogy (1907, 1907, 1908), described by Conrad as 'a noble conception—the swan song of Historical Romance', describes in ornate and colourful prose the fate of Catherine Howard, wife of *Henry VIII, portrayed as an earnest, innocent Catholic idealist. In 1908 Ford embarked on two significant enterprises, an affair with the glamorous and emancipated novelist Violet *Hunt, which was to involve him in scandal and in complex, unsuccessful divorce proceedings; and the founding of the *English Review, which he edited for 15 months, with much éclat but also with much financial and personal stress.

In 1915 Ford published what he himself regarded as his finest achievement, his 'one novel', *The Good Soldier, and in the same year enlisted in the army: he was invalided home from France in 1917 and changed his name from Hueffer to Ford in 1919. The war inspired a volume of poems (1918), sketches, and propaganda pieces written for his friend *Masterman; also, more significantly, his other major work of fiction now known as *Parade's End (or sometimes, after its hero, as the 'Tietjens' tetralogy), which was published in four parts between 1924 and 1928. Ford began writing it in Paris, whither he moved in 1922 and where he founded in 1924 the *Transatlantic Review, in which he published work by *Joyce, *Pound, G. *Stein, E. E. *Cummings, and others. During his last years, which were spent in France and America, he published several volumes of autobiography and reminiscence (including Return to Yesterday, 1931, and It Was the Nightingale, 1933) and a final characteristically personal and ambitious volume of criticism, The March of Literature (1938). He died in Deauville. As a writer he has been more studied than read, a neglect due partly, perhaps, to the diversity of his output, and partly to his own unsettled emotional and eccentric personality, which has somehow obscured the outlines of his achievements; as an editor he has long been regarded as a highly influential figure whose devotion to literature and ready appreciation of originality and quality in others (see MODERNISM) did much to shape the course of 20th-cent. writing. See The Saddest Story (1971), a biography by A. Mizener.

FORD, John (1586–after 1639), born in Devon, and admitted to the Middle Temple in 1602. He probably spent many years there, since he is called 'Master John Ford, of the Middle Temple' as late as 1638. His earliest work was non-dramatic (1606–20), but he wrote all or a substantial part of 18 plays, of which seven have been lost. Between 1621 and 1625 he collaborated with *Dekker and others in at least five plays including *The Witch of Edmonton. After 1625 Ford probably worked alone. His chief plays are *The Lover's Melancholy (1629), *Love's Sacrifice (1633), *'Tis Pity She's a Whore (1633), *The Broken Heart (1633), *Perkin Warbeck (1634), The Lady's Trial (1639). Ford's plays are predominantly concerned with human dignity, courage, and endurance in suffering. He explores melancholy, torture, incest, delusion, but always seriously and objectively, through 'the distinct personal rhythm in blank verse which could be no one's but his alone' (T. S. *Eliot). He is described in William Heminges's 'Elegy on Randolph's Finger':

> Deep in a dump Jack Ford alone was got
> With folded arms and melancholy hat.

The standard edition is still The Works of John Ford, ed. Gifford, rev. Dyce (1869), but there are modern editions of 'Tis Pity She's a Whore (ed. Bawcutt, 1966; Morris, 1968; Roper, 1975), The Broken Heart (ed. Spencer, 1980), Perkin Warbeck (ed. Anderson, 1965).

FORD, Richard (1796–1858), educated at Winchester and Trinity College, Oxford. He contributed to various periodicals; in articles published in the *Quarterly Review and Penny Magazine he was largely responsible for introducing English readers to Velázquez. He is remembered as author of the remarkable A Handbook for Travellers in Spain (1845) which owes its survival to his unrivalled knowledge of the Spain of his day, acquired through travels, often on horseback, between 1830 and 1834, and to its individual style, rich with anecdote and local idiom, with frequent allusions to the Peninsular War. Ford was a friend of *Borrow, encouraged him with *The Bible in Spain and Zincali, and recommended Murray to publish these works.

FORD, Richard (1944–   ), American novelist and writer of short stories, born in Jackson, Mississippi. He is best known for his novel The Sportswriter (1986) and its sequel Independence Day, for which he was awarded the *Pulitzer Prize for fiction (1995). These two novels, wistfully lyrical and sharply realistic by turns, tell the story of Frank Bascombe, novelist turned eponymous sportswriter, who by the second novel has quit his job and moved into the real estate market. Ford is the author of three other novels, including The Ultimate Good Luck (1981). His collection of short *stories Rock Spring (1988) has much in common with the *'Dirty Realism' of Raymond *Carver and others.

Foresight, the foolish old astrologer in Congreve's *Love for Love.

Forest, The, a collection of miscellaneous short poems, odes, epistles, and songs, by *Jonson, printed in the folio of 1616, including 'To Penshurst' and the songs 'Drink to me only with thine eyes' and, from *Volpone, 'Come, my Celia, let us prove'. The title was suggested by Latin silva, which can mean both 'collection' and 'wood'.

FORESTER, C(ecil) S(cott) (Cecil Lewis Troughton Smith) (1899–1966), principally remembered for his seafaring novels set during the Napoleonic wars, featuring Horatio Hornblower, introduced in 1937 in The Happy Return, and rising by degrees over subsequent volumes to the rank of admiral. Forester gives an account of his own creation in The Hornblower Companion (1964). His other works include Brown on Resolution (1929) and The African Queen (1935; filmed 1951, with a screenplay by J. *Agee).

formalism, a term applied, usually pejoratively, to any creative performance in which technique or manner seems to have been cultivated at the expense of substance; or to critical approaches that disregard the subject matter of a work in favour of discussing its formal or stylistic features. More positively, formalism as a critical principle may be defended as a way of understanding art or literature primarily through its techniques rather than as a mere vehicle for personal expression or for moral and political doctrines. Formalism thus exists in continuous dispute with a range of biographical, social, and religious modes of criticism that show more interest in the 'message' of an art than in the medium. Just as in literary *Modernism a 'formalist' emphasis on creative technical experiment is prominent, so in modern literary criticism formalism has been a powerful principle, notably in the *New Criticism of the mid-20th cent. Outside the English-speaking world, the most important such critical tradition has been that of the 'Russian formalists'— a label applied to two groups of linguistic and literary scholars active in St Petersburg and Moscow in the period 1915–30, led by Roman Jakobson (1896–1982) and Victor Shklovsky (1893–1984). Repudiating the mainly psychological and historical methods of previous Russian critics, they inaugurated a new 'scientific' approach to literature that focused upon the linguistic 'devices' and conventions—from metre to plot-structure—by which literature distinguishes itself from ordinary uses of language. They thus attempted to arrive at an objective account of 'literariness' through formal linguistic analysis, and of its principal effects through the concept of *defamiliarization. Stalin's suppression of intellectual life led to a recantation by Shklovsky in 1930, but Jakobson had earlier emigrated to Czechoslovakia, where he helped to found in 1926 the Prague Linguistic Circle, which became a major link between Russian formalism and the emergence of the broader *structuralist movement. Meanwhile in Russia the arguments of the formalists had influenced, partly through strong disagreement, the work of *Bakhtin and his group. In the West, the work of Shklovsky and his associates, Boris Tomashevsky, Boris Eikhenbaum, and Vladimir Propp, was rediscovered in the 1960s; Propp's work in particular encouraged the development of *narratology.

FORMAN, Simon (1552–1611), physician and astrologer, who in his *Bock of Plaies* (preserved in a manuscript in the Bodleian Library, Oxford) records and comments on visits to performances of Shakespeare's *Macbeth* and *The Winter's Tale* at the Globe Theatre in 1611 and to an unspecified *Cymbeline. See also ROWSE.

Fors Clavigera; *Letters to the Workmen and Labourers of Great Britain*, by *Ruskin, was issued monthly from Jan. 1871 to March 1878, then at irregular intervals: two numbers appeared in 1880, four in 1883, the last three in 1884.

Fors Clavigera was a continual challenge, deliberate and serious, to the supporters of and apologists for a capitalist economy. The obscurity of the title suggests how little he wished to ingratiate himself with the working classes; he analyses the letters of 'clerks, manufacturers and other' in the 'Notes and Correspondence' section as mercilessly as the writings and speeches of his more famous enemies; only *Whistler sued for libel. Ruskin's tactics were demonstrative rather than discursive. He delivers lessons in 'the principles and plans of political economy' by setting events from contemporary history and his own immediate experience against the nobler human possibilities expressed in literature and art. *Fors Clavigera* became the mouthpiece of Ruskin's Guild of St George.

FORSTER, E(dward) M(organ) (1879–1970), the only child of Edward Morgan Forster, architect, who died in 1880, and of Alice 'Lily' Whichelo (1855–1945). His boyhood was dominated by women, among them his influential great-aunt and benefactress Marianne Thornton, whose father had been a leading member of the *'Clapham Sect'; on her death in 1887 she left him £8,000 in trust. His happiest childhood years (1883–93) were spent at Rooksnest, Stevenage, a house he evokes in *Howards End. In 1893 he and his mother moved to Tonbridge, and Forster attended Tonbridge School, where he was deeply unhappy and developed a lasting dislike of public-school values. In 1897 he went to King's College, Cambridge, where he found congenial friends; the atmosphere of free intellectual discussion, and a stress on the importance of personal relationships inspired partly by G. E. *Moore, was to have a profound influence on his work. In 1901 he was elected to the *Apostles and largely through them was later drawn into closer contact with *Bloomsbury. A year of travel in Italy with his mother and a cruise to Greece followed, providing material for his early novels, which satirize the attitudes of English tourists abroad, Baedeker in hand, clinging to English *pensioni*, and suspicious of anything foreign. On his return from Greece he began to write for the new *Independent Review*, launched in 1903 by a group of Cambridge friends, led by G. M. *Trevelyan; in 1904 it published his first short story, 'The Story of a Panic'. In 1905 he completed *Where Angels Fear to Tread*, which was published the same year, and spent some months in Germany as tutor to the children of the Countess *von Arnim. In 1906, now established with his mother in Weybridge, he became tutor to Syed Ross Masood, a striking and colourful Indian Muslim patriot, for whom Forster developed an intense affection. *The Longest Journey* appeared in 1907, *A Room with a View* in 1908, and *Howards End*, which established Forster as a writer of importance, in 1910. In 1911 he published a collection of short stories, mostly pastoral and whimsical in tone and subject matter, *The Celestial Omnibus*. In 1912–13 he visited India for some months, meeting Masood in Aligarh and travelling with him. In 1913 another significant visit to the home of E. *Carpenter near Chesterfield resulted in his writing *Maurice*, a novel with a homosexual theme which he circulated privately; it was published posthumously in 1971. It did not as he had hoped open a new vein of creativity, and the outbreak of war further impeded his career. He worked for a while at the National Gallery, then went to Alexandria in 1915 for the Red Cross; his *Alexandria: A History and a Guide* was published somewhat abortively in 1922 (almost the entire stock was burned) and reprinted in revised form in 1938. In Alexandria he met *Cavafy, whose works, on his return to England in 1919, he helped to introduce; an essay on Cavafy appears in *Pharos and Pharillon* (1923). In 1921-2 he revisited India, working as personal secretary for the maharajah of the native state of Dewas Senior for several months. The completion of **A Passage to India* (1922-4), which he had begun before the war, was overshadowed by the death of his closest Egyptian friend Mohammed, but when the novel appeared in June 1924 it was highly acclaimed. Forster's fears that this would be his last novel proved correct, and the remainder of his life was devoted to a wide range of literary activities; over many years he took a firm stand against censorship, involving himself in the work of PEN and the NCCL, of which he became the first president, campaigning in 1928 against the suppression of R. *Hall's *The Well of Loneliness*, and appearing in 1960 as a witness for the defence in the trial of the publishers of **Lady Chatterley's Lover*. In 1927 he delivered the Clark Lectures at Cambridge printed the same year as *Aspects of the Novel*; his tone in these was in his own words 'informal, indeed talkative', and they contain the celebrated comment, 'Yes—oh dear yes—the novel tells a story.' *Leavis, representing the new school of Cambridge criticism, found the lectures 'intellectually null', but they were a popular success, and King's offered him a three-year fellowship and, in 1946, an honorary fellowship and a permanent home. In 1928 *The Eternal Moment*, a volume of pre-1914 short stories, whimsical and dealing with the supernatural, appeared. He wrote two biographies, *Goldsworthy Lowes Dickinson* (1934) and *Marianne Thornton* (1956). *Abinger Harvest*, essays named after the village in Surrey in which Forster inherited a house in 1924, appeared in 1936, *Two Cheers for Democracy* in 1951, *The Hill of Devi*, a portrait of India through letters and commentary, in 1953. Between 1949 and 1951 he worked with Eric Crozier on the libretto for *Britten's opera *Billy Budd*. He spent his last years in King's College, and was awarded the OM in 1969. *Maurice* was followed by another posthumous publication, *The Life to Come* (1972), a collection of short stories, many with homosexual themes, including the tragic story 'The Other Boat' written 1957-8. See biography by P. N. Furbank (2 vols, 1977-8); *Selected Letters*, ed. M. Lago and P. N. Furbank (1983, 1985).

FORSTER, John (1812-76), educated at Newcastle Grammar School, University College London, and the Inner Temple, and called to the bar in 1843. His career in journalism began as editor of the short-lived *Reflector* owned by E. *Moxon and he became drama critic for *True Sun* in 1832, eventually leading to editorship of *Foreign Quarterly Review*, 1842-3, *Daily News*, 1846, and *Examiner*, 1847-55. He was engaged for a short time in 1835 to Letitia *Landon, but married Eliza Colburn, the wealthy widow of the publisher Henry Colburn, in 1856. He was the literary associate and close friend of Leigh *Hunt, C. *Lamb, W. S. *Landor, *Bulwer-Lytton, and *Dickens: from 1837 on he read in manuscript or proof everything Dickens wrote. His earliest biographical work, *Lives of Eminent British Statesmen* (1836-9) in Lardner's *Cyclopedia*, was followed by various political lives partly reprinted as *Historical and Biographical Essays* (1858). His popular literary biographies include *Life and Adventures of Oliver Goldsmith* (1848; rev. 2 vols, 1854), *Landor* (2 vols, 1869), *Dickens* (3 vols, 1872-4), and the first volume of a scholarly life of *Swift (1875). He is recognized as the first professional biographer of 19th-cent. England. His business acumen plus activities as a man of letters made his assistance valued by many. Landor, Dickens, and *Carlyle appointed him their literary executor.

FORSTER, Margaret (1938-), novelist and biographer, born in Carlisle, educated at Carlisle County High School and at Somerville College, Oxford. Her first novel, *Dame's Delight* (1964), was followed by the highly successful *Georgy Girl* (1965; film script with P. *Nichols 1966), the story of a large and awkward young woman who wins unexpected admiration. Several comedies of contemporary life and manners followed, but she reached a new plane with later works, such as *Mother Can You Hear Me?* (1979), a sombre evocation of motherhood, portrayed through the intense but painful cross-generation connections between frustrated, working-class, dying Mother, living in the West Country, her London-based schoolteacher daughter Angela, and Angela's daughter Sadie. *Have the Men Had Enough?* (1989) is an even more painful and angry account of old age and senile dementia and their impact on family life, as Grandma, a Scottish Presbyterian, deteriorates from a semi-independent routine of devoted home care to death in a psychiatric geriatric hospital. Non-fiction works include an 'autobiography' of *Thackeray (1978) and lives of E. B. *Browning (1988) and D. *du Maurier. *Hidden Lives* (1995) is a poignant family memoir, and *Shadow Baby* (1996) is a fictional offshoot from it. She is married to Hunter Davies (1936-), author, walker, Wordsworthian, broadcaster, journalist.

Forsyte Saga, The, a sequence by J. *Galsworthy, published 1922.

The three novels containing the story, *The Man of Property* (1906), *In Chancery* (1920), and *To Let* (1921), with two interludes, 'Indian Summer of a Forsyte' (1918), and *Awakening* (1920), appeared together in

1922 as *The Forsyte Saga*, tracing the fortunes of three generations of the Forsyte family. The Forsyte sequence *A Modern Comedy* (1929) is often (but incorrectly) included under the title of the *Saga*. In his preface Galsworthy describes his use of the word 'saga' as ironic, yet at the same time indicates that he is exposing a primal tribal and acquisitive urge.

Soames Forsyte, a successful solicitor, the nephew of 'old Jolyon', lives in London surrounded by his prosperous old uncles and their families. He marries the penniless Irene and builds a country house for her, Robin Hill; when she falls in love with its architect, Bosinney, Soames asserts his rights over his property and rapes her. Bosinney is killed in a street accident and Irene returns to Soames. *In Chancery* describes the growing love of young Jolyon, Soames's cousin, for Irene; Irene's divorce from Soames and her happy marriage with Jolyon; and the birth of their son Jon. Meanwhile Soames marries Annette Lamotte and they have a daughter, Fleur. In *To Let* Fleur and Jon fall in love; Jon's father feels compelled to reveal the past of Irene and Soames, and the agonized Jon, in spite of Fleur's Forsyte determination, rejects her. She marries Michael Mont, the heir to a baronetcy, and when young Jolyon dies Irene leaves to join Jon in America. The desolate Soames learns that his wife is having an affair with a Belgian, and discovers that Irene's house, Robin Hill, is empty and to let. *The Forsyte Saga* was successfully serialized for television in 1967.

FORSYTH, Frederick, see SPY FICTION.

FORTESCUE, Sir John (?1394–?1476), chief justice of the King's Bench under Henry VI, and the earliest English constitutional lawyer. He was a Lancastrian during the Wars of the Roses but, having been captured at Tewkesbury in 1471, was pardoned and made a member of the council on recognizing Edward IV (1471). His principal works were a Latin treatise, *De Natura Legis Naturae* (1461–3), distinguishing absolute from constitutional monarchy; an English treatise on the same subject (*Monarchia or The Difference between an Absolute and a Limited Monarchy*); a Latin treatise, *De Laudibus Legum Angliae* (1471); and an English work, *On the Governance of England* (1470s; ed. C. Plummer, 1885). His recantation of his Lancastrian views is contained in *A Declaration upon Certain Wrytinges* (1471–3). See *Works*, ed. Lord Clermont (2 vols, 1869), containing a short biography.

Fortinbras, prince of Norway in Shakespeare's *Hamlet*, whose name, 'strong-in-arm', suits his military temperament.

FORTINI, Franco, pseudonym of Franco Lattes (1917–1994), Italian poet and Modernist critic. His poems have been translated by M. *Hamburger; the best are in *Foglio di via* (*Expulsion Order*, 1946), *Poesia ed errore* (*Poetry and Error*, 1959), *Una volta per sempre* (*Once and for All*, 1963), and *Questo muro* (*This Wall*, 1973). His essays and his left-wing critique of communism, and especially of *Socialist Realism, have posed the problem of poetry and political commitment.

Fortnightly Review (1865–1934), an influential and respected literary periodical, which retained its high standard throughout its existence. G. H. *Lewes, the first editor, required that all articles be signed, thus breaking a long tradition of anonymity in reviews. The contents were miscellaneous, but the *Review* is largely remembered for its literary value. Almost all numbers ran a serialized novel; the first contained a chapter of Trollope's *The Belton Estate* and a part of *Bagehot's *The English Constitution*. Positivist and anti-orthodox, Lewes and his successor John *Morley published work by *Thackeray, G. *Eliot, M. *Arnold, T. H. *Huxley, *Meredith, D. G. *Rossetti, L. *Stephen, *Pater, and *Hardy, among others. In the 20th cent. work published included that of H. *James, *Gissing, *Kipling, H. G. *Wells, *Joyce, and *Pound. In 1934 it changed its name to the *Fortnightly*, under which title it survived until 1954. It was then incorporated in the *Contemporary Review*.

Fortunate Mistress, The, see ROXANA.

Fortunatus' purse, the subject of a European 15th-cent. romance, translated into many languages and dramatized by *Dekker. For the story see OLD FORTUNATUS.

Fortunes of Nigel, The, a novel by Sir W. *Scott, published 1822.

The novel is set in 17th-cent. London and tells the story of a young Scots nobleman, Nigel Olifaunt, who comes to claim repayment of a debt owed to his father by the king, James VI and I. The king's portrait is one of the book's highlights, as are those of the other historical characters and the vivid descriptions of Alsatia drawn by Scott from his reading of the Elizabethan and Jacobean dramatists.

Fosco, Count, a character in Wilkie Collins's *The Woman in White*.

FOSCOLO, Ugo (1778–1827), Italian poet, tragedian, and critic. He was the first modern Italian poet of exile, and the writer of his generation who was most sensitive to the crisis of his age. In 1797 he wrote an ode to Bonaparte as Liberator, but when later that year Napoleon's Treaty of Campoformio handed over Venetian independence to the Austrians, Foscolo was bitter at the betrayal. Nevertheless he fought with the French throughout Napoleon's occupation of northern Italy. In 1804, with the plan to invade England, he was stationed in northern France where he fell in love with an Englishwoman by whom he had a daughter, 'Floriana'. After Napoleon's defeat and the reoccupation of northern Italy by the Austrians in 1814, Foscolo went into exile, first in Switzerland; then, from 1816, in London where, tended by his daughter, he was to die in poverty. He wrote tragedies in imitation of *Alfieri and intensely lyrical neo-classical sonnets (1802). In the first Romantic Italian novel, *Ultime lettere di Jacopo Ortis* (*Last Letters of Jacopo Ortis*, 1802, rev. 1814), inspired by Goethe's *Werther* (see WERTHERISM), the hero chooses suicide, having lost both his love and his political hopes after the Treaty of Campoformio. His greatest work is *Dei sepolcri* (*Of Sepulchres*, 1807), a 295-line poem influenced by T. *Gray. This poem deals with the tension between the modern poet's prophetic 'interrogation' of history and his exile from the society with which he is at odds. In his last years he contributed critical essays—notably on *Dante, *Petrarch, and *Tasso—to the *Edinburgh Review*, *Quarterly Review*, and *New Monthly Review*. He died in Turnham Green, London.

FOUCAULT, Michel (1926–84), French historian, born in Poitiers. He studied in Paris at the École Normale Supérieure before pursuing a varied academic career in Poland, Sweden, Tunisia, and France, culminating in his chair in the history of systems of thought at the Collège de France. His early work, notably *Folie et déraison: histoire de la folie à l'âge classique* (*Madness and Civilization*, 1961), *Les Mots et les choses* (*The Order of Things*, 1966), and *L'Archéologie du savoir* (*The Archaeology of Knowledge*, 1969), is devoted to the history of institutions (scientific, medical, penal, etc.) and the *discourses on which their power is founded. It expresses a libertarian distrust of the ways in which modern institutions since the *Enlightenment regulate knowledge and submit people to the control of 'experts'. His *Surveiller et punir* (*Discipline and Punish*, 1975) examines the history of punishment and imprisonment in this light. His later work includes an incomplete project for a history of sexuality: the first volume (1976) argues against the Freudian view that sexuality was 'repressed' in the 19th cent., proposing instead that sex became controlled by medical discourse. His visiting professorships in California furthered his strong influence on American historical and literary studies, notably the *New Historicism and the work of *Said. He died of an AIDS-related illness. See STRUCTURALISM AND POST-STRUCTURALISM.

FOULIS (originally Faulls), Robert (1707–76), a barber's apprentice in Glasgow. With his brother Andrew he visited Oxford and France in 1738–40, collecting rare books, and started as bookseller and printer in Glasgow. He printed for the university their first Greek book (1743) and the 'immaculate' *Horace (1744). He issued a number of other remarkable books, the fine folio *Iliad* of 1756, the *Odyssey* (1758), the Olivet *Cicero (1748–9), the small folio *Callimachus (1755), the quarto edition of *Gray (1768), and *Paradise Lost* (1770). (See James MacLehose, *The Glasgow University Press*, 1931, and Philip Gaskell, *A Bibliography of the Foulis Press*, 2nd edn 1986.)

'Four Ages of Poetry, The', a literary essay by *Peacock, published 1820. It makes ironic use of the argument advanced by 18th-cent. cultural historians such as *Winckelmann, that as society progresses, poetry deteriorates in inevitable stages. Shelley's reply, a *Defence of Poetry*, takes Peacock's charges seriously, and argues that poetry in modern times continues to play an important social role, through advocating the ideal and stimulating the life of the mind.

FOURIER, Charles (1772–1837), French social reformer. Persuaded that the competitive principles of civilization had created unhappiness by establishing inequality of wealth and repressing human passions, Fourier advocated a system of social reorganization, generally known as *Fouriérisme*, which was to ensure the maximum of co-operation in the interests of personal and collective harmony. To this end he proposed the regrouping of society into communities, or *phalanges*, of about 1,600 persons. Each *phalange* was to be a co-operative enterprise providing for the subsistence of all its members, and dividing its remaining revenues among them according to capital invested, labour, and talent. The internal organization of the community would allow for variety of occupation and a large measure of sexual freedom. Fourier's major works are *Théorie des quatre mouvements* (1808), *Traité de l'association domestique agricole* (1822), *Le Nouveau Monde industriel* (1829–30).

Four Quartets, a poem in four parts by T. S. *Eliot, published as a whole in New York in 1943. The first part, 'Burnt Norton', was the final poem in *Collected Poems 1909–35* (1936); 'East Coker', 'The Dry Salvages', and 'Little Gidding' first appeared in the *New English Weekly* in 1940, 1941, and 1942 respectively, and were then published separately in pamphlet form by Faber and Faber.

The four quartets represent the four seasons and the four elements; the imagery of the first centres on a Cotswold garden, that of the second round a Somerset village (whence Eliot's own ancestor had departed in 1669 for the New World), the third mingles the landscapes of Missouri and New England, the landscapes of Eliot's youth; and the fourth uses as symbol *Little Gidding, the home of N. *Ferrar. But all are concerned with time past and time present, with the wartime London of the Blitz as well as the England of *Julian of Norwich and Sir T. *Elyot. These were the first of Eliot's poems to reach a wide public (they were seen as a unifying force in the war years), and they succeeded in communicating in modern idiom the fundamentals of Christian faith and experience. For a discussion of their sources and composition, see H. *Gardner, *The Composition of Four Quartets* (1978), in which she describes the whole work as an 'austere and rigorously philosophic poem on time and time's losses and gains'.

Four Sons of Aymon, see AYMON.

Fourth Estate, the, the press. The use of the expression in this sense is attributed by *Carlyle (*On* *Heroes and Hero-Worship*) to *Burke, but not traced in his speeches. A correspondent to *N. & Q.* (1st series, 11. 452) attributes it to *Brougham.

Four Zoas, The, a symbolic poem by *Blake, originally entitled *Vala*, written and revised 1795–1804, described by John Beer (*Blake's Humanism*, 1968) as 'a heroic attempt to write the first psychological epic'. It presents characters familiar from Blake's earlier symbolic works (*Urizen, *Los, *Enitharmon, *Orc, and others), elaborating his cosmic mythology in a framework of a 'Dream of Nine Nights'; this framework was possibly suggested by Young's *Night Thoughts*, which Blake was illustrating at the same period. The Four Zoas appear to represent the four human faculties, once united, but then at war with one another until the final radiant vision of joy and peace when the eyes of the Eternal Man 'behold the depths of wondorous worlds' and around his tent 'the little children play among the wooly flocks'.

FOWLER, Henry Watson (1858–1933) and Francis George (1870–1918), lexicographers and grammarians; joint authors of *The King's English* (1906), *The Concise Oxford Dictionary* (1911), and *The Pocket Oxford Dictionary* (1924). *A Dictionary of Modern English Usage* (1926; 2nd edn 1965, ed. Sir E. Gowers) is the work of H. W. Fowler.

FOWLES, John Robert (1926–   ), novelist, educated at Bedford School and New College, Oxford, where he read French. He worked as a schoolteacher before embarking on a career as a full-time writer. His first novel, *The Collector* (1963), a psychological thriller, consists largely of the laconic first-person narration of a repressed clerk and butterfly collector who spends a fortune won on the football pools on the kidnapping of an art student, Miranda; the novel ends with her death and his plans to add another specimen to his collection. This was followed by *The Aristos* (1965), an idiosyncratic collection of notes and aphorisms aimed at a 'personal philosophy', and *The Magus* (1966, revised version 1977), a novel set largely on the Greek island of 'Phraxos', where British schoolmaster Nicholas D'Urfe, half guest and half victim, is subjected to a series of mysterious apparitions and tableaux which, despite their naturalistic explanations, give the novel a narrative complexity and mythological dimension faintly suggestive of *magic realism. *The French Lieutenant's Woman* (1969) is a semi-historical novel, set largely in Lyme Regis in 1867; wealthy amateur palaeontologist Charles Smithson, engaged to conventional Ernestina Freeman, falls under the spell of eccentric, sensual, apparently 'fallen' Sarah Woodruff, a lady's companion, who is believed to have been deserted by the French lover of the title. His pursuit of Sarah breaks his engagement, but Sarah eludes him, and when he finds her again (in the protection of D. G. *Rossetti) she has

become a *New Woman. The novel is notable for the author's intrusive commentary and suggestion of alternative endings, an aspect represented in *Pinter's screenplay by a double action of film-within-film. *The Ebony Tower* (1974) is a collection of novellas; *Daniel Martin* (1977) is a long, self-searching, semi-naturalistic, semi-experimental account of screenwriter Daniel and his relationships with Hollywood, capitalism, art, and his sister-in-law, set in a wide variety of locations, ranging from opening sequences in Devon and Oxford to a closing sequence in the ruins of Palmyra; *Mantissa* (1982) consists largely of extended erotic fantasy on the subject of *la femme inspiratrice*, with mythological undertones. *A Maggot* (1985) is an 18th-cent. murder mystery that makes use of contemporary documents. *The Tree* (1992), which contains recollections of Fowles's childhood and explores the impact of nature on his life and work, was followed by *Tessera* (1993).

FOX, Caroline (1819–71), diarist, of an old Quaker family, born at Falmouth, whose *Memories of Old Friends* (1882, ed. Horace N. Pym: extracts from journals and letters which cover the years 1835–71) contains vivid recollections of *Sterling, the *Carlyles, Elizabeth Fry, the Coleridges, and other eminent Victorians. Her turn of mind was predominantly serious and reflective, but she could also be very entertaining, as her account of an evening in 1842 with the Carlyles discussing *Swedenborg bears witness.

FOX, Charles James (1749–1806), a great Whig statesman and orator, who first made his mark by speeches against *Wilkes in 1769. He was one of the managers of the proceedings against *Hastings, and a constant opponent of the policy of *Pitt. Sir G. *Trevelyan described him as 'our first great statesman of the modern school' (*The Early History of Charles James Fox*, 1880). He was a man of great personal charm, noted for his scholarship but also for his gambling and drinking and the bad influence he exercised over the prince of Wales. He was elected a member of Dr Johnson's *Club (1774). See *Charles James Fox* (1992) by L. G. Mitchell.

FOX, George (1624–91), son of a Leicestershire weaver and founder of the Society of *Friends, or Quakers. Fox abandoned church attendance and left home in 1643 in search of enlightenment. As an itinerant apostle he preached the Inner Light of Christ, interrupting church services and causing riots and disturbances: he was a magnetic preacher and attracted a large following. Margaret *Fell's home at Swarthmoor, Ulverston, became his headquarters from 1652 and he married her in 1669. He travelled widely in the British Isles, the New World, and Holland and suffered imprisonments at Launceston, Lancaster, Scarborough, and Worcester. He was a compulsive controversialist, attacking the *Ranters, the state Church, the law, and prejudice against women preachers in innumerable epistles and pamphlets. His *Journal*, revised by a committee under the superintendence of *Penn and published in 1694, describes in vividly idiomatic and abrasive prose his spiritual journey and the trials and schisms of the movement.

FOXE, John (1516–87), the martyrologist, was born at Boston, Lincolnshire, and was educated at Oxford, where he became a fellow of Magdalen College but resigned his fellowship in 1545, being unwilling to conform to the statutes in religious matters. In 1554 he retired to the Continent, and issued at Strasbourg his *Commentarii* (the earliest draft of his *Actes and Monuments*). From 1555 to 1559 he was employed at Basle as reader of the press by Oporinus (Herbst), who published Foxe's verse drama *Christus Triumphans* in 1556, his appeal to the English nobility on toleration in 1557, and the first issue of his *Rerum in Ecclesia Gestarum … Commentarii* in 1559. On his return to England he was ordained priest by Grindal in 1560, and in 1564 joined John *Day, the printer, who in 1563 had issued the English version of the *Rerum in Ecclesia Gestarum … Commentarii* as *Actes and Monuments*, popularly known as the *Book of Martyrs*. He became a canon of Salisbury in 1563, but objected to the use of the surplice and to contributing to the repairs of the cathedral. He preached at Paul's Cross a famous sermon, 'Of Christ Crucified', in 1570. His edition of the canon laws *Reformatio Legum* appeared in 1571. He was buried in St Giles's Church, Cripplegate. Four editions of the *Actes and Monuments* (1563, 1570, 1576, and 1583) appeared in the author's lifetime; of the posthumous issues, that of 1641 contains a memoir of Foxe, attributed to his son.

FOX, William Johnson (1786–1864), independent Unitarian preacher, orator, journalist, drama critic, and editor. He was important in a literary context for his association with the *Monthly Repository*, originally a Unitarian periodical, but which under his ownership and editorship (from 1831) encouraged and published many of the leading writers of the day, including *Browning, *Martineau, and J. S. *Mill. He sold it in 1836 to his friend and protégé R. H. *Horne. He continued to write and speak extensively and effectively on public matters, and in 1847 became MP for Oldham.

Fradubio, in Spenser's *Faerie Queene* (i. ii. 32 *et seq.*), 'the doubter', the lover of Fraelissa; he doubts whether her beauty is equal to that of *Duessa. Duessa transforms Fraelissa into a tree, obtains Fradubio's love, and when he discovers her deformity, turns him also into a tree.

FRAME, Janet Paterson (1924–2004), New Zealand novelist, poet, and short story writer, born in Oamaru of Scottish parentage. Her childhood was overshadowed by the death (by drowning) of her two sisters. She was educated at Otago University and trained as a teacher at Dunedin Teachers' Training College but was misdiagnosed as a schizophrenic and spent several harrowing years undergoing treatment, including long spells in hospital and electric shock therapy, experiences that coloured her subsequent work as a writer. Her first book, *The Lagoon* (1952), was a collection of stories and was followed by a novel, *Owls Do Cry* (1957, published in Britain in 1961), in which many of the circumstances of her own life are mirrored in those of the Withers family, who are also the subject of *Faces in the Water* (1961) and *The Edge of the Alphabet* (1962). On a grant from the New Zealand Literary Fund she travelled to Europe and spent a number of years living in England before returning to New Zealand after the death of her father. *Scented Gardens for the Blind* appeared in 1963. Subsequent novels, all of which display her gifts as a stylist, are *The Adaptable Man* (1965), *A State of Siege* (1966), *The Rainbirds* (1968), the futuristic *Intensive Care* (1970), *Daughter Buffalo* (1972), *Living in the Maniototo* (1979), and *The Carpathians* (1988). She published three volumes of autobiography—*To the Island* (1982), *An Angel at My Table* (1984), and *The Envoy from Mirror City* (1985). These were made into a film by Jane Campion under the title of the second volume. Two further collections of short stories were published as *The Reservoir and Other Stories* (1966) and *You Are Now Entering the Human Heart* (1983). Her only volume of poetry, *The Pocket Mirror*, appeared in 1967.

Framley Parsonage, a novel by A. *Trollope first published 1861, the fourth in the *'Barsetshire' series.

Mark Robarts is an ambitious young clergyman. At the age of 26 Lady Lufton helped him to the comfortable living at Framley, but he has now become involved with the unreliable Whig member of Parliament, Mr Sowerby of Chaldicotes, and hopes for further preferment from Sowerby's patron, the duke of Omnium. Robarts rashly guarantees some bills for Sowerby, and as an indirect gesture of gratitude Sowerby pulls strings to acquire for Robarts a prebendary stall at Barchester, but when the bills fall due, Sowerby makes no attempt to pay them. He is by this time in considerable financial difficulty and, after an abortive attempt to marry the money of the patent-medicine heiress Miss Dunstable, his career ends in ruin. Mark Robarts becomes liable for the full amount of the debts and has to appeal to his original patron, Lady Lufton.

This is doubly embarrassing for the Luftons, as young Lord Lufton has fallen in love with Robarts's sister Lucy. At first Lady Lufton vehemently opposes the match, and hopes to interest her son in Griselda Grantly, daughter of the archdeacon. Griselda, however, marries the wealthy Lord Dumbello, and Lady Lufton and Lucy are thrown together by the illness of Mrs Crawley, wife of a neighbouring clergyman. In nursing her Lucy shows her true worth, and Lady Lufton removes her opposition to the match; Mark Robarts's debts are paid as a gesture of goodwill. The novel is remarkable for the first appearance of the proud, impoverished curate Mr Crawley.

FRANCE, Anatole, the pseudonym of Jacques-Anatole-François Thibault (1844–1924), French novelist and man of letters, the son of a Parisian bookseller. As writer, journalist, and editor he became a leading figure in French literary life from about 1890. His first successful novel, *Le Crime de Sylvestre Bonnard* (1881), was followed by *La Rôtisserie de la reine Pédauque* (1893) which, with its companion volume *Les Opinions de M. Jérôme Coignard* (1893), attempts a fictionalized revival of the mind and sensibility of 18th-cent. France. Social and political satire dominate the four novels which introduce the observant and disenchanted provincial professor M. Bergeret and which together form the *Histoire contemporaine* (1897–1901). *L'Île des pingouins* (1908) gives a fanciful and satirical version of the evolution of human society and institutions. Many consider *Les Dieux ont soif* (1912), a study of fanaticism during the French Revolution, to be his finest novel. His numerous tales, variously exotic, philosophical, and satirical, were collected in, notably: *L'Étui de nacre* (1892), *Crainquebille* (1901), and *Sur la pierre blanche* (1905). Anatole France provided a somewhat fictionalized account of his childhood and early years in *Le Livre de mon ami* (1885), *Pierre Nozière* (1899), *Le Petit Pierre* (1918), and *La Vie en fleur* (1922). He was awarded the *Nobel Prize for literature in 1921.

Francesca da Rimini, see PAOLO AND FRANCESCA.

FRANCIS, Sir Philip (1740–1818), the son of the Philip Francis who was *Gibbon's schoolmaster. He was educated at St Paul's School with Woodfall, subsequently publisher of the letters of *Junius. From 1762 to 1772 he was a clerk in the war office, and became one of the four newly appointed councillors of the governor-general of India in 1774. He left India in 1780 and assisted *Burke in preparing the charges against *Hastings.

Recent research tends to confirm the long-standing identification of Francis as the author of the letters of Junius, although Woodfall always denied it, and the letters themselves show some malignity towards Francis's friends and benefactors.

FRANCIS OF ASSISI, St, Giovanni Francesco Bernardone (1181/2–1226). He experienced as a young man two serious illnesses and a spiritual crisis on a military expedition, in consequence of which he lived for a time in solitude and prayer and devoted himself to the relief of the poor, the sick, and the lepers. He was joined by disciples, the first members of the Franciscan order for which he drew up the rule in 1209, the principal characteristic of which was humility, in token of which they called themselves 'Friari Minori'. He preached in Italy, and went to the Holy Land and Spain. The special notes of his teaching were poverty and love of nature (St Francis preaching to the birds is a favourite painter's subject). Two years before his death, after a period of fasting on Mount Alverno, he is said to have

discovered on his body the stigmata, the marks made by the nails of Christ's Crucifixion. Two 13th-cent. biographies of him were written, by Bonaventura and by Thomas of Celano. The *Fioretti de San Francisco* (*Little Flowers of St Francis*) is a 14th-cent. Italian narrative, partly legendary, of the doings of St Francis and his first disciples. See *Penguin Book of Italian Verse* (ed. G. Kay, 1958) for his 'Cantico delle creature'. He occurs with St Dominic, the founder of the Dominicans, in *Dante's *Paradiso*, xii. See A. Fortini, *Francis of Assisi*, trans. H. Moak (1981); *Little Flowers of St Francis*, trans. H. E. Manning (1864), rev. R. Huddleston (1926, 1953).

Frankenstein, or *The Modern Prometheus*, a *Gothic tale of terror by M. *Shelley, published 1818. In her preface she records that she, *Shelley, and *Byron had spent the wet summer of 1816 in Switzerland reading German ghost stories; all three agreed to write tales of the supernatural, of which hers was the only one to be completed. She also records that the original concept came to her in a half-waking nightmare.

Technically an *epistolary novel, told through the letters of Walton, an English explorer in the Arctic, the tale relates the exploits of Frankenstein, an idealistic Genevan student of natural philosophy, who discovers at the University of Ingolstadt the secret of imparting life to inanimate matter. Collecting bones from charnel-houses, he constructs the semblance of a human being and gives it life. The creature, endowed with supernatural strength and size and terrible in appearance, inspires loathing in whoever sees it. Lonely and miserable (and educated in human emotion by studies of *Goethe, *Plutarch, and *Paradise Lost), it turns upon its creator, and, failing to persuade him to provide a female counterpart, eventually murders his brother, his friend Clerval, and his bride Elizabeth. Frankenstein pursues it to the Arctic to destroy it, but dies in the pursuit, after relating his story to Walton. The monster declares that Frankenstein will be its last victim, and disappears to end its own life. This tale inspired many film versions, and has been regarded as the origin of modern *science fiction, though it is also a version of the myth of the *Noble Savage, in which a nature essentially good is corrupted by ill-treatment. It is also remarkable for its description of nature, which owes much to the Shelleys' admiration for *Wordsworth, *Coleridge, and in particular the *Ancient Mariner*.

FRANKLIN, Benjamin (1706–90), born in Boston, Massachusetts, the son of a tallow chandler, largely self-educated. He was apprenticed at the age of 12 to his half-brother, a printer, to whose *New England Courant* he contributed, but they later quarrelled and he went off to seek independence in Philadelphia. In 1724 he travelled to England, hoping to buy equipment for his own printing press, and worked in a London printing house for some months, returning to Philadelphia in 1726. Four years later he set up his own press, from which he issued the *Pennsylvania Gazette*, and, by thrift and hard work, became prosperous. He acquired a wide reputation by his occasional writings, especially *Poor Richard's Almanack* (1733–58), the best known of American *almanacs, which followed the British pattern of mixing practical information with satiric prognostications, aphorisms, proverbs, etc. He was active as a public figure, founding the American Philosophical Society and the academy that became the University of Pennsylvania, and he also became well known for his practical interest in natural philosophy; his experiment with lightning and electricity, using a kite to demonstrate their identity, was famous, and he also invented the Franklin stove and a new kind of clock. In 1757 he travelled to England as agent for the colonies, where he mixed widely in intellectual society (his friends including *Burke, *Hume, Adam *Smith, *Strahan, and J. *Priestley) and contributed greatly to the controversies that caused the breach with England; he returned home in 1774 and, after helping to draft the Declaration of Independence, travelled to France as ambassador, where he was enthusiastically welcomed. Upon his return in 1785 he continued to be active in public affairs, and signed the Constitution as a member of the Federal Constitutional Convention. His *Autobiography*, which he began to write in England, at Twyford, in 1771, and which breaks off with an account of his return to England in 1757, was published in England in 1793 (translated from the French), in America in 1818. Franklin's prose was much admired in England; *Jeffery (1806, *Edinburgh Review*) praised its 'force and clearness', and *Lecky (*History of England in the Eighteenth Century*) described it as 'always terse, luminous, simple, pregnant with meaning, eminently persuasive'. D. H. *Lawrence, however, deplored 'middle-sized, sturdy, snuff-coloured Doctor Franklin' and his thrift and orderliness: 'He tries to take away my wholeness and my dark forest, my freedom' (*Studies in Classic American Literature*, 1923).

FRANKLIN, Sir John (1786–1847), Arctic explorer, and author of two *Narratives* (1823 and 1828) of voyages to the Polar Sea. His final voyage of discovery in *Erebus* and *Terror* in search of the North-West Passage began in 1845, and resulted in disaster. Numerous relief expeditions were sent out including one organized by his widow which found a record of the expedition proving that Franklin had discovered the North-West Passage.

'Franklin's Tale, The,' see CANTERBURY TALES, 12.

FRASER, Lady Antonia, née Pakenham (1932–), biographer, broadcaster, anthologist, and writer of mystery stories, educated at Lady Margaret Hall, Oxford. She married H. *Pinter in 1980. Her readable and scholarly biographies include lives of *Mary Queen of Scots (1969), *Cromwell (1973), and Marie Antoinette (2001). Her female detective Jemima Shore was introduced in *Quiet as a Nun* (1977), and has since appeared in several mystery

novels and in a television series. *The Gunpowder Plot: Terror and Faith in 1605* was published in 1997.

FRASER, George MacDonald, see HISTORICAL FICTION.

FRASER, George Sutherland, see NEW APOCALYPSE.

Fraser's Magazine (1830–82), a general and literary Tory journal of high standing, founded by *Maginn and Hugh Fraser, which provided some competition for *Blackwood's*. Unlike *Blackwood's*, the *Edinburgh*, or the *Quarterly* it was not owned by a publisher of books, and prided itself that it could not therefore be accused of partisanship in its reviews. Among notable contributors were J. *Hogg, *Coleridge, *Southey, *Peacock, *Carlyle, *Ainsworth, *Thackeray, and *Ruskin. J. A. *Froude was editor from 1860 to 1874, but the journal had by then declined in influence and repute.

Fraternitie of Vacabondes, a tract printed by John Awdely (fl. 1559, d. 1575), published in 1565 in two parts, the first dealing with thieves' cant and the devices of beggars to excite compassion; the second with the methods employed by well-dressed impostors.

FRAUNCE, Abraham (?1558–92/3), educated at Shrewsbury School. Under the patronage of P. *Sidney he involved himself in contemporary movements, such as Ramism (see RAMUS), in logic, rhetoric, and metrics. His most interesting work, *The Arcadian Rhetorike* (1588), illustrates rhetorical tropes with examples from Sidney's *Arcadia, side by side with *Tasso, *Du Bartas, and *Boscán. Other works include *The Lawiers Logike* (1588), *The Countesse of Pembrokes Emanuel* (1591), and *The Countesse of Pembrokes Yvychurch* (1591).

FRAYN, Michael (1933–), novelist and playwright, educated at Kingston Grammar School and Emmanuel College, Cambridge. He worked for some years as a humorous columnist for the *Manchester Guardian*, then for the *Observer*. His novels include *The Russian Interpreter* (1966), *Towards the End of the Morning* (1967, a comedy of Fleet Street life and London middle-class domestic *mores*), *A Very Private Life* (1968, a satiric anti-utopian fantasy), *Sweet Dreams* (1973), *The Trick of It* (1989), and *Headlong* (1999). His stage comedies include *Alphabetical Order* (1975, pub. 1976), again with a background of journalism; *Donkeys' Years* (1976, pub. 1977), based on a college reunion; *Noises Off* (1982), a farce of theatre life; *Benefactors* (1984); and *Wild Honey* (pub. 1984, perf. 1986), adapted from an untitled play by Anton *Chekhov. *Copenhagen* (1998) is a tense, lucid drama about the unexplained meeting in 1941 in occupied Denmark of German physicist Werner Heisenberg and his Danish mentor Niels Bohr; *Democracy* (2003) is a drama set in 1969 and based on the career of German Chancellor Willy Brandt.

FRAZER, Sir James George (1854–1941). He was appointed to the first named chair of social anthropology in Liverpool, in 1907, but spent most of his life in Cambridge, where he was fellow of Trinity from 1879. Often regarded as one of the founders of modern anthropology, he did much to popularize his own field of study and to make its agnostic tendencies acceptable, although his methods (he relied on secondary sources) and many of his conclusions are now unacceptable. *The Golden Bough* (of which the first volume appeared in 1890, and the twelfth and last in 1915, followed by *Aftermath, a Supplement* in 1936) is a vast and enterprising comparative study of the beliefs and institutions of mankind, offering the thesis that man progresses from magical through religious to scientific thought. Its discussion of fertility rites, the sacrificial killing of kings, the dying god, the scapegoat, etc., and its analysis of the primitive mind, caught the literary imagination, and its influence may perhaps be seen more lastingly in the works of D. H. *Lawrence, T. S. *Eliot, *Pound, and others than in works of scholarly anthropology. Frazer's many other works include *Totemism and Exogamy* (1910) and *Folklore in the Old Testament* (1918), and he also published translations with commentary of Pausanias (1898) and the *Fasti* of *Ovid (1929).

Frederick, the usurping duke in Shakespeare's *As You Like It.*

FREDERICK THE GREAT, of Prussia (1712–86), military genius, able administrator, and a man of considerable culture, who established the nationhood of Prussia. He has strong links with the French Enlightenment: *Rousseau kept Frederick's picture in his room, and *Voltaire and Frederick were for a time mutually admiring correspondents. Several of his poems were published in London with great success. He was the subject of a biography by T. *Carlyle, entitled *The History of Frederick II of Prussia Called Frederick the Great* (6 vols, 1858–65), in which he is described as 'a questionable hero' who nevertheless was able to emerge from a 'century opulent in accumulated falsities'. The work was a labour of many years of what Carlyle himself described as 'horrid struggles'; after finishing it, characteristically, he says he 'sank into new depths of stupefaction and dull misery of body and mind'.

free indirect style, a way of narrating characters' thoughts or utterances that combines some of the features of third-person report with some features of first-person direct speech, allowing a flexible and sometimes ironic overlapping of internal and external perspectives. Free indirect style (a translation of French *style indirecte libre*) dispenses with tag-phrases ('she thought', etc.), and adopts the idiom of the character's own thoughts, including indicators of time and place, as *She'd leave here tomorrow*, rather than 'She decided to leave that place the next day'. The device was exploited by some 19th-cent. novelists such as *Austen and *Flaubert, and has been widely adopted thereafter.

FREEMAN, E(dward) A(ugustus) (1823–92), historian and controversialist. Endowed with private means, which he supplemented by regular writing for the *Saturday Review*, he spent much of his life in the study of medieval and ancient history, but he was handicapped by prolixity and a marked aversion to public libraries, a trait shared by many Victorian scholars (e.g. *Carlyle, *Buckle). His best-known work is his gigantic *History of the Norman Conquest* (5 vols, 1867–79), and its sequel on *The Reign of William Rufus* (2 vols, 1882). Here his Whig belief in the excellence of the British constitution as it had developed from the Conquest was at odds with his deep affection and respect for Anglo-Saxon culture, which also led him to write in a curiously archaic style, eschewing Latin derivations wherever possible. In his hands, therefore, the events of 1066 emerge as a happy tragedy. He was a man of violent temperament and warm emotions, capable of close friendships (for instance with W. *Stubbs and J. R. *Green), but guilty of almost paranoid hatreds which are not rationally explicable, particularly for C. *Kingsley and J. A. *Froude. His aversion to blood sports also involved him in public controversy with A. *Trollope, and all his work is infected with anti-Semitism and a violent though selective xenophobia.

free verse, a term loosely used from the early years of the 20th cent. to describe many forms of irregular, syllabic, or unrhymed verse, freed from the traditional demands of *metre: also known as *vers libre*. The origins of free verse have been variously described, but its widespread adoption in English is commonly associated with *Imagism. Practitioners have included poets as varied as *Rilke, T. S. *Eliot, *Pound, and D. H. *Lawrence.

French Revolution, The: *A History*, the work by which T. *Carlyle established his reputation, written in London 1834–7, published 1837.

It is in three volumes, 'The Bastille', 'The Constitution', and 'The Guillotine'; it opens with the death of Louis XV in 1774, covers the reign of Louis XVI, the period which included the assembly of the States General, the fall of the Bastille, the Constituent and Legislative Assemblies, the flight of the king to Varennes, the Convention, the trial and execution of the king and queen, the reign of terror, the fall of Robespierre, and extends to 5 Oct. 1795, when Bonaparte quelled the insurrection of the Vendémiaire, the title of the last chapter being 'The Whiff of Grapeshot'. It is a work of great narrative and descriptive power, with a notable gallery of portraits (Mirabeau, Lafayette, Danton, Robespierre), and impressive set pieces; it was greatly admired by *Dickens, and was in part the inspiration of *A Tale of Two Cities.

French Revolution, *Reflections on the,* by E. Burke, see REVOLUTION IN FRANCE.

FRENEAU, Philip Morin (1752–1832), the 'poet of the American Revolution', and miscellaneous writer, editor, and journalist, born in New York and educated at the College of New Jersey (later Princeton). He lived for a while (1775–8) in the West Indies, where he wrote poems inspired by the tropical atmosphere and landscape, and in 1780 during the Revolutionary War was captured by the British, an experience which prompted the bitter satire of his poem *The British Prison-Ship* (1781), one of his many attacks on the British. His not wholly prosperous career as a writer was interspersed with periods at sea as a ship's master (1784–90 and 1803–7). His first collection of verse, *Poems* (1786), was followed by various volumes of essays, poems, etc., and he wrote widely for newspapers and periodicals, some of which he also edited. His verse ranged from the satirical and patriotic to works such as 'The Wild Honey Suckle' (1786), a nature poem of delicacy and sensitivity which heralds *Romanticism.

FRERE, John Hookham (1769–1846), educated at Eton and Caius College, Cambridge. He was a friend of *Canning, an MP, and an official of the Foreign Office, who occupied many important positions at home and abroad. While at Eton Frere wrote a translation of *Brunanburh, and was one of the founders of the *Microcosm* periodical (1786–7). He contributed some accomplished humorous verse to the *Anti-Jacobin, including most of 'The Loves of the Triangles' (a parody of E. *Darwin). He collaborated in *Ellis's *Specimens of the Early English Poets* (1801), and in *Southey's *Chronicle of the Cid* (1808); his translations from the *Poema del Cid* were said by *Coleridge to be 'incomparable'. He was one of the founders of the *Quarterly Review* in 1809, and an adviser to John *Murray the publisher. He is, however, chiefly remembered as the inspirer of the style, stanza, and idiom of Byron's *Beppo* and *Don Juan. In the Italian verses of *Pulci he found a verse form and a colloquial voice which he felt could be adapted to English, and in 1817 he published the first two cantos of his mock-epic *Prospectus and Specimen of an Intended National Work . . . by William and Robert Whistlecraft . . . Relating to King Arthur and His Round Table.* It gave *Byron what he wanted, and he describes *Beppo* as 'in or after the excellent manner of Mr Whistlecraft'. Frere also published lively metrical versions of *Aristophanes: *Frogs* (1839); *Acharnians, Knights,* and *Birds* in 1840; and *Theognis Restitutus* (1842).

FREUD, Esther (1963–   ), novelist, born in London, a former actress who achieved immediate success with her first novel *Hideous Kinky* (1992). It tells of a child's upbringing in Morocco at the hands of her bohemian mother, and was widely praised for the authenticity of its young narrator's voice. Set in an abandoned London tower block, *Peerless Flats* (1993) offered a slightly bleaker portrait of dysfunctional families. *Gaglow* (1997) told the parallel stories of an impoverished single mother and her East German ancestors, and like its predecessors was distinguished by a prevailing generosity of spirit, pierced by frequent shafts of irony.

FREUD, Sigmund (1856–1939), born at Freiberg in Moravia, and known as the creator of psychoanalysis, a science (or, as some claim, a mythology) which has had an incalculable effect both on literature and on literary theory. Freud, after studying with the neurologist Charcot in Paris, practised for many years in Vienna, until Hitler's invasion of Austria drove him to London, where he died. His theories of the normal and abnormal mind were evolved originally from his study of neurotic ailments. His many contributions to knowledge include his studies of the development of the sexual instinct in children, his descriptions of the workings of the unconscious mind and of the nature of repression, and his examinations and interpretations of dreams. Many of his concepts have become universally familiar in a vulgarized form, e.g. the Oedipus complex, the death wish, the family romance, penis envy, *phallic symbolism, and the formulation of the divisions between the 'Id, the Ego and the Superego'. Such phrases rapidly acquired a currency even among those who had not read the works of Freud, and direct or indirect influence is frequently hard to ascertain. A characteristic case is that of D. H. Lawrence's *Sons and Lovers* (1913), considered by many a classic example of a novel about the Oedipus complex; Lawrence himself claimed not to have read Freud, and dismissed the theory of complexes as 'vicious half-statements of the Freudians' (1916, on a review in the *Psychoanalytic Review*), but his wife Frieda was greatly interested in psychoanalysis and claimed that they discussed Freud's theories together. L. *Strachey, in *Elizabeth and Essex* (1928), produced what is possibly the first consciously Freud-oriented biography; its many successors include Leon Edel's life of H. *James. The significance for both biographers and novelists of Freud's stress on the formative experiences of childhood is obvious; equally obvious is the importance to poets and prose writers such as *Joyce of Freud's theories of word association, although Joyce (possibly for Freudian reasons) always indignantly repudiated the influence of Freud, whose work he certainly knew. Freud's works were made available in English by James Strachey, Lytton's brother, who was responsible for the *Standard Edition of the Complete Psychological Works of Sigmund Freud* (24 vols, 1953–73). The works reveal Freud himself as a writer of great distinction. (See PSYCHOANALYTIC CRITICISM.) See also Ernest Jones, *The Life and Works of Sigmund Freud* (1953–7) and R. Clark, *Freud: The Man and the Cause* (1980).

Friar Bacon and Friar Bungay, see FRIER BACON, AND FRIER BONGAY.

'Friar's Tale, The', see CANTERBURY TALES, 7.

Friar Tuck, one of the principal characters in the legend of *Robin Hood; the fat, jovial, and pugnacious father confessor of the outlaw chief. He figures in Scott's *Ivanhoe* and in Peacock's *Maid Marian*. See *Ritson's *Robin Hood* (2 vols, 1795, a collection of songs, ballads, etc., with a full introduction) and *The Outlaws of Medieval England* (1961) by M. Keen. (See also BALLAD.)

Friday, Man, see ROBINSON CRUSOE.

FRIEL, Brian (1929–   ), Irish playwright, born Omagh, Co. Tyrone. The suspicious, often despairing, sensibility of Brian Friel's plays may be traced to the experience of growing up as a Catholic outsider in Protestant-dominated Northern Ireland. His great theme is the gulf between private experience and the public world. The public record history, theory, shared memories, even language itself is, in his work, always untrustworthy. Friel began as a short story writer and retains a strong interest in monologue and direct narration, evident in such plays as *Faith Healer* (1979) and *Molly Sweeney* (1994). His first international success, *Philadelphia, Here I Come!* (1964), in which different actors play the main character's public and private selves, established both his reputation and his central concerns. Typically, as in *Translations* (1980) and *Dancing at Lughnasa* (1990), the world on stage is about to implode, a way of seeing that gives substance to his identification as an Irish *Chekhov. He has also adapted works by Chekhov and *Turgenev.

Friend, a weekly periodical edited and largely written by S. T. *Coleridge in the Lake District, 1809–10.

It was the first to publish early sections of Wordsworth's *Prelude*. In its final three-volume book form of 1818, Coleridge transformed it into a substantial series of interlinked essays 'to aid in the formation of fixed principles in politics, morals, and religion, with literary amusements interspersed'. Vol. i contains a notable defence of 'free communication' in the press; vol. ii attacks Jacobin theories of the 'Rights of Man'; vol. iii expounds the 'Principles of Method'.

Friends, Society of, a religious society founded in 1648–50 by G. *Fox, distinguished by faith in the Inner Light; the spiritual equality of men and women; refusal of oaths; plain egalitarian dress, language, and manners; and antagonism to paid clergy and forms of worship. The movement was regarded as subversive by both the Protectorate and the restored monarchy, and heavily persecuted. Each member was also a minister, and the message was carried to Holland, Rome, America, and Turkey. Margaret *Fell first enunciated the peace principle for which Friends are famous, at the Restoration, when a quietist ethic succeeded the revolutionary phase. Quakerism encouraged literacy among people of all ranks: 650 Friends published 3,853 documents before 1700, 82 of the authors being women. The Society has pioneered social reform. Its nickname 'Quakers' reflected the derisive public reaction to the 'quaking' convulsions of early Friends when seized by the power of the Inner Light. See also: PENN, NAYLER, BARCLAY, R.

Friendship's Garland, a collection of essays in letter form by M. *Arnold, originally printed in the *Pall Mall Gazette*, published 1871.

The principal imaginary correspondent is a Prussian, Arminius, Baron von Thunder-ten-Tronckh (a descendant of a character in Voltaire's *Candide*), and through him Arnold expresses his mockery of the English *philistine as represented by Bottles, a wealthy manufacturer; of narrow Liberal reform as represented by the 'deceased-wife's-sister' Act; of the *Daily Telegraph* and its naïve patriotism, and of English foreign and educational policy. Arminius believes in the application of 'Geist' or 'Intelligence', which the English persistently undervalue, and teases 'poor Arnold' for his supposed 'infatuation about everything English'.

Frier Bacon, and Frier Bongay, The Honorable Historie of, a comedy in verse and prose by R. *Greene, acted 1594. The play is partially based on a prose pamphlet *The Famous Historie of Fryer Bacon*, embodying legends relating to R. *Bacon and T. *Bungay.

Bacon with the help of Friar Bungay makes a head of brass, and, conjuring up the devil, learns how to give it speech. It is to speak within a month, but 'if they heard it not before it had done speaking, all their labour should be lost'. After watching day and night for three weeks, Bacon hands over the duty to his servant Miles and falls asleep. The head speaks two words, 'Time is'. Miles, thinking his master would be angry if waked for so little, lets him sleep. The head presently speaks again, 'Time was'; and finally, 'Time is past', when it falls down and breaks. Bacon awakes, and heaps curses on Miles's head. The tale is diversified with the pleasant story of the loves of Edward prince of Wales (afterwards Edward I) and Lord Lacy for the fair Margaret, the keeper's daughter of Fressingfield, and the prince's surrender of her to Lacy. There is also an amusing scene where Bacon, Bungay, and a German rival display their respective powers before the German emperor and the kings of England and Castile.

FRISCH, Max (1911–91), Swiss playwright, diarist, and novelist, also a qualified architect. His best-known plays are *Biedermann und die Brandstifter* (originally written for radio: *The Fire-Raisers*, 1958), a satire on the passivity of the middle class as represented by the man who tolerates, even abets, criminal arson in his own home, and *Andorra* (1961). The novel *Homo Faber* (1957) concerns the helplessness of a technologist to control the events of his life. Coincidences which defy statistical analysis pursue him like the Furies in a Greek tragedy. From the 1960s onwards Frisch published several short stories and essays of an autobiographical nature. His diaries, some previously published, appeared as *Tagebuch 1946–49* (1950) and *Tagebuch 1966–71* (1972).

FROISSART, Jean (*c*.1337–*c*.1410), French chronicler and poet. He travelled widely in western Europe, collecting material for his future histories. In 1361 he was received in England by Edward III, and visited Scotland. In 1366 he accompanied the *Black Prince to Bordeaux, and in 1368 the duke of Clarence to Milan. He revisited England in 1394–5. His chronicles record the chivalric exploits of the nobles of England and France from 1325 to 1400. They were translated into English by John Bourchier (Lord *Berners) in 1523–5. As author of lively personal *lais* and ballades he had some influence on *Chaucer.

FROST, Robert Lee (1874–1963), poet, born in San Francisco of New England stock. He was taken at the age of 10 to the New England farm country of which his poetry was to be so deeply expressive. He spent some time at both Dartmouth College and Harvard, but left to teach, edit a country paper, learn to make shoes, and to farm. In 1912 he came to England with his wife and family, where he published his first volumes of poems, *A Boy's Will* (1913) and *North of Boston* (1914), which contains 'Mending Wall' and 'The Death of the Hired Man'; he met the *Georgian poets, and formed a particularly close and fruitful friendship with E. *Thomas, whom he was to describe as 'the only brother I ever had'. Upon his return to New England in 1915 he settled in New Hampshire and continued to write poetry, supporting himself by successive teaching appointments in several colleges. His volumes include *Mountain Interval* (1916), which contains 'Birches' and 'The Road Not Taken'; *New Hampshire* (1923); *Collected Poems* (1930); *A Witness Tree* (1942); and *In the Clearing* (1962). He established himself as one of the most popular of 20th-cent. American poets, admired for the blend of colloquial and traditional in his verse, and hailed as a fitting heir, in his response to the natural world, of *Wordsworth and *Emerson; his dramatic monologues and pastorals have been particularly popular. But beneath the country lore and wisdom hailed in a 1913 review of his first book by N. *Douglas as his 'simple woodland philosophy' lay a more troubled, combative, at times destructive spirit, both in his life and work, expressed in such poems as 'Fire and Ice' (1923) and 'Bereft' (1928), which led to *Trilling's praise of him, on the occasion of his 85th birthday, as a 'poet of terror'. His *Selected Letters*, ed. L. Thompson, were published in 1965.

'Frost at Midnight', a blank-verse poem by S. T. *Coleridge written at Stowey, Somerset, in Feb. 1798. Addressed to his sleeping child Hartley *Coleridge, it meditates on the poet's own boyhood, and magically evokes the countryside, ending on a note of rare and thrilling happiness. It is possibly the finest of Coleridge's series of 'conversation' poems.

Froth, Lord and Lady, characters in Congreve's *The Double Dealer*.

FROUDE, J(ames) A(nthony) (1818–94), historian. Educated at Westminster and Oriel College, Oxford, he was an early casualty of the *Oxford movement. Surrendering to the charismatic leadership of J. H. *Newman, he lost his faith when Newman reneged on the Church of England in 1845. Out of his religious agonies and his sexual frustrations he wrote a bad but spectacular novel, *The Nemesis of Faith* (1849), which obliged him to resign his fellowship at Exeter College and leave for London, where he maintained himself by journalism; he wrote for several of the reviews, and edited *Fraser's Magazine* 1860–74. He now fell under the influence of *Carlyle, and became one of his most faithful companions, though with no apparent effect on his own work; he was also a friend of A. H. *Clough and C. *Kingsley (later his brother-in-law). His *History of England from the Death of Cardinal Wolsey to the Defeat of the Spanish Armada* (12 vols, 1856–70) was a distinguished work of scholarship on which all subsequent Tudor studies rest, and he was the first English historian to make a thorough and systematic use of archive material in the manner laid down by Ranke. He was also the first to publicize and glorify the deeds of the Elizabethan seamen, a topic to which he returned in his Oxford lectures on *English Seamen in the Sixteenth Century* (1892–4, pub. 1895). All his books were highly successful, even his collected essays, *Short Studies in Great Subjects* (4 vols, 1867–83); but he was criticized for his partisan treatment of the English Reformation and his attempt to rehabilitate Henry VIII, and the accuracy of his scholarship was unjustly impugned by E. A. *Freeman, whose charges seem to have been accepted by the profession, especially when Froude went on to publish a slipshod history of 18th-cent. Ireland (2 vols, 1872–4). Latterly he seemed to attract public controversy; his American lecture tour in 1872 was cut short by Irish nationalist agitation, his attempt to intervene in South African politics in 1874–5 provoked a storm, and even his visit to the West Indies in 1886–7 had political repercussions. But this was nothing to the uproar which greeted his *Reminiscences* of Carlyle (1881) and his *Letters and Memorials* of Jane Welsh *Carlyle (1883), which were distinguished by their shattering frankness. Nevertheless, in 1892 Lord Salisbury offered him the Regius chair of modern history at Oxford, an appointment which met with a distinctly mixed reception. He was a brilliant public speaker and his lectures attracted large audiences, but he died after only two years in office.

See Herbert Paul's *Life of Froude* (1907) and Waldo Hilary Dunn's biography (1961–3).

FROUDE, R(ichard) H(urrell) (1803–36), Tractarian, brother of J. A. *Froude, educated at Oriel College, Oxford, where he became a fellow. He was intimate with *Newman with whom he collaborated in the early stages of the *Oxford movement. He contributed three of the *Tracts for the Times* and wrote poems contained in *Lyra Apostolica*. His *Remains* (1838–9), including strictures on the Reformers, aroused public hostility against the movement.

Frugal, Sir John and Luke, characters in Massinger's *The City Madam.*

FRY, Christopher (Harris) (1907–2005), born in Bristol of Quaker stock. He worked as schoolmaster, actor, and theatre director before making his name as a playwright with works that were hailed in the late 1940s as a sign of a new renaissance of poetic drama; his mystical and religious plays (*The Boy with a Cart*, 1939; *The Firstborn*, 1946; *Thor with Angels*, 1949; *A Sleep of Prisoners*, 1951) were frequently compared to those of T. S. *Eliot, though the theatre-going public tended to prefer the ebullient optimism and exuberant word-play of his comedies, e.g. *A Phoenix Too Frequent* (1946, based on *Petronius), *The Lady's Not for Burning* (1949, set in the Middle Ages), and *Venus Observed* (1950, a romantic château comedy). *The Dark is Light Enough* (1954) was less successful; the vogue for poetic drama proved short-lived, giving way to the *kitchen sink school, and *Curtmantle* (1962), about *Becket, struck critics as dated. Fry also wrote several screenplays, including that of *Ben-Hur* (1959), and successful translations and adaptations of *Anouilh (*Ring round the Moon*, 1950; *The Lark*, 1955) and *Giraudoux (*Tiger at the Gates*, 1955; *Duel of Angels*, 1958).

FRY, Roger Eliot (1866–1934), art critic and painter, born in London of a Quaker family, educated at Clifton and King's College, Cambridge, where he read natural sciences and became a member of the *Apostles. He became art critic of the *Athenaeum* in 1901, helped to establish the *Burlington Magazine* in 1903, and from 1906 to 1910 was employed by the Metropolitan Museum of Art in New York. On his return to England he organized two highly influential and controversial exhibitions of 'Post-Impressionist' paintings (a term he coined himself) at the Grafton Galleries in 1910 and 1912, and his collected essays (*Vision and Design*, 1920; *Transformations*, 1926) were also instrumental in spreading his enthusiasm for modern French painting. He was closely associated with the *Bloomsbury Group, and his biography was written by V. *Woolf (1940).

FRYE, Northrop (1912–91), Canadian critic. Born in Sherbrooke, Quebec, he studied at Victoria College, University of Toronto, and, after ordination in the United Church of Canada, at Oxford. Returning to Toronto as a lecturer, he wrote *Fearful Symmetry* (1947), an influential defence of William *Blake's allegorical system. His most important book is *Anatomy of Criticism* (1957), which redirected American literary theory away from the 'close reading' of *New Criticism and towards the larger meanings of literary genres, modes, and *archetypes. Rejecting critical evaluation in favour of a value-free literary science, Frye elaborates here a comprehensive map of the literary 'universe' in a boldly schematic series of

classifications. His early work did much to redeem the genre of romance, the subject of his later book *The Secular Scripture* (1976). He wrote three books on Shakespeare, two collections of essays on Canadian literature, and the more ambitious work *The Great Code: The Bible and Literature* (1982), among many other writings. His emphasis on the deeper 'codes' or generic structures under the surface of literature foreshadowed the later turn to *structuralism in literary studies.

Fudge Family in Paris, The, verses by T. *Moore, under the pseudonym of Thomas Brown the Younger, published 1818.

In these light verses the author endeavoured to collect 'the concentrated essence of the various forms of cockneyism and nonsense of those groups of ridiculous English who were at that time swarming in all directions throughout Paris'. They take the form of letters written by or to various members of the Fudge family when visiting Paris in 1817, shortly after the restoration of the Bourbons. They include inane descriptions by the mindless Fudges, and pompous, sycophantic letters from Mr Fudge to *Castlereagh.

FUENTES, Carlos (1928–   ), Mexican writer and critic, who was born in Panama City and grew up speaking excellent English. His first novel, *La región más transparente* (1958; *Where the Air is Clear*), explores the expanding megapolis Mexico City. *La muerte de Artemio Cruz* (1962; *The Death of Artemio Cruz*) narrates the failure of the Mexican Revolution. His prolific output includes *Terra nostra* (1975; *Terra Nostra*, 1976), *Gringo viejo* (1985; *Old Gringo*,1986), *Cristóbal Nonato* (1985; *Christopher Unborn*), *Constancia y otras novelas para vírgenes* (1989; *Constancia and Other Stories for Virgins*, 1990); *La campaña* (1990; *The Campaign*, 1991), *El naranjo* (1988; *The Orange Tree*, 1994), *Diana o la cazadora solitaria* (1994; *Diana: The Goddess Who Hunts Alone*, 1995) and *La frontera de cristal* (1996; *The Crystal Frontier: A Novel in 9 Stories*, 1998). He combines vivid realism with a baroque verbal fantasy and is a satirist and acute political commentator.

FUGARD, Athol (1932–   ), South African playwright, born in Middlesburg, the son of a small shopowner; he was brought up in Port Elizabeth and educated there and at Cape Town University. After various jobs, some connected with the theatre, he moved in 1958 with his actress wife to Johannesburg, where he worked for some time as clerk to the Native Commissioner's Court, an experience which greatly sharpened his awareness of racial tension and inequality, the subject of much of his drama. His plays include *The Blood Knot* (1961, pub. 1963), about the fraught relationship of two coloured brothers; *Boesman and Lena* (1968, pub. 1969), a sombre work figuring a derelict middle-aged couple of Coloured migrant workers, whose presence as they set up their shelter on the open stage has a symbolic quality akin to that of the characters of *Beckett; *Sizwe Bansi is Dead* (1972, pub. 1974, written with John Kani and Winston Ntshona), based on the problems created by the pass laws; *A Lesson from Aloes* (1980, pub. 1981), which contrasts the political attitudes, ranging from stoicism to defeat, of an Afrikaner, his wife, and their Coloured friends; and *'Master Harold' . . . and the Boys* (1982, pub. 1983), portraying the relationship between a white South African teenager and two black family servants, 'the boys'.

Fugard's career has been greatly complicated by the politics of racialism; he was in 1962 active in encouraging a boycott of South African theatre by overseas English-speaking playwrights, insisting that plays should be performed before non-segregated audiences, but later modified this attitude in view of the complexities and necessities of a situation which his own works vividly evoke.

FULBRIGHT, James William (1905–95), American senator educated at Arkansas and Oxford, who in 1946 established the programme that provided government grants for the international exchange of students, a programme extravagantly described as 'the largest and most significant movement of scholars across the face of the earth since the fall of Constantinople in 1453'.

Fulgens and Lucrece, a late 15th-cent. *interlude by Henry Medwall (fl. 1486), regarded as the earliest known purely secular play in English. It has been edited by G. Wickham in *English Moral Interludes* (1976).

FULLER, John Leopold (1937–   ), poet and novelist, son of Roy *Fuller. His several volumes of poetry include *Fairground Music* (1961), *The Tree that Walked* (1967), *Cannibals and Missionaries* (1972), *Lies and Secrets* (1979, which contains one of his most sustained works, 'The Most Difficult Position', about the non-confrontation of two 19th-cent. chess masters), *The Illusionists* (1980), a satiric narrative in stanza form of contemporary life, and *Selected Poems 1954–1982* (1985). His poems range from lyrics to pastiche verse epistles, from sonnets to long unrhymed monologues, and his subjects are also diverse. In collaboration with J. *Fenton he wrote a collection of satirical poems, *Partingtime Hall* (1987). His *Collected Poems* were published in 1996. His novel *Flying to Nowhere* (1983), set on a Welsh island, is a fantasy about a 16th-cent. abbot who thinks he has discovered, through surgical dissection, the seat of the soul. Other novels include *The Adventures of Speedfall* (1985), *Tell It Me Again* (1988), *The Burning Boys* (1989).

FULLER, (Sarah) Margaret (1810–50), American author and feminist, born in Massachusetts, whose name is associated with the New England Transcendentalists; she helped to found the *Dial, which she edited for two years from 1840 to 1842, and at the same period (1839–44) conducted a series of conversations or seminars for educated women in Boston. One of the

products of these discussions was her influential feminist tract *Women in the Nineteenth Century* (1845). In 1844 she moved to New York, where she wrote for Greeley's *New York Tribune*, and in 1846 she went to Europe and settled in Italy, where she married one of Mazzini's followers, the Marquis Ossoli. Sailing from Livorno to America in 1850, she and her husband were drowned when their ship was wrecked just short of its destination. Her *Memoirs* (1852) were edited by *Emerson, W. H. Channing, and J. F. Clarke. She is said to have suggested the character of the magnetic and passionate Zenobia in Hawthorne's *The Blithedale Romance*.

FULLER, Roy Broadbent (1912–91), poet and novelist, born near and brought up in Oldham, the son of a director of a rubber-proofing company. He was educated at Blackpool High School, and then became a solicitor, working for many years for a building society. During the 1930s he contributed to left-wing literary magazines, including *New Verse, and his first volume, *Poems* (1939), shows the influence of *Auden and *Spender. This was followed by several collections of poetry: *Collected Poems 1936–1961* (1962), with work from several previous volumes, forms a link between the poets of the 1930s and the poets of the *Movement, in its lucid, ironic, detached tone, and its formal accomplishment. His later volumes, which include *From the Joke Shop* (1975) and *The Reign of Sparrows* (1980), while displaying an equal interest in technique, frequently strike a more personal note, particularly in the many sardonic reflections on old age and the ageing process. Fuller also published several novels, including, notably, *Image of a Society* (1956), which is a portrait of personal and professional conflicts in a northern provincial building society, narrated in a low-key, naturalistic, yet ironic manner. He was professor of poetry at Oxford, 1968–73, and *Owls and Artificers* (1971) and *Professors and Gods* (1973) are collections of his Oxford lectures. He also published three volumes of memoirs, *Souvenirs* (1980), *Vamp till Ready* (1982), and *Home and Dry* (1984).

FULLER, Thomas (1608–61), born at Aldwinkle St Peter's in Northamptonshire and educated at Queens' and Sidney Sussex colleges, Cambridge. He became rector of Broadwindsor, Dorset, in 1634, and shortly before the Civil War was made a preacher at the Savoy. A moderate Royalist, he followed the war as chaplain to Sir Ralph Hopton and during his travels conceived the idea of 'a more exact collection' of the worthies of England. After the Restoration he became 'chaplain in extraordinary' to the king. He published *The Historie of the Holy Warre* (i.e. of the Crusades) in 1639; *The Holy State and the Profane State* in 1642; *Good Thoughts in Bad Times* in 1645 (followed by two sequels); *A Pisgah-Sight of Palestine*, a topographical and historical work, in 1650. His *The Church-History of Britain; with the History of the University of Cambridge* (1655), which covers from the birth of Christ to the execution of

Charles I, was criticized (by *Heylyn, among others) for its 'puns and quibbles' and its 'trencher-jests', but was widely read and enjoyed. *The History of the *Worthies of England*, his best-known and most characteristic work, appeared after his death in 1662, and was the fruit of much research; in his own words, 'My pains have been scattered all over the land, by riding, writing, going, sending, chiding, begging, praying, and sometimes paying too, to procure manuscript material.' *Lamb referred to him as 'the dear, fine, silly, old angel', and he was much admired by *Coleridge. His writings are marked by a lively and eccentric curiosity, by 'fantastic caprices' (L. *Stephen), and by a fondness for aphorisms.

Funeral, The, or *Grief à-la-Mode*, a comedy by R. *Steele, produced 1701.

Lord Brumpton has disinherited his son Lord Hardy, owing to the misrepresentations of his wife, the young man's stepmother; he has left her all his property, as well as two wards, the ladies Sharlot and Harriot. When the play opens Lord Brumpton has, as is generally believed, just died. He has in fact, however, recovered from a 'lethargic slumber', a fact known only to himself and his steward Trusty (and the audience). At Trusty's instance he remains in concealment, and thus discovers his supposed widow's unseemly rejoicing at her release, her machinations against her stepson, and her unscrupulous design to dispose profitably of Sharlot and Harriot. The widow is exposed, Lord Hardy reinstated, and the ladies bestowed on their true lovers, Lord Hardy and his friend. The devices by which these results are effected are somewhat clumsy; but the play is notable as marking a change of moral tone in the drama after the licentiousness of the *Restoration.

Fungoso, a foolish law student in Jonson's *Every Man out of His Humour*, obsessed with courtly fashion.

FURNIVALL, Frederick James (1825–1910), educated at University College London and Trinity College, Cambridge. He began his career as a barrister, but soon devoted his great energy to educational, philological, and literary pursuits. He was from 1847 a member of the *Philological Society, and became its secretary; in 1861 he became editor of the proposed New English Dictionary which developed into the *Oxford English Dictionary*. He founded the *Early English Text Society (1864), the Chaucer Society (1868), the Ballad Society (1869), the New Shakspere Society (1873), the Wyclif Society (1881), the Browning Society (1881), and the Shelley Society (1886), and himself edited many texts. He was also a leader in the move for popular education, supported women's rights, and taught grammar at the Working Men's College founded in 1854.

FUSELI, or **FÜSSLI,** Henry (1741–1825), Swiss artist who came to England in 1764; after studying in Rome (1770–8) he settled in London. Fuseli's works show the powerful attraction that Burke's *sublime of terror held for early Romantic artists. He was fascinated by the supernatural and by the darkest of human passions; the disturbing intensity of his works depends on sudden contrasts of scale, and on the frenzied expressions and muscular energy of his stylized figures. Fuseli drew his subjects from Shakespeare, *Milton, *Dante, *Ossian, and other poets. His were the most brilliant contributions to *Boydell's Shakespeare Gallery; a monumental series of illustrations to Milton reflect the Romantic conception of Satan as hero. The fame of the *Nightmare* (1782; the earliest version is in Detroit, Institute of Arts), a work full of Gothic horror, spread throughout Europe. Fuseli, who began his career as a translator, was a learned artist who shone in literary and artistic society in London. His extravagant wit is recorded by many of his contemporaries and his lectures and essays illumine the intellectual life of his times. Both *Hazlitt and *Coleridge despised his nightmare fantasy, but *Blake, a constant friend, wrote: 'The only man that e'er I knew | Who did not make me almost spew | Was Fuseli.' The two artists admired each other and worked together: Blake engraved some of Fuseli's designs and Fuseli wrote the preface to Blake's edition of *Blair's *The Grave*. Mary *Wollstonecraft suffered from an obsessive passion for Fuseli.

FUST, Johann (d. 1467), German goldsmith. He financed *Gutenberg's experiments in printing, but the partnership between them was dissolved probably in 1455 and Fust carried on with his son-in-law Peter Schöffer. Their Latin Psalter of 1457 is the first to bear a printer's imprint and date. R. *Browning wrote a dialogue, 'Fust and His Friends' (in *Parleyings with Certain People*).

Futurism, a 20th-cent. avant-garde movement in Italian art, literature, and music, promoted by *Marinetti and others. Its programme, outlined in the *Futurist Manifesto* (1909), was to break with the past and its academic culture and to celebrate technology, dynamism, and power. In language and in poetry it advocated the destruction of traditional syntax, metre, and punctuation in the name of the 'free word'. The *Manifesto of Futurist Painting* (1910), by Boccioni, Carrà, Balla, Russolo, and Severini, advocated a new art which represented nature in a dynamic state and in simultaneous movements. The movement petered out during the 1930s after Marinetti's incorporation into Fascist academic culture. (For Russian Futurism, see MAYAKOVSKY.)

G

GABORIAU, Émile (1832–73), French writer of crime fiction, considered to be the first practitioner in France of the *roman policier*. He created two famous characters, the professional detective Monsieur Lecoq and the amateur Le Père Tabaret. Gaboriau's best-known works are: *L'Affaire Lerouge* (1866), *Le Crime d'Orcival* (1867), *Le Dossier No. 113* (1867), *Monsieur Lecoq* (1869), *Les Esclaves de Paris* (1869).

Gabriel, the name of one of the archangels (Dan. 9: 21 and Luke 1: 19, 26). The name means 'strength of God' in Hebrew. In Islam he is Jibril, the angel who dictated the *Koran to Muhammad. Milton makes him 'Chief of the angelic guards' (*Paradise Lost, IV. 550).

GADBURY, John, see ALMANACS.

GADDA, Carlo Emilio (1893–1973), Italian novelist. His most important novels are *Il castello di Udine* (*The Castle of Udine*, 1934), a memoir of his experience in the First World War; *Adalgisa* (1944), a critique of contemporary Milanese society; and the unfinished *Cognizione del dolore* (*The Cognizance of Sorrow*, 1963, written 1938–41). Also unfinished is *Quel pasticciaccio brutto de via Merulana* (*That Dreadful Mess on the Via Merulana*, 1957), which uses the conventions of the thriller to dissect Roman society under Fascism. That his two major works are incomplete is not accidental: in *Cognizione* the relationship between the protagonist and his mother is irresolvable, and *Pasticciaccio* stops short of revealing the murderer. His style is remarkable for its grotesquerie, its implicit use of European philosophy, and its pastiches of different languages and dialects.

GADDIS, William (1922–98), American novelist, born in New York and educated at Harvard where he briefly edited the *Harvard Lampoon*. His four novels, three of them epic in scope and all published at extremely long intervals, give him a unique place in contemporary world literature: an unforgiving satirist possessed of an almost Victorian moral sternness, combined with the bracingly experimental technique of the true modernist. The hero of his enormous first novel *The Recognitions* (1955) is Wyatt Gwyon, who has abandoned his training as a priest to become a forger of Old Masters. The book offers a disquisition on real and false spiritual values which is highly complex, but at least written in conventional prose. For *J.R.* (1975) Gaddis gave up this approach and instead told his story of an 11-year-old stockmarket dealer entirely in fractured, overlapping, often incoherent dialogue. Both *J.R.* and the smaller-scale *Carpenter's Gothic* (1985) are bleak, dismayed, but bitterly funny portraits of a society driven mad by material greed and spiritual emptiness. The more jaunty *A Frolic of His Own* (1994), a satire on America's obsession with litigation, is perhaps the best place to start exploring this most pleasurably daunting of modern writers.

Gadshill, near Rochester, the scene of Prince *Hal's joke robbery of *Falstaff in Shakespeare's *1 *Henry IV* (II. ii); confusingly, one of Falstaff's companions also has the name Gadshill. Gadshill was the home of *Dickens in his later years.

Gaheris, Sir, in *Malory, the fourth and youngest son of King Lot of Orkney and Arthur's sister Morgawse. He killed his mother when he found her in bed with Lamorak. He was accidentally killed by Launcelot, an event which led to the implacable hatred of his brother Gawain for Launcelot. Variant forms of his name are confusable with variants of Gareth (Gaheret) his brother, so the two may be archetypally identical.

GAIMAR, Geoffrei (fl. *c.*1140), author of *L'Estoire des Engleis*, an Anglo-Norman romance history in octosyllabic rhymed couplets covering the period from the Anglo-Saxon settlements to the death of William Rufus. An earlier section, beginning (like *Geoffrey of Monmouth's contemporary *History*) with the fall of Troy, has been lost, probably as a consequence of being replaced in the manuscripts by the more fashionable account by *Wace. It contains the Lincolnshire story of Havelok, corresponding to the Anglo-Norman *Le Lai d'Havelok*. Gaimar was probably a secular clerk of Norman blood; his work has no great historical authority. His patron was Ralph FitzGilbert of Lincolnshire and Hampshire, areas in which Gaimar displays particular interest. See *L'Estoire des Engleis*, ed. A. Bell (Anglo-Norman Texts Soc., 1960); English trans. by T. D. Hardy and C. T. Martin (Rolls Series, 1888–9).

GAINSBOROUGH, Thomas (1727–88), portrait and landscape painter; after training in London he returned to his native Suffolk (1748). He painted landscapes and small portrait groups in landscape settings, of which the most famous is *Mr and Mrs Andrews* (*c.*1748, London, National Gallery). From 1774 he worked in London where he became a fashionable portrait painter, and his varied landscapes included rococo idylls, seascapes, and pictures of mountain grandeur—in 1783 he planned a visit to the Lakes 'to show you that your Grays and Dr Brownes were tawdry fan-Painters'. The 'fancy pictures', Arcadian rustic themes like the *Peasant Girl Gathering Sticks*, led on to the sentiment of early *Romanticism. Gainsborough, in both style and temperament, is quite unlike his rival *Reynolds, although Reynolds's *Fourteenth Discourse* is a fine appreciation of his art. Gainsborough's biographer and friend William Jackson wrote that he 'avoided the company of literary men, who were his aversion . . . he detested reading . . .'. Yet Jackson compared the style of Gainsborough's letters to that of *Sterne and the letters—spontaneous, vivid, and intimate—create a strong sense of character.

Gai saber, the title of a 13th-cent. society in Toulouse which devoted itself to a consideration and cultivation of the courtly troubadour idea of 'jois', 'exaltation'.

Galafron, or **Galaphron,** in *Orlando innamorato* and *Orlando furioso*, the king of Cathay and father of *Angelica.

Galahad, Sir (The Haute Prince), in *Malory, is (by enchantment) the son of *Launcelot and *Elaine, daughter of King *Pelles. He is predestined by his immaculate purity to achieve the Siege Perilous (see ROUND TABLE) and the *Grail, after the vision of which he dies in ecstasy.

GALDÓS, Benito Pérez (1843–1920), Spanish novelist, playwright, and journalist, born in the Canary Islands, who spent most of his life in Madrid, a city of which he became the chronicler. His output was vast: he published a series of 46 historical novels between 1873 and 1912, to which he gave the general title of *Episodios nacionales*. Of his novels of contemporary life, the best known is his masterpiece, *Fortunata y Jacinta* (1887), an extraordinarily rich, realistic, densely populated panoramic work which follows the fortunes of two contrasted women, but also explores Spanish society, history, and politics. Galdós published a translation of Dickens's *Pickwick Papers* in 1868: he greatly admired both Dickens and Shakespeare, and made many visits to England, where he was elected fellow of the *Royal Society of Literature.

Galehaut (or **Galehault**) of Surluse and the Long Isles, a highly significant character in the story of the love of Launcelot and Guinevere as described in the early 13th-cent. French prose 'Vulgate' cycle. He was a close friend of Launcelot who demanded tribute from Arthur; he first introduced the lovers but later became jealous of the queen's influence over Launcelot. He is most famous as the Galeotto in *Dante's reference to this story in the episode of Paolo and Francesca (*Inferno*, v. 137). *Malory wrongly calls him 'the Haute Prince' through a confusion with the similar name *Galahad. See J. Frappier, 'The Vulgate Cycle' in R. S. Loomis (ed.), *Arthurian Literature in the Middle Ages* (1959), 299.

GALEN (Claudius Galenus) (*c.* AD 129–99), perhaps the most influential of ancient physicians. He is reputed to have written some 500 treatises in Greek, a number of which have survived. Translated into Latin during the 11th and 12th cents, his writings dominated the development of medieval medicine, and in the 16th cent. he was greatly esteemed also as an exponent of scientific method. *Linacre translated six of his works and there are references to him in *Chaucer, F. *Bacon, and Sir T. *Browne.

Galeotto, see GALEHAUT.

GALIGNANI, Giovanni Antonio (1757–1821). With his English wife Anne Parsons he set up an English bookshop and circulating library in Paris *c.*1799, and in 1814 founded a newspaper, *Galignani's Messenger*, which had a wide circulation among English residents on the Continent. The paper was carried on by his sons John Anthony (1796–1873) and William (1798–1882), who were born in London. As publishers in Paris they issued reprints of English books, and guides to Paris, Switzerland, etc. There is a bookshop of this name on the rue de Rivoli in Paris.

GALILEO GALILEI (1564–1642), Italian astronomer and physicist, born in Pisa of a Florentine family. In 1604 he demonstrated that unequal weights drop with equal velocity, an observation apocryphally said to be based on the dropping of weights from the leaning Tower of Pisa. In 1609 he assembled a telescope on the basis of reports of such an instrument in Holland, and so discovered the moons of Jupiter, the phases of Venus, the configuration of the Moon, and the stars invisible to the naked eye, all of which were described in *Sidereus Nuncius* ('Starry Messenger', 1610). His two principal works were *Dialogo sopra i due massimi sistemi del mondo* (1632), in which Copernicanism is shown to be superior to the Ptolemaic cosmology, and *Due nuove scienze*, an exposition of the mathematics of moving bodies. Galileo's publications led him into conflict with the Inquisition; in 1616 he was forbidden to teach Copernican cosmology and in 1634 he was compelled to repudiate it and sentenced to life imprisonment, commuted to house arrest. (The story of his muttering 'eppur si muove'—'yet it does move'—after his recantation is also apocryphal.) Milton records his meeting with Galileo in *Areopagitica and recalls the 'optic glass' of 'the Tuscan artist' in *Paradise Lost* I.

Galliambic, the metre of the *Attis* of *Catullus, so called because it was the metre used by the Galli, or priests of Cybele, in their songs. It was imitated by *Tennyson in his 'Boadicea':

> So the Queen Boädicéa, standing loftily charioted,
> Brandishing in her hand a dart and rolling glances lioness-like,
> Yell'd and shriek'd between her daughters in her fierce volubility.

GALLOWAY, Janice (1956–   ), Scottish novelist and short story writer, born in Ayrshire, where she worked as a teacher before becoming a full-time writer. Her first novel, *The Trick is to Keep Breathing* (1990), a typographically experimental and psychologically intense story of mental breakdown, was followed by *Blood* (1991), a collection of short stories (some very short) which combine sharp observation of daily life, predominantly urban, with a sense of the imminent uncanny. Later works, which include *Foreign Parts* (1994, novel) and *Where You Find It* (1996, interlinked short stories), continue to explore with sharp immediacy inner states, sexual obsessions, and contemporary mores.

GALSWORTHY, John (1867–1933), educated at Harrow and New College, Oxford, and trained for the law. But a chance meeting with *Conrad, and the strong influence of his future wife, turned him to writing, in which career he was greatly assisted by a long association, beginning in 1900, with E. *Garnett. His first volume of stories, *From the Four Winds*, appeared in 1897 and in 1898 his first novel, *Jocelyn*, which he never republished. The first appearance of the Forsyte family was in one of the stories in *Man of Devon* (1901). In 1902 he married Ada, his cousin's wife, with whom he had been living for ten years. *The Island Pharisees* (1904), a novel revealing his abiding interest in the effects of poverty and the constraints of convention, was much praised and other novels followed including *Fraternity* (1909), which attacked the artificial veneer of urban life, and *The Dark Flower* (1913), about the creative and disruptive effects of love. The first of the Forsyte novels, *The Man of Property*, appeared in 1906, followed by *In Chancery* (1920) and *To Let* (1921) which, together with two interludes, appeared collectively as *The Forsyte Saga* in 1922. The second part of the Forsyte chronicles, containing *The White Monkey* (1924), *The Silver Spoon* (1926), *Swan Song* (1928), and the two interludes 'A Silent Wooing' and 'Passers By', was published as *A Modern Comedy* in 1929. In 1931 Galsworthy followed the immense success of the Forsyte books with a further collection of stories, *On Forsyte Change*.

Galsworthy began his playwriting career in 1906 with *The Silver Box*—a play about theft in which he employed a favourite device of 'parallel' families, one rich and one poor. This was the first of a long line of plays on social and moral themes. His reputation as a dramatist became firmly established with *Strife* (1909), an examination of men and managers in industry, which was followed by *Justice* (1910), in which a minor felon is ground down by the cruel majesty of the law; the play was part of Galsworthy's long campaign against the practice of solitary confinement, a campaign which strongly influenced the Home Office. His later plays include *The Skin Game* (1920), tracing the rivalry between a nouveau riche manufacturer and an aristocrat; *Loyalties* (1922); and *Old English* (1924). Posthumous publications included *Collected Poems* (1934) and in 1935 *The End of the Chapter*, consisting of *Maid in Waiting* (1931), *The Flowering Wilderness* (1932), and *Over the River* (1933), relating the family history of the Charwells, cousins of the younger Forsytes. Galsworthy was awarded the *Nobel Prize for literature in 1932; he was already an OM, and received many other honours.

GALT, John (1779–1839), born in Ayrshire, employed for some time in the customs house at Greenock. While travelling on the Continent he made the acquaintance of *Byron (of whom he published a life in 1830) and later of *Carlyle, who admired his work. From 1824 to 1827 he was secretary of the Canada Company, and between 1825 and 1829 he visited Canada as a member of a government commission to evaluate the price of land, but these enterprises proved unprofitable and he returned to England to meet heavy debts and to make his living by his pen. Galt produced a good deal of miscellaneous writing, including poems, dramas, historical novels, and travel books, but is chiefly remembered for his studies of country life in Scotland: *The Ayrshire Legatees* (1821), *Annals of the Parish* (1821), *The Entail* (1823), *The Provost* (1822), and *The Member* (1832). The last two were reprinted in 1973 and 1975 respectively, edited by Ian A. Gordon, who also published *John Galt: The Life of a Writer* (1972). Galt was not greatly admired in his own time, but he made a unique contribution to fiction with the subtlety and irony of his writing in the first person, and he was an acute observer of social change. He wished his most important fiction to be regarded not as 'novels' but as 'theoretical histories'.

Game and Playe of the Chesse, The, a translation by *Caxton from Vignay's French version of the *Liber de ludo scacchorum* of Jacobus de Cessolis, probably the second book printed at Caxton's press in Bruges, 1474.

Game at Chesse, A, a comedy by T. *Middleton, produced 1624, when it successfully ran for nine nights at the Globe until suppressed by the authorities.

It deals allegorically with the rivalry of England and Spain (the White House and the Black House) and the project of the 'Spanish Marriage' (1623), the failed plan for Prince Charles to marry the Spanish infanta in 1623. The play places on the stage the sovereigns of the two countries, Charles, prince of Wales, Buckingham, and the Spanish ambassador *Gondomar, and represents the discomfiture of the Black House. The play, reflecting the popular aversion to the Spanish match, was enthusiastically received, but gave great offence to the Spanish ambassador and to King James.

Gamelyn, The Tale of, a verse romance of the mid-14th cent. from the East Midlands, in 902 lines of long couplets. It is found in a number of manuscripts of *The Canterbury Tales*, usually assigned to the Cook, and it is possible that Chaucer did intend to write a version of it for use as the Cook's tale. It is included in *Skeat's *Chaucerian and Other Pieces*, appended as vol. vii to his edition of Chaucer.

Gamelyn is the youngest of three brothers whose father leaves them his property in equal shares but whose eldest brother cheats him of his entitlement. Like Orlando in *As You Like It* (which is clearly related to it), Gamelyn overthrows the court wrestler and flees to the forest, from where he wages a campaign to recover his birthright, ultimately with success. The story also has striking affinities with the legends of *Robin Hood. It has been edited by D. B. Sands in *Middle English Verse Romances* (1966).

Gamester, The, a comedy by J. *Shirley, acted 1633, printed 1637.

This was one of Shirley's most popular plays, adapted (and sentimentalized) by C. *Johnson in 1712 as *The Wife's Relief* and by *Garrick in 1758 as *The Gamesters*. Its main plot is taken from the *Heptameron* of Marguerite of Navarre.

Wilding, the title character, tells his wife of his intention to make love to his ward, her relation Penelope, and makes an assignation with the girl. Mrs Wilding takes Penelope's place; Wilding, who has just lost heavily to his friend Hazard, sends him in his place as a way of paying his debt. Naturally, when husband and wife compare notes, he is appalled at the revelation of the double bed-trick. To save his honour and conceal his own cuckolding, he arranges for Hazard to marry Penelope; it then turns out that everyone's honour has been preserved anyway, so he has cheated himself twice. There is a romantic sub-plot, and a comic one featuring young Barnacle, a citizen's son who wants to learn the art of being a 'roaring boy'.

The Gamester is also the title of a play by Mrs *Centlivre and of a tragedy by E. *Moore.

Gammer Gurtons Nedle, the second English comedy in verse (the first being *Ralph Roister Doister*), published 1575, having been acted 1566, at Christ's College, Cambridge. Its authorship has been attributed either to J. Still, fellow of Christ's College, or to William Stevenson, also a fellow of the college and one of its leading spirits in dramatic activities.

It is written in rhymed long doggerel, and deals farcically with the losing and finding of the needle used to mend the garments of Hodge, Gammer Gurton's man. The other characters, besides Hodge and the Gammer, are Tib and Cock, their maid and boy; Diccon the Bedlem; Dame Chatte and Doll, her maid; Master Baylye and his servant Scapethryft; Doctor Rat the curate; and Gyb the cat. The mischievous Diccon persuades the Gammer that Dame Chatte has taken the needle; a quarrel ensues and Doctor Rat is called in, but gets his head broken. Finally Hodge becomes acutely aware that the needle is in the seat of his breeches. The play includes the famous old drinking song with the refrain:

> Back and syde go bare, go bare,
> booth foote and hande go colde:
> But Bellye god sende thee good ale ynoughe,
> whether it be newe or olde.

Gamp, Sarah, a character in Dickens's *Martin Chuzzlewit*. Her large cotton umbrella has given rise to the expression 'a gamp' for an umbrella, especially an untidy one; also for a midwife.

Gandalin, in *Amadis of Gaul*, the son of a knight of Scotland and squire of Amadis. In *Don Quixote* (I. xx) the Don reminds Sancho that Gandalin 'always spoke to his master cap in hand, his head inclined and his body bent, in the Turkish fashion'.

Ganelon, or **Gano,** in the *Charlemagne romances and the *Morgante maggiori* of *Pulci, the count of Mayence, the villain and traitor who schemes for the defeat of the rearguard at Roncesvalles (see ROLAND). He figures among the traitors in *Dante's *Inferno* (xxxii. 122) and in *Chaucer's 'Nun's Priest's Tale' (see CANTERBURY TALES, 20).

GARAMOND, Claude (d. 1561), French typefounder, noted for his elegant roman types, inspired by one cut for *Aldus in 1495, and for his 'Grecs du roi', the Greek type he cut for Francis I for use by R. *Estienne, the king's printer.

GARCÍA LORCA, Federico (1898–1936), Spanish poet and dramatist, born in Fuente Vaqueros, near Granada. He spent his first 11 years in the region. Such immersion in the language and ways of the Andalusian countryside profoundly influenced his sensibility. In Granada he began writing poetry, became an excellent pianist, and studied without much enthusiasm at the university. Lorca's early prose and poetry is pervaded with intense erotic anxiety and anticlerical anger, and shows that by 1918 he was aware of being homosexual. In 1921 he published a selection of verse, *Libro de poemas*, in Madrid, where for several years he lived sporadically at the famous, Europe-oriented students' residence, and became close friends with Luis Buñuel and Salvador *Dali (whom he celebrated in a distinguished ode). In 1927 he staged *Mariana Pineda* and published his second volume of poems, *Canciones* (*Songs*). A collection of gypsy ballads, *Romancero gitano*, catapulted him to fame the following year. Tired of his 'gypsy myth', and by then within the orbit of *Surrealism, Lorca fled to New York in 1929, where he produced the anguished compositions published posthumously as *Poeta en Nueva York* (1940), wrote a film script, *Viaje a la luna* (*Trip to the Moon*, written 1929), and began a revolutionary play, *The Audience* (*El público*), which back in Spain he described as 'explicitly homosexual'. In 1932 he was appointed director of Madrid University's moving theatre, La Barraca, with which he took Spanish classical plays out into the provinces. Unable to stage *The Audience* and its successor, *Así que pasen cinco años* (*When Five Years Pass*, 1931), he exploited his rural vein in the tragedies *Bodas de sangre* (*Blood Wedding*, perf. 1933) and *Yerma* (perf. 1934). *Llanto por Ignacio Sánchez Mejías* (1934), written for a friend who was a bullfighter, is one of the finest elegies in the Spanish language. *Doña Rosita la soltera* (*Doña Rosita the Spinster*, perf. 1935) expresses Lorca's desolate view of Granada. His last play, *La casa de Bernarda Alba* (*The House of Bernarda Alba*), was completed just before his return to the city in July 1936 and the outbreak of the Civil War: it was published posthumously in 1945. That August he was murdered by the Fascists. See Ian Gibson, *Federico García Lorca: A Life* (1989).

GARCÍA MÁRQUEZ, Gabriel (1928–), Colombian novelist, born in Aracataca, and educated at the Jesuit College in Bogotá. After beginning a career as a journalist, he came to Europe in 1955 for the Liberal newspaper *El espectador.* It was during this period that he published his first novel, *La hojarasca* (1955; *Leaf Storm,* 1972); it introduces the village of Macondo, which was to become the setting for his most famous novel *Cien años de soledad* (1967; *One Hundred Years of Solitude,* 1970). This account of the small, remote, decaying village is presented through the eyes of seven generations of the much intermarried and incestuous Buendía family; a classic work of *magic realism, it mingles the ordinary and the miraculous, the semi-supernatural and the concrete detail, in a kaleidoscopic survey in which time, numbers, repetition, superstitions, magic, and natural phenomena are all charged with a curiously heightened power and colour. This was followed in 1975 by *El otoño del patriarca* (*The Autumn of the Patriarch,* 1977), by *Crónica de una muerte anunciada* in 1981 (*Chronicle of a Death Foretold,* 1982); and in 1985 he published the acclaimed *El amor en los tiempos de cólera* (1988; *Love in the Time of Cholera,* 1988), an evocative and wistful story examining love in its various forms and the changing power of memory. His later work includes *Del amor y otros demonios* (1994; *Of Love and Other Demons,* 1995), *El general en su laberinto* (1989; *The General in His Labyrinth,* 1990), and *Noticias de un secuestro* (1996; *News of a Kidnapping,* 1997), a journalistic enquiry into a kidnapping in Bogotá. He has also published several collections of short stories, among them *Doce cuentos peregrinos* (1992; *Strange Pilgrims,* 1993). There is a multi-volume edition of his collected journalism, *Obra periodística* (1991–). He was awarded the *Nobel Prize for literature in 1982.

GARCILASO DE LA VEGA (?1501–36), Spanish poet and friend of *Boscán; the names of the two poets are coupled in Byron's *Don Juan* (i. 95). His sonnets, eclogues, and odes won the praise of Cervantes (*Don Quixote,* II. lviii) and inaugurated the Golden Age of Spanish poetry.

GARDAM, Jane (1928–), novelist, children's writer, and short story writer, born in Coatham, North Yorkshire. Her first novel, *God on the Rocks* (1978), set in a summer between the wars, depicts the growth of Margaret Marsh towards adult experience and loss of faith. Gardam has written many collections of short stories, among them *The Sidmouth Letters,* whose title story explores the much-discussed subject of Jane Austen's love life with subtlety and imaginative tact; other stories create the lives of varied characters with similar economy, observant detail, and dexterous art.

Like *God on the Rocks,* her novel *Bilgewater* (1976) is a journey of enlightenment through the snares of adolescence, whose dangers Gardam portrays with extraordinary insight. *The Queen of the Tambourine* (1991) returns to the religious topic of *God on the Rocks.* It depicts in a psychological thriller the obsessively zealous Eliza Peabody at her sinister work amidst suburbia. Eliza's delusions are powerfully created and sustained by Gardam and the book is perhaps her most accomplished to date. *Missing the Midnight: Hauntings and Grotesques* appeared in 1997.

Garden of Cyrus, The, by Sir T. *Browne, the companion piece to *Hydriotaphia,* published 1658, treats of the occurrence of the quincunx (:·:) or lozenge and the number five in man-made objects, primarily the plantations of the ancients, and then their buildings, other artefacts, and customs, in plants, in animals, and in traditional philosophy and theology. He chooses his 'bye and barren theme' partly to please the dedicatee, an ardent horticulturist, partly because 'Paradise succeeds the Grave'. By intertwining many heterogeneous observations he playfully demonstrates his ability to elaborate and digress.

GARDINER, Samuel Rawson (1829–1902), educated at Winchester and Christ Church, Oxford. He settled in London to study the history of the Puritan revolution, supporting himself meanwhile by teaching. In 1872 he became lecturer and subsequently professor of modern history at King's College, London. The first instalment of his great *History* of the first Stuarts and Cromwell appeared in 1863; successive instalments followed, and in 1883–4 appeared a second edition of all these, entitled a *History of England from the Accession of James I to the Outbreak of the Civil War 1603–42. The History of the Great Civil War (1886–91)* and the *History of the Commonwealth and Protectorate* (1894–1901) carried the record down to the year 1656 (an additional chapter was published posthumously). Gardiner's historical writing shows minute accuracy and impartiality, but is, perhaps necessarily, lacking in picturesque quality. He was very proud of his descent from Bridget, daughter of Oliver *Cromwell and wife of Henry Ireton.

GARDNER, Dame Helen Louise (1908–86), scholar and critic, educated at North London Collegiate School and St Hilda's College, Oxford. Her works include an important edition of *The Divine Poems of John Donne* (1952, 2nd edn 1978), other editions of the *metaphysical poets, and a revealing study of T. S. *Eliot's work, *The Composition of Four Quartets* (1978). She also edited *The Faber Book of Religious Verse* (1972) and *The New Oxford Book of English Verse 1250–1950* (1972).

'Gareth and Lynette', one of Tennyson's *Idylls of the King,* published 1872. It describes Gareth's disguise as a scullion at court, and his winning of Lynette through his rescue of her besieged sister Lyonors.

Gareth of Orkney (or **Gaheret**), Sir, the third son of King Lot of Orkney and Arthur's sister Morgawse who, on his arrival at Camelot, is made to work in the kitchen and nicknamed by Kay 'Beaumains'. The fourth of *Malory's eight *Works* as edited by Vinaver is named *Sir Gareth of Orkney* and the book (VII in *Caxton) is largely concerned with his rescue of the lady Lyonesse from Ironsyde and his being brought there by the haughty Lynette. Malory's exact source for this book is not known. See GARETH AND LYNETTE.

Gargantua, Pantagruel, etc., by F. *Rabelais, the first two volumes published under the anagrammatical pseudonym Alcofribas Nasier.

Gargantua (1534) introduces Pantagruel's father: his birth, early education, and attendance at the University of Paris, his successful defence of the paternal territories against military invasion, his foundation of a commemorative abbey. The book evokes the province of Rabelais's birth, parodies and criticizes various kinds of education, attacks aggressive war, commends the virtues of the *vita activa*, and defines ecclesiastical and communal ideals (the abbey of Thélème).

Pantagruel (1532 or 1533), the first of the sequence to be written, celebrates the prodigious strength and appetite of a popular giant. It describes his fantastic birth and childhood, his tour of the French universities, his experience of Paris, his employment of the rascally Panurge, and his military exploits in the remote Utopia. These events become opportunities for parading Renaissance exuberance, burlesquing medieval learning and literature, mocking classical and ecclesiastical authority, and affirming humanist values.

The *Tiers Livre* (1546) turns Pantagruel into a sensible and humorous prince and Panurge into a voluble buffoon. The action centres on a variety of attempts by the latter, who is now the spendthrift governor of an independent province, to discover whether he should marry. This produces a highly inventive, anti-feminist contribution to a current debate on women and marriage. The *Quart Livre* (ch. 1–11, 1548, the remainder 1552) relates Pantagruel's journey to the oracle of the 'Dive Bouteille' (or 'divine bottle') in Cathay in quest of a solution for Panurge's dilemma. Drawing on narratives of voyages to the North-West Passage and on the satirical possibilities of travel literature in general, it mocks a whole variety of contemporary abuses, including the worship of Rome and the greed and idleness of monks. The *Cinquième Livre* (published posthumously, ch. 1–16 as *L'Isle Sonnante*, 1562, the whole 1564) conducts the travellers to their destination. This book, the authenticity of which has been questioned, shows evidence of decline, the satire of the administration of justice never rising above crudity and the material of the second part consisting for the most part of mere translations and imitations.

Gargery, Joe, a character in Dickens's *Great Expectations.*

GARIOCH, Robert, the pen-name of Robert Garioch Sutherland (1909–81), Scottish poet, born and educated in Edinburgh, who worked for many years in England as a schoolmaster. He is known principally for his witty and satiric poems in *Scots. His first volume, published in 1940 in collaboration with S. *Maclean (*17 Poems for 6d: In Gaelic, Lowland Scots and English*), was followed by several other volumes, including *The Masque of Edinburgh* (1954), and his *Collected Poems* appeared in 1977. He also translated into Scots *Pindar, G. *Buchanan, *Belli, *Apollinaire, and others. *Two Men and a Blanket* (1975) is a prose work describing his experiences as a prisoner of war in Italy and Germany. His *Complete Poetical Works*, ed. R. Fulton, was published in 1983.

Garland, (1) Mr and Mrs, characters in Dickens's *The Old Curiosity Shop*; (2) Anne, a character in Hardy's *The Trumpet Major.*

GARNER, Alan, see CHILDREN'S LITERATURE.

GARNETT, Constance (1861–1946), wife of E. *Garnett, educated at Newnham College, Cambridge. She began to study Russian while awaiting the birth of her son David (below), and became a distinguished translator, responsible for introducing many of the great Russian classics to English readers. She translated *Turgenev, *Tolstoy, *Dostoevsky, *Chekhov, *Gogol, and *Herzen, and although her versions have in many cases been superseded (and criticized in some quarters as banal or prudish) they had enormous impact and influence in their day; K. *Mansfield wrote to her in 1921 that 'the younger generation owe you more than we ourselves are able to realise. These books have changed our lives, no less.' See *Constance Garnett: A Heroic Life* (1991) by Richard Garnett.

GARNETT, David (1892–1981), novelist and critic, son of E. and C. *Garnett, and friend and associate of the *Bloomsbury Group. He studied botany for some years at the Royal College of Science, was a conscientious objector and farm labourer during the First World War, then opened a bookshop in Soho in association with Francis Birrell, son of A. *Birrell. His first short novel, *Lady into Fox* (1922), an enigmatic fable about a young wife transformed into a vixen, had a considerable success, and was followed by another fable, *A Man in the Zoo* (1924), about a thwarted lover who donates himself as a specimen of *homo sapiens* for exhibition in the zoo. *The Sailor's Return* (1925) describes the conflict between a sailor and his black African wife and the Dorset villagers among whom they settle. Other works include a biography, *Pocahontas: or The Nonpareil of Virginia* (1933), the semifictional *Beany-eye* (1935), and three volumes of autobiography, *The Golden Echo* (1953), *The Flowers of the Forest* (1955), and *The Familiar Faces* (1962). Garnett also edited the letters of T. E. *Lawrence (1938), the novels of *Peacock (1948), and his own correspondence with T. H. *White (1968). His early works were memorably illustrated by his first wife Rachel Alice ('Ray' Marshall, d. 1940). His second wife Angelica was the daughter of V. *Bell.

GARNETT, Edward (1868–1937), son of R. *Garnett and husband of C. *Garnett. He published several volumes, including novels, plays, and critical works, but is chiefly remembered as publisher's reader for several successive firms, the last of which was Jonathan Cape. In this role he encouraged and advised many of the most important writers of the period, amongst them *Conrad, D. H. *Lawrence, D. *Richardson, E. M. *Forster, and W. H. *Hudson.

GARNETT, Richard (1835–1906), the son of Richard Garnett (1789–1850), linguist, philologist, and from 1838 assistant keeper of printed books at the British Museum. The younger Richard also worked at the British Museum, where his erudition became legendary; he was superintendent of the Reading Room from 1875, a post from which he resigned in 1884 to become chief editor of the library's first printed catalogue. He published several volumes of original and translated verse, several biographies, and edited many works, including *Relics of Shelley* (1862). He is best remembered as a writer for his collection of pagan tales *The Twilight of the Gods* (1888), some of which originally appeared in the *Yellow Book*. See also GARNETT, E.

GARRICK, David (1717–79), of Huguenot descent, born in Hereford, the son of a recruiting officer, and educated in Lichfield, where he became a pupil of Dr *Johnson at Edial. He accompanied Johnson to London, and set up briefly with his brother in the wine trade before turning to the stage. His mythological burlesque *Lethe* was performed at Drury Lane in 1740, and in 1741 he appeared as an actor at Ipswich in Southerne's *Oroonoko*. Later that year he made his London début as Richard III at Goodman's Fields, with great success, and subsequently proved his versatility by many successes in both comic and tragic parts, ranging from Abel Drugger and Sir John Brute to Lear (in the version by Nahum *Tate). He wrote a number of lively farces, including *The Lying Valet* (1741), *Miss in Her Teens* (1747), *A Peep behind the Curtain* (1767), and *Bon Ton, or High Life above Stairs* (1775), and collaborated with *Colman in writing *The Clandestine Marriage* (1766). He also wrote many prologues and epilogues. In 1747 he joined Lacy in the management of Drury Lane, where he produced many of Shakespeare's dramas; he made his last appearance in 1776, when he sold his share of the patent to *Sheridan and two others for £35,000. In 1769 he organized a grand 'Shakespeare Jubilee' at Stratford-upon-Avon, but lost over £2,000 when heavy rain forced him to cancel most of the three-day event. In 1773 he was elected a member of Johnson's *Club; his correspondence with many of the most distinguished men of his

day was published in 1831–2 and in a greatly enlarged collection, edited by D. M. Little and G. M. Kahrl, in 1963. Garrick's fame as an actor was unsurpassed, and there are many contemporary tributes and descriptions, including those by *Boswell, *Lichtenberg, F. *Burney, H. *More, and *Burke. He was also painted by many of his celebrated contemporaries, including *Reynolds, *Hogarth, *Gainsborough, and Zoffany. A life by T. *Davies appeared in 1780, shortly after Garrick's sudden death, and another in 1801 by A. *Murphy. His widow, the dancer Eva-Maria Violetti, long outlived him, dying in 1822; they were childless.

Garrick Club, founded in 1831 as a club in which 'actors and men of education and refinement might meet on equal terms'. Its original premises were at 35 King Street, London. *Barham, *d'Orsay, and S. *Rogers were among its first members. It was much frequented by *Thackeray, and possesses a famous collection of portraits of actors and actresses and theatrical memorabilia.

Garsington Manor, the Oxfordshire home of Ottoline *Morrell from 1915 to 1927, where she and her husband entertained many distinguished guests from the political and artistic worlds.

GARTH, Sir Samuel (1661–1719), a physician, freethinker, and member of the *Kit-Cat Club, remembered as the author of *The Dispensary* (1699), a burlesque poem in which he ridiculed the opposition of apothecaries to the supply of medicines to out-patients' dispensaries. He also wrote a prospect poem, *Claremont* (1715), in the vein of his friend Pope's *Windsor Forest*. *Pope described him as 'the best good Christian without knowing it'. See TOPOGRAPHICAL POETRY and MOCK-EPIC.

GASCOIGNE, George (c.1534–77), soldier and poet. He came from a good Bedfordshire family. He may have been educated at Trinity College, Cambridge, entered Gray's Inn in 1555, and spent more than ten years there. In 1561 his marriage to the already-married Elizabeth Boyes, mother of the poet N. *Breton, initiated a series of legal and financial difficulties, culminating in a spell in debtors' jail in Bedford in 1570. From 1572 to 1574 he was a soldier in the Netherlands, spending four months as a prisoner of the Spanish. His poems and plays were published during his absence, supposedly without his authority, as *A Hundreth Sundrie Flowres* (1573); on his return he brought out a corrected and augmented edition under the title of *The Posies of George Gascoigne*. In the last two years of his life he achieved some success as a court poet.

Many of Gascoigne's works were contained in *The Posies*: a variety of secular and devotional verse, including 'The Delectable History of Dan Bartholmew of Bathe'; a verse account of his adventures in the Netherlands, 'The Fruites of Warre', dedicated to Lord Grey de Wilton; two plays written for performance at

Gray's Inn in 1566, *Supposes*, a prose comedy based on *Ariosto's I suppositi*, and *Jocasta*, a blank verse tragedy supposedly based on *Euripides but actually translated from Lodovico Dolce; a strange Chaucerian novella, *The Adventures of Master *F.J.*, whose Italian source, if it existed, has never been found; and *Certayne Notes of Instruction Concerning the Making of Verse or Ryme in English*, a pithy but pioneering account of English versification. Gascoigne's other works include *The Glasse of Governement: A Tragicall Comedie* (1575), *The Droomme of Doomes Day* (1576), and *The Steele Glas: A Satyre* (1576). He presented to Queen *Elizabeth on I Jan. 1576 an illustrated autograph manuscript of his translations into Latin, Italian, and French of the anonymous *Tale of Hemetes the Heremyte*, which had originally been part of the royal entertainment at Woodstock in 1575. Gascoigne's achievement has been overshadowed by the later Elizabethan poets who were to tread hard on his heels, such as *Spenser, *Marlowe, and *Sidney, but he was an innovator in a wide variety of literary forms. His novella of sexual intrigue *The Adventures of Master F.J.* is the only one of his works to have commanded much interest in the 20th cent. His works were edited by J. W. Cunliffe (1907–10), and there is a book on him by C. T. Prouty (1942).

GASCOIGNE, Sir William (?1350–1419), appointed lord chief justice of the King's Bench in 1400 by Henry IV, he figures in that capacity in Shakespeare's *Henry IV*. Shakespeare follows *Holinshed's apparently apocryphal story (told in *Elyot's *Governour*) that Prince Hal struck Gascoigne when he was chief justice for attempting to arrest one of the prince's unruly followers, whereupon Gascoigne arrested the prince himself. Hal, when Henry V, praises Gascoigne when confirming him in office for this fearless and even-handed administration of justice. See *1 Henry IV*, III. ii. 32–3 and *2 Henry IV*, v. ii. 65 ff.

GASCOYNE, David (1916–2001), poet, who published his first volume, *Roman Balcony* (1932), when only 16, and in 1935 *A Short Survey of Surrealism*, which established him as a champion of *Surrealism and a writer unusually aware of European literature. He translated many of the French surrealists, and his own work shows the influence of and pays tribute to artists and writers such as Max Ernst, Magritte, *Éluard, *Apollinaire, Tzara, and Djuna *Barnes. His work includes *Man's Life Is His Meat* (1936), *Hölderlin's Madness* (1938), *Poems 1937–1942* (1943, illustrated by Graham Sutherland), and *Night Thoughts*, a long poem commissioned by the BBC, broadcast 1955, published 1956.

Gashford, a character in Dickens's *Barnaby Rudge*.

GASKELL, Mrs Elizabeth Cleghorn (1810–65), daughter of William Stevenson, a Unitarian minister and later a treasury official and journalist; she was brought up by her aunt in Knutsford, Cheshire (the original of 'Cranford' and of 'Hollingford' in *Wives and Daugh-

ters). In 1832 she married William Gaskell, minister at the Cross Street Unitarian Chapel in Manchester; they had four daughters and a son who died in infancy. As a distraction from her sorrow at his death she wrote her first novel, *Mary Barton* (1848). It won the attention of *Dickens, at whose invitation much of her work was first published in *Household Words* and *All the Year Round*. Her other full-length novels were *Cranford* (1853), *Ruth* (1853), *North and South* (1855), *Sylvia's Lovers* (1863), and *Wives and Daughters* (1866), which was left unfinished when Mrs Gaskell died suddenly of heart failure at the Hampshire house she had just bought for her husband's retirement. She also wrote the first and most celebrated biography of C. *Brontë—which caused a furore because it contained some allegedly libellous statements which had to be withdrawn—and many vivid and warm-hearted short stories and novellas, of which the finest was *Cousin Phillis* (1864).

Mrs Gaskell was an active humanitarian and the message of several of her novels was the need for social reconciliation, for better understanding between employers and workers, between the respectable and the outcasts of society. She was a keen observer of human behaviour and speech, among both industrial workers in Manchester and farming and country-town communities, and a careful researcher of the background and technicalities of her novels. She had a natural gift for storytelling, although she was at first rather uncertain in plot creation and given to melodramatic devices. She was a beautiful and much-liked woman, at ease in any company and a devoted wife and mother, with many friends who included (besides Charlotte Brontë) *Ruskin, *Milnes, the *Carlyles, *Kingsley, C. E. *Norton, the Howitts, Mme Mohl, and Florence Nightingale. Her relations with Dickens were chiefly professional, as their characters were not congenial: on one occasion, exasperated by her waywardness as a contributor, he exclaimed to his sub-editor: 'If I were Mr G. Oh Heaven how I would beat her!' Her contemporaries classed her as a novelist with the Brontës and G. *Eliot, but although *Cranford* has always remained a favourite with the general reader her other novels were underrated in critical esteem for a full century after her death. See *Elizabeth Gaskell: A Habit of Stories* (1993) by Jenny Uglow.

GATTO, Alfonso (1909–76), Italian poet, communist, and Resistance fighter. Like many other writers of his generation he left the Party shortly after the Second World War. His poetry is highly lyrical, condensing hermetic symbolism with autobiographical, political, and social motifs. His best poems are in *Isola* (*Island*, 1930), *Il capo sulla neve* (*Head down on the Snow*, 1949; 1st pub. clandestinely); his Resistance poems *Storia delle vittime* (*History of Victims*, 1960); and *Poesie d'amore* (*Love Poems*, 1973).

GAUDEN, Dr J., see EIKON BASILIKE.

GAUDIER-BRZESKA, Henri (1891–1915), French sculptor and draughtsman, who came to London in 1910, where he became associated with the most avant-garde artists and writers. His most brilliantly accomplished works are his pen and pencil line drawings, some of which were published in *Rhythm*. Gaudier, with W. *Lewis and *Pound, founded the Vorticist group in 1914 (see VORTICISM), and contributed a Vorticist history of sculpture to *Blast No. 1* which exalts the energy and intensity of primitive art and condemns the ideals of the Greeks and the Renaissance. In 1914 Gaudier enlisted in the French army and he was killed in action. In 1916 Pound's *Gaudier-Brzeska: A Memoir* republished several of his writings. Pound stressed that Gaudier had given him 'a new sense of form' and of 'planes in relation': Gaudier's immense marble head of Pound is on loan to the Tate Gallery, London, which also houses his celebrated *Red Stone Dancer*.

GAUNT, John of, see JOHN OF GAUNT.

GAUTIER, Théophile (1811–72), French poet, novelist, critic, and journalist. He was an admirer of *Hugo, and played a prominent role in the Romantic movement in the 1830s (his *Histoire du romantisme* appeared in 1874). He was closely associated with the doctrine of *l'art pour l'art* (*'art for art's sake'), expounded in the preface to his novel *Mademoiselle de Maupin* (1835). His best-known collection of poems is *Émaux et camées* (1852), which exercised considerable influence on the *Parnassians. He had a long career in journalism, and wrote widely on travel, art, ballet, and the theatre.

Gawain, Sir (Walwain), the eldest of the four sons of King Lot of Orkney and Arthur's sister Morgawse. His wife, in some stories, was Dame Ragnell and their son was Ginglain, the Fair Unknown (*Libeaus Desconus); he also had two natural sons. In the Arthurian legends he is prominent from the first 12th-cent. stories in which he is the leading knight, courageous, pure, and courteous. In later versions his excellence was surpassed by that of Launcelot and his character becomes harsher, more ruthless, and often philandering. In *Geoffrey of Monmouth he is Arthur's ambassador to Rome; in *Malory he becomes at the end the bitter enemy of Launcelot who has accidentally killed Gawain's beloved youngest brother Gaheris and who also killed Gareth (who tries to avenge Gaheris) and Agravain, the witness and betrayer of the affair between Launcelot and Guinevere. Gawain is killed when Arthur lands at Dover before the final battle with Mordred. He is related to Gwalchmei, the sun-god of Welsh mythology, and elements of this relation surface in many stories about Gawain (possibly including the most admired, Sir *Gawain and the Green Knight*: see essay by John Speirs in *Medieval English Poetry*, 1957); in Malory too there is allusion to Gawain's strength waxing and waning with the sun (see R. S. Loomis, *Arthurian Tradition and Chrétien de Troyes*, 1949, 146–55). The most celebrated single adventure of Gawain is the one described in *Sir Gawain and the Green Knight*. In Malory his characterization varies according to the source being followed; for example his status is not very high in *The Book of Sir Tristram de Lyones* (the fourth of the eight Works in Vinaver), but he is great again in the eighth, the *Morte Arthur Saunz Guerdon*.

J. L. Weston, *The Legend of Sir Gawain* (1897); *The Wedding of Sir Gawain and Dame Ragnell* (15th-cent. east Midland) and *Sir Gawain and the Carl of Carlisle* (late 15th-cent. northern), ed. in D. B. Sands, *Middle English Verse Romances* (1966).

Gawain and the Green Knight, Sir, a greatly admired alliterative poem from the north-west Midlands, dating from the second half of the 14th cent. (some authorities date it around 1375), the only manuscript of which is the famous Cotton Nero A. X which is also the sole manuscript of *Pearl, *Patience, and *Cleanness. The poem is in 2,530 lines in long-lined alliterative stanzas of varying length, each ending with a *'bob and wheel'. Most modern critics regard the four poems in the manuscript as the work of a single poet; but as far as the interpretation of this poem is concerned, the question of single authorship is largely irrelevant, so different is its subject from the three doctrinal pieces.

The story of the poem is as follows (under the headings of its four 'fitts', narrative divisions). *Fitt 1*: Arthur and his court are seated at a New Year's feast in Camelot waiting for a marvel when a huge green man enters, bearing an axe and a holly bough. He challenges a knight to cut his head off on condition that the knight agrees to have his head cut off a year hence. Gawain accepts the challenge and cuts the green knight's head off; the knight picks it up and rides away. *Fitt 2*: A year later Gawain sets off to keep his side of the bargain. After riding through grim landscapes in wintry weather, on Christmas Eve Gawain comes upon a beautiful castle where he is graciously received. The lord of the castle makes an agreement with Gawain that each day he himself will hunt in the fields and Gawain in the castle; at the end of the day they will exchange spoils. *Fitt 3*: For three consecutive days, the lord hunts and Gawain, famous for his skill and prowess in love, is amorously approached by the beautiful lady of the castle, who gives him one kiss on the first day, two on the second, and on the third day three kisses and a girdle which has magic properties that will save his life. Each evening Gawain exchanges the kisses with his host for the animals slain in the hunt; but on the third evening he keeps the girdle (thus breaking his bargain), to protect him in the imminent meeting with the green knight. *Fitt 4*: Gawain is directed to the green knight's chapel where he kneels to receive his blow. Twice the knight feints at him, and the third time he makes a slight cut in Gawain's neck. Then he explains that he is the knight of the castle in a different form, and that the cut in the neck was sustained because of Gawain's infidelity in keeping the girdle. Gawain bitterly curses his failing and the snares of women; but the green knight applauds him and, on Gawain's return to Arthur's court, they declare that they will all wear a green girdle in honour of his achievement. The poem may be connected with the founding of the Order of the Garter. The elegance of the construction of the narrative, as well as the vivid language of the poem, are universally admired, and this is agreed to be one of the greatest poems in Middle English. Interpretation of its somewhat enigmatic raison d'être has been more varying; Speirs stressed its connection with some unexpressed archetypal story of seasons and vegetation; John Burrow concentrates on the moral seriousness underlying its colourful romantic exterior; modern critics, such as E. Wilson, see it in relation to the other Christian poems in the manuscript.

Ed. J. R. R. *Tolkien, E. V. Gordon, and N. Davis (2nd edn, 1967); J. A. Burrow, A Reading of Sir Gawain and the Green Knight (1965); J. Speirs, Medieval English Poetry (1957), 215–51; A. C. Spearing, The Gawain Poet (1970), ch. 5; E. Wilson, The Gawain-Poet (1976); W. R. J. Barron, Trawthe and Treason (1980); D. R. Howard and C. K. Zacher (eds), Critical Studies of Sir Gawain and the Green Knight (1968).

GAY, John (1685–1732), born at Barnstaple, apprenticed for a time to a London mercer. In 1708 he published a burlesque poem, Wine, and in 1713 Rural Sports, on the model of his friend Pope's *Windsor Forest, and The Fan, which is in the mock-heroic style of *The Rape of the Lock. *The Shepherd's Week (1714) was the first poem to show his real ability. His first play, The What D'ye Call It, a satirical farce, was produced in 1715, and *Trivia appeared in 1716. With *Pope and *Arbuthnot he wrote a comedy, Three Hours after Marriage, which was acted in 1717. He speculated disastrously in *South Sea funds with the proceeds of his Poems (1720) and his hopes of advancement under the new king were disappointed; he was intermittently helped in his early career by various patrons, and eventually became an inmate of the household of the duke of Queensberry, who was to be his literary executor. The first series of his popular Fables appeared in 1727, but real success came in 1728 with *The Beggar's Opera and its sequel *Polly, which was banned from the stage but earned a considerable sum on publication in 1729. These two plays contain many of Gay's best-known ballads, but 'Sweet William's Farewell to Black-Eyed Susan' was published in Poems (1720) and 'Twas when the seas were roaring' is from his first play. He also wrote, c.1718, the librettos of *Handel's Acis and Galatea (pub. 1732) and Achilles, an opera produced at Covent Garden in 1733. His poem in ottava rima, 'Mr Pope's Welcome from Greece', first published in 1776, was written to celebrate his friend's finishing his translation of The Iliad; it gives a vivid picture of the members of the *Scriblerus Club (Pope, *Swift, Arbuthnot, and *Parnell) and of many other contemporary figures. Gay was a genial and much-

loved man, but his health appears to have been undermined by financial anxieties and he died of an old intestinal disorder; he was buried in Westminster Abbey, accompanied by his own epitaph:

> Life is a jest, and all things show it;
> I thought so once, and now I know it.

The duke of Queensberry attended to various posthumous publications, including the second series of Fables (1738). Gay's Poetry and Prose, ed. V. A. Dearing and C. E. Beckwith, was published in two volumes (1974).

Gay, Walter, a character in Dickens's *Dombey and Son.

gay and lesbian literature consists of texts by homosexual/bisexual writers and texts amenable to gay/lesbian readings. The central controversy in the defining of gay literature concerns Shakespeare's *sonnets (1609), the first 126 of which are addressed to a young man. Their homoeroticism was troublesome from the start: John Benson republished them in 1640, leaving out some sonnets altogether and even heterosexualizing others by regendering their pronouns. Modern readers continue to debate whether the poems express platonic friendship or sexual love.

Most male homosexual writing in English before the 20th cent. is based on a narrow range of classical precedents: Plato's *Symposium, the erotic epigrams of the Greek *Anthology, the homosexual narratives from *Ovid's Metamorphoses. The English tradition of male friendship elegies invariably contains echoes of *Theocritus' Idylls and the second of *Virgil's Eclogues. These classical authors offered persuasive alternatives to the hellfire warnings of Leviticus and the Sodom myth. Their influence is pervasive from Edmund Spenser's *Shepheardes Calender (1579) and the poems of Richard *Barnfield to the bucolic nostalgia of A. E. *Housman and the poetry of the First World War.

With the exception of the residua of *Sappho, lesbian writing lacks these strong classical precedents. Apart from extraordinary early figures like 'the English Sappho', Katherine *Philips, lesbian literature was born among the 'ephemera' in which women privately wrote down their affections for each other: letters, diaries, commonplace books. Among the most celebrated of these are the diaries of Eleanor *Butler (?1739–1829) and Anne Lister (1791–1840).

The influence of bisexual libertines like *Rochester (1647–80) and the Marquis de *Sade (1740–1814) looms over the atmosphere and many of the characters of the Gothic novel, which ultimately helps shape the homosexual villain of mid-20th-cent. fiction.

But homosexual literature proper dates from the late 19th cent., expressing the newly pathologized concept of homosexuality as a lifelong condition. Although cowed by the prosecutions of Oscar *Wilde and of Radclyffe *Hall's The Well of Loneliness (1928), homosexual/bisexual authors began to voice the newly defined identity in coded ways. Such playful texts as Virginia Woolf's *Orlando* (1928) and the fiction of Ronald *Firbank (1886–1926) effected a transition from decadence to camp modernism.

E. M. *Forster's *Maurice*, written in 1913 but unpublished until 1972, argues for the normality of homosexuality and sets itself in opposition to decadence, effeminacy, and camp. This anticipates the American-influenced mid-century period, which produced much didactic, often apologetic fiction in which a central character was used to represent homosexual people in general. Many such novels ended in death. One English novelist who did much to break this tendency was Angus *Wilson.

In the 1970s a more outspoken generation of writers emerged from the women's and gay liberation movements. Among other tendencies of their self-celebratory texts has been a determined appropriation of popular genres. This generation includes Adam *Mars-Jones (1954–   ), meticulously attentive to narrow stretches of a universe transformed by AIDS; Neil Bartlett (1958–   ), who applies a detailed map of homosexual history to the cityscapes of postmodern queerness; and Jeanette *Winterson (1959–   ), whose robustly physical language tells extravagant fables of gender ambiguity.

The most comprehensive summaries of a fast-developing field are Lillian Faderman's *Surpassing the Love of Men* (1979) and Gregory Woods's *A History of Gay Literature: The Male Tradition* (1998). On modern drama, see Alan Sinfield, *Out on Stage* (1999). Recent critical writing has been dominated by queer theory, which calls into question conventional versions of both sexual identity and literary value.

gazette, from Italian *gazzetta*, apparently so called from the coin of that name, which may have been the sum paid either for the paper itself or for the privilege of reading it [*OED*]. The *gazzetta* was a news-sheet first published in Venice about the middle of the 16th cent., and similar news-sheets (see CORANTO, and NEWSPAPERS, ORIGINS OF) appeared in England from the 17th cent., giving news from foreign parts.

gazetteer, a geographical index or dictionary. A work of this kind by L. Echard (2nd edn, 1693) bore the title *The Gazetteer's or Newsman's Interpreter; Being a Geographical Index*, intended for the use of 'gazetteers' or journalists.

GEDDES, Alexander (1737–1802), Catholic priest, linguist, and biblical scholar. He wrote a 'Dissertation on the Scoto-Saxon Dialect' which appeared in the *Transactions of the Society of Antiquaries of Scotland* (1792), in which he discusses the theory and practice of the *Scots language, and complains of the new vogue for introducing 'low words and trite proverbial phrases' instead of seeking the 'genuine Scottish idiom'.

GEE, Maggie (1948–   ), novelist, born in Poole, Dorset. Her first novel, *Dying, in Other Words* was followed by

The Burning Book in 1983, a family saga covering three generations, set against the backdrop of nuclear destruction in Japan. *Light Years* appeared in 1985, a love story charting an estranged married couple's year-long search for reconciliation. *Grace* (1988) also presents the redeeming power of love in a ruthless and violent world. Powerful and holding, the book sees the future in the form of a fearless child in the womb, burrowing its way to the light. *Where Are the Snows* (1991) reconsiders the twists and turns of a love affair, narrating a couple's separations, struggles for individual fulfilment, and, finally, their shared journey 'over the snows towards the light'. Recent novels include *The White Family* (2002) and its sequel *The Flood* (2004), which explores issues of racism and global warming in contemporary London.

GELLIUS, Aulus (2nd cent. AD), Roman man of letters, the author of a miscellany, *Noctes Atticae*, which contains extracts from many authors, anecdotes, and short discussions on a variety of topics. Twelve of the stories in Painter's *Palace of Pleasure* are taken from Gellius.

Gem, (1) a literary annual, edited by T. *Hood, 1829–32; (2) a weekly paper for boys, largely written by C. *Hamilton under the pen-name Martin Clifford, 1907–39.

Generydes, a late Middle English romance surviving in two forms: 10,000 short rhyming lines and 7,000 lines of rhyme-royal, perhaps from the first part of the 15th cent. It tells of the love of Generydes and Clarionas who, after his exile, cures and marries him.

Genesis, an Old English poem of 2,396 lines in the *Junius manuscript and previously attributed hypothetically to *Cædmon. Lines 235–851 are an interpolated section (usually called 'Genesis B') translated from a continental Saxon original which deals in a dramatic and vivid manner with the Fall of the Angels (the title of this excerpt in Sweet's *Anglo-Saxon Reader*). It has often been suggested that this section may have been the Old English poem on the subject that *Milton knew and that it may therefore have been a seminal influence on *Paradise Lost*. There are also some echoes of it in the early poems of *Auden. Ed. ASPR 1 (1931); see also *The Later Genesis*, ed. B. J. Timmer (1948).

Genesis and Exodus, a Middle English poem in just over 4,000 lines of rhyming couplets, written about the middle of the 13th cent. in Norfolk. It relates scriptural history from the Creation to the death of Moses in popular form, based partly on the Bible but mostly on the *Historia Scholastica* of *Comestor. The poem, particularly in its early sections, has a lively vigour. It has been edited by O. Arngart (Lund Studies in English 36, 1968).

GENEST, John (1764–1839), educated at Westminster and Cambridge, cleric, and author of *Some Account of the English Stage from the Restoration in 1660 to 1830*

(10 vols, 1832), an accurate and comprehensive work of reference.

GENET, Jean (1910–86), French novelist and dramatist. Much of the earlier part of his life was spent in reformatories or in prison, and his literary work is clearly marked by those experiences. He has published the autobiographical *Journal du voleur* (1949; *The Thief's Journal*, 1954), and novels such as *Notre-Dame des fleurs* (1944; *Our Lady of the Flowers*, 1948), and *Miracle de la rose* (1946; *Miracle of the Rose*, 1965). His plays include *Les Bonnes* (perf. 1946; *The Maids*, pub. 1954), *Le Balcon* (pub. 1956; *The Balcony*, 1957), and *Les Nègres* (pub. 1958; perf. 1959). He is the subject of *Sartre's *Saint Genet, comédien et martyr* (1952; *Saint Genet, Actor and Martyr*, 1964). There is a life by Edmund *White (1993).

Genevieve, the heroine of S. T. *Coleridge's poem 'Love', first published in the *Morning Star* (1799) and included in the second edition of *Lyrical Ballads*.

Gentleman Dancing-Master, The, a comedy by *Wycherley, probably performed 1671, published 1673. It is loosely based on *Calderón's *El maestro de danzar*.

Hippolita, who has been closely confined from the world by her aunt Mrs Caution, at the instigation of her father Mr Formal, is wooed by her cousin, the affected, Frenchified Monsieur de Paris. She prefers young Gerrard, and persuades him to present himself as her dancing-master, with Monsieur's gullible connivance. Gerrard's incompetence in this role is many times on the point of betraying him, and in the final confusion he and Hippolita contrive to get themselves married by the parson who had intended to marry her to Monsieur. The moral of the play appears to be contained in the final verse of Act II:

> Our Parents who restrain our liberty
> But take the course to make us sooner free,
> Though all we gain be but new slavery;
> We leave our Fathers, and to Husbands fly.

Gentleman's Journal, a periodical edited by *Motteux from 1692 to 1694, containing the news of the month and miscellaneous prose and poetry. It was the germ of the modern magazine.

Gentleman's Magazine (1731–1914), a periodical founded by *Cave under the pseudonym Sylvanus Urban.

Its original aim was to produce monthly, from the innumerable daily and weekly news-sheets and journals, interesting news, essays, anecdotes, and information. Cave's appears to be the first use of the word 'magazine' to describe a journal. By about 1739 original contributions had largely replaced news-digests; the magazine, while remaining general in scope, began to include serious works of criticism, essays, a record of publications, and parliamentary reports. Dr *Johnson, a friend of Cave, was a regular contributor and had a great influence on the management of the *Magazine*;

with Cave he devised a means of evading the official ban on parliamentary reporting by pretending his reports were from 'Lilliput'. J. *Nichols was an effective editor from 1792 to 1826, but although he published some work of *Lamb and other young contemporaries the *Magazine* seemed antiquated to the young writers of the day, and *Hazlitt's comments on it, written in 1823, sound a valedictory note. However, as a journal of general interest the *Gentleman's* lasted nearly another century.

Gentleman Usher, The, a tragi-comedy, by *Chapman, probably acted c.1602, printed 1606.

The duke Alphonso and his son Vincentio are both in love with Margaret, daughter of Earl Lasso. The daughter loves Vincentio, who is ordered into exile. Margaret in despair disfigures herself with a poisonous unguent. The remorseful duke surrenders Margaret, who on account of her disfigurement refuses to marry Vincentio. The doctor provides a remedy and solves the difficulty. The name of the play is taken from the usher, Bassiolo, a conceited major-domo, possibly based on *Malvolio, who acts as go-between for the lovers and is fooled and made ridiculous.

GEOFFREY OF MONMOUTH (Gaufridus Monemutensis) (d. 1155), probably a Benedictine monk of Monmouth, studied and worked at Oxford and was attached to *Robert, earl of Gloucester. He is said to have been archdeacon of Llandaff, and he was appointed bishop of St Asaph in 1152. In his *Historia Regum Britanniae* (c.1138) he purports to give an account of the kings who dwelt in Britain since before the Incarnation of Christ, extending over a period of 1,900 years, from Brutus (see BRUT), the great-grandson of Aeneas, to Cadwallader (AD 689), 'and especially of Arthur and the many others who succeeded him'. For this purpose he states that he drew upon a 'most ancient book in the British tongue' (presumably early Welsh), handed to him by Walter, archdeacon of Oxford (also known as *Calenius); but this book is unknown to any chronicler of the time. It is possible that this alleged work is an invention; *William of Newburgh condemns it as such in strong terms, in about 1198, and Geoffrey's veracity was also questioned by *Higden in *Polychronicon*. He drew on *Bede and *Nennius, on British traditions, perhaps on Welsh documents now lost, and probably for the rest on a romantic imagination. The life and clarity of his writing contributed substantially to the popularity of the Arthurian legends. The *Historia* was translated into Anglo-Norman by *Gaimar and *Wace, and into English verse by *Laȝamon and by *Robert of Gloucester; its translation into French was a major factor in the dissemination of the Arthurian legend because of the hegemony of French courtly literature. Geoffrey's Section Five is *The Prophecies of Merlin*, originally printed separately (1603). (See also ANGLO-LATIN LITERATURE.) There is a translation by Lewis Thorpe (1966) and a discussion by J. J. Parry and R. A. Caldwell in R. S.

Loomis (ed.), *Arthurian Literature in the Middle Ages* (1959), ch. 8.

GEOFFREY DE VINSAUF (fl. *c.*1200), an English rhetorician, author of *Nova Poetria* and *Summa de Coloribus Rhetoricis*, which were the standard and much-cited textbooks of poetic rhetoric in the later Middle Ages. Chaucer (in 'The Nun's Priest's Tale', *Canterbury Tales*, VII. 3347) laments his lack of the skill to apostrophize the downfall of the cock Chauntecleer with which Geoffrey in the *Nova Poetria* addressed the Friday on which Richard I died (in 1199): 'O Veneris lacrimosa dies!' His works have usually been dismissed as tedious catalogues of figures; recently they have begun to be taken more seriously as poetic aesthetics. (See also ANGLO-LATIN LITERATURE.)

GEORGE, Henry (1839–97), American writer on political economy, who advocated the nationalization of land and a 'single tax' on its increment value. Although not himself a socialist, he considerably influenced the British socialist movement and the *Fabian Society. G. B. *Shaw heard him speak in 1882, and claimed that at that point 'the importance of the economic basis dawned' on him; he was led on to *Marx and *Proudhon. H. G. *Wells bought a sixpenny paperback copy of George's bestselling *Progress and Poverty* (1879) when a young man in Midhurst and records its 'fermenting influence' upon his mind. Marx himself described George's proposals as 'the capitalist's last ditch'.

George-a'-Green, the merry pinner or pinder (pound-keeper) of Wakefield. The story is given in W. C. *Hazlitt's *Tales and Legends*. George-a'-Green wins the pindership by defeating all competitors at quarterstaff, defies the messenger who comes from Prince John (during Richard I's absence) demanding a contribution from Wakefield, and elopes with Justice Grymes's daughter. *Maid Marian provokes *Robin Hood to challenge him, but George-a'-Green defeats both Robin and his companions.

He is the subject of a play (entered for publication, 1595; the earliest known edition is that of 1599) probably by R. *Greene.

George Barnwell, *The History of, or The London Merchant*, a domestic tragedy in prose by *Lillo, produced 1731.

In this play, for the first time, everyday commercial life is made the theme of tragedy. The play was a great success, was translated into French, German, and Dutch, and was highly commended by G. E. *Lessing and *Diderot, who used it as a model for *Miss Sara Sampson* (1755) and *Le Fils naturel* (1757) respectively. *Goldsmith mocked it as a 'Tradesman's Tragedy' but *Pope admired it greatly. Based on an old ballad, it tells the story of an innocent young apprentice, Barnwell, who is seduced by a heartless courtesan, Millwood. She encourages him to rob his employer, Thorowgood, and to murder his uncle, for which crime both are brought to execution, he profoundly penitent and she defiant. It was frequently performed at holidays for apprentices as a moral warning.

Georgian, a term applied in a literary sense to the writers of the reign of George V (1910–36), and usually indicating poetry of a pastoral or, as later critics asserted, an escapist nature. (See GEORGIAN POETRY.) When applied to architecture, the term suggests the earlier period of the reigns of George I to George IV (1714–1830), when *Palladian principles of classical proportions were adapted to an unpretentious, refined, and discreet style suited to the needs of the rising middle classes.

Georgian Poetry, a series of volumes of verse planned by R. *Brooke, H. *Monro, and E. *Marsh. The series appeared in five volumes between 1912 and 1922, edited by Marsh and published by Monro at the Poetry Bookshop. The early volumes were widely influential and successful, bringing a fresh vision and manner into the tired poetry of the time. Writers represented in the first volume included Brooke, W. H. *Davies, *Masefield, D. H. *Lawrence, *de la Mare, *Abercrombie, *Bottomley, and *Drinkwater; R. *Hodgson and others were added for the second volume. Later volumes contained the work of *Blunden, *Sassoon, Robert *Graves, and *Rosenberg. However, the poems of quality were fewer in the volumes of 1919 and 1922; several poets (including Graves, Sassoon, and Blunden) objected to being identified as 'Georgian', in the company of J. C. *Squire, *Baring, and other traditionalists; and the term acquired a pejorative sense. *Pound, T. S. *Eliot, and the *Sitwells attacked the entire series, though some of the poets represented are now of high repute.

Georgics, The, see VIRGIL.

'Geraint and Enid', one of Tennyson's *Idylls of the King*, first published under this title 1886. It originally formed with 'The Marriage of Geraint' a single idyll, published in 1859 as 'Enid' and divided in 1873. Geraint, suspecting his wife's virtue, subjects her to various trials, from which she emerges patient and triumphant.

Geraldine, (1) the hero of T. Heywood's *The English Traveller*; (2) the name under which Elizabeth Fitzgerald, daughter of the ninth earl of Kildare, is traditionally held to have been courted by *Surrey: the connection is extremely tenuous; (3) the beautiful but malignant enchantress in Coleridge's *'Christabel'.

Gerard, (1) the hero of Reade's *The Cloister and the Hearth*; (2) Brigadier Gerard, the hero of historical romances by A. C. *Doyle.

GERARD, Alexander (1728–95), theological and philosophical writer, professor of moral philosophy and logic at Marischal College, and later professor of divinity at King's College, Aberdeen. He published two analytical studies which contributed to the development of aesthetics in Britain: 'An Essay on Taste' (1759, augmented 1780) and 'An Essay on Genius' (1774).

GERARD, John (1545–1612), a herbalist and superintendent of Burghley's gardens, and author of the celebrated *Herball or Generall Historie of Plantes* (1597), in a large measure adapted from the *Pemptades* of Rembert Dodoens. A revised edition of the *Herball* was issued by Thomas Johnson in 1633. The work gives a description of each plant, the localities in which it is found, and its medical virtues (correcting superstitions, e.g. about the mandrake); discusses nomenclature; and contains a large number of beautiful woodcuts, many of which had appeared in an earlier work.

GERHARDIE (originally Gerhardi), William Alexander (1895–1977), born of English parents in St Petersburg. During the First World War he served in the British embassy at Petrograd, then with the British military mission in Siberia. He then attended Worcester College, Oxford, where he wrote the first English book on *Chekhov, Anton Chehov* (1923), and his first novel, *Futility: A Novel on Russian Themes* (1922). During the next 15 years he produced many other novels admired by, among others, H. G. *Wells, E. *Waugh, *Beaverbrook, and O. *Manning. They include *The Polyglots* (1925), perhaps his best-known work, the bizarre narrative of a wildly egocentric young officer who on a military mission in the Far East comes into contact with a highly eccentric Belgian family, the Vanderflints; the intermingling of comedy and tragedy, of events of historical significance and the utmost human triviality, of Belgians, British, Russians, and Japanese, of love and war, create an oblique, lyrical, inconsequential world which is characteristic of Gerhardie, and largely autobiographical in content. Other novels include *Pending Heaven* (1930), *Resurrection* (1934), and *Of Mortal Love* (1936). *Meet Yourself As You Really Are* (1936, written with Prince Leopold of Loewenstein) is an interesting early example of *hypertext: it consists of a questionnaire which leads along many different interactive paths to self-knowledge. His autobiography *Memoirs of a Polyglot* appeared in 1931, and in 1940 a historical study, *The Romanovs*. For the rest of his life he lived increasingly as a recluse, planning novels, but, it seems, not writing them. *God's Fifth Column*, a biography of the age 1890–1940, ed. Michael *Holroyd and Robert Skidelsky, was published in 1981. His name was spelt Gerhardie for the first time on the revised Collected Edition of his works, published in ten volumes in the early 1970s. There is a life by Dido Davies (1990).

Germ, *Thoughts towards Nature in Poetry, Literature and Art*, a periodical of which the first issue appeared on 1 Jan. 1850. Edited by W. M. *Rossetti, it was the organ of the *Pre-Raphaelite Brotherhood, and ran for four issues, the last appearing on 30 Apr. 1850; the last two were renamed *Art and Poetry, Being Thoughts towards Nature*. It contained work by D. G. *Rossetti (including 'The Blessed Damozel'), C. *Rossetti, *Patmore, F. M. Brown, W. B. *Scott, and others and was credited by W. M. Rossetti as the inspiration behind W. *Morris's *Oxford and Cambridge Magazine* (1856) which continued the Pre-Raphaelite impetus.

Gerontius, *The Dream of*, see NEWMAN, J. H.

Gertrude, in Shakespeare's *Hamlet*, mother of Hamlet and married to her late husband's brother *Claudius.

Gertrude of Wyoming, a poem by T. *Campbell, in Spenserian stanzas, published 1809.

The poem, which was immensely popular, centres on a historical event. It describes the destruction of the settlement of Wyoming in Pennsylvania by a force of Indians under the Mohawk Brandt, and the destruction of the happiness of a home by the death of Gertrude, the newly married wife of Sir Henry Waldegrave, and of her father Albert. Campbell later withdrew the charge of cruelty against Brandt.

Gerusalemme liberata, see JERUSALEM DELIVERED.

Geryoneo, in Spenser's *Faerie Queene* (V. x and xi), a three-bodied giant who represents Philip II's power which controlled Spain, Portugal, and the Low Countries.

Gesta Francorum, a chronicle in medieval Latin, the first known to have been written by a layman. It gives the story of the First Crusade. Its actual author is unknown. It has been edited with a translation by Rosalind Hill (Nelson's Medieval Texts, 1962).

Gesta Romanorum, a collection of fictitious stories in Latin, probably compiled in England in the late 13th cent. The stories and fables have an attached moralization, like the *bestiaries and *allegories. Some of the stories are of oriental origin. There are about 165 manuscripts of the Latin versions, and the immense popularity of the work is shown by the existence of 15th-cent. versions in many European languages and by its influence on later medieval writers such as *Boccaccio, *Chaucer, *Hoccleve, and *Lydgate. See *Early English Versions of the Gesta Romanorum*, ed. S. J. Herrtage (EETS ES 33, 1879; repr. 1962).

ghost stories, see overleaf.

ghost-words, a term used by *Skeat to signify words which have no real existence, 'coinages due to the blunders of printers or scribes, or to the perfervid imaginations of ignorant or blundering editors' (*Trans. Philol. Soc.*, 1885–7, ii. 350).

Giant Pope, in Bunyan's *Pilgrim's Progress*, a satiric personification of the papacy, sardonically presented as a senile cave-dweller, 'grown . . . crazy and stiff in his joints', who is too weak and enfeebled to entrap the pilgrims.

Giaour, The, a poem by *Byron, published 1813. Eight editions of the work appeared in the last seven months of that year, and the length was increased from 685 to 1,334 lines.

The story is of a female slave, Leila, who loves the Giaour, a true *'Byronic' hero, and is in consequence bound and thrown in a sack into the sea by her Turkish lord, Hassan. The Giaour avenges her by killing Hassan, then in grief and remorse banishes himself to a monastery.

An indication of the romantic passions aroused by the poem may be found in the response of Captain Benwick in *Persuasion (ch. ii) whose interest in 'hopeless agony' and broken hearts leads Anne to say 'that she thought it was the misfortune of poetry, to be seldom safely enjoyed by those who enjoyed it completely'.

GIBBINGS, Robert, see GOLDEN COCKEREL PRESS.

GIBBON, Edward (1737–94), born in Putney of a good family. He was a sickly child and his education at Westminster and at Magdalen College, Oxford, was irregular; in his posthumously published *Memoirs* he paints a vivid portrait of the 'narrow, lazy and oppressive' spirit of Oxford, and of the 'idle and unprofitable' time he spent there. He became a Catholic convert at the age of 16, perhaps through reading C. *Middleton and *Bossuet, perhaps through reading the works of the Elizabethan Jesuit Robert Parsons, and was sent off to Lausanne by his father, where he was reconverted to Protestantism. There he continued to read voraciously, as he had done since boyhood, his 'blind and boyish taste' for exotic history maturing into serious study of French and Latin classics; he also became attached to Suzanne Curchod (later Mme *Necker, mother of Mme de *Staël), but his father persuaded him to break off the engagement and he returned to England in 1758 after an absence of nearly five years. In 1761 he published his *Essai sur l'étude de la littérature*, of which an English version appeared in 1764. From 1759 he served as a captain in the Hampshire Militia until he left again for the Continent in 1763; it was in Italy, while 'musing amid the ruins of the Capitol' that he formed the plan of his *The History of the *Decline and Fall of the Roman Empire*. His improvident father's death left him in some difficulties, but he was able to settle in London in 1772 to proceed with his great work.

He entered Parliament in 1774, voted steadily for Lord North, and was made a commissioner of trade and plantations, but his parliamentary career added nothing to his reputation. He was also elected to Dr Johnson's *Club in 1774. In 1776 appeared the first volume of the *History* which was very favourably received, although his chapters on the growth of Christianity provoked criticisms from those he mock-

ingly dubbed the 'Watchmen of the Holy City'. To these theological critics Gibbon replied in 1779 in *A Vindication of Some Passages in the XVth and XVIth Chapters*. The second and third volumes appeared in 1781, but were less warmly received; he himself suspected he had become prolix through 'superfluous diligence'. He retired to Lausanne in 1783 to share the home of his old friend Deyverdun, who died not long afterwards. There Gibbon completed the work; he wrote as memorably of its completion as of its inception, describing his sense of freedom followed by a sober melancholy at taking 'an everlasting leave of an old and agreeable companion'. The last three volumes were published in 1788. He returned to England and spent most of his remaining days in the home of his friend the earl of Sheffield (John Baker Holroyd), who put together his remarkable *Memoirs* from various drafts and fragments, publishing them in 1796 with his *Miscellaneous Works*. The memoirs reveal Gibbon's sense of vocation as a historian, and record on several occasions his gratitude at having been born 'in a free and enlightened country'. The *Decline and Fall* is a work which responds to the full range of the culture of the *Enlightenment, in both its English and its European aspects, and Gibbon has been seen as one of the last of the great Augustans. The standard edition of the *History* is by David Womersley (1994) and the standard biography is by Patricia Craddock: see also the life by D. M. Low (1937).

GIBBON, Lewis Grassic, the pen-name of James Leslie Mitchell (1901–35), born on his father's farm near Auchterless, Aberdeenshire; he was educated at Arbuthnott School and (stormily and briefly) at Mackie Academy, Stonehaven. He then worked as a journalist in Glasgow, and in 1919 joined the Royal Army Service Corps; from 1923 to 1929 he was a clerk in the RAF. The army offered him opportunities to travel which resulted in various works written under his own name, including *The Calends of Cairo* (1931), and he also published fiction under the same name, including *Stained Radiance* (1930), his first novel, and *Spartacus* (1933). He worked productively but not with great financial success in his last years, with the encouragement of H. G. *Wells, *MacDiarmid, and others, and published works on exploration, archaeology, etc., but is now remembered principally for his trilogy *A Scots Quair*, published under this collective title in 1946. It consists of *Sunset Song* (1932), *Cloud Howe* (1933), and *Grey Granite* (1934), novels which relate the life of Chris Guthrie from girlhood on her father's farm, through three marriages, the First World War, the Depression, her son's commitment to the Communist Party, etc. All three were published under the name of Grassic Gibbon, taken from his mother's maiden name, and written in a powerful, idiosyncratic, lyrical prose, with a highly personal use of Scottish dialect and archaisms; the narrator shares his heroine's mixture of

(cont. on p.406)

The ghost story genre may be broadly defined as comprising short stories or, less commonly, novels or novellas which have as their central theme the power of the dead to return and confront the living. The ghost in fiction is, on the whole, to be distinguished from the manifestations described in the veridical literature of psychical research. 'Real' ghosts, according to testimony and report, are often spasmodic, mute, and obedient to simple laws (a murder to be revealed, a warning to be given). But in fiction, ghosts become empowered with a variety of active qualities and appear to operate within a moral and physical universe that interpenetrates our own but whose workings are wholly inexplicable to us. Moreover fictional ghosts take many forms, from the recognizably human to the fearfully alien: insubstantial wraiths, or corporeal creatures with the ability to inflict gross physical harm. Or they may never reveal themselves at all, relying instead on an ability to infect and control the minds of the living, or to achieve their ends through inanimate objects—be it a typewriter, a telephone, or a feather boa.

Rooted in immemorial folk beliefs, ghost stories, as a literary genre, have their own conventions and are a comparatively recent development. It is true that spectacles of the returning dead are common in classical and early modern literature—as in *Chaucer's 'Nun's Priest's Tale', when Chanticleer the cock tells how the ghost of a murdered man revealed the circumstances of his death to his sleeping companion ('And truste wel, his dreem he foond ful trewe'). But such moments are both qualitatively and structurally different from the way the supernatural is deployed in the literary ghost story. Before the 19th cent., ghosts are, in themselves, generally less important than the prophetic or revelatory information they convey; and though they naturally excite fear and wonder, their introduction is not deliberately designed to unsettle. In the literary ghost story, at least in many of its classic manifestations, the ghost is all, and the deliberate arousal of fear is the story's primary purpose. There are certainly benevolent ghosts in the literature; but the most memorable stories are those in which the supernatural is presented in a malevolent or predatory aspect.

Literary ghost stories were largely a Victorian creation, part of a wider engagement with the unseen and the uncanny—like the craze for spiritualism—that provided a counterbalance to the prevailing forces of secularism and science. Ghost stories often included admonitions to rationalism; others took account of attempts to establish the objective existence of supernatural phenomena by devising narratives in which the author posed as the reporter or recorder of events, as in *The Night-Side of Nature* (1848) by Catherine Crowe (1790–1876), a popular collection of tales and incidents claiming to be based on actual experiences.

The ghost story's immediate literary antecedents were the *Gothic short stories and fragments common in English magazines during the late 18th and early 19th cents.; but while the short story remained the genre's dominant form, 19th-cent. ghost stories were quite different in character and intention from their Gothic predecessors. Where early Gothic fiction had been, sometimes risibly, unconcerned with either historical detail or present realities, the best Victorian writers of ghost stories set supernatural incidents in solid everyday settings, the very banality of which made such violations of normality all the more convincing.

There is a parallel here with *sensation fiction, another literary vogue of the 1860s and 1870s, in which criminality lurks beneath the surface decorums of daily life.

An early example of a story which struck a new and distinctly anti-Gothic note was Sir Walter *Scott's 'The Tapestried Chamber' (1828). The story takes place in a castle, but it is an English castle, 'rich in all the bizarrerie of the Elizabethan school', set in a real English landscape in the recent past; and its ghost, encountered by General Browne in the tapestried chamber of the title, is disturbingly palpable. Such characteristics became fully developed in the stories of J. S. *Le Fanu, who created the most consistently impressive body of short ghost fiction in the Victorian period. Le Fanu gave his most effective stories credible settings and characters and was adept at creating ghosts that induced physical fear—like the famous spectral monkey in 'Green Tea' (1869). His first collection, *Ghost Stories and Tales of Mystery* (1851), though it made little impact at the time, inaugurated the golden age of the Victorian ghost story, and for the next 20 years or so ghost stories were produced in abundance, helped by a boom in magazine publishing during the 1860s. It was in the pages of monthlies such as *Temple Bar, Tinsley's, *Belgravia*, and *All the Year Round* (owned and edited by Charles *Dickens) that the Victorian ghost story flourished, with special Christmas numbers offering a seasonal opportunity to satisfy a growing public taste for tales of the supernatural. Dickens himself was responsible for one of the most anthologized of all ghost stories, 'The Signalman' (1866), though his role as popularizer of Christmas and its association with the telling of ghost stories was of far greater importance. Many writers of magazine ghost stories were women, amongst them Amelia B. Edwards (1831–92), whose famous story 'The Phantom Coach' first appeared in *All the Year Round* in 1864; Mary Elizabeth *Braddon, author of 'The Cold Embrace' (1860) and 'Eveline's Visitant' (1867), both published in *Belgravia*; Rhoda *Broughton (*Tales for Christmas Eve*, 1873); and Mrs J. H. Riddell (1832–1906: *Weird Stories*, 1882). The same dominance continued through the 1890s and into the 20th cent., with writers such as 'Vernon *Lee' (*Hauntings*, 1890), Edith *Wharton (*Tales of Men and Ghosts*, 1910), Violet *Hunt (*Tales of the Uneasy*, 1911), Marjorie *Bowen (*Curious Happenings*, 1917), and May *Sinclair (*Uncanny Stories*, 1923), amongst others, contributing notably to the genre's development.

Le Fanu's heir, and the great exponent of the factualizing narrative, in which ancient objects and historical and bibliographical references are used to reinforce a sense of actuality and provide a conduit between past and present, was M. R. *James. His antiquarian ghost stories, the first of which, 'Canon Alberic's Scrap-Book', was published in 1895, drew on his own formidable learning and were so convincing that some readers believed them to be factual accounts. His four collections, beginning with *Ghost Stories of an Antiquary* in 1904, were built on solid Victorian foundations but were far from offering a conventional view of the supernatural. Even more than Le Fanu, James excelled at conveying physical, particularly tactile, horror. His ingeniously plotted stories, some of which drew on themes from English and Scandinavian folklore, typically portrayed safe and ordered worlds invaded by terrifying agents of unappeasable supernatural malice. James's style was emulated by a number of younger contemporaries, some of whom had known him personally, including E. G. Swain (1861–1938: *The Stoneground Ghost Tales*, 1912), R. H. Malden (1879–1951: *Nine Ghosts*, 1943), and A. N. L. Munby (1913–74: *The Alabaster Hand*, 1949). Among contemporary authors in whom the Jamesian influence is still detectable are Ramsey *Campbell and Susan *Hill, whose richly atmospheric novel *The Woman in Black* (1983) has been

successfully adapted for both the stage and television.

If M. R. James is the master of the direct ghost story, in which the intrusion of the supernatural is objective and incontrovertible, his namesake Henry *James created, in *The Turn of the Screw* (1898), a potent reinterpretation of Victorian conventions, which begins with a deliberately Dickensian evocation—ghost stories being told round the fire at Christmas—but develops into an ambiguous narrative that blurs the boundary between subjective and objective phenomena. Other well-known stories in which nuance and indirectness predominate over blatancy include 'How Love Came to Professor Guildea' (in *Tongues of Conscience*, 1900) by Robert *Hichens and 'The Beckoning Fair One' (in *Widdershins*, 1911) by Oliver *Onions. An even more complete acceptance of the inconclusive characterizes the ghost stories of Walter *de la Mare (e.g. 'Out of the Deep', in *The Riddle*, 1923); more recently, the enigmatic stories of Robert Aickman (1914–81), in *Powers of Darkness* (1966), *Cold Hand in Mine* (1975), and other collections, fuse traditional elements of ghost fiction with oblique narrations that are concerned not with appearance and consistency, but with 'the void behind the face of order'.

The 20th cent.—perhaps surprisingly—has been prolific in ghost stories. The first 30 years of the century saw the rise of specialist ghost story writers such as Algernon *Blackwood (*The Listener*, 1907); W. F. Harvey (1885–1937: *Midnight House*, 1910); E. F. *Benson (*The Room in the Tower*, 1912); A. M. Burrage (1889–1956: *Some Ghost Stories*, 1927); and H. Russell Wakefield (1888–1964: *They Return at Evening*, 1928). Like their Victorian predecessors, these writers show us ordinary men and women confronted by mysteries that are beyond nature and reason. Though their number may have declined, ghost stories continue to be written and read, their resilience and adaptability testifying to the tenacity of what Virginia Woolf called 'the strange human craving for the pleasure of feeling afraid'. See also GOTHIC FICTION.

J. Briggs, *Night Visitors: The Rise and Fall of the English Ghost Story* (1977); J. Sullivan, *Elegant Nightmares: The English Ghost Story from Le Fanu to Blackwood* (1978); E. F. Bleiler, *The Checklist of Science Fiction and Supernatural Fiction* (1978); M. Cox and R. A. Gilbert (eds.), *The Oxford Book of English Ghost Stories* (1986, 1989).

love and hatred for their ancestral land, 'the red clay of the Mearns', and the plot abounds in lurid and violent incident, as well as in impassioned description. *Sunset Song* was hailed as the first really Scottish novel since *Galt, though many objected to its rawness and frankness. Mitchell died of a perforated ulcer in Welwyn Garden City, where he had been living since 1931. There is a life by I. S. Munro (1966).

GIBBONS, Orlando (1583–1625), English composer. After some early years as a chorister at Cambridge, Gibbons became a gentleman of the Chapel Royal and later its senior organist, as well as organist of Westminster Abbey. The largest part of his output is instrumental or sacred vocal music, but he published one book of secular vocal works, *The First Set of Madrigals and Mottets, Apt for Viols and Voyces* (1612), one of the best of the later *madrigal collections. The tone here is predominantly serious, and poems like *Ralegh's 'What is our life', or 'Oh! deare heart' (attributed to *Donne), are typical of the set and indicative of the temperament of the composer. 'The Silver Swan', one of the best-known of all English madrigals, is in this collection.

GIBBONS, Stella, see COLD COMFORT FARM.

Gibson, Dr, Mrs, and Molly, characters in Mrs Gaskell's *Wives and Daughters*.

GIBSON, Wilfrid Wilson (1878–1962), poet, born in Hexham, Northumberland. He moved to London in 1912, where he met E. *Marsh (to whose *Georgian Poetry* he contributed) and R. *Brooke, who made him one of his heirs. Gibson published many volumes of verse and verse drama, much of it dealing with Northern rural themes; his experiences in the First World War inspired several shorter, sharper battle pieces, such as 'Breakfast'. His *Collected Poems 1905–25* appeared in 1926.

GIDE, André (1869–1951), French novelist, essayist, critic, and dramatist. He published a number of short novels, including *L'Immoraliste* (1902; *The Immoralist*, 1930), *La Porte étroite* (1909; *Strait is the Gate*, 1924), and *La Symphonie pastorale* (1919; *The Pastoral Symphony*, 1931); two longer novels, *Les Caves du Vatican* (1914; translated under various titles: *The Vatican Swindle*, 1925; *Lafcadio's Adventures*, 1928; *The Vatican Cellars*, 1952) and *Les Fauxmonnayeurs* (1925; *The Counterfeiters*, 1927); and a number of autobiographical works, including *Si le grain ne meurt* . . . (1926; *If it Die* . . ., 1935), which describes his revolt against his Protestant upbringing, and his *Journal* for the years 1889 to 1949 (*The Journals of André Gide*, 1947–51). He was awarded the *Nobel Prize for literature in 1947. His recorded disillusion with the Soviet Union, which he visited in 1936, was edited by E. *Starkie from his *Retour de l'U.R.S.S.* (1936) and *Retouches à mon retour* (trans. as *Afterthoughts: A Sequel*, 1938) for inclusion in *The God that Failed* (1950).

GIFFORD, William (1756–1826), the son of a glazier and himself a shoemaker's apprentice. He was sent with the help of a friendly surgeon to Oxford, after which he became tutor to the son of Lord Grosvenor. He published in 1791 and 1795 two satires, *The Baviad* and *The Maeviad*, the first directed against the *Della Cruscan school of poetry, and the second divided between the Della Cruscans and the contemporary drama. In 1797–8 he was editor of the *Anti-Jacobin*. In 1809 he was appointed the first editor of the *Quarterly Review*, a post he held until 1824. He bitterly attacked most of the young innovating writers of his time; among many instances, he wholly altered the warm tone of *Lamb's essay on Wordsworth's *The Excursion* and published J. W. *Croker's virulent attack on Keats's *Endymion*. His character and inadequacies are mercilessly exposed by Hazlitt in *The Spirit of the Age*. He translated the satires of *Juvenal (1802) and of *Persius (1821), and edited the works of *Massinger, *Jonson, *Ford, and *Shirley. A short autobiography is prefixed to the 1827 edition of Juvenal.

GILBERT, William (1540–1603), physician to *Elizabeth I and James I. He declared the earth to be a magnet in his *De Magnete* (1600), so explaining the behaviour of the compass needle. He was the first scientist to distinguish between electricity and magnetism and the first advocate of Copernicanism in England.

GILBERT, Sir William Schwenck (1836–1911), educated at King's College, London, and afterwards employed as a clerk at the Privy Council office. He resigned after four years to study law; he practised as a barrister for several years, without success. In 1861 he began contributing regular columns of comic verse, with his own illustrations, to the magazine *Fun*; this was the beginning of the *Bab Ballads* (collected under this title in 1869), which laid the foundation of his fame on the stage and which became the source of some of his operatic plots. Here he showed his ingenious metrical skill and sketched out his fantasy world, turning the odd into the ordinary, calling it 'Topsy-Turvydom'. The ballads became the favourite literature of sailors, soldiers, lawyers, doctors, and other non-literary people, though Gilbert had a low opinion of his own work: 'I am a doggerel bard', runs the refrain in one of them. Encouraged by T. W. *Robertson he produced his first dramatic work, *Dulcamara* (1866), a burlesque based on *Donizetti's opera *L'elisir d'amore*, followed by several other light stage works. His second period, which began with *The Palace of Truth* (1870), a poetical fantasy based on a novel by Mme de Genlis and influenced by the fairy work of *Planché, included the verse plays *Pygmalion and Galatea* (1871); *The Wicked World* (1873) and a burlesque version, *The Happy Land* (1873), in collaboration with Gilbert Arthur *à Becket; and *The Princess* (1870), a 'respectful perversion' of *Tennyson's poem.

Gilbert was a great verbal rhythmist; his true province was satirical light verse, frequently topical and absurdly funny; and in his third period he found his true genius in comic opera. He met *Sullivan in 1869 and their first collaboration was *Thespis* (1871), but it was not until 1874 that Gilbert met D'Oyly Carte. For him they wrote *Trial by Jury* (1875), which began the series of light operas which was permanently to link the names of Gilbert and Sullivan (see GILBERT AND SULLIVAN OPERAS). D'Oyly Carte leased the old Opéra Comique for their productions and in 1881 built the Savoy Theatre especially for the D'Oyly Carte company. The collaboration lasted for over 20 years, though after *The Gondoliers* (1889) there was a rift resulting from a business transaction in which Sullivan sided with D'Oyly Carte. *Utopia, Limited* (1893) healed the breach. *The Grand Duke* (1896), the only unsuccessful Savoy opera, was the last. Gilbert continued writing plays and operas without Sullivan; among them *Rosencrantz and Guildenstern* (1891), *Fallen Fairies* (1909), with music by E. German, and *The Hooligans* (1911), his last play. He was knighted in 1907, and died of a heart attack while attempting to rescue a young woman who had fallen into a lake. He used the profits from his plays to build the Garrick Theatre.

Gilbert was an outstanding figure in a period which had witnessed a decline in the literary quality of drama; 'and it may be that in the remote future that laughter will still be heard, when all the voices of that age are silent' (G. K. *Chesterton, in his introduction to A. H. Godwin's *Gilbert and Sullivan*, 1926; see also *W. S. Gilbert: A Century of Scholarship and Commentary*, ed. J. B. Jones, 1970).

Gilbert and Sullivan operas, comic operas containing much social satire, the librettos of which were written by Sir W. S. *Gilbert, and the music by Sir A. *Sullivan, for D'Oyly Carte. The operas are: *Trial by Jury* (1875); *The Sorcerer* (1877); *H.M.S. Pinafore* (1878); *The Pirates of Penzance* (1879, NY; 1880, London); *Patience* (1881); *Iolanthe* (1882), probably the cleverest; *Princess Ida* (1884), a satire on feminism suggested by Tennyson's *The Princess*; *The Mikado* (1885); *Ruddigore* (1887); *The Yeomen of the Guard* (1888); *The Gondoliers* (1889); *Utopia, Limited* (1893); and *The Grand Duke* (1896). They are sometimes known as the 'Savoy Operas' because from *Iolanthe* onwards they were produced at the Savoy Theatre.

Gilbert Markham, in A. Brontë's *The Tenant of Wildfell Hall*, the narrator.

Gil Blas, see LESAGE.

GILCHRIST, Anne, née Burrow (1828–85), the wife of Alexander Gilchrist (1828–61), author of a *Life of Etty* (1855) and a life of the then largely unrecognized *Blake, on which he was working when he died. She finished it, and it was published in 1863; it made a considerable contribution to the awakening of interest in Blake's work in the late 19th cent. Anne Gilchrist was friendly with the *Carlyles, and with W. M. *Rossetti (also an admirer of Blake), who imparted to her his admiration for *Whitman. She corresponded passionately with Whitman (who occasionally replied), wrote appreciations of his work, and visited him in America in 1876–9. She also wrote a life of Mary *Lamb (1883) and various articles, sketches, etc. See *Anne Gilchrist: Her Life and Writings*, ed. H. H. Gilchrist (1887).

GILDAS (d. 570), a British historian who lived in the west of England and wrote shortly before 547 a Latin sketch of the history of Britain, *De Excidio et Conquestu Britanniae*, followed by a castigation of the degraded rulers and priests of his day. In the historical section he says nothing of Arthur, but he does refer to the victory of Mt *Badon. He is the first writer of history in Britain; his work is impoverished by insufficiency of dating and by ignorance of the Anglo-Saxons, against whose invasions he shows the 5th-cent. Britons appealing. But he was an important source for later historians from *Bede onwards. *Geoffrey of Monmouth mentions his 'excellent book' in the first sentence of his *Historia Regum Britanniae*.

Gilfil, the Revd Maynard, see SCENES OF CLERICAL LIFE.

GILFILLAN, George (1813–78), a Scottish Dissenting minister, literary critic, and editor, who for a brief period in the mid-19th cent. exercised considerable influence, particularly as the champion of the *Spasmodic school. He was befriended by *Carlyle, who found his prose 'full of fervour, and crude, gloomy fire—a kind of opium style'. His *A Gallery of Literary Portraits* ran to three series, 1845, 1850, 1854, with essays on the Spasmodics, *Macaulay, Carlyle, etc., and he also edited many useful volumes of minor British poets, with notes and memoirs.

GILL, (Arthur) Eric (Rowton) (1882–1940), stone-carver, engraver, and typographer, who cut lettering and designed types, among them Perpetua and Gill Sans-serif. He settled in Ditchling in 1907, where a community of craftsmen and artists began to gather round him; D. *Jones was there for four years from 1921. In 1913 Gill became a Roman Catholic, and he worked for some years from 1914 on a commission to carve the Stations of the Cross for Westminster Cathedral. His statue of Prospero and Ariel carved on site on Broadcasting House in Upper Regent Street is a well-known landmark. From 1924 he was associated with the *Golden Cockerel Press, for which he illustrated many books, including *The Four Gospels* and Chaucer's *Troilus and Criseyde*. Gill wrote many essays, pamphlets, and books on art, sculpture, typography, etc., proclaiming the religious basis of art, the validity of craftsmanship in the machine age, and the holiness of the body (many of his early works were erotic and his own sexual life highly unorthodox); his works include *Art-Nonsense and Other Essays* (1929), *The Necessity of Belief* (1936), and an *Autobiography* (1940). A life by Fiona MacCarthy was published in 1989.

GILLRAY, James (1757–1815), caricaturist. He used his mordant wit and political independence to show up the abuses and vices of Parliament and the royal family, and his often vicious caricatures of Napoleon helped to rouse the patriotism of the country to the threat of invasion.

Gills, Solomon, a character in Dickens's *Dombey and Son*.

GILMAN, Charlotte Anna Perkins (1860–1935), born in Connecticut, American feminist and journalist, and author of *Women and Economics* (1898), *Concerning Children* (1900), *The Home: Its Work and Influence* (1903). She wrote several novels, but is best remembered for her disturbing short story 'The Yellow Wallpaper', published May 1892 in the *New England Magazine*. It is the first-person narration of a young mother isolated in a country colonial mansion, under the supervision of a nurse, on the authority of her physician husband John: she is largely confined to a room with paper of 'a smouldering unclean yellow', in which she discerns sinister patterns and, eventually, the movements of imprisoned women. The story chronicles her descent into madness, and may be read as a simple ghost story or as a feminist text.

Gil Morrice, the subject of an old Scottish ballad, included in Percy's *Reliques*. He is the natural son of an earl and Lady Barnard. A message he sends to his mother leads Lord Barnard to think that he is his wife's lover, and to kill him. The ballad is the same as that of *Child Maurice* in the *Oxford Book of Ballads*, where 'Lord Barnard' is 'John Steward'.

Gilpin, John, see JOHN GILPIN.

GILPIN, William (1724–1804), educated at The Queen's College, Oxford, and subsequently a schoolmaster and vicar of Boldre, is remembered for his extremely influential writings on the *picturesque, which did much to form the taste in landscape, art, and the literary treatment of nature in the later 18th cent. and which some have seen as heralds of *Romanticism. From 1768 onwards he embarked on various travels in search of the picturesque, visiting many parts of the British Isles, and produced the series of illustrated tours parodied by *Combe in his *Dr Syntax*. These include accounts of Wye and south Wales (1782), the Lake District (1789), and the Highlands (1800). His theoretical principles are set out in his *Three Essays: On Picturesque Beauty; On Picturesque Travel; and On Sketching Landscape* (1792), in which he defines the characteristics of the picturesque. See W. D. Templeman, *The Life and Work of William Gilpin* (1939).

Ginevra, (1) a character in *Orlando furioso*, whose story is that of Hero in *Much Ado about Nothing*; (2) the subject of a section of S. *Rogers's poem *Italy*, in which a young bride on her wedding day in playful mood hides herself inside a trunk, of which the lid is closed with a spring lock. Fifty years later her skeleton is discovered there. Rogers notes, 'The story is, I believe, founded on fact; though the time and the place are uncertain. Many old houses lay claim to it.' It is retold by *Bayly in his ballad 'The Mistletoe Bough'; (3) Ginevra Fanshawe, in *Villette* by C. Brontë.

GINSBERG, Allen (1926–97), American *Beat poet born in New Jersey and educated at Columbia University, New York. He took the democratic spirit of *Whitman and applied it to his own experiences of homosexuality and madness. His major poems *Howl* (1956) and *Kaddish* (1960) are composed according to the dictates of breath and are both long laments for an America which has disowned its own more marginalized figures (Trotskyites, Wobblies, Hell's Angels, Junkies, Queers). His empathy for the outcast made him an ideal figurehead for the counter-culture of the 1960s and he wrote and campaigned tirelessly against the Vietnam War, in support of the drug LSD and cannabis, and in defence of such contemporaries as Abbie Hoffman, Timothy Leary, and *Burroughs. His later work, *Mind Breaths* (1978) and *Plutonium Ode and Other Poems* (1982), display less of the urgency of his earlier work, yet still maintain a confessional tone wherein his most private concerns are addressed as a statement about the nation. Along with Ann Waldman he founded the Jack Kerouac School of Disembodied Poetics at the Naropa Institute in Boulder, Colorado.

'Gioconda Smile, The', see LEONARDO DA VINCI and HUXLEY, A.

GIORGIONE DA CASTELFRANCO (1476–1510), Venetian painter, to whom only three pictures—the Castelfranco altarpiece, the *Three Philosophers*, and the *Tempest* (c.1504)—are universally attributed. Yet, since *Vasari, his importance has been recognized; he introduced a new kind of painting in his small oils of pastoral subjects, where the figures and hazy landscape create a poignant, dreamy mood. Ruskin in *Modern Painters* ('The Two Boyhoods') compared him with *Turner. In the later 19th cent. literary interest in Giorgione was intense, although it centred on a picture, the *Fête champêtre* (c.1510, now known as the *Concert champêtre*), which many scholars now give to *Titian. It shows young men making music with naked girls in an idyllically sunny landscape, and was evoked by D. G. *Rossetti's sonnet 'For a Venetian Pastoral by Giorgione' (1850, rev. 1870); thereafter it inspired *Pater's 'The School of Giorgione' (1877) with its celebrated dictum, 'All art constantly aspires to the condition of music.'

GIOTTO DI BONDONE (c.1267–1337), the most celebrated of the early Italian painters, whose art marks a turning away from Byzantine tradition to the clear space and dignified human figures of Renaissance art; his undisputed works are frescos in the Arena Chapel at Padua (1303–13) and in the Peruzzi and Bardi chapels in Sta Croce, Florence. Giotto was the first artist to be celebrated by literary men in his own day; praised by *Dante, *Boccaccio, and *Petrarch, and his epitaph written by *Poliziano, he was seen as the start of a new artistic era and rapidly became a legendary figure. Yet there followed a long period of neglect, until the late 19th cent. when he was admired by *Ruskin, followed by R. *Fry and *Berenson. E. M. Forster, in *A Room with a View*, wittily describes a scene in Sta Croce, where his heroine looks for Giotto's 'tactile values'—a phrase made famous by Berenson's essay *The Florentine Painters*.

Gipsies Metamorphosed, The, a masque by *Jonson, performed before James I 1621, printed 1640. It is the most elaborate of his masques, and unusual in its assigning of principal parts to members of the court. The chief event is the telling of the king's fortune by the gypsy captain, a part taken by the duke of *Buckingham.

GIRALDUS CAMBRENSIS (de Barri) (?1146–1220), a native of Pembrokeshire and son of Nest, a Welsh princess. He studied at Paris before 1176 and again 1177–80. As a churchman he had a stormy career. He was archdeacon of Brecon, and twice (1176 and 1198) a nominee for the see of St David's, but was rejected, as a Welshman, first by Henry II, then by Archbishop Hubert. He appealed to Rome, sought the support of the Welsh, was outlawed, fled abroad, and was imprisoned at Châtillon. He was finally reconciled to the king and archbishop and was buried at St David's. In 1184 he accompanied Prince John to Ireland. From 1196 to 1198 he led a student's life at Lincoln.

His works (ed. J. S. Brewer and J. F. Dimock, 1861–77) include *Topographia Hibernica*, *Expugnatio Hibernica*, *Itinerarium Cambriae*, *Gemma Ecclesiastica*, *De Rebus a se Gestis*, and lives of St *Hugh of Lincoln, St David, and others. The *Topographia*, which he read aloud to the assembled masters at Oxford in 1184 or 1185, is an account of the geography, fauna, marvels, and early history of Ireland; the *Expugnatio* a narrative of the partial conquest of Ireland (1169–85); the *Itinerarium* (the most important of his works) a description of the topography of Wales; the *Gemma* a charge to the clergy of his district, affording interesting information as to the conditions then prevailing. (See also ANGLO-LATIN LITERATURE.)

The Historical Works of Giraldus Cambrensis, ed. T. Wright (1905); The Autobiography of Giraldus Cambrensis, ed. and trans. H. E. Butler (1937); R. Bartlett, Gerald of Wales (1982).

GIRAUDOUX, Jean (1882–1944), French diplomat, novelist, and playwright; his first novel, *Suzanne et le Pacifique*, was published in 1921. In 1928 the novel *Siegfried et le Limousin* (1922) was successfully adapted for the stage. Thereafter the drama became the most suitable medium for Giraudoux's gifts of irony and paradox; his plots are frequently stylized and modernized versions of biblical or classical legend. His plays include *Amphitryon 38* (1929), *Judith* (1931), *La Guerre* de Troie n'aura pas lieu (1935; trans. 1955 by C. *Fry as *Tiger at the Gates*), *Ondine* (1939), and *Pour Lucrèce* (1953, trans. by Fry as *Duel of Angels*, 1958).

GIRODIAS, Maurice, see OLYMPIA PRESS.

GISBORNE, Maria, née James (1770–1836). She refused *Godwin, and married John Gisborne in 1800. Both she and her husband were close friends of *Shelley. They lent him their Italian villa when they were in London, and in 1820 he published his buoyant 'Letter to Maria Gisborne', written to London from the workshop of the villa.

Gismond of Salerne, see TANCRED AND GISMUND.

GISSING, George Robert (1857–1903), educated at a Quaker school, Alderley Edge, Cheshire, and Owens College, Manchester. Caught stealing from school friends to support a prostitute, Nell Harrison, he was sentenced to a month's hard labour. He subsequently worked as a teacher and a photographer's assistant in America, and published his first short stories, later collected in *Brownie* (1931). In 1877, Gissing moved to London, and married Nell. The marriage was not a success, largely due to her chronic alcoholism; they separated by 1883, and Nell died in 1888. Gissing's first novel, *Workers in the Dawn*, was published in 1880, followed by *The Unclassed* (1884, rev. 1895), *Isabel Clarendon* and *Demos* (1886), *Thyrza* (1887; rev. 1891), *A Life's Morning* (1888), and *The Nether World* (1889). After a trip to Italy, Gissing turned away from the working-class subjects that had been predominant in his earlier fiction, writing *The Emancipated* (1890; revised 1893) and his best-known work, *New Grub Street* (1891). Gissing still felt unable to support a middle-class woman, so in 1890 married the artisan's daughter Edith. Though the marriage produced Gissing's sons Walter and Alfred, it was also unsuccessful. Gissing and Edith parted in 1897, and in 1902 she was committed to an asylum. Gissing wrote in a letter to his friend Morley Roberts in 1895, 'the most characteristic, the most important part of my work is that which deals with a class of young men distinctive of our time—well-educated, fairly bred but *without money*. It is this fact of the *poverty* of my people which tells against their recognition as civilised beings.' The most characteristic of these heroes is Godwin Peak, the hero of 1892's *Born in Exile*; Gissing writes in a similar vein about the Woman Question in *The Odd Women* (1893). Though never highly successful, Gissing began to gain more recognition with *Denzil Quarrier* (1892), *In the Year of Jubilee* (1894), *Sleeping Fires*, *Eve's Ransom*, *The Paying Guest* (1895), *The Whirlpool* (1897), and *The Town Traveller* (1898); he was also commissioned to produce more short stories, collected in *Human Odds and Ends* (1897) and *Charles Dickens: A Critical Study* (1898). George *Meredith had been an early supporter of Gissing's work; Gissing also met Thomas *Hardy and became friendly with W. H. *Hudson and H. G. *Wells. In 1897, Gissing met

Gabrielle Fleury, with whom he fell in love. Unable to obtain a divorce, Gissing moved to France to live as man and wife with Gabrielle. Subsequent novels are *The Crown of Life* (1899) and *Our Friend the Charlatan* (1901); also the travel book *By the Ionian Sea* (1901) and an abridgement of John *Forster's *Life of Dickens* (1903). *The Private Papers of Henry Ryecroft* (1902), a mock-autobiography, has remained popular. Troubled by lung disease, Gissing returned occasionally to Britain to recuperate, but died at St Jean-Pied-de-Port in southern France. Posthumously published were *Veranilda* (1904), a classically set romance, *Will Warburton* (1905), *The Immortal Dickens* (1925), *Notes on Social Democracy* (1968), and the short story collections *The House of Cobwebs* (1906), *The Sins of the Fathers* (1924), and *A Victim of Circumstances* (1927). Gissing's notebooks and diary have been published; also nine volumes of his *Letters* (completed 1997). Morley Roberts wrote the affectionate but inaccurate portrait *The Private Life of Henry Maitland* (1912); modern biographies are by Jacob Korg (1963) and John Halperin (1982).

GITTINGS, Robert William (1911–92), poet and biographer, born in Portsmouth, the son of a naval surgeon, and educated at Jesus College, Cambridge. His first volume of poetry, *The Roman Road and Other Poems* (1932), was followed by several volumes of poems and plays, and a *Collected Poems* (1976). His biographical works include *John Keats* (1968) and a two-volume life of *Hardy (1975, 1978); and a study (based on lectures delivered at the University of Washington), *The Nature of Biography* (1978). With his biographer wife Jo (Joan Grenville) Manton he wrote *Claire Clairmont and the Shelleys*, published posthumously in 1992.

GIULIO ROMANO (?1499–1546), Italian mannerist painter and architect, and the most important of *Raphael's pupils; his most famous works were created for Federigo Gonzaga at Mantua and include the Palazzo del Te (begun 1526)—where the frescos in the Sala dei Giganti and the witty, erotic decoration of the Sala de Psiche are most notable—and decorations in the Ducal Palace. Giulio is the only Renaissance artist mentioned by Shakespeare, who apparently thought that he was a sculptor: in *The Winter's Tale* (v. ii) he mentions 'that rare Italian master, Julio Romano'. *Aretino wrote obscene verses to accompany engravings made after pornographic drawings by Giulio; 'Aretine's pictures' are mentioned by *Jonson, *Donne, and *Pope, who perhaps knew them by repute.

GLADSTONE, William Ewart (1809–98), the great Liberal statesman, born in Liverpool, the son of a prosperous tradesman; he was educated at Eton (where one of his close friends was A. H. *Hallam) and at Oxford, where he distinguished himself as an orator, although it took him some time to determine on a career as politician rather than churchman. He is remembered in literary history for his *Studies on Homer and the Homeric Age* (1858), a subject further dealt with in his *Juventus Mundi* (1869) and *Homeric Synchronism* (1876). He firmly maintained his belief in a personal *Homer and 'a solid nucleus of fact in his account of the Trojan war', and sought to justify classical studies as the basis of a Christian education. (For an account of Gladstone as classical scholar, see J. N. L. Myres, *Homer and His Critics*, 1958.) His political writings include *The State in its Relations with the Church* (1838), in which he defended the principle of a single state religion, and his impassioned *Bulgarian Horrors and the Question of the East* (1876). His minor political writings and contributions to periodicals were republished as *Gleanings of Past Years* (7 vols, 1879, with a supplementary vol. 1890). J. *Morley's *The Life of Gladstone*, 3 vols, was published in 1903; see also a life by R. Shannon (vol. I, 1982). *The Gladstone Diaries* (1968–94, 14 vols), ed. M. R. D. Foot and H. C. G. Matthew, shed new light on his complex personality, particularly on his interest in prostitutes, which expressed itself in a zeal for 'rescuing' them and was associated with bouts of self-flagellation, dutifully recorded in what Matthew describes as 'a classic of mid-Victorian self-analysis of guilt'. The diaries (which are for the most part restrained and factual) also illustrate Gladstone's literary tastes; he read *Marmion, *Lalla Rookh, and his own verses to his wife immediately after their marriage, was given to reading Tennyson's *The Princess* and *Guinevere* to his rescue cases, and found *Ainsworth's *Jack Shepherd* 'dangerous' reading for the masses.

GLAISTER, Lesley (1956–), novelist, born in Wellingborough, and brought up in Suffolk. She was educated at the Open University and the University of Sheffield, and teaches a master's degree in writing at Sheffield Hallam University. Her first novel, *Honour Thy Father* (1990), was a dark rural *Gothic story, set in the East Anglian fens, narrated by Milly, one of four ageing sisters, looking back on a life of murder, secrets, and incest: this was followed by several others, including *Partial Eclipse* (1994), which is the story of Jennifer, a woman prisoner leading a fantasy life through her ancestor, who had been transported to Botany Bay. Later books include *The Private Parts of Women* (1996), *Easy Peasy* (1997), and *Sheer Blue Bliss* (1999). Her work is dark, brooding, and powerfully realized, particularly, as in *Easy Peasy*, when evoking the fearful and secret world of children, or the darker side of female sexuality.

GLANVILL, Joseph (1636–80), educated at Exeter College and Lincoln College, Oxford. He was rector of the abbey church at Bath, and held other benefices. He attacked the scholastic philosophy in *The Vanity of Dogmatizing* (1661), a work that contains the story of *'The Scholar-Gipsy'. He defended belief in the pre-existence of souls in *Lux Orientalis* (1662) and belief in witchcraft in *Saducismus Triumphatus* (1681).

GLANVILLE, Ranulf de (d. 1190), chief justiciar of England. The authorship of the first great treatise on the laws of England, *Tractatus de Legibus et Consuetudinibus Angliae*, has been doubtfully ascribed to him on the evidence of *Hoveden.

Glasgerion, an old English ballad of a king's son who is a harper and wins the favour of the king's daughter of Normandy. By a trick his page takes his place at an assignation. When the lady learns the deceit she takes her own life, and Glasgerion cuts off the lad's head and kills himself. The ballad is included in Percy's *Reliques.*

GLASGOW, Ellen Anderson Gholson (1873–1945), American novelist, born in Richmond, Virginia, where she spent most of her life, and which formed the setting of much of her work. In 1896 she took the first of many trips to Europe, and in 1897 published (anonymously) her first novel, *The Descendant*, which was followed by many other works; most critics agree with her own judgement that she began to write her best books in the 1920s, despite ill health, increasing deafness, and much domestic and emotional trouble. She was a woman of advanced views, a supporter of *women's suffrage, attracted by *Fabianism; in her fiction she attempted to show realistically the social and political conflicts of her native region, perceived through a sharp, informed, at times lyrical, and somewhat isolated sensibility. Her novels include *The Voice of the People* (1900); *Virginia* (1913); *Barren Ground* (1925; the story of farmer's daughter Dorinda Oakley, a tough survivor of misfortune); *The Romantic Comedians* (1926); *They Stooped to Folly* (1929); and *The Sheltered Life* (1932), a tragi-comedy set in quiet Queensborough, where beautiful Eva Birdsong clings to past romance and elegance through straitened circumstances, ill health, and the philanderings of her husband George, observed by her neighbours, the dangerously awakening adolescent Jenny Blair and Jenny's grandfather, old General Archbald, symbol of a dying chivalry. *Vein of Iron* (1935) is the story of another survivor, the spirited Ada Fincastle of Shut-In Valley, Virginia, who lives through the First World War, an illegitimate baby, a difficult marriage, and the Depression. *In This Our Life* (1941) describes an aristocratic Virginian family in decline, and *The Woman Within* (1954) is a posthumously published autobiography.

Glastonbury, in Somerset, the abbey of which was said to have been founded by Joseph of Arimathea, according to the *Grail legends (for example in the *Joseph d'Arimathie* of Robert de *Boron, c.1200). The abbey certainly pre-dates the 10th cent. *William of Malmesbury, in his *De Antiquitate Glastoniensis Ecclesiae* (c.1140), suggests that it may have been one of the first Christianized areas in England, founded by French monks. *Giraldus Cambrensis tells the story of the discovery there by the monks of the bodies of Arthur and Guinevere in the 1180s, confirming the story of 'a certain Breton poet' who, according to Henry II, said they were buried there. This led to the identification of Glastonbury with *Avalon. It has been suggested that Henry II arranged the finding of Arthur's body to scotch the tradition that the British king would return to claim his throne. The tradition of the foundation by Joseph of Arimathea advanced to the point in the late 14th cent. where it was claimed by John of Glastonbury that his bones had been found there. See J. A. Robinson, *Two Glastonbury Legends* (1926); R. S. Loomis, *The Grail from Celtic Myth to Christian Symbol* (1963), ch. 15, 250–70.

Glatysaunt Beast, the, the creature in Malory's *Morte D'Arthur* which is the original of *Spenser's 'blatant beast'. The word is from an Old French term meaning 'baying', 'barking'. In Malory it is pursued by Palomydes the Saracen. See BLATANT BEAST; QUESTING BEAST.

Glaucé, in Spenser's *Faerie Queene* (III. ii. 30, etc.), the nurse of *Britomart.

Glegg, Mr and Mrs, characters in G. Eliot's *The Mill on the Floss.*

GLENDINNING, Victoria, née Seebohm (1937–), biographer and novelist, author of *A Suppressed Cry* (1969), a portrait of the Quaker Seebohm family and the short life of her great-aunt Winnie, one of the first students to attend Newnham College, Cambridge: the research for this inspired her historical novel *Electricity* (1995). Other works include lives of Elizabeth *Bowen (1977), Edith *Sitwell (1981), Vita *Sackville-West (1983), Rebecca *West (1987), Anthony *Trollope (1992), and Jonathan *Swift (1998). She was from 1982 until his death married to Irish critic and novelist Terence de Vere White.

GLENDOWER, Owen (?1359–?1416), Welsh rebel leader who in Shakespeare's 1 *Henry IV* allies himself with *Hotspur and *Mortimer to divide the kingdom between them. The chroniclers associate him with wizardry and prophecy, which Shakespeare presents sympathetically. His failure to appear at the battle of Shrewsbury contributes to Hotspur's defeat.

Globe Theatre, the *Burbages' theatre on Bankside in Southwark, erected in 1599 with materials from the old Theatre on the north side of the river. It was a large polygonal building, thatched, with the centre open to the sky. The thatch caught fire in 1613, owing to the discharge of a peal of ordnance at an entry of the king in *Henry VIII*, and the whole building was destroyed. It was rebuilt in 1614 and demolished in 1644. Shakespeare had a share in the theatre and acted there. Shakespeare's Globe, which opened in 1996 close to the original site of the Globe, includes a full-sized reconstruction of the theatre, built in oak and using Elizabethan construction techniques, based on excavations carried out on

Bankside: the driving force behind the building of this new theatre, opened by Elizabeth II in 1997, was American actor-director Sam Wanamaker (1919–93).

Gloriana, one of the names under which Queen *Elizabeth I is indicated in Spenser's *Faerie Queene*, and the title of the opera composed by *Britten for the coronation of Elizabeth II (1953), with a libretto by *Plomer.

Gloucester, earl of, in Shakespeare's *King Lear*, father of *Edgar and the bastard *Edmund. *Regan and Cornwall blind him (on stage) because they suspect him of supporting *Cordelia's French troops. See also RICHARD III.

GLOVER, Richard (1712–85), MP for Weymouth, 1761–85, and an opponent of R. *Walpole. He published much blank verse including *Leonidas* (9 books, 1737) and *The Athenaid* (30 books, 1788), but was long remembered as the author of the ballad 'Admiral Hosier's Ghost' (1740) which was included in Percy's *Reliques*. This was a party song, contrasting the fate of Admiral Hosier (sent in 1726 with a fleet to the Spanish West Indies but obliged to remain there inactive till most of his men perished and he himself died of a broken heart) with the successful attack of Admiral Vernon on Portobello in 1739.

Glumdalclitch, in *Gulliver's Travels*, the farmer's daughter who attended on Gulliver during his visit to Brobdingnag.

GLYN, Elinor, née Sutherland (1864–1943), author of many sensational and romantic novels, of which the best known is *Three Weeks* (1907), a *succès de scandale*, which features illicit passion in Venice on a tiger skin. As exotic as her characters in appearance, she and adaptations of her works achieved great success in Hollywood during the silent movie era.

Gnosticism, a a religious movement which in the 2nd cent. developed into a Christian heresy; its name is taken from the Greek word for knowledge, with reference to the knowledge of God revealed by the founders of various Gnostic sects. Gnosticism was long known only through hostile patristic sources, but 44 early Gnostic documents (in Coptic) were found in Upper Egypt in 1946. Gnostic teaching distinguished between a perfect and remote divine being and an imperfect demiurge who had created suffering. This dualism was represented in the image of a struggle between a spiritual world of light and a material world of darkness. Gnosticism eventually declined and was replaced by Manichaeism, founded by Mani (martyred c.AD 276): this was a religion of personal redemption in which the dualistic myth underlay an ascetic ethic. It has been claimed that *Comenius, Henry More (see CAMBRIDGE PLATONISTS), and *Blake were familiar with Gnosticism.

Gobbo, Launcelot, the 'clown' and servant to *Shylock in Shakespeare's *The Merchant of Venice*; he teases his father, Old Gobbo, who is 'sand-blind' (II. ii).

Go-Between, The, a novel by L. P. *Hartley.

Goblin Market, a poem by C. *Rossetti, published 1862. It is a fairy tale which has been subjected to many interpretations, some seeing it as religious allegory, others as sexual symbolism.

The story tells, in short, irregularly rhymed verses, of two sisters, Lizzie and Laura, both tempted by goblins selling forbidden fruit. Laura yields, eats, and pines for more; she falls sick, unable to hear the song of the goblins, which still haunts Lizzie. Lizzie, for Laura's sake, braves their temptations, while refusing to eat herself, and redeems her sister by carrying back the juices of the fruits which the goblins have crushed upon her in vain.

GODDEN, Rumer (1907–98), novelist and children's writer, born in Sussex. She spent her childhood in India, coming to England for her education, and later returning to open a dance school in Calcutta. Her novels include *Black Narcissus* (1939), about life in a convent in the Himalayas, which was made into a successful film (Michael Powell, 1946); *The River* (1946), set in India; and *The Greengage Summer* (1958, filmed 1961), about children discovering the sexual intensity of the adult world. Her children's books include *The Diddakoi* (1972), *Thursday's Children* (1984), and *Great Grandfather's House* (1992). She also wrote autobiographical works, including *Two under the Indian Sun* (1966), co-written with her novelist sister Jon Godden.

GODFREY OF BOUILLON, see BOUILLON; FAIRFAX.

GODIVA, the wife of Leofric, ealdorman of Mercia, one of Edward the Confessor's great earls. According to legend, her husband having imposed a tax on the inhabitants of Coventry, she begged him to remit it, which he jestingly promised to do if she would ride naked through the streets at noonday. She took him at his word, directed the people to stay indoors and shut their windows, and complied with his condition. Peeping Tom, who looked out, was struck blind.

The story is told by Drayton in his *Poly-Olbion*, xiii; by Leigh *Hunt; and by *Tennyson in 'Godiva'. Lady Godiva figures as the mother of Hereward in C. *Kingsley's *Hereward the Wake* and in one of Landor's *Imaginary Conversations*.

GODLEY, A(lfred) D(enis) (1856–1925), classical scholar and writer of light verse, public orator of Oxford, 1910–25, and joint editor of the *Classical Review*, 1910–20. He translated *Horace's Odes (1898) and *Herodotus' Works (Loeb Series, 1921–3). His volumes of verse, much of which deals with university life, include *Verses to Order* (1892), *Lyra Frivola* (1899), and *Reliquiae A. D. Godley* (1926).

GODOLPHIN, Sidney (1610–43), poet and Royalist, a friend of *Falkland and described by *Suckling as 'little Sid'. He was killed at Chagford. His poems, not collected during his life, were edited by W. Dighton (1931). Hobbes dedicated *Leviathan to his brother Francis.

God that Failed, The: *Six Studies in Communism*, a volume published in 1950, edited by R. H. S. Crossman, which marked a significant point in the reaction against the pro-communist mood of the 1930s. It contained contributions by three ex-communists, *Koestler, *Silone, and R. *Wright, and by three sympathizers, *Gide (presented by Enid *Starkie), Louis Fischer, and *Spender (who had been a party member for a matter of weeks only).

GODWIN, William (1756–1836), educated at Hoxton Academy. He was at first a Dissenting minister, but became an atheist and philosopher of anarchical views. He believed that men acted according to reason, that it was impossible to be rationally persuaded and not to act accordingly, that reason taught benevolence, and that therefore rational creatures could live in harmony without laws and institutions. He married Mary *Wollstonecraft in 1797; she died at the birth of their daughter Mary, the future wife of *Shelley, and Godwin subsequently married Mrs Clairmont, whose daughter by her first marriage, Claire *Clairmont, bore a daughter, Allegra, to Lord *Byron.

Godwin produced in 1793 his *Enquiry Concerning Political Justice*, in which he proclaimed that 'Truth is omnipotent ... Man is perfectible, or in other words susceptible of perpetual improvement.' In 1794 he published The Adventures of *Caleb Williams and Cursory Strictures, a pamphlet defending twelve radicals, including his friends *Tooke and *Holcroft, against the charge of high treason. His life of Mary Wollstonecraft, *Memoirs of the Author of a Vindication of the Rights of Woman*, appeared in 1798; and there is a portrait of her in his novel *St Leon* (1799). He wrote several other novels (*Fleetwood*, 1805; *Mandeville*, 1817; *Cloudesley*, 1830; *Deloraine*, 1833) and a life of *Chaucer (1803–4).

Göemot, the name under which *Gogmagog figures in Spenser's *Faerie Queene.

Goesler, Madame Marie Max, a character of importance in the *'Palliser' novels of A. Trollope.

GOETHE, Johann Wolfgang von (1749–1832), born at Frankfurt am Main, trained for the law against his inclination. In 1775 he was invited by the duke of Weimar, Karl August, to his court, and thereafter spent most of his life in Weimar: he was raised to the nobility in 1782. In 1791 he was appointed director of the Weimar court theatre, a post he held for many years. Throughout his life he was interested in a variety of pursuits, including painting, for which he had only a mediocre gift, though his scattered critical remarks on the visual arts are of great interest. In the field of scientific research he evolved a new theory of the character of light, expounded in the *Farbenlehre* (*Treatise on Colour*, 1810). He also made important discoveries in connection with plant and animal life.

His most famous literary work was the poetic drama in two parts, *Faust. His first important work was *Götz von Berlichingen mit der eisernen Hand* (1773), a drama written under the influence of his friend and critic *Herder. This rough, exuberant play excited Sir W. *Scott, who translated it (inaccurately) in 1799, and it was adapted for the English stage by J. *Arden under the title *Iron Hand* (1965). *Die Leiden des jungen Werthers* (*The Sorrows of Young Werther*, 1774) is a semi-autobiographical *epistolary novel. Werther is a sensitive artist, ill at ease in society and in love with Charlotte (Lotte), who is engaged to someone else. This novel, with the eventual suicide of the hero, caused a sensation throughout Europe (see WERTHERISM). In 1786 Goethe made the first of two visits to Italy, which he recorded in *Italienische Reise* (*Italian Journey*, 1816–17, trans. W. H. *Auden and Elizabeth Mayer, 1962). He returned with his ideas about art radically changed in favour of 'classicism' and cured of his early *Sturm und Drang tendencies. In 1787 there appeared his drama *Iphigenia auf Tauris* based on *Euripides. *Tasso* (1790) dramatizes the problems of the artist in society and is based, like all Goethe's works, partly on his own experience as resident poet in Weimar. In 1795 Goethe published the *Römische Elegien* (*Roman Elegies*), sensuous poems relating partly to Christiane Vulpius, who became Goethe's mistress in 1789 and whom he married in 1806. *Hermann und Dorothea* (1797) is a pastoral epic. *Die Wahlverwandtschaften* (*Elective Affinities*) appeared in 1809, a novel dealing in a strikingly unmoralistic way with the mutual attraction of a married couple for two other persons. Goethe modelled his collection of poems *Der west-östliche Divan* (*East-West Divan*, 1819) on the Divan of the Persian poet *Hāfiz. In the successive volumes of *Dichtung und Wahrheit* (*Poetry and Truth*), which were published between 1811 and 1832, Goethe recalled and reshaped those experiences in his life which had most influenced his artistic development. Along with the *Conversations with Goethe* published by his secretary Eckermann, these were the source of much interest in Goethe's life in England as well as Germany. The 'Wilhelm Meister' novels, written at intervals between 1777 and 1829, are the prototype of the German *Bildungsroman. The first part, *Wilhelm Meisters Lehrjahre* (*Wilhelm Meister's Apprenticeship*) (1795–6), translated into English by *Carlyle in 1824, deals with the disillusioning experiences of the stage-struck youth as he travels the country with a theatrical company. In the sequel, *Wilhelm Meisters Wanderjahre* (*Wilhelm Meister's Travels*; 1821, expanded 1829), also translated by Carlyle (in a volume of stories translated from the German, *German Romance*, 1827), Wilhelm's education for life is completed. Goethe was also a lyric poet of great genius. Many of his poems, as well as the songs from 'Wilhelm Meister', were set to music by German Romantic composers.

In Britain, Goethe exercised an enormous influence on Carlyle, who elevated him to the status of 'the Wisest of our Time' (*Sartor Resartus*). Through Carlyle a whole generation of Victorians turned their attention to Goethe, and eminent authors like G. *Eliot and M. *Arnold paid tribute to his genius both in essays on Goethe and in their creative works (for example, the dénouement of *The Mill on the Floss* may owe something to that of *Elective Affinities*, and the chapter epigraphs of *Middlemarch* and *Daniel Deronda* are frequently quotations from Goethe). G. H. *Lewes wrote the first full biography of Goethe in any language (*The Life and Works of Goethe*, 1855), a book he researched, with George Eliot's help, in Weimar in 1854. The impact of Goethe's *Faust* was curiously delayed, however; *Coleridge never undertook a projected version, and although it was finely translated into French by de *Nerval (1828), no major English poet produced a version until *MacNeice (1951).

GOGARTY, Oliver Joseph St John (1878–1957), poet, surgeon, and for some time a close friend of *Joyce who portrayed him in *Ulysses* as 'stately, plump Buck Mulligan'. He published several novels and volumes of verse, and *Yeats, who included 17 of his poems in *The Oxford Book of Modern Verse* (1936), rated his work highly.

Gogmagog, according to *Geoffrey of Monmouth's *History* (i. 16), a 12-foot member of the tribe of giants who occupied Britain before the coming of Brutus (*Brut). He attacked Brutus and the settlers, killing many of them. Brutus told the avenging Britons to spare Gogmagog so that he could wrestle with Brutus' ally Corineus (a companion of Antenor who joined Brutus at the Pillars of Hercules; Geoffrey, i. 12). Corineus defeats the giant, throwing him to his death far out in the sea. See Spenser, *Faerie Queene* (III. ix. 50). The hills near Cambridge are called the Gogmagog Hills.

The name was divided between two giant figures of wicker and plaster, Gog and Magog, which were carried in the lord mayor's procession through the City of London from the 15th cent. Carved wooden copies 14 ft 6 in high were placed flanking the Guildhall's council chamber door in 1708: these were destroyed in the Second World War, and modern copies now stand in the west gallery.

GOGOL, Nikolai Vasilevich (1809–52), Russian prose writer and dramatist. Born in the Ukraine, which he used as a setting for his early writings, he left for St Petersburg in 1828. His first collection of stories, *Evenings on a Farm near Dikanka*, appeared in 1831–2. His collections *Mirgorod* and *Arabesques* (1835) were followed by the play *The Government Inspector* (or *The Inspector-General*) (1836), a savagely

satirical picture of life in a provincial Russian town. His brilliant St Petersburg stories, 'Nevsky Prospekt' (1835), 'Notes of a Madman' (1835), 'The Portrait' (1835), 'The Nose' (1836), and 'The Greatcoat' (1842), are set in a mad city where nothing is what it seems. From 1836 to 1848 Gogol lived mainly abroad, spending most of his time in Rome. During this period he was at work on his masterpiece, the comic epic *Dead Souls*; the first part was published in 1842, but in 1845, during a developing spiritual crisis, he burnt the drafts of the second part. In 1847 he published an intended moral testament, the *Selected Passages from Correspondence with Friends*, to almost universal rebuke, especially from *Belinsky and *Aksakov. In 1848 he made a pilgrimage to Jerusalem. On his return he continued with *Dead Souls*, but by now he had fallen under the influence of Father Matvei Konstantinovsky, who encouraged him to renounce literature. In Feb. 1852, during a regime of fasting and prayer, Gogol burnt the manuscript of part two of *Dead Souls* and ten days later he died.

Gogol's prose is characterized by extraordinary imaginative power and linguistic originality. Among English writers, he was an admirer of Shakespeare, *Fielding, *De Quincey, Sir W. *Scott, and particularly *Sterne, who may have influenced him. He was himself much admired by the young *Dostoevsky, and has been claimed as precursor by many significant writers. 'The Portrait' was translated into English in 1847, in *Blackwood's*. The most complete early translation is by C. *Garnett (1922–8).

Golagros and Gawain, a 15th-cent Scottish poem of 1,362 lines in 13-line alliterative stanzas, printed in a pamphlet in Edinburgh in 1508, and having some similarities to *The Awntyrs of Arthure*. It is loosely based on the French prose *Perceval* and is concerned with a journey of Arthur and his knights to the Holy Land. There are two episodes, both demonstrating the courtesy of Gawain: in the first, Kay churlishly and Gawain courteously ask for hospitality; in the second Arthur unwisely lays siege to the stronghold of Golagros and Gawain fights in single combat against the latter, ending with Golagros's defeat and reflections on the vagaries of fortune. But the stress throughout is on chivalry, especially that of Gawain. See edition by F. J. Amours, *Scottish Alliterative Poems* (STS, 1897).

Golden, a term used by C. S. *Lewis (*English Literature in the Sixteenth Century*, Introduction) to distinguish the literature of the later Elizabethan period from its predecessors in the *'Drab' age. According to Lewis, 'for a few years nothing more is needed than to play out again and again the strong, simple music of the uncontorted line and to load one's poem with all that is naturally delightful.' The 'Golden' period may be seen as running roughly from Lyly's *Euphues* (1579) to the death of Queen *Elizabeth in 1603. All the major works of *Spenser, *Sidney, and *Marlowe fall within this period, as does two-thirds of the work of Shakespeare. The term suggests a certain bright, innocent, repetitive beauty, which one might see exemplified in such poems as T. *Campion's:

> There is a Garden in her face,
> Where Roses and white Lillies grow;
> A heav'nly paradise is that place,
> Wherein all pleasant fruits doe flow.

But the limited applicability of the term will be realized when we remember that *Hamlet, *Dr Faustus, and much of the poetry of *Donne were among the works written within the period of so-called 'Golden' poetry.

Golden Age, The, see GRAHAME.

Golden Ass, The, see APULEIUS.

Golden Bough, The, see FRAZER.

Golden Bowl, The, the last completed novel of H. *James, published 1904.

The widowed American Adam Verver is in Europe with his daughter Maggie. They are rich, finely appreciative of European art and culture, and deeply attached to each other. Maggie has all the innocent charm of so many of James's young American heroines. She is engaged to Amerigo, an impoverished Italian prince; he must marry money and, as his name suggests, an American heiress is the perfect solution. The golden bowl, first seen in a London curio shop, is used emblematically throughout the novel. Not solid gold but gilded crystal, the perfect surface conceals a flaw; it is symbolic of the relationship between the main characters and of the world in which they move.

Also in Europe is an old friend of Maggie's, Charlotte Stant, a girl of great charm and independence, and Maggie is blindly ignorant of the fact that she and the prince are lovers. Maggie and Amerigo are married and have a son, but Maggie remains dependent for real intimacy on her father, and she and Amerigo grow increasingly apart. Feeling that her father has suffered a loss through her marriage Maggie decides to find him a wife, and her choice falls on Charlotte. The affair with the prince continues and Adam Verver seems to Charlotte to be a suitable and convenient match. When Maggie herself finally comes into possession of the golden bowl the flaw is revealed to her, and, inadvertently, the truth about Amerigo and Charlotte. Fanny Ashingham (an older woman, aware of the truth from the beginning) deliberately breaks the bowl, and this marks the end of Maggie's 'innocence'. She is no pathetic heroine-victim. Abstaining from outcry and outrage, she takes the reins and manœuvres people and events. She still wants Amerigo but he must continue to be worth having and they must all be saved further humiliations and indignities. To be a wife she must cease to be a daughter; Adam Verver and the unhappy Charlotte are banished forever to America, and the new Maggie will establish a real marriage with Amerigo.

Golden Cockerel Press, a *private press founded in 1920 at Waltham St Lawrence, Berkshire, by Harold Taylor, and taken over in 1924 by Robert Gibbings (1889–1958), wood-engraver, illustrator, and writer of travel books. The Golden Cockerel type was designed by *Gill, who was associated with the press from 1924 and designed one of its most celebrated productions, *The Four Gospels* (1941).

Golden Grove, The, see TAYLOR, JEREMY.

Golden Legend, The, a medieval manual of ecclesiastical lore: lives of saints, commentary on church services, homilies for saints' days, and so on. A version in English of this compilation from various sources was published by *Caxton in 1483 and was his most popular production, often reprinted. One of its most important sources was the *Legenda Aurea* in Latin by Jacobus de Voragine (1230–98), an Italian Dominican friar who became archbishop of Genoa. Caxton's version was edited by F. S. Ellis (3 vols, 1892; Temple Classics 1900); selections ed. G. V. O'Neill (1914).

Golden Notebook, The, a novel by D. *Lessing published in 1962. Regarded as one of the key texts of the Women's movement of the 1960s, it opens in London in 1957 with a section ironically entitled 'Free Women', a realistic account of a conversation between two old friends, writer Anna Wulf, mother of Janet, and Molly, divorced from Richard, and mother of disturbed son Tommy, who will later attempt suicide. The novel then fragments into the four sections of Anna's 'Notebooks'—a black notebook, in which Anna has been recording her memories of her emotional and political life in Central Africa during the war, experiences which inspired her own successful novel *Frontiers of War*; a red notebook, in which she describes the activities of and her relationship with the British Communist Party, of which both she and Molly are members; a yellow notebook, which is a fictional interpretation and recreation of Anna's reality (including the painful ending of a serious love affair) through 'the shadow' of alter ego Ella; and a blue notebook, in which Anna records memories, dreams, world events, her own emotional life, and the progress of her psychoanalysis with Mrs Marks ('Mother Sugar'). This pattern of five non-chronological overlapping sections is repeated four times, as it tracks both the past and the present, and although one of Lessing's concerns is to expose the dangers of fragmentation, she also builds up through pastiche and parody, and through many refractions and mergings, a remarkably coherent and detailed account of her protagonists and the world they inhabit. Women who take responsibility for their own lives are seen grappling independently with the conflicts of work, sexuality, maternity, and contemporary politics. In the last section of the blue notebook, Anna takes young American Saul Green as lodger, and falls in love with him: their affair, which descends into a mutual madness, releases

Anna from her 'writer's block' and she determines to put 'all of myself in one book'—this is 'The Golden Notebook', which liberates both Anna and Saul. The conventional narrative ends more prosaically with Anna's declaration that she is about to join the Labour Party.

Golden Treasury, see PALGRAVE, F. T.

GOLDING, Arthur (?1536–?1605), translator of Latin and French works, including *Ovid's *Metamorphoses* (1565, 1567), *Caesar's *Gallic War* (1565), Justin's abbreviation of Trogus Pompeius (1564), and Philippe de Mornay's *A Woorke Concerning the Trewnesse of the Christian Religion* (1587), which had originally been undertaken by Sir P. *Sidney. His translations are clear, faithful, and fluent; his Ovid was known to Shakespeare.

GOLDING, Sir William (1911–93), born in Cornwall and educated at Marlborough Grammar School and Brasenose College, Oxford. He worked as a writer, actor, and producer with small theatre companies and then as a teacher; during the war he served in the Royal Navy and was lieutenant in command of a rocket ship. After the war he returned to writing and teaching. He had published a volume, *Poems*, in 1935 but his first novel, *Lord of the Flies*, did not appear until 1954 when it was an immediate success. *The Inheritors* (1955) tells of man's brutal extermination of his gentler ancestors; the intrinsic cruelty of man is at the heart of many of Golding's novels. *Pincher Martin* (1956), *The Brass Butterfly* (a play, 1958), *Free Fall* (1959), *The Spire* (1964), were followed by a collection of essays, *The Hot Gates* (1965). His other novels are *The Pyramid* (1967), *The Scorpion God* (three novellas, 1971), *Darkness Visible* (1979), and *Rites of Passage* (1980, *Booker Prize). Golding often presents isolated individuals or small groups in extreme situations dealing with man in his basic condition stripped of trappings, creating the quality of a fable. His novels are remarkable for their strikingly varied settings.

Golding was awarded the *Nobel Prize in 1983, and his novel *The Paper Men* (1984), which describes the pursuit of world-famous English novelist Wilfred Barclay by American academic Rick L. Turner, echoes some of the author's previously expressed irritation at finding himself 'the raw material of an academic light industry'. (See the title lecture, delivered in 1976, of a collection of lectures and essays, *A Moving Target*, 1982.) *Close Quarters* (1987) and *Fire down below* (1989) complete the historical trilogy begun with *Rites of Passage. The Double Tongue*, left in draft at his death, was published in 1995. He was knighted in 1988.

GOLDONI, Carlo (1707–93), Italian dramatist, whose comedy is based on the society of his native Venice. He renewed stage comedy, which had been dominated by the *commedia dell'arte. He wrote 250 plays, of which 150 are comedies. In 1762 he settled in Paris, where after writing two successful plays, *Il ventaglio* (*The Fan*)

and *Le Bourru bienfaisant* (*The Beneficent Grumbler*), he died a pauper. The majority of his plays, many of which satirize the aristocracy, fall into three categories: comedies retaining the masked characters of the *commedia dell'arte*, who speak in their traditional dialects, e.g. *La vedova scaltra* (*The Clever Widow*); Italian comedies of manners without masks, e.g. *La locandiera* (*The Mistress of the Inn*), *La bottega del caffè* (*The Coffee-Shop*); and comedies in Venetian dialect, generally considered his best, e.g. *I rusteghi* (*The Tyrants*).

GOLDSMITH, Oliver (?1730–74), the second son of an Anglo-Irish clergyman, born probably at Pallas, Co. Longford, or perhaps at Elphin, Roscommon. He spent much of his childhood at Lissoy, and is thought to have drawn on his memories of it when writing *The Deserted Village*. He was educated at Trinity College, Dublin, and graduated after some upheavals in 1750; he then presented himself for ordination, was rejected, and went to Edinburgh, where he studied medicine but took no degree. He studied in Leiden, and during 1755–6 wandered about France, Switzerland, and Italy, reaching London destitute in 1756, where he supported himself with difficulty as a physician in Southwark and as an usher in Peckham; he may at this period have received a medical degree from Trinity, though this remains unclear. He applied for a medical post in India, but failed to obtain it; meanwhile he had embarked on a literary career as reviewer and hack-writer for Griffith's *Monthly Review, one of his early pieces being a favourable review of Burke's *Philosophical Enquiry . . . into the *Sublime and Beautiful; *Burke was to become a close friend. In 1758 he published, under the pseudonym 'James Willington', his translation of *The Memoirs of a Protestant, Condemned to the Galleys of France for his Religion* (by Jean Marteilhe of Bergerac, a victim of the Edict of Nantes), and in 1759 his first substantial work, *An Enquiry into the Present State of Polite Learning in Europe. It was at this period he met *Percy, later bishop of Dromore, who was to become a loyal friend and also his biographer. He was by now contributing to many periodicals (the *Busy Body*, the *Monthly Review*, the *Critical Review, the *Ladies' Magazine*, etc.), and during Oct. and Nov. 1759 published his own little periodical, the *Bee*, in which appeared his 'Elegy on Mrs Mary Blaize' (a pawnbroker) and 'A City Night-Piece'. He contributed to *Smollett's *British Magazine*, started in 1760, and was also employed by *Newbery, for whose new *Public Ledger* he wrote his 'Chinese Letters', subsequently republished as *The Citizen of the World* in 1762; he is also said to have written the nursery tale *Goody Two-Shoes*. In 1761 he met Dr *Johnson, who admired his work; he became one of the original members of Johnson's *Club. Johnson remained his friend and champion, and in 1762 sold for him the (possibly unfinished) manuscript of *The Vicar of Wakefield* to Newbery, thereby saving him from arrest for debt.

Goldsmith was still struggling as a writer, and making his living with a variety of hack-work in the form of biographies, compilations, translations, abridgements, etc.: these include lives of *Voltaire (1761) and Beau *Nash (1762), an abridgement of *Plutarch (1762), a *History of England in a Series of Letters from a Nobleman to his Son* (1764), a *Roman History* (1769), a *Grecian History* (1774), lives of T. *Parnell and *Bolingbroke (1770), etc.—in all more than 40 volumes. But he first achieved literary distinction with his poem *The Traveller* (1764) which also introduced him to his only patron, Lord Clare; it was his first signed work, and was much admired by Johnson and *Fox among others. *The Vicar of Wakefield* (1766), which was to become one of the most popular works of fiction in the language, was slower to find its audience, possibly because it was, as the *Monthly Review* commented, 'difficult to characterize'.

Goldsmith's first comedy, *The Good-Natur'd Man*, was rejected by *Garrick but produced at Covent Garden in 1768 with moderate success; *She Stoops to Conquer* followed in 1773 with immense success. Goldsmith had criticized the vogue for *sentimental comedy and the prejudice against laughter (see CHESTERFIELD) in an essay in the *Westminster Magazine* entitled 'A Comparison between Laughing and Sentimental Comedy' (1773); his own play's lasting popularity justified his comments.

His best-known poem, *The Deserted Village*, was published in 1770; his lighter verses include *Retaliation (1774) and the posthumously published *The Haunch of Venison* (1776), written to thank Lord Clare for a gift of game from his estate. His *An History of the Earth and Animated Nature* (1774), also published posthumously, in eight volumes adapted from *Buffon, *Linnaeus, *Ray, and others, inventively portrays 'tygers' in Canada, and squirrels migrating on bark boats in Lapland, fanning themselves along with their tails.

There are many anecdotes about Goldsmith in Boswell's *Life of *Johnson*, which represent him as ridiculous, vain, extravagantly dressed, improvident, and naïve, but also as tender-hearted, simple, and generous, with flashes of brilliance in conversation (despite Garrick's gibe that he 'wrote like an angel, but talked like poor Poll'). He was regarded with much affection; Johnson, in his Latin epitaph, stated that he adorned whatever he touched. He never married, and his relationship with Mary Horneck, his 'Jessamy bride', remains mysterious. He was introduced to the Horneck family by *Reynolds in 1766, when Mary was 14, and accompanied Mrs Horneck, Mary, and her other daughter Catherine ('Little Comedy', who married H. W. *Bunbury) to Paris in 1770; in 1773 he attacked Thomas Evans for publishing in the *London Packet* a letter from 'Tom Tickler' mocking his feelings for 'the lovely H——k'. She long outlived him, and provided material for J. Prior's life (1837); another biographer, W. *Irving (1844), concluded that Gold-

smith had suffered from unrequited love, but this has been much disputed.

The 1801 *Miscellaneous Works* contain Percy's memoir, and there are other lives by J. *Forster (1848) and Ralph M. Wardle (1957). *The Collected Works* (5 vols, 1966) were edited by A. Friedman, and the correspondence by K. C. Balderston (1928).

Goliard, Goliardic, see GOLIAS.

Golias, or **Goliardus,** the name found attached in English manuscripts of the 12th and 13th cents to Latin poems of a satirical and profane kind, the most famous of these being the so-called 'Apocalypse of Golias', for which no certain evidence of authorship can be claimed. According to F. J. E. Raby (*A History of Secular Latin Poetry in the Middle Ages*; 2 vols, 1934), the conception of Golias as 'Bishop' or 'Archpoet' is a myth, largely of English creation. The 'Goliards' are, it seems, to be linked with Golias, Goliath of Gath, the symbol of lawlessness and of evil, though the original derivation may have been from 'gula', on account of their gluttony. The famous 'Goliardic' measure or 'Vagantenstrophe' appears to have passed from secular into religious verse. See CARMINA BURANA.

GOLLANCZ, Sir Israel (1863–1930). After lecturing at University College London, 1892–6, he was appointed in 1896 as the first lecturer in English at Cambridge. In 1905 he became professor of English at King's College, London, a post he held until his death. He followed *Furnivall as director of the Early English Text Society, and he was one of the founders and original fellows of the *British Academy (1902). He was an outstanding medieval and Shakespearian scholar and editor. As well as editing several texts in Old and Middle English, he was the general editor of the Temple Shakespeare and of Temple Classics. A British Academy lectureship and prize were founded in his memory. He was one of the most active and distinguished members of the British Jewish community, promoting Jewish cultural causes.

GOLLANCZ, Sir Victor (1893–1967), nephew of Sir I. *Gollancz, publisher; he founded his own firm in 1928, and in 1936 the *Left Book Club. He was well known for his progressive views, his resistance to Fascism, his 'Save Europe Now' movement in 1945 to relieve starving Germany, and his opposition to capital punishment; these were reflected in his firm's publications.

GOMBRICH, Sir Ernst (1909–2001), distinguished British art historian, long associated with the Warburg Institute in the University of London, as director and as professor of the history of the classical tradition. His immensely popular work *The Story of Art* (1950) is now widely used as a textbook by many schools and universities. He wrote extensively on the theory of art and on the psychology of pictorial representation; three volumes of essays, *Studies in the Art of the Renaissance* (1966, 1972, 1976), discuss the style of

Renaissance painting, its symbolism, and its relationship to the classical tradition.

GONCHAROV, Ivan Aleksandrovich (1812–91), Russian prose writer. From 1834 to 1867 he worked in the Russian bureaucracy, serving from 1855 as an official censor. In 1852–4 he journeyed round the world as secretary to an admiral. The book he wrote about his travels, *The Frigate Pallas*, contains impressions of England and of English colonialism. Goncharov's most important works are the novels *An Ordinary Story* (1847; trans. C. *Garnett, 1894), *The Ravine* (1869; trans. 1915), and his masterpiece *Oblomov* (1859; trans. 1915), where in the portrait of a man who disdains to get out of bed he created a literary archetype admired the world over.

GONCOURT, Edmond and Jules de (1822–96 and 1830–70), French authors, brothers, who wrote in close collaboration. Their earliest interests were art criticism, in which field they published several works (including the important *L'Art du dixhuitième siècle*, 1859–75), and French social history. From 1851 they wrote novels, painstakingly documented studies which they regarded as a form of contemporary social history. *Sœur Philomène* (1861), *Germinie Lacerteux* (1864), and *Madame Gervaisais* (1869) are among the best known. Their *écriture artiste*, an impressionistic, highly mannered style, elaborate in syntax and vocabulary, is well exemplified in *Manette Salomon* (1867), a novel of artist life. Some years after Jules's death Edmond returned to novel writing with, for example, *Les Frères Zemganno* (1879). The famous *Journal des Goncourt* is a richly detailed record of literary life in Paris between 1851 and 1896. Several volumes were published, omitting many passages likely to shock or give offence, during Edmond de Goncourt's lifetime. An integral edition appeared between 1956 and 1959. The Académie Goncourt, founded under the will of Edmond de Goncourt, is a body of ten men or women of letters which awards an annual money prize (Prix Goncourt) for imaginative prose. (See also NATURALISM.)

Gondal, see ANGRIA AND GONDAL.

Gondibert, an uncompleted romantic epic by *D'Avenant, published 1651, consisting of some 1,700 quatrains.

It is a tale of chivalry, set in Lombardy; Duke Gondibert loves Birtha, and is therefore impervious to the love of Rhodalind, the king's daughter, who is in turn loved by Oswald, but before these issues are resolved the author declares himself bored with the poem. D. F. Gladish in his 1971 edition describes it as 'a poetic museum of seventeenth-century literature and theory'.

GONDOMAR, Don Diego Sarmiento de Acuña, marquis de, the Spanish ambassador in the reign of James I.

He was the enemy of *Ralegh, and caused *Middleton to be imprisoned for his play *A Game at Chesse*.

Goneril, in Shakespeare's *King Lear*, the king's eldest daughter, who is married to *Albany.

Gongorism, an affected type of diction and style introduced into Spanish literature in the 16th cent. by the poet Luis de Góngora y Argote (1561–1627), a style akin to Euphuism in England and Marinism in Italy (see EUPHUES and MARINO). Góngora was none the less a poet of genius, and both his earlier and his latest verses were simple and unaffected.

Gonzalo, 'an honest old Councellor' loyal to *Prospero and part of Antonio's company in *The Tempest*.

Good-Natur'd Man, The, a comedy by *Goldsmith, produced 1768.

Mr Honeywood is an open-hearted but foolishly good-natured and credulous young man, who gives away to the importunate what he owes to his creditors. His uncle Sir William Honeywood decides to teach him a lesson by having him arrested for debt and letting him see who are his true friends. Young Honeywood is in love with Miss Richland, a lady of fortune, and she with him, but he is too diffident to propose to her. He even recommends to her the suit of Lofty, a government official to whom he believes himself indebted for release from arrest. In fact it is Miss Richland who has secured the release, and Lofty is exposed; Honeywood, cured from his folly, is united with Miss Richland. There is a sub-plot turning on a love affair between Leontine, the son of Croaker, Miss Richland's doleful guardian, and Olivia; these two are also united through the intervention of Sir William. The character of Croaker, 'always lamenting misfortunes he never knew' (T. *Davies), was taken from Suspirius, in the *Rambler* No. 59, according to *Boswell. The theme of excessive generosity was treated several times by Goldsmith and, according to Davies, he himself, 'rather than not relieve the distressed, would borrow'. (See also *Citizen of the World*, 'The Man in Black'.) In a preface Goldsmith attacks 'genteel comedy' and praises the comedy of 'nature and humour'.

Good Soldier, The: *A Tale of Passion*, a novel by F. M. *Ford, published 1915; an earlier version of the first part of the novel appeared in *Blast*, 20 June 1914, as 'The saddest story'.

Generally considered Ford's finest technical achievement, it consists of the first-person narration of American John Dowell (an archetypally unreliable narrator), who relates the history of relationships that begin in 1904, when he and his wife Florence meet Edward and Leonora Ashburnham in a hotel in Nauheim. The two couples form a foursome, and meet regularly. In August 1913 the Ashburnhams take their young ward Nancy Rufford to Nauheim with them, and Florence commits suicide. Later that year the Ashburnhams send Nancy to India (where she goes mad) and Edward also commits suicide. Dowell becomes Nancy's 'male sick nurse'; Leonora remarries. The substance of the novel lies in Dowell's growing understanding of the intrigues that lay behind the orderly Edwardian façade both couples had presented to the world; the carefully plotted time-scheme (orchestrated round the fatal date of 4 August, Florence's wedding day and death day) introduces the 'facts' (that Edward and Florence had been lovers, that both Edward and Dowell were in love with Nancy and Nancy with Edward) in an apparently casual, haphazard way that lends plausibility to an essentially melodramatic tale. The frequent time-shifts show an affinity with Ford's one-time collaborator *Conrad.

Good Thoughts in Bad Times, a collection of reflections by T. *Fuller, published 1645 at Exeter, where Fuller was living as chaplain to Sir Ralph Hopton. It was followed in 1647 by *Good Thoughts in Worse Times*, and in 1660, at the Restoration, by *Mixt Contemplations in Better Times*. The work consists of meditations on his own shortcomings, observations of passages of Scripture, and applications of historical incidents and anecdotes to current events, and is marked by his usual good humour.

Goody Two-Shoes, a moralistic nursery tale, said to have been written by *Goldsmith, published by *Newbery.

GOOGE, Barnabe (1540–94), a member of both universities, a kinsman of Sir William Cecil, who employed him in Ireland, 1547 and 1582–5. He published *Eglogs, Epytaphes, and Sonnetes* (1563; ed. J. M. Kennedy, 1989), and translations, including Heresbach's *Foure Bookes of Husbandry* (1577). His eclogues are of interest as being, with those of *Barclay, the earliest examples of pastorals in English.

Gorboduc, or *Ferrex and Porrex*, one of the earliest of English tragedies, of which the first three acts are by Thomas Norton (1532–84) and the last two by T. *Sackville. It was acted in the Inner Temple Hall on Twelfth Night 1561. The play is constructed on the model of a Senecan tragedy, and the subject is taken from the legendary chronicles of Britain.

Gorboduc and Videna are king and queen, Ferrex and Porrex are their two sons, and the dukes of Cornwall, Albany, Logres, and Cumberland are the other chief characters. Ferrex and Porrex quarrel over the division of the kingdom. Ferrex is killed by Porrex, and Porrex is murdered in revenge by his mother. The duke of Albany tries to seize the kingdom and civil war breaks out. There is no action on the stage, the events being narrated in blank verse. Sidney praised the play in his *Defence of Poetry* as being 'full of stately speeches and well-sounding phrases'.

The legend of Gorboduc is told by *Geoffrey of Monmouth, and figures in Spenser's *Faerie Queene* (II. x. 34 and 35), where Gorboduc is called Gorbogud.

GORDIMER, Nadine (1923–   ), South African novelist and short story writer, awarded the *Nobel Prize for literature in 1991. Most of her work is concerned with the political situation in her native land; her protests against apartheid and censorship were outspoken. Her collections of stories include *The Soft Voice of the Serpent* (1953), *Friday's Footprint* (1960), *Livingstone's Companions* (1972), and *Jump* (1991); her novels include *A Guest of Honour* (1970), in which an English colonial administrator returns to the complexities of a newly independent African country from which he had been previously expelled for his sympathies with the black population; *The Conservationist* (1974, joint winner of the *Booker Prize); *Burger's Daughter* (1979), which describes the personal and political heritage of Rosa Burger, whose communist father had died in prison; and *July's People* (1981), a novella set in the future, in which a white family on the run from civil war find themselves dependent on their black servant. Later novels include *A Sport of Nature* (1987), *My Son's Story* (1990), *None to Accompany Me* (1994), which focuses on the period leading up to democratic elections in South Africa, and *The House Gun* (1996), which investigates a crime of passion in post-apartheid South Africa. *The Essential Gesture* (1988) and *Writing and Being* (1997) are collections of essays. See Stephen Clingman, *The Novels of Nadine Gordimer: History from the Inside* (1993). See also POST-COLONIAL LITERATURE.

GORE, Mrs Catherine Grace Frances, née Moody (1799–1861), a novelist of the *silver-fork school, who published about 70 novels between 1824 and 1862, many anonymously; they include *Mothers and Daughters* (1830) and *Mrs Armytage: or Female Domination* (1836), generally considered her best; *Cecil, or The Adventures of a Coxcomb* (1841); and *The Banker's Wife, or Court and City* (1843). She also wrote several plays and many short stories. Her novels, with their marked predilection for titled ladies and fashionable life, were parodied by *Thackeray in 'Lords and Liveries', one of *Mr Punch's Prize Novelists*.

GORE, Charles (1853–1932), bishop of Oxford 1911–19. He wrote a number of works on religious subjects and edited and contributed to *Lux Mundi* (1889), a collection of essays on the Christian faith written by various hands which attempted 'to put the Catholic faith into its right relation to modern intellectual and moral problems'; the book caused some distress among the older and more conservative school of High Churchmen.

GORGES, Sir Arthur (1557–1625), courtier and poet, educated at Oxford, and from 1580 a gentleman pensioner at court. He was a close friend of *Ralegh. His grief for the death of his young wife Douglas Howard was depicted by *Spenser in *Daphnaïda* (1591). His love poems *Vannetyes and Toyes of Yowth* were not published until 1953; other works include *The Olympian Catastrophe* (1612), an elegy on Prince Henry; *Lucans Pharsalia* (1614), a powerful rendering of *Lucan's epic into rhyming tetrameters; and a translation of F. *Bacon's *Wisedome of the Ancients* in 1619. His English poems were edited by H. E. Sandison (1953).

GORKY, Maxim (Aleksei Maksimovich Peshkov) (1868–1936), Russian prose writer and playwright. Obliged to work for his living from the age of 8, Gorky roamed all over Russia. He was self-educated and read voraciously. He suffered for his radical views and after taking part in the 1905 Revolution he went abroad to collect funds for the revolutionary movement. After the 1917 Revolution his independent views and increasing ill health led, in 1921, to his leaving Russia for Italy. In 1928 he returned to the Soviet Union as supporter of the government. His position in the last years of his life is paradoxical and obscure. He was partly responsible for the formulation of the doctrine of *Socialist Realism, and in 1934 he became first president of the Union of Soviet Writers. Yet he is also said to have intervened to protect writers who came under attack. The circumstances of his death, too, remain mysterious.

His first story was 'Makar Chudra' (1892), but it was 'Chelkash' (1895) which established his reputation. His best-known works are *Twenty-Six Men and a Girl* (1899), *Foma Gordeev* (1899), *The Mother* (1906–7), the story of the radicalization of an uneducated woman that was later taken as a model for the Socialist Realist novel, and his autobiographical masterpieces *Childhood* (1913), *Among People* (1915), *My Universities* (1923). Then came *The Artamonov Business* (1925) which traced the decline of a mercantile family, and the unfinished cycle of novels *The Life of Klim Samgin* (1925–36), on the emergence of the revolutionary spirit in Russia. His plays, of which the most famous are *Philistines* and *The Lower Depths* (both 1902), are still performed regularly in Russia and abroad.

Gorlois, in the Arthurian legend, duke of Cornwall and husband of *Igraine.

Gormenghast, see PEAKE.

GOSSE, Sir Edmund William (1849–1928), the son of Philip Henry Gosse (1810–88), eminent zoologist and fanatical fundamentalist Christian, his relations with whom he describes in *Father and Son* (1907), his masterpiece. This is in Gosse's own words 'the record of a struggle between two temperaments, two consciences and almost two epochs', as well as a moving and amusing study of an individual childhood.

Gosse came to London from Devon in 1867 to work as a transcriber at the British Museum. In 1875, the year of his marriage, he became a translator at the board of trade. He saw himself as a poet and made early acquaintance with the *Pre-Raphaelites. *Swinburne became a close friend. When Gosse applied for the post of Clark lecturer at Cambridge in 1883, he was able to give *Tennyson, R. *Browning, and M. *Arnold as references. A great deal of his early critical work was devoted to Scandinavian literature and he was the first to introduce *Ibsen's name to England. A successful lecture tour of America in 1884–5 was followed by Churton *Collins's attack on his published lectures *From Shakespeare to Pope*, an indictment of his carelessness which shadowed the rest of his life.

His books include lives of *Gray (1882), *Congreve (1888), P. H. Gosse (1890), *Donne (1899), Jeremy *Taylor (1904), *Patmore (1905), Ibsen (1907), and Swinburne (1917), as well as collections of poems and critical essays. He introduced *Gide to England and was honoured by the *Académie française for his services to the literature of France. His close friends included R. L. *Stevenson, H. *James, and *Hardy. From 1904 he was librarian of the House of Lords and exercised considerable power and influence: H. G. *Wells dubbed him the 'official British man of letters'. He was writing regularly for the *Sunday Times* until his death. A biography by Ann Thwaite appeared in 1984.

GOSSON, Stephen (1554–1624), educated at Corpus Christi College, Oxford. His plays are not now extant, but were ranked by *Meres among 'the best for pastorall': however, he soon became a leader of the Puritan attacks on plays and players. His *Schoole of Abuse* (1579) was dedicated to *Sidney, as was a romance, *The Ephemerides of Phialo*, to which he appended *An Apologie of the Schoole of Abuse* (both also 1579). Whether or not he was 'scorned' by Sidney as *Spenser claimed in a letter to *Harvey, his *Schoole of Abuse* helped to stimulate Sidney to write his *Defence of Poetry. T. *Lodge replied more directly to Gosson in *A Defence of Stage Plays*, provoking a reply from Gosson in *Playes Confuted in Five Actions* (1582). Gosson's attacks on the stage were edited by A. F. Kinney under the title *Markets of Bawdrie* (1974).

Gotham, a village near Nottingham traditionally famed for the simplicity of its inhabitants: the origins of the tradition are obscure, but there is a reference to it in the Towneley *mysteries, and related stories appeared in a collection of the *Merie Tales of the Mad Men of Gotam Gathered Together by A.B.* of which a 1630 edition is extant. A reprint of a copy (probably 1565) was published in 1965, ed. S. J. Kahrl. Washington *Irving introduced the term Gotham as a sobriquet for New York (*Salmagundi*, 1807–8), and the New York identification stuck. Gotham was most readily recognized in the late 20th cent. as the skyscraper city of the exploits of the long-lived and famous comic strip hero Batman, created in the 1930s by Bob Kane (d. 1998). Batman and his friend Robin had originally lived in a Gothic mansion complete with Batcave on the outskirts of the city, but they moved into a modern penthouse in the heart of the metropolis in the 1960s. See also CHURCHILL, CHARLES.

Gothic fiction, see overleaf.

Gothic Revival, a revival of the Gothic style of architecture which began in the late 18th cent. with a new romantic interest in the medieval, and produced Walpole's *Strawberry Hill and *Beckford's Fonthill. This was followed in the 19th cent. by a more scholarly study of Gothic, expressed in the works of *Pugin and the writings of *Ruskin. The widespread adoption of the Gothic style transformed the appearance of English towns and cities, not always, it was long thought, for the better; its leading architects (William Butterfield, 1814–1900; G. E. Street, 1824–81; Gilbert Scott, 1811–78) had many less successful imitators. See K. *Clark, *The Gothic Revival*, first published 1928, reprinted 1950 with a foreword by the author crediting *Betjeman with initiating a change of taste and a new respect for Victorian architecture.

GOULD, Nat(haniel) (1857–1919), journalist and novelist, born in Manchester; from 1884 he spent 11 years in Australia, and his first book, *The Double Event* (1891), was published while he was there. Most of his novels (about 130) were concerned with horse racing, and he also wrote two books of Australian life, *On and Off the Turf in Australia* (1895) and *Town and Bush* (1896).

GOUNOD, Charles François (1818–93), French composer, whose four-year stay in England (1870–4) produced a considerable number of settings of English poetry, from *Wordsworth, *Byron, and *Shelley to *Palgrave and Mrs C. F. Alexander: Gounod was not proof against the Victorian fondness for sentimental and pious ballades, and his later oratorios for the English market catered for a similar taste. In his earlier manner, however, his *Roméo et Juliette* (1867) is one of the more successful Shakespearian adaptations: the libretto, by Barbier and Carré, stays reasonably close to Shakespeare's intention, and the love music is handled with delicacy and a sense of character.

Gower, in Shakespeare: (1) a Welsh captain, friend of Fluellen, in *Henry V; (2) the poet Gower (below), who acts as Chorus and narrator in *Pericles.

GOWER, John (?1330–1408), of a family of gentry who owned land in Kent and Yorkshire. He probably lived in Kent throughout the first half of his life. He may have been trained in the law, but from about 1377 to his death he lived at the priory of St Mary Overies in Southwark, devoted to his writing. He was married (perhaps for the second time) in 1398 when he was probably nearly 70; he went blind in about 1400. He was a friend of Chaucer and (jointly with *Strode) the dedicatee of *Troilus and Criseyde (see V. 1856); it is possible that the two authors became estranged, because a tribute to Chaucer in the first version of *Confessio Amantis* is removed in a later one. In his revision of the *Confessio* (in the early 1390s, while Richard II was still on the throne) he removed the

praises of King Richard at its conclusion and dedicated the final version to Henry of Lancaster (later Henry IV).

Gower's considerable learning is attested by his writing with accomplishment in three languages. In French he wrote his *Cinkante Balades* (written in *Anglo-Norman before 1374, and presented to Henry IV in 1400) and, his first large-scale work, the *Mirour de l'omme* (*Speculum Meditantis*), an allegory written c.1376–8 in about 32,000 lines of octosyllabics in twelve-line stanzas, concerned with fallen man, his virtues and vices. His second major work was the much more considerable Latin *Vox Clamantis* (c.1385), an apocalyptic poem of seven books in 10,265 lines of elegiac couplets, dealing with politics and kingship and containing reflections on the disturbances of the early years of Richard II and the Peasants' Revolt of 1381. In English he wrote the late poem 'In Praise of Peace' (which influenced the closing section of *Hoccleve's *Regiment of Princes*, 5020–5439) in 55 stanzas of rhyme-royal, as well as his principal work, the *Confessio Amantis*.

The *Confessio* exists in three manuscript versions from the 1390s, the first of which, published in 1390, is the most commonly attested amongst the 49 manuscripts. It is over 33,000 lines long, containing 141 stories in octosyllabic couplets which are handled with a metrical sophistication and skill unsurpassed in English. The framework of the poem is the confession of a lover, Amans, to Genius, a priest of Venus; the confessor helps to examine the lover's conscience and tells him exemplary stories of behaviour and fortune in love, organized under the headings of the *Seven Deadly Sins and drawing widely on classical story (most prominently *Ovid) and medieval romance. There are eight books: one for each of the sins, and one (Book VII) which gives an encyclopaedic account of philosophy and morals. Although the framework is a container for stories (like *The Canterbury Tales or *Decameron), it is as interesting for its Prologue and admirable Epilogue, and for its exchanges between the priest and lover, as it is for the narratives themselves. At the end, when the lover has been entirely shriven of his sins and his grasp of the ethics of love is complete, the confessor tells him that he is too old for love and disappears. After pondering his abandonment, the lover sees the reason in this and

Homward a softe pas y wente (VIII. 2967):

a conclusion which has been seen as a comment on the longueurs of the lover's apprenticeship in the self-perfecting of courtly love. Several of the exemplary tales are paralleled by stories in *The Canterbury Tales* and other works of Chaucer: for example, the story of Florent (I. 1407–1861) corresponds to 'The Wife of Bath's Tale' (*CT*, 6); Constance (II. 587–1612) to 'The Man of Law's Tale' (*CT*, 5); Phebus and Cornide (III. 768–835) to 'The Manciple's Tale' (*CT*, 23); Pyramus and Thisbe (III. 1331–1494) to Chaucer's 'Legend of
(cont. on p.424)

Frightening or horrifying stories of various kinds have been told in all ages, but the literary tradition confusingly designated as 'Gothic' is a distinct modern development in which the characteristic theme is the stranglehold of the past upon the present, or the encroachment of the 'dark' ages of oppression upon the 'enlightened' modern era. In Gothic romances and tales this theme is embodied typically in enclosed and haunted settings such as castles, crypts, convents, or gloomy mansions, in images of ruin and decay, and in episodes of imprisonment, cruelty, and persecution. The first important experiment in the genre, written half in jest, was Horace *Walpole's *The Castle of Otranto (1764, subtitled A Gothic Story in the 2nd edn, 1765), which tells a pseudo-Shakespearian tale of a family curse that eliminates the princely dynasty of the usurper Manfred in 12th-cent. Italy, foiling his incestuous attempt to marry his dead son's fiancée.

The great vogue for Gothic novels occurred in Britain and Ireland in the three decades after 1790, culminating in the appearance of C. R. *Maturin's *Melmoth the Wanderer (1820). During this period, the leading practitioner of the new genre was Ann *Radcliffe, whose major works The Romance of the Forest (1791), *The Mysteries of Udolpho (1794), and The Italian (1797) were decorous in their exhibitions of refined sensibility and of virtue in distress. Udolpho in particular established the genre's central figure: that of the apprehensive heroine exploring a sinister building in which she is trapped by the aristocratic villain. Radcliffe's formula was followed by numerous clumsy plagiarists in the popular market for chapbooks and 'shilling shockers', but she also inspired a few more talented imitators. Of these, the most striking is Matthew G. *Lewis, whose novel *The Monk (1796) cast aside Radcliffe's decorum in its sensational depictions of diabolism and incestuous rape.

The term 'Gothic' in this context means 'medieval', and by implication barbaric. In the late 18th cent. it was applied loosely to the centuries preceding the enlightened Protestant era that began with the Glorious Revolution of 1689. Radcliffe, Lewis, and Maturin set their novels in the Catholic countries of southern Europe in the 16th and 17th cents., alarming their readers with tales of the Spanish Inquisition and of villainous, hypocritical monks and nuns. While drawing upon the imaginative liberties of greater English writers of the 'Gothic' age—principally *Shakespeare's use of ghosts and omens, and *Milton's portrait of Satan—the Gothic novelists deplored the cruelty and arbitrary power of barons and monks, and mocked the superstitious credulity of the peasants. In this sceptical Protestant attitude to the past, they differ significantly from the genuinely nostalgic medievalism of *Pugin and other advocates of the later *Gothic Revival in architecture. Radcliffe in particular was careful to distance herself from vulgar belief in ghosts or supernatural marvels, by providing rational explanations for the apparitions and nocturnal groans that frighten her heroines.

Some of Radcliffe's contemporaries and immediate successors managed to achieve comparable effects of apprehension and claustrophobia in novels with more modern settings: William *Godwin in The Adventures of *Caleb Williams (1794), his daughter Mary *Shelley in *Frankenstein; or The Modern Prometheus (1818), and the Scottish writer James *Hogg in *The Private Memoirs and Confessions of a Justified Sinner (1824) all evoked powerful unease without employing medieval trappings. Although each of these three novels includes prominent prison scenes, the principal strength is the evocation of psychological torment, guilt, self-division, and paranoid delusion. There are some grounds for excluding these works from the strictest definitions of Gothic fiction, but they are none the less commonly grouped with the work of Radcliffe, Lewis, and Maturin.

By the 1820s, the Gothic novel had given way to the more credible historical novels of *Scott, its clichés by now provoking less terror than affectionate amusement, as in Jane *Austen's parody *Northanger Abbey (1818). Some of the tales of terror published by *Blackwood's Magazine and its London rival the *New Monthly Magazine, however, retained the Gothic flavour in more concentrated forms, and John *Polidori's story 'The Vampyre' (1819) launched the powerful new Gothic sub-genre of vampiric fiction, which commonly expresses middle-class suspicion of the decadent aristocracy. From these sources the first master of American Gothic writing, Edgar Allan *Poe, developed a more intensely hysterical style of short Gothic narrative, of which his story 'The Fall of the House of Usher' (1839) is the classic model. Since Poe's time, the strong tradition of American short story writing, from *Hawthorne to Joyce Carol *Oates, has frequently resorted to Gothic themes and conventions.

In English and Anglo-Irish fiction of the Victorian period, the Gothic influence is pervasive, not just among minor authors such as *Bulwer-Lytton and Bram *Stoker but among some major figures: the novels of the *Brontë sisters are strongly Gothic in flavour, Charlotte Brontë's *Villette (1853) being a late example of the overtly anti-Catholic strain in this tradition. Charles *Dickens favoured such settings as prisons and gloomy houses, while his characterization employs a Gothic logic that highlights cursed families and individuals who are paralysed by their pasts: the significantly named Dedlock family in *Bleak House (1852–3) and Miss Havisham in *Great Expectations (1860–1) are among the best-known examples, but similar emphases prevail throughout his œuvre. Somewhat closer to the spirit of the original Gothic novels are the so-called *sensation novels of the 1860s, notably Wilkie *Collins's *The Woman in White (1860), and Sheridan *Le Fanu's *Uncle Silas (1864), which is descended directly from Radcliffe's Udolpho in its use of the imprisoned heiress. Le Fanu's ghost stories and tales of terror, along with those of Elizabeth *Gaskell and others, are also significant contributions to the Victorian Gothic tradition. The last decades of the Victorian period witnessed a curious revival of Gothic writing by Irish- and Scottish-born authors in which the haunted house seemed to give way to the possessed body, as in *Stevenson's The Strange Case of *Dr Jekyll and Mr Hyde (1886), *Wilde's The Picture of Dorian Gray (1890), and Stoker's vampire classic *Dracula (1897). At the turn of the century, more traditional Gothic settings and effects are found in such mystery stories as Henry *James's *The Turn of the Screw (1898), which again refers back to Udolpho, and Conan *Doyle's The Hound of the Baskervilles (1902).

In the first part of the 20th cent. the Gothic tradition was continued principally by writers of ghost stories, such as M. R. *James and Algernon *Blackwood, and by fantasy writers, of whom Mervyn *Peake is the most distinctive. A major exception in the realm of higher literary achievement is the work of William *Faulkner, which renews and transcends the Gothic genre in its preoccupation with the doomed landowning dynasties of the American South. His novel Sanctuary (1931) is still a shocking exercise in Gothic sensationalism, surpassed by the tragic depth of his Absalom, Absalom! (1936) and by several of his shorter stories. The English writer Daphne *du Maurier meanwhile opened a new vein of popular Gothic romance with *Rebecca (1938), which revived the motif of the defenceless heroine virtually imprisoned in the house of a secretive masterfigure, inspiring countless formulaic imitations in the popular paperback market. The Hollywood cinema did even more to grant Gothic narrative a favoured place in the popular imagination, through its various adaptations of Dracula, Frankenstein, and other literary works.

In the 1960s a few of the leading English novelists, including Iris *Murdoch, John *Fowles, and David *Storey, experimented with Gothic effects in some of their works. As a taste for non-realistic forms of fiction established itself, Gothic settings and character-types reappeared regularly as part of the repertoire of serious fiction. The novels and stories of Angela *Carter, notably The Magic Toyshop (1967) and The Bloody Chamber & Other Stories (1979), showed how Gothic images of sexuality and domestic confinement could be used imaginatively to explore the concerns of contemporary feminism. In the 1980s, several of the finest novels in English were clearly derived from the Gothic tradition: Graham *Swift's Waterland (1983) and Toni *Morrison's *Beloved (1987), for example, both encapsulate their larger tragic and historical themes within the convention of the dreadful family secret and the haunted house. American writers specializing in Gothic fiction at the end of the 20th cent. included the English-born novelist Patrick *McGrath, whose The Grotesque (1989) and later works display a mood of macabre humour, the hugely popular horror writer Stephen King, and the vampire romancer Anne Rice, who also has a cult following associated with the 'Goth' youth subculture.

The critical fortunes of Gothic writing since Walpole's time have swung intermittently between derision of its hoary clichés and enthusiasm for its atmospheric, psychologically suggestive power. From either side, the Gothic tradition is usually considered a junior or marginal rival to the mainstream of fictional *realism. Walpole inaugurated the tradition in the hope that the lifelike solidity of realism might be reconciled with the imaginative range of romance. It fell to his greater successors—the Brontë sisters, Dickens, and Faulkner—to fulfil this promise. See also GHOST STORIES.

See: D. Punter, The Literature of Terror (1980, rev. edn, 1996); C. Baldick (ed.), The Oxford Book of Gothic Tales (1992); F. Botting, Gothic (1996).

Thisbe' (*The Legend of Good Women, II. 706–923); Ceix and Alceone (IV. 2927–3123) to *The Book of the Duchess (62–220); Tarquin and his son Aruns (VII. 4593–5123) to the 'Legend of Lucrece' (LGW, V. 1680–1885). The pairs of narrative are usually compared to Gower's disadvantage, because his stories lack the development and dramatic scope of Chaucer's; but the lucidity and pointedness, as well as the stylistic accomplishment, of Gower are admirable too. Moreover the stories in common with Chaucer are not, in general, Gower's best; 'Jason and Medea' (V. 3247–4222) and some of the shorter stories ('Narcissus', I. 2275–2358; 'Canace and Machaire', III. 143–336; 'Rosiphilee', IV. 1245–1446) are slight masterpieces of the classical narrative. Up to the 17th cent. almost every writer who praised Chaucer coupled his name with Gower's (see C. F. E. Spurgeon, *500 Years of Chaucer Criticism and Allusion*, 1925, vol. i); he has more examples than any other writer in *Jonson's Grammar*, and he speaks the Prologue to Shakespeare's *Pericles*, part of the story of which is taken from Gower's 'Apollonius of Tyre' (CA, VIII. 271–2008). Perhaps his significance as an English writer is to have brought into the mainstream of the canon of the literature the disparate narratives of the classics and the popular romances. (See also ANGLO-LATIN LITERATURE.)

Works (French, Latin, and English), ed. G. C. Macaulay (1899–1902); trans. of *Vox Clamantis* in E. W. Stockton, *The Major Latin Works of John Gower* (1962); selections from *Confessio Amantis* by J. A. W. Bennett (1968) and R. A. Peck (1968). For criticism and discussion see introduction to Macaulay's edition of the *Confessio*; W. P. Ker, *Essays on Medieval Literature* (1905), ch. 5; J. H. Fisher, *John Gower: Moral Philosopher and Friend of Chaucer* (1964); D. A. Pearsall, 'Gower's Narrative Art' (PMLA 81, 1966, 475–84).

Grace Abounding to the Chief of Sinners, or *The Brief Relation of the Exceeding Mercy of God in Christ to his Poor Servant John Bunyan* (1666), a Puritan conversion narrative by *Bunyan, testifying to the focal events in his journey to assurance of salvation. Its pastoral purpose was to comfort his flock at Bedford during his imprisonment. The author bound himself to the Puritan 'plain style', for 'God did not play in convincing of me . . . I may not play in relating'. The document chronicles anguished oscillation between suicidal despair and contrite reassurance and bears witness to the inner struggle of moods ('up and down twenty times in an hour') which typified Puritan experience. External events (military service in the Civil War, marriage, etc.) are subordinate to inner and spiritual events, as Bunyan struggles against the lure of church bells, the doctrines of the *Ranters, Sabbath recreations, dancing, swearing and blaspheming—even against envy of toads and dogs as being exempt from God's wrath. It details his joining of the Bedford church, call to the ministry, and trials.

Gradasso, in *Orlando innamorato and *Orlando furioso, the king of Sericane, who invades Spain, overcomes its king Marsilio, and presses Charlemagne back to Paris. His object is to secure *Bayard and *Durindana, which he succeeds in doing, but not by his prowess. He is killed with *Agramant by Orlando, in the great fight at Lipadusa.

Gradgrind, Mr, Louisa, and Tom, leading characters in Dickens's *Hard Times.

GRAEVIUS (Latinized form of Greffe), Johann Georg (1632–1703), Dutch scholar and antiquary, professor at Utrecht, the foremost Latinist of his day, a friend of Richard *Bentley.

GRAHAM, R. B. Cunninghame, see CUNNINGHAME GRAHAM, R. B.

GRAHAM, William Sydney (1918–86), Scottish poet, born in Greenock, and brought up on Clydeside; he was educated at Greenock High School, and worked as an engineer as a young man. He later settled in Cornwall, which provides the landscape for many of his later poems. His first volume, *Cage without Grievance* (1942), shows considerable verbal energy and a debt to Dylan *Thomas; his own voice emerges more clearly by *The White Threshold* (1949), through which the image of drowning and the seascapes of his youth resound. The poems in *The Night-Fishing* (1955) range from its long and complex title poem, which uses the metaphor of a herring fishing expedition to explore the poet's struggle with language and vocation, to the grim but lively ballad 'The Broad Close' (which evokes his grandfather, 'the rude oak of his day'). Later collections, *Malcolm Mooney's Land* (1970) and *Implements in Their Places* (1977), continue the same preoccupations with the metaphors of sea and language, and the embattled struggle of artistic creation, often with a sense that the language itself is alive, hostile, independently animate, or else 'a frozen tundra of the lexicon and the dictionary'. Graham's *Collected Poems 1942–1977* were published in 1979.

GRAHAM OF CLAVERHOUSE, John (?1649–89), first viscount Dundee, a Royalist officer employed by the Scottish Privy Council in executing the severities of the government in Scotland during the reigns of Charles II and James II. In 1688, when James 'forsook his own cause', Graham's life was in danger even in Scotland; he determined to raise the Highlands for James (after the manner of his collateral, Montrose, in 1644) and was killed at the battle of Killiecrankie. He figures prominently in Scott's *Old Mortality; see also *Wordsworth's sonnet 'In the Pass of Killiecranky' (written 1803, pub. 1807).

GRAHAME, Kenneth (1859–1932), born in Edinburgh. After school in Oxford he entered the Bank of England, where he became secretary in 1898. As a young man he contributed to the *Yellow Book and was encouraged by W. E. *Henley, who published many of the essays which later appeared in *Pagan Papers* in 1893. Six of the 'papers' described the life of a family of five orphans, whose activities then filled the chapters of *The Golden Age* (1895) and its continuation, *Dream Days* (1898). The sharp, authentic vision of childhood, and the shrewd observation of the child narrator, were widely praised, not least by *Swinburne, and brought Grahame great success in both England and the USA. *The Wind in the Willows*, based largely on bedtime stories and letters to his son, was never intended by Grahame to become a published work; the manuscript was given reluctantly to an importunate American publisher, who then rejected it. Published in England in 1908, its reception was muted, and it was not for some years that the story of Rat, Mole, Badger, and Toad, and their life by the river, became established as a children's classic. The book was dramatized by A. A. *Milne in 1929, and has been performed widely since.

Grail, the Holy, in Arthurian legend, a symbol of perfection sought by the knights of the *Round Table. In the latest development of the legend it is identified as the cup of the Last Supper in which Joseph of Arimathea caught the blood of the crucified Christ and which, in some versions, he brought to north Wales at the end of his lengthy wanderings. The legend has a long history, drawing on Celtic elements as well as Middle Eastern ones, and it is most familiar in English in the version of *Malory which is mostly an abridgement of the stories contained in three of the romances of the early 13th-cent. French prose 'Vulgate' cycle. R. S. Loomis notes that, in spite of its long history, the ten principal versions of the legend were written in a period of about 50 years, between 1180 (*Chrétien de Troyes) and 1230 (Gerbert). As well as Chrétien's *Perceval* or *Conte del Graal* and the Vulgate versions, there is a third major version in that period, the *Parzival* of *Wolfram von Eschenbach (*c*.1205) which was the inspiration for *Wagner's *Parsifal*. Von Eschenbach's and Chrétien's story, in which Perceval is the successful quester, may be regarded as related to the original and more 'authentic' Grail myth which was joined by accretions and euhemerization of a Christian kind until, by Malory's time, it was very far removed from its archetype.

In Malory's *Tale of the Sankgreal* (the sixth of Vinaver's eight *Works*) *Launcelot fathers *Galahad on *Elaine, the daughter of the Grail King *Pelles. On the feast of Pentecost Galahad is brought to the Round Table and seated at the Siege Perilous; the Grail appears, accompanied by lightning, but the knights cannot see it. Led by *Gawain they set off in search of it. Launcelot fails in the Quest, despite several glimpses, because of the sin of his amour with *Guinevere; Gawain gives up the quest. Three knights distinguished by great purity, Galahad, Bors, and Perceval, come to the castle of *Corbenic where they have a vision of Christ and receive the Eucharist from him; they take the Grail from him and carry it to Sarras.

Galahad dies in ecstasy; Perceval becomes a monk and dies two months later; Bors returns to Logrus and reports their adventures in Camelot, in particular telling Launcelot of the eminence of his son Galahad.

The origins and motivation of the Grail have been explained in three principal ways: (1) as a Christian legend from the first, which altered only in detail through its history (J. D. Bruce, *The Evolution of Arthurian Romance*, 1923); (2) as a pagan fertility ritual, 'the horn of plenty', related to the devastation of the land of King Pellam and its redemption—a connection made briefly by Malory (see DOLOROUS STROKE; J. L. Weston, *From Ritual to Romance*, 1920; and the essays on Arthurian romances in J. Speirs, *Medieval English Poetry*, 1957); (3) as a Celtic story, already mythological in its origins in Irish, transmitted through Welsh (see MABINOGION) and Breton to the French romance tradition and gradually Christianized (Loomis). There is disagreement too as to whether a fairly coherent myth has been constructed out of a series of originally disparate elements (Vinaver), or an originally coherent myth has been obscured by misunderstandings and mistranslations of elements in it (Loomis). Loomis believes, for example, that the horn of plenty (*cor*) of Celtic myth has been misinterpreted as the body (*cors*) of Christ, and that the phrase *San Graal* (Holy Grail, derived possibly from the Latin word for dish) has been wrongly divided *Sang real* (royal blood, for the Eucharist). It is likely that the symbol was effective, in the Middle Ages as now, precisely as a 'heap of broken images' (T. S. *Eliot) whose crypticism made it particularly apt as the object of a romance quest, a genre whose creators were constantly in search of difficult tasks. See R. S. Loomis, *The Grail from Celtic Myth to Christian Symbol* (1963); C. L. Brown, *The Origin of the Grail Legend* (1943).

GRAINGER, James (?1721–66), physician and man of letters, who emigrated to the West Indies in 1759. His didactic poem *Sugar Cane* (1764) pleased many, but not Dr *Johnson, who said to Boswell, 'One might as well write "The Parsley-bed, a Poem", or "The Cabbage-garden, a Poem".'

GRAINGER, Percy (1882–1961), Australian composer, pianist, and folk-song collector. He settled in London in 1901 as a concert pianist and in 1905 became a member of the English Folk-Song Society, in which capacity he was active as a collector of folk songs, working alongside figures like *Vaughan Williams and C. *Sharp in this field and being the first to introduce the wax cylinder phonograph as a means of recording his discoveries. He later made many very original and very beautiful folk-song settings, although his most famous work *Country Gardens*, based on a morris dance sent to him by C. Sharp, is simply a variant of the well-known tune of *'The Vicar of Bray'. He also made, at various periods of his life, a great many settings of *Kipling.

Grainne, in the legends relating to the Irish hero *Finn, the daughter of King Cormac. Finn, though a great warrior and hunter, was unfortunate in love. He sought to marry Grainne, but she fell in love with Finn's nephew Diarmait O'Duibhne and eloped with him. The long story of their flight and Finn's unsuccessful pursuit ends in Finn's temporary acceptance of the situation; but Finn finally causes the death of Diarmait.

Gramont, *Mémoires de la vie du comte de*, published anonymously at Cologne, 1713, was written by Anthony Hamilton (?1646–1720), third son of Sir George Hamilton and grandson of the earl of Abercorn. Anthony Hamilton was the brother-in-law of the comte de Gramont, who married Elizabeth Hamilton in 1663. The memoirs were edited (in French) by Horace *Walpole and translated into English (with many errors) by *Boyer in 1714; and this translation, revised and annotated by Sir W. *Scott, was reissued in 1811. A new translation was made in 1930 by *Quennell, with an introduction and commentary by C. H. Hartmann.

The first part of the memoirs, dealing with Gramont's life on the Continent down to the time of his banishment from the French court, was probably dictated by Gramont to Hamilton. The second part, relating to the English court, appears to be Hamilton's own work. It is an important source of information, but its trustworthiness on details is doubtful.

GRAMSCI, Antonio (1891–1937), founder of the Italian Communist Party (1921) and, through his ideas on culture, an important factor in its appeal. Born in Sardinia, son of a minor civil servant, he read literature and philology at Turin University. Elected to Parliament in 1924, he was arrested in 1926, sentenced to 20 years in jail by the Fascist Special Tribunal, and died from illnesses contracted in prison. His *Quaderni del carcere* (*Prison Notebooks*, 1948–56) deal with philosophy, history, culture, folklore, literature, language, and the role of the intellectuals. They include his theatre criticism, and journalism for *Ordine nuovo* (*New Order*), which he founded. His letters from prison are a classic of Italian prose.

GRAND, Sarah (1854–1943), the pseudonym of novelist Frances Elizabeth Bellenden McFall, née Clarke, adopted in 1893 after she had left her surgeon husband and published several volumes anonymously. She achieved sensational success with *The Heavenly Twins* (1893), which attacked the sexual double standard in marriage and dealt frankly with the dangers of syphilis and the immorality of the Contagious Diseases Act. This novel launched her on a public career as a *New Woman (a phrase she was said to have coined in 1894); she lectured and wrote extensively, and was for six years (1922–9) mayoress of Bath. *The Beth Book* (1897), a semi-autobiographical novel, describes with much spirit (and occasional lapses into melodramatic absurdity) the girlhood, disillusioning marriage, liter-

ary aspirations, and eventual independence of its heroine. See G. Kersley, *Darling Madame: Sarah Grand and Devoted Friend* (1983).

Grandison, Sir Charles, a novel by S. *Richardson, published 1754.

Urged by many friends, Richardson had been thinking since about 1749 of the portrayal of a 'Good Man', to balance his female creations in *Pamela* and *Clarissa*. In his usual manner he took much advice. The novel, again epistolary in form, ranges far more widely in scene and has more characters and a looser plot than his earlier works. It is also the only one set in aristocratic and wealthy society, of which Richardson had little personal knowledge.

Harriet, described as the most beautiful woman in England, attracts many admirers, among them the wealthy and unscrupulous Sir Hargreve Pollexfen. When she refuses his advances he has her abducted from a masquerade, then after the failure of a secret marriage ceremony has her carried off into the country. Sir Charles, hearing her cries from the coach, rescues her and gives her into the care of his kindly married sister. He and Harriet fall in love, but on the day she learns of his love for her he has to set out for Italy. There, in the past, he has become involved with one of the noblest-born women in Europe, Clementina Porretta, but religious differences have kept them apart. Clementina's unhappiness has deranged her mind, and her parents, now prepared to accept any terms for the cure of their daughter, summon Sir Charles to Italy. As she recovers, however, Clementina reaffirms that she cannot marry a heretic, and Sir Charles, released, returns to England to marry Harriet. Three months later Clementina appears, declaring that she wishes to become a nun but that her parents wish her to marry another suitor. Her parents and suitor then appear, but Sir Charles is able to arrange everything to everyone's satisfaction, and Harriet, he, and Clementina swear eternal friendship.

The book is faster-moving and less analytical than Richardson's previous novels, but the 'sense of reality' on which Richardson had so often been complimented is somewhat lacking. Richardson was anxious to avoid all stricture, and as a result Sir Charles is a paragon of honour, wisdom, and all the virtues. However, the book was very popular, and J. *Austen, who held it in high esteem, dramatized scenes from it for family performance: see *Jane Austen's 'Sir Charles Grandison'*, ed. B. Southam (1980).

Grand Tour, the, which began in the 16th cent. and became a fashion in 18th-cent. England. It was a leisurely journey through Europe, perhaps of two or three years, during which the sons of the aristocracy enriched their knowledge of the classical past and developed the socially desirable skills of the connoisseur. By the mid-1760s the educated middle classes were also travelling, and a colony of British painters and architects was studying in Rome. Travellers followed a well-established route, musing—more enthusiastically as the century wore on—on the sublime landscape of the Alps, with the glories of ancient Rome and Naples as their main aim; Herculaneum was excavated from 1711 onwards, and Pompeii from 1733. Travellers admired the works of the great Venetians and of 17th-cent. Bolognese painters; they sat to Pompeo Batoni or Rosalba Carriera, and were caricatured by Thomas Patch; Canaletto, Panini, and Piranesi satisfied a taste for souvenir cityscapes. Celebrated collections of antiquities, among them those of Charles Townley, Sir W. *Hamilton, and T. *Hope, were made in this period; back in England the Palladian villa and Claudian garden suggest an English nostalgia for Italian grace. Guidebook writing flourished; *Addison's *Remarks on Several Parts of Italy* (1705) was a frequent companion in the first half of the century; J. *Richardson's (father and son) *An Account of the Statues, Bas-Reliefs, Drawings and Pictures in Italy, France, etc.* (1722) is the first English guidebook to the works of art in Italy; the exclamatory *Letters from Italy* of Mariana Starke (?1762–1838; written in 1797 and 1815) is a forerunner of *Baedeker and the *Guide bleu*. The letters of *Gray and Horace *Walpole describe the Grand Tour that they made together in 1739–41; among very many repetitive travel writings, accounts by *Boswell, *Gibbon, and *Beckford stand out. *Smollett's *Travels through France and Italy* (1766) is a cross, original account (his dislike of the Medici Venus was notorious) which was satirized in Sterne's *A Sentimental Journey through France and Italy* (1768).

GRANGE, John (c.1557–1611), educated at the Queen's College, Oxford, and the Inns of Court. He wrote *The Golden Aphroditis* (1577). This novel of romantic intrigue, comparable to G. Gascoigne's *Adventures of Master *F.J.*, is largely made up of speeches, moral discourses, letters, and poems and concerns the courting of Lady A.O. (who turns out to be the daughter of Diana and Endymion) by Sir N.O.

Granger, Edith, in Dickens's *Dombey and Son*, the daughter of the Hon. Mrs Skewton, and Dombey's second wife.

Grania, see GRAINNE.

Granta, a Cambridge University undergraduate periodical started in 1889 by Murray Guthrie to replace the *Gadfly*, which came to an end owing to an article of a personal character. The name 'Granta' was appropriated by Guthrie from O. *Browning, who intended it for a paper that he was about to edit. Guthrie, the first editor, was succeeded by R. C. Lehmann, and the last editor before the First World War was John Norman of Emmanuel College, who was killed at the Dardanelles in 1915. It subsequently went through various transformations, looking at times like a boy's school magazine, at other times like an amateur *Punch, and in the 1950s and 1960s was edited as a literary magazine

devoted to publishing poetry and fiction by promising young students (who included S. *Plath and Ted *Hughes). After some years' disappearance it re-emerged in 1979 as an avant-garde literary periodical, publishing work by G. *Steiner, A. *Sillitoe, Angela *Carter, E. *Tennant, Salman *Rushdie, and others; its editor Bill Buford described it in 1983 as 'an international paperback magazine of contemporary fiction and cultural journalism'. In 1983 appeared *Granta* No. 7, *Best of Young British Novelists*, its first in association with *Penguin Books, with work by Martin *Amis, Ian *McEwan, A. N. *Wilson, and others.

Grantly, the Revd Theophilus, Mrs, and their daughter Griselda, in the *'Barsetshire' novels of A. Trollope.

Grantorto, in Spenser's *Faerie Queene* (V. xii), the tyrant from whom Sir *Artegall rescues *Irena (Ireland). He probably represents the spirit of rebellion.

GRANVILLE-BARKER, Harley (1877–1946), born in London, where his mother taught elocution. He became an actor at the age of 14, and quickly gained recognition. From 1904 to 1907 he directed with brilliant success at the *Royal Court Theatre, producing Shakespeare, many classics, the work of moderns (such as *Galsworthy, and his own *The Voysey Inheritance*, 1905), and above all establishing the reputation of G. B. *Shaw. His own play, *Waste*, was banned in 1907 by the Lord Chamberlain. In 1910 he produced his own *The Madras House* and Galsworthy's *Justice* at the Duke of York's; then in 1912 two productions, *The Winter's Tale* and *Twelfth Night*, which revolutionized the presentation of Shakespeare. An apron stage, simple settings, an authentic text, and swift continuity of action were new to critics and public, and not until a similar production of *A Midsummer Night's Dream* in 1914 did Barker meet with any general acclaim. In the same year he produced a version of Hardy's *The Dynasts*, which was a failure, and he spent much of the years 1914–18 producing in New York. After the war he retired from the stage (and hyphenated his name), but in 1919 became president of the new British Drama League, and in 1923 began his Prefaces to the new *Players' Shakespeare*. The project was abandoned, but Barker continued with his Prefaces, of which he eventually published five series between 1927 and 1947, covering ten plays. These studies, which broke new ground in presenting the producer's rather than the scholar's point of view, are generally held to be the best of his written work. Among much other writing, lectures, and broadcasts he published *On Dramatic Method* (1931); *On Poetry in Drama* (1937), and *The Use of Drama* (1946).

GRASS, Günter (1927–   ), German novelist and outspoken socialist, born in Danzig. His long, humorous, experimental novels (sometimes called 'Rabelaisian' by critics) include *Die Blechtrommel* (*The Tin Drum*, 1959), *Hundejahre* (*Dog Years*, 1963), *Der Butt* (*The Flounder*, 1977), and *Das Treffen in Telgte* (*The Meeting* *at Telgte*, 1979). He was awarded the *Nobel Prize for Literature in 1999.

Gratiano, in Shakespeare's *The Merchant of Venice*, one of Antonio's friends, who marries *Portia's servant Nerissa.

Grave, The, see BLAIR, R.

GRAVES, Alfred Perceval (1846–1931), born in Dublin, an inspector of schools, 1875–1910, who published many volumes of Irish songs and ballads, and an autobiography, *To Return to All That* (1930). He composed the popular 'Father O'Flynn', written in 1875, first published in the *Spectator*.

GRAVES, Richard (1715–1804), a highly educated and cultivated West Country cleric, who was a close friend of *Shenstone and R. *Allen, taught the young *Malthus at his rectory school and wrote successful novels, verses, and articles. He is now chiefly remembered for his lively novel *The Spiritual Quixote, or the Summer's Ramble of Mr Geoffry Wildgoose* (1773), which ran into several editions. The eccentric Methodist Wildgoose travels, with many ludicrous adventures, through the West Country and to the Peak District, encountering (and refuting) everywhere the 'enthusiasm' of the new Methodists, whose intrusion into religious life Graves greatly resented. Graves's old acquaintance, the Methodist *Whitefield, is satirized in the book. His other chief novels, *Columella* (1779), based on the life of Shenstone, and *Eugenius* (1785), are illuminating on social manners and conditions of the time. He published *Recollections of William Shenstone* in 1788.

GRAVES, Robert van Ranke (1895–1985), son of A. P. *Graves, born in London and educated at Charterhouse; he joined the army in 1914 and his first poetry appeared (with the encouragement of E. *Marsh) while he was serving in the First World War (*Over the Brazier*, 1916; *Fairies and Fusiliers*, 1917); his poems also appeared in *Georgian Poetry. In 1918 he married, and in 1919 went to St John's College, Oxford, to read English, though he left without taking a degree, later successfully submitting a critical work, *Poetic Unreason and Other Studies* (1925), as a thesis for a B.Litt. In 1926, accompanied by his wife and a new acquaintance, Laura *Riding, he went briefly to Egypt as professor of literature. He was to live and work with Laura Riding in Majorca, then Brittany, until 1939, publishing various works in collaboration with her, including *A Survey of Modernist Poetry* (1927). He spent the Second World War in England, then returned to Majorca in 1946 with his second wife Beryl Hodge, and settled there permanently.

Graves's output was prodigious; he wrote many volumes of poetry, essays, fiction, biography, and works for children, and published many free translations from various languages. He saw himself primarily as a poet, and wrote some of his prose reluctantly, for financial reasons, but much of it is of lasting quality. His powerful autobiography, *Goodbye to All That* (1929), which describes his unhappy schooldays and the horrors of the trenches, and gives a frank account of the breakdown of his first marriage, is an outstanding example of the new freedom and passionate disillusion of the post-war generation. He wrote many novels, most of them with a historical basis; they include *I, Claudius* and *Claudius the God* (both 1934), narrated in the imaginatively and idiosyncratically conceived persona of the Emperor Claudius (10 BC–AD 54); *Antigua, Penny, Puce* (1936), a barbed tale of sibling rivalry; and the controversial *The Story of Marie Powell, Wife to Mr Milton* (1943). Notable amongst his non-fiction works is *The White Goddess: A Historical Grammar of Poetic Myth* (1948), which argues that true poets derive their gifts from the Muse, the primitive, matriarchal Moon Goddess, the female principle, once dominant but now disastrously dispossessed by male values of reason and logic. Graves's often unorthodox interpretation of myth may also be seen in his *The Greek Myths* (1955), *The Hebrew Myths* (1963, with R. Patai), and other works.

A personal mythology also manifests itself, although not to the point of obscurity, in much of his poetry. His volumes of verse appeared regularly over the years, and his *Collected Poems* of 1955 confirmed a worldwide reputation; the most recent volume of *Collected Poems* appeared in 1975. Since his early days, when he rid himself of tendencies towards Georgian poetic diction, Graves (partly through voluntary exile) avoided identification with any school or movement, speaking increasingly with a highly individual yet ordered voice in which lucidity and intensity combine to a remarkable degree. His love poetry, some of his best known and most distinctive work, is at once cynical and passionate, romantic and erotic, personal and universal. He has also written ballads, songs for children, dramatic monologues, narratives, and poetic anecdotes; his technique is not experimental, but the classical precision of his verse is rarely archaic.

Graves received many honours, and refused many. He was professor of poetry at Oxford from 1961 to 1966, and various of his essays and lectures have been published in *Poetic Craft and Principle* (1967), *The Crane Bag and Other Disputed Subjects* (1969), and other works. There is a life by M. Seymour-Smith (1982), and a volume of letters, *In Broken Images: Selected Letters 1914–1946* (1982, ed. P. O'Prey).

graveyard poets, a term applied to 18th-cent. poets who wrote melancholy, reflective works, often set in graveyards, on the theme of human mortality. Examples include T. *Parnell's 'Night-Piece on Death' (1721), E. Young's *Night Thoughts* (1742), and R. *Blair's *The Grave* (1743). See also Gray's *Elegy Written in a Country Church-Yard* (1751), the best-known product of this kind of sensibility.

GRAY, Alasdair James (1934–   ), Scottish novelist, playwright, and painter, born in Glasgow, educated at

Whitehill Secondary School and the Glasgow School of Art. For several years he worked as an art teacher and then as a theatrical scene-painter. His début novel, *Lanark: A Life in Four Books*, a vast picaresque fable in which Glasgow is reinvented as the apocalyptic Unthank, was not published until 1981 (although begun several years earlier), but immediately established him as a leading figure in contemporary Scottish writing. Gray's fiction, in which fantasy is given a firmly realistic underpinning, is inventively unconventional in both structure and style and eclectic in its references. At the same time it displays a sharp, and at times savage, turn of humour and deploys its effects on a grand scale. *Unlikely Stories*, Mostly appeared in 1983, followed by *1982*, Janine (1984), the sadomasochistic musings of a character called Jock McLeish, and *The Fall of Kelvin Walker* (1985). In *Something Leather* (1990) Received Pronunciation is explicated as if it were a regional accent, a device used elsewhere in Gray's work. *McGrotty and Ludmilla* (1990) is a political satire set in Whitehall, while in *Poor Things* (1992), a pastiche of the Victorian mystery novel, with echoes of *Stevenson and Conan *Doyle and subtitled *Episodes from the Early Life of Archibald McCandles MD, Scottish Public Health Officer*, he returned to the fantastic neo-Gothic mode of *Lanark*. *A History Maker* (1994) is a futuristic tale set in the border region of Scotland during the 23rd cent. Other works include a volume of poetry, *Old Negatives* (1989); *Lean Tales* (1985), written with James *Kelman and Agnes Owen; *Ten Tales Tall and True* (1993); and *Mavis Belfrage: With Five Shorter Tales* (1996).

GRAY, David (1838–61), Scottish poet, born in Duntiblae, the son of a handloom weaver, and educated at the University of Glasgow. Befriended by R. *Buchanan and *Milnes, he aspired to be a poet, but was struck by consumption; he lived just long enough to see the proofs of *The Luggie and Other Poems* (1862), the title poem of which is a blank verse celebration of the river Luggie. The sonnets he wrote while approaching death have many echoes of *Keats, whom he greatly admired.

GRAY, John Henry (1866–1934), poet, born in Woolwich of a Nonconformist background. He became a Roman Catholic, was ordained in 1901, and spent many years as rector of St Peter's in Edinburgh. He was a friend of *Wilde, who urged on the publication of his first volume of poetry, *Silverpoints* (1893), which contained translations from *Verlaine and *Mallarmé. He published other volumes of poetry, booklets of devotional verse, and a surreal novel, *Park: A Fantastic Story* (1932), set in the future. His best long poem, 'The Flying Fish', first appeared in the *Dial* in 1896, and was republished in *The Long Road* (1926). A life by B. Sewell, *In the Dorian Mode*, was published in 1983.

GRAY, Simon James Holliday (1936–   ), playwright, director, novelist, and radio and television script-writer, educated at Dalhousie University, Halifax, Nova Scotia, and at Trinity College, Cambridge. He is best known for his plays about the problems and contradictions of middle-class and academic life, many of which show a clear debt to his Cambridge years: these include *Butley* (1971), *Otherwise Engaged* (1975), *Close of Play* (1978), *Wise Child* (1981), *The Common Pursuit* (1984; the title an oblique tribute to F. R. *Leavis), and *Hidden Laughter* (1990). His novels include *Colmain* (1963), *Simple People* (1965), and *Little Portia* (1967): the last of these was inspired by his time as a language teacher in Cambridge, as was his play *Quartermaine's Terms* (1981). He has also written autobiographical accounts of his career: *Fat Chance* (1995) tells the disastrous story of the production and collapse of his play about espionage, *Cell Mates* (1995), and *The Smoking Diaries* (2004) is equally frank about his addictions, phobias, failures, and triumphs.

GRAY, Thomas (1716–71), born in London, the son of a scrivener; his mother and aunt kept a milliner's shop. He was educated at Eton, with Horace *Walpole, and at Peterhouse, Cambridge. He accompanied Walpole on a tour of France and Italy in 1739–41 (see GRAND TOUR), but they quarrelled and returned home separately. Also in 1741 his father died, leaving the family financially insecure. In 1742 Gray moved to Cambridge, where he was to live, apart from travels and visits, for the rest of his life, first at Peterhouse, then from 1756 at Pembroke College; in 1741–2 he began to write English rather than Latin poetry, producing a fragment of a Racinian tragedy, *Agrippina* (first published 1775), and his first odes, including *Ode on a Distant Prospect of Eton College* (1747), the first of his works to appear in print. In June 1742 his Etonian friend Richard *West died, just after Gray had sent him 'Ode on the Spring' (1748); Gray paid tribute in 'Sonnet on the Death of West' (1775) and in some lines of his Latin poem *De Principiis Cogitandi*. He was reconciled with Walpole in 1745, and the following year showed him some of his earlier poetry, including probably the beginning of his *Elegy Written in a Country Church-Yard* (1751); in 1750 he completed the elegy at Stoke Poges, where his mother and aunt had lived since 1742. He sent Walpole in 1747 his 'Ode on the Death of a Favourite Cat' (1748).

In 1754 Gray finished his Pindaric *ode on *The Progress of Poesy*, and in 1757 a second Pindaric ode, *The Bard*, both remarkably ambitious and intense, and marking a clear shift from *neo-classical lucidity towards the obscure and the *sublime; both were published by Walpole in 1757, the first works printed by the *Strawberry Hill Press. These were his last major poems, but by this time, owing largely to the *Elegy*, his poetry was extremely popular, and on the death of *Cibber (1757) he was offered the laureateship, which he declined. His remaining years were devoted largely to antiquarian and botanical studies and to travels to Scotland and the Lake District in search of the *picturesque; he was deeply interested in new discoveries of Old Norse and Welsh poetry (including *Macpherson's) and produced various imitations, including 'The Fatal Sisters' and 'The Descent of Odin' (written 1761, pub. 1768). One of the best of his later poems is the satiric 'On Lord Holland's Seat near Margate, Kent' (1769). His *Journal* (published 1775) is an account of his visit to the Lakes, kept for Dr Thomas Wharton, who had hoped to accompany him, and his letters (3 vols, 1935, ed. P. Toynbee and L. Whibley) are an interesting mixture of erudition, affectionate informality, and enthusiasm for nature and literature. The standard editions of the poems are by H. W. Starr and J. R. Hendrickson (1966) and R. Lonsdale (with W. *Collins, 1977).

Great Expectations, a novel by *Dickens, which first appeared in *All the Year Round* 1860–1, published in book form in the latter year.

It recounts the development of the character of the narrator, Philip Pirrip, commonly known as 'Pip', a village boy brought up by his termagant sister, the wife of the gentle, humorous, kindly blacksmith Joe Gargery. He is introduced to the house of Miss Havisham, a lady half-crazed by the desertion of her lover on her bridal night, who, in a spirit of revenge, has brought up the girl Estella to use her beauty as a means of torturing men. Pip falls in love with Estella, and aspires to become a gentleman. Money and expectations of more wealth come to him from a mysterious source, which he believes to be Miss Havisham. He goes to London, and in his new mode of life meanly abandons the devoted Joe Gargery, a humble connection of whom he is now ashamed. Misfortunes come upon him. His benefactor proves to be an escaped convict, Abel Magwitch, whom he, as a boy, had helped; his great expectations fade away and he is penniless. Estella marries his sulky enemy Bentley Drummle, by whom she is cruelly ill-treated. Taught by adversity, Pip returns to Joe Gargery and honest labour, and is finally reunited to Estella who has also learnt her lesson. Other notable characters in the book are Joe's uncle, the impudent old impostor Pumblechook; Jaggers, the skilful Old Bailey lawyer, and his good-hearted clerk Wemmick; and Pip's friend in London, Herbert Pocket.

It appears from *Forster's life of Dickens that the author originally devised a less happy ending to the story, which he altered in deference to the advice of *Bulwer-Lytton.

Great-heart, in the second part of Bunyan's *Pilgrim's Progress*, the escort of Christiana and her children on their pilgrimage, who represents the pastor of a militant Nonconformist church.

Greaves, Sir Launcelot, a novel by T. *Smollett, published 1762.

Smollett's shortest novel, this is a neglected and interesting work, which was written in episodes (many of them in prison in 1760) for Smollett's monthly *British Magazine*. He describes it as 'an agreeable medley of mirth and madness', but his purpose is serious in examining various states of madness and questioning conventional definitions of sanity. Launcelot is a paragon, handsome, learned, good, robust, but when the book opens he is already crazed by the loss of his love Aurelia, who has been compelled to break with him by her vindictive uncle Darnel. Together with his absurd cowardly squire Crabshaw, and his horse Bronzomarte, the half-mad Launcelot undertakes a quixotic life of knight-errantry, warring against the enemies of virtue and reason. During his adventure on the road between London and York he is involved in many brawls in the cause of justice; he is trapped and abducted; embroiled in a violent election; challenged to a tourney; denounced by the misanthropic charlatan Ferret; and thrown into the prison of the atrocious Judge Gobble. His friends include a lawyer, Tom Clarke, and Clarke's uncle, the nautical Crowe. After a terrible period in a madhouse, Launcelot recovers his sanity and Aurelia is at last restored to him.

The well-known words 'I think for my part one half of the nation is mad—and the other half not very sound' are spoken by Crowe.

GREEN, Henry (1905–73), novelist and industrialist, born Henry Vincent Yorke, the son of a wealthy and well-connected Midlands industrialist, and educated at Eton and Magdalen College, Oxford. His first novel, *Blindness* (1926), was published while he was still an undergraduate, when, in his aesthete phase, he was a contemporary of E. *Waugh and H. *Acton. His second novel, *Living* (1929), in marked contrast, describes life on the factory floor in Birmingham, and is based on his own experiences working for the family firm, H. Pontifex and Sons; he himself rose from the shop floor to become managing director, and the novel vividly records working-class dialogue, as well as the reactions of the manager's son, Dupret. It also manifests the idiosyncrasies of prose—dropped articles, sentences without verbs, a highly individual use of colloquial language in both narrative and dialogue—which contribute to his work's distinctive quality. *Party Going* (1939), describing a group of rich, idle young people, delayed at a railway station in fog on the brink of departure for a winter holiday, has strong symbolic suggestions in an apparently trivial narrative. This was followed by his autobiographical *Pack My Bag: A Self-Portrait* (1940) and several other novels: *Caught* (1943); *Loving* (1945), one of his most admired works, which describes life above and below stairs in an Irish country house during wartime, with a notable portrait of the butler, Raunce; *Back* (1946); *Concluding* (1948); *Nothing* (1950); and *Doting* (1952), the latter two written almost wholly in dialogue. His wartime service in the ranks of the NFS provided him with new social experiences and further widened his range. Although he liked to describe himself as 'a business man whose pastime was romancing over a bottle to a good band',

431   GREEN | GREENE

he was a highly conscious and original artist, who commanded more admiration from fellow writers (including E. *Bowen, A. *Wilson, and W. H. *Auden) than from the common reader.

GREEN, John Richard (1837–83), educated at Magdalen College School and at Jesus College, Oxford, where he was unhappy and did badly. After a spell as a curate in the East End of London he took to journalism, contributing frequently to the *Saturday Review. He is best known for his *Short History of the English People* (1874), dedicated to *Stubbs and *Freeman, who encouraged his career as a historian. This work, which was immensely popular, was remarkable for its broad approach, simple style, generosity of outlook, and attention to the social, economic, and intellectual aspects of national history; Green aimed to chart 'the growth . . . of the people itself' and to produce an account in which 'Aidan and Bede would claim more space than the wars of the Anglo-Saxon kingdoms.' It was enlarged in *The History of the English People* (1877–80).

GREEN, Matthew (1697–1737), poet. Little is known of his life; he appears to have been of Quaker background, and was employed at the Customs House; his only literary friend was *Glover, to whom he left his manuscripts. He is remembered for his poem *The Spleen* (1737), which praises in fluent octosyllabics the simple life and describes his dream of 'a farm some twenty miles from town' where he could live (with occasional visits to London) on 'two hundred pounds half-yearly paid'.

GREEN, Thomas Hill (1836–82), educated at Rugby and Balliol College, Oxford, fellow of Balliol, 1866–78 (the first fellow not in orders), appointed White's professor of moral philosophy in 1878. Green's philosophical publications began with a criticism of *Locke, *Hume, and *Berkeley in the form of two very full introductions to a new edition of Hume's *Treatise.* His philosophical views as set forth in his *Prolegomena to Ethics* (1883) and his collected *Works* (1885–8) show a qualified acceptance of the doctrines of *Hegel as speculatively true but requiring to be supplemented for practical purposes.

Mrs H. *Ward pays tribute to his moral influence in her sympathetic portrait of him as Henry Grey in *Robert Elsmere* (1888); she quotes from his *The Witness of God, and Faith: Two Lay Sermons* (1883) and describes him as one who held 'a special place in the hearts of men who can neither accept fairy tales, nor reconcile themselves to a world without faith'.

GREENAWAY, Kate (1846–1901), writer and illustrator of children's picture books. Her drawings suggest an idyllic world, where quaintly dressed children play amid flowery meadows and trim gardens. Her first success was *Under the Window* (1878), a collection of rhymes for children which she both wrote and illustrated. Her many later works include *Marigold Garden* (1885)—another collection of verses and pictures—and her illustrated edition of *The Pied Piper of Hamelin* (1888) by R. *Browning. She was encouraged by *Ruskin, whom she met in 1882 and with whom she corresponded. Ruskin lectured on her art at Oxford in 1883; he praised the innocence of her vision of childhood—'no gasworks! no waterworks, no mowing machines, no sewing machines, no telegraph poles . . .' Her books and watercolour drawings were immensely popular and influenced contemporary design.

GREENE, (Henry) Graham (1904–91), novelist and playwright, educated at Berkhamsted School, where his father was headmaster, then at Balliol College, Oxford; a book of verse, *Babbling April* (1925), was published while he was still at Oxford. He joined the Roman Catholic Church in 1926, married in 1927, and was from 1926 to 1930 on the staff of *The Times, which he left in order to attempt to make a living as a writer. His first three novels (1929–31), which he later disclaimed, made little impression, but *Stamboul Train* (1932) sold well and was followed by many increasingly successful novels, short stories, books of reportage and travel, plays, children's books, etc. Greene describes his own early years in *A Sort of Life* (1971), which gives a vivid impression of a manic-depressive temperament tempted by deadly nightshade and Russian roulette, and a literary imagination nourished by influences as diverse as *Weyman, M. *Bowen, and R. *Browning: Greene states, 'if I were to choose an epigraph for all the novels I have written, it would be from *Bishop Blougram's Apology*:

> Our interest's on the dangerous edge of things,
> The honest thief, the tender murderer,
> The superstitious atheist . . .

His pursuit of danger (despite quieter interludes, e.g. as literary editor on the *Spectator and *Night and Day) dominated much of his life and travels, as described in his second volume of autobiography, *Ways of Escape* (1980). His novels include *England Made Me* (1935); *The Power and the Glory* (1940); *The Heart of the Matter* (1948); *The End of the Affair* (1951; a wartime love affair with strong religious-supernatural touches modified by Greene himself in a later version); *The Quiet American* (1955, set in Vietnam); *A Burnt-out Case* (1961, set in a leper colony in the Congo); *The Honorary Consul* (1973, set in Argentina); and *The Human Factor* (1978, a secret service novel). Other works of fiction he classed as 'entertainments': these include *Brighton Rock* (1938, paradoxically the first novel in which critics detected a strong Catholic message, not surprisingly, in view of the fact that it introduces what was to be his central concept of 'the appalling strangeness of the mercy of God'); *The Confidential Agent* (1939); *Loser Takes All* (1955); and *Our Man in Havana* (1958). *The Third Man* (1950), also described as an entertainment, was originally written as a screenplay and filmed (1949) by Carol Reed (see EXPRESSIONISM). Greene's plays include

The Living Room (1953), *The Potting Shed* (1957), and *The Complaisant Lover* (1959). He also published travel books, describing journeys in Liberia (*Journey without Maps*, 1936), Mexico (*The Lawless Roads*, 1939), and Africa (*In Search of a Character: Two African Journals*, 1961). His *Collected Essays* appeared in 1969. His range as a writer is wide, both geographically and in variations of tone, but his preoccupations with moral dilemma (personal, religious, and political), his attempts to distinguish 'good-or-evil' from 'right-or-wrong', and his persistent choice of 'seedy' (a word which he was to regret popularizing) locations give his work a highly distinctive and recognizable quality, while his skilful variations of popular forms (the thriller, the detective story) have brought him a rare combination of critical and popular admiration. There is a biography by Norman Sherry (2 vols, 1989, 1994).

GREENE, Robert (1558–92), born in Norwich, educated at St John's College and Clare Hall, Cambridge, from 1575 until 1583, and incorporated at Oxford in 1588. From about 1585 he lived mainly in London. Although he liked to stress his connections with both universities, his later literary persona was that of a feckless drunkard, who abandoned his wife and children to throw himself on the mercies of tavern hostesses and courtesans; writing pamphlets and plays was supposedly a last resort when his credit failed. He is said to have died of a surfeit of Rhenish wine and pickled herrings, though it may more likely have been plague, of which there was a severe outbreak in 1592. Greene was attacked at length by G. *Harvey in *Foure Letters* (1592) as the 'Ape of Euphues' and 'Patriarch of shifters'; *Nashe defended him in *Strange Newes* in the same year, acknowledging Greene to have been a drunkard and a debtor, but claiming that 'Hee inherited more vertues than vices.' Greene's 37 publications, progressing from moral dialogues to prose romances, romantic plays, and finally realistic accounts of underworld life, bear out Nashe's assertion that printers were only too glad 'to pay him deare for the very dregs of his wit'. The sententious moral tone of his works suggests that his personal fecklessness and deathbed repentance may have been partly a pose.

Among the more attractive of his romances are the Lylyan sequel *Euphues his Censure to Philautus* (1587); *Pandosto: The Triumph of Time* and *Perimedes the Blacke-Smith* (1588); *Menaphon* (1589). Among his 'repentance' pamphlets are *Greenes Mourning Garment* and *Greenes Never too Late* (1590) and the work attributed to him, *Greenes Groats-Worth of Witte* (1592). *Greenes Vision* (1592) is a fictionalized account of his deathbed repentance in which he receives advice from *Chaucer, *Gower, and King Solomon. The low-life pamphlets include *A Notable Discovery of Coosenage* (1591) and three 'conny-catching' pamphlets in the same years 1591–2. His eight plays were all published posthumously. The best known are *Orlando furioso* (1594), *Frier Bacon, and Frier Bongay* (1594),

and *James the Fourth* (1598), of which there are editions by J. A. Lavin and N. Sanders.

Greene is now best known for his connections with Shakespeare. The attack on him in the *Groats-Worth of Witte* (below) as an 'upstart Crow, beautified with our feathers' is the first reference to Shakespeare as a London dramatist; and his *Pandosto* provided Shakespeare with the source for *The Winter's Tale*. The voluminousness of Greene's works and the supposed profligacy of his life have caused him to be identified with the typical Elizabethan hack-writer; he probably provided a name and a model for the swaggering Nick Greene in V. *Woolf's *Orlando* (1928). Greene's works were edited in 15 volumes by *Grosart (1881–6).

Greenes Groats-Worth of Witte, *Bought with a Million of Repentance*, a prose tract attributed to R. *Greene, but edited and perhaps written by H. *Chettle, published 1592.

It begins with the death of the miser Gorinius, who leaves the bulk of his large fortune to his elder son Lucanio, and only 'an old groat' to the younger, Roberto (i.e. the author), 'wherewith I wish him to buy a groats-worth of wit'. Roberto conspires with a courtesan to fleece his brother, but the courtesan betrays him, subsequently ruining Lucanio for her sole profit. The gradual degradation of Roberto is then narrated, and the tract ends with the curious 'Address' to his fellow playwrights *Marlowe, *Lodge, and *Peele, urging them to spend their wits to better purpose than the making of plays. It contains the well-known passage about the 'upstart Crow, beautified with our feathers', the *'Johannes *fac totum*', who 'is in his owne conceit the onely Shake-scene in a countrey', which probably refers to Shakespeare as a non-graduate dramatist newly arrived in London.

Green Knight, see GAWAIN AND THE GREEN KNIGHT, SIR.

GREENLAW, Lavinia (1962–), poet, born in London. Her first collection, *Night Photograph* (1993), contains many poems on scientific subjects and reveals a combination of measured, precise tone with an undiminished sense of wonder. Her second collection, *A World Where News Travelled Slowly* (1997), refines the taut, controlled style for which she is noted and returns often to the themes of communication in societal and personal contexts, love and travel.

Green Mansions, a novel by W. H. *Hudson, published 1904.

The young hero, Abel, fleeing from persecution in Venezuela, travels into the vast jungle (the 'green mansions'). Eventually he settles with the tribe of Runi, an Indian friend. Finding that one part of the forest is mysteriously forbidden, he investigates and becomes haunted by the recurring cry, half bird, half human, which terrifies the Indians. He finds the caller, Rima, a wild and beautiful girl of the woods, and meets her grandfather, Nuflo. Abel and Rima fall in love, and the three of them set out on a long journey to find her mother. They fail, and impetuously Rima returns home first; when Nuflo and Abel arrive they discover that the Indians have burned her on a great pyre built round a forest tree. In anguish Abel kills Runi and his friends, and makes a long, desolate journey, carrying Rima's ashes, back to the coast. The animistic overtones of the book, and its intimations of love and death, made a deep impression.

The sculpture of Rima in London's Hyde Park is by Sir Jacob Epstein (1880–1959).

Green-sleeves, the name of an inconstant lady-love, who is the subject of a ballad surviving in a complete form, published in 1584. This, and the tune to which it was sung, became and remain very popular; both are mentioned by Shakespeare (*The Merry Wives of Windsor*, II. i and v. v).

GREENWELL, Dora (1821–82), poet and essayist, who published seven volumes of poetry between 1848–71, of which *Carmina Crucis* (1869), described by her as 'roadside songs with both joy and sorrow in them', was particularly admired. An evangelical Anglican, her longer prose works were on religious subjects, but her essays covered a variety of social causes including women's education, child labour, and the education of the learning disabled. In this latter cause she edited a series of stories for children urging decent treatment for 'imbeciles'. She was a friend of Josephine Butler, met E. B. *Browning, and corresponded with C. *Rossetti; *Whittier wrote the introduction to the US edition of one of her prose works, but for the most part she led a secluded and inconspicuous life.

GREENWOOD, Walter (1903–74), novelist, born in Salford of radical working-class parents, who is remembered for his classic novel of life in a northern town during the depression, *Love on the Dole* (1933; dramatized 1934; filmed 1941). He wrote several other novels and a volume of autobiography, *There Was a Time* (1967).

GREER, Germaine (1939–   ), feminist, polemicist, and critic, born in Melbourne, and educated at the universities of Melbourne, Sydney, and Cambridge; she settled in Europe in 1964. Her first book, *The Female Eunuch* (1970), opened a new area of feminist debate about the role of women in a male-dominated culture: this was followed by *The Obstacle Race* (1979), a discussion of the social and financial difficulties of women painters, and the reluctance to grant their achievements proper recognition; *Sex and Destiny* (1984); and other sociological works. *Slip-Shod Sibyls: Recognition, Rejection and the Woman Poet* (1995) is a challenging view of women poets, known and little known, which does not spare what Greer sees as their failings as writers. *The Madwoman's Underclothes* (1986) is a collection of essays and occasional pieces (1968–85), some previously unpublished, some culled from the mainstream press, and some from underground periodicals such as *Oz and the late 1960s *Suck*.

Daddy We Hardly Knew You (1989) is a family memoir and *The Whole Woman* (1999) reconsiders the progress of feminism.

GREG, Sir Walter Wilson (1875–1959), scholar and bibliographer, educated at Harrow and Trinity College, Cambridge, where he came to know *McKerrow. His first substantial publication (1900) was a finding-list of English plays written before 1700 which was the beginning of his more important work, *A Bibliography of the English Printed Drama to the Restoration* (1939–59). In 1906 he founded, and was general editor of (1906–39), the *Malone Society, for the exact reproduction of English plays and dramatic documents before 1640. His edition of *Henslowe's Diary and Papers (1904–8) is an outstanding example of his skill in palaeography and his knowledge of Elizabethan theatrical history, which he further developed in later works. Greg raised the standards of bibliography and textual criticism in his constructive reviews, and in editions of manuscript plays, notably *Sir Thomas *More* (1911), and in his works, including *Dramatic Documents from the Elizabethan Playhouses* (1931) and *English Literary Autographs 1550–1650* (1925–32). In his last and most fruitful years he published, in addition to his *Bibliography*, a remarkable edition of 'Doctor Faustus' 1604–1616 (1950), *The Editorial Problem in Shakespeare* (1942), *The Shakespeare First Folio* (1955), and *Some Aspects and Problems of London Publishing between 1550 and 1650* (1956).

Gregorian Calendar, see CALENDAR.

GREGORY I, St (Gregory the Great) (540–604), one of the greatest of the early popes (from 590), a reformer of monastic discipline and a prolific writer whose works include the *Cura Pastoralis* (see ALFRED), the *Dialogues*, and famous collections of letters and sermons. He sent *Augustine to England. *Bede (*Ecclesiastical History*, II. i) tells the story of him that, seeing Anglo-Saxon boys for sale in the slave-market at Rome, he remarked: 'Not Angli but Angeli, if they were Christians.' The story that he delivered the Emperor Trajan from hell by his prayers, touched by his humility and justice, is mentioned by *Aquinas, by *Dante more than once, and by Langland (*Piers Plowman*, B XI. 140 ff.). See *Dialogues*, trans. O. J. Zimmerman (1959); P. Batiffol, *Saint Gregory the Great*, trans. J. L. Stoddard (1929).

GREGORY, (Isabella) Augusta, Lady, née Persse (1852–1932), born at Roxborough, Co. Galway. She married the former MP and governor of Ceylon Sir William Gregory of nearby *Coole Park, in 1880, and was widowed in 1892. They had one child (see below). A leading figure in the *Irish Revival, she assisted *Yeats and *Martyn in the foundation of the *Irish Literary Theatre, forerunner of the *Abbey Theatre, for which she became playwright, director, and patent holder. She helped popularize Irish legends with her translations *Cuchulain of Muirthemne* (1902) and *Gods and Fighting Men* (1904), and Irish folklore with *Poets and

Dreamers (1903), *A Book of Saints and Wonders* (1906, enl. 1907), and *Visions and Beliefs in the West of Ireland* (1920). Lady Gregory's idiomatic style (often called 'Kiltartanese') and knowledge of folklore were assets in her collaboration with Yeats on several plays including *Cathleen ni Houlihan* (1902) and *The Unicorn from the Stars* (1908). Excelling in the one-act form, with plays such as *Spreading the News*, *The Workhouse Ward*, *The Rising of the Moon*, and *The Gaol Gate*, Lady Gregory wrote or translated over 40 plays, mostly published in *Seven Short Plays* (1909), *The Kiltartan Molière* (1910), *Irish Folk History Plays* (1912), *New Comedies* (1913), *Three Wonder Plays* (1922), *The Image and Other Plays* (1922), and *Three Last Plays* (1928). Her *Our Irish Theatre* (1913) is a somewhat biased account of the Abbey's early years, but her defence of Synge's **Playboy of the Western World*, G. B. **Shaw's *The Shewing up of Blanco Posnet*, and **O'Casey's *The Plough and the Stars* typifies her tenacious work. Lady Gregory's stance as a cultural nationalist culminated in her fight for the return to Ireland of 39 French Impressionist pictures collected by her nephew Sir Hugh Lane, who drowned in the sinking of the *Lusitania* in 1915 leaving an unwitnessed codicil to his will, a campaign she partly recorded in *Hugh Lane's Life and Achievement* (1921). Her collected works are published in the Coole Edition (1970–82), ed. Colin Smythe.

GREGORY, (William) Robert (1881–1918), artist. The son of Sir William and Lady **Gregory, he designed sets for early **Abbey Theatre productions. In 1916 he joined the RFC and was killed in action. **Yeats wrote several commemorative poems about him, including 'An Irish Airman Foresees his Death' and 'In Memory of Major Robert Gregory'.

GREGORY OF TOURS (*c*.540–94), bishop of Tours, whose *Historia Francorum* is the chief authority for the early Merovingian period of French history. He places in 520 the raid against the Frisian territory of the Franks by a Scandinavian leader 'Chochilaicus' (in Latin) who has been identified with the Geatish king Hygelac in **Beowulf*; the raid is mentioned in *Beowulf* at lines 1207, 2357, 2503, and 2912. Gregory's identification provides the only historical corroboration for any character or event in the poem. The *Historia* has been translated by O. M. Dalton (1927).

Gregynog Press, a **private press founded in 1923 at Gregynog Hall, near Newtown, Montgomeryshire, and endowed by Miss Gwendoline and Miss Margaret Davies as part of their plan to establish an arts and crafts centre. It excelled in the fineness of its bindings, and survived until 1940. It was revived in 1974.

Grendel, see BEOWULF.

GRENFELL, Julian (1888–1915), educated at Eton, where he began to publish, and at Balliol College, Oxford; he joined the regular army in 1910 and in 1914 was sent to France, where he won the DSO and was killed at Ypres. His celebrated poem 'Into Battle' appeared in **The Times* in 1915 and has been much anthologized. There is a life by N. **Mosley (1976).

GRESHAM, Sir Thomas (?1519–79), a celebrated financier and financial agent of the Crown, and an intimate friend of Sir William Cecil. He was the son of Sir Richard Gresham (?1485–1549), lord mayor of London, who initiated the design of the Royal Exchange. This was built at the expense of Sir Thomas Gresham, who also made provision in his will for the founding of Gresham College. Gresham's School, Holt, which was founded by his uncle John, has produced such distinguished figures as **Britten and **Auden.

GREVILLE, Charles Cavendish Fulke (1794–1865), politician and man of public affairs, who was for many years clerk to the Privy Council. From 1820 to 1860 he kept a detailed diary of his life in the inner circles of politics and power. He was the friend and trusted confidant of both Whigs and Tories, and includes in his work many lively portraits of friends and colleagues, such as the duke of **Wellington and Lord Palmerston. His *Memoirs* were first edited and published in 1874–87. See DIARIES.

GREVILLE, Sir Fulke, first Baron Brooke (1554–1628), educated at Shrewsbury School, where he was an exact contemporary of P. **Sidney, and at Jesus College, Cambridge. From the mid-1560s he was at court, where he had a long and moderately successful career, culminating in his peerage in 1621, when he was granted Warwick Castle and Knowle Park by James I. It was in Warwick Castle that he died, mysteriously murdered by a servant who went on to stab himself.

Greville began to write poetry during Sidney's lifetime and was intimately concerned with the first plans for posthumous publication of his friend's works. Poems written after Sidney's death in 1586, gathered together with earlier ones in his sequence *Caelica*, show him moving away from secular love towards broader political and religious themes. His neo-Stoic *Letter to an Honourable Lady* belongs to 1589; and his two Senecan tragedies *Mustapha* (published 1609) and *Alaham*, in their earliest versions, before the fall of **Essex in February 1601; the verse *Treatise of Monarchy* about 1600; and his major prose work, *A Dedication to Sir Philip Sidney*, was probably begun in 1610. Greville was a compulsive reviser of his own work, however, and many of his works survive in versions which reflect different stages of revision. Often he seems to change his mind about his central theme or purpose. The *Dedication to Sir Philip Sidney* is as much about Greville's own political ideals and disappointments as about his friend's career, and in its printed version (1652, as *The Life of Sir Philip Sidney*) it incorporates judgements of **Elizabeth I and her reign which he had originally hoped to include in a life of that monarch.

Type-casting of the poetry of this period as either 'Elizabethan' or 'metaphysical' has not helped Greville's literary reputation, but a movement led by *Winters, characterizing Greville as a master of the 'plain style', has stimulated admiration among a sizeable minority of critics. C. S. *Lewis saw him as a writer of 'genuinely didactic verse, verse utterly unadorned and dependent for interest almost exclusively on its intellectual content'. These qualities are well reflected in Greville's best-known lines, from the 'Chorus Sacerdotum' in *Mustapha*:

> Oh wearisome Condition of Humanity!
> Borne under one Law, to another bound:
> Vainely begot, and yet forbidden vanity,
> Created sicke, commanded to be sound.

His *Poems and Dramas* have been edited by G. *Bullough (1939); *The Remains* by G. Wilkes (1965); the *Life of Sir Philip Sidney* by D. Nowell Smith (1907); *Prose Works* by J. Gouws (1986). There is a life by R. A. Rebholz (1971).

Greville Memoirs, The, see GREVILLE, CHARLES CAVENDISH FULKE.

Grewgious, Mr, a character in Dickens's *Edwin Drood*.

Gride, Arthur, a character in Dickens's *Nicholas Nickleby*.

GRIERSON, Sir Herbert John Clifford (1866–1960), first professor of English literature at Aberdeen University, 1894–1915, and succeeded *Saintsbury as professor of rhetoric and English literature at Edinburgh University, 1915–35. He advanced the study of the *metaphysical poets in his well-annotated edition of *Donne's poems (1912) and in *Metaphysical Lyrics and Poems of the Seventeenth Century* (1921), and was co-editor of a 12-volume edition of Sir W. *Scott's letters (1932–7). He published a biography of Scott (1938).

GRIFFIN, Gerald (1803–40), Irish dramatist, novelist, and poet, remembered chiefly for his impressive social novel *The Collegians* (1829), in which young Cregan, allured by wealth and beauty, permits the murder of his humble country wife. *Boucicault made it the basis of a very successful play, *The Colleen Bawn*, in 1860. Griffin's play *Gisippus*, a blank verse drama of classical times, was produced at Drury Lane in 1842. A biography by J. Cronin was published in 1978.

Griffith Gaunt, or *Jealousy*, a novel by C. *Reade, published 1866.

The story is set in the 18th cent. Griffith Gaunt, an impoverished gentleman of Cumberland, wishes to marry Kate Payton, a spirited and ardent young Roman Catholic, who dreams of taking the veil but feels at the same time bound to the world. She prefers her other suitor, George Neville, but when Griffith loses his inheritance for her sake she accepts him, hoping for a contented marriage without undue submission. After some happy years, in which children are born, Griffith begins to drink heavily, and does not perceive Kate's disguised but growing passion for her new spiritual director, the exalted Father Leonard. She cannot eat after listening to his sermons, her glove is found secreted in his room, and it becomes clear that their religious ardours stem from human love. The envious housekeeper goads Griffith into a jealous fury, and he drags Leonard through a horse-pond. When he finds Kate and the priest walking together in a grove, at a time when Kate is supposed to be ill in her room, he attacks Leonard with demonic violence and the terrified Kate renounces her love. Griffith gallops away, and in his fever is nursed by Mercy Vint, an innkeeper's daughter, whom he eventually bigamously marries. When he briefly returns home to fetch some money the frenzied Kate tries to stab him, and although he escapes a disfigured body is later found in a mere and Kate is tried for murder. Mercy Vint walks miles alone with her child to save Kate. Eventually Kate and Griffith are happily reconciled, Mercy marries Kate's old suitor Neville, and the four live as neighbours, ostracized but happy in their good works.

The novel, based on a story by Wilkie *Collins, was unusually frank for its time and Reade was prosecuted in a case in which *Dickens ('as a husband and father') refused to help defend him. Reade's interest lay clearly not only in the theme of jealousy, both male and female, but in the sexual nature of Kate.

GRIGSON, Geoffrey Edward Harvey (1905–85), poet, critic, and editor of many publications, including the influential *New Verse* (1933–9), which he founded. His first volume of poetry, *Several Observations* (1939), was followed by others, including *Under the Cliff* (1943), *The Isles of Scilly* (1946), *Collected Poems 1924–1962* (1963), *Angles and Circles* (1974), and *History of Him* (1980). Much of his work celebrates his native Cornwall, and his collections of essays, which contributed to his reputation as a fierce controversialist, include *The Harp of Aeolus* (1947) and *The Contrary View* (1974). He also edited selections of work by W. *Barnes (1950), J. *Clare (1950), W. S. *Landor (1964), C. *Cotton (1975), and others, and his eclectic reading is expressed in several Faber anthologies.

GRIGSON, Jane (née MacIntyre) (1928–90), writer on cookery and food, born in Gloucestershire and educated at Newnham College, Cambridge, where she read English. She began her literary career as a translator from Italian, and in 1968 became cookery writer for the *Observer*, for which she wrote until her death. Her first book, *Charcuterie and French Pork Cookery* (1967), was followed by many classics of the kitchen, including *Good Things* (1971), *Fish Cookery* (1973), *The Mushroom Feast* (1975), a *Vegetable Book* (1978), and a *Fruit Book* (1982). She wrote in scholarly and elegant prose, and her recipes were always carefully tested. She was married to G. *Grigson.

Grim, see HAVELOK THE DANE.

GRIMALD, Nicholas (*c.*1519–*c.*1562), of Christ's College, Cambridge, chaplain to Bishop *Ridley. He contributed 40 poems to *Tottel's *Miscellany* and assisted in its compilation. He made translations from *Virgil (a Latin paraphrase of the *Eclogues*) and *Cicero (*De Officiis*), and wrote two Latin plays. He was admiringly commemorated in an elegy by *Googe.

GRIMALDI, Joseph (1779–1837), a celebrated clown and pantomimist, who first appeared as an infant dancer at Sadler's Wells, and acted there and at Drury Lane for many years. He had a son of the same name who succeeded him as pantomimist and died in 1863. Grimaldi's *Memoirs* were edited (without much enthusiasm) by *Dickens, with illustrations by *Cruikshank (2 vols, 1838).

GRIMBALD, or **GRIMBOLD, St** (?820–903), a native of Flanders and a monk of St Bertin's at St Omer. King *Alfred summoned him to England for the promotion of learning and appointed him abbot of the new minster at Winchester. Alfred mentions him as one of his teachers in the Preface to the *Cura Pastoralis*. A hagiographical *Life of Grimbald* survives in the 13th-cent. breviary of Hyde Abbey; but the events of his life are notoriously confused.

Grimes, (1) Peter, see PETER GRIMES; (2) Thomas, chimney-sweep, Tom's employer in C. Kingsley's *The Water-Babies.*

GRIMM, Jacob Ludwig Carl (1785–1863) and Wilhelm Carl (1786–1859), German brothers who pioneered the study of German philology, law, mythology, and folklore. They are chiefly known in England for their collection of *fairy tales, *Kinder- und Hausmärchen* (1812–14), of which an English translation by Edgar Taylor, illustrated by *Cruikshank, was published in 1823 under the title *German Popular Stories*. The brothers also began the German etymological dictionary *Deutsches Wörterbuch*, the German equivalent of the *OED*, in 1852. The work was continued by later scholars, and brought to completion in 1960. Jacob Grimm formulated 'Grimm's Law' of the mutations of the consonants in the several Aryan languages.

GRIMMELSHAUSEN, Johannes Jacob Christoffel von (*c.*1621–76), German writer, author of the picaresque novel *Simplicissimus* and, among other things, of a novel from which *Brecht took the story of his *Mother Courage.*

Grimwig, Mr, a character in Dickens's *Oliver Twist.*

Gringolet, or **Gryngolet,** Gawain's horse, in *Chrétien (*Erec et Enide*, l. 3935), *Le Chevalier à l'épée* (l. 226), *Sir *Gawain and the Green Knight* (l. 597), etc. Speght, in his 1598 edition of Chaucer, gives it as the name of *Wade's infamous boat.

Griselda, the type of long-suffering female fortitude; see PATIENT GRISSIL.

Groats-Worth of Witte, see GREENES GROATS-WORTH OF WITTE.

Grobian (German *Grobheit*, rudeness), an imaginary personage often referred to by writers of the 15th and 16th cents in Germany as a type of boorishness. Sebastian Brant in his *Narrenschiff* (see SHIP OF FOOLS) invented St Grobianus as typical of ill-mannered and indecent behaviour. In 1549 F. Dedekind, a German student, wrote a poem in Latin elegiacs, *Grobianus, de Morum Simplicitate*, a burlesque of the generally uncivilized social conditions then prevailing in Germany, in the form of ironical advice on conduct given to a gallant. This was translated into German by Kaspar Scheidt, and into English, and suggested to Dekker his *Guls Horne-Booke.*

GROCYN, William (1449–1519), educated at Winchester and New College, Oxford. He held various ecclesiastical preferments. He studied in Italy with *Linacre under *Poliziano and Chalcondyles, and was instrumental in introducing the study of Greek at Oxford.

Grongar Hill, see DYER, J.

GRONNIOSAW, Ukawsaw, see BLACK BRITISH LITERATURE.

GRONOVIUS, Johann Friedrich (1611–71), a Dutch scholar and editor of Greek and Roman classics. His son, Jakob Gronovius (1645–1716), was professor of Greek at Leiden, and, like his father, an editor of classical authors.

GROSART, Alexander Balloch (1827–99), editor remembered for his reprints of rare Elizabethan and Jacobean literature; between 1868 and 1896 he edited more than 130 volumes.

GROSSETESTE, Robert (1175–1253), bishop of Lincoln and the first chancellor of Oxford University. He was the author of translations from the Greek, including *Aristotle's *Ethics* and the works of Pseudo-Dionysius (see DIONYSIUS THE AREOPAGITE). Though closely connected with the Franciscans in thought, he remained a secular throughout his life. He was a major figure in the development of the Augustinian philosophical tradition, and he was largely responsible for the Oxford emphasis on the development of the natural sciences; it is likely that he passed on to his pupil R. *Bacon his knowledge of and interest in experimental science, especially optics and mathematics. Influenced by the Platonic tradition of the Arabs, he developed his light-metaphysic in his work *De Luce*, which identifies a form of corporaneity as the most important of forms and makes the individual the essence of the form. See *Writings*, ed. S. H. Thompson (1940); James McEvoy, *The Philosophy of Robert Grosseteste* (1983).

GROSSMITH, George (1847–1912) and Weedon (1852–1919), brothers whose father was a friend of H. *Irving, the *Terry family, and other theatrical people. Both pursued successful theatrical careers. *The Diary of a Nobody* (1892), which appeared in *Punch, was written by both brothers, and illustrated by Weedon. Its popularity with a wide range of readership was immediate, and has not faltered. See DIARIES.

Grosvenor Gallery, the, Bond Street, London, for the exhibition of pictures of the modern school, erected by Sir Coutts Lindsay in 1876. It was especially associated for a time with the *Aesthetic movement. Bunthorne in *Gilbert and Sullivan's *Patience* describes himself as:

> A pallid and thin young man,
> A haggard and lank young man,
> A greenery-yallery, Grosvenor Gallery,
> Foot-in-the-grave young man.

The Gallery closed in 1890.

GROTE, George (1794–1871), banker, educated at Charterhouse, MP for the City of London, 1832–41. He took an active part in favour of the Reform movement, publishing a pamphlet on the subject in 1820 and another in 1831. His outlook was much influenced by James *Mill and *utilitarianism. He retired from Parliament in order to devote himself to historical work. His famous *History of Greece*, in eight volumes, on which he had been intermittently at work since 1823, was published in 1846–56, and achieved immediate success. Grote's other works include studies of *Plato (1865) and *Aristotle (1872), and various papers and essays on philosophical and ethical subjects.

GROTIUS, Hugo (1583–1645), Dutch statesman and jurist. He was born at Delft, studied law at Orleans and Leiden, and became the leader of the bar at The Hague. He wrote in 1601 a sacred drama in Latin, *Adamus Exsul*, with which Milton was probably familiar when he wrote *Paradise Lost. Grotius was on a deputation to London in 1613, but his intimacy with Barnavelt (who was executed in 1619 for conspiracy against the state) led to his condemnation to imprisonment for life. From this he escaped in a large box in which books were sent to him for the purpose of study, and took refuge in Paris. He became the ambassador of Queen Christina of Sweden at the French court, and died, after shipwreck, in her service. He wrote a large number of works, including a Latin history of the revolt of the Netherlands. But his principal title to fame is his great treatise of international law, the *De Jure Belli ac Pacis*, published in 1625. In the midst of the Thirty Years War (1618–48) he asserted in this work the principle of a rule of law binding upon nations in their relations with one another.

Group, the, an informal association of writers, mostly poets, set up in London by Philip *Hobsbaum, with his then wife, poet Hannah Kelly, in 1955. A number of poems or a chapter of a novel (which had been previously distributed to other participants) would be read aloud by the author and discussed by all present. Membership was by invitation of the chairman, and during the formative years, 1956–7, most of the key figures were recruited: these included *Redgrove, P. *Porter, *Lucie-Smith, and G. *MacBeth. Lucie-Smith took over as chairman in 1959, and the group expanded to include F. *Adcock, B. S. *Johnson, and others. An anthology of the Group's writings, edited by Hobsbaum and Lucie-Smith, appeared in 1963 (*A Group Anthology*). In 1965 the Group was restructured into a more formal organization called the Writers' Workshop, but its basic purpose, to expose the work of young writers to their peers, remained constant: it would be considered, not as a movement in poetry, but as a critical approach.

GROVE, George, see MUSIC, LITERATURE OF.

Grubbinol, a shepherd in Gay's *The Shepherd's Week*.

Grub Street, London, according to Dr *Johnson was 'originally the name of a street near Moorfields in London, much inhabited by writers of small histories, dictionaries, and temporary poems, whence any mean production is called *grubstreet*' (*Dictionary*). The name of the street was changed in the 19th cent. to Milton Street (Cripplegate). 'Grub Street' is current in modern usage as an epithet meaning 'of the nature of literary hack-work'. See Pat Rogers, *Grub Street* (1972).

Grub Street Journal, a weekly literary newspaper, highly satirical in tone, which ran from Jan. 1730 to Dec. 1737; its targets included the *Gentleman's Magazine* and the *Bee*, 'Orator' *Henley's *Hyp-Doctor*, *Theobald, *Cibber, *Eusden, and *Curll. *Pope (whose enemies were reviled as 'Knights of the Bathos') is thought to have had a hand in it, although the connection has not been established. See James T. Hillhouse, *The Grub Street Journal* (1928).

Grueby, John, a character in Dickens's *Barnaby Rudge*, servant to Lord George Gordon.

Grundy, Mrs, the symbol of rigid conventional propriety. For the origin of the name see MORTON, T.

Gryll, in Spenser's *Faerie Queene* (II. xii. 86), the hog in the Bower of *Acrasia who repined greatly at being changed back into a man. The incident is based on a dialogue of *Plutarch, in which Gryllus is one of the Greeks transformed into swine by Circe.

Gryll Grange, the last satirical novel of T. L. *Peacock, serialized 1860, issued as a book 1861.

The main plot concerns Mr Falconer, idealist, ascetic, and classicist, who lives in a tower attended by seven virgins, but is persuaded to join a convivial house party at Gryll Grange, where he woos and wins its presiding genius, Morgana Gryll. A second plot concerns the courtship of the scientific, outgoing Lord Curryfin, and the musical, meditative Alice Niphet. The characters debate many mid-Victorian issues, often criticizing the misuse of science. As part of the Christmas festivities they act an Aristophanic play which parodies the competitive examinations newly introduced into the civil service: Hannibal, Richard Cœur de Lion, and Oliver Cromwell are all failed. Notable characters include the Revd Dr Opimian, an agreeable gourmet with conservative views, and Miss Ilex, a wise and cheerful spinster. Perhaps the most urbane and polished of Peacock's books, *Gryll Grange* upholds civilization, harmony, and completeness against both technology and religious asceticism, two dominant strands of mid-Victorian thought.

Guardian, (1) a periodical started by *Steele in March 1713. It professed at the outset to abstain from political questions, and *Addison contributed 51 papers to it. It included also among its contributors *Berkeley, *Pope, and *Gay. But Steele soon launched into political controversy, falling foul of the Tory *Examiner*. Owing to some disagreement with Tonson, the publisher, the *Guardian* came to an abrupt end in Oct. 1713 and was succeeded by the *Englishman*. See *The Guardian* (1983), ed. J. C. Stephens. (2) a national daily paper originally published as the *Manchester Guardian*.

GUARINI, Giovanni Battista (1538–1612), born at Ferrara, author of the pastoral drama *Il pastor fido* (1589), written in emulation of *Tasso's *Aminta*. It had a considerable vogue in England in the 17th cent., where it was translated many times; notably by Sir Richard *Fanshawe in 1647 as *The Faithfull Shepherd* (ed. W. F. Staton and W. E. Simeone, 1964). Guarini also wrote an influential defence of tragi-comedy, the *Compendio della poesia tragicomica* (1601).

Gudrun, (1) in the *Vǫlsunga saga* and in W. Morris's *Sigurd the Volsung*, the daughter of the king of the Niblungs; (2) the heroine of the *Laxdaela saga* (see SAGA), who appears in Morris's version, 'The Lovers of Gudrun', in *The Earthly Paradise*; (3) Gudrun Brangwen, one of the two sisters in D. H. Lawrence's *Women in Love*.

Guest, Stephen, a character in G. Eliot's *The Mill on the Floss*.

GUICCIARDINI, Francesco (1483–1540), Florentine historian and statesman, employed by the Medici and the papacy. His *Storia d'Italia*, a history of Italy from 1492 to 1534, was translated into English (from a French version) by Sir Geoffrey Fenton, and is of lasting significance; passages from it were inserted in the second edition of *Holinshed's Chronicles. Both *Ralegh and F. *Bacon knew the work well, and *Gibbon proclaimed it 'from the point of view of intellectual power, the most important work to have issued from an Italian mind'. The *Ricordi*, a collection of aphorisms, also had a wide diffusion.

Guiderius, in Shakespeare's *Cymbeline*, elder son of the king, who in mountain exile bears the name Polydore. The supplements to *A Mirror for Magis-*trates* contained two 'tragedies' of Guiderius, presenting him as a powerful opponent of the Romans.

GUIDO delle COLONNE, a 13th-cent. Sicilian writer of Latin romances, author of the *Historia Destructionis Troiae* which was in fact a prose version of a poem by *Benoît de Sainte-Maure, though Guido did not acknowledge this. His romance was used as a source in poems attributed to *Barbour and *Huchown, and by *Lydgate in his *Troy Book*. The story of Troilus and Cressida, taken by Guido from Benoît, was in turn developed by *Boccaccio, *Chaucer, *Henryson, and Shakespeare. Muriel Bowden, in *A Commentary on the General Prologue to the Canterbury Tales* (1948, 20), shows that the famous opening of the *Prologue* corresponds very closely to a passage in Guido.

Guignol, the chief character in the popular French puppet-show of that name, similar to the English Punch and Judy show: Guignol is a variant (from Lyons) of the character of Polichinelle, who became Anglicized as *Punch. The word Guignol is also used for the theatre where the show is performed. Grand Guignol is a term applied to a theatre presenting plays of a gruesome character.

Guildenstern, see ROSENCRANTZ.

GUILLAUME de LORRIS, see ROMAN DE LA ROSE.

GUILLAUME de MACHAUT (c.1300–77), French musician and poet. He was prominent in the development of the ballade and the rondeau, and one of the most widely celebrated composers in the field of polyphonic songwriting. His poetry influenced Chaucer, particularly in *The Book of the Duchess*.

GUILPIN, Everard (b. ?1572), presumed to be the author of *Skialetheia: Or, A Shadowe of Truth, in Certaine Epigrams and Satyres* (1598), which has interesting affinities with the satires of *Marston and *Donne. It has been edited by D. Allen Carroll (1974).

Guinevere, the wife of King *Arthur in the Arthurian legend. The name figures in various forms: in *Geoffrey of Monmouth she is 'Guanhamara', of a noble Roman family, brought up in the household of Cador, duke of Cornwall. In the *Brut* of *Laȝamon she is 'Wenhaver', a relative of Cador; in *Sir *Gawain and the Green Knight* she is Wenore, Guenore, Gwenore, and Gaynor (the form also in *The Awntyrs of Arthure*). The most prevailing form of both her name and her story developed in the French tradition, in *Chrétien's *Lancelot* (1170s) and the related early 13th-cent. prose *Lancelot* of the Vulgate cycle, where the queen Guenièvre is the lover of Lancelot, with disastrous consequences: Lancelot fails to achieve the *Grail, and in the final confrontation with Modred he arrives too late to save Arthur, finding that the queen has become a nun. This traces only the main tradition of Guinevere, from Chrétien to Malory; there is also a more disreputable version of her as unfaithful and vengeful, reflected in such poems as *Sir Launfal*. But in this main tradition, the tragic love of Guinevere and Lancelot is one of the classics of *courtly love.

'Guinevere', one of Tennyson's *Idylls of the King*, published 1859. It describes Guinevere's growing repentance, her parting with Launcelot, her last meeting with Arthur, and her death as abbess of the nunnery of Almesbury.

Gulliver's Travels, a satire by *Swift, published 1726 as *Travels into Several Remote Nations of the World 'By Lemuel Gulliver'*.

Swift probably got the idea of a satire in the form of a narrative of travels at the meetings of the *Scriblerus Club, and intended it to form part of the 'Memoirs of Scriblerus'; indeed Scriblerus is described in the 'Memoirs' as visiting the same countries as Gulliver. Swift appears to have worked at the book from as early as 1720.

In the first part Lemuel Gulliver, a surgeon on a merchant ship, relates his shipwreck on the island of Lilliput, the inhabitants of which are 6 inches high, everything on the island being in the proportion of an inch to a foot as compared with things as we know them. Owing to this diminutive scale, the pomp of the emperor, the civil feuds of the inhabitants, the war with their neighbours across the channel, are made to look ridiculous. The English political parties and religious denominations are satirized in the description of the wearers of high heels and low heels, and of the controversy on the question whether eggs should be broken at the big or small end.

In the second part Gulliver is accidentally left ashore on Brobdingnag, where the inhabitants are as tall as steeples, and everything else is in proportion. Here the king, after enquiring into the manners, government, and learning of Europe, sums up his impression of what Gulliver tells him as follows: 'By what I have gathered from your own relation . . . I cannot but conclude the bulk of your natives to be the most pernicious race of little odious vermin that nature ever suffered to crawl upon the surface of the earth.'

The third part (which was written last) is occupied with a visit to the flying island of Laputa, and its neighbouring continent and capital Lagado. Here the satire is directed against philosophers, men of science—especially members of the *Royal Society—historians, and projectors, with special reference to the *South Sea Company. In Laputa Gulliver finds the wise men so wrapped up in their speculations as to be utter dotards in practical affairs. At Lagado he visits the Academy of Projectors, where professors are engaged in extracting sunshine from cucumbers and similar absurd enterprises. In the Island of Sorcerers he is enabled to call up the great men of old, and discovers, from their answers to his questions, the deceptions of history. The Struldbrugs, a race endowed with im-

mortality, so far from finding this a boon, turn out to be the most miserable of mankind.

In the fourth part Swift describes the country of the Houyhnhnms, who are horses endowed with reason; their rational, clean, and simple society is contrasted with the filthiness and brutality of the Yahoos, beasts in human shape whose human vices Gulliver is reluctantly forced to recognize. So alienated is he from his own species that when he finally returns home he recoils from his own family in disgust.

Gulliver's Travels, the only work for which Swift received payment, was an immediate success and was read (in the words of *Pope and *Gay) 'from the cabinet council to the nursery'; it continues to appeal to readers of all ages, both as a travel book and as a powerful satire, although many find themselves repelled or disturbed by the darkness of Swift's vision, particularly in the last book, which *Thackeray described as 'furious, raging, obscene', and L. *Stephen found 'painful and repulsive'. Like much else in the book, the textual history of *Gulliver* is far from straightforward, most scholars finding the widely varying editions published by Benjamin Motte and George Faulkner difficult, if not impossible, to reconcile.

Guls Horne-Booke, The, a satirical book of manners by *Dekker, published 1609.

It is an attack on the fops and gallants of the day under the guise of ironical instructions how they may make themselves conspicuous in places of public resort by their offensive conduct. The occupations of a young man of leisure are described; his dressing, his walk in 'Paul's', his meal at the 'ordinary', the visit to the playhouse, etc. It is a parody of the *courtesy books of the period, and was suggested by a German original (see GROBIAN).

GUMILEV, Nikolai Stepanovich (1886–1921), Russian poet and critic, born at Kronstadt and educated at Tsarskoe Selo, where in 1903 he met *Akhmatova, whom he was to marry in 1910. His first book of poetry, *The Path of the Conquistadors*, was published in 1905. In 1911 he founded the Guild of Poets, which brought together the members of the school of Russian *Acmeism, whose poetic ideals were clarity and precision. After serving with the Uhlans from 1914 he visited England in June 1917 and again in Jan.–Apr. 1918. He met R. *Fry and A. *Huxley, and visited *Garsington in June 1917. He also met G. K. *Chesterton and during an air raid made a 'mad' speech suggesting that countries should be ruled by poets and offering Chesterton the crown of England. He made the acquaintance of most of the writers associated with *Orage's The New Age, which frequently published translations from and articles about Russian writers. From England he returned to Russia; he was divorced from Akhmatova in 1918. On 3 Aug. 1921 he was arrested for alleged participation in the so-called 'Tagantsev conspiracy', a pro-monarchist plot, and he was executed later that month. The major English edition is *Selected Works of Nikolai S. Gumilev* (trans. Burton Raffel and Alla Burago, 1972).

Gummidge, Mrs, a character in Dickens's **David Copperfield*, a 'lone lorn creetur'.

GUNN, Neil Miller (1891–1973), Scottish novelist, short story writer, and playwright, born and brought up in Caithness. His first novel *The Grey Coast* (1926), short stories, and several of his plays contemplate Highland life in decline but *Morning Tide* (1931) introduces more Gunnian characteristics: a sensuous lyricism, remarkable evocations of childhood and of the sea, and a hard-won confidence in humankind. Two historical novels followed: *Sun Circle* (1933), about a Viking invasion, and *Butcher's Broom* (1934), a powerful testament to the Highland Clearances. The modernist *Highland River* (1937) maps the life of its hero, Kenn, on to his experience of the river of his childhood. *The Silver Darlings* (1941) is set in Caithness immediately after the Napoleonic wars, synthesizing folk song, historical detail, acute psychological observation, and symphonic recurrences of almost supernatural experiences. *Young Art and Old Hector* (1942) explores the shared experience of a child and an old man. In *The Green Isle of the Great Deep* (1944) the duo return, but to a dystopian Celtic heaven. *The Serpent* and *The Key of the Chest* scrutinize homespun values more critically, while *The Silver Bough* (1948) and *The Well at the World's End* (1951) gently satirize those who wish to observe 'primitive communities'. The thriller *Bloodhunt* (1952) and the metaphysical *The Other Landscape* (1954) envisage rehabilitation after violence. *The Atom of Delight* (1956), Gunn's last book, analyses incidents in the first two decades of his life.

GUNN, Thom(son William) (1929–2004), poet, born in Gravesend, the son of a journalist, and educated at University College School and Trinity College, Cambridge, where he was a contemporary of Ted **Hughes. His first volume of poems, *Fighting Terms*, was published in 1954; shortly afterwards he took up a fellowship at Stanford University, California (where he came under the influence of **Winters), and in 1960 he settled permanently in San Francisco, gradually relinquishing the academic life for a full-time career as a writer. His collections include *The Sense of Movement* (1957), *My Sad Captains* (1961), *Moly* (1971), and *Jack Straw's Castle* (1976). His celebration of men of action (soldiers, motorcyclists, tough boys), his fascination with violence, his gallery of heroes (who range from Elvis Presley to Caravaggio), together with his predominantly low-key, rational, laconic, colloquial manner provide an interesting synthesis of the English **Movement and the romantic elements of American **Beat poetry. Other volumes include *Selected Poems 1950–1975* (1979); *The Passages of Joy* (1982), in which his homosexuality was openly acknowledged; *The Man with Night Sweats* (1992), containing several powerful poems about AIDS; and *Collected Poems* (1993). The

Occasions of Poetry: Essays in Criticism and Autobiography, ed. Clive Wilmer, appeared in 1982 (enl. 1985).

GUNNING, Susannah (?1740–1800). She lived a difficult life, largely in high London society, with a turbulent army husband, a beautiful high-spirited daughter, and a countess and a duchess for sisters-in-law. **Walpole referred to the notorious family as 'the Gunningiad'. She wrote some poetry, and from 1763 onwards produced almost a dozen unmemorable novels, many of them successful, including *Barford Abbey* (1768) and *The Heir Apparent* (1802).

Guppy, a character in Dickens's **Bleak House*.

GURDJIEFF, Georgei Ivanovitch (?1874–1949), esoteric thinker and teacher, son of a Greek father and Armenian mother, born at Alexandrople, just inside Armenia on the Turkish frontier. He claimed to have spent his youth travelling in Central Asia, India, and Tibet with a company of fellow seekers acquiring occult knowledge. In 1910 he appeared in St Petersburg practising as a healer with theosophical leanings, and in 1914 met **Ouspensky, who became his principal disciple and recorded his teaching in *In Search of the Miraculous* (1950). He moved to the Caucasus during the revolution, then via Constantinople and Berlin to France, where in 1922, from mysterious funds, he set up the Institute for the Harmonious Development of Man at Fontainebleau, where K. **Mansfield died in 1923. His ideas influenced A. **Huxley (*After Many a Summer*, 1939, and *The Doors of Perception*, 1954) and **Isherwood. **Orage, editor of the *New Age*, was a disciple, followed him to Fontainebleau in 1922, and spent some years teaching the doctrine, raising funds, and organizing groups. A powerful and hypnotic personality, often labelled as a charlatan, Gurdjieff insisted that his knowledge was more a method than a doctrine, and could only be acquired by initiates through long discipline and a technique of self-observation.

GURNEY, Ivor (Bertie) (1890–1937), poet and composer, born in Gloucester, the son of a tailor. He was awarded a scholarship in composition at the Royal College of Music, which he attended from 1911. He volunteered at the outbreak of the First World War, served on the Western Front as a private from 1915 to 1917, and was wounded and gassed. He published two volumes of verse, *Severn and Somme* (1917) and *War's Embers* (1919). After the war he became increasingly unsettled, and worked at various jobs, at times sleeping rough, and taking night-walks back to Gloucestershire from London. He was committed to a mental institution in 1922, and spent the rest of his life in care, dying in the City of London Mental Hospital. He continued in these later years to compose and to write poetry of growing individuality. He set few of his own poems to music, but produced two A. E. **Housman cycles (*Ludlow and Teme* and *The Western Playland*, both 1919) and a set of six E. **Thomas songs, *Lights Out*

(1918–25). In the short time at his disposal he produced altogether nearly 300 songs. *Blunden made a selection of his post-1919 poems, published 1954, and Leonard Clark published a larger selection in 1973. Interest in his verse—with its memories of the war, its evocations of Gloucestershire, and descriptions of his own mental state—continued to grow, and his *Collected Poems*, edited and with an introduction by P. J. Kavanagh, appeared in 1982. See also M. Hurd's biography, *The Ordeal of Ivor Gurney* (1978).

GURNEY, Thomas (1705–70), shorthand writer at the Old Bailey, the first shorthand writer to hold an official appointment. His *Brachygraphy* (1750), originally an improvement of W. Mason's *Shorthand*, has been frequently reissued and improved. His grandson, William Brodie Gurney, shorthand writer to the Houses of Parliament (1813), is referred to by Byron in *Don Juan* (i. 189).

Guster, a character in Dickens's *Bleak House*.

GUTENBERG, Johann (c.1400–?68), the inventor of printing with movable type. Born at Mainz, he learned printing skills in Strasbourg, where he lived from 1434 until he returned to Mainz in 1444. In 1436 he founded a press in partnership with *Fust, who provided the capital. Fust dissolved the partnership acrimoniously in 1455 and took possession of the implements and stock. Books published up to 1455 cannot be assigned with confidence to Gutenberg or Fust or Fust's son-in-law Peter Schöffer, but the 42-line Latin Bible known as the 'Gutenberg Bible', printed at Mainz 1453–5, is usually attributed to Gutenberg. See Albert Kapr, *Johannes Gutenberg* (Eng. trans. 1996).

GUTHLAC, St (d. 714/15), a young nobleman of Mercia who reacted against his military life and became a hermit at Crowland (or Croyland) in Lincolnshire. Æthelbald, king of Mercia, had a church built over his tomb, which later became the abbey of Crowland. Not long after his death was written the Latin *Vita Sancti Guthlaci* (c.740) by Felix of Croyland, which is in the tradition of Latin saints' lives such as Evagrius's *Vita Sancti Antonii*, and of which there is a late Old English prose version from Mercia. Two adjacent poems in Old English, found in the *Exeter Book, known as *Guthlac A* and *Guthlac B*, are distinguished from each other in style and in the degree of their dependence on Felix: B is much more closely copied from him and is written in a more elaborate, Cynewulfian style than A. The poems used to be attributed to *Cynewulf and they are thought to date originally from the late 9th cent. See W. de G. Birch (ed.), *Memorials of St Guthlac* (Wisbech, 1881).

Guy Mannering, a novel by Sir W. *Scott, published 1815. This, the first novel published by Scott after *Waverley*'s success, is concerned, like so many of Scott's best books, with old loyalties and the transition in Scotland from the old customs to the new. The story,

set in the 18th cent., narrates the fortunes of Harry Bertram, son of the laird of Ellangowan in Dumfriesshire, who is kidnapped as a child and carried to Holland at the instigation of a dishonest lawyer, Glossin, who hopes to acquire the Ellangowan estate on easy terms if there is no male heir. Bertram, ignorant of his parentage, goes to India as Vanbeest Brown, joins the army, and serves with distinction under Colonel Guy Mannering. He is suspected by Mannering of paying attentions to his wife, is wounded by him in a duel, and left for dead. In reality, Bertram loves Julia, Mannering's daughter. Recovering from his wound, he follows her to Ellangowan. Glossin, who has seized the Ellangowan estate, is alarmed by the possibility that Bertram may learn the secret of his parentage. He plots with Dirk Hatteraick, the smuggler who kidnapped him as a child, to carry him off again and kill him. But Bertram is recognized by an old gipsy, Meg Merrilies, who had loved him as a child and, despite having been evicted from the estate by Bertram's father with all her clan, devotes herself to securing his restoration. She frustrates the plot, with the help of Dandie Dinmont, a sturdy Lowland farmer, but loses her own life. Hatteraick and Glossin are captured and Hatteraick, after murdering Glossin in prison, kills himself. Bertram is restored to his property, reconciled with Mannering, and marries Julia. Mannering's part in the plot is emphasized by the fact that he had happened to be stormstayed at Ellangowan on the night of Bertram's birth and diverted himself by casting (accurately) the horoscope of the newborn child.

Guy of Gisborne, see ROBIN HOOD AND GUY OF GISBORNE.

Guy of Warwick, a very popular verse romance of about 1300, based on an Anglo-Norman original (of which there are 13 manuscripts), occurring in four manuscripts ranging from 7,000 to 12,000 lines.

Guy is the son of Siward, steward of Rohand, earl of Warwick, and the romance tells of the exploits he performs in order to win the hand of the earl's daughter Fenice. He rescues the daughter of the emperor of Germany, fights the Saracens, and slays the Soldan. He returns to England where he is honourably received by King Athelstan and marries Fenice, but soon returns to the Holy Land where he performs more great exploits. He comes back again to England and fights the Danish giant Colbrand in a famous combat, slays the Dun Cow of Dunsmore, and vanquishes a winged dragon in Northumberland. He becomes a hermit and is fed by Fenice who does not recognize him until he sends her his ring from his deathbed.

The romance served as a patriotic rallying-poem because of its celebration of Athelstan's resistance to the Danes, and its popularity was enhanced by its nature as saint's life combined with violent adventure story. The legend was accepted as authentic by chroniclers and versified by *Lydgate (c.1450); the Beauchamp earls claimed descent from Guy. The story of the encounter between Guy and Colbrand is told in Drayton's *Poly-Olbion*, xii. 129 ff., which describes other feats of Guy in xiii. 327 ff. See edition by J. Zupitza (3 vols, EETS ES, 42, 49, 59, 1883–91).

Guyon, Sir, in Spenser's *Faerie Queene*, the knight of Temperance. His various exploits, the conquest of *Pyrochles, the visit to the cave of *Mammon, the capture of *Acrasia, and the destruction of her *Bower of Bliss, are related in II. v–xii.

Guzmán de Alfarache, a Spanish *picaresque romance, the second of its kind (the successor of *Lazarillo de Tormes*) by Mateo Alemán (1547–c.1614). It was translated into English (as *The*

Rogue) in 1622 and published with an introductory poem by *Jonson.

Guzmán is by turns scullion, thief, gentleman, beggar, soldier, and page.

Gwendolen, (1) in *Geoffrey of Monmouth's *History*, the daughter of Corineus and wife of King *Locrine who threw *Estrildis and Sabrina (Habren) into the Severn. (2) Gwendolen Harleth, a character in G. Eliot's *Daniel Deronda*.

GWYN, Eleanor ('Nell') (1650–87), orange-seller, actress, and mistress of Charles II; her best role seems to have been the 'breeches part' of Florimel in *Dryden's *Secret Love*. One of her sons was created duke of St Albans in 1684.

H

Habbakkuk Hilding, the name given to *Fielding in a scurrilous pamphlet of 1752, possibly by *Smollett.

HABINGTON, William (1605–54), of an old Catholic family, educated at St Omer and Paris. He married Lucy Herbert, daughter of the first Baron Powis, and celebrated her in *Castara* (1634, anon.), a collection of love poems. A later edition (1635) contained in addition some elegies on a friend, and the edition of 1640 a number of sacred poems. He also wrote a tragi-comedy, *The Queene of Arragon* (1640). His poems were edited by Kenneth Allott (1948), with a life.

HĀFIZ, Shams ud-din Muhammad (d. *c*.1390), a famous Persian poet and philosopher, born at Shiraz, whose poems sing of love and flowers and wine and nightingales. His principal work is the *Divan*, a collection of short lyrics called *ghazals*, or *ghasels*, in which some commentators see a mystical meaning. Translations of his works include *Odes of Hafez* (1774) by J. Richardson, and versions by Sir W. *Jones, G. *Bell (*Poems from the Divan of Hafiz*, 1897), and R. *Le Gallienne (1905). See also *Persian Poems*, ed. A. J. Arberry (1954). Hāfiz and *Sa'dī were buried near one another at Shiraz.

HAGGARD, Sir H(enry) Rider (1856–1925), sixth son of a Norfolk squire. He spent six years in South Africa as a young man, and later served on official commissions concerned with agriculture, forestry, and emigration, and wrote books on South African history and on farming; but it was his 34 adventure novels that made him famous. These were notable chiefly for weird invention and spellbinding narrative, and were diversely set in Iceland, Mexico, Constantinople, and Ancient Egypt; but his best novels—of which *King Solomon's Mines* (1886) and *She* (1887) are the most celebrated—were set in Africa, and vividly conveyed the fascination he found in its landscape, wildlife, tribal society, and mysterious past. *Kipling and *Lang were close friends of his, and he had a worldwide readership which included *Jung, who used *She* as a striking example of the anima concept. Haggard's novels have remained continuously popular, and several of them have been filmed. *The Days of My Life: An Autobiography* appeared in 1926, and there is a biography by Morton Cohen (1960).

Haidée, a character in Byron's *Don Juan*.

haiku, a Japanese lyric form of 17 syllables in lines of 5, 7, 5 syllables. It emerged in the 16th cent. and flourished from the 17th to the 19th cent., and dealt traditionally with images of the natural world; in this century it has been much imitated in Western literature.

Hajji Baba of Ispahan, The Adventures of, see MORIER.

HAKLUYT (pron. Haklit), Richard (1552–1616), of a Herefordshire family, educated at Westminster and Christ Church, Oxford. He was chaplain to Sir Edward Stafford, ambassador at Paris, 1583–8. Here he learnt much of the maritime enterprises of other nations, and found that the English were reputed for 'their sluggish security'. He accordingly decided to devote himself to collecting and publishing the accounts of English explorations, and to this purpose he gave the remainder of his life. He had already been amassing material, for in 1582 he published *Divers Voyages Touching the Discoverie of America*. In 1587 he published in Paris a revised edition of the *De Orbe Novo* of Peter Martyr of Anghiera (subsequently translated into English by Michael Lok), and in the same year appeared his *A Notable Historie, Containing Foure Voyages Made by Certayne French Captaynes unto Florida*, a translation of René de Laudonnière. His *Principall Navigations, Voiages, and Discoveries of the English Nation* was issued in 1589, and, much enlarged, in three volumes, 1598–1600. It contained some account of the voyages of the Cabots, and narratives of Sir Hugh Willoughby's voyage to the Near East in search of Cathay, Sir John *Hawkins's voyages to Guinea and the West Indies, *Drake's voyages of 1570–2 and his circumnavigation, Sir Humphrey Gilbert's last voyage in which he perished, Martin Frobisher's search for the North-West Passage, John Davys's Arctic voyages, and the voyages of *Ralegh, James Lancaster, and others. He thus brought to light the hitherto obscure achievements of English navigators, and gave a great impetus to discovery and colonization. He was closely associated with *Sidney in the last years of his life, and from 1582 with Ralegh (particularly between 1583 and 1590). He is referred to by many contemporary scholars and writers, some of whom were his personal friends, including *Camden, Gabriel and Richard *Harvey, *Mulcaster, *Nashe, and *Drayton. He was a pluralist, holding prebendaryships at Bristol and Westminster; he was rector of Wetheringsett, 1590–1616, and of Gedney, 1612–16. He left unpublished a number of papers which came into the hands of *Purchas.

The Hakluyt Society was founded in 1846 as an offshoot of the (Royal) Geographical Society to publish voyages and travels, which it has done at the rate of at least two volumes a year since then. Its publications include reissues and re-editions of Hakluyt's writings, and very many original narratives. Its history and that of its founder are succinctly set out in D. B. Quinn (ed.), *The Hakluyt Handbook* (2 vols, 1974).

Hal, Prince, in Shakespeare's *1* and *2* *Henry IV*, the prince of Wales who later becomes Henry V.

HALDANE, J(ohn) B(urdon) S(anderson) (1892–1964), geneticist and brother of N. *Mitchison. He was professor of genetics, then of biometry, at University College London, and, 1940–9, chairman of the editorial board of the communist *Daily Worker*, to which he contributed hundreds of articles. He became known to a large public as a witty popularizer of science with such works as *Daedalus* (1924), *Possible Worlds* (1927, in the forewords of which he stresses the public's 'right to know'), *Animal Biology* (with J. *Huxley, 1927), and a collection of children's stories, *My Friend Mr Leakey* (1937). His scientific but imaginative speculations about the future have much in common with those in *Brave New World*, and Haldane himself appears as Shearwater, a biologist with a flighty wife, in A. *Huxley's *Antic Hay*. A Marxist from the 1930s, Haldane resigned from the Communist Party *c.*1950 on the issue of Lysenko's claims to have manipulated the genetic structure of plants and '*Stalin's interference with science'. See a life by R. Clark (1968).

HALE, Sir Matthew (1609–76), educated at Oxford. He became lord chief justice and was a voluminous writer on many subjects, but much of his best work was left in manuscript and published long after his death. His works include a *History of the Common Law* (1713) and an unfinished *History of the Pleas of the Crown* (1736), the first history of English criminal law. He was a friend and admirer of *Selden and G. *Burnet wrote his biography.

Hale, Mr, Mrs, Margaret, and Frederick, characters in E. Gaskell's *North and South*.

HALÉVY, Élie (1870–1937), French social and political historian, author of *Histoire du peuple anglais au XIXe siècle*, a study of political, economic, and religious change in England after 1815. Having dealt with the period 1815–41 in three volumes (1913–23), Halévy went on to write a further two (1926–32) on the years 1895–1915 before turning his attention to the middle of the century. His last work (1946), on the years 1841–52, was published after his death.

HALIBURTON, Thomas Chandler (1796–1865), born at Windsor, Nova Scotia, became a judge of the supreme court of the province. As a writer he became known for his *The Clockmaker; or, The Sayings and Doings of Samuel Slick, of Slickville* (1836; London, 1837), a satirical and humorous work of fiction published anonymously which had a great vogue in England. It was followed by other works in the same series, including *The Attaché or Sam Slick in England* (1843–4), designed to stimulate political reform through the

satirical observations of the character Sam Slick, a Yankee from Ohio. See V. L. O. Chittick, *Thomas Chandler Haliburton: A Study in Provincial Toryism* (1924).

HALIFAX, George Savile, marquess of (1633–95), a powerful influence in the court of Charles II, and a noted anti-Catholic, chiefly remembered for his *Character of a Trimmer*, published 1688 but previously circulated in manuscript, in which he urged the king to free himself from his brother's influence and advocated compromise and moderation. His political tracts (which include his subtle piece of argument *The Anatomy of an Equivalent*, 1688) were reprinted in 1898. He also wrote some much-reprinted essays, *A Lady's New Year's Gift, or Advice to a Daughter* (1688). His other works include *A Letter to a Dissenter upon Occasion of His Majesties Late Gracious Declaration of Indulgence* (1687) and *A Character of King Charles II* (printed with *Political, Moral, and Miscellaneous Reflexions* in 1750). He saved the throne by his resolute opposition to the Exclusion Bill. He is the 'Jotham' of Dryden's *Absalom and Achitophel*.

Hali Meiŏhad (Holy Maidenhood), a prose treatise on virginity from the west Midlands, written in the period 1190–1225. It occurs in two manuscripts which also contain *Sawles Warde* and one or more members of the group of saints' lives known as the *Katherine Group. It is vigorously written in an accomplished style, very reminiscent of that of *Ancrene Wisse*, but it takes an extreme, dualist position on its subject. There is an edition by B. Millett (EETS 284, 1982).

HALL, or **HALLE,** Edward (d. 1547), educated at Eton and King's College, Cambridge, the author of a chronicle glorifying the House of Tudor entitled *The Union of the Two Noble and Illustre Families of Lancastre and York*, which was prohibited by Queen Mary and which is interesting for the account it gives of the times of Henry VIII and the vivid description of his court and of the Field of the Cloth of Gold. It was used by Shakespeare as a source in his early history plays.

HALL, Joseph (1574–1656), educated at Ashby-de-la-Zouch and Emmanuel College, Cambridge. He was successively bishop of Exeter (1627) and Norwich (1641). He was imprisoned in 1641 in the course of the attack on episcopacy, and released after five months. In 1643 he was sequestered at Norwich, his revenues and bishop's palace seized, his cathedral desecrated. As a student at Cambridge he published two volumes of satires, *Virgidemiarum, Sex Libri*; a semi-bawdy satirical novel in Latin, *Mundus Alter et Idem*; and, very probably, the last play in the St John's College *Parnassus Plays. He is responsible for initiating several literary genres: the first to publish his epistles in English (1608–10); the beginner of the mode of *character-writing (1608); the introducer of Juvenalian satire; the first to mine his own sermons for his great meditations written for Protestants to counter the popular Ignatian mode of meditation on the Continent. A favourite of King James, he was sent three times on royal embassies abroad; and he was employed as a controversialist by the king and later by *Laud against *Smectymnuus. His collected works fill ten volumes, and he is famous for his plain, Senecan prose style. *A Biographical and Critical Study* by F. Huntley was published in 1979.

HALL, Sir Peter (1930–), director of plays, operas, and films. He was born in Suffolk and educated at St Catharine's College, Cambridge, where he came under the spell of F. R. *Leavis, whose rigorous textual analysis influenced his later career. Hall directed the British première of *Waiting for Godot* in 1955, founded the Royal Shakespeare Company in 1960, laying great emphasis on intelligent verse-speaking, and was director of the *National Theatre from 1973 to 1988. He has shaped post-war British subsidized theatre and applied the same classical rigour to *Beckett, *Pinter, and *Albee as to Stratford Shakespeare, where his joint production, with John Barton, of the history-cycle *The Wars of the Roses* (1963) remains a modern landmark. His *Diaries* were published in 1983.

HALL, Radclyffe (1883–1943), the pen-name of Marguerite Radclyffe-Hall, born in Bournemouth, and educated erratically by governesses. She published several volumes of verse and eight volumes of fiction, including *The Unlit Lamp* (1924) and *Adam's Breed* (1926). Her open treatment of lesbianism in *The Well of Loneliness* (1928) occasioned a trial for obscenity; it was banned and an appeal refused, despite the support of many eminent writers including E. M. *Forster, L. and V. *Woolf, and Arnold *Bennett. It has been many times republished, and other titles were reissued, notably by Virago. There is a life by S. Cline (1997).

HALL, Willis (1929–2005), playwright, born and educated in Leeds at Cockburn High School. His successful play *The Long and the Short and the Tall* (1958, pub. 1959), set in 1942 in the Malayan jungle during the Japanese advance on Singapore, was followed by many other works for stage, screen, and television, many written in collaboration with K. *Waterhouse. He also wrote many books for children.

HALLAM, Arthur Henry (1811–33), educated at Eton and Trinity College, Cambridge, where he became a close friend of *Tennyson and after his early death the subject of Tennyson's poem *In Memoriam*. He was a young man of great promise, an Italian scholar, and an ardent admirer of the Romantic poets. His *Remains*, edited by his father Henry *Hallam in 1834, contain work of distinction in poetry, philosophy, and criticism.

HALLAM, Henry (1777–1859), historian, and the father of *Tennyson's friend Arthur *Hallam, educated at Eton and Christ Church, Oxford. He became a

barrister and a commissioner of stamps. He spent some ten years on the preparation of his first published work, *A View of the State of Europe during the Middle Ages* (1818), in which he attempts 'a comprehensive survey of the chief circumstances that can interest a philosophical enquirer'. Hallam's best-known work, his *Constitutional History of England* (1827), to the death of George II, became a work of great and prolonged influence. The work was continued by Sir T. E. May. In 1834 he edited, with a memoir, the verse and prose of his son Arthur. His last great work was *An Introduction to the Literature of Europe during the Fifteenth*, Sixteenth, and Seventeenth Centuries (1837–9), the sweep of which covers not only creative literature but the literature of the classics, mathematics, theology, science, and, most notably, of philosophy and thought.

HALLIWELL (later Halliwell-Phillipps), James Orchard (1820–89), a noted Shakespearian scholar. He entered Trinity College, Cambridge, in 1837 where he had unlimited access to the locked-up manuscripts. After it was discovered that 17 volumes were missing, he transferred to Jesus College. He was elected a fellow of the *Royal Society before he was 19 and was a founder member of the Shakespeare Society. In 1842 he married Henrietta, daughter of Sir T. *Phillipps, whose surname he later added to his own. His published works include *The Life of William Shakespeare* (1848), *Observations on the Shakespearean Forgeries at Bridgewater House* (1853), on the J. P. *Collier controversy, *A Dictionary of Old English Plays* (1860), *Outlines of the Life of Shakespeare* (1881–7), which became a primary source for subsequent 19th-cent. Shakespeare biographies. He edited the *Works* of Shakespeare (16 vols, 1853–65) and some 150 volumes, mainly of 17th-cent. literature (some in collaboration with T. *Wright), and did much work for the *Percy Society, notably editing *The Nursery Rhymes of England* (1842–6), a pioneering study which remained standard until that of the *Opies, and for the *Camden Society.

HALL-STEVENSON, John (1718–85), the friend of *Sterne, traditionally said to be the original of Eugenius in *Tristram Shandy* and *A Sentimental Journey*. He was squire of Skelton Castle, near Saltburn-by-the-Sea, Yorkshire, where he was host to a circle of literary friends, 'the Demoniacs', which included Sterne. He published *Fables for Grown Gentlemen* (1761), *Crazy Tales* (1762), and other coarse, sometimes indecent, verse satires done in what he conceived to be imitations of French *fabliaux. He was not, as has been said, the author of *A Sentimental Journey Continued* (1769). His *Works*, edited carefully though anonymously, appeared in 1795.

Hamartia, see POETICS, THE.

HAMBURGER, Michael Peter Leopold (1924–), poet and translator, born in Berlin of a German family which emigrated to England in 1933; his brother is publisher Paul Hamlyn. His own collections of poetry include *Flowering Cactus* (1950), *Weather and Season* (1963) (which contains his sequence, 'In a Cold Season', on the Eichmann trial), and *Ownerless Earth: New and Selected Poems* (1973), and his many distinguished translations include versions of *Hofmannsthal (1961), *Grass (1966), and, notably, the *Poems and Fragments* of *Hölderlin (1966). His *Collected Poems* appeared in 1984 and an autobiography, *A Mug's Game*, in 1983. Later volumes include *Roots in the Air* (1991) and *Late* (1997).

HAMILTON, Anthony, see GRAMONT.

HAMILTON, Charles Harold St John (1876–1961), born in Ealing, the son of a journalist. His first boys' story was published when he was 17, and he was to become for half a century the world's most prolific author for boys. He wrote under many different pen-names, but was most renowned as 'Frank Richards' of the *Magnet* (1908–40) and 'Martin Clifford' of the *Gem* (1907–39). The *Magnet*'s Greyfriars School included, among other household names, Billy Bunter, who survived with his friends, after the *Magnet*'s closure, in book form, on television, and in the theatre. *Orwell, writing in *Horizon* in 1939, objected to the snobbery, insularity, dated slang, and tedious style of this exclusively male world, but Hamilton's game reply conceded nothing.

HAMILTON, Cicely, see WOMEN'S SUFFRAGE.

HAMILTON, Ian (1938–2001), poet, editor, biographer, and essayist, educated at Darlington Grammar School and Keble College, Oxford. He published collections of poetry, *The Visit* (1970), *Returning* (1976), and *Fifty Poems* (1988); other works include *The Little Magazines* (1976); a life of R. *Lowell (1983); and *In Search of J. D. Salinger* (1988), a compelling account of the difficulties he encountered in writing about his elusive subject, which he describes as 'a kind of *Quest for Corvo*, with *Salinger as quarry'. This investigation led to *Keepers of the Flame: Literary Estates and the Rise of Biography* (1992), in which he discusses historical, legal, and ethical questions associated with the growing interest in literary biography. He edited the *New Review* (1974–9) and *The Oxford Companion to Twentieth Century Poetry in English* (1994). *Walking Possession* (1994) collects essays and reviews 1968–93.

HAMILTON, (Anthony Walter) Patrick (1904–62), the son of an eccentric clergyman. He worked for a time as a repertory actor and wrote several successful plays, including *Rope* (1929) and *Gas Light* (1939), both thrillers, and *The Duke in Darkness* (1943), a historical drama. He also wrote radio plays. His novels include *Craven House* (1926), the story of the inmates of a boarding house; *The Midnight Bell* (1929), *The Siege of Pleasure* (1932), and *The Plains of Cement* (1934), a trilogy published in 1935 as *Twenty Thousand Streets under the Sky*, which deals respectively with the interlocking lives of Bob, a waiter, Jenny, a prostitute,

and Ella, a barmaid; *Hangover Square* (1941), a thriller set in Earls Court dealing with George Harvey Bone's fatal passion for destructive Netta; and *The Slaves of Solitude* (1947), also set in a boarding house, which centres on the wartime experiences of the quiet spinster Miss Roach. Hamilton's particular gift is for describing, in the words of J. B. *Priestley, 'a kind of No-Man's-Land of shabby hotels, dingy boarding-houses and all those saloon bars where the homeless can meet' (1972); *Holroyd praises his 'invention of the monster-bore—that terrible mixture of the banal and the sinister who entertains the reader by driving the other characters in the book to distraction' (*Unreceived Opinions*, 1973). All the novels show a preoccupation with the perils and pleasures of drinking, and Hamilton's Marxism is expressed in his compassion for the hopelessness of his characters' lives.

HAMILTON, William, of Bangour (1704–54), Scottish *Jacobite patriot and poet, who commemorated the battle of Gladsmuir in an ode and fought at Culloden. He is chiefly remembered for his song 'The Braes of Yarrow' ('Busk ye, busk ye, my bony bony bride'), published in *Ramsay's *Miscellany*.

HAMILTON, Sir William (1730–1803), diplomat, archaeologist, and collector, and British envoy and plenipotentiary at Naples from 1764, where his embassy became a cultural and musical centre; he entertained many travellers on the *Grand Tour, studied Vesuvius (recording his observations in *Campi Phlegraei: Observations on the Volcanos of the Two Sicilies*, 1776), collected so-called Etruscan vases and paintings, and in 1791 married, as his second wife, Emma Hart (born Amy Lyon), who was to achieve notoriety as the mistress of Nelson. The Hamiltons were recalled to England in 1800, where Sir William died, with both Emma and Nelson attending his deathbed. His friends and correspondents included *Beckford and Horace *Walpole, and his collections exerted a wide influence on *neo-classicism in Britain; one of his most important collections of vases, terracottas, coins, etc., sold to the British Museum in 1771, laid the foundation for its department of classical antiquities. There is a fictionalized account of his life, *The Volcano Lover* (1992), by S. *Sontag.

HAMILTON, Sir William (1788–1856), educated at Glasgow and Balliol College, Oxford. His philosophical reputation was made by a number of articles which appeared in the *Edinburgh Review*, 1829–36 (republished in 1852 as *Discussions on Philosophy and Literature, Education and University Reform*), of which the most important were those on 'the Philosophy of the Unconditioned', 'the Philosophy of Perfection', and 'Logic'. He was elected to the chair of logic and metaphysics at Edinburgh in 1836. His *Lectures on Metaphysics and Logic* appeared in 1859–60, after his death.

A man of great philosophical erudition rather than a great philosophical thinker, Hamilton represents the influence of *Kant upon the commonsense philosophy of the Scottish school set forth by *Reid. He maintained that we have immediate perception of external objects, or rather of their primary and real qualities; he also expounded the doctrine of the phenomenal and relative quality of all knowledge, according to which we must remain ignorant of ultimate reality, since knowledge, whether of mind or matter, must be conditioned by the knowing mind, and cannot therefore be knowledge of the thing-in-itself. If we attempt to think of things not so conditioned, we are faced by two contradictory propositions, both inconceivable, and one of which must be true; for example, time must be either finite or infinite, but we cannot conceive of it as either.

In logic, Hamilton introduced a modification of the traditional doctrine, known as the 'Quantification of the Predicate'. His philosophical views were vigorously attacked by J. S. *Mill in his *Examination of Sir William Hamilton's Philosophy.

HAMILTON, William Gerard (1729–96), known as 'Single-Speech Hamilton' from his celebrated three-hour maiden speech in 1755 as MP for Petersfield. His friend Dr *Johnson was for a time his unofficial adviser and *Burke was his private assistant from 1759 to 1765. Some of his contemporaries claimed he was *'Junius'. His works were published after his death by *Malone under the title *Parliamentary Logick*.

HAMILTON, Sir William Rowan (1805–65), a distinguished mathematician whose fame rests principally on his discovery of the science of quaternions, a higher branch of calculus. He was also an amateur poet, and friend and correspondent of *Wordsworth, *;Coleridge, M. *Edgeworth, and other literary figures.

Hamlet, a tragedy by *Shakespeare, written perhaps, in its first version, in mid-1599, probably completed by 1601: it was registered as 'latelie Acted' in July 1602. A short text probably reconstructed from memory by actors was published 1603 and a good text, almost twice as long, 1604–5. The *Folio text (1623) adds some passages not in the second quarto, and omits others. References by *Nashe, *Lodge, and others show that a play on the same subject (now lost) preceded Shakespeare's; it was presumably a source. His chief non-dramatic source was *Saxo Grammaticus's narrative in his *Historiae Danicae*, as retold by Belleforest in his *Histoires tragiques*.

Old Hamlet, king of Denmark, is recently dead, and his brother Claudius has assumed the throne and married his widow Gertrude. Young Hamlet, returning from university at Wittenberg, learns from the ghost of his father that Claudius murdered him by pouring poison into his ear, and is commanded to avenge the murder without injuring Gertrude. Hamlet warns his friend Horatio and the guard Marcellus (who have also seen the apparition) that he intends to feign madness,

and swears them to secrecy. Immediately after his famous speech of deliberation beginning 'To be, or not to be' (III. i) he repudiates Ophelia, whom he has loved, while spied on by Claudius and by Ophelia's father Polonius. He welcomes a troupe of visiting players, and arranges a performance of a play ('the Mouse-trap') about fratricide, which Claudius breaks off, in apparently guilty and fearful fury, when the player Lucianus appears to murder his uncle by pouring poison into his ear. Hamlet refrains from killing Claudius while he is at prayer, but stabs through the arras in his mother's bedroom, killing the old counsellor Polonius, before reprimanding his mother for her affection for Claudius. Claudius sends Hamlet to England with sealed orders that he should be killed on arrival. Hamlet outwits him, however, returning to Denmark, having arranged the deaths of his old friends Rosencrantz and Guildenstern, who were his uncle's agents. During Hamlet's absence Ophelia has gone mad with grief from Hamlet's rejection of her and her father's death, and is found drowned. Her brother Laertes, having returned from France, determines to avenge his sister's death. Hamlet and Laertes meet in the graveyard where Ophelia is to be buried, and fight in her grave. Claudius arranges a fencing match between Hamlet and Laertes, giving the latter a poisoned foil; an exchange of weapons results in the deaths of both combatants, not before Gertrude has drunk a poisoned cup intended for her son, and the dying Hamlet has succeeded in killing Claudius. Fortinbras, prince of Norway, whose resolute military heroism has been alluded to throughout the play, appears fresh from wars with Poland and gives Hamlet a military funeral. (See also OBJECTIVE CORRELATIVE.)

Hamley, Squire, Mrs, and their sons Osborne and Roger, in *Wives and Daughters* by E. Gaskell.

HAMMETT, (Samuel) Dashiell (1894–1961), American writer of detective fiction, whose tough, realistic works (*Red Harvest*, 1929; *The Maltese Falcon*, 1930; *The Glass Key*, 1931; *The Thin Man*, 1932; etc.), based in part on his own experiences as a detective in San Francisco, created a vogue for a new kind of hard-boiled hero and seedy locale. Many of his stories were filmed, and he himself worked as a screenwriter in Hollywood; in 1951, in the McCarthy era, he was imprisoned for 'un-American activities'. He was for many years the friend and companion of the playwright Lillian *Hellman (1905–84), whom he met in 1930. See a life by Diane *Johnson, published in 1983.

HAMMICK, Georgina (1939–   ), novelist and short story writer, born in Hampshire and educated at schools in England and Kenya before attending the Académie Julian, Paris, and the Salisbury School of Art. The author of two volumes of short stories, *People for Lunch* (1987) and *Spoilt* (1992), and a novel, *The Arizona Game* (1996), she explores emotional terrain with acuity and an ironic wit which illuminates the dark corners of relationships. Her faithfulness to language and shades of meaning is evident throughout her work. She is one of five poets in *A Poetry Quintet* and edited an anthology, *The Virago Book of Love and Loss* (1992).

HAMPDEN, John (1594–1643), a respected leader of the parliamentary opposition and later of the Long Parliament, famous for his historic refusal in 1636 to pay the ship money exacted by Charles I. His attempted seizure in 1642 was one of the events that led to the Civil War. He was mortally wounded at Chalgrove Field, near Oxford. His status as a byword for civic resistance owes much to Gray's reference in his *Elegy Written in a Country Church-Yard* to 'some village-Hampden, that with dauntless breast I The little tyrant of his fields withstood'.

HAMPTON, Christopher James (1946–   ), playwright, screenwriter, and translator, who was born in the Azores, and travelled widely with his family as a child: he was educated at Lancing and New College, Oxford, where he read modern languages. His first play *When Did You Last See My Mother?* (1966), written when he was 18, was performed by OUDS (the Oxford University Dramatic Society) and later at the *Royal Court. This was followed by *Total Eclipse* (1968, pub. 1969, based on the tormented relationship of *Verlaine and *Rimbaud). *The Philanthropist* (1970) is an elegant and epigrammatic comedy, which alludes in its title to *Molière's *Le Misanthrope*: it features as hero Philip, a lecturer in philology who suffers from 'compulsive amiability'. *Savages* (1972) is a political and ecological drama set in the Amazon, protesting against genocide and other atrocities in Brazil. *Treats* (1976) is a provoking study of sexual behaviour, responding to the rising tide of feminist orthodoxy; *Tales from Hollywood* (1982) describes the lives of the German literary refugees (including Thomas and Heinrich *Mann and Lion *Feuchtwanger) and their attempts to survive in Hollywood in the 1930s, using the device of a (dead) narrator, the playwright Ödön von Horváth (1901–38), whose *Tales from the Vienna Woods* Hampton had translated from the German for the *National Theatre (1977). *The White Chameleon* (1991) is based on his childhood memories of Egypt at the time of the Suez crisis; *The Talking Cure* (2002), set in 1904–13, documents the relationships of *Freud, *Jung, and patient Sabina Spielrein. Hampton has also made many translations and stage and screen adaptations of works by *Bradbury (see *The History Man*), *Steiner (*The Portage to San Cristobal of A.H.*, 1982), *Conrad, *Greene, and *Ibsen. He adapted *Laclos's *Les Liaisons dangereuses* for both stage (1985) and screen (1989): its great success he attributed to the work having found a new life in the amoral atmosphere of the 1980s. He adapted and directed the film *Carrington* (1995), based on *Holroyd's life of *Strachey, and translated for the stage *Art* (1996) and *The Unexpected Man* (1998) by French dramatist

Yasmina Reza. Most of his original work is marked by an ironic, good-humoured, and humane detachment, though paradoxically he is also strongly drawn to the Modernist experiments and violent visions of Conrad.

Hampton Court Conference, held in 1604 to settle points of dispute between the church party and the Puritans, out of which arose the preparation of the Authorized Version of the Bible. See BIBLE, THE ENGLISH.

HAMSUN, Knut (1859–1952), Norwegian novelist, poet, and dramatist, born Knut Petersen in central Norway. He is best known for his novel *Hunger* (1890), set in Christiania (now Oslo), in which his narrator suffers the state of semi-starvation which Hamsun himself had endured during ten years of hardship and work as a labourer in Norway and the USA; its nervous, hallucinatory quality and abrupt, vivid prose made a considerable impact, and he followed its success with many other works of fiction, including *Mysteries* (1892), *Pan* (1894), *Victoria* (1898), *Under the Autumn Star* (1906), *Wanderer Plays on Muted Strings* (1909), *Growth of the Soil* (1917), and *Wayfarer* (1929). He was awarded the *Nobel Prize for literature in 1920, and continued to write almost to the end of his life, although he alienated many of his followers by his support of Hitler during the Second World War. The influence of his early work was, however, great; I. B. *Singer has stated that 'the whole modern school of fiction in the twentieth century stems from Hamsun' ('Knut Hamsun, Artist of Skepticism', 1967). *Hunger* was originally translated by G. *Egerton (1899).

HANDEL, George Frideric (1685–1759), composer of German birth who settled in London at the age of 27 and became a naturalized Englishman 15 years later. He scored an immediate triumph with *Rinaldo* (1711), which was written to an Italian text in the manner of Italian *opera seria*, a convention with which he never really broke in his work for the secular stage. His earliest setting of English words, a little cantata by John Hughes, dates from the same period. The masque *Acis and Galatea* (1718) was written for performance at Cannons, the seat of Lord Carnarvon. The libretto of *Acis* was by *Gay, and other members of Gay's circle may have had a hand in the masque of *Esther* (?1720), also written for Cannons. A revised version of *Esther* was given in London in 1732, not, as originally intended, by the children of the Chapel Royal, but in concert performance, with professional adult singers. Its success encouraged Handel to produce *Deborah* and *Athalia* in the following year. Thus began the series of 'oratorios or sacred dramas' which were the glory of his later years, and his chief contribution to English music. *Saul* (1739), and immediately after it *Israel in Egypt* (1739), both had texts by the wealthy amateur Charles Jennens, who also provided the composer with the brilliantly constructed anthology from Old and New Testaments which he called *Messiah* (1742). Its successor *Samson* (1743), from *Milton, is a strong dramatic work effective in stage performances. Jennens was librettist for *Belshazzar* (1745), but was then succeeded as Handel's main collaborator by Thomas Morell, who wrote most of the remaining oratorio texts, including *Judas Maccabaeus* (1747) and the masterpieces of Handel's old age, *Theodora* (1750) and *Jephtha* (1752). Of the secular odes and oratorios, *Semele* (1743) is a setting of a *Congreve text originally designed for music and now adapted for Handel by *Pope; *Alexander's Feast* (1736), an adaptation of *Dryden's Cecilian ode, is one of Handel's most successful works, and was followed by *Ode for St Cecilia's Day* (1739), also from Dryden. There is also a setting of *L'Allegro, il Penseroso e il Moderato* (1740–1), in which an adaptation of Milton's two poems is followed by a third section (which Handel later dropped) by Jennens in praise of moderation.

Handful of Dust, A, a novel by E. *Waugh, published 1934.

It describes the infatuation of Lady Brenda Last with an idle, parasitic young man-about-town, John Beaver, which leads her to neglect her 'madly feudal' husband Tony, her son, and her country home of Hetton. When her son is killed in a hunting accident, Brenda leaves Tony, expecting him to grant her a divorce, but after an 'arranged' visit to Brighton to acquire evidence of adultery Tony realizes that he will lose Hetton if he meets Brenda's alimony demands. He departs instead up the Amazon, where he is rescued from the brink of death by the old mad recluse Mr Todd, and consigned to a fate of reading *Dickens aloud forever to his host, who keeps him captive. Hetton passes to cousins and Brenda is remarried, but not to Beaver. The epigraph and title are from *The Waste Land*, and although the novel resembles Waugh's earlier comic works, it has also been seen as a serious comment on the empty morality and shifting values of the 1930s.

Handlyng Synne, by *Mannyng of Brunne, a verse treatise on sin, written in rough octosyllabics in lively narrative and begun in 1303. It is based on the French *Manuel des pechez*, written in the north of England by William of Wadington. It deals with sin under various headings: the Ten Commandments, the Seven Deadly Sins, Sacrilege, and the Sacraments, culminating with Penance. Each sin is illustrated by a story, rather in the manner of *Gower's *Confessio Amantis*, and the value of the work lies in Mannyng's narrative vigour. His most familiar and often anthologized story is 'The Dancers of Colbek' (item one, for example, in Sisam's *Fourteenth Century Verse and Prose*), which tells of some churchyard revellers, including the priest's daughter, who would not stop dancing when the priest bade them do so and whom he cursed, condemning them to dance incessantly for a year. They do this, and at the end of the year the priest's daughter drops dead. There is an edition by F. J. *Furnivall (EETS OS 119 and 123, 1901 and 1903).

Hand of Ethelberta, The, a novel by T. *Hardy, published 1876.

As the author states in his preface, this is 'a somewhat frivolous narrative'. Ethelberta is one of the numerous family of Chickerel, a butler. She marries the son of the house where she is governess, and is soon left a widow at 21. Her spirited efforts to maintain her social position, while concealing her relationship to the butler (and yet helping her brothers and sisters), account for most of the story. She finally secures a wicked old peer for a husband, while her faithful admirer, the musician Christopher Julian, is left to marry her sister Picotee.

HANLEY, James (1901–85), Irish novelist, short story writer, and playwright, born in Dublin but brought up in Liverpool. He went to sea at the age of 14 and his subsequent experiences were often incorporated into his fiction, including *Boy* (1931). He made a name, and gained some notoriety, as an uncompromising realist, though his style could be laboured and diffuse. The lives of the Dublin poor were portrayed in *The Furys* (1935), *Secret Journey* (1936), and *Our Time Is Gone* (1940). His other novels include *Captain Bottell* (1933), *Quartermaster Clausen* (1934), *Hollow Sea* (1938), *The Ocean* (1941), *The Closed Harbour* (1952), and *A Woman in the Sky* (1973). His short stories can be found in *Men in Darkness* (1931), *People Are Curious* (1938), and *A Walk in the Wilderness* (1950). A volume of autobiography, *Broken Water*, was published in 1937.

Hansard, the official reports of the proceedings of the Houses of Parliament, colloquially so called because they were for a long period compiled by Messrs Hansard. Luke Hansard (1752–1828) commenced printing the *Journal of the House of Commons* in 1774. The name disappeared from the title-page of the Reports in 1892, but was restored during the Second World War. The Reports were published by Reuter's Telegram Company in 1892, Eyre & Spottiswoode, 1893–4, and subsequently by a number of other firms in succession; they are now a regular publication of HM Stationery Office.

HANWAY, Mary Ann, see ROMANTIC FICTION.

hapax legomenon (from Greek *apax*, 'on one occasion', and *legomenon*, 'something said'), a piece of text which has only one attested occurrence. Sometimes reduced to 'hapax', the term has been used in English (though very infrequently and only in scholarly contexts) since the 17th cent. The corresponding English term, equally uncommon, is 'nonce usage'.

Harapha, in Milton's *Samson Agonistes*, the giant of Gath who comes to mock the blind Samson in prison. His name is derived from a problematic word occurring in 2 Sam. 21: 16–22.

Hard Cash: *A Matter of Fact Romance*, a *sensation novel by C. *Reade, published 1863 (published in serial form as *Very Hard Cash*). Reade's novel attacks mid-

Victorian Britain's poorly regulated asylum system through two main plot strands. The first concerns Alfred Hardie, wrongfully incarcerated in an insane asylum by his father Richard, in order to conceal a banking fraud. Alfred is terrorized by the mental pathologist Dr Wycherly (an unflattering portrait of the eminent Dr John Conolly), and escapes only when a fellow inmate sets the institution on fire. A second plot involves a genuine case of insanity, David Dodd, a sea-captain ruined by Richard Hardie's scheme. Dodd is also the hero of Reade's *Love Me Little, Love Me Long* (1859). The novel concludes with a request for information relating to the wrongful committal of other sane persons—in response to which Rosina *Bulwer-Lytton wrote her memoir, *A Blighted Life* (1880).

Hardcastle, Squire, Mrs, and Miss, characters in Goldsmith's *She Stoops to Conquer*.

HARDENBERG, Friedrich Leopold von (1772–1801), known as 'Novalis', German Romantic poet and novelist, author of poems religious, mystic, and secular, including *Hymnen an die Nacht* (*Hymns to the Night*, 1800), laments on the death of his young fiancée Sophie von Kuhn, and the unfinished novels *Heinrich von Ofterdingen* (1802) and *Die Lehrlinge zu Sais* (*The Disciples at Sais*, 1802). Novalis was influenced by the idealism of *Fichte, and was the subject of an enthusiastic essay by *Carlyle in the *Foreign Review*, 1829; he had a powerful influence on German poets and artists, on *Leopardi, and on a later generation of English poets, including James *Thomson, who translated his 'Hymns to Night' (pub. 1995, ed. Simon Reynolds). P. *Fitzgerald's novel *The Blue Flower* was based on his life: the title image of 'die blaue Blume', the grail of German Romanticism, is taken from *Heinrich von Ofterdingen*.

Harding, the Revd Septimus, a character in the *'Barsetshire' novels of A. Trollope. He is most prominent in *The Warden* and *Barchester Towers*.

Hard Times, a novel by *Dickens, published 1854.

Thomas Gradgrind, a citizen of Coketown, a northern industrial city (based on impressions of Preston, which Dickens visited in 1854), is a misguided exponent of *utilitarianism, an 'eminently practical man', who believes in facts and statistics and brings up his children Louisa and Tom accordingly, ruthlessly suppressing the imaginative sides of their nature. He marries Louisa to Josiah Bounderby, a manufacturer 30 years older than herself. Louisa consents partly from the indifference and cynicism engendered by her father's treatment, partly from a desire to help her brother, who is employed by Bounderby and who is the only person she loves. James Harthouse, a young politician without heart or principles, comes to Coketown and, taking advantage of her unhappy life with Bounderby, attempts to seduce her. The better side of her nature is awakened at this experience, and at the crisis she flees for protection to her father, who in turn

is awakened to the folly of his system. He shelters her from Bounderby and the couple are permanently separated. But further trouble is in store for Gradgrind. Tom has robbed the bank of his employer, and though he contrives for a time to throw suspicion on a blameless artisan, Stephen Blackpool, he is finally detected and hustled out of the country. Among the notable minor characters are Sleary, the proprietor of a circus, and Cissy Jupe, whose father had been a performer in his troupe, whose generous hearts are contrasted with the harshness of Gradgrind's regime; also Mrs Sparsit, Bounderby's venomous and intriguing housekeeper.

Condemned by *Macaulay for its 'sullen socialism', the novel was not in its day greatly popular, but gained a considerable reputation in this century partly through the admiration of G. B. *Shaw (who published a preface, 1912) and *Leavis (*The Great Tradition*, 1947), who saw Dickens in this work 'for once possessed by a comprehensive vision'.

HARDY, Thomas (1840–1928), born at Higher Bockhampton, near Dorchester in Dorset, son of a stonemason, whose family had known better days. His father taught Hardy the violin and his mother greatly encouraged his early interest in books. He attended school in Dorchester and at 16 was articled to John Hicks, a local architect. At the age of 22 he went to London, where he worked for the architect Arthur Blomfield, pursued a hectic London life, and also found time for extensive reading. During this time he lost the religious faith which had once led him to consider taking holy orders. He returned home in 1867 to continue architectural work in Dorchester, and began his first (unpublished) novel, *The Poor Man and the Lady*. At this time he probably fell in love with Tryphena Sparks, a girl of 16 who was regarded as his cousin but may have been his niece. The history of his relationship with her, and of her relationship with Hardy's great friend Horace Moule, continues to be the subject of considerable speculation. In 1868 he was sent on an architectural mission to St Juliot, Cornwall, where he met the rector's sister-in-law, Emma Gifford. His first published novel, *Desperate Remedies*, appeared in 1871, to be followed by *Under the Greenwood Tree* (1872), *A Pair of Blue Eyes* (1873), and *Far from the Madding Crowd* (1874). The success of the last enabled him, in 1874, to give up architecture for writing, and to marry Emma Gifford. The marriage soon produced intolerable strains, but it also produced, after Emma's death in 1912, some of Hardy's most moving poems. Between 1874 and the publication of *Jude the Obscure* in 1895 Hardy wrote 12 other novels (see below), as well as many short stories and poems. He and his wife travelled in Europe and Hardy spent several months of nearly every year in London. In 1885 they moved into Max Gate, near Dorchester, a forbidding house, now shrouded by trees and shrubberies, to Hardy's own design. During this time Hardy became both famous and infamous. He greatly enjoyed the admiration of London's literary and aristocratic society; what he did not enjoy was the constant carping of reviewers on his 'pessimism' and 'immorality', culminating in the bitterly hostile reception of *Tess of the D'Urbervilles in 1891 and Jude the Obscure in 1895. He gave up the writing of fiction (which he had always regarded as inferior to poetry) and began to assemble his first volume of verse, Wessex Poems (1898). His successive collections, ending with Winter Words in 1928, were received without enthusiasm, except by a discerning few. In 1912 Emma died and in 1914 Hardy married Florence Dugdale. She, together with the terrier Wessex, did much to protect Hardy from the adulation of his admirers. Public honours fell upon him, among them the OM, honorary degrees from Cambridge and Oxford, a visit from the prince of Wales, the gold medal of the *Royal Society of Literature. Among the pall-bearers at his funeral in Westminster Abbey were *Barrie, *Galsworthy, *Gosse, A. E. *Housman, *Kipling, and G. B. *Shaw.

The underlying theme of many of the novels, the short poems, and the epic drama *The Dynasts is, in *Binyon's words, 'the implanted crookedness of things'; the struggle of man against the indifferent force that rules the world and inflicts on him the sufferings and ironies of life and love. Hardy's sharp sense of the humorous and absurd finds expression largely in the affectionate presentation of the rustic characters in the novels. Most of the poems and novels reveal Hardy's love and observation of the natural world, often with strong symbolic effect.

Hardy's novels and short stories, according to his own classification, fall into three groups; most of them are described separately under their titles:

Novels of Character and Environment: Under the Greenwood Tree (1872); Far from the Madding Crowd (1874); *The Return of the Native (1878); *The Mayor of Casterbridge (1886); *The Woodlanders (1887); Wessex Tales (1888); Tess of the D'Urbervilles (1891); Life's Little Ironies (1894); Jude the Obscure (1896, in the edition of the Works of that year).

Romances and Fantasies: A Pair of Blue Eyes (1873); *The Trumpet Major (1880); *Two on a Tower (1882); A Group of Noble Dames (1891); *The Well-Beloved (published serially 1892, revised and reissued 1897).

Novels of Ingenuity: Desperate Remedies (1891); *The Hand of Ethelberta (1876); A Laodicean (1881).

A Changed Man, The Waiting Supper, and Other Tales (1913) is a reprint of 'a dozen minor novels' belonging to the various groups.

Hardy published eight volumes of poetry: Wessex Poems (1898); Poems of the Past and Present (1902); Time's Laughingstocks (1909); Satires of Circumstance (1914); Moments of Vision (1917); Late Lyrics and Earlier (1922); Human Shows (1925); Winter Words (1928). The Collected Poems (1930), published posthumously, contain over 900 poems of great variety and individuality, yet consistent over more than 60 years in their attitudes to life and fate. Probably the most remarkable are in the group of poems written in recollection of his first wife ('Poems of 1912–13' in Satires of Circumstance). Hardy followed *Wordsworth and R. *Browning in his endeavour to write in a language close to that of speech, and he abhorred, to use his own words, 'the jewelled line'. He experimented constantly with rhythms and stresses and verse forms, disliking and avoiding any facile flow. Gosse, *Blunden, and *Strachey were of the small band who greatly admired his poetry, but not until long after his death did it begin to receive general critical acclaim.

He published over 40 short stories, most of which were collected in Wessex Tales (1888); A Group of Noble Dames (1891); Life's Little Ironies (1894); and A Changed Man . . . (1913). The stories vary considerably in content, form, and style, and in many cases demonstrate a high degree of skill, but Hardy's reputation in this field has never approached his reputation as a novelist or poet.

The Dynasts, a vast work in blank verse and prose, occupied him for many years, and was published in three volumes, 1904, 1906, and 1908. He wrote one other poetic drama, The Famous Tragedy of the *Queen of Cornwall (1923).

Hardy continues to attract a great deal of biographical and critical attention: recent works include a critical biography by J. I. M. *Stewart (1971); a two-volume life by R. *Gittings (Young Thomas Hardy, 1975; The Older Hardy, 1980); An Essay on Thomas Hardy (1978) by J. Bayley; and Thomas Hardy (1982) by M. Millgate.

HARDYNG, John (1378–c.1465), author of The Chronicle of John Hardyng in verse which was written between the years 1440 and 1457. The Chronicle covers the period from Brutus (see BRUT) to 1437 and argues the claims of English kings (in the interests of Henry V and Henry VI) to overlordship of Scotland. A second version revises the work in the Yorkist interest, expunging the earlier eulogy of Henry V and declaring Henry VI to be 'of small intelligence'; this is perhaps the (dubious) authority for that prevailing view of him. It was edited by H. Ellis (1812, repr. New York, 1974); see A. Gransden, Historical Writing in England II (1982), 274 ff.

HARE, Sir David (1947–), dramatist and director, born in Bexhill. After some time in fringe theatre, during which he co-founded (with Tony Bicat) the Portable Theatre Company, he succeeded Christopher *Hampton as resident dramatist at the *Royal Court Theatre in London in 1970–1, moving to a residence at the Nottingham Playhouse in 1973. Slag (1970), The Great Exhibition (1972), and Knuckle (1974) marked him out as a powerful and original talent with a keen eye for both the iniquities of social privilege and the contradictions of radical idealism. Class antagonism at Cambridge, when a rock band plays at a May Ball at Jesus College, was the subject of Teeth n' Smiles (1976), first produced at the Royal Court in September 1975 with Helen Mirren in the role of Maggie, the band's singer. In *Plenty* (1978), produced at the *National Theatre, Hare provides a metaphor of the economic and ideological decline of post-war Britain through the experiences of Susan Traherne, a former courier in occupied France who seeks in vain for an outlet for her wartime idealism. *Pravda* (1985, rev. 1986), a political satire concerning two national newspapers, was co-written with Howard Brenton, with whom he had previously collaborated on *Brassneck* (1973) and *England's Ireland* (1972). His acclaimed trilogy of plays on British institutions began with *Racing Demon* (1990), about four south London clergymen trying to make sense of their vocations at a time of crisis for the Church of England. This was followed by *Murmuring Judges* (1991), a critique of the British criminal justice system, and *The Absence of War* (1993), about the Labour Party. *Amy's View* (1997) contrasts the values of an ageing actress with those of her daughter's partner, who represents the media. *The Permanent Way* (2003) documents the troubled privatization of British Rail; *Stuff Happens* (2005) takes its title from a remark by US Secretary of Defense Donald Rumsfeld, and dramatizes issues surrounding the invasion of Iraq in 2003.

HARE, Julius Charles (1795–1855), educated at Trinity College, Cambridge. He was elected fellow in 1818 and became an intimate companion of *Whewell. He was ordained in 1826 and in 1832 appointed rector of Herstmonceaux. Through travel in Germany he became influenced by German scholars and theologians. He was author, with his brother Augustus William Hare (1792–1834, biographer and compiler of travel books), of the popular *Guesses at Truth* (1827), a collection of observations on philosophy, religion, literature, language, and related subjects. He translated with *Thirlwall *Niebuhr's *History of Rome* (1828–42), which was vehemently attacked for its scepticism in the *Quarterly Review*, prompting the translators to publish a *Vindication of Niebuhr's History* (1829). Also with Thirlwall he was joint editor of the *Philological Museum* (1832–3), which made some effort to introduce the much neglected new continental philology of *Grimm. He edited *Sterling's *Essays and Tales* (1848) with a memoir which treated Sterling chiefly as a cleric who deserted his vocation; *Carlyle replied with his *Life of John Sterling* (1851).

Haredale, Geoffrey and Emma, characters in Dickens's *Barnaby Rudge*.

HARINGTON, James, see HARRINGTON.

HARINGTON, Sir John (1560–1612), godson of Queen *Elizabeth I, educated at Eton and King's College, Cambridge. Supposedly at the command of the queen, he translated Ariosto's *Orlando furioso* (1591), retaining the *ottava rima* of the original and providing A *Preface or rather Briefe Apologie of Poetrie*, closely modelled on Sidney's *Defence of Poetry*, and interesting, often gossipy notes referring to such stray figures as his own pet dog Bungy, who is also depicted on the title-page. Though *Jonson claimed 'that John Haringtones *Ariosto*, under all translations was the worst', it has been read and enjoyed by many generations of readers including, in modern times, A. *Powell. Harington's next work, *A New Discourse of a Stale Subject, Called the Metamorphosis of Ajax* (1596) (a proposal for the introduction of water closets), was an ill-judged bid for royal favour; together with other satires and epigrams it led to a period of exile from court. In 1599 Harington accompanied *Essex to Ireland, and was deputed by him to appease the queen's anger on his return, without success. His letters and miscellaneous writings were collected in Henry Harington's *Nugae Antiquae* (1769–75); N. E. McClure edited his letters and epigrams (1930); Robert McNulty edited the *Orlando furioso* (1972); E. S. Donno *The Metamorphosis of Ajax* (1962); and S. Cauchi the translation of *Virgil's *Aeneid Bk VI* (1991). The lasting interest of Harington's writings lies in his lively personality and ability to record detailed impressions of his world. He gives, for instance, an account of a visit to the queen a few weeks before her death, in which she said to him, 'When thou doste feele creepinge tyme at thye gate, these fooleries will please thee lesse.'

HARLAND, Henry (1861–1905), American author who wrote several novels about Jewish immigrant life under the pseudonym of Sidney Luska. In 1889 he moved to Paris, and in 1890 to London, where he became editor of the *Yellow Book*. He published several romances during his London period, including the popular *The Cardinal's Snuff-Box* (1900).

Harleian Manuscripts, the, a collection of manuscripts made by R. *Harley, first earl of Oxford, and augmented by his son Edward, the second earl (1689–1741). It consisted of some 50,000 books, 350,000 pamphlets, and over 7,000 volumes of manuscripts, including early biblical texts in Greek, Latin, and Hebrew, texts of classical authors and church Fathers, papal bulls and registers, deeds, charters, state papers, etc. The manuscripts were bought by Parliament in 1753 after Edward's death and placed in the British Museum: they are now in the British Library. The Harleian Society was founded in 1869 for the publication of heraldic visitations, pedigrees, etc.

Harleian Miscellany, The, a reprint of a selection of tracts from the *Harleian manuscripts, edited by *Oldys and Dr *Johnson, published 1744–6 by T. *Osborne.

Harleth, Gwendolen, the heroine of G. Eliot's *Daniel Deronda*.

Harley, (1) the principal character in *The Man of Feeling* by H. Mackenzie; (2) Adrian Harley, in Meredith's *The Ordeal of Richard Feverel*, the cynical 'wise youth' and tutor of Richard, drawn from Meredith's friend Maurice Fitz-Gerald.

HARLEY, Robert, first earl of Oxford (1661–1724), Tory statesman and bibliophile. He frequented the *Scriblerus Club, and several verse invitations to him composed by *Pope, *Swift, and others survive. He acquired a great library of books and manuscripts, which his son inherited: see HARLEIAN MANUSCRIPTS.

Harley Lyrics, a collection of 32 Middle English lyrics occurring with other material in the manuscript Harley 2253, from the west Midlands (though the poems are thought to be originally from various parts of the country) dated c.1340. W. P. Ker says the manuscript contains 'everything best worth remembering in the old lyrical poetry' and, although we might add other individual poems, his high assessment of them finds general assent. Among the most celebrated poems in the collection are 'Alysoun', 'Lenten ys come with love to toune', 'Blow, Northerne Wynd', 'Wynter wakeneth al my care', and 'The Man in the Moon'. In spite of their liveliness the poems are highly sophisticated in themes, diction, and literary forms. They have been edited by G. L. Brook (1956).

Harlot's Progress, The, see HOGARTH, W.

Harlowe, Clarissa, see CLARISSA.

Harmon, John, alias John Rokesmith, alias Julius Handford, the hero of Dickens's *Our Mutual Friend.

HARMSWORTH, Alfred Charles William, first Viscount Northcliffe (1865–1922), born in Dublin, the eldest of five brothers who were distinguished as newspaper magnates and politicians. He was largely self-educated, rejecting Cambridge and the bar for journalism, and in 1887 formed, with his brother Harold, a publishing business which issued a growing number of periodicals including the popular *Answers* (1888), which laid the foundations of his career. In 1894 the brothers acquired the *Evening News* and in 1896 Alfred started the *Daily Mail*, which changed the course of English journalism. In 1903 he added to his empire the *Daily Mirror*, the first newspaper devoted exclusively to women's interests, and in 1908 he became chief proprietor of *The Times. In 1917 Lloyd George appointed him to lead a war mission to the USA and in 1918 he directed British propaganda in enemy countries. He was created baronet in 1903, baron in 1905, and viscount in 1917.

HAROUN-al-RASCHID, see HĀRŪN AL-RASHĪD.

Harper's Monthly Magazine, founded in 1850 by Messrs Harper & Brothers of New York, originally for the avowed purpose of reproducing in America the work of distinguished English contributors to magazines (including *Dickens, *Thackeray, and *Bulwer-Lytton). It subsequently became more American in character, publishing work by *Melville, *Howells, S. O. *Jewett, and many others. From 1900 to 1925 it was known as *Harper's New Monthly Magazine*, and subsequently as *Harper's Magazine*.

Harper's Weekly (1857–1916), an illustrated political and literary journal, published in New York, best known for its engravings and woodcuts. It also serialized novels by *Dickens, Mrs *Gaskell, and others, and later published work by *Kipling, H. *James, A. C. *Doyle, etc.

HARPSFIELD, Nicholas (c.1519–75), educated at Winchester and New College, Oxford. A lawyer by training, he attached himself to Cardinal Pole, but was imprisoned in the Fleet, 1562–74. As well as controversial works and a history of the English Church, he wrote (c.1557) an important life of Sir T. *More, first published in full in 1932.

Harriet Smith, a character in J. Austen's *Emma.

HARRINGTON, or **HARINGTON,** James (1611–77), born in Northampton of an ancient family, and educated at Trinity College, Oxford, where he took no degree; he subsequently travelled on the Continent, and attended the court of the elector palatine. During the Civil War he attended Charles I in his captivity (1647–8), and a tradition (through *Aubrey and *Wood) was established that his deep personal devotion to the monarch plunged him into years of profound melancholy on his execution; some have seen this as one of the impulses behind his great republican work *The Commonwealth of Oceana* (1656). Harrington also wrote several tracts in defence of this work, and other political works (*The Prerogative of Popular Government*, 1657–8; *The Art of Law-Giving*, 1659; *Aphorisms Political*, 1659) in all of which he expounds his concept of a republic or commonwealth, advocates the ballot, rotation of officers, indirect elections, etc. In 1659 he founded the Rota, a *coffee-house academy which met for political discussion, and the first of its kind in England. In 1661 he was arrested and imprisoned on a charge of treason, defended himself ably, and was later released, but by this time his health was in decline, and little is known of the remaining years of his life. Harrington has never been considered a great stylist (*Hume described his prose as 'altogether stiff and pedantic') but he had many admirers, including *Wordsworth and *Coleridge, and his shrewd historical analysis and political projections have increasingly attracted attention. See *The Political Works of James Harrington* ed. J. G. A. Pocock (1977).

HARRINGTON, Sir John, see HARINGTON.

HARRIOT, or **HARIOT,** Thomas (1560/61–1621), mathematician and astronomer. He was taken into the household of *Ralegh, c.1580, as mathematical tutor, and in 1585 went on Ralegh's expedition to Virginia, where he stayed for a year. His *A Briefe and True Report of the New Found Land of Virginia*, one of the earliest examples of a large-scale economic and statistical survey, was published in 1588 and printed by *Hakluyt. From 1591 he lived at Syon House in Isleworth as part of the household of Henry Percy, earl of North-umberland. He corresponded with Kepler and is thought to have influenced *Descartes. His name was popularly associated with atheism and necro-mancy; the judge at Ralegh's trial in 1603 referred to him as 'that devil Harriot' and *Kyd, while himself attempting to evade an accusation of atheism, claimed that *Marlowe had been one of his intimates. He was thought by some to have been the leading spirit of the so-called *'School of Night', but appears to have been a faithful believer.

HARRIS, Benjamin, see CHILDREN'S LITERATURE.

HARRIS, Frank (really James Thomas) (1856–1931). Born in Galway, he went to America at the age of 14, then travelled on the Continent before settling in London, where he soon made his mark in the literary world. He edited the *Evening News* (1882–6), the *Fortnightly Review* (1886–94), and, most significantly, the *Saturday Review* (1894–8), in which he published, among others, G. B. *Shaw (as dramatic critic), H. G. *Wells, and *Beerbohm, all of whom left vivid recol-lections of him. As an editor he had great flair, though his extrovert arrogance made him as many enemies as friends; Wells described him as 'too loud and vain . . . to be a proper scoundrel', but a scandalous reputation gathered round him, occasioned by his fight against Victorian prudery, by his decreasingly respectable role as editor (of such periodicals as the *Candid Friend, Vanity Fair*, and *Hearth and Home*), by his champion-ship of Germany while in America during the First World War, and by his sexually boastful, explicit (and unreliable) memoirs, *My Life and Loves* (4 vols, 1922–7). His other publications include volumes of short stories, a novel (*The Bomb*, 1908, set in Chicago), two plays, one of them (*Mr and Mrs Daventry*, 1900; pub. 1956) based on a scenario by his friend *Wilde, and lives of Shakespeare, Wilde (1916), and Shaw (1931). He advertised himself with characteristic bravado as the greatest Shakespearian of his day, and his *The Man Shakespeare and His Tragic Life-story* (1909), though derided by scholars, had a considerable impact; like his other biographies, it reveals more about its author than its subject. Harris remains an enigmatic and contro-versial figure, whose personality continues to attract attention and whose real achievements tend to be obscured by his persistent and self-destructive self-aggrandizement. There is a lively biography by his one-time admirer and employee *Kingsmill, published 1932. See also Philippa Pullar, *Frank Harris* (1975).

HARRIS, Joel Chandler (1848–1908), American author, born at Eatonton, Georgia, and devoted from child-hood to English literature. To this taste he added an extraordinary knowledge of black American myth and custom and of black dialect and idiom, which he reproduced in his famous 'Uncle Remus' series. These contain a great number of folklore tales, relating to a variety of animals, with the rabbit as hero and the fox

next in importance, told by a 'Negro' to a little boy and interspersed with comments on many other subjects. The principal volumes of this series were *Uncle Remus, His Songs and Sayings* (1881), *Uncle Remus and His Friends* (1892), *Mr. Rabbit at Home* (1895), *The Tar-Baby* (1904), *Told by Uncle Remus* (1905), *Uncle Remus and Brer Rabbit* (1906), *Uncle Remus and the Little Boy* (1910). See also CULTURAL APPROPRIATION.

HARRIS, John (1820–84), Cornish poet and miner, born at Bollenowe, near Camborne, who published several volumes of poetry celebrating his native landscapes, including *Lays from the Mine, the Moor and the Mountains* (1853) and *A Story of Carn Brea* (1863). *Songs from the Earth*, a selection (1977), has an introduction by D. M. *Thomas which praises his 'Romantic visionary quality which breathes life into an Augustan vocabulary'.

HARRIS, John, see CHILDREN'S LITERATURE.

HARRIS, (Theodore) Wilson (1921–), Guyanese-born novelist, educated at Queen's College, George-town, British Guiana, where he qualified and subse-quently worked as a land surveyor before coming to England in 1959. His 'Guyana Quartet' consists of *Palace of the Peacock* (1960), *The Far Journey of Oudin* (1961), *The Whole Armour* (1962), and *The Secret Ladder* (1963), and his later works include *The Waiting Room* (1967), *The Age of the Rainmakers* (1971), and *The Tree of the Sun* (1978). His fiction is experimental in form, built on a complex, poetic structure, interweav-ing history, mythology, and the contemporary world. *The Infinite Rehearsal* (1987) is a 'fictional autobio-graphy'. (See POST COLONIAL LITERATURE.)

HARRISON, Carey (1944–), British novelist, born in London, the son of actors Rex Harrison and Lilli Palmer. A writer of numerous radio and television plays, he turned to the novel in 1984 with *Freud*, an adaptation of his own six-part television biography. Since then he has published the ambitious, sprawling *Richard's Feet* (1990, winner of the Encore Award), *Cley* (1991), and *Egon* (1993): three parts of a massive tetralogy which proposes to examine European post-war history on a scale and with a narrative complexity almost without comparison in recent British fiction.

HARRISON, Frederic (1831–1923), educated at King's College School, London, and Wadham College, Oxford, professor of jurisprudence and international law to the Inns of Court (1877–89), and from 1880 to 1905 president of the English Positivist Committee, formed to disseminate the doctrines of *Comte. He was the author of many works on historical, political, and literary subjects, and attracted the censure of M. Arnold in *Culture and Anarchy* for his challenging remarks on culture: 'The man of culture is in politics one of the poorest mortals alive. For simple pedantry and want of good sense no man is his equal . . .', a view which roused Arnold to his own defence of the meaning of culture.

HARRISON, G(eorge) B(agshawe) (1894–1991), author of a wide range of scholarly publications on Shakespeare and his world. His *Elizabethan* and *Jacobean Journals* (1938 and 1941/58) gather up in chronological sequence much primary material from the years 1591–1610. He was general editor of the Penguin Shakespeare (1937–59), producing extremely useful old-spelling texts. With *Granville-Barker he edited *A Companion to Shakespeare Studies* (1934).

HARRISON, Tony (1937–   ), poet and translator, born in Leeds, and educated at Leeds Grammar School and Leeds University; memories of his working-class childhood and family life provide the material for much of his poetry, although he has travelled widely and his works also reflect experiences of Africa, the Soviet Union, and America. His volumes include *The Loiners* (1970), *From 'The School of Eloquence' and Other Poems* (1978), and *Continuous* (1981), and he has also written theatrically effective verse translations of *Molière's *The Misanthrope* (1973), *Racine's *Phèdre* (*Phaedra Britannica*, 1975), and the *Oresteia* (1981). Both his original works and his translations show a great facility in rhyme and a skilful adaptation of colloquial speech. Other volumes include *V* (1985, broadcast on television in 1987), written during the miners' strike of 1984–5, *Loving Memory* (1987), *The Blasphemers' Banquet* (1989), *Selected Poems* (1984; rev. 1987), *V and Other Poems* (1990, containing some previously uncollected work), *A Cold Coming: Gulf War Poems* (1992), and *The Gaze of the Gorgon* (1992), which won the Whitbread Award for poetry. Harrison is renowned for his independent voice and impassioned commentary on public affairs.

HARRISON, William (1535–93), born in London and educated at St Paul's and Westminster schools and Christ Church, Oxford, rector of Radwinter and canon of Windsor. He was the author of the admirable *Description of England* and translator of *Bellenden's Scottish version of *Boece's *Description of Scotland*, both included in the *Chronicles of *Holinshed.

Harrowing of Hell, a semi-dramatic poem of 250 lines in octosyllabic couplets from about 1250, based on the legend (very popular in the Middle Ages) that Christ descended into hell to lead out the souls of the just condemned there by the closing of the gates of heaven by Adam's sin. The legend derives from the account in the Apocryphal Gospel of Nicodemus (2nd–3rd cents AD). There are also versions in Old and Middle English prose and in *Piers Plowman*, as well as recurrent appearances as one of the most popular scenarios in the *mystery plays. In the poem a narrative introduction is followed by speeches assigned to Christ, Satan, the doorkeeper of hell, and some of the souls in Hell: Adam, Eve, Abraham, David, John, and Moses. Christ reproves Satan and claims Adam; Satan replies that he

will win one of mankind on earth for every soul released. But Christ breaks down the door, binds Satan, and frees his servants. See W. H. Hulme (ed.), *The Middle English Harrowing of Hell and Gospel of Nicodemus* (EETS ES 100, 1907); A. W. Pollard, *English Miracle Plays* (1927, 8th edn).

Harry Richmond, *The Adventures of*, a novel by G. *Meredith, published 1871.

This began as 'an autobiographical study', and the early part of the book describes his schooldays near Petersfield in some detail. More deeply autobiographical, however, is the father–son relationship portrayed (which may also reflect on Meredith's relationship with his own son Arthur). Richmond Roy, the father of Harry, is the son of an actress and a mysterious royal personage. Although a flamboyant and romantic figure, he is in fact only an indigent teacher of singing, once employed by Squire Beltham of Riversley, one of whose daughters he carried off and married. She shortly dies, and young Harry, their son, is dramatically captured by his father from his grandfather's house. At this point the narrative adroitly switches to the first person, and the rest of the story is related by Harry. The conflict between his father and grandfather, and his father's obsessive determination to marry him well, are important themes in the book. Harry loves his tempestuous father, but as he matures he realizes that he must escape the 'dreadful devotion' of his parent. Richmond Roy lives a life of splendour in the courts of petty German princes, interrupted by periods in a debtors' prison. At one of these courts Harry and the beautiful Princess Ottilia fall in love; the determined and outrageous manœuvres of Harry's father to settle the unlikely match, and the many humiliations to which Harry is exposed, are related with much comic-grotesque detail. Harry also encounters the fascinating gypsy Kioni in one of the novel's many picaresque and implausible sub-plots, but in the end marries an English girl, Janet Ilchester, whom his grandfather had long wished to see as Harry's wife. Roy dies melodramatically in the last chapter, perishing in the flames of Riversley Grange while seeking to save Harry's ever-loyal Aunt Dorothy.

HART-DAVIS, Sir Rupert (1907–99), publisher and author, educated at Eton and Balliol College, Oxford, and founder of the publishing house of Rupert Hart-Davis Ltd in 1946. His works include a life of Hugh *Walpole (1952), and he also edited several volumes (*The Letters of Oscar Wilde*, 1962; *The Autobiography of Arthur Ransome*, 1976). He became widely known for his correspondence with his one-time schoolmaster George Lyttelton (1863–1962), begun in 1955, and published in six volumes 1978–84, which are full of literary and social gossip and anecdote, sometimes indulgent, sometimes malicious.

HARTE, (Francis) Bret (1836–1902), born at Albany, New York, and taken to California at 18, where he saw something of mining life. He worked on various newspapers and periodicals in San Francisco, to which he contributed some excellent writing including the short stories which made him famous. Notable among these were 'The Luck of Roaring Camp' (1868), and 'Tennessee's Partner' and 'The Outcasts of Poker Flat', which were included in *The Luck of Roaring Camp and Other Sketches* (1870). His humorous–pathetic verse includes 'Plain Language from Truthful James' (1870), often referred to as 'The Heathen Chinee'. Bret Harte was American consul at Crefeld in Germany (1878–80) and at Glasgow (1880–5), after which he lived in England, where his repetitive and inferior later work was more readily accepted by literary editors than in his own country, where his popularity had declined.

Harthouse, James, a character in Dickens's *Hard Times*.

HARTLEY, David (1705–57), educated at Bradford Grammar School and Jesus College, Cambridge. He practised as a physician. In his *Observations on Man, His Frame, His Duty and His Expectations*, published 1749, he repudiated the view of *Shaftesbury and *Hutcheson that the 'moral sense' is instinctively innate in us, and attributed it to the association of ideas, i.e. the tendency of ideas which have occurred together, or in immediate succession, to recall one another. From this association of the ideas of pain and pleasure with certain actions, he traces the evolution of the higher pleasures out of the lower, until the mind is carried to 'the pure love of God, as our highest and ultimate perfection'. With this psychological doctrine he combined a physical theory of 'vibrations' or 'vibratiuncles' in the 'medullary substance' of the brain. This mechanistic theory of the processes of the imagination was popularized by Joseph *Priestley in *Lectures on Oratory and Criticism* and influenced the development of critical theory up to the time of *Coleridge. It replaced the psychology of 'animal spirits' and 'traces' found in Cartesian philosophers and in *Mandeville and *Hume. Coleridge named his first son Hartley in honour of the philosopher, and many of his poems (e.g. 'The Nightingale' and *'Frost at Midnight') show that he took the theory of association in a touchingly literal sense; indeed, it considerably influenced the Romantic view of man's relationship with the natural world. (See ROMANTICISM.)

HARTLEY, L(eslie) P(oles) (1895–1972), novelist. He was the son of a solicitor who became the director of a brickworks, and he spent his childhood at the family home, Fletton Towers, near Peterborough. He was educated at Harrow and Balliol College, Oxford. He began his literary career as a writer of short stories and as a fiction reviewer; his stories were published as *Night Fears* (1924) and *The Killing Bottle* (1932); *Simonetta Perkins*, a novella set in Venice (where Hartley spent much of his time) describing a young

Bostonian's adventure with a gondolier, appeared in 1925. His first full-length novel, *The Shrimp and the Anemone* (1944), was followed by *The Sixth Heaven* (1946) and *Eustace and Hilda* (1947), the last being the title by which the trilogy is known: the first volume is a powerfully evocative account of a childhood summer by the sea in Norfolk, at the end of which Eustace unexpectedly inherits a small fortune, and the two subsequent volumes take him through fashionable Oxford undergraduate life to Venice and the Continent, as he struggles with his complex, intense relationship with his elder sister Hilda. Hartley's best-known novel is *The Go-Between* (1953), narrated in the first person by an elderly man recalling in 1952 the events of the hot summer of 1900, when, staying with a schoolfriend in a Norfolk country house for the holidays, he innocently carried letters between the friend's sister and the local farmer with whom she was having an affair. As the story progresses, it becomes clear that this distant holiday has marked him for life. The portrayal of leisurely Edwardian England, with its cricket matches, bathing parties, and lurking social embarrassments, is masterly. Hartley's other novels include *A Perfect Woman* (1955); *The Hireling* (1957), which takes up the recurrent theme of dangerous inter-class sexual relationships in its story of the widowed Lady Franklin and her friendship with her driver; *The Brickfield* (1964); and *The Love-Adept* (1969).

HARTLIB, Samuel (d. 1662), born in Prussia and educated in Silesia; he studied at Cambridge from 1621 to 1626, and settled in England in 1628. In 1637 he made contact with *Comenius whom he published. He was a promoter of useful inventions, interested in science and educational reform, a patron of Robert *Boyle, and a friend of *Milton, who addressed his *Of Education* (1644) to him. His *A Description of the Famous Kingdom of Macaria* (1641) is a utopian vision of a reformed society. His vast archive, now in Sheffield University, was published on CD-ROM in 1995.

HĀRŪN-al-RASHĪD, or **HAROUN-** (d. 809), Abbasid caliph of Baghdad, whose powerful rule extended from India to Africa. He entertained friendly relations with *Charlemagne, who was almost his exact contemporary. He figures in many of the tales of the *Arabian Nights*, together with Jaffar (or Ja'afar), his vizier.

HARVEY, Gabriel (c.1550–1631), son of a Saffron Walden rope-maker, educated at Christ's College, Cambridge. Elected a fellow of Pembroke Hall, he became the friend of *Spenser and was probably his tutor. The poet remembered him in his sonnet 'Harvey, the happy above happiest men'. He benefited from the patronage of Sir Thomas Smith, whom he commemorated in a series of Latin elegies *Smithus* (1578), which may have influenced the form of Spenser's 'Teares of the Muses'. After a brilliant but troubled academic career, mainly concerned with rhetoric, Ramism (see RAMUS), civil law, and Latin poetry, he turned his interests towards the court and the vernacular. In his exchange of *Letters* with Spenser (1580) he sensibly indicated the difficulties and limitations of writing English verse in classical metres, but also delivered his famous judgement of *The Faerie Queene*, as it then existed, as 'Hobgoblin runne away with the Garland from Apollo'. He was in trouble with the university and the government for these *Letters*, which included satirical verses on the earl of *Oxford, but was protected by the earl of *Leicester, for whom he worked for a time. His attack on the dying *Greene in *Foure Letters* (1592) provoked *Nashe's stinging replies which Harvey's *Pierces Supererogation* (1593) did not mitigate. With his old-fashioned humanist values and often awkward prose style Harvey came off worse in the controversy, and spent the last 30 years of his life in retirement at Saffron Walden, probably practising medicine.

Harvey's extraordinarily wide range of interests is reflected in the marginalia beautifully written in the books he owned. Many of these survive and record penetrating comments and notes on rhetoric, mathematics and navigation, astrology, medicine, his contemporaries, and literature, including references to Shakespeare and his friends *Sidney and Spenser. His English works were edited by A. B. *Grosart in 1884–5 and there is a life and an account of his library by V. F. Stern (1979).

HARVEY, Sir (Henry) Paul (1869–1948), scholar and diplomat, educated at Rugby and New College, Oxford. He was orphaned at an early age, and the first stages of his distinguished career were watched over with interest by H. *James and Lady *Gregory, both friends who had known him since boyhood. He was the compiler of *The Oxford Companion to English Literature* (1932), the first of the Oxford *Companions*, the idea for which originated in a suggestion from Kenneth Sisam at the *Oxford University Press in 1927–8. It was conceived as a reference book on the lines of *Brewer's *Dictionary of Phrase and Fable*, to contain English authors, plots of their works, and characters; foreign authors commonly quoted; legendary characters; a little classical background; and allusions, such as 'The Wise Men of Gotham'. Somewhat to Harvey's dismay, the project grew to include literary terms, periodicals, social clubs, etc., and the pressure of work obliged him to concede that he could not on the average deal with more than three five-act plays a day 'and to do this is a burden; the shorter the article, the greater the labour of condensation'. The result of his labours was a much-loved and idiosyncratic volume, with a very wide range of reference and some masterly plot summaries, which went through four editions. After his death, the volume was updated by Dorothy Eagle. Harvey went on to compile the *Oxford Companions* to *Classical Literature* (1937) and *French Literature*, completed by Janet E. Heseltine (1959).

HARVEY, William (1578–1657), the eldest son in a large family from Folkestone, which enjoyed ever-growing prosperity owing to involvement in Levant trade. Educated at King's School, Canterbury, and Caius College, Cambridge, he obtained his MD at Padua, then at the height of its reputation as a centre for medical research. He practised in London, became influential in the College of Physicians, and acted as physician to James I and Charles I. His career and researches were completely disrupted by the Civil War; when the court moved to Oxford the king presented him with the wardenship of Merton College; but he was compelled to retire to London under the Commonwealth.

Harvey's discovery of the circulation of blood was announced in *De Motu Cordis* (1628; English trans. 1653). He then worked on a major embryological treatise which was left incomplete, but a fragment, *De Generatione* (1651; trans. 1653), was published by his disciple George Ent. Despite its innovatory nature, Harvey's work was rapidly accepted by the medical establishment. Harvey drew on circle symbolism, and metaphysical poets such as H. *Vaughan and Henry More made use of the imagery of Harveian circulation. Harvey's work was also actively exploited by his fellow physician Sir T. *Browne. Harvey, like the *Cambridge Platonists, resisted trends towards mechanization of the world-view.

HARVEY, W. F., see GHOST STORIES.

HARWOOD, Ronald (1934–   ), South African playwright, screenwriter, and novelist, who came to London as an actor in 1953 and turned to writing in the early 1960s. His best-known play, *The Dresser* (1983), is a partly autobiographical account of the months he spent on tour with actor Sir Donald Wolfit, of whom he also published a biography in 1971, subtitled 'His Life and Work in the Unfashionable Theatre'. Since then, several of Harwood's works have had a South African theme, sometimes related to his family upbringing, but in a varied stage and screen career he has also worked on the musical adaptation of *Priestley's *Good Companions*, E. *Waugh's *The Ordeal of Gilbert Pinfold*, and *Chekhov's *Ivanov*. His theatre life has often been linked to the careers of actors Albert Finney and Tom Courtenay, and he has been an active campaigner for civil rights. His fiction includes *The Girl in Melanie Klein* (1969) and the movie satire *One Interior Day* (1978). He also wrote and presented a BBC TV series on the history of World Theatre (1984). Harwood was one of the founding playwrights of the Royal Exchange, Manchester, where three of his plays were premièred.

HAŠEK, Jaroslav (1883–1923), Czech writer, born in Prague, remembered for his creation of the character of 'the good soldier Švejk' (or Schweik), a subversive, irreverent, opportunistic figure, a 'wise fool', who appeared in several narratives, most notably in the long rambling work bearing his name, published

1921–3. Hašek's works have been translated into English by Cecil Parrott.

HASSALL, Christopher Vernon (1912–63), poet, songwriter, and biographer, born in London, the son of painter and illustrator John Hassall, and educated at Wadham College, Oxford. He was encouraged when young by E. *Marsh, published his first of several books of verse in 1935 (*Poems of Two Years*), and wrote the lyrics for several musicals for Ivor Novello in the 1930s. He also wrote librettos for W. *Walton (*Troilus and Cressida*, 1954) and *Bliss. His biography *Edward Marsh, Patron of the Arts* (1959) was followed by a life of R. *Brooke (1964).

Hastings, a character in Goldsmith's *She Stoops to Conquer*.

HASTINGS, Warren (1732–1818), the first governor-general of British India. He left India in 1785, was impeached on the ground of cruelty and corruption in his administration, and acquitted after a trial of 145 days, extending, with long intervals, from 1788 to 1795. *Burke and C. J. *Fox were among the prosecutors.

HATHAWAY, Anne (1555/6–1623). She married *Shakespeare in Nov. 1582. Her family home, 'Anne Hathaway's cottage', is still to be seen in Shottery, on the edge of Stratford-upon-Avon.

HATTON, Sir Christopher (1540–91), said to have attracted the attention of Queen *Elizabeth I by his graceful dancing (alluded to by Sheridan, *The Critic*, II. ii). He became her favourite, and received grants of offices and estates (including Ely Place, now the site of Hatton Garden). Hatton was lord chancellor, 1587–91, and chancellor of Oxford University, 1588. He was the friend and patron of *Spenser and *Churchyard, and wrote Act IV of *Tancred and Gismund*.

Haunch of Venison, The, a poetical epistle to Lord Clare by *Goldsmith, written about 1770, published 1776.

Haunted Man and the Ghost's Bargain, The, a Christmas book by *Dickens, published 1848.

Redlaw, a learned man in chemistry, is haunted by the memories of a life blighted by sorrow and wrong. His evil genius tempts him to think that these memories are his curse, and makes a bargain with him by which he shall forget them; but on condition that he communicates this power of oblivion to all with whom he comes in contact. He discovers with horror that with remembrance of the past he blots out from his own life and the lives of those about him (in particular the delightful Tetterbys) gratitude, repentance, compassion, and forbearance. He prays to be released from his bargain, which is effected by the influence of the good angel Milly Swidger.

HAUPTMANN, Gerhart (1862–1946), German dramatist from Silesia. His first play *Vor Sonnenaufgang* (*Before Sunrise*, 1889) was the first German naturalistic play to be produced and, together with a production of *Ibsen's *Ghosts* in the same theatre the previous month, introduced *naturalism to the German stage. His other important play of this period was *Die Weber* (*The Weavers*, 1892). With *Hanneles Himmelfahrt* (*The Ascension of Joan*, 1893) he began to move towards a new symbolism, returning from time to time to more realistic drama. His narrative works, of which the two novellas of 1888, *Bahnwärter Thiel* (*Signalman Thiel*) and *Fasching* (Shrovetide), are the outstanding examples, are dark naturalistic tales with some symbolic elements. He won the *Nobel Prize for literature in 1912. Hauptmann was much admired by *Joyce, who translated two of his plays and described *The Weavers* as a masterpiece: 'a little immortal thing'.

Haut-ton, Sir Oran, the orang-utan in Peacock's *Melincourt*, in which Peacock makes satiric use of *Monboddo's claim that the higher primates have most of the essential qualities of human beings, except speech.

Havelok the Dane, The Lay of, a 13th-cent. romance (before 1272) from Lincolnshire, in 3,000 lines of rhyming octosyllables. There is an Anglo-Norman version from c.1130–40 which has resemblances to the 800-line account in Anglo-Norman at the beginning of *Gaimar's *Histoire des Engles* (c.1150). The story tells of the dispossessed Havelok, prince of Denmark, and his marriage to Goldborough, the dispossessed daughter of King Athelwold of England. Havelok is brought up at Grimsby by the eponymous fisherman Grim and becomes kitchen-boy in the household of Godrich, the treacherous guardian of Goldborough. His noble origins are twice declared, once to Grim and once to Goldborough, by a mystical light that shines over his head. At the end all three return to Denmark, defeat and hang Havelok's usurping guardian Godard, and reclaim the throne. The story has parallels with events in English and Norwegian history: Havelok has been etymologically identified with Anlaf Cuaran, the son of a Viking chief Sihtric, king of Northumberland in 925, who was defeated with King Constantine of Scotland in 937 at *Brunanburh; but most of its material and themes are legendary. It is one of the most admired of all Middle English romances nowadays, because of its narrative coherence and life and the sustained interest of its action. The loss of the story was lamented by *Tyrwhitt in the 1770s and by *Ritson just afterwards; the manuscript was discovered only by a happy accident in the Bodleian Library. It was edited by W. W. *Skeat, rev. K. Sisam (1967).

Havisham, Miss, a character in Dickens's *Great Expectations*.

HAWES, Stephen (c.1475–1511), a poet of the school of *Chaucer and *Lydgate, groom of the chamber to Henry VII. His *Passetyme of Pleasure or The Historie of Graunde Amoure and La Bell Pucel* was first printed by Wynkyn de *Worde, 1509. His *Example of Vertu*, a poem in rhyme-royal, an allegory of life spent in the pursuit of purity, much after the manner of the *Passetyme of Pleasure*, was also printed by de Worde in 1512.

Hawk, Sir Mulberry, a character in Dickens's *Nicholas Nickleby*.

HAWKER, R(obert) S(tephen) (1803–75), educated at Pembroke College, Oxford, and from 1834 vicar of Morwenstow in Cornwall; much of his poetry was inspired by Cornish landscape and legend, and by the frequent shipwrecks off the dangerous coast of his parish. He was an isolated and eccentric figure, though the portrait drawn in *Baring-Gould's *The Vicar of Morwenstow* (1875) has been modified by Piers Brendon's *Hawker of Morwenstow* (1975). He was the author of 'The Song of the Western Men', first published anonymously in 1825; based on an old Cornish ballad, it has the refrain: 'And shall Trelawney die?' He published various volumes of poetry, including in 1864 part of a projected long blank-verse Arthurian poem, *The Quest of the Sangraal*, which has passages of visionary power attributed by some to his opium addiction.

HAWKES, Jacquetta, née Hopkins (1910–96). She studied archaeology at Newnham College, Cambridge, and subsequently took part in many excavations. Her first work, *The Archaeology of Jersey* (1939), was followed by many others, written in a style which successfully conveys her enthusiasm to a lay reader; the best known is *A Land* (1951), with drawings by H. *Moore, a personal evocation of the geological shaping of Britain. She collaborated with her first husband, Christopher Hawkes, in *Prehistoric Britain* (1944), and with her second husband, J. B. *Priestley, in *Journey down a Rainbow* (1955), an account of travels in New Mexico and Texas.

HAWKESWORTH, John (1715–73), schoolmaster and writer of miscellaneous essays, plays, stories, and general journalism. With the considerable assistance of his friend Dr *Johnson, and of J. *Warton, he successfully conducted the *Adventurer*, a bi-weekly successor to the *Rambler*, 1752–4. He produced a reliable edition of *Swift, with a biography, in 1754–5, and in 1766 an edition of Swift's letters. His highly successful *Almoran and Hamet* (1761) is an exotic *Oriental tale. Untrammelled by space or time, Almoran can change into any shape to pursue his strange, and often supernatural, adventures among magnificent heroes and base villains. Hawkesworth edited and annotated various journals, including *Cook's and Carteret's, for his *Account of the Voyages . . . in the Southern Hemisphere* (1773). His sympathy with the native inhabitants of the Pacific Islands led him to convey a picture of innocent indulgence which was widely condemned as indecent. There is a biography by J. L. Abbott (1982).

HAWKINS, Sir Anthony Hope (1863–1933), barrister and author, who gave up the law after the success of *The Prisoner of Zenda* (1894), published under the pseudonym 'Anthony Hope'. A sequel, *Rupert of Hentzau*, followed in 1898. Hawkins also published several other novels and plays, and *The Dolly Dialogues* (1894), reprinted from the *Westminster Gazette*, which is a series of light-hearted conversations featuring a flirtation between Samuel Carter, a bachelor, and Dolly Foster, who in chapter 5 marries Lord Mickleham.

HAWKINS, Sir John (1532–95), naval commander, who led expeditions in 1562, 1564, and 1567 to the West African and Spanish-American coasts, slave-trading and fighting the Spaniards, and published an account of his voyages in 1569.

HAWKINS, Sir John (1719–89), a lawyer and magistrate who devoted much of his life to music and literature. He was a friend of Dr *Johnson, who, however, found him 'a most unclubable man', an opinion endorsed by most of his contemporaries. Johnson made him an executor, and Hawkins wrote his biography, a work of considerable merit (although later overshadowed by *Boswell's), published 1787: he also edited Johnson's works in 15 volumes, 1787–8. His scholarly *General History of the Science and Practice of Music* (5 volumes, 1776), based on 16 years of research, had a similar misfortune in that it appeared in the same year as, and was seen as the rival of, Dr *Burney's history: these were the first two histories of music in England of their kind. There is a life by B. H. Davis (1973). (See MUSIC, LITERATURE OF.)

HAWKSMOOR, Nicholas (1661–1736), the most original and dramatic of English baroque architects, except for *Vanbrugh, for whom he worked from 1690 to c.1702, after training with Sir Christopher *Wren. His masterpieces are the six London churches he designed after 1711, as joint surveyor of Queen Anne's new churches; four of these are still extant. They are remarkable for their originality, their combination of classical and Gothic features, and their theatricality: Christchurch, Spitalfields (1723–39), being outstanding. His reclusive character and the perversity of some of his architectural practice inspired the metaphysical thriller *Hawksmoor* (1985) by P. *Ackroyd.

HAWKWOOD, Sir John (1320–94), a famous *condottiere*, who figures in *Froissart as 'Haccoude'. *Machiavelli calls him 'Giovanni Acuto'. He was the leader of the body of English mercenaries known as the White Company and fought for one Italian city or another, and for pope or prince, from 1360 to 1390. He was finally commander-in-chief of the Florentine forces, died at Florence, and was buried in the Duomo, where Paolo Uccello painted a commemorative equestrian portrait in 1436.

HAWTHORNE, Nathaniel (1804–64), American novelist and short story writer, born at Salem, Massachusetts. He was a descendant of Major William Hathorne (1607–81), one of the Puritan settlers in America, the 'grave, bearded, sable-cloaked and steeple-crowned progenitor' whose portrait is drawn in the introductory chapter of *The Scarlet Letter*: he was remembered for his persecution of the Quakers, as his son John Hathorne, also a magistrate, was remembered for his persecution of the so-called Witches of Salem. Hawthorne (who adopted this spelling of the family name) spent a solitary childhood with his mother, a widowed recluse, during which he read widely; he was educated at Bowdoin College, Brunswick (with *Longfellow), then returned to Salem, where he began to write stories and sketches and published a novel, *Fanshawe* (1828), at his own expense. His stories began to appear in periodicals (notably in S. G. Goodrich's *Token*) and were collected in *Twice-Told Tales* (1837) and later volumes, including *Mosses from an Old Manse* (1846) and *The Snow-Image and Other Twice-Told Tales* (1851); he also did a considerable amount of hack-work as writer and editor, and wrote some lasting works for children, including *A Wonder Book* and *Tanglewood Tales* (1852 and 1853, stories from Greek mythology).

He was, however, slow to earn his living as a writer; he was employed for some time as measurer at the Boston custom house (1839–41), then spent in 1841 several months at Brook Farm, an experience on which he based *The Blithedale Romance* (1852), a novel which conveys his mixed response to the *Transcendentalists. He married in 1842 and settled in Concord; from 1846 to 1849 he was surveyor of the port of Salem. He lost his post through a change of administration, and then wrote *The Scarlet Letter* (1850), a classic enquiry into the nature of American Puritanism and the New England conscience, and *The House of the Seven Gables* (1851), a study in ancestral guilt and expiation, also deeply rooted in New England and his own family history. In 1850 he met *Melville, who admired Hawthorne's work enormously, and indeed wrote an enthusiastic review comparing him to the Shakespeare of the tragedies. From 1853 to 1857 Hawthorne was in England, as American consul at Liverpool; he then spent two years in Italy, which provided the setting and inspiration for *The Marble Faun* (1860), returning in 1860 to Concord, where he spent his last years, which were marked by declining creative powers. *Our Old Home*, sketches of his life in England, appeared in 1863.

Hawthorne has long been recognized as one of the greatest of American writers, a moralist and allegorist much preoccupied with the mystery of sin, the paradox of its occasionally regenerative power, and the compensation for unmerited suffering and crime. The optimistic answers of *Emerson to these questions left him unconvinced, and the 'darkness' of his genius, first noted by Melville, found a ready response in the 20th cent. A study of his life and work by H. *James, published in 1879 in the 'English Men of Letters' series, is remarkable for the light that it sheds on both author and subject; James's comments on Hawthorne's 'exaggerated, painful, morbid national consciousness' clearly relate to James's own relation to his American and European experiences, and sense of national identity; he wrote of *The Scarlet Letter*: 'Something might at last be sent to Europe as exquisite in quality as anything that had been received, and the best of it was that the thing was absolutely American . . . it came out of the very heart of New England.'

HAYDN, (Franz) Joseph (1732–1809), Austrian composer. He kept his interests predominantly local for most of his life, but made two triumphant visits to London, in 1791–2 and 1794–5, undertaken at the invitation of the concert manager Johann Peter Salomon. These provided new inspiration and stimulus. The oratorio *Die Schöpfung* (*The Creation*, 1798) was written to a text compiled from the first Chapter of Genesis and Books VII and VIII of *Paradise Lost*, translated into German by Baron van Swieten. It is said that the original version of this text had been intended for *Handel, and there is a strongly Handelian feel about this masterpiece of Haydn's old age. (The English version now normally sung outside the German-speaking countries is a retranslation from van Swieten and not without its absurdities.) The success of *The Creation* encouraged Haydn to compose *Die Jahreszeiten* (1801) with a text (again by van Swieten) drawn from Thomson's *The Seasons*. Haydn also made some 125 arrangements with instrumental accompaniment of Scottish and Welsh folk songs: after his return to Vienna he made another 250 of these for the Scottish publishers Whyte and Thomson.

HAYDON, Benjamin Robert (1786–1846), a historical painter but best known for his posthumously published *Autobiography and Journals* (selections ed. Tom *Taylor, 1853; complete text in 5 vols, ed. W. B. Pope, 1960, 1963). Haydon, son of a Plymouth bookseller, at first had some success with his large paintings of biblical and classical subjects, but quarrelled with most of his patrons, fell deeply in debt, and finally committed suicide. His vigorous advocacy helped to secure the Elgin Marbles for the British Museum, and his pioneering theories on art education, industrial design, and state patronage of the arts, expressed in his *Lectures on Painting and Design* (1846), had much influence. He was a friend of *Keats, *Wordsworth, *Hazlitt, Leigh *Hunt, M. R. *Mitford, and Elizabeth Barrett (*Browning), and his vivid and vehement journals contain many interesting anecdotes and pen-portraits of his contemporaries. His outrageous personality has interested many novelists, notably Dickens who used him (combined with Leigh Hunt) as the model for Harold Skimpole in *Bleak House*, and A. *Huxley, whose Casimir Lypiatt in *Antic Hay* is based on Haydon. See *A Sultry Month: Scenes of London*

Literary Life in 1846 (1965) by Alethea Hayter, which gives a vivid portrait of his last days.

HAYES, J. Milton (1884–1940), remembered as the author of 'The Green Eye of the Yellow God', a rousing poem (often assumed to be by *Kipling) first published in 1911, which begins 'There's a one-eyed yellow idol to the north of Khatmandu' and tells the tale of the idol's revenge on Mad Carew, who steals the eye at the behest of his beloved, and leaves her forever broken-hearted at his grave.

HAYLEY, William (1745–1820), a prolific poet, whose most ambitious works, *The Triumphs of Temper* (1781) and *The Triumphs of Music* (1804), were ridiculed by *Byron as 'Forever feeble and for ever tame', but were nevertheless popular. In 1805 his *Ballads on . . . Animals* was illustrated by *Blake, who was at that time his friend and protégé, although the two were not always in sympathy. He was a close friend of *Cowper, whose *Life* he published in 1803; he also published lives of *Milton (1804) and *Romney (1809). His friend *Southey commented that 'Everything about that man is good except his poetry.' He was nevertheless offered the laureateship in 1790, but declined it.

Haymarket, the, London, so called from the Hay Market established there in 1664, and maintained until 1830. Her Majesty's Theatre, Haymarket (called also the Opera House), was the first opera house in London (1705). The first performances in England of *Handel's operas were given there. The Haymarket Theatre, on the opposite side of the street, also built at the beginning of the 18th cent., was *Foote's theatre from 1747, and later that of the Bancrofts.

HAYWARD, Abraham (1801–84), essayist, called to the bar in 1832, author of *The Art of Dining* (1852); his gastronomic dinners in his chambers were famous for their distinguished company which included *Lockhart and *Macaulay. Some of his essays and reviews including *More about Junius* (1868), a vigorous attack on the Franciscan theory of *'Junius', and an account of the life and work of J. S. *Mill (1873) provoked acute controversy. His articles appeared in the leading periodicals of his day and many were collected in five volumes of *Biographical and Critical Essays* (1858–74). He also published biographical and legal works and a translation of Goethe's *Faust*.

HAYWARD, Sir John (?1564–1627), educated at Pembroke College, Cambridge, the author of various historical works, in which he emulated the style of the great Roman historians. His *First Part of the Life, and Raigne of Henrie the IIII* (1599), dedicated to *Essex, gave offence to *Elizabeth I and led to his imprisonment. His other chief works were the *Lives of the III Normans, Kings of England* (1613), the *Life and Raigne of King Edward the Sixt* (1630), and *The Beginning of the Reigne of Queene Elizabeth* (1636).

HAYWOOD, Eliza (?1693–1756), an actress and author of several plays and many novels. She conducted a periodical, the *Female Spectator*, 1744–6, and in 1751 published the most memorable of her novels, *The History of Miss Betty Thoughtless*, followed in 1753 by *Jenny and Jemmy Jessamy*. Among her other writings are *Anti-Pamela* (1741) and *The Fortunate Foundlings* (1744). Her writing has vivacity, particularly in situations of high emotion, but her licentiousness and her habit of thinly disguising figures of society brought denunciations by *Swift, Horace *Walpole, and others. *Pope cited her in the *Dunciad*, and in a note described her as 'a shameless scribbler'.

HAZLITT, William (1778–1830), critic, *theatre critic, and essayist, born in Maidstone, the son of a Unitarian minister of Irish birth who sympathized with the American Revolution. His infancy was passed in Ireland and in New England, his youth in the Shropshire village of Wem. He attended the New Unitarian College at Hackney, London, absorbing *Enlightenment philosophy and radical politics. He refused to enter the ministry, entertaining hopes of becoming a philosopher or, like his brother John, a painter. The influences of S. T. *Coleridge, W. *Wordsworth, and C. *Lamb turned him away from painting and towards writing, although he deplored the Lake poets' betrayal of their early radicalism. Hazlitt's first books were political studies: *An Essay on the Principles of Human Action* (1805) disputes *Hobbes's account of self-interested motives; it was followed by a polemic against *Malthus, *A Reply to the Essay on Population* (1807), and by *The Eloquence of the British Senate* (1807), containing studies of contemporary political leaders. He married Sarah Stoddart in 1808, settling near Salisbury. Four years later, he moved to London and launched his career as a public lecturer, political journalist, and critic of painting, drama, and poetry, writing for the *Morning Chronicle*, for Leigh *Hunt's *Examiner*, and for the *Edinburgh Review*. His book *Characters of Shakespear's Plays* appeared in 1817, as did *The Round Table*, containing general essays such as 'On Gusto'. In the following year he published his theatre reviews as *A View of the English Stage*, and gave two series of literary lectures at the Surrey Institution, the first of which was attended by *Keats and published as *Lectures on the English Poets* (1818); its sequel was *Lectures on the English Comic Writers* (1819). His *Political Essays* (1819) include remarkable studies of E. *Burke, whom he honoured as a man of genius while abhorring his political conservatism. *Lectures Chiefly on the Dramatic Literature of the Age of Elizabeth* (1820) was followed by a two-volume collection of general essays, *Table Talk* (1821–2).

Meanwhile his personal affairs were thrown into turmoil by an obsessive infatuation with his landlord's daughter, Sarah Walker; in the deluded hope of marrying her, he divorced his wife in 1822. *Liber Amoris* (1823), his confessional account of this episode, damaged his public reputation. After taking Isabella Bridgewater as his second wife in 1824 he produced two of his best works, *The Spirit of the Age* (1825) and *The Plain Speaker* (1826). Lesser works of this period are the collection of aphorisms, *Characteristics* (1823), and *Notes of a Journey through France and Italy* (1826). His last years were spent on his four-volume *Life of Napoleon Buonaparte* (1828–30), a tribute to his political idol. He died in Soho, and is buried in St Anne's churchyard. Posthumous works include *Literary Remains* (1836), containing two of his most striking essays, 'My First Acquaintance with Poets' and 'The Fight'.

Hazlitt is now acknowledged as the first original master of English prose in the 19th cent. and as a serious rival to Coleridge in the value of his critical writings. His prose style is variable, moving from the pugnacious to the seductive, from allusive subtlety to democratic plainness, but always stamped with personality and passion. He revived the art of the essay, and brought new psychological and political insight into literary criticism. Devoted to the ideals of the French Revolution, he nonetheless grasped the imaginative force of conservatism, whether in *Shakespeare or in W. *Scott and Wordsworth; this tension between rational enlightenment and the power of 'genius' animates much of his work. The standard edition is the *Complete Works* (ed. P. P. Howe, 21 vols, 1930–4). The standard biography is S. Jones, *Hazlitt, A Life* (1989). See also D. Bromwich, *Hazlitt: The Mind of a Critic* (1983) and T. *Paulin, *The Day-Star of Liberty* (1998).

HAZLITT, William Carew (1834–1913), bibliographer, grandson of William *Hazlitt. Among his works are a *Hand-Book to the Popular Poetical and Dramatic Literature of Great Britain, from the Invention of Printing to the Restoration* (1867), *Bibliographical Collections and Notes* (1876–89, 3 series), and memoirs of his grandfather (1867). His editorial work included *English Proverbs and Proverbial Phrases Collected from the Most Authentic Sources* (1869, for which H. G. *Bohn accused him of plagiarism), *Letters of Charles Lamb* (1886), reprints of Hazlitt, *Herrick, *Suckling, and a translation of *Montaigne. His *Confessions of a Collector* appeared in 1897. *Schoenbaum describes him as 'unreliable' and 'an antiquarian bumbler'.

HAZZARD, Shirley (1931–), novelist and short story writer, born Sydney, Australia. Her work at the United Nations headquarters in New York 1951–61 provided material for her satirical linked short stories, *People in Glass Houses* (1967). She had already published a short story collection, *Cliffs of Fall* (1963), and *The Evening of the Holiday* (1966), a novel exploring the fruitful theme of northern Europeans in Italy. *The Bay of Noon* (1970), set in Naples just after the Second World War, pursues this theme. It is in Hazzard's dense, multi-layered survey of the post-war world *The Transit of Venus* (1980) that her preoccupations with ideas, politics, and complex human emotions reach their fullest expression. It follows the loves and careers of Australian sisters Caro and Grace, along with the British working-class astronomer Ted Tice, from post-war England through ensuing decades. *The Great Fire* (2003), set in the aftermath of the Second World War, charts the delicate but passionate love affair of Major Leith and 17-year-old Helen from New Zealand, and vividly evokes post-Hiroshima Japan and Hong Kong.

H.D., see DOOLITTLE, H.

HEAD, Bessie Amelia (1937–86), writer, born in South Africa out of wedlock to a 'white' mother and 'black' father under apartheid classification; she lived as a refugee in Botswana from the age of 26. Her major work was written and set in Botswana. *When Rain Clouds Gather* (1968) addresses the rural community's ability to survive economic hardship and the autocracy of their chief, while *Maru* (1971) and *A Question of Power* (1973) present a young woman's struggle against the racism and sexism in the Botswana community. The latter novel, with its autobiographical rendering of psychological breakdown, also turns back to the remembered effects of apartheid. In her later, less introspective phase, Head's stories *The Collector of Treasures* (1977) develop the themes gleaned from interviews with villagers—these interviews were published later as *Serowe: Village of the Rain Wind* (1981)—and her social history *A Bewitched Crossroad* (1984) augments fact with fiction in order to counter the European version of Botswana's past. Additional stories and essays, early and late, have been collected in *Tales of Tenderness and Power* (1989) and *A Woman Alone* (1990). Overall, Head's major interest is in envisioning an Africa free of inherited and imported oppressions, hospitable to European thinking yet strongly enough informed with communal rural traditions to resist the social breakdown and materialism of post-colonial life. The small selection of her letters hitherto published in *A Gesture of Belonging* (1991) recount an often lonely life funded by meagre royalties and refugee subsidies. Today, her pioneering, deeply engaged narratives have earned her an international reputation. See Gillian Stead Eilersen, *Bessie Head: Thunder Behind Her Ears* (1995).

Headlong Hall, a satire by T. L. *Peacock, published 1816, the first of the series of books in which Peacock adapts the Socratic dialogue as a tool for satirizing contemporary culture.

Mr Foster the optimist, Mr Escot the pessimist, Mr Jenkinson the status-quo-ite, Dr Gaster, a gluttonous cleric, Mr Milestone, a landscape gardener, and many others gather at the Welsh country house of Squire Headlong to eat, drink, and discuss the arts. In the central comic episode, Mr Milestone blows up part of the grounds in order to achieve the smooth effect preferred by his real-life prototype, Repton. The debates of the philosophers enact the clash between the optimism of Condorcet and *Godwin and the pessimism of *Malthus. See also PICTURESQUE.

Headstone, Bradley, a character in Dickens's *Our Mutual Friend.*

HEANEY, Seamus Justin (1939–   ), Irish poet, educated at St Columb's College, Derry, and Queen's University, Belfast. In the 1960s he belonged to a group of poets in Belfast, who, he said, 'used to talk poetry day after day with an intensity and prejudice that cannot but have left a mark on all of us'. After lecturing on poetry at Queen's for six years he moved in 1972 to the Republic of Ireland, living first in Co. Wicklow and then in Dublin. His early poetry is rooted in the farmland of his youth, and communicates a strong physical sense of environment with subtlety and economy of words, as in *Eleven Poems* (1965), *Death of a Naturalist* (1966), and *Door into the Dark* (1969). His later work, densely written and often poignant, as in *Wintering Out* (1972), *North* (1975), and *Field Work* (1979), broods on the cultural and historical implications of words and explores their use in wider social and political contexts. *Selected Poems, 1965–1975* was published in 1980. *Preoccupations* (1980), a collection of essays and lectures from 1968 to 1978, includes 'The Fire i' the Flint: Reflections on the Poetry of Gerard Manley Hopkins' (Chatterton Lecture, 1975). In 1989 he was appointed professor of poetry at Oxford. *Station Island* (1984), which contains a sequence of poems on Lough Derg and includes a ghostly encounter with James *Joyce, was followed by *Sweeney Astray* (1984), a version of the medieval Irish ballad *Buile Suibhne*, and *The Haw Lantern* (1987), which includes a moving sonnet sequence on the death of his mother. Recent volumes include *Seeing Things* (1991), and *Sweeney's Flight* (1992). *The Government of the Tongue*, a collection of essays, was published in 1988. He was awarded the *Nobel Prize for Literature in 1995: his Nobel Lecture, *Crediting Poetry* (1995), was included in his *Collected Poems 1966–96* (1999). His highly praised translation of *Beowulf* appeared in 1999.

HEARD, Gerald, see HUXLEY, A.

HEARN, Lafcadio (1850–1904), born in Santa Maura (Levkas), one of the Ionian Islands, of Irish-Greek parentage, and educated in England, where he lost through an accident the sight of one eye. In 1869 he left penniless for America, where he worked as a journalist in Cincinnati and incurred scandal by living openly with a mulatto woman; he also translated from the French, and his own works show the influence of the exoticism of Pierre Loti, *Baudelaire, and *Gautier. He then lived in Martinique, an experience which produced *Two Years in the French West Indies* (1890) and a novel, *Youma* (1890). In 1890 he went to Japan, where he spent the rest of his life. He married a Japanese wife, took the name of Yakumo Koizumi, and adopted Japanese dress, though he never mastered the language. He taught at a school in Matsue, and from 1896 to 1903 lectured on English literature at the Imperial University, Tokyo. He published several works which affectionately and vividly evoke the landscapes, mythology, and customs of his adopted country, including *Glimpses of Unfamiliar Japan* (1894), *Out of the East* (1895), and *Japan: An Attempt at Interpretation* (1904). See lives by E. Bisland (1906) and E. Stevenson (1961).

HEARNE, Thomas (1678–1735), historical antiquary, author of *Reliquiae Bodleianae* (1703) and editor of a valuable collection of early English chronicles, of *Leland's *Itinerary*, *Camden's *Annales*, and other works. He was the 'Wormius' of Pope's *Dunciad. He might have held high office in Oxford University but for his staunch Jacobitism: as a nonjuror he refused to take the oath of allegiance to George I. See C. E. Doble et al. (eds), *Remarks and Collections of Thomas Hearne* (11 vols, 1885–1921).

Heartbreak House: *A Fantasia in the Russian Manner on English Themes*, a play by Bernard *Shaw, first performed in New York 1920, published there 1919; probably written 1916–17, despite Shaw's claims that he began it before the war.

It describes the impact of Ellie Dunn, daughter of the idealistic and unworldly Mazzini Dunn, upon the eccentric, complacent, and 'horribly Bohemian' household of 88-year-old Captain Shotover, with whom she strikes up an alliance: the inmates include energetic, beautiful, dominating Hesione Hushabye (determined Ellie shall not marry the ageing business magnate Boss Mangan); her husband, the romantic liar and fantasist Hector Hushabye; her sister, the apparently conventional, newly returned Lady Utterword; and Lady Utterword's devoted brother-in-law Randall, prototype of the useless artist. Shaw appears to be portraying, in 'this silly house, this strangely happy house, this agonizing house, this house without foundations', an aspect of British (or European) civilization (suggested in part by the *Bloomsbury Group, in part by the society portrayed by *Chekhov), about to run on the rocks or blow itself up through lack of direction and lack of grasp of economic reality, but, after various Shavian debates on money, marriage, and morality, the play ends in deep ambiguity: an air raid destroys Boss Mangan, the practical man (who takes refuge in a gravel pit where the captain stores dynamite), and is greeted with exhilarated rapture by Hesione and Ellie ('It's splendid: it's like an orchestra: it's like Beethoven'), who with the rest of the household refuse to take shelter, and survive.

Heartfree, (1) a character in Vanbrugh's *The Provok'd Wife*; (2) Heartfree and Mrs Heartfree, characters in Fielding's *Jonathan Wild.*

'Heart of Darkness', a tale by J. *Conrad, published 1902. On board a boat anchored peacefully in the Thames the narrator, Marlow, tells the story of his journey on another river.

Travelling in Africa to join a cargo boat, Marlow grows disgusted by what he sees of the greed of the ivory traders and their brutal exploitation of the natives. At a company station he hears of the remarkable Mr Kurtz who is stationed in the very heart of the ivory country and is the company's most successful agent. Leaving the river, Marlow makes a long and arduous cross-country trek to join the steamboat which he will command on an ivory collecting journey into the interior, but at the Central Station he finds that his boat has been mysteriously wrecked. He learns that Kurtz has dismissed his assistant and is seriously ill. The other agents, jealous of Kurtz's success and possible promotion, hope that he will not recover and it becomes clear that Marlow's arrival at the Inner Station is being deliberately delayed. With repairs finally completed Marlow sets off on the two-month journey towards Kurtz. The river passage through the heavy motionless forest fills Marlow with a growing sense of dread. The journey is 'like travelling back to the earliest beginnings of the world'. Ominous drumming is heard and dark forms glimpsed among the trees. Nearing its destination the boat is attacked by tribesmen and a helmsman is killed. At the Inner Station Marlow is met by a naïve young Russian sailor who tells Marlow of Kurtz's brilliance and the semi-divine power he exercises over the natives. A row of severed heads on stakes round the hut give an intimation of the barbaric rites by which Kurtz has achieved his ascendancy. Ritual dancing has been followed with human sacrifice and, without the restraints imposed by his society, Kurtz, an educated and civilized man, has used his knowledge and his gun to reign over this dark kingdom. While Marlow attempts to get Kurtz back down the river Kurtz tries to justify his actions and his motives: he has seen into the very heart of things. But dying his last words are: 'The horror! The horror!' Marlow is left with two packages to deliver, Kurtz's report for the Society for Suppression of Savage Customs, and some letters for his girlfriend. Faced with the girl's grief Marlow tells her simply that Kurtz died with her name on his lips. This short novel has become one of the most-discussed texts in *postcolonial literary studies: it also inspired Coppola's post-Vietnam film *Apocalypse Now* (1979).

Heart of Midlothian, The, a novel by Sir W. *Scott, published 1818, as the 2nd series of *Tales of My Landlord*.

Scott has built one of his greatest novels on two historical incidents: the Porteous riots, in which John Porteous, commander of the Edinburgh City Guard, is dragged from the Edinburgh Tolbooth ('the Heart of Midlothian') and hanged by a mob after he has been pardoned for firing on the citizens at the hanging of Wilson, a convicted robber; and the story of Isobel Walker whose pardon for child murder, for which she had been sentenced to death, is obtained by her sister Helen, who walks to London to intercede for her with the duke of Argyle. In the novel, the riot is engineered by George Staunton, an accomplice, under the name of Robertson, of the hanged Wilson, to release his lover Effie Deans, who is imprisoned in the Tolbooth for child murder. Effie refuses to escape, stands trial, and, since her sister Jeanie refuses to perjure herself to save her, is, like Isobel Walker, condemned to death. Jeanie sets out on foot for London to plead for her life and, after various vicissitudes and through the mediation of the duke of Argyle, secures her sister's pardon from Queen Caroline. Effie, like her real-life model, eventually marries her seducer but, unlike her, did not actually kill her child, which was sold by the midwife to a vagrant woman whose daughter, Madge Wildfire, Staunton had also seduced. The child later unwittingly becomes his father's assassin. Jeanie eventually marries her faithful suitor, the Presbyterian minister Reuben Butler.

Scott had given a picture of the sterner, crueller side of strict Cameronian Presbyterianism two years earlier in *Old Mortality*; in this novel, the rigid tenets of Davie Deans, father of Jeanie and Effie, are seen through more compassionate eyes. Jeanie inherits his unbending rectitude, but demonstrates the heights to which it can rise through love as opposed to those to which it can be driven by fanaticism and torture. Jeanie has none of the normal attributes of a fictional heroine; she is not well educated, pretty, or witty. Presented with a dilemma as crucial to her as that of Isabella in *Measure for Measure* (and as alien to the understanding of our own times), and with only her own integrity to guide her, she achieves her goal by simple, uncompromising dignity and goodness.

Heart of the Matter, The, a novel by G. *Greene, published 1948.

Set in West Africa, 'the white man's grave', during the Second World War, it describes how the deputy commissioner of police, Scobie, a just and honourable man, is led to make various false moves, initially by pity for his unhappy, hysterical, 'literary' wife Louise, then through a mixture of pity and love for a 19-year-old widow, Helen, with whom he has an affair. He borrows money, compromises himself, is indirectly responsible for the death of his faithful servant Ali, and finally, with much deliberation, commits suicide, a mortal sin which, as a Catholic, he attempts to conceal from his wife by laying a false trail in his diary. The deceit is posthumously exposed by the young intelligence agent Wilson, who has been watching his every move, motivated partly through his own love for Scobie's wife. The novel vividly evokes an area of 'Greeneland' characterized by intense heat, vultures, cockroaches, rats, heavy drinking, corruption, and a painful struggle to maintain faith, in a hostile environment, with concepts of justice and religion.

Heartwell, the title role in Congreve's comedy *The Old Bachelor*.

Heathcliff, the central figure in E. Brontë's *Wuthering Heights*.

HEATH-STUBBS, John Francis Alexander (1918–   ), poet and critic, educated at Worcester College for the Blind and at the Queen's College, Oxford, where his first published poems appeared in *Eight Oxford Poets* (1941, ed. S. *Keyes and M. Meyer). He describes himself as a traditionalist in literature, who believes that traditional values can only be maintained at the price of continual change and flexibility. His inspiration comes chiefly from Ancient Greece, Rome, Alexandria, classical myth, Christian legend, and works of art and scholarship, and his poetry includes translations from *Hāfiz and *Leopardi. But he is also a poet of contemporary urban society, and in *A Charm against the Toothache* (1954) the megalopolis is modern London. His principal works include poetry: *Wounded Thammuz* (1942), *Beauty and the Beast* (1943), *The Divided Ways* (1946), *The Swarming of the Bees* (1950), *The Blue-Fly in His Head* (1962), *Artorius* (an epic poem on Arthurian legend, 1972), and *Naming the Beasts* (a collection, 1982); and criticism: *The Darkling Plain* (a study of Victorian Romantic poetry, 1950) and *Charles Williams* (a monograph, 1955). His *Collected Poems 1943–1987* was published in 1988, and a volume of *Selected Poems* in 1990. His autobiography, *Hindsights*, appeared in 1993.

Heaven and Earth, a poetic drama by Lord *Byron, published in the *Liberal*, 1822. Like its predecessor *Cain*, it is subtitled 'A Mystery', and questions God's choice to create only to destroy. The story, suggested by Genesis 6, tells of the marriage of rebel angels and mortal women: Japhet, son of Noah, loves Anah, but she and her sister Aholibamah are carried away by their immortal lovers, the spirits Azaziel and Samiasa. The drama ends as the flood sweeps over the earth, and Japhet remains upon a rock as the Ark floats towards him.

HEBER, Reginald (1783–1826), educated at Oxford; in 1822 he became bishop of Calcutta. He published various works, including *Poems and Translations* (1812); an edition of the works of Jeremy *Taylor (1822), and his *Life* (1824); various hymns of his own authorship, including 'Brightest and best of the sons of the morning', 'From Greenland's icy mountains', and 'Holy, holy, holy' in 1827; *Narrative of a Journey through India* (1828); and his *Poetical Works* (1841).

HEBER, Richard (1777–1833), half-brother of Reginald *Heber, a devoted bibliophile; he travelled widely to collect his library of 150,000 volumes, and edited *Persius and other classical authors. He is the 'Atticus' of T. F. *Dibdin's *Bibliomania.

Hebrew Melodies, a collection of short poems by *Byron, some written during the early days of his marriage, published 1815. Many are on scriptural subjects, but some are love songs and lyrics: the volume was published by Jewish composer Isaac Nathan (?1791–1864) who arranged some to traditional Heb-

rew melodies. The poems include 'She walks in beauty' and 'The Assyrian came down like the wolf on the fold'.

Hebrides, *The Journal of a Tour to the*, see JOURNAL OF A TOUR TO THE HEBRIDES, THE. See also JOURNEY TO THE WESTERN ISLANDS OF SCOTLAND, A.

HECHT, Anthony (1923–2004), American poet, born in New York, whose volumes include *The Hard Hours* (1967), *The Venetian Vespers* (1979), and *The Transparent Man* (1989). At ease with both light and sombre verse, and writing with a mastery of classical and traditional forms, his work dwells on art, landscape, love, and loss: many of his poems evoke an intense experience of Europe, often linked to a restrained and poignant *confessional mode.

Hector, Sir, see ECTOR.

Heep, Uriah, a character in Dickens's *David Copperfield.

HEGEL, Georg Wilhelm Friedrich (1770–1831), German philosopher. His first important work was *Phänomenologie des Geistes* (*Phenomenology of Spirit*, 1807), followed by his *Logik* (1812–16), and later by the *Philosophie des Rechts* (*Philosophy of Right*, 1820), embodying his political views. *Kant had left an essential dualism in his philosophy, nature opposed to spirit, object opposed to subject, the outer world composed of isolated unrelated substances whose nature is beyond the reach of knowledge. Hegel endeavours to bridge the gulf and reduce duality to unity. He shows that all difference presupposes a unity, that a definite thought cannot be separated from its opposite, that the idea of fullness, for example, cannot be separated from that of emptiness, that they are identical in difference. Duality and unity are blended in consciousness and the boundaries between mind and matter set aside. Hegel's central idea is the dialectic of thesis–antithesis–synthesis, which he applied to the problem of historical evolution as represented by the *Weltgeist* or World Spirit. His dialectical method was adopted by political thinkers of both right and left, those who supported authoritarian rule in Prussia in the 19th cent. and those, like *Feuerbach, *Marx, and *Engels, who advocated reform and revolution. As Engels said, his doctrine was large enough to give shelter to the ideas of the most varied groups. Hegel enjoyed a vogue in philosophical circles in England, particularly at Oxford, in the 1880s and 1890s.

HEGLEY, John, see PERFORMANCE POETRY.

HEIDEGGER, Martin (1889–1976), German philosopher, educated at Freiburg Jesuit Seminary and Freiburg University. Heidegger was primarily concerned with the question of being; in his formulation, he dealt with the question 'what is "is"?' Heidegger used the word *Dasein* to refer to specifically human modes of being; *Dasein* is, for him, self-conscious and involves not only Being but also the very Question of Being. In his most famous work *Sein und Zeit* (1927; *Being and Time*, 1962), he studies *Dasein* in relation to time, asking how Being deals with its temporality, including the fear of being 'thrown into Being'. *Sartre published his response in *L'Être et le néant*, in 1943 (*Being and Nothingness*, 1956). Heidegger believed that Being can only be articulated through language; he defined as 'poetry' that language capable of doing this, language which is responsive to Being. He admired *Rilke and, especially, *Hölderlin, as they can help us to escape from 'forgetfulness of Being'. Heidegger continued to write and lecture extensively on this subject for the following eight years. For Heidegger, the representation of things estranges us from the things themselves; in his famous example of Van Gogh's painting of a pair of peasant shoes he describes how the act of estranging us from the shoes themselves serves to show us their essential 'shoeness'. Although Heidegger's writing is often abstruse, and in spite of the backlash against him due to his sympathies with Nazism, his writings had enormous influence on 20th-cent. thought and literary theory. He was a crucial influence for 20th-cent. *existentialism (especially Sartre), one of the founders (with Hans-Georg Gadamer) of *hermeneutic criticism, and his work was a starting point for Jacques *Derrida's development of *deconstruction. A collection of his work on the nature of thought, language, and poetry has been translated as *Poetry, Language, Thought* (1971). There is a study by George *Steiner (1978).

Heidelberg, Mrs, a character in Colman and Garrick's *The Clandestine Marriage*. Her illiteracy and mispronunciation of words bring her into some sort of kinship with Mrs *Malaprop.

Heimskringla, a series of short sagas making up a history of the kings of Norway from mythical times to the year 1177, written by *Snorri Sturluson. It is of more value for its high literary quality than for its historicity, although it is basically reliable and its political analyses are illuminating. It has a bearing on English history, covering as it does the reign of the Danish king *Canute (Knútr) and describing Viking expeditions to England. Its title is taken from its opening words, 'Kringla heimsins'—'orb of the world'. See *The Olaf Sagas from Heimskringla*, trans. S. Laing (1914, etc.).

HEINE, Heinrich (1797–1856), German poet, born of Jewish parents in Düsseldorf. Disappointed in his hopes of a liberal regime in Germany after the expulsion of Napoleon, he emigrated in 1831 to Paris, where he remained for the rest of his life. His political works show him a radical and a cosmopolitan (he wrote both in German and in French), but he was most famous as a lyric poet, many of whose songs were set to music by German composers in the 19th cent. He called himself 'the last Romantic', and his lyrics are characterized by a combination of self-indulgent emotion and sharp self-criticism and deflating irony. His chief works include the *Buch der Lieder* (*Book of Songs*, 1827), one of the most widely read and influential books of poetry in Germany, combining *Romanticism with irony; the satirical travel sketches in his *Reisebilder* (*Travel Pictures*, 1826–31); and his savage and witty attacks on German thought and literature in *Zur Geschichte der Religion und Philosophie in Deutschland* (*On the History of Religion and Philosophy in Germany*, 1834) and *Die romantische Schule* (*The Romantic School*, 1836). In 1835 his works were officially condemned in Germany, but he renewed his attack in two verse satires, *Atta Troll* (1843) and *Deutschland: Ein Wintermärchen* (1844). In 1848 he became paralysed by spinal tuberculosis and was bedridden for the rest of his life. G. *Eliot wrote critical essays on his works, as did M. *Arnold (*Essays in Criticism*, 1st series).

HEINLEIN, Robert, see FANTASY FICTION; SCIENCE FICTION.

HEINSIUS, Daniel (1580–1655), Dutch scholar, editor of Aristotle's *Poetics* (1611) and author of *De Tragoediae Constitutione* (1611), a Latin work on tragedy which had a significant effect on French classical theatre. His son Nicolaas Heinsius (1620–81), also a famous scholar, published critical editions of Roman poets and travelled in England. Daniel Heinsius' edition of *Virgil (1636) is his most famous work.

Heir-at-Law, The, a comedy by G. *Colman the younger.

Heiress, The, a comedy by *Burgoyne.

Heir of Redclyffe, The, a novel by C. M. *Yonge, published 1853.
 This novel, illustrating the contrast between real and apparent goodness of character, is the story of the cousins Guy and Philip Morville; the former—who is the heir of a baronetcy and an ancient house—is hot-tempered but generous, the latter a much-admired prig. Philip, by passing on ill-founded suspicions about Guy, at first succeeds in thwarting Guy's marriage to his guardian's daughter Amy, but Guy's character is eventually vindicated and he marries Amy. On their honeymoon they find Philip severely ill with fever; Guy nurses him through the fever, catches it himself, and dies, whereby the now repentant Philip inherits Redclyffe.

He Knew He Was Right, a novel by A. *Trollope, published 1869.
 Louis Trevelyan, on a visit to the Mandarin Islands, marries Emily Rowley, daughter of the governor. The couple return to England, where Trevelyan begins to be troubled by visits from the governor's old friend, the ageing philanderer Colonel Osborne. Osborne enjoys the sensation he creates, and continues to call; Emily's pride gives her husband further fuel for his jealousy. Partly as a result of misunderstanding, partly as a result of Trevelyan's morbid instability of temperament, a

separation ensues, and Bozzle, a private detective, becomes the only mediator between the couple. Trevelyan abducts his son and takes him off to Italy. In time Emily pursues them, only to find her husband in a state of complete mental breakdown. There is a partial reconciliation between husband and wife, but Trevelyan dies soon after his return to England.

The Italian scenes allow Trollope time to caricature the transatlantic feminism of Miss Wallachia Petrie and to marry off the English aristocrat Mr Glascock to the charming American Caroline Spalding. The novel also contains the story of old Aunt Stanbury of the cathedral close at Exeter, with her protégés, particularly her nephew Hugh, whose engagement to Emily's sister Nora temporarily angers her.

Helena, (1) the taller of the two young heroines in Shakespeare's *A Midsummer Night's Dream* and lover of Demetrius; (2) the heroine of his *All's Well that Ends Well*, whose name may derive from the Queen Helen in Sidney's *Arcadia*, who is unhappily in love and skilled in surgery; (3) Helen of Troy in Goethe's *Faust*.

Helen of Kirkconnell, the subject of an old ballad (included in Sir W. Scott's *Minstrelsy of the Scottish Border* and F. T. *Palgrave's Golden Treasury*), who throws herself before her lover when his rival fires at him, and dies to save him. The story is also the subject of *Wordsworth's 'Ellen Irwin'.

Heliand, The, an Old Saxon paraphrase in alliterative verse of the NT, dating from the 9th cent.

HELIODORUS, see AETHIOPICA.

Hellas, a lyrical drama by P. B. *Shelley written at Pisa in late 1821, the last work to be published in his lifetime, 1822. Based in form on the *Persians* of *Aeschylus, it was inspired by news of the Greek War of Independence against the Turkish Empire, and dedicated to their national leader, Prince Mavrocordato, whom Shelley had known at Pisa.

The action, 'a series of lyric pictures', is set at Constantinople, where the Turkish Sultan Mahmud receives a number of messengers reporting the insurrection, and prophesying Greek victory. Shelley uses visionary figures—Christ, Mahomet, Ahasuerus the *Wandering Jew, and the phantom of Mahomet II—to explore a cyclical philosophy of history. But the main interest lies in the choruses, composed like songs for opera, and concluding with the celebrated poem, 'The world's great age begins anew'. Shelley's preface, his last great appeal for political liberty in Europe, remains a classic statement of English philhellenism: 'We are all Greeks.'

Hellenistic, a term that in the 20th cent. came to replace the earlier adjective 'Alexandrian', applied to the civilization, language, art, and literature of the Graecized lands of the eastern Mediterranean from the death of *Alexander (323 BC) to that of Cleopatra (31 BC). In the creative arts Hellenism was distinguished by a preference for small, delicate, and highly decorated products intended to please a public of connoisseurs. Hellenistic literature displayed (sometimes in one and the same work) a mandarin artificiality full of recondite, learned allusions and a lively, realistic interest in everyday life. Its treatment of the gods of Greece showed at times genuine religious feeling, but was often playful and mocking, marked by a preoccupation with the excitements of sex that bordered on the pornographic. Subtly ironic, highly polished, it seems in spite of its sincerities to hold life at arm's length. Much of this literature has perished, and what we possess of it today is, thanks to papyrus discoveries, far more than was available during the *Renaissance. But the Hellenistic tradition had a marked influence on the Latin poets of the late Republic and the *Augustan age and so exercised a far-reaching, if indirect, influence.

Hellenore, in Spenser's *Faerie Queene (III. x), the wife of *Malbecco, who elopes with *Paridell.

HELLER, Joseph (1923–99), novelist, born in New York. He served as a bombardier in the air force during the Second World War, an experience which resurfaced in his first novel, *Catch-22 (1961), a satire on the absurdity of war which took him eight years to write and brought him instant fame. His second novel, *Something Happened* (1974), is the domestic tragi-comedy of a middle-aged New York executive, Bob Slocum, and *Good as Gold* (1979) a surreal and comic satire about Jewish New York and Washington politics. *God Knows* (1984), a monologue spoken by the biblical King David, was followed by *Picture This* (1988) and *Closing Time* (1994), a sequel to *Catch-22* in which several of the original characters reappear, including the bombardier Yossarian.

HELLMAN, Lillian (1905–84), American dramatist, screenwriter, librettist, and writer of memoirs, born in New Orleans. She was for many years the partner of Dashiell *Hammett, and with him was accused of un-American activities during the McCarthy period. Her plays include *The Children's Hour* (1934), set in a girls' school, in which two teachers are accused by a malicious pupil of having a lesbian relationship, and lose the libel action they take against her grandmother; *The Little Foxes* (1939), a family melodrama set in 1900 in the deep South, and *Watch on the Rhine* (1941), an anti-Nazi war drama set near Washington. Other works include *Pentimento: A Book of Portraits* (1973), an account of friendships with various people, including 'Julia', filmed as *Julia* (1977), with Vanessa Redgrave.

HÉLOÏSE, or **ELOISA,** see ABELARD.

HELVÉTIUS, Claude Arien, see PHILOSOPHES.

HEMANS, Mrs Felicia Dorothea, née Browne (1793–1835), a precocious and copious poet of intermittent but often considerable skill, who was born in Liverpool and educated at home. She published her first volume of *Poems* when she was 15, and in 1812 married Captain Hemans, from whom she lived apart from 1818, though they had five sons. From the publication of *The Domestic Affections* in 1812 she produced further volumes, exhibiting a wide range of subject and style, almost every year until her death: these include many historical poems, a volume of patriotic *Welsh Melodies* (1822: she lived with her mother and sons for some years in Flintshire, Wales) and *Records of Woman* (1828), evoking legendary and historical women. She made many translations from *Camões and other Portuguese or Spanish poets, including *Translations from Camoens and Other Poets* (1818). Her works were very popular, especially in America. The most famous of her poems, 'Casabianca', beginning 'The boy stood on the burning deck', appeared in *The Forest Sanctuary* (2nd edn, 1829).

HEMINGES, or **HEMING,** John (1566–1630), and **CONDELL,** Henry (d. 1627), fellow actors of Shakespeare and joint editors of the First *Folio of his plays (1623). Heminges is said to have been the first player of *Falstaff.

HEMINGWAY, Ernest Miller (1899–1961), American short story writer and novelist, born in Illinois, the son of a doctor. After working as a Kansas City reporter he served in 1918 as a volunteer with an ambulance unit on the Italian front, where he was wounded, then worked as a reporter for the Toronto *Star* before settling in Paris among the American expatriate literary group, where he met *Pound, G. *Stein, F. M. *Ford, and others described in his posthumously published *A Moveable Feast* (1964). His *Three Stories and Ten Poems* (1923) was followed by *In Our Time* (1923; stories) and two novels, the satirical *The Torrents of Spring* (1926) and the more characteristic *The Sun Also Rises* (1926; in England, as *Fiesta*, 1927), with which he made his name. It catches the post-war mood of disillusion of the so-called 'lost generation' through its portrayal of the wanderings of Lady Brett Ashley and her entourage, which includes the war-wounded, impotent American reporter Jake Barnes; its economy of style and characterization and its 'toughness' of attitude made a great impression. *A Farewell to Arms* (1929), the story of a love affair between an American lieutenant and an English nurse during the war on the Italian front, confirmed his position as one of the most influential writers of the time. He has been considered a finer writer of short stories than of novels, and his collections *Men without Women* (1927) and *Winner Take Nothing* (1933) are especially notable. His growing dissatisfaction with contemporary culture was shown by his deliberate cultivation of the brutal and the primitive; he celebrated bullfighting in *Death in the Afternoon* (1932) and big game hunting in *The Green Hills of Africa* (1935). He actively supported the Republicans during the Spanish Civil War, and *For Whom the Bell Tolls* (1940) is set against its background.

He was a war correspondent in Europe in the Second World War. In his later years he lived mostly in Cuba, where his passion for deep-sea fishing provided the setting for his most successful later work, *The Old Man and the Sea* (1952), a parable-novella about man's struggle against nature. He was awarded the *Nobel Prize in 1954 and wrote little thereafter; he shot himself in July 1961, having been seriously ill for some time. Various posthumous publications followed, including volumes of selected journalism and his *Selected Letters* (1981).

Henchard, Michael, the mayor in Hardy's *The Mayor of Casterbridge.*

hendecasyllabic, a verse line of 11 syllables (¯ ¯ ¯ ˘ ˘ ¯ ˘ ¯ ˘ ¯ ¯), used by *Catullus and imitated by *Tennyson:

> O you chorus of indolent reviewers.

hendiadys, from the Greek words meaning 'one by means of two', a figure of speech by which a single complex idea is expressed by two words joined by a conjunction, e.g. 'sound and fury' for 'furious sound'.

HENDRY, James Findlay, see NEW APOCALYPSE.

HENGIST and **HORSA,** the traditional leaders of the Jutes who, according to *Bede (*Ecclesiastical History*, I. 15), landed at Ebbsfleet in 449 and were given by *Vortigern the Isle of Thanet for a dwelling-place. Horsa was killed in battle against Vortigern in 455, but Hengist was the progenitor of a line of Kentish kings through his son Æsc.

HENLEY, John (1692–1756), an eccentric preacher, generally known as 'Orator' Henley, who published works on oratory, theology, and grammar. From Dec. 1730 to Jan. 1741 he single-handedly authored the *Hyp-Doctor*, a pro-government weekly periodical which had the *Craftsman* as its main target. Infamous for his *mock-biblical political preaching, he was caricatured by *Hogarth and ridiculed in *Pope's *Dunciad. See G. Midgley, *The Life of Orator Henley* (1973).

HENLEY, W(illiam) E(rnest) (1849–1903), son of a Gloucester bookseller, and pupil there of T. E. *Brown. He suffered from boyhood from tubercular arthritis and had a foot amputated; to save the other he went in 1873 to Edinburgh where he spent a year in the Infirmary under the care of Lister. His 'Hospital Sketches', a sequence of poems first published in the *Cornhill* in 1875 and subsequently revised, are a striking record of this grim ordeal, and his best-known poem, the defiant and stoic 'Invictus' ('Out of the night that covers me'), was written in 1875. While in hospital he was introduced by L. *Stephen to R. L. *Stevenson, who became a close friend and with whom he collaborated in the plays *Deacon Brodie* (1880), *Admiral Guinea* (1884), *Beau Austin* (1884), and *Macaire* (1885), none of which had much success. He did a great deal of miscellaneous literary work, much of it as editor of the *Magazine of Art* (1881–6), the *Scots Observer*, continued as the *National Observer* (1888–94), and the *New Review* (1895–8); he was a courageous and independent editor, publishing important work by *Hardy, *Kipling, Stevenson, *Yeats, H. *James, and H. G. *Wells, among many others. He also compiled anthologies, and edited *Slang and Its Analogues* (7 vols, 1890–1904). A powerful and flamboyant personality, described by Stevenson (in his portrait of him as 'Burly' in his essay 'Talk and Talkers') as 'boisterous and piratic', he had considerable influence on his contemporaries, particularly in his defence of realism and activism, although his literary judgements were not always dictated by his strong Tory imperial views. His volumes of poetry include *A Book of Verses* (1888), *The Song of the Sword and Other Verses* (1892), *London Voluntaries* (1893), and *For England's Sake* (1900), some of which, notably the last, expound his jingoistic patriotism. But he also wrote ballads, lyrics, and impressionistic free verse; he dedicated an evocation of the Thames ('Under a stagnant sky') to *Whistler, whose work he had consistently championed. Stevenson acknowledged him as the inspiration behind the creation of Long John Silver in *Treasure Island*. There are lives by L. C. Cornford (1913), K. Williamson (1930), and J. H. Buckley (1945).

HENRI, Adrian Maurice (1932–2000), poet and painter, born in Birkenhead and educated at the University of Durham, where he studied fine art. He settled in Liverpool in 1957, and during the 1960s was known (with Roger McGough and Brian Patten) as one of the *'Liverpool poets'; from 1967 to 1970 he led the poetry/rock group 'Liverpool Scene'. His own collections of poetry include *Tonight at Noon* (1968), *City* (1969), *From the Loveless Motel* (1980), *Penny Arcade* (1983), and *Collected Poems 1967–1985* (1986).

HENRY II (1133–89), king of England 1154–89. His literary occurrences tend to be related to his order (traditionally regarded as misinterpreted) to kill *Becket.

Henry IV, King, Parts 1 and 2, historical plays by *Shakespeare, written and performed about 1597. Part 1 was printed in quarto 1598, Part 2 1600. The chief sources are the chronicles of *Hall and *Holinshed, and *Daniel's historical poem *The Civil Wars*. The contemporary popularity of the plays on the stage was recorded by Leonard Digges (printed 1640 but written before 1635):

> let but *Falstaffe* come,
> *Hall, Poines,* the rest you scarce shall have a roome
> All is so pester'd.

They have been popular fairly continuously ever since.

The subject of Pt 1 is the rebellion of the Percys, assisted by Douglas and in concert with Mortimer and Glendower; and its defeat by the king and Prince Hal, the prince of Wales, at Shrewsbury (1403). *Falstaff first appears in this play. The prince of Wales associates with him and his boon companions, Poins, Bardolph, and Peto, in their riotous life. Poins and the prince contrive that the others shall set on some travellers at Gadshill and rob them, and be robbed in their turn by themselves. The plot succeeds, and leads to Falstaff's well-known fabrication to explain the loss of the booty, and his exposure. At the battle of Shrewsbury, Prince Hal kills *Hotspur in a heroic single combat, and then discovers Falstaff feigning death, whom he mourns with the words, 'I could have better spar'd a better man.' After Hal's exit Falstaff resourcefully claims credit for having slain Hotspur.

Pt 2 deals with the rebellion of Archbishop Scroop, Mowbray, and Hastings; while in the comic underplot the story of Falstaff's doings is continued, with those of the prince, *Pistol, Poins, Mistress *Quickly, and Doll Tearsheet. Falstaff, summoned to the army for the repression of the rebellion, falls in with Justices *Shallow and *Silence in the course of his recruiting, makes a butt of them, and extracts £1,000 from the former. Henry IV dies, reconciled to his son, and Falstaff hastens from Gloucestershire to London to greet the newly crowned king, who rejects him in the speech beginning 'I know thee not, old man. Fall to thy prayers', banishing him from his presence but allowing him 'competence of life'.

Henry V, King, a historical drama by *Shakespeare, written, as the reference to *Essex in Ireland (v. chorus, 30–2) indicates, in the spring or summer of 1599. It was printed in 1600 from what may be a memorial reconstruction; the First *Folio text (1623) is based on Shakespeare's own papers. Its chief sources are the chronicles of *Hall and *Holinshed. The play has most often been popular in time of national crisis, as in the film version made in 1944 with Laurence Olivier as Henry. Kenneth Branagh's 1989 film (which he directed and in which he played the leading role) presented a harsher and more questioning view of the play.

The play opens with the newly ascended Henry astonishing clergy and courtiers by his piety and statecraft (cf. Prince *Hal). The archbishop of Canterbury demonstrates, in the long 'Salic Law' speech, Henry's claim to the throne of France, and the dauphin's jesting gift of tennis balls gives him an immediate pretext for invasion. Henry unmasks the three traitors, Scrope, Grey, and Cambridge, and sets out for France; he besieges and captures Harfleur, and achieves a resounding victory at Agincourt (1415), a battle for which he prepares his soldiers in the 'Crispin Crispian' speech. Comic relief is provided by the old tavern companions of *Falstaff, who have fallen on hard times, and by some of Henry's soldiers, especially the pedantic but courageous Welsh captain Fluellen. The new, patriotic, comic characters symbolically defeat the old when Fluellen compels the braggart Pistol to eat a leek (v. i). The last act is given to Henry's wooing of Katherine of France.

Henry VI, King, Parts 1, 2 and 3, sections of a historical tetralogy (completed by *Richard III*) by *Shakespeare written between 1590 and the summer of 1592. Part 1 was not published until the First *Folio (1623), but Part 2 was published anonymously in 1594 under the title 'The First Part of the Contention betwixt the Two Famous Houses of Yorke and Lancaster . . .', and Part 3 in 1595 as 'The True Tragedie of Richard Duke of Yorke, and the Death of Good King Henrie the Sixt'. Shakespeare's authorship of the plays, especially of Part 1, was doubted throughout the 18th and 19th cents, on the grounds that they were artistically unworthy of him. In the 20th cent., however, although scholars have made increasingly confident claims for his sole authorship, others have argued that parts of the plays were written in collaboration, especially that most of the first act of 1 Henry VI was by T. *Nashe. Reference to 'an upstart Crow' in *Greenes Groats-Worth of Witte used to be taken as evidence of plagiarism, but is now generally read as merely the malice of a rival dramatist. The plays' chief sources are the chronicles of *Hall and *Holinshed.

Pt 1, opening with the funeral of Henry V, deals with wars in France in which the gallant Talbot is a powerful leader on the English side, and the witchlike *Joan of Arc, 'La Pucelle', on the French. After a series of encounters Talbot, together with his valiant son John Talbot, are killed near Bordeaux (IV. vii). A crucial scene (II. iv) is that in the Temple garden, in which the plucking of red and white roses establishes the opposition of Plantagenet and York in the subsequent wars. In the fifth act the earl of Suffolk arranges a marriage between the young Henry VI and *Margaret of Anjou, daughter of the king of Naples, vowing ominously to rule king, queen, and kingdom.

Pt 2 shows Henry's marriage to Margaret. The giving of Anjou and Maine to her father as a price for her marriage angers *Humphrey, duke of Gloucester, the lord protector; his wife Eleanor is banished as a witch (II. iii) and he is arrested on a charge of high treason, against the king's better judgement, and murdered. Suffolk is banished and, after a touching farewell to Queen Margaret, murdered by pirates on the Kent coast. Richard, duke of York, pretender to the throne, stirs up Jack Cade to rebellion (IV): after considerable success, Cade is eventually killed by Alexander Iden, a Kentish gentleman. The final act concerns the battle of St Albans (1455), in which Somerset is killed, a victory for the Yorkists.

Pt 3 opens with Henry's attempt to buy peace by making the duke of York his heir, thus disinheriting his son by Margaret. Savagery and strife proliferate, however; Margaret, enraged and eloquent, instigates the murder of the boy Rutland, York's youngest son, by Clifford, and the mock-coronation and murder of York himself, who addresses to her the line that *Greene was to parody, 'O tiger's heart wrapp'd in a woman's hide!' Clifford is killed at the battle of Towton, which also includes a scene symbolic of the horrors of civil war in

which a son who has killed his father encounters a father who has killed his son. Henry VI is captured and Edward (IV) declared king; he marries the dowerless widow Elizabeth Grey, though previously promised to Bona, the French king's sister. Richard, duke of Gloucester (later Richard III), emerges as an ambitious *Machiavelli. Warwick, a powerful contriver on the Lancastrian side, is killed at Barnet by King Edward; the battle of Tewkesbury is a decisive victory for Edward, and Margaret's young son (also an Edward) is killed in cold blood by Edward, Richard, duke of Gloucester, and George, duke of Clarence. King Henry, imprisoned in the Tower, is murdered by Richard.

Henry VII, The History of the Reign of, by F. *Bacon, published in 1622. It marked a new era in English historiography. Rejecting the medieval chronicle form and the providential concept of history still popular in the 17th cent., Bacon blended elements from the Italian Renaissance and classical antiquity. He followed *Machiavelli and *Guicciardini in concentrating on political events, fusing their tendency to explain historical change in terms of the main actors with *Tacitus' emphasis on the causes and motives which determine events. Bacon used the standard historical sources—the Anglicae Historiae Libri XXVI (1534, rev. edn 1555) of Polydore *Vergil, and E. *Hall's The Union of the Two Noble and Illustre Families of Lancastre and York (1548)—but interpreted the material to show how the king's behaviour was affected by his personality. The fact that Henry (a Lancastrian, descended from *John of Gaunt through the illegitimate Beauforts) succeeded to the throne after deposing *Richard III, although his dynastic claims were weaker than those of his Yorkist wife, Bacon argued, accounted for the insecurity which made him 'a dark prince, and infinitely suspicious'. His dubious title to the throne explains the numerous rebellions and conspiracies that his reign witnessed, including the claims of two royal impostors, Lambert Simnell and the more famous Perkin Warbeck (this episode was the source for Ford's play *Perkin Warbeck). Bacon also emphasized the king's avarice. Earlier historians assigned this to Henry's late years, but Bacon showed it to have been constant throughout his life, taking many forms: high taxes, raising money for wars but keeping it in his coffers, and oppressing the rich with illegal extortions. (Modern scholarship has endorsed Bacon's analysis.) Bacon ends with a penetrating summing up of the king's character, who brought peace by uniting the houses of York and Lancaster, yet never escaped the effects of civil war and many years spent in exile: reserved, distrustful, hungry for money and power, winning fear and respect from his subjects, but not love.

HENRY VIII (1491–1547), king of England, from 1509. His life was written by Lord *Herbert of Cherbury. His book A Defence of the Seven Sacraments, directed against *Luther's teaching, was printed in 1521 and presented to *Leo X, who thereupon conferred on Henry the title 'Defender of the Faith'. Henry was also an accomplished musician and poet, and several of his compositions survive, including 'Pastyme with good companye', 'Alas, what shall I do for love?', and 'O my hart and O my hart'. His lyrics deal with courtly and chivalric themes, with one known exception, the sacred composition 'Quam pulcra es'. (See J. Stevens, *Music and Poetry in the Early Tudor Court*, 1961.) *Holbein was painter at Henry's court, and drew and painted many of his circle, as well as the king himself. Henry's private life became the subject of many dramas and works of fiction, including a work by Shakespeare and *Fletcher (below), and he remains legendary on account of his six wives, who were, successively, Catherine of Aragon (m. 1509), Anne Boleyn, mother of *Elizabeth I (m. 1533), Jane Seymour (m. 1536), Anne of Cleves (m. 1539), Catherine Howard (m. 1540), and Catherine Parr (m. 1543).

Henry VIII, a historical drama also known to contemporaries as 'All is True'. Shakespeare has been claimed as its sole author, but it is usually held that he was responsible for less than half of the play, the remainder being written by J. *Fletcher, whose hand in it was originally suggested by *Tennyson. Its early production may have been connected with the marriage in February 1613 of Frederick, the elector palatine, and Princess Elizabeth, daughter of James I and Anne of Denmark. Its performance in June 1613 resulted in the burning down of the *Globe Theatre.

It deals with the fall and execution of the duke of Buckingham; the question of the royal divorce (vividly depicting the dignity and resignation of Queen Catherine); the pride and fall of Cardinal Wolsey and his death; the advancement and coronation of Anne Boleyn; the triumph of Cranmer over his enemies; and the christening of the Princess Elizabeth.

The chief sources of the play are *Holinshed's *Chronicles* and Foxe's *Actes and Monuments* (or *Book of Martyrs*).

HENRY, O., pseudonym of William Sydney Porter (1862–1910), American short story writer, born in North Carolina. He had a chequered early career, which included a term in prison for embezzlement (1896). He began to write short stories in prison, based on his observations of life, and published the first of his many collections, *Cabbages and Kings*, in 1904. He was prolific, humorous, and highly ingenious, especially in his use of coincidence, and became the most famous writer of his kind of the day.

HENRY OF HUNTINGDON (?1084–1155), archdeacon of Huntingdon, compiled at the request of Bishop Alexander of Lincoln a *Historia Anglorum*, which in its latest form extends to 1154.

HENRY THE MINSTREL, or **BLIND HARRY** or **HARY** (?1440–?92), a half-legendary Scottish poet, perhaps a native of Lothian, who wrote in about 1460 *The Wallace*, one of the most famous of all *Scots poems. This vigorous poem consists of about 12,000 lines in heroic couplets concerning the martial feats of William Wallace, who was executed by the English in 1305. It claims to be based on a work of John Blair, Wallace's chaplain. The earliest text is a manuscript (in the Scottish National Library) written in 1488 by John Ramsay, the scribe of *Barbour's *The Bruce*. A popular version of the poem was a rewriting in 1722 by William Hamilton of Gilbertfield, which inflamed *Burns. See *Hary's Wallace*, ed. M. P. McDiarmid (STS, 2 vols, 1968–9).

HENRYSON, Robert (?1424–?1506), a Scottish poet of the school known until recently as 'Scottish *Chaucerians', and, along with *Dunbar, its most prominent member. His dependence on Chaucer is not now much stressed. His most important poems are *The Testament of Cresseid*, written as a moralizing but sympathetic sequel to Chaucer's *Troilus and Criseyde* and printed with editions of Chaucer as its Book VI until the 18th cent., and his *Morall Fabillis of Esope*. Henryson was a schoolteacher from Dunfermline; his distinctive virtue is the combination of stern morality with humane sympathy.

Ed. H. Harvey Wood (Edinburgh, 1933; rev. 1958); J. Speirs, *The Scots Literary Tradition* (1940); M. W. Stearns, *Robert Henryson* (1949); Douglas Gray, *Robert Henryson* (1979).

HENSHER, Philip (1965–   ), novelist and journalist, educated at the universities of Oxford and Cambridge; he worked for some years as a clerk in the House of Commons. His first novel, *Other Lulus* (1994), was followed by the much-praised *Kitchen Venom* (1996), a moody family drama based in part on his experiences at Westminster at the time of Mrs Thatcher's defeat. *Pleasured* (1998) is set in Berlin just before the collapse of communism and the fall of the wall, and offers a bleak, comic, and poignant account of lives caught up in urban terrorism and espionage. *The Mulberry Empire* (2002) is a historical novel set largely in 19th-cent. Afghanistan.

HENSLOWE, Philip (c.1557–1616). He built the *Rose Theatre on Bankside in 1587, and thereafter was involved in theatrical affairs as financier, manager, and owner until his death. With his stepson-in-law *Alleyn he was involved in the affairs of several important companies of actors, notably the Lord Admiral's Men, and in the building of the Fortune and *Hope theatres. Most of the dramatists of the period, apart from Shakespeare, at some time wrote for his companies. His *Diary* (ed. R. A. Foakes and R. T. Rickert, 1961) contains a mass of information about theatrical life, and about dramatists and their methods of writing plays.

HENTY, G(eorge) A(lfred) (1832–1902), novelist. He enlisted as a soldier in the Crimea, where he became a war correspondent, a career he followed subsequently in Italy, Abyssinia, Ashanti, Spain, India, and in Paris during the Commune. He wrote without success some dozen novels for adults, including *Colonel Thorndyke's Secret* (1898), but was very successful for many years as the author of stories for boys, mainly based on military history. *Out in the Pampas* (1868) was followed by some 35 other books, sometimes at the rate of three or four a year. Most ran to several editions, and some are still available. Among the best remembered are *The Young Buglers* (1880), *Under Drake's Flag* (1883), *With Clive in India* (1884), and *The Lion of St Mark's* (1889). The didactic influence, conveyed largely through the manly characters of the heroes, is supported by strong narrative and an appearance of historical fidelity.

HENZE, Hans Werner (1926–   ), German composer. His very substantial list of works includes two operas to librettos by W. H. *Auden and Chester Kallman, *Elegy for Young Lovers* (1961) and *The Bassarids* (1966), and *Moralities* (1968), a set of three scenic cantatas with texts by Auden after *Aesop. There is an early *Whitman cantata and one unusual Shakespearian work, *Royal Winter Music* (1976), a sonata for guitar in which each movement is concerned with a character from one of the plays. Henze's large-scale stage work *We Come to the River*, described as 'actions for music' with a text by E. *Bond, was written for the Royal Opera House, Covent Garden (1976).

Heorot, see BEOWULF.

Heptameron, The, a collection of tales of love (depicted as a serious and sometimes tragic passion) linked by the fiction that the narrators are travellers detained in an inn by a flood. It was composed by Marguerite, sister of Francis I and queen of Navarre (1492–1549). Only 72 of the intended 100 tales were completed. The name 'Heptameron', 'seven days', was first given to the collection in 1559, on the analogy of Boccaccio's *Decameron*.

HERACLITUS of Ephesus (fl. *c*.500 BC), a philosopher who maintained that all things are in a state of flux, coming into existence and passing away. He condemned thinkers who sought for permanence in the universe. F. *Bacon calls him 'the profound', but more generally he was called 'the weeping philosopher' because of his conviction that nothing lasts.

Herball or Generall Historie of Plantes, see GERARD, J.

HERBERT, A(lan) P(atrick) (1890–1971), a writer of great versatility and humour, who contributed to *Punch* for many years. His works include *The Secret Battle* (1919), a stirring account of the horrors of war; *Misleading Cases in the Common Law* (1929), which ridiculed some absurdities in court procedure; *A Book of Ballads* (1949); and *Independent Member* (1950), describing his experiences as MP for Oxford University (1935–50). Herbert campaigned for several causes, such as reform in the divorce laws (a theme treated in *Holy Deadlock*, 1934), reform in English spelling (in *What a Word*, 1935), improving author's rights,

changes in the obscenity laws, and water-buses on the Thames. *Riverside Nights* (1926; a revue) and his best-known novel *The Water Gipsies* (1930) reflect his affection for the Thames. He was knighted in 1945. His autobiography, *My Life and Times*, appeared in 1970.

HERBERT, George (1593–1633), fifth son of Sir Richard and Magdalen Herbert and younger brother of Lord *Herbert of Cherbury, born in Montgomery into a prominent family. His father died when he was 3, and in 1608 his mother, the patron of *Donne, remarried Sir John Danvers, who was 20 years her junior. Educated at Westminster School where he was named king's scholar, and Trinity College, Cambridge, George published his first poems (two sets of memorial verses in Latin) in a volume mourning Prince Henry's death in 1612. But he had already, according to his earliest biographer, I. *Walton, sent his mother at the start of 1610 a New Year's letter dedicating his poetic powers to God and enclosing two sonnets ('My God, where is that ancient heat towards thee?' and 'Sure, Lord, there is enough in thee to dry'). In 1616 he was elected a major fellow of Trinity, and in 1618 appointed reader in rhetoric. In 1620 he became public orator at the university (holding this distinguished position until his resignation in 1627). He seems at this period to have been rather pushing, keen on making the acquaintance of the great and conscious of his distinction of birth. F. *Bacon and Donne were among his friends, and the public oratorship introduced him to men of influence at court. Although he was obliged, by the terms of his fellowship, to take orders within seven years, he seems to have gravitated towards a secular career, leaving his university duties to be performed by proxies. In 1624, and again in 1625, he represented Montgomery in Parliament. This fairly brief experience of worldly ambition seems, however, to have disillusioned him. He was ordained deacon, probably before the end of 1624, and installed in 1626 as a canon of Lincoln Cathedral and prebendary of Leighton Bromswold in Huntingdonshire, near *Little Gidding, where *Ferrar, whom Herbert had known at Cambridge, had recently established a religious community. Once installed, Herbert set about restoring the ruined church at Leighton. His mother died in 1627, and his *Memoriae Matris Sacrum* was published in the volume containing Donne's commemoration sermon. In March 1629 Herbert married his stepfather's cousin, Jane Danvers, and they adopted two orphaned nieces of Herbert's. He became rector of Bemerton, near Salisbury, in April 1630, being ordained priest the following September. In his short priesthood he gained a reputation for humility, energy, and charity. He was also a keen musician, and would go twice a week to hear the singing in Salisbury Cathedral which was, he said, 'Heaven upon earth'. He died of consumption shortly before his 40th birthday. When he realized he was dying he sent his English poems to his friend Ferrar with instructions to publish them, if he thought they might 'turn to the advantage of any dejected soul', and otherwise to burn them. *The Temple*, containing nearly all his surviving English poems, was published in 1633, *Outlandish Proverbs* (a collection of foreign proverbs in translation) in 1640, and Herbert's prose picture of the model country parson, *A Priest to the Temple*, in 1652, as part of *Herbert's Remains*. His translation of Luigi Cornaro's *Trattato de la vita sobria* appeared in 1634, and his 'Brief Notes' on Juan de Valdés's *Hundred and Ten Considerations* in 1638. He told Ferrar that his poems represented 'a picture of the many spiritual conflicts that have passed betwixt God and my soul'. They were much admired in the 17th cent. and 13 editions of *The Temple* came out between 1633 and 1679. In the 18th cent. Herbert went out of fashion, though J. *Wesley adapted some of his poems. The Romantic age saw a revival, and the appreciative notice in Coleridge's *Biographia Literaria* (1817) enhanced Herbert's reputation. Modern critics have noted the subtlety rather than the simplicity of his poems, seeing them as an attempt to express the ultimately ineffable complications of the spiritual life. The precise nature of Herbert's relationship to Calvinism has also generated debate. See *Works* (ed. F. E. Hutchinson, 1941); Amy M. Charles, *Life* (1977).

HERBERT, Mary, see PEMBROKE.

HERBERT, Zbigniew (1924–98), Polish poet and essayist, born in Lvov, whose predominantly political poetry has appeared in English as *Selected Poems* (1968, repr. 1985, translated by *Milosz and Peter Dale Scott) and in another selection by John and Bogdana Carpenter (published 1977) who also translated his collection *Report from the Besieged City*, which appeared in English in 1985. His last collection, *The Epilogue of the Storm*, appeared in 1998.

HERBERT of Cherbury, Edward, Lord (1582–1648), elder brother of G. *Herbert, born at Eyton-on-Severn, Shropshire, into one of the foremost families of the Welsh border. In 1596, aged 14, he was enrolled as gentleman commoner at University College, Oxford. That year his father died, and Herbert became ward of Sir George Moore (later *Donne's father-in-law). At 16 he was married to his cousin Mary, daughter of Sir William Herbert of St Julians, five years Edward's senior and heiress to her father's estates in England, Wales, and Ireland. By the time he was 21 the couple had had, he reports, 'divers children', of whom none survived him. He was created knight of the Bath in 1603. His adventures are recounted by Herbert in his *Life*, a remarkable document, not least for its unabashed presentation of its author's martial valour, success with women, truthfulness, sweetness of breath, and other virtues. Herbert aspired to a career in public service and spent much of the time from 1608 to 1618 in France, getting to know the French aristocracy and court. He also travelled in Italy and the Low Countries, fighting at the siege of Juliers (1610).

In 1619 he became ambassador to France, on *Buckingham's recommendation. His most famous philosophical work, *De Veritate*, was published in Paris in 1624. He was recalled to London in 1624, where he unsuccessfully petitioned for high office. Although he joined Charles's council of war in 1629, becoming Baron Herbert of Cherbury, recognition still eluded him. To attract royal notice he wrote, in 1630, *The Expedition to the Isle of Rhé*, which tries to justify Buckingham's calamitous generalship, and in 1632 he began a detailed 'official' history of *Henry VIII's reign, assisted by Thomas Masters, which was published in 1649. At the outbreak of the Civil War he retired to Montgomery Castle and declined to become involved. The castle was threatened by Royalists in 1644, and he admitted a parliamentary garrison, under Sir Thomas Myddleton, in exchange for the return of his books, which had been seized. He moved to his London house in Queen Street, St Giles, and dedicated himself to philosophy, supplementing his *De Veritate* with *De Causis Errorum* and *De Religione Laici*, both published in 1645, and writing besides *De Religione Gentilium* and his autobiography (begun in 1643). In 1647 he visited Gassendi in Paris.

Herbert's *De Veritate* postulates that religion is common to all men and that, stripped of superfluous priestly accretions, it can be reduced to five universal innate ideas: that there is a God; that he should be worshipped; that virtue and piety are essential to worship; that man should repent of his sins; and that there are rewards and punishments after this life. It gained Herbert the title of father of English *Deism. It was widely read in the 17th cent., earning the attention and disagreement of Mersenne, Gassendi, *Descartes, and *Locke. Herbert also wrote poetry which is obscure and metrically contorted, evidently influenced by his friend Donne, but he also wrote some tender and musical love lyrics. (See also METAPHYSICAL POETS.)

Life, ed. S. Lee (1886, rev. 1906), and ed. J. M. Shuttleworth (1976); *Poems English and Latin*, ed. G. C. Moore Smith (1923); *De Veritate*, ed. and trans. M. H. Carré (1937); *De Religione Laici*, ed. and trans. H. R. Hutcheson (1944); R. D. Bedford, *The Defence of Truth* (1979).

HERD, David (1732–1810), an Edinburgh clerk and antiquary, who produced in 1769 a collection of *Scots songs, which appeared in 1776 in a two-volume revised version in 1776 as *Ancient and Modern Scottish Songs*. Unlike many of his contemporaries, Herd was faithful to the texts as he found them, and his section of 'fragments of comic and humorous songs' provided *Burns with many suggestions.

HERDER, Johann Gottfried (1744–1803), German philosopher and critic, who decisively influenced *Goethe during the latter's early *Sturm und Drang* period. He was an ardent collector of folk song, publishing two volumes of *Volkslieder* (1778–9); an investigator of problems of language, *Über den Ursprung der Sprache*

(*On the Origin of Language*, 1772); an enthusiastic critic of Shakespeare, essay in *Von deutscher Art und Kunst* (*Of German Art*, 1773); and a philosopher of history, *Ideen zur Philosophie der Geschichte der Menschheit* (*Ideas towards the Philosophy of Mankind*, 1784–91). As a philosopher Herder's chief contribution lay in his recognition of historical evolution.

HEREWARD THE WAKE (fl. 1070), a Lincolnshire outlaw, a legendary account of whose exploits is given by the 15th-cent. forger who calls himself Ingulf of Croyland in his *Gesta Herewardi*. He headed a rising of the English, aided by a Danish fleet, against William the Conqueror in 1070. He is said to have been pardoned by William and (according to *Gaimar) killed by Normans at Maine. C. *Kingsley tells a legendary version of the story of Hereward and his wife Torfrida (1866). His mare was Swallow.

Hergest, *Red Book of*, see MABINOGION.

hermeneutics, a term for the theory of interpretation, employed at first in biblical scholarship, but then also more generally in the humanities and social sciences. In modern literary theory and related fields, the term refers to a philosophical tradition, predominantly German, in which certain general problems of interpretation arise. It originates in the lectures of the theologian Friedrich Schleiermacher (1768–1834), who proposed that comprehension of the grammatical sense of a text was insufficient without a larger intuitive grasp of the author's intention. The philosopher Wilhelm Dilthey (1833–1911) later developed the implications of this idea, and formulated the problem of the 'hermeneutic circle': that we cannot understand any part of a text or of a historical period without understanding the whole, yet we cannot understand the whole without understanding its parts. His answer to the conundrum is that we reconcile part and whole through successively adjusted provisional understandings or intuitive projections. In the philosophical tradition of Martin *Heidegger (1889–1976) and his followers, hermeneutics reaches far beyond mere interpretation, as 'understanding' is held to precede its objects. In modern literary theory, a return to hermeneutic problems is found in E. D. Hirsch's *Validity in Interpretation* (1967), which distinguishes between a work's determinate 'meaning' and its variable 'significance', and in various alternatives to his view (for which, see READER-RESPONSE THEORY). An especially influential modern hermeneuticist is the French philosopher Paul Ricœur (1913–), who has noted a distinction between the religious 'hermeneutics of the sacred', which seeks to restore an original meaning that has become obscured, and the modern 'hermeneutics of suspicion', which seeks (as in *Marx and *Freud) a concealed meaning behind misleading appearances.

Hermengyld, in Chaucer's 'Man of Law's Tale' (see CANTERBURY TALES, 5), the wife of the constable of Northumberland, to the coast of which Constance is borne when set adrift on the sea.

Hermes Trismegistus, the 'thrice great Hermes' of Milton's *'Il Penseroso', the name given by the *Neoplatonists and the devotees of mysticism and alchemy to the Egyptian god Thoth, regarded as more or less identical with the Grecian Hermes, and as the author of all mystical doctrines. From the 3rd cent. onwards the name was applied to the author of various Neoplatonic writings, including one *On the Divine Intelligence*. This work, translated by *Ficino (*c.*1490) into Latin and by John Everard (1650) into English, made a notable impact on 16th- and 17th-cent. minds. Its influence cannot, however, be isolated from the general one exercised by the Neoplatonist, cabbalistic, and occultist tradition which had such a marked effect on writers like G. *Chapman (*Euthymiae Raptus; or The Teares of Peace*, 1609), H. *Vaughan, Sir T. *Browne, *Comenius, and the *Cambridge Platonists.

hermeticism, a *Modernist trend in Italian poetry, practised by *Ungaretti, *Quasimodo and, later, *Gatto, Sereni, and Luzi. Influenced by French *Symbolism and the ideal of *la poésie pure*, it concentrated on extreme precision and intensity of language. This tended to obscurity and to drastic concision, focusing on a single image, isolating phrases or even simple words (compare *Imagism). Uneasily related to the poetics of *Marinetti, the formalism of the hermeticists allowed them to work through the Fascist period unscathed by political censorship; but this was later held against them by writers associating themselves with the Resistance.

Hermia, one of the two young heroines, the lover of Lysander, in Shakespeare's *A Midsummer Night's Dream*, the smaller in stature.

Hermione, (1) daughter of Menelaus and Helen, the wife first of Neoptolemus, then of Orestes; (2) in Shakespeare's *The Winter's Tale*, the wife of Leontes.

'Hermit, The, or Edwin and Angelina', a ballad by *Goldsmith, written 1764 and included in *The Vicar of Wakefield*. Angelina, benighted in the wilderness, and sorrowing for her lost Edwin, whom she believes dead, is welcomed to the Hermit's cell and in answer to his question reveals the cause of her sorrow. Whereupon the Hermit acknowledges himself to be Edwin. (See BALLAD.)

'The Hermit' is also the title of a poem by T. *Parnell.

Hermit of Hampole, see ROLLE.

Hermit of Warkworth, The, a Northumberland *ballad by T. *Percy.

Hermsprong, *or Man as He Is Not*, a novel by R. *Bage, published 1796.

Hermsprong, who as a boy and youth has been brought up among Native Americans, finds himself in England in the conventional and wealthy circle of Lord

Grondale. The originality of his views on, for instance, the equality of women or the class divisions of society shock the company in which he moves, and lead him into much trouble. He does not drink, play cards, or eat more than he strictly needs, and he fervently hopes that these indulgences, and the horrors of disease, will be kept away from the land of his boyhood. In the end his engaging manner and his manly, benevolent nature win him the hand of Lord Grondale's daughter. (See PRIMITIVISM.) There is a critical edition by S. Tave (1981).

Herne the Hunter, a spectral hunter said to have been in medieval times a keeper in Windsor Forest, who hanged himself from the tree known as Herne's (or, later, Falstaff's) oak, and thereafter haunted the forest; the origins of the story are uncertain, though it bears some resemblance to the tale of the *Wild Huntsman, and a version of it is related by Mrs Page in *The Merry Wives of Windsor* (IV. iv). *Falstaff dresses as Herne, for the denouement at Herne's oak. Herne also appears in *Ainsworth's historical romance *Windsor Castle* (1843), with vivid illustrations by *Cruikshank.

Hero, the beloved of Claudio in Shakespeare's *Much Ado about Nothing.*

Hero and Leander, the tragic story of Leander's love for Hero, the priestess of Aphrodite: he is drowned while swimming to her at night across the Hellespont, and she then in despair throws herself into the sea. This story has been made the subject of poems by *Marlowe and T. *Hood, and of a burlesque by T. *Nashe in his *Lenten Stuffe.*

HERODOTUS (*c*.480–*c*.425 BC), a Greek historian, often referred to as the 'father of history' since he was the first to collect his materials systematically, test their accuracy as far as he was able, and arrange them agreeably. His work, the first masterpiece of Greek prose, takes as its main theme the struggle between Asia and Europe which culminated in the Persian invasions of Greece. His 'fabulosities', as Sir T. *Browne called them, provided material for miscellanists like *Painter (1566, 1567) and Thomas Milles (1613, 1619) and later for *Landor in some early works, for *Beddoes in *Death's Jest-Book* and for M. *Arnold's 'Mycerinus' (1849).

Heroes, Hero-Worship and the Heroic in History, On, a course of six lectures by T. *Carlyle, delivered 1840, published 1841. In this series Carlyle elaborates his view that 'Universal History, the history of what man has accomplished in this world, is at bottom the History of . . . Great Men', and chooses for his examples the Hero as Divinity (e.g. Odin, the 'Type Norseman'); the Hero as Prophet (e.g. Muhammad); the Hero as Poet (e.g. *Dante, Shakespeare); the Hero as Priest (e.g. *Luther, *Knox); the Hero as Man of Letters (e.g. Dr *Johnson, *Rousseau, *Burns); and the Hero as King (e.g. *Cromwell, Napoleon).

heroic couplet, a pair of rhymed lines of iambic pentameter. The form was introduced into English by *Chaucer, and widely used subsequently, reaching a height of popularity and sophistication in the works of *Dryden and *Pope.

heroic poetry, the same as *epic.

heroic verse, that used in *epic poetry: in Greek and Latin poetry, the hexameter; in English, the iambic of five feet or ten syllables; in French, the alexandrine of 12 syllables.

HERRICK, Robert (1591–1674), seventh child of Nicholas Herrick, a prosperous goldsmith who migrated to London from Leicester, and of Julian, daughter of a London mercer, William Stone, whom Nicholas married in 1582. In Nov. 1592, 16 months after Robert's birth, and two days after making his will, Herrick's father fell to his death from a fourth-floor window in his London house. Suicide was suspected, but being 'moved with charity' the queen's almoner did not confiscate the Herrick estate for the Crown, as was usual with suicides. There is no record of Robert attending school, but the family was wealthy and the classical bent of his poetry makes it likely he had a grammar-school education. In 1607 he was apprenticed to his uncle Sir William Herrick, goldsmith, a man of mark who was MP for Leicester, owned land in 13 counties, and had been knighted in 1605. Herrick's earliest datable poem was written about 1610 to his brother Thomas on his leaving London to farm in Leicestershire ('A Country Life: To his Brother M. Tho. Herrick'). 'To my dearest Sister M. Mercie Herrick' must also have been written before 1612.

In 1613, having obtained release from his apprenticeship, he entered St John's College, Cambridge, as a fellow commoner, a status reserved for sons of wealthy families, which entailed double fees and privileges such as dining at high table. He lived lavishly at university and, despite his private income, frequently sent to his uncle William for additional funds. College friends included Clipsby Crew (knighted 1620) to whom he addressed several poems including the outstanding 'Nuptiall Song'. Herrick moved to Trinity Hall, graduating BA in 1617, MA in 1620. In 1623 he was ordained priest. He evidently mixed with literary circles in London, particularly the group around *Jonson, and was well known as a poet by 1625 when Richard James in 'The Muses' Dirge' ranked him beside Jonson and *Drayton. Friends included *Fletcher, W. *Browne, *Selden, *Corbett, Mildmay Fane (second earl of Westmorland), and W. and H. *Lawes. In 1627 he was one of the army chaplains on the duke of *Buckingham's disastrous expedition to the Isle of Rhé, in aid of the Protestants of La Rochelle. In reward for his services he received the living of Dean Prior, a village deep in the south Devon countryside, taking up the living in Sept. 1630.

Repelled by the barren isolation of rural life at first, he developed, as his poems show, a feeling for folk customs and festivals like May Day and Harvest Home, which appealed partly because the Puritans tried to suppress them. He also made friends among the country gentry, writing poems to their daughters. He left Dean Prior for a period, without permission from his bishop, and lived in Westminster with Tomasin Parsons, daughter of a musician and 27 years younger than Herrick, by whom he may have had an illegitimate daughter. An ardent loyalist, Herrick was ejected from his living by Parliament in 1647 and returned to London, where the following year his poems *Hesperides*, together with his religious poems *Noble Numbers*, were published. During the Commonwealth he probably subsisted on the charity of his relations and in 1660 was reinstated at Dean Prior where he remained for the rest of his life, writing, apparently, no more poems, and being buried in an unmarked grave in the churchyard.

Herrick's secular poems are mostly exercises in miniature, very highly polished (as comparison with surviving earlier versions shows) and employing meticulous displacements of syntax and word order so as to give diminutive, aesthetic grace to the great chaotic subjects—sex, transience, death—that obsess him. He is one of the finest English lyric poets, and has a faultless ear. His religious poems have generally been derided as childish, but more recent scholarship has seen them as part of a calculated 17th-cent. Anglican attempt to idealize childhood in face of the Puritan emphasis on original sin. See *Works*, ed. L. C. Martin (1956); *Complete Poetry*, ed. J. Max Patrick (1963); G. W. Scott, *Robert Herrick* (1974).

HERVEY, James (1714–58), rector of Collingtree and Weston Favell in Northamptonshire, prominent in the early Methodist movement. His prose poems *Meditations among the Tombs, Reflections on a Flower Garden, Contemplations on the Night*, etc. (1746–7) were extremely popular, and bear some affinity to the works of the *graveyard school.

HERVEY, John, Baron Hervey of Ickworth (1696–1743). As vice-chamberlain he exercised great influence over Queen Caroline. He was a close friend of Lady M. W. *Montagu and collaborated with her in response to attacks from *Pope. He was satirized by Pope in various works from 1732 onwards, at first with mildness, as 'Lord Fanny', an idle versifier, and then with increasing bitterness in *The Dunciad and as *'Sporus' in the *Epistle to Dr Arbuthnot* ('this painted child of dirt, that stinks and stings'). He also appears in other works under the names Narcissus and Adonis; his effeminacy was a particular target. Many of Hervey's poems appeared in *Dodsley's *Collection of Poems by Several Hands* (1748–58). His *Memoirs of the Reign of George II*, first published in 1848, edited by J. W. *Croker, give a vivid satirical picture of the court. A new edition in three volumes by R. Sedgwick was published in 1931.

HERZEN, Alexander Ivanovich (1812–70), leading Russian revolutionary thinker, born in Moscow, the son of a wealthy Russian nobleman. His early involvement in radical politics led to two periods of exile in Russia. He emigrated to the West in 1847, at first to Italy, France, and Switzerland, and to London in 1852. The Romantic and idealist philosophy of *Goethe and *Schelling and the French utopian socialism of *Proudhon were early influences on Herzen's thought. However, the failure of the revolutions of 1848 and the tragedies and turbulence of his private life deeply affected his political outlook. His disillusionment (described in *From the Other Shore*, 1850) led him to embrace a more nationalistic and agrarian kind of socialism. In London he established the first Free Russian Press (1853) and in 1857, with Ogarev, published two journals, the *Polar Star* and the *Bell*, which were smuggled into Russia, where they became a major influence on radical opinion towards the establishment of reform and emancipation of the serfs. His major work was his classic autobiography, *My Past and Thoughts* (1885), in which his personal life is interwoven with the development of his political ideology. Herzen also wrote an important critique of *Hegel from a Russian left standpoint; a novel, *Who Is to Blame* (1847); numerous essays on historical, philosophical, and political subjects; and short fictions.

HESIOD (8th cent. BC), an early Greek epic poet. The *Theogony* contains an account of the origins of the world and the genealogy of the gods. *Works and Days* gives an account of a farmer's life that was to serve *Virgil for a model in the *Georgics*. The *Shield of Heracles* is modelled in part on Achilles' shield in *Iliad 18. There are references to Hesiod in *Sidney, *Chapman, and *Dryden, and both *Spenser and *Milton made use of him.

Hesperides, see HERRICK.

HESSE, Hermann (1877–1962), German/Swiss author of several mystical novels which attracted a revival of interest in Germany and Britain in the 1960s. *Siddhartha* (1922) is rooted in Hesse's study of Indian religions and describes the quest of two Hindu friends for spiritual and sexual fulfilment; it was later adopted as a *New Age cult book. *Der Steppenwolf* (1927) came into vogue with the cult of 'the outsider' initiated in part by C. *Wilson. The latter reflects Hesse's interest in double personalities (a legacy of *Romanticism also connected with Hesse's interest in psychoanalysis). *Narziss und Goldmund* (1930) is a surrealist work set in the Middle Ages and *Das Glasperlenspiel* (*The Glass Bead Game*, 1943), Hesse's last novel, envisages a philosophical utopia under the control of a quasi-monastic élite, and was based on *Hardenberg's novel *Die Lehrlinge zu Sais* (1802). Hesse's books were banned in Germany in 1943; he was awarded the *Nobel Prize for literature in 1946.

Hetty Sorrel, a character in G. Eliot's *Adam Bede*.

HEWLETT, Maurice Henry (1861–1923), novelist, poet, and essayist, who became known for his romantic novel of the Middle Ages, *The Forest Lovers* (1898), which was followed by other historical novels, including *The Queen's Quair* (1904); three books, *Halfway House* (1908), *The Open Country* (1909), and *Rest Harrow* (1910), of which the imaginary gypsy scholar John Maxwell Senhouse is the central figure; and various volumes of poetry, including *The Song of the Plow* (1916), a long poem which recounts the history of the 'governed race' in England and particularly of Hodge, the agricultural labourer, from the Norman Conquest. He joined the *Fabian Society in 1917, and worked on a report on wages for the Board of Agriculture.

hexameter, a verse of six metrical feet, which in the typical form consists of five dactyls and a trochee or spondee; for any of the dactyls a spondee may be substituted, except in the fifth foot, where a spondee is rare. It is not frequently used in English, but has sometimes been employed, as in *Clough's *The Bothie of Tober-na-Vuolich*, to considerable effect. (See METRE.)

HEYER, Georgette (1902–74), writer of detective stories and *historical fiction; she was best known for her Regency romances, which included *Devil's Cub* (1934), *Regency Buck* (1935), and *Faro's Daughter* (1941).

Hey for Honesty, Down with Knavery, a comedy by T. *Randolph, printed 1651.

'Chremylus, an honest decayed gentleman, willing to become rich, repaireth to the oracle of Apollo, to inquire how he might compass his design. The oracle enjoineth him to follow that man whom he first met with, and never part from his company. The man whom he met is the old blind God of Wealth disguised. After this Chremylus calleth his poor (but honest) neighbours to partake of his happiness. The honest party rejoice at the news; rascals only and vicious persons are discontented. Plutus is led to the temple of Esculapius and recovers his eyesight. At this knaves are even mad, they murmur and complain exceedingly. Nay the pope himself is even starved. Lastly to vex them more, the God of Wealth is introduced, married to Honesty' (argument prefixed to the play). The play is a free adaptation of *Aristophanes' *Plutus*, and contains allusions to current events and recent plays, including mentions of *Falstaff, *Hamlet's ghost, and Shakespeare himself.

HEYLYN, Peter (1600–62), an Anglican controversialist and writer of ecclesiastical history, whose works include a defence of *Laud (*Cyprianus Anglicus*, 1668), histories of the Reformation (1661) and Presbyterianism (1670), and a *Cosmographie* (1652).

HEYWOOD, John (?1497–?1580), probably born in London. He married Elizabeth Rastell, niece of Sir T. *More. Under *Henry VIII he was a singer and player on the virginals. He was much favoured by Queen Mary, and on her death withdrew to Malines, and afterwards to Antwerp and Louvain. He published *interludes, substituting the human comedy of contemporary types for the allegory and instructive purpose of the *morality; but he did this in the form of narrative and debate rather than of plot and action. His principal works were *The Foure PP* (first printed ?1544), *The Play of the Wether* (1533), in which Jupiter takes the conflicting opinions of various persons regarding the kind of weather to be supplied, and *A Play of Love* (1534). He may also have been the author of *The Pardoner and the Frere* and *Johan Johan the Husbande, Tyb his Wyfe & Syr Jhān the Preest*, comedies of a wider scope. Heywood also wrote a dialogue called *Witty and Witless*, collections of proverbs and epigrams, and a long satirical poem, *The Spider and the Flie* (1556).

HEYWOOD, Thomas (c1573–1641), dramatist, a Lincolnshire man, and a student at Cambridge. He was writing for *Henslowe's Admiral's Men in 1596, and later became a leading dramatist of Queen Anne's and Lady Elizabeth's Men at the Red Bull and Cockpit theatres. He claimed to have written over 200 plays, many of which are lost; his chief strength lay in domestic drama. His best plays are *A Woman Killed with Kindness* (acted 1603, printed 1607), *The Fair Maid of the West* (printed 1631), and *The English Traveller* (printed 1633). His other chief plays were *The Four Prentices of London* (produced c.1600, printed 1615), ridiculed in Beaumont's *Knight of the Burning Pestle* (?1607); *Edward IV* (two parts, 1599); *The Rape of Lucrece* (1608); *The Royal King and the Loyal Subject* (printed 1637); *The Wise Woman of Hogsdon* (c.1604, printed 1638); and perhaps the *Fair Maid of the Exchange* (printed 1607), whose attribution is questioned. *The Golden Age* (1611), *The Brazen Age* and *The Silver Age* (1613), and *The Iron Age* (two parts, 1632) are a panoramic dramatization of classical mythology. His *An Apology for Actors* (1612) is the best Jacobean summary of traditional arguments in defence of the stage, and has some good anecdotes. He also translated *Sallust and published poems (including *The Hierarchy of the Blessed Angels*, 1635), translations, and pageants for seven lord mayor's shows. Two plays, *The Captives* (1624) and *The Escapes of Jupiter* (a mildly erotic cut version of the golden and silver *Ages*), survive in his own hand.

Hiawatha, The Song of, a narrative poem in unrhymed trochaic tetrameter, by *Longfellow, published 1855, reproducing Native American stories which centre in the life and death of Hiawatha, reared by his grandmother Nokomis on the shores of Lake Superior. He marries Minnehaha ('laughing water'), the Dacotah maiden, and after various adventures departs for the Isles of the Blest to rule the kingdom of the Northwest Wind. Longfellow took nothing but the name from the historical figure of Hiawatha (fl. c.1570), an Indian statesman, probably a Mohawk.

The poem's incantatory metre and novel subject matter made it immensely popular, and attracted many parodies and imitations.

Hibernia, one of the Latin names for Ireland, *Ptolemy's Ἰουερνία, a corruption of 'Iverna' the equivalent of an old Celtic word, whence 'Erin' is derived. *Claudian used the form 'Ierne'.

HICHENS, Robert Smythe (1864–1950), novelist, short story writer, and music critic, remembered for *The Green Carnation* (1894), a sub-Wildean novel of fashionable London society, and for the best-selling *The Garden of Allah* (1904), a romance of the desert set in North Africa.

HICKES, George (1642–1715), Anglo-Saxon scholar and nonjuring divine, and a passionate controversialist. He was the acknowledged leader of the first great generation of Anglo-Saxon scholars which included the *Elstobs, *Wanley, William Nicholson (1655–1727), and Edmund Gibson (1669–1748). He published the first Anglo-Saxon grammar in 1689. The climax of his work was the *Linguarum Veterum Septentrionalium Thesaurus*—the Treasury of the Northern Tongues (1703–5), a comparative grammar of Old English and the related Germanic tongues, for which he acquainted himself with almost every Teutonic manuscript of northern Europe. Its examination of the manuscript sources of Anglo-Saxon history had a deep influence upon the study of the whole Old English past. See D. C. Douglas, *English Scholars* (1939).

HICKEY, William (?1749–1830), son of the Joseph Hickey who figures in Goldsmith's *Retaliation*, and the author of entertaining *Memoirs*, 1749–1809 (first pub. 1913–25), in which he describes his numerous voyages to India and other parts of the world, his chequered career as an attorney, and, with great frankness, his weakness for women and claret.

Hieronimo, the principal character in Kyd's *The Spanish Tragedy*.

HIERONYMUS, see JEROME, ST.

Higden, Mrs Betty, a character in Dickens's *Our Mutual Friend*.

HIGDEN, Ranulf (d. 1364), a Benedictine of St Werburg's, Chester, credited by popular tradition with the composition of the Chester cycle of *mystery plays. He wrote in Latin prose *Polychronicon*, a universal history extending down to 1327, which was translated by John of *Trevisa in 1387 and printed by *Caxton in 1482. It was very popular in the 14th cent. and influenced such works as the *Stanzaic Life of Christ*.

HIGGINS, Aidan (1927–), novelist, born in Celbridge, Co. Kildare, and best known for the novel *Langrishe, Go Down* (1966), a pungent contribution to the Irish 'big house' genre. Set in the 1930s, in a disintegrating mansion, it has at its centre a trio of ageing sisters, with the emphasis falling on the youngest, Imogen Langrishe, and her affair with a German student. The theme is hitched not only to Irish, but to European malaise. *Balcony of Europe* (1972) is a very ambitious novel, which makes up in intellectual scope for what it lacks in form. Higgins has also produced some striking travel writing, and a couple of exercises in autobiography, *Donkey's Years* (1995) and *Dog Days* (1997).

HIGGINS, Frederick Robert (1896–1941), Irish lyric poet, whose volumes of poetry include *Island Blood* (1925, with a foreword by 'Æ', G. W. *Russell), *The Dark Breed* (1927), and *Arable Holdings* (1933); most of his poems deal with rural life, landscape, and legend.

Higgins, Henry, the phonetician in Shaw's *Pygmalion*, modelled on H. *Sweet.

HIGGINS, Matthew James (1810–68), known as 'Jacob Omnium', a prominent journalist who contributed to *The Times*, *Punch*, and the *Cornhill Magazine*; his articles, which often exposed abuses of social and public life, brought him into contact with *Thackeray, who dedicated his *Adventures of Philip* to Higgins. His *Essays on Social Subjects* was published in 1875.

Highland Widow, The, a short tale by Sir W. *Scott, one of the stories in *The Chronicles of the Canongate*, published 1827. The story of the widow of a Highland cateran, killed by government soldiers after the '45 rebellion, and the circumstances in which she brings about the death of her only son, is one of Scott's few excursions into unrelieved tragedy. Ostensibly told by Mrs Bethune Baliol to Chrystal Croftangry, it is, like most of the *Chronicles of the Canongate*, a lament for a forgotten world, for 'manners, long since changed and gone'.

High Life above Stairs, the subtitle of *Bon Ton*, a farce by *Garrick, performed 1775.

High Life below Stairs, a comedy by the Revd J. *Townley, produced 1759.

Lovel, a rich young West Indian merchant, receives warning that he is being outrageously robbed by his servants. He pretends to go to Devon, but returns, assumes the character of a country lad who seeks to be trained as a servant, and obtains employment under his own butler. We are presented with the gay doings below stairs, in which the servants ape the vices and follies of their masters until, the iniquities of most of his staff having been revealed to him, Lovel reveals himself and packs them off. *Wordsworth, who saw the play performed in London in 1812, wrote to his wife describing it as 'very entertaining; it is an excellent Piece' (*The Love Letters of William and Mary Wordsworth*, 1982).

HIGHSMITH, Patricia (1921–95), writer of mixed German and English–Scots parentage, educated at Barnard College at Columbia University, New York. Her stylish crime novels have a distinctively black humour: the best known (*The Talented Mr Ripley*, 1956; *Ripley under Ground*, 1971; *Ripley's Game*, 1974, etc.) feature her amoral anti-hero, the leisure-loving amateur villain Tom Ripley, resident in France. *The Price of Salt*, a novel with a lesbian theme and a happy ending, was published pseudonymously (under the name of Claire Morgan) in 1952, and appeared under her own name in 1990, retitled *Carol*. Her last novel, *Small g: A Summer Idyll*, about a bohemian café in Zurich, was published in 1995.

Hildebrandslied, a 68-line fragment of an alliterative poem in Old High German, thought to date from about 800, consisting of a dialogue between Hildebrand, a follower of Theodoric, who is returning home after many years' absence, and a young knight who challenges him. Hildebrand tries to avert a fight but fails; and, just as it transpires that the young knight is Hadubrand, his son, the poem breaks off. The manuscript disappeared in 1946 but the two sheets reappeared in America in 1950 and 1972 and are now in Kassel; the text is in Klaeber's *Beowulf* (app. 4, 290–2).

HILL, Aaron (1685–1750), poet, dramatist, theatre-manager, and projector, who wrote a much criticized history of the Ottoman Empire (1709), the libretto for *Handel's Rinaldo* (1711), and an unfinished epic poem, *Gideon* (1749). He was satirized by Pope in *The Dunciad* and elsewhere, and responded in *The Progress of Wit* (1730). He was responsible for launching the *Plain Dealer* (1724), a bi-weekly, and also dabbled in various commercial concerns, such as clearing the river Spey of rocks and manufacturing potash at Plaistow. He had a wide circle of literary friends, including *Dyer, Charles *Churchill, and James *Thomson, and *A Collection of Letters between Mr Aaron Hill, Pope and Others* (1751) is an interesting record of the period. He also edited with *Popple a bi-weekly theatrical periodical, the *Prompter* (1734–6; selection ed. W. Appleton and K. A. Burnim, 1966). See THEATRE CRITICISM.

HILL, (John Edward) Christopher (1912–2003), Marxist historian, educated at St Peter's School, York, and Balliol College, Oxford; he was for many years a fellow, then (1965–78) master of Balliol. His many works on the period of the Civil War include *The World Turned upside down: Radical Ideas during the English Revolution* (1972), which provides a lively introduction to the prose of many of the lesser known and radical writers of the period, including *Clarkson, *Coppe, *Walwyn, *Winstanley, and the anonymous author of *Tyranipocrit Discovered*. He also edited the works of Winstanley, and wrote studies of *Cromwell (*God's Englishman*, 1970), *Milton (*Milton and the English Revolution*, 1977), and *Bunyan (*A Turbulent, Seditious and Factious People: John Bunyan and His Church*, 1988).

HILL, Geoffrey (1932–   ), poet and lecturer, born in Bromsgrove and educated there and at Keble College, Oxford. His first volume of poetry was *For the Unfallen* (1959), followed by *King Log* (1968), *Mercian Hymns* (1971), which consists of prose poems celebrating Offa, 'a presiding genius of the West Midlands', and *Tenebrae* (1978). His early works show the influence of *Blake and A. E. *Housman; his language is rich and complex, and his themes predominantly historical and religious, many of the poems brooding over the violence of the near and distant past. His long poem *The Mystery of the Charity of Charles Péguy* (1983) is a densely allusive meditation on the life, faith, and death of the French poet *Péguy. *Canaan* (1996), a volume in which distinct poetic sequences are interwoven, mulls over the political and religious history of England, and denounces what it takes to be the corruption of recent public life. Hill has written two books of literary criticism, *The Lords of Limit* (1984) and *The Enemy's Country* (1991), in which the social context of poetry, and therefore the responsibilities of the poet, are minutely described. His version of *Ibsen's *Brand* was produced at the *National Theatre in 1978. His *Collected Poems* were published in 1994.

HILL, G(eorge) B(irkbeck Norman) (1835–1903), educated at Pembroke College, Oxford, chiefly remembered as the editor of Dr *Johnson. After his resignation as a headmaster in 1869 he wrote for the *Saturday Review* and began work on Johnson and other 18th-cent. writers. *Dr Johnson, His Friends and Critics* appeared in 1878, and a *Life of Rowland Hill* in 1880. *Jowett's encouragement led to a six-volume edition in 1887 of Boswell's *Life of *Johnson*, generally regarded as a masterpiece of editing. This was followed by editions of *Johnson's Letters* (1892), *Miscellanies* (1897), and *Lives of the Poets* (1905). He also edited the letters of *Swift, and the *Memoirs* of *Gibbon, wrote a memoir of Gibbon, and produced editions of the works of *Goldsmith and *Chesterfield.

HILL, Selima (1945–   ), poet, educated at Cambridge, now living in Dorset. In early collections, *Saying Hello at the Station* (1984) and *My Darling Camel* (1988), it is possible to trace the development of Hill's singular poetic landscape where the everyday is invested with wild flights of imagination, often through her signature use of surreal, extended similes. Her book-length poem, *The Accumulation of Small Acts of Kindness* (1989), charts a young woman's journey through mental breakdown and recovery, and *A Little Book of Meat* (1993) focuses on lust and Catholicism through the voice of a farm girl loosely inspired by Flannery *O'Connor and her works. Her other collections are *Trembling Hearts in the Bodies of Dogs* (1994) and *Violet* (1997).

HILL, Susan Elizabeth (1942–   ), novelist, children's writer, and radio playwright, born in Scarborough and educated at King's College, London. Her first novel, *The Enclosure* (1961), was published while she was still a student. This was followed by *Gentlemen and Ladies* (1968), in which tension is precipitated by the arrival of a stranger at a funeral; *A Change for the Better* (1969), which has an English seaside setting; *I'm the King of the Castle* (1970), a powerful evocation of childhood terrors which won the Somerset *Maugham Award; *Strange Meeting* (1971), which tells the story of a young subaltern returning to the Western Front during the First World War; and *The Bird of Night* (1972), which won the Whitbread Award. *In the Springtime of the Year* (1974) is a novel about bereavement. Throughout her work Susan Hill shows a sensitivity to atmosphere and to the nuances of the physical environment. This was used to good effect in *The Woman in Black* (1983), a successful recreation of the ambience of the Victorian ghost story that was later adapted for both the stage and for television, and *The Mist in the Mirror* (1992). *Air and Angels* (1991) is the story of a middle-aged academic's passion for a young girl. In 1993 she published *Mrs de Winter*, a sequel to Daphne *du Maurier's *Rebecca*. A collection of short stories, *The Albatross*, appeared in 1971 and a collection of her plays for radio, *The Cold Country*, in 1975. She has also published two autobiographical volumes, *The Magic Apple Tree* (1982) and *Family* (1989), and several books for children, including *Can It Be True?* (1988), *Susie's Shoes* (1989), *The Glass Angels* (1991), and *King of Kings* (1993). She is married to the Shakespearian scholar Stanley Wells.

HILLARY, Richard Hope (1919–43), RAF fighter pilot who was horribly wounded and disfigured in combat in 1940, underwent painful and lengthy surgery, and died in a flying accident. He is remembered as a writer for his account of his wartime experiences *The Last Enemy* (1942).

HILLIARD, Nicholas (*c.*1547–1619), miniaturist, patronized by *Elizabeth I from the early 1570s and later by James I. His gorgeously patterned portraits of the queen and of courtiers evoke the poetic mythology that surrounded the Virgin Queen. His miniatures, which often bear inscriptions and emblems, played a part in the ceremonies of love at the Elizabethan court; his famous *An Unknown Youth Leaning against a Tree amongst Roses* (London, Victoria and Albert Museum) suggests the delicate beauty of the Elizabethan lyric. Hilliard was the first British painter who won widespread fame and was accepted as an equal by a cultivated society; he was eulogized by contemporary poets, including H. *Constable and *Donne. Between 1589 and 1603 he wrote a treatise, the *Art of Limning*, influenced by *Alberti, Lomazzo, and *Castiglione's *Book of the Courtier*; Hilliard argues that limning is a noble art, 'fittest for gentlemen'. The treatise mentions an artistic discussion with Sir P. *Sidney, and a conversation about shadow with Elizabeth I. Hilliard

found the more prosaic court of James I less stimulating, and his art declines after 1600.

HILTON, James (1900–54), novelist, remembered principally for *Lost Horizon* (1933), set in the Tibetan lamasery of Shangri-La (the origin of this well-known term) where the inmates enjoy extended youth, and *Good-bye Mr Chips* (1934), a novella about an old schoolmaster. Hilton became a Hollywood scriptwriter and died in California.

HILTON, Walter (d. 1396), an Augustinian canon of Thurgarton, near Newark, in Nottinghamshire, the mystical author of *The Scale of Perfection* and perhaps of a number of lesser works (see D. Jones, *Minor Works of Walter Hilton*, 1929). The *Scale*, which is addressed to a single woman recluse, has some things in common with *Rolle and *The Cloud of Unknowing* (Hilton used to be considered as a possible author of the latter), but it is the most approachable and least esoteric of the celebrated 14th-cent. English mystical texts. It was edited by E. Guy (1869) and translated by G. Sitwell (1953).

Hind and the Panther, The, a poem by *Dryden, published 1687.

Dryden became a Catholic in 1685, and the poem represents an attempt to reconcile Anglican and Catholic political interests, while at the same time defending Catholic doctrine. The first part describes various religious sects under the guise of different beasts, and in particular the Catholic Church and the Church of England as the Hind and the Panther respectively. The second part is occupied with arguments about church authority and transubstantiation, issues full of political as well as ecclesiological implications. This leads into the third part, which constitutes half the poem, and is designed to recommend a political alliance between both Churches and the Crown against Whigs and Dissenters. It contains two celebrated fables, that of the swallows and that of the doves. However the balance of the latter, and so of the whole poem, may have been upset by James II's Second Declaration of Indulgence, which appealed to dissenting Protestant sects over the heads of the Anglican establishment.

HINES, Barry (1939–), novelist, children's writer, and television playwright, born near Barnsley, Yorkshire, and educated at Ecclesfield Grammar School. His first novel *The Blinder* (1966), about a talented but rebellious schoolboy footballer, was followed by *A Kestrel for a Knave* (1968; filmed by Ken Loach as *Kes*, 1969, and thereafter republished under this title) which tells the story of schoolboy Billy Caspar on an estate in a Yorkshire mining village who finds a temporary escape from a dead-end future in his passion for the bird he has trained. Other works include *First Signs* (1972), *The Gamekeeper* (1975), *The Price of Coal* (1979), and *Looks and Smiles* (1981).

HINMAN, Charlton (1911–77), a modern pioneer in the study of Shakespeare's texts. His two-volume *The Printing and Proof-Reading of the First Folio* (1963) offers a detailed analysis of how the *Folio was printed, based on a close comparison of 55 copies of the First Folio in the Folger Library aided by a machine of his own invention, the Hinman Collator. In particular, his work has shown how the shares of individual compositors who set up the type in different sections may be distinguished and characterized.

HIPPOCRATES (*c.*469–399 BC), born in the island of Cos, one of the Cyclades, the most celebrated physician of antiquity. Of the *Corpus Hippocraticum*, or collection of Greek medical works of various dates which have come down to us, none can be attributed to Hippocrates himself. The 'Hippocratic Oath' was for centuries used as an initiation oath for the medical profession.

Hippolyta, a queen of the Amazons given in marriage to *Theseus by Hercules, who had conquered her and taken away her girdle, the achievement being one of his 12 labours. She had a son by Theseus called *Hippolytus. According to another version she was slain by Hercules, and it was her sister Antiope that was the wife of Theseus. She and Theseus frame the action in Shakespeare's *A Midsummer Night's Dream*.

Hippolytus, a son of *Theseus and *Hippolyta. The fatal passion of Phaedra for her stepson Hippolytus is the subject of one of *Racine's dramas, *Phèdre*.

Historia Ecclesiastica Gentis Anglorum, the most famous work of *Bede, was finished in 731. It is a Latin history of the English people, in five books, from the invasion of Julius Caesar, beginning with a description of Britain and ending with an account of the state of the country in 731. The author draws on *Pliny and other Latin authors, and on *Gildas and probably the *Historia Britonum* of *Nennius. In the second book, in connection with the consultation between Edwin of Northumbria and his nobles whether they shall accept the gospel as preached by Paulinus, occurs the famous simile of the life of man as a sparrow flying out of the night into the lighted hall, and out again into the night. There is a version of this in *Wordsworth's *Ecclesiastical Sonnets*, entitled 'Persuasion'. The *Historia* was translated into Old English in the 890s, in the course of the programme of translations inaugurated by *Alfred. There is a modern translation by L. Sherley-Price (1955).

historical fiction, see overleaf.

Historic Doubts on . . . Richard III, see WALPOLE, HORACE.

History Man, The, a novel by Malcolm *Bradbury published in 1975. Set in the new University of Watermouth, it describes the sexual and political intrigues of manipulative radical sociologist Howard Kirk, long married to Barbara: now in their mid-thirties, they and their marriage have undergone a radical transformation since their early days as northern grammar-school students, and Bradbury charts with a precise satiric wit the collapse of the early idealism of the 1960s, the triumph of trend and form over content, the progress of student unrest and sexual liberation, the moral inconsistencies of the Kirk position, and the power of the new orthodoxies. The party-giving Kirk seems to be riding high on the tide of history, despite attempts by a disaffected student to convict him of gross moral turpitude. The large cast includes Henry Beamish, an accident-prone 'liberal reactionary'; his unhappy wife Myra; and social psychologist Flora Beniform, who bestows sex as therapy.

History of Henry Esmond, Esquire, The, a historical novel by *Thackeray, set during the reign of Queen Anne, published 1852.

Henry Esmond, who tells his own story, mainly in the third person, is the (supposed illegitimate) son of the third Viscount Castlewood, who dies at the battle of the Boyne. Henry, a serious, lonely boy, much influenced by his tutor, the Jesuit priest and Jacobite spy Father Holt, continues to live at Castlewood House under the protection of the fourth viscount, his father's cousin, and his young wife Rachel. (The skilfully oblique narration, and a preface by 'Rachel Esmond Warrington', make it clear that Henry will love Rachel, and eventually marry her.) Rachel and her husband have two children, Frank, the heir, and Beatrix, a beautiful but wilful girl. Henry is devoted to Lady Castlewood, who treats him with much kindness. The Castlewoods become estranged after Lady Castlewood catches smallpox, inadvertently brought to the household by Henry, and loses much of her beauty. The wicked Lord Mohun takes advantage of Castlewood's neglect of his wife to attempt to seduce her. There is a duel and Castlewood is killed. On his deathbed he reveals to Henry that he is in fact legitimate and the rightful heir, but Henry keeps silent for the sake of Lady Castlewood and her son. He is imprisoned for a year for having acted as Castlewood's second in the duel, for which Lady Castlewood bitterly reproaches him, and on his release joins the army and fights in the war of the Spanish Succession. On a visit to England, in a dramatic scene set in Winchester Cathedral, he is reconciled to Lady Castlewood, who is secretly in love with him: Henry falls in love with the vain and dazzling Beatrix, now grown up. But Beatrix is too ambitious to consider a man who has no fortune or position in society. Henry goes back to the wars and fights in Marlborough's Flemish campaign. The wayward Beatrix becomes engaged, first to Lord Ashburnham, then to the much older duke of Hamilton, who fights a duel with Lord Mohun, in which both are killed. Beatrix and her brother Frank, now the fifth viscount, are ardent

(cont. on p.484)

The origins of the British historical novel are congenital with those of the Gothic novel, in the larger-than-life conceptions of Elizabethan and 'heroic' *Restoration drama. Deeper roots can be traced in medieval *romances of chivalry. A convenient generic starting point is Horace *Walpole's *The Castle of Otranto (1764). As Walter *Scott noted, this was 'the first attempt to found a tale of amusing fiction upon the ancient romances of chivalry'. Walpole's antiquarian enthusiasm for mossy old castles was much copied by his disciples. Otranto patented many of the conventional devices of the *Gothic–historical tale— the ruined but menacing castle with its labyrinthine passageways, secret compartments, hideous dungeons, haunted suites, trapdoors, oratories, and chambers of horrors. Clara *Reeve frankly proclaimed her The Old English Baron (1778) to be a 'literary offspring of The Castle of Otranto'. Following Walpole the Gothic pile was adopted as a main element in the décor of the emergent historical novel (see, for instance, Scott's *Kenilworth, 1821; *Woodstock, 1826). Precise generic description was slow in emerging. In the mid-18th cent., 'romance' tended to denote a specific corpus of sagas of chivalry (works such as *Amadis of Gaul). Charlotte *Lennox's anti-romance The Female Quixote (1752) satirizes the heroine Arabella's dangerous infatuation with these 'old tales' (as does the opening chapter of Scott's *Waverley, 1814). With Clara Reeve's authoritative distinction (in The Progress of Romance, 1785) 'romance' was identified as a narrative set in the past, as opposed to the '*novel' which is set in the present (this, broadly, seems to have been the definition accepted by Scott and his many followers).

'Historical romance' is thus a term with something of the tautology about it. A distinctive turn to the embryo historical novel was given by the 'national tale'. Fiction was routinely used in the late 18th and early 19th cents to advance nationalist causes and sentiment—principally by cherishing or inventing myths about the nation's glorious past. A useful starting point for the English national tale is Thomas Leland's Longsword, Earl of Salisbury: An Historical Romance (1762), set in the 13th cent. and chauvinistically 'English'. Clara Reeve's The Old English Baron (1778) was the most influential and reprinted work in this vein, and anticipates in some respects Scott's *Ivanhoe (1819). These 'national

tales' celebrate the peculiar virtues of English (more specifically, much-romanticized 'Saxon') democracy, as founded and defended by English knights and barons. The Scottish national tale was popularized by Jane *Porter's The Scottish Chiefs (1810), a precursor of Scott's efforts in the sub-genre. After Scotland and England, Ireland furnished the richest crop of national tales. Lady *Morgan's The Wild Irish Girl (1806, subtitled A National Tale) has, at its centre, a long disquisition on the aboriginal culture of the pre-colonial Irish civilization. The 'Irish national tale' was a sub-genre which always sold well in England. The greatest of them is the earliest: Maria *Edgeworth's *Castle Rackrent (1800). This powerful depiction of Irish life in the mid-18th cent. was an influence which Scott acknowledged in his afterword to Waverley. It is a moot point as to which of these novels, Edgeworth's or Scott's, should properly be regarded as the first 'historical novel' in English. There is no dispute, however, that the success of Scott's 25 Waverley novels (1814–32) established the historical novel as the dominant style of fiction in the first half of the 19th cent. Scott's range of historical setting is remarkable, ranging from the early 'Scottish novels' (e.g. *The Heart of Midlothian, 1818; *Rob Roy, 1817), through the English Middle Ages (Ivanhoe), Jacobethan England (*The Fortunes of Nigel, 1822; Kenilworth), medieval France (*Quentin Durward, 1823), the Middle East of the Crusades (*The Talisman, 1825), and even the Roman Empire (*Count Robert of Paris, 1831). Scott stands in the same relation to the British historical novel as does Shakespeare to English tragedy.

For most of the Victorian period the historical novel retained its Scott-established status as the most respected of fiction's genres. Genuflecting to 'the author of Waverley', all the great Victorian novelists tried their hand at the form. The roll-call of titles includes: W. M. Thackeray's The History of *Henry Esmond (1852), Charles Dickens's *A Tale of Two Cities (1859), Anthony *Trollope's La Vendée (1850), Wilkie *Collins's Antonina (1850), George Eliot's *Romola (1863), Elizabeth Gaskell's *Sylvia's Lovers (1863), Hardy's *The Trumpet Major (1880), Charles Reade's *The Cloister and the Hearth (1861), and Charles *Kingsley's Hereward the Wake (1866). As with Scott, these novelists ranged freely through the British and European past, strictly observing his rule that authentically 'historical' personages should be introduced only as supporting characters. The respectability of the historical novel for school-children (on the Carlylean grounds that it instructed as well as entertained) meant that these titles became the best-known works of these authors.

The respectability of historical fiction was boosted by factual works such as *Macaulay's *History of England* (1848). The Victorians would have rated much higher than posterity the efforts of Edward *Bulwer-Lytton, whose *The Last Days of Pompeii* (1834) ranks as one of the handful of successful historical novels with a Graeco-Roman classical setting, along with Walter *Pater's eccentric *Marius the Epicurean* (1855) and Charles Kingsley's ferociously racist *Hypatia* (1853). Less successful was Bulwer-Lytton's attempt to promote his political opinions with the pro-Saxon *Harold* (1848). Catering at a lower level for the popular audience, G. P. R. *James wrote more historical (mostly sub-*Quentin Durward*) novels than anyone has been able to count; more interestingly, W. H. *Ainsworth pointed the so-called 'Newgate' novel (e.g. *Jack Sheppard*, 1840) towards crime fiction. Ainsworth also drew on Victor *Hugo's example in *The Hunchback of Notre Dame* (1830) with English 'topographical' romances such as *The Tower of London* (1840) and *Windsor Castle* (1843). An uncategorizable masterpiece is J. H. *Shorthouse's *John Inglesant* (1880), set in the English Civil War period.

At the end of the 19th cent., a number of distinguished novelists explored the romantic potential of the genre, notably R. L. *Stevenson with adventure tales such as *Kidnapped* (1886) and dark studies in psychology such as *The Master of Ballantrae* (1889). In the 19th cent. (particularly after the Education Act of 1870) there was a huge market in 'manly' historical yarns for boys, often with a strong imperialist tendency. The most famous exponents were G. A. *Henty ('the boys' Dumas') and his disciple G. Manville Fenn. H. Rider *Haggard and Stanley *Weyman straddled the adult and boys' market. Following Scott, there remained a strong link between historical and regional fiction; *Blackmore's tale of 17th-cent. Devon, *Lorna Doone* (1869), is a late flowering of this branch, as are S. R. *Crockett's tales of Lowland Scotland.

The sense that historical fiction had sunk to the condition of adventure stories for boys, and romance for the millions, cast a blight on the genre in the 20th cent. Ambitious literary writers like Aldous

*Huxley or George *Orwell were more inclined to dabble in 'future history', with science fiction (see *Brave New World*, 1932; *Nineteen Eighty-Four*, 1949). Ford Madox *Ford's Catherine Howard trilogy (1906–8) was hailed by Joseph *Conrad as the 'swan song of historical romance'. Although he had high hopes for the historical fiction over which he laboured (such as *Sir Nigel*, 1906) Arthur Conan *Doyle discovered to his chagrin that readers preferred Sherlock *Holmes. The historical fiction which the masses did like was 'Regency romances', such as Jeffrey *Farnol's *The Broad Highway* (1910) and *The Amateur Gentleman* (1913), a sub-genre whose popularity was continued later in the century by Georgette *Heyer and Barbara Cartland. Baroness *Orczy's *The Scarlet Pimpernel* (1905)—a romanticization of Dickens's French Revolution melodrama *A Tale of Two Cities*—was wildly popular, spawning a sequence of successors and film adaptations. Drawing on the nautical–historical novel pioneered by Captain Frederick *Marryat (in the 1830s), C. S. *Forester launched his middlebrow Hornblower sequence (set in the Napoleonic wars) in 1937. Mary *Renault's novels of ancient Greece (for example *The King Must Die*, 1958) appealed to the same public.

It was a feature of popular historical fiction in the 20th cent. that its practitioners have been hyperproductive. Barbara Cartland tops the list with 600 or so titles. More impressive is the work of Eleanor Hibbert, who has written her hundred or more historical novels (mainly for a female readership) as 'Jean Plaidy', 'Victoria Holt', and 'Philippa Carr'. New directions in historical fiction as an ambitious literary genre were indicated by John *Fowles's Victorian romance crossed with French *nouveau roman*, *The French Lieutenant's Woman* (1969). George MacDonald Fraser's Flashman series adopted the schoolboy villain of *Tom Brown's Schooldays* (1857), more to the taste of the 1970s and 1980s than Thomas *Hughes's paragon. That there remains literary life in the form is indicated by historical novels which have won the Booker Prize: J. G. *Farrell's *The Siege of Krishnapur* (1973), A. S. *Byatt's *Possession* (1990), and Barry *Unsworth's *Sacred Hunger* (1992). Rose *Tremain's *Restoration* (1989) has a lighter touch than these, but is a major achievement, as are the historical fantasias of Peter *Ackroyd. The genre of scholarly historical pastiche has been continued by C. *Palliser and L. *Norfolk.

Jacobites, and Esmond becomes involved with them in a plot to restore James Edward Stuart, the old pretender, to the throne on the death of Queen Anne. The plot fails because Beatrix is carrying on an intrigue with the pretender, and at the moment when he should be in London he is at Castlewood, 'dangling after Trix'. Esmond, disillusioned with Beatrix and the Jacobite cause, marries her mother Rachel and they emigrate to Virginia. The later history of the family in America and England is told in *The Virginians.

History of the Rebellion and Civil Wars, see CLARENDON.

Histriomastix, see PRYNNE, W.

HOADLY, Benjamin (1676–1761), bishop successively of Bangor, Hereford, Salisbury, and Winchester, a Low Church divine much in favour with the Whigs and Queen Caroline, whose famous sermon 'The Nature of the Kingdom or Church of Christ' (1717) initiated the *Bangorian Controversy.

HOADLY, Dr Benjamin (1706–57), son of Bishop Hoadly (above). He was a physician and (with his brother John Chancellor Hoadly) the author of one comedy, *The Suspicious Husband (1747). Verses by the Hoadly brothers appear in *Dodsley's Collection of Poems by Several Hands (1748–58).

HOBAN, Russell Conwell (1925–), American novelist and writer for children, born in Pennsylvania. In 1959 he wrote the first of more than 50 books for children, the best known being The Mouse and His Child (1967). He moved to London in 1969. Hoban's fables have affinities with *magic realism: set in bizarre but internally consistent worlds, they feature characters on strange quests, allusions to classical mythology, extensive anthropomorphism, bleak humour, and erudite wordplay. His first novel, The Lion of Boaz-Jachin and Jachin-Boaz (1973), is a fantasy drawing on Sumerian mythology. Kleinzeit (1974) is the surreal tale of a mid-life crisis set in a dreamlike London. Turtle Diary (1975), in which two disaffected people share an obsession with freeing turtles from London Zoo, was filmed in 1985 with a screenplay by H. *Pinter. Riddley Walker (1980) is set in south-east England thousands of years after a nuclear holocaust. The myths, laws, and rituals of this barbaric, post-literate society are debased versions of our own, and the story is rendered in a degenerate English vernacular of Hoban's invention. Pilgermann (1983) is a complex and scholarly allegory set during the First Crusade of 1098. The myth of Orpheus and Eurydice is a key theme in The Medusa Frequency (1987). Fremder (1996) is a dystopian science fiction novel. Mr Rinyo-Clacton's Offer (1998), a tale of damnation with echoes of the *Faust legend, is set in a precisely rendered but strangely transformed London. He wrote the libretto for Harrison Birtwistle's opera The Second Mrs Kong (1994).

HOBBES, John Oliver (1867–1906), the pseudonym of Mrs Pearl Mary Teresa Craigie. She began writing articles and criticisms for various journals. After an unhappy marriage she turned to Roman Catholicism, adding 'Mary Teresa' to her name. Her first novel, Some Emotions and a Moral (1891), established her reputation as a serious novelist. Others followed including The Sinner's Comedy (1892), Robert Orange (1899), The Serious Wooing (1901), and several plays, the most successful of which was The Ambassador (1898). She also wrote critical essays on G. *Eliot (1901, for the 10th edn of EB) and G. *Sand (1902).

HOBBES, Thomas (1588–1679), philosopher, born at Malmesbury and educated at Magdalen Hall, Oxford. For a great part of his life he was in the service of the Cavendish family, and in 1647 was appointed mathematical tutor to the prince of Wales. At some time (probably between 1621 and 1626) he was in contact with F. *Bacon, translated some of his essays into Latin, and took down his thoughts from his dictation. On three occasions he travelled on the Continent with a pupil, and met *Galileo, Gassendi, *Descartes, and the French mathematician Mersenne. On his return to England he submitted to the Council of State in 1652, and was pensioned after the Restoration. He was intimate with W. *Harvey, *Jonson, *Cowley, *Aubrey, *Waller, and *Godolphin.

As a philosopher Hobbes resembles Bacon in the practical or utilitarian importance that he attaches to knowledge. Nature and man are the objects of his enquiry. But he does not share Bacon's enthusiasm for the inductive method; he regards science as essentially deductive, and the geometrical method of demonstration as the true scientific method. Hobbes has been generally described as a Nominalist, owing to the importance he attaches to the definition of the meaning of terms. But he does not deny the reality of the common element entitling things to the same name. The basis of all knowledge, according to him, is sensation, and the causes of all sensations are the 'several motions of matter, by which it presseth on our various organs diversely'. Motion is the one universal cause, and our appetites are our reactions, in the direction of self-preservation, to external motions. Accordingly man is essentially a selfish unit. Upon this theory Hobbes bases the political philosophy expounded in De Corpore Politico (1650, originally Elements of Law), De Cive (Latin 1642, English 1651), and *Leviathan (English 1651, definitive Latin text 1668). This brought him into general disfavour on both political and religious grounds; and, indeed, the Royalists had some reason to regard Leviathan as designed to induce *Cromwell to take the crown.

Hobbes's philosophical works, founded on a comprehensive plan in which matter, human nature, and society were successively to be dealt with, include Human Nature (1650), De Corpore (Latin 1655, English 1656), and De Homine (1658). (See J. W. N. Watkins,

Hobbes's System of Ideas, 1965, and M. M. Goldsmith, *Hobbes's Science of Politics*, 1966.) He published a translation of *Thucydides in 1629, and of *Homer in quatrains (1674–5); also a sketch of the Civil Wars, *Behemoth, or The Long Parliament* (1680), which was suppressed. His reply to *D'Avenant's dedication of *Gondibert*, published in 1650, expresses his theory; he believes poetry 'should avert men from vice and incline them to virtuous and honourable literary actions', holds that 'Judgement begets the strength and structure, and Fancy … the ornaments of a Poem', and wittily applauds D'Avenant for neglecting the customary and in his view meaningless invocation of a Muse. His prose is masterly, distinguished by economy, directness, a highly effective use of metaphor, and passages of sustained and inventive irony, such as that in *Leviathan*, chapter 47, which compares the papacy with the kingdom of the fairies. The aphorism which expresses a central tenet of his philosophy, that the life of man in a state of nature is 'solitary, poore, nasty, brutish and short', has had an incalculable influence on later writers.

His complete works were edited by Sir William Molesworth (1839–45), his *Correspondence* by Noel Malcolm (1994).

Hobbinol, in *Spenser's writings, the poet's friend G. *Harvey.

Hobbit, The, see TOLKIEN.

HOBHOUSE, John Cam (1786–1869), a politician, and close friend of Lord *Byron, one of whose executors he became. His *Imitations and Translations from the Ancient and Modern Classics* (1809) contains nine poems by Byron, with whom he travelled in Europe; his *Journey through Albania* (1813) describes the same journey that appears in Byron's *Childe Harold*. In 1818 he produced the 'Historical Illustrations' to Canto IV of that poem, and the canto is dedicated to him. He was an adviser to John *Murray, who published most of Byron's work, and he ensured that Byron's *Memoirs* were burnt immediately after the poet's death. In 1865 appeared his *Recollections of a Long Life*, which contains much material relating to Byron.

HOBSBAUM, Philip Dennis (1932–2005), poet and lecturer, educated at Downing College, Cambridge. He was the founder of the *Group; a poem by M. *Bell, 'Mr Hobsbaum's Monday Evening Meeting', celebrates its gatherings, over which: 'Below the ceiling, guardian of the Grail | The ghost of Dr Leavis floats.'

HOBSBAWM, Eric J(ohn) (1917–   ), historian, born in Alexandria, and educated in Vienna, Berlin, London, and Cambridge. His widely read works, written from a Marxist viewpoint and showing a strong sympathy for the proletariat, include *The Age of Revolution 1789–1848* (1962), *The Age of Capital 1848–1875* (1975), *The Age of Empire 1875–1914* (1987), and *The Age of Extremes: The Short Twentieth Century 1914–1991*

(1994). He also wrote *The Jazz Scene*, originally published under the pseudonym of Francis Newton in 1959.

HOBSON, a Cambridge carrier, who 'sickened in the time of his vacancy, being forbidden to go to London by reason of the plague'. He died in Jan. 1630–1. *Milton wrote two epitaphs on him, and his name survives in the phrase 'Hobson's choice', which refers to his custom of letting out his horses in rotation, and not allowing his customers to choose among them. (See *Spectator*, No. 509.)

Hobson's Choice (1916), by Harold Brighouse (1882–1958), the most successful and often revived play of the *Manchester school.

HOBY, Sir Thomas (1530–66), educated at St John's College, Cambridge; from 1547 to 1555 he made frequent visits to the Continent and his notebook covering the years 1547–64, with interesting accounts of Italy, was published by the *Camden Society (1902). In 1552–3, while staying in Paris, he translated *Castiglione's *Il cortegiano*, as *The Courtyer*, though it was not published until 1561. It became immediately popular, even being translated into Latin in 1577, and was an important influence on such writers as *Spenser, *Jonson, and Shakespeare. It was edited by W. *Raleigh (1900).

HOCCLEVE, or **OCCLEVE,** Thomas (?1369–1426), apart from *Lydgate the most significant named English poet of the 15th cent. He was a clerk in the office of the privy seal and, although most of his small corpus is taken up with moral writings, a significant part of his output describes (ostensibly at least) the events of his own life, in 'La Male Regle de Thomas Hoccleve', the prologue to *The Regiment of Princes* (1411–12), and in a number of his 'Series Poems', such as 'The Complaint' and 'The Dialogue with a Friend' (linked into a series by the device of an interchange with a friend who discusses the poems). Of his 'autobiographical' writings, the most interesting deal with his mental breakdown. Traditionally he has been regarded as a poor imitator of *Chaucer; more sympathetic recent accounts (such as that of Mitchell) examine him in his own right and find him less wanting.

Ed. in two EETS volumes (ES 61 and 73, by F. J. *Furnivall and I. *Gollancz, rev. A. I. Doyle and J. Mitchell 1970, and ES 72, 'The Regiment of Princes', etc. by F. J. Furnivall, 1897); convenient selections by M. C. Seymour (1981) and B. O'Donoghue (1982); J. Mitchell, *Thomas Hoccleve: A Study in Early Fifteenth-Century English Poetic* (1968).

Hock-Tuesday play, an early English mimetic performance, perhaps of ritual origin, representing the defeat of the Danes by the English. It was revived during the festival given to *Elizabeth I at Kenilworth in 1575, and knowledge of it is chiefly based on descriptions of this. Hock Tuesday, or Hocktide, is the second Tuesday after Easter Sunday.

Hodge, a familiar adaptation of Roger, used as a typical name for the English rustic. Also the name of Dr *Johnson's cat.

HODGSON, Ralph Edwin (1871–1962), born in Co. Durham, the son of a coal merchant, and brought up in the south, where his lifelong love and observation of the natural world took root. He worked in the theatre in New York, then as an artist in London in the 1890s. His first collection of poems, *The Last Blackbird*, appeared in 1907, but his reputation was not established until 1917, when he published *Poems*, a volume which contains one of his most ambitious, visionary works, 'A Song of Honour'. In 1913 he founded a publishing house, 'The Sign of the Flying Fame', which had some influence on contemporary typography. Hodgson was much encouraged by friends such as *de la Mare, *Sassoon, and T. S. *Eliot, as well as by E. *Marsh who published some of his work in *Georgian Poetry. He lectured in Japan, 1924–38, and spent the rest of his life in the USA. *The Skylark and Other Poems*, which appeared in 1958, contained, among many shorter works, two important long poems: 'To Deck a Woman' (a new version of 'The Last Blackbird'), a passionate protest against man's cruelty to the animal world, and 'The Muse and the Mastiff'. The *Collected Poems* were published in 1961. The widely anthologized poems, which include 'Stupidity Street' and 'The Bells of Heaven', are not generally thought to do justice to the author of such poems as 'To vegetate', 'The Moor', 'Of Nature, write', and the longer poems.

HODGSON, Shadworth Holloway (1832–1912), educated at Rugby and Corpus Christi College, Oxford. He devoted his life, after the death of his wife and child in 1858, to the study of philosophy. He regarded himself as continuing and improving on the work of *Hume and *Kant, and was the first president and leading spirit of the Aristotelian Society, whose proceedings contain many addresses by him.

HOFFMANN, Ernst Theodor Amadeus (originally Wilhelm) (1776–1822), German Romantic writer and music critic. His works include the extravagantly fantastic *Fantasiestücke* (1814–15) and *Elixiere des Teufels* (*The Devil's Elixir*, 1815–16). His stories and his wild unhappy life provided the inspiration for Offenbach's *Tales of Hoffmann*.

HOFMANN, Michael (1957–), poet and translator, son of German novelist and playwright Gert Hofmann (1931–93). Michael Hofmann was born in Freiburg and educated in the United States and England: he came to England in 1961, studied English at Cambridge, and later settled in London. He is bilingual, and has translated *Kafka, *Rilke, *Brecht, and Joseph *Roth: his own volumes of verse are *Nights in the Iron Hotel* (1983), *Acrimony* (1986: Part 2 of which, 'My

Father's House', is a powerful and moving sequence to his father, that 'indulgent patriarch') and *Corona, Corona* (1993). *Approximately Nowhere* (1999) returns to the subject of his father. His poems, both European and American in manner and content, dwell on themes of travel, displacement, and love, often invoking contemporary landscapes of casual urban disorder and disconnection.

HOFMANNSTHAL, Hugo von (1874–1929), Austrian poet, dramatist, and essayist. Among his earlier plays are *Gestern* (*Yesterday*, 1891), *Oedipus und die Sphinx* (*Oedipus and the Sphinx*, 1906). *Jedermann* (*Everyman*, 1911), a modernization of the old morality play destined to become a regular feature (originally in Max Reinhardt's production) of the Salzburg Festival (which Hofmannsthal helped to found), prefigures *Das Salzburger grosse Welttheater* (*The Great Salzburg World Theatre*, 1922) and inaugurated Hofmannsthal's increasing tendency towards a religious art with strongly Roman Catholic associations. He wrote the librettos for six of R. *Strauss's operas, including *Der Rosenkavalier* (1911), *Ariadne auf Naxos* (1912), and *Arabella* (1933), and his correspondence with Strauss (1926) is of both literary and musical interest. His last play *Der Turm* (*The Tower*, 1925), influenced (like some of his other works) by *Calderón, completed Hofmannsthal's development away from *fin-de-siècle* aestheticism to the idea of literature as carrying a social and religious message.

HOGARTH, David George (1862–1927), archaeologist and authority on Near Eastern affairs. From 1908 until his death he was keeper of the Ashmolean Museum at Oxford. His publications include *A Wandering Scholar in the Levant* (1896), *The Penetration of Arabia* (1904), and *The Life of C. M. Doughty* (1928). One of his disciples at Oxford was T. E. *Lawrence, who came very much under his influence and who was later to write of him, 'He is the man to whom I owe everything I have had since I was seventeen.' See P. Knightley and C. Simpson, *The Secret Lives of Lawrence of Arabia* (1969).

HOGARTH, William (1697–1764), British painter and engraver. He was apprenticed to a goldsmith and began engraving c.1720. In 1726 he designed 12 large engravings for Butler's *Hudibras; his earliest paintings were conversation pieces, and he also painted portraits. In 1732 *The Harlot's Progress* introduced his 'modern moral subjects'; it was followed by *The Rake's Progress* (1733–5) and *Marriage à la Mode* (1743–5; London, National Gallery). This highly original genre consisted of a series of paintings, popularized through engravings, which tell a story that is topical, erotic, spiced with contemporary portraits, and yet comments with humanity and passion on social and political vices and corruption. Hogarth's later engravings, the *Industry and Idleness* series (1747) and the prints *Beer Street* and *Gin Lane* (1750–1), are coarser, and their harsher morality is aimed at a mass market. Hogarth also published a work on aesthetics, *The Analysis of Beauty* (1753).

His series of engravings were immensely successful and immediately inspired numerous plays and novels; his success was such that his work was pirated and he was instrumental in obtaining the passage of 'Hogarth's Act' (1735) protecting the copyright of engravers. *Fielding became Hogarth's friend and collaborator in the early 1730s; in his preface to *Joseph Andrews* (1742) he describes Hogarth as a 'Comic History-Painter', defending him against critics who attacked his work as mere caricature or burlesque. Fielding, and later *Smollett, compared characters and scenes in their novels to the prints of Hogarth. The artist aroused less interest in the late 18th cent. but his popularity soared in the early 19th cent., with essays by *Hazlitt and *Lamb that emphasized his literary qualities. Both *Dickens and *Thackeray admired and were influenced by him; Dickens, in the preface to *Oliver Twist*, writes that he had never met 'the miserable reality' of low-life London except in Hogarth. No other British painter has had such close connections with literature; Hogarth's *Portrait of the Painter and His Pug* (1745, London, Tate Gallery) shows his aggressive image resting on volumes of Shakespeare, *Milton, and *Swift and lays claim to his place within a British artistic tradition. See R. E. Moore, *Hogarth's Literary Relationships* (1948). There is a biography by Jenny Uglow (1997).

Hogarth Press, the, founded in 1917 by L. and V. *Woolf at their home, Hogarth House, Richmond; their earliest publications included K. *Mansfield's *Prelude* (1918), V. Woolf's *Kew Gardens* (1919, illustrated with woodcuts by V. *Bell), and T. S. *Eliot's *Poems* (1919). Their policy was to publish new and experimental work; they also published translations of *Gorky, *Chekhov, *Tolstoy, *Dostoevsky, *Bunin, *Rilke, and *Svevo. They were the first to introduce the work of *Jeffers, J. C. *Ransom, and E. A. *Robinson in England. Until 1923 they operated on a subscription basis. In 1924 they moved to Tavistock Square, where J. *Lehmann became assistant (1931–2), and then part-owner (1938–46). The press also published papers and pamphlets on psychoanalysis, politics, aesthetics, economics, and disarmament, and with its outstanding list of authors made a major contribution to the literary and intellectual life of the nation. The present Hogarth Press has been an allied company of Chatto and Windus since 1947.

HOGG, James (1770–1835), poet, who was born in Ettrick Forest and became a shepherd: after he began to write he became known as the 'Ettrick Shepherd'. His poetic gift was discovered by Sir W. *Scott, to whom he had sent poems for *The Minstrelsy of the Scottish Border* and who remained his friend. His early ballads were published as *The Mountain Bard* (1807). He came to Edinburgh in 1810, and in 1813 made his reputation as a poet with *The Queen's Wake*. He became the friend

of *Byron, *Wordsworth, *Southey, John *Murray, and other literary figures. He was on the editorial board of *Blackwood's Edinburgh Magazine*, to which he frequently contributed, notably to the 'Noctes Ambrosianae'; and he conceived the idea of the notorious *'Chaldee Manuscript' of 1817. In 1816 he was granted a farm in Yarrow and here he mainly lived for the rest of his life, combining farming with writing. He published *Pilgrims of the Sun* in 1815 and *The Jacobite Relics of Scotland* (with music) in 1819. His chief prose works are *The Three Perils of Man* (1822), *The Private Memoirs and Confessions of a Justified Sinner* (1824; now considered his most important work), and *The Domestic Manners and Private Life of Sir Walter Scott* (1834). With *Motherwell he published an edition of *Burns (1834–5). He was well thought of by his contemporaries, and Wordsworth wrote a poem 'Upon the Death of James Hogg'. See E. C. Batho, *The Ettrick Shepherd* (1927); L. Simpson, *James Hogg: A Critical Study* (1962).

HOGG, Thomas Jefferson (1792–1862), educated at Oxford with *Shelley and sent down with his friend on the publication of the latter's *Necessity of *Atheism*. He was one of the circle of Shelley, *Peacock, and other friends who about 1820 referred to themselves as 'The Athenians'. In 1832 he contributed reminiscences of Shelley at Oxford to the *New Monthly Magazine*, and these later formed a part of his *Life of Shelley* (1858). Peacock, in his *Memorials of Shelley*, felt obliged to question and revise many of Hogg's observations.

HOGGART, Richard (1918–), scholar and writer, brought up in Leeds and educated at Leeds University. He has held many academic and public appointments, and was warden of Goldsmith's College, London, 1976–84. His interest in literature, education, and the means of communication was expressed in his influential work *The Uses of Literacy* (1957), which has been followed by many other works of literary criticism and sociology and three volumes of memoirs, *A Local Habitation* (1988), *A Sort of Clowning* (1990), and *An Imagined Life* (1992).

HOLBACH, Paul Henri, Baron d' (1723–89), see PHILOSOPHES.

HOLBEIN, Hans, the younger (1497/8–1543), German painter, born in Augsburg; by 1515 he was in Basle, where he designed woodcuts for the publisher Johannes Froben and met *Erasmus. In 1516 he made a series of marginal drawings in Erasmus' *The Praise of Folly* and painted Erasmus several times. His religious paintings include the unflinchingly realistic *Dead Christ* (1521); c.1525 he designed a series of woodcuts, *The Dance of Death*. Erasmus recommended Holbein to Sir T. *More, and he spent the years 1526–8 in England, probably staying at More's house in Chelsea; he painted the friends and patrons of Erasmus and More and his family. Holbein settled in England in 1532, when Thomas *Cromwell seized on his potential as a court painter. His drawings and paintings of the period include many literary figures—Sir T. *Wyatt, *Surrey, Sir Thomas and Lady *Elyot, and Sir Philip Hoby, friend of *Titian and *Aretino. Holbein created the massive, overpowering image of *Henry VIII; contemporaries were 'abashed and annihilated' before the mural painting of the king and his parents at Whitehall Palace (1537; destroyed; part of the cartoon is in the National Portrait Gallery). The 19th cent. was fascinated by his *Dance of Death*: *Dickens bought a set in 1841; and W. *Cather took from it the title of *Death Comes for the Archbishop*.

HOLCOT, Robert (d. 1349, probably young), a Dominican, perhaps born at Northampton where he spent the last seven years of his life; he studied and taught at Oxford from *c.*1326 to 1334. Theologically, he was a follower of *Ockham in his insistence on human free will, in opposition to his contemporary *Bradwardine (Holcot may have been one of his 'New Pelagians'). The canon of his works is large but uncertain; his most important work is his *Moralitates Historiarum*, a series of metaphorical stories (corresponding to Ridevall's *Fulgentius Metaforalis*, but much more vivid) which were very influential on the *Gesta Romanorum*. Throughout his work he alluded to and used 'pictures', metaphorical representations of abstract phenomena, in a lively and literary way. See Beryl Smalley, *English Friars and Antiquity in the Early Fourteenth Century* (1960), 133–202.

HOLCROFT, Thomas (1745–1809), successively stable-boy, shoemaker, actor, and author. He was largely self-educated, a militant atheist, and believed fervently in man's capacity for self-improvement. His varied and energetic life is described in his *Memoirs* (edited and completed by his friend *Hazlitt), which contain early reminiscences of *Foote and the aged *Macklin, and later accounts of radical associates such as *Godwin and *Tooke. He was acquitted for high treason in 1794, and spent eight weeks in Newgate before being discharged. He wrote a number of sentimental plays, of which the best known was *The Road to Ruin* (1792); also several novels, including *Anna St Ives* (1792) and *The Adventures of Hugh Trevor* (1794), both of them influenced by Godwin's radical philosophy, but less successful as literature than *Caleb Williams*. After the hostile reception of his play *Knave or Not?* in 1798, Holcroft, plagued by debt, moved to Hamburg, then Paris, returning to England in 1802; he died in London after a long illness, during which he dictated a large part of his *Memoirs*. *Anna St Ives* (ed. P. Faulkner) and *Hugh Trevor* (ed. S. Deane) were reissued in 1970 and 1973 respectively.

HÖLDERLIN, Friedrich (1770–1843), German poet and friend of *Hegel and *Schelling. He suffered from insanity from 1802. His only novel, *Hyperion* (1797, 1799), is an *epistolary work set in contemporary Greece. He wrote poems on classical subjects, in which he expressed a hopeless, romantic yearning for ancient Greek harmony with nature and beauty in classical verse forms. His works have been finely translated by M. *Hamburger (1966).

HOLINSHED, Raphael (d. ?1580), historian, who was of a Cheshire family and is said by Anthony *Wood to have been a 'minister of God's word'. He came to London early in the reign of *Elizabeth I, and was employed as a translator by Reyner *Wolfe, the printer and publisher. While in his employ he planned the *Chronicles* (1577) which are known by his name and are by several hands. They form the first authoritative vernacular and continuous account of the whole of English history. The *Historie of England* was written by Holinshed himself. The *Description of England*, a vivid account, not devoid of humour, of English towns, villages, crops, customs, etc., of the day, was written by W. *Harrison. The *History and Description of Scotland* and the *History of Ireland* were translations or adaptations, and the *Description of Ireland* was written by Richard Stanyhurst and E. *Campion. A few passages in the *History of Ireland* offended the queen and her ministers, and were expunged. The *Chronicle* was reissued, with continuation, edited by John Hooker, alias Vowell, in 1587, and politically offensive passages again taken out. This edition was widely used by Shakespeare and other dramatists.

HOLLAND, Philemon (1552–1637), master of the free school at Coventry from 1628, celebrated for his translations of *Livy (1600), *Pliny's *Natural History* (1601), *Plutarch's *Moralia* (1603), *Suetonius (1606), Ammianus Marcellinus (1609), Camden's *Britannia* (1610), and *Xenophon's *Cyropaedia* (1632). His knowledge of Greek and Latin was accurate and profound, and his renderings are made in a vivid, familiar, and somewhat ornamented English.

Holland House, Kensington, London, built at the beginning of the 17th cent. for Sir Walter Cope, passed by marriage into the possession of Henry Rich (son of Penelope *Rich), first earl of Holland, who took his title from the 'parts of Holland' in Lincolnshire; he was executed in 1649. In 1767 it was acquired by Henry Fox, First Baron Holland, who entertained Horace *Walpole and George Selwyn there. In the time of his grandson, the third baron (1773–1840), Holland House became a great political, literary, and artistic centre, and many eminent authors, such as *Sheridan, T. *Moore, T. *Campbell, S. *Rogers, *Macaulay, *Grote, *Dickens, and *Thackeray, were received there. *Addison, who had married the widow of one of the earls of Warwick and Holland, died at Holland House in 1719.

HOLLINGHURST, Alan (1954–), novelist, born in Stroud and educated at Magdalen College, Oxford. His first novel, *The Swimming-Pool Library* (1988), is narrated by 25-year-old gay Oxford graduate William Beckwith, who by a chance encounter in a public lavatory saves the life of octogenarian Lord Nantwich and is subsequently asked to write his memoirs: the request reveals much to Will about his own family history. The book explores with elegance and *Firbankian panache the changing dangers and pleasures of the homosexual alternative culture of the public school and of the London club. *The Folding Star* (1994) takes voyeuristic narrator Edward Manners to a Belgian town where he falls in love with one of his private pupils, Luc: the novel interweaves the incongruously youthful gay life of an ancient and silent city with Edward's own erotic memories, with sudden death, and with the story of a celebrated Belgian symbolist *fin-de-siècle* painter who had himself suffered a sexual obsession. A somewhat desolate but lyrical sense of place pervades the work. *The Spell* (1998) presents a gay anatomy of a modern Britain of London clubs and country-house parties, a project pursued to tragic effect in *The Line of Beauty* (2004, *Booker Prize), set in Notting Hill in an era of AIDS and Thatcherism.

HOLME, Constance (1881–1955), novelist, born in Westmorland, where her successful and realistic *regional novels were set; they include *The Lonely Plough* (1914), *The Splendid Fairing* (1919), and *The Trumpet in the Dust* (1921).

HOLMES, Oliver Wendell (1809–94), born at Cambridge, Massachusetts, professor of anatomy and physiology at Harvard University from 1847 to 1882. His *Autocrat of the Breakfast-Table* appeared in the *Atlantic Monthly* in 1857–8, *The Professor at the Breakfast-Table* in 1860, *The Poet at the Breakfast-Table* in 1872, and *Over the Tea-Cups* in 1891. He also wrote novels, poems, and essays, and memoirs of *Emerson and *Motley. He also wrote a considerable quantity of mainly light and occasional verse, collected in many volumes; among the best known are 'The Last Leaf' (1831), on an aged survivor of the Boston Tea Party; 'The Deacon's Masterpiece; or, The Wonderful "One-Hoss Shay"' (1857), a comic tale; and 'Dorothy Q' (1871), inspired by a family portrait.

HOLMES, Richard (1945–), biographer, born in London and educated at Downside School and Churchill College, Cambridge. He published a volume of poems, *One for Sorrow, Two for Joy*, in 1970, and in 1974 his first major biography, *Shelley: The Pursuit*, appeared to great acclaim. This was followed by other works including the semi-autobiographical *Footsteps: Adventures of a Romantic Biographer* (1985), which broke new ground in its account of Holmes's personal experiences and travels in the course of pursuing, sometimes unsuccessfully, subjects which included Gerard de *Nerval and R. L. *Stevenson: this influential work was instrumental in creating a more personal approach to the art of *biography, in which the narrator feels able to intrude his or her own thoughts and feelings. *Dr Johnson and Mr Savage* (1993) was another unorthodox work, exploring the relationship of the two poets, and their early days of poverty

together in London, and seeking to reinterpret *Johnson's attitude to *Savage. His two-volume biography of *Coleridge, *Early Visions* (1989) and *Darker Reflections* (1998), is a magisterial, scholarly, and deeply sympathetic account, written with sensitivity, colour, and passion.

Holmes, Sherlock, the private detective who appears in *The Adventures of Sherlock Holmes* and other books by A. C. *Doyle.

Holocaust, literature of the. The racialized mass murder committed by the Nazis during the Second World War has been the subject of a great variety of written work, ranging from diaries, testimonies, and memoirs, to fiction, poetry, and drama. Diaries are often seen as most authentically concerned with the events they describe: both personal diaries, and those written in ghettos by self-styled archivists driven to record the enormities they witnessed every day (for instance, Emanuel Ringelblum's *Notes from the Warsaw Ghetto*, 1958, and David Sierakowiak's *Five Notebooks from the Lódz Ghetto*, 1996: neither writer survived). Immediately after the war Holocaust writing was not popular; Elie Wiesel was unable to find a publisher for his long, Yiddish account of Auschwitz, *And the World Was Silent*, which was eventually published in French as a slim volume entitled *Night* in 1958. However, Anne Frank's *The Diary of a Young Girl*, published in English in 1952, did much to increase the general public's interest in the Holocaust—even if the death of the *Diary*'s author at the age of 15 in Bergen-Belsen was received in ways critics have seen as inappropriately humanist or even Christian. The trial of Adolf Eichmann in 1961 also added to general knowledge of the Holocaust (see ARENDT). Sylvia *Plath, most notably in poems such as 'Daddy' and 'Lady Lazarus', was one of the first non-survivors to write about the Holocaust, to the chagrin of critics such as *Steiner who saw these poems as enlisting an unprecedented tragedy to prop up personal angst. Others have seen her work, like that of Geoffrey *Hill and Randall *Jarrell, as the effort of a poet to represent a historicized subjectivity. Among the canonical works written in the first decades after the war's end Primo *Levi's *If This Is a Man* (1961) is probably the best known, and his essays, particularly *The Drowned and the Saved* (1988), and his autobiography, *The Periodic Table* (1986), have contributed to his high reputation. Very quickly a tradition among survivor-writers arose for generic and narrative experimentation in order to represent the Holocaust years: André Schwarz-Bart's novel *The Last of the Just* (1960) draws upon Jewish tradition to represent Auschwitz in magic realist vein; while Piotr Rawicz's nightmarish black comedy *Blood from the Sky* (1964) describes life in hiding in Nazi-occupied Ukraine. Jiri Weil's allegorical novel *Life with a Star* (1989) renders the Nazi occupation of Prague without naming any of the different groups of protagonists; Jakov Lind's 1966 novel *Landscape in Con-*

crete is a Kafkaesque portrayal of a German soldier who 'only follows orders'; while Aharon Appelfeld's novels (*Badenheim 1939*, 1990; *To the Land of the Reeds*, 1994) are stylized accounts of the Holocaust years which imply but do not actually describe the facts of mass murder. More recently, both Ida Fink (*A Scrap of Time*, 1989) and Louis Begley (*Wartime Lies*, 1991) have published fictionalized autobiographies of their experiences in hiding during the war: written by survivors, these works gain from the leeway of novelization. The work of non-Jewish survivors has also been characterized by formal and generic experimentation; such writers include Charlotte Delbo, a French political prisoner whose memoir *Life after Auschwitz* (1996) considers the problem of memory and subjectivity, and Tadeusz Borowski, a Polish political prisoner whose blackly comic fictionalized vignettes in *This Way for the Gas, Ladies and Gentlemen* (1976) disconcertingly describe the life of a guard in Auschwitz. Such experimentation exists alongside a tradition of 'documentary fiction', in which the techniques of the novel are combined with eyewitness accounts or other historical material. Such works include Jean-François Steiner's *Treblinka* (1967) and Anatolii Kuznetsov's *Babi Yar: A Document in the Form of a Novel* (1970). This tendency not to trust outright invention continues even in works written more than 50 years after the events of the Holocaust: *Keneally's Schindler's List* (1982) is described as 'faction', while even novels which take the Holocaust simply as the trigger for fiction, such as William *Styron's Sophie's Choice* (1979), Martin *Amis's Time's Arrow* (1991), and D. M. *Thomas's The White Hotel* (1981), all draw upon historical sources. Critical reactions to anything but the most scrupulously factual and respectful novels by non-survivors about the Holocaust have tended to be explosive—see for instance the response to Rolf Hochhuth's 1964 play *The Deputy*, about the role of Pope Pius XII in the Holocaust; by contrast, the poetic approach of Anne Michaels's prize-winning novel *Fugitive Pieces* (1996) was seen by many to be appropriate to its subject, although others judged it to be over-aestheticized. Art Spiegelman's *Maus* (1986, 1991), a two-volume cartoon history of Spiegelman's efforts to record his father's story of imprisonment in Auschwitz, perfectly illustrates the difficulties Holocaust writing presents to existing literary categories: the first volume appeared simultaneously in the fiction and non-fiction best-seller lists of the *New York Times* in 1986. Poetry has not been as popular a medium for representing the Holocaust, although the poetry of survivor P. *Celan is a striking exception. *The Poems of Paul Celan*, translated by M. *Hamburger (1988, 1994), is a collection of elliptical, powerful lyrics, and his 'Death Fugue' is, alongside Nelly Sachs's 'O the chimneys' (*Selected Poems*, 1968), and Itzhak Katzenelson's long poem *Song of the Murdered Jewish People* (1980), the best-known poetic treatment of the subject. Writing by and about other groups of victims has been far less extensive. In the case of the gypsies, written records formed little part of their tradition (though see Alexander Ramati's documentary novel *And the Violins Stopped Playing*, 1989); and in the case of gay men, homosexuality remained illegal until the 1970s in Germany and Austria (see Heinz Heger's account of an anonymous eyewitness, *The Men with the Pink Triangle*, 1980, and Martin Sherman's fictional 1979 play *Bent*, which takes the events of Nazi persecution as an allegory for identity politics).

Holofernes, (1) Nebuchadnezzar's general, who was decapitated by Judith (Judith 4), a subject often treated by Renaissance painters; (2) the great doctor in theology (Tubal Holofernes) who instructed the youthful Gargantua (*Rabelais, i. xiv); (3) the pedantic schoolmaster in Shakespeare's *Love's Labour's Lost*.

HOLROYD, Michael de Courcy Fraser (1935–), author and biographer, born in London and educated at Eton. His first book was a critical biography of *Kingsmill, which was followed by a two-volume life of L. *Strachey (*The Unknown Years*, 1967; *The Years of Achievement*, 1968), a work which greatly contributed to a revival of interest in the *Bloomsbury Group and to a new interest in the art of *biography, and which incidentally achieved a remarkable recovery of the personality of Strachey's friend and companion, the painter Dora *Carrington (1893–1932). Other works followed, including a major two-volume biography of Augustus *John (1974, 1975). His biography of Bernard *Shaw was published in three separate volumes: *The Search for Love* (1988), *The Pursuit of Power* (1989), and *The Lure of Fantasy* (1991). There are revised one-volume editions of Strachey (1994), John (1996), and Shaw (1997). *Basil Street Blues* (1999) and *Mosaic* (2004) record the decline and fall of the Holroyd family. He is married to the novelist Margaret *Drabble.

HOLST, Gustav (1874–1934), English composer, who, with *Vaughan Williams, was involved in the folk-song movement and was attracted to the Elizabethan composers and *Purcell, influences which guided him in his search for 'the musical idiom of the English language'. His earlier works, including a first *Whitman setting, *The Mystic Trumpeter* (1904), show traces of *Wagner-worship, and even *The Planets* (1917) is not one of his best pieces. But from the same year *The Hymn of Jesus*, a setting from the apocryphal Acts of St John, is a masterpiece, and the *Four Songs for Voice and Violin* on medieval texts show that he could already produce a masterly fusion of language and melodic line. Later choral works include a setting of Whitman's *Ode to Death* (1919) and the *First Choral Symphony* (1924) to poems of *Keats. The last of the big choral works was the *Choral Fantasia* (1930) with words by his friend *Bridges, who also provided the words for the *Seven Partsongs* (1926) for soprano, female chorus, and strings.

Holst's next purely orchestral composition was *Egdon Heath* (1927), a spare but evocative score headed with a quotation from Hardy's *The Return of the Native*, describing the heath's 'swarthy monotony'. Holst wrote librettos for three of his operas: *Savitri* (1909), a one-act chamber opera of great originality; *The Perfect Fool* (1923); and *At the Boar's Head* (1925), in which the tavern scenes from both parts of *Henry IV* were strung together and set to traditional country dances and folk tunes with great ingenuity but little theatrical appeal. His last opera, *The Wandering Scholar* (1930), has a libretto by Clifford Bax after H. *Waddell.

HOLTBY, Winifred (1898–1935), writer, born in the East Riding of Yorkshire. She broke off her studies at Oxford to serve in France with the WAAC, an experience which led her to devote much time to lecturing on international questions. She was also a vocal feminist. She published several novels, the best known of which is her last, *South Riding* (1936), set in Yorkshire, which is at once the story of enterprising headmistress Sarah Burton and a portrait of a whole community. Her other novels include *Anderby Wold* (1923), *The Crowded Street* (1924), *The Land of Green Ginger* (1927), and *Mandoa, Mandoa!* (1933). She was a prolific journalist, contributing to the *Manchester Guardian, *Time and Tide*, and many other periodicals. For an account of her life and early death after a long illness, see V. *Brittain, *Testament of Friendship* (1940).

HOLUB, Miroslav (1923–98), poet and scientist, born in Pilsen, Czechoslovakia, equally famed internationally for his poetry and work in the field of immunology. Holub began publishing poetry in 1958 and was first introduced to English readers when *Selected Poems* (1967) was published in the Penguin Modern European Poets series. *Although* (1971) and *Notes of a Clay Pigeon* (1977) followed in Britain, with two selections *The Fly* (1987) and *On the Contrary* (1984) appearing in the 1980s. Collected English translations were finally published in *Poems before & after* (1990), due to opposition from the Czech authorities which had led to its previous publication in two halves in 1984 and 1987. *Before* refers to the stifling pre-1968 climate and the poems from this period are often expressed allegorically in lean, free forms suffused with Holub's mordant wit. The poems of *After* show a movement to more expansive and dramatic structures, including the puppet poems of *Interferon, or On Theatre* (1986) which provide an absurdist vehicle for Holub's political satire. His subsequent collections are *Vanishing Lung Syndrome* (1990), *Supposed to Fly* (1996), and *The Rampage* (1997). Prose works include *The Dimension of the Present Moment* (1990) and *The Jingle Bell Principle* (1990).

'Holy Fair, The', a satirical poem by *Burns, published 1786, in which the poet contrasts the conviviality of the young parishioners assembled for a prayer meeting with the exhortations of the ministers and elders, preaching of damnation and hell-fire.

Holy Grail, see GRAIL.

'Holy Grail, The' one of Tennyson's *Idylls of the King*, published 1869, in which Sir Percivale, now a monk, describes the quest of the Holy Grail, and the differing degrees of failure of himself, Bors, Gawain, and Launcelot.

Holy Living and ***Holy Dying,*** see TAYLOR, JEREMY.

Holy State and the Profane State, The, by T. *Fuller, published 1642, the most popular of his works during his life, a mixture of *character-writing, essays, and 30 short biographies; the characters include, for example, 'The Good Widow', 'The Good Merchant', and 'The True Gentleman'.

Holy War, The, a Puritan prose allegory by *Bunyan, published 1682.

The author narrates how Diabolus gets possession by his wiles of the city Mansoul (i.e. soul of man), the metropolis of the universe. Thereupon King Shaddai, the builder of the city, sends Boanerges and three other captains to recover it, and finally his own son Emmanuel to lead the besieging army. The vicissitudes of the siege are recounted with much spirit. The city falls to the assault conducted by Emmanuel, after much parley between the defenders ('Diabolonians') and the besiegers. But when the power of the king has been re-established, the city presently relapses into evil ways. Diabolus recaptures the city but cannot take the citadel, and is presently defeated by Emmanuel. Bunyan in this allegory evidently drew upon his experience as a soldier in the Parliamentary war. It is an allegory both of the progress of the Christian soul and of the history of the Christian Church.

'Holy Willie's Prayer', a satirical poem by *Burns, published 1799, takes the form of a dramatic monologue by an elder in Burns's parish of Mauchline. In the course of his musings Holy Willie unconsciously reveals his selfish hypocrisy. The poem was not included in the Kilmarnock edition of 1786 for fear of giving offence.

Homage to Catalonia, (1938), G. *Orwell's account of his participation in the Spanish Civil War, describes his months fighting for the workers' cause, with inadequate ammunition amongst ill-trained ragged volunteers: an experience which nevertheless gave him a sense of the meaning of socialism in action, and of the possibility of belonging to a classless society. The tone is laconic, stoic, disillusioned, and anti-heroic, yet nevertheless admits to moments of great 'fun' amidst the misery, and to some sense of making history. The narration covers the fall of Malaga to the Fascists, the street fighting in Barcelona, and the increasing fragmentation of the left: Orwell describes his own wounding (he was shot through the throat by a sniper) and his escape with his wife to France, and then to the 'deep, deep sleep' of the English landscape.

'Homage to Sextus Propertius', see POUND.

HOME, Daniel Dunglas (1833–86), a spiritualistic medium, whose seances in England in 1855 and subsequent years were attended by well-known people including R. *Browning, who, unlike his wife, remained sceptical (see his 'Mr Sludge, "The Medium" '). He published *Incidents of My Life* (1863, 1872).

HOME, Henry, Lord Kames (1696–1782), Scottish judge and landowner, keenly interested in agricultural improvement and philosophy. A representative figure of the *Scottish Enlightenment, he wrote on law, history, natural religion, and farming; his works, much read in his day, include *Elements of Criticism* (1762) and *Sketches of the History of Man* (1774). He was a member of the *Select Society.

HOME, John (1722–1808), playwright, who succeeded R. *Blair as minister of Athelstaneford, and later became secretary to Bute and tutor to the prince of Wales. His friends included *Hume, Adam *Smith, W. *Collins, and W. *Robertson. His first tragedy, *Agis*, was initially rejected by *Garrick, but *Douglas* was performed with much success at Edinburgh in 1756, and at Covent Garden in 1757. His later tragedies were less successful. He was a friend of *Macpherson and a firm believer in the authenticity of 'Ossian'.

Homecoming, The, a play by H. *Pinter, performed and published 1965.

A black Freudian family drama, the play presents the return to his north London home and ostentatiously womanless family of Teddy, an academic, and his wife of six years, Ruth, once a photographic model. The patriarch, Mac, a butcher, is alternately violent and cringing in manner, and the other two sons, Lenny and Joey, in a very short time make sexual overtures to Ruth, who calmly accepts them; by the end of the play Teddy has decided to leave her with the family, who intend to establish her as a professional prostitute. The tone is dark, erotic, and threatening; the shocking and the banal are sharply juxtaposed throughout. Ruth's acceptance of her role as mother, mistress, and possibly breadwinner for her new family, and her rejection of her husband, are intricately connected with the enigmatic figure of the long-dead mother, Jessie, who is both reviled and idolized by her survivors.

HOMER (c. 9th–8th cent. BC), the supposed author of two famous early Greek epics, *The Iliad* and *The Odyssey*. Homer occupied in the culture of ancient Greece a position even more central than Shakespeare's in England, since his works provided everyone's elementary education. No one in antiquity questioned his claim to be the greatest of poets, and his reputation survived in the Middle Ages even in the Latin West where his works were unknown. When the humanists began to learn Greek in the 14th

cent. they turned eagerly to *The Iliad*, but found its directness and realism disappointing. The study of Homer stagnated, and a serious interest in his work did not show itself, in spite of G. *Chapman's heroic versions (*Il.* ?1611, *Od.* ?1615), until *Hobbes's and *Dryden's attempts at translation towards the end of the century. The 18th-cent. interest in Homer had a number of different causes. There was the natural wish to make an ancient masterpiece available to contemporary readers which produced *Pope's *Iliad* (1715–20); there was the new view of poetic inspiration fostered by *'Longinus', which justified the 'fire' Pope found in Homer; there was the cult of *primitivism as an alternative to the corruptions of civilization, which was to lead to the veneration of 'Ossian', and which prepared the ground for F. A. Wolf's theory (1795) that *The Iliad* consisted of bardic lays woven roughly together, a theory that produced a long (and still undecided) struggle between 'analysts' and 'unitarians'. In the 19th cent. some poets like *Tennyson (in 'The Lotos-Eaters') made use of a Homeric story for unhomeric purposes, while others, like M. *Arnold or *Kingsley, attempted (unsuccessfully) to write in a Homeric manner; but it is Arnold's lectures 'On Translating Homer' that indicate most forcefully the almost extravagant worship that the poet inspired in cultivated Englishmen of the Victorian age, including *Gladstone, who wrote several works on Homer.

In the 20th cent. the most widely read English translations were those of E. V. Rieu, whose prose version of the *Odyssey* was the first *Penguin Classic in 1946, but there have also been several attempts at verse, including those of Richmond Lattimore (1965–7) and C. *Logue, and a 'plain prose' adaptation by I. A. *Richards (1950).

Homeric Hymns, of unknown authorship and various dates, are ancient Greek hymns, addressed to various deities and recounting legends relating to them. The hymns were composed by various poets (not including Homer) from the 8th to the 6th cents BC. They do not figure seriously in English literature until the 19th cent., when *Shelley, *Peacock, *Tennyson, *Swinburne, and *Bridges are all indebted to them in particular poems.

Homilies, Books of, a title applied in the Church of England to two books of Homilies, published 1547 and 1563, appointed to be read in the churches. The second Book of Homilies is mentioned in Article 35 of the Thirty-Nine Articles in the Book of *Common Prayer.

HONE, William (1780–1842), author and bookseller, who published numerous political satires, parodies, and pamphlets, some illustrated by *Cruikshank. He was prosecuted for his *Political Litany* (1817). He published his *Every-Day Book*, which was dedicated to *Lamb and praised by Sir W. *Scott and *Southey, in 1826–7; his *Table-Book* in 1827–8; and *The Early Life* in

1841. See Marcus Wood, *Radical Satire and Print Culture 1790–1822* (1994) and *The Laughter of Triumph* (2005) by Ben Wilson.

Honest Whore, The, a play by *Dekker in two parts, both written *c.*1604/5, of which the first was printed 1604, the second 1630. It appears from *Henslowe's diary that *Middleton collaborated in writing the first part.

In Pt I Count Hippolito, making the acquaintance of Bellafront, and discovering that she is a harlot, upbraids her bitterly for her mode of life and converts her to honesty. She falls in love with Hippolito, who repels her and marries Infelice, daughter of the duke of Milan. Bellafront is married to Matheo, who had caused her downfall.

In Pt II we find the converted Bellafront as the devoted wife of the worthless Matheo, who, to get money for his vices, is prepared to see her return to her old way of life. Hippolito, now falling in love with her, tries to seduce her. She stoutly resists temptation and is finally rescued from misery by her father, Orlando Friscobaldo. The painful character of the play, one of the great dramas of the age, heightened by Dekker's powerful treatment and by scenes in Bedlam and Bridewell, is somewhat alleviated by the admirable character Orlando Friscobaldo, and by the comic underplot, dealing with the eccentricities of the patient husband Candido, the linen draper.

Honeycomb, Will, in the *Spectator*, introduced in No. 2 as an expert in 'the female world' of fashion and conversation.

Honeywood, Mr and Sir William, characters in Goldsmith's *The Good-Natur'd Man*.

Honorificabilitudinitatibus, the long word in Shakespeare's *Love's Labour's Lost* (V. i), in which Baconians see a cryptogram indicating that Bacon was the author of the works attributed to Shakespeare. (See BACONIAN THEORY.)

HOOD, Thomas (1799–1845), born in London, the son of a bookseller, assistant editor of the *London Magazine*, 1821–3, and the friend of *Lamb, *Hazlitt, *De Quincey, and other literary men. He edited various periodicals: the *Gem* (1829), the *Comic Annual* (1830), the *New Monthly Magazine* (1841–3), and *Hood's Magazine* (1843). He and J. H. *Reynolds published *Odes and Addresses to Great People* (1825), a series of satires and parodies which sold well. He wrote much humorous and satirical verse, often making use of his remarkable skill with puns, but his satire lacked bite. Lamb, recognizing this lack, and referring to Hood's attempts to do in verse for London what W. *Hogarth had done with engraving, called him 'our half-Hogarth'. His serious poems include *'The Song of the Shirt', which was immensely successful; *'The Bridge of Sighs', and 'The Dream of Eugene Aram', the first about a suicide by drowning, the second about a

murder; 'The Last Man'; 'The Plea of the Mid-summer Fairies' (which includes 'I remember, I remember'); and shorter pieces, such as 'The Death-bed'. He wrote a comedy, *York and Lancaster*, and in *Hood's Own* (1839) published a lively account of an assembly at the Lambs' house. He received a Civil List pension not long before his death.

HOOD, Thomas, the younger (1835–74), a talented humorous writer and artist, known as Tom Hood, the son of Thomas *Hood. The first of his illustrated books, *Pen and Pencil Pictures*, was published in 1857. He became editor of *Fun* in 1865, in which year he published the most successful of his six novels, *Captain Master's Children*. In 1867 he founded *Tom Hood's Comic Annual*, which continued after his death. He wrote and illustrated many children's books; his collected verse, *Favourite Poems*, was published in 1877.

HOOK, Theodore Edward (1788–1841), remembered as a wit, a writer of light verses and dramas, a successful editor of the Tory *John Bull*, and a prolific and popular novelist. He was the most successful of the writers of the *'fashionable novel'. As a friend of the prince of Wales Hook knew the fashionable world, and he described it admiringly in his novels, which were read in large numbers by those aspiring to social fashion. Among his various novels *Sayings and Doings* (1824–8), *Maxwell* (1830), *Gilbert Gurney* (1836), *Jack Brag* (1837), and *Gurney Married* (1838) were all popular; but their interest is now chiefly for the social historian.

HOOKER, Richard (?1554–1600), theologian, born at Exeter of poor parents, and by Bishop Jewel's patronage sent to Corpus Christi College, Oxford, where he remained till 1584, becoming a fellow and deputy professor of Hebrew. He was appointed to the living of Drayton-Beauchamp in 1584, master of the Temple 1585, rector of Boscombe in Wiltshire, and of Bishopsbourne in Kent, where he died and where the inscription on his monument first called him 'Judicious'. Of his great prose classic, the defence of the Church of England as established in Queen Elizabeth's reign entitled *Of the *Laws of Ecclesiastical Politie*, four books appeared in 1593, the fifth in 1597. Other works by Hooker were issued at Oxford in 1612–14. A pleasant biography of Hooker was written by I. *Walton and published with the 1666 edition of his *Works*. There is some reason to credit Hooker with the first steps towards making known in England the theory of 'original contract' as a basis of sovereignty.

HOPE, A(lec) D(erwent) (1907–2000), Australian poet, born New South Wales, and educated at the universities of Sydney and Oxford. His first collection, *The Wandering Islands* (1955) was followed by *Poems* (1960), *Collected Poems 1930–1965* (1966, rev. 1972), and other volumes, but much of his work was written and published before his first book appeared. His work is technically accomplished, witty, and allusive, abounding in references to the Bible and classical mythology: he pays homage to *Byron, *Coleridge, *Yeats, and other colleagues in the trade. He displays a formidable command of traditional verse forms, and his salute to *ottava rima* in 'A Letter from Rome' (1958) hits a characteristic informal ironic note, but he also explored more sombre themes, often with a detached gravity: see for example 'The Death of the Bird' (1948) on a last migration, or 'Meditation on a Bone' (1956), on scholarship and passion.

HOPE, Anthony, see HAWKINS, A. H.

HOPE, Christopher (1944–), South African-born poet, children's writer, short story writer, and novelist, educated at the universities of Witwatersrand and Natal, who moved to London in 1975, where he worked for a while as a teacher before becoming a full-time writer. His first volume of poetry, *Cape Drives* (1974), evoked the landscapes and racial tensions of South Africa, as does much of his later work: it was followed by his first novel, *A Separate Development* (1980), the story of Harry Moto, a white teenage South African outsider who ends up in jail writing his memoirs, and *In the Country of the Black Pig* (poems, 1981). Hope's output has been varied in subjects and settings: other titles include *Kruger's Alp* (1984), a historical satire about the aftermath of the Boer War; *My Chocolate Redeemer* (1989), set in France; *Learning to Fly* (1990, short stories); *Serenity House* (1992), which deals with the legacy of the Holocaust as Max Montfalcon awaits death in an old people's home in north London; and *Me, the Moon and Elvis Presley* (1997), a novel about post-apartheid problems.

HOPE, Laurence, the pseudonym of Adela Florence Cory; see INDIAN LOVE LYRICS.

HOPE, Thomas (?1770–1831), a man of great wealth, architect, art historian, and traveller, and the author of the once popular novel *Anastasius*, published in 1819 and at first attributed to Lord *Byron, who wished he had written it. It tells, at considerable length, the story of a brave but unscrupulous Greek who, in the 18th cent., travels in the Middle East and becomes involved in a variety of escapades. It is possible that the story influenced the later cantos of *Don Juan*.

Hope Theatre, on Bankside, Southwark, built in 1613 by *Henslowe as a bear-garden, with a movable stage on which plays could be performed. Jonson's *Bartholomew Fair* was acted there in 1614.

HOPKINS, Gerard Manley (1844–89), born in Stratford, Essex, the eldest of nine children in the High Anglican, artistically minded home of Kate and Manley Hopkins. He attended Highgate School, where he showed academic and artistic promise as well as a 'nervous grace' and distinctive independence. In 1863 he went to Balliol College, Oxford, as an exhibitioner. The 'star of Balliol' was tutored by B.

*Jowett and T. H. *Green among others; *Pater coached him for his Greats examinations. His intellectual interests ranged from *Heraclitus to *Hegel, and a friendship with R. *Bridges began. Hopkins was seeking deeper religious certainties; the University, still responding to the *Oxford movement, was embroiled in controversy. With *Newman's guidance, he was received into the Roman Catholic Church in 1866. In 1867 he completed his degree (a double first), then taught for a year at Newman's Oratory school, Birmingham. In 1868 he entered the Society of Jesus (Jesuits) as a candidate for priesthood. Jesuit 'formation' included life as a novice (Roehampton, 1868–70), scholastic (Stonyhurst, 1870–3), 'Regent' (professor of rhetoric, Roehampton, 1873–4), and 'theologian' (St Beuno's in north Wales, 1874–7, where he also learned Welsh). His pastoral talents were never as great as his remarkable faith. Following ordination in 1877, he had a peripatetic pastoral career. Frequent transfers were necessitated by short-staffing in Jesuit parishes and schools, and his own shortcomings as preacher, administrator, and teacher. He worked in Chesterfield and London before being sent to Oxford, 1878–9; any hopes that he would be Newman-like in the community were not realized. Parish life in industrial Liverpool (1880–1) and Glasgow overwhelmed him; he resumed teaching at Roehampton and Stonyhurst. In 1884 he was appointed to the chair of Greek and Latin at University College, Dublin. At this 'third remove' from homeland, family, and friends, he experienced extreme desolation. Yet life in Dublin was renewed by friendship with Katharine *Tynan and others, travels, and visits to Monasterevan. He died of typhoid in June 1889.

The earliest poems express a Keatsian sensuousness and a Ruskinian zest for natural detail, but a distinctive flair for aural and rhythmic effects is also evident. Oxford texts such as 'Heaven-Haven' and 'Easter Communion' trace his desire and need to convert. Always too scrupulous and self-critical, Hopkins never reconciled writing poetry and serving God. When he joined the Jesuits, he symbolically burned his poems, though he sent some copies to Bridges for safe keeping. The writing stopped for eight years, but language and poetic theorizing did not. Ironically, a disaster at sea in 1875 revived his creativity and produced '*The Wreck of the Deutschland'. While studying for ordination, inspired by 'God's grandeur' in Wales, he composed a remarkable series of sonnets including 'The Windhover', 'Spring', and 'Pied Beauty'. Aesthetic and moral questions intensify in subsequent poems such as 'Henry Purcell' and 'Binsey Poplars'. Feeling exiled in Dublin, 'selfwrung, selfstrung', he composed the 'terrible sonnets' such as 'Carrion Comfort' and 'No worst, there is none', and 'Spelt from Sibyl's Leaves'. But he was also inspired to write 'That Nature is a Heraclitean Fire' and 'To R.B.'

Schooled to discern the 'science of aspects', Hopkins developed theories of natural essence and expressiveness, and of metre, and coined the terms 'inscape', 'instress', and 'sprung rhythm', respectively, to define them. 'Inscape' refers to 'the individual or essential quality of the thing' or 'individually-distinctive beauty of style'. 'Instress' is the force or energy which sustains an inscape; it originates in the Creator and is felt by the responsive perceiver. (Hopkins uses 'pitch' to express *Duns Scotus' concept of *haecceitas*, or 'thisness'.) *Sprung rhythm, which he believed 'gives back to poetry its true soul and self', is distinguished from regular or 'running rhythm' (with its regular metrical feet) because it involves writing and scanning by number of stresses rather than by counting syllables.

Surviving journals, notebooks, and letters articulate his profound responsiveness to nature and beauty, his acumen as a literary critic and theorist of prosody, his playful wit and devoted friendliness. His sermons and spiritual writings are extraordinary for their style and insights informed by the *Spiritual Exercises* of *Ignatius Loyola. The visual arts were crucial to his refined aesthetic sensibilities. He was a keen enthusiast of the *Pre-Raphaelites, whose works he first saw at Oxford. His own talents as a sketch artist were encouraged by studies of *Ruskin, the example of his aunt, painter Frances Hopkins, and his brothers, Arthur and Everard, illustrators. Yet disturbed by the 'dangerous' potential of mortal (especially masculine) beauty, he gave up sketching. In later years he explored musical theory and composition.

His first surviving poem, 'The Escorial', won the schoolboy a prize; acceptance of his works would never again happen so readily. Poetic fame was posthumous and gradual. In 1881 R. W. *Dixon (a devoted admirer, who had taught Hopkins briefly at Highgate) persuaded Hopkins to submit some sonnets to an anthology which *Caine was preparing, but they were rejected. Bridges became the guardian of the manuscripts after Hopkins's death; he doubted public receptiveness. A few texts were placed in anthologies, including Bridges's own *The Spirit of Man* (1916), but an edition of *Poems* was delayed until 1918. Only the second edition, produced by C. *Williams in 1930, attracted the attention of readers such as *Auden, *Spender, and *Thomas, and critics such as F. R. *Leavis. T. S. *Eliot was persuaded to publish excerpts from the letters and notebooks in the *Criterion*.

Poetical Works of Gerard Manley Hopkins, ed. N. H. Mackenzie (1990); *Early Poetic Manuscripts and Note-Books . . . in Facsimile* (1989) and *Later Poetic Manuscripts* (1991), ed. N. H. Mackenzie; *Note-Books and Papers of Hopkins*, ed. H. House (1937; rev. and enl. as *Journals and Papers*, 1959, ed. H. House and G. Storey); *Sermons and Devotional Writings*, ed. C. Devlin, SJ (1959); *Letters of Hopkins to Robert Bridges* (1935, rev. 1955), *Correspondence of Hopkins and Richard Watson Dixon* (1935, rev. 1955) and *Further Letters* (1938, rev. 1956), ed. C. C. Abbott. The major biographies are by R. B. Martin (1991) and N. White (1992).

HOPKINS, Matthew (d. 1647), the witch-finder, said to have been a lawyer at Ipswich and Manningtree. He initiated many prosecutions, and procured a special judicial commission under which 60 women were hanged in Essex in one year, and many in Norfolk and Huntingdonshire. His *The Discovery of Witches* was published in 1647. See C. L'Estrange Ewen, *Witch Hunting and Witch Trials* (1929), Keith Thomas, *Religion and the Decline of Magic* (1971), and Robin Briggs, *Witches and Neighbours* (1996).

HORACE (Quintus Horatius Flaccus) (65–8 BC), Latin poet, a member of the literary circle round Augustus' minister Maecenas. Like his friend *Virgil, he joined in celebrating the restoration of order after the civil wars and worked to lift Latin literature to the level of Greek. In his *Odes* he imitated the lyric poets of early Greece. His *Satires* and *Epistles* were characterized by perceptive realism and by an ironical approach, novel at the time, in that the persona of the satirist was mocked as well as his ostensible victims. His critical works, notably the *Ars Poetica*, supplemented and in some cases distorted the teachings of *Aristotle. English satire from *Wyatt to Dr *Johnson derives much of its manner and aims from Horace. The writers of formal *odes, *Marvell and *Dryden in particular, are also indebted to him and the critical writings of Dryden and the *Augustans plainly reveal the influence of his *Ars Poetica*. Horace's poems, taught with great thoroughness in every school, formed during the 17th and 18th cents an essential element in the pattern of English culture, as testified by the vogue for Horatian imitations in the 18th cent.

Horatian ode, see ODE.

Horatio, in Shakespeare's *Hamlet*, the university friend of Hamlet who is left alive 'To tell my story' at the end of the play. For another version of this narrative, see Alethea Hayter's novel *Horatio's Version* (1972).

Horizon, a literary magazine founded in 1939 by *Connolly, *Spender, and Peter Watson, which ran from 1940 to 1950. It was edited throughout by Connolly, and published works by *Orwell, *Waugh, Angus *Wilson, L. *Lee, *Auden, and *Grigson, amongst others.

HORMAN, William (c.1458–1535), fellow of New College, Oxford, and headmaster of Winchester and Eton, of which he became vice-provost, author of *Vulgaria*, Latin aphorisms for boys to learn. It was printed by Pynson (1519), Wynkyn de *Worde (1530), and for the Roxburghe Club (ed. M. R. *James, 1926); a most remarkable book.

hornbook, a leaf of paper containing the alphabet (often with the addition of the ten digits, some elements of spelling, and the Lord's Prayer) protected by a thin plate of translucent horn, and mounted on a tablet of wood with a projecting piece for a handle, used for teaching children to read. A simpler and later form of this, consisting of the tablet without the horn covering, or a piece of stiff cardboard varnished, was also called a battledore. For an exhaustive account see A. W. Tuer, *History of the Hornbook* (1896).

HORNBY, Nick (1957–), novelist and autobiographer, born in Redhill, Surrey. He began by writing journalism, some of it collected in *Contemporary American Fiction* (1992), a book of essays. The same year he published *Fever Pitch*, a hugely successful and influential memoir about his years as a supporter of Arsenal football club, which opened the floodgates for a whole new genre of male *confessional writing. He then edited *My Favourite Year* (1993), an anthology of football pieces, and wrote two warm-hearted comic novels, *High Fidelity* (1995) and *About a Boy* (1998), which confirmed his position as the spokesman for a generation of emotionally bewildered young men. See also LADS' LITERATURE.

Horn Childe, a northern verse romance from the period 1290–1340 of 1,136 lines in tail-rhyme stanza. The plot is broadly similar to that of *King Horn* though different in some details. Horn is a prince in the north of England who flees with his teacher and companions to the south where a king's daughter, Rimnild, falls in love with him. Two of Horn's companions betray the lovers to the king, and Horn flees to Wales and Ireland, taking Rimnild's magic ring with him. After ridding Ireland of the pagans, he returns to England, where he is revenged on his treacherous companions and marries Rimnild. There is a ballad of 'Hind Horn', and it is believed that *Horn Childe* is the version of the romance referred to in 'Sir Thopas' (see CANTERBURY TALES, 17); it is certainly the kind of romance that Chaucer's satire was aimed at. Ed. in *King Horn* by J. Hall (1901).

HORNE, John, see TOOKE.

HORNE, Richard Henry or Hengist (1802–84), educated at Sandhurst; he served in the Mexican navy, and, in his own words, 'took up scribbling' when he was 30. He made his name with *Orion*, an allegorical epic which he published in 1843 at a farthing 'to mark the public contempt into which epic poetry had fallen', and also no doubt through a desire for notoriety. The poem deals with the myth of Orion, portrayed as 'a Worker and a Builder for his fellow men', and contrasted with Akinetos, the 'Great Unmoved', or Apathy. It was much praised by *Carlyle, *Lewes, and *Poe, who found it 'one of the noblest, if not the very noblest poetical work of the age'; contemporary reviewers compared it not unfavourably with Keats's *Hyperion and *Endymion. Horne wrote several blank-verse tragedies, influenced by *Webster, and adapted various plays for the stage, including *The Duchess of Malfi. He contributed many articles to Dickens's *Daily News and *Household Words, published other volumes of verse, and in 1852, in the midst of the gold fever, went to Australia (leaving his wife behind) where he stayed until 1869.

His varied adventures there are described in the autobiographical preface to his *Australian Facts and Prospects* (1859). From 1839 he corresponded with E. B. *Browning (whom he first met in 1851), and he published two volumes of her letters to him (1877). She collaborated with him in his *A New Spirit of the Age* (1844). See *The Farthing Poet* (1968) by Anne Blaine.

Horner, a character in Wycherley's *The Country Wife.

HORNIMAN, Annie Elizabeth Fredericka (1860–1937), a pioneer supporter of the modern English drama, founder of Miss Horniman's Company of Actors, and of the Manchester Repertory Theatre, for the purposes of which she acquired the Gaiety Theatre in that town in 1908. By her generous assistance the Irish National Theatre Society was provided with a permanent home in the *Abbey Theatre, Dublin.

HORNUNG, E(rnest) W(illiam) (1866–1921), novelist, remembered as the creator of Raffles, the gentleman burglar, public-school man, and cricketer who appeared in *The Amateur Cracksman* (1899), *The Black Mask* (1901), *A Thief in the Night* (1905), and *Mr Justice Raffles* (1909), narrated by his admiring assistant and ex-fag Bunny. See 'Raffles and Miss Blandish' (1944) by G. *Orwell. (See also DETECTIVE FICTION.)

HOROVITZ, Frances, née Hooker (1938–83), poet, actress, and broadcaster, whose volumes of poetry *Water over Stone* (1980) and *Snow Light, Water Light* (1983) provide intense, lyrical evocations of the landscapes of Gloucestershire, where she lived for some years, and of Northumberland, where she lived shortly before her death from cancer. Her work also appeared in *New Departures*, edited by her husband Michael *Horovitz.

HOROVITZ, Michael (1935–), poet, performance artist, and editor, born in Frankfurt. He emigrated to England with his family as a child, and was educated at Brasenose College, Oxford. He was one of the earliest British exponents of the counter-culture and *Beat Generation, editing important anthologies of new work for *New Departures* including *Children of Albion: Poetry of the 'Underground'* (1969), organizing many poetry readings and events (including the celebrated poetry festival at the Royal Albert Hall in June 1965), and encouraging many young poets, whose work appears in *Grandchildren of Albion* (1997).

horror and fantasy have been with us, in one form or another, for as long as literature has existed. Mary Shelley's *Frankenstein* (1818), Robert Louis Stevenson's *The Strange Case of *Dr Jekyll and Mr Hyde* (1886), and Bram Stoker's *Dracula* (1897) are landmarks in horror/fantasy, but then so, too, it could be argued, are certain plays by Shakespeare, *Marlowe, and *Webster. But the horror/fantasy tradition goes back further, to *Beowulf*, the most important poem in Old English, dating from the 10th cent., and indeed beyond to the bloody visions of *Sophocles (496–406 BC) and others. More directly influential on the horror/ fantasy fiction of the 20th cent. was *Romanticism and the *Gothic, in particular *Blake, Monk *Lewis, Ludwig Tieck, Clemens Brentano, and of course the early masters of the macabre short story, *Bierce, *Le Fanu, *Poe, M. R. *James, and *Machen. In terms of longer work, *Peake's Gormenghast trilogy (1946–59) has become a cult classic. H. P. (Howard Phillips) Lovecraft (1890–1937) is probably the most influential horror writer of the first half of the 20th cent., although his work lacked the intellectual thrill of *Borges and the emotional engagement of Ray *Bradbury. Horror as a trade category has one or two problems, chief among them the fact that many potential readers are put off by the name. Robert Aickman preferred to call his horror tales 'strange stories'. Chris Morgan may have coined the short-lived tag 'dark fantasy' in his anthology *Dark Fantasies* (1989). Ramsey *Campbell, on the other hand, has never shied away from the term 'horror' and he is Britain's most respected living horror writer. If there is a ghetto mentality, one horror writer who has smashed his way out of it to head the world's best-seller lists is Stephen King. But for every King there are a dozen or more knaves hacking away at the coalface of horror. In the USA, Dennis Etchison, Peter Straub, Poppy Z. Brite, Steve Rasnic Tem, and British-born Clive Barker, among others, consistently produce notable work; in the UK, a new generation of horror writers has grown up reading the subtly weird stories and novels of Campbell (who also edited an outstanding, intelligent anthology in *New Terrors*), Aickman, and M. John Harrison on the one hand and *The Pan Book of Horror Stories* on the other. In the 1980s and 1990s the most notable new writers of horror/fantasy included Joel Lane, Michael Marshall Smith, Mark Morris, Conrad Williams, Kim Newman, Christopher Fowler, Elizabeth Young, and Graham Joyce. Certain anthologies such as Christopher Kenworthy's *The Sun Rises Red, Sugar Sleep,* and *The Science of Sadness*, Nicholas Royle's *Darklands* and *Darklands 2,* Stephen Jones and David Sutton's *Dark Terrors* series, Stephen Jones's *The Mammoth Book of Best New Horror,* and Ellen Datlow and Terri Windling's *The Year's Best Fantasy and Horror* have encouraged these new writers to develop a voice at the same time as continuing to support veterans such as John Burke, Basil Copper, and R. Chetwynd-Hayes. Although there may always be a baying pack of gorehounds and a (limited) market for their splatter-filled tales (Shaun Hutson and James Herbert have both been moving away from their trademark graphic horror towards thrillers), it is with regard to the subtler, more imaginative writers that it may be true to say that of the popular genres, horror is arguably the one that runs closest to the literary mainstream and most interestingly subverts it.

Hortensio, friend to Petruchio and suitor of Bianca in Shakespeare's *The Taming of the Shrew*.

HOSKYNS, John (1566–1638), born in Monmouthshire and educated at Winchester and New College, Oxford, a lawyer who enjoyed a high reputation for wit and learning. He is best known for his *Directions for Speech and Style,* drawn on by *Jonson in his *Timber, or Discoveries,* but not published in full until 1935 (ed. H. H. Hudson). The *Directions* were written in 1599; most of Hoskyns's examples are drawn from Sidney's *Arcadia,* but he also makes interesting use of other authors of the previous 20 years.

HOSPITAL, Janette Turner (1942–   ), novelist and short story writer, born in Melbourne, Australia, who studied at the University of Queensland and at Queen's University, Canada. She has taught in universities in Australia, Canada, the USA, and the UK. Her novels include *The Ivory Swing* (1982), *The Tiger in the Tigerpit* (1983), *Borderline* (1985), *Charades* (1988), *The Last Magician* (1992), *Oyster* (1996), and *Due Preparations for the Plague* (2003), which interweaves a plot of post 9/11 terrorism with references to the Black Death. Her allusive, lyrical prose and intricate narratives have been much admired. The theme of dislocation—both cultural and emotional—is recurrent in her work, as is the damage wrought by secrecy, and the ways in which the past influences and can discolour the present. She elaborates these themes in her collections of short stories, *Dislocations* (1986) and *Isobars* (1990). Her *Collected Stories* (including seven previously uncollected) appeared in Australia in 1995.

HOTSON, Leslie (1897–1992), Canadian scholar and literary detective who specialized in the minute examination of Shakespeare's life and times. He made some notable discoveries (including vital material relating to *Marlowe's death), but many of his theories and conclusions about Shakespeare's works have not gained widespread acceptance.

HOTSPUR, nickname of Sir Henry Percy (1364–1403), eldest son of the first earl of Northumberland. He figures in Shakespeare's *Richard II* and 1 *Henry IV*. Shakespeare changes his age (following *Daniel) to make him as young as Prince *Hal, and stresses his fiery, impetuous valour as contrasted with Hal's apparent idleness.

HOUGHTON, Baron, see MILNES.

HOUGHTON, William Stanley (1881–1913), born in Manchester, where he worked in the cotton trade while pursuing his passion for the theatre. He did much dramatic criticism in Manchester, then in 1908 had his play *The Dear Departed* performed by Miss *Horniman's Repertory Theatre. *Independent Means* (1909), *The Younger Generation* (1910), *Master of the House* (1910), and *Fancy-Free* (1911) led up to the great and lasting success of his satiric comedy *Hindle Wakes* (1912), a play which mocks the small-minded people of the Lancastrian manufacturing town of Hindle, and their deep attachment to property and propriety. Most of Houghton's plays centre, with sympathy and insight, on problems of homely Lancashire life, and are strongly influenced by *Ibsen, both in theme and manner. (See MANCHESTER SCHOOL.)

'Hound of Heaven, The', a poem by Francis *Thompson.

Hours of Idleness, a collection of poems by *Byron, published 1807. The first of Byron's works for general rather than private publication, these poems show a wide variety of attitudes, from the light to the sentimental and the solemnly nostalgic, and hint at the tone and technical range of his mature work. But their quality is uneven and the volume was bitterly attacked by *Brougham in the *Edinburgh Review* as 'so much stagnant water'. Byron responded in *English Bards and Scotch Reviewers*.

HOUSEHOLD, Geoffrey (Edward West) (1900–88), novelist, educated at Clifton and Magdalen College, Oxford, and the author of many successful adventure stories in the tradition of *Buchan. The most characteristic (including his best known, *Rogue Male*, 1939, and its sequel *Rogue Justice*, 1982) pit a sporting, well-bred, lonely adventurer against the forces of darkness in the modern world (e.g. Nazis and Nazi agents), and depend on the suspense of pursuit and revenge. Other titles include *Watcher in the Shadows* (1960), and *Dance of the Dwarfs* (1968).

Household Words, a weekly periodical started in 1850 by *Dickens, and incorporated in 1859 into *All the Year Round*, which he edited until his death. It was aimed at a large audience, carried contributions from well-known writers such as Mrs *Gaskell, *Reade, and *Bulwer-Lytton, established the reputation of Wilkie *Collins, and published poems by the young *Meredith and *Patmore, as well as much of Dickens's own work. Although its attacks on the abuses of the day (poor sanitation, slums, factory accidents) were radical and persistent, its subject matter was varied and entertaining, and it captivated a vast readership.

House of Fame, The, an unfinished dream-poem by *Chaucer, composed at some time between 1374 and 1385. There are three books, in 2,158 lines of octosyllabics; it is believed to be Chaucer's last poem in that French form. The poem remains cryptic, and it is uncertain what its purpose or extent would have been (though the poem says that the third book will, in fact, be the final one).

After the prologue on dreams and the invocation to the god of sleep, Bk I says the poet fell asleep and dreamt that he was in a Temple of Glass where he saw depicted Aeneas and Dido (based on *Aeneid*, 4); the dream moves on to deal more briefly with other parts of the *Aeneid*. At the end of Bk I the poet sees an eagle who alights by him and is his guide through the House of Fame in Bk II (initially suggested, perhaps, by *Fama*, Rumour, in *Aeneid*, 4. 173 ff.). The eagle explains, philosophically and at length, how Fame works in its arbitrary ways and the book ends with a vision of the world (thought by some to be amongst Chaucer's most inspired writing: 896–1045). The eagle departs and at the beginning of Bk III Chaucer enters the Palace of Fame (Rumour) where he sees the famous of both classical and biblical lore. Eolus blows a trumpet to summon up the various celebrities who introduce themselves in categories reminiscent of the souls in Dante's *Divina commedia*. Towards the end of the poem comes a vision of bearers of false tidings: shipmen, pilgrims, pardoners, and messengers, whose confusion seems to be about to be resolved by the appearance of 'A man of gret auctorite . . .'; but there the poem ends. The identity of this figure has been much discussed; *Boethius seems the most plausible suggestion. Versions of the poem were made by *Lydgate (in *The Temple of Glas*), *Douglas, and *Skelton.

See J. A. W. Bennett, *Chaucer's Book of Fame* (1968); S. Delaney, *Chaucer's House of Fame* (1972); P. Boitani, *Chaucer and the Imaginary World of Fame* (1984); also *The Riverside Chaucer*, ed. L. D. Benson et al. (1988).

'House of Life, The', a sonnet sequence by D. G. *Rossetti, written over a long period, and published in two parts in *Poems* (1870) and *Ballads and Sonnets* (1881).

Rossetti described these sonnets as an evocation of 'life representative, as associated with love and death, with aspiration and foreboding, or with ideal art and beauty'. They have been seen both as a record of his love for his dead wife and sorrow over her death, and as a record of his passion for W. *Morris's wife Jane. Their emphasis on secrecy, delayed union, and 'regenerate rapture' would seem to support the latter view, though both Rossetti and his brother William were at pains to avoid a biographical interpretation.

House of the Seven Gables, The, a novel by N. *Hawthorne, published 1851.

It deals with the problem of hereditary guilt, unmerited misfortune, and unexpiated crime, through the story of the Pyncheon family, suffering from generation to generation from the curse of old Maule, the dispossessed owner of the Pyncheon property; persecuted as a wizard, Maule on the scaffold curses Colonel Pyncheon, with the words 'God will give him blood to drink!' Pyncheon's descendant Hepzibah Pyncheon is a poor, grotesque old spinster inhabiting the decayed paternal mansion of the title; under stress of poverty, she is obliged to do violence to family pride by opening a small shop. At this moment, to add to her anxieties, her brother Clifford Pyncheon, an amiable, epicurean, weak-minded bachelor, who has spent long years in prison for a crime of which he has been unjustly convicted by the machinations of his cousin Judge Pyncheon, returns home. On the other hand, a young country cousin, Phoebe, arrives to lighten the gloom of the old house. Judge Pyncheon, a bland, prosperous hypocrite, diffusing a 'sultry' benevolence, continues his persecution of Clifford; but this is arrested by the judge's sudden death. With the help of Holgrave, a young daguerreotypist, a descendant of 'old Wizard Maule', Clifford is rehabilitated; Holgrave, who has fallen in love with Phoebe, marries her, and the curse appears to be lifted. The semi-allegorical treatment of the theme of the 'transmitted vices of society' is characteristic of Hawthorne, and manifests his acute sensitivity about his own Puritan ancestry.

HOUSMAN, A(lfred) E(dward) (1859–1936), educated at Bromsgrove and St John's College, Oxford. While at university he formed a passionate attachment to his contemporary Moses Jackson, who became an important inspiration of his later verse. For unexplained reasons the brilliant Housman failed his finals and became for ten years a clerk in the Patent Office in London, during which time he worked on *Propertius, *Ovid, *Juvenal, and other classical authors, publishing articles when he could. In 1887 Jackson emigrated to India, then married, and soon afterwards the anguished Housman (who had not written verse since his schooldays) began to experiment, composing poems which he wrote, rewrote, and completed in notebooks which have been preserved, and which he continued until Jackson's death in 1923. In 1892 he was appointed a professor of Latin at University College London, where he began to produce his definitive edition of Manilius, which appeared in five volumes, 1903–30. In 1896 he published, at his own expense, *A Shropshire Lad*, a series of 63 spare and nostalgic verses, based largely on ballad forms, and mainly set in a half-imaginary Shropshire, a 'land of lost content', and often addressed to, or spoken by, a farm-boy or a soldier. Housman met with little encouragement, and made the barest profit from the publication. However, *Le Gallienne found the verse of 'exquisite simplicity', and another reviewer noted its 'heart-penetrating quality'; public indifference slowly gave way to interest, and sales mounted steadily. In 1911 Housman was appointed professor of Latin at Cambridge, and during the years of the First World War *A Shropshire Lad* became hugely popular. The notebooks then yielded *Last Poems* (1922), whose 41 poems met with great acclaim. In 1931 Housman published, in Germany, *Praefanda*, a collection of glosses and commentaries on bawdy and obscene passages from Latin authors. His lecture 'The Name and Nature of Poetry', given in 1933, was partly based on observations in his notebooks, which provide illuminating comments on the process of poetic creation. In 1936 *More Poems* appeared, from work in the notebooks, 18 further poems were printed in L. *Housman's *Memoir* of his brother (1937), and *Collected Poems* appeared in 1939. A volume of letters, ed. H. Maas, was published in 1971; see also R. P. Graves, *A. E. Housman: The Scholar Poet* (1979). He is the principal character in *Stoppard's play *The Invention of Love* (1997).

HOUSMAN, Laurence (1865–1959), brother of A. E. *Housman. He trained as an artist, wrote art criticism, and illustrated books throughout his life, but is remembered chiefly as a writer and dramatist. He published many stories, for both children and adults, and wrote much on feminism and on socialist and pacifist themes. Among his works were volumes of somewhat derivative poems, including *Green Arras* (1896) and *Spikenard* (1898); *An Englishwoman's Love-letters* (1900), which enjoyed some notoriety and was widely parodied; and several successful novels, among them a political satire, *Trimblerigg* (1924), directed against Lloyd George, and *The Duke of Flamborough* (1928). His first play, *Bethlehem*, was banned in 1902, as were many later plays on religious or royal figures. *The Little Plays of St Francis* (1922), together with further plays on the same theme and on St Clare, were well received and much performed for many years. *Angels and Ministers* (1921), consisting of gently mocking scenes laid in the court of Queen Victoria, were collected with further royal playlets into *Victoria Regina* (1934); when the lord chamberlain's ban on the impersonation of members of the royal family was lifted in 1937 the play enjoyed great success. In 1937 Housman published an autobiography, *The Unexpected Years*, and in the same year produced *A. E. Housman*, a volume which contained some new poems, some letters, and a valuable *Memoir* of his brother.

Houyhnhnms, the talking horses in *Gulliver's Travels* by Swift.

HOVEDON, or **HOWDEN,** Roger of (d. ?1201), a Yorkshireman and a chronicler who lived in the reign of Henry II. He was the author of both the main chronicles of the reigns of Henry II and Richard I, the *Gesta Regis Henrici*, which long went under the name of Benedict of Peterborough, and the *Chronica*.

HOWARD, Elizabeth Jane (1923–), novelist and short story writer, born in London. She was an actress and model before becoming a full-time writer. Her third marriage, dissolved in 1983, was to Kingsley *Amis. Her first novel, *The Beautiful Visit* (1950), was set during the First World War and its aftermath. Well crafted and strongly evocative of place and time, her novels of English middle-class life have continued to attract a large readership. They include *The Long View* (1956), *The Sea Change* (1959), *After Julius* (1965), *Something in Disguise* (1969), *Odd Girl Out* (1975), and *Getting It Right* (1982). *The Light Years* (1990), *Marking Time* (1991), *Confusion* (1993), and *Casting Off* (1995) together form the saga of the Cazalet family from 1937 to the post-war period. A collection of short stories, *Mr Wrong* (1975), contains her well-known ghost story 'Three Miles up', first published in *We Are for the Dark* (1951), a collaborative volume of ghost stories written with Robert Aickman. Her many plays for television include adaptations of *After Julius* and *Something in Disguise*. *Slipstream*, a revealing memoir, appeared in 2002.

HOWARD, Henry, see SURREY.

HOWARD, John (1726–90), philanthropist and prison reformer, born in London, the son of a prosperous upholsterer, and educated in Dissenting circles. In 1773 he became sheriff of Bedford, where an inspection of the local jail quickened his interest in the sufferings of prisoners. He devoted the rest of his life to visiting prisons both in England and on the Continent; his great work *The State of the Prisons in England and Wales, and an Account of Some Foreign Prisons and Hospitals* was published in 1777; a subsequent work on lazarettos appeared in 1789. He died of typhoid at Kherson in the Ukraine. A Howard Association was formed in 1866, which merged in 1921 with the Penal Reform League to become the Howard League for Penal Reform, which concerns itself with many aspects of criminal justice.

HOWARD, Robert E., see FANTASY FICTION.

Howards End, a novel by E. M. *Forster, published 1910, deals with personal relationships and conflicting values.

On the one hand are the Schlegel sisters, Margaret and Helen, and their brother Tibby, who care about civilized living, music, literature, and conversation with their friends; on the other, the Wilcoxes, Henry and his children Charles, Paul, and Evie, who are concerned with the business side of life and distrust emotions and imagination. Helen Schlegel is drawn to the Wilcox family, falls briefly in and out of love with Paul Wilcox, and thereafter reacts away from them. Margaret becomes more deeply involved. She is stimulated by the very differences of their way of life and acknowledges the debt of intellectuals to the men of affairs who guarantee stability, whose virtues of 'neatness, decision and obedience . . . keep the soul from becoming sloppy'. She marries Henry Wilcox, to the consternation of both families, and her love and steadiness of purpose are tested by the ensuing strains and misunderstandings, which include the revelation that Helen has been made pregnant by Leonard Bast, a young, married, lower-class but intellectually aspiring clerk whom the Schlegels had briefly befriended. Her marriage cracks but does not break. In the end, torn between her sister and her husband, she succeeds in bridging the mistrust that divides them. Howards End, where the story begins and ends, is the house that belonged to Henry Wilcox's first wife, and is a symbol of human dignity and endurance.

Howe, Anna, the heroine's principal correspondent in Richardson's *Clarissa.*

HOWELL, James (?1593–1666). Of Welsh descent, he held diplomatic and administrative posts under Charles I and was imprisoned in the Fleet as a Royalist, 1643–51; at the Restoration he became historiographer royal. His *Dodona's Grove* (1640) is a political allegory, and in 1642 he published his entertaining *Instructions for Forreine Travell.* A violently anti-Scots pamphlet, *A Perfect Description of the Country of Scotland,* reprint-ed in the *North Briton,* No. 31, was attributed to him, but its authorship is disputed. Howell wrote many other works, including poems and historical pamphlets, but is chiefly remembered for his *Epistolae Ho-Elianae: Familiar Letters Domestic and Forren* (1645–55), reprinted many times, ed. J. Jacobs (1890–2). These letters to correspondents, most of whom are imaginary, were written largely during his imprisonment; their intimate 'back-stairs' view of history had a lasting appeal, and *Thackeray wrote of them, 'Montaigne and Howell's *Letters* are my bedside books . . . I like to hear them tell their old stories over and over again.'

HOWELL, Thomas (fl. 1568–81), a minor Tudor poet patronized by the Herbert family. His *Devises* (1581) contains the earliest printed reference to P. Sidney's *Arcadia.*

HOWELLS, William Dean (1837–1920), American novelist, who was born in Ohio, and began life as a printer and journalist. He was American consul at Venice, 1861–5, an experience reflected in his *Venetian Life* (1866) and *Italian Journeys* (1867). He was sub-editor of the *Atlantic Monthly,* 1866–71, and chief editor 1871–81, and was associate editor of *Harper's Magazine,* 1886–91, to which periodicals he contributed many articles on literary subjects. His numerous romances include *Their Wedding Journey* (1872), *The Lady of the Aroostook* (1879), *The Undiscovered Country* (1880), *A Modern Instance* (1882), *The Rise of Silas Lapham* (1885; his greatest work), *Indian Summer* (1886; another charming book), and *A Hazard of New Fortunes* (1890), which shows the effect of his political and critical moves towards socialism and social realism. His works of criticism and reminiscence include *Criticism and Fiction* (1891), *My Literary Passions* (1895), *Literary Friends and Acquaintances* (1900), *Literature and Life* (1902). He also wrote several dramas. His industry and his influence made him the leading American man of letters of his age, and he did much to encourage H. *James and other writers.

Howleglass, see EULENSPIEGEL.

Hoyden, Miss, a character in Vanbrugh's *The Relapse* and in Sheridan's *A Trip to Scarborough.*

HRABAL, Bohumil (1914–97), born in Brno, Czechoslovakia. He trained as a lawyer but was unable to practise under communist rule. His writing career began only in his late forties, with *Dancing Lessons for the Advanced in Age* (Czech, 1964; English, 1995), the reminiscences of a nostalgic roué, unfolding in a single sentence more than 100 pages long. *Closely Observed Trains* (1965; 1968) is a tragi-comic novella about a young railway worker in Nazi-occupied Czechoslovakia. The Oscar-winning film version, directed by Jiri Menzel, brought Hrabal to international notice, but he was then unable to publish in his own country for many years. *Too Loud a Solitude* (1980; 1990), the charming fictional memoirs of a book-pulper, preceded Hrabal's masterpiece *I Served the King of England* (1982; 1989), the life story of a self-interested waiter, which ranges over most of pre- and post-war European history. His shorter pieces *The Death of Mr Baltisberger* (1966; 1975) and *The Little Town Where Time Stood Still* (1982; 1993) seem minor by comparison.

Hrothgar, see BEOWULF.

HROTSVITHA, or **ROSWITHA** (fl. 10th cent.), a Benedictine abbess of Gandersheim in Saxony, who adapted the comedies of *Terence for the use of her convent, an example of the survival of classical influence in the Middle Ages.

hubris, see POETICS, THE.

HUCHOWN (fl. 14th cent.), apparently a northern alliterative poet. 'Huchown of the Awle Ryale' is mentioned by Andrew of *Wyntoun, *c*.1400, who claims that 'He made the gret Gest of Arthure | And the Anteris of Gawane, | The Epistill als of Suete Susane.' These poems have been tentatively identified as respectively the alliterative *Morte Arthure*, *The Awntyrs of Arthure*, and *The Pistyll of Susan*. Huchown was declared by G. Neilson (1902) to be the Scot Sir Hew of Eglinton, famous from the reference to him in *Dunbar's 'Lament for the Makaris' (53); but there is little advantage in postulating a particular poet since so little is known of him. It has been argued that the named poems are unlikely to be the work of the same writer; on the other hand, it is hard to see why Andrew of Wyntoun should invent a poetic canon more or less contemporary with himself. In the past other works were, with little justification, added to the canon, of which the most distinguished were the four poems in the manuscript containing *Pearl*.

Huckleberry Finn, The Adventures of, a novel by Mark *Twain, published 1884, as a sequel to *Tom Sawyer*, and generally accepted as his masterpiece and one of the great works of American fiction.

Huck Finn, the narrator, recounts his adventures after being taken away from the Widow Douglas's by his drunken and brutal father. He escapes from his father, faking his own death, and joins up with a runaway slave, Jim, and together they make their way down the Mississippi on a raft. The picaresque device of a journey serves to introduce a number of events and a variety of characters: Huck becomes a witness of the feud between the Grangerford and Shepherdson families; he and Jim are joined by two villainous confidence men, the 'Duke' and the 'Dauphin', who sell Jim into captivity again, but at the end of the book Tom reappears in time to help Huck to rescue him in a characteristically romantic and quixotic manner (unnecessarily, as it turns out, for Jim had earlier and unknowingly been given his freedom). Perennially popular as an adventure story, the novel is also a profound moral commentary on the nature of the

'American experience' and the institution of slavery, and a vital contribution to the myth of the frontier, told with a freshness and raciness that shocked some of its readers, and has given rise to many theses on the subject of 'Southern Humour'. Twain's use of the innocent narrator to present oblique moral judgement is masterly, and his use of the vernacular extremely sensitive; he claimed in a preface to have used 'the Missouri Negro dialect; the extremest form of the backwoods South-Western dialect; and four modified varieties of this last', and the flexibility and power of his narrative is in no way impeded by this adherence to realistic speech. Among many tributes to the novel's imaginative power might be mentioned Jonathan Raban's *Old Glory* (1981), an account of a boyhood passion that resulted in a lone Mississippi voyage.

Hudibras, or **Huddibras,** in Spenser's *Faerie Queene* (II. ii. 17), the lover of Elissa,

an hardy man;   Yet not so good of deedes, as great of name,
Which he by many rash adventures wan.

Another Huddibras, in II. x. 25 of the same poem, is a legendary king of Britain.

Hudibras, a satire in three parts, each containing three cantos, written by Samuel *Butler (1613–80). Part I, dated 1663, appeared in Dec. 1662, Part II, dated 1664, was published 1663, and a revised version of both parts came out in 1674. Part III was published 1680.

Its narrative form is that of a mock romance, derived from *Don Quixote, in which a grotesque Presbyterian knight, Sir Hudibras, and his sectarian squire Ralpho set out on horseback and encounter a bear-baiting mob who, after a comic skirmish, imprison them in the stocks. In the second part a widow, whom Hudibras hopes to marry for the sake of her jointure, agrees to release them on condition that the knight undergoes a whipping for her sake. They visit Sidrophel, a charlatan posing as an astrologer, whom Hudibras assaults and leaves for dead. In Part III Hudibras returns to the widow and claims that he has fulfilled his promise to whip himself, but is interrupted by a gang which he mistakes for Sidrophel's supernatural agents. They cudgel him and force him to confess to his iniquities. He consults a lawyer, who advises him to write love letters to the widow in order to inveigle her in her replies. The second canto of Part III has no connection with the rest of the poem but consists of an account of political events between the death of *Cromwell and the restoration of Charles II and a dialogue between two politicians, one of them modelled on *Shaftesbury.

The loose narrative framework of the poem allows Butler ample opportunity to digress; in fact the digressions form the substance of the poem. They deal with academic pedantry, the theological differences between the Presbyterians and independent sectarians, Aristotelian logic, the hermetic philosophy, the politics of the civil war period, the ethics of oath-breaking, witchcraft, alchemy, astrology, and the nature of marriage. *Hudibras* is the most learnedly allusive poem in English but Butler treats all erudition with contempt. His most powerful satirical weapon is his style, the deliberately cumbersome octosyllabic metre and comic rhymes of which render absurd every subject to which they are applied.

Hudibrastic, in the style of Butler's **Hudibras*; in octosyllabic couplets and with comic rhymes.

HUDSON, W(illiam) H(enry) (1841–1922), born near Buenos Aires, the son of poor American parents of English descent who had moved to the Argentine to farm. His education was haphazard and he ran wild on the family ranch. Rheumatic fever at 15 disabled him for the outdoor life he had intended, and his lifelong interest in birds intensified. He began to publish stories and articles on natural history in both English and Argentine journals, then in 1874 came to London, where he remained, often in poverty, for the rest of his life. He wrote prolifically, but until his last decade his work was little regarded. In 1885 he published *The Purple Land*, a series of strange and vivid stories set in South America, and *Belloc expressed great admiration for *The Crystal Age* (1887), an account of a utopian land where the sex impulse has burned out and society is therefore at last stable and at peace. In 1888 a standard work, *Argentine Ornithology*, of which Hudson was part-author, appeared. A. R. *Wallace praised *The Naturalist in La Plata* (1892), the first of Hudson's books to enjoy some success. In 1895 his *British Birds* appeared. In 1901 he met R. *Garnett, who henceforth greatly encouraged him, and in the same year he was awarded a Civil List pension of £150. *Idle Days in Patagonia*, an engaging work of travel and natural lore, appeared in 1893, and in 1900 *Nature in Downland*. His novel **Green Mansions* (probably the best known of his books) was published in 1904; success came slowly, but in the course of the next ten years the book made huge sales in both England and America. *A Shepherd's Life* (1910), which some hold to be his finest book, describes Caleb Bawcombe, a Wiltshire shepherd, who lives night and day, through all seasons, with his sheep and dogs among the people and the wild life of the downs. By now E. *Thomas, *Galsworthy, and others were ensuring that Hudson's work was widely noticed; *Adventures among Birds* (1913) was much praised, and the joyful account of his boyhood, *Far Away and Long Ago* (1918), received great acclaim. Another standard work, *Birds of La Plata*, appeared in 1920. New editions of Hudson's earlier books now began to appear, and by the time of his death he was generally recognized as a masterly writer on the natural world.

Hugh, in Dickens's **Barnaby Rudge*, the ostler of the Maypole Inn.

HUGH OF LINCOLN, Little St (?1246–55), a child supposed to have been crucified by a Jew named Copin or Joppin at Lincoln, after having been starved and tortured. The body is said to have been discovered in a well and buried near that of *Grosseteste in the cathedral, and to have been the cause of several miracles. The story, a frequent theme for medieval poets, and often related with strong anti-Semitic overtones, is referred to by Chaucer ('The Prioress's Tale', see CANTERBURY TALES, 16) and by Marlowe in **The Jew of Malta*. See also the ballad of 'The Jew's Daughter' in Percy's **Reliques*.

HUGHES, Langston, see JAZZ POETRY and PERFORMANCE POETRY.

HUGHES, Richard Arthur Warren (1900–76), writer of Welsh descent, born in Surrey and educated at Charterhouse and Oriel College, Oxford. He began writing at an early age and while at Oxford published a volume of poems, *Gipsy Night* (1922). In the same year his one-act play *The Sister's Tragedy*, sponsored by *Masefield, was performed at the *Royal Court, London. He travelled widely in Canada, the West Indies, and America before settling in 1934 in Wales. His first ambition was to be a dramatist and he was commissioned by the *BBC to write the first original radio play, *Danger*, produced by Nigel Playfair in 1924; in the same year a full-length play, *A Comedy of Good and Evil*, appeared at the Royal Court. *Confessio Juvenis* (collected poems) appeared in 1926. He gained fame with his first novel, *A High Wind in Jamaica* (1929), the story of the adventures of a family of children bound for England and captured by pirates. His unconventional and unsentimental treatment of childhood in this novel is said to have ended the Victorian myth of childhood, and paved the way for works such as Golding's **Lord of the Flies*. *In Hazard* (1938), a seafaring novel, contains a brilliant description of a hurricane which prompted comparisons with *Conrad. He produced three volumes of short stories, *A Moment of Time* (1926), *The Spider's Palace* (1931), and *Don't Blame Me* (1940), the last two for children. He worked for the admiralty during the war, and in 1961 broke a long silence with *The Fox in the Attic*, the first volume of an ambitious new project, 'The Human Predicament', a long historical sequence which was to cover the rise of Nazism and end with the Second World War. Opening in Wales just after the First World War, it mingles real and fictional characters, both German and British, ending with Hitler's Munich putsch. The second volume, *The Wooden Shepherdess* (1973), ends with the murder of Röhm, and was less well received. Hughes was a highly original and idiosyncratic writer, and his influence can be traced in the novels of J. G. *Farrell.

HUGHES, Robert (1938–), Australian art critic and historian, born in Sydney. He has written extensively and influentially on Australian, European, and American art: his publications include *Heaven and Hell in Western Art* (1969), *The Shock of the New* (1980), and *Culture of Complaint: The Fraying of America* (1993).

He is perhaps most widely known for his substantial, gripping, controversial, and scholarly history of the founding of Australia, *The Fatal Shore* (1987).

HUGHES, Ted (Edward James) (1930–98), poet, born in west Yorkshire, the son of a carpenter, and educated at Mexborough Grammar School, then at Pembroke College, Cambridge, where he met Sylvia *Plath, whom he married in 1956. As a boy he spent much time on shooting and fishing expeditions with his brother, and his obsession with animals and his sense of the beauty and violence of the natural world appear in his first volume, *The Hawk in the Rain* (1957). This was followed by *Lupercal* (1960), *Wodwo* (1967, prose and verse), and several books of children's verse. *Crow* (1970) is a sequence of poems introducing the central symbol of the crow (partly inspired by a meeting with the American artist Leonard Baskin, who has illustrated much of Hughes's work), which recurs frequently in subsequent volumes. Hughes retells the legends of creation and birth through the dark vision of predatory, mocking, indestructible crow, 'screaming for blood' amidst 'the horror of creation'. Later volumes include *Cave Birds* (1975), *Season Songs* (1976), and *Moortown* (1979), the last of these containing the sequence 'Prometheus on his crag', written in Iran in 1971, on his expedition with the stage director Peter *Brook, during which he also wrote *Orghast*, a play in an invented language. He also published plays for children, a version of *Seneca's *Oedipus* (1968), and edited various anthologies. *Remains of Elmet* (1979), with photographs by Fay Godwin, celebrates the landscapes of his youth in the Calder valley, which he describes as 'the last ditch of Elmet, the last British kingdom to fall to the Angles'; *River* (1983), with photographs by P. Keen, is a sequence of poems invoking riverside and river life. Together these volumes constitute interesting examples of the renewed vogue for *topographical poetry (with illustrations) that arose in the environment-conscious second half of the 20th cent. Hughes's stress on the physical, animal, and subconscious is in marked contrast to the urbane tone of the *Movement, and his poetry, hailed as vital and original, has also been described as excessively brutal and violent. He was appointed poet laureate in 1984. More recent volumes include *Wolfwatching* (1989), *Rain-Charm for the Duchy and Other Laureate Poems* (1992), and *New Selected Poems* (1995). A prose work, *Shakespeare and the Goddess of Complete Being*, was published in 1992 and *Winter Pollen*, a collection of occasional prose, in 1995. *Tales from Ovid* (1997), which won the Whitbread Prize, contains a selection of free verse translations from *Ovid's *Metamorphoses*, and *Birthday Letters* (1998) consists of 88 poems describing his relationship with Plath: it is dedicated to their two children.

HUGHES, Thomas (1822–96), educated at Rugby and Oriel College, Oxford. He was a barrister and Liberal MP, and, under the influence of F. D. *Maurice, devoted much energy to working men's education, the Co-operative movement, etc. He is remembered as the author of *Tom Brown's Schooldays* (1857, by 'An Old Boy'), which evokes the Rugby of his youth and his veneration for its headmaster, Dr T. *Arnold. Hughes condemned, in the character of the tyrannical Flashman, the bullying prevalent in public schools of the day, and advocated a form of what came to be known as 'muscular Christianity', which attempted to combine Christian principles with physical courage, self-reliance, love of sport, school loyalty, and patriotism, a mixture that had much impact on the public-school ethos. Its detractors found it philistine, and indeed there are few mentions in the novel of any intellectual pursuits. The sequel, *Tom Brown at Oxford* (1861), is less interesting. Hughes wrote several biographies and memoirs, one other novel (*The Scouring of the White Horse*, 1859), and published various sermons and addresses, including *The Manliness of Christ* (1879), which attacks the view that Christianity is a religion for the timid and fearful. There is a life by E. C. Mack and W. H. G. Armytage (1953).

Hugh Selwyn Mauberley, see POUND.

HUGO, Victor(-Marie) (1802–85), poet, novelist, and dramatist, the central figure of the Romantic movement in France. Coming late to active political life, he was elected to the Assembly in 1848, but spent the years 1851–70 in exile, the greater part of the time in Guernsey. He returned to Paris in 1870 and was again chosen as a deputy, later becoming a senator of the Third Republic. He had been elected to *Académie française in 1841. Hugo is one of the masters of French poetry, to which he brought a new freedom of subject, diction, and versification. His many collections include: *Odes et poésies diverses* (1822), *Odes et ballades* (1826), *Les Orientales* (1829), *Les Feuilles d'automne* (1831), *Les Chants du crépuscule* (1835), *Les Voix intérieures* (1837), *Les Rayons et les ombres* (1840), and *Le Rhin* (1842). His daughter and her husband were drowned in 1843, and a long silence followed. *Les Châtiments*, a violent satire against Louis Napoleon, written in exile, appeared in 1853. Spiritual and cosmic themes come to the fore in *Les Contemplations* (1856). The poems of *La Légende des siècles* (1859, 1877, 1883) compose an epic and prophetic treatment of history, of which the posthumously published *La Fin de Satan* (1886) and *Dieu* (1891) were intended to form the final parts. Of Hugo's plays, *Cromwell* (1827), *Hernani* (1830), and *Ruy Blas* (1838) are variously important; the first because of its preface, which became a manifesto of the French Romantic movement. The first two performances of *Hernani*, taking place amidst the vociferous manifestations of the partisans and opponents of the new drama, mark an epoch in the French theatre and have entered its mythology. *Ruy Blas* continued his success in verse drama. Besides his well-known *Notre Dame de Paris* (1831) and *Les Misérables* (1862), Hugo wrote a number of other novels, e.g., *Les Travailleurs de la mer* (1866, set in Guernsey) and *Quatre-vingt-treize* (1874, royalist insurrections in Brittany and the Vendée during the French Revolution).

HUIZINGA, Johan (1872–1945), Dutch historian, chiefly known in Britain for four books, *Homo Ludens* (1938; trans. 1949), *Erasmus of Rotterdam* (1924; trans. 1924), *In the Shadow of Tomorrow* (1935; trans. 1936), and *The Waning of the Middle Ages* (1919; trans. 1924), and perhaps principally for the last of these, a cultural history which, in opposition to *Burckhardt's model of a cultural shift, emphasizes the continuity of the medieval tradition.

HULL, E. M., see ROMANTIC FICTION.

HULME, Keri (1947–   ), New Zealand poet and novelist, author of *The Bone People* (1985, *Booker Prize), a poetic, impassioned account of the relationship between Kerewin Holmes and a mute wild boy, Simon Gillalyey, who invades her solitary artist's life in a tower on the seashore: she becomes deeply involved with Simon's Maori foster father Joe, who had rescued him from shipwreck. Hulme's colourful vocabulary is enriched by Maori words and phrases, integrated into a text which gives a vivid account of contemporary New Zealand life, myth, landscape, and seascape. Other works include *The Silences Between: Moeraki Conversations* (1982, poems) and *Lost Possessions* (1985). *Te Kaihau/The Windeater* (1986) is a collection of short stories, poems, and prose poems dealing with the street, the sea, fish gutting, and the 'city underbelly', embracing the lives both of Maori and Pakeha (i.e. non-Maori white New Zealanders).

HULME, T(homas) E(rnest) (1883–1917), poet, essayist, and (in his own phrase) 'philosophic amateur', whose reaction against *Romanticism and advocacy of the 'hard dry image' influenced *Imagism. His essay 'Romanticism and Classicism' defines Romanticism as 'split religion', and predicts a new 'cheerful, dry and sophisticated' poetry; similarly, in the visual arts, he predicted the triumph of precise, abstract geometric form. (His friends included Jacob Epstein and *Gaudier-Brzeska.) His own poems (of which only six were published in his lifetime, five in *Orage's *The New Age*, 1912, as 'The Complete Poetical Works of T. E. Hulme') largely bear out his thesis; several of the handful that survive are short, provocative treatments of the subject of 'Sunset'. Hulme also contributed regularly to the *New Age*, notably in his essays on *Bergson, whom he also translated. He was killed in action, and much of his work survived only in notebooks. *Speculations: Essays on Humanism and the Philosophy of Art* (1924) and *Notes on Language and Style* (1929) were edited by *Read. Hulme's double role as conservative and Modernist had considerable influence on the development of 20th-cent. taste; T. S. *Eliot described him in 1924 as 'classical, reactionary and revolutionary . . . the antipodes of the eccentric, tolerant and democratic mind

of the end of the century', and Hulme's stress on original sin and man's 'extraordinarily fixed and limited nature' finds echoes in Eliot's own work. See A. R. Jones, *The Life and Opinions of T. E. Hulme* (1960).

Human Understanding, *Enquiry Concerning*, see HUME.

Humber, in *Geoffrey of Monmouth's *History* (ii. 1–2), a king of the Huns who invaded northern Britain in the reign of *Locrine, who defeated him and drowned him in the river Albus which afterwards bore his name. He brought to England *Estrildis with whom Locrine fell in love. The story is told in Spenser's *Faerie Queene* (II. x. 15–16).

HUMBOLDT, (Friedrich Heinrich) Alexander von (1769–1859), German traveller and scientist, and brother of Wilhelm (see below). He published a series of works embodying the results of a scientific expedition to South America and Mexico, which were translated into English (1814–21). His greatest work was the *Cosmos* (published in German, 1845–62), a physical description of the universe, passing from celestial phenomena to the earth and its atmosphere, and finally to organic life.

HUMBOLDT, Wilhelm von (1767–1835), German writer, philologist, and educationalist. He introduced educational reforms in Prussia in the early 19th cent., his particular achievement being the founding of the University of Berlin on the principle of 'akademische Freiheit' ('academic freedom'). Students were to be educated on a humanist model, based on the study of the classical languages; universities were to be autonomous; and students were to be free to migrate from one university to another to complete their degrees. This was the basis of higher education in modern Germany.

HUME, David (1711–76), born and educated at Edinburgh. He developed early in life a passion for philosophy. He spent three years (1734–7) in private study in France, and in 1739 published anonymously his *Treatise of Human Nature* in two volumes, a third volume and a promotional *Abstract* appearing in 1740. During his lifetime it sold poorly and was generally received with hostility, but its doctrines had an important impact on H. *Home and Adam *Smith. Hume's *Essays Moral and Political* (1741–2) was more successful. *A Letter from a Gentleman to His Friend in Edinburgh* (1745) includes Hume's defence of his *Treatise* when he contended unsuccessfully for the moral philosophy chair at Edinburgh, against the opposition of *Hutcheson and *Wishart. He accompanied General St Clair as judge-advocate in the expedition to Port L'Orient in 1747 and on a mission to Vienna and Turin in 1748. His *Enquiry Concerning Human Understanding* (originally entitled *Philosophical Essays*) appeared in 1748 and his *Enquiry Con-

cerning the Principles of Morals in 1751. In 1752 he published his *Political Discourses*, which was translated into French and made Hume famous on the Continent. In the same year he was appointed advocates' librarian in Edinburgh, subsequently surrendering the stipend to the poet *Blacklock. In 1754 appeared the first volume of his *History of Great Britain*, devoted to the early Stuarts, followed by further volumes in 1757, 1759, and 1762; publication was initially obstructed by the London book trade, but the work became immensely popular both in Britain and abroad, was extolled by *Gibbon and *Voltaire, and appeared in nearly 200 lifetime and posthumous editions. *Four Dissertations*, dedicated to J. *Home, was published in 1757, after the prudential suppression of controversial essays on suicide and immortality. From 1763 to 1765 Hume was secretary to the embassy in Paris, where he was well received by the court and by literary society. He brought back *Rousseau to England and befriended him, but Rousseau's suspicious nature presently led to a quarrel, Hume's account of which was published in 1766. Hume was under-secretary of state in 1767–8, and after this finally settled in Edinburgh. After his death, his friend Adam Smith published his autobiography with a eulogy (1777). Hume's *Dialogues Concerning Natural Religion* was published in 1779 by his nephew. A collection of letters to him was published by J. H. Burton in 1849, and collections of letters from him by J. Y. T. Greig in 1932 and R. Klibansky and E. C. Mossner in 1954.

For Hume's philosophical views, see TREATISE OF HUMAN NATURE. His views on religion are contained, (*a*) in sections X–XI of *An Enquiry Concerning Human Understanding*, in which he argues that the evidence for miracles is necessarily inferior to the evidence for the 'laws of nature' established by uniform experience of which they purport to be a violation, and that our belief in a supreme intelligence is founded not in the rational but in the imaginative faculty; (*b*) in the dissertation entitled *The Natural History of Religion*, in which he investigates its origin in human nature and traces its development from polytheism to monotheism and its inevitable degeneration; (*c*) in the *Dialogues Concerning Natural Religion*, of which the cautious and ambiguous conclusion is 'that the cause or causes of order in the universe probably bear some remote analogy to human intelligence'.

Hume's writings on politics and history show a strong interest in human character and motivation. Though a believer in civil liberties (except freedom of divorce), and an opponent of 'divine right', he also defended the characters of the Stuart kings; and he rejected the social contract theory of society and social obligation as historically unrealistic, tracing these instead to custom and convenience. By deliberately steering between the extremes of prevailing Whig and Tory philosophies he incurred the complaints of both sides. As a political economist Hume attacked the mercantile system, and in general anticipated the

views of later economists in the tradition of Adam Smith.

Hume was an early friend of James *Thomson and of the family of *Ramsay. He was a consummate stylist, but personal partialities made him an erratic judge of others. His high opinion of the writing of John Home and *Wilkie, and low opinion of A. *Ferguson, have not been supported by later critics. He preferred the classical style of *Milton, *Racine, and *Pope, to what he saw as the linguistic liberties of Shakespeare. In aesthetic theory he followed *Dubos. The standard biography is Ernest C. Mossner, *The Life of David Hume* (2nd rev. edn., 1980) though John Hill Burton's *Life and Correspondence* (2 vols, 1846, repr. 1983) remains useful. See also A. J. *Ayer, *Hume* (1980).

Humorous Lieutenant, The, a comedy by J. *Fletcher, produced about 1619.

Prince Demetrius is in love with Celia, a captive. His father Antigonus, king of Syria, also falls in love with her, and during his son's absence at the wars, tries to seduce her, but she remains faithful to Demetrius. On Demetrius' return from victory, Antigonus informs him that Celia is dead, and while Demetrius shuts himself up in despair, tries to obtain her affection by a love-philtre. But the plot miscarries, and finally Celia's virtue and loyalty prevail on the king to surrender her to his son.

The title is taken from an eccentric lieutenant, suffering from an infirmity which stimulates him to wonderful deeds of courage in war. When cured, his courage fails him; and it comes again when he is deluded into thinking himself sick once more. By accident he drinks the love-philtre intended for Celia, and in consequence falls grotesquely in love with the king.

humours, comedy of, a term applied especially to the type of comic drama written by *Jonson, where a 'humour' is the embodiment in one of the characters of some dominating individual passion or propensity. The cardinal humours, whose balance was thought to determine a man's nature, were blood, phlegm, choler, and melancholy or black choler.

HUMPHREY, duke of Gloucester (1391–1447), youngest son of Henry IV, 'the Good Duke Humphrey', was, according to *Bale, educated at Balliol College, Oxford. He was appointed protector on the death of Henry V in 1422 and acted as regent, 1420–1 and periodically until 1431, in place of his brother, the duke of Bedford, who was abroad in the French wars much of the time. Politically he was naïvely ambitious and factious; he owes the epithet 'Good' only to his patronage of men of letters, including *Lydgate and *Capgrave. He read Latin and Italian literature, and he promoted Renaissance humanism in England. He collected books from his youth and gave the first books for a library at Oxford; still named after him is the oldest part of the Bodleian which was built to house his bequest in the

15th cent. He married the luckless Jacqueline of Bavaria late in 1422 (Lydgate wrote a ballad in celebration of the wedding), but he abandoned her in Burgundy in 1425 in favour of Eleanor Cobham, and the marriage was annulled in 1428. He married Eleanor before 1431; in the 1440s she was repeatedly tried for witchcraft (it seems that she did experiment with black magic), and she was finally imprisoned on the Isle of Man in 1446. He and his wife appear in Shakespeare's history plays.

HUMPHREYS, Emyr (1919–   ), Welsh novelist and poet. Born in Prestatyn, Flintshire, he served with the Save the Children Fund under the aegis of the UNO in Italy during the Second World War. He worked as a drama producer in radio and television, and his many novels include *Hear and Forgive* (1952), *A Toy Epic* (1958), *Outside the House of Baal* (1965), and a septet, the last of which is *Bonds of Attachment* (1991). He has been engaged in writing 'the Protestant novel', examining the means by which good is or is not passed on from generation to generation. Although true to the tradition of the realist novel, his work has a complexity of narrative, an ever-enlarging time-scheme, uninterrupted dialogue, severely episodic cutting, a surface wit, and a lyrical quality which have enabled many readers to enjoy it without engaging with its underlying concerns. He has also published four volumes of verse, a selection of which appeared in the *Penguin Modern Poets* series in 1979.

HUMPHRIES, (John) Barry (1934–   ), Australian satirist, comedian, and performer, born in Melbourne, began his theatrical career in 1955 with a touring company after cutting short his studies at Melbourne University. His most famous creation, Edna Everage, was first seen in December 1955, and made her Sydney debut in 1956. Humphries came to England in 1959, where he worked in Joan *Littlewood's company and the West End. Edna appeared in 1963 at the Establishment, a Soho club owned by comedian Peter Cook: the act was not an immediate success, but became immensely popular, and the monstrous, sadistic, and bizarrely apparelled Dame Edna became a household name. Humphries is also remembered for his collaboration with cartoonist Nicholas Garland in the 1960s strip cartoon *The Adventures of Barry McKenzie*, which offered a satiric view of Australian national characteristics.

Humphry Clinker, The Expedition of, a novel by T. *Smollett, published 1771.

The mellowest and most accomplished of Smollett's works, the novel achieves its effects by a new and pointed economy. It is *epistolary in form, describing, in the words of Sir W. *Scott (who published a memoir of Smollett in 1821), 'the various effects produced upon different members of the same family by the same objects'. Nearly two-thirds of the letters are either from Matthew Bramble to his friend and doctor Lewis, or from young squire Jery Melford (Bramble's nephew) to his friend Phillips at Oxford; the rest are from Bramble's sister Tabitha to her housekeeper Mrs Gwyllim at Brambleton-hall; from Bramble's niece Lydia to her school friend Letty; and from the wildly illiterate Winifred Jenkins, Tabitha's servant, to Molly, a maid at the hall. The two principal non-letter writers are Clinker himself and the Scot Lismahago. The narrative is simple, covering a round trip from Wales to London, to Scotland and back again, and its principal interest lies in the interplay of characters, whose mutual hostility is resolved by the end of the journey into general amity, or, as Winifred puts it, 'a family of love'.

The letters begin in Gloucester, whence the party proceeds to Clifton. Here Lydia first meets Wilson, apparently a mere strolling player, whom the outraged Jery challenges to a duel. After a stay at Bristol the party travels to Bath, which enchants Lydia and where the husband-hunting Tabitha fastens on Sir Ulic MacKilligut, but which is castigated by Bramble as 'a sink of profligacy and extortion'. On the journey to London the carriage overturns, Thomas the postilion is bitten by Tabitha's ferocious and much-loved cur Chowder, and the destitute Humphry is engaged in Thomas's place. In London Humphry is detected by Bramble preaching Methodism among servants at court, on the streets, and later (when he has been mistaken for a felon) in prison; he is outraged, but Lydia, Tabitha, and Win are moved, and Bramble is reconciled to Humphry's simple sincerity. The party then leaves for the north. At Harrogate they encounter the de Melvils and a reformed Count Fathom (see FERDINAND COUNT FATHOM) and at Scarborough Humphry 'rescues' his master from an enjoyable sea-bathe. At Durham they meet the disputatious Lismahago, his face 'half a yard in length', and hear of his exotic history, during which he was scalped by Red Indians. Tabitha scents a husband and prepares her pursuit. Once in Scotland Bramble recovers his health and Lydia becomes the toast of Edinburgh, a city which, however, disgusts them by its filth. Praise for Glasgow is followed by an Arcadian interlude by Loch Lomond. Returning by Carlisle, they meet Lismahago again and he and Tabitha become engaged. Various tumultuous and ludicrous events interrupt the journey south; Lydia catches sight of her beloved Wilson, but Jery will not permit them to meet. The carriage in which the party is travelling overturns in a river, and Humphry saves the life of the drowning Bramble. Shortly afterwards, through a chance encounter with Bramble's old friend Dennison, Humphry is revealed as Bramble's natural son, and Wilson as the son of Dennison. At the end of the story Bramble, filled with new vigour and magnanimity, is delighted to be on the way back to Brambleton-hall; Lydia is united with Wilson, Tabitha with Lismahago, and Humphry with Winifred. While none have been improbably transformed, all have advanced considerably in understanding of themselves and of the world.

Huncamunca, a character in Fielding's *Tom Thumb*. (See also SOPHONISBA.)

HUNT, (William) Holman (1827–1910), painter, and founder member of the *Pre-Raphaelite Brotherhood. Many of his most famous paintings (*The Scapegoat, The Light of the World*) have a strong religious inspiration, though he also painted many literary and historical subjects from Shakespeare, *Tennyson, *Keats, *Bulwer-Lytton, etc. His autobiographical *Pre-Raphaelitism and the Pre-Raphaelite Brotherhood* (1905) is a full but personal history of the movement.

HUNT, John (1775–1848), the brother of Leigh *Hunt. He was a courageous and enterprising publisher who was prosecuted, threatened with legal actions, and fined many times. In 1805 he founded a short-lived paper, the *News*, then in 1808 he and Leigh established the very successful *Examiner*, a general weekly independent paper devoted to liberal and reforming causes, which ran for many years and was frequently threatened with actions for libel. In 1810 he started a quarterly, the *Reflector* (with Leigh as editor), in which several essays by *Lamb appeared, but it ran for only four numbers. He was prosecuted in 1811 for an article against military flogging and was successfully defended by *Brougham. But in 1813 he and Leigh were both sentenced to two years' imprisonment in separate jails and fined £500 apiece for a libel on the prince regent. Both men refused a guarantee to abstain from further attacks on the prince. In 1815–17 John published those essays of his brother and of *Hazlitt which were collected as *The Round Table* (1817). Hazlitt, in dedicating his *Political Essays* of 1819 to John Hunt, described him as 'the tried, steady, zealous and conscientious advocate of the liberty of his country'. He was the publisher and Leigh the editor of the short-lived but brilliant *Liberal*, founded in 1822, in which *Byron published *The Vision of Judgement*, a work which had been refused by Byron's publisher, John *Murray. John was prosecuted for 'a seditious libel' on the late king, but Byron's executors settled the costs and the fine of £100. In the same year John published in the *Liberal* all the later cantos of *Don Juan (from Canto VI), which Murray had again refused. The *Literary Examiner*, founded in 1823, was short-lived, and in the same year John's long collaboration with his unbusinesslike brother, who owed him large sums, ended in unhappy litigation.

HUNT, (James Henry) Leigh (1784–1859), born at Southgate, the son of a poor clergyman. Hunt received his schooling as a charity boy at *Christ's Hospital. His first collection of poems appeared in 1807. In 1808 he founded and edited, with his brother John (above), the *Examiner*, the first of many journals he was to initiate. He was to write poetry and drama, but the bulk of his large output was in the form of essays on a wide variety of subjects, many of which were published in his journals. The *Reflector*, in which he published

*Lamb's essays on Shakespeare and *Hogarth, appeared in 1810. In 1813 he and his brother were fined £500 and sentenced to two years' imprisonment for a libel in the *Examiner* on the prince regent. While in jail he was allowed to have his family with him, to continue to write and edit the *Examiner*, and to receive visits from friends, who included *Byron, *Moore, the *Lambs, *Bentham, James *Mill, and *Brougham. In 1816 he printed *Keats's early sonnet 'O Solitude' in the *Examiner*, and began his vigorous and lifelong support of Keats, *Shelley, and the *Romantic poets; his name was linked with that of Keats and *Hazlitt in attacks on the so-called *Cockney School. He published his influential poem *The Story of Rimini* in the same year. His verses appeared in a volume, *Foliage* (1818), and in 1819 he published his poems *Hero and Leander* and *Bacchus and Ariadne*. In his journal the *Indicator* he published in 1821 Keats's *'La Belle Dame sans Merci', and in a journal founded jointly with Byron, the *Liberal*, appeared in 1822 *The Vision of Judgement*, and in the three subsequent numbers works by Byron, Shelley, Hazlitt, Hunt, *Hogg, and others. The *Companion*, a magazine which contains some of Hunt's best work, appeared in 1828, his *Tatler* in 1830–2, and his *London Journal* in 1834–5. *Captain Sword and Captain Pen* (1835) is an effective poem describing the horrors of war. 'Abou Ben Adhem' (probably, with 'Jenny kissed me', Hunt's best-known poem) was published in an anthology, the *Book of Gems* (1838). Hunt's play *A Legend of Florence* (1840), a semi-Elizabethan tragedy, was produced at Covent Garden and was well received: he wrote many others without success. In the same year he published an edition of Restoration dramatists. In 1844 appeared his *Poetical Works* and *Imagination and Fancy*, in which he usefully compares painting and poetry; in 1846 an anthology, *Wit and Humour*, and *Stories from Italian Poets*; in 1847 (the year in which he received a Civil List pension) appeared *Men, Women, and Books*; in 1848 *A Jar of Honey from Mount Hybla* and *The Town*, an evocation of London; in 1850 a lively *Autobiography*, much admired by *Carlyle and others; in 1851 *Table Talk*; in 1853 *The Religion of the Heart*; in 1855 *The Old Court Suburb*, essays on Kensington, and a bowdlerized edition of *Beaumont and *Fletcher.

Hunt's essays, although much influenced by the essayists of the previous century, were not moral in intent. His aim was to convey appreciation and enjoyment ('to reap pleasure from every object in creation'), and his pleasure in literature, drama, music, and friendship is agreeably infectious. (See THEATRE CRITICISM.) His gift for detecting talent, from Keats to *Tennyson, and his determined support for it, made him an invaluable editor. His sunny, optimistic nature is sketched in the early character of Skimpole in *Bleak House*. See *Fiery Heart: The First Life of Leigh Hunt* (2005) by Nicolas Roe.

HUNT, Thornton Leigh (1810–73), journalist and editor, the eldest son of Leigh *Hunt. He was, with G. H.

*Lewes, joint founder of the *Leader*, and in 1855 joined the staff of the new *Daily Telegraph*, of which he became the virtual editor. His prolonged relationship with Lewes's wife Agnes, who bore him four children, was the indirect cause of the unorthodoxy of the union of Lewes with George *Eliot.

HUNT, (Isobel) Violet (1866–1942), novelist, born in Durham, the daughter of artist Alfred Hunt and novelist Margaret Hunt. She was for some years the companion of F. M. *Ford. A flamboyant feminist, a supporter of *women's suffrage, and a friend of H. G. *Wells, H. *James, and many others in the literary world, she published several novels (including *The Maiden's Progress*, 1894, and *White Rose of Weary Leaf*, 1908) and an autobiography, *The Flurried Years* (1926). M. *Sinclair, in the *English Review* (1922), attempts to qualify the novels' reputation for 'a merely hard yet superficial cleverness', praises her 'gallery of *demi-vierges*', and singles out her macabre *Tales of the Uneasy* (1911).

HUNTER, Sir William Wilson (1840–1900), born in Glasgow, educated there and in Paris and Bonn. He entered the Indian civil service in 1862. He was a man of broad cultural interests and was author of several notable volumes mainly on Indian historical subjects including *Annals of Rural Bengal* (1868), *Orissa* (1872), *The Imperial Gazetteer of India* (1881), *The Old Missionary* (1895), and *The Thackerays in India* (1897). He had completed only two volumes of his *History of British India* (1899–1900) at his death.

Huntingdon, Arthur and Helen (Graham), leading characters in A. Brontë's *The Tenant of Wildfell Hall*.

HUNTINGDON, Robert, earl of, see ROBIN HOOD.

HUNTINGDON, Selina Hastings, countess of (1707–91), founder of the group of Calvinistic Methodists known as 'Lady Huntingdon's Connexion', and warm supporter of *Whitefield. She was largely responsible for introducing Methodism to the upper classes.

Hunting of the Snark, The, a *mock-heroic nonsense poem by Lewis Carroll (C. L. *Dodgson), published 1876. Dodgson said that the poem sprang from 'one line of verse—one solitary line—"For the Snark *was* a Boojum, you see"' that came to him one day in 1874 while he was out walking: to questions asking whether the poem was an allegory, or a political satire, or contained some hidden moral, he claimed to have 'but one answer, "I don't know!"' (*The Theatre*, Apr. 1887).

Huon of Bordeaux, the hero of a French 13th-cent. *chanson de geste*. He has the misfortune to kill Charlot, son of *Charlemagne, in an affray, not knowing who his assailant is. He is thereupon condemned to death by the emperor, but reprieved on condition that he will go to the court of Gaudisse, amir of Babylon, bring back a handful of his hair and four of his teeth, kill his doughtiest knight, and kiss Esclarmonde his daughter.

By the help of the fairy Oberon, Huon achieves the adventure. The work was translated by Lord *Berners and printed in about 1515. Huon's adventure is the theme of Weber's opera *Oberon*.

HURD, Richard (1720–1808), son of a Staffordshire farmer, bishop successively of Lichfield and Worcester. He produced an edition of *Horace's *Ars Poetica* (1749) and *Epistola ad Augustum* (1751), adding to the second his 'A Discourse Concerning Poetical Imitation'. His *Moral and Political Dialogues* appeared in 1759, with dialogues between, for example, A. *Cowley and *Sprat. *Letters on Chivalry and Romance* (1762) is an important reassessment of Elizabethan literature: Hurd was notably sympathetic to *Spenser, argued that the 'Gothic' was more poetic than the 'Grecian', and that *neo-classical rules were inappropriately applied to chivalric romances, which were composed on different but no less artistic principles. The 'revolution' in taste of the *Augustan age had produced 'a great deal of good sense', but, 'What we have lost is a world of fine fabling.' His ideas on the classic and the romantic were developed by T. *Warton. Hurd was a friend and correspondent of W. *Mason and T. *Gray; the letters were edited by E. H. Pearce and L. Whibley (1932).

HURDIS, James (1763–1801), minor poet, and friend and correspondent of *Cowper. He was professor of poetry at Oxford in 1793. His best-known work is *The Village Curate: A Poem* (1788). See A. P. Whitaker, *James Hurdis, His Life and Writings* (1960).

Hurlothrumbo (1729), a popular burlesque by Samuel Johnson (1691–1773), a Manchester dancing master; it was described by his fellow Mancunian *Byrom (who also wrote an epilogue for it) as full of 'oddities, out-of-the-waynesses, flights, madness, comicalities etc.'

HURSTON, Zora Neale (c.1891–1960), American novelist, folklorist, journalist, and critic, born in Eatonville, Florida, the first incorporated all-black town in America. She worked her way through university, where she studied cultural anthropology. She was a prolific writer during the 1920s and 1930s, prominent within the Harlem Renaissance: her works include *Mules and Men* (1935), a study of black American folklore in the South; the novel for which she is best known, *Their Eyes Were Watching God* (1937); plays, short stories, and *Dust Tracks on a Road* (1942), an 'autobiography'. Writers such as Alice *Walker and T. *Morrison acknowledge their debt to her.

Husband's Message, The, an Old English poem of 53 lines in the *Exeter Book, one of the group usually called 'elegies'. Its ostensible form is a message to a woman from her husband who has had to leave his own country because of a feud, telling her of his prosperity in another land and asking her to join him. The text of the poem is the inscription itself which bears the message, and it is sometimes thought to be the continuation of the riddle (No. 60, the Reed) which it follows in the *Exeter Book*. It has also, not too implausibly, been interpreted in a religious sense, perhaps as an address from Christ to the Church.

Ed. and trans. R. Hamer, in *A Choice of Anglo-Saxon Verse* (1970); ed. R. F. Leslie in *Three Old English Elegies* (1961).

HUTCHESON, Francis (1694–1746), an Ulsterman, educated at Glasgow University, professor of moral philosophy at Glasgow from 1729 until his death. Before this he had published aesthetic, moral, and political essays in the Dublin and London press, and two books, *An Inquiry into the Original of Our Ideas of Beauty and Virtue* (1725) and *An Essay on the Nature and Conduct of the Passions and Affections with Illustrations on the Moral Sense* (1728), both subsequently revised. His posthumous *System of Moral Philosophy* was published in 1755 with a biography by William Leechman.

A protégé of *Molesworth, Hutcheson introduced the civic humanist tradition into higher education: he trained a whole generation of students, among them Adam *Smith, in the Whig philosophy of personal liberty and government restraint, and his progressive views on social justice, representative government, colonial autonomy, and the rejection of slavery, were influential among Scots émigrés to America. In ethics he developed the ideas of *Shaftesbury on the moral sense into a fully-fledged system. He saw a close relation between aesthetic and moral perception, by which we come to be aware of providentially designed order. We have a 'moral sense of beauty in actions and affections' which is stimulated by contemplating benevolence directed at another person. Virtue is identical with benevolence insofar as it gives disinterested pleasure, that action being best which aims at the greatest happiness of the greatest number. This view anticipates *utilitarianism.

Hutcheson was instrumental in helping to establish the publishing and printing business of the *Foulis brothers.

HUTCHINSON, Lucy (1620–after 1675), daughter of Sir Allen Apsley, and wife of John Hutchinson (1615–64). She was the author of *Memoirs of the Life of Colonel Hutchinson,* which she wrote after his death to preserve his memory for her children; it is a classic account of the state of the country at the outbreak of civil war and of the conflict in the vicinity of Nottingham, told from the point of view of the radical Puritan high gentry. John Hutchinson held Nottingham for Parliament as governor, signed the king's death warrant, was imprisoned at the Restoration, and saved from execution partly through his wife's intervention. Her narrative was first published in 1806, ed. J. Hutchinson, with a brief 'Fragment' of her own life, in which she records with satisfaction that she 'out-stripped' her brothers in intellectual achievement. Lucy Hutchinson's trenchant writing, with its mastery of the grand sweep

as well as the fine nuance of history, is at odds with her grief-stricken disavowal of autonomy as her husband's mere 'mirror' and 'shadow'. See *Memoirs of the Life of Colonel Hutchinson,* ed. N. H. Keeble (1995).

HUTCHINSON, R(ay) C(oryton) (1907–75), novelist, educated at Oriel College, Oxford; he worked for some years in the advertising department of Colman's at Norwich before becoming a full-time writer. His works include *The Unforgotten Prisoner* (1933), a powerful portrayal of revenge and conciliation in the aftermath of the First World War, seen partly through the sufferings of young Klaus, half English and half German, a victim of the conflicts of his parents and of his country; *Testament* (1938), set in Russia at the time of the revolution; *The Stepmother* (1955); and *Rising* (1976), a historical novel set in South America.

Hutchinsonians, (1) the followers of Mrs Anne Hutchinson (1591–1643), who emigrated from England to Massachusetts, where she founded an Antinomian sect, was banished from the colony, and eventually massacred by Native Americans at Hell Gate, New York county, with all but one of her family; (2) the followers of John Hutchinson (1674–1737), whose chief work, *Moses's Principia* (1724), maintained that Hebrew was the primitive language of mankind and the key to all knowledge. It was written as an attack on I. *Newton's *Principia,* and is thought to have influenced *Smart.

HUTTEN, Ulrich von, see EPISTOLAE OBSCURORUM VIRORUM.

HUTTON, Richard Holt (1826–97), educated at University College London, prepared for the Unitarian ministry at Manchester New College. He became joint editor with his friend *Bagehot of the *National Review* (1855–64). From 1861 until his death he was joint editor of the *Spectator,* and under his control the journal wielded great influence. His works, most of which show his theological inclinations, include *Essays, Theological and Literary* (1871), a volume on *Newman (1891), *Criticisms on Contemporary Thought* (1894), and *Aspects of Religious and Scientific Thought* (1899).

HUXLEY, Aldous Leonard (1894–1963), grandson of T. H. *Huxley and brother of Julian *Huxley; his mother died when he was 14, and when he was 16 at Eton he developed serious eye trouble which made him nearly blind and prevented any possibility of a scientific career, though he recovered sufficiently to read English at Balliol College, Oxford. During the war he met Lady O. *Morrell and visited Garsington frequently; she and other literary figures that he met there were to appear, not always to their own satisfaction, in his early satirical novels. By 1919, when he began to write for *Murry in the *Athenaeum,* he had already published three volumes of verse; a volume of stories, *Limbo* (1920), was followed by *Crome Yellow* (1921), a country-house satire which earned him a reputation for precocious brilliance and cynicism, and much offended Lady Ottoline. During the 1920s and 1930s Huxley and his wife Maria lived in Italy, then France; during this period he wrote much fiction, including *Mortal Coils* (1922, stories; includes 'The Gioconda Smile'); *Antic Hay* (1923, set in post-war London's nihilistic bohemia); *Those Barren Leaves* (1925, set in Italy); and *Point Counter Point* (1928), in which were recognized portraits of his friend D. H. *Lawrence as Rampion and Murry as Burlap. *Brave New World* (1932), his most enduringly popular work, was followed by *Eyeless in Gaza* (1936). Huxley's literary reputation deteriorated when he left in 1937 for California, partly for the sake of his eyes, partly in disillusion with the failure of the peace movements of Europe, partly in search (with his friend Gerald Heard) of new spiritual direction. He continued to write in many genres: novels include *After Many a Summer* (1939), in which Heard appears as the mystic Propter, and *Island* (1962), an optimistic Utopia; and other works include essays, historical studies, travel works, and *The Devils of Loudon* (1952), a study in sexual hysteria which became the basis of *Whiting's play *The Devils*. He became deeply interested in mysticism and parapsychology; *The Doors of Perception* (1954) and *Heaven and Hell* (1956) describe his experiments with mescalin and LSD.

Although *Brave New World* has an assured place as a popular classic, Huxley's other novels have proved difficult to 'place' as literature. Their mixture of satire and earnestness, of apparent brutality and humanity, have led some to dismiss them as smart and superficial, a symptom rather than an interpretation of a hollow age; others have seen them as brilliant and provocative 'novels of ideas' written by a man who was not by nature a novelist, but who (according to *Berlin) helped to liberate a generation by shedding light 'in dark places'. A biography by S. *Bedford (2 vols) was published 1973–4.

HUXLEY, Sir Julian Sorell (1887–1975), biologist and writer, brother of Aldous *Huxley, educated at Eton and Balliol College, Oxford. He won the Newdigate Prize for poetry in 1908, and published a small collection of verse, *The Captive Shrew and Other Poems of a Biologist* (1932), which shows, though less vividly than some of his scientific works, his keen interest in and love of the natural world, particularly of birds. He held many important appointments, was professor of zoology at King's College, London, 1925–7, professor of physiology in the Royal Institution, 1926–9, and secretary of the Zoological Society, 1935–42. He was well known as a writer and broadcaster, and, like his grandfather T. H. *Huxley, had a gift for popular exposition which did not impede the rigours of his scientific work. His writings include *Essays of a Biologist* (1923), *Animal Biology* (with J. B. S. *Haldane, 1927), *The Science of Life* (with H. G. and G. P. *Wells,

1929), and *Soviet Genetics and World Science* (on the Lysenko controversy, 1949). See R. W. Clark, *The Huxleys* (1968).

HUXLEY, T(homas) H(enry) (1825–95). He studied at Charing Cross Hospital and was assistant surgeon on HMS *Rattlesnake*, 1846–50. His surveys of marine life on the Australian Barrier Reef appeared as papers for the *Royal and Linnean Societies (see LINNAEUS), he was elected FRS in 1851, and in 1854 became professor of natural history at the Royal School of Mines. He wrote extensively on specialist subjects, but was also widely known and admired as a lecturer to lay audiences, often of working men; he aimed to avoid 'technical dialect' and had a gift for explaining complicated scientific points in language that was generally intelligible. His views on religion, education, philosophy, and evolution, and on man's newly conceived place in the universe (e.g. in *Evidence as to Man's Place in Nature*, 1863, *Evolution and Ethics*, 1893, and other essays) had a profound impact on 19th-cent. thought. He was a friend of *Darwin, and an influential though discriminating supporter of his theories. He coined the word 'agnostic' to describe his own philosophical position, which he expounded at the *Metaphysical Society and in the *Nineteenth Century*. A vigorous though courteous disputant, he engaged in controversy with *Owen, *Gladstone, and other critics of evolutionary theory. His *Collected Essays* were published in 1893–4, his *Scientific Memoirs* in 1898–1903, and his *Life and Letters*, edited by his son Leonard, in 1900–3.

HUYSMANS, Joris-Karl (1848–1907), French novelist. After a number of early novels in a naturalistic vein (e.g. *Marthe, histoire d'une fille*, 1876; *En ménage*, 1881), he adopted another mode in *A rebours* (1884; *Against the Grain*, 1922, trans. J. Howard; *Against Nature*, 1959, trans. R. Baldick), the work for which he is now chiefly remembered. Introducing the neuraesthenic aristocrat Des Esseintes, who turns his back on the world as he finds it to create a world of sensuousness and artifice within which to cultivate extremes of self-awareness, *À rebours* has been regarded as a manual of the extravagant aestheticism of the *fin de siècle*. It was much admired by *Wilde, who introduces it into *The Picture of Dorian Gray* as the 'yellow book' given to Dorian by Lord Henry Wotton. Huysmans' later work includes four novels which follow the spiritual progress of the central character Durtal towards Roman Catholicism: *Là-bas* (1891), *En route* (1895), *La Cathédrale* (1898), *L'Oblat* (1903).

HYDE, Douglas (1860–1949), Irish writer and ardent pioneer in the *Irish Revival, who became the first professor of Irish at the National University in 1908. He founded the Gaelic League in 1893 and was its president until 1915. Several of his writings, including in particular *Love Songs of Connacht* (1893) and *A Literary History of Ireland* (1899), together with several volumes of verse translations from the Gaelic, were highly influential. In 1901 the *Irish Literary Theatre produced Hyde's Gaelic *Casadh*, and he later became one of the vice-presidents of the *Abbey Theatre company. He was the first president of Eire, holding office from 1938 to 1945. A biography by G. W. Dunleavy appeared in 1974.

HYDE, Edward, see CLARENDON.

Hyde Park, a comedy by J. *Shirley, acted 1632, printed 1637.

This comedy seems to have been written for performance at the time of the annual opening of the park, and it exploits the topical appeal of the subject. The fourth act features horse racing; when *Pepys saw a revival of the play after the Restoration, horses were actually led across the stage. Apart from the local colour, there is a plot about the return of a long-lost husband in disguise; another plot, sometimes seen as a foreshadowing of *Restoration comedy, is the courtship of the witty Carol and her no less witty suitor Fairfield, culminating in what is probably the earliest example of a 'proviso scene' (i.e. a scene of premarital negotiation) such as Congreve was to develop more fully in *The Way of the World*.

Hydriotaphia, or *Urn Burial*, by Sir T. *Browne, the companion piece to *The Garden of Cyrus*, published 1658, has been called the first archaeological treatise in English. He takes the discovery of some burial urns in a Norfolk field as the occasion for a wide-ranging meditation on the funeral procedures of many nations. The fragility of all relics and monuments prompts him to turn to the Christian doctrine of resurrection as the only lasting hope. From the first words of the 'Epistle Dedicatory', 'When the Funerall pyre was out, and the last valediction over', to the solemn splendour of the closing pages, beginning 'But the iniquity of oblivion blindely scattereth her poppy', Browne achieves the 'high style' demanded by his subject with a richness of diction and rhythmical power seldom if ever equalled in English prose.

Hye Way to the Spyttell House, The, a tract printed and adapted from a French work by Robert Copland (fl. 1508–48), describing the beggars and other types of the poorer classes who visit the hospital, in the form of a dialogue between the author and the porter of the hospital. It throws a vivid light on the poverty prevailing in the early 16th cent.

HYGINUS, *Gaius Julius*, an immensely erudite freedman whom the Emperor Augustus (d. AD 14) put in charge of the Palatine Library. He was a prolific author, but the astronomical treatise with stellar myths and the book of legends that now bear his name are probably no more than incompetent summaries of two of his works. They remain, however, our sole authorities for a number of legends and were widely used by later mythographers.

Hymenaei, a marriage masque by *Jonson, performed at Whitehall on Twelfth Night 1606, and printed in that year, with the theme of union. The marriage was that of the earl of Essex and Lady Frances Howard, the murderer of *Overbury. It ended in scandal and divorce.

hymns. The Greek *hymnos* means a 'song of praise', honouring gods or heroes. In the Christian tradition, hymns are songs of worship, sung by congregation and choir. They are often based on the Bible but, unlike canticles such as the 'Magnificat' or 'Nunc Dimittis', they are not settings of biblical texts. Hymn-singing was revived in 16th-cent. Germany by the Lutherans and English hymns were first written for Dissenting churches—by Isaac *Watts, an Independent minister, who published *Hymns and Spiritual Songs* (1707); by C. *Wesley in *Hymns and Sacred Poems* (1739); and by W. *Cowper and John *Newton in *Olney Hymns* (1779). Typically, these hymns resemble ballads in their four-line verses and simple metres. Before 1820, only the singing of Psalms was permitted in the Church of England. After 1820, there was a great revival of Anglican hymnody, leading to *Hymns Ancient and Modern* (1861), edited by the Revd Sir H. W. Baker (1821–77). As well as new compositions (by Mrs C. F. Alexander, 1823–95, and *Newman). 'A&M' was notable for its translations from Latin hymns. In the *Yattendon Hymnal* (1899), edited by R. *Bridges, and *The English Hymnal* (1906), edited by Sir Percy Dearmer (1867–1936) and *Vaughan Williams, English folk melodies were frequently employed, as hymn-singing was connected to nationalist ideas of Englishness. Since the 1960s, pop lyrics have become the dominant idiom for hymns, most successfully in the work of Graham Kendrick.

'Hymn to the Naiads', see AKENSIDE.

hypallage, from a Greek word meaning 'exchange', a transference of epithet, as 'Sansfoy's dead dowry' for 'dead Sansfoy's dowry' (*Spenser).

hyperbole, the use of exaggerated terms not in order to deceive but to emphasize the importance or extent of something. *Puttenham translated it as 'the over reacher', which in turn provides the title of H. Levin's study of *Marlowe, *The Overreacher* (1952), Marlowe having been particularly addicted to this figure of speech: e.g. 'Was this the face that launched a thousand ships? | And burnt the topless towers of Ilium?' (*Dr Faustus*).

Hyperion: *A Fragment* and *The Fall of Hyperion*, fragments of epic poems by *Keats written 1818–19. *Hyperion* was published 1820, *The Fall of Hyperion* not until 1856. In 1818 Keats gave up the effort to finish *Hyperion*, then began to rewrite and recast it as *The Fall of Hyperion*, but once again the effort was abandoned.

In the first version, written as direct narrative, the tremendous figure of the fallen Saturn, conquered by

Jove, mourns the loss of his kingdom and debates with his fallen fellow Titans, in their craggy lair, how he may regain his kingdom. They conclude that only the magnificent Hyperion, who is still unfallen, will be able to help them. In Bk III the golden Apollo, god of music, poetry, and knowledge, speaks to the goddess Mnemosyne of his inexplicable anguish; then, at the moment of his deification, the fragment ends. In the second version, the poet is in a luxuriant garden, where he drinks an elixir which induces a vision. He finds himself in a vast domed monument, then proceeds with pain and difficulty to climb the stair to the shrine of the priestess Moneta. Together they find the agonized fallen Saturn, and with Mnemosyne and Thea they speak to him of his pain and loss. In despair he leaves with Thea to comfort his fellow Titans, while the poet and Moneta watch the magnificent, but much troubled, Hyperion blaze into the west. The precise meaning of the allegory is not always clear, but both poems have as their general theme the nature of poetry and the nature and development of the poet. It is not known why Keats abandoned what was to have been his great work, but one of his fears, expressed in a letter to his friend *Reynolds, was that his writing was too Miltonic.

hypertext. Printed literature is not linear. A rich network of paths exists both within works (indexes, contents tables, cross-references) and between works (citations, bibliographies, catalogues). To follow some of the longer paths, however, required intercontinental travel, until the advent of literary machines. The magic lantern and the cinema spawned the microfilm reader. Television and the typewriter led to the computer terminal which could rapidly retrieve information from distant shores. Inspired by microfilm, Vannevar Bush in 1945 envisioned a 'private file and library' with screen and keyboard, with facilities for finding documents and linking them together to form branching 'trails'. In 1968 Douglas Engelbart of Stanford Research Institute demonstrated NLS, a computer system with many revolutionary features including facilities for editing non-sequential text. Cinema and television were the inspiration for Theodor H. Nelson, who in 1965 coined the term 'hypertext' for linked literature, or 'hypermedia' if sound and moving pictures were included. He saw that networks of computers could nurture a worldwide 'docuverse'. His 1980 Xanadu proposal included a scheme for managing copyright and payments. Paperback 'game-books' for young readers, such as the *Fighting Fantasy* series edited by Steve Jackson and Ian Livingstone, flourished in the 1980s. These showed the influence of computer games such as *Adventure* and were essen-

tially hypertext stories in print. In 1987 Apple Computer released HyperCard, a hypertext reading and authoring programme which was included with every Apple Macintosh computer sold. The world community of hypertext readers and authors expanded rapidly. Other notable pre-1990 hypertext systems include Intermedia, developed at Brown University; Guide, from Owl International; and NoteCards, from Xerox Corporation. More recently, millions have used Windows help, a simple hypertext system delivered with the Microsoft Windows operating system. Hypertext or hypermedia are the basis of most computer-based learning materials. The *World Wide Web, invented in 1990, realized much of Nelson's vision. This time an infrastructure was ready: universities and research institutes were connected to the Internet, as were some companies and private individuals, who used it for electronic mail and other purposes. Soon the Web became the Internet's main attraction for millions of new users. Compared with Xanadu, the Web was crude: it left users to make their own arrangements for protecting copyright and collecting fees. But people and organizations happily published material on the Web in order to spread their ideas, enhance their reputations, or sell their products. Reference works translate successfully into hypertext on the Web or on *CD-ROM. Writers working singly or co-operatively have also experimented with *interactive fiction which permits many different readings of the same story. Computer games such as Myst (Broderbund, 1995) and Resident Evil (Capcom, 1996) have complex plots and may be regarded as popular hypermedia novels. See V. Bush, 'As We May Think', *Atlantic Monthly* (July 1945), 101–8; T. H. Nelson, *Literary Machines* (1981); various authors, *Communications of the ACM*, 31/7 (July 1988).

hypotaxis (from Greek, 'subjection') is the frequent use of relative and dependent clauses (subordination), as in 'When I came, then I saw, and, having seen, I conquered'. The adjectival form is 'hypotactic'. (See PARATAXIS.)

hysteron-proteron, in grammar and rhetoric, a figure of speech in which the word or phrase that should properly come last is put first; in general, 'putting the cart before the horse': 'let us die and rush into the heart of battle.'

Hythloday, Raphael, in More's *Utopia*, the traveller in whose mouth the author places the criticisms of English institutions, and the description of the 'wise and godly ordinances' of the Utopians.

Iachimo, the villain in Shakespeare's *Cymbeline*, whose name, a diminutive of Iago (see below), may recall the villain in *Othello*.

Iago, the villainous ensign in Shakespeare's *Othello*. The equivalent character in the source was nameless. His character has often been seen as problematic, *Coleridge speaking in a famous phrase of the 'motive-hunting of motiveless malignity'.

iamb, iambic pentameter, see METRE.

IBSEN, Henrik (1828–1906), Norwegian dramatist, generally acknowledged as the founder of modern prose drama. His first successes, *Brand* (1866) and *Peer Gynt* (1867), both 'dramatic poems', created his name in Scandinavia, but it was over 20 years before the work of *Gosse and *Archer (and later the support of *Hardy, W. *James, G. B. *Shaw, and others) established him as a major dramatist in England. In 1872 Gosse wrote a review of *Poems* of the unknown Ibsen, and in 1872 translated an early play (*Love's Comedy*) and published an enthusiastic account of Ibsen's work. In the same year Archer read Ibsen's *Emperor and Galilean*, and his translation of *The Pillars of Society* was used for the first performance of Ibsen in England in 1880 (a single matinée) which was largely ignored. Archer introduced and read Ibsen to the young Shaw, who became deeply interested. By the end of the 1880s Archer's few translations were selling well, and in 1889 a long review of Ibsen's work by Gosse in the *Fortnightly Review* was followed by a highly successful production of Archer's translation of *A Doll's House* (1889). In 1890 Shaw gave a lecture which he published in 1891 as *The Quintessence of Ibsenism*, and the first volumes of Archer's translation of Ibsen's collected works were well received. In 1891 a single performance of *Ghosts* (1881) and a commercial production of *Hedda Gabler* (1890) both caused a storm of outrage; in 1893 a production of *The Master Builder* was reviled by critics but supported by the public. In the course of the next ten years Ibsen became established in England as a major dramatist and an important influence, both through Archer's continuing translations and through productions of many of the plays. In 1900 the *Fortnightly Review* contained an enthusiastic review of *When We Dead Awaken* (1899) by the 18-year-old *Joyce, who became a lifelong admirer.

Ibsen's earlier plays (such as *Ghosts* and *An Enemy of the People*, 1882) were concerned largely with social and political themes, but the last six (*The Wild Duck*, 1885; *Rosmersholm*, 1886; *The Lady from the Sea*, 1888; *The Master Builder; Little Eyolf*, 1894; and *John Gabriel*

Borkman, 1896) are more deeply concerned with the forces of the unconscious, and were greatly admired by *Freud. At the end of his life Ibsen commented that he was 'more of a poet and less of a social philosopher than people . . . suppose', and also declared that his interest was not so much in women's rights as in human rights. Ibsen created new attitudes to drama, and is credited with being the first major dramatist to write tragedy about ordinary people in prose. The quality of his dialogue, and his discarding of traditional theatrical effects, demanded and achieved a new style of performance. All his great prose dramas are now in the standard English-language repertoire, and *Peer Gynt* is also frequently revived; there have been many translations since Archer's, including versions by Una Ellis-Fermor, M. Meyer, R. Farquharson Sharp, J. W. McFarlane, and Peter Watts, and recent stage adaptations include those by A. *Miller, J. *Osborne, C. *Fry, A. *Jellicoe, G. *Hill, and Christopher *Hampton. There is a life by M. Meyer (3 vols, 1967–71).

Ida, Princess, the heroine of Tennyson's *The Princess*, which is the basis of the *Gilbert and Sullivan opera *Princess Ida*.

Idea, a sonnet sequence by M. *Drayton, first published as *Ideas Mirrour* in 1594, much revised and expanded, reaching its final form of 63 sonnets in 1619.

idealism, in philosophy, the view that minds or spirits are the only, or the fundamental, entities in the world, material things being unreal or in some way parasitical upon the mental. There are several varieties of idealist philosophy, and their most notable exponents include *Berkeley, *Kant, and *Hegel.

Idea of a University, The, see NEWMAN, J. H.

Idea: The Shepheards Garland, see DRAYTON.

'Idiot Boy, The', a ballad by *Wordsworth, first published in *Lyrical Ballads* (1798). One of the most characteristic and controversial of the poet's early works, it takes as hero the idiot son of a poor countrywoman, Betty Foy, who is sent off on horseback by night to fetch the doctor for a sick neighbour. He is so long gone that his mother sets out to seek him, and finds him at last by a waterfall, whither the pony has wandered freely through the moonlight, to the boy's delight. The neighbour recovers and sets out to meet mother and son, and all three are happily reunited; the boy's description of his adventures,

> 'The cocks did crow to-whoo, to-whoo,
> And the sun did shine so cold',

fittingly illustrate Wordsworth's intention of 'giving the charm of novelty to things of everyday'. Wordsworth ably defended his choice of subject matter (which offended many) in a letter to John *Wilson, June 1802, attacking the 'false delicacy' of his detractors, and praising the natural humanity of the poor: 'I have indeed, often looked upon the conduct of fathers and mothers of the lower classes of society towards idiots as the great triumph of the human heart.'

Idler, (1) a series of papers contributed by Dr *Johnson to the *Universal Chronicle: or Weekly Gazette* between 15 Apr. 1758 and 5 Apr. 1760. These papers are shorter and lighter than those of the *Rambler*, but their general character is the same. They include the well-known sketches of Dick Minim, the critic, of Mr Sober (the author himself), Jack Whirler (*Newbery the publisher), and Tom Restless. Twelve were by other contributors, including three by *Reynolds and three by T. *Warton the younger. (2) a monthly journal edited by J. K. *Jerome and Robert Barr, 1892–1911.

idylls, see ECLOGUE.

Idylls of the King, a series of 12 connected poems by *Tennyson, of which *'Morte d'Arthur', subsequently incorporated in 'The Passing of Arthur', was composed in 1833 after A. H. *Hallam's death and published in 1842. It was a project that preoccupied Tennyson over many years, during which he studied *Malory, *The Mabinogion, *Laȝamon, and other sources of Arthurian legend. In 1855–6 he began writing the first Idyll, which was to become 'Merlin and Vivien', which he followed with 'Enid', later divided into 'The Marriage of Geraint' and 'Geraint and Enid'. The first four were published in 1859 as 'Enid', 'Vivien', 'Elaine', and 'Guinevere' and constituted, though with many revisions, roughly half of the final version. They were extremely successful, selling 10,000 copies in six weeks. In 1869 followed 'The Coming of Arthur', 'The Holy Grail', 'Pelleas and Ettarre', and 'The Passing of Arthur'. 'The Last Tournament' was published in the *Contemporary Review* in 1871, then, with 'Gareth and Lynette', in 1872. 'Balin and Balan', written 1872–4, did not appear until 1885. The sequence as now printed first appeared in 1891.

The poems present the story of *Arthur, from his first meeting with Guinevere to the ruin of his kingdom and his death in the 'last, dim, weird battle of the west'. The protagonists are Arthur and Guinevere, Launcelot and Elaine, but the design embraces the fates of various minor characters. The adultery of Guinevere and Launcelot is seen as one of the forces that destroys the idealism and bright hopes of the Round Table, and the scene in which the guilty Guinevere 'grovelled with her face against the floor' before Arthur to listen to his long denunciatory speech was received with great enthusiasm; his forgiveness of her ('Lo! I forgive thee, as Eternal God | Forgives') moved the poet himself to tears. But even in his day some critics found the poems abstract, shadowy, and defective in dramatic power, the scenes of violence false, and the medieval costume trappings absurd; *Swinburne commented ironically on the fact that 'our Laureate should find in the ideal cuckold his type of the ideal man'. These doubts have been endorsed by most subsequent criticism, though some, following Tennyson's own hint that 'there is an allegorical or perhaps rather a parabolic drift in the poem', have argued in favour of the *Idylls* as 'a dramatic parable of enormous variety, richness and complexity' (F. E. L. Priestley, 1973) or as a new and therefore perplexing genre, a symbolist vision of apocalyptic doom (Rosenberg, *The Fall of Camelot*, 1973).

IGNATIEFF, Michael (1947–), cultural historian and novelist. He was born in Toronto, Canada, but has made his home largely in England. His first substantive work was a sociological examination of prisons during the Industrial Revolution, *A Just Measure of Pain* (1978). He has also produced works of fiction (e.g. *Asya*, 1991; *Scar Tissue*, 1993), political theory, combinations of biography and history (*The Russian Album*, 1987; *Isaiah Berlin*, 1998), and has co-written (with Hugh Brody) an exceptional film *Nineteen Nineteen* (1985), based upon a fictitious meeting between two of *Freud's patients. One of Ignatieff's most characteristic themes is reflection upon the nature of pathos through the examination of past lives: he has also shown a continuing concern (which might be seen as part of his mixed Russian-Canadian inheritance) with questions of liberalism, nationalism, national identity, and multiculturalism.

IGNATIUS LOYOLA, St (1491–1556), a page to Ferdinand II of Aragon, and subsequently an officer in the Spanish army. He was wounded at the siege of Pampeluna (Pamplona) (1521), and thereafter devoted himself to religion. He constituted himself the Knight of the Blessed Virgin, went on a pilgrimage to the Holy Land in 1523, returned in 1526 to study at Barcelona and Alcalá, and in 1534 founded in Paris the Society of Jesus (Jesuits), bound by vows of chastity, poverty, obedience, and submission to the holy see, and authorized by papal bull in 1540. Its principal activities were preaching, instruction, and confession, and it formed a spiritual army bound to obedience. The object of the society was to support the Roman Church in its conflict with the 16th-cent. reformers and to propagate its faith. Francis *Xavier and other missionaries carried on the latter work in the most distant parts of the world. Loyola's *Exercitia* (*Spiritual Exercises*), a manual of devotion and of rules for meditation and prayer, was published in Rome in 1548.

Ignoge, in *Geoffrey of Monmouth's *History* (i. 2), the daughter of the Greek king Pandrasus, abducted and married by Brutus (*Brut). She was the mother of *Locrine, *Camber, and Albanactus. Spenser (*Faerie Queene*, II. x. 13) calls her Inogene of Italy.

Ignoramus, a famous university farcical play in Latin by George Ruggle (1575–1622), a fellow of Clare College, Cambridge, produced in 1615 before James I, an adaptation of an Italian comedy by della Porta. The title part is a burlesque of the recorder of Cambridge, Brackyn, who is subjected to various humiliations; he falls in love with the heroine Rosabella, but is fobbed off with the virago Polla, belaboured, thought to be possessed by evil spirits, subjected to exorcism, and finally carried off to a monastery for treatment. Brackyn had already been held up to ridicule in the last part of *The Parnassus Plays*.

Igraine, in Arthurian legend, the wife of *Gorlois of Cornwall, taken as his wife by Uther *Pendragon who assumed the likeness of Gorlois by Merlin's magic. *Arthur was the child of this union.

Iliad, The, a Greek epic poem attributed to *Homer, describing the war waged by Achaean princes against Troy for the purpose of recovering Helen, wife of Menelaus, whom Paris, son of King Priam of Troy, had carried off. In particular it deals with the wrath of Achilles, the special hero of the poem, at the slight put upon him by Agamemnon, leader of the host, and his final return to the field and slaying of Hector.

'Il Penseroso', a poem in rhymed octosyllabics (with a ten-line prelude) by *Milton, written ?1631, printed 1645. The title means 'the contemplative man'. The poem is an invocation to the goddess Melancholy, bidding her bring Peace, Quiet, Leisure, and Contemplation. It describes the pleasures of the studious, meditative life, of tragedy, epic poetry, and music. It had a considerable influence on the meditative *graveyard poems of the 18th cent., and there are echoes in Pope's *'Eloisa to Abelard', and later *Gothic works. It is a companion piece to *'L'Allegro'.

Imaginary Conversations of Literary Men and Statesmen, by W. S. *Landor, published 1824–9, followed by Imaginary Conversations of Greeks and Romans, published 1853.

The conversations are between characters from classical times to the 19th cent.; some are dramatic, some idyllic, some satirical. There are some 150 dialogues and the quality is very uneven, for Landor's own passionate and often prejudiced views tend to obtrude. *Wordsworth observed that the dialogues between classical characters, such as between Cicero and his brother, were often the best.

Imagism, a movement of English and American poets in revolt from *Romanticism, which flourished c.1910–17, and derived in part from the aesthetic philosophy of T. E. *Hulme. Its first anthology, Des Imagistes (1914), edited by *Pound, had eleven contributors: R. *Aldington, H. *Doolittle, F. S. Flint, Skipwith Cannell, A. *Lowell, W. C. *Williams, *Joyce, Pound, F. M. Hueffer (*Ford), Allen Upward, and John Cournos. Some of D. H. *Lawrence's poems of

this period may also be described as Imagist. The characteristic products of the movement are more easily recognized than its theories defined: they tend to be short, composed of short lines of musical cadence rather than metrical regularity, to avoid abstraction, and to treat the image with a hard, clear precision rather than with overt symbolic intent. (Pound: 'the natural object is always the adequate symbol.') The influence of Japanese forms (tanka and *haiku) is obvious in many. Amy Lowell succeeded Pound as spokesperson of the group, and was responsible for several Imagist anthologies.

Imitation of Christ, or De Imitatione Christi, see THOMAS À KEMPIS.

Imlac, a character in Dr Johnson's *Rasselas.

Imogen, the heroine of Shakespeare's *Cymbeline. Her name may be the result of a typographical error by the printers of the First *Folio; *A Mirror for Magistrates, *Holinshed, and *Forman all give the name as 'Innogen', which is also that of *Leonato's silent wife in *Much Ado about Nothing.

Imoinda, see OROONOKO.

Impertinent, The Curious, see CURIOUS IMPERTINENT, THE.

Importance of Being Earnest, The: A Trivial Comedy for Serious People, a play by O. *Wilde, first performed at the St James's Theatre, London, on 14 Feb. 1895.

Wilde's most dazzling and epigrammatic work, it describes the courtships and betrothals of two young men-about-town, John Worthing (Jack) and Algernon (Algy) Moncrieff, who are in pursuit respectively of Gwendolen Fairfax (Algy's cousin) and Jack's ward, Cecily Cardew. Both young men lead double lives, in that Jack is known in town under the name of Ernest, while representing to his ward Cecily in the country that he has a wicked brother Ernest; Algy, to cover his own diversions, has created a fictitious character, the sickly Bunbury, whose ill health requires a visit whenever engagements in town (particularly those with his formidable aunt Lady Bracknell) render his absence desirable. After many confusions of identity, during which it transpires that Cecily's governess, Miss Prism, had once mislaid Jack as a baby in a handbag at Victoria Station, it is revealed that Jack and Algy are in fact brothers, and that Jack's name is indeed Ernest. All objections, both financial and genealogical, to both matches, are thus overcome, and Gwendolen's addiction to the very name of 'Ernest' is satisfied, so all ends happily.

Impressionism, the name given in derision (from a painting by Monet called Impression: soleil levant) to the work of a group of French painters who held their first exhibition in 1874. Their aim was to render the effects of light on objects rather than the objects themselves. Claude Monet (1840–1926), Alfred Sisley

(1839–99), and Camille Pissarro (1831–1903) carried out their aims most completely. Auguste Renoir (1841–1919) reacted against the spontaneity of the movement in the early 1880s, while Paul Cézanne (1839–1906) became increasingly interested in an analysis of form that led on to Cubism. The term is used by transference in literature and music.

Impressions of Theophrastus Such, The, a volume of essays by G. *Eliot, published 1879. Most of the 18 essays are character studies loosely based on the model of *Theophrastus; the author writes in the character of the bachelor son of a Tory Midlands country parson, himself a Londoner, and reflects on various contemporary types, such as the carping and arrogant Lentulus and the ever-youthful though ageing Ganymede. The last chapter echoes *Daniel Deronda* in its defence of Jewish nationalism and its attack on various manifestations of anti-Semitism.

In a Glass Darkly, a collection of stories by J. S. *Le Fanu, published 1872. They purport to be cases from the papers of 'Dr Martin Hesselius, the German Physician'—the first of a long line of psychic investigators in English literature. Of the five stories the best known are 'Green Tea', featuring an apparition in the form of a malignant monkey, and 'Carmilla', an extremely powerful tale of a female vampire which antedates Stoker's *Dracula* by 25 years and was adapted by Carl Dreyer in his film *Vampyr* (1932).

INCHBALD, Mrs Elizabeth, née Simpson (1753–1821), a novelist, dramatist, and actress, and a close friend of *Godwin until his marriage with Mary *Wollstonecraft. She is chiefly remembered for her two prose romances, **A Simple Story* (1791) and **Nature and Art* (1796), both of which display skill in character and narration and illustrate her faith in natural upbringing (see PRIMITIVISM); and her play **Lovers' Vows* (1798), which retains its fame as the drama enacted by the Bertram family in J. Austen's *Mansfield Park*. Her most successful play was *I'll Tell You What*, produced in 1785. She edited *The British Theatre*, a large collection of plays, both old and new, in 1806–9.

'Inchcape Rock, The', a ballad by R. *Southey, written 1796–8, published 1802. Because the rock, off the Firth of Tay, was dangerous to mariners, the abbot of Arbroath, or Aberbrothock, fixed a warning bell upon it. A piratical character, Sir Ralph the Rover, in order to plague the abbot, cuts the bell from its float and later, on his homeward way, is wrecked upon the rock.

incunabula, incunables, books printed before the 16th cent., from the Latin word for 'swaddling clothes', hence 'infancy'.

Index Expurgatorius, strictly, an authoritative specification of the passages to be expunged or altered in works otherwise permitted to be read by Roman Catholics. The term is frequently used in England to cover the 'Index Librorum Prohibitorum', or list of forbidden books (not authors, as sometimes thought). Rules for the formation of this list and of the 'Index Expurgatorius' were drawn up by the Council of Trent, and successive editions of the former have been published from time to time [OED]. The 'Index Expurgatorius' and the 'Index Librorum Prohibitorum' were abrogated in 1966.

Index on Censorship, a periodical founded in 1972 by Writers and Scholars International, a group of writers, scholars, artists, and intellectuals concerned with the promotion of free expression, formed largely at the instigation of the Soviet dissident Pavel Litvinov and S. *Spender. It monitors censorship throughout the world, publishing comment, analysis, testimony, and reports, as well as original poetry and prose by authors many of whom are suppressed in their own countries.

Indian Love Lyrics, the name under which the popular poems and songs of Adela Florence Cory, later Nicolson (1865–1904), were generally known. Cory, who wrote as Laurence Hope, was born in England but spent most of her life in India: she published *The Garden of Kama* (1902), *Stars of the Desert* (1903), and *Indian Love* (1905). Some of her impassioned and romantic Oriental verse was set to music (Kashmiri Song—'Pale hands I loved') by Amy Woodforde Finden.

Indicator (1819–21), a periodical established and edited by Leigh *Hunt. It was non-political and entirely devoted to literary matters. Hunt and his friends, notably *Hazlitt and *Lamb, thought it Hunt's happiest venture in periodical publishing. It published the work of the young poets, including Keats's *'La Belle Dame sans Merci', and introduced much foreign literature. Although short-lived, it sold well.

Indo-European, the name applied to the great family of cognate languages (formerly called Indo-Germanic and Aryan) spoken over most of Europe and extending into Asia as far as northern India. Much of the energy of the 19th-cent. Comparative Philologists was devoted to illustrating the cognations between these groups of languages of which fourteen are distinguished by W. B. Lockwood in *A Panorama of Indo-European Languages* (1972).

Iñez, a character in Byron's *Don Juan*.

IÑEZ DE CASTRO, the daughter of a Castilian nobleman attached to the court of Alphonso IV of Portugal. Prince Pedro married her secretly, and lived with her in happy seclusion. When the marriage was discovered, the king authorized the murder of Iñez. On the accession (1357) of Pedro, who had been reduced to despair by the death of his wife, his first measure was to take vengeance on her murderers. The subject has been treated by various poets and dramatists, including *Camões, *Landor, and, more recently, *Montherlant.

Inferno, The, of Dante, see DIVINA COMMEDIA.

INGE, William Ralph (1860–1954), dean of St Paul's, 1911–34, dubbed 'the gloomy dean' by the *Daily Mail* in 1911 for his pessimistic views on democracy, progress, education, etc. He became a well-known public figure, partly through his journalism (principally for the *Evening Standard*), and he also published diaries, memoirs, and many volumes on religion, politics, and philosophy.

INGELOW, Jean (1820–97), poet, born in Boston, Lincolnshire. She published several volumes of verse, some stories for children (including *Mopsa the Fairy*, 1869), and some adult prose fiction; her best-known poems are 'Divided', a poem of lost love, and 'The High Tide on the Coast of Lincolnshire, 1571', a vivid evocation of a natural disaster in 1571 in which the narrator laments the drowning of 'my sonne's faire wife, Elizabeth', both in *Poems* (1863).

Ingoldsby Legends, The, see BARHAM, R. H.

Inheritance, The, a novel by S. *Ferrier, published 1824.

The novel relates, in an improbably complex plot, but with much humour, the fortunes of Gertrude St Clair, granddaughter of the earl of Rossville and heiress presumptive to his estate. On the death of her father (who had been repudiated by the earl) she and her mother are admitted to Rossville Castle and encounter the earl, a conceited tyrant. Gertrude falls in love with her fascinating cousin Colonel Delmour and after the earl's death becomes engaged to him, to the despair of all who care for her, and in particular of another cousin, Edward Lyndsay, who loves Gertrude with self-effacing humility. A vulgar American now comes forward and claims to be Gertrude's father. It is revealed that the ambitious Mrs St Clair, despairing of children, has adopted the daughter of a servant and passed her off as her own. Gertrude, having lost title and fortune, is abandoned by Colonel Delmour, and the faithful Edward Lyndsay gradually wins her love. Miss Pratt, a garrulous and eccentric spinster, is a memorable character.

inkhorn, a term originating in the 16th cent., applied to excessively literary, bookish, or pedantic language: see WILSON, T., for an example.

Inkle and Yarico, a romantic musical comedy by G. *Colman the younger, performed 1787.

The young Londoner Inkle, saved from cannibals on a voyage to Barbados by the beautiful native girl Yarico, has to decide between fidelity to her and a wealthy marriage to Narcissa, the governor's daughter; he chooses the latter and is punished for his ingratitude. *Burns, on seeing Mrs *Kemble as Yarico in Dumfries in 1794, wrote, 'At Yarico's sweet notes of grief | The rocks with tears had flowed.' The plot is based on a story in the *Spectator* (No. 11), which had been versified by Frances Thynne Seymour, the duchess of Somerset, as 'The Story of Inkle and Yarrico' (1738). (See PRIMITIVISM.)

'Inklings, The', a group of friends who gathered round C. S. *Lewis at Oxford from the 1930s to the 1960s, and read aloud their original compositions, often at the Eagle and Child public house. Members included J. R. R. *Tolkien and C. *Williams. See *The Inklings* (1978) by Humphrey Carpenter.

In Memoriam A.H.H., a poem by *Tennyson, written between 1833 and 1850 and published anonymously in the latter year. The poem was written in memory of A. H. *Hallam, the son of H. *Hallam, a young man of great promise and an intimate friend of Tennyson, who died at Vienna aged 22. It is written in stanzas of four octosyllabic lines rhyming a b b a, and is divided into 132 sections of varying length.

It is not so much a single elegy as a series of poems written over a considerable period, inspired by the changing moods of the author's regret for his lost friend, and expressing his own anxieties about change, evolution, and immortality, the last a subject which continued to perturb him deeply. The epilogue is a marriage song on the occasion of the wedding of the poet's sister Cecilia to Edward Lushington; Hallam had himself been engaged to his sister Emily. A critical and popular success (G. H. *Lewes referred to it as 'the solace and delight of every house where poetry is loved'), it was widely regarded as a message of hope and an affirmation of faith; but T. S. *Eliot commented in 1936: 'It is not religious because of the quality of its faith, but because of the quality of its doubt. Its faith is a poor thing, but its doubt is a very intense experience. *In Memoriam* is a poem of despair, but of despair of a religious kind.'

Inn Album, The, a poem of approximately 3,000 lines, in blank verse, by R. *Browning, published 1875. Browning originally intended to write a play on the subject, but changed his mind to avoid competing with *Tennyson's forthcoming *Queen Mary*. The poem has affinities with drama in its use of long passages of dialogue, but the whole is more like a short novel.

The story is based on the career of a famous Regency rake, Lord de Ros, but was influenced by the trial of the Tichborne Claimant which had just ended, and has a contemporary setting. It is an intricate melodrama, involving a spendthrift aristocrat, his cast-off mistress, his wealthy young protégé and dupe, and the pure young girl to whom the younger man has cynically become engaged; it concludes with blackmail, suicide, and murder. At another level this sensational tale of social and psychological corruption, treated with the satirical realism of *Red Cotton Night-Cap Country*, may be read as a bleak fable of the dualism of human art, its self-destructive combination of ideal and material elements.

INNES, Michael, the pseudonym of J. I. M. *Stewart.

Innisfail, a poetic name for Ireland.

Innocence, Songs of, see SONGS OF INNOCENCE.

Innocents Abroad, The, a satirical account by Mark *Twain, published 1869 (in England, 1870, as *The New Pilgrim's Progress*), of a cruise on the *Quaker City* to the Mediterranean with a company of Americans in 1867. The comedy lies in seeing Europe, its scenes, customs, and religious rites and attitudes, through the irreverent and chauvinist eyes of an American 'innocent', and is at the expense both of the Old World and the New. The work, originally published as travel letters in New York and Californian newspapers, was a great success on both sides of the Atlantic, despite some reviews which took its satire at face value, the *Saturday Review* describing Twain as 'a very offensive specimen of the vulgarest kind of Yankee'.

Inogene, see IGNOGE and IMOGEN.

inscape, instress, see HOPKINS, G. M.

Intelligencer, see L'ESTRANGE.

Intelligent Woman's Guide to Socialism and Capitalism, The (1928), G. B. *Shaw's answer, 200,000 words long, to a request for 'a few ideas on socialism' from his sister-in-law, to whom the book is dedicated. This closely argued and passionately felt political testament treats women as the have-nots of a male culture and traces specific social evils to inequality of income. A new edition, with two additional chapters and retitled *The Intelligent Woman's Guide to Socialism, Capitalism, Sovietism and Fascism*, was published in 1937 as the first two Pelican Books (see PENGUIN BOOKS).

intentional fallacy, a phrase coined by the American *New Critics W. K. Wimsatt Jr and Monroe C. Beardsley in an essay of 1946 to describe the common assumption that an author's declared or assumed intention in writing a work is a proper basis for deciding upon the work's meaning or value. These critics argued that once a work is published, it has an objective status and that its meanings belong to the reading public. Any surmise about the author's intention thus has to be tested against the evidence of the text itself.

interactive fiction is a term encompassing a range of experimental approaches to both fictional form and the writing process. Formal developments range from text-based role-playing games to complex *hypertext novels, and include material published in both print and electronic media. The defining feature of this work is that the author relinquishes to the reader a degree of control over the text, opening it to a range of readings. Notable examples, which demonstrate that narrative is merely one way in which fiction can comment on the world, include: *Hopscotch* (1963), in which Julio *Cortázar proposed two 'approved' sequences for

his 155 chapters while inviting the reader to impose alternative patterns; B. S. *Johnson's *The Unfortunates* (1969), which consisted of a box of 27 unbound sections, with only the beginning and end segments designated by the author; and Milorad Pavic's *Dictionary of the Kazars* (1988), a pastiche reference book in the form of three dictionaries representing separate cultural traditions, which enabled a linear reading, random consultation, or the tracing of themes and events across the texts. Developments in hypertext, *CD-ROM, and *World Wide Web (WWW) technologies enabled further exploration of the relationship between author and reader. The original WWW version of Geoff *Ryman's *253* (1996) exploited the interconnectivity of hypertext, leading readers to approach the piece as a fictional encyclopaedia—browsing randomly or according to interest through a series of linked documents—rather than treating it as a traditional narrative. In terms of interactivity in the creative process, the tradition of collaborative authorship was well established by the time *Dickens and *Collins worked together on stories for *Household Words* in the 1850s. In the 1930s Charles Henri Ford, American surrealist poet and editor, organized international chainpoems to tap into 'a hypothetical joint imagination': an opening was written, then each of Ford's collaborators (including members of the *New Apocalypse) added a line to build up the poem. Multiple author fiction is seen by some writers as a means of enriching their storytelling through exposure to alternative styles, associations, and points of view—but others feel the lack of a unified vision makes it virtually unreadable. New forms of interactive authorship have been made possible by the development of the MOO—a computer-based technology (Multiple User Dungeons, Object-Oriented) enabling individual users to create imaginary spaces, roles, and personalities. These virtual writing communities often combine elements of the creative writing workshop, role-playing game, literary discussion forum and experiment in literary collaboration. Typically, they aspire to the production of authorless texts and are characterized by loose editorial control and a blurring of the boundaries between the role of writer, reader, and critic. Examples can be found at *Lingua MOO* (1995), created and administered by Cynthia Haynes and Jan Rune Holmevik at the University of Texas at Dallas [www location: http://lingua.utdallas.edu/]; and the *trAce International Online Writing Community*, co-ordinated by Sue Thomas at Nottingham Trent University [www location: http://trace.ntu.ac.uk]. In the popular *trAce* 'Noon Quilt' experiment (1998) contributors from all over the world were invited to submit 100-word impressions of the view through their window at noon.

interior monologue, an extended representation in prose or verse of a character's unspoken thoughts, memories, and impressions, rendered as if directly 'overheard' by the reader without the intervention of a summarizing narrator. The device is distinguished from the *dramatic monologue by the fact that the thoughts are unspoken, rather than addressed to an auditor. Many modern poems make use of this convention, and it is widely employed in modern fiction, notably in the deliberately incoherent *'stream-of-consciousness' style adopted by D. *Richardson, J. *Joyce, and others.

interludes were plays performed at court, in the halls of the nobles, at the Inns of Court, and in colleges, generally but not exclusively by professional actors, dealing with a short episode and involving a limited number of characters. That interludes were sometimes performed by villagers we know from 'Pyramus and Thisbe' in *A Midsummer Night's Dream. Their vogue was chiefly in the 15th and 16th cents. They succeeded *morality plays in the history of the drama, and are not always clearly distinguishable from them. The characters are still frequently allegorical, but the comic or farcical element is more prevalent, the versification tends to doggerel, and they are shorter than the moralities. There are good examples by *Heywood, *Rastell, and H. Medwall. The origin of the name is obscure. The *OED* speaks of interludes as 'commonly introduced between the acts of long mystery-plays or moralities'; Ward finds the probable origin in the fact that interludes were 'occasionally performed in the intervals of banquets and entertainments'. E. K. *Chambers gives reasons for questioning both these explanations. He is inclined to interpret *interludium* not as a *ludus* in the intervals of something else, but as a *ludus* carried on between two or more performers, and as primarily applicable to any kind of dramatic performance. See *English Moral Interludes*, ed. G. Wickham (1976).

intertextuality, the sum of relationships between and among writings. This modern critical term usually covers the range of ways in which one 'text' may respond to, allude to, derive from, mimic, or adapt another. The concept has been used in various ways under the influence of *structuralism and post-structuralism, often in reaction against the *New Criticism and its assumption that a literary work is a self-contained object. The idea that poems are made from other poems has been proclaimed by *Frye, *Barthes, and H. *Bloom, among others.

In the Year of Jubilee, a novel by George *Gissing, published in three volumes in 1894 by Lawrence and Bullen, and in a censored version by Appleton in the USA in 1895. The novel tells the story of a group of young upper- and lower-middle-class people at the time of Queen Victoria's Golden Jubilee. The superficially educated Nancy Lord falls in love with Lionel Tarrant; after a sexual encounter in a seaside resort, they have to marry. Nancy's father dies before learning of their marriage, leaving a will that prohibits Nancy

from marrying before she is 30. Lionel's inheritance also disappears; after separation, hardship, estrangement, and disinheritance, the Tarrants are happily reconciled, but live separately in London. Gissing's heavy irony condemns, but is resigned to, the emergent mass culture portrayed in the novel.

'Intimations of Immortality from Recollections of Early Childhood', an ode by *Wordsworth, composed 1802–4/6, published 1807.

It is Wordsworth's most profound and memorable exploration of the significance of the intensity of childhood experience of the natural world (which suggests to him a state of pre-existence), of its gradual fading into 'the light of common day', and of the consolations of maturity, where man can still retain 'shadowy recollections' of former glory, and can still have sight, if only by glimpses, 'of that immortal sea which brought us hither'. The poem ends with a moving affirmation of the poet's faith in the powers of the philosophic mind and the human heart. The tone throughout is tentative rather than dogmatic, and Wordsworth was later to insist that he used the concept of pre-existence (which had both a popular and a Platonic basis) not as a philosopher but as a poet, using his own peculiarly vivid childhood recollections of 'a splendour in the objects of sense' and his conviction of personal immortality.

Invisible Man, a Kafkaesque and claustrophobic novel by American writer R.W. *Ellison (1914–94), 1952, which describes the life of a young black man in New York City.

Invisible Man, The, a science fiction romance by H. G. *Wells, published 1897, about a scientist who fatally stumbles upon the secret of invisibility.

IONESCO, Eugène, see ABSURD, THEATRE OF THE.

Ipomadon, a Middle English romance, taken from the French of Huon de Rotelande (*c.*1190). There are three English versions: one in prose which seems to be early 14th cent.; the most famous, in 8,890 lines of 12-line, tail-rhyme stanzas, thought to be from Lancashire of the mid-14th cent.; and a more condensed version in rhyming couplets in a 15th-cent. manuscript. Ipomadon is a prince of Apulia who wins by his exploits (mostly in disguise) the love of La Fière, the disdainful duchess of Calabria.

Ed. H. Weber, *Metrical Romances of the XIII, XIV and XV Centuries* (1810); selections in W. E. French and C. B. Hale, *Middle English Metrical Romances* (1930), and in *Medieval English Romances*, Part II, ed. A. V. C. Schmidt and N. Jacobs (1980).

IQBAL, Sir Muhammad (1875–1938), poet and philosopher, born in the Punjab, where his education began. He continued his studies in England, where he was called to the bar, and in Germany, before returning home to practise as a lawyer. As a poet, he worked primarily in two veins, the first in the tradition of the

Farsi-derived lyric poem, often with metaphysical or allegorical content, and the second in a more directly political mode, as in his Urdu poem *Lenin's Interview with God* (1935, in *Bal-I-Jibril*). Writing in both Persian and Urdu, he soon became a leader of Islamic modernism not only in India but elsewhere in the Islamic world. He emphasized the international character of Islam but eventually concluded that it could only find expression in the free association of Muslim states. As president of the Muslim League in 1930 he advocated the creation of the separate Muslim state in north-west India.

Iras, in Shakespeare's **Antony and Cleopatra*, one of Cleopatra's attendants. Her name is in *Plutarch's *Life of Antony*.

IRELAND, John (1761–1842), the son of an Ashburton butcher, bible-clerk at Oriel College, Oxford, who became dean of Westminster, and founded a professorship of biblical exegesis and the Ireland scholarship for classics at Oxford.

IRELAND, William Henry (1777–1835), remembered chiefly as a forger of Shakespeare manuscripts. He began his audacious series of deceptions at the age of 17, when he was working in a lawyer's office with easy access to old parchment, deeds, and antiquated forms of writing. An exhibition of his forgeries of poems and deeds, arranged in 1794 by his innocent and excited father, wholly deceived the general public, and *Boswell kissed the parchments. A facsimile edition of the 'works' was published in 1795, and other works, including the plays *Vortigern and Rowena* and *Henry II*, made their appearance. However, strong doubts were expressed, *Kemble's production of *Vortigern* was jeered, and in 1796 *Malone published *An Inquiry into the Authenticity* . . . . In the same year Ireland admitted to the forgeries, and embarked on a more conventional literary career. He published two volumes of poems, then in 1808 *The Fisher Boy*, which, like *Bloomfield's earlier *Farmer's Boy*, satisfied the fashion for tales of rural life. *The Sailor Boy* (1809) relates the rise of humble Dick to be a captain at Trafalgar. In 1815 he published *Scribbleomania*, a doggerel collection of entertaining but frequently inaccurate descriptions of his contemporaries.

Irena, in Spenser's **Faerie Queene* (Bk V), personifies Ireland, oppressed by *Grantorto and righted by Sir *Artegall.

Irene, a blank verse tragedy by Dr *Johnson, written 1736, performed 1749, without much success.

The story, taken from *Knolles's history of the Turks, concerns the fate of Irene, a Greek slave loved by the Emperor Mahomet, in Knolles's account a helpless victim, but in Johnson's the victim of her own weakness. It cost its author much effort, but remained frigid and static.

Irish Literary Theatre was founded by W. B. *Yeats, Lady *Gregory, and E. *Martyn in 1899 to encourage Irish drama. It eventually became the Irish National Theatre Society in 1903, with Yeats as president, and moved into the new *Abbey Theatre in 1904.

Irish playwrights, new. In the early 1990s, a new generation of Irish dramatists, many in their twenties, began to find an international audience. The London-Irish writer Martin McDonagh produced a remarkable trilogy of black comedies on life in the west of Ireland, of which *The Beauty Queen of Leenane* (1997) was the most immediately successful. Marina Carr's *Portia Coughlin* and *The Bog of Cats* marked her as a distinctive voice and as the first significant Irish woman playwright since Lady *Gregory. Conor McPherson's *The Weir*, a huge success in 1998, best captured the sensibility of this new generation with its playful yet elegiac approach to a traditional culture that is all but dead but that still haunts the imagination of these writers.

Irish Revival, a resurgence of Irish nationalism and culture which began in the last quarter of the 19th cent. and flourished until the 1920s. Among the books which fostered the revival were translations and retellings of Irish legend, folklore, and poetry, such as S. *Ferguson's *Lays of the Western Gael* (1865) and D. *Hyde's *Love Songs of Connacht* (1893). Histories, such as Standish O'Grady's bardic *History of Ireland* (1880) and Hyde's *Literary History of Ireland* (1892), were also highly influential. The *Irish Literary Theatre, founded by W. B. *Yeats and others in 1899, developed eventually into the important *Abbey Theatre company. Plays by Yeats, *Synge, G. B. *Shaw, and *O'Casey made the Abbey renowned. Meanwhile the poetry of Yeats and the prose work of G. *Moore, *Joyce, and many others established the new literary stature of Irish writing. See also CELTIC LITERATURE.

IRVING, Sir Henry (1838–1905), originally John Henry Brodribb, who achieved fame as an actor for his performance in **The Bells* (1871–2), and afterwards scored successes in a large number of Shakespearian and other parts, his impersonation of *Tennyson's *Becket* being one of his chief triumphs. His management of the Lyceum Theatre in association with Ellen *Terry, 1878–1902, was distinguished, and he revived popular interest in Shakespeare. He was a romantic actor, highly intellectual, of magnetic personality and originality of conception, but of mannered elocution and gait.

IRVING, John Winslow (1942–), American novelist, born in Exeter, New Hampshire, educated locally and at the universities of Pittsburgh, Vienna, New Hampshire, and Iowa. From 1967 to 1972, and again from 1975 to 1978, he was an assistant professor of English at Mount Holyoke College. His serio-comic novels, which display great individuality of style and imagination, began with *Setting Free the Bears* (1968), about two young men on a motorcycle tour of Austria who plot to free all the animals in the Vienna Zoo. This was followed by *The Water-Method Man* (1972) and *The 158-Pound Marriage* (1974). These made little impact, but with *The World According to Garp* (1978), the comic biography of a writer, he achieved spectacular international success. After this came *The Hotel New Hampshire* (1981), *The Cider House Rules* (1985), *A Prayer for Owen Meaney* (1989), and *A Son of the Circus* (1994), about an expatriate Parsi surgeon who returns to India and becomes involved in the repercussions of two murders committed 20 years earlier. *Trying to Save Piggy Sneed*, published in 1993, is a collection of short stories.

IRVING, Washington (1783–1859), born in New York, the son of a wealthy British merchant who had sided with the rebels in the Revolution. After training as a lawyer, Irving turned to a literary career, writing for various newspapers, and publishing (1807–8), with his brother William Irving and friend J. K. Paulding, a series of whimsical and satirical essays and poems, collected in book form as *Salmagundi: or, The Whim-Whams and Opinions of Launcelot Langstaff, Esq. and Others* (1808). This was followed by his highly successful burlesque *A History of New York from the Beginning of the World to the End of the Dutch Dynasty*, by 'Diedrich Knickerbocker' a pseudonym chosen to represent the solid, phlegmatic Dutch burgher created by Irving; the name became synonymous with the descendants of the original Dutch settlers of the New Netherlands in America. Over the next years Irving struggled (unsuccessfully) to save the family business from bankruptcy, visiting England and making the acquaintance of Sir W. *Scott, T. *Moore, T. *Campbell, John *Murray, and others during the process; on his return, encouraged by Scott he wrote *The Sketch Book*, essays and tales under the pseudonym 'Geoffrey Crayon, Gent.', published serially in the USA (1819–20) and in book form in England (1820). This work, which contains sketches of English life ('The Christmas Dinner', 'Westminster Abbey', etc.), essays on American subjects, and American adaptations of German folk tales (including *'Rip Van Winkle' and 'The Legend of *Sleepy Hollow'), made him a celebrity in both continents. It was followed by other popular works, including *Bracebridge Hall* (1822), which features Squire Bracebridge, a sort of 19th-cent. de *Coverley. Some of his subsequent works were inspired by his period as diplomatic attaché in Spain (1826–9), including *Legends of the Alhambra* (1832). He rejoined the London literary world of London as secretary to the US legation (1829–32), and returned to America in 1832 to an enthusiastic welcome as the first American author to have achieved international fame. His later works include *The Crayon Miscellany* (1835), *Astoria* (1836; an account of John Jacob Astor's development of the fur trade), and his monumental five-volume life of George Washington (1855–9).

Isabella, (1) in *Orlando furioso*, daughter of a Saracen king of Spain, with whom the Scottish prince *Zerbino fell in love. After his death she fell into the power of *Rodomont, and to protect her honour caused him by guile to slay her; (2) in Kyd's *Spanish Tragedy*, wife to Hieronimo; (3) queen to Marlowe's *Edward II*; (4) the heroine of Shakespeare's *Measure for Measure*.

'Isabella, or The Pot of Basil', a narrative poem by *Keats, written 1818, published 1820.

The poem is based on a story in Boccaccio's *Decameron*. The worldly, ambitious brothers of Isabella intend that she shall marry a nobleman. When they discover her love for the humble Lorenzo they lure him away, murder him, and bury his body in a forest. His ghost then appears to Isabella and tells her where he is buried. With the help of her old nurse she finds his body, severs the head, and places it in a pot with a plant of basil over it. Her brothers, observing how she cherishes the plant, steal the pot, discover the mouldering head, and fly, conscience-stricken, into banishment. Pathetically Isabella mourns her loss, pines away, and dies. The poem reflects a contemporary fashion for the macabre, and *Lamb pronounced it the best work in the volume of poems of 1820, but Keats himself very soon came to dislike it.

Isengrym, or **Isengrin,** the wolf in *Reynard the Fox.

Iseult the Fair (also Isolde, Isoud, Isode, Ysoude), the daughter of the king of Ireland in Arthurian legend. She is the lover of *Tristram (Tristan) who has been sent by his uncle King Mark of Cornwall to bring Iseult as his wife. The story of Tristram and Iseult is the great classic of doomed love; Tristram is the slayer of her uncle Marhaus and they are fated to love each other by drinking in error the potion which was meant to have been shared by Mark and Iseult on their wedding night, binding them in everlasting love. Her mother is also called Iseult (even sometimes Iseult the Fair), and in some versions of the story it is she, the sister of Marhaus, who becomes Tristram's lover. No doubt the two, as well as their rival *Iseult of the White Hands, are archetypally related.

Iseult of the White Hands, in Arthurian legend, daughter of the ruler of Brittany, with whom *Tristram falls in love and whom he marries after his banishment by King Mark. But Iseult of Brittany does not succeed in erasing the memory of *Iseult the Fair; when Tristram is dying, he sends for his first Iseult by ship; if she is on the ship on its return from Ireland it is to fly a white flag: if not a black one. The white flag is flown; but Iseult of the White Hands tells Tristram it is black, whereupon he dies.

ISHERWOOD, Christopher William Bradshaw (1904–86), novelist, born in Cheshire, the son of an army officer who was killed in the First World War. He made the acquaintance of *Auden at preparatory school, and of *Upward at Repton; he and Upward were at

Cambridge together, where both began to write. His first novels, *All the Conspirators* (1928) and *The Memorial* (1932), show the influence (as he acknowledged) of E. M. *Forster and V. *Woolf; his own voice appears distinctly in *Mr Norris Changes Trains* (1935) and *Goodbye to Berlin* (1939), works which reflect his experiences of living in Berlin, 1929–33, where he supported himself by giving English lessons. They were planned as part of a long novel, to be entitled *The Lost*, which was never written, and are largely autobiographical in manner and content, although the narrator appears as Bradshaw in the first and as Isherwood in the second, and the overlapping cast of characters shows a certain fictional inconsistency. The first is a novel about a conman and double agent, the corrupt, seedy, emotional, and engaging Arthur Norris, and his adventures in the criminal and political underworld; the second is a series of sketches, some of which were originally published in *New Writing*, and of which the best known is the section 'Sally Bowles' (published independently in 1937). Sally is a cabaret artist of more beauty, eccentricity, and wit than talent, and her bohemian enterprises were later successfully dramatized in 1951 by John Van Druten as *I Am a Camera*, and turned into a stage musical in 1968 as *Cabaret*. Both novels give a vivid portrait of Germany on the eve of Hitler's rise to power. Isherwood travelled widely in Europe after leaving Berlin, went to China with Auden in 1938, and in 1939 went with him to America; he became an American citizen in 1946.

During the 1930s he collaborated with Auden in the writing of *The Ascent of F6* and several other works (see under AUDEN), and wrote the semi-autobiographical *Lions and Shadows* (1938), in which his friends (Auden, *Spender, Upward, V. *Watkins, and others) appear under fictitious names. After settling near Hollywood, where he worked as a scriptwriter, he became interested in Hindu philosophy and Vedanta, influenced partly by A. *Huxley and Gerald Heard, and edited various works on the subject (*Vedanta for the Western World*, 1945, etc.) and translated the *Bhagavad-gītā* (1944, with Swami Prabhavananda) and other Hindu classics. Novels written in America include *Down There on a Visit* (1962) and *A Single Man* (1964); *Kathleen and Frank* (1972) is an account of his parents, and *Christopher and His Kind* (1977) is a frank account of the homosexual affairs of his young manhood. *Diaries*, i: 1939–1960, ed. K. Bucknell, appeared in 1996. See *Isherwood: A Life Revealed* (2004) by Peter Parker.

ISHIGURO, Kazuo (1954–   ), novelist. He was born in Nagasaki but came to England in 1960 and studied at the universities of Kent and East Anglia. His first novel, *A Pale View of Hills* (1982), about a Japanese widow living in England who is haunted by memories of her daughter's suicide, has been translated into over a dozen languages. *An Artist of the Floating World* (1986) is the story of an ageing Japanese artist who looks back on his life in the aftermath of the Second World War. He came to prominence with his 1989 novel *The Remains of the Day*, a subtle and moving story of an ageing butler's memories of his life in the service which won the *Booker Prize and was made into a successful film. *The Unconsoled* (1995), a Kafkaesque novel about the sense of displacement of an international musician, is set in contemporary Europe. The same theme is pursued in *When We Were Orphans* (2001). *Never Let Me Go* (2005) deals with mortal fragility through the ethics of human cloning.

ISIDORE OF SEVILLE (570–636), archbishop of Seville, an encyclopaedic writer much admired in the Middle Ages, author of *Origines* or *Etymologiae* in 20 books (ed. W. M. Lindsay, 2 vols, 1910). This work argues that the natures of all things can be derived etymologically from their names. Much of it is fantastic, but it remained popular down to the 14th cent. and can be seen as one of the first texts in the encyclopaedic tradition in medieval literature.

Island, The, a poem by Lord *Byron, published 1823. The poem, a mixture of romance and humour, is based on the story of the mutiny on HMS *Bounty*, and idolizes nature at the expense of society.

Island in the Moon, An, an untitled burlesque fragment by W. *Blake, written c.1784–5, first printed (though inaccurately) in 1907 by E. J. Ellis in *The Real Blake*. It is a satirical portrait of scientific and cultural dilettantism and pretension, interspersed with songs (some of them bawdy) including the fragment with the lines 'Winking and blinking | Like Doctor Johnson'; its characters include 'Sipsop the Pythagorean' and 'Inflammable Gas', the latter probably inspired by J. *Priestley.

Island of Dr Moreau, The, a *science fiction tale by H. G. *Wells, published 1896. It is an evolutionary fantasy about a shipwrecked naturalist who becomes involved in an experiment to 'humanize' animals by surgery. The theme was developed by *Aldiss.

isocolon, a rhetorical figure in which the same grammatical form is repeated in different words, as in 'Fair to no purpose, artful to no end, | Young without lovers, old without a friend' (A. *Pope).

Isumbras, Sir, a verse romance in 804 lines of twelve-line tail-rhyme stanzas, from the north-east Midlands, popular before 1320 and mentioned in *Cursor Mundi*. Its theme is that of 'the man tried by fate' of which the model is St Eustace, of Eastern origin. Isumbras is strong, handsome, and prosperous, but also proud and arrogant. A bird sent by God offers him the choice of suffering in youth or old age, and he chooses the former. He loses his wife, children, and possessions, and suffers for 21 years among the Saracens. But he bears all patiently, and at the end of that period an angel tells him that his sins are expiated and he is restored to his family and possessions. Its moral theme is typical of the concern of the 14th-cent. tail-rhyme romances.

Ed. M. Mills in *Six Middle English Romances* (1973); discussion by A. McI. Trounce, 'The English Tail-Rhyme Romances' (*Medium Aevum*, 1, 2, and 3, 1932–4).

Iuliene, St, see KATHERINE GROUP.

Ivanhoe, a novel by Sir W. *Scott, published 1819. The first of Scott's novels to deal with an English, rather than Scottish subject, *Ivanhoe* is also one of his best constructed. In Rebecca, the beautiful Jewess, he produced a heroine as virtuous and strong-minded as Jeanie Deans (*Heart of Midlothian*), but with all the graces which Jeanie lacked, and had the resolution to deprive her of the conventional happy ending. The story deals, somewhat anachronistically, with the antagonism in England between Saxon and Norman during the reign of Richard I. The hero, Wilfred of Ivanhoe, has been disowned by his father Cedric the Saxon because of his love for Cedric's ward, the lady Rowena, and has joined King Richard on crusade; Prince John, taking advantage of the king's absence, is endeavouring to seize the throne himself. The story hinges on two main episodes: the famous tournament at Ashby-de-la-Zouche where Ivanhoe, returned in disguise from the Crusade, and supported by an equally disguised Richard, defeats all challengers, including the Templar Sir Brian de Bois-Guilbert, and Sir Reginald Front-de-Bœuf; and the siege of Front-de-Bœuf's castle of Torquilstone to which he and Bois-Guilbert have carried off Isaac the Jew and his daughter Rebecca. The main plot thereafter concerns the passion of the Templar for Rebecca, and her resistance to his dishonourable advances. Bois-Guilbert dies in combat with Ivanhoe, who, reconciled to his father, marries Rowena; Rebecca, suppressing her love for Ivanhoe, leaves England with her father. The novel was a great success, the first edition selling out within the week. Thackeray's *Rebecca and Rowena* is an amusing sequel to, and critical reinterpretation of, Scott's tale.

J

Jabberwock, a fictitious monster, the subject of the poem 'Jabberwocky' in Lewis Carroll's *Through the Looking-Glass*. The story, told in an invented vocabulary, begins: ' 'Twas brillig and the slithy toves'. *Tenniel's drawing of the Jabberwock, originally intended as a frontispiece, was considered so terrifying by *Dodgson that it was printed by the ballad in the volume; the White Knight became the frontispiece.

Jack, Colonel, see COLONEL JACK.

Jack of Dover, in the prologue to Chaucer's 'Cook's Tale' (*Canterbury Tales*, ll. 4347–8), refers probably to a pie (or, less probably, fish) that has been reheated. In 'Jack of Dover, his quest of Inquirie' (1604), reprinted in W. C. *Hazlitt's *Shakespeare Jest-Books*, Jack travels in search of a greater fool than himself, and fails to find one.

Jack Horner, the subject of a nursery rhyme ('Little Jack Horner sat in a corner', etc.) which occurs in an 18th-cent. chapbook, *The Pleasant History of Jack Horner, Containing his Witty Tricks, etc*. The rhyme is also referred to by H. *Carey in 1725.

Jack of Newbery, or **Newbury,** John Winchcombe, alias Smallwood (d. 1520), a clothier of Newbury, whose wealth inspired the authors of numerous chapbook stories. According to legend he led 100 or 250 men, equipped at his own expense, at the battle of *Flodden Field and entertained *Henry VIII and Catherine of Aragon in his house. (See DELONEY.)

Jack the Ripper, the name given to a murderer who, between 1888 and 1891, killed and eviscerated several prostitutes (at least five, possibly more) in the Whitechapel area of London. Attempts to guess his identity have included a Harley Street surgeon, a mad midwife, a Russian anarchist, the duke of Clarence (1864–92), and J. K. *Stephen. He has been the subject of many novels and films, including Mrs Belloc Lowndes's *The Lodger* (1913) and C. *Wilson's *Ritual in the Dark* (1960), in which he appears as a homosexual sadist, and his presence is also felt in the works of P. *Ackroyd and Iain *Sinclair.

Jack Straw, the leader of a party of insurgents from Essex in the Peasants' Revolt of 1381. A *macaronic poem on him is included in *Medieval English*, ed. R. Kaiser (3rd edn, 1958), 386.

Jacke Wilton, The Life of, see UNFORTUNATE TRAVELLER, THE.

Jacobean, in literary terms, applies to writing of the period of *James I of England, who succeeded Eliza-beth I in 1603: most commonly used of 'Jacobean tragedy'. (See MIDDLETON, TOURNEUR, WEBSTER, REVENGE TRAGEDY.)

Jacobin, originally a name of the French friars of the order of St Dominic, so called because the church of Saint-Jacques in Paris was given to them and they built their first convent near it. From them the name was transferred to the members of a political club established in 1789, in Paris, in the old convent of the Jacobins, to maintain extreme democratic and egalitarian principles. It was applied in a transferred sense to sympathizers with their principles, and about 1800 became a nickname for any radical political reformer.

Jacobite, a term used to describe supporters of James II of England (1633–1701), his son James (1688–1766), known as the old pretender, and his son Charles Edward Stuart (1720–88), known as 'the young pretender', 'the young chevalier', and 'Bonnie Prince Charlie'. Jacobite hopes were effectively crushed in the brutal defeat of the Highland revolt at Culloden in 1746 by troops led by the duke of ('Butcher') Cumberland (1721–65). The Jacobite cause was taken up by many writers (including C. *Nairne, whose songs were celebrated) and provided material for innumerable *historical novels.

JACOBS, W(illiam) W(ymark) (1863–1943), born in Wapping, the son of a wharf manager. He became a clerk in the civil service. He began to publish stories in J. K. *Jerome's *Idler* and the *Strand Magazine* in the 1890s, and in 1896 published his first collection, *Many Cargoes*, the success of which led to his resignation from his clerkship. He wrote several novels, including *At Sunwich Port* (1902) and *Dialstone Lane* (1904), but it was chiefly his short stories which established his popularity. These fall roughly into two groups: those dealing humorously with the escapades of sailors on shore (as well as at sea) and of country characters and rogues, as in the highly successful 'Claybury' stories; and tales of the macabre, such as the celebrated 'The Monkey's Paw', which was dramatized with great success. *Light Freights*, often held to be the best of his collections, appeared in 1901; *The Lady of the Barge* in 1902; and *Night Watches* in 1914.

Jacob's Room, see WOOLF, V.

JACOBSON, Dan (1929–), novelist and critic, born in Johannesburg, but for many years settled in England, where he taught at University College London. His first novel, *The Trap* (1955), was followed by several others, many of them set in South Africa. They include *The

Price of Diamonds (1957); *The Beginners* (1966), a richly peopled family saga which opens in South Africa after the Second World War and moves to England; *The Confessions of Joseph Baisz* (1977); and *The Rape of Tamar* (1970), based on the biblical story from 2 Samuel, about the rape of King David's daughter by her brother Amnon, and the revenge of Absalom. *The Story of the Stories* (1982) is an examination of the Bible as narrative, emphasizing the power of a sustaining plot, and the novel *Her Story* (1987) pursues the biblical theme and the mystery of religious fanaticism in a story-within-a-story, set both in the future (AD 2296) and in the distant past at the time of the crucifixion of Christ. *Time and Time Again* (1985) is a collection of autobiographical essays, with a memorable chapter on *Leavis, and *Heshel's Kingdom* (1998) vividly and movingly re-examines the question of Jewish history and destiny through a quest for Jacobson's grandfather, a Lithuanian rabbi whose early death had paradoxically rescued his family from the Holocaust by sending them as emigrants to South Africa.

JACOBSON, Howard (1942–), novelist, born in Manchester and educated at Cambridge. His first novel, *Coming from Behind* (1983), a sparkling *campus satire set in the Midlands polytechnic of Wrottesley, was followed by *Peeping Tom* (1984), an intertextual comedy which moves between north London and Cornwall and interweaves a provocative commentary on Thomas *Hardy's voyeurist sexuality with the exploits of the narrator, emphatically Jewish Barney Fugelman of Finchley. *Redback* (1987) takes its narrator from the north of England, via a double first in moral decencies at Cambridge, to Australia, which also is the subject of a volume of travel writing, *In the Land of Oz*, published in the same year. *The Very Model of a Man* (1992) is a novel on the biblical theme of Cain and Abel. *No More Mr Nice Guy* (1998) is a macho comedy, and *The Making of Henry* (2004) embraces romance, bathos, and middle age in St Johns Wood. *Roots Schmoots: Journeys Among Jews* (1993) is an exploration of Jewish identity.

Jacobus de Voragine, see GOLDEN LEGEND, THE.

JAGGARD, William (fl. 1594–1623) and Isaac (fl. 1613–27), London printers and principal publishers of the Shakespeare First Folio (see FOLIOS AND QUARTOS, SHAKESPEARIAN).

Jaggers, Mr, a character in Dickens's *Great Expectations*.

JAGO, Richard (1715–81), of Cornish descent, born in Warwickshire, and holder of three livings in that county. He was the author of *Edge-Hill* (1767), a *topographical poem in four books describing, with many digressions, the views seen at morning, noon, afternoon, and evening, as he looks from that famous spot over his favourite county. Several of his verses were published in *Dodsley's *Collection of Poems*

(1748–58). John Scot Hylton composed a life of Jago for a posthumous edition of his *Poems* (1784).

Jakin, Bob, a character in G. Eliot's *The Mill on the Floss*.

JAKOBSON, Roman, see STRUCTURALISM AND POST-STRUCTURALISM.

JAMES I (1394–1437), king of Scotland. He was captured while on his way to France by an English ship, probably in 1406. He was detained in England for 19 years and well educated; he was a captive at the court at the same time as another famous literary hostage, *Charles d'Orléans. In 1424 he married Lady Jane Beaufort, daughter of the earl of Somerset and granddaughter of *John of Gaunt, who is the heroine of James's famous poem *The Kingis Quair*, which he composed in England. He was assassinated at Perth by Sir Robert Graham (see SHIRLEY, JOHN). The authorship of *The Kingis Quair* has been doubted, but there seems no good reason to deny it to James. One or two other poems have been doubtfully attributed to him: 'The Ballad of Good Counsel', *'Christis Kirk on the Green', and 'Peblis to the Play'. *Skeat attributed to him the 'B' section of the Middle English *Romaunt of the Rose* (ll. 1706–5810), but this is very unlikely to be his. See E. W. M. Balfour-Melville, *James I, King of Scots 1406–37* (1936).

JAMES I (James VI of Scotland) (1566–1625), king of England 1603–25. He is reputedly the author of *True Lawe of Free Monarchies* (1598), a reply to the argument of G. *Buchanan in his *De Jure Regni* that the king is elected by and responsible to the people. He wrote *Basilikon Doron* (1599, precepts on the art of government, addressed to his son); *A Counterblaste to Tobacco* (1604), a good many theological works, and poetry in Scots, Latin, and English. His works include metrical versions of 30 psalms, translations of *du Bartas and *Lucan, a long poem on the battle of Lepanto, numerous occasional songs and sonnets, and a short treatise on the rules for writing *Scots poetry.

JAMES, C(yril) L(ionel) R(obert) (1901–89), historian, novelist, cricket enthusiast, born in Tunapuna near Port of Spain, Trinidad. His many works include *Minty Alley* (1936), a low-key realist novel which describes the intrigues amongst the mixed-race lodgers in a West Indian boarding house, seen largely through the eyes of 20-year-old Haynes, who has moved in from a more educated background; *The Black Jacobins* (1938), an important study of the revolution led by *Toussaint L'Ouverture in Haiti, and *Beyond the Boundary* (1963), essays on politics and cricket.

JAMES, George Payne Rainsford (1799–1860). He travelled widely, served in the Napoleonic wars, held various diplomatic posts, and was appointed historiographer royal by William IV. Influenced by Sir W. *Scott he wrote numerous romantic novels, biographies, and popular historical works, including

Richelieu (1829), Darnley (1830), and Life of Edward the Black Prince (1836). *Thackeray parodied him as 'the solitary horseman' in his burlesque Barbazure, by G. P. R. Jeames, esq. for the two horsemen who were a frequent beginning to his romances.

JAMES, Henry (1843–1916), born in New York of ancestry originally both Irish and Scottish. His father, Henry James senior, was a remarkable writer on questions of theology and a follower of *Swedenborg. His elder brother William (below) was a distinguished philosopher. After a desultory education in New York, London, Paris, and Geneva, Henry James entered the law school at Harvard in 1862. He settled in Europe in 1875. From 1865 he was a regular contributor of reviews and short stories to American periodicals and owed much to his friendship with W. D. *Howells. His first considerable piece of fiction, Watch and Ward, appeared serially in 1871; this was followed by Trans-atlantic Sketches and A Passionate Pilgrim in 1875, and his first important novel *Roderick Hudson in 1876 (in the *Atlantic Monthly, 1875). For more than 20 years he lived in London, and in 1898 moved to Lamb House, Rye, where his later novels were written. He at first chiefly concerned himself with the impact of the older civilization of Europe upon American life, and to this period belong his novels Roderick Hudson, The American (1877), *Daisy Miller (1879), and *Portrait of a Lady (1881). He next turned to a more exclusively English stage in The Tragic Muse (1890), The Spoils of Poynton (1897), and The Awkward Age (1899), in which he analysed English character with extreme subtlety, verging at times on obscurity. *What Maisie Knew appeared in 1897. In his last three great novels, *The Wings of the Dove (1902), *The Ambassadors (1903), and *The Golden Bowl (1904), he returned to the 'international' theme of the contrast of American and European character. In 1914 he began work on two novels, The Ivory Tower and The Sense of the Past, which remained unfinished at his death and were published in fragments in 1917. For the revised collection of his fiction, of which the issue began in 1907, James wrote a series of prefaces of high interest. In his critical essays James concentrated on the 19th-cent. novel. He felt that *Dickens was limited by his failure to see below the surface of things; he was a firm admirer of G. *Eliot; but his hero was *Balzac whom he called 'the master of us all'.

Besides more than 100 short stories (including the well-known ghost story *The Turn of the Screw, 1898), James wrote several volumes of sketches of travel (Portraits of Places, 1883; A Little Tour in France, 1884). He wrote a number of plays, of which the few that were acted were not successful. At the opening of Guy Domville in 1895 James was booed by the audience and although the play was praised by some critics, including G. B. *Shaw, its failure plunged James into a severe depression. For the English Men of Letters series he wrote a life of *Hawthorne; and in The American Scene

(1906) a record of the impressions produced on him by a visit to America after an absence of nearly 20 years. A Small Boy and Others (1913) and Notes of a Son and a Brother (1914) are evocations of his early days in New York and Europe. A short story called 'The Middle Years' appeared in the volume Terminations in 1895. The autobiographical work of the same title is a fragment (published posthumously, 1917) 'representing all that James lived to write of a volume of autobiographical reminiscences to which he had given the name of one of his own short stories' (from the prefatory note to the autobiographical fragment).

In addition to the works referred to above, the following may be mentioned: Madonna of the Future (1879), *Washington Square (1881), The Siege of London (1883), *The Bostonians (1886), The Princess Casamassima (1886), The Reverberator (1888), The Aspern Papers (1888), The Real Thing (1893), Embarrassments (1896), The Other House (1896), In the Cage (1898), The Two Magics (1898), The Better Sort (1903).

In 1915 James became a British subject, and in 1916 was awarded the OM. Two volumes of his letters were published in 1920, and re-edited by Leon Edel (1975, 1980); Edel's comprehensive biography in five volumes (1953–72) is of the *Freudian school.

JAMES, M(ontague) R(hodes) (1862–1936), born near Bury St Edmunds, a brilliant linguist, palaeographer, medievalist, and biblical scholar, successively provost of King's College, Cambridge, and (from 1918) of Eton. His memoirs, Eton and King's, were published in 1926. He edited works by *Le Fanu, whom he greatly admired, and himself wrote several volumes of distinguished *ghost stories, many with East Anglian settings, including 'Oh, Whistle, and I'll Come to You, My Lad', which appeared in Ghost Stories of an Antiquary (1904). More Ghost Stories of an Antiquary appeared in 1911, followed by A Thin Ghost and Others (1919), A Warning to the Curious (1925), and his collected stories in 1931. The masterly combination of scholarly control and antiquarian detail with suggestions of underlying supernatural horror have made them lastingly popular. See Michael Cox, M. R. James: An Informal Portrait (1983).

JAMES, P(hyllis) D(orothy), Baroness James of Holland Park (1920–   ), crime writer, born in Oxford. She was educated at Cambridge Girls' High School, after which she worked in a tax office. She also worked as a hospital administrator, and in 1968 took a job in the Home Office, where she became involved with forensic investigations: in consequence her fiction is underpinned by strong factual detail. Her first novel, Cover Her Face (1962), introduced the character of the romantic Adam Dalgleish, a police detective who is also a published poet. Dalgleish also appears in A Mind to Murder (1963), Unnatural Causes (1967), Shroud for a Nightingale (1971), The Black Tower (1975), Death of an Expert Witness (1977), A Taste for Death (1986), Devices *and Desires* (1989), and *Original Sin* (1994), which is set in a long-established but financially ailing publishing company. Her other main character, the private detective Cordelia Gray, features in *An Unsuitable Job for a Woman* (1972) and *The Skull beneath the Skin* (1982). *Innocent Blood* (1980) is a psychological thriller, while *The Children of Men* (1992) is a dystopian novel set in the year 2021 in a world in which no children have been born for 25 years. She was made a life peer in 1991.

JAMES, William (1842–1910), American philosopher, the son of Henry James senior (a Swedenborgian philosopher), and elder brother of Henry *James. He was at first a student of art and then a teacher of physiology, but turned his attention to psychology. His views are embodied in his *Principles of Psychology* (1890), and show a tendency to subordinate logical proof to intuitive conviction. He was a vigorous antagonist of the idealistic school of *Kant and *Hegel, and an empiricist who made empiricism more radical by treating pure experience as the very substance of the world. Yet he was not a monist but a pluralist, 'willing to believe that there may ultimately never be an all-form at all, that the substance of reality may never get totally collected . . . and that a distributive form of reality, the each-form, is as acceptable as the all-form' (*Pluralistic Universe*, 34). Pragmatism, for which he is best remembered by philosophers, was his method of approach to metaphysics: abstract ideas are true if 'they work', if they harmonize with our other experience and accepted ideas. James's principal works were, besides the *Principles of Psychology*, *Varieties of Religious Experience* (1902), *Pragmatism* (1907), *The Meaning of Truth* (1909), *A Pluralistic Universe* (1909), *Essays in Radical Empiricism* (1912). The conclusions of his *Varieties of Religious Experience* are notable: 'the visible world is part of a more spiritual universe from which it draws its chief significance; union with the higher universe is our true end; spiritual energy flows in and produces effects within the phenomenal world.' He coined the phrase *'stream of consciousness'* now widely used as a literary term.

JAMESON, Anna Brownell (1794–1860). She began adult life as a governess. Friendship with the *Kembles, and a long visit to Germany, brought her into contact with literary society, and she became a close friend of the *Brownings, of M. R. *Mitford, and eventually of the *Carlyles. She first attracted attention in 1826 with *A Lady's Diary* (later retitled *The Diary of an Ennuyée*), describing a visit to Italy. From that time on she produced many highly respected works of art history and criticism, biography, theology, history, travel, social comment, and general essays, some of which exhibited a strong interest in the position and education of women. The work for which she is now chiefly remembered is *Characteristics of Women* (1832, later known as *Shakespeare's Heroines*), dedicated to Fanny *Kemble, and illustrated with her own etchings.

Shakespeare she saw as 'the Poet of Womankind', whose heroines display all the aspects and complexities of womanhood. She divides the 25 heroines of her book into four groups: the characters of intellect, such as Portia; those of passion and imagination, such as Viola; those of the affections, such as Desdemona; and those from history, such as Cleopatra and Lady Macbeth. In preparation Mrs Jameson read Dr *Johnson, *Hazlitt, *Coleridge, *Lamb, and other major critics, as well as relevant European and Greek drama, and thoroughly investigated the sources of the histories. Although she makes little attempt to relate character to context, her interpretations, many of which are very detailed, were considered illuminating, and the work was received with considerable respect, G. M. *Hopkins placing her among the most eminent of Shakespeare's critics.

JAMESON, (Margaret) Storm (1891–1986), born in Whitby, the daughter of a sea captain, and educated at Leeds University; her first novel, *The Pot Boils* (1919), was followed by many other works of fiction, including *Women against Men* (1933, stories), *Company Parade* (1934), *Love in Winter* (1935), and *None Turn Back* (1936), the last three forming a trilogy. She also published poems, essays, and biographies, and several volumes of autobiography, including *Journey from the North* (1969), describing her time during the Second World War as president of *PEN. Her second husband was the historian and author Guy Chapman (1889–1972), remembered for his vivid personal account of trench warfare in France, *A Passionate Prodigality* (1933).

James the Fourth, The Scottish Historie of, a play by R. *Greene, published posthumously 1598. In spite of the title, this is a fictionalized romantic comedy, framed by the comments of Oberon, king of fairies. James, king of Scots, marries the English princess Dorothea, but is in love with Ida, daughter of the countess of Arran. Dorothea remains constant in her love for the king, disguising herself as a man when she learns that he seeks her life; she is wounded, but survives to be reconciled to the king after Ida has married the English lord Eustace. Notable among the minor characters are the *Machiavellian counsellor Ateukin and the affectionate dwarf Nano.

JAMIE, Kathleen (1962–), Scottish poet and travel writer, born in Renfrewshire, whose works include *A Flame in your Heart* (1986, with poet and mountaineer Andrew Greig), a sequence of love poems set in the summer of 1940; *The Way We Live* (1987), her first full-length collection; and *The Queen of Sheba* (1994), which shows her increasingly strong lyric command of Scottish themes and language. *The Golden Peak* (1992) describes travels in northern Pakistan, and *The Autonomous Region* (1993, with photographs by Sean Mayne Smith) contains poems inspired by a 1989 journey to Tibet. *Full Strength Angels* (1996, ed., with

James McGonigal) is an anthology of new Scottish prose and verse.

JAMIESON, John (1759–1838), lexicographer and antiquary, a friend of Sir W. *Scott. His chief work was the *Etymological Dictionary of the Scottish Language*, which first appeared in 1808.

Jane Eyre, a novel by C. *Brontë, published 1847.

The heroine, a penniless orphan, has been left to the care of her aunt Mrs Reed. Harsh and unsympathetic treatment rouses her defiant spirit, and a passionate outbreak leads to her consignment to Lowood Institution (based on Cowan Bridge, which the author herself briefly attended). There, consoled for the severity of the regime by the kindness of the superintendent Miss Temple and a fellow orphan, Helen Burns, who dies in Jane's arms of consumption, she spends some miserable years, eventually becoming a teacher. On Miss Temple's marriage she obtains a post as governess at Thornfield Hall to Adèle, the illegitimate daughter of Mr Rochester, a *Byronic hero of grim aspect and sardonic temper. Rochester, despite Jane's plainness, is fascinated by her sharp wit and independence, and they fall in love. After much resistance she agrees to marry him, but on the eve of their wedding her wedding veil is rent by an intruder who Rochester assures her is a servant, Grace Poole, but who is the next day revealed to be his mad Creole wife Bertha, confined to the upper regions of the Hall for years, whose unseen presence has long disturbed Jane. The marriage ceremony is interrupted by Mrs Rochester's brother from the West Indies and, despite Rochester's full confession and pleadings with Jane to stay with him, she flees. After nearly perishing on the moors, she is taken in and cared for by the Revd St John Rivers and his sisters Mary and Diana. It emerges that they are her cousins, and that Jane has inherited money from an uncle; the legacy is equally divided between the four. Under pressure from the earnest appeals and strong personality of the dedicated Rivers, she nearly consents to marry him and share his missionary vocation in India, but is prevented by a telepathic appeal from Rochester. She returns to Thornfield Hall to find the building burned, and Rochester blinded and maimed from his attempt to save his wife from the flames. She marries him, and in the last chapter we learn that his sight is partially restored.

From its first publication, the novel's exceptional emotional and narrative power made it a success, though, despite its strict adherence to conventional moral standards, it was considered by many to be unsuitable for young ladies; more recently its strong sexual undercurrents have subjected it to many *Freudian interpretations encouraged by the author's frequent use of dream imagery. Additional scandal attended the publication of the second edition, which Charlotte dedicated to *Thackeray, unaware that he too had a wife certified as insane. The story of the first Mrs Rochester was told by J. *Rhys in *Wide Sargasso Sea*.

'Janet's Repentance', see SCENES OF CLERICAL LIFE.

JANEWAY, James, see CHILDREN'S LITERATURE.

'January and May', a version by *Pope of Chaucer's 'Merchant's Tale' (see CANTERBURY TALES, 10).

Jaquenetta, a country wench loved by *Armado in Shakespeare's *Love's Labour's Lost*.

Jaques, a discontented lord attending the banished duke in Shakespeare's *As You Like It*. Many of the play's most memorable lines are his, including the speech beginning 'All the world's a stage' (II. vii). His name is clearly to be pronounced as two syllables. A second Jaques, 'the second son of old Sir Rowland', appears in the final scene of the play.

Jarley, Mrs, in Dickens's *The Old Curiosity Shop*, the proprietor of a travelling waxworks show.

Jarndyce, John, a character in Dickens's *Bleak House*.

JARRELL, Randall (1914–65), American poet and critic, born in Nashville, Tennessee; he taught for many years in various colleges, and his one novel, *Pictures from an Institution* (1954), is a satire on life in a progressive women's college and an early example of a *campus novel. He published several volumes of poetry, from his first, *Blood for a Stranger* (1942), to *The Lost World*, published posthumously in 1966 with a memoir by his friend R. *Lowell.

JARRY, Alfred, see ABSURD, THEATRE OF THE.

jazz poetry, a genre presaged in the USA by (Nicholas) Vachel Lindsay (1879–1931) with his incantatory ballads 'General William Booth' (1913), 'The Congo' (1914), *The Daniel Jazz* (1920), etc.; and then by (James) Langston Hughes (1902–67), who was probably the first to pitch his verse in conjunction with musicians in the late 1930s. The fusion was developed in the 1950s by Kenneth Patchen (1911–72), Kenneth Rexroth (1905–82), Amiri Baraka (adopted name of black militant writer Everett Le Roi Jones, 1934–), and the poets of the American *Beat Generation; and in Britain from the mid-1950s to the 1980s by C. *Logue, Roy Fisher (1930–), Michael *Horovitz, Pete Brown (1940–), Spike Hawkins (1942–), and others. Various permutations of primarily non-academic, often regional, entertainers and singer-songwriters have proliferated since, with the punk-rock, post-punk, and 'new wave' voices of John Cooper Clarke, Paul Weller of The Jam, and the Rastafarian and reggae-cadenced contributions of Anglo-Jamaican poets such as James *Berry, E. K. *Brathwaite, Linton Kwesi *Johnson, and Benjamin *Zephaniah. See also UNDERGROUND POETRY.

JEA, John, see BLACK BRITISH LITERATURE.

JEAN de MEUN, see ROMAN DE LA ROSE.

Jean Paul, an abbreviation frequently used in the 19th cent. of the name of J. P. F. *Richter.

JEBB, Richard Claverhouse (1841–1905), professor of Greek at Glasgow University 1874, Regius professor at Cambridge 1889. Unfriendly reviewers of his first major work, *The Attic Orators* (1876), saw no merit in it beyond diligence and a certain elegance, and in a way this verdict holds good for all his writings. The critical editions familiar to generations of students show that his knowledge of ancient Greece and its language was voluminous and exact. His style reflected the fastidiousness which we know from his wife's witty letters to have characterized him as a man. But when there was need for literary criticism or for an understanding of human nature, he could produce nothing but generalities. That his career was markedly successful in spite of these shortcomings—he became MP for his university (1891) and received the OM and a knighthood in 1900—sheds an interesting light on the character of late Victorian scholarship.

Jeeves, in many of P. G. *Wodehouse's stories, the omniscient and resourceful valet.

JEFFERIES, Richard (1848–87), writer and naturalist, the son of a Wiltshire farmer. As a boy of 16 he attempted to run away to Moscow or perhaps America, but only got as far as Liverpool. He began his literary career as a local reporter in Wiltshire, and from then on he wrote much, including novels (which had no success), works of natural history and country life, and essays in journals and magazines. The books for which he is remembered combine his love of the natural world with a poetic apprehension and individuality of thought which blur the usual literary distinctions. He first attracted attention with *The Gamekeeper at Home: Sketches of Natural History and Rural Life* (1878), published first in the *Pall Mall Gazette*. This, together with *Hodge and his Masters* (1880), appears to have influenced *Hardy's article of 1883 on 'The Dorsetshire Labourer'. For these books, as for most of his others, Jefferies relied greatly on 'field notebooks', where he entered his meticulous observations on the life of the countryside. *Wild Life in a Southern County*, in which the author, sitting on a Wiltshire down, observes in ever widening circles the fields, woods, animals, and human inhabitants below him, was published with success in 1879, as was *The Amateur Poacher. Wood Magic* (1881), in which a solitary boy lives in a magical world of speaking wild animals, was followed in 1882 by *Bevis: The Story of a Boy*, an evocation (for both adults and children) of his country childhood (see CHILDREN'S LITERATURE). The book for which he is probably best known, *The Story of My Heart*, tracing the growth of his unorthodox beliefs, caused some scandal on its publication in 1883. *After London*, a savage vision of the future, in which London is a poisonous swamp inhabited by cruel dwarfs, followed in 1885, as did a collection of essays much reprinted, *The Open Air*. Published in the year of his death, *Amaryllis at the Fair*, though lacking narrative, contains in Iden an impressive portrait of Jefferies's father. See *Richard Jefferies* (1965) by S. J. Looker and C. Porteous; there is also a life (1909) by E. *Thomas.

JEFFERS, (John) Robinson (1887–1962), American poet, born in Pittsburgh, the son of a professor of biblical languages. He travelled widely with his parents as a boy until they settled in California, then studied at Occidental College and other universities before himself settling, with his wife Una, at Carmel on the Californian coast, where they lived in seclusion, in a granite house on the cliffs facing the sea. The scenery of the redwood and seashore inspires much of his works, and one of his dominant themes is what he called 'Inhumanism'—the insignificance of man, contrasted with the vast, merciless, enduring processes of nature and the animal kingdom; the hawk provides one of his most strikingly recurrent symbols. After two minor volumes he made his name with *Tamar and Other Poems* (1924), of which the title poem is a tragic narrative of family passion and incest in a wild Californian setting; this was followed by other volumes, many of them of a similar pattern—a long narrative, together with shorter lyrics. These include *The Women at Point Sur* (1927), *Cawdor and Other Poems* (1928), *Thurso's Landing and Other Poems* (1932), and, in 1938, *Selected Poetry*. He suffered a certain lapse in popularity due to his wartime espousal of an attitude of isolationism, expressed in 'The Eye', written during the war; the eye is the Pacific, to which 'our ships, planes, wars are perfectly irrelevant'. He had a stage success with his adaption of *Euripides' Medea* in 1947, and his last volume of poetry, *Hungerfield and Other Poems*, appeared in 1954.

JEFFREY, Francis, Lord (1773–1850), educated at Edinburgh and Glasgow Universities, a Whig who became a Scottish judge and an MP. He is remembered in a literary connection as the founder, with Sydney *Smith, of the *Edinburgh Review* in 1802, as its editor until 1829, and as a stern but judicious critic of the writers of his day. Although he was often severe (and was challenged to a duel by T. *Moore), he nevertheless wrote appreciatively of many writers, including *Crabbe, Sir W. *Scott, *Byron, and, most notably *Keats, in whose *Poems* of 1820 he discerned genius. *Hazlitt thought him an admirable editor, perceptive and just, with 'a great range of knowledge, an incessant activity of mind'. His inability to understand Wordsworth—his review of *The Excursion* in 1814 begins: 'This will never do'—led to a series of attacks on 'a *sect* of poets' designated as *'The Lake Poets'. Smith complained, 'The whole effect of your mind is to destroy', but this seems no more just than Byron's lampoons in *English Bards and Scotch Reviewers* on 'the self-constituted judge of poesy'.

Jekyll and Hyde, see DR JEKYLL AND MR HYDE.

JELLICOE, (Patricia) Ann (1927–), playwright and director, trained as an actress at the Central School of

Speech and Drama. She was associated for some years with the *English Stage Company, which in 1958 put on the play which made her name, *The Sport of My Mad Mother*, an experimental drama about a London street gang described by *Tynan as a '*tour de force*'. This was followed by *The Knack* (1962) and *Shelley* (1965). She has also written plays for children and drama-documentaries on historical themes performed by the local West Country community, including *The Reckoning* (1978), set in Lyme Regis and based on the 1685 Monmouth Rebellion. In 1985 she worked with David *Edgar on his community play *Entertaining Strangers* in Dorchester.

Jellyby, Mrs, a character in Dickens's *Bleak House*.

Jenkyns, Deborah, Matilda, and Peter, characters in Mrs Gaskell's *Cranford*.

JENNINGS, Elizabeth (1926–2001), poet, born in Boston, Lincolnshire, of a Roman Catholic family, and educated at St Anne's College, Oxford. She worked as a library assistant, in advertising, and in publishing, while publishing her early collections of poetry, *Poems* (1953), *A Way of Looking* (1955), and *A Sense of the World* (1958). She was somewhat arbitrarily associated with the *Movement, through Robert Conquest's inclusion of some of her work in *New Lines* (1956), but her subsequent volumes of verse (e.g. *Recoveries*, 1964; *The Mind has Mountains*, 1966) are highly personal and confessional accounts of mental breakdown and hospital treatment, very far removed in tone from the laconic detachment of the more representative Movement poets. Her *Collected Poems* were published in 1967 (revised and extended 1987) and she subsequently published several more volumes, including *Lucidities* (1970) and *Moments of Grace* (1979), which manifest her quiet and sensitive control of, and openness towards, experiences of suffering, loneliness, friendship, and religious faith. Other volumes include *Celebrations and Elegies* (1982), *Extending the Territory* (1985), *Tributes* (1989), *Times and Seasons* (1992), and *Familiar Spirits* (1994). She also published two volumes of prose, *Every Changing Shape* (critical essays, 1961) and *Christianity and Poetry* (1965).

Jennings, Mrs, (1) a character in J. Austen's *Sense and Sensibility*; (2) the mother of *Keats, as she became by her second marriage.

'Jenny', a poem by D. G. *Rossetti, first published 1870, although he had been working on it for many years, and was further to revise it. It was one of the poems buried with his wife Lizzie in 1862. The poet describes a night spent in the chamber of a prostitute, golden-haired Jenny; she falls asleep against his knees and at dawn he leaves her, after much meditation on her thoughtless gaiety, shame, and beauty, and on the toad Lust which has ruined her. Fallen women and prostitutes were favourite subjects with the Pre-Raphael-ites: e.g. Rossetti's painting *Found* and H. *Hunt's *The Awakening Conscience*. This poem roused the indignation of those like R. W. *Buchanan who thought Rossetti's work too sensual, and *Ruskin greatly disliked it.

JENYNS, Soame (1704–87), MP and minor poet, chiefly remembered for his *A Free Enquiry into the Nature and Origin of Evil* (1757), which elicited a brilliant and scathing attack from Dr *Johnson in the *Literary Magazine*. Jenyns's work is a classic statement of the more facile elements of 18th-cent. philosophical optimism, justifying evil and suffering by their place in the 'scale of Being' and ignorance as the 'opiate' of the poor: 'the sufferings of individuals are absolutely necessary to universal happiness.' Johnson poured scorn on a philosophy which envisaged superior beings laughing at human misery, and links Jenyns's view with that of *Pope (see ESSAY ON MAN): 'This author and Pope perhaps never saw the miseries which they imagine thus easily to be borne.'

jeremiad, a doleful complaint, in allusion to the Lamentations of Jeremiah in the OT.

JEROME, St (Hieronymus) (c.342–420), one of the four early Latin 'Doctors of the Church', born at Strido near Aquileia, educated at Rome, and baptized in 360. He visited Gaul and Asia Minor, and after a period of dissipation (perhaps conventional) he practised asceticism. He lived as a hermit near Chalcis (south-east of Antioch), spent the years 382–5 at Rome, where he was the spiritual counsellor of some noble Roman ladies, and in 386 settled at Bethlehem, where he died in 420 after 25 years of writing and translation. His principal works were a translation and continuation of the chronicles of *Eusebius and the Latin version of the Scriptures which came to be known as the *Vulgate, afterwards the standard Latin version up to the Renaissance.

   Dogmatic and Political Works (including *Against Rufinus* and *Against the Pelagians*), trans. J. N. Hritzu (1965); J. Steinmann, *Saint Jerome*, trans. R. Matthews (1959).

JEROME, Jerome K(lapka) (1859–1927), brought up in east London, the son of an unsuccessful ironmonger, became an actor and published a volume of humorous pieces about the theatre, *On the Stage and Off* (1885), and another collection of light essays, *Idle Thoughts of an Idle Fellow* (1886). He achieved lasting fame with *Three Men in a Boat* (1889), the comic story of three young men and their dog who take a rowing holiday on the Thames. In 1892 Jerome and some friends founded the *Idler*, a humorous magazine which published work by *Harte, *Twain, and W. W. *Jacobs, among others. *Three Men on the Bummel*, describing a tour in Germany, appeared in 1900, and in 1902 *Paul Klever*, an autobiographical novel. Jerome also wrote many plays, in the manner of his friend *Barrie, including the most memorable, *The Passing of the Third Floor Back* (1908). There is a life by J. Connolly (1982).

Jeronimo, or **Hieronimo,** the chief character in Kyd's *The Spanish Tragedy.*

JERROLD, Douglas William (1803–57), the son of an actor-manager. He served in the navy, was apprenticed to a printer, and became dramatic author of the Surrey Theatre before making his name in the theatre with *Black-Ey'd Susan* (1829), founded on *Gay's ballad; other successful plays included *Fifteen Years of a Drunken's Life* (1828), *The Rent Day* (1832), and *The Prisoner of War* (1842). He was a friend of *Dickens. In his later years Jerrold turned to journalism; he was associated with *Punch* from its beginnings and became a regular contributor, writing several serial works, including social political articles signed 'Q' which gave *Punch* a liberal trend in politics and *Mrs Caudle's Curtain Lectures* (issued as a book in 1846), which greatly added to the journal's popularity. From 1845 he ran *Douglas Jerrold's Shilling Magazine* and from 1846 *Douglas Jerrold's Weekly Newspaper.* He wrote several novels and his studies of *Men of Character* (1838) were illustrated by *Thackeray.

JERROLD, William Blanchard (1826–84), son of D. *Jerrold; journalist, playwright, biographer, and writer of miscellaneous works on food, travel, etc. He wrote the text of *London* (1872), illustrated by *Doré, and wrote a life of Doré (1891).

Jerusalem: *The Emanation of the Giant Albion,* a prophetic poem by *Blake, written and etched, with 100 plates, 1804–20. (It is not to be confused with the short poem beginning 'And did those feet . . .', commonly known as 'Jerusalem', which appears at the beginning of Blake's *Milton.) After a preface in which he defends his use of free verse ('Poetry Fetter'd Fetters the Human Race') Blake proceeds to personify England as the fallen giant *Albion, and to summon him to the 'awakening of Eternal Life' which lies beyond the Vegetable Universe, and to reunion with his banished emanation, the lovely Jerusalem. Blake mingles prophecy with social criticism, biblical legend with legends of Druids and of Gog and Magog (see GOGMAGOG), and references to 'Hampstead, Highgate, Finchley, Hendon, Muswell Hill' with descriptions of *Los labouring in his furnace to build the city of Golgonooza. The long poem ends with a 'fourfold vision' of regeneration, 'rejoicing in Unity in the Four Senses' and in the 'Forgiveness of Sins which is Self-Annihilation'.

Jerusalem Delivered (*Gerusalemme liberata*), a poem by *Tasso, published without his consent 1580, in authorized form 1581. (Tasso later rewrote the poem, giving it a more 'regular' structure and a more austere moral tone, and changing the title to *Gerusalemme conquistata.* The new work, published 1593, was inferior to the original.)

The poem is an epic of the First Crusade, with the addition of romantic and fabulous elements. By the side of Godfrey of Bouillon, the leader of the Christian host besieging Jerusalem, and other historical characters, we have the romantic figures of Sofronia and her lover Olindo, who are prepared to face martyrdom to save the Christians in the beleaguered city; the warlike Clorinda, who is beloved by Tancred the Norman, and killed by him unwittingly; and Armida, the niece of the king of Damascus, who lures away the Christians to her enchanted gardens. Rinaldo, prince of Este (an imaginary personage, introduced as a way of extolling the author's patron), rescues the prisoners of Armida, and Armida falls in love with him. By her enchantments they live happily together until Rinaldo is summoned away to help the army by slaying the devil-enchanted wood. He takes part in the capture of Jerusalem, and at last marries a repentant Armida.

The poem was translated into English in 1594 by R. Carew (1555–1620), and in 1600 by *Fairfax as *Godfrey of Bulloigne.* Spenser's description of Acrasia's *Bower of Bliss (*Faerie Queene*, II. xii) was modelled on the gardens of Armida, and the poem considerably influenced *Milton and others (see TASSO).

JESPERSEN, Jens Otto Harry (1860–1943), Danish philologist, educated at Copenhagen, where he became professor of English in 1893. He wrote many philological books, the most important perhaps being *A Modern English Grammar on Historical Principles* (Parts 1–7, 1909–49); *The Growth and Structure of the English Language* (1909; 9th edn 1938); *Essentials of English Grammar* (1933). But he also wrote works more concerned with the theoretical analysis of language, the principal ones being *The Philosophy of Grammar* (1929), *Analytic Syntax* (1937), and, most importantly, *Language, Its Nature, Development and Origin* (1922).

Jessamy Bride, the, the name given by *Goldsmith to the younger Miss Horneck, with whom he is supposed to have been in love.

Jessica, Shylock's daughter in Shakespeare's *The Merchant of Venice.*

jest book literature, collections of 'merie Tales', 'quicke answeres', and 'pleasant conceites' popular throughout the 16th and 17th cents and later. Their authorship was often ascribed to witty writers such as *Skelton and *Peele or to famous jesters such as J. *Scogan and R. Armin. The genre is related to the apophthegm and adage, popularized by *Erasmus, and to *rogue literature, and can be detected in some early fiction, for example in the opening of T. Nashe's *The Unfortunate Traveller.* (See also JOE MILLER'S JESTS.)

Jew, the Wandering, see WANDERING JEW.

JEWETT, Sarah Orne (1849–1909), American novelist and short story writer, born in Maine, the daughter of a doctor. She was inspired when young by H. B. *Stowe's novel set in Maine, *The Pearl of Orris Island,* to write about her native region of New England, and began her career by publishing short stories in the *Atlantic Monthly. Her volumes include Deephaven (1877), A Country Doctor (1884), A White Heron (1886; short stories), and The Country of the Pointed Firs (1896), which describes daily life in a decaying Maine seaport town. Her precise, realistic, subdued portraits of ordinary people and her sense of community and place bear witness to her admiration for *Flaubert as an artist, and won her an enduring reputation; W. *Cather records her debt to her in Not under Forty.

Jew of Malta, The, a drama in blank verse by *Marlowe, performed about 1592, not published until 1633.

The grand seignior of Turkey having demanded the tribute of Malta, the governor of Malta decides that it shall be paid by the Jews of the island. Barabas, a rich Jew who resists the edict, has all his wealth impounded and his house turned into a nunnery. In revenge he indulges in an orgy of slaughter, procuring the death of his daughter Abigail's lover among others, and poisoning Abigail herself. Malta being besieged by the Turks, he betrays the fortress to them and, as a reward, is made its governor. He now plots the destruction of the Turkish commander and his force at a banquet by means of a collapsible floor; but is himself betrayed and hurled through this same floor into a cauldron, where he dies. The prologue to the play is spoken by 'Machevil', and Barabas is one of the prototypes for unscrupulous *Machiavellian villains in later Elizabethan and Jacobean drama. His praise of gold and precious stones as 'Infinite riches in a little roome' is often quoted.

JEWSBURY, Geraldine Endsor (1812–80), an intimate friend of the *Carlyles. Her brilliant wit and conversation made her house in Manchester, and later in London, a centre for such eminent visitors as the Carlyles, J. A. *Froude, T. H. *Huxley, *Ruskin, D. G. *Rossetti, and *Thirlwall. Besides contributing articles and reviews to the *Athenaeum, the *Westminster Review, and other journals, she wrote six novels, including Zöe (1845), The Half Sisters (1848), and Marian Withers (1851), and two stories for children. A Selection from the Letters of Geraldine Jewsbury to Jane Carlyle (1892, edited with a memoir by Mrs A. Ireland) gave undue emphasis to the emotional element of the friendship between the two women and was the subject of an interesting article by V. *Woolf ('Geraldine and Jane', TLS, 28 Feb. 1929). Jewsbury had destroyed all the letters to her from Jane Carlyle, except for one which was published in Mrs Ireland's Life of Jane Welsh Carlyle (1891); it was the wish of both women that their letters be destroyed.

JEWSBURY, Maria Jane (1800–33), poet, and sister of G. *Jewsbury: she was the daughter of a cotton manufacturer and kept house for him in Manchester after her mother's death, until her marriage in 1832 to W. K. Fletcher, a chaplain with the East India Company. She

published poetry and essays, contributed to the Manchester Courier and the *Athenaeum, and was a close friend of the *Wordsworths. Her most remarkable work was perhaps the 'Oceanides', a poem which she wrote on her voyage out to India, 1832–3, and which was published in twelve sections in the Athenaeum; the poem vividly celebrates the stages and changing moods of the voyage. She died of cholera not long after her arrival.

JHABVALA, Ruth Prawer (1927–), novelist, born in Germany, the daughter of a Polish Jewish solicitor; she came to England in 1939 as a refugee and was educated in London. In 1951 she married an Indian architect, and subsequently lived for 24 years in India, where she wrote several novels including Esmond in India (1958), A New Dominion (1973), and Heat and Dust (1975, *Booker Prize), all of which reflect her mingled affection for and impatience with her adopted country and show intimate knowledge of the lives of both Indian and European families. She published volumes of short stories and wrote several original screenplays, including Shakespeare-Wallah (1965), the story of a troupe of travelling actors, and adaptations of E. M. Forster's *A Room with a View and *Howards End. In 1975 she moved to New York, where her novel In Search of Love and Beauty (1983) and later works are set.

jig, 'an afterpiece in the form of a brief farce which was sung and accompanied by dancing', popular in the Elizabethan and Jacobean theatre. Few have survived, but there are numerous references to them in contemporary literature and both W. *Kemp and *Tarlton performed them with great success. Cf. *Hamlet's comment on Polonius: 'he's for a jig, or a tale of bawdry, or he sleeps' (II. ii. 494).

Jimson, Gulley, the bohemian artist hero of J. *Cary's novel The Horse's Mouth. Although popularly supposed to be based on the painter Stanley *Spencer (1891–1959), he also contains some of the characteristics of Augustus *John, including the urge to paint large murals.

Jingle, Alfred, a character in Dickens's *Pickwick Papers.

Jiniwin, Mrs, in Dickens's *The Old Curiosity Shop, the mother of Mrs Quilp.

JOAN OF ARC, St (1412–31), Jeanne D'Arc, or more correctly Jeanne Darc, as it was spelt in all contemporary documents (Littré), the daughter of Jacques Darc, a farmer of Domrémy in the valley of the Meuse, an illiterate girl who contributed powerfully to liberate France from the English in the reign of Charles VII. Inspired, she claimed, by the voices of Sts Michael, Catherine, and Margaret, her mission was a double one, to raise the siege of Orléans, and to conduct Charles to his coronation at Rheims. She accomplished both these tasks and then wished to return home; but she yielded to the demands of the French patriots and was taken prisoner by the Burgundians, who handed her over to the English. But it was a French court of ecclesiastics (with the help of the Inquisition) who sentenced her as a heretic, and the English who burned her at Rouen. She was canonized in 1920. She appears in Shakespeare's *1 Henry VI*, and is the subject of Voltaire's *La *Pucelle*, of a tragedy by *Schiller, of a poem by *Southey, and of dramas by G. B. *Shaw and *Anouilh. See also Marina *Warner's *Joan of Arc: The Image of Female Heroism* (1981) for a discussion of St Joan's changing function as national and political symbol.

Job Trotter, a character in Dickens's *Pickwick Papers*.

Jocasta, a tragedy in blank verse, translated from an Italian adaptation of the *Phoenissae* of *Euripides, by G. *Gascoigne and F. Kinwelmarshe, included in Gascoigne's *Posies* (1575).

JOCELIN DE BRAKELOND (fl. 1200), a monk of Bury St Edmunds, whose chronicle of his abbey (1173–1202) inspired *Carlyle's *Past and Present*.

Jocoseria, a volume of ten poems of various lengths and metres by R. *Browning, published 1883. The collection is consciously a miscellany; Browning borrowed the title from Otto Melander's book of jokes and stories (1597) to suggest its lightweight character, though several of the poems ('Donald', 'Cristina and Monaldeschi', 'Ixion') do not bear out this judgement. The volume contains the much-parodied lyric 'Wanting is—what?', an exquisite miniature of Browning's whole philosophy of art as a mode of desire.

Joe Gargery, a character in Dickens's *Great Expectations*.

Joe Miller's Jests: or *The Wit's Vade-Mecum* (1739), a *jest-book by J. *Mottley. The name is taken from Joseph Miller (1684–1738), an actor in the Drury Lane company, and a reputed humorist. It was a childhood favourite of G. *Eliot.

Johannes Factotum, 'John Do-everything', a Jack of all trades, a would-be universal genius. The phrase, as also *Dominus Factotum, Magister Factotum,* and the corresponding Italian *fa il tutto,* is found in the 16th cent. It occurs in *Greenes Groats-Worth of Witte, Bought with a Million of Repentance*, attacking Shakespeare:

> . . . beeing an absolute *Johannes fac totum,* is in his owne conceit the onely Shake-scene in a countrey.

JOHN, Augustus (Edwin), OM (1878–1961), painter, born at Tenby, the son of a solicitor, and trained at the Slade School. His autobiography, *Chiaroscuro* (1952), contains many good anecdotes about writers whom he met or knew as friends (including *Wilde, G. B. *Shaw, *Joyce, and W. *Lewis), and he also painted some remarkable portraits of literary figures, including *Yeats, Shaw, Dylan *Thomas, T. E. *Lawrence, *Fir-

bank, and Joyce. M. *Holroyd's two-volume biography (1974–5) gives a full account of John's flamboyant personality and unorthodox domestic life, and suggests various fictitious characters who were partly based on John, including Struthers in D. H. *Lawrence's *Aaron's Rod*, Albert Sanger in M. *Kennedy's *The Constant Nymph*, Gulley Jimson in *Cary's *The Horse's Mouth*, and the younger Strickland in *Maugham's *The Moon and Sixpence*. His sister Gwen John (1876–1939) was also a painter of distinction.

JOHN OF AUSTRIA, Don (1547–78), a natural son of Charles V. He defeated the Turkish fleet at Lepanto (1571), a victory celebrated in *Chesterton's popular narrative poem 'Lepanto'.

JOHN OF THE CROSS, St (Juan de la Cruz) (1542–91), a friar of the Carmelite order, and, with the encouragement of his fellow Carmelite St *Teresa of Ávila, who considerably influenced his spiritual and practical understanding, a joint founder of the Discalced Carmelites. A major figure of the Counter-Reformation, he was imprisoned in Toledo in 1577 for his reformist views, an experience which inspired some of his finest mystical writing. Fewer than a thousand lines of his poetry survive, but they are regarded as some of the greatest in the Spanish language; particularly well known are his *Cántico espiritual* (Spiritual Canticle), most of which was composed in prison; his *En una noche oscura* (The Dark Night), composed shortly afterwards; and *Llama de amor viva* (The Living Flame of Love), written c.1583–4. He writes of the stages of union of the soul with God, and of the ecstasy of that union, in a language both erotic and spiritual, and of an exceptional power, grace, and intensity. His work has been translated by E. Allison Peers (1934–5), and a selection of his poems by R. *Campbell (1951); there is a study by G. *Brenan (1972).

JOHN OF GAUNT (1340–99), duke of Lancaster, the fourth and longest-lived son of Edward III and the father of Henry IV, named from his birthplace Ghent (Gaunt). He was first the regent, in effect, during the early years of the reign of the young Richard II and afterwards his bitter enemy. He was the dominant figure in English politics during much of Richard's reign, and his oppressive rule was repeatedly but unsuccessfully opposed, first by his eldest brother the *Black Prince in the year of his death and of the 'Good Parliament' (1376). He was the employer of *Wyclif and the patron of Chaucer whose *Book of the Duchess* is commonly believed to be an elegy for the death of Gaunt's duchess Blanche in 1369. He is a major figure in Shakespeare's *Richard II*.

JOHN OF HOVEDEN, see ANGLO-LATIN LITERATURE.

JOHN OF SALISBURY (fl. 1120–80). He was born at Salisbury and studied at Paris under *Abelard and at Chartres. He returned to England in 1154, remaining mostly at Canterbury where he was secretary to

Archbishop Theobald and was sent on missions to Rome. He was also secretary to *Becket with whom he was exiled when he fell into disfavour with Henry II. John retired to Rheims, where he composed his *Historia Pontificalis*. He is said to have been present in Canterbury Cathedral when Becket was assassinated; he wrote a life of Becket (and of *Anselm), arguing for the canonization of both. He became bishop of Chartres in 1176. He was the most learned classical writer of his time, often seen as the principal humanist inspiration in 'the twelfth-century Renaissance'. Among his many works, the principal items are the *Polycraticus* (or *De Nugis Curialium*), on the vanities of the court and miscellaneous questions on philosophy, and the *Metalogicon*, a treatise on logic and an account of Aristotle's treatment of the subject. (See also ANGLO-LATIN LITERATURE.)

Ed. C. C. J. Webb, *Polycraticus* (1909) and *Metalogicon* (1929); C. C. J. Webb, *John of Salisbury* (1932).

John Bull, *The History of*, a collection of pamphlets by *Arbuthnot, issued 1712, rearranged and republished in *Pope and *Swift's *Miscellanies* of 1727.

The pamphlets (of which the first, *Law is a Bottomless Pit*, appeared on 6 Mar. 1712) were designed to advocate the cessation of war with France, and introduced the allegorical character John Bull, who represents England; he is 'an honest plain-dealing fellow, choleric, bold, and of a very inconstant temper . . . very apt to quarrel with his best friends, especially if they pretend to govern him . . . a boon companion, loving his bottle and his diversion'. Other characters are Nicholas Frog (the Dutch), Lord Strutt (Philip of Spain), Lewis Baboon (Louis XIV of France), and Humphrey Hocus, an attorney (the duke of Marlborough). Ed. A. W. Bower and R. A. Erickson (1976).

John Bull is also the title of a play by G. *Colman the younger.

John Bull's Other Island, an ironic description of Ireland deriving from Leon Paul Blouet's *John Bull and His Island* (1884) and used by G. B. *Shaw as the title of a play (1904) written at the request of *Yeats 'as a patriotic contribution to the repertory of the Irish Literary Theatre'.

John Buncle Esq, The Life and Opinions of, a novel by T. *Amory, published in two volumes (1756, 1766).

Buncle, a man of passionate temperament and a highly original turn of mind, sets out on a journey through the more magnificent and dangerous landscapes of northern England. Among the moors and mountains he comes upon small centres of civilized elegance and culture, in many of which he encounters beautiful and learned women, seven of whom (with the intervention of successive deaths) he marries. Miss Spence, with 'the head of Aristotle, the heart of a primitive Christian, and the form of Venus de Medicis', who discusses differential calculus after dinner, is typical of his wives. But the bulk of the book is taken up with eloquent discussion and digression on religious, scientific, and literary subjects, descriptions of awesome scenery, and much eating and drinking. How far the author is in humorous command of his material, and how far subject to his own fantasy, is difficult to establish. *Hazlitt, who enjoyed the book, found 'the soul of Rabelais' in it.

'John Gilpin, The Diverting History of', a poem by *Cowper, first published anonymously in the *Public Advertiser*, reprinted in chapbook form, and included in the same volume as *The Task* (1785). The story of John Gilpin was told to Cowper by Lady Austen to divert him from melancholy. He laughed over it during the night and next day had turned it into a ballad.

John Gilpin, a 'linen-draper bold' of Cheapside, and his wife decide to celebrate their 20th wedding anniversary by a trip to the Bell at Edmonton, he on a borrowed horse, she, her sister, and the children in a chaise and pair. But John loses control of his horse, and the poem describes his headlong career to Edmonton, 10 miles beyond it to Ware, and then back again.

John Halifax, Gentleman, a novel by Mrs *Craik published 1856.

The story, set between the Bredon hills and Tewkesbury, tells of the poor honest orphan John, who finds employment with the tanner Abel Fletcher and is befriended by Abel's weakling son Phineas, improves his position, and marries the book's heroine, Ursula March. John's status as 'gentleman' is earned not by birth and wealth but by his own integrity and worth. The book was immensely successful both in England and America, and ran into numerous editions over many years. Long after Mrs Craik's death American tourists would visit the 'Halifax country' of Tewkesbury.

JOHNSON, Amryl, see BLACK BRITISH LITERATURE.

JOHNSON, B(ryan) S(tanley William) (1933–73), novelist, poet, and film-maker, born in Hammersmith, London. After graduating from King's College, London, he published seven novels, each highly adventurous in form. *Travelling People* (1963) is a lightweight novel of comic misadventures, each chapter written in a different style; *Albert Angelo* (1964) vividly evokes the London of its era, and has holes cut through the pages to provide a 'flashforward' to future events. *Trawl* (1967) and *The Unfortunates* (1969) are autobiographical pieces, the latter consisting of unbound sections presented in a box. (See INTERACTIVE FICTION.) *House Mother Normal* (1971), *Christie Malry's Own Double Entry* (1973), and *See the Old Lady Decently* (1975) continue his passionate crusade against realism. Johnson's work has an emotional candour and directness unusual in a so-called 'experimental' writer; the same qualities are to be found in his two volumes of poetry. He committed suicide at the age of 40. See *Like a Fiery Elephant* (2004) by J. *Coe.

JOHNSON, Charles (1679–1748), dramatist, the author of 18 plays, including *The Wife's Relief* (1712), adapted from Shirley's *The Gamester, and The Country Lasses (1715), his most successful comedy. He was ridiculed by Pope in the early version of *The Dunciad for the fatness of his person, his prolific output, and his plagiaries.

JOHNSON, Diane (1934–), American novelist and biographer, born in Illinois and educated at the universities of Utah and California. Her ironic and observant novels, many of which have a hint of thriller suspense, include *Fair Game* (1965); *The Shadow Knows* (1972), about a woman pursued and victimized; *Persian Nights* (1987), set in Persia on the eve of revolution, seen through the eyes of an innocent American abroad; *Health and Happiness* (1990), a chilling tale of medical misadventure set in San Francisco; and *Le Divorce* (1997), *Le Mariage* (2000) and *L'Affaire* (2003), a Jamesian trilogy of manners set in Paris. She has also written an innovative feminist life of Mary Ellen Peacock, wife of G. *Meredith (*Lesser Lives*, 1972) and a life of D. *Hammett (1983).

JOHNSON, Joseph (1738–1809), a radical bookseller and publisher of St Paul's Churchyard, who encouraged and published many writers, including *Wordsworth (*Descriptive Sketches*, 1793), *Cowper, E. *Darwin, and M. *Wollstonecraft. He held literary dinners over the shop, where his guests included *Blake, *Fuseli, *Godwin, J. *Priestley, and *Paine. From 1788 to 1799 he published the scientific and literary monthly the *Analytical Review. Although his shop served as an important meeting place, he himself had the reputation of a retiring and self-effacing man.

Johnson, The Life of Samuel, by *Boswell, published 1791.

Boswell informed Dr *Johnson in 1772 of his intention to write his life, and had been collecting materials for this purpose since their first meeting in 1763. After Johnson's death in 1784 he set to work arranging and adding to the 'prodigious multiplicity of materials', a task which, he writes in 1789, involved him in great labour, perplexity, and vexation. The result was the most celebrated biography in the English language. Boswell learned much from his master's own love of the art of biography, and brought to the task boundless curiosity, persistence, and zest. His portrait is vivid and intimate, in his own words a 'Flemish picture' made up of trifling incidents as well as significant events, and Boswell's skill in stage-managing encounters (as with *Wilkes or, in contrast, Johnson's old fellow collegian, the modest Mr Edwards) adds greatly to the liveliness of the whole. The final edition, after Boswell's death, was revised by *Malone, who assisted Boswell considerably in his biographical labours. The standard edition (G. B. *Hill, 6 vols, 1887) has been revised by L. F. Powell (1934–50; 1964). See also *The Correspondence and Other Papers of James Boswell: Relating to the Making of the Life of Johnson*, ed. M. Waingrow (2 vols., 1969) and *James Boswell's Life of Johnson: An Edition of the Original Manuscript*, ed. M. Waingrow and B. Redford, 2 vols (1994–). (See also BIOGRAPHY.)

JOHNSON, Linton Kwesi (1952–), poet, performer, and reggae artist, born in Jamaica. He came to England in 1963 to join his mother who had emigrated two years earlier, went to school in south London, and studied sociology at Goldsmith's College. *Dread Beat an' Blood* (1975), his first album, introduced his characteristic voice of disaffected dissent, with bleak and powerful lyrics. In 1977 he was writer in residence in the London borough of Lambeth. Later volumes of verse and albums include *Forces of Victory* (1979), *Bass Culture* (1980), *Inglan Is a Bitch* (1980), and *Making History* (1984). His work (*Tings an' Times*, CD, 1991, and *More Time*, CD, 1998, with its haunting single 'Liesense Fi Kill') continues to show a strong political commitment to the cause of black rights.

JOHNSON, Lionel Pigot (1867–1902), educated at Winchester and New College, Oxford. He became an influential man of letters, and one of the notable Catholic converts of his day. A perceptive supporter of *Hardy, his *The Art of Thomas Hardy* (1894) was one of the first full-length studies to appear. His *Poems* appeared in 1895, *Ireland and Other Poems* in 1897, and *Post Liminium*, a posthumous collection of essays, in 1911. He was a member of the *Rhymers Club and a friend of *Yeats, who much admired his poetry; there is an account of his personality and decline into alcoholism in Yeats's *Autobiographies*. See also ART FOR ART'S SAKE.

JOHNSON, Pamela Hansford (1912–81), critic and novelist, the granddaughter of H. *Irving's treasurer, brought up in Clapham, a district evoked in several of her many works, from her first novel, *This Bed Thy Centre* (1935), to her last, *The Bonfire* (1981). In 1950 she married C. P. *Snow. She is perhaps most widely known for her comic 'Dorothy Merlin' trilogy, a satire on the pretensions of literary life, which consists of *The Unspeakable Skipton* (1959), *Night and Silence, Who Is Here* (1962), and *Cork Street, Next to the Hatter's* (1965).

JOHNSON, Paul (Bede) (1928–), journalist and historian, educated at Magdalen College, Oxford. He was editor of the *New Statesman from 1965 to 1970, since which period his political views have moved to the independent right. His publications include *Merrie England* (1964, a novel); *The Offshore Islanders* (1972); *Elizabeth I* (1974); *Pope John XXIII* (1975); and his idiosyncratic and polemic *A History of the Modern World*, from 1917 to the 1980s (1983). *A History of the American People* appeared in 1997.

JOHNSON, Richard (1573–?1659), the author of *The Most Famous History of the Seaven Champions of Christendome* (1596–7), a widely read romance of chivalric legend, which influenced *Spenser; *The Nine Worthies of London* (1592); *The Crowne-Garland of Golden Roses* (ballads, 1612, repr. by the *Percy Society); *Tom a Lincolne*, a romance of Arthurian times dating from 1599, of which the earliest surviving edition is 1631; and *Pleasant Conceites of Old Hobson* (1607, repr. 1843).

JOHNSON, Samuel (1709–84), born at Lichfield of elderly parents; his father was a bookseller. When 3 years old he was brought to London to be touched for the king's evil (scrofula) by Queen Anne; the illness seriously affected his sight, but he was from an early age an avid reader. He was educated at Lichfield Grammar School and Pembroke College, Oxford, where he spent 14 months, 1728–9, but took no degree, despite evidence of creative and scholastic powers; his college days were marred by poverty, and during the scantily documented period between leaving Oxford and his father's death in 1731 he appears to have suffered acute mental stress; bouts of melancholia were to recur in later life and gave him much sympathy with those similarly afflicted, such as W. *Collins and *Smart. He worked briefly and unhappily as an undermaster at Market Bosworth, then moved to Birmingham, where he contributed essays (none of which survive) to the *Birmingham Journal*, and translated and abridged from the French an account (originally in Portuguese) of Father Lobo's *Voyage to Abyssinia*; his version appeared anonymously in 1735. In the same year he married Mrs Elizabeth Porter, a widow considerably older than himself, and started a private school at Edial, near Lichfield. This was not a success; Johnson's lack of a degree and convulsive mannerisms hindered his prospects as a teacher, and in 1737 he set off with one of his few pupils, *Garrick, to try his fortune in London, where his wife shortly joined him. He entered the service of Edward Cave (whom he had already approached in Birmingham), the founder of the *Gentleman's Magazine*, to which he contributed regularly for years; he did editorial work and prefaces, and wrote essays, poems, Latin verses, biographies, and, most notably, his *Parliamentary Debates*, which were widely accepted as authentic speeches by the great politicians of the day. In 1738 he published his poem *London*, which may record his friendship with the poet *Savage, whose nocturnal wanderings he often shared during this period of poverty and hackwork; his *Life of Mr Richard Savage* (1744) is a vivid evocation of *Grub Street and a notable stage in the evolution of the art of biography. It was subsequently included in his *The Lives of the English Poets*. In 1747 he issued the 'Plan' of his Dictionary (see JOHNSON'S DICTIONARY), on which he had already started work at his new home in Gough Square; he dedicated it to *Chesterfield, with results recorded under the latter's name. In 1749 he published *The Vanity of Human Wishes*, the first work to bear his own name, and in the same year Garrick produced his tragedy *Irene*, written

in 1736 at Edial; it brought him almost £300. In 1750 he started the *Rambler*, a periodical written almost entirely by himself, partly for money and partly for 'relief' from the *Dictionary*. His wife died in 1752, a loss which caused him great and prolonged grief, bequeathing to his care her blind friend Anna Williams, who became an inmate of his home; another dependant was Robert Levet, an obscure physician and friend of the poor, on whose death in 1783 Johnson was to write the elegy beginning 'Condemned to hope's delusive mine'. From Mar. 1753 to Mar. 1754 Johnson contributed regularly to *Hawkesworth's *Adventurer*; in 1754 his biography of his old employer Cave appeared in the *Gentleman's Magazine*. His *Dictionary* was published in 1755, after nine years of labour; it firmly established his reputation, and also brought him, just before publication and through the support of Francis Wise and T. *Warton, the Oxford degree he had failed to achieve earlier. He continued to write essays, reviews, and political articles for various periodicals, and during 1758–60 contributed the *Idler* series of papers to the *Universal Chronicle*. In 1759 appeared *Rasselas, Prince of Abyssinia*. In 1762 Johnson was relieved of much of the drudgery of hack-work by the receipt of a crown pension of £300 a year, and the following year he met his biographer, *Boswell, in the bookshop of his friend T. *Davies.

From this period onwards we have Boswell's account of Johnson's life as one of the most eminent literary figures of his day, and also vivid portraits of his contemporaries, notably of the members of the *Club (later known as the 'Literary Club'), founded in 1764. These include *Reynolds, *Burke, and *Goldsmith; Garrick, C. J. *Fox, *Gibbon, and Boswell were later added. Although Johnson himself was a fervent Tory, it is interesting to note that he was on friendly and intimate terms with several well-known Whigs. In Jan. 1765 he met the *Thrales, in whose town and country houses he found much comfort and companionship. Later that year appeared his edition of Shakespeare, on which he had been at work for some years; in the last months he received help from *Steevens. Although superseded by later scholarship, it contained valuable notes and emendations, and its preface is regarded as one of his finest works of critical prose. In 1773 he travelled with Boswell to Scotland and the Hebrides, a journey recorded in his *A Journey to the Western Islands of Scotland* (1775) and Boswell's *Journal of a Tour to the Hebrides* (1785); in 1774 he visited north Wales with the Thrales, and in 1775 went with them to Paris, his only visit to the Continent. In 1777 he undertook, at the request of a number of booksellers, to write *The Lives of the English Poets*, the crowning work of his old age (1779–81). In 1784, saddened by the deaths of Levet and Thrale and by his estrangement from Mrs Thrale, he died at his house in Bolt Court and was buried in Westminster Abbey.

Johnson's reputation rests not only on his works but also on Boswell's evocation of his brilliant conversation, his eccentricities and opinionated outbursts (against Scots, Whigs, Americans, players, etc.), his interest in the supernatural (see COCK LANE GHOST), his generosity and humanity, and many other aspects of his large personality. His profound but melancholy religious faith is revealed also in his diaries and meditations, and in his attacks on the facile optimism of mid-18th-cent. thought (see JENYNS, S.). Two useful accounts appeared before Boswell's: *Anecdotes of the Late Samuel Johnson* (1786) by Mrs Piozzi, formerly Mrs Thrale, and a life by Sir John *Hawkins (1787). For a 20th-cent. assessment of Johnson, see T. S. *Eliot's essay 'Johnson as Critic and Poet' (1944).

Johnson's other works include: *Marmor Norfolciense* (1739), an ironical political pamphlet attacking Robert *Walpole; *The Compleat Vindication of the Licensers of the Stage* (1739), an ironic 'defence' of the Stage Licensing Act of 1737 by which Walpole's government in 1739 banned H. *Brooke's *Gustavus Vasa*; his work with *Oldys in 1743–4 on the *Harleian Miscellany*; *Miscellaneous Observations on the Tragedy of Macbeth* (1745), praised by *Warburton; 'The Vision of Theodore, Hermit of Teneriffe', contributed in 1748 to *Dodsley's *The Preceptor*, an allegory about the power of habit, which he described to *Percy, somewhat misleadingly, as the best thing he ever wrote; a dedication to C. Lennox's *The Female Quixote* and many other prologues, dedications, etc.; and four political pamphlets, *The False Alarm* (1770), against *Wilkes; *Thoughts . . . Respecting Falkland's Islands* (1771); *The Patriot* (1774); and *Taxation No Tyranny* (1775), on the question of American taxation and representation: Johnson supported taxation as warmly as he opposed slavery. His remarkable *Prayers and Meditations* were published in 1785, his diaries of his visits to Wales and France in 1816. His correspondence was edited by R. W. Chapman (3 vols, 1952) and the Yale edition of his works (vol. i, 1958–vol. xv, 1985, continuing) is under the editorship of A. T. Hazen and J. H. Middendorf. There are biographies by J. *Wain (1974) and W. J. Bate (1978).

JOHNSON, Terry (1955–), playwright and theatre director, born in Middlesex and educated in Birmingham. *Insignificance* (1982), like much of his later work, is peopled with real characters: the play evokes a (fictional) meeting between Marilyn Monroe, Albert Einstein, Joe DiMaggio, and Senator McCarthy in a New York hotel room in 1953. This was followed in 1984 by *Unsuitable for Adults*, the first of his trilogy of plays examining the relationship between the British and their comic icons. The serious questions raised by these plays are belied by the comedy, which often extends to pure slapstick or farce. In *Hysteria* (1993), *Freud and *Dali are among the characters thrown together, as the latter appears in the London consulting-room of the former, in what turns out to be a nightmarish reincarnation of a Freudian case history. Johnson continued his sequence on British comedy

with *Dead Funny* (1994), and completed it in 1998 with *Cleo, Camping, Emmanuelle and Dick*, a behind-the-scenes look at the making of four 'Carry On' films. He has directed extensively at the *Royal Court Theatre and the Bristol Old Vic, and has directed much of his own work at the *National Theatre, including his version of *London Cuckolds* (1998). His other plays include *Cries from the Mammal House* (1984) and *Imagine Drowning* (1991).

'Johnson's Dictionary', *A Dictionary of the English Language*, by S. *Johnson, published 1755.

Johnson entered into an agreement in 1746 with *Dodsley and others to write a dictionary, the first of its kind in English, and started work with six humble assistants in newly rented premises in Gough Square. A 'Plan' and dedication to *Chesterfield followed in 1747. Johnson said his object was to produce 'a dictionary by which the pronunciation of our language may be fixed, and its attainment facilitated; by which its purity may be preserved, its use ascertained, and its duration lengthened'. He wrote the definitions of over 40,000 words, illustrating them with about 114,000 quotations drawn from every field of learning and literature from the time of *Sidney onwards; his derivations suffer from the scantiness of etymological knowledge in his day, but the work as a whole remained without rival until the creation of the *Oxford English Dictionary. Five editions were published in his own lifetime. His well-known playful definitions (e.g. *lexicographer*, 'a writer of dictionaries, a harmless drudge') represent a mere handful in the body of this enormous achievement. (See also DICTIONARY.)

JOHNSTON, (William) Denis (1901–84), playwright, critic, director of the Dublin Gate Theatre, and mystical philosopher. He is best known for his plays, which include *The Old Lady Says 'No!'* (1929), *The Moon in the Yellow River* (1931), *A Bride for the Unicorn* (1933), his adaptation of *Toller's *Die blinde Göttin* as *Blind Man's Buff* (1936), and *The Scythe and the Sunset* (1958). He wrote many plays for radio and television, and his non-dramatic writings include *In Search of Swift* (1959) and *The Brazen Horn* (1976).

JOHNSTON, Jennifer (1930–), Irish novelist, daughter of playwright Denis *Johnston, born in Dublin; her novels have explored in spare and lyrical prose the troubled legacy of Irish history, its *Troubles, its divided loyalties, and its land- and seascapes. She moved to Derry in Northern Ireland in the 1970s. Her works include *The Gates* (1973), a poignant elegiac description of young Minnie MacMahon's return from schooling in England to her decaying family home, her failing alcoholic uncle, and confrontations with the past and a restless young local admirer. Other titles include *Shadows on Our Skin* (1977), a sensitive coming-of-age novel set in Derry which explores sectarian imperatives; *The Old Jest* (1979); and *The*

Railway Station Man (1984), which is the story of middle-aged violently widowed Helen, who retreats to the north-west coast of Ireland to paint, and falls in love there with another semi-recluse, a wounded English war-hero. The heroine of *The Invisible Worm* (1991) is trapped childless in a sterile marriage and a large house by the sea; *Two Moons* (1998) is a three-generation three-women novel of retrospect, love, and ageing, in which the central figure, actress Helen, is appearing as Gertrude in *Hamlet* at the *Abbey Theatre in Dublin.

JOHNSTONE, Charles (?1719–1800). He was educated in Dublin and became a lawyer. He travelled in 1782 to Calcutta, where he remained as a journalist and later as a prosperous newspaper proprietor. His best-known work is *Chrysal, or The Adventures of a Guinea* (1760–5). 'Chrysal' is the articulate spirit of gold in the guinea, whose progress from hand to hand, through some six different countries, serves to link various inventive and satirical episodes, including a section on the Hell-Fire Club at *Medmenham Abbey. Various characters, good and bad, from high life and low (many of whom were libellously identified with characters of the day), covet and become corrupted by the golden coin. *The History of Arsaces, Prince of Betlis* (1774) is an *Oriental tale, in which thinly disguised comment on the struggle between Great Britain and its American colonies leans strongly towards sympathy with the latter. *The Pilgrim* followed in 1775 and *John Juniper* in 1781.

JOLLEY, Elizabeth (1923–), Australian novelist, poet, and playwright, born in Birmingham. She moved to Western Australia in 1959 with her family. Her first book was not published until 1976, but since then she has produced three short story collections, 11 novels, two non-fiction works, and several radio plays. Her writing is characterized by a recurring sense of alienation and displacement, its source revealed in the semi-autobiographical trilogy *My Father's Moon* (1989), *Cabin Fever* (1990), and *George's Wife* (1993). Here as in other novels the tone is one of deep sadness, the protagonist, Vera, intensely lonely, and the structure is musical, employing repetitions, recurring moods and images to build a resonant symbolism. Many of her earlier novels combine dark comedy, often centred on eccentricity and bizarre behaviour in characters who are invariably outsiders, with Gothic plots and surprises.

'Jolly Beggars, The', a poem by *Burns, written 1786. A company of vagrants meet and carouse, with their female companions, in an alehouse kept by Poosie Nancy, in Burns's parish of Mauchline. A maimed soldier, his girl, a strolling player, a thief, a fiddler, and a ballad singer each sing a song in character, and the songs are connected by descriptions of the various rogues. Burns thought poorly of the work and it was not printed in his lifetime. However, both *Carlyle and M. *Arnold regarded it as the most original of his works.

Jonathan Wild the Great, The Life of, a short novel by H. *Fielding, published as the third volume of his *Miscellanies*, 1743, based on the life of a notorious thief-taker, Jonathan *Wild.

It is a satire on the figure of the 'Great Man', in low life or in high, who is held up to our admiration for his clever practice of avarice, corruption, and cruelty, which so often achieve success at the expense of the simple and the good. Fielding's hatred of hypocrisy here finds its most mordant expression. The quality Wild most values in himself and in others is 'that of hypocrisy'. His own position as the Great Man among thieves, cheats, and bullies is constantly compared, directly and by implication, with that of the Great Man among public figures of power (with Sir Robert *Walpole as a particular target), whose palaces are no more than 'Newgate with the mask on'. The name and something of the history of Jonathan Wild are borrowed from a thief and thief-taker who was hanged in 1725. The life of Fielding's Wild is traced from his birth to his death on the gallows, through a series of episodes involving thieves, highwaymen, whores, cheats, murderers, and the corrupt and brutal officers of Newgate.

As a young man Wild enters a career of professional crime under the direction of the corrupt Mr Snap, a sheriff's officer, thief-taker, and receiver of stolen goods, whose shrewish daughter Wild eventually marries. After becoming an expert pickpocket Wild organizes a gang of thieves, whose goods he receives and sells at huge profit to himself. Fireblood, Blueskin, Count la Ruse, and his own unfeeling daughters Tishy and Doshy are a few of the people he dominates and whose criminal activities he directs. He begins to live in style, dressing finely as a gentleman, and cunningly keeping himself beyond the reach of the law. If one of his men defies him, as Blueskin does, Wild denounces him and sees him hanged. He determines to ensnare an old schoolfellow, Heartfree, an innocent and gullible jeweller, who lives happily with his wife and children and his amiable apprentice Friendly. He arranges that Heartfree shall be robbed, then ensures that he is imprisoned as a bankrupt. Once the Heartfrees are ruined, Wild plans for the attractive and innocent Mrs Heartfree to become entangled in the underworld of vice, and has her abducted to Holland. Heartfree escapes Wild's malevolence, only to be implicated by Wild in a robbery, which means he is convicted and likely to be hanged. Only at this point, when he has apparently entirely destroyed the Heartfrees, does Wild feel a glimmer of remorse. By this time his embittered gang are turning on him, and eventually, in a foolish confusion over a piece of lace, he is committed to Newgate. Heartfree is pardoned and his wife returns unharmed, but Wild is condemned and meets his end with the same bravura with which he has lived his destructive life.

JONES, David Michael (1895–1974), poet and artist, born in Kent; his Welsh father gave him his strong sense of identity with Wales, although he lived there only from 1924 to 1927. After art school he served in the trenches throughout the First World War, an experience which produced one of his major works and left him with a lifelong interest in warfare and soldiers. In 1921 he became a Roman Catholic and in 1922 began a long association with *Gill. He preferred that his work in engraving, watercolour, and drawing should be intimately combined with his own writing, or the writing of others. The Welsh *Mabinogion*, the *'matter of Britain' (centring on King *Arthur), and the Bible provided much of the material and the background for his poetry. In 1927 he began *In Parenthesis*, an epic work of mixed poetry and prose on the subject of the war, which was published in 1937. The personal story and terrible sufferings of Private John Ball are related to the long history of war, and embedded in Welsh legend and the work of *Malory. A few, including T. S. *Eliot and H. *Read, admired it greatly. In 1952 Jones published *The Anathemata*, a long, complex work of poetry and prose, part chronicle, part incantation, celebrating in richly allusive language the ancient 'matter of Britain'. The small circle of admirers, including K. *Raine and E. *Muir, grew considerably. *The Sleeping Lord* (1974) is a collection of complete fragments of a projected work centred on the Crucifixion, and the lives of Roman soldiers at the time. Jones received the CH in 1974. *The Dying Gaul*, a selection of his writing, was published posthumously in 1978. There is a life by D. Blamires (1971).

JONES, Glyn (1905–95), Welsh poet, short story writer, and novelist, born in Merthyr Tydfil, Glamorgan, which he made the setting for many of his stories and novels. He drew on his experience of teaching at primary schools in Cardiff in writing *The Dream of Jake Hopkins* (1944), a long poem for radio, and *The Learning Lark* (1960), which pillories the widespread corruption in teaching appointments in south Wales. His *Collected Poems* (ed. Meic Stephens) appeared in 1996 and his volumes of short stories *The Blue Bed* (1937), *The Water Music* (1944), and *Welsh Heirs* (1977) were edited by Tony Brown and published as *Collected Short Stories* in 1998. His novels are *The Valley, the City, the Village* (1956) and *The Island of Apples* (1965; new edn with an introduction by Belinda Humfrey, 1992). His semi-autobiographical book *The Dragon Has Two Tongues* (1968) is a seminal account of Welsh writing in English, and a valuable memoir of the many writers he knew. *A People's Poetry* is a selection of Welsh harpstanzas in English translation.

JONES, Gwyn (1907–99), Welsh short story writer, novelist, and Viking scholar, born in New Tredagar, Monmouthshire, a collier's son. From 1939 to 1948 he was editor of the *Welsh Review*. He was professor of English at the University of Wales, Aberystwyth (1940–64), and at University College, Cardiff (1954–75). Of his many works of scholarship, *A History of the Vikings* brought him international acclaim. His most important novels are *Richard Savage* (1935), *Times Like These* (1936), *A Garland of Bays* (1938), and *The Flowers beneath the Scythe* (1952). His *Selected Short Stories* appeared in 1974 and his *Collected Stories* in 1997. With his colleague Thomas Jones he translated the *Mabinogion*, first published by the Golden Cockerel Press in 1948 (new edn Everyman, 1993). He also edited a number of anthologies including *The Oxford Book of Welsh Verse in English* (1977).

JONES, Henry Arthur (1851–1929). He left school at 12, and worked as a draper's assistant and warehouseman before his first play was produced in 1878. His first London production, in 1882, was *The Silver King*, which met with instant success. A friend and contemporary of *Pinero, Jones also was a prolific playwright, who did much to re-establish serious themes in the theatre. As a young man he was greatly encouraged by G. B. *Shaw and *Beerbohm. Although he wrote many comedies (including *The Liars*, 1897; *Dolly Reforming Herself*, 1908; *Mary Goes First*, 1913), his most influential plays treated social themes, often the double standards of behaviour expected of men and of women; *The Dancing Girl* (1891), *The Case of Rebellious Susan* (1894), *Mrs Dane's Defence* (1900), and *The Lie* (1923) were considered among the most effective. *Archer judged Jones the most popular playwright of the 1890s, but his popularity, like that of Pinero, faded. As well as writing plays, pamphleteering, lecturing, and managing a theatre, Jones fought for the abolition of censorship, for the publication of plays, and for a new dignity for the theatre.

JONES, Inigo (1573–1652), architect, stage designer, painter, mathematician, and man of letters, whose depth of knowledge of Roman and Italian art and of Renaissance theory was new in England, and whose revolutionary buildings brought the classical style to this country. Little is known of his early career; he travelled abroad some time between 1598 and 1604, and again in 1613–14, when he developed a deep admiration for *Palladio, met Scamozzi, and copied ancient Roman monuments. In 1615 he became surveyor of the King's Works; his most famous buildings are the Queen's House, Greenwich (1616–18 and 1629–35), and the Banqueting Hall, Whitehall (1619–22), both lucid, classic, harmonious buildings with crisp detail which mark a turning point in English architecture. Jones's career as a designer of *masques opened in 1605, and many of his drawings for costume and scenery—influenced by his European counterparts, among them Buontalenti and Callot—survive. A stormy but fruitful collaboration with *Jonson began in 1605 with *The Masque of Blacknesse*, and lasted until 1630/1; their quarrel about the rival claims of the visual arts and literature was also long standing, and became notorious. Later Jones worked with other poets, producing with T. *Carew, in *Coelum Britannicum* (1634), perhaps the most brilliant of later Caroline masques. Jones's fame in England soared between 1710 and 1760, when, with Palladio, he became one of the heroes of the Palladian movement, revered by Lord Burlington and *Pope. Many of his designs were published in two folio volumes, edited by William Kent (1727). See *Inigo Jones: The Theatre of the Stuart Court* (1973) by S. Orgel and R. Strong.

JONES, Russell Celyn (1955–), Welsh writer, born in London and raised in Swansea. His novels include *Soldiers and Innocents* (1990), about an army officer who goes on the run with his child; *Small Times* (1992) which charts a romance between a petty thief and an actress; *An Interference of Light* (1995), describing a homosexual affair in a Welsh mining community; *The Eros Hunter* (1998), a *policier* set in contemporary London; and *Ten Seconds from the Sun* (2005), about a child killer living a morally resurrected life under a new identity. His work is notable for its pungent laconic prose and rueful investigation of masculine values, with an emphasis on fathers and sons.

JONES, Sir William (1746–94), a distinguished orientalist and brilliant jurist, and a friend of Dr *Johnson, *Gibbon, and *Burke. He was judge of the high court at Calcutta from 1783 till his death. A master of Sanskrit and a pioneer in the science of comparative philology, he did much to make Indian literature and learning known in Europe, and is remembered for his translations (including *The Moâllakát*, 1782, from the Arabic, and *Sacontala, or The Fatal Ring: An Indian Drama*, 1789), and for the well-known 'A Persian Song of Hafez' (*Poems Consisting Chiefly of Translations from the Asiatic Languages*, 1772). He had considerable influence on the Oriental themes of the Romantic poets such as *Byron, *Southey, and T. *Moore. His collected works were edited by Lord Teignmouth (6 vols, 1799) and his letters by G. H. Cannon (2 vols, 1970). There is a life, *Oriental Jones*, by G. H. Cannon (1964).

JONSON, Ben(jamin) (1572/3–1637), dramatist, poet, scholar, and writer of court *masques. He was of Border descent, but was born in or near London, the posthumous son of a clergyman. He was educated at Westminster School under *Camden. During the early 1590s he worked as a bricklayer in his stepfather's employ, saw military service in Flanders, where he killed an enemy champion in single combat, and joined a strolling company of players for whom he acted the part of Hieronimo in *The Spanish Tragedy*, a play for which he wrote additional scenes in 1601–2. In 1597 he began to work for *Henslowe's companies as player and playwright, and was imprisoned for his share in *The Isle of Dogs*, a satire now lost 'containing very seditious and slandrous matter' (see SWAN THEATRE). In 1598 he killed a fellow actor in a duel, but escaped hanging by pleading benefit of clergy, being branded instead as a felon. He became a Roman Catholic during imprisonment, but returned to Anglicanism 12 years later. His first important play, *Every Man in His Humour*, with Shakespeare in the cast, was performed by the Lord Chamberlain's Company at the Curtain in 1598, and *Every Man out of His Humour* at the Globe in 1599. *Cynthia's Revels* (1600) and *Poetaster* (1600–1, attacking *Dekker and *Marston) were performed by the Children of the Queen's Chapel. His first extant tragedy, *Sejanus*, was given at the Globe by Shakespeare's company, 1603; his first court masque, *The Masque of Blackness*, written to accommodate Queen Anne's desire to appear as a Negress, was given on Twelfth Night, 1605. In that year he was imprisoned, and in danger of having his nose and ears slit, for his share in *Eastward Hoe*, and gave evidence to the Privy Council concerning the Gunpowder Plot. Then followed the period of his major plays: *Volpone, acted at both the Globe and the two universities, 1605–6; *Epicene, or The Silent Woman*, 1609–10; *The Alchemist*, 1610; and *Bartholomew Fair*, 1614. In 1612–13 he was in France as tutor to *Ralegh's son, and in 1618–19 journeyed on foot to Scotland, where he stayed with *Drummond of Hawthornden, who recorded their conversation.

Though not formally appointed the first *poet laureate, the essentials of the position were conferred on Jonson in 1616, when a pension was granted to him by James I. In the same year he published a folio edition of his *Works*, which raised the drama to a new level of literary respectability, received an honorary MA from the Oxford University, and about this date became lecturer in rhetoric at Gresham College in London. He was elected chronologer of London in 1628. After *The Devil Is an Ass* (1616), he abandoned the public stage for ten years, and his later plays, *The Staple of News* (1626), *The New Inn* (1629), *The Magnetic Lady* (1631), and *A Tale of a Tub* (1633), show a relatively unsuccessful reliance on allegory and symbolism; *Dryden called them his 'dotages'. From 1605 onwards Jonson was constantly producing masques for the court, with scenery by I. *Jones. This form of entertainment reached its highest elaboration in Jonson's hands. He introduced into it the 'antimasque', an antithetical, usually disorderly, prelude to the main action which served to highlight by contrast the central theme of political and social harmony. There are examples of this in *The Masque of Queens* (1609), *Love Restored* (1612), *Mercury Vindicated from the Alchemists at Court* (1616), *Pleasure Reconciled to Virtue* (1618, which gave Milton his idea for *Comus), and *Neptune's Triumph for the Return of Albion* (1624). After *Chloridia* (1631), his collaboration with Jones ended with a famous quarrel, which Jonson treated in several vituperative poems, concerning the relative priority of verbal and thematic content and spectacle. His last masques were produced in 1633–4. His non-dramatic verse includes *Epigrammes* and *The Forest*, printed in the folio of 1616: notable among his epigrams are two tender and moving epitaphs, Nos xxii and xlv, 'On My First Daughter' (*c*.1595) and 'On His First Sonne' (1603) ('Farewell, thou child of my right hand, and joy'). *The Underwood* and a translation of *Horace's *Ars Poetica* were printed in 1640. His chief prose works are *The English Grammar* and *Timber, or Discoveries*, printed in 1640.

During the reign of James I Jonson's literary prestige and influence were unrivalled. He presided over a literary circle which met at the *Mermaid Tavern, and later in the Apollo Room of the Devil and St Dunstan Tavern, where his *leges convivales* or 'social rules' were inscribed over the mantelpiece. His friends included Shakespeare, whom he loved 'on this side idolatry', *Donne, F. *Bacon, George *Chapman, *Beaumont, *Fletcher, *Cotton, and *Selden, and among the younger writers (who styled themselves the 'sons' or 'tribe of Ben') R. *Brome, *Carew, *Cartwright, Sir K. *Digby, Lord *Falkland, *Herrick, Nabbes, *Randolph, and *Suckling. His chief patrons were the *Sidney family, the earl of Pembroke, the countess of Bedford, and the duke and duchess of Newcastle. Jonson suffered a stroke in 1628, after which he was perhaps permanently bedridden until his death in August 1637. He was buried in Westminster Abbey under a tombstone bearing the inscription 'O rare Ben Jonson', and celebrated in a collection of elegies entitled *Jonsonus Virbius* (1638). As a man Jonson was arrogant and quarrelsome, but fearless, warm-hearted, and intellectually honest. His reputation declined sharply from about 1700, as Shakespeare's, with whom he was inevitably compared, increased, but in this century it has revived, thanks partly to the comprehensive edition of C. H. Herford and P. and E. Simpson (11 vols, 1925–52), vols i and ii of which contain the standard biography.

JORDAN, Dorothy, née Phillips (1761–1816), actress, who made her first stage appearance in 1779 in Dublin under the name of Miss Francis. She came to England and adopted the name of Mrs Jordan, under which she appeared as Calista in *The Fair Penitent* at Leeds in 1782. She made her début at Drury Lane as Peggy in *Garrick's *The Country Girl* in 1785, and took many parts there, at the Haymarket, and at Covent Garden, Lady Teazle in *The School for Scandal* being one of her finest roles. Her last London performance was in 1814 and her final stage appearance at Margate in 1815. She was much praised by *Hazlitt, *Lamb, Leigh *Hunt, etc. She was for long mistress of the duke of Clarence (William IV), and bore him ten children. She went to France in 1815 and died at Saint- Cloud. There is a life by C. *Tomalin.

Jorkins, see SPENLOW AND JORKINS.

Jorrocks, Mr, see SURTEES, R. S.

JOSEPH, Jenny (1932–   ), poet, born in Birmingham and educated at St Hilda's College, Oxford. Her early poems were published by J. *Lehmann and her first collection, *The Unlooked-for Season*, appeared in 1960. This was followed by *Rose in the Afternoon* (1974) which contains her well-known poem 'Warning', about the joys of defying old age. Other collections include *The Thinking Heart* (1978), *Beyond Descartes* (1983), and *Ghosts and Other Company* (1932). She employs fable, dramatic monologue, and myth to illumine with unromantic precision a recognizable but not always comfortable everyday world.

Joseph Andrews, The History of the Adventures of, and of His Friend Mr Abraham Adams, a novel by H. *Fielding, published 1742.

In an important preface Fielding relates his book to classical forms; he describes it as a 'comic romance', and outlines his purpose in devising 'this kind of writing, which I do not remember to have seen hitherto attempted in our language'. His declared object is to defend what is good by displaying the Ridiculous, which he believes arises from Affectation, and ultimately from Vanity and Hypocrisy.

The work begins as a parody of Richardson's *Pamela*, with Joseph as Pamela's brother and 'Mr B.' appearing as young Booby. But it soon outgrows its origins in parody, and its deepest roots lie in *Cervantes and in *Marivaux. The son of the humble Gaffer and Gammer Andrews, Joseph becomes at 10 years old stable-boy to Sir Thomas Booby. His supposed sister Pamela lives at the home of young Squire Booby, nephew to Sir Thomas. Parson Adams, poor, learned, and innocently certain that everyone is as good as himself, takes an interest in the boy. Eventually Joseph falls in love with Fanny, a milkmaid, becomes footman to Sir Thomas and Lady Booby, and, together with Mrs Slipslop the chambermaid, attends them for their season in London. After Sir Thomas's death Lady Booby makes amorous advances to Joseph, and when he stoutly rejects them he is thrown out. He sets off on foot to return to the seat of the Boobys in Somerset. After he has been robbed and stripped naked he is taken to an inn kept by the Towwouses, where he encounters Parson Adams, now on his way to London in the hope of having his sermons published. However, finding he has forgotten to bring them, Adams turns back with Joseph towards Somerset. Adams rescues a girl from an attack in a wood, only to find that she is Fanny, on her way to look for Joseph, and both become embroiled in a farcical scene before a JP. The three travellers, Joseph, Fanny, and Adams, constantly in trouble and short of money, are on almost every occasion rescued by some fellow traveller equally poor, such as a poacher or a coachman; their application for assistance from the prosperous Parson Trulliber is sanctimoniously refused. When almost destitute they are given hospitality by Mr Wilson, a country gentleman who tells them the story of his life. This tale, with its recollections of poverty, the iniquities of London life, the vanities of the playhouse, and a brief scene of idyllic marriage, clearly echoes much of Fielding's own experience. Mr Wilson describes how his baby son was stolen by gypsies, and hopes to re-encounter Joseph and Adams when he is next in Somerset. After further adventures the party returns at last to Booby Hall, where Lady Booby, in a desperate attempt to secure Joseph, tries to have Fanny committed to Bridewell. Eventually both Fanny and Joseph are arraigned and convicted for cutting and bearing off a hazel twig. But Parson Adams calls their banns, young Squire Booby appears with Pamela, now his wife, and a series of events reveals that Joseph is the son of Wilson and Fanny is Pamela's sister. Joseph and Fanny are joyfully married, and Adams is given a handsome living.

The novel, a major innovation in form and style, was only moderately successful, and was considerably less popular than *Pamela* which it set out to mock. However, a few discerning critics, including E. *Carter, privately gave it high praise, and the greater success of *Tom Jones* in 1749 probably owed much to the establishment of the form in *Joseph Andrews*.

Joseph of Arimathea. For the legend of Joseph and the Holy Grail, see GRAIL and GLASTONBURY. According to fable, St Philip sent 12 disciples into Britain to preach Christianity, of whom Joseph of Arimathea was the leader. They founded at Glastonbury the first primitive church, which subsequently was developed into Glastonbury Abbey. Here Joseph was buried. His staff, planted in the ground, became the famous Glastonbury Thorn, which flowered at Christmas (*William of Malmesbury, *De Antiquitate Glastoniensis Ecclesiae*). The fullest version of the Joseph Grail story is Robert de *Boron's *Joseph d'Arimathie* (Burgundy, c.1200), for which see ch. 19 in R. S. Loomis (ed.), *Arthurian Literature in the Middle Ages* (1959), 251–62.

JOSEPHUS, Flavius (AD 37–c.98), a celebrated Jew, who proved his military abilities by supporting against Vespasian a siege of 47 days in a small town in Galilee. He obtained the esteem of Vespasian by foretelling that he would one day become ruler of the Roman Empire. He was present at the siege of Jerusalem by Titus, and received from the conqueror the gift of certain sacred books that it contained, besides an estate in Judaea. He came to Rome with Titus, was honoured with Roman citizenship, and devoted himself to study. He wrote in Greek a *History of the Jewish War* and *Jewish Antiquities*, which is a history of the Jews down to AD 66.

JOSIPOVICI, Gabriel (1940–   ), novelist, playwright, and critic, born in Nice, and educated at Victoria College, Cairo, and Oxford University. His critical works include *The World and the Book* (1971), in which he discusses writers ranging from *Rabelais to *Bellow; *The Lessons of Modernism* (1977); and an examination of the Bible, *The Book of God* (1988). His fiction is innovative and experimental, and includes *The Inventory* (1968), in which a man takes an inventory of the belongings of a dead man; *Words* (1971); *Migrations* (1977); *Moo Park* (1994); and *Now* (1998)

which consists almost entirely of dialogue. In *Steps: Selected Fiction and Drama* (1990) Josipovici states his interest in creating 'something impossible to imagine . . . which it might just be possible to make'.

Journal of a Disappointed Man, The, see CUMMINGS, B. F.

Journal of a Tour to the Hebrides, The, by *Boswell, published 1785. It is a narrative of the journey taken by Boswell and Dr *Johnson in Scotland and the Hebrides in 1773, recording Johnson's encounters with Boswell's family and eminent Scottish literati, including W. *Robertson, *Dalrymple, *Monboddo, and *Blacklock. It also describes Johnson's responses to Scottish landscape and traditions, his sceptical enquiries about Ossian (see MACPHERSON), and his remarkable physical fortitude. Boswell's manuscript, which Johnson and others read, was discovered at Malahide Castle with other private papers. There is a scholarly edition by F. A. Pottle and C. H. Bennett (1961). Boswell's manuscript journal reveals that he chose not to publish about a third of the material he wrote in the Hebrides.

Journal of a Voyage to Lisbon, The, a work by H. *Fielding, published posthumously 1755.

When he set out for Portugal in 1754, in the vain hope of recovering his health, Fielding was suffering so greatly from gout, dropsy, asthma, and other complications that he had to be carried aboard the *Queen of Portugal*. In his preface to the *Journal*, which he then began, he declares that he is once again attempting something that has not been done before, in that he proposes to write a work of travel which leaves out all fabulous adventures, monsters, and tedious detail. He writes of the daily events of the difficult voyage, the eccentricities of Captain Veal, the abuses suffered by the sailors, the devotion of his wife and daughter, the terror of storms, a sunset and moonrise at sea, and the details of his food and drink. The most personal and most painful of his works, the *Journal*, which he describes as 'possibly the production of the most disagreeable hours which ever haunted the author', reflects his shifting moods of stoicism, good humour, irritability, and the deep despondency of patience stretched beyond endurance. He described it as 'a novel without a Plot', and had prepared it for the press before he died in Lisbon in October. There is a fine edition edited by Tom Keymer (1996).

Journal of the Plague Year, A, see PLAGUE YEAR.

Journey from this World to the Next, A, the second volume of *Miscellanies* by H. *Fielding, published 1743.

The author purports to have found an almost indecipherable manuscript, consisting of a series of 'Epistles', which was left in an attic by someone now departed to the West Indies. The soul leaves the body in its lodgings in Cheapside and finds itself, guided by Mercury, in a stage-coach with other departing souls.

They pass through the City of Diseases and past the black marble Palace of Death, on to the Wheel of Fortune. At the door of Elysium Minos dictates who shall be permitted to enter; the generous and the honest are favoured, whatever their station, while the cruel and hypocritical are rejected. In the Elysian Fields heroes and writers of antiquity converse animatedly with Shakespeare, *Milton, *Dryden, *Addison, Fielding's own *Tom Thumb, and many others. The spirit of Julian the Apostate appears and, for the major part of the book, discourses in several guises as slave, Jew, courtier, and statesman. The tale (the last part of which, about Anne Boleyn, may have been by Sarah *Fielding) comes to a somewhat haphazard end with the excuse that the rest of the 'manuscript' has been unfortunately burned. It was edited by C. Rawson, 1973; the best text is found in *Miscellanies by Henry Fielding*, ed. Hugh Amory and Bertrand A. Goldgar (vol. ii, 1993).

Journey's End, see SHERRIFF.

Journey to London, The, see PROVOK'D HUSBAND, THE.

Journey to the Western Islands of Scotland, A, by Dr *Johnson, published 1775. It is a narrative of the tour undertaken by *Boswell and Johnson in 1773 in Scotland and the Hebrides. (For Boswell's account, see JOURNAL OF A TOUR TO THE HEBRIDES, THE.) It describes Johnson's response to Scottish history, culture, and landscape, and on publication aroused the wrath of *Macpherson because of its sceptical comments on the authenticity of 'Ossian'. Macpherson demanded, unsuccessfully, a cancellation or a revision, and received instead a letter from Johnson saying, 'What shall I retract? I thought your book an imposture from the beginning, I think it upon yet surer reasons an imposture still.'

Joviall Crew, A, or *The Merry Beggars*, a romantic comedy by R. *Brome, produced 1641.

Oldrents, a rich and kindly country squire, has been thrown into melancholy by a gypsy's prediction that his two daughters must be beggars. Springlove, an honest vagabond whom Oldrents has tried to reclaim to a settled life by making him his steward, is seized each spring with a desire to return to his wandering life, and rejoins a party of beggars, whom Oldrents from kindness of heart entertains in his barn. Oldrents's daughters, wearied by their father's melancholy, decide to join the beggars for a frolic, with their two lovers. They thus give effect to the gypsy's prediction, but their begging exposes them to unforeseen dangers. Meanwhile Justice Clack's niece has run away with the Justice's clerk, and they too fall in with the beggars. The search for the runaways, and the apprehension of the beggars, give occasion for exuberantly comic scenes, and all ends well.

The play, Brome's masterpiece, is highly original in its picture of Oldrents's compassion for the poor and Springlove's longing for a vagabond life and response to the call of the spring.

JOWETT, Benjamin (1817–93), one of the legendary figures of late Victorian Oxford, famed for his 'cherubic chirp', long silences, and occasional devastating rudeness. He was professor of Greek from 1855 and master of Balliol College from 1870. A Broad Churchman in the tradition of T. *Arnold, he outraged the Tractarians with the common sense of his *Epistles of Paul* (1855), came near to being charged with heresy before the vice-chancellor because of his contribution to *Essays and Reviews* (1860), and was successful in promoting the Act that abolished religious tests for university degrees (1871). His translations of *Plato (1871), *Thucydides (1881), and Aristotle's *Poetics* (1885), criticized by scholars, charmed the public. But he was primarily a teacher of genius. He held that the purpose of university education was the personal development of each student and hoped more particularly to form future statesmen. As Asquith, Milner, Grey, and *Curzon were among his pupils, he may be fairly regarded as a founding father of Edwardian England.

JOYCE, James Augustine Aloysius (1882–1941), novelist, born at Rathgar, Dublin, and educated at the Jesuit schools Clongowes Wood College and Belvedere College, and at University College, Dublin, where *Gogarty was a fellow student. A good linguist, from an early age he read and studied widely, and in 1901 wrote a letter of profound admiration in Dano-Norwegian to *Ibsen. Other early influences included *Hauptmann, *Dante, G. *Moore, and *Yeats; Yeats was to treat him with considerable personal kindness. Dissatisfied with the narrowness and bigotry of Irish Catholicism, as he saw it, Joyce went to Paris for a year in 1902, where he lived in poverty, wrote verse, and discovered Dujardin's novel *Les Lauriers sont coupés* (1888), which he was later to credit as the source of his own use of *interior monologue. He returned to Dublin for his mother's death, stayed briefly in the Martello tower of *Ulysses* with Gogarty, then left Ireland more or less for good with Nora Barnacle, the woman with whom he spent the rest of his life, and who bore him a son and a daughter. They lived at Trieste for some years, where Joyce taught English at the Berlitz school and made the acquaintance of *Svevo, whose writing he encouraged; they moved in 1915 to Zurich, and settled finally after the war in Paris. His first published work was a volume of verse, *Chamber Music* (1907), followed by *Dubliners* (1914), a volume of short stories published after great delays and difficulties, culminating in his final visit to Ireland in 1912, when the sheets were destroyed through the prospective publisher's fear of libel. When the stories at last appeared they were greeted with enthusiasm by *Pound, in a review in the *Egoist*. Pound's friendship and support greatly encouraged Joyce's career and reputation. Another important ally gained at this period was Harriet Shaw *Weaver, business manager and then editor of the *Egoist*, and a lifelong benefactress of Joyce. Difficulties also attended the performance and publication of Joyce's play *Exiles*: it was published in 1918 and staged unsuccessfully the same year in Munich, then first performed in London by the Stage Society in 1926 after years of hesitation. It was revived and directed by *Pinter in 1970. *A Portrait of the Artist as a Young Man*, a largely autobiographical work, was published serially in the *Egoist*, 1914–15 (part of a first draft, *Stephen Hero*, appeared in 1944). With strong backing from Yeats and Pound, Joyce received a grant from the *Royal Literary Fund in 1915, and shortly after a grant from the Civil List. Despite growing recognition, he continued to struggle against poverty, and also suffered from increasing eye trouble; a severe attack of glaucoma in 1917 led to years of pain and several operations. He was also much troubled in later years by his daughter's mental illness.

His famous novel *Ulysses* was first published in Paris on 2 Feb. 1922, his 40th birthday, and was received as a work of genius by writers as varied as T. S. *Eliot, *Hemingway, and Arnold *Bennett; others (*Claudel, V. *Woolf, G. *Stein) were less admiring. The first UK edition appeared in 1936. Another small volume of verse, *Pomes Penyeach*, appeared in 1927, and his second great work, *Finnegans Wake*, extracts of which had already appeared as 'Work in Progress', was published in its complete form in 1939. *Ulysses* and *Finnegans Wake* revolutionized the form and structure of the novel, decisively influenced the development of the 'stream of consciousness' or 'interior monologue' (see also RICHARDSON, D.), and pushed language and linguistic experiment (particularly in the latter work) to the extreme limits of communication. (See MODERNISM.) They have also produced a mass of critical commentary in many languages, covering Joyce's use of Homeric myth, puns, Catholicism, Irish folklore, Scholastic philosophy, etc. There is a full life by R. *Ellmann (1959, 2nd edn 1982).

JOYCE, Patrick Weston (1827–1914), author, among other works, of *Irish Names of Places* (1869–1913), *A Grammar of the Irish Language* (1878), *Old Celtic Romances* (1879, 1894, from which *Tennyson drew his 'Voyage of Maeldune'), and a *Social History of Ireland* (1903–20), all highly influential in the *Irish Revival. He also published *Irish Peasant Songs* (1906) and contributed folk songs to Petrie's *Ancient Music of Ireland*.

Joyous Gard, the castle of Launcelot in Arthurian legend. It is situated somewhere in the north, and *Malory says it has been variously identified as Alnwick or Bamburgh (near Berwick-on-Tweed). Tristram once keeps Isoud there for three years (see TRISTRAM AND ISOUD); after Launcelot has to surrender Guinevere it is renamed 'Dolorus Gard'.

Jubilate Agno, see SMART, C.

JUDD, Alan (1945–), novelist and biographer, born in Kent, who turned to writing after a varied career serving with the army in Northern Ireland, in the foreign office, and other less regular occupations. His first novel, *A Breed of Heroes* (1981), is set in Northern Ireland and shows the conflict from the point of view of Charles Thoroughgood, an innocent young graduate officer who becomes involved in the action. This was followed by *Short of Glory* (1988), set in Africa, and *The Noonday Devil* (1987), set in Oxford. *Tango* (1989) moves to an unnamed South American country, where its unheroic hero William, ostensibly running a loss-making British bookshop, is recruited as a spy and takes part in a coup. Judd published a life of Ford Madox *Ford in 1990.

Jude the Obscure, a novel by T. *Hardy, originally printed in abridged form in *Harper's New Monthly Magazine* (1894–5, as *Hearts Insurgent*), then in the 1895 edition of his works.

In the author's words, it is a story 'of a deadly war waged between flesh and spirit'. Jude Fawley, a young Wessex villager of exceptional intellectual promise, is encouraged by the schoolmaster Phillotson, and conceives the ambition of studying at Christminster (which represents Oxford). But he is trapped into marriage by the coarse, handsome barmaid Arabella Donn, who feigns pregnancy to win him, and shortly afterwards deserts him. He moves to Christminster, earning his living as a stonemason and continuing his studies, hoping one day to be admitted to the university, the vision of which still dominates him. He meets his cousin, Sue Bridehead, an unconventional, hypersensitive, *Swinburne-quoting young woman who works in a shop selling ecclesiastical ornaments: they fall in love, despite efforts on both sides to avoid one another, and Sue, in what appears to be a fit of desperate masochism, suddenly marries Phillotson, who had long been interested in her. She is driven from him by physical revulsion, and flies to Jude; they begin to live together in Christminster, but do not consummate their love until Arabella reappears on the scene. Jude, who had been planning to enter the priesthood as a licentiate, as a substitute for his thwarted intellectual ambitions, is now doubly defeated. He and Sue become free to marry, but Sue shrinks from the step, partly because of her apprehension that a conventional union will destroy love, and partly from a superstitious fear that the Fawley family is doomed to marry unhappily: she at one point compares the family to the house of Atreus, and Jude compares it to the house of Jeroboam, an interchange which reflects the theme of Hellenism and Hebraism prominent throughout the novel.

Under the pressure of poverty and social disapproval their relationship deteriorates, and tragedy overtakes them in the death of their children: the eldest, 'Old Father Time', son of Jude and Arabella, hangs the two babies and himself, leaving a note saying, 'Done because we are too menny.' In an agony of remorse and self-abasement, Sue returns to Phillotson and the Church, and Jude, deeply shocked by her abandoning of her freethinking principles, begins drinking heavily (a weakness to which he had always been susceptible) and is inveigled back by Arabella. He dies wretchedly, not yet 30, and his last words are: 'Wherefore is light given to him that is in misery, and life unto the bitter in soul?'

The novel caused an uproar, and the *Pall Mall Gazette set the tone by castigating it as 'dirt, drivel and damnation'; even Hardy's friend *Gosse found it 'grimy' and 'indecent'. Hardy describes in the preface to the 1912 edition how the work was 'burnt by a bishop—probably in his despair at not being able to burn me'. The reception of the book was no doubt one of the several reasons why Hardy wrote no more fiction.

Judith, a 350-line poem in Old English, fragmentary at the beginning, found in the *Beowulf manuscript (ASPR 4), probably dating from the late 9th cent. The poem tells the story of the Apocryphal Book of Judith, and the surviving sections (numbered in divisions x, xi, and xii, presumably preceded by the last part of ix) correspond to about the last quarter of the biblical book. It describes the banquet in the Assyrian camp, the bringing of Judith to the drunken Holofernes, her beheading of him and escape, and the defeat and flight of the Assyrians. The language of the poem is opulent and its battle description is celebrated; critical discussion of it has largely been confined to deliberations about what proportion of the original the surviving fragment. There is an edition by B. J. Timmer (1952).

Julia, the faithful lover of Proteus in Shakespeare's *The Two Gentlemen of Verona.

Julia, Donna, in Byron's *Don Juan, a lady of Seville, whose love for the hero is the first incident in his career.

Julia de Roubigné, a novel by H. *Mackenzie.

'Julian and Maddalo: A Conversation', a poem partly in dialogue form by P. B. *Shelley, written at Venice and Este in 1818, published 1824. It is the most naturalistic of Shelley's long poems, deliberately opposed to the 'idealism' of his dramas.

Julian (Shelley) and Count Maddalo (*Byron) ride and boat through 'bright Venice', discussing problems of free will, progress, and religious belief. They visit a 'Maniac', confined in elegant rooms in an island asylum in the Venetian lagoon, whose tortured and confused monologue shows how superficial their arguments have been. The Maniac, partly based on *Tasso and partly on Shelley himself, has suffered some profound 'wrong' in love. His presence, like the uncensored outpourings of the Freudian unconscious, deepens and darkens the terms of the debate: he provides 'the text of every heart'. A little child, based on Claire Clairmont's baby Allegra, is also introduced to show the powers of innocence and good: though the outcome of the 'conversation' is not entirely optimistic. This is one of Shelley's most subtle studies of human

affections and hopes. It is composed in fluent, almost chatty couplets, with marvellous evocations of the deserted Venetian lido and twinkling lagoon: 'I love all waste | And solitary places; where we taste | The pleasure of believing what we see | Is boundless, as we wish our souls to be.' It powerfully influenced Browning's *dramatic monologues.

JULIAN OF NORWICH (c.1342–after 1416), a recluse in a cell attached to the church of St Julian at Norwich. She wrote, 20 years after the events they describe, her Sixteen Revelations of Divine Love which describes visions revealed to her during her illness in 1373 and her reflections on them. She is well known now because of the quotation of a sentence from the Revelations in T. S. *Eliot's 'Little Gidding': 'Sin is Behovely, but | All shall be well, and | All manner of thing shall be well.' See Julian's Showings, Parts 1 and 2 (Short and Long Texts), ed. E. Colledge and J. Walsh (1978); P. Molinari, Julian of Norwich (1958, trans. C. Wolters, 1966).

Julie, the heroine of La Nouvelle Héloïse of *Rousseau, loved by Saint-Preux.

Juliet, (1) the heroine of Shakespeare's *Romeo and Juliet; (2) the lover of *Claudio in his *Measure for Measure.

Julius Caesar, a Roman tragedy by *Shakespeare, probably written and performed 1599, not printed until the First *Folio (1623). Its major source is *North's translation of *Plutarch's Lives. The play seems to have been a popular one.

It begins with the events of the year 44 BC, after Caesar, already endowed with the dictatorship, had returned to Rome from a successful campaign in Spain, and when there are fears that he will allow himself to be crowned king. Distrust of Caesar's ambition gives rise to a conspiracy against him among Roman lovers of freedom, notably Cassius and Casca; they win over to their cause Brutus, who reluctantly joins them from a sense of duty to the republic. Caesar is slain by the conspirators in the senate house. Antony, Caesar's friend, stirs the people to fury against the conspirators by a skilful speech at Caesar's funeral. Octavius, nephew of Julius Caesar, Antony, and Lepidus, united as triumvirs, oppose the forces raised by Brutus and Cassius. The quarrel and reconciliation of Brutus and Cassius, with the news of the death of Portia, wife of Brutus, provide one of the finest scenes in the play (IV.iii). Brutus and Cassius are defeated at the battle of Philippi (42 BC), and kill themselves.

Jumpers, a comedy by T. *Stoppard performed and published 1972.

The play's central character is a professor of moral philosophy, George Moore, who shares with G. E. *Moore not only his name but also his intuitionist ethics. The physical acrobatics of the jumpers of the title parallel the 'verbal gymnastics' of Moore's lengthy speeches, which are brilliantly witty parodies of academic philosophy.

JUNG, Carl Gustav (1875–1961), Swiss psychiatrist, whose professional career began at the Burghölzli mental hospital in Zurich, where he was the first to apply psychoanalytic ideas to the study of schizophrenia. He collaborated with *Freud 1907–13, but then parted with him to found his own school of 'Analytical Psychology'. Jung introduced into psychology the terms 'complex', 'collective unconscious', 'extrovert'–'introvert', *'archetype', and 'individuation', and his concept of psychological types has been taken over by the experimental psychologists. His notion of the mind as a self-regulating system is in line with modern ideas on cybernetics. In emphasizing the importance of man's search for meaning in life, he anticipated *Existentialism. Jung specialized in the treatment of older patients, and his main contribution to psychotherapy was to the study of adult development. The central theme of his work is the idea that mental illness is characterized by disunity of the personality, while mental health is manifested by unity, towards which the personality is striving.

Jung's influence has been felt in many fields outside psychiatry. The physicist Wolfgang Pauli, the art historian H. *Read, and the composer M. *Tippett have all acknowledged their debt to Jung. J. B. *Priestley made use of his ideas in *Literature and Western Man*; the title of Maud Bodkin's *Archetypal Patterns in Poetry* (1934) is directly derived from Jung; and his influence pervades the criticism of the Canadian critic Northrop Frye (1912–91). Alex Aronson's *Psyche and Symbol in Shakespeare* (1972) is an interpretation of Shakespearian drama in terms of Jungian psychology. *Hesse made use of Jung's concepts in his novels, and Jung himself wrote an essay on Joyce's *Ulysses*.

Jungle Book, The (1894), and *The Second Jungle Book* (1895), stories by *Kipling, which tell how the child Mowgli was brought up by wolves and was taught by Baloo, the bear, and Bagheera, the black panther, the law and business of the jungle.

JUNIUS, the pseudonymous author of a series of letters that appeared in the *Public Advertiser*, Jan. 1769–Jan. 1772, attacking, with bitter scorn and invective, among others, the duke of Grafton, Lord Mansfield, and George III himself. Junius also takes an active part on behalf of *Wilkes. Both before 1769 and after 1771 political letters under other pseudonyms, which have been traced to the same hand, appeared in the public press. Though personal invective is the cheap weapon of Junius, his political arguments, written from the Whig standpoint, are shrewd and lucidly expressed,

and he shows himself well read in *Hobbes and *Locke. The identity of Junius, which he concealed with great skill, has never been definitely established, and many candidates were offered during his lifetime and later, including Lord *Temple, *Lyttleton, *Gibbon, *Burke, W. *Hamilton (1729–96), and Wilkes himself. He is now generally thought to have been Sir Philip *Francis. There is a full discussion in Alvar Ellegård's *Who Was Junius?* (1962), which argues conclusively for Francis on the basis of statistico-linguistic tests.

JUNIUS, Francis, or Du Jon, François (1589–1677), philologist and antiquary, born at Heidelberg, a friend of *Milton, and librarian and tutor in the household of Thomas Howard, earl of Arundel. His *Etymologicum Anglicanum* (1743) was used by Dr *Johnson. He gave Anglo-Saxon manuscripts, including the so-called *Cædmon manuscript (see below), to the Bodleian Library (see LIBRARIES), and to the *Oxford University Press materials for printing in Gothic, Runic, Anglo-Saxon, and Roman founts. He published an edition of Cædmon in 1655.

Junius manuscript, the, one of the four major manuscripts containing Old English poetry, named after the editor (above) who first printed it at Amsterdam in 1655, calling it 'Cædmon the monk's poetical paraphrase of Genesis, etc.' The biblical poetry in the manuscript (*Genesis A and B*, *Exodus*, *Daniel*, and *Christ and Satan*) continued to be associated with the name of *Cædmon for some time, but it is clear that it is unconnected with him; the title 'The Cædmon Manuscript' has proved tenacious however. See editions by G. V. Krapp and E. V. Dobbie, *Anglo-Saxon Poetic Records*, Vol. i (1931), and in facsimile by I. *Gollancz (British Academy, 1927).

Juno and the Paycock, see O'CASEY.

Jupe, Cissy, a character in Dickens's *Hard Times*.

JUVENAL (Decimus Junius Juvenalis) (c. AD 60–c.136), Roman satirist, whose 16 satires are bitter denunciations of greed, stupidity, vulgarity, and immorality. His great merit as a poet is his ability to depict with unusual vividness scenes that arouse his anger. Imitations of his work are found in J. *Hall, *Jonson, *Oldham, and Dr *Johnson. *Dryden edited and wrote in part a translation of Juvenal's Satires to which he prefixed his long discourse on satire (1693). The references to 'the English Juvenal' in Scott's *Waverley* and to 'the British Juvenal' in *The Heart of Midlothian* are to *Crabbe. The former title has also been applied to Oldham.

K

KAFKA, Franz (1883–1924), German-speaking Jewish novelist, born in Prague. He is the author of three novels, *Der Prozess* (*The Trial*, 1925), *Das Schloss* (*The Castle*, 1926), and the unfinished *Amerika* (1927), and also a large number of short stories, of which 'Die Verwandlung' ('The Metamorphosis', 1915) and 'Das Urteil' ('The Judgement', 1913) are among the best known. His novels were first published after his death, by his friend Max Brod, and were translated into English by E. and W. *Muir, beginning with *The Trial* in 1930. Kafka's letters and diaries contain interesting insights into his complex relationship with his father and with Felice Bauer, to whom he was twice briefly engaged. Characteristic of Kafka's work is the portrayal of an enigmatic reality, in which the individual is seen as lonely, perplexed, and threatened, and guilt is one of his major themes. The opening sentence of *The Trial* gives a sense of the combination of the ordinary and the sinister in his works: 'Someone must have slandered Joseph K., because one morning, without his having done anything wrong, he was arrested.' The word 'Kafkaesque' is frequently used to describe work which employs similar narrative techniques, and evokes a similarly uneasy response.

Kailyard school, from 'Kail-yard' (cabbage patch), a term applied to a group of Scottish writers who exploited a sentimental and romantic image of small-town life in Scotland, with much use of the vernacular; the vogue lasted from about 1888 to 1896. Leading writers in this vein were J. M. *Barrie, 'Ian Maclaren' (John Watson, 1850–1907), and S. R. Crockett (1860–1914). These false notions of Scottish life were shattered by G. *Douglas in *The House with the Green Shutters* (1901); in J. B. *Priestley's words, 'into this cosy chamber of fiction Brown let in the East wind.' See G. Blake, *Barrie and the Kailyard School* (1951).

KAISER, Georg (1878–1945), German dramatist, who died in exile, author of *Die Bürger von Calais* (*The Burghers of Calais*, 1914), *Gas 1* (1918), and *Gas 2* (1920, which ends with the end of the world), leading examples of the German Expressionist theatre (see EXPRESSIONISM). He was a prolific and inventive writer, author of some 60 plays.

Kalevala, 'Land of Heroes', the national epic poem of Finland, transmitted orally until 1822, when a pioneering first collection was published by physician Zacharius (Sakari) Topelius (1782–1831). A fuller version was collected and published in 1835 by Elias Lönnrot (1802–84), who was influenced in his task by an admiration for *Macpherson's creation of

Ossian. It was translated into English by W. M. Crawford in 1887, and tone-poems have been composed around some of the myths by Sibelius.

KĀLIDĀSA, a great Indian poet and dramatist, best known for his play *Shakūntalā*, which was translated from the Sanskrit by Sir W. *Jones (1789). Kālidāsa probably lived in the 3rd cent. AD, but there is a diversity of opinion on this point.

Kama Sutra, see BURTON, SIR R.

KAMES, Lord, see HOME, H.

KANE, Sarah (1971–99), playwright, brought up in Essex and educated at Bristol University. Her first play, *Blasted* (1996), performed at the *Royal Court, was a violent drama which brought her success and notoriety: this was followed by *Phaedra's Love* (1997, performed at the Gate); *Cleansed* (1998) set in a concentration camp; and *Crave* (1998), on the theme of obsessional love. Her dark and unsparing vision won her an international reputation before her death by suicide.

Kangaroo (1923), a novel by D. H. *Lawrence, based on the Lawrences' visit to Australia in 1922.

Richard Lovat Somers, a writer, and his wife Harriet are in Sydney for an indefinite period. Through their neighbour Jack Calcott, Somers makes the acquaintance of 'Kangaroo' Ben Cooley, a Jewish barrister involved in radical politics. He tries to enlist Somers's sympathy for his programme, but fails, and the novel ends with his death after a violent Labour meeting at Canberra Hall (at which Calcott claimed to have killed a demonstrator) and the departure of the Somers for America. The book mingles political outbursts and meditations with observant evocation of Australian life and landscape. Chapter 10, 'The Nightmare', describes Lawrence's own wartime confrontations with authority in Cornwall and his humiliating examinations, in Bodmin and Derby, for military service. Like Somers, he was rejected as unfit.

KANT, Immanuel (1724–1804), second son of a leatherworker (of Scottish descent), of Königsberg in Prussia. He was educated at the university of that town, and supported himself as a tutor. He published his first considerable work, *A General Natural History of the Heavens*, in 1755, and in that year became a lecturer at Königsberg, an unsalaried post in which he remained for 15 years, during which he published a number of minor philosophical treatises. In 1770 he became professor of logic and metaphysics at Königsberg, retaining the appointment until his death. He remained unmarried. His *Critique of Pure Reason* appeared in 1781, *Prolegomena to Any Future Metaphysics* in 1783, *Fundamental Principles of the Metaphysic of Ethics* in 1785, *Metaphysical Rudiments of Natural Philosophy* in 1786, the second edition of the *Critique of Pure Reason* in 1787, the *Critique of Practical Reason* in 1788, and the *Critique of Judgement* in 1790. His *Religion within the Boundaries of Pure Reason* (1793) called down on him the censure of the government.

In Kant's philosophy, knowledge is the outcome of two factors, the senses and the understanding. Sensations are the starting point of knowledge. Space and time are essential conditions of our sensuous perception, the forms under which our sensations are translated into consciousness. Therefore space and time are essential conditions of knowledge, although they exist only as forms of our consciousness. These forms, continuous and infinite, provide the possibility of unifying our individual perceptions, and the unification is effected by the understanding. This act of synthesis Kant analyses into 12 principles or 'categories', or laws of thought. The categories are to the understanding very much what time and space are to the consciousness. They include such notions as quality, quantity, and, notably, causation. The external world is thus the product of sensations conditioned by the forms of consciousness and linked by thought according to its own laws. It consists of appearances, 'phenomena'; but the causes of these appearances, 'noumena', things in themselves, lie beyond the limits of knowledge, nor can we, by the aid of reason alone, apart from appearances, arrive at absolute truth, for reason leads to certain insoluble contradictions, or 'antinomies', such as the impossibility of conceiving either limited or unlimited space.

Where metaphysics fails us, practical reason comes to our aid. The moral consciousness assents to certain 'categorical imperatives', such as 'do not lie'. From this follow the conviction that man is in a certain sense free, the belief in immortality (because self-realization within any finite period is impossible), and the belief in God. We are driven by the nature of our minds to see design in nature, and man as the centre of that design. Though the advantages resulting from obedience to particular moral laws can be shown, the moral obligation itself is a categorical imperative, something that we feel but cannot explain. Interpreted as a practical rule of conduct, the moral law bids you 'act as if the principle by which you act were about to be turned into a universal law of nature', and do all in your power to promote the highest good of all human beings. This highest good is not realizable unless the course of the world is itself guided by moral law, that is to say by a moral Master of the universe, whose existence we are driven to assume. But metaphysics places religion and morality outside the province of knowledge, and in the region of faith.

Kant's philosophy was developed and profoundly modified by *Fichte, *Schelling, and *Hegel. In Britain, *Coleridge and *Carlyle valued Kant's criticism of the empirical philosophy (and the atheism) of the 18th cent., particularly that of *Hume.

KARAMZIN, Nikolai Mikhailovich (1766–1826), Russian prose writer and historian. Born into the provincial gentry, Karamzin spent most of his life in Moscow and St Petersburg. In his writings he is associated with the reform of the Russian language under French influence and with the growth of Sentimentalism, particularly in his most famous stories *Poor Liza* and *Natalya, the Boyar's Daughter* (both 1792, first English trans. John Battersby Elrington, 1803). Later he turned to writing history and his *History of the Russian State* appeared in 12 volumes (1818–29). Karamzin's enthusiasm for England and English literature was immense. His first published book was a translation of *Julius Caesar* (1787) and his consistent admiration for Shakespeare as psychologist did much to advance Shakespeare's reputation in Russia. He also from his early years admired *Milton, *Young, *Thomson (whose *The Seasons* he translated in 1787), and *Macpherson's Ossian. In 1789–90 he travelled to western Europe, including England, and his *Letters of a Russian Traveller* (1797–1801), trans. Florence Jonas, 1957) describe his disillusionment with the English and their 'sluggish blood', but his fascination with English eccentricity.

Kastril, the rustic lad in Jonson's *The Alchemist*, who comes to London to learn the speech of the roaring boys.

Katharina, the 'shrew', or self-willed girl, in Shakespeare's *The Taming of the Shrew*.

Katherine, (1) a character in Shakespeare's *Love's Labour's Lost*; (2) in his *Henry V*, the daughter of the king of France.

Katherine Group, the, the name given to five Middle English works of devotional prose found together in the manuscript Bodley 34, dating from c.1190–1225: *Seinte Marherete*, *Seinte Iuliene*, *Seinte Katerine*, *Sawles Warde*, and *Hali Meðhad*. They come from Herefordshire, and their common language is also, for the most part, shared with *Ancrene Wisse and therefore called 'Language AB' from the first letter of that text combined with that of Bodley 34. It is a distinctive and interesting language from a transitional period of English; but the interest of the works in the group is not only philological: they are all written in a lively, often colloquial style, with vivid details of illustration. They use alliteration and rhythmic art in a way that has been compared to the prose of *Ælfric. The three saints' lives are all concerned with heroic virgins who were frequently exalted in medieval writings: St Catherine of Alexandria, St Juliana of Nicomedia, and St Margaret of Antioch, who were all believed to have suffered from the persecutions of Diocletian in the first decade of the 4th cent. The most

549 | KAUFFER | KEACH

celebrated English life of one of them is the Old English *Juliana* by *Cynewulf.

See N. R. Ker, *Facsimile of MS Bodley 34* (EETS 247, 1960); S. R. T. O. d'Ardenne and E. J. Dobson, *Seinte Katerine* (EETS SS 7, 1981); S. R. T. O. d'Ardenne, *The Liflade and te Passiun of Seinte Iuliene* (EETS 248, 1961); F. M. Mack, *Seinte Marherete* (EETS 193, 1934).

KAUFFER, E(dward) McKnight (1890–1954), American-born artist and illustrator, who settled in England in 1914, and won great praise for his posters and commercial designs, notably for the London Transport Board and the Great Western Railway: Arnold *Bennett (*Evening Standard*, 1928) wrote that he had 'changed the face of London streets' and that his success 'proves that popular taste is on the up-grade'. He also illustrated various works by T. S. *Eliot, including the 'Ariel Poems' series (1927–31). He moved back to America in 1940 and died in New York.

KAVAN, Anna (1901–68), novelist and short story writer, born of English parents in Cannes. A heroin addict for 30 years, she died in London. Best known for the short, apocalyptic novel *Ice* (1967), she published numerous novels and short story collections under the name Anna Kavan (having changed the name she was born with, Helen Emily Woods, by deed poll), as well as several earlier, more traditional, romantic novels under her married name, Helen Ferguson. Kavan's *Sleep Has His House* (1948; *The House of Sleep* in the USA) is a unique blend of dream diary, visionary fiction, and autobiography.

KAVANAGH, Julia (1824–77), born in Thurles, educated at home. She spent much of her youth in France, which gave her an insight into French life and character which she conveyed faithfully in her novels and tales. Of the novels the best known were *Madeleine* (1848), *Nathalie* (1850), and *Adèle* (1858). Then followed *French Women of Letters* (1862) and *English Women of Letters* (1863), biographical sketches, both of which received high praise. *Forget-me-nots* (1878) is a collection of short stories.

KAVANAGH, Patrick (1905–67), Irish poet, born in Co. Monaghan, the son of a small farmer and shoemaker; after some years of farming he went to Dublin in 1939 and embarked on a literary career as journalist and poet. His works include *Ploughman and Other Poems* (1936), *A Soul for Sale* (1947), *Tarry Flynn* (1948, a novel set on a small farm in his home county), and *Collected Poems* (1964). His best-known work is probably *The Great Hunger* (1942), a long poem contrasting the realities of life for an archetypal peasant, Patrick Maguire (figuratively 'locked in a stable with pigs and cows forever', and in fact dominated by an elderly mother, and suffering from sexual and intellectual hunger, as well as a humdrum poverty), with the more conventional idealized peasant of the *Irish Revival, with his 'little lyrical fields'. Much of Kavanagh's work is concerned with the relationship between Irish archetype and stereotype; he rejected the 'stage-Irish' of some of his early work, but nevertheless turned himself into a kind of caricature of the hard-drinking Irish poet. His *Collected Pruse* (sic, 1967) includes autobiographical essays and articles from the periodical *Kavanagh's Weekly*, which he produced with his brother Peter in 1952.

KAVANAGH, P(atrick) J(oseph) (1931–), poet, novelist, and editor, born in Worthing and educated at Merton College, Cambridge. His volumes of poetry include *One and One* (1960, his first), *Edward Thomas in Heaven* (1974), and *An Enchantment* (1991); his *Collected Poems* was published in 1992. Novels include *A Song and Dance* (1968), *A Happy Man* (1972), *Rebel for Good* (1980), and *Only by Mistake* (1986). *The Perfect Stranger* (1966) is a moving account of his life up to the sudden death of his first wife Sally, daughter of Rosamond *Lehmann, in 1958, and *Finding Connections* (1990) pursues his family's past in Australia and New Zealand. He edited the *Collected Poems of Ivor Gurney* (1982).

KAWABATA, Yasunari (1899–1972), Japanese novelist. After a Modernist early period, Kawabata developed a fascination with death, eroticism, and traditional Japanese aesthetics. A well-known early book is *Izu Dancer* (1926). *Snow Country* (1948) is another classic. Kawabata became the second Asian writer (after *Tagore) to win the *Nobel Prize for literature, in 1968. He committed suicide four years later.

Kay, Sir, in the Arthurian legend (as in *Malory), Arthur's steward, a brave but churlish knight. He was the son of Sir *Ector and therefore the foster-brother of Arthur. His churlishness is accounted for in the Merlin legends by the fact that he was supplanted by Arthur at his mother's breast and brought up by a rough-speaking nurse. His most famous churlish greetings are those accorded to Sir *Gareth and Sir *Perceval.

KAY, Jackie (1961–), Scottish poet, dramatist, and novelist. Her first collection, *The Adoption Papers* (1991), introduces themes of racial and sexual identity, class and Scottishness, which have remained central to Kay's writing. *Other Lovers* (1993) includes a sequence on blues singer Bessie Smith, of whom she has also written a biography. Her first novel, *Trumpet* (1998), employs various narrative perspectives to tell the story of a male jazz musician who is discovered, after his death, to have been a woman. She has also published poetry for children.

KAYE-SMITH, Sheila (1887–1956), born in Sussex, where she spent all her life; her successful *regional novels are precisely located, principally on the Kent–Sussex border, and include *Starbrace* (1909) and *Joanna Godden* (1921). Hers was the genre of novel satirized by Stella Gibbons in *Cold Comfort Farm*.

KEACH, Benjamin, see CHILDREN'S LITERATURE.

KEAN, Edmund (1787/90–1833), actor of uncertain parentage, whose adventurous childhood gave rise to innumerable legends. He was befriended by various guardians, including Moses Kean, a mimic and ventriloquist, and worked on stage as infant prodigy and strolling player before achieving fame in 1814 as Shylock in *The Merchant of Venice*, a performance recorded by *Hazlitt. He was a great tragic actor, whose numerous successes included Richard III, Hamlet, Othello, Iago, Macbeth, Lear, and *Marlowe's Jew of Malta. *Dumas *père* wrote a play based on his colourful life which was subsequently adapted by *Sartre (1954). His son Charles John Kean (1811–68) was also an actor, and manager of the Princess's Theatre, 1851–9.

KEANE, Molly (1904–96), novelist and playwright, born in Co. Kildare, into a leisured Anglo-Irish world. She was educated by governesses and spent a brief period at a boarding school. At the age of 17 she wrote her first novel, choosing the pseudonym M. J. Farrell (which she took from a public house) to hide her literary side from her sporting friends. Between 1928 and 1952 she published ten others, including *Devoted Ladies* (1934), *The Rising Tide* (1937), and *Two Days in Aragon* (1941.) She also wrote successful plays (with John Parry) such as *Spring Meeting* (1938) and *Treasure Hunt* (1949). Her work chronicles the manners and *mores* of Anglo-Irish life, especially the thrill of the chase, both sexual and sporting. Characterized by a detailed evocation of place and a bittersweet flavour, it is underlined by an awareness of the cruelties, snobberies, and evasions of that narrow world, seen most notably in *Good Behaviour* (1981). Published under her own name and written after a long gap following her husband's death, the novel brought her work to a new audience. *Time after Time* (1983) and *Loving and Giving* (1988) followed. She also published *Nursery Cooking* (1985, illustrated by Linda Smith).

KEATS, John (1795–1821), the son of the manager of a livery stables in Moorfields, who died when he was 8; his mother remarried, but died of tuberculosis when he was 14. The oldest of the family, he remained deeply attached to his brothers George and Tom and to his sister Fanny. He was well educated at Clarke's school, Enfield, where he began a translation of the *Aeneid*, and in 1810 was apprenticed to an apothecary-surgeon. His first efforts at writing poetry appear to date from 1814, and include an 'Imitation of Spenser'; his school friend Cowden-*Clarke recorded the profound effect of early reading of *Spenser. In 1815 Keats cancelled his fifth year of apprenticeship and became a student at Guy's Hospital; to the same year belong 'Ode to Apollo' and 'Hymn to Apollo'. In 1816 he was licensed to practise as an apothecary, but in spite of precarious finances abandoned the profession for poetry. In 1816 he also met Leigh *Hunt, who published in the same year in the *Examiner* Keats's poem, 'O Solitude', and in the course of a survey of young poets in the same journal he included Keats's sonnet 'On First Looking

into Chapman's Homer'. Keats met *Shelley and *Haydon, began to plan *Endymion, and wrote 'I stood tiptoe upon a little hill' as a first effort towards that poem. His first volume of poems was published in March 1817. It included, among sonnets, epistles, and miscellaneous poems, 'I stood tiptoe upon a little hill' and 'Sleep and Poetry'. There were at first some pleasing reviews, but public interest was not aroused and sales were meagre; and in the autumn came the first of *Lockhart's harsh attacks in *Blackwood's, labelling Keats and his associates as members of the so-called *Cockney School. He finished the first draft of *Endymion* and during the winter of 1817–18 saw something of *Wordsworth and *Hazlitt, both of whom much influenced his thought and practice. In December Haydon gave his 'immortal dinner', whose guests included Wordsworth, *Lamb, and Keats. *Endymion*, dedicated to *Chatterton, whom Keats greatly admired, was published in the spring of 1818, and *'Isabella, or The Pot of Basil' finished in May. With his friend Charles Armitage Brown (1786–1842) Keats then toured the Lakes, spent July and August in Scotland, and included a brief visit to Northern Ireland. He had travelled frequently in southern England but he had never before seen scenery of rugged grandeur. It moved him deeply and he made full use of it when he came to write *Hyperion. Bitter attacks on *Endymion* came in the autumn from Lockhart in *Blackwood's* and from the *Quarterly Review. For the time being Keats concealed his pain and wrote to his brother George that, in spite of the reviews, 'I think I shall be among the English poets after my death', but his friends believed the wound was very deep. Meanwhile his brother Tom was very ill and Keats spent much time with him. When Tom died in December Keats moved into his friend Brown's house in Hampstead, now known as Keats House. There, in the early winter, he met Fanny *Brawne, with whom he fell deeply in love, and with whom he remained in love until his death. During the course of the summer and autumn of 1818 his sore throats had become more frequent and persistent. Nevertheless September 1818 marked the beginning of what is sometimes referred to as the Great Year; he began *Hyperion* in its first version, abandoning it a year later; he wrote, consecutively, *'The Eve of St Agnes', 'The Eve of St Mark', the 'Ode to Psyche', *'La Belle Dame sans Merci', *'Ode to a Nightingale', and probably at about the same time the *'Ode on a Grecian Urn', 'Ode on Melancholy', and 'Ode on Indolence'; *'Lamia Part I', *'Otho the Great' (in collaboration with Brown); the second version of *Hyperion*, called *The Fall of Hyperion*, *'To Autumn', and 'Lamia Part II'. During this year he was beset with financial problems, both his own and those of his friends and relations, and intensely preoccupied with his love for Fanny, to whom he became engaged. In the winter of 1819 he began the unfinished 'The Cap and Bells', but he became increasingly ill with tuberculosis and his great creative work was now over. His second volume of poems, *Lamia, Isabella, The Eve of St Agnes, and Other Poems*, was published in July 1820, and included, as well as the title poems, five odes, *Hyperion*, 'Fancy', and other works. The volume was generally well received, gaining much praise in some quarters, with criticism from *Blackwood's* much muted, but the sales were very slow. Shelley invited Keats to Italy and in September, after sorting out his copyrights and financial affairs, Keats set off with his friend *Severn. They did not go to the Shelleys but settled in Rome, where Keats died the following February.

Keats has always been regarded as one of the principal figures in the *Romantic movement, and his stature as a poet has grown steadily through all changes of fashion. *Tennyson considered him the greatest poet of the 19th cent., and M. *Arnold commended his 'intellectual and spiritual passion' for beauty; in the 20th cent. he has been discussed and reconsidered by critics from T. S. *Eliot and *Leavis to *Trilling (*The Opposing Self*, 1955) and Christopher Ricks (*Keats and Embarrassment*, 1974).

His letters, published in 1848 and 1878, have come to be regarded with almost the admiration given to his poetry, to which many of them act as a valuable commentary. He wrote fully and revealingly to Fanny Brawne, to his brothers and sister, to Shelley, Leigh Hunt, Haydon, Severn, and many others, mixing the everyday events of his own life with a lively and delicate interest in that of his correspondents, and displaying wit and high spirits as well as his profoundest thoughts on love, poetry, and the nature of man. T. S. Eliot described the letters as 'certainly the most notable and most important ever written by any English poet' (*The Use of Poetry and the Use of Criticism*, 1933). The major biographies are by W. J. Bate (1963), R. *Gittings (1968), and Andrew *Motion (1997).

KEBLE, John (1792–1866), educated at Corpus Christi College, Oxford. He became fellow and tutor at Oriel College (where *Newman and *Pusey were also fellows) and professor of poetry at Oxford, 1831–41. His sermon on national apostasy in 1833 was considered the start of the *Oxford movement, which he also supported by nine of the *Tracts for the Times*. Although a leading figure in Oxford intellectual life, he was personally unambitious, and from 1836 until his death was vicar of the country parish of Hursley. His volume of sacred verse *The Christian Year*, published anonymously in 1827, had an immense success, and was widely admired, not only by those with Tractarian leanings, but also by *evangelical and *Broad Church readers; intended as a guide to devotion and a commentary on the Book of Common Prayer, it shows the influence of G. *Herbert and, in its feeling for the natural world, of *Wordsworth, and combines Keble's considerable scholarship with deep personal feeling. A second volume, *Lyra Innocentium* (1846), was less popular, and was criticized by some for its undue reverence for the Virgin Mary. C. M. *Yonge was a pupil of his, and

drew a vivid character sketch in *Musings over the Christian Year . . . with a Few Gleanings of Recollections of Keble* (1871). Keble also edited *Hooker (1836), helped Newman with *Froude's *Remains*, contributed to *Lyra Apostolica*, and published a life of Bishop Thomas Wilson. Keble College, Oxford, was founded in his memory in 1870. There are lives by W. Lock (1893) and G. Battiscombe (1963).

Kells, Book of, an 8th- to 9th-cent. manuscript of the four Gospels, with prefaces, summaries, and canon tables; seven charters of the abbey of Kells have been added on blank pages. It is written in Irish majuscule and has magnificent illustrations consisting of intricate patterns made up of abstract and animal forms. It was probably written at Kells in Co. Meath, the headquarters of the Columban community after the sack of Iona in 806. It was collated by *Ussher in 1621 and presented to Trinity College, Dublin, after the Restoration.

KELLY, Hugh (1739–77), an Irishman who came to London in 1760, edited the *Court Magazine* and the *Lady's Museum*, and afterwards the *Public Ledger*. His *False Delicacy*, produced by *Garrick in 1768, is a *sentimental comedy with a triple plot in which the mistakes arise from excessive tact or delicacy, which keeps the three couples apart until the misunderstandings are resolved through the intervention of the down-to-earth Mrs Harley: 'Your people of refined sentiments are the most troublesome creatures in the world to deal with,' she declares. Kelly also wrote *A Word to the Wise* (1770) and *The School for Wives* (1773). In 1774 he was called to the bar and gave up literature.

KELMAN, James (1946–   ), Scottish novelist, short story writer, and dramatist, born in Glasgow. He left school at the age of 15, and after a brief period living in America, where his family had emigrated, he returned to Scotland and a succession of temporary jobs, alternating with periods of unemployment. For a time he studied philosophy at the University of Strathclyde, though he left without taking a degree. In 1983 he published a collection of stories, *Not Not While the Giro*, in which urban Scottish working-class life is depicted with terse touches of humour using the authentic language of the streets. This uncompromising demotic style was further developed in his first novel, *The Busconductor Hines* (1984), *A Chancer* (1985), *Greyhound for Breakfast* (stories, 1987), *A Disaffection* (1989), a powerful portrayal of an alcoholic secondary-school teacher which was shortlisted for the *Booker Prize, and *The Burn* (stories, 1991). His fourth novel, *How Late It Was, How Late* (1994), which won the Booker Prize, is the story of an unemployed Glaswegian construction worker and petty crook who comes round after a two-day drinking bout to find himself blind and in police custody: his mixture of aggression and stoic acceptance in the face of authority is expressed in vivid narration which successfully reproduces the interior monologue of largely inarticulate struggle. *Hardie and Baird and Other Plays* was published in 1991. *The Good Times* (1998) consists of 20 first-person narratives.

Kelmscott Press, see MORRIS, W.

KEMBLE, Charles (1775–1854), son of a strolling actor-manager, Roger Kemble (1721–1802), and brother of Sarah *Siddons, J. P. *Kemble, Stephen Kemble, and other theatrical siblings; father of Fanny *Kemble and the scholar J. M. *Kemble. A leading actor for some 25 years, he was a respected member of London society. His voice was light, and his most successful roles were of young men, such as Mirabell in *The Way of the World*, Mercutio, Orlando, Benedick, and, most especially, Romeo. His range was considerable in comedy and romance, but he did not often attempt tragedy.

KEMBLE, Fanny (Frances Anne) (1809–93), daughter of Charles *Kemble, a very beautiful and accomplished actress. She first appeared under her father's management at Covent Garden in 1829, when she played Juliet to his Mercutio. She played comedy and tragedy with equal success, and added most of the great roles to her repertoire, including Portia, Lady Macbeth, Beatrice, Lady Teazle in *The School for Scandal*, Belvidera in *Venice Preserv'd*, and many others. She published a volume of poems in 1844 and *Records of a Later Life* in 1882.

KEMBLE, John Mitchell (1807–57), historian and philologist, elder son of Charles *Kemble, educated at Trinity College, Cambridge, where he was a member of the *Apostles and a friend of R. C. *Trench, *Milnes, and *Tennyson. He later studied in Germany, where he became a close friend of *Grimm and was converted to the new continental philology, which he supported on his return. His text of *Beowulf* (1833), dedicated to Grimm, aroused much controversy, and he did useful work on the early history of England.

KEMBLE, John Philip (1757–1823), eldest brother of Charles *Kemble. He achieved success as a formal tragic actor, and was particularly renowned in the roles of Coriolanus and Hamlet, in which part *Hazlitt particularly admired him.

KEMBLE, Sarah, see SIDDONS, S.

KEMP, William (fl. 1600), a comic actor and dancer, who acted in plays by Shakespeare and *Jonson. In 1599 he danced a morris dance from London to Norwich, in *Rowley's words a 'wild morrige to Norridge'; his own account, *Kemps Nine Daies Wonder*, was published in 1600.

KEMPE, Margery (c.1373–c.1439), a mystic, daughter of John Brunham who was once mayor of King's Lynn in Norfolk. She married John Kempe of Lynn c.1393. She gave up married life to devote herself to religion and she travelled widely on pilgrimage: to Jerusalem, Rome, Compostela, and Wilsnack in Poland. She

dictated, probably in the 1420s, her *Book of Margery Kempe* which recounts with great vividness her visions and experiencess of a more general kind: her temptations to lechery, her travels, and her trial for heresy. Though the work is not a strictly mystical text (like *The Cloud of Unknowing*), it is a vigorous and readable piece of early autobiography with considerable appeal. Ed. S. B. Meech and E. H. Allen (EETS OS 212, 1940).

KEMPIS, Thomas à, see THOMAS À KEMPIS.

Kemp Owyne, an old ballad in *Child's collection, from an Icelandic source. Isabel, who has been transformed into a monster by a wicked stepmother, is released from the enchantment by three kisses of her lover, Kemp Owyne. In modern versions of the ballad he is 'Kempion'.

KEN, Thomas (1637–1711), fellow of Winchester and New College, Oxford, who became bishop of Bath and Wells. He was a writer of devotional prose and verse; his works include *The Practice of Divine Love* (1685), the extremely popular *A Manual of Prayers for the Use of Scholars of Winchester College* (1674), and some well-known hymns, including 'Awake, my soul, and with the sun'. His works were collected by W. Hawkins in 1721.

KENEALLY, Thomas (1935–   ), Australian novelist, born in Sydney. He began training as a Catholic priest at the age of 17 but in 1960 abandoned his intention to become ordained. He then worked as a schoolteacher, turning to writing full-time after the publication of his first novel, *The Place at Whitton*, in 1964. This was followed by *The Fear* (1965), a condensed version of which was published as *By the Line* in 1989. He has travelled widely in Australia, Europe, and the USA and published several accounts of his journeys, including *Now and in Time to Be: Ireland and the Irish* (1991), and *The Place Where Souls Are Born* (1992), about the American south-west. His first major success came with the publication of *Bring Larks and Heroes* (1967), a historical novel whose protagonist, an Irish Catholic marine, Phelim Halloran, is detached to serve in a British penal colony. Subsequent novels included *Three Cheers for the Paraclete* (1968); *The Chant of Jimmie Blacksmith* (1972), the main character of which is the son of an Aboriginal mother and a white father; *Blood Red, Sister Rose* (1974), a historical novel about *Joan of Arc; *Confederates* (1979), set during the American Civil War; *A Family Madness* (1985), which interweaves ordinary lives in contemporary Sydney with terrible events in Belorussia during the Second World War; *The Playmaker* (1987), set in 1789 and dealing with the first dramatic production in Australia (adapted for the stage by T. *Wertenbaker as *Our Country's Good*); and *Towards Asmara* (1988), which reflects his experiences of the Eritrean War. His most celebrated work to date, *Schindler's Ark* (1982), which won the *Booker Prize, is the moving story of a German industrialist, Oskar Schindler, who risked his life saving Jews in Nazi-occupied Poland during the Second World War. It was subsequently filmed by Steven Spielberg under the title *Schindler's List*. Other novels include *Flying Hero Class* (1991), about a group of Palestinian terrorists who hijack an airliner on which is a troupe of Aboriginal dancers, displaced and dispossessed like the hijackers; *Woman of the Inner Sea* (1992), the tale of a disastrous marriage and a nightmarish flight into the Australian interior; *Jacko, the Great Intruder* (1993); and *A River Town* (1995), set in late 19th-cent. Australia and based on his grandfather's life. He has also written a children's fantasy, *Ned Kelly and the City of the Bees* (1978), and two novels under the pseudonym William Coyle, *Act of Grace* (1988) and *Chief of Staff* (1991).

Kenilworth, a novel by Sir W. *Scott, published 1821.
   The novel is a celebration of the glories of the Elizabethan age. The fact that the plot is riddled with anachronisms did nothing to impair its popularity with the public; published in the year of the coronation of George IV, the story of Elizabeth and her favourite Leicester and of the betrayal and murder of Leicester's wife Amy Robsart caught the national mood. Shakespeare, *Spenser, and Sir Walter *Ralegh all appear, and the climax of the novel is the great pageant at Kenilworth in July 1575.

KENNEDY, A(lison) L(ouise) (1965–   ), Scottish writer, born in Dundee, who moves almost seamlessly between the novel and the short story. Her novels— *Looking for the Possible Dance* (1993), *So I Am Glad* (1995), *Everything You Need* (1999), *Paradise* (2004)— are freeform, while her story collections—*Night Geometry and the Garscadden Trains* (1990), *Now That You're Back* (1994), and *Original Bliss* (1997)— seem novelistic in their fullness of human detail. The typical Kennedy character, male or female, is usually incomprehending, deep in pain, and adrift in a purposeless world: Nathan Staples, the wretched, self-loathing protagonist of *Everything You Need*, being perhaps the most extreme example. Her writing is characterized by bleak humour, an intense lyricism, political awareness and, increasingly, a preoccupation with derangement and sexual obsession. Kennedy has also written a screenplay, *Stella Does Tricks* (1998), and a long autobiographical essay on Michael Powell's film *The Life and Death of Colonel Blimp* (1997).

Kennedy, Lady Laura, a character in A. Trollope's novels *Phineas Finn* and *Phineas Redux*.

KENNEDY, Margaret Moore (1896–1967), novelist, remembered principally for her highly praised bestseller *The Constant Nymph* (1924), which was dramatized (1926) and filmed several times.

KENNEDY, Walter (?1460–?1508), a Scottish poet, the rival (ostensibly at least, and probably in reality) of *Dunbar in 'The *Flyting of Dunbar and Kennedie' (1508) and mentioned by him in his 'Lament for the Makaris' (ll. 89–91) as being on the point of death. The few poems by him that survive were edited by J. Schipper in *Denkschriften der kaiserlichen Akademie der Wissenschaften*, 48 (1902).

kenning, a poetic compound, made up of two or more nouns standing for another noun, occurring in ancient Germanic languages, notably Old Norse (Icelandic) and Old English. According to the strictest deffinitions it must be metaphorical (or, in technical semantic terms, exocentric) in that the poetic compound must not be literally identical to any of its components; thus, to take a familiar Old English example, 'arrow' in *Judith* is represented by *hildenaerdre*, 'battle-arrow'. The Old Norse examples are the most important and the most elaborate, especially in *skaldic verse. *Snorri Sturluson gives the authoritative discussion in his *Edda*; he urges against kenning having more than six noun-components. Obviously, in poetry where this was one of the most important mechanisms, the kennings for very common nouns (such as 'man' or 'woman') are various and inventive. To take one example of each: 'man' is represented as 'tree-of-the-storm-of-Othinn': Othinn (*Wagner's Wotan) is the god of battle (as well as poetry and death), and 'tree' (something straight and upright) is a common element in 'person' kennings. 'Woman' is 'fir-tree-of-the-ember-of-the-wave': Gunnar throws the Nibelungs' treasure into the Rhine (the *Rheingold*), so the glowing ember in the water is gold, which this person (fir-tree) might wear as decoration. Clearly the resolution of some ingenious kennings is conjectural. Some of the Old English ones are metonymic and not required to be literally distinct: 'swanroad', 'whaleroad', and 'gannet's bath' (sea); 'voice-bearers' (people).

Kent, earl of, loyal follower of the king in Shakespeare's *King Lear*; he is banished in the opening scene, but continues to attend him in disguise.

KENT, William (1685–1748), painter, architect, decorator, and landscape gardener, best known through his association from 1719 with his major patron, the *Palladio enthusiast the third earl of Burlington (1694–1753). His imaginative, informal, and Arcadian garden designs, the archetype for the English *landscape garden, were highly influential and praised by his peers, including Horace *Walpole, who recognized Kent's originality. The best known, although subsequently altered, was the garden at Stowe. Although an indifferent painter he has the distinction of being the earliest painter of medieval subjects, those of Henry V (c.1730; Royal Collection) painted for Queen Caroline.

KENTIGERN, St (St Mungo) (?518–603), brought up in the monastic school of Culross in Scotland, where he received the name 'Mungo', a corruption of the Gaelic for 'my love'. He was a missionary to the Strathclyde Britons, from whom he proceeded to evangelize in Cumberland and Wales. He founded the monastery of Llanelwy, later named St *Asaph's after its first abbot

He was recalled to Strathclyde and settled at Glasgow where he is buried in the crypt of the cathedral, named St Mungo's after him.

Kenwigs, Mr and Mrs, a genteel couple in Dickens's *Nicholas Nickleby*.

KER, William Paton (1855–1923), born in Glasgow, a fellow of All Souls College, Oxford, from 1879 to his death. He was professor of literature at Cardiff from 1883 to 1889 when he became Quain professor at London. In 1917 he became director of the Scandinavian Studies School and in 1920 Oxford professor of poetry. He is buried in Italy where he died on holiday. He is celebrated for the width of his humane criticism in English, Norse, and Scottish literature. His *Collected Essays* were edited by C. Whibley and published in 1925. His other most admired works are *Epic and Romance* (1897) and *The Dark Ages* (1904), both often republished.

KERMODE, Sir Frank (1919–), literary critic, was born in Douglas, Isle of Man. He studied at the University of Liverpool, and served in the Royal Navy in the Second World War. He held a succession of academic posts at the universities of Newcastle, Reading, Manchester, Bristol, London, and Cambridge, resigning in 1982. His critical studies have alternated between the English Renaissance—beginning with an edition of *The Tempest* (1954)—and 20th-cent. literature, in which he has championed the works of Wallace *Stevens and F. M. *Ford. His most influential early books are *Romantic Image* (1957), which demonstrates continuities between late Romantic and early Modernist uses of enigmatic symbols, and *The Sense of an Ending* (1967), which explores the ways in which narrative fiction makes sense of linear time. Through his editorship of the Fontana Modern Masters series and his seminars on literary theory at University College London, he helped to inject fresh currents of European thought into literary studies in Britain. His later books include *The Classic* (1975), *The Genesis of Secrecy* (1979), *Essays on Fiction* (1983), *An Appetite for Poetry* (1989), and a memoir, *Not Entitled* (1997). He was knighted in 1991.

KEROUAC, Jack (1922–69), American novelist, born in Massachusetts of French Canadian parents, and educated at Columbia University. His first novel, *The Town and the City* (1950), was written under the influence of Thomas *Wolfe and it was only with *On the Road* (1957) that he constructed his image as the hip-flask swinging hobo. Thinly disguising himself as Sal Paradise, he describes his cross-county excursions with his friend Neal Cassady (Dean Moriarty in the book). Written in a three-week frenzy, the novel is a hymn to the freedom of American geography—its promises and possibilities, its unique wonder at itself. Much to Kerouac's irritation, the work would be heralded as the forerunner of the counter-culture, whereas he saw it as reclaiming the rugged individu-

alism of the 19th cent. Further books (*The Subterraneans*, 1958; *The Dharma Bums*, 1958) continued in this autobiographical mode, mythologizing his *Beat friends and their relentless pursuit of the moment (what he simply called 'It'). In his essays 'Essentials of Spontaneous Prose' (1953) and 'Belief & Technique for Modern Prose' (*Evergreen Review*, 1959), he outlined a philosophy of writing that refused all revision and was more akin to the free association and improvisation of jazz. His later years were spent in alcoholic decline, a process that effectively alienated him from the group he helped to define. *Selected Letters*, ed A. Charters, appeared in 1995.

KEYES, Sidney Arthur Kilworth (1922–43), poet, born in Dartford, the son of an army officer. He was brought up largely by his grandfather, whom he commemorates in several poems, and was educated at Tonbridge School, where he began to write poetry, and at Oxford, where he became friendly with *Heath-Stubbs, and edited, with Michael Meyer, *Eight Oxford Poets* (1941), which contains some of his own work. His first collection, *The Iron Laurel*, appeared in 1942; in the same year he joined the army. His second, *The Cruel Solstice*, appeared in 1943, after his presumed death in Tunisia. He was awarded the Hawthornden Prize posthumously in 1944, and his *Collected Poems*, with a Memoir by M. Meyer, appeared in 1945. He himself claimed as his major influences *Wordsworth, *Yeats, *Rilke, and *Jung; H. *Read described his characteristic note as 'elegiac'.

KEYNES, Sir Geoffrey Langdon (1887–1982), surgeon, scholar, and bibliographer, born in Cambridge, the brother of J. M. *Keynes, and educated at Rugby and Pembroke College, Cambridge. His works include bibliographies of *Donne, *Evelyn, and notably *Blake (1921, 1953); his editions of Blake (1925–66, and various studies) were a major contribution towards the 20th-cent. reappraisal of Blake's work. His autobiography *The Gates of Memory* was published in 1981.

KEYNES, John Maynard, first Baron Keynes of Tilton (1883–1946), a distinguished economist, whose book *A General Theory of Employment, Interest, and Money* (1936) revolutionized economic theory by showing how unemployment could occur 'involuntarily'. For 30 years after the Second World War governments of western nations pursued 'Keynesian' full-employment policies. He regarded economists as the 'trustees . . . of the possibility of civilisation', and in his essay 'The Future Possibilities for Our Grandchildren' wrote that with the coming of economic abundance man would for the first time be faced with his 'real, his permanent problem . . . how to occupy the leisure, which science and compound interest will have won for him, to live wisely and agreeably and well'. Keynes was a member of the *Bloomsbury Group and a noted patron of the arts. He founded and endowed the Arts Theatre at

Cambridge, and was chairman of CEMA (Council for the Encouragement of Music and the Arts) in 1942 and the first chairman when it became the *Arts Council of Great Britain in 1945. At its best Keynes's writing had a strong visual sense, and he was a fine phrase-maker. His portraits of President Woodrow Wilson, Georges Clemenceau, and Lloyd George (the first two of which appeared in his book *The Economic Consequences of the Peace*, 1919) are justly famous; V. *Woolf was much impressed by his 'method of character drawing' in his essay 'Dr Melchior: A Defeated Enemy' which he read to Bloomsbury's Memoir Club in 1921. The latter, together with 'My Early Beliefs', was published posthumously in 1949. Keynes's *Collected Writings* have been issued by the Royal Economic Society. Robert Skidelsky's three-volume biography (*Hopes Betrayed*, 1983; *The Economist as Saviour*, 1992; *Fighting for Britain*, 2000) appeared in a single volume as *John Maynard Keynes: Economist, Philosopher, Statesman* in 2003.

KID, Thomas, see KYD.

Kidnapped and *Catriona* (Gaelic for Catherine and pronounced Catreena), a novel and its sequel by R. L. *Stevenson, published in 1886 and 1893.

The central incident in the story is the murder of Colin Campbell, the 'Red Fox' of Glenure, the king's factor on the forfeited estate of Ardshiel: this is a historical event. The young David Balfour, left in poverty on the death of his father, goes for assistance to his uncle Ebenezer, a miserly old villain who has illegally taken control of the Balfour estate. Having failed to effect the death of David, Ebenezer has him kidnapped on a ship to be carried off to the Carolinas. On the voyage Alan Breck is picked up from a sinking boat. He is 'one of those honest gentlemen that were in trouble about the years forty-five and six', a Jacobite who 'wearies for the heather and the deer'. The ship is wrecked on the coast of Mull, and David and Alan journey together. They are witnesses of the murder of Colin Campbell, and suspicion falls on them. After a perilous journey across the Highlands they escape across the Forth, and the first novel ends with the discomfiture of Ebenezer and David's recovery of his rights.

Catriona is principally occupied with the unsuccessful attempt of David Balfour to secure, at the risk of his own life and freedom, the acquittal of James Stewart of the Glens, who is falsely accused, from political motives, of the murder of Colin Campbell; with the escape of Alan Breck to the Continent; and with David's love affair with Catriona Drummond, the daughter of the renegade James More.

KIERKEGAARD, Søren Aabye (1813–55), Danish philosopher and theologian. His life was tortured and unhappy, but within its short span he managed to write a very large number of books on a wide variety of topics. Thus, although he is now chiefly remembered and referred to as having initiated much that is characteristic of existentialist trends in modern philosophy (e.g. *Concluding Unscientific Postscript*, trans. W. Lowrie and D. F. Swenson, 1941), he was also the author of works whose themes were primarily religious, psychological, or literary (e.g. *The Concept of Dread* and *Fear and Trembling*, both trans. W. Lowrie, 1944); moreover, his satirical gifts made him a formidable social critic, witness his essay on *The Present Age* (trans. A. Dru, 1962), reminiscent in some respects of *Carlyle's polemics. Yet, for all their diversity of subject, his writings have certain distinctive common features: a distrust of abstract dogma and a correlative emphasis upon the particular case or concrete example; an acute and imaginative concern with the forms under which human character and motivation may manifest themselves; and a passionate belief in the value of individual choice and judgement as contrasted with tame acquiescence in established opinions and norms. It was precisely his insistence upon the importance of personal decision, direct and unmediated by artifiicial ratiocination, that lay at the root of his rejection of *Hegel. For he saw in Hegelianism a philosophy which tended to obliterate, in the name of pretended metaphysical demonstrations, the element of subjective commitment and 'risk' implicit in every valid act of faith, and which sought to submerge the unique and unassimilable consciousiness of the individual beneath a welter of universal categories. To all such speculative attempts to conceal or explain away what is central to human existence as genuinely understood and known, Kierkegaard opposed the conception of authentic choice, the explicit self-commitment of a person who stakes his whole being and future upon a belief which he cannot prove but which he maintains in the face of all intellectual doubt and uncertainty. This idea finds forceful exemplification in the religious sphere, but it also applies within other domains of experience, e.g. the ethical. Some of Kierkegaard's most penetrating psychological observations occur in his descriptions of the 'leap of faith' and in his analyses of the state of 'dread' (*Angst*) which precedes and accompanies it; in such passages, too, one is made aware of the peculiar significance he attached to the notion of freedom. The stress upon freedom in his sense, as an inescapable condition of life and action and as something which both fascinates and repels the choosing individual, represents perhaps the clearest link between his philosophical ideas and the doctrines of his existentialist successors. (See EXISTENTIALISM.)

Killigrew, Mrs Anne, To the Pious Memory of, see DRYDEN.

KILLIGREW, Henry (1613–1700), brother of T. *Killigrew the elder, educated at Christ Church, Oxford, master of the Savoy Hospital in 1663, the author of one play, *The Conspiracy* (1638). He was the father of Anne Killigrew (1660–85; see DRYDEN).

KILLIGREW, Thomas, the elder (1612–83), page to Charles I and groom of the bedchamber and a favourite companion of Charles II. With *D'Avenant he held the monopoly of acting in Restoration London. He built a playhouse on the site of the present Theatre Royal Drury Lane, in 1663, and was master of the revels in 1679. His most popular play, *The Parson's Wedding*, a bawdy farcical comedy, was first performed 1640/1 and printed in 1664 with his other plays, which include *The Princess*, *The Prisoners*, *Claracilla*, and *Thomaso, or The Wanderer* (in two parts), on the last of which A. *Behn based her successful adaptation *The Rover*. *Cecilia and Clorinda*, a tragi-comedy in two parts, is based on a subject from *Artamène, ou le Grand Cyrus* by *Scudéry.

KILLIGREW, Thomas, the younger (1657–1719), son of T. *Killigrew the elder, and gentleman of the bed-chamber to George II when prince of Wales. He was the author of *Chit Chat*, a comedy acted in 1719.

KILLIGREW, Sir William (?1606–95), brother of T. *Killigrew the elder and author of *Selindra* and *Ormasdes, or Love and Friendship*, tragi-comedies, and *Pandora*, a comedy, published in 1664; and of *The Siege of Urbin*, a tragi-comedy, published in 1666. *Pandora* and *Selindra* were acted, and there is reason to think (*TLS* 18 Oct. 1928) that *The Siege of Urbin* was also acted.

Killing No Murder, a pamphlet ironically dedicated to *Cromwell, 'the true father of your country; for while you live we can call nothing ours, and it is from your death that we hope for our inheritances'; it advocates his assassination. It was written by the Leveller Edward Sexby (d. 1658) and printed in 1657 in Holland. The name on the title-page is that of William Allen, who had been one of Cromwell's Ironsides. See *Des révolutions d'Angleterre à la révolution française: le tyrannicide et Killing No Murder* (1973) by O. Lutaud.

Kilmeny, the subject of the 13th bard's haunting supernatural song in *The Queen's Wake* by J. Hogg. The girl Kilmeny goes up the glen, does not return, and is mourned for dead. At last she comes back. She had been carried away from the troubles of men to 'ane land of love, and ane land of lychte', from which she had a vision of war and sin in the world below. She asked to return to tell her friends what she had seen, and she returns transformed and sanctified; but after a month and a day she disappears and passes again to another world.

KILVERT, (Robert) Francis (1840–79), curate at Langley Burrell, Wiltshire, then at Clyro, Radnorshire; he was briefly vicar at Saint Harmon, Radnorshire, then became vicar of Bredwardine, Herefordshire, in 1877. He is remembered for his diary, kept with no thought of publication, from 1870 until his death; it was first published in a three-volume selection edited by W. *Plomer (1938–40), and has become established

as a classic of its kind. His wife, whom he married only five weeks before his death of peritonitis, destroyed large portions of it, but enough is left to provide a full portrait of the author and the remote and beautiful region of the Welsh borders where he lived and worked. He records the landscape which he loved and through which he indefatigably walked; the distresses of his parishioners; the life of the gentry, with their balls and conversaziones; and the beauty of girls, from early childhood to young womanhood, in clear and vivid prose, with much sensitivity and memorable detail. Two encounters of great importance to him were with the niece of *Wordsworth, who told him that her uncle 'could not bear the act of writing', and with W. *Barnes, 'the great idyllic Poet of England'.

Kim, a novel by *Kipling, published 1901.
   Kimball O'Hara, the orphaned son of a sergeant in an Irish regiment, spends his childhood as a vagabond in Lahore, until he meets an old lama from Tibet and accompanies him in his travels. He falls into the hands of his father's old regiment, is adopted, and sent to school, resuming his wanderings in his holidays. Colonel Creighton of the Ethnological Survey remarks his aptitude for secret service ('the Great Game'), and on this he embarks under the directions of the native agent Hurree Babu. While still a lad he distinguishes himself by capturing the papers of a couple of Russian spies in the Himalayas. The book presents a vivid picture of India, its teeming populations, religions and superstitions, and the life of the bazaars and the road.

KINCAID, Jamaica (1949–), novelist and short story writer, born Elaine Potter Richardson in Antigua. Her first work, *At the Bottom of the River* (1983), was a volume of short stories based on childhood in the Caribbean: her first novel, *Annie John* (1985), set in Antigua, explores the fierce vicissitudes of a daughter's love for her mother and her homeland; *Lucy* (1990) describes a girl leaving Antigua for America, and *The Autobiography of my Mother* (1995) is a first-person narrative in which a woman looks back on her troubled life. *A Small Place* (1988) describes Antigua. Some of her works were first published in the *New Yorker*, where she worked (1976–95) as a staff writer.

Kind Harts Dreame, a pamphlet by *Chettle, registered Dec. 1592, noteworthy for its allusion to Shakespeare.

Kind of Loving, A, a novel by S. *Barstow.

KING, Edward (1612–37), a contemporary of Milton at Cambridge and commemorated by him in *Lycidas*. There is no evidence that they were close friends.

KING, Francis Henry (1923–), novelist, short story writer, and critic, born in Switzerland, and brought up partly in Switzerland and India. He was educated at Shrewsbury School and Balliol College, Oxford, and for some years (1949–63) worked abroad for the British Council; several of his novels have foreign settings, notably Japan and Greece. They include *To the Dark Tower* (1946), *The Dividing Stream* (1951), *The Widow* (1957), *The Custom House* (1961), *Flights* (1973), and *The Action* (1979), and are marked by a cool and ironic detachment, close analysis of human motivation (particularly in some of its less admirable aspects), and an unobtrusive technical elegance. *Act of Darkness* (1983) is a psychological thriller, set largely in India; it describes, with considerable narrative power and an insight into perverse and pathological behaviour, the murder of a small boy. *The Nick of Time* (2003) describes the dubious but comic adventures of charming Albanian con-man, Mehmet. Volumes of short stories, which show the influence of *Chekhov and K. *Mansfield, include *The Brighton Belle and Other Stories* (1968) and *Hard Feelings and Other Stories* (1976). He has also written travel books, and a study of E. M. *Forster (*E. M. Forster and His World*, 1978), to whose work, in terms of social comedy and nuance and narrative lucidity, his own bears some similarity. *Yesterday Came Suddenly* (1993) is a spirited volume of autobiography.

KING, Henry (1592–1669), educated at Westminster and Christ Church, Oxford. He became bishop of Chichester and was the friend of *Donne and I. *Walton. He published poems sacred and profane, an unauthorized volume appearing in 1657. His best-known poem is 'An Exequy to his Matchless Never to be Forgotten Friend', written for his wife Anne who died in 1624. An edition of his poems, with a life, ed. Margaret Crum, appeared in 1965.

KING, Jessie, see ART NOUVEAU.

KING, Stephen, see GOTHIC FICTION and HORROR.

KING, William (1650–1729), archbishop of Dublin, author of *State of the Protestants in Ireland under the Late King James's Government* (1691) and *De Origine Mali* (1702).

KING, William (1663–1712), educated at Westminster and Christ Church, Oxford, an advocate at Doctors' Commons, a High Church Tory, and a writer of burlesques, satires, and light verse, much of which was published anonymously. In his *Dialogues of the Dead* (1699) he joined Charles Boyle in the attack on *Bentley. (See BATTLE OF THE BOOKS, THE.) Other works include *The Furmetary* (1699), *The Transactioneer* (1700, a satire on Sir H. *Sloane), and *The Art of Cookery, in Imitation of Horace's Art of Poetry* (1708).

King Alisaunder, an early 14th-cent. romance, probably from London, in 8,034 lines of short couplets, based on the late 12th-cent. Anglo-Norman *Roman de toute chevalerie* (which is unpublished). Passing remarks suggest that it was composed for oral delivery, though it also suggests wide literary range. It is based on a legend according to which Alexander was not the son of Philip of Macedon but of the Egyptian king Nectanabus who tricked Philip's wife by magic into

sleeping with him. The poem deals with the birth and youth of Alexander, his succession to Philip's throne, his conquest of Carthage and other cities, and his wars with Darius. The latter parts of the poem deal with his perils and conquests in the Far East (describing the geography and wonders of those regions), his seduction by Candace, and his death by poison. Though somewhat rambling in structure, the work is written in a lively verse and flexible metre that make it more compelling than most English romances of its period. Ed. G. V. Smithers (EETS os 227, 1952, and 237, 1957).

King and No King, A, a tragi-comedy by *Beaumont and *Fletcher (probably largely by Beaumont), performed 1611, printed 1619; it was one of their most successful dramas.

The emotional and erratic Arbaces, king of Iberia, has defeated Tigranes, king of Armenia, in single combat, thus bringing to an end a long war. Arbaces offers his prisoner freedom if he will marry his sister Panthea, who has grown up to womanhood during his long absence, but Tigranes loves Spaconia, an Armenian lady, declines the offer, and sends Spaconia to engage Panthea to oppose the match. However, when Tigranes and Arbaces meet Panthea, they are both so smitten by her beauty that they both fall violently in love with her. Arbaces encourages his own incestuous passion, and Panthea appears to return it; all seems set for sin, retribution, and tragedy when, in the last act, the lord protector of the kingdom, Gobrias, confesses that Arbaces is in fact his own son, therefore 'no king', and Panthea the true queen of Iberia. Arbaces and Panthea react to this news with joy and are united; Tigranes repents of his infidelity, takes Spaconia as his queen, and is released from captivity. Comic relief throughout is provided by Bessus, a cowardly braggart captain in Arbaces' army, who brings to mind *Parolles in *All's Well that Ends Well*, a play which has other similarities of plot and tone.

Dryden, in *Of Dramatick Poesy*, praises the play warmly for its skilful and theatrically effective denouement, and for the complex character of Arbaces ('that strange mixture of a man', derived, he supposes, from the extravagances of Alexander the Great); he writes, 'I find it moving when it is read', and concludes that the 'lively touches' of passion overcome the faults of the plot.

There is a modern edition by R. K. Turner (1964).

King Charles's head, a phrase taken from Mr Dick's obsession in *David Copperfield*, and thence used to describe any recurrent and irrational obsession.

King Horn, the earliest surviving English verse romance, of about 1,500 lines, dating from about 1225. The story is substantially the same as that of the later *Horn Childe*, concerning Horn, the son of the king and queen of Suddene, who is turned adrift by invading Saracens and falls in love with Rymenhild, the daughter of the king of Westernesse. Horn's companion Fikenhild betrays the lovers, has Horn banished to

Ireland, and marries Rymenhild. After spectacular deeds of prowess in Ireland, Horn returns to Westernesse in disguise and makes himself known to Rymenhild. Then, having recovered his land of Suddene, he kills Fikenhild and marries Rymenhild who becomes his queen. The plot is over-elaborate and the style is rudimentary, but the romance is full of life and traditional motifs. Ed. in W. H. French, *Essays on King Horn* (1940); the three manuscripts are edited together in J. Hall's edition, *King Horn* (1901).

Kingis Quair, The, 'The King's Book', a poem of 379 lines of rhyme-royal (so called because of its employment in this king's poem but previously used in Chaucer's *Troilus and Criseyde* and elsewhere), by *James I of Scotland while he was a prisoner in England and about the time of his marriage (*c*.1424) to Lady Jane Beaufort, the poem's heroine. It was discovered and printed by Lord Woodhouselee in 1783. It is one of the works traditionally described as 'Scottish *Chaucerian', and it does show the influence of Chaucer. C. S. *Lewis calls it the first poem in celebration of married love (though there are German poems of this kind about 1200, including a famous one by *Wolfram von Eschenbach, 'Der helden Minne'). The royal prisoner, lamenting his fortune, sees (like the noble prisoners in 'The Knight's Tale', *Canterbury Tales*, I) a beautiful lady walking in the garden below, and is smitten with love. He visits the empire of Venus and the palace of Minerva, goddess of wisdom; he speaks with the goddess Fortuna, and finally is assured by Venus of the ultimate success of his suit. *Rossetti quotes from the poem in *The King's Tragedy*. Ed. J. Norton-Smith (1971); W. A. Craigie, 'The Language of the *King's Quhair' (*Essays and Studies*, 25, 1940).

King John, a historical drama written in a first version before 1536, by *Bale.

King John, *The Life and Death of*, a historical play by *Shakespeare, possibly based on an anonymous play, *The Troublesome Raigne of John King of England* (1591), though the latter may be a derivative rather than a source. The date of Shakespeare's play is uncertain. It was first printed in the *Folio of 1623.

The play, with some departures from historical accuracy, deals with various events in King John's reign, and principally with the tragedy of young Arthur. It ends with the death of John at Swinstead Abbey. It is striking that no mention of Magna Carta appears in it. The tragic quality of the play, the poignant grief of Constance, Arthur's mother, and the political complications depicted are relieved by the wit, humour, and gallantry of the Bastard, supposed son of Faulconbridge, actually the son of Richard Cœur de Lion.

KINGLAKE, Alexander William (1809–91), educated at Eton and Trinity College, Cambridge. He published anonymously in 1844 *Eōthen: or Traces of Travel Brought Home from the East*, an account of a journey taken some ten years earlier which achieved instant success and is regarded as a classic of its genre. In his preface Kinglake explains that after several false starts he decided to cast his account in the form of a personal communication to a friend, which would aim at intimacy and avoid antiquarian research, statistics, and all display of 'sound learning, and religious knowledge'. The result is a lively description of his travels, giving his own reactions to, for example, the desert, the relics of the Holy Land, and the plague in Cairo; his friend B. E. G. *Warburton said it evoked 'the East itself in vital actual reality', and critics have often compared its familiar tone with that of Sterne's *Sentimental Journey*. He followed the British expedition to the Crimea in 1854, and devoted many years to an exhaustive history of the Crimean War (1863–87) which shows his great admiration for Lord Raglan.

King Lear, a tragedy by *Shakespeare, dating from 1604–5, performed at court 1606. The quarto printed in 1608 (reprinted 1619) is now thought to have been badly printed from Shakespeare's original manuscript, and the text of the First *Folio (1623) appears to represent a revision from a few years later. The play's sources include a chronicle play, *King Leir* (performed 1594, printed 1605), the chronicles of *Holinshed, and the *Mirror for Magistrates*. The Gloucester sub-plot derives from Sidney's *Arcadia*.

Lear, king of Britain, a petulant and unwise old man, has three daughters: Goneril, wife of the duke of Albany; Regan, wife of the duke of Cornwall; and Cordelia, for whom the king of France and duke of Burgundy are suitors. Intending to divide his kingdom among his daughters according to their affection for him, he bids them say which loves him most. Goneril and Regan make profession of extreme affection, and each receives one-third of the kingdom. Cordelia, self-willed, and disgusted with their hollow flattery, says she loves him according to her duty, not more nor less. Infuriated with this reply, Lear divides her portion between his other daughters, with the condition that himself with 100 knights shall be maintained by each daughter in turn. Burgundy withdraws his suit for Cordelia, and the king of France accepts her without dowry. The earl of Kent, taking her part, is banished. Goneril and Regan reveal their heartless character by grudging their father the maintenance that he had stipulated for, until, enraged, he rushes out of doors in a storm. The earl of Gloucester shows pity for the old king, and is suspected of complicity with the French, who have landed in England. His eyes are put out by Cornwall, who receives a death-wound in the affray. Gloucester's son Edgar, who has been traduced to his father by his bastard brother Edmund, takes the disguise of a lunatic beggar, and tends his father till the latter's death. Lear, whom rage and ill-treatment have deprived of his wits, is conveyed to Dover by the faithful Kent in disguise, where Cordelia receives him.

Meanwhile Goneril and Regan have both turned their affections to Edmund. Embittered by this rivalry, Goneril poisons Regan, and takes her own life. The English forces under Edmund and Albany defeat the French, and Lear and Cordelia are imprisoned; by Edmund's order Cordelia is hanged, and Lear dies from grief. The treachery of Edmund is proved by his brother Edgar. Gloucester's heart has "Twixt two extremes of passion, joy and grief, | Burst smilingly'. Albany, who has not abetted Goneril in her cruel treatment of Lear, takes over the kingdom.

KINGSLEY, Charles (1819–75), novelist and social reformer, born at Holme in Devon, where his father was curate-in-charge, was educated at Helston Grammar School (where Derwent Coleridge was headmaster), at King's College, London, and at Magdalene College, Cambridge. He became curate and subsequently, in 1844 (the year of his marriage to Frances Grenfell), rector of Eversley in Hampshire. During his engagement to her he had been working on a version of the life of St Elizabeth of Hungary which finally appeared as a blank verse drama, *The Saint's Tragedy*, in 1848; it deals with the conflict between natural affections and asceticism, and in a characteristically militant introduction Kingsley attacks 'those miserable dilettanti, who in books and sermons are whimpering meagre second-hand praises of celibacy', thus striking early in his career an anti-Tractarian note that recurs throughout his work. At this period he was much influenced by F. D. *Maurice and the writings of *Carlyle; he took a vigorous interest in the movement for social reform, while condemning the violent policies of the *Chartists. He contributed, over the signature 'Parson Lot', to *Politics for the People* in 1848, and to its successor, *The Christian Socialist*, in 1850–1.

His first novel, *Yeast*, was serialized in *Fraser's Magazine* in 1848, and published in book form in 1851; *Alton Locke* appeared in 1850. Both are reforming novels, showing his concern with the sufferings of the working classes. A visit to Germany in 1851 inspired his first historical novel, *Hypatia, or New Foes with Old Faces*, published in *Fraser's* in 1851 and in book form in 1853; set in 5th-cent. Alexandria, it exalts the Greek Neoplatonic philosopher Hypatia who was torn to pieces in AD 415 by a mob of infuriated Christians, and condemns the ignorant fanaticism of the Alexandrian monks. It had a mixed reception; many complained of its violence, its anachronisms, and its emphasis on Hypatia's nakedness at death; and *Newman's *Callista* was written in part to correct its hostile portrait of the early Church. His next novel, *Westward Ho!* (1855), was inspired by an upsurge of patriotism with which he greeted the Crimean War; set in the Elizabethan period, its hero, Devon seaman Amyas Leigh, wages war against the Armada and the Spanish captain Don Guzman, his rival in love. Its violent anti-Catholicism and bloodthirsty narrative shocked some readers, but delighted more; G. *Eliot's judgement in the *West-

minster Review was that Kingsley 'sees, feels and paints vividly, but he theorizes illogically and moralizes absurdly'. *Two Years Ago* (1857) returns to the theme of social reform and *Hereward the Wake* (1866) is a historical novel based on the exploits of the legendary outlaw, in Kingsley's version the son of Leofric of Mercia and Lady Godiva, who attempts to save England from the Normans.

Kingsley's other works include *The Heroes* (1856), in which he tells for young readers the stories of Perseus, Theseus, and the Argonauts, and *The Water-Babies* (1863), also for the young. The latter displays his profound and sympathetic interest in underwater and seashore life, as does his earlier work (which contains several tributes to his friend and fellow naturalist P. H. Gosse, father of E. *Gosse) *Glaucus: or The Wonders of the Shore* (1855). Of his poetry, the hexameters of 'Andromeda' (1858) and the dying monologue in blank verse of Saint Maura (1858), though psychologically revealing, are forgotten, whereas many of his songs and ballads remain popular; these include 'Airly Beacon' and 'The Sands of Dee', and many of his lines, such as 'Be Good, sweet maid, and let who can be clever' (quoted in *Two Years Ago*) and 'For men must work and women must weep', from 'The Three Fishers', have become proverbial. Kingsley also wrote tracts on many topics, published lectures and sermons, and his *At Last* (1871) is a record of a long-desired visit to the West Indies.

Kingsley in his lifetime was a celebrated and revered figure, who gained towards the end of his life (as professor of modern history at Cambridge, 1860–9, and as canon of Chester and Westminster) a high degree of public and indeed royal approval, but he remained the centre of controversy. His leanings towards polemics were most damagingly displayed in his celebrated confrontation with Newman, which was initiated by Kingsley's review in *Macmillan's Magazine* (Jan. 1864) of *Froude's *History of England*, vols vii and viii; in this he misrepresented Newman's sermon on 'Wisdom and Innocence' in support of his own statement that 'Truth for its own sake has never been a virtue of the Roman clergy.' After some correspondence, Newman's crushing rejoinder appeared in the form of his *Apologia*, and he was widely considered the victor of the exchange.

Although Kingsley's works are now read largely for their social interest and admired for their brilliantly evocative descriptive passages, his complex personality continues to interest biographers, and he seems to represent some of the central paradoxes of his age. A keen sportsman who was tender to animals, a champion of the working man who despised Negroes, a muscular Christian who wrote much (like his friend T. *Hughes) of the virtues of 'manliness' and who nevertheless held an unusually explicit physical passion for his wife, an admirer of physical prowess who himself suffered from an acute stammer and occasional nervous breakdowns, he was both Philistine and artist; his strong didacticism, while it mars many of his works, is inseparable from them. See R. B. Martin, *The Dust of Combat* (1959); Susan Chitty, *The Beast and the Monk* (1974); Brenda Colloms, *Charles Kingsley* (1975).

KINGSLEY, Henry (1830–76), younger brother of C. *Kingsley, was born at Barnack, Northamptonshire, where his father was rector. He spent his childhood at Clovelly, in Devon, and in Chelsea. He was educated at King's College School, London, and at Worcester College, Oxford, which he left without taking a degree. From 1853 to 1858 he was in Australia, at the gold-diggings and as a trooper in the Sydney Mounted Police. His Australian experiences provided the basis for two of his best novels, *Geoffry Hamlyn* (1859) and *The Hillyars and the Burtons* (1865), which have been influential in Australian literary history. After his return to England in 1858 he married his cousin Sarah Haselwood and lived at Wargrave, Berkshire, making a precarious living as a novelist and journalist (after his first four novels his popularity waned). For a time he was editor of the *Edinburgh Daily Review*, and was its correspondent at the Franco-Prussian War.

Ravenshoe (1862), the best-known of his 21 books, is a story of inheritance intrigues in a Roman Catholic landed family in Devon, and includes Crimean War scenes. Kingsley's best novels are distinguished for admirable descriptions of landscape in England and Australia, for engrossing accounts of storms and cyclones, attacks and alarms, and for humorous and well-observed character sketches. He was less skilled at sustained narration and at devising convincing plots, and was somewhat obsessed by his ideal of the virile and athletic 'English gentleman'. He was himself a keen athlete who once at Oxford, for a bet, ran a mile, rowed a mile, and trotted a mile, all within 15 minutes. His premature departure from Oxford, where he was a founder-member of an extremely misogynist club, has sometimes been attributed to homosexual tendencies, and he was also rumoured to have been an alcoholic in his later years, but there is no firm evidence on either of these points. Kingsley, an impulsive, convivial but insecure man, was a friend of M. *Arnold, *Swinburne, Lewis Carroll (*Dodgson), and Anne Thackeray (*Ritchie). His relations with his brother Charles in later life were soured by his frequent requests for money loans. See S. M. Ellis, *Henry Kingsley: Towards a Vindication* (1931); W. H. Scheuerle, *The Neglected Brother: A Study of Henry Kingsley* (1971).

KINGSLEY, Mary Henrietta (1862–1900), niece of C. *Kingsley. She was largely self-educated, and until the death of her parents in 1892 devoted herself to caring for them. In 1893 she made her first journey to West Africa, returning in 1894. *Travels in West Africa* (1897) is an account of her travels and ethnological researches, written in a lively, witty, and informal style, expressing her admiration for the peoples and landscape of the country, and recommending a closer understanding of African culture to its British

rulers. She went to South Africa in 1900 to nurse Boer prisoners of war, and died at Simonstown of enteric fever.

KINGSMILL, Hugh (Hugh Kingsmill Lunn) (1889–1949), anthologist, biographer, literary critic, novelist, and parodist, whose lives of M. *Arnold (1928), *Dickens (1935), and D. H. *Lawrence (1938) gave him a reputation for iconoclasm. He also wrote a life of F. *Harris (1932), with whom he had worked in 1912 on *Hearth and Home*. His other works include *The Return of William Shakespeare* (1929, a fictional fantasy with some perceptive literary criticism), and *The Progress of a Biographer* (1949, collected literary criticism). See M. *Holroyd, *Hugh Kingsmill: A Critical Biography* (1964); *The Best of Kingsmill*, ed. Holroyd (1970).

KINGSTON, W(illiam) H(enry) G(iles) (1814–80), an extremely prolific and successful writer of stories for boys, covering adventures in all continents, at sea, in history, at school, and elsewhere. Much of his work was published by the Society for Promoting Christian Knowledge, and a strong patriotic and didactic message is evident.

KIPLING, Rudyard (1865–1936), born in Bombay, son of John Lockwood Kipling, author and illustrator of *Beast and Man in India* (1891), and Alice Kipling, sister-in-law of *Burne-Jones. He was brought to England in 1871, where he spent five years living unhappily with a family in Southsea with his younger sister, separated from his parents, a period recalled with bitterness in his short story 'Baa, Baa, Black Sheep' (1888) and his novel *The Light that Failed* (1890). From 1878 to 1882 he attended the United Services College, Westward Ho!, later depicted in his schoolboy tales *Stalky & Co.* (1899). From 1882 to 1889 he worked as a journalist in India; many of his early poems and stories were originally published in newspapers or for the Indian Railway Library, and were later collected under various titles, which include *Departmental Ditties* (1886), *Plain Tales from the Hills* (1888), *Soldiers Three* (1890, in which the three soldiers are the three privates Learoyd, Mulvaney, and Ortheris), and *Wee Willie Winkie* (1890). In 1889 he came to London, where he achieved instant literary celebrity, aided by *Henley's publication in his *Scots Observer* of many of the poems ('Danny Deever', 'Mandalay', etc.) later collected as *Barrack-Room Ballads* (1892). In 1892 he married Caroline Balestier, sister of his American agent *Balestier (with whom he had written *The Naulahka*, 1892); from 1892 to 1896 the Kiplings lived on Balestier homeground at Brattleboro, Vermont. In 1896 they returned to England, settling finally at 'Bateman's' in Sussex in 1902, though Kipling continued to travel extensively, spending much time in South Africa, which he first visited in 1900 during the Boer War, where he had his first sight of warfare. Widely regarded as unofficial poet laureate, he refused many honours; in 1907 he was the first English writer to receive the *Nobel Prize.

Kipling's output was vast and varied, and has been variously judged. His early tales of the Raj, praised for their cynical realism, were compared to those of *Maupassant, but his growing reputation as the poet of empire cut both ways. His poem 'Recessional', written for Jubilee Day 1897, was acclaimed for catching the mood of the moment, but the mood changed. Kipling retained his popularity with the common soldier and reader, and his verse has added many phrases to the language (including, significantly, 'the white man's burden'), but he was increasingly accused of vulgarity and jingoism in aesthetic and anti-imperialist circles. His fluent versification, with its powerful echoes of hymns and ballads, and his use in both prose and verse of colloquial speech, impressed many but alienated others; even such admirers as H. *James, *Yeats, and T. S. *Eliot were uneasy about the nature of his art. His most uncontroversial and durable achievements are perhaps his tales for children (principally *The Jungle Book, 1894; Just So Stories, 1902; Puck of Pook's Hill, 1906; and Rewards and Fairies, 1910) and his picaresque novel of India *Kim, generally considered his masterpiece. His autobiographical fragment Something of Myself was published in 1937, and there are biographies by C. Carrington (1955), Angus *Wilson (1977), and Lord Birkenhead (1978).

Kipps, a novel by H. G. *Wells.

KIRK, Robert, see SECRET COMMONWEALTH OF ELVES, FAUNS AND FAIRIES, THE.

KIRKE, Edward (1553–1613), a friend of *Spenser, educated at Pembroke Hall and Caius College, Cambridge. He probably wrote the preface, the arguments, and a verbal commentary to Spenser's *Shepheardes Calender, under the initials 'E.K.' (1579). Modern critics have, on insufficient grounds, sought to prove that 'E.K.' was Spenser himself.

Kirkrapine, in Spenser's *Faerie Queene (I. iii), 'a stout and sturdie thiefe' of the Church, who is destroyed by *Una's lion.

KIRKUP, James (1918–), poet, translator, and travel writer, born in South Shields and educated at South Shields High School and Durham University; he has held many academic posts in England and abroad, notably in Japan and Malaya. His volumes of poetry include A Correct Compassion (1952, of which the title poem celebrates the precision of a surgical operation), The Descent into the Cave (1957), Paper Windows (1968), and A Bewick Bestiary (1971). In 1977 his poem 'The love that dares to speak its name' (which deals with the homosexual love of one of the Roman centurions for Christ) became the subject of the first prosecution for blasphemous libel for over 50 years, and as a result the editor of Gay News, the periodical which published the poem, was fined and given a suspended prison sentence. Kirkup's autobiographical The Only Child (1957) is an evocative account of a working-class northern childhood, and he has also published many books on Japan, and translated works by *Dürrenmatt, *Ibsen (with C. *Fry), *Valéry, and others. He has also published several books on Japan, and startlingly frank memoirs detailing his literary and homosexual adventures (A Poet Could Not But Be Gay, 1991; Me All Over, 1993).

Kit-Cat Club, founded in the early part of the 18th cent. by leading Whigs, including (according to *Pope) *Steele, *Addison, *Congreve, *Garth, and *Vanbrugh. *Tonson, the publisher, was for many years its secretary and moving spirit. It met at the house of Christopher Cat (or Kat), a pastrycook, in Shire Lane (which ran north from Temple Bar). Cat's mutton-pies were called Kit-cats, hence the name of the club (*Spectator, No. 9). The club subsequently met at Tonson's house at Barn Elms. The portraits of the members (painted by *Kneller and now in the possession of the National Portrait Gallery) had to be less than half-length because the dining-room was too low for half-size portraits. The term 'kit-cat' is in consequence still used for portraits of this size, with one arm shown.

kitchen sink drama, a term applied in the late 1950s to the plays of writers such as *Wesker, S. *Delaney, and J. *Osborne, which portrayed working-class or lower-middle-class life, with an emphasis on domestic realism. These plays were written in part as a reaction against the drawing-room comedies and middle-class dramas of *Coward and *Rattigan, and also undermined the popularity of the verse drama of T. S. *Eliot and C. *Fry. *Tynan was a principal advocate of this new group of writers.

KITCHIN, Clifford Henry Benn (1895–1967), novelist and barrister, educated at Exeter College, Oxford, whose great gifts as a chess player, bridge player, pianist, author, and investor of an inherited fortune led his close friend L. P. *Hartley to describe him as 'the most talented man I have ever known'. His early novels, Streamers Waving (1925) and Mr Balcony (1927), were witty and allusive, with a strong element of fantasy; the later ones, such as The Birthday Party (1938) and The Secret River (1956), were works of settled accomplishment. He also wrote several detective stories, including the well-known Death of My Aunt (1929).

Kite, Sergeant, one of the chief characters in Farquhar's *The Recruiting Officer. One of his songs is the well-known 'Over the hills and far away'.

Kitely, the jealous husband of Jonson's *Every Man in His Humour.

Kit Nubbles, a character in Dickens's *The Old Curiosity Shop.

KLOPSTOCK, Friedrich Gottlieb (1724–1803), German poet, famous for his patriotic odes and his great religious epic *Der Messias* (*The Messiah*), inspired by Milton's *Paradise Lost*, of which the first three cantos were published in 1748 and the last in 1773, and which is characterized by its pietistic delight in sentiment and its disregard for action.

Knag, Miss, in Dickens's *Nicholas Nickleby*, Madame Mantalini's forewoman.

KNELLER, Godfrey (1646/9–1723), portrait-painter born in Lübeck, trained in Holland and Italy, and arrived in England in 1676. His immensely successful career at the English court spans the reigns of five monarchs; he was knighted in 1692 and made a baronet in 1715. *Addison's poem on his picture of George I looks back at his portraits of earlier rulers, and is a witty résumé of the entire era recorded by the artist. Kneller painted many hundreds of portraits, of royalty, of the 'beauties' of the court, of admirals and generals, and of men eminent in the world of affairs and in literary life. Kneller's finest achievements are the *Kit-Cat series (1702–17; London, National Portrait Gallery) and several related portraits of scholars and poets. At their best, these works, sharp and direct in their portrayal of individual personality, reflect the sophisticated urbanity and rational temper of the 18th-cent. man of letters; outstanding are the portraits of *Dryden (c.1698) and *Prior (1700) (both Trinity College, Cambridge). Kneller, who lived in a grand house at Whitton, a neighbour of *Pope at Twickenham, knew most of the leading literary figures of the day. He was constantly flattered by poets, among them Dryden, Prior, and *Gay.

Knickerbocker Magazine, founded in New York City, 1 Jan. 1833, under the editorship of Charles Fenno Hoffman (1806–84). From that date until it was discontinued in 1865 the *Knickerbocker* numbered many of the foremost American writers among its contributors, including W. *Irving, H. W. *Longfellow, W. C. *Bryant, O. W. *Holmes, J. R. *Lowell, H. *Greeley, and J. F. *Cooper.

KNIGHT, Charles (1791–1873), son of a bookseller, an industrious and influential publisher who did much to introduce the sale of cheap books. He worked diligently to make knowledge available to the poor; and greatly assisted in creating, from the 1820s onwards, an entirely new class of reader. He was publisher to the 'Society for the Diffusion of Useful Knowledge', for whom he produced the *Penny Magazine*, the *Penny Cyclopaedia*, and other works, including 'The Library of Useful Knowledge'. Christopher Thomson, who in 1847 published his *Autobiography of an Artisan*, described how he went without sugar in his tea in order to afford the *Penny Magazine*. In 1825 Knight published his *Library of Entertaining Knowledge* and in 1842 his *Store of Knowledge*. His popular illustrated history of London appeared between 1841 and 1844, when his series 'Weekly Volumes', containing contributions from H. *Martineau, was published; in 1842

and 1844 his biographies of Shakespeare, of whose works he had produced a popular pictorial edition (1839–41), and *Caxton; and in 1856–62 *The Popular History of England*. His admirable *Passages of a Working Life* (1864–5) contains valuable information about the writers and the publishing trade of his time.

KNIGHT, G(eorge Richard) Wilson (1897–1985), Shakespeare scholar and critic. His poetic and symbolic approach to Shakespeare is perhaps seen at its best in *The Wheel of Fire* (1930), *The Imperial Theme* (1931), and *The Crown of Life* (1947), among many other publications. *The Starlit Dome* (1941) is a study of *Wordsworth, *Coleridge, *Shelley, and *Keats. Knight exercised considerable influence on Shakespearian production, himself giving memorable solo performances as *Timon and *Caliban.

KNIGHT, William Payne, see PICTURESQUE.

Knightley, George, and John, his brother, characters in J. Austen's *Emma*.

Knight of the Burning Pestle, The, a comedy now thought to be the unaided work of *Beaumont, but formerly generally attributed to Beaumont and *Fletcher; it was probably performed 1607–8, and was printed (anonymously) 1613. The most successful of Beaumont's plays, it is a high-spirited comedy of manners, and a burlesque of knight-errantry and of such fabulous and patriotic plays as *Heywood's *The Four Prentices of London* and *The Travels of the Three English Brothers* by *Day, *Rowley, and George Wilkins. It has clear echoes of *Don Quixote*, both in attitude and incident, and satirizes the middle-class taste for such popular and improbable romances as *Palmerin of England*.

It takes the form of a play-within-a-play: a grocer and his wife, members of an audience about to watch a drama called 'The London Merchant', interrupt the prologue to insist that their apprentice Rafe have a part. He therefore becomes a Grocer Errant, with a Burning Pestle portrayed on his shield, and undertakes various absurd adventures, including the release of patients held captive by a barber, Barbarossa. These are interspersed with the real plot, in which Jasper, a merchant's apprentice, woos, and after much opposition wins, his master's daughter Luce.

There is a modern edition by S. P. Zitner (1984).

Knight of the Rueful (or **Sad,** or **Woeful,** or **Sorrowful**) **Countenance,** *Don Quixote.

KNIGHTS, L(ionel) C(harles) (1906–97), Shakespeare critic, and for 22 years member of the editorial board of *Scrutiny*. His longer books include *Drama and Society in the Age of Jonson* (1937) and *Some Shakespearean Themes* (1959). One of his best-known essays is 'How many children had Lady Macbeth?' (1933), a celebrated attack on the style of criticism represented by A. C. *Bradley.

Knights of the Round Table, see ROUND TABLE.

'Knight's Tale, The', see CANTERBURY TALES, 1.

KNOLLES, Richard (?1550–1610), author of *The Generall Historie of the Turkes* (1603), which was much admired by Dr *Johnson (who took from it the plot of his *Irene*), and also by *Byron, who credited it with inspiring the 'oriental colouring' of his poetry.

Knowell, in Jonson's *Every Man in His Humour*, Edward's over-solicitous father.

KNOWLES, James Sheridan (1784–1862). After trying the army, medicine, and teaching, he became an actor and verse dramatist, and was described by the *Edinburgh Review* in 1833 as 'the most successful dramatist of the day'. His *Virginius* was produced at Covent Garden with C. *Kemble and *Macready in 1820; *Caius Gracchus* in 1823 (1815 Belfast); *William Tell* in 1825. His greatest success was *The Hunchback*, produced in 1832; *The Wife*, with Prologue and Epilogue by *Lamb, followed in 1833, and in 1837 his highly successful *The Love Chase*. His friend *Hazlitt described Knowles as 'the first tragic writer of his time', and he was the recipient of many of the letters in Hazlitt's *Liber Amoris*.

KNOWLES, Sir James Thomas (1831–1908), editor, architect, and a friend of *Tennyson. He published in 1862 *The Story of King Arthur and His Knights* from Malory's *Morte D'Arthur*. He founded the *Metaphysical Society, became editor of the *Contemporary Review* in 1870, and in 1877 founded the *Nineteenth Century*.

KNOX, Edmund George Valpy ('Evoe') (1881–1971), essayist, humorist, and parodist, brother of R. A. *Knox. He contributed to *Punch* as 'Evoe', and was editor 1932–49.

KNOX, John (c.1513–72), educated at Haddington School and Glasgow University. He was called to the ministry and began preaching for the reformed religion in 1547. In 1551 he became chaplain to Edward VI. He went abroad at the accession of Mary Tudor, wrote his 'Epistle on Justification by Faith' in 1548, met *Calvin at Geneva in 1554, was pastor of the English congregation at Frankfurt am Main, 1554–5, and from 1556 to 1558 lived at Geneva. Thence he addressed epistles to his brethren in England suffering under the rule of Mary Tudor, and in Scotland under the regency of Mary of Lorraine. It was this situation which led to the publication of his *First Blast of the Trumpet against the Monstrous Regiment of Women* (1558), of which the title, *Saintsbury remarks, was the best part. (The phrase is often now misapplied: 'Regiment' here has its old sense of 'rule, magisterial authority', and has no connection with the later sense of 'large body of troops'.) In 1559 appeared the *First Book of Discipline*, of which Knox was part-author, advocating a national system of education ranging from a school in every

parish to the three universities. His *Treatise on Predestination* was published in 1560. In 1572 he was appointed minister at Edinburgh, where he died. His *History of the Reformation of Religion within the Realm of Scotland* was first printed in 1587 (the best edition of this is in the first two vols of Laing's edition of Knox's *Works*, 1846–8). It contains, in its fourth book, the notable account of the return of Mary Stuart to Scotland, of Knox's interviews with her, and his fierce denunciations from the pulpit of St Giles.

KNOX, the Rt Revd Monsignor Ronald Arbuthnott (1888–1957), educated at Eton and Balliol College, Oxford, where he acquired a reputation as a writer of witty light verse. He was fellow of Trinity, 1910–17, when he was received into the Church of Rome. His autobiographical *A Spiritual Aeneid* (1918) describes his conversion. Knox wrote many theological works, published a new translation of the Bible, based on the *Vulgate (1945–9), and acquired a wide reputation as journalist and broadcaster. He also wrote six detective stories. *Let Dons Delight* (1939), a work for which he himself had a particular affection, uses a dream framework to describe, through conversations in an Oxford senior common room at 50-year intervals, the process of specialization and fragmentation that leads to the loss of a common culture. After the Second World War he became a close friend of E. *Waugh, who wrote his official biography (1959); see also *The Knox Brothers* (1977) by Penelope *Fitzgerald, daughter of E. G. V. *Knox.

KNOX, Vicesimus (1752–1821), educated at St John's College, Oxford, remembered as the compiler of *Elegant Extracts* (1784), an anthology of passages from H. *Blair, *Hurd, *Sterne, *Smollett, etc. He was author of *Essays, Moral and Literary* (1778).

KNYVETT, Thomas (1596–1658), born at Ashwellthorpe in Norfolk, and educated at Emmanuel College, Cambridge. He was a landowner in the eastern counties, and a Royalist in sympathy during the Civil War. His letters to his wife, which have been preserved, throw light on the life of the period. They have been edited by B. Schofield (1949).

KOESTLER, Arthur (1905–83), author, born in Budapest and educated at the University of Vienna. He worked as foreign correspondent in the Middle East, Paris, and Berlin. In 1932 he joined the Communist Party and travelled in the USSR; he was imprisoned under Franco during the Spanish Civil War and broke from the Party in 1938. In 1940 he came to England, adopting the language with his first book written in English, *Scum of the Earth* (1941). His publications manifest a wide range of political, scientific, and literary interests, and include *Darkness at Noon* (1940), *Arrival and Departure* (1943), and *Thieves in the Night* (1946), novels concerned with the ethics of revolution and survival. Non-fiction includes *The Yogi and the Commissar and Other Essays* (1945), *The Trail of* the Dinosaur and Other Essays (1955), and The Act of Creation (1964). The Roots of Coincidence (1972) reflects his interest in parapsychology. He was one of the contributors to *The God that Failed: Six Studies in Communism (1950). He died by suicide with his wife, having frequently expressed a belief in the right to euthanasia.

Koran, or **Qur'ān,** the sacred book of Islam, regarded by Muslims as the final revelation of God to humankind, passed by the archangel Gabriel in Arabic to Muhammad, the last of the prophets. It consists of 114 chapters or sūras which contain narratives of Arab legend, Old Testament stories (notably Moses and Abraham), New Testament stories (especially Mary and Jesus), and Christian legend (e.g. the *Seven Sleepers of Ephesus). The style of the Koran is by turns gnomic, admonitory, dramatic, and legalistic; the early Meccan material is terse and dense, and the later Medinan material diffuse and evocative in substance but rendered coherent in Arabic by the rhetorical use of assonance. Such factors convince orthodox Muslims that the Koran cannot be translated accurately, and should therefore not be translated. There have nonetheless been a few translations into English by Arabs and some 35 translations by Muslims in the Indian subcontinent. Such translations are usually called 'interpretations', partly because translation is not thought possible, but also because the original Kufic script had neither vowels nor diacritical marks, and so meaning has been mediated through a long tradition of learned commentary which renders the text intelligible.

In Britain there have been several complete translations by non-Muslims and one by an expatriate Muslim convert. The first translation, by Alexander Ross (1649), was based on a French version, and its interest is historical rather than literary. The first translation from Arabic was that of George Sale (1734), who was followed by John Rodwell (1861; now the Everyman text), Edward Palmer (1880), Richard Bell (1937–9), Arthur Arberry (1955, now the Oxford text), and N. J. Dawood (1956, rev. 1974; the Penguin text). Of these the most successful are the translations by Arberry, who recreates the rhapsodic character of the Arabic by setting out his rhythmical prose as if it were poetry, and Dawood, who translates into contemporary English. The finest and most influential translation, by virtue of the dignity and fluidity of its prose and the resourcefulness with which it evokes the tone of the Arabic by recourse to the cadences of Jacobean English, is that of Muhammed Marmaduke Pickthall (1930), an English convert to Islam who spent much of his life in the service of the Nizam of Hyderabad.

KOTZEBUE, August von (1761–1819), German dramatist, author of a large number of sentimental plays which had considerable vogue in their day and influenced the English stage. His Menschenhass und Reue (1789) enjoyed great popularity as The Stranger, brought out by *Sheridan in 1798, the story of a wife duped and erring, her husband in consequence turned misanthropical, the wife's repentance, the reconciliation, and the husband's return to sanity. *Lovers' Vows, made famous by J. Austen's *Mansfield Park, was adapted by Mrs *Inchbald from Kotzebue's Das Kind der Liebe (1790). Sheridan adapted Die Spanier in Peru (1797) as Pizarro.

'Kraken, The', a short poem by *Tennyson, published in Poems, Chiefly Lyrical (1830). It describes the mythical sea-monster mentioned by *Pontoppidan, sleeping in the depths of the sea 'his ancient, dreamless, uninvaded sleep', and waiting only to rise and die; Christopher Ricks (Tennyson, 1972) describes it as an example of the poet's 'pained fascination with the thought of a life which somehow is not life at all'.

Krook, a character in Dickens's *Bleak House.

KRYLOV, Ivan Andreevich (1769–1844), Russian writer of fables. He entered the civil service at an early age, but soon turned to satirical journalism. When the journal he edited, the St Petersburg Mercury, was closed down, he abandoned literature until 1805, when he translated his first fable by *La Fontaine. In 1809 a book of 23 fables, some still based on La Fontaine, met with enormous success. He wrote nine books of fables in all, and their common sense, universality, and linguistic vigour has secured their continuing popularity. Many of their conclusions and morals have become proverbial in Russia. The fables were first translated by W. R. S. Ralston in 1869, and are now most accessible in the translations of Sir Bernard Pares (1926, etc.).

'Kubla Khan: A Vision in a Dream', a poem by S. T. *Coleridge, published 1816.

In 1797, while living near the *Wordsworths in Somerset, Coleridge took opium and fell asleep when reading a passage in Purchas his Pilgrimage (see PURCHAS), relating to the Khan Kubla and the palace that he commanded to be built. He claimed that on awaking he was conscious of having composed in his sleep two or three hundred lines on this theme, and eagerly began to set down the lines that form this fragment. He was then unfortunately interrupted by 'a person . . . from Porlock', and, on returning to his task an hour later, found that almost the entire remainder of the poem had slipped from his memory. The poem has no narrative line, but consists of a series of potent visionary images, suggesting themes of eternity and change. Alph, the sacred river, flung up in a tremendous fountain, connects Khan's 'stately pleasure-dome', great caverns, and the 'sunless sea'. Within the gardens of the pleasure-dome is growth and sunlight and colour. There are hints of death and war, the vision of a damsel with a dulcimer, and of the frenzy of the poet who has drunk 'the milk of Paradise'. Coleridge thought the poem 'a psychological curiosity', but later in his work on literary criticism vigorously defended poetic images 'just on the vestibule of Consciousness'. *Lowes, in *The Road to Xanadu* (1927), traces the varied sources of Coleridge's imagery. See also Alethea Hayter, *Opium and the Romantic Imagination* (1968).

KUNDERA, Milan (1929–   ), Czech novelist, born in Brno, and educated in Prague, where he later taught at the Institute for Advanced Cinematographic Studies. He lost his post after the Russian invasion in 1968, and in 1975 settled in Paris. His first novel, *Zert*, was published in 1967 (English trans., *The Joke*, 1969). His other novels (which have not been published in his own country) include *The Farewell Party* (1976, English trans. 1977) and *The Book of Laughter and Forgetting* (French, 1979; English, 1980), a semi-fictional, semi-autobiographical evocation of the cultural, political, and sexual life of post-war Europe, seen partly through Kundera's own eyes, partly through those of several of the 'two or three new fictional characters baptized on earth every second'. Other novels include *Life is Elsewhere* (French, 1973; English, 1986), in which the central characters are an aspiring poet and his mother, and *The Unbearable Lightness of Being* (English, 1984), a classic of *magic realism. *Laughable Loves* (Czech, 1969; English, 1991) is a collection of stories. He has also written on *The Art of the Novel* (French, 1986; English, 1988).

KUREISHI, Hanif (1954–   ), screenwriter and novelist, born in Bromley, south London, and educated at King's College, London. His mother is English, his father Pakistani. His screenplays include *My Beautiful Laundrette* (1986) and *Sammy and Rosie Get Laid* (1987). His first novel, *The Buddha of Suburbia* (1990), is a spirited narration by bisexual Karim Amir, 'an Englishman born and bred, almost', whose father Haroon came to England from Bombay in 1950. It offers a comic, idiosyncratic, and startling panorama of multicultural south London suburban life, adolescent and middle-aged sex, party going, and yoga—a world in which Muslim patriarchal attitudes and the arranged marriage (of Jamila, daughter of Uncle Anwar of Paradise Stores) coexist with Karim's ambitions as an actor and his friend Charlie's success as a rock-star in New York.

Other works include the novel *The Black Album* (1995), dealing with race and religion in contemporary London, and *Love in a Blue Time* (short stories, 1997). *My Son the Fanatic* (screenplay, pub. 1998, based on one of these stories) portrays the conflict between a liberal-minded north country immigrant taxi-driver and his fundamentalist convert son. *Intimacy* (1998) is a confessional novella narrated by a man about to leave his partner and sons.

Kurtz, a character in Conrad's *'Heart of Darkness' whose epitaph, 'Mistah Kurtz—he dead', provides the epigraph for T. S. *Eliot's 'The Hollow Men'.

KYD, or **KID,** Thomas (1558–94), dramatist, born in London. He was educated at *Merchant Taylors' School, London, whose headmaster was *Mulcaster; he may have worked for a time as a scrivener. He wrote (now lost) plays for the Queen's Men c.1583–5 and was in the service of an unknown lord 1587–93. He seems to have been associated with *Marlowe, with whom he shared lodgings in 1591, and whose 'atheistical' writings led to Kyd's suffering a period of torture and imprisonment in 1593. His *Spanish Tragedy (c.1587) was published anonymously in 1592. The play proved exceptionally popular on the Elizabethan stage and passed through eleven printed editions by 1633. The only work published under his name was a translation of Robert Garnier's neo-Senecan *Cornelia (1594), reissued in 1595 as *Pompey the Great, His Faire Corneliaes Tragedie. The First Part of Ieronimo* (printed 1605) is probably a burlesque adaptation of a fore-piece to *The Spanish Tragedy. Other works Kyd is likely to have written are a lost pre-Shakespearian play on the subject of Hamlet, *The Householders Philosophie* (a prose translation from *Tasso) and *The Tragedye of Solyman and Perseda* (printed 1592).

KYRLE, John, the Man of Ross (1637–1724). He lived very simply upon his estates at Ross and devoted his surplus income to charity. *Pope's portrait of him in his *Epistle to Bathurst* (see MORAL ESSAYS) was based on information supplied by the elder *Tonson, who had an estate in Ledbury. There is a later account in the *Gentleman's Magazine* (1786) by 'Viator'.

L

'**La Belle Dame sans Merci'**, a ballad by *Keats, written 1819, published 1820, which describes a knight fatally enthralled by an elfin woman. Although Keats himself spoke of it lightly, critics and biographers have written of it at length, many concurring with Robert *Graves (*The White Goddess*, 1948) that 'the Belle Dame represented Love, Death by Consumption . . . and Poetry all at once'. It was much admired by the *Pre-Raphaelites and W. *Morris asserted that 'it was the germ from which all the poetry of his group had sprung.'

La Belle Dame sans mercy is also the title of a poem translated from *Chartier, attributed at one time to *Chaucer, but now thought to be the work of Sir Richard Ros.

LA BRUYÈRE, Jean de (1645–96), French satiric moralist, author of *Les Caractères ou les mœurs de ce siècle* (1688; *The Characters, or The Manners of the Age*, 1699). The work, consisting of short portrait sketches revelatory of the vanity and corruption in human behaviour, was published as an appendage to La Bruyère's translation of the *Characters* of *Theophrastus from which it derives its method. It was immediately successful on publication, and has been widely admired by such writers as *Flaubert, *Gide, and *Proust. See also CHARACTER WRITING.

LA CALPRENÈDE, Gauthier de Costes de (1614–63), French novelist. His heroic romances achieved an immense international vogue, and had a marked effect on the heroic drama of high classicism in France and of the English Restoration. They divide into three cycles: *Cassandre* (10 vols, 1644–50), trans. Sir Charles Cotterell (1667), centred on the life of the daughter of Darius, wife of Alexander the Great; *Cléopâtre* (12 vols, 1647–56), trans. R. Loveday and others (1652–9), describing the adventures of the daughter of Antony and Cleopatra; and *Pharamond* (12 vols, 1661–70), first four vols trans. John Davies (1662), narrating the loves of the first French kings for the Cambrian princess Rosemonde.

LACAN, Jacques, see STRUCTURALISM and MARXIST LITERARY CRITICISM.

LACLOS, Pierre Choderlos de (1741–1803), French novelist. His masterpiece, *Les Liaisons dangereuses* (1782), influenced by *Richardson's epistolary novels, records the unscrupulous seductions of Valmont, aided by his accomplice Mme de Merteuil. In depicting the moral and sexual raids of a cynical aristocratic couple on an unsuspecting society, it remarkably combines searching psychological analysis in the manner of 17th-cent. drama, the assumptions of 18th-cent. philosophical sensationalism, and intimations of demonic Romantic revolt. It was successfully adapted for stage and screen by C. *Hampton, whose work caught the mood of the cynical 1980s.

La Creevy, Miss, the cheerful little miniature-painter in Dickens's *Nicholas Nickleby*.

Ladislaw, Will, a character in G. Eliot's *Middlemarch*.

Lads' literature. By the mid-1990s, most of the feminist battles of the last three decades seemed to have been won, at least in the rather rarefied circles inhabited by writers and publishers. It was time for a backlash. Sections of the media now began to exalt an old-fashioned, unreconstructed model of the British male, for whom the female body was once again relentlessly objectified and the ideal of serious commitment to emotional relationships was jettisoned in favour of a sort of boorish hedonism centred around sport, drinking, and recreational sex. Propaganda along these lines was issued, beneath a cheery veneer of *postmodern irony, by a new rash of men's magazines including *Loaded*, *Arena*, and *FHM*.

The 'New Lad' was born, and soon established his own, quite distinct tastes in literature. Among the key texts are Nick *Hornby's *Fever Pitch* (1992) and *High Fidelity* (1995), which show how the languages of football and record collecting can function as a code in which men discuss their feelings; *A White Merc with Fins* (1996) and *Rancid Aluminium* (1997) by James Hawes, notable both for their laconic, wisecracking style and their emphasis on violence as a means of resolving conflict (they owe a strong debt to Quentin Tarantino, the New Lad's favourite film director); John King's *The Football Factory* (1996), *Headhunters* (1997), and *England Away* (1998), which have attracted many male readers by offering a vicarious insight into the world of football hooligans; and, from a slightly earlier era, Bret Easton Ellis's *American Psycho* (1991), in which the female body is repeatedly mutilated and dismembered in the name of social satire.

In 1996 a backlash-against-the-backlash was instigated by *Bridget Jones's Diary*, an immensely successful novel in *diary form by Helen Fielding, whose heroine's frustration at the emotional fecklessness of her various boyfriends struck a chord with thousands of female readers.

Lady Audley's Secret, see BRADDON.

Lady Chatterley's Lover, a novel by D. H. *Lawrence
(privately printed, Florence, 1928; expurgated version,
London, 1932; full text, London, 1960).

Constance Chatterley is married to Sir Clifford,
writer, intellectual, and landowner, of Wragby Hall in
the Midlands. He is confined to a wheelchair through
injuries from the First World War. She has an
unsatisfying affair with a successful playwright,
Michaelis, followed by a passionate love relationship
with gamekeeper Oliver Mellors, son of a miner and ex-
officer from the Indian army. She becomes pregnant by
him, goes to Venice with her sister Hilda partly to
obscure the baby's parentage, but returns and tells her
husband the truth, spurred on by the knowledge that
Mellors's estranged wife Bertha has been stirring
scandal in an effort to reclaim him. The novel ends
with the temporary separation of the lovers, as they
hopefully await divorce and a new life together.

Lawrence's detailed and poetic descriptions of sexual union, and his uncompromising use of four-letter
words, caused the book (long available in foreign
editions) to be unpublishable in full in England until
1960 when *Penguin Books took the risk of producing
a complete text. They were prosecuted under the
Obscene Publications Act 1959, and acquitted after a
celebrated trial during which many eminent authors
(including E. M. *Forster, R. *Hoggart, H. *Gardner)
appeared as witnesses for the defence, a victory which
had a profound effect on both writing and publishing
in subsequent decades.

Lady of May, The, a short pastoral entertainment by P.
*Sidney. It consists of a dispute between a shepherd
and a forester for the hand of the rustic May Lady, and
was performed under the aegis of the earl of *Leicester
for *Elizabeth I when she visited him at Wanstead in
1578 or 1579. The character of the pedantic schoolmaster Rombus may have suggested that of Holofernes
in *Love's Labour's Lost.

Lady of Pleasure, The, a comedy by J. *Shirley, acted
1635, printed 1637.

In the central plot Lady Bornwell is cured of her
desire to live a life of thoughtless pleasure, partly by the
discovery of the worthlessness of her foppish suitors
and partly by her husband's pretence that he too means
to live extravagantly. The play's scenes of fashionable
conversation, the contrast between the manners of the
true gentleman and lady of the sub-plot and the
affected main-plot characters, and the rapid transformation of the scholarly bashfulness of Lady Bornwell's nephew Frederick into town debauchery, are a
cross between *Jonson's comedy of humours and
*Restoration comedy of manners; the moral tone of the
ending, in which Lady Bornwell decides to return to the
country, contrasts with the largely amoral tone of much
that has gone before.

'Lady of Shalott, The', a poem by *Tennyson, published 1832, much revised for the 1842 *Poems*.

Tennyson said of it 'I met the story first in some
Italian novelle: but the web, mirror, island etc. were my
own. Indeed, I doubt whether I should ever have put it
into that shape if I had then been aware of the Maid of
Astolat in Mort Arthur.' (Quoted by F. J. *Furnivall,
1868.) The story bears little resemblance to his subsequent treatment of it in 'Lancelot and Elaine' of the
Idylls of the King. The Lady, like *Mariana, was one of
several enchanted or imprisoned maidens to capture
the Victorian imagination, and was the subject of
many illustrations, including a notable one by Holman
*Hunt.

Lady of the Idle Lake, see PHAEDRIA.

Lady of the Lake, in the Arthurian legends, a rather
shifting supernatural character. In *Malory she gives
Arthur the sword Excalibur, but when she asks for the
head of Balyn as payment Balyn strikes off her head, for
which deed he is banished from the court. Also called
the Lady of the Lake (in Malory 'chief' lady, suggesting
more than one) is Nimiane (Nymue and, probably by
scribal misreading, Vivien), the wife of Pelleas, who
loves Merlin, whom she tricks into revealing his magic
arts and then imprisons in a tower of air in the forest of
*Broceliande from which he never escapes. In Malory
she is said to have accompanied the three queens who
bore Arthur away by ship after his death. In Celtic
origin she may derive from Morgan, the archetypal
lake lady.

Lady of the Lake, The, a poem in six cantos by Sir W.
*Scott, published 1810.

The action takes place chiefly on and around Loch
Katrine in Perthshire, and involves the wooing of Ellen
Douglas, the lady of the title and daughter of the
outlawed Lord James of Douglas: she is courted by
various suitors, including a mysterious wandering
huntsman-knight whom she ferries to the island in the
lake, and who after various adventures and skirmishes
is revealed at court, as she seeks her father's pardon, to
be King James V himself. The lively narrative evokes
highland scenery and manners, and contains various
poetic interludes, including the *coronach (Canto III)
'He is gone on the mountain' and the ballad (Canto IV)
'Alice Brand', which tells the story of Alice's lost
brother, transformed by the Elf King into a hideous
dwarf, and redeemed by his sister's courage. The poem
was immensely popular, and inspired several composers, including *Schubert and *Rossini.

Lady's Not for Burning, The, a play by C. *Fry,
performed 1948, published 1949. A springtime romantic comedy in verse, set in 1400, it introduces
Jennet Jourdemayne, young, beautiful, and accused of
witchcraft, to world-weary ex-soldier Thomas Mendip
who insists he wishes to be hanged. They fall in love
and all ends happily. Full of verbal invention and word-
play, it was one of the most enjoyable and successful
works of the post-war revival of verse drama.

Lady Susan, a novel by J. *Austen, written probably 1793–4, published 1871, from an untitled manuscript dated 1805: the manuscript is a fair copy, and the date of composition is discussed by B. C. Southam, *Jane Austen's Literary Manuscripts* (1964). It is Jane Austen's only *epistolary novel, although her first version of *Sense and Sensibility*, called *Elinor and Marianne*, was also in letter form.

The story consists of letters, written chiefly between the kindly Mrs Vernon and her mother Lady de Courcy, and between Lady Susan and her London friend Mrs Johnson. The events occur mainly at Churchill, the country house of the Vernons. Lady Susan, the widow of Mr Vernon's brother, is beautiful, selfish, and unscrupulous. She has had to leave the house of the Mainwarings, where both Mr Mainwaring and his sister's suitor Sir James Martin have fallen in love with her. At Churchill she meets Reginald de Courcy, Mrs Vernon's brother, young and gullible, who also succumbs to her superficial charms. Lady Susan's 16-year-old daughter Frederica is terrorized by her mother, and becomes so distraught when learning of her mother's plan to marry her off to Sir James Martin that she begs Reginald de Courcy to intercede for her. The story then breaks off and the author appends a 'Conclusion', informing the reader that Lady Susan herself married Sir James Martin; that Frederica went to live at Churchill and would in time marry Reginald; and that 'this correspondence [i.e. the novel] . . . could not, to the great detriment of the Post Office revenue, be continued any longer'.

Laertes, in Shakespeare's *Hamlet*, the brother of Ophelia.

LA FAYETTE, Marie-Madeleine de La Vergue, comtesse de (1634–93), French novelist. The centre of a select circle in Paris which included Mme de *Sévigné and *La Rochefoucauld, she published three novels, the third of which, *La Princesse de Clèves* (1678), ensured her place in French literature. It is concerned with its heroine's overwhelming passion for an outsider from the point of view of its effects on her otherwise successful marriage. Written with harmonious sobriety and unaffected sympathy, *La Princesse* transformed the novel of romance, as practised by Mme de *Scudéry and *La Calprenède, into the novel of character. It was translated into English in 1679.

Lafeu, an old lord in Shakespeare's *All's Well that Ends Well*.

La Fleur, Yorick's French servant in Sterne's *A Sentimental Journey*.

LA FONTAINE, Jean de (1621–95), French poet, author of the *Fables*, a collection of some 240 poems, published in 12 books between 1668 and 1694 (English trans., 1734). The material for the fables is drawn from Eastern, classical, and modern sources, and a number of them, such as 'La Cigale et la fourmi' ('The Grass-

hopper and the Ant') or 'Le Corbeau et le renard' ('The Crow and the Fox'), have long enjoyed widespread popularity in France.

LAFORGUE, Jules (1860–87), French poet, prominent in the development of *vers libre*, author of *Les Complaintes* (1885), *L'Imitation de Notre-Dame la Lune* (1886), and the posthumously published *Derniers Vers* (1890). The characteristic tone of his poetry is one of ironic self-deprecation. He was an important influence on the early work of T. S. *Eliot, and on the poetry of *Pound (see *Canto* CXVI). Three of his poems were translated by H. *Crane (1922). He also published a collection of short stories, *Moralités légendaires* (1887).

Lagado, see GULLIVER'S TRAVELS.

LAING, R(onald) D(avid) (1927–89), author, poet, psychoanalyst, born in Glasgow. He studied medicine at Glasgow University. His works include *The Divided Self* (1960), *Sanity, Madness and the Family* (1964), and *The Politics of Experience and the Bird of Paradise* (1967). *Knots* (1970) is a collection of poem-pattern-dialogues revealing the 'knots, tangles. . . impasses, disjunctions' of various forms of what he describes as human bondage. His radical ideas on madness, family dynamics, and care in the community made a considerable impact on the counter-culture of the 1960s, and his work has continued to exert an influence. Mary Barnes, one of his patients at his experimental therapeutic centre, Kingsley Hall, was to be the subject of a play by David *Edgar.

Lake Poets, Lake School, terms applied to *Coleridge, *Southey, *Wordsworth, and sometimes to *De Quincey, who lived in the Lake District at the beginning of the 19th cent. The expression 'Lake School' seems first to appear in the *Edinburgh Review* of Aug. 1817. *Byron makes play with the term, and in the dedication to *Don Juan* (1819) refers slightingly to 'all the Lakers'. In his *Recollections of the Lake Poets* De Quincey denies the existence of any such 'school'.

Lallans, see SCOTS.

Lalla Rookh, a series of *Oriental tales in verse connected by a story in prose, by T. *Moore, published 1817. The first of the tales is written in heroic couplets, the others in stanzas of varied metre. The work enjoyed immense popularity, and went into 20 editions by 1840.

The frame story tells of the journey of Lalla Rookh ('Tulip Cheek'), the daughter of the emperor, from Delhi to Kashmir, to be married to the king of Bucharia. On the way she and her train are diverted by four verse tales told by Feramorz, a young Kashmiri poet, with whom she falls in love and who turns out, on her arrival, to be the king of Bucharia himself. A series of accidents on the way throws the pompous chamberlain Fadladeen into a bad temper, which he vents in pungent criticisms of the young man's verse, in the style of the *Edinburgh Review*.

'L'Allegro', a poem in rhymed octosyllabics with a ten-line prelude by *Milton, written ?1631, printed 1645. The Italian title means 'the cheerful man', and this idyll is an invocation to the goddess Mirth to allow the poet to live with her, first amid the delights of pastoral scenes, then amid those of 'towered cities' and the 'busy hum of men'. It is a companion piece to *'Il Penseroso'.

LAMARCK, Jean Baptiste de Monet, chevalier de (1744–1829), French naturalist. He advanced the view that species were not unalterable, and that the higher and more complex forms of life were derived from lower and simpler forms; that environment and new needs led to new actions and hence to organic modifications or the creation of new organs, and that these were transmitted to descendants. C. *Darwin introduced Lamarckian ideas into later editions of his work, having retreated from his original position on natural selection.

LAMARTINE, Alphonse de (1790–1869), French poet and politician. In addition to the poetry which, from the *Méditations poétiques* of 1820, established him as one of the leading figures in the French Romantic movement, he produced many volumes of biography, memoirs, political and historical works, novels, and travel writing. His work, both literary and historical, was widely translated into English from the late 1820s. His other collections of poetry include the *Nouvelles Méditations poétiques* (1823), the *Harmonies poétiques et religieuses* (1830), and the *Recueillements poétiques* (1839); he also published two fragments of a projected epic poem, *Jocelyn* (1836) and *La Chute d'un ange* (1838), while in 1835 he published his account of a journey to Syria, Lebanon, and the Holy Land. In the provisional government of 1848 he served as minister of foreign affairs (*Trois Mois au pouvoir*, 1848), withdrawing from public life in 1851. His historical works include the *Histoire des Girondins* (1847) and the *Histoire de la Révolution de 1848* (1849).

LAMB, Lady Caroline (1785–1828), daughter of the third earl of Bessborough. She married William Lamb, afterwards second Viscount Melbourne. In 1812, shortly after her marriage, she became infatuated with *Byron, and about the same time began to show signs of serious mental instability. Her first novel, *Glenarvon*, published anonymously in 1816 after Byron had broken with her, is a wild *Gothic extravaganza, in which she herself is cast as the dashing Calantha and Byron as the fated, fascinating Glenarvon. The novel enjoyed a tremendous but brief *succès de scandale*. Neither *Graham Hamilton* (1822) nor *Ada Reis* (1823) is remembered. Her accidental meeting with Byron's funeral procession on its way to Hucknall Torkard in 1824 further provoked the disintegration of her mind.

LAMB, Charles (1775–1834), born in London. His father, the Lovel of 'The Old Benchers of the Inner Temple' in *Essays of Elia, was the clerk to Samuel Salt, a lawyer, whose house in Crown Office Row was Lamb's birthplace and his home during his youth. He was educated at *Christ's Hospital, where he formed an enduring admiration for S. T. *Coleridge. After a few months at the South Sea House (see ESSAYS OF ELIA), he obtained at 17 an appointment in the East India House, where he remained until his retirement in 1825. For a short time in 1795–6 he was mentally deranged, and the threat of madness became a shadow on his life. In 1796 his sister Mary, in a fit of insanity, killed their mother. Lamb undertook the charge of his sister, who remained liable to periodic breakdowns, and she repaid him with great sympathy and affection. They lived in London, which Lamb loved, then from 1823 in Islington, Enfield, and Edmonton, where Lamb died. Four sonnets of Lamb's appeared in 1796 in a volume of poems by Coleridge, who became a lifelong friend. In 1798 appeared *Blank Verse* by Charles Lloyd and Charles Lamb, which included the poem 'The Old Familiar Faces'. In the same year appeared the *Tale of Rosamund Gray and Old Blind Margaret*, a melodramatic, sentimental village tragedy, in which Rosamund meets a fate worse than death, then death itself. In 1802 Lamb published *John Woodvil* (at first called *Pride's Cure*), an ineffective tragedy in the Elizabethan style; and in 1806 his farce *Mr H* proved a failure at Drury Lane. With his sister he wrote *Tales from Shakespear* (1807), designed to make the stories of Shakespeare's plays familiar to the young; and also *Mrs Leicester's School* (1809), a collection of original stories. *The Adventures of Ulysses* (1808) was an attempt to do for the *Odyssey* what they had done for Shakespeare. In 1808 he published *Specimens of English Dramatic Poets who Lived about the Time of Shakespeare. Between 1810 and 1820 his literary output was not great. It includes the essays 'On the Tragedies of Shakespeare', which presents the characters of the tragedies as individual 'objects of meditation', stripped of their dramatic function; and an admiring analysis 'On the Genius and Character of Hogarth' in 1811. He wrote for Leigh Hunt's *Reflector and for the *Examiner, and in 1814 contributed to the *Quarterly Review an article (much altered by *Gifford, the editor) on Wordsworth's *The Excursion, commending the originality of Wordsworth's genius, as well as his high seriousness. A collection of his miscellaneous writings in prose and verse appeared in 1818. From 1820 to 1823 Lamb was a regular contributor to the *London Magazine, in which appeared the first series of essays known as *Essays of Elia*, published in a collected volume in 1823. The second series was published in 1833. Of his poems the best known are 'The Old Familiar Faces', the lyrical ballad 'Hester' (1803), and an elegy 'On an Infant Dying as Soon as Born' (1827), probably his finest poem. *Album Verses* (1830) includes many other lyrics and sonnets.

A. C. *Bradley regarded Lamb as the greatest critic of his century, but few would follow Bradley quite so far. Lamb's literary criticism is scattered and small in volume. He had no interest in critical theory, and a poor sense of structure; as he wrote to *Godwin: 'I cannot grasp at a whole.' But his sympathies were wide and his sensitivity acute; while careful always to approve moral worth he also enjoys 'an airing beyond the diocese of strict conscience', as into the then little read Jacobean or Restoration drama. His habit of brief but accurate characterization, and of generalized but perceptive comment (such as he employs in his *Specimens*) results in original and illuminating work. He was a prolific letter writer of great charm and quality, and many of his observations on literature are scattered throughout the letters. He was much loved, and his various homes were a meeting place for Coleridge, *Wordsworth, Leigh *Hunt, *Hazlitt, *Southey, and other literary men. His *Letters* have been edited by E. W. Marrs (3 vols, 1975–8); see also D. *Cecil, *A Portrait of Charles Lamb* (1983) and the standard life by E. V. *Lucas (1905).

LAMB, Mary Ann (1764–1847), the sister of Charles *Lamb, under whose name the facts of her life will be found. She collaborated with her brother in writing for children the prose *Tales from Shakespear* (1807), and she wrote the greater part of *Mrs Leicester's School* (1809), a book of stories for children containing many autobiographical details, to which her brother contributed three tales.

LAMBERT, Constant (1905–51), English composer, conductor, and writer on music. Like W. *Walton, Lambert was a member of the *Sitwell circle, and his best-known work, *The Rio Grande* (1928), is a jazzy setting for piano solo, chorus, contralto, and orchestra of a poem by Sacheverell Sitwell. In a different vein is the masque to words from *Nashe's 'pleasant comedy' *Summer's Last Will and Testament* (1936), and there is a version of the dirge from *Cymbeline, 'Fear no more the heat of the sun' (1940). Only marginally connected with Shakespeare is the ballet *Romeo and Juliet* (written for Diaghilev in 1926), in which an actor and actress, rehearsing Shakespeare's play, themselves fall in love and eventually elope in an aeroplane.

As a writer Lambert's stimulating but controversial book *Music Ho!* (1934), subtitled 'A Study of Music in Decline', was enthusiastically acclaimed in its day: it retains its status as a classic of its period and a testimony of an exceptional musical and critical intelligence. (See also MUSIC, LITERATURE OF.)

Lambeth Books, a name sometimes given to the symbolic poems which *Blake wrote and etched while living at Lambeth (1790–1800). They include *America, *Europe, and *The Song of Los.

Lament of Tasso, The, a dramatic monologue by *Byron, published in 1817, inspired by Byron's visit to 'much decayed' Ferrara in that year, and written on the way to Florence. It is based on the legend of *Tasso's tragic love for Leonora d'Este: the narrator describes his imprisonment in a madhouse in Ferrara, and

asserts his own enduring fame, which will outlive that of the city which has incarcerated him.

'Lamia', a narrative poem by *Keats, written 1819, published 1820.

The story was taken from Burton's *Anatomy of Melancholy*, there quoted from Philostratus. Lamia, a sorceress, is transformed by Hermes from a serpent into a beautiful woman. She loves the serious young Corinthian Lycius, and he, spellbound by her beauty and believing her human, falls in love with her. They retire to her secret and sumptuous palace in Corinth. Here, not content with his happiness and against Lamia's wishes, Lycius orders a magnificent bridal feast and summons his friends. Among them, though uninvited, comes his old guide and mentor, the sage Apollonius, who pierces Lamia's disguise and calls her by her name. Her beauty withers, with a frightful scream she vanishes, and Lycius dies in a frenzy of grief. Keats wrote to his brother George that he believed the poem had 'a sort of fire in it' and that it would please a sensation-loving public. Interpretations of the work vary considerably, but it is clearly connected with Keats's persistent theme of the relationship between the real and the ideal.

LAMMING, George Eric (1927–), novelist and poet, born in Barbados. His first novel, *In the Castle of My Skin* (1953), is the story of a boy's adolescence in a small peasant village in Barbados, and of his growing awareness of the colonial situation; this was followed by *The Emigrants* (1954), which describes the voyage to and arrival in Britain of a group of West Indians. *Of Age and Innocence* (1958) and *Season of Adventure* (1960) are more optimistic works, set on the imaginary island of San Cristobal. Other works include *Water with Berries* (1971) and *Natives of My Person* (1972). *Thiong'o commented (*Homecomings*, 1972) that Lamming's novels are dominated by the theme of 'exile as a universal experience'.

Lammle, Alfred and Sophronia, in Dickens's *Our Mutual Friend, unscrupulous social adventurers.

Lamorak de Galis (of Wales), Sir, in *Malory, the brother of Percivale (Perceval) and son of Pellinore. Just as his father kills King Lot of Orkney and is killed by Lot's son Gawayne (*Gawain), he is slain by the four sons of King Lot because of his adultery with Arthur's sister Morgawse, the wife of King Lot. In some versions he is treacherously stabbed in the back by Mordred (Modred); in others he is slain without ignobility by Gawain.

LAMPEDUSA, Giuseppe Tomasi Di (1896–1957), Sicilian aristocrat, author of a remarkable novel, *Il gattopardo* (*The Leopard*, 1955–6), which describes the reactions of a noble Sicilian family to the political and social changes following Garibaldi's annexation of Sicily in 1860.

LANCASTER, Joseph (1778–1838), the founder of a system of education, based 'on general Christian principles' (i.e. undenominational), in schools organized 'on the monitorial or mutual system', described in *Improvements in Education* (1803). The proposal gave rise to heated controversy, of which the outcome was the 'voluntary system' of elementary schools that endured until 1870.

LANCASTER, Sir Osbert (1908–96), writer, artist, cartoonist, and theatre designer, educated at Charterhouse and Lincoln College, Oxford. He is remembered for his many illustrated works which gently mock the English way of life: he was particularly good at country-house and upper-class architecture and mannerisms, but also had a sharp eye for suburbia. Titles include *Pillar to Post* (1938) and *Homes Sweet Homes* (1939), which record architectural history and fashion, and books based on Draynflete, the ancestral village of the Littlehampton family, which include *Draynflete Revealed* (1949) and *The Life and Times of Maudie Littlehampton* (1982).

Lancelot, see LAUNCELOT OF THE LAKE.

Lancelot du Lake, Sir, a ballad included in Percy's *Reliques*, recounting the adventure of Lancelot with Tarquin, who had in prison threescore of Arthur's knights. Lancelot kills him and liberates the knights. Falstaff sings a snatch from this ballad in Shakespeare's 2 *Henry IV* (II. iv).

Landeval, Sir, see SIR LAUNFAL.

Landfall, the most important of New Zealand's literary periodicals, founded in 1947 as a quarterly.

Landless, Neville and Helena, characters in Dickens's *Edwin Drood*.

LANDON, Letitia Elizabeth (1802–38), who wrote under the initials L.E.L., and supported herself from an early age by her writing. She published between 1821 and her death a number of volumes of poetry, contributed to periodicals, and wrote several novels, of which the best is *Ethel Churchill* (1837). Her unprotected position as a woman in the literary world gave rise to various vague scandals linking her name to *Maginn and, less certainly, to *Bulwer-Lytton, who appears with his wife Rosina in her novel *Romance and Reality* (1831). Such rumours caused her to break off her engagement to J. *Forster, and she later married George Maclean, with whom she travelled to West Africa, where she died shortly afterwards in mysterious circumstances, either by suicide or accident, from swallowing prussic acid.

LANDOR, Robert Eyres (1781–1869), a cleric, youngest brother of W. S. *Landor. He was the author of five tragedies, including *The Count of Arezzi* (1823), which was attributed to *Byron and enjoyed a brief success for that reason. He also published a poem, *The Impious Feast* (1828); a fantastic prose story, *The Fawn of

Sertorius (1846); and *The Fountain of Arethusa* (1848), dialogues between a certain Anthony Lugwardine and famous men of classical times.

LANDOR, Walter Savage (1775–1864), educated at Rugby and at Trinity College, Oxford, where he was rusticated. An intractable temper involved him in trouble throughout his life. As a young man he fought as a volunteer in Spain against the French. In 1795 he published a miscellany of verses, *Poems*, and in 1798 an epic poem in seven books, *Gebir*. In 1802 followed *Poetry by the Author of Gebir*, and in 1806 another collection of poems, *Simonidea*, which included *'Rose Aylmer'. In 1811 he married Julia Thuillier. A dramatic tragedy, *Count Julian*, followed in 1812, but was never staged. In the same year Landor's intemperate 'Commentary on the Memoirs of Mr Fox' had to be suppressed. In 1815 he began a long residence in Italy, which did not end until 1835, when he separated from his wife. The *Imaginary Conversations of Literary Men and Statesmen* appeared 1824–9. In 1834 he published the light-hearted *Citation and Examination of William Shakespeare Touching Deer-Stealing. *Pericles and Aspasia*, a full-length work which grew out of an imaginary conversation, appeared in 1836, and in 1837 *The Pentameron*, in which *Boccaccio and *Petrarch discuss the poetry of *Dante. The trilogy *Andrea of Hungary, Giovanna of Naples*, and *Fra Rupert*, set in the 14th cent., was published in 1839–40, and *The Hellenics*, a retelling in verse of various Greek myths, completed in 1847. In 1853 appeared *Imaginary Conversations of Greeks and Romans*. His work was much admired by R. *Browning and many others. Boythorn in Dickens's *Bleak House* is a genial caricature of Landor. See *Landor: A Replevin* (1958) by M. Elwin.

landscape gardening. The pioneer landscape gardener in England was Charles Bridgeman or Bridgman (fl. 1709–38), a pivotal figure in the change from the formal garden designs of Le Nôtre to the 'natural' style inspired by the paintings of *Claude and classical writers. In a letter to *Prior of 1724, *Pope described him as 'a man of the virtuoso class as well as I'. Bridgeman influenced W. *Kent who, according to *Walpole, 'leaped the fence and saw that all Nature was a garden' (*Essay on Modern Gardening*, 1780), an almost literal description as Kent championed the Ha-Ha, a shallow ditch which separated house and park without the need for intrusive wall or railings. Kent's assistant Lancelot 'Capability' *Brown and his follower Humphry Repton (1752–1818) continued the Claudean tradition, combining the formal and informal in carefully composed 'natural' compositions. Repton is recommended to 'improve' the grounds of Sotherton in *Mansfield Park* (1814). Brown was criticized from 1784 by Payne Knight and Uvedale Price, champions of the *picturesque, categorized by *Gilpin as lying between the beautiful and the *sublime. The picturesque style was more dramatic than the Arcadian, more Gothic than classical; its principal practitioner was Gilpin's nephew William Sawrey Gilpin, fashionable 1820–40.

From the 1720s to the 1820s English gardening and literature had a virtually symbiotic relationship, each feeding the other. Writers were inspired by the artificial creations of gardeners, and vice versa, most notably by Thomson's poem *The Seasons* (1726–30), which influenced landscape design well into the 19th cent.

LANDSEER, Sir Edwin Henry (1802–73), painter, the son of an engraver. A visit to Sir W. *Scott in 1824 introduced him to the landscapes of Scotland, which featured prominently in his work. Professional and social success came rapidly to him; he enjoyed the favour of Queen Victoria, and his friends included *Dickens, *Thackeray, *Macready, and *d'Orsay. Although he painted portraits, historical scenes (mostly from Scott), and, in his late days, some strange allegorical works, he is best remembered for his animal paintings, such as *The Monarch of the Glen* (1851) and *Dignity and Impudence* (1839).

LANE, Allen (1902–70), publisher. He was born Allen Lane Williams, in Bristol, and took the name Allen Lane when he went to London to work at the Bodley Head for his distant cousin, 'Uncle John' *Lane. With the foundation in 1935 of the *Penguin series, he became a pioneer in the paperback revolution in publishing. See *Penguin Special* (2005) by Jeremy Lewis.

LANE, Edward William (1801–76), Arabic scholar. He published in 1836 *An Account of the Manners and Customs of the Modern Egyptians* and in 1838–40 a translation of *The Thousand and One Nights* (see ARABIAN NIGHTS ENTERTAINMENTS), an expurgated but scholarly version with copious notes illustrating his profound knowledge of Egyptian customs and beliefs. His publishers resisted his attempts to reproduce authentic Arabic names and spellings, preferring the more familiar Anglicized versions. Sir R. *Burton attacked his and other early translations as 'garbled and mutilated, unsexed and unsouled'.

LANE, John (1854–1925), *fin-de-siècle* publisher who, with Charles Elkin Mathews, established the Bodley Head in 1887. Authors who appeared under its imprint included *Davidson, *Dowson, *Le Gallienne, J. A. *Symonds, and *Wilde. The firm gained a high reputation for the quality of its publications, and as publisher of the *Yellow Book* it became the centre of ferment in art and letters in the 1890s.

LANEHAM, or **LANGHAM,** Robert, the name of the author of the letter describing some of the entertainments put on by the earl of *Leicester for the queen's visit to Kenilworth in 1575. Shakespeare may have remembered the shows in *A Midsummer Night's Dream* (ii. i. 148–68) and Scott used the description in *Kenilworth*. The list of Captain Cox's books which

'Laneham' gives is an important source for the titles of ballads, romances, and other popular literature still read at this time. The ghost of Captain Cox appears again in *Jonson's *Masque of Owles* (1624). There is an edition of the letter by R. J. P. Kuin (1983).

LANFRANC (*c*.1015–89), born in Pavia, archbishop of Canterbury from 1070 to his death, whereupon William Rufus left the see vacant until the appointment of *Anselm in 1093. He was a man of wide secular and classical learning (including Greek) who worked successfully with William the Conqueror and rebuilt the cathedral at Canterbury which had been burnt down in 1067. He was a celebrated teacher who had preceded Anselm as prior of Bec, from 1045 to 1070. See A. J. Macdonald, *Lanfranc* (1926).

LANG, Andrew (1844–1912), born at Selkirk, educated at St Andrews University and at Oxford, where he became a fellow of Merton. In 1875 he settled down in London to a life of journalism and letters, becoming one of the most prolific writers of his day

His first book of verse, *Ballads and Lyrics of Old France* (1872), was followed by others, including *Ballades in Blue China* (1880, 1881), *Rhymes à la Mode* (1884), and *Grass of Parnassus* (1888). Many of his poems were written in the old French forms of *rondeau, *triolet, etc. The poor reception of his ambitious narrative poem *Helen of Troy* (1882) discouraged him from serious poetry, and his verse became increasingly lightweight. His *Collected Poems* (4 vols) was published in 1923.

Lang appears to have valued himself most as an anthropologist. His first book on folklore, *Custom and Myth*, did not appear until 1884, but contained papers written and printed much earlier. *Myth Ritual and Religion*, dealing chiefly with totemism, was published in 1887, and *The Making of Religion* in 1898, the second edition of *Myth, Ritual and Religion* in 1899 being drastically rehandled to harmonize with his more developed views. *Freud's *Totem and Taboo* refers to Lang's work in this field.

As a Greek scholar Lang devoted himself largely to *Homer. He was one of the joint authors (with S. H. Butcher) of prose versions of the *Odyssey* (1879, preceded by his well-known sonnet 'The Odyssey'), and (with W. Leaf and E. Myers) of the *Iliad* (1883). He wrote on the Homeric question, arguing the unity of Homer. He also took part in the *Baconian controversy, arguing in favour of Shakespearian authorship, in *Shakespeare, Bacon and the Great Unknown* (1912).

His many works of belles-lettres, imaginary letters and dialogues, etc. are now largely forgotten, as are his melodramatic novels, which include *The Mark of Cain* (1886) and *The Disentanglers* (1902). He collaborated with H. R. *Haggard in *The World's Desire* (1891) and with A. E. W. *Mason in *Parson Kelly* (1899). He is best remembered for his own *fairy tales, which include *The Gold of Fairnilee* (1888, set in Scotland) and *Prince Prigio* (1889, set in Pantouflia), and for his collections, each volume named after a different colour; the first was *The Blue Fairy Book* (1889). These did much to stimulate interest in fairy tales. In their compilation Lang was greatly aided by his wife Leonora (née Alleyne). See also Lang's introduction to *Perrault's Popular Tales* (1888, see PERRAULT).

LANGHORNE, John (1735–79). He worked first as a tutor near Ripon, in 1768 became rector of Blagdon, Somerset, and was from 1772 a justice of the peace. He published several volumes of poetry, an *Oriental tale, and a reply to Charles *Churchill's *Prophecy of Famine* entitled *Genius and Valour: A Scotch Pastoral* (1764). He edited the works of W. *Collins (1765) and, with his brother William (1721–72), translated *Plutarch's *Lives* (1770). His best-remembered poem is *The Country Justice* (1774), which was praised by *Wordsworth for bringing 'the Muse into the Company of Common Life', and by *Davie in the introduction to his anthology *The Late Augustans* (1958) for its earnest and informed response to 'the strain of historical change'.

LANGLAND, William (perhaps *c*.1330–*c*.1386), the author of *Piers Plowman*, of whose identity and life very little is known for certain. That the 'lives' of Langland reconstructed from internal evidence in the poem were highly dubious was demonstrated by George Kane in *Piers Plowman: The Evidence for Authorship* (1965). It seems that Langland lived in London, but that he had lived in the Malvern district of the west Midlands. Kane takes seriously the evidence of the Trinity College, Dublin, manuscript of the C-text, that Langland was the son of Stacy de Rokayle of Shipton-under-Wychwood in Oxfordshire. He was probably in minor orders. No other poem is now attributed to him; *Skeat's parallel-text edition of the poem is still printed with *Richard the Redeless* which Skeat believed was by Langland but cannot be his, being part of *Mum and the Sothsegger*, which dates from the very early 15th cent.

langue d'oïl, the language of the north of France during the medieval period, so called to distinguish it from the *langue d'oc* (see PROVENÇAL), the distinction being based on the particle of affirmation: late Latin 'hoc ille' for 'yes' became 'o'il' in the north and 'oc' in the south. The distinction of language corresponded to a difference of culture and literature, the *langue d'oïl* being the literary medium of the *trouvères, the *langue d'oc*, or Provençal, that of the *troubadours. The dialects of the *langue d'oïl*, particularly Norman, Picard, and Francien (the language of the Paris region), each had some literary independence during the 12th and 13th cents, but Francien gradually became the standard language, and is the ancestor of modern standard French.

Languish, Lydia, the heroine of Sheridan's *The Rivals*.

LANIER, or **LANYER,** Emilia, née Bassano (1569–1645), a member of a large Italian family of musicians and instrument-makers living in London; she married a penurious civil servant Alfonso Lanier in 1592. Her collection of poems *Salve Deus Rex Judaeorum* (1611) is chiefly religious, but includes 'The Description of Cooke-ham', a country-house poem celebrating the patronage of Margaret Clifford, countess of Cumberland, and her daughter Anne: a very early example of the genre, the poem may pre-date *Jonson's 'To Penshurst'. There is no documentary proof to support *Rowse's contention that Lanier was the dark lady of Shakespeare's sonnets. There is an edition of the poems by S. Woods (1993).

LANIER, Sidney (1842–81), American poet and critic, born in Georgia. After serving in the Confederate army during the Civil War, he devoted himself to poetry, in spite of ill health and poverty. He published his *Poems* in 1877; a complete *Poems* appeared in 1884, with further additions in subsequent editions. His lyrical and metrically experimental verse is strongly influenced by his knowledge and practice of music. He became a lecturer in English at Johns Hopkins University in 1879, and his critical writings include *The Science of English Verse* (1880).

Laodicean, A, a novel by T. *Hardy, published 1881.
    Paula Power is a vacillating young woman, the Laodicean of the title. Faced with the ordeal of total immersion, according to her father's Baptist faith, she cannot take the plunge. She wavers between her love for George Somerset, a young architect, and Captain de Stancy, the heir of an ancient family which once owned the castle in which she now lives. She accepts the more romantic captain, but discovers in time a plot hatched by Willy Dare, his illegitimate son, to blacken the character of George Somerset. She finally marries Somerset, her ancient castle is burned to the ground, and she remains a Laodicean to the end.

Laokoon, an essay in literary and artistic criticism by G. E. *Lessing, published 1766. It takes its title from the celebrated group of statuary disinterred at Rome in the 16th cent. representing Laocoön and his sons in the coils of serpents. Adopting this group and the Horatian formula 'ut pictura poesis' ('poetry resembles painting') as the initial subject of discussion, Lessing examines the grounds for the divergence in the treatment of the scene by the artist and by *Virgil who described it (*Aeneid* Bk 2), and develops the essential differences between the art of poetry and the plastic arts. The work was left unfinished.

'Laon and Cythna', see REVOLT OF ISLAM, THE.

Laputa, see GULLIVER'S TRAVELS.

Lara, a poem by Lord *Byron, published 1814.
    Lara is in fact Conrad of *The Corsair* returned to his domains in Spain accompanied by his page Kaled, who is his love, the slave Gulnare, in disguise. Lara lives, like other *'Byronic' heroes, aloof and alien, shrouded in mystery. He is, however, recognized as Conrad, and

becomes involved in a feud in which he is finally killed, dying in the arms of Kaled.

LARKIN, Philip Arthur (1922–85), poet and novelist, born in Coventry and educated at King Henry VIII School, Coventry, and at St John's College, Oxford, where he was a contemporary of K. *Amis and developed an interest in jazz which was later to produce a volume of essays, *All What Jazz* (1970). From 1943 he worked in various libraries before becoming librarian of the Brynmor Jones Library in Hull. Larkin's early poems appeared in an anthology, *Poetry from Oxford in Wartime* (1944), and a collection, *The North Ship* (1945), and were, by his own account, much influenced by *Yeats. He then published *Jill* (1946), set in wartime Oxford, a novel which describes the undergraduate career of John Kemp, a working-class boy from Lancashire, and his encounters with the world of traditional privilege; 'Jill' is the fantasy sister he creates, who is transformed into a teasing reality. A second novel, *A Girl in Winter* (1947), relates a day in the life of refugee librarian Katherine Lind, working in a drab English provincial town, with a lengthy flashback to an abortive adolescent romance with a penfriend. Larkin's own poetic voice (with a new allegiance to *Hardy rather than Yeats) became distinct in *The Less Deceived* (1955), where the colloquial bravura of a poem like 'Toads' is offset by the half-tones and somewhat bitter lyricism of other pieces; his name was at this time associated with the *Movement, and his work appeared in *New Lines* (1956). *The Whitsun Weddings* (1964) adds a range of melancholy urban and suburban provincial landscapes, a satiric sociological commentary, and more stoic wit, manifested in 'Toads Revisited', with its characteristic Larkin conclusion: 'Give me your arm, old toad; | Help me down Cemetery Road.' Many of the poems in *High Windows* (1974), notably 'The Old Fools', show a preoccupation with death and transience; in 'Annus Mirabilis' and 'Posterity' the poet ironically places himself as somewhat defiantly out of date; in the words of his fictitious American biographer: 'One of those old-type *natural* fouled-up guys.' Throughout his work, the adaptation of contemporary speech rhythms and vocabulary to an unobtrusive metrical elegance is highly distinctive. Larkin edited *The Oxford Book of Twentieth-Century English Verse* (1973). A volume of essays, *Required Writing*, was published in 1983. See *Philip Larkin: A Writer's Life* by A. *Motion (1993) and his *Selected Letters* (1992), edited by A. *Thwaite: both volumes shed a startling new light on his personality and opinions.

LA ROCHEFOUCAULD, François de Marsillac, duc de (1613–80), French courtier, soldier, and moralist, author of *Réflexions ou sentences et maximes morales* (1665), usually known as *Maximes*. By the fifth (1678) edition, the *Maximes* consisted of 504 brief reflections of extreme concision and finish which range widely over human nature and society, investigating and extending the sense of such traditional moral concepts as love, friendship, wit and folly, virtue and vice, happiness and misfortune. The epigraph to the collection, 'Our virtues are mostly vices in disguise', expresses one of its leading themes; another is the discovery of the springs of men's actions in their vanity, self-interest, desire for praise, and readiness to deceive themselves. The possibility of noble conduct and genuine worth is admitted, but most men and women are judged to be ruled by circumstances and their passions. There were several English translations of the *Maximes* in the 17th and 18th cents, including one by A. *Behn: *Reflections on Morality or Seneca Unmasqued* (1685).

LAROUSSE, Pierre (1817–75), French grammarian, lexicographer, and encyclopaedist. He edited and (in part) compiled the *Grand Dictionnaire universel du XIXe siècle* (1866–76), a vast encyclopaedia which aimed to comprehend every department of human knowledge. In 1852 he founded, together with Augustin Boyer, the publishing house of Larousse, which continues to issue the dictionaries and reference works that bear its name.

La Saisiaz and ***The Two Poets of Croisic,*** two long poems by R. *Browning, published 1878, the third and final such pairing in his work.

La Saisiaz is a philosophical elegy prompted by the sudden death of a close friend of Browning's, with whom he had been holidaying in a chalet called 'La Saisiaz' (the sun) near Geneva. It deals with the central religious question 'Does the soul survive the body? Is there God's self, no or yes?', though the terms are equally applicable to the creative imagination; the poem, like *In Memoriam, is as much a self-scrutiny as a tribute to the dead. *The Two Poets of Croisic* is much less solemn in tone than *La Saisiaz*: it tells the stories of two obscure poets associated with the small village of Croisic in Brittany, each of the stories illustrating, in comic and grotesque vein, the folly of human (and specifically poetic) aspiration. Coming immediately after *La Saisiaz*, in which Browning had asserted (however equivocally) his own status as a visionary poet, *The Two Poets of Croisic* makes a strong and effective contrast.

LAS CASAS, Bartolomé de (?1474–1566), Spanish historian and bishop of Chiapas (Mexico), famous for his protest against the ill-treatment by his countrymen of the native people of South America, in his *Very Brief Account of the Ruin of the Indies* (1542). He also wrote an unfinished general *History of the Indies*.

LASKI, Marghanita (1915–88), novelist, critic, secularist, and broadcaster, born in London but brought up in Manchester, and educated there and at Somerville College, Oxford. She was the niece of Harold Laski (1893–1950), Manchester-born political theorist and teacher, and professor of political science at the London School of Economics from 1926: the Laskis were a prominent Liberal Jewish family. Her novels include *Little Boy Lost* (1949), which describes a father's search for his son in a France still ravaged by war and overshadowed by the Occupation, and a short time-travel fiction, *The Victorian Chaise Longue* (1953). *The Offshore Island* (BBC, 1959) is an admonitory television play about an isolated family's struggle for survival ten years after the horrors of the nuclear devastation of Europe, and *Ecstasy* (1961) is a study of mystical and religious experience.

Last Chronicle of Barset, The, a novel by A. *Trollope, published 1867, the last of the *'Barsetshire' series.

The Revd Josiah Crawley is accused of fraudulently acquiring a cheque for £20, and using it to pay off the debts he inevitably incurs in an attempt to subsist on his meagre curate's income. As ever, Crawley broods deeply over his wrongs, but he cannot remember the exact origin of the cheque and is thus committed for trial. Even before the sessions come on the autocratic Mrs Proudie pre-judges his case, and attempts to oust Crawley from his church. Matters are not finally cleared up in Crawley's favour until Dean Arabin's family are recalled from the Continent, whereupon Mrs Arabin explains her part in the muddle. At the close of the novel the Crawley fortunes brighten decidedly: Mr Crawley is presented with the fatter living of St Ewold's, and the archdeacon finally removes his opposition to the marriage of Grace Crawley and his son Major Grantly.

Interleaved with the theme of Crawley's cheque is the London life of Johnny Eames and his continuing love for Lily Dale despite his unfortunate flirtation with Madalina Demolines; and the deaths of Mrs Proudie and Mr Harding, once warden of Hiram's Hospital.

Last Days of Pompeii, The, a novel by *Bulwer-Lytton.

Last Man, The, (1) a collection of poems by T. *Campbell and T. *Hood; (2) a novel by M. *Shelley.

Last of the Mohicans, The, a novel by J. F. *Cooper.

LATIMER, Hugh (?1492–1555). He was educated at Cambridge, took priest's orders, and became known as a preacher. He was accused of heresy, brought before convocation, and absolved on making a complete submission, 1532. He was appointed bishop of Worcester in 1535, but resigned his bishopric and was kept in custody for a year because he could not support the Act of the Six Articles, 1539. His famous sermon 'of the plough' was preached in 1548. Latimer was committed to the Tower on Mary's accession, 1553; was sent to Oxford with *Ridley and *Cranmer to defend his views before the leading divines of the university, 1554; and was condemned as a heretic and burnt at Oxford with Ridley on 16 Oct. 1555. His extant writings were edited for the Parker Society in 1844–5. They are notable for a simple vernacular style and for their graphic and vivid illustrations.

LAUD, William (1573–1645), educated at St John's College, Oxford. He became predominant in the Church of England at Charles I's accession, being at the time bishop of St David's. He was promoted successively to the sees of Bath and Wells and London, and became archbishop of Canterbury (1633). He supported the king in his struggle with the Commons and adopted the policy of enforcing uniformity in the Church of England. He was impeached of high treason by the Long Parliament in 1640, committed to the Tower in 1641, tried in 1644, condemned, and beheaded. A few of his sermons were published in 1651, and a collected edition of his works in 1696–1700. In these he shows himself a sturdy defender of the Anglican Church as a national institution, resisting the claim of the Church of Rome to universality and infallibility, and equally resisting the claims of Puritanism. A former chancellor of Oxford University, Laud gave some 1,300 manuscripts in 18 different languages, and his collection of coins, to the Bodleian Library.

LAUDER, William (d. 1771), literary forger and good classical scholar. He was proved to have interpolated in the works of Masenius and Staphorstius (17th-cent. Latin poets) extracts from a Latin verse rendering of *Paradise Lost*. Incidentally he proved that *Milton had deeply studied the works of modern Latin poets.

Launce, clownish servant to *Proteus in Shakespeare's *Two Gentlemen of Verona*.

Launcelot Gobbo, see GOBBO.

Launcelot Greaves, see GREAVES, SIR LAUNCELOT.

Launcelot of the Lake, Sir, the greatest and most romantic of the knights of the Round Table, son of King *Ban of Benwick in Brittany, father of *Galahad by *Elaine Sans Pere (daughter of King *Pelles), and the lover of *Guinevere. He is a relatively late development in the English Arthurian tradition, not appearing at length before the 14th cent., although the story of his love for Guinevere is the subject of *Chrétien de Troyes's *Lancelot* (c.1170s) and of the early 13th-cent. French prose 'Vulgate' *Lancelot* (and there is a lost Anglo-Norman story earlier than these). His name, which probably has Welsh etymological connections, refers to a tradition that he was abducted at birth and brought up by a lake-lady, before being brought by a hermit to Arthur's court. Chrétien's romance *Lancelot*, or *Le Chevalier de la charrette*, is concerned exclusively with the love of Lancelot and Guinevere, presented faithfully as a *courtly love affair, to an extent that has been thought to be self-parodying by some critics. The main elements of the Launcelot story are found in the three romances of the French prose cycle: *Lancelot*; the *Queste del Saint Graal*; and the *Mort Artu* (for these, see ch. 22, 'The Vulgate Cycle', by Jean Frappier in R. S. Loomis (ed.), *Arthurian Literature in the Middle Ages*, 1959). *Malory's treatment of Launcelot is closely based on this: Launcelot's love for the queen is again central; it is strained by his relations with Elaine the Fair Maid of Astolat whose death ends Guinevere's jealousy. Their love is betrayed by *Agravain; the lovers flee to Launcelot's castle of *Joyous Gard and, after a siege, the queen is restored to Arthur. Launcelot withdraws to Brittany where he is pursued by Arthur and Gawain; in the ensuing clash Launcelot injures Gawain. Arthur returns to Dover to fight the usurping Mordred (*Modred) and Gawain is killed. Launcelot comes back to help the king, but arrives too late for the final battle in Cornwall in which both Arthur and Mordred die. He finds that Guinevere has become a nun, so he becomes a priest. On his death he is carried to Joyous Gard where visions suggest that he is taken to heaven. He is very prominent in Malory who stresses the tragedy of his imperfection (his courtly amour with the queen) which prevents his full achievement of the *Grail, though he has glimpses of it. Malory also makes much of his later bitter hatred by Gawain because of his killing of Gawain's brothers; the implacability of Gawain's hatred prevents Arthur from making a peace with Launcelot which might have enabled them to ally to defeat Mordred. See T. P. Cross and W. A. Nitze, *Lancelot and Guenevere* (1930).

Launfal, Sir, see SIR LAUNFAL.

Laura, (1) see PETRARCH; (2) the wife of Beppo in Byron's poem *Beppo*.

Laurence, Friar, in Shakespeare's *Romeo and Juliet*, counsellor and confessor to the lovers, who performs their marriage at the end of Act II.

LAURENCE, Margaret (Jean Margaret Wemys) (1926–87), Canadian novelist and short story writer, born in the prairie town of Neepawa, Manitoba (inspiration for the fictional Manawaka). Her mother died when she was 4, and after her father's death in 1935 she was brought up by her stepmother (her natural mother's elder sister). She attended the local high school, at which she began to write stories, and studied at United College (now the University of), Winnipeg. In 1947 she married John Laurence, a civil engineer, whose work later took them to live in Africa for five years. Her time there inspired *A Tree for Poverty* (1954), a translated selection of Somali poetry; *The Prophet's Camel Bell* (1963), a memoir of her life in Somaliland; her first novel, *This Side Jordan* (1960), set in Ghana; a collection of stories set in West Africa, *The Tomorrow-Tamer* (1963); and a critical work on contemporary Nigerian dramatists and novelists, *Long Drums and Cannons* (1968). In 1962 she moved to England with her two children after separating from her husband, and it was at Penn in Buckinghamshire that she began the series of four books based on her home town, renamed Manawaka, for which she is now best known: *The Stone Angel* (1964); *A Jest of God* (1966), retitled *Now I Lay Me Down* for British publication, filmed as *Rachel, Rachel* (1968), and later reissued under that title; *The*

Fire-Dwellers (1969); and *The Diviners* (1974). *A Bird in the House* (1970), a collection of linked short stories, is also part of the Manawaka sequence. She returned to Canada in 1974. *Heart of a Stranger* (1976) is a collection of essays. A draft of her memoirs, *Dance on the Earth*, edited by her daughter, was published in 1989.

LAURIE, Annie (1682–1764), the subject of the famous Scottish song that bears her name. She was the daughter of Sir Robert Laurie of Maxwelton, Dumfriesshire, and married Alexander Ferguson. The song was written by her rejected lover William Douglas. It was revised and set to music by Lady John Scott in 1835.

LAUTRÉAMONT, comte de, the pseudonym of Isidore-Lucien Ducasse (1846–70), French writer of prose poems. Little is known of his life, and his reputation depends largely on the prominence given to his work by the *surrealists. *Les Chants de Maldoror*, a work of violent and anguished inspiration, appeared in 1868, and his *Poésies* in 1870.

LAVATER, Johann Kaspar (1741–1801), Swiss theologian and poet, and a close friend of *Fuseli. He is chiefly remembered in connection with the new science of phrenology (or Physiognomy, as he called it), which had many adherents, including the young G. *Eliot and her friend Charles Bray. See *Physiognomy in the European Novel* (1982) by G. Tytler.

Lavengro: *The Scholar—the Gypsy—the Priest*, a narrative by G. *Borrow, published 1851. 'Lavengro', in Romany language, means 'philologist'. The name was applied to Borrow in his youth by Ambrose Smith, who figures in this work as Jasper Petulengro.

This work purports to be the story of Borrow's own wandering, restless life, but in it, as in his other works, fact is mingled with fiction. The son of a professional soldier, he had followed his parents while they moved from station to station around England, Scotland, and Ireland, visiting strange places and striking up unusual friendships on his travels—he became attached to a family of gypsies and met tinkers, including the Flaming Tinman, with whom he had a memorable fight, horse-copers, an old apple-woman (also a receiver of stolen goods), and a brace of future murderers. He tells the reader much of his comparative study of languages (though his scholarship is often suspect); he had violent prejudices, including a savage hatred of the Roman Catholic Church, that frequently overflow into his books. The book closes in the midst of the romantic episode with Belle Berners, an Amazonian vagrant, which is resumed in *The Romany Rye*.

LAVIN, Mary (1912–96), short story writer and novelist. She was born in Massachusetts, but spent most of her life, from 1921, in Ireland. Her first collection was *Tales from Bective Bridge* (1942), ten stories based in and around Bective, an Irish village on the Boyne: other collections include *The Long Ago and Other Stories* (1944), of which the title story describes the friendship of three women tugged towards the past; *The Becker Wives and Other Stories* (1946), of which the title story evokes a family of Dublin corn merchants and their 'fat, heavy and furred' women; and *The Shrine and Other Stories* (1977). Family relationships, domestic conflicts over class, religion, and property are recurrent issues, treated with irony and pathos. Her novels are *The House in Clewe Street* (1945), a three-generation family saga set largely in a small Irish town with small-town morals and values, which exerts a powerful and retarding influence on its inhabitants, and *Mary O'Grady* (1950), which follows its protagonist from Tullamore in the early 1900s to Dublin. *A Likely Story* (1957) is a children's tale set in Bective.

Lavinia, Titus's daughter, who is raped and mutilated in Shakespeare's *Titus Andronicus.*

LAW, William (1686–1761), born at King's Cliffe in Northamptonshire, the son of a grocer. He was elected a fellow of Emmanuel College, Cambridge, but, declining to take the oath of allegiance to George I, lost his fellowship. Edward Gibbon made him the tutor of his son, the father of the historian *Gibbon, in *c*.1727 and he remained as an honoured friend of the family in their Putney home until 1740, when he returned to King's Cliffe and became the centre of a small spiritual community which included the historian's aunt Hester.

Law's earlier writings are of a controversial nature; he replied to Bishop *Hoadly's latitudinarian doctrine in *Three Letters to the Bishop of Bangor* (1717–19, see BANGORIAN CONTROVERSY); attacked *Mandeville in *Remarks upon the Fable of the Bees* (1723); outdid *Collier in his condemnation of the theatre in *Absolute Unlawfulness of the Stage-Entertainment* (1726); and attacked the *Deists and particularly Tindal in *The Case for Reason* (1731). But he is chiefly remembered for his treatises of practical morality, *A Practical Treatise on Christian Perfection* (1726), and more particularly *A Serious Call to a Devout and Holy Life* (1728). This work greatly influenced Law's friend J. *Wesley, who said it 'will hardly be excelled, if it be equalled in the English tongue, either for beauty of expression or for justice and depth of thought'. It had an equally profound effect on Dr *Johnson, who read it while at Oxford and told *Boswell that it was 'the first occasion of my thinking in earnest of religion'. It is addressed to believers, and urges them to a simple and pious way of life, with emphasis on private rather than public prayer; it is enlivened with many satiric character portraits of, for example, Calidus the business man, forced to live, eat, drink, pray, and take his pleasures at a great pace, and of Flavia, worldly, vain, but with 'an expensive collection of all our English poets'. Gibbon, whose *Autobiography* contains some interesting comments on Law, thought his Characters

as good as those of *La Bruyère. See also BYROM for other aspects of his personality.

In later life Law became increasingly interested in mysticism and in the writings of *Boehme; some critics have seen in *The Spirit of Prayer* (1749–50) and *The Spirit of Love* (1752–4) a foreshadowing of *Blake's attacks on materialism and reason.

LAWES, Henry (1596–1662) and William (1602–1645), English composers. Henry was widely recognized in his day as the most important songwriter after *Dowland: his 430-odd songs include settings of *Carew (38), *Waller (16), *Herrick (14), *Suckling, *Lovelace, and *Milton, the best probably written after his entry into court circles as one of Charles I's musicians in 1631. As a particular friend of Milton, he arranged the original performance of *Comus, for which he wrote the songs.

His brother William was more versatile; he wrote a great deal of instrumental music and contributed to the music of many stage works during the period immediately before the establishment of opera in England. He composed a large part of the music for the most sumptuous of English masques, Shirley's *The Triumph of Peace* (1634), and composed incidental music for several of the masques and plays of *D'Avenant. Both brothers experimented with a declamatory style on the lines of the new 'stile recitative', and in so doing paved the way for the operatic developments of *Locke, *Blow, and *Purcell.

LAWLESS, Emily (1845–1913), daughter of an Irish peer, author of the successful Irish novels *Hurrish* (1886), a peasant story set in Clare, and *Grania* (1892), set on the Aran Islands. She also wrote *With Essex in Ireland* (1890); a collection of poems, *With the Wild Geese* (1902); and a *Life of Maria Edgeworth* (1904).

LAWRENCE, D(avid) H(erbert) (1885–1930), born at Eastwood, Nottinghamshire, one of five children of a miner and an ex-schoolteacher. He was often ill as a child (he was later to develop tuberculosis) and grew up in considerable poverty. His ill-suited parents quarrelled continually, and a passionate bond grew between Lawrence and his mother; she was determined to keep him out of the mines and encouraged him at school. This love for his mother had a crucial effect on his early life and work. With the help of a scholarship he attended Nottingham High School for three years, but at 15 was forced to give up his education and take a job for a short time as a clerk in a surgical goods factory and then became a pupil-teacher. At this time he formed a close friendship with Jessie Chambers, a local farmer's daughter, the Miriam of *Sons and Lovers. In 1906, having worked to save the necessary £20 fee, he took up a scholarship at Nottingham University College to study for a teacher's certificate.

He was already writing poetry and short stories and he now began his first novel *The White Peacock* (1911), which was followed by *The Trespasser* (1912). He taught for two years at an elementary school in

Croydon but after the death of his mother he became seriously ill and was advised to give up teaching. His first major novel, *Sons and Lovers* (1913), is a faithful autobiographical account of these early years, though he was later to think he had been unjustly harsh about his father. In 1912 he met Frieda Weekley (née von Richthofen), wife of his old professor at Nottingham. Six years older than Lawrence and mother of three children, she was dissatisfied with her marriage and suffocated by life in Nottingham. They fell in love and eloped to Germany. They were always on the move, always short of money, and their life together was passionate and stormy. Lawrence's nomadic life supplied him with material for much of his writing and he wrote four travel books of a very personal kind. He spent the war years in England and began to form friendships in literary and intellectual circles: A. *Huxley and his wife Maria, D. *Garnett, Lady O. *Morrell, J. M. Murry and K. *Mansfield, *Aldington, and B. *Russell (with whom he was later to quarrel bitterly). His next novel, *The Rainbow* (1915), was seized by the police and declared obscene; his frankness about sex, and his use of four-letter words, was to keep him in constant trouble with the law. He was outspoken in his criticism of the war (he was unfit for service); while living in Cornwall he and his German-born wife were persecuted as suspected German agents and he felt life in England to be intolerable. In 1917 he published a volume of poems, *Look! We Have Come through!* and in 1919 he and Frieda left for Italy. He had finished his novel *Women in Love* in 1916 but was unable to find a publisher until 1920 in New York, where an action against it failed, and 1921 in London. In 1920 *The Lost Girl* (begun before the war) won the James Tait Black Memorial Prize, the only official honour he was to receive during his lifetime. *Aaron's Rod*, which shows the influence of *Nietzsche, followed in 1922 and the same year he began his serious travels, to Ceylon and Australia and finally to America and Mexico. While in Australia he wrote *Kangaroo*, which appeared in 1923, the same year as a critical book, *Studies in Classic American Literature*.

Lawrence's output was remarkable considering his unsettled life, his poor health, and his now increasingly fraught relationship with his wife. He lived in constant anxiety about money, struggling to publish a few stories and articles in various periodicals, and was sometimes helped by well-to-do friends or admirers. While in Mexico he began work on *The Plumed Serpent* (1926) and wrote many short stories and poems. In 1923 Frieda returned to Europe alone, and after an exchange of tug-of-war letters Lawrence joined her in England. But he was miserable there and early the next year they were back in New Mexico at the Kiowa Ranch, where Lawrence had hoped to found Rananim, his ideal community. While on a visit to Old Mexico he fell desperately ill and was told that he was in an advanced state of tuberculosis, with two years to live. They returned to Italy, via England and Germany,

settling first at the Villa Bernardo at Spotorno and finally near Florence at the Villa Mirenda. He became seriously interested in painting: in 1929, at an exhibition in London, 13 pictures were removed by the police and pronounced obscene. At the Villa Mirenda he also finished *Lady Chatterley's Lover*, his last novel and the one that was to cause more furore than any other. It was privately printed in Florence in 1928 by his good friend Pino Orioli and was finally published in unexpurgated editions in the United States and England over 30 years later, after unsuccessful prosecutions for obscenity. It had become clear that he was dying and Frieda took him first to Germany and then to the south of France in search of what could only have been a miraculous cure. He died in Vence on 2 Mar. 1930.

It is difficult now to understand the outrage occasioned by Lawrence's work which blinded many readers to its lasting value. He was a moralist (and at his worst a preacher); he believed that modern man was in danger of losing his ability to experience the quality of life. Passionately involved with his characters and the physical world of nature, he wrote of them with a fresh immediacy and vividness. His reputation as a short story writer has always been high, many stories appearing first in small collections (*The Prussian Officer*, 1914; *England, My England*, 1922; *The Woman Who Rode Away*, 1928) and in a complete edition in three volumes, 1955. His travel books, containing a great deal of personal narrative, are *Twilight in Italy* (1916), *Sea and Sardinia* (1921), *Mornings in Mexico* (1927), and *Etruscan Places* (1932).

In his poems Lawrence wanted to be free of the weight of formalism but not, as he said, to 'dish up the fragments as a new substance'. At times uneven, his poetry always has the immediate and personal quality of his prose. His volumes include *Love Poems* (1913), *Amores* (1916), *Look! We Have Come through!* (1917), *Birds, Beasts and Flowers* (1923), *Pansies* (1929), *Complete Poems* (3 vols, 1957).

Other non-fiction works include *Movements in European History* (1921), *Psychoanalysis and the Unconscious* (1921), *Fantasia of the Unconscious* (1922), *Studies in Classic American Literature* (1923), and *Apocalypse* (1931). *The Boy in the Bush* (1924) is a novel he wrote in conjunction with M. L. Skinner. A first collection of *The Letters of D. H. Lawrence* (1932) was edited by A. *Huxley. A new edition, ed. J. T. Boulton, was published in seven vols, 1979–93.

LAWRENCE, George Alfred (1827–76), educated at Rugby and Balliol College, Oxford. He was called to the bar but abandoned law for a literary career. His first and best-known novel, *Guy Livingstone* (1857), was an immediate and lasting success; its glorification of brute strength and questionable morality provoked criticism from those who objected to endowing the immoral, blood-lusting Livingstone with 'heroic qualities and social aplomb', but won applause from others for its lack of hypocrisy. As an example of 'muscular black-guardism', the novel showed a revolt against the 'muscular Christianity' of the time, and set a fashion not only in literature (*'Ouida' was a notable disciple) but even in the mode of dress and behaviour of the young men of the period. *Sword and Gown* followed in 1859, and *Border and Bastille* in 1863, which describes Lawrence's adventures when he attempted to join the Confederate forces during the American Civil War, was captured by Northern authorities, and sent back to England. He continued producing successful novels almost every other year. *Guy Livingstone* was parodied by *Harte in his 'Guy Heaveystone'.

LAWRENCE, Sir Thomas (1769–1830), painter. His portraits are distinguished for their courtliness and social elegance. He painted portraits for the Waterloo Chamber at Windsor of persons who took part in the defeat of Napoleon.

LAWRENCE, T(homas) E(dward) (1888–1935), the illegitimate son of an Anglo-Irish landowner, educated at Jesus College, Oxford, where, under the guidance of D. G. *Hogarth, he became deeply interested in both archaeology and the Middle East. He studied Arabic, read *Doughty, travelled to Syria in 1909, and from 1910 to 1914 worked on the excavation of Carchemish, on the banks of the Euphrates. During this period he became involved with British Intelligence, and his daring exploits during the First World War won him the confidence and admiration of the Arabs, and later made him, as 'Lawrence of Arabia', a mythical figure in his own country. He entered Damascus in 1918 with the Arab forces after the defeat of the Turks, and after the war spent some time as adviser to the Colonial Office, resigning in 1922. His subsequent career was marked by mental breakdown, self-accusation, and anxiety about his own legend; he enlisted in the RAF in 1922 as an aircraft hand under the name of John Hume Ross, and a year later joined the tank corps as T. E. Shaw, a name he adopted by deed poll in 1927. He later returned to the RAF, retiring from it shortly before he was killed in a motorcycle accident near his home at Clouds Hill, Dorset.

He began writing *The Seven Pillars of Wisdom*, his account of the Arab Revolt and his own part in it, shortly after the war (after claiming to lose much of the text, which he later rewrote, while changing trains at Reading in 1919); he sought literary advice from E. M. *Forster (who found his style 'granular') and G. B. *Shaw, both of whom encouraged him greatly, and became close friends. (He formed an even closer friendship with Shaw's wife Charlotte, to whom he confided his most intimate anxieties.) It was printed for private circulation in a limited edition in 1926 (pub. 1935); a shortened version, *Revolt in the Desert*, was published in 1927. It has been described as the last great romantic war book, and W. S. *Churchill declared it one of 'the greatest books ever written in the English language'. Meanwhile Lawrence was working on a documentary account of army life, sketches of which he showed to Forster who found in them 'a world of infinite suffering, but of limited cruelty' (1928); these were published posthumously in 1936 (New York) and 1955 (England) as *The Mint*, by '352087 A/c Ross'.

Lawrence's complex personality and multiple roles as man of action, poet, ascetic, neurotic, and leader of men fascinated friends, writers, and the general public, and his many biographers have suggested various explanations for both his masochism and his heroism. *Auden (who based *The Ascent of F6* in part on the Lawrence legend) described his life in a review of Liddell Hart's biography in *Now and Then* (1934) as 'an allegory of the transformation of the Truly Weak Man into the Truly Strong Man'. He appeared, complete with motor cycle, as Private Meek in Shaw's *Too True to be Good* (performed 1932); in *Rattigan's play *Ross* (1960); and as the hero of the popular film *Lawrence of Arabia* (1962). His friend Henry *Williamson imagined him as a leader who might have formed with Hitler an Anglo-German alliance. It has been suggested that he was all things to all men, a character who acted as a mirror to those who wrote of him. Robert *Graves wrote the first authorized life (1927); *Aldington's in 1955 caused outrage by its iconoclastic portrayal of him as a hysterical homosexual. More recent attempts (e.g. *The Secret Lives of Lawrence of Arabia*, 1969, by P. Knightley and Simpson) have attempted to present a more balanced picture. See also his *Letters* (1938), ed. D. *Garnett, his introductions to Doughty (1921) and R. *Garnett (1924), and his essay on *Flecker (1937).

Laws of Ecclesiastical Politie, Of the, by R. *Hooker, a philosophical and theological treatise of which four books appeared in 1593, the fifth in 1597. The sixth and eighth appeared in 1648, the seventh was first included in Gauden's edition of 1661–2. These last three books, as we have them, not published until after Hooker's death, do not represent work prepared by him for the press. The whole was reissued with a life of Hooker by I. *Walton in 1666.

The work is a defence, written in a dignified and harmonious prose, of the position of the Anglican Church against the attacks of the Puritans. The first book is a philosophical discussion of the origin and nature of law in general, as governing the universe and human society, and of the distinction between laws of a permanent and of a temporary character. The second, third, and fourth books deal with the assertion of the Puritan party that Scripture is the sole guide in determining the actions of a Christian and the form of church polity, and that the Anglican Church is corrupted with popish rites and ceremonies. The fifth book is a defence of the Book of *Common Prayer. According to Hooker's scheme, the last three books were to deal with church discipline, the power of jurisdiction (whether of the bishops or lay elders), and the nature of the king's supreme authority. The principal characteristics of the work are its breadth of outlook and tolerant spirit, and its advocacy of intellectual liberty against the dogmatism of *Calvin and the ecclesiastical despotism recommended in the *Admonition to Parliament*, a statement of the Puritan case by John Field and Thomas Wilcox (1572).

lay, a short lyric or narrative poem intended to be sung; originally applied specifically to the poems, usually dealing with matters of history or romantic adventure, which were sung by minstrels.

Lay of the Last Minstrel, The, a poem in six cantos by Sir W. *Scott, published in 1805. Scott's first important original work, it is a metrical romance in irregular stanzas (much of it in rhymed octosyllabics) put in the mouth of an ancient minstrel, the last of his race, who bewails the decline of his art and his nation as he tells a Border tale of feud and witchcraft and frustrated love set in the mid-16th cent. The story is involved and violent, featuring the vengeful Lady of Branksome Hall, her daughter Margaret, the 'stark moss-trooping' Deloraine, and the legend of the wizard Michael *Scott: it contains the well-remembered invocation of Melrose (Canto Second), 'If thou wouldst view fair Melrose aright, | Go visit it by pale moonlight', and (Canto Sixth) the minstrel's passionately patriotic lines 'O Caledonia! Stern and wild, | Meet nurse for a poetic child! | Land of brown heath and shaggy wood, | Land of the mountain and the flood.' The narrative also encloses several ballads, and ends with a version of the 'Dies Irae'.

Lays of Ancient Rome, a collection of poems by *Macaulay, published 1842, in which Macaulay takes episodes from Roman history (some from *Livy) such as the defence of the bridge leading to Rome against the Tuscans ('Horatius'); 'The Battle of Lake Regillus'; and *'Virginia'. These rattling ballads with their hypnotic rhythms and heroic patriotic attitudes were immensely popular and are still remembered. Later editions included rousing poems from British history written in Macaulay's youth which were first published in *Knight's Quarterly Magazine* (1823–4): these include 'The Battle of Naseby', 'Ivry', and 'Moncontour'. 'Epitaph of a Jacobite', a touching lament by a follower of James II, was written later, in 1847, and was later included with the *Lays*.

LAȜAMON (fl. early 13th cent.), according to his own testimony a priest of Ernley (Arley Regis in Worcestershire). He wrote the *Brut*, a history of England from the arrival of the legendary Brutus to *Cadwallader (AD 689), based mostly on Wace's French version of *Geoffrey of Monmouth's *Historia Regum Britanniae* (1155). There are additions from other sources which are uncertain; they are not from *Bede and St *Alban and St *Augustine, as he claims himself. The *Brut* gives for the first time in English not only the story of Arthur but also those of Lear, Cymbeline, and other figures prominent in later English literature. The poem is in 32,241 short lines, corresponding broadly to the later,

debased Old English alliterating half-line with occasional rhyme; it also employs some of the epic formulas and other stylistic features of Old English, which contribute to the poem's energy and vigour. It is in some ways a transitional work, and one of the earliest major works in Middle English. (See BRUT.) There are two 13th-cent. manuscripts, both of which are in the edition by F. Madden (3 vols, 1847); see ed. G. L. Brook and R. F. Leslie, EETS OS 250, 277 (1963, 1978).

Lazarillo de Tormes, the first of the Spanish *picaresque romances, of uncertain authorship, printed 1553. It is the autobiography of the son of a miller, who lived on the banks of the Tormes, near Salamanca. The boy begins his career of wit and fraud as a blind man's guide whose money and victuals he steals. He passes into the service of various poverty-stricken or rascally employers, and ultimately reaches the position of town-crier of Toledo. His career provides occasion for many satirical portraits of Spanish types.

LEACH, Edmund (1910–89), social anthropologist. An irreverent disciple of *Malinowski, Leach turned to the analysis of structure and process rather than the then dominant functional analysis, from his *Political Systems of Highland Burma* (1954) onwards. A prolific writer, he disseminated the structuralist ideas of *Lévi-Strauss to English readers (see *Genesis and Myth*, 1969) and was a serious popularizer of anthropology in for example *A Runaway World?* (1967: *BBC's Reith Lectures) and *Social Anthropology* (1982).

LEACOCK, Stephen Butler (1869–1944), political economist and humorist, born in Britain but brought up and educated in Canada, where he was for many years lecturer, then professor, at McGill University, Montreal. His many volumes of collected humorous essays and stories include *Literary Lapses* (1910), *Nonsense Novels* (1911), *Sunshine Sketches of a Little Town* (1912), *Arcadian Adventures with the Idle Rich* (1914), and *Frenzied Fiction* (1918). J. B. *Priestley described his best work as 'balanced between cutting satire and sheer absurdity' (introduction to *The Bodley Head Leacock*, 1957).

Leader, a weekly periodical started in 1850 by *Lewes and T. L. *Hunt, to which Lewes contributed satirical pieces and lively theatre reviews under the pseudonym of 'Vivian'. The staff included *Spencer and *Kinglake. It ran until 1866, in its later issues as *Saturday Analyst and Leader*.

Leander, see HERO AND LEANDER.

LEAPOR, Mary (1722–46), poet, born in Northamptonshire, the daughter of a gardener who worked first on the estate of Sir John Blencowe, then as a nursery gardener. She was in early years discouraged from writing and 'overstudying', but despite considerable domestic duties, perhaps working at one time as a cook-maid in the neighbourhood, she produced a distinguished body of work which attracted the attention of

Bridget Fremantle, a rector's daughter, who persuaded her to consider publication. Leapor died of measles before this plan was executed, but her *Poems upon Several Occasions* appeared in 1748 and received praise and support from S. *Richardson and his friends. Her work, which in recent years has been much admired, is confident, witty, and predominantly satiric in tone: its heroic couplets declare her admiration for *Pope, as do her sharply drawn and realized characters, but she also writes with feeling about her own position as a woman writer who runs the risk of being thought 'mighty proud' by her neighbours, and who has to endure the condescension of patrons less sensitive than Miss Fremantle (whom she addresses as 'Artemesia'). Her verses 'Upon her Play Being Returned to her, Stained with Claret' elegantly demonstrate both her good humour and her sense of her own worth.

LEAR, Edward (1812–88), artist, traveller, and writer, born in Holloway, the 20th child of a stockbroker, and brought up largely by his elder sister Ann. He worked as a zoological draughtsman until he came under the patronage of the earl of Derby, for whose grandchildren he wrote *A Book of Nonsense* (1845), with his own *limericks and illustrations. He travelled widely, and published accounts of Italy (1846), Albania and Illyria (1851), Calabria (1852), and Corsica (1870); he also visited and sketched Egypt, the Holy Land, Greece, and India. He settled in 1871 in San Remo and died there. His posthumous reputation as a watercolourist has risen steadily and as a writer he is remembered for his nonsense verses, with their linguistic fantasies and inventiveness and their occasional touches of underlying melancholy; Lear suffered from epilepsy and depression, and despite many close friends (including *Tennyson's wife Emily) from loneliness. Later nonsense volumes were *Nonsense Songs, Stories, Botany and Alphabets* (1871), which contains 'The Owl and the Pussy-Cat' and 'The Jumblies'; *More Nonsense, Pictures, Rhymes, Botany etc.* (1871); and *Laughable Lyrics* (1877), with the Dong, the Yonghy-Bonghy-Bò, and the Pobble who has no toes. There are lives by Angus Davidson (1938) and Vivien Noakes (1968).

Lear, King, see KING LEAR.

Leasowes, the, see SHENSTONE.

LEAVIS, F(rank) R(aymond) (1895–1978), critic, Cambridge born, bred, and educated. He read history, then English, at Emmanuel College, was appointed probationary lecturer 1927–31, and a college lecturer at Downing in 1935. He continued to teach in Cambridge until 1964, establishing a new critical approach that largely superseded the historical and narrative type of literary history favoured by Émile Legouis, Oliver Elton, and *Saintsbury. As a young man he attended and contributed to the Practical Criticism courses of I. A. *Richards, which encouraged close attention to the text. In 1929 he married Q. D. *Leavis, From 1932 to 1953 he was chief editor of the quarterly *Scrutiny*, a

periodical which was a vehicle for the new Cambridge criticism, upholding rigorous intellectual standards and attacking the dilettante élitism which he believed to characterize the *Bloomsbury Group. *For Continuity* (1933), *Culture and Environment* (1933, with Q. D. Leavis and Denys Thompson), followed by *Education and the University* (1943), stress the importance of creating within universities, and particularly within English departments, an informed, discriminating, and highly trained intellectual élite whose task it would be to preserve the cultural continuity of English life and literature, a continuity he believed to be threatened by mass media, technology, and advertising. *New Bearings in English Poetry* (1932) attacked Tennysonian and Swinburnian 'late Victorian poetastry' and Georgian verse, presenting in their place the claims of E. *Thomas, T. S. *Eliot, *Pound, and (with qualifications) *Yeats: he also made an important reassessment of G. M. *Hopkins. *Revaluation* (1936) continued to reshape the main line of English poetry, tracing it through *Donne, *Pope, and Dr *Johnson to Hopkins and Eliot, and producing iconoclastic attacks on *Spenser, *Milton, and *Shelley. In 1948 he turned his attention to fiction in *The Great Tradition*, possibly his finest work; he traced this tradition through J. *Austen, G. *Eliot, H. *James, and *Conrad, dismissing other major authors (e.g. *Sterne and *Hardy) in a somewhat summary fashion. In later years he changed his position on *Dickens, whose *Hard Times* was the only novel to win unqualified admiration in this volume. (See *Dickens the Novelist*, with Q. D. Leavis, 1970.) *D. H. Lawrence: Novelist* (1955) presented the claims of *Lawrence, then much underrated, as a great English writer and moralist.

Leavis in his writing thus radically altered the literary map of the past and laid out new patterns for the future; but perhaps his most vital contribution lay not in his assessment of individual authors, but in his introduction of a new seriousness into English studies. As a teacher he was admired and revered, and his influence spread throughout the educational world. His vehement dismissal of opposing views earned him much hostility, notably on the occasion of his response to C. P. Snow's Rede Lecture on *'The Two Cultures': *Two Cultures? The Significance of C. P. Snow* (1962). He was a controversial figure who inspired both deep devotion and profound antagonism, and occasionally a mixture of the two.

LEAVIS, Queenie Dorothy, née Roth (1906–81), scholar and critic, educated at Girton College, Cambridge. She married F. R. *Leavis in 1929, and they worked for many years together in close partnership. Her influential and pioneering study *Fiction and the Reading Public* (1932), which originated in a thesis under the supervision of I. A. *Richards, investigated the changes in reading habits since the 18th cent., and their connection with lending libraries, book clubs, mass culture, film, film novelizations, and the state of literary journalism: her 'anthropological' approach included the sending of a questionnaire to 60 best-selling authors asking their opinions on popular taste, literary influences, and other matters. She collaborated with Leavis and Denys Thomson in *Culture and Environment* (1933), and worked 1932–53 as a sub-editor for *Scrutiny*, a task she had to abandon partly through ill health. She collaborated with her husband in their book on *Dickens, Dickens the Novelist* (1970), and after his death continued to write and to lecture extensively.

LE CARRÉ, John, pseudonym of David John Moore Cornwell (1931–), who was educated at Oxford, taught briefly at Eton, then joined the Foreign Office. His earliest novels were conventional thrillers; the first, *Call for the Dead* (1961), introduced the mild-mannered mastermind and secret agent George Smi-ley, who appears in many of his later books. *The Spy Who Came in from the Cold* (1963), a Cold War thriller inspired by the Berlin Wall (described by G. *Greene as the best *spy story he had ever read), brought Le Carré immediate fame. Its successors, *The Looking Glass War* (1965), *A Small Town in Germany* (1968), *Tinker, Tailor, Soldier, Spy* (1974), *The Honourable Schoolboy* (1977), *Smiley's People* (1980), *The Little Drummer Girl* (1983), *A Perfect Spy* (1986), *The Russia House* (1989), *The Secret Pilgrim* (1992), and *The Night Manager* (1993), have confirmed his reputation as a storyteller who mixes grim and realistic detail with byzantine elab-oration of plot. (Le Carré has described the spy stories of I. *Fleming as 'candyfloss'.) *Our Game* (1995) is set in the aftermath of the break-up of the Soviet Union.

LECKY, William Edward Hartpole (1838–1903), his-torian, born in Co. Dublin and educated at Trinity College, Dublin. He published anonymously in 1860 *The Religious Tendencies of the Age* and in 1861 *Leaders of Public Opinion in Ireland*, which at the time met with little success. His *History of the Rise and Influence of Rationalism in Europe*, published in 1865 after visits to Spain and Italy, attracted much attention; in it he traced the progress of the spirit of rationalism from religious dogmatism and persecution to tolerance. His *History of European Morals from Augustus to Charle-magne* (1869) discussed the relationship of morality and theology, and was also widely read. His *History of England in the Eighteenth Century* (1878–92) was concerned primarily with the history of political ideas and institutions, and social and economic history; the last volumes are devoted to the history of Ireland, and designed to refute *Froude's misstatements.

LECONTE de LISLE, Charles-Marie-René (1818–94), French poet and leader of the *Parnassians. He pub-lished a number of collections, including *Poèmes antiques* (1852), *Poèmes barbares* (1862), and *Poèmes tragiques* (1884).

Lectures on the English Poets, a critical work by W. *Hazlitt, delivered as public lectures in 1818 and published that year. The series begins with *Chaucer and *Spenser, concluding with W. *Wordsworth and S. T. *Coleridge. By contrast with these *Lake poets, *Shakespeare is praised for his lack of egotism, and immersion in his characters. This view influenced the poetics of *Keats, who attended the lectures. Hazlitt's critical observations are made with his usual vivacity: 'The characteristic of Chaucer is intensity, of Spenser, remoteness; of Milton, elevation; of Shakspeare, every thing.'

LEDGWIDGE, Francis (1891–1917), Irish poet, born in Slane, Co. Meath. He was encouraged and befriended by *Dunsany, who saw in his work promise of the authentic Irish rural voice, and wrote introductions for his three volumes of poetry, *Songs of the Field* (1916), *Songs of the Peace* (1917), and *Last Songs* (1918). The poems are chiefly lyrics of the countryside, although there are some that deal with Irish mythology and folklore, reminiscent of the *Celtic Twilight period of *Yeats. He was killed in action in Flanders.

LEE, Harriet (1757–1851), daughter of an actor, who ran a private school in Bath with her sister Sophia *Lee. She became both dramatist and novelist, but succeed-ed only as the latter. An *epistolary novel, *Errors of Innocence*, appeared in 1786; *Clare Lennox* in 1797; and her very successful *Canterbury Tales* (in part a collab-oration with Sophia) in 1798, with three further volumes in 1805. The twelve stories of the *Tales*, told by travellers accidentally thrown together, include 'Kruitzner', on which Byron based his verse drama *Werner*, with acknowledgement. Her own adaptation of the story for the stage was briefly performed. She was a friend of Jane and Anna *Porter; of Sir T. *Lawrence, who presented the sisters with several important portraits of actors; and of *Godwin, who proposed to her in 1798.

LEE, Sir Henry (1531–1611), master of the armoury and ranger of Woodstock. Lee was closely involved in much Elizabethan pageantry and probably initiated around 1570 the celebration of the queen's accession day (17 Nov.) with tilts and allegorical devices: some of these are reflected in Sidney's revised *Arcadia*. He played a part in the Woodstock entertainments of 1575 and 1592, and his own retirement as queen's champion in 1590, when what has been claimed as his own poem, 'His Golden lockes, | Time hath to Silver turn'd', was sung, was commemorated by G. Peele in his *Poly-hymnia*. He appears in Scott's *Woodstock*.

LEE, Laurie (1914–97), writer, born in Gloucestershire and educated at Slad Village School and Stroud Central School. He worked for some time in an office in Stroud before travelling in Europe from 1935 to 1939, and then worked in various film units, for the Ministry of Information, the Festival of Britain, etc. His volumes of poetry (*The Sun my Monument*, 1944; *The Bloom of Candles*, 1947; *My Many-Coated Man*, 1955) show a rich sensuous apprehension of the natural world, as does his best-known work, the widely popular *Cider with Rosie* (1959), a highly evocative and nostalgic account of his country boyhood in a secluded Cotswold valley. It describes a vanished rural world of home-made wine, village school, church outings, 'a world of silence . . . of hard work and necessary patience . . . of white roads, rutted by hooves and cartwheels, innocent of oil and petrol'; Lee described himself as a chance witness of 'the end of a thousand years' life'. The 'Rosie' of the title is a village girl who 'baptized [him] with her cidrous kisses' behind a haycock. A second autobiographical volume, *As I Walked out One Midsummer Morning* (1969), describes his departure from Stroud, his walk to London, and his months in Spain on the eve of the Spanish Civil War. *A Moment of War* (1991) is a sequel. His other works include screenplays, travel books, and an essay on the birth of his daughter, *The Firstborn* (1964).

LEE, Nathaniel (?1649–92), educated at Westminster School and Trinity College, Cambridge, a failed actor turned playwright, whose tragedies, marked by extravagance and passion, were long popular. They include *Nero* (1675), *Sophonisba* and *Gloriana* (1676), all in heroics; his best-known tragedy, *The Rival Queens* (1677), in blank verse; *Theodosius* (1680); and one of his most serious dramas, *Lucius Junius Brutus*, which was banned for its anti-monarchical speeches after only three performances. He collaborated with *Dryden in *Oedipus* (1679) and *The Duke of Guise* (1682), and wrote one comedy, *The Princess of Cleve* (?1681), which is nearly as extreme as his tragedies. He lost his reason, was confined to Bedlam 1684–9, and died after a drinking bout. Several editions of his collected plays appeared in the 18th cent., and an edition in 2 vols, ed. T. B. Stroup and A. L. Cooke, in 1954–5.

LEE, Sir Sidney (1859–1926), born Solomon Lazarus Levi, educated at City of London School and Balliol College, Oxford, a member of the editorial staff of the *DNB* from the beginning in 1882, joint editor in 1890, and sole editor from 1891. His publications include *Stratford-on-Avon from the Earliest Times to the Death of Shakespeare* (1885; new edn 1906), *Life of William Shakespeare* (1898; rev. edn 1925), *Life of Queen Victoria* (1902), *Great Englishmen of the 16th Century* (1904), *Elizabethan Sonnets* (1904), *Shakespeare and the Modern Stage* (1906), *The French Renaissance in England* (1910), *Principles of Biography* (1911), *Shakespeare and the Italian Renaissance* (1915), *Life of King Edward VII* (1925–7).

LEE, Sophia (1750–1824), daughter of an actor, who ran a private school in Bath with her sister Harriet *Lee. She had some success as both dramatist and novelist. Her play *The Chapter of Accidents* (1780) was frequently staged; and her first novel, *The Recess* (1783–5), a form of early historical novel, sold well and was

translated into French. A long ballad, *The Hermit's Tale*, followed in 1787, and a verse tragedy, *Almeyda, Queen of Grenada*, with *Kemble and Mrs *Siddons, was staged in 1796. She contributed to her sister's *Canterbury Tales* (1798), and published an epistolary autobiographical novel, *The Life of a Lover* (1804).

LEE, Vernon, pseudonym of Violet Paget (1856–1935), essayist and novelist, who spent most of her life in Italy. She published some 45 volumes, including essays on Italian history, art, aesthetics, and travel; her travel writings (*Genius Loci*, 1899; *The Sentimental Traveller*, 1908; etc.) were much admired by A. *Huxley, whereas H. *James described her novel *Miss Brown* (1884) as 'a deplorable mistake'. A biography by P. Gunn was published in 1964.

LEECH, John (1817–64), caricaturist and illustrator, who formed a lifelong friendship with *Thackeray at Charterhouse; he was also a close friend of *Dickens, whose *A Christmas Carol* and other Christmas books he illustrated. From 1841 until his death he contributed to *Punch* political cartoons and scenes of everyday middle-class life. He drew for a number of other magazines, and illustrated the works of *Surtees.

'Leech Gatherer, The', see RESOLUTION AND INDEPENDENCE.

Le FANU (pron. Léff-anew), J(oseph) S(heridan) (1814–73), journalist, newspaper proprietor, and writer of novels and tales of mystery and the supernatural, who came of a well-educated Dublin family of Huguenot origins, connected by marriage with the Sheridans; Joseph's paternal grandmother was the sister of R. B. *Sheridan. After graduating at Trinity College, Dublin, Le Fanu was called to the bar, but never practised. By 1840 he had published a dozen or so stories (including 'A Strange Event in the Life of Schalken the Painter', rated by M. R. *James as 'one of the best of Le Fanu's good things') in the *Dublin University Magazine*, which had been founded in 1833 by a group of young Trinity College men with strong literary interests. From 1840 onwards he became increasingly involved in Irish journalism as editor of the *Warden* and owner or part-owner of that and other papers. His first two novels, *The Cock and Anchor* (1845) and *Torlogh O'Brien* (1847), were in the tradition of Sir W. *Scott and *Ainsworth; and it was not until 1861, three years after his wife's death, that his main output began with the serialization in the *Dublin University Magazine*, which he acquired in that year, of *The House by the Churchyard*. There followed *Wylder's Hand* (issued in book form in 1864), *Uncle Silas* (1864), *Guy Deverell* (1865), *The Tenants of Malory* (1867), *A Lost Name* (1868), *The Wyvern Mystery* (1869), *Checkmate* (1871), *The Rose and the Key* (1871), and *Willing to Die* (1873). In 1872 appeared the remarkable collection of stories entitled *In a Glass Darkly*.

Le Fanu was one of the best-sellers of the 1860s–1880s, and in a story published in 1888 H. *James wrote: 'There was the customary novel of Mr Le Fanu for the bedside; the ideal reading in a country house for the hours after midnight.' But thereafter he entered a period of what has been called 'unmitigated famelessness'. This century's revival of interest dates from the publication in 1923 of *Madam Crowl's Ghost and Other Tales of Mystery*, a collection of forgotten tales by Le Fanu edited by M. R. James, who considered that Le Fanu 'stands absolutely in the first rank as a writer of *ghost stories'. Since then Le Fanu's reputation has steadily risen, and he is now recognized as the equal of Wilkie *Collins as a writer of mysteries, and as occupying a place all of his own in the field of the sinister and the supernatural.

Le Fever, and his son, the subjects of a story related in Sterne's *Tristram Shandy*.

Left Book Club, a publishing venture founded by V. *Gollancz in association with John Strachey and Harold Laski; modelled on commercial book club lines, its educational aim was to resist the rise of Fascism and Nazism by providing, as Gollancz wrote in the first issue of *Left Book Club News*, 'the indispensable basis of *knowledge* without which a really effective United Front of all men and women cannot be built'. It flourished as a movement, circulating political books to some 50,000 members; the vast majority were factual (though three novels and one play, *Waiting for Lefty*, 1937, by *Odets, were included). The best-known title today is *Orwell's *The Road to Wigan Pier* (1937), which appeared with an introduction by Gollancz warning readers against the provocative second half of the book in which Orwell, he claimed, appeared as 'devil's advocate for the case against Socialism'. The Club defended Stalin over the Moscow show trials, but was divided on the Nazi–Soviet pact of 1939, and was dissolved in 1948.

Le GALLIENNE, Richard (1866–1947), of Channel Islands descent, born in Liverpool where he was an apprentice accountant for seven years. His first volume, *My Ladies' Sonnets and Other 'Vain and Amatorious' Verses*, was printed privately in Liverpool in 1887 and in 1888 he left for London with the ambition of becoming a man of letters. There he became attached to the *fin-de-siècle* group which centred on *Beardsley; he was an original member of the *Rhymers Club with *Yeats, *Wilde, L. *Johnson, and others. He contributed to the *Yellow Book*, and throughout the 1890s wrote verse and literary criticism; he published several romantic novels, including *The Quest for the Golden Girl* (1896); *The Romance of Zion Chapel* (1898); and *Young Lives* (1899), which describes the early London years of his first marriage. (His wife Mildred died of typhoid in 1894: he was to remarry twice.) *The Romantic '90s* (1926) is an account of this period. In 1901 he settled in the United States, returning to Europe in 1927 to spend his last years in the south of France.

Legenda Aurea, see GOLDEN LEGEND, THE.

Legend of Good Women, The, written by *Chaucer between 1372 and 1386, based on such works as *Ovid's *Heroides*, and *Boccaccio's *De Claris Mulieribus* and *Vitae Virorum et Feminarum Illustrium*. The prologue is more admired than the stories which make up the body of the poem. This prologue occurs in two forms, the dates and order of precedence of which have been disputed; the prevailing modern view is that the one known as 'F' dates from 1385–6 and 'G' from 1394. It opens with some famous lines in praise of the daisy (conforming to the tradition of 'Marguerite' poems in French) and continues with a description of the rebuking of the sleeping narrator by the god of love because of the things he had written in dispraise of women (another commonplace convention). Chaucer vows to make amends by composing this work in praise of women celebrated for their fidelity in love, as directed by the queen of love, Alceste (who has been identified as Anne of Bohemia). The poem (which is unfinished) contains nine stories of famous women (the narratives lacking the expansiveness and wit of the best of the *Canterbury Tales*): Cleopatra, Thisbe, Dido, Hypsipyle and Medea, Lucrece, Ariadne, Philomela, Phyllis, and Hypermnestra. The poem is significant, as well as for the charm of its prologue, for the fact that it is the first attested use of the heroic couplet in Chaucer (and, as far as is known, in English poetry). *Tennyson refers to it in his 'A Dream of Fair Women'. See H. Phillips and N. Havely, *Chaucer's Dream Poetry* (1997).

Legend of Montrose, A, a novel by Sir W. *Scott, published 1819, in *Tales of My Landlord*, 3rd series. The novel is based on an episode in the earl of Montrose's campaign of 1644 to raise Scotland for Charles I against the Covenant forces led by the marquis of Argyle. The love of Allan McAulay for the mysterious Annot Lyle is the main theme, but the most interesting part of the story is the character of Dugald Dalgetty, the pedantic mercenary who, like so many of his 17th-cent. compatriots, had served in the Thirty Years War and will fight for either king or Covenant, whichever pays best.

Le GUIN, Ursula K(roeber) (1929–   ), American novelist and short story writer, born in Berkeley, California. She has published many works of *science fiction and *fantasy, for both children and adults, and her works have been widely admired for their distinguished prose, as well as their imagination and thoughtful speculations. They include the 'Hainish' trilogy (*Rocannon's World*, 1966; *Planet of Exile*, 1966; and *City of Illusions*, 1967) and the Earthsea Tetralogy (*A Wizard of Earthsea*, 1968; *The Tombs of Atuan*, 1971; *The Farthest Shore*, 1972; *Tehanu*, 1991).

LEHMANN, (Rudolph) John (Frederick) (1907–87), poet, publisher, and editor, brother of Rosamond *Lehmann, educated at Eton and Trinity College,

Cambridge, where he became friendly with Julian Bell, nephew of V. *Woolf; from 1931 he was associated with the *Hogarth Press, of which he became a partner in 1938. It published his first book of poems, *A Garden Revisited* (1931), and several others. His *Collected Poems 1930–63* appeared in 1963. Lehmann is probably best known as the editor of *New Writing* and of the *London Magazine*. His three volumes of autobiography, *The Whispering Gallery* (1951), *I am my Brother* (1960), and *The Ample Proposition* (1966), record a life rich in literary friendships and activity, as do his several volumes of reminiscence and biography, which include works on the *Sitwells (1968), the Woolfs, and R. *Brooke (1980).

LEHMANN, Rosamond Nina (1901–90), novelist, sister of John *Lehmann, born in Buckinghamshire, the second daughter of a Liberal MP and contributor to *Punch*. She was educated privately and at Girton College, Cambridge, and shortly after her first marriage achieved a *succès de scandale* with her first novel, *Dusty Answer* (1927), which describes the awakening into womanhood of 18-year-old Judith Earle, through Cambridge and through her emotional entanglements with a neighbouring family of cousins. In 1928 she married the painter Wogan Philipps. Her second novel, *A Note in Music* (1930), also created a stir with its frank treatment of homosexuality. *Invitation to the Waltz* (1932) describes the impact on innocent 17-year-old Olivia Curtis of her first dance; its sequel, *The Weather in the Streets* (1936), shocked some of its readers by taking Olivia through a failed marriage, an adulterous love affair, and an abortion. *The Ballad and the Source* (1944) is a child's eye view of adult passion: 10-year-old Rebecca Landon listens entranced to the experienced and enigmatic Sybil Jardine. (Both characters reappear in R. Lehmann's later novel *A Sea-Grape Tree*, 1976.) *The Echoing Grove* (1953), a novel about the relationship of two sisters, one of whom had had an affair with the other's husband, was followed by a long silence, then by *The Swan in the Evening: Fragments of an Inner Life* (1967). This short autobiographical testament opens by recalling her own childhood, then describes her reactions to the sudden death from poliomyelitis of her daughter Sally in Java in 1958; her spiritual experiences (she quotes *Jung and F. W. H. *Myers in support) convinced her of her daughter's survival after death, and of their continuing relationship.

Rosamond Lehmann's novels, in their insistence on the emotional and sensuous aspects of life, have fairly been described as romantic and female, by both admirers and critics, qualifications that led in part to their neglect; the new wave of *feminist criticism which inspired many reprints in the 1980s prefers to point to their pioneering frankness and faith in the importance of women's lives. There is a biography by Selina Hastings (2002).

LEIBNIZ, Gottfried Wilhelm (1646–1716), German philosopher and mathematician, born at Leipzig, the founder of the Society (later Academy) of Sciences at Berlin. He discovered the infinitesimal calculus at about the same time as I. *Newton, but by a different method. As a philosopher he was inspired by *Descartes, *Spinoza, and *Hobbes, but broke away from Descartes's mechanical conception of the universe. Matter he regarded as a multitude of monads, each a nucleus of force and a microcosm or concentration of the universe. Admitting that the interaction of spirit and matter is inexplicable, he assumed a 'pre-established harmony' between them: the spirit is modified by final causes, bodies by efficient causes; the two series are brought together, like two clocks ticking in unison (the simile is *Voltaire's), by a harmony established from all time by God, the supreme monad and perfect exemplar of the human soul. Voltaire satirized his 'optimism' in *Candide*. His system is embodied in his *Théodicée* (1710) and *Monadologie* (1714), written in French. Leibniz was one of the chief forces in the German *Enlightenment.

LEICESTER, Robert Dudley, earl of (?1532–88), the favourite of *Elizabeth I, who figures in Scott's *Kenilworth* as the husband of the unfortunate Amy Robsart.

LEIGH, Augusta (1784–1851), half-sister of Lord *Byron, daughter of his father by the latter's earlier marriage to Lady Carmarthen. Augusta's relations with Byron have been the subject of much speculation, and it is probable that he was the father of her daughter Elizabeth Medora, born in 1814.

LEIGH, Mike (1943–   ), writer and stage and film director, one of the few outstanding, individual British auteurs, who evolved a unique way of creating his work in extended periods of intense improvisation and rehearsal in close collaboration with actors. Raised in Salford, Lancashire, Leigh trained at RADA, the London International Film School, and the Central School of Art and Design. A gifted cartoonist and obsessively outsider-ish Jew with a proudly ambivalent attitude to both his background and his fellow humans, his work has the vivacity, humour, and social detail of a latterday *Hogarth or *Dickens. His theatre work was a preparation for a prodigious output of brilliant television and feature films ranging from the suburban bleakness of *Bleak Moments* (1971) to the inner city anomie of *Meantime* (1983). The tragicomedy *Abigail's Party* (1977) is his best-known stage play, a classic of social embarrassment and observation. *Life is Sweet* (1990), the tumultuous, Dostoevskian *Naked* (1993), and the richly poignant *Secrets and Lies* (1996) are among the best British films of their era. In print, Leigh is represented by *Abigail's Party* and *Goose-Pimples* (1983), *Smelling a Rat* and *Ecstasy* (1989), and *Naked and Other Screenplays* (1995). Michael Coveney's critical biography, *The World According to Mike Leigh*, was published in 1996.

LEIGHTON, Frederic, Lord (1830–96), Victorian classical artist, born at Scarborough, but educated on the

Continent, at Florence, Frankfurt, and Rome. In 1855 his *Cimabue's Celebrated Madonna Carried in Procession through the Streets of Florence* (1855) was shown at the *Royal Academy; his first exhibit, it was immensely successful, and was bought by Queen Victoria and praised by *Ruskin. Thereafter the handsome and utterly respectable Leighton occupied a privileged position in the art establishment; he became president of the Royal Academy in 1878, a peer in 1896. His interest in Florentine Renaissance subjects led to his commission to illustrate *Romola. In Rome in the early 1850s he moved in the circle of A. *Sartoris, and was to appear as the exuberant Mr Kiowski in her *A Week in a French Country House* (1867); he also met there R. *Browning and *Thackeray, and suggested aspects of Clive Newcome, 'the cock of the whole painting school, the favourite of all', in *The Newcomes*. He appeared as Gaston Phoebus in Disraeli's *Lothair, and less sympathetically as the public artist Lord Mellifont in H. *James's story 'The Private Life' (1892). The parties at his exotic Moorish house in Holland Park are recalled in many memoirs of the period. See L. and R. Ormond, *Lord Leighton* (1975).

Leila, (1) in Byron's *Don Juan, the Muslim child whom Juan rescues at the siege of Ismail; (2) in his *The Giaour, the unfortunate heroine.

Leinster, Book of, an Irish manuscript of the 12th cent., containing stories of Gaelic mythology, in particular the feats of *Cuchulain.

L.E.L., see LANDON.

LELAND, John (c.1506–52), the earliest of modern English antiquaries, educated at St Paul's School and Christ's College, Cambridge. He studied at Paris, took holy orders, and by 1530 was involved with the royal libraries, and claimed he received a commission in 1533 to search monastic and collegiate libraries for old authors. He made a tour through England in 1535–43, intending his researches to be the basis of a great work on the 'History and Antiquities of this Nation', but he left merely a mass of undigested notes. In *A Newe Yeares Gyfte* (1549) he described to the king the manner and aims of his researches. He became insane in 1550. *Leland's Itinerary* was first published at Oxford, in nine volumes, by *Hearne in 1710–12; and his *Collectanea* in six (1715). Leland claimed to have 'conservid many good autors, the which other wise had beene like to have perischid', in the dissolution of the religious houses. There is an edition of the *Itinerary* by Lucy Toulmin Smith (1906–10).

LELAND, Thomas, see HISTORICAL FICTION.

LELY, Sir Peter (1618–80), British portrait painter, of Dutch origin, who is best known as the painter of the voluptuous beauties who graced the court of Charles II. He became principal painter to the king in 1661 and his style is a vulgarized version of *Van Dyck's. Lely was a friend of *Lovelace, who eulogized him in verse. Lely's poignant double portrait of *Charles I and the Duke of York* (1647) inspired Lovelace's poem 'See what a clouded majesty', which contains the somewhat unexpected praise: 'None but my Lilly ever drew a mind.' His most characteristic works are the *Windsor Beauties* (Hampton Court).

LEMON, Mark (1809–70), a founder, first joint-editor, then editor of *Punch, from 1841 until his death, and contributor to other periodicals. He wrote prolifically for the stage, and performed in *Dickens's private theatricals. He collaborated with Dickens in *Mr Nightingale's Diary* (1851), a one-act farce with both authors in the cast.

LEMPRIÈRE, John (d. 1824), classical scholar; author of a standard classical dictionary, *Bibliotheca Classica*, which has frequently been enlarged and revised and is still in use. He features as a character in a novel by L. *Norfolk.

LENCLOS, Anne, known as Ninon de Lenclos (1620–1705), a Frenchwoman noted for her beauty and wit, which she retained to a very advanced age, depicted by Mlle *Scudéry as 'Clarisse' in her *Clélie*. She had many celebrities for her lovers, and her *salon* was frequented by *Saint-Evrémond, *Molière, the youthful *Voltaire, etc.

LENNOX, Charlotte née Ramsay (?1729–1804), novelist, essayist, translator, editor, and poet. She was the daughter of an army officer, and spent some of her childhood in New York Province. When she came to England she failed as an actress and turned to a hardworking and not very remunerative life as a writer. Her first novel, the *Life of Harriot Stuart*, appeared in 1750, and in 1752 her most important work, *The Female Quixote*, which established her name and was praised by *Fielding. Her collection and translation of the sources of Shakespeare's plays appeared as *Shakespear Illustrated* (1752–3), and *Henrietta* (1758), a novel concerned with female dependence, was dramatized as *The Sisters*, with an epilogue by *Goldsmith: it had one performance in 1769. She also translated many works from the French. Dr *Johnson, a friend and admirer of her work, cited her under 'Talent' in his *Dictionary*. She was skilled in discerning and describing fleeting moments of emotion, and may be grouped with practitioners of the novel of *sentiment. The poverty of her later years entitled her to become one of the early beneficiaries of the *Royal Literary Fund.

'Lenore' (1774), a celebrated ballad by the German poet Gottfried August Bürger (1747–94), based on the Scottish ballad 'Sweet William's Ghost'. Lenore is carried off on horseback by the spectre of her lover after his death and married by him at the graveside. It was translated first by W. *Taylor, whose version circulated in manuscript and was published in 1797 in the *Monthly Magazine; Mrs *Barbauld said Sir W. *Scott told her that he had been inspired by a reading of

Taylor's translation, and his own version (with the borrowing of two lines from Taylor acknowledged) appeared also in 1797, anonymously, as 'William and Helen' in *The Chase and William and Helen*. The two poets corresponded about their versions: see J. W. Robberds's *Memoir* of Taylor (1843). Other imitations of 'Lenore' appeared almost simultaneously, and a parody, 'Miss Kitty' (1797). As late as 1872 the ballad provided the programme for Joachim Raff's Fifth ('Lenore') Symphony, very popular in its time. (See also WILD HUNTSMAN.)

LEO X, Giovanni de' Medici (1475–1521), pope 1513–21, a patron of literature and art, notably of *Raphael. It fell to him to deal with the theses of *Luther, whom he excommunicated in 1521. It was he who gave *Henry VIII the title of 'Defender of the Faith'.

Leo Hunter, Mrs, a character in Dickens's *Pickwick Papers*.

Leodegrance ('Leodegan' elsewhere in the Arthurian cycles), in *Malory, king of Cameliard and father of *Guinevere.

LEÓN, Fray Luis de (?1527–91), a Spanish Augustinian monk, and professor for nearly 30 years at the University of Salamanca; like his near contemporary *John of the Cross, he endured imprisonment for his beliefs. Known as a scholar in his lifetime, he subsequently became known as a mystic poet. See a life by A. F. G. Bell (1925).

LEONARD, Elmore (1925–   ), American writer, born in New Orleans, and educated at the University of Detroit. He began his literary career writing westerns: his first short story, 'Trail of the Apache', appeared in *Argosy* in Dec. 1951. *Hombre* (1961) was filmed in 1966 with Paul Newman. He later moved to crime writing, as the cult of the western declined, and produced many titles including *City Primeval* (1980), *Glitz* (1985), *Freaky Deaky* (1988), *Get Shorty* (1990), and *Rum Punch* (1992). Admired for his terse dialogue, vividly observed locations, laconic wit, and short scenes of direct action, he has been acclaimed as the heir to *Hammett and *Chandler, and many of his works have been successfully filmed.

LEONARD, Tom (1944–   ), Scottish poet, performance poet, critic, essayist, and radical polemicist, born in Glasgow, and educated at the University of Glasgow. His free-style, highly personal writings cover a wide range of topics, both Scottish and international, in both prose and verse, ranging from *Satires and Profanities* (1984) to acerbic domestic and existential meditations (*Nora's Place*, 1990), and the Gulf War (*On the Mass Bombing of Iraq and Kuwait*, 1991). He has written powerfully about the Scottish voice, in essays such as 'On Reclaiming the Local', written while compiling his anthology *Radical Renfrew* (1990), which collected lost or marginalized work written largely in the 19th cent. by 'poets born, or sometime resident' in the county of

Renfrew. He himself has made inventive and witty use of the Glasgow dialect in much of his work. *Reports from the Present: Selected Works 1982–94* (1995) collects prose and verse. He has also written on James *Thomson ('B.V.') (*Places of the Mind*, 1993).

LEONARDO da VINCI (1452–1519), Florentine painter, sculptor, musician, scientist, and thinker, who developed in his painting greater complexity in composition, chiaroscuro, and psychological insight than had ever been achieved before; his *sfumato* technique was deeply influential. *The Last Supper* (c.1495) and the *Mona Lisa* (c.1503) are perhaps the two most celebrated pictures in the Western tradition. In 1481/2 Leonardo went to Milan, and remained in the employ of Ludovico Sforza until 1499; he was then in Florence, Rome, and Milan again, and finally in France, where he died near Amboise. In the 19th cent. the enigmatic charm of Leonardo's women mesmerized writers; *Gautier and the *Goncourt brothers pondered over the subtle smile of the *Mona Lisa*, the 'Gioconda smile'; in the second half of the century her beauty was seen as darker and tinged with evil, and was most powerfully evoked in a famous passage by *Pater, in an essay which owes something to D. G. *Rossetti's early sonnet 'Our Lady of the Rocks' and to *Swinburne's descriptions of Fatal Women. Pater's 'Lady Lisa' popularized the Fatal Women whose development has been outlined by *Praz, and echoes of her fascination recur through Decadent poetry until she is parodied by A. *Huxley in 'The Gioconda Smile'.

Leonato, in Shakespeare's *Much Ado about Nothing*, the father of Hero and uncle of Beatrice.

Leonatus, Posthumus, see POSTHUMUS LEONATUS.

leonine verse, a kind of Latin verse much used in the Middle Ages, consisting of hexameters, or alternate hexameters and pentameters, in which the last word rhymes with that preceding the caesura; for instance:

> His replicans clare tres causas explico quare
> More Leonino dicere metra sino.

The term is applied to English verse of which the middle and last syllables rhyme. It is derived, according to Du Cange, from the name of a certain poet Leo, who lived about the time of Louis VII of France (1137–80) or his successor Philippe-Auguste (1180–1223).

LEONORA d'ESTE, sister of Alfonso II, duke of Ferrara, with whom, according to legend, the poet *Tasso fell in love, and was in consequence imprisoned in a madhouse. This story is the foundation of Byron's *The Lament of Tasso*.

LEONOV, Leonid Maksimovich (1899–1994), Russian novelist. His first two novels, *The Badgers* (1924), a Dostoevskian study of a counter-revolutionary woman, and *The Thief* (1927), which tells the story of an anti-Soviet band of criminals, are suffused with the experimentalism of 1920s Russian prose and brought him great prestige. With his third novel, *Sot* (1929), he wrote one of the best examples of the so-called 'five-year plan novel' about the building of a papermill on a northern river, but in the early 1930s the novel came under attack, as did his next novels, *Skutarevsky* (1932) and *The Road to the Ocean* (1935). *The Russian Forest* (1953), combining the story of the first year of the Russo-German War, 1941–2, with a description of the hero's life stretching back before the revolution, is held by many to be his best work. English translations of *The Thief* (by H. Butler) and *The River Sot* (by Ivor Montagu and S. S. Nolbandov) appeared in 1931.

Leontes, in Shakespeare's **The Winter's Tale*, the husband of Hermione.

LEOPARDI, Giacamo (1798–1837), the greatest Italian Romantic poet. His richly suggestive lyrics (*Canti*, 1831, 1845) were written between 1816 and 1837. In 1824 he turned his attention to philosophical prose, notably the ironical dialogues *Operette morali* (*Moral Tales*, 1827). The 'cosmic pessimism' of his poems is often attributed to chronic illness, but it was also an intensely intellectual and even scholarly development. In his early thought, based on *Vico and the classics, poetry is given the task of recovering the freshness of the Greek response to nature. Later he was to see nature as purposeless, indifferent, or even cruel—the 'stepmother' of humanity; and he elaborated a Romantic poetics based on the tension between past and present, childhood innocence and adult awareness of insignificance, illusions and their loss. This gave rise to a wistful poetry of images he called 'vague', in that they evoke memory: the present is too precise to be beautiful. Both *Pound and R. *Lowell produced versions of his poems.

Le QUEUX, William Tufnell, see SPY FICTION.

Lêr, or **Lir,** in Gaelic mythology, the sea-god, one of the *Tuatha Dé Danann; perhaps to be identified with the British sea-god Llyr. He was the father of *Manannán.

According to the story of 'The Children of Lêr', one of the 'three sorrowful tales of Erin', Lêr had one daughter, Fionnuala, and three sons. These were changed into swans by their jealous stepmother Aoife, and condemned to spend 900 years on the seas and lakes of Ireland. Before the end of this period St Patrick arrived, the old gods were swept away, and the swans were able to return to their home. They were converted to Christianity and restored to human shape; but were now old people and soon died.

LERMONTOV, Mikhail Yurevich (1814–41), Russian Romantic poet and novelist. Descended from a Scottish officer and adventurer, Captain George Learmont, who entered the Russian service in the early 17th cent., Lermontov was himself an army officer. Strongly influenced by *Byron, he wrote lyric and narrative poetry on the themes of disillusionment, rebellion, and

personal freedom. He was killed in a duel. His best-known poems are 'A Wish' (1831), in which he expresses nostalgia for Scotland, 'The Sail' and 'No, I am not Byron' (both 1832), 'The Death of a Poet' (1837), which bemoans the death of *Pushkin, the bitter 'Gratitude' (1840), and the romantic narratives 'Mtsyri' ('The Novice', 1840) and 'The Demon' (1829–41). His prose masterpiece, the novel *A Hero of Our Time*, first translated in 1854, is his lasting monument.

LESAGE, Alain-René (1668–1747), French novelist and playwright. Generally regarded as the first major writer in France to live entirely by his pen, he produced over 60 farces and librettos. He specialized in picaresque narratives: *Le Diable boiteux* (1707) and his masterpiece *Gil Blas* (1715–35) are notable for their narrative brio and their shrewd, good-humoured presentation of human nature. *Gil Blas* was translated by *Smollett in 1749: with **Don Quixote* and *Rabelais, it can be considered the greatest foreign influence on 18th-cent. English comic fiction.

LESKOV, Nikolai Semenovich (1831–95), Russian prose writer, born near Orel in central Russia. His maternal uncle, Alexander Scott, was a Russianized British Protestant, and between 1857 and 1860 Leskov travelled widely in provincial Russia for the agricultural firm of Scott and Wilkins. After this he turned to journalism, his first work appearing in 1860 and his first story in 1862. Leskov's major themes, provincial Russia and Russian religion, expressed with an uncanny ear for the speech of ordinary people, are perhaps best seen in his stories 'The Musk-Ox' (1863), 'Lady Macbeth of the Mtsensk District' (1865), 'The Sealed Angel' and 'The Enchanted Wanderer' (both 1874), and his major long work, the 'chronicle' *Cathedral Folk* (1872). In his most famous story 'Lefty' (1881) the eponymous Russian craftsman is sent by Tsar Alexander I to England to match his skills against English rivals. The first translations of Leskov into English, by A. E. Chamot, appeared in 1922.

LESSING, Doris May, née Tayler (1919–), novelist and short story writer, born in Persia of British parents who moved when she was 5 to a farm in Southern Rhodesia. She left school at 15 and worked as a nursemaid, then as a shorthand-typist and telephone operator in Salisbury. After the break-up of her first marriage she became involved in radical politics. She remarried in 1945, but in 1949 left for England with her youngest child and the manuscript of her first novel to be published, *The Grass is Singing* (1950), the story of the complex relationship between a white farmer's wife and her black servant, and its violent conclusion. From this period she supported herself and her son by her writing. Her quintet *Children of Violence* is a **Bildungsroman*, tracing the history of Martha Quest from her childhood in Rhodesia, through post-war Britain, to an apocalyptic ending in AD 2000 (*Martha*

Quest, 1952; *A Proper Marriage*, 1954; *A Ripple from the Storm*, 1958; *Landlocked*, 1965; and *The Four-Gated City*, 1969). Perhaps her best-known book, **The Golden Notebook* (1962) is a lengthy and ambitious novel which was hailed as a landmark by the women's movement. Later novels, *Briefing for a Descent into Hell* (1971) and *Memoirs of a Survivor* (1975), enter the realm of 'inner space fiction', exploring mental breakdown and the breakdown of society. The sequence collectively entitled *Canopus in Argus Archives* (*Re: Colonised Planet 5, Shikasta*, 1979; *The Marriages between Zones Three, Four and Five*, 1980; *The Sirian Experiments*, 1981; *The Making of the Representative for Planet 8*, 1982; *Documents Relating to the Sentimental Agents in the Volyen Empire*, 1983) marks a complete break with traditional realism, describing the epic and mythic events of a fictional universe with a remarkable freedom of invention. Other novels include *The Good Terrorist* (1985), describing the behaviour of a group of middle-class revolutionaries in a London squat; *The Fifth Child* (1988), a nightmarish fable about the effect on an ordinary couple of an ugly and violent child; *Love, Again* (1996); and *Mara and Dann* (1999) and its sequel *The Story of General Dann* (2005), set in a bleak and apocalyptic future of war and regression. The first volume of her autobiography, *Under My Skin*, was published in 1994, and the second, *Waiting in the Shade: 1949–1962*, in 1997. She has written many other works of fiction and non-fiction, displaying her concern with politics, with the changing destiny of women, with a fear of technological disaster, and has also written of her interest in Sufi thought and the works of I. *Shah. Her *Collected Stories* (2 vols, 1978) show a similarly broad range of interests, from the feminism of 'One off the Short List' to meditations on the material and spiritual life in 'The Temptation of Jack Orkney'; they include her much-anthologized evocation of childhood bravado, 'Through the Tunnel'. She has also published two 'romantic' and realistic novels, *Diary of a Good Neighbour* (1983) and *If the Old Could* (1984) under the pseudonym of Jane Somers.

LESSING, Gotthold Ephraim (1729–81), German critic and dramatist. He was educated at Leipzig University, was the literary adviser of the National Theatre at Hamburg (1765–9), and in 1770 became librarian to the duke of Brunswick at Wolfenbüttel, where he died. As a dramatist his principal works were: the serious comedy *Minna von Barnhelm* (1767); *Emilia Galotti* (1772), a tragedy on a social theme; and *Nathan der Weise* (1779), a plea for religious tolerance. *Miss Sara Sampson* (1755), the first significant domestic tragedy in German, was modelled on Lillo's **George Barnwell* (1731). Lessing was, in the words of *Macaulay, 'beyond all dispute, the first critic in Europe', who emancipated German literature from the narrow conventions of the French classical school, suggesting that German writers look instead to Shakespeare and English literature as more congenial models. His

chief critical works were the *Briefe die neueste Litteratur betreffend* (*Letters Relating to Recent Literature*, 1759–65), the **Laokoon* (1766), on the limits of the several arts, and the *Hamburgische Dramaturgie* (1767–9). In England, Lessing was much admired not only by Macaulay, but also by *Coleridge, G. *Eliot, and G. H. *Lewes, both for his humane and liberal beliefs and for the clarity of his prose style.

L'ESTRANGE, Sir Roger (1616–1704), journalist and pamphleteer, and an active royalist, obliged to flee to the Continent in 1648. After the Restoration he was appointed surveyor of printing presses and licenser of the press. He issued the *News* and the *Intelligencer* (1663–6) which were ousted by the *London Gazette* of *Muddiman; also many political pamphlets, one of the earliest being a reply to *Milton, *No Blind Guides* (1660). In his periodical the *Observator* (1681–7) he attacked the Whigs, *Oates, and Dissenters, often employing a lively dialogue form of question and answer; his prose is colloquial, forceful, and conversational. He was knighted by James II in 1685, but after the revolution was regarded by the Whigs as a grave threat to liberty, and was several times imprisoned; he thereafter supported himself by translations which include *The Visions of Quevedo* (1667), *Aesop's *Fables* (1692), and the works of *Josephus (1702).

Letter on the Spirit of Patriotism, A, see BOLINGBROKE, H. ST J.

Letters on a Regicide Peace, see REGICIDE PEACE.

Letters on the Study and Use of History, see BOLINGBROKE, H. ST J.

Letter to a Noble Lord *on the Attacks Made upon Him and His Pension in the House of Lords by the Duke of Bedford and the Earl of Lauderdale*, by E. *Burke, published 1796.

Burke retired from Parliament in 1794 and received a pension from the government of *Pitt. This grant was criticized in the House of Lords, principally by the peers above named, as excessive in amount and inconsistent with Burke's own principles of economical reform. Burke replied in one of the greatest masterpieces of irony and feeling in the English language, comparing his own services to the state with those rendered by the duke of Bedford and his house, which had been the recipient of enormous grants from the Crown.

Letter to Sir William Wyndham, A, see BOLINGBROKE, H. ST J.

Letter to the Sheriffs of Bristol, A, by E. *Burke, published 1777.

The American war had at this time followed its disastrous course for two years. The letter begins with a protest against certain Acts of Parliament subjecting the rebels to exceptional legal disabilities, treating them in fact as traitors, and passes to a review of the current humiliating situation. Burke goes on to defend the course that he has taken. Asserting his zeal for the supremacy of Parliament, he defines the problem which the exercise of this supremacy involves: 'to conform our government to the character and circumstances of the several people who compose this mighty and strangely diversified' empire. The scheme of taxing America is incompatible with this conception of imperial policy, and Burke consequently voted for the pacification of 1766, and even for the surrender of the whole right of taxation.

LEVER, Charles (1806–72), born and educated in Dublin. He qualified as an MD and practised in Ireland. He became a prolific and successful novelist, writing chiefly of military and Irish life. His first novels, *Harry Lorrequer* (1839), *Charles O'Malley* (1841), and *Jack Hinton the Guardsman* (1843), were extremely popular, and in 1842 he gave up medicine for the editorship of the *Dublin University Magazine*. *Tom Burke of Ours* (1844) and a historical novel, *The Knight of Gwynne* (1847), were notable among the stream of his racy, anecdotal works. In 1845 he left Ireland and eventually settled in Italy. *The Martins of Cro'Martin* (1847) provides a spirited portrait of life in the west of Ireland, and *The Dodd Family Abroad* (1852–4) an account of an English family's vicissitudes on the Continent. His later novels were more carefully constructed; *Sir Jasper Carew* (1855), *The Fortunes of Glencore* (1857), and *Lord Kilgobbin* (1872) are considered among the best of this period. Lever received much encouragement and advice from *Thackeray, and was admired by G. *Eliot and A. *Trollope.

LEVERSON, Ada (1862–1933), whose novels enjoyed a belated vogue in the 1960s. She is chiefly remembered for her association with *Wilde, who named her 'The Sphinx'. She sheltered him during his trials, and his letters to her were published in a limited edition in 1930. For some years she held a salon frequented by the *Sitwells, *Beerbohm, the novelist G. *Moore, and H. *Acton. Her novels, set in fashionable London society, include *Love's Shadow* (1908), *Tenterhooks* (1912), and *Love at Second Sight* (1916), all of which feature Edith Ottley as protagonist; they were published in one volume in 1962 as *The Little Ottleys*, with a foreword by C. *MacInnes, praising her as 'the classic author of the comedy of manners'.

LEVERTOV, Denise (1923–97), British/American poet, born in Ilford, Essex; she published the neo-Romantic *The Double Image* in 1947. In 1948 she moved to America where she held a variety of academic posts. She became a central figure in the *Black Mountain group, and maintained their Modernist aims in an unceasing flow of volumes from 1958 to 1996. Her search for the mystic and for 'organic form' led her to use free verse as she addressed family relationships, the natural world, and politics, notably the Vietnam War. *The Sorrow Dance* (1967) and *Selected Poems* (Bloodaxe, 1986) contain some of her best work.

LEVI, Carlo (1902–75), Italian writer and painter. His best-known work is *Cristo si è fermato a Eboli* (*Christ Stopped at Eboli*, 1945) based on his experience in southern Italy where he had been condemned to internal exile as an opponent of the Fascist regime. His other works are: *Le parole sono pietre* (*Words are Stones*, 1955) on Sicily; *Il futuro ha un cuore antico* (*The Future Has an Ancient Heart*, 1956) on the Soviet Union; *La doppia notte dei tigli* (*The Two-fold Night*, 1959) on Germany.

LEVI, Peter Chad Tigar (1931–2000), poet, translator, classical scholar, travel writer, and archaeologist, born in Ruislip, near London, and educated at Campion Hall, Oxford, where he was tutor and lecturer, 1965–77; he was a Jesuit priest from 1964 to 1977, when he resigned the priesthood. His first volume of poetry, *The Gravel Ponds* (1960), was followed by several others, including a *Collected Poems 1955–1975* (1976); his poems mingle imagery and themes from classical antiquity, British history and prehistory, Christianity, and domestic life. Notable among his translations is Pausanias' *Guide to Greece* (1971). A volume of autobiography, *The Flutes of Autumn* (1983), concludes with an eloquent tribute to David *Jones. Levi was professor of poetry at Oxford, 1984–2000.

LEVI, Primo (1919–87), Italian writer of memoirs, fiction, essays, and poetry, born in Turin. His greatest works are his first, *Se questo è un uomo* (1947; *If This is a Man*, 1960), his memoir of Auschwitz, and *La tregua* (1963; *The Truce*, 1965), the story of his journey home; and his last, *I sommersi e i salvati* (1985; *The Drowned and the Saved*, 1988), essays which return to Auschwitz, and to the question of what it means to be human. Levi shared Turin's traditions of science, modesty, and melancholy, and worked there as an industrial chemist; not until he retired did he admit to being as much a writer as a chemist. In 1943 he was captured as a partisan and sent as a Jew to Auschwitz. His scientific training and self-effacing nature made him an observant and objective witness. To these gifts he added clarity of expression, ironic humour, and metaphorical imagination, which make his 'chemist's autobiography', *Il sistema periodico* (1975; *The Periodic Table*, 1985), the equal, for many readers, of his darker meditations. He also wrote two novels, *La chiave a stella* (1978; *The Wrench*, 1987) and *Se non ora, quando?* (1982; *If Not Now, When?*); two books of poetry (*L'osteria di Brema*, 1975, and *Ad ora incerta*, 1984) and five collections of stories. He took his own life on 11 Apr. 1987. See HOLOCAUST, LITERATURE OF THE.

Leviathan, or *The Matter, Form, and Power of a Commonwealth, Ecclesiastical and Civil*, a treatise of political philosophy by *Hobbes, published 1651, Latin text 1668.

By 'The Leviathan' the author signified sovereign power. The basis of his political philosophy is that man is not, as *Aristotle held, naturally a social being, recognizing the claims of the community upon him and sharing in its prosperity, but a purely selfish creature, seeking only his own advantage. The state of nature is one of general war, and 'the notions of Right and Wrong, Justice and Injustice, have there no place.' There is 'continuall feare . . . And the life of man [is] solitary, poore, nasty, brutish and short.' To escape these conditions man has adopted certain 'articles of peace', those 'Laws of Nature', by which a man is forbidden to do 'that which is destructive of his life' and of which the science is 'true moral philosophy'. Virtue is the means of 'peaceful, sociable and comfortable living'. The first law of nature is, 'that every man ought to endeavour Peace'. The second is, 'That a man be willing, when others are so too . . . to lay down his right to all things; and be contented with so much liberty against other men, as he would allow other men against himselfe.' The third is, 'that men performe their Covenants made'.

To enforce these covenants it is necessary to establish an external power, which shall punish their infraction; accordingly all individuals must enter into a contract 'to conferre all their power and strength upon one Man, or upon one Assembly of men'. 'This done, the Multitude so united in one Person, is called a Common-Wealth.' This representative person is sovereign, and his power is inalienable. The contract is not between the subjects and the sovereign, but only between the subjects. The sovereign power is indivisible; it cannot for instance be divided between king and parliament. Hobbes is careful to repudiate the rival claim of the Church to control over the citizen, which involves either a division of sovereign power, or the absorption of the state in the Church. He accordingly makes the Church subordinate to the state.

The absolute power thus given to the sovereign is, however, subject to certain limits. There is liberty to refuse obedience if the command of the sovereign frustrates the end for which the sovereignty was ordained, i.e. the preservation of the life of the individual. Moreover, the obligation of subjects to the sovereign is understood to last so long as, and no longer than, 'the power lasteth, by which he is able to protect them'. The sovereign finally is responsible to God, if not to his subjects, for the proper discharge of his office.

LÉVI-STRAUSS, Claude (1908–   ), French anthropologist, born in Brussels and educated in Paris, taking degrees in law and philosophy. From 1934 to 1939 he taught at the University of São Paolo, Brazil, becoming interested in anthropology and pursuing some fieldwork in Amazonia. During the 1940s he taught in New York and worked at the French embassy in Washington. Returning to Paris, he taught at the École Pratique des Hautes Études, and then as the first professor of social anthropology at the Collège de France. His principal early works are the analysis of kinship systems in *Les Structures élémentaires de la parenté* (*Elementary Structures of Kinship*, 1949) and the autobiographical travelogue *Tristes tropiques* (1955). *Le Totémisme aujourd'hui* and *La Pensée sauvage* (*Totemism* and *The Savage Mind*, both 1962) are notable defences of the complex thinking practised by 'primitive' peoples. His major contributions to the analysis of myths appear in *Anthropologie structurale* (1958), *Le Cru et le cuit* (*The Raw and the Cooked*, 1964), and the four volumes of *Mythologiques* (1964–72). After *Saussure, he has been the chief exponent of *structuralism in the 'human sciences', seeking the underlying codes, rules, or systems of meaning that can explain the workings of the human mind behind the variety of cultural appearances. His influence not just in anthropology but upon French philosophy, psychoanalysis, and literary theory, has been extensive.

LEVY, Amy (1861–89), poet, novelist, and feminist, born in Clapham, London, and educated at Newnham College, Cambridge. Her collections are *Xantippe and Other Verse* (1881, of which the title poem is a dramatic monologue spoken by the allegedly shrewish wife of Socrates), *A Minor Poet and Other Verse* (1884), and the posthumously published *A London Plane-Tree and Other Verse* (1889). Her observant novel *Reuben Sachs: A Sketch* (1888) roused indignation for its lightly satirical portrayal of London Jewish social life, but was widely read and translated into German by her friend Eleanor Marx. Levy was a friend of O. *Schreiner and other prominent feminists. Of a morbidly sensitive temperament, and suffering from deafness, she committed suicide by inhaling charcoal fumes at her London home.

LEWES, G(eorge) H(enry) (1817–78), a writer of extraordinarily varied interests and talents, best known in his secondary role as 'husband' and encourager of the diffident George *Eliot. When he met her in 1851, however, he already had behind him a varied career as comic dramatist, actor, essayist on subjects ranging from *Hegel's aesthetics (his was the first proselytizing article on the subject in England) to Spanish drama, and author of a novel in imitation of *Goethe, *Ranthorpe* (1847). He wrote one of the first books in English on *Comte's positivist philosophy (1853), and a popular history of philosophy from F. *Bacon to Comte (*Biographical History of Philosophy*, 1845–6). His liaison with George Eliot, dating from 1854, could not be regularized because he had condoned the adultery of his wife Agnes with T. L. *Hunt; admirers of *Shelley, the Leweses believed in free love, and when Agnes bore the first of her four children by Hunt in 1850 Lewes registered the boy as his own. By the time he met George Eliot, he was estranged from Agnes, but unable to obtain a divorce.

Lewes's most distinguished work is his still valuable *Life of Goethe* (1855), which he researched, with George

Eliot's help, in Weimar and Berlin in 1854–5. Lewes turned his attention increasingly to science: his later works range from biological works like *Seaside Studies* (1858) and *The Physiology of Common Life* (1859) to his ambitious attempt at psychology, *Problems of Life and Mind* (1873–9), the last volume of which was completed by George Eliot after his death. That George Eliot benefited not only from his encouragement of her talents but also from his studies is evident from the scientific metaphors which inform her works.

Lewesdon Hill, a *topographical poem by William Crowe (1745–1829), published 1788, in the style of James *Thomson.

LEWIS, Alun (1915–44), born in a Welsh mining village. He went to university at Aberystwyth and trained as a teacher before joining the army (after much hesitation) in 1940. His first volume of poems, *Raiders' Dawn*, appeared in 1942, and in 1943 a volume of stories, *The Last Inspection*, most of which deal with army life in England, 'the rootless life of soldiers having no enemy', as does his most anthologized poem, 'All Day it has Rained...', first published in 1941. Lewis was killed in Burma. Letters and stories were collected in *In the Green Tree* (1948); *Selected Poetry and Prose*, with a biographical introduction by Ian Hamilton, appeared in 1966, and a paperback selection by J. Hooker and G. Lewis in 1981. Many of Lewis's poems show a recurring obsession with the themes of isolation and death, and a debt to E. *Thomas, to whom one of his best poems is addressed.

LEWIS, Cecil Day, see DAY-LEWIS.

LEWIS, C(live) S(taples) (1898–1963), literary scholar, critic, and novelist, fellow of Magdalen College, Oxford, 1925–54, and afterwards professor of medieval and Renaissance English at Cambridge. His critical works include *The Allegory of Love* (1936) and *English Literature in the Sixteenth Century* (vol. iii in the *Oxford History of English Literature*, 1954). He is more widely known for his popular religious and moral writings, such as *The Problem of Pain* (1940), *The Screwtape Letters* (1940), and *The Four Loves* (1960). *Out of the Silent Planet* (1938) is the first of three science fiction novels with a strong Christian flavour, influenced by his friendship with *Tolkien and C. *Williams. With *The Lion, the Witch, and the Wardrobe* (1950) he began a series of seven 'Narnia' stories for children. *Surprised by Joy* (1955) is his spiritual autobiography. 'The Inklings', a group of his friends, met in his Oxford rooms for many years to talk and read aloud their compositions. In 1956 he married Helen Joy Davidman, an American, to protect her from extradition: she died in 1960 and he wrote of their marriage in *A Grief Observed* (1961). Their relationship became the subject of a successful stage play and film, *Shadowlands* (1989) by William Nicholson. See Walter Hooper, *C. S. Lewis; A Companion and Guide* (1996).

LEWIS, M(atthew) G(regory) (1775–1818), educated at Westminster and Christ Church, Oxford, remembered as the author of *The Monk* (1796), a representative *Gothic novel, from which his nickname 'Monk' Lewis was derived. Lewis was greatly influenced by German Romanticism, and wrote numerous dramas. His verses (of which 'Alonzo the Brave and the Fair Imogine', which appears in *The Monk*, is probably the best known) had some influence on Sir W. *Scott's early poetry.

LEWIS, Norman (1908–2003), novelist and travel writer, born in Enfield, north London. His novels of action and adventure include *The Day of the Fox* (1955), set in the aftermath of the Spanish Civil War, *The Volcanoes above Us* (1957), set during a South American revolution, and *A Suitable Case for Corruption* (1984), set in the Middle East. His travel writings include journeys through Indo-China and Burma (*A Dragon Apparent*, 1951; *Golden Earth*, 1952), the Mediterranean, India, and Cuba, and combine vivid evocation of place with acute political analysis. A notable piece of reportage was his influential article 'Genocide in Brazil' (*Sunday Times*, 1968), which drew attention to the plight of the near-extinction of the native population. (See also C. *Hampton's play *Savages*.) His autobiography, *Jackdaw Cade*, was published in 1987.

LEWIS, (Harry) Sinclair (1885–1951), American novelist, born in Minnesota. After graduating from Yale he spent some years in journalism and published several novels, but none was of much importance until *Main Street* which scored an enormous success upon its appearance in 1920. In it he described with realism and satire the dullness of life in a small Midwestern town called Gopher Prairie. He strengthened his reputation as the most widely read and controversial of American writers with *Babbitt* (1922), the story of George Babbitt, a prosperous and self-satisfied house agent in the Midwestern town of Zenith, who comes to doubt the conventions of middle-class society, but who is eventually reabsorbed after a period of defiance and ostracism; *Arrowsmith* (1925), which describes the career of a bacteriologist and, like many of Lewis's works, is based on considerable research; *Elmer Gantry* (1927), a satiric view of Midwestern religious evangelism; and *Dodsworth* (1929), which describes the marital relations of a middle-aged American industrialist and his adventures in Europe. Lewis was awarded the *Nobel Prize in 1930.

LEWIS, (Percy) Wyndham (1882–1957), artist, novelist, and critic. He was born in Canada but came to England as a child and studied at the Slade School of Art, then, from 1901 to 1908, on the Continent, based in Paris. He was a leader of the *Vorticist movement and, with *Pound, edited *Blast: The Review of the Great English Vortex* (1914–15). His novels include *Tarr* (1918), *The Apes of God* (1930), *The Revenge for Love* (1937), and *Self Condemned* (1957); his projected four-part work *The Human Age* (*The Childermass*, 1928; *Monstre Gai* and *Malign Fiesta*, both 1955) remained unfinished. Essays and criticism include *Time and Western Man* (1927), *The Lion and the Fox: The Role of Hero in the Plays of Shakespeare* (1927), and *The Writer and the Absolute* (1952). *Blasting and Bombardiering* (1937) and *Rude Assignment* (1950) are autobiographies. Although his criticism of the increasing hollowness and mechanization of 20th-cent. civilization has affinities with the ideas of Pound, T. S. *Eliot and D. H. *Lawrence, his savage satirical attacks on his contemporaries (particularly the *Bloomsbury Group), his association with the British Fascist party, and his praise of Hitler alienated him from the literary world, and his biographer Jeffrey Meyers (*The Enemy*, 1980) describes him as 'one of the loneliest figures in the intellectual history of the thirties'. The title of the biography is taken from Lewis's own little magazine *The Enemy*, which appeared in three book-length issues, 1927–9, written largely by himself (with poems by L. *Riding and R. *Campbell): it contained the text of the volume published as *Time and Western Man* and three of his most important essays, 'Paleface', 'The Diabolical Principle', and 'The Revolutionary Simpleton'. (He is not to be confused with D. B. Wyndham Lewis, 1891–1969, the Catholic biographer and journalist who also wrote as *'Beachcomber'.)

LEYDEN, John (1775–1811), Scottish antiquary, physician, poet, and orientalist, who was equally inspired by Border ballads and the travels of Mungo *Park. He assisted Sir W. *Scott in *Minstrelsy of the Scottish Border*, contributed to M. G. *Lewis's *Tales of Wonder* (1801), and in 1803 set off for India and the Far East; he died at Batavia, Java, having mastered many oriental languages and having set himself up somewhat prematurely as the rival of Sir W. *Jones. Scott mourned his 'bright and brief career' in *The Lord of the Isles* (Canto IV. xi), and contributed a Memoir to the *Edinburgh Annual Register*, 1811, dwelling on his friend's colourful eccentricities. This was reproduced with Leyden's *Poems and Ballads* (1858, 1875). He published several treatises on oriental languages, and translated the Malay Annals (1821) and the *Commentaries of Baber* (1826).

Libeaus Desconus (a corruption of *le bel inconnu*, the fair unknown), a late 14th-cent. romance in 2,250 lines of 12-line, tail-rhyme stanzas, surviving in six manuscripts, and previously attributed to Thomas Chestre (see SIR LAUNFAL). Gingelein, the son of Gawain and Dame Ragnell, asks Arthur for knighthood and, since his name is unknown, he is knighted as *Li Beaus Desconus*. The poem is concerned with his adventures in rescuing the imprisoned Lady of Sinadoune. In *Chaucer's 'Sir Thopas' the knight's name, whether satirically or not, is given simply as 'Sir Lybeux' (see CANTERBURY TALES, 17) and it has been argued that this romance is the closest in form to 'Thopas'. See edition

by M. Mills, EETS OS 261, 1969); W. H. Schofield, *Studies on the Libeaus Desconus* (1895).

Libelle of Englyshe Polycye, The ('The Little Book of English Policy'), a political poem of about 2,250 lines written c.1436, in which the author exhorts his countrymen to regard the sea as the source of national strength, discusses commercial relations with other countries, and urges the importance of retaining Ireland, Calais, and Wales. The poem was included by *Hakluyt, and it has been doubtfully attributed to Adam Moleyns or Molyneaux (d. 1450), clerk of the king's council. See T. Wright, *Political Poems and Songs . . . Edward III to Richard III* (Rolls Series vol. ii, 1861); best edn by F. G. Warner (1926).

Liberal (1822–4), a magazine of four issues only but of great brilliance. Conceived by *Shelley, the plan was carried out after his death by *Byron and Leigh *Hunt from Pisa. Byron's *The Vision of Judgement* first appeared in its pages, as did his *Heaven and Earth*, and much other work by Shelley, Hunt, *Hazlitt, J. *Hogg, and others. Libel problems with *The Vision of Judgement*, and the incompatibility of Byron and Hunt, brought the magazine to an untimely close.

Liber Albus, see CARPENTER, J.

Liber Amoris; or, *The New Pygmalion*, an autobiographical prose work by W. *Hazlitt, published anonymously in 1823. It records in letters and dialogues the frenzied infatuation Hazlitt conceived at the age of 43 for a 19-year-old girl, Sarah Walker, who waited at table in his London lodgings, and who eventually rejected him for another suitor. The fevered tone of the book, and its humiliating self-exposure, distressed Hazlitt's friends and gave ammunition to his various enemies, his anonymity having been seen through at once. Unwholesomely absorbing, it fails to achieve the balanced self-analysis found in the *Confessions* of J.-J. *Rousseau, whom Hazlitt revered.

Liberty, On, an essay by *J. S. Mill, published 1859. In this work Mill examines the proper relations of society to the individual. In his view, 'the sole end for which mankind are warranted, individually or collectively, in interfering with liberty of action of any of their number, is self-protection.' The only part of the conduct of anyone, for which he is amenable to society, is that which concerns others. A man's own good, either physical or moral, is not a sufficient warrant for the interference of society. 'Mankind are greater gainers by suffering each other to live as seems good to themselves, than by compelling each to live as seems good to the rest.'

libraries: a listing of major university libraries and national collections in England, Ireland, Scotland, and Wales, with some details of holdings:

Aberdeen University Library. A 12th-cent. bestiary, Jacobite literature, extensive minor literature of the 18th and 19th cents.

Ashley Library. Private library collected by *Wise. First editions from *Jonson onwards. Acquired by the British Museum in 1937.

Bodleian Library, Oxford. Founded by Sir T. *Bodley. In 1610 the *Stationers' Company undertook to give the library a copy of every book printed in England. It received also important gifts of books and manuscripts from *Laud, *Cromwell, F. *Junius, and Robert *Burton. Other considerable accessions included *Selden's library, in 1659, the Tanner, Rawlinson, Gough, Malone, and Douce collections of manuscripts, and John Nichols's collection of newspapers in more recent times. Many of the manuscripts of *Locke were acquired in 1947, and the collections of manuscripts, both oriental and western, are being continually extended. Copyright library.

British Library. The national library for the United Kingdom. It was established in 1973 under Act of Parliament by the amalgamation of the library departments of the *British Museum and other organizations, as the national centre for reference, lending, bibliographical, and other information services based on its vast collections of books, manuscripts, maps, music, periodicals, and other material. It moved to St Pancras in 1998. Copyright library.

Cambridge University Library. The Royal (Bishop Moore's) Library, presented by King George I; the Bradshaw Collection of Irish Books; Taylor-Schechter collection of Hebraica; papers of C. *Darwin. Incunables include a *Gutenberg Bible and unique *Caxton items; *Codex Bezae Cantabrigiensis*, a 5th-cent. manuscript of the Gospels and Acts in Greek and Latin. Copyright library.

Durham University Library. Middle English manuscripts; letters of G. M. *Hopkins, the *Rossettis, E. *Thomas; manuscripts of *Plomer, and letters to him from *Britten, E. M. *Forster, etc. Printed books 16th–18th cent.

Glasgow University Library. 1.3 million volumes, including 350 medieval manuscripts, 1,100 incunabula. Research collections include: *emblem literature, Sir T. *Browne's works, broadside ballads, Scottish theatre archives, 19th-cent. art and literature.

National Library of Scotland, Edinburgh. Founded by Sir George Mackenzie of Rosehaugh (1636–91) as library of the Faculty of Advocates, opened in 1689. Became the National Library of Scotland in 1925. Four million printed items, one million maps, and 34,000 manuscripts, mainly of Scottish interest. Also modern foreign literature. Copyright library.

National Library of Wales, Aberystwyth. Manuscripts, books, maps, prints, and drawings relating to Wales and the Celtic peoples. Copyright library.

Queen's University of Belfast, The. University library. Hibernica Collection (Irish literature and history), Macdouall Collection (philology), Hamilton Harty Collection (music), and Thomas Percy Library.

St Andrews University Library, Scotland. First four

Shakespeare Folios on permanent loan from the Folger Library; Bibles; first editions of Galileo.

Trinity College Library, University of Dublin. Largest research library in Ireland. Important collection of manuscripts, including Book of *Kells.

libraries, circulating, libraries from which, for a fee, books were borrowed by the public. The first appears to have been A. *Ramsay's, founded in Edinburgh in 1726, and the system flourished for over two centuries, at its most dominant in the second half of the 18th and the latter part of the 19th cents. It greatly stimulated the production of books, particularly of novels, though not all approved of this development; the light romantic novels provided by such successful libraries as those of William Lane in the mid-18th cent. were often considered improper, and Sir Anthony Absolute declared, in Sheridan's *The Rivals*, 'A circulating library. . . is an evergreen tree of diabolical knowledge.' But there was also a strong link between Dissent, the self-education of the lower classes, and the circulating library, as J. *Priestley noted. The great new libraries of the 19th cent., *Mudie's, W. H. *Smith's, and *Boots, exercised a powerful censorship; Smith's refused Moore's *Esther Waters* in 1894, and in this century most circulating libraries banned some of the works of H. G. *Wells, *Caine, D. H. *Lawrence, and others. The three-volume novel of the middle and late 19th cent. was largely supported by these libraries, and died out at the end of the century when they no longer wanted it. The chief circulating libraries of this century (Boots, the Times Book Club, the Army and Navy, Mills and Boon, Harrods, etc.) enjoyed great success in the 1920s and 1930s, but all were closed by 1970, and replaced by the system of Book Clubs. (See VIZETELLY.)

libraries, copyright, see COPYRIGHT LIBRARIES.

libraries, public. The first British public libraries were established under the Museum Act, in Canterbury (1847), Warrington (1848), and Salford (1850). A library service was begun in Brighton in 1850 by a private Act. The 1850 Public Libraries Act, piloted by William Ewart against stiff opposition, empowered borough councils in England and Wales (extended to Scotland in 1853, where growth followed a parallel but different course) with a population of 10,000 plus to spend a halfpenny rate on libraries and museums, thus establishing a principle though imposing severe restrictions in practice. In 1855 this was raised to a penny rate and the population limit was lowered to 5,000; in 1866 the population limit was removed. Norwich was the first authority to adopt the 1850 Act, but provided no services until 1857. Winchester was the first library opened under the Act, in 1851, followed the next year by Manchester, then Liverpool (by a special Act), Sheffield, and Birmingham. St Margaret and St John's at Westminster was London's only public library from 1857 until 1885, when another was opened in Wandsworth. Growth was slow at first, only 48 libraries being established before 1870, chiefly in England, but also in Wales and Scotland. Thereafter growth was faster, and by the turn of the century some 400 libraries had been set up. The supporters of the Public Libraries Acts hoped that they would encourage working people in refinement, thrift, and sobriety; opponents objected to the burden on the rates and expected the libraries to lead to idleness and discontent.

Public meanness was shamed by private generosity. By 1913 the American philanthropist *Carnegie had given £2m for public libraries and, through the Carnegie UK Trust set up in that year, he continued to give important and influential support. John Passmore Edwards supported 24 libraries, chiefly in and around London and his native Cornwall. After the First World War, the Public Libraries Act of 1919 removed the rate limitation and extended library powers to the counties. By 1928, with the help of the Carnegie Trust, most counties had started a library service. The Mitchell Report of 1924 and the Kenyon Report of 1927 reflected an increasing interest in library development, and marked a stage in the development of libraries for all. Village reading rooms were set up, and library provisions were made for children. The Public Library service continued to grow despite being set back by the depression of 1931–3, helped by the overall increase of local government spending on libraries between 1928 and 1939 (£1.8m to £3.2m). The growth of the county library service was a notable feature of the post-war years, until it was arrested by the recession of the early 1980s. Attempts (some of them controversial) were also made from the 1960s onwards to make libraries attractive as community centres, and to extend their activities to include exhibitions of art and photography, schemes for loaning both reproductions of and original works of art, poetry readings, book order points, etc.; also to attract a larger readership of children through storytelling sessions, school visits, etc.

Library, a journal of bibliography and literature, published from 1889 to 1898 as the organ of the Library Association, and from 1899 to 1918 as an independent journal. In 1920 it was merged with the *Transactions* of the *Bibliographical Society, though retaining its original title.

libretto, the Italian word for the 'little book' in which the text of an opera (or oratorio) was printed, and hence the text itself. A few composers (*Berlioz, *Wagner, *Tippett) have written their own librettos, one or two have set stage plays more or less as they stood (*Debussy, R. *Strauss), but the majority have used a poet or professional librettist.

A libretto must provide the composer with a core of character, situation, and plot; a framework of words laid out for musical treatment; and language that will stimulate the imagination. Few writers have succeeded in satisfying all these requirements. The fact that a libretto possesses beauty of language—as with, e.g., *Hofmannsthal's librettos for Strauss, *Boito's for *Verdi's *Falstaff,* or *Auden's for *Stravinsky's *The Rake's Progress*—is a bonus, but the other elements must also be present. Nor is the language necessarily to be evaluated in terms of conventional literary criticism: *Tate's libretto for *Purcell's *Dido and Aeneas,* which has been much attacked on literary grounds, nevertheless succeeded in firing Purcell's imagination, and its naïvely florid imagery is transmuted by his setting.

Tate is generally held to have been preceded by *D'Avenant with *The Siege of Rhodes.* Other early English librettists include *Shadwell, whose *Psyche* (1675, music by M. *Locke) was an adaptation from *Molière, and *Dryden, whose *Albion and Albanius* (1685) ended up as a tedious political allegory set to feeble music by Louis Grabu.

In the 18th cent. the taste for Italian music gained ground in England, and the future of the English libretto was threatened. *Addison's single attempt, *Rosamond,* met with a disastrous failure in Clayton's setting in 1707, and with *Handel's arrival in London in 1710 the fate of English opera was sealed. Only in the lighter field did the English libretto survive; the *ballad operas which followed Gay's *The Beggar's Opera* were effectively straight plays interspersed with music, and nearer to the true libretto were the many comic opera texts produced by I. *Bickerstaffe in the 1760s and 1770s, set mainly by *Arne and *Dibdin, often, as was the custom, at least partly as *pasticcios.* In the same vein is Sheridan's *The Duenna* (1775).

Handel's oratorios gave rise to an English libretto of a different character and quality, which however also pointed the way for the Victorian oratorio: the texts for works by Balfe, Benedict, and Vincent Wallace by librettists like Alfred Bunn and Edward Fitzball have become bywords for absurdity. It was not until 1871 that the first of the *Gilbert and Sullivan operas introduced an invigorating new talent. Many 20th-cent. composers have taken an active part in the preparation of their own librettos, and the professional librettist has disappeared; in his place appear names like *Hardy, *Synge, A. P. *Herbert, Clifford Bax, J. B. *Priestley, and *Plomer. *Auden, in his librettos for *Britten, Stravinsky, and *Henze, established himself as an important writer in the form. J. *Fenton contributed material to the libretto of the immensely successful musical adaptation of *Hugo's *Les Misérables* (perf. UK 1985).

LICHTENBERG, Georg Christoph (1742–99), born in Hessen, educated and later a professor at Göttingen. A distinguished scientist, but interested also in philosophy (a disciple of *Kant), he twice visited England, in 1770 and 1774–5, and was a guest at Kew of George III. He was an ardent admirer of English institutions and literature and a keen dramatic critic. His letters from England to his friends in Germany (*Lichtenberg's Visits* *to England*, 1938) contain shrewd comments on the acting of *Garrick, *Macklin, etc., and throw an interesting light on contemporary English manners. He also published (1794–9) in Germany explanations of W. *Hogarth's engravings. His aphorisms, collected in nine volumes after his death (1800–5), are considered his finest literary achievement.

LIDDELL, Henry George (1811–98), born into a family with substantial aristocratic connections; he became successively headmaster of Westminster School (1846) and dean of Christ Church, Oxford (1855). A lifelong friend of *Ruskin, he did much to reform both these institutions. Earlier he had compiled with Robert Scott (1811–87) the famous Greek lexicon, which, repeatedly revised, is still in use today. Held in the highest esteem by his contemporaries, he is chiefly remembered now as the father of the little girl who served Lewis Carroll (C. L. *Dodgson) as a model for Alice.

LIDDELL, Robert (1908–92), novelist and critic, who spent his early childhood in Cairo. He was educated at Corpus Christi, Oxford, and worked for a time in the Bodleian before travelling eastwards to lecture in Cairo and Athens. His novels include the trilogy *Kind Relations* (1939), *Stepsons* (1969), and *The Last Enchantments* (1948, set in Oxford), following the boyhood and youth of two brothers, and dwelling on the theme of domestic tyranny. A second trilogy comprises *An Object for a Walk* (1966), *Unreal City* (1952, set in the Alexandria of *Cavafy towards the end of the Second World War), and *The Rivers of Babylon* (1959). Liddell also wrote of his friendship with E. *Taylor and I. *Compton-Burnett in *Elizabeth and Ivy* (1986).

Life and Adventures of Sir Launcelot Greaves, The, see GREAVES, SIR LAUNCELOT, THE LIFE AND ADVENTURES OF.

Life and Labour *of the People in London*, see BOOTH, C.

Life and Letters, a literary monthly periodical founded and edited from 1928 to 1933 by D. *MacCarthy. It subsequently continued as *Life and Letters Today*, and in 1939 absorbed the *London Mercury* and *Bookman*, reverting from 1945 to 1950 to its original title. The final issue appeared in June 1950. Early issues contained essays, reviews, fiction, passages of autobiography, etc., from many distinguished contributors, including *Beerbohm, A. *Huxley, C. *Bell, V. *Woolf, and C. *Connolly; poetry was better represented in its later years by G. *Barker, V. *Watkins, and others.

Life in London, see EGAN.

LIGHTFOOT, John (1602–75), biblical and rabbinic scholar, and from 1643 master of Catharine Hall, Cambridge. His best-known work is his series of *Horae Hebraicae et Talmudicae* (1658–78), which relates Jewish studies to the interpretation of the New Testament. He assisted Brian Walton with the *Polyglot Bible.

Light Shining in Buckinghamshire, (1) the title of an anonymous pamphlet issued by the Levellers in 1648, attacking monarchy and calling for equality of property; it was followed by a sequel, *More Light Shining in Buckinghamshire* (1649) (see PAMPHLETEERING, ORIGINS OF); (2) the title of a play by Caryl *Churchill, staged in 1976 by Joint Stock at the Theatre Upstairs at the *Royal Court Theatre for the *English Stage Company.

Light that Failed, The, a novel by R. *Kipling, published in *Lippincott's Monthly Magazine* (New York, 1890), and in 1891 with a fuller text and different ending. Dick Heldar and Maisie meet as children as miserable fellow lodgers in a boarding house by the sea. Dick as an adventurous adult goes off to the Sudan campaign, survives a head wound, and returns to London as a precociously successful military artist. Maisie, now a New Woman, is struggling to become a painter. They meet by chance, and the novel traces their mutual attraction and professional rivalry: both attempt a *fin-de-siècle* painting of Melancolia, after *Dürer. While Maisie is in France studying with an Impressionist master, Dick becomes blind as a result of the old head wound. In the earlier version, Maisie returns and marries him: in the later, she returns, is appalled by his state of mind (which she misconceives through a misunderstanding) and departs. Dick then returns to the Sudan, where he dies in combat in the arms of his close friend, special correspondent Torpenhow.

LILBURNE, John (c.1614–57), pamphleteer, political agitator, and Leveller. He was brought before the Star Chamber in 1638 for printing an unlicensed book, and imprisoned; *A Work of the Beast* (1638) gives an account of his barbarous treatment. He fought with distinction in the Parliamentary army, but repeatedly criticized the army officers and was repeatedly imprisoned; he was banished in 1652 but returned the following year. In 1655 he became a Quaker. In his many pamphlets he speaks for the rights of the common man, describing his followers as 'clubs and clouted shoon', for God 'doth not choose many rich, nor many wise . . . but the fools, idiots, base and contemptible poor men and women in the esteem of the world', but he never advocated communism. He published pamphlets jointly with *Overton and *Walwyn. A life by P. Gregg was published in 1961.

'Lilli-Burlero Bullen-a-la!' 'said to have been the words of distinction used among the Irish Papists in their massacre of the Protestants in 1641' (*Percy). They were made the refrain of a song, attributed to Lord Wharton, satirizing the earl of Tyrconnel on the occasion of his going to Ireland in Jan. 1686–7 as James II's papist lieutenant. The song is given in Percy's *Reliques*. According to Chappell's *Popular Music of the Olden Time*, the tune of 'Lillibulero' was included, in 1689, in the second part of *Music's Handmaid* as 'a new Irish Tune' by 'Mr Purcell', but it occurs in *The Delightful Companion* of 1686.

Lilliput, see GULLIVER'S TRAVELS.

LILLO, George (1693–1739), the author of the famous prose domestic tragedy *The London Merchant, or The History of**George Barnwell*, produced in 1731. Little is known of his life; he is said to have been a jeweller of Flemish descent, praised by *Fielding as 'content with his little state of life'. His other plays include *The Christian Hero*, produced in 1735, **The Fatal Curiosity* (1736), and a tragedy on the subject of *Arden of Feversham (also 1736). Lillo's introduction of middle-class domestic tragedy had an influence which extended beyond English literature: see LESSING, G. E., and DIDEROT.

LILLY, William (1602–81), a noted astrologer, patronized by *Ashmole, who built up a highly successful London practice, and managed to survive the political upheavals of the period despite several arrests; he supported Parliament during the 1640s and was favoured by the Protectorate, but wrote with some sympathy of Charles I as 'not the worst, but the most unfortunate, of Kings' (*Monarchy or No Monarchy in England*, 1651) and from 1660 protested loyalty to the Crown. He published almanacs yearly from 1644 until his death (issued from 1647 under the title *Merlini Anglici Aphemeris*) and by 1659 these were selling in vast quantities of *c.*300,000 a year. His *Christian Astrology* (1647) was the standard guide to the subject for those who could read only English. He is thought to have been in part the model for Sidrophel in *Hudibras. The case-books recording his consultations survive in the Ashmole manuscripts of the Bodleian library, and his autobiography appears with Ashmole's *Memoirs*, in the 1774 edition. (See ALMANACS.)

Lillyvick, Mr, a character in Dickens's **Nicholas Nickleby*.

LILY, William (*c.*1468–1522), friend of *Colet and Sir T. *More, grandfather of J. *Lyly, and a leader of the revival of Greek studies in England. Though married and a layman, he was made first high master of St *Paul's School. He contributed a short Latin syntax, with the rules in English, to the Latin grammar by Colet and *Erasmus, *c.*1509. This, with another grammar, was the basis of the work known as *Lily's Grammar* which was long familiar to English schoolboys; cf. the Latin lesson in **The Merry Wives of Windsor*, IV. i. On the complete history of his grammatical writings, see C. G. Allen in the *Library* (June 1954).

limerick, a form of jingle, of which the first instances occur in *The History of Sixteen Wonderful Old Women* (1820) and *Anecdotes and Adventures of Fifteen Gentlemen* (*c.*1821), subsequently popularized by *Lear in his *Book of Nonsense*.

In the older form of limerick, as written by Lear, D. G. *Rossetti, and others, the first and last lines usually ended with the same word, but in more recent examples, such as the following comment on G. *Berkeley's philosophy by R. *Knox, and those written by W. H. *Auden, G. *Ewart, O. *Nash, N. *Douglas, R. *Conquest, and others, a third rhyming word is supplied:

> There once was a man who said: 'God
> Must think it exceedingly odd
> If he finds that this tree
> Continues to be
> When there's no-one about in the Quad.'

LINACRE, Thomas (?1460–1524), physician and classical scholar, educated at Oxford and a fellow of All Souls College. He was MD of Padua, and became one of *Henry VIII's physicians. Later he was Latin tutor to the Princess Mary, for whom he composed a Latin grammar, *Rudimenta Grammatices*. He was mainly instrumental in founding the College of Physicians in 1518. He wrote grammatical and medical works, and translated from the Greek, mainly from *Galen.

Lindisfarne Gospels, a manuscript of the four Gospels in the *Vulgate text, probably written in honour of the canonization of St *Cuthbert (698). The script is Anglo-Saxon majuscule and there are magnificent illuminations and decorative capitals. An Anglo-Saxon gloss was added in the late 10th cent. in Northumbrian dialect with a colophon stating that the text was written by Eadfrith, bishop of Lindisfarne 698–721, and naming the binder, the goldsmith who ornamented the binding, and the translator, Aldred of Chester-le-Street. See Janet Backhouse, *The Lindisfarne Gospels* (1981).

LINDSAY, Lady Anne (1750–1825), daughter of the fifth earl of Balcarres. She wrote in 1771 the immensely popular ballad 'Auld Robin Gray', in which young Jamie goes off to sea to make his fortune: his sweetheart, supposing him drowned, and her family hard pressed by poverty, marries 'old Robin Gray' four weeks before Jamie comes back to claim her. Lady Anne did not acknowledge authorship until two years before her death when *Scott prompted her to reveal her secret. She became by marriage Lady Anne Barnard, and accompanied her husband (who was younger and poorer than she) to South Africa, where she wrote the journals *Lady Anne Barnard at the Cape, 1797–1802*, which provide important authority for events during the first British occupation of Cape Town. After the death of her husband she returned home, and with her sister established a literary salon in London.

LINDSAY, or **LYNDSAY,** Sir David (*c.*1486–1555), Scottish poet and Lyon king-of-arms; usher to Prince James (afterwards James V). His first poem, 'The Dreme', written in 1528 but not printed till after his death, is an allegorical lament on the misgovernment of the realm, followed by a vigorous exhortation to the king. In 1529 he wrote the *Complaynt to the King*, in octosyllabic couplets, commenting on the improved social condition of the realm except as regards the Church, lamenting that others have been preferred before him at court, and requesting the king that he 'wyll uther geve or len me' 'off gold ane thousand pound, or tway'. The *Testament, and Complaynt, of Our Soverane Lordis Papyngo* (finished 1530, printed 1538) combines advice to the king, put in the mouth of his parrot, with a warning to courtiers drawn from the examples of Scottish history, and with a satire on ecclesiastics in the form of a conference between the dying parrot and its 'Holye Executouris'. Lindsay's principal poem, *Ane *Pleasant Satyre of the Thrie Estaitis*, a morality, was produced in 1540 before the king and court. Other poems by Lindsay include *The Monarchie* (*Ane Dialog betwix Experience and ane Courteour, off the Miserabyll Estait of the Warld*) (1554) and the *Historie of Squyer Meldrum* (first extant edition of 1582), a spirited verse romance on the career and exploits of a Scottish laird.

Works, ed. D. Hamar (STS, 3rd series, 1, 2, 6, 8, 1931–6); selection ed. M. Lindsay (Saltire Society Classics, 1948); *The Thrie Estaitis*, ed. J. Kinsley (1954) and by P. Happé in *Four Morality Plays* (1979).

LINDSAY, Robert (?1500–?65), of Pitscottie, author of *The Historie and Croniclis of Scotland* from the reign of James II, one of Sir W. *Scott's principal sources for the period.

LINDSAY, Vachel, see JAZZ POETRY, PERFORMANCE POETRY, and FILM, LITERATURE OF.

LINGARD, John (1771–1851), a Roman Catholic priest, author of *The Antiquities of the Anglo-Saxon Church* (1806); and, more importantly, of a *History of England* (1819–30), the principal object of which is to emphasize the disastrous effects of the Reformation. His idealized portrait of the Middle Ages had considerable influence on writers and thinkers as diverse as W. *Morris and the founders of the *Oxford movement.

linguistics (also 'theoretical' or 'general' linguistics), a term used to characterize the study of language in the 20th cent. owing much to the Swiss linguist *Saussure; it distinguishes itself from earlier language study by concentrating on the language at a particular time ('synchronic') rather than the history of language and languages ('diachronic'). It claims to be the principal new science, and its method has been influential in several other areas (anthropology, sociology, mathematics, and literary criticism, for example). For major practitioners, see SAUSSURE; BLOOMFIELD, L.; CHOMSKY. See also STRUCTURALISM.

Linkinwater, Tim, in Dickens's *Nicholas Nickleby*, clerk to the brothers Cheeryble.

LINKLATER, Eric (1899–1974), brought up in Wales and Orkney. He served in the First World War, and after graduating from Aberdeen University became assistant editor to the *Times of Bombay*. In 1928–30, he was in the USA as Commonwealth fellow, where he gathered material for *Juan in America* (1930), a satirical novel which brought him immediate fame. Other works include *The Men of Ness* (1932) and *Magnus Merriman* (1934), both Orkney-based; *Private Angelo* (1946) describing the campaign in Italy; and *The Wind on the Moon* (1944), perhaps his most successful children's book. See a life by M. Parnell (1984).

LINNAEUS, Latinized form of Linné, Carl von (1707–78), Swedish botanist and founder of a pioneering binomial system of plant classification according to genus and species. His international reputation was established in 1735 with the publication (in Latin) of *Systema Naturae*, and he continued to develop his theory of plant classification; its final form is contained in the last edition of *Genera Plantarum* (1771). From 1741 he was professor of medicine and then botany at Uppsala, and began to write the evocative and lyrical travel books which are regarded as masterpieces of Swedish prose. These include accounts of journeys to Öland, Gotland, Lapland, and Dalarna. The Linnean Society of London was founded in 1788, and the library and herbarium of Linnaeus were purchased for it by public subscription; they are now in Burlington House.

Linton, Edgar, Isabella, and Catherine, characters in E. Brontë's *Wuthering Heights*.

LINTON, Eliza Lynn, née Lynn (1822–98), English novelist and journalist, born in Keswick, who launched herself on a London literary career with two historical novels (*Azeth the Egyptian*, 1846; *Amymone*, 1848), which she followed with many more successful novels of contemporary life, such as *Rebel of the Family* (1880). She offended many of her female contemporaries by her essays attacking feminism and the *New Woman, some of which were collected from the *Saturday Review as The Girl of the Period* (1883). Her posthumously published memoir *My Literary Life* (1899) contains a notably hostile portrait of G. *Eliot.

LINTOT, or **LINTOTT,** Barnaby Bernard (1675–1736), bookseller and printer. He published a *Miscellaneous Poems and Translations by Several Hands* (1712), which contained the first version of *The Rape of the Lock*. He published other works by *Pope (who compared his uncouth appearance to that of a dabchick in the *Dunciad*, ii. 63), and poems and plays by *Gay, *Farquhar, *Steele, *Rowe, and others.

LIPSIUS, Justus, or Joest Lips (1547–1606), a Flemish humanist, who adopted the Lutheran faith while professor at Jena (1572–5), turned to Calvinism when professor at Leiden (1579–91), and reverted to the Catholicism of his youth when he became professor at Louvain in 1592. His principal works were editions of *Tacitus and *Seneca, which contributed greatly to the development of neo-Stoicism, and a treatise on politics in which he advocated the suppression by fire and sword of religious dissidence.

Lir, see LÊR.

Lisle Letters, a collection of some 3,000 letters written to and from Arthur Plantagenet, Viscount Lisle (an illegitimate son of Edward IV), his family, and household, while he was lord deputy of Calais from 1533 to 1540. They give a vivid picture of the political and domestic life of the time; the originals are in the Public Record Office and have been edited by Muriel St Clare Byrne (6 vols, 1981), with a one-volume abridgement by B. Boland (1983).

Lismahago, Obadiah, a character in Smollett's *Humphry Clinker.*

Listener, a BBC weekly magazine, of which the first number appeared on 16 Jan. 1929, the last in 1991; it published reviews, broadcasts, essays, poetry, etc. Its literary editor from 1935 to 1959 was J. R. *Ackerley, who attracted work from many distinguished writers. *The Music of What Happens: Poems from the Listener* (1981), edited by Derwent May, poet and novelist, and literary editor from 1965, contains work by Stevie *Smith, P. *Larkin, P. *Porter, Ted *Hughes, S. *Heaney, and others.

LISTER, Thomas Henry (1800–42), the first registrar-general of England and Wales. He was a neglected but very accomplished novelist, much influenced by J. *Austen, whose tone he noticeably adopts and the names of whose characters he sometimes uses. Although they contain certain overdramatic incidents, *Granby* (1826), *Herbert Lacy* (1828), and *Arlington* (1832) are all shrewd and animated works, which describe with an ironic eye the aristocratic and upper-middle-class society of the time.

LISZT, Franz (1811–86), Hungarian composer and pianist and a central figure in the musical Romantic movement. His qualities as a composer have been disputed, though it is generally conceded that he was a figure of importance and originality. English literary influences are not strong in his work, but his series of 12 'symphonic poems' (1848–58) ends with a *Hamlet*, originally planned as an overture to the play. *Byron also hovers as an influence. There is a single delicate English setting, *Tennyson's 'Go not, happy day', and, more surprisingly, a late choral work, *Die Glocken des Strasburger Münsters* (1875), based on an episode from *Longfellow's *Golden Legend.* When Liszt died, G. B. *Shaw described him as 'a man who loved his art, despised money, attracted everybody worth knowing in the nineteenth century, lived through the worst of it, and got away from it at last with his hands unstained'.

Literary Anecdotes of the Eighteenth Century, see NICHOLS, J.

Literary Club, see CLUB.

Literary Gazette (1817–62), a very successful journal founded by *Colburn, with William Jerdan as editor. It aimed at a very wide coverage of books, fine arts, and sciences, but most of the space was given to book reviews and long extracts from the works reviewed. Early contributors, in the days of its greatest success, included *Crabbe, M. R. *Mitford, *Cornwall, and L. E. *Landon.

Literary Magazine or *Universal Review,* a periodical started in 1756, nominally edited by the printer William Faden, but in practice conducted largely by Dr *Johnson, who contributed many articles, including, notably, his review of *Jenyns's *A Free Enquiry into the Nature and Origin of Evil* (1757). The magazine was discontinued in 1758.

literati, a term introduced into English in 1624 by Robert *Burton to refer to the literate class in China, and later applied to the writers and readers of fashionable literature in other communities, often by contrast with the practical scientists, or virtuosi. The term is now frequently used to identify those who frequented the literary clubs of 18th-cent. Edinburgh, and the bookshops of *Ramsay, Creech, and Kincaid. They included resident literary figures like R. *Fergusson, A. *Cockburn, *Boswell, and H. *Mackenzie, and temporary residents like *Gay, *Defoe, *Goldsmith, and *Smollett. But it is more particularly applied to a group of professional men, mostly lawyers and clergy, and mostly supporters of or supported by the Moderate party in the Scottish Church; at a time when vernacular writing was in decline, they self-consciously cultivated an English writing style, both to make a cultural impact on London society and to cement the political union with England. They included the lawyers H. *Home and *Monboddo, the philosophers *Hume and Adam *Smith, and the clerical coterie of H. *Blair, A. *Carlyle, A. *Ferguson, J. *Home, W. *Robertson, and *Wilkie, several of whom were associated with the abortive first *Edinburgh Review.* Although their writings were primarily on history, philosophy, and the theory of criticism, many of them also supported the legalization and revival of the legitimate theatre, against fierce Calvinist opposition. Hume in 1752 and *Beattie in 1779 assisted the movement for stylistic improvement by publishing collections of unacceptable 'Scotticisms'; and Thomas Sheridan, father of the dramatist, lectured to men's and women's classes on English elocution in 1761 under the auspices of the *Select Society. (See also SCOTTISH ENLIGHTENMENT.)

litotes, a figure of speech in which an affirmative is expressed by the negative of the contrary, e.g. 'a citizen of no mean city'; 'a not unhandsome man'; an ironical understatement.

Littimer, in Dickens's *David Copperfield,* Steerforth's hypocritical valet.

Little Billee, a humorous ballad of three sailors of Bristol, of whom Little Billee is the youngest. When provisions fail he narrowly escapes being eaten by the other two. *Thackeray wrote a version of the ballad. 'Little Billee' was the nickname of the hero of Du Maurier's *Trilby.

Little Dorrit, a novel by *Dickens, published in monthly parts, 1855–7.

William Dorrit has been so long in the Marshalsea prison for debtors that he has become the 'Father of the Marshalsea'. He has had the misfortune to be responsible for an uncompleted contract with the Circumlocution Office (a satirical portrait of the government departments of the day, with their incompetent and obstructive officials typified in the Barnacles). His lot is alleviated by the devotion of Amy, his youngest daughter, 'Little Dorrit', born in the Marshalsea, whose diminutive stature is compensated by the greatness of her heart. Amy has a snobbish sister Fanny, a theatrical dancer, and a scapegrace brother, Tip. Old Dorrit and Amy are befriended by Arthur Clennam, the middle-aged hero, for whom Little Dorrit conceives a deep passion, at first unrequited. The unexpected discovery that William Dorrit is heir to a fortune raises the family to affluence. Except Little Dorrit, they become arrogant and purse-proud. Clennam, on the other hand, owing to an unfortunate speculation, is brought in turn to the debtor's prison, and is found in the Marshalsea, sick and despairing, by Little Dorrit, who tenderly nurses him and consoles him. He has meanwhile learnt the value of her love, but her fortune stands in the way of his asking her to marry him. The loss of it makes their union possible, on Clennam's release.

With this main theme is wound the thread of an elaborate mystery. Clennam has long suspected that his mother, a grim old puritanical paralysed woman, living in a gloomy house with a former attendant and present partner, Flintwinch, has done some wrong to Little Dorrit. Through the agency of a stagy villain, Rigaud, alias Blandois, this is brought to light, and it appears that Mrs Clennam is not Arthur's mother, and that her religious principles have not prevented her from suppressing a codicil in a will that benefited the Dorrit family.

There are a host of minor characters in the work, of whom the most notable are the worthy Pancks, rent-collector to the humbug Casby; Casby's voluble daughter Flora Finching, the early love of Arthur Clennam; her eccentric relative 'Mr F's Aunt'; Merdle, the swindling financier, and Mrs Merdle, who 'piques herself on being society'; Affery, the villain Flintwinch's wife; 'Young John' Chivery, the son of the Marshalsea warder; and the Meagles and Gowan households.

Little Dorrit was heavily criticized on publication, largely for its sombre tone and complex plot, but later critics such as G. B. *Shaw (his 'masterpiece among many masterpieces'), *Trilling, and Angus *Wilson have done much to reverse this judgement.

Little Eva, the saintly child Evangeline St Clair in H. B. *Stowe's *Uncle Tom's Cabin* whose deathbed scene rivals in sentiment the death of Little Nell in *The Old Curiosity Shop.

Little Gidding, a manor in Huntingdonshire where N. *Ferrar and his family established, 1625–46, a religious community of some 40 members, following a systematic rule of private devotion, public charity, and study. The house was visited by Charles I, *Crashaw, and G. *Herbert, and *Shorthouse's novel *John Inglesant* (1881) portrays its life vividly. It was raided by Cromwell's soldiers in 1646, and the community dispersed. T. S. Eliot celebrates it in 'Little Gidding', one of the *Four Quartets, and a record of its activities survives in *The Little Gidding Story Books*, five manuscript volumes bound by Mary Collett, part of which was printed in 1899, ed. E. C. Sharland.

Little John, one of the companions of *Robin Hood in the legends relating to that outlaw. He was a sturdy yeoman and a skilled archer, originally called John Little. He figures in Sir W. Scott's *Ivanhoe.

Little Lord Fauntleroy, see BURNETT.

little magazines, a term used to describe minority literary and artistic periodicals, possibly derived from one of the better known of such publications, the *Little Review*. English 'little magazines' include the *Savoy, *Rhythm, Blast, *New Verse, the *Review and its successor the *New Review*, *Stand, *Ambit, and *Agenda.

Little Musgrave and Lady Barnard, an ancient ballad, given in Percy's *Reliques, which tells how Lady Barnard, loving Little Musgrave, invited him to pass the night with her in her bower at Bucklesford-Bury. A little foot-page overhears the assignation and tells Lord Barnard. He finds the lovers together, fights with Musgrave and kills him, then kills his wife and is afterwards filled with remorse.

Musgrave is referred to in Beaumont and Fletcher's *The Knight of the Burning Pestle*, Act V, and in D'Avenant's *The Wits*, III. iii.

Little Nell (Trent), the heroine of Dickens's *The Old Curiosity Shop.

Little Review, an American monthly magazine founded in Chicago in 1914 by Margaret Anderson. In 1916 it came under the influence of *Pound, who was foreign editor from 1917 to 1919; it published *Yeats, W. *Lewis, T. S. *Eliot, F. M. *Ford, and, notably, from 1918, chapters of Joyce's *Ulysses. It later became a quarterly published from Paris (1924–9), edited principally by Jane Heap and including work by *Hemingway, *Cummings, H. *Crane, etc. It folded in 1929 with Jane Heap's statement: 'For years we offered the *Little Review* as a trial-track for racers . . . But you can't get race horses from mules. We have given space in the *Little Review* to 23 new systems of art (all now dead), representing 19 countries. In all of this we have not brought forward anything approaching a masterpiece except the *Ulysses* of Mr Joyce.'

Little Women, by L. M. *Alcott, one of the most popular juvenile books ever written, published 1868–9, and based on the author's memories of her childhood home. The story concerns the daily lives of four girls— Jo March, who aspires to be a writer, and her sisters Meg, Beth, and Amy—in a New England family in the mid-19th cent. Their mother is cheerful and uncomplaining, their father an improvident army chaplain in the Civil War.

LITTLEWOOD, Joan (1914–2002), director whose company, Theatre Workshop, had a strong influence on post-war British theatre. Trained as an actress and at one time a BBC radio producer, Littlewood created in 1936 a left-wing touring company, Theatre Union. Out of this evolved Theatre Workshop, which combined a radical social conscience with an exuberant musical style. Based at the Theatre Royal, Stratford East, from 1953, the company staged rare English and foreign classics, new works by Shelagh *Delaney and Brendan *Behan, and popular musicals by Lionel Bart. Littlewood's most celebrated production was *Oh, What a Lovely War!* (1963): a documentary satire counterpointing the grim statistics of First World War carnage with the affirmative popular songs of the period.

LITTRÉ, Émile (1801–81), French scholar, philosopher, and lexicographer, who began work on his great dictionary of the French language in 1846. It was published in four volumes (1863–72), with a supplementary volume in 1877. The whole work was reprinted in 1950. Littré was a follower of *Comte, after whose death he became the leading exponent of the positive philosophy, publishing *Auguste Comte et la philosophie positive* in 1863. In 1867 he founded with G. N. Wyrouboff, the Russian positivist, the *Revue de philosophie positive*. Littré also edited and translated the works of *Hippocrates (1839–61) and wrote an *Histoire de la langue française* (1862).

LIVELY, Penelope Margaret, née Greer (1933–   ), novelist and children's writer, born in Cairo, educated at St Anne's College, Oxford, where she read history. In 1957 she married Jack Lively, tutor in politics at St Peter's College, Oxford. The intrusion of the past upon the present is a recurrent theme in her work. She began by writing a number of successful novels for children, including *Astercote* (1970), *The Whispering Knights* (1971), *The Ghost of Thomas Kempe* (1973), which won the Carnegie Medal, *Going Back* (1975), and *A Stitch in Time* (1976). Her first adult novel was *The Road to Lichfield* (1977), which juxtaposes a woman's visits to her dying father with a summer love affair. *Treasures of Time* (1979) brings past and present together through the figure of a distinguished archaeologist and the site in Wiltshire that made him famous, while in *Judgement Day* (1980) the action centres on English village

life and the quatercentenary of the local church. *Next to Nature, Art* (1982), set in a Creative Study centre, was followed by *Perfect Happiness* (1983), about a woman who finds a new life after the death of her famous husband, and *According to Mark* (1984), in which a married biographer falls in love with his subject's granddaughter. *Moon Tiger* (1987), which won the *Booker Prize, presents the recollections of a dying woman, a successful historian, from her childhood just after the First World War to the 1970s, the central emotional focus being a love affair in wartime Egypt. Her other novels are *Passing On* (1989), which examines family relationships after the death of a mother; *City of the Mind* (1991), a multi-layered vision of London seen through the eyes of an architect; *Cleopatra's Sister* (1993), which is set in the imaginary country of Callimbia and in which history, politics, and myth are skilfully woven together; and *Heatwave* (1996), a powerful study of mother love. Her collected short stories were published in 1986 as *Pack of Cards*. A memoir, *Oleander, Jacaranda* (1994) was followed by an experimental alternative autobiography, *Making it Up* (2005).

Liverpool poets, the name given to a group of three poets, Adrian *Henri, Roger *McGough, and Brian *Patten, who came together in the 1960s in the period of the Liverpool euphoria generated partly by the success of the *Beatles. They performed together, and published together in various periodicals and anthologies including *The Mersey Sound* (1967), *The Liverpool Scene* (1967), and *New Volume* (1983). The combined tone of their work was pop, urban, anti-academic, good-humoured, and vocal: poetry was conceived by them as a medium for public rather than private consumption, a *performance art.

Lives of the English Poets, The, a work by Dr *Johnson, originally entitled *Prefaces Biographical and Critical to the Works of the English Poets*, published 1779–81.

Johnson was invited in 1777 by a deputation of London booksellers to provide biographical prefaces for an edition of the works of various English poets, from the period of *Milton onwards; the selection was made by them, and includes poets of very differing merit. The final total was 52, including four minor poets suggested by Johnson himself (*Blackmore, *Watts, *Pomfret, and Thomas Yalden). When the work was completed the prefaces were issued without the texts as *Lives of the Poets*. The *Lives* contain much interesting biographical matter, but are not always trustworthy. The criticism has been considered unequal, particularly in respect of its strictures on Milton's *Lycidas, *Gray's Odes, and its evident prejudice against *Swift; Johnson's hostile analysis of the *metaphysical style, in his life of *Cowley, became notorious. But the work remains a classic, important both as a landmark in the history of critical taste and judgement, and for its own insights; T. S. *Eliot ('Johnson as Critic and Poet', 1944) credited it 'with a coherence, as well as an amplitude, which no other English criticism can claim'.

Lives of the Poets, see LIVES OF THE ENGLISH POETS, THE.

LIVINGSTONE, David (1813–73), Scottish missionary and explorer. From the age of 10 he worked in a cotton factory, while educating himself. He took his medical degree in 1840 and in the same year was ordained under the London Missionary Society and embarked for the Cape of Good Hope. In the following 30 years he travelled across more than one-third of the African continent gathering important information about the country, its products, its native tribes, and the slave trade. His expeditions are described in *Missionary Travels and Researches in South Africa* (1857) and *Narrative of an Expedition to the Zambesi and its Tributaries and the Discovery of the Lakes of Shirwa and Nyassa* (1865, in collaboration with his brother Charles). During his final expedition, to discover the sources of the Nile, he was rescued, almost dying, by H. M. *Stanley in Ujiji in 1871; he resumed his explorations but never recovered his health. His *Last Journals of David Livingstone in Central Africa from 1865 to his Death* appeared posthumously in 1874.

LIVY (Titus Livius) (59 BC–?AD 17), Roman historian whose great work related the history of Rome from its beginnings to 9 BC. Of its 142 books only 35 have survived, the best known of which give us the legendary history of early Rome and the second Punic War. His *History* became a set text for Roman schoolboys, and most of what now survives was recovered by *Petrarch. *Boccaccio translated much of Livy: *Machiavelli wrote *Discoures on Livy*, and P. *Holland translated Livy into English. Livy's stories of Rome's beginnings provided material for Painter's *Palace of Pleasure* (1566, 1567) and *Pettie's similar work of 1576, for Shakespeare's *Rape of Lucrece* (1594), and later for Macaulay's *Lays of Ancient Rome* (1842).

Lizzie Hexam, a character in Dickens's *Our Mutual Friend*.

Llangollen, the Ladies of, Lady Eleanor Butler (?1739–1829) and Miss Sarah Ponsonby (?1735–1831), two devoted friends who left their families (against strong opposition) to set up a lifelong residence together in Plas Newydd in Llangollen Vale. Their house, adorned in the *Gothic style, became a place of admiration and curiosity far beyond its neighbourhood, visited by distinguished guests, including *Wordsworth (who wrote them a sonnet), A. *Seward (who commemorated them in her poem 'Llangollen Vale', 1975), *Burke, and Mme de Genlis. See *The Hamwood Papers of the Ladies of Llangollen and Caroline Hamilton* (1930), ed. Mrs G. H. Bell, and 'Living the Gothic Pastoral Romance' (1949, *Modern Language Review*; reprinted in *Women and Literature*, 1982) by M. C. *Bradbrook.

Llyr, see MABINOGION. Perhaps to be identified with Lir (see LÊR).

LOCHHEAD, Liz (1947–), Scottish poet and dramatist, born in Motherwell, Lanarkshire. From 1965 to 1970 she studied at the Glasgow School of Art and then worked as an art teacher in Glasgow. Her characteristically ironic style as a poet is displayed in collections such as *Memo for Spring* (1972), *The Grimm Sisters* (1981), *Dreaming Frankenstein and Collected Poems* (1984), and *True Confessions and New Clichés* (1985). She has also written plays inspired by literature and history, including *Blood and Ice* (1982), based on the life of Mary *Shelley; a version of Bram Stoker's *Dracula* (1985); and *Mary Queen of Scots Got Her Head Chopped off* (1987). She has also translated Molière's *Tartuffe* into Glaswegian vernacular (1989). *Perfect Days* (1998) is a comedy dealing with the ironies of modern maternity in the age of surrogacy.

Lochinvar, the hero of a ballad included in the fifth canto of Scott's *Marmion*. His fair Ellen is about to be married to 'a laggard in love and a dastard in war', when the brave Lochinvar arrives at the bridal feast, claims a dance with her, and, as they reach the hall door, swings the lady onto his horse, and rides off with her.

LOCKE, John (1632–1704), born at Wrington, Somerset, educated at Westminster and Christ Church, Oxford. He held various academic posts at that university, and became physician to the household of the first earl of *Shaftesbury in 1667. He held official positions and subsequently lived at Oxford, then fled to Holland in 1683 as a consequence of Shaftesbury's plotting for Monmouth; how far he was himself involved is not certain. In 1687 he joined William of Orange at Rotterdam; on his return to England he became commissioner of appeals and member of the council of trade. His last years were spent in Essex in the home of Sir Francis and Lady Masham, the latter being the daughter of Ralph Cudworth, one of the *Cambridge Platonists.

Locke's principal philosophical work is the *Essay Concerning Human Understanding* (1690), a work which led J. S. *Mill to call him the 'unquestioned founder of the analytic philosophy of mind'. Always critical of 'enthusiasm', he was originally opposed to freedom of religion, and never supported Catholic emancipation; but in his maturity he defended the rights of the Dissenters on both moral and economic grounds. He published three *Letters* on Toleration between 1689 and 1692; a fourth was left unfinished at his death. His defence of simple biblical religion in *The Reasonableness of Christianity* (1695), without resort to creed or tradition, led to a charge of *Socinianism, which Locke replied to in two *Vindications* (1695, 1697). He was also involved in an extensive pamphlet war with Edward Stillingfleet (1696–8) over the alleged compatibility of his *Essay* with Socinianism and *Deism.

Locke published in 1690 two *Treatises of Government* designed to combat the theory of the divine right of kings. He finds the origin of the civil state in a contract. The 'legislative', or government, 'being only a fiduciary power to act for certain ends, there remains still in the people the supreme power to remove or alter the legislative when they find the legislative act contrary to the trust reposed in them'. Throughout, Locke in his theory of the 'Original Contract' opposes absolutism; the first *Treatise* is specifically an attack on Sir Robert Filmer's *Patriarcha*. Although Locke in his early manuscripts was closer to *Hobbes's authoritarianism and continues to share with Hobbes the view that civil obligations are founded in contract, he strongly rejected Hobbes's view that the sovereign is above the law and no party to the contract. He published a volume on education in 1693, and on the rate of interest and the value of money in 1692 and 1695. The first edition of his collected works appeared in 1714. A full critical edition of his works, including eight volumes of correspondence, was launched in 1975.

Locke's writings had an immense influence on the literature of succeeding generations, and he was very widely read; his *Thoughts Concerning Education*, which are concerned with practical advice on the upbringing of 'sons of gentlemen', were given to *Richardson's Pamela by Mr B—, and to his son by *Chesterfield, and their influence is seen in *Rousseau's *Émile*; his view of the child's mind as a *tabula rasa*, and his distinctions between wit and judgement, were the subject of much discussion in the *Augustan age. The anti-philosophy jokes of the *Scriblerus Club demonstrate the currency of his ideas; *Addison was his champion in many essays. But perhaps his greatest impact was on *Sterne, who quotes him frequently in *Tristram Shandy*, and who was deeply interested in his theories of the random association of ideas, of the measuring of time, of the nature of sensation, etc. On this subject, see Kenneth MacLean, *John Locke and English Literature of the Eighteenth Century* (1936).

An Essay Concerning Human Understanding (1975), ed. Peter H. Nidditch; *A Paraphrase and Notes on the Epistles of St Paul*, ed. Arthur W. Wainwright (2 vols, 1987); *The Correspondence of John Locke*, ed. E. S. De Beer (8 vols, 1976–89). (See also RESTORATION.)

LOCKE, Matthew (1621–77), the most eminent composer of the early Restoration, prolific in many forms and of the first importance as a producer of music for the stage during the period when opera was on the verge of being introduced into England. His earliest work of this type was the music for *Shirley's masque *Cupid and Death* (1653), written in collaboration with Christopher Gibbons (Orlando *Gibbons's son): this is the only work of its kind of which the complete score has survived, and is particularly interesting for its use of the declamatory, recitative style of word setting, the essential feature upon which the future development

of opera was to depend. The music he wrote, with four other composers, for what is generally regarded as the first English opera, *D'Avenant's *The Siege of Rhodes* (1656), is all lost; and what was for years considered one of the classics of Shakespearian incidental music, for D'Avenant's version of *Macbeth*, is now known not to have been by Locke. But he made another contribution to the development of opera in his music for *Shadwell's *Psyche* (1675), grandly entitled in the libretto 'The English Opera . . .', though it is in fact clearly based on a *tragédie-ballet* by *Molière of four years earlier and does not step over the borderline that divides the courtly *masque from its operatic successors.

LOCKER-LAMPSON, Frederick (1821–95), born Locker, remembered for his light verse, included in *London Lyrics* (1857), *Lyra Elegantiarum* (1867, an anthology, which, in its preface, offers a description of *vers de société*, in which 'sentiment never surges into passion, and where humour never overflows into boisterous merriment'), and *Patchwork* (1879), a miscellany of prose and verse. He formed an important collection of books (the Rowfant Library), concentrating on English and continental literature.

LOCKHART, John Gibson (1794–1854), born at Cambusnethan, educated at Glasgow University and Balliol College, Oxford. He was called to the Scottish bar, and became one of the principal contributors to *Blackwood's Magazine*. In 1817 he began a long series of attacks on, in particular, Leigh *Hunt, *Keats, and *Hazlitt, castigating them as the low-born *'Cockney School of Poetry' and treating their work with great harshness. He did, however, support *Wordsworth and *Coleridge. In 1818 he translated *Schlegel's *Geschichte der alten und neuen Literatur* as *Lectures on the History of Literature, Ancient and Modern*, and he contributed several important articles on German literature to *Blackwood's* during the 1820s. From 1825 to 1853 he was editor of the *Quarterly Review*, and his ferocity as a critic was well reflected in his chosen nickname, 'The Scorpion'. He published a wide range of books. *Peter's Letters to his Kinsfolk* (1819) contains spirited sketches of life in Edinburgh and Glasgow. In 1821 he published *Valerius*, a simple tale of Rome under Trajan; in 1822 came his novel *Some Passages in the Life of Adam Blair*, a dark and disquieting story of a Scots minister. This was followed in 1823 by a conventional and popular romance, *Reginald Dalton*, and by his translations of *Ancient Spanish Ballads*. In 1824 he published another arresting novel, *Matthew Wald*, about the love of cousins. His *Life of Burns* appeared in 1828, and in 1837–8 his *Memoirs of the Life of Sir Walter Scott* (his father-in-law), which is comprehensive, methodical, and full of personal detail.

Lockit, and his daughter Lucy, characters in Gay's *The Beggar's Opera*.

Locksley, the name under which *Robin Hood figures in Scott's *Ivanhoe*. *Ritson states that Robin Hood was born at Locksley in Nottinghamshire.

Locksley Hall, a poem in trochaics by *Tennyson, published 1842, probably written 1837–8. It consists of a monologue spoken by a disappointed lover, revisiting the desolate moorland home by the sea where he had been brought up by an unsympathetic uncle, and where he fell in love with his cousin Amy; she returned his love, but, through family pressure, accepted another suitor. The narrator proceeds to rail against the modern world of steamship and railway, and ends with an ambiguous acceptance of 'the ringing grooves of change'—a phrase that the notoriously poor-sighted Tennyson wrote while under the impression that the new railways ran in grooves, not on rails.

Lockwood, the narrator of E. Brontë's *Wuthering Heights*.

Locrine, or **Logrin,** according to *Geoffrey of Monmouth's *History* (ii. 1–5), the eldest son of Brutus (*Brut) and *Ignoge. He rules over Loegria (*Logres) which is named after him, as his inherited third of his father's kingdom. He married Gwendolen but abandoned her for *Estrildis and was the father of her daughter Sabrina. He is mentioned by Spenser in *The Faerie Queene* (II. x. 13–18). T. *Lodge's 'The Complaynt of Elstred' (1593) tells the story of his unhappy mistress Estrildis, and *Swinburne wrote a play on the subject (*Locrine*, 1887).

Locrine, *The Lamentable Tragedie of*, a play published in 1595, and included in the third Shakespeare Folio. The authorship is unknown. The play deals with the legend of *Locrine, king of England, his queen Gwendolen, and *Estrildis.

LODGE, David John (1935–), critic and novelist, born in London and educated at University College London; he has held several academic appointments and in 1976 became professor of modern English literature at the University of Birmingham. His critical works (*Language of Fiction*, 1966; *The Novelist at the Crossroads*, 1971; *The Modes of Modern Writing*, 1977; *Working with Structuralism*, 1981; *After Bakhtin*, 1990) display his gift for lucid exposition, and he has done much to introduce and explain continental literary theory in Britain, while maintaining for himself 'a modest affirmation of faith in the future of realistic fiction'. His novels include *The British Museum is Falling Down* (1965); *Changing Places* (1975; a satirical 'two-*campus novel' about a transatlantic academic exchange); and *How Far Can You Go?* (1980), a novel which charts the response over two decades of an interconnected group of Roman Catholics to moral and sociological change both inside and outside the Church. *Small World* (1984) reintroduces the American academic Morris Zapp and the English professor Philip Swallow from *Changing Places*, in a jet-set world of international conferences, academic gamesmanship, and romantic pursuits. The novels' relationship to

traditional realism is ironic and oblique, as Lodge employs an intrusive narrator, jokes about omniscience, film techniques, and other fictive devices to establish a tone of detachment that serves to intensify an underlying seriousness of intention. The plot of *Nice Work* (1988) turns on the relationship between Vic Wilcox, the managing director of a small engineering firm, and Dr Robyn Penrose, a lecturer in English. In *Paradise News* (1991), an agnostic theologian, Bernard Walsh, accompanies his father Jack to Hawaii to the deathbed of Jack's estranged sister. Later novels include *Therapy* (1995), about a male mid-life crisis; *Thinks …* (2001), which explores the nature of consciousness; and *Author, Author* (2004), based on the life of H. *James and his friendship with G. *du Maurier.

LODGE, Sir Oliver, see SOCIETY FOR PSYCHICAL RESEARCH.

LODGE, Thomas (1558–1625), son of Sir Thomas Lodge, lord mayor of London, educated at Merchant Taylors' School, London, and Trinity College, Oxford. He was a student of Lincoln's Inn in 1578. In 1579–80 he published an anonymous *Defence of Poetry, Music and Stage Plays*, a reply to *Gosson's *Schoole of Abuse*, and in 1584 *An Alarum against Usurers* (dedicated to Sir P. *Sidney), depicting the dangers that moneylenders present to young spendthrifts. Appended to it was a prose romance *Forbonius and Prisceria*. *Scillaes Metamorphosis*, an Ovidian verse fable, was published in 1589. In about 1586 Lodge sailed on a privateering expedition to the Terceras and the Canaries, and in 1591–3 to South America. On the earlier voyage he wrote his best-known romance *Rosalynde* (1590), 'hatcht in the stormes of the Ocean, and feathered in the surges of many perillous seas'. After four more minor prose romances he published *Phillis: Honoured with Pastorall Sonnets, Elegies, and Amorous Delights* (1593), including many poems adapted from Italian and French models, to which was appended 'The Complaynt of Elstred', the story of the unhappy mistress of King *Locrine. His play *The Wounds of Civill War* (1594), about Marius and Sulla, had been performed by the Lord Admiral's Men; he also wrote *A Looking Glasse for London and England* (1594), in collaboration with R. *Greene. It is not clear whether he wrote any other plays. *A Fig for Momus* (1595) was a miscellaneous collection of satirical poems including epistles addressed to S. *Daniel and M. *Drayton. *Wits Miserie, and the Worlds Madnesse: Discovering the Devils Incarnat of this Age* was published in 1596, as was a remarkable romance, *A Margarite of America*, written during his second voyage, under Thomas Cavendish, while they were near the Magellan Straits. Lodge soon after this became a Roman Catholic, and studied medicine at Avignon; he was incorporated MD at Oxford in 1602, and in the next year published *A Treatise of the Plague*. He completed two major works of translation: *The Famous and Memorable Workes of Josephus* (1602), which was frequently reprinted, and *The Workes of Lucius Annaeus Seneca* (1614). His last work was a translation of Goulart's commentary on

*Du Bartas (1621). Lodge is now mainly remembered for *Rosalynde* and for the lyrics scattered throughout his romances. His works were edited by E. *Gosse (4 vols, 1883).

Loegria, see LOGRES.

LOFFT, Capel (1751–1824), barrister, reformer, and eccentric, who lived on his family estate near Bury St Edmunds and corresponded with many eminent literary figures. He published poems, essays, etc., but is perhaps best remembered for his support of R. *Bloomfield, whose poem *The Farmer's Boy* (1800) he edited (claiming to have made only 'occasional corrections . . . with respect to orthography and sometimes in the grammatical construction'). His son, also Capel Lofft (1806–73) and also somewhat eccentric, complained that his father's 'love of literature was excessive' in his own 'mental autobiography', *Self-Formation* (1837); he also wrote an epic on *Chartism called *Ernest* (1839).

LOFTING, Hugh, see CHILDREN'S LITERATURE.

Logic, A System of, Ratiocinative and Inductive, a treatise by J. S. *Mill, published 1843, revised and enlarged in the editions of 1850 and 1872.

The importance of Mill's *Logic* lies in the fact that it supplied, to use the author's own words (*Autobiography*), 'a text-book of the opposite doctrine [to the a priori view of human knowledge put forward by the German school]—that which derives all knowledge from experience, and all moral and intellectual qualities principally from the direction given to the associations'. In this work Mill stressed the importance of inductive methods, while, unlike F. *Bacon, giving its proper share to deduction. He lays down methods for investigating the causal relations of phenomena, assuming the causal principle, in defence of which he can only say that 'the belief we entertain in the universality, throughout nature, of the law of cause and effect, is itself an instance of induction', constantly verified by experience; if there were an exception to this law, we should probably have discovered it.

In attributing to experience and association our belief in mathematical and physical laws, he came into conflict with the intuitional philosophers, and gave his own explanation 'of that peculiar character of what are called necessary truths, which is adduced as proof that their evidence must come from a deeper source than experience'. This peculiar certainty, he holds, is 'an illusion, in order to sustain which it is necessary to suppose that those truths relate to, and express the properties of purely imaginary objects' as in the laws of geometry, which are only approximately true in the real world. Geometry being built on hypotheses, 'it owes to this alone the peculiar certainty supposed to distinguish it'. This conflict with the intuitional school is further developed in Mill's *Examination of Sir William Hamilton's Philosophy.*

Logistilla, in *Orlando furioso*, a beneficent witch who defends *Rogero against her wicked sisters *Alcina and Morgana, and gives *Astolfo his magic horn and book.

Logres, according to *Geoffrey of Monmouth's *History* (where it is called Loegria), the part of Brutus' kingdom assigned to his eldest son *Locrine, i.e. England. It is the usual term for Arthur's kingdom in medieval romance from *Chrétien de Troyes onwards. Spenser calls it 'Logris' (*Faerie Queene*, II. x. 14).

Logrin, see LOCRINE.

Logris, see LOGRES.

LOGUE, Christopher (1926–   ), poet, playwright, journalist, and actor. He lived in Paris for a while during the 1950s, where he co-edited with A. *Trocchi the short-lived but influential magazine *Merlin* (1952–5) which published work by *Beckett, *Genet, *Neruda, and others. He was associated with the early years of the *English Stage Company, which put on several of his plays, including the Brechtian musical *The Lily White Boys* (1960, with H. Cookson). He was a pioneer in the *jazz poetry movement, and experimented with publishing his poems as Verse Posters. His volumes of poetry include *Wand and Quartet* (1953), *Songs* (1959), *New Numbers* (1969), and *Ode to the Dodo: Poems from 1953–1978* (1981); he has also adapted sections of the *Iliad, collected in *War Music* (1981), *Kings* (1991), and *The Husbands* (1994), and written several screenplays.

Lohengrin, the son of *Perceval, first mentioned in the *Parzival* (*c.*1205) of *Wolfram von Eschenbach, and in Wolfram's incomplete epic *Titurel*. According to legend he is summoned from the temple of the *Grail at Montsalvatsch (possibly Montserrat in Catalonia) and borne in a swan-boat to Antwerp. He saves Princess Elsa of Brabant from Frederick of Telramund who wants to marry her against her wishes. Lohengrin will marry Elsa if she does not ask what his race is; but she does, and the swan-boat carries him back to the Grail castle. The story is the subject of *Wagner's opera (1850). In early forms of the legend the Knight of the Swan is called Helias (Helis in Icelandic).

Lolita, a novel by V. *Nabokov.

Lollards, from Dutch *lollaerd*, 'mumbler', applied to a heretical sect devoted to piety, implying pretentions to great virtue; it was borrowed in late 14th-cent. English to apply with the same connotations to the Wyclifites, but originally with a commoner variant from 'loller' which *Skeat says (in his note to *Piers Plowman* C X. 213) was deliberately confused in writers such as *Langland and *Chaucer with an earlier English sense 'one who lolls around'. But the verb 'to loll around' was new in English of that period, and the entries in the *OED* leave the question open. See WYCLIF and OLD-CASTLE.

LOLLIUS, an unknown author mentioned three times by Chaucer in connection with the Trojan War (*Troilus and Criseyde*, I. 394, V. 1653, and *The House of Fame*, l. 1468), once regarded as a great puzzle, but no doubt correctly explained (by R. G. Latham in 1868) as a misreading of *Horace, Epistles*, 1. 2. 1: 'Troiani belli scriptorem, Maxime Lolli, . . . relegi', where 'Lolli' is the vocative for the addressee of the letter, not the *scriptor*. Lollius came by this misreading to be regarded as a writer on the Trojan War whose work, naturally, was missing and he thus provided a useful fiction as Chaucer's source. The *scriptor* in Horace is Homer, and *Maxime* is a cognomen.

LOMBARD, Peter, see PETER LOMBARD.

LOMONOSOV, Mikhailo Vasilevich (1711–65), Russian poet, historian, chemist, physicist, mathematician, mining engineer; he has been described as the founder of modern Russian literature and of modern Russian culture. His greatest literary achievements are in the ode, both sacred and panegyrical; 'Ode on the Taking of Khotin' (1739), 'Ode on the Accession of the Empress Elizaveta Petrovna' (1747), 'Ode, Selected from Job, Chapters XXXVIII–XLI' (1750). His poetry was first translated by John Bowring in 1821.

London, a poem by Dr *Johnson, published anonymously 1738, in imitation of the Third Satire of *Juvenal. *Pope predicted its unknown author would soon be 'déterré'. Thales (perhaps *Savage), disgusted with London, and about to leave for Wales, reflects on London's vices and affectations, and on the oppression of the poor—'All crimes are safe, but hated poverty.' Johnson attacks Sir R. *Walpole's administration in his allusions to excise, the abuse of pensions, and the new stage licensing laws; the poem's success was in part political.

LONDON, Jack (John) Griffith (1876–1916), American novelist, born in San Francisco, the son of an itinerant astrologer and a spiritualist mother; he took the name of his stepfather John London. He grew up in poverty, scratching a living in various legal and illegal ways— robbing the oyster beds, working in a canning factory and a jute mill, serving aged 17 as a common sailor, and taking part in the Klondike gold rush of 1897. These various experiences provided the material for his works, and made him a socialist; as he was later to write, he had seen as a youth 'the cellar of society . . . the pit, the abyss, the human cess-pool', and he was to attack capitalism and exploitation with great vigour, while maintaining, to the embarrassment of some of his comrades, some markedly chauvinist and racist attitudes. *The Son of the Wolf* (1900), the first of his many collections of tales, is based upon life in the far north, as is the book that brought him recognition, *The Call of the Wild* (1903), which tells the story of the dog Buck, who, after his master's death, is lured back to the primitive world to lead a wolf pack. In the same year appeared *The People of the Abyss*, an emotive docu-mentary based on some weeks spent in the slums of London's East End. Many other tales of struggle, travel, and adventure followed, including *The Sea-Wolf* (1904), *White Fang* (1906, another tale with dog as hero), *South Sea Tales* (1911), and *Jerry of the South Seas* (1917). *The Iron Heel* (1908) is a novel about the class struggle, which prophesies a Fascist revolution; *The Valley of the Moon* (1913) advocates a return to the land in an ideal community. One of London's most interesting novels is the semi-autobiographical *Martin Eden* (1909), which describes the struggles of the protagonist, a sailor and labourer, to acquire education and to become a writer, inspired partly by his love for Ruth Morse, a girl of education and what appears to him to be refinement; he succeeds, spectacularly, only to find himself disillusioned with her and the world he has entered, and he drowns himself on the way to the South Seas. *John Barleycorn* (1913), also semi-autobiographical, is a record of London's own struggle against alcohol. He also wrote socialist treatises, autobiographical essays, and a good deal of journalism in his short but intensely active life, and was remembered by his friend U. *Sinclair as 'one of the great revolutionary figures' of America's history.

London, Survey of, see STOW.

London Assurance, see BOUCICAULT.

London Cuckolds, The, a rollicking farce by Edward Ravenscroft (fl. 1671–97), which was first produced at the Dorset Gardens theatre in 1681 and annually revived on Lord Mayor's Day (9 Nov.) for nearly a century. An adaptation by Terry *Johnson was performed at the National Theatre in 1998.

London Gazette, see under OXFORD GAZETTE.

London Labour and the London Poor, see MAYHEW.

London Library, the, was founded in 1840, largely at the instance of *Carlyle, with the support and encouragement of many eminent men of letters of the day, including *Gladstone, *Grote, H. *Hallam, and Mazzini; the manifesto, published on 15 Feb. 1841, deplored the dearth of libraries in London, and carried a quotation from *Gibbon stating that: 'The greatest city in the world is destitute of that useful institution, a public library.' It opened on 3 May 1841, in two rooms in Pall Mall, with a stock of 3,000 volumes and with John George Cochrane (1761–1852) as its first librarian. Its initial subscribers included *Dickens, *Macaulay, and *Macready. It moved to its present premises in St James's Square in 1845, and continues to be much valued by its many members. See *The London Library* by Miron Grindea, first published in 1977 as Nos 387–400 of *Adam International Review*.

London Magazine, (1) a periodical which ran from 1732 to 1785, founded in opposition to the *Gentleman's Magazine*. (2) a magazine of great brilliance (1820–9), established under the editorship of John

*Scott on roughly the same miscellany plan as *Black-wood's*, except that it was non-political and gave a large proportion of its space to writers and books. Scott championed the work of the younger writers, including *Wordsworth, *Lamb, *De Quincey, *Clare, *Hood, *Carlyle, and in particular the *'Cockney School' (*Keats, Leigh *Hunt, and *Hazlitt). But he was soon provoked into attacks on *Blackwood's*, which bitterly derided most of his writers, and he was killed in a duel by a representative of that magazine. John *Taylor then took over the editorship with the assistance of Hood; but, although the magazine continued successfully for another eight years, Taylor's habit of editorial interference angered his writers, and many, including Lamb and Hazlitt, withdrew their work; see J. Bauer, *The London Magazine 1820–29* (1953). (3) a monthly literary magazine founded in 1954 by J. *Lehmann, and edited by him until 1961. It was welcomed in its first issue by T. S. *Eliot as a non-university-based periodical that would 'boldly assume the existence of a public interested in serious literature'. It aimed to avoid being 'narrowly British' or political in content; Lehmann (*The Ample Proposition*, 1966) writes that he aimed to create 'the London magazine, and not the Magazine of Oxford, or Cambridge, or Redbrick', and to reach Dr *Johnson's 'common reader'. He was succeeded as editor by Alan *Ross, who enlarged the magazine's range to cover other arts, including photography.

London Merchant, The, or *The History of George Barnwell*, see GEORGE BARNWELL.

London Mercury, a monthly literary periodical founded in 1919 by J. C. *Squire, who edited it until 1934, and used it in its early days as a vehicle to condemn *Modernism and what he described as 'anarchical cleverness'; it published fiction, poetry, reviews, etc., and contributors included *de la Mare, *Chesterton, *Belloc, W. H. *Davies, *Yeats, and D. H. *Lawrence. In 1939 it was incorporated in *Life and Letters*.

London Prodigal, The, a comedy published in 1605, attributed to Shakespeare in the title of the quarto edition of that year and included in the third and fourth Folios, but undoubtedly by some other hand.

The play is a comedy of London manners, and deals with the reclaiming of the prodigal young Flowerdale by the fidelity of his wife.

London Review of Books, a literary and cultural review founded in 1979 and edited by Karl Miller (1931–   ), professor of modern English literature at University College London, in conscious emulation of the *New York Review of Books* (founded 1963) in both design and editorial approach. It has published critical essays and articles by many of the most prominent critics and scholars of the day, including Christopher Ricks, John *Bayley, Frank *Kermode, A. J. P. *Taylor, D. *Lodge, Sir Peter Medawar, and Dan *Jacobson, and

has published poems and fiction by S. *Heaney, N. *Gordimer, G. *Ewart, Douglas *Dunn, Tom *Paulin, Ted *Hughes, P. *Redgrove, D. *Walcott, and many others.

Loneliness of the Long Distance Runner, The, a novella by A. *Sillitoe.

Longaville, in Shakespeare's *Love's Labour's Lost*, one of the three lords attending on the king of Navarre.

Longest Journey, The (1907), a novel by E. M. *Forster.
Rickie Elliot, a sensitive and lame young man, escapes from suburban misery and public school bullying to Cambridge, where he finds sympathetic friends, including Ansell, a grocer's son, and attempts to become a writer. But he is attracted to and eventually marries Agnes, whose athletic fiancé has been killed in a football match: she proves to be mean-spirited and conventional and he finds he has condemned himself to a life of petty jealousy and domesticity. He is killed while trying to rescue his drunken, healthy, 'pagan' half-brother Stephen, whom Agnes had rejected as a family disgrace. This was Forster's favourite of his works: he admitted its faults of construction (and the number of accidental deaths is high even by Forsterian standards) but nevertheless felt that in Stephen he had created a living being who expressed some of his own feelings for the English landscape.

LONGFELLOW, Henry Wadsworth (1807–82), American poet, born in Maine and educated at Bowdoin, where he was the classmate of *Hawthorne. The offer of a professorship of modern languages at Bowdoin took him to Europe to study, 1826–9; after lecturing at Bowdoin he returned to Europe again to prepare for the post of professor at Harvard. His wife, travelling with him, died in Holland in 1835. In 1836 he began his many influential years of teaching at Harvard.

His prose romance *Hyperion* (1839), a product of his bereavement, is the tale of a young man who seeks to forget sorrow in travel, a thread on which are hung philosophical discourses, poems, and legends. In the same year was published *Voices of the Night*, which includes his didactic pieces 'A Psalm of Life', 'Footsteps of Angels', and 'The Reaper and the Flowers'. In 1841 appeared *Ballads and Other Poems*, with such well-known pieces as 'The Wreck of the Hesperus' and 'The Village Blacksmith'. In 1842 he met *Dickens in America, and visited him in London later in the same year; on his voyage home he wrote his *Poems on Slavery* (1842). In 1843 he married Frances Appleton, an event foreshadowed in *Hyperion*. By this time he was already one of the most widely read poets in America, and subsequent volumes confirmed his reputation in the English-speaking world as second only to that of *Tennyson in popularity; these include *The Belfry of Bruges and Other Poems* (1847); *Evangeline* (1849; a narrative poem in hexameters, set in Acadia, now Nova Scotia, with some fine evocations of 'the forest primeval' to balance the sentimentality of the tale); *The Song of *Hiawatha* (1858); and *The Courtship of Miles Standish* (1858; another long hexameter narrative, based on a New England legend). In 1854 he had resigned his professorship, but his peaceful creative life was tragically interrupted in 1861 by the death of his second wife, who was burned to death in a domestic accident. *Tales of a Wayside Inn* (1863, 1st series; with the rousing 'Paul Revere's Ride' and 'The Song of King Olaf') follows the form of the *Canterbury Tales* and the *Decameron*; a group of travellers, in the 'old-fashioned, quaint abode' of the inn, pass the evening by telling tales, directed by the landlord. Much of this was written before his wife's death, and an increased sombreness may be seen in his translation of *Dante (1867) and his trilogy *Christus* (1872; incorporating the earlier *Golden Legend* of 1851), which he considered his masterpiece. Other 'Tales of a Wayside Inn' followed in 1872 (in *Three Books of Song*) and in 1874 (in *Aftermath*). His last volumes, *The Masque of Pandora* (1875), *Ultima Thule* (1880), and *In the Harbor* (1882), contain some poignant autumnal reflections on old age, including his 'Morituri Salutamus' (1875), written for the 50th anniversary of the class of 1825 at Bowdoin.

LONGINUS, the name bestowed by a scribe's error on the author of the Greek critical treatise περὶ ὕψους (On the Sublime) written probably in the 1st cent. AD. It locates the sources of poetic excellence in the profundity of the writer's emotions and the seriousness of his thought. The first English translation, by John Hall, appeared in 1652, but it was not until the appearance of *Boileau's French version (1674) and its influence on *Dryden that the concept of creative fire became popular. 'Longinus' had a marked effect on 18th-cent. critics and aestheticians. *Dennis, *Shaftesbury, and even *Pope were influenced by him, while the later Primitivists like John Brown and William Duff, as well as J. *Warton, fell wholly under his spell. The cult of the *sublime did much to prepare the way for *Romanticism.

Longinus ('Longeus' in *Malory), the traditional name of the Roman soldier who pierced with his spear the side of Christ at the Crucifixion. The lance in the *Grail legend is sometimes identified as his spear, as by Malory (Vinaver, *Works*, 54). See chapter 21 in R. S. Loomis (ed.), *Arthurian Literature in the Middle Ages* (1959).

Long John Silver, a character in Stevenson's *Treasure Island*.

LONGLEY, Michael (1939–   ), Irish poet, born in Belfast, educated at Trinity College, Dublin. Longley is one of the triumvirate of important Northern Irish poets (see also Seamus *Heaney and Derek *Mahon) who emerged in the 1960s. A classicist by training, Longley began as a formalist ('Circe') with *No Continuing City* (1969). His natural role as love poet and observer of nature has been challenged by the horrors of the post-1969 *Troubles. 'Wounds' encompasses both the fate of the Ulster Division at the Somme in 1916 and recent sectarian atrocity. Longley is a fine monologuist, as exemplified by 'Arrest' and 'Peace (After Tibullus)' from *The Echo Gate* (1979). His poems from the rural fastness of Co. Mayo show him to be a fine natural historian and elegist. Married to the critic Edna Longley, he shares her admiration of Louis *MacNeice and edited an edition of MacNeice's *Selected Poems* (1988).

LONGMAN, Thomas (1699–1755). He established the long surviving family firm of publishers; the original Thomas published various important works of reference, including a share in *Johnson's Dictionary*. Thomas III (1771–1842) published, among other work, that of *Wordsworth, *Coleridge, T. *Moore, *Southey, and Sir W. *Scott, and became the proprietor of the *Edinburgh Review*. See Harold Cox and John E. Chandler, *The House of Longman, 1724–1924* (1925) and Philip Wallis, *At the Sign of the Ship, 1724–1974* (1974).

Longman's Magazine, a family magazine, a successor to *Fraser's, which ran from 1882 to 1905. It published short stories, serialized novels, poetry, and reviews, and contributors included A. *Dobson, G. *Allen, *Kipling, Mrs *Oliphant, *Newbolt, and *Hardy.

LONSDALE, Frederick (1881–1954), playwright, born Lionel Frederick Leonard, in St Helier, Jersey, the son of a seaman. His many successful, worldly, witty, and light-hearted drawing-room comedies include *Aren't We All?* (perf. 1923), *The Last of Mrs Cheyney* (1925), and *On Approval* (1927). He also wrote musical comedies. See *Freddy Lonsdale* (1957) by his daughter Frances Donaldson.

Look Back in Anger, a play by J. *Osborne, first produced by the *English Stage Company at the Royal Court Theatre on 8 May 1956, published 1957. It proved a landmark in the history of the theatre, a focus for reaction against a previous generation (see KITCHEN SINK DRAMA), and a decisive contribution to the corporate image of the *Angry Young Man.

The action takes place in a Midlands town, in the one-room flat of Jimmy and Alison Porter, and centres on their marital conflicts, which appear to arise largely from Jimmy's sense of their social incompatibility: he is a jazz-playing ex-student from a 'white tile' university, working on a market sweet stall, she is a colonel's daughter. He is by turns violent, sentimental, maudlin, self-pitying, and sadistic, and has a fine line in rhetoric. The first act opens as Alison stands ironing the clothes of Jimmy and their lodger Cliff, as Jimmy reads the Sunday papers and abuses her and the 'Edwardian brigade' which her parents represent. In the second act the battle intensifies, as Alison's friend Helena attempts to rescue her from her disastrous marriage; Alison departs with her father, and Helena falls into Jimmy's arms. The third act opens with Helena at the ironing board; Alison returns, having lost the baby she was expecting, and she and Jimmy find a manner of reconciliation through humiliation and games-playing fantasy. In its use of social milieu, its iconoclastic social attitudes, and its exploration of sadomasochistic relationships, the play was highly influential.

Looking Backward, a novel by E. *Bellamy.

LOOS, Anita (1893–1981), American novelist and screenwriter, born in California, best remembered for her classic comedy *Gentlemen Prefer Blondes: The Illuminating Diary of a Professional Lady* (1925), in which the ambitious Lorelei Lee from Little Rock, Arkansas, describes in *faux-naïf* prose her adventures, ambitions, and conquests.

LOPE DE VEGA, see VEGA CARPIO.

LORCA, Federico García, see GARCÍA LORCA.

Lord Jim, a novel by J. *Conrad, published 1900.
    Jim is chief mate on board the *Patna*, an ill-manned ship carrying a party of pilgrims in Eastern waters. He is young, idealistic, and a dreamer of heroic deeds. When the *Patna* threatens to sink and the cowardly officers decide to save their own skins and escape in the few lifeboats, Jim despises them, but at the last moment, dazed by the horror and confusion of the moment, he joins them. He acts without conscious decision and his last-minute jump into the boat is almost involuntary. The *Patna* does not sink and the pilgrims are rescued. What happens to Jim thereafter is related by an observer, Marlow. Jim, alone among the crew, remains to face the court of enquiry, deeply disturbed at his defection from a code of conduct dear to him. Condemned by the court and stripped of his papers, he tries to disappear, moving from place to place whenever his past threatens to catch up with him. He searches for anonymity and the chance to redeem himself. Through Marlow's intervention Jim is sent to a remote trading station in Patusan. His efforts create order and well-being in a previously chaotic community and he wins the respect and affection of the people for whom he becomes Tuan—or Lord Jim. He has achieved some sense of peace, but the memory of his jump is still with him. When Gentleman Brown and his gang of thieves arrive to disrupt and plunder the village Jim begs the chiefs to spare them, pledging his own life against their departure. But Brown behaves treacherously and a massacre takes place. Jim feels he has only one course of action; rejecting the idea of flight he delivers himself up to Chief Doramin, whose son was a victim of the massacre. Doramin shoots him and Jim willingly accepts this honourable death.

Lord of the Flies (1954), a novel by W. *Golding.
    An aeroplane carrying a party of schoolboys crashes on a desert island. The boys' attempts, led by Ralph and Piggy, to set up a democratically run society quickly fail and the savagery which in Golding's work underlies man's true nature takes over. Terror rules under the dictator Jack, and two boys are killed; it is only with the arrival of a shocked rescue officer that a mask of civilization returns. It is a savage reply to the naïve optimism of *Ballantyne's *The Coral Island*. (See also BEELZEBUB.)

Lord of the Isles, The a poem in six cantos by Sir W. *Scott, published 1815. It is set at the time of the battle of Bannockburn, and deals with the return of Robert Bruce to Scotland in 1307. Interwoven with the historical drama is the story of the love of Edith of Lorn for Lord Ronald, the Lord of the Isles: Edith, disguised as a page, manages to save both Bruce and Ronald, and her devotion wins Lord Ronald's heart.

Lord of the Rings, The, see TOLKIEN.

'Lord Ullin's Daughter', a ballad by T. *Campbell.

Lorel, the swineherd in Jonson's *The Sad Shepherd.

Lorenzo, (1) son of the duke of Castile in Kyd's *The Spanish Tragedy*; (2) the lover of *Jessica in Shakespeare's *The Merchant of Venice.

Lorna Doone, a novel by R. D. *Blackmore, published 1869.
    This celebrated and continuously popular story is set in the later 17th cent. on Exmoor, where an outlawed family, the Doones, and their retainers terrorize the surrounding countryside. They murder a farmer, father of the novel's hero John Ridd, a boy of 12 when the story starts. He secretly discovers the child Lorna, who has been kidnapped by the Doones, and they grow up to love each other. John Ridd, by now a giant in height and strength, is involved in adventures with the highwayman Tom Faggus, who marries his sister Annie, in the events leading up to Monmouth's rebellion, and in a rivalry with the villainous Carver Doone, from whom he rescues Lorna during a superbly described blizzard. The Doones are eventually destroyed, Lorna turns out not to be a Doone but an heiress of noble family, and she and John are married; but Carver Doone shoots her at the altar. John avenges her, she recovers, and the story ends happily. The infamous Judge Jeffreys plays a part in the action, and John Ridd and Tom Faggus are also based on historical characters.

LORRIS, Guillaume de, see ROMAN DE LA ROSE.

Lorry, Jarvis, a character in Dickens's *A Tale of Two Cities*.

Los, one of the principal characters in the symbolic books of *Blake, a complex and ambiguous figure, described in the opening of *The Song of Los* (1795) as 'the Eternal Prophet'. He is usually portrayed as the antagonist of *Urizen; in his role as blacksmith (which links him with the Loki of northern mythology, and the Roman Vulcan) he is portrayed in *The Book of Los* (1795) binding Urizen in iron links forged in his glowing furnace, and in earlier poems of the cycle (and also in *The Four Zoas*) he binds his own son, the rebellious *Orc. He represents the artist, and also Time; his female counterpart is *Enitharmon (Inspiration, and Space); his periods of estrangement from her spell disaster for the universe. His character changes during the evolution of Blake's mythology, and he finally becomes in *Jerusalem a great heroic force of energy, while remaining morally ambiguous. An insight into the nature of Blake's vision is offered in his verse epistle to his friend Butts (dated 22 Nov. 1802) in which he describes Los descending before his face 'in fierce flames; in my double sight | 'Twas outward a Sun: inward Los in his might'.

'Lost Leader, The', a poem by R. *Browning (1845) deploring *Wordsworth's political change of heart, and suggesting that he abandoned his radical views 'just for a handful of silver' and 'just for a riband to stick in his coat'.

Lost World, The, an adventure story by Conan *Doyle, published in 1912. It is the first of his stories to feature the irascible, vast, and bearded zoologist and explorer Professor George Edward Challenger, who leads an expedition to South America to an almost inaccessible plateau where prehistoric creatures survive from the Jurassic period. He and his comrades (the journalist narrator Malone, the big game hunter Lord John Roxton, and anatomist Summerlee) survive many perils and eventually return to London with evidence in the form of a living pterodactyl, which dramatically escapes during a meeting at the Zoological Institute. Other Challenger stories include *The Poison Belt* (1913) and *The Land of Mist* (1926).

Lot, king of Orkney in the Arthurian legends, is the husband of Arthur's sister or half-sister *Morgawse. Their sons are *Gawain, *Agravain, *Gareth, and *Gaheris, as well as *Modred in the earlier versions (before Arthur was made his unwitting, incestuous father). The feud between his family and *Pellinore's is one of the running themes in *Malory.

Lothair, a novel by B. *Disraeli, published 1870.

Like the hero of *Tancred, Lothair is a young man determined to seek the true path. He is a wealthy nobleman, left, when his parents died, in the joint guardianship of Lord Culloden, a member of the Scottish Kirk, and the brilliant cleric Grandison, who adopts the Catholic faith and rapidly becomes a cardinal. A deep interest in the merits of the Anglican and Catholic faiths, and their shared background in Judaism, pervades the book. At about the time of Lothair's coming of age in 1866 the forces of Garibaldi were confronting the papacy, and for most of the rest of the book both the Catholics and the Italian patriots struggle and manœuvre for control of the wealthy and influential Lothair. Like *Endymion (in the novel of that name), Lothair is reflective rather than active and is much influenced by three women, the beautiful Catholic Clare Arundel, the charming Lady Corisande, and the stormy Italian patriot Theodora. Lothair joins

Theodora in Italy, but she is killed at Viterbo and he is himself wounded at Mentana. Lothair continues his search for the first 'cradle' of Christianity, and in Jerusalem the mystic Paraclete gives him a revelation of the origins of Christianity. The cardinal and fellow prelates struggle to convince and convert Lothair, but he resists, realizing that the fanaticism of both the Catholics and the Italian patriots is corrupting. After further travels he returns home, confirmed in his Anglicanism, and marries Lady Corisande.

The wit and irony of the scenes of high social life are thought by some to foreshadow *Wilde. Various memorable incidental characters include the radiant artist Mr Phoebus, modelled on *Leighton, and Lord St Aldegonde, the aristocratic republican opposed to all privileges except those of dukes, and in favour of the equal division of all property except land. 'Lothair-mania' swept England, the USA, and Europe; although the book was poorly reviewed (and said to lack *gravitas*), the first edition sold out in two days and there were eight editions in 1870 alone.

Lothario, (1) the heartless libertine (proverbial as 'the Gay Lothario') in Rowe's *The Fair Penitent*; (2) a character in the episode of *The Curious Impertinent* in *Don Quixote*; (3) a character in *Goethe's *Wilhelm Meister*.

Lotte, the heroine of *Goethe's *The Sorrows of Werther*. She was drawn from Lotte Buff, with whom Goethe fell in love at Wetzlar and who married Goethe's friend Kestner.

Lousiad, The, a *mock-heroic poem by J. *Wolcot (Peter Pindar), published 1785–95.

The subject of this exuberant mockery is the appearance of a louse in a dish of peas served to George III, the king's feelings on the discovery, and his subsequent order that all the servants in the kitchen should have their heads shaved.

LOVE, Nicholas (fl. 1410), prior of the Carthusian House of Mount Grace near Middlesbrough, author before 1410 of *The Mirrour of the Blessed Lyf of Iesu Christ,* an accomplished prose translation of the *Meditationes Vitae Christi* attributed to Bonaventura. It has been edited by L. F. Powell (1908).

Love à la Mode, a comedy by *Macklin, produced 1759.

Four suitors, an Englishman, an Irishman, a Scot, and a Jew, are rivals for the hand of the heroine. Their quality is tested by the pretence that she has lost her fortune. The play is famous for the characters of Sir Archy MacSarcasm and Sir Callaghan O'Brallaghan.

LOVECRAFT, H. P., see FANTASY FICTION and HORROR.

Loveday, John and Bob, brothers in Hardy's *The Trumpet Major.

Love for Love, a comedy by *Congreve, performed 1695.

Valentine has fallen under the displeasure of his father by his extravagance, and is besieged by duns. His father, Sir Sampson Legend, offers him £4,000 (only enough to pay his debts) if he will sign a bond engaging to make over his inheritance to his younger brother Ben. Valentine, to escape from his embarrassment, signs the bond. He is in love with Angelica, who possesses a fortune of her own, but she has hitherto not yielded to his suit. Sir Sampson has arranged a match between Ben, who is at sea, and Miss Prue, an awkward country girl, the daughter of Foresight, a superstitious old fool who claims to be an astrologer. Valentine, realizing the ruin entailed by the signature of the bond, tries to move his father by submission, and fails; then pretends to be mad and unable to sign the final deed of conveyance to his brother. Finally Angelica intervenes. She induces Sir Sampson to propose marriage to her, pretends to accept, and gets possession of Valentine's bond. Valentine, finding that Angelica is about to marry his father, generously declares himself ready to sign the conveyance in order to make her happy. She reveals the plot, tears up the bond, and declares her love for Valentine.

The comedy is enlivened by its witty dialogue and its humorous characters. Among these are Jeremy, Valentine's resourceful servant; Sir Sampson, with his 'blunt vivacity'; Ben, the rough and stupid young sailor, who intends to marry whom he chooses; Miss Prue, only too ready to learn the lessons in love given her by Tattle, the vain, half-witted beau, who finds himself married to Mrs Frail, the lady of easy virtue, when he thinks he has captured Angelica; and Foresight, the gullible old astrologer.

Love in a Tub, see COMICAL REVENGE, THE.

Lovel the Widower, a story by *Thackeray, published in the *Cornhill Magazine, 1860.

The story is told by Lovel's friend Mr Batchelor, who is more than half in love with the young governess Bessy Prior, who copes tactfully with Lovel's spoiled children, his interfering mother-in-law Lady Baker, her own greedy relatives, and her other suitors, who include the highly educated butler Bedford. Lady Baker discovers that Miss Prior once earned her living as a dancer in the theatre and orders her out of the house, but Lovel finally asserts himself and asks Bessy to marry him.

LOVELACE, Richard (1618–57/8), educated at Charterhouse School and Gloucester Hall, Oxford, the heir to great estates in Kent. Wealthy, handsome, and elegant, he was a courtier, and served in the Scottish expeditions of 1639. Having presented a 'Kentish Petition' to the House of Commons in 1642, he was thrown into the Gatehouse prison, where he is supposed to have written the song 'To Althea' ('Stone walls do not a prison make'). He rejoined Charles I in 1645, and served with the French king in 1646. According to A. *Wood, his betrothed Lucy Sacheverell married another on a false report of his death. He was imprisoned again in 1648 and in prison prepared for the press his *Lucasta: Epodes, Odes, Sonnets, Songs etc.* which includes the well-known lyric 'On Going to the Wars'. He died in extreme poverty. After his death his brother published his remaining verses, *Lucasta: Posthume Poems.* He wrote two plays, now lost. During the earlier part of the 18th cent. his work was entirely neglected, until Percy reprinted two of his lyrics in his *Reliques (1765), since when his reputation as a *Cavalier poet has steadily increased. His works were edited by C. H. Wilkinson (2 vols, 1925).

Lovelace, Robert, a character in Richardson's *Clarissa.

Loveless, a character in Vanbrugh's *The Relapse and Sheridan's *A Trip to Scarborough.

Lovell, Lord, a character in Massinger's *A New Way to Pay Old Debts.

Love on the Dole, a novel by W. *Greenwood.

'Lover's Complaint, A', a poem in rhyme-royal appended to Shakespeare's *Sonnets (1609). In it a nameless maiden complains, in a rustic setting, of her seduction by a charming but untrustworthy young man.

Lover's Melancholy, The, a romantic comedy by J. *Ford, printed 1629.

Palador, prince of Cyprus, has been betrothed to Eroclea, daughter of Meleander, an old lord; but, to escape the evil designs of Palador's father, she has been conveyed away to Greece, where she has remained disguised as a boy. Meleander has been accused of treason, imprisoned, and driven to madness. Palador, after his father's death, is left in a state of hopeless melancholy. Eroclea returns to Cyprus as the page of Menaphon. Thamasta, cousin of the prince, falls in love with her in this disguise, and to escape her attentions Eroclea is obliged to reveal her identity. She is then restored to Palador; Meleander is released and cured; Thamasta marries Menaphon; and all ends happily. The play contains a version of Strada's contest of the lute player and the nightingale, which is also dealt with by *Crashaw.

The conventional romantic plot is the framework for Ford's analysis of love melancholy, strongly influenced by Burton's *Anatomy of Melancholy. The scene in which Eroclea is recognized by Palador contains some of Ford's finest poetry ('Minutes are numbered by the fall of sands, | As by an hourglass').

Lovers' Progress, The, a romantic drama by J. *Fletcher, produced 1623, revised 1634 as *The Wandering Lovers* by *Massinger, printed 1647.

Lidian and Clarangè, devoted friends, are both in love with Olinda. Clarangè lets it be believed that he is dead, and finally turns friar, in order to surrender Olinda to Lidian. The plot is complicated with another illustration of the conflict of love and friendship. Lisander loves the virtuous Calista, wife of his friend Cleander. Cleander is killed by a servant. The imprudent but not criminal conduct of Lisander and Calista throws grave suspicion on them, and they narrowly escape condemnation for the murder.

Lovers' Vows, a play by Mrs *Inchbald, adapted from *Das Kind der Liebe* by *Kotzebue, acted 1798. The play is chiefly of interest because of the place it occupies in the story of J. Austen's *Mansfield Park*.

Baron Wildenhaim has in his youth seduced and deserted Agatha and married another woman. When the play opens Agatha is reduced to destitution, in which state she is found by her son Frederic, who now for the first time learns the story of his birth. To assist his mother's needs he goes out to beg, chances upon his unknown father, and attempts to rob him. He is arrested, discovers who the baron is, reveals his own identity and his mother's, and finally, with the aid of the pastor Anhalt, persuades the baron to marry Agatha. The baron consents also to the marriage of his daughter Amelia to Anhalt, instead of the wealthy Count Cassell.

Love's Labour's Lost, a comedy by *Shakespeare, probably written and performed about 1595, printed in quarto 1598. No major sources for it have been identified. It has often been felt to contain topical references (see SCHOOL OF NIGHT), but none of these has been firmly established.

The king of Navarre and three of his lords have sworn for three years to keep from the sight of woman and to live studying and fasting. The arrival of the princess of France on an embassy, with her attendant ladies, obliges them 'of mere necessity' to disregard their vows. The king is soon in love with the princess, his lords with her ladies, and the courting proceeds amidst disguises and merriment, to which the other characters contribute: Don Adriano de Armado, the Spaniard, a master of extravagant language, Holofernes the schoolmaster, Dull the constable, Sir Nathaniel the curate, and Costard the clown. News of the death of the princess's father interrupts the wooing, and the ladies impose a year's ordeal on their lovers. The play ends with the beautiful songs of the cuckoo and the owl, 'When daisies pied and violets blue' and 'When icicles hang by the wall'.

Loves of the Angels, The, a poem by T. *Moore, published 1823.

The poem, founded on the *Oriental tale of Harût and Marût and certain rabbinical fictions, recounts the loves of three fallen angels for mortal women, and illustrates the decline of the soul from purity. The first angel loved Lea, and taught her the spell which opens the gate of heaven. At once she uttered it and rose to the stars. The second angel loved Lilis; he came to her in his full celestial glory and she was burned to death. The third, Zaraph, loved Nama; they were condemned to live in imperfect happiness among mortals, but would ultimately be admitted to immortality.

This was Moore's last long poem, and it enjoyed great popularity as well as provoking much stricture.

Loves of the Plants, The, see DARWIN, E.

'Loves of the Triangles, The', a clever parody by G. *Canning and J. H. *Frere in the *Anti-Jacobin in 1798 of E. *Darwin's *The Loves of the Plants*. Darwin good-humouredly acknowledged its skill.

Love's Sacrifice, a tragedy by J. *Ford, printed 1633.

Fernando, favourite of the duke of Pavia, falls in love with Bianca, the duchess. He declares his love, but is repulsed. Presently, however, the duchess, in whom he has awakened a strong passion, comes to his room and offers herself to him, but warns him that she will not survive her shame, but take her own life before morning. Fernando masters his passion and determines to remain her distant lover. Fiormonda, the duke's sister, who has vainly importuned Fernando with her love for him, discovers his affection for Bianca, and pursues her vengeance. With the help of D'Avolos, the duke's base secretary, she stirs up the duke's jealousy, and a trap is laid for Fernando and Bianca. The duke finds them together, and kills Bianca. Convinced too late, by Fernando's declarations and Bianca's manner of meeting her death, of her innocence, he stabs himself, and Fernando takes poison in Bianca's tomb.

Less wide-ranging than *'Tis Pity She's a Whore, the play's main theme is the folly of love, including the platonic love cult, fashionable at the Caroline court. Its tone has aroused critical perplexity: 'In the beginning of it everyone knows what is decent; in the middle Fernando and Bianca grow sceptical as to what is decent; in the end no one knows what is decent—not even the author' (Stuart Sherman).

LOWELL, Amy Lawrence (1874–1925), American poet, born in Massachusetts. Her first volume of poetry, *A Dome of Many-Coloured Glass* (1912), was relatively conventional; shortly thereafter she took up *Imagism and in 1913 and 1914 visited England, where she met *Pound, D. H. *Lawrence, 'H.D.' (Hilda *Doolittle), and other writers active in or on the fringes of the movement, becoming so active in it herself that Pound spoke of 'Amy-gism'. Her subsequent volumes, which include *Sword Blades and Poppy Seed* (1914), *Men, Women and Ghosts* (1916; which contains 'Patterns'), and *Can Grande's Castle* (1918), show her experiments in what she called 'polyphonic prose' as well as her allegiance to Imagism; her love of New England is expressed in two of her own favourite pieces, 'Lilacs' and 'Purple Grackles', published in *What's O'Clock* (1925). She became well known as a public figure, vast and cigar-smoking, through her lectures and readings in America.

LOWELL, James Russell (1819–91), born in Cambridge, Massachusetts, and educated at Harvard. He succeeded *Longfellow as professor of French and Spanish in 1855, and was American minister in Spain, 1877–80, and in England, 1880–5. He was editor of the *Atlantic Monthly* in 1857, and subsequently (1864), with C. E. *Norton, of the *North American Review*. His works include several volumes of verse, the satirical *Biglow Papers* (1848 and 1867, prose and verse), and memorial odes after the Civil War; and various volumes of essays, including *Among My Books* (1870) and *My Study Window* (1871). His *Letters*, ed. C. E. Norton, appeared in 1894.

LOWELL, Robert Traill Spence (1917–77), American poet, born in Boston, of venerable New England families on both his father's and his mother's side. He was educated at Kenyon College, where he became friendly with R. *Jarrell and J. C. *Ransom, of whose influence he later wrote (*Kenyon Collegia*, 1974) 'The kind of poet I am was largely determined by the fact that I grew up in the heyday of the New Criticism. From the beginning, I was preoccupied with technique, fascinated by the past, tempted by other languages.' In 1940 he married his first wife, the novelist Jean Stafford, and became a fanatical convert to Roman Catholicism: his first volume of verse, *Land of Unlikeness* (1944), betrays the conflict of Catholicism and his Boston ancestry. He was jailed for six months during the Second World War as, in effect, a conscientious objector. His second volume, *Lord Weary's Castle* (1946), which contains 'The Quaker Graveyard in Nantucket' and 'Mr Edwards and the Spider', was hailed in extravagant terms. In 1949, having divorced, he married the writer Elizabeth Hardwick. *The Mills of the Kavanaughs* (1951) has as its title poem a meditation by a Catholic widow, Anne Kavanaugh, reflecting on the past in her ancestral home in Maine; this was followed by *Life Studies* (1959), *For the Union Dead* (1964), *Near the Ocean* (1967), and volumes of translation, plays, etc. He reached the height of his public fame during his opposition to the Vietnam War and support of Senator Eugene McCarthy, as his *Notebook 1967–1968* (1968) records; but he had long been suffering bouts of manic illness and heavy drinking, and a visit to Britain (at the invitation of All Souls, Oxford, and Essex University) in 1970 increased the disorder of his private life. His highly personal, confessional volume of poetry *The Dolphin* (1973) caused scandal with its revelations of martial anguish and discord. He married the writer Caroline *Blackwood in 1973, but later returned to America, where he died: *Day by Day*, a last collection, was published just before his death. A legendary figure in his lifetime, both *poète maudit* and aristocrat, both classic and romantic, he suffered from the claims made on his behalf as the greatest American poet of his time, a heroic myth-maker whose work was compared favourably with that of *Yeats, an ironic intellectual whose ambiguous, complex imagery satisfied the demands of the *New Criticism; the response to Ian Hamilton's frank biography, published in 1982, bore witness to a sense of the need for reassessment.

LOWES, J(ohn) L(ivingston) (1867–1945), professor of English in several American universities and at Harvard from 1918. He is best known for three of his books: *Convention and Revolt in Poetry* (1919); his brilliant study of *Coleridge, *The Road to Xanadu* (1927); and *The Art of Geoffrey Chaucer* (1931). He is a greatly admired critic of 14th-cent. English, especially *Chaucer.

LOWNDES, William Thomas (d. 1843), author of *The Bibliographer's Manual of English Literature* (1838) and *The British Librarian* (1839), early bibliographical works of importance. The former was revised and enlarged (1857–8) by H. G. *Bohn.

LOWRY, (Clarence) Malcolm (1909–57), novelist, born in Cheshire, the fourth son of a wealthy cotton broker. Under the influence of *Melville, *O'Neill, *Conrad, and Jack *London he went to sea on leaving school, travelling to the Far East, then returned to take a degree at Cambridge. In 1933 he published *Ultramarine*, which shows a considerable debt to *Blue Voyage* by his friend *Aiken, in whose autobiography *Ushant* (1952) he was to appear as Hambro. He travelled widely in Europe and the USA, settling in Mexico with his first wife Jan from 1936 to 1938, where he worked on *Under the Volcano*, published 1947. Various manuscripts were meanwhile rejected. In 1940 he settled in Dollarton, British Columbia, with his second wife, ex-starlet Margerie. His last years were spent in England, and he died 'by misadventure' in Sussex. He was a chronic alcoholic, as are many of his characters, and had severe problems in disciplining his work, which went through innumerable revisions, many with Margerie's help. His posthumous publications include: *Hear Us O Lord from Heaven Thy Dwelling Place* (1961), *Selected Poems*, ed. Earle Birney and M. B. Lowry (1962), *Dark as the Grave Wherein My Friend Is Laid* (1968), and *October Ferry to Gabriola* (1970). There is a biography by Gordon Bowker (1993): see also *Collected Letters* (1995, 1996), edited by Sherrill Grace.

LOY, Mina (1882–1966), poet and artist, born Mina Gertrude Lowy in London of Jewish parents; she attended art school in Munich and Paris, and exhibited her paintings in Paris. On moving to Italy in 1907 she became acquainted with Mabel Dodge and Gertrude *Stein, and with the Italian *Futurists. She continued to paint and began writing, both 'manifestos' and poetry. The publication of her 'Love Songs' (in *Others*, NY 1915, 1917) caused, as W. C. *Williams remarked, 'wild enthusiasm among free-verse writers . . . and really quite a stir in the country at large'. Loy's work was noticed for its 'radical' social views and its innovative forms. Her *Lunar Baedecker*, a landmark in *Modernist poetry, was published in 1923, and her long Modernist autobiographical poem *Anglo-Mongrels and the Rose* between 1923 and 1925. She settled in New York in 1937, then moved to Aspen, Colorado, in 1953, where she continued to write and sculpt. See Carolyn Burke, *Becoming Modern: The Life of Mina Loy* (1996).

Loyal Subject, The, a drama by J. *Fletcher, produced 1618.

The subject is the jealousy shown by the duke of Muscovy of his late father's loyal general, Archas, whom he dismisses and replaces by an incompetent flatterer, Boroskie. The young Archas, son of the general, disguised as a girl (Alinda), is placed in the service of Olympia, the duke's sister, wins her affection, and attracts the duke's love. On an invasion of the Tartars Boroskie feigns sickness, Archas is recalled and conquers. But Boroskie inflames the duke's suspicion of Archas. On signs of the disaffection of the troops, who are devoted to him, Archas is carried off to torture. The infuriated troops attack the palace, and then march away to join the Tartars, but are brought back to submission by Archas, fresh from the rack. The repentant duke marries Honora, daughter of Archas. The identity of Alinda, who has been dismissed by Olympia on suspicion of yielding to the duke's advances, is now declared, and the young Archas is married to Olympia.

LOYOLA, St Ignatius, see IGNATIUS LOYOLA, ST.

LUBBOCK, Percy (1879–1965), critic and biographer, whose works include *Earlham* (1922), an account of his own Norfolk childhood holidays; *Roman Pictures* (1923), which describes an English tourist's responses to Rome; *Shades of Eton* (1923), recollections of his schooldays; and *Portrait of Edith Wharton* (1947). He was a friend of H. *James, and edited a selection of his letters (1920); also of A. C. *Benson, a selection from whose diary he edited (1926). His *The Craft of Fiction* (1921), which analyses the techniques of *Tolstoy, *Flaubert, James, etc., appears to have been closely studied by G. *Greene, who describes it as an 'admirable primer' in *Ways of Escape* (1980).

LUCAN (Marcus Annaeus Lucanus) (AD 39–65), a Roman poet of Spanish origin, the brother of *Seneca. Favoured by Nero, then estranged from him, Lucan joined Piso's conspiracy and was forced on its discovery to commit suicide. The only one of his works to have survived is a historical epic in ten books about the Civil Wars called the *Pharsalia* or the *Bellum Civile*. This work shows he had a remarkable skill in the depiction of character, a mastery of epigram, and a passionate love of freedom, but he set no limits on his unruly imagination and liking for bombast. He was widely read in the Middle Ages, and his influence can be felt in the poetry and drama of the English Renaissance, particularly on Senecan tragedy. *Dryden thought him lacking in artistic judgement, but *Shelley and *Macaulay were firm admirers. There are

important translations by A. *Gorges, T. *May, and N. *Rowe.

LUCAS, E(dward) V(errall) (1868–1938), journalist and essayist. He acquired much of his education working in a Brighton bookshop, and thereafter wrote prolifically on a great variety of subjects, including art, literature, and travel. His works include biographies, novels, and romances (such as *Over Bemerton's*, 1908, set over an antiquarian bookshop); he edited the works and letters of Charles and Mary *Lamb (1903–35) and many popular anthologies, contributed to *Punch, and was a member of its staff for some time. His autobiographical *Reading, Writing and Remembering* (1932) describes some odd corners of the book world, and a life which combined hard work and amateur inaccuracy.

LUCAS, F(rank) L(aurence) (1894–1967), scholar, critic, and poet, educated at Colfe's Grammar School, Lewisham, at Rugby, and at Trinity College, Cambridge; he became a fellow of King's, Cambridge. His critical works include *Tragedy in Relation to Aristotle's Poetics* (1927) and *The Decline and Fall of the Romantic Ideal* (1936), and he edited an edition of J. *Webster (4 vols, 1927). He also published several volumes of verse and translations from the classics, and edited various anthologies.

Lucasta, see LOVELACE, RICHARD.

Lucentio, successful suitor of *Bianca in Shakespeare's *The Taming of the Shrew*.

LUCIAN OF SAMOSATA (AD *c*.125–*c*.200), writer of prose satires in Greek. Many of his works are dialogues where mythical or historical figures are placed in ridiculous situations, and the contrast between their traditional dignity and what they are made to say or do becomes a fruitful source of irony. Lucian was popular with the humanists. Sir T. *More put some of his dialogues into Latin, and *Erasmus' mock encomium the *Praise of Folly* made his irony familiar to the whole of Europe. But the piece by Lucian that had perhaps the most influence was *The True History* which claimed to describe a visit to the moon and inspired a long series of imaginary voyages from J. *Hall's *Mundus Alter et Idem* (1605) to S. Butler's *Erewhon* (1872), Swift's *Gulliver's Travels* (1726) being the most eminent example of the genre. Among modern authors, *Fielding has been Lucian's greatest champion.

LUCIE-SMITH, (John) Edward Mackenzie (1933–), poet and art critic, born in Jamaica. *A Tropical Childhood and Other Poems* appeared in 1961, and in the early 1960s Lucie-Smith was associated with the *Group, but since then has moved more towards literary journalism; his works include various editions of contemporary poetry, works of art history and criticism, a life of *Joan of Arc (1976), *The Burnt Child* (autobiography, 1975), etc.

Lucifera, in Spenser's *Faerie Queene* (I. iv. 12), the symbol of baseless pride and worldliness.

Lucina, in *Orlando innamorato* and *Orlando furioso*, a lady in the power of a cruel monster called an orc, released by *Mandricardo and *Gradasso.

Lucius, (1) a mythical king of Britain, supposed to have been the first to receive Christianity: see Spenser, *The Faerie Queene* (II. x. 53); (2) Lucius (Iberius) is the Roman emperor who demands tribute from King Arthur, who makes war on Rome (in e.g. Malory's Second Romance in Vinaver's edition); in *Malory he is slain by Arthur, in other versions by Gawain. In *Geoffrey of Monmouth's *History* he is slain by an unknown hand when on the territorial offensive against Arthur. (3) Brutus' page in Shakespeare's *Julius Caesar*; (4) a character in his *Timon of Athens*; (5) a character in his *Titus Andronicus*; (6) in his *Cymbeline*, Caius Lucius is 'General of the Roman Forces'.

Luck of Barry Lyndon, The, a satirical *historical novel by *Thackeray, published in *Fraser's Magazine* 1844, republished under the title *The Memoirs of Barry Lyndon, Esquire, by Himself* (1852, New York).

It is the picaresque story of an Irish adventurer who unconsciously reveals his villainy while attempting self-justification. Redmond Barry flees from Ireland after a duel, having been tricked into believing he has killed his opponent. He serves in the Seven Years War, first in the English, then in the Prussian, army. He is set to spy upon the Chevalier de Balibari, who turns out to be his uncle Cornelius Barry. The two set up as card-sharpers, and Barry becomes a successful gambler and man of fashion. He marries a wealthy, foolish widow, the countess of Lyndon, and takes her name. He spends her fortune and ill-treats her and her son, showing affection only to his old mother and his own son Bryan, whom he indulges until the boy is killed in a riding accident. Finally the countess, with the help of her son Viscount Bullingdon, now grown up and no longer susceptible to his stepfather's bullying, is released from Barry's hold over her. Barry is forced to live abroad on a pension, and when left penniless after the countess's death ends his life miserably in the Fleet Prison, prematurely senile and cared for by his devoted old mother. The novel was filmed in 1975 by Stanley Kubrick.

Lucky Jim, a novel by K. *Amis.

Lucrece, The Rape of, see RAPE OF LUCRECE, THE.

Lucretia, or **Lucrece,** a celebrated Roman lady, daughter of Lucretius and wife of Tarquinius Collatinus, whose beauty inflamed the passion of Sextus (son of Tarquin, king of Rome), who raped her. Lucretia, after informing her father and husband of what had passed and entreating them to avenge her indignities, took her own life. The outrage committed by Sextus, coupled with the oppression of the king, led to the expulsion of the Tarquins from Rome, and the introduction of republican government. See also RAPE OF LUCRECE, THE.

LUCRETIUS, (Titus Lucretius Carus) (probably c.99–55 BC), Roman poet. His chief work is a philosophical poem in hexameters, in six books, *De Rerum Natura*. He adopts the atomic theory of the universe of *Epicurus, and seeks to show that the course of the world can be explained without resorting to divine intervention, his object being to free mankind from terror of the gods. The work is marked by passages of great poetical beauty. Echoes of Lucretius can be found in *Spenser, *Hobbes, *Dryden, who produced some vigorous translations, and *Shelley; but the finest poem inspired by his work is *Tennyson's 'Lucretius' (1869).

Lucy poems, the, name given to a group of poems by *Wordsworth, most of which were written in Germany in the exceptionally cold winter of 1798–9. 'She dwelt among the untrodden ways' and 'Strange fits of passion have I known' were sent to *Coleridge in a letter, as was 'A slumber did my spirit seal'; 'Three years she grew in sun and shower' was written a little later, in the spring. All four were published in the *Lyrical Ballads* of 1800. A fifth poem, 'I travelled among unknown men', was sent in a letter in 1801 to Mary Hutchinson (later Wordsworth's wife), and published in 1807. The poems are remarkable for their lyric intensity and purity, and the identity of Lucy has aroused much speculation; in 'Strange Fits of Passion' she appears to be identified with Dorothy *Wordsworth (who was with him in Germany), but in other poems she is presented as having died. Coleridge reflected that, 'Most probably, in some gloomier moment he had fancied the moment in which his sister might die' (Letter to T. Poole, 1799). The name Lucy is used in the ballad 'Lucy Gray' also written in Germany and published in 1800, where it is also associated with death and solitude. See also H. W. Garrod's essay on 'Wordsworth's Lucy' in *Wordsworth* (1927).

Lucy Snowe, the narrator of *Villette*.

Lud, a mythical king of Britain, according to *Geoffrey of Monmouth's *History* (i. 17) the eldest brother of *Cassivelaunus. He built walls around the city of Brutus (Trinovantum) and renamed it Caerlud (Lud's city) from which derives its modern name London. Geoffrey says that *Gildas recounts at length the quarrel that ensued between Lud and his brother Nennius because of the impiety of renaming their father's city.

Luddites, a band of English craftsmen and labourers, organized 1811–16, who felt their livelihoods threatened by machinery and set about its destruction. The name is said to have come from Ned Ludd, who lived about 1779, and who in a rage smashed two frames of a 'stockinger'. Luddites appear in *Shirley* by C. Brontë, and *Byron wrote 'A Song for the Luddites', published

1830. The term is now commonly applied to any person who resists technological change.

LUDLOW, Edmund (?1617–92), Puritan general and regicide, author of *Memoirs*, first printed 1698–9, which cover the course of the Civil War and the Protectorate, and his own flight to Geneva in 1660. He died at Vevey.

Ludus Coventriae, see MYSTERY PLAYS.

LUKÁCS, Georg (1885–1971), Hungarian critic and philosopher. He was born in Budapest, the son of a Jewish banker, and studied at Berlin and Heidelberg, where he wrote *The Theory of the Novel* (1916) under the philosophical influence of *Hegel. Returning to Hungary, he became a communist, serving as an education commissar under the short-lived revolutionary government of 1918–19; then went into exile in Vienna, where he wrote his major work of Marxist political philosophy, *History and Class Consciousness* (1923). After moving back to Berlin, he spent the period 1933–45 in Moscow, where he engaged in debates in *Marxist literary criticism and wrote his major literary study *The Historical Novel* (1955). This work examines the historical awareness of W. *Scott, *Balzac, and other 19th-cent. authors. After the Second World War, he returned to Hungary as professor at the University of Budapest and as a member of the national assembly. He took part in the Nagy government of 1956, and was sent into exile in Romania when the Soviet invasion removed it. He was allowed to return as a private scholar, devoting himself to a long work on aesthetics. The most influential of Marxist critics, he valued highly the 'bourgeois' tradition of fictional *realism for its understanding of social and historical dynamics. While distancing himself from the official doctrine of *Socialist Realism, he deplored the alleged nihilism of *Modernist experimentation in literature, notably in *The Meaning of Contemporary Realism* (1958).

LULLY, Raymond (Raimon Lull) (*c*.1235–1315), a Catalan born in Majorca, who, after visions of Christ crucified, became a Franciscan, a mystic, a philosopher, a missionary to the Arabs, an author of controversial treatises, and a poet. He urged on the Council of Vienne the establishment of schools for missionary languages and obtained a decree for the foundation of chairs of Hebrew, Greek, Chaldee, and Arabic at various universities (including Oxford; *Rashdall, ii. 459). He died of wounds received in a missionary crusade in North Africa, undertaken in his 80th year, after he had been twice expelled from Barbary. Most of his writing was in Latin, but he was the first great writer of poetry and prose fiction in Catalan.

Lumpkin, Tony, a character in Goldsmith's *She Stoops to Conquer.*

Luria, a tragedy in blank verse by R. *Browning, published 1846, together with *A Soul's Tragedy*, as No. VIII of *Bells and Pomegranates*. It was written,

Browning told Elizabeth Barrett (see BROWNING, E. B.), 'for a purely imaginary stage', and is set in the 15th cent. during the conflict between Florence and Pisa, though the actual episode is unhistorical. The plot concerns the fall of the noble-hearted Florentine commander Luria, a Moorish mercenary (Browning acknowledged the influence of *Othello) who, at the height of his triumph, is falsely accused of plotting a coup against the Republic. The failure of political idealism, consummated and transcended by a heroic death, relates the play to Browning's earlier *Sordello.*

LURIE, Alison (1926–   ), American novelist and critic, born in Chicago, and for some years a member of the English department at Cornell. Her sharply satiric and sociologically observant novels include *Love and Friendship* (1962), *Imaginary Friends* (1967), and *The War between the Tates* (1974), a *campus novel involving student politics, teenage revolt, and marital anguish and infidelity. *Foreign Affairs* (1985) brings to England two Americans, middle-aged scholar of children's literature, Vinnie Miner, and handsome academic Fred Turner, where both find a kind of romance. *The Truth about Lorin Jones* (1988) is a novel of biographical quest, *Women and Ghosts* (1994) is a collection of short stories, and *The Last Resort* (1998) is a benign comedy of death and love set in Key West, Florida, where Jenny Walker, the hitherto docile wife of an ageing eco-celebrity professor, finds herself happily involved in a lesbian affair: it reintroduces characters from earlier novels, including the long-running literary critic, L. D. Zimmern, who first appeared in *Real People* (1969) *Truth and Consequences* (2005) is a campus novel dealing with the effects of chronic pain on relationships and the creative process.

Lusiads, The, see CAMÕES.

Lussurioso, a character in *The Revenger's Tragedy.*

LUTHER, Martin (1483–1546), the leader of the Reformation in Germany. He was born of humble parents at Eisleben, and entered the Augustinian order. As a monk he visited Rome, and his experience of the corruption in high ecclesiastical places influenced his future career. He attacked the principle of papal indulgences by nailing his famous *Theses* to the door of the church at Wittenberg, and as a consequence the papal ban was pronounced on him (1521) at the Diet of Worms. He left the monastic order and married, and devoted himself to forming the League of Protestantism. His chief literary work, apart from polemical treatises, was his translation into German of the Old and New Testaments, known as the Lutheran Bible (1534; portions had appeared earlier). He also composed hymns of great popularity in Germany, notably 'Ein' feste Burg'.

Luther's power lay in these hymns of joy and strength and in his revival of the doctrine of justification by the faith of the individual, implying religious liberty and attacking the scandal of indulgences.

He is the subject of a play by J. *Osborne, *Luther* (1961), which traces his career from 1506, when he is received into the Augustinian Order of Eremites, to 1530, when, married, he has settled into 'the tired pain of middle age'.

LUTTRELL, Henry (?1765–1851), wit and member of the *Holland House circle, author of clever and lively verses, including *Advice to Julia*, admired by *Byron.

LUTTRELL, Narcissus (1657–1732), annalist and bibliographer. He compiled *A Brief Historical Relation of State Affairs from September 1678 to April 1714*, published in 1857 (6 vols), after *Macaulay had drawn attention to the manuscript in All Souls College, Oxford. His collection of pamphlets (1679–1722), all annotated with the first date of issue, is a valuable resource for book history and allied fields; see Steven Parks, *The Luttrell File* (1998).

Luve Ron, or 'the Love Song', traditionally but wrongly called 'the Love Rune', a mystical love poem in 210 lines by the Franciscan Thomas de Hales, written probably in the second part of the 13th cent. It describes to a young woman novice the love of Christ and the joy of mystical union with him. Ed. in *An Old English Miscellany* by R. Morris (1872), EETS OS 49, 93–9.

LYALL, Edna, the pseudonym of Ada Ellen Bayly (1857–1903), novelist and supporter of political liberal causes including women's emancipation. Her convictions were expounded in many of her novels. She admired *Bradlaugh, whose life is vaguely reflected in her first success, *We Two* (1884), the sequel to *Donovan* (1882). Her other novels include *In the Golden Days* (1885), which was the last book to be read to *Ruskin on his deathbed, and *Doreen* (1895), which strongly states the case for Home Rule for Ireland, and won praise from *Gladstone.

Lycidas, a pastoral elegy by *Milton, written 1637, at Horton, published the following year. It is a pastoral elegy on the death of Edward *King, a fellow of Christ's College, Cambridge, who had been a student there at the same time as Milton, though not, it would appear, a close friend. Like Milton himself, he had aspirations as a poet and as a clergyman. He was drowned while crossing from Chester Bay to Dublin, his ship having struck a rock and foundered in calm weather. Milton, in lamenting his premature death and the uncertainty of life, suggests deep anxieties about his own ambitions and unfulfilled promise; his apparent digression when, in the voice of St Peter, he violently attacks the unworthy clergy whose 'hungry Sheep look up, and are not fed' (a passage which unites the Christian pastoral tradition with the pagan) may refer to his mixed feelings about and delay in entering the ministry. The poem ends with a moving expression of faith in resurrection and redemption. It has been subjected to innumerable conflicting interpretations, but most critics agree that it is one of the finest elegies in the English language, and a work of great originality.

LYDGATE, John (?1370–1449), born in Lydgate, Suffolk, and admitted to the monastery of Bury St Edmunds in about 1385. He was in Paris in about 1426, and was briefly abbot of Hatfield Broadoak in Essex shortly before that; otherwise he spent nearly all his life in the monastery at Bury. He is one of the most voluminous of all English poets, with a corpus of well over 100,000 lines. Of his more readable poems, most were written in the first decade of the 15th cent. in a Chaucerian vein: *The Complaint of the Black Knight* (originally called *A Complaynt of a Loveres Lyfe* and modelled on Chaucer's *The Book of the Duchess*); *The Temple of Glas* (indebted to *The House of Fame*); *The Floure of Curtesy* (like *The Parliament of Fowls*, a Valentine's Day poem); and the allegorical *Reason and Sensuality*. His short poems tend to be the best; as he got older, his poems grew progressively longer, and it is on the later poetry that *Ritson's harsh characterization of him is based: 'a voluminous, prosaick and drivelling monk'. His bulkiest works are his *Troy Book* (1412–20), a 30,000-line translation of *Guido delle Colonne; *The Siege of Thebes* (1420–2), translated from a French prose redaction of the *Roman de Thebes; The Pilgrimage of Man* (1426–30), translated from Deguileville, which comprises 24,000 lines of octosyllabic couplets; and, last and longest, *The Fall of Princes* (1431–8), which is a translation in 36,000 lines of a French version of *Boccaccio's *De Casibus Virorum Illustrium*. There have been some recent attempts, notably by D. A. Pearsall, to re-elevate the reputation of Lydgate to the stature he enjoyed up to the 17th cent., until which time he was almost invariably coupled for praise with *Chaucer and *Gower.

For editions of the various poems and discussion, see D. A. Pearsall, *John Lydgate* (1970), 301; see also A. Renoir, *The Poetry of John Lydgate* (1967); W. F. Schirmer, *John Lydgate: A Study in the Culture of the XVth Century* (in German 1952; trans. A. E. Keep, 1961); there is a convenient selection of *Poems*, ed. J. Norton-Smith (1966).

Lydgate, Tertius, a character in G. Eliot's *Middlemarch*.

LYELL, Sir Charles, see DARWIN, C., and SCIENCE, LITERATURE OF.

LYLY, John (?1554–1606), the grandson of W. *Lily. He was educated possibly at the King's School, Canterbury, then at Magdalen College, Oxford; he studied also at Cambridge. He was MP successively for Hindon, Aylesbury, and Appleby (1589–1601), and supported the cause of the bishops in the *Martin Marprelate controversy in a satirical pamphlet, *Pappe with an Hatchet* (1589). The first part of his *Euphues: The Anatomy of Wit* appeared in 1578, and the second part, *Euphues and His England*, in 1580. Its peculiar style came to be known as 'Euphuism'. Among Lyly's plays, all of which were written for performance by boy actors to courtly audiences, are *Alexander, Campaspe and Diogenes* (see under CAMPASPE, its later title); *Sapho and Phao* (1584); **Endimion* (1591); **Midas* (1592); *Mother Bombie* (1594, see under BUMBY). The attractive songs in the plays, including such well-known lyrics as 'Cupid and my Campaspe played', were first printed in Blount's collected edition of 1632: it is doubtful to what extent they are the work of Lyly. Although *Euphues* was Lyly's most popular and influential work in the Elizabethan period, his plays are now admired for their flexible use of dramatic prose and the elegant patterning of their construction. R. W. Bond edited Lyly's works in 1902, and there is a good study of him by G. K. Hunter, *John Lyly: The Humanist as Courtier* (1962).

LYND, Robert Wilson (1879–1949), journalist and essayist, described by L. *Woolf as 'one of those impeccable journalists who every week for 30 or 40 years turn out an impeccable essay (called in the technical jargon of journalism a "middle") like an impeccable sausage, about anything or everything or nothing' (*Beginning Again*, 1964). Born in Belfast, and educated there at Queen's College, Lynd came to England in 1901, and worked as a freelance journalist before joining the **Daily News* in 1908 to which he contributed until 1947. He was best known for his weekly articles in the *Nation*, then in the **New Statesman*, signed 'Y.Y.', which were collected in various volumes with titles such as *The Pleasures of Ignorance* (1921), *The Green Man* (1928), and *In Defence of Pink* (1937).

LYNDSAY, Sir David, see LINDSAY, SIR D.

Lynet, Linet, Lunet, or the *Saveage Damsel*, in *Malory, is the sister of the lady *Lyones who brings Gareth to fight Ironsyde, liberating Lyones who marries Gareth. Another lady of the same name (also called the Saveage Damsel once) is the Lunete in *Chrétien's *Yvain* (and in the English **Ywain and Gawain*) who is also an intermediary; she commends Ywain to Laudine (Alundyne) whom he marries. Chrétien explains her name by reference to the moon. See GARETH AND LYNETTE.

Lyones, Liones, and, in *Malory, **Lyonesse,** (1) the sister of *Lynet, imprisoned by Ironsyde in the Castle Perilous and freed by *Gareth whom she marries; (2) in Malory, the region of origin of Tristram; the name is also geographical in *Tennyson who makes it the place of the last battle between Arthur and Mordred. It is traditionally said to be a tract of land between the Isles of Scilly and Land's End, now submerged.

Lyonesse, see LYONES.

Lyra Apostolica, a collection of sacred poems contributed originally to the **British Magazine* and reprinted in a separate volume in 1836. The poems, 179 in all, appeared anonymously, the six authors each being designated by a Greek letter: J. W. Bowden (α) contributed six, R. H. *Froude (β) eight, *Keble (γ) 46, *Newman (δ) 109, R. I. Wilberforce (ϵ) one, and I. *Williams (ζ) nine. All the writers were associated with the *Oxford movement.

lyric, lyric poetry, derived from the Greek adjective λυρικός ('for the lyre'), was the name given in ancient Greece to verses sung to a lyre, whether as a solo performance (*Sappho) or by a choir (*Pindar). The Greek lyrists were then imitated in Latin at an artistic level by *Catullus and *Horace, but what appears to have been more important for the development of the genre was the tradition of popular song which existed both in Rome and among the German tribes. This continued to flourish in spite of the Church's disapproval and produced in all the medieval literatures of western Europe a lyric harvest that ranged from hymns to bawdy drinking songs and drew its authors from every social category. In England lyric poems flourished in the Middle English period (in such manuscript collections as the **Harley Lyrics*), and in the 16th-cent. heyday of humanism this already quite sophisticated lyric tradition was enriched by the direct imitation of ancient models and reached perfection in the songbooks and plays of the Elizabethan age. During the next 200 years the link between poetry and music was gradually broken, and the term 'lyric' came to be applied to short poems expressive of a poet's thoughts or feelings, and which could not be classed under another heading. The convention that a poem communicates its author's feelings to a reader reached the high point of its popularity in the Romantic period, but soon after *Baudelaire introduced the modern form of lyric poetry in which the poet seems to struggle to express for his own satisfaction psychic experiences whose nature he at times only half understands: the lyric of *Mallarmé, *Rilke, *Yeats, and T. S. *Eliot.

Lyrical Ballads, with a Few Other Poems, a collection of poems by *Wordsworth and *Coleridge, of which the first edition appeared 1798, the second with new poems and a preface (known as the 1800 edition) Jan. 1801, and a third 1802.

The book was a landmark of English *Romanticism and the beginning of a new age. The poems were written largely in Somerset, and Coleridge, in the *Biographia Literaria* (ch. xiv), describes the nature of their collaboration: 'it was agreed that my endeavours should be directed to persons and characters supernatural or at least romantic . . . Mr Wordsworth, on the other hand, was to propose to himself as his object, to give the charm of novelty to things of everyday.' Coleridge's contributions to the first edition were *The Rime of the *Ancient Mariner*, 'The Foster-Mother's Tale', 'The Nightingale', and 'The Dungeon'; Wordsworth's include ballads and narratives such as 'The Thorn', *'The Idiot Boy', and 'Simon Lee, the Old Huntsman', and more personal poems such as 'Lines Written in Early Spring' and 'Lines Written a Few Miles above *Tintern Abbey'. They appeared with a brief 'Advertisement' by Wordsworth, stating his theory of *poetic diction and attacking the 'gaudy and inane phraseology of many modern writers'; his views were much expanded in his important preface to the second edition, and enlarged again in 1802. The poems themselves, with their 'low' subjects and language and their alleged banality and repetitions, were subjected to much ridicule, as was Wordsworth's confident and unperturbed maintaining of his own position, which had little of the defensive in its attitude. The second volume of the second edition added many of Wordsworth's most characteristic works, including the so-called *'Lucy poems', 'The Old Cumberland Beggar', and *'Michael, a Pastoral'.

Lysander, a character in Shakespeare's *A Midsummer Night's Dream.

LYTTELTON, George, first Baron Lyttelton (1709–73), a prominent politician, and an opponent of Sir R. *Walpole, also a friend of *Pope, *Shenstone, and *Fielding, and a liberal patron of literature. It is he whom Thomson addresses in *The Seasons and who procured the poet a pension; he also contributed a stanza to *The Castle of Indolence. He assisted *Dodsley in editing the celebrated Collection of Poems (1748–58), to which he contributed. Other works include Dialogues of the Dead (1760), and a history of Henry II (1767–71). Of the Dialogues, the last three were by Mrs *Montagu. He was caricatured by Smollett as Scragg in *Peregrine Pickle.

LYTTON, Edward Earle Lytton Bulwer-, see BULWER-LYTTON.

LYTTON, Edward Robert Bulwer, first earl of Lytton (1831–91), son of E. *Bulwer-Lytton, was educated at Harrow and Bonn; his childhood was overshadowed by the quarrels of his parents, and he relied much on the protective interest of his father's friend J. *Forster, who encouraged his literary efforts. After a successful career in the diplomatic service he became viceroy of India (1876–80), where his 'Forward' policy aroused much opposition. He published several volumes of verse, at first under the pseudonym 'Owen Meredith'. Clytemnestra, The Earl's Return, The Artist and Other Poems (1855) was followed by The Wanderer (1858); both show talent, and the Wanderer's mildly *Byronic and lyrical continental adventures had some success. His later volumes, which include two long verse romances, are marred by prolixity and facile versification. His own favourite, King Poppy: A Story without End, an obscure, fanciful, and lengthy blank verse allegory, was circulated privately to his friends in 1875, constantly revised over many years, and published in 1892. Lytton seems to have found his dual career as statesman and poet problematic, and to have sensed his own failure in the latter role: in 'Last Words of a Sensitive Second-Rate Poet', published in Chronicles and Characters (1868), the poor reception of which much distressed him, he writes, 'Talk not of genius baffled. Genius is master of man. | Genius does what it must, and Talent does what it can.' There is a critical biography by A. B. Harlan (1946).

M

MABBE, James (1572–?1642), educated at, and fellow of, Magdalen College, Oxford. He became a lay prebendary of Wells. He is remembered for his translations of Fernando de Rojas's *Celestina and of The Spanish Ladye*, one of *Cervantes's 'Exemplary Novels'. Mabbe Hispanicized his name as 'Puede-Ser' (may-be).

Mabinogion, The, strictly, the first four Welsh tales contained in the collection of Lady Charlotte Guest, made in 1838–49. The four are preserved in two Welsh manuscripts: The White Book of Rhydderch (1300–25) and The Red Book of Hergest (1375–1425). 'Mab' is the word for 'youth', but, even by the time of the medieval title, it is likely that the word meant nothing much more precise than 'story'. In the four stories it is likely that the original common element was the hero Pryderi; as they survive their subjects are (1) Pwyll, the father of Pryderi; (2) Branwen, the daughter of Llyr and her marriage to the Irish king Matholwch; (3) Manawyddan, the son of Llyr and his association with Pryderi; (4) the death of Pryderi in battle with the nephews of Math who had cheated him. There is no mention of *Arthur in these four branches of the Mabinogion proper; but five of the other seven tales published by Guest from The Red Book of Hergest deal indirectly with him: *The Lady of the Fountain; Peredur, Gereint,* three romances from French originals; *Culhwch and Olwen;* and *The Dream of Rhonabwy;* the latter two native tales are perhaps the most appealing of the collection. The other two tales in Guest's collection are *The Dream of Macsen Wledig* and *Lludd and Llefelys.*

Trans. by Gwyn Jones and Thomas Jones (1949). *Math vab Mathonwy* by W. J. Gruffydd (1928); I. L. Foster, chs 4 and 16 in R. S. Loomis (ed.), *Arthurian Literature in the Middle Ages* (1959).

macaronic verse, a term used to designate a burlesque form of verse in which vernacular words are introduced into a Latin context with Latin terminations and in Latin constructions and *loosely* to any form of verse in which two or more languages are mingled together [OED]. The chief writer of macaronic verse was *Folengo.

MACAULAY, Catherine, afterwards Graham (1731–91), republican historian, whose *History of England* in eight volumes appeared 1763–83, and in a French translation 1791–2. Dr *Johnson mocked her radical views, but she was much admired in France. Mary *Wollstonecraft praised her highly, and *Lecky was to write with respect of her ability.

MACAULAY, Dame (Emilie) Rose (1881–1958), novelist, essayist, and travel writer, whose many works include *Potterism* (1920), *They Were Defeated* (1932), both fiction, and *Pleasures of Ruins* (1953). Her best-known novels, *The World My Wilderness* (1950) and *The Towers of Trebizond* (1956), appeared after a decade in which she wrote no fiction, and followed her return to the Anglican faith, from which she had been long estranged through her love for a married man who died in 1942. Her religious revival was inspired partly by the Revd J. H. C. Johnson, and her correspondence with him was published after her death in two volumes, 1961–2, as *Letters to a Friend.*

MACAULAY, Thomas Babington (1800–59), politician and historian, son of the philanthropist and reformer Zachary Macaulay. After graduating at Trinity College, Cambridge, he was called to the bar, but his essay on *Milton for the *Edinburgh Review* in Aug. 1825 brought him instant fame, and for the next 20 years he wrote many articles on historical and literary topics (Horace *Walpole, Chatham (*Pitt), Sir F. *Bacon, etc.) for the *Review.* In 1830 he entered Parliament as a Whig, first for Calne (Wiltshire), then for Leeds, and took an active part in the passing of the Reform Bill. But in 1834, in order to achieve financial independence, he took up a post on the Supreme Council of India, where his Minutes on Law and Education had a decisive influence on the development of the subcontinent. On his return in 1838 he began to write a detailed history of England from the revolution of 1688. He was elected MP for Edinburgh in 1839 and again in 1852; he was a secretary at war 1839–41 and paymaster-general 1846–7. But by now his literary fame was such that everything he published was a 'dazzling success', beginning in 1842 with *Lays of Ancient Rome.* His collected *Essays Critical and Historical* (1843) sold steadily down the century. *Acton called them 'A key to half the prejudices of our age'; but their urgent, declamatory style, their self-confidence and biting wit, endeared them to the reading public all over the world. His *History of England* (vols i–ii, 1849; vols iii–iv, 1855) was more restrained and more deeply researched. Macaulay took an immense pride in the English constitution, and shared with many Victorians an exaltation at the material advances of the 19th cent., under the shadow of the French Revolution, and the purpose of the *History* was strictly defensive—to demonstrate that revolution on the continental model was unnecessary in England because of the statesmanlike precautions taken in 1688. He used a wide range of manuscript

sources with great skill. He also affected an interest in
social history, though this was focused on his superficial and discredited chapter III, on 'The Condition of
England in 1685'. He acknowledged a great debt to Sir
W. *Scott, which is evident in his habit of exploring on
the ground all the places in which his narrative was set.
His descriptive power was one of his great assets;
another was the narrative momentum he was able to
achieve. The *History* was one of the best-sellers of the
century, and it has never since gone out of print. It
brought him wealth and, in 1857, a peerage. He at first
intended to take the *History* up to 1830, but when he
died in 1859 he had only reached 1697. Macaulay was
always criticized for his philistinism and his overweening self-confidence; Lord Melbourne once said, 'I
wish I was as cocksure of anything as Tom Macaulay is
of everything.' Certainly his literary brilliance has
always been such as to disarm criticism, which explains Lord Acton's paradoxical judgement: 'He remains to me one of the greatest of all writers and
masters, although I think him base, contemptible and
odious.'

He was the subject of one of the best Victorian
biographies, by his nephew, Sir G. O. *Trevelyan
(1876). See also John Clive, *Thomas Babington Macaulay: The Shaping of the Historian* (1973). The best
literary study is by Jane Millgate (1973). His letters
have been edited by Thomas Pinney (6 vols, 1974–81).

Macbeth, a tragedy by *Shakespeare, probably written and first performed at the *Globe in 1606, but not
printed until the First *Folio (1623). The text is an
unusually brief one, and has often been thought to
contain some non-Shakespearian material, probably
by *Middleton. Two songs certainly by him were added
to the play. It may have been performed before James I,
who had a strong interest in witches and was supposedly a descendant of Banquo.

Macbeth and Banquo, generals of Duncan, king of
Scotland, returning from a victorious campaign
against rebels, encounter three weird sisters, or
witches, upon a heath, who prophesy that Macbeth
shall be thane of Cawdor, and king hereafter, and that
Banquo shall beget kings though he be none. Immediately afterwards comes the news that the king has
created Macbeth thane of Cawdor. Stimulated by the
prophecy, and spurred on by Lady Macbeth, Macbeth
murders Duncan, who is on a visit to his castle.
Duncan's sons Malcolm and Donalbain escape, and
Macbeth assumes the crown. To defeat the prophecy of
the witches regarding Banquo, he orders the murder of
Banquo and his son Fleance, but the latter escapes.
Haunted by the ghost of Banquo, Macbeth consults the
weird sisters, and is told to beware of Macduff, the
thane of Fife; that none born of woman has power to
harm Macbeth; and that he never will be vanquished
till Birnam Wood shall come to Dunsinane. Learning
that Macduff has joined Malcolm, who is gathering an
army in England, he surprises the castle of Macduff and

causes Lady Macduff and her children to be slaughtered. Lady Macbeth goes mad and dies. The army of
Malcolm and Macduff attacks Macbeth; passing
through Birnam Wood every man cuts a bough and
under these 'leavy screens' marches on Dunsinane.
Macduff, who was 'from his mother's womb|Untimely
ripp'd', kills Macbeth. Malcolm is hailed king of
Scotland.

MacBETH, George Mann (1932–92), poet, born in
Lanarkshire, but educated in England. From 1955 to
1976 he produced programmes on poetry and the arts
for the BBC, and he has also edited various anthologies.
He was a member of the *Group during the 1950s, and
in the 1960s was associated with the vogue for poetry
in performance. His early work was experimental, and
at times macabre and violent in its preoccupations;
later collections show (in his own words) fewer 'comic
and performance and experimental elements' (foreword to *Poems from Oby*, 1982). His works include *A
Form of Words* (1954), *The Colour of Blood* (1967), and
Collected Poems 1958–1970 (1971). He has also published novels.

Macbeth, Lady, ambitious wife of Macbeth in Shakespeare's play; a favourite role among 18th- and 19th-
cent. actresses, for example Mrs *Siddons. L. C.
*Knights's essay 'How many children had Lady
Macbeth?' (1933) is a teasing riposte to the sort of
biographical speculation favoured by A. C. *Bradley.

McCABE, Patrick (1955–   ), Irish novelist. A year after
publishing a children's story, *The Adventures of Shay
Mouse* (1985), McCabe published his first novel, *Music
on Clinton Street* (1986), set in rural Ireland during the
1960s and 1970s, a time when Irish life was beginning
to feel the encroaching presence of American culture.
This was followed by *Carn* (1989) and *The Butcher Boy*
(1992), a disturbing story told in the voice of Francis
Brady, an engaging but disturbed (and ultimately
homicidal) boy in an unnamed small town in Ireland;
we follow his loosening hold on reality and increasing
inability to respond appropriately to the society into
which he was born. McCabe's virtuoso use of his
character's voice plays back and forth between humour
and horror, while remaining realistic and compelling
throughout. It is a technique McCabe attempts to
develop in *Breakfast on Pluto* (1998); here the principal
character is Patrick 'Pussy' Braden, a transvestite boy
who escapes to London, only to become involved in
prostitution and the affairs of the IRA.

MacCAIG, Norman Alexander (1910–96), Scottish
poet, born and educated in Edinburgh, who worked
for many years as a schoolmaster, and afterwards as a
lecturer at the University of Stirling. His first volume of
poetry, *Far Cry* (1943), was followed by many others
which (notably in the 1960s) showed an increasing
discipline and sensitivity; they include *Measures*
(1965), *Rings on a Tree* (1968), and *A Man in My
Position* (1969). His *Selected Poems* appeared in 1971,

and he also edited two anthologies of Scottish poetry, *Honour'd Shade* (1959) and (with Alexander Scott) *Contemporary Scottish Verse 1959–1969* (1970). Much of his own poetry was inspired by the landscapes of the West Highlands and the life of Edinburgh, but his inspiration is less exclusively Scottish than that of many of his contemporaries. Other volumes: *The Equal Skies* (1980), *Collected Poems* (1985, republished 1990, revised and expanded edition 1993), *Voice-Over* (1988).

MacCARTHY, Sir (Charles Otto) Desmond (1877–1952), educated at Cambridge, where he was an *Apostle, and later on friendly terms with the *Bloomsbury Group. He is remembered largely for his perceptive theatre criticism, some of it collected in *The Court Theatre, 1904–7* (1907), *Drama* (1940), and *Shaw* (1951). He described himself as a 'literary journalist', was dramatic critic then literary editor of the *New Statesman* (1913–27), and from 1928 to 1952 wrote weekly for the *Sunday Times*. He also edited *Life and Letters* from 1928 to 1933.

McCARTHY, Mary (1912–89), novelist, short story writer, and critic, born in Seattle and orphaned at the age of 6. She was raised by an aunt and uncle and two sets of grandparents of Catholic, Jewish, and Protestant backgrounds, a mixture that she describes in *Memoirs of a Catholic Girlhood* (1957). After graduating from Vassar she worked as a drama critic, then taught for some years at Bard College and Sarah Lawrence College, experiences she used in her satirical *campus novel *The Groves of Academe* (NY 1952, London 1953), which describes the political persecutions of the McCarthy period. Her first novel, *The Company She Keeps* (1942), is a portrait of a bohemian intellectual, and *The Oasis* (1949, London 1950, as *A Source of Embarrassment*) describes the failure of a New England utopia. *Cast a Cold Eye* (1950, short stories) and *A Charmed Life* (1955, novel) were followed by *The Group* (1963), a study of the lives and careers of eight Vassar girls, which caused some stir when published in England because of its frank and amusing descriptions of contraception, breastfeeding, and other gynaecological matters. She published two volumes of reportage, *Vietnam* (1967) and *Hanoi* (1968), protesting against American involvement in Vietnam. *Birds of America* (1971) is a novel written from the point of view of an idealistic, ecology-conscious young American boy living in Paris and Rome, deploring the effects of the growing tourist industry. *Cannibals and Missionaries* (1980) deals with a hijacking in Holland, in which a group of art-collectors and would-be philanthropists are held hostage by terrorists; it explores the conflicting values of art, élitism, and democracy. She also published several volumes of essays and criticism. Her second husband was Edmund *Wilson. Her correspondence with Hannah *Arendt was published in 1995.

McCULLERS, Carson née Smith (Lula) (1917–67),

American novelist and short story writer, born in Georgia, where most of her works are set. These include *The Heart Is a Lonely Hunter* (1940), *Reflections in a Golden Eye* (1941), *The Member of the Wedding* (1946; dramatized by the author, 1950), and a collection, *The Ballad of the Sad Café* (1951), of which the title story was dramatized by *Albee, 1963. Critics have detected *Gothic elements in her work, which is frequently tinged with the macabre; she herself wrote that her central theme was 'spiritual isolation'.

MacDIARMID, Hugh, the pseudonym of Christopher Murray Grieve (1892–1978), poet and critic, a founder (in 1928) of the National Party of Scotland. In 1922, influenced by the prose experimentation of *Ulysses, he adopted the pseudonym and began to write lyrics in a synthetic Scots that drew on various dialects and fortified the oral idiom with words preserved in *Jamieson's etymological dictionary. MacDiarmid deplored the sentimentality of post-Burnsian verse and wanted to renew the poetic tradition once carried by 'makars' like *Dunbar: 'Not Burns—Dunbar!' was one of his many mottoes. His masterpiece, *A Drunk Man Looks at the Thistle* (1926), presents a vision that remakes Scotland in the MacDiarmidian image; a drunk man comes to consciousness on a hillside and has to contend with the huge thistle that confronts him symbolically in the moonlight before he can resume his odyssey to the arms of his wife Jean. In the process the alcoholic spirit wears off and is replaced by a spiritual awareness of what Scotland can be: 'The thistle rises and forever will, | Getherin' the generations under't. | This is the monument o' a' they were, | And a' they hoped and wondered.' MacDiarmid's Scots literary renaissance of the 1920s was followed by his political poetry of the 1930s; in 1931 he published his *First Hymn to Lenin* and thereby initiated the leftist verse of the decade. Expelled from the National Party in 1933, he joined the Communist Party the following year: in 1938 he was expelled from the Communist Party, which he rejoined in 1956. A powerful polemicist, MacDiarmid delighted in causing controversy: his autobiography *Lucky Poet* (1943) offended the officials of his native Langholm, so he was never offered the freedom of the burgh, despite his achievements. MacDiarmid scored some of his greatest poetic triumphs in English, albeit a synthetic English. His long meditative poem 'On a Raised Beach', from *Stony Limits* (1934), is a subtle statement of the MacDiarmidian metaphysic: 'I will have nothing interposed | Between my sensitiveness and the barren but beautiful reality.' His later work comprises a series of long, linguistically dense, poems amounting to a modern epic of the Celtic consciousness. MacDiarmid's *Complete Poems 1920–1976*, edited by Michael Grieve and W. R. Aitken, appeared (posthumously) in 1978. See Alan Bold, *MacDiarmid: The Terrible Crystal* (1983) and *The Letters of Hugh MacDiarmid* (ed. A. Bold, 1984). (See also SCOTS.)

MacDONALD, George (1824–1905), son of a Scottish miller, was briefly a Congregationalist minister, but was rejected by his congregation, and thereafter struggled to support his family of 11 children by writing. In his own day he was celebrated chiefly as poet, preacher, and lecturer, and as the author of numerous novels, including *David Elginbrod* (1863), *Alec Forbes of Howglen* (1865), and *Robert Falconer* (1868), often with banal melodramatic plots and cardboard villains, but illuminated by compassionate affection for humanity and nature. The Scottish setting of his best novels helped to found the *'Kailyard school' of fiction. MacDonald is now best known for his children's stories, including *At the Back of the North Wind* (1871) and *The Princess and the Goblin* (1872), memorably illustrated by Arthur Hughes, and for his two allegorical fantasies for adults, *Phantastes* (1858) and *Lilith* (1895), in which he creates dream worlds of power and vivid strangeness, influenced by his study of *Novalis and E. T. A. *Hoffmann, and in turn strongly influencing G. K. *Chesterton, W. H. *Auden, and C. S. *Lewis. There are biographies by Greville MacDonald (*George MacDonald and His Wife*, 1924) and R. H. Reis (1972). (See CHILDREN'S LITERATURE.)

MACDONELL, A. G., see ENGLAND, THEIR ENGLAND.

Macduff and Lady Macduff, characters in Shakespeare's *Macbeth*. Macbeth's murder of Lady Macduff and her children ('What, all my pretty chickens and their dam | At one fell swoop?') precipitates the play's denouement.

McEWAN, Ian (Russell) (1948–), novelist and short story writer, born in Aldershot, the son of an army NCO, educated at the University of Sussex and later at the *University of East Anglia, where he was the first graduate of the new creative writing department. He came to immediate notice with his first short story collections, *First Love, Last Rites* (1975), which won the Somerset *Maugham Award, and *In Between the Sheets* (1977), both of which displayed his gift for the macabre. His first novel, *The Cement Garden* (1978), a *Gothic story about an orphaned family of children, was followed by *The Comfort of Strangers*, a tale of sexual menace, set in Venice (1981), which was adapted for the cinema by Harold *Pinter. *The Child in Time* (1987) concerns the emotional consequences for a couple whose baby daughter is abducted, and explores notion of time and synchronicity. *The Innocent* (1990), subsequently filmed, is based on the true story of the Berlin Tunnel and is set during the early years of Cold War espionage. *Black Dogs* (1992) is a powerful parable of evil in which an English couple on honeymoon in France soon after the Second World War have an encounter with two terrifying dogs. *Enduring Love* (1997) opens with a bravura account of a fatal helium balloon accident, and traces its effects on surviving witnesses. *Amsterdam* won the 1998 *Booker Prize. *Atonement* (2001) covers a long historical time span, from 1935 to 1990, and centres on the Second World War, whereas *Saturday* (2005) concentrates on the events of a single day in London in 2003. McEwan has also written the libretto for Michael Berkeley's anti-nuclear oratorio, *Or Shall We Die?* (1982); a television play, *The Imitation Game* (1981), about the Bletchley Park code-breaking centre during the Second World War; and the screenplay of the film *The Ploughman's Lunch* (1983).

Mac Flecknoe, or *A Satyr upon the True-Blew-Protestant Poet, T. S.*, a *mock-epic poem by *Dryden published 1682, and in a definitive edition, 1684.

The outcome of a series of disagreements, personal, professional, and critical, between Dryden and *Shadwell, the poem represents the latter as heir to the kingdom of poetic dullness, currently governed by the minor writer *Flecknoe. It brilliantly exploits the crudity of Shadwell's farces (notably *The Virtuoso*) and critical writings; while the range of its allusions to 17th-cent. theatre demonstrates the complexity of Dryden's critical thought and, since he satirizes his own work (notably *Tyrannick Love*) as well as Shadwell's, his humility towards the tradition in which he was working. *Mac Flecknoe* was a vital inspiration for Pope's *Dunciad.

McGAHERN, John (1934–), Irish novelist and short story writer, born in Dublin, and educated at University College, Dublin; most of his work is set in Ireland, though he has travelled and worked abroad. His novels are *The Barracks* (1962), *The Dark* (1965), *The Leave-taking* (1974), *The Pornographer* (1979), and *Amongst Women* (1990). He worked in Dublin as a teacher until the publication of *The Dark*, a novel of adolescent sexuality, guilt, and awakening, describing a boy's intense relationship with his widowed father, his schoolteacher, and a priest. McGahern has also published collections of short stories, including *High Ground* (1985); his *Collected Stories* was published in 1992.

McGONAGALL, William (1825 or 1830–1902), the son of an Irish weaver, who attracted a certain following in Edinburgh with his readings in public houses and his broadsheets of topical verse. His naïve and unscanned doggerel continues to entertain, and he now enjoys a reputation as the world's worst poet.

McGOUGH, Roger, (1937–), poet, born in Liverpool, and educated at St Mary's College and the University of Hull. He worked as a teacher before becoming a member of the music/poetry group the Scaffold, best remembered for the hit record 'Lily the Pink' (1969). The emphasis on *performance poetry became a hallmark of his style and in 1967 he published (with *Patten and *Henri) *The Mersey Sound*: this was followed by another group work, *The New Volume* (1983). He has written many volumes of poetry for both adults and children, as well as fiction and plays, distinguished by high spirits, wit, and accessibility:

works include *Watchwords* (1969, poems); *In the Glassroom* (1976, poems) and *The Great Smile Robbery* (1982, children's fiction). His *Selected Poems 1967–1987* appeared in 1989, followed by a second selection, *You at the Back* (1991).

McGrath, John Peter (1935–2002), playwright and director, educated in Mold and at Oxford, whose first success was the play *Events while Guarding the Bofors Gun* (pub. 1966). He founded in 1971 the theatre group 7 : 84, through which he explored and expressed his belief in the possibility of a genuine working-class theatre, characterized by 'directness, comedy, music, emotion, variety, effect, immediacy', and often with a strong local or community interest (*A Good Night Out*, 1981). The group, which later divided into separate English and Scottish companies, presented plays by McGrath himself (including *The Cheviot, the Stag and the Black, Black Oil*, 1974; *Little Red Hen*, 1977; both dealing with Scottish politics) and by others, including *Arden, Trevor Griffiths, and A. *Mitchell. McGrath also wrote, directed, and produced extensively for film and television.

McGrath, Patrick (1950–), novelist, born in London. His father was a superintendent at Broadmoor, and McGrath grew up in the grounds of this institution, surrounded by the criminally insane. His early fiction tended towards the bizarre and neo-Gothic: *Blood and Water* (1988) is a sometimes lurid collection of short stories; *The Grotesque* (1989) a morally serious parody of English *Gothic fiction; and *Spider* (1990) a disconcerting account of a schizophrenic's return to the scene of his brutal London childhood. With Bradford Morrow he co-edited an anthology of the New Gothic in 1991, but his subsequent novels show him moving beyond this genre. *Dr Haggard's Disease* (1993) and *Asylum* (1996) are both studies in romantic obsession: the latter, in a tour de force of unreliable narration, tells of a psychiatrist, Peter Cleave, whose colleague's wife becomes destructively infatuated with one of his most dangerous patients. A film version of *Asylum* (screenplay by playwright Patrick Marber) was released in 2005.

McGUINNESS, Frank (1953–), Irish playwright, born Buncrana, Co. Donegal. Having grown up on the border between the Republic of Ireland and Northern Ireland, McGuinness seems drawn to people isolated by conflict and violence. His first play, the vivid and angry *Factory Girls* (1982), deals with a group of women barricaded into a factory. His next major work, *Observe the Sons of Ulster Marching towards the Somme* (1985), enacts the experience of Ulster loyalists in the First World War, and is remarkable as a Catholic writer's attempt to come to terms with a key myth of Protestant Ireland. The fact that the cast of one play is almost entirely female and the other entirely male reflects both McGuinness's interest in gay themes and the sense of division that also underlies *Mary and Lizzie* (1989), *The Breadman* (1990), and *Someone*

Who'll Watch over Me (1992), which deals with a group of hostages in Beirut.

MACHADO, Antonio (1875–1939), Spanish poet. In his most famous collection, *Campos de Castilla* (1912), he reflects on the landscape of Castile and his childhood in Seville. He published his final volume of poetry, *Nuevas canciones*, in 1924, before turning to prose, adopting a variety of pseudonyms to allow himself to explore more freely a variety of philosophical subjects and tones. Throughout his life he had been a spokesman for the Republican cause, and he died in France in flight from the Fascists. After his death his work was suppressed by Franco, not regaining prominence until the mid-1960s. His poems have inspired numerous English versions, and *The Eyes*, a collection of versions by Don *Paterson, was published in 1999.

MACHAUT, Guillaume de, see GUILLAUME DE MACHAUT.

Macheath, Captain, the hero of Gay's *The Beggar's Opera*.

MACHEN, Arthur Llewellyn (1863–1947), son of a Welsh clergyman, deeply influenced by his lonely childhood, the Welsh landscape, and local folklore. He left for London in 1880 and a period of employment as a cataloguer of diabolistic and occult books introduced him to various secret sects and societies (he later joined the Order of the Golden Dawn of which *Yeats and *Crowley became members). He translated *The Heptameron* (1886) and *The Memoirs of Casanova* (1894) and began writing the mystic, supernatural tales of evil and *horror for which he is best remembered. The most successful of these were written in the 1890s (some were published later), including *The Great God Pan* (1894), *The Hill of Dreams* (1907), and *The Three Impostors* (1895). He spent several years from 1901 as an actor in Sir Frank Benson's Shakespeare Repertory Company and in 1910 joined the London *Evening News*, which led to his rediscovery and the publication in 1923 of the Caerleon Edition of his works. His short story 'The Bowmen', published in the *Evening News* in Sept. 1914, was responsible for the legend of 'The Angels of Mons', which were said to have saved the retreating British forces. Machen's belated recognition came when his creative powers had waned and his later works were less successful. Other works include *Hieroglyphics* (1902, criticism); and *Far off Things* (1922) and *Things Near and Far* (1923), both autobiographical.

MACHIAVELLI, Niccolò (1469–1527), a Florentine dramatist and political theorist. After holding office in the restored Florentine republic and discharging various missions abroad, he was exiled on suspicion of conspiracy against the Medici, but was subsequently restored to some degree of favour. He turned his experience to advantage in his writings, which include *Arte della guerra* (*The Art of War*, written 1517–20; English trans. 1560–2) and a history of Florence (*Storie*

Fiorentine, 1520–5; trans. 1595). His comedy *Mandragola*, probably written in 1518, is a powerful satire. His best-known work was *Il principe* (*The Prince*, written 1513, pub. 1532), a treatise on statecraft by an acute observer of the contemporary political scene with an idealistic vision of an Italian saviour who should expel all foreign usurpers. He teaches that the lessons of the past (of Roman history in particular) should be applied to the present, and that the acquisition and effective use of power may necessitate unethical methods not in themselves desirable. In 1640 Edward Dacres published the first English translation of *The Prince*, but it was well known both by repute and in Italian and Latin texts throughout the previous century. It is repeatedly referred to in Elizabethan drama, and influenced the policy of Thomas *Cromwell, Cecil, and Leicester. It was appreciated critically by F. *Bacon; exploited intelligently by *Marlowe; used guardedly in the Maxims of State wrongly attributed to *Ralegh by *Milton, who in 1658 published the collection as *The Cabinet-Council*. Selected maxims from *Il principe* were translated into French and refuted by Gentillet, a French Huguenot, in 1576; there was an English translation, by Simon Paterick, in 1602.

In Elizabethan and Jacobean drama, Machiavellian villains and anti-heroes abound, appearing in many guises, as pandar, atheist, poisoner, politician, miser, and revenger, and the name of Machiavelli himself is frequently invoked: for example by Gloucester, who resolved in 3 *Henry VI* 'to set the murtherous Machiavel to school' (III. ii. 193), by Flamineo in *The White Devil*, who rejoices in 'the rare trickes of a Machivillian' (V. iii. 193), and in the prologue to *The Jew of Malta* by the spirit of Machiavelli himself. There is a sketch of his character in G. Eliot's *Romola*.

McILVANNEY, William (1936–   ), novelist, poet, and journalist, born in Kilmarnock, Ayrshire, the son of an ex-miner, and educated at Kilmarnock Academy and Glasgow University. His first novels, *Remedy is None* (1967) and *A Gift of Nessus* (1968), were followed by the widely praised *Docherty* (1975), set in the fictional mining town of Graithnock in the first quarter of the 20th cent., drawing on his own family history. The Inspector Jack Laidlaw novels (*Laidlaw*, 1977; *The Papers of Tony Veitch*, 1983; *Strange Loyalties*, 1991), set mainly in Glasgow, have affinities with the work of *Chandler and focus on Laidlaw's subversive outlook and the psychological, social, and political roots of crime. *The Big Man* (1985), a parable of the break-up of working-class communities, tells the story of an ex-miner lured into illegal prize fighting. *Walking Wounded* (1989) is a series of linked stories of drifting lives and diminished dreams, blending angry compassion and black comedy. *The Kiln* (1996) continues the history of the Docherty family. McIlvanney's work is characterized by his socialist perspective, pared-down prose, bleak wit, and a fine ear for the cadences of modern speech.

MacINNES, Colin (1914–76), novelist, the son of singer James McInnes (*sic*: Colin altered the spelling of his name) and Angela *Thirkell, brought up partly in Australia; on his return to England, after a period in art school and (during the war) the army, he embarked on a career as a writer and journalist. His first novel, *To the Victors the Spoils* (1950), was followed by *June in Her Spring* (1952, set in Australia) and the novels for which he is best remembered, *City of Spades* (1957) and *Absolute Beginners* (1959). These describe teenage and black immigrant culture, and the new bohemian underworld of Notting Hill, coffee bars, jazz clubs, drink, and homosexuality. MacInnes called himself an 'anarchist sympathizer' and defended several of the causes of the 1960s, including Black Power and the writers of *Oz. His relations with his mother were less than friendly: he despised her writing (a 'sterile, life-denying vision of our land': *New Statesman*, June 1963) and she cut him out of her will. See *Inside Outsider* (1983), a biography by T. Gould.

MACKAY, Shena (1944–   ), Scottish novelist and short story writer, born in Edinburgh. Her first two very short novels, *Toddler on the Run* and *Dust Falls on Eugene Schlumberger*, were published together in 1964, when she was only 19. Their successors *Music Upstairs* (1965), *Old Crow* (1967), and *An Advent Calendar* (1971) established her mastery of brief, perfectly judged comic narratives, in which bizarre sequences of events often flow from tiny accidents, and where beneath the offhand ironies one can also detect Mackay's profound sympathy for her characters' damaged lives. A long literary silence was broken by a story collection, *Babies in Rhinestones* (1983), then the novels *A Bowl of Cherries* (1984) and *Redhill Rococo* (1986). In *Dunedin* (1992), a more ambitious work, the narrative swings from the beginning to the end of the twentieth century, providing a hellish vision of contemporary suburban London along the way. *The Orchard on Fire* (1996), an elegiac farce about childhood friendship, is compact and exquisite, while *The Artist's Widow* (1998), a satire on modern artistic values, is one of her most astringent novels. Mackay's full range is perhaps best explored in the *Collected Short Stories*, which appeared in 1994.

McKENDRICK, Jamie (1955–   ), English poet, born in Liverpool, educated at Nottingham University. McKendrick, who taught in Italy, is drawn to the Mediterranean, where 'the soul speaks Latin | with a Gothic slur'. *The Sirocco Room* (1991) and *The Kiosk on the Brink* (1993) are pungent, sardonic, anxious books whose promise is fulfilled in *The Marble Fly* (1997), where meditations on art and history ('Paestum', 'Ancient History') mingle with winningly bleak humour. McKendrick has developed a richly suggestive but economical idiom with strong millennial overtones.

MACKENZIE, Sir (Edward Montague) Compton (1883–1972). He was educated at St Paul's and Magdalen College, Oxford, and became a prolific writer, who produced books of travel, biography, essays, poems, and much journalism, as well as the novels for which he is best remembered. He lived at various times on Capri, in the Channel Islands, and in Scotland, all of which provided settings for his work. The most notable of the novels include *Carnival* (1912), a grim story of Jenny, an actress and singer, who settles for the chorus-line and makes a disastrous marriage; then in 1913 and 1914 Mackenzie published *Sinister Street* (2 vols) which presents a semi-autobiographical figure, Michael Fane, 'handicapped by a public school and university education', passing through school, Oxford, and low life in London. For many years the book was widely popular; F. M. *Ford found it 'the history of a whole class . . . during a whole period of life'; and Scott *Fitzgerald acknowledged its deep influence on his early work. In 1915 Mackenzie fought at Gallipoli and after the war continued to write prolifically in all genres. In 1927 he published *Vestal Fire*, a story based on real events, of two cousins, Maimie and Virginia, who take up residence on the Mediterranean island of Sirene, find their Anglo-Saxon attitudes loosening delightfully, and become disastrously devoted to the scandalous Count Marsac. Mackenzie came near to prosecution for *Extraordinary Women* (1928), again set on Sirene, in which various absurd lesbian entanglements are set against a brittle hedonistic society. In 1929 and 1932 he published two volumes of war memoirs, *Gallipoli Memoirs* and *Greek Memories*. During 1937–45 appeared the six volumes of *The Four Winds of Love*, his most ambitious work, tracing the life of John Ogilvie, a pensive and individualistic Scot, from the time of the Boer War to the emergence of Scottish nationalism in 1945. *Whisky Galore* (1947), a fictional account of an actual wreck of a ship loaded with whisky on Eriskay, was made into a highly successful film. *Thin Ice*, a perceptive story of two homosexuals and their fate, appeared in 1956, and in 1963–71 the ten 'Octaves' of *My Life and Times*, a rambling, entertaining autobiography which met with much popular and critical success. Mackenzie was knighted and became a CH.

MACKENZIE, Henry (1745–1831), a lawyer, educated in Edinburgh, who held the position of Comptroller of the Taxes for Scotland. He was the author of a highly influential novel, *The Man of Feeling* (1771), in which the refined and gentle hero is presented in a series of sketches loosely woven together, somewhat in the manner of *Addison's essays on Sir Roger de *Coverley. Mackenzie's book was greatly admired by the young C. *Lamb and was one of *Burns's 'bosom favourites'. In 1773 he published *The Man of the World*, in which the protagonist is a villain; and in 1777 *Julia de Roubigné*, a novel in the manner of Richardson's *Clarissa*. Mackenzie also wrote a play, *The Prince of Tunis* (1773); was chairman of the committee that investigated *Macpherson's 'Ossian'; and edited two periodicals, the *Mirror* and the *Lounger*, to both of which he also frequently contributed. He has been referred to as 'the Addison of the North'. (See SENTIMENT, NOVEL OF.) See H. W. Thompson, *A Scottish Man of Feeling* (1931).

McKERROW, Ronald Brunlees (1872–1940), bibliographer and editor, co-founder of the *Malone Society, 1906. He became joint secretary of the *Bibliographical Society, 1912, and in 1925 founded the *Review of English Studies*. His best-known works were an important edition of the works of T. *Nashe (1904–10) and *An Introduction to Bibliography for Literary Students* (1927).

MACKINTOSH, Sir James (1765–1832), educated at Aberdeen University, a doctor, philosopher, disputant, and barrister, and the author of the highly successful *Vindiciae Gallicae* (1791), a reasoned defence of the French Revolution. Mackintosh later recanted his views, in a lecture attended by a disapproving *Hazlitt. He published a *Dissertation on the Progress of Ethical Philosophy* (1830) and wrote the first three volumes of a *History of England* (1830–1) for Lardner's *Cabinet Cyclopaedia*, as well as an unfinished *History of the Revolution in England in 1688* (1834).

MACKLIN, Charles (MacLaughlin) (?1699–1797), an Irish-born actor who made his reputation by his impersonation of Shylock, a role he first played in 1741. He wrote several plays, of which the most successful were *Love à la Mode*, performed 1759, and *The Man of the World*, performed 1781, with himself in the leading role. He continued to act until a failing memory drove him from the stage in 1789.

MACKMURDO, A. H., see ART NOUVEAU.

MACLAREN, Ian, see KAILYARD SCHOOL.

MacLAVERTY, Bernard (1942–   ), novelist and short story writer, born in Belfast. He worked as a laboratory technician for ten years before reading English at the Queen's University, Belfast. He then moved to Scotland, working as a teacher, and writing his first collection of stories, *Secrets* (1977). His first novel, *Lamb* (1980), is the tragic tale of a Christian Brother who flees a dismal reformatory, taking with him an abused 12-year-old boy. *A Time to Dance* (stories, 1982) was followed by *Cal* (1983), a novel of the *Troubles which combines thriller elements with the lyrical tale of a doomed affair between a reluctant IRA man and the widow of one of his victims. This was followed by two more story collections, *The Great Profundo* (1987) and *Walking the Dog* (1994). His third novel, *Grace Notes* (1997), a softly spoken reflection on the power of art to transform experience, is rooted in Irish identity and culture: a young composer escapes a repressive Catholic upbringing and the 'troubles' of Ulster, finally coming to terms through her work with the tormented

627

history of her birthplace. MacLaverty's work for film includes adaptations of *Cal* (1984) and *Lamb* (1986) and an original screenplay, *Hostages* (1993).

MACLEAN, Sorley (Somhairle MacGill-Eain) (1911–96), Gaelic poet, born on the island of Raasay and educated on Skye and at the University of Edinburgh. He was one of the leading writers in Gaelic of the 20th-cent. Scottish Renaissance. *From Wood to Ridge: Collected Poems in Gaelic and English* (1989), with his own translations, gathers work from 1932 to 1977, and includes lyrics of lansdscape and love, and poems lamenting Scottish history and the 20th-cent. wars of Europe.

MacLEISH, Archibald (1892–1982), American poet and dramatist, born in Illinois and educated at Yale and Harvard. He was one of the American expatriates in Paris in the 1920s, and was strongly influenced by *Pound and T. S. *Eliot. His volumes of verse include *The Pot of Earth* (1924); *The Hamlet of A. MacLeish* (1928); *New Found Land* (1930); the narrative poem *Conquistador* (1932); and his *Collected Poems, 1917–1933* (1933). Among his verse dramas are *Panic* (1935), the anti-totalitarian *The Fall of the City* (1937), and the successfully staged *J.B.* (1958), an updating of the trials of Job. After his return to America at the end of the 1920s, MacLeish became an increasingly public figure, holding many important posts; he was Librarian of Congress (1939–44), assistant secretary of state (1944–5), and Boylston professor at Harvard (1949–62).

MACLEOD, Fiona, see SHARP, W.

MACLISE, Daniel (1806–70), Irish portrait and history painter; he sketched Sir W. *Scott in 1825, when Scott was visiting Cork with Maria *Edgeworth. In 1827 he settled in London where he moved in literary circles and became a close friend of *Dickens and of J. *Forster; his well-known portrait of Dickens is in the National Portrait Gallery, London (1839). He contributed a brilliant series of caricatures of celebrated authors to *Fraser's Magazine*.

McLUHAN, (Herbert) Marshall (1911–80), Canadian scholar, born in Edmonton, and educated at the universities of Manitoba and Cambridge. His studies of the media of communication and the role of technology in society proved highly influential: these include *The Mechanical Bride: Folklore of Industrial Man* (1951); *The Gutenberg Galaxy: The Making of Typographic Man* (1962), which introduced the concept of the 'global village' created by electronic interdependence, and *Understanding the Media* (1964), which explored the proposal that 'The Medium is the Message'.

Macmillan's Magazine, a periodical founded in 1859, and edited successively by D. *Masson (1859–68), George Grove (1868–83), J. *Morley (1883–5), and Mowbray Morris (1885–1907). It was one of the first magazines to use signed articles only, and published a wide variety of material, including poetry, serialized fiction, articles on politics, travel, etc. Contributors included *Tennyson, Thomas *Hughes, *Milnes, and F. D. *Maurice.

Macmorris, Captain, in Shakespeare's *Henry V*, the only Irishman presented in Shakespeare's plays.

MacNEICE, (Frederick) Louis (1907–63), poet, born in Belfast, the son of the rector of Holy Trinity, later bishop of Down, Connor, and Dromore. He left Ulster for Sherborne preparatory school, Marlborough, and Merton College, Oxford, where he took a first in Greats, made the acquaintance of *Auden and *Spender, and published a book of poems, *Blind Fireworks* (1929). After lecturing in classics at Birmingham University and Bedford College he joined the *BBC Features Department in 1941 as writer-producer. Meanwhile he had made several unsuccessful attempts at writing for the theatre, including *Station Bell* (1935) and *Out of the Picture* (1937); produced a fine verse translation of the *Agamemnon* (1936); and was becoming known as a poet through his contributions to *New Verse* and his *Poems* (1935). *Letters from Iceland* (1937) was written in collaboration with Auden. Subsequent volumes of poetry include *The Earth Compels* (1938); *Autumn Journal* (1939), a long personal and political meditation on the events leading up to Munich; *Plant and Phantom* (1941); *Springboard* (1944); *Holes in the Sky* (1948); *Autumn Sequel* (1954); and *The Burning Perch* (1963).

His early work revealed a technical virtuosity, a painter's eye for an image, humour, and an impulse towards making sense of what he later called the 'drunkenness of things being various'; suspicious of all rigid systems, whether political or philosophical, he worked to establish some pattern from life's flux. He used most of the classic verse forms, but his distinctive contribution was his deployment of assonance, internal rhymes, and half-rhymes, and ballad-like repetitions that he had absorbed from the Irishry of his childhood. He was also renowned as an outstanding writer of radio documentaries and radio parable plays; these include *Christopher Columbus* (1944) and his most powerful dramatic work, *The Dark Tower* (1947). He also published a pseudonymous novel (*Roundabout Way*, 1932, by 'Louis Malone'), various potboilers, a book on *Yeats (1941), and a translation of an abridged version of *Goethe's *Faust* (1951); *Varieties of Parable* (from the 1963 Clark lectures) and a volume of autobiography, *The Strings are False*, both appeared posthumously in 1965. Although overshadowed in the 1930s and 1940s by Auden, and later by critical fashion, his reputation was revived by the publication in 1966 of his *Collected Poems*, edited by E. R. Dodds. See *Louis MacNeice* (1995) by J. *Stallworthy.

MACPHERSON, James (1736–96), born near Kingussie, the son of a farmer, educated at Aberdeen and Edinburgh universities. In 1758 he published *The Highlander*, a heroic poem in six cantos. In 1759 he met

John *Home, for whom he produced his first 'Ossianic' fragment 'The Death of Oscar'; encouraged by Home and Hugh *Blair he then produced *Fragments of Ancient Poetry, Collected in the Highlands of Scotland, and Translated from the Galic or Erse Language* (1760). Interest in *primitivism was at this period considerable, and rumours that a Gaelic epic existed aroused much curiosity and enthusiasm; pressed on by his admirers, Macpherson travelled round Scotland collecting the materials for *Fingal, an Ancient Epic Poem, in Six Books*, which appeared in 1762. It purported to be Macpherson's faithful translation of an epic by Ossian, the son of Finn (or, in this version, Fingal), dating from some vague but remote period of early Scottish history. A second epic, *Temora* (1763), soon followed. These works created a great sensation; patriotic Scots, delighted at the revelation of so rich a national treasure, praised them highly. *Hume and Adam *Smith were at first convinced by them: Home and Blair remained so. Ossian's fame spread to the Continent, where *Klopstock, *Schiller, and *Goethe joined in the chorus of praise. Goethe quoted Ossian at length in *The Sorrows of Young Werther*, which, with Ossian, was to be one of the favourite works of Napoleon. Ossian also had an influence on national consciousness in Scandinavia: Macpherson was translated by the Danish writer *Blicher, and helped to inspire efforts to record the Finnish *Kalevala*. But at home doubts of the poems' authenticity sprang up almost at once, with Dr *Johnson as the most formidable of sceptics; his enquiries during his tour of Scotland and remarks published in his *Journey to the Western Islands* (1775) were highly critical. Macpherson, when called upon to produce his originals, was obliged to fabricate them. A committee appointed after his death, chaired by Henry *Mackenzie, investigated the mystery and reported in 1805 that Macpherson had liberally edited Gaelic poems and inserted passages of his own; subsequent investigation supports this view. The immense popularity of the poetry survived the exposure of its origins; as late as 1866 M. *Arnold in his lectures on Celtic literature was defending its 'vein of piercing regret and sadness'; 'Choose any of the better passages in Macpherson's *Ossian* and you can see even at this time of day what an apparition of newness and power such a strain must have been to the eighteenth century.'

Macpherson's other works include a prose translation of the *Iliad* (1773) and a *History of Great Britain* (1775). He wrote in defence of Lord North's ministry, was MP for Camelford from 1780, and was buried in Westminster Abbey at his own expense. See *The Poems of Ossian and Related Works*, ed. Howard Gaskill (1996).

MACREADY, William Charles (1793–1873), son of a provincial actor-manager, educated at Rugby. He achieved a considerable reputation in the provinces before appearing at Covent Garden in 1816. By 1819 he was an established rival of *Kean, appearing regularly at both Covent Garden and Drury Lane; he was manager of both theatres at various times, where he sought to improve standards of production and made many reforms in both acting and the texts. In 1837 he appeared in *Strafford*, which *Browning had written for him, and in 1838 in *Byron's *Two Foscari*; but it was in the roles of Lear, Hamlet, and Macbeth that he gained eminence as a tragic actor. He enjoyed the society of some of the most important writers of his day and was a friend of *Dickens. His last performance was as Macbeth in 1851 and *Tennyson wrote a sonnet to mark the occasion.

Macro Plays, the, three *morality plays (*The Castle of Perseverance*, *Mankind*, and *Wisdom*) named after their 18th-cent. owner. Ed. Mark Eccles in *The Macro Plays* (EETS 262, 1969).

MacStinger, Mrs, in Dickens's *Dombey and Son*, Captain Cuttle's termagant landlady.

McTAGGART, John McTaggart Ellis (1866–1925), philosopher, fellow of Trinity College, Cambridge, and lecturer in moral sciences 1897–1923. He was an exponent of *Hegel's *Logic*, and published several studies of Hegel. His massive treatise *The Nature of Existence* was published in two volumes, 1921–7. He is now chiefly remembered, perhaps, for his arguments about the nature of time, which issued in the conclusion that it did not exist.

McWILLIAM, Candia (1955–), novelist, born in Edinburgh and educated at Girton College, Cambridge. Her first novel, *A Case of Knives* (1988), is a dark tale of sexual intrigue and manipulation, featuring a homosexual heart surgeon, a titled Scottish lady, and an enigmatic young woman who becomes engaged to marry the surgeon's lover: all four tell their own stories. The prose is carefully wrought and the *Firbankian interest in haute couture connects with a violent subplot of Animal Rights terrorism. *A Little Stranger* (1989) describes the tensions between the narrator and her 5-year-old son's conventional but mysteriously threatening nanny: *Debatable Land* (1994) evokes a voyage from Tahiti to New Zealand, and into the past of its six characters. *Wait Till I Tell You* (1997) is a collection of short stories.

MADGE, Charles Henry (1912–96), poet and sociologist, whose left-wing sympathies were manifested in his poetry (his first volume was *The Disappearing Castle*, 1937) and other work and writings. His second volume of verse, *The Father Found* (1941), was followed by a gap of 50 years until *Of Love, Time and Places* (1993), a selection from the earlier volumes together with more recent work. In 1937 with Humphrey Jennings and Tom Harrisson he founded Mass-Observation, a scheme which recruited hundreds of observers (including poets and novelists) to collect accurate sociological data about everyday life and popular culture. His first wife was Kathleen *Raine.

Madoc, a narrative poem by *Southey, published 1805.

Madoc is the youngest son of Owen Gwyneth, king of Wales (d. 1169). He has left Wales and sailed to a western land across the ocean where he has founded a settlement and defeated the Aztecas. He returns to Wales for a fresh supply of adventurers and tells his tale. After his return to the settlement in Aztlan, war breaks out again with the Aztecas. Madoc is ambushed and captured, chained by the foot to the stone of human sacrifice, and required to fight in succession six Azteca champions. After much fighting the Aztecas are finally defeated and migrate to another country. The poem gave its title to *Madoc: A Mystery* (1990) by Paul *Muldoon.

madrigal, originally a short lyrical poem of amatory character, but used in musical terminology to describe a type of part-song, or short polyphonic composition, to secular words and usually without instrumental accompaniment, designed on the whole for amateur performance. The madrigal originated in Italy; it reached England from Europe in the 1530s but developed its own native style in the 1580s with the poetic experiments of the *'Golden Age'. It was first widely disseminated in this country in *Musica Transalpina* (1588), an anthology of 57 Italian madrigals with English texts and the most influential of the five such volumes which appeared in England between 1588 and 1598. Native composers rapidly took over the form, some (like *Morley, the first in the field, or Farnaby, Farmer, and Bennet) staying fairly close to the Italian model, others (like *Weelkes and *Wilbye) adapting it to a more serious and specifically English manner. By the beginning of the 17th cent. practically all English composers (with the exception of the rather older *Byrd) were producing works in the new form, and when Morley brought out the famous madrigal collection *The Triumphes of Oriana* as a tribute to *Elizabeth I in 1601 he was able to include contributions by no fewer than 24 musicians. The marvellous flowering of the English madrigal was of short duration, however, and the quality of many individual pieces in later collections by masters like *Gibbons (1612), Ward (1613), or *Tomkins (1622) does not alter the fact that by this time there was much in them that was old-fashioned; by the third decade of the 17th cent. the madrigal as the Elizabethans understood it was effectively dead. See *English Madrigal Verse*, ed. E. H. Fellowes (1967, 3rd edn).

Mad World, My Masters, A, a comedy by T. *Middleton, written 1604–7, printed 1608.

In a complex plot of deceits and disguises, the impecunious young Follywit seeks to pre-empt his inheritance by robbing his wealthy old grandfather, Sir Bounteous Progress; and Penitent Brothel seeks to seduce the wife of the jealous and suspicious citizen Hairbrain. A courtesan, Gullman, the mistress of Sir Bounteous, plays a part in both actions, and in the last act Follywit (who has married her, believing her to be a virgin) finds himself the gull, married to his grandfather's whore. But she protests reform, Sir Bounteous generously endows the young couple, and all ends reasonably happily. There is an edition by S. Henning (1965).

MAETERLINCK, Maurice (1862–1949), Belgian poetic dramatist and essayist. He wrote in French, establishing himself as one of the leading figures in the *symbolist movement with his play *La Princesse Maleine* (1889; English trans. 1892). In 1892 *Pelléas et Mélisande* appeared (trans. 1894), the work for which he is now chiefly remembered and the source of *Debussy's opera of the same name (1902). He also achieved great contemporary popularity with *L'Oiseau bleu* (1908; *The Blue Bird*, 1909) and was awarded the *Nobel Prize in 1911. He drew heavily on traditions of romance and *fairy tale, and the characteristic tone of much of his drama is one of doom-laden mystery and timeless melancholy. He also produced a number of essays of a philosophical nature, including *La Vie des abeilles* (1901; *The Life of the Bee*, 1901) and *L'Intelligence des fleurs* (1907; *The Intelligence of Flowers*, 1907).

Maeve, or **Medb** (pron. Maeve), in the Ulster cycle, queen of Connaught. See under CUCHULAIN and TAIN-BO-CUAILGNE.

magazine, originally a place where goods are stored, now also a periodical publication containing articles by different authors. Thus the *Gentleman's Magazine* in the introduction to its first number (1731) described itself as 'a Monthly Collection to store up, as in a Magazine, the most remarkable Pieces on the Subjects above-mentioned'. The word had been used before this for a storehouse of information.

magic realism, a term coined by Franz Roh (*Nachexpressionismus, magischer Realismus: Probleme der neuesten europäischer Malerei*, 1925), to describe tendencies in the work of certain German artists of the *neue Sachlichkeit* (new objectivity), characterized by clear, cool, static, thinly painted, sharp-focus images, frequently portraying the imaginary, the improbable, or the fantastic in a realistic or rational manner. The term was adopted in the United States with the 1943 exhibition (containing work by Charles Sheeler, 1883–1965, and Edward Hopper, 1882–1967) at the New York Museum of Modern Art, entitled 'American Realists and Magic Realists'. The term has subsequently been used to describe the works of such Latin American authors as *Borges, *García Márquez, and Alejo Carpentier (1904–80), and elements of it have been noted in *Grass, *Calvino, *Fowles, and other European writers. In the 1970s and 1980s it was adopted in Britain by several of the most original younger fiction writers, including, notably, Emma *Tennant, Angela *Carter, and Salman *Rushdie. Magic realist novels and stories have, typically, a strong narrative drive, in which the recognizably realistic mingles with the unexpected and the inexplicable, and in which elements of dream, fairy story, or mythology combine with the everyday, often in a mosaic or kaleidoscopic pattern of refraction and recurrence. English magic realism also has some affinity with the neo-*Gothic.

MAGINN, William (1793–1842), Irish writer, born in Cork and educated at Trinity College, Dublin. He came to London in 1823, where he wrote under various pseudonyms including 'Ensign Morgan O'Doherty', in whose persona he produced memoirs, anecdotes, and verses in English, Latin, and Greek for the *Literary Gazette* and other journals. He was an important and prolific contributor to *Blackwood's* notably to the *Noctes Ambrosianae,* in the devising of which he seems to have had some part. He became assistant editor of the *Evening Standard,* and in 1830 helped in the establishing of *Fraser's Magazine,* in which much of his best work, including *Homeric Ballads* and *A Gallery of Literary Characters,* appeared. His wit and learning are evident in his parodies of Sir W. *Scott, *Coleridge, T. *Moore, *La Rochefoucauld, *Disraeli, *Carlyle, and many others. He wrote seriously and well on Shakespeare and others, and his 'A Story without a Tail' (1834) is still admired; but he never fulfilled his early promise. He was the original of Captain Shandon in Thackeray's *Pendennis.*

Magnet, see HAMILTON, C.

Magnetic Lady, The, or Humours Reconciled, a comedy by *Jonson, performed 1632, printed 1641.

Lady Loadstone, the 'Magnetic Lady', who 'draws unto her guests of all sorts', has a niece Placentia, of age to be married. The girl is pursued by various suitors until, after an argument between two of them, she goes into labour and gives birth. Her uncle, the usurer Sir Moth Interest, uses this as an excuse to take possession of her dowry. However, Compass, the play's hero, learns that Lady Loadstone's real niece is her waiting-woman Pleasance, who had been exchanged with Placentia when the two were infants. He marries Pleasance, whom he loves, reveals her true identity, and receives her dowry. Placentia is married to the father of her child, Lady Loadstone's steward Needle, and Lady Loadstone marries Compass's brother Captain Ironside. Between the acts there is an interlude of debate about the theatre between a boy actor and two scoffing gallants, Probee and Damplay.

Magnus, Mr Peter, a character in Dickens's *Pickwick Papers.*

Magnyfycence, (1516) a morality play by *Skelton. Magnyfycence, symbolizing a generous prince, is ruined by mistaken liberality and bad counsellors, but restored by Good-hope, Perseverance, and other similar figures. The play was edited by Paula Neuss (1980).

Magwitch, Abel, a character in Dickens's *Great Expectations.*

Mahābhārata, The, an epic Hindu poem, written in Sanskrit, reputedly over 100,000 stanzas long, describing the war between two groups of cousins, the Pandavas and the Kauravas. It dates in its earliest written forms to the 5th or 6th cent. BC. The work was introduced to an English-speaking readership in 1785 when a section, the *Bhagavad-gītā,* translated by Charles Wilkins, was published. Since then there have been numerous translations of sections of the poem, notably by *Isherwood and Swami Prabhavananda (American edition, 1944; introduction by A. *Huxley). *The Mahabharata* became well known in Britain with Peter *Brook's stage adaptation of 1985, which went to Glasgow in 1988. Brook worked closely with French writer Jean-Claude Carrière, and their production attracted enormous public interest, sparking off lively and sometimes fierce debate about *'cultural appropriation': see 'A View from India' (1988) by Rustom Barucha in David Williams (ed.), *Peter Brook and the Mahabharata: Critical Perspectives* (1991).

MAHFOUZ, Naguib (1911–), Egyptian novelist, born in Cairo, who was awarded the *Nobel Prize for literature in 1988. He has written many novels in several genres—historical, realist, and experimental—but is best known internationally for the 'Cairo trilogy', which manifests admiration for the tradition of *Tolstoy, *Balzac, and *Zola. It consists of *Palace Walk* (1956), *Palace of Desire* (1957), and *Sugar Street* (1957) and traces with a broad humane sympathy the fate of the Al Jawad family over three generations, and its many connections and ramifications: the books present a portrait of a city, particularly of its old quarter, of a nation's changing identity, and of many individuals (both men and women) caught in the web of history, between tradition and modernity, religion and national politics, repression and a yearning for self-fulfilment. Dominant among the characters is the ageing patriarch Ahmad, whose virtues are very mixed. The time spanned is from 1902 to the victories of Nasser in the 1950s.

MAHON, Derek (1941–), poet, born in Belfast, educated at Trinity College, Dublin. In the 1960s he became associated, together with Seamus *Heaney and Michael *Longley, with the group known as the Northern Poets. His poetry, often bleak and uncompromising in its portrayal of urban squalor and deprivation, is influenced by the work of *MacNeice and *Auden. His first collection, *Twelve Poems* (1965), was followed by *Night-Crossing* (1968), *The Snow Party* (1975), *The Hunt by Night* (1982), *A Kensington Notebook* (1984), and *Antarctica* (1985). A collected volume, *Poems 1962–1975* appeared in 1979, *Selected Poems* in 1991. He has also translated *Molière's *School for Wives* (1986) and the *Bacchae* of *Euripides (1991).

MAHONY, Francis Sylvester (1804–66), born in Cork, best known by his pseudonym Father Prout, a Jesuit priest who admitted he had mistaken his vocation and left the order for a career as a journalist and poet. He contributed many lively papers and poems to *Fraser's Magazine* and *Bentley's Miscellany*. These included translations from *Horace, *Béranger, *Hugo, etc., and, interspersed amongst them, mystifications in the form of invented 'originals' in French, Latin, and Greek for well-known poems by T. *Moore, C. *Wolfe, and others. He travelled much abroad, and was Paris correspondent for the *Globe*, 1858–66. The contributions to *Fraser's* were collected in 1836 as *The Reliques of Father Prout*.

Maid Marian, a female personage in the May-game (see MAY DAY) and *morris dance. In the later forms of the story of *Robin Hood she appears as the companion of the outlaw, the association having probably been suggested by the fact that the two were both represented in the May day pageants [*OED*]. According to one version of the legend she was Matilda, the daughter of Lord Fitzwater.

Maid Marian, a medieval romance by *Peacock largely written 1819, published 1822. It features *Robin Hood, *Maid Marian, *Friar Tuck, and Prince John, while lampooning institutions such as the monarchy and the Church in the post-Napoleonic era. The irreverent treatment of Prince John's government also mocks the idealized medievalism newly fashionable among conservative propagandists, artists, and historians. Peacock wrote *Maid Marian* at a time when he had fallen under the spell of the new Italian opera of *Rossini, *Bellini, and *Donizetti. Many scenes already seem cast as duets or quartets, and the book was later adapted as a popular operetta.

'Maid of Athens', a poem by Lord *Byron, written 1810.

The 'Maid' is said to have been the 12-year-old daughter of Mrs Macri, a widow whose husband had been vice-consul in Athens.

Maid of Honour, The, a romantic drama by *Massinger, acted about 1621–2, published 1632. It is based on a story by *Boccaccio.

Bertoldo, natural brother of the king of Sicily and a knight of Malta, is in love with Camiola. Departing on an expedition to aid the duke of Urbino against the duchess of Siena, he asks for her hand, but she refuses on the ground of the disparity of their station and his oath as a knight of Malta not to marry. Bertoldo is taken prisoner by the Sienese, cast into prison, and held to ransom for a large sum, which the king of Sicily, being incensed against Bertoldo, forbids anyone to pay. Camiola directs her follower Adorni, who is passionately devoted to her, to carry the ransom (which she provides from her own estate) to Bertoldo, and to require of him a contract to marry her. Adorni, though it means the defeat of his own hopes, faithfully

discharges his mission; Bertoldo is released and signs the contract. But the duchess of Siena falls in love with him, and he yields to her wooing. They are on the point of being married when Camiola interposes and pleads her cause with spirit, so that all, including the duchess, condemn the ingratitude of Bertoldo and the marriage is broken off. Camiola, 'the Maid of Honour', takes the veil, and the humiliated and repentant Bertoldo resumes his vocation as a knight of Malta. Camiola is Massinger's best female character, and the play contains some of his finest scenes.

Maid of Norway, see SIR PATRICK SPENS.

Maid's Tragedy, The, a tragedy by *Beaumont and *Fletcher, written ?1610–11, published 1619, generally considered one of their best works.

Amintor, a gentleman of Rhodes, breaks his engagement to Aspatia at the king's request and in her stead marries Evadne, sister to his friend Melantius. On their wedding night, in a powerful confrontation, Evadne reveals that she is the king's mistress and refuses to sleep with him. Amintor initially agrees to conceal the position and present a mock marriage to the world; but later he reveals the truth to Melantius, who passionately reproaches the by now penitent Evadne, and persuades her to murder the king. Meanwhile the desolate Aspatia laments her loss in some of the finest verse in the play (II. ii); her lines 'And the trees about me, | Let them be dry and leafless; let the rocks | Groan with continual surges; and behind me | Make all a desolation. Look, look, wenches!' were used by T. S. *Eliot as an epigraph to 'Sweeney Erect'; the speech is also quoted by Emily *Eden in *The Semi-detached House* (ch. 20). Aspatia later takes action by disguising herself as her brother and provoking the reluctant Amintor to a duel. He wounds her; as she lies dying Evadne arrives, fresh from the king's murder, hoping to be pardoned by Amintor. He rejects her; she commits suicide; Aspatia reveals herself and dies; Amintor takes his own life. The last act of the play was rewritten by E. *Waller, with a happy ending in which Amintor marries Aspatia. There is a modern edition by T. W. Craik (1988).

MAILER, Norman Kingsley (1923–   ), American novelist and essayist, educated at Harvard, whose naturalistic first novel *The Naked and the Dead* (1948) was based on his experiences with the army in the Pacific. It was followed by other novels, including *Barbary Shore* (1951), *The Deer Park* (1955), and *An American Dream* (1965). Most of his work is of a more unorthodox genre, mixing journalism, autobiography, political commentary, and fictional passages in a wide range of styles. (See *Advertisements for Myself*, 1959; *The Presidential Papers*, 1963; *The Armies of the Night*, 1968; and many other titles.) *The Executioner's Song* (1979), a lengthy non-fiction account of a murderer, bears some resemblance to *In Cold Blood* by *Capote. (See also FACTION.) His lengthy and ambitious novel *Ancient Evenings*

(1983; described by A. *Burgess as possibly 'one of the great works of contemporary mythopoesis') is set in ancient Egypt (1290–1100 BC). His other novels include: *Tough Guys Don't Dance* (1984), a thriller; *Harlot's Ghost* (1991), an analysis of the CIA; and *The Gospel According to the Son* (1997), a first-person account of the life of Jesus, whom he portrays as engaging and very human as well as deeply pious and divine. He is also the author of a number of biographies, including studies of Lee Harvey Oswald (*Oswald's Story: An American Mystery*, 1995) and of the early life of Picasso (*Portrait of Picasso as a Young Man*, 1995). *Time of Our Time*, a retrospective anthology of his writings, was published in 1998.

MAIMONIDES (1135–1204), a Jew of Córdoba who went to Fez and Cairo when the Jews were expelled from Spain. His chief work was *The Guide for the Perplexed* of which there are English, French, and German translations. This work influenced *Aquinas (who drew on it in the course of his proofs of the existence of God) and other *Scholastic theologians; its endeavour was to reconcile Talmudic Scripture with the philosophy of *Aristotle.

MAITLAND, Sara (1950–   ), novelist and short story writer, born in Scotland, and educated at Oxford University. Her first novel, *Daughter of Jerusalem* (1979), was followed by *Virgin Territory* in 1984, a perceptive and compelling story about a nun, Sister Anna, who leaves her convent in South America and moves to London, where she finds her vows and faith under threat. Attracted to Karen, a 'freelance feminist intellectual', but pursued by the repressive voices of patriarchal control, she searches for meaning in an alien world. *Archy Types* (1987) is a flamboyant and colourful feminist epistolary novel, written with Michelene Wandor; *Home Truths* (1993) is perhaps her most powerful and searching work to date. Set in a comfortable family house in the Scottish Highlands, the novel centres on Clare, a photographer, returned home after the sudden death in Zimbabwe of her partner. No one, except perhaps Clare, knows the cause of his death; the book charts the protagonist's painful attempts to understand her reasons for forgetting. Maitland explores with characteristic intelligence and idiosyncratic verve the emergence of truth from concealment and the proximity of danger and life. Maitland has also written on women and Christianity in *A Map of the New Country*, a book of theology, *A Big-Enough God*, and a collection of religious short stories, *Angel and Me* (1995).

MAJOR, or **MAIR,** John (c.1467–1550), born near Berwick. He has been called 'the last of the schoolmen'. He studied at Cambridge and Paris, where he became doctor of theology. He lectured on Scholastic logic and theology at Glasgow and St Andrews from 1518 to 1525, and then returned to Paris, where he was regarded as the most eminent exponent of medieval learning. He published between 1509 and 1517 a Latin *Commentary on the Sentences of Peter Lombard* and in 1521 a Latin *History of Greater Britain, both England and Scotland*, in which he showed himself in advance of his times by advocating the union of the two kingdoms.

According to *Rabelais (II. vii), among the books found by Pantagruel in the library of St Victor was a treatise by Major, *De Modo Faciendi Puddinos* ('On the art of making black-puddings').

Major Barbara, a play by Bernard *Shaw performed 1905, published 1907.

It portrays the conflict between spiritual and worldly power embodied in Barbara, a major in the Salvation Army, and her machiavellian father, millionaire armaments manufacturer Andrew Undershaft. While visiting her East End shelter for the poor, as part of a bargain struck between them, he reveals that the shelter's benefactor, Lord Saxmundham, made his money through 'Bodgers' whisky', and she suffers a crisis of faith as she glimpses the possibility that all salvation and philanthropy are tainted at the source: the next day, visiting his factory with her mother Lady Britomart and her fiancé, classical scholar Adolphus Cusins, she is further shaken to discover her father is a model employer. Cusins enters the debate, reveals that he is technically a foundling and therefore eligible to inherit the Undershaft empire (as Undershaft's own children are not), strikes a hard bargain with his prospective father-in-law, and agrees to enter the business, partly persuaded by Undershaft's quoting of *Plato to the effect that 'society cannot be saved until either the Professors of Greek take to making gunpowder, or else the makers of gunpowder become Professors of Greek'. Barbara, recovering her spirits, embraces this synthesis as a possibility of hope for the future. The portrait of Cusins is based on G. *Murray.

MAKIN, Bathsua (fl. 1640s–1673), sister of mathematician John Pell, and tutor to Princess Elizabeth, daughter of Charles I. A correspondent of the Dutch polymath Anna Maria van Schurman, Makin was an educationalist and practising poet, whose panegyric to the dowager countess of Huntingdon emphasizes her 'learning humane and divine . . . French, Italian, Hebrue, Latin, Greek'. Her *Essay to Revive the Antient Education of Gentlewomen* (1673) insists that the whole 'encyclopaedia of learning' be opened to women. Makin asserts that 'women are not such silly giddy creatures as many proud ignorant men would make them' but will become more malleable through education. The moderation of her claims may have been linked with a wish to dissociate herself from Henry Care's 1670 translation of Cornelius *Agrippa's inflammatory feminist *Female Pre-eminence: or The Dignity and Excellence of that Sex, above the Male*.

Malagigi, in *Orlando innamorato*, a cousin of *Rinaldo, possessed of magic lore, who detects the wiles of

*Angelica and attempts to slay her, but is taken prisoner and carried to Cathay. He is released on condition that he shall lure Rinaldo to her.

MALAMUD, Bernard (1914–86), American novelist, born in Brooklyn, best known for his novel *The Fixer* (1967), the story of a Jewish handyman or 'fixer' in tsarist Russia just before the First World War, who is falsely accused of murder and turned into the scapegoat for anti-Semitic feeling in his neighbourhood. Other works include *A New Life* (1961), *The Tenants* (1971), *Dubin's Lives* (1979), and *God's Grace* (1982). He has also published volumes of short stories.

Malaprop, Mrs, in Sheridan's *The Rivals*, the aunt and guardian of Lydia Languish, noted for her aptitude in misapplying words; for instance (among many brilliant inventions of Sheridan's) 'as headstrong as an allegory on the banks of the Nile' or 'He is the very pineapple of politeness.' Her solecisms have given the word 'malapropism' to the language.

Malbecco, in Spenser's *Faerie Queene* (III. ix, x), a 'cancred crabbed Carle', jealous and avaricious, married to the lovely *Hellenore. *Paridell elopes with her, and Malbecco, unable to escape from his jealous thoughts, throws himself from a rock. But his 'aery Spright' lives for ever, under the name of Jealousy.

Malcontent, The, a tragi-comedy by *Marston, and generally considered his best play, published 1604 (with additions by *Webster), written not earlier than 1602.

The central character is Altofronto, banished duke of Genoa, disguised as the malcontent Malevole; in this role he reveals to his successor Pietro that he is being deceived by his wife Aurelia, and watches over the attempts of the Machiavellian Mendoza to supplant Pietro, to banish Aurelia, and to marry Altofronto's own wife Maria. After much intrigue Altofronto reveals himself to the by now penitent Pietro, and the two expose Mendoza's villainy and regain their own wives. The plot resembles that of *Measure for Measure* in several respects, but the exposure of court corruption, lust, and greed is more harshly satiric, reflecting (in *Swinburne's view) 'the poet's own ambitions and dissatisfied intelligence'. There is a modern edition by T. W. Craik (1988).

Maldon, Battle of, a 325-line poem in Old English, incomplete at the beginning and the end, probably written c.1000, dealing with the battle fought in 991 at Maldon in Essex against Danish raiders. The Danes are drawn up on the shore of the river Pant (Blackwater), opposed by Byrhtnoth (c.926–91), ealdorman of Essex since 956, who rejects the demand for tribute by the Danes. In the fight Byrhtnoth is killed and the English are defeated, partly because some of his men flee but partly too because of Byrhtnoth's 'ofermod', his excessive pride, in yielding ground to the Danes as a gesture of magnanimity. The second half of the poem,

concerned with the loyalty of the followers of Byrhtnoth to their dead leader, is a powerful statement of fidelity and determination to avenge his death. The poem survives only in a transcript, fortunately made by John Elphinston, under-keeper of the Cotton Library (1677–1729), because the manuscript was destroyed in the fire at the Cotton Library in 1731. Ed. E. V. Gordon (1937, etc.).

Maldon, Jack, in Dickens's *David Copperfield*, the scapegrace cousin of Mrs Strong.

Malecasta, 'unchaste', in Spenser's *Faerie Queene* (III. i), the lady of Castle Joyeous.

Maleger, in Spenser's *Faerie Queene* (II. xi), the captain of twelve troops, the seven deadly sins and the evil passions that assail the five senses. He is lean and ghostlike, and Prince *Arthur's sword has no effect on him. Finally, remembering that earth is his mother and that he draws his strength from her, Arthur lifts him up and squeezes the life out of him.

Malengin, in Spenser's *Faerie Queene* (V. ix), the personification of guile. Sought out by Prince *Arthur and *Artegall, he runs away assuming various disguises, but is destroyed by *Talus.

Male Règle, La, see HOCCLEVE.

MALINOWSKI, Bronislaw (1884–1942), social anthropologist, born in Poland. He came to the London School of Economics in 1910 (as professor, 1927) and did fieldwork in New Guinea and Melanesia. He was the most important figure in the early development of British social anthropology, establishing a method of detailed observation and description of cultures, based on residence with the people studied and fluency in their language. He developed functional analysis based on the assumption that cultural arrangements were related to human needs and drew, initially, on Freudian ideas to relate psychological attributes of the mind to social institutions. His monographs (most importantly *Argonauts of the Western Pacific*, 1922; *Sexual Life of Savages in North Western Melanesia*, 1929; and *Coral Gardens and Their Magic*, 1935) were characterized by clarity and elegance of expression. These and his theoretical works (*Magic, Science and Religion*, 1925; *Crime and Custom in Savage Society*, 1926; and *Sex and Repression in Savage So*ciety, 1927) were read by a wide public and novelists and poets of the period made frequent allusion to his ideas.

MALLARMÉ, Stéphane (1842–98), French poet, one of the founders of modern European poetry, and more recently one of the heroes of *structuralism. He spent the years 1862–3 in London; thereafter he taught English in various lycées, mostly in Paris. The hermetic preciousness of his later verse made him the object of a cult. Two of his longer pieces, the icily poised 'Hérodiade' (c.1864) and the sensuously textured 'Prélude à l'après-midi d'un faune' (c.1865), celebrate the hidden virtues of deferment and absence against the vulgarity of possession and plenitude. His pursuit of a perfection realizable only through renunciation of the actual demanded a new effort of language: the rare, intensely wrought lyrics, sonnets, and elegies gathered in *Poésies* (1887) and *Vers et prose* (1893) attempt a science of suggestion through the exploitation of syntactical and metaphoric ambiguities and of the formal and aural properties of verse. These tendencies reach their culmination in 'Un coup de dés jamais n'abolira le hasard' (1897), a poem which makes revolutionary use of typographical possibilities to suggest a musical score and to indicate what he called the 'prismatic subdivisions of the idea'.

MALLET, or **MALLOCH,** David (?1705–65), Scottish author, who Anglicized his name, to the disapproval of *Boswell. He wrote the well-known ballad *'William and Margaret', *The Excursion* (1728, a poem), and various tragedies, including *Elvira* (1763) which was admired by his friend *Gibbon but criticized in *Critical Strictures* by Boswell and others. He collaborated with *Thomson in the masque of *Alfred* (1740), wrote a *Life of Francis Bacon* (1740), and edited *Bolingbroke's *Works* (5 vols, 1754).

Malleus Maleficarum, or *Hexenhammer*, the 'Hammer of Witches', published in 1486? by Jakob Sprenger, the Dominican inquisitor of Cologne, and Heinrich Krämer, prior of Cologne. It was the textbook of the day on witchcraft, setting out how it may be discovered and how it should be punished.

MALLOCH, David, see MALLET.

MALLOCK, William Hurrell (1849–1923), the nephew of R. H. and J. A. *Froude, educated at Balliol College, Oxford, is best known as author of *The New Republic: or Culture, Faith and Philosophy in an English Country House* (1877), a lively satire on English society and ideas, in which *Ruskin figures as Mr Herbert, and *Jowett, M. *Arnold, *Pater, T. H. *Huxley, and *Tyndall appear under thin disguises among the other characters. He published various other works, including poems, novels, and memoirs; a High Anglican Tory, he attacked socialism and the *Fabian Society in several studies of social and economic science, and was himself attacked for his views by G. B. *Shaw in the *Fortnightly Review*, Apr. 1894.

MALMESBURY, William of, see WILLIAM OF MALMESBURY.

MALONE, Edmond (1741–1812), literary critic and Shakespearian scholar, educated at Trinity College, Dublin, who came to London in 1777 and established himself as a writer and as a friend of Dr *Johnson, Sir J. *Reynolds, *Burke, and many others. He published in 1778 his *An Attempt to Ascertain the Order in Which the Plays Attributed to Shakespeare Were Written*, and edited the works of *Goldsmith (1780), Reynolds (1791), and the prose works of *Dryden (1800). A friend of *Boswell, and a member of the *Club, he

revised the *Journal of a Tour to the Hebrides* (1785) while it was going through the press, and gave great assistance with Boswell's *Life of Samuel *Johnson* (1791), of which he edited the third to sixth editions. He exposed the forgeries of *Chatterton and *Ireland. His new edition of Shakespeare was issued posthumously in 1821 in 21 volumes by James Boswell the younger.

Malone Society, the, founded by *Greg and *McKerrow in 1906 for the purpose of making accessible materials for the study of early English drama, by printing dramatic texts and documents. Its name is taken from E. *Malone.

MALORY, Sir Thomas (d. 1471), author of *Le *Morte D'Arthur*. Although his exact identity is uncertain, he is identified by his editor Vinaver as Sir Thomas Malory of Newbold Revel, Warwickshire, who was a knight before 1442. The *Morte D'Arthur* was written in prison and we know that Malory of Newbold Revel was charged with crimes of violence, theft, and rape after 1450. For a Yorkshire identification see W. M. Matthews, *The Ill-Framed Knight* (1966). The fact that much of the work was translated from a 'French book' has led to a proposed identification as a hostage held in France during the French wars. But the identity remains a matter of conjecture. See P. J. C. Field, *The Life and Times of Sir Thomas Malory* (1993).

MALOUF, David (1934–   ), Australian poet and novelist, born in Brisbane of English and Lebanese parents, educated at Brisbane Grammar School and the University of Queensland. After a period living and working in Europe he taught English at the University of Sydney from 1968 to 1977. His first volume of poems, *Bicycle and Other Poems*, was published in 1970 and was followed by *Neighbours in a Thicket* (1974), *Poems 1975–76* (1976), *Wild Lemons* (1980), *First Things Last* (1980), *Selected Poems* (1981), and *Selected Poems 1959–1989* (1994). His autobiographical novel *Johnno* (1975) is set in wartime Brisbane, while *An Imaginary Life* (1978) is a lyrical prose meditation on the last years of the Roman poet *Ovid and his obsession with a wolf-child. He has also published four novellas: *Child's Play*, the story of a terrorist assassin assessing his victim and written in a restrained documentary style, which was published together with *Fly away Peter* (set in Queensland before the First World War and originally entitled *The Bread of Time to Come*) in 1981 and republished separately in 1982; and *The Prowler* and *Eustace*, which appeared with *Child's Play* in 1982. Other novels: *Harland's Half Acre* (1984), the central figure of which is an artist who is obsessed by a desire to reclaim his family's lost inheritance; *The Great World* (1990), which is about the experiences of two friends as prisoners of war in Singapore and Thailand during the Second World War and which won the Commonwealth Writers Prize; and *Remembering Babylon* (1993), set in Queensland during the mid-19th cent. *Antipodes* (1985) is a collection of short stories. A selection of autobiographical essays was also published in 1985 as *12 Edmondstone Street*. Malouf has been the recipient of many awards, including the Australian Literature Society's Gold Medal for *Child's Play* and *Fly away Peter*. A play, *Blood Relations*, was published in 1988, and he wrote the libretto for Michael Berkeley's *Baa Baa Black Sheep*, adapted from *Kipling's short story, performed in Cheltenham, 1994.

MALRAUX, André (1901–76), French novelist, essayist, and art critic. Out of his experiences as a political activist, in China in the 1920s and in Spain during the Civil War, he wrote a number of novels on revolutionary themes, including *Les Conquérants* (1928; *The Conquerors*, 1929), *La Condition humaine* (1933; trans. under various titles: *Storm in Shanghai*, 1934, *Man's Fate*, 1934, *Man's Estate*, 1948), and *L'Espoir* (1937; *Days of Hope*, 1938, *Man's Hope*, 1938). His writings on art include *Les Voix du silence* (1951; *The Voices of Silence*, 1953). In 1967 his *Antimémoires* appeared (*Anti-memoirs*, 1968).

MALTHUS, Thomas Robert (1766–1834), educated at Cambridge, where he had a brilliant student career. He became curate of Albury in Surrey in 1798. In that year, provoked by *Godwin's *Political Justice* of 1793, he published *An Essay on the Principle of Population*, in which he argued that population (growing geometrically) would soon increase beyond the means of subsistence (which grew only arithmetically), and that checks in the form of poverty, disease, and starvation were necessary. After he had collected a great deal of further information from travels in northern Europe, the *Essay* was heavily recast in a second edition of 1803; in this Malthus modified his conclusions, suggesting that the regulation of greed and sexual activity would act as more acceptable checks on population growth. His work was vigorously attacked by Godwin, *Cobbett, *Hazlitt, and others, but it exerted a powerful influence on social thought in the 19th cent. C. *Darwin declared in his *Life* that Malthus's *Essay* helped to point him towards his own theory of evolution.

Malvolio, in Shakespeare's *Twelfth Night*, the joyless steward whose gulling forms the play's secondary plot. His name, which denotes 'ill will', has on occasion (e.g. at court, 1623) been used as the play's title.

MAMET, David (1947–), Chicago-born dramatist whose work is distinguished by its attentions to the rhythms of blue-collar speech and the theme of how low-life criminality mirrors the world of big business. *American Buffalo* (1975) follows the bungled attempts of three petty crooks to pull off a robbery, while *Glengarry Glen Ross* (1983) adapts a similar plot to a bunch of real-estate salesmen. Often criticized for sexism, his work is unafraid to address crises in gender relations, with plays such as *Sexual Perversity in Chicago* (1974), which satirizes the vacuity of male sexual bravado. *Oleanna* (1992) dramatized the misunderstandings between a professor and his student in a complex narrative of sexual harassment. He has written widely for the cinema, providing scripts for *The Postman Always Rings Twice* (1981), *The Verdict* (1982), and *The Untouchables* (1983). He went on to direct films of his own, including the highly acclaimed *House of Games* (1987), *Homicide* (1991), and *The Spanish Prisoner* (1998). He has also written two novels, *The Village* (1994), a portrayal of hunting which recalls *Hemingway, and *The Old Religion* (1997), a fictional reconstruction of the lynching of a Jewish factory owner falsely accused of the rape and murder of a southern white girl.

Mammon, the Cave of, described in Spenser's *Faerie Queene* (II. vii). It is the treasure-house of the god of wealth, visited by Sir Guyon. Milton in his *Areopagitica* uses the example of Spenser making Guyon visit the cave of Mammon 'that he might see and know, and yet abstain'.

Mammon, Sir Epicure, in Jonson's *The Alchemist*, a voluptuous, gourmandizing knight, one of Jonson's greatest characters.

Man and Superman: *A Comedy and a Philosophy*, a play by Bernard *Shaw, first published 1903, first performed (without Act III) in 1905 by the Stage Society at the Court Theatre.

The play is Shaw's paradoxical version of the *Don Juan story, in which his hero John Tanner (Don Juan Tenorio), provocative, eloquent, and witty ideologue and author of the *Revolutionist's Handbook* (a work which appears in full as an appendix to the play), is relentlessly if obliquely pursued by Ann Whitefield, who is more interested in him as a potential husband than she is in his political theories. Ann has been entrusted as ward by her dead father jointly to Tanner and to the elderly respectable Ramsden, who expects her to marry the devoted and poetic Octavius. Tanner is made aware of Ann's intentions by his chauffeur Straker (the New Man of the polytechnic revolution), and flees to Spain whither he is pursued by Ann and her entourage, which includes her mother and Octavius's sister Violet, who demonstrates, through a matrimonial sub-plot, the superior force of women. Act III consists of a dream sequence set in hell in which Tanner, captured by the brigand Mendoza, becomes his ancestor Don Juan, Mendoza the Devil, Ramsden 'the Statue', and Ann becomes Ana: in one of Shaw's most characteristic 'Shavio-Socratic' debates, the four characters discuss the nature of progress, evolution, and the Life Force, the Devil arguing powerfully that man is essentially destructive, and Don Juan arguing for the saving power of ideas and rational effort, for the philosopher as 'nature's pilot'. In the last act Ann achieves her object, despite Tanner's struggles; the play ends with the announcement of their impending marriage and Tanner's submission to the Life Force.

The concept of the Life Force bears some similarity to *Bergson's 'élan vital', although Shaw was not at the time familiar with Bergson's work: the echo in his 'Superman' of *Nietzsche's 'Übermensch' (*Also sprach Zarathustra*) is, however, deliberate.

Manannán, the son of *Lêr, a highly popular god of the old Gaelic pantheon, the subject of many legends and the patron of sailors and merchants. The Isle of Man was his favourite abode, and is said to take its name from him. There he has degenerated into a legendary giant, with three legs (seen revolving in the coat of arms of the island).

Manawyddan, see MABINOGION.

Manchester Guardian, founded in 1821 as a weekly, and in 1855 as a daily paper; the principal Liberal organ outside London, edited 1872–1929 by Charles Prestwich Scott (1846–1932). Its title was changed to the *Guardian* in 1959; since 1961 it has been published from London.

Manchester School, the name first applied by *Disraeli to the political party, led by *Cobden and *Bright, who advocated the principles of free trade. It was afterwards extended to the party who supported those leaders on other questions of policy. 'Manchester policy' was used derisively to signify a policy of *laissez-faire* and self-interest. The 'Manchester School' of drama refers loosely to the playwrights associated with Miss *Horniman's repertory seasons at the Gaiety Theatre, Manchester, 1907–14, including Harold Brighouse (1882–1958), W. S. *Houghton, and Allan Monkhouse (1858–1936).

'Manciple's Tale, The', see CANTERBURY TALES, 23.

mandarin, used as an adjective to describe esoteric, highly decorative, or highbrow prose. According to C. *Connolly, those favouring it included *Donne, *Addison, and *De Quincey, and its last great exponents were *Pater and H. *James (*Enemies of Promise*, 1938).

MANDELSTAM, Osip Emilevich (1891–?1938), Russian poet, born into the family of a Jewish leather merchant in Warsaw and brought up in St Petersburg. He spent most of 1907–10 in western Europe, particularly Paris, and then studied at St Petersburg University. His first poems appeared in 1910. In 1911 he joined the Acmeist 'Guild of Poets' with *Akhmatova and *Gumilev, and the poems of his first collection, *Stone* (1913), are marked by Acmeist brevity and clarity. He met Nadezhda Yakovlevna Khazina (b. 1899) in Kiev in 1919 and married her in 1922. His second collection, *Tristia* (1922), confirmed his status while considerably widening his range. During the 1920s Mandelstam came under increasing attack for being 'out of step' with the new Soviet age, and his ruminations on the subject produced such important poems as 'The Age' and 'The Slate Ode'. His third volume, *Poems*, and collections of prose and criticism

appeared in 1928. In 1930 he made a long visit to Armenia, from which emerged *The Journey to Armenia*, a major prose piece (trans. Clarence Brown, 1980), his last work to be published in the Soviet Union for 30 years. His first arrest, in 1934, resulted from his recitation of his famous poem denouncing Stalin. Prison was followed by internal exile and attempted suicide. In exile he wrote his important late poetry the 'Voronezh Notebooks'. Arrested again in 1938, he was sentenced to five years' hard labour and died of a heart attack on the way to the camps (the exact date of his death has not been established). His collected works have only been published abroad, though a complete edition of his poetry appeared in Leningrad in 1973. The two volumes of memoirs by Nadezhda Mandelstam, *Hope against Hope* (1971) and *Hope Abandoned* (1974), are not only the main source of information on the poet but also a powerful and harrowing description of the experience of 20th-cent. totalitarianism: she died in 1980 and her work remained unpublished in Russia during her lifetime. Mandelstam's reputation continues to grow, and he is now regarded as one of the major poets of the 20th cent. He has been widely translated into English, notably by Clarence Brown and W. S. Merwin (*Selected Poems*, 1973) and by David McDuff (*Selected Poems*, 1973).

MANDEVILLE, Bernard de (1670–1733), born in Holland. He trained as a physician at Leiden, settled in London, and published *A Treatise of the Hypochondriack and Hysterick Passions* (1711, expanded into three dialogues, 1730). His other prose works include *The Virgin Unmasked* (1709, 1714), arguing for a better status and better education for women; *Free Thoughts on Religion, the Church and National Happiness* (1720), a defence of *Deism and an attack on clericalism; *A Modest Defence of Public Stews* (1724), recommending governmental regulation of bawdy-houses; and *An Enquiry into the Origin of Honour* (1732), distinguishing self-esteem from self-love. Of his moral and satirical verse the best known is 'The Grumbling Hive, or Knaves Turn'd Honest' (1705), which was incorporated with various prose supplements into *The Fable of the Bees, or Private Vices, Public Benefits* (1714, 1723). Mandeville here rejects the optimistic view of benevolent human nature put forward by *Shaftesbury, and argues that the mutual help on which society thrives like a colony of bees is due to personal acquisitiveness and the love of luxury: a 'virtuous' society, where only subsistence needs are satisfied, would lack both culture and trade and would collapse from want of employment. Mandeville's writing was admired by *Defoe, and later by Dr *Johnson and *Hume, but his ironic use of the language of 'vice' and 'virtue' was widely misconstrued. He was attacked by W. *Law (*Remarks upon a Late Book*, 1723), *Dennis (*Vice and Luxury Public Mischiefs*, 1724), *Hutcheson (letters in the *Dublin Journal*, 1726), *Watts (*An Essay towards the Encouragement of Charity Schools*, 1728), and G. *Berkeley (*Alciphron*, 1732), Mandeville himself responding to the last in *A Letter to Dion* (1732). Mandeville was a literary target in Pope's *Dunciad* and Fielding's *Amelia*, but is favourably portrayed in R. *Browning's *Parleyings with Certain People of Importance*.

MANDEVILLE, Sir John, the ostensible author of the famous book of *Travels* which is found in many European languages after its first appearance in Anglo-Norman French in 1356–7. There are a number of English manuscripts, one of a metrical version from Coventry, and the first probably coming from Lincolnshire c.1375. Jean d'Outremeuse, a historian from Liège, tells us that he knew the writer, who left his native St Albans in 1322 and died in Liège in 1372. Until J. W. Bennett's *The Rediscovery of Sir John Mandeville* (1954), Jean d'Outremeuse himself was believed to be the writer of the work. The book purports to be an account of the author's journeys in the East, but it is really a compilation, drawn especially from William of Boldensele and Friar Odoric of Pordenone, and from the *Speculum Majus* of *Vincent of Beauvais. It claims to be a guide, both geographical and ethical, for pilgrims to the Holy Land, but it carries the reader far off course, to Turkey, Tartary, Persia, Egypt, and India. It is a highly entertaining work, combining geography and natural history with romance and marvels, such as the fountain of youth and the ant-hills of gold-dust. It was an important influence on subsequent English writers from *Chaucer to Shakespeare, and was the prototype in English of the popular genre of the fabulous travel book.

Ed. C. W. R. D. Moseley (1983); metrical version ed. M. C. Seymour (EETS OS 269, 1973).

Mandricardo, in *Orlando furioso*, the son of *Agrican, king of Tartary. He wears the armour of Hector, and comes to Europe to secure Hector's sword *Durindana, now in the possession of Orlando, and to avenge his father's death. He carries off Doralis, who is betrothed to *Rodomont, meets Orlando and fights with him (but the fight is broken off), gets Durindana after Orlando in his madness has thrown it away, and is finally killed by *Rogero.

Manette, Dr and Lucie, characters in Dickens's *A Tale of Two Cities*.

Manfred, a poetic drama by Lord *Byron, published 1817.

Manfred, a Faustian figure, 'half-dust, half deity', lives alone as an outcast in a castle in the Alps, and is tortured by guilt for 'some half-maddening sin'. He summons the spirits of the universe, who offer him everything except the oblivion he seeks. Eventually, overcoming his terror of death, he tries to hurl himself from an alpine crag, but is dragged back by a hunter. He invokes the Witch of the Alps and reveals his sin—his incestuous love for his sister Astarte. He descends to the underworld, the Hall of Arimanes, and encounters a vision of Astarte, who promises him death on the morrow. Back in his castle an abbot begs him to repent, but he cannot. He denies the power of the demons who summon him, and when they vanish he dies.

Byron was deeply interested in the idea of supermen, half-way between gods and mortals, and was to return to the theme in *Heaven and Earth*. But he was dissatisfied with *Manfred* and did not wish it ever to be performed, a wish which was ignored after his death. Aspects of the drama were satirized in *Nightmare Abbey* by T. L. Peacock, but its power as an archetypal statement of romantic rebellion lived on, and inspired musical compositions by *Schumann, *Balakirev, and *Tchaikovsky.

MANGAN, James Clarence (1803–49), Irish poet, born in Dublin, whose life was plagued by poverty and alcohol, despite the efforts of friends who found him occasional employment in the library of Trinity College, Dublin. Under various pseudonyms he published prose and verse in newspapers and periodicals and is chiefly remembered for a few powerful ballads and songs including 'Dark Rosaleen' and 'The Nameless One' ('Roll forth, my song, like the rushing river'). He died of malnutrition in extreme destitution. His tragic career suggested part of the theme of B. *Moore's *The Mangan Inheritance* (1979).

Manichaeism, see GNOSTICISM.

Mankind, a morality play in 914 lines from East Anglia, dating from c.1465, one of the group called *Macro plays after their 18th-cent. owner (the others are *Wisdom and *The Castle of Perseverance). Its principal theme is Sloth (*Accidia*), and it is written in the Low Style with much employment of obscenity. Earlier critics and editors regarded the play with some primness, declaring it to be 'unprintable' in parts; more recently it has been admired for its dramatic vigour and for its ingenious structure. Ed. G. Wickham in *English Moral Interludes* (1976); it is discussed briefly by Richard Axton in 'The Morality Tradition' (*Pelican Guide to English Literature* i. 340–52, 2nd edn, 1982).

MANLEY, Mrs (Mary?) Delarivière (1663–1724). She had a colourful life, which included a bigamous marriage with her cousin John Manley and some years as mistress of the warden of the Fleet Prison, John Tilly. She published several novels and memoirs, including *The New Atalantis* (1709), a *roman à clef (published with a Key to its characters) in which she attacked various Whigs and people of note. Her *The Adventures of Rivella* (1714) is largely autobiographical. She also wrote several plays. In 1711 she succeeded *Swift as editor of the *Examiner. Swift wrote of her (*Journal to Stella*, Jan. 1711/12), 'she has very generous principles, for one of her sort; and a great deal of sense and invention'. Her novels, with an introduction by P. Koster, were reproduced in facsimile in 1971.

Manly, (1) a character in Wycherley's *The Plain Dealer*; (2) a character in Vanbrugh and Cibber's *The Provok'd Husband*.

MANN, Heinrich (1871–1950), German novelist, brother of Thomas *Mann. His early work includes some notable satirical novels directed against life and institutions in Wilhelmine Germany: *Professor Unrat* (1905) and *Der Untertan* (*The Subject*, 1918), for example. More politically engaged than his brother in the period before 1918, and standing more to the left, he provided the model for the type of 'Zivilisations-literat' with whom his brother took issue in his *Betrachtungen eines Unpolitischen* (*Observations of an Unpolitical Man*, 1918). Like his brother, he emigrated from Nazi Germany.

MANN, Sir Horace (1701–86), British envoy at Florence, where the Young Pretender was residing. Horace *Walpole made his acquaintance there in 1739, and they became correspondents for 45 years, although they never met again. Walpole requested the return of his letters and used them in his historical works, as well as retouching them for publication.

MANN, Thomas (1875–1955), German novelist and essayist. Born in Lübeck, he went into emigration (most of the time in the United States) in the Nazi period. *Buddenbrooks*, a novel on the theme of the decay of a family, with strongly autobiographical features, appeared in 1901 and quickly made him famous. *Tonio Kröger* (1903), one of his most celebrated novellas, is, like so many of his works, about the nature of the artist. *Der Tod in Venedig* (*Death in Venice*, 1912), influenced particularly by the thought of *Schopenhauer and *Nietzsche, presents the artist and artistic creation in a highly ironic light. Originally a man of rather conservative sympathies, as expressed in *Betrachtungen eines Unpolitischen* (*Observations of an Unpolitical Man*, 1918), he caused surprise by quickly lending his public support to the Weimar Republic. *Der Zauberberg* (*The Magic Mountain*) appeared in 1924, the 'Joseph' novels (in four parts) in 1933–43, during which time he also published his novel *Lotte in Weimar*, expanding on a brief episode in the life of *Goethe, the writer whom Mann most admired and whom he resembled in the ironic detachment of his writing. Constantly concerned with the character and role of the artist, particularly in what Mann saw as his culpable, even criminal, relation to society, he linked this theme with the problem of Nazism in *Dr Faustus* (1947), also elaborating the subject in a book about this novel, *Die Entstehung des Dr Faustus* (*The Genesis of Dr Faustus*, 1949). His last full-length novel derived from the picaresque tradition: *Die Bekenntnisse des Hochstaplers Felix Krull* (*The Confessions of the Confidence Trickster Felix Krull*, 1954). He was awarded the *Nobel Prize in 1929.

mannerism, a term used to describe any stylistic habit that becomes exaggerated or is carried to excess, but more specifically applied to the style of Italian art of c.1520–c.1600, between the High Renaissance and the baroque. A powerful and disturbing effect is achieved by distorted or elongated figures, violent perspective, and unexpected colour harmonies. The beginning of the style can be seen in the late work of *Michelangelo and *Raphael; it was developed by Tintoretto, El Greco, Bronzino, *Vasari, and others.

MANNING, Frederic (1882–1935), novelist, born in Sydney, who spent his adult life in England. He served in the First World War on the Somme and Ancre fronts as a private with the King's Shropshire Light Infantry, an experience which inspired his novel *The Middle Parts of Fortune*, published anonymously in 1929, and in 1930 in expurgated form as *Her Privates We* by 'Private 19022'. The full text was published again in 1977 with his full name. It is a powerful account of camaraderie, military inefficiency, and squalor in and behind the trenches, seen through the eyes of Private Bourne (named after the Lincolnshire town which Manning had made his home). Bourne's death ends the narrative.

MANNING, Henry Edward (1808–92), educated at Balliol College, Oxford. He became archdeacon of Chichester (1840) and succeeded *Newman as one of the leaders of the *Oxford movement. He joined the Roman Catholic Church in 1851, and became archbishop of Westminster in 1865 and cardinal in 1875. He published many religious and polemical works, was a great preacher and ecclesiastical statesman, and a subtle controversialist. He is one of the subjects of L. *Strachey's *Eminent Victorians*.

MANNING, Olivia (1908–80), novelist, brought up in Portsmouth, the daughter of a naval officer of small means. Her first novel, *The Wind Changes* (1937), was set in Dublin. In 1939 she married R. D. Smith, then a British Council lecturer, subsequently a BBC producer, and at the outbreak of war travelled with him to Bucharest. Her experiences there, and later in Greece, Egypt, and Jerusalem, inspired the works for which she is best remembered, *The Balkan Trilogy* (*The Great Fortune*, 1960; *The Spoilt City*, 1962; *Friends and Heroes*, 1965) and *The Levant Trilogy* (*The Danger Tree*, 1977; *The Battle Lost and Won*, 1978; and *The Sum of Things*, 1980). This sequence opens with the experiences of the newly married Guy and Harriet Pringle in rumour-filled Romania, surrounded by a crowd of vividly drawn minor characters and hangers-on, most memorable among them an amiable scrounger, the Russian émigré Prince Yakimov, now down-at-heel but trailing dubious memories of a glorious past. Harriet spends much of her time trying to protect Guy and herself from Guy's impulsive generosity. As the German army advances the couple flee to Athens, and the second trilogy finds them in Egypt. The novels are a fine portrait of the tragi-comedy of war and of its effects on civilian life, and give a vivid sense of place and period; *The Battle Lost and Won* also contains a striking account of the battle of Alamein seen through the eyes of Simon Boulderstone, a young British officer. Olivia Manning wrote five other novels and two volumes of short stories (*Growing up*, 1948; *A Romantic Hero*, 1966). The *Balkan Trilogy* was adapted for television by Alan *Plater.

MANNINGHAM, John (*c*.1575–1622), a barrister whose diary or commonplace book (among the *Harleian manuscripts in the British Library) records a performance at the Middle Temple in 1602 of Shakespeare's *Twelfth Night*, which he compares to *The Comedy of Errors*, and the only known and probably authentic contemporary anecdote about Shakespeare.

MANNYNG, Robert, of Brunne (Bourne) in Lincolnshire (fl. 1288–1338), is known only from what he tells us of himself in the Prologues to his two works, his verse *Chronicle of England* (finished 1338) and *Handlyng Synne*. He was a member of the Gilbertine Order. Part I of *Chronicles*, ed. F. J. *Furnivall (Rolls Series), 2 vols (1887).

Man of Feeling, The, a novel by H. *Mackenzie, published 1771.

The work is generally considered to have been the most influential 'novel of *sentiment'. The author deliberately fragments the story, with the explanation that the manuscript has been mutilated, so that the effect is of a series of abrupt but concentrated episodes. Harley, the hero, is the man of feeling, whose unwavering benevolence and acute, often tearful, sensibility are demonstrated through various scenes in which he assists the down-trodden, loses his love, and fails to achieve worldly success.

'Man of Law's Tale, The', see CANTERBURY TALES, 5.

Man of Mode, The, the last and finest comedy of *Etherege, first performed at court 1676. It was an immediate success, and remains a classic of the *Restoration period. *Steele singled it out for attack in the *Spectator*, 65, and *Dennis provided a spirited defence.

There are two main plots, neatly interwoven. Dorimant rids himself of his mistress Mrs Loveit, with the aid of faint-hearted Bellinda whom he seduces in the process. In doing so he meets the heiress Harriet Woodvil, with whom he appears to fall in love. She is wise enough to keep him at arm's length until he proposes marriage, and even then requires him to follow her into the country, there to receive her answer after the play is ended. In counterpoint, Young Bellair has been ordered by his father to marry Harriet; but he loves Emilia, who with the help of his aunt Lady Towneley enables him to outwit the old man, who has fallen for Emilia. The revelation of his own dotage induces Old Bellair to give his blessing to his son's marriage.

Slight though the action is, it is natural and easy, and

Etherege sustains interest through his unsentimental views, eloquent dialogue, and telling social detail. Dorimant was said to be drawn after *Rochester, and Dennis considered that the comedy 'so burnished his vices that they appeared as virtues', though a modern reader might find the play's values more ambiguous, and the satire directed not only at Sir Fopling Flutter, 'the prince of fops' who gives the drama its name.

Man of Ross, The, see KYRLE.

Man of the World, The, (1) a novel by H. *Mackenzie; (2) a comedy by *Macklin, performed 1781, and adapted from his own earlier unpublished work *The True Born Scotchman*, performed 1764. It had long been refused a licence because of its satire on the Scots, though Macklin claimed in a preface that his intention was only to 'explode the reciprocal national prejudices that equally soured and disgraced the minds of both English and Scots men'.

A Scottish politician, Sir Pertinax Mac-Sycophant (originally played by the author), has risen to parliamentary eminence through pliability and flattery, and now seeks to gain control of three parliamentary boroughs by marrying his eldest son Egerton to Lady Rodolpha, the daughter of another servile but needy politician, Lord Lambercourt. The young couple, at their parents' insistence, reluctantly embark on a scene of courtship, to find to their mutual relief that both have affections otherwise engaged, and they combine to defeat their parents' purposes. Rodolpha, who secretly loves Egerton's younger brother, is ordered to marry him, which suits all concerned; Egerton marries his own choice, his father's ward Constantia.

Manon Lescaut, see PRÉVOST.

MANSFIELD, Katherine, pseudonym of Kathleen Mansfield Beauchamp (1888–1923), born in Wellington, New Zealand, educated at Queen's College, London, 1903–6. She returned to New Zealand to study music for two years, then came back to London in 1908. In 1909 she married, but left her husband after a few days; she became pregnant by another man and gave birth to a stillborn child in Bavaria, an experience that formed the background to her first collection of stories *In a German Pension* (1911), most of which were previously published in *Orage's *New Age*. In 1911 she met John Middleton *Murry, whom she was to marry in 1918; he was editing *Rhythm*, to which, and to its successor the *Blue Review*, she also contributed stories, many based on her New Zealand childhood. In 1915 she and Murry spent some weeks in Zennor, Cornwall, in close and sometimes strained proximity to their friends D. H. *Lawrence and Frieda; in 1916 she, Murry, and Lawrence founded a magazine, *Signature*, which survived for only three issues. From this period she knew that she was suffering from tuberculosis, and spent part of every year abroad in the south of France and Switzerland. In 1918 'Prelude' was published by the *Hogarth Press, and later in a collection, *Bliss, and*

Other Stories (1920). She was increasingly recognized as an original and experimental writer, whose stories were the first in English to show the influence of *Chekhov, whom she greatly admired. Her success aroused the jealousy of V. *Woolf, who began to describe her work as 'hard' and 'shallow'. *The Garden Party, and Other Stories* (1922) was the third and last collection to be published in her lifetime: in that year she entered the institute run by *Gurdjieff near Fontainebleau, hoping to regain spiritual and physical health, and died the following January. Her stories vary greatly in length and tone, from long, impressionistic, delicate evocations of family life ('At the Bay', 'Prelude') to short, sharp sketches such as 'Miss Brill'. Two collections were published posthumously (*The Dove's Nest*, 1923; *Something Childish*, 1924) as well as various collections of letters, extracts from her journal, etc.; a biography by A. Alpers appeared in 1980, superseding his own earlier version of 1954. Four vols of her *Collected Letters* (1903–21), ed. V. O'Sullivan and M. Scott, have been published 1984–96. There is also a life by C. *Tomalin (1987).

Mansfield Park, a novel by J. *Austen, begun 1811, published 1814.

Sir Thomas Bertram of Mansfield Park, a stern but kind-hearted man, has two sons, Tom and Edmund, and two daughters, Maria and Julia. His wife, a charming, indolent woman, has two sisters: Mrs Norris, a near neighbour, who is spiteful and selfish, and Mrs Price, the wife of an impecunious officer of marines, with a large family of young children. In order to assist the Prices, Sir Thomas undertakes the charge of their eldest daughter Fanny, a timid child of 9. In spite of her humble situation and the cruelty of Mrs Norris, Fanny, by her gentle and modest disposition, gradually becomes an indispensable part of the household. The strength and earnestness of her character is particularly shown during Sir Thomas's absence in the West Indies, when family discipline is considerably relaxed, forbidden private theatricals are mounted, and an unseemly flirtation begins between Maria Bertram, who is already engaged to marry Mr Rushworth, and Henry Crawford, the attractive, worldly brother-in-law of the parson of Mansfield. Against all this Fanny resolutely sets her face. Loving her cousin Edmund, she grieves greatly to see him fascinated by the frivolous Mary Crawford, sister of Henry. Maria having become Mrs Rushworth, Henry turns his attention to Fanny, to his own and her astonishment falls in love with her, and proposes marriage. Fanny unhesitatingly rejects him, incurring the grave displeasure of Sir Thomas for what he regards as a piece of ungrateful perversity. During a visit paid by Fanny to her own home in Portsmouth matters come to a crisis. Henry, accidentally encountering Maria Rushworth again, runs away with her; and Julia elopes with a foolish and unsuitable suitor, Mr Yates. Mary Crawford's failure to condemn her brother's conduct,

together with her aversion to marrying a clergyman (for Edmund has by now taken orders), finally opens Edmund's eyes to her true character. He turns for comfort to Fanny, falls in love, and they are married.

Mantalini, Madame, in Dickens's *Nicholas Nickleby*, a fashionable dressmaker. Her husband Mr Mantalini, a selfish, affected fop, lives on her earnings and ruins her.

MANTEL, Hilary (1952–), novelist, born in Hadfield, Derbyshire, and educated at the London School of Economics and Sheffield University. She married Gerald McEwan in 1972 and lived in Botswana 1977–82, then in Jeddah, Saudi Arabia, until 1986; this experience produced her essay 'Last Months in Al Hamra', which won the Shiva Naipaul Memorial Prize in 1987, and the finely atmospheric psychological thriller *Eight Months on Ghazzah Street* (1988). Mantel's other novels include *Every Day is Mother's Day* (1985), a story of a mother and daughter, Muriel and Evelyn Axon, living together in retreat from the outside world, and *Vacant Possession* (1986), which continues Muriel's story as she returns from a mental hospital and enters 'care in the community'. *Fludd* (1989), a comedy set in the north of England, uses motifs and memories from the author's Catholic childhood and explores the meanings of alchemy. Her broadly ranging historical novel *A Place of Greater Safety* (1992) is set in the French Revolution. *A Change of Climate* (1994) depicts the return of two former missionaries in southern Africa to Norfolk, where an old secret surfaces. *Giving Up the Ghost* (2003) is a memoir vividly describing childhood trauma and adult ill health, and *Beyond Black* (2005) follows the dark adventures through suburban England of medium Alison and her companion Colette.

MANTUAN, or **MANTUANUS** (1448–1516), Johannes Baptista Spagnolo, a Carmelite of Mantua who wrote Latin eclogues. These had a considerable vogue in England and influenced the pastorals of *Barclay and *Spenser. He is the 'good old Mantuan' quoted by Holofernes in *Love's Labour's Lost* (IV. ii).

MANUTIUS, Aldus, see ALDUS MANUTIUS.

MANZONI, Alessandro (1785–1873), Italian novelist, author of *I promessi sposi* (*The Betrothed*), a work of unique historical significance. In a long series of painstaking revisions from its first published version (1825–7) to its final form (1840–2), it forged from Tuscan the literary Italian which, after the unification of Italy (1870), became standard Italian. It is also remarkable for its powerfully characterized historical reconstruction of 17th-cent. Lombardy, under Spanish domination and ravaged by plague. The simple attempts of two poor silkweavers to marry are used to explore the corrupt and oppressive rule of the Spaniards and, by implication, of the later Austrians. Manzoni also wrote two historical tragedies in verse, *Il conte di Carmagnola* (*The Count of Carmagnola*, 1820) and *Adelchi* (1822), which deal with the relationship between oppressed and oppressors, and the role of divine providence in history. He was greatly admired by Sir W. *Scott, and was the subject of a great Requiem Mass by *Verdi.

MAP, Walter (*c*.1140–*c*.1209), a Welshman who was archdeacon of Oxford in the time of Henry II and the author between 1181 and 1192 of a satirical and entertaining miscellany *De Nugis Curialium*, 'Courtiers' Trifles', which contains the disquisition formerly attributed to St *Augustine, 'Dissuasio Valerii ad Rufinum de non ducenda uxore', referred to by Chaucer in the 'Prologue to the Wife of Bath's Tale' (*Canterbury Tales*, III. 671). Some Goliardic poems have been doubtfully attributed to him, as well as a lost Latin original of the prose *Lancelot*. He was highly regarded as a poet in his own day and he used to be identified as *Golias and hence the author of all the Goliardic poems; this is certainly not right, though he must have been the composer of more works than the small certain *œuvre* that survives. (See also ANGLO-LATIN LITERATURE.)

De Nugis Curialium, trans. F. Tupper and M. B. Ogle (1924). Ed. T. Wright, *The Latin Poems Commonly Attributed to Walter Mapes* (Camden Soc. 1841: inauthentic works).

MARANA, Giovanni Paolo, see TURKISH SPY.

Marble Faun, The, a novel by *Hawthorne, published 1860 (in England as *Transformation*). It is the product of Hawthorne's two years in Italy; the scene is laid in Rome, and the title is taken from the resemblance of one of the principal characters, Count Donatello, to the Marble Faun of Praxiteles.

Donatello is in love with the liberated young American art student Miriam, who is being persecuted by a mysterious stranger—a 'dusty, death-scented apparition', with whom she has some guilty connection. Roused to sudden fury when encountering her with him on a moonlight expedition, Donatello murders him, with her unspoken assent, thus binding them together in a relationship 'cemented by blood'. A subplot describes the relationship of a sculptor, Kenyon, and Miriam's art student friend Hilda, 'the Dove'; Hilda, although herself totally innocent, feels herself under a 'mysterious shadow of guilt', by connection with Miriam. Hawthorne uses the image of Beatrice Cenci, in the painting attributed to *Reni, which Hilda is engaged in copying, as a symbol for the mystery of sin, which, in the character of Donatello, has a purifying power. He surrenders himself to justice, and Kenyon's reflection is, 'Sin has educated Donatello, and elevated him. Is sin, then . . . merely an element in human education?'

MARCEL, Gabriel (1889–1973), French Catholic existentialist. Following *Kierkegaard and Jaspers, he repudiated abstraction, generalization, categorization,

in favour of individual authenticity. From *Être et avoir* (1935) to *Le Mystère de l'être* (1951), he argued that being is a concept that cannot be analysed, only recognized, and that man has to confront it not as a problem to be posed or conceived, but as an experience to be lived and explored.

Marchioness, the, a character in Dickens's *The Old Curiosity Shop*.

MARCIAN, see MARTIANUS CAPELLA.

MARCO POLO, see POLO.

MARCUS AURELIUS ANTONINUS (AD 121–80), Roman emperor 161–80 and Stoic philosopher, the author of 12 books of 'Meditations'. The *Meditations* were not printed till 1555, but a Spanish counterfeit by Antonio da Guevara purporting to be a life of Marcus Aurelius was translated by J. *Berners as *The Golden Boke* (1535) and by T. *North as the *Diall of Princes* (1557), and enjoyed great public favour. But so did Jeremy *Collier's translation (1701) of the authentic *Meditations* which saw 58 editions before the end of the century. They were highly valued also by M. *Arnold and had a further spell of popularity in the decades preceding the First World War. For his philosophy, see STOICISM.

Marfisa, in *Orlando innamorato* and *Orlando furioso*, the warrior sister of *Rogero. Brought up by an African magician, she becomes queen of India, and leads an army to the relief of *Angelica besieged in Albracca. Later, discovering her own Christian parentage, Marfisa joins Charlemagne and is baptized. She falls in love with Rogero before discovering that he is her brother.

Marforio, see PASQUIL.

Margaret, (1) in Shakespeare's *Much Ado about Nothing*, a gentlewoman attendant on *Hero; (2) in Goethe's *Faust*, the principal female character ('Gretchen') of Part I, a girl of humble station, simple, confiding, and affectionate.

MARGARET OF ANJOU (1430–82), the 'She-wolf of France', daughter of Reignier, king of Naples, who is a dominant character in Shakespeare's *1, 2,* and *3 *Henry VI* and *Richard III*. In *1* and *2 Henry VI* she is the mistress of Suffolk, though married to Henry; in *3 Henry VI* her role as a termagant develops, with her mocking and murder of York, and in *Richard III* she is a powerful prophetess of doom. The historical Margaret remained in France after her defeat at the battle of Tewkesbury. Peggy Ashcroft played the role memorably in John Barton's adaptation of the four plays as *The Wars of the Roses* (1963). She figures also in Scott's *Anne of Geierstein*.

Margarete, St, see KATHERINE GROUP.

Margarite of America, A, a prose romance by T. *Lodge published 1596, but written during his voyage to South America under Thomas Cavendish in 1591–3. It describes the tragic love of Margarite, daughter of the king of Muscovy, for the treacherous and violent Arsadachus, son of the emperor of Cusco, who eventually kills her, together with his wife Diana and their child. It is notable for its variety of visual spectacle and pageantry, its highly patterned poems and songs, and the unsparing savagery of many of the incidents. It was edited by G. B. *Harrison (1927).

Marguerite of Navarre, see HEPTAMERON.

Maria, (1) one of the ladies attending the princess in Shakespeare's *Love's Labour's Lost*; (2) Olivia's waiting woman in his *Twelfth Night*; (3) a character in Sterne's *Tristram Shandy* (vol. vii) and *A Sentimental Journey*; (4) a character in Sheridan's *The School for Scandal*.

Mariana, (1) Diana's friend in Shakespeare's *All's Well that Ends Well*; (2) in his *Measure for Measure*, a lady betrothed to *Angelo, but cast off by him. The duke describes her as living 'dejected' 'at the moated grange' (III. i. 255), the phrase which suggested *Tennyson's poems (below).

'Mariana' (1830) and **'Mariana in the South'** (1832), two poems by *Tennyson, suggested by Shakespeare's Mariana of 'the moated grange' in *Measure for Measure*. Both describe women waiting hopelessly and in desolate loneliness for their lovers; the first inspired *Millais's painting of 1851, and the landscape of the second was drawn from Tennyson's journey with A. H. *Hallam in 1832. Tennyson appears to have invented the stanza form.

MARIANA, Juan de (1535–1624), a Spanish Jesuit who taught theology at Rome and Paris, and then settled at Toledo, and wrote a long and remarkable history of Spain. He also wrote a notable Latin treatise *De Rege et Regis Institutione* (Toledo, 1599), in which he spoke with approval of the assassination of Henry III of France by Jacques Clément and defined the circumstances in which it was legitimate to get rid, even by violence, of a tyrannical prince. This book was condemned in Paris to be burnt by the public executioner immediately after the assassination of Henry IV by Ravaillac in 1610, and encouraged the belief in England that the Jesuits were responsible for the Gunpowder Plot of 1605.

MARÍAS, Javier (1951–), Spanish novelist and translator, born in Madrid. He has published several novels including *Todas las almas* (*All Souls*, 1992), an academic comedy set in Oxford, and *Corazón tan blanco* (1992; *A Heart so White*, 1995), a complex and carefully plotted novel of jealousy and passion, packed with Shakespearian allusions, set in Cuba, New York, and Madrid, dealing with the honeymoon and marriage of two Spanish translators, and interwoven revelations of family tragedy and violence.

MARIE DE CHAMPAGNE, daughter of *Eleanor of Aquitaine and her first husband Louis VII of France,

became countess of Champagne in 1164 on her marriage to Count Henry, and regent there on his death in 1181. She set up at Troyes from the 1160s onwards a cultural centre modelled on that of her mother at Poitiers. Her most famous protégé was *Chrétien de Troyes who attributes to her the *sen* and *matière* of his *Lancelot* in the first lines of the poem. *Andreas Capellanus also claims to be a courtier of hers.

MARIE DE FRANCE (fl. 1160–90), a French poet of whom little certain is known, the author of twelve *Lais*, a series of apparently Celtic stories told in Anglo-Norman couplets. She appears to have been born in France and to have done much or all of her literary work in England. She knew Latin and English as well as French, and she wrote a French version of the Latin *St *Patrick's Purgatory*. As well as her famous *Lais*, some of which were copied in English (see BRETON LAYS), she wrote a collection of *Aesop's Fables which she called *Isopet* and which she says she translated from English. See *Lais*, ed. A. Ewert (1944); E. Rickert, *Marie de France: Seven of Her Lays Done into English* (1901).

Marina, in Shakespeare's *Pericles*, the daughter of Pericles, whose name alludes to her being born at sea. She inspired T. S. *Eliot's poem 'Marina' (1930).

Marinell, see FLORIMELL.

MARINETTI, Filippo Tommaso (1876–1944), Italian dramatist, novelist, and poet, who launched *Futurism in 1909. In his poems he anticipated the *Dada technique of juxtaposing words without syntactical links. In his plays he abandoned verisimilitude and traditional methods of characterization and plot development. His innovations include: the use of automatons; the simultaneous staging of unrelated actions; the 'drama of objects', in which human interlocutors play no significant part. He shared with Fascism the glorification of virility, nationalism, and war.

MARINO, Giambattista (1569–1625), Neapolitan poet, best known for his *Adone* (1623), a long poem on the love of Venus and Adonis. The term *marinismo* (or sometimes *secentismo*) denotes the flamboyant style of Marino and his 17th-cent. imitators, with its extravagant imagery, excessive ornamentation, and verbal conceits. *Crashaw was profoundly influenced by Marino. See *Secentismo e marinismo* (1925) by M. *Praz.

Marino Faliero, *Doge of Venice*, a drama in blank verse by *Byron, published 1821 and produced in the same year at Drury Lane, against Byron's wishes. The play, based upon historical facts and inspired by Byron's 1816–17 period in Venice, is set in 1355. The elderly but vigorous and passionate Faliero, recently elected doge, is outraged by the inadequate punishment imposed upon a young patrician who has grossly insulted Faliero's young, beautiful, and innocent wife. In revenge Faliero joins a popular insurrection in an attempt to overthrow the constitution and its corrupt officers, but the plot is discovered, and he is executed, unrepentant and defiant to the last. This conspiracy was also the subject of a tragedy by *Swinburne, 1885.

Marius the Epicurean, a philosophical romance by *Pater, published 1885.

Pater describes the boyhood, education, and young manhood of Marius, a serious young Roman imbued with a 'morbid religious idealism'. With his friend Flavian (who, like so many of Pater's characters, dies young) he discovers the 'jewelled' delights of *Apuleius, in particular of the story of *Cupid and Psyche, then progresses through the philosophies of *Heraclitus, Aristippus, and *Marcus Aurelius to Christianity. He dies more or less a martyr to save a Christian friend. The work is a vehicle for Pater's own reflections on pagan and Christian art and religion; T. S. *Eliot in his essay 'Arnold and Pater' (1930) quotes with approval A. C. *Benson's view that Pater's true interest was in the sensuous appeal and liturgical solemnities of religion, and concludes that the book documents an important historical moment in the process whereby 'religion became morals, religion became art, religion became science and philosophy'.

MARIVAUX, Pierre (1688–1763), French playwright. After the loss of his provincial inheritance he lived by his pen and frequented the literary salons of Paris. In 1722 he founded a *Spectateur français* in imitation of Addison's *Spectator. In all he produced about 30 comedies, the intrigues of which are motivated by social and psychological obstacles to the union of lovers. The refined and subtle analysis of sentiment known as *marivaudage* which is his trademark as a dramatist is best revealed in *Le Jeu de l'amour et du hasard* (1730) and *Les Fausses Confidences* (1737). His plays have held the French stage ever since.

Mark, King, in Arthurian legend, the king of Cornwall and the husband of Isoud of Ireland, who is brought to Mark by her lover *Tristram; in some versions Tristram is the son of Mark's sister Elizabeth. Various Tristram stories represent the king as nobly trusting, or as a treacherous coward. See TRISTRAM AND ISOUD.

MARKANDAYA, Kamala (1923–2004), British novelist, born and educated in India. *Nectar in a Sieve* (1954) established her as the first notable woman novelist from the Indian subcontinent. The impact of new economic and political ideas on traditional Indian society was Markandaya's main theme in *A Silence of Desire* (1960), *Possession* (1963), *A Handful of Rice* (1966), and *The Coffer Dams* (1969). *The Nowhere Man* (1972) transports the clash of cultures to England, where Markandaya settled in the early 1960s. *Two Virgins* (1973) marks a radical change, showing a much more experimental style and a more positive view of modernization. Her most ambitious novel was *The Golden Honeycomb* (1977)—a historical look at how the coming of Indian independence affected a native or princely state. *Pleasure City* (1982) provides a subtle and ironic view of a friendship between Rikki, a local fisherboy, and Tully, a representative of the multinational company which builds a modern holiday resort next to Rikki's village.

MARKHAM, E(dward) A(rchibald) (1939–   ), poet, editor, and short story writer, born on Montserrat; he came to England in 1956. His volumes of poetry include *Human Rites* (1984), *Living in Disguise* (1986), *Towards the End of a Century* (1989), and *Misapprehensions* (1995). His work frequently returns (though without sentimental nostalgia) to the theme of his Montserrat childhood and his grandmother's house. *A Papua New Guinea Sojourn* (1998) describes his life as media coordinator in New Guinea in the 1980s. He has edited *Hinterland* (Caribbean poetry, 1989) and *The Penguin Book of Caribbean Short Stories* (1996). Since 1997 he has been professor of creative writing at Sheffield Hallam University; most recently he has published *Marking Time* (1999), a campus novel.

MARKHAM, Gervase (1568–1637), who wrote on country pursuits, the art of war, and horsemanship; also plays and poems. His principal works on horses are *A Discource of Horsmanshippe* (1593), *Cavelarice, or The English Horseman* (1607), *Markham's Methode or Epitome* (?1616), and *Markhams Faithful Farrier* (1629). His chief work on country occupations, *A Way to Get Wealth* (1623), contains treatises on 'Cheap and Good Husbandry' (the management of domestic animals); 'Country Contentments' (hunting, hawking, fishing), with a section on the 'English Huswife' (cooking, dairying, physic); and agriculture and horticulture. (These treatises had been separately published earlier.) Other works include a poem about Sir Richard Grenville (1595) and *The English Arcadia* (prose, 1607). There is a bibliography by F. N. L. Poynter (1962).

MARKHAM, Mrs, pseudonym of Mrs Elizabeth Penrose (1780–1837), who wrote for children, and published two very popular school histories, of England (1823) and of France (1828), from which she carefully omitted all instances of cruelty and deception.

Markleham, Mrs, in Dickens's *David Copperfield, familiarly known as the 'Old Soldier', the mother-in-law of Copperfield's old schoolmaster at Canterbury, Dr Strong. Her nickname was due to the 'skill with which she marshalled great forces of relations against the Doctor'.

Mark Tapley, in Dickens's *Martin Chuzzlewit, servant at the Dragon Inn, who leaves it to find some position in which it will be a credit to show his indomitable good humour. He becomes the devoted attendant of Martin during his American tour.

Marley, Jacob, in Dickens's *A Christmas Carol*, Scrooge's late partner, whose ghost appears.

Marlow, (1) a character in and part-narrator of several of the works of J. *Conrad, including *Lord Jim*, *'Heart of Darkness', Youth*, and *Chance*; (2) Sir Charles and his son, characters in Goldsmith's *She Stoops to Conquer*.

MARLOWE, Christopher (1564–93), son of a Canterbury shoemaker, educated at the King's School, Canterbury, and Corpus Christi College, Cambridge. He became a BA in 1584, and MA, after some difficulty, in 1587. Though of excellent classical attainments, as his writings make clear, he seems to have been of a violent and at times criminal temperament. It is not clear whether visits he made to the Continent related to espionage. In 1589 he was involved in a street fight in which the poet T. *Watson killed a man; an injunction was brought against him by the constable of Shoreditch three years later. Early in 1592 he was deported from the Netherlands for attempting to issue forged gold coins. On 30 May 1593 he was killed by one Ingram Frizer (as *Hotson discovered) in a Deptford tavern after a quarrel over the bill; Marlowe was at the time under warrant to appear before the Privy Council on unknown charges. *Kyd and another friend, Richard Baines, testified after his death to his blasphemy and outrageous beliefs.

*The Tragedie of *Dido, Queene of Carthage*, published in 1594, may have been written while Marlowe was still at Cambridge, and in collaboration with *Nashe. Part I of *Tamburlaine* was written not later than 1587, and Part II in the following year; it was published in 1590. The next plays may have been *The Jew of Malta*, not published until 1633, and *Edward II*, published in 1594. The highly topical *Massacre at Paris*, which survives only in a fragmentary and undated text, and *Dr Faustus*, published 1604, may both belong to the last year of Marlowe's life. At various times he translated *Ovid's Amores*, published without date as *All Ovids Elegies*, together with some of Sir John *Davies's 'Epigrammes'; wrote two books of an erotic narrative poem *Hero and Leander*, which was completed by G. *Chapman and published in 1598; made a fine blank verse rendering of *Lucans First Booke*, Book 1 of *Lucan's *Pharsalia*; and wrote the song 'Come live with me and be my love', published in *The Passionate Pilgrim* (1599) and *England's Helicon* (1600), with a reply by *Ralegh. In spite of his violent life Marlowe was an admired and highly influential figure: within weeks of his death *Peele paid tribute to him as 'Marley, the Muses darling for thy verse'. Shakespeare's early histories are strongly influenced by Marlowe, and he paid tribute to him in *As You Like It* as the 'dead shepherd'. *Jonson referred to 'Marlowes mighty line', and among others who praised him were Nashe, Chapman, G. *Harvey, and *Drayton. There are many modern editions of his plays and poems: the Revels Plays editions of the plays are to be recom-

mended, and in the same series, Millar Maclure's edition of the *Poems* (1968).

MARLOWE, Derek (1938–96), novelist and screenwriter, born in Perivale, Middlesex. His first novel, the spy thriller *A Dandy in Aspic* (1966), remains the best known of his nine novels, although his later work is more ambitious. *Do You Remember England?* (1972), in some ways his most autobiographical work, is both the story of a tragic love affair and a revealing picture of the idle rich at play. His fiction is marked equally by his elegant style as by his facility for byzantine plotting. He spent his last ten years screenwriting in Hollywood. A tenth novel was started but never finished.

MARMION, Shackerley (1603–39), educated at Wadham College, Oxford. He served in the Netherlands, and joined *Suckling's expedition to Scotland in 1638, though he became ill en route and returned to London. He wrote three plays, *Hollands Leaguer* (1632), *A Fine Companion* (1633), and, his best, *The Antiquary* (perf ?1635, printed 1641). He also wrote a long verse narrative in heroic couplets, *Cupid and Psyche* (1637), and contributed verse to the *Annalia Dubrensia* (see COTSWOLD OLIMPICK GAMES).

Marmion: *A Tale of Flodden Field*, a poem in six cantos by Sir W. *Scott, published in 1808. Marmion is a fictitious character of mixed qualities, a favourite of Henry VIII, proud, ambitious, and treacherous, who has tired of one love (a perjured nun, Constance of Beverley, who is walled up alive in a scene of Gothic horror) and is in pursuit of the wealthy Lady Clare, who is herself in love with Ralph de Wilton. After much intrigue and disguise (during which Clare herself takes to the convent for a while in refuge from Marmion, and Wilton passes for a palmer) the action moves to Flodden, with stirring descriptions of the encamped armies, and then of the battle, during which Marmion is mortally wounded: Clare, who has watched the fight from a nearby hill, succours the dying man with water from a fountain, an incident which provokes some of the best-known lines of the poem (Canto VI)—'O, woman! in our hours of ease, | Uncertain, coy and hard to please . . . When pain and anguish wring the brow, | A ministering angel thou!' Clare is finally united with Wilton, with the blessing of 'bluff King Hal'. The poem contains the Song of *Lochinvar (Canto V).

MAROT, Clément (1496–1544), French poet. He spent the greater part of his life in court service, and from 1527 was *valet de chambre* to Francis I. His Protestant sympathies led to arrest or exile on several occasions, and he spent some time in Italy and Geneva. He enjoyed great popularity in the 16th cent., developed the rondeau and ballade, and introduced a number of new forms into French poetry, including the elegy, the eclogue, the epigram, the epithalamium, and (probably) the Petrarchan sonnet. His translations of the Psalms were much admired by *Calvin, and were very frequently reprinted for some 200 years after his death.

Marplot, a character in Mrs Centlivre's *The Busie Body*.

Marprelate Controversy, see MARTIN MARPRELATE.

MÁRQUEZ, Gabriel García, see GARCÍA MÁRQUEZ.

MARQUIS, Don (1879–1937), Illinois-born American journalist and writer of light verse, known internationally for his creation of archy the cockroach, a *vers libre* bard writing in lower case because he cannot work the typewriter's shift key, and his friend mehitabel the alley cat, with her slogans 'wotthehell' and 'toujours gai, archy, toujours gai'. These characters first appeared in the New York *Sun*, then in the New York *Herald Tribune* and *Collier's Weekly*, and in various collections from *archy and mehitabel* (1927) onwards.

Marriage, a novel by S. *Ferrier, published 1818.

Lady Juliana, the foolish and romantic daughter of the earl of Courtland, elopes with a penniless young officer, Henry Douglas, who takes her to his Highland home, a gaunt, lonely house, where she is greeted by 'three long-chinned spinsters' and 'five awkward purple girls'. The dismay of the worldly Juliana, and the characters of the household and of the neighbouring gentry, are presented with liveliness and wit. Lady Juliana gives birth to twin daughters, the climax of her misfortunes. The couple move to London, and Henry eventually joins a regiment in India, permanently separating from his wife. Of the twins, Mary is brought up in Scotland, and grows into a plain but a wise and sensible girl. She rejects her mother's choice of a wealthy husband for her, marries happily, and settles in Scotland. Adelaide, her sister, marries an ageing duke, and eventually elopes with a man as heartless as herself. The novel, which Sir W. *Scott greatly admired, is clearly intended to commend prudent marriage.

Marriage-à-la-Mode, a tragi-comedy by *Dryden produced 1672, published 1673.

The main plot concerns a usurper's discovery that his daughter and his (lawful) predecessor's son have been secretly reared together in rural seclusion, and have fallen idealistically in love. The comic plot is a double intrigue involving two friends and their pursuit respectively of the wife of the one and the betrothed of the other. The counterpointing of these contrasting plots is particularly striking, especially as each ends anticlimactically, the lawful heir being restored to his throne in an overtly stagy manner, and the adulterous lovers failing to consummate their affairs. The play contains some of Dryden's finest songs, and embodies the principles of comic writing outlined in his preface to *An Evening's Love*.

Marriage of Heaven and Hell, The, a prose work by W. *Blake, etched c.1790–3, introduced by a short poem ('Rintrah roars and shakes his fires in the burden'd air'). It consists of a sequence of paradoxical aphorisms in which Blake turns conventional morality on its head,

claiming that man does not consist of the duality of Soul = Reason and Body = Evil, but that 'Man has no Body distinct from his Soul . . . Energy is the only life, and is from the Body . . . Energy is Eternal Delight.' He proceeds to claim that *Milton's Satan was truly his Messiah, and that Milton 'was a true Poet and of the Devils party without knowing it', and to produce a series of 'Proverbs of Hell' ('Sooner murder an infant in its cradle than nurse unacted desires' being one of the most notorious), which also celebrate the holiness of the natural world. He then moves to a sequence of visionary encounters with angels and prophets, in the course of which he dismisses the writings of *Swedenborg (whom he had greatly admired) as 'a recapitulation of all superficial opinions', accuses him of not having conversed sufficiently with Devils but only with Angels, and ends with an evocation of an Angel turned Devil 'who is my particular friend; we often read the Bible together in its infernal or diabolical sense . . . .' The aphorisms, both in form and content, resemble the paradoxes of G. B. *Shaw, who greatly admired Blake and was much influenced by his doctrine of contraries; they were also adopted by those active in the counter-culture movement of the 1960s: see under UNDERGROUND POETRY.

MARRYAT, Captain Frederick (1792–1848), author, naval captain, and FRS. His first novel, *The Naval Officer: or Scenes and Adventures in the Life of Frank Mildmay* (1829), a partly autobiographical story of adventure at sea, was a success, and he resigned his commission in 1830, after which he wrote another 15 novels as well as many miscellaneous essays and articles. Among his most successful works, *Peter Simple* (1834), *Jacob Faithful* (1834), and *Mr *Midshipman Easy* (1836), all sea stories, were followed in 1836 by *Japhet in Search of a Father*, the story of the struggles of a foundling. In 1837 came *Snarleyyow*, the tale of an indestructible dog, in 1839 *The Phantom Ship*, and in 1840 *Poor Jack*. Between writing his novels he travelled widely in Europe, America, and Canada. With *Masterman Ready* (1841) he turned his attention to children's books, and it is chiefly for these he is remembered. *The Settlers in Canada* (1844) was followed by *The Children of the New Forest* (1847), a historical novel about the adventures of the four Beverley children, orphaned during the Civil War, who take refuge with and learn the arts of survival from Jacob Armitage, a poor forester.

MARSH, Sir Edward Howard (1872–1953), classicist, scholar, patron of modern poetry and painting, a lifelong and eminent civil servant. An early champion of *Ibsen, he became a friend and executor of Rupert *Brooke, and between 1912 and 1922 edited five highly influential volumes of *Georgian Poetry. He edited Brooke's *Collected Poems*, with a long Memoir, in 1918; made many translations of classical and French authors, including *La Fontaine; and in 1939 published *A Number of People*, reminiscences of his many friends in the literary and political worlds. See C. Hassall, *Edward Marsh, Patron of the Arts* (1959).

MARSH, Dame Ngaio (pron. Ny-o) Edith (1899–1982), writer of *detective fiction, born at Christchurch, New Zealand. When young she worked as an actress and devoted much time in later life to theatre in New Zealand, an interest reflected in many of her novels. Her hero, Chief Detective Inspector Roderick Alleyn, first appears in *A Man Lay Dead* (1934); other titles include *Vintage Murder* (1937), *Surfeit of Lampreys* (1941), *Died in the Wool* (1945), and *Final Curtain* (1947). (See DETECTIVE FICTION.)

MARS-JONES, Adam (1954–), London-born novelist, short story writer and critic, educated at Cambridge, whose fiction includes *Lantern Lecture* (1981), a collection of three stories, one of which, 'Hoosh-Mi', features the queen and her corgis in fatal conjunction; *Monopolies of Loss* (1992), stories in a more sombre and predominantly realist vein, based on the AIDS epidemic, some of which first appeared in *The Darker Proof: Stories from a Crisis* (1987, with Edmund *White), and a novel, *The Waters of Thirst* (1993), a poignant gay suburban tragi-comedy about sexual obsession and kidney failure. He edited *Mae West is Dead: Recent Lesbian and Gay Fiction* (1983).

MARSTON, John (1576–1634), dramatist, whose mother was Italian. He graduated from Oxford in 1594, and joined his father, a lawyer, in the Middle Temple, where he maintained rooms until 1606. There he began to write satirical verse and plays for the new professional children's companies, playing at private indoor theatres. He took orders in 1609 and was incumbent of Christchurch, Hampshire, 1616–31. His *The Metamorphosis of Pigmalion's Image: And Certaine Satyres* and *The Scourge of Villanie* (both 1598) were published under the pseudonym Kinsayder, under which name he figures in *The Returne from Parnassus* (see PARNASSUS PLAYS, THE). Some of these satires were directed against literary rivals, including Bishop J. *Hall, and were burned by order of the archbishop of Canterbury in 1599. Marston's quarrel with *Jonson resulted in his portrayal as Crispinus in *Poetaster, but the two became friends again. His dramatic works were printed as follows: *The History of *Antonio and Mellida* (1602), of which *Antonio's Revenge* is the second part; *The Malcontent* (1604), with additions by *Webster; *Eastward Hoe* (1605), a comedy, written with Jonson and *Chapman; *The Dutch Courtezan* in the same year; *The Parasitaster, or The Fawner*, a comedy, and *Sophonisba*, a tragedy (both 1606); *What You Will* (1607), a comedy; and *The Insatiate Countesse* (1613), a tragedy (possibly completed by William Barksted). The plays were edited by H. H. Wood (1934–9) (including the doubtfully assigned *Histriomastix*, 1610), the poems by A. Davenport (1961). Wood, in line with most current critical opinion, gave highest praise to *The Malcontent* as 'one of the most original plays of

its period', but T. S. *Eliot ('John Marston', 1934) somewhat eccentrically singled out *Sophonisba* for its 'exceptional consistency of texture' and 'underlying serenity'. There is a life by P. J. Finkelpearl (1969).

MARSTON, John Westland (1819–90), dramatic poet and critic, who contributed to the *Athenaeum, wrote several critical works, and more than a dozen plays, including the successful *The Patrician's Daughter*, which was performed at Drury Lane in 1842. His son Philip Bourke Marston (1850–87), blinded in infancy, published several volumes of poems and short stories (*Collected Poems*, 1892). Their London home was a meeting place for many eminent friends in the theatrical and literary world, including *Kean, *Macready, *Dickens, *Swinburne, and D. G. *Rossetti.

Martext, Sir Oliver, vicar of a country parish in Shakespeare's *As You Like It*.

MARTIAL (Marcus Valerius Martialis) (*c.* AD 40–104), Roman epigrammatist of Spanish origin. His 1,500 epigrams, mostly satirical and often coarse, are very witty and have a great formal perfection. He found a translator in *May (1629) and was popular throughout the 17th cent. He influenced T. *Campion, *Jonson, *Herrick, and *Cowley. *Dryden thought him much inferior to *Virgil and *Lucan, but nevertheless quoted him a good deal. More recently he has been translated by P. *Porter (*After Martial*, 1972).

Martian school of poetry, see RAINE, C.

MARTIANUS CAPELLA (Marcian) (fl. 410–39), a North African writer, celebrated in the Middle Ages. He was the author of *De Nuptiis Philologiae et Mercurii* in nine books of prose and verse. The first two deal with the wooing (in a wide, metaphorical sense) of Philology by Mercury, and the last seven are an allegorical encyclopaedia of the Seven Liberal Arts (see TRIVIUM and QUADRIVIUM). This allegorization, together with that of the contemporary Prudentius, remained popular up to the Renaissance. Marcian is referred to by Chaucer in 'The Merchant's Tale' (*Canterbury Tales*, IV. 1732 ff.) and in *The House of Fame* (985). *Mulcaster is still using Martianus's method in his allegorizing of Philology in *The First Part of the Elementarie* (1582).

Martin, (1) in Dryden's *The Hind and the Panther*, symbolizes the Lutheran party; (2) in Swift's *A Tale of a Tub*, the Anglican Church, the allusion being to Martin Luther.

MARTIN, John (1789–1854), painter, who came to London from Northumberland in 1806. He specialized in pictures showing the sensational destruction of the legendary cities of antiquity—of Babylon, Nineveh, Sodom, and Gomorrah; these are vast paintings, where nightmare is made concrete by elaborate architectural detail. Martin's relationship with literature was close; he illustrated Milton's *Paradise Lost* (1823–7); he drew subjects from *Gray, *Byron, and Mary *Shelley;

he was extravagantly admired by poets and writers. It has been suggested that his *Sadak in Search of the Waters of Oblivion* (1812, Southampton Art Gallery) may have inspired a passage in Keats's **Hyperion*; P. B. *Shelley wrote a poem to accompany the engraving, published in 1828. *Beckford took Martin to Fonthill (1823); the descriptions of gloom and grandeur in **Vathek* (1782) are close to the vision of the painter. *Bulwer-Lytton enthused over his works, and his *Last Days of Pompeii* (1834) is indebted to Martin. Through his prints Martin became a widely popular artist; they were copied by both Branwell and Charlotte *Brontë, and Martin's fantastic cities influenced the imagery of their juvenilia: Martin himself plays a role as Edward de Lisle of Verdopolis, painter of Babylon. He was widely acclaimed in France; *Hugo drew images from him; Romantic writers use the word 'Martinien' to describe the spectacular and grandiose. Martin's paintings are the swansong of the taste for the Burkeian *sublime: something of his magnificence lingered on in the lavish films of Cecil B. de Mille.

MARTIN, Sir Theodore (1816–1909), educated at Edinburgh University, practised as a solicitor in Edinburgh and moved to London in 1846. He contributed, under the pseudonym *'Bon Gaultier', to *Tait's Magazine* and **Fraser's Magazine*, and collaborated with W. E. *Aytoun in the writing of the 'Bon Gaultier ballads', published in 1845. He also translated many works from German, Latin, Danish, and Italian, wrote a life of Prince Albert (5 vols, 1875–80) and reminiscences of Queen *Victoria (*Queen Victoria as I Knew Her*, 1902).

Martin Chuzzlewit, The Life and Adventures of, a novel by *Dickens, published 1843–4.

Martin, the hero, is the grandson of old Martin Chuzzlewit, a wealthy gentleman made misanthropical by the greed of his family. The old man has reared Mary Graham, a young orphan, to look after him, and regards her as his daughter. Young Martin is in love with Mary; but the grandfather, mistrusting his selfish character, repudiates him and gets him dismissed from his position as pupil to his cousin Mr Pecksniff, architect and arch-hypocrite. Martin, accompanied by the indomitably cheerful Mark Tapley as his servant, sails for America to seek his fortune. He goes as an architect to the fraudulent Eden Land Corporation, where he loses his money and nearly dies of fever. (This part gave great offence in the USA.) He then returns to England, his experiences having reformed his selfish attitudes. His grandfather has meanwhile established himself and Mary in Pecksniff's household and pretended to place himself under his direction, thus satisfying himself of Pecksniff's meanness and treachery. (Pecksniff tries to inveigle and bully Mary into marrying him.) He exposes the hypocrite, restores his grandson to favour, and gives him Mary's hand.

A sub-plot concerns Jonas Chuzzlewit, the son of old Martin's brother, a character of almost incredible villainy. He murders his father (in intention if not in fact); marries Mercy Pecksniff and treats her with the utmost brutality; murders the director of a bogus insurance company, by whom he has been taken in and blackmailed; is detected; and finally poisons himself.

The book contains many memorable minor characters: Tom Pinch, Pecksniff's gentle loyal assistant, and his sister Ruth; Pecksniff's daughters Charity and Mercy (Cherry and Merry); and Mrs Gamp, the disreputable old nurse; while 'Todgers's' is an eccentric London boarding house.

MARTIN DU GARD, Roger, see ROMAN FLEUVE.

MARTINEAU, Harriet (1802–76), born in Norwich; her childhood and youth were dogged by illness and poverty. A devout Unitarian in youth, her first published work was *Devotional Exercises* (1823), from which time she wrote indefatigably for the rest of her life. She began to review for the *Monthly Repository*, then in 1830 won all three prizes in an essay competition set by the Unitarians. Between 1832 and 1834 she published a series of stories, *Illustrations of Political Economy*, revealing both her passion for social reform and the influence of *Bentham and J. S. *Mill. The stories were immensely successful, as were her tales for *Brougham's Society for the Diffusion of Useful Knowledge, and she became a literary celebrity, including among her friends *Malthus, Sydney *Smith, and *Milnes, as well as politicians who consulted her on economic and social matters. In 1834 she travelled in America, and supported the abolitionists at some personal risk. *Society in America* appeared in 1837, and her first novel, *Deerbrook* (always her favourite among her works), in 1839. *The Hour and the Man*, a biography of *Toussaint L'Ouverture, came out in 1840, and a book of children's stories, *The Playfellow*, in 1841. In 1845 she settled in the Lake District and became a friend of the *Wordsworths. She had by now repudiated her Unitarian faith, and indeed all religious belief. Her radical *History of the Thirty Years' Peace* was published in 1849, and her anti-theological *Laws of Man's Social Nature* in 1851. Her translation and condensation of *Comte, *The Philosophy of Comte*, appeared in 1853. For most of the rest of her life she continued energetically with her journalism, and wrote a book which appeared posthumously as *An Autobiographical Memoir*, containing many observations on public and literary figures of her day. On several occasions she refused the offer of a Civil List pension, feeling it would compromise her independence.

MARTINEAU, James (1805–1900), brother of Harriet *Martineau, educated at Norwich Grammar School and Manchester New College, where, after working as a Unitarian minister at Dublin and Liverpool, he was appointed professor of moral philosophy in 1840; he was principal of the college from 1869 to 1885. He was an ardent upholder of the theist position, a powerful critic of materialism and naturalism, and was prompt to recognize the claims of the Darwinian philosophy of evolution. His chief books, mainly philosophical religious works, were mostly published after his 80th year. These include *Types of Ethical Theory* (1885), *A Study in Religion* (1887), and *The Seat of Authority in Religion* (1890). He was joint editor of the *Prospective Review* (1845–54). (See UNITARIANISM.)

MARTIN MARPRELATE, the name assumed by the authors of a number of anonymous pamphlets (seven are extant) issued in 1588–9 from a secret press, containing attacks in a railing, rollicking style on the bishops, and defending the Presbyterian system of discipline. They were stimulated by Archbishop Whitgift's attempts to impose uniformity in liturgical practice and to promote royal supremacy and the authority of the Articles.

The Marprelate tracts are among the best prose satires of the Elizabethan age. Their titles (in abbreviated form) are: *The Epistle*, *The Epitome*, *Minerall and Metaphisicall Schoolpoints*, *Hay Any Worke for Cooper* (a familiar street cry, here alluding to Thomas Cooper, bishop of Westminster), *Martin Junior*, *Martin Senior*, and *The Protestatyon*. As well as ballads, rhymes, and plays, they provoked replies from such noted writers as *Lyly and *Nashe; Richard and Gabriel *Harvey later became involved in the controversy. But the replies are on the whole less entertaining than the original pamphlets. *Hooker's work eventually settled the matter for the Church. The suspected authors, a Welshman named Penry and a clergyman named Udall, were arrested. The latter died in prison, the former was executed. Their collaborator, Job Throckmorton, denied his complicity at the trial of Penry, and escaped punishment.

Martinus Scriblerus, Memoirs of, a satirical work, directed against 'false tastes in learning', initiated by the *Scriblerus Club and written mainly by *Arbuthnot. It was printed in the second volume of *Pope's prose works in 1741. Martinus is the son of Cornelius, an antiquary of Munster, and the description of his birth, christening, education, and travels is a burlesque on various forms of contemporary pedantry.

The name 'Martin Scriblerus' was occasionally used by Pope as a pseudonym, and by *Crabbe in some of his earlier poems. Ed. Charles Kerby-Miller (1950, 1988).

MARTYN, Edward (1859–1923), born in the west of Ireland and educated in England; he was one of the founders of the *Irish Literary Theatre in 1899, as well as an ardent supporter of Irish educational and musical activities. His best-known plays are *The Heather Field* (chosen as one of the plays to open the Literary Theatre in 1899) and *Maeve* (1899), a drama of Anglo-Irish antagonism. He is caricatured as 'dear Edward' in G. A. *Moore's *Hail and Farewell*.

MARVELL, Andrew (1621–78), son of the Revd Andrew Marvell, born at Winstead in Holderness, Yorkshire. In 1624 the family moved to Hull on his father's appointment as lecturer at Holy Trinity Church. Marvell attended Hull Grammar School. He matriculated at Trinity College, Cambridge, as a sizar in Dec. 1633, and graduated in 1639. In 1637 he had contributed Greek and Latin verses to a Cambridge volume congratulating Charles I on the birth of a daughter. His mother died in Apr. 1638, his father remarrying in November. Around 1639 Marvell may have come under the influence of Roman Catholic proselytizers: according to one story he went to London with them and was fetched back by his father. In January 1641 his father was drowned while crossing the Humber, and soon after Marvell left Cambridge for London. Between 1643 and 1647 he travelled for four years in Holland, France, Italy, and Spain, learning languages and fencing, and perhaps deliberately avoiding the Civil War (he said later that 'the Cause was too good to have been fought for'). On his return from the Continent he apparently moved in London literary circles and had friends among Royalists. His poems to *Lovelace ('his Noble Friend') and on the death of Lord Hastings were published in 1649. In the early summer of 1650 he wrote 'An Horatian Ode upon Cromwell's Return from Ireland', perhaps the greatest political poem in English.

From 1650 to 1652 Marvell tutored young Mary Fairfax, daughter of the Parliamentarian general, at Nun Appleton in Yorkshire. In this period, it is usually assumed, he wrote 'Upon Appleton House' and lyrics such as 'The Garden' and the Mower poems. In 1653 he was appointed tutor to Cromwell's ward William Dutton, and moved to John Oxenbridge's house at Eton, where he probably wrote 'Bermudas'. In 1654 with 'The First Anniversary' (published 1655) he began his career as unofficial laureate to *Cromwell, and was appointed in 1657 Latin secretary to the council of state (a post previously occupied by his friend and sponsor *Milton, now blind). For eight months during 1656 Marvell was in Saumur with Dutton, where he was described as 'a notable English Italo-Machiavellian'. He mourned Cromwell in 'Upon the Death of His Late Highness the Lord Protector' (1658) and took part in the funeral procession. The following year (January) he was elected MP for Hull, and remained one of the Hull members until his death. At the Restoration his influence secured Milton's release from prison.

From June 1662 to April 1663 Marvell was in Holland on unknown political business, and in July 1663 he travelled with the earl of Carlisle as private secretary on his embassy to Russia, Sweden, and Denmark, returning in January 1665. His satires against *Clarendon were written and published in 1667. Later that year he composed his finest satire 'Last Instructions to a Painter', attacking financial and sexual corruption at court and in Parliament, and took part in the impeachment of Clarendon. *The*

Rehearsal Transpros'd, a controversial *mock-biblical prose work advocating toleration for Dissenters, which set new standards of irony and urbanity, appeared in 1672 (Pt II, 1673). Gilbert *Burnet called these 'the wittiest books that have appeared in this age', and Charles II apparently read them 'over and over again'. According to the report of government spies, Marvell (under the codename 'Mr Thomas') was during 1674 a member of a fifth column promoting Dutch interests in England, and in touch with Dutch secret agents. The second edition of *Paradise Lost* contained a commendatory poem by Marvell, and in his prose works he continued to wage war against arbitrary royal power. *Mr Smirk, or The Divine in Mode* and *A Short Historical Essay Concerning General Councils* (both 1676), and *An Account of the Growth of Popery and Arbitrary Government in England* (1677), were all Marvell's though prudently published anonymously. The *London Gazette* offered a reward, in Mar. 1678, for information about the author or printer of *An Account*. That August, however, Marvell died in his house in Great Russell Street from medical treatment prescribed for a tertian ague. His *Miscellaneous Poems* appeared in 1681, printed from papers found in his rooms by his housekeeper Mary Palmer, who gave herself out to be his widow and signed the preface 'Mary Marvell' in order to get her hands on £500 which Marvell had been keeping for two bankrupt friends. This volume did not contain the satires (the authorship of some of which is still disputed): these appeared in *Poems on Affairs of State* (1689–97).

Famed in his day as patriot, satirist, and foe to tyranny, Marvell was virtually unknown as a lyric poet. C. *Lamb started a gradual revival, but Marvell's poems were more appreciated in 19th-cent. America than in England. It was not until after the First World War, with *Grierson's *Metaphysical Lyrics* and T. S. *Eliot's 'Andrew Marvell', that the modern high estimation of his poetry began to prevail. In the second half of the 20th cent. his small body of lyrics was subjected to more exegetical effort than the work of any other *metaphysical poet. His oblique and finally enigmatic way of treating what are often quite conventional poetic materials (as in 'The Nymph Complaining for the Death of Her Faun' or 'To His Coy Mistress') has especially intrigued the modern mind.

Poems and Letters, ed. H. M. Margoliouth, 3rd edn rev. P. Legouis and E. E. Duncan-Jones (2 vols, 1971); *Latin Poems*, ed. and trans. W. A. McQueen and K. A. Rockwell (1964); *The Rehearsal Transpros'd*, ed. D. E. B. Smith (1971); P. Legouis, *Andrew Marvell: Poet, Puritan, Patriot* (2nd edn, 1968); H. Kelliher, *Andrew Marvell: Poet and Politician* (1978); J. B. Leishman, *The Art of Marvell's Poetry* (1966).

Marwood, Mrs, a character in Congreve's *The Way of the World*.

MARX, Karl (1818–83), born in Rhenish Prussia, of Jewish descent, editor of the *Rheinische Zeitung* at Cologne in 1842. His extreme radical views led to the suppression of the paper, and Marx went to Paris, where he met *Engels and collaborated with him in works of political philosophy. He was expelled from Paris, moved to Brussels, and at the time of the revolutionary movement of 1848 returned to Cologne, where, with Engels, he again conducted a newspaper, the *Neue Rheinische Zeitung*. His revolutionary and communistic views caused him to be once more expelled, and he finally settled in London. He and Engels wrote about contemporary politics and society in England, finding in *Carlyle's works, particularly *Latter-Day Pamphlets* (1850), the only example of proper concern on the part of a British writer for the social condition of workers. They adopted Carlyle's rhetoric about the 'cash nexus' connecting worker, product, and manufacturer, but they differed radically from Carlyle's proposed solution to the misery of the working class in a return to a feudal system of government.

In 1867 appeared the first volume of Marx's treatise *Das Kapital*, in which he propounded his theory of political economy. After the death of Marx this was completed from his papers by Engels. It is a criticism of the capitalistic system under which, according to Marx, a diminishing number of capitalists appropriate the benefits of improved industrial methods, while the labouring class are left in increasing dependency and misery. Marx holds the view that the price of a commodity should be the remuneration of the labour required to produce it, and that it fails to be this because capital exacts a share of the price, while competition among the workers obliges them to accept less than their proper due. The remedy for this state of things Marx finds in the total abolition of private property, to be effected by the class war. When the community has acquired possession of all property and the means of production, it will distribute work to each individual and provide him with the means of sustenance: 'From everyone according to his faculties, to everyone according to his needs.'

Marx was the principal creator of the First International Working Men's Council.

Marxist literary criticism, a critical tradition that seeks to understand literature from the perspective of the 'historical materialism' developed by *Marx and *Engels; that is, as a changing form of material production that participates in and illuminates the processes of history. Marx himself was deeply versed in world literature, and drew upon his favourite authors (*Aeschylus, Shakespeare, *Goethe) even in his economic writings. Neither he nor Engels, though, bequeathed a critical or aesthetic theory, but they suggested that authors such as *Balzac who held conservative political views could nonetheless, as artists, reveal the true tendencies of history, and more convincingly than socialist writers of a propagandist type; and further, that art is not tied directly to phases of economic development but has a certain autonomy. These principles are upheld in 'classical' Marxism, by G. Plekhanov (1856–1918), Lenin, Trotsky, and *Lukács, against tendencies in more mechanistic applications of Marxism to reduce art to its economic circumstances or to dismiss the great achievements of bourgeois culture in favour of some purely 'proletarian' art. Of these writers, it was Lukács who eventually developed a consistent Marxist critical position, one that stressed the value of 19th-cent. *realism. In the Soviet Union under the tyranny of Stalin, the crudely prescriptive policy of *Socialist Realism obstructed more independent critical thinking, except in the little-known *Bakhtin circle. The first significant Marxist criticism in the English-speaking world emerged within the doctrinaire constraints of Communist Party orthodoxy: Granville Hicks (1901–82) in the USA and the more imaginative *Caudwell in England assessed literature in terms of its usefulness as a weapon in the class struggle. The German Marxists *Benjamin and *Brecht provided far more sophisticated and influential views, seeing literature less as a 'reflection' of history than as a 'production' of new meanings. In significant disagreement with Lukács, Brecht distrusted the 'illusionism' of realistic or naturalistic art, and claimed political value for his own kind of *Modernist experiment. His influence has been strong upon *Barthes and other critics who have brought about alliances among Marxist, *formalist, and post-*structuralist literary theory, usually of a kind that regards realism as inherently conservative. In the English-speaking world since 1968, the foremost Marxist critics have been R. *Williams, who discarded the traditional metaphor of economic 'base' and cultural 'superstructure', Terry Eagleton (1943–), whose work since the 1970s has approached literature through the contradictions of 'ideology', and Fredric Jameson (1934–), who has developed from Lukács's work a broader system for the analysis of literary and cultural forms. Resisting the assumption that Marxist criticism is pertinent only to overtly 'sociological' features of literature, Eagleton and Jameson have both employed its methods to illuminate general problems of literary theory and the phenomenon of *postmodernism. Since the 1930s, elements of Marxist theory have often been combined with those of other critical schools such as *psychoanalytic criticism, *feminist criticism, structuralism, and *deconstruction.

Mary Barton: *A Tale of Manchester Life*, a novel by Mrs *Gaskell, published 1848.

The entirely working-class cast of characters in this novel was then an innovation. The background of the story is Manchester in the 'hungry forties' and the acute poverty of the unemployed mill-hands. Mary Barton is the daughter of an active and embittered worker and trade unionist, John Barton. She has attracted Henry Carson, son of one of the employers,

and, flattered by his attentions and the hope of a grand marriage, has repulsed in his favour her faithful admirer Jem Wilson, a young engineering worker. A group of workmen, exasperated by the failure of the employers to consider their grievances, decide to kill young Carson (who has mocked their attempts to reach an understanding), as a warning to his class, and the lot falls on Barton to do the deed. When Carson is shot dead suspicion falls on Jem Wilson as his rival with Mary, and she, who has by now realized that it is Jem whom she loves, discovers that her father is the real murderer. Jem is tried for his life, and is saved by Mary's frantic and finally successful efforts to prove his innocence without betraying her father. Made desperate by his guilt, John Barton confesses to the fiercely vindictive old father of Henry Carson, and wins his forgiveness as he dies.

The book was violently attacked by Manchester mill-owners and the Tory press as being biased against the employers, but it was admired by *Carlyle and *Dickens and was translated into many languages, including Finnish and Hungarian.

Mary Magdalene, Play of, the only surviving play in late medieval English drama which is based on the legend of a saint, presenting events in the saint's life both before the Resurrection and during her subsequent legendary residence in Provence. It is a very long play, in the Digby set, in two parts, 52 scenes and 2,144 lines. It has some claims to sophistication and is dedicated to 'Miles Blomefylde' whose name appears as *Poeta* in the Digby 'The Conversion of St Paul'.

Digby Plays, ed. F. J. *Furnivall (EETS ES 70, 1896, repr. 1967, 55–136); D. L. Jeffrey, 'English Saints' Plays' in N. Denny (ed.), *Medieval Drama* (1973).

'Mary Morison', a lyric by *Burns, published 1786, possibly addressed to Alison Begbie, one of his youthful loves.

MARY QUEEN OF SCOTS (Mary Stuart) (1542–87), daughter of James V of Scotland, who married Francis II of France (1558), Lord Darnley (1565), and Bothwell (1567). She was imprisoned by *Elizabeth I and finally beheaded on a charge of conspiring against the latter's life. She appears as *Duessa in *The Faerie Queene*, and she and her four attendants, The *Queen's Maries, appear in many ballads: She figures in *Scott's *The Abbot*, and is the subject of a tragedy by *Schiller (in which she and Elizabeth meet, as they did not in real life). J. *Hogg celebrates her memory in *The Queen's Wake* (1813). She also appears in a trilogy of plays by *Swinburne, and a novel by M. *Hewlett. More recently her conflict with Elizabeth has been dramatized by R. *Bolt in *Vivat, Vivat Regina* (1970) and Liz *Lochhead in *Mary Queen of Scots Got Her Head Chopped off* (1987). There is a biography by Antonia *Fraser (1969).

MASEFIELD, John Edward (1878–1967), born in Herefordshire; his idyllic early childhood was vital to his later work, but in 1884 his mother died and in 1891, after severe mental breakdown, he was brought up by relatives who did not prove sympathetic. School in Warwick was followed at the age of 13 by training for the merchant navy. In 1894 Masefield sailed for Chile, suffered acutely from sea-sickness, and was returned home. He sailed again across the Atlantic, but at the age of 17 deserted ship and became a vagrant in America, taking what jobs he could find, reading voraciously, and writing verse. Back in England he began his prolific writing career, which included poetry, plays, novels, essays, children's stories, and, at the end of his life, memoirs. *Salt-Water Ballads* (which included 'I must to the seas again') was received with interest in 1902: one of its dedicatees, a teacher 11 years older than himself, Constance de Cherois Crommelin, became his wife. (Masefield's well-known line was altered to the more familiar 'I must go down to the seas again' for the convenience of the musical setting.) *Ballads and Poems*, which contained 'Cargoes', appeared in 1910, but in this year another nervous crisis began, only resolved when the first lines of *The Everlasting Mercy* (1911) came to him on a country walk: this narrative poem, with its account of the conversion of the rough Saul Kane, provoked indignation and admiration. *The Widow in the Bye Street* (1912) was another novel of Herefordshire low life, with a strong erotic theme, and *Reynard the Fox* (1919) was a rattling verse tale set in the rural world of Masefield's childhood. Meanwhile he had produced collections of shorter verse, as well as stories, novels, and plays: his *Collected Poems* (1923) sold in great numbers, as did the novels *Sard Harker* (1924), *Odtaa* (1926), *The Bird of Dawning* (1933), and his story for children *The Midnight Folk* (1927). In 1930 Masefield became *poet laureate and in 1935 received the OM. He continued to write with energy, producing more volumes of poetry, the sea-novels *Dead Ned* (1938) and *Live and Kicking Ned* (1939), and the autobiographical *So Long to Learn* (1952). A final luminous fragment of autobiography, describing his country childhood up to his mother's death, appeared in 1966 as *Grace before Ploughing*. There is a life by C. Babington Smith, published 1978: see also *An Endless Quiet Valley* (1998) by Paul Binding.

Mask of Anarchy, The, a poem of political protest by P. B. *Shelley, written in response to the 'Peterloo Massacre' at Manchester in August 1819, published 1832.

Composed at speed and in anger, the poem uses the popular ballad form with immense power and sometimes surreal effect. The 'mask' is a pageant, or masquerade, of British political leaders—Castlereagh, Eldon, Sidmouth—whom Shelley blames not only for the killing and wounding of some 500 people at a public demonstration for parliamentary reform, but also for the general conditions of harshness and oppression in England: what he calls the 'triumph of Anarchy' (compare *The Triumph of Life). Anarchy

rides on a horse: 'He was pale even to the lips, | Like Death in the Apocalypse.' His bloody progress is only prevented by Hope, 'a Maniac maid', who throws herself under the trampling hooves. The poem ends with a celebration of freedom, and Shelley's historic appeal for non-violent mass political protest in a great assembly of working people: 'Rise like lions after slumber | In unvanquishable number.'

masks, see MASQUES.

Maskwell, the *'Double Dealer' in Congreve's comedy of that name, 'a sedate, thinking villain, whose black blood runs temperately bad'.

MASON, A(lfred) E(dward) W(oodley) (1865–1948), failed actor turned successful novelist, best remembered for *The Four Feathers* (1902; film version 1939), the story of Harry Feversham's heroism in redeeming himself from the accusation of cowardice in the eyes of three fellow officers and his beloved, Ethne Eustace. His many other popular works include the series featuring Inspector Hanaud, which began with *At the Villa Rose* (1910).

Mason, Mary, Lady, the principal character in A. Trollope's novel *Orley Farm*.

MASON, William (1724–97), poet, and friend of T. *Gray and Horace *Walpole, with both of whom he corresponded; he became Gray's executor, edited his poems and letters, and wrote his life. Many of his poems, like Gray's, were printed in *Dodsley's *Collection of Poems* (1748–58). His own work includes the tragedies *Elfrida* (1751) and *Caractacus* (1759); the latter clearly shows the influence of Gray's interest in *primitivism in its subject, its Pindaric *odes, and its chorus of bards. He also wrote a long blank verse poem on landscape gardening, *The English Garden* (4 books, 1771–81), which expresses his enthusiasm for the *picturesque.

masques, or **masks,** dramatic entertainments involving dances and disguises, in which the spectacular and musical elements predominated over plot and character. They were acted indoors by amateurs, and were designed to include their spectators in the action, sometimes simply by a concluding dance. As they were usually performed at court, often at very great expense, many have political overtones. They were perhaps of Italian origin, but assumed a distinctive character in England in the 16th and 17th cents. Many of the great poets and dramatists, S. *Daniel, T. *Campion, G. *Chapman, and T. *Middleton, wrote masques, and they reached their highest degree of elaboration in the hands of *Jonson who introduced the 'anti-masque' as a comic and grotesque foil to the main spectacle. The great architect Inigo *Jones designed the machinery or decoration (the 'Painting and carpentry' as Jonson scathingly dismissed them) for some of them. Jonson's *The Sad Shepherd*, Milton's *A Maske*, better known as *Comus*, and other such works often called masques, can only be loosely assigned to the genre, and are closer to *pastoral dramas.

Massacre at Paris, The, a play by *Marlowe written c.1592. The undated first edition (c.1593/4) describes it as having been acted by the Admiral's Men. It is a short and poor text, probably representing a mangled version of what Marlowe wrote. A single leaf surviving in manuscript used to be thought to be a forgery by J. P. *Collier, but is now considered a genuine contemporary copy of part of one scene.

The play deals with the massacre of Protestants in Paris on St Bartholomew's day, 24 Aug. 1572 (an event witnessed by P. *Sidney, who was staying in Paris at the time). Its most memorable character is the Machiavellian duke of Guise, whose high aspiring language seems to have influenced Shakespeare in his early history plays. The massacre is depicted in a series of short episodes, a notable one being that in which the rhetorician *Ramus is killed after a verbal onslaught by the Guise on his emendations of Aristotle. The Guise himself is eventually murdered at the behest of Henry III, dying on the lines:

> *Vive la messe!* Perish Huguenots!
> Thus Caesar did go forth, and thus he died.

whose relationship to Shakespeare's *Julius Caesar (II. ii. 10, 28, 48) has not been satisfactorily explained. Leaping over 17 years, the play concludes with the murder of Henry III and the succession of the (then) Protestant Henry of Navarre. It is difficult to tell whether the frequent comic effect of the play is authorially intended or is the result of the incompleteness of the text. Ed. H. J. Oliver (1968).

Massacre of St Bartholomew, see BARTHOLOMEW, MASSACRE OF ST.

MASSIE, Allan (1938–), novelist, critic, and reviewer, born in Singapore. His first novel, *Change and Decay in All Around I See* (1978) was followed by *The Last Peacock* (1980) and *The Death of Men* (1981), a thriller. A trilogy of novels set in imperial Rome, *Augustus* (1989), *Tiberius* (1990), and *Caesar* (1993), established him as one of the best historical novelists of his generation. *Antony* (1997) completed the series. In *A Question of Loyalties* (1989) a Frenchman, Étienne de Balafré, reconstructs the career of a father he hardly knows, a former supporter of the Vichy regime during the Second World War. *The Hanging Tree* (1990) returns to a historical setting, this time the 15th cent. *The Sins of the Father* (1991) is a love story set against the legacy of the Holocaust, while *These Enchanted Woods* (1993) presents a rags-to-riches love story set in rural Perthshire. *The Ragged Lion* (1994), a recreation of the life of Sir Walter *Scott, was followed by *King David* (1995), a fictional study of the biblical monarch.

MASSINGER, Philip (1583–1640), born at Salisbury, and educated at St Alban Hall, Oxford. His father was the trusted agent of the Herbert family, to members of which the playwright addressed various dedications and poems. He became the chief collaborator of J. *Fletcher after the withdrawal of *Beaumont, and on Fletcher's death in 1625 he became the principal dramatist of the King's Men. He was buried in Fletcher's grave at St Saviour's, Southwark (now Southwark Cathedral).

He is known to have written or shared in the writing of 55 plays. Of these 22 are lost. Of the extant plays 15 are of his sole composition, 16 were written in collaboration with Fletcher, and two in collaboration with others. Massinger's share in the Fletcher plays was given no acknowledgement in the Beaumont and Fletcher folios, but has been identified with reasonable accuracy by modern scholars. He shared with Fletcher the writing of such plays as *The Custom of the Country (?1619–22), Sir John van Olden *Barnavelt (1619), The Double Marriage (?1621), *The Beggar's Bush (?1622) and A Very Woman (?1625) and with Fletcher and others collaborated in *The Bloody Brother (c.1616). With *Dekker he shared the writing of a religious play, *The Virgin Martyr, a work uncharacteristic of both men. With N. *Field he wrote *The Fatal Dowry, in which his high romantic seriousness blends strikingly with Field's satire.

He wrote only two social comedies, *A New Way to Pay Old Debts and *The City Madam. A New Way was a mainstay of the English stage in the late 18th and early 19th cents, with the villainous Sir Giles Overreach providing a vehicle for the talents of a long line of actors including J. P. *Kemble and *Kean. Both plays are inspired by his patrician contempt for the ambitions and affectations of the rising mercantile classes in the city. Two amusing and sophisticated but much more romantic comedies are *The Guardian* (1633) and his feminist play *The Picture* (1629).

He wrote several excellent tragedies. The early *Duke of Milan, a tragedy of jealousy, was followed by *The Roman Actor, which was his favourite play. It makes remarkable use of plays-within-the-play, and in the person of Paris the actor he was able to show something of his own prolonged difficulties with political censorship. Because of this censorship he was forced to do a complete rewriting of *Believe as You List, perhaps his greatest tragedy. It is a powerful story of a returned nationalist leader failing to get support and being hounded by the imperial authorities.

The remainder of his plays are in the Fletcherian vein of tragi-comedy. These include *The Maid of Honour, *The Bondman, The Renegado, and The Great Duke of Florence (perf. 1627, printed 1636).

The equable and lucid verse of Massinger's plays, once a big point in their favour, went out of fashion when *Webster and *Tourneur became better known, and it may well be that a lack of interest in the linguistic texture of his plays is the reason for the present comparative neglect of one of the most serious professional dramatists of the post-Shakespearian period.

The standard edition of Massinger's plays is by Philip Edwards and Colin Gibson (5 vols, 1976). The most recent biographical and critical study is T. A. Dunn, *Philip Massinger* (1957).

MASSINGHAM, H(arold) J(ohn) (1888–1952), eldest son of H. W. *Massingham. He published many works reflecting a deep appreciation of many aspects of the English countryside and natural history; they include *The English Countryman* (1942).

MASSINGHAM, H(enry) W(illiam) (1860–1924), described by his friend G. B. *Shaw as 'the perfect master journalist'. He was the influential editor of the *Nation* from 1907 to 1923, when he resigned in response to a change in its political intentions.

Mass Observation, see MADGE.

MASSON, David (1822–1907), biographer, critic, journalist, successively professor of English literature at University College London (1853) and Edinburgh University (1865). He is remembered for his *Life of Milton* (7 vols, 1859–94). He was a disciple of *Carlyle, and became the founder and editor of *Macmillan's Magazine* (1859). His other works include biographies of *Drummond of Hawthornden (1873) and *De Quincey (1881), editions of *Milton, *Goldsmith, and De Quincey, and *Essays Biographical and Critical* (1856). His *Edinburgh Sketches and Memories* (1892), *Memories of London in the Forties* (1908), and *Memories of Two Cities* (1911) are accounts of literary circles in mid-century London and Scotland.

Master Humphrey's Clock, a weekly founded by *Dickens in 1840, originally intended as a miscellany which would contain a continuous narrative (*The Old Curiosity Shop*) linked by the reminiscences of the narrator, Master Humphrey. This device was soon dropped, as was the periodical's title after the publication in weekly numbers of *Barnaby Rudge* (1841).

MASTERMAN, C(harles) F(rederick) G(urney) (1874–1927), Liberal politician, author, and journalist, whose writings describe, with a mixture of Christian Socialist sympathy, Edwardian–Georgian nostalgia, and apprehension, the changing social conditions of England. *From the Abyss* (1902) is an impressionistic collection of essays about slum life; *In Peril of Change* (1905) collects essays on literary and social topics, including the telling piece 'In Dejection near Tooting', in which he reflects on the ravaged landscape and hideous architecture of London's dumping ground; *The Condition of England* (1909) expresses fears for a nation acquiring social improvements without spiritual renewal. Samuel Hynes, in *The Edwardian Turn of Mind* (1968), suggests that part of Masterman's weakness as a practical politician lay in his dependence on imaginative literature rather than politics or economics. He was a friend of F. M. *Ford, and inspired the portrait of the Liberal minister Waterhouse in *Parade's End*.

Master of Ballantrae, The: *A Winter's Tale*, a novel by R. L. *Stevenson, published 1889.

It is the story of the lifelong feud between the master of Ballantrae, violent, unscrupulous, elegant, and courageous, and his younger brother Henry, at the outset a quiet, dull, honest fellow. The master joins Prince Charles Edward in the '45 rebellion, disappears after Culloden, and is believed dead. After many adventures the master returns, with a price on his head, to find that Henry has succeeded to his place and the woman whom he was to have married. Embittered by misfortune, he embarks on a course of persecution, first in Scotland then in America, which brings both brothers to an untimely grave in the Adirondacks, where Stevenson first conceived the story. The extravagant action and the hints of the supernatural are rendered more plausible by the character of the dour narrator, the unimaginative but loyal Ephraim Mackellar.

MASTERS, Edgar Lee (?1868–1950), American poet and novelist, born in Kansas, who is best known for his collection of poems *Spoon River Anthology* (1915), which consists of dramatic monologues spoken from beyond the grave by the inhabitants of a Midwestern cemetery.

MATHER, Cotton (1663–1728), Presbyterian divine of Boston, Massachusetts, a narrow, self-righteous minister and voluminous writer, one of the best-known examples of the tyrannical Puritan ministers of his time in New England. He was noted for the part he played in the Salem witchcraft trials of 1692, on which he commented in his best-known work, *Magnalia Christi Americana* (1702).

MATHEWS, Harry (1930–   ), the only American member of *OuLiPo. His early fictions, such as *The Conversions* (1962) and *Tlooth* (1966), offer a compendium of eccentric narratives and sophisticated word-play. His recent novels, *Cigarettes* (1987) and *The Journalist* (1994), are just as inventive and bewildering, but explore more recognizable American contexts. In these works Mathews disguises the formal constraints underlying his plots and characters. Mathews has also written a number of shorter, more obviously experimental texts such as 'Their Words, for You' (1977) which consists wholly of scrambled proverbs. Mathews's poetry (collected in *A Mid-Season Sky*, 1992) again employs rigid conventions as a means of embodying the surrealism of everyday life.

MATHIAS, Thomas James (?1754–1835). He published anonymously in 1794 the first part of *The Pursuits of Literature*, a work which went through 16 editions, in which he satirizes many contemporary authors, most of them radicals; other parts followed in 1797. He became librarian at Buckingham Palace in 1812. In 1817, pursuing an ardent love of Italy and Italian literature, he moved to the Continent, and spent his last years at Naples.

'matter of Britain, the', the term used by Jean Bodel (late 12th–early 13th cent.) in a French verse romance about *Charlemagne (dating from the late 12th cent.) to describe the subject matter of the romances concerned with the Arthurian legends, as distinct from those concerned with classical stories (the *matter of Rome), or with Charlemagne and his circle (the *matter of France). The 'matter of Britain' was a source of inspiration in the 20th cent. for D. *Jones and C. *Williams.

'matter of England, the', a term sometimes used by 20th-cent. scholars to refer to romances concerned with English heroes or localized in England (such as *King Horn or *Havelok the Dane), which therefore fall outside the three subject matters said by Jean Bodel to be the only ones: the matters of Britain (above), Rome, and France (below).

'matter of France, the', the term used by Jean Bodel, a late 12th-cent. romance writer, to refer to the romances based on stories about *Charlemagne and his circle, as distinct from those based on Arthurian (the *matter of Britain) or classical (the *matter of Rome) legend.

'matter of Rome, the', the term used by Jean Bodel, a late 12th-cent. French romance writer, to refer to those romances concerned with classical stories, as distinct from Arthurian (the *matter of Britain) or *Charlemagne legends (the *matter of France).

MATTHEW PARIS, see PARIS, M.

Matty, Miss (Matilda Jenkyns), the principal character in Mrs Gaskell's *Cranford.

MATURIN, Charles Robert (1782–1824), educated at Trinity College, Dublin. He took orders and for a time kept a school. He was one of the most important writers of the *'Gothic' novel. He published The Fatal Revenge in 1807; The Wild Irish Boy in 1808; and The Milesian Chief in 1811. In 1816 his tragedy *Bertram was produced by *Kean at Drury Lane, on the recommendation of Sir W. *Scott and *Byron, with great success. His next two tragedies, Manuel (1817) and Fredolfo (1819), were failures. He then returned to novels, publishing Women, or Pour et Contre (1818) and his most memorable work *Melmoth the Wanderer (1820). His last novel, The Albigenses, appeared in 1824.

Maud, a poem by *Tennyson, published 1855, composed 1854, but springing from the germ of the lyric 'Oh! that 'twere possible', composed 1833–4.

The poem is a monodrama in sections of different metres, in which the narrator, a man of morbid temperament, describes the progress of his emotions: first describing his father's death and his family's ruin, both contrived by the old lord of the Hall; then expressing his growing love for Maud, the old lord's daughter, and the scorn of her brother, who wishes her to marry a vapid 'new-made' lord; his triumph at winning Maud; their surprisal and her

brother's death in a duel; his own flight abroad and ensuing madness; and his final reawakening to hope in the service of his country. The poem contains several of Tennyson's best lyrics ('I have led her home', 'Come into the garden, Maud'), but some contemporary critics found it obscure or morbid; G. *Eliot protested against its 'faith in war as the unique social regenerator', and *Gladstone disliked the emphasis on bloodshedding as a cure for disappointed love, writing, 'We do not recollect that 1855 was a season of serious danger from a mania for peace and its pursuits.'

MAUGHAM, W(illiam) Somerset (1874–1965), novelist and playwright, born in Paris, the fourth surviving son of a lawyer attached to the British embassy: his mother died when he was 8, and his father in 1884. William was sent to Whitstable to live with an aunt and uncle, and was educated at the King's School, Canterbury, and at Heidelberg. He then trained in London as a doctor and his first 'new realist' novel, Liza of Lambeth (1897), drew on his experiences of slum life as an obstetric clerk. He achieved fame in 1907 with Lady Frederick, a comedy of marriage and money, and in 1908 had four plays running in London. In 1911 he met Syrie Wellcome: their daughter Liza was born in 1915, and he married Syrie in 1917. Their marriage was unorthodox, and they spent most of their time apart. In 1914 Maugham met Gerald Haxton in Flanders, where both were working for an ambulance unit: Haxton became his secretary and companion, and in 1916 they set off on the first of many journeys together, this time to the South Seas. Further travels to China, Asia, and Mexico followed. In 1926 Maugham bought a house at Cap Ferrat on the French Riviera, which became a meeting place for writers and politicians. In 1954 he was created a Companion of Honour.

Maugham's plays include The Circle (1921), the story of a young wife who elopes with a rubber planter from Malaya; Our Betters (1917), a satire on title-hunting Americans; Home and Beauty (1919); East of Suez (1922), which impressed audiences with spectacular evocations of Peking; The Constant Wife (1926) in which a woman takes revenge on her unfaithful husband and departs for Italy with an old admirer; The Sacred Flame (1928); and the anti-war drama For Services Rendered (1932). His best-known novel, Of Human Bondage (1915), describes Philip Carey's lonely boyhood in Whitstable (disguised as Blackstable) and subsequent adventures: Carey is handicapped by a club foot as Maugham was by a severe stammer. The Moon and Sixpence (1919) recounts the life in Tahiti of Charles Strickland, a Gauguinesque artist who neglects duty for art. Cakes and Ale (1930) is a comedy about good-natured Rosie Driffield married to a Grand Old Man of letters, who most took to be *Hardy. The Razor's Edge (1944) takes a mystical turn, as its American hero learns the value of non-attachment in an Indian ashram. A Writer's Notebook (1949) consists of extracts from notes which Maugham had kept from the age of 18, and shows him as sharp, worldly, and observant.

He also wrote many successful short stories: 'Rain', set in Samoa (*The Trembling of a Leaf*, 1921), tells of the conflict between a life-affirming prostitute, Sadie Thompson, and a repressed missionary: it was staged, and filmed several times. 'The Alien Corn' (*Six Stories in the First Person Singular*, 1931), about a pianist who commits suicide when he realizes he will never transcend the second-rate, is also well remembered. Maugham claimed to take the view expressed in his autobiography, *The Summing Up* (1938), that he himself stood 'in the very first row of the second-raters', a view which has been largely endorsed by critics. Despite a lack of serious recognition, his works remain popular, and his plays performed.

Maule, Matthew, a character in Hawthorne's *The House of the Seven Gables*, whose curse at the point of execution condemns the house of Pyncheon for its persecution of him.

MAUPASSANT, Guy de (1850–93), French short story writer and novelist, a literary disciple of *Flaubert and one of the group of young *naturalistic writers that formed around *Zola. To their collection of tales *Les Soirées de Médan*, he contributed 'Boule de suif', a story of the Franco-Prussian War that many regard as his finest. The hundreds of stories, simply and directly told, that he published in a brief creative life typically deal with country folk or urban employees and civil servants, though other social groups (aristocrats, prostitutes, soldiers) also appear regularly. *La Maison Tellier* (1881), *Clair de lune* (1884), *Miss Harriet* (1884), *Le Horla* (1887), *L'Inutile Beauté* (1890) are among his many collections. Besides his stories he wrote six novels, of which the best known are *Une vie* (1883), *Bel-Ami* (1885), and *Pierre et Jean* (1888).

MAUPIN, Armistead (1944–   ), American writer, best known for a sequence of six comic novels depicting alternative lifestyles in San Francisco: *Tales of the City* (1978), *More Tales of the City* (1980), *Further Tales of the City* (1982), *Babycakes* (1984), *Significant Others* (1987), and *Sure of You* (1989). Beginning life as a daily newspaper serial, this joyous *roman fleuve* about the inhabitants of a bohemian boarding house broke new ground in its high-spirited celebration of gay subcultures. Maupin was also one of the first writers to chronicle the AIDS epidemic. *Maybe the Moon* (1992) was a more muted satire on hypocrisy in the film business.

MAURIAC, François (1885–1970), French novelist, dramatist, and critic, author of *Thérèse Desqueyroux* (1927) and other short psychological tales set usually in the 'Landes' country round Bordeaux; *Le Nœud de vipères* (1932) and *Le Mystère Frontenac* (1933), longer studies of family life; *Asmodée* (1937) and *Les Mal Aimés* (1945), dramas; etc. His characters are fettered by prosperous bourgeois convention and by religion and human frailty. He was awarded the *Nobel Prize in 1952.

MAURICE, (John) F(rederick) D(enison) (1805–72), educated at Trinity Hall, Cambridge. He joined the Church of England in 1830 and was ordained in 1834. *The Kingdom of Christ* (1838) was a plea for Christian unity. In 1840 he became professor of English literature and history at King's College, London. His belief in the application of Christian principles to social reform gained him many followers; he became a leader of the Christian Socialist movement which brought him into close contact with C. *Kingsley. His *Theological Essays* (1835) presented his unorthodox views on Eternal Punishment and caused his dismissal from King's College. In 1854 he founded a Working Men's College, and was its first principal. In 1866 he became professor of moral philosophy at Cambridge. *Tennyson's lyric inviting him to visit the Isle of Wight ('Come, when no graver cares employ') was well known.

MAUROIS, André (1885–1967), French author of *biography: *Ariel* (1923, of *Shelley; the first *Penguin paperback, 1935), *Disraëli* (1927), *Byron* (1930), *A la recherche de Marcel Proust* (1949), *Lélia* (i.e. George *Sand, 1952), etc.; histories of England (1937) and the United States (1948); novels: *Climats* (1928), *Le Cercle de famille* (1932), etc.; also of the early *Les Silences du Colonel Bramble* (1918), sketches of an English officers' mess.

MAX MÜLLER, Friedrich (1823–1900), son of the German poet Wilhelm Müller. He came to England in 1846 and became a British subject. He was commissioned by the East India Company to bring out an edition of the Sanskrit *Rigveda* which was published in 1849–73. He settled in Oxford in 1848 and was Taylorian professor of modern European languages from 1854 to 1868, and one of the curators of the Bodleian Library, 1856–63 and 1881–94. Max Müller delivered two remarkable courses of lectures on 'The Science of Languages' at the Royal Institution in 1861–4, and was professor of comparative philology at Oxford from 1868 until his death. He devoted much attention to comparative mythology and the comparative study of religions. A full edition of his works was published in 1903.

MAXWELL, Gavin (1914–69), writer, traveller, and conservationist, educated at Stowe and Hertford College, Oxford, where he studied estate management. He is best remembered for *Ring of Bright Water* (1960), a poignant evocation of life on the remote Scottish coast and of his relationship with two semi-tame otters; his other works include travel writings and the autobiographical *The House of Elrig* (1965).

MAXWELL, Glyn (1962–   ), poet and dramatist, born in Welwyn Garden City and educated at Oxford. Versatile, bold, unexpected, and prolific, he followed his first collection *Tale of the Mayor's Son* (1990) with

Out of the Rain (1992), and *Rest for the Wicked* (1995): both his subject matter and his tone are vastly varied, ranging from classical myth (in his 'Phaeton' sequence, on male ambition, in his third collection) to contemporary satire and surreal speculation. Many of the poems in *The Breakage* (1998) dwell on the First World War: it contains a sequence written in homage to Edward *Thomas. His novel *Blue Burneau* (1994) is a Ruritanian political fantasia set on the imaginary Island of Badeo. He has written several verse dramas, encouraged by *Walcott, with whom he studied at Boston: three of them were published as *Gnyss the Magnificent* (1995). *Wolfpit* (1996) was performed at the Edinburgh Fringe and is based on the legend of the Green Children of Suffolk. *Moon Country* (1996) describes a journey to Iceland with S. *Armitage.

MAY, Thomas (1595–1650), educated at Sidney Sussex College, Cambridge. He adopted the parliamentary cause and was secretary for the Parliament (1646). He was author of two narrative poems on the reigns of Edward III and Henry II and of a history of the Long Parliament (1647). He also wrote translations of *Virgil's *The Georgics* and *Lucan's *Pharsalia* (which were praised by *Jonson), two comedies, *The Heir* and *The Old Couple* (c.1620), and three tragedies on classical subjects. It appears that he had hoped to succeed Jonson as laureate in 1637, and transferred his allegiance from court to Parliament when *D'Avenant obtained the post; it is for this reason that *Marvell in his poem 'Tom May's Death' (1681) writes of his 'Most servile wit and Mercenary Pen'.

MAYAKOVSKY, Vladimir Vladimirovich (1893–1930), Russian *Futurist poet. Born in Georgia, he grew up in Moscow, where in 1908 he joined the Bolshevik Party. He was arrested for revolutionary activities three times in 1908–9, spending his time in prison reading widely and beginning to write poetry. In 1910 he and a group of other painter-poets published the first Russian Futurist collection *A Trap for Judges*, and in 1912 signed the Futurist manifesto 'A Slap in the Face for Public Taste'. His first long poem, *A Cloud in Trousers* (1914–15), began a series of masterpieces on his main theme, impossible fate and impossible love. In July 1915 he met Lili Brik, the great love of his life, to whom his long love and fate poems *The Backbone-Flute* (1915), *Man* (1916–17), *About That* (1923) are dedicated. Mayakovsky greeted the revolution and expected the Futurists to provide the vanguard of the new state's art, but the Futurists found little favour with the communist authorities, Lenin in particular finding Mayakovsky's *150,000,000* (1920) 'incomprehensible rubbish'. In 1923 Mayakovsky was one of the founders of LEF (the Left Front of the Arts), but this was forced to disband in 1925 (to re-emerge briefly as 'New Lef', 1927–8). His work in the 1920s shows a constant tension between the personal and the civic, between his hopes from the revolution and his awareness that nothing had changed. By the end of the decade

Mayakovsky was in a state of crisis; his relationship with Lili Brik and her husband had soured, he had fallen in love with an émigrée, Tatyana Yakovleva, who refused to return to Russia, his plays *The Bedbug* and *The Bath-House* (both 1929) had been disastrous. He shot himself on 14 Apr. 1930. The suicide cast a shadow on his official reputation, until some years later when Stalin declared that 'Mayakovsky was and remains the best and most talented poet of our Soviet epoch.' English translations of Mayakovsky include versions by Herbert Marshall (*Mayakovsky*, 1965, etc.) and G. Reavey and M. Hayward (*The Bedbug and Selected Poetry*, 1960).

May Day, 1 May, celebrated with garlands and dancing, the choice of a queen of the May (gaily dressed and crowned with flowers), the erection of a Maypole (painted with spiral stripes and decked with flowers) to dance round, and so forth. Perhaps derived from the Roman *Floralia*. The May-game was a set performance in the May Day festivities, in which *Robin Hood and *Maid Marian figured. May Day was adopted in 1889 as the international Labour holiday.

MAYHEW, Henry (1812–87), the son of a London solicitor, educated at Westminster School, from which he ran away. He was briefly articled to his father before becoming a dramatist and journalist. The first of his many plays and farces (some very successful) was *The Wandering Minstrel* (1834). In 1841 he was a co-founder and briefly a joint editor of *Punch. He wrote many novels and stories, as well as books on science, religion, education, and travel, including works on Germany and the Rhine (where he briefly lived), and *The Boyhood of Martin Luther* (1865). But he is chiefly remembered for the philanthropic journalism to which he turned at the end of the 1840s; his remarkable series of 82 articles, couched as lengthy 'letters', in the *Morning Chronicle* were published with some alterations as *London Labour and the London Poor* (1851). His painstaking and compassionate investigations into the plight of the London poor revealed the extent to which starvation, disease, and transportation were daily horrors. He performed similar work on the subject of prisons, publishing *The Criminal Prisons of London* (1862) and *London Children* (1874), illustrated by W. S. *Gilbert. His plain but harrowing descriptions, often told in the words of those he spoke with, did much to stir the public conscience towards reform.

Maylie, Mrs and Harry, characters in Dickens's *Oliver Twist*.

Mayor of Casterbridge, The: *A Story of Character*, a novel by T. *Hardy, published 1886.

Michael Henchard, a hay-trusser, gets drunk at a fair and sells his wife and child for 5 guineas to a sailor, Newson. When sober again he takes a solemn vow not to touch alcohol for 20 years. By his energy and acumen he becomes rich, respected, and eventually the mayor of Casterbridge. After 18 years his wife returns, supposing Newson dead, and is reunited with her husband. She brings with her her daughter Elizabeth-Jane, and Henchard is led to believe that she is his child, whereas she is in fact Newson's. Through a combination of unhappy circumstances, and the impulsive obstinacy of Henchard, troubles accumulate. He quarrels with his capable young assistant in his corn business, Donald Farfrae. Mrs Henchard dies and Henchard learns the truth about the girl. Farfrae becomes his successful rival, both in business and in love, and marries Lucetta, whom Henchard had hoped to win. Soon Henchard's business is ruined, the story of the sale of his wife is revealed, and he takes again to heavy drinking. Farfrae now has Henchard's business, his house, and Lucetta, while Henchard works as a labourer in his yard. Eventually Farfrae becomes mayor, the office Henchard once held. His stepdaughter is his only comfort, then Newson returns and claims her and after Lucetta's death Farfrae marries her. Thus he possesses all that was once Henchard's. Henchard becomes lonelier and more desolate, and dies wretchedly in a hut on Egdon Heath.

Mazeppa, a poem by Lord *Byron, published 1819.

The poem, which forms an interesting transition between Byron's romantic and colloquial styles, is founded on a passage in *Voltaire's *Charles XII*. While *Charles, king of Sweden, and his men rest after their defeat at Pultowa, one of the king's officers, Mazeppa, tells a tale of his early life. Being detected in an intrigue, he had been bound naked onto the back of a wild horse from the Ukraine, which was then loosed and lashed into madness. The horse galloped off, through forest and river, carrying its fainting rider, and never stopped until it reached the plains of the Ukraine, where it fell dead. Mazeppa, at the point of death, was rescued by Cossack peasants.

Meagles, Mr, Mrs, and their daughter Pet, characters in Dickens's *Little Dorrit*.

Meanjin (pron. Me-an-jin) **Quarterly,** a review of literature and art in Australia, founded in 1940 and edited by C. B. Christesen. The title is taken from the Aboriginal name for Brisbane, where the magazine was first published.

Measure for Measure, a tragi-comedy by *Shakespeare, written probably in the summer of 1604, but not printed until the First *Folio (1623). Its chief source is *Whetstone's play *Promos and Cassandra*, itself based on a story in *Cinthio's *Hecatommithi*. It has often been categorized as a 'problem play' because of the unpleasantness of its subject matter and the complexity of its plot and themes.

The duke of Vienna, on the pretext of a journey to Poland, hands over the government to his virtuous-seeming deputy Angelo, who enforces strict laws against sexual licence which for the past 14 years had been neglected. Angelo at once sentences to death Claudio, a young gentleman who has got his betrothed Julietta with child. Claudio's sister Isabella, who is a novice in a sisterhood of nuns, pleads with Angelo for her brother's life, urged on by Claudio's friend Lucio. In response to her repeated pleas, Angelo offers to spare Claudio's life if she will consent to be his mistress. Isabella refuses, and will not be persuaded even by the desperate entreaties of Claudio in prison. The duke, disguised as a friar, has made a visit of spiritual comfort to Claudio, and now devises a way of saving his life. Isabella is to agree to a midnight assignation with Angelo, but her place is to be taken by Mariana, who was betrothed to Angelo and still loves him. Mariana is first seen (IV. i) listening to the song 'Take, O, take those lips away'. This scheme is successful, but Angelo still proceeds with the order for Claudio's execution, though unknown to Isabella Claudio is saved by the substitution of the head of Ragozine, a pirate, who has died that night in the same prison. The duke lays by his disguise, simulates a return to Vienna, and pretends to disbelieve the complaints of Isabella and suit of Mariana, in favour of Angelo's hypocritical denial. When Angelo is forced to confess, both Mariana and Isabella plead for his life; Mariana is married to Angelo, Lucio to a whore, and at the end of a baffling final speech the duke appears to propose marriage to the novice Isabella.

Medall, The, a poem by *Dryden, published 1682.

The earl of *Shaftesbury, who is represented in *Absalom and Achitophel* and possibly in *Mr Limberham*, was acquitted of charges of high treason in 1681, and a medal was struck to commemorate the event. Dryden's response includes savage attacks on Shaftesbury himself, the City, and the Commons. It predicts with some accuracy the constitutional instability which was to beset the country in the ensuing 30 years. *Shadwell and Samuel Pordage (1633–?91) both wrote replies.

Medici, the, the family that were rulers of Florence from 1434 and grand dukes of Tuscany from 1569 to 1737. The earlier Medici were great patrons of art and literature, chief among them Cosimo (1389–1464) and Lorenzo 'the Magnificent' (c.1449–92), founders of the Medicean or Laurentian Library. The latter, himself a poet, was father of Pope *Leo X. Cathérine de Médicis, as she is known in France (1519–89), daughter of the grandson of Lorenzo the Magnificent, was consort of Henry II of France, and regent during the minority of Charles IX; her rule there was the source of much of the anti-Italian feeling embodied in the myth of the *Machiavellian politician. Marie de Médicis (1573–1642), niece of the grand duke of Tuscany, was consort of Henry IV of France from 1600 and regent 1610–17. There is a life of Lorenzo by W. *Roscoe (1795).

Medina, in Spenser's *Faerie Queene* (II. ii), represents the golden mean of sensibility, her sisters *Elissa and Perissa representing its extremes.

Medmenham Abbey, a ruined Cistercian abbey on the Thames near Marlow, rebuilt as a residence and notorious in the 18th cent. as the meeting place of a convivial club known as the Franciscans or the Hell-Fire Club. This was founded by Sir Francis Dashwood, and *Wilkes and *Dodington were among its members. Its motto 'Fay ce que voudras' ('Do what you like') was adopted from that of *Rabelais's abbey of Thelema. There is a good deal about it in *Johnstone's *Chrysal, or The Adventures of a Guinea* (III. ii, chs 17 *et seq.*).

Medoro, in *Orlando furioso*, a young Moor of humble birth, with whom *Angelica falls in love and whom she marries, thereby causing the despair and madness of Orlando.

MEDWALL, Henry, see FULGENS AND LUCRECE.

MEHTA, Gita, see ANGLO-INDIAN LITERATURE.

MEHTA, Ved Parkash (1934–), Indian writer and journalist (now an American citizen), born near Lahore, and educated at Balliol College, Oxford, and at Harvard. His works include several studies of Indian life and autobiographical and biographical memoirs, including *Face to Face* (1957); *Daddyji* (1972); *Mamaji* (1979); *Vedi; My Early Education in an Indian Orphanage for the Blind* (1982), *The Ledge between the Streams* (1984), *Sound-Shadows of the New World* (1986), and *The Stolen Light* (1989)—the whole series now collectively entitled *Continents of Exile*. *Fly and the Fly-Bottle* (1963) is a personal account of meetings with various British intellectuals, including I. *Berlin, A. J. *Ayer, A. J. P. *Taylor, and I. *Murdoch, originally published in the *New Yorker*, to which he was a regular contributor.

meiosis, an understatement, sometimes ironical or humorous and intended to emphasize the size, importance, etc., of what is belittled. Except in *litotes, which is a form of meiosis, the use of meiosis is chiefly colloquial; e.g. 'He's doing all right out of it'; 'That must be worth a few bob.'

Meistersinger, a title taken in the 15th cent. by certain professional German poets of high skill and culture, to distinguish themselves from the wandering gleemen. They were often craftsmen in their ordinary avocations—smiths, weavers, and the like. They represent a phase of the development of German verse from the minnesang (see MINNESINGERS). The Meistersang and singer were governed by an elaborate set of rules and organization, which are depicted in *Wagner's opera *Die Meistersinger von Nürnberg*, produced in 1868.

MELANCHTHON, the Graecized name of Philip Schwartzerd (1497–1560), German humanist who was professor of Greek at Wittenberg University; one of the principal advocates of the *Reformation.

Melbury, Grace, a character in Hardy's *The Wood-landers*.

Meleagant (Mellyagaunce, Mellygaunt, etc., in *Malory), in the Arthurian legends, the evil son of the good king Bademagus (Baudemagus) of Gorre. He abducts Guinevere after winning her by a trick at Arthur's court and is pursued by Arthur's knights, most significantly by Lancelot. Their conflict is the central story in the *Lancelot* of *Chrétien de Troyes.

'Melibeus, The Tale of', see CANTERBURY TALES, 18.

Melincourt, or *Sir Oran Haut-ton*, a satire by *Peacock, published 1817.

One of the longest and most ambitious of Peacock's books, it has a more novelistic plot than the others, which features the wooing by various suitors of a rich young heiress, Anthelia Melincourt, her abduction by a villainous peer, Lord Anophel Achthar, and his friend, the Revd Mr Grovelgrub, and her rescue when she is about to be raped by Lord Anophel. The plot, which is indebted to Richardson's *Clarissa* and to *Holcroft's *Anna St Ives*, has strong feminist connotations. Anthelia is ultimately rescued by a humorous variant on the Noble Savage, Sir Oran *Haut-ton (see MONBODDO), an orang-utan whom the hero, Mr Sylvan Forester, has educated to everything except speech, and for whom he has bought a seat in Parliament. Sir Oran is affectionate and chivalrous and plays delightfully on the flute. His virtues show up the corruptions of 'advanced' society, as Forester, an idealistic primitivist, intends. Forester, whose views resemble *Shelley's literary brand of radicalism, debates with Mr Fax, a Malthusian economist, such causes as rotten boroughs, paper currency, slavery, and the recent conservatism of the Lake poets. Provoked by an article by *Southey in the *Quarterly Review*, vol. 16 (1816), Peacock censures Southey himself (Mr Feathernest), *Coleridge (Mr Mystic), *Wordsworth (Mr Paperstamp), and *Gifford, the editor of the *Quarterly* (Mr Vamp), as a group of political renegades. The central set piece is the election in the borough of One-Vote, in which Sir Oran Haut-ton is returned to Parliament by the single, bought vote of Mr Christopher Corporate.

Melissa, in *Orlando furioso*, the beneficent witch who releases *Rogero from the power of *Alcina.

Mell, Mr, in Dickens's *David Copperfield*, the poor usher at Creakle's school.

Mellefont, a character in Congreve's *The Double Dealer*.

Melmoth the Wanderer, a novel by C. R. *Maturin, published 1820.

This novel, which was praised by writers as diverse as *Thackeray, D. G. *Rossetti, and *Baudelaire, was in effect the last, and also one of the most effective, of the *'Gothic' school. The tale rushes energetically through every kind of horror and iniquity, and has moments of genuine power. Melmoth, who has sold his soul for the promise of prolonged life, offers relief from suffering to each of the characters, whose terrible stories succeed one another, if they will take over his bargain with the Devil. But Stanton, imprisoned in the cell of a raving lunatic; Moncada in the hands of the Inquisition; Walberg, who sees his children dying of hunger; and many other sufferers, all reject the proposed bargain.

After his trial *Wilde adopted the name Sebastian Melmoth.

Melmotte, Augustus, a financial speculator, one of the principal characters in A. Trollope's novel *The Way We Live Now.

melodrama, in early 19th-cent. use, a stage play (usually romantic and sensational in plot and incident) in which songs and music were interspersed. In later use the musical element gradually ceased to be an essential feature, and the name now denotes a dramatic piece characterized by sensational incident and violent appeals to the emotions, but with a happy ending [OED].

Melvil, Count de, and his son Renaldo, in Smollett's *Ferdinand Count Fathom.

MELVILLE, Herman (1819–91), American novelist and poet, born in New York City, a product of the American mercantile gentry. After his father's business failure and death in 1832, however, Melville left school and was largely an autodidact, devouring Shakespeare, the Authorized Version of the Bible, and 17th-cent. meditative writers such as Sir T. *Browne, as well as the numerous historical, anthropological, and technical works which he used to supplement his experiences when he wrote. After sailing as a 'boy' on a packet to Liverpool in 1839, Melville shipped in 1841 on the whaler *Acushnet* for the South Seas, where he jumped ship, joined the US navy, and finally returned three years later to begin writing.

The fictionalized travel narrative of *Typee or A Peep at Polynesian Life* (1846) was Melville's most popular book during his lifetime. Like most of his works, *Typee* was published first in Britain, for prestige and to guard against piracy, and throughout his career Melville enjoyed a rather higher estimation in Britain than in America. After a well-received sequel, *Omoo: A Narrative of Adventures in the South Seas* (1847), the perfunctorily plotted *Mardi and a Voyage Thither* (1849), an allegorical romance with philosophical meditations, fared less well.

Having married Elizabeth Shaw, daughter of the chief justice of Massachusetts, in 1847, and with a mother, sisters, and eventually four children to support, Melville wrote the realistic sea stories *Redburn: His First Voyage* (1849) and *White-Jacket; or The World in a Man-of-War* (1850), which he considered potboilers. Inspired by the achievement of *Hawthorne, Melville changed his next sea tale into *Moby-Dick, or, The Whale* (1851), whose brilliance was noted at the time by some critics and very few readers.

After the critical disaster of *Pierre, or The Ambiguities* (1852), a *Gothic romance with Shelleyan over-tones and a satire on the literary profession, Melville wrote anonymous magazine stories, among them *'Bartleby the Scrivener' and *'Benito Cereno', which were collected in *The Piazza Tales* (1856), and the historical novel *Israel Potter: His Fifty Years of Exile* (1855) about a neglected hero of the American Revolution. To recover from a breakdown he undertook a long journey to Europe and the Holy Land (depicted in the narrative poem *Clarel*, 1876). Sceptical and tormented, but unable to discard his Manichaean view of God, Melville remarked while visiting Hawthorne in Liverpool in 1856, 'I have just about made up my mind to be annihilated.'

The Confidence-Man: His Masquerade (1857), a mordantly nihilistic satire of human gullibility, was Melville's last novel. After unsuccessful lecture tours, he worked as customs officer in New York harbour, where he wrote *Battle-Pieces and Aspects of the War* (1865), trenchant poems of disillusion with Civil War era America. *John Marr and Other Sailors* (1888) and *Timoleon* (1891) were privately printed. Despite some revival of interest in Britain, Melville died virtually forgotten, with *Billy Budd, Foretopman* still in manuscript: contemporary misunderstanding, censorship, and neglect, and the subsequent revision of Melville's reputation since the 1920s, have made him a classic case of the artist as reviled Titan. He enlarged the stylistic range and metaphysical concerns of fiction while helping to create the characteristically American mixed-genre, symbolic novel which Hawthorne called 'romance'; and *Moby-Dick* is the closest approach the United States has had to a national prose epic.

Melyodas, in *Malory, king of Lyones, the father of Tristram by his first wife Elizabeth, the sister of King Mark.

memoir-novel, an early form of the novel, purporting to be true autobiographical history, often including diaries and journals, but in fact largely or wholly fictitious. The author appears, if at all, merely as 'editor' of another's memoirs. The form arose in 17th-cent. France, and *Defoe, with *Robinson Crusoe* (1719) and *Moll Flanders* (1722), was the first English master. During the 18th cent. the author's claim to be presenting a genuine (as opposed to a fictional) memoir dwindled to a literary convention; Smollett's *Roderick Random, Goldsmith's *The Vicar of Wakefield, Mackenzie's *The Man of Feeling, M. Edgeworth's *Castle Rackrent, and many others were presented as memoirs under only the thinnest disguise. The popularity of the form declined sharply in the 19th cent., but Hogg's *Private Memoirs and Confessions of a Justified Sinner, Dickens's *David Copperfield, Melville's *Moby-Dick, C. Brontë's *Jane Eyre, and several novels of Thackeray (notably *The History of Henry Esmond) are outstanding examples. (See also NOVEL, RISE OF THE.)

Memoirs of a Cavalier, a historical romance most probably by *Defoe, published 1724.

The pretended author, 'Col. Andrew Newport', a young English gentleman born in 1608, travels on the Continent, starting in 1630, goes to Vienna, and accompanies the army of the emperor, being present at the siege and sack of Magdeburg, which is vividly presented. He then joins the army of Gustavus Adolphus, remaining with it until the death of that king and taking part in a number of engagements which he describes in detail. After his return to England he joins the king's army, first against the Scots, then against the forces of Parliament, being present at the battle of Edgehill, which he fully describes, the relief of York, and the battle of Naseby.

Memoirs of a Woman of Pleasure, often known as *Fanny Hill*, a work by J. *Cleland, published 1748–9.

Unlike, for instance, her predecessor *Moll Flanders, Fanny Hill is only narrowly developed as a character. However, Cleland employs her cleverly, in breathless epistle and journal, as a vehicle for his absorbed examination of sexuality, in both men and women, in its many varieties and in minute physiological detail. His occasional pretence of moral indignation, and use of euphemistic language, add an ironic and spurious respectability to his work.

Memoirs of Captain Carleton, a narrative published 1728 as *The Memoirs of an English Officer*, by Captain George Carleton. It was once thought to be by *Defoe, but is now known not to be by him or *Swift, to whom the work was sometimes groundlessly attributed. Captain Carleton, who unquestionably existed, is the subject of an attractive tale of soldierly adventure. Sir W. *Scott, who regarded the *Memoirs* as Carleton's own work, brought out a new edition in 1808.

Carleton volunteers on board the *London* on the declaration of war with the Dutch in 1672. In 1674 he enters the service of the prince of Orange, remaining there until the peace of Nijmegen. Returning to England, he receives a commission from James II and serves in Scotland and then in Flanders until the peace of Ryswick. The most interesting part of the memoirs follows. Carleton embarks with Lord Peterborough for Spain in 1705, and gives a stirring narrative of the siege, capture, and subsequent relief of Barcelona and of the campaign by which Peterborough, with scanty resources, temporarily placed the Archduke Charles on the throne of Spain. This is followed by some account of various parts of Spain visited by the author as a prisoner of war. See Steig Hargevick, *The Disputed Assignment of 'Memoirs of an English Officer' to Daniel Defoe* (2 vols; 1972, 1974).

MENANDER (c.342–292 BC), an Athenian dramatic poet, was the most distinguished writer of New Comedy, which, with its trend towards realistic fiction based on contemporary life, gave a pattern for much light drama from the Renaissance onwards, making its influence felt through Latin adaptations by *Plautus and *Terence, at least eight from Menander himself.

No play survived the Dark Ages; but *Dyskolos* (or *Misanthrope*), a light-hearted early play, and large parts of others were recovered from papyri in the 20th cent.; they show at first hand something of the blend of amusement and perceptive human sympathy which earned Menander his reputation.

Men and Women, a collection of 51 poems by R. *Browning, published in two volumes, 1855. The poems date from the period after Browning's marriage in 1846, and express a new-found energy and confidence—'poems of all sorts and sizes and styles and subjects', as he said, adding, 'I hope to be listened to, this time.' But the volumes made their way slowly. The poems show Browning's mind at its most multitudinous and eclectic, ranging over history, art, philosophy, and religion; they include many of his finest dramatic monologues, such as 'Fra Lippo Lippi', 'Bishop Blougram's Apology', 'Andrea del Sarto', and 'Cleon', whose effect is based on the fusion of an intensely realized situation with an unsurpassed feeling for the cadences of the speaking voice. The collection also includes Browning's most famous love poem 'Love among the Ruins', and the problematic *'Childe Roland to the Dark Tower Came'. The collection closes with an address to Elizabeth Barrett (*Browning), 'One Word More' (a phrase picked up during their correspondence in 1845–6).

Menaphon, a prose romance with interludes of verse by R. *Greene, published 1589. *Nashe's preface to the first edition offered a satirical survey of contemporary literature.

The romance tells the adventures of the princess Sephestia, shipwrecked on the coast of Arcadia. The convention of impenetrable disguise is taken to ridiculous lengths as Sephestia, disguised as Samela, is wooed simultaneously by her father and her teenage son, while herself carrying on a love affair with her (disguised) husband. Her fourth lover is the shepherd Menaphon of the title. Some charming lyrics, including the cradle song 'Weepe not my wanton, smile upon my knee', diversify the intricate narrative.

MENCKEN, H(enry) L(ouis) (1880–1956), American journalist and critic, born in Baltimore, who, as literary editor from 1908, then as co-editor, 1914–23 (with G. J. *Nathan), of *The Smart Set* exercised a great influence on American taste, upholding the iconoclasm of writers as diverse as G. B. *Shaw, *Ibsen, *Nietzsche, *Zola, and *Twain, and attacking the 'ferocious intolerance', 'snouting Puritanism', and 'literary standards derived from the *Ladies' Home Journal*' which prevailed in America. Nevertheless he strongly opposed European 'patronage' of America, and supported such native writers as *Dreiser and S. Anderson. In 1924 he founded with Nathan the *American Mercury*, which he edited until 1933, and in which he continued to satirize and goad his countrymen. His many books include *The American Language* (1919), in which he defends the developing vigour and versatility of colloquial American usage. There is a life by D. C. Stenerson (1971).

MENDELSSOHN(-BARTHOLDY), Felix (1809–47), German composer, whose most popular work is one of the most famous compositions inspired by Shakespeare, the incidental music to *A Midsummer Night's Dream*. Mendelssohn had known Shakespeare through the *Schlegel translations from an early age, and wrote the overture when only 17 for piano performance within the family, though he orchestrated it immediately afterwards. The remaining numbers, including the Scherzo, the Nocturne, and the ubiquitous Wedding March, were added for a stage performance in Berlin in 1843. This remained Mendelssohn's only contribution to Shakespeare music: an early project for an opera on *The Tempest* never came to fruition.

Mendelssohn made many visits to Britain, the first of which included a trip to Scotland which inspired the overture *The Hebrides* and the 'Scottish' Symphony: the latter, not finished until 1842, was dedicated to Queen *Victoria who had twice received the composer in London that year. Another outcome of his English connection was the oratorio *Elijah* (1846), an essay in the Handelian tradition, though originally written to a German text. He wrote several anthems and psalms to English (biblical) words, of which 'Hear My Prayer' (containing the popular 'O for the wings of a dove') is the best known. There are surprisingly few songs with English texts, but the eight books of *Songs without Words* for piano solo were staple piano fodder in the Victorian drawing room; over-popularity has made it difficult to hear them for the distinguished compositions that the best of them are.

MENEGHELLO, Luigi (1922–), Italian novelist, emeritus professor at the University of Reading. His novels *Libera nos a malo* (*Free us from Evil*, 1963) and *I piccoli maestri* (*The Outlaws*, 1964), and *Pomo pero* (*Eeny Meeny*, 1974, a commentary on *Libera nos a malo*), deal with memories, including the Resistance against Fascism. His extreme linguistic self-consciousness draws on a variety of stylistic registers and language (including English), making him one of the most original writers to have emerged from postwar Italy.

Men's Wives, stories by *Thackeray, which appeared in *Fraser's Magazine*, 1843.

They are concerned with different kinds of unhappy marriage, and the exploitation of one partner by the other. The longest and most fully developed story, 'The Ravenswing', concerns Morgiana Crump ('The Ravenswing'), who possesses beautiful hair and a beautiful singing voice, marries the profligate Captain Walker, and supports him by singing.

Mephistopheles, a word of unknown origin, which appears first in the German *Faustbuch* of 1587 as 'Mephostophiles'. It is the name of the evil spirit to whom *Faust was said in the German legend to have sold his soul. Shakespeare, in *The Merry Wives of Windsor* (I. i), mentions 'Mephostophilus'.

Mercator, a trade journal edited by *Defoe. It succeeded the *Review* in 1713 and continued till the following year.

MERCATOR, Gerardus, the Latinized form of the name of Gerhard Kremer (1512–94), a Flemish geographer who devised the form of map known as 'Mercator's Projection', in which the meridians of longitude are shown at right angles to the parallels of latitude, enabling the navigator to plot the correct compass bearing for a direct course from one point to another.

MERCER, David (1928–80), playwright, born in Wakefield, the son of an engine-driver. After attempts at various careers he achieved recognition with his trilogy of television plays *Where the Difference Begins* (1961), *A Climate of Fear* (1962), and *The Birth of a Private Man* (1963), published together as *The Generations* in 1964. The trilogy is primarily concerned with problems of left-wing political commitment; it opens in a Yorkshire working-class home, and ends with death on the Berlin Wall. Mental disturbance, alienation, class conflict, generation conflict (particularly between working-class father and educated son), and the meaning of Marxism, both British and continental, are recurrent themes in many subsequent works for stage, screen, and television, which include *A Suitable Case for Treatment* (TV 1962, published in *Three TV Comedies*, 1966, filmed as *Morgan*, 1965); *After Haggerty*, staged and published in 1970, which has as protagonist a Marxist theatre critic; and *Shooting the Chandelier* (TV 1977, pub. 1978). Mercer was one of the first playwrights to appreciate the possibilities of television as a writer's medium.

Merchant of Venice, The, a comedy by *Shakespeare written between 1596 and 1598. It was printed in 1600, and this text was reprinted in the First *Folio (1623). Its chief source is the first story of the fourth day in *Il pecorone*, Giovanni Fiorentino's collection of *novelle*. Other sources include *Munday's *Zelauto* and the *Gesta Romanorum*. In performance *Shylock, treated sometimes comically, sometimes tragically, has often been made into the central character. An adaptation by George Granville, *The Jew of Venice*, was the normal stage version from 1701 to 1741.

Bassanio, a noble but poor Venetian, asks his friend Antonio, a rich merchant, for 3,000 ducats to enable him to prosecute fittingly his suit of the rich heiress Portia at Belmont. Antonio, whose money is all employed in foreign ventures, undertakes to borrow the sum from Shylock, a Jewish usurer, whom he has abused for his extortions. Shylock consents to lend the money against a bond by which, if the sum is not repaid at the appointed day, Antonio shall forfeit a pound of his flesh. By her father's will Portia is to marry that suitor who selects of three caskets (one of gold, one of silver, one of lead) that which contains her portrait. Bassanio makes the right choice—the leaden casket—and is wedded to Portia, and his friend Gratiano to her maid Nerissa. News comes that Antonio's ships have been wrecked, that the debt has not been repaid when due, and that Shylock claims his pound of flesh. The matter is brought before the duke. Portia disguises herself as an advocate, Balthazar, and Nerissa as her clerk, and they come to the court to defend Antonio, unknown to their husbands. Failing in her appeal to Shylock for mercy, Portia admits the validity of his claim, but warns him that his life is forfeit if he spills one drop of blood, since his bond gives him right to nothing beyond the flesh. Pursuing her advantage, she argues that Shylock's life is forfeit for having conspired against the life of a Venetian citizen. The duke grants Shylock his life, but gives half his wealth to Antonio, half to the state. Antonio surrenders his claim if Shylock will turn Christian and make over his property on his death to his daughter Jessica, who has run away and married a Christian and been disinherited; to which Shylock agrees. Portia and Nerissa ask as rewards from Bassanio and Gratiano the rings that their wives have given them, which they have promised never to part with. Reluctantly they give them up, and are taken to task accordingly on their return home. The play ends with news of the safe arrival of Antonio's ships.

'Merchant's Tale, The', see CANTERBURY TALES, 10.

Mercilla, in Spenser's *Faerie Queene* (V. viii), 'a mayden Queene of high renowne' (Queen *Elizabeth I), whose crown the *soldan seeks to subvert.

Mercurius Aulicus, see BERKENHEAD.

Mercurius Librarius: or A Catalogue of Books, a booksellers' trade journal founded in 1668 by two stationers, John Starkey and Robert Clavell, described by Walter Graham (*The Beginnings of English Literary Periodicals*, 1926) as 'in a very limited sense. . . entitled to be regarded as the first literary periodical published in England'. It survived until 1709, and a reprint (as *Term Catalogue*), edited by *Arber, was published in 1903. A second *Mercurius Librarius: or A Faithful Account of All Books and Pamphlets* began as a weekly in 1680, but does not appear to have lasted long.

Mercutio, in Shakespeare's *Romeo and Juliet*, the lively, cynical friend of Romeo who is killed in a brawl by Juliet's cousin Tybalt. It is he who speaks the famous 'Queen Mab' speech (I. iv. 53–94).

Merdle and Mrs Merdle, characters in Dickens's *Little Dorrit*.

MEREDITH, George (1828–1909). He had a precarious childhood in Portsmouth as the son of an indigent, but flamboyant and extravagant, tailor who was early a widower—a background which Meredith was later at pains to conceal, although he made use of it in several of his novels. He was intermittently educated in Portsmouth and Southsea, and then with much success at the unusual school of the Moravians at Neuwied in Germany. In London, after a period with a solicitor, he began his long literary career with 'Chillianwallah', a poem published in 1849. In the same year he married Mary Ellen Nicholls, the widowed daughter of T. L. *Peacock, and in 1851 paid for the publication of his own *Poems*, a volume he later disowned but which was praised by *Tennyson and C. *Kingsley. The Shaving of Shagpat (1856 for 1855), a series of *Oriental fantasies about a vain, bewhiskered enchanter whose power resides in one hair on his head, was well received by the critics but did not sell well. In the same year he sat as the model for Henry Wallis's painting The Death of Chatterton. In 1857 his wife left him for Wallis, and *Farina*, a German burlesque reminiscent of *Shagpat*, appeared. His first major novel, *The Ordeal of Richard Feverel*, was published in 1859; it sold poorly, caused much scandal, and *Mudie's cancelled its order of 300 copies, but it brought praise in *The Times* and the *Athenaeum*, as well as the friendship of *Carlyle and the *Pre-Raphaelites.

Meredith was now contributing to many periodicals, including the *Fortnightly Review*, in which *Evan Harrington* began to appear in 1860: the novel has many elements of autobiography, for its hero, like the author himself, is the son of a tailor, the handsome and dashing Melchizedek Harrington of Lymport. (Meredith's grandfather was also a tailor, known as the 'Great Mel'). Evan's sisters have married advantageously and wish their brother to do likewise: the problems of social class and the concept of being a gentleman are explored (often comically) as Evan is implored by one side of the family to launch himself in high society, and by his mother to carry on the debt-ridden family business. Meredith wished the book to be a popular success, and it is accordingly written in a plainer style, without the 'lumen purpureum' which he usually liked his prose to cast.

In 1860 Meredith also became a reader for *Chapman and Hall (a post he retained until 1894) and a regular compiler of news for the *Ipswich Chronicle*, a task he endured for eight years. *Modern Love and Poems of the Roadside appeared in 1862. In 1864 he published Emilia in England (retitled Sandra Belloni in 1886) and married his second wife, Marie Vulliamy. Rhoda Fleming (1865), one of his shorter 'plain' works, is a regional novel with a farmer's daughter as its central character: Vittoria, a sequel to Sandra Belloni, began to appear in 1866, but was enlarged, after Meredith had spent a brief inactive period as a war correspondent in Italy, before its publication in book form in 1867: the novels trace the career of Emilia Sandra Belloni, a singer and the daughter of an Italian musician, first against an English backdrop, then in northern Italy during the failed revolution of 1848–9, led by Mazzini, who appears as a heroic figure. Few of these works brought much profit, but Meredith's reputation was growing steadily with the discerning public. *The Adventures of *Harry Richmond* (1871) brought some success, and the friendship of the influential *Milnes. A political novel, *Beauchamp's Career*, followed in 1876, and in 1877 Meredith delivered a lecture on 'The Idea of Comedy' which was published in 1897 and enjoyed a long reputation.

The novel for which he was chiefly celebrated, *The Egoist*, appeared in 1879. *The Tragic Comedians*, a novella based on an episode in the life of the German socialist Ferdinand Lassalle, appeared in 1880 and *Poems and Lyrics of the Joy of Earth*, often held to include his best poetry, including the final version of 'Love in a Valley', in 1883. The only novel to meet with general popularity, though exhibiting the growing preciosity of Meredith's style, was *Diana of the Crossways*, which ran to three editions in 1885 alone, and a century later found a new lease of life with the critical approval of the feminist movement. Among other volumes of verse were *Ballads . . . of Tragic Life* (1887) and *A Reading of Earth* (1888): then came three more novels, *One of Our Conquerors* (1891), Meredith's convoluted study of the woes that are in marriage and the minimal pleasures that may eventually be gained from it; *Lord Ormont and his Aminta* (1894), another study of unhappy marriage, with more exotic settings and a more aristocratic milieu than normal in Meredith's work; and *The Amazing Marriage* (1895), his last novel and considered by some his most impenetrable. A collection of short stories, including the celebrated 'The Case of General Ople and Lady Camper', appeared in 1898, as did *Odes . . . of French History*; *A Reading of Life* followed in 1901 and *Last Poems* in 1909. *Celt and Saxon*, an unfinished story, was published posthumously in 1910, and a conversational comedy, *The Sentimentalists*, was produced in the same year.

By the time he died Meredith had written steadily for 50 years, had received the OM and an Oxford DCL, was president of the *Society of Authors, and had become a greatly revered man of letters, sought out by many younger poets and novelists, such as H. *James, *Hardy, and R. L. *Stevenson, as well as by the rich and famous. He himself felt he was a poet first and a novelist after, but that was not the verdict of his readers. His reputation stood very high well into the 20th cent., with his perceptive portrayal of women, his narrative skill, and his incisive dialogue receiving most praise; but the deliberate intricacy of much of his prose (twisted, as *Trollope wrote, 'into curl-papers') defeats many modern readers, and for the last 50 years or so neither his poetry nor his novels have received any great popular or critical acclaim. See L. Stevenson, *The Ordeal of George Meredith* (1954) and G. Beer, *Meredith: A Change of Masks* (1970).

MEREDITH, Owen, see LYTTON, E. R. B.

MERES, Francis (1565–1647), educated at Pembroke College, Cambridge, and rector and schoolmaster at Wing. He was author of *Palladis Tamia. Wits Treasury* (1598), containing quotations and maxims from various writers. In this Meres reviewed all literary effort from the time of *Chaucer to his own day, contrasting each English author with a writer of like character in Latin, Greek, or Italian. He thus commemorates 125 Englishmen; his list of Shakespeare's works with his commendation of the dramatist's 'fine filed phrase' and his account of *Marlowe's death are notable elements in English literary history. The section on 'Poetrie' was edited by D. C. Allen (1933).

MÉRIMÉE, Prosper (1803–70), French novelist, playwright, and writer of short fiction. One of the earliest of the French Romantic dramatists, he successfully passed off the six short plays of *Le Théâtre de Clara Gazul* (1825) as having been written by the imaginary Spanish actress of the title. Another hoax was *La Guzla*, a collection of supposed translations of Illyrian poetry, in reality his own inventions. *La Jacquerie* (1828) was a series of dramatic scenes of medieval life; *La Chronique du règne de Charles IX* (1829) a historical novel of the religious wars of the 16th cent. Mérimée's short stories—he is a recognized master of the form—include 'Matteo Falcone' (1829), 'La Vision de Charles XI' (1829), 'La Vénus d'Ille' (1837), 'Colomba' (1840), 'Carmen' (1845), which inspired Bizet's opera, and 'Lokis' (1869). His *Lettres à une inconnue* (written to Mlle 'Jenny' Dacquin) display his critical and ironic temperament.

Merle, Madame, a character in H. James's *The Portrait of a Lady*.

MERLEAU-PONTY, Maurice (1908–61), French philosopher. With *Sartre, co-editor of *Les Temps modernes*, he dominated French intellectual life during the post-war period. Reacting against Cartesian idealism, he based his epistemology on the relationship between consciousness and the world. His main work *Phénoménologie de la perception* (1945; English trans. C. Smith, 1962), attempts to do equal justice to the mind's constructive powers in perception and to the independence of the object of perception, arguing that the structure of consciousness is neither discernible from first principles nor dependent on causal mechanisms, but exhibited in the mind's actual encounters with the world.

Merlin, the magician who guides the destinies of *Arthur and his predecessor *Uther, though the range of his activities extends beyond this feature of him for which he is most celebrated now. His story is first set out by *Geoffrey of Monmouth in his *Vita Merlini* (c.1150), which draws on the story of Ambrosius told by *Nennius. Merlin is born of a devil and a virtuous maiden and is named after his maternal grandfather. He is superhumanly precocious and hairy but, although wilful, not malevolent as his diabolical father intended. He grows infatuated with Nimiane (Nimue or Vivien: see LADY OF THE LAKE), who imprisons him in a forest of air in Broceliande where he dies. He is also linked to the Welsh bard Myrddhin and is credited, like him, with a series of prophecies. He predicts to *Vortigern (as Ambrosius did in Nennius) the triumph of the Britons over the Saxons, as a gloss on the killing of a white dragon by a red one after the two creatures are released by the digging of the foundations of a citadel from which Vortigern is to fight the Saxons. In Geoffrey of Monmouth's *Historia Regum Britanniae* (Book viii) he aids Uther in the deceit by which he marries Igraine (Ygerna) and fathers Arthur, and he helps by magic to bring the great stones of Stonehenge from Naas in Ireland. The Arthurian stories connected with him form a very important part of the whole tradition in French in the Middle Ages, particularly as transmitted by the (fragmentary) stories of Merlin by Robert de *Boron, c.1200, the prose Vulgate *Merlin* and the *Suite du Merlin* (*Huth Merlin*); the latter two are related to de Boron. See R. S. Loomis (ed.), *Arthurian Literature in the Middle Ages* (1959), chapters 8, 19, 23, and 24, for a series of detailed accounts.

'Merlin and Vivien', one of Tennyson's *Idylls of the King*, published 1859 as 'Vivien', retitled 1870. The wily Vivien, filled with hatred for Arthur and his court, seduces the aged Merlin and imprisons him forever in an old oak.

Mermaid Series, the, a series of unexpurgated reprints of early English dramatists, published originally by *Vizetelly, at the suggestion of Havelock *Ellis, who edited the series from 1887 to 1889. It continued through various transformations, and became in 1964 the New Mermaid Series, under the general editorship of Philip Brockbank, later with Brian Morris. The series now includes English plays from the late medieval period up to the time of *Synge and *Wilde.

Mermaid Tavern, a tavern that stood in Bread Street (with an entrance in Friday Street), London. It was frequented by *Beaumont, *Donne, I. *Jones, and others who may have included Shakespeare, and according to *Coryate a 'Fraternitie of Sirenaical Gentlemen' met there 'the first Friday of every Moneth', but the membership of the 'club' is not clear. The tavern is celebrated by Beaumont in the fine lines ('Master Francis Beaumont to Ben Jonson'):

> What things have we seen
> Done at the Mermaid! heard words that have been
> So nimble, and so full of subtle flame,
> As if that every one from whence they came
> Had meant to put his whole wit in a jest,
> And had resolved to live a fool the rest
> Of his dull life.

*Keats also wrote 'Lines on the Mermaid Tavern' beginning: 'Souls of poets dead and gone'.

Merrilies, Meg, the old gypsy woman in Scott's *Guy Mannering*. She is the subject of a poem by *Keats, 'Old Meg she was a gipsy'.

MERRY, Robert, see DELLA CRUSCANS.

Merry Devil of Edmonton, The, a romantic comedy published 1608, authorship unknown. C. *Lamb, who praised it highly, suggested *Drayton as the possible author. It was included in a volume in Charles II's library entitled 'Shakespeare' but there is no evidence in support of this attribution.

The prologue presents Peter Fabel of Edmonton, a magician, who has made a compact with the devil. The period of it has run out, and the fiend comes to claim Fabel. He is, however, tricked into sitting down in a necromantic chair, where he is held fast and is obliged to give a respite. The play itself, in which the magical element is practically absent, deals with the attempt of Sir Arthur Clare and his wife to break off the match between their daughter Millicent and Raymond Mounchensey, and its defeat by the elopement of the young couple, aided by the kindly magician Fabel.

Merry Wives of Windsor, The, a comedy by *Shakespeare, possibly written or adapted for the occasion of George Carey, Lord Hunsdon's installation as a knight of the Garter on 23 Apr. 1597. Various topical allusions have been discerned in the play, but the tradition that it was written at the request of *Elizabeth I for a play showing *Falstaff in love is documented no earlier than 1702 (by J. *Dennis). The passage alluding to the Garter Feast is found only in the *Folio text (1623), which is twice the length of the 'bad' quarto (1602); the latter appears to be based on a report of a less courtly performance.

Falstaff, who is 'out at heels', determines to make love to the wives of Ford and Page, two gentlemen dwelling at Windsor, because they have the rule of their husbands' purses. Nym and Pistol, the discarded followers of Falstaff, warn the husbands. Falstaff sends identical love letters to Mrs Ford and Mrs Page, who contrive the discomfiture of the knight. At a first assignation at Ford's house, on the arrival of the husband, they hide Falstaff in a basket, cover him with foul linen, and have him tipped into a muddy ditch. At a second assignation, they disguise him as the 'fat woman of Brainford', in which character he is soundly beaten by Ford. The jealous husband having also been twice fooled, the plot is now revealed to him, and a final assignation is given to Falstaff in Windsor Forest at Herne's oak (see HERNE THE HUNTER), where he is beset and pinched by mock fairies and finally seized and exposed by Ford and Page.

The sub-plot is concerned with the wooing of Anne, the daughter of Page, by three suitors: Doctor Caius, a French physician, Slender, the foolish cousin of Justice Shallow, and Fenton, a wild young gentleman, whom Anne loves. Mistress Quickly, servant to Dr Caius, acts as go-between for all three suitors, and encourages them all impartially. Sir Hugh Evans, a Welsh parson, interferes on behalf of Slender and receives a challenge from the irascible Dr Caius, but hostilities are confined to the 'hacking' of the English tongue. At the final assignation with Falstaff in the forest, Page, who favours Slender, arranges that the latter shall carry off his daughter, who is to be dressed in white; while Mrs Page, who favours Dr Caius, arranges that he shall carry her off dressed in green. In the event both find themselves fobbed off with a boy in disguise, while Fenton has run away with and married the true Anne.

Messiah, (1) an oratorio by *Handel; (2) a religious epic (*Messias*) by *Klopstock; (3) a sacred eclogue by *Pope published in the *Spectator* in May 1712, embodying in verse the Messianic prophecies of Isaiah.

Messianic Eclogue, see VIRGIL'S FOURTH OR MESSIANIC ECLOGUE.

metafiction, a kind of fiction that openly draws attention to its own fictional status. *Sterne's *Tristram Shandy* (1759–67) is the classic English example. *Postmodernist novelists' and storytellers' tales often resort to metafiction: a notable example is *Borges.

Metamorphoses, see APULEIUS and OVID.

metaphor, the transfer of a name or descriptive term to an object different from, but analogous to, that to which it is properly applicable, e.g. 'abysmal ignorance'. Mixed metaphor is the application of two inconsistent metaphors to one object.
   *Empson defines metaphor as the first of his *Seven Types of Ambiguity.

metaphysical poets. Poets generally grouped under this label include *Donne (who is regarded as founder of the 'school'), G. *Herbert, *Crashaw, H. *Vaughan, *Marvell, and *Traherne, together with lesser figures like *Benlowes, *Herbert of Cherbury, H. *King, A. *Cowley, and *Cleveland. The label was first used (disparagingly) by Dr *Johnson in his 'Life of Cowley' (written in 1777), where he identifies them as a 'race of writers' who display their learning, use far-fetched comparisons, and lack feeling. But *Pope partly anticipated Johnson when he spoke (Spence's *Anecdotes*) of Cowley borrowing his 'metaphysical' style from Donne, and earlier *Dryden had complained that Donne 'affects the metaphysics', perplexing the minds of the fair sex with 'nice speculations of philosophy'. Earlier still W. *Drummond, probably with Donne in mind, censured poetic innovators who employed 'Metaphysical Ideas and Scholastical Quiddities'. The label is misleading, since none of these poets is seriously interested in metaphysics (except Herbert of Cherbury, and even he excludes the interest from his poetry). Further, these poets have in reality little in common: the features their work is generally taken to display are sustained dialectic, paradox, novelty, incongruity, 'muscular' rhythms, giving the effect of a 'speaking voice', and the use of 'conceits', or comparisons in which tenor and vehicle can be related only by ingenious pseudologic.

With the new taste for clarity and the impatience with figurative language that prevailed after the *Restoration, their reputation dwindled and, though their 'quaintness' earned some recognition from critics, their revival was delayed until after the First World War. When it came, however, it was dramatic: indeed, the revaluation of metaphysical poetry, and the related downgrading of the *Romantics and *Milton, was the major feature of the rewriting of English literary history in the first half of the 20th cent. Key documents in the revival were H. J. C. *Grierson's *Metaphysical Lyrics and Poems of the Seventeenth Century* (1921) and T. S. *Eliot's essay 'Metaphysical Poets', which first appeared as a review of Grierson's collection (*TLS*, 20 Oct. 1921). According to Eliot these poets had the advantage of writing at a time when thought and feeling were closely fused, before the *'dissociation of sensibility' set in about the time of Milton. Their virtues of difficulty and tough newness were felt to relate them closely to the Modernists—*Pound, *Yeats, and Eliot himself. Some more recent critics, notably Tuve, have questioned this. Modern scholarship has also followed Johnson's hint and related the English metaphysicals to *Marino, *Gongorism, and the European baroque generally.
   Rosemond Tuve, *Elizabethan and Metaphysical Imagery* (1947); J. E. Duncan, *The Revival of Metaphysical Poetry* (1959); F. J. Warnke, *European Metaphysical Poetry* (1961); L. Nelson, *Baroque Lyric Poetry* (1961); J. M. Cohen, *The Baroque Lyric* (1963).

Metaphysical Society, the, was founded in 1869 by Sir J. T. *Knowles. It lasted until 1880 and brought together for discussion meetings most of the leaders of English thought of the period, of all shades of opinion, including T. H. *Huxley, *Tyndall, *Manning, *Gladstone, and *Tennyson.

metathesis, the transposition of letters or sounds in a word. When the transposition is between the letters or sounds of two words, it is popularly known as a 'Spoonerism', of which a well-known specimen, attributed to the Revd W. A. Spooner (1844–1930), warden of New College, Oxford, is 'Kinquering congs their titles take'.

metonymy, a figure of speech which substitutes a quality or attribute of something for the thing itself, as *the fair* to mean 'the fair sex', *the deep* to mean 'the deep sea', *the bench* for the judiciary, or *Shakespeare* to mean the works of Shakespeare. In such examples, metonymy works by a kind of conventional abbreviation. A closely related figure is that of synecdoche, in which a part is substituted for the whole (*per head*, to mean 'per person'), or a whole is substituted for a part (*Pakistan*, to mean the Pakistani cricket team).

metre, see overleaf.

Metroland, Margot (originally Margot Beste-Chetwynde), a character in E. Waugh's *Decline and Fall*, *Vile Bodies*, *Scoop*, and other novels.

The metre of a poem, or the 'measure', as it used to be known, is the more or less regular pattern formed by its sequence of syllables. Poems in which the sound patterns are not perceptibly formed from similar groupings of syllables are regarded as non-metrical, and thus placed in the category of *free verse. The largest body of traditional verse, however, in both the high literary and the popular traditions, observes some form of metrical regularity. The particular forms of such regularity vary from one language to another: in ancient Greek and Latin, lines of verse were made from fixed numbers of 'feet', a foot being a combination of syllables regarded as either long or short; while in French and in Japanese what is measured is simply the number of syllables that make up the line, without distinctions of length or stress. These metrical systems are known as 'quantitative' and 'syllabic' respectively. Verse written in English almost always employs a different principle, one that relies on a distinction perceived between stressed (●) and unstressed (○) syllables. English verse lines are measured either principally or wholly by the number of stresses (i.e. stressed syllables) they are expected to contain. They may also observe further regularities in the total number of syllables, stressed or unstressed, that each line may include. The two major tendencies or traditions of English verse metre may be differentiated according to whether this inclusive syllable-count applies.

The older of the two dominant metrical systems in English counts only the number of stresses in a line, and so allows variation in the number of unstressed syllables. This is called 'accentual metre', or 'strong-stress metre'. It was the standard metrical principle of Old English verse, and was still vigorous in 14th-cent. literature, notably in the works of *Langland and the anonymous author of *Sir *Gawain and the Green Knight*. Following the example of *Chaucer, most learned poets in English since that time have counted their syllables and thus departed to some degree from the pure accentual principle, at least in the more elevated kinds of formal verse composition. Accentual verse has continued to flourish, however, in a wide range of popular songs, hymns, ballads, and nursery rhymes. A conscious effort to revive it for more complex lyrical uses was made in the late 19th cent. by G. M. *Hopkins, who referred to the effect of his accentual experiments as 'sprung rhythm'.

The second English metrical system is known as the 'accentual-syllabic', because it counts both the number of stresses and the total number of syllables in a line, thus restricting the use of unstressed syllables. So, in the standard line of post-Chaucerian English verse, the iambic pentameter, we expect to find ten syllables, of which five are stressed; in the perfectly regular version of this line, the unstressed and stressed syllables will alternate so as to conclude with a stress (○●○●○●○●○●):

If Winter comes, can Spring be far behind?

It should be remembered that such a pattern is not a rule but an expectation, and that accentual-syllabic verse of any sophistication requires variety in the placing both of the stressed syllables and of the pause ('*caesura') within the line. Given the restriction that accentual-syllabic metres place upon the use of unstressed syllables, they fall into two basic kinds, known as duple and triple. By far the more commonly used are the duple metres, in which stressed syllables alternate with single unstressed syllables, as in the iambic metre illustrated above. In triple metres, pairs of unstressed syllables alternate with the stresses, as in *Hardy's dactylic tetrameter (●○○●○○●○○●○)

Woman much missed, how you call to me, call to me

The predominance of the duple metres in English gives the use of triple metres the appearance of being a special or even comical device, as in the anapaestic metre of the limerick (○●○○●○○●):

There was an Old Man in a tree

Of the two duple metres, the iambic, in which unstressed syllables are heard to precede the stresses, is the standard. The less commonly used trochaic metre gives the impression that the stresses precede the unstressed syllables (●○●○●○●○):

Ye whose hearts are fresh and simple

Trochaic metre is unusual in that its regular form, illustrated in the tetrameter by *Longfellow above, is quite rare by comparison with an irregular (truncated, or 'catalectic') version in which the final unstressed syllable is not used, allowing the line to end with a stress (●○●○●○):

Tyger, tyger, burning bright

Similar forms of truncation are found in the triple metres.

Setting aside the distinction between accentual and accentual-syllabic metres for a moment, the simplest description of the metre in a given line of verse is given by the number of stresses we expect it to include. In English, the two standard lines are the four-stress (tetrameter) and the five-stress (pentameter); in accentual-syllabic terms these standard lines may be described as octosyllabic and decasyllabic, if we take the use of duple metre for granted. The four-stress line is the older and the more persistent in all popular forms of verse and song, being easily compatible with the regularity of musical beats. It is also the natural line for accentual metres. The five-stress line has the effect of loosening or suppressing the assertive beat, and approximating itself to the rhythms of speech. Less frequently found as the regular basis of verse are the three-stress (trimeter) and two stress (dimeter) lines on the one hand, or the six-stress (hexameter) and seven-stress (heptameter) lines on the other. Two-, three-, and six-stress lines find their usual place in verse forms that mix longer and shorter lines: the 'Burns stanza' employs dimeters for its fourth and sixth lines, the limerick for its third and fourth, while the Spenserian stanza has a hexameter as its final line. Trimeters alternate with tetrameters in the usual form of the ballad metre. Iambic heptameters, known as 'fourteeners' from their syllabic count, were employed by a number of poets in the 15th and 16th cents, for example in *Chapman's translation of *Homer. Several English poets have attempted extended composition in hexameters, the dactylic hexameter having been the epic metre of Homer; the hexametric experiments of *Clough are among the more successful.

The theory of metre, known as prosody or metrics, has been bedevilled by the survival of terminology and concepts derived from ancient Greek practice, despite the radical difference between Greek quantitative principles and English stress patterns. The ways in which stressed and unstressed syllables can be arranged in English verse have come to be named after the various kinds of Greek 'foot' they seem to resemble, when one mistranslates 'long syllable' as 'stressed syllable'. Many modern metricians regard the concept of the foot as a positive hindrance to the understanding of English metre and especially of accentual verse, but the names have stuck, and the analysis (scansion) of English lines as sequences of 'feet' is still attempted. Four principal kinds of metrical pattern in English are accordingly named after the *iamb* (○●), the *trochee* (●○), the *anapaest* (○○●), and the *dactyl* (●○○). Two other feet are sometimes invoked in scansion of English verse: the *spondee* (●●) and the *pyrrhic* (○○); among several others that are of relevance to ancient Greek verse but only very rarely to English are the *amphibrach* (○●○), the *amphimacer* (●○●), and the *choriamb* (●○○●).

Understanding the metrical effects of English verse requires some appreciation of the many variations that poets can play upon a regular metrical pattern. In the case of the iambic pentameter, especially, the scope for such variation is so wide that completely regular lines like P. *Shelley's 'If Winter comes, can Spring be far behind?' will be outnumbered by irregular versions. The principal variant upon the standard pentameter involves what is (in traditional foot-based scansion) known as 'initial trochaic inversion' because the line starts with a stress but 'compensates' for this with an unstressed syllable (●○○●●○●●○●):

Far on the ringing plains of windy Troy

Similar inversions may be found in later positions in a line. Other permissible variations include the use of an unstressed syllable where a stress is expected, thus speeding up the line (e.g. ○●○●○●○○○●):

A horse! a horse! My kingdom for a horse!

or the addition of an eleventh, unstressed syllable:

To be or not to be, that is the question

The pentameter also offers several different positions at which the caesura, if any, may be placed. In this it contrasts with the accentual four-stress line of Old English and Middle English *alliterative verse, in which the caesura is expected to fall in the middle of the line.

See P. *Hobsbaum, *Metre, Rhythm and Verse Form* (1996), D. Attridge, *Poetic Rhythm: An Introduction* (1995), D. Attridge, *The Rhythms of English Verse* (1982).

MEUN, Jean de, see ROMAN DE LA ROSE.

MEW, Charlotte Mary (1869–1928), poet and short story writer, the daughter of a prosperous London architect, born in Bloomsbury where she spent most of her life. Although stubborn and reserved in temperament, she accepted a civil list pension procured for her by *Hardy, but, beset by increasing family and financial problems that stifled her literary output, she eventually committed suicide. Her short story 'Passed' appeared in the *Yellow Book* in 1894, but she did not become well known until her first volume of poetry, *The Farmer's Bride* (1915). Her second volume, *The Rambling Sailor*, appeared posthumously in 1929. Her poems are notable for a restraint of expression combined with a powerful and passionate content which distinguish her from many of her Georgian contemporaries. Her collected poems and prose was edited by V. Warner, 1981; see also P. *Fitzgerald, *Charlotte Mew and her Friends* (1984).

MEYNELL, Alice, née Thompson (1847–1922). She became a Roman Catholic in 1868, and in 1875 published her first volume of poetry, *Preludes*, which attracted the attention of Wilfrid Meynell (1852–1948), author and editor, whom she married in 1877. She had many friends in the literary world, including F. *Thompson, *Meredith, and *Patmore, and a busy domestic life. Her poetic inspiration was intermittent, but her several volumes of verse, which include *Poems* (1893), *Later Poems* (1902), and *Last Poems* (1923), won her a considerable reputation; many of her most successful poems deal with the theme of religious mystery. She is perhaps now more admired for her essays, introductions, and anthologies, which, despite her prolific output, manifest independence and sensitivity of critical judgement; her essays, published in the *National Observer*, the *Pall Mall Gazette*, the *Tablet*, and other periodicals, were collected under various titles, which include *The Rhythm of Life* (1893), *The Colour of Life* (1896), and *The Spirit of Place* (1899). There is a life by J. Badeni (1981).

MEYNELL, Sir Francis Meredith Wilfrid (1891–1975), book designer, publisher, and journalist, and son of Wilfrid and Alice *Meynell. He was founder and director of the *Nonesuch Press, and his autobiography *My Lives* was published in 1971.

Micawber, Wilkins and Mrs, characters in Dickens's *David Copperfield*.

'Michael', a pastoral poem by *Wordsworth, written and published 1800. The poem is a narrative in blank verse, describing, with a moving strength and simplicity, the lonely life in Grasmere of the old shepherd Michael, his wife, and his beloved son Luke. Because of family misfortune Luke is sent away to a dissolute city, where he disgraces himself; he eventually disappears abroad. Michael dies in grief and the cottage and pasture become a ruin.

MICHAEL, Livi (Olivia) (1960–), novelist, educated at Fairfield High School, Droysden, Manchester, and at the University of Leeds. Her first novel, *Under a Thin Moon* (1992), was followed by *Their Angel Reach* (1994), five interlinked stories evoking with lyrical realism the often depressing lives of women in and around the fictitious Lancashire village of Marley. *All the Dark Air* (1997) is an unsentimental, socially acute, and poignant portrayal of Julie, young and confused, adrift in a world of unemployment, homelessness, drugs, and doubt.

Michaelmas Terme, see MIDDLETON, T.

MICHELANGELO BUONARROTI (1475–1564), Florentine painter, sculptor, architect, and poet, who worked also in Rome, and whose artistic legacy includes some of the greatest works of the Renaissance, including the Pietà (completed 1499; St Peter's, Rome) and the ceiling of the Sistine Chapel (1508–12). He also left around 300 poems and many letters. Amongst them are many love poems, full of Platonic imagery, to the beautiful Tommaso de' Cavalieri, whom he had met in 1532. Others, intensely spiritual, are addressed to Vittoria *Colonna. The poems of his later years express fears of sin and salvation.

Michelangelo's contemporaries idolized 'il divino Michelangelo' and his biography was written in his lifetime: *Vasari described him as towering over the Greeks and the Romans and bringing to perfection the artistic tradition that had opened with Cimabue. Yet by the 1540s he came under attack: *Aretino, in a famous letter of 1545, poured scurrilous abuse on his character and work. Throughout the 17th and 18th cents, classicists felt uneasy with his individuality and tended to favour *Raphael. A change may be sensed in the late 18th cent., when Sir J. *Reynolds praised him in his last discourse, and his work was increasingly esteemed by followers of the cult of the Romantic and the *sublime. The writings and drawings of *Fuseli and *Blake, and of *Goethe, Delacroix, and *Stendhal in Europe, bear witness to a passionate admiration. In the late 19th cent. scholarly editions of the poems and letters were published, and a lavishly documented, albeit romantic, biography was written by J. A. *Symonds (1893). The legend of tormented genius lingers on in Irving Stone's novel *The Agony and the Ecstasy* (1961).

MICHELET, Jules (1798–1874), French historian, keeper of National Historical Archives (1831–52), professor at the Collège de France (1838–51). His principal work, *L'Histoire de France* (vols i–vi, 1833–43; vols vii–xvii, 1855–67), is remarkable for its luminous and eloquent style, its aim to recreate the past in its complex fullness, and for the part that the author attributes to geographical and racial factors in forming the men who were the agents of historical change. Michelet's fervent republicanism is evident in his other major work, *La Révolution française* (7 vols, 1847–53). He also wrote a number of monographs and shorter studies on subjects allied to history in his broad conception of it: e.g. *Les Jésuites* (1843, with Edgar Quinet), *Du prêtre, de la femme, de la famille* (1845), *Le Peuple* (1846), *La Femme* (1860).

MICKIEWICZ, Adam (1798–1855), Polish poet, born near Nowogródek, and educated at the University of Wilno (now Vilnius), where he became involved in nationalist politics, was imprisoned, and then exiled in 1824 to Russia for five years by the Russian authorities. He subsequently lived in Dresden, Paris, and Rome, and died in Constantinople. His first collection of poems, published 1822, contained his poetic manifesto, an essay 'On Romantic Poetry'; in the same year he studied English and became a devoted admirer of *Byron, whose struggles for freedom strongly influenced him. His passionately patriotic works include *Konrad Wallenrod* (1828), a narrative poem presenting in historical guise the enduring hostility between Russia and Poland, and *Dziady* (*Forefathers' Eve*), an extremely complex and baffling work, of which the first part appeared in 1823, and the third and greatest in 1832. Part 3 is a poetic drama (unfinished), in which the central character, Gustav, awakens to political and prophetic consciousness; it is based on Mickiewicz's own political experiences at Wilno. *Pan Tadeusz* (1834) is an epic poem set in Lithuania on the eve of Napoleon's expedition to Russia in 1812: it has been adapted by D. *Davie.

Microcosm of London, The, see ACKERMANN.

Microcosmographie, see EARLE.

Midas, a prose play by *Lyly, published 1592, on the legend of Midas, king of Phrygia.

Middle Ages, the period from the Roman decadence (5th cent. AD) to the Renaissance (about 1500), to designate the period between the end of classical culture proper and its revival at the Renaissance. The high point of its culture is the 12th and 13th cents, with the growth of vernacular literature around 1200 and the Scholastic compendia of theology and philosophy in the 13th cent. The earliest use yet discovered of 'Middle Age' in this sense is in one of *Donne's sermons (1621), but the corresponding Latin terms, *medium aevum, media aetas*, etc., are found in the 16th cent. The term is sometimes restricted to the 11th–15th cents, the earlier part of the period being called the Dark Ages.

Middle English, see ENGLISH.

Middlemarch: *A Study of Provincial Life*, a novel by G. *Eliot, published 1871–2.

The scene is laid in the provincial town of Middlemarch, Loamshire, during the years of the agitation immediately preceding the first *Reform Bill. It has a multiple plot, with several interlocking sets of characters. Dorothea Brooke, an ardent, intelligent, ideal-istic young woman, under the negligent though affable care of her eccentric uncle, marries the elderly pedant Mr Casaubon, despite the doubts of her sister Celia, her neighbour and suitor Sir James Chettam (who later marries Celia), and Mrs Cadwallader, the rector's outspoken wife. The marriage proves intensely unhappy; Dorothea realizes during a disastrous honeymoon in Rome that Casaubon's scholarly plans to write a great work, a 'Key to all Mythologies', are doomed, as are her own aspirations to share and aid her husband's intellectual life, and her respect for him gradually turns to pity. She is sustained by the friendship of Casaubon's young cousin Will Ladislaw, a lively, light-hearted, good-natured young man, detested by Casaubon, who begins to suspect that Dorothea's feelings for Ladislaw are questionable; his irritation is increased by the fact that he fears he has acted justly but not generously by his impoverished kinsman. Shortly before he dies, with characteristic meanness, he adds a codicil to his will by which Dorothea forfeits her fortune if she marries Ladislaw.

Meanwhile other threads have been added to the remarkably broad canvas of the novel. We follow the fortunes of Fred and Rosamund Vincy, son and daughter of the mayor of Middlemarch; the extrovert Fred, unsuitably destined to be a clergyman, is in love with his childhood sweetheart Mary Garth, a practical, shrewd young woman, daughter of Caleb Garth, a land agent. Mary, who at the opening of the novel is nursing her disagreeable and aged relative Mr Featherstone, will not pledge herself to Fred unless he abandons his father's plan for him to enter the Church and proves himself stable and self-sufficient. Rosamund, the town's beauty, sets herself to capture the ambitious, idealistic, and well-connected doctor Tertius Lydgate; she succeeds, and their marriage, wrecked by her selfishness, insensitivity, and materialism, proves as unhappy as the Casaubons'. Lydgate finds himself heavily in debt, and against his better judgement borrows money from Mr Bulstrode, the mayor's brother-in-law, a religious hypocrite; Lydgate's career is ruined when he finds himself involved in a scandal concerning the death of Raffles, an unwelcome visitor from Bulstrode's shady past. Only Dorothea, now widowed, maintains faith in him, but she is severely shocked to find Ladislaw and Rosamund together in what seem to be compromising circumstances. Rosamund finally rises above self-interest to reveal that Ladislaw has remained faithful to the memory of Dorothea, though with no prospect of any happy outcome. Dorothea and Ladislaw at last confess their love to one another; she renounces Casaubon's fortune and marries him. Fred, partly sobered by the spectacle of Lydgate's decline, and encouraged by Caleb Garth to enter his own profession, marries Mary. Lydgate is condemned to a successful and fashionable practice and dies at 50, his ambitions frustrated.

Through the histories of these characters, George Eliot analyses and comments upon the social and political upheavals of the period, contrasting the staunch Tory attitudes of Chettam and the Cadwalladers with the growing demand for Reform, somewhat unsatisfactorily espoused by Mr Brooke, more satisfactorily by Ladislaw, who in the last chapter becomes 'an ardent public man' and a member of Parliament, with Dorothea's support. The importance of marital loyalty is also widely illustrated, not least in Mrs Bulstrode's support of her husband in his disgrace.

George Eliot's reputation reached its height with *Middlemarch*, despite some complaints that the action was slow or the tone didactic; H. *James found faults in its organization, but concluded, 'It sets a limit . . . to the development of the old-fashioned English novel' (1874). Its status as one of the greatest works of English fiction was confirmed by *Leavis (*The Great Tradition*, 1948), despite his doubts about the indulgent portrayal of Dorothea.

MIDDLETON, Conyers (1683–1750), a fellow of Trinity College, Cambridge, and proto-bibliothecarius of the University Library. His *Letter from Rome* was published in 1729, and his life of Cicero in 1741. His *A Free Inquiry into the Miraculous Powers which Are Supposed to Have Subsisted in the Christian Church* (1749), which attacked the authenticity of post-apostolic miracles, caused much controversy; ironically, it was partly responsible for *Gibbon's temporary conversion to Catholicism, but is quoted to very different effect in chapter XV of *The Decline and Fall of the Roman Empire*.

MIDDLETON, Stanley (1919–), novelist, born in Nottingham where all of his fiction is set. Maintaining an even output of one novel a year, Middleton has spent four decades chronicling English provincial family life. His work is untouched by literary fashion: dogged social realism prevails in *Harris's Requiem* (1960), *Live and Learn* (1996), and everything in between, including *Holiday* (*Booker Prize, 1974).

MIDDLETON, Thomas (1580–1627), the son of a prosperous London bricklayer. He matriculated at Oxford but probably did not take a degree. His first published work was a long and undistinguished poem, *The Wisdome of Solomon Paraphrased* (1597), which was followed by other verses and prose pamphlets. By 1600 he was in London, 'daylie accompaninge the players', and by 1603 he was writing for *Henslowe, collaborating with J. *Webster, *Dekker, *Rowley, *Munday, and others; many of these works are now lost. He collaborated with Dekker in writing the first part of *The Honest Whore* (1604) and wrote many successful comedies of city life, including *The Familie of Love* (with Dekker?, written 1602, published 1608), *The Roaring Girle* (with Dekker, written 1604–8?, pub. 1611), *Michaelmas Terme* (written 1604–6, published 1607), *A Trick to Catch the Old-One* (written 1604–7, pub. 1608), *A Mad World, My Masters* (written 1604–7, pub. 1608), *A Chaste Mayd in Cheap-side*

(written 1613, pub. 1630), and *The Mayor of Quinborough* (written 1615–20, pub. 1661). *A Fair Quarrel*, a tragi-comedy written with Rowley (c.1615–16, pub. 1617), a play in a very different genre, discusses the ethics of duelling: *The Spanish Gipsy*, also with Rowley (and possibly *Ford, written 1623, pub. 1625) is a romantic comedy based on two plots from *Cervantes. Other plays include *The Witch* (written 1609–16, pub. 1778); *Anything for a Quiet Life* (with Webster?, written ?1621); he probably contributed to Shakespeare's *Macbeth* and *Timon of Athens* and was responsible for *A Yorkshire Tragedy* (c.1605).

A writer of great versatility, Middleton also wrote many pageants and masques for city occasions, and was appointed city chronologer in 1620. His political satire *A Game at Chesse* (written 1624, published 1625) created a furore, and caused him and the actors to be summoned before the Privy Council: it was described by T. S. *Eliot as 'a perfect piece of literary political art'. But Middleton is now best known for his two great tragedies, *The Changeling* (with Rowley, written 1622, pub. 1653) and *Women Beware Women* (written 1620–7, pub. 1657), both of which were highly praised by Eliot in his influential essay on Middleton (1927). Both have been successfully revived on stage in recent years. Many scholars now also consider that *The Revenger's Tragedy* (1607) is certainly by Middleton (see D. J. Lake, *The Canon of Thomas Middleton's Plays*, 1975), but this and many other suggested attributions are still disputed. The works were edited by A. H. Bullen (8 vols, 1885–6), and there are several recent single editions in the New *Mermaid Series. For an account of the life see R. H. Barker, *Thomas Middleton* (1958).

Midshipman Easy, Mr, a novel by *Marryat, published 1836.

Jack Easy is the son of a wealthy gentleman who brings his boy up to believe that all men are equal, a notion which causes considerable problems to Jack as a midshipman. But he is heir to a fortune and this, together with his cheerful honesty and the help of his Ashanti friend Mesty, help him through many clashes, encounters, and adventures. Hawkins, the bellicose chaplain, Mr Biggs the boatswain, and Mr Pottyfar, the lieutenant who kills himself with his own universal medicine, are notable among the ship's company.

Midsummer Night's Dream, A, a comedy by *Shakespeare, written probably about 1595 or 1596. It was printed in quarto in 1600 and 1619. The play has often been thought to be associated with a courtly marriage but scholarly opinion is undecided as to which of several possible weddings it may celebrate. It has no single major source, but Shakespeare drew, among other authors, on *Chaucer, A. *Golding's translation of *Ovid, and *Apuleius' *Golden Ass*.

Hermia, ordered by her father Egeus to marry Demetrius, refuses, because she loves Lysander, while Demetrius has formerly professed love for her friend Helena, and Helena loves Demetrius. Under the law of Athens, Theseus, the duke, gives Hermia four days in which to obey her father; else she must suffer death or enter a nunnery. Hermia and Lysander agree to leave Athens secretly in order to be married where the Athenian law cannot pursue them, and to meet in a wood a mile outside the city. Hermia tells Helena of the project, and the latter tells Demetrius. Demetrius pursues Hermia to the wood, and Helena Demetrius, so that all four are there that night. This wood is the favourite haunt of the fairies.

Oberon and Titania, king and queen of the fairies, have quarrelled, because Titania refuses to give up to him a little changeling boy for a page. Oberon tells Puck, a mischievous sprite, to fetch him a certain magic flower, of which he will press the juice on the eyes of Titania while she sleeps, so that she may fall in love with what she first sees when she wakes. Overhearing Demetrius in the wood reproaching Helena for following him, and desirous to reconcile them, Oberon orders Puck to place some of the love-juice on Demetrius' eyes, but so that Helena shall be near him when he does it. Puck, mistaking Lysander for Demetrius, applies the charm to him, and as Helena is the first person Lysander sees he at once woos her, enraging her because she thinks she is being made a jest of. Oberon, discovering Puck's mistake, now places some of the juice on Demetrius' eyes; he on waking also first sees Helena, so that both Lysander and Demetrius are now wooing her. The ladies begin to abuse one another and the men go off to fight for Helena.

Meanwhile Oberon has placed the love-juice on Titania's eyelids, who wakes to find Bottom the weaver near her, wearing an ass's head (Bottom and a company of Athenian tradesmen are in the wood to rehearse a play for the duke's wedding, and Puck has put an ass's head on Bottom); Titania at once becomes enamoured of him, and toys with his 'amiable cheeks' and 'fair large ears'. Oberon, finding them together, reproaches Titania for bestowing her love on an ass, and again demands the changeling boy, whom she in her confusion surrenders; whereupon Oberon releases her from the charm. Puck at Oberon's orders throws a thick fog about the human lovers, and brings them all together, unknown to one another, and they fall asleep. He applies a remedy to Lysander's eyes, so that when he awakes he returns to his former love. Theseus and Egeus appear on the scene, the runaways are forgiven, and the couples married. The play ends with the 'play' of 'Pyramus and Thisbe', comically acted by Bottom and his fellow tradesmen, to grace these nuptials and those of Theseus and Hippolyta.

Miggs, Miss, in Dickens's *Barnaby Rudge*, the shrewish maidservant of Mrs Varden.

MIGNE, Jacques-Paul (1800–75), French priest and publisher. He founded a printing house to make theological works available at moderate prices. His most famous publication was the *Patrologiae Cursus Completus* ('Complete Course of the Teachings of the Church Fathers'), comprising the *Patrologia Latina* ('Collection of the Latin Fathers', 221 vols, 1844–64), the works of Latin ecclesiastical writers from the earliest known to Innocent III (d. 1216), and the *Patrologia Graeca* ('Collection of the Greek Fathers', 161 vols, 1857–66), the writings of Christian Greeks down to the time of the Council of Florence (1438–9).

miles gloriosus, the braggart soldier, a stock character in Greek and Roman comedy, and also the title of a play by *Plautus, which contains a prototype of the role in its protagonist, Pyrgopolynices. Elements of the miles gloriosus may be found in Shakespeare's *Parolles, *Pistol, and *Falstaff, in Jonson's Captain *Bobadill, and in Beaumont and Fletcher's *Bessus.

Milesians, the people of Miledh, a fabulous Spanish king, whose sons are said to have invaded Ireland about 1300 BC. They represent probably the first Gaelic invaders of the country. See FIR BOLGS.

Milesian Tales, a collection, now lost, of short Greek stories of love and adventure, of a generally bawdy character, by Aristides of Miletus of the 2nd cent. BC.

MILL, James (1773–1836), born near Forfar, the son of a shoemaker. He was educated for the ministry, but came to London in 1802 and took up journalism. He published in 1817 a *History of British India* which obtained him a high post in the East India Company's service. He was closely associated with *Bentham and *Ricardo, whose views in philosophy and political economy, respectively, he adopted. He published his *Elements of Political Economy* in 1821, *Analysis of the Phenomena of the Human Mind* in 1829, and *Fragment on Mackintosh* in 1835. In the *Analysis* he provided, by an elaboration of *Hartley's theory of association, a psychological basis for Bentham's utilitarianism: associations may become inseparable and transform what had merely been means into ends sought on their account, thus explaining disinterested conduct by the egoistic individual. He also endeavoured to found on the association of ultimate sensations a theory of knowledge and reality. The *Fragment on Mackintosh* is a rejoinder to the attack on the utilitarians contained in the *Dissertation on the Progress of Ethical Philosophy* of *Mackintosh. Mill helped to found and contributed to the *Westminster Review. An interesting picture of his austere personality is given in the *Autobiography* (1873) of his son J. S. *Mill.

MILL, John Stuart (1806–73), son of James *Mill, by whom he was rigorously educated from a very early age, and by whose influence he obtained a clerkship in the India House. He formed the Utilitarian Society which met during 1823–6 to read essays and discuss them, and in 1825 edited *Bentham's *Treatise upon Evidence*. In 1826 an acute mental crisis caused him to reconsider his own aims and those of the Benthamite school; he found a new will to live in poetry, particularly in that of *Wordsworth, who brought him 'a greatly increased interest in the common feelings and common destiny of human beings'. In 1831 he met Harriet Taylor, whom he saw constantly for the next 20 years and who was, in his view, the chief inspiration of his philosophy; after her husband's death they married in 1851. His divergence from strict Benthamite doctrine is shown in his essays on 'Bentham' and '*Coleridge' (1838, 1840, *London and Westminster Review*) whom he describes as 'the two great seminal minds of England in this age'; and, later, in *Utilitarianism* (1861). In 1843 he published his *System of *Logic* and in 1848 *Principles of Political Economy*. In 1859 appeared his essay on *Liberty* and two volumes of *Dissertations and Discussions*, and in 1865 his *Examination of Sir William Hamilton's Philosophy*. Among other works may be mentioned *Thoughts on Parliamentary Reform* (1859), *Representative Government* (1861), *Auguste Comte and Positivism* (1865), his *Inaugural Address* on being installed rector of the University of St Andrews in 1867, and *The Subjection of Women* (1869). His *Autobiography* (1873), a classic of its genre, describes his intellectual and moral development from his earliest years to his maturity.

On the dissolution of the East India Company in 1858 he retired with a pension, and was independent MP for Westminster 1865–8. He passed most of the remainder of his life in France, and died at Avignon.

MILLAIS, Sir John Everett (1829–96). He began his career as child prodigy and finished as president of the *Royal Academy (1896); he is best known as a founder member of the *Pre-Raphaelite Brotherhood. His *Lorenzo and Isabella* (1848–9; Liverpool, Walker Art Gallery), from *Keats's poem, is one of the earliest Pre-Raphaelite works; the startling realism of his *Christ in the House of His Parents* (1849–50) was brutally attacked by *Dickens in *Household Words* in 1850. *Ophelia* (1851–2), *Mariana* (1851), which was exhibited with lines from *Tennyson's poem, and the poignant, melancholy *Autumn Leaves* (1856; Manchester, City Art Gallery) display his brilliant technique and fresh, precise detail. His portrait of his champion *Ruskin was painted in Scotland in 1853; Millais fell in love with Effie Ruskin on this holiday and married her in 1855. Millais made a distinguished contribution to the revival of book illustration in the 1860s; he had contributed to E. *Moxon's edition of Tennyson in 1857; he illustrated several of *Trollope's novels with sharply observed scenes from contemporary Victorian life and became a close friend of Trollope. He also became a friend of Dickens and drew him the day after the novelist's death. *Bubbles* (1886; A. and F. Pears Ltd) became celebrated as a soap advertisement.

Millamant, the heroine of Congreve's *The Way of the World*, a witty coquette, who is at the same time a lady of fashion, the author's most vivid creation.

MILLAY, Edna St Vincent (1892–1950), American poet, born in Maine and educated at Vassar. Her first volume, *Renascence and Other Poems* (1917), was followed by *A Few Figs from Thistles* (1920), which established her persona as a reckless, romantic, cynical, 'naughty' New Woman with such poems as 'The Penitent' and 'My Candle Burns at Both Ends'. This was followed by many other volumes, including dramatic pieces; her *Collected Poems* were published in 1956. Her impact on a whole generation was recorded by D. *Parker, who wrote, 'We all wandered in after Miss Millay. We were all being dashing and gallant, declaring that we weren't virgins, whether we were or not. Beautiful as she was, Miss Millay did a great deal of harm with her double-burning candles... made poetry seem so easy that we could all do it. But, of course, we couldn't.'

MILLER, Arthur (1915–2005), American playwright, born in New York and educated at the University of Michigan, where he began to write plays. He made his name with *All My Sons* (1947), an Ibsenesque drama about a manufacturer of defective aeroplane parts, and established himself as a leading dramatist with *Death of a Salesman* (1949), in which a travelling salesman, Willie Loman, is brought to disaster by accepting the false values of contemporary society. This was followed by *The Crucible* (1952), in which the Salem witchcraft trials of 1692 are used as a parable for McCarthyism in America in the 1950s. *A View from the Bridge* (1955) is a tragedy of family honour and revenge, sparked by the presence in longshoreman Eddie's apartment of two illegal Italian immigrants; the lawyer Alfieri comments as chorus on the inevitability of the action. *The Misfits* (1961) is a screenplay written for his then wife Marilyn Monroe. *After the Fall* (1964) presents the semi-autobiographical figure of Quentin, seeking to comprehend the meaning of his own past relationships, and *The Price* (1968) contrasts the lives and opinions of two long-estranged brothers, who meet to dispose of the old family house. Other plays include *The American Clock* (1980), *Playing for Time* (1981), *The Last Yankee* (1993), *Broken Glass* (1994) and his last work, a surreal political satire *Resurrection Blues* (2003). Miller published short stories and essays, and adapted *Ibsen's *An Enemy of the People* (1951). Although most of Miller's plays are set in contemporary America, and on the whole offer a realistic portrayal of life and society, the overtones from Ibsen and Greek tragedy are frequently conspicuous, and the theme of self-realization is recurrent; in some of the works, symbolism and naturalism are unobtrusively combined. A volume of criticism, *Theatre Essays*, was published in 1971, and an autobiography, *Timebends*, in 1987.

MILLER, Henry Valentine (1891–1980), American novelist and essayist, born in New York, the son of a middle-class tailor of German origin. He was brought up in Brooklyn, early acquiring the intensely individualistic and rebellious spirit that led him to reject

673 | MILLER | MILLS AND BOON

university in favour of a sequence of odd jobs and intellectual, sexual, and literary enterprises. He left America for Europe in 1930, and his autobiographical novel *Tropic of Cancer* was published in Paris in 1934 by the Obelisk Press, the predecessor of the *Olympia Press, which was also to publish him: it is a frank and lively account of an American artist's adventures in Paris, and was banned for decades (as were many of his works) in Britain and the USA. This was followed by many other works which mingled metaphysical speculation (he was interested in both theosophy and astrology) with sexually explicit scenes, surreal passages, and scenes of grotesque comedy; they include *Tropic of Capricorn* (France 1939; USA 1962), *The Colossus of Maroussi* (1941), *The Air-Conditioned Nightmare* (1945, reflections on a return to America), and a sequence of three works, *Sexus* (1949), *Plexus* (1953), and *Nexus* (1960), known together as *The Rosy Crucifixion*. In 1944 he settled in Big Sur, near Carmel, California, and despite continuing attacks from censors in various countries, including his own, he gradually became accepted as a major figure in the fight for literary and personal freedom, and a spiritual sage who greatly influenced the *Beat Generation in its search for salvation through extremes of experience. Works which had been previously condemned as pornographic are now widely described as works of 'innocent eroticism', although modern *feminist criticism (while recognizing his importance) has strongly attacked the sexism of his obsession with male potency and female masochism.

MILLER, Hugh (1802–56), born in Cromarty. He began to write poetry while working as a stonemason (*Poems Written in the Leisure Hours of a Journeyman Mason*, 1829), but made a more lasting mark as journalist and as self-educated palaeontologist. From 1840 he was editor of the *Witness*, a radical and evangelical twice-weekly for which he wrote on many subjects, including rural poverty, geology, and foreign affairs. His books include *The Old Red Sandstone, or New Walks in an Old Field* (1841), a vivid account of his sense of excitement and discovery when, as a young man, he learned to look for fossils in the sandstone quarries; it became a Victorian classic, highly regarded both for its learning and its lucidity of expression. His autobiographical *My Schools and Schoolmasters* (1854) also enjoyed a considerable success. In *The Footprints of the Creator* (1849), which was an attack on R. Chambers's *The Vestiges of Creation*, Miller expounded his own God-centred and pre-Darwinian views of evolution, and argued that evolutionary change took place not slowly but suddenly. He shot himself on Christmas Eve 1856, after recording 'a fearful dream'. See George Rosie, *Hugh Miller: Outrage and Order* (1981).

MILLER, James, see BLACK BRITISH LITERATURE.

'Miller of Dee, The', see BICKERSTAFFE.

'Miller's Tale, The', see CANTERBURY TALES, 2.

Mill on the Floss, The, a novel by G. *Eliot, published 1860.

Tom and Maggie, the principal characters, are the children of the honest but ignorant and obstinate Mr Tulliver, the miller of Dorlcote Mill on the Floss. Tom is a prosaic youth, narrow of imagination and intellect, animated by conscious rectitude and a disposition to control others. Maggie in contrast is highly strung, intelligent, emotional, and, as a child, rebellious. From this conflict of temperaments, and from Maggie's frustrated sense of purpose, spring much of her unhappiness and the ultimate tragedy. Her deep love of her brother is thwarted by his lack of understanding, and she turns to Philip Wakem, the deformed son of a neighbouring lawyer, for intellectual and emotional companionship. Unfortunately lawyer Wakem is the object of Mr Tulliver's suspicion and dislike, which develop into hatred when Tulliver is made bankrupt as a result of litigation in which Wakem is on the other side. Tom, loyal to his father, discovers the secret friendship of Maggie and Philip, and forbids their meetings: Maggie reluctantly complies. After Mr Tulliver's death, accelerated by a scene of violence in which he thrashes the lawyer, Maggie leaves the mill for a visit at St Ogg's to her cousin Lucy Deane, who is to marry the handsome and agreeable Stephen Guest. Stephen, though loyal in intention to Lucy, is attracted by Maggie, and she by him. A boating expedition on the river leads, partly by Stephen's design, partly by accident, to Maggie's being irremediably compromised; Stephen implores her to marry him, but she refuses. Her brother turns her out of the house, and the society of St Ogg's ostracizes her. She and her mother take refuge with the loyal friend of her childhood, the packman Bob Jakins. Only Lucy, Philip, and the clergyman Dr Kenn show sympathy. The situation seems without issue, but in the last chapter a flood descends upon the town, and Maggie, whose first thought is of her brother's safety, courageously rescues him from the mill. There is a moment of recognition and reconciliation before the boat overturns, and both, locked in a final embrace, are drowned.

The portrayal of childhood, of rural life, and the subsidiary characters of Mrs Tulliver's sisters, the strong-minded Mrs Glegg and the melancholy Mrs Pullett, with their respective spouses, delighted most critics, though the book was felt to lack the charm of *Adam Bede*; Maggie's lapse into passion, the character of the lightweight Stephen, and the arbitrary tragedy of the denouement enraged others. It remains, however, one of the most widely read of her works.

Mills, Miss, in Dickens's *David Copperfield*, Dora's friend.

Mills and Boon, a publishing company founded in 1908; its early authors included P. G. *Wodehouse and Jack *London, and it launched the career of Georgette *Heyer. Its name has since become almost synonymous with popular *romantic fiction; as the circulating *libraries declined in the 1950s and paperback fiction became more popular, Mills and Boon (in association with a Canadian company, Harlequin) published increasing quantities of light romances, doctor/nurse romances, and historical fiction, selling not only in bookshops, but also in supermarkets, newsagents, etc.

MILMAN, Henry Hart (1791–1868), educated at Eton and Brasenose College, Oxford. He became incumbent of St Mary's, Reading, then professor of poetry at Oxford (1821–31) and dean of St Paul's (1849). He wrote a number of verse dramas, of which *Fazio* (1815), a neo-Jacobean tragedy set in Italy, proved successful on the stage; also a Miltonic epic, *Samor* (1818), set in 5th-cent. Britain. His historical writings include *The History of the Jews* (1829) and *History of Latin Christianity* (6 vols, 1854–5).

MILNE, A(lan) A(lexander) (1882–1956), educated at Westminster School and Trinity College, Cambridge. He became a prolific author of plays, novels, poetry, short stories, and essays, all of which have been overshadowed by his children's books. After freelance work in London he became from 1906 to 1914 assistant editor of **Punch*; and after the First World War began a successful career as playwright with *Mr Pim Passes by* (1919; pub. 1921), *The Truth about Blayds* (1921; pub. 1922), *The Dover Road* (1921; pub. 1922), and *Toad of Toad Hall* (1929; a dramatization of **Grahame's* The Wind in the Willows*). In 1924 his book of verses for children *When We Were Very Young* was immediately successful, outdone only by the phenomenal and abiding success of *Winnie-the-Pooh* (1926). Further popular verses, *Now We Are Six* (1927), were followed in 1928 by *The House at Pooh Corner*, no less successful than its predecessor. There is a life by Ann Thwaite (1990). (See CHILDREN'S LITERATURE.)

MILNES, (Richard) Monckton (1809–85), later Baron Houghton, educated at Trinity College, Cambridge, where he became the friend of **Tennyson, A. H. **Hallam, and **Thackeray, the first of many close literary friendships, which included, most notably, **Swinburne (whom he greatly assisted), **Burton, the **Brownings, **Patmore, W. S. **Landor, and many others. In 1837 he became an MP and worked for various reforming causes, including the Copyright Act and the establishment of Mechanics' Institutes. He published his first volume of verse in 1838 and *Palm Leaves* in 1844, following these with works of biography, history, sociology, and Boswelliana. His major work was probably his *Life and Letters of Keats* (1848), a poet whom he consistently championed. He also did much to enhance the reputation of **Blake, and in 1875 edited the works of T. L. **Peacock. His own collected *Poetical Works* appeared in 1876. His large collection of erotic books included the first serious collection of de **Sade. See J. Pope-Hennessy, *Monckton Milnes* (2 vols, 1950–2).

MIŁOSZ, Czesław (1911–2004), Polish poet and writer, born on the Polish–Lithuanian borderland of Wilno (Vilnius). He was a leader of the Polish literary avant-garde in the 1930s, and prominent in the Resistance movement. After some years in the diplomatic service, he emigrated to America, settling in California, and teaching at Berkeley. His works include novels, volumes of essays, and poetry, and *The Captive Mind* (1951), an apologia for his withdrawal from Poland. He has also translated Shakespeare, **Milton, and T. S. **Eliot into Polish. He was awarded the **Nobel Prize for literature in 1980. A volume of *Collected Poems 1931–1987* was published in 1988.

Milton, a poem in two books by W. **Blake, written and etched 1804–8, one of his longest and most complex mythological works, which is prefaced by his well-known lines 'And did those feet in ancient time', commonly known as 'Jerusalem'. It uses the mythological and allegorical framework of his earlier poems and also develops Blake's own extremely powerful and personal response to **Paradise Lost* and its author, which had affected and perplexed his imagination for years (see also under MARRIAGE OF HEAVEN AND HELL, The). Blake appears to suggest that he himself becomes imbued with the spirit of **Milton, who descends to earth in order to save **Albion through the power of Imagination: the bizarre and the sublime mingle, as Blake describes the spirit of Milton entering his foot— 'and all this Vegetable World appear'd on my left Foot | As a bright sandal form'd immortal of precious stones and gold. | I stooped down and bound it to walk forward through eternity' (Bk I, Pt 21, ll. 12–14). Blake imagines himself carried from Lambeth to Felpham by **Los, where, walking in his cottage garden, he is visited by the Virgin Ololon (Bk II, Pt 36), in search of Milton, and the poem draws to an end with Milton's address to Ololon, in which he proclaims his mission of regeneration, 'To cast off the rotten rags of Memory by Inspiration | To cast off Bacon, Locke and Newton from Albion's covering', and prophesies the purging away by Jesus of the 'sexual garments' which hide 'the human lineaments'. The final section is an apocalyptic vision, in which Jesus 'wept and walked forth | From Felpham's Vale clothed in Clouds of blood', from which Blake returns to his 'mortal state' to hear the mounting lark. The mythology of the poem is obscure, but much of it clearly relates to the experiences of his time at Felpham, and some of the descriptive passages (notably of **Beulah, at the opening of Bk II) show a magnificent combination of mystic vision and natural observation.

MILTON, John (1608–74), born in Bread Street, Cheapside, at the Sign of the Spread Eagle, the house of his father John Milton the elder, a scrivener and composer of music. He was educated at St **Paul's School, where he became friendly with **Diodati, then at Christ's College, Cambridge, where he acquired the nickname 'the Lady of Christ's', and may have alienated his fellow students by, in his own words, 'a certain niceness of nature, an honest haughtiness'. He was briefly rusticated, probably in 1626, became BA in 1629, and MA in 1632. During his Cambridge period, while considering himself destined for the ministry, he began to write poetry in Latin and Italian, and also in English, on both sacred and secular themes. His first known attempt at English verse, 'On the Death of a Fair Infant' (in a complex stanza repeated in the opening of the 'Nativity Ode'), was probably written in 1628 on the death of his niece Anne Phillips and 'At a Vacation Exercise' belongs to the same year. His first distinctively Miltonic work, 'On the Morning of Christs Nativity', written at Christmas 1629, shows a growing mastery of stanza and structure, an exuberant and at times baroque use of imagery, and the love of resounding proper names so marked in his later work. His fragmentary 'The Passion' was probably written at Easter 1630, and the *'Arcades' probably in 1632. 'On Shakespeare', his two epitaphs for *Hobson, the university carrier, and 'An Epitaph on the Marchioness of Winchester' belong to 1631. His twin poems, *'L'Allegro' and *'Il Penseroso', may have been written at Cambridge, or possibly at Hammersmith, where Milton the elder moved 1631/2: Milton himself on leaving Cambridge adopted no profession, but embarked on an ambitious course of private study at his father's home in preparation for a future as poet or clergyman; his Latin poem 'Ad Patrem' (?1634) appears to be an attempt to persuade his father that the two pursuits were reconcilable. His 'masque' *Comus, published anonymously in 1637, was written, and performed at Ludlow, in 1634. In 1636 the Miltons moved to Horton, then in Buckinghamshire, where John pursued his studies in Greek, Latin, and Italian, devoting much time to the Church Fathers. In 1637 he wrote *Lycidas, a pastoral elegy, which dwells on fears of premature death, unfulfilled ambition, and wasted dedication; during the 20 years that elapsed between this and his composition of *Paradise Lost Milton wrote no poetry, apart from some Latin and Italian pieces, and some sonnets, of which the most notable are those 'On the late Massacre in Piedmont', on his blindness, on his deceased wife (whether the first or second wife is disputed), his addresses to *Cromwell, Fairfax, and Vane, and those to *Lawes (with whom he had collaborated on the 'Arcades' and Comus) and to his young friends and students Edward Lawrence and Cyriack *Skinner. From 1638 to 1639 Milton travelled abroad, chiefly in Italy; he met *Grotius in Paris and *Galileo, still under official condemnation, at his villa just outside Florence. On his return he established himself in London and became tutor to his nephews Edward and John *Phillips; he appears at this time to have been contemplating an epic on an Arthurian theme, which he mentions in his Latin epitaph on his friend Diodati, Epitaphium Damonis; Diodati died while Milton was abroad. The epitaph was written in 1639, and privately printed and distributed.

His attentions were now diverted by historical events to many years of pamphleteering and political activity, and to a tireless defence of religious, civil, and domestic liberties. In 1641 he published a series of five pamphlets against episcopacy, engaging in controversy with bishops *Hall and *Ussher, and displaying from the first (Of Reformation in England and the Causes that Hitherto Have Hindered It) a vigorous, colourful Ciceronian prose, and a keenly polemic spirit which could yet rise to visions of apocalyptic grandeur. The Reason of Church Government (1642) was the first to which he put his name; it was followed in the same year by An Apology against a Pamphlet . . . against *Smectymnuus, which contains interesting autobiographical details. In July 1642 Milton married Mary Powell, daughter of Royalist parents; he was 33, she 17. Within six weeks he consented to her going home to her parents at Forest Hill, near Oxford (the Royalist stronghold), on condition that she returned by Michaelmas. She did not do so, for reasons perhaps connected with the outbreak of the Civil War as well as personal antipathy and sexual incompatibility. Taking advantage of the breakdown in censorship, Milton published in 1643 The Doctrine and Discipline of Divorce, arguing among other points that a true marriage was of mind as well as of body, and that the chaste and modest were more likely to find themselves 'chained unnaturally together' in unsuitable unions than those who had in youth lived loosely. This pamphlet made him notorious, but he pursued his arguments in three more on the subject of divorce in 1644–5, including *Tetrachordon, and also published in his own support a translation of Martin Bucer's views on the same theme. Of Education, addressed to his friend *Hartlib, appeared in 1644, as did his great defence of the liberty of the press, *Areopagitica. During this period he became aware of his growing blindness; by 1652 he was to be totally blind. His wife rejoined him in 1645, and their first daughter Anne was born a year later: a second daughter Mary was born in 1648 and Deborah in 1652. A son, John, born 1651, died in infancy.

After the execution of Charles I, Milton published The Tenure of Kings and Magistrates (1649), arguing in general terms that a people 'free by nature' had a right to depose and punish tyrants, and attacking the Presbyterians, whose belief in church discipline and state authority posed in his view a growing threat to freedom. He was appointed Latin secretary to the newly formed Council of State. He replied officially to *Eikon Basilike in Eikonoklastes (i.e. Image Breaker, 1649), and to *Salmasius in Pro Populo Anglicano Defensio (1651, A Defence of the English People), a work which created a furore on the Continent and was publicly burned in Paris and Toulouse; also to Du Moulin's Clamor (which he attributed to Alexander More, or Morus) in Defensio Secunda (1654), which contains some self-defensive autobiographical passages and reflections on his blindness. He was now assisted in his secretarial duties successively by G. R. Weckherlin, Philip Meadows, and *Marvell. His first wife died in 1652, three days after the birth of their third daughter, and in 1656 he married Katherine Woodcock, then aged 28, who died in 1658, having given birth to a daughter who survived only a few months. He retained his post as Latin secretary until the Restoration, having lived during most of this period at Petty France, Westminster. On the eve of the Restoration, he boldly published *The Ready and Easy Way to Establish a Free Commonwealth* (1660), a last-minute attempt to defend the 'Good old Cause' of republicanism and to halt the growing tide of Royalism and the 'defection of the misguided and abused multitude'. At the Restoration he went into hiding briefly, then was arrested, fined, and released: *D'Avenant and Marvell are said to have interceded on his behalf. He now returned to poetry and set about the composition of *Paradise Lost*; he had shown his nephews a sketch of lines from Book IV as early as 1642, and his notebooks show that he had earlier contemplated a drama on a similar theme. In 1663 he married his third wife, Elizabeth Minshull (who survived him by more than 50 years), and moved to what is now Bunhill Row, where he spent the remaining years of his life, apart from a brief visit to Chalfont St Giles in 1665, to avoid the plague, organized by his Quaker friend *Ellwood. *Paradise Lost* is said by *Aubrey to have been finished in 1663, but the agreement for his copyright was not signed until 1667. *Paradise Regained* was published in 1671 with *Samson Agonistes*: the composition dates of the latter have been much discussed, and the assumption that it was his last, or even one of his latest poems has been challenged. In these late years he also published various works written earlier in his life, including a *History of Britain* (1670), from legendary times to the Norman Conquest, and a compendium of *Ramus' Logic* (1672). In 1673 appeared a second edition of his *Poems*, originally published in 1645, including most of his minor verse. His *A Brief History of Moscovia*, drawn from the *Hakluyt and *Purchas collections, appeared posthumously in 1682.

Of Milton's Latin poems, the finest is his epitaph to Diodati, but his epistle 'Ad Patrem' and his address to 'Mansus' (Giovanni Battista Manso, intimate friend of *Tasso and *Marino) also have great interest: the latter was probably written in 1639.

The State Papers that he wrote as Latin secretary (discovered in 1743) are mostly concerned with the routine work of diplomacy, but include an interesting series of dispatches, 1655–8, on the subject of the expulsion and massacre of the Protestant Vaudois by the orders of the prince of Savoy, who had commanded them to abandon their faith. These breathe the same indignation that found more impassioned expression in his sonnet 'Avenge O Lord thy slaughter'd Saints'. The canon of his prose writings long included *De Doctrina Christiana*, an unorthodox theological trea-

tise first printed in 1825. His *Commonplace Book*, with interesting insights into his studies and plans for composition, came to light in 1874.

Milton died from 'gout struck in' (probably of renal failure associated with gout) and was buried beside his father in St Giles', Cripplegate. There are full biographies by D. *Masson (1859–94) and W. R. Parker (2 vols, 1968, rev. 1996 by G. Campbell); see also a Chronology (1997) by G. Campbell. His personality continues to arouse as much discussion as his works; as a man he has been variously presented as sociable, good-natured, and increasingly serene, as a domestic tyrant who bullied his daughters, as a strict Puritan, a misogynist, a libertine, and as a radical heretic. (See C. *Hill, *Milton and the English Revolution*, 1977.) As a writer, his towering stature was recognized early. Although appreciated as a master of polemical prose as well as of subtle lyric harmony, his reputation rests largely on *Paradise Lost*, which *Dryden (who made a rhymed version of it) was describing by 1677 as 'one of the greatest, most noble and sublime poems which either this age or nation has produced'. Poets and critics in the 18th cent. were profoundly influenced by Milton's use of blank verse (previously confined largely to drama) and his treatment of the *sublime, and he inspired many serious and burlesque imitations and adaptations. (See THOMSON, J., 1700–48; COWPER; PHILLIPS, J.; SOMERVILE.) But even at this period there were murmurs of dissent: Dr *Johnson complained that Milton used 'English words with a foreign idiom'. He found *Lycidas* 'harsh', and noted Milton's misogyny. *Addison, although greatly admiring, felt that 'our language sunk under him', and *Bentley's revisions were notorious for their insensitivity. Blake's famous dictum from *The Marriage of Heaven and Hell* (1790) that Milton was 'a true Poet and of the Devils party without knowing it' preceded the Romantic version, disseminated principally by *Shelley, which represented Satan the Arch-Rebel as the true hero of *Paradise Lost*, and its God as either dull or wicked; critics (and notably C. S. *Lewis, *A Preface to Paradise Lost*, 1942) have endeavoured in vain to dismiss this notion, which continues to attract students and creative writers, including *Empson (*Milton's God*, 1961). A different controversy, echoing the older complaints of Johnson and Addison, was brought into focus by T. S. *Eliot's attack, in 1936, in which he described Milton as one whose sensuousness had been 'withered by book-learning' and further impaired by blindness, who wrote English 'like a dead language'. He claimed that Milton's poetry 'could *only* be an influence for the worse'. He modified these views later, but they were endorsed by *Leavis, who condemned the rhythmic deadness, mechanical externality, and Latinate syntax of the later works, praising in contrast the sensuous Spenserian richness of the earlier. The debate continued in e.g. *Milton's Grand Style* by C. Ricks (1963), which claims that Milton's verse, although powerful, is also subtle and suggestive. Modern readings have explored Milton's conflicting feelings in portraying gender (see J. Wittreich, *Feminist Milton*, 1987, and S. Davies, *John Milton*, 1991); and the complex stresses of his political affiliations (see *Surprised by Sin*, 1968; 2nd edn 1998, by Stanley Fish).

mime, in modern usage, a term used to describe a kind of theatrical performance without words, in which meaning is conveyed by gesture and movement. As an art form it flourishes more on the Continent, in the work of such performers and writer-performers as Marcel Marceau (1923–) and Dario *Fo, than in England.

The earliest form of mime was the dramatic scenes from middle-class life, realistic and often, though not invariably, obscene, first composed in the 5th cent. BC by the Athenian Sophron, who is said to have served *Plato as a model for the writing of dialogue. His works have not survived, and the only known Greek mimes (by *Theocritus and Herodas) date from two centuries later. How they were presented is not known, but it seems probable that they were declaimed to a musical accompaniment by a single actor with appropriate gestures. Later still, in Rome, sketches of low life performed by several actors with masks and scenic effects became so popular that they drove both tragedy and comedy from the stage. After an interlude in the Middle Ages, the genre flourished again in the 16th cent. with the *commedia dell'arte in which the actors relied mainly on dumb-show though they did extemporize snatches of dialogue. Divertissements with music, dancing, and mime were also much in fashion from the Renaissance onwards and contributed to the development of ballet, opera, and the English *pantomime.

mimesis, see POETICS, THE. See also under AUERBACH.

Minnesingers, German lyric poets of the late 12th to the 14th cent., so called because love (*Minne*) was the principal subject of their poetry. They correspond to the Provençal troubadours (who influenced them) and the northern French trouvères. The Minnesang flourished at its best in the period called the Blütezeit, *c.*1200; after the first quarter of the 13th cent. it degenerated (as did the contemporary French lyric poetry), and the later Meistersang lacks the inspiration of the earlier singers (the theme of *Wagner's *Die Meistersinger von Nürnberg*). Some of the greatest Minnesingers were also writers of epic: Hartmann von Aue, *Wolfram von Eschenbach, and Gottlieb von Strassburg. The other most admired exponents of the *Minne* lyric are Reinmar von Hagenau, Heinrich von Morungen, and Walther von der Vogelweide. See Olive Sayce (ed.), *Poets of the Minnesang* (1967).

MINOT, Laurence, probably a soldier, the author (of whom nothing is known) of a series of spirited and patriotic war songs, written about 1352, concerning events of the period 1333–52 in the English wars against the Scots and French. There are poems on

Crécy, Halidon Hill, the sieges of Berwick and Calais, and such victorious topics. The poems give some suggestion of what medieval warfare was like, but they have little claim to literary distinction. They were edited by J. Hall (1897; 3rd edn rev. 1914).

Minstrel, The, see BEATTIE.

Minstrelsy of the Scottish Border (3 vols, 1802–3), a collection of *ballads compiled by Sir W. *Scott, who divided them into three sections, Historical Ballads, Romantic Ballads, and Imitations of the Ancient Ballad. He was aided by various friends and advisers, who included *Leyden, J. *Hogg, R. *Surtees, and many old women (including Hogg's mother) who kept alive the oral traditions. The extent to which Scott himself altered and improved on the texts has been much discussed; it appears to vary from minor adjustments to the insertion of whole lines and stanzas. In his introduction Scott stated a patriotic intention: 'By such efforts, feeble as they are, I may contribute somewhat to the history of my native country; the peculiar features of whose manners and character are daily melting and dissolving into those of her sister and ally.' According to *Motherwell, Scott later in life regretted the extent of his editorial work; 'In fact, I think I did wrong myself in endeavouring to make the best possible set of an ancient ballad out of several copies obtained from different quarters, and that, in many respects, if I improved the poetry, I spoiled the simplicity of the old song.' The volumes contain many well-known ballads, including 'The Wife of Usher's Well' (its first printing) and 'The Twa Corbies', in a version that M. J. C. Hodgart (*The Ballads*, 1950) claims is 'largely of Scott's making'.

Mirabell, (1) the hero of J. Fletcher's *Wilde Goose Chase*; (2) in Congreve's *The Way of the World*, the lover of Millamant.

Mirabilia Urbis Romae, a medieval guidebook to Rome. Its first form probably dates from the 12th cent., and it was perhaps 'kept up to date' till the 15th. There is a translation by F. Nichols (1889).

miracle plays, see MYSTERY PLAYS.

Miranda, in Shakespeare's *The Tempest*, the daughter of *Prospero. Her name means 'To be wondered at'.

Mirour de l'Omme (*Speculum Meditantis*), see GOWER, J.

mirror (mirour), as a literary term, based on the medieval Latin use of the word *speculum* (e.g. *Speculum Historiale* of *Vincent of Beauvais or *Speculum Meditantis* of *Gower, translated into French as *Mirour de l'omme*) to mean a true reflection or description of a particular subject, hence compendium. Thus there are titles such as *Mirrour of the Blessed Lyf of Iesu Christ* by N. *Love, the *Mirrour of the World* (translated by *Caxton from French), the *Mirror of Fools* (translation of the late 12th-cent. *Speculum Stultorum* by *Wireker), and, in the Renaissance, *A Mirror for Magistrates*.

Mirror for Magistrates, A, a work planned by George Ferrers, Master of the King's Pastimes in the reign of Henry VIII, and William Baldwin of Oxford. In it various famous men and women, most of them characters in English history, recount their downfall in verse. The book was originally begun as a continuation of *Lydgate's *The Fall of Princes*, itself based on *Boccaccio's *De Casibus*. After a suppressed edition of ?1554 it first appeared in 1559, containing 20 tragedies by various authors. In the enlarged edition of 1563 T. *Sackville contributed the 'Induction', set in deep winter, in which Sorrow leads the poet to the realms of the dead, and the *Complaint of Buckingham*. Further editions, with more tragedies added, were published in 1571, 1574, 1575, 1578, 1587, and 1609–10. John Higgins, compiler of the 1574–87 additions, added complaints by figures from early or mythical British history, such as Locrinus, Elstride, and Cordila, as well as Roman history, e.g. Julius Caesar, Nero.

Though the *Mirror* may not seem to offer much to a modern reader, it was one of the major achievements of what C. S. Lewis called the *'Drab Age', and provided source material for many major writers, including *Spenser, Shakespeare, *Daniel, and *Drayton. The *Mirror* and its continuations were edited by L. B. Campbell (1938–46).

Mirror of Fools (*Speculum Stultorum*), see WIREKER.

MIRSKY, D. S. (Prince Dmitry Petrovich Svyatopolk-Mirsky) (1890–1939), literary historian and critic, and in the inter-war period the most influential interpreter of Russian literature to the British. He left his native Russia in 1920 and taught Russian literature and literary criticism from 1922 at the University of London, until he was dismissed in 1932, whereupon he returned to the Soviet Union. There he continued to publish on Russian and English literature, and to engage in literary polemics. His *The Intelligentsia of Great Britain*, including estimates of G. B. *Shaw, *Wells, B. *Russell, D. H. *Lawrence, A. *Huxley, V. *Woolf, W. *Lewis, and others, caused a scandal on its London publication in 1935. In 1937 he was arrested and sent to Siberia, where he died in a prison hospital.

Misfortunes of Elphin, The, a satirical romance by *Peacock, published 1829.

It is an ingenious blend of Welsh Arthurian legend, in which Peacock was learned, and current political debate about reform. Elphin is king of Ceredigion in western Wales, but the bulk of his territory has been engulfed by the sea, owing to the drunkenness of Seithenyn, who was in charge of the embankment to keep out the waves. The 'inundation of Gwaelod', in the generation before the main action, becomes an allegory for the French revolution. Elphin succeeds to the diminished kingdom and is imprisoned by a powerful neighbour, whereupon his bard Taliesin sets out to rescue him through the poetic gifts of divination, or, since Peacock remains a sceptic, truth-telling. In Seithenyn the book contains what is perhaps Peacock's finest political parody, the celebrated drunken speech about the wall ('the parts that are rotten give elasticity to those that are sound'), which imitates a speech made by *Canning in 1822 in defence of the existing constitution. The book contains the celebrated 'War Song of Dinas Vawr', in context a sly comment on political opportunism, and a clever bardic contest in which the current Romantic fashion for escapist themes is gently mocked.

MISHIMA, Yukio (1925–70), Japanese novelist. Although married, with children, Mishima's work is suffused with a strong homoerotic sensibility. His first—and some say his best—novel, *Confessions of a Mask* (1949), deals directly with homosexuality, as does *Forbidden Colours* (1954). Even his later, political activities, culminating in his ritual samurai-style suicide, reflect his aesthetic and sexual preoccupations.

Misrule, King, Lord, or **Abbot of,** at the end of the 15th and beginning of the 16th cents, an officer appointed at court to superintend the Christmas revels. At the Scottish court he was called the 'Abbot of Unreason'. Lords of Misrule were also appointed in some of the university colleges and Inns of Court.

'Mistletoe Bough, The', see GINEVRA.

MISTRAL, Frédéric, see FÉLIBRIGE.

MISTRY, Rohinton (1952–), Indian writer, born in Bombay but based in Canada since 1975. Mistry is a former bank clerk whose first book was *Tales from Firozsha Baag* (1987), a collection of linked short stories set among the Parsi residents of a Bombay apartment building. More the portrait of a whole community than a series of discrete narratives, it paved the way for the novel *Such a Long Journey* (1991) in which the hero, Gustad Noble, works in a Bombay bank and becomes unwittingly involved in a scheme to divert funds into an illegal government account. Set against the backdrop of the creation of Bangladesh, it shows history as a juggernaut destroying and sweeping aside the lives of ordinary people, a theme also treated in the even more expansive *A Fine Balance* (1996). This heartbreaking account of poverty and thwarted ambition concerns two brothers working as tailors during the 1970s State of Emergency: by the end of the novel, official corruption and their own naïvety have left them not just penniless but physically maimed. Unlike his countryman Salman *Rushdie, Mistry eschews magical realism and instead favours traditional, 19th-cent. storytelling on a Dickensian scale. His attention to detail is delightful, the bleakness of his vision somewhat overwhelming.

MITCHEL, John (1815–75), Irish nationalist and solicitor, editor of the influential *Nation*, and later of the *United Irishman*. He was tried for sedition for his part in the rising of 1848, and transported to Tasmania to serve a 14-year sentence. In his *Jail Journal, or Five Years in British Prisons* (1854) he left a vivid account of his experiences. He escaped to America, where he again became editor of various journals. His work also includes a *Life and Times of Aodh O'Neill, Earl of Tyrone* (1845) and *The History of Ireland* (1869).

MITCHELL, Adrian (1932–   ), poet, novelist and playwright, born in London and educated at Christ Church, Oxford. He was associated with the pacifism, social protest, and free verse forms of *underground poetry; his collections of verse include *Out Loud* (1969), *Ride the Nightmare* (1971), and *For Beauty Douglas; Collected Poems and Songs* (1981). Other volumes: *On the Beach at Cambridge* (1986), *Love Songs of World War II* (1989), *Greatest Hits* (1991). His novels include *If You See Me Comin'* (1962) and *Wartime* (1973), and his many plays and stage adaptations, which make considerable use of songs and lyrics, an adaptation of Peter *Weiss's *Marat/Sade* (1966), *Tyger* (1971), based on the life and work of *Blake, and *Man Friday* (1973). *Heart on the Left: Poems 1953–1984* appeared in 1997.

MITCHELL, Julian (1935–   ), novelist, playwright, and screenwriter, educated at Winchester and Wadham College, Oxford. His novels include *Imaginary Toys* (1961), *The White Father* (1964, set in Africa), and the more experimental *The Undiscovered Country* (1968), in which a narrator, 'Julian Mitchell', in an apparently straight autobiographical mode, tells the story of his school and university days, and describes his relationship with 'Charles Humphries', a boyhood friend who, on his suicide, leaves Julian the manuscript of his novel *A New Satyricon*, which he proceeds to transcribe. Mitchell then turned to the theatre and television, adapting the novels of I. *Compton-Burnett for the stage and achieving West End success with *Half-Life* (1977), a play about an ageing archaeologist, and *Another Country* (1981, pub. 1982, filmed 1984), set in a public school, which examines the pressures and conflicts that turned some of the young intellectuals of the 1930s towards Marxism, and made one of them a potential spy. Later plays include *Francis* (1983), based on the life of Francis of Assisi, and *After Aida* (1986); screenplays include a study of Oscar *Wilde, played by Stephen Fry (1998), and TV adaptations of Colin Dexter's 'Inspector Morse' Oxford *detective stories.

MITCHELL, Margaret (1900–49), American novelist, whose one novel, the best-selling and Pulitzer Prize-winning *Gone with the Wind*, was published in 1936; the equally popular film was released in 1939. Set in Georgia at the time of the Civil War, it is the story of headstrong Scarlett O'Hara, her three marriages, and her determination to keep her father's property of Tara, despite the vicissitudes of war and passion.

MITCHISON, Naomi Mary Margaret (1897–1999), novelist, and sister of J. B. S. *Haldane, born in Edinburgh and brought up in Oxford. In 1916 she married the barrister and future Labour politician G. R. Mitchison. She began early to write both prose and verse, and her many works of fiction include *The Corn*

King and the Spring Queen (1931), a historical novel set in Greece and the eastern Mediterranean countries in 228–187 BC, *The Blood of the Martyrs* (1939), and *The Big House* (1950). Her non-fiction works, including three volumes of autobiography (*Small Talk*, 1973; *All Change Here*, 1975; *You May Well Ask*, 1979), illustrate her own commitment to the progressive political and social causes of the intellectual circles in which she moved.

MITFORD, Jessica Lucy (1917–96), writer, journalist, and sister of Nancy *Mitford. She early adopted left-wing views, and during the Spanish Civil War became a Republican sympathizer, eloped to Spain to join her cousin Esmond Romilly, and married him there in 1937: after his death (in 1941 in Hamburg) she married in 1943 American lawyer Bob Treuhaft, and settled with him in California. Together they joined the Communist Party, and maintained a lifelong support of civil rights and other radical and sometimes unpopular causes. Her vivid and entertaining account of her early family life, *Hons and Rebels* (1960), was followed by many other works of polemic and biography, and by campaigning documentaries, ranging from *The American Way of Death* (1963), a spirited exposé of the funeral industry, to *The American Way of Birth* (1992), attacking childbirth technology.

MITFORD, Mary Russell (1787–1855), born of a father whose extravagance and gambling compelled her to try to earn a living as a writer. She published a volume of verse in 1810, and was encouraged to continue writing by *Coleridge. Further volumes of poems appeared, and various essays in magazines, then in 1823 her drama *Julian*, with *Macready in the title role, was produced successfully at Covent Garden, and was followed by the even more successful *Foscari* in 1826 and *Rienzi* in 1828. She wrote other historical dramas, but meanwhile, in 1824, she had begun a series of sketches and stories which made up *Our Village* (1832), the work by which she is justly remembered. This was followed by *Belford Regis* (1835), a portrait of Reading; *Country Stories* (1837); and *Recollections of a Literary Life* (1852); a novel, *Atherton, and Other Tales*, was published in 1854, but, as the author confessed, prose fiction was not her *métier*. Her fluent letters, to *Lamb, *Haydon, *Horne, *Ruskin, Elizabeth Barrett (*Browning), W. S. *Landor, and many others, reveal an intense enjoyment of people and places and a sunny, affectionate nature: they were published in a selection ed. A. G. L'Estrange (*Life of M. R. Mitford in a Selection from Her Letters to Her Friends*, 3 vols, 1870) and in *Letters of M. R. Mitford, 2nd Series*, ed. H. Chorley (2 vols, 1872). See also a life by V. Watson (1949).

MITFORD, Nancy Freeman (1904–73), daughter of the second Lord Redesdale, who appears in many of her novels as the eccentric 'Uncle Matthew'. She published three novels before her first popular success, *The Pursuit of Love* (1945), in which the sensible Fanny, daughter of the irresponsible Bolter, describes the affairs of her six Radlett cousins, and in particular the progress of the lovely Linda through several marriages and passions to a premature death. Subsequent works (*Love in a Cold Climate*, 1949; *The Blessing*, 1951; *Don't Tell Alfred*, 1960) accompany the family and its associates through various social and amatory trials and triumphs; the appeal of the novels lies in the reckless upper-class bohemianism of many of the characters, determined to find life 'amusing' at all costs, and in Nancy Mitford's sharp ear for dialogue. *Noblesse Oblige: An Enquiry into the Identifiable Characteristics of the English Aristocracy* (1956, with A. S. C. Ross et al.), also a manifestation of her sense of social nuance, provoked a debate on 'U' and 'Non-U' vocabulary, terms she had herself promoted in *Encounter (1955). She also wrote several historical biographies (chiefly French), and edited two volumes of family correspondence (*The Ladies of Alderley*, 1938; *The Stanleys of Alderley*, 1939). Her *Letters* (1993), including many to her close friend and literary mentor Evelyn *Waugh, were edited by Charlotte Mosley.

MO, Timothy (1950–   ), novelist, born in Hong Kong, the son of a Chinese father and an English mother. His first novel was *The Monkey King* (1978), set in Hong Kong's business community; it was followed by *Sour Sweet* (1982), which describes the fortunes of a Chinese family who emigrate to London in the 1960s to open a restaurant and become caught up with Triad criminals. It was shortlisted for the *Booker Prize and subsequently adapted by Ian *McEwan for a film (1988). His most ambitious work to date, *An Insular Possession* (1986), is set during the opium wars of the 19th cent. between Britain and China. *The Redundancy of Courage* (1991), also shortlisted for the Booker, is a powerful political thriller telling the story of a young Chinese hotelier, Adolph Ng, whose life is transformed by violent events.

Moby-Dick, or, The Whale (1851), a novel by H. *Melville, first published in Britain, as *The Whale*, and slightly later in New York. It is made up of 135 chapters, written in an extraordinary variety of styles, from sailors' slang to biblical prophecy and Shakespearian rant.

Inspired by his friend *Hawthorne to say 'NO! in thunder' to Christianity, Melville fused his original *Bildungsroman with the tragic quest narrative of 'stricken' Captain Ahab seeking revenge on the white whale that has bitten off his leg. 'Call me Ishmael', is the striking opening phrase of a story that takes the young narrator to sea on the doomed whaler *Pequod*. Both Ahab and Ishmael seek knowledge, but while Ishmael learns love and humanity 'monomaniacal Ahab' pursues a demonic God behind the 'hooded phantom' or 'unreasoning mask' of the symbolic whale. The *Pequod* is a male microcosm with, among others, the 'soothing savage' harpooner Queequeg, 'right-minded' first mate Starbuck, jolly Stubb, and Pip the cabin boy, driven

prophetically mad, all involved in the whale fishery whose adventures and rituals Melville energetically describes. He interrupts the narrative with facts, tales, and soliloquies, including Father Mapple's sermon on the Leviathan, the Town-Ho's story, a dissertation on whales ('Cetology'), and a metaphysical dissertation on the ambiguous 'whiteness of the whale'. After a fierce three-day chase Moby-Dick destroys the *Pequod*. Ishmael survives the vortex, buoyed up on Queequeg's coffin: 'And only I am escaped alone to tell thee', begins his epilogue, citing the Book of Job.

Moby-Dick had some initial critical appreciation, particularly in Britain, but only since the 1920s has it been recognized as a masterpiece, an epic tragedy of tremendous dramatic power and narrative drive.

mock-biblical, a rhetorical strategy in which scriptural quotations, typologies, or tropes are used for satirical ends. Appropriating the Bible to satirize the maculate world of human vice and folly typically gives the mock-biblical a special sting because scriptural texts cannot be wholly divorced from their authoritative context. The Bible as the lingua franca of English culture provides a recognizable stock of images, catchphrases, and characters: two squabbling authors might be cast as Cain and Abel, or a foundering prime minister portrayed as Moses in the wilderness. Although the *mock-epic also exploits disjunctions between text and context, mock-biblical satire differs significantly in that it rarely parodies the Bible itself. Mock-biblical satire may be traced back to medieval writings against ignorance and corruption in the Roman Catholic Church. *Skelton's *Speak, Parrot* (1552) is one of the earliest instances in English of biblical images directed towards satirizing secular affairs. During the Reformation Lucas Cranach ('the Elder'), working in consort with *Luther, effectively deployed the mock-biblical against Rome in satirical woodcuts. It is during the 18th cent. that the genre reached its apogee as a mode of popular political satire. A cluster of writings surrounding the *Popish Plot trials of 1679 and the Exclusion crisis of 1681—most notably Dryden's *Absalom and Achitophel (1681)— propelled the mock-biblical into the mainstream of partisan political writing. A flood of typological, political, and ecclesiastical satire followed Dryden's success, even as his *Mac Flecknoe, with its likening of *Shadwell's success to that of Elisha (2 Kgs 2) highlighted the comic dimensions of the genre. That the Bible was satirically exploited by Anglicans, Dissenters, and Roman Catholics alike is evidenced by Swift's *Tale of a Tub (1704), *Drapier's Letters (1724), and other political pamphlets: *Defoe's *True-Born Englishman* (1701) and *Iure Divino* (1706); and *Pope's 'First Psalm' (1716), *Epistle to Bathurst* (1733), and the conclusion of *The Dunciad (1728, 1742). The mock-biblical engravings of *Hogarth, including *An Emblematical Print of the South Sea Scheme* (1721) and *The Harlot's Progress* (1732), gave popular English expression to a common feature of Dutch satirical prints. Mock-biblical satire became part of the 18th-cent. journalistic stock-in-trade and figured prominently during the Excise crisis (1733), the 'Jew Bill' (1753), the 'prime ministry' of Bute (1761–3), the Westminster election of 1784, and other secular events. Charles *Churchill's *Prophecy of Famine* (1763) and Blake's *Marriage of Heaven and Hell* (1790–3) and *The Book of *Los* (1793) testify to the ongoing vitality of this satirical species. The fashion for pseudo-biblical 'Chapters', 'Chronicles', 'Books', and 'Lessons' inspired by R. *Dodsley's *Chronicle of the Kings of England* (1740) and Horace *Walpole's *Lessons for the Day* (1742) culminated in the publication of '*The Chaldee MS' (1817) in *Blackwood's Magazine*, to a storm of controversy. In the Romantic period, many of the most vibrant mock-biblical satires were found in the political prints of *Rowlandson, *Cruikshank, William Dent, and James Gillray.

mock-epic, or **mock-heroic,** a satirical form that produces ridicule and humour by the presentation of low characters or trivial subjects in the lofty style of classical epic or heroic poems. The disjunction between matter and manner—as a sprig of common herbs is substituted for the golden bough that protected Aeneas in the underworld, or a petticoat is likened to a warrior's shield—both parodies the conventions of epic poetry and satirizes the people and events so depicted. Almost invariably a poem in heroic couplets, the mock epic typically employs elevated *poetic diction (which *Pope said should generate 'pompous expressions'), focuses on a single 'heroic' incident or action, and incorporates selected elements from the machinery of classical epic: the proposition, invocation, and inscription; the challenge; battles; the acclamation of the hero; games and other tests of prowess; perilous journeys; *epic similes; prayers and sacrifices to gods and/or goddesses, and their subsequent intervention; the visit to the underworld; and the vision of future glories.

Although the mock-epic satirical poem, which flourished in the later 17th and 18th cents, portrayed real characters and events (often thinly disguised) in contemporary and local settings, its literary ancestry may be traced back to classical antiquity. The pseudo-Homeric *Batrachomyomachia* ('Battle of the Frogs and Mice') and *Margites* (unfortunately lost), *Virgil's mock-heroic aggrandizing of the bees ('little Romans') in *Georgic IV*, and the pseudo-Virgilian *Culex* (in which a shepherd kills a gnat that has saved his life), though lacking any satirical design, supplied precedents for the display of trivial subjects comically elevated by the heroic manner, and for the heroic manner comically debased by trivial subjects. More recent forebears include Vida's *Scacchia Ludus* (1537), which describes a game of chess between Apollo and Mercury with the pantheon as spectators; Tassoni's *Secchia rapita* (1622), in which the citizens of Modena and Bologna in the guise of epic heroes war over a stolen bucket; *Scarron's *Virgile travesti* (1648–52), and Charles *Cotton's creative adaptation, *Scarronides* (1664).

An accomplished medley of burlesque, farce, parody, satire, and moral seriousness in which two ecclesiastical dignitaries fight over the placement of a lectern, *Boileau's *Le Lutrin* (1674, 1683) is a tour de force. Second only to the *Dunciad* in its adroit integration of mock-heroic elements, it was widely influential in England. Dryden's *Mac Flecknoe* (1682), a pyrotechnic demolition of his rival *Shadwell, and *Garth's *The Dispensary* (1699), which satirically chronicles a dispute between the College of Physicians and the Company of Apothecaries over the dispensing of medication, are the most important mock-heroic poems between Boileau and Pope. The two mock epics by the acknowledged master of the form, Pope's ingenious *Rape of the Lock* (1712, 1714) and the more satirically aggressive *Dunciad* (1728, 1742–3), are among the greatest comic poems in English.

Other noteworthy examples of the mock epic include Paul Whitehead's *The Gymnasiad: or, Boxing Match* (1744), R. O. Cambridge's *The Scribleriad* (1751), C. *Smart's *The Hilliad* (1753), C. *Churchill's *Rosciad* (1761), *Chatterton's *Consuliad* (1770), and *The Lousiad* (1785 *et seq.*) of 'Peter Pindar' (John *Wolcot). Generally speaking, mock-heroic poetry after Pope increasingly abandons its epic machinery, sacrificing its learned and comic qualities for a mode of personal and political satire that is more accessible and truculent, but less parodic and genuinely inventive. *The Eighteenth-Century Mock-Heroic Poem* (1990) by Ulrich Broich is the best guide to the genre, though R. P. Bond's *English Burlesque Poetry 1700–1750* (1932, repr. 1964) remains useful. See also G. C. Colomb, *Designs on Truth: The Poetics of the Augustan Mock-Epic* (1992).

Modernism, see overleaf.

Modern Love, a poem by G. *Meredith, published 1862.

An intense, innovative work of 50 poems, each of 16 lines; spoken by a narrator who painfully discovers how unreal are his ideas of women, the verses are connected as much by theme as by direct sequence of events. They unfold the disillusionment of passionate married love slowly giving place to discord, jealousy, and intense unhappiness, ending in the separation and wreck of two ill-assorted lives, and the death by poison of the wife, the 'Madam' who has given way to the narrator's mistress, the 'Lady'. The sequence clearly reflects Meredith's own unhappy experience in his first marriage to Mary Ellen Peacock, who died of kidney failure in 1861: some have read it as an exercise in confessional self-justification, but it also evidences a tortured sense of regret.

Modern Painters, by *Ruskin, a work of encyclopaedic range which filled five volumes: i, 1843; ii, 1846; iii and iv, 1856; v, 1860.   (*cont. on p.684*)

Modernism may be seen as a literary movement, spanning the period from the last quarter of the 19th cent. in France and from 1890 in Great Britain and Germany to the start of the Second World War. It may also be viewed as a collective term for the remarkable variety of contending groups, movements, and schools in literature, art, and music throughout Europe over the same period: *Symbolism, Post-Impressionism, Decadence, Fauvism, Cubism, *Expressionism, *Imagism, *Vorticism, *Futurism, *Dada, *Surrealism, and so on. The period was a time of confrontation with the public, typified by the issuing of manifestos, the proliferation of 'little magazines', and the rapid dissemination of avant-garde works and ideas across national borders or linguistic barriers.

The Modernist novel is often non-chronological, with experiments in the representation of time such as sudden jumps, temporal juxtapositions, or 'spatialization of time', in Joseph Frank's phrase (in which many different moments of time are presented with an effect of simultaneity), or studies of duration (making a great deal occur within a small amount of text, or stretching a small amount of action over a large textual space). Instead of upholding the realist illusion, the Modernists break narrative frames or move from one level of narration to another without warning; the works may be reflexive, about their own writing, or they may place one story inside another (a device known as interior duplication or *mise-en-abyme*, placing into the abyss). Instead of plot events, there is an emphasis on characters' consciousness, unconsciousness, memory, and perception (after 1900, the ideas of the philosopher Henri *Bergson and the psychoanalyst Sigmund *Freud became important tools and points of departure for writers and artists). Works are often oriented around a centre or centres of consciousness, and characterized by the use of such techniques as *free indirect style and *stream of consciousness. The narrators are often strangely limited third-person or unreliable first-person narrators, or there are multiple, shifting narrators. Instead of using closure and the fulfilment of reader expectations, or following genre conventions and formulas, Modernists often work towards open endings or unique forms: they utilize enigma, the ellipsis, the narrative gap, and they value ambiguity and complexity. Modernist poetry follows similar lines, overthrowing the rhyme and traditional forms and moving towards fragmentation, juxtaposition of images from widely scattered times and cultures, complex intertextual allusion and patterning, and personal discourse, often purposefully obscure.

Each national experience of Modernism is unique. For English literature, the beginning of Modernism is associated with French-influenced *fin-de-siècle* movements such as *naturalism, Symbolism, Decadence, and Aestheticism. Together with the aesthetic theories of Walter *Pater, the work of *Baudelaire, *Laforgue, *Mallarmé, Corbière, and *Valéry had a profound influence on the British Decadent poets of the 1890s, Oscar *Wilde, Ernest *Dowson, Arthur *Symons, Lionel *Johnson, and W. B. *Yeats. *Flaubert, *Huysmans, and the Russians *Turgenev and *Dostoevsky were important influences for such fiction writers as James *Joyce, D. H. *Lawrence, Virginia *Woolf, Ford Madox *Ford, and others, as well as the Americans Henry *James and Stephen *Crane, and the Polish-born Joseph *Conrad, resident in England.

Realistic fiction writers from the late 1890s to the Edwardian period wrote about modern life and often portrayed subjects such as extreme poverty, sexual misadventure, or the remote reaches of the British Empire (e.g. Arnold *Bennett, John *Galsworthy, H. Rider *Haggard, Rudyard *Kipling, *Ouida, William Somerset *Maugham, Edwin Pugh, and Arthur *Morrison). But they were following the general lines of the Victorian novel and were neither innovative in technique nor experimental in language. Even a writer as self-consciously modern and future-oriented as H. G. *Wells was traditional in his style and techniques, as well as outwardly focused in his fiction.

But in the late 1890s the novels of Henry James signalled a new direction, becoming increasingly complex, dense, and ambiguous. In his 'late style', as it appears in *The Wings of the Dove* (1902), *The Ambassadors* (1903), and *The Golden Bowl* (1904), with his convoluted, overly qualified sentences filled with parenthetical statements, self-interruptions, and indirection, James achieves such nuance and subtlety that his writing takes on an overheated opacity, both gripping and enervating. James was a model for Crane, Conrad, and Ford Madox Ford, and certainly had an impact on Virginia Woolf. Of the writers who began their careers in the 1890s, Conrad appears now to be the most fully Modernist. His remarkable series of novels, especially *'Heart of Darkness' (1899), *Nostromo* (1904), *The Secret Agent* (1907), and *Under Western Eyes* (1911), constantly experiment with abrupt temporal and spatial shifts in the presentation of narrative information, with many long gaps in exposition or seeming digressions; they also employ a dense, nervous, and shifting prose style characterized by overdetermination, ambiguity, and repetition and by the use of multiple narrators and narrative frames. At the same time, the works are engaged with important areas of *fin-de-siècle* anxiety: the corruption of imperialism and colonialism, urban chaos, political extremism (whether extreme nationalism or anarchism), racism, the apparatus of secret police and surveillance, and the inability to discover the truth of events.

James Joyce began with naturalism and urban realism in his story collection *Dubliners* (1914), but in *A Portrait of the Artist as a Young Man* (1916) started to experiment with interior monologue and free indirect discourse (in which the style shifts to match the 'centre of consciousness' on that page, changing in complexity and reference as the character develops). *Ulysses* (1922) focuses on one day in the lives of two Dubliners, using a mixture of multiple narrators (including many different third-person narrative voices), interior monologue, stream of consciousness, literary parodies, constant stylistic and technical changes. *Finnegans Wake* (1939) takes experimentation to the extreme, providing a one-night study of a Dublin pub-owner and his family told in a multilingual, multiple-punning, endlessly intertextual dream-speech.

Virginia Woolf and D. H. Lawrence, though very different in the milieux they depict, were psychological novelists much influenced by Freud. Woolf is experimental in technique and narrative structure, and focused in subject matter, in such novels as *Mrs Dalloway* (1925), *To the Lighthouse* (1927), *The Waves* (1931), *The Years* (1937), and *Between the Acts* (1941). Lawrence is traditional in narrative form but poetic and emotional in his style and daring in his subject matter, especially concerning sexual relations, in works like *Sons and Lovers* (1913), *The Rainbow* (1915), and *Women in Love* (1920).

Much British poetry of the modern period is self-consciously traditional in form and subject matter, especially the *Georgian poets just prior to the First World War (such as Rupert *Brooke, Edward *Marsh, J. C. *Squire, Robert *Graves, and John *Drinkwater). The soldier-poets (Wilfred *Owen, Isaac *Rosenberg, Siegfried *Sassoon, Ivor *Gurney) who wrote at the front line about the horrors of war were far more striking, their work becoming increasingly horrific and disillusioned as the war went on. David *Jones, in his long memoir-poems *In Parenthesis* (1937) and *The Anathemata* (1952), was the most experimental of these writers. But it was three outsiders to England who are the most important figures in Modernist poetry: the Irish W. B. Yeats and the Americans Ezra *Pound and T. S. *Eliot.

Yeats drew from mystical or occult traditions, Irish history and mythology, Japanese *Nōh theatre, and his own life and passions. Pound was the greatest promoter of Modernism in London, where he lived from 1908 to 1920. He declared the start of Imagism with his own famous two-line poem 'In a Station of the Metro' and the publication of a group of poems by H.D. (Hilda *Doolittle) and Richard *Aldington. Pound's own poetry shifted from imitation of *Browning and medieval forms, through imitation of Japanese poetic structures and the minimalist writing of Imagism, to Vorticism and, with the *Cantos* (on which he worked from 1915 to 1969), the epic poem. This extremely complex 'poem with history' is almost 800 pages long, and has many sections of Confucianism, 18th-cent. American history, Renaissance Italian portions, and elliptical personal memoirs. Making no concessions to the reader, it includes untranslated Chinese, Italian, Greek, Latin, French, and Provençal. T. S. Eliot arrived in London in 1914 and published *Prufrock and Other Observations* in 1917. Eliot's poetry was marked by its juxtaposition of fragments, its humorous mixture of forms and linguistic registers, its *intertextuality, and its use of personas and bleak, urban settings. His masterpiece was *The Waste Land* (1922), which utilized all of these features and, in both its sweep through time and space and in its indirection and ambiguity, captured the largest audience of any 20th-cent. English-language poem. Its despairing mood, gallows humour, and seemingly hopeful ending appealed to many readers just after the First World War.

The writers of the 1930s set themselves apart from the earlier Modernists by their involvement with political, especially left-wing, causes, in response to the threats of Fascism and Nazism and the experience of the Spanish Civil War. W. H. *Auden, C. *Day-Lewis, Christopher *Isherwood, Stephen *Spender, and Louis *MacNeice are among the most important of these. Novelists Malcolm *Lowry and Flann *O'Brien, and the young Samuel *Beckett, continued the experiments of Joyce.

See: M. *Bradbury and J. McFarlan (eds), *Modernism 1890–1930* (1976); Michael H. Levenson, *The Genealogy of Modernism* (1984); W. R. Everdell, *The First Moderns* (1997).

It began as a defence of contemporary landscape artists, especially *Turner. Ruskin's plan was to show his artists' 'Superiority in the Art of Landscape Painting to all the Ancient Masters Proved by Examples of the True, the Beautiful and the Intellectual'. Volume i deals with the true. Turner had been accused of defying nature. For Ruskin he was the first painter in history to have given 'an entire transcript of the whole system of nature'. Knowledge is to be attained not from the traditions of 17th-cent. landscape but from direct observation of the facts of nature.

In vol. ii the logical framework of ideas was rapidly constructed. Beauty is perceived by the 'theoretic', i.e. contemplative faculty (as opposed to the aesthetic, which is sensual and base). It consists of the varied manifestations, in natural forms, of the attributes of God. But Ruskin now wanted to write, not of 'party or person' but of the functions of all art. Two years' study of old art brought revelations: Tuscan painting and sculpture of the 13th and 14th cents, Venetian Gothic architecture, and oil painting of the Renaissance. The outcome was that *Modern Painters* ii belies its title and exalts the 'great men of old time'.

In the third and subsequent volumes the earlier systematic treatment gives way to a looser structure. An unrelentingly detailed analysis of mountain beauty takes up most of *Modern Painters* iv, to Ruskin 'the beginning and the end of all natural scenery'. Part of Turner's greatness lies in his representation of the gloom and glory of mountains to express the wrath of God.

Modern Painters v is the work of a man embarking on a vital old age, not a little eccentric. He concludes his investigation of natural beauty. The volume reflects a new interest in myth as a source of wisdom and instrument of interpretation. A history of *Invention Spiritual* from ancient Greece to the present ends in the defeat of man's spiritual and intellectual powers by the 'deathful selfishness' of modern Europe. Turner's greatness is finally revealed in his mythological paintings, which express despair at the triumph of mortifying labour over beauty.

Modest Proposal, A, *for Preventing the Children of Poor People in Ireland, from Being a Burden to Their Parents or Country; and for Making Them Beneficial to the Publick* (1729), a satirical pamphlet by *Swift in which he suggests that the children of the poor should be fattened to feed the rich, an offer he describes as 'innocent, cheap, easy and effectual'. It is one of his most savage and powerful tracts, a masterpiece of ironic logic.

Modred, in the Arthurian legends, the nephew of King *Arthur, the son of King Lot of Orkney and Arthur's sister *Morgawse or Morcades (sometimes Anna; see PENDRAGON). *Geoffrey of Monmouth makes him the son of Arthur and his sister by an illicit union; he is accordingly the brother or half-brother of Gawain and his brothers. During Arthur's absence on a Roman war he treacherously seizes the queen (with her compliance, according to Geoffrey of Monmouth and his followers, such as *Laȝamon and *Wace) and the kingdom. In the final battle in Cornwall he is slain by Arthur but deals the king his death blow. He is alluded to as a definitive traitor in the *Divina commedia* (*Inferno,* xxxii. 61–2). The form of his name from *Malory to *Tennyson is Mordred.

MOIR, David Macbeth (1798–1851), a Scottish doctor, who signed himself Δ, Delta, published a number of volumes of poems, and contributed much prose and verse to *Blackwood's Magazine* and to many other periodicals. He is chiefly remembered as the author of *Mansie Wauch,* Tailor in Dalkeith (1828), which is an imaginary autobiography, in the manner of Moir's friend, *Galt, revealing a comically parochial view of the world, and satirizing the rising fashion for *autobiography. Moir also published works on medicine, and in 1851 *Lectures on Poetical Literature.*

MOLESWORTH, Mary Louisa, née Stewart (1839–1921). She wrote novels under the pseudonym Ennis Graham, but is known for her much-loved children's books, fairy tales, including *The Cuckoo Clock* (1877) and *The Tapestry Room* (1879), and realistic studies of child psychology in everyday life such as *Carrots* (1876) and *Two Little Waifs* (1883). The effect of her stories was much enhanced by illustrations by W. *Crane. See Roger Lancelyn Green, *Mrs Molesworth* (1961). (See CHILDREN'S LITERATURE.)

MOLESWORTH, Robert, first Viscount (1656–1725), diplomatist and political writer, born and died in Dublin. His publication in 1694 of *An Account of Denmark as It Was in the Year 1692,* extolling the liberty of post-revolution England in comparison with political and clerical 'tyranny' in Denmark, brought him to the notice of *Locke, led to a lifelong friendship with *Shaftesbury, and caused a diplomatic storm. He was answered by W. *King (1663–1712) in *Animadversions upon the Pretended Account of Denmark*. In a subsequent controversy in 1713 *Steele wrote in his defence in *The Crisis* and *Swift responded in *The Public Spirit of the Whigs*. Swift nevertheless admired him as an Irish patriot and later dedicated to him the fifth of *The Drapier's Letters*. As leading spokesman for the 'Old Whigs' or 'Commonwealth Men', Molesworth was the common patron of the different groups of Shaftesbury's followers among the English *Deists (Anthony *Collins, *Toland), the Irish Presbyterians (*Arbuckle, *Hutcheson), and the Edinburgh *Rankenian club (*Turnbull, *Wishart).

MOLIÈRE, pseudonym of Jean-Baptiste Poquelin (1622–73), French comic playwright and actor. Son of the court furnisher, he was educated at the Jesuit Collège de Clermont, but at the age of 21 abandoned his commercial prospects in order to found a professional theatre. From 1645 to 1658 he toured the provinces. Returning to Paris he was granted by royal favour the use of the Théâtre du Petit-Bourbon. For the next 15 years he played regularly before city and court audiences, his troupe being adopted by the king in 1665. He was at once enormously popular and the object of professional and ecclesiastical malice. Equally gifted as actor, director, and playwright, he was the creator of French classical comedy, bringing to a new synthesis the major comic traditions at his disposal: the high comedy of *Corneille and Rotrou, the Latin comedy of *Plautus and *Terence, and the improvisatory farce of the *commedia dell'arte. The 30 comedies that he composed after his return to Paris reveal an art capable of admitting serious and even tragic experience without sacrificing the laughter, gaiety, and exuberance proper to comedy. He has a profound understanding of the incongruities of human life. Whether dealing with the conflicts between husbands and wives (L'École des maris, 1661, and L'École des femmes, 1662), between youth and age (L'Avare, 1669), between artifice and nature (Les Précieuses ridicules, 1659, and Les Femmes savantes, 1672), between professional and domestic life (Le Tartuffe, 1664, and Le Malade imaginaire, 1673), between master and servant (Sganarelle, 1660, and Le Bourgeois Gentilhomme, 1660), between nobleman and peasant (Don Juan, 1665), or even between moral principle and relativism (Le Misanthrope, 1666), he shows an unwavering insight into human falsity and an equally undeviating delight in the generous virtues. He possessed an unrivalled knowledge of French society in the second half of the 17th cent. and has left a comprehensive gallery of portraits and types. He possessed an equally unrivalled ear for the rhythms of dialogue, the flavours of patois, and the extravagances of jargon. His major plays show that he was saturated in *Montaigne; and although he is less sceptical than Montaigne and more confident in man's powers of renewal, he has a similar capacity for reconciling the comic and the intellectual. His influence on English *Restoration comedy exceeded that of *Jonson: dramatists like *D'Avenant, *Dryden, *Wycherley, *Vanbrugh, and *Shadwell quarried his plays for characters and situations.

MOLINA, Tirso de, see TIRSO.

MOLINOS, Miguel de (1628–96), priest, founder of *Quietism. His Guía espiritual (Spiritual Guide) was published in 1675. It was proscribed in 1687 and Molinos was imprisoned for the rest of his life.

Moll Flanders, The Fortunes and Misfortunes of the Famous, a romance by *Defoe, published 1722.

This purports to be the autobiography of the daughter of a woman who had been transported to Virginia for theft soon after her child's birth. The child, abandoned in England, is brought up in the house of the compassionate mayor of Colchester. The story relates her seduction, her subsequent marriages and liaisons, and her visit to Virginia, where she finds her mother and discovers that she has unwittingly married her own brother. After leaving him and returning to England, she is presently reduced to destitution. She becomes an extremely successful pickpocket and thief, but is presently detected and transported to Virginia in company with one of her former husbands, a highwayman. With the funds that each has amassed they set up as planters, and Moll moreover finds that she has inherited a plantation from her mother. She and her husband spend their declining years in an atmosphere of prosperity and ostensible penitence.

Molly Mog, or The Fair Maid of the Inn, a *crambo ballad probably by *Gay, with *Pope and *Swift possibly as part authors. It first appeared in Mist's Weekly Journal in 1726, with a note to the effect that 'it was writ by two or three Men of Wit . . . upon the Occasion of their lying at a certain Inn at Ockingham, where the Daughter of the House was remarkably pretty, and whose Name is Molly Mog.'

Moloch, or **Molech,** the name of a Canaanite idol, to whom children were sacrificed as burnt offerings (Lev. 18: 21 and 2 Kgs 23: 10), represented by Milton (*Paradise Lost, I. 392) as one of the chief of the fallen angels. Hence applied to an object to which horrible sacrifices are made.

Monastery, The, a novel by Sir W. *Scott, published 1820. The Monastery followed the success of Ivanhoe, but did not equal its sales. Set in the abbey of Melrose (renamed Kennaquhair) in the Scotland of the early Reformation, it gives a vivid picture of the decline of the unreformed Catholic Church, but was the first of Scott's novels to be considered a failure. A sequel, The Abbot, followed in 1820 with greater success.

MONBODDO, James Burnett, Lord (1714–99), a Scottish judge and pioneer in anthropology, who published Of the Origin and Progress of Language (1773–92) and Ancient Metaphysics (1779–99). An admirer of *Rousseau, he was deeply interested in primitive societies; he himself lived an eccentrically austere life, believing civilization caused corruption and degeneracy. The orang-utan for which he is remembered figures in both these works as an example of 'the infantine state of our species', who was gentle, sociable, and intelligent, could play the flute, but never learned to speak; he suggested to *Peacock the character of Sir Oran Haut-ton in *Melincourt. Some writers consider Monboddo a precursor of C. *Darwin, and although he was mocked in his day for his gullibility and his keen interest in whether or not primitive men possessed vestigial tails, he was a prominent member of Scottish literary and intellectual life, and a member of the *Select Society. (See also PRIMITIVISM.)

Money, a comedy by *Bulwer-Lytton, produced 1840.

Alfred Evelyn, private secretary to the worldly-wise Sir John Vesey, loves Clara Douglas, as poor as himself. She refuses him, not wishing to involve him in her own poverty. Evelyn comes into a large fortune, and, stung by Clara's refusal, which he attributes to the wrong motive, proposes to the worldly Georgina, daughter of Sir John; but soon has reason to regret the step. To test her affection and her father's loyalty, he pretends to be ruined by gambling and the breaking of a bank. Thereupon Georgina promptly transfers the promise of her hand to a rival suitor, while Clara comes forward to help Evelyn. Thus released, and earlier misconceptions removed, Evelyn marries Clara.

Monimia, (1) the heroine of Otway's *The Orphan*; (2) a character in Smollett's *Ferdinand Count Fathom*.

Monitor, a short-lived thrice-weekly folio half-sheet, which appeared in 1713, written entirely in verse (much of it by N. *Tate) of a morally uplifting intent, on themes such as 'The Upright Man', 'The Gamester', etc. The name was adopted by several equally short-lived successors. The *Monitor: or British Freeholder*, a weekly political paper founded in 1755 by Richard Beckford, a London merchant, and edited by John Entick, in the Whig interest, lasted for ten years; *Wilkes contributed to it, and it was prosecuted for its attacks on Lord Bute's government.

Monk, The, a novel by M. G. *Lewis, published 1796.
   Ambrosio, the worthy superior of the Capuchins of Madrid, falls to the temptations of Matilda, a fiend-inspired wanton who, disguised as a boy, has entered his monastery as a novice. Now utterly depraved, Ambrosio falls in love with one of his penitents, pursues the girl with the help of magic and murder, and finally kills her in an effort to escape detection. But he is discovered, tortured by the Inquisition, and sentenced to death, finally compounding with the devil for escape from burning, only to be hurled by him to destruction and damnation. Although extravagant in its mixture of the supernatural, the terrible, and the indecent, the book contains scenes of great effect. It enjoyed a considerable contemporary vogue.

'Monk' Lewis, the sobriquet of M. G. *Lewis, author of *The Monk*.

Monks, a character in Dickens's *Oliver Twist*.

'Monk's Tale, The', see CANTERBURY TALES, 19.

MONRO, H(arold) E(dward) (1879–1932), chiefly remembered for his Poetry Bookshop which he founded in 1913 to publish poetry, to encourage its sale, and to promote poetry readings; and for publishing the series *Georgian Poetry*, edited by E. *Marsh. He founded and edited the *Poetry Review*, among other journals and broadsheets, and wrote poetry himself; his *Collected Poems*, introduced by T. S. *Eliot, appeared in 1933. His poems 'Bitter Sanctuary' and 'Milk for the Cat' appear in many anthologies.

MONROE, Harriet, see POETRY: A MAGAZINE OF VERSE.

MONSARRAT, Nicholas John Turney (1910–79), novelist, best remembered for his highly successful novel *The Cruel Sea* (1951), based on his wartime experiences at sea; his other works include *The Tribe that Lost Its Head* (1956), about the struggle for independence in an African state, and two volumes of autobiography (1966–70).

Monsieur D'Olive, a comedy by *Chapman, published 1606, acted a few years before. The plot is of little interest, but the play is enlivened by the remarkable character D'Olive, 'the perfect model of an impudent upstart', fluent, self-confident, good-humoured, witty, 'a mongrel of a gull and a villain'.

MONTAGU, Basil (1770–1851), the natural son of John, fourth earl of Sandwich, and his mistress Martha Ray, the singer. He met *Wordsworth in 1795, and became friendly with him, *Coleridge, and *Godwin, sharing their youthful radical views; his young son, also Basil Montagu, lived with William and Dorothy Wordsworth during their West Country period, and inspired William's poem, 'Anecdote for Fathers'. Montagu became a successful barrister and author, published many legal and political works on such subjects as bankruptcy, copyright, the death penalty, etc.; edited F. *Bacon (1825–37); and in 1846 published a little volume of mock-heroic couplets, *Railroad Eclogues*, in which he describes the advent of the railways in rural England, the effects of speculation, and so on.

MONTAGU, Mrs Elizabeth, née Robinson (1720–1800), a celebrated member of the *Blue Stocking Circle. She was an impressive woman, married to the wealthy grandson of the earl of Sandwich. After a markedly precocious childhood, she became a woman of great learning and wit. Dr *Johnson was amazed by her 'radiations of intellectual excellence' and dubbed her 'Queen of the Blues'. Her receptions, begun in the early 1750s, were more formal than Mrs *Vesey's, with the guests ranged in a half-circle around their hostess. She told *Garrick that, whatever their birth, wealth, or fame, 'I never invite idiots.' F. *Burney, a younger member of the circle, writing late in the century, found Mrs Montagu 'brilliant in diamonds, solid in judgement, and critical in talk'. She was generous and charitable, and deeply interested in literature; many young authors, such as *Beattie and R. *Price, were befriended with hospitality, encouragement, and gifts of money. Hannah *More described her as 'the female Maecenas of Hill St'. She wrote the first three of George Lyttelton's *Dialogues of the Dead* (1760), but only one, between Mercury and Mrs Modish, reflects anything of her learning and wit. In 1769 appeared her *Essay on the Writings and Genius of Shakespeare*, refuting the strictures of *Voltaire. It was received with general acclaim, Dr Johnson being apparently the only critic to perceive its weakness, and it made her a celebrity when she visited Paris in 1776. She retained her position as 'Queen of the Blues' for almost 50 years. Her sister, Sarah *Scott, was a novelist.

MONTAGU, Lady Mary Wortley, née Pierrepont (1689–1762), daughter of the fifth earl and first duke of Kingston. Her mother died in 1694, and she early became acquainted with social and literary life; she wrote verses while young and taught herself Latin. In 1712 she secretly married Edward Wortley Montagu, and accompanied him in 1716 when he went to Constantinople as ambassador. She wrote there her celebrated 'Turkish Letters' (published in 1763 after her death), and introduced into England on her return in 1718 the practice of inoculation against smallpox, an illness by which she herself had been badly marked in 1715. For the next two decades she was a leading member of society, famed for her wit. In 1716 *Curll piratically published some of her *Town Eclogues* and *Court Poems*; the *Eclogues* with other poems were republished in 1747. In 1737–8 she wrote an anonymous periodical, the *Nonsense of Common-Sense* (ed. R. Halsband, 1947), and in 1739 left England and her husband to live abroad for nearly 23 years in France and Italy, spending ten years near Brescia; during this period she wrote many letters, mostly to her daughter, Lady Bute. She returned to England shortly before her death. She is remembered principally for her letters, which are erudite as well as entertaining (though she disliked the label of *Blue Stocking attached to Mrs E. *Montagu and others); *Voltaire praised them above those of Mme de *Sévigné. But she is also known for her quarrels with *Pope, with whom she was on terms of close friendship before her visit to Turkey, and for some time after. The reasons for their rupture are not clear, but in later works he was to attack her viciously, and she unwisely joined with Pope's enemy *Hervey in *Verses Addressed to the Imitator of Horace* (1733) which understandably increased Pope's animosity. Her *Letters and Works*, ed. Lord Wharncliffe, appeared in 1837; R. Halsband published a life (1956) and edited the *Complete Letters* (1965–7). *Essays and Poems and Simplicity, a Comedy* (1977) was edited by R. Halsband and Isobel Grundy.

MONTAGUE, C(harles) E(dward) (1867–1928), educated at Balliol College, Oxford. He joined the staff of the *Manchester Guardian* in 1890 and later became assistant editor. He earned a considerable reputation as a reviewer and dramatic critic, and wrote several novels, including *A Hind Let Loose* (1910), *Rough Justice* (1926), and *Right off the Map* (1927). *Disenchantment* (1922) is his bitter account of the First World War in which he served as a private soldier.

MONTAGUE, John Patrick (1929–   ), Irish poet, born in New York, and educated at St Patrick's College, Armagh, and University College, Dublin. His volumes of poetry include *Forms of Exile* (1958), *Poisoned Lands* (1961), *A Chosen Light* (1967), *Tides* (1970), *The Great Cloak* (1978), and *Selected Poems* (1982). *New Selected Poems* was published in 1990. Many of his short, intense lyrics evoke the landscapes and heritage of rural Ireland, in a fine, spare diction; other poems recall periods spent in France and America and personal moments of family history. He has also edited various anthologies of Irish literature, and published short stories and a play.

Montagues, the, in Shakespeare's *Romeo and Juliet*, see under CAPULETS.

MONTAIGNE, Michel Eyquem de (1533–92), French moralist and essayist. He is generally regarded as the inventor of the modern 'essay', a genre which he fashioned out of the late medieval 'compilation', transforming it into a personal test of ideas and experience. The first two books of his *Essais* appeared in 1580, the fifth edition, containing the third book, in 1588, and a posthumous edition in 1595, each successive version containing extensive additions to the existing material. The first English translator was *Florio (1603). Traditionally the *Essais* are held to exhibit three stages of development, leading from an early Stoicism, under the influence of *Seneca, to a philosophical scepticism (*Apologie de Raimond Sebond*, II. 12), and finally to a moderate Epicureanism, but such an outline does only partial justice to a complex process. The *Apologie*, his most sustained piece, is a comprehensive attack on reason as a source of presumption in man, and its challenge was taken up by a number of later thinkers, including *Descartes, *Pascal, and F. *Bacon. Other notable readers of his work have been Robert *Burton, Sir T. *Browne, *Swift, and *Peacock. His essay 'Des cannibales' (I. 31) was a source, via Florio, of Shakespeare's *The Tempest*.

Montalban, in *Orlando innamorato*, the home of *Rinaldo, and the scene of a great battle, in which the Christians under Charlemagne are driven back by the Saracens under Marsilio. See *Paradise Lost*, I. 583.

MONTALE, Eugenio (1896–1981), the greatest Italian poet of the 20th cent., recipient of the *Nobel Prize (1975). He draws on an extreme range of language from the prosaic to the lyrical—from naval and biological terminology to the dialect of Genoa, his native city—and on all the strains in Italian literary tradition, recovering 'dead' words, coining new ones, and subjecting every word to intense multiplicity of meaning. This linguistic engagement means that he rejected the aloof 'Petrarchan' role for the poet, although his wariness of moral keys has often attracted the accusation of apoliticality. His main books of poems (now all included in the critical edn approved by him shortly before his death, *E. M.: l'opera in versi*, ed. F. Contini, 1980) are: *Ossi di seppia* (*Cuttle-Fish Bones*, 1925), *Le occasioni* (*Occasions*, 1932), *La bufera e altro* (*The Storm and Others*, 1943–54), *Satura* (1962), *Diario del '71 e del '72* (*Diary of 1971 and 1972*, 1973). His translations of Shakespeare, G. M. *Hopkins, *Yeats, and T. S. *Eliot are in *Quaderno di traduzioni* (*Translator's Notebook*, 1975). He has been translated by R. *Lowell and by E. *Morgan.

MONTEMAYOR, Jorge de (1519–61), a Portuguese poet and author who wrote mostly in Spanish. His chief work is *Diana* (?1559), a prose pastoral interspersed with verses, in which he transferred Arcadia to the heart of Spain. It was extremely popular and was translated into French, German, and English. The English translation was by B. *Yonge (1598); the episode of Felix and Felismena in Yonge's version is almost certainly the direct source of much of the plot of Shakespeare's *The Two Gentlemen of Verona*. The scene is laid at the foot of the mountains of León and the pastoral is occupied with the misfortunes of Sereno and Sylvanus, two shepherd lovers of the fair Diana, a shepherdess; and the loves, transfers of affection, and disguises of various other shepherds and shepherd-esses. Happiness is finally restored by the agency of enchanted potions. A continuation (or, as has recently been argued, a rejoinder), *Diana enamorada* by Gaspar Gil Polo (c.1519–85), appeared in 1564, and was also very popular.

MONTESQUIEU, Charles-Louis de Secondat (1689–1755), French social and political philosopher. A member of the lesser nobility of Guyenne, he trained as a lawyer and served as president of the Bordeaux *Parlement*. He made his name as a writer with the publication of *Lettres persanes* (1721; English trans. Ozell, 1722), in which the correspondence of two Persian visitors to Paris occasions a satirical review of French legal and political institutions. His masterpiece, *De l'esprit des lois* (1748), is the first European work to employ a recognizable sociological method. It analyses a variety of political constitutions, and advocates a liberal constitutional monarchy on the English model. He lived in England during 1729–31, and he travelled in western Europe in the company of Lord *Chester-field.

MONTGOMERIE, Alexander (c.1545–c.1598), a Scot-tish poet, who held office in the Scottish court in 1578 and received a pension from James VI in 1583. He left to travel abroad in 1586, having got into trouble. His principal work is *The Cherry and the Slae*, a long allegorical poem on the contrast between the cherry growing high up and valued, and the sloe growing close at hand and despised, in which Hope, Experience, Cupid, etc., take part in the conversation. It was published twice in 1597, the first edition being un-finished and corrupt. He also wrote a *Flyting of Montgomerie and Polwart* (pub. 1621), sonnets, and miscellaneous poems.

MONTHERLANT, Henry de (1896–1972), French nov-elist and dramatist. Born of an aristocratic and Roman Catholic family, he showed himself receptive to the ideas of *Barrès, *d'Annunzio, and *Gide, evolving in his early novels—notably *Les Célibataires* (1934)—an ideology of chivalric ardour and masculine disdain. His major plays, which include *La Reine morte* (1942), *Le Maître de Santiago* (1947), *La Ville dont le prince est un* *enfant* (1951), and *Port-Royal* (1954), exhibit his gifts for mordant writing and heroic intensity. His culmin-ating work, the novel *Le Chaos et la nuit* (1963), evokes the proud and austere isolation of an exiled Spanish anarchist. He travelled widely and sometimes dan-gerously during his early life. An extreme right-winger in politics, he consistently rejected modern French democracy. His work has been translated into English by T. Kilmartin and J. Griffin.

Monthly Magazine, an influential radical publication founded in 1796 by Richard Phillips, a Jacobin and a supporter of *Paine. Contributors included *Godwin, *Malthus, *Hazlitt, *Southey, and W. *Taylor. The magazine had an encyclopaedic range, covering lit-erature (including German, Spanish, and oriental literature), science, politics, philosophy, etc. Its first editor was Dr J. *Aikin (to whom *Coleridge originally intended to send the *Ancient Mariner); its last (in 1825) was *Thelwall. Both the *Anti-Jacobin and the *New Monthly Magazine were founded to oppose the views of the *Monthly*.

Monthly Review, (1749–1845), founded by the book-seller Ralph Griffiths, began as a series of digests of miscellaneous matters, but about 1780 became the first of the influential literary reviews. It was liberal in outlook, and its standard of contributions, from *Sheridan, Dr C. *Burney, *Goldsmith, and others, was very high. Its attempt, by 1790, to review all publications in each month gives it considerable bibliographical interest. The term 'autobiography' seems first to have appeared in its columns, in Dec. 1797.

MONTROSE, James Graham, fifth earl and first mar-quis of (1612–50), Royalist and general, is remembered as a poet for a few songs and epigrams (printed in Mark Napier's *Memoirs of Montrose*, 1856, and since much anthologized), including 'My dear and only love' and lines said to have been written on his prison window the night before his execution in Edinburgh.

MOODY and SANKEY, Dwight Lyman Moody (1837–99) and Ira David Sankey (1840–1908), American evangelists. After undergoing 'conversion' as a young man, Moody began his evangelizing activities by starting a Sunday school in Chicago. He devoted himself to missionary work there and among soldiers during the American Civil War. With Sankey as singer and organist, they carried on a revival campaign in America and England. The compilation of the *Sankey and Moody Hymn Book* (1873) and its many subsequent editions (as *Sacred Songs and Solos*, etc.) was due to Sankey.

Moonstone, The, a novel by Wilkie *Collins, pub-lished 1868. The moonstone, an enormous diamond originally stolen from an Indian shrine, is given to an English girl, Rachel Verrinder, on her 18th birthday, but disappears the same night. Under suspicion of stealing it are Rosanna Spearman, a hunchbacked housemaid, formerly a thief; a troop of Indian jugglers; Franklin Blake, Rachel's cousin; and Rachel herself. A detective, Sergeant Cuff, is called in to solve the mystery, and is aided by the house steward Gabriel Betteredge, principal narrator of the story, but thwarted by Rachel's reticence and by the tragic suicide of Rosanna. It is eventually discovered that Franklin Blake was seen by Rachel to take the diamond, that at the time he was sleepwalking under the influence of opium, that it was taken from him by Rachel's other suitor, Godfrey Ablewhite, a sanctimonious hypocrite, and finally secured (by the murder of Ablewhite) and returned to the shrine by the Indian jugglers, who were high-caste Brahmans in disguise.

MOORCOCK, Michael (1939–   ), one of the most prominent of the 'New Wave' *science fiction writers of the 1960s, part of whose aim was to invest the genre with literary merit. He edited New Worlds from 1964 to 1971, and has also edited many collections of short stories. A prolific and versatile writer, his own works include the Cornelius Quartet (The Final Programme, 1969; A Cure for Cancer, 1971; The English Assassin, 1972; The Condition of Muzak, 1977), whose central character, Jerry Cornelius, was described by Brian *Aldiss as the meeting point of 'the world of Ronald *Firbank and Ian *Fleming'. An omnibus edition was published in 1993. The Colonel Pyat books (three novels of a projected quartet, Byzantium Endures, 1981; The Laughter of Carthage, 1984; Jerusalem Commands, 1992) explore the development of Fascism and the Jewish Holocaust through the unreliable memoirs of a self-deceiving Russian émigré snob, racist, charlatan, and cocaine addict: they take Pyat from childhood in pre-revolutionary Russia to bitter exile in 1970s London. The poignant and optimistic Mother London (1988) celebrates the adaptability and vitality of London's people, landscape, history, and mythology through a dense non-linear narrative tracking the stories of a group of psychiatric outpatients from the Blitz to the 1980s. Other works of note include The Brothel in Rosenstrasse (1982), Blood: A Southern Fantasy (1995), and War amongst the Angels (1996).

MOORE, Brian (1921–99), novelist, born and educated in Belfast, the son of a Roman Catholic surgeon of strong Irish nationalist views. He emigrated in 1948 to Canada and subsequently moved to the USA. Some early pot-boilers were published pseudonymously. The first serious work under his own name was Judith Hearne (1955; published in the USA as The Lonely Passion of Judith Hearne, 1956), a poignant story of a lonely Belfast spinster who takes refuge in alcohol. His subsequent works, many of which deal with transatlantic migrations, include The Feast of Lupercal (1957, set in Belfast); The Luck of Ginger Coffey (1960, describing the misfortunes and daydreams of an Irish immigrant in Canada); I am Mary Dunne (1968, a first-person female narration set in America),

Catholics (1972, a papal representative visiting an Irish religious community some time in the future), and The Mangan Inheritance (1979, an American journalist in search of his Irish heritage and the poète maudit J. C. *Mangan). Other works include The Black Robe (1983), a violent historical novel set in 17th-cent. Quebec; Lies of Silence (1990), a novel of the *Troubles, in which a hotel manager finds himself in the hands of gunmen; and The Magician's Wife (1997), a historical novel set in France and Algeria in the 1850s. Critics have praised both the versatility of his subject matter and the economy and understatement of his style.

MOORE, Edward (1712–57), a linen draper turned author, who contributed to the *Gentleman's Magazine and other periodicals, wrote poems and fables which show a debt to *Gay, and edited the *World, 1753–6, which included *Walpole and *Chesterfield among its contributors. Though himself a contributor to *Dodsley's Collection of Poems (1748–58), he is best remembered as a dramatist. His first comedy, The Foundling (1748), may owe something to Richardson's *Pamela, and was warmly praised by *Fielding. Gil Blas (1751) is a lively comedy of intrigue, the plot of which is taken from *Lesage's Gil Blas of Santillane (IV. iii et seq.) where a lady masquerades as a student in order to get acquainted with a young man who has taken her fancy, maintains by a series of quick changes the dual role of lady and student, and achieves her object of winning the young man's heart. His most successful play, however, was a domestic prose tragedy, The Gamester (1753), an exposure of the vice of gambling, through which the weak creature Beverley is lured to ruin and death by the villain Stukeley; this play was widely translated, and was described by Moore's biographer J. H. Caskey (The Life and Works of Moore, 1927) as 'the most modern English tragedy written in the eighteenth century'. It was adapted by *Diderot.

MOORE, Francis, see OLD MOORE.

MOORE, George Augustus (1852–1933), Anglo-Irish novelist, born at Moore Hall in Co. Mayo; his father's racing stables provided background for his most successful novel, *Esther Waters. He studied painting in Paris for some years and the knowledge of French writing he gained there stood him in good stead when, returning to England c.1880, he set about revitalizing the Victorian novel with naturalistic and, later, realistic techniques borrowed from *Balzac, *Zola, and the *Goncourts. His first novel, A Modern Lover (1883), set in artistic bohemian society, was banned by the circulating *libraries, a circumstance which confirmed Moore in his outspoken battle against prudery and censorship. It was followed by A Mummer's Wife (1885), set in the Potteries, which influenced Arnold *Bennett); Esther Waters (1894); Evelyn Innes (1898) and its sequel Sister Teresa (1901). The Untilled Field (1903) is a collection of short stories strongly influenced by *Turgenev and *Dostoevsky. In his later novels, e.g.

The Brook Kerith (1916), which unfolds the interwoven lives of Christ (who survives the Cross), St Paul, and *Joseph of Arimathea, and Heloïse and Abelard (1921), he aimed at epic effect. Confessions of a Young Man (1888), Memoirs of my Dead Life (1906), and Hail and Farewell (3 vols, 1911–14) are all autobiographical; the last is an important though unreliable source for the history of the *Irish Revival. Moore collaborated in the planning of the Irish National Theatre (see ABBEY THEATRE), a work which, in the words of *Yeats, 'could not have been done at all without Moore's knowledge of the stage'. His collection of short stories Celibate Lives (1927) shows the influence of *Flaubert, not only in subject (all five tales deal with the state of celibacy) but also in their careful reworking and publishing of earlier material. The Ebury edition of Moore's works (20 vols, 1936–8) owes its name to 121 Ebury Street ('that long, lack-lustre street', in his own words), where he lived from 1911 until his death, an object of pilgrimage for many younger writers and admirers. See J. M. Hone, The Life of Moore (1936). (See VIZETELLY.)

MOORE, G(eorge) E(dward) (1873–1958), brother of T. Sturge *Moore, educated at Dulwich College and Trinity College, Cambridge. He was professor of philosophy in the University of Cambridge, 1925–39. His Principia Ethica (1903) inaugurated a new era in British moral philosophy, and also had great influence outside academic philosophy, particularly on the *Bloomsbury Group, who adopted its emphasis on 'the pleasures of human intercourse and the enjoyment of beautiful objects'. His other writings, which include Philosophical Studies (1922) and Some Main Problems of Philosophy (1953), have had a great, but more narrowly confined, influence. For an account of his personal influence (which, despite his modest nature, was profound) see P. Levy, G. E. Moore and the Cambridge Apostles (1979). (See also APOSTLES.)

MOORE, John (1729–1802). He studied medicine at Glasgow, and practised in the army and in London as a surgeon until 1772. He then travelled in Europe for several years, publishing accounts of his journeys in 1779, 1781, and 1793. In 1786 he published a successful novel, *Zeluco, the history of a wicked man; Edward (1796), in sharp contrast, redressed the balance by telling the story of a thoroughly good one, and was clearly influenced by *Marivaux's Vie de Marianne. In 1797 he produced a collected edition of *Smollett, who had been a friend and patient, and provided a brief biography. *Mordaunt, an *epistolary novel of some quality, was published in 1800. Moore was the father of Sir John *Moore of Corunna.

MOORE, Sir John (1761–1809), lieutenant-general, son of the above. He became commander-in-chief in the Peninsula on the recall of Sir Harry Burrard (1808). He led the historic retreat to Corunna during the winter of 1808–9 and began the embarkation of the British force on 13 Jan. The French, who now appeared, were repulsed, but Moore was mortally wounded, and buried at midnight of 16 Jan. 1809, in the citadel of Corunna. He is the subject of the famous elegy by C. *Wolfe.

MOORE, Marianne Craig (1887–1972), American poet, born in Missouri. From 1925 to 1929 she was editor of the *Dial, and contributed greatly to its distinction. Her first volume, Poems (1921), was followed by Observations (1924), Selected Poems (1935, with an introduction by T. S. *Eliot), The Pangolin, and Other Verse (1936), and other collections; her Collected Poems appeared in 1951. Her early work was well known in Britain, admired by I. A. *Richards, and anthologized by Michael *Roberts. Her tone is characteristically urbane, sophisticated, and conversational, her observations detailed and precise, and her poems are composed for the page with a strong sense of visual effect. Her subject matter—animals, both homely and exotic, baseball matches, art galleries, catalogues, etc.—is idiosyncratic and has been described as 'incontrovertibly American'.

MOORE, Thomas (1779–1852), born in Dublin, the son of a grocer. He was educated at Trinity College, Dublin, and entered at the Middle Temple. In 1801 he published a collection of indifferent poems, The Poetical Works of the Late Thomas Little, under which pseudonym Byron refers to him in *English Bards and Scotch Reviewers. In 1803 he was appointed admiralty registrar in Bermuda, a post which he briefly occupied before transferring it to a deputy. In 1806 appeared Epistles, Odes, and Other Poems which *Jeffrey brought to general notice by his strictures in the *Edinburgh Review. From 1808 to 1834 Moore continued to add to his Irish Melodies, which established him as the national bard of Ireland. He was a good musician and a skilful writer of patriotic and often nostalgic songs, which he set to Irish tunes, mainly of the 18th cent. He himself felt he had 'an instinctive turn for rhyme and song'. Among his more famous songs are 'The Harp that once through Tara's Halls', 'The Minstrel Boy', and 'The Last Rose of Summer'. In 1813 he issued The Twopenny Post Bag, a collection of satires directed against the prince regent. He acquired fame and a European reputation with the publication of *Lalla Rookh (1817). In 1818 appeared the satirical and entertaining *The Fudge Family in Paris. His deputy in Bermuda then defaulted, leaving Moore to meet a debt of £6,000. He left England for Italy, returning in 1822 when the debt had been paid. *The Loves of the Angels (1823) enjoyed a considerable vogue and caused some scandal. In 1824 he was prevailed upon to permit the burning of *Byron's Memoirs, which Byron (a close friend) had given to him. In 1825 there appeared a life of Sheridan; in 1827 The Epicurean, a novel about a Greek philosopher; in 1830 a life of Byron; and in 1831 a Life of Lord Edward Fitzgerald. He was awarded a literary pension in 1835, and in the same year published *The Fudges in England*, a light satire on an Irish priest turned Protestant evangelist and on the sentimental literary absurdities of the day. His *History of Ireland* (1835–46) was not a success. He was awarded a Civil List pension in 1850.

Moore's *Letters* were edited by W. S. Dowden (2 vols, 1964); see also *The Journal of Thomas Moore*, ed. P. *Quennell (1964).

MOORE, T(homas) Sturge (1870–1944), poet, woodengraver, and illustrator, and brother of G. E. *Moore; he was a friend of *Ricketts and Shannon, and also of *Yeats, his correspondence with whom was published in 1953, and for whom he designed several books. His first volume of verse, *The Vinedresser and Other Poems* (1899), was followed by several others, and by various verse dramas, including *Tragic Mothers: Medea, Niobe, Tyrfing* (1920).

Mopsa, a character in Sidney's *Arcadia*.

MORAES, Dom (1938–2004), prolific and widely travelled Indian poet and writer. He was born in Bombay and read English at Jesus College, Oxford. *A Beginning* (1957), his first book of poems, made him the youngest poet to win the Hawthornden Prize. His other volumes of poetry include *John Nobody* (1965) and *Bedlam and Others* (1967); his autobiographical memoir *My Father's Son* (1968) was hailed as a minor classic by S. *Spender. Moraes also co-translated with Aryeh Sivan an anthology of *Modern Hebrew Peace Poetry* (1998).

Moral Essays, four ethical poems by *Pope, published 1731–5; the collective title was added later by Pope's editor *Warburton. Pope himself called the poems 'Epistles to Several Persons', for each work is a familiar letter in verse addressed to someone he knew well and admired.

They were inspired by *Bolingbroke and take the form of four epistles. Epistle I (1734), addressed to Viscount Cobham, deals with the knowledge and characters of men; it sets forth the difficulties in judging a man's character and finds their solution in the discovery of the ruling passion, which 'clue once found unravels all the rest'. Epistle II (1735), addressed to Martha *Blount, deals with the characters of women. Atossa was intended either for Sarah, duchess of Marlborough, or for Katherine, duchess of Buckinghamshire; *Chloe for Lady Suffolk; Philomodé for Henrietta, duchess of Marlborough. These three portraits were suppressed at the last moment, and withheld until 1744; it was rumoured that Pope received £1,000 for the suppression. Epistle III (1733), to Lord Bathurst, deals with the use of riches, which is understood by few, neither the avaricious nor the prodigal deriving happiness from them. The Epistle contains the famous characters of the 'Man of Ross' (see KYRLE) and 'Sir *Balaam'. Epistle IV (1731), to Lord Burlington, originally subtitled 'Of False Taste', deals with the same subject as Epistle III, giving instances of the tasteless use of wealth, particularly in architecture and gardening; where nature should be followed, and ending with advice on the proper use of wealth. Pope told his friend *Swift that he intended the four poems to comprise the last part of his 'opus magnum', a 'system of ethics in the Horatian way', but this ambitious project was never completed. See Miriam Leranbaum, *Alexander Pope's 'Opus Magnum', 1729–1744* (1977).

morality plays, medieval allegorical plays in which personified human qualities are acted and disputed, mostly coming from the 15th cent. They developed into the *interludes, from which it is not always possible to distinguish them and hence had a considerable influence on the development of Elizabethan drama. They lost popularity with the development of naturalistic drama, but interest in them revived in the 20th cent., prompted by a new interest in more mannered, pageant-like theatre, such as the Japanese *Nōh theatre and the plays of *Yeats and *Brecht. Among the most celebrated English examples are *Everyman; Ane *Pleasant Satyre of the Thrie Estaitis by Sir D. Lindsay; *Magnyfycence by Skelton; King John by *Bale; *Mankind; *The Castle of Perseverance. See P. Happé (ed.), *Four Morality Plays* (1979); G. Wickham (ed.), *English Moral Interludes* (1976).

Moral Ode, The, see POEMA MORALE.

MORAVIA, Alberto, pseudonym of Alberto Pincherle (1907–90), Italian novelist. He played a major part in shaping *neo-realism in Italian fiction after the Second World War. His first novel, *Gli indifferenti* (*The Time of Indifference*, 1929), portrayed a middle-class society sick with a moral inertia which favoured the rise of Fascism. *La ciociara* (*Two Women*, 1957), the most lyrical and complex of his novels, deals with the close of the war, when Italy was occupied by both Germans and Allies. *La romana* (*The Woman of Rome*, 1947) and *Racconti romani* (*Roman Tales*, 1957) draw on the language and culture of Roman plebeians in order to criticize middle-class values. Other full-length novels, notably *Il conformista* (*The Conformist*, 1951) and *1934* (1983), explore the psychosexual basis of politics.

Mordaunt, a novel by J. *Moore, published 1800.

This *epistolary novel, of considerable quality, falls uneasily into three parts; in the first the cool but kindly Mordaunt describes his travels through Europe; in the second a French marquise relates her fearful experiences during the Terror; and in the third various friends and acquaintances of Mordaunt reveal their lives and characters in correspondence. The hypocrite Mrs Demure and her friend the spiteful countess, the charming spinster Lady Franklin and her young friend Horatia Clifford, together with Mordaunt himself, are the chief letter writers. To his own amused surprise, Mordaunt falls in love with Miss Clifford and the novel ends with their betrothal.

Morddure, in Spenser's *Faerie Queene* (II. viii. 20–1), the name of the sword made by Merlin for Prince Arthur. Its more general name is *Excalibur.

Mordred, see MODRED.

MORE, Hannah (1745–1833), an eminent member of the *Blue Stocking Circle. She was educated at her sister's boarding school in Bristol: there, and at home, she acquired French, Italian, Spanish, Latin, and mathematics. In 1773 she published *The Search for Happiness*, a pastoral play for schools. She came to London in 1774, where she became very friendly with *Garrick and his wife, who in 1776 offered her a suite of rooms in their house. She became the friend of *Burke, Dr *Johnson, S. *Richardson, J. *Reynolds, *Percy, Mrs *Montagu, and all the Blue Stocking ladies. She was greatly esteemed by Horace *Walpole, who honoured her in 1781 by printing her *Bishop Bonner's Ghost* on his press at *Strawberry Hill. Her tragedy *Percy* was produced by Garrick in 1777, and established her as a social as well as a literary success. It was followed by another tragedy, *The Fatal Falsehood* (1779). Her poem *Bas Bleu*, written some years earlier, was published in 1786, and vividly describes the charm of Blue Stocking society. Meanwhile she had begun to write tracts directed towards the reform of the conditions of the poor; *Village Politics* appeared in 1793, and in 1795–8 *Cheap Repository Tracts* (of which the best known is *The Shepherd of Salisbury Plain*), which sold 2 million copies in four years and led to the formation of the Religious Tract Society in 1799. Her *Thoughts on the Importance of the Manners of the Great* (1788) also went into many large editions. In 1809 she published an immensely successful novel, *Coelebs in Search of a Wife*, the sale of which was not apparently affected by the strictures of Sydney *Smith in the *Edinburgh Review*. She was a lively letter writer, and her letters give a full and entertaining picture of the intellectual and social world she frequented. See M. G. Jones, *Hannah More* (1952).

MORE, Henry, see CAMBRIDGE PLATONISTS.

MORE, Sir Thomas (St) (?1477–1535), son of Sir John More, a judge, educated at St Antony's School, Threadneedle Street, London, and at Canterbury College (now Christ Church), Oxford. He was for a time in youth in the household of Cardinal Morton, and it was probably from Morton's information that he derived his account of Richard III's murder of the princes, etc. He was called to the bar, where he was brilliantly successful. He devoted his leisure to literature, becoming intimate with *Colet, *Lily, and, in 1499, *Erasmus, who afterwards stayed frequently at his house. He entered Parliament in 1504. During an absence as envoy to Flanders he sketched his description (in Latin) of the imaginary island of *Utopia, which he completed and published in 1516. He became master of requests and privy counsellor in 1517, being treated by *Henry VIII with exceptional courtesy

during his residence at court. He was present at the Field of the Cloth of Gold, 1520, where he met *Budé, the greatest Greek scholar of the age. He completed his *Dialogue*, his first controversial book in English (directed mainly against *Tyndale's writings), in 1528. He succeeded Wolsey as lord chancellor in 1529, but resigned in 1532 and lived for some time in retirement, mainly engaged in controversy with Tyndale and Frith.

Although willing to swear fidelity to the new Act of Succession, More refused to take any oath that should impugn the pope's authority, or assume the justice of the king's divorce from Queen Catherine, 1534; he was therefore committed to the Tower of London with John *Fisher, bishop of Rochester, who had assumed a like attitude. During the first days of his imprisonment he prepared a *Dialoge of Comfort against Tribulacion* and treatises on Christ's passion. He was indicted of high treason, found guilty, and beheaded in 1535. His body was buried in St Peter's in the Tower and, according to Thomas Stapleton, his head exhibited on London Bridge. The head was later buried in the *Roper vault in St Dunstan's, Canterbury.

More was a critic and a patron of art, and *Holbein is said to have stayed in his house at Chelsea, and painted portraits of More and his family during his first English visit in 1526–8. More's other chief English works are his *Lyfe of Johan Picus Erle of Mirandula* (printed by John *Rastell, *c.*1510), his *History of Richard the Thirde* (printed imperfectly in Grafton's *Chronicle* 1543, used by *Hall, and printed fully by William Rastell in 1557), *Supplycacyon of Soulys* (1529), *Confutacyon of Tyndales Answere* (1532), and *The Apologye of Syr Thomas More* (1533). His English works were collected in 1557. His Latin publications (collected 1563, etc.) included, besides the *Utopia*, four dialogues of *Lucian, epigrams, and controversial tracts in divinity. There is a pleasant description of More in his Chelsea home in the epistle of Erasmus to Ulrich Hutten, 23 July 1519. He was beatified by the Church of Rome in 1886, and canonized in 1935. *Bolt's play about More, *A Man for All Seasons* (1960), was also made into a successful film. There is a life by P. *Ackroyd (1998).

More, Sir Thomas, a play based on *Hall's Chronicle and biographies of *More, surviving in an incomplete transcript with additions in various hands (British Library, Harley MS 7368) which was submitted to Sir Edmund Tilney, master of the revels, probably about 1593. The scribe, *Munday, is likely to have been at least part-author of the original play. Tilney required major changes before granting permission to perform. The revisions (which may date from 1593–4 or 1603–4) are in five different hands, probably including those of *Chettle, *Heywood, *Dekker, and a playhouse scribe known to have worked for both Strange's Men and the Admiral's Men. The fifth ('Hand D') has been claimed, with strong support, as Shakespeare's. If so, this is his only surviving literary manuscript. A scene of three pages, it depicts More, as sheriff of London, pacifying apprentices in a May Day rebellion against foreigners. *More* was first printed in 1844; there is a scholarly transcript in the *Malone Society reprints (1911, repr. 1961) and an edition by V. Gabrielli and G. Mechiori (1990). The first known professional performance was in London in 1954; it was seen at the Nottingham Playhouse in 1964, directed by Frank Dunlop, with Ian McKellen as More.

MORGAN, Charles Langbridge (1894–1958), novelist and dramatist, and from 1926 to 1939 dramatic critic of *The Times*. His novels include *The Fountain* (1932), *Sparkenbroke* (1936), *The Judge's Story* (1947), and *The River Line* (1949, dramatized 1952). The last is set against a background of the French Resistance; Morgan's status as a writer has been and remains significantly higher in France than in Britain.

MORGAN, Edwin George (1920–   ), Scottish poet and translator, educated at the University of Glasgow and professor of English there from 1975. He has published several volumes of poetry, from *The Vision of Cathkin Braes* (1952) onwards, in which he mingles traditional forms with experimental and *concrete poems such as 'The Computer's First Christmas Card, December 1963'; many of his poems, such as *Glasgow Sonnets* (1972), evoke Scottish urban landscape. He has also translated the poetry of *Montale, *Mayakovsky, *Neruda, and others. Other volumes include *Sonnets from Scotland* (1984), *From the Video Box* (1986), *Collected Poems* (1990), and *You: Anti-War Poetry* (1991). *Crossing the Border* (critical essays) was published in 1990. He has adapted Edmond *Rostand's *Cyrano de Bergerac* into Glaswegian demotic (1992). Poems set to music by jazz musician Tommy Smith include 'Beasts of Scotland' (1996), 'Planet Wave' (1997), and 'Monte Cristo' (1998).

MORGAN, Lady, née Sydney Owenson (1776–1859), a prolific and popular writer, who published ten novels, as well as volumes of poetry, biography, and memoirs. She made her name in 1806 with a work of *historical fiction, *The Wild Irish Girl*, and was paid £1,200 (a huge sum) by her publisher for *Florence Macarthy* in 1818. *France* (1817) and *Italy* (1821) were both highly successful.

MORGAN, William De, see DE MORGAN.

Morgan le Fay, queen of *Avalon, the daughter of Arthur's mother Igerne and therefore his half-sister; she is derived from a figure in Welsh and Irish (the Morrigan) mythology, and has a curiously ambivalent attitude to Arthur. In *Malory she attempts to kill Arthur through the agency of her lover Sir Accolon, but she is also the leader of the queens who carries him away to cure his wounds. She is sometimes represented as the bitter enemy of Guinevere (a tradition indicated by the end of *Sir *Gawain and the Green Knight*, where it is said that she instigated the beheading game to frighten Guinevere to death). *Geof-frey of Monmouth calls the fairy lady who takes Arthur off to Avalon Argante, but all later accounts (such as *Giraldus Cambrensis and the prose Vulgate cycles) call her Morgan. A related figure occurs in the *Orlando innamorato* and *Orlando furioso*, called 'Morgana' there and being a *Lady of the Lake. The term *Fata Morgana* (*fata* means 'fairy' in Italian) is given in Sicily to a vision traditionally seen at sea from the Calabrian coast. See MORGAWSE.

MORGANN, Maurice (1726–1802), secretary to the embassy for peace with America in 1782, and author of various political pamphlets. He is remembered chiefly as the author of an *Essay on the Dramatic Character of Sir John Falstaff* (1777) in which he defends *Falstaff from the charge of cowardice, and points to 'a certain roundness and integrity in the forms of Shakespeare, which give them an independence'. A. C. *Bradley said of it: 'There is no better piece of Shakespeare criticism in the world.'

Morgante maggiore, a poem by *Pulci which recast, with humorous additions and alterations, the popular epic *Orlando* (see ROLAND). Orlando (Roland) encounters three giants. He slays two and subdues the third, Morgante, converts him, and makes him his brother in arms. *Byron translated the first canto.

Morgawse, or **Morcades,** half-sister of Arthur, the wife of King Lot of Orkney, and mother of *Modred, *Gawain, *Agravain, *Gareth, and *Gaheris. She seems to be in some ways identical in origin with *Morgan le Fay; in later versions Arthur sleeps with her in disguise, thus begetting Modred. She is called 'Anna' in *Geof-frey of Monmouth, though Anna is otherwise attested as Arthur's full sister.

Morglay, the name of the sword of *Bevis of Hampton, sometimes used allusively for a sword in general.

Moriarty, Professor, the enemy of Sherlock *Holmes, a character created by A. C. *Doyle.

MORIER, James Justinian (?1780–1849), born in Smyrna, educated at Harrow. He joined the diplomatic service in 1807. He became attached to Sir Harford Jones's mission to Persia, during which he collected valuable information about a country little known at that time. His account of these travels appeared in *A Journey through Persia, Armenia and Asia Minor to Constantinople in the Years 1808–1809* (1812); *A Second Journey through Persia* appeared in 1818. He retired from the foreign office in 1817 to devote his time to literature. He published a number of *Oriental romances including the popular *The Adventures of Hajji Baba of Ispahan* (1824), a picaresque tale (the hero undergoes amusing vicissitudes, becoming successively barber, doctor, and assistant executioner) which gives a colourful and accurate presentation of life in Persia during the early 19th cent. Its sequel *The Adventures of Hajji Baba in England* (1828) was less successful. His later works, including *Ayesha* (1834) which introduced the Turkish word 'bosh' into the English language, did not reach the level of his earlier ones.

Morland, Catherine, a character in J. Austen's *Northanger Abbey*.

MORLEY, Henry (1822–94). He turned from medicine to journalism, joined the staff of *Household Words* at Dickens's invitation, edited the *Examiner*, and devoted much of his career to the development of English literature as an academic subject. He published biographies of Palissy the Potter (1852), Cardano (1854), and *Agrippa (1856), wrote *A First Sketch of English Literature* (1873), 11 volumes of *English Writers* (1887–95), and edited cheap editions of English classics in Morley's Universal Library (1883–8) and Cassell's National Library (1886–92).

MORLEY, Henry Parker, Lord (1476–1556), a successful courtier and diplomat under Henry VIII. His *Exposition and Declaration* of Psalm 94 was really a defence of Henry's position as head of the Church of England; better known now is his other published work, a translation of *Petrarch's *Trionfi* (c.1553), which has been edited by D. Carnicelli (1971).

MORLEY, John, first Viscount Morley of Blackburn (1838–1923), educated at Cheltenham College and Lincoln College, Oxford. He began his literary career as a journalist, writing chiefly for the *Fortnightly Review*, of which he was editor (1867–82), and became a friend of *Meredith and J. S. *Mill; he was editor of the *Pall Mall Gazette* 1881–3. His literary achievements, chiefly biographical, include *Edmund Burke: An Historical Study* (1867), *Voltaire* (1872), *Rousseau* (1873), *On Compromise* (1874), *Burke* (1879), *The Life of Richard Cobden* (1881), *Oliver Cromwell* (1900), *Life of Gladstone* (1903), and he edited the English Men of Letters series. He was a Liberal MP (1883–1908) and a close supporter of *Gladstone; he was chief secretary for Ireland (1886 and 1892–5) and secretary of state for India (1905–10). From 1910 he was lord president of the council but resigned at the outbreak of war.

MORLEY, Thomas (1557/18–1602), English composer, organist, and writer. He studied under *Byrd, to whom he later dedicated his successful treatise *A Plaine and Easie Introduction to Praticall Musicke* (1597), the first work of its kind in the English language and still one of the most famous. He became organist of St Paul's and a gentleman of the Chapel Royal, and in his later years was much involved in the printing and publishing of music. Morley's historical importance stemmed from his championship of the Italian *madrigal, and his role in the development of its English counterpart. His first two publications, the *Canzonets, Or Little Short Songs to Three Voyces* (1593) and the first book of *Madrigalls to Foure Voyces* (1594), contain the best of his own work in this form, brightly Italianate in style yet finished

with the seriousness proper to a pupil of Byrd. The famous 'Aprill is in my mistris face' (1594) is characteristic. The two volumes of *Balletts* and *Canzonets* which followed in 1595 were largely free transcriptions of pieces by contemporary Italian composers, and were printed in both Italian and English—'Now is the month of maying', for example, appearing also as 'Se ben mi ch'ha bon tempo' (after Orazio Vecchi). He was the moving spirit behind *The Triumph of Oriana* (1601), a collection of madrigals by 24 English composers in honour of *Elizabeth I. Most of Morley's madrigal texts are either from Italian originals or from anonymous sources. His own book of *Ayres . . . to the Lute* (1600), however, contains a setting of 'It was a lover and his lass' which is apparently the earliest Shakespeare setting to survive, though it is not known whether it was ever used in a production of *As You Like It*. Shakespeare and Morley lived for some time in the same London parish and the possibility of a connection between the two men has been much debated.

Morning Chronicle, a Whig journal founded by the printer William Woodfall (1746–1803) in 1769, and successfully conducted by him for 20 years. It rose to importance when James Perry became chief proprietor and editor in 1789. Its staff then included *Sheridan, *Lamb, T. *Campbell, Sir J. *Mackintosh, *Brougham, T. *Moore, and *Ricardo. Perry was succeeded by John Black (1783–1855), scholar, Scotsman, and friend of James *Mill; J. S. *Mill described Black as 'the first journalist who carried criticism and the Spirit of Reform into the details of English institutions . . . Black was the writer who carried the warfare into those subjects, and by doing so he broke the spell.' Both Mills were among his contributors, *Dickens was one of his reporters, and *Thackeray his art critic. The *Morning Chronicle* came to an end in 1862.

Morning Herald and Public Advertiser, a London newspaper that ran from 1780 to 1869; it published the mock criticisms of the mock epic *The Rolliad* in 1784. One of its special features for a time was a selection of reports of police cases, illustrated by *Cruikshank.

Morning Post, a London daily newspaper founded in 1772. Under the management of D. *Stuart, Sir J. *Mackintosh and S. T. *Coleridge were enlisted in its service, and *Southey, *Wordsworth, and A. *Young were also contributors. After a period of decline, it recovered its position under the direction of Peter Borthwick and his son Algernon Borthwick (Lord Glenesk, 1830–1908). It was amalgamated with the *Daily Telegraph* in 1937.

Morose, in Jonson's *Epicene*, a crabbed old bachelor who hates noise.

MORRELL, Lady Ottoline (1873–1938), daughter of Lieutenant-General Arthur Bentinck and half-sister of the duke of Portland. She married Philip Morrell, shortly to become a Liberal MP, in 1902. From 1908 she entertained a wide circle of political and literary celebrities at her Thursday evening gatherings at 44 Bedford Square, and continued her career as hostess and patron of the arts at *Garsington Manor, Oxfordshire, between 1915 and 1927. Her friends and guests included Asquith, H. *James, L. *Strachey, B. *Russell, V. *Woolf, T. S. *Eliot, *Yeats, D. H. *Lawrence, and A. *Huxley. Tall, striking, and eccentric, she appeared as a character in several works of fiction by her protégés, most memorably in Lawrence's *Women in Love and Huxley's Crome Yellow. Both portraits caused considerable offence. Her Memoirs, edited by Robert Gathorne-Hardy, appeared in two volumes in 1963 and 1974.

Morrice, Gil, see GIL MORRICE.

Morris, Dinah, a character in G. Eliot's *Adam Bede.

MORRIS, Jan, formerly James (1926–   ), travel writer and novelist, born in Somerset of Anglo-Welsh descent, educated at the Cathedral Choir School, Oxford, Lancing College, and Christ Church, Oxford. As James Morris, Morris served in the army with the 9th Lancers, then travelled widely while working (until 1961) as a foreign correspondent. Her many travel books range from the Middle East, Everest, Hong Kong, Sydney, Venice, Oxford, and Spain to Manhattan and beyond; the 'Pax Britannica' trilogy (Pax Britannica, 1968; Heaven's Command, 1973, Farewell the Trumpets, 1978) chronicles with elegiac sympathy the decay of British imperialism. Conundrum (1974) is an account of her transsexuality, her happy marriage as a man, and her journey towards and after the surgery that enabled her to become a woman. Last Letters from Hav (1985) is a novel, and Fisher's Face (1995) an idiosyncratic biography of the charismatic J. A. Fisher, admiral of the fleet.

MORRIS, Sir Lewis (1833–1907), born at Carmarthen and educated at Oxford. He contributed actively to the establishment of the University of Wales. He published several volumes of mediocre verse, imitative of *Tennyson; the most popular were Songs of Two Worlds (1871) and The Epic of Hades (1876–7). The latter, which consists of monologues by various characters from Greek mythology, owes much to Tennyson's A Dream of Fair Women.

MORRIS, William (1834–96), the son of a successful business man, educated at Marlborough School and Exeter College, Oxford. He was articled to the architect G. E. Street, and in 1858 worked with *Rossetti, *Burne-Jones, and others on the frescos in the Oxford Union. He was one of the originators of the *Oxford and Cambridge Magazine (1856), to which he contributed poems, essays, and tales. In 1858 he published The Defence of Guenevere and Other Poems, which contains much of his best work, including 'The Haystack in the Floods', 'Concerning Geffray Teste Noire', 'Shameful

Death', and 'Golden Wings', poems marked by a striking mixture of beauty and brutality, all with medieval settings. In 1859 he married Jane Burden, one of the most painted Pre-Raphaelite 'stunners'; their home, Red House at Bexley, was designed by Philip Webb, and was an important landmark in domestic architecture, adapting late Gothic methods to 19th-cent. needs; it was described as 'grand and severely simple'. The failure to find suitable furniture for it strengthened Morris's growing hatred of industrial 'shoddy', and led to the founding, together with Rossetti, Burne-Jones, Webb, Madox Brown, and others, of the firm of Morris, Marshall, Faulkner and Co. This firm produced furniture, printed textiles, tapestries, wallpapers, and stained glass; its designs brought about a complete revolution in public taste, though Morris was well aware of the irony that only the rich could afford its products. In 1867 he published The Life and Death of Jason, a poem in heroic couplets based on the story of Jason, Medea, and the Argonauts; in 1868–70 appeared *The Earthly Paradise, which established him as one of the most popular poets of the day, though critics now condemn its verse as archaic and escapist, compared with the freshness of his early work. In 1871 he took a joint tenancy of Kelmscott Manor with Rossetti, wrote the poem Love is Enough (1872), and visited Iceland, which stimulated his interest in the heroic themes of Icelandic literature. His epic *Sigurd the Volsung appeared in 1876. In 1877 he founded the Society for the Protection of Ancient Buildings (the 'Antiscrape Society') in protest against the destruction being caused by the restorers. From this time on he turned increasingly towards political activity; in 1883 he joined the Social Democratic Federation, the doctrine of which, largely under his leadership, developed into socialism. On its disruption in 1884 he became head of the seceders, who organized themselves as the Socialist League, and was to lecture and write for the cause with great energy. The verse tale 'The Pilgrims of Hope' appeared in the League's magazine Commonweal in 1885. His later works, with the exception of Poems by the Way (1891) and Chants for Socialists (1884–5), were mainly in prose, and most remarkable among them were *A Dream of John Ball (1888) and *News from Nowhere (1891), both socialist fantasies cast in a dream setting. He also wrote several historical romances set in the distant past of northern Europe. These include The House of the Wolfings (1889), which he said was 'meant to illustrate the melting of the individual into the society of the tribes', The Roots of the Mountains (1890), The Story of the Glittering Plain (1890), The Wood beyond the World (1894), and the work which he completed just before his death, The Sundering Flood (1898). All were published by the Kelmscott Press, which he had founded at Hammersmith in 1890, and for which he designed founts of type and ornamental letters and borders. The Press also published other works by Morris, reprints of English classics (including *Caxton's The Golden Le-

gend and the Kelmscott *Chaucer), and various smaller books by other authors, including poems by *Blunt. Morris's later romances were described by G. B. *Shaw as 'a startling relapse into literary Pre-Raphaelitism', but they were admired by *Yeats, who was much influenced in his early years by Morris. On his death Morris was widely mourned as 'our best man' by his fellow socialists, by whom he was deeply revered; his view that 'the true incentive to useful and happy labour is, and must be, 'pleasure in the work itself' links his political and artistic aspirations, both of which have remained profoundly influential. Morris published many other works, including lectures on art, architecture, and politics, and various translations, including the *Aeneid* (1875) and the *Odyssey* (1887); he collaborated with E. Magnusson in translations from the Icelandic. See F. MacCarthy, *William Morris: A Life for Our Time* (1994). E. P. *Thompson's *Morris: Romantic to Revolutionary* (1961) gives a detailed appraisal of his political development. His letters were edited by P. Henderson (1950).

morris dance, an English form of folk dance associated since at least the 15th cent. with seasonal festivities such as May Day and Christmas, but now commonly performed throughout the summer months. Morris, or 'morisco' ('Moorish') dancers dress in striking, sometimes grotesque, uniforms, usually with bells attached to legs or arms; the name may refer to the habit of some traditions of blackening the face. Dances often involve the waving of handkerchiefs or clashing of sticks. See under KEMP, and *The Morris Book* by Cecil J. Sharp and H. C. MacIlwaine (1907).

MORRISON, Arthur (1863–1945), novelist, whose 'realist' tales of East End life in London were first published in *Macmillan's Magazine* and later collected as *Tales of Mean Streets* (1894). He is chiefly remembered for his novel *A Child of the Jago* (1896). He devoted the latter part of his life to the study and collection of oriental art.

MORRISON, (Philip) Blake (1950–), journalist and poet, born in Skipton, Yorkshire, and educated at Nottingham University. He worked as poetry and fiction editor of the *Times Literary Supplement* from 1978 to 1981, before joining the staff of the *Observer*, where he became literary editor, a post he took over in the *Independent on Sunday* in 1990. During this time he published two collections of poetry, *Dark Glasses* (1984) and *The Ballad of the Yorkshire Ripper* (1987), and edited *The Penguin Book of Contemporary British Poetry* (1982) with Andrew *Motion.

His first book of narrative writing, *And when did you last see your father?* (1993) was followed in 2002, by an equally candid, *confessional and more revelatory memoir of his mother, *Things My Mother Never Told Me*. In 1997 he published *As If*, a personal response to the murder trial of two 10-year-old boys, drawing on his own experience of parenthood as well as the month he spent covering the trial for an American magazine.

He has also published critical studies of Seamus *Heaney (1982) and *The Movement: English Poetry and Fiction of the 1950s* (1980) (see MOVEMENT), and a book for children, *The Yellow House* (1987).

A selection of his short fiction and journalism has been collected in *Too True* (1998).

MORRISON, Toni (Chloe Anthony), née Wofford (1931–), American novelist, born in Lorain, Ohio, educated at Howard University, where she later taught, and at Cornell. She married Howard Morrison, a Jamaican architect, but separated from him in 1964. Before becoming a professional writer she worked in publishing, as an editor for Random House. Her novels deal with the historical experiences of black Americans within a white social and cultural environment. *The Bluest Eye* (1970) recounts a year in the life of Pecola Breedlove, a victim of rape by her father. Succeeding novels included *Sula* (1974), the story of two young black girls, one of whom leaves the small Ohio community of their birth and returns ten years later; *Song of Solomon* (1977); and *Tar Baby* (1981). *Beloved* (1987) was set in the 19th cent. and is the story of a runaway slave who kills her daughter rather than see her brought up to slavery. (See SLAVERY, LITERATURE OF.) Her other work includes *Jazz* (1992) and a study of the significance of African-Americans in American literature, *Playing in the Dark: Whiteness and the Literary Imagination* (1992). She was awarded the *Nobel Prize for literature in 1993.

***Morte Arthure,** The Alliterative*, a 14th-cent. poem of 'the *Alliterative Revival' in 4,346 alliterative long lines, used as a source by *Malory in his Book I, the story of Arthur and Lucius. It used to be identified wrongly as 'the gret Gest off Arthure' by *Huchown. Correspondences with the *Roman de Brut* by *Wace suggest that, directly or indirectly (perhaps mediated through *Mannyng), this may have been the poet's principal source. The poem has claims to be regarded (as it was by R. W. *Chambers) as the most powerful epic narrative in Middle English. Its material corresponds roughly to Malory's first, second, and eighth romances (in Vinaver's numbering): the early exploits of Arthur, his European ventures, and the final battle with Modred. The obscurity of its dialect makes it somewhat forbidding (though it is less difficult than the popular *Sir *Gawain and the Green Knight*). At any rate it is one of the most important and influential Middle English poems, the influence of which has been detected in Malory, *Cleanness*, *The Awntyrs of Arthur*, *Henry the Minstrel's *Wallace*, and elsewhere.

Selections ed. J. Finlayson (1967); ed. L. D. Benson in *King Arthur's Death* (1976). For discussion, see J. L. N. O'Loughlin in R. S. Loomis (ed.), *Arthurian Literature in the Middle Ages* (1959), 522–6, and T. Turville-Petre, *The Alliterative Revival* (1977).

Morte Arthur, Le (The Stanzaic Morte Arthur), a late 14th-cent. poem from the north-west Midlands in 3,834 lines of eight-line rhyming stanzas surviving in one manuscript, and the source (directly or indirectly) for the sections in *Malory leading up to and dealing with the death of Arthur (i.e. the last two *Works* in Vinaver's edition; though in these it is clear that Malory was also using a French text). It deals with Launcelot's love affairs with Guinevere and the Maid of Astolat, with Arthur's last battles, and with the king's being borne away to *Avalon.

Ed. L. D. Benson in *King Arthur's Death* (1976); J. D. Bruce, EETS es 88 (1903).

Morte D'Arthur, Le, the title generally given to the lengthy cycle of Arthurian legends by *Malory, finished in 1470 and printed by *Caxton in 1485, divided into 21 books. But in 1934 W. F. Oakeshott discovered in Winchester College Library a manuscript of the same period as Caxton's but without his division into 21 books and without several of his colophons. This superior manuscript, dividing the whole into eight parts, was used by Vinaver as the basis of his new standard edition of Malory. Though Malory refers throughout to a 'French book' as his source, it is clear that his sources were more various than this implies. Vinaver divides the cycle into eight *Works* which he wishes to treat as separate romances: (1) The Tale of Arthur and Lucius, based principally on the Alliterative English *Morte Arthure; (2) The Book of King Arthur, based largely on the *Suite du Merlin* (Huth Merlin) (see MERLIN). The *Suite* is believed to be a later rewriting of part of the 13th-cent. prose Vulgate cycle; (3) The Tale of Sir Launcelot du Lake, mostly from two sections of the prose *Lancelot* in the Vulgate cycle; (4) Sir Gareth of Orkney, the precise source of which is not known; (5) Tristram de Lyones, thought to be a translation of part of a lost 13th-cent. prose *Tristan* in French; (6) The Quest of the Holy Grail, principally from the prose Vulgate *Queste del Saint Graal* (see GRAIL); (7) Launcelot and Guinevere; and (8) The Morte Arthur, both based to a considerable degree on the French Vulgate *Mort Artu*, and the 15th-cent. English stanzaic *Le Morte Arthur* (above). Since the publication of Vinaver's three-volume edition in 1947 criticism of Malory has concentrated on the rather terminological matter of whether his work is to be regarded as a single 'whole Book' (see Lumiansky and Moorman below) or as eight *Works* (Vinaver), a middle position being taken by C. S. *Lewis and by D. S. Brewer (see Bennett below). Although Vinaver's edition is now regarded as authoritative, the traditional view of Malory as a single whole, compounded of disparate parts, is the prevailing one.

The Works of Sir Thomas Malory, ed. E. Vinaver (2nd edn 1968); in one volume as *Malory: Works* (2nd edn 1971). Caxton's edition, ed. J. Cowen (Penguin, 2 vols, 1969); J. A. W. Bennett (ed.), *Essays on Malory* (1963); R. M. Lumiansky (ed.), *Malory's Originality* (1964); C.

Moorman, *The Book of Kyng Arthur* (1965); T. Takimaya and D. S. Brewer (eds), *Aspects of Malory* (1982); E. Archibald and A. S. G. Edwards, *A Companion to Malory* (1996).

'Morte d'Arthur', a poem by *Tennyson, written 1833–4, published 1842, subsequently incorporated in 'The Passing of Arthur' (1869), preceded by 169 lines and followed by 29, where it formed one of the *Idylls of the King*, though it continued to be published separately as well. Tennyson's first major Arthurian work, it describes the last moments of Arthur after the battle with Mordred's forces, and includes his elegy on the Round Table, delivered to Sir Bedivere: 'The old order changeth, yielding place to new . . . '.

Mortimer, a character in Marlowe's *Edward II.

MORTIMER, John Clifford (1923–   ), novelist, barrister, and playwright, formerly married to novelist Penelope *Mortimer. Well known in the legal and literary worlds for his stand against censorship, he gained a wide readership for his stories, many of which were adapted for television, about an eccentric defence barrister, Horace Rumpole, who appears in *Rumpole of the Bailey* (1978) and many subsequent volumes. Other works of fiction include *Paradise Postponed* (1985), a comic saga of English life from 1945 to the 1980s which charts the rise of the odious Tory politician Leslie Titmuss, and its sequel, *Titmuss Regained* (1990); *Dunster* (1992), and *Under the Hammer* (1994), stories set in a London auction house. *In Character* (1983) and *Character Parts* (1986) are collections of interviews, mainly from the *Sunday Times*. His plays include *The Dock Brief* (produced for both radio and television in 1957, pub. 1958) and the autobiographical *A Voyage Round My Father* (perf. 1970, pub. 1971), a powerful and poignant portrait of his blind and histrionic barrister father. A volume of autobiography, *Clinging to the Wreckage*, appeared in 1982 and *Murderers and Other Friends* (further recollections) in 1994.

MORTIMER, Penelope Ruth, née Fletcher (1918–1999), novelist, born in north Wales and educated at London University: her works, with their emphasis on frankness about female experience, contributed to the development of the woman's novel in the 1960s. They include *The Pumpkin Eater* (1962, her seventh book: filmed 1964, script by *Pinter), *My Friend Says It's Bulletproof* (1967, which tackled the taboo subject of breast cancer), *The Home* (1971), *Long Distance* (1974), and *The Handyman* (1983). A volume of autobiography, *About Time*, appeared in 1979.

Mortimer His Fall, fragments of a tragedy by *Jonson, printed in 1640, concerning the earl of Mortimer, the murderer of Edward II. Only the Argument and the opening speeches survive.

MORTON, John Maddison (1811–91), son of the dramatist T. *Morton, educated in France. He wrote *farces and showed a special gift for adaptations from the French. His most successful piece was *Box and Cox* (1847); *Done on Both Sides* appeared in the same year.

MORTON, Thomas (?1764–1838). He entered Lincoln's Inn in 1784, and was the author of three successful comedies, *The Way to Get Married* (1796), *A Cure for Heartache* (1797), and *Speed the Plough* (1798). The last of these introduced the name and character of 'Mrs Grundy', and the conception of Grundyism as the extreme of moral rigidity.

Mosca, Volpone's parasite in Jonson's **Volpone*.

MOSCHUS (fl. *c.*150 BC), a pastoral poet of Syracuse. The beautiful *Lament for Bion*, doubtfully attributed to Moschus, is a dirge for the author's friend and teacher. There is an echo of it in **Milton's Latin *Epitaphium Damonis*, in his **Lycidas*, in Shelley's **Adonais*, and in M. Arnold's **'Thyrsis'.

MOSELEY, Humphrey (fl. 1627, d. 1661), a London bookseller and the chief literary publisher of his time, who published the first collected edition of **Milton's *Poems* (1645) which contains the unflattering portrait engraved by William Marshall. Moseley also published the 1647 folio of **Beaumont and **Fletcher, and work by **Crashaw, **D'Avenant, **Denham, **Donne, **Waller, and many others.

MOSLEY, Nicholas, third Baron Ravensdale (1923–), novelist and biographer, educated at Eton and Balliol College, Oxford. His highly intellectual, experimental, and metaphysical novels include *Accident* (1964) and *Impossible Object* (1968), both of which were filmed; *Natalie Natalia* (1971); and *Catastrophe Practice* (1979), a complex network of three plays with prefaces and a short novel, built on the mathematical 'catastrophe theory' of the 1970s, applied here to human relationships and identity. Other novels: *Imago Bird* (1980), *Serpent* (1981), *Judith* (1986). His biographies include a life of J. **Grenfell (1976) and a two-volume study of his father, *Rules of the Game: Sir Oswald and Lady Cynthia Mosley 1896–1933* (1982) and *Beyond the Pale: Sir Oswald Mosley 1933–1980* (1983). He won the Whitbread Prize for his much-praised panoramic novel *Hopeful Monsters* (1990).

Mosses from an Old Manse, published 1846, a collection of tales and sketches by N. **Hawthorne. The Old Manse itself is the author's Concord home, and best known among the book's contents are 'Young Goodman Brown', 'Rappaccini's Daughter', and 'Roger Malvin's Burial'.

Moth, (1) in Shakespeare's **Love's Labour's Lost*, **Armado's page; (2) in his **A Midsummer Night's Dream*, one of the fairies. The name, interchangeable aurally with 'mote', suggested diminutive size.

Mother Goose, a traditional name for a narrator of nursery rhymes and **fairy stories. She came into the English language through the frontispiece of **Perrault's tales in 1729: the name was taken up by children's publisher John **Newbery and others in various collections of rhymes and tales, and she became a well-known figure of folklore in both Britain and North America, appearing as a comic, wise, and occasionally bawdy old crone with a witch's hat and hooked nose and chin.

Mother Hubbard, the subject of a nursery rhyme attributed to Sarah Catherine Martin (1768–1826) and published in 1805, but probably based on oral tradition.

'Mother Hubberds Tale', or *'Prosopopoia'*, a satire in rhymed couplets, by **Spenser, included in the volume of *Complaints* published in 1591. The ape and the fox, 'disliking of their evill | And hard estate', determine to seek their fortunes abroad, and assume the disguises first of an old soldier and his dog, then of a parish priest and his clerk, then of a courtier and his groom; their knaveries in these characters are recounted. Finally they steal the lion's crown and sceptre and abuse the regal power, until Jove intervenes and exposes them. The poem is a satire on the abuses of the Church and the evils of the court.

MOTHERWELL, William (1797–1835), a native of Glasgow, who became editor of the *Paisley Advertiser* and *Glasgow Courier*. In 1827 he published a collection of ballads, *Minstrelsy Ancient and Modern*, and in 1832 *Poems Narrative and Lyrical*, of which the best known and least characteristic is 'Jeanie Morrison', addressed to a childhood sweetheart. With **Hogg he issued an edition of **Burns's works in 1834–5.

motion, the name given to puppet-plays in the 16th and 17th cents. These dealt originally with scriptural subjects, but their scope was afterwards extended. Shakespeare in **The Winter's Tale* (IV. iii) refers to a 'motion of the Prodigal Son', and there are references to 'motions' in Jonson's **Bartholomew Fair*, **A Tale of a Tub*, and **Every Man out of His Humour*.

MOTION, Andrew (1952–), poet, novelist, and biographer, born in London, educated at Radley College and at University College, Oxford, where he won the **Newdigate Prize. His first collection, mostly lyrical in character and showing the influence of **Larkin, *The Pleasure Steamers* (1978), was a great critical success. *Independence* (1981) uses the device of a narrator both to evoke the ending of British rule in India and to tell the story of a relationship cut short by death. His next collection, *Secret Narratives* (1983), contains a sequence of short narrations told within an enigmatic context. *Dangerous Play* (1984) brought together selections from his first three volumes with new poems and an autobiographical prose piece, 'Skating'. This was followed by *Natural Causes* (1987); *Love in a Life* (1991), a narrative in which the stories of two marriages gradually emerge and are brought together; and *Salt Water* (1997). *The Price of Everything* (1994) contains two long poems, 'Lines of Desire' and 'Joe

Soap'. He is the author of biographies of Larkin (1993) and
*Keats (1997), and two novels, *The Pale Companion* (1989)
and *Famous for the Creatures* (1991). Since his appointment as *poet laureate in 1999 he has published and
broadcast many poems on public issues, ranging from
war in Iraq to the marriage of Prince Charles in 2005.

MOTLEY, John Lothrop (1814–77), born in Massachusetts, educated at Harvard, Göttingen, and Berlin
(where he formed a lifelong friendship with Bismarck).
He was American minister to Austria, 1861–7, and to
Great Britain, 1869–70. He is chiefly remembered as a
historian and author of *The Rise of the Dutch Republic*
(1855). This was followed by the *History of the United
Netherlands* (1860–7) and *The Life and Death of John
Barneveld* (1874).

MOTTEUX, Peter Anthony (1660–1718). He was born at
Rouen and came to England after the revocation of the
Edict of Nantes (1685). He edited and wrote much of
the *Gentleman's Journal*, completed Sir T. *Urquhart's
translation of Rabelais (1693–4), and published a free
translation of *Don Quixote* (1700–3).

MOTTLEY, John (1692–1750), author of several plays
and lives of Peter the Great and Catherine I, remembered as having published *Joe Miller's Jests: or The
Wit's Vade-Mecum* (1739).

MOTTRAM, R(alph) H(ale) (1883–1971), novelist, born
in Norwich, where his family had long worked for
Gurney's Bank; he himself worked as a bank clerk
before establishing himself as a novelist with, principally, *The Spanish Farm Trilogy* (1927), a sequence of
novels based on his own experiences in France and
Flanders while serving in the First World War. It
consists of *The Spanish Farm* (1924), *Sixty-Four, Ninety-
Four* (1925), and *The Crime at Vanderlynden's* (1926),
and is set in northern France on the 'Ferme Espagnole'
of Flemish-speaking, French-writing farmer Jerome
Vanderlynden and his daughter Madeleine.

Mouldy, Ralph, in Shakespeare's 2 *Henry IV* (III. ii),
one of Falstaff's recruits.

Mourning Bride, The, a tragedy by *Congreve, produced 1697. This was the author's only attempt at
tragedy, and was received with enthusiasm.

Almeria, daughter of Manuel, king of Granada, has
secretly married Alphonso, prince of the enemy state of
Valencia. He becomes a captive of Manuel. The
discovery of his marriage to Almeria infuriates the
king, who orders the immediate murder of Alphonso
and, further to punish his daughter, decides to impersonate the captive in his cell, so that when she
comes to save him he may mock her disappointment.
As a result he is by mistake killed instead, and
decapitated. Zara, a Moorish queen, a fellow captive
in love with Alphonso but repulsed by him, finding the
headless body, takes poison in despair. A revolt against
Manuel releases the true Alphonso, and he and
Almeria are reunited.

The play contains lines that are widely known, such
as the first in the play:

> Music has charms to soothe a savage breast,

and those which close the third act:

> Heaven has no rage, like love to hatred turned,
> Nor hell a fury, like a woman scorned.

'Mouse, To a' ('Wee, sleekit, cow'rin', tim'rous beastie
...'), a poem by *Burns, published in 1786; one of a
small group of tender, unsentimental poems about
animals, which include 'Poor Mailie's Elegy', 'The Twa
Dogs', and 'The Auld Farmer's ... Salutation to his ...
Mare, Maggie'.

Movement, the, a term coined by J. D. Scott, literary
editor of the *Spectator*, in 1954 to describe a group of
writers including K. *Amis, *Larkin, *Davie, *Enright,
*Wain, E. *Jennings, and *Conquest. Two anthologies
(Enright's *Poets of the 1950s*, 1955, and Conquest's *New
Lines*, 1956) illustrate the Movement's predominantly
anti-romantic, witty, rational, sardonic tone; its fictional heroes (e.g. Larkin's John Kemp in *Jill*, 1946, and
Amis's Dixon in *Lucky Jim*, 1954) tended to be lower-
middle-class scholarship boys. Definitions of its aims
were negative (Conquest: 'a negative determination to
avoid bad principles') and by 1957 its members began
to disown it, claiming, in Wain's words, 'its work is
done'. See Blake *Morrison, *The Movement* (1980).

Mowcher, Miss, in Dickens's *David *Copperfield*, a
humorous and good-hearted dwarf, a hairdresser and
manicurist.

Mowgli, the child brought up by wolves in R. Kipling's
The Jungle Book.

MOXON, Edward (1801–58). He became a distinguished London publisher and bookseller, and a
less distinguished poet: Leigh *Hunt described him
as 'a bookseller among poets, and a poet among
booksellers'. Various volumes of his poems were
published between 1826 and 1835, and his chief
interest in publishing was in poetry. He became a
close friend of *Lamb, who introduced him to many of
the writers of his day and whose 'adopted' daughter,
Emma Isola, he married. He set up his own business
in 1830, when he proceeded to build a remarkable
list which included *Shelley, *Clare, *Wordsworth,
*Coleridge, Lamb, Hunt, *Keats, *Southey, R. *Brown-
ing, *Patmore, and *Longfellow, as well as *Tennyson,
whose close friend he became and whose work he
continued to champion and publish until his death.
Hunt wrote that 'Moxon has no connection but with
the select of the earth.' In 1831 he established the
Englishman's Magazine, in which he published much
of the work of the writers he supported, and in which
he defended them against the attacks of *Blackwood's,
and the *Edinburgh* and *Quarterly Reviews*. Apart
from their literary qualities, his publications were
famed for a high standard of typography and binding.

MOXON, Joseph (1627–91), maker of globes and mathematical instruments, printer and typefounder, born in Wakefield, the son of a printer. He wrote *Mechanick Exercises; Or, The Doctrine of Hand-Works Applied to the Art of Printing* (1683–4; ed. Herbert Davis and Harry Carter, 1958), the first manual of printing and typefounding in any language, and probably the first book to be published serially.

MOZART, Wolfgang Amadeus (1756–91), Austrian composer. He visited London with his parents and sister when he was 8: he was received three times by George III, and was later systematically 'tested' by *Barrington, whose 'Account of a Very Remarkable Young Musician' appeared in the *Philosophical Transactions* of the *Royal Society, 1770. The first two Mozart symphonies were written in Ebury Street (then Ebury Row), and before he left London in July 1765 he composed and presented to the British Museum his first vocal work, the unaccompanied motet 'God is our refuge'. Mozart never came to England again, nor did he set any more music to English words. He certainly knew some Shakespeare, but does not seem to have considered him as an operatic source until the end of his life, when he is said to have accepted a libretto based on *The Tempest* by F. H. von Einsiedel, with revisions by F. W. Gotter. The text, which *Goethe called a masterpiece, was eventually set by no fewer than four composers in 1798. Mozart and his contemporary Salieri appear as the principal characters in *Amadeus* by P. *Shaffer.

'Mr Gilfil's Love-Story', see SCENES OF CLERICAL LIFE.

Mr Limberham, or *The Kind Keeper*, a comedy by *Dryden, produced 1679, published 1680.

The play was banned by royal decree after three performances and has been execrated since, but Dryden nonetheless thought highly of it. The title role is possibly based on *Shaftesbury. Limberham is an impotent masochist, who is cuckolded by the oversexed hero Woodall, to whom every woman in the play succumbs. In this Woodall (who has been brought up abroad and is under an assumed name) is enthusiastically abetted by his unknowing father, Aldo. By implication the play attacks the patriarchism of a sexually corrupt court, the blind hedonism of the nobility, and the hypocrisy of Dissenters.

Mr Scarborough's Family, a novel by A. *Trollope, published 1883.

John Scarborough has gone through two marriage ceremonies, and by producing the certificate of either earlier or later date can pronounce his eldest son and heir Mountjoy legitimate or illegitimate as he pleases. When he hears that Mountjoy has been passing post-obits on his estate, Scarborough takes a summary revenge: Mountjoy is declared illegitimate and his younger brother Augustus is named as heir. Augustus, however, begins to show an ill-concealed impatience to inherit, and, by now on his deathbed, Scarborough again alters the will. At first Augustus is to keep the entail, the moveable property reverting to Mountjoy; then the fatal first marriage certificate is produced, and Augustus is completely disinherited. In the last pages of the novel Mountjoy returns to the moneylenders, and sets about mortgaging the property to the hilt.

Mrs Caudle's Curtain Lectures, see JERROLD, D. W.

Mrs Dalloway, a novel by V. *Woolf, published 1925.

The action is restricted to the events of one day in central London, punctuated by the chimes of Big Ben; it opens on a June morning in Westminster as Clarissa Dalloway, wife of Richard Dalloway MP (both had appeared briefly and enigmatically in an earlier novel, *The Voyage Out*), sets off to buy flowers for her party that evening, the party which provides the culmination and ending of the book. Her *interior monologue, interwoven with the sights and sounds of the urban scene, is handled with a technical confidence and bravura that herald a new phase in Woolf's mastery of the novel. Clarissa herself—51 years old, fashionable, worldly, wealthy, the 'perfect hostess' who possesses a 'virginity preserved through childbirth'—is captured in her many shifting moods and recollections, and contrasted with and seen through the eyes of many other characters, including her one-time suitor Peter Walsh, returned after five years in India; her girlhood friend Sally Seton; her daughter Elizabeth and her dowdy and envious spinster tutor, Miss Kilman; the political hostess, Lady Bruton. Her day is also contrasted with that of the shell-shocked Septimus Warren Smith, who hears the sparrows sing in Greek in Regent's Park, and who at the end of the day commits suicide by hurling himself from a window; news of his death intrudes upon Clarissa's party, brought by the Harley Street doctor whom he had uselessly consulted. Woolf insisted upon the mutual dependence of these two characters, noting in her workbook, 'Mrs D. seeing the truth. SS seeing the insane truth.' Accused by some (including *Strachey) of triviality, the novel was generally well received, and sold well; it succeeds as a richly textured impression of the cross-currents of sophisticated social life, as a celebration of the mysterious growth and change of human relationships and personality (for so brief a work its sense of the passage of time is remarkable), and as a portrait of a type of society woman who both fascinated and alarmed her creator. Woolf's doubts that she was making Clarissa 'too stiff, too glittering and tinsely' have not been reflected in its popularity as one of her most accessible works.

Mrs Lirriper's Lodgings and **Mrs Lirriper's Legacy,** Christmas stories by *Dickens, which appeared in *All the Year Round*, 1863 and 1864. Mrs Lirriper lets lodgings in Norfolk Street, Strand, and her lodgers and past lodgers tell their stories.

'Mr Sludge, the "Medium"', a poem by R. *Browning, included in *Dramatis Personae*.

Mucedorus, A Comedie of, a play of uncertain authorship, published 1598, and included in the Shakespeare apocrypha.

Mucedorus, prince of Valencia, in order to discover the virtues of Amadine, the daughter of the king of Arragon, assumes the disguise of a shepherd, saves her from a bear, and falls in love with her. Banished from her father's court, he next appears as a hermit, saves Amadine from a 'wild man', reveals his identity to her father, and is now successful in his suit.

Much, in the *Robin Hood legend, a miller's son, one of the outlaw's companions. He figures in *A Lytell Geste of Robyn Hode* (*Ritson's collection of ballads).

Much Ado about Nothing, a comedy by *Shakespeare, written probably 1598–9, first printed 1600. Its chief sources are a novella by *Bandello and an episode in Ariosto's *Orlando furioso*. The play has always been a popular one in performance.

The prince of Arragon, with Claudio and Benedick in his suite, visits Leonato, duke of Messina, father of Hero and uncle of Beatrice. The sprightly Beatrice has a teasing relationship with the sworn bachelor Benedick. Beatrice and Benedick are each tricked into believing the other in love, and this brings about a genuine sympathy between them. Meanwhile Don John, the malcontented brother of the prince, thwarts Claudio's marriage by arranging for him to see Hero apparently wooed by his friend Borachio on her balcony—it is really her maidservant Margaret in disguise. Hero is publicly denounced by Claudio on her wedding day, falls into a swoon, and apparently dies. Benedick proves his love for Beatrice by challenging Claudio to a duel. The plot by Don John and Borachio is unmasked by the 'shallow fools' Dogberry and Verges, the local constables. Claudio promises to make Leonato amends for his daughter's death, and is asked to marry a cousin of Hero's; the veiled lady turns out to be Hero herself. Benedick asks to be married at the same time; Beatrice, 'upon great persuasion; and partly to save your life, for I was told you were in a consumption', agrees, and the play ends with a dance.

MUDDIMAN, Henry (b. 1629), a pensioner at St John's College, Cambridge. He was authorized as a journalist by the Rump Parliament, at the request of General Monck, in 1659, in which year he started the *Parliamentary Intelligencer* and *Mercurius Publicus*. He became the most famous of the 17th-cent. journalists, and his *newsletters in manuscript, sent twice a week to subscribers all over the kingdom, were an important political feature of the day. One of his principal rivals was *L'Estrange, whose papers, however, he drove from the field. In 1665, under the direction of his patron, Sir J. Williamson (1633–1701), he started the *Oxford Gazette* (the predecessor of the *London Gazette*), the court being then at Oxford on account of the great plague. (See also GAZETTE and NEWSPAPERS, ORIGINS OF.)

MUDIE, Charles Edward (1818–90), the founder of Mudie's Lending Library (see LIBRARIES, CIRCULATING), the son of a bookseller. He embarked on a career as bookseller, stationer, and lender of books in Bloomsbury; the lending proved so successful that he opened premises in Oxford Street in 1852, where the business prospered for many years, despite frequent complaints about Mudie's moral scruples in selecting his stock, which amounted, some claimed, to a form of censorship. G. A. *Moore was a particularly outspoken adversary.

MUGGERIDGE, Malcolm (1903–90), journalist and broadcaster, born in Croydon and educated at Selwyn College, Cambridge. He published novels, plays, reportage, and memoirs, and from 1953 to 1957 was a successful editor of *Punch*, but is principally remembered as a pundit and controversialist. In his youth he shocked liberals and the left by his exposé of the Soviet Union (*Winter in Moscow*, 1934) and in later years, while remaining iconoclastic, he became a well-known television performer and an outspoken Christian apologist.

Muggletonians, a sect founded *c.*1651 by Lodowicke Muggleton, a tailor (1609–98), and his cousin John Reeve (1608–58), who claimed to be the 'two witnesses' of Rev. 11: 3–6. They denied the doctrine of the Trinity, and taught that matter was eternal and reason the creation of the devil.

Muiopotmos, or *The Fate of the Butterflie*, a mythological poem by *Spenser published among his *Complaints* (1591). It describes the destruction of the butterfly Clarion by the jealous spider Aragnoll, and contains the lines:

> What more felicitie can fall to creature,
> Than to enjoy delight with libertie?

MUIR, Edwin (1887–1959), poet, son of a tenant farmer, born in Orkney, where he spent his childhood. His family moved to Glasgow when he was 14, and within five years both parents and two of his brothers were dead; he himself suffered poor physical and mental health, and while working as office boy and clerk he turned to socialism (through the writings of *Blatchford) and to the works of *Nietzsche. He began to write, contributing to *Orage's *New Age*, and in 1919 married Willa Anderson (1890–1970); they moved to London, where Muir became assistant to Orage, and underwent a course of psychoanalysis which profoundly affected his writing. In 1921 the Muirs went to Prague, and remained in Europe for four years, a period that later produced their collaborative translations from the German (notably of *Kafka, 1930–49). More importantly, it freed Muir's imagination as a poet. *First Poems* (1925) was followed by several other collections, including *Chorus of the Newly Dead* (1926), *The Labyrinth* (1949), and *Collected Poems 1921–1951* (1952). Muir's poetry is traditional rather than experimental in form, and much of his imagery is rooted in the landscapes of his childhood; a recurrent theme is the dream journey through time and place, and the narrative of the poet's own life lends itself naturally to the myth of an Eden threatened by various forms of catastrophe or expulsion. A sense of subdued menace lies beneath many of his quiet and orderly poems, which sometimes (as in his well-known piece 'The Horses') achieve the *apocalyptic. Muir also published three novels, a number of critical works, and a highly evocative autobiography (again with much emphasis on the significance of dreams), published in 1940 as *The Story and the Fable* and revised as *An Autobiography* in 1954. See also P. H. Butter, *Edwin Muir: Man and Poet* (1966), and *Belonging: A Memoir* (1968) by Willa Muir.

MUIR, Kenneth (1907–96), professor of English literature at Liverpool University (1951–74). As well as *Wyatt's poems and letters, he edited many of Shakespeare's plays and did much work on their sources.

MULCASTER, Richard (c.1531–1611), educated at Eton, King's College, Cambridge, and Christ Church, Oxford. He was the first headmaster of Merchant Taylors' School, London, where his pupils included *Spenser, *Kyd, *Lodge, and *Andrewes, and he was later high master of St *Paul's. He wrote two books on education, *Positions* (1581), dedicated to *Elizabeth I, and *The Elementarie* (1582). Both books show his humanist interests and ideals, such as his suggestion that gentlewomen should be educated in school, though only up to the age of 13 or 14, and his stress on physical exercise, music, and vernacular literature, including the writing of English verse. Presumably the future poets who attended his school benefited from this last. He also published Latin and English verses on the queen's death (1603), and helped devise City shows and pageants.

MULDOON, Paul (1951–), poet, born in Moy, Co. Armagh, educated at the Queen's University, Belfast. He worked for the BBC in Northern Ireland, resigning in 1985. He now lives in America and teaches at Princeton University. *New Weather* (1973), his first volume of poems, marked him out as a distinctive and important new voice: ironic, allusive, technically adept, and verbally inventive. This was followed by the enigmatically entitled *Why Brownlee Left* (1980) and by *Quoof* (1983), which firmly established his reputation. His *Selected Poems 1968–1983* appeared in 1986. In the first work published after his move to America, *Madoc: A Mystery* (1990), a poem in 247 chapters, the idealistic social philosophy of *Pantisocracy, as expounded by Samuel Taylor *Coleridge and *Southey (whose poem *Madoc* is referred to in the title), inspires a dazzling, though ultimately baffling, mélange of allusions, correspondences, and fragmented storylines. His most substantial and important work

to date, *The Annals of Chile* (1994), contains a number of poems, including 'Yarrow' and 'Incantata', an elegy for the artist Mary Farl Powers, that confirm and extend Muldoon's position as one of the most original poetic talents of his generation. Later collections include *Hay* (1998) and *Moy Sand and Gravel* (2002).

MULGRAVE, earl of, see SHEFFIELD.

Mulla, frequently referred to in *Spenser's poems, is the river Mulla or Awbeg, a tributary of the Blackwater in Ireland, near which stood Kilcolman Castle, his residence when he composed much of *The Faerie Queene*.

MÜLLER, Friedrich Max, see MAX MÜLLER.

Mulliner, Mr, (1) in Mrs Gaskell's *Cranford*, the Hon. Mrs Jamieson's butler; (2) the teller of some of the stories by P. G. *Wodehouse.

MULOCK, Dinah Maria, see CRAIK.

MULSO, Hester, see CHAPONE.

Mum and the Sothsegger, an alliterative poem of c.1403–6, bewailing the follies of Richard II and offering advice to Henry IV. Two sections survive with a gap between them: the first of 857 lines (the Cambridge manuscript) was previously called *Richard the Redeless* and edited by *Skeat with *Piers Plowman* which it resembles in language and in its division into prologue and four *passus*; the second of 1,751 lines (in a British Library manuscript). Skeat and Jusserand believed, probably wrongly, that the poem was by *Langland. Mum (as in 'keep mum') remains silent in evil days, such as those of Richard II, while the Truthteller is ignored as he speaks the unwelcome truth. Ed. M. Day and R. Steele (EETS os 199, 1936; repr. Kraus 1971).

MUMBY, Frank A. (1872–1954), journalist and historian of the British book trade, whose *Romance of Bookselling* (1910) was the basis of *Publishing and Bookselling: A History from the Earliest Times to the Present Day* (1930). This became a standard work and was revised by Ian Norrie, who wrote a new second section, 1870–1970, which was itself revised as *Mumby's Publishing and Bookselling in the Twentieth Century*. Mumby, who also wrote a history of Routledge and Kegan Paul and other volumes of publishing history, was on the staff of the *Times Literary Supplement* from 1923 to 1940.

mummers' play, or **St George play,** folk play evolved from the *sword-dance, widespread through England, Scotland, Ireland, and Wales. The play, in its characters and detailed action, varies in different localities, but the main lines are as follows. The principal characters are St George (Sir George, King George, Prince George), the Turkish knight, Captain Slasher, and the Doctor. Minor personages bear, according to the different versions, a great variety of names. After a brief prologue, the fighting characters advance and introduce themselves, or are introduced, in vaunting rhymes. A duel or several duels follow, and one or other of the combatants is killed. The Doctor then enters, boasts his skill, and resuscitates the slain. Supernumerary grotesque characters are then presented, and a collection is made. The central incident of the play is doubtless connected with the celebration of the death of the year and its resurrection in the spring. See E. K. *Chambers, *The English Folk-Play* (1933).

A celebrated description of mumming occurs in Bk II, ch. 4–6 of Hardy's *The Return of the Native*, in which Eustacia Vye disguises herself as the Turkish knight, in the place of the young lad Charley, in order to engineer a meeting with Clym Yeobright.

MUNBY, Arthur Joseph (1828–1910), educated at Trinity College, Cambridge. He published various volumes of verse, including *Verses New and Old* (1865) and *Relicta* (1909), but is now chiefly remembered for his diaries and notebooks, used by Derek Hudson as the basis of his *Munby: Man of Two Worlds* (1972). These give an interesting picture of Victorian literary and social life; they also reveal Munby's obsession with working women and the story of his secret marriage to a maidservant, Hannah, which explain some of the allusions in his poems.

Munchausen, Baron, *Narrative of His Marvellous Travels*, by Rudolf Erich Raspe, published 1785.

The original Baron Münchhausen is said to have lived 1720–97, to have served in the Russian army against the Turks, and to have been in the habit of grossly exaggerating his experiences. Raspe (1737–94) was a Hanoverian who, when librarian at Cassel, stole gems from the Landgraf's collection, fled to England to escape the consequences, and added to his resources by publishing in English a version of the baron's narratives. They include such stories as that of the horse who was cut in two, drank of a fountain, and was sewn up again; of the stag that the baron shot with a cherry-stone, and afterwards found with a cherry-tree growing out of its forehead; and so forth.

MUNDAY, Anthony (1560–1633), hack-writer. He wrote or collaborated in a number of plays, and was ridiculed by *Jonson as Antonio Balladino in *The Case Is Altered*. Among his plays are *John a Kent and John a Cumber* (written c.1589–90, dealing with a conflict between two wizards of those names): he also collaborated in the writing of *Sir Thomas *More* and in *The Downfall of Robert, Earle of Huntington* (printed 1601), followed by *The Death* of the same, of which the subject is the legend of *Robin Hood, with whom the earl is identified. Munday wrote ballads, which are lost, and as 'Shepheard Tonie' contributed several poems to *Englands Helicon* (1600). He also translated popular romances, including the *Palmerin cycle (1581–1602), *Palladine of England* (1588), and *Amadis of Gaul* (?1590), and wrote City pageants from 1605. His

experiences as a student at the English College in Rome during 1579 are the basis for his *The English Romayne Lyfe* (1582).

Mundungus, the ill-tempered author (possibly Dr Sharp) of a travel book satirized by Sterne in *A Sentimental Journey*.

Munera, the Lady, in Spenser's *Faerie Queene* (v. ii), the daughter of the Saracen Pollente, the personification of ill-gotten wealth, whom Sir *Artegall besieges and whom *Talus drowns in the moat of her castle after chopping off her golden hands and feet.

Mungo, see Bickerstaffe's PADLOCK, THE.

MUNGO, St, see KENTIGERN.

MUNRO, Alice (1931–   ), Canadian short story writer, born in Wingham, Ontario, where she grew up. She spent two years at the University of Ontario, married, and moved to British Columbia. Each of her collections, *Dance of the Happy Shades* (1968), *Who Do You Think You Are?* (1978), published in Britain as *The Beggar Maid*, and *The Progress of Love* (1986), won the Governor General's Award. Her other collections include *Friends of my Youth* (1973), *Open Secrets* (1994), and *Runaway* (2004). Munro describes herself as writing about 'places where your roots are', in her case, small-town southern Ontario, whose texture and unremarkable lives engage her imaginative sympathy. Her writing is characterized by, above all, superb and precise mastery of the short story form; both lucid and compellingly mysterious, the stories combine poetic intensity and economy with the surprising scope and depth of a novel.

MUNRO, H(ector) H(ugh), see SAKI.

MURASAKI, Lady, see TALE OF GENJI, THE.

Murder in the Cathedral, a verse drama by T. S. *Eliot, written for performance at the Canterbury Festival, June 1935, and published the same year. Drawing on Greek tragedy, Christian liturgy, and biblical imagery, it is based on the martyrdom of St Thomas *Becket, who returns to Canterbury after a seven-year absence: he receives visits from four Tempters, the last of whom tempts him to spiritual pride ('to do the right deed for the wrong reason'). In an interlude he preaches to the people (Christmas Morning, 1170) and in Part II he is murdered by four knights, who later prosaically justify their actions. A chorus of townswomen opens and closes the drama, and comments on the action: these speeches contain some of Eliot's most memorable and haunting dramatic verse.

MURDOCH, Dame Iris Jean (1919–99), novelist and philosopher, born in Dublin of Anglo-Irish parents, and educated at Badminton School and Somerville College, Oxford. She worked for some time in the civil service, then lectured in philosophy in Oxford and London; her works on philosophy include *Sartre,*

Romantic Rationalist (1953) and *The Sovereignty of Good* (1970). In 1956 she married the literary critic John *Bayley. Her first novel, *Under the Net* (1954), a first-person male narration, was followed by many other successful works, including *The Bell* (1958, set in a lay community in a country house); *A Severed Head* (1961, dramatized 1963 by J. B. *Priestley); *The Red and the Green* (1965, set in Ireland); *The Time of the Angels* (1968, set in a murky vicarage in the City, dominated by a satanic priest); *Bruno's Dream* (1969); *The Black Prince* (1973, with an unreliable 58-year-old male narrator, in love with a 20-year-old, who becomes involved in scenes of domestic violence and tragedy); *A Word Child* (1975); *The Sea, the Sea* (1978, a novel about a theatre director and his childhood love, with strong echoes of *The Tempest*, which won the *Booker Prize); and *The Philosopher's Pupil* (1983, her 21st novel). She also wrote three plays. Her novels, which have been described as psychological detective stories, portray complicated and sophisticated sexual relationships (usually, but not exclusively, amongst the professional classes), and her plots have an operatic quality, combining comic, bizarre, and macabre incidents in a highly patterned symbolic structure. Though clearly not intended as strictly realistic, her portrayal of 20th-cent. middle-class and intellectual life shows acute observation as well as a wealth of invention, and has baffled critics by its evasion of recognized fictional genres. Her narrative skill conceals (or effortlessly conveys) the seriousness and abstraction of her preoccupations—with the nature of good and evil, the religious life, the sacred and the taboo, the nature of sexuality and Freudian determinism—and has brought her a wide readership. She herself several times declared her allegiance to the large, realistic tradition of the Anglo-Russian novel; in 'Against Dryness' (*Encounter*, Jan. 1961) she distinguished between the 'crystalline' novels which exhibit 'smallness, clearness, self-containedness', and the 'large, shapeless, quasi-documentary' novel, and her own works may be seen as an attempt to resolve the contradictions between the 'fantasy-myths' of the one form, and the 'unfashionable naturalistic idea of character', which brings vitality to the other. Later novels include *The Good Apprentice* (1985), *The Book and the Brotherhood* (1987), *The Message to the Planet* (1989), and *The Green Knight* (1993), a dense allegory based on the medieval poem *Sir *Gawain and the Green Knight*. *Metaphysics as a Guide to Morals* (1992) is a survey of ethics in an age of religious decline. See *Iris Murdoch: A Life* (2001) by Peter J. Conradi.

Murdstone, Edward and Jane, characters in Dickens's *David Copperfield*.

MURPHY, Arthur (1727–1805), barrister, journalist, actor, and playwright. He wrote over 20 farces, comedies, and tragedies, including adaptations of *Molière and *Voltaire; his better-known pieces include *The Way to Keep Him* (1760), *Three Weeks after Marriage* (1764), and *Know Your Own Mind* (1777). He also wrote lives of *Fielding (1792), Dr *Johnson (1792), and *Garrick (1801). He and Johnson became lifelong friends after their first meeting in 1754, which arose from Murphy's inadvertent borrowing of a tale from the *Rambler*; Murphy was later responsible for introducing Johnson to the *Thrales.

MURPHY, Richard (1927–   ), Irish poet, born in Co. Mayo, who spent his early childhood in Ceylon, and was educated at Magdalen College, Oxford, and the Sorbonne. Much of his poetry portrays the landscapes, and more particularly the seascapes, of Ireland; his publications include *The Archeology of Love* (1955), *Sailing to an Island* (1963, which contains his long narrative poem about a fishing tragedy, 'The Cleggan Disaster', and other sea tales), *The Battle of Aughrim* (1968), a poetic non-partisan evocation, interweaving past and present, of the battle of 1691, first broadcast in 1968 with Ted *Hughes and *Day-Lewis among its readers; *Selected Poems* (1979); *The Price of Stone* (1985); and *New Selected Poems* and *Mirror Wall* (both 1989).

MURPHY, Tom (1935–   ), Irish playwright, born Tuam, Co. Galway. When Murphy submitted his first full-length play, the ferocious *A Whistle in the Dark* (1961), to the *Abbey Theatre, he was told that such people as the violent family of the play did not exist in Ireland. Since then, Murphy has continued to create the kind of characters that are not supposed to exist. Angry and hilarious portraits of small-town hypocrisy make up a realistic strain of social drama in *A Crucial Week in the Life of a Grocer's Assistant* (1969) and *Conversations on a Homecoming* (1985). But the work that places Murphy in the front rank of modern dramatists fuses these elements of realism with baroque dialogue, surreal comedy, and a yearning for transcendence. In at least two plays, *The Gigli Concert* (1983) and *Bailegangaire* (1985), Murphy's extraordinary ambition is completely and vividly fulfilled.

MURPHY, (George) Gilbert (Aimé) (1866–1957), perhaps the most brilliant Greek scholar of his generation in England and the model for Adolphus Cusins in Shaw's *Major Barbara*. Born in Sydney, New South Wales, he became professor of Greek at Glasgow in 1889 and was Regius professor of Greek at Oxford 1908–36. Although he possessed a thorough mastery of the techniques of Greek scholarship fashionable in his day, his claim to brilliance lay rather in his ability to make the ancient world sensitively real to his contemporaries; and while he produced influential studies in Greek epic and drama, he is best remembered for his translations of *Euripides, which, by romanticizing their originals, appealed to a wide, if unacademic, public. Murray had, however, many interests beyond scholarship and the stage. Always an eloquent champion of women's rights and other liberal causes, he devoted his energies after 1918 to the furtherance of peace, and as chairman of the League of Nations Union (1922–38) he struggled without much hope to save Europe from war.

MURRAY, Sir James Augustus Henry (1837–1915), the son of a clothier from Hawick. He was educated at Cavers School, near his native village of Denholm, and at Minto School, but his great philological and antiquarian knowledge was acquired largely through his own studies. He became a schoolmaster and moved to London in 1864, where he worked for some years as a bank clerk before returning to his earlier profession at Mill Hill. Throughout these years he pursued his philological interests and made the acquaintance of many scholars with similar preoccupations, including *Skeat, *Sweet, and *Furnivall; he became a member of the *Philological Society, to which he delivered in 1868 papers later printed as *The Dialect of the Southern Counties of Scotland* (1873) which were received with much respect. In 1879, after lengthy negotiation and much hesitation, he was appointed editor of the *Oxford English Dictionary*, a monumental work which was to occupy the rest of his life. He laid down the lines on which the work was to be compiled, and persevered through many difficulties (some financial), resisting suggestions that the work be completed more rapidly. There is a detailed account of the dictionary's composition in *Caught in the Web of Words* (1977) by his granddaughter K. M. E. Murray, which also gives a vivid portrait of his industrious personality, his high moral standards and sense of responsibility, and his happy family life. He was the father of 11 children, several of whom aided him considerably in the great work that dominated their early lives.

MURRAY, John (1778–1843), the son of John Murray I (1745–93), who founded the publishing house still in existence. The second John Murray was one of those who, together with the reviews such as the *Edinburgh* and the *Quarterly*, began to substitute for the dying system of personal patronage his own personal encouragement and commercial expertise. His publishing house became a social meeting place for many of the literary figures of his time, and it is probable that the plan for the founding of the Athenaeum club was devised in his rooms. With the help and encouragement of Sir W. *Scott he established the Tory *Quarterly Review* in 1809, and took a close interest in its management. He gave up the London agency of *Blackwood's* in protest at its attacks on the *Cockney School. He was the friend and publisher of *Byron, who was his single most important author. *Childe Harold* appeared under his imprint, as did most of Byron's other work. But he was so apprehensive of the public reception of *Don Juan* that he published only the early cantos, and those without his imprint; the later cantos were published by John *Hunt, who also produced *The Vision of Judgement*, which Murray had refused. Murray bought Byron's memoirs of 1818–21 from T. *Moore, and reluctantly consented to having

them burned in his grate at Albemarle Street. His other authors included J. *Austen, *Crabbe, *Coleridge, *Southey, Leigh *Hunt, and *Borrow. Mariana Starke's *Guide for Travellers on the Continent* (1820) led to a long and profitable series of guidebooks, several of which were written by John Murray III (1808–92). In the publishing slump of the late 1820s and 1830s Murray noted, 'the taste for literature is ebbing', and he sold his copyright of Jane Austen's novels.

The John Murray succession, and the firm's independence, continues.

MURRAY, Les(lie) Allan (1938–   ), Australian poet, born in Nabiac, in the Manning River area of New South Wales, who spent his childhood and adolescence on his grandfather's dairy farm. He attended the University of Sydney, though he left without taking a degree, and, after marrying in 1962, worked as a translator. His first published work as a poet, *The Ilex Tree* (1965), was written in collaboration with Geoffrey Lehmann. For a time he lived with his wife and two children in England and Europe, returning eventually to Sydney to pursue a career as a full-time writer. From 1973 to 1979 he was editor of *Poetry Australia*, during which time he attempted to hold out against the inroads of the postmodernistic New Poetry, his instincts being always for poetry that communicated to a broad readership rather than to coteries of intellectuals. He was appointed writer-in-residence at the University of New England in 1978 and over the next decade established himself as one of Australia's leading poets and literary personalities. From 1976 to 1991 he was poetry editor for the publishers Angus & Robertson and in 1990 became literary editor of the magazine *Quadrant*. In 1975 he had bought back part of his family's former farm in the Bunyah district of NSW and in 1985 returned to live there permanently. At the heart of Murray's poetry is a profound response, expressing itself through a rich visual imagination and meticulously crafted language, to the Australian bush and the ideals and values of the pioneer settlers. His many volumes include *The Weatherboard Cathedral* (1969), *Poems against Economics* (1972), *Lunch and Counterlunch* (1974), *Ethnic Radio* (1977), *The Boys Who Stole the Funeral* (1980, a novel-in-verse comprising 140 sonnets), *The People's Otherworld* (1983), *Dog Fox Field* (1990), and *Translations from the Natural World* (1992). His reviews and articles have been collected in *The Peasant Mandarin* (1978), *Persistence in Folly* (1984), *Blocks and Tackles* (1990), and *The Paperbark Tree* (1992). He is the editor of *The New Oxford Book of Australian Verse* and an anthology of Australian religious poetry (both 1986).

MURRAY, Lindley (1745–1826), Quaker grammarian, born in Pennsylvania, who came to England in 1784 and settled in York. He published an English grammar in 1795, a reader in 1799, and a spelling book in 1804, which were widely used in schools and earned him the title of 'the father of English grammar'. He wrote many other educational works, and his *Memoirs*, in epistolary form, were published in 1826.

MURRY, John Middleton (1889–1957), born in Peckham of ambitious lower-middle-class parents. He made his mark while still an Oxford undergraduate as editor of the *Modernist periodical *Rhythm* (1911–13), through which he met in 1912 Katherine *Mansfield, whom he was later (in 1918) to marry. In 1914 he met D. H. *Lawrence, who greatly influenced him; the relationship of the Lawrences and the Murrys was intense and tempestuous, particularly during the war years, and is reflected in *Women in Love*. From 1919 to 1921 Murry was editor of the *Athenaeum*, in which he published an impressive range of writers, including V. *Woolf, T. S. *Eliot, and Valéry, and in which he himself attacked *Georgian poetry. In 1923, the year of his wife's death, he founded the *Adelphi*; although he was to marry again three times, he continued to dwell on her memory, editing her works, publishing reminiscences, letters, etc. His many critical works include *Fyodor Dostoevsky* (1916), *The Problem of Style* (1922), *Countries of the Mind* (1922, 1931), *Keats and Shakespeare* (1925), and *Son of Woman: The Story of D. H. Lawrence* (1931). He also wrote many works of a semimystical nature, and became deeply interested in the concept of an ideal community (a concern dating back to the days when he and Lawrence had planned the utopian community of 'Rananim') and in pacifism. Throughout his turbulent emotional and professional life he was attracted to the extreme and the romantic, seeing life as a spiritual search; his reputation as a critic declined in a new age of specialization and professionalism, but he remains an important figure in literary history. See his autobiography, *Between Two Worlds* (1935), and the standard life by F. A. Lea (1959).

MUSAEUS, (1) a legendary Greek poet, said to have been a pupil of *Orpheus; (2) a Greek poet, who perhaps lived about AD 500, the author of a poem on the story of *Hero and Leander which provided the groundwork for *Marlowe's poem.

Muses Lookinge-Glasse, The, a defence of the drama, in the form of a play, by *Randolph, printed 1638.

'The scene lies in the playhouse at Blackfriars. Bird and Mistress Flowerdew, two Puritans, who serve the theatre with feathers and other small wares, enter; they express their abhorrence of playhouses; Roscius joins them; he prevails on them to see the representation of the play; Roscius explains the drift of it to them as it proceeds. This play has no plot; the object of it is to show that all virtues, and every commendable passion, proceed from mediocrity or a just medium between two extremes. At the conclusion Bird and Mistress Flowerdew agree that a play may be productive of moral good' (*Genest).

Musgrove, Mr and Mrs, their son Charles and his wife Mary (née Elliot), and their daughters Henrietta and Louisa, characters in J. Austen's *Persuasion*.

music, literature of. The first important English contribution to musical literature is T. *Morley's *Plaine and Easie Introduction to Practicall Musicke, Set Down in Forme of a Dialogue* (1597), for many years the standard work in its field. There is a chapter on music in *Peacham's *Compleat Gentleman* (1622), but on the whole the musical writings of the 17th cent. were technical and instructional, rather than literary, as in the publications of John Playford, whose *Breefe Introduction to the Skill of Musicke* (1654) continued to appear in new editions until well into the 18th cent. An exception, of somewhat idiosyncratic literary charm, is Thomas Mace's *Musick's Monument; or, A Remembrancer of the Best Practical Musick, both Divine, and Civil, that Has Ever been Known, to Have Been in the World* (1676).

An interesting figure in the early 18th cent. is R. *North, whose treatises *The Musicall Grammarian* and *Memoires of Musick* remained in manuscript at his death in 1734 and have been collected in a modern edition (1959): his personal approach to the theory and aesthetics of music was carried on, almost to excess, in Charles Avison's controversial *An Essay on Musical Expression* (1752). The later 18th cent. produced the two great histories of music by Dr C. *Burney and Sir J. *Hawkins. Burney published the first volume of *A General History of Music from the Earliest Ages to the Present Period* in 1776, only to see it followed some nine months later by Hawkins's *A General History of the Science and Practice of Music* complete in five volumes (also 1776); Burney's remaining three volumes came out in 1782 and 1789. Hawkins is stronger on the earlier periods, while Burney is more personal and readable: it was preceded by much travelling to collect material, recounted with perspicacity and humour in *The Present State of Music in France and Italy* (1771) and *The Present State of Music in Germany, the Netherlands and the United Provinces* (1773). Addison's essays on opera in the early issues of the *Spectator are among the first of interest in any language, but the polemics that flourished later in the century in France and Italy had little counterpart in England, where the best writing in this field was more personal: the *Musical Reminiscences* of Lord Mount-Edgcumbe (1825), the *Reminiscences* of the Irish tenor Michael Kelly (1826), George Hogarth's *Memoirs of the Opera* (1838), and the chronicles of theatrical managers like Ebers, Lumley, Mapleson, etc.

The first monograph devoted to a single composer was by an Englishman, John Mainwaring's *Memoirs of the Life of the Late George Frederic Handel* (1760). Hawkins and Burney also made contributions in this field, the former on *Corelli* (1777) and the latter on *Handel* (1785, in connection with the *Handel commemoration in Westminster Abbey in the previous year). Occasional works of this kind appeared during the next half-century, including Edward Holmes's still valuable *Life of Mozart* (1845) and the monumental *Life of Beethoven* by the American Alexander Wheelock Thayer, begun in 1849 but not published in England until 1921. Most of the important biographical work in the 19th cent. was done outside England, but growing interest in musical scholarship produced the four volumes of George Grove's *Dictionary of Music and Musicians* (1879–89), not the first compilation of its kind but by far the most comprehensive—as, in the 20 volumes of the sixth edition (*The New Grove*, 1980), it remains. The same stimulus inspired *The Oxford History of Music* (6 vols, 1901–5), now superseded by *The New Oxford History of Music* (designed in 11 volumes, of which nine appeared 1954–90). Both of these were collaborative efforts: Percy Scholes's *Oxford Companion to Music* (1938; 11th edn, the *New Oxford Companion to Music*, ed. Denis Arnold, 1983) remains an unrivalled personal lexicographical tour de force.

The conclusion of Grove's great enterprise saw the rise of G. B. *Shaw as music critic. His work in this field was collected as *London Music in 1888–89 as Heard by Corno di Bassetto* (1937) and *Music in London* (3 vols, 1932), and provides some of the most stimulating reading in all musical literature; his major essay, *The Perfect Wagnerite*, came out in 1898. Another Wagnerian landmark, *A Study of Wagner*, appeared the following year by a young critic writing under the pseudonym of Ernest Newman (William Roberts, 1868–1959); this was the first of his several treatments of the subject which culminated in the four-volume *Life of Richard Wagner* (1933–47), the most important of many books written by Newman in his long and active career. The 20th cent. saw a vast increase in books on every aspect of musical activity, from which one might select Edward Dent's *Mozart's Operas* (1913) and his study of Scarlatti (1905); Edmund Fellowes's pioneering biographies of native composers, *Orlando Gibbons* (1925), *William Byrd* (1936), the *English Madrigal Composers* (1921); Frank Walker's *Hugo Wolf* (1951) and *The Man Verdi* (1962); the seven volumes of Donald Tovey's *Essays in Musical Analysis* (1933–9); and even such an occasional squib as *Music Ho!* (1934) by Constant *Lambert.

Musidorus ('gifted by the Muses'), the young duke of Thessalia in Sidney's *Arcadia*.

MUSIL, Robert Elder von (1880–1942), born in Klagenfurt of Austrian and partly Czech descent, best known for his massive (and unfinished) novel, *Der Mann ohne Eigenschaften* (1930–2), which appeared in an English translation by E. Wilkins and E. Kaiser as *The Man without Qualities* (1953–60). He trained as an engineer and then had a brief career in the army before turning to writing. His first novel *Young Törless* (1906) was followed by various short works of fiction and two plays, but Musil then devoted the rest of his life to his great work. Despite its daunting scale, *The Man without Qualities* is witty and approachable: its main narrative strands concern Ulrich, the indecisive hero, and his bestial counterpart, the murderer Moosbrugger. A new translation by Sophie Wilkins and Burton Pike, pub-

lished in 1995, included a vast amount of previously unseen, incomplete, and fragmented material, which confirmed the novel's stature and enduring relevance.

'Musophilus, or A Generall Defence of Learning', a verse dialogue in six- and eight-line stanzas by S. *Daniel, dedicated to his friend Fulke *Greville, published 1599.

Musophilus defends the claims of culture against the worldly arts practised by Philocosmus, the unlettered man of action. The poem shows at its best Daniel's gift for moral reflection in dignified but plain language, and his faith in a poetic vocation independent of worldly recognition: neglect cannot undo 'The love I beare unto this holy skill; | This is the thing that I was borne to do, | This is my Scene, this part must I fulfill' (ll. 576–9). The poem also contains a notable description of Stonehenge (l. 337 ff.) and ends with a fine invocation of 'heavenly Eloquence' and the prophetic lines:

> And who in time knowes whither we may vent
> The treasure of our tongue, to what strange shores
> This gaine of our best glorie shal be sent,
> T'inrich unknowing Nations with our stores?
> What worlds in th'yet unformed Occident
> May come refin'd with th'accents that are ours?

MUSSET, Alfred de (1810–57), French poet and playwright. His first published work was a free translation of *De Quincey's *Opium Eater* (1828). His career as a *littérateur* was enlivened by a notorious liaison with G. *Sand (1833–5). His most famous poems, *Souvenir* (1841), occasioned by a chance meeting with Sand in a theatre foyer, and *Les Nuits* (1835–7), rehearse the central Romantic motif of lost love. His most original achievements are his plays, in particular *Fantasio, On ne badine pas avec l'amour*, and *Lorenzaccio* (all 1834), which blend irony, fantasy, and psychological penetration. Even his liveliest work is seldom free from the melancholy and anxiety known as the *mal du siècle*.

Mustapha, (1) a tragedy (1609) by Sir F. *Greville; (2) a heroic play (1665) by R. *Boyle, based on *Ibrahim* by Mlle de Scudéry.

'Mutabilitie Cantos', name given to the fragmentary 'Book VII' of Spenser's *Faerie Queene*: two cantos only, first published with the folio edition of *The Faerie Queene* in 1609. They describe the challenge of the Titaness Mutabilitie to the cosmic government of Jove. (The first canto includes the charming topographical fable of Faunus and Molanna, which reflects Spenser's affection for his Irish home.) The goddess Nature vindicates Jove's rule, displaying its orderly beauty in a procession of Seasons and Months, asserting finally that natural things 'are not changed from their first estate | But by their change their being doe dilate'. The cantos can be seen as an epilogue to *The Faerie Queene*, ending with the poet's prayer:

O! that great Sabaoth God, graunt me that
    Sabaoths sight.

MYERS, F(rederic) W(illiam) H(enry) (1843–1901),
poet and inspector of schools, educated at Cambridge,
where he spent much of his life. He published several
volumes of poetry and critical essays; his essay on G.
*Eliot, first published in the *Century Magazine* in 1881
(and reprinted in *Essays Classical and Modern*, 1883),
describes the celebrated incident in which she spoke to
him of '*God, Immortality, Duty*', and declared 'how
inconceivable was the *first*, how unbelievable the
second, and yet how peremptory and absolute the
third'. Myers's own childhood obsession with the
possibility of survival after death led to his involvement with the *Society for Psychical Research, of
which he was a founder; he was joint author (with E.
Gurney and F. Podmore) of *Phantasms of the Living*
(1886), a two-volume work dealing largely with telepathy, which embodied the first considerable results
of the society's labours.

MYERS, L(eopold) H(amilton) (1881–1944), novelist,
the son of F. W. H. *Myers. His novels are concerned
with the problem of how human beings can live rightly
in society if they exclude spirituality, which, to his
mind, was an activity as natural as sex. In his troubled
personal life he failed to reconcile the flesh and the
spirit, but he believed deeply that society would find a
way to transcend itself. Here he was in violent opposition to humanism and to the values of the
*Bloomsbury Group, which he thought were a denial
of life. After trying several political solutions he
became a communist. Apart from the *Orissers*
(1922), *The 'Clio'* (1925), and *Strange Glory* (1936),
the novels are set in an imaginary 16th-cent. India: *The
Near and the Far* (1929), *Prince Jali* (1931), *The Root and
the Flower* (1935), and *The Pool of Vishnu* (1940); all
collected under the title *The Near and the Far* (1943). He
died from an overdose of veronal.

'My Mind to me a Kingdom is' the first line of a poem
on contentment which was first printed in *Byrd's
Psalmes, Sonets, & Songs (1588). It was frequently
referred to in the 16th and 17th cents, and often
attributed to Sir E. *Dyer. It is more probably by the earl
of *Oxford.

Mysteries of Udolpho, The, a novel by A. *Radcliffe,
published 1794.
    The orphaned Emily St Aubert is carried off by her
aunt's villainous husband Montoni to a remote castle
in the Apennines, where her life, honour, and fortune
are threatened and she is surrounded by apparently
supernatural terrors. These are later explained as due
to human agency and Emily escapes, returns to France
and, after further mysteries and misunderstandings, is
reunited with her lover Valancourt. The book plays an
important part in J. Austen's *Northanger Abbey*.

Mysterious Mother, The, a tragedy in blank verse by
Horace *Walpole, printed at *Strawberry Hill in 1768.
    It deals with the remorse of a mother (the countess of
Narbonne) for an act of incest committed many years
before. Under the calamity of the marriage of her son
Edmund, who had been the unwitting partner of her
crime, with the girl Adeliza (brought up as her ward,
but in fact the fruit of their union) she takes her own
life. The theme of incest shocked many of his admirers
but greatly interested *Byron, who described the play
as 'a tragedy of the highest order, and not a puling love-
play'.

mystery plays, biblical dramas popular in England
from the 13th to the later 16th cent., take their name
from the *mestier* (*métier* or trade) of their performers;
they were previously called 'miracle plays' which,
strictly, are enactments of the miracles performed by
the saints. The mysteries enact the events of the Bible
from the Creation to the Ascension (and in some cases
later). Their origin is much disputed; one of the earliest
is the Anglo-Norman *Jeu d'Adam* (see ADAM), and there
were cycles in many countries: France, Italy, Ireland,
and Germany (surviving in the Oberammergau Passion Play). Though it is clear from their archives that
many English towns had them, only four complete
cycles survive: York, Chester, Wakefield (also called
Towneley from the owners of the manuscript), and the
Ludus Coventriae, also called the Hegge cycle, and N-
town because it is not known where it comes from. The
argument over their origins is whether they were
derived from Latin liturgical pageants or developed as
new vernacular drama. They are connected with the
feast day of Corpus Christi (the Thursday after Trinity
Sunday) which was declared in 1264 and first observed
as a holy day in 1311. The various pageants (whose
number varies from 25 in Chester to nearly 50 in York)
were each assigned to a particular trade-guild, often
with a humorous or macabre connection between the
métier and the play: the York Shipwrights enact the
story of Noah, for instance. Their great popularity in
England from the time of *Chaucer to Shakespeare is
repeatedly attested by those writers, among others.
Their end was no doubt mainly caused by Reformation
distaste for idols and religious pageantry (an attitude
occasionally manifested earlier), though there are
some signs of decadence, in the later Digby plays, for
example (see MARY MAGDALENE). Their great
interest is as an early, popular form of theatre, manifesting energy, humour, and seriousness; it is not
accurate to think of their composers as unlearned, as is
clear from the group of six plays in the Towneley cycle
assigned to a presumed author known as 'the Wakefield Master'. The latter's most celebrated play is the
Second Shepherd's Play in which the Nativity is
parodied by and collocated with a contemporary
case of sheep stealing. It was not these plays, so
much as the moralities and *interludes, which affected
the development of Elizabethan drama. But they had a

considerable vogue in the 20th cent., with its interest in popular, less articulated forms of drama (such as *Nōh plays from Japan); evidence of this is *Britten's *Noye's Fludde*, and revivals of performances of the cycles, most notably at York.

There are editions of the Cycles in EETS ES Chester, nos. 62 and 115, ed. H. Deimling and J. Matthews (1892 and 1914); Wakefield, no. 71 (1897, reprinted 1973), ed. G. England and A. W. Pollard; *Ludus Coventriae*, no. 120 (1917), ed. K. S. Block. L. Toulmin Smith (ed.); *The York Plays* (1885, repr. 1963). See also E. K. *Chambers, *The Mediaeval Stage* (2 vols, 1903); V. A. Kolve, *The Play Called Corpus Christi* (1966); R. E. Woolf, *The English Mystery Plays* (1972). For a very useful selected edition, see P. Happé, *The English Mystery Plays* (1975).

Mystic, Mr, a character in Peacock's *Melincourt*, a caricature of *Coleridge.

myth criticism, an area of literary investigation and commentary that deals with the relations between 'myth'—in the positive sense of a traditional story— and literature, often drawing upon anthropology, psychology, and studies of folklore. Myth criticism is usually concerned to demonstrate that literary works draw upon a common reservoir of *archetypes or recurrent images, or that their narrative patterns repeat those of ancient myths or religious rituals, as in quests for sacred objects, or cycles of death and rebirth. Much *psychoanalytic criticism overlaps with myth criticism, not just in the tradition of *Jung but in that of *Freud, who interpreted literary texts as well as dreams and neurotic symptoms as echoes of the Oedipus myth. Jung, however, is the principal founder of the school of myth critics which flourished from the 1930s to the 1960s. An early study in this vein is Maud Bodkin's *Archetypal Patterns in Poetry* (1934); other notable works are Richard Chase's *Quest for Myth* (1946), Robert *Graves's *The White Goddess* (1948), W. H. *Auden's *The Enchafèd Flood* (1951), and C. L. Barber's *Shakespeare's Festive Comedy* (1959). A more elaborate theoretical foundation for myth criticism was proposed by *Frye in his *Anatomy of Criticism* (1957). This tradition of literary study came under repeated attack for dealing only with the 'contents' of literary works and ignoring all questions of language and style; and it declined in the 1960s as new theoretical agendas redefined the relations between anthropological and literary study (see STRUCTURALISM AND POST-STRUCTURALISM). Some of its concerns survive in the writings of the American critic Leslie Fiedler (1917–), and in the questions posed by the French anthropologist René Girard (1923–), whose studies of scapegoating and sacrificial victims have excited interest among students of dramatic tragedy.

N

NABOKOV, Vladimir Vladimirovich (1899–1977), Russian novelist, poet, and literary scholar. The son of a leading member of the Cadet party and of the Kerensky government, Nabokov had published only a small volume of poetry when his family left Russia for Germany in 1919. After studying French and Russian literature at Trinity College, Cambridge (1919–23), Nabokov lived in Berlin (1923–37) and Paris (1937–40), writing mainly in Russian, under the pseudonym 'Sirin'. In 1940 he moved to the USA, working as a lecturer at Wellesley College (1941–8) and as professor of Russian literature at Cornell University (1948–59). From then on all his novels were written in English. The outstanding success of his novel *Lolita* (USA, 1958) enabled him to give up teaching and devote himself fully to writing. From 1959 he lived in Montreux, in Switzerland, where he died.

Nabokov's reputation as one of the major, most original prose writers of the 20th cent., a stylist with extraordinary narrative and descriptive skill and a wonderful linguistic inventiveness in two languages, is based on his achievement in the novels *Mary* (1926), *King, Queen, Knave* (1928), *The Eye* (1930), *The Defence* (1930), *Glory* (1932), *Laughter in the Dark* (1932), *Despair* (1936), *Invitation to a Beheading* (1938), *The Gift* (1938), *The Real Life of Sebastian Knight* (1941), *Bend Sinister* (1947), *Lolita* (1955), *Pnin* (1957), *Pale Fire* (1962), *Ada* (1969), *Transparent Things* (1972), and *Look at the Harlequins!* (1974), and on several volumes of short stories. All his works first written in Russian were translated into English with his own collaboration, and the English novels into Russian. Nabokov's admiration for *Dickens, R. L. *Stevenson, and *Joyce, among English writing, and his unease with J. *Austen, can be seen in his *Lectures on Literature* (1980).

NAIPAUL, Shiva (1945–85), novelist and travel writer, born in Port of Spain and educated in Trinidad and at University College, Oxford, where he read classical Chinese. His first novel, *Fireflies* (1970), was set in Trinidad, as was *The Chip-Chip Gatherers* (1973), a sombre family drama in which Wilbert eventually inherits the small estate, business, and problems of his successful but mean father Egbert. *North of South* (1978) is an account of a journey through Africa. *Black and White* (1980) investigates a mass suicide in Guyana instigated by American religious fanatic Jim Jones, and *A Hot Country* (1983) is a novel set in a fictitious South American state, Cuyama, which much resembles Guyana. *Beyond the Dragon's Mouth* (1984), a collection of fictional and travel pieces, was published in 1984,

and *An Unfinished Journey* (1986) collects travel and personal memoirs, including an essay on his relationship with V. S. *Naipaul, 'My Brother and I'. Naipaul died suddenly of thrombosis in London.

NAIPAUL, Sir V(idiadhar) S(urajprasad) (1932–), novelist, born in Trinidad of a Brahman family, the son of a journalist. He was educated at Queen's Royal College, Port of Spain, and University College, Oxford. He settled in England, married in 1955, and embarked on a career of literary journalism. His first three books, *The Mystic Masseur* (1957), *The Suffrage of Elvira* (1958), and *Miguel Street* (short stories, 1959), are comedies of manners, all set in Trinidad. His next novel, *A House for Mr Biswas* (1961), also set in Trinidad, traces the fortunes of its mild hero (a portrait inspired by Naipaul's father) from birth to death; he progresses from the job of sign-writer to that of journalist, is trapped into marriage and almost absorbed by his wife's vast family, the Tulsis, but continues to bid for independence, symbolized by the house which he acquires shortly before his death. The novel describes the dissolution of a whole way of life, as the younger members of the family depart for new educational opportunities in Europe. *Mr Stone and the Knights Companion* (1963), his only novel set in London, was followed by *The Mimic Men* (1967), set on a fictitious Caribbean island and narrated by failed politician and visionary Ralph Singh. *A Flag on the Island* (1967) is a collection of short stories set in the West Indies and London. From this time Naipaul's work becomes more overtly political and pessimistic. *In a Free State* (1971, *Booker Prize) explores problems of nationality and identity through three linked narratives, all describing displaced characters—a servant from Bombay transported to Washington, a lost and angry West Indian youth in London, two whites in a hostile African state. *Guerrillas* (1975) is a portrait of political and sexual violence in the Caribbean; *A Bend in the River* (1979) is an equally horrifying portrait of emergent Africa. Naipaul's intense, broad, and predominantly melancholy experience of human nature in the modern world may also be seen in the travel books and works of political journalism which have provided a background for his fiction; these include *The Middle Passage* (1962), on the Caribbean; *An Area of Darkness* (1964), his highly controversial and critical account of India; *The Return of Eva Peron* (1980); *Among the Believers: An Islamic Journey* (1981); and *A Turn in the South* (1989), about evangelical Christianity in the southern states of the USA. *The Overcrowded Barracoon* (1972) is a collection of personal and political articles. Naipaul's recurrent themes of political violence, innate homelessness, and alienation inevitably give rise to comparisons with *Conrad. *The Enigma of Arrival* (1987), which shows a softening of mood and tone, is a semi-autobiographical novel describing a young Trinidadian's arrival in post-imperial England, and his sense of settling into a rural landscape which he had previously known only through literature and art: Naipaul himself, like his narrator, lived for many years in rural Wiltshire on a decaying estate. Naipaul was knighted in 1990. *A Way in the World,* a memoir, was published in 1994. He was awarded the *Nobel Prize in 2001. See also ANGLO-INDIAN LITERATURE; BLACK BRITISH LITERATURE; POST-COLONIAL LITERATURE.

NAIRNE, Carolina, Baroness, née Oliphant (1766–1845), the author of many spirited and well-known *Jacobite songs, including 'Will ye no come back again?' and 'Charlie is my darling'; also of humorous and pathetic ballads, such as 'The Laird of Cockpen' (suggested by an older song) and 'The Land o' the Leal'. She concealed her authorship during her lifetime, and her poems were collected and published as *Lays from Strathearn* in 1846.

Namancos, in Milton's *Lycidas,* 'Where the great vision of the guarded mount | Looks toward Namancos and Bayona's hold', is a place in Galicia, near Cape Finisterre, shown in *Mercator's Atlas of 1623. The castle of Bayona is shown near it. A line from the 'guarded mount' (St Michael's Mount in Cornwall) to Finisterre passes clear of Ushant.

Namby-Pamby, see PHILIPS, A.

NAMIER, Sir Lewis Bernstein (1888–1960), historian, born in Poland of a Jewish family; his father was a Roman Catholic convert. Namier came to England and was educated at the London School of Economics and Balliol College, Oxford; in 1913 he became a British subject and in 1931 professor of modern history at Manchester. His major works include *The Structure of Politics at the Accession of George III* (1929) and *England in the Age of the American Revolution* (1930). During the 1930s he became deeply involved with the plight of Jewish refugees and with Zionism, to which he devoted much energy. He was an admirer of *Freud, and stressed Freud's importance in historical and biographical science; *Berlin, in *Personal Impressions* (1980), gives a vivid account of his personality, explains his twofold reputation as a dazzling talker and a bore, and contrasts his 'desire to reduce both the general propositions and the impressions of historians to pellet-like "facts"' with the romantic, nationalist elements in his character.

Nancy, in Dickens's *Oliver Twist,* the fancy woman of Bill Sikes.

Nandy, John Edward, in Dickens's *Little Dorrit,* the father of Mrs Plornish.

NAPIER, John (1550–1617), laird of Merchiston, near Edinburgh, educated at St Andrews. A mathematician and inventor, he devised logarithms, the nature of which he explained in his *Mirifici Logarithmorum Canonis Descriptio* (1614). His *Rabdologia* (1617) explains the use of numerating rods ('Napier's bones') and metal plates for effecting multiplications and divisions—the earliest form of calculating machine. He also invented the present notation of decimal fractions.

NARAYAN, R(asipuram) K(rishnaswami) (1906–2001), Indian novelist writing in English; he was born in Madras, and educated at the Collegiate High School in Mysore, where his father was headmaster, then at Maharaja's College, Mysore. He worked (very briefly) as a teacher, then as a journalist, before publishing his first novel, *Swami and Friends* (1935), in which he created the imaginary small town of Malgudi, which he was to map out and populate in several succeeding novels, including *The Bachelor of Arts* (1937), *The English Teacher* (1945), *Mr Sampath* (1949), *The Financial Expert* (1952), *The Vendor of Sweets* (1967), *The Painter of Signs* (1977), *A Tiger for Malgudi* (1983), and *The Grandmother's Tale and Other Stories* (1993). His fictional world is peopled with characters—journalists, printers, professors, financial experts, lawyers, dreamers—portrayed with a gentle irony as they struggle to accommodate tradition with Western attitudes inherited from the British. G. *Greene, who recommended his first novel for publication, compared the tragi-comedy, pathos, and frequently disappointed aspirations of his characters to those of *Chekhov's, and commented that Narayan's particular comic gift flourished in 'the strong framework of social convention'. Narayan's other publications include short stories (*An Astrologer's Day and Other Stories,* 1947; *Lawley Road,* 1956; *A Horse and Two Goats,* 1970; *Malgudi Days,* 1982) and a memoir, *My Days* (1975). See ANGLO-INDIAN LITERATURE.

Narcissa, (1) in Pope's *Moral Essays* is Anne *Oldfield; (2) Roderick's love in Smollett's *Roderick Random;* (3) one of the persons mourned in Young's *Night Thoughts.*

narratology, the term applied since 1969 to the formal analysis of narratives. Although in principle applicable to ancient theories of storytelling such as *Aristotle's, the term is applied to the modern tradition, of which the Russian scholar Vladimir Propp's *Morphology of the Folktale* (1928) is taken to be the founding work. Narratology rests upon certain basic distinctions between what is narrated (e.g. events, characters, and settings of a story) and how it is narrated (e.g. by what kind of narrator, in what order, at what time). Different narratological approaches pursue each of these questions. Investigations into the narrated materials commonly seek the elementary units that are common to all narratives: Propp's work on Russian folk tales proposed that there were no more than 31 such basic elements or 'functions', and that they always appeared in the same order. Likewise, the French narratologist A. J. Greimas proposed that there are only six basic roles (or 'actants') in stories: subject, object, sender, receiver, helper, and opponent. This kind of folkloric analysis has no necessary interest in literary technique. On the other hand, studies of narration, that is, how stories are told, have an obvious relevance to literary fictions. In this field, there is an English-speaking tradition of narratology, originating in the theory and practice of H. *James, and codified in terms of narrative 'point of view' by his disciple P. *Lubbock in *The Craft of Fiction* (1921); other notable early contributions were E. M. *Forster's *Aspects of the Novel* (1927), and E. *Muir's *The Structure of the Novel* (1928). More convincing than these works was W. C. Booth's *The Rhetoric of Fiction* (1961), which introduced important new distinctions such as those between the real author and the 'implied author' of a novel, and between reliable and unreliable narrators. The most comprehensive analyses of the various kinds of possible narrator and narrative order appear in the works of the French narratologist Gérard Genette (1930–), especially his *Figures III* (1972; partly translated as *Narrative Discourse*, 1980).

Narrenschiff, see SHIP OF FOOLS.

NASH, Ogden (1902–71), American writer of sophisticated light verse, renowned for his puns, epigrams, elaborate rhymes, elaborate lack of rhymes, wildly asymmetrical lines, and other verbal fancies. His verse appeared in many collections from 1931 onwards.

NASH, Richard, 'Beau' (1674–1761), born at Swansea, educated at Carmarthen Grammar School and for a time at Jesus College, Oxford. He supported himself in London as a gamester, and went to Bath in 1705, where he established the Assembly Rooms, drew up a code of etiquette and dress, and became unquestioned autocrat of society. The gambling laws of 1740–5 deprived him of his source of income, and his popularity waned after 1745. In 1758 he was allowed 10 guineas a month by the corporation of Bath. *Goldsmith's life of Nash, published 1762, was probably written without personal knowledge of its subject, despite Goldsmith's hints to the contrary.

NASHE, Thomas (1567–1601), a sizar of St John's College, Cambridge. By 1588 he had settled in London. His first publication was a preface to Greene's *Menaphon*, 1589, surveying the follies of contemporary literature; he expanded this theme in *The Anatomie of Absurditie* later in the same year. His hatred of Puritanism drew him into the *Martin Marprelate controversy, but it is not clear which of the seven or more unascribed anti-Martinist pamphlets were his work. In 1592 Nashe replied to the savage denunciations of Richard Harvey, astrologer and brother of Gabriel *Harvey, with *Pierce Penniless His Supplica-

tion to the Divell, which he claimed was translated into French. In the same year he avenged Gabriel Harvey's attack on R. *Greene with *Strange Newes, of the Intercepting Certaine Letters*. A florid religious meditation, *Christs Teares over Jerusalem*, dedicated to Lady Elizabeth Carey, was published in 1593, and in the following year *The Terrors of the Night*, a discourse on dreams and nightmares, was dedicated to her daughter, to whom he may have acted as tutor for a time.

The Unfortunate Traveller: Or The Life of Jacke Wilton also appeared in 1594, described in the dedication to the earl of Southampton as 'being a cleane different vaine from other my former courses of writing'. It is a medley of picaresque narrative, literary parody, and mock-historical fantasy. Nashe returned to satire with *Have with You to Saffron-Walden: Or, Gabriell Harveys Hunt Is up* (1596), to which Harvey replied; in 1599 Archbishop Whitgift ordered that the works of both writers should be suppressed. Nashe's lost satirical comedy *The Isle of Dogs* also led to trouble with the authorities, and though it is not clear whether Nashe, like his collaborator *Jonson, had a spell in prison, he was forced to flee London for Great Yarmouth. *Nashes Lenten Stuffe* (1599), a mock encomium of the red herring (or kipper), includes a burlesque version of the story of *Hero and Leander. In 1600 *Summers Last Will and Testament* was published, though it had probably been written in the plague year of 1592–3, when the archbishop's household was removed to Croydon. Nashe had a share in Marlowe's *Dido, Queene of Carthage*, and probably other plays now lost. He was amusingly satirized as 'Ingenioso', a Cambridge graduate who lost favour with his patrons and turned to satire, in the three *Parnassus Plays* (1598–1606). *The Unfortunate Traveller* and the satirical works were much admired in the 20th cent. The entire works were definitively edited by R. B. *McKerrow in 1904–10 and revised with corrections and additions by F. P. Wilson in 1958; see also a life by C. Nicholl, *A Cup of News* (1984).

NASO, see OVID. The word means 'nose', to which Holofernes alludes in Shakespeare's *Love's Labour's Lost* (IV. ii).

Nasrudin, a semi-legendary Turkish sage and folk hero, around whose name has gathered a body of jokes, stories, and anecdotes. They have been collected and translated many times: for recent versions, see *The Pleasantries of the Incredible Mulla Nasrudin* (1968) and *The Subtleties of the Inimitable Mulla Nasrudin* (1973) by I. *Shah.

NATHAN, George Jean (1882–1958), American essayist, drama critic, and polemicist, co-founder in 1924 with H. L. *Mencken of the *American Mercury*, a lively monthly cultural magazine, of which he remained an editor until 1930. He published many collections of theatre criticism and essays, including *The Popular Theatre* (1918), *The Critic and the Drama* (1922), and

Art of the Night (1938), which show him as an early supporter of the works of *O'Neill.

Nathaniel, Sir, in Shakespeare's *Love's Labour's Lost*, a curate and friend to Holofernes.

National Anthem, the. The first recorded public performance of 'God Save the King' took place at Drury Lane Theatre on 28 Sept. 1745, during the excitement and alarm caused by the *Jacobite invasion of that year. It was an unannounced addition by the actors to the ordinary programme of the day. The score used on this occasion was prepared by *Arne, leader of the orchestra at the theatre and composer of *'Rule, Britannia'. The example set at Drury Lane was followed at other theatres and the song was soon very popular. It became customary about 1747 or 1748 to greet the king with it when he entered a place of public entertainment. In George III's reign it figured as a political battle-song in connection with the regency troubles and later during the dissensions aroused by the French Revolution. It was sung at the coronation banquet of George IV and the description of it as 'National Anthem' appears to have been adopted early in the 19th cent. Variant versions, imitations, and parodies have been very numerous; among the imitations may be mentioned the 'New National Anthem' written by *Shelley in 1819 after Peterloo, and the 'New National Anthem' of E. *Elliott, the Corn Law Rhymer (1830).

The remoter origin of 'God save the King' is obscure. Before being sung at Drury Lane, words and tune, with slight differences, had appeared in *Thesaurus Musicus*, a song collection published in 1744. There is good evidence that the song was originally written in favour of James II in 1688 (when the invasion by the prince of Orange was threatening) or possibly of Charles II in 1681; but the author is unknown. Various 17th-cent. tunes of the same rhythm more or less resemble that of 'God save the King'. The closest resemblance is that of a galliard composed by John *Bull in the early 17th cent. But this may be the keyboard setting of some folk tune or other well-known air of the time, and the tune of 'God save the King' may have been drawn directly from that original.

For a fuller treatment of the subject see Percy Scholes, *God save the King* (1942), on which the above article is based.

National Theatre, a three-auditorium complex on London's South Bank devoted to the spectrum of world drama. Initially proposed by a London publisher, Effingham Wilson, in 1848, the idea of a National Theatre Company only became a living reality at the Old Vic in 1963 under the direction of Laurence Olivier: its early successes included standard classics by Shakespeare, *Farquhar, *Chekhov, and *Shaw as well as new plays by Tom *Stoppard, Peter *Shaffer, and Peter *Nichols. In 1976 it moved into its South Bank home designed by Sir Denys Lasdun where, under the direction of Sir Peter *Hall, Sir Richard Eyre,

and Trevor Nunn, it has provided an eclectic mixture of world drama, new writing, and popular musicals. Its repertoire has ranged from *Aeschylus and *Sophocles to *Brecht and *O'Casey but it has achieved particular success with new plays including the David *Hare Trilogy, charting the decline of British institutions under Thatcherism, *The Madness of George III* by Alan *Bennett, *Arcadia* by Tom Stoppard, *Angels in America* by Tony Kushner, and *Closer* by Patrick Marber. It became officially known as the Royal National Theatre in October 1988.

naturalism, as a term of literary history, primarily a French movement in prose fiction and (to a lesser extent) the drama during the final third of the 19th cent., although it is also applied to similar movements or groups of writers in other countries (e.g. Germany, the USA) in the latter decades of the 19th and early years of the 20th cents. In France *Zola was the dominant practitioner of naturalism in prose fiction and the chief exponent of its doctrines. His novel *Thérèse Raquin* (1867), together with the *Goncourts' *Germinie Lacerteux* (1865), are considered as marking the beginnings of the movement; its most substantial and important achievement in fiction is the series of 20 novels written by Zola between 1871 and 1893 under the general title of *Les Rougon-Macquart*. Other writers who shared, in a greater or lesser degree, the ideas and aims of naturalism are *Daudet, *Maupassant and, in his early fiction, *Huysmans.

Broadly speaking, naturalism is characterized by a refusal to idealize experience and by the persuasion that human life is strictly subject to natural laws. The naturalists shared with the earlier realists the conviction that the everyday life of the middle and lower classes of their own day provided subjects worthy of serious literary treatment. These were to be rendered so far as possible without artificiality of plot and with scrupulous care for *documentation*, i.e. for the authenticity and accuracy of detail, thus investing the novel with the value of social history. Emphasis was laid on the influence of the material and economic environment on behaviour, and, especially in Zola, on the determining effects of physical and hereditary factors in forming the individual temperament.

Many of the naturalists wrote for the theatre, sometimes adapting their own fiction for stage presentation; these plays, and more especially those of the dramatist Henri Becque (1837–99), enlarged the scope of the movement, which was promoted in the Théâtre Libre (1887–94) of André Antoine. In Germany, the movement flourished from c.1885 until the 1890s, largely in the theatre, influenced both by *Ibsen (whose interest in heredity was easily explicable in naturalist terms) and by the Théâtre Libre, which visited Berlin in 1889; one of its principal exponents was *Hauptmann. See also REALISM.

Nature and Art, a romance by Elizabeth *Inchbald, published 1796, the story of two contrasted brothers,

William and Henry, and their equally contrasting sons. The story illustrates the wholesome effects of a natural and simple upbringing compared with the warping effects of civilization.

NAYLER, James (1616/17–60), a Quaker who had served in the Parliamentary army, converted by G. *Fox in 1651. He describes 'being at the plough' and hearing a voice telling him 'Get thee out from thy kindred' (*Saul's Errand to Damascus*, 1654). His gifts of eloquence and tenderness of heart won him many disciples, especially disaffected women, with whom he challenged Fox for the leadership. His entry into Bristol on a donkey in 1656 accompanied by followers shouting 'Hosannah' brought him before the House of Commons on a charge of blasphemy, for which he was cruelly punished and imprisoned in Bridewell. Though his schism had split the movement, his contrite release in 1659 brought reconciliation with Fox. He wrote pamphlets of striking beauty and depth, especially *Milk for Babes* (pub. 1661). Quaker history blamed Nayler's fall on the women surrounding him, particularly Martha Simmons, described by M. Brailsford in a life of Nayler (1927) as 'the villain of this piece', but recent scholarship has recognized Nayler's disciples as casualties of complex historical conditions which refused females parity as leaders. See P. Mack, *Visionary Women* (1992), P. Crawford, *Women and Religion in England 1500–1720* (1993), and S. Davies, *Unbridled Spirits* (1998).

NEALE, J(ohn) M(ason) (1818–66), educated at Trinity College, Cambridge, founder of the Cambridge *Camden Society. He was author of *The History of the Holy Eastern Church* (1847–73), and many hymns (some of them translations from Greek, medieval Latin, and Eastern sources) including 'O happy band of pilgrims', 'Art thou weary', and 'Jerusalem the Golden'; *Hymns Ancient and Modern* owes much to his inspiration.

NECKER, Mme, née Suzanne Curchod (1739–94), a Swiss woman, at one time engaged to *Gibbon; she became the wife of Jacques Necker, the French financier and statesman. She was prominent in French literary circles of the period preceding the revolution. Her daughter became Mme de *Staël.

Neckett, Mr, the sheriff's officer in Dickens's *Bleak House*, generally referred to as Coavinses, the name of the sponging-house which he keeps. He has three children, Tom, Emma, and Charlotte (known as 'Charley'), who becomes Esther Summerson's maid.

NEDHAM, or **NEEDHAM,** Marchamont (1620–78), journalist, and chief author of *Mercurius Britanicus* (1643–6), the arch-enemy of the Royalist *Mercurius Aulicus* of *Berkenhead. His subsequent professional career showed shifting loyalties, and he was several times imprisoned. In 1660, after some years of considerable power as editor of *Mercurius Politicus*, he fled to Holland, obtained a pardon, and returned to England, where he practised medicine and continued to write pamphlets. He was also the author of verses and a translation of *Selden's *Mare Clausum* (1652). His prose was powerful, and *Milton was not implausibly credited with some of his anonymous works. (See also NEWSPAPERS, ORIGINS OF.)

negative capability, a phrase coined by *Keats to describe his conception of the receptivity necessary to the process of poetic creativity, which draws on *Coleridge's formulation of 'Negative Belief' or 'willing suspension of disbelief'. In a letter to Benjamin Bailey (22 Nov. 1817) Keats wrote, 'If a Sparrow come before my Window I take part in its existence and pick about the Gravel', and a month later (22 Dec. 1817) he wrote to his brothers George and Thomas defining his new concept: '*Negative Capability*, that is when man is capable of being in uncertainties, Mysteries, doubts, without any irritable reaching after fact and reason—'. Keats regarded Shakespeare as the prime example of negative capability, attributing to him the ability to identify completely with his characters, and to write about them with empathy and understanding; he contrasts this with the partisan approach of *Milton and the 'wordsworthian or egotistical sublime' (Letter to Woodhouse, 27 Oct. 1818) of *Wordsworth. However, he was ambivalent about his own attitude, and sometimes expressed admiration for the Miltonic approach; Douglas Bush ('Keats and his Ideas', *English Romantic Poets*, ed. M. H. Abrams, 1960) writes, 'As artist he fluctuates—and is aware of his fluctuations—between belief in the poetic efficacy of a wise passiveness, and belief in the active pursuit of rational knowledge and philosophy.'

Négritude, a term used to denote a movement in literature that dates from the 1930s, and which derived its impetus from French-speaking African and Caribbean writers. It was a movement that sought to recover and define the richness of black cultural values in the face of the dominant values of European colonialism, and it emerged specifically as a protest against French colonial rule and the French policy of assimilation. Prominent amongst its members were the poet and essayist Léopold Sédar Senghor (1906–2001), who became, in 1960, the first president of the Republic of Senegal; Aimé Césaire (1913–   ), poet and dramatist from Martinique (*Cahier d'un retour au pays natal*, 1939; English trans., *Return to My Native Land*, 1968); and Léon Damas (1912–78), from French Guiana.

NEKRASOV, Nikolai Alekseyevich (1821–77), Russian poet and editor. His first poems were published in 1838. In 1840 his first collection *Dreams and Sounds* appeared, with little success, and he began work as a journalist. As an editor he showed extraordinary discernment. In 1846 he edited the *Petersburg Collection*, which included 'Poor Folk', the first work by *Dostoevsky to be published. From 1847 to 1866 he was editor of the leading review of the day, the

Contemporary, which in 1852 contained the first published work by *Tolstoy, *Childhood*, and also published *Turgenev, *Ostrovsky, and other major figures. His second collection, *The Poems of Nikolai Nekrasov* (1856), brought him great success, despite heavy censorship. In 1857 he visited London in an attempt to see *Herzen. After the closure of the *Contemporary* he was editor, from 1868 until his death, of the radical review *Notes of the Fatherland*, jointly with *Saltykov-Shchedrin. Nekrasov is considered the greatest of Russia's 'civic' poets: in his 1856 poetic dialogue, 'The Poet and the Citizen', the Citizen famously contends that 'You do not have to be a poet, l But you must be a citizen'; but Turgenev considered that 'poetry never so much as spent a night in his [Nekrasov's] verse'. In poetry his main theme is the life of the Russian peasant. His major works are the narrative poems *The Peddlers* (1861), *Red-Nosed Frost* (1862–3), *The Railway* (1864), *Who Is Happy in Russia?* (1865–77), and *Russian Women* (1871–2). *Red-Nosed Frost* appeared in a translation by J. Sumner Smith in 1886.

Nelly Dean, a character in E. Brontë's *Wuthering Heights*.

Nemesis of Faith, The, a novel by J. A. *Froude.

Nemo (1) the law-writer in Dickens's *Bleak House*; (2) Captain Nemo, in *Verne's *Twenty Thousand Leagues under the Sea*, commander of the submarine *Nautilus*.

NENNIUS (fl. *c*.830), the author or reviser of the *Historia Britonum*. He lived on the borders of Mercia in Brecknock or Radnor and was a pupil of Elfodd, bishop of Bangor (d. *c*.811). The 33 surviving manuscripts enshrine several versions: the north-west, the south-west, the Irish, and the English. It is a collection of notes, drawn from various sources including *Gildas and (perhaps indirectly) *Bede, on the history and geography of Britain, and is interesting for the account it purports to give of the historical *Arthur who, as *dux bellorum*, after Hengist's death led the Britons against the Saxons in 12 battles (including Mt Badon) which Nennius enumerates. It is one of the sources on which *Geoffrey of Monmouth drew for his *Historia Regum Britanniae*. A mixture of legend and history, it is characterized by pride in the Celtic people of Britain and interest in its topography. See A. Gransden, *Historical Writing in England c.550–c.1307* (1974), 5–12.

neo-classicism, in literature, the habit of imitating the great authors of antiquity (notably its poets and dramatists) as a matter of aesthetic principle; and the acceptance of the critical precepts which emerged to guide that imitation. Medieval writers had often used classical works for models, but *Petrarch in the 14th cent. was the first to do so because he considered it the only way to produce great literature; and where he led a host of later authors followed. The *epic, *eclogue,

*elegy, *ode, *satire, *tragedy, *comedy, and *epigram of ancient times all found imitators, first in Latin, then in the vernaculars, and eventually practice was succeeded by precept. At the beginning of the 16th cent. the recovery of the previously neglected *Poetics of Aristotle provoked an attempt to establish rules for the use of the ancient genres. The *Poetics* itself was repeatedly edited, translated, and supplied with commentaries, the most popular being the one by *Castelvetro (1570), and there also appeared a number of treatises on poetry, culminating in J. C. *Scaliger's controversial *Poëtice* (1561). These theoreticians imprisoned imitation within a rigid framework of rules, for which the flexibility of ancient practice offered little precedent. The most famous of their inventions was the observance of the dramatic *unities of time, place, and action, which won great support in France where a new generation of playwrights in the 1620s and 1630s was eager to attract a more educated public. A noisy battle over *Corneille's popular tragi-comedy *Le Cid* (1637), which was blamed for breaking the rules, ended in an acceptance of the unities, and during the next 30 years a succession of critics, the best known of whom was *Boileau, extended the scope of their prescriptions from drama to all other major genres.

Up to the last quarter of the 17th cent. neo-classicism had little influence in England. The imitation of classical models was less common than on the Continent and, except for *Jonson, no important writer paid strict attention to the rules humanist critics had formulated. But at that point, unsettled perhaps by the successes of their colleagues in France, playwrights responded to the urgings of *Rymer and began to take neo-classical theories more seriously. Translations and adaptations of Corneille and *Racine enjoyed some popularity. Dryden produced *All for Love* (1677) and Addison his *Cato* (1713), which has been called the only correct neo-classical tragedy in English; but the fashion was not to last.

The usual excuse for the rules was that they helped writers to be true to nature. *Pope wrote,

> Those RULES of old *discover'd*, not *devis'd*,
> Are *Nature* still, but *Nature methodiz'd*,

and implicit in his view was the assumption that 'nature' consisted in what was generally true. But this assumption, advanced first by Scaliger and echoed much later by Dr *Johnson, had never commanded unquestioning support. As early as the beginning of the 17th cent. *Cervantes had argued for the representation of true facts of an exceptional nature, even though they were implausible, and 100 years later it had become clear to everybody that extraordinary phenomena furnished literary material of considerable value. The scope of what could be regarded as natural was steadily growing, and simultaneously the difficulty *Homer's readers experienced in appreciating his poems made them aware of the fact that behaviour usual in one age could prove unacceptable in another. What is natural came to be seen no longer as an absolute, but as historically conditioned. What undermined neo-classicism most decisively however in the 18th cent. was the changing view of the goal of literary creation provoked by Boileau's translation (1674) of the pseudo-Longinian treatise of the *sublime. A cult of sublimity—greatness of conception and emotion—replaced the wish to produce a just representation of general reality, and the way to *Romanticism lay open.

In the context of art history, the term 'neo-classical' generally refers to the style and aesthetics of a somewhat later period (mid- to late 18th cent.), when an emphasis on the 'antique' ideals of harmony and grandeur (see WINCKELMANN) emerged in part as a reaction against the excesses of *baroque and the triviality of rococo.

Neoplatonism, a philosophical and religious system, combining Platonic ideas with oriental mysticism, which originated at Alexandria in the 3rd cent. and is especially represented in the writings of *Plotinus, Porphyry, and Proclus. This system of thought, which thanks to *Augustine left a deep mark on Christianity, combined in the 5th and 6th cents AD with survivals of *Gnosticism and persisted in this form through the Middle Ages. It experienced a notable revival in the 15th cent., associated with *Ficino, *Pico della Mirandola, *Agrippa, and *Paracelsus. The conglomeration of ideas found in the works of these writers extends well beyond Neoplatonism, but is often given that name, and it influenced literature in a number of distinct ways. (1) The 'Neoplatonic' theory of love rested on the beliefs that earthly beauty was an image of absolute beauty and that spiritual graces in a beloved were even more important than bodily ones. These beliefs find frequent expression in the poetry of the Renaissance and recur in *Shelley. (2) Belief in the existence of airy creatures that could be invisible, and that served or crossed mankind, appears in Dr *Dee's familiar, Prospero's Ariel in *The Tempest, or on a humorous level the sylphs of *The Rape of the Lock. (3) The attempt to bring together all systems of belief— Christian, Neoplatonist, Cabbalistic—that maintained the power of spirit over matter appears in poets like T. *Vaughan and in the writings of the *Cambridge Platonists. (4) There was the view that both Art and Nature are copies of the same supersensuous reality and that Art could be the better copy, a view that appealed to *Sidney and *Spenser.

neo-realism, a movement in the post-war Italian novel and film which may be seen as a continuation of *verismo. While its narratives were naturalistic on the surface, the works were imbued with a lyrical populism that was occasionally sentimental and even owed something to the style of films made under Fascism. As Fascism collapsed, the Resistance emerged as the theme of neo-realist novels by Beppe Fenoglio (1922–63), Elio Vittorini (1908–66), and the young

*Calvino, and of films by Rossellini, whose *Roma città aperta* (*Rome Open City*, 1945) is a classic of this genre. At the same time, neo-realism documented the lives of poor people in the underdeveloped south or struggling in northern cities: this strand is represented by the novels of Carlo Levi (1902–75) and *Pavese, and by the films of De Sica (e.g. *Bicycle Thieves*, 1948), Olmi, Rosi, and the young Visconti.

Nerissa, in Shakespeare's *The Merchant of Venice*, Portia's waiting-woman, who marries Gratiano.

NERUDA, Pablo (1904–73), the pen-name (adopted by deed poll in 1946, after the Czech poet Jan Neruda, 1834–91) of Chilean poet and diplomat Ricardo Eliecer Neftali Reyes, born in Parral, Chile, the son of a railwayman. He travelled widely in the diplomatic service from 1927 to 1938 (in south-east Asia and Spain), and after the Second World War (having joined the Communist Party in 1939) he visited the USSR, China, and eastern Europe. His poetry, which ranges from short, intense personal lyrics to odes, political meditations, and various autobiographical works, both in prose and verse, won him an international reputation, and, in 1971, the *Nobel Prize for literature. A political activist and in many ways the prototype of the committed poet, he supported the socialist president Allende, and was Chilean ambassador to Paris in 1970. He died in Santiago shortly after Allende's own death.

NERVAL, Gérard de (1808–55), French poet and prose writer, best known for his sonnet sequence *Les Chimères* (1854). He also produced a number of short stories, including 'Sylvie' (1853), a considerable amount of journalism, and an account of a journey to the Middle East, *Le Voyage en Orient* (1851). Much of his later life was dominated by his struggle against mental instability, of which he gives an account in *Aurélia* (1855). The deeply private, elusive, and visionary quality of much of his work exercised an influence over the adherents of both *Symbolism and *Surrealism.

NESBIT, E(dith) (1858–1924). She enjoyed as a girl the society of her sister Mary's friends, who included *Swinburne, the *Rossettis, and W. *Morris. Her husband Hubert Bland was a founder member of the *Fabian Society and a noted philanderer; after the failure of his health and business she was obliged to abandon her aspirations as a poet and write potboilers in order to support her family. She is remembered, however, for her children's books, tales of everyday family life sometimes mingled with magic. In 1898 her first stories about the young Bastables appeared with such success that she published three 'Bastable' novels in quick succession: *The Story of the Treasure-Seekers* (1899), *The Wouldbegoods* (1901), and *The New Treasure-Seekers* (1904). Other well-known titles with a lasting appeal include *Five Children and It* (1902), *The Phoenix and the Carpet* (1904), *The Railway Children* (1906), and *The Enchanted Castle* (1907).

Neville, Miss, a character in Goldsmith's *She Stoops to Conquer.*

New Age, the, a phrase and concept which became current in the 1960s ('the age of Aquarius', so called for astrological reasons). New Age thinking manifests itself in forms of Oriental mysticism, in yoga, Zen Buddhism, and the cult of the guru and the ashram: *Hesse's *Siddhartha* was adopted as a key text, as were the writings of Lebanese mystic Kahlil Gibran (1883–1931) and those of Carlos Castaneda (?1925–98), who explored shamanistic practices and the use of drugs (peyote) in Mexico through the wisdom of 'Don Juan'. *Tolkien's *fantasies were also admired, and produced many imitations. The New Age found a home in Britain in ecological and spiritual communities (Findhorn, Arthurian cults associated with Glastonbury), and in the USA (notably in California) in various groups seeking spiritual and psychological self-help and self-realization. *The New Age* was also the title of a periodical edited by A. R. *Orage (1907–22), whose interest in *Gurdjieff has a connection with these later spiritual movements. A. *Huxley and *Isherwood may also be seen as links in a chain of continuing interest in heightened states of consciousness.

New Apocalypse, the, a group of writers who flourished briefly as a movement in the 1940s, united by a romantic reaction against what they saw as the 'classicism' of *Auden; it expressed itself in wild, turbulent, and at times surreal imagery. Their work appeared in three anthologies, *The New Apocalypse: An Anthology of Criticism,* Poems and Stories (1940), edited by James Findlay Hendry (1912–   ); *The White Horseman: Prose and Verse of the New Apocalypse* (1941), edited by Hendry and Henry Treece (1911–66), with an introduction by George Sutherland Fraser (1915–80), and *The Crown and the Sickle* (1945), also edited by Hendry and Treece. They described themselves as 'anti-cerebral', claimed a 'large, accepting attitude to life', invoked the name of D. H. *Lawrence, and approved of Dylan *Thomas; G. *Barker and V. *Watkins also were associated with the movement.

New Atalantis, The, see MANLEY, Mrs.

New Atlantis, The, an unfinished work by F. *Bacon, posthumously published at the end of a volume containing his *Sylva Sylvarum; or A Natural Historie* (1627; some copies dated 1626). William Rawley, Bacon's chaplain and literary executor, called it a 'fable' devised to describe 'a college instituted for the interpreting of nature and the producing of great and marvellous works for the benefit of men, under the name of Salomon's House, or the College of the Six Days' Works'—alluding to the biblical account of the Creation. A hybrid, it begins with the narrative of a sea voyage in the Pacific, in which a ship gets blown off course into unknown waters near Peru, and lands on an island resembling the lost island of Atlantis, as described by *Plato in the *Timaeus* and *Critias.* A native explains to the travellers how a King Solamona had reigned there 'about 1900 years ago', and had set up a scientific research institute with the goal of discovering 'the knowledge of causes and secret motions of things; and the enlarging of the bounds of human empire, to the effecting of all things possible'. The 'Father' or director of the institute describes a wide range of laboratories for physical experiments at low temperatures, for conservation of food, medical research, biology and chemistry, optics and acoustics, each with the appropriate technologies. He also describes the personnel, hierarchically divided: collectors of scientific information, experimenters, theorists, and philosophers. The whole work expressed Bacon's forward-looking belief that scientific research could flourish only as a collective pursuit, and its vision had an inspiring effect in the mid-17th cent., acknowledged by those associated with the *Royal Society such as Robert Hooke, W. *Petty, *Evelyn, *Sprat, and *Glanvill.

NEWBERY, John (1713–67), publisher and bookseller, who established himself in 1744 in St Paul's Churchyard, and was one of the earliest and best-known publishers of children's books. He produced and partly wrote many books of riddles, fables, stories, etc. *Goldsmith was one of his authors, and may have written the much-imitated *Goody Two-Shoes* for him: he contributed his *Chinese Letters* (later *The Citizen of the World*) to Newbery's *Public Ledger* (1760). Newbery also published *Smart, who married one of his step-daughters. He was a friend of Dr *Johnson, and appears as 'Jack Whirler' in the *Idler;* he features as 'the philanthropic bookseller' in *The Vicar of Wakefield.* He also ran a profitable business in patent medicines. See *John Newbery and His Successors 1740–1814: A Bibliography* (1973). (See CHILDREN'S LITERATURE.)

NEWBOLT, Sir Henry John (1862–1938), barrister, poet, and man of letters, educated at Clifton and Corpus Christi College, Oxford, remembered principally for his rousing patriotic nautical ballads, which include 'Drake's Drum', published in *Admirals All and Other Verses* (1897). His other collections include lyrics and satires, and he also published novels, short stories, and *A Naval History of the War, 1914–18* (1920). He was benevolent and active in public life, and served on many committees, including that of the *Royal Literary Fund.

NEWBY Percy Howard (1918–97), broadcaster and novelist, born in Sussex. He served as stretcher-bearer and then as a lecturer in Egypt during the Second World War and his first two novels, *A Journey to the Interior* (1945) and *Agents and Witnesses* (1947), draw on his wartime experiences and broad knowledge of Egyptian society. Other works include *A Step to Silence* (1952), *The Retreat* (1953), *Something to Answer for* (1968, which won the first *Booker Prize), and *Feelings*

Have Changed (1981), which gives an insight into his years with the Third Programme of the *BBC.

NEWCASTLE, Margaret Cavendish, duchess of (1623–73), daughter of Sir Thomas Lucas, the second wife of William Cavendish (below), whom she met in Paris during his exile. Her first volume of verse, *Poems and Fancies* (1653), which displays her interest in chemistry and natural philosophy, was followed by many other works, including plays, letters, and an affectionate, vivid, and informal biography of her husband (1667). Dismissed as 'mad, conceited and ridiculous' by *Pepys and as 'airy, empty, whimsical and rambling' by *Evelyn's wife, she was nevertheless praised (and influenced) by *Hobbes, and both *Lamb and V. *Woolf wrote of her with sympathy. Her intellectual curiosity was omnivorous, and she was one of the first women to attend a meeting of the *Royal Society. Her *autobiography, *A True Relation of My Birth, Breeding and Life*, was appended to her collection of fictions, *Nature's Pictures* (1656): here she diplomatically dismissed her writing as 'scribbling' but justified her forwardness in writing her own life on the grounds that 'Caesar, Ovid and many more' had done so. She dressed eccentrically, and regarded the female intelligence as distinguished by its fantastical quality. See E. Graham *et al.* (eds.) *Her Own Life* (1989) and *Mad Madge* (2003) by Katie Whitaker.

NEWCASTLE, William Cavendish, first duke of (1592–1676), husband of Margaret Cavendish (above). He supported the king generously during the Civil War, and from 1644 lived abroad, often in much poverty, until the Restoration. He was the author of several poems and plays, collaborating in the latter with *Shirley, whose patron he was, and with *Dryden and *Shadwell.

Newcomes, The, a novel by *Thackeray, published in numbers 1853–5.

The story, told by Arthur Pendennis, is concerned with the descendants of a self-made man, Thomas Newcome. His eldest son, Colonel Thomas Newcome, is a simple, unworldly soldier, who has lived most of his life in India. In contrast, his half-brothers Hobson and Brian are wealthy and pretentious. Colonel Newcome is a widower, and his only son Clive is sent home to England to be educated. When Clive is almost grown up, his father returns from India, and indulgently allows him to become an art student. Clive loves his cousin Ethel, daughter of Sir Brian Newcome, but Ethel's brother Barnes and her grandmother Lady Kew intend her to make a grand marriage. Ethel is intelligent and independent-minded, but finds it difficult to fight the pressures of the marriage-market; she allows herself to become engaged first to her cousin, Lord Kew, and, after that match is broken off, to Lord Farintosh. The disastrously unhappy marriage of Barnes, who treats his wife so badly that she runs away with a former admirer, Jack Belsize, makes Ethel

decide that she will not marry at all, but will devote herself to her brother's children. Meanwhile Clive has been manœuvred into marriage to a pretty, superficial girl, Rosey Mackenzie. When Colonel Newcome's fortune is lost with the failure of the Bundelcund Bank, he and Clive and Rosey are reduced to extreme poverty, and Rosey's mother makes life so intolerable for the Colonel with her accusations and reproaches that he finally takes refuge from her by becoming a pensioner in the Grey Friars almshouse, where he dies. Rosey has also died, and Thackeray allows the reader to assume that Clive and Ethel will get married. Certain aspects of Clive's character were suggested by *Leighton, whom Thackeray met in Rome.

New Country, an anthology of prose and verse published 1933, edited by M. *Roberts, with contributions by *Auden, *Spender, *Day-Lewis, *Empson, *Isherwood, *Upward, and R. *Warner. Its tone was highly political, verging on the revolutionary: Roberts wrote in his preface, 'It is time that those who would conserve something which is still valuable in England began to see that only a revolution can save their standards.' A collection with many of the same contributors, *New Signatures*, also edited by Roberts, had appeared in 1932.

New Criticism, an important movement in American literary criticism in the period 1935–60, characterized by close attention to the verbal nuances of lyric poems, considered as self-suffiicient objects detached from their biographical and historical origins. In reaction against the then dominant routines of academic literary history, the New Critics insisted that a poem should not be reduced to its paraphrased 'content', but understood in its own terms as a complex unity of verbal ironies, ambiguities, and paradoxes. They repudiated what they called the 'extrinsic' approaches to poetry—historical, psychological, or sociological—and cultivated an 'intrinsic' understanding of the actual 'words on the page', while defending poetry as a richer form of knowledge than that offered by scientific abstraction.

The early phase of the New Critical campaign was led by Southern poets and university teachers: J. C. *Ransom and his former student Allen *Tate, along with R. P. *Warren and Cleanth *Brooks, editors of the *Southern Review* (1935–42). The name applied to this movement comes from the title of Ransom's book *The New Criticism* (1941), which surveys the critical work of T. S. *Eliot, I. A. *Richards, and W. *Empson in Britain, from which the New Critics clearly derived their inspiration. While Ransom and Tate formulated the theoretical principles, Brooks and Warren, notably in their textbook *Understanding Poetry* (1938), applied them to the teaching of literature in universities. More marginal contributions to the cause came from R. P. *Blackmur (*The Double Agent*, 1935) and Y. *Winters (*Primitivism and Decadence*, 1937).

From 1939, when Ransom founded the *Kenyon Review* and Brooks published his *Modern Poetry and the Tradition*, the New Criticism made important headway in replacing 'extrinsic' approaches with critical analysis in the universities; notably at Yale, where a second wave of New Critical theory was represented by René Wellek and Austin Warren's *Theory of Literature* (1949) and by W. K. Wimsatt's *The Verbal Icon* (1954). The latter work includes essays written with M. C. Beardsley on the critical 'fallacies' involved in judging a work according to its author's intentions (see INTENTIONAL FALLACY) or its readers' impressions. In this period, the most celebrated work of 'applied' New Criticism was Brooks's *The Well Wrought Urn* (1947).

By the late 1950s, New Criticism had become an academic orthodoxy which younger critics found to be not only inapplicable to genres other than lyric poetry but narrow in its exclusion of social and historical dimensions of literature. Nonetheless, some of its methods and strictures have survived as essential precautions against clumsy misreadings of poems.

NEWDIGATE, Sir Roger (1719–1806), educated at Westminster School and University College, Oxford, MP successively for Middlesex and Oxford University, and founder of the Newdigate Prize at Oxford for English verse (1805).

Newgate Calendar, The, published about 1773 in 5 vols, recording notorious crimes from 1700 to that date. Similar compilations appeared in the next 50 years under varying titles, including *The Malefactor's Register* (1779); Andrew Knapp and William Baldwin, attorneys-at-law, issued *Criminal Chronology* (1809), *The Newgate Calendar* (1824–6), and *The New Newgate Calendar* (1826). All the Newgate Calendars began in 1700 and they continued until before or a little after 1820. Plots derived from Newgate Calendars appear in novels by *Ainsworth (*Jack Sheppard* and *Rookwood*), *Bulwer-Lytton (**Pelham* and **Eugene Aram*), *Fielding (**Jonathan Wild*), *Godwin (**Caleb Williams*), and in *Hood's poem 'The Dream of Eugene Aram'. See also Thackeray's **Catherine* and Dickens's **Oliver Twist*. *Celebrated Trials*, attributed to *Borrow, is a selection of trials from about 1413 to 1825. See Rayner Heppenstall, *Reflections on the Newgate Calendar* (1975).

Newgate Novel, see HISTORICAL FICTION.

New Grub Street, a novel by *Gissing, published 1891.

In this work Gissing depicts the struggle for life, the jealousies, and intrigues of the literary world of his time, and the blighting effect of poverty on artistic endeavour. The main theme is the contrast of the career of Jasper Milvain, the facile, clever, selfish, and unscrupulous writer of reviews (who accepts the materialistic conditions of literary success), with those of more artistic temperaments. Among these are Edwin Reardon, the author of two fine works, who is hampered by poverty and by the lack of sympathy of his worldly wife, and the generous Harold Biffen, a poor scholar, the author of a work of 'absolute realism in the sphere of the ignobly decent'. The literary world is presented in a multitude of characters, of which one of the best is the learned pedant Alfred Yule, rendered rancorous and sardonic by constant disappointment. Jasper is attracted to Yule's daughter and assistant Marian, who passionately loves him; but he proposes to her only when she inherits a legacy of £5,000. When this legacy proves not to be forthcoming, he shabbily withdraws, and marries Amy Reardon, the young widow of Edwin, whom failure and his wife's desertion have driven to an early grave. The sombre story ends with Jasper's success, the triumph of self-advertisement over artistic conscience.

New Historicism, a term applied to a trend in American academic literary studies in the 1980s that emphasized the historical nature of literary texts and at the same time (in contradistinction from 'old' historicisms) the 'textual' nature of history. As part of a wider reaction against purely formal or linguistic critical approaches such as the *New Criticism and *deconstruction, the New Historicists, led by Stephen Greenblatt, drew new connections between literary and non-literary texts, breaking down the familiar distinctions between a text and its historical 'background' as conceived in previous historical forms of criticism. Inspired by *Foucault's concepts of *discourse and power, they attempted to show in detail how literary works are entangled in the power relations of their time, not as secondary 'reflections' of any coherent world-view but as active participants in the continual remaking of meanings. New Historicism is less a system of interpretation than a set of shared assumptions about the relationship between literature and history, and an essayistic style that often develops general reflections from a startling historical or anthropological anecdote. Greenblatt's books *Renaissance Self-Fashioning* (1980) and *Shakespearean Negotiations* (1988) are the exemplary models. Other scholars of Renaissance (or 'early modern') culture associated with him include Jonathan Goldberg, Stephen Orgel, and Louis Montrose. The term has been applied to similar developments in the study of *Romanticism, such as the work of Jerome McGann and Marjorie Levinson. While American New Historicism, following Foucault, tends to argue that literary dissent is harmlessly contained by 'power', the otherwise similar movement in Britain known as 'cultural materialism' parts company with it on this point, insisting that no ruling authority can neutralize every form of cultural subversion. The cultural materialists, such as Jonathan Dollimore and Alan Sinfield, although indebted to Foucault, are more closely aligned with *Marxist literary criticism, notably through the work of R. *Williams.

New Inn, The, or *The Light Heart*, a comedy by *Jonson, performed in 1629 by the King's Men, printed 1631.

Frances, the young Lady Frampul, invites some lords and gentlemen to make merry at the New Inn at Barnet. One of the guests, Lord Beaufort, falls in love with, and is promptly married to, the son of the innkeeper, who has been dressed up as a girl, while Frances falls in love with Lovel, a melancholy gentleman staying at the inn. In a succession of discovered identities it is learnt that the innkeeper's son really is a girl and, moreover, Frances's sister Laetitia; that the innkeeper is Frances's long-lost father; and that the son's old Irish nurse is the father's long-lost wife and Frances's mother. Jonson records in his dedication that the play was hissed at its first performance.

New Lines (1956), an anthology edited by R. *Conquest, containing work by himself, E. *Jennings, John Holloway (1920–   ), *Larkin, *Gunn, *Amis, *Enright, *Davie, and J. *Wain, poets associated with the *Movement. In his introduction Conquest attacked obscure and over-metaphorical poetry, presenting the claims of 'rational structure and comprehensible language'. New Lines Volume II (1963) added other poets including *Thwaite, *Scannell, and G. *MacBeth.

NEWMAN, Andrea (1938–   ), novelist and television writer, born in Dover, and educated at London University. Her early novels, acclaimed for their frank treatment of women's lives and needs, include A Share of the World (1964), Mirage (1965), The Cage (1966), Alexa (1968), Three into Two Won't Go (1967, filmed by Peter *Hall, 1969), and A Bouquet of Barbed Wire (1969). She has also written many successful TV series and adaptations from her own work, featuring byzantine and carefully patterned plots of sexual intrigue, and stressing the amorality of the demands of the erotic life.

NEWMAN, Ernest, see MUSIC, LITERATURE OF.

NEWMAN, John Henry (1801–90), educated privately at Ealing and at Trinity College, Oxford. He became a fellow of Oriel, where he came in contact with *Keble and *Pusey and later with R. H. *Froude. In 1828 he was presented to the vicarage of St Mary's, Oxford, where his 4 o'clock Sunday sermons attracted much attention. In 1832 he went to the south of Europe with Froude, and with him in Rome wrote much of the *Lyra Apostolica; 'Lead, kindly Light', which appeared in this collection, was composed during a passage from Palermo to Marseilles in 1833. In the same year he resolved with William Palmer (1803–85), Froude, and A. P. Perceval (1799–1853) to fight for the doctrine of apostolic succession and the integrity of the Prayer Book, and began Tracts for the Times (see OXFORD MOVEMENT). He was moving slowly towards the Roman Catholic Church, and in 1841 his celebrated Tract XC, on the compatibility of the Articles with Catholic theology, roused great opposition and brought the Tractarians under official ban. He retired to Littlemore in 1842, where he adopted a semi-monastic way of life;

he had always favoured celibacy and argued in its defence. In 1843 he resigned the living of St Mary's, preaching his last sermon there in September of that year, and in 1845 he joined the Church of Rome, a move which profoundly shocked many of his fellow Tractarians, caused a rift with Keble and Pusey, and isolated him from his old Oxford life. He went to Rome in 1846 and was ordained; on his return in 1847 he established the Oratory in Birmingham. He was in Ireland as rector of the new Catholic University in Dublin, 1854–8; his lectures and essays on university education appeared in various forms from 1852, and finally as The Idea of a University Defined and Illustrated (1873). In these he maintained that the duty of a university is instruction rather than research, and to train the mind rather than to diffuse useful knowledge; he also defended theological teaching and the tutorial system. In 1864 appeared his Apologia pro Vita Sua, in answer to C. *Kingsley, who had remarked in Macmillan's Magazine, misrepresenting Newman, that Newman did not consider truth a necessary virtue. The Apologia came out serially, and was not so entitled until it appeared in volume form. It is an exposition of his spiritual history, written with much sincerity and feeling, which also displays his formidable powers of argument. It made a profound impression on many who did not share his religious convictions, including G. *Eliot (who said it had 'breathed much life' into her), and is now recognized as a literary masterpiece. His poem The Dream of Gerontius (later set to music by *Elgar) appeared in the Month in 1865, and in book form in 1866; it is a vision of a just soul leaving the body at death, with choruses of angels, demons, etc., and includes the well-known hymn 'Praise to the Holiest in the height'. In 1870 Newman published The Grammar of Assent, an examination of the nature of belief, which argues that we reach certainties not through logic but through intuitive perception; the real universe is not logical, and the premisses of logic are not realities but assumptions. In 1879 Newman was created a cardinal.

Newman also published two novels, both anonymously. Loss and Gain (1848) gives a vivid portrait of the religious ferment of Oxford at the period of the Oxford movement; his protagonist, Charles Reding, undergraduate son of a clergyman, is gradually drawn towards the Roman Catholic Church, despite the efforts of friends, teachers, and advisers, many of whom are drawn with satiric wit; the absurdities and weaknesses of the opposition are set against the loneliness and sacrifice involved in Reding's conversion. Callista (1856), a less interesting work, describes the persecution and martyrdom of a Christian convert, the sculptor Callista, in the 3rd cent. Newman also published many volumes of sermons, lectures, lives of saints, etc. Although he himself argued that most of his writing was prompted by occasion and duty, and that he found the process of writing painful 'like gestation or childbirth', many of his works have long outlived the occasions that prompted them, and remain a powerful intellectual and emotional influence. There is a life by Ian Ker (1988).

New Monthly Magazine (1814–84), a periodical founded by *Colburn in opposition to the *Jacobin *Monthly Magazine*, whose 'political poison' it attacked over many years. Under T. *Campbell, who took over the editorship in 1821, it became more literary in interest. Colburn's tendency to promote his own publications became less apparent, and much literary work of distinction appeared. *Talfourd wrote well on *Wordsworth, *Lamb, *Keats, and others; and among other distinguished editors were *Bulwer-Lytton (for three stormy years), *Hood, and *Ainsworth.

NEWNES, Sir George (1851–1910), publisher and magazine proprietor, who founded *Tit-Bits* in 1881, and in 1890, with his old school friend W. T. *Stead, the *Review of Reviews*. Stead took over the latter, and Newnes proceeded to found the *Strand Magazine* and other publications, including the liberal daily the *Westminster Gazette* (1893).

New Review, (1) a literary review edited by Archibald Grove from 1889 to 1894, and then, with much éclat, by W. E. *Henley, from 1895 to 1897, who serialized H. G. *Wells's *The Time Machine* (1895), A. Morrison's *A Child of the Jago* (1896), and H. James's *What Maisie Knew* (1897), and published poetry by *Verlaine, *Kipling, R. L. *Stevenson, and others. (2) The successor to the *Review*, edited from 1974 to 1979 by Ian *Hamilton.

newsbooks, or **diurnalls,** the successors of the *corantos in the evolution of the newspaper. Newsbooks consisting of one printed sheet (eight pages) and later of two printed sheets (16 pages) were issued during the period 1641–54, then gave place to the *Oxford* (later *London*) *Gazette*. (See also GAZETTE; NEWSPAPERS, ORIGINS OF; BERKENHEAD; MUDDIMAN; and NEDHAM.)

News Chronicle, see DAILY NEWS.

News from Nowhere, a utopian socialist fantasy by W. *Morris, first published in *Commonweal*, Jan.–Oct. 1890, in volume form 1891.

The narrator falls asleep in the 'shabby London suburb' of Chiswick, after an evening at the Socialist League spent discussing the Morrow of the Revolution, and wakes in the future, to find London and its surroundings transformed into a communist paradise where men and women are free, healthy, and equal, the countryside reclaimed from industrial squalor, and money, prisons, formal education, and central government abolished. In a lengthy conversation with the old historian Hammond, he learns of the struggles and bloodshed (which took place in 1952) that achieved this happy state. There is a characteristic Morris stress on the beauty of the new craftsmanship in comparison with the shoddiness of the 19th cent., and a powerful poetic evocation of a journey up the Thames through the restored landscape. At the close he fades back into the past, inspired by the vision of what he has seen and the need to work for its fulfilment. *News from Nowhere* was in part a critical response to *Bellamy's *Looking Backward*, a utopian portrait of a state socialist future dominated by machinery.

newsletters, a term specially applied to the manuscript records of parliamentary and court news, sent twice a week to subscribers from the London office of *Muddiman in the second half of the 17th cent.

New Society, a weekly periodical founded in 1962, edited by Timothy Raison, 1962–8, then by Paul Barker, and merged with the *New Statesman* in 1988. It covered the social sciences, social policy, documentary reportage, and the arts, and reviewed books of a wide range of interest.

Newsome, Chad, a leading character in H. James's *The Ambassadors*.

newspapers, origins of. The direct ancestors of newspapers devoted to English news were the Dutch *corantos, newsbooks dealing with foreign events. The first to appear in English was a single-sheet publication, *The New Tydings out of Italie Are Not Yet Com* (Amsterdam, 2 Dec. 1620), followed by a second number, *Corrant out of Italy, Germany &c* (Amsterdam, 23 Dec. 1620), printed by Joris Veseler for Dutch map-engraver Pieter van der Keere. The first English weekly of home news appeared in Nov. 1641 (*Heads of Severall Proceedings in This Present Parliament*), shortly followed by various other publications, mostly eight pages, e.g. Samuel Pecke's *A Perfect Diurnall*, Colling's *Kingdomes Weekly Intelligencer*, *Berkenhead's *Mercurius Aulicus* edited from the Royalist headquarters in Oxford, *Mercurius Civicus*, which was the first to be illustrated with woodcuts, and, perhaps the most popular, *Mercurius Britanicus*, edited by Thomas Audley and the most professional journalist of the period, *Nedham. Decreasingly efficient censorship and the stirring political climate stimulated demand for news, and by 1645 fourteen papers were on sale in English in London, including Dillingham's *Moderate Intelligencer*. In 1647 appeared the pro-Royalist *Mercurius Pragmaticus*, edited by Nedham, *Cleveland, and the minor poet Samuel Sheppard: in 1648 the *Moderate*, edited by chief censor Gilbert Mabbott, became the first paper consistently to preach a radical programme. This period of rapid journalistic expansion also saw the birth of many unlicensed, short-lived, and counterfeit newsbooks, as well as the publication of literally thousands of pamphlets (see PAMPHLETEERING, ORIGINS OF). The style of the newsbooks ranges from the baldly informative, through attempts at non-controversial objectivity, to the colourful, scurrilous, and highly polemical; Colling's prose was perhaps the most consciously literary, and his paper contains the only Interregnum newspaper reference to *Chaucer yet discovered. The thirst for information introduced many new readers to familiarity with the printed word and created a new class of professional journalist: the newsbooks introduced many of the ingredients of modern journalism, such as features, fillers, advertising, human-interest items, as well as news and political argument. This vigorous proliferation came to a sudden end in Sept. 1649 when Parliament, irritated by the onslaughts of both radical pamphleteers and Royalist mercuries, and anxious about public reaction to the massacre at Drogheda, passed a stringent printing law with heavy fines which effectively silenced all the licensed weeklies, while authorizing two new papers, one to deal with army news, the other with news from Westminster. Both were predictably cautious, as were other new publications that slowly surfaced, and a period of press docility followed, leaving Nedham with a virtual monopoly of information in his official 16-page *Mercurius Politicus* and its close relation the *Publik Intelligencer* (1650–60): Nedham, having offended various shades of political opinion, fled to Holland in 1660. His place was taken by *Muddiman, who started his career as spokesman for the revived monarchy in 1659 with the *Parliamentary Intelligencer*, later *Kingdomes Intelligencer*. In 1665 he founded the *Oxford Gazette*, the first real newspaper. (See GAZETTE, also L'ESTRANGE.) See J. Frank, *The Beginnings of the English Newspaper 1620–1660* (1961).

New Statesman, a weekly journal of politics, art, and letters, originally planned as an organ of the *Fabian Society, socialist in standing but independent in party. It was first published in 1913 with Clifford Sharp as editor, J. C. *Squire as literary editor, and the *Webbs and G. B. *Shaw as regular contributors. The journal, which merged with *New Society in 1988, has maintained its policy of 'dissent, of scepticism, of inquiry, of nonconformity' under subsequent editors, who include Kingsley Martin (1931–60), John Freeman (1961–5), P. *Johnson (1965–70), R. H. S. Crossman (1970–2), Anthony Howard (1972–8). Among other writers connected with the journal have been J. M. *Keynes, L. *Woolf, G. D. H. *Cole, Raymond Mortimer, J. B. *Priestley, and V. S. *Pritchett.

NEWTON, Sir Isaac (1642–1727), the only child of a humble family from Woolsthorpe, near Grantham. His career was uneventful; he was attached to Trinity College, Cambridge, from 1661 to 1696; the rest of his life was spent in London as master of the mint and president of the *Royal Society, being knighted in 1705. Newton was unmarried and averse to luxury. He had few friends, but was not intellectually isolated; his vast correspondence kept together a band of dedicated disciples, some of whom were used as intermediaries in his debates with philosophical adversaries such as *Leibniz. Newton's intellect was quite as formidable as his flatterers maintained. Modern scholarship has not seriously affected his stature in the fields of mathematics, dynamics, celestial mechanics, astronomy, optics, natural philosophy, or cosmology. We now appreciate more fully the extent of his dedication to theology, biblical chronology, prophecy, and alchemy. In these latter spheres, Newton relates to the *Cambridge Platonists, especially More and Cudworth. Newtonianism was based on just three major works by Newton: *Philosophiae Naturalis Principia Mathematica* (1687), the *Opticks* (1704), and *Arithmetica Universalis* (1707). Newton's ideas were diffused through popularizations such as Henry Pemberton's *View of Sir Isaac Newton's Philosophy* (1728). Newtonianism was the dominant philosophy of the *Enlightenment, influencing all fields of science, and finding its way into the poetry of *Pope, J. *Thomson, and E. *Young, but eventually producing a reaction from *Goethe and *Blake. The latter could not have known from his public reputation that Newton had written more than two million words on alchemy; he was as steeped in the hermetic tradition as themselves. F. *Bacon and Newton were fused together to become the twin deity of English science in the 19th cent. under the banner 'inductive philosophy'.

NEWTON, John (1725–1807), an evangelical minister who went to sea as a boy and worked in the slave trade. His *An Authentic Narrative* (1764) gives a vivid picture of his ordeals and slowly growing doubts about the morality of his occupation. He became curate of Olney in 1764 and with *Cowper (on whom his powerful faith and at times overbearing personality had a profound influence) wrote *Olney Hymns* (1779). His *Journal* for 1750–4 was edited by B. Martin and M. Spurrell (1962). See HYMNS.

New Verse, a little magazine edited 1933–9 by its founder G. *Grigson. It included work by *Auden, *MacNeice, G. *Barker, *Empson, R. *Fuller, and the young *Ewart, and attacked, among other objects, the drowsy poeticism of the preceding century and the 'self-righteous' *Scrutiny.

New Way to Pay Old Debts, A, a comedy by *Massinger, acted probably in 1625–6, published 1633, perhaps the best known of his works.

The play deals with the discomfiture of Sir Giles Overreach, a character based in part on the notorious extortioner Sir Giles Mompesson (1584–?1651). The cruel and rapacious Overreach, having got possession of the property of his prodigal nephew Frank Wellborn and reduced him to utter poverty, treats him contemptuously. Lady Allworth, a rich widow, to whose husband Wellborn had rendered important services, agrees to help him by pretending she is about to marry him. Overreach, deceived, changes his attitude and helps Wellborn. Tom Allworth, Lady Allworth's stepson and page to Lord Lovell, is in love with Overreach's daughter Margaret, who returns his love. Overreach is determined that his daughter shall marry Lord Lovell and become 'right honourable'. Lovell consents to help

Allworth to win Margaret, and a trick is played on Overreach by which he helps the marriage along, thinking that Lord Lovell is to be the bridegroom. Overreach goes mad on discovering the deceit and on finding that his claim to Wellborn's property cannot be maintained; he is sent to Bedlam. Wellborn receives a company in Lord Lovell's regiment, and Lovell marries Lady Allworth.

New Woman fiction, a term used to describe late 19th-cent. writings which foreground the ideas and actions of the 'New Woman', a phrase said to have been coined by *Ouida when responding to S. *Grand's article 'The New Aspects of the Woman Question', 1894. Grand's own novels, like *The Heavenly Twins* (1893) and *The Beth Book* (1897), include many elements associated with this agent and representative of social change: attacks on sexual double standards; demands for better employment and educational opportunities for women; frankness about matters like venereal disease and sex education; and questioning of traditional attitudes towards marriage and woman's place in the family and in relation to motherhood. The first example of the genre is probably O. *Schreiner's *Story of an African Farm* (1883). Other notable writers include E. F. *Brooke, M. *Caird, E. H. *Dixon, G. *Egerton, M. M. *Dowie. Many novelists also published journalism dealing with further related issues within the growing women's movement of the period, such as rational dress and *women's suffrage. *Ibsen and *Gissing (*The Odd Women*, 1893) are among the male writers who addressed similar themes: less sympathetic fictional treatments came from both men (G. *Allen, *The Woman Who Did*, 1895) and women, like E. Lynn *Linton.

New Writing, a book-periodical edited by J. *Lehmann, first published in 1936 and afterwards at approximately half-yearly intervals until 1940. It published imaginative writing, mainly by young authors (including *Spender, *Auden, *Isherwood, *Upward, *Anand, *Pritchett), and particularly those whose work was too unorthodox for the established magazines. New contributors were recruited from many parts of Europe, India, New Zealand, South Africa, China, and Russia. In 1940 it came out as *Folios of New Writing*; it became *New Writing and Daylight* in 1942 and this lasted until 1946. Meanwhile *Penguin New Writing* appeared in 1940, first as a monthly paperback and then in 1942 as a quarterly. It reprinted some work from *New Writing*, but relied more and more on new material. A series of 11 articles based on personal experience of the upheavals of war, all published in 1941, was especially notable. The title was revived in 1992 for an annual anthology of new work, initiated by the British Council's literature department: the first volume was edited by Malcolm *Bradbury and Judy Cooke, and it and subsequent issues have contained work by established writers and new names.

New Yorker, an American weekly magazine founded in 1925 by Harold Ross (1892–1951). It is sophisticated, satirical, and urbane, and although famed for its humour has also published distinguished articles of reportage, such as, notably, 'Hiroshima' by John Hersey (1914–93), which occupied an entire issue in 1946. Writers and cartoonists associated with the magazine include *Thurber, O. *Nash, Charles Addams, Saul Steinberg, *O'Hara, S. J. Perelman (1904–79), and *Updike. Its editors have been William Shawn (1952–87), Robert Gottlieb (1987–92), Tina Brown (1992–8), and David Remnick (1998–   ).

NGUGI, James, see THIONG'O.

Niamh, in the second or southern cycle of Irish mythology, the daughter of *Manannán, the sea-god. She fell in love with *Oisin, the son of *Finn, carried him off over the sea, and kept him with her for 300 years. She then let him return to his own country, mounted on a magic steed, but on condition that he should not set foot on earth. Oisin disregarded the caution, immediately lost his youth, and became a blind, decrepit old man.

Nibelung, Niblung, or **Niebelung,** in the Norse *sagas and German *Nibelungenlied*, a mythical king of a race of dwarfs, the Nibelungs, who dwelt in Norway. The Nibelung kings and people also figure in W. Morris's *Sigurd the Volsung*.

Nibelungenlied, a German poem of the 13th cent. embodying a story found in primitive shape in both forms of the *Edda. In these the story is substantially as told by W. Morris in *Sigurd the Volsung*, Sigurd being the Siegfried of the German poem.

In the *Nibelungenlied* the story is somewhat different. Siegfried, son of Siegmund and Sieglind, king and queen of the Netherlands, having got possession of the Nibelung hoard guarded by Alberich, rides to woo Kriemhild, a Burgundian princess, sister of Gunther, Gernot, and Giselher. Hagen, their grim retainer, warns them against Siegfried, but the match is arranged, and the hoard is given to Kriemhild as marriage portion. Siegfried undertakes to help Gunther to win Brunhild, queen of Issland, by defeating her in trials of skill and strength, which he succeeds in doing. The double marriage takes place, but Brunhild remains suspicious and ill-humoured, and Siegfried, called in by Gunther to subdue her, does so in Gunther's semblance and takes away her ring and girdle, which he gives to Kriemhild. The two queens quarrel, and Kriemhild reveals to Brunhild the trick that has been played on her. Hagen, who thinks his master's honour injured by Siegfried, treacherously kills the latter at a hunt.

Kriemhild later marries Etzel (Attila), king of the Huns, and in order to avenge her husband and secure the hoard, which her brothers have seized and sunk in the Rhine, persuades them to visit Etzel's court. There they are set upon and overcome, but refuse to betray the hiding-place of the hoard, and are slain. Hagen, the last survivor of the party who knows the secret, is killed by Kriemhild with Siegfried's sword; and Kriemhild herself is slain by Hildebrand, a knight of *Dietrich of Bern. See RING DES NIBELUNGEN for *Wagner's version.

Nicholas Nickleby, a novel by *Dickens, published 1838–9.

Nicholas, a generous, high-spirited lad of 19, his mother, and his gentle sister Kate are left penniless on the death of his father. They appeal for assistance to his uncle, Ralph Nickleby, a griping usurer, of whom Nicholas at once makes an enemy by his independent bearing. He is sent as usher to Dotheboys Hall, where Wackford Squeers starves and maltreats 40 urchins under pretence of education. His special cruelty is expended on Smike, a half-witted lad left on his hands and employed as a drudge. Nicholas, infuriated by what he witnesses, thrashes Squeers and escapes with Smike, who becomes his devoted friend. For a time he supports himself and Smike as an actor in the provincial company of Vincent Crummles; he then enters the service of the brothers Cheeryble, whose benevolence and good humour spread happiness around them. Meanwhile Kate, apprenticed to Madame Mantalini, dressmaker, is by her uncle's designs exposed to the gross insults of Sir Mulberry Hawk, one of his associates. From this persecution she is released by Nicholas, who breaks Sir Mulberry's head and makes a home for his mother and sister. Nicholas himself falls in love with Madeline Bray, the support of a selfish father and the object of a conspiracy of Ralph Nickleby and another revolting old usurer, Gride, to marry her to the latter. Ralph, whose hatred for Nicholas has been intensified by the failure of his plans, knowing Nicholas's affection for Smike, conspires to remove the latter from him; his plots are thwarted with the help of Newman Noggs, his eccentric clerk, but nevertheless Smike falls a victim to consumption, and eventually dies in the arms of Nicholas. Confronted with ruin and exposure, and finally shattered by the discovery that Smike was his own son, Ralph hangs himself. Nicholas, befriended by the Cheerybles, marries Madeline, and Kate marries the Cheerybles' nephew Frank. Squeers is transported, and Gride is murdered.

NICHOLS, Grace (1950–   ), poet, born at Stanleyville, East Coast, Demerara, in British Guiana (now Guyana). In 1977 she moved to London and began a successful career as a travelling poet in Britain and the world. Her first collection of poetry *I Is a Long-Memoried Woman* (1983) established her reputation instantly as a Caribbean poet with a gift for blending Caribbean Creole and Standard English, and demonstrating the literary qualities of Creole for exploring Caribbean history, folklore, and myth. She has done this consistently in all her work including *The Fat Black Woman's Poems* (1984), *Lazy Thoughts of a Lazy Woman* (1989), *Sunris* (1996). She has written one novel, *Whole of a Morning Sky* (1986). She is also a prolific writer of children's stories and poems.

NICHOLS, John (1745–1826), printer, author, and devoted antiquary, who joined in the management of the *Gentleman's Magazine* in 1778 and became its manager and editor from 1792 until his death. In the pages of the *Magazine* he built up his digressive, disordered, but invaluable work, *Literary Anecdotes of the Eighteenth Century* (published as a collection 1812–16); and his *Illustrations of the Literary History of the Eighteenth Century* which was published 1817–58, having been continued after his death by his son. He also collected *The Progresses and Public Processions of Queen Elizabeth* (which was used by Scott for *Kenilworth*); published *Anecdotes of Mr Hogarth* (1780); an edition of *Swift (1801); and a massive *History and Antiquities of the County of Leicester* (1795–1815). His valuable collection of newspapers is in the Bodleian Library, Oxford.

NICHOLS, Peter Richard (1927–   ), playwright, born and educated in Bristol. He served with the RAF in the Far East, then returned to train and work as an actor and teacher before making his name with both stage and television plays. His works include *A Day in the Death of Joe Egg* (1967), in which schoolteacher Bri and his wife Sheila struggle to share the burden of their handicapped daughter Joe; *The National Health* (1969, pub. 1970), a satirical hospital comedy which contrasts reality with soap opera; *Forget-Me-Not-Lane* (1971), a family drama set during the Second World War; *Privates on Parade* (1977, set in Malaya); and *Passion Play* (1980, pub. 1981), a marital tragicomedy. *Feeling You're Behind* (1984) is an autobiography.

NICHOLS, Robert Malise Bowyer (1893–1944), educated at Winchester and Oxford, fought in France in the First World War; his volumes of poems, *Invocation* (1915) and *Ardours and Endurances* (1917), were highly regarded; he appeared in *Georgian Poetry, and was thought by some to be another R. *Brooke. But *Aurelia* (1920) was his last volume of lyrics, after which he taught for many years in Tokyo and concentrated on writing plays, where he believed his talent lay. However, *Guilty Souls* (1922), *Wings over Europe* (1930), and other dramas met with little success. *Such Was My Singing* (1942) contained fragments from two vast projected works, *Don Juan Tenorio the Great*, on the subject of *Don Juan, and *The Solitudes of the Sun*, a series of vigorous poems and monologues by the romantic Prince Axel. Neither work was ever finished.

NICHOLSON, Norman (1914–87), poet, born in the working-class iron town of Millom, Cumberland, where he lived all his life (apart from a long spell in a sanatorium, suffering from tuberculosis, when he was in his late teens) and which became the theme of most of his work. He evokes its buildings, its dying industry, its people, its geology, and the surrounding rural landscape in several volumes of verse, including *Five Rivers* (1944), *The Pot Geranium* (1954), and *A Local Habitation* (1972), the title of which indicates the intense, precise rootedness of his poetry. His *Collected Poems* (ed. Neil Curry) appeared in 1994.

NÍ CHUILLEANÁIN, Eiléan (1942–   ), poet, born in Cork, now resident in Dublin, where she edits the poetry magazine *Cyphers*. Intelligent, anecdotal, sometimes drily humorous, her work conjures up an enigmatic world in which closely observed or vividly imagined details can assume the dimensions of parable or myth. This distinctive voice was already fully present in her first collection, *Acts and Monuments* (1972), which was followed by *Site of Ambush* (1975), *The Second Voyage* (1977), and *The Rose Geranium* (1981). More recently, *The Magdalene Sermon* (1989) and *The Brazen Serpent* (1994) take their focus from ironic hagiographies and agnostic studies of the miraculous.

Nicolette, see AUCASSIN AND NICOLETTE.

NICOLSON, Sir Harold George (1886–1968), born in Teheran, Persia. The son of a diplomat, he himself became a diplomat and, less successfully, a politician. He published critical and biographical works (on *Verlaine, 1921; *Swinburne, 1926; *Constant, 1945; King George V, 1952; and others), travel books, books on diplomacy, essays, etc., and some fiction: *Some People* (1927), a series of nine closely observed, semi-fictitious, semi-autobiographical sketches, is perhaps his most memorable work. He married V. *Sackville-West in 1913, and his *diaries were edited (3 vols, 1966–8) by his son Nigel Nicolson.

NÍ DHOMHNAILL, Nuala (1952–   ), poet, born in Lancashire, and fostered out to Irish-speaking relatives in Kerry at the age of 5. Her collections include *An Dealg Droighin* (1981), *Féar Suaithinseach* (1984), and *Feis* (1991). Deeply rooted in the Gaelic tradition, her voice is yet utterly contemporary, and can be by turns passionate, acerbic, lyrical, and satirical. Her wide range of idiom has attracted many poet translators: *Pharaoh's Daughter* (1990) includes translations by, among others, S. *Heaney, M. *Longley, Medbh McGuckian, J. *Montague, and Eiléan *Ní Chuilleanáin. Often, the Irish language itself can be read as a metaphor for an alternative reality, an 'Otherworld', and the title of *The Astrakhan Cloak* (1991), with translations by Paul *Muldoon, plays on the Irish word for translation, *aistriúchán*. Her *Selected Poems: Rogha Dánta* (1986; dual language, 1988, 1993) has translations by poet Michael Hartnett.

Niebelung, see NIBELUNG.

NIEBUHR, Barthold Georg (1776–1831), the son of a distinguished German traveller, educated at Kiel; he studied physical science at Edinburgh in 1798. His great *History of Rome*, which originally took the form of lectures delivered at Berlin in 1810–12, appeared in 1827–8. Niebuhr was the first historian to deal with the subject in a scientific spirit, discussing critically the early Roman legends and paying more attention to the

development of institutions and to social characteristics than to individuals and incidents. The *History* was translated into English by J. C. *Hare and *Thirlwall in 1828–42.

NIETZSCHE, Friedrich Wilhelm (1844–1900), German philosopher and poet, educated at the ancient grammar school of Schulpforta and appointed very young to a professorship of classical philology at Basle. He resigned because of ill health and in 1889 suffered a mental breakdown from which he never properly recovered. His first work, *Die Geburt der Tragödie* (*The Birth of Tragedy*, 1872), was of revolutionary importance, challenging the accepted tradition of classical scholarship; it argued against the 'Apollonian' views associated with *Winckelmann in favour of a 'Dionysiac' interpretation which allowed for pessimism and passion as central features of Greek literature. In *Unzeitgemässe Betrachtungen* (*Thoughts out of Season*, 1873–6) he heavily criticized the complacency of German culture in the age of Bismarck. For his general philosophical position, his most important works were *Also sprach Zarathustra* (*Thus Spake Zarathustra*, 1883–92), *Jenseits von Gut und Böse* (*Beyond Good and Evil*, 1886), and *Der Wille zur Macht* (*The Will to Power*) (published posthumously from fragments). His basic ideas are the affirmation of the Superman, the rejection of Christian morality as the morality of the slave, the doctrine of power, and the 'revision of all values'. Nietzsche began as a disciple of *Schopenhauer, but later rejected his pessimism and quietism. For some time he was an admirer of *Wagner, but was eventually unable to accept the Christian and nationalist elements in Wagner's outlook, and a breach between the two men took place. T. *Mann's works show the influence of Nietzsche's thought, as do D. H. *Lawrence's (see, for example, the repudiation of Christianity and the doctrine of power, particularly in *Aaron's Rod*, 1922, and *Apocalypse*, 1931). A version of Nietzsche's 'Übermensch' (from *Also sprach Zarathustra*) appears in Shaw's *Man and Superman*.

Nigger of the 'Narcissus', The, a novel by J. *Conrad, published 1897.

The voyage of the *Narcissus* from Bombay to London is disrupted by two new hands, James Wait, the 'nigger' of the title, and Donkin, a compulsive troublemaker. During a ferocious gale Wait has to be rescued from his sickbed; and in the ensuing calm Donkin tries unsuccessfully to incite the crew to mutiny. Finally, as predicted by Singleton, 'the oldest able seaman in the ship', Wait dies, the wind rises, and the *Narcissus* is able to dock in London.

Described by H. *James as 'the very finest and strongest picture of the sea and sea life that our language possesses', the novel is generally regarded as Conrad's first masterpiece. Its preface contains perhaps the clearest expression of the author's artistic aims and beliefs.

Night and Day, (1) a novel by V. *Woolf; (2) a weekly periodical which ran from July to Dec. 1937, edited by John Marks and G. *Greene, with contributions by *Betjeman, E. *Bowen, *Kingsmill, E. *Waugh, H. *Read, and others. It folded as the result of a libel action arising from a review written by Greene of a film adaptation of *Kipling's story *Wee Willie Winkie*, in which he was alleged to have insulted Shirley Temple. See Greene, *Ways of Escape* (1980, ch. 2); (3) a play by T. *Stoppard.

Nightmare Abbey, a satire by *Peacock, published 1818.

The most literary of Peacock's satires, it mocks the modish gloom infecting contemporary literature: *Coleridge's German transcendentalism is the prime example, but *Byron's self-dramatizing and *Shelley's esotericism are also ridiculed. In imitation of the opening of *Godwin's novel *Mandeville* (1817), Mr Glowry's isolated house is staffed by servants with long faces and names like Diggory Deaths-head. He gives a house party attended by Mr Toobad, the millenarian pessimist, Mr Flosky (Coleridge), Mr Cypress (Byron), and Mr Listless, the common reader, who is currently immersed in the blue devils. Two guests remain unfashionably cheerful, Mr Asterias the scientist and Mr Hilary, whose literary tastes come from the Greeks. Scythrop Glowry, the son of the house, a young writer who resembles Shelley, cannot decide between his frivolous cousin Marionetta and Mr Toobad's sybilline daughter Stella. Peacock seems to have intended to present, in amusing contemporary terms, the dilemma facing the young Milton in *'L'Allegro' and *'Il Penseroso'. In a classic comic denouement, in which the ladies are discovered to one another, Scythrop loses both. He briefly contemplates suicide in Werther's manner (see WERTHERISM), but calls instead for a bottle of Madeira.

'Night-Piece on Death', see PARNELL, T.

Night Thoughts on Life, Death, and Immortality, *The Complaint or*, a didactic and reflective poem of some 10,000 lines of blank verse, in nine books, by E. *Young, published 1742–5.

This work was extremely popular and had considerable influence in Europe, where it was admired by *Klopstock, *Diderot, and Robespierre, among others. It is a long and somewhat rambling meditation on life's vicissitudes, death, and immortality, and includes lines which have become proverbial, such as 'Procrastination is the thief of time' (Bk I, l. 393). The poet deplores the deaths of Lucia, Narcissa, and Philander, loosely identified as his wife, his stepdaughter, and her husband; he also addresses much reproof and exhortation to the worldly and infidel young Lorenzo, a character unlikely to be based on his own son, as many supposed, for the boy was only 8 when the poem was begun. Thus a certain narrative and autobiographical

interest is added to his evocations of 'delightful gloom' and the 'populous grave'.

nihilism (Latin *nihil*, nothing), originally a movement in Russia repudiating the customary social institutions, such as marriage and parental authority. The term was introduced by *Turgenev. It was extended to a secret revolutionary movement, social and political, which developed in the middle of the 19th cent.

Nimphidia, a fairy poem by *Drayton which appeared in 1627.

Nimphidia, a fairy attendant on Queen Mab, reports to the poet the doings at the fairy court. It appears that Pigwiggin has fallen in love with Mab and made an assignation to meet her in a cowslip. The queen in her snail-shell coach, and the maids of honour hurrying after her on a grasshopper and shrouded with a spider's web, set off for the cowslip. King Oberon, roused to frenzy by the loss of his queen, and armed with an acorn cup, goes in pursuit, belabouring whomsoever he finds and meeting with mortifying adventures. He comes upon the faithful Puck (or Hobgoblin) and sends him to continue the search. Meanwhile Pigwiggin sends a challenge to Oberon, and a combat ensues between the two, mounted on earwigs. Proserpina, goddess of fairyland, intervenes, with mist and Lethe water, and restores harmony.

Nimue or **Nimiane,** see LADY OF THE LAKE.

Nineteen Eighty-Four, a novel by G. *Orwell, published 1949.

It is a nightmare story of totalitarianism of the future and one man's hopeless struggle against it and final defeat by acceptance. Winston Smith, the hero, has no heroic qualities, only a wistful longing for truth and decency. But in a social system where there is no privacy and to have unorthodox ideas incurs the death penalty he knows that there is no hope for him. His brief love affair ends in arrest by the Thought Police, and when, after months of torture and brainwashing, he is released, he makes his final submission of his own accord. The book is a warning of the possibilities of the police state brought to perfection, where power is the only thing that counts, where the past is constantly being modified to fit the present, where the official language, 'Newspeak', progressively narrows the range of ideas and independent thought, and where Doublethink becomes a necessary habit of mind. It is a society dominated by slogans—'War is Peace, Freedom is Slavery, Ignorance is Strength'—and controlled by compulsory worship of the head of the Party, *Big Brother. The novel had an extraordinary impact, and many of its phrases and coinages (including its title) passed into the common language, although the precise implications of Orwell's warning (and it was a warning, rather than a prophecy) have been subjected to many different political interpretations.

Nineteenth Century, a monthly review founded in 1877 by J. T. *Knowles, who was its first editor. It was more impartial in its attitude than the *Fortnightly*, bringing together in its pages the most eminent advocates of conflicting views; one of its celebrated controversies (1890–1) was that between *Gladstone and T. H. *Huxley on the subject of the miracle of the Gadarene Swine. Other contributors included *Ruskin, B. *Webb, W. *Morris, *Ouida, and *Wilde. *Tennyson, a friend of Knowles, provided a prefatory sonnet for the first issue, welcoming contributions from the faithful and from 'wilder comrades' seeking a harbour 'In seas of Death and sunless Gulfs of Doubt'. When the century of the title ended, the review added to its old title 'And After', and changed the whole title to the *Twentieth Century* in 1951. See *Nineteenth Century Opinion* (1951), a selection from the years 1877–1901, edited by Michael Goodwin.

Nine Worthies, the, see WORTHIES OF THE WORLD.

Nipper, Susan, a character in Dickens's *Dombey and Son*.

Nobel Prizes were established under the will of Alfred Bernhard Nobel (1833–96), a Swedish chemist distinguished in the development of explosives, by which the interest on the greater part of his large fortune is distributed in annual prizes for the most important discoveries in physics, chemistry, and physiology or medicine respectively, to the person who shall have most promoted 'the fraternity of nations' (the Nobel Peace Prize), and to the 'person who shall have produced in the field of literature the most outstanding work of an idealistic tendency'. (See Appendix 3 (*a*) for a list of winners.)

Noble Savage, see PRIMITIVISM.

Noctes Ambrosianae, a series of dialogues, which appeared in *Blackwood's Edinburgh Magazine* from 1822 to 1835. The series was devised by J. G. *Lockhart, and bears some resemblance to his own *Peter's Letters to His Kinsfolk*, in which the scene of the *Noctes*, *Ambrose's Tavern, first appears. The conversations take place between various friends, largely based on real people, such as the 'Shepherd' (J. *Hogg) and 'Christopher North' (John *Wilson). Wilson wrote more than half the 71 dialogues, but Lockhart, Hogg, and *Maginn also contributed. The conversations, which cover a wide range of subjects, and present a romanticized and whimsical view of Scotland, were extremely popular.

NOEL, Roden Berkely Wriothesley (1834–94), the author of several volumes of verse, including *A Little Child's Monument* (1881), inspired by the death of his son Eric, and *Songs of the Heights and Deeps* (1885). His collected works were issued in 1902.

Noggs, Newman, in Dickens's *Nicholas Nickleby*, Ralph Nickleby's clerk, who has seen better days.

Nōh plays, a form of traditional, ceremonial, or ritualistic drama peculiar to Japan, symbolical and spiritual in character. It was evolved from religious rites of Shinto worship, was perfected in the 15th cent., and flourished during the Tokugawa period (1652–1868). It has since been revived. The plays are short (one or two acts), in prose and verse, and a chorus contributes poetical comments. They were formerly acted as a rule only at the Shōgun's court, five or six in succession, presenting a complete life drama, beginning with a play of the divine age, then a battle piece, a 'play of women', a psychological piece (dealing with the sins and struggles of mortals), a morality, and finally a congratulatory piece, praising the lords and the reign. The text was helped out by symbolic gestures and chanting. About 200 Nōh plays are extant. Of these the most interesting are the psychological pieces, in which some type of human character or some intense emotion is taken as the subject. In various respects the Nōh plays are comparable with the early Greek drama (see 'Noh, or Accomplishment', by Ernest Fenollosa and Ezra Pound, 1916).

Both *Pound and *Yeats were much influenced by the Nōh theatre: Yeats in his essay 'Certain Noble Plays of Japan' (1916) describes the impact of its ritual, simplicity, and stylization on his own plays, and compared its treatment of the supernatural with that of Lady *Gregory.

NOLLEKENS, Joseph (1737–1823), sculptor, born in London, the son of Antwerp-born painter Joseph Francis Nollekens ('Old Nollekens', 1702–48). His many busts of statesmen, aristocrats, and writers were lively, and his career was immensely successful. An eccentric figure, he is frequently mentioned in the literature of the period, and was a friend of Dr *Johnson and *Reynolds. Fanny *Burney drew on him for the character of Briggs in *Cecilia*.

Nominalism (as opposed to *Realism), the view of those Scholastics and later philosophers who regarded universals or abstract conceptions as a 'flatus vocis', mere names without any corresponding reality. The founder of the school of thought is usually said to be Roscelin (*c*.1050–1125) whose view (as well as its extreme opposite Realist view) was opposed by *Abelard. Its anti-Platonic emphasis on Individuals has some affinity with later Empiricist philosophy.

No Name (1862), a novel by Wilkie *Collins.

When her parents die, the spirited Magdalen Vanstone, a talented amateur actress, discovers that she and her sister Norah are illegitimate and penniless. Their father's fortune goes to a cousin, Noel Vanstone, a querulous invalid. Norah finds a post as a governess, but Magdalen is determined to have justice. With the help of an amiable rogue, Captain Wragge, she gets access in disguise to Noel Vanstone, and eventually charms him into marrying her under an assumed name. His French housekeeper discovers and reveals the deception, and persuades him to alter his will, leaving his money in a secret trust. Vanstone dies, and Magdalen, disguising herself as a parlourmaid, penetrates the house of the trustee of his will to find the document which reveals the legatee. She is frustrated yet again, but the money finally returns to the sisters through Norah's love match with Vanstone's heir.

Nonesuch Press, a publishing firm established in 1923 by F. *Meynell, Vera Mendel, and D. *Garnett, for the production of books of high quality of content and presentation, at a moderate price. Not strictly a *private press, it shared many of the aims of the private presses. See *The Nonesuch Century* (1936), by A. J. A. *Symons, Desmond Flower, and F. Meynell, which describes the first 100 books and 12 years of the press's life.

NOONAN, Robert, see under TRESSELL.

NORFOLK, Lawrence (1963–), novelist, born in London, brought up partly in Iraq, and educated at King's College, London. He achieved instant success with his lengthy *historical novel *Lemprière's Dictionary* (1991), a bizarre and erudite work full of pageantry set largely in the 18th cent. in Jersey, London, and Paris, which traces the fortunes of a Jersey family, using the figure of dictionary compiler John *Lemprière as protagonist. It is a storehouse of esoteric information about the East India Company, navigation, the siege of La Rochelle, *Jacobin revolt, classical mythology, and much else: the complicated plot has elements of the *sensational novel and of *detective fiction. *The Pope's Rhinoceros* (1996) is in a similar genre, describing with poetry, scholarship, and relish the violence of Europe during the Renaissance, and a quest for the fabulous beast in Africa.

NORRIS, Frank (Benjamin Franklin Norris) (1870–1902), American novelist, born in Chicago, the son of a wholesale jeweller, but brought up partly in San Francisco, and educated at the University of California and in Paris, where he studied art. The influence of *Zola and *naturalism is seen in his best work, which includes *McTeague* (1899), a tragic account of violence, greed, and treachery in San Francisco, in which McTeague, an unlicensed dentist, becomes both thief and murderer; and in his unfinished trilogy *The Epic of the Wheat*: the masterly first two volumes, *The Octopus* (1901) and *The Pit* (1903), describe the raising of wheat in California and speculation on the Chicago wheat exchange. A projected third volume, *The Wolf*, to be set in famine-stricken Europe, was never written.

NORRIS, John (1657–1711), poet, philosopher, and from 1691 rector of Bemerton; he is considered as the last of the *Cambridge Platonists, and is remembered for his *An Essay towards the Theory of the Ideal or Intelligible World* (1701–4), in which he shows himself a supporter of Malebranche's development of the theories of *Descartes. His poems were edited by A. B. *Grosart (1871).

Norris, Mrs, a character in J. Austen's *Mansfield Park*.

NORTH, Christopher, a pseudonym used by John *Wilson (1785–1854).

NORTH, Roger (1653–1734), youngest son of Dudley, fourth Baron North, and great-great-nephew of Sir T. *North. Educated at Jesus College, Cambridge, he had a successful career as a lawyer which came to an end with the accession of William of Orange. He is remembered as the author of interesting biographies, published in 1742–4, of three of his brothers, Francis North, Lord Guildford, keeper of the great seal; Dudley North, the great Turkey merchant; and John North, master of Trinity College, Cambridge. They are enriched by much affectionate personal detail. His own *Autobiography* was published in 1887. For an account of his posthumously published musical treatises, see under MUSIC, LITERATURE OF.

NORTH, Sir Thomas (1523–?1601), son of Edward North; first Baron North; he perhaps studied at Peterhouse, Cambridge. He entered Lincoln's Inn, was knighted in 1591, and pensioned by *Elizabeth I in 1601. He is famous for his translations, which include the *Diall of Princes* from Guevara's *El relox de principes* with *The Famous Booke of Marcus Aurelius*, *The Morall Philosophie of Doni*, from the Italian (1570, see BIDPAI), and *Plutarch's *Lives* from the French of *Amyot (1579), to which he made additions from other authors in 1595 and 1603. His Plutarch, written in a noble and vivid English, formed Shakespeare's chief storehouse of classical history and exerted a powerful influence on Elizabethan prose.

North American Review (1815–1939), a Boston quarterly, later monthly, review of the old solid type, and one of the most distinguished of American periodicals. Its editors included C. E. *Norton, J. R. *Lowell, and H. *Adams, and its contributors ranged from *Emerson, W. *Irving, *Parkman, and *Longfellow in its earlier days, to H. *James, *Wells and *Twain towards the end of the century. It then declined, and was revived again as a quarterly in 1963 by the University of Northern Iowa.

North and South, a novel by Mrs *Gaskell, published serially in *Household Words* 1854–5, in volume form 1855.

This novel is a study of the contrast between the values and habits of rural southern England and industrial northern England. The heroine, Margaret Hale, is the daughter of a parson whose religious doubts force him to resign his Hampshire living and to move with his family to a sooty cotton-spinning northern city. Here, at a moment of conflict between workers and employers, Margaret meets the grim, intolerant Mrs Thornton and her son, an able, stubborn manufacturer, whose lack of sympathy for the workers

Margaret at first finds unattractive. When she endangers herself to protect him from a mob of strikers he misunderstands her motives and offers marriage, which she refuses. But when he suspects her of an intrigue with another man (in fact her brother, whom she has to shield as he is in danger of arrest), and shows his suspicion, her unhappiness reveals to her that she really loves him. It is not till after a series of deaths and other misfortunes that Margaret and Thornton are finally united. The theme in the title is gradually worked out as Margaret—at first aristocratically repelled by 'trade' and its practitioners—comes to know and respect the ideas and the family life of both mill-hands and mill-owners.

Northanger Abbey, a novel by J. *Austen, begun 1798, sold to a publisher 1803, but not published until 1818, when it appeared posthumously with *Persuasion. It is probably the earliest of her completed works.

The purpose of the novel is to ridicule the popular tales of romance and terror, such as Mrs Radcliffe's *Mysteries of Udolpho, and to contrast with these the normal realities of life. Catherine Morland, the daughter of a well-to-do clergyman, is taken to Bath for the season by her friends, Mr and Mrs Allen. Here she makes the acquaintance of Henry Tilney (son of the eccentric General Tilney) and his pleasant sister Eleanor. Catherine falls in love with Henry, and has the good fortune to gain his father's approval, which is founded upon the exaggerated report of her parents' wealth given him by the foolish young John Thorpe, brother of Catherine's friend Isabella. Catherine is invited to Northanger Abbey, the medieval seat of the Tilneys. Somewhat unbalanced by a too assiduous reading of Mrs Radcliffe's novels, Catherine imagines a mystery in which General Tilney is criminally involved, and suffers severe mortification when her suspicions are discovered. General Tilney, having now received a second report from John Thorpe as misleading as the first, representing Catherine's parents as extremely humble, packs her off back to her family and forbids Henry to have any further thoughts of her. Henry, disobeying his father, follows Catherine to her home, proposes, and is accepted. General Tilney's consent is obtained at a time when his humour has been greatly improved by the marriage of his daughter Eleanor to a peer, and his discovery of the true financial position of Catherine's family.

Interwoven with the main plot is the flirtation of Captain Tilney, Henry's elder brother, and the vulgar Isabella Thorpe, who is engaged to Catherine's brother; the consequent breaking of the engagement, and the rupture of the friendship between Catherine and Isabella; and Isabella's failure to secure Captain Tilney.

North Briton, a weekly political periodical founded in 1762 by *Wilkes, in opposition to the *Briton*, which *Smollett was conducting in the interests of Lord Bute. In this venture Wilkes was assisted by Charles *Churchill, the author of the *Rosciad. The North

Briton purports ironically to be edited by a Scotsman, who rejoices in Lord Bute's success and the ousting of the English from power. Wilkes's attacks on the government grew bolder, and in No. 45, in an article on the speech from the throne, he exposed himself to prosecution for libel. Though Wilkes was discharged on the ground of privilege, the North Briton was suppressed. See The North Briton: A Study in Political Propaganda (1939), by G. Nobbe.

NORTHCLIFFE, Viscount, see HARMSWORTH.

Northern Lass, The, a comedy by *Brome, printed 1632.

This is the earliest of Brome's extant plays, and was very popular. Sir Philip Luckless is about to marry the rich city widow Fitchow, when he receives a letter from Constance, the 'northern lass', reminding him of her love for him. Mistaking the writer for another Constance of a less reputable character, he disregards the letter and marries the widow, only to discover his mistake too late. The play is occupied with the devices by which the widow is induced to agree to a divorce, while her foolish brother, whom she tries to marry to Constance, is fobbed off with an inferior substitute, and Luckless and the true Constance are united.

Northward Hoe, a comedy by *Webster and *Dekker, written 1605, printed 1607.

Greenshield, having failed to seduce Mayberry's wife, but having obtained by force her ring, to avenge himself produces the ring to her husband as evidence of her infidelity. The husband, assisted by the little old poet Bellamont, a genial caricature of *Chapman, becomes convinced of her innocence, and obtains an appropriate revenge on Greenshield and his confederate Featherstone.

The play was a good-humoured retort to the *Eastward Hoe of Chapman, Jonson, and Marston. Like *Westward Hoe it presents a curious picture of the manners of the day.

NORTON, the Hon. Mrs Caroline, née Sheridan (1808–77), poet, novelist, editor, and political hostess: she was a granddaughter of R. *Sheridan. She married the Hon. George Norton in 1827 and in 1836 became involved in a notorious divorce action (her husband unsuccessfully citing Lord Melbourne) and in a spirited and influential battle for the custody of her children and a revision of the laws relating to married women's property. She successfully supported her family by writing, and published several volumes of Byronic verse; the first appeared anonymously, in 1829 and was followed by The Undying One, and Other Poems (1830), of which the title poem is a spirited four-canto version of the legend of the *Wandering Jew. She also published stories, essays, and novels, including Lost and Saved (3 vols, 1863). She served as a model for the heroine of Meredith's *Diana of the Crossways.

NORTON, Charles Eliot (1827–1908), born in Cambridge, Massachusetts, and educated at Harvard, where he was professor of fine arts from 1873 to 1898. Although his direct contributions to literature were small, he was an intellectual leader of great influence beyond the confines of the university. His aim was, in his own words, to arouse in his countrymen 'the sense of connection with the past and gratitude for the efforts and labours of other nations and former generations'. He was a frequent contributor to the *Atlantic Monthly,* joint editor of the *North American Review* (1864–8), and founder and co-editor of the *Nation* (1865). His many friendships with English writers and artists (including *Clough, Mrs *Gaskell, the *Brownings, *Carlyle, and L. *Stephen) are recorded in his *Letters,* ed. S. Norton and M. A. D. Howe (1913).

NORTON, Mary, see CHILDREN'S LITERATURE.

Norval, see DOUGLAS (the tragedy).

NOSTRADAMUS (1503–66), French astrologer and physician, whose enigmatic prophecies, cast in the form of rhymed quatrains grouped in sets of 100 and published under the title *Centuries* (1556, English trans. 1672), enjoyed widespread popularity during the Renaissance.

Nostromo, a novel by J. *Conrad, published 1904.

In an imaginary South American country, Costaguana, Charles Gould runs a silver mine of national importance in the province of Sulaco. He is married to Emilia, a woman of charm and intelligence, whose arrival has been of great benefit to the local people. In a time of political unrest and revolution the dictator President Ribiera is forced to flee the country and the opposing factions struggle for control. Nostromo ('our man' or 'boatswain') is an Italian sailor, now Capataz de Cargadores, handsome, courageous, strong, and a hero to all. When the silver from the mine is in danger of being seized by the rebel forces, Gould becomes obsessed with the idea of saving it. He enlists the help of Decoud, the cynical, Paris-influenced journalist suitor of Antonia Avellanos (daughter of Don José Avellanos, the 'hereditary friend' of the Gould family), and of an older man, Dr Monygham, who was tortured under the previous regime and is a fond admirer of Emilia, and together they appeal to Nostromo. With great daring Decoud and Nostromo sail off with the treasure. Their silent journey through the night, their collision with an enemy boat, and their eventual arrival at a nearby island where they bury the treasure are vividly described. Decoud is left on guard while Nostromo returns to Sulaco. Alone on the deserted island Decoud loses his mind and, after shooting himself, drowns, his body weighted with silver. Nostromo learns that the woman to whom he has refused the offices of a priest has died, and is filled with a superstitious dread that this offence will threaten the whole venture and his own future. The common assumption is that the silver was lost at sea and the temptation proves too much for Nostromo, who decides to steal it. His old friend Viola, an ex-Garibaldino, is appointed lighthouse keeper on the island and, unwittingly, guard for the silver. Nostromo trifles with Viola's two infatuated daughters, grows rich as he gradually pilfers the silver, and is finally shot when mistaken for an intruder. Mortally wounded, he sends for Emilia, and confesses his crime in the hope of absolution, but dies without revealing the whereabouts of the treasure; as the 'incorruptible' Emilia, appalled by the destruction it has caused and by Nostromo's miserable subjection to his obsession, declares: 'No one misses it now. Let it be lost forever.'

Notebooks, The, a modern edition edited by Coleridge scholar Kathleen Coburn (1905–91) of the personal notebooks and journals of S. T. *Coleridge, of which four volumes, 1794–1826, consisting of separate Text and Notes, have been published (1956–): they supersede the *Anima Poetae* edited by E. H. Coleridge in 1895. They consist of Coleridge's sometimes daily comments on his life, travels, writing, and dreams: full of his anxiety and self-consciousness, they throw remarkable light on the raw materials of his thought and art. Biographically, they reveal his struggle with opium, and the tortuous side of his relations with the *Wordsworths and his beloved Sara Hutchinson ('Asra').

Notes and Queries, a periodical founded in 1849 by *Thoms, designed to furnish a means for the interchange of thought and information among those engaged in literature, art, and science, and a medium of communication with each other. Its motto was (until 1923) Captain Cuttle's 'When found, make a note of' (see DOMBEY AND SON).

nouveau roman ('new novel'), a term applied to the work of a wide range of modern French novelists, including Nathalie Sarraute (1902–1999), Claude Simon (1913–2005), Marguerite *Duras, Robert Pinget (1919–97), Alain *Robbe-Grillet, and *Butor. What distinguishes these novelists is primarily a shared conviction as to the inadequacies of the traditional novel. Thus Robbe-Grillet (*Pour un nouveau roman,* 1963; English trans., *Snapshots, and Towards a New Novel,* 1965) argues that the traditional novel, with its dependence on an omniscient narrator, creates an illusion of order and significance which is denied by the reality of experience. The task of the new novel is therefore to foster change by dispensing with any technique which imposes a particular interpretation on events, or which organizes events in such a way as to endow them with a collective significance.

Nouvelle Héloïse, La, see ROUSSEAU.

Nouvelle Revue française, La, a monthly review of literature, drama, and the other arts, founded in 1909 by a group that included *Gide, the novelist Jean

Schlumberger, and the actor and theatre director Jacques Copeau. A publishing enterprise associated with the review, the 'maison d'éditions de la nrf', was started soon afterwards. The *NRF* published a number of little-known writers later to become famous, including *Valéry, *Giraudoux, *Claudel, *Montherlant, and *Mauriac, and made efforts to introduce German, Russian, and English authors to French readers. Valéry Larbaud's celebrated lecture on Joyce's *Ulysses, delivered in Adrienne Monnier's bookshop, La Maison des Amis des Livres, on 7 Dec. 1921, appeared in the *NRF* in April 1922. Publication was interrupted during the First World War and ceased in 1943, to recommence in 1953 as *La Nouvelle Nouvelle Revue française*. In 1959 the original title was readopted, under which it continues to appear.

NOVALIS, pseudonym of *Hardenberg.

***Nova Solyma,** the Ideal City; or Jerusalem Regained*: an anonymous Latin romance written in the time of Charles I, probably by Samuel Gott. It contains a notable scheme of education.

novel, rise of the. The word 'novellae' was employed in the 16th cent. to describe the short tales of the *Decameron* and the *Heptameron*, and others like them. Used in a recognizably modern sense, the word 'novel' appears in England in the mid-17th cent., when it was chiefly associated with romances of illicit love. For this reason the word 'history' was more often favoured to describe the long prose fictions of the 18th cent. which were the precursors of the modern novel. The novel form developed slowly, through the memoir-novel and the epistolary novel of the 16th and 17th cents to the novel of the omniscient third-person narrator, which has dominated from the late 18th cent. to the present time. The chief novelists of the 18th cent. (*Defoe, *Richardson, *Fielding, *Smollett, and *Sterne) so greatly and rapidly developed the form that by the early 19th cent. J. *Austen could write (albeit with a hint of irony) in *Northanger Abbey*, that in the novel 'the greatest powers of the mind are displayed'. Form, style, and subject matter varied considerably, but by 1824 Sir W. *Scott could confidently define the novel as 'a fictitious narrative . . . accommodated to the ordinary train of human events', a definition which may be allowed to stand today. (See also EPISTOLARY NOVEL; FASHIONABLE NOVEL; HISTORICAL NOVEL; MEMOIR-NOVEL; ORIENTAL NOVEL; SENTIMENT, NOVEL OF.)

Novum Organum, a Latin treatise on scientific method, which F. *Bacon included in his *Instauratio Magna* (1620). This 'great renewal' of natural philosophy (which Bacon never completed) involved a systematic methodology, starting with fresh observation of natural phenomena, followed by carefully controlled experiments, to provide data from which scientific laws could be formulated. The 'new instrument' outlined here (the title alludes to the corpus of Aristotelian philosophy, known as the *Organon*) abandoned the main tool of logic, the syllogism, which Bacon criticized as a self-contained verbal procedure starting from an a priori premiss. Instead, he advocated an inductive method, generalizing upward from experimental results, tested by the use of 'negative instances' (if 100 white swans are observed, the discovery of a single black one is enough to falsify the thesis that all swans are white).

Book I of the *Novum Organum* restates in the form of detached aphorisms Bacon's fundamental criticisms of science and his plans for its renewal. Calling for the direct observation of nature (rather than recycling *Aristotle's texts), Bacon was nonetheless aware of the possible distortions involved, brilliantly analysing the four 'Idols' (from the Greek εἴδωλα, illusions) to which human beings are prone. These are the Idols of the Tribe, Cave, Market Place, and Theatre: respectively, the distortions caused by sense perception, which are common to all; distortions caused by differences of temperament and education, arising from particular circumstances of each individual; distortions arising from the treacherous medium of language; and the illusions of philosophic systems, these systems being in Bacon's view like so many stage plays, representing imaginary worlds of their own manufacture. In the more technical Book II Bacon gives a worked example of inductive method as applied to heat, using experimental data to construct tables of absence and presence, concluding that heat is a form of motion. Bacon's inductive method has often been misrepresented as a purely mechanical procedure, but recent research has shown that it includes hypothetico-deductive elements, representing a substantial contribution to natural science.

Now and Then, a house periodical published from 1921 till 1944 by Jonathan Cape, the publishing company, which contained poems, essays, and reviews by W. H. *Davies, *Auden, *Spender, D. H. *Lawrence, H. *Read, and many others. A selection taken from its first 50 issues was published in 1935 as *Then and Now*.

NOYES, Alfred (1880–1959), poet, playwright, novelist, and anthologist, who held violently anti-*Modernist views on literature; his own collections of verse (many of them about seafaring) include *Drake* (1908), an epic, and *Tales of the Mermaid Tavern* (1913). His anecdotal autobiography, *Two Worlds for Memory*, appeared in 1953.

Nubbles, Mrs and Kit, characters in Dickens's *The Old Curiosity Shop*.

'Nun's Priest's Tale, The', see CANTERBURY TALES, 20.

Nupkins, Mr, a character in Dickens's *Pickwick Papers*.

Nurse, the loquacious and humorous attendant of *Juliet in Shakespeare's *Romeo and Juliet*. She acts as a go-between for the lovers. Her name may have been Angelica (IV. iv. 5).

'Nut-Brown Maid, The', a 15th-cent. poem in praise of woman's fidelity. The lover, to prove the Maid, tells her that he must to the greenwood go, 'alone, a banyshed man' and live the life of an outlaw. She declares her intention of accompanying him, nor can be dissuaded by the prospect of hardships and humiliations. The lover finally reveals his deceit and that he is an earl's son 'and not a banyshed man'. The poem is included in Percy's *Reliques*. It is the foundation of *Prior's 'Henry and Emma'.

NUTTALL, Jeff, see UNDERGROUND POETRY.

Nuyorican Poets Café, see PERFORMANCE POETRY.

NYE, Robert (1939–   ), novelist, poet, playwright, and critic, born in London and educated at Southend High School. His exuberant early poems, collected in *Juvenilia 1* (1961) and *Juvenilia 2* (1963), exhibit the influence of Robert *Graves and *de la Mare. Later work is more austere: the approach to his key themes of love and guilt is literary, allegorical, and eccentrically humorous. Nye's first novel was the *Joycean *Doubtfire* (1967), but he is best known for his sequence of pastiche biographies of characters from literature, folklore, and history: their mix of poetic language, learning, and bawdy humour has led to comparisons with *Rabelais. The first, *Falstaff* (1976), was described by *Burgess as 'an indication of what the novel can do

when freed from the constraints of the *Jamesian tradition'. These idiosyncratic portraits continued with *Merlin* (1978), *Faust* (1980), *The Voyage of the Destiny* (1982; Nye's rendition of the life of *Ralegh), *The Memoirs of Lord Byron* (1989), *The Life and Death of My Lord Gilles de Rais* (1990), *Mrs Shakespeare* (1993), and *The Late Mr Shakespeare* (1998). Nye has also written radio and stage plays, and books for children. His short stories were collected as *Tales I Told My Mother* (1969) and *The Facts of Life* (1983). A *Collection of Poems 1955–1988* (1989) includes new poems and revised versions of early pieces.

Nym, Corporal, appears in Shakespeare's *Merry Wives of Windsor* and *Henry V* as a follower of *Falstaff, a rogue and thief, obsessed with 'Humours'. To 'nim' was slang for to steal.

Nymphidia, see NIMPHIDIA.

nymphs, see PARACELSUS.

NYREN, John (1764–1837), a famous early cricketer and cricket chronicler. He belonged to the celebrated Hambledon Club, which flourished c.1750–91, and was a left-handed batsman of average ability and a fine fielder at point and mid-wicket. His recollections were published in *The Young Cricketer's Tutor* (1833, edited by C. C. *Clarke), which includes some history of the game, reminiscences of great games and 'cricketers I have known', advice on tactics, etc.

O

Oak, Gabriel, a character in Hardy's *Far from the Madding Crowd*.

OATES, Joyce Carol (1938–), American novelist, short story writer, poet, and critic, born in Lockport, New York, educated at Syracuse University and the University of Wisconsin. A former professor of English at the University of Detroit (a city which provides the setting for much of her work), she is a prolific novelist whose fiction portrays intense individual experiences as expressions of the dark and violent heart of American society. Her novels—predominantly naturalistic but with suggestions of the neo-*Gothic—include *With Shuddering Fall* (1964), *A Garden of Earthly Delights* (1967), *Expensive People* (1968), *them* (1969), *Wonderland* (1971), *Do With Me What You Will* (1973), *The Assassins* (1975), *The Childwold* (1976), *The Triumph of the Spider Monkey* (1977), *Son of the Morning* (1978), *Bellefleur* (1980), *A Bloodsmoor Romance* (1982), *Mysteries of Winterhurn* (1984), *Solstice* (1985), *Marya: A Life* (1986), *You Must Remember This* (1989), *American Appetites* (1989), and *Because It Is Bitter, Because It Is My Heart* (1990). *Black Water* (1992), set on an island off the coast of Maine, is the story, told in 32 short episodes, of a young woman's meeting with a US Senator at a beach party and her subsequent death by drowning. *Foxfire* (1993) is a powerful portrayal of a teenage girl-gang in upstate New York during the 1950s. *What I Lived for* (1994) is about the public and private faces of a property millionaire and city councillor. Her many short stories have been collected in *By the North Gate* (1963), *Upon the Sweeping Flood* (1966), *The Wheel of Love* (1970), *Marriages and Infidelities* (1972), *The Hungry Ghosts* (1974), *The Goddess and Other Women* (1974), *The Poisoned Kiss* (1975), *The Seduction* (1975), *Crossing the Border* (1976), *Night-Side* (1977), and *Last Days* (1984). Her poetry collections include *Women in Love* (1968), *Angel Fire* (1973), and *Dreaming in America* (1973). Selections of essays and critical writings can be found in *The Edge of Impossibility* (1971), *The Hostile Sun* (1973), and *Contraries* (1981), amongst other volumes. Her monograph *On Boxing* was published in 1987.

OATES, Titus (1649–1705), the fabricator of the *Popish Plot (1678), the 'Corah' of Dryden's *Absalom and Achitophel*.

Obadiah, the manservant of the Shandy family in Sterne's *Tristram Shandy*.

Obermann, see SENANCOUR.

Oberon, in Shakespeare's *A Midsummer Night's Dream*, the king of the fairies and husband of *Titania. He also appears in R. Greene's play *James the Fourth and is the eponymous hero of a *masque by *Jonson and an opera by *Weber.

objective correlative, a term used by T. S. *Eliot in his essay 'Hamlet and His Problems' (1919; included in *The Sacred Wood*, 1920). Eliot ascribes the alleged 'artistic failure' of the play *Hamlet to the fact that Hamlet himself is 'dominated by an emotion which is inexpressible, because it is in *excess* of the facts as they appear . . . The only way of expressing emotion in the form of art is by finding an "objective correlative"; in other words, a set of objects, a situation, a chain of events which shall be the formula of that *particular* emotion.' This phrase, like *'dissociation of sensibility', became very fashionable, and was doubtless one of those to which Eliot referred in a lecture in 1956 ('The Frontiers of Criticism') when he spoke of 'a few notorious phrases which have had a truly embarrassing success in the world'.

Objectivism, see ZUKOFSKY.

O'Brallaghan, Sir Callaghan, a character in *Love à la Mode* by Macklin.

O'BRIEN, Edna (1932–), Irish novelist and short story writer, born in the west of Ireland. Her first novel *The Country Girls* (1960) describes the girlhood of Caithleen Brady (Kate) and Bridget Brennan (Baba), who escape from their country homes and convent education to the addictive 'crowds and lights and noise' of Dublin. They continue their search for experience through *The Lonely Girl* (1962, in which Kate falls in love with film director Eugene Gaillard) and *Girls in Their Married Bliss* (1963, in which both have moved to London). Her subsequent novels include *August is a Wicked Month* (1964), *A Pagan Place* (1971, an evocation of rural Ireland), *Night* (1972, the sombre, impassioned, monologue of middle-aged Mary Hooligan), *Johnny I Hardly Knew You* (1977, a tale of *crime passionnel*), *Time and Tide* (1992), and *House of Splendid Isolation* (1994). Her themes are female sensuality, male treachery, Irish nostalgia, and celebration of the intermittent 'good times' which even her much abused and self-abusing heroines enjoy, and her lyrical descriptive powers and lack of inhibition have led to comparisons with *Colette. Her short story collections include *A Scandalous Woman* (1974), *Mrs Reinhardt* (1978), *Returning* (1982), and *Lantern Slides* (1990). *A Fanatic Heart* (1984 USA, 1985 UK) reprints stories from earlier collections with four new stories.

Mother Ireland (1976), with photographs by Fergus Bourke, is an autobiographical evocation of her native country.

O'BRIEN, Flann, pseudonym of Brian O'Nolan or Ó Nualláin (1911–66), born at Strabane, Co. Tyrone, and educated at University College, Dublin. He worked for the Irish civil service until his retirement through ill health in 1953, and also for many years contributed a satiric weekly column under the name 'Myles na Gopaleen' to the *Irish Times.* His first novel, *At Swim-Two-Birds* (1939), is an exuberant work, operating on several levels of invention: the narrator, a young Dublin student living with his uncle, offers variants of reality which include a naturalistic portrayal of student and lower-middle-class life; a 'novel-within-a-novel' written by 'eccentric author Dermot Trellis' which deals with the legendary Irish hero *Finn Mac Cool; and a layer of Irish folklore rendered in terms of farce, featuring the Pooka, the Good Fairy, etc. The effect is a multidimensional exploration of Irish culture and of the nature of fiction, much influenced by *Joyce. O'Brien's second novel, *An Béal Bocht* (1941), was written in Gaelic, translated into English in 1973 as *The Poor Mouth.* The best known of his other works is *The Third Policeman* (written 1940, pub. 1967), which *Wain (*Encounter,* 1967) found 'tense, grim and threatening', closer in tone to *Beckett than his 'hilarious, elegiac, sarcastic, relaxed and genial' first novel.

O'BRIEN, Kate (1897–1974), novelist, born in Limerick, Ireland, and educated at University College, Dublin. She found initial success as a playwright with *Distinguished Villa* (1926) and *The Bridge* (1927), among others. *Without My Cloak* (1931), a saga of the Irish bourgeoisie, immediately established her reputation as a novelist. *Mary Lavelle* (1936), the most romantic of her nine novels, drew on a year spent as a governess in Spain following university. Her knowledge of Spain also upholds *That Lady* (1946). A distinguished historical novel, set in the 16th cent., it brought her wide critical acclaim, as did *The Land of Spices* (1942), a notable portrait of convent life, which (like *Mary Lavelle*) was censored for 'immorality' by the Irish Censorship Board. Conflicts between the Catholic conscience and the self are a keynote of her fiction. Her other work includes *Farewell Spain* (1937), a travel book and elegy to the country from which she was barred for Republican sympathies; a monograph on *Teresa of Avila* (1951); the novel *As Music and Splendour* (1958), the portrait of a relationship between two women; and *Presentation Parlour* (1963), a book of reminiscences.

O'BRIEN, Sean (1952–   ), poet and critic, born in London, brought up in Hull, and educated at Cambridge; he taught for some time at the University of Sussex, and has more recently lived in Newcastle upon Tyne. His volumes include *The Indoor Park* (1983), *The Frighteners* (1987), *HMS Glasshouse* (1991), and *Ghost Train* (1995). His poetry, colloquial yet at times formal, and characteristically driven by a strong rhythmic energy and beat, evokes contemporary (particularly northern) urban landscapes and popular culture, reinforced by strong literary and painterly allusions: the effect is of a slightly surreal, displaced, offbeat portrait of a late 20th-cent. Britain uncertainly on the move.

Observations on the Present State of the Nation, see PRESENT STATE OF THE NATION.

Observator, see L'ESTRANGE.

Observer, a Sunday paper founded in 1791 by W. S. Bourne, and now Britain's oldest national Sunday paper. In 1814 it passed into the control of William Innell Clement (1770–1852), a powerful newspaper proprietor, under whose charge it flourished, partly through its pioneering use of woodcut illustrations to report sensational incidents (e.g. notably, the Cato Street conspiracy in 1820). It declined after Clement's death, reviving in the last decades of the century with Julius Beer (1837–80) as proprietor and Edward Dicey (1832–1911) as editor. It was bought by *Harmsworth in 1905, and edited from 1905 to 1908 by Austin Harrison (1873–1928), then from 1908 to 1942 by James Louis Garvin (1868–1947), who impressed his own personality and professional judgement deeply on the paper during his lengthy period as editor. The paper was bought in 1911 by William Waldorf Astor (1848–1919), and edited from 1948 to 1975 by David Astor (1912–2001). In 1994 the *Observer* was bought by the group owning the *Guardian.*

O'CASEY, Sean (John Casey) (1880–1964), Irish playwright, born in Dublin of Protestant parents, educated, according to his own autobiographies, in the streets of Dublin. He worked from the age of 14 at a variety of jobs, spending nine years from 1903 as a labourer on the Great Northern Railway of Ireland, meanwhile learning Irish, joining the Gaelic League and the Irish Republican League, and developing an enthusiasm for the theatre through amateur dramatics and the plays of *Boucicault. He began to publish articles, songs, and broadsheets under the name of Sean O Cathasaigh; his first plays were rejected by the *Abbey Theatre, but he received encouragement from Lady *Gregory and Lennox *Robinson, and *The Shadow of a Gunman* was performed in 1923, followed by *Juno and the Paycock* in 1924; they were published together as *Two Plays* (1925). *The Plough and the Stars* provoked nationalist riots at the Abbey in 1926. All three plays deal realistically with the rhetoric and dangers of Irish patriotism, with tenement life, self-deception, and survival; they are tragi-comedies in which violent death throws into relief the blustering masculine bravado of e.g. Jack Boyle and Joxer Daly in *Juno,* and the heroic resilience of Juno herself, or of Bessie Burgess in *The Plough.* O'Casey moved to England in 1926, and settled there permanently; his alienation from Ireland was confirmed by a rift with *Yeats and the Abbey over its rejection of *The Silver Tassie* (1928), an experimental anti-war play about an injured footballer, which introduced the symbolic *Expressionist techniques employed in his later works. These include *Within the Gates* (1933), *Red Roses for Me* (1942), *Cock-a-Doodle Dandy* (1949), and *The Bishop's Bonfire* (1955); although none achieved the popularity of his 'Abbey' plays, O'Casey continued to arouse both controversy and admiration, on stage and off. He also published a much-praised series of autobiographies, in six volumes, beginning with *I Knock at the Door* (1939) and ending with *Sunset and Evening Star* (1954). See David Krause, *Sean O'Casey: The Man and His Work* (1960); Eileen O'Casey, *Sean* (1971); and his *Letters* (ed. D. Krause; 4 vols, 1975–92).

OCCAM, and **Occam's Razor,** see OCKHAM.

OCCLEVE, see HOCCLEVE.

Oceana, see COMMONWEALTH OF OCEANA, THE.

OCKHAM, William of (1285–1349), born at Ockham in Surrey. He joined the Franciscans and studied at Oxford, where he wrote a Commentary on the *Sentences* of *Peter Lombard, Book I. In 1324 he was summoned by the pope to Avignon to answer charges of unorthodoxy, and several of his writings were condemned in 1326. In 1328 he fled from Avignon along with the Franciscan general, Michael of Cesena, having taken the side of the Spiritual Franciscans in their dispute with Pope John XXII. Thereafter he remained with the emperor, Louis of Bavaria, concerned with the question of papal power until his death (possibly of the plague) in 1349 or 1350. His importance is as a theologian with a strongly developed interest in logical method, and whose approach (characteristic of his century, perhaps) was critical rather than system-building. He is usually said to have been the most important figure in the breakdown of the Thomist synthesis between Aristotelian philosophy and Christian theology, though he always shied away from the radicalism of this division. The logical axiom associated with him is Ockham's 'Razor', that 'entities (*entia*) must not be unnecessarily multiplied', an attack on the postulation of Universals by the *Realists. The logical precision of his theory of language has been much admired (and, to some extent, copied) by 20th-cent. theoretical linguists and linguistic philosophers. His importance for literature in the century of *Langland lies in his stress on the Augustinian/Franciscan pre-eminence of Faith and the relative relegation of philosophical 'Reason', founded on Aristotle. See *Ockham: Philosophical Writings; A Selection*, ed. P. Boehner (1957); G. Leff, *William of Ockham* (1975).

O'CONNOR, (Mary) Flannery (1925–64), American novelist and short story writer, born in Georgia, whose works may be described as examples of Southern *Gothic. *Wise Blood* (1952) is a novel about a violent young religious extremist and *The Violent Bear It Away* (1960) also deals with fanaticism, as do many of her short stories, collected as *The Complete Stories* (1971). E. *Bishop described her work as 'clear, hard, vivid, and full of . . . more real poetry than a dozen books of poems'.

O'CONNOR, Frank, pseudonym of Michael Francis O'Donovan (1903–66), born in Cork, the son of a soldier; his work includes two novels, a life of Michael Collins (1937), translations from the Irish, literary criticism, and dramatizations, but he is best known for his short stories, many of them much revised and rewritten. Collections include *Bones of Contention* (1936), *Crab Apple Jelly* (1944), *Traveller's Samples* (1951), and *Domestic Relations* (1957). Realistic and closely observed, they offer a full portrait of the middle and lower classes of Ireland, and of the 'warm dim odorous feckless evasive southern quality' of his native Cork, which as a young man he had shocked by his productions of plays by *Ibsen and *Chekhov, and by his support of *Joyce (whose art, however, he was later to conclude, was too removed from life). He also wrote two volumes of autobiography, *An Only Child* (1961) and *My Father's Son* (1969), and his critical works include *The Lonely Voice: A Study of the Short Story* (1962).

O'CONNOR, Thomas Power (1848–1929), journalist and politician, supporter of *Parnell. His first book, *Lord Beaconsfield* (1879, first appeared in serial form anonymously, 1876), attracted much attention for its unsparing attack on *Disraeli. He was founder of the *Star* (1887), the *Sun* (1893), and *T.P.'s Weekly* (1902–16), a penny literary paper of some merit.

Octavia, the sister of Octavian (Augustus) and Mark Antony's wife, figures in Shakespeare's *Antony and Cleopatra* and Dryden's *All for Love.*

octosyllabics, consisting of eight syllables, usually applied to the eight-syllabled rhyming iambic metre of, e.g. Milton's *'Il Penseroso'.

Odd Women, The, a novel by George *Gissing, published in 1893. To escape the drudgery of her life in a draper's, Monica Madden, impoverished by the sudden death of her father, marries Edmund Widdowson, who proves to be a jealous tyrant. Wrongly suspected by him of adultery, she dies giving birth to his daughter. Monica's sisters become respectively an alcoholic and foolishly religious. While containing a portrayal of an establishment that promotes women's independence, the novel is a grim look at the possible fates of England's half a million more women than men, the 'Odd Women' of the title.

ode (from Greek, 'song'), a lyric poem of some length and elevated style on a serious subject. Odes are generally classified as either Pindaric or Horatian, depending upon their stanzaic structure and tone. The Pindaric ode—which is typically passionate, visionary, and sonorous—is modelled on the lyrics of *Pindar.

Designed to be sung and danced by the Greek chorus either at a public festival or in a theatre, these lyrics were written in complex stanzas which mirror the pattern of the dance and have a triadic structure: dancing to the left, the chorus chanted the strophe; dancing to the right, they repeated the pattern in the antistrophe; standing still, they brought the intricate pattern to a close in the epode, which had a different length and arrangement.

Unlike Pindarics, the Horatian ode (named after *Horace) tends to be meditative, tranquil, and colloquial. Horatian odes are almost always homostrophic, repeating a single stanzaic form, and typically shorter than the more declamatory Pindaric ode. Among the best-known Horatian odes are *Marvell's *An Horation Ode upon Cromwell's Return from Ireland*, T. *Gray's *Ode on a Distant Prospect of Eton College*, and Keats's *'To Autumn'.

The first outstanding imitation of Pindar was *Jonson's 'To the Immortal Memory . . . of . . . Sir Lucius Cary and Sir H. Morison' (1629), with the three parts renamed as 'turn', 'counter-turn', and 'stand'. This was a 'regular ode' in that it closely followed Pindar's scheme of all strophes and antistrophes conforming to one stanzaic pattern, and all epodes following another. The Pindaric ode gained popularity in English with the publication of *Cowley's *Pindarique Odes* (1656), which attempted to capture the spirit of Pindar, rather than furnish an exact translation or slavish imitation. In this work and in his original Pindaric compositions, beginning with the *Ode, upon the Blessed Restoration and Return of His Sacred Majesty* (1660), Cowley developed the 'irregular ode', which abandoned Pindar's stanzaic rules. Instead, Cowley invented a form without fixed forms, each stanza developing its own pattern of rhythm, rhyme, and number of lines.

*Dryden's odes, 'To the Pious Memory . . . of Mrs. Anne Killigrew' (1686), 'Ode in Honour of St. Cecilia's Day' (1687), and *Alexander's Feast: or The Power of Musique* (1697), which he thought his best poem, added to the reputation of the irregular Pindaric. Promising the would-be poet a freedom from formal constraints, the irregular ode, with its lofty manner, prosodic liberty, and intensity of feeling, attracted many writers, most of whom were not equipped for its demands. 'All the boys and girls caught the pleasing fashion, and they that could do nothing else could write like Pindar', Dr *Johnson wryly commented in his *Life of Cowley*. Accordingly, the irregular Pindaric ode was both the subject of critical censure and the object of parody, though the 18th cent. produced some fine examples, most notably W. *Collins's 'Ode to Liberty' (1746). Writing regular Pindaric odes, *Congreve and Gray worked against the prevailing trend; Gray's *The Progress of Poesy* and *The Bard* are two of the finest such works in English. From the mid-18th cent. onwards, it often becomes more difficult and less useful to distinguish between the Pindaric and Horatian styles, as poems indebted to both traditions became increasingly common.

The Romantic poets produced a remarkable number of outstanding odes, including Coleridge's *'Dejection: An Ode'; Wordsworth's *'Intimations of Immortality'; Shelley's *'Ode to the West Wind' and 'To a Sky-Lark'; and Keats's *'Ode to a Nightingale' and *'Ode on a Grecian Urn'. With a few notable exceptions, such as *Tennyson's *Ode on the Death of the Duke of Wellington* (1852), the Pindaric ode was not congenial to Victorian sensibilities, nor was it revived with much success in the 20th cent. One of the most successful modern examples of the form is Allen *Tate's 'Ode to the Confederate Dead' (1927, 1937). See George N. Shuster, *The English Ode from Milton to Keats* (1940, repr. 1964); Carol Maddison, *Apollo and the Nine: A History of the Ode* (1960); and John D. Jump, *The Ode* (1974).

'Ode on a Grecian Urn', a poem by *Keats, written 1819, published 1820.

While he describes the various pastoral scenes of love, beauty, and joy illustrated on the urn, the poet reflects on the eternal quality of art and the fleeting nature of human love and happiness. The last two lines are particularly well known and their meaning much debated:

> 'Beauty is truth, truth beauty,'—that is all
> Ye know on earth, and all ye need to know.

'Ode to a Nightingale', a poem by *Keats, written 1819, published 1820.

Keats's friend Charles Brown relates that a nightingale had nested near his house in Hampstead (now known as Keats House), and that one morning Keats sat under a plum-tree in the garden composing his ode on 'some scraps of paper'. Briefly, the poem is a meditation on the immortal beauty of the nightingale's song and the sadness of the observer, who must in the end accept sorrow and mortality.

'Ode to Autumn', see TO AUTUMN.

'Ode to the West Wind', a poem by P. B. *Shelley, 'chiefly written in a wood that skirts the Arno, near Florence' in Oct. 1819, published 1820.

The ode is a passionate invocation to the spirit of the West Wind, both 'Destroyer and Preserver'. It is composed in five sweeping stanzaic movements, each taking the form of a sonnet, but with complex musical patterns of internal rhyme and run-on lines, culminating in a breathless series of cries or questions. The symbolism is rich. The Wind is the seasonal force of renewal in Nature; it is also the power that produces self-sacrifice (even self-destruction) in personal life; the 'unextinguished' political hopes that drive continually over the 'unawakened Earth'; and the very passion of the ideal—aspiration, creativity—itself. Shelley's minute observations of wind, water, wood, cloud, and sky combine imagery which is simultaneously scientific, mythical, and even biblical.

The total effect is one of transcendent hope and energy, achieved through suffering and despair.

ODETS, Clifford (1906–63), American dramatist, born in Philadelphia. He was a founder member in 1931 of the Group Theatre, which followed the naturalistic methods of the Moscow Art Theatre, and his reputation was made when it performed his short play *Waiting for Lefty* (1935), about a taxi-drivers' strike. This was followed in the same year by two other dramas of social conflict, *Till the Day I Die*, about the German communists and the rise of the Nazis, and *Awake and Sing!*, portraying struggle and tragedy in a poor Jewish family in the Bronx. Later works include *Clash by Night* (1941), *The Big Knife* (1948, an attack on the corruptions of Hollywood), and *The Country Girl* (1950, first known in Britain as *Winter Journey*) about an alcoholic actor's marriage.

O'DONOGHUE, Bernard (1945–), Irish poet, born in Co. Cork, fellow of Magdalen College, Oxford. O'Donoghue combines work as a teacher of medieval literature with work as a poet and critic of contemporary poetry. *The Weakness* (1991) and *Gunpowder* (1995) are driven by a fascination with the unknowable nature of the poet's fellow humans, whether grotesques ('O'Regan the Amateur Anatomist') or innocents ('A Nun Takes the Veil'). O'Donoghue's clarity and modesty repeatedly expose the reader to the limits of the understanding while retaining a compassionate curiosity. *Here nor There* (1999) looks, back to childhood in Cork, and *Outliving* (2004) also explores themes of exile, Irish history, and family memory. O'Donoghue is also the author of an important critical book, *Seamus Heaney and the Language of Poetry* (1994).

O'Dowd, Major and Mrs, characters in Thackeray's **Vanity Fair.*

Odyssey, The, a Greek epic poem attributed to *Homer describing the adventures of Odysseus in the course of his return from the Trojan War to his kingdom of Ithaca.

OË, Kenzaburo (1935–), Japanese author who was awarded the *Nobel Prize for literature in 1994. His best-known work in the West is *A Personal Matter* (1964), the shocking, powerful, and frank account of a teacher's discovery that he has become the father of a seriously brain-damaged child.

OED, see OXFORD ENGLISH DICTIONARY, The.

O'FAOLAIN, Julia (1932–), novelist and historian, daughter of S. *O'Faolain, born in London but brought up in Dublin. She has lived in Ireland, England, Italy, and the United States. Her fiction includes a collection of short stories and eight novels, among which are *Women in the Wall* (1975), set in 6th-cent. Gaul and examining the phenomenon of nuns voluntarily immuring themselves; *No Country for Young Men* (1980), about history's difficult legacy in contemporary Ire-

land's private and public life; *The Obedient Wife* (1982); *The Irish Signorina* (1984); and *The Judas Cloth* (1992), a sweeping saga reconstructing the controversial career of the 19th-cent. pope Pius IX.

O'FAOLAIN, Sean (1900–91), Irish novelist and short story writer, born in Cork, the son of a police constable. He was educated at the National University of Ireland, was a member of the Irish Republican Army during the Troubles, studied at Harvard for three years from 1926, then taught at Strawberry Hill Training College before returning to Ireland in 1933, where, with the encouragement of E. *Garnett, and a subsidy from Jonathan Cape, he settled as a writer, having already published his first collection, *Midsummer Night Madness and Other Stories* (1932). This was followed by other collections, by three novels (*A Nest of Simple Folk*, 1934; *Bird Alone*, 1936; and *Come Back to Erin*, 1940; all of which deal with the frustrations of Irish society and the doomed aspirations of Irish nationalists), biographies of Constance Markiewicz (1934), Daniel O'Connell (1938), de Valera (1939), and Hugh O'Neill (1942), and a study of the Irish people, *The Irish* (1947). His autobiography *Vive-moi!* was published in 1964, and his *Collected Stories* in 1981. He is best known for his short stories, many of which evoke frustrated lives, missed opportunities, characters limited by their environment (as he had felt himself to be by provincial Cork), and which clearly demonstrate O'Faolain's allegiance to *Chekhov; later stories (*The Heat of the Sun: Stories and Tales*, 1966; *The Talking Trees*, 1971) tend to be dryer, more amusing, and more resilient in tone.

Of Dramatick Poesy: *An Essay* by *Dryden, published 1668.

The essay is in the form of a dialogue between Eugenius (C. *Sackville), Crites (Sir Robert Howard), Lisideius (*Sedley), and Neander (Dryden himself), who take a boat on the Thames on the day of the battle between the English and Dutch navies in June 1665, and subsequently discuss the comparative merits of English and French drama, and of the old and new in English drama. The essay is largely concerned with justifying Dryden's current practice as a playwright. It also contains admirable appreciations of Shakespeare, J. *Fletcher, and *Jonson.

O'FLAHERTY, Liam (1896–1984), Irish nationalist, novelist, and short story writer, who was born in the Aran Islands. His first novel, *The Neighbour's Wife* (1923), was published with the encouragement of E. *Garnett, and followed by several others, notably *The Informer* (1925), *The Puritan* (1931), and *Famine* (1937). But he is best known for his short stories, published in many periodicals and several volumes including *Spring Sowing* (1924), *The Tent* (1926), *Two Lovely Beasts* (1948), etc. Characteristic stories are those which deal unsentimentally with life, or more often death, from an animal's point of view, e.g. 'The Cow's

Death' (1923), 'The Wounded Cormorant' (1925), and 'The Seal' (1948). O'Flaherty published three volumes of flamboyant and inventive memoirs of his restless life: *Two Years* (1930), *I Went to Russia* (1931), and *Shame the Devil* (1934). He was described by S. *O'Faolain as 'an inverted romantic'. A life by P. A. Doyle was published in 1971.

Og, Dryden's name for *Shadwell in *The Second Part of *Absalom and Achitophel.*

ogham, or **ogam,** an alphabet of 20 characters used by the ancient British and Irish, consisting of conjunctions of upright and sloping strokes, and dots. It is found in inscriptions on stone and wood.

Ogier the Dane, a hero of the *Charlemagne romances, identified with a Frankish warrior, Autgarius, who fought against Charlemagne and then submitted to him. According to the romances, he is hostage for his father Gaufrey of Dannemarch at Charlemagne's court, and there are a number of legends about him, some of them including him as one of the *Paladins. It is doubtful if he had anything to do with Denmark; 'Dannemarch' perhaps signifies the marches of the Ardennes. Nevertheless, as Holger Danské he became the subject of Danish folk song, identified as a national hero who fought with the Ostrogoth *Dietrich of Bern (c.500).

OGILBY, John (1600–76), Scottish author, topographer, and printer, who published verse translations of *Virgil, *Aesop, and *Homer; also maps, atlases, and *Road Books of England and Wales*, the last of which were constantly revised until they faded into Mogg's *Road Books*.

O'HARA, John (Henry) (1905–70), American novelist, born in Pennsylvania, the son of a doctor. More than 200 of his sharp, satiric short stories were published in the *New Yorker*, and contributed to its characteristic tone; they were later collected under many different titles, from *The Doctor's Son* (1935) onwards. His novels, which gained wide popularity with their toughness, frankness, and sophistication, include *Appointment in Samarra* (1934), set in the country club and cocktail belt; *Butterfield 8* (1935), which evokes the promiscuity, violence, and hard drinking of Manhattan under prohibition; *Pal Joey* (1940; later a musical), told in the form of letters from a nightclub singer; *A Rage to Live* (1949), presenting the torments of a faithless wife; and many others, of generally decreasing interest and increasing prolixity.

Oisin, a legendary Gaelic warrior and bard, known also as Ossian (see MACPHERSON and FINGAL). In *The Wanderings of Oisin* (1889), a narrative poem by *Yeats, the bard tells St Patrick the story of his love for *Niamh, the daughter of the sea-god Manannán.

O'KEEFFE, John (1747–1833), Irish actor and dramatist, who wrote his first play at the age of 15. He produced his *Tony Lumpkin in Town* in 1778, after which he wrote some 50 farces and musical pieces. Of these the best known are *The Castle of Andalusia* (1782); *The Poor Soldier* (1783), which had great success in America; and *Wild Oats*, a romp of much skill and wit, produced at Covent Garden in 1791, and successfully revived in London in the late 1970s. O'Keeffe was the author of the song 'I am a friar of orders grey' (from his opera *Merry Sherwood*). *Hazlitt described him as 'the English Molière', but the compliment seems excessive.

OKRI, Ben(jamin) (1959–), Nigerian-born novelist and poet, born in Lagos, and educated at Urhobo College, Warri, and the University of Essex. His first novel, *Flowers and Shadows* (1980), was followed by *The Landscapes Within* (1981). *The Famished Road* (*Booker Prize, 1991) is a large, poetic, colourful novel narrated by a 'spirit child', Azaro, which blends myth, harsh contemporary reality, and a strong and epic sense of African place: *Songs of Enchantment* (1993) is a sequel. Other prose works include the mythic *Astonishing the Gods* (1995) and the more realistic *Dangerous Love* (1996). *Incidents at the Shrine* (1986) and *Stars of the New Curfew* (1989) are collections of short stories. *An African Elegy* (1992) is a collection of poetry. Okri is known for his political and social concerns as well as for his distinctively glowing prose, often composed of short, light, arresting sentences, which move from closely observed detail to the visionary and strange. He has also written occasional verse on topical issues.

OLCOTT, Colonel H. S., see BLAVATSKY.

Old Bachelor, The, the first comedy of *Congreve, produced 1693.

The 'Old Bachelor' is Heartwell, a 'surly old pretended woman-hater', who falls in love with Silvia, not knowing her to be the forsaken mistress of Vainlove, and is inveigled into marrying her, only discovering her true character afterwards from the gibes of his acquaintances. The parson who has been brought in to marry them, however, is in fact Vainlove's friend Bellmour, who has assumed the disguise for the purpose of an intrigue with Laetitia, the young wife of an uxorious old banker, Fondlewife; and Heartwell is relieved to find the marriage is only a pretence. The comedy includes the amusing characters of Sir Joseph Wittol, a foolish knight, who allows himself to be really married to Silvia, under the impression that she is the wealthy Araminta; and his companion, the cowardly bully Captain Bluffe, who under the same delusion is married to Silvia's maid. Bellmour in the end marries Belinda, whom he has been courting, in spite of her affectations, but Vainlove, who loves women only as long as they refuse him, finds that Araminta will not yet agree to marry him.

Oldcastle, The First Part of Sir John, a play first printed in 1600, reprinted in 1619 as Shakespeare's, and included in the Third and Fourth Folios of his plays. It is certainly not by him, though the historical John Oldcastle seems to have been Shakespeare's original model for *Falstaff. It is a collaborative work in which *Munday and *Drayton among others had a hand.

The play deals with the proceedings in Henry V's reign against Oldcastle as the chief supporter of the Lollards. Its true authorship is unknown.

Old Curiosity Shop, The, a novel by *Dickens, published as a separate volume in 1841. It was originally intended to be fitted into the framework of *Master Humphrey's Clock (1840–1), and Master Humphrey is, in fact, the narrator of the first few chapters, but this idea was soon abandoned.

Little Nell Trent lives in the gloomy atmosphere of the old curiosity shop kept by her grandfather, whom she tends with devotion. Reduced to poverty by a spendthrift son-in-law, and his remaining means drained by Nell's profligate brother Fred, he has borrowed money from Daniel Quilp, a hideous dwarf and a monster of iniquity, and this money he secretly expends in gambling, in the vain hope of retrieving his fortunes, for Little Nell's sake. Quilp, who believes him a rich miser, at last discovers where the borrowed money has gone, and seizes the shop. The old man and the child flee and wander about the country, suffering great hardships and haunted by the fear of being discovered by Quilp, who pursues them with unremitting hatred. They at last find a haven in a cottage by a country church, which they are appointed to look after. The grandfather's brother, returning from abroad, and anxious to relieve their needs, has great difficulty in tracing them. At last he finds them, but Nell, worn out with her troubles, has just died, and the grandfather soon follows her.

The novel contains a number of well known characters. Besides the loathsome and grotesque Quilp (who is drowned when on the point of being arrested for felony), there are his associates, the attorney Sampson Brass and his grim sister Sally; the honest lad Kit Nubbles, devoted to Little Nell, who incurs the hatred of Quilp and is nearly transported through his machinations; Mr and Mrs Garland, the kindly old couple who befriend Kit; Dick Swiveller, the disreputable facetious friend of Fred Trent, placed by Quilp for his own purposes as clerk to Brass; 'the Marchioness', the half-starved drudge in the Brass household (she marries Dick in the end); Codlin and Short, the Punch and Judy men, whom Little Nell and her grandfather accompany for a time in their wanderings; and Mrs Jarley, of the waxworks.

The death of Little Nell, in its day one of the most celebrated scenes in fiction, later became the focus of much of the reaction against Dickens's use of pathos. See G. H. Ford, *Dickens and His Readers* (1955), ch. iv.

Old English, see ENGLISH.

OLDFIELD, Anne (1683–1730), an actress who excelled in both tragedy and comedy. She first made her mark as Lady Betty Modish in Cibber's *The Careless Husband*, but her best parts are said to have been Calista (in Rowe's *The Fair Penitent*) and Lady Townly (in Cibber's *The Provok'd Husband*). She was buried in Westminster Abbey, beneath *Congreve's monument. She is the 'Narcissa' of Pope's *Moral Essays*.

Old Fortunatus, a comedy by *Dekker, published 1600, based on a story contained in a German 'Volksbuch' of 1509 and dramatized by *Sachs in 1553.

The beggar Fortunatus, encountering Fortune, is offered the choice between wisdom, strength, health, beauty, long life, and riches, and chooses the last. He receives a purse from which he can at any time draw ten pieces of gold. He goes on his travels, in the course of which he secures the marvellous hat of the Soldan of Turkey, which transports the wearer wherever he wishes to go. But at the height of his success Fortune steps in and puts an end to his life. His son Andelocia, refusing to take warning by his father's fate and equipped with the purse and hat, goes through a series of adventures at the court of Athelstane, is finally deprived of his talismans, and meets a miserable death.

The character of Orléans, the 'frantic lover' of Athelstane's daughter, was much praised by C. *Lamb.

OLDHAM, John (1653–83), educated at St Edmund Hall, Oxford. He published several Pindaric *odes, but is chiefly remembered for his ironical *Satire against Virtue* (1679) and *Satires upon the Jesuits* (1681). He also translated and wrote imitations of *Juvenal, *Horace, *Bion, *Moschus, and *Boileau. His *Poems and Translations* were collected in 1683. He died young of smallpox, and *Dryden commemorated him and his verse in the well-known lines beginning 'Farewell, too little and too lately known'.

OLDMIXON, John (?1673–1742), Whig historian and pamphleteer, who also wrote plays, poems, and pastorals. He published *The British Empire in America* (1708), *The Secret History of Europe* (1712–15, anonymously), and histories of England during the Stuart reigns (1729) and those of William III, Anne, and George I (1735–9). By his 'Essay on Criticism', prefixed to the third edition (1728) of his *Critical History of England* (1724–6) he incurred the hostility of *Pope, who pilloried him in *The Dunciad* and *Peri Bathous*.

OLD MOORE, Francis Moore (1657–1714), astrologer, licensed physician, and Whig partisan, who had an astrological practice in Lambeth, later in Southwark. His *Vox Stellarum, an Almanac for 1698 with Astrological Observations* appeared in 1697. *Old Moore's Almanac* long outlived its creator, and sold extremely well throughout the 18th and 19th cents, and it still thrives thanks to its reputation for sensationalism and prophecy; its print-order in 1999 ran to 800,000 copies. (See also ALMANACS.)

Old Mortality, a novel by Sir W. *Scott, published in 1816 in *Tales of My Landlord*, 1st series.

'Old Mortality' is the nickname of a certain Robert Paterson who, towards the end of the 18th cent., wandered about Scotland cleaning and repairing the tombs of the Cameronians, a sect of fanatical Covenanters who took up arms for their religion against Charles II. The novel, one of Scott's masterpieces, tells the story of young Henry Morton of Milnwood, a moderate Presbyterian of courage and integrity who, like so many of Scott's heroes, finds himself drawn into a struggle which at first he only imperfectly understands and where his sympathies are divided between the opposing parties. The action takes place in the period between the uprising of the Covenanters at Drumclog and their defeat at Bothwell Bridge three weeks later, with a final section several years after. At the outset, Morton is arrested by John Grahame of Claverhouse's dragoons for harbouring an old friend of his father's, John Balfour of Burley, unaware that Burley had just taken part in the assassination of Archbishop Sharpe. Morton narrowly escapes execution and, spurred by this injustice, coupled with a sense of his countrymen's wrongs, joins the insurgent Covenanters, little though he shares their more extreme opinions. This brings him into conflict with the family of Lady Margaret Bellenden, the Royalist owner of Tillietudlem Castle and grandmother of Edith Bellenden whom he loves, and who is loved by Lord Evandale who is serving under Claverhouse. Morton and Evandale in turn, by rival acts of generosity, save each other's lives, and Morton maintains his place in Edith's heart; but the defeat of the Covenanters at Bothwell Bridge and his capture and banishment divide him from her for many years. She, believing him dead, is on the point of marrying Evandale when the accession of William III enables Morton to return; Evandale's death in a skirmish with fanatics finally makes it possible for her to marry Morton. The high points of the novel are the contrasting portraits of the ruthless but chivalrous Claverhouse and the devious Burley, each in their different ways fanatical, the descriptions of the two battles and the siege of Tillietudlem, and the trial of Ephraim Macbriar, one of the leading Covenanters; but Cuddie Headrigg, Morton's self-appointed squire, and his Cameronian old mother add memorably to Scott's gallery of lower-class Scottish characters.

Old Possum's Book of Practical Cats, a volume of verse for children, by T. S. *Eliot, on which the long-running musical *Cats* was based.

Old Q, the nickname of William Douglas, third earl of March and fourth duke of Queensberry (1724–1810), a friend of the prince of Wales, notorious for his escapades and dissolute life, much interested in horse racing. He was satirized by *Burns, and is the 'degenerate Douglas' of *Wordsworth's sonnet.

OLDS, Sharon (1942–   ), American poet, born in San Francisco, educated at Stanford and Columbia universities. She now lives in New York. Her collections include *Satan Says* (1980), *The Dead and the Living* (1984) and *The Gold Cell* (1987) and a Selected Poems, *The Sign of Saturn*, was published in Britain in 1991, where her reputation has since been firmly established. Olds is widely regarded as heir to the *confessional tradition of *Lowell, *Plath, and *Sexton. Her fluid, descriptive free verse forms are consistently rich in metaphor, and display her power to transform an often harsh reality through startling imagery into the kind of art that transcends the personal. The self-knowledge that can be drawn from the wrongs of the past and the hope contained for us in the future can be seen reflected in Olds's many studies of her parents and her children. *The Father* (1992), perhaps her finest work to date, is the poetic narrative of her father's illness and death from cancer. *The Wellspring* (1996) explores themes of sex, love, and mortality, and continues the poet's celebratory expression of life and the redemptive power of love.

Old Vic Theatre (previously the Royal Victoria), a theatre in the Waterloo Road, London, long famous for its notable productions of Shakespeare's plays under the management of Lilian Baylis (1874–1937), who took it over in 1912.

Old Wives Tale, The, a play largely in prose by *Peele, published 1595.

The play is a satire on the romantic dramas of the time, the first English work of this kind. Two brothers are searching for their sister Delia, who is held captive by the magician Sacrapant. The brothers also fall into his hands. They are all rescued by the knight Eumenides aided by Jack's ghost, who is impelled by motives of gratitude, because the knight had borne the expense of Jack's funeral. The play is rich in songs and magical invocations such as: 'Gently dippe, but not too deepe, | For feare thou make the goulden beard to weep.'

Old Wives' Tale, The, a novel by Arnold *Bennett, published 1908.

It is the long chronicle of the lives of two sisters, Constance and Sophia Baines, daughters of a draper of Bursley (Burslem, one of Bennett's Five Towns), from ardent girlhood, through disillusionment, to death. The drab life of the draper's shop, its trivial incidents, are made interesting and important. Constance, a staid and sensible young woman, marries the estimable and superficially insignificant Samuel Povey, the chief assistant in the shop, and spends all her life in Bursley. The more passionate and imaginative Sophia elopes with the fascinating Gerald Scales, a commercial traveller who has come into a fortune. He is an unprincipled blackguard, has to be forced to marry her, carries her to Paris, where she is exposed to indignities, and finally deserts her. She struggles to success as a lodging-house keeper in Paris, where she lives through the siege of 1870. The sisters are reunited, and spend their last years together in Bursley.

OLDYS, William (1696–1761), antiquary, and editor of the *Harleian Miscellany*. His principal interest was biography, and his *Life of Sir Walter Raleigh* was prefixed to the 1736 edition of *Ralegh's *History of the World*. He contributed many biographies to and was general editor of the *Biographia Britannica* (6 vols, 1747–66). He also wrote the poem 'Busy, curious, thirsty fly', first published in 1732. He was relieved from poverty and the Fleet Prison by being appointed Norroy king-of-arms.

Olindo, the lover of Sofronia in Tasso's *Jerusalem Delivered*.

OLIPHANT, Laurence (1829–88), born at Cape Town of Scottish descent; after a desultory education and extensive travel with his parents, he became a barrister in Ceylon, where his father was chief justice. *A Journey to Khatmandu* (1852) and *The Russian Shores of the Black Sea* (1853–4) are accounts of some of his early adventures. He was secretary to Lord Elgin in Washington, Canada, and China; the latter is described in *A Narrative of the Earl of Elgin's Mission to China 1857–9* (1859). He acted as *The Times* correspondent in Circassia during the war and again during the Franco-Prussian War. He is then heard of as plotting with Garibaldi in Italy, as secretary of a legation in Japan, and in other parts of the world. His novel *Piccadilly* (1870) is a satirical exposure of the venal side of London society. He was an MP during 1865–7 and high office appeared within his grasp, but by 1867 he had come under the influence of the spurious American 'prophet' Thomas Lake Harris, joined his Brotherhood of New Life in New York state, and surrendered to him most of his property. His allegiance to Harris ended in 1882 and in that year Oliphant and his wife founded a community for Jewish immigrants in Haifa. There he wrote his second novel, *Altiora Peto* (1883), and the strange *Sympneumata* (1885) which was dictated by his wife as if possessed by a spirit. M. *Oliphant (no relation) published his biography in 1891. A recent biography by Anne Taylor (1982) suggests that Oliphant's crazed behaviour was attributable to inherited syphilis.

OLIPHANT, Margaret (M.O.W.), née Wilson (1828–97), a prolific Scots writer, author of well over 100 books and innumerable articles. Early widowed, she was compelled to write for an income, both for her own and for her brother's families. In 1849 she published *Passages in the Life of Mrs Margaret Maitland*, a tale of Scotland which had an encouraging reception; *Caleb Field*, a historical novel, appeared in 1851; and among her many domestic romances *The Athelings* (1857) was probably the most interesting. In 1862 appeared her biography of the brilliant heretical preacher Edward Irving and in 1891 a life of Laurence *Oliphant (no relation). But it is for her 'Chronicles of Carlingford' series that she is best remembered. Carlingford is a quiet country town near London, and this series of novels (the most notable of which are *Salem Chapel*, 1863; *The Perpetual Curate*, 1864; *Miss Marjoribanks*, 1866; and *Phoebe Junior*, 1876) is set among the aristocracy, professional families, and tradesmen of the town. Religious themes predominate, but the books are sharp and humorous. In 1868 Mrs Oliphant was awarded a civil list pension of £100 a year. Her other most interesting group of books, *Stories of the Seen and Unseen*, all connected in some way with death and the experience of the soul, began with *A Beleaguered City* (1880) which was followed by *A Little Pilgrim* (1882) and others. Her astute *Literary History of England* (1882) earned much praise, but the continuing stream of undemanding romances and novels of domestic life brought little further success. Her long association with *Blackwood's* was commemorated in the posthumous *Annals of a Publishing House* (1897). Her autobiography (1899) poignantly describes the destructive necessity of having to write so much.

Olivant, the ivory horn (from *Oliphaunt*) of *Roland.

Oliver, in the *Charlemagne cycle of legends, one of Charlemagne's *Paladins. He is the close friend of *Roland, with whom he has a prolonged and undecided single combat (the origin of their comradeship), and is his equal in bravery, but more prudent. At the battle of Roncesvalles he urges Roland to summon help by sounding his horn, but Roland postpones doing so till too late. Oliver's sister Aude is betrothed to Roland.

Oliver de Boys, Orlando's elder brother in Shakespeare's *As You Like It*, who marries *Celia.

Oliver Twist, a novel by *Dickens, published 1837–8.

Oliver Twist is the name given to a child of unknown parentage born in a workhouse and brought up under the cruel conditions to which pauper children were formerly exposed, the tyrant at whose hands he especially suffers being Bumble, the parish beadle. After experience of an unhappy apprenticeship, he runs away, reaches London, and falls into the hands of a gang of thieves, at the head of which is the old Jew Fagin, and whose other chief members are the burglar Bill Sikes, his mistress Nancy, and 'the Artful Dodger', an impudent young pickpocket. Every effort is made to convert Oliver into a thief. He is temporarily rescued by the benevolent Mr Brownlow, but kidnapped by the gang, whose interest in his retention has been increased by the offers of a sinister person named Monks, who has a special interest in Oliver's perversion. Oliver is now made to accompany Bill Sikes on a burgling expedition, in the course of which he receives a gunshot wound, and comes into the hands of Mrs Maylie and her protégée Rose, by whom he is kindly treated and brought up. After a time, Nancy, who develops some redeeming traits, reveals to Rose that

Monks is aware of Oliver's parentage, and wishes all proof of it destroyed; also that there is some relationship between Oliver and Rose herself. Enquiry is set on foot. In the course of it Nancy's action is discovered by the gang, and she is brutally murdered by Bill Sikes. A hue and cry is raised; Sikes, trying to escape, accidentally hangs himself, and the rest of the gang are secured and Fagin executed. Monks, found and threatened with exposure, confesses what remains unknown. He is the half-brother of Oliver, and has pursued his ruin, animated by hatred and the desire to retain the whole of his father's property. Rose is the sister of Oliver's unfortunate mother. Oliver is adopted by Mr Brownlow. Monks emigrates and dies in prison. Bumble ends his career in the workhouse over which he formerly ruled.

Dickens resented the implication that this work made crime glamorous, and in a preface to the third edition (Apr. 1841) tactfully dissociated it from the popular *'Newgate novels' of the period, by *Ainsworth, *Bulwer-Lytton, and others.

Olivia, (1) the wealthy Illyrian countess in Shakespeare's *Twelfth Night*; (2) a character in Wycherley's *The Plain Dealer*; (3) the elder daughter of Dr Primrose, in Goldsmith's *The Vicar of Wakefield*.

Olney Hymns, see COWPER and NEWTON, J.

OLSON, Charles, see BLACK MOUNTAIN POETS.

Olympian Odes, The, see PINDAR.

Olympia Press, a Paris-based imprint founded in 1953 by Maurice Girodias (1920–90), son of writer and publisher Jack Kahane, owner of the Obelisk Press. It published many English-language literary and pornographic works then censored in England, some of which were pseudonymous, including books by C. *Logue and A. *Trocchi. Girodias also published *Nabokov's *Lolita* (1955), *Burroughs's *Naked Lunch* (1959), and work by H. *Miller and British experimentalist P. *Ableman. Olympia Press eventually merged in the late 1960s with the US-based Grove Press.

Omar Khayyám, The Rubáiyát of, a translation by E. *FitzGerald of the *rubais* or quatrains of the 12th-cent. Persian poet. The translation was first published anonymously in 1859; FitzGerald produced further editions, revised and with added quatrains, in 1868, 1872, and 1879. FitzGerald's translation preserved the stanza form of the original, but adapted the quatrains into a connected theme, sceptical of divine providence, mocking the transience of human grandeur, and concentrating on the pleasures of the fleeting moment. The felicitously phrased aphorisms of this cynical yet genial poetic sequence are among the most frequently quoted lines in English poetry.

Omnium, duke and duchess of (Plantagenet Palliser and Lady Glencora), leading characters in the *'Palliser'

novels of A. Trollope; in his view Plantagenet was 'a perfect gentleman'.

ONDAATJE, Michael (1943–   ), Canadian poet and novelist, born in Sri Lanka (formerly Ceylon). He moved to Canada in 1962 and was educated at the University of Toronto and at Queen's University, Kingston, Ontario. He taught English at the University of Western Ontario from 1967 to 1970 and then at Glendon College, York University, Toronto. He first came to critical notice as a poet with *The Dainty Monsters* (1967), *The Man with Seven Toes* (1969), *Rat Jelly* (1973), and *There's a Trick with a Knife I'm Learning to Do* (1979). In *The Collected Works of Billy the Kid* (1970), a collage of poetry and prose and visual devices, he uses temporal dislocation and multiple viewpoints to present a paradoxical amalgamation of history, fiction, and autobiography. *Coming through Slaughter* (1976) is a fictionalized life of the legendary jazz musician Charles 'Buddy' Bolden (1876–1931). In *Running in the Family* (1982), though blurring the boundaries between autobiography and fiction, Ondaatje drew on his family's Sri Lankan past to produce 'not a history but a portrait or "gesture"'. *The English Patient* (1992), set at the end of the Second World War, won the *Booker Prize and was made into a hugely successful film directed by Anthony Minghella. He has also edited three anthologies: *The Broken Ark* (1971, a collection of animal poems), *Personal Fictions* (1977), and *The Long Poem Anthology* (1979). A new collection of poems, *Handwriting*, appeared in 1998.

O'NEILL, Eugene (1888–1953), American dramatist, born in New York. The son of a well-known romantic actor, he had a varied career (as seaman, gold prospector, journalist, and actor) before associating himself (1916) with the experimental theatre group the Provincetown Players, which staged several of his early one-act plays, including *Bound East for Cardiff* (1916) and *The Moon of the Caribbees* (1918). His first big success was the full-length naturalistic drama *Beyond the Horizon* (1920), which was followed in the same year by his expressionistic *The Emperor Jones*, a tragedy which describes the rise and fall of the Negro 'emperor' of a West Indian island, and *Anna Christie* (1921), a naturalistic study of a prostitute on the New York waterfront and her redemption. Among other important plays of this period were *The Hairy Ape* (1922), *All God's Chillun Got Wings* (1924), and *Desire under the Elms* (1924). O'Neill's criticism of contemporary materialistic values was powerfully and poetically expressed in *The Fountain* (1925), *The Great God Brown* (1926), *Lazarus Laughed* (1927), and *Marco Millions* (1927). He experimented with a *stream-of-consciousness technique in *Strange Interlude* (1928), and adapted the theme of the *Oresteia to the aftermath of the American Civil War in his trilogy *Mourning Becomes Electra* (1931). *Ah! Wilderness* (1932) and *Days without End* (1934) were followed by a long absence from the stage, during which he was awarded the

*Nobel Prize (1936) and worked on several plays, including *The Iceman Cometh* (1946), a lengthy naturalistic tragedy set in Harry Hope's Bowery saloon, where a collection of down-and-out alcoholics nourish their illusions ('pipe dreams') with the aid of an extrovert, apparently cheerful salesman, Hickey. His masterpiece, *Long Day's Journey into Night*, was written in 1940–1, and posthumously produced and published in 1956; it is a semi-autobiographical family tragedy, portraying the mutually destructive relationships of drug-addicted Mary Tyrone, her ex-actor husband James, and their two sons, hard-drinking Jamie and intellectual Edmund. His last play, *A Moon for the Misbegotten*, was written by 1943 and produced in 1947; it portrays, with humour and lyricism, the relationship of Phil Hogan, tenant farmer, with his spirited and allegedly promiscuous daughter Josie, and Josie's chaste and compassionate love for their self-tormenting, haunted, dissolute landlord, James Tyrone. Despite occasional lapses into melodrama and rhetoric, O'Neill's plays remain powerfully theatrical and original; he transcends his debt to *Ibsen and *Strindberg, producing an *œuvre* in which the struggle between self-destruction, self-deception, and redemption is presented as essentially dramatic in nature.

ONIONS, C(harles) T(albut) (1873–1965), grammarian and lexicographer, co-editor of the *Oxford English Dictionary* and its original *Supplement*, 1914–33; editor of *A Shakespeare Glossary* (1911), *The Shorter Oxford English Dictionary* (1932), *The Oxford Dictionary of English Etymology* (1966); author of *An Advanced English Syntax* (1904: rev. edn, *Modern English Syntax*, 1971).

ONIONS, George Oliver (1873–1961), novelist and short story writer born in Bradford, whose works include *The Compleat Bachelor* (1900), *Widdershins* (1911, tales of the uncanny), and *The Story of Ragged Robyn* (1945). He changed his name by deed poll in 1918 to George Oliver. He was married to the romantic novelist Berta Ruck (1878–1978), whose name appeared inadvertently in V. *Woolf's *Jacob's Room*, thus occasioning first a dispute, then an acquaintance between the two women.

onomatopoeia, the formation of a word by an imitation of the sound associated with the object or action designated: as 'hurlyburly', 'buzz', 'creak'. The term is also applied to the use of a combination of words to evoke by sound a certain image or mood, the most frequently quoted example being *Tennyson's 'murmuring of innumerable bees'.

opera, a dramatic performance in which music forms an essential part, consisting of recitatives, arias, and choruses, with orchestral accompaniment and scenery; also, a dramatic or musical composition intended for this, a libretto or score [*OED*]. The most important word in this definition is 'essential', for it is precisely the integration of music into the substance of the drama that differentiates opera from the *masque (in which the music is generally episodic and accompanimental) or the straight play with incidental music. This integration, and hence the first operas, developed out of the experiments in the *stile recitativo* (the 'reciting style') made by a group of cultured intellectuals at the Medici court in Florence towards the end of the 16th cent.: the distinctive combination of elements in which it results has been differently balanced at different times and in different countries, though usually with music in a dominant role.

In England, in spite of a continuous and often passionate interest in imported foreign examples, opera never established itself as an indigenous form in the way that it did in Italy, France, and Germany—a comment on the way the English feel about music which isolated exceptions like *Purcell in the 17th cent. or *Britten in the 20th do not really disprove. The first attempts at opera in English were somewhat obstructed by the 'Puritan interregnum' and the closing of the public theatres under *Cromwell. It is difficult at this stage to distinguish between opera and masque, but the first English work that is normally regarded as an opera is *The Siege of Rhodes* (1656), of which the text was by *D'Avenant: the music is lost, and was anyhow a collective effort by a number of different composers. The first English example of which the music has survived is John *Blow's *Venus and Adonis* (*c*.1684), a genuine opera in miniature which preceded Purcell's *Dido and Aeneas* by some five years. See also LIBRETTO.

Ophelia, in Shakespeare's *Hamlet*, the daughter of Polonius.

OPIE, Mrs Amelia (1769–1853), wife of John Opie the painter, and friend of Sydney *Smith, *Sheridan, Mme de *Staël, and many other members of literary society. She was a copious novelist and poet, and was satirized by T. L. Peacock in *Headlong Hall* as Miss Poppyseed, 'an indefatigable compounder of novels'. Her works include: *Poems* (1802); *Adeline Mowbray* (suggested by the story of Mary *Wollstonecraft) (1804); *Simple Tales* (1806); a *Memoir* of her husband in 1809; and *Lays for the Dead* in 1833.

OPIE, Peter Mason (1918–82), author and folklorist, and his wife Iona Margaret Balfour Opie (1923–). They produced, after many years of research together, such distinguished works as the *Oxford Dictionary of Nursery Rhymes* (1951), *The Lore and Language of Schoolchildren* (1959), and *Children's Games in Street and Playground* (1969). They also edited anthologies, including *The Oxford Book of Children's Verse* (1973).

Opimian, the Revd Dr Theophilus, a character in Peacock's *Gryll Grange*. According to Lewis and Short's Latin-English Dictionary *Opimianum* was a celebrated wine of the vintage of AUC 633 = 121 BC, when Opimius was consul.

OPPENHEIM, E. Phillips, see SPY FICTION.

ORAGE, Alfred Richard (1875–1934), born in York-shire, the son of a schoolmaster. He became himself a schoolmaster in Leeds, where he joined the *Fabian Society, and was active in a wide range of artistic, political, and intellectual activities. He came to London in 1906, and from 1907 till 1922, partly financed by G. B. *Shaw and assisted initially by Holbrook Jackson (1874–1948), edited the *New Age*, a periodical which acquired during this period much political and literary prestige. His contributors include both the established (Shaw, Arnold *Bennett, *Wells, and others) and the as yet unknown (including *Pound, K. *Mansfield, *Al-dington, and T. E. *Hulme). He was an advocate of Social Credit, and in later years came under the influence of *Gurdjieff; after leaving the *New Age* in 1922 he went to Fontainebleau, then New York, as a Gurdjieff disciple, returning to England in 1931 to found a new paper, the *New English Weekly*, which he edited until his death. See the life by Philip Mairet (1936) and *'The New Age' under Orage* (1967) by W. Martin.

Oran Haut-ton, see HAUT-TON.

Orc, (1) a mythical sea-monster mentioned by *Ar-iosto, *Drayton, *Milton, and others, from the Latin 'orca', a kind of whale; (2) in the Prophetic Books of *Blake, the symbol of rebellion and anarchy, the son of *Los and *Enitharmon, who is chained, like *Pro-metheus, to a rock in *The Book of *Urizen*, and who bursts his bonds in *America: A Prophecy* to fight and defeat Albion's Angel; (3) in the personal mythology of J. R. R. *Tolkien, orcs are the evil and hideous creations of the rebellious Vala, Melkor.

ORCZY, Baroness (Mrs Montague Barstow) (1865–1947), Hungarian-born novelist who lived from the age of 15 in London. She achieved fame with her romantic novel *The Scarlet Pimpernel* (1905), the story of the League of the Scarlet Pimpernel, a band of Englishmen pledged to rescue the innocent victims of the reign of terror in Paris. Its leader, Sir Percy Blakeney, outwits his opponents—in particular the wily Chauvelin—by means of his courage and ingenious disguises, at the same time concealing his identity from his friends in England. The success of the novel followed its success in a dramatized version, written in collaboration with her husband, in which Fred Terry took the leading part. It was performed first in Nottingham in 1903, then, to great acclaim, in London in 1905. She wrote many other historical and romantic novels, including several sequels to *The Scarlet Pimpernel*.

Ordeal of Richard Feverel, The, a novel by G. *Meredith, published 1859.

This book, in which Meredith found his strength as a novelist, was written just after the painful collapse of his first marriage; it exhibits clearly for the first time his theory of 'comedy', and the growing luxuriance of his style. Sir Austin Feverel's wife has run off with a poet, leaving him with their son Richard. Sir Austin, arro-gant and obtuse, devises a 'System' for Richard's education, which consists in keeping the boy at home (for schools are corrupting) and in trusting to authoritarian parental vigilance. The slow collapse of the 'System', and Richard's struggle for freedom and knowledge, form the underlying theme of the book. Richard and Lucy Desborough, a neighbouring farm-er's niece, fall in love at first sight, and an idyllic courtship ends in the discovery of their attachment. Lucy has every natural charm, but not the birth Sir Austin requires for his son. His attempts to break their relationship result in their secret marriage and the fury of the possessive Sir Austin, who cruelly ensures the separation of the young couple by playing on Richard's love and duty. Ordered to await his father in London, Richard earnestly sets about the redemption of ladies of pleasure, succeeding only in falling a temporary victim to the beautiful Bella Mount, who falls equally in love with him. Initially Bella has acted at the instigation of the predatory Lord Mountfalcon, who has plans to ensnare Lucy. Richard becomes increasingly over-whelmed with shame at his treatment of his wife, then hears that he is a father and that Lucy and Sir Austin are reconciled. But as soon as he returns to her he learns of the designs of Lord Mountfalcon; he furiously challenges him to a duel and is seriously wounded. In the succeeding fever his confusions are stripped away and he is finally freed of his devouring father. But the shock of events proves overwhelming for Lucy, who loses her mind and eventually dies.

ORDERICUS VITALIS (1075–1142/3), born near Shrewsbury of a Norman father and probably English mother, a monk of Saint Évroul in Normandy. He wrote between 1114 and 1141 his *Ecclesiastical History of England and Normandy* in Latin, covering events from the beginning of the Christian era down to 1141, which is one of the standard authorities for the Norman period. His accounts of the Conquest and other events show a lively sympathy with the English and a predominant interest in English matters.

Oresteia, The, a trilogy of plays by *Aeschylus.

Agamemnon describes the return to Argos after the Trojan War of the victorious Agamemnon, brother of Helen's husband Menelaus, and his murder by his wife Clytemnestra foretold by his captive, the prophet Cassandra, daughter of King Priam of Troy. The *Choephoroe* (or *The Libation Bearers*) portrays the vengeance of the son and daughter of Agamemnon, Orestes and Electra: Orestes murders Clytemnestra and her lover Aegisthus, and is himself pursued by the Eumenides, or Furies. The *Eumenides* shows the Furies in pursuit of Orestes, who is protected by the younger god Apollo. Orestes is tried, Athena, goddess of wisdom, delivers her casting vote on his behalf, and he goes free, released from the ancient blood vengeance: Athena reconciles the Furies to the new

Law, and they are transformed into the Kindly Ones, who bless the city of Athens and the land.

Other versions of the story appear in the works of *Sophocles (who wrote *Electra*) and *Euripides, and it reappears in many forms throughout Western literature; there are notable 20th-cent. dramatic versions by T. S. *Eliot (*The Family Reunion*, 1939), *O'Neill (*Mourning Becomes Electra*, 1931), and *Sartre (*Les Mouches*, 1942).

Orfeo, Sir, a metrical romance of the early 14th cent. in about 600 lines (the poem varies considerably in its three manuscript versions), identified in its prologue as a *Breton lay. It represents the story of Orpheus and Eurydice (see ORPHEUS) in a Celtic guise: Queen Heurodys is carried off to fairyland and pursued by King Orfeo whose melodious playing of his harp succeeds in bringing her back to the world of men. The Middle English version (to which *Child's ballad 'King Orfeo' is related) ends happily: the queen's return is permanent, and the steward left in charge of the kingdom by Orfeo during his absence passes the romance test of his fidelity. The poem is much admired as one of the most charming and interesting of Middle English romances. Ed. A. J. Bliss (1954; rev. 1966).

Orgoglio (Italian, signifying haughtiness), in Spenser's *Faerie Queene* (I. vii, viii), captures the *Redcrosse Knight, and is slain by Prince *Arthur.

Oriana, (1) see under AMADIS OF GAUL; (2) a name frequently applied by poets to *Elizabeth I, as in T. *Morley's collection of madrigals *The Triumphes of Oriana* (1601); (3) the heroine of Fletcher's *The Wild-Goose Chase*; (4) the subject of an early ballad by *Tennyson.

Oriental (or Eastern) **novel** (or tale), a class of story exotically set in the Middle or Far East, and varying greatly in tone, from Johnson's *Rasselas* to Beckford's *Vathek* and Byron's *The Corsair* and *The Giaour. Many of the tales (such as those of *Dow, *Hawkesworth, *Ridley, and F. *Sheridan) relate the flamboyant adventures of well-defined heroes and villains, often with the intervention of the supernatural; others (such as *Southey's poem *The Curse of Kehama* or Moore's *Lalla Rookh*) are more complex. These tales enjoyed great popularity in the second half of the 18th and the early part of the 19th cents. Public interest in the Orient was no doubt greatly stimulated by the translation into English in 1705–8 of the *Arabian Nights*; by *Knolles's history of the Turks (much admired by both Dr *Johnson and *Byron); and by the translations of Sir W. *Jones. (See also NOVEL, RISE OF THE.)

ORIGEN (*c*.185–*c*.253), a great Christian thinker and scholar in the Alexandrian school, the author of many theological works and compiler of the famous *Hexapla* versions of the Old Testament (see BIBLE). He studied under Ammonius, sometimes regarded as the founder of *Neoplatonism, and he is of great importance as the introducer of Neoplatonic elements into Christianity. His *Principles*, which were rejected by church orthodoxy, were translated by *Jerome and quoted by St *Bernard, and he influenced the allegorical method of literary criticism developed by *Augustine. See J. Daniélou, *Origen*, trans. W. Mitchell (1955).

Origin of Species, *On the*, the great work of C. *Darwin, published 1859. Its full title was *On the Origin of Species by Means of Natural Selection, or the Preservation of Favoured Races in the Struggle for Life.*

ORIGO, Iris (1902–88), British historian and biographer, married to Marchese Antonio Origo. Among her twelve books in English are a biography of *Leopardi (1935, rev. 1953); *War in Val d'Orcia* (1947), a vivid and moving account of wartime events in her part of Italy; *The Last Attachment* (1949), chronicling *Byron's last years; and *The Merchant of Prato* (1957), a lively and meticulous study of the eponymous 14th-cent. merchant.

Orinda, the Matchless, see PHILIPS, K.

Orlando, (1) the Italian form of *Roland, a hero of the *Charlemagne romances (see also ORLANDO FURIOSO and ORLANDO INNAMORATO); (2) in Shakespeare's *As You Like It*, the lover of Rosalind; (3) the title of a novel by V. *Woolf.

Orlando furioso, a poem by *Ariosto, published in its complete form in 1532, designed to exalt the house of Este and its legendary ancestor *Rogero (Ruggiero) and to continue the story of Orlando's love for *Angelica begun by Boiardo in *Orlando innamorato.*

The main theme of the poem is this: Saracens and Christians, in the days of *Charlemagne, are at war for the possession of Europe. The Saracens under *Agramant, king of Africa, are besieging Charlemagne in Paris with the help of Marsilio, the Moorish king of Spain, and two mighty warriors, *Rodomont and *Mandricardo. Christendom is imperilled. Angelica, who at the end of Boiardo's poem had been consigned by Charlemagne to the care of Namo, escapes. Orlando, chief of the Paladins, a perfect knight, invincible and invulnerable, is lured by her beauty to forget his duty and pursue her. Angelica meets with various adventures, finally coming upon the wounded Moorish youth *Medoro, whom she tends, falls in love with, and marries. A charming description follows of their honeymoon in the woods. Orlando, arriving there by chance and learning their story, is seized with a furious and grotesque madness, runs naked through the country, destroying everything in his path, and at last returns to Charlemagne's camp, where he is finally cured of his madness and his love and in a great conclusive battle kills Agramant.

Although the madness of Orlando gives the poem its name, a not less important theme in it is the love of Rogero for *Bradamante, a maiden warrior, sister of *Rinaldo, and the many adventures and vicissitudes that interrupt the course of true love. Other notable episodes in the work are the voyage of *Astolfo on the hippogriff to the moon, whence he brings back the lost wits of Orlando; and the self-immolation of *Isabella, the widow of the Scottish prince *Zerbino, to escape the attentions of the pagan king Rodomont. Orlando's horse is Brigliandoro; his sword Durindana.

Spenser, in *The Faerie Queene, aimed to 'overgo' Ariosto's epic, and owes much to it for his characters and form of narration. The first complete English version 'in English Heroical Verse' is that of Sir J. Harington (1591; ed. R. McNulty, 1972). John Hoole's translation (1783) was read and enjoyed by *Scott and *Southey. A version by W. S. Rose (8 vols, 1823–31) in *ottava rima*, though less amusing than Harington's, is more faithful, and was highly praised by Rose's friend *Foscolo. Recent versions are by G. Waldman (1974) and B. Reynolds (1975).

Orlando innamorato, a poem by *Boiardo published 1487, on the subject of the falling in love of *Orlando (the Roland of the *Charlemagne cycle) with *Angelica, daughter of *Galafron, king of Cathay. She arrives at the court of Charlemagne, with her brother *Argalia, under false pretences, to carry off the Christian knights to her father's country. Several knights attempt to win her, the chief among them being *Astolfo, *Ferrau, *Rinaldo, and Orlando. Argalia is slain and Angelica flees, but, drinking of an enchanted fountain, falls in love with Rinaldo, who, drinking of another enchanted fountain, conceives a violent aversion to her. He runs away, pursued by her, and they reach her father's country, where she is besieged in the capital, Albracca, by *Agrican, king of Tartary, to whom her hand had been promised (an incident to which Milton refers in *Paradise Regained, III. 337 ff.). Orlando comes to Angelica's rescue, slays Agrican, and carries Angelica off to France whither he has been summoned to assist Charlemagne against *Agramant, king of the Moors. Owing once more to enchanted waters, Rinaldo this time falls in love with Angelica, and Angelica into hatred of him. A fierce combat ensues between Orlando and Rinaldo, suppressed by Charlemagne, who entrusts Angelica to Namo, duke of Bavaria.

The poem, which was left unfinished, was refashioned by *Berni, and translated into English by W. S. Rose (1823). There is some slight evidence that *Spenser knew Boiardo's poem as well as Ariosto's sequel, *Orlando furioso. See M. Murrin, *The Allegorical Epic* (1980).

Orley Farm, a novel by A. *Trollope, published 1862.

While Joseph Mason of Groby Park inherits the bulk of his father's property, the small estate at Orley Farm goes unexpectedly to Lucius Mason, the old man's son by his second marriage. The will is unsuccessfully contested, and matters hang fire for many years until discontented Samuel Dockwrath, formerly a tenant at Orley Farm, discovers important irregularities in the evidence brought before the court. The suspicion

grows that the codicil attached to Sir Joseph's will was forged by Lucius's mother, Lady Mason, still living at Orley Farm. The case is reopened, and though the verdict is in Lady Mason's favour, this is largely due to the professional skill of the lawyers who represent her, including the indefatigable Chaffanbrass. Lady Mason confesses her guilt to her aged lover Sir Peregrine Orme and to his daughter Edith, her closest friend, and surrenders the property. Mother and son embrace voluntary exile in Germany.

Ormond, a novel by M. *Edgeworth, published 1817.

This is largely a tale of life in Ireland, but also of fashionable Paris society in the 18th cent. The main characters are Harry Ormond, an orphan; his fascinating but unprincipled guardian Sir Ulick O'Shane; the kind-hearted eccentric Cornelius O'Shane, the 'king of the Black Islands'; and his daughter Dora, who has been plighted before her birth to one or other of the twin sons of Cornelius's companion Connal, with disastrous results.

Ormulum, The, a Middle English poem of which about 20,000 short lines survive, written in the east Midlands in the late 12th cent. by an Augustinian canon called Orm. It purports to consist of paraphrases of the Gospels for the year as arranged in the mass book, supplemented by a homily on each; but in fact it is a series of sermons arranged chronologically around the Gospel versions of the life of Christ. In any case what we have is only about an eighth of the writer's ambitious scheme. Its literary merit is inconsiderable, but it is of great linguistic interest, particularly for the semi-phonetic spelling system devised by the writer (largely a matter of doubling consonants after short vowels). Ed. R. M. White and R. Holt (1878).

Oroonoko, or The History of the Royal Slave, a novel by A. *Behn, published c.1688, adapted for the stage by *Southerne, 1695.

Oroonoko, grandson and heir of an African king, loves and wins Imoinda, daughter of the king's general. The king, who also loves her, is enraged and orders her to be sold as a slave. Oroonoko himself is trapped by the captain of an English slave-trading ship and carried off to Surinam, then an English colony, where he is reunited with Imoinda and renamed Caesar by his owners. He rouses his fellow slaves to revolt, is deceived into surrender by deputy governor Byam (a historical figure), and brutally whipped. Oroonoko, determined on revenge but not hoping for victory, kills Imoinda, who dies willingly. He is discovered by her dead body and cruelly executed.

The novel is remarkable as an early protest against the slave trade, and as a description of primitive people in 'the first state of innocence, before men knew how to sin'; the author comments on the superior simplicity and morality of both African slaves and the indigenous Indians, whose Christian oppressors are shown as treacherous and hypocritical. Afra Behn's memories of her own visit to Surinam in 1663 provide a vivid background, and much of the story is narrated as by a personal witness. Southerne's tragedy follows the broad lines of the novel, but the deputy governor's passion for Imoinda is made a chief motive of action, Imoinda herself is presented as the daughter of a white European, and Oroonoko dies by his own hand, alterations which decrease the violence of the story and increase its intended pathos.

OROSIUS (fl. early 5th cent.), a priest of Tarragona in Spain, disciple of St *Augustine and friend of St *Jerome, author of the *Historia Adversus Paganos*, a universal history and geography which was translated by the circle of King *Alfred in the 890s. See *Seven Books of History against the Pagans*, trans. I. W. Raymond (1936).

Orphan, The, a tragedy in blank verse by *Otway, produced 1680.

Castalio and Polydore are the twin sons of Acasto. Monimia, the orphan daughter of a friend of Acasto's, has been brought up with them. Castalio and Polydore, loyally devoted to one another, have both fallen in love with Monimia, who returns the love of Castalio. But the latter, out of mistaken consideration for his brother, feigns indifference for Monimia. Chamont, an honest but rough and tactless soldier, brother of Monimia, comes as a guest to Acasto's house; he suspects that Monimia has been wronged by one of the young men, and annoys her with his questions. Castalio and Monimia thereupon are secretly married. Polydore, ignorant of this and overhearing them arranging for a meeting in the night, takes Castalio's place in the darkness, and is not detected. Castalio, coming later, is shut out, and curses his wife for what he supposes to be her heartless and rebellious conduct. The truth being discovered through Chamont, the brothers fall into despair. Both kill themselves, and Monimia takes poison.

The play proved a great success, and was frequently revived. Monimia was one of Mrs *Barry's most celebrated parts.

Orpheus, a legendary Greek hero, son of Apollo (or according to some authorities of a Thracian king Oeagrus) by the Muse Callipe, was renowned as a musician, a religious leader, and a seer. He was reputed to have made trees and rocks follow his singing, been one of the Argonauts, visited Egypt, and founded mystery cults in several parts of Greece. He was eventually torn to pieces by Maenads (frenzied votaresses of Dionysus); and his head and lyre, thrown into the river Hebrus, drifted to Lesbos where the head became an oracle, while Apollo placed the lyre among the stars. The relationship of Orpheus to Dionysus remains puzzling. The Maenads are said to have attacked him because as a priest of Apollo he censured their orgiastic rites. Orphic beliefs seem however to have been rooted in the assumption that 'the body is

the tomb of the soul', so that one's aim in life must be to free oneself from an endless series of reincarnations, not only by moral and physical purity, but also through certain rites which involved eating the flesh of a sacrifice that represented the god; and on such occasions the god in question was always Dionysus.

Orphism had a decisive influence on Pythagoreanism and through this on Platonism and *Neoplatonism. There existed many writings ascribed to Orpheus and his son Musaeus, which are quoted by ancient writers; but the Orphic literature that survives belongs probably to the 5th cent. AD, though this was not established until Gottfried Hermann's edition of 1805.

The legend which found most favour in later literature was, oddly, one of which there is no early record: the story of Orpheus going down into hell, persuading Hades to let him have back his wife, Eurydice, and then losing her because he disregarded the instruction not to look back before they reached the light of day. The popularity of this legend was due perhaps to its presence in poems that were widely read in the Middle Ages: *Virgil, *Georgics*, 4. 454–527, *Ovid, *Metamorphoses*, 10. 1–85, and especially *Boethius, *De Consolatione Philosophiae*, iii. 12, so that it appears in the English *Sir *Orfeo*, in the 14th-cent. *King Orfew*, and in Italy *Poliziano chose it as the subject of his pastoral play *Orfeo* (1480). Robert *Burton cites it as evidence that beasts respond to music, and it inspired one of *Poussin's finest paintings. But appropriately enough opera has been the genre that has made most use of the Orpheus story in modern times. The first opera of which the complete music exists is an *Euridice* that Peri based on an Italian poem by Ottavio Rinuccini (1600). This was followed by Monteverdi's more competent *Orfeo* (1607). Gluck's opera with the same title appeared in 1762, and in a lighter vein there is Crémieux and Offenbach's *Orpheus in the Underworld* (1858). The best-known modern version is *Cocteau's tragedy *Orphée* (1927), filmed in 1950. The legend has exercised a spell that is not immediately easy to explain.

Orpheus Caledonius: or *A Collection of the Best Scotch Songs* (1725), the first printed collection of Scots airs for the voice, collected by William Thomson, which contains many of the songs first printed by *Ramsay.

ORRERY, earls of, see BOYLE.

Orsino, the duke of Illyria in Shakespeare's *Twelfth Night*, whose words 'If music be the food of love, play on' begin the play.

ORTEGA Y GASSET, José (1883–1955), Spanish writer and philosopher, born in Madrid. He studied philosophy in Germany and was professor of metaphysics in Madrid University 1910–36. He was a bitter opponent of the dictator Primo de Rivera, and was elected to the Constituent Cortes of the Second Republic. During the Civil War he went into voluntary exile, finally returning to Spain in 1945. He was a prolific and versatile writer of essays on philosophy, literature, and politics; from 1902 he published a series of essays in Madrid journals on Spanish writers (including A. *Machado and Ramón del Valle Inclán) and their works, in which he advocated the development of a social, moral, 'human' literature, rather than the self-indulgent aestheticism then prevalent; his later articles and journal *Revista de Occidente* (1923–35) were influential in introducing European writers to Spain. In his first book, *Meditaciones del Quijote* (1914; *Meditations on the Quixote*, 1963), he examines the novel as a form and *Don Quixote in particular, using this study as a basis for the development of his philosophy. In this book, as in other works, there are clear signs of the influence of *Unamuno, whom he much admired. *La deshumanización del arte* (1925) discusses the nature of *Modernism and the hostility it inspires, and introduces his ideas on *Mallarmé, who is, he suggests, a paradigm of what poetry should be. He is now best known for *La rebelión de las masas* (1929; *The Revolt of the Masses*, 1932), which continues the socio-historical arguments of *España invertebrada*, deploring the lack of intellectual leadership in Spain, and advocating a United States of Europe.

ORTELIUS, Abraham (1527–98), a geographer and scholar of Antwerp, who visited England and became familiar with *Camden. He published his atlas, *Theatrum Orbis Terrarum*, in 1570.

ORTON, Joe (1933–67), playwright and novelist, born in Leicester. He left school at 16 to train as an actor. His comedies, which include *Entertaining Mr Sloane* (1964), *Loot* (1965), and the posthumously performed *What the Butler Saw* (1969), are black, stylish, satirical, farcical, and violent, and their emphasis on corruption and sexual perversion made them a *succès de scandale*. Orton was battered to death in his Islington home by his friend and companion Kenneth Halliwell, who then committed suicide. See *Prick up Your Ears* (1978), a biography by John Lahr, which formed the basis of a film scripted (1987) by Alan *Bennett. Lahr also edited Orton's *diaries (1986). Orton's novel *Between Us Girls*, written in 1957, was published in 1998.

Orville, Lord, the hero of F. Burney's *Evelina*.

ORWELL, George, the pen-name of Eric Arthur Blair (1903–50), who was born in Bengal, brought to England at an early age, and educated at St Cyprian's (of which his account, 'Such, such were the joys', was considered too libellous to print in this country until 1968) and then at Eton, at both with C. *Connolly. His first patriotic poem appeared in a local Henley paper in 1914. He served with the Indian Imperial Police in Burma, 1922–7, and his experiences are reflected in his first novel, *Burmese Days* (1934); he resigned 'to escape not merely from imperialism but from every form of man's dominion over man', as he later put it, and returned to Europe where he worked in Paris and London in a series of ill-paid jobs in a state of 'fairly

severe poverty' (see *Down and Out in Paris and London*, 1933), struggling with rejection of his work. His second novel, *A Clergyman's Daughter* (1935), describes the adventures of Dorothy, who through loss of memory briefly escapes from her narrow spinster's life to join the tramps and hop-pickers; in style it somewhat uneasily mixes realism with Joycean experiment. *Keep the Aspidistra Flying* (1936), which he wrote while working in a Hampstead bookshop, recounts the literary aspirations, financial humiliations, and shotgun wedding of Gordon Comstock, bookseller's assistant. A journey north in 1936, commissioned (like J. B. *Priestley's *English Journey*) by *Gollancz, produced his vivid and impassioned documentary of unemployment and proletarian life *The Road to Wigan Pier* (1937, published by the *Left Book Club), and the Spanish Civil War (in which he fought for the Republicans and was wounded) intensified his political preoccupations and produced *Homage to Catalonia* (1938). The threat of the coming war hung over his next novel, *Coming up for Air* (1939), which deals with suburban frustration and Georgian nostalgia in the person of insurance man George Bowling. By this stage Orwell saw himself primarily as a political writer, a democratic socialist who avoided party labels, hated totalitarianism, and was to become more and more disillusioned with the methods of communism; his plain, colloquial style made him highly effective as pamphleteer and journalist (he was literary editor of *Tribune*, 1943–5, and contributed regularly to it and other papers). V. S. *Pritchett, reviewing his *The Lion and the Unicorn: Socialism and the English Genius* (1941), compared him to *Defoe and *Cobbett both for his 'subversive, nonconforming brand of patriotism' and for his 'lucid conversational style'. His collections of essays include *Inside the Whale* (1940), *Critical Essays* (1946), and *Shooting an Elephant* (1950). But his most popular works were undoubtedly his political satires *Animal Farm* (1945) and *Nineteen Eighty-Four* (1949), which brought inevitable comparisons with *Swift. His first wife, Eileen, died in 1945, and he married Sonia Mary Brownell in 1949, shortly before his death from tuberculosis, an illness from which he had suffered for many years. His *Collected Essays, Journalism and Letters* (4 vols, ed. S. Orwell and I. Angus) appeared in 1968 and his *Complete Works* (20 vols, ed. Peter Davison) in 1998; see also *George Orwell: A Life* by Bernard Crick (1980).

OSBORNE, Dorothy (1627–95). She met William *Temple on the Isle of Wight in 1648, when she was 21, he 20. After considerable family opposition they married in 1654. Her letters to him during the period 1652–4, most of them written from her family home of Chicksands, came to light when T. P. Courtenay published some in an appendix to his life of Temple in 1836; *Macaulay singled them out for praise and Parry's edition (1888) was followed by G. C. Moore Smith's more scholarly edition in 1928. The letters are lively and witty, though occasionally solemn in their reflections; she believed that letters 'should be as free and easy as one's discourse'. They provide an intimate picture of the life, manners, and reading habits of the times, of the relations between the sexes, and particularly of a woman's attitudes to marriage and filial duty.

OSBORNE, John James (1929–94), playwright, born in Fulham, London, the son of a commercial artist who died in 1940; the first volume of his autobiography, *A Better Class of Person* (1981), describes his childhood in suburbia, his brief spell as a journalist, and his years as an actor in provincial repertory, during which he began to write plays, the first of which was performed in 1950. He made his name with *Look back in Anger* (1956, pub. 1957), which was followed by *Epitaph for George Dillon* (1957, pub. 1958; written in the mid-1950s in collaboration with Anthony Creighton); *The Entertainer* (1957, which starred Laurence Olivier as Archie Rice, a faded survivor of the great days of music hall); *Luther* (1961, based on the life of Martin *Luther, with much emphasis on his physical as well as his spiritual problems); *Inadmissible Evidence* (1964, the tragedy of a down-at-heel solicitor, Bill Maitland, plunging rhetorically towards self-destruction); and *A Patriot for Me* (1965, a highly theatrical piece set in Vienna, based on the rise and fall of Redl, a homosexual officer in the Austro-Hungarian army, ruined by blackmail). Iconoclastic, energetic, and impassioned, Osborne's works at their most positive praise the qualities of loyalty, tolerance, and friendship, but his later works (which include *West of Suez*, 1971; *A Sense of Detachment*, 1972; *Watch It Come down*, 1976) became increasingly vituperative in tone, and the objects of his invective apparently more arbitrary; his outbursts of rage against contemporary society are frequently exhilarating, for the anger that made him known as an *'Angry Young Man' remained one of his strongest theatrical weapons, but he also expressed from time to time an ambivalent nostalgia for the past that his own work did so much to alter. His last play, *Déjàvu* (1991), is a sequel to *Look back in Anger*, presenting the same characters in their regrouped, bad-tempered, but occasionally companionable middle age. *Almost a Gentleman* (1991) was a second volume of autobiography; *Damn You, England* (1994) a miscellany of reviews and letters to the press. (See also KITCHEN SINK DRAMA.)

Osborne, Mr, his offspring George, Maria and Jane, characters in Thackeray's *Vanity Fair*.

OSBORNE, Thomas (d. 1767), bookseller, remembered as having issued Richardson's *Pamela*, and published the *Harleian Miscellany*. He was beaten by Dr *Johnson for impertinence and ridiculed by *Pope.

O'SHAUGHNESSY, Arthur William Edgar (1844–81), poet and friend of D. G. *Rossetti, who worked at the British Museum in the department of printed books and the natural history department. He published several volumes of poetry; his best-known piece, 'Ode' ('We are the music-makers'), appeared in *Music and Moonlight* (1874) and has been noted as a characteristic example of Victorian escapist verse. There is a setting of it by *Elgar.

OSLER, Sir William (1849–1919), distinguished physician, born in Canada, was professor of medicine at McGill, Pennsylvania, and Johns Hopkins universities and Regius professor of medicine at Oxford (1905–11). His many published works include the notable *Principles of Practice of Medicine* (1892) and his valuable medical library is now at McGill University, Montreal.

OSORIO DA FONSECA, Jeronimo (1506–80), Portuguese historian, born in Lisbon, and educated at the universities of Salamanca, Paris, and Bologna. He was for a time professor of theology at Coimbra and, from 1564, bishop of Silves. He wrote in Latin (and was dubbed the 'Portuguese Cicero'); his *De Rebus Emmanuelis Regis Lusitaniae* (1571) was much admired. In 1562 he wrote an attack on the English Reformation, which was answered by Haddon, master of requests to Elizabeth, and continued by *Foxe (1577; English trans. 1581). His library was seized on the occasion of Essex's expedition of 1596 and subsequently given to the newly founded Bodleian (see LIBRARIES).

Osric, an affected courtier in Shakespeare's *Hamlet, referred to as 'a Bragart Gentleman' in the first quarto.

Ossian, the name commonly given to *Oisin, a legendary Gaelic warrior and bard. See MACPHERSON and FINGAL.

OSTROVSKY, Alexander Nikolaevich (1823–86), Russian playwright, was born into a merchant family in Moscow. The first of his plays to be staged was *The Poor Bride* (1853), and by the time of his death he had produced about 40 prose plays and eight in blank verse. He translated *The Taming of the Shrew* (1865) and was working on a translation of *Antony and Cleopatra* when he died. His main subject matter is the life of Muscovite and provincial merchants and lower officialdom. Among his best plays are *It's a Family Affair—We'll Settle It Ourselves* (1850), *The Poor Bride* (pub. 1852), *The Dowerless Girl* (1879), and his two acknowledged masterpieces, *The Storm* (1860, an intensely poetical work) and *The Forest* (1871). *A Domestic Picture* (1847) and *Incompatibility of Temper* (1858) appeared in English translation by E. *Voynich in 1895, and C. *Garnett's translation of *The Storm* in 1898. Since then a number of his plays have appeared in English, and have been successfully performed on the English stage.

OSWALD, St (d. 992), one of the three leading figures (along with *Dunstan and *Æthelwold) in the 10th-cent. Benedictine Revival in England, became a Benedictine monk at Fleury and accompanied Oskitel, archbishop of York, to Rome. On Dunstan's initiative he was appointed bishop of Worcester in 961. He founded monasteries at Westbury, Worcester, Winchcombe, and on the Isle of Ramsey. In 972 he was made archbishop of York, but (like his successor *Wulfstan) retained the see of Worcester as well, for which he had a special affection and where he is buried in the church of St Mary.

Othello, *the Moor of Venice*, a tragedy by *Shakespeare, written between 1602 and 1604 when it was performed before James I at Whitehall. It was first printed in quarto in 1622, and again in a different version in the *Folio of 1623. The story is taken from *Cinthio, which Shakespeare could have read in Italian or French.

The play's first act (which *Verdi's opera *Otello* omits) is set in Venice. Desdemona, the daughter of Brabantio, a Venetian senator, has secretly married Othello, a Moor in the service of the state. Accused before the duke and senators of having stolen Brabantio's daughter, Othello explains and justifies his conduct, and is asked by the Senate to lead the Venetian forces against the Turks who are about to attack Cyprus.

In the middle of a storm which disperses the Turkish fleet, Othello lands on Cyprus with Desdemona, Cassio, a young Florentine, who helped him court his wife and whom he has now promoted to be his lieutenant, and Iago, an older soldier, bitterly resentful of being passed over for promotion, who now plans his revenge. Iago uses Roderigo, 'a gull'd Gentleman' in love with Desdemona, to fight with Cassio after he has got him drunk, so that Othello deprives him of his new rank. He then persuades Cassio to ask Desdemona to plead in his favour with Othello, which she warmly does. At the same time he suggests to Othello that Cassio is, and has been, Desdemona's lover, finally arranging through his wife Emilia, who is Desdemona's waiting-woman, that Othello should see Cassio in possession of a handkerchief which he had given to his bride. Othello is taken in by Iago's promptings and in frenzied jealousy smothers Desdemona in her bed. Iago sets Roderigo to murder Cassio, but when Roderigo fails to do this Iago kills him and Emilia as well, after she has proved Desdemona's innocence to Othello. Emilia's evidence and letters found on Roderigo prove Iago's guilt; he is arrested, and Othello, having tried to stab him, kills himself.

According to *Rymer one of the play's morals was 'a warning to all good wives that they look well to their linen'. *Coleridge in a famous phrase described Iago's soliloquy at the end of I. iii as 'the motive-hunting of motiveless malignity'.

Otho the Great: *A Tragedy in Five Acts*, a play written by *Keats in 1819, in collaboration with his friend Charles Brown, who planned its construction. The plot is based on the history of the rebellion against Otho, during his Hungarian wars, by his son Ludolf and the Red Duke Conrad of Lorraine. For both artistic and financial reasons Keats had hoped that *Kean would undertake the part of Ludolf, but the hope was not fulfilled.

O'Trigger, Sir Lucius, a character in Sheridan's *The Rivals.*

ottava rima, an Italian stanza of eight 11-syllable lines, rhyming a b a b a b c c, employed by *Tasso, *Ariosto, etc. It was introduced into England by *Wyatt, and used to great effect by Byron in *Don Juan*, with a ten-syllable iambic line.

Otter, Captain Thomas and Mistress, the ill-matched husband and wife in Jonson's *Epicene*. Charles II, joking about the henpecked state of his brother the duke of York, christened him Tom Otter.

Otterbourne, The Battle of, one of the earliest of English ballads, included in Percy's *Reliques.*

The Scots in 1388, returning from a raid into England, attacked the castle of Otterburn in Northumberland, and after an unsuccessful assault were surprised in their camp by Henry *Hotspur, Lord Percy. In the ensuing engagement James, earl of Douglas, commanding the Scottish force, was killed, and Percy taken prisoner. These events are the subject of the ballad.

Otuel, Sir, a pagan knight, miraculously converted, who became one of *Charlemagne's *Paladins. He is the nephew of Vernagu, killed in combat by *Roland as recounted in the English romance *Roland and Vernagu*. The Otuel story is told in three English romances: *Otuel*, in four-stress couplets in the Auchinlech manuscript (EETS ES 39, ed. S. J. Herrtage, 1882); *Duke Rowland and Sir Otuell of Spayne* (EETS ES 35, ed. S. J. Herrtage, 1880); the Fillingham Otuel and Roland (EETS OS 198, ed. M. O'Sullivan, 1934).

OTWAY, Thomas (1652–85), born at Milland near Trotton in Sussex, educated at Winchester and Christ Church, Oxford. He appeared unsuccessfully on the stage, being given a part by the kindness of A. *Behn. In 1678 he enlisted in the army in Holland and received a commission, but soon returned. He died in destitution at the age of 33.

Of his three great tragedies, *Don Carlos*, in rhymed verse, was produced in 1676; *The Orphan*, in blank verse, in 1680; and *Venice Preserv'd*, also in blank verse, in 1682. Of his other plays *Alcibiades*, a tragedy, was produced in 1675 (and provided Mrs *Barry, for whom Otway cherished an unrequited passion, with her first successful part); *Titus and Berenice*, adapted from a tragedy by *Racine, and *The Cheats of Scapin*, from a comedy by *Molière, in 1676; *The History and Fall of Caius Marius*, an adaptation of *Romeo and Juliet*, in 1679; *Friendship in Fashion*, a comedy, in 1681; *The Atheist*, also a comedy, in 1683. He also wrote prologues, epilogues, and a few poems. The standard edition of Otway, ed. J. C. Ghosh, was published in 1932.

OUIDA, pen-name of Marie Louise de la Ramée (1839–1908), born in Bury St Edmunds; her mother was English and her father, Louis Ramée, a teacher of French. Her pseudonym is a childish mispronunciation of 'Louise'. She began her career contributing stories to *Bentley's Miscellany* (1859–60) encouraged by its editor *Ainsworth. Her first real success was *Held in Bondage* (1863), which was followed by *Strathmore* (1865). By this time her reputation was established. She spent much time in Italy from 1860 and in 1874 settled in Florence where she pursued her work as a novelist while living in lavish style. Her other popular novels included *Under Two Flags* (1867), perhaps her most famous, *Folle-Farine* (1871), which *Bulwer-Lytton considered 'a triumph of modern English fiction', *Two Little Wooden Shoes* (1874), *Moths* (1880), *A Village Commune* (1881), and *In Maremma* (1882). Her 45 novels, often set in a fashionable world far removed from reality, show a spirit of rebellion against the moral ideals reflected in much of the fiction of the time. She suffered frequent ridicule for her extravagantly portrayed heroes, often languid guardsmen, miracles of strength, courage, and beauty, and for her inaccuracies in matters of men's sports and occupations; but her faults were redeemed by her narrative power and emotional energy. She wrote several animal stories, including *A Dog of Flanders* (1872) and *Bimbi, Stories for Children* (1882). After 1890 her popularity waned and she wrote chiefly critical and social articles for magazines. When her literary profits declined, she fell into debt, moved to Lucca in 1894, and from 1904 lived in destitution in Viareggio.

OuLiPo (an acronym for Ouvroir de Littérature Potentielle) was a French movement founded in 1960 by Raymond Queneau (1903–76) and François Le Lionnais. Oulipians are dedicated to exploring connections between mathematics and the formal constraints inherent in literature. Its members have included Georges Perec, Harry *Mathews, and Italo *Calvino. An example of their practice is the lipogram, which is a text from which one or more letters of the alphabet have been excluded. The best-known lipogram is Perec's *La Disparition* (1969), a 300-page novel in which the letter *e* is not once used (translated into English, without *es*, by Gilbert Adair as *A Void*, 1994). Perec's masterpiece, *La Vie: mode d'emploi* (1978), more fully illustrates the ways in which an arbitrary set of constraints can serve as a catalyst for the imagination. Other Oulipian developments include poems in which the vowels *a e i o u* always occur in that order, and narratives predicated on algorithms, such as Harry Mathews's *Cigarettes* (1987).

Our Mutual Friend, a novel by *Dickens, published in monthly parts between May 1864 and Nov. 1865.

John Harmon returns from the exile to which he has been sent by a harsh father, a rich dust-contractor; he expects to receive the inheritance to which his father has attached the condition that he shall marry a certain girl, Bella Wilfer. Bella is unknown to him, and he confides to a mate of the ship which is bringing him home his intention of concealing his identity until he has formed some judgement of his allotted wife. The mate lures him to a riverside haunt, attempts to murder him, throws his body into the river, and is in turn murdered and his body likewise thrown into the river. Harmon recovers and escapes; the mate's body is found after some days, and, owing to Harmon's papers found upon it, it is taken to be that of Harmon. Harmon's intention of remaining unknown is thus facilitated; he assumes the name of John Rokesmith and becomes the secretary of the kindly, disinterested Mr Boffin, old Harmon's foreman, who, in default of young Harmon, inherits the property. He is thrown into close contact with Bella, a flighty minx, who is adopted by Boffin and who is turned by her first taste of wealth into an arrogant, mercenary jade. Rokesmith nevertheless falls in love with her and is contemptuously rejected. Harmon's identity is now discovered by the amiable Mrs Boffin, and the Boffins, devoted to their old master's son and convinced of Bella's soundness of heart, contrive a plot to prove her. Boffin pretends to be transformed by his wealth into a hard and griping miser, and heaps indignities on Harmon, who is finally dismissed with contumely. Bella, awakened to the evils of wealth and to the merits of Rokesmith, flies from the Boffins and marries her suitor. His identity presently comes to light, and with his assistance the scheme of a one-legged old villain, Silas Wegg, to blackmail Boffin is exposed.

Concurrently with this main theme runs the story of the love of Eugene Wrayburn, a careless, insolent young barrister, for Lizzie Hexam, daughter of a disreputable boatman. His rival for her affections, Bradley Headstone, a schoolmaster, attempts to murder Wrayburn. The latter is saved by Lizzie and marries her. Among the notable characters in the book are the Veneerings, types of social parvenus; the good Jew Riah; the blackmailing waterside villain Rogue Riderhood; Jenny Wren, the dolls' dressmaker; Bella Wilfer's grotesque father, mother, and sister; and the spirited Betty Higden, an old woman with a haunting dread of the workhouse.

Many early reviewers agreed with H. *James, who found the novel 'forced' and 'wanting in inspiration', but later critics (including Humphry House and E. *Wilson) have praised it highly, stressing in particular the complex use of the dirt–money symbolism.

Our Village: *Sketches of Rural Life, Character, and Scenery*, by M. R. *Mitford, published 1832.

The sketches, episodes, and descriptions which make up the book were written between 1824 and 1832, most of them appearing in the *Lady's Magazine*. *The Sketch Book* of W. *Irving provided her with the original idea. The village is based on Three Mile Cross, near Reading, where she and her father lived for 30 years, but other locations and memories are also used.

The author declared, before beginning the series, that it was to describe 'country scenery and country manners', and that she abhorred sentimentality and pathos. Seasons, places, events, and people are sharply observed and precisely described, with affection and humour. Her lucid, unpretentious prose was evidently the result of diligence, for she wrote that 'what looks like ease in my style is labour'.

OUSPENSKY, Peter Demianovich (1878–1947), journalist and unorthodox philosopher. He was born in Moscow, and, although a brilliant student, refused to take regular courses, though he attended the university as a 'free listener'. He met *Gurdjieff in 1914 and became a disciple, devoted to disseminating his doctrines.

Outsider, The, (1) a novel by American author R. *Wright, published 1953; (2) a study by C. *Wilson published 1956.

OVERBURY, Sir Thomas (1581–1613). He was educated at The Queen's College, Oxford, and went to the Middle Temple. He opposed the marriage of his patron Robert Carr (afterwards earl of Somerset) with the divorced countess of Essex, and on the pretext of his refusal of diplomatic employment was sent to the Tower, where he was slowly poisoned by the agents of Lady Essex. Four of these were hanged; Somerset and his wife were convicted and pardoned. The prosecution was conducted by F. *Bacon. The whole business remains a historical mystery. Overbury's poem *A Wife* appeared in 1614, and with its second edition the Theophrastian 'Characters' by which he is chiefly remembered. Later editions added new characters, some by J. *Webster and some by *Dekker (see W. J. Taylor's edition, *The Overburian Characters*, 1936). The types include 'A Roaring Boy', 'A Puny Clerk', 'A Mere Scholar', and few are as benign as the portrait of a milkmaid; *Earles responded to their harsh and anti-scholastic tone in his own *Microcosmographie*. (See CHARACTER-WRITING.)

Overdo, Justice Adam, the busy seeker-out of 'enormities' in Jonson's *Bartholomew Fair*.

Overreach, Sir Giles, a character in Massinger's *A New Way to Pay Old Debts*.

OVERTON, Richard (fl. 1646), printer and leader of the Leveller movement, a prolific, forceful, and versatile pamphleteer, much of whose work was published anonymously, and some under the pseudonym of Martin Marpriest, in the tradition of *Martin Marprelate. A tract on the immortality of the soul, *Man's Mortality* (1643), aroused much controversy, and he was imprisoned many times for his unorthodox religious and radical political views. He adopted *Lilburne's cause and was imprisoned in 1649 with him, Prince, and *Walwyn. His writing displays a firm faith in human reason, a colourful and often caustic prose (Walwyn praised his 'comic' and 'satiric' pen), and some powerful arguments for religious tolerance.

OVID (Publius Ovidius Naso) (43 BC–AD 18), Roman writer of love elegies (*Amores*), who then experimented with the imaginary letter (*Heroides*), mock didactic verse (*Ars Amatoria*), 'collective' narrative relating disconnected stories inside a large historical (*Metamorphoses*) or chronological (*Fasti*) frame, and finally with elegies of nostalgic complaint (*Tristia, Epistulae ex Ponto*), when Augustus had exiled him in AD 8 to the Black Sea for some mysterious indiscretion. Ovid continued in favour with writers and public so long as Rome was pagan, but the Christian Church disapproved of his immorality, so that little is heard of him during the six centuries that followed the conversion of Constantine. His works were certainly copied, and interest in them revived with the 11th cent. Poets in the cathedral schools took him for a model. The *Metamorphoses*, rendered edifying by moralization, were widely read (see e.g. OVIDE MORALISÉ). During the Renaissance Ovid enjoyed great favour with writers and painters alike. *Chaucer and *Gower both borrowed his stories. But the late 16th and early 17th cents were England's Ovidian Age when T. *Lodge, *Marlowe, *Spenser, Shakespeare, G. *Chapman, *Drayton, T. *Heywood, were all indebted to him directly or through A. *Golding's translation of the *Metamorphoses* (1565–7). Themes from the *Metamorphoses* were handled by W. *King ('Orpheus and Eurydice', 1704), Swift (*Baucis and Philemon*), *Prior ('Daphne and Apollo', 1740), *Shelley (*Arethusa*, 1820), Morris ('Pygmalion' in *The Earthly Paradise*, 1868–70), Swinburne (*Atalanta in Calydon*, 1865), and Shaw (*Pygmalion*, 1916), but they stray very far from their originals. Ted *Hughes produced some free and powerful verse translations in *Tales from Ovid* (1997).

Ovide moralisé, a French work influential on *Chaucer and on the *Ovidius Moralizatus* by Pierre Bersuire (d. 1362) which is Book XV of his huge *Reductorium Morale*, completed in 1340. It moralizes 15 books of the *Metamorphoses* and is highly significant in the development of late medieval and Renaissance literature by bringing secular literature into the official canon. Cf. *Fulgentius Metaforalis* by Ridewall (*c.*1330) for the practice of allegorizing the stories of classical authors.

OWEN, Alun (1925–94), Welsh-Liverpudlian playwright, actor, and television scriptwriter, born in Menai Bridge, north Wales, and educated at Oulton High School, Liverpool. During the war he worked as a Bevin Boy down the coal mines. He is principally remembered for his gritty, realist television dramas, which helped to shape the emerging style of TV drama in the 1960s: these include *No Trams to Lime Street* (1959), and *After the Funeral* (1960); *A Little Winter Love* (1964) was a stage play. He also wrote the screenplay for the *Beatles' film *A Hard Day's Night* (1964).

OWEN, John (?1563–1622), educated at Winchester and New College, Oxford, the author of several volumes of Latin epigrams, mostly in elegiac couplets, which were translated into several languages and frequently reprinted down to the 19th cent.

OWEN, Sir Richard (1804–92), educated at Lancaster School with *Whewell. He became conservator of the Hunterian museum and first Hunterian professor of comparative anatomy and physiology. He opposed C. *Darwin's views on evolution, and was a fierce controversialist.

OWEN, Robert (1771–1858), socialist and philanthropist. He was born in Wales, the son of a shopkeeper, and became the wealthy owner of cotton-spinning mills in Manchester. In 1799 he purchased the New Lanark mills in Scotland, and proceeded to set up there his model community and model village, organized on principles of mutual co-operation, as well as infant schools and other educational institutions. His example was largely instrumental in bringing about the Factory Act of 1819, although, disappointed with the slow rate of reform, he left Britain in 1821 for some years to set up another model community, New Harmony, in America. Owen was the pioneer of co-operation between workers and consumers, and his ideas strengthened the growing co-operative movement. He published *A New View of Society* in 1813 and *The Revolution in Mind and Practice of the Human Race* in 1849. There is a life by G. D. H. *Cole, published 1925. (See also SOCIALISM.)

OWEN, Wilfred (1893–1918), born in Shropshire, where his father was a station-master, educated in Birkenhead and at Shrewsbury Technical College. He began to experiment with verse from an early age, and read widely. After a period assisting in a poor country parish, he left in 1913 to teach English in Bordeaux, then returned in 1915 to join the army, in which he was soon commissioned. After concussion and trench-fever on the Somme he was invalided to hospital in Edinburgh, where he was greatly encouraged in his writing by *Sassoon. He returned to France in 1918, won the MC, and was killed on the Sambre Canal a week before the Armistice. He found his own voice as a poet in the trenches, and most of the poems for which he is remembered were written in a creative burst between the summer of 1917 and the autumn of the next year. Only five of his poems were published in his lifetime, and they made little mark on a public revering Rupert *Brooke. However, his reputation slowly grew, greatly assisted by *Blunden's edition of his poems, with a memoir, in 1931, and he is now generally regarded as a war poet of the first rank. His bleak realism, his energy and indignation, his compassion, and his high technical skills (he was a master of metrical variety and of assonance) are evident in most of his work. His poems were chosen by *Britten for the *War Requiem*. The poems were collected again in 1963, edited by *Day-Lewis; *Collected Letters* (ed. H. Owen and J. Bell) appeared in 1967, and a biography by Jon *Stallworthy in 1974.

OWENSON, Sydney, see MORGAN, LADY.

Owl and the Nightingale, The, an early Middle English poem of 1,794 lines of octosyllabic couplets, probably from the beginning of the 13th cent., two of the three known manuscripts of which survive. It is a debate between the grave owl and the gay nightingale as to the benefits each confers on mankind, the symbolic implications of which have been much disputed; they have been said, for example, to represent the religious poet and the love poet. It is a very learned work which touches with light, scholastic legalism on many matters of serious contemporary interest: foreknowledge, music, confession, papal missions, and so on. It is a virtuoso poem, highly accomplished in its style and in its humorous tone, which reaches no definite conclusion. The debate is to be submitted at the end to the judgement of one Nicholas of Guildford who is likely to be the author; a certain John of Guildford, who is known to have written c.1225, has also been proposed. See editions by E. G. Stanley (1960), J. W. Atkins (1922, with translation); see also K. Hume, *The Owl and the Nightingale: The Poem and its Critics* (1975).

Owlglass, see EULENSPIEGEL.

OXFORD, Edward De Vere, 17th earl of (1550–1604), educated at Cambridge. A. *Golding, the translator of Ovid, was his uncle. He married Lord Burleigh's daughter, and high hopes were placed on him as a courtier and patron, but they were dissipated as his capricious and quarrelsome temperament became apparent. His most famous quarrel was with *Sidney, whom, according to *Greville, he addressed as 'puppy' in a dispute at the tennis court in 1579; there is also some evidence that he planned to kill him. It is perhaps appropriate that one of the 15 or so surviving poems attributed to him is entitled 'Love compared to a tennis playe'. By some his literary capacities have been highly regarded: J. T. Looney identified him in 1920 as the author of Shakespeare's plays, and a sizeable body of 'Oxfordians' have since built on this claim. (See also BACONIAN THEORY.)

OXFORD, Robert, first earl of, see HARLEY, R.

Oxford and Cambridge Magazine, a periodical of the year 1856, of which 12 monthly numbers appeared, financed mainly by W. *Morris. Among its (anonymous) contributors were Morris and *Burne-Jones (of Oxford), and Henry Lushington (1812–55) of Cambridge, and by invitation D. G. *Rossetti, whose 'Burden of Nineveh' appeared in its pages. The contents were predominantly literary, and included poems, tales, fairy stories, essays, and reviews.

Oxford English Dictionary, The. The scheme of 'a completely new English Dictionary' was conceived in 1858, chiefly as the result of the reading of two papers 'On some Deficiencies in Our English Dictionaries' by Dr R. C. *Trench to the *Philological Society in 1857.

Herbert Coleridge (1830–61), and after him Dr F. J. *Furnivall, were the first editors. Their work, which covered 20 years, consisted mainly in the collection of materials, and it was not until Dr J. A. H. *Murray took the matter up in 1878 that the preparation of the dictionary began to take active form. The first part (A–Ant) was published in 1884, at which time Murray estimated that the whole might be completed in another 12 years. It was not in fact finished until 1928, 70 years from the inception of the undertaking. Murray, who laid down the lines of the work, did not live to see it completed (at his death, T had been reached); but more than half was produced under his personal editorship. His co-editors were Dr H. *Bradley (from 1888), Dr W. A. *Craigie (from 1901), and Dr C. T. *Onions (from 1914).

The essential feature of the dictionary is its historical method, by which the meaning and form of the words are traced from their earliest appearance on the basis of an immense number of quotations, collected by more than 800 voluntary workers. The dictionary contains a record of 414,825 words, whose history is illustrated by 1,827,306 quotations. A supplement of 867 pages appeared in 1933. In 1957 work began, under the editorship of R. W. *Burchfield, on the new supplement, superseding that of 1933, and treating all the vocabulary which came into use while the main dictionary was being published or after its completion. The outcome of this work, entitled *A Supplement to the Oxford English Dictionary*, contains a record of approximately 120,000 words and is about one-third of the length of the main dictionary. The second edition, by J. Simpson and E. Weiner, was published in 1989. It is also available in electronic form on CD-ROM. The original title of the main work was 'A New English Dictionary on Historical Principles' (abbreviated as *NED*). The title *The Oxford English Dictionary* first appeared in the reprint of 1933.

Oxford Gazette, the first real newspaper, other than a newsletter, to be published in England. It appeared in Nov. 1665, the court being then at Oxford owing to the great plague, and was started by H. *Muddiman under the direction of his patron Sir Joseph Williamson. It became the *London Gazette* in 1666. It still survives, not now a newspaper, but a record of official appointments, notices of bankruptcy, etc., having passed in 1923 into the keeping of the Stationery Office. See P. M. Handover, *A History of the London Gazette 1665–1965* (1965), in which she describes its slow evolution to its present form, and describes its anomalies and eccentricities as 'relics of ancient pride and state'.

Oxford, or **Tractarian, movement,** a movement of thought and doctrine within the Church of England, centred at Oxford, the impulse of which was the Assize Sermon on National Apostasy preached by *Keble in 1833. This criticized the prevalent Erastian and latitudinarian tendencies of the Anglican Church, and generated an investigation into the nature of the Church. The movement aimed to defend the Church of England as a divine institution with an independent spiritual status, and to revive the High Church traditions of the 17th cent.; the Reform Act of 1832, and the views of *Broad Church supporters such as T. *Arnold, had led many to believe that the Church was in danger of increasing subordination to the state. Keble's sermon inspired *Newman, R. H. *Froude, and others to launch their series *Tracts for the Times* in 1833 (which gave the Tractarian movement its name); the series gained the influential support of *Pusey, who gave the movement cohesion and authority. The tracts varied from short leaflets to learned treatises, and covered a wide range of theological issues; it was Newman's famous Tract XC (1841) on the compatibility of the Thirty-Nine Articles with Roman Catholic theology that brought the Tractarians under official ban, but hostility had already been aroused by the publication of the first volumes of Froude's *Literary Remains* in 1838, with its strictures on the Reformation. W. G. *Ward's *The Ideal of a Christian Church* (1844), with its praise of the Roman Catholic Church, intensified hostility, and led to suspicions that the Tractarians (and principally Newman) were subversively leading their followers towards Rome. Newman himself became a Roman Catholic in 1845, a decision which dealt a severe blow to the unity of the movement. There is a notable and sympathetic history of the movement, *The Oxford Movement, Twelve Years, 1833–1845* (1891) by Richard William Church (1815–90), dean of St Paul's; see also Newman's *Apologia pro Vita Sua* (1864), the autobiography of I. *Williams, and *Pattison's Memoirs. (Pattison, a hostile witness, recalled that 'the "Tracts" desolated Oxford life, and suspended, for an indefinite period, all science, humane letters, and the first strivings of intellectual freedom'.) Other leaders of the movement included J. W. Bowden, W. Palmer, and A. P. Perceval.

The impact of the Tractarians was immense. In literary terms, the revival of interest in the medieval and 17th-cent. Church influenced *Tennyson, W. *Morris and the *Pre-Raphaelites, C. *Rossetti, and C. M. *Yonge, among others; it also strengthened the revival of *Gothic architecture associated with *Pugin.

Oxford University Press, a publishing and printing business owned by the university and directed by its delegates of the press, of whom the vice-chancellor is *ex officio* chairman. Its aims are to produce books of religious, scholarly, and educational value, and, its surplus profits being devoted to financing the editing and production of unremunerative works of this kind, its status is that of a charity.

Printing in Oxford by independent craftsmen began in the 15th cent. (see UNIVERSITY PRESSES), and in 1584 one of these was appointed 'Printer to the University'. This title was borne by a succession of printers in the 17th cent. and was revived in 1925 for the head of the printing department of the press. One press at Oxford was excepted from the prohibition of printing outside London by a decree of the Star Chamber in 1586, and in 1632 a royal charter allowed the university three presses and to print and sell 'all manner of books'. *Laud in 1634 bound the university to provide itself with a printing house; but a press under its immediate control did not come into being until 1690. In the meantime *Fell had won an international reputation for Oxford books by his exercise of the university's privilege of printing, let to him in 1672. By his bequest his unsold books and printing equipment became the property of the university in 1690.

Under the management of the delegates since then the press has produced such famous books as *Clarendon's *History* (1702), *Blackstone's *Commentaries* (1769), Kennicott's Hebrew Bible (1780), Clerk Maxwell's *Treatise on Electricity and Magnetism* (1873), the Revised Version of the English Bible (1885), and *The Oxford English Dictionary*, completed in 1928, besides many millions of Bibles and prayer books and, in recent times, of standard classical and modern texts, schoolbooks, and English and bilingual dictionaries.

The copyright in Clarendon's works, once very profitable, is secured to the university in perpetuity, and in his honour the building to which the press moved in 1829 was named 'the Clarendon Press'. This is the imprint given to learned books published under the supervision of the secretary to the delegates at Oxford. Books of more general appeal, including verse anthologies and reference books covering a wide range of topics, were published between 1880 and 1976 from the press's London offices, subsequently from Oxford.

oxymoron, from two Greek words meaning 'sharp', 'dull', a rhetorical figure by which two incongruous or contradictory terms are united in an expression so as to give it point; e.g. 'Faith unfaithful kept him falsely true' (Tennyson, *Idylls of the King*).

Oz, an underground magazine started in Sydney, Australia (1963–6), by Richard Neville (1941–   ), and relaunched by him in London in 1966 with Jim Anderson and Felix Dennis. The 'Schoolkids' issue (No. 28) was the occasion of a notorious trial during which the editors were convicted of issuing a publication likely to 'corrupt public morals', but were freed on appeal. *Oz* faded away in the winter of 1973, having reached a peak print-run of 70,000 in 1971.

OZ, Amos (1939–   ), Israeli novelist and political commentator, born in Jerusalem. His first novel to be widely translated from the Hebrew was *My Michael* (1968; trans. 1972), set in the 1950s and narrated by Hannah Gonen, who describes her hesitant student marriage to a young geologist, set against the background of the struggles of a newly independent nation: it gives a vivid portrait of her own unsettling fantasies and of the changing city of Jerusalem. Oz's fictional works (titles include *A Perfect Peace*, 1982, dealing with kibbutz life, and *Fima*, 1991, about a failed middle-aged poet) build up a strong physical and political sense of a developing country, and his reportage (see *In the Land of Israel*, 1983) gives a voice to its varied cultures and inhabitants.

P

Pacchiarotto *and How He Worked in Distemper: With Other Poems*, a collection of 19 poems, in various metres, by R. *Browning, published 1876. The title poem, the three which follow it, and the epilogue, were directed at Browning's critics, in satirical or serious vein; the remaining poems are a miscellany on topics of religion, love, and art. 'Numpholeptos', 'St Martin's Summer', and 'A Forgiveness' deserve particular mention. The most unusual poem in the volume is, however, the ballad 'Hervé Riel', about the heroic exploit of a French sailor in a fight against the British.

PADEL, Ruth (1946–   ), poet and classical scholar, born in London and educated at the Sorbonne, the Free University, Berlin, and Oxford University. Her volumes of poetry are *Alibi* (1985), *Summer Snow* (1990, with poems invoking Crete and the 'summer snow deep in the mountain' of Mount Ida), *Angel* (1993), *Fusewire* (1996), and *Rembrandt Would Have Loved You* (1995), which is an intimate exploration of a love affair. Her verse combines classical allusion with an increasingly contemporary idiom. Scholarly works include *In and Out of the Mind: Greek Images of the Tragic Self* (1992) and *Whom Gods Destroy: Elements of Greek and Tragic Madness* (1995).

Padlock, The, a comic opera by *Bickerstaffe, with music by *Dibdin, performed with much success in 1768.

The elderly Don Diego is the temporary guardian of the young Leonora and is about to make her his wife. But, in spite of a large padlock on the door, Leander, a young lover, presents himself during Diego's absence, cajoles the duenna and Mungo, the Negro servant, and gains admission to the lady. Diego returns unexpectedly, but sensibly accepts the situation and handsomely endows Leonora. The story is taken from one of *Cervantes's novels.

The part of Mungo (taken in the original production by Dibdin himself) provided the London stage with its first black-faced comedian, and created a sensation: for a while his lines 'Mungo here, Mungo dere, Mungo every where' were a catchphrase. As feeling for the oppressed Negro grew, the role appears to have been played with increasing stress on sentiment.

paean, a song of thanksgiving for deliverance from evil or danger, addressed usually to Apollo who, as god of healing, was given the name Paean. Later the word is used for a shout or song of triumph.

Page, Mrs Page, and Anne Page, their daughter, characters in Shakespeare's *The Merry Wives of Windsor.

PAGET, Violet, see LEE, V.

PAINE, Thomas (1737–1809), son of a Quaker staymaker of Thetford, who followed various pursuits before being dismissed as an exciseman in 1774 for agitating for an increase in excisemen's pay. At the suggestion of his friend Benjamin *Franklin he sailed for America, where he published in 1776 his pamphlet *Common Sense* and in 1776–83 a series of pamphlets, *The Crisis*, encouraging American independence and resistance to England; he also wrote against slavery and in favour of the emancipation of women. In 1787 he returned to England (via France), and published in 1791 the first part of *The Rights of Man* in reply to Burke's *Reflections on the *Revolution in France*. The second part appeared in 1792, when, alerted by *Blake of an impending arrest, Paine left for France, where he was warmly received and elected a member of the Convention. However, he opposed the execution of Louis XVI, was imprisoned for nearly a year, and narrowly escaped the guillotine. *The Age of Reason* (1793), an attack on Christianity and the Bible from a Deist point of view, greatly increased the violent hatred with which he was regarded in England, where his effigy and books were repeatedly burned; he was attacked in print by R. *Watson, bishop of Llandaff, and many others. He returned to America in 1802, where his views on religion and his opposition to Washington had made him unpopular, and his last years were saddened by ill health and neglect. He was buried at his farm in New Rochelle; ten years later *Cobbett, who had once vehemently opposed Paine, exhumed his bones and brought them back to England, planning some kind of memorial as reparation, but they were eventually mislaid.

Paine's early biographers did their best to denigrate him, but his writings became a textbook for the radical party in England and were extremely influential; his connection with the American struggle and the French Revolution gave him a unique position as an upholder of the politics of the *Enlightenment. His prose is plainer, more colloquial, and less rhetorical than that of *Burke, whose 'high-toned exclamation' he despised. He gave away most of the considerable earnings from his pen, in part to the Society of Constitutional Information, founded in 1780.

PAINTER, George, see BIOGRAPHY.

PAINTER, William, see PALACE OF PLEASURE.

Pair of Blue Eyes, A, a novel by T. *Hardy, published 1873.

The scene is the northern coast of Cornwall. Stephen

Smith, a young architect, comes to Endelstow to restore the church tower and falls in love with Elfride Swancourt, the blue-eyed daughter of the vicar. Her father is incensed that someone of Stephen's humble origin should claim his daughter. Elfride and Stephen run away together, but Elfride vacillates over marriage, and Stephen, hoping to better himself, accepts a post in India. Henry Knight, Stephen's friend and patron, then meets Elfride, and after she has saved his life on a cliff they become engaged. However, Knight is horrified to hear of Elfride's truancy with Stephen and is convinced that they must have been lovers. He harshly breaks off the engagement leaving Elfride heartbroken. Eventually he and Stephen meet; Stephen learns that Elfride is still unmarried and Knight learns the innocent facts of her past escapade with Stephen. But the train which carries them both to Cornwall is also carrying Elfride's dead body. They learn when they arrive at Endelstow that she has died, and that she had recently married Lord Luxellian.

Palace of Pleasure, a collection of translations into English of 'Pleasant Histories and excellent Novelles . . . out of divers good and commendable Authors', made by William Painter (c.1525–95), Clerk of the Ordnance, and published in 1566, 1567, and 1575. Many of the translations are from *Boccaccio, *Bandello, and Marguerite of Navarre (see HEPTAMERON), but Painter also drew on *Herodotus, *Livy, and *Gellius. The book provided a storehouse of plots for Elizabethan writers, especially dramatists; Shakespeare probably used it for *The Rape of Lucrece and *All's Well that Ends Well, and Webster certainly drew the plot of *The Duchess of Malfi from it. It was edited by Joseph Jacobs (1890).

Paladins, the, in the cycle of *Charlemagne legends, the 12 peers who accompanied the king. The origin of the conception is seen in the *Chanson de Roland* (see ROLAND), where the 12 peers are merely an association of particularly brave warriors, under the leadership of Roland and *Oliver, who all perish at Roncesvalles. From the Spanish war the idea was transported by later writers to other parts of the cycle, and Charlemagne is found always surrounded by 12 peers. The names of the 12 are differently stated by different authors, most of the original names given by the *Chanson de Roland* being forgotten by them; but Roland and Oliver figure in all the enumerations. Among the best known are *Otuel, Fierabras or *Ferumbras, *Ogier the Dane, and the count palatine. In the early 13th cent. there was a French court, comprising six ecclesiastics and six laymen, known as 'the Twelve Peers of France'; this court in 1202 declared King John deprived of his fiefs in France. Since the 16th cent. the word is applied to any great knightly champion (cf. the word 'Peer').

palaeography, see WANLEY, H.

Palamon and Arcite, the two Theban princes whose love for Emelye is the subject of Chaucer's 'The Knight's Tale' (see CANTERBURY TALES, 1), following the *Teseida* of *Boccaccio. The tale was paraphrased in heroic couplets by *Dryden under the title 'Palamon and Arcite'. It is also the subject of *The Two Noble Kinsmen*.

PALEY, Grace (1922–   ), American short story writer and poet, who grew up in the Bronx, New York city, the daughter of Russian-Jewish parents. She was taught Russian and Yiddish by her father and attended but did not complete courses at Hunter College and New York University. She is the author of three acclaimed volumes of short stories: *The Little Disturbances of Man* (1959); *Enormous Changes at the Last Minute* (1974); and *Later the Same Day* (1985). Pungent and laconic, her tragi-comic stories resound with the cadences of the city where she was raised and are carried by the spoken word. All embrace 'the open destiny of life' and the politics of dailiness. Paley has long campaigned on behalf of anti-war movements, nuclear disarmament, and women's rights. Her essays and articles on family, community, and politics are collected in *Just as I Thought* (1997). *Begin Again: New and Collected Poems* (1992) features poems written from the 1950s onwards.

PALEY, William (1743–1805), educated at Christ's College, Cambridge, of which he became fellow. He was one of the principal exponents of theological utilitarianism of which his *Moral and Political Philosophy* (1785), based largely on the doctrine of *Tucker, is the textbook; an attack on private property in Book III, drawing an analogy between human greed and the behaviour of a flock of pigeons, gave him his nickname 'Pigeon' Paley. In *Evidences of Christianity* (1794) and *Natural Theology* (1802) he finds proof of the existence of God in the design apparent in natural phenomena, and particularly in the mechanisms of the human body; the opening pages of *Natural Theology* introduce the celebrated analogy of an abandoned watch found upon a heath, from which he argues the existence of God as designer, for as 'the watch must have had a maker', so must the natural world.

PALGRAVE, Francis Turner (1824–97), son of barrister, historian, and antiquary Sir Francis Palgrave (1788–1861), who had changed his name from Cohen when he converted to Christianity in 1823. F. T. Palgrave was educated at Balliol College, Oxford, was an official in the education department 1855–84, and professor of poetry at Oxford, 1885–95. He is chiefly remembered for his anthology *The Golden Treasury of Best Songs and Lyrical Poems in the English Language* (1861, and much reprinted; 2nd series, 1897). In the selection for the first edition Palgrave was advised by his close friend *Tennyson; it contained no work by living poets, and is a reflection of the taste of the age (e.g. no *Donne and no *Blake, though work by these poets was added to subsequent editions). New and enlarged editions with poems by later writers have since appeared; the most recent in 1965, with a fifth book selected by John Press. Palgrave compiled other anthologies and selections, and published several volumes of his own verse.

PALGRAVE, William Gifford (1826–88), son of Sir F. Palgrave, educated at Trinity College, Oxford. He became a Jesuit missionary in Syria and Arabia. After undertaking a daring journey through Arabia for Napoleon III, in the guise of a doctor, he wrote *Narrative of a Year's Journey through Central and Eastern Arabia* (1865), his interesting but somewhat unreliable reminiscences of this expedition. He then left the Jesuits to join the diplomatic service in which he held various posts from 1865. Shortly before his death he became reconciled to the Church.

palimpsest, from πάλιν, 'again', and ψηστός, 'rubbed smooth', a manuscript in which a later writing is superimposed on an effaced earlier writing. Of frequent occurrence in the early Middle Ages because of the cost of parchment.

palindrome, from παλίνδρομος, 'running back again', a word, verse, or sentence that reads the same forwards or backwards, e.g.:

> Lewd did I live & evil I did dwel
> > (Phillips, 1706)

and the Latin line descriptive of moths:

> In girum imus noctes et consumimur igni.

palinode, from παλινῳδία, 'singing over again', a poem of recantation. 'Palinode' is the name of the Catholic shepherd in the fifth eclogue of Spenser's *The Shepheardes Calender*.

Palinurus, see CONNOLLY.

Palladianism, a revival of the style and ideas of *Palladio and of his English follower I. *Jones, dominated English architectural theory from c.1720 to 1770. The Whig aristocrat and man of taste admired the rationality and the mathematical proportions of Palladio's buildings; the movement marks a turning away from the panache of *Hawksmoor and *Vanbrugh towards a purer form of classicism. Palladianism opened with two publications: Colen Campbell's *Vitruvius Britannicus* (1st vol. 1715), a collection of engravings of English buildings inspired by antiquity, and Giacomo Leoni's English version of Palladio's *I quattro libri dell'architettura* (1st vol. 1715). In the 1720s the architect-earl Lord Burlington dominated; his Chiswick House (1725–9), deeply influenced by Palladio's Villa Rotonda and by Inigo Jones, epitomizes the Palladian movement in England. *Pope was a Palladian enthusiast; his *Epistle to Burlington* (1731) both satirizes its excesses and sums up its aspirations; he invites the earl to:

> Erect new wonders, and the old repair
> Jones and Palladio to themselves restore,
> And be whate'er Vitruvius was before.
> > (192–4)

PALLADIO, Andrea (1508–80), highly influential Italian architect of the late Renaissance, whose elegant style was formed by his passion for the buildings of antiquity, by his knowledge of *Vitruvius, and by his response to High Renaissance and mannerist architects. The name Palladio (from Pallas Athena) was given him by the humanist Giangiorgio Trissino of Vicenza, who sensed in him a renewal of Greek wisdom and beauty. Palladio was unrivalled in his ability to express the ideas of antiquity in a modern idiom, yet he was a sophisticated mannerist architect, and as his career progressed his treatment of classical themes became increasingly imaginative. Palladio designed the churches of San Giorgio Maggiore (1566–80) and Il Redentore (begun 1577) in Venice, but most of his works are in and around Vicenza; they include many town palaces, the Teatro Olimpico (begun 1580; finished by Scamozzi), and many country houses and villas which were to affect English architecture in the early 18th cent. The characteristic Palladian villa has a symmetrically planned central block, with a portico deriving from a classical temple front and low wings. The most famous is the untypical Villa Rotonda (1550–1). Palladio's buildings became widely known through his *Quattro libri dell'architettura* (1570). (See also PALLADIANISM.)

Palladis Tamia, see MERES.

PALLISER, Charles (1947–), American novelist, born in Holyoke, Massachusetts, but resident in Britain since the age of 10. *The Quincunx* (1989) is a monumental and explicit *hommage* to *Dickens which matches his atmosphere, sense of place, and hatred of poverty and social injustice to an extraordinary degree. It was followed by a modernist novella (*The Sensationalist*, 1990) and an intricate book of parodies (*Betrayals*, 1994), but in *The Unburied* (1999) Palliser finally returned to the Victorian setting and neo-Gothic mode for which he has such a singular gift.

Palliser Novels, the, a term used to describe the political novels of A. *Trollope, which are: *Can You Forgive Her?*, *Phineas Finn*, *The Eustace Diamonds*, *Phineas Redux*, *The Prime Minister*, and *The Duke's Children*.

Pall Mall Gazette, an evening paper founded in 1865 by Frederick Greenwood (1830–1909) and George *Smith to combine the features of a newspaper with the literary features of the *Spectator and the *Saturday Review. Its name was taken from Thackeray's *Pendennis, where Captain Shandon in the Marshalsea prepares the prospectus of 'The Pall Mall Gazette', 'written by gentlemen for gentlemen'. Its early contributors included Sir Henry Maine (1822–88), *Trollope, Sir J. F. *Stephen, L. *Stephen, and M. *Arnold (whose *Friendship's Garland* first appeared in it); in 1880 Smith parted with it to his Liberal son-in-law, and J. *Morley took over as editor, to be succeeded

(1883–9) by W. T. *Stead, whose sensational journalism altered the character of the paper. Greenwood produced instead the newly founded Conservative *St James's Gazette*.

PALMER, Samuel (1805–81), Romantic painter and etcher, born in Newington, London, the son of a bookseller. His early aspirations were literary, and he greatly admired *Blake, to whom he was introduced in 1824 by the painter John Linnell (1792–1882). He settled for some years, 1826–32, in Shoreham, Kent, where he painted some of his most celebrated visionary pastoral landscapes. He later travelled in north Wales, Devon, and Italy, all of which provided inspiration. Some of his subjects were drawn from the Bible and the classics (he produced an English translation of *Virgil's *Eclogues*, published 1881), but he also looked to English literature, and produced illustrations for the work of *Bunyan and *Dickens (*Pictures from Italy*, 1846), among others. His fine watercolours on the themes of Milton's *'L'Allegro' and *'Il Penseroso' belong to his later years, he worked on them from 1868 onwards. His powerfully poetic imagination has won the admiration of many writers. See *The Followers of William Blake* (1925) by L. *Binyon and *Samuel Palmer: The Visionary Years* by G. *Grigson (1947).

Palmerin of England (*Palmerín de Inglaterra*), a chivalric romance attributed to the 16th-cent. Portuguese writer Francisco de Moraes.

The 'Palmerins' consist of eight books dealing with the exploits and loves of Palmerin d'Oliva, emperor of Constantinople, and his various descendants, of which Palmerin of England is the subject of the sixth. The daughter of Palmerin d'Oliva, Flerida by name, married Don Duardos, son of Fadrique, king of Great Britain, and became the mother of Palmerin of England and his brother Floriano of the Desert. Duardos having been imprisoned in the castle of the giant Dramusiando by Eutropa, a magician, a savage carries off Palmerin and Floriano intending them as food for his hunting lions, but his wife insists on bringing them up. Palmerin is taken to Constantinople and appointed to wait on his cousin Polinarda, with whom he falls in love; while Floriano is taken to London and appointed to wait on Flerida. Palmerin and Floriano undertake the quest of Don Duardos, and the former is successful. Thereafter the identity of the brothers is revealed and Palmerin marries Polinarda. Then the soldan advances against the Christians and demands the surrender of Polinarda as a condition of peace. Finally the Turks attack Constantinople; all the Turks and most of the Christians perish, but Palmerin survives.

*Munday translated the Palmerin cycle into English (through a French intermediary), 1581–95. It was highly popular with the Elizabethan middle classes, and there are many references to Palmerin in the plays of the time (e.g. *The Knight of the Burning Pestle*, where the vogue for such chivalric fantasies is mocked). A revised translation by *Southey appeared in 1807, in which Southey suggests debts to Palmerin from Shakespeare, *Spenser, and *Sidney. See *The Palmerin Romances in Elizabethan Prose Fiction* by M. Tatchell (1947).

Palmerin of England and *Amadis of Gaul* were two romances of chivalry specially excepted from the holocaust of such works carried out by the curate and the barber in *Don Quixote*.

Palomydes the Saracen, in *Malory, a prominent knight and great fighter who follows the *Questing Beast and who once abducts *Iseult, for whom he entertains an unrequited and mostly selfless passion. He is the great friend of Tristram who has him christened at the end. The French prose romance *Palamedes* seems to have been written as an addition to the Vulgate *Tristan* and *Lancelot* in the early 13th cent.; it achieved enormous popularity in the later Middle Ages and influenced *Boiardo and *Ariosto, who said it was his favourite among the Arthurian romances.

PALTOCK, Robert (1697–1767), author of *Peter Wilkins*. He was an attorney of Clement's Inn.

Pamela, the heir to the dukedom of Arcadia in the romance of *Sidney. Richardson took her name for the heroine of his first novel (below).

Pamela, *or Virtue Rewarded*, a novel by S. *Richardson, published 1740–1.

The first of Richardson's three novels, *Pamela* consists, like them, entirely of letters and journals, of which Richardson presents himself as the 'editor'. He believed he had hit upon 'a new species of writing' but he was not the inventor of the *epistolary novel, several of which already existed in English and French. He did however raise the form to a level hitherto unknown, and transformed it to display his own particular skills.

There are six correspondents in *Pamela*, most with their own particular style and point of view, but Pamela herself provides most of the letters and journals, with the 'hero', Mr B., having only two. Pamela Andrews is a handsome, intelligent girl of 15 when her kind employer Lady B. dies. Penniless and without protection, Pamela is pursued by Mr B., Lady B.'s son, but she repulses him and remains determined to retain her chastity and her unsullied conscience. Letters reveal Mr B.'s cruel dominance and pride, but also Pamela's half-acknowledged tenderness for him, as well as her vanity, prudence, and calculation. Angrily Mr B. separates her from her friends, Mrs Jervis the housekeeper and Mr Longman the steward, and dispatches her to B—Hall, his remote house in Lincolnshire, where she is imprisoned, guarded, and threatened by the cruel Mrs Jewkes. Only the chaplain, Mr Williams, is her friend, but he is powerless to help. For 40 days, allowed no visits or correspondence, she keeps a detailed journal, analysing her situation and her feelings, and at the same time revealing her faults of prudence and pride. She despairs, and begins to think of suicide. Mr

B., supposing her spirit must now be broken, arrives at B— Hall, and, thinking himself generous, offers to make her his mistress and keep her in style. She refuses indignantly, and he later attempts to rape her and then to arrange a mock-marriage. Two scenes by the pond mark a turning point in their relationship. Both begin to be aware of their faults, and of the genuine nature of their affection. However, Pamela again retreats and refuses his proposal of marriage. She is sent away from B— Hall, but a message gives her a last chance. Overcoming her pride and caution, she decides to trust him, accepts his offer, and they are married. In the remaining third of the book Pamela's goodness wins over even Lady Davers, Mr B.'s supercilious sister, and becomes a model of virtue to her circle of admiring friends; but (as in *Pamela, Part II*) the author's creative drive becomes overwhelmed by his urge to moralize.

The book was highly successful and fashionable, and further editions were soon called for. Richardson felt obliged to continue his story, not only because of the success of *Pamela* but because of the number of forged continuations that began to appear. *Pamela, Part II* appeared in 1741. Here Pamela is exhibited, through various small and separate instances, as the perfect wife, patiently leading her profligate husband to reform; a mother who adores (and breastfeeds) her children; and a friend who is at the disposal of all, and who brings about the penitence of the wicked. Much space is given over to discussion of moral, domestic, and general subjects.

Shamela (1741, almost certainly by *Fielding) vigorously mocked what the author regarded as the hypocritical morality of *Pamela*; and Fielding's *Joseph Andrews*, which begins as a parody of *Pamela*, appeared in 1742.

pamphleteering, origins of. The word 'pamphlet' appears to derive, curiously, from the generalized use of the title of a popular 12th-cent. Latin love poem called *Pamphilus, seu de Amore*, which was adapted to 'Pamphilet'. *Orwell, in his introduction to *British Pamphleteers* (vol. i, 1948), describes a pamphlet as 'a short piece of polemical writing, printed in the form of a booklet and aimed at a large public', usually of 5,000–10,000 words, and without hard covers. Pamphleteering may be said to have started with the Reformation, and during the 16th cent. became widespread (see Nashe, Dekker, and Martin Marprelate); J. *Knox's *First Blast of the Trumpet against the Monstrous Regiment* (i.e. 'government') *of Women* (1558) was perhaps the first British political pamphlet. In the 17th cent. the religious and political ferment that gave rise to the Civil War produced many thousands of pamphlets, some of high literary quality; *Milton's are perhaps the best known, but see also Winstanley, Overton, Walwyn, Clarkson, Coppe, Lilburne, Nedham, and Berkenhead. *Tyranipocrit Discovered* and *Light Shining in Buckinghamshire* (1648) were both anonymous, as were many others. These writers

played an important part in the transition from the learned, allusive prose of men like *Donne, *Andrewes, and Sir T. *Browne to the plain, clear, and colloquial style recommended by the *Royal Society. (See C. *Hill, *The World Turned upside down*, 1972.) In the 18th cent., though important works in pamphlet form were produced by writers as considerable as *Defoe and *Swift, the rise of weekly periodicals tended to reduce the demand for this form of communication. The form was revived in the 19th cent. by two important intellectual movements, the *Oxford movement, and the *Fabian Society, both of which used the pamphlet (or tract) extensively and to much effect.

Pancks, a character in Dickens's *Little Dorrit*.

Pandarus, in classical legend, a son of Lycaon who assisted the Trojans in their war against the Greeks. The role that he plays in *Chaucer's and Shakespeare's stories of Troilus and Criseyde (Cressida) was the invention of *Boccaccio in his *Filostrato* (where he is called Pandaro; see N. R. Havely, *Chaucer's Boccaccio*, 1980). In Boccaccio he is the cousin of Cressida, presumably much the same age as her and Troilus; Chaucer strikingly changes him from her cousin to her uncle and guardian, for reasons that are not entirely clear but whose effect is to increase the sense of irresponsibility towards her in arranging their love affair. His role plays a striking part in the atmosphere of sourness in which the events of Shakespeare's play occur. The word 'pander' (as Shakespeare says: V. x. 34) derives from his role as go-between for Troilus and Criseyde.

Pandemonium, a word coined by *Milton, the abode of all the demons; a place represented by Milton (*Paradise Lost*, I. 756) as the capital of Hell, containing the council-chamber of the Evil Spirits.

Pandosto, or *The Triumph of Time*, a prose romance by R. *Greene published 1588. It went through nine editions up to 1632, but is now best known as the source for *The Winter's Tale*. Shakespeare followed Greene's romance closely, except that he preserved the life of Hermione (Bellaria in *Pandosto*), and made Leontes, not Hermione/Bellaria, appeal to the oracle. Pandosto, the Leontes figure, is killed at the end of the romance, 'to close up the Comedie with a Tragicall stratageme'. *Pandosto* is one of Greene's best narratives, and of understandable popularity in its time.

Pandulph, Cardinal, the papal legate in Shakespeare's *King John*.

Pangloss, Dr, (1) in *Candide by *Voltaire, an optimistic philosopher who holds that all is for the best in the best of all possible worlds, in spite of a series of most distressing adventures (including unsuccessful hanging by the Inquisition and subsequent dissection). He is brought, however, to recognize that, to be happy, man must work and must 'cultivate his garden'.

The intended object of the satire was *Leibniz. (2) In *The Heir-at-Law* by G. *Colman the younger, a pompous pedant.

PANIZZI, Antonio (later Sir Anthony) (1797–1879), born in Italy. He fled to England as a political exile in 1823, where he was befriended by *Foscolo, W. *Roscoe, and Lord *Brougham. He taught Italian before obtaining a post in the *British Museum, where he eventually became (in 1856) principal librarian. He had a great talent for administration, and among many achievements was responsible for the preparation of a new catalogue and for the plans of the celebrated circular domed Reading Room which he opened personally in 1857. The Panizzi Lectures on *book history are delivered annually at the British Library; D. F. McKenzie delivered the inaugural lecture in 1985.

PANKHURST, Emmeline and Christabel, see WOMEN'S SUFFRAGE.

Panopticon, J. *Bentham's term (1843) for a proposed type of prison, consisting of cells ranged round a central point from which a warder could observe the prisoners while they could see neither him nor their fellow prisoners in adjacent cells. *Foucault took up the idea in *Discipline and Punish* (1975), his study of the change in the way power was exercised after the 16th cent. Before this he claims power was exerted through violence and coercion of the body, whereas the body was subsequently schooled to discipline itself. The Panopticon exemplifies this change; the prisoner, unable to see the guard and know whether observation is taking place at any given time, exercises self-control over behaviour and demeanour.

Pantagruel, see GARGANTUA.

Pantisocracy, a utopian scheme invented by *Coleridge and *Southey in 1794–5, to set up an egalitarian commune of six families 'on the banks of the Susquehanna' in New England, based on a joint-stock farm.

pantomime, (1) originally a Roman actor, who performed in dumb show, representing by mimicry various characters and scenes; (2) an English dramatic performance, originally consisting of action without speech, but in its further development consisting of a dramatized traditional fairy tale, with singing, dancing, acrobatics, clowning, topical jokes, a transformation scene, and certain stock roles, especially the 'principal boy' (i.e. hero) acted by a woman and the 'dame' acted by a man. (See MIME.)

Panurge, one of the principal characters in Rabelais's *Pantagruel* (see GARGANTUA), a cunning, voluble, witty, and in the later books cowardly buffoon, 'and a very dissolute and debauched fellow, if there were any in Paris: otherwise and in all matters else, the best and most virtuous man in the world; and he was still contriving some plot, and devising mischief against the serjeants and the watch'.

Paolo and Francesca. Francesca, daughter of Giovanni da Polenta, count of Ravenna, was given in marriage by him to Giovanni (Sciancato, the Lame) Malatesta, of Rimini, an ill-favoured man, in return for his military services. She fell in love with Paolo, her husband's brother, and, their relations being discovered, the two lovers were put to death in 1289. *Dante, at the end of the fifth canto of the *Inferno*, relates his conversation with Francesca, who told him how her fall was occasioned by the reading of the tale of Launcelot and Guinevere. The 'Galeotto' mentioned by Dante is Galahault, the prince who, in the story of the early loves of Launcelot and Guinevere, not included in *Malory, introduces Launcelot to the queen. The story of Paolo and Francesca was the subject of the poem *The Story of Rimini* by Leigh *Hunt, and it remained popular throughout the 19th cent., most famously in *Tchaikovsky's symphonic fantasy *Francesca da Rimini*.

Paper Money Lyrics, burlesque poems by *Peacock, ridiculing political economists and bankers. They were written in the late 1820s, but not published until 1837, after the death of J. *Mill, Peacock's immediate superior at the India Office.

Pappe with an Hatchet, the title of a tract contributed in 1589 by *Lyly to the Marprelate controversy (see MARTIN MARPRELATE) on the side of the bishops. The sense of the expression appears to be 'the administration of punishment under the ironical style of a kindness or benefit' [*OED*]. Lyly's pamphlet is a mixture of abuse and ribaldry.

PARACELSUS (Theophrast Bombast von Hohenheim) (1493–1541), Swiss-born physician. He lectured on medicine in Basle in 1527–8, but instead of lecturing in Latin on *Avicenna and *Galen, as was required, lectured in German on his own experience of medical disorders. He quarrelled with the faculty and thereafter led a wandering life. He was attracted to alchemy, astrology, and mysticism, but was nevertheless credited with remarkable cures, had a genuinely original and enquiring mind, and initiated improvements in pharmacy and therapeutics. His arrogance, unconventionality, and ambiguous philosophy won him many enemies, and led to his being pronounced a charlatan, but he also had many followers and exerted considerable influence, particularly through the *Rosicrucian movement. He believed in the divine alchemy of the Creation, in which God (the Divine Artificer) separated by chemical process the elements from the primal matter, the Mysterium Magnum: he supported the notion of the four Aristotelian elements (earth, air, fire, water), and added the concept of the 'three principles' of sulphur, mercury, and salt. The elements were inhabited by spirits—the air by sylphs, the water by nymphs or undines, the earth by gnomes, the fire by salamanders—and by many other spiritual or super-natural beings, such as syrens, nenuphar, lorins, etc. (Paracelsus: *De Nymphis Pygmiis, Salamandris, De Homonculis et Monstris*, etc., *Works*, 1658). This mytho-logical machinery was borrowed by Pope, via the Rosicrucians, in **The Rape of the Lock*. Paracelsus died shortly after being offered a permanent post in Salzburg in 1541. He was the subject of a poem by **Browning (below). See also A. Debus, *The English Paracelsians* (1965); F. **Yates, *The Rosicrucian Enlight-enment* (1972).

Paracelsus, a dramatic poem in blank verse by R. *Browning, published 1835. The career of the histor-ical *Paracelsus serves Browning, despite his claim to the contrary, as a stalking-horse for his own explor-ation of the processes of the creative imagination, in particular the conflict between 'Love' (self-forgetting) and 'Knowledge' (self-assertion) in the mind of the artist. The poem's critical success introduced Brown-ing to literary London and launched his career, at first in the (unhappy) direction of the theatre. Browning's works up to the end of **Bells and Pomegranates* were published as by 'Robert Browning, author of Para-celsus'.

Parade's End, a tetralogy by F. M. *Ford, now known under this collective title, but originally published as *Some Do Not . . .* (1924), *No More Parades* (1925), *A Man Could Stand up* (1926), and *Last Post* (1928).

The hero is Christopher Tietjens of Groby, a Tory Yorkshire squire and younger son, married to the neurotic, beautiful, unfaithful Catholic Sylvia. In the first volume Christopher agrees to take back his wife and to conceal her adultery; meanwhile he himself falls in love with a young suffragette schoolteacher, Val-entine Wannop, but the affair is not consummated. The next two volumes cover his wartime experiences and his resolution, on Armistice Day, to leave Sylvia and make Valentine his mistress. In *Last Post* Valentine is pregnant, Christopher is making his living by restoring antiques, and his older brother Mark is dying; Sylvia eventually agrees to divorce Christopher. Other major characters include the Pre-Raphaelite hostess Edith Ethel Duchemin, both elegant and vulgar, who has an affair with and later marries Christopher's friend, critic and writer Vincent Macmaster. The subject of the novel appears to be the breakdown of the accepted standards of the old world and the necessary emer-gence of a new order; the breadth of Ford's canvas, his impressionistic and highly idiosyncratic narrative technique, and his creation of the deeply English 'saintly mealsack' Tietjens have been admired by many (including G. *Greene), although others are made uneasy by a sense of unresolved conflict, narrative inconsistency, and emotional posturing.

Paradise Lost, an epic poem by *Milton, originally in ten books, subsequently rearranged in 12, first printed 1667.

Milton formed the intention of writing a great epic poem, as he tells us, as early as 1639. A list of possible subjects, some of them scriptural, some from British history, written in his own hand about 1640–1, still exists, with drafts of the scheme of a poem on 'Paradise Lost'. The work was not, however, begun in earnest until 1658, and it was finished, according to *Aubrey, in 1663. It was licensed for publication by the Revd Thomas Tomkyns, chaplain to the archbishop of Canterbury. Milton entered into an agreement for the copyright with Samuel Simmons by which he received £5 down, and a further £5 when the first impression of 1,300 copies was exhausted. His widow subsequently parted with all further claims for the sum of £8.

Milton added to later copies of the first edition not only an 'Argument', summarizing the contents of each of the books, but also a spirited defence of his choice of blank verse, 'Rime being no necessary Adjunct or true Ornament of Poem or good Verse, in longer works especially, but the Invention of a barbarous Age, to set off wretched matter and lame Meeter'.

Book I. The poet, invoking the 'Heav'nly Muse', states his theme, the Fall of Man through disobedience, and his aim, which is no less than to 'justifie the wayes of God to men'. He then presents the defeated arch-angel Satan, with *Beelzebub, his second-in-command, and his rebellious angels, lying on the burning lake of hell. Satan awakens his legions, rouses their spirits, and summons a council. The palace of Satan, *Pan-demonium (a word coined by Milton), is built.

Book II. The council debates whether another battle for the recovery of Heaven be hazarded, *Moloc recommending open war, *Belial and Mammon rec-ommending peace in order to avoid worse torments. Beelzebub announces the creation of 'another World, the happy seat | Of som new Race call'd *Man*', which may prove a means of revenge. Satan undertakes to visit it alone, and passes through hell-gates, guarded by Sin and Death, and passes upward through the realm of Chaos.

Book III. Milton invokes celestial light to illumine the 'ever-during dark' of his own blindness, then describes God, who sees Satan's flight towards our world, and foretells his success and the fall and punishment of man, emphasizing that man will fall not through predestination but through free will. The Son of God offers himself as a ransom, is accepted, and exalted as the Saviour. Satan alights on the outer convex of our universe, 'a Limbo large and broad, since call'd | The Paradise of Fools'. He finds the stairs leading up to heaven, descends to the sun, disguises himself as 'a stripling Cherube', and in this shape is directed to earth by Uriel, where he alights on Mt Niphates in Armenia.

Book IV. Satan, at first tormented by doubts, resolves 'Evil be thou my Good' and journeys on towards the garden of Eden, where he first sees Adam and Eve 'in naked Majestie', and overhears their discourse about the forbidden Tree of Knowledge. He resolves to tempt them to disobey the prohibition but is discovered by the guardian angels Ithuriel and Zephon as he squats like a toad near the ear of Eve, and expelled from the garden by their commander, *Gabriel.

Book V. Eve relates to Adam the disquieting dream of temptation which Satan had inspired. He comforts her, and they set about their daily tasks. Raphael, sent by God, comes to paradise, warns Adam, and enjoins obedience. They discourse of reason, free will, and predestination, and Raphael, at Adam's request, relates how Satan, inspired by hatred and envy of the newly anointed Messiah, inspired his legions to revolt, resisted only by Abdiel—'Among the faithless, faithful only hee'.

Book VI. Raphael continues his narrative, telling how Michael and Gabriel were sent to fight against Satan. After indecisive battles the Son of God himself, alone, attacked the hosts of Satan, and, driving them to the verge of heaven, forced them to leap down through chaos into the deep.

Book VII. Milton evokes Urania (in classical times the Muse of Astronomy, but perhaps here the Christian Muse: a much disputed passage), and requests her to aid him to 'fit audience find, though few', in the evil days on which he has fallen; then continues Raphael's narrative, with an account of God's decision to send his Son to create another world from the vast abyss. He describes the six days of creation, ending with the creation of man, and a renewed warning to Adam that death will be the penalty for eating of the fruit of the tree of knowledge.

Book VIII. Adam enquires concerning the motions of the heavenly bodies, and is answered 'doubtfully'. (The controversy regarding the Ptolemaic and Copernican systems was at its height when *Paradise Lost* was written, and Milton was unable to decide between them, as seen in X. 668 ff.) Adam relates what he remembers since his own creation, notably his own need for rational fellowship, and his plea to his Maker for a companion, which is answered by the creation of Eve. Adam and Raphael talk of the relations between the sexes, then, with a final warning to 'take heed least Passion sway | Thy Judgement', Raphael departs.

Book IX. Insisting that his argument is 'not less but more Heroic' than the themes of *Homer and *Virgil, Milton describes Satan's entry into the body of the serpent, in which form he finds Eve, she having insisted, despite Adam's warnings, on pursuing her labours alone. He persuades her to eat of the Tree of Knowledge. Eve relates to Adam what has passed and brings him of the fruit. Adam, recognizing that she is doomed, resolves to perish with her: 'If Death | Consort with thee, Death is to mee as Life; | So forcible within my heart I feel | The Bond of Nature draw me to my owne.' He also eats of the fruit, and after initial intoxication in their lost innocence, they cover their nakedness and fall to mutual accusation.

Book X. God sends his Son to judge the transgressors. They greet him with guilt and shame, and confess, and

he pronounces his sentence. Sin and Death resolve to come to this world, and make a broad highway thither from hell. Satan returns to hell and announces his victory, whereupon he and his angels are temporarily transformed into serpents. Adam, recognizing that in him 'all Posteritie stands curst', at first reproaches Eve, but then, reconciled, they together resolve to seek mercy from the Son of God.

Book XI. The Son of God, seeing their penitence, intercedes. God decrees that they must leave paradise, and sends down Michael to carry out his command. Eve laments; Adam pleads not to be banished from the 'bright appearances' of God, but Michael reassures him that God is omnipresent, then unfolds to him the future, revealing to him the consequences of his original sin in the death of Abel and the future miseries of mankind, ending with the Flood and the new Covenant.

Book XII. Michael relates the subsequent history of the Old Testament, then describes the coming of the Messiah, his incarnation, death, resurrection, and ascension, which leads Adam to rejoice over so much good sprung from his own sin. Michael also foretells the corrupt state of the Church until the Second Coming. Eve meanwhile, during these revelations, has been comforted by a dream presaging 'some great good'. Resolved on obedience and submission, and assured that they may possess 'a Paradise within', they are led out of the Garden.

Paradise Lost has inspired a mass of critical commentary and histories of critical commentary, theological discussion, imitations and adaptations, and illustrations. (For bibliography, see under MILTON.) Illustrators include *Fuseli, 1802; *Blake, 1806; J. *Martin, 1827, 1846, 1847, etc.; *Turner, 1835; and *Doré, 1866. See *Milton and English Art* by Marcia Pointon (1970).

Paradise Regained, an epic poem in four books by *Milton, published 1671. (See ELLWOOD.)

It is a sequel to *Paradise Lost*, and deals exclusively with the temptation of Jesus in the wilderness. According to the poet's conception, whereas Paradise was lost by the yielding of Adam and Eve to Satan's temptation, so it was regained by the resistance of the Son of God to the temptation of the same spirit. Satan is here represented not in the majestic lineaments of *Paradise Lost*, but as a cunning, smooth, and dissembling creature, a 'Spirit unfortunate', as he describes himself. There is a comparative scarcity of similes and ornament, and only a vivid and ingenious expansion of the biblical texts.

Book I relates the baptism of Jesus by John at Bethabara, and the proclamation from heaven that he is the Son of God. Satan, alarmed, summons a council of his peers, and undertakes his temptation. Jesus is led into the wilderness, where, after 40 days, Satan in the guise of 'an aged man in rural weeds' approaches him and suggests that he, being now hungry, should prove his divine character by turning the stones around him into bread. Jesus, seeing through his guile, sternly replies. Night falls on the desert.

Books II and III. Meanwhile Andrew and Simon seek Jesus, and Mary is troubled at his absence. Satan confers again with his council. He once more tries the hunger temptation, placing before the eyes of Jesus a 'table richly spread', which is contemptuously rejected. He then appeals to the higher appetites for wealth and power, and a disputation follows as to the real value of earthly glory. Satan, confuted, next reminds Jesus that the kingdom of David is now under the Roman yoke, and suggests that he should free it. He takes Jesus to a high mountain and shows him the kingdoms of the earth. A description follows (III. 251–346) of the contemporary state of the eastern world, divided between the powers of Rome and of the Parthians, as seen in this vision. Satan offers an alliance with, or conquest of, the Parthians, and the liberation of the Jews then in captivity.

Book IV. Jesus remaining unmoved by Satan's 'politic maxims', the tempter, turning to the western side, draws his attention to Rome and proposes the expulsion of the wicked emperor Tiberius; and finally, pointing out Athens, urges the attractions of her poets, orators, and philosophers. All these failing, Satan brings Jesus back to the wilderness, and the second night falls. On the third morning, confessing Jesus proof against all temptation, Satan carries him to the highest pinnacle of the temple and bids him cast himself down, 'to know what more he is than man', only to receive the well-known answer, 'Tempt not the Lord thy God'. Satan falls dismayed, and angels bear Jesus away.

Paradise of Dainty Devises, The, a collection of works by minor poets of the 1560s and 1570s: they include Lord *Vaux, the earl of *Oxford, *Churchyard, and William Hunnis. The volume was compiled by R. *Edwards, published after his death (1576), and frequently reprinted. It was edited by H. E. Rollins (1927).

Paradiso, of Dante, see DIVINA COMMEDIA.

paraleipsis, a rhetorical figure (sometimes called 'preterition') of apparent omission in which a speaker pretends to pass over what he actually calls to mind, as in 'I shall not mention my opponent's criminal record'.

Parasitaster, The, or *The Fawn*, a comedy by J. *Marston, published 1606.

Hercules, the widowed duke of Ferrara, wishes his son Tiberio to marry Dulcimel, daughter of a neighbouring prince, and, in order to defeat his unwillingness, declares that he will marry Dulcimel himself. He sends Tiberio to negotiate the marriage, and under the name of Faunus follows in disguise to see how matters develop. Dulcimel falls in love with Tiberio and, being a woman of wit and resource, manages to win him.

parataxis is the absence of relative or dependent clauses (subordination), as in 'I came, I saw, I conquered'. The adjectival form is 'paratactic'. See HYPOTAXIS.

Pardiggle, Mrs, in Dickens's *Bleak House*, a lady 'distinguished for rapacious benevolence'.

'Pardoner's Tale, The', see CANTERBURY TALES, 14.

Paridell, in Spenser's *Faerie Queene*, a false and libertine knight (III. viii, ix, x, and IV. i, ii) who consorts with *Duessa and elopes with *Hellenore, the wife of *Malbecco.

Paris, Count, a Capulet and suitor of *Juliet in Shakespeare's *Romeo and Juliet*.

PARIS, Matthew (d. 1259), monk and historian, who entered the monastery of St Albans in 1217, succeeding *Roger of Wendover as chronicler, and compiling the *Chronica Majora*, his greatest work, there from 1235 to 1259. He extends the range of the chronicle to include foreign events; as well as its great historical value, the work is outstanding for its expressive liveliness. He also wrote the *Historia Minor* (or *Historia Anglorum*), a summary of events in England from 1200 to 1250, and the *Vitae Abbatum S. Albani*, the lives of the first 23 abbots up to 1255, the last two or three of which were composed by him. It is unlikely that the *Vitae Duorum Offarum*, which are found with manuscripts of the *Chronica*, are by him. He went to Norway on a papal visit in 1248 and he knew French, which has been taken by some to suggest a period spent in Paris to explain his name. But Paris was an English surname in the 13th cent., especially in Lincolnshire.

'Parish Register, The', a poem by *Crabbe, published 1807.

Developing the form of *The Village*, 'The Parish Register' relates the memories of a country parson, as he looks through the entries in his registers of births, marriages, and deaths. The work first revealed Crabbe's gift for narrative, and reaffirmed his determination to present the truth, however sordid. The tales include the story of Phoebe Dawson, which pleased Sir W. *Scott and C. J. *Fox; and the terrible account, written in stanzas (and possibly under the effect of opium) in 'Sir Eustace Grey', of a patient in a madhouse.

Parisina, a poem by *Byron, published 1816, founded on a passage in *Gibbon's *Antiquities of the House of Brunswick*.

When his beloved wife Parisina murmurs the name of Hugo in her sleep, Prince Azo learns of her incestuous love for his bastard son. Hugo is a noble youth, loved by his father, but he must suffer death for his sin. Wild with grief, Parisina departs to an unknown fate, and Azo is left embittered and wretched.

PARK, Mungo (1771–1806), born near Selkirk. He was educated at Edinburgh and became a surgeon in the mercantile marine. He explored the course of the Niger and became famous by his vivid account of his travels, *Travels in the Interior Districts of Africa . . . in the Years 1795, 1796 and 1797*, published on his return in 1799. He went back to the Niger in 1805, and was killed in an attack on his party in the rapids of Boussa (now submerged in Kainji Reservoir, Nigeria). He was a friend of Sir W. *Scott. See K. Lupton, *Mungo Park, the African Traveler* (1979).

PARKER, Dorothy (Rothschild) (1893–1967), New York-born American humorist and journalist, legendary for her instant wit and for her satirical verses; she also wrote sketches and short stories, many of them published in the *New Yorker* and various collections.

PARKER, Matthew (1504–75), educated at St Mary's Hostel and Corpus Christi College, Cambridge. He was in 1544 elected master of the college, where he reformed the library, to which he was to bequeath his fine manuscripts. He fled to Frankfurt am Main during Queen Mary's reign, reluctantly accepted the archbishopric of Canterbury on Elizabeth's accession, and was consecrated at Lambeth in 1559. He identified himself with the party (afterwards known as the Anglican party) which sought to establish a *via media* between Romanism and Puritanism. From 1563 to 1568 he was occupied with the production of the Bishop's Bible (see BIBLE, THE ENGLISH), his most distinguished service to the theological studies of the day. In his later years he retired more and more from society, being conscious of the strength of the opposing current, headed by Leicester. He was buried in his private chapel at Lambeth. In 1648 his remains were disinterred and buried under a dunghill, but after the Restoration they were restored to their original resting place. He was a great benefactor to his college and to the University of Cambridge, where he constructed a handsome new street, which he named University Street, leading from the schools to Great St Mary's. To his efforts we are indebted for the earliest editions of *Asser, *Ælfric, the *Flores Historiarum* of Matthew of Westminster, *Paris, and other early chroniclers (an important manuscript of the *Anglo-Saxon Chronicle*, given by him to Corpus Christi College, is known as the 'Parker Chronicle'). In spite of Queen Elizabeth's dislike of clerical matrimony, he was married, and left one son. His *De Antiquitate Britannicae Ecclesiae et Privilegiis Ecclesiae Cantuariensis cum Archiepiscopis eiusdem 70* (1572–4) is said to be the first book privately printed in England.

PARKINSON, John (1567–1650), apothecary to James I, herbalist, author of *Paradisi in Sole Paradisus Terrestris, or A Garden of All Sorts of Pleasant Flowers which Our English Ayre will Permitt to Be Noursed up . . .* (1629), with woodcuts; also of a great herbal, *Theatrum Botanicum* (1640).

PARKMAN, Francis (1823–93), American historian, born in Boston. After graduation from Harvard he travelled in Europe, then journeyed out to Wyoming to study Indian life, giving an account of his journey in *The Oregon Trail* (1849), which was dictated, owing to his own ill health, to his cousin and companion Quincy A. Shaw. His history of the struggle of the English and French for dominion in North America was published in a series of studies, beginning with his *History of the Conspiracy of the Pontiac* (1851) and continuing through several volumes, concluding with *A Half-Century of Conflict* (1892). D. *Davie pays tribute to Parkman's distinguished prose in *A Sequence for Francis Parkman* (1961), inspired by Parkman's vivid evocation of Lasalle, Frontenac, Montcalm, Wolfe, Pontiac, and others.

Parleyings with Certain People of Importance in Their Day, a volume of poems in blank verse by R. *Browning, published 1887. The phrase 'certain people of importance' derives from a passage in *Dante's *Vita nuova*. Browning refers to a number of obscure historical figures whose works he had studied in his youth, and who had contributed to the formation of his mind. Each of these figures is matched by a contemporary of Browning's, and Browning 'parleys' with them in a renewed consideration of the central topics of art and life that had preoccupied him since the beginning of his career. The collection therefore constitutes an oblique autobiography and personal testament, and is of unique value to an understanding both of the sources of Browning's art and of the mature processes of that art. Perhaps the finest of the 'Parleyings' are the two concluding ones, with 'Gérard de Lairesse' and 'Charles Avison'.

Parliament of Fowls, The, a dream-poem by *Chaucer in 699 lines of rhyme-royal, centring on a conference of birds to choose their mates on St Valentine's day; it has accordingly been thought to be a poem in celebration of a marriage, perhaps the marriage of the young Richard II to Anne of Bohemia in 1382. This date would accord with the Italian influences on the poem, which otherwise cannot be dated more closely than between 1372 and 1386.

The poet falls asleep after a prologue in which he makes the Boethian lament that he has not what he wants, and has what he does not want (this usually refers to unrequited love in medieval writing). He then has a vision of a garden of the kind which is the setting for the *Roman de la rose* and in which the goddess Nature presides over the choosing of mates. Three tercel eagles pay court to a beautiful 'formel' (female) and there follows a long dispute about the criteria for success in a love suit, the argument of which centres on the opposition between the courtly love approach of the noble eagles and the pragmatism of the duck (whose worldly advice has been called 'bourgeois'): 'But she will love him, let him take another.' The debate is unresolved, and the birds agree to assemble again a year later to decide. Although the argument is inconclusive, the poem itself has a rounded completeness which makes it almost unique in Chaucer's works.

Ed. H. Phillips and N. Havely, *Chaucer's Dream Poetry* (1997). J. A. W. Bennett, *The Parlement of Fowles* (1957).

Parnassians, a group of French poets, headed by *Leconte de Lisle, who sought restraint, precision, and objectivity in poetry, in reaction to the emotional extravagances of Romanticism. Their name derives from the three collections of their work published under the title *Le Parnasse contemporain*, in 1866, 1871, and 1876. Associated with the group, besides Leconte de Lisle, were José-Maria de Heredia (1842–1905), whose collection *Les Trophées* appeared in 1893, Catulle Mendès (1841–1909), and René-François-Armand Sully-Prudhomme (1839–1907).

Parnassus Plays, The, the name given to a trilogy produced between 1598 and 1602 by students of St John's College, Cambridge, consisting of *The Pilgrimage to Parnassus* and *The Returne from Parnassus*, the latter apparently in two parts. Authorship has not been established, but they seem to be the work of two dramatists, unusually writing academic drama in the vernacular; they have been attributed to J. *Day and, more recently, to John Weever of Queen's and J. *Hall. They treat amusingly of the attempts of a group of young men (one apparently modelled on *Nashe) to resist temptation and to gain preferment or at least a livelihood, and are full of allusions to contemporary literature. In the third more satirical section the students are shown on their way to London, learning how to catch a patron or cheat a tradesman, and following menial occupations, which they finally abandon in discouragement and 'returne' to Cambridge. They were first published together in 1886 and edited by J. B. Leishman (1949).

PARNELL, Charles Stewart (1846–91), born at Avondale, Co. Wicklow, educated at Magdalene College, Cambridge. He became MP for Meath in 1875 and was elected chairman of the Home Rule party in its fight for Irish self-government, in spite of being a Protestant himself, and exerted enormous influence outside the House. In 1878 he was elected president of the Irish National Land League. Parnell formulated the tactic of 'boycotting' in 1880. He was imprisoned in Kilmainham Jail in 1881 for his incendiary speeches, and gained the title of 'uncrowned king of Ireland'. He converted *Gladstone and the Liberal Party to the idea of Home Rule and overthrew the Tory government in 1886. In an article published by *The Times, 'Parnellism and Crime' (1887), he was accused of connivance with outrage and crime, but he vindicated himself of the charges in 1888–9. His career was ruined by his appearance as co-respondent in a divorce case brought by Capt. O'Shea against his wife; the scandal turned the Irish Catholics against him and contributed to a split amongst the Irish nationalists. He died five months after his marriage to Mrs O'Shea.

PARNELL, Thomas (1679–1718), born in Dublin and educated at Trinity College, Dublin. He was archdeacon of Clogher and a friend of *Swift and *Pope (to whose *Iliad* he contributed an introductory essay). He was a member of the *Scriblerus Club. His 'Hymn to Contentment' was published in *Steele's *Poetical Miscellanies* (1714) and his mock-heroic *Homer's Battle of the Frogs and Mice with the Remarks of Zoilus* in 1717 (see BATRACHOMYOMACHIA), but most of his work was published posthumously by Pope in 1721. His poems include 'The Hermit', a moral narrative in heroic couplets, in which the mysterious ways of God are revealed to the hermit by the apparently ruthless and amoral actions of a disguised angel, and 'Night-Piece on Death', in fluent octosyllabics, perhaps the first of the 18th-cent. *graveyard poems (though reminiscent of *'Il Penseroso') which in *Goldsmith's view inspired 'all those night-pieces and churchyard scenes that have since appeared' (Goldsmith's *Life of Parnell*, 1770). Dr *Johnson praised 'the easy sweetness of his diction'. The first complete edition of his poems, ed. C. Rawson and F. P. Lock, was published in 1985.

parody, from the Greek παρῳδία, normally held to have meant a song sung counter to or alongside another song. The term parody first referred to a narrative poem in epic metre, but is not generally restricted in later use. The parodist must both imitate and create incongruity in relation to the pretext, and parody has, contrary to pastiche, traditionally had a comic dimension. Parody should be distinguished from *satire: the former targets a pre-existing text, the latter persons or events in the real world. Parody is a double-coded form of discourse. The classical mock-epic tradition and *Aristophanes' parodies of *Euripides' tragedies provide early examples of the genre. Liturgical parody and parodies of sacred texts flourished in the Middle Ages, and Chaucer's *Canterbury Tales* contains parodic elements. Cervantes's *Don Quixote* is an outstanding example of what has been called 'general parody', a form in which parody is central to the plot and structure of the whole work. Sterne's *Tristram Shandy* and Joyce's *Ulysses* are celebrated examples of such parody. Often writing in the mock-epic tradition, *Swift, *Pope, *Sterne, and *Fielding all used parody. *Shamela*, attributed to Fielding, is an example of parody's potential as criticism. *Rejected Addresses* (1812), by James and Horace Smith, was influential in its time, and there was a strong popular tradition of parody in the 19th cent. William *Hone was acquitted in three famous trials after having parodied the litany, the Athanasian Creed, and the church catechism. There were innumerable short parodies of Shakespeare's work, and *Carroll's nonsense verse is often parodic. *Beerbohm is perhaps the finest prose parodist in the language. The second half of the 20th cent. witnessed a renewed interest in parody—see NABOKOV, FOWLES, STOPPARD.

Parolles, the cowardly follower of Bertram in Shakespeare's *All's Well that Ends Well*; his name means 'words' and suggests that he promises more talk than action.

paronomasia, a play on words, a kind of *pun, in which the repeated words are similar but not identical; e.g. Lady Macbeth: 'I'll gild the faces of the grooms withal, | For it must seem their guilt.'

PARR, Samuel (1747–1825), a fine Latin scholar, who excelled as a writer of Latin epitaphs, and wrote that on Dr *Johnson in St Paul's. He was regarded as 'the Whig Johnson' (*DNB*), but his conversation was apparently far inferior to that of his model, and his works (collected in 8 vols, 1828) are marked by verbosity and mannerism.

PARRY, Sir Hubert (1848–1918), English composer and teacher, who, with *Stanford, began to put new life and standards into English music after the doldrums of the Victorian period. The year 1880 which saw the first performance of Parry's Piano Concerto and the cantata *Scenes from Prometheus Unbound* (*Shelley) marked the beginning of a musical renascence, and the choral settings of *Milton which followed, *Blessed Pair of Sirens* (1887) and *L'Allegro ed Il Penseroso* (1890) confirmed Parry's position as its figurehead: the former is generally considered his masterpiece. The later choral works sound more conventional, though there is a nice vein of humour in *The Pied Piper of Hamelin* (1905), and the six *Songs of Farewell* (1916, with words by *Vaughan, John *Davies, *Campion, *Lockhart, and *Donne) are outstanding. On a smaller scale he produced 12 sets of *English Lyrics* for solo voice and piano settings of some of the greatest poems in the language. Parry by now is best known for the unison setting, made in the hardest days of the First World War, of *Blake's short poem commonly known as 'Jerusalem'.

PARRY, Sir William Edward (1790–1855), Arctic explorer, whose expeditions are described in his three *Journals* of voyages for the discovery of a North-West Passage, undertaken between 1819 and 1825 (published 1821, 1824, 1826) and in his *Narrative of an Attempt to Reach the North Pole, 1827* (1828).

Parsifal, see PERCEVAL.

'Parson's Tale, The', see CANTERBURY TALES, 24.

Parthenissa, see BOYLE, Roger.

Parthenophil and Parthenophe, a collection of sonnets by B. *Barnes, issued in 1593, notable as one of the first of such collections to appear after Sidney's *Astrophel and Stella.*

Partlet, the hen in the tale of *Reynard the Fox and in Chaucer's 'The Nun's Priest's Tale' (see CANTERBURY TALES, 20) as Pertelote. 'Sister Partlet with her hooded head' in Dryden's *The Hind and the Panther* stands for Catholic nuns.

Partridge, a character in Fielding's *Tom Jones.*

PARTRIDGE, Frances (Catherine) (1900–2004), diarist and translator, educated at Bedales and Newnham College, Cambridge. She became with her husband Ralph Partridge assistant editor of *The *Greville Memoirs* (ed. L. *Strachey and Roger Fulford, 8 vols, 1938). Six volumes of her own diaries, covering her experiences in and beyond the *Bloomsbury Group between the late 1930s and mid-1970s, gained her a wide readership late in life.

PARTRIDGE, John (1644–1715), the victim of a mystification by *Swift. See BICKERSTAFF and ALMANACS.

Parzifal, an epic by *Wolfram von Eschenbach, composed early in the 13th cent. on the subject of the legend of *Perceval and the Holy *Grail. (See also TITUREL.)

PASCAL, Blaise (1623–62), French mathematician, physicist, and moralist. As gifted in science as in letters, he did important work in geometry, hydrodynamics, and atmospheric pressure, and invented a calculating machine, a syringe, and a hydraulic press. He came under the influence of Jansenism from around 1646, and entered the convent of Port-Royal in 1655. His literary fame rests on two works, *Les Provinciales* (1656–7, English trans., 1657), polemical letters directed against the casuistry of the Jesuits, and the posthumously published *Pensées* (1670, trans., 1688), fragments of an uncompleted defence of the Christian religion. These form a survey of the contradictions of human existence, pursued with an intensity of logic and passion characteristic of all his work, and encompassing all the major branches of knowledge, from history and ethics to rhetoric and psychology. He exercised an influence on a number of later thinkers, notably *Rousseau, *Bergson, and the *existentialists.

PASCOLI, Giovanni (1855–1912), the major precursor of *Modernism in Italian poetry. A socialist sympathizer, he was imprisoned for some months after demonstrations in 1879. Nature and simple things often provide his themes, but he draws from Symbolism the suggestion of enigma and evanescence. His language spans the range from pure sound (animal- and baby-talk) to the literary conventions of lyric tradition. He translated from the classics and English Romantic poets. The essential Pascoli is in *Myricae* (1891–1905) and *Canti di Castelvecchio* (1903).

PASOLINI, Pier Paolo (1922–75), Italian poet, novelist, critic, and film director. Much of his work deals with the theme of innocence corrupted by capitalism. In his films he challenged *neo-realism with its conventions of sentimentalism and linear narrative. His main films are: *Accattone* (1961), *Mamma Roma* (1962), *The Gospel According to Saint Matthew* (1964), *Oedipus Rex* (1967), *Theorem* (1968), *Pigsty* (1969), *Medea* (1970), *Decameron* (1971), *Canterbury Tales* (1973), *Arabian Nights* (1974), *Salò* (1975). In Italy he was also known for his novels *Ragazzi di vita* (*The Ragazzi*, 1955) and *Una vita violenta* (*A Violent Life*, 1958), in which he explores the culture and language of outcast plebeians of the Roman shanty suburbs (he was murdered in such a setting); and for his anti-establishment polemics, as in *Scritti corsari* (*Pirate Writings*, 1975). His best critical essays are in *Passione e ideologia* (*Passion and Ideology*, 1960) and his best poetry is in *Le ceneri di Gramsci* (*Gramsci's Ashes*, 1957).

Pasquil, or **Pasquin.** 'Pasquino' or 'Pasquillo' was the name popularly given to a mutilated statue disinterred at Rome in 1501, and set up by Cardinal Caraffa at the corner of his palace near the Piazza Navona. It became the custom to salute Pasquin on St Mark's day in Latin verses. In process of time these *pasquinate* or pasquinades tended to become satirical, and the term began to be applied, not only in Rome but in other countries, to satirical compositions and lampoons, political, ecclesiastical, or personal. According to Mazocchi, the name Pasquino originated in that of a schoolmaster who lived opposite the spot where the statue was found; a later tradition made Pasquino a caustic tailor or shoemaker; another calls him a barber [*OED*]. Replies to the pasquinades used to be attached to the *Marforio*, an ancient statue of a river-god, thought to be of Mars.

PASQUIN, Anthony, see WILLIAMS, J.

Passage to India, A, a novel by E. M. *Forster, published 1924. It is a picture of society in India under the British Raj, of the clash between East and West, and of the prejudices and misunderstandings that foredoomed goodwill. Criticized at first for anti-British and possibly inaccurate bias, it has been praised as a superb character study of the people of one race by a writer of another.

The story is told in three parts, I, *Mosque*, II, *Caves*, III, *Temple*, and concerns Aziz, a young Muslim doctor, whose friendliness and enthusiasm for the British turn to bitterness and disillusionment when his pride is injured. A sympathy springs up between him and the elderly Mrs Moore, who has come to visit her son, the city magistrate. Accompanying her is Adela Quested, young, earnest, and charmless, who longs to know the 'real' India and tries to disregard the taboos and snobberies of the British circle. Aziz organizes an expedition for the visitors to the famous Caves of Marabar, where an unforeseen development plunges him into disgrace and rouses deep antagonism between the two races. Adela accuses him of insulting her in the Caves, he is committed to prison and stands trial. Adela withdraws her charge, but Aziz turns furiously away from the British, towards a Hindu–Muslim *entente*. In the third part of the book he has moved to a post in a native state, and is bringing up his family in peace, writing poetry and reading Persian. He is visited by his friend Mr Fielding, the former principal of the Government College, an intelligent, hard-bitten man. They discuss the future of India and Aziz prophesies that only when the British are driven out can he and Fielding really be friends. Among the many characters is Professor Godbole, the detached and saintly Brahman who is the innocent cause of the contretemps, and who makes his final appearance in supreme tranquillity at the festival of the Hindu temple.

Passetyme of Pleasure, or *The Historie of Graunde Amoure and La Bell Pucel*, an allegorical poem in rhyme-royal and decasyllabic couplets by *Hawes, written about 1506 and first printed by Wynkyn de *Worde in 1509 (edited by *Southey, 1831, and by *Wright for the Percy Society, 1845). It describes the education of a certain Graunde Amour in the accomplishments required to make a knight perfect and worthy of the love of La Bell Pucel, and narrates his encounters with giants (representing the vices), his marriage, and his death; the whole constituting an allegory of life in the form of a romance of chivalry. It contains a well-known couplet in perhaps its original form:

> For though the day be never so longe,
> At last the belles ryngeth to evensonge.

'Passing of Arthur, The', see MORTE D'ARTHUR.

Passionate Pilgrim, The, an unauthorized anthology of poems by various authors, published by *Jaggard in 1599, and attributed on the title-page to Shakespeare, but containing only a few authentic poems by him.

PASTERNAK, Boris Leonidovich (1890–1960), Russian poet and prose writer, born in Moscow. In his youth he became involved with the Russian Futurist poets and published his first verse collection *A Twin in the Clouds* (1914). A second volume, *Above the Barriers*, appeared in 1917, but it was his third collection, *My Sister Life* (the poems of 1917, pub. 1922), which established his reputation. It was followed by a number of important publications, the collection *Themes and Variations* (1923), a collection of *Stories* (1925), the long poems *The Year 1905* and *Lieutenant Shmidt* (both 1927), and *Spektorsky* (1931). In 1931 he also published his first autobiography *A Safe Conduct*, followed by another major verse collection *Second Birth* (1932), associated with his meeting with his second wife, Zinaida Neigauz. In the 1930s Pasternak's position became increasingly difficult. After a doomed effort to become a 'Soviet writer', he began what he described as his 'long silent duel' with Stalin. After 1933 no original work by Pasternak could be published for ten years, when two further poetry collections, *On Early Trains* (1943) and *The Breadth of the Earth* (1945), appeared. During this time he earned his living by translating, notably Goethe's *Faust*, the poetry of *Ralegh, *Jonson, *Shelley, *Byron, and *Keats, and Shakespeare. His excellent translations of *Hamlet, *Othello, *Romeo and Juliet, *King Lear, *Macbeth, *Antony and Cleopatra, and 1 and 2 *Henry IV* are highly valued in Russia.

His main literary concern in the final decades of his life, however, was feverish activity, despite declining health, on the work he intended to be his testament, a witness to the experience of the Russian intelligentsia before, during and after the revolution, the novel *Doctor Zhivago*. In October 1946 he met Olga Ivinskaya, who was to become the companion of his last years and on whom Lara, the heroine of *Doctor Zhivago*, is largely based. Despairing of publication in the USSR, he gave permission for publication in Italy, where the novel appeared in 1957. In 1958 he wrote a second 'Autobiographical sketch', and was awarded the *Nobel Prize for literature. This led to a vehement and shameful campaign against him, the so-called 'Pasternak affair', and he declined the prize. Ivinskaya was arrested and imprisoned. Publication of Pasternak's poetry resumed in the USSR soon after his death, and a volume of his short prose appeared in 1982. But *Doctor Zhivago*, on which his worldwide fame is based, was not published in Russia until 1987, where his reputation depends on the poetic achievement of *My Sister Life* and *Second Birth*.

pastiche, a literary composition made up from various authors or sources, or in imitation of the style of another author; or a picture made up of fragments pieced together or copied with modification from an original, or in professed imitation of the style of another artist: the imitative intention is now the most usual meaning.

Paston Letters, the, a collection of letters preserved by the Pastons, a well-to-do Norfolk family, written between c.1420 and 1504. They are of great value for the evidence they give of the language of their time, but even more for the general historical, political, and social interest they provide. They concern three generations of the family, and most were written in the reigns of Henry VI, Edward IV, and Richard III. They are unique as historical material, showing the violence and anarchy of 15th-cent. England and the domestic conditions in which a family of this class lived. The letters were published in three volumes, in 1787, 1789, and 1823. The originals were recovered in the second half of the 19th cent.
   Ed. Norman Davis (1971, 1976); *Selections* (1958); *Selections* (modernized) (1963).

pastoral, a form of escape literature concerned with country pleasures, which is found in poetry, drama, and prose fiction. Its earliest examples appear in the *Idylls* of *Theocritus in which shepherds lead a sunlit, idealized existence of love and song. The eclogues of *Virgil and Longus' romance *Daphnis and Chloe* blended the idealization with a more authentic picture of country life, and Virgil added an important new feature to the tradition in making his poems a vehicle for social comment. Neglected during the Middle Ages, the pastoral reappeared during the Renaissance when *Petrarch and his imitators composed eclogues in Latin and in the vernaculars. These were often more realistic and richer in contemporary references than their Virgilian models; but it was with drama (*Tasso, *Guarini, *Fletcher) and the prose romance (*Sannazar, *Cervantes, *Sidney, *d'Urfé) that pastoral attained the peak of its popularity. In the 17th cent., however, the Theocritean vision which had so far satisfied men's desire to escape from the pressures of urban life gave place to a more realistic dream of enjoying a rural retreat. Poets like James *Thomson extolled country pleasures and represented rural trades as enjoyable, until *Crabbe showed that their descriptions were divorced from reality, and *Wordsworth taught men to seek comfort in a Nature endowed with visionary power. The pastoral in its traditional form died with the rise of *Romanticism.

Pastorella, in Spenser's *Faerie Queene* (VI. ix–xii), a shepherdess, loved by Coridon the shepherd and by Sir *Calidore, believed to be the daughter of Meliboe. She is carried off by brigands, rescued by Sir Calidore, and discovered to be the daughter of Sir Bellamour and the Lady Claribell.

pastor fido, Il, see GUARINI.

Patelin, see PATHELIN.

PATER, Walter Horatio (1839–94), born in Stepney, the son of a surgeon who died in 1842; his mother died in 1854. From 1869 he lived with his unmarried sisters Hester and Clara (one of the founders of Somerville College, Oxford). After a childhood in rural Enfield, he was educated at King's School, Canterbury, and The Queen's College, Oxford, where his interests in Hellenism, pre-Socratic and German philosophy, European art and literature were encouraged, variously, by B. *Jowett, W. W. Capes, and M. *Arnold. He became a fellow of Brasenose in 1864; his Oxford career was marked by personal and professional controversies. Jowett blocked a university appointment when he suspected Pater's involvement with a student; colleagues attacked the 'Conclusion' to *Studies in the History of the Renaissance* (1873) because it postulated the relativity of existence ('that strange, perpetual, weaving and unweaving of ourselves'), celebrated 'pagan' art, and 'the love of art for its own sake', and advised 'To burn always with this hard gem-like flame, to maintain this ecstasy, is success in life.' Many of his writings on art provide a counterpoint to those of *Ruskin, then Oxford's Slade professor of art. *Hopkins was among the students who appreciated his critical and aesthetic independence.
   Early essays for the *Westminster Review* and the *Fortnightly Review* articulated a radical critique of absolutism and expressed admiration for Hellenic homoerotic discourse and culture. *Studies in the History of the Renaissance*, later acclaimed by *Wilde and others as 'the holy writ of beauty', traces the rebirth of Hellenism in medieval France, the art of

*Botticelli, *Leonardo, and *Michelangelo, and the classicism of *Winckelmann.

Pater's prose fiction examines the possibilities of subjectivity within a specific historical and cultural milieu. The quality of life is always measured against the fact of death; the 'aesthetics of pain' is paramount. *Marius the Epicurean* (1885) is set in the days of Marcus Aurelius; *Gaston de Latour* (published 'unfinished' in 1896 but reissued with new materials in 1995) in the era of *Montaigne and the religious controversies of 16th-cent. France. 'The Child in the House' (*Macmillan's Magazine*, 1878) is one of many texts blurring the boundaries between autobiography and fiction. Four *Imaginary Portraits* (1887) are experiments in genre-blending. Narratives such as 'Apollo in Picardy' (*Harper's New Monthly*, 1893) exploit the rebirth/twilight of the gods motif. *Appreciations: With an Essay on Style* (1889) and *Essays from the Guardian* (1896) encapsulate his engagement with Victorian periodical journalism and belles-lettres. *Plato and Platonism* (1893), based on lectures and scholarly essays, represents an eclectic synthesis of ancient and then-contemporary philosophy, and justifies a homoerotic sensibility. 'Demeter and Persephone', an 1876 lecture later published in *Greek Studies* (1895), praises ancient matriarchal religious practices; Modernists such as *Doolittle and V. *Woolf were influenced by its revisionary myth-making and the story of female empowerment.

Pater's works have long been associated with the *'art for art's sake' movement, and the cultivation of decadence in the 1880s and 1890s. *Yeats insisted that Pater's writings were 'permanent in our literature' because of their 'revolutionary importance'. In the decades immediately following the Wilde trial, many male Modernists, including T. E. *Hulme, T. S. *Eliot and W. *Lewis, felt compelled to denigrate Pater's writings, but his contribution to Modernist aesthetics and theories of subjectivity, his importance to *Joyce, Woolf, and others, have been reconsidered by critics such as F. McGrath (*The Sensible Spirit*, 1986). See *Letters of Walter Pater*, ed. L. Evans (1970); M. Levey, *The Case of Walter Pater* (1978); R. Seiler (ed.), *Walter Pater: A Life Remembered* (1987); L. Brake, *Walter Pater* (1994).

PATERSON, Don (1963–), poet and jazz musician, born in Dundee. His much-praised first collection, *Nil Nil* (1993), introduced his distinctive style, mingling demotic and recondite vocabulary in tightly wrought, often oblique poems about love, families, reading, and fear of parenthood. In *God's Gift to Women* (1997), which won the T. S. Eliot prize, a more supple and confident lyric voice emerges in a variety of forms. Poems about memory—notably 'A Private Bottling'—childhood, failed relationships, and versions of (sometimes fictional) foreign writers are loosely connected by the structuring device of a train journey. His highly praised volume *Landing Light* (2003) also won the T. S. Eliot Prize.

Pathelin, La Farce de Maistre Pierre, the most celebrated of the medieval French *farces, dating from before 1470, of uncertain authorship, and written in octosyllabic couplets. Its central figure is the duplicitous lawyer Pathelin, who is himself finally duped by the shepherd Aignelet.

pathetic fallacy, a phrase coined by *Ruskin in 'Of the Pathetic Fallacy' (*Modern Painters*, iii, 1856, ch. 12), indicating the tendency of writers and artists to ascribe human emotions and sympathies to nature. Ruskin sees in it morbidity and 'a falseness in all our impressions of external things', preferring the 'very plain and leafy fact' of a primrose to those poets (e.g. Wordsworth in *Peter Bell*) 'to whom the primrose is anything else than a primrose'. The technique was extensively used in the late 18th and 19th cents by *Goethe, *Gray, *Collins, *Cowper, *Wordsworth, *Shelley, and *Tennyson: Shelley's *Adonais* and Tennyson's *In Memoriam* contain notable examples. Wordsworth in particular used the pathetic fallacy with great seriousness, not as a decorative device, but its use declined after Ruskin's formulation. Nevertheless it is still widely though perhaps not so conspicuously employed. See J. Miles, *Pathetic Fallacy in the Nineteenth Century* (1942); J. D. Thomas, 'Poetic Truth and Pathetic Fallacy', *Texas Studies in Literature and Language*, 3 (1961).

Path to Rome, The, see BELLOC.

Patience, an alliterative poem in 531 lines from the second half of the 14th cent., the only manuscript of which is the famous Cotton Nero A. X which is also the sole manuscript of *Pearl*, *Cleanness*, and *Sir *Gawain and the Green Knight*. It tells in a vigorous and humorous way the story of Jonah and his trials sent by God. Modern critical practice usually treats the four poems in the manuscript as the work of a single author, and there are some affinities between them (particularly between *Patience* and *Pearl*) which make this not implausible. Ed. J. J. Anderson (1969).

Patience, an opera by *Gilbert and *Sullivan produced in 1881, a deliberate satire on the *Aesthetic movement, in which *Bunthorne is said to be modelled on *Wilde and Grosvenor on *Swinburne.

Patient Grissil, a comedy by *Dekker in collaboration with *Chettle and Haughton, written 1600, printed 1603.

The marquess of Salucia, smitten with the beauty of Grissil, the virtuous daughter of a poor basket-maker, makes her his bride. Wishing to try her patience, he subjects her to a series of humiliations and cruelties, robbing her of her children and making her believe them dead, and finally pretending to take another wife and making her attend upon the new bride. All these trials she bears submissively. The new bride is revealed to be Grissil's daughter, and Grissil is restored to honour. The play contains the well-known songs 'Art thou poore yet hast thou golden slumbers, | O sweet content' and 'Golden slumbers kisse your eyes'.

The same subject is treated in Chaucer's 'Clerk's Tale' (see CANTERBURY TALES, 9). It was taken originally from the *Decameron (Day 10, Tale 10). *Perrault also wrote a playful version of it.

PATMORE, Coventry Kersey Dighton (1823–96), son of P. G. *Patmore. He published his first volume of *Poems* (including 'The Woodman's Daughter', later the subject of a well-known painting by *Millais) in 1844. In 1846, after his father's financial collapse, he became assistant in the printed book department of the British Museum, on the recommendation of *Milnes. His work was much admired by the *Pre-Raphaelites, with whom he became acquainted, and he contributed to the *Germ. In 1847 he married his first wife Emily, who inspired his long and popular sequence of poems in praise of married love, *The Angel in the House (1854–63); together the Patmores represented an image of the ideal Victorian couple, and in this role entertained many eminent literary figures, including *Tennyson, *Ruskin, and R. *Browning, who wrote a poem to Emily. Emily died in 1862, leaving him with six children. In 1864 he travelled to Rome, where he met his second wife Marianne, a Roman Catholic, and was himself converted to Catholicism, factors which may have contributed to his decline in popularity as a poet; *The Unknown Eros* (1877) was received with much less enthusiasm than his previous work. It contains odes marked by an erotic mysticism, but also some more autobiographical pieces (now the most anthologized), including 'The Azalea', 'Departure', 'A Farewell', directly inspired by Emily's illness and death, and 'The Toys', inspired by a moment of anger and grief aroused by one of his sons. *Amelia, Tamerton Church-Tower, etc.*, with a preface on English metrical law, appeared in 1878. His second wife died in 1880 and he married Harriet, the governess of his children, who survived him. In his later years he formed new friendships, predominantly with other Catholic writers including G. M. *Hopkins, F. *Thompson, and A. *Meynell, who helped to revive interest in his poetry. His *The Rod, the Root and the Flower* (1895) is chiefly meditations on religious subjects.

PATMORE, Peter George (1786–1855), the father of C. *Patmore, a close friend of *Lamb and *Hazlitt, and an active journalist. He was editor of the *New Monthly Magazine*, 1841–53, and among other varied works published in 1854 *My Friends and Acquaintances*, a lively, unreliable account of Lamb, Hazlitt, T. *Campbell, *Sheridan, and others. Many of the intimate letters in Hazlitt's *Liber Amoris* are addressed to him.

PATON, Alan (1903–88), the author of *Cry, the Beloved Country*.

PATRICK, St (c.389–c.461), the patron saint of Ireland, the son of a Roman decurion, was probably born in Scotland (or Wales). He was taken captive to Ireland when he was a child, and returned there voluntarily to preach the gospel in 432, after years of study in Gaul, directed by Martin of Tours. He journeyed first through Ulster and then, it is said, through the whole of Ireland. Many stories, legends, and purported writings of his are current in Ireland. See J. T. McNeill, *The Celtic Churches: A History A.D. 200 to 1200* (1974), ch. 4; R. P. C. Hanson, *St Patrick, His Origins and Career* (1968).

Patriot King, The Idea of a, see BOLINGBROKE, H. ST J.

patronage, literary, traditionally, individual patronage, in the form of financial help, payment in kind, or more indirect assistance, exercised by royalty and the wealthy in return for dedications, entertainment, and prestige (as well as sometimes for more altruistic motives). Among innumerable examples, *Chaucer was assisted by *John of Gaunt, Shakespeare by the earl of Southampton, *Donne by Sir Robert Drury, Dr *Johnson (belatedly) by the earl of *Chesterfield, *Wordsworth by Sir G. *Beaumont. The relationship was not always happy, as Johnson's definition of a patron as 'a wretch who supports with insolence, and is paid with flattery' suggests, but it also directly inspired many fine works, such as *Jonson's tribute to the *Sidneys in his 'country house poem' 'To Penshurst' (see PENSHURST PLACE).

Patronage was also exercised through the gift of clerical livings; *Crabbe, befriended by the duke of Rutland, wrote of the possible misfortunes of such an experience in 'The Patron' (1812). (See also PUBLISHING, SUBSCRIPTION.)

Early in the 18th cent. new sources of support for authors began to develop. The circulating *libraries offered new openings for sales, and the rising success of *periodicals provided more work until well into the 20th cent. So in the course of the 18th cent. patronage passed largely from men of individual wealth to men of professional power or commercial interest, such as literary editors and library owners and suppliers. Dr *Johnson, for example, called the bookseller R. *Dodsley 'my patron'. *Goldsmith commented that 'the few poets of England no longer depend on the great for subsistence; they have now no other patrons than the public.'

In 1790 David Williams founded the *Royal Literary Fund, and in 1837 the Civil List Act permitted the treasury to assist authors by the grant of pensions (and by the occasional gift of a 'bounty'), provided they could demonstrate 'desert and distress'. Over 750 authors (and their dependants) have benefited, including Wordsworth, *Tennyson, M. *Arnold, W. H. *Hudson, W. B. *Yeats, and T. F. *Powys. *Conrad eventually returned his pension; Mrs *Craik set hers aside for less fortunate authors; and H. *Martineau refused several offers, fearing they would compromise her independence. The proportion of the Civil List monies awarded to authors has declined from over 40 per cent in the last century, to around 35 per cent, and the pension is now worth on average only £600 p.a. It is awarded on the recommendation of the Royal Literary Fund, the *Society of Authors, the *Poetry Society, and other bodies. The *Arts Council also has provided grants to individual writers, as well as assisting literature in more indirect ways through grants to bodies, support for schemes such as 'Writers in Schools', 'Writers in Residence', etc., support for periodicals, and other projects.

PATTEN, Brian (1946–   ), poet, born and educated in Liverpool, where he became one of the group known as the *Liverpool poets. He published with R. *McGough and A. *Henri in *The Mersey Sound* (1967), and has many subsequent volumes of his own, including *Little John's Confession* (1967), *Vanishing Trick* (1976), and *Armada* (1996). He also writes prolifically for children, in both prose and verse: titles include *Mr Moon's Last Case* (1977), *Gangsters, Ghosts and Dragon Flies* (1981), and *Impossible Parents* (1994).

Patterne, Sir Willoughby, Eleanor and Isabel, Lieutenant, and Crossjay, characters in Meredith's *The Egoist*.

PATTISON, Mark (1813–84), educated at Oriel College, Oxford, a supporter of Newman and the *Oxford movement until Newman's departure for Rome. He was ordained priest in 1843 and became successively fellow and tutor (1843–55) of Lincoln College, Oxford; he would have been elected rector in 1851 but for an intrigue among the reactionary fellows of the college. He was an influential tutor, keenly interested in university reform, and travelled to Germany to study continental systems of education. His ideas on education can be found in *Oxford Studies* (1855) and *Suggestions on Academical Organisation* (1868); his life work—a history of European learning surrounding a biography of *Scaliger—was never completed. His best-known work was his classic life of *Issac Casaubon 1559–1614* (1875). His other published works included a contribution to *Essays and Reviews on the Tendencies of Religious Thought in England, 1688–1750* (1860), a short life of *Milton (1879), editions of certain of *Pope's and Milton's poems, and contributions to the *Encyclopaedia Britannica*, articles on *Erasmus, Sir T. *More, and *Grotius. In 1861, still embittered from his earlier rejection, he was finally elected rector of Lincoln. In the same year he married Emilia Francis Strong (later Lady *Dilke) who was 27 years his junior; this and the fact that both parties remained apart as far as convention would allow gave rise to the famous theory that Mr and Mrs Pattison were the originals of Casaubon and Dorothea in G. Eliot's *Middlemarch*. The question has been often debated and produced many differences of learned opinion. His *Memoirs* (1885) are an important study of 19th-cent. Oxford.

PAUL THE DEACON (Paulus Diaconus) (c.725–97), a Lombard who was at one time an inmate of the Benedictine house of Monte Cassino, where he met *Charlemagne. He is one of the best chroniclers of the Dark Ages, author of the *Historia Lombardorum*, and an important figure in the Carolingian Renaissance.

Paul Emmanuel, a character in *Villette* by C. Brontë.

Paul and Virginie, see BERNARDIN DE SAINT-PIERRE.

PAULIN, Tom (1949–   ), Northern Irish poet, born in Leeds, educated at Hull and Oxford, lecturer in English at Hertford College, Oxford. With Paul *Muldoon, Paulin is a leading member of the second generation of important post-war Northern Irish poets. He is the most overtly 'political' Ulster poet, imagining a form of non-sectarian Republican socialism deriving from the Protestant political radicalism which climaxed in the 1798 revolt. *A State of Justice* (1977) and *The Strange Museum* (1980) drew on *Auden and Douglas *Dunn, while in *Liberty Tree* (1983) Paulin's language took in Ulster dialect and assumed a jagged, improvised 'spoken' quality which is both compelling and forbidding, ranging from revolutionary France to the Second World War. See *Selected Poems 1972–1990* (1993) and *Walking a Line* (1994). Poetry and criticism seem continuous for Paulin. Prose includes *Writing to the Moment: Selected Critical Essays 1980–1996* (1996) and *The Day Star of Liberty: William Hazlitt's Radical Style* (1998).

Paulina, the wife of *Antigonus and loyal defender of *Hermione in Shakespeare's *The Winter's Tale*.

Pauline, a poem in blank verse, the first poem to be published by R. *Browning; it appeared anonymously in 1833. Subtitled 'A Fragment of a Confession', it is marked by the influence of Browning's Romantic predecessors, notably *Shelley; but its form and theme already declare Browning's independence. The 'confession' is addressed to Pauline by the first in a long series of 'fallen' speakers whose ambivalent rhetoric combines self-reproach and self-justification. The poem was barely noticed, but an important commentary by J. S. *Mill, in the form of an annotated copy, reached Browning through their common friend W. J. *Fox. Mill assumed the speaker of the poem to be the author, and severely criticized his morbidity and self-regard. Partly in response to this misunderstanding of the poem's 'dramatic' form, Browning suppressed it for over 30 years, finally acknowledging it 'with extreme repugnance' in the collected edition of 1867, to avoid the threat of pirate publication.

Paul's, Children of, a company of boy actors, recruited from the choristers of St Paul's Cathedral, whose performances enjoyed great popularity at the end of the 16th and beginning of the 17th cents. They performed among others the plays of *Lyly. The Children of the Chapel, recruited from the choristers of the Chapel Royal, was another company enjoying popular favour at the same time. Their rivalry with men actors is alluded to in *Hamlet (II. ii).

Paul's Letters to his Kinsfolk, a series of letters by Sir

W. *Scott, published in 1816, describing a visit by the author to Brussels, Waterloo, and Paris a few weeks after the battle of Waterloo. The account of the battle is interesting for the details it contains, some of them obtained from Napoleon's Belgian guide.

Paul's School, St, founded between 1509 and 1512 by *Colet. *Lily was its first high master. The school was removed from St Paul's Churchyard to Hammersmith in 1884, and to Barnes in 1968. Among its many distinguished scholars may be mentioned *Camden, *Milton, *Pepys, Sir P. *Francis, G. K. *Chesterton, and E. *Thomas.

PAVESE, Cesare (1908–50), Italian novelist and poet, whose last novel, *La luna e i falò* (*The Moon and the Bonfire*, 1950), is his finest. Realism and myth, lyrical memoir and contemporary reality, combine in the highly individual texture of his prose, which expresses the heart-searchings of a solitary man with a restless social conscience. Other main novels are: *Il compagno* (*The Comrade*, 1947), *Prima che il gallo canti* (*Before Cock-Crow*, 1949), *La bella estate* (*The Beautiful Summer*, 1949). His best poems are in *Lavorare stanca* (*Work Wearies*, 1936). He made many translations from English and American authors (*Joyce, *Faulkner, etc.) who influenced him; his translation of Melville's *Moby-Dick* is definitive. His suicide was seen as representative of intellectuals broken by the tensions of post-war Europe.

PAYN, James (1830–98), educated at Trinity College, Cambridge. He was a regular contributor to *Household Words* and became editor of *Chambers's Journal* (1859–74) and the *Cornhill Magazine* (1882–96). He published a volume of poems in 1853 and several volumes of essays, including *Some Private Views* (1894), *Some Literary Recollections* (1884), *Gleams of Memory* (1894), and *The Backwater of Life* (1899), with an introduction by Sir L. *Stephen. He wrote 100 novels of which *Lost Sir Massingberd* (1864) and *By Proxy* (1878) were the most popular.

PAZ, Octavio (1914–98), poet, who was born and died in Mexico City. He made his name interrogating Mexican identity and history in *El laberinto de la soledad* (1950; *The Labyrinth of Solitude: Life and Thought in Mexico*, 1961). *Águila o sol?* (1951; *Eagle or Sun?*, 1970) and *Piedra de sol* (1957; *Sun Stone*, 1962) explore Mexican motifs guided by a fascination with how the mind perceives through language and how poetry and eroticism defeat history, collected in *Poemas (1935–1975)* (1979; *The Collected Poems of Octavio Paz, 1957–1987*, 1987). His best works are his journey-meditation *El mono gramático* (1974; *The Monkey Grammarian*) and his biography of the Mexican nun *Sor Juana o las trampas de la fe* (1986; *Sor Juana: or, The Traps of Faith*, 1988). Paz was a political commentator, an art critic, a translator, and editor of distinguished magazines. He was awarded the *Nobel Prize in 1990.

PEACHAM, Henry (1578–?1643), educated at Trinity College, Cambridge, an author and a man of very varied talents. He published in 1606 *The Art of Drawing with the Pen*, a practical treatise on art, issued in 1612 as *Graphice*, and in many subsequent editions under the title *The Gentleman's Exercise*. He published *The Compleat Gentleman*, the work by which he is best known, in 1622. From the last edition of this (1661) Dr *Johnson drew all the heraldic definitions in his dictionary.

Peachum, and his daughter Polly, characters in Gay's *The Beggar's Opera*.

PEACOCK, Thomas Love (1785–1866), satirist, essayist, and poet, the son of a London glass merchant, though brought up by his mother. He inherited private means just sufficient to enable him to live as a man of letters. He had published two volumes of verse when, in 1812, he met *Shelley, whose close friend he afterwards remained. Peacock's prose satires, *Headlong Hall* (1816), *Melincourt* (1817), and *Nightmare Abbey* (1818), survey the contemporary political and cultural scene from a radical viewpoint. Formally they owe most to two classical genres: the 'Anatomy', or miscellaneous prose satire, and the Socratic dialogue, especially perhaps Plato's *Symposium* which, like many of Peacock's convivial arguments, takes place over a dinner table. The satiric debate is diversified by a romantic love-plot, increasingly important in *Crotchet Castle* (1831) and *Gryll Grange* (1860–1), and by amusing, clever songs. Peacock's fictional world is an exceptionally pleasant one, for he assembles his characters in English country houses, and sends them on excursions into mountain and forest scenery. In *Maid Marian* (1822) and *The Misfortunes of Elphin* (1829) he varies his format by employing a historical setting, 12th-cent. England and 6th-cent. Wales, but the topical satirical reference remains unmistakable. Peacock's early volumes of poetry are of antiquarian interest, but *Rhododaphne* (1818) is a fine and historically important poem, in the mythological manner of Keats's *'Lamia'; Peacock also wrote some touching lyrics, especially 'Long Night Succeeds Thy Little Day' (1826) and 'Newark Abbey' (1842). Of his satirical poems and squibs, *The Paper Money Lyrics* (1837) lampoon the dogmas of political economists and the malpractices of bankers. Peacock's sceptical attitude to the fashionable cult of the arts is apparent in his two most sustained critical essays, 'Essay on Fashionable Literature' (a fragment, written 1818) and *'The Four Ages of Poetry' (1820), to which Shelley replied in a *Defence of Poetry. In 1819 Peacock married Jane Gryffydh, the 'White Snowdonian antelope' of Shelley's 'Letter to Maria Gisborne'; she suffered a breakdown at the death of their third daughter in 1826, though she lived on until 1851. His favourite child was his eldest daughter Mary Ellen, who became the first wife of G. *Meredith, and features in Meredith's sonnet sequence *Modern Love. Peacock entered the East India Company's service in

1819 and worked immediately under J. *Mill until the latter's death in 1836, when he succeeded to the responsible position of examiner.

The standard books on Peacock are the life by C. van Doren (1911), and M. Butler's *Peacock Displayed* (1979). The best editions are the *Halliford Edition of the Works of T. L. Peacock*, ed. H. F. B. Brett-Smith and C. E. Jones (10 vols, 1924–34), and *The Novels*, ed. D. *Garnett (2 vols, 1948).

PEAKE, Mervyn Laurence (1911–68), novelist, poet, and artist, born at Kuling in China, the son of a medical missionary; he came to England aged 11, was educated at Eltham College, Kent, then attended the Royal Academy Schools. He spent three years from 1934 with a group of artists on the island of Sark, then returned to London, where he taught art, exhibited his own work and illustrated books, published verse and stories for children, etc. He was invalided out of the army in 1943 after a nervous breakdown, but was later commissioned as a war artist, and also visited Belsen in 1945 on a journalistic expedition for the *Leader*, an experience which profoundly affected him. Meanwhile he was working on a novel, *Titus Groan*, which was published in 1946; it was followed by *Gormenghast* (1950) and *Titus Alone* (1959), which as a trilogy form the work for which Peake is best remembered, a creation of grotesque yet precise Gothic *fantasy, recounting the life of Titus, 77th earl of Groan, in his crumbling castle of Gormenghast, surrounded by a cast of characters which includes the colourful Fuchsia, Dr Prunesquallor, and the melancholy Muzzlehatch. Peake's poetry includes *The Glassblowers* (1950) and *The Rhyme of the Flying Bomb* (1962), a ballad of the Blitz; he illustrated most of his own work, and also produced memorable drawings for *The Rime of the *Ancient Mariner* (1943), *Treasure Island* (1949), and other works. A lighter side of his prolific imagination is seen in his posthumous *A Book of Nonsense* (1972). The last years of his life were overshadowed by Parkinson's disease, as described by his widow Maeve Gilmore in her memoir *A World Away* (1970). For an account of the relationship between his drawings and his prose, see Hilary Spurling's introduction to *The Drawings of Mervyn Peake* (1974).

PEARCE, Philippa A., see CHILDREN'S LITERATURE.

Pearl, an alliterative poem in 1,212 lines of twelve-line octosyllabic stanzas from the second half of the 14th cent., the only manuscript of which is the famous Cotton Nero A. X which is also the sole manuscript of *Patience*, *Cleanness*, and *Sir *Gawain and the Green Knight* and which comes from the north-west Midlands. Pearl was the author's daughter and only child who has died before she was 2 years old. Wandering in misery in the garden where she is buried, he has a vision of a river beyond which lies paradise. Here he sees a maiden seated whom he recognizes as his daughter. She chides him for his excessive grief and

describes her blessed state. He argues with her about the justice that makes her queen of heaven when she died so young. Convinced by her, he plunges into the river in an attempt to join her, and awakes, comforted and reassured of his faith in God. Discussion of the poem has centred on the extent to which it is to be interpreted literally, as elegy, or allegorically. The form and language of the poem are extremely brilliant, and its literary relations apparently not confined to England: *Boccaccio's *Olympia* and the earthly paradise sections of *Dante's *Purgatorio* (from Canto xxviii to the end) seem to be parallels to the poem. Ed. E. V. Gordon (1953); P. M. Kean, *The Pearl: An Interpretation* (1967).

PEARS, Tim (1956–), novelist, born in Tunbridge Wells, Kent. His first novel, *In the Place of Fallen Leaves* (1993), was set in an English village during the long drought of 1984, and provided a gentle counterblast to the prevailingly urban fiction of his contemporaries. *In a Land of Plenty* (1997) was a family saga on the grand scale, an epic of English provincial life, peopled by warmly sympathetic characters. Pears has also written a screenplay, *Loop*, filmed in 1996.

PEARSON, Sir (Cyril) Arthur (1866–1921), newspaper magnate, educated at Winchester, who embarked on a career in journalism with *Tit-Bits, inspired by his own passion for quizzes and puzzles. He soon set up a successful rival to *Tit-Bits* in the form of *Pearson's Weekly*, in 1890, and in 1900 founded the *Daily Express*. He went blind, and was more widely honoured for his work for the blind than for his journalistic talents.

PEARSON, (Edward) Hesketh (Gibbons) (1887–1964), actor and biographer, who joined the company of Beerbohm *Tree as a young man, and whose first book, *Modern Men and Mummers* (1921), contained portraits of many of the theatre personalities of the time. *The Whispering Gallery* (1926), an anonymous work purporting to be 'leaves from the diary of an ex-diplomat', occasioned a scandal, a court case, and an acquittal for Pearson, who went on to write many lively and widely read biographies, of (for example) *Hazlitt (1934), Sydney *Smith (*The Smith of Smiths*, 1934), G. B. *Shaw (1942), *Wilde (1946), Beerbohm Tree (1956), and several others. He also wrote literary travel books in collaboration with *Kingsmill, and his autobiography, *Hesketh Pearson by Himself*, appeared posthumously in 1965.

PEARSON, John (1613–86), educated at Eton and Cambridge, a Royalist chaplain during the Civil War, and after the Restoration master of Jesus College, then of Trinity, Cambridge. He became bishop of Chester in 1673. From 1654 he preached at St Clement's, Eastcheap, the series of lectures which he published in 1659 as his classic *Exposition of the Creed*, the notes of which are a rich mine of patristic learning. He was one of the most erudite theologians of his age.

Peasants' Revolt, the popular insurrection of the labourers of Essex and Kent which began in May 1381, provoked in part by the tyrannies of *John of Gaunt. While the Kentish leader Wat Tyler was treating with the king, the 14-year-old Richard II, he was pulled from his horse and killed by Walworth, the mayor of London. The rebels dispersed and by the end of June the revolt had been repressed with ferocity everywhere. Its principal motivation—the wish of tenants to end repressive feudal rights—is reflected in literature, most famously in the couplet of the preacher John Ball (who was condemned after the revolt):

> When Adam delved and Eve span
> Who was then a gentleman?

The introduction of the fable of Belling the Cat into the later B and C texts of *Piers Plowman* is thought to be a response to the revolt and accordingly to date those later texts after 1381. See R. B. Dobson, *The Peasants' Revolt of 1381* (1970).

Pecksniff, Mr, a character in Dickens's *Martin Chuzzlewit.*

PECOCK, Reginald (1395–c.1460), a Welshman who became bishop successively of St Asaph and Chichester. Most of his writings employ the syllogistic logic of the *Scholastics (in a somewhat debased form), and many were directed against the *Lollards, notably his *Repressor of Over Much Blaming of the Clergy* (1455), a monument of 15th-cent. English prose of considerable eloquence and lexical variety. His *Book of Faith*, also in English, was issued in 1456, and in his *Donet* and the *Folewer to the Donet* he sought to define a body of faith acceptable to all. He alienated by his writings all sections of theological opinion in England, was arraigned before the archbishop of Canterbury, and obliged to resign his bishopric and recant his opinions (1458), whereupon he was sent to Thorney Abbey where he probably lived in seclusion. His work has considerable importance from a literary viewpoint for its development of the English vocabulary, which he added to, both by loan-translations such as 'unto-bethoughtupon' (*imponderabile*) and by borrowings such as 'anagogy' and 'tropology'.

EETS OS editions: *The Donet*, ed. E. V. Hitchcock (No. 156, 1918); *The Folewer to the Donet*, ed. E. V. Hitchcock (No. 164, 1923); *The Reule of Christen Religioun*, ed. W. C. Greet (No. 171, 1926). See also *The Repressor*, ed. C. Babington (2 vols, 1860); V. H. H. Green, *Bishop Reginald Pecock* (1945).

Pecunia, Lady, the rich heiress in Jonson's *The Staple of News.*

Pedro, Don, the prince of Aragon who has defeated his illegitimate brother Don John and who woos *Hero on Claudio's behalf in Shakespeare's *Much Ado about Nothing.*

PEELE, George (1556–96), the son of James Peele, clerk of Christ's Hospital and author of city pageants and books on accountancy. He was educated at *Christ's Hospital, Broadgates Hall (Pembroke College), and Christ Church, Oxford. From about 1581 he was mainly resident in London, and pursuing an active and varied literary career. He was an associate of many other writers of the period, such as T. *Watson and R. *Greene. His works fall into three main categories: plays, pageants, and 'gratulatory' and miscellaneous verse. His surviving plays are *The Araygnement of Paris* (1584); *Edward I* (1593); *The Battle of Alcazar* (1594); *The Old Wives Tale* (1595); and *David and Fair Bethsabe* (1599). His miscellaneous verse includes *Polyhymnia* (1590) and *The Honour of the Garter* (1593), a gratulatory poem to the Earl of Northumberland. Peele's work is dominated by courtly and patriotic themes, and his technical achievements include extending the range of non-dramatic blank verse. The jest book *The Merrie Conceited Jests of George Peele* (1607) seems to bear little relation to Peele's actual personality. His *Life and Works* were edited by C. T. Prouty (3 vols, 1952–70).

Peggotty, Daniel, Clara, and Ham, characters in Dickens's *David Copperfield.*

Pegler, Mrs, in Dickens's *Hard Times*, Bounderby's mother.

PÉGUY, Charles (1875–1914), French poet and essayist. Profoundly responsive to traditional French forms of life, he expressed his nonconformist Catholic faith in such poems as the biblical *Le Porche du mystère de la deuxième vertu* (1911) and the fresco-like stanzas of *Sainte Geneviève* (1912) and *Ève* (1913). His death at Villeroy, the first battle on the Marne, only served to deepen the effect of his almost mystical vision of France on his contemporaries. He is the subject of a long poem by G. *Hill, published 1983, *The Mystery of the Charity of Charles Péguy.*

Peg Woffington, a novel by C. *Reade, based on an episode in the life of Peg *Woffington, and adapted from his play *Masks and Faces.*

Pelagian, derived from **Pelagius,** the Latinized form of the name of a British monk, Morgan, of the 4th and 5th cents whose doctrines were fiercely combated by Germanus, bishop of Auxerre, and by St *Augustine, and condemned by Pope Zosimus in 418. The Pelagians denied the doctrine of original sin, asserting that Adam's fall did not involve his posterity, and maintained that the human will is itself capable of good without the assistance of divine grace. In spite of their condemnation, their beliefs died slowly and were only finally defeated by the Augustinian view at the Council of Orange (529) that grace is God-given. Even so, the voluntarist tendency of Pelagianism revived in the Middle Ages; many of the thinkers opposed by *Bradwardine (d. 1349) he called 'modern Pelagians' in their attempts to qualify the immanence of God's grace by their views of free will. See R. E. Evans, *Pelagius, Inquiries and Appraisals* (1968).

Pelham: *or The Adventures of a Gentleman*, a novel by *Bulwer-Lytton, published 1828. This was his second novel, and is generally considered his best.

It recounts the adventures of Henry Pelham, a young dandy, wit, and aspiring politician, who falls in love with Ellen, sister of his old friend from Eton days, Reginald Glanville. The latter is falsely suspected of a murder, and tells his story to Pelham, who unearths the real murderer, Thornton, a character drawn from the well-known murderer Thurtell. But the interest of the novel lies in its lively portrayal of fashionable society, in English country houses, in Paris, in Cheltenham, in London, etc., and in such minor characters as Lady Frances, Pelham's worldly mother, and Lord Vincent, whose conversation is laced with puns, largely in Latin. Bulwer-Lytton mocks the genre of the *fashionable novel even while employing it, which adds to the tone of sparkling cynicism which captivated contemporary readers and made his hero's name a catchphrase.

Pell, Solomon, in Dickens's *Pickwick Papers*, an attorney in the Insolvent Court.

Pellam, King, 'the Maimed King', in Arthurian legend, father of the Grail King, *Pelles. Wounded by Balyn's *'Dolorous Stroke', he is healed by his great-grandson Galahad in the Grail quest.

Pelleas, Sir, 'the Noble Knight', in Arthurian legend the lover of Ettarde. After her death he marries Nimue, the *Lady of the Lake.

'Pelleas and Ettarre', one of Tennyson's *Idylls of the King*, published 1869. Pelleas woos the heartless Ettarre, is tricked by Gawain, learns of the adultery of Lancelot and Guinevere, and vows to avenge the treasons of the Round Table.

Pelléas et Mélisande, see MAETERLINCK.

Pelles, King, 'the Grail King', in *Malory, one of the Fisher Kings and said to be 'cousin nigh unto Joseph of Arimathie'. He is maimed for drawing the sword of David on the mysterious ship. Founded perhaps on *Pwyll of Welsh mythology, he was the father of Elaine who was the mother of Galahad by Launcelot.

Pellinore, King, 'the King of the Waste Lands', in *Malory the father of Sir Lamorak, Sir Perceval, and Sir Torre, and the brother of King *Pelles. He follows the *Questing Beast and kills King Lot of Orkney, because of which ten years later he is killed by Lot's son Gawain. Charles Moorman (in *The Book of Kyng Arthur*, 1965) believes that the rivalry between the houses of King Lot and King Pellinore is one of the three principal running themes in Malory.

PEMBROKE, Mary Herbert, countess of (1561–1621), the younger sister of P. *Sidney, whose first version of the *Arcadia* was written for her at Wilton early in her married life. After her brother's death in 1586 she became in effect his literary executrix, overseeing the publication of the *Arcadia* and the rest of his works for the editions of 1593 and 1598 and undertaking literary projects of which he would have approved. She completed the *Psalms*, of which Sidney had translated only the first 42, rendering them in a very wide variety of English verse forms; they were not published as a whole until the edition of J. C. A. Rathmell (1963), but *Ruskin, who much admired them, made a selection from them under the title of *Rock Honeycomb* (1877). She translated Du Plessis Mornay's *Discourse of Life and Death* and R. Garnier's Senecan tragedy *Antonius* (both published in 1592; the latter also published as *Antonie*, 1595), and at an unknown date she translated *Petrarch's *Trionfo della morte*. Her reputation as a patroness perhaps outstripped her specific achievements (T. S. *Eliot's essay 'Apology for the Countess of Pembroke', 1932, implies a deliberate control of a literary clique which she probably never had); but she certainly had links with such writers as S. *Daniel, N. *Breton, and Sir J. *Harington. A letter from her once seen at Wilton by *Cory said 'we have the man Shakespeare with us'; it has since disappeared, and her connection with Shakespeare, if any, cannot be proved. The epitaph on her by W. *Browne was popular throughout the 17th cent.:

> Underneath this sable herse
> Lies the subject of all verse:
> Sidney's sister, Pembroke's mother:
> Death, ere thou hast slain another,
> Fair, and learn'd, and good as she,
> Time shall throw a dart at thee.

There is an edition of her works by Margaret P. Hannay, Noel J. Kinnamon, and Michael G. Brennan (2 vols, 1998).

PEN, an international association of Poets, Playwrights, Editors, Essayists, and Novelists founded in 1921 by Mrs Dawson-Scott, under the presidency of J. *Galsworthy, to promote co-operation between writers all over the world in the interests of literature, freedom of expression, and international goodwill.

Pendennis, The History of, a novel by *Thackeray, serialized in numbers Nov. 1848–Dec. 1850, and illustrated by himself. Its publication was interrupted by the serious illness of its author, who fell ill with cholera in 1849, and the second half of the novel, after its hero's own illness, is correspondingly more sombre in tone. It is a *Bildungsroman in which the main character, Arthur Pendennis, who has many of Thackeray's own traits, is the only son of a devoted and unworldly widow, Helen. As a very young man he falls in love with an actress, Emily Costigan ('Miss Fotheringay'), and is only rescued from an unsuitable marriage by the tactful intervention of his uncle, Major Pendennis, who persuades her disreputable old father, Captain Costigan, that Arthur has no money of his own.

Pendennis then goes to the university of Oxbridge, where he runs up bills and has to be rescued by a loan from Helen's adopted daughter Laura Bell. Helen hopes that Laura and her son will marry, but Pendennis's next entanglement is with Blanche Amory, an affected and hard-hearted girl, the daughter of the rich, vulgar Lady Clavering by her first husband. Major Pendennis encourages a match between his nephew and Blanche, although he is secretly aware that Blanche's father is an escaped convict who is still alive and is blackmailing Sir Francis Clavering.

Pendennis goes to London and is supposed to be reading for the bar. He shares chambers with George Warrington (descended from the Warringtons in *The Virginians*), who starts him on a literary career by introducing him to Captain Shandon, a debt-ridden Irish journalist (based on *Maginn) who is editing a new magazine, the 'Pall Mall Gazette', from prison. Pendennis has a mild flirtation with a working-class girl, Fanny Bolton, and, when he falls ill, Fanny nurses him devotedly. Helen Pendennis jumps to the false conclusion that Fanny is Pendennis's mistress, and treats the girl very unkindly. Pendennis is so indignant when he discovers this, that he threatens to marry Fanny, but is dissuaded by Warrington, who tells the story of his own unfortunate early marriage. Fanny soon finds consolation with Sam Huxter, a medical student, but Blanche is harder to shake off. After the exposure of the existence of her villainous father, Pendennis feels obliged to go through with an engagement to her, although he does not really care for her. Fortunately Blanche decides in favour of Harry Foker, heir to a brewing fortune, and Pendennis and Laura finally marry, after Helen's death.

Pendragon, a title given to an ancient British or Welsh chief holding or claiming supreme power. In English chiefly known as the title of Uther Pendragon, father of *Arthur. The word means 'chief dragon', the dragon being the war standard.

Penguin Books, the name first given to a series of paperback books published in 1935 by A. *Lane, and established in its own right as a publishing company in 1936. The first ten titles, which sold for sixpence each, included *Ariel* by *Maurois (No. 1), and fiction by A. *Christie, *Hemingway, D. L. *Sayers and M. *Webb. In 1937 the non-fiction Pelican series was launched with the publication, in two parts, of Shaw's *Intelligent Woman's Guide to Socialism*, and Puffin Picture Books for children followed in 1940. Other notable ventures include the Penguin Classics, edited for many years by E. V. Rieu (1887–1972), whose own translation of the *Odyssey* (1946) was its first and best-selling volume; *Pevsner's series *The Buildings of England* (1951–74); and the first unexpurgated edition of *Lady Chatterley's Lover* (1960), which led to a celebrated trial and acquittal at the Old Bailey.

PENN, William (1644–1718), a Quaker and founder of Pennsylvania, son of the admiral Sir William Penn. He was committed to the Tower in 1668 for publishing *The Sandy Foundation Shaken* (an attack on orthodox doctrines of the Trinity and the Atonement, and on the Calvinist theory of justification) and there wrote *No Cross, No Crown* (1669), an eloquent and learned dissertation on Christian duty and a Quaker classic. He suffered frequent persecutions, turned his thoughts to America as a refuge for his faith, and in 1682 obtained grants of East New Jersey and Pennsylvania, and framed, possibly in concert with A. *Sidney, a new constitution for the colony by which religious toleration would be secured. He travelled twice to America, returning in 1701 to spend the rest of his life in England. *Some Fruits of Solitude*, a collection of aphorisms praised by R. L. *Stevenson, was published anonymously in 1693.

PENNANT, Thomas (1726–98), naturalist, antiquary, and traveller. He published *A Tour in Scotland* in 1771, *A Tour in Wales* in 1778–81, *A Tour in Scotland and Voyage to the Hebrides* in 1774–6, and *The Journey from Chester to London* in 1782. His travel writings were admired by Dr *Johnson, though *Boswell disapproved of his portrait of Scotland. He was also a distinguished zoologist, and figures in G. *White's *Selborne* as one of the author's correspondents. *Literary Life of the Late Thomas Pennant, Esq., by Himself* appeared in 1793.

Penny Magazine, see KNIGHT, C.

Penshurst Place, in Kent, has been in the possession of the Sidney family since 1552, and was the birthplace of Sir P. *Sidney. Many writers enjoyed its hospitality, including *Jonson, who paid a graceful tribute in 'To Penshurst' (*The Forest*, 1616), praising the fruitfulness of the landscape and the gardens, the 'high huswifery' of its lady, the generosity of its lord, and the virtues of the whole household, who learned there 'the mysteries of manners, armes and arts'. (See also PATRONAGE.)

Pentameron, The, a prose work by W. S. *Landor, published 1837, an expression of Landor's admiration of *Boccaccio. The book consists of imaginary conversations between *Petrarch and Boccaccio, while the latter lies ill at his village near Certaldo, and Petrarch visits him on five successive days. They speak mainly of Dante's *Divina commedia*; but Petrarch also reproves Boccaccio for the licentious character of some of his tales.

pentameter, see METRE and BLANK VERSE.

Penthea, a character in Ford's *The Broken Heart*.

PEPYS (pron. Peeps or Peppis), Samuel (1633–1703), son of John Pepys, a London tailor, educated at St *Paul's School, London, and at Magdalene College, Cambridge. In 1655, when 22, he married Elizabeth St Michel, a girl of 15, the daughter of a French father and

English mother. He entered the household of Sir Edward Montagu (afterwards first earl of Sandwich), his father's first cousin, in 1656; and his subsequent successful career was largely due to Montagu's patronage. His famous *Diary* opens on 1 Jan. 1660, when Pepys was living in Axe Yard, Westminster, and was very poor. Soon after this he was appointed 'clerk of the King's ships' and clerk of the privy seal, with a salary of £350 (supplemented by fees). In 1665 he became surveyor-general of the victualling office, in which capacity he showed himself an energetic official and a zealous reformer of abuses. Owing to an unfounded fear of failing eyesight he closed his diary on 31 May 1669, and in the same year his wife died. In 1672 he was appointed secretary to the admiralty. He was committed to the Tower on a charge of complicity in the *'Popish Plot' in 1679 and deprived of his office, but was soon set free. In 1683 he was sent to Tangier with Lord Dartmouth and wrote an interesting diary while there. In 1684 he was reappointed secretary to the admiralty, a post which he held until the revolution, labouring hard to provide the country with an efficient fleet. At the revolution he was deprived of his appointment and afterwards lived in retirement, principally at Clapham. His *Diary* remained in cipher (a system of shorthand) at Magdalene College, Cambridge, until 1825, when it was deciphered by John Smith and edited by Lord Braybrooke. An enlarged edition by Mynors Bright appeared in 1875–9, and an edition in ten volumes (1893–9) by Henry B. Wheatley remained the standard text until the appearance of a new and unbowdlerized transcription by R. Latham and W. Matthews (11 vols, 1970–83). On his death his friend and fellow diarist *Evelyn remembered him as 'a very worthy, industrious and curious person, none in England exceeding him in knowledge of the navy . . . universally beloved, hospitable, generous, learned in many things, skilled in music, a very great cherisher of learned men'. Pepys's *Memoirs of the Navy, 1690* were edited by J. R. Tanner (1906). There is a good biography: *Pepys* by Richard Ollard (rev. edn 1984). (See also RESTORATION.)

Perceforest, a vast French prose romance of the 14th cent., in which the author seeks to link the legends of *Alexander and *Arthur. Alexander, after the conquest of India, is driven by a storm on the coast of England, and makes one of his followers (called Perceforest because he has killed a magician in an impenetrable forest) king of the land. Under the latter's grandson the *Grail is brought to England.

Perceval, Sir, probably to be identified with Peredur of the *Mabinogion. He is a legendary figure of great antiquity, first found in European poetry in the 9,000-line, incomplete *Perceval, ou le conte del Graal* of *Chrétien de Troyes (c.1182) and the German *Parzival* (c.1205) of *Wolfram von Eschenbach (which was the inspiration for *Wagner's opera). In English he appears in *Sir Perceval of Galles,* a 2,288-line romance, in

16-line stanzas in tail-rhyme from the 15th cent. (ed. W. H. French and C. B. Hale, *Middle English Metrical Romances,* 1930) and in *Malory. The former tells of the childhood of Perceval and his being knighted by Arthur, without any allusion to the *Grail. Malory makes him a son of King *Pellinore, describing his success in the quest for the Grail with Galahad and Bors. In the French prose Vulgate *La Queste del Saint Graal,* the three successful questers are joined on Solomon's ship by Perceval's sister who dies by giving her blood to heal a lady suffering from a great illness, and is committed to the waves in a boat; her body is found and buried in the Grail land of Sarras where the three are borne in Solomon's boat.

Percy, a tragedy by Hannah *More.

PERCY, Thomas, born Piercy (1729–1811), son of a Bridgnorth grocer. He was educated at Oxford and became bishop of Dromore in 1782. He was a man of varied intellectual and antiquarian interests; in 1761 he published a translation (from the Portuguese) of the first Chinese novel to appear in English, *Hau Kiou Choaan,* and in 1763 his *Five Pieces of Runic Poetry Translated from the Islandic Language,* including the 'Incantation of Hervor' and the 'Death-Song of Ragnar Lodbrog'. The latter had a considerable influence on the study of ancient Norse in England. Percy also published poetry (including his ballad *The Hermit of Warkworth,* 1771), translated from the Hebrew and Spanish, and wrote a *Memoir of Goldsmith* (1801). He is best known for his celebrated collection *Reliques of Ancient English Poetry* (3 vols, 1765), which was attacked by later writers (see RITSON) as unscholarly, but which nevertheless contributed greatly to the understanding of and enthusiasm for the older English poetry, reached a fourth edition by 1794, and has since been several times re-edited. (See also PERCY FOLIO and BALLAD.)

Percy Folio, the, a manuscript in mid-17th-cent. handwriting, which belonged to Humphrey Pitt of Shifnal, the most important source of our *ballad literature and the basis of *Child's collection. From it T. *Percy drew the ballads included in his *Reliques. It also contains the 14th-cent. alliterative allegorical poem 'Death and Liffe' (modelled on *Piers Plowman) and 'Scottish Feilde' (mainly on the battle of *Flodden). The Percy Folio was printed in its entirety by Hales and *Furnivall in 1867–8. It is now in the British Library.

Percy Society, the, founded in 1840 by T. C. *Croker, *Dyce, *Halliwell-Phillipps, and J. P. *Collier, for the purpose of publishing old English lyrics and ballads. It was named in honour of T. *Percy.

Percy's Reliques, see RELIQUES OF ANCIENT ENGLISH POETRY.

Perdita, the daughter of *Hermione and *Leontes, brought up in Bohemia, in Shakespeare's *The Winter's Tale;* her name means 'the lost one'.

PEREC, G., see OuLiPo.

Peredur, the Arthurian subject of one of the seven tales added by Lady Charlotte Guest to the *Mabinogion* proper and now, accordingly, normally included in it. The Welsh *Peredur* is found most completely in the White Book, rather than the Red Book used by Guest (see MABINOGION), and it is found in two additional manuscripts. The story corresponds closely to the *Perceval* of *Chrétien de Troyes, from which however it departs in a number of ways, and it corresponds too to a number of other Arthurian texts, such as *Perlesvaus* (ed. F. Nitze et al., 1932).

Peregrine Pickle, The Adventures of, a novel by T. *Smollett, published 1751.

Unlike *Roderick Random*, this lengthy novel is told by an omniscient narrator, and its principal target appears to be Pride, in all its manifestations. Peregrine's circle is introduced, principally his apathetic father Gamaliel, his fanciful mother, and his parents' friends, the Trunnions. Commodore Hawser Trunnion, one of Smollett's happiest creations, lives in a house known as 'the garrison', and has as his comrades the boatswain Pipes and Lieutenant Hatchway, who become friends of Peregrine. Even as a boy Peregrine shows 'a certain oddity of disposition' which manifests itself in arrogant behaviour and ferocious practical jokes. At Winchester and at Oxford Peregrine plunges into hectic living, and develops further his violent vein of humour. He meets Emilia, with whom he falls abruptly in love, and who remains throughout the book, and through all his wanderings, a fixed point to which he always returns. But she is beneath him in fortune and in rank, and pride forbids him to court her. He meets Godfrey, Emilia's brother, and together they share a long series of wild japes and adventures.

Peregrine's *Grand Tour provides opportunity for heavy satire on foreign lands. Peregrine, a 'professed enemy to all oppression' (by which he means all authority), behaves with violent aggression and suffers imprisonment in the Bastille. Affectation and ignorance are ridiculed in the figures of the tutor Jolter, the artist Pallet, and the didactic Doctor, all of whom are involved with Peregrine in a gross feast in the style of the ancients. His tempestuous and often frustrated adventures with women, such as Mrs Hornbeck and a high-born Flemish lady, succeed each other pell-mell, and his brief repentances are always overcome by the next violent passion.

Far gone in degradation, Peregrine returns to England. He allies himself in Bath with the misanthrope Crabtree, but demonstrates that he has not yet lost all generous feeling when Trunnion is ill. He nurses the old man lovingly and is filled with grief at his death. But with the money Trunnion has left him he reverts to profligacy and becomes obsessed with his object of seducing Emilia. When perjury and drugging fail he becomes almost mad, and develops a dangerous fever.

At this point, the lengthy, scandalous, and erotic memoirs of Lady *Vane are inserted into the narrative. The story is broken, but the tale of a life of pleasure is not irrelevant to Peregrine's own. Debauchery now takes almost complete hold on Peregrine. Emilia again rejects him, he loses a vast sum in an attempt to enter politics, and is eventually sent to prison for a gross libel. Another long story, of the unfortunate poet Mackercher, whose generous character contrasts strongly with those of both Peregrine and Lady Vane, is interpolated at this point. In prison Peregrine becomes morose and withdrawn, quarrels with the faithful Pipes and Hatchway, and begins to long for death. But this is the beginning of repentance. He is rescued by Godfrey, Emilia returns to him, and he inherits his father's fortune. When he and Emilia marry he rejects the fashionable urban world, pays his debts, and retires with her to the country.

The novel, which contained many savage caricatures of, for instance, *Fielding as Mr Spondy, *Garrick as Marmozet, and *Akenside as the Doctor, was only moderately successful, and was modified both in form and tone for the second edition of 1758.

perfectibilism, the doctrine that man, individual and social, is capable of progressing indefinitely towards physical, mental, and moral perfection. Mr Foster, in Peacock's *Headlong Hall*, was a 'perfectibilian'.

performance poetry, a term applied to poetry specifically written to be performed out loud. The work may sometimes transfer successfully to the printed page, but its true power usually lies in the moment of public performance.

Often with an anti-establishment edge, performance poetry covers a wide range of poetic activity, from topical satire and burlesque to ranting and agitprop, including avant-garde sound poetry and mixings of word and music. Usually performed from memory, rather than read, it can be accompanied by highly choreographed gestures and subtle voice techniques, leading to accusations (not always unjust) of style over substance. A term also in vogue is 'Spoken Word'.

'It is very important to get poetry out of the hands of the professors and out of the hands of the squares,' declared American jazz poet Kenneth Rexroth (1905–82) in 1958. 'We simply want to make poetry a part of show business.' Rexroth's motivation to broaden the audience remains at the heart of performance poetry today. Performing poets are less likely to appear at literary clubs than in music venues, bars, comedy festivals, and on radio; they may issue a *CD before a book.

Jazz (see JAZZ POETRY) has been a consistently dominant influence, starting with Langston Hughes (1902–67) and Vachel Lindsay (1879–1931); to Rexroth's 1950s jazz-poetry collaborations with *Ferlinghetti; and continuing since the 1970s, with Amiri Baraka (b. Everett LeRoi Jones, 1934–   ), Jayne Cortez

(1936–), Gil Scott Heron (1949–), and the Last Poets, through to contemporary hip-hop poetry.

In the 1960s, Allen *Ginsberg took oral poetry into coffee houses, pop festivals, and art happenings. In Britain, the spirit was spread by Michael *Horovitz, Adrian *Mitchell, and the *Liverpool poets. Maverick figures with a music-hall tilt followed, including Glaswegian absurdist Ivor Cutler (1923–); then, in the mid-1970s, punky quickfire monologuist John Cooper Clarke (1950–), and from the mid-1980s cabaret scene, John Hegley (1953–).

Performance poetry has become most closely identified with black writers such as Benjamin *Zephaniah, Linton Kwesi *Johnson, and the more playful Guyanese-born poet John Agard (1949–).

Most recently, performance activity has been sparked by New York's Nuyorican Poets Café, home of the Poetry Slam, a raucous stand-up poetry talent contest.

Perfumed Garden, The, see BURTON, SIR R.

Peri Bathous, or The Art of Sinking in Poetry (1727), a treatise by *Pope, in which he examines bathos, or the insipid, in poetry, illustrating his work with examples from his contemporaries, including R. *Blackmore, John *Dennis, A. *Phillips, and Lewis *Theobald. Pope's satirical treatise and the outraged replies it engendered led to the publication of the *Dunciad.

Pericles and Aspasia, a prose work by W. S. *Landor, published 1836.

The book consists of imaginary letters, the bulk of them from Aspasia to her friend Cleone, together with Cleone's replies. Others are addressed by Pericles to Aspasia, or by her to him; while others again are from or to prominent figures of the time, such as Anaxagoras and Alcibiades. The letters, which end with the death of Pericles, include discussions of artistic, literary, religious, philosophical, and political subjects.

Pericles, Prince of Tyre, a romantic drama by *Shakespeare, the first two acts probably written by George Wilkins: there may have been an element of collaboration between the two men. It was composed between 1606 and 1608, when it was registered and when Wilkins's prose narrative The Painfull Adventures of Pericles Prince of Tyre, which was based on a performance of the play, was published. A textually corrupt quarto of Pericles appeared in 1609 and was reprinted five times; the play was omitted from the First *Folio of 1623, but was included in the second issue of the third Folio of 1664. The play is based on the story of Apollonius of Tyre in *Gower's Confessio Amantis and a prose version (itself derived from the *Gesta Romanorum), The Patterne of Painefull Adventures, registered 1576 and reprinted 1607, by Laurence Twyne.

The play is presented by Gower, who acts as chorus throughout, and tells how, having solved the riddle set by King Antiochus and discovered his incestuous relationship with his daughter, Pericles, prince of Tyre, finds his life in danger. He leaves his government in the hands of his honest minister, Helicanus, and sails from Tyre to Tarsus where he relieves a famine. Off the coast of Pentapolis Pericles alone survives the wreck of his ship, and in a tournament defeats the suitors for the hand of Thaisa, daughter of King Simonides, whom he marries.

Hearing that Antiochus has died, Pericles sets sail for Tyre, and during a storm on the voyage Thaisa gives birth to a daughter, Marina, and faints. Apparently dead, Thaisa is buried at sea in a chest, which is cast ashore at Ephesus, where Cerimon, a physician, opens it and restores Thaisa to life. She, thinking her husband drowned, becomes a priestess in the temple of Diana. Pericles takes Marina to Tarsus, where he leaves her with its governor Cleon and his wife Dionyza.

When the child grows up Dionyza, jealous of her being more favoured than her own daughter, seeks to kill her; but Marina is carried off by pirates and sold in Mytilene to a brothel, where her purity and piety win the admiration of Lysimachus, the governor of the city, and the respect of the brothel-keeper's servant, Boult, and secure her release. In a vision Pericles is shown Marina's tomb, deceivingly erected by Cleon and Dionyza. He puts to sea again and lands at Mytilene, where through Lysimachus and to his intense joy Pericles discovers his daughter. In a second vision, Diana directs him to go to her temple at Ephesus and there recount the story of his life. In doing this, the priestess Thaisa, his lost wife, recognizes him, and is reunited with her husband and daughter. At the end of the play the chorus tells how Cleon and Dionyza are burnt by the citizens of Tarsus as a penalty for their wickedness.

Perilous Chair, the 'Siege Perilous' at the *Round Table.

periodical, literary, a term here taken to describe any repeating series of literary journal, magazine, or review. From the beginning of the 18th cent. until the beginning of the Second World War the literary periodical flourished, and contributed greatly to the development of creative writing and criticism. It stemmed from 17th-cent. abstracts of books and comments on publishers' puffs. The *Mercurius Librarius of 1668 was the first periodical to catalogue books, and the Universal Historical Bibliotheque of 1687 the first publication to invite contributions and include rudimentary comments on essays and other recent writings. At about this time periodical publications began to divide into two main types; the first to become established was the magazine miscellany, whose contents were partly but not exclusively literary. The Gentleman's Journal of 1692 is generally held to be the first established ancestor of this abiding form which developed (to take only a few notable examples) through the *Tatler (1709–11) of *Addison and *Steele, *Cave's influential *Gentleman's Magazine, and the

Analytical Review (1788–99); to the 19th-cent. *Black-wood's Magazine* (1817–1980), the *London Magazine* (1820–9), and *Bentley's Miscellany* (1837–69); and on to the 20th-cent. *Monthly Review* (1900–7), *John O'London's* (1919–54), the *London Mercury* (1919–39), and many others.

The second type of periodical was the review, with which may be grouped the weekly journal of original, critical, and general literary work. The *Monthly Review* (1749–1845), Smollett's *Critical Review* (1756–90), and the *Analytical Review* established a form which culminated in the magisterial and influential reviews of the 19th cent.—the *Edinburgh Review* (1802–1929), the *Quarterly Review* (1809–1967), the *Examiner* (1808–81), the *Westminster Review* (1824–1914), the *Athenaeum* (1828–1921), the *Cornhill Magazine* (1860–1975), the *Fortnightly Review* (1865–1934), and others, including the notorious *Yellow Book* (1894–7). Although by this time the distinction between miscellany and review was blurring, these led directly to the significant periodicals of this century, such as the *Bookman* (1891–1934), the *English Review* (1908–37), the *Times Literary Supplement* (1902–   ), the *Criterion* (1922–39), and many others, including in particular *Horizon* (1940–50) and the post-war *Encounter* (1953–   ), *London Magazine* (1954–   ), and the *London Review of Books*. Specialist reviews, such as *Scrutiny* (1932–53), designed for the more academic reader, have exerted great critical influence.

The single-essay (or serial-essay) publication, best represented by the most celebrated of all periodicals, Steele's *Spectator* (1711–12, 1714) and Johnson's *Rambler* (1750–2), had immeasurable literary influence and reputation, but the form did not last beyond the end of the 18th cent.

Although for almost a century before 1800 the periodical had encouraged many talents, including those of *Defoe, *Swift, *Fielding, *Smollett, and *Goldsmith, by the beginning of the 19th cent. the dying system of personal *patronage was largely replaced by the support of the literary periodicals and their editors (such as Leigh *Hunt and John *Scott). The work of the *Romantics, and of the Victorian poets and novelists, was greatly encouraged and widely published. For the first part of the 20th cent. new weeklies and periodicals joined others living on from the 19th cent. in supporting a wide range of new writers. But economic problems have compelled the closure of many periodicals, and it seems likely that their three centuries of influence and support has largely come to an end.

(See also ANTI-JACOBIN; CHAMPION; ENGLISHMAN'S MAGAZINE; FRASER'S MAGAZINE; FRIEND; INDICATOR; LIBERAL; LITERARY GAZETTE; MONTHLY MAGAZINE; NEW MONTHLY MAGAZINE; POLITICAL REGISTER; RETROSPECTIVE REVIEW; WATCHMAN.)

peripeteia, see POETICS, THE.

Perissa, in Spenser's *Faerie Queene*, see MEDINA.

Perker, Mr, in Dickens's *Pickwick Papers*.

Perkin Warbeck, a historical play by J. *Ford, printed 1634: its source is an episode in F. *Bacon's *Henry VII*.

The play deals with the arrival of Warbeck at the court of King James IV of Scotland and his marriage, at the king's instance and against her father's wish, to Lady Katherine Gordon; the treason of Sir William Stanley and his execution; the expedition of James IV with Warbeck into England; the desertion of Warbeck's cause by James; Warbeck's landing in Cornwall, his defeat, capture, and execution.

Ford takes up, in a new key, the much earlier fashion for plays in English history, but departs from his sources in making Perkin convinced that he actually is duke of York, not an impostor. Thus Perkin is a victim, not a villain, and the play is a study of delusion rather than ambition.

PERRAULT, Charles (1628–1703), French writer. Although known in his lifetime for his participation in the quarrel between the ancients and the moderns (see CORNEILLE), he is remembered today for a collection of *fairy tales published under the name (and possibly with the collaboration of) his son Pierre: *Histoires ou contes du temps passé* (1697), subtitled 'Contes de ma Mère l'Oye'. These tales, based on French popular tradition, were very popular in sophisticated court circles, and contributed greatly to the vogue for such works: they were translated into English as 'Mother Goose Tales' by Robert Samber in 1729. The original tales were 'Le Petit Poucet' (Hop o' my Thumb); 'Cendrillon, ou la petite pantoufle de verre' (Cinderella); 'La Belle au bois dormant' (Sleeping Beauty); 'La Barbe Bleue' (Blue Beard); 'Les Fées' (The Fairies, or 'Diamonds and Toads': a tale of two sisters, one good, one bad, from whose mouths issue the appropriate objects); 'Le Chat botté' (Puss in Boots); 'Le Petit Chaperon rouge' (Little Red Riding-Hood); and 'Riquet à la houppe' (Ricky with the Tuft, the story of a hideous but intelligent prince and his marriage choice between a beautiful and stupid woman and her intelligent, ugly sister: he selects the former). These were accompanied by three ironic verse tales, 'Griséli-dis' (the story of Patient Griselda), 'Peau d'Asne' (or 'Donkeyskin', in which a princess flees the incestuous advances of her widowed father disguised as a kitchen maid wrapped in a donkey-skin), and 'Les Souhaits ridicules' (in which Jupiter grants three disastrous wishes to a man and his wife).

PERSAUD, Lakshmi, see BLACK BRITISH LITERATURE.

PERSIUS (Aulus Persius Flaccus) (AD 34–62), Roman satirist, author of six satires, which show the influence of *Horace and of *Stoicism and which were imitated by *Donne and translated by *Dryden (1692).

personification, or **prosopopeia,** a figure of speech in which inanimate objects or abstractions are endowed with human qualities or represented as possessing human form, as in 'Let us flee this cruel shore', or 'The leaves laughed in the trees'.

Persuasion, a novel by J. *Austen, written 1815–16, published posthumously 1818.

Sir Walter Elliot, a spendthrift baronet and widower, with a swollen sense of his social importance and personal elegance, is obliged to retrench and let his seat, Kellynch Hall. His eldest daughter Elizabeth, haughty and unmarried, is now 29; the second, Anne, who is pretty, intelligent, and amiable, had some years before been engaged to a young naval officer, Frederick Wentworth, but had been persuaded by her trusted friend Lady Russell to break off the engagement, because of his lack of fortune and a misunderstanding of his easy nature. The breach had brought great unhappiness to Anne, and caused angry indignation in Wentworth. When the story opens Anne is 27, and the bloom of her youth is gone. Captain Wentworth, who has had a successful career and is now prosperous, is thrown again into Anne's society by the letting of Kellynch to Admiral and Mrs Croft, his sister and brother-in-law. Sir Walter's youngest daughter Mary is married to Charles Musgrove, the heir of a neighbouring landowner. Wentworth is attracted by Charles's sisters Louisa and Henrietta, and in time becomes involved with Louisa. During a visit of the party to Lyme Regis, Louisa, being 'jumped down' from the Cobb by Wentworth, falls and is badly injured. Wentworth's partial responsibility for the accident makes him feel an increased obligation to Louisa at the very time that his feelings are being drawn back to Anne. However, during her convalescence Louisa becomes engaged to Captain Benwick, another naval officer, and Wentworth is free to proceed with his courtship. He goes to Bath, where Sir Walter is now established with his two elder daughters and Elizabeth's companion Mrs Clay, an artful woman with matrimonial designs on Sir Walter. There Wentworth finds another suitor for Anne's hand, her cousin William Elliot, the heir to the Kellynch estate, who is also indulging in an intrigue with Mrs Clay, in order to detach her from Sir Walter. Anne has remained unshaken in her love for Wentworth and moreover learns about the duplicity of William Elliot. Accidentally made aware of Anne's constancy, Wentworth renews his offer of marriage and is accepted.

In this, Jane Austen's last completed work, satire and ridicule take a milder form, and the tone is more grave and tender. There is a tradition—poorly substantiated—that a love story of her own life is reflected in Anne Elliot's, although she wrote to her niece Fanny, 'You may *perhaps* like the heroine, as she is almost too good for me.'

Pertelote, the hen in Chaucer's 'Nun's Priest's Tale' (see CANTERBURY TALES, 20); also the wife of Chanticleer in *Reynard the Fox (see PARTLET). The word in Old French was a female proper name.

PETER OF BLOIS, see ANGLO-LATIN LITERATURE.

PETER LOMBARD (*c*.1100–60), *Magister Sententiarum*, or Master of the Sentences, born at Novara and educated at Bologna. He came to Paris where he became professor of theology and, in 1159, bishop. The *Sententiae* were written between 1145 and 1150. They are a collection of opinions on the Church Fathers, dealing with God, the Creation, the Redemption, and (most importantly) the nature of the Sacraments. It was very popular and became the standard theological textbook of the 13th cent., upon which all those with aspirations to theological authority had to write a commentary: see COMESTOR; ALEXANDER OF HALES; SCOTUS; OCKHAM.

PETER MARTYR (1499–62), Pietro Vermigli, born in Florence, an Augustinian monk, who accepted the Reformed faith, fled from Italy in 1542 to Switzerland, and subsequently to England, and became Regius professor of divinity at Oxford (1548). He helped *Cranmer in the preparation of the second *Book of Common Prayer* and was responsible for an important collection of *Loci Communes*. In 1553 he escaped to Strasbourg and died at Zurich. His wife is buried in Christ Church Cathedral, Oxford. See *Peter Martyr in Italy* (1967) by Philip McNair.

PETER PINDAR, see WOLCOT.

Peter Porcupine, see COBBETT.

Peter Bell, a poem by *Wordsworth, written 1798, published with a dedication to *Southey 1819.

Peter Bell is a potter, a lawless, roving man, insensible to the beauty of nature. Coming to the edge of the Swale he sees a solitary ass and hopes to steal it. The ass is gazing into the water at some object, which turns out to be the dead body of its owner. After a series of supernatural events Peter mounts the ass, which eventually leads him to the cottage of the drowned man's widow. Peter's spiritual and supernatural experiences on this ride make him a reformed man. The ludicrous nature of part of the poem diverted attention from its merits, and it was made the subject of many parodies, including one by Shelley, *Peter Bell the Third*.

Peter Bell the Third, a satirical poem by P. B. *Shelley written at Florence 1819, published 1839.

It is a demonic parody of *Wordsworth's poem of the same title (above). A second 'Peter Bell' had already been published by *Keats's friend J. H. *Reynolds. Shelley uses inventive doggerel, outrageous rhymes, and effervescent social satire to mock Wordsworth's 'defection' from the radical cause—'a solemn and unsexual man'. He follows Peter's progress through a black, comic underworld, described in seven sections: 'Death', 'The Devil', 'Hell', 'Sin', 'Grace', 'Damnation', and 'Double Damnation'. Part III begins with the celebrated, 'Hell is a city much like London'; while Part V draws a surprisingly sympathetic cartoon of Peter the poet, who remembered 'Many a ditch and quick-set fence; | Of Lakes he had intelligence'.

Peterborough Chronicle, The, the last part of the Laud manuscript of the *Anglo-Saxon Chronicle*, written in Peterborough at various times between 1121 and 1154, the date of its last annual. It is the only part of the chronicle to extend beyond 1080, and is of great linguistic interest in exemplifying the developments between Old and Middle English. The 12th-cent. entries, in particular, as they describe the disasters and hardships of Stephen's reign, have a vigour and circumstantiality far beyond the earlier parts of the chronicle. See C. Clark, *The Peterborough Chronicle 1070–1154* (1958); facsimile edn D. Whitelock (1954); trans. G. N. Garmonsway (1953).

'Peter Grimes', one of the tales in Crabbe's *The Borough*. Grimes is a fisherman who 'fish'd by water and who filch'd by land' and killed his apprentices by ill-treatment, until, becoming suspect and forbidden to keep apprentices, he lived and worked in solitude. Under the pressure of guilt and remorse he became insane, and died after enduring terrible imagined terrors. He is the principal figure in *Britten's opera Peter Grimes.

Peter Pan, or, *The Boy Who Would Not Grow up*, a play by J. M. *Barrie, written for the sons of Arthur and Sylvia Llewlyn Davies, and first performed on 27 Dec. 1904 with Gerald du Maurier playing both Mr Darling and Captain Hook. Peter Pan, the eternal boy, flies off from a London nursery to the Never Never Land with Wendy, John, and Michael Darling, where Wendy becomes a mother to Peter's tribe of Lost Boys. Barrie's original subtitle was 'The Boy Who Hated Mothers' and there is an interesting subtext of jealousy, possessiveness, and family conflict which explains some of the work's enduring appeal, although it also has the more evident attractions of the dog-nurse Nana, exotic scenery, flying ballet, a crocodile which devours Captain Hook, and a disembodied fairy, Tinkerbell. The name 'Wendy' was coined by Barrie from the childish mispronunciation of 'Fwend' or 'Fwendy' (for 'friend') of W. E. *Henley's daughter Margaret, who died when she was 6. *Peter Pan in Kensington Gardens* (1906, with illustrations by A. *Rackham), took stories from an earlier novel, *The Little White Bird* (1902), about a lonely bachelor who meets a boy in Kensington Gardens. The play itself has been through many versions and adaptations, and was first published in book form in 1911.

PETERS, Ellis, see DETECTIVE FICTION.

Peter Wilkins, a Cornishman, The Life and Adventures of (1751), a romance by *Paltock.

This is the tale of a shipwrecked mariner, in the manner of but more fantastic than *Robinson Crusoe. Wilkins is shipwrecked in the Antarctic region and reaches a land where the inhabitants can fly. One of

them, the beautiful Youwarkee, falls outside his hut, and he takes her up, tends her, and eventually marries her. This work was much admired in the Romantic period by *Southey, *Coleridge, *Shelley, *Lamb, and Sir W. *Scott.

PETHICK-LAWRENCE, E., see WOMEN'S SUFFRAGE.

Peto, a crony of *Falstaff's in Shakespeare's *1* and *2* *Henry IV*.

Petowker, Henrietta, a character in Dickens's *Nicholas Nickleby*. She marries Mr Lillyvick.

'Petra', see BURGON.

PETRARCH (Francesco Petrarca) (1304–74), Italian poet and humanist, and the most popular Italian poet of the English Renaissance. He was born at Arezzo, the son of a notary who was expelled from Florence (in the same year as *Dante) by the Black Guelfs and migrated to Avignon in 1312. Here in 1327 Petrarch first saw the woman who inspired his love poetry. He calls her Laura; her true identity is unknown. Until 1353 Petrarch's life was centred in Provence (Avignon and his beloved retreat at Vaucluse), but he made extended visits to Italy, on the first of which, in 1341, he was crowned poet laureate in Rome, for him the most memorable episode of his life. From 1353 onwards he resided in Italy, though he travelled widely, both on his own account and at the instance of his patrons. He died in Arquà in the Euganean Hills near Padua.

Today Petrarch is best known for the collection of Italian lyrics variously known as the *Canzoniere* or the 'Rime sparse', which includes the long series of poems in praise of Laura, now regarded as the fountainhead of the European lyric; but to his contemporaries and the generations that immediately succeeded him he was best known as a devoted student of classical antiquity. This enthusiasm he shared with his friend *Boccaccio. The encouragement which Petrarch gave to Cola di Rienzo in 1347, at the time of the restitution of the Roman republic, may be seen as an expression of the humanist spirit with which he was imbued, and in accordance with which he wrote the majority of his works in Latin. These include: a large number of letters and treatises (*De Vita Solitaria, De Remediis Utriusque Fortunae*, etc.); a Latin epic, *Africa*, on the struggle between Rome and Carthage; and the *Secretum*, a self-analysis in the form of a dialogue between himself and St *Augustine.

Petrarch is justly regarded as the father of Italian humanism and the initiator of the revived study of Greek and Latin literature, but for English writers his chief inspiration was to the early sonneteers (see under SONNET); he was imitated and translated by *Surrey, *Wyatt, T. *Watson, and, later, by *Drummond of Hawthornden. *Sidney, while mocking the poets who slavishly echoed 'poor Petrarch's long deceased woes', yet bears witness to his powerful and pervasive influence. (See George Watson, *The English Petrarch-ans*, 1967.) Henry Parker, Lord Morley (1476–1556), translated at some point before 1546 his *Trionfi* as *The Tryumphes of Fraunces Petrarcke* (?1555; ed. D. D. Carnicelli, 1971), and the countess of *Pembroke translated the *Trionfo della morte* into *terza rima*. The Petrarchan vogue declined in the 17th cent. with the waning popularity of the sonnet sequence, and in 1756 J. *Warton in his essay on *Pope dismissed Petrarch as 'metaphysical and far fetched'. *Gray, in a note on the last stanza of his *Elegy*, credits Petrarch with his phrase 'trembling hope' (*paventosa speme*), which indicates a renewal of interest in the later 18th cent.

PETRONIUS, the author of the *Satyricon*, a realistic novel of low life, sexually explicit, but written in a pure and elegant Latin, interspersed with verses and con-taining a great deal of parody. He is traditionally identified with the Gaius Petronius Arbiter who having been one of Nero's favourites was forced to commit suicide AD 65. Internal evidence certainly suggests that the novel was written in Nero's reign. Only excerpts have survived, the most striking of which are *Cena Trimalchionis* (Trimalchio's Banquet), the description of a dinner given by a rich freedman, a poem on the Civil War covering the same ground as *Lucan, and a story, *The Matron of Ephesus*. After a long period of obscurity during the Middle Ages, the *Cena* was discovered by the Florentine collector Poggio, copied in 1423, and promptly lost again, and until its rediscovery and its publication in 1650 only the smaller excerpts were known. Petronius is mentioned by religious writers like John Hales and Jeremy *Taylor in the first half of the 17th cent. and by *Dryden in his critical works. The first English translation was William Burnaby's in 1694. A passage about death was imitated by Peacock in *Rhododaphne* (1818). But the piece which aroused most interest was *The Matron of Ephesus* which inspired Walter Charleton's *Ephesian Matron* (1659) and *Fry's one-act play *A Phoenix Too Frequent* (1946).

Petruchio, a gentleman of Verona and suitor to *Katharina in Shakespeare's *The Taming of the Shrew*.

PETTIE, George (*c*.1548–89), educated at Christ Church, Oxford. His *A Petite Pallace of Pettie His Pleasure*, first published in 1576, was often reprinted. This collection of 12 'pretie Hystories' concerns lovers, and all but one derive from classical sources. They are mainly made up of long speeches with little action, and their style to some extent anticipates *Lyly's euphuism. Writing about 100 years after their first publication, Pettie's grand-nephew A. *Wood calls them 'more fit to be read by a schoolboy, or rustical amoratto, than by a gent. of mode or language'. Pettie's work follows on from Painter's *Palace of Pleasure* from which he derived his title, and his translation of most of Guazzo's

Civile Conversation (1581) contributed to the Eliza-bethan vogue for *courtesy literature and fiction.

PETTY, Sir William (1623–76), a political economist who studied on the Continent and became the friend of *Hobbes. He executed for the Commonwealth the 'Down Survey' of forfeited lands in Ireland, the first attempt on a large scale at carrying out a survey scientifically. Petty acquiesced in the Restoration, and was knighted and made an original member of the *Royal Society in 1662. He published economic treat-ises, the principal of which was entitled *Political Arithmetic* (1690), a term signifying that which we now call statistics. *Swift parodied this work in *A Modest Proposal*. Petty examined, by the quantitative method, the current allegations of national decay. He rejected the old 'prohibitory' system, and showed the error of the supporters of the 'mercantile' system in regarding the abundance of precious metals as the standard of prosperity. He traced the sources of wealth to labour and land.

Petulengro, Jasper, the principal gypsy character in Borrow's *Lavengro and *The Romany Rye*, founded upon the Norfolk gypsy Ambrose Smith, with whom Borrow was acquainted in his youth. 'Petulengro' means 'shoeing smith'.

Peveril of the Peak, a novel by Sir W. *Scott, published 1823.

The novel is set in the Restoration England of Titus Oates's *Popish Plot, and its plotting was described by Lockhart as 'clumsy and perplexed'. The action is chiefly concerned with corruption at the court of Charles II, with fanaticism turned sour, and with conflicting loyalties. These are worked out most effectively in the characters of Major Bridgenorth and young Julian Peveril, in both of whom there is profound psychological development. The part played by the apparent deaf-mute, Fenella, is less convincing.

PEVSNER, Sir Nikolaus Bernhard Leon (1902–83), architectural historian, born in Germany and educated at the universities of Leipzig, Munich, Berlin, and Frankfurt. He lectured for four years at Göttingen before the rise of Hitler brought him to England, where he became in 1941 associated with *Penguin Books, as editor of King Penguins and of his celebrated county-by-county series *The Buildings of England* (1951–74). His association with Birkbeck College began formally in 1942, where he continued to teach until 1967, and he was professor of fine art at Cambridge (1949–55) and at Oxford (1968–9). His many works on art, design, and architecture include *Pioneers of the Modern Movement, from William Morris to Walter Gropius* (1936), *High Victorian Design* (1951), and *The Englishness of English Art* (1956).

Pew, the blind buccaneer in Stevenson's *Treasure Island*.

PFEFFERKORN, Johannes (c.1469–c.1522), a Jewish-born Christian convert, the associate of the Dominicans in their controversy with *Reuchlin regarding the proposed destruction of works of Jewish literature and philosophy, which he keenly approved. See EPISTOLAE OBSCURORUM VIRORUM.

Phaedria, in Spenser's *Faerie Queene* (II. vi), the Lady of the Idle Lake, symbolizing immodest mirth.

Phalaris, Epistles of, letters attributed to Phalaris, a tyrant of Acragas in Sicily (6th cent. BC), with a reputation for extreme cruelty. They were edited by Charles Boyle, fourth earl of Orrery (1676–1731) in 1695, and praised by Sir W. *Temple. R. *Bentley proved that they were spurious and dated from perhaps the 2nd cent. AD. There is an echo of the controversy in Swift's *The Battle of the Books.

phallic symbols, objects used, in Freudian theory, to represent the phallus, which itself is in its original sense a representation or image of the penis, symbolizing male or regenerative power. Any erect and pointed object may be a phallic symbol: Freud himself in case histories cites objects such as swords, knives, pens, flames, closed umbrellas, and screwdrivers. *Psychoanalytic criticism frequently applies itself to the detection of such symbols, whether consciously or unconsciously deployed, as an aid to interpretation.

Phaon, (1) in Spenser's *Faerie Queene* (II. iv), the unfortunate squire who, deceived by Philemon and under the influence of Furor (mad rage), slays Claribel and poisons Philemon; (2) in classical mythology, the boatman with whom *Sappho is said to have fallen in love. *Lyly wrote a play on the subject (*Sapho and Phao*).

Pharsalia, see LUCAN.

Phebe, a shepherdess in Shakespeare's *As You Like It* who marries Silvius.

Phèdre, see RACINE and HIPPOLYTUS.

philander, to, to play the trifling and even promiscuous lover. Philander, in an old ballad, was the lover of Phillis; and in *Beaumont and *Fletcher's *Laws of Candy* the lover of Erota.

Philaster, or *Love Lies a-Bleeding*, a romantic tragicomedy by *Beaumont and *Fletcher (see FLETCHER, J.), written ?1609, printed 1620. One of the most successful of the Beaumont and Fletcher collaborations, the play draws on the conventions of the prose romances, notably on *Montemayor's *Diana* and Sidney's *Arcadia.

The king of Calabria has usurped the crown of Sicily. The rightful heir, Philaster, loves and is loved by Arethusa, daughter of the usurper, but the latter intends to marry her to Pharamond, prince of Spain. To maintain contact with her, Philaster places his page Bellario in her service, Arethusa reveals to the king that Pharamond (made impatient by her own frigid reception of him) has embarked on an affair with Megra, a lady of the court; Megra in turn accuses Arethusa of misconduct with the handsome young Bellario. After various pastoral pursuits and disasters, during which Bellario touchingly and constantly demonstrates devotion to Philaster, and Philaster himself manifests a marked lack of chivalry, it is revealed that Bellario is in fact Euphrasia, daughter of a Sicilian lord, in love with Philaster. Reassured thus of Arethusa's virtue, Philaster regains both his loved one and his kingdom, whereas Bellario is left with their gratitude, to devote herself to a life of chastity.

An edition in the Revels series by Andrew Gurr was published in 1969.

Philip, see ADVENTURES OF PHILIP, THE.

philippics, see CICERO and DEMOSTHENES.

Philip Quarll, The Adventures of, an adventure story originally published as *The Hermit* (1727) by 'Edward Dorrington', but generally attributed to Peter Longueville, though some authorities ascribe it to Alexander Bicknell. A derivative of *Robinson Crusoe, it describes Quarll's 50 years of solitude and suffering on a South Sea island. It went through many editions, and was much adapted for children.

PHILIPS, Ambrose (1674–1749), poet, and fellow of St John's College, Cambridge, was a member of *Addison's circle. He wrote *The Distrest Mother* (1712), a successful adaptation of *Racine's *Andromaque*, but is remembered chiefly for his quarrel with *Pope over the relative merits of their pastorals. Pope drew, in the *Guardian* (No. 40, 1713), 'a comparison of Philips's performance with his own, in which, with an unexampled and unequalled artifice of irony, though he has himself always the advantage, he gives the preference to Philips' (Johnson, *Lives of the English Poets*). Philips's 'Epistle to the Earl of Dorset' (1709) memorably evokes the frozen landscape of Denmark. His infantile trochaics addressed to children ('Dimply damsel, sweetly smiling', etc.) earned him the nickname of 'Namby Pamby', though Johnson described them as his pleasantest pieces. For the 'pastoral war', see also Gay's *The Shepherd's Week.

PHILIPS, John (1676–1709), educated at Christ Church, Oxford. He was the author of *The Splendid Shilling* (unauthorized 1701, authorized 1705), a burlesque in Miltonic blank verse, in which Philips contrasts the happy possessor of the splendid shilling, who 'nor hears with pain | New oysters cry'd, nor sighs for chearful ale', with the poor poet in his garret, hungry and thirsty, and beset by creditors. In 1705 he published *Blenheim*, written at the suggestion of *Harley and *Bolingbroke, as a Tory counterpart to *The Campaign* of *Addison. *Cyder* (1708), a poem in blank verse written in imitation of *Virgil's *Georgics*, celebrates the cultivation, manufacture, and virtues of cider; it provided a model for later blank verse georgics, such as *Smart's *The Hop-Garden* and parts of Thomson's **The Seasons*. Thomson, in 'Autumn', salutes 'Philips, Pomona's bard' both for his 'native theme' and for his 'rhyme-unfetter'd verse' (ll. 640–50), and later critics have endorsed this view of his place in literary tradition. There is an edition by M. G. L. Thomas (1927).

PHILIPS, Katherine (1631–64), known as the 'Match-less Orinda', the daughter of Royalist John Fowler, a London merchant. She lived in London until the age of 15, attending Mrs Salmon's School, Hackney. Upon her father's death her mother married a Welsh baronet, whose castle in Pembrokeshire became Katherine's home. In 1648 she married Parliamentarian James Philips of Cardigan: he was 59, she 17. Her poems were widely circulated in manuscript, inspiring eulogies by H. *Vaughan ('It was thy light showed me the way' in *Olor Iscanus* and *Thalia Rediviva*); a commendatory poem by 'Orinda' was prefixed to the latter volume. Her translation of *Corneille's *Pompée* was acted in Dublin with great success in 1663, and her version of *Horace*, completed by *Denham, in 1668. Her collected poems appeared unauthorized in 1664. She died of smallpox, and was mourned in elegies by *Cowley and Sir W. *Temple; her collected poems were published in 1667. They memorialize a coterie, a Platonic Society of Friendship, whose members were known by poetic sobriquets, including Anne Owen (Lucasia), Mary Aubrey (Rosania), John *Berkenhead (Cratander), and Sir Charles Cotterell (Polliarchus), her correspond-ence with whom was published as *Letters from Orinda to Poliarchus* in 1705. These letters show Philips's careful construction of the persona of 'Orinda'. She was pre-eminently a poet of female friendship. Her lyrics, marrying Cavalier and metaphysical influences, ap-plied Petrachan love conventions to present women's friendship as an ideal. Friendship is 'our passion ... the strongest thing I know'. See P. W. Souers, *The Matchless Orinda* (1931); E. Hobby, *The Virtue of Necessity* (1988); G. *Greer, *Kissing the Rod* (1988).

Philip Sparrow, see PHYLLYP SPAROWE.

Philistine, the name of an alien warlike people who in early biblical times constantly harassed the Israelites. The name is applied, (1) humorously or otherwise to persons regarded as 'the enemy' into whose hands one may fall, bailiffs, literary critics, etc.; (2) to persons deficient in liberal culture and enlightenment, from *philister*, the term applied by German students to one who is not a student at the university, but a townsman. In sense (2) the word was introduced into English by M. *Arnold ('Heine', *Essays in Criticism*); he describes *Heine as a progressive, a lover of ideas and hater of philistinism, and the English as a nation dominated by 'inveterate inaccessibility to ideas'. In other works, notably *Culture and Anarchy*, he develops the concept; the English middle classes are predominantly philis-tine, whereas the aristocracy, with its love of field sports, physical prowess, and external graces, is de-scribed as 'Barbarian'. The working classes are de-scribed as the 'Populace'.

PHILLIPPS, Sir Thomas (1792–1872), educated at Rugby and University College, Oxford. He early de-veloped a passion for collecting books and, more particularly, manuscripts (he described himself as 'a perfect vello-maniac'), and assembled an extremely valuable library at his home in Broadway, Worcester-shire. He also established there a private printing press, the Middle Hill Press, where he printed visitations, extracts from registers, cartularies, etc. In 1863 he moved his library to Thirlestaine House, Cheltenham, and on his death left it to his youngest daughter Mrs Fenwick (his eldest, Henrietta, had married the Shakespearian scholar J. O. *Halliwell): it has been gradually dispersed in sales to public institutions at home and abroad and to private collectors. Some unique items (such as the manuscript of part of a translation of *Ovid's *Metamorphoses* associated with *Caxton) came to light as late as 1964: the Caxton manuscript is now reunited with its other half, which had been in the possession of *Pepys, in the Pepys Library at Magdalene College, Cambridge. See A. N. L. *Munby, *Phillipps Studies* (1951–60); N. J. Barker, *Portrait of an Obsession* (1967).

PHILLIPS, Caryl (1958–), novelist and playwright, born in St Kitts, West Indies. He came to England with his family as a baby and was educated in Leeds, Birmingham, and at Oxford University. Early plays include *Strange Fruit* (1980) and *The Shelter* (1983). His first novel, *The Final Passage* (1985), described the experiences in Britain of the post-war immigrant generation: later works include *A State of Independ-ence* (1986), in which the protagonist returns to his West Indian home, with a severe sense of dislocation, and *Higher Ground* (1989). *Cambridge* (1991) is a tour de force of *historical fiction set in the West Indies just after the abolition of the slave trade: much of the novel is narrated by English visitor Emily Cartwright, who is disturbed and shocked by the brutal world she enters, but we also hear other voices, including that of Cambridge himself, an educated plantation slave. *Crossing the River* (1994) is a many-layered polyphonic narration, linking past and present, Africa and Eng-land, which celebrates the difficulties and triumph of a mixed-race love affair during the Second World War; this was followed by *The Nature of Blood* (1997), a novel which deals with the consequences of the *Holocaust. *A Distant Shore* (2003) is a tragic story of loneliness, immigration, and racism in contemporary Britain. Non fiction works include *The European Tribe* (1987); he also edited *Extravagant Strangers* (1997), a survey of non-British born writers and their invigorating contribution to Britain's literary tradition.

PHILLIPS, Edward (1630–?96), brother of John Phil-lips (below) and nephew of *Milton, by whom he was educated. He was tutor to the son of *Evelyn, and then to Philip Herbert, afterwards seventh earl of Pembroke. His various literary works include an edition of the poems of *Drummond of Hawthornden (1656); a popular philological dictionary called *The New World of English Words* (1658); and *Theatrum Poetarum* (1675), a collection of literary biographies in the preface to which some have seen the hand of Milton. He also wrote a short life of his uncle, published 1694. *Lives of Edward and John Phillips* by W. *Godwin was published in 1815.

PHILLIPS, John (1631–1706), younger brother of Edward Phillips (above) and nephew of *Milton, by whom he was educated. He wrote a scathing attack on Puritanism in his poem *A Satyr against Hypocrites* (1655), supported Charles II and *Oates, and worked as translator and hack-writer; he translated *La Calprenède's *Pharamond*, *Scudéry's *Almahide*, and wrote a travesty of *Don Quixote* (1687) in which he mentions *Paradise Lost*, but his biographer *Godwin (who much prefers his elder brother Edward) was unable to determine whether the reference was 'intended as a compliment or a slur'.

PHILLIPS, Stephen (1864–1915), actor and poet, who resolved, after the success of his *Poems* (1898), to revive poetic drama; his *Paolo and Francesca* (pub. 1900, perf. 1902) was received with great enthusiasm and compared by serious critics to *Sophocles and Shakespeare. *Herod* (1901), *Ulysses* (1902), and *Nero* (1906) were also well received, but his later plays were failures.

Phillotson, Richard, a character in Hardy's *Jude the Obscure*.

PHILLPOTTS, Eden (1862–1960), prolific and popular novelist, playwright, and poet, most of whose many novels are set in Dartmoor. He collaborated as playwright with Arnold *Bennett and J. K. *Jerome.

Philoclea, younger sister of Pamela in Sidney's *Arcadia*.

Philological Society, the, founded in its present form in 1842 to investigate and to promote the study and knowledge of the structure, the affinities, and the history of language. Active in its formation were *Thirlwall, A. P. *Stanley, and T. *Arnold; prominent members were to include *Furnivall, *Trench, and James *Murray, all of whom were involved in the creation of the *Oxford English Dictionary. See H. Aarsleff, *The Study of Language in England 1780–1860* (1967).

Philosophes, the collective name of a group of 18th-cent. writers and thinkers united by their faith in the efficacy of reason and their dislike of repressive traditions. Its most significant representatives included *Montesquieu, *Voltaire, *Diderot, *Rousseau, *Buffon, *Condillac, Condorcet, *d'Alembert, d'Holbach, and Helvétius. They inclined to scepticism in religion, materialism in philosophy, and hedonism in ethics.

Philosophical Enquiry into the Origin of Our Ideas of the Sublime and Beautiful, see SUBLIME AND BEAUTIFUL.

Philosophical View of Reform, A, a political essay by P. B. *Shelley, written at Pisa 1820, not published until 1920.

Intended as an 'instructive and readable' octavo booklet, this was Shelley's most mature political statement about Liberty, Revolution, and Reform: it confirms his position as a radical (rather than a liberal)—but not a revolutionary. Chapter 1 is a historical sketch of the continuous overthrow of imperial powers in Europe; it argues that periods of great literary creativity have always coincided with libertarian movements. Chapter 2 describes conditions of political and economic oppression in contemporary Britain and proposes specific measures of radical change, including parliamentary reform and alteration of laws regarding marriage, property inheritance, capital investment, and working hours. Chapter 3 (unfinished) suggests actual means of enforcing political change, including non-violent protest, the intervention of 'poets and philosophers', and the 'last resort' of resistance which is 'undoubtedly insurrection'. The essay illuminates the thinking behind Shelley's political poems of 1817–20, and provided much material for the *Defence of Poetry, such as the concept of 'unacknowledged legislators'.

Philotas, a Senecan tragedy in blank verse by S. *Daniel, published 1605.

Philotas, a gallant and bountiful soldier held in high estimation among the Macedonians, incurs the suspicion of Alexander by his boasts. He is accused of concealing his knowledge of a conspiracy against the king, is tortured, and, having confessed, is stoned to death.

The author had subsequently to defend himself against the charge of covertly defending, by this play, the rebellion of Essex. Performance of the play was suppressed in 1604.

Phineas Finn, the Irish Member, a novel by A. *Trollope, published 1869, the second of the *'Palliser' series.

Phineas Finn, a young Irish barrister, catches the eye of Lord Tulla and is elected to Parliament for the family seat of Loughshane. In London Phineas wins friends on all sides, is admitted to high society, and falls in love with the politically minded Lady Laura Standish. Lady Laura's personal fortune is considerably diminished after paying the debts of her brother Lord Chiltern, and she feels she must marry money, in the person of the chilly but wealthy Mr Kennedy. Phineas is at first disappointed, and is later deeply grieved at the unhappiness and finally the collapse of the Kennedy marriage, but turns for consolation elsewhere. He first pursues Violet Effingham, Lord Chiltern's childhood sweetheart, but after a brief quarrel between the two suitors (featuring a duel fought in Belgium), Violet settles for Chiltern, and they are married. Madame Max Goesler, the rich widow of a Viennese banker, is Phineas's next favourite. Phineas has lost his government salary by sticking to his principles over the issue of Irish Tenant Right, and has no money to cover the cost of re-election. Madame Max offers to help him out, and when Phineas refuses she offers him her hand in marriage and her fortune to finance a fresh political career. This he is too scrupulous to accept in view of his prior engagement to a pretty Irish girl, Mary Flood-Jones, and he returns to Ireland.

Phineas Redux, a novel by A. *Trollope, published 1874, the fourth in the *'Palliser' series.

Phineas Finn returns to politics in time for the fall of Mr Daubeny's government, and earnestly hopes for office under Mr Gresham. Unhappily a series of quarrels makes his progress anything but smooth. First Mr Kennedy, outraged at Phineas's visit to his wife Lady Laura in her Dresden exile, unsuccessfully tries to shoot him. Then Phineas exchanges heated words with the president of the board of trade, Mr Bonteen, and when, later that night, Bonteen is murdered, the burden of circumstantial evidence against Phineas is very strong. He is arrested and remanded for trial, and only the spirited efforts of Madame Max in discovering the true culprit, and a brilliant courtroom performance by Chaffanbrass in presenting her findings, succeed in getting him off. For a time Phineas is shattered by his experiences, but towards the end of the novel he rallies, returns to politics, and marries Madame Max.

In this novel the old duke of Omnium dies, and Plantagenet and Lady Glencora become duke and duchess. Madame Max, the old duke's favourite, is left some valuable jewellery in his will, but refuses to accept it. Instead the legacy is made over to Plantagenet's cousin Adelaide Palliser, who is thus able to marry the impoverished Gerard Maule.

Bonteen's murderer turns out to have been the Revd Mr Emilius, the converted Jew who married Lizzie *Eustace. Emilius, who has a previous wife still living at Prague, is convicted of bigamy and imprisoned, but there is insufficient evidence to hang him.

Phiz, see BROWN, H. K.

Phoenix, The, an Old English poem of 677 lines, found in the *Exeter Book and possibly written in the later 9th cent. It is a beast allegory of the kind found in the *bestiaries but developed over a greater length than usual. The descriptive part of the poem is closely based on Carmen de Ave Phoenice, probably by Lactantius (d. c.340), and the later allegorizing section has not been attributed to any certain source. The poem is admired for the vividness of its imagery and the accomplishment of its syntax. Ed. N. F. Blake (1964).

'Phoenix and the Turtle, The', an allegorical elegy ascribed to Shakespeare which was included in Robert Chester's collection Love's Martyr (1601).

Phoenix Nest, The, a poetic miscellany published in 1593 and compiled by one R.S., who has never been identified. It includes poems by *Ralegh, *Lodge, and *Breton, and opens with three elegies on *Sidney, the 'Phoenix' of the title. It was edited by H. E. Rollins (1931).

Phunky, Mr, in Dickens's *Pickwick Papers, Serjeant Snubbin's junior in the case of Bardell v. Pickwick.

Phyllyp Sparowe, a poem by *Skelton.

'Physician's Tale, The', see CANTERBURY TALES, 13.

physiocrat, one of a school of political economists founded by François Quesnay (1694–1774) in France in the 18th cent. They maintained that society should be governed according to an inherent natural order, that the soil is the sole source of wealth and the only proper object of taxation, and that security of property and freedom of industry and exchange are essential [OED]. The other principal exponents of the physiocrat doctrines were Jacques Turgot (1727–81), an able financier, whose dismissal in 1776 from the post of controller-general of the finances was the prelude of the French national bankruptcy; and Victor de Riquetti, marquis de Mirabeau (1715–89), the author of L'Ami des hommes and father of the revolutionary statesman. Adam *Smith, though no physiocrat in the technical sense of the word, was strongly influenced by the school.

Physiologus, see BESTIARIES.

picaresque, from the Spanish pícaro, a wily trickster; the form of novel accurately described as 'picaresque' first appeared in 16th-cent. Spain with the anonymous *Lazarillo de Tormes (1553) and Alemán's *Guzmán de Alfarache (1599–1604), which relate the histories of ingenious rogues, the servants of several masters, who eventually repent the error of their ways; examples of their descendants in English would be *Moll Flanders, *Roderick Random, and *Tom Jones. The term was apparently first used in England in the 19th cent.; Sir W. *Scott, for example, writing in 1829, describes the Memoirs of Vidoq as 'a pickaresque tale . . . a romance of roguery', and The Bookman in 1895 defined a picaresque tale as that of a 'trickster'. Nowadays the term is commonly, and loosely, applied to episodic novels, especially those of *Fielding, *Smollett, and others of the 18th cent. which describe the adventures of a lively and resourceful hero on a journey. The Golden Ass of *Apuleius is regarded as a forerunner of the picaresque novel, while Nashe's *The Unfortunate Traveller (1594) is commonly accepted as the first picaresque romance in English.

PICCOLOMINI, Aeneas Silvius (1405–64), Pope Pius II from 1458, was a patron of letters and author of a romance in Latin, *Eurialus and Lucretia*, of treatises on many subjects, and of commentaries on his times. His secular works include the *Miseriae Curialium*, which provided one of the models for the **Eclogues* of A. *Barclay. He visited Scotland in 1435, and wrote a somewhat hostile report of its poverty-stricken condition. His third-person autobiography was translated as *Memoirs of a Renaissance Pope* by F. A. Gragg (1959).

PICKARD, Tom (1946–   ), poet, born in Gateshead, Newcastle upon Tyne: in 1963 he instigated a celebrated series of poetry readings and performances at the Mordern Tower in Newcastle, including a reading by Basil *Bunting, whose work he did much to revive. He has published several collections, from *High on the Walls* (1967) to *Tiepin Eros: New and Selected Poems* (1994). See UNDERGROUND POETRY.

PICKERING, William (1796–1854), publisher, commenced business in London in 1820, and did much to raise the standard of design in printing. He published the 'Diamond Classics' 1821–31, and in 1830 adopted the trademark of the Aldine Press (see ALDUS MANUTIUS). He increased his reputation by his Aldine edition of the English poets in 53 vols.

Pickwick Papers (*The Posthumous Papers of the Pickwick Club*), a novel by *Dickens, first issued in 20 monthly parts Apr. 1836–Nov. 1837, and as a volume in 1837 (when Dickens was only 25 years old).

Mr Samuel Pickwick, general chairman of the Pickwick Club which he has founded, Messrs Tracy Tupman, Augustus Snodgrass, and Nathaniel Winkle, members of the club, are constituted a Corresponding Society of the Club to report to it their journeys and adventures, and observations of characters and manners. This is the basis on which the novel is constructed, and the Club serves to link a series of detached incidents and changing characters, without elaborate plot. The entertaining adventures with which Mr Pickwick and his associates meet are interspersed with incidental tales contributed by various characters. The principal elements in the story are: (1) the visit of Pickwick and his friends to Rochester and their falling in with the specious rascal Jingle, who gets Winkle involved in the prospect of a duel (fortunately averted). (2) The visit to Dingley Dell, the home of the hospitable Mr Wardle; the elopement of Jingle with Wardle's sister, their pursuit by Wardle and Pickwick, and the recovery of the lady; followed by the engagement of Sam Weller as Pickwick's servant. (3) The visit to Eatanswill, where a parliamentary election is in progress, and Mr Pickwick makes the acquaintance of Pott, editor of a political newspaper, and Mrs Leo Hunter. (4) The visit to Bury St Edmunds, where Mr Pickwick and Sam Weller are fooled by Jingle and his servant Job Trotter. (5) The pursuit of Jingle to Ipswich, where Mr Pickwick inadvertently enters the bedroom of a middle-aged lady at night; is in consequence involved in a quarrel with Mr Peter Magnus, her admirer; is brought before Mr Nupkins, the magistrate, on a charge of intending to fight a duel; and obtains his release on exposing the nefarious designs of Jingle on Nupkins's daughter. (6) The Christmas festivities at Dingley Dell. (7) The misapprehension of Mrs Bardell, Mr Pickwick's landlady, regarding her lodger's intentions, which leads to the famous action of *Bardell v. Pickwick* for breach of promise of marriage, in which judgement is given for the plaintiff, with damages £750. (8) The visit to Bath, in which Winkle figures prominently, first in the adventure with the blustering Dowler, and secondly in his courtship of Arabella Allen. (9) The period of Mr Pickwick's imprisonment in the Fleet in consequence of his refusal to pay the damages and costs of his action; and the discovery of Jingle and Job Trotter in that prison, and their relief by Mr Pickwick. (10) The affairs of Tony Weller (Sam's father) and the second Mrs Weller, ending in the death of the latter and the discomfiture of the pious humbug and greedy drunkard Stiggins, deputy shepherd in the Ebenezer Temperance Association. (11) The affairs of Bob Sawyer and Benjamin Allen, medical students and subsequently struggling practitioners. The novel ends with the happy marriage of Emily Wardle and Augustus Snodgrass.

PICO DELLA MIRANDOLA, Giovanni (1463–94), an Italian humanist and philosopher, born at Mirandola, of which his family were the lords. He spent part of his short life at Florence in the circle of Lorenzo de' *Medici. In 1486 he published 900 theses, offering to maintain them at Rome, but some of his propositions were pronounced heretical and the public debate did not take place. The famous oration *De Dignitate Hominis*, with which he intended to introduce the debate, is one of the most important philosophical works of the 15th cent. Pico was a daring syncretist, who vainly tried to make a synthesis of Christianity, Platonism, Aristotelianism, and the Jewish cabbala. As a pioneer in the study of Hebrew philosophy he influenced *Reuchlin. His life (*The Lyfe of Johan Picus, Erle of Myrandula a Grete Lorde of Italy*) and some of his pious writings were translated by Sir T. *More. *Colet was influenced by Pico.

picturesque, a term which came into fashion in the late 18th cent., principally to describe a certain kind of scenery. Writers on the picturesque include W. *Gilpin, W. *Mason, William Payne Knight (1750–1824, who published *The Landscape* in 1794), Uvedale Price (1747–1829, who published *Essays on the Picturesque*, 1794), and the landscape gardener Humphry Repton (1752–1818) (see LANDSCAPE GARDENING). The impact of these writers on the sensibility and vocabulary of writers of the 19th cent. was considerable. The 'picturesque', as defined by Price, was a new aesthetic category, to be added to *Burke's recently established categories of the *sublime and the beautiful; its attributes were roughness and irregularity, and its most complete exponent in terms of painting was

*Rosa, whose works enjoyed much popularity at this period; Constable described him as 'a great favourite with novel writers, particularly the ladies'. Mrs *Radcliffe's works dwell frequently on the picturesque, and J. *Austen and many of her characters were familiar with the works of Gilpin; in *Mansfield Park she mocks the spirit of 'improvement' in the character of the foolish Mr Rushworth. The entertaining aesthetic disputes of Price and Knight, both of whom owned estates near the Welsh borders, are satirized in Peacock's *Headlong Hall, and *Combe's adventures of Dr Syntax are aimed at the movement in general and Gilpin in particular. Although the excesses of picturesque theory became a popular target for satire, these writers made a lasting contribution to our vision, and writers as diverse as *Dickens, G. *Eliot, and H. *James found the term useful. The development of the picturesque movement into *Romanticism is a subject of much complexity and literary interest. See C. Hussey, *The Picturesque* (1927, 1967).

'Pied Piper of Hamelin, The: A Child's Story', a poem by R. Browning, included in *Dramatic Lyrics*.

Pierce Penniless, *His Supplication to the Divell*, a fantastic prose satire by T. *Nashe, published 1592. The author, in the form of a humorous complaint to the devil, discourses on the vices of the day, throwing interesting light on the customs of his time. One of the best passages is that relating to the recently developed practice of excessive drinking, 'a sinne, that ever since we have mixt our selves with the Low-countries, is counted honourable', and containing a description of the various types of drunkards, drawn with a coarse Rabelaisian humour and vigour. The work is directed in part against Richard Harvey the astrologer (brother of Gabriel *Harvey) and the Martinists (see MARTIN MARPRELATE). It ends with a discussion of hell and devils.

Pierce the Ploughman's Crede, an alliterative poem dating from the last decade of the 14th cent., influenced by *Langland, to whom it pays tribute, and attacking the friars. It is as evocative and forceful as Langland himself, and it contains the most effective piece of social criticism in Middle English, in its lines describing the hardships of the ploughman and his wife (ll. 420–42). Ed. W. W. *Skeat (EETS 30, 1867: repr. 1973).

PIERO DELLA FRANCESCA (?1416–92), Italian painter, whose most celebrated works, *The History of the True Cross* (1452–64; Arezzo, San Francesco), *The Resurrection* (Borgo, San Sepolcro), and the *Madonna del Parto* (Monterchi, Chapel of the Cemetery), are now perhaps the most revered of all Renaissance frescos. Yet Piero was almost ignored until the 20th cent.; *Ruskin scarcely mentions him, and it was left to the generation that followed Cézanne to rediscover the formal beauties of his works. A. *Huxley, in *Along the Road*, describes the *Resurrection* as 'The greatest picture in the world': in *Ape and Essence* he imagines

a composition by Piero—'luminously explicit, an equation in balanced voids and solids, in harmonising and contrasting hues'.

Piers Plowman, the greatest poem of the Middle English *Alliterative Revival, by *Langland. It survives in about 50 manuscripts, in three widely varying versions, known as the A, B, and C texts. The A-text, totalling 2,567 lines in its longest version, was probably written about 1367–70; the B-text, a very considerable extension of the A-text which both rewrites the parts of the poem that occur in the A-text and adds more than as much again to the end of it, extends to 7,277 lines (or more) and probably dates from about 1377–9; and the C-text is a substantial revision of the B-text, about the same length, dating from about 1385–6. It is now generally agreed (following Kane, *Piers Plowman: The Evidence for Authorship*, 1965, and Donaldson, *Piers Plowman: The C-Text and Its Poet*, 1949) that the three versions were all the work of Langland, who would, therefore, have been occupied with the work and its revisions for at least the last 20 years of his life. Structurally, the poem is divided in a number of ways which are also problematical because the evidence of the manuscripts is conflicting. The principal division of the poem has been into two parts, the 'Visio' and the 'Vita', the 'Visio' comprising the prologue and the first seven *passus* ('step': the term used in the poem for the section divisions, varying from 129 to 642 lines in length) in the B-text (prologue and the first eight in A; the first ten *passus* in C which sometimes does not have a prologue). This 'Visio'–'Vita' distinction has been seen to be of such importance by some critics that they have argued that they are properly to be regarded as two distinct poems (see T. P. Dunning, *Piers Plowman: An Interpretation of the A-Text*, rev. T. P. Dolan, 1980); but the distinction is not found in B manuscripts at all (see Schmidt's edition, 1978, p. xx). There has been argument too whether B or C is to be taken as the more authoritative text; C is the latest and in many places clarifies points which remained obscure in B, but its revisions have damaged the shape of the poem at some points so that it no longer divides into coherent visions, describing falling asleep—vision—awakening. B has the advantage of being complete and coherent in this way (and it can also be claimed that some of the very obscurities that C clarifies, such as the tearing of the pardon in *Passus* VII, display great imaginative power). A, though some claims have been made for its integrity as a poem, may be regarded as superseded by the other versions. The following account follows the B-text (where there is any divergence in plot), in its division into eight separate visions.

Vision 1. While wandering on the Malvern Hills, the narrator (who, it transpires later, is called Will) falls asleep and has a vision of a Tower where Truth dwells, a deep Dungeon, and between them 'a fair feeld ful of folk' (prologue, 17) where all the order of human society can be seen about their business. The worldly values thus raised are expounded by Lady Holy Church in *Passus* I; the theme is sustained by the analytical trial of Lady Meed in *Passus* II–IV which considers whether Meed (Reward or payment) is to be given to Wrong or according to Conscience and Reason.

Vision 2. The narrator observes what J. A. Burrow has shown to be an established sequence of events: Sermon (preached here by Reason); Confession (by the Seven Deadly Sins, colourfully personified in *Passus* V, the longest in the poem); Pilgrimage (to Truth, led by Piers the Plowman who first appears as the just leader on the road to Salvation; and Pardon (a paper pardon sent to Piers by Truth, but torn up by him when its validity is questioned by a priest, who rejects it as a moral statement rather than a papal document). The conflict with the priest awakens the dreamer; this is the end of the 'Visio' as distinct from 'Vita', if such a distinction is indicated (as in A and C manuscripts).

Vision 3 shows Will turning to the faculties and sources of knowledge and understanding, as the search for Truth (now referred to as 'Dowel') becomes individualized. In *Passus* VIII–XII Will progressively consults Thought, Wit, Study, Clergy, Scripture, Ymagynatyf (Imagination—linked with Nature in an inner dream containing an inspired description of the workings of nature, ll. 326–67), and Reason.

Visions 4 and 5. The theme of these visions is Charity, and *Passus* XIII–XVII attempt to show in action the ideas concerning doing well which were offered in Vision 3. Piers Plowman reappears, in a transfigured form in which his action is indistinguishable from that of Christ.

Vision 6. The Passion of Christ is described as the culmination of doing well in *Passus* XVIII, where the death of Christ is evoked with great power (ll. 57–63), and after his death the *Harrowing of Hell.

Visions 7 and 8. These *Passus* (XIX and XX) continue with the liturgical cycle begun in Lent in *Passus* XVI (l. 172) and show the attempts to put into practice the lessons gained from observing the saving actions of Christ. The attempts to perfect the Church are still frustrated by evildoers, as Piers Plowman had first been in *Passus* VI as he set out on his first pilgrimage, and the poem ends with Conscience setting out to find Piers, to lead the perfected search for salvation.

The strength of *Piers Plowman* does not lie in its structure or argument, both of which are often confusing and uncertain. The same crypticism that often results in sublimely imaginative poetry often blocks a literal understanding (as Rosemary Woolf says). But the passages of greatest imaginative power (such as those mentioned in *Passus* XI and XVIII, or the metaphor of 'the plant of peace' 1148–57) have a sublimity beyond the reach of any other medieval English writer.

The 'official' editions, based on all the manuscripts, are *Piers Plowman: The A Version*, ed. G. Kane (1960), *Piers Plowman: The B Version*, ed. G. Kane and E. T. Donaldson (1975), and *Piers Plowman: The C Version*,

ed. G. Russell and G. Kane (1997). The most useful editions are *The Vision of Piers Plowman: A Complete Edition of the B-Text*, ed. A. V. C. Schmidt (1978), and *Piers Plowman: An Edition of the C-Text*, ed. D. A. Pearsall (1978). Translation by Terence Tiller (1981).

Pierston, Jocelyn, a character in Hardy's *The Well-Beloved*.

Pigwiggin, a character in Drayton's *Nimphidia*.

Pilgrim's Progress, The, *from This World to That Which Is to Come*, a prose allegory by *Bunyan, Part I published 1678 (a second edition with additions appeared in the same year, and a third in 1679), Part II 1684.

The allegory takes the form of a dream by the author. In this he sees *Christian, with a burden on his back and reading in a book, from which he learns that the city in which he and his family dwell will be burned with fire. On the advice of Evangelist, Christian flees from the *City of Destruction, having failed to persuade his wife and children to accompany him. Pt I describes his pilgrimage through the *Slough of Despond, the Interpreter's House, the House Beautiful, the *Valley of Humiliation, the *Valley of the Shadow of Death, *Vanity Fair, *Doubting Castle, the *Delectable Mountains, the country of *Beulah, to the *Celestial City. On the way he encounters various allegorical personages, among them Mr *Worldly Wiseman, *Faithful (who accompanies Christian on his way but is put to death in Vanity Fair), Hopeful (who next joins Christian), Giant *Despair, the foul fiend *Apollyon, and many others.

Pt II relates how Christian's wife Christiana, moved by a vision, sets out with her children on the same pilgrimage, accompanied by her neighbour Mercy, despite the objections of Mrs Timorous and others. They are escorted by *Great-heart, who overcomes Giant Despair and other monsters and brings them to their destination. The work is a development of the Puritan conversion narrative (see GRACE ABOUNDING), drawing on popular literature such as *emblem books and *chapbooks, as well as *Foxe's *Book of Martyrs* and the Bible. It is remarkable for the beauty and simplicity of its language (Bunyan was permeated with the English of the Bible, though he was also a master of the colloquial English of his own time), the vividness and reality of the characterization, and the author's sense of humour and feeling for the world of nature. It circulated at first mainly in uneducated circles, and its wide appeal is shown by the fact that it has been translated into well over 100 languages. It became a children's classic, regarded by generations of parents as a manual of moral instruction and an aid to literacy, as well as a delightful tale. It was a seminal text in the development of the realistic novel, and Bunyan's humorously caustic development of the tradition of name symbolism influenced *Dickens, *Trollope, and *Thackeray.

PILKINGTON, Laetitia (?1709–50), Irish autobiographer and poet, the daughter of the distinguished Dublin physician John Van Lewen and successively a friend of J. *Swift, C. *Cibber, and S. *Richardson. She turned to verse, playwriting, autobiography, and miscellaneous ghost-writing when her father died unexpectedly poor in 1737 and her ambitious husband, the Revd Matthew Pilkington (below), promptly divorced her. Between 1739 and 1747, when she returned for good to Ireland, she lived in London supporting herself largely through Cibber and his circle of friends at White's. Appearing in stages between 1748 and 1754 after she returned to Dublin, her three-volume *Memoirs* incorporate a fragmentary tragedy and almost all her known poems. The unfinished last volume appeared posthumously in 1754, with a supplementary appendix by her son John Carteret Pilkington (1730–63). Celebrated for their vignettes of Swift as she knew him in private life, the *Memoirs* exhibit a breezy conversational style and a mastery of dialogue uncommon in narrative at so early a date. Ten years after her death John tried to repeat her success with *The Real Story of John Carteret Pilkington*, a *picaresque account of his boyhood travels after he escaped from the scullery of his father's house in 1740 or 1741 until 1744, a year or two before he was reunited with his mother in London. See *Memoirs of Laetitia Pilkington*, ed. A. C. Elias (2 vols, 1997).

PILKINGTON, Matthew (1701–74), Irish poet turned art historian. Educated at Trinity College, Dublin, and ordained in 1723, he began to publish verse as early as 1725. J. *Swift helped him to revise his collected *Poems on Several Occasions* (1730) and procured his appointment as chaplain to the lord mayor of London for 1732–3. In London Pilkington successfully passed off as Swift's one of his own satires, *An Infallible Scheme to Pay the Public Debt of This Nation in Six Months*, wrote a libellous short biography of the mayor, and apparently turned government informer when arrested for his part in publishing Swift's *Epistle to a Lady* (1734). Growing notoriety at home, where in 1738 he divorced his wife Laetitia (see above), seems to have cut short his literary career. By the mid-1750s he had re-emerged as a leading authority on Old Master paintings. In 1770 he published his classic reference work, *The Gentleman's and Connoisseur's Dictionary of Painters* which, periodically revised, expanded, and retitled, held its own for nearly a century.

Pills to Purge Melancholy, see D'URFEY.

Pimlyco, *or Runne Red-Cap*, a satirical pamphlet, published 1609, of unknown authorship, in which the poet describes a crowd of persons of all classes of society, from courtiers to 'greasie lownes', pressing towards Hogsden to drink Pimlico ale.

Pinch, Tom and Ruth, characters in Dickens's *Martin Chuzzlewit*.

Pinchwife, a character in Wycherley's *The Country Wife*.

PINDAR (*c.*522–443 BC), Greek lyric poet, the majority of whose surviving works are odes celebrating victories in the games at Olympia and elsewhere. Antiquity's most notable exponent of the Greater Ode, he served as an inspiration to all subsequent poets attempting this difficult genre. His compositions were elevated and formal, distinguished by the boldness of their metaphors and a marked reliance on myth and gnomic utterance. He used a framework of strophe, antistrophe, and epode which his imitators sought to copy, but in Pindar this framework rested on an elaborate prosodic structure that remained unknown until it was worked out by August Boeckh in his edition of the Odes (1811). The 17th- and 18th-cent. writers of Pindarics—*Cowley, *Dryden, *Pope, *Gray—employed a much looser prosodic system, so that their odes, although elevated and rich in metaphor, lack Pindar's architectural quality. See also ODE.

PINDAR, Peter, see WOLCOT.

Pindaric, see ODE.

PINERO, Sir Arthur Wing (1855–1934). He left school at 10 to work in his father's solicitor's practice, but, stage-struck from youth, became an actor, and was noticed by H. *Irving who later produced some of his plays. His first one-act play, *Two Hundred a Year*, performed in 1877, heralded a successful and prolific career. The first of his *farces, *The Magistrate* (perf. 1885), involves a series of ludicrous confusions between Mr Posket, the magistrate, and his family; it brought Pinero both fame and wealth. Later farces, such as *The School-Mistress* (1887), did nearly as well, as did his sentimental comedy *Sweet Lavender* (1888). His first serious play, on what was to be the recurrent theme of double standards for men and women, was *The Profligate* (1889); it was praised by *Archer, and noted not only for its frankness but also for its absence of the standard devices of soliloquy and aside. *Lady Bountiful* (1891) was the first of the 'social' plays in which Pinero was deemed to display his understanding of women. *The Second Mrs Tanqueray* (1893), returning to the theme of double standards, was a lasting success. *The Notorious Mrs Ebbsmith* (1895) again dealt with a woman's dubious past. *Trelawny of the 'Wells'* (1898), a sentimental comedy nostalgically recalling his own passion for the theatre he had haunted as a boy, also had great success. He continued to write, but, although knighted in 1909, lived through many years of dwindling reputation and disillusion, eclipsed by the rising popularity of the new theatre of *Ibsen and G. B. *Shaw.

PINKER, J. B., see AGENTS, LITERARY.

Pinkerton, the Misses, characters in Thackeray's *Vanity Fair*.

Pinner of Wakefield, the, see GEORGE-A'-GREEN.

PINTER, Harold (1930–   ), poet and playwright, born in east London, the son of a Jewish tailor, and educated at Hackney Downs Grammar School. He began to publish poetry in periodicals before he was 20, then became a professional actor, working mainly in repertory. His first play, *The Room*, was performed in Bristol in 1957, followed in 1958 by a London production of *The Birthday Party*, in which Stanley, an out-of-work pianist in a seaside boarding house, is mysteriously threatened and taken over by two intruders, an Irishman and a Jew, who present him with a Kafkaesque indictment of unexplained crimes. Pinter's distinctive voice was soon recognized, and many critical and commercial successes followed, including *The Caretaker* (1960), *The Lover* (1963), *The Homecoming* (1965), *Old Times* (1971), and *No Man's Land* (1975). *Betrayal* (1978; film, 1982) is an ironic tragedy which ends in beginning and traces in a reversed chronology the development of a love affair between a man and his best friend's wife. Later plays include *A Kind of Alaska* (1982), based on a work by O. *Sacks, *One for the Road* (1984), *Mountain Language* (1988), *Party Time* (1991), and *Ashes to Ashes* (1996, a short drama of the *Holocaust). Pinter's gift for portraying, by means of dialogue which realistically produces the nuances of colloquial speech, the difficulties of communication and the many layers of meaning in language, pause, and silence, have created a style labelled by the popular imagination as 'Pinteresque', and his themes—nameless menace, erotic fantasy, obsession and jealousy, family hatreds, and mental disturbance—are equally recognizable. Pinter has also written extensively for radio and television, directed plays, and written several screenplays, which include versions of L. P. *Hartley's *The Go-Between* (1969), and J. *Fowles's *The French Lieutenant's Woman* (1982). *Poems and Prose, 1947–1977* was published in 1978. See *The Life and Work of Harold Pinter* (1996) by Michael Billington. He was awarded the *Nobel Prize in 2005.

PINTO, Fernão Mendes (?1509–83), a Portuguese traveller in the East, who left a narrative of his voyages (*Peregrinação*, 1614), marked by a vivid imagination. It was translated by Henry Cogan (1653). *Cervantes calls him the 'Prince of Liars', and Congreve in *Love for Love* (II. i) couples his name with that of *Mandeville when describing a 'Lyar of the first Magnitude'.

PIOZZI, Mrs, see THRALE.

Pip, in Dickens's *Great Expectations*, the name by which the hero, Philip Pirrip, is commonly known.

Pipchin, Mrs, in Dickens's *Dombey and Son*, a boarding-house keeper in Brighton.

Pippa Passes, by R. *Browning, published 1841 as No. I of the series *Bells and Pomegranates*. Although subtitled 'A Drama', it was not written for the stage. In its final version it consists of an 'Introduction', in verse and four parts, entitled 'Morning', 'Noon', 'Evening', and 'Night'. The first two parts have a verse section followed by one in prose; the third part has two verse sections; the fourth part has a prose section followed by one in verse. (This combination of verse and prose was influenced by Browning's study of Elizabethan and Jacobean drama; see also SOUL'S TRAGEDY, A.)

The play is set in and around Asolo, a small town near Venice which Browning visited in 1838 (see ASOLANDO). The plot is a web of dramatic ironies. The Introduction shows Pippa, a young silk-worker, waking up on the morning of her annual holiday. She contrasts the life of 'Asolo's Four Happiest Ones' with her own, and decides to 'pass' by them all in the course of the day. These four constitute an ascending scale of value, from carnal love (Ottima, wife of a rich silk merchant, and her lover Sebald), through married love (Jules, a sculptor, and his bride), filial love (the young patriot Luigi and his mother), reaching at last the love of God (the good bishop). Each life turns out to be different from Pippa's imagining of it, though she herself does not realize this. Ottima and Sebald are quarrelling after their murder of Ottima's husband; Jules's bride turns out not to be the cultivated patrician he thought her, but an ignorant peasant girl; Luigi and his mother are disputing over his intention to carry out a political assassination; and the bishop is negotiating with a corrupt official about the destruction of Pippa herself, who turns out to be his own lost niece, heiress to a fortune he might otherwise appropriate. Pippa 'passes' by each of the four main scenes in turn, singing as she goes; each song, ironically juxtaposed with the action, effects a moral revolution in the characters concerned. (The famous concluding lines of Pippa's first song, 'God's in his heaven—All's right with the world!', are often quoted out of context as evidence of Browning's own naïve optimism.) At the end of the drama we see Pippa back in her room at nightfall, unaware of the day's events. The focus of modern criticism is the ambivalent moral and aesthetic value of Pippa's 'innocence', a theme repeated in the figure of Pompilia in *The Ring and the Book.

PIRANDELLO, Luigi (1867–1936), Italian dramatist, short story writer, and novelist, awarded the *Nobel Prize in 1934. He exercised a pervasive influence on European drama by challenging the conventions of *naturalism. Among his plays, ten of which he published as *Maschere nude* (*Naked Masks*, 1918–22), the best known are: *Così è* (*se vi pare*) (*Right You Are, If You Think You Are*, 1917), *Sei personaggi in cerca di autore* (*Six Characters in Search of an Author*, 1921), and *Enrico IV* (*Henry IV*, 1922). In these plays he anticipated the anti-illusionist theatre of *Brecht, *Wilder, and *Weiss; his exploration of the disintegration of personality foreshadowed *Beckett; his probing of the conflict between reality and appearance has echoes in the work of *O'Neill; and his examination of the relationship between self and persona, actor and character, face and mask, is a precursor of the work of *Anouilh, *Giraudoux, and *Genet. Yet much of Pirandello's best work is to be found in his very short stories (28 of which were dramatized), where themes in common with his plays are more deeply explored. His main full-length novels are: *L'esclusa* (*The Outcast*, 1901), which deals with a woman's desire for independence within patriarchal Sicilian society; *Il fu Mattia Pascal* (*The Late Mattia Pascal*, 1904), where Pascal goes home to discover it is impossible to alter his status as 'deceased'; and *I vecchi e i giovani* (*The Old and The Young*, 1909), dealing with the effects of the unification of Italy on Sicily at the turn of the century.

PIRANESI, Giovanni Battista (1720–78), an Italian architect, who published many dramatic etchings of the ruins of classical Rome. In literary circles Piranesi is most famous for the *Carceri d'invenzione* (c.1745; rev. edn c.1761), dark visions of Roman prisons where chains and instruments of torture swing before massive arches, and isolated figures wander aimlessly along stairs, ladders, and bridges that lead nowhere. Before his death his works were already popular in England, where they were associated with the Burkeian *sublime; Horace *Walpole wrote of 'the sublime dreams of Piranesi . . . He piles palaces on bridges, and temples on palaces, and scales Heaven with mountains of edifices'; *The Castle of Otranto* perhaps shows this influence. Piranesi's deepest influence was on the Romantics. In *Confessions of an English Opium Eater* (1821) De Quincey compared Piranesi's prisons with the illusions induced by opium: 'With the same power of endless growth and self-reproduction did my architecture proceed in dreams.' Curiously, he had not seen the etchings but had listened to *Coleridge's description of a print showing Piranesi groping up endless flights of stairs. This passage became famous in France, where *Musset, *Gautier, and *Hugo were fascinated by Piranesi. Later Piranesi appealed to writers who saw the *Carceri* as symbolizing metaphysical despair.

Pirate, The, a novel by Sir W. *Scott, published 1821. Set in 17th-cent. Shetland, the plot deals with the tension between long-established tradition and new ideas brought into a closed community by outsiders. Mordaunt Mertoun, though the son of an outsider, has been reared in Shetland, and occupies a half-way house between tradition and common sense, familiar to many of Scott's heroes. The heroines, Minna and Brenda Troil, embody an equally familiar contrast between romance and realism. Fantasy is supplied by the half-crazed seer Norna of the Fitful Head, whose machinations control the plot.

Pisanio, in Shakespeare's *Cymbeline*, the servant *Posthumus leaves to *Imogen's service when he is banished.

Pistol, Ancient or Ensign, in Shakespeare's 2 *Henry IV*, *Henry V*, and *The Merry Wives of Windsor*, one of Falstaff's associates, a braggart with a fine command of bombastic language.

Pistyl of Susan (or *The Pistel of Swete Susan*), meaning 'the epistle of Susanna', a northern alliterative poem, c.1350–60, in 364 lines of 13-line tail-rhyme stanzas, telling the story of Susanna and the Elders (Dan. 13). Up to recently, though no longer, scholars accepted the attribution of the work to *Huchown made in the *Orygynale Cronykil* (c.1420) of Andrew of *Wyntoun. Ed. H. Koster, *Huchown's Pistel of Swete Susan* (*Quellen und Forschungen* LXXVI, 1895).

PITT, William, first earl of Chatham (1708–78), a great Whig statesman and orator, who entered Parliament in 1735. He was secretary of state in 1765–7, but his fame as a great administrator rests on the period that immediately followed, when Pitt and Newcastle were the chief ministers in the coalition. He strenuously opposed from 1774 onwards the harsh measures taken against the American colonies, though unwilling to recognize their independence. His speeches were marked by lofty and impassioned eloquence and, judged by their effect on their hearers, place him among the greatest orators, but only fragments have survived.

PITT, William, 'the Younger' (1759–1806), second son of the first earl of Chatham. He became chancellor of the exchequer in his 22nd year and prime minister in 1783 in his 25th year, and retained the position until 1801. He returned to office in 1804, formed the third coalition, and died shortly after the battle of Austerlitz.

PITT-KETHLEY, (Helen) Fiona (1954–   ), poet, travel writer, novelist, and journalist, best known for her outspoken writing about sex. Her satirical poetry collections include *Sky Ray Lolly* (1986), *Private Parts* (1987), *The Perfect Man* (1989), *Dogs* (1996), and her travel books are *Journeys to the Underworld* (1988) and *The Pan Principle* (1994). She has also produced an anthology with some of her own translations from Latin, Greek, Italian, and French, *The Literary Companion to Sex* (1992), and essays on red light districts around the world. She is married to the grandmaster and former British chess champion James Plaskett.

Pizarro, a tragedy adapted by *Sheridan from a German play by *Kotzebue, on the Spanish conqueror of Peru (1471–1541).

Plagiary, Sir Fretful, a character in Sheridan's *The Critic*, a caricature of R. *Cumberland.

Plague Year, A Journal of the, a historical fiction by *Defoe, published 1722.

It purports to be the narrative of a resident in London during 1664–5, the year of the Great Plague; the initials 'H.F.' which conclude it have been taken to refer to Defoe's uncle Henry Foe, a saddler, from whom the author may have heard some of the details he describes. It tells of the gradual spread of the plague, the terror of the inhabitants, and the steps taken by the authorities, such as the shutting up of infected houses and the prohibition of public gatherings. The symptoms of the disease, the circulation of the dead-carts, the burials in mass graves, and the terrible scenes witnessed by the supposed narrator are described with extraordinary vividness. The general effects of the epidemic, notably in the closing down of trading and the flight from the city, are also related, and an estimate of the total number of deaths is made. *The Journal* embodied information from various sources, including official documents; some scenes appear to have been borrowed from *Dekker's *The Wonderfull Yeare* (1603). Defoe's subject was suggested by fears of another outbreak, following the one in Marseilles in 1721 which occasioned Sir R. *Walpole's unpopular Quarantine Act. *Hazlitt ascribed to the work 'an epic grandeur, as well as heart-breaking familiarity'.

Plain-Dealer, The, a comedy by *Wycherley, probably performed 1676, published 1677. It was highly praised by *Dryden and *Dennis, though from the start it was criticized for obscenity, and in the 18th cent. was performed in a version bowdlerized by *Bickerstaffe.

It is loosely based on *Molière's *Le Misanthrope*; Wycherley's hero Manly, an honest misanthropic sea-captain (from whom the playwright took the nickname 'Manly' Wycherley), corresponds to Molière's Alceste, and his treacherous, worldly beloved Olivia to Célimène. Manly, returned from the Dutch wars, has lost faith in all but Olivia, to whom he has confided his money, and his friend Vernish: he finds Olivia married to Vernish, and faithless even to him. Manly is beloved by Fidelia, a young woman who has followed him to sea in man's clothes; she intercedes with Olivia on his behalf, in a scene reminiscent of the Olivia–Viola scene in *Twelfth Night*, is discovered by Vernish, who attempts to rape her, and is finally wounded in an attempt to defend Manly from Vernish. Manly forswears Olivia and pledges himself to Fidelia. There is a sub-plot in which the litigious widow Blackacre, who has a passion for legal jargon, trains up her son Jerry (a literary ancestor of Tony Lumpkin in *She Stoops to Conquer*) in her footsteps, and thereby overreaches herself.

The *Plain Dealer* is also the name of a periodical established by A. *Hill.

Plain Speaker, The, a volume of essays by W. *Hazlitt, published in 1826, the last such collection to appear before his death. The title fittingly captures his gift for forthright assertion and invective. The collection includes several of his finest pieces, such as 'On Dreams' ('We are not hypocrites in our sleep') and 'On the Pleasures of Hating', which concludes with Hazlitt's self-description as 'the dupe of friendship, and the fool of love'.

PLANCHÉ, James Robinson (1796–1880), prolific dramatist of Huguenot descent. Besides his many original pieces for the stage, mainly burlesques and extravaganzas, he made translations and adaptations from French, Spanish, and Italian authors, including *fairy tales by the Countess d'Aulnoy (1855) and by *Perrault (1858). His stage works include *The Vampyre; or The Bride of the Isles* (1820), an adaptation of a French melodrama which introduced the 'vampire' trap to the English stage, and *The Island of Jewels* (1849). He wrote several opera librettos including *Maid Marian* (1822) adapted from a tale by *Peacock, *Weber's *Oberon* (1826), and English versions of *William Tell* and *The Magic Flute*. Planché also made a reputation as an antiquary and a scholar of heraldry and costume; his *History of British Costumes* (1834) long remained a standard work; he also published an edition of Strutt's *Regal and Ecclesiastical Antiquities of England* (1842). He was appointed Somerset herald in 1866.

Plantagenet Palliser, see OMNIUM, DUKE OF.

PLATER, Alan (1935–), writer, born in Jarrow and educated at Kingston High School, Hull, and King's College, Newcastle upon Tyne. After contributing many episodes to BBC TV's *Z Cars* and its sequel *Softly Softly* in the 1960s, several stage plays followed: the moving *Close the Coalhouse Door* (1972, from a story by ex-miner and novelist Sid Chaplin) heralded the effects of pit closures upon regional communities. Life in the north-east, sport, and jazz feature in his considerable television output, the first predominant in *Seventeen Per Cent Said Push Off* (1972) and *The Land of Green Ginger* (1974), Rugby League featuring in *Trinity Tales* (1975, a 'Chaucerian' pilgrimage of supporters to a cup final) and the recordings of cornet-player Bix Beiderbecke inspiring *The Beiderbecke Affair* (1985). His adaptations for the small screen include A. *Trollope's *Barchester Chronicles* (1982) and O. *Manning's *The Fortunes of War* (1987) (from her *Balkan Trilogy*). *All Credit to the Lads* (1998) is a stage play about football.

PLATH, Sylvia (1932–63), poet and novelist, born in Boston, Massachusetts, the daughter of a German immigrant professor and entomologist, who died when she was 8. She was educated at Smith College, Massachusetts, and Newnham College, Cambridge. She married Ted *Hughes in 1956. After teaching for a while in America, she and Hughes returned to England in 1959, where they lived in London before moving to Devon in 1961. Her first volume of poetry, *The Colossus*, appeared in 1960, and in 1963 her only novel *The Bell Jar*. Less than a month after its publication, in the coldest February for many years, she committed suicide in London. In 1965 appeared her best-known collection, *Ariel*, which established her reputation with its courageous and controlled treatment of extreme and painful states of mind. Much of her symbolism was deeply rooted in actuality; the poems on bee-keeping ('The Bee Meeting', 'The Arrival of the Bee Box', etc.) are based on her own attempts to keep bees in Devon, and other poems—'Elm', 'Letter in November', 'The Moon and the Yew Tree'—describe the physical surroundings of the house and the views from it. Other poems refer directly to her own experiences: 'Lady Lazarus' is based on her two previous suicide attempts, 'Daddy' on the early loss of her father, 'Tulips' on a week spent in hospital undergoing an appendectomy: in the first of these two she uses powerful imagery drawn from the *Holocaust, though she was not herself Jewish. Other posthumous volumes include *Crossing the Water* and *Winter Trees* (both 1971); *Johnny Panic and the Bible of Dreams* (1977, collected prose pieces); and *Collected Poems* (1981, with an introduction by T. Hughes). A volume of letters, *Letters Home*, edited by her mother, A. S. Plath, with a commentary, appeared in 1975. Although her best-known poems deal with illness, suffering, and death, others (particularly those addressed to her two children, such as 'Morning Song' and 'You're') are exhilarating, tender, and affectionate, and her tone is frequently witty as well as disturbing. There is a biography, *Bitter Fame*, by the poet Anne *Stevenson (1989), written with the approval of the Plath estate.

PLATO (*c*.428/7–*c*.348/7 BC), Greek philosopher, eminent for the profundity of his thought, the number of his surviving writings, and the extent of his influence. Born in Athens of an aristocratic family, he was a friend and admirer of *Socrates, after whose death in 399 BC he went into exile; he returned to Athens in the 380s and set up a school which was then or at a later stage known as the Academy. The majority of his works are in dialogue form and may have been intended for public performance or for performance to a select audience of pupils. The principal speaker is nearly always Socrates, but it is impossible to say how close Plato's 'Socrates' stands to the real man either in character or in his teaching. The dialogues fall roughly into three groups. About a dozen demonstrate what has been called the Socratic Method. Socrates plies his interlocutors with a chain of questions, and their replies trap them into self-contradiction. These dialogues, the best known of which are the *Ion*, *Euthyphro*, *Protagoras*, and *Gorgias*, are considered Plato's earliest work. The second group includes the *Crito*, *Apology*, *Phaedo*, *Symposium*; these do not employ the Socratic Method and are considered to have been written between 371 and 367 BC. Finally, the profound and technically subtle dialogues such as the *Theaetetus*, *Parmenides*, *Timaeus*, *Sophistes*, *Philebus* are the products of Plato's old age. There are also two monumental treatises, *The Republic* and *The Laws*, which were probably compiled over a period, *The Laws* being the later.

Plato's ideas have had a lasting appeal for philosophers, and some of them also caught the popular imagination. Notable among these were: (1) the Theory of Forms which is best illustrated by an example. The concept 'cat' is derived from our knowledge of particular cats. Plato held that concepts of this nature have a real existence outside the world of sense, and this belief served to reinforce men's hope that there existed an eternal order. (2) The project of establishing philosopher-kings which produced a multitude of schemes for the education of princes. (3) *Platonic love, a devotion inspired by the best qualities of the beloved and aiming at their further development, was formulated originally by Plato in the context of a homosexual relationship, but by the 16th cent. it was applied to a heterosexual love that could rise above sexual desire.

Plato has played a markedly vitalizing role in the history of European thought. Through *Augustine he came to exercise a formative influence on Christianity. Through the Florentine Platonists of the 15th cent. he made a manifold impact on art and ideas in the major countries of Europe. It is impossible, however, to separate Plato's direct from his indirect influence. Platonic themes appear in many writers—*Spenser, *Chapman, *Donne, *Marvell, and later *Wordsworth, *Bridges—the extent of whose reading of Plato must remain in doubt, as well as in the work of his attested students such as the *Cambridge Platonists, *Milton, *Gray, *Shelley, E. B. *Browning, M. *Arnold, and *Pater. But what we find in all these cases are just generalities that could have issued from a Christian or *Neoplatonist source as surely as from a reading of Plato himself.

platonic love, now used to mean love of a purely spiritual character, free from sensual desire. *Amor Platonicus* was used by *Ficino synonymously with *Amor Socraticus* to denote the kind of interest in young men which was imputed to Socrates; cf. the last few pages of Plato's *Symposium*. As thus originally used it had no reference to women, but by the 16th cent. it was extended to include heterosexual love that rose above sensual desire (see e.g. CASTIGLIONE). The ennobling and idealizing aspects of the homosexual Platonic concept appear in many English writers, however, particularly towards the end of the 19th and the beginning of the 20th cents; the 'love that dared not speak its name' appeared frequently in a pagan-Hellenic context, consciously or subconsciously, in the works of *Pater, J. A. *Symonds, F. *Reid, E. M. *Forster, and many others.

Platonists, Cambridge, see CAMBRIDGE PLATONISTS.

PLATONOV, Andrei Platonovich (A. P. Klimentov) (1899–1951), Russian prose writer. He was born in Voronezh in central Russia and from the age of 13 had various manual jobs. He fought for the Bolsheviks in the Civil War and then qualified as an engineer. In 1927 he gave up his job to devote himself to literature. His first collection of stories, *The Epifan Locks*, appeared in 1927. During 1928–30 he wrote his most important works, *Chevengur*, which relates with bitter irony the tale of a group of proletarians who dream of building a communist utopia and choose the steppe town of Chevengur for their experiment, and *Kotlovan* (*The Foundation Pit*), in which the inhabitants of a village plan to build a house for communal living but get no further than the enormous foundation pit. Both these works have now been published abroad (1972, 1968) and translated into English (1978, 1973), but they did not appear in the Soviet Union. The publication of his story 'For Future Use: A Poor Farmhand's Chronicle' (1931) led to accusations of 'kulak tendencies' and a ban on his work till 1936, and he was again in disfavour from 1946 until his death. He began to be published again in 1958.

PLAUTUS, Titus Maccius (*c.*254–184 BC), early Roman dramatist who adapted the Greek New Comedy for the Roman stage. The extent of his originality remains uncertain. He does not seem to have translated exactly, but he certainly worked within the Greek convention using the same stock characters—miserly fathers, spendthrift sons, boastful soldiers, resourceful parasites, courtesans, and slaves—and often borrowing the plots of his Greek models. Twenty of his plays have survived, and it was from him and from his successor *Terence that Europe learned about ancient comedy. His direct influence on English literature is slight, though Udall was indebted to him in *Ralph Roister Doister*, Shakespeare adapted his *Menaechmi* in *The Comedy of Errors*, Jonson conflated the *Captivi* and the *Aulularia* in *The Case Is Altered*, and Dryden adapted his *Amphitryon*; but the tradition he represented is responsible for the form taken by English comedy up to the 19th cent.

Playboy of the Western World, The, a comedy by *Synge, performed and published 1907.

Christy Mahon, 'a slight young man, very tired and frightened', arrives at a village in Mayo. He gives out that he is a fugitive from justice, who in a quarrel has killed his bullying father, splitting him to the chin with a single blow. He is hospitably entertained, and his character as a dare-devil gives him a great advantage with the women (notably Pegeen Mike and Widow Quin) over the milder-spirited lads of the place. But admiration gives place to angry contempt when the father himself arrives in pursuit of the fugitive, who has merely given him a crack on the head and run away. The implication that Irish peasants would condone a murder and the frankness of some of the language (Christy speaks of 'all the girls in Mayo . . . standing before me in their shifts') caused outrage and riots when the play was first performed at the *Abbey Theatre. In his preface, Synge compares the 'joyless and pallid' language of the naturalistic theatre of *Ibsen with the 'rich and living' imagination and language of the Irish people, and this play is his best-known effort to fuse the language of ordinary people with a dramatic rhetoric of his own making.

Pleasant Satyre of the Thrie Estaitis, Ane, in *Commendatioun of Vertew and Vituperatioun of Vyce*, a morality play by Sir D. *Lindsay, produced 1540.

Pt I represents the temptation of Rex Humanitas by Sensuality, Wantonness, Solace, and other evil companions, while Good Counsel is hustled away, Verity is put in the stocks, and Chastity is warned off. An interlude follows in which are described the adventures of Chastity among humbler folks, a tailor, a soutar, and their wives. Then Chastity is put in the stocks. But the arrival of Correction alters the situation. Verity, Good Counsel, and Chastity are admitted to the king, and Sensuality is banished.

After an interlude in which an impoverished farmer exposes his sufferings at the hands of the ecclesiastics and a pardoner's trade is ridiculed, Pt II presents the Three Estates summoned before the king, and their misdeeds denounced by John the Common Weal. The Lords and Commons repent, but the clergy remain impenitent, are exposed, and the malefactors brought to the scaffold.

The play, which is extremely long and exists in three different versions, is written in various metres, eight- and six-lined stanzas and couplets. It is, as a dramatic representation, in advance of all contemporary English plays, and gives an interesting picture of the Scottish life of the time.

Pleasures of Hope, The, a poem by T. *Campbell published 1799.

In Pt I the poet considers the consolation and inspiration of Hope and by contrast the hard fate of a people deprived of it, described in a passage on the downfall of Poland. In Pt II he reflects on Love in combination with Hope, and on the belief in a future life.

Pleasures of Imagination, The, a philosophical poem by *Akenside, published 1744; it was completely rewritten and issued as *The Pleasures of the Imagination* in 1757.

The poem is based on the philosophical and aesthetic doctrines and distinctions of *Addison, *Shaftesbury, and *Hutcheson; *Gray found it 'too much infected with the Hutchesonian jargon'. It examines the primary and secondary pleasures of the imagination, the first connected with the *sublime, the wonderful, and the beautiful, the second with passion and sense. Akenside's speculations, which many found obscure (and Dr *Johnson 'loquacious'), range from Platonic theories of form and essence to I. *Newton's account of the rainbow. Mrs *Barbauld in her 1794 edition gives a sympathetic and useful interpretation.

Pleasures of Memory, The, see ROGERS, S.

Pléiade, la, a group of seven French writers of the 16th cent., led by *Ronsard. The name, deriving ultimately from the seven stars of the constellation of the Pleiades, had originally been applied by Alexandrian critics to a group of seven poets from the reign of Ptolemy II.

Ronsard's use of the term dates from 1556. The other members of the group were *du Bellay, Pontus de Tyard, Jean-Antoine de Baïf, Étienne Jodelle, Remi Belleau, and either Peletier du Mans or, according to some authorities, Jean Dorat. The group, inspired by a common interest in the literatures of antiquity and of the Italian Renaissance, sought to promote the claims of the French language to a comparably dignified status as a medium for literary expression, and their aims were set forth in du Bellay's *Deffence et illustration de la langue françoyse* of 1549. The Pléiade were largely responsible for the acclimatization of the sonnet form in France, and for the establishment of the alexandrine as the dominant metrical form for much later French poetry. Indeed, the group did much, in ways both formal and intuitive, to create the conditions for the emergence of modern poetry in France.

pleonasm, a rhetorical figure characterized by the use of superfluous words, as in 'I saw the wound, I saw it with mine eyes' (*Romeo and Juliet*, III. ii. 52) or 'Th'inaudible and noiseless foot of time' (*All's Well that Ends Well*, V. iii. 41).

Pliable, in Bunyan's *Pilgrim's Progress*, one of *Christian's companions, who turns back at the *Slough of Despond.

Pliant, Dame, the rich widow in Jonson's *The Alchemist*.

PLINY THE ELDER (Gaius Plinius Secundus) (AD 23–79), Roman compiler of a *Natural History*, which is an encyclopaedic rag-bag of popular science. Widely read in the Middle Ages, it provided a cosmology for *Du Bartas's *La Semaine, ou création du monde* (1578), which *Sylvester's translation established for the 17th cent. as an English classic. The *Natural History* was translated by Philemon *Holland in 1601.

PLINY THE YOUNGER (Gaius Plinius Caecilius Secundus) (AD 62–c.112), Roman letter writer, nephew of the above. The vogue for letter writing in the 1690s led to the translation of some of his correspondence, and William Melmoth produced a full but inaccurate version in 1746. Pliny was a more formal writer than *Cicero, and is remembered mainly for his description of the eruption of Vesuvius and his official correspondence with Trajan.

PLOMER, William Charles Franklyn (1903–73), poet and novelist, was born in Pietersberg, S. Africa, of British parents, and several of his works, including his first novel, the savagely satirical *Turbott Wolfe*, published in 1926 by the *Hogarth Press, are portraits of South African life. In 1926, with R. *Campbell, he founded a magazine, *Voorslag* (Whiplash); they were joined in the enterprise by L. *van der Post. Plomer then spent some two years teaching in Japan, an experience reflected in his poems, in *Paper Houses* (1929, stories), and in *Sado* (a novel, 1931). He came to

England in 1929 and settled in Bloomsbury, where he was befriended by L. and V. *Woolf, and in 1937 succeeded E. *Garnett as principal reader to Jonathan Cape. His first volume of poetry, *Notes for Poems* (1927), was followed by several others, and his *Collected Poems* appeared in 1973. His poems are largely satirical and urbane, with a sharp eye for character and social setting; many of them, like the title piece of *The Dorking Thigh* (1945), are modern ballads with a macabre touch. His edition of *Kilvert's *Diary* appeared in three volumes, 1938–40. He wrote the librettos for several of *Britten's operas, including *Gloriana*, which is based on L. *Strachey's *Elizabeth and Essex*.

Plornish, Mr and Mrs, in Dickens's *Little Dorrit*, a plasterer and his wife who lived in Bleeding Heart Yard. Mrs Plornish was a notable interpreter of the Italian language.

PLOTINUS (AD c.203–62), Greek philosopher, the chief exponent of *Neoplatonism. His *Enneads* did much to shape Christian theology in the 4th cent. and also exercised a wide influence on Renaissance thought through *Ficino's translation (1492). They were studied by the *Cambridge Platonists. The concept of the Chain of Being which Plotinus elaborated was generally accepted until the end of the 18th cent., as was the principle, which *Sidney learnt from *Scaliger, that a poet is a second creator, Art reascending to the Ideas from which Nature is derived.

Plough and the Stars, The, see O'CASEY.

Plough Monday play, a folk drama of the east Midlands, surviving in versions from Cropwell in Nottinghamshire and from Lincolnshire. Like the St George play, the Plough Monday play probably symbolizes in its central incident the death and resurrection of the year. See E. K. *Chambers, *The Mediaeval Stage* (2 vols, 1903) and *The English Folk-Play* (1933).

Plowman's Tale, The, an early 15th-cent. poem in 1,380 lines of eight-line stanzas rhyming on alternate lines, of Wycliffite sympathies. It was (improbably, on stylistic grounds) attributed to *Chaucer and included in earlier editions of his works. It was relegated by Skeat to the seventh volume of his *Works of Geoffrey Chaucer* (1897), amongst the 'Chaucerian and other Pieces', and its text is still to be found there.

Plume, Captain, a character in Farquhar's *The Recruiting Officer*.

Plumed Serpent, The, a novel by D. H. *Lawrence, published 1926.

Kate Leslie, an Irish widow of 40, weary of Europe, arrives in Mexico at a turning point in her life. She has had lovers and children, and loved her husband Joachim 'to the bounds of human love'. The theme of the novel is Kate's struggle for deliverance, for a mystical rebirth. She meets and is drawn to General

Don Cipriano Viedma, who introduces her to Don Ramón Carrasco, a mystic and revolutionary leader, reviver of the cult of the ancient god Quetzalcoatl, the plumed serpent. The book contains scenes of violent Aztec 'blood-lust' (Cipriano ceremoniously stabbing half-naked prisoners, the drinking of the victims' blood); Kate, though repelled, is fascinated by the darkness and elemental power of Mexico and its people, and herself enters the cult as the fertility goddess Malintzi and the bride of Cipriano. The novel ends with her acceptance of the subjugation and loss-of-self demanded of her by Cipriano and her hopes for fulfilment. This is the Lawrence of 'dark gods' and 'phallic power', containing besides much of his usual vivid descriptive writing.

Plurabelle, Anna Livia, a character in Joyce's *Finnegans Wake*, and also the title of a section of the novel published as 'Work in Progress' (1928), with an introduction by P. *Colum.

PLUTARCH (AD *c*.50–*c*.125), biographer and moralist, the most popular of Greek authors at the time of the Renaissance. His *Parallel Lives* exemplified the tradition of biography associated with the Peripatetic school, illustrating the moral character of his subjects through a series of anecdotes. Translated by T. *North (1579), they served as a source-book for Shakespeare's Roman plays and later for *Otway's *Caius Marius* and Addison's *Cato*. They also served as a model for I. *Walton's *Lives* (1670). Sir T. *Browne gave them to his sons to read, *Dryden gave a pioneer analysis of their style and structure in his *Life of Plutarch* (1683), and in America the Founding Fathers turned to them for models of republican virtue.

The *Moral Essays* provide a compendium of ancient wisdom on a variety of topics: moral philosophy, religious belief, education, health, literary criticism, and social customs. Individual essays were translated into English during the 16th cent., including the probably pseudonymous love stories (by James Sanford, 1567), and material from Plutarch's Morals can be found in a number of Elizabethan authors: *Elyot, *Painter, *Lyly, Thomas Fenne, *Meres, Sir Thomas Cornwallis the younger, *Chapman. The first complete version in English, by *Holland, appeared in 1603, when its popularity was enhanced by the almost simultaneous publication of *Florio's translation of *Montaigne, for the latter cites Plutarch on nearly every page. After the middle years of the 17th cent., when they were read by Jeremy *Taylor and *Milton, the popularity of the *Moral Essays* declined. By then there were more recent examples of the genre with which they could not compete. (See also BIOGRAPHY.)

Plymley, Letters of Peter, by Sydney *Smith, published 1807-8.

The letters purport to be written by Peter Plymley to his brother in the country, the Revd Abraham Plymley ('a bit of a goose'), in favour of Catholic emancipation. The arguments, both serious and absurd, of the Revd Abraham for maintaining the disabilities of the Catholics are taken one by one, and demolished with sense, wit, and humour; while at the same time the author makes his own Anglican position plain, and ridicules the 'nonsense' of the Roman Catholic Church.

POCAHONTAS, or **MATOAKA** (1595–1617), a Native American princess, the daughter of Powhattan, a chief in Virginia. According to Capt. John *Smith, one of the Virginia colonists who had been taken prisoner by the Native Americans, he was rescued by her when her father was about to kill him in 1607 (she was then only 12). In 1612 she was seized as a hostage by the colonists for the good behaviour of the indigenous tribes (or for the restitution of English captives), became a Christian, was named Rebecca, and married a colonist, John Rolfe. She was brought to England in 1616, where she at first attracted considerable attention, but died neglected. Those who claim descent from her are legion. She is introduced by Jonson in his *The Staple of News*, II. i. George Warrington in Thackeray's *The Virginians* composes a tragedy on her, and she becomes a national symbol in H. *Crane's *The Bridge* (1930).

Pocket, Herbert, a character in Dickens's *Great Expectations*.

Podsnap, Mr, a character in Dickens's *Our Mutual Friend*, a type of self-satisfaction and self-importance.

POE, Edgar Allan (1809–49), born in Boston, Massachusetts, the son of itinerant actors. He became an orphan in early childhood, and was taken into the household of John Allan, a tobacco exporter of Richmond; he took his foster-father's name as his middle name from 1824 onwards. He came to England with the Allans (1815–20) and attended Manor House school at Stoke Newington (which he describes, in an imaginative manner but with some accurate detail, in his *Doppelgänger* story 'William Wilson', 1839); he spent a year at the University of Virginia, which he left after incurring debts and gambling to relieve them. He published his first volume of verse, *Tamerlane and Other Poems* (1827), anonymously and at his own expense; then enlisted in the US army under the name of Edgar A. Perry. He was sent to Sullivan's Island, South Carolina, which provided settings for 'The Gold Bug' (1843) and 'The Balloon Hoax' (1844). Allan (from whom he had been estranged) procured his discharge from the army, and he entered West Point in 1830, having published a second volume of verse, *Al Aaraaf* (1829); he was dishonourably discharged in 1831, for intentional neglect of his duties, and published a third volume of *Poems* (containing 'To Helen') in the same year. He now turned to journalism, living from 1831 to 1835 with a relative, Mrs Clemm, in Baltimore, whose 13-year-old daughter, his cousin Virginia, he married in 1836. He worked as editor on various papers, including the *Southern Literary Messenger*, and began to publish his stories in magazines. His first collection, *Tales of the Grotesque and Arabesque* (1839, for 1840), contains one of his most famous works, 'The Fall of the House of Usher', a *Gothic romance in which the narrator visits the crumbling mansion of his childhood companion, Roderick Usher, to find both Usher and his twin sister Madeline in the last stages of mental and physical weakness; Madeline is buried alive while in a trance, arises, and carries her brother to death 'in her violent and now final death agonies', whereupon the house itself splits asunder and sinks into the tarn. In 1845 his poem 'The Raven', published in a New York paper and then as the title poem of *The Raven and Other Poems* (1845), brought him fame, but not security; he and his ménage continued to suffer poverty and ill health, his wife dying in 1847 and he himself struggling with alcohol addiction and nervous instability. His end was characteristically tragic; he died in Baltimore, five days after having been found semi-conscious and delirious, from alcohol, heart failure, epilepsy, or a combination of these. His posthumous reputation and influence have been great; he was much admired by *Baudelaire, who translated many of his works, and in Britain by *Swinburne, *Wilde, *Rossetti, and *Yeats. *Freudian critics (and Freud himself) have been intrigued by the macabre and pathological elements in his work, ranging from hints of necrophilia in his poem 'Annabel Lee' (1849) to the indulgent sadism of 'The Pit and the Pendulum' (1843); *Existentialism has been detected in the motiveless obsession in such stories as 'The Cask of Amontillado' (1846). *Borges, R. L. *Stevenson, and a vast general readership have been impressed by the cryptograms and mysteries of the stories which feature Poe's detective Dupin ('The Murders in the Rue Morgue', 1841; 'The Purloined Letter', 1845) and the morbid metaphysical speculation of 'The Facts in the Case of M. Waldemar' (1845). His critical writings include 'The Philosophy of Composition' (1846, which includes the statement: 'The death of a beautiful woman is, unquestionably, the most poetical topic in the world') and 'The Poetic Principle' (1850, originally a lecture) which preaches a form of *art for art's sake.

Poema Morale (or 'The Moral Ode'), a southern poem in early Middle English of about 400 lines, surviving in seven manuscripts, and dating from *c*.1175. It is a vigorous work on the themes of transience and repentance, and is very early in the Middle English period after the transition from Old English. Ed. in J. Hall, *Selections from Early Middle English* (1920).

Poetaster, a comedy by *Jonson, performed by the Children of the Queen's Chapel 1601, printed 1602.
Set in the court of the Emperor Augustus, the main plot concerns the conspiracy of the poetaster Crispinus and his friend Demetrius (who represent Jonson's contemporaries *Marston and *Dekker) and a swaggering captain, Pantilius Tucca, to defame Horace, who represents Jonson. The matter is tried before Augustus,

with Virgil as judge. Horace is acquitted, the 'dresser of plays' Demetrius is made to wear a fool's coat and cap, and Crispinus is given a purge of hellebore and made to vomit up his windy rhetoric. A secondary plot concerns Ovid's love for the daughter of Augustus, and his subsequent banishment. Marston and Dekker replied to the attack in *Satiromastix*, where the main characters of this play reappear.

Poetical Rhapsody, A, a collection of Elizabethan verse published by Francis Davison (?1575–?1619) in 1602, 'Containing, Diverse Sonnets, Odes, Elegies, Madrigalls and other Poesies' (2nd edn 1608, 3rd edn 1611, 4th edn 1621), and edited by H. E. Rollins in 2 vols (1931–2). It includes 'The Lie', attributed to *Ralegh; the song 'In Praise of a Beggar's Life' quoted in *The Compleat Angler*; and poems by *Greene, *Wotton, *Sidney, *Spenser, *Donne, and others.

poetic diction, a term used to mean language and usage peculiar to poetry, which came into prominence with *Wordsworth's discussion in his preface (1800) to the *Lyrical Ballads*, in which he claims to have taken pains to avoid 'what is usually called poetic diction', and asserts that there is and should be no essential difference between the language of prose and the language of metrical composition. Wordsworth thus implies that there should be no such thing as 'language and usage peculiar to poetry', and illustrates his point by attacking a sonnet of *Gray (who had, he said, attempted to widen the gap between poetry and prose); Gray himself had declared (1742, letter to West) that 'the language of the age is never the language of poetry.' Wordsworth's attack on *neo-classicism, archaisms, abstractions, personifications, etc., was both forceful and revolutionary, although it is noticeable that he himself did not always consider it necessary to use 'the real language of men', and his views were later repudiated by *Coleridge; moreover, although poetry became less stilted in its language, its vocabulary remained on the whole distinctive throughout the Romantic and Victorian periods, and few followed Wordsworth in his faith that the language of low and rustic life is plainer, more emphatic, and more philosophical than the 'gaudiness and inane phraseology' which he condemned. *Clare is a rare and isolated example of a poet capable of resisting conventional notions of 'poetic diction' and writing in his own idiom; it was not until the 20th cent. and the advent of *Modernism in the works of *Yeats, T. S. *Eliot, *Pound, and others that another major attempt to enlarge the poetic vocabulary and bring it closer to ordinary speech was made.

Poetics, The, a fragment of a treatise by *Aristotle which greatly influenced the theory of *neo-classicism. It is the source of the principles elaborated by later critics as the *unities, and it also introduced many much-discussed concepts related to the theory of tragedy, such as *mimesis* (imitation); *catharsis* (purification or purgation); *peripeteia* (reversal); and *hamartia* (either 'tragic flaw' or, more accurately, 'error of judgement'). *Hubris* (overweening pride or confidence) was a form of *hamartia*.

poet laureate, the title given to a poet who receives a stipend as an officer of the royal household, his duty (no longer enforced) being to write court odes, etc. The title was sometimes conferred by certain universities. For a list of poets laureate see Appendix 2. The title of poet laureate in the USA was established in 1985 by the US Senate: the salaried post has been held by, among others, R. *Wilbur (1987), J. *Brodsky (1991), and R. *Dove (1993).

Poetry: A Magazine of Verse (1912–   ), founded at Chicago by the American poet and critic Harriet Monroe (1860–1936), who edited it until her death. In its early days it published work by E. *Pound, A. *Lowell, T. S. *Eliot, *Frost, H.D. (Hilda *Doolittle), F. M. *Ford, and others, and has continued to flourish, publishing work by nearly every major American poet of the 20th cent.

Poetry Bookshop, see MONRO.

Poetry London, a bi-monthly which became the leading poetry magazine of the 1940s. It was conceived by a group of four, Dylan *Thomas, James Meary Tambimuttu (1915–83), Anthony Dickins, and Keidrych Rhys, and edited by Tambimuttu, who had arrived in 1938 from Ceylon, almost penniless, and entered the literary London of Soho and *Fitzrovia. The first issue appeared in Feb. 1939; Tambimuttu produced 15 numbers, and it was subsequently edited by Richard Marsh and Nicholas Moore. It published work by G. *Barker, V. *Watkins, G. *Ewart, H. *Pinter, C. *Tomlinson, D. *Gascoyne, L. *Durrell, and many others.

Poetry Nation, a twice-yearly poetry magazine edited by C. B. Cox and Michael Schmidt (6 issues, 1973–6), founded in sympathy with what its first editorial described as 'a renewed popularity and practice of clearly formal writing, a common bridling at vacuous public and private rhetoric'. Contributors included C. *Tomlinson, P. *Porter, E. *Jennings, G. *Hill, and Douglas *Dunn; D. *Davie and C. H. *Sisson became co-editors of its thrice-yearly successor, *PN Review* (1976–   ).

Poetry Review, see MONRO and POETRY SOCIETY.

Poetry Society, the, a society founded in 1909 (as the Poetry Recital Society) for the promotion of poetry and the art of speaking verse, and sponsored by many figures in the literary world, including G. *Murray, A. P. *Graves, Sturge *Moore, *Gosse, *Newbolt, Arnold *Bennett, E. V. *Lucas, and A. C. *Benson. Its many activities now include the organization of poetry competitions, workshop sessions, and examinations in and awards for the speaking of verse and prose. Its

journal, *Poetry Review,* was founded in 1912; its first editor was H. E. *Monro.

Poets' Corner, part of the south transept of Westminster Abbey containing the tombs or monuments of *Chaucer, *Spenser, Shakespeare, *Jonson, *Milton, *Drayton, Samuel *Butler, A. *Behn, *Gay, and many later distinguished poets and authors. Many of the monuments are by *Rysbrack.

Poins, in Shakespeare's *1* and *2 *Henry IV,* one of Prince Henry's companions.

POLIDORI, John William (1795–1821), physician and literary fellow traveller. The son of an Italian translator, he was educated at Ampleforth before taking an Edinburgh medical degree at the age of 19. In 1816 he was hired by Lord *Byron as personal physician and travelling companion for a few months; and kept a journal of this association, much later published as his *Diary* (1911). He participated in the famous ghost story competition in June 1816 that gave rise to M. *Shelley's *Frankenstein* and eventually to Polidori's only novel, *Ernestus Berchtold* (1819). Byron's incomplete tale 'Augustus Darvell' provided the basis for Polidori's story 'The Vampyre', written in 1816 and misleadingly published under Byron's name in 1819 by the *New Monthly Magazine.* Frequently reprinted and adapted for the stage in the 1820s, 'The Vampyre' laid the foundations of modern vampire fiction, notably in the use of an aristocratic villain, Lord Ruthven, evidently modelled upon Byron himself. Polidori established an unsuccessful medical practice in Norwich, and committed suicide in 1821.

Polite Learning, An Enquiry into the Present State of, see ENQUIRY INTO THE PRESENT STATE OF POLITE LEARNING, AN.

POLITIAN, see POLIZIANO.

Political Register (1802–35), a weekly newspaper founded by *Cobbett. It began as a Tory paper but by 1809 was thoroughly Radical. He continued to issue it even when committed to prison for an article condemning military flogging. His new version of the paper produced in 1816 at 2d. reached a remarkable circulation of 40,000–50,000 a week. In 1821 *Rural Rides* began to appear serially. Cobbett continued the paper until his death.

Politic Would-be, Sir and Lady, the foolish traveller and his loquacious wife in Jonson's *Volpone.*

Polixenes, the king of Bohemia in Shakespeare's *The Winter's Tale.*

POLIZIANO (in English Politian), Angelo (1454–94), the name assumed from his birthplace, Montepulciano, by Angelo Ambrogini, Italian humanist and friend of Lorenzo the Magnificent, in whose household in Florence he lived as tutor and scholar. In this period he combined philological studies with the composition of poetry in Latin and Italian. In 1479 he moved to Mantua, where he wrote *Orfeo*, the first pastoral drama in Italian. The following year he returned to the chair of Greek and Latin at the University of Florence. The two volumes of editorial and philological studies that he published at this period established him as the greatest textual scholar of his time, and his Greek epigrams showed him to be the first Italian humanist with the fluency in Greek requisite for the composition of poetry of real quality. *Linacre was one of his students, and G. *Chapman translated and imitated his verse.

POLLARD, A(lfred) W(illiam) (1859–1944), honorary secretary of the *Bibliographical Society, keeper of the Department of Printed Books at the *British Museum, 1919–24. He was an authority on *Chaucer and Shakespeare, edited several volumes of Chaucer's *Canterbury Tales* (1886–7) and the 'Globe' Chaucer (1898), and published other pioneering works which influenced the study of medieval literature. His important contributions to Shakespearian criticism included *Shakespeare's Folios and Quartos 1594–1685* (1909) and *Shakespeare's Fight with the Pirates* (1917). He was largely responsible for the completion of the *Short-Title Catalogue of Books Printed in England, Scotland and Ireland . . . 1475–1640* (1926).

Pollente, in Spenser's *Faerie Queene* (V. ii), the 'cruell Sarazin' who holds a bridge and despoils those who pass over it, the father of *Munera. He is slain by Sir *Artegall.

Polly, a musical play by J. *Gay, published 1729, the sequel to *The Beggar's Opera*. Its performance on stage was prohibited by the Lord Chamberlain.

Macheath has been transported to the West Indies, and has escaped from the plantation; he is disguised as Morano, chief of the pirates. Polly comes to seek him, but is trapped in the household of an amorous planter, whose advances she escapes owing to an attack by the pirates. Disguised as a man, she joins the loyal Indians, helps to beat off the attack, takes Morano prisoner, discovers his identity too late to save him from execution, and marries an Indian prince. *Polly* brought Gay nearly £1,200 in subscriptions.

POLO, Marco (1254–1324), a member of a patrician family of Venice, who accompanied his father and uncle in 1271 on an embassy from the pope to Kublai, grand khan of Tartary. They travelled overland to China, where they were well received by the emperor. After 17 years in the territories of the grand khan, the Polos obtained permission to return home, which they did by sea to the Persian Gulf, eventually reaching Venice after an absence of 24 years. Marco Polo's account of his travels was written while imprisoned by the Genoese, by whom he had been captured in a sea-fight with the Venetians. The original text appears to have been in French, but it was widely read in Latin and in various vernacular translations. The existence of other and wilder romances of Eastern travel (such as

*Mandeville, etc.) tended to make Polo 'suspect', at least in places; but there is no reason for any such suspicion. The work was Englished by John Frampton in 1579; but the first serious English translation was by W. Marsden early in the 19th cent.

Polonius, the lord chamberlain, father of *Ophelia and *Laertes in Shakespeare's *Hamlet*. Dr *Johnson described him as 'a man bred in courts, exercised in business, stored with observation, confident of his knowledge, proud of his eloquence, and declining into dotage'.

Polychronicon, The, see HIGDEN, R.

Polydore, (1) in Shakespeare's *Cymbeline*, the name borne by Guiderius while in the Welsh forest; (2) a character in Otway's *The Orphan*; (3) a character in J. *Fletcher's *The Mad Lover*.

POLYDORE VERGIL, see VERGIL, P.

Polyglot Bible, the, edited in 1653–7 by Brian Walton (?1600–61), bishop of Chester, with the help of many scholars. It contains various oriental texts of the Bible with Latin translations, and a critical apparatus.

Polyhymnia, a poem by *Peele written in 1590 commemorating the retirement of Sir H. *Lee from the office of queen's champion, and describing the ceremonies that took place on this occasion. It contains at the end the beautiful song 'His Golden lockes, | Time hath to Silver turn'd' made widely known by Thackeray's quotation of part of it in *The Newcomes*, ch. 76.

Poly-Olbion, The (this is the spelling of the 1st edn), the most ambitious work of *Drayton. It was written between 1598 and 1622 and consists of 30 'Songs' each of 300–500 lines, in hexameter couplets, in which the author endeavours to awaken his readers to the beauties and glories of their country.

Travelling from the south-west to Chester, down through the Midlands to London, up the eastern counties to Lincoln, and then through Lancashire and Yorkshire to Northumberland and Westmorland, he describes, or at least enumerates, the principal topographical features of the country, but chiefly the rivers and rivulets, interspersing in the appropriate places, legends, fragments of history, catalogues of British saints and hermits, of great discoverers, of birds, fishes, and plants with their properties. The first part, published 1612–13, was annotated by *Selden. The word 'poly-olbion' (from the Greek) means 'having many blessings'.

polyptoton is the repetition of the same word or root with varying grammatical inflections, as in 'And singing still dost soar, and soaring ever singest' (*Shelley), or 'Love is an irresistible desire to be irresistibly desired' (Robert *Frost).

polysyndeton (from Greek, 'using many connectives') is the repetition of conjunctions in close succession for rhetorical effect, as in 'Since brass, nor stone, nor earth, nor boundless sea' (Shakespeare, Sonnet 65).

POMFRET, John (1667–1702), a Bedfordshire vicar remembered for his poem *The Choice* (1700), derived from *Horace, Satire 6, which describes the pleasures of a quiet country estate where the author 'might live genteelly, but not great'. It enjoyed considerable success, and secured its author inclusion in Johnson's *Lives of the English Poets*, where Pomfret's choice was described as 'such a state as affords plenty and tranquillity, without exclusion of intellectual pleasures'.

Pompey the Great, *His Faire Corneliaes Tragedie*, see CORNELIA.

Pompey the Little, The History of, see COVENTRY, F.

PONSONBY, Sarah, see LLANGOLLEN, THE LADIES OF.

PONTOPPIDAN, Erik (1698–1764), a Danish author and bishop of Bergen in Norway. His principal works are the *Gesta et Vestigia Danorum extra Daniam* (1740), and a *Natural History of Norway* (1755), frequently mentioned on account of its description of the *kraken.

POOLE, John (?1786–1872), a dramatist of great success, who also produced poems and essays and wrote for many years for the *New Monthly Magazine*. His comedies and farces were produced at Drury Lane, Covent Garden, and the Haymarket, with C. *Kemble and other well-known actors. There were few years between 1813 and 1829 when no play of his was produced. The most successful were *Paul Pry* (1825), *'Twixt the Cup and the Lip* (1826), and *Lodgings for a Single Gentleman* (1829). Later in his life *Dickens obtained him a state pension of £100 p.a.

POOLE, Thomas (1765–1837), farmer and tanner, born at Nether Stowey; he became a close friend of *Coleridge and *Wordsworth, and assisted them both in finding homes to rent in his neighbourhood in 1796–7. Coleridge wrote 'This lime tree bower my prison' in Poole's garden, and Sara Coleridge corresponded with him for many years. Another of his friends was Sir H. *Davy. He was a man of progressive and generous spirit; Wordsworth said of him, 'he felt for all men as his brothers.'

Poor Tom, a name assumed by one who feigns madness in the *Fraternitie of Vacabondes*, and by *Edgar in Shakespeare's *King Lear* (II. iii).

Pooter, the archetypally suburban protagonist of *The Diary of a Nobody* by G. and W. Grossmith.

POPE, Alexander (1688–1744), the son of a Roman Catholic linen draper of London. His health was ruined and his growth stunted by a severe illness at the age of 12 (probably Pott's disease, a tubercular affection of the spine). He lived with his parents at Binfield in Windsor Forest and was largely self-educated. He showed his precocious metrical skill in his 'Pastorals'

written, according to himself, when he was 16, and published in *Tonson's *Miscellany* (vol. vi) in 1709. (For Pope's quarrel with Ambrose Philips on this subject see under PHILIPS, A.) He became intimate with *Wycherley, who introduced him to London life. His *Essay on Criticism* (1711) made him known to *Addison's circle, and his *'Messiah' was published in the *Spectator* in 1712. *The Rape of the Lock* appeared in *Lintot's *Miscellanies* in the same year and was republished, enlarged, in 1714. His *Ode for Music on St Cecilia's Day* (1713), one of his rare attempts at lyric, shows that his gifts did not lie in this direction. In 1713 he also published *Windsor Forest*, which appealed to the Tories by its references to the Peace of Utrecht, and won him the friendship of *Swift. He drifted away from Addison's 'little senate' and became a member of the *Scriblerus Club, an association that included Swift, *Gay, *Arbuthnot, and others. He issued in 1715 the first volume of his translation in heroic couplets of Homer's *Iliad. This work, completed in 1720, is more *Augustan than Homeric in spirit and diction, but has nevertheless been much admired; *Coleridge thought it an 'astonishing product of matchless talent and ingenuity'. It was supplemented in 1725–6 by a translation of the *Odyssey, in which he was assisted by William Broome and Elijah Fenton. The two translations brought him financial independence. He moved in 1718 with his mother to Twickenham, where he spent the rest of his life, devoting much time to his garden and grotto; he was keenly interested in *landscape gardening and committed to the principle 'Consult the Genius of the Place in all'.

In 1717 had appeared a collection of his works containing two poems dealing, alone among his works, with the passion of love. They are 'Verses to the Memory of an Unfortunate Lady', an elegy on a fictitious lady who had killed herself through hopeless love, and *'Eloisa to Abelard', in which Eloisa describes her inner conflicts after the loss of her lover. About this time he became strongly attached to Martha *Blount, with whom his friendship continued throughout his life, and to Lady M. W. *Montagu, whom in later years he assailed with bitterness; Lady Mary left for Turkey in July 1716 and Pope sent her 'Eloisa to Abelard' with a letter suggesting that he was passionately grieved by her absence.

Pope assisted Gay in writing the comedy *Three Hours after Marriage* (1717), but made no other attempt at drama. In 1723, four years after Addison's death, appeared (in a miscellany called *Cytherea*) Pope's portrait of *Atticus, a satire on Addison written in 1715. An extended version appeared as 'A Fragment of a Satire' in a 1727 volume of *Miscellanies* (by Pope, Swift, Arbuthnot, and Gay), and took its final form in *An Epistle to Dr Arbuthnot* (1735). In the same *Miscellanies* volume Pope published his prose treatise *Peri Bathous, or The Art of Sinking in Poetry*, ridiculing among others Ambrose Philips, *Theobald, and J.

*Dennis. In 1725 Pope published an edition of Shakespeare, the errors in which were pointed out in a pamphlet by Theobald, *Shakespeare Restored* (1726). This led to Pope's selection of Theobald as hero of his *Dunciad*, a satire on Dullness in three books, on which he had been at work for some time; the first volume appeared anonymously in 1728. Swift, who spent some months with Pope in Twickenham in 1726, provided much encouragement for this work, of which a further enlarged edition was published in 1729. An additional book, *The New Dunciad*, was published in 1742, prompted this time, it appears, by *Warburton. The complete *Dunciad* in four books, in which C. *Cibber replaces Theobald as hero, appeared in 1743. Influenced in part by the philosophy of his friend *Bolingbroke, Pope published a series of moral and philosophical poems, *Essay on Man* (1733–4), consisting of four Epistles; and *Moral Essays* (1731–5), four in number: *Of the Knowledge and Characters of Men*, *Of the Characters of Women*, and two on the subject *Of the Use of Riches*. A fifth epistle was added, addressed to Addison, occasioned by his dialogue on medals. This was originally written in Addison's lifetime, c.1716. In 1733 Pope published the first of his miscellaneous satires, *Imitations of Horace*, entitled 'Satire I', a paraphrase of the first satire of the second book of Horace, in the form of a dialogue between the poet and William Fortescue, the lawyer. In it Pope defends himself against the charge of Malignity, and professes to be inspired only by love of virtue. He inserts, however, a gross attack on his former friend Lady Mary Wortley Montagu as 'Sappho'. He followed this up with his *Imitations* of Horace's Satires 2. 2 and 1. 2 ('Sober Advice from Horace'), in 1734, and of Epistles 1. 6; 2. 2; 2. 1; and 1. 1, in 1737. Horace's Epistle 1. 7 and the latter part of Satire 2. 6, 'imitated in the manner of Dr Swift', appeared in 1738. The year 1735 saw the appearance of the *Epistle to Dr Arbuthnot*, the prologue to the above Satires, one of Pope's most brilliant pieces of irony and invective, mingled with autobiography. It contains the famous portraits of Addison (ll. 193–214) and Lord *Hervey, and lashes his minor critics, Dennis, Cibber, *Curll, Theobald, etc. In 1738 appeared *One Thousand Seven Hundred and Thirty Eight*, two satirical dialogues. These satires, and the 'Satires (2 and 4) of Dr Donne Versified' (1735), with the *New Dunciad*, closed his literary career.

He was partly occupied during his later years with the publication of his earlier correspondence, which he edited and amended in such a manner as to misrepresent the literary history of the time. He also employed discreditable artifices to make it appear that it was published against his wish. Thus he procured the publication by Curll of his 'Literary Correspondence' in 1735, and then endeavoured to disavow him.

With the growth of *Romanticism Pope's poetry was increasingly seen as artificial; Coleridge commented that Pope's thoughts were 'translated into the language of poetry', *Hazlitt called him 'the poet not of nature

but of art', and W. L. *Bowles compared his work to 'a game of cards'; *Byron, however, was highly laudatory: 'Pope's pure strain | Sought the rapt soul to charm, nor sought in vain.' M. *Arnold's famous comment, 'Dryden and Pope are not classics of our poetry, they are classics of our prose' (*Essays in Criticism*, 1880), summed up much 19th-cent. opinion, and it was not until *Leavis and *Empson that a serious attempt was made to rediscover Pope's richness, variety, and complexity.

Minor works that deserve mention are:

Verse: the Epistles 'To a Young Lady [Miss Blount] with the Works of Voiture' (1712), to the same 'On her Leaving the Town after the Coronation' (1717); 'To Mr Jervas with Dryden's Translation of Fresnoy's Art of Painting' (1716) and 'To Robert, Earl of Oxford and Earl Mortimer' (1721); 'Vertumnus and Pomona', 'Sappho to Phaon', and 'The Fable of Dryope', translations from *Ovid (1712); *'January and May', 'The Wife of Bath, her Prologue', and *The Temple of Fame*, from *Chaucer (1709, 1714, 1715).

Prose: *The Narrative of Dr Robert Norris* (1713), a satirical attack on Dennis; *A Full and True Account of a Horrid and Barbarous Revenge by Poison, on . . . Mr Edmund Curll* (1716), an attack on Curll (to whom he had secretly administered an emetic).

The standard edn of Pope's poetry is the Twickenham Edition, under the general editorship of J. Butt (11 vols plus Index, 1940–69); see also G. Sherburn, *The Early Career of Alexander Pope* (1934); N. Ault, *New Light on Pope* (1949); P. *Quennell, *Alexander Pope: The Education of a Genius* (1968); M. Mack, *The Garden and the City* (1969) and *Alexander Pope: A Life* (1985); Morris R. Brownell, *Alexander Pope and the Arts of Georgian England* (1978).

Popish Plot, a plot fabricated in 1678 by Titus *Oates. He deposed at the end of September before the Middlesex magistrate Sir Edmond Berry Godfrey that it was intended to murder Charles II, place James on the throne, and suppress Protestantism. Godfrey disappeared on 12 Oct. and was found murdered on 17 Oct. The existence of the plot was widely believed and great excitement prevailed. Many persons, especially Catholics, were falsely accused and executed. These events occasioned John Caryll's poem *Naboth's Vineyard* (1679) which was an important predecessor of *Absalom and Achitophel* and thus contributed to the efflorescence of the *mock-biblical as a satirical mode.

POPPER, Sir Karl Raimund (1902–94), Austrian philosopher of science, born in Vienna, and originally connected with the Vienna circle, the source of logical positivism. He left Vienna for New Zealand on Hitler's rise to power, and came to England in 1946, where, in 1949, he was appointed professor of logic and scientific method at the London School of Economics. Popper asserted that a statement, if it is to count as scientific rather than merely metaphysical, must be falsifiable:

such that the conditions that would make it false are clearly known. His philosophy of science claimed to solve the problem of induction: the problem of extrapolating from past to future, or, more precisely, from limited evidence to a general conclusion. This work appealed greatly to many scientists. He also contributed to political philosophy and a defence of free will and the 'self-conscious mind'. His works include *The Logic of Scientific Discovery* (*Logik der Forschung*, 1934); *The Open Society and Its Enemies* (1945), and *The Self and Its Brain* (1977, with John C. Eccles).

POPPLE, William (1701–64), dramatist, *theatre critic, and friend of A. *Hill, with whom he edited the *Prompter* (1734–6), a bi-weekly theatrical periodical (selection ed. W. Appleton and K. A. Burnim, 1966). He wrote two comedies, *The Lady's Revenge* (1734) and *The Double Deceit: or A Cure for Jealousy* (1735), in which two young men, intended to marry two heiresses, conspire to avoid their fate by exchanging places with their valets. The ladies, apprised of the trick, exchange places with their maids, the pseudo-valets fall in love with the pseudo-maids, and all ends well.

PORSON, Richard (1759–1808), a distinguished classical scholar, who was elected Regius professor of Greek at Cambridge in 1792. He edited four plays of *Euripides (most notably *Hecuba*), and advanced Greek scholarship by his elucidation of Greek idiom and usage, by his study of Greek metres, and by his emendation of texts. He is also remembered for various witticisms and for contributions to the *Gentleman's Magazine*, in which appeared in 1787 letters ironically praising *Hawkins's *Life of Johnson* and in 1788–9 his *Letters to Mr Archdeacon Travis* (repr. separately 1790) on the authenticity of the contentious proof text of the Trinity known as the Johannine Comma (1 John 5: 7, 'For there are three that bear record in heaven.'). There is a life by M. L. Clarke (1937).

Porter, in Shakespeare's *Macbeth*; he lets *Macduff and Lennox into Macbeth's castle (II. iii), and is the subject of *De Quincey's essay 'On the Knocking at the Gate'.

PORTER, Anna Maria (1780–1832), poet and novelist, whose martial tale of the French Revolution, *The Hungarian Brothers* (1807), was a considerable success and went into several editions. She published *Don Sebastian* in 1809, and several other novels, as well as ballads and poems.

PORTER, Endymion (1587–1649), groom of the bedchamber to Charles I, and the friend and patron of painters and poets. He was painted by *Van Dyck, and *Jonson, *Herrick, *D'Avenant, and *Dekker, among others, celebrated him in verse. He sat in the Long Parliament but was expelled, lived abroad in poverty, and compounded with the Parliament for a small fine in 1649.

PORTER, Jane (1776–1850), sister of A. M. *Porter. She published in 1803 *Thaddeus of Warsaw*, which was immensely successful and led to friendship with one of its heroes, the Polish General Kosciuszko: it describes the adventures of a young Polish nobleman who accompanies his grandfather to join the army of King Stanislas against the invading Russians. In 1810 she published *The Scottish Chiefs*, a story of William Wallace, which ends with the battle of Bannockburn. This was also successful, and was translated into German and Russian: it is of interest as a precursor of the *historical fiction of Sir W. *Scott. *The Pastor's Fireside* (1815) is a story of the later Stuarts. Her tragedy *Switzerland*, produced in 1819 with *Kean and C. *Kemble, was a disastrous failure. Among several other volumes she produced *Sir Edward Seaward's Narrative*, on Caribbean exploration, a work which purported to be a genuine diary but which was almost certainly largely fictitious.

PORTER, Katherine Anne (1890–1980), Texan-born short story writer and novelist whose collections of short stories include *Flowering Judas* (1930), *Pale Horse, Pale Rider* (1939), and *The Leaning Tower* (1944). Her novel *Ship of Fools* (1962) is a heavily allegorical treatment of a voyage from Mexico to Germany on the eve of Hitler's rise to power.

PORTER, Peter Neville Frederick (1929–   ), poet, born and educated in Brisbane, where he worked as a journalist before coming to England in 1951. Since then he has worked as clerk, bookseller, and as copywriter in an advertising agency (in the company of G. *Ewart, P. *Redgrove, and other poets), before becoming a full-time writer, broadcaster, and critic in 1968. He was briefly associated with the *Group in the 1960s, and the work in his early collections (*Once Bitten, Twice Bitten*, 1961; *Poems, Ancient and Modern*, 1964; *The Last of England*, 1970) provides a sharply satiric portrait of London in the 'swinging sixties', with a gallery of fops, publishers, concrete poets, filmmakers, etc. In the 1970s, his work became more meditative, complex, and allusive, though no less colloquial and urbane; its learned references to a vast range of subjects, from Italian baroque to classical mythology, opera, and German Romanticism, add both richness and obscurity. His technical command of complex stanza forms, sometimes used parodically, is striking. *The Cost of Seriousness* (1978) and *English Subtitles* (1981) introduce a new and sombre exploration of the poet's conflicting responsibilities to his art and to others. *After Martial* (1972) is a volume of translations. Later volumes include *Fast Forward* (1984), *The Automatic Oracle* (1987), *Possible Worlds* (1989), *The Chair of Babel* (1992), *A Porter Selected* (1989), *Millennial Fables* (1994), and *Collected Poems 1961–1999* (2 vols, 1999). A critical biography by Bruce Bennett, *Spirit in Exile*, appeared in 1991.

Portia, (1) the heroine of Shakespeare's *The Merchant of Venice*; (2) in his *Julius Caesar*, the wife of Brutus.

Portrait of a Lady, The, a novel by H. *James, published 1881.

This is one of the best of James's early works, in which he presents various types of American character transplanted into a European environment. The story centres on Isabel Archer, the 'Lady', an attractive American girl. Around her we have the placid old American banker, Mr Touchett; his hard repellent wife; his ugly invalid, witty, charming son Ralph, whom England has thoroughly assimilated; and the outspoken, brilliant, indomitably American journalist Henrietta Stackpole. Isabel refuses the offer of marriage of a typical English peer, the excellent Lord Warburton, and of a bulldog-like New Englander, Caspar Goodwood, to fall a victim, under the influence of the slightly sinister Madame Merle (another cosmopolitan American), to a worthless and spiteful dilettante, Gilbert Osmond, who marries her for her fortune and ruins her life; but to whom she remains loyal in spite of her realization of his vileness.

Portrait of the Artist as a Young Dog (1940), a collection of stories by Dylan *Thomas.

Portrait of the Artist as a Young Man, A, an autobiographical novel by J. *Joyce, first published in the *Egoist*, 1914–15.

It describes the development of Stephen Dedalus (who reappears in *Ulysses* in a slightly different incarnation) from his early boyhood, through bullying at school and an adolescent crisis of faith inspired partly by the famous 'hellfire sermon' preached by the Jesuit Father Arnall (ch. 3) and partly by the guilt of his own precocious sexual adventures, to student days and a gradual sense of his own destiny as poet, patriot, and unbeliever, who paradoxically must leave his own land in order to 'encounter . . . the reality of experience and to forge in the smithy of my soul the uncreated conscience of my race'. Though not as innovative as the later work (its experimentation lies principally in its prose style changing as the novel progresses to mirror the growth and development of Stephen's mind), the novel foreshadows many of the themes and verbal complexities of *Ulysses*.

positivist philosophy, see COMTE.

post-colonial literature, see overleaf.

Posthumus Leonatus, the hero of Shakespeare's *Cymbeline* and husband of *Imogen; 'The fit and apt construction' of his name, as the Soothsayer partially explains, is that he was the last-born of his father Sicilius Leonatus and his mother, who died in labour.

postmodernism, the term applied by some commentators since the early 1980s to the ensemble of cultural features characteristic of Western societies in the aftermath of artistic *Modernism. In this view, 'postmodernity' asserts itself from about 1956 with the exhaustion of the high Modernist project, reflected in the work of S. *Beckett among others, and the huge cultural impact of television and popular music. The term has been applied as a 'period' label more confidently by architectural historians than by students of literature, and many disputants maintain that artistic or literary works described as 'postmodernist' are really continuations of the Modernist tradition. Nevertheless, some general literary features of the period have been identified as tendencies to parody, pastiche, scepticism, irony, fatalism, the mixing of 'high' and 'low' cultural allusions, and an indifference to the redemptive mission of Art as conceived by the Modernist pioneers. Postmodernism thus favours random play rather than purposeful action, surface rather than depth. The kinds of literary work that have been described as postmodernist include the Theatre of the *Absurd and some experimental poetry. Most commonly, though, it is prose fiction that is held to exemplify the postmodernist mood or style, notably in works by American novelists such as V. *Nabokov, J. *Barth, T. *Pynchon, and K. *Vonnegut, and by the British authors J. *Fowles, A. *Carter, S. *Rushdie, J. *Barnes, P. *Ackroyd, and J. *Winterson. Outside the English-speaking world, the fictions of J. L. *Borges and the later work of I. *Calvino show similar tendencies. Distinctive features of this school include switching between orders of reality and fantasy (see MAGIC REALISM), resort to *metafiction, and the playful undermining of supposedly objective kinds of knowledge such as biography and history.

'Pot of Basil, The', see ISABELLA.

Pott, Mr, in Dickens's *Pickwick Papers*, the editor of the 'Eatanswill Gazette'.

POTTER, (Helen) Beatrix (1866–1943), born in Kensington to wealthy parents and never sent to school. She grew up a lonely child. She taught herself to draw and paint small natural objects and as a young woman did serious work dissecting, drawing, and classifying fungi. She invented a cipher so elaborate that the half-million words she wrote in it were not deciphered until Leslie Linder broke the code and published *The Journal of Beatrix Potter* (1966). In a letter to the son of her former governess in 1893 she began *The Tale of Peter Rabbit*, and other books began in the same way. Copied out and more fully illustrated, *Peter Rabbit* was published at her own expense in 1901 and *The Tailor of Gloucester* in 1902. Warne then took over publication and in 1903 *Squirrel Nutkin* was her first great success. Her farm at Sawrey in the Lake District, which she bought in 1905, became the background for six of her books. In 1913 she married William Heelis, a Lakeland solicitor, and for the rest of her life devoted herself almost entirely to her farms and the new National Trust. *Johnny Town-Mouse* (1918) was the last of her books in the old style; those later written for the USA, such as *The Fairy Caravan* (1928), are of little interest. A biography by Margaret Lane appeared in 1968 (rev. edn 1985); see also *Beatrix Potter* (rev. edn 1996) by Judy Taylor.

POTTER, Dennis Christopher George (1935–94), playwright, born in the Forest of Dean, the son of a miner. He was educated at New College, Oxford, where he became involved in left-wing politics, and subsequently worked as journalist and critic; *The Glittering Coffin* (1960) is an analysis of the Labour Party and the political climate of the time. He wrote fiction, stage plays, screenplays, and adapted works for television but is best known for his own television plays, which show an original and inventive use of the medium. These include two plays dealing with the career of an aspiring working-class, Oxford-educated politician, *Vote, Vote, Vote for Nigel Barton* (1965) and *Stand up, Nigel Barton* (1965), published together in 1968; *Pennies from Heaven*, a six-part serial (1978, pub. 1981); and *Blue Remembered Hills* (1979, a tragic evocation of childhood). *Brimstone and Treacle* (1978) was first performed on stage after being banned for television performance. Potter's experience of psoriatic arthropothy, a debilitating condition affecting skin and joints, is central to his six-part serial *The Singing Detective* (1986), widely held to be his finest work: this is a multi-layered narrative, moving between a moody 1940s thriller and incorporating songs of that period, and a present-day hospital ward where Philip Marlow, hero of both sequences, is suffering from a skin disease: it dwells on key themes of childhood trauma, disillusion, betrayal, love, and guilt. *Blackeyes* (1989) is a study of sexual exploitation and *Lipstick on Your Collar* (1993) is a musical black comedy based on Potter's National Service experiences. His final work was a pair of linked serials completed weeks before his death from cancer: *Karaoke* is a nightmarish thriller, full of ironic self-references, and *Cold Lazarus* is a futuristic and dystopian confrontation of imminent death and the meaning of memory.

POTTER, Stephen Meredith (1900–69), writer, editor, and radio producer, whose book *The Theory and Practice of Gamesmanship; or The Art of Winning Games without Actually Cheating* (1947) had a great vogue and added a new word and concept to the language; he followed it with *Some Notes on Lifemanship* (1950), *One-Upmanship* (1952), and *Supermanship* (1958). His other works include an edition of Sara *Coleridge's letters to T. *Poole, published as *Minnow among Tritons* (1934).

poulter's measure, a fanciful name for a metre consisting of lines of 12 and 14 syllables alternately. Poulter = poulterer.

> Poulter's measure, which giveth xii for one dozen, and xiiij for another.

(*Gascoigne, *Certayne notes of instruction*)

POUND, Ezra Weston Loomis (1885–1972), American poet born in Idaho, of Quaker ancestry; he studied at the University of Pennsylvania, where he met Hilda *Doolittle. He taught briefly in Indiana, but was asked to resign, and in 1908 came to Europe and published his first volume of poems, *A Lume Spento* (1908), at his own expense in Italy; he then moved to London, where he lectured for a time in medieval Romance literature at the Regent Street Polytechnic and soon became prominent in literary circles. He published several other volumes of verse, including *Personae* (1909), *Canzoni* (1911), *Ripostes* (1912), and *Lustra* (1916). Together with F. S. Flint, R. *Aldington, and Hilda Doolittle he founded the *Imagist school of poets, advocating the use of free rhythms, concreteness, and concision of language and imagery; in 1914 he edited *Des Imagistes: An Anthology*. Pound also championed the *Modernist work of avant-garde writers and artists like *Joyce, W. *Lewis, *Gaudier-Brzeska, and T. S. *Eliot, whom he was always ready to assist critically and materially; Eliot, who described him as 'more responsible for the XXth Century revolution in poetry than any other individual', greatly valued his advice, as may be seen from the history of the composition of *The Waste Land*. Further volumes of poetry include *Quia Pauper Amavi* (1919, which contains 'Homage to Sextus Propertius') and *Hugh Selwyn Mauberley* (1920). Pound was now increasingly turning away from the constrictions of Imagism, and finding freedom partly through translations; his early volumes had contained adaptations from Provençal and early Italian, a version of the Old English *The Seafarer*, and in 1915 *Cathay*, translations from the Chinese of Li Po, via a transliteration. Pound was thus moving towards the rich, grandly allusive, multicultural world of the *Cantos*, his most ambitious achievement; the first three Cantos appeared in 1917 in *Poetry*. In 1920 Pound left London for Paris with his English wife Dorothy Shakespear, where he lived until 1924, finding a new literary scene figuring Gertrude *Stein, *Hemingway, etc.; in 1925 he settled permanently in Rapallo, where he continued to work on the Cantos, which appeared intermittently over the next decades until the appearance of the final *Drafts and Fragments of Cantos CX to CXVII* (1970).

In Italy Pound became increasingly preoccupied with economics, embraced Social Credit theories, and was persuaded that 'Usura', or credit capitalism, lay at the root of all social and spiritual evils. (See Canto XLV for his violent attack on usury.) His own interpretations of these theories led him into anti-Semitism and at least partial support for Mussolini's social programme. During the Second World War he broadcast over Italian radio: in 1945 he was arrested at Genoa, then sent to a US Army Disciplinary Training Centre near Pisa, a period which produced the much-admired *Pisan Cantos* (1948). He was then moved to Washington, found unfit to plead, and confined to a mental

(*cont. on p.810*)

Post-colonial literature consists of a body of writing emanating from Europe's former colonies which addresses questions of history, identity, ethnicity, gender, and language. The term should be used loosely and hesitantly, for it is replete with contradictions and conundrums. What, for instance, is the difference, if any, between imperialism and colonialism? Were not the forms of colonial rule and the processes of decolonization too varied to admit of a single definition? Is the literature of the United States of America to be included in such a body? Why does the once favoured term 'Commonwealth literature' no longer seem appropriate? Is it that it contains too many implied assumptions of a multicultural community in which each country is working towards a sense of shared enterprise and common purpose? Did empire end with Indian independence in 1947, or in 1956 with Suez, or was it later, when many of the African countries gained their independence, or in 1970 or 1973 when Fiji and the Bahamas respectively were granted theirs?

Such questions abound, but the term 'post-colonial literature' is to date the most convenient way of embracing the powerful and diverse body of literary responses to the challenges presented by decolonization and the transitions to independence and post-independence in a wide variety of political and cultural contexts.

Of course criticism of empire and imperial practices is not a 20th-cent. phenomenon, but originated among the colonists themselves. Recusants such as Bartolomé de las Casas and the Dominican Antonio Montesinos were busy challenging the savage practices which were to depopulate vast swathes of the Caribbean of their indigenous inhabitants. When in 1511 Montesinos asked whether the Indians were not themselves men, his intervention was greeted by the almost unanimous demand from his fellow colonists that he be forced to recant and be repatriated to Spain. Any opposition from the indigenous population was met with more summary treatment.

Out of the circumstances of this first colonial encounter was born an argument which has continued to be rehearsed right up to the present day. The dispute has been conducted around the contrast between natural and artificial societies: on one side, *Montaigne argued that primitive peoples were more virtuous by reason of their uncorrupted existence in nature. As he put it in his famous essay 'Of Cannibals', 'there is no reason, art should gaine the point of honour of our great and puissant mother nature'. On the other side, the social achievement of art and its superiority over nature was stressed:

> not all That beare the name of men. . .
> . . .Are for to be accounted men: but such as under awe
> Of reasons rule continually doo live in vertues law,
> And that the rest doo differ nought from beast, but rather be
> Much woorse than beasts, bicause they do not abace theyr
>   owne degree.

The terms of the debate, then, were already well established by the time Shakespeare wrote *The Tempest*, in which there emerges the recognizable paradigm of the native who is first amicable, only later to become duplicitous and require the correcting hand of the 'cultivated' man. This theme was to continue, with few exceptions, to the fiction of the present day through *Robinson Crusoe* and the writings of *Kipling, who, in conceding the passing of the British Empire, could exhort the United States of America to take up the moral duty of the 'White Man's Burden' and bring the backward races to maturity. *'Heart of Darkness' (1899) marks a key moment in colonial literature, Joseph *Conrad questioning the certainties about racial superiority which underpinned white rule. Simple greed is what motivates empire, Conrad suggests, the quest for money making Europeans more barbarous than the supposed black cannibals they governed and worked to death.

Post-colonial authors have advanced Conrad's perspectives, contesting European versions of the colonial experience: 'the Empire writes back', as Salman *Rushdie puts it. The forms of retaliation are manifold. Post-colonial literature, in seeking to awaken political and cultural nationalism, has dwelt on popular revolts against colonial rule, exposing the lie of the passive native. Writers like the Trinidadian C. L. R. *James have brought to the fore neglected black heroes like *Toussaint L'Ouverture, who led the greatest slave revolt in history, defeating French, Spanish, and British military forces to set up Haiti, the first free black republic in the West. History, however, is not an epic narrative of kings and rebels, but a record of the day-to-day existence of the common people; the cane-cutters for instance, whose labour produced the sugar which not only boosted the profits of imperial commerce but, in the 18th cent., created a taste among the gentry for taking sweetened tea. By giving voice and character to cane-cutters and the like, post-colonial writers point to the people who truly mattered to history but who, for political and related reasons, were written out. The world-view of such 'lowly' people, expressed in their myths and legends, is also given space, writers like the Guyanese Wilson *Harris arguing that Amerindian mythology reveals values and perspectives as complex and mysterious as any originating from the Graeco-Roman or Judaeo-Christian traditions. There is a corresponding reappraisal of oral expression, the riddles and proverbs and songs and stories handed down over generations and shared by the whole community. These forms of orality are often spurned by literary academics as lesser forms of 'literature' and relegated to the dubious category of 'folk tale'. But as the Nigerian writer Chinweizu reminds us, the African folk tale is a product of ancient traditions of eloquence and rhetoric, created for courtship or wedding ceremonies, or ceremonies marking birth and death. The folk tale is therefore an 'integral part of the fabric of personal and social life', often with profound religious significance. To ignore it is to ignore the cultural history of a nation.

Western power has been most seriously challenged by being placed in a new historical perspective. In 1992, despite the almost deafening propaganda organized by the government of the USA, the 500th anniversary celebrations of Columbus's arrival in the Americas were significantly contested by a vast array of post-colonial writing which repudiated the very idea that the Americas were 'discovered' or 'brought into discursive being' by the appearance of European adventurers. Amongst many other examples, they pointed out that, at the height of the Aztec civilization, the capital Tenochtitlan was five times larger than Madrid at the time of the Spanish conquest, while, on the other side of the world, Akbar, the Mughal emperor of India, had, at the same time that Elizabeth I allowed the founding of the East India Company, established dominion over a much larger trading area than his English contemporary.

Repositioning the co-ordinates of history has also involved coming to terms with the language of expression itself. Language is inextricably bound up with culture and identity, and as the colonizers attempted, with varying degrees of success, to impose the English language on subject peoples, the response from the formerly colonized has ranged from the outright rejection of English as a medium through which to exercise their art to the appropriation of it with subversive intent. After first using English as the medium for his novel, the Kenyan writer Ngugi wa *Thiong'o finally decided

to reject it. For him 'language is at the heart of the two contending forces in the Africa of the 20th century' and is crucial to maintaining control over one's own culture and mental universe. For others, such as the Nigerian writer Chinua *Achebe, English has been a means of uniting peoples across continents and of reaching a wider audience than would have been possible in their own mother tongues. However, whether or not the English language is capable of supplying the rhythms and cadences necessary to dramatize foreign landscapes, this has not prevented writers from doing 'unheard of things with it'; certainly Caribbeanists like Derek *Walcott and V. S. *Naipaul have used techniques such as switching in and out of standard English and local Creoles to emphasize that the post-Columbian world is irrevocably multicultural and hybridized. The debate continues to rage, and, although the view is by no means universally shared, there are now many people in all parts of the world who see English as having become detached from Britain or Britishness. They claim the language as their own property, for they have moulded and refashioned it to make it bear the weight of their own experience.

Another important progression has been the acknowledgement and reappearance of women's experience after being hidden from the histories of colonial societies. Many of the fixed representations of non-Western women have been powerfully rejected in a host of contemporary writings, most of which in their different ways refute imaginings deeply rooted in Western narrations and their subsequent over-simplistic depictions. The 1997 winner of the *Booker Prize, Arundhati Roy, is only the latest to join a distinguished list of women writers which already includes Jean *Rhys, Anita *Desai, Buchi *Emecheta, Olive *Senior, Nadine *Gordimer, and Grace *Nichols. Such writers have placed women at the centre of history, as makers and agents of history, not silent witnesses to it.

Whatever the irony contained in the fact that very many post-colonial writers choose both to write in English, the language of their former colonizers, and in the literary forms, such as the novel, developed in European societies, there is no doubt that the new literatures in English constitute a body of exciting and dynamic texts capable at once of forcing a reassessment of the traditional canon and of providing a vigorous alternative to what are often regarded as rather defensive and introspective English texts.

institution; he was released in 1958 and returned to Italy, where he died.

Inevitably, Pound's literary reputation was obscured by the tragedy of his last decades, and also by the difficulty of the work itself, which resides principally in its astonishingly wide range of reference and assimilation of cultures; *Hugh Selwyn Mauberley*, despite the advocacy of Eliot and *Leavis (who described it as 'the summit of Mr Pound's superbly supple and varied art'), never quite reached the 'popular classic' status of *The Waste Land*, and the *Cantos* remain formidable both in style and content. As Eliot said, Pound suffers from being seen as 'objectionably modern' and 'objectionably antiquarian' at the same time. Nevertheless, he is widely accepted both as a great master of traditional verse forms and as the man who regenerated the poetic idiom of his day.

See *Literary Essays of Ezra Pound* (1954; collected critical writings, with an introduction by T. S. Eliot); *Letters of Ezra Pound 1907–1941* (1950, ed. D. D. Paige); N. Stock, *The Life of Ezra Pound* (1970); H. Carpenter, *A Serious Character* (1988).

POUSSIN, Nicolas (1593/4–1665), French painter, who worked mainly in Rome. His early works are romantic treatments of subjects from *Ovid and *Tasso; later he developed an austerely classical style. In the early 18th cent. Poussin was deeply admired by English men of letters, and many of his greatest works were in English collections. James *Thomson's descriptions of landscape are indebted to Poussin and, in the second half of the century, poets, travellers, and landscape gardeners frequently contrast the nobility of Poussin's landscapes with the wildness of *Rosa and the beauty of *Claude. In the late 18th cent. Poussin's most severe works were most admired. *Hazlitt wrote many passionate descriptions of his painting; *Keats was inspired by the lyrical Ovidian pictures; *Ruskin described the *Triumph of Flora* (Paris, Louvre) as 'a Keats-like revel of body and soul of most heavenly creatures'. The picture most admired by literary men was Poussin's second treatment of the theme 'Et in Arcadia Ego', *The Shepherds of Arcady*, c.1650–5 (Paris, Louvre), a picture which fascinated later writers and painters. It has been suggested that *Gray thought of it when he wrote his *Elegy* (1751); *The Monument in Arcadia: A Dramatic Poem* (1773) by the minor poet and dilettante George Keate (1729–97) derives from it. English admiration paused with *Ruskin, but revived in the late 19th cent. when he was most admired for his formal brilliance. *Powell's image of *A Dance to the Music of Time* was inspired by Poussin's picture in the Wallace Collection, London.

POWELL, Anthony Dymoke (1905–2000), novelist, whose initial reputation as a satirist and light comedian rests on five pre-war books, beginning with *Afternoon Men* (1931) which maps a characteristically seedy section of pleasure-loving, party-going London: a territory contiguous with E. *Waugh's, bounded at opposite extremes by N. *Mitford and by Powell's Oxford contemporary and friend, Henry *Green.

After the war he embarked on a more ambitious sequence of twelve novels, *A Dance to the Music of Time* (named after *Poussin's painting, with which the sequence shares a certain classical severity as well as an architectural command of structural rhythm). They are: *A Question of Upbringing* (1951), *A Buyer's Market* (1952), *The Acceptance World* (1955), *At Lady Molly's* (1957), *Casanova's Chinese Restaurant* (1960), *The Kindly Ones* (1962), *The Valley of Bones* (1964), *The Soldier's Art* (1966), *The Military Philosophers* (1968), *Books Do Furnish a Room* (1971), *Temporary Kings* (1973), and *Hearing Secret Harmonies* (1975). The whole cycle is framed and distanced through the eyes of a narrator, Nicholas Jenkins, whose generation grew up in the shadow of the First World War to find their lives dislocated by the Second. Jenkins's canvas, following the perspectives of time rather than space, is hospitable and broad, especially rich in literary and artistic hangers-on, stiffened by a solid contingent from society, politics, and the City, enlivened and sometimes convulsed by eccentrics, derelicts, and drop-outs of all classes and conditions from the socialist peer Erridge to a shifty crew of baleful, semi-fraudulent gurus and seers. Against these looms Kenneth Widmerpool, one of the most memorable characters of 20th-cent. fiction, whose ruthless pursuit of power, which carries him from innately ludicrous beginnings to a position of increasingly formidable, eventually sinister, authority, is the chief of many threads binding this higgledy-piggledy, jampacked, panoramic view of England.

The narrative is part humorous, part melancholy, and at times so funny that readers have tended if anything to underrate its sombre, even tragic, sweep and range. Powell's naturalism takes on the almost surrealistic overtones implicit in Jenkins's rule of thumb: 'All human beings, driven as they are at different speeds by the same Furies, are at close range equally extraordinary.' Powell's memoirs, which shed considerable light on the creation of the characters of his fictional world, were published in four vols, 1976–82, under the general title *To Keep the Ball Rolling*. Later works include the novels *O, How the Wheel Becomes It!* (1983) and *The Fisher King* (1986), two volumes of criticism, *Miscellaneous Verdicts* (1990) and *Under Review* (1992), and *Journals 1982–6* (1995).

Power and the Glory, The, a novel by G. *Greene, published 1940.

Set in Mexico (which Greene had visited in 1938) at a time of religious persecution in the name of revolution, it describes the desperate last wanderings of a whisky priest as outlaw in his own state, who, despite a sense of his own worthlessness (he drinks, and has fathered a bastard daughter), is determined to continue to function as priest until captured. He is contrasted with

Padre José, a priest who has accepted marriage and humiliation; with 'the gringo', bank robber, murderer, and materialist, also on the run; and with the lieutenant, portrayed as an angry idealist and 'a good man', who pursues the priest and corners him when he is drawn back (by the Judas-figure of a half-caste) to offer the last rites to the dying gringo, just as he has reached safety over the border. His execution (and martyrdom?) is witnessed by the grotesque expatriate dentist Mr Tench, and the final episode indicates that the Church will survive its persecution. Greene describes it as his only novel 'written to a thesis'; it was condemned as 'paradoxical' by the Holy Office, but not publicly. Like many of Greene's works, it combines a conspicuous Christian theme and symbolism with the elements of a thriller.

POWYS, John Cowper (1872–1963), the son of a country parson, brother of Llewelyn and Theodore Powys (below), brought up in the Dorset–Somerset countryside which was to become of great importance in his later writing, even though he spent much of his life in the USA. Educated at Sherborne and Corpus Christi College, Cambridge, he became a prolific writer, including poetry and many essays on philosophy, religion, literature, and the arts of living among his publications, as well as a remarkable *Autobiography* (1934). It is, however, for his highly individual novels that he is chiefly remembered; the first, *Wood and Stone* (1915, NY; 1917, London) contains many hints of the powerful characters and intense relationships, the attachment to place, and the arresting oddity of personal names which were more fully developed in later works. *Rodmoor* (1916) was followed by *Ducdame* (1925), one of the simplest of his novels, with a single plot, relating a hapless Dorset love story. His first major novel, and major success, was *Wolf Solent* (1929), a crowded work, set again in the West Country, of many interweaving stories, but chiefly concerning Wolf and Gerda, and the destructive pull of opposites. *A Glastonbury Romance* (1932, NY; 1933, London), probably the best known of Powys's novels, is a work on a huge scale, in which *Glastonbury and its legends, both Christian and pagan, exert a supernatural influence on the life of the town—on the religious revival led by Johnny Geard, on the hard commercial interests of Phil Crow, on the communist workers, and on the complex loves, both sacred and sexual, of the town's inhabitants. *Weymouth Sands* (1934, NY) had, because of a libel action, to be recast as *Jobber Skald* (1935), but was restored and republished as *Weymouth Sands* in 1963. Against a sombre background of Portland and the sea, the human struggle centres on Jobber, his love for Perdita and his hatred of Dog Cattistock, and on the final relinquishing of dream in favour of the possible. *Maiden Castle* (1936, NY; 1937, London), set in Dorchester and among the excavations of the fort, follows the interlocking loves of several couples, no longer young; dominated by Dud No-man,

and the girl Wizzie, the lives of the protagonists move towards disillusion and endurance. Most of the later novels, written after Powys had settled in Wales, share an extravagance of subject and style and strong elements of the supernatural. In *Morwyn* (1937), cast as a letter from the narrator to his son, the theme of man's cruelty, to his fellows and to animals, is carried through various meetings with characters from history. *Owen Glendower* (1940, NY; 1941, London), the most successful of his historical novels, describes the confused events and passions surrounding Owen and his cousin Rhisiart. Set in the Dark Ages of Wales, *Porius* (1951) presents a fraught world of giants, Mithraic cults, and Arthurian legend filling the void the Romans have left. This was followed by *The Inmates* (1952), on the theme of madness; *Atlantis* (1954), containing Powys's most extreme flight of imagination, in which Odysseus, returned from Troy, sets out again through a world of giants, heroes, talking animals, and inanimate objects, to discover the continent of America, where he settles; and *The Brazen Head* (1956), on the subject of Roger *Bacon.

Much controversy centres on Powys's stature as a writer. Some regard him as unjustly neglected, an arresting and major novelist, while others find his talent spurious and verbose. See *The Brothers Powys* (1983), a life of all three brothers by R. P. Graves.

POWYS, Llewelyn (1884–1939), brother of John Cowper and Theodore *Powys. He was educated at Sherborne and Corpus Christi College, Cambridge, and shared his brothers' individuality of temperament. He was a prolific essayist and journalist: the best of his many books and collections are generally thought to be *Skin for Skin* (1925), a sombre account of the course of his tuberculosis and the idyllic Dorset interludes when it seemed to be cured; *Impassioned Clay* (1931), an intensely personal account of the human predicament, the Epicurean ethic, and the confrontation with death; and *Love and Death* (1939), an eloquent 'imaginary autobiography', on the theme of his lost first love and his approaching death. Apart from these works, and among many others, was a novel, *Apples Be Ripe* (1930), and two volumes, *Earth Memories* (1934) and *Dorset Essays* (1935), the essays in which had originally achieved wide circulation in London newspapers. *Damnable Opinions* (1935) presented many of the radical, iconoclastic views he shared with his brothers.

POWYS, T(heodore) F(rancis) (1875–1953), brother of John Cowper and Llewelyn Powys (above). He was sent away from the West Country to school in East Anglia, where he later farmed. But in 1902 he returned to Dorset and settled in East Chaldon, whose local landscape became the significant background to almost all his novels and stories. His first book, *Soliloquies of a Hermit* (1916), a series of brief meditations, gave notice of a highly original, idiosyncratic mind. A collection of three long stories, *The Left Leg* (1923), was followed by the novels *Black Bryony* (1923), *Mark Only*

(1924), and *Mr Tasker's Gods* (1925), pessimistic tales of village life in which the author's sensitivity to cruelty and injustice sets the prevailing tone. *Mockery Gap* (1923) and *Innocent Birds* (1926) develop his religious concerns and include elements of the fable and the supernatural. They were followed in 1927 by the novel for which Powys is best remembered, *Mr Weston's Good Wine*. In this vivid allegory Mr Weston (or God) comes to the worldly village of Folly Down, selling from his old van his vintages of Love and Death; after his departure he leaves no paradise, but the good are happier, and the evil (such as Mrs Vosper, the procuress) are vanquished. *Fables* (1929), in which Powys's beliefs are most clearly exposed, was followed by his other major novel, *Unclay* (1931), in which John Death (or the archangel Michael) arrives in Dodder with instructions from God to 'unclay', or kill, various people; however, he loses his instructions, is unsettled by the mysterious Tinker Jar, and falls in love with a village girl. The most complex of Powys's works, it interlocks the stories of several bizarre characters, innocent, evil, and mad, whose lives and loves are altered by Death's arrival. Other volumes of short stories, including the melancholy *Bottle's Path* (1946) and the sunnier *God's Eyes A-Twinkle* (1947), followed, but Powys almost stopped writing about 1940.

Poyser, Martin and Mrs, characters in G. Eliot's *Adam Bede*.

practical criticism, the term used in academic literary studies for an exercise in which students are required to comment upon a poem or short prose passage without knowledge of its authorship, date, or circumstances of composition. This procedure encourages attention to form, diction, and style rather than 'extraneous' associations. It was adopted by I. A. *Richards at the University of Cambridge in the 1920s as an experiment which he records and analyses in his book *Practical Criticism* (1929). Thereafter it became a standard exercise, especially under the influence of the *New Criticism in America. In a more general sense, the term has been used, by S. T. *Coleridge and others, to designate the applied uses of criticism as distinct from the purely theoretical.

PRAED, Winthrop Mackworth (1802–39), educated at Eton, where he founded the *Etonian*, and at Trinity College, Cambridge. He was called to the bar, then went into Parliament, and was appointed secretary to the board of control in 1834. He is remembered principally as a humorous poet and composer of elegant *vers de société*; 'The County Ball', 'A Letter of Advice', 'Stanzas on Seeing the Speaker Asleep', and 'The Vicar' are characteristic examples of his light verse. Like *Hood, with whom he is often compared, he sometimes uses humour to clothe a grim subject, as in 'The Red Fisherman'. He also wrote verse epistles, some to his sister, and historical ballads similar to those of his Cambridge friend *Macaulay, e.g. 'Sir Nicholas at Marston Moor'. His verse was published largely in periodicals and annuals, and his early death from consumption prevented him from taking an interest in more formal publication, but his inoffensive satire, gentle wit, and fluent metrical variations assured him a more lasting readership; his *Poems*, with a memoir by his friend Derwent Coleridge, appeared in 1864. See also D. Hudson, *A Poet in Parliament* (1939).

Praeterita, see RUSKIN, J.

pragmatism, in philosophy, the doctrine that the test of the value of any assertion lies in its practical consequences, i.e. in its practical bearing upon human interests and purposes. See JAMES, W.

Prague Circle, see STRUCTURALISM.

PRATCHETT, Terry, see FANTASY FICTION; SCIENCE FICTION.

PRATT, Samuel Jackson (1749–1814), who wrote as 'Courtney Melmoth'. He was a failed actor who became a voluminous and popular writer of poetry, essays, biography, travel, letters, plays, and anthologies. A play, *The Fair Circassian* (1781, based on *Hawkesworth's *Almoran and Hamet*), was a success, but his novel *Shenstone-Green* (1779), together with his many other novels of *sentiment, made no permanent mark, and his work in general was much criticized, by *Byron and *Lamb among others.

PRAZ, Mario (1896–1982), Italian critic and scholar, born in Rome, who spent ten years in England, in Liverpool and Manchester (1924–34), as senior lecturer, then professor, of Italian studies, before returning to Rome as professor of English literature. He wrote on many aspects of English literature and the connections between the English and Italian traditions; his best-known work is *La carne, la morte e il diavolo nella letteratura romantica* (1930; published in a translation by Angus Davidson as *The Romantic Agony*, 1933) in which he explores the legacy of de *Sade, the perverse and pathological elements in *Poe, *Swinburne, *Wilde, etc., and the cult of the Fatal Woman. His other works include *The Flaming Heart* (1958; essays on *Crashaw, *Machiavelli, T. S. *Eliot, and others) and *La casa della fama* (1952; as *The House of Life*, 1958).

Précieuse, the French equivalent of the English *Blue Stocking. The circle of the marquise de Rambouillet was mocked by *Molière in *Les Précieuses ridicules*.

Prelude, The: or, *Growth of a Poet's Mind*, an autobiographical poem in blank verse by *Wordsworth, addressed to *Coleridge, and begun in 1798–9; a complete draft in 13 books was finished in 1805, but it was several times remodelled, and published posthumously in its final version in 1850, with its present title, suggested by Mary Wordsworth. The full text, showing the work of Wordsworth on it in his later years (which increased the number of books to 14, toned down some of the earlier political views, tidied up structure, syntax, etc.), was published by de Selincourt in 1926. The poem was originally intended as an introduction to 'The Recluse', a vast work which Wordsworth planned but never completed (see Ex-CURSION, THE).

The Prelude is thus composed of passages written at various periods, and sometimes with another purpose; in the first book Wordsworth describes his search for a conventional epic theme, and moves from this to an evocation of his own childhood which leads him less by logic than by imaginative association to his central subject, his own development as a poet and the forces that shaped his imagination. Although profoundly autobiographical, the poem does not proceed in terms of strict chronology; it deals with infancy, school days, Cambridge, his walking tour through the Alps, his political awakening in France, and consequent horrors, etc., but (for example) the passage describing the 'visionary dreariness' of a highly charged moment in his early boyhood is delayed until Book XI ('Imagination, How Impaired and Restored') and the landscape there described is immediately linked in the immediate past with his sister Dorothy and Coleridge, both of whom are intermittently addressed throughout the work. The tone is similarly flexible and variable; conversational and informal in some passages, narrative and naturalistic in others, it rises at points to an impassioned loftiness. A constant theme throughout is Wordsworth's sense of himself as a chosen being, with an overriding duty to his poetic vocation. Wordsworth was aware that his choice of subject (highly original in its day, when the confessional mode in poetry was little developed) might be construed as 'self-conceit', but he insisted that he wrote thus through 'real humility' and 'diffidence'. Apart from its poetic quality, the work is remarkable for its psychological insight into the significance of childhood experience, a theme dear to *Romanticism, but rarely treated with such power and precision. There is an edition by S. M. Parrish (1977).

Premium, Mr, the name taken by Sir Oliver Surface in Sheridan's *The School for Scandal*.

Pre-Raphaelite Brotherhood, a group of artists, poets, and critics—J. E. *Millais, D. G. *Rossetti, W. Holman *Hunt, W. M. *Rossetti, T. *Woolner, Frederic George Stephens (1828–1907), and James Collinson (1825–81)—who first met as a group, led by the first three, in 1848. Various derivations have been assigned to the term 'Pre-Raphaelite', which indicated the group's admiration for the Italian quattrocento and its defiance of the authority both of *Raphael as a master and of 19th-cent. academic painting. The initials 'P.R.B.' first appeared on their work in the RA exhibition of 1849. As its periodical the *Germ (1850) suggests, the movement was strongly literary, and some of its most striking paintings were inspired by *Keats (see Millais's *Isabella*), *Dante, Shakespeare,

and *Tennyson. Common aspirations of the group included fidelity to nature (manifested in clarity, brightness, detailed first-hand observation of flora, etc.), and moral seriousness, in some expressed in religious themes or symbolic mystical iconography. Many of the subjects were medieval as well as literary, and the movement (much influenced by *Ruskin, who became its champion) saw itself in part as a revolt against the ugliness of modern life and dress. Its revolutionary aims thus became in some of its products inextricably mingled with nostalgia. Artists connected with the PRB include Ford Madox Brown, W. B. *Scott, William Dyce, Henry Wallis, Arthur Hughes, *Burne-Jones, and *De Morgan. In literary terms, the movement's most important recruits were perhaps W. *Morris and, more indirectly, *Pater. The brotherhood dissolved in the 1850s, and the original members went their different ways, some achieving considerable commercial success, but its influence was enduring, and the term 'Pre-Raphaelite' has come to denote a distinctive style of appearance, décor, design, etc.

PRESCOTT, William Hickling (1796–1859), born at Salem, Massachusetts, and educated at Harvard. He had his sight affected by an accident while at college, but nevertheless devoted himself, with the help of a reader, to the study of ancient and modern literature. His first work, *The History of Ferdinand and Isabella*, appeared in 1838. It was followed by the *History of the Conquest of Mexico* (1843) and the *History of the Conquest of Peru* (1847). The first two volumes of his unfinished *History of Philip II, King of Spain* appeared in 1855, the third in 1858.

Present Discontents, Thoughts on the Cause of the, a political treatise by E. *Burke, published 1770.

The occasion of this work was the turbulence that had attended and followed the expulsion of *Wilkes from Parliament after his election for Middlesex, and in it Burke expounds for the first time his constitutional creed. He attributes the convulsions in the country to the control of Parliament by the cabal known as the 'King's friends', a system of favouritism essentially at variance with the constitution. Burke considers in detail the Wilkes case, of which the importance lies in its being a test whether the favour of the people or of the court is the surer road to positions of trust. He dismisses various remedies that have been proposed, as endangering the constitution, which 'stands on a nice equipoise'. He thinks the first requirement is the restoration of the right of free election, and looks for further safeguards in the 'interposition of the body of the people itself' to secure decent attention to public interests, and in the restoration of party government.

Present State of the Nation, Observations on a Late Publication Intituled the, a political treatise by E. *Burke, published 1769.

This was Burke's first controversial publication on

political matters. It is a reply to an anonymous pamphlet attributed to George Grenville, in which the decision of the Grenville administration to tax America was defended on the ground that the charges left by the war had made this course necessary. Burke reviews the economic condition of England and France, and defends the repeal of the Stamp Act by the Rockingham administration for the reason that 'politics should be adjusted, not to human reasonings, but to human nature', and that 'people must be governed in a manner agreeable to their temper and disposition'.

PRESTON, Thomas (1537–98), a fellow of King's College, Cambridge, master of Trinity Hall, and vice-chancellor of Cambridge, 1589–90. He is thought to have been the Thomas Preston who wrote *A Lamentable Tragedie Mixed Ful of Pleasant Mirth, Conteyning the Life of Cambises King of Percia* (?1570) (see CAMBYSES).

PRÉVOST, Antoine-François, l'Abbé (1697–1763), French novelist. Successively Jesuit novice, professional soldier, Benedictine priest, Protestant convert, and literary hack, he is remembered today for one novel, *Manon Lescaut* (1731), the story of a mutually destructive passion between a refined but weak nobleman (des Grieux) and a bewitching demi-mondaine. Although classical in form, the novel was romantic in substance, and acquired a huge readership: it formed the basis of operas by Massenet and Puccini. Prévost translated *Richardson's Pamela* (1742), *Clarissa* (1751), and *Histoire du Chevalier Grandisson* (1755–8).

Price, Fanny, a character in J. Austen's *Mansfield Park*.

PRICE, Richard (1723–91), a Dissenting minister who became, with his friend Joseph *Priestley, one of the original members of the Unitarian Society in 1791; he was from 1758 minister at Newington Green, which had been a centre of Dissent for many years, where he influenced many younger writers, including S. *Rogers and M. *Wollstonecraft. He published in 1756 his best-known work, *A Review of the Principal Questions in Morals*, in which he questions *Hutcheson's doctrine of 'moral sense', and argues that the rightness and wrongness of an action belong to it intrinsically. (See BUTLER, J., with whose natural theology and views on conscience he was in sympathy.) He was a close friend of *Franklin, and supported the cause of American independence; he also supported the French Revolution, and his sermon delivered on 4 Nov. 1789, celebrating 'the ardour for liberty' of the French, provoked Burke to write his *Reflections on the *Revolution in France*.

PRICE, Uvedale, see PICTURESQUE.

Pride and Prejudice, a novel by J. *Austen, published 1813. It was originally a youthful work entitled 'First Impressions' and was refused by Cadell, a London publisher, in 1797.

Mr and Mrs Bennet live with their five daughters at Longbourn in Hertfordshire. In the absence of a male heir, the property is due to pass by entail to a cousin, William Collins. Through the patronage of the haughty Lady Catherine de Bourgh, Collins has been presented with a living near Rosings, the Kentish seat of Lady Catherine. Charles Bingley, a rich young bachelor, takes Netherfield, a house near Longbourn, bringing with him his two sisters and his friend Fitzwilliam Darcy, nephew of Lady Catherine. Bingley and Jane, the eldest of the Bennet girls, very soon fall in love. Darcy, though attracted to the next sister, the lively and spirited Elizabeth, greatly offends her by his supercilious behaviour at a ball. This dislike is increased by the account given her by George Wickham, a dashing young militia officer (and son of the late steward of the Darcy property), of the unjust treatment he has met with at Darcy's hands. The aversion is further intensified when Darcy and Bingley's two sisters, disgusted with the vulgarity of Mrs Bennet and her two youngest daughters, effectively separate Bingley from Jane.

Meanwhile the fatuous Mr Collins, urged to marry by Lady Catherine (for whom he shows the most grovelling and obsequious respect), and thinking to remedy the hardship caused to the Bennet girls by the entail, proposes to Elizabeth. When firmly rejected he promptly transfers his affections to Charlotte Lucas, a friend of Elizabeth's, who accepts him. Staying with the newly married couple in their parsonage, Elizabeth again encounters Darcy, who is visiting Lady Catherine. Captivated by her in spite of himself, Darcy proposes to her in terms which do not conceal the violence the proposal does to his self-esteem. Elizabeth indignantly rejects him, on the grounds of his overweening pride, the part he has played in separating Jane from Bingley, and his alleged treatment of Wickham. Greatly mortified, Darcy in a letter justifies the separation of his friend and Jane, and makes it clear that Wickham is, in fact, an unprincipled adventurer.

On an expedition to the north of England with her uncle and aunt, Mr and Mrs Gardiner, Elizabeth visits Pemberley, Darcy's seat in Derbyshire, believing Darcy to be absent. However, Darcy appears, welcomes the visitors, and introduces them to his sister. His manner, though still grave, is now gentle and attentive. At this point news reaches Elizabeth that her youngest sister Lydia has eloped with Wickham. With considerable help from Darcy, the fugitives are traced, their marriage is arranged, and (again through Darcy) they are suitably provided for. Bingley and Jane are reunited and become engaged. In spite, and indeed in consequence, of the insolent intervention of Lady Catherine, Darcy and Elizabeth also become engaged. The story ends with both their marriages, an indication of their subsequent happiness, and an eventual reconciliation with Lady Catherine.

Jane Austen regarded Elizabeth Bennet as her favourite among all her heroines.

PRIEST, Christopher (1943–), novelist and short story writer, born in Cheshire. Like Geoff *Ryman and M. John Harrison, Priest was first published as a *science fiction writer, with *Indoctrinaire* (1970), *Fugue for a Darkening Island* (1972), and *The Inverted World* (1974), but by the early 1980s he was edging towards the mainstream. In *The Affirmation* (1981), in which a lottery winner is promised eternal life, he patrols the frontier between sanity and insanity, rendering his narrator's fantasy world more real than the 'real' world. *The Glamour* (1984) explored not dissimilar psychological territory in a world where little is what it seems. *The Prestige* (1995) is a compelling tale of doppelgängers and magicians, while *The Extremes* (1998) takes a Priestian look at virtual reality, which essentially has been his subject since the beginning. In an interview in *The Third Alternative* in 1998 he stated: 'Perception of memory, and understanding it, is probably the central theme in most of my novels.'

PRIESTLEY, J(ohn) B(oynton) (1894–1984). He was born in Bradford, the son of a schoolmaster, and worked as junior clerk in a wool office before serving in the infantry in the First World War; he then took a degree at Trinity Hall, Cambridge, and in 1922 settled in London, where he quickly made a name as journalist and critic. His first major popular success as a novelist was with the high-spirited, rambling *The Good Companions* (1929), an account of theatrical adventures on the road, which was followed by the grimmer, somewhat self-consciously *'realist' novel of London life, *Angel Pavement* (1930). His many other novels, which vary greatly in scope, include *Bright Day* (1946), *Festival at Farbridge* (1951), *Lost Empires* (1965), and *The Image Men* (1968). Priestley also wrote some 50 plays and dramatic adaptations; amongst the best known are his 'Time' plays, influenced by the theories of J. W. *Dunne (*Dangerous Corner*, 1932; *I Have Been Here Before*, 1937; *Time and the Conways*, 1937), his psychological mystery drama *An Inspector Calls* (1947), and his West Riding farce *When We Are Married* (1938). He also published dozens of miscellaneous works, ranging from *English Journey* (1934, an acutely observant documentary account of his own travels through England, which foreshadowed *Orwell's *Road to Wigan Pier*) to collections of his popular and influential wartime broadcasts (*Britain Speaks*, 1940; *All England Listened*, 1968); from the ambitious, *Jungian *Literature and Western Man* (1960) to informal social histories and commentaries, many of which attempt to define the Englishness of the English, such as *The Edwardians* (1970) and *The English* (1973). He also wrote *Journey down a Rainbow* (1955) with his wife, Jacquetta *Hawkes, describing travels in New Mexico; and several volumes of autobiography, including *Margin Released* (1962) and *Instead of the Trees* (1977). He was awarded the OM in 1977.

Priestley consciously cultivated various poses—of grumbling patriot, cosmopolitan Yorkshireman, pro-fessional amateur, cultured philistine, reactionary radical, etc. He much admired H. G. *Wells (whose spirited disregard of the 'mandarin conventions' of the literary novel he applauded), and in a sense inherited his role as Man of Letters, who remained nevertheless a spokesman for the common sense of the common man. His plays continue to be successfully revived.

PRIESTLEY, Joseph (1733–1804), the son of a Yorkshire cloth-dresser. He became Presbyterian minister at Nantwich and other places, but his views grew increasingly unorthodox and he became with his friend R. *Price one of the original members of the Unitarian Society in 1791. In politics he was a radical, labelled 'Gunpowder' Priestley for his remarks about laying gunpowder 'under the old building of error and superstition'; on 14 July 1791 his Birmingham house was wrecked by a mob outraged by his public support of the French Revolution and his attacks on *Burke. Finding life in England uncomfortable, he emigrated to America in 1794, and died there ten years later.

He wrote on theology, grammar, education, government, psychology, and other subjects; his *Essay on the First Principles of Government* (1768) considerably influenced *Bentham's development of the principle of utilitarianism. He was himself influenced by *Hartley. His work as a chemist was of the first importance; he was the discoverer of oxygen and the author of various valuable scientific works. *Coleridge, in describing him as 'Patriot, and Saint, and Sage' ('Religious Musings', 1796), expresses the esteem in which he was held by radical Dissenters.

Prig, Betsey, a character in Dickens's *Martin Chuzzlewit*, who nurses in partnership with Mrs Gamp, until her remark concerning the apocryphal Mrs Harris, 'I don't believe there's no sich person', causes a difference between them.

Primas, the name (meaning 'first', 'chief') given to Hugh of Orléans, a canon of Orléans c.1140 and a *Goliardic poet who excelled in Latin lyrics which reveal both scholarship and a libertine disposition. Although he taught in Paris and Orléans and was admired by his contemporaries, his career was erratic and he died in the *Hospitium* amongst the destitute. See K. Langosch, *Hymnen und Vagantenlieder* (Basle, 1954), 170 ff.

Prime Minister, The, a novel by A. *Trollope, published 1876, the fifth in the *'Palliser' series.

Ferdinand Lopez is disappointed in his marriage to Emily Wharton. He had hoped it would bring him money and social position, but Emily's father ties up her fortune, and Lopez is revealed as an improvident adventurer. The duchess of Omnium promises Lopez support in the Silverbridge by-election, but the duke, who is now prime minister, refuses to exert his influence. Lopez claims he has been cheated, and presses the duke to pay his election expenses, to the duke's political embarrassment. But even this effrontery does not save Lopez from financial ruin. Briefly flirting with the idea of managing a Guatemalan mine, he prefers death to exile, and walks in front of an express train.

The novel also records the history of the duke of Omnium's ministry. He is appointed head of a rickety coalition, which few observers believe will last long, but which he holds together for three years, while the duchess makes a determined attempt to support the ministry by a programme of lavish entertainment.

Prime of Miss Jean Brodie, The, a novel by M. *Spark, published 1961.

Set in Edinburgh during the 1930s, it describes the career of eccentric and egotistical Miss Brodie, teacher at the Marcia Blaine School for Girls, and her domination of her 'set' of 16-year-olds, Monica Douglas ('famous mostly for mathematics'), Rose Stanley ('famous for sex'), Eunice Gardiner ('spritely gymnastics and glamorous swimming'), Jenny Gray (an intended actress), Mary Macgregor (famed as 'silent lump' and scapegoat), and Sandy Stewart, who becomes Miss Brodie's betrayer. With many flashes back and forward, it describes the manner in which Miss Brodie fascinates her disciples, who are particularly intrigued by her relationships with two male teachers, the married and Catholic art master, Mr Lloyd, and the bachelor Church of Scotland singing master, Mr Lowther, who, rejected after much dalliance by Miss Brodie, in despair marries the science mistress. Sandy (rather than Rose, as Miss Brodie plans) has an affair with Mr Lloyd while Miss Brodie is away in the summer of 1938 touring Hitler's Germany; the results of this are that Sandy becomes a Catholic and arranges the dismissal of Miss Brodie on the grounds of her sympathy with Fascism, manifested not only in her enthusiasm for Hitler but also in her indirect responsibility for the death of another schoolgirl, not one of 'the set', who had died on a journey to Spain in the Spanish Civil War, encouraged by Miss Brodie to support Franco. Miss Brodie herself, dangerous but compelling, 'an Edinburgh Festival all on her own', is the centre of the novel's considerable moral ambiguity and complexity; she is seen most clearly through the 'treacherous' little eyes of Sandy, who, we are told in the second chapter, in a characteristic omniscient narrative leap, becomes a nun and writes a 'psychological treatise on the nature of moral perception, called "The Transfiguration of the Commonplace"'.

primer, a term in English from the 14th cent. (used by both *Chaucer and *Langland) for a first reading-book of prayers. Because it was used as the basic instruction in reading for children, the term gradually came to be applied to a book containing the rudiments of instruction in reading or any language, an elementary schoolbook. This sense survived up to the 20th cent. (archaically pronounced 'primmer'), in the titles of works such as the *Anglo-Saxon Primer* of *Sweet.

primitivism, and the cult of 'the Noble Savage', have been closely associated with the 18th cent., though they are clearly in some aspects descended from the classical concept of the Golden Age, and preceded by individual works like A. Behn's *Oroonoko* (which was extremely successful during the 18th cent. in *Southerne's stage version). Primitivism took the form of a revolt against luxury (see Goldsmith's *The Deserted Village*), against sophistication (see Colman's *Inkle and Yarico*, Cumberland's *The West Indian*, Mrs *Inchbald's *The Child of Nature*, Bage's *Hermsprong*, all works which stress the superiority of a simple education), and, in terms of critical theory, against *Neoclassicism. (See HURD; GRAY, T.; HERDER.) Primitivism proposed a belief in man's natural goodness, and in the inevitable corruptions of civilization. Interest in the educational and philosophic theories of *Rousseau was accompanied by great enthusiasm for travel writings and for real-life South Sea Islanders, Eskimos, Lapplanders, Negroes, etc.; the South Sea Islander Omai from Tahiti received a warm welcome in London in 1776 from men of the world like *Boswell, who found him 'elegant'. *Reynolds's portrait of Omai is a powerful emblem of this fascination with so-called 'primitives'. There was also much curiosity about the phenomenon of the 'wild child' (which found recent versions in *Kipling's Mowgli, *Burroughs's Tarzan, Truffaut's film *L'Enfant sauvage*, and Jill Paton *Walsh's *Knowledge of Angels*; *Monboddo, a keen disciple of Rousseau, wrote a preface to a French case history of a 'savage girl' in 1768. Home-grown primitives were also in demand, and 'peasant' poets such as S. *Duck and A. *Yearsley were taken up by eager patrons: the notorious fake primitives *Macpherson and *Chatterton enjoyed a considerable vogue. They in turn were stimulated by the scholarly researches of *Percy and *Ritson, who revived an interest in early English poetry. One of the most important figures in the movement was Gray, whose poems *The Bard* and *The Progress of Poesy* reflect his own interest in and feelings for the non-classical past: a note on the latter insisted on the 'extensive influence of poetic genius over the remotest and most uncivilized nations; its connection with liberty, and the virtues that naturally attend on it' (see also STUKELEY). It was in the cause of liberty that writers such as *Cowper and T. *Day defended the Noble Savage and attacked the slave trade. The ideas embodied in primitivism were in many ways continued in the *Romantic movement, with its stress on Nature, freedom (both political and artistic), and the natural man. (See SLAVERY, LITERATURE OF, and C. B. Tinker, *Nature's Simple Plan* (1922); H. N. Fairchild, *The Noble Savage* (1928); L. Whitney, *Primitivism and the Idea of Progress* (1934).) In recent years writers like Edward *Said took exception to the Eurocentric implications that the concept of primitivism carried, and the subject has been redefined in the context of *post-colonial studies. See *The Myth of Primitivism: Perspectives on Art* (1991) by Susan Hiller and *The Last of the Race: The Growth of a Myth from Milton to Darwin* by Fiona J. Stafford (1994).

PRIMROSE, Diana (fl. 1630), possibly a daughter or daughter-in-law of James Primrose, clerk of the Privy Council of Scotland. Her poem-sequence *Chaine of Pearle. Or a Memoriall of … Queene Elizabeth* (1630), based on *Camden's *Annals of Queen Elizabeth* (1615), is a nostalgic panegyric on a Protestant queen, obliquely angled at King Charles I's pro-Catholic policies. 'Shee banged the Pope, and took the Gospells part' is the core of her message. The poem, in serviceable rhyming pentameter, consists of a chain of ten 'pearls', dealing with Elizabeth's virtues.

Primrose, Dr, the vicar of Wakefield in *Goldsmith's novel of that name. His family consists of his wife Deborah; daughters Olivia and Sophia; sons George and Moses; and two younger boys.

Prince, The, see MACHIAVELLI.

PRINCE, F(rank) T(empleton) (1912–2003), poet, born in South Africa, and educated there and at Balliol College, Oxford, and Princeton. From 1957 to 1974 he was professor of English at Southampton University. His collections of poetry include *Poems* (1938), *Soldiers Bathing and Other Poems* (1954), and *The Doors of Stone: Poems 1938–62* (1963); his *Collected Poems* appeared in 1979. His poems range from dramatic monologues ('The Old Age of Michelangelo') to long meditations on R. *Brooke (*Afterword on Rupert Brooke*, 1977) and on *Sterne's *Eliza* ('A Last Attachment', 1979); from technical experiments with little-used verse forms (e.g. the Italian *strambotto*) to the wartime immediacy and pictorial qualities of the title poem of *Soldiers Bathing*.

PRINCE Mary, see BLACK BRITISH LITERATURE.

Prince Hohenstiel-Schwangau, *Suviour of Society*, a poem in blank verse by R. *Browning, written and published 1871. The prince is based on the Emperor Napoleon III.

The title 'saviour of society' was often used of Napoleon by his adherents; Browning makes ironic use of it in his depiction of a statesman who reviews his long career of compromise and tergiversation, ostensibly addressing himself to his mistress in a hotel in Leicester Square, where he is living in exile and disgrace, and justifying his conduct by appeal to a pragmatism which he believes is inherent in the relation between humanity and God. But the last lines of the poem reveal that the prince has been fantasizing the whole episode; that he has been meditating, on the brink of an important political decision, what he *would* say if his plans failed and he were forced into exile. Thus, while the poem alludes in detail to Napoleon III's career, its form also raises questions about truth and imagination which are central to Browning's aesthetics: political and poetic

idealism, opposed to and yet dependent on the materialism of action and language, mirror one another.

Princess, The: *A Medley*, a poem by *Tennyson, published 1847. Some of the well-known lyrics ('The splendour falls', 'Ask me no more: the moon may draw the sea') were added in the third edition of 1850, but others, including 'Tears, idle tears' (composed in 1834 at Tintern) and 'Now sleeps the crimson petal, now the white', were included in the first. The poem, which opens with a description of a summer fête based on an event at the Lushingtons' home Park House, near Maidstone, purports to be a tale of fancy composed in turn by some young people, based on an old chronicle.

A prince has been betrothed since childhood to Princess Ida, daughter of neighbouring King Gama. She becomes a devotee of women's rights, abjures marriage, and founds a university. The prince and two companions, Cyril and Florian, gain admission to the university dressed as women, and are detected by the two tutors, Lady Psyche and Lady Blanche, who from different motives conceal their knowledge. The deceit is presently detected by Ida, but not before the prince has had occasion to rescue her from drowning. Her determination is unshaken, and a combat ensues, between fifty warriors led by the prince and fifty led by Gama's son, during which the three comrades are wounded. The university is turned into a hospital, the prince urges his suit, and he wins Ida, envisaging a future in which 'The man [may] be more of woman, she of man'; the epilogue is a plea for gradual social reform: 'Maybe wildest dreams | Are but the needful prelude of the truth.' The work was well received on the whole, though Tennyson wrote of it to his friend E. *FitzGerald 'I hate it and so will you', and subjected it to considerable revision. It formed the basis of the satirical *Gilbert and Sullivan opera *Princess Ida*.

Princesse de Clèves, La, see LA FAYETTE.

principe, Il, see MACHIAVELLI.

Principia Ethica, see MOORE, G. E.

Principia Mathematica, see NEWTON, I., and RUSSELL, B.

PRINGLE, Thomas (1789–1834). He studied at Edinburgh University, became a friend of Sir W. *Scott, and was for a short time editor of the *Edinburgh Monthly Magazine*, the first of several editorships of various journals. In 1809 he published his first volume of poems, which included 'The Emigrant's Farewell', and emigrated to South Africa. He is remembered chiefly as a poet of that country. His *Ephemerides* (1828) and *African Sketches* (1834) reveal his sympathetic interest in the native races and the wildlife of Africa, and contain some poems of quality, such as 'The Hottentot' and 'Afar in the Desert', which was highly praised by *Coleridge.

PRIOR, Matthew (1664–1721), the son of a joiner of Wimborne, Dorset, educated at Westminster School and St John's College, Cambridge. He began writing early, and joined with Charles Montagu (later earl of Halifax) in *The Hind and the Panther Transvers'd to the Story of the Country Mouse and the City Mouse* (1687, see TOWN MOUSE AND COUNTRY MOUSE), a satire on Dryden's *The Hind and the Panther*. He was appointed secretary to the ambassador at The Hague and employed in the negotiations for the Treaty of Ryswick; his poem 'The Secretary' (1696) gives a lively picture of this period of his life. He joined the Tories and in 1711 was sent to Paris as a secret agent at the time of the peace negotiations, the subsequent Treaty of Utrecht (1713) being popularly known as 'Matt's Peace'. He was recalled on Queen Anne's death and imprisoned for over a year. A handsome folio edition of his poems was brought out in 1718 after his release, by which he gained 4,000 guineas in subscriptions; *Harley gave him £4,000 for the purchase of Down Hall in Essex. Prior is best remembered for his brilliant occasional verses, epigrams, and familiar pieces ('My noble, lovely, little Peggy' and 'Jinny the Just', for example, in which he combines lightness of touch with mock seriousness), but also wrote longer works in various styles. *Carmen Seculare* (1700) is an ode celebrating the arrival of William III; 'Alma; or the Progress of the Mind' (1718) is a *Hudibrastic dialogue ridiculing various systems of philosophy; and 'Solomon on the Vanity of the World' (1718) is a long soliloquy in heroic couplets on the same theme. 'Hans Carvel' (1701) and 'The Ladle' (1718) are narratives ending with coarse jests, in a genre popular at the time, whereas 'Henry and Emma' (1709) (described by *Cowper as 'enchanting') is a sentimental burlesque of the old ballad *'The Nut-Brown Maid'. *Down-Hall, a Ballad* (1723), a lively account of a trip to Essex, also deserves mention. His prose works include an *Essay upon Learning*, an *Essay upon Opinion*, and *Four *Dialogues of the Dead*, which were not published until A. R. Waller's two-volume edition of 1905–7. His *Literary Works*, ed. H. B. Wright and M. K. Spears, were published in two volumes, 1959.

'Prioress's Tale, The', see CANTERBURY TALES, 16.

Prisoner of Chillon, The, a dramatic monologue principally in rhymed octosyllabics by *Byron, written in 1816 after a visit with *Shelley to the castle of Chillon on Lake Geneva, and published in the same year. It presents the imprisonment of a historical character, the Swiss patriot François de Bonnivard (1496–1570), who in the poem describes his years spent chained with his two brothers in the castle's dungeons. He survives their slow deaths, and in time his guards relax their vigilance, and he is able to glimpse the outside world from his barred windows. At first tormented by the vision of the lake, the mountains, and the joy of nature, he becomes at last reconciled to his fate, a friend in 'long communion'

of his fellow inmates, the mice and the spiders: when he is released he leaves his hermitage and regains his freedom 'with a sigh'. This simple and powerful work of dignified resignation became one of Byron's most popular poems.

Prisoner of Zenda, The, and its sequel *Rupert of Hentzau*, novels by Anthony Hope (*Hawkins), published 1894 and 1898.

They deal with the perilous and romantic adventures of Rudolf Rassendyll, an English gentleman, in Ruritania, where, by impersonating the king (to whom he bears a marked physical resemblance), he defeats a plot to oust him from the throne. He falls in love with the king's betrothed, Princess Flavia, and she with him, but gallantly relinquishes her to the restored king. In the sequel he defeats a plot of the villain Rupert of Hentzau against Flavia, now the unhappy wife of the king, and has another chance of taking the throne and of marrying Flavia. But he is assassinated before his decision is known.

PRITCHETT, Sir V(ictor) S(awdon) (1900–97), novelist, critic, and short story writer. He was born in Ipswich, the son of a travelling salesman, and spent a peripatetic childhood in the provinces and various London suburbs before attending Alleyn's School, Dulwich, which he left at 15 to work in the leather trade. He went to Paris at the age of 21, where he worked in the photographic trade; he then became a journalist, writing for the *Christian Science Monitor* in Ireland, then Spain, before settling to a literary life in London. His first novel, *Clare Drummer* (1929), was followed by several others, but Pritchett is principally known for his short stories, the first of which appeared in the *Cornhill, the *New Statesman*, etc., in the 1920s; his first collection, *The Spanish Virgin and Other Stories* (1930), was followed by many others, including *You Make Your Own Life* (1938), *When My Girl Comes Home* (1961), and *The Camberwell Beauty* (1974). Two volumes of *Collected Stories* appeared (1982, 1983). They are distinguished by their wide social range, shrewd observation of the quirks of human nature, and humane irony. Pritchett's other works include *The Living Novel* (1946), studies of *Balzac (1973) and *Turgenev (1977), and two volumes of much-praised autobiography, *The Cab at the Door: Early Years* (1968, of which the title refers to his household's frequent removals, which he claimed gave him a lifelong love of travel) and *Midnight Oil* (1971), which ends with the Second World War. He also edited the *Oxford Book of Short Stories* (1981). As critic he contributed most regularly to the *New Statesman*, of which he became a director in 1946.

Private Memoirs and Confessions of a Justified Sinner, The, a novel by J. *Hogg, published 1824, a macabre and highly original tale, inviting psychological as well as literary interpretation.

In the first part of the book Colwan, believing

himself to be one of the 'saved' (according to the Calvinist doctrine of predestination), and under the influence of a malign stranger who may be interpreted as his evil alter ego, commits a series of horrifying crimes, including the murder of his half-brother. The second section of the book purports to be a memoir written by Colwan, and discovered when his grave was opened a century after his suicide. This reveals that he also murdered his mother, a girl, and a preacher, all under the supposed auspices of divine justice, before coming eventually to believe that the stranger who haunts him is in fact the devil. His skull, on exhumation, is found to have two horn-like protuberances.

private presses are distinguished by aims that are aesthetic rather than commercial and by printing for the gratification of their owners rather than to order. Many such have been set up since the 17th cent. by amateurs of books or printing: that of Horace *Walpole at *Strawberry Hill (1757–97) is a well-known example. At the end of the 19th cent. presses of this kind were intended as a protest against the low artistic standards and degradation of labour in the printing trade. W. *Morris set up the Kelmscott Press (1891–8) with this object; and others, notably C. H. St John Hornby (the Ashendene Press, 1895), *Ricketts (the Vale Press, 1896), and T. J. Cobden-Sanderson and Emery Walker (the Doves Press, 1900), followed him. The *Cuala Press was founded in Ireland in 1902. The 1920s saw the foundation of the *Golden Cockerel Press, the *Gregynog Press, and the *Nonesuch Press, and a considerable revival of interest in the art of wood engraving. The term 'private press' is sometimes applied, perhaps unjustifiably, to such publishing companies as the Nonesuch, which used commercial printers and called itself 'architects rather than builders' of books. See W. Ransom, *Private Presses and Their Books* (1929) and Roderick Cave, *The Private Press* (1971).

PROCTER, Adelaide Anne (1825–64), daughter of B. W. Procter (Barry *Cornwall). She was *Dickens's most published poet in *Household Words*. She lived in London and was a leading member of the Society for Promoting the Employment of Women as well as supporting a hostel for homeless women and children in east London. In addition to her popular devotional lyrics Procter wrote witty, ironic poems about women's position ('A Woman's Last Word' is a rewriting of Robert *Browning's poem of the same title) and some lyrical ballads which draw attention to the position of fallen and single women at mid-19th cent. She also wrote some humane lyrics about the Crimean War. Her most famous poem 'A Lost Chord' (*Legends and Lyrics*, 1858–61) was set to music by Arthur *Sullivan. The poem combines conventional devotional sentiment with a more unconventional concern that a woman's expressive voice be heard. See Gill Gregory, *The Life and Work of Adelaide Procter: Poetry, Feminism and Fathers* (1998).

PROCTER, Brian Waller, see CORNWALL.

Prodigal Son, the, the general subject of a group of plays written about 1540–75, showing the influence of the continental neo-classic writers of the period, particularly Gnaphaeus in his *Acolastus*, on the early Tudor dramatists and novelists. The chief of these are *Misogonus*, dating from about 1560 (author unknown), *Jacke Jugeler* (?1562), and *Gascoigne's *Glasse of Government* (1575). The parable of the Prodigal Son is in Luke 15: 11–32.

Professor, The, a novel by C. *Brontë, written 1846 (before *Jane Eyre*), but not published until 1857.

The story is based, like *Villette*, on the author's experiences in Brussels, and uses much of the same material, though the two principal characters are transposed. William Crimsworth, an orphan, after trying his hand at trade in the north of England, goes to seek his fortune in Brussels. At the girls' school where he teaches English he falls in love with Frances Henri, an Anglo-Swiss pupil-teacher and lace mender, whose Protestant honesty and modesty are contrasted with the manipulating duplicity of the Catholic headmistress, Zoraide Reuter. Crimsworth resists Mlle Reuter's overtures; she marries the headmaster of the neighbouring boys' school, M. Pelet, Crimsworth resigns his post, and, after finding a new and better one, is able to marry Frances.

Progress of Poesy, The, a Pindaric *ode by T. *Gray, published 1757. Gray describes the different kinds of poetry, its varying powers, its primitive origins, and its connections with political liberty. He recounts its progress from Greece, to Italy, to Britain, paying homage to Shakespeare, *Milton, and *Dryden—a footnote singling out Dryden's *'Sublime' 'Ode on St Cecilia's Day'—and concludes that no one in his day can equal them. Dr *Johnson found the poem obscure. (See also BARD, THE.)

PROKOFIEV, Sergei (1891–1953), Russian composer. His first composition with English connections was a Soviet commission towards the end of his time abroad (1918–36), the music for a theatrical experiment combining excerpts from G. B. *Shaw's *Caesar and Cleopatra*, Shakespeare's *Antony and Cleopatra*, and *Pushkin's *Egyptian Nights*, given in Moscow in 1935 with little success.

In the same year the first version of Prokofiev's ballet *Romeo and Juliet* was heard by the directors of the Bolshoi Theatre and turned down as unsuitable for dancing: the composer revised and improved his score (restoring the tragic ending, which he had originally altered because of the difficulty of dancing it), but he had to wait until 1940 for the first performance in his own country of this classically beautiful score. Another Shakespearian enterprise was the incidental music for *Hamlet (1939), but more important was the opera *Betrothal in a Monastery*, based on Sheridan's *The Duenna*. Here Prokofiev laid aside the well-meaning

*Socialist Realism of more recent compositions and produced a brightly lyrical score which perfectly matches Sheridan's play. It was completed by 1941, but not performed until 1946, after the première of the composer's greatest opera, the epic adaptation of *Tolstoy's *War and Peace*.

prolepsis (from Greek, 'to anticipate'), the assignment of something, such as an event or a name, to a time that precedes it, as in 'If you tell the cops, you're a dead man'; the use of a descriptive word in anticipation of the act or circumstances that would make it applicable, as in 'overwhelm the sunken ships' for 'overwhelm and sink the ships'.

Prometheus (the name means 'Forethought') appears in Greek myth as a divine being, one of the Titans, descended from the original union of the Sky God with the Earth Mother. In some stories he is the creator of mankind and he is always their champion. He is supposed to have stolen fire for them from heaven when they were denied it by Zeus, and to have been punished by being fastened to a cliff in the Caucasus where an eagle tore daily at his liver. *Hesiod explains Zeus' enmity to Prometheus and his human dependants by stating that Prometheus had played a trick on him over a sacrifice, but this story, like so many in Hesiod, has the air of a rationalization. It is certainly possible that behind the rebellious Titan of *Aeschylus there lurks an early Greek or Indo-European divinity, a benevolent demiurge, whom the Olympians supplanted. But even if we allow for a measure of distortion in the story as we know it, this primitive deity must have been an ambivalent figure. The fire and the skills which were his gifts to mankind were not an unmixed blessing, since they were also the source of work and war. It is interesting that Prometheus seems as a god to have been firmly rooted in the real world of effort, danger, and pain, while the Olympians who successfully supplanted him were the products of an idealizing daydream, beautiful, potent, happy, and free from suffering and death.

The modern popularity of the Promethean myth dates from the 1770s when *Goethe came to see in the Titan a symbol of man's creative striving and of his revolt against the restraints of society and life. Goethe set the pattern which the 19th cent. followed. Shelley's *Prometheus Unbound* (1820) glorified the virtues of revolt, representing authority as responsible for man's sufferings. *Coleridge wrote an essay on the *Prometheus* of Aeschylus (1825), Elizabeth Barrett (*Browning) translated the play (1833), and *Bridges wrote a version called *Prometheus the Firegiver* (1883). In the 20th cent., *Gide's enigmatic *Prométhée mal enchaîné* presented a hero who is still a symbol of mankind's quest to transcend the obvious.

Prometheus Unbound, a lyrical drama in four acts by P. B. *Shelley, written in Italy 1818–19, published 1820.

A great but uneven work that orchestrates all Shelley's aspirations, and contradictions, as a poet and radical, it is partly mythical drama (or 'psychodrama') and partly political allegory. Shelley began with the idea of completing the Aeschylian story of *Prometheus the firebringer and champion of mankind, who is bound to his rock for all eternity by a jealous Jupiter. He combined this with his view of Satan as the hero of *Paradise Lost*, and of God as the Oppressor. Boldly rewriting or updating these two myths, he presents a Prometheus–Lucifer figure of moral perfection and 'truest motives', who is liberated by 'alternative' and benign forces in the universe and triumphs over Tyranny in the name of all mankind. The work is executed in a bewildering variety of verse forms, some more successful than others: rhetorical soliloquies, dramatic dialogues, love songs, dream visions, lyric choruses, and prophecies.

Act I shows Prometheus chained in agony, 'in a ravine of Icy rocks in the Indian Caucasus', comforted by his mother Earth, but tempted to yield to Jupiter's tyranny by Mercury and the Furies. Act II introduces Asia and Panthea, the lovely daughters of Ocean, who determine to release Prometheus by confronting the ultimate source of power, *Demogorgon, a volcanic force dwelling in a shadowy underworld. Act III abruptly presents Jupiter vanquished by the eruption of Demogorgon, and Prometheus released and united with his beloved Asia. Their child, the Spirit of the Hour, prophesies the liberation of mankind. Act IV is a cosmic coda, or epithalamium, sung by a chorus of Hours, Spirits, Earth, and Moon.

The sexual, scientific, and political symbolism of the drama have been variously interpreted: but the concept of liberation is central. Act II sc. iv in which Asia (the Spirit of Love) confronts and questions Demogorgon (Fate, Historical Necessity, or perhaps 'the People-Monster') must count among Shelley's poetic masterpieces. The work has an important preface on the role of poetry in reforming society, which links with the *Defence of Poetry*.

PROPERTIUS, Sextus (*c*.50–*c*.16 BC), Roman poet, whose four books of poetry celebrate his passion for the lover whom he calls Cynthia. His poetry ranges from poems of rare elegance and refinement to allusively mythological pieces in the Hellenistic tradition to which he is deeply indebted. Echoes of his verse can be found in B. *Barnes and T. *Campion and he is the subject of *Pound's 'Homage to Sextus Propertius' (1919).

Prophecy of Famine, The, see CHURCHILL, CHARLES.

Prophetic Books, the name sometimes given to the symbolic and prophetic poems of *Blake, e.g. *The Book of *Urizen*, *The Book of *Los*, *Milton*, and *Jerusalem*.

Prose Brut, The, see BRUT, THE PROSE.

prosody, see METRE.

prosopopeia, see PERSONIFICATION.

'Prosopopoia', the subtitle of Spenser's *'Mother Hubberds Tale'.

Prospero, (1) in Shakespeare's *The Tempest*, the usurped duke of Milan and father of *Miranda; (2) a character in Jonson's *Every Man in His Humour*, a play in which Shakespeare himself acted.

Proteus, one of *The Two Gentlemen of Verona* in Shakespeare's play; his name suggests his fickle and changing nature.

Prothalamion, a 'Spousall Verse' written by *Spenser, published 1596, in celebration of the double marriage of the Lady Elizabeth and the Lady Katherine Somerset, daughters of the earl of Worcester. The name was invented by Spenser on the model of his *Epithalamion*.

PROUDHON, Pierre-Joseph (1809–65), French social philosopher and political activist. His writings laid the basis for the organized anarchist movement in France, and exercised considerable influence on the thought and practice of anarchist and socialist movements throughout Europe. He published a large number of works, including *Qu'est-ce que la propriété?* (1840; *What is Property?*, 1876), which begins with the celebrated paradox 'La propriété, c'est le vol!'; *Idée générale de la révolution au XIXe siècle* (1851); *De la justice dans la révolution et dans l'église* (1858); and *De la capacité politique des classes ouvrières* (1865). His prose style was admired by *Baudelaire and *Flaubert, and his influence extended to such figures as Courbet and *Tolstoy, as well as to large numbers of political activists in Italy, Spain, Russia, and elsewhere.

Proudie, Mrs, the violently evangelical wife of the bishop of Barchester, and a leading character in the *'Barsetshire' novels of A. Trollope.

PROULX, E(dna) Annie (1935–   ), American novelist who has achieved critical and commercial success since her first novel, *Postcards* (1991), made her the first woman to win the PEN/Faulkner prize. Her second, *The Shipping News* (1993), won her other awards and a large British readership. In both of these, in *Accordion Crimes* (1996), and in her collected short stories (*Hearts Songs and Other Stories*, USA 1998; *Heart Songs*, UK 1995) she combines two powerful strands of American writing: a regionalist emphasis on particular places and an encyclopaedic attempt to grasp the diversity of America. For her short story 'Brokeback Mountain' (1997) she dropped the E and published as Annie Proulx.

PROUST, Marcel (1871–1922), French novelist, essayist, and critic, author of *A la recherche du temps perdu* (1913–27; *Remembrance of Things Past*, 1922–31). In the 1890s Proust moved in the most fashionable Parisian circles, but in later years became a virtual recluse, dedicating himself to the completion of *A la recherche*, which occupied him till the end of his life. In 1896 he published a collection of essays, poems, and short stories, *Les Plaisirs et les jours* (*Pleasures and Regrets*, 1948), and in the period *c.*1896–1900 worked on an early version of *A la recherche* which was published posthumously, as *Jean Santeuil*, in 1952 (English trans. 1955). He was actively involved, on the side of *Dreyfus, in the Dreyfus case of 1897–9. Around 1899 he discovered *Ruskin's art criticism, and subsequently translated Ruskin's *The Bible of Amiens* and *Sesame and Lilies* into French. In 1919 he published a collection of literary parodies, *Pastiches et mélanges*. He explored his own literary aesthetic in *Contre Sainte-Beuve* (1954; *By Way of Sainte-Beuve*, 1958), where he defines the artist's task as the releasing of the creative energies of past experience from the hidden store of the unconscious, an aesthetic which found its most developed literary expression in *A la recherche*.

Prout, Father, see MAHONY.

Provençal, or *langue d'oc* (as distinct from the *langue d'oïl*), the language of the southern part of France, and the literary medium of the *troubadours. Their language was a *koiné*, a class language avoiding marked regional features; it was known as *lemosi* (Limousin), probably because some of the most famous troubadours came from the area around Limoges. Provençal declined as a literary language after the defeat of the south in the Albigensian War. The language is now generally called *occitan*, though the terms Provençal and *langue d'oc* are still in use (but see also under FÉLIBRIGE).

   Provençal literature in the medieval period consisted chiefly of the lyric poetry composed by the troubadours for the feudal courts of the Midi, northern Italy, and Spain. The *canso*, the love song in the courtly style which was the troubadours' special achievement, was known all over western Europe, and inspired the courtly poetry of northern France, the minnesang of Germany, and the Petrarchan poetry of Italy. The sirventes, the satirical poem mostly on political or moral themes, was also much cultivated by the troubadours. There is little literature of an epic kind, or literature in prose, extant in Old Provençal, and Provençal was considered the language *par excellence* of lyric poetry, courtly in content and very elaborate in style. This poetic flowering came to an end with the decline, after the Albigensian crusade, of the aristocratic society which had produced it.

   Ed. A. R. Press, *Anthology of Troubadour Lyric Poetry* (1971).

Proverbs of Alfred, The, an early Middle English poem, dating, in the form in which it has reached us, from the 13th cent., though probably composed about 1150–80. The poem's 600 lines begin by giving an account of Alfred and proceed to a series of 35 sayings, each beginning 'Thus quath Alfred', containing proverbial instructions. The attribution of the proverbs to Alfred is no more than traditional: many different proverbs are attributed to him in *The Owl and the Nightingale*: see H. P. South's edition (1931), 43–63.

'Proverbs of Hell', see MARRIAGE OF HEAVEN AND HELL, THE.

Provok'd Husband, The, or *A Journey to London*, a comedy by *Vanbrugh, finished by C. *Cibber, produced 1728.

The 'provok'd husband' is Lord Townly, who, driven to desperation by the extravagance of his wife, decides to separate from her and to make his reasons public. The sentence (according to Cibber's ending) brings Lady Townly to her senses, and a reconciliation is promoted by Manly, Lord Townly's sensible friend and the successful suitor of Lady Grace, Lord Townly's exemplary sister. A second element in the plot is the visit to London of Sir Francis Wronghead, a simple country gentleman, with his wife, a foolish, extravagant woman who wants to be a fine lady, and their son and daughter. Count Basset, an unprincipled gamester, under cover of courting Lady Wronghead, plans to entice her daughter into a secret marriage, and to effect a match between her son and his own cast-off mistress. The plot nearly succeeds, but is frustrated by Manly.

Provok'd Wife, The, a comedy by *Vanbrugh, produced 1697, but possibly written before *The Relapse*.

Sir John Brute, a debauched man of quality, married his wife for love, but is now disillusioned with her and with matrimony, and rails against both. Lady Brute married for money, but has remained technically faithful; she is courted by Constant, whose cynical friend Heartfree falls in love with her niece Belinda. The two ladies, for a frolic, invite Constant and Heartfree to meet them in Spring Garden. Here Lady Brute is on the point of yielding to Constant when they are interrupted by the jealous and affected Lady Fancyfull. The two couples return to Lady Brute's house and sit down to cards, confident that Sir John will not return from a drinking bout for some hours. Sir John, however, having been arrested by the watch for brawling in the streets disguised in a parson's gown, has been dismissed by the magistrate. (Vanbrugh rewrote scenes i and iii of Act IV for the 1725/6 revival and had Sir John put on 'a light lady's short cloak and wrapping goun' and call himself 'Bonduca, Queen of the Welchmen' when arrested, but 'Lady Brute' before the justice.) He comes home unexpectedly, finds the two men hidden in a closet, but declines the duel offered by Constant. The presence of the men is attributed to the proposed marriage of Heartfree and Belinda, and in spite of Lady Fancyfull's attempts to make mischief all ends relatively well, though the problems of the Brutes clearly remain unresolved.

Provost, The, a novel by J. *Galt, published 1822, a book in which Galt's particular skills are at their best.

The Provost, Mr Pawkie, reflects on the arts of authority and rule, and his own successful manipulation of them throughout his life. The ironic revelation of his self-righteous, contriving character is of more importance in this work than the Scottish social scene he describes.

PRUDENTIUS (Aurelius Prudentius Clemens) (348–post-405), a Christian Latin poet born in Spain, the composer of many hymns and of the *Psychomachia*, an allegorical account of the battle for the soul of man which was a very important influence on the development of medieval and Renaissance allegorical works. It is given extended attention in *The Allegory of Love* by C. S. *Lewis, who had little admiration for the work. It is translated (along with some of the hymns) in H. Isbell's *The Last Poets of Imperial Rome* (1971).

'Prufrock, The Love Song of J. Alfred', a *dramatic monologue by T. S. *Eliot.

Pryderi, see MABINOGION.

Prynne, Hester, the heroine of Hawthorne's *The Scarlet Letter*.

PRYNNE, William (1600–69), Puritan pamphleteer. He was educated at Bath grammar school and Oriel College, Oxford, and was a barrister of Lincoln's Inn. He wrote against *Arminianism from 1627, and endeavoured to reform the manners of his age. He published *Histriomastix*, an enormous work attacking stage plays, in 1633. For a supposed aspersion on Charles I and his queen in it he was sentenced by the Star Chamber, in 1634, to be imprisoned during life, to be fined £5,000, and to lose both his ears in the pillory. He continued to write in the Tower of London, and in 1637 was again fined £5,000, deprived of the remainder of his ears, and branded on the cheeks with the letters S. L. ('seditious libeller') which Prynne humorously asserted to mean 'Stigmata Laudis' (i.e. of Archbishop *Laud). He was released by the Long Parliament, and his sentences declared illegal in Nov. 1640. He continued an active paper warfare, attacking Laud, then the independents, then the army (1647), then, after being arrested by Pride, the government. In 1660 he asserted the rights of Charles II, and was thanked by him. He was MP for Bath in the Convention Parliament and was appointed keeper of the records in the Tower of London. He published his most valuable work, *Brevia Parliamentaria Rediviva*, in 1662. He published altogether about 200 books and pamphlets.

Psalms, the, the Book of Psalms, one of the books of the Old Testament, often called the Psalms of David, in accordance with the belief that they, or part of them, were composed by David, king of Israel. This belief, maintained by many of the Latin Fathers (e.g. St *Ambrose and St *Augustine), was largely dismissed in the 19th cent., although modern scholars assign some to him and date many from the early years of the monarchy. The Psalms were the basis of the medieval church services, probably the only book in the Bible on the use of which, by the laity, the medieval Church imposed no veto at all. The Prayer Book version of them, attributed to *Coverdale, is one of our greatest literary inheritances. *A Metrical Version* of the Psalms was begun by *Sternhold and Hopkins (2nd edn, 1551), and continued at Geneva during Mary's reign by Protestant refugees. The complete *Old Version* (metrical) was published in 1562. *The New Version* by *Tate and Brady appeared in 1696. The Psalms have been translated and adapted by many English poets, including *Wyatt, P. *Sidney, the countess of *Pembroke, G. *Herbert, *Addison, *Smart (whose *A Song to David* celebrates their supposed author, and whose *Jubilate Agno* displays many characteristics of antiphonal psalms), and *Watts.

PSEUDO-DIONYSIUS, see DIONYSIUS THE AREOPAGITE.

Pseudodoxia Epidemica: *or, Enquiries into Very Many Received Tenets, and Commonly Presumed Truths,* often referred to as *Vulgar Errors,* by Sir T. *Browne, first published 1646, revised and augmented 1650, 1658, and 1672.

Whereas *Religio Medici* made him famous for wit, this, his longest work, established him as a man of learning. Fulfilling Bacon's desire in *The Advancement of Learning* for a 'Calendar of Dubitations, or Problemes' and a 'Calendar of Falshoods, and of popular Errors', it comprises one general book, treating of the sources and propagation of error—original sin, popular gullibility, logical fallacy, learned credulity and laziness, reverence for antiquity and authority, influential authors, and Satan—and six particular books, three on natural history—mineralogy, botany, zoology, physiology—and three on civil, ecclesiastical, and literary history—iconography, magic and folklore, chronology, historical geography, and biblical, classical, and medieval history. Browne examines more than 100 problems in the light of his extensive learning, the verdicts of reasoned argument, and the results of his own experiments and observations. The standard edition, comprising a critical text with introduction and full commentary, is by Robin Robbins (1981).

psychoanalytic criticism, a form of literary interpretation that employs the terms of psychoanalysis (the unconscious, repression, the Oedipus complex, etc.) in order to illuminate aspects of literature in its connection with conflicting psychological states. The beginnings of this modern tradition are found in *Freud's *The Interpretation of Dreams* (1900), which provides a method of interpreting apparently unimportant details of narratives as 'displacements' of repressed wishes or anxieties. Freud often acknowledged his debts to the poets, and his theory of the Oedipus complex is itself a sort of commentary upon *Sophocles' drama. He also attempted posthumous analyses of *Michelangelo, Shakespeare, E. *Hoffmann, and other artists. Ambitious interpretations of literary works as symptoms betraying the authors' neuroses are found in 'psychobiographies' of writers, such as Marie

Bonaparte's *Edgar Poe* (1933), which diagnoses sadistic necrophilia as the problem underlying Poe's tales. A more sophisticated study in this vein is E. *Wilson's *The Wound and the Bow* (1941). As L. *Trilling and others have objected, this approach risks reducing art to pathology. More profitable are analyses of fictional characters, beginning with Freud's own suggestions about Prince Hamlet, later developed by his British disciple Ernest Jones: Hamlet feels unable to kill his uncle because Claudius's crimes embody his own repressed incestuous and patricidal wishes, in a perfect illustration of the Oedipus complex. A comparable exercise is Wilson's essay 'The Ambiguity of Henry James' (1934), which interprets the ghosts in *The Turn of the Screw* as imaginary projections of the governess's repressed sexual desires. A third possible object of analysis, after the author and the fictional protagonist, is the readership. Here the question is why certain kinds of story have such a powerful appeal to us, and numerous answers have been given in Freudian terms, usually focusing on the overcoming of fears (as in *Gothic fiction) or the resolution of conflicting desires (as in comedy and romance). Although Freud's writings are the most influential, some interpretations employ the concepts of heretical psychoanalysts, notably Adler, *Jung, and Klein. Since the 1970s, the theories of Jacques Lacan (1901–81) have inspired a new school of psychoanalytic critics who illustrate the laws of 'desire' through a focus upon the language of literary texts. In Lacan's very complicated scheme, literary works may embody a quest for an imaginary wholeness that we, as 'split' subjects, have lost upon our entry into the linguistic world of differences and distinctions. The advent of post-*structuralism has tended to cast doubt upon the authority of the psychoanalytic critic who claims to unveil a true 'latent' meaning behind the disguises of a text's 'manifest' contents. The subtler forms of psychoanalytic criticism make allowance for ambiguous and contradictory significances, rather than merely discover hidden sexual symbolism in literary works.

PTOLEMY (Claudius Ptolemaeus), who lived at Alexandria in the 2nd cent. AD, was a celebrated mathematician, astronomer, and geographer. He devised the system of astronomy (according to which the sun, planets, and stars revolved round the earth) which was generally accepted until displaced by that of *Copernicus. Combined with *Aristotle's natural philosophy, which saw Nature as orderly, hierarchical, and teleological, Ptolemaic astronomy when suitably Christianized formed the core of the medieval world picture. Ptolemy's work on this subject is generally known by its Arabic name of *Almagest*. His great geographical treatise remained a textbook until superseded by the discoveries of the 15th cent. Ptolemy compiled a map of the world in which both the parallels and the meridians are curved.

Public Advertiser, originally the *London Daily Post and*

General Advertiser, started in 1752 and expired in 1798. From 1758 to 1793 it was edited by Henry Sampson Woodfall (1739–1805), who published the famous letters of *'Junius'. It contained home and foreign intelligence, and correspondence, mainly political, from writers of all shades of opinion. *Wilkes and *Tooke carried on a dispute in its columns. The notable pamphlets of 'Candor' against Lord Mansfield (1764) also appeared originally as letters to the *Public Advertiser*. The author of these is unknown.

Public Lending Right, a right achieved by Act of Parliament in 1979. The idea that the author of a book (in copyright) should be paid for its use by a public, commercial, or other kind of lending library was first advanced by the novelist John Brophy in 1951. It was then formally adopted by the *Society of Authors which conducted a prolonged campaign—for what became known as 'Public Lending Right' (PLR). The campaign was reinforced and brought ultimately to a successful conclusion by the Writers' Action Group— which was set up in 1972 by Brigid *Brophy (daughter of the campaign's originator) and Maureen *Duffy. Initially the campaign was opposed by many librarians, who feared that the payments to authors would have to come from library budgets. There was also disagreement among authors themselves over the nature of the proposed right and how the payments should be calculated.

PLR was finally secured, not by amendment to the Copyright Act, but by a separate statute, followed three years later by the PLR scheme which set out detailed arrangements for the operation of the new right. The scheme is administered by the Registrar of PLR from an office in Stockton-on-Tees and is financed by a central government grant. Qualifying authors received their first payments in 1984.

publishing, subscription, a system by which the author (sometimes with his publishers' help) collected a pre-publication list of buyers prepared to pay for his book in advance and usually at a reduced rate. The first book known to be published by a fully developed form of this system was John Minsheu's lexicographical *Guide into Tongues* of 1617, but it is known that *Caxton, in the late 15th cent., acquired promises of sales before producing his major works. The system flourished most widely in the 18th cent. when authors frequently issued 'Proposals' for future works and collected subscribers; for instance, *Pope enlisted *Swift's help in obtaining subscribers for his *Iliad*; Dr *Johnson, who had great trouble with the list for his edition of Shakespeare, said, 'he that asks subscriptions soon finds that he has enemies'; *Burns, proposing to issue the Kilmarnock second edition of his poems, was delighted to obtain a list of over 300 subscribers; and the name of the young J. *Austen appears in 1796 on a subscription list for F. *Burney's forthcoming *Camilla*. Subscription publishing was still flourishing at the end of the 19th cent. and survives in a modified form in certain areas of scholarly and technical publishing.

PUCCINI, Giacomo (1858–1924), Italian composer, almost exclusively of opera. Only two of his completed operas have any connection with English literature: both *Madame Butterfly* (1904) and *La Fanciulla del West* (1910, from *The Girl of the Golden West*) are based on plays by the American actor-manager and playwright David Belasco, the former taken in its turn from a magazine story by John Luther Long. The uncompleted operas, however, included, at various stages of his career, works based on *Enoch Arden*, *Oliver Twist*, works by *Wilde and Shakespeare, *Bulwer-Lytton's *Last Days of Pompeii*, *Lorna Doone*, and *Trilby*.

Pucelle, La (*The Maid*), a burlesque epic by *Voltaire on the subject of *Joan of Arc, published 1755. Joan is called 'la Pucelle' in Shakespeare's 1 *Henry VI*.

Puck, originally an evil or malicious spirit or demon of popular superstition; from the 16th cent. the name of a mischievous or tricksy goblin or sprite, called also Robin Goodfellow and Hobgoblin. In this character he figures in Shakespeare's *A Midsummer Night's Dream* (II. i. 40) and Drayton's *Nimphidia* (xxxvi).

PUDNEY, John Sleigh (1909–77), poet, novelist, and journalist, born at Langley, Buckinghamshire, and educated at Gresham's School, Holt, where he was a contemporary and friend of *Auden and B. *Britten. His first volume of verse, *Spring Encounter* (1933), was followed by ten works of fiction, but he is principally remembered for his poem lamenting pilots who died in the war, 'For Johnny' ('Do not despair | For Johnny-head-in-air'), written while he was an intelligence officer with the RAF in 1941, and first published in the *News Chronicle*. It became one of the most quoted poems of the Second World War.

Puff, Mr, a character in Sheridan's *The Critic*.

PUGH, Sheenagh (1950–   ), poet and translator, born in Birmingham and educated at the University of Bristol: she now lives in Wales. Her volumes include *Crowded by Shadows* (1977); *Earth Studies and Other Voyages* (1982), the title section of which is a geographical-ecological meditation in the form of a 19-poem sequence, celebrating the beauty and fragility of the earth and its inhabitants; *Beware Falling Tortoises* (1987), which wryly questions accidental death and individual worth and survival; and *Sing for the Taxman* (1993). Her poetry springs from saga, ancient history, contemporary politics, and everyday life, and is marked by a lyrical detachment. *Prisoners of Transience* (1985) contains translations from *Christine de Pisan, *Charles d'Orléans, and German poets of the Thirty Years War.

PUGIN, Augustus Welby Northmore (1812–52), architect, son of the French artist Auguste-Charles Pugin (1762–1832). He was the protagonist and theorist of the *Gothic Revival, and developed his thesis that Gothic was the only proper Christian architecture in *Contrasts: or, A Parallel between the Noble Edifices of the Fourteenth and Fifteenth Centuries and Similar Buildings of the Present Day, Shewing the Present Decay of Taste* (1836), an important work that foreshadowed *Ruskin and *Carlyle's *Past and Present*. He wrote various other works on architectural and ecclesiastical matters, including *An Apology for the Revival of Christian Architecture in England* (1843), and was also responsible for designing the decorations and furniture for Barry's Houses of Parliament.

PULCI, Luigi (1432–84), Florentine poet of the circle of Lorenzo de' *Medici. His poem *Morgante maggiore* was the first romantic epic to be written by an Italian *letterato*, and was a major source for *Rabelais.

Pulitzer Prizes, annual prizes established under the will of Joseph Pulitzer (1847–1911), an American newspaper proprietor of Hungarian birth, who used sensational journalism for the correction of social abuses. The prizes, which are confined to American citizens, are offered in the interest of letters (American history and biography, poetry, drama, and novel writing), music, and good newspaper work. A fund of $500,000 was set aside for the prizes, which are controlled by the School of Journalism (also founded under the terms of Pulitzer's will) at Columbia University.

Pullet, Mr and Mrs, characters in G. Eliot's *The Mill on the Floss*.

PULLMAN, Philip, see CHILDREN'S LITERATURE.

Pumblechook, Mr, a character in Dickens's *Great Expectations*.

pun, a play on words, depending on similarity of sound and difference in meaning. Shakespeare was greatly given to punning, both in comic and in serious contexts: for an example of the latter, see Sonnet 138, 'Therefore I lie with her, and she with me, | And in our faults by lies we flattered be.' The pun fell into disrepute in the 18th and 19th cents, but was reinstated as a form of ambiguity in W. Empson's *Seven Types of Ambiguity*. (See also PARONOMASIA.)

Punch, the principal character in the most famous of English puppet plays, distinguished by humped back, hooked nose, and a tendency to beat his wife Judy and other victims: he is accompanied by his faithful dog Toby. The name of Punch came into the language after the Restoration through Pulcinella, a similar character in the *commedia dell'arte*. See also GUIGNOL.

Punch, or *The London Charivari*, an illustrated weekly comic periodical, founded 1841; at first a rather strongly radical paper, gradually becoming more bland and less political. It suspended publication in 1992, and was revived in 1996.

Various accounts have been given of the birth of this famous paper. One or two illustrated comic papers had already appeared in London, notably Gilbert Abbott *à Beckett's *Figaro in London* (1831) and *Punchinello* (1832), illustrated by *Cruikshank. It appears that the idea of starting in London a comic paper somewhat on the lines of Philippon's Paris *Charivari* first occurred to Ebenezer Landells, draughtsman and wood-engraver, who submitted it to *Mayhew. Mayhew took up the proposal and enlisted the support of *Lemon and Joseph Stirling Coyne (1803–68), who became the first joint editors. The first number was issued on 17 July 1841. Joseph Last was the first printer, and Landells the first engraver. À Beckett and *Jerrold were among the original staff, soon joined by *Thackeray, *Hood, *Leech, and *Tenniel, among others. Shirley Brooks (1816–74) became editor in 1870, Tom *Taylor in 1874, and *Burnand in 1880. Sir Owen Seaman was editor from 1906 to 1932; he was succeeded by E. V. *Knox, 1932–49. Kenneth Bird (better known as the cartoonist 'Fougasse') was editor from 1949 to 1952; Malcolm *Muggeridge 1953–7; Bernard Hollowood 1958–68; William Davis 1969–78; and Alan Coren (who introduced full colour cartoon covers) from 1978. Recent regular contributors have included M. *Bragg, Hunter Davies, Benny Green, and Alan Brien.

Among other famous draughtsmen of the past may be mentioned Charles Keene (1823–91), whose first drawing in *Punch* appeared in 1851 and who joined the staff in 1860; and G. *du Maurier, who contributed drawings from 1860 and joined the staff in 1864. The most famous drawing for the cover, by R. *Doyle, was used from 1849 to 1956, when it was replaced by a full-colour design, different each week. The Punch figure and the dog Toby usually appeared in the design on the front cover until 1969, and the last vestige of the original Doyle frieze disappeared from the inside pages in 1978. Amongst the many eminent cartoonists of later years, mention may be made of Ronald Searle, Bill Tidy, Michael Heath, Norman Thelwell, and Gerald Scarfe.

puppet-play, see MOTION.

PURCELL, Henry (1659–95), English composer, who began his musical career as a chorister and later organist of the Chapel Royal, and at the age of 20 succeeded *Blow as organist at Westminster Abbey. A considerable part of his output consisted of anthems and other sacred works, the former to texts from the Bible or Book of *Common Prayer, the latter with words by *Cowley, *Tate, *Quarles, *Flatman, and others. Comparable to these in the secular field are the various Odes and Welcome songs, written mainly for royal occasions to texts in courtly language, which drew from the composer music that was often splendid but generally uncomplicated in style.

The mixture of instrumental, choral, and vocal styles in works like these is complex and varied, yet throughout it is the solo vocal line, idiomatic, flexible, and richly coloured by a vivid harmonic sense, that most profoundly influenced later composers. His 250 solo songs range from simple, almost folk song-like tunes to elaborate sequences of recitative and aria that develop and improve on the declamatory style introduced from Italy by *Lawes and M. *Locke; some of these were independent compositions, but many more were written for the 49 stage works (by *Dryden, *Shadwell, *D'Urfey, *Southerne, and others) for which Purcell is known to have provided music. 'The Author's extraordinary Talent in all sorts of Musick is sufficiently known', wrote musician John Playford in 1698, 'but he was especially admir'd for the *Vocal*, having a peculiar Genius to express the Energy of *English* Words, whereby he mov'd the Passions of all his Auditors.'

It was this distinctive gift that assured the position of Purcell's one opera *Dido and Aeneas* (modelled in part on Blow's *Venus and Adonis*) in the history of music. It was written to a libretto by Tate for performance by the young gentlewomen of Josias Priest's boarding school at Chelsea in 1689. Though short and restricted in theatrical scope, *Dido* achieves an astonishing range of dramatic expression: from the ribald vitality of the sailors to the fiery exchanges between Dido and Aeneas and the noble resignation of Dido's lament, 'When I am laid in earth', there is a sureness of characterization and depth of human understanding that justifies the work's place as the most famous of English operas.

It was Purcell's only opera in the strict sense of the word, but he also provided music for five 'semi-operas' in the last five years of his life. Of these, only *King Arthur* (by Dryden, 1691) was written with Purcell's music in mind, and it is therefore perhaps the most satisfactory whole; the song 'Fairest Isle' comes in the fifth act. The music for *The Prophetess, or The History of Dioclesian* (1690), adapted from *Beaumont and *Fletcher by *Betterton, includes a much admired *masque that is complete in itself, and *The Fairy Queen* (1692), an elaboration of **A Midsummer Night's Dream*, consists almost entirely of masques, to the virtual exclusion of Shakespeare's play. (This is the longest of Purcell's dramatic works, but it contains no setting of Shakespeare's words.) The two last stage works, *The Indian Queen* and a final Shakespearian adaptation, Shadwell's arrangement of Dryden and *D'Avenant's version of **The Tempest*, were both written in the last year of Purcell's life. They exhibit the composer's dramatic and musical gifts at their highest, yet they remain obstinately hybrid period pieces. (See also LIBRETTO; OPERA.)

PURCHAS, Samuel (1577–1626), educated at St John's College, Cambridge, and rector of St Martin's, Ludgate. He published in 1613 *Purchas His Pilgrimage. Or Relations of the World and the Religions Observed in All Ages*; in 1619 *Purchas His Pilgrim*; and in 1625 *Hakluytus Post-humus, or Purchas His Pilgrimes, Contayning a History of the World in Sea Voyages and Land Travell by Englishmen and Others*. This last is in part based on manuscripts left by *Hakluyt, and consists of

two sections, each of ten books. The first section, after an introductory book, contains accounts of voyages to India, China, Japan, Africa, and the Mediterranean. The second part deals with attempts to discover the North-West Passage, the Muscovy expeditions, and explorations of the West Indies and Florida. Among the best narratives are William Adams's description of his voyage to Japan and residence there and William Hawkins's account of his visit to the court of the great mogul at Agra. *Coleridge, according to his own account, was reading about Kubla Khan in Purchas when he fell into the trance that produced his own poem on the subject, and J. L. *Lowes in *The Road to Xanadu* (1927) further traces his debt. (See also ROMANTICISM.)

Purgatorio, The, of Dante, see DIVINA COMMEDIA.

Puritan, The, or *The Widow of Watling-Street*, a comedy published in 1607 as 'written by W.S.' and included in the third and fourth Shakespeare folios, but by some other hand, almost certainly *Middleton's.

The play is a farcical comedy of London manners, and sets forth the tricks played on the widow and her daughter by Captain Idle and George Pye-board in order to win their hands, with scenes in the Marshalsea.

Purley, *The Diversions of*, see TOOKE and ACKROYD.

Purple Island, The, see FLETCHER, P.

Pursuits of Literature, The, see MATHIAS.

PUSEY, Edward Bouverie (1800–82), educated at Christ Church, Oxford, elected a fellow of Oriel College in 1823. In 1828 he was ordained deacon and priest, and appointed Regius professor of Hebrew. He became attached to the *Oxford movement in 1833 and joined *Keble and *Newman in contributing, in 1834, No. 18 for *Tracts for the Times* and Nos 67–9, in 1836, on 'Scriptural Views of Holy Baptism'; Pusey gave the movement cohesion and prestige by his erudition, and in 1841 when Newman withdrew he became its leader. His most influential activity was preaching and his sermon on 'The Holy Eucharist, a Comfort to the Penitent' (1843) caused his suspension for heresy from the office of university preacher for two years. The condemnation drew him wide publicity and attracted attention to the doctrine of the Real Presence of which he was a devoted defender. He was a principal defender of the doctrines of the High Church movement, a passionate believer in the union of the English and Roman Churches, and endeavoured to hinder secessions to the Roman Catholic Church which prevailed at that time.

PUSHKIN, Alexander Sergeyevich (1799–1837), widely considered Russia's greatest poet. Born in Moscow into an ancient gentry family, he attended the Lyceum at Tsarskoe Selo, outside St Petersburg, where he began to write poetry. He worked in government service, but was expelled from St Petersburg in 1820 for writing revolutionary epigrams. In August 1824 he was dismissed from the civil service for atheistic writings, and his seclusion at his mother's estate prevented him from taking part in the revolt of the Decembrists, with whom he sympathized. In 1832 he married a young beauty, Natalia Goncharova. The attentions paid to his wife by Baron Georges D'Anthès, a French royalist in the Russian Service, caused him to challenge D'Anthès to a duel, in which Pushkin was fatally wounded.

Pushkin wrote in a variety of genres: lyric poems, among the most important of which are 'Winter Evening' (1825), 'The Prophet' (1826), 'I remember a wondrous moment' (1827), 'The Poet' (1827), 'The Upastree' (1828), and 'I loved you' (1829); narrative poems in various styles, including *Ruslan and Ludmilla* (1820), a Romantic epic, *The Prisoner of the Caucasus* (1820–1) and *The Fountain of Bakhchisarai* (1822), which examine Romantic and *Byronic themes, *The Gypsies* (1824), in which Romantic influences are discarded, the comic *Count Nulin* (1825) and *The Little House in Kolomna* (1830), the historical *Poltava* (1829), and *The Bronze Horseman* (1833), in which the statue of Peter the Great chases the clerk Evgeny through St Petersburg during the flood of 1824; the novel in verse *Eugene Onegin* (1823–31), his greatest and most sophisticated work; plays, including the blank verse historical drama *Boris Godunov* (1825) and the four 'Little Tragedies': 'Mozart and Salieri', 'The Covetous Knight', 'The Stone Guest', and 'The Feast during the Plague' (all 1830); and prose, on which he concentrated after 1830, *The Tales of Belkin* (1830), *The Queen of Spades* (1834), and *The Captain's Daughter* (1836).

Pushkin was widely read in English literature, and particularly interested in Shakespeare, *Sterne, *Richardson, *Byron, and Sir W. *Scott. The first English translation, by G. *Borrow, was *The Talisman: From the Russian of Alexander Pushkin. With Other Pieces* (St Petersburg, 1835). Recent translations include those by John Fennell (1964), Gillon Aitken (*The Complete Prose Tales*, 1962, etc.), Antony Wood (1982), and D. M. *Thomas (1982). *Nabokov's controversial but scholarly translation (in unrhymed iambics) of *Eugene Onegin* appeared in 1964 (rev. edn 1977, when it was described by R. *Lowell as a work of 'fascinating eccentricity'); it was followed by Sir Charles Johnston's stanzaic version, which also appeared in 1977.

PUTTENHAM, George (c.1529–91), a nephew of Sir T. *Elyot, and almost certainly author of *The Arte of English Poesie*, sometimes ascribed to his brother Richard. It appeared anonymously in 1589, but is thought to have been in manuscript in some form perhaps 20 years earlier. It is a critical treatise in three books, *Of Poets and Poesie*, *Of Proportion*, and *Of Ornament*, important as a record of Elizabethan taste and theory, and lively in its own right. The author's tone is personal, and he mingles anecdotes with serious appraisal, illustrating the view that epitaphs should be

brief by telling us that he was locked up in a cathedral by the sexton while reading a long one. He condemns *Gower for 'false orthographie', finds *Skelton 'a rude rayling rimer and all his doings ridiculous', and praises *Wyatt and *Surrey as the stars of a 'new company of courtly makers'. In the second book he discusses 'courtly trifles' such as anagrams, *emblems, and posies, showing a fondness for 'ocular representations'—in particular for poems shaped liked eggs and pillars. The third book defines and illustrates various figures of speech and suggests vulgar names for Greek and Latin originals, e.g. 'single supply, ringleader and middlemarcher' (zeugma, prozeugma, and mezozeugma), 'the drie mock' (irony), 'the bitter taunt' (sarcasm), and 'the over reacher' (hyperbole). He attacks excessive use of foreign words, but was aware of the rapidly changing vernacular. The *Arte* was edited by G. D. Willcock and Alice Walker (1936). George Puttenham may also be the author of a royal panegyric, *Partheniades*.

Pwyll, in Welsh mythology, prince of Dyfed and 'Head of Hades', the subject of the first story in the *Mabinogion. The stories of Sir *Pelleas and King *Pelles in *Malory are perhaps connected with his myth. See J. Rhys, *Studies in the Arthurian Legend* (1891).

PYCLETIUS (c.116–c.163), Graeco-Spanish geographer and traveller, trading ambassador in Spain for Antoninus Pius. His wise and subversive *Histories* record with unflinching though unreliable authority details of Mediterranean life under the Romans in the 2nd cent. AD. Amongst his discoveries were lands 'where citizens are as dextrous with their toes as with their fingers'. Stylistically, Pycletius is judged an early *magic realist, with tributes to his work by *Calvino, Emile dell'Ova, and *Borges. A second manuscript, discovered in 1787, *Hoc Genus Omne*, was published in verse translation by the minor English poet Abraham Howper. It provides evidence that the *Histories* might have been wholly invented and that Pycletius never travelled beyond his home town of Carthago Nova (Carthagena). Contemporary commentators, however, considered *Hoc Genus Omne* to be the work of Howper himself, a fantasist.

PYE, Henry James (1745–1813). He became *poet laureate in 1790, and was the constant butt of contemporary ridicule.

Pygmalion, one of the most popular plays of Bernard *Shaw, first performed 1913 in Vienna, published in London, 1916.

It describes the transformation of a Cockney flowerseller, Eliza Doolittle, into a passable imitation of a duchess by the phonetician Professor Henry Higgins (modelled in part on H. *Sweet, and played by Beerbohm *Tree), who undertakes this task in order to win a bet and to prove his own points about English speech and the class system: he teaches her to speak standard English and introduces her successfully to social life, thus winning his bet, but she rebels against his dictatorial and thoughtless behaviour, and 'bolts' from his tyranny. The play ends with a truce between the two of them, as Higgins acknowledges that she has achieved freedom and independence, and emerged from his treatment as a 'tower of strength: a consort battleship': in his postscript Shaw tells us that she marries the docile and devoted Freddy Eynsford Hill. *My Fair Lady*, the 1957 musical version, makes the relationship between Eliza and Higgins significantly more romantic.

Pygmalion, in classical legend, was the king of Cyprus, who fell in love with his own sculpture; Aphrodite endowed the statue with life and transformed it into the flesh-and-blood of Galatea.

Pyke and **Pluck,** in Dickens's *Nicholas Nickleby*, the toadies of Sir Mulberry Hawk.

Pylon school, a nickname for the group of younger left-wing poets of the 1930s, chiefly *Auden, *Day-Lewis, *MacNeice, and *Spender, alluding to the rather self-conscious use of industrial imagery in their work. Spender's poem 'The Pylons' was published in 1933, and pylons and skyscrapers appear in Day-Lewis's poem to Auden ('Look west, Wystan, lone flyers') in *The Magnetic Mountain* (1933); Auden's own verse features power stations ('Out on the lawn I lie in bed', 1933), and landscapes of arterial roads and filling stations are evoked in, e.g., Auden and *Isherwood's *The Dog beneath the Skin* (1935), whereas MacNeice's early work has a high preponderance of poems about trains and trams.

PYM, Barbara Mary Crampton (1913–80), novelist, the daughter of a Shropshire solicitor. She was educated at St Hilda's College, Oxford, and later worked at the International African Institute in London. Her novels include *Excellent Women* (1952), *Less than Angels* (1955), *A Glass of Blessings* (1958, described by *Larkin as 'the subtlest of her books'), and *Quartet in Autumn* (1977). They are satirical tragi-comedies of middle-class life, and contain some distinctive portraits of church-going spinsters and charismatic priests; many of the relationships described consist of a kind of celibate flirtation.

Pyncheon, Hepzibah, a character in Hawthorne's *The House of the Seven Gables*.

PYNCHON, Thomas (1937–), American novelist, born on Long Island, New York, and educated at Cornell. His novels are less concerned with character than with the effects of historical and political processes on individual behaviour. Their fragmented *picaresque narratives, often based around outlandish quests, blend paranoia, literary game-playing, bawdy humour, social satire, and fantasy: science provides an important source of metaphor and subject matter. He began his first novel while working as a technical

writer for the Boeing Aircraft Corporation. This was *V* (1963), a long and complex allegorical fable interweaving the picaresque adventures of a group of contemporary Americans with the secret history of a shape-changing spy, 'V', who represents a series of female archetypes. *The Crying of Lot 49* (1966, UK 1967) is a paranoid mystery story mixing philosophical speculation with satirical observation of American culture in the 1960s. *Gravity's Rainbow* (1973) is a multi-layered black comedy set at the close of the Second World War: its convoluted plots and conspiracies reflect the socio-political processes threatening personal freedom. In *Vineland* (1990), a darkly humorous conspiracy thriller, participants in the 'counter-culture' of the 1960s face up to the conservative political scene of the 1980s. *Mason & Dixon* (1997) is a pastiche historical novel, based on the adventures of the two 18th-cent. British surveyors who established the Mason–Dixon line, drawing parallels between the political and scientific upheavals of the Age of Reason and those of the late 20th cent.

Pyrochles, in Spenser's *Faerie Queene*, symbolizes rage. He is the brother of *Cymochles, the son of 'old Acrates and Despight' (II. iv. 41). On his shield is a flaming fire, with the words *'Burnt I do burne'*. He is overcome by Sir *Guyon (II. v), and tries to drown himself in a lake to quench his flames. He is rescued and healed by *Archimago (II. vi. 42–51), and finally killed by Prince *Arthur (II. viii).

Pyrocles, the young prince of Macedon in Sidney's *Arcadia*, who adopts a disguise as an Amazon in order to woo Philoclea.

PYTHAGORAS, a Greek philosopher, native of Samos, who lived in the second half of the 6th cent. BC. He settled in Cortona in Italy where he founded a brotherhood who combined ascetic practices and mystical beliefs with the study of mathematics. Pythagoras is credited with the discovery of the proof of the proposition that the square on the hypotenuse of a right-angled triangle is equal to the sum of the squares on the other two sides, which is called therefore the Pythagorean Theorem. He worked out a mathematical basis for music and supposed the heavenly bodies to be divided by intervals according to the laws of musical harmony, whence arose the idea of the harmony of the spheres. He discovered the rotation of the earth on its axis and found in this the causes of day and night. His religious teaching centred on the doctrine of metempsychosis, or the transmigration of souls from man to man, man to animal, or animal to man in a process of purification or punishment. There are references to this Pythagorean doctrine in the dialogue between Feste and Malvolio (*Twelfth Night*, IV. ii), in *The Merchant of Venice* (IV. i), and in *As You Like It* (III. ii); and Faustus, in *Marlowe's tragedy, cries in his last moments of anguish, 'Ah, Pythagoras' *metempsychosis*, were that true | This soul should fly from me' (*Dr Faustus*, V. ii). The *Pythagorean Letter* is the Greek letter upsilon *Y* used as symbol of the divergent paths of vice and virtue. His teachings exerted a marked influence on later Greek philosophers and notably on *Plato.

Pythias, see DAMON AND PITHIAS.

Q

Q, the initial of German *Quelle*, 'source', is the symbol used, in the comparative study of the synoptic Gospels, to designate a supposed Greek translation of a collection attributed to Matthew of the *logia* of Christ, from which the parts common to the Gospels of Matthew and Luke, but omitted from Mark, are derived. It is supposed to have contained certain narrative parts, but not the Passion.

'Q', see JERROLD, D. W., and QUILLER-COUCH.

Quadrivium, the higher division of the Seven Liberal Arts, comprising the sciences, arithmetic, geometry, astronomy, and music (as distinct from the methodological subjects of the *Trivium, grammar, rhetoric, and logic). Although the Liberal Arts in groupings of this kind were a staple of Greek and Roman education, the Quadrivium as such originates with *Martianus Capella (early 5th cent.), followed by *Boethius and his pupil Cassiodorus whose 6th-cent. *On the Arts and Disciplines of the Liberal Letters* was the definitive text for the Middle Ages. The Quadrivium had great importance for the writers of Chartres in the 11th–12th cents; it was neglected by the metaphysical synthesists of the 13th cent., and became associated thereafter with Oxford rather than with the Schools of continental Europe, which were less interested in the material sciences. (See BACON, R.) See G. Leff, *Medieval Thought: St Augustine to Ockham* (1958), *passim*.

Quakers, members of the Society of *Friends.

QUARITCH, Bernard (1819–99), bookseller. At first employed by *Bohn, he started his own firm in 1847. He was the first to publish FitzGerald's *The Rubáiyát of *Omar Khayyám (1859). He was the author of the valuable bibliographical work *A General Catalogue* (1887–97). His interests were wide and above all he was known as a collector of incunabula, fine manuscripts, Bibles, Shakespeariana, early English literature, and cartography.

QUARLES, Francis (1592–1644), born near Romford in Essex, was educated at Christ's College, Cambridge, and at Lincoln's Inn. He made his reputation in the 1620s by a series of biblical paraphrases (e.g. *A Feast for Wormes*, 1620), and in 1629 published a 'vain amatory poem', *Argalus and Parthenia*, based on an episode in Sidney's *Arcadia. He is chiefly remembered for his extremely successful and popular *Emblemes* (1635) and *Hieroglyphikes of the Life of Man* (1638). In 1639 he was appointed chronologer to the City of London. From 1640 he turned to prose, publishing pamphlets, some anonymous, holding a constitutionalist–royalist position. A petition circulated against him in 1644 accused him of popery, but A. *Wood declared that he was a Puritan. *Eclogues* (1646) and a comedy, *The Virgin Widow* (1649), were published posthumously. A nearly complete collection of his works was edited by *Grosart (3 vols, 1880–1) and additional poems by J. Hordern (1960).

Quarterly Review (1809–1967), founded by John *Murray as a Tory rival to the Whig *Edinburgh Review*. Sir W. *Scott, who had been harshly reviewed in the *Edinburgh*, became an ardent supporter of the venture but refused the editorship. The journal stood for the defence of the established order, Church, and Crown; its unwavering adherence to the bishops and the Church was satirized by Peacock in *Melincourt. Its tone was magisterial from the beginning, and its influence, both literary and political, was for the best part of the century matched only by that of the *Edinburgh*. The first editor, *Gifford, brought with him several clever writers from the *Anti-Jacobin, including *Canning and *Frere, but the quality of his chief writers (largely Scott and *Southey) could not match that of the *Edinburgh*, who had *Hazlitt, *Macaulay, *Carlyle, and *Jeffrey, among many others. The *Quarterly*'s enemies averred that its political bias strongly affected its literary criticism. However, unlike the *Edinburgh*, it supported the *'Lake school' and *Byron, although it fiercely condemned *Keats, *Hunt, Hazlitt, *Lamb, *Shelley, and later *Tennyson, Macaulay, *Dickens, and C. *Brontë. Two of its more famous early articles were those of Scott in praise of J. Austen's *Emma; and *Croker's review of Keats's *'Endymion'. Gifford was succeeded as editor in 1825 by *Lockhart, who was followed by a distinguished line, including members of the Murray family.

QUASIMODO, Salvatore (1901–68), Italian poet associated with *hermeticism, awarded the *Nobel Prize (1959). His main collections are *Acque e terre* (*Water and Land*, 1930), *Oboe sommerso* (*Sunken Oboe*, 1932), and *Ed è subito sera* (*And it's Suddenly Evening*, 1942). After the Second World War his hermeticism yielded to a more extrovert poetry of social conscience, as in *Con il piede straniero sopra il cuore* (*With the Alien Foot on Our Heart*, 1946), *La vita non è sogno* (*Life Is Not Dream*, 1949), and *Dare e avere* (*Giving and Having*, 1966). He has been translated by R. *Wilbur.

Queen Mab, a visionary and ideological poem by P. B. *Shelley, written in England and Wales during his early period of political activism, published privately 1813, when he was 21.

The poem is in nine cantos, using 'didactic and descriptive' blank verse greatly indebted to *Milton and to Southey's *Thalaba. Despite its lyrical opening, invoking 'Death and his brother Sleep' and Mab the Fairy Queen in her time-chariot (Cantos I and II), the poem largely consists of attacks on Monarchy (III), War (IV), Commerce (V), and Religion (VI and VII). In place of these Shelley celebrates a future of Republicanism, Free Love, Atheism, and Vegetarianism. The verse is furious and polemical in style, with occasional passages of grandiloquent beauty, such as Canto VIII, presaging Asia's speeches in *Prometheus Unbound. Seventeen remarkable prose Notes are attached as Appendices, many of them substantial essays, 'against Jesus Christ, & God the Father, & the King, & the Bishops, & Marriage, & the Devil knows what', as Shelley himself later put it. They are often better than the poetry: Note 9 on Free Love is especially striking, showing the influence of *Hume, *Godwin, *Wollstonecraft, and *Rousseau. The work was extremely popular among working-class radicals, and ran to 14 cheap editions by 1840.

Queen of Cornwall, The Famous Tragedy of the, a poetic drama by T. *Hardy, published 1923.

The play is a retelling of the old story of King Mark, the two Iseults, and Tristram. The events are conjured up by Merlin, and the Chanters perform as chorus. Queen Iseult has been to seek her love Tristram in Brittany, but is told that he is dead. Tristram discovers that his wife, Iseult of Brittany, had deceived him in telling him that the queen would not come to him. Disguised as a harper, he travels to Cornwall, followed by his wife. King Mark, the jealous husband of Queen Iseult, discovers his wife with Tristram and kills him. The queen then stabs Mark and leaps over a cliff to her death. The play was first produced in 1923 by the Hardy Players in Dorchester.

Queen of the May, see MAY DAY.

Queen's Maries, or **Marys, the,** the four ladies named Mary attendant on *Mary Queen of Scots. The list is variously given, including: Mary Seton, Mary Beaton, Mary Livingstone, Mary Fleming, Mary Hamilton, and Mary Carmichael. They are frequently mentioned in Scottish ballads.

Queen's Wake, The, a poem by J. *Hogg, published 1813. Queen Mary of Scotland holds her 'wake' at Holyrood, during which seventeen bards, including Rizzio, sing their songs in competition. These are verse tales in various styles: martial, comic, horrible, or mystical. The most memorable is the tale of *Kilmeny, but 'The Witch of Fife' is also an effective work.

QUENNELL, Peter (1905–94), poet, biographer, and editor, and the son of social historians Marjorie and C. H. B. Quennell, educated at Berkhamsted Grammar School and Balliol College, Oxford. He was editor of the *Cornhill Magazine (1944–51). His first volume,

Masques and Poems (1922), was followed by many other works, including *Four Portraits* (1945; studies of *Boswell, *Gibbon, *Sterne, and *Wilkes) and works on *Pope, *Byron, *Ruskin, and Dr *Johnson. *The Marble Foot* (1976) is a volume of autobiography.

Quentin Durward, a novel by Sir W. *Scott, published 1823.

One of the most vigorous and readable of Scott's novels, *Quentin Durward* is set in 15th-cent. France and Burgundy. It was Scott's first venture onto the mainland of Europe, and his story of a young Scots soldier of fortune serving in the guard of Louis XI had an enthusiastic reception in Paris. As in many of Scott's novels, the plot deals with the breakdown of traditional chivalric values and the opposition (and here, the reconciliation) of romance and reality.

Querno, in Pope's *Dunciad (II. 15), was an Apulian poet to whom the author compares C. *Cibber. According to Paulus Jovius, Querno, hearing that Pope Leo X patronized literature, set out for Rome where he recited some 20,000 lines of his *Alexias* and was made poet laureate as a joke.

Quest for Corvo, The: *An Experiment in Biography*, a life of Frederick *Rolfe by A. J. A. *Symons, published in 1934. This account dwells as much on the author's pursuit of his evasive and eccentric subject as on his findings, and was a pioneer in what was to be a new genre of biography, in which the biographer's difficulties and setbacks were to become part of the story: see Ian *Hamilton's life of *Salinger, and R. *Holmes, *Footsteps* (1985).

Questing Beast, the, in *Malory, pursued by *Palomydes the Saracen. See GLATYSAUNT BEAST.

QUEVEDO Y VILLEGAS, Francisco de (1580–1645), great Spanish satirist, author of the picaresque novel *La vida del Buscón* (1626), translated into English (through a French intermediary) by John Davies of Kidwelly as *The Life and Adventures of Buscan* (1657), and later by J. Stevens as *The Life of Paul the Spanish Sharper* (1707). His *Sueños* (1627), which are biting satiric portraits of members of all classes of society, were translated by Richard Croshawe of the Inner Temple (from the French) as *Visions, or, Hels Kingdom* (1640), and later by *L'Estrange (1667). Quevedo also wrote political works, satirical poetry, etc.

Quickly, Mistress, in Shakespeare's *1* and *2* *Henry IV, hostess of the Boar's Head Tavern in Eastcheap; *Falstaff is betrothed and in debt to her. In *The Merry Wives of Windsor* she is housekeeper to Dr Caius. In *Henry V she is married to *Pistol and describes Falstaff's death (II. iii).

Quietism, a form of religious mysticism (originated before 1675 by *Molinos), consisting in passive devotional contemplation, with extinction of the will and withdrawal from all things of the senses [OED]. One of the best-known exponents of Quietist doctrines was *Fénelon, whose *Maximes des saints*, embodying his opinions, was condemned by Rome. Another noted Quietist was Mme Guyon (1648–1717).

QUILLER-COUCH, Sir Arthur Thomas (1863–1944), son of a Cornish doctor, educated at Clifton and Oxford, where he began writing parodies under the pseudonym 'Q', which he used all his life. His prolific literary career opened with the publication of a novel of adventure, *Dead Man's Rock* (1887), after which followed a vast output of criticism, fiction, verse, anthologies, and literary journalism. In 1900 he edited the first *Oxford Book of English Verse*, which had considerable influence and large international sales. A knighthood in 1910 was followed in 1912 by the chair of English at Cambridge, where in 1917 he established the final honours school in that subject. Two influential volumes of lectures, *On the Art of Writing* and *On the Art of Reading*, appeared in 1916 and 1920, and his edition of the *New Cambridge Shakespeare* began to appear in 1921. In 1928 his collected novels and stories appeared in 30 volumes. The first volume of his unfinished autobiography, *Memories and Opinions* (1944), covers his early years. See a life by F. Brittain (1947).

Quilp, Daniel and Mrs, characters in Dickens's *The Old Curiosity Shop*.

QUILTER, Roger (1877–1953), English composer, remembered chiefly for his many songs, which were fluently and sensitively written and very popular in their day. His *Three Shakespeare Songs* (1905) are outstanding among his many Shakespeare settings, and songs like 'Love's Philosophy' (*Shelley) and 'Now sleeps the crimson petal' (Tennyson, *The Princess*) were staple recital diet during the first half of the 20th cent.

QUIN, Ann (1936–73), novelist, born in Brighton, Sussex. Her best-known novel is *Berg* (1964), the story of a young man who travels to an English seaside resort in order to murder his father. Like *Three* (1966), *Passages* (1969), and *Tripticks* (1972), it is unorthodox in form, owing more to the French *nouveau roman* than the English social realist novel. Quin's lifelong struggle against depression ended in suicide at the age of 37.

QUIN, James (1693–1766), an actor who first made his name playing Bajazet in Rowe's *Tamerlane*. He took leading parts in tragedy at Drury Lane, Lincoln's Inn Fields, and Covent Garden. He was the last of the old school of actors, which gave place to that of *Garrick. Smollett introduces him in *Humphry Clinker*.

Quinbus Flestrin, 'the Great Man-Mountain', the name by which Gulliver was known in Lilliput (*Gulliver's Travels*, ch. 2), and sometimes used as a pseudonym in magazines of the period.

Quince, Peter, in Shakespeare's *A Midsummer Night's Dream*, a carpenter, the stage manager of the interlude 'Pyramus and Thisbe'.

QUINE, Willard Van Orman (1908–2000), American mathematical logician and philosopher, born in Ohio and educated at Harvard, where he became Edgar Pierce professor of philosophy. He defended a system of logic, inspired by B. *Russell, where singular terms are eliminated in favour of general terms. He argued against the existence of a sharp distinction between analytic truths (e.g. 'All bachelors are unmarried') and synthetic truths (e.g. 'Hume was a bachelor'). He also doubted the extent to which translation is possible between languages. His slogan, 'To be is to be the value of a variable', is a logician's criterion of what it is for something to exist. Quine's works include *Methods of Logic* (1950), *From a Logical Point of View* (1953), and *Word and Object* (1960).

QUINTILIAN (Marcus Fabius Quintilianus) (AD *c*.35–*c*.100), Roman rhetorician, educationist, and literary critic. His monumental *De Institutione Oratoria* (On the Education of an Orator) is not only a treatise on rhetoric, but discusses also the training of an ideal orator for whom Quintilian like Cicero advocates a wide general education; Book 10 contains a critical history of Greek and Roman literature. *Petrarch lamented in his *Epistle to Quintilian* that 'he came torn and mangled into my hands'; the complete text of the *Institutio* became known only after Poggio Bracciolini unearthed a complete text in St Gall in 1416, after which it served the humanists as a guide on all literary and educational matters. Jonson excerpted it in *Timber*, Milton referred to it in the *Tetrachordon* sonnet, and *Dryden cited it on a number of points.

Quinze Joyes de mariage, Les, a French anti-feminist satire, of unknown authorship, dating from the early 15th cent. Several English versions of the work were made in the 17th and 18th cents, including one by *Dekker entitled *The Batchelars Banquet* (1603), and a 1682 version called *The Fifteen Comforts of Rash and Inconsiderate Marriage*.

Quixote, see DON QUIXOTE.

R

RABAN, Jonathan (1942–), travel writer, sailor, and novelist, born in Norfolk, the son of an Anglican clergyman, and educated at the University of Hull; he subsequently lectured at the universities of Aberystwyth and East Anglia. His works include *Soft City* (1974), a study of city life, particularly in London and New York; *Arabia through the Looking Glass* (1979); and *Old Glory* (1982), an account of a voyage down the Mississippi. *Coasting* (1986) is an account of a 1982 journey by ketch round the British Isles, which combines autobiography, marine scholarship, and sharp political commentary. *Foreign Land* (1985) is a novel which also returns to England, seen through the eyes of a returning exile. *For Love and Money* (1987) combines essays and autobiography. *Hunting Mister Heartbreak* (1990) is a journey exploring American emigration and identity, and *Bad Land: An American Romance* (1996) is an account of the settling of Montana by aspiring immigrant farmers and homesteaders, and of the disillusionment that overcame so many of them when beset by drought. Both are characteristic mixtures of a first-hand exploration and reading of the landscape, interviews, personal encounters, and imaginative interpretation of documentary sources: they manifest Raban's understanding of adventurers and loners, pitted against powerful natural forces. Raban edited *The Oxford Book of the Sea* (1992).

RABELAIS, François (*c.*1494–*c.*1553), French physician, humanist, and satirist. The son of a Touraine lawyer, he became successively a Franciscan monk, the secretary of the bishop of Maillezais (*c.*1524), and a bachelor of medicine from Montpellier (1530). He published various works on archaeology and medicine in Latin, and in French the satirical entertainments with the popular giants *Gargantua and Pantagruel for which he is remembered. He travelled regularly in France and Italy, and acquired a widespread reputation for his erudition and medical skill. For much of his life he enjoyed the patronage of Cardinal Jean du Bellay and the protection of Francis I, but he was subject to frequent proscriptions and condemnations. Rabelais' great prose work is a unique expression of Renaissance energy and plenitude. His comic inventiveness, ranging from obscenity, wit, and jokes to parody, invective, and fantasy, is inexhaustible. His intellectual curiosity, which encompasses virtually all the sciences and techniques of his age—theology, law, medicine, natural science, politics, military art, navigation, botany, Hebrew, Basque, etc.—is insatiable. His knowledge of contemporary life and society, from rustics, artisans, and monks to merchants, landowners, and academics, is without rival. His command of the vernacular, sustained by an encyclopaedic vocabulary and a virtuoso's rhetorical repertoire, and extending beyond French and its dialects to a dozen contemporary languages, remains unique in French literature. His realism recognizes the physical functions of mankind, affirms its uncorrupted origins, trusts in the effectiveness of virtuous action, and urges gaiety of mind as a supreme good. Although he was known to G. *Harvey and F. *Bacon, he was not translated into English until *Urquhart's magisterial version of 1653 (Books I and II) and 1693–4 (Book III together with *Motteux's translation of Books IV and V). Thereafter his influence on English literature was widespread, though particularly marked on S. *Butler, *Swift, *Sterne, *Peacock, and *Joyce.

RACINE, Jean (1639–99), French tragic dramatist. He was informally educated by the Jansenists of Port-Royal, but was estranged from them between 1666 and 1677, during which time he wrote the majority of his plays. His tragedies derive from various sources: from Greek and Roman literature, *Andromaque* (1667), *Iphigénie* (1674), and *Phèdre* (1677); from Roman history, *Britannicus* (1669), *Bérénice* (1670), and *Mithridate* (1673); from recent Turkish history, *Bajazet* (1672); and from the Bible, *Esther* (1689) and *Athalie* (1691). He also wrote one comedy, *Les Plaideurs* (1668), drawn from *Aristophanes. Central to the majority of the tragedies is a perception of the blind folly of human passion, continually enslaved to the pursuit of its object and destined always to be unsatisfied. The plays were extensively translated into English from the 1670s, but differences in national tastes and dramatic conventions have rendered most English versions wildly unfaithful to their originals. The most famous of these versions was *The Distrest Mother*, an adaptation of *Andromaque* by A. *Philips, which ran to many editions between 1712 and the 1820s. There are modern versions of *Phèdre* by R. *Lowell (1961) and T. *Harrison (1975).

RACKHAM, Arthur (1867–1939), children's book illustrator. Amongst his most successful works are *Fairy Tales of the Brothers Grimm* (1900), *Rip Van Winkle* (1905), which established him as the fashionable illustrator of his time, and *Peter Pan in Kensington Gardens* (1906). Rackham's vein of fantasy is Nordic—he created a sinister world, full of the twisting roots and tendrils of gnarled trees with gnome-like faces, and peopled by goblins, birds, mice, and monsters. Rackham believed passionately in 'the stimulating and educative power of fantastic and playful pictures and writings for children in their impressionable years'. See also FAIRY STORIES.

RADCLIFFE, Mrs Ann (1764–1823), daughter of a London tradesman, William Ward; she married in 1786 William Radcliffe, manager of the *English Chronicle*. In the next twelve years she published five novels, *The Castles of Athlin and Dunbayne* (1789), *A Sicilian Romance* (1790), *The Romance of the Forest* (1791), *The Mysteries of Udolpho* (1794), and *The Italian* (1797), and a description of journeys to Holland, Germany, and the Lake District. A further romance, *Gaston de Blondeville*, and her journals of travels in southern England were published after her death. She and her husband led such a retired life that unfounded rumours that she was already dead or insane circulated towards the end of her life. She suffered much from asthma, and died of pneumonia.

She was the leading exponent of the *Gothic novel, which relates terrifying adventures in lonely castles. On human relationships she was unconvincing, but her portrayals of the raptures and terrors of her characters' imagination in solitude are compelling, and she was one of the first novelists to include vivid descriptions of landscape, weather, and effects of light. Her plots were wild and improbable, but she was expert at maintaining suspense and devising striking incidents. Her novels were immensely popular throughout Europe, and were much imitated. The £500 advance which she received for *Udolpho* was then unprecedented for a novel. See *Memoir* by T. N. *Talfourd, in *Posthumous Works of Ann Radcliffe* (1833); Aline Grant, *Ann Radcliffe* (1951).

Radigund, in Spenser's *Faerie Queene* (V. iv–vii), a queen of the Amazons, who subdues *Artegall and forces him to spin flax and tow until he is rescued by *Britomart.

Raffles, see HORNUNG.

Ragged Trousered Philanthropists, The, see TRESSELL.

Rainbow, The, a novel by D. H. *Lawrence, published 1915.

It opens as a family chronicle relating the history of the long-established Brangwen family of Marsh Farm, on the Derbyshire–Nottinghamshire border. Tom Brangwen marries the vicar's housekeeper, a Polish widow who already has a daughter, Anna, by her first marriage. Tom takes the child to his heart. Anna marries Will Brangwen, Tom's nephew, a craftsman and draughtsman at a lace factory; they move into Yew Tree Cottage, Cossethay, and produce over the succeeding years a large family, of which the two eldest are Ursula and Gudrun of *Women in Love*. Ursula becomes the 'child of her father's heart', and the interest of the novel gradually shifts to her developing consciousness. When she is about 8 her grandfather is drowned one night when the canal embankment

bursts, and Ursula grows close to her grandmother Lydia at the Marsh, intrigued by her Polish heritage; her interest is reinforced when she meets Anton, son of a Polish émigré friend of Lydia's, Baron Skrebensky, who had married an English girl late in life. Ursula and Anton fall in love, but he, a subaltern, departs for the Boer War, leaving her to finish school. She has a brief but intense relationship with a schoolmistress (Winifred, who marries her uncle, colliery manager Tom Brangwen), then matriculates, and resolves to earn her living as a teacher, somewhat against her parents' wishes. Her struggles at a poor school in Ilkeston are based on Lawrence's own teaching experience there (1902–6). Will Brangwen is appointed Art and Handwork Instructor for the county of Nottingham, and the whole family move to Beldover, Ursula embarking on a three-year BA course and Gudrun on studies at the Art School. Anton returns, and they renew their relationship, become engaged, and plan to go out to India together, but Ursula breaks away, and Anton abruptly marries his colonel's daughter. The novel ends with Ursula emerging from a spell of illness and suffering (and an implied miscarriage) to contemplate a rainbow arching symbolically over the ugly industrial landscape. The book is remarkable for its study of the 'recurrence of love and conflict' within the marriages it describes; for its attempt to capture the flux of human personality; and for its sense of a mystic procreative continuity within the 'rhythm of eternity' both of the seasons and the Christian year.

RAINE, Craig Anthony (1944–   ), poet, born in Bishop Auckland, Co. Durham, educated at Barnard Castle School and Exeter College, Oxford, where he became a lecturer. He subsequently lectured at Lincoln College and at Christ Church, Oxford. In 1981 he became poetry editor at Faber & Faber, returning to Oxford in 1991 as a fellow of New College. From 1971 to 1981 he combined his career as a don with journalism, writing and reviewing for the *New Review*, *Quarto*, and the *New Statesman*. A collection of his critical work from this period, together with later pieces, was published as *Haydn and the Valve Trumpet* (1990). In 1972 he married Ann Pasternak Slater. His first collection of poetry, *The Onion, Memory*, was published in 1978 and attracted a good deal of critical attention, as did his second volume, *A Martian Sends a Postcard Home* (1979). In both books he displayed great metaphoric vitality and individuality and as a result of his inventive transformations of the everyday was credited by some critics with having instigated a 'Martian' school of poetry. The same approach continued in *A Free Translation* (1981) and *Rich* (1984), in which his father appears in a central prose account of his childhood, 'A Silver Plate'. *1953* (1990) was a version of *Racine's *Andromaque*. *History: The Home Movie* (1994) is a 'novel' in verse, a chronicle of the Raine and Pasternak families set against the background of 20th-cent. European history. *Clay: Whereabouts Unknown* appeared in 1996. He also wrote *The Electrification of the Soviet Union*, an adaptation of Boris *Pasternak's *The Last Summer*, as a libretto for an opera by Nigel Osborne (1986).

Raine, Kathleen Jessie (1908–2003), poet and critic, the daughter of a Scottish mother and a Northumbrian father, and educated at Girton College, Cambridge. She was formerly married to Charles *Madge. She published many collections of poetry, from her first, *Stone and Flower* (1943), to her *Collected Poems* of 1981, and also three volumes of autobiography, *Farewell Happy Fields* (1973), *The Land Unknown* (1975), and *The Lion's Mouth* (1977). Later collections include *The Oracle in the Heart* (1980), *The Presence: Poems 1984–7* (1988), and *Living with Mystery: Poems 1987–91* (1992). Much of her poetry is inspired by the landscapes of Scotland, particularly of Wester Ross, and has what she describes as 'a sense of the sacred', an intense and mystic vision of the vitality of the natural world which also informs her critical work on *Blake and the *Neoplatonic tradition. In 1981 she founded the review *Temenos*.

Rainolds, John (1549–1607), an Oxford academic among whose pupils was R. *Hooker. As well as composing Latin lectures on Aristotle which contributed to the development of euphuism (see EUPHUES), and controversial works and Protestant apologetics, including his *De Romanae Ecclesiae Idolatria* (1596), he also took part in a controversy over the lawfulness of acting plays. His contributions to this were published in *Th 'Overthrow of Stage-Plays* (1599).

Rake's Progress, The, a series of engravings by *Hogarth which inspired an opera by *Stravinsky of the same title with a libretto by W. H. *Auden in collaboration with Chester Kallman.

Ralegh, Sir Walter (1554–1618), born at Hayes Barton in south Devon; the sailor Sir Humfrey Gilbert was his half-brother. After little more than a year at Oriel College, Oxford, he spent four years as a volunteer with the Huguenot forces in France, being present at the battle of Montcontour in 1569. After a period in London loosely attached to the Middle Temple, Ralegh began his long career as an explorer and colonizer. In Ireland in 1580 he became acquainted with *Spenser, who approved of Ralegh's commanding role in the massacre of Smerwick, in which 600 Spanish mercenaries were killed. Throughout the 1580s he seems to have enjoyed royal favour, though *Fuller's story of his throwing a plush cloak over a puddle for the queen to tread on is most unlikely to be true. His marriage to Elizabeth Throckmorton, one of the maids of honour, led to a period of imprisonment in the summer of 1592. The journey to Guiana (now Venezuela) in 1595 in search of gold was in part a bid for royal favour; his leadership of the expedition to sack Cadiz harbour in June 1596 was a more successful one, and by adroitly dissociating himself from the earl of *Essex he maintained a strong position until the queen's death.

Ralegh's trial, on largely trumped-up charges of high treason, was one of the first events of James I's reign, and from 1603 to 1616 he was imprisoned in the Tower with his wife and family, a dead man in the eyes of the law. He was released to search out the gold mine he claimed to have discovered in Guiana 20 years before. On returning from this disastrous expedition, in which his eldest son was killed and his chief lieutenant, Keymis, committed suicide, a commission of inquiry set up under Spanish pressure determined that the gold mine was a fabrication, the old charge of treason was renewed, and on 29 Oct. 1618 Ralegh was executed.

His poems are beset by uncertainties as to date and authenticity, though a few of them, including the fragmentary '21th: and last booke of the Ocean to Scinthia', survive in his own handwriting. Two well-known poems formerly attributed to him, 'Walsingham' ('As you came from the holy land') and 'The Passionate Mans Pilgrimage' ('Give me my Scallop shell of quiet'), are not now thought to be his work. Among the authentic poems are his 'An Epitaph upon Sir Philip Sidney' and the prefatory sonnet to *The Faerie Queene* which begins, 'Methought I saw the grave, where *Laura* lay'. There are numerous prose works. His *Report of the Truth of the Fight about the Iles of Acores* (1591) was a source of *Tennyson's 'The Revenge' (1878). His *Discoverie of Guiana* (1596) includes a description of 'Eldorado', and describes the plain-lands as a natural Eden:

> still as we rowed, the deer came down feeding by the water's side, as if they had been used to a keeper's call.

The History of the World (1614), written during Ralegh's long imprisonment, was originally intended for Henry, prince of Wales (d. 1612). This ambitious book, which Ralegh worked on with the help of several assistants, deals with Greek, Egyptian, and biblical history up to 168 BC. The preface, at the beginning of which he affirms his 'fidelity towards Her, whom I must still honor in the dust', summarizes modern European history, demonstrating the unchangeableness of God's judgement. The *History* contains many reflective passages, most characteristically elegiac in tone:

> For this tide of mans life, after it once turneth and declineth, ever runneth, with a perpetuall ebbe and falling streame, but never floweth againe: our leafe once fallen, springeth no more, neither doth the Sunne or the Summer adorne us againe, with the garments of new leaves and flowers.

The best-known such passage comes on the final page:

> O eloquent, just and mightie Death! whom none could advise, thou hast perswaded; what none hath dared, thou hast done; and whom all the world hath flattered, thou only hast cast out of the world and despised: thou hast drawne together all the farre stretched great-nesse, all the pride, crueltie, and ambition of man, and covered it all over with these two narrow words, *Hic iacet*.

The poems have been edited by A. Latham (1951); Pierre Lefranc's *Sir Walter Ralegh, écrivain* (1968) offers detailed theories about the relationship of the poems to the life; C. A. Patrides has edited selections from *The History of the World* (1971).

RALEIGH, Sir Walter Alexander (1861–1922). After holding chairs at Liverpool and Glasgow, he became in 1904 the first holder of the chair of English literature at Oxford. Among his works are *Style* (1897), *Milton* (1900), and *Shakespeare* (1907), but in his day he was renowned more as a stimulating if informal lecturer than as a critic. He wrote the first volume of the official *The War in the Air* (1922), and his selected letters were published in 1926.

Ralpho, the squire in Butler's **Hudibras*. (See VAUGHAN, T.)

Ralph Roister Doister, the earliest known English comedy, by *Udall, probably performed about 1552 and printed about 1566, and perhaps played by Westminster boys while Udall was headmaster of that school. The play, in short rhymed doggerel, represents the courting of the widow Christian Custance, who is betrothed to Gawin Goodlucke, an absent merchant, by Roister, a swaggering simpleton, instigated thereto by the mischievous Mathewe Merygreeke. Roister is repulsed and beaten by Custance and her maids; and Goodlucke, after being deceived by false reports, is reconciled to her. The play shows similarity to the comedies of *Plautus and *Terence.

Rambler, a twice-weekly periodical in 208 numbers issued by Dr *Johnson from 20 Mar. 1750 to 14 Mar. 1752.

The contents are essays on all kinds of subjects, character studies, allegories, Eastern fables, criticisms, etc., and were, with the exception of five, written by Johnson himself. The moral seriousness of his enterprise is indicated by the fact that he wrote a prayer on beginning the work, and in the last paper he claimed never to have exploited 'the topic of the day'. The other contributors were *Richardson, E. *Carter, Mrs *Chapone, and Catherine Talbot (1720–70). Despite initial protests against its 'solemn' tone, the *Rambler* was pirated and imitated, and went through ten numbered reprintings in Johnson's lifetime.

RAMSAY, Allan (1686–1758), Scottish poet, born in Lanarkshire, who came to Edinburgh where he spent most of his life. He was a wigmaker, then a bookseller, and an important figure in Edinburgh literary society; he opened the first circulating library in Edinburgh in 1726 (see LIBRARIES, CIRCULATING). In 1718 he brought out anonymously several editions of **Christis Kirk on the Green*, with supplementary verses of his own in fake antique *Scots, and also various vernacular mock elegies. A collection of his elegies and satires appeared in 1721. In 1724–37 he issued *The Tea-Table Miscellany*, one of the more famous 18th-cent. collections of songs

and ballads, and in 1724 *The Ever Green*, which contained work by the great poets of late medieval Scotland, notably *Dunbar and *Henryson, though with revisions and additions of his own. These contributed much to the revival of vernacular Scottish poetry, and in his preface to the latter Ramsay makes clear his patriotic intentions: 'When these good old Bards wrote, we had not yet made Use of imported Trimming'. Ramsay's pastoral comedy *The Gentle Shepherd* (1725), with its Scots songs, was very successful and much admired by *Boswell among others for its 'beautiful rural imagery' and its 'real picture of manners'. His son, also Allan (1713–84), became a well-known portrait painter; *Hume and *Rousseau were among his subjects.

RAMUS, Petrus (Latin form of Pierre de la Ramée) (1515–72), French philosopher and grammarian. A supporter of the Protestant faith, he perished in the massacre of St *Bartholomew, an event portrayed by Marlowe in **The Massacre at Paris*. His *Dialectique* of 1555, the first work of its kind to be written in French, systematically challenged Aristotelian and *Scholastic logic. It was introduced into England in the late 16th cent. and obtained wide academic currency, especially at Cambridge. His followers were known as Ramists and his anti-Scholastic system of logic as Ramism. Walter J. Ong has written historical studies of Ramus and edited several of his Latin works.

RANDOLPH, Thomas (1605–35), educated at Westminster School and Trinity College, Cambridge, where he became known as a writer in English and Latin verse. He returned to London in 1632. His principal plays are *Amyntas*, a pastoral comedy, and **The Muses Lookinge-Glasse*, printed 1638; and **Hey for Honesty*, printed 1651. He wrote an eclogue included in *Annalia Dubrensia*, verses in celebration of the *Cotswold Games. His plays and poems were edited by W. C. *Hazlitt (1875).

RANDS, William Brighty (1823–82), the 'laureate of the nursery', who wrote sometimes under the pseudonyms Henry Holbeach and Matthew Browne. His best-known work was *Lilliput Levee* (1864), a book of verse for children with illustrations by *Millais and G. J. Pinwell, which was followed by *Lilliput Lectures* (1871, mostly prose), and *Lilliput Legends* (1872). All three were published anonymously. He was a reporter in the House of Commons, and also wrote a good deal of miscellaneous journalism.

Rankenian Club, one of the most influential 18th-cent. Edinburgh clubs, founded *c.*1717 by a group of radical divinity students who were admirers of the moral and political writings of the third earl of *Shaftesbury. Its leading members rose to prominence in the universities, the Church, medicine, and the law, and were influential in the improvement of literary style in Edinburgh. Lord Auchinleck, father of *Boswell, was a member.

RANSOM, John Crowe (1888–1974), American poet and critic, born in Tennessee, the son of a Methodist minister, and educated there and at Oxford. From 1937 to 1958 he was a professor at Kenyon College, Ohio, where he founded and edited the important *Kenyon Review*, a scholarly publication committed to the close textual analysis associated with the *New Criticism. His critical works include *God without Thunder* (1930) and *The New Criticism* (1941), the latter an independent survey of the works of I. A. *Richards, Y. *Winters, and others. His period of activity as a poet was relatively brief, but his output, notably in *Chills and Fever* (1924) and *Two Gentlemen in Bonds* (1927), is impressive, and he is particularly remembered for his formal, subtle, taut ballad-portraits and elegies, which include 'Captain Carpenter' and 'Bells for John Whiteside's Daughter'.

RANSOME, Arthur Michell (1884–1967), journalist and author, born in Leeds, the son of a professor of history, and educated at Rugby. He started work in London as office boy for Grant *Richards, then graduated to ghost-writing, reviewing, and short story writing, and eventually became a reporter, first for the *Daily News*, then (in 1919) for the *Manchester Guardian*. He went to Russia in 1913 to learn the language, and covered the revolution at first hand for the *Daily News*; his collection of Russian legends and fairy stories, *Old Peter's Russian Tales* (1916), had a considerable success. In 1924 he married, as his second wife, Evgenia Shelepin, who had been Trotsky's secretary. He is best remembered for his classic sequence of novels for children, which reflect his keen interest in sailing, fishing, and the countryside: beginning with *Swallows and Amazons* (1930) and ending with *Great Northern?* (1947), it describes the adventures of the Walker (Swallow) and Blackett (Amazon) families, and various of their friends, in the Lake District, the Norfolk Broads, and other vividly drawn locations. See *The Autobiography of Arthur Ransome* (1976), ed. Rupert Hart-Davis, and a biography by Hugh Brogan (1984). (See CHILDREN'S LITERATURE.)

Ranters, a miscellaneous sect of heretical Puritan extremists whose heresies, which mushroomed in the late 1640s and early 1650s, were founded on the Inner Light and included freedom from the moral law (antinomianism), community of goods and women, abolition of tithes, the futility of the Bible, the non-existence of hell, the excellence of tobacco and alcohol, and mystical Pantheism (Jacob Bauthumley's 'God in an ivy-leaf'). Notorious Ranters included L. *Clarkson, A. *Coppe, Richard Coppin, and Joseph Salmon. Hackwriters exploited their reputation for orgiastic sex by inventing sensational reports, leading some modern historians to claim that 'there was no Ranter movement' (J. C. Davis, *Fear, Myth and History*). However, C. *Hill has written persuasively about their revolutionary anarchism in *The World Turned upside down* (1972).

RAO, Raja (1909–   ), Indian writer, born at Hassan, Karnataka, and educated at Nizam College, Hyderabad, and the universities of Montpellier and the Sorbonne. His first novel, *Kanthapura* (1938), an account of the Independence movement seen from the perspective of a small south Indian village grandmother, attempts to forge an Indian idiom and tempo through the medium of the English language. This was followed by the more sophisticated *The Serpent and the Rope* (1960), the story of a young Indian Brahman intellectual, Rama, and his French wife Madeleine in their search for spiritual truth in India, France, and England. Rao's stories have been collected in *The Cow of the Barricades* (1947) and *The Policeman and the Rose* (1978) and *On the Ganga Ghat* (stories, 1989). Later works include *The Chessmaker and His Moves* (1988). See ANGLO-INDIAN LITERATURE.

rap, the performance of a rhythmic monologue over a pre-recorded instrumental backing. Rap was developed in the dance halls and clubs of North America as a way of exciting the crowds and allowing the rappers to show off their ability to rhyme. Rap studio recordings are now recognized as a legitimate branch of popular music. Many of the poets now referred to as rap poets are concerned not only with their rhyming skills but also with lyrical content.

Rape of Lucrece, The, a poem in rhyme-royal by *Shakespeare, published 1594 and dedicated to Henry Wriothesley, earl of Southampton. It is presumably the 'graver labour' which he promised to the earl in the dedication of *Venus and Adonis* the previous year. It is a highly rhetorical expansion of the story as told by *Livy. See LUCRETIA.

Rape of the Lock, The, a poem by *Pope, in two cantos, published in *Lintot's *Miscellany* 1712 as 'The Rape of the Locke'; subsequently enlarged to five cantos and thus published 1714.

When Lord Petre forcibly cut off a lock of Miss Arabella Fermor's hair, the incident gave rise to a quarrel between the families. With the idea of allaying this, Pope treated the subject in a playful *mock-heroic poem, on the model of *Boileau's *Le Lutrin*. He presents Belinda at her toilet, a game of ombre, the snipping of the lock while Belinda sips her coffee, the wrath of Belinda and her demand that the lock be restored, the final wafting of the lock, as a new star, to adorn the skies. The poem was published in its original form with Miss Fermor's permission. Pope then expanded the sketch by introducing the machinery of sylphs and gnomes, adapted from a light erotic French work, *Le Comte de Gabalis*, a series of five discourses by the Abbé de Montfaucon de Villars, which appeared in English in 1680; in his dedication he credits both *Gabalis* and the *Rosicrucians. (See also PARACELSUS.) One of Pope's most brilliant performances, it has also been one of his most popular; Dr *Johnson called it 'the most attractive of all ludicrous compositions', in which

'New things are made familiar and familiar things are made new'.

RAPHAEL (Raffaello Sanzio) (1483–1520), Italian painter, born in Urbino. He worked in Perugino's studio and then in Florence, and succeeded Bramante as architect of St Peter's. Throughout the 17th, 18th, and 19th cents Raphael was generally revered as the greatest of all painters; his supremacy was challenged by the romantic admirers of Michelangelo, and in the 19th cent. the *Pre-Raphaelites revolted—somewhat vaguely—against his authority.

RAPHAEL, Frederic (1931–   ), novelist, short story writer, and screenwriter, born in Chicago, educated at St John's College, Cambridge, and long resident in England. His novels, many of which deal with the dilemmas of educated middle-class life, include *Obbligato* (1956), *The Limits of Love* (1960, set partly in Jewish north London), and *The Graduate Wife* (1962). *Lindmann* (1963) is based on the historical incident of the break-up of the illegal immigrant ship, the SS *Broda*, in 1942, off the Turkish coast: in Raphael's version, the 'courteous and sad and homeless' Austrian Lindmann survives, and the tragedy is re-examined through the device of a screenplay written by London-based writer Dick Milstein. Other novels include *Orchestra and Beginners* (1967), *Heaven and Earth* (1985), and *Coast to Coast* (1998). Raphael's screenplays include *Darling* (1965, directed by John Schlesinger), a satire of life in the Swinging Sixties, and a six-part TV series, *The Glittering Prizes* (1976), which follows the careers of a group of artistic and theatrical Cambridge undergraduates from 1952 to the 1970s. Raphael also translated *Catullus (1978, with K. McLeish) and *Aeschylus (1991).

RASHDALL, Hastings (1858–1924), philosopher and theologian, educated at New College, Oxford. His most important work, *The Theory of Good and Evil* (1907), expounds his own version of what he called 'ideal utilitarianism'. *The Universities of Europe in the Middle Ages* (1895; new edn, ed. Powicke and Emden, 1936) is a standard work.

RASPE, Rudolf Erich, see Munchausen.

Rasselas, Prince of Abyssinia, The History of, a didactic romance by Dr *Johnson, published 1759, and composed during the evenings of a week to help his dying mother and eventually to pay for her funeral. It is an essay on the 'choice of life', a phrase repeated throughout the work, usually in italics.

Rasselas, a son of the emperor of Abyssinia, weary of the joys of the 'happy valley' where the inhabitants know only 'the soft vicissitudes of pleasure and repose', escapes to Egypt, accompanied by his sister Nekayah, her attendant Pekuah, and the much-travelled old philosopher Imlac. Here they study the various conditions of men's lives, and after a few incidents of no great importance resolve to return to Abyssinia, in a

'conclusion, in which nothing is concluded'. The charm of the work lies not in its plot, which is minimal, but in its wise and humane melancholy; in many ways it echoes the theme of *The Vanity of Human Wishes*, stressing that earthly happiness is unobtainable, and demonstrating that philosophers, hermits, and the wealthy all fail to achieve it. 'Harmless pleasures', Imlac concludes, are very rare. Thus, in the concluding chapters of the work, the emphasis shifts from 'the choice of life' to 'the choice of eternity'. Imlac also produces Johnson's celebrated definition of the 'business of a poet', which is to 'examine not the individual, but the species . . . he does not number the streaks of the tulip'; and to write 'as the interpreter of nature, and the legislator of mankind . . . presiding over the thoughts and manners of future generations' (ch. X)—a phrase that anticipated Shelley's arguments in his *Defence of Poetry. Rasselas*, though much milder in tone, bears some resemblance in plan to *Voltaire's *Candide*, published in the same year but not read by Johnson until later, when he himself commented on the similarity.

RASTELL, John (c.1475–1536), printer, barrister, playwright, and brother-in-law of Sir T. *More. He wrote and published an interlude called *Four Elements* (c.1520), and two comedies of c.1525, *Calisto and Melebea* and *Gentleness and Nobility*. The latter has been attributed to Rastell's son-in-law J. *Heywood.

Rat, the Cat, and Lovel the dog, the, in the political rhyme:

> The Rat, the Cat, and Lovel the dog
> Rule all England under the Hog,

refer to three adherents of Richard III: Sir Richard Ratcliffe (killed at Bosworth, 1485), Sir John Catesby (d. 1486), and Francis, first Viscount Lovell (1454–?88; his skeleton was found in a vault, where he had evidently starved to death). The Hog is a reference to the boar that figured as one of the supporters of the royal arms.

RATTIGAN, Sir Terence Mervyn (1911–77), the son of a diplomat. He was educated at Harrow and Trinity College, Oxford, and early embarked on a career as a playwright. His first West End success was a comedy, *French without Tears* (1936, pub. 1937). This was followed by many other works, including *The Winslow Boy* (1946), a drama in which a father fights to clear his naval-cadet son of the accusation of petty theft, and *The Browning Version* (1948), about Crocker-Harris, a repressed and unpopular schoolmaster with a faithless wife: the title refers to Browning's *Agamemnon of Aeschylus*, presented to Crocker-Harris as a leaving present by his pupil Taplow. The heroine of *The Deep Blue Sea* (1952) is a judge's wife suffering from passion for a test pilot. *Separate Tables* (1954, pub. 1955) comprises two one-act plays set in a hotel, both studies of emotional failure and inadequacy; *Ross* (1960) is based on the life of T. E. *Lawrence; and *Cause Célèbre* (1977, pub. 1978) is based on an actual murder trial.

When Rattigan's *Collected Works* were published in 1953, he wrote a preface to the second volume in which he created the character of 'Aunt Edna', the average middle-brow matinée attender whom playwrights must take into account, and critics were later to use this light-hearted invention as a focus for their complaints about the middle-class, middle-brow nature of his own plays; the so-called *kitchen sink dramatists of the 1950s and 1960s reacted against Rattigan (expressly, in the case of S. *Delaney), but his works are still much performed and admired, and *Rudkin in a BBC Radio 3 programme in 1976 stressed not his celebrated 'craftsmanship' but his sense of 'existential bleakness and irresolvable carnal solitude'. A biography by M. Darlow and G. Hodson (1979) gives an account of his troubled personal life and successful career.

Rauf Coilyear, a rhymed poem of the *Charlemagne cycle, in stanzas of 13 lines, of which a copy survives, printed in Scotland in 1572 (written probably c.1475). This humorous poem tells how Charlemagne loses his way and takes refuge in the hut of Rauf, a plain-spoken and self-willed charcoal-burner who treats him hospitably but with excessive freedom. Ed. S. J. Herrtage (EETS ES 39, 1882).

RAVEN, Simon Noël (1927–2001), novelist, educated at Charterhouse and King's College, Cambridge. In 1957 he resigned his infantry commission to become a professional writer and reviewer. His first novel, *The Feathers of Death* (1959), brought him instant recognition. His major work is a ten-volume series of novels, *Alms for Oblivion*, consisting of *The Rich Pay Late* (1964), *Friends in Low Places* (1965), *The Sabre Squadron* (1966), *Fielding Gray* (1967, chronologically the first in the series), *The Judas Boy* (1968), *Places Where They Sing* (1970), *Sound the Retreat* (1971), *Come Like Shadows* (1972), *Bring Forth the Body* (1974), and *The Survivors* (1976). The sequence presents an uncompromising panorama of post-war life from 1945 to 1973 through the lives and vicissitudes of the same group of characters. Some of these also appear in the seven-volume series *The First-Born of Egypt*, which began with *Morning Star* (1984) and concluded with *The Troubadour* (1992). *The Old School* (1986), a work of non-fiction, reflects Raven's ambivalent attitude to the British public school system, which he found at once detestable and fascinating. He also published plays and essays.

'Raven, The', a poem by E. A. *Poe.

Ravenshoe, a novel by H. *Kingsley.

RAVERAT, Gwen(dolen Mary), née Darwin (1885–1957), wood-engraver and granddaughter of C. *Darwin, born in Cambridge; her childhood is described in her autobiographical *Period Piece* (1952). Works illustrated by her include *Spring Morning* (1915) by her cousin F. *Cornford, and various anthologies in asso-

ciation with K. *Grahame. Her husband Jacques Raverat (d. 1925) was a correspondent of V. *Woolf.

RAWLINSON, Thomas (1681–1725), educated at Eton and St John's College, Oxford, a book-collector, whose manuscripts are in the Bodleian Library. He was satirized by Addison in the *Tatler* (No. 158) as 'Tom Folio'.

RAWLS, John (1921–2002), American political philosopher, at Harvard since 1962, whose seminal *A Theory of Justice* (1971) transformed the discipline by mounting a systematic defence of egalitarian liberalism under the label 'justice as fairness'. This presents valid principles of social justice as those that would be agreed to by people in the 'original position', behind a 'veil of ignorance' that deprives them of knowledge about their own particular characteristics and ethical beliefs. His *Political Liberalism* (1993) develops and qualifies the theory, emphasizing the extent to which it builds upon ideas implicit in the public political cultures of, and is applicable specifically to, liberal democracies.

RAY, John (1627–1705), the son of a blacksmith, who became one of England's greatest naturalists. He was pre-eminently a botanist (he originated the division of plants into monocotyledons and dicotyledons), but also took up the unfinished zoological work of his friend Francis Willughby. His *Historia Plantarum* was published 1686–1704, and his *Wisdom of God Manifested in the Works of Creation* (1691) went through many editions. He also published *A Collection of English Proverbs* (1670) and was keenly interested in philology.

READ, Sir Herbert Edward (1893–1968), born in Yorkshire, and educated at Leeds University; he served in France throughout the First World War. He worked in the Victoria and Albert Museum, 1922–31, as professor of fine art in Edinburgh, 1931–3, and as editor of the *Burlington Magazine*, 1933–9. The first volumes of his spare, taut poems (much influenced by *Imagism) were *Songs of Chaos* (1915) and *Naked Warriors* (1919), largely based on the war; these were followed by various volumes of collected poems, a long poem, *The End of a War* (1933), and the final *Collected Poems* of 1966. His critical work includes studies of *Wordsworth, *Malory, *Sterne, and others; *Form in Modern Poetry* (1932), *The True Voice of Feeling* (1953), and *Essays in Literary Criticism* (1969) contain much of his most valuable work. Many publications on art include *Art and Industry* (1934) and *Education through Art* (1943). His personal prose writing includes two records of trench life, *In Retreat* (1925) and *Ambush* (1930); *The Innocent Eye* (1933), a brief autobiography of his Yorkshire childhood, and a full autobiography in 1963, *The Contrary Experience*; and his only novel, *The Green Child* (1935), an allegorical fantasy, based on a folk tale, of the return to innocence. He also edited works by T. E. *Hulme, *Orage, Kropotkin, and *Jung, and various anthologies.

READ, Piers Paul (1941–), novelist, son of Sir H. *Read, educated at Ampleforth and St John's College, Cambridge. His novels, which combine the psychological thriller and strong narrative with political questioning, a well-travelled eye, Catholic apologia, and sharp analysis of the English class structure, include *Game in Heaven with Tussy Marx* (1966), *The Junkers* (1968, set in Germany), *Monk Dawson*, (1969, the story of a defecting monk), and *The Professor's Daughter* (1971, set in America, as a wealthy liberal Harvard academic becomes fatally involved in student revolt at the time of Vietnam). *The Upstart* (1973) is the story of Hilary Fletcher, son of a parson, who turns to crime and pursues a protracted revenge upon the aristocratic Yorkshire family which had humiliated him socially in his youth. Later works range widely, taking in settings in the Soviet Union (*The Villa Golitsyn*) and in post-Soviet Europe (*A Patriot in Berlin*, 1995). Read has also written books of reportage, including *Alive: The Story of the Andes Survivors* (1974), based on an air crash and the cannibalism of its survivors, and *The Train Robbers* (1978).

READE, Charles (1814–84), born at Ipsden, in Oxfordshire, the son of a solidly respectable country squire. In 1831 he won a demyship to Magdalen College, Oxford, beginning a long association which brought him a fellowship and various important college offices over the years. The effects of enforced celibacy (as required by college life) provided an important theme in several of his novels. He travelled abroad, then in 1842 began to study for the bar; in 1846 he tried studying medicine in Edinburgh; and in 1847, the year in which he obtained a DCL, he began to deal in violins, on which he was an expert. He began his literary career publishing a stage version of Smollett's *Peregrine Pickle* in 1851, and in 1852 entered on his long career as theatre manager and dramatist. *Masks and Faces*, successfully produced in that year, became a novel, *Peg Woffington*, in 1853. In that year he also published *Christie Johnstone*, the first of his 'reforming' novels, urging the reform of prisons and the treatment of criminals, which was followed in 1856 by *It Is Never Too Late to Mend*, a highly successful work in the same genre, which was later dramatized. *Gold!*, a play converted in 1869 into the novel *Foul Play*, also appeared in this prolific year. At the same time Reade was also writing short stories, working as a journalist, and writing plays. In 1854 he met the actress Mrs Seymour, with whom he lived until her death in 1879. *The Autobiography of a Thief* and *Jack of All Trades* (both greatly admired by *Orwell) appeared in 1858; *Love Me Little, Love Me Long* in 1859; and in 1861 the work for which he is chiefly remembered, *The Cloister and the Hearth*. *Hard Cash*, a novel exposing the scandal of lunatic asylums (which Reade considered 'my best production'), appeared in 1863, and in 1866 *Griffith Gaunt*,

which some judge superior to *The Cloister and the Hearth*. The frankness of its attitude to sexual problems provoked scandal and considerable litigation, in which Reade pugnaciously defended himself against 'the Prurient Prudes'. For much of the rest of his life he was engaged in various personal and legal controversies. A long collaboration with *Boucicault, a highly successful adapter of plays and novels, began in 1867, and the last of Reade's major novels, *Put Yourself in His Place*, attacking the trade union practice of 'rattening' or enforcing membership, appeared in 1870. In 1871 he published another novel, *A Terrible Temptation*, and in 1872 quarrelled with *Trollope over the adaptation of one of Trollope's novels, following this with a libel action in 1873 over his own new novel, *The Simpleton*. *The Wandering Heir* (1873), suggested by the Tichborne trial, was again both novel and play; Reade persuaded Ellen *Terry to emerge from retirement to perform in the stage version. He continued to produce short stories, journalistic work, and plays for his touring company, and to be embroiled in disputes and legal actions. By the time he published *A Woman Hater* (1877) he had lost his determination to present honestly the problems of sex in society, and meekly agreed to all *Blackwood's objections. After the death of Mrs Seymour in 1879 he wrote little, turned to religion, and in 1882 gave up theatrical management. *A Perilous Secret* appeared posthumously in 1884.

Reade enjoyed great fame and success, and was accepted by the public as the natural successor of *Dickens (whose novels had considerably influenced him). Among critics, both the young H. *James and *Swinburne regarded him as a novelist of genius, and placed his work above that of G. *Eliot (a view which at the time did not apparently seem eccentric). But his reputation has considerably dimmed, and he is now remembered only for *The Cloister and the Hearth* and *Griffith Gaunt*. The 'realism' of his novels was based on immense research, recorded in intricate detail in his mass of notebooks; for *The Cloister and the Hearth*, he read *Erasmus, *Froissart, *Luther, *chronicles, *jest books, and all the records he could find. He wished by this method to impart an authentic reality to his work, and also to discipline the 'inner consciousness', which he distrusted; but the detail of information is often thought to overwhelm his considerable narrative power. His expression of sexual frustration and fantasy (celibacy, he wrote, is 'an invention wholly devilish'), and its place in religious feeling, was much stifled by the proprieties of the time. See M. Elwin, *Charles Reade* (1931); W. Burns, *Charles Reade: A Study in Victorian Authorship* (1961).

READE, William Winwood (1838–75), explorer, novelist, and nephew of C. *Reade. His explorations in West and South-West Africa are described in *Savage Africa* (1863), *The African Sketchbook* (1873), and *The Story of the Ashanti Campaign* (1874). His other works, which aroused some controversy for their criticism of religion, included the notable *The Martyrdom of Man* (1872), which exposes the author's atheistical views and influenced H. G. *Wells who described it as 'an extraordinarily inspiring presentation of human history as one consistent process'.

reader-response theory, a body of literary investigations, chiefly German and American, into the nature of the reader's activity in the process of understanding literary texts. A major contribution to debates on this topic was made by Wolfgang Iser (1926–   ), whose books *The Implied Reader* (1974) and *The Act of Reading* (1979) argue that a literary work is incomplete until the reader has 'actualized' those elements that are left to her imagination. The American psychologist Norman H. Holland (1927–   ) attempted to demonstrate in *Five Readers Reading* (1975) that individual interpretations of the same text vary according to the reader's 'identity theme'. The more controversial arguments of Stanley Fish (1938–   ) in his essays collected as *Is There a Text in This Class?* (1980) include the claim that literary texts are produced by the strategies of interpretation that guide us to seek certain meanings in them; and that the way we read poems is determined by the 'interpretive community' in which we are trained. See also HERMENEUTICS.

READING, Peter (1946–   ), poet, born in Liverpool. He has published several volumes of poetry: *Water and Waste* (1970), was followed by *For the Municipality's Elderly* (1974), which strikes in its title poem a note of subdued, realist resignation as it describes an everyday scene in a provincial town: later volumes were increasingly to display inventiveness and aggression in typography, verse form, and subject matter. Titles include *Nothing for Anyone* (1977), *C* (1984, a grim meditation on cancer), and *Ukulele Music* (1985). Reading contrasts a reporter's unsparing evocation of the underside and underclass of non-metropolitan contemporary Britain—pub life, domestic brutality, street violence—with a mocking command of classical metrics: ' "Unemployed/Hopeless" doesn't sufficiently | Serve to explain Cro Magnon atrocities' (*Stet*, 1986). *Final Demands* (1988) combined prose and verse, past and present, peace and war in an unsettling collage of different typefaces. The gallows-humour assault on decay and self-destruction continued in *Perduta Gente* (1989), *Evagatory* (1992), *Work in Regress* (1997), and other volumes.

Ready-to-halt, Mr, in Bunyan's *Pilgrim's Progress*, a pilgrim who follows Mr *Great-heart, though upon crutches. When he comes to the land of *Beulah and is about to cross the river, he bequeaths his crutches to his son, for he sees chariots and horses ready to carry him into the City.

Real Charlotte, The, see SOMERVILLE AND ROSS.

Realism, in *Scholastic philosophy, the doctrine that attributes objective or absolute existence to universals, the principal exponent of which was St Thomas *Aquinas. The opposite view is *Nominalism which regards universals simply as words, a *flatus vocis*.

realism, a literary term so widely used as to be more or less meaningless except when used in contradistinction to some other movement, e.g. *naturalism, *Expressionism, *Surrealism. Sir P. *Harvey's original definition was 'a loosely used term meaning truth to the observed facts of life (especially when they are gloomy)', which would seem to indicate that he had in mind such post-French-realist works as those of *Gissing, A. *Morrison, G. A. *Moore, *Maugham's *Liza of Lambeth*, etc., most of which have proletarian or lower-middle-class settings. The French realist school of the mid-19th cent. (for which the novelist Champfleury, 1821–89, produced a manifesto, *Le Réalisme*, 1857) stressed 'sincerity' as opposed to the 'liberty' proclaimed by the Romantics; it insisted on accurate documentation, sociological insight, an accumulation of the details of material fact, an avoidance of poetic diction, idealization, exaggeration, melodrama, etc.; and subjects were to be taken from everyday life, preferably from lower-class life. This emphasis clearly reflected the interests of an increasingly positivist and scientific age. *Balzac and *Stendhal were seen as the great precursors of realism; *Flaubert (though he disliked the label, and was also claimed by the naturalists) and the *Goncourts as among its practitioners. French realism developed into naturalism, an associated but more scientifically applied and elaborated doctrine, seen by some later critics (notably *Marxist critics) as degenerate. In England, the French realists were imitated consciously and notably by Moore and Arnold *Bennett, but the English novel from the time of *Defoe had had its own unlabelled strain of realism, and the term is thus applied to English literature in varying senses and contexts, sometimes qualified as 'social' or 'psychological' realism etc. (See also SOCIALIST REALISM.)

Reasonableness of Christianity, see ESSAY CONCERNING HUMAN UNDERSTANDING.

Rebecca, (1) the name given (in allusion to Gen. 24: 60) to the leader, in woman's attire, of the rioters who demolished tollgates in south Wales in 1843–4; (2) a character in Scott's *Ivanhoe*; (3) a novel by D. *du Maurier (see below).

Rebecca, a popular romantic novel by D. *du Maurier, published in 1938. A cinematic adaptation was directed by Alfred Hitchcock in 1940. The unnamed narrator is plucked from obscurity as a lady's companion to become the second wife of the wealthy widower Maxim de Winter, and mistress of Manderley, his Cornish estate. Insecure in the role created by Maxim's glamorous first wife, Rebecca, she is tormented for her failure to match her predecessor's social confidence, especially by the servant Mrs Danvers, who remains obsessively loyal to Rebecca's memory. Having assumed that Maxim too adored his first wife, the narrator discovers that in fact he hated and indeed—provoked by her shameless adultery— murdered Rebecca, disguising her death as a boating accident. The belated discovery of Rebecca's boat threatens to expose Maxim's guilt, but the coroner is led to record a verdict of suicide. The de Winters go into exile after Mrs Danvers sets fire to Manderley. The novel has echoes of C. *Brontë's *Jane Eyre and of the wider *Gothic tradition. Although Maxim's character is weakly drawn, the sinister Mrs Danvers remains a memorable creation.

Rebecca and Rowena, a humorous sequel by *Thackeray to Scott's *Ivanhoe, in which Ivanhoe tires of domestic life with Rowena, and after various comic vicissitudes is reunited with Rebecca.

'Recluse, The', see EXCURSION, THE.

Recruiting Officer, The, a comedy by *Farquhar, produced 1706.

It deals with the humours of recruiting in a country town, with a vividness suggesting that the author drew on his own experience. The plot is slender; it presents Captain Plume making love to the women in order to secure their followers as recruits; Kite, his resourceful sergeant, employing his wiles and assuming the character of an astrologer, for the same purpose; while Sylvia, daughter of Justice Ballance, who is in love with Plume but has promised not to marry him without her father's consent, runs away from home disguised as a man, gets herself arrested for scandalous conduct, is brought before her father, and delivered over by him to Captain Plume, as a recruit. Captain Brazen, a rival recruiting officer, who boasts of battles and friends in every quarter of the globe, endeavours to marry the rich Melinda, but finds himself fobbed off with her maid.

recusant, a term used to describe those who from Elizabeth's reign to about the end of the 18th cent. refused to attend the services of the Church of England. It was especially applied to Roman Catholics.

Red Book of Hergest, see MABINOGION.

Red Cotton Night-Cap Country or Turf and Towers, a poem in blank verse by R. *Browning, published 1873. The title refers ironically to the description by Browning's friend Anne Thackeray (*Ritchie) of a district in Normandy as 'white cotton night-cap country'; Browning undertakes to show that the 'red' of passion and violence should replace the 'white'.

The story is based on a contemporary cause célèbre, involving the wealthy heir to a Paris jewellery business, Antoine Mellerio (in the poem, Léonce Miranda). As Browning tells it, Miranda's life was dominated by the opposed principles of sensual indulgence and religious fanaticism, symbolized by the 'turf' and 'towers' of the subtitle. He lived with his mistress Anna (in the poem, Clara) at a luxurious estate in Normandy, to which he had added a grandiose belvedere. His mother's death in Paris occasioned a fit of violent remorse, in which he renounced Clara and mutilated himself by burning off both his hands. However, he soon resumed his relationship with Clara and, in the period before his death, made extravagant donations to a convent near his estate, which housed a famous statue of the Virgin. He died by a fall from the top of his belvedere, leaving his fortune to the convent, with a life interest for Clara. The will was challenged by his family, but their suit was comprehensively rejected by the courts, who upheld the will and declared Miranda's death to be due to an accident. Browning, however, maintains that Miranda leapt from the tower in a deliberate test of the power of the Virgin to save him, and thus resolve the struggle in his spirit between idealism and materialism. This struggle is the real topic of the poem: Miranda, weak-headed victim of a self-imposed dualism, is a nightmare parody of the figure of the artist in Browning. The poem has never been popular, because of its sordid plot and harsh, sardonic style; but contains, in Miranda's long interior monologue before he jumps, one of the most powerful single passages of Browning's late work.

Redcrosse Knight, the, in Bk I of Spenser's *Faerie Queene, St George, the patron saint of England. He is the 'patron' or champion of Holiness, and represents the Anglican Church. He is separated from *Una (the true religion) by the wiles of *Archimago (hypocrisy), and is led away by *Duessa (the Roman Catholic religion) to the House of Pride. He drinks of an enchanted stream, loses his strength, and is made captive by the giant *Orgoglio (pride). Orgoglio is slain by Prince *Arthur, and Una leads her knight to the House of Holiness, to learn repentance and be healed. The Knight and Una are finally betrothed, after he has killed the dragon which besieged her parents' castle.

Redgauntlet, a novel by Sir W. *Scott, published 1824.

In this novel, Scott returns after several years and with triumphant success to the period and setting in which he was always most happily at home. The plot concerns an apocryphal attempt by Prince Charles Edward to regain the throne, 20 years after 1745. Under the name of Herries of Birrenswork, Hugh Redgauntlet, a fanatical Jacobite, leads the attempt and kidnaps his nephew Darsie Latimer (unknown to himself, Sir Arthur Darsie Redgauntlet and head of the family) in order to strengthen the cause. Darsie has been brought up, in ignorance of his background and of his father's forfeiture after the 1745 rebellion, in the household of Saunders Fairford, an Edinburgh writer to the signet, and in companionship with his son Alan who, like the young Scott, was studying to become an advocate. Alan, alarmed at the disappearance of his friend, goes in search of him and their joint experiences make up the substance of the novel. The plot collapses with the realization by the conspirators that the Hanoverian government does not take them seriously enough even to arrest them; that, in the words of Redgauntlet, the cause is lost forever. Apart from Darsie and Alan, each of whom portrays different aspects of the young Scott, the novel contains some memorable characters, notably Redgauntlet himself, the Quaker Joshua Geddes, the crazy litigant Peter Peebles (a parody of the situation of the Young Pretender) and particularly Saunders Fairford, an affectionate and probably accurate portrait of Scott's own father; it also contains, embedded in the centre of the novel and thematically linked to it, one of the finest short stories in the language, 'Wandering Willie's Tale'.

REDGROVE, Peter William (1932–2003), poet and novelist, educated at Taunton School, Somerset, and at Queens' College, Cambridge, where he read natural sciences. He worked as a scientific journalist, and wrote some *science fiction. In 1966 he became resident author at Falmouth School of Art, Cornwall, a county that appears in many of his landscapes and seascapes. A founder member of the *Group, his first volume of poetry, *The Collector and Other Poems* (1960), was followed by many others, including *The Force and Other Poems* (1966), *Sons of My Skin: Selected Poems 1954–74* (1975), *The Weddings at Nether Powers* (1979), and *The Moon Disposes: Poems 1954–1987* (1987, enlarged 1989), and *My Father's Trapdoor* (1994). His poetry is marked by a richness of visual imagery, a sense of physical immediacy, and a deep preoccupation with religious and sexual mysteries. His novels, which include *In the Country of the Skin* (1973) and *The Beekeepers* (1980), are also rich in imagery, written in a highly poetic prose. He wrote several works in collaboration with Penelope *Shuttle; these include *The Terrors of Dr Treviles* (1974), a novel of the occult and the psychic, of dream and identity, based on the relationship of psychologist Gregory Treviles and his witch-wife Robyn; and *The Wise Wound* (1978), a study of the mythology and reality of menstruation. Although Redgrove's work has some affinity with that of the *magic realists, it appears to spring from a different, possibly less cerebral source; with him, the artist as magician is less of a conjurer, more of a mystic.

REDI, Francesco (1626–98), physician to the grand duke of Tuscany and author of a spirited dithyrambic poem, *Bacco in Toscana* (*Bacchus in Tuscany*, 1685), which Leigh *Hunt translated. It may have helped to inspire *Dryden's *Alexander's Feast*.

REED, Henry (1914–86), poet, translator, and radio dramatist, educated at the University of Birmingham. He is best known for his book of verse *A Map of Verona* (1946), which contained his much-anthologized poem, inspired by his wartime experiences, 'Naming of Parts'. His plays made a notable contribution to *BBC radio drama in the 1950s, and two collections have been published: *The Streets of Pompeii* (1971), which contains five verse plays, and *Hilda Tablet and Others* (1971), which contains his four prose comedies of

contemporary cultural life, based on the central character of composer Hilda Tablet.

REED, Isaac (1742–1807), biographer, editor, and bibliophile. He was born in London, the son of a baker, and practised, reluctantly, as a conveyancer, devoting the greatest part of his energy to literature: his works include a new edition of *Dodsley's *Select Collection of Old Plays* (1780); *Biographica Dramatica* (2 vols, 1782, biographies of English dramatists); contributions to Dr Johnson's *The Lives of the English Poets*; and a 'first variorum' edition of Shakespeare (21 vols, 1803). He was a modest and good-natured man, generous with his large library and much liked by his contemporaries; the only scholar to find fault with him was the irritable *Ritson. See *The Reed Diaries 1762–1804*, ed. C. E. Jones (1946), and Arthur Sherbo, *Isaac Reed: Editorial Factotum* (1989).

REEVE, Clara (1729–1807), novelist, who was born and died in Ipswich. *The Champion of Virtue: A Gothic Story*, published 1777, was reprinted in 1778 as *The Old English Baron*, and met with tremendous success. The author acknowledged her debt to Walpole's *The Castle of Otranto*, but found its machinery so violent that it destroyed its own effect; to which Walpole replied that he found her novel 'insipid'. Her hero, the virtuous and noble Edmund, moves resolutely through many adventures of romantic horror in order to obtain his rightful heritage, but the ghost of the murdered baron provides the only element of the supernatural. The story concludes with a dramatic day of retribution. Clara Reeve wrote several other novels, and a critical dialogue on *The Progress of Romance* (1785). See ROMANTIC FICTION.

'Reeve's Tale, The', see CANTERBURY TALES, 3.

Reflections on the Revolution in France, see REVOLUTION IN FRANCE.

Reflector (1810–11), founded and edited by Leigh *Hunt, a literary and political quarterly consisting of 'a collection of essays'. Hunt and *Lamb were the principal contributors, and in its pages Lamb's essays on *Hogarth and on the plays of Shakespeare first appeared.

Reformation, the, the great religious movement of the 16th cent., aiming to reform the doctrines and practices of the Church of Rome, and ending in the establishment of the various Reformed or Protestant churches of central and north-western Europe. Its principal leaders were *Luther in Germany, *Calvin in Geneva, *Zwingli in Zurich, and J. *Knox in Scotland. The principal points contended for by the reformers were the general use and authority of the Scriptures and the need of justification by faith; they repudiated the doctrine of transubstantiation, the veneration of the Virgin Mary, and the supremacy of the pope.

Reformation, History of the, see KNOX, J.

Reform Bills. The Reform Bill of 1832 widened the parliamentary franchise by extending the vote to include the rich middle classes, and removed some of the inequalities in the system of representation by redistributing members of Parliament to correspond with the great centres of population. The Bill was introduced by Lord John Russell (1792–1878) in 1831, and carried in 1832. The Reform Bill of 1867, which more than doubled the electorate, extended the franchise to include many male members of the industrial working class, and the Bill of 1884 took in (with the exception of certain categories, i.e. lunatics, convicted criminals, and peers) all males over 21. In 1872 voting by ballot was introduced. Women over 30 were enfranchised in 1918; and women over 21 received the vote in 1928. (See also WOMEN'S SUFFRAGE.) In 1969 an Act was passed which lowered the age of all voters to 18. The question of reform is a principal theme in many Victorian novels, notably in G. Eliot's *Middlemarch* and *Felix Holt*.

Regan, in Shakespeare's *King Lear*, the second of Lear's daughters, who is married to Cornwall.

Regicide Peace, *Letters on a,* by E. *Burke, the first two published 1796, the third 1797, the fourth posthumously in the collected works.

The theme of these letters, which purport to be addressed to a member of Parliament, is the necessity for stamping out the Jacobin government of France, that 'vast tremendous unformed spectre'; and the ability of England from an economic standpoint to carry on the struggle. Burke describes Jacobinism as 'the spirit of ambition' which had overtaken the swelling middle classes, and which caused them to assert their pretensions against the propertied classes, impatient of 'the places which settled society prescribes to them', in an attempt to destroy pre-existing laws and institutions.

regional novel, a novel describing people and landscape of an actual locality outside the metropolis. Early examples are set in Ireland (M. Edgeworth, *Castle Rackrent*) and Scotland (J. Galt, *The Provost*) and are primarily studies of individual societies and characters. The regional novels of Sir W. *Scott however combine a historically informed feeling for local customs with an aesthetic appreciation of natural scenery. By the mid-19th cent. the localities described are often smaller and more exact, the focus being partly sociological, as in C. Brontë's *Shirley*, and in the rural fiction of Mrs *Gaskell (Cheshire) and G. *Eliot (the Midlands). The genre achieved maturity in the works of *Hardy, set in a fictive Wessex where an appreciation of both aesthetic and geological aspects of landscape complements a concern with agricultural and economic issues. Thenceforward these two approaches tend to diverge. In the mid-19th cent., industrial or urban novels set in a specific town or city included Gaskell's *Mary Barton*, Dickens's *Hard Times*, and Eliot's *Middlemarch*, and the tradition continued in the 20th cent. in the work of *Joyce. Following E. Brontë's *Wuthering Heights* and R. D. Blackmore's portrayal of Exmoor in *Lorna Doone*, other novelists adopted remote locations as settings for romantic dramas (S. R. Crockett's Galloway, Eden *Phillpotts's Dartmoor, Sir H. *Walpole's Cumberland). The popularity of regional novels is reflected in the invention of fictional counties (A. *Trollope's Barset, W. *Holtby's South Riding) or towns (M. *Oliphant's Carlingford). The genuinely regional work of R. *Jefferies (Wiltshire), C. Holme (Westmorland), and F. Brett Young (Worcestershire) combines social analysis with a celebration of domestic allegiances, as do the domestic novels set in Radstowe (Bristol) of E. H. Young (1880–1947). More didactically slanted accounts of particular regions are found in the Shropshire romances of Mary *Webb and the early work of H. Williamson (Devon) in which country life is contrasted favourably with that of towns. The continued oscillation between romantic and realistic handling of regionalism in the 20th cent. is reflected in the enormous popularity enjoyed by the Cornish novels of D. *du Maurier and the Tyneside ones of Catherine *Cookson (1906–98): Winston Graham (1909–2003) gained a considerable following for his *historical Cornish novels, the Poldark series, of which the first (*Ross Poldark*) appeared in 1945. Examples of regionalism of an exclusively naturalistic kind are A. *Bennett's tales of the Staffordshire 'Five Towns' and the accounts of farming life of S. *Kaye-Smith (Kent and Sussex) and Adrian Bell (1901–80, Suffolk). Emphasis on social realism becomes more pronounced in the 1920s in the work of Phyllis Bentley (1894–1977), born in Halifax, who wrote of the textile industry in the West Riding of Yorkshire in many works including *Inheritance* (1932), a family saga; and H. E. *Bates (Northamptonshire). In D. H. *Lawrence's *The Rainbow* (Nottinghamshire) and *A Glastonbury Romance* by J. C. *Powys the potential limitations of the genre are surmounted through the integration of particular landscapes and places with individual psychological, religious, and emotional experience. In the second half of the 20th cent. regional writers continued to favour a realist approach, as in the work of Leo Walmsley (1892–1966), Yorkshire novelist born at Robin Hood's Bay, whose works include the saga *Three Fevers* (1932), *Phantom Lobster* (1933), and *Sally Lunn* (1937), a trilogy set on the north Yorkshire coast dealing with the lives of fishermen and their families; John Moore (1907–67) with works based in Gloucestershire, Tewkesbury, and the surrounding villages (see the 'Brensham trilogy', 1946–8, and others); and John Toft (1933–), Staffordshire. In particular the regional novel has become a sociologically attuned vehicle for working-class concerns, *A Scots Quair* by Lewis Grassic *Gibbon anticipating the novels of Durham-born ex-miner Sid Chaplin (1916–86: see his *The Day of the Sardine*,

1961), A. *Sillitoe, and S. *Barstow in replacing nostalgia with radical questioning and social realism.

Register, Stationers', see STATIONERS' COMPANY.

Rehearsal, The, a farcical comedy attributed to George Villiers, second duke of *Buckingham, but probably written by him in collaboration with others, among whom are mentioned S. *Butler and Martin Clifford, master of the Charterhouse; printed 1672.

The play satirizes the heroic tragedies of the day, and consists of a series of parodies of passages from these, strung together in an absurd heroic plot. The author of the mock play is evidently a laureate (hence his name 'Bayes'), and *D'Avenant was probably intended; but there are also hits at *Dryden (particularly his *Conquest of Granada*) and his brothers-in-law, Edward and Robert Howard. Bayes takes two friends, Smith and Johnson, to see the rehearsal of his play, and the absurdity of this work (which includes the two kings of Brentford, entering hand in hand), coupled with the comments of Bayes, his instructions to the actors, and the remarks of Smith and Johnson, remains highly entertaining. Prince Pretty-man, Prince Volscius, and *Drawcansir are among the characters. It was one of the earliest of English dramatic *burlesques, and was much performed during the 18th cent., during which period the genre developed to one of its highest points in Sheridan's *The Critic*. The work helped to inspire *Marvell's *The Rehearsal Transpros'd* (1672; Pt II, 1673).

REID, Forrest (1875–1947), Ulster novelist, whose uneventful life was spent in and near Belfast. His fiction includes *The Kingdom of Twilight* (1904), *The Garden God: A Tale of Two Boys* (1905), *Following Darkness* (1912), and a trilogy, *Uncle Stephen* (1931), *The Retreat* (1934), and *Young Tom* (1944); the last three were published in one volume in 1955 as *Tom Barber*, with an introduction by Reid's friend E. M. *Forster. Reid's dominant subject is boyhood and the longing for an ideal dream playmate; he evokes a pagan, lyrical world of 'lonely garden and sombre grove', in which hints of the supernatural are contrasted with the realities of everyday. His autobiographies, *Apostate* (1926) and *Private Road* (1940), vividly describe his sense of the numinous in nature. See *The Green Avenue* (1980), a critical biography by B. Taylor.

REID, Thomas (1710–96), philosopher, who graduated from Marischal College, Aberdeen, in 1726. He was elected regent in philosophy at King's College, Aberdeen, in 1751, and he succeeded Adam *Smith as professor of moral philosophy at Glasgow in 1764, largely through the influence of his patron Henry *Home, Lord Kames. While at King's he composed his first major work, *An Inquiry into the Human Mind, on the Principles of Common Sense* (1764), and after retiring from active teaching at Glasgow in 1780 he published his *Essays on the Intellectual Powers of Man* (1785) and *Essays on the Active Powers of Man* (1788).

His lectures on the fine arts were first published in 1973. Reid was perhaps the most notable 18th-cent. exponent of the philosophy of common sense, by which phrase he meant both a faculty of the mind, and a set of incontrovertible beliefs implanted in the human mind by God. He also questioned the widely held theory that the immediate objects of perception are 'ideas', arguing that we directly perceive external objects rather than mental representations of them. Aesthetic qualities he conceived either as intrinsic qualities of mind, or, derivatively, as the qualities of objects of design. He was a vigorous critic of the writings of *Hume, and, later in life, J. *Priestley, and he championed the inductive methods of F. Bacon and I.*Newton. Reid was an accomplished mathematician and scientist as well as a philosopher, contributing 'An Essay on Quantity' to the *Philosophical Transactions of the Royal Society of London* in 1748. The Scottish poet Thomas *Campbell was named after him.

Rejected Addresses, by James and Horatio *Smith, published 1812.

A competition was held to find a suitable address to celebrate the opening of the new *Drury Lane Theatre in 1812. James and Horatio Smith produced a large batch of bogus entries, purporting to be by *Wordsworth, *Byron, T. *Moore, *Southey, *Coleridge, *Crabbe, Sir W. *Scott, *Cobbett, and others. The parodies are mixed in quality, but the brilliance of some made the Smiths famous, and caused T. *Campbell to feel annoyed that he had been left out.

Relapse, The, or *Virtue in Danger*, the highly successful first play of *Vanbrugh, produced 1696.

It is an avowed continuation of *Love's Last Shift* by C. *Cibber, some of the characters being retained, though more effectively presented. It contains two plots, very slenderly related to each other. Loveless, a reformed libertine, living happily in the country with his wife Amanda, is obliged to go with her to London, where he suffers a relapse under the temptation of Berinthia, an unscrupulous young widow. Worthy, a former lover of Berinthia, prevails on her to favour Loveless's suit and to persuade Amanda of the infidelity of her husband, in order to promote his own chances of seducing Amanda. But Amanda, though bitterly resenting her husband's faithlessness, remains firm in her virtue.

The second plot is more entertaining. Sir Novelty Fashion, the perfect beau, who has just become (by purchase) Lord Foppington, is about to marry Miss Hoyden, daughter of Sir Tunbelly Clumsey, a country squire, neither father nor daughter having yet seen him. Foppington's younger brother, Young Fashion, having overspent his allowance, vainly appeals to Foppington for help. To revenge himself and rehabilitate his fortunes, he decides to go down to Sir Tunbelly's house, impersonate his brother, and marry the heiress. The plot is at first successful. Sir Tunbelly welcomes him unsuspectingly, and Miss Hoyden is only too ready to marry him next morning;

but Sir Tunbelly will not hear of the marriage for a week, so Fashion bribes the nurse and parson, and a secret marriage is at once celebrated. Foppington arrives, is treated as an impostor, and subjected to indignities, until a neighbour vouches for his identity. Meanwhile young Fashion escapes. Hoyden, the parson, and the nurse decide to say nothing of the former marriage, and Hoyden is married to Foppington, who immediately brings his wife to London. Here young Fashion claims his bride, the nurse and parson are bullied and cajoled into admitting the earlier marriage, and Hoyden is reconciled to her lot on learning that Fashion is Lord Foppington's brother.

The play was adapted by Sheridan as *A Trip to Scarborough.

Religio Laici, a poem by *Dryden, published 1682.

Written in defence of Anglicanism against Deist, Catholic, and Dissenting arguments, *Religio Laici* combines an exalted recognition of religious sublimity with a defence of a 'layman's' reasonable and straightforward religious attitudes. The poem's opening lines, beginning 'Dim as the borrow'd Beams of Moon and Stars', are among the finest Dryden wrote.

Religio Medici, a self-directed stocktaking by Sir T. *Browne of his attitudes as a Christian and a doctor towards God and the Church, faith and reason, the classical tradition, private friendship, and national prejudice, first published in an unauthorized edition 1642, reprinted 1643 with some authorial corrections, revisions, and additions.

Written in about 1635, after experience of life in Ireland, France, Italy, and Holland, the work is divided into two parts, relating broadly to God and to man. The first treats of matters of faith, the hostilities among rival sects and religions, and man as microcosm. Its breadth of vision and tolerance are matched in the second part, where he expresses love for all sorts and conditions of men, English or foreign, rich or poor, learned or ignorant, friend or foe, good or bad. While based on biblical teaching, the arguments are reinforced and widened with citations of classical philosophers, historians, and poets. Often reprinted, and translated into many languages, *Religio Medici* quickly made the author famous as much by its wit and style as by its piety.

Reliques of Ancient English Poetry, a collection of ballads, sonnets, historical songs, and metrical romances published in 1765 by T. *Percy. The majority of them were extracted from the *Percy Folio and edited and 'restored' by Percy. They were of very different periods, some of great antiquity, some as recent as the reign of Charles I. Ancient poems drawn from other sources and a few of more modern date (including works by *Wither, *Dryden, *Lovelace, *Shenstone, and *Glover) were added by the editor. The antiquary J. *Ritson was sharply critical of Percy's editorial method. The editions of 1767, 1775, and 1794 each contained new matter. See the facsimile edition of the *Reliques*, introd. N. M. Groom (1996).

REMARQUE, Erich Maria (1898–1970), German novelist, author of *Im Westen nichts Neues* (*All Quiet on the Western Front*, 1929), a fictionalized acount of his experiences in the First World War which was translated into many languages, but in Germany was denounced for its pacifism and burnt publicly (1933) by the Nazis. Remarque left Germany in 1938, and in 1939 moved permanently to the United States; many of his later novels centre on the theme of exile.

Remorse, a tragedy by S. T. *Coleridge, written in 1797 as *Osorio*, produced at Drury Lane 1813.

The story, set in Granada at the time of the Spanish Inquisition, tells of the slow corruption of the character of Osorio, a man who supposed himself strong but who is gradually led by temptations and events into guilt and evil.

Renaissance, the great flowering of art, architecture, politics, and the study of literature, usually seen as the end of the Middle Ages and the beginning of the modern world, which came about under the influence of Greek and Roman models. It began in Italy in the late 14th cent., culminated in the High Renaissance in the early 16th cent. (the period of *Michelangelo and *Machiavelli), and spread to the rest of Europe in the 15th cent. and afterwards. Its emphasis was humanist: that is, on regarding the human figure and reason without a necessary relating of it to the superhuman; but much of its energy also came from the *Neoplatonic tradition in writers such as *Pico della Mirandola. The word Renaissance has been applied in the 20th cent. to earlier periods which manifested a new interest in and study of the classics, such as the 12th cent. and the period of Charlemagne. But the Italian Renaissance is still seen as a watershed in the development of civilization, both because of its extent and because of its emphasis on the human, whether independent of or in association with the divine. See J. A. *Symonds, *History of the Renaissance in Italy* (1875–86); W. *Pater, *Studies in the History of the Renaissance* (1873); J. *Burckhardt, *The Civilization of the Renaissance in Italy* (English trans., S. G. C. Middlemore, 1929).

RENAN, Ernest (1823–92), French Hebraist, historian, and archaeologist. After a childhood spent in his native Brittany he studied for the priesthood in Paris, but withdrew because of doubts about the divinity of Jesus and the divine inspiration of the Bible. His eccentric sexuality, which was aroused by the veiled and the inaccessible, seems eventually to have focused on his sister Henriette, about whom he was to write rhapsodically years after her death in *Ma Sœur Henriette* (1895), not least for her role in the preparation of his masterpiece, *Vie de Jésus* (1863), the first of a seven-volume account of the historical origins of Christianity

(*Histoire des origines du Christianisme*). The *Life of Jesus* is a fusion of Renan's romantic Christianity, which centred on its aesthetic and emotional significance, and his solid historical scholarship, which led him to subject the biblical accounts of the life of Jesus to sceptical scrutiny. It earned him both fame and persecution. Besides his historical and philological works, Renan published a number of critical, reflective, and prophetic essays, among them: *Essais de morale et de critique* (1859), *La Réforme intellectuelle et morale* (1871), *Examen de conscience philosophique* (1888), *L'Avenir de la science* (written 1848–9, pub. 1890). His early years are recalled in *Souvenirs d'enfance et de jeunesse* (1883).

Renaud, in the *chansons de geste* a rebel against *Charlemagne, better known under the Italian name of *Rinaldo.

RENAULT, Mary, pseudonym of Mary Challans (1905–83), novelist, known principally for her *historical novels, most of which are lively first-person narratives set in Ancient Greece or Asia Minor, incorporating the new anthropological and historical insights of the 20th cent. They include *The King Must Die* (1958) and *The Bull from the Sea* (1962), both retelling the legend of Theseus, and *The Persian Boy* (1972), set in the time of Alexander the Great.

RENDELL, Dame Ruth Barbara, née Grasemann (1930–), prolific writer of detective fiction and psychological thrillers, many of which have been successfully adapted for television. Educated at Loughton High School, Essex, she worked as a reporter and sub-editor for several years before becoming a full-time writer. Her fiction consists of three main strands, the most popular, and structurally conventional, of which is the series of novels based round the character of Detective Chief Inspector Reginald Wexford and his colleague Mike Burden, who work in the fictional English town of Kingsmarkham. The first Wexford novel, *From Doon with Death* (1964), was followed by many others, including *No More Dying Then* (1971), *The Speaker of Mandarin* (1983), *Kissing the Gunner's Daughter* (1991), *Simisola* (1994), and *Road Rage* (1997). A collection of Wexford short stories, *Means of Evil*, was published in 1979, and another story is contained in the collection *The Copper Peacock* (1991). A second strand of psychological thrillers explores more oblique and ambiguous scenarios and aberrant psychologies. These include *The Lake of Darkness* (1980), *Master of the Moor* (1982), and *The Crocodile Bird* (1993). Under the pseudonym Barbara Vine this strand is further developed in *A Dark-Adapted Eye* (1986), *A Fatal Inversion* (1987), *The House of Stairs* (1988), *Gallowglass* (1990), *Asta's Book* (1993), and *No Night is Too Long* (1994). A volume of *Collected Short Stories* was published in 1987. Her many awards include four Gold Daggers from the Crime Writers

Association and three Edgar Allen *Poe awards from the Mystery Writers of America.

RENÉ OF PROVENCE, duc d'Anjou and comte de Provence (1408–80), known as 'le bon Roi René', son of Louis II, duke of Anjou, was titular king of Naples, the two Sicilies, and Jerusalem, 'whose large style agrees not with the leanness of his purse' (Shakespeare, 2 *Henry VI*, I. i). His daughter *Margaret of Anjou was wife of Henry VI. As count of Provence, he gave free play to his love of music and poetry, tilting and hunting, minstrels and knight-errants, and showed indifference to political affairs. There is a picture of his court in Scott's *Anne of Geierstein*. He figures in *Henry VI* as 'Reignier'. He left some prose and verse romances, pastorals, and allegories.

RENI, Guido (1575–1642), Bolognese painter much admired in England in the 18th and early 19th cents, when he was ranked second only to *Raphael; Horace *Walpole's comment in *Aedes Walpolianae* (1747)— 'all the qualities of a perfect painter never met but in Raphael, Guido and Carracci'—typifies the response of this period. *Shelley, in Bologna in 1818, wrote rapturously to *Peacock of the Guidos in the Pinacoteca, and from Rome (1819) exclaimed that only Raphael, Guido, and *Rosa could sustain comparison with antiquity. A painting traditionally described as a portrait of Beatrice Cenci, almost certainly not by Reni himself but loosely derived from his *St Andrew Led to Martyrdom* (1608), cast a spell over the Romantics: Shelley describes it in his preface to *The Cenci, and later it fascinated *De Quincey, *Dickens, *Swinburne, *Melville, and many others: Hawthorne uses it and Reni's *Archangel Michael* in *The Marble Faun to symbolize various aspects of his central characters. But *Keats disliked his 'melodramatic mawkishness' and his reputation plunged with *Ruskin: only recently has the true stature of his work again been recognized.

REPTON, Humphry, see PICTURESQUE.

Republic, The, one of the dialogues of *Plato, in which *Socrates is represented as eliciting, in the course of a discussion on justice, the ideal type of state. In this the perfect forms of goodness, truth, and beauty are cultivated, and everything repugnant to them excluded. The famous fable of the men who live bound in a cavern, so that they can see only the shadows of real objects projected by a bright fire on its inner wall, occurs in Book 7.

Republic of Letters, the, the collective body of those engaged in literary pursuits. The expression occurs first in *Addison's *Dialogues upon Ancient Medals* (i. 19).

'Resolution and Independence', a poem by *Wordsworth, written 1802, published 1807, sometimes known as 'The Leech Gatherer'.

The poet describes his own elation as he walks over the moors on a fine spring morning after a storm, and his sudden descent into apprehension and dejection, as he ponders the fate of earlier poets, such as *Chatterton: 'We Poets in our youth begin in gladness, | But thereof come in the end despondency and Madness.' At this stage he comes upon the aged leech gatherer, whom he cross-questions in characteristically Wordsworthian manner about his way of life: the old man responds with cheerful dignity, and the poet resolves to remember him as an admonishment. The poem was based on a meeting recorded in Dorothy *Wordsworth's *Journal*, 3 Oct. 1800, with an 'old man almost double', whose trade was to gather leeches. Its mixture of elevated language and sentiment with prosaic detail is peculiarly Wordsworthian, and led *Coleridge to comment on its 'inconstancy of style'. Wordsworth's own comments on his use of imagery in the poem and 'the conferring, the abstracting, and the modifying powers of the Imagination' in his 1815 preface are of great interest.

RESTIF de la BRETONNE, Nicolas (1734–1806), French novelist. His vast, rambling output reflects the dissipations of his life as a peasant adrift in Paris. Long forgotten, he has recently been restored to critical favour for his knowledge of the life of the humble classes (*Le Paysan perverti*, 1775, and *Monsieur Nicholas*, 1794), and by his understanding of rural values (*La Vie de mon père*, 1779).

Restoration, the re-establishment of monarchy in England, with the return of Charles II (1660); also the period marked by this event of which the chief literary figures are *Dryden, *Rochester, *Bunyan, *Pepys, *Locke, and the Restoration dramatists. One of the characteristic genres of the period is Restoration comedy, or the comedy of manners, which developed upon the reopening of the theatres. Its principal writers were *Congreve, *Etherege, *Farquhar, *Vanbrugh, and *Wycherley, and its predominant tone was witty, bawdy, cynical, and amoral. The plays were mainly in prose, with passages of verse for the more romantic moments; the plots were complex and usually double, sometimes triple, though repartee and discussions of marital behaviour provide much of the interest, reflecting the fashionable manners of the day. Standard characters include fops, bawds, scheming valets, country squires, and sexually voracious young widows and older women; the principal theme is sexual intrigue, either for its own sake or for money. Playwrights came under heavy attack for frivolity, blasphemy, and immorality (see COLLIER, JEREMY): they and their subsequent admirers defended their works as serious social criticism, and mirrors to the age. During the 18th cent. the plays were presented in more 'genteel' versions, and in the 19th cent. hardly at all: the 20th cent. saw a considerable revival of interest, with such notable productions as *The Way of the World*, one of the masterpieces of the period, in 1924 with Edith Evans as Millamant.

Retaliation, an unfinished poem by *Goldsmith, published 1774, consisting of a string of humorous and critical epitaphs on *Garrick, Sir J. *Reynolds, *Burke, and other friends, in reply to their similar efforts directed against himself. Of the latter Garrick's is the best known:

> Here lies Nolly Goldsmith, for shortness called Noll,
> Who wrote like an angel, but talked like poor Poll.

Retrospective Review (1820–8), founded by Henry Southern (1799–1853), its first editor, as a 'Review of past literature', the object of which was 'to exhibit a bird's-eye view of the rise and progress of our literature' and to rouse interest 'in the old and venerable literature of the country'. Extracts from poetry, essays, drama, and other prose, chiefly drawn from the 16th and 17th cents, included the work of F. *Bacon, Sir T. *Browne, G. *Chapman, G. *Herbert, *Jonson, *Vaughan, and many others. Some three-quarters of the work was English; the rest consisted of translations from past European literature. Another of the founder's objects was to question the deference accorded to contemporary critics, such as those of the *Quarterly* and the *Edinburgh*, and to expose their substitution of prejudice for true critical principles. The method of the *Review* was to consider each piece or extract as if it were just from the press, and sometimes to compare the quality of the old with some work of the 'moderns'. The *Review* was briefly revived in 1853–4.

Return of the Druses, The, a tragedy in blank verse by R. *Browning, published 1843 as No. IV of *Bells and Pomegranates*. It was written for the stage, but was rejected by *Macready, although Browning had created the role of Djabal with him in mind.

The action of the play is unhistorical. Browning places the religious sect of the Druses in exile and subjection on a small Aegean island, and the plot concerns the downfall of the impostor Djabal, who claims to be the incarnation of Hakeem, divine founder of the sect, in order both to liberate his people from their oppressors and to gain the love of Anael. Djabal and Anael both perish in the end, but the 'return of the Druses' to their homeland, the Lebanon, is assured.

Return of the Native, The, a novel by T. *Hardy, published 1878.

The scene is the sombre Egdon Heath, powerfully and symbolically present throughout the novel. Damon Wildeve, once an engineer but now a publican, dallies between the two women by whom he is loved—the gentle Thomasin Yeobright and the wild, capricious Eustacia Vye. Thomasin rejects her humble suitor Diggory Venn, a reddleman, and is eventually married to Wildeve, who takes her less for love than from a wish to hurt Eustacia. Thomasin's cousin Clym Yeobright, a diamond merchant in Paris, disgusted with the worthlessness of his occupation, returns to Egdon intending to become a schoolmaster in his native heath. He falls in love with Eustacia, and she in a brief infatuation marries him, hoping to induce him to return to Paris, thus escaping from Egdon, which she detests. But to her despair he will not return; his sight fails and he becomes a furze-cutter on the heath. She becomes the cause of estrangement between Clym and his beloved mother, and unintentionally causes the mother's death. This, together with the discovery that Eustacia's relationship with Wildeve has not ceased, leads to a violent scene between Clym and his wife, and ultimately to Eustacia's flight, in the course of which both she and Wildeve are drowned. Clym, blaming himself for the death of his mother and his wife, becomes an itinerant preacher, and the widowed Thomasin marries Diggory Venn.

REUCHLIN, Johann (1455–1522), born at Pforzheim, a celebrated humanist and the foremost Hebraist of his day. Braving the powerful Dominicans, he published in 1494 his *De Verbo Mirifico*, defending Jewish literature and philosophy, and became the centre of an acute controversy in which he was opposed by *Pfefferkorn and which was the occasion of the publication of the *Epistolae Obscurorum Virorum*. Reuchlin was author of the first Hebrew grammar.

Revelation, Book of, see APOCALYPSE.

revels, master of the, an officer appointed to superintend *masques and other entertainments at court. He is first mentioned in the reign of Henry VII. The first permanent master of the revels was Sir Thomas Cawarden, appointed in 1545. Holders of the office in Shakespeare's day were Edmund Tilney, 1579–1610, and Sir George Buc, 1610–22 (he had been deputy master since 1603).

Revenge of Bussy D'Ambois, The, a tragedy by G. *Chapman, written 1610/11, printed 1613, a sequel to *Bussy D'Ambois*.

Clermont D'Ambois, brother of Bussy, described by his close friend the duc de Guise as the ideal 'Senecal [i.e. Stoical] man', gentle, noble, generous, and 'fix'd in himself', is urged by his brother's ghost to avenge his murder, but will only do so by the honourable method of a duel. He sends a challenge to Montsurry, who evades it; urged again by the ghost, he introduces himself to Montsurry's house, forces him to fight, and kills him. He then learns of the assassination of the Guise, and, refusing to live amid 'all the horrors of the vicious time' as 'the slave of power', he kills himself. The hero's reluctance to exact revenge recalls certain aspects of *Hamlet*. (See also REVENGE TRAGEDY.)

Revenger's Tragedy, The, a tragedy published anonymously in 1607, and from 1656 ascribed to *Tourneur; its authorship has been disputed since 1891, with some scholars defending the traditional attribution and others championing the rival claims of *Middleton and others.

The central character is Vendice (or Vindice), intent on revenging the death of his mistress, poisoned by the lecherous old duke. The court is a centre of vice and intrigue; the duchess's youngest son is convicted of rape, she herself seduces Spurio, the duke's bastard, and her two older sons, the duke's stepsons, plot against each other and against Lussurioso, the duke's heir. Vendice, disguised as Piato, appears to attempt to procure his own sister Castiza for Lussurioso; she resists, but their mother Gratiana temporarily succumbs to his bribes and agrees to play the bawd. Vendice murders the duke by tricking him into kissing the poisoned skull of his mistress, and most of the remaining characters kill one another or are killed in a final masque of revengers and murderers; Vendice, who survives the bloodbath, owns up to the murder of the duke, and is promptly condemned to death with his brother and accomplice Hippolite by the duke's successor, old Antonio. He is led off to execution, content to 'die after a nest of dukes'. The play is marked by a tragic intensity of feeling, a powerfully satiric wit, and passages of great poetic richness, all combined, for example, in Vendice's address to 'the bony lady', his dead mistress: 'Does the silkworm expend her yellow labours | For thee?' (III. v. 71 ff.). (See also REVENGE TRAGEDY.)

revenge tragedy, a dramatic genre that flourished in the late Elizabethan and Jacobean period, sometimes known as 'the tragedy of blood'. Kyd's *The Spanish Tragedy* (c.1587), a much quoted prototype, helped to establish a demand for this popular form; later examples are Marlowe's *The Jew of Malta*, Shakespeare's *Titus Andronicus*, *The Revenger's Tragedy*, and, most notably, *Hamlet*; there are also strong revenge elements in *Webster. Common ingredients include: the hero's quest for vengeance, often at the prompting of the ghost of a murdered kinsman or loved one; scenes of real or feigned insanity; a play-within-a-play; scenes in graveyards, severed limbs, scenes of carnage and mutilation, etc. Many of these items were inherited from Senecan drama, with the difference that in revenge tragedy violence was not reported but took place on stage: as Vendice in *The Revenger's Tragedy* rather baldly puts it, while in the process of slowly murdering the duke, 'When the bad bleeds, then is the tragedy good.' The revenge code also produced counter-attacks, as in *The Atheist's Tragedy*, in Chapman's *The Revenge of Bussy D'Ambois*, and again in *Hamlet*, in which the heroes refuse or hesitate to follow the convention.

Revesby play, the, a folk drama acted by morris dancers at Revesby in Lincolnshire at the end of the 18th cent. The characters are the Fool and his sons— Pickle Herring, Blue Breeches, Pepper Breeches, Ginger Breeches—and Mr Allspice and Cicely. The Fool fights with a hobby-horse and a dragon. The sons decide to kill the Fool; he kneels down, the swords of the dancers are locked around his neck, and he is slain. He revives when Pickle Herring stamps his foot. Sword-dances and the wooing of Cicely by the Fool and his sons conclude the play. The central incident no doubt symbolizes the death of the year and its resuscitation in the spring. The text is given by T. F. Ordish in the *Folk-Lore Journal*, 7. 338. See also E. K. *CHAMBERS, *The Mediaeval Stage* (2 vols, 1903).

Review, (1) a periodical started by *Defoe in 1704, under the title of *A Weekly Review of the Affairs of France*, which after various transformations became *A Review of the State of the British Nation* in 1707; it lasted until 1713. It was a non-partisan paper, an organ of the commercial interests of the nation; it appeared thrice weekly and was written, practically in its entirety, by Defoe himself, who expressed in it his opinions on all current political topics, thus initiating the political leading article. It also had lighter articles on love, marriage, gambling, etc.; Defoe's attitude to his readers was that he strove to '*wheedle them in* (if it may be allowed that expression) to the knowledge of the world; who, rather than take more pains, would be content with their ignorance, and search into nothing'. (2) A quarterly magazine of poetry and criticism, founded in 1962 and edited by Ian *Hamilton. It ran for 30 issues, and was succeeded by the *New Review*, also edited by Hamilton, which ran from 1974 to 1979.

Review of English Studies, a scholarly quarterly published by the *Oxford University Press devoted to historical scholarship in English language and literature, founded by R. B. *McKerrow. The first issue appeared in Jan. 1925, and the present New Series began in 1950.

Revolt of Islam, The, an epic political poem by P. B. *Shelley, written at Great Marlow in 1817 (under the title 'Laon and Cythna: or The Revolution in the Golden City, A Vision of the Nineteenth Century'), published 1818.

The poem is Shelley's idealized and highly idiosyncratic version of the French Revolution, transposed to an Oriental setting. It is composed in Spenserian stanzas (too ornate for effective narrative), forming twelve cantos. The revolt is organized by a brother and sister, Laon and Cythna, whose temporary success is celebrated in incestuous love-making (Canto VI). But the tyrants recover power, and Islam is subject to plague and famine, vividly described (Canto X). Brother and sister are burnt at the stake, but sail together with an illegitimate child to a visionary Hesperides (Canto XII). Though cumbersome, diffuse, and obsessive (there is much disguised autobiography), the poem contains powerful images of struggle and renewal which are brilliantly clarified in Shelley's poems of 1819. The figure of Cythna, the revolutionary feminist, is of historical interest; and the prose preface, concerning reactions to the French Revolution, is impressively argued.

Revolution in France, *Reflections on the*, by E. *Burke, published 1790.

This treatise was provoked by a sermon preached by R. *Price in Nov. 1789, in which he exulted in the French Revolution and asserted that the king of England owes his throne to the choice of the people, who are at liberty to cashier him for misconduct. Burke repudiates this constitutional doctrine, and contrasts the inherited rights of which the English are tenacious with the 'rights of man' of the French revolutionaries, based on 'extravagant and presumptuous speculations', inconsistent with an ordered society and leading to poverty and chaos. He examines the character of the men who made the French Revolution, and the proceedings of their National Assembly, a 'profane burlesque of that sacred institute'. The well-known eloquent passage on the downfall of Marie Antoinette leads to the lament that 'the age of chivalry is gone . . . All the decent drapery of life is to be rudely torn off' in deference to 'the new conquering empire of light and reason'. His general conclusion is that the defective institutions of the old regime should have been reformed, not destroyed.

Revue des deux mondes, La, a celebrated French monthly review which first appeared in 1829 and which continues to be published today. Under the editorship (1831–77) of François Buloz it became one of the leading periodicals of its kind in Europe, dealing with foreign and domestic politics as well as literature, philosophy, and the fine arts, and attracting contributions from such writers as *Balzac, *Sainte-Beuve, *Dumas *père*, *Hugo, *Vigny, and G. *Sand.

REXROTH, Kenneth, see PERFORMANCE POETRY.

Reynard the Fox, the central character in the *Roman de Renart*, a series of popular satirical fables, related to the *bestiaries and the tradition from *Aesop's Fables, written in France at various times *c*.1175–1250. The first known cycle is the Latin one by Nivard of Ghent, *Ysengrimus* (*c*.1148), and this was followed by the Middle High German *Reinhard Fuchs* (*c*.1180). There is a Flemish version from *c*.1250; another Flemish version (now lost) was translated into English and printed by *Caxton in 1481. In these anthropomorphic stories, the fox is the man who preys on society, is brought to justice, but escapes by his cunning. The popularity of the series was most marked in French (which took from it the German word *Regin-hart*, 'strong in counsel', for 'fox' in place of its etymological *goupil* which is found in some of the earlier stories), but there are some derived and related English works. The most important of these is the Middle English 'The Fox and the Wolf' (in *Early Middle English Verse and Prose*, ed. J. A. W. Bennett and G. V. Smithers, 2nd edn 1968, 67–76). Other related works in English are Chaucer's 'The Nun's Priest's Tale' (see CANTERBURY TALES, 20), some of *Henryson's 'Morall Fabillis of Esope' (where the fox is called Lowrence), and J. C. *Harris's Uncle Remus stories (where the role of the fox is taken by *Brer Rabbit). The principal characters in Caxton's version are: Reynard the Fox, King Noble the Lion,

851

REYNOLDS | RHODODAPHNE

Isengrym the Wolf, Courtoys the Hound, Bruin the Bear, Tybert the Cat, Grymbert the Badger, Coart (or Cuwaert) the Hare, Bellyn the Ram, Martin and Dame Rukenawe the Apes, Chanticleer the Cock, Partlet the Hen. Ermeline is Reynard's wife and Malperdy (*Malpertuis*) his castle.

Le Roman de Renart, Branche II (ed. M. Roques, Classiques Français du Moyen Âge, 79, Paris, 1951); L. Flinn, *Le 'Roman de Renart' dans la littérature française et dans les littératures étrangères au moyen âge* (Paris, 1963); *The History of Reynard the Fox Translated from the Dutch Original by William Caxton*, ed. N. F. Blake (EETS OS 263, 1970).

REYNOLDS, John Hamilton (1796–1852), poet, and a close friend and correspondent of *Keats. (Keats's letter to Reynolds of May 1818 on *The Fall of *Hyperion* is particularly important.) In 1814 Reynolds published *Safie*, an *Oriental novel reminiscent of *Byron, and *The Eden of the Imagination*, which echoes late 18th-cent. verse. *The Garden of Florence* (1821) contains his most effective serious work, and includes two verse tales from *Boccaccio, as part of a Boccaccio volume he and Keats intended to write together, and for which Keats originally produced *'Isabella'. He had great skill in parody and comic verse; his parody of Wordsworth's *Peter Bell* appeared in 1819, *The Fancy* in 1820, and *Odes and Addresses* (with T. *Hood) in 1825.

REYNOLDS, Sir Joshua (1723–92), painter, born in Devon. He was apprenticed in London (1740–4) and studied in Italy (1750–2); on his return to London (1753) he swiftly became the most successful portrait painter of his age. Reynolds sought to give new dignity to British portraiture by relating it to the Grand Style of European art. His portraits are immensely varied and enriched by allusions to the antique and to Renaissance and 17th-cent. Italian art. He was a distinguished man of letters; it was he who suggested the idea of the *Club to his friend Dr *Johnson. He painted Johnson at least five times and wrote a memoir of him and two Johnsonian dialogues; *Boswell dedicated his *Life of Johnson* to the painter. Goldsmith dedicated *The Deserted Village* to him. Reynolds's first literary works were three essays published in the *Idler* (1759). In 1768 he was made first president of the Royal Academy and his *Discourses*, delivered to the students (1769–90), are his most significant achievement as a writer. He supported the values of academic art, and stressed the importance of study of the great masters of the past. Yet the *Discourses* reveal that he was sensitive to the new ideals of Romantic art; the last is a tribute to *Michelangelo, whose sublimity Reynolds had come to value above the perfection of *Raphael. *Hazlitt pointed out the contradictions in the *Discourses* and *Blake, in a series of annotations to his copy of the *Works*, attacked Reynolds for his lack of faith in the inspiration of genius—on the title page he wrote, 'This man was hired to depress art.' Yet he was admired by *Constable, *Turner, and *Ruskin, and

*Wordsworth paid tribute to him in lines on Sir G. *Beaumont's cenotaph to his memory at Coleorton. See *Discourses on Art*, ed. Robert R. Wark (1975; repr. 1997); Nicholas Penny, *Reynolds* (1986); and Richard Wendorf, *Sir Joshua Reynolds: The Painter in Society* (1996).

rhetoric, in Greek, the art of speaking so as to persuade, was from the first tied up with ethics (persuasion of what is true) and literature (use of language in order to please). It was a branch of the medieval *Trivium and therefore an important part of the school syllabus up to the 17th cent. Literary rhetoric is concerned with the organization (*inventio* and *dispositio*) and embellishment (*elocutio*) of works. The first of these is prominent in many 18th-cent. works (*Tristram Shandy* and *A Tale of a Tub*, for instance), and the second is important in its provision of poetic 'devices' (figures and tropes) in poets from *Chaucer to the present day. The study of rhetoric—encompassing *Plato and *Aristotle, *Cicero and *Quintillian, *Boethius and *Bede, *Erasmus and *Ramus, *Bacon and *Locke, *Burke and H. *Blair, *Joyce and *Golding—is an increasingly vital and important area in literary studies. See B. Vickers, *Classical Rhetoric in English* (1970) and *In Defence of Rhetoric* (1988); G. A. Kennedy, *Classical Rhetoric and Its Christian and Secular Tradition* (1980) and *A New History of Classical Rhetoric* (1994); and T. M. Conley, *Rhetoric and the European Tradition* (1990).

RHODES, Cecil John (1853–1902), born in Bishop's Stortford. He gained a degree at Oriel College, Oxford, after some delay, and made a fortune at the diamond fields of Kimberley. He became a statesman of South Africa and was instrumental in securing part of Bechuanaland for the Cape government (1884) and later (1887) the charter for the British South Africa Co. whose territory became known as Rhodesia. He was prime minister of Cape Colony from 1890, but was forced to resign in 1896 because of an unauthorized raid into the Transvaal (the 'Jameson raid'). In his will he endowed 170 scholarships at Oxford, for students from the British Empire, America, and Germany.

RHODES, William Barnes (1772–1826), a bank teller, who translated the *Satires* of *Juvenal in 1801 and the *Epigrams* in 1803. He did not acknowledge his authorship of his highly successful farce *Bombastes Furioso* (1810) until 1822. Rhodes collected volumes of plays, old and new, and bought heavily at the *Roxburghe sale in 1812.

Rhododaphne, a narrative poem in octosyllabics by *Peacock, published 1818.

In ancient Thessaly, the shepherd boy Anthemion is torn between the mortal girl Calliroë and the nymph Rhododaphne. Calliroë appears to die, and Rhododaphne takes Anthemion to an enchanted palace (anticipating the one built by Keats's *Lamia), but Rhododaphne is struck down by the spirit of Heavenly Love, and Calliroë is restored.

rhyme. 'Male' or 'masculine' rhymes or endings are those having a final accented syllable, as distinguished from 'female' or 'feminine' rhymes or endings in which the last syllable is unaccented.

rhyme-royal, or **rime royal,** a seven-line stanza form of iambic pentameter, rhyming a b a b b c c, used for narrative poetry from Chaucer (*Troilus and Criseyde*) to William *Morris.

Rhymers Club, a group of poets that met at the *Cheshire Cheese in Fleet Street for two or three years, from 1891, to read poetry. Members and associates included *Yeats, Ernest Rhys (1859–1946, poet and editor of the *Everyman's Library), *Le Gallienne, *Dowson, L. *Johnson, Arthur *Symons, and J. *Davidson. It published two collections of verse, 1892 and 1894.

Rhyming Poem, The, an Old English poem from the *Exeter Book and therefore not later than the 10th cent., striking for the fact that the two halves of its alliterating lines rhyme (as happens sporadically in later Old English poetry). It is a loose discussion of the vicissitudes of life, contrasting the misfortunes of a fallen king with his past glory, a common Boethian, elegiac theme in Old English. The form is autobiographical but the speaker is not individuated to any extent; it has been suggested that the poem is a paraphrase of Job 29 and 30. See ASPR 4.

RHYS, Ernest, see RHYMERS CLUB and EVERYMAN'S LIBRARY.

RHYS, Jean (Ella Gwendolen Rees Williams) (1890–1979), novelist, born in Dominica, the daughter of a Welsh doctor; she came to England in 1907. She briefly attended the Perse School, Cambridge, and the Academy of Dramatic Art, then worked as chorus girl and film extra, and, during the First World War, as volunteer cook. In 1919 she left England to marry the first of three husbands, Jean Lenglet, and remained abroad for many years, living mainly in Paris, where she began to write and where much of her early work is set. *The Left Bank: Sketches and Studies of Present-Day Bohemian Paris* appeared in 1927 with an introduction by F. M. *Ford, followed by *Postures* (1928, reprinted 1969 as *Quartet*) and *After Leaving Mr Mackenzie* (1930). *Voyage in the Dark* (1934) is a first-person account of 19-year-old Anna Morgan's experiences as a chorus girl in London and on tour, and *Good Morning, Midnight* (1939) is the story, also told in the first person, of middle-aged Sasha Jensen, lonely and adrift in Paris, with a dead marriage and a dead baby behind her, seeking ambiguous consolation in a relationship with a gigolo. A long silence followed, during which Jean Rhys returned to England, living quietly in the West Country, until a radio adaptation of *Good Morning, Midnight* in 1958 brought her back to public attention. *Wide Sargasso Sea* (1966), set in Dominica and Jamaica during the 1830s, presents the life of the mad Mrs Rochester from *Jane Eyre*, a Creole heiress here called Antoinette Cosway; in the brief last section she is imprisoned in the attic in Thornfield Hall. This book was very well received and reprints of earlier novels were issued, to much praise of their 'bitter poetry', and were followed by two collections of short stories, *Tigers Are Better Looking* (1968) and *Sleep It off, Lady* (1976), and an unfinished autobiography, *Smile Please* (1979). Her *Letters 1931–66*, ed. F. Wyndham and D. Melly, were published in 1984, and a biography, *Jean Rhys Life and Work*, by Carole Angier in 1990.

RHYS, John Llewellyn (1910–40), killed in action with the RAF, author of three books, all reflecting his passion for flying and his life as a pilot: they are *The Flying Shadow* (1936), *The World Owes Me a Living* (1939), and *England Is My Village*, a volume of short stories, for which he was posthumously awarded the Hawthornden Prize. His widow established in 1942 the prize that bears his name. Originally awarded to writers under 30, it is now available to writers under 35. Winners include Alun *Lewis (1944), V. S. *Naipaul (1958), Dan *Jacobson (1959), David *Storey (1961), Nell *Dunn (1964), Angela *Carter (1968), Andrew *Motion (1984), and Jonathan *Coe (1994).

Rhythm (1911–13, superseded 1913 by the *Blue Review*), a periodical edited by J. M. *Murry, with M. *Sadleir and K. *Mansfield. Murry conceived it as 'The Yellow Book of the modern movement', and in it appeared work by D. H. *Lawrence, Mansfield, F. M. *Ford, *Picasso, *Gaudier-Brzeska, and others.

Riah, the Jew in Dickens's *Our Mutual Friend*.

RICARDO, David (1772–1823), English economist, of Dutch-Jewish family, who made a fortune on the London stock exchange, and then, under the influence of Adam *Smith, devoted himself to the study of political economy. In 1811 he met James *Mill, who became a close friend, and encouraged him in the composition and publication of his chief work, *On the Principles of Political Economy and Taxation* (1817), in which he sets forward his views on prices, wages, and profits, and his theory of rent. Again with Mill's encouragement, he became a member of Parliament for Pontarlington in 1819. J. S. *Mill, who was as a boy obliged by his father to learn the rudiments of political economy from Ricardo's works, described him as 'the most modest of men' (*Autobiography*, ch. 1), but his personal and social interests and sympathies appear to have been narrow, and in many ways he represents the archetypal 'Dryasdust' economist, concerned only with facts and statistics, of *Carlyle's diatribes.

RICE, Anne, see GOTHIC FICTION.

RICE, Elmer (1892–1967), American dramatist, born Elmer Reizenstein in New York. His first major play was the expressionist drama *The Adding Machine* (1923), which satirized increasing regimentation and mechanization through the posthumous adventures of

Mr Zero, a bookkeeper. His plays of the 1930s (*We, the People*, 1933; *Judgment Day*, 1934; *Between Two Worlds*, 1934) are a response to the Depression and international ideological conflict. Rice was a campaigner for social justice and an outspoken critic of censorship. He wrote many other plays, some of them farces and melodramas, four novels, and a memoir, *Minority Report* (1963).

RICE, James (1843–82), novelist and journalist, educated at Queens' College, Cambridge. While editing the failing periodical *Once a Week* he made the acquaintance of Walter *Besant, and proposed to him that they should collaborate in writing a novel: the result was *Ready-Money Mortiboy* (1872), the tale of a Prodigal Son who returns home 'ten times worse than when he went away' and proceeds to ruin his father. Their successful association produced several novels and volumes of short stories.

RICH, Adrienne Cecille (1929–   ), American poet, essayist, and critic, born in 1929; she graduated from Radcliffe College in 1951. She has held a variety of academic posts, most recently professor in Stanford, California. Rich has published steadily since *A Change of World* (1951), though it was only with her third collection, *Snapshots of a Daughter in Law* (1956), that her characteristic, fractured, free verse, frequently in lengthy sequences, began to emerge. Rich's volumes through the 1960s, 1970s, and 1980s keep pace with her own increasing politicization and involvement with first the anti-war movement, and then lesbian/feminist politics, making them valuable representative documents of their times. Her poetry allies the personal ever more closely with the political, typically juxtaposing scenes of domestic life with reminders of horrifying instances of history. *Diving into the Wreck* (1971) and *The Dream of a Common Language* (1978) are outstanding collections, while *The Fact of a Doorframe: Poems Selected and New, 1950–1984* presents much of her most achieved work. Rich's essays, particularly *Compulsory Heterosexuality and Lesbian Existence* (1981), have been seminal for her generation of feminists. Some of her prose work is published in *Lies, Secrets and Silence* (1978) and in *Bread, Blood, and Poetry* (1984).

RICH, Barnaby (1542–1617). He fought at Le Havre, in Ireland, and in the Netherlands, rising to the rank of captain; from 1574 he turned to literature, writing romances in the style of Lyly's *Euphues, pamphlets, and reminiscences. From 1587 he received a pension. His best-known romance is *Riche His Farewell to Militarie Profession* (1581), which includes 'Apolonius and Silla', the source of Shakespeare's *Twelfth Night. It was edited by T. M. Cranfill (1959).

RICH, John (?1692–1761), theatrical producer, and son of the notoriously mean manager of Drury Lane, Christopher Rich (d. 1714). John opened the New Theatre in Lincoln's Inn Fields in 1714, where he had

much success with pantomime. In 1728 he produced Gay's *Beggar's Opera which was popularly said to have 'made Gay rich and Rich gay'. He became manager of Covent Garden in 1732, and in 1735 founded the Sublime Society of Beef Steaks, a club with many eminent members which met and dined in a room at the theatre.

RICH, Penelope (*c*.1562–1607), the sister of Robert Devereux, earl of *Essex, *Elizabeth I's last favourite. Her father's dying wish, when she was only 13 or 14, that she should marry *Sidney, came to nothing; in 1581 she was unhappily married to Lord Rich, and soon after provided the model for Sidney's 'Stella'. The exact nature of their relationship can never be known, but details in some sonnets, e.g. the comment that Stella 'Hath no misfortune, but that Rich she is', make it clear that she is the lady in question. After bearing Lord Rich seven children she became the mistress of Charles Blount, Lord Mountjoy (later earl of Devonshire), bearing him five or six children: they were married, after she had been legally separated from Lord Rich, by *Laud, but the legality of the match was not accepted, and both died soon after. She was a famous beauty and a good linguist, especially in Spanish; took part in masques by *Jonson and *Daniel; and was addressed by other poets besides Sidney, e.g. *Constable. According to Fr John Gerrard, she died in the Roman Catholic faith.

RICHARD I (1157–99), 'Cœur de Lion', king of England 1189–99, was one of the leaders of the Third Crusade and became a figure of romantic admiration in England (in the *Robin Hood legends, for instance, and in Scott's *The Talisman and *Ivanhoe*), in spite of the fact that only six months of his ten-year reign were spent in England. For the Middle English verse romance see RICHARD CŒUR DE LION.

Richard II, King, a historical tragedy by *Shakespeare, probably written and acted 1595. It was an immediate success and the first quarto of 1597 was followed by two more in 1598. After the death of *Elizabeth I a fourth quarto was issued in 1608, which contained the first appearance in print of the deposition scene (IV. i. 154–318), probably previously suppressed because of the politically contentious subject of the queen's succession, upon which it could be taken to reflect. The scene was included in the text of the play printed in the First *Folio of 1623. Shakespeare's main source was the *Chronicles* of *Holinshed, but he appears possibly to have known the anonymous play about Richard II called *Woodstock*, and to have drawn on S. Daniel's narrative poem *The Civil Wars*.

The play begins with the quarrel between Henry Bolingbroke, son of John of Gaunt, and Thomas Mowbray, duke of Norfolk, which King Richard resolves arbitrarily by exiling Mowbray for life and Bolingbroke for ten years. When 'time-honoured' John of Gaunt dies Richard confiscates his property to pay for his Irish wars, for which he leaves the country. Bolingbroke returns to claim his inheritance and takes Berkeley Castle, which the duke of York has as regent to yield him. The king returns to Wales, hears that his Welsh supporters have deserted him and that Bolingbroke has executed the king's favourites Bushy and Green; accompanied by York's son Aumerle, he withdraws to Flint Castle, where Bolingbroke accepts his surrender. The first half of the play ends with a discussion between a gardener and Richard's Queen Isabel about the government of the garden-state and the possibility of the king's deposition (III. iv).

In London Richard relinquishes his crown to Bolingbroke, who sends him to the Tower. The earl of Carlisle's and Aumerle's plot to kill Bolingbroke, who has now proclaimed himself Henry IV, is foiled by York. Richard is transferred to Pomfret Castle, where he hears of Henry's coronation and is murdered by Sir Pierce of Exton.

Richard II, like *1 *Henry VI* and *King John*, is written entirely in verse and it contains some of Shakespeare's most famous speeches, including John of Gaunt's evocation of England as 'This royal throne of kings, this scept'rd isle'. Its telling 'sad stories of the death of kings' contributed to its potent appeal. On the day before the earl of *Essex's planned revolt in 1601 his supporters paid for a performance of a play about Richard II, which was almost certainly Shakespeare's.

Richard III, King, a historical tragedy by *Shakespeare, probably written and performed 1591. It was first published in a quarto in 1597, which was reprinted five times before it appeared again, in a fuller and more reliable text in the First *Folio of 1623. The play's chief sources are the chronicles of R. *Holinshed and E. *Hall which contained material from *Vergil's *Anglicae Historiae* and Sir T. More's *The History of King *Richard the Thirde*.

The play completes the tetralogy whose first three parts are the *Henry VI* plays. It centres on the character of Richard of Gloucester, afterwards King Richard III, ambitious and bloody, bold and subtle, treacherous, yet brave in battle, a murderer, and usurper of the crown. The play begins with the deformed Richard's announcement: 'Now is the winter of our discontent | Made glorious summer by this sun of York', that is the king, Edward IV, who is dying. Richard is determined that he shall succeed to the crown and sets out to eliminate any opposition to this and to secure his position. He has his brother the duke of Clarence, who has been imprisoned in the Tower, murdered. As she accompanies the corpse of her dead father-in-law Henry VI, Anne, the widow of Edward, prince of Wales, is wooed by Richard, and they are later married.

When the king dies Richard begins his attack on Queen Elizabeth's family and supporters, with the help of the duke of Buckingham. Hastings, Rivers, and Grey are all executed, and Buckingham persuades the citizens of London to proclaim Richard king. After his coronation he murders his nephews, the princes in the Tower, and following the death of his wife Anne, which he encourages, tries to marry his niece, Elizabeth of York. However, Buckingham rebels and goes to join Henry Tudor, earl of Richmond, who has landed in Wales at Milford Haven to claim the crown. Buckingham is captured and Richard has him executed, but he now has to face Richmond's army at Bosworth. On the night before the battle the ghosts of those whom Richard has killed appear to him and foretell his defeat. In the battle the next day he loses his horse and is killed by Richmond, who is then proclaimed Henry VII, the first of the Tudor monarchs.

RICHARD DE BURY, see BURY, RICHARD DE.

Richard Cœur de Lion, a verse romance in 7,136 lines of short couplets dating from the early 14th cent., which some scholars suggest may be by the same writer as two other long romances of the same period, *Of *Arthour and of Merlin* and *King Alisaunder* (see introduction to the latter by G. V. Smithers for discussion of authorship). The writer says he is taking his poem from a French source, but it is marked by spirited English patriotism and contempt for the French King Philip. It is assumed that the source is Anglo-Norman, dating from about 1230–50. The poem describes the discomfiture of the Saracens in the course of the Third Crusade and breaks off, unfinished, when a three-year truce is arranged. There are several manuscripts and fragments. Quotations from it are found in the notes to Scott's *The Talisman*, referring to the cooking and eating of the Saracen's head, and of the heads served to the Paynim ambassadors. The edition by K. Brunner (Vienna, 1913) is a critical edition of the seven manuscripts then known.

RICHARDS, Alun (1929–2004), Welsh short story writer, novelist, and playwright, born in Pontypridd, Glamorgan. Drawing on his experiences as a probation officer and teacher, he was concerned with the contemporary, post-industrial valleys of Wales. His two volumes of stories are *Dai Country* (1973) and *The Former Miss Merthyr Tydfil* (1976); his *Selected Stories* appeared in 1995. Among his novels are *The Home Patch* (1966), *A Woman of Experience* (1969), and *Home to an Empty House* (1973). He has written plays for television, notably *The Onegin Line*, and also for the stage. His autobiography, *Days of Absence*, was published in 1986, and he edited the *Penguin Book of Welsh Short Stories* (1976; new edn 1993).

RICHARDS, Frank, see HAMILTON, CHARLES.

RICHARDS, (Thomas Franklin) Grant (1872–1948), publisher and author, son of an Oxford don; he worked for W. T. *Stead on the *Review of Reviews* before setting up as a publisher himself. His *Memories of a Misspent Youth* (1932) and *Author Hunting* (1934) describe a life devoted to literature, and to the support of authors as diverse as A. E. *Housman, *Firbank, *Tressell, and

*Dreiser; he was more adventurous and enthusiastic than financially prudent, and *Shaw wrote to him (23 May 1934), 'You should call your book The Tragedy of a Publisher who Allowed Himself to Fall in Love with Literature.' He was the founder, in 1901, of the *World's Classics series.

RICHARDS, I(vor) A(rmstrong) (1893–1979), critic and poet, educated at Clifton and Magdalene College, Cambridge, where he became a fellow; in 1929 he travelled to China, then in 1939 moved to Harvard, where he devoted many years to the study of linguistics and education. He was the founder, with Charles Kay Ogden (1889–1957), of Basic English, 'an auxiliary international language comprising 850 words arranged in a system in which everything may be said for all the purposes of everyday language'; Richards and Ogden published two works together, *The Foundations of Aesthetics* (1922, with J. Wood) and *The Meaning of Meaning* (1923). In a literary context Richards is best known for his *Principles of Literary Criticism* (1924), *Science and Poetry* (1926), and above all *Practical Criticism: A Study of Literary Judgement* (1929), a work which revolutionized the teaching and study of English. It was based on an experiment conducted by Richards in Cambridge in which he issued unsigned poems to students and asked for their written comments; the results were both entertaining and alarming, revealing that a majority of readers condemned poems by *Donne, D. H. *Lawrence, and G. M. *Hopkins, while praising highly the work of G. A. Studdert Kennedy ('Woodbine Willie') and J. D. C. Pellow. In his commentary, Richards analyses the stock responses, preconceptions, metrical insensitivities, lack of attentive reading, etc., of his guinea-pigs, and, while he refrains from concluding that 'a man who is stupid with poetry *must* be stupid with life', he does assert that 'a general insensitivity to poetry does witness a low level of general imaginative life'. Richards's attacks on vagueness, sentimentality, and laziness in poets and readers, his praise of irony ('a characteristic of poetry of the highest order'), ambiguity, complexity, and allusiveness, did much to create the climate which accepted *Modernism, and greatly influenced *Empson (his student from 1928 to 1929) and *Leavis; but perhaps his greatest contribution lay in his emphasis on the importance of close textual study and the danger of random generalization. His methods have now become standard classroom procedure in many schools and universities (see NEW CRITICISM and PRACTICAL CRITICISM). Richards's views on scientific and emotive language, and on the nature of the status of statements (or pseudo-statements) in poetry have been less widely accepted. Richards also published several volumes of poetry; a collection, *Internal Colloquies: Poems and Plays*, appeared in 1972.

RICHARDSON, Dorothy Miller (1873–1957), novelist, the third of four daughters of an impoverished gentleman. She was obliged to earn her living from an early age, first as governess, then as secretary, translator, and journalist. She became an intimate friend of H. G. *Wells and other avant-garde thinkers of the day who encouraged her to write. In 1915 appeared *Pointed Roofs*, the first of a sequence of highly autobiographical novels entitled *Pilgrimage*, of which the last volume, *March Moonlight*, first appeared posthumously in 1967. She was a pioneer of the *stream-of-consciousness technique, narrating the action through the mind of her heroine Miriam. She believed in 'unpunctuated' female prose (citing *Joyce in support), and V. *Woolf credited her with inventing 'the psychological sentence of the feminine gender'.

The formidable length of her great work deterred many readers, but interest revived in the 1960s and 1970s with the growth of *feminist criticism. Angus *Wilson ('Sexual Revolution', *Listener*, Oct. 1968) acclaimed her as a defiant writer who 'enters more fully than any novelist I know into the material and spiritual struggles of a young, very gifted, but at the same time utterly underprivileged woman in a world made by men for men'. *Pilgrimage* was reissued in 1979 in four volumes by the Virago Press, and a critical biography by John Rosenberg appeared in 1973.

RICHARDSON, Henry Handel, the pen-name of Ethel Florence Lindesay Richardson (1870–1946), novelist, born in Melbourne, Australia; her father, an Edinburgh-educated Irish doctor, and her English mother married after emigrating during the gold rushes. Her mother worked as postmistress after her father's death in 1879. Ethel was educated at the Presbyterian Ladies College in Melbourne, then, from 1888, in Leipzig, where she studied music. In 1895 she married John George Robertson, a philologist, and from 1904 (with one brief return visit to Australia in 1912) she lived in England. Her first novel, *Maurice Guest* (1908), is a tale of *grande passion* set in Leipzig, with an English provincial schoolmaster, studying music, as protagonist. Her second, and most economical, *The Getting of Wisdom* (1910), describes her Australian schooldays in the person of Laura Rambotham, an intelligent child caught between rebellion and the desire to please, between ambition and reality, who makes the discovery that the art of fiction is the art of lying plausibly. Her most ambitious work, the trilogy *The Fortunes of Richard Mahony*, consists of *Australia Felix* (1917), *The Way Home* (1925), and *Ultima Thule* (1929), of which the last was the most successful. Clearly rooted in the biography of her own parents, it traces the fluctuating progress of Mahony, from storekeeper in a rough mining settlement, through a prosperous medical career and even more prosperous financial speculation, to bankruptcy, madness, and death; throughout he is loyally supported by his wife Mary, who is finally obliged to work as a postmistress to support her small children. In its epic sweep it is at once the history of a man, a marriage, and a continent, capturing with imaginative recollection the landscapes, developing social attitudes, and growing prosperity and respectability of Australia. Her last novel, *The Young Cosima* (1939), returns to a musical theme, and is based on a life of Cosima Wagner; her autobiography, *Myself when Young* (1948), was unfinished at her death.

RICHARDSON, Jonathan, the elder (1665–1745), British portrait painter, who was highly successful in his own day. Yet his portraits are less interesting than his writings on art, and on the science of connoisseurship. His *Theory of Painting* (1715) was the first significant work on aesthetic theory by an English author; in the second edition, 1725, he added an influential essay on the *sublime. He was himself a discriminating connoisseur with a superlative collection of drawings; he had a wide circle of literary friends, amongst them *Pope, *Gay, and *Prior, and with his son wrote a book *Explanatory Notes on Paradise Lost* (1734). He drew and painted Pope and his family many times. His son did the research for a guidebook to Italy which was a popular companion on the *Grand Tour.

RICHARDSON, Samuel (1689–1761), the son of a joiner, born near Derby, where his parents lived briefly before returning to London. Little is known of his boyhood, but because of his father's comparative poverty he appears to have received (in his own words) 'only common School-learning'. The tradition that he attended either Merchant Taylors' or *Christ's Hospital cannot be substantiated. As a boy he read widely, told stories to his friends, and by the age of 13 was employed writing letters for young lovers. In 1706 he was apprenticed to a printer (as his father could not afford to enter him for the Church), and in 1715 he was admitted a freeman of the *Stationers' Company. He set up in business on his own in 1721, in which year he married Martha Wilde, the daughter of his former master. All his working life he was extremely industrious, and his business prospered and expanded steadily. Like all printers of his time, he combined printing and publishing, producing books, journals, advertisement posters, and much miscellaneous work. In 1723 he took over the printing of an influential Tory journal, the *True Briton*, and by 1727 was sufficiently established in his profession to be appointed renter warden of the Stationers' Company. In the 1720s and early 1730s he suffered the early deaths of all his six children, and in 1731 that of his wife. He attributed the nervous disorders of his later life to the shock of these deaths. In 1733 he married Elizabeth Leake, the daughter of a fellow printer, and four of the daughters of their marriage survived. In the same year he published his *The Apprentice's Vade Mecum*, a book of advice on morals and conduct. In 1738 he purchased in Fulham a weekend 'country' house, which he always referred to as 'North End', and which later became famous for his readings and literary parties. He published in 1739 his own version, pointedly moral, of *Aesop's Fables*, and, more importantly, he began *Pamela*.

Inspiration for the novel initially came from a series of 'familiar letters' which fellow printers had encouraged him to write on the problems and concerns of everyday life. While these eventually grew into *Pamela*, they were also published separately as *Letters . . . to and for Particular Friends* (1741). *Pamela* was written in two months, between November 1739 and January 1740, and was published later in that year, to very considerable acclaim. The morality and realism of the work were particularly praised, as Richardson had hoped. However, complaints of its impropriety persuaded him to revise his second edition considerably. The work had a great vogue abroad, and was soon adapted for the stage in France. Imitations and forged 'continuations' persuaded Richardson to go on with the story, and volumes iii and iv (*Pamela II*) were published in 1741. In that year there appeared a stinging parody called *An Apology for the Life of Mrs *Shamela Andrews*, which Richardson believed to be by *Fielding (as it almost certainly was) and which he never forgave. Fielding's *Joseph Andrews*, which begins as a parody of *Pamela*, was published in 1742 but did not affect the popularity of *Pamela II*.

Richardson's business continued to prosper, although his health was beginning to cause him great concern, and he extended his publications in religion, history, biography, and literature. In 1733 he had begun printing for the House of Commons and in 1742 he secured the lucrative post of printer of its journals. His circle of friends had by now vastly increased, and included many admiring young ladies, known as his 'songbirds' or 'honorary daughters'.

During the writing of *Clarissa, which was probably begun in 1744, he endlessly asked his friends for comments and advice, and read passages aloud to them in his 'grotto' (or summer house) at North End. The first two volumes of *Clarissa* appeared in 1747 and were very favourably received. After heavy revision, and determined efforts to prune, a further five volumes appeared in 1748. Correspondents and the circle of friends continued to grow and now included the *Bluestocking ladies Mrs *Delany, Mrs *Carter, and later Mrs *Chapone. *Clarissa* was an undoubted success but there were complaints about both its length and its indecency, and it was not reprinted as often as *Pamela*. However, it also became very popular abroad and was translated into French, Dutch, and German.

Urged by friends, Richardson began thinking, in about 1750, of the portrayal of a 'Good Man'. He asked for the views of his extensive acquaintance and began experimenting with the 'letters' of Harriet, who was to become one of the heroines of his next novel. His illnesses and general malaise, which appear to have included a form of Parkinson's disease, increased steadily but he persevered strenuously both with his business and his writing. His authors in the 1750s included C. *Lennox, S. *Fielding, E. *Young, and G. *Lyttelton. He had by now become friendly with Dr *Johnson, to whose *Rambler he contributed in

1750 and whom he helped with money in 1751. In 1752 Johnson (together with many of Richardson's other friends) read the draft of *Sir Charles *Grandison*, and Richardson printed the fourth volume of the *Rambler*. In 1753 he travelled to Bath and Cheltenham, which was as far as he had ever gone, and in 1753–4 he published the seven volumes of *Sir Charles Grandison*. The book sold well and rapidly became fashionable, but was assailed in various critical pamphlets for length, tedium, and doubtful morality.

In 1754–5 Richardson was master of the Stationers' Company. He published in 1755 *A Collection of the Moral and Instructive Sentiments . . . in the Histories of Pamela, Clarissa, and Sir Charles Grandison*, a book which he considered contained the pith of all his work. In the same year Dr Johnson published the *Dictionary*, which contained 97 citations from *Clarissa*. In 1756 Richardson was asked by *Blackstone for advice on the reform of the *Oxford University Press. Towards the end of his life Richardson wrote a few 'letters' to, from, and about Mrs Beaumont, a minor character from *Sir Charles Grandison*, who had been someone of mysterious importance in his early life. He continued to revise his novels heavily, and remained active in his business until his death.

Richardson is generally agreed to be one of the chief founders of the modern novel. All his novels were *epistolary, a form he took from earlier works in English and French, which he appreciated for its immediacy ('writing to the moment' as he called it), and which he raised to a level not attained by any of his predecessors. The 'letters', of which his novels consist, contain many long transcriptions of conversations, and the kinship with drama seems very strong. He was acutely aware of the problems of prolixity ('Length, is my principle Disgust') and worked hard to prune his original drafts, but his interest in minute analysis led inevitably to an expansive style.

A selection of his letters (6 vols, 1804) was edited by Mrs *Barbauld: see also *Selected Letters of Samuel Richardson*, ed. J. Carroll (1964). There is a life by T. C. D. Eaves and B. D. Kimpel (1971); see also M. Kinkead-Weekes, *Samuel Richardson, Dramatic Novelist* (1973); M. A. Doody, *A Natural Passion* (1974).

Richard the Redeless, see MUM AND THE SOTHSEGGER.

Richard the Thirde, The History of King, by Sir T. *More, written in English and Latin and included in his *Workes* (1557) and the *Latina Opera* (1565). It is distinguished from earlier English chronicles by its unity of scheme and dramatic effectiveness. Shakespeare probably used More's work only as filtered through *Hall and *Holinshed; it was More, however, who was ultimately responsible for the image of Richard as a *Machiavellian tyrant which Shakespeare transmits in *Richard III*. (See also BIOGRAPHY.)

RICHELIEU, Armand Jean du Plessis, Cardinal and duc de (1585–1642), one of the greatest of French states-men, who first came into prominence as bishop of Luçon, and became prime minister of Louis XIII in 1624. He disciplined the nobles by a series of executions, destroyed the political importance of the Protestants by the siege and capture of La Rochelle (1628), and intervened successfully in the Thirty Years War. He was the founder of the *Académie française. He figures in *The Three Musketeers* of *Dumas, and is the anti-hero of a blank verse drama by *Bulwer-Lytton and a novel by *Vigny.

RICHLER, Mordecai (1931–2001), Canadian novelist and screenwriter, born in Montreal, who from 1959 spent some years working in England, returning to Canada in 1972. His first novel, *The Acrobats* (1954), was followed by others, including, notably, *The Apprenticeship of Duddy Kravitz* (1959) which describes a Jewish boyhood in Montreal. *The Incomparable Atuk* (1963) is a satire on popular culture, and *Cocksure* (1968) is an extravaganza set in theatrical London of the Swinging Sixties, in which English gentleman publisher Mortimer Griffin confronts multicultural-ism, cinema starlets, and pornography: this was followed by *St Urbain's Horseman* (1971) also set in London, in which Jake Hersh, Jewish-Canadian film director, is acquitted from a rape charge. His many other exuberant, witty, and irreverent novels include *Solomon Gursky Was Here* (1989), which many consider his masterpiece: this is an ambitious and epic work which interweaves Jewish themes and Inuit folklore in an extraordinary and gripping exploration of Canada's historic multicultural roots, by means of the mysterious family saga of the wealthy Gurskys. *Barney's Version* (1997) recounts the unreliable and outrageous memories of Barney Panofsky in Montreal, London, and Paris.

RICHMOND, Sir Bruce (1871–1964), educated at Winchester and New College, Oxford; he joined *The Times* in 1899, and for 35 years was editor of the *Times Literary Supplement* from its first production in 1902.

RICHMOND, Legh (1772–1827), an evangelical divine who lived in the Isle of Wight, where he collected the material for his immensely successful pious tales of country life, published between 1809 and 1814, *The Dairyman's Daughter*, *The Young Cottager*, and *The Negro Slave*. He gave money for the establishment of a library, which still exists, on the island of Iona.

RICHTER, Johann Paul Friedrich (1763–1825), German Romantic novelist, who wrote under the name 'Jean Paul'. Reared in humble village surroundings, he was at his best in idyllic representations of the life he knew. His combination of humour with mystic idealism appealed to *Carlyle and *De Quincey, both of whom translated stories by 'Jean Paul' and wrote appreciations of his works. His best-known works are: *Hesperus* (1795), *Quintus Fixlein* (1796), *Siebenkäs* (1796–7), *Vorschule der Ästhetik* (*Introduction to Aesthetics*, 1804), and the unfinished *Flegeljahre* (1804–5).

RICKETTS, Charles (1866–1931), English aesthete, illustrator, designer, and painter. His brilliant conversation and rarefied tastes attracted many writers to his house in the Vale, Chelsea, and later to Townshend House; among his friends were *Wilde, J. H. *Gray, *Yeats, G. B. *Shaw, 'Michael *Field' (Edith Cooper and Katherine Bradley), and *Binyon. Ricketts illustrated and designed many of Wilde's books; most beautiful are *A House of Pomegranates* (1891) and *The Sphinx* (1894). After Wilde's death he wrote a memoir of him, *Recollections of Oscar Wilde* (1932). With Charles Shannon, Ricketts edited the *Dial* (1889–97), a lavishly illustrated literary magazine deeply influenced by the then little-known works of French and Belgian symbolists. His Vale Press, founded in 1896, was one of the most important of the *private presses. Later Ricketts worked as a stage designer; Shaw's *Saint Joan* (1924) was his most successful production. Ricketts was a distinguished collector, connoisseur, and writer on art, and in his last years designed and illustrated two of his own prose works, *Beyond the Threshold* (1929) and *Unrecorded Histories* (1933).

RICKWORD, Edgell (1898–1982), poet, critic, and radical, who edited from 1925 to 1927 the *Calendar of Modern Letters*, an influential literary periodical which helped to form the critical attitudes of *Leavis. He also edited two volumes of *Scrutiny* (1928–32), the *Left Review* (1936–8), and *Our Time* (1944–7), and edited the essays of *Caudwell (1949). *Essays and Opinions* (1921–51), edited by A. Young, appeared in 1974, and *Collected Poems* in 1976.

Riddle of the Sands, The, see CHILDERS.

Riderhood, Rogue, a character in Dickens's *Our Mutual Friend*.

RIDING, Laura (1901–91), American poet and critic, who lived and worked with Robert *Graves from 1927 until 1939. She was well represented in the *Faber Book of Modern Verse* (1936) and her elliptical verses were brought together in *Collected Poems* (1938). Critical works include (with Graves) *A Survey of Modernist Poetry* (1927) and *Contemporaries and Snobs* (1928). A novel, *A Trojan Ending*, appeared in 1937, and *Lives of Wives*, on various marriages in history, in 1939.

RIDLER, Anne, née Bradby (1912–2001), lyric and religious poet and verse dramatist, born in Rugby, the daughter of a housemaster at Rugby School, educated at King's College, London. She worked for a time at Faber and Faber, at one point as assistant to T. S. *Eliot, whose Anglican faith she shared. Her volumes include *Poems* (1939), *The Nine Bright Shiners* (1943), *The Golden Bird* (1951, which contains her poem on the theme of 'Deus Absconditus') and *Some Time After* (1972). Her poetic dramas include *The Mask* (1950) and *The Trial of Thomas Cranmer* (1956). Her *Collected Poems*, published in 1994, shows the range of her devotional verse, ballads, and lyrics, and contains some of her later *libretti* or 'Words for Music'.

RIDLEY, James (1736–65), a cleric, remembered for his *Tales of the Genii*, published in 1764. As often with *Oriental novels, the author purports to be merely the discoverer and translator, in this case 'Sir Charles Morell', ambassador to the great mogul. Many of these curious and exotic tales are modelled on those of the *Arabian Nights*. The book enjoyed a great and abiding success; it was later bowdlerized, and read by several generations of children, including the young *Dickens, who founded his youthful tragedy *Misnar* on one of the tales.

RIDLEY, Nicholas (?1500–55), bishop successively of Rochester and London, and a fellow of Pembroke Hall, Cambridge. He became one of *Cranmer's chaplains and began gradually to reject many Roman doctrines. If any hand beside that of Cranmer can be detected in the two Prayer Books of Edward VI, it is believed to be Ridley's. As bishop of London he exerted himself to propagate reformed opinions. On Edward VI's death he denounced Queen Mary and Elizabeth as illegitimate at St Paul's Cross, London. He was sent to the Tower in June 1553 and deprived of his bishopric. In September 1555 he was condemned on the charge of heresy and burnt alive with *Latimer at Oxford, 16 Oct. He wrote several theological treatises, which appeared after his death. In 1841 the *Works of Nicholas Ridley* were edited for the Parker Society by Henry Christmas.

Rience, see RYENCE.

RIEU, E(mile) V(ictor), see PENGUIN BOOKS.

Rigaud, a character in Dickens's *Little Dorrit*.

Rights of Man, The, a political treatise by T. *Paine in two parts, published 1791 and 1792.

Pt I is in the main a reply to Burke's *Reflections on the *Revolution in France*. Paine accuses *Burke of 'rancour, prejudice and ignorance', of seeking theatrical effects at the expense of truth, and of disorderly arguments: 'Mr Burke should recollect that he is writing history, and not *plays*.' He denies that one generation can bind another as regards the form of government, and argues that the constitution of a country is an act of the people constituting the government. He traces the incidents of the French Revolution up to the adoption of the Declaration of the Rights of Man by the National Assembly, and criticizes Burke's account of these incidents as over-emotional and inaccurate; he alleges that Burke cares only for the forms of chivalry, and not for the nation. 'He pities the plumage, and forgets the dying bird.'

Pt II touches on Burke's *Appeal from the New to the Old Whigs*, then passes to a comparison of the new French and American constitutions with those of British institutions, to the disadvantage of the latter. The work also contains Paine's far-sighted proposals for reform of taxation, family allowances, maternity grants, etc.

Rights of Woman, Vindication of the, see WOLLSTONE-CRAFT.

RILEY, Joan, see BLACK BRITISH LITERATURE.

RILKE, Rainer Maria (1875–1926), German lyric poet, a member of the German-speaking minority in Prague. Of decisive importance were his two visits to Russia which, deepening his religious experience, led to *Das Stunden-buch* (*The Book of Hours*, 1905), in which death is the central theme, handled in a highly individual way. The subjective emotionalism of the early work began to give way to poetry of a more objective type, the transition to which is seen in *Das Buch der Bilder* (*The Book of Pictures*, 1902) and which finds its mature expression in the *Neue Gedichte* (*New Poems*, 1907–8). The latter was greatly influenced by the French sculptor Rodin, whose secretary Rilke was for a time. In 1910 appeared a full-scale prose work, *Die Aufzeichnungen des Malte Laurids Brigge* (*Sketches of Malte Laurids Brigge*), in which Rilke explored the relationship between a sensitive poet and a threatening environment. The *Duineser Elegien* (1923; *Duino Elegies*), begun shortly before the First World War and completed not long afterwards, arose from Rilke's endeavour to discover for himself as a poet a satisfactory spiritual position amid the decay of reality; and the *Die Sonette an Orpheus* (*Sonnets to Orpheus*, 1923), written in a sudden frenzy of inspiration, are the jubilant outcome of that endeavour. His extensive correspondence is of great literary interest. He is one of the most important lyric poets of the 20th cent., and his poetry has been translated into many languages—various collections have appeared in English translated by J. B. Leishman, sometimes in collaboration with *Spender.

RIMBAUD, Arthur (1854–91), French poet. One of the most revolutionary figures in 19th-cent. literature, he was by the age of 16 in full revolt against every form of authority. Expressing the exhilaration of his regular escapes from maternal discipline and his fascination with cabbalistic and alchemical imagery, his verse was already fiercely independent of religious, political, and literary orthodoxy. By the age of 17 he had written his most famous poem, 'Le Bateau ivre', a hymn to the quest of unknown realities, which became a sacred text for the next two generations of writers. Between 1871 and 1873—the period of his association with *Verlaine and his sojourns in England—he undertook a programme of 'disorientation of the senses' in order to try to turn himself into a voyant or seer. This resulted in his most original work, two collections of prose poems, *Les Illuminations*, which explored the visionary possibilities of this experiment, and *Une saison en enfer*, recording its moral and psychological failure. By the time he was 19, his poetic career was over. The remainder of his life has been described as a prolonged act of passive resistance. Having repudiated poetry, he gave himself up to vagabondage, first in Europe, and later in Aden and north-east Africa. His poems have been translated into prose versions by poet Oliver Bernard (1962).

'Rime of the Ancient Mariner, The', see ANCIENT MARINER, THE RIME OF THE.

rime royal, see RHYME-ROYAL.

Rimini, The Story of, see STORY OF RIMINI, THE.

Rinaldo, or **Renaud,** first figures under the latter name in the *Charlemagne cycle of legends as the eldest of the Four Sons of *Aymon, who were first the enemies of Charlemagne but later pardoned on condition that Renaud goes to Palestine to fight the Saracens and surrenders his horse Bayard. Renaud complies and becomes a hermit in Palestine; but Bayard will allow no one else to mount him. As Rinaldo, he figures in Boiardo's *Orlando innamorato*, Ariosto's *Orlando furioso*, and Tasso's *Gerusalemme liberata*: in the first two as the cousin of Orlando and the suitor of Angelica; in the third as a prince of Este, the lover of Armida and the victor in the battle for Jerusalem.

Ring and the Book, The, a poem in blank verse, in 12 books, totalling over 21,000 lines, by R. *Browning, published in four monthly instalments Nov. 1868–Feb. 1869. The poem was a critical and popular success, and established Browning's contemporary reputation.

The 'Ring' of the title is a figure for the process by which the artist transmutes the 'pure crude fact' of historical events into living forms; the 'Book' is a collection of documents relating to the Italian murder trial of the late 17th cent. on which the poem is based. Browning found the volume on a market stall in Florence, and offered it to several of his acquaintances (including *Tennyson and *Trollope) before finally deciding to use it himself.

The story in bare outline is as follows. Pietro and Violante Comparini were a middle-aged childless couple living in Rome. Their income could only be secured after Pietro's death if they had a child; so Violante bought the child of a prostitute and passed it off as her own. This child, Pompilia, was eventually married to Count Guido Franceschini, an impoverished nobleman from Arezzo. The marriage was unhappy, and the Comparini, disappointed by life in Arezzo, returned to Rome, where they sued Guido for the restoration of Pompilia's dowry on the grounds of her illegitimacy, which Violante now revealed. Pompilia herself eventually fled from Arezzo in the company of a young priest, Giuseppe Caponsacchi. Guido pursued them and had them arrested on the outskirts of Rome; as a result, Caponsacchi was exiled to Civita Vecchia for three years, and Pompilia was sent to a convent while the lawsuits were decided. But then, because she was pregnant, she was released into the custody of the Comparini. A fortnight after the birth of her child, Guido and four accomplices murdered her and her putative parents. They were arrested and tried for the murder, Guido claiming justification on the grounds of his wife's adultery with Caponsacchi; nevertheless he and his accomplices were convicted and sentenced to death. Guido then pleaded exemption for himself, but his appeal was rejected and the five were executed.

In Browning's poem, the story is told by a succession of speakers—citizens of Rome, the participants themselves, the lawyers, and the pope—each of whose single, insufficient perceptions combines with the others to form the 'ring' of the truth. This design represents Browning's response to a number of pressing concerns in his own creative life and in contemporary philosophies of art and religion. He saw 'truth' as both absolute (in its divine essence) and relative (in its human manifestation); the artist partakes of either quality, all means of expression (such as language) being an inadequate 'witness' to the true life of the imagination, just as historical witnesses give a partial and inadequate account of 'real' events.

In its immense but ordered size and scope; in the vitality of its characters and the rich evocation of time and place; and in its magnificently troubled exposition of the relation between sign and significance, the poem stands at the centre of Browning's achievement.

Ring des Nibelungen, Der, a series of four music dramas by *Wagner, based indirectly on the *Nibelungenlied*, composed 1853–70, produced 1869–76.

Das Rheingold tells the story of the stealing of the gold of the Rhine maidens by Alberich, king of the Nibelungs, and the forging and theft (by Wotan) of the magic ring. *Die Walküre* (*The Valkyrie*) deals with the love of Sieglinde and Siegmund, and of the laying to sleep of Brünnhilde the Valkyrie by Wotan, who surrounds her with a ring of fire. In *Siegfried* the son of Siegmund and Sieglinde obtains the magic ring and passes through the flames to awaken Brünnhilde. In *Götterdämmerung* (*The Twilight of the Gods*) Siegfried betrays Brünnhilde for Gutrune, under the influence of a magic potion, and is slain: Brünnhilde places the ring on her finger and throws herself on Siegfried's pyre, whereupon the ring is recovered by the Rhine maidens.

'Rip Van Winkle', a story by W. *Irving attributed to 'Diedrich *Knickerbocker' and included in *The Sketch Book* (1820).

Rip Van Winkle, taking refuge from a termagant wife in a solitary ramble in the Catskill mountains, falls asleep, and awakens after 20 years, to find his wife dead, his house in ruins, and the world completely changed.

RITCHIE, Anne Isabella Thackeray, Lady (1837–1919), elder daughter of *Thackeray. She wrote novels of an impressionistic kind which influenced her stepniece V. *Woolf, who drew a portrait of her in *Night and Day* as 'Mrs Hilbery'. *Old Kensington* (1873) and *Mrs Dymond* (1885) are probably the best remembered of her novels today. She also wrote reminiscences of the literary figures she had known in her youth: *Records of Tennyson, Ruskin and Robert and Elizabeth Browning* (1892) and *Chapters from Some Memoirs* (1894), among others. A biography of her by Winifred Gérin was published in 1981.

Ritho, see RYENCE.

RITSON, Joseph (1752–1803), literary antiquary, vegetarian, republican, and eccentric, and a friend of Sir W. *Scott, who consulted him while working on his *Border Minstrelsy*. Ritson was a man of an irritable and bitter nature, exacerbated by ill health, which expressed itself in his attacks (often justified) on the works of fellow scholars: he challenged T. *Warton's *History of English Poetry* (1782) and also Dr *Johnson's and *Steevens's edition of Shakespeare. In 1783 he published *A Select Collection of English Songs* containing strictures on Percy's *Reliques*, accusing *Percy of corrupting texts 'to give the quotations an air of antiquity, which it was not intitl'd to', and of other 'monstrous lies' and misrepresentations. In 1795 he published *Robin Hood: A Collection of All the Ancient Poems, Songs and Ballads Now Extant Relative to That Outlaw*, with illustrations by *Bewick: Scott attributed a 'superstitious scrupulosity' to this work, which he thought excessively comprehensive. His *Ancient English Metrical Romances* appeared in 1802. Ritson also published several popular collections and anthologies of songs, children's verses, fairy stories, etc. He became increasingly odd in later life, more and more fanatically vegetarian (his diet was originally inspired by reading *Mandeville), and finally insane. (See also PRIMITIVISM and BALLAD.)

Rival Queens, The: *or The Death of Alexander the Great*, a tragedy by N. *Lee, founded on the *Cassandre* of *La Calprenède, produced 1677. C. *Cibber attributed its success to the performance of *Betterton, but it held the stage for 100 years.

Statira, daughter of Darius and wife of Alexander, learning that Alexander has again fallen a victim to the charms of his first wife Roxana, whom he had promised to discard, vows never to see him again. Alexander, returning from his campaign and passionately loving Statira, is deeply distressed. Roxana goads Statira to fury, Statira revokes her vow, and Alexander banishes Roxana, who later stabs her rival to death. Alexander is poisoned by the conspirator Cassander.

Rivals, The, a comedy by R. B. *Sheridan, produced 1775.

This was Sheridan's first play, written rapidly when he was only 23, yet it is generally agreed to be one of the most engaging and accomplished of English comedies. It is set in Bath, where Sheridan lived from 1770 to 1772. Captain Absolute, son of Sir Anthony Absolute, a warm-hearted but demanding old gentleman who

861   RIZPAH | ROBERT THE DEVIL

requires absolute obedience from his son, is in love with Lydia Languish, the niece of Mrs Malaprop. As he knows the romantic Lydia prefers a poor half-pay lieutenant to the heir of a baronet with £3,000 a year, he has assumed for the purposes of courtship the character of Ensign Beverley, and in this guise he is favourably received. But Lydia will lose half her fortune if she marries without her aunt's consent, and Mrs Malaprop will not approve of an indigent ensign. Sir Anthony arrives in Bath to propose a match between his son and Lydia Languish, a proposal welcomed by Mrs Malaprop. Captain Absolute is now afraid of revealing his deception to Lydia in case he loses her; while Bob Acres, who is also Lydia's suitor and has heard of Beverley's courtship, is provoked by the fiery Irishman Sir Lucius O'Trigger to ask Captain Absolute to carry a challenge to Beverley. Sir Lucius himself, who has been deluded into thinking that some love letters received by him from Mrs Malaprop are really from Lydia, likewise finds Captain Absolute in his path, and challenges him. But when Acres finds that Beverley is in fact his friend Absolute, he declines his duel with relief and resigns all claim to Lydia. Sir Lucius's misapprehension is removed by the arrival of Mrs Malaprop, and Lydia, after a pretty quarrel with her lover for shattering her hopes of a romantic elopement, finally forgives him. Another plot, neatly interwoven with the rest, concerns the love affair of the perverse and jealous Faulkland with Lydia's friend Julia Melville.

'Rizpah', a poem by *Tennyson, published in *Ballads and Other Poems* (1880), the monologue of a mother who collects the unhallowed bones of her son night by night from the foot of the gallows and buries them secretly in the churchyard. Her claim that the bones are hers because 'they had moved in my side' gave to *Swinburne 'perfect proof once more of the deep truth that great poets are bisexual'.

Road to Oxiana, The, see BYRON, R.

Road to Ruin, The, see HOLCROFT.

Road to Wigan Pier, The, see ORWELL and LEFT BOOK CLUB.

Roaring Girle, The, or *Moll Cut-Purse*, a comedy by T. *Middleton and *Dekker, written ?1604–8, published 1611.

In this play Moll Cutpurse, a notorious thief in real life, is portrayed as an honest girl, who helps lovers in distress and defends her virtue with her sword. Sebastian Wentgrave is in love with and betrothed to Mary Fitzallard, but his covetous father forbids the match. Sebastian pretends he has fallen desperately in love with Moll Cutpurse and is about to marry her; and Moll good-naturedly lends herself to the deception. Old Wentgrave, distracted at the prospect, is only too glad to give his blessing when the real bride turns out to be Mary Fitzallard. There are some pleasant bustling

scenes in which the life of the London streets is vividly presented, shopkeepers selling tobacco and feathers, their wives intriguing with gallants, and Moll talking thieves' cant and discomfiting overbold admirers. The play was highly praised by T. S. *Eliot.

ROBBE-GRILLET, Alain (1922–), French novelist and leading proponent of the *nouveau roman*, also a screenwriter and film-maker, born in Brest. In *Les Gommes* (1953), the erasers of the title represent the erasure of one version of events and its replacement by another. The title of *Le Voyeur* (1955) refers equally to author, narrator, and reader. In *La Jalousie* (1957) the narrator allows his presence to be inferred only from significant details in the descriptive passages. *L'Année dernière à Marienbad* (1961), a *ciné-roman*, is the screenplay for Alain Resnais's landmark film. Robbe-Grillet's first novel, *Un régicide*, written in 1949 but not published until 1978, has yet to appear in English; it is one of his most accessible and enjoyable books, while no less 'important' than the more challenging novels of the 1970s, including *Topologie d'une cité fantôme* (1976) and *Souvenirs du triangle d'or* (1978). In the 1980s he produced three volumes of novelistic memoirs, including, most recently, *Les Dernier Jours de Corinthe* (1994).

Robene and Makyne, a pastoral by *Henryson, on the model of the French *pastourelle* rather than the classical *eclogue, included in Percy's *Reliques. Robene is a shepherd, and Makyne (a form of Malkin, a diminutive of Matilda which seems to have been a stereotypical name for an unattractive woman: see *Piers Plowman B I. 184) loves him. He rejects her advances and she goes away. Robene changes his mind and appeals to her, whereupon she delivers the Henrysonian moral:

> Robene, thow hes hard soung and say
> In gestis and storeis auld:
> The man that will nocht quhen he may
> Sall haif nocht quhen he wald (ll. 89–92).

ROBERT, earl of Gloucester (d. 1147), a natural son of Henry I, and the chief supporter of Matilda against Stephen. He was a patron of literature, in particular of *William of Malmesbury, *Henry of Huntingdon, and *Geoffrey of Monmouth. Geoffrey's *History* is dedicated to him.

Robert the Devil, sixth duke of Normandy and father of William the Conqueror, a personage about whom many legends gathered in consequence of his violence and cruelty. In *The Life of Robert the Devil*, Robert is represented as having been devoted soul and body to Satan by his mother, who had long been childless and prayed to the devil to give her a son; but as finally repenting of his misdeeds and marrying the emperor's daughter (he in fact died on a pilgrimage to Palestine). This verse tale is a translation from the French and was printed in about 1500 by Wynkyn de *Worde. T. *Lodge wrote a prose account of the same subject.

ROBERT OF GLOUCESTER (fl. 1260–1300), the reputed author of a metrical Chronicle of England from Brutus to Henry III, for much of which he drew upon *Laȝamon. It is written in long lines, running to 14 syllables and more, and is not the work of a single hand, though probably the whole was composed in the abbey of Gloucester. It contains among passages of special interest a famous description of the death of Simon de Montfort at the battle of Evesham and a section in praise of England beginning: 'Engelond his a wel god lond.' Ed. W. A. Wright, Rolls Series 86 (1887).

Robert Elsmere, see WARD, M. A.

ROBERTS, Michael William Edward (1902–48), poet, critic, editor, and teacher of mathematics, whose anthologies *New Signatures* (1932) and *New Country* (1933), containing work by *Auden, *Day-Lewis, *Empson, *Spender, and others, established him, in T. S. *Eliot's phrase, as 'expositor and interpreter of the poetry of his generation'. *The Recovery of the West* (1941) is a study of the ills of Western civilization and *The Estate of Man* (1951), written in 1947–8, shows him as a pioneer ecologist, issuing a then unfashionable warning about the devastation of the earth's resources. He also edited the influential *Faber Book of Modern Verse* (1936). See *Michael Roberts: Selected Poems and Prose*, ed. F. Grubb (1980).

ROBERTS, Michèle (1949–   ), novelist and poet, who became one of the leading literary writers of the women's liberation movement of the 1970s: from 1975 to 1977 she was poetry editor of the feminist magazine *Spare Rib*, and her first novel, *A Piece of the Night* (1978), was the first original fiction published by the Women's Press. This introduced several of the themes that were to inform her later work: its heroine, Julie Fanchot, is French born but English convent educated, and the story takes her back to Normandy to care for her mother, and to meditate on her French childhood, her Oxford experiences, marriage and motherhood, female friendship, and her struggle to emerge as an independent woman. This was followed by *The Visitation* (1983), with a theme of gender and twinning; and *The Wild Girl* (1984). *The Book of Mrs Noah* (1987) is set partly in Venice and partly on a surreal voyage in a Women's Ark, where various women writers gather to create their own dream environment: the narrator, like the author, had trained as a librarian, which lends the fantasy a Borgesian bibliographical touch. *In the Red Kitchen* (1990) was followed by *Daughters of the House* (1992), a family drama set in France. *Flesh and Blood* (1994) is a series of parodistic highly coloured erotic-historical stories, linked in *Scheherazade style, beginning and ending in London of the 1960s, and *Impossible Saints* (1997) explores female religious faith and ritual and was inspired in part by the life of St *Teresa of Ávila. *During Mother's Absence* (1993)

is a collection of short stories. Her poetry includes *The Mirror of the Mother: Selected Poems 1975–1985* (1986), *Psyche and the Hurricane* (1991) and *All the Selves I Was: New and Selected Poems* (1995). Both her poetry and her prose are distinguished by a warm, sensuous richness, whether she is writing about sex, food, or motherhood, and she draws with equal ease on classical and biblical legend. Her work offers on the whole a positive, optimistic, yet sharply observant version of women's experience at the end of the 20th century.

ROBERTSON, T(homas) W(illiam) (1829–71). He began life as an actor, but retired from the stage and became a dramatist. His plays *Society* (1865), *Ours* (1866), *Caste* (1867), *Play* (1868), *School* (1869), and *M.P.* (1870) introduced a new and more natural type of comedy to the English stage than had been seen during the first half of the century. His earlier drama *David Garrick* (1864) was also well received. Marie Wilton (Lady Bancroft) was the great exponent of Robertson's best female characters.

ROBERTSON, William (1721–93), educated at Edinburgh University, of which, after some time as a Presbyterian parish minister, he became principal in 1762. He achieved fame on the publication of his *History of Scotland during the Reign of Queen Mary and of King James VI* (1759), which was followed by his history of the reign of Charles V (1769), *The History of America* (1777), and a *Disquisition Concerning the Knowledge which the Ancients Had of India* (1791). Both in style and in scholarship his work is comparable with that of *Hume. (Dr *Johnson found it had too much 'painting' and verbiage.) Robertson was a member of the *Select Society, and an account of his life and writings was published in 1801 by D. *Stewart.

Robin Hood, a legendary outlaw. The name is part of the designation of places and plants in every part of England. The facts behind the legend are uncertain. In the portion of the Pipe *Roll of 1230 relating to Yorkshire there is mention of a 'Robertus Hood fugitivus'. Robin Hood is referred to in *Piers Plowman*. As a historical character he appears in *Wyntoun's *The Orygynale Cronykil* (c.1420), and is referred to as a ballad hero by Abbot Bower (d. 1449), *Major, and *Stow. The first detailed history, *Lytell Geste of Robyn Hode* (printed c.1500), locates him in south-west Yorkshire; later writers place him in Sherwood and Plumpton Park (Cumberland), and finally make him earl of Huntingdon. *Ritson, who collected all the ancient songs and ballads about Robin Hood, says definitely that he was born at Locksley in Nottinghamshire about 1160, that his true name was Robert Fitz-Ooth, and that he was commonly reputed to have been earl of Huntingdon. There is a pleasant account of the activities of his band in Drayton's *Poly-Olbion*, song 26. According to Stow, there were about the year 1190 many robbers and outlaws, among whom were Robin

Hood and Little John, who lived in the woods, robbing the rich, but killing only in self-defence, allowing no woman to be molested, and sparing poor men's goods. A date for his death (18 Nov. 1247) was given by Martin Parker (*True Tale*, c.1632) and by the antiquary Ralph Thoresby (1658–1725), and his pedigree was supplied by *Stukeley. Legend says that he was bled to death by a treacherous nun at Kirklees in Yorkshire. According to Joseph Hunter (antiquary, 1783–1861), with support from the court rolls of the manor of Wakefield in Yorkshire, he was a contemporary of Edward II (1307–27) and adherent of Thomas of Lancaster. He is the centre of a whole cycle of ballads, one of the best of which is *Robin Hood and Guy of Gisborne, printed in Percy's *Reliques, and his legend shows affinity with Chaucer's 'Cook's Tale of Gamelyn' (see GAMELYN) and with the tales of other legendary outlaws such as Clym of the Clough and *Adam Bell. Popular plays embodying the legend appear to have been developed out of the village *May Day game, the king and queen of May giving place to Robin and Maid Marian. Works dealing with the same theme were written by *Munday, *Chettle, *Tennyson, and others. The *True Tale of Robbin Hood* was published c.1632, *Robin Hood's Garland* in 1670, and a prose narrative in 1678. He figures in Peacock's *Maid Marian, and Scott's *Ivanhoe as Locksley.

Robin Hood and Guy of Gisborne, one of the best known of the ballads of the *Robin Hood cycle. Robin Hood and Little John having gone on their separate ways in the forest, the latter is arrested by the sheriff of Nottingham and tied to a tree. Meanwhile Robin Hood meets with Guy of Gisborne, who has sworn to take Robin; they fight and Guy is slain. Robin puts on the horse-hide with which Guy was clad, takes his arms, and blows a blast on his horn. The sheriff mistakes him for Guy, thinks he has killed Robin, and gives him permission, as a reward, to kill Little John. Robin releases Little John, gives him Guy's bow, and the sheriff and his company take to their heels.

ROBINS, Elizabeth, see WOMEN'S SUFFRAGE.

ROBINSON, A. Mary F. (later Darmesteter, later Duclaux) (1857–1944), poet, born at Leamington Spa and educated at University College London. Her first husband was professor of Persian in Paris, where she lived until his death in 1894: she remarried in 1904 and moved to Olmet. She published several collections of poetry, reflective and lyrical, including *Songs, Ballads, and a Garden Play* (1889) and *Retrospect and Other Poems* (1893).

ROBINSON, E(dwin) A(rlington) (1869–1935), American poet, born at Head Tide, Maine, the son of a general merchant and lumber dealer. He records that at the age of 17 he became 'violently excited over the structure and music of English blank verse', and his admiration for *Hardy, *Crabbe, and R. *Browning is manifest in his many volumes of poetry about New England life,

beginning with *The Torrent and the Night Before* (1896) and *The Children of the Night* (1897), which introduce, often through dramatic monologues, the population of his fictitious and representative Tilbury Town. His predominantly dry, restrained, ironic tone continues through most of his prolific output, in which he employs traditional forms with a delicate and original skill. As well as the New England character sketches for which he is best remembered in Britain, he also wrote several long blank-verse narratives, including an Arthurian trilogy (*Merlin*, 1917; *Lancelot*, 1920; *Tristram*, 1927) and *The Man Who Died Twice* (1924), a tale of genius destroyed. He was introduced in England by a *Collected Poems* (1922) with an introduction by *Drinkwater.

ROBINSON, Henry Crabb (1775–1867), a solicitor and later a barrister, but chiefly remembered for his diaries, reading-lists, and letters, first collected in 1869, which provide valuable information about the writers and events of his time. He was the friend of *Wordsworth, *Coleridge, *Lamb, *Hazlitt, and later *Carlyle, and because of his indefatigable attendance at public lectures was able to provide useful descriptions of the lecturing of Coleridge (with his 'immethodical rhapsody'), Hazlitt, and others. He was an admirer of the German writers, of *Goethe in particular, travelled in Germany, and did much to popularize German culture in England. For many years he wrote for *The Times, at home and abroad, and he was one of the founders of both University College London, and the Athenaeum Club.

ROBINSON, (Esmé Stuart) Lennox (1886–1958), prolific Irish dramatist, who was also manager of the *Abbey Theatre, 1910–14 and 1919–23, when he became the director until his death. Among his best-known plays are *The Clancy Name* (1911); the patriotic *Harvest* (1911) and *Patriots* (1912); *The Whiteheaded Boy*, a comedy (1920); *Crabbed Youth and Age* (1924); the ambitious *The Big House* (1928), on the changing state of Ireland; and two successful later comedies, *The Far-off Hills* (1931) and *Church Street* (1955). He also edited the *Oxford Book of Irish Verse* (with D. MacDonagh, 1958) and other anthologies; and wrote *The Irish Theatre* (1939) and *Ireland's Abbey Theatre. A History* (1951).

ROBINSON, Mary, née Darby (1758–1800), writer and actress, educated in Bristol, Chelsea and lastly Marylebone. In 1774 she married Thomas Robinson, who incurred debts. She published *Poems* (1775) and became mistress of the prince of Wales (George IV) in 1779. Poverty provoked a large number of publications in the 1790s, among them *Sappho and Phaon* (1796), a collection of sonnets, and several novels, including the popular *Vancenza* (1792) and *The Natural Daughter* (1799). Her poetry was admired by *Coleridge and her *Lyrical Tales* (1800) were influenced by the *Lyrical Ballads. Her daughter edited her

Memoirs, with Some Posthumous Pieces (1801) and her *Poetical Works* (1806). After her death, her work declined in popularity because of her reputation for loose morality, but its energy and lively social awareness recommend it to modern readers. See *Perdita* (2005) by Sarah Gristwood.

ROBINSON, William Heath (1872–1944), illustrator and artist, born in Islington, London, whose 'Heath Robinson contraptions' remain distinctive and instantly recognizable: he delighted in creating elaborate, unlikely, and absurd devices, often for absurd purposes, such as putting mites into cheese. He parodied the machine age with wit and style, and his drawings appeared in many magazines and were collected in volume form.

Robinson Crusoe, *The Life and Strange and Surprising Adventures of,* a romance by *Defoe, published 1719.

In 1704 Alexander *Selkirk, who had run away to sea and joined a privateering expedition under *Dampier, after a quarrel with his captain was put ashore on the uninhabited island of Juan Fernández. He was rescued in 1709 by Woodes *Rogers. Defoe was probably familiar with several versions of this tale, and added many incidents from his own imagination to his account of Crusoe, presenting it as a true story. The extraordinarily convincing account of the shipwrecked Crusoe's successful efforts to make himself a tolerable existence in his solitude first revealed Defoe's genius for vivid fiction; it has a claim to be the first English novel. Defoe was nearly 60 when he wrote it.

The author tells how, with the help of a few stores and utensils saved from the wreck and the exercise of infinite ingenuity, Crusoe built himself a house, domesticated goats, and made himself a boat. He describes his struggle to accept the workings of Providence, the perturbation of his mind caused by a visit of cannibals, his rescue from death of an indigenous native he later names Friday, and finally the coming of an English ship whose crew are in a state of mutiny, the subduing of the mutineers, and Crusoe's rescue.

The book had immediate and permanent success, was translated into many languages, and inspired many imitations, known generically as 'Robinsonnades', including *Philip Quarll, *Peter Wilkins, and *The Swiss Family Robinson. Defoe followed it with *The Farther Adventures of Robinson Crusoe* (1719), in which with Friday he revisits his island, is attacked by a fleet of canoes on his departure, and loses Friday in the encounter. *Serious Reflections . . . of Robinson Crusoe . . . with His Vision of the Angelick World,* which is more a manual of piety than a work of fiction, appeared in 1720, and was never as popular. The influence of *Robinson Crusoe* has been very great. *Rousseau in *Émile* recommended it as the first book that should be studied by a growing boy, *Coleridge praised its evocation of 'the universal man', and *Marx in *Das Kapital* used it to illustrate economic theory in action.

In recent years 'Man (later Girl) Friday' came to describe a lowly assistant performing a multiplicity of tasks.

In *The Rise of the Novel* (1957) and other essays Ian Watt provides one of the most controversial modern interpretations, relating Crusoe's predicament to the rise of bourgeois individualism, division of labour, and social and spiritual alienation. See David Blewett, *The Illustration of Robinson Crusoe, 1719–1920* (1995).

Rob Roy, a novel by Sir W. *Scott, published 1817.

The novel, set in the period preceding the Jacobite rebellion of 1715, celebrates the new predominance of a prosperous Whig mercantile class, personified here by Francis Osbaldistone and Bailie Nicol Jarvie, over the fox-hunting, Tory world of Osbaldistone Hall, ruled by Francis's elder brother Sir Hildebrand Osbaldistone. Francis's son Frank, on refusing to enter his father's business, Osbaldistone and Tresham, is exiled to Osbaldistone Hall; in exchange, his father decides to give his youngest nephew, Rashleigh, the place designed for his son. The plot is complicated by Frank's and Rashleigh's rival interest in their cousin Diana Vernon, one of Scott's most successful and delightful heroines. Rashleigh, unknown to his uncle, is deeply embroiled in plans for the forthcoming rebellion and uses his place in the firm to rob and ruin Francis Osbaldistone. Frank, in an attempt to save his father's credit, goes to Scotland to seek the help of the firm's Scottish correspondent, Bailie Nicol Jarvie, the real hero of the novel, and, with him, ventures into the Highlands in search of Rob Roy. Jarvie's defence of the practical benefits to Scotland of the Union is set against a striking picture of the ignorance, brutality, and squalor of the Highlands which Scott is too often accused of romanticizing. The titular hero does not appear *in propria persona* to take a prominent part in the action until late in the novel, though he appears in disguise earlier. Rob Roy Macgregor, a historical figure and member of a proscribed clan, has been driven by injustice to outlawry but is still capable of generosity. A Jacobite, he is involved in Rashleigh's plans for the rebellion, but Frank needs his help to frustrate his cousin's designs. In the end the rebellion fails, Rashleigh is killed by Rob Roy, and Frank inherits Osbaldistone Hall and marries Diana. His incorrigible manservant Andrew Fairservice is one of Scott's great characters.

ROBSART, Amy, daughter of Sir John Robsart, married to Sir R. *Dudley, afterwards earl of Leicester, in 1549; she figures in Scott's *Kenilworth.

Rochester, Edward Fairfax, the hero of C. Brontë's *Jane Eyre.

ROCHESTER, John Wilmot, second earl of (1647–80), lyric poet, satirist, and a leading member of the group of 'court wits' surrounding Charles II. He was born at Ditchley in Oxfordshire, his father a Cavalier hero and his mother a deeply religious woman related to many prominent Puritans. In his early teens he was sent to Wadham College, Oxford, the home of the *Royal Society, and then went on a European tour, returning to the court late in 1664. At the age of 18 he romantically abducted the sought-after heiress Elizabeth Malet in a coach-and-six. Despite the resistance of her family, and after a delay of 18 months (during which Rochester fought with conspicuous gallantry in the naval wars against the Dutch), she married him. Subsequently his time was divided between periods of domesticity with Elizabeth at his mother's home in the country (the couple had four children), and fashionable life in London with, among several mistresses, the brilliant actress Elizabeth *Barry, and his riotous male friends, who included the earl of Dorset (C. *Sackville) and the duke of *Buckingham. Wherever he was staying he tried to keep up the other side of his life through letters, many of which survive.

Although Dr *Johnson dismissed Rochester's lyrics, their wit and emotional complexity give him some claim to be considered one of the last important *Metaphysical poets of the 17th cent., and he was one of the first of the *Augustans, with his social and literary verse satires. He wrote scurrilous lampoons—some of them impromptu—dramatic prologues and epilogues, 'imitations' and translations of classical authors, and several other brilliant poems which are hard to categorize, such as his tough self-dramatization 'The Maimed Debauchee' and the grimly funny 'Upon Nothing'. He wrote more frankly about sex than anyone in English before the 20th cent., and is one of the most witty poets in the language. Although his output was small (he died young), it was very varied. *Marvell admired him, *Dryden, *Swift, and *Pope were all influenced by him (he was Dryden's patron for a time), and he has made an impression on many subsequent poets—*Goethe and *Tennyson, for example, and in modern Britain, *Empson and P. *Porter.

Rochester is famous for having, in Johnson's words, 'blazed out his youth and health in lavish voluptuousness'. He became very ill in his early thirties and engaged in discussions and correspondence with a number of theologians, particularly the deist Charles Blount and the rising Anglican churchman G. *Burnet, an outspoken royal chaplain who superintended and subsequently wrote up the poet's deathbed conversion. It was the final contradiction in a personality whose many oppositions—often elegantly or comically half-concealed—produced an important body of poems. See Complete Poems, ed. D. M. Vieth (1968); Poems, ed. K. Walker (1984); Letters, ed. J. Treglown (1980). There is a life by V. de Sola Pinto (1953, 2nd edn 1964); see also Lord Rochester's Monkey (1974) by G. *Greene.

Roderick Hudson, the first novel of H. *James, published in book form 1876. It is the story of a young man transplanted from a lawyer's office in a Massachusetts town to a sculptor's studio in Rome. Incapable of adjustment to his environment, he fails in both art and love, and meets a tragic end in Switzerland. The leading female character, Christina Light, was taken up again by the author in a later novel, The Princess Casamassima.

Roderick Random, The Adventures of, by T. *Smollett, published 1748.

Smollett's first novel, narrated with rampant, youthful vigour in the first person, is strongly influenced by *Lesage's Gil Blas. In his preface the author declares his wish to arouse 'generous indignation . . . against the vicious disposition of the world'. Roderick is combative, often violent, but capable of great affection and generosity. His father had been disinherited and has left Scotland, leaving his young son penniless with a neglectful grandfather. Roderick is befriended and rescued by his uncle, Lieutenant Tom Bowling of the navy. After a brief apprenticeship to a surgeon, and accompanied by an old schoolfellow, Strap, the innocent Roderick travels to London, where he encounters various rogues. Eventually, after struggling against assault, deception, and other tribulations, he qualifies as a surgeon's mate. He is then pressed as a common sailor aboard a man-of-war, the Thunderer, where he eventually becomes mate to the ebullient Welsh surgeon Morgan. They are present at the siege of Cartagena, and after much suffering and ill-treatment (which he does not accept supinely) Roderick returns to England. Here he lives under a false name as a footman, falls in love with Narcissa, and is once again kidnapped, this time by smugglers, who bear him off to France. He finds and helps his uncle, Tom Bowling, joins the French army, and fights at Dettingen. He again encounters his generous friend Strap, who arranges his release from the army and undertakes to serve Roderick as his valet. The two return to England, where Roderick intends to marry a lady of fortune. Again in London, he becomes embroiled in riotous life, amatory adventures, and fiery debates on a great range of subjects. He courts, among others, Miss Melinda Goosetrap, but does not succeed in deceiving her mother; other matrimonial enterprises are no more successful. Again he meets Narcissa, but he is shortly in prison for debt, and on his release, when he cannot find her, he sinks into despair. He is rescued by Tom Bowling, and embarks as surgeon on a ship under Bowling's command; in the course of the voyage he meets Don Roderigo, who turns out to be his long-lost father, now a wealthy merchant. When they return to England Roderick marries Narcissa, and Strap marries her maid, Miss Williams. Two long digressive stories are inserted into the narrative, the history of Miss Williams, who had earlier been a prostitute; and the story of Melopoyn, based on Smollett's own experience in trying to get his The Regicide accepted for the stage.

Roderigo, *Iago's gull in Shakespeare's *Othello.

Rodomont, in *Orlando innamorato and *Orlando furioso, the king of Sarza, arrogant and valiant, the doughtiest of the followers of *Agramant. His boastfulness gave rise to the word 'rodomontade'. He leads the first Saracen invasion into France. Doralis, princess of Granada, is betrothed to him, but falls into the power of *Mandricardo. After an indecisive duel between the two Saracen heroes, the conflict is referred to the princess herself, who, to Rodomont's surprise, expresses her preference for Mandricardo. Rodomont retires in disgust to the south of France. Here *Isabella falls into his power and, preferring death, by guile causes him to slay her. In remorse, in order to commemorate her, he builds a bridge and takes toll of all who pass that way. Orlando, coming in his madness to the bridge, throws Rodomont into the river. Rodomont is also defeated by *Bradamante. Thus humiliated he temporarily retires from arms, emerges once more, and is finally killed by *Rogero.

ROETHKE, Theodore (1908–63), American poet born in Michigan, who taught from 1947 at the University of Washington. His first book of poems, *Open House* (1941), already displays characteristic imagery of vegetable growth and decay, rooted in childhood memories of the greenhouses of his father, who was a keen horticulturalist. It was followed by various volumes including *The Lost Son* (1948), *Praise to the End* (1951), a book of light verse (divided into 'Nonsense' and 'Greenhouse' poems) called *I Am! Says the Lamb* (1961), and a posthumous collection, *The Far Field* (1964). His work has affinity with both *Yeats and *Blake, and influenced the early poetry of S. *Plath.

Roger, the name of the London cook (from Ware) in Chaucer's *Canterbury Tales*. His name may have been Roger Knight; see note ix, 50 in Robinson's edition, 763–4.

Roger de Coverley, Sir, see COVERLEY.

ROGER OF WENDOVER (d. 1236), monk and chronicler at St Albans; his *Flores Historiarum* was a history of the world from the Creation to AD 1235, compiled from many different sources. He was succeeded as chronicler by M. *Paris.

Rogero, or **Ruggiero,** the legendary ancestor of the house of Este, extolled in *Orlando furioso*. He is the son of a Christian knight and a Saracen lady of royal birth, brought up in Africa, and taken by *Agramant on the expedition against Charlemagne, where he falls in love with the warrior maiden *Bradamante and she with him. He falls into the power of *Alcina and is released by *Melissa. He then, mounted on the hippogriff, rescues *Angelica from the Orc. Bradamante has also an active rival in *Marfisa, a lady fighting on the Moorish side, who is smitten with love for Rogero, but eventually turns out to be his sister. Finally, after the retreat of Agramant, Rogero joins Charlemagne and is baptized. He now hopes to marry Bradamante, but her ambitious parents vigorously oppose the match. Bradamante, to secure her lover without openly op-

posing her parents, declares, with Charlemagne's approval, that she will marry no one who has not withstood her in battle for a whole day. This Rogero alone does, and after many vicissitudes the lovers are united. In a final duel Rogero slays *Rodomont. Some elements of the Bradamante/Rogero romance can be discerned in the relationship between *Spenser's Britomart and Artegall.

ROGERS, James Edwin Thorold (1825–90), educated at King's College, London, and Oxford, professor of political economy at Oxford in 1862–7 and again in 1888. He had been a strong *Tractarian until about 1860, but put off his orders and swung right round, being the first clergyman to take advantage of the Clerical Disabilities Relief Act of 1870. He was Radical MP for Southwark, 1880–6, and a father figure of economic history; all subsequent studies of inflation rest on his *A History of Agriculture and Prices in England . . . from 1259–1793* (1866–87).

ROGERS, Jane, (1952–), novelist, born in London. She read English at Cambridge and took a postgraduate teaching certificate at Leicester University. She has worked in secondary education and in the tertiary sector at Cambridge and Sheffield. Her novels include *Her Living Image* (1984), an account of Carolyn, a wife and mother, and her feminist alter ego Caro, 'transparent but unpredictable', who lives in a women's refuge with her friend Clare. Clare enables Carolyn to escape from the tedium and pettiness of her home; their relationship becomes the forum for a humane and thoughtful engagement with feminist arguments and concerns. Rogers's other publications include *Separate Tracks* (1983), *The Ice is Singing* (1987), and *Mr Wroe's Virgins* (1991) which has been adapted for television. Her 1995 novel *Promised Lands* interweaves contemporary lives and the first year of settlement in a nineteenth-century convict colony to produce a powerful and intricately plotted work on an epic scale.

ROGERS, Samuel (1763–1855), the son of a banker and himself a banker for some years, in his lifetime a highly successful poet, and well known as an art collector and for the celebrated 'breakfasts' which he held for over 40 years. In 1792 he published *The Pleasures of Memory*, in which the author wanders reflectively round the villages of his childhood. The work went into four editions in its first year, and by 1816 over 23,000 copies had been sold. In 1810 he published a fragmentary epic, *Columbus*; in 1814 *Jacqueline*; in 1822–8 *Italy*, a collection of verse tales; and in 1832 *Poems*. His work was praised by *Jeffrey and admired by *Byron, who came to believe that only Rogers and *Crabbe were free from 'a wrong revolutionary system'. But *Hazlitt spoke for many younger writers when he declared in a lecture in 1818 that in Rogers's work 'the decomposition of prose is substituted for the composition of poetry'.

ROGERS, Woodes (d. 1732), commander of a privateering expedition (1708–11) in which *Dampier was pilot, and in the course of which *Selkirk was discovered on the island of Juan Fernandez and rescued, the town of Guayaquil was taken and held to ransom, and a Manila ship captured. These incidents are described in Rogers's entertaining journal, *A Cruizing Voyage round the World* (1712).

Roget's Thesaurus of *English Words and Phrases*, by Dr Peter Mark Roget (1779–1879), English physician and scholar, is a compilation of words classified in groups according to the ideas they express, the purpose of which is to supply a word, or words, which most aptly express a given idea; conversely, a dictionary explains the meaning of words by supplying the ideas they are meant to convey. The volume, first published in 1852, has been followed by many successive revised editions: by Roget's son John Lewis Roget (from 1879), and his grandson Samuel Romilly Roget (from 1933). The family connection came to an end with the death of Samuel Roget in 1953.

rogue literature, a very popular type of underworld writing in the 16th and 17th cents. Its practitioners include the Kentish magistrate Thomas Harman, whose a *Caveat for Commen Cursetors* appeared in 1567; R. Copland (see under HYE WAY TO THE SPYTTELL HOUSE, THE); R. *Greene, whose pamphlets describe 'coneycatching', that is, the deception of innocents; and T. *Dekker. Rogue literature is generally vividly descriptive and often confessional, providing an important source for our knowledge of everyday common life and its language, as well as for the canting terms of thieves and beggars. It can be related to stories about *Robin Hood, *jest book literature, and early attempts at writing fiction and autobiography. A large collection of such tracts was edited by A. V. Judges in 1930.

ROJAS, Fernando de (c.1465–1541), a Spanish author born at Puebla de Montalbán, near Toledo, his family being *conversos*, or Jews converted to Christianity. He studied law at the University of Salamanca and, in spite of difficulties owing to his racial origin, rose to the position of *alcalde* (mayor) of Talavera. He is remembered for his masterpiece *Celestina*, but there is no record of any other work by his hand.

Rokeby, a poem in six cantos by Sir W. *Scott, published 1813.
The scene is laid chiefly at Rokeby near Greta Bridge in Yorkshire, and the time is immediately after the battle of Marston Moor (1644). The complicated plot involves conspiracy, attempted murder, and disguise: young Redmond O'Neale, who has helped to frustrate an attack on Rokeby Castle, is finally revealed as the lost son of Philip of Mortham, and marries Matilda, daughter of Lord Rokeby. The poem contains (Canto III) the songs 'A weary lot is thine, fair maid', 'Allan-a-Dale', and 'Brignal Banks'—

O, Brignal banks are fresh and fair,
And Greta woods are green,
I'd rather rove with Edmund there,
Than reign our English queen.

Rokesmith, John, in Dickens's *Our Mutual Friend*, the name assumed by John Harmon.

Roland, the most famous of the *Paladins of Charlemagne. According to the chronicler Einhard, his legend has the following basis of fact. In August 778 the rearguard of the French army of Charlemagne was returning through the Pyrenees from a successful expedition in the north of Spain, when it was surprised in the valley of Roncevaux by the Basque inhabitants of the mountains; the baggage was looted and all the rearguard killed, including Hrodland, count of the Breton marches. The story of this disaster was developed by the imagination of numerous poets. For the Basques were substituted the Saracens. Roland becomes the commander of the rearguard, appointed to the post at the instance of the traitor Ganelon, who is in league with the Saracen king Marsile. Oliver is introduced, Roland's companion in arms and the brother of Aude, Roland's betrothed. Oliver thrice urges Roland to summon aid by sounding his horn, but Roland from excess of pride defers doing so until too late. Charlemagne returns and destroys the pagan army. Ganelon is tried and executed. The legend has been handed down in three principal forms: in the fabricated Latin chronicle of the 12th cent. erroneously attributed to Archbishop Turpin (d. *c.*800); in the *Carmen de Proditione Guenonis* of the same epoch; and in the *Chanson de Roland*, in medieval French, also of the early 12th cent. It is a well-known tradition that Taillefer, a *jongleur* in the army of William the Conqueror, sang a poem on Roncesvalles at the battle of Hastings (1066), possibly an earlier version of the extant *Chanson*. Roland, as Orlando, is the hero of Boiardo's *Orlando innamorato* and Ariosto's *Orlando furioso*. Roland's sword was called 'Durandal' or 'Durindana', and his horn 'Olivant'. (See also OLIVER.)

Roland, Childe, see CHILDE ROLAND.

Roland de Vaux, (1) the baron of Triermain, in Scott's *The Bridal of Triermain*; (2) in Coleridge's *'Christabel'*, the estranged friend of Christabel's father.

ROLFE, Frederick William (1860–1913), who liked to call himself 'Baron Corvo', or, equally misleadingly, Fr Rolfe, by turns schoolmaster, painter, and writer. From a Dissenting background, he was a convert to Roman Catholicism and an unsuccessful candidate for the priesthood; his most outstanding novel, *Hadrian the Seventh* (1904), appears to be a dramatized autobiography—a self-justification and a dream of wish-fulfilment, in which Rolfe's protagonist, George Arthur Rose, is rescued from a life of literary poverty and elected pope. His other writings include *Stories Toto Told Me* (published in 1898, after first appearing in the

Yellow Book), *Chronicles of the House of Borgia* (1901, an eccentric historical study), *Don Tarquinio: A Kataleptic Phantasmatic Romance* (1905, a novel relating 24 hours in the life of a young nobleman in the company of the Borgias in 1495), and *The Desire and Pursuit of the Whole: A Romance of Modern Venice* (1934). This last work was written largely in 1909; Rolfe moved to Venice (where he died) in 1908, and he here describes his own poverty, his homosexual fantasies, and the beauties of Venice, as well as abusing in characteristic vein many of those who had previously befriended him, including R. H. *Benson; *Auden in a 1961 foreword describes him as 'one of the great masters of vituperation'. Two other novels (*Nicholas Crabbe; or The One and the Many*, 1958; *Don Renato: An Ideal Content*, 1963) and several fragments were published posthumously. Rolfe's style is highly ornate and idiosyncratic; his vocabulary is arcane, his allusions erudite, and although he had admirers during his lifetime, he alienated most of them by his persistent paranoia and requests for financial support. The story of his unhappy life is told by A. J. A. *Symons in *The Quest for Corvo: An Experiment in Biography* (1934). See also D. Weeks, *Corvo* (1971).

Roll, Ragman, a set of rolls in the Public Record Office, in which are recorded the instruments of homage made to Edward I by the Scottish king (Balliol), nobles, etc., at the Parliament of Berwick in 1296; so called apparently from the pendent seals attached.

ROLLAND, Romain, see ROMAN FLEUVE.

ROLLE, Richard, of Hampole (*c.*1300–49), one of the principal 14th-cent. English mystical writers, in prose and poetry. He was born at Thornton in north Yorkshire and is said to have left Oxford in his 19th year to become a hermit. He lived at various places in Yorkshire, finally at Hampole where he died, near a Cistercian nunnery where he had disciples. Among these was Margaret Kirkeby who became an anchoress in his neighbourhood and to whom a number of his major English works (notably *The Forme of Perfect Living*) are addressed. He wrote in the Yorkshire dialect, in a somewhat mannered, rhetorical language which makes much use of alliteration. The essential element in his mysticism is personal enthusiasm, rather than the rationalism of the more classical mystical writings; the echoing words he returns to are *calor, canor, dulcor*: warmth, melodiousness, sweetness. One of his earliest English writings is the *Meditations on the Passion*, and among the most familiar, later works are *Ego Dormio* and *The Commandment of Love*. The canon of his works, in Latin as well as English, is very large. (See also ANGLO-LATIN LITERATURE.) See H. E. Allen, *Writings Ascribed to Richard Rolle* (1927); *The English Writings of Richard Rolle*, ed. H. E. Allen (1931); *Yorkshire Writers: Rolle and His Followers*, C. T. Horstman (2 vols, 1895–6).

Rolliad, *Criticism on the,* a collection of Whig political satires directed against the younger *Pitt and his followers after their success at the election of 1784, first published in the *Morning Herald and Daily Advertiser* during that year. The authors, members of the 'Esto Perpetua' club, are not known with certainty, but among them were Dr French Laurence, who became Regius professor of civil law at Oxford; G. *Ellis; General Richard Fitzpatrick; and Lord John Townshend. The satires originally took the form of reviews of an imaginary epic, 'The Rolliad', which took its name from John Rolle, MP, one of Pitt's supporters, and dealt with the adventures of a mythical Norman duke, Rollo, his ancestor. These were followed by 'Political Eclogues', 'Probationary Odes' for the vacant laureateship, and 'Political Miscellanies', all directed to the same purpose, the ridicule of the Tories. A complete collection was published in 1791.

Rollo Duke of Normandy, see BLOODY BROTHER, THE.

Rolls, Pipe, the great rolls of the exchequer, comprising the various 'pipes', or enrolled accounts, of sheriffs and others for a financial year. The complete series of Pipe Rolls dates from the reign of Henry II (1155–89), but there is an isolated one (of the highest importance) of the year 1130.

Rolls Series, otherwise *Chronicles and Memorials of Great Britain and Ireland from the Invasion of the Romans to the Reign of Henry VIII*. Their publication was authorized by governments in 1847 on the suggestion of Joseph Stevenson, the archivist, and the recommendation of Sir John Romilly, master of the rolls, and it produced texts of many of the most important literary and historical writings of the Middle Ages and Renaissance. Among its most celebrated editors were the historians James Gairdner (1828–1912) and J. H. Round (1854–1928).

ROMAINS, Jules, see ROMAN FLEUVE.

roman à clef, i.e. a 'novel with a key', in which the reader (or some readers) is intended to identify real characters under fictitious names. The key is sometimes literal, sometimes figurative, and sometimes provided by the author, as in the case of Mrs *Manley's *The New Atalantis*, sometimes published separately by others, as in the case of Disraeli's *Coningsby*.

Roman Actor, The, a tragedy by *Massinger, acted 1626, printed 1629. The play is based on the life of the Emperor Domitian as told by *Suetonius and Dio Cassius.

The cruel and licentious Domitian forcibly takes from Aelius Lamia, a Roman senator, his wife Domitia. He executes Lamia and makes her his empress. He dotes on her, but she falls in love with the actor Paris. So well does he act before her a scene in which, as Iphis scorned by Anaxarete, he threatens to take his life, that she betrays her feelings to her enemies, who warn Domitian. The emperor finds her wooing Paris, and kills the actor with his own hand in the course of a play in which he takes the part of an injured husband and Paris the part of a false servant. Domitia escapes punishment but, incensed at the death of Paris and presuming on her power over the emperor, she rails at and taunts him. At last he writes down her name in a list of those marked for death. Domitia finds the list while he sleeps, and joins others whose names are there in a conspiracy. Domitian is lured from the protection of his guards and assassinated.

romance, derived from the medieval Latin word *romanice*, 'in the Roman language'. The word *roman* in Old French was applied to the popular courtly stories in verse which dealt with three traditional subjects: the legends about Arthur; Charlemagne and his knights; and stories of classical heroes especially Alexander (see MATTER). English correspondents, almost always translations, are found from the 13th cent. onwards. Some of the most distinguished include *King Horn, *Havelok, Sir *Gawain and the Green Knight, Sir *Orfeo (see also BRETON LAYS). Defining them by theme is very difficult; they usually involve the suspension of the restrictions normally attendant on human actions (often through magic) in order to illustrate a moral point. From the 15th cent. onwards English romances are mostly in prose, and some 16th-cent. examples were the inspiration for *Spenser and Shakespeare (as, for instance, *Pandosto by R. Greene was used by Shakespeare in *The Winter's Tale). A new interest in the medieval romance (in writers such as Sir W. *Scott and *Keats) contributed to the naming of 19th-cent. *Romanticism, though the term was also used to embrace some sentimental novels from the 18th cent. onwards, as in the *Mills and Boon romances of the modern era.

Romance languages, the group of modern languages descended from Latin (which itself joins with them to form the branch of *Indo-European known as Italic), the chief of which are French, Italian, Spanish, Portuguese, and Romanian (and, of literary-historical importance, *Provençal).

Roman d'Alexandre, see ALEXANDER THE GREAT.

Roman de Brut and ***Roman de Rou,*** see WACE.

Roman de la rose. The first 4,058 lines of this allegorical romance were written c.1230 by Guillaume de Lorris (d. 1237) to expound 'the whole art of love'; the remaining 17,622 lines were composed c.1275 by Jean de Meun as a more wide-ranging anatomy of love within a social and philosophical framework. The story in de Lorris's part of the poem is an allegorical presentation of *courtly love; the allegorical figures mostly embody various aspects of the lady whom the lover-narrator meets in his endeavours to reach the rose which symbolizes the lady's love. The story is set in the walled garden of the god of love, the unpleasant realities of life being depicted on the walls outside. In the second part Jean de Meun shows love in a wider context of scholarship, philosophy, and morals, shifting the work from the courtly to the encyclopaedic literary tradition, in line with the rationalist and compendious spirit of the 13th cent. The poem, in its allegorical dream form and in its presentation of both the courtly and the philosophical discussions of love, remained an immense literary influence all through the later Middle Ages, both inside and outside France. About one-third of the whole (ll. 1–5,154 and 10,679–12,360) is translated in the Middle English *The Romaunt of the Rose, the first part of which may be by *Chaucer. The *Roman* was much the most important literary influence on writings in English in the 14th cent.

Ed. D. Poiriou (Paris, 1974); trans. C. Dahlberg (1971); A. M. F. Gunn, *The Mirror of Love: A Reinterpretation of the Romance of the Rose* (1952).

Roman de Renart, see REYNARD THE FOX.

roman fleuve, the French term for a novel sequence. The practice of pursuing a family story through a number of related novels in order to render a comprehensive account of a social period ultimately derives from *Balzac and *Zola, but it reached its culmination between 1900 and 1940. Its major exemplars were: Romain Rolland (1866–1944), whose *Jean Christophe* (10 vols, 1905–12) describes the career of a musical genius; Roger Martin du Gard (1881–1958), whose *Les Thibault* (10 vols, 1922–40) explores the reaction of two brothers against their bourgeois inheritance; Georges Duhamel (1884–1966), whose *Chronique des Pasquiers* (10 vols, 1933–41) traces the moral and cultural development of a Parisian family; and Jules Romains (1885–1972), whose *Les Hommes de bonne volonté* (27 vols, 1932–47) offers a panorama of French society between 1910 and 1940. Translations of these works have been popular in England, but the English version of the phenomenon, descending from *Trollope and including such novelists as *Galsworthy and C. P. *Snow, did not have the same conviction and consistency.

romantic fiction, see p.870.

Romanticism, see p.872.

Romany Rye, The, a novel by *Borrow, published 1857. 'Romany Rye' in Romany language means 'Gypsy Gentleman', a name applied to Borrow from his youth by Ambrose Smith, the Norfolk gypsy. This book is a sequel to *Lavengro, and continues in a less accomplished style the story of the author's wanderings and adventures.

Romaunt of the Rose, The, a translation into Middle English octosyllabics of about one-third of the *Roman de la rose, lines 1–5,154 and 10,679–12,360, made in the time of *Chaucer and usually included in editions of his Works (such as the Riverside) because previously
(cont. on p.874)

(*cont. on p.874*)

A capacious and much-contested category, romantic fiction could be said to pre-date the novel—as in the medieval verses of courtly love written in the vernacular, the 'popular' languages derived from Latin—or to coincide with its origins in the 17th cent., when the first novels are romances of illicit love. If the English novel's literary canon begins in the 18th cent. with Samuel *Richardson's *Pamela and *Clarissa, these, too, are classic romantic fictions: the first, a story in which our heroine tames the rapacious rake through her intelligence and virtue; the latter, one in which she fails to do so and must, tragically, pay with her life. In the same way that Richardson's *Pamela* becomes, in the hands of the inventor of the modern novel Henry *Fielding, the satire *Shamela Andrews, the novel emerges as a literary form only in its constantly renewed attempt to distinguish itself from romantic fiction—an increasingly scapegoated genre, soon irretrievably gendered female.

As literary generations succeed one another, there is a tendency for the realism of one epoch to look like romance to the readers and writers of the next. Currencies or novelties grow remote, past social forms seem exotic or idealized, language overblown. Remoteness, exoticism, idealization, excess in language or emotion are all characteristics which render fiction romantic. In her literary history of 1785, *The Progress of Romance*, Clara *Reeve already makes a distinction between the 'novel' which deals with everyday life and the 'romance', a more elevated form concerned with high emotion, high life, and past times.

Nonetheless, the term romantic fiction remains slippery and its use through time replete with ironies. The venerable Sir Walter *Scott, who self-consciously wrote romances, criticized Jane *Austen for not being romantic enough. Cupid, he complained in a review of *Emma, was unfairly left out of popular novels. Romance can render young men's characters 'honourable, dignified and disinterested'. This latter thought would surely startle today's male critics, as much as the former would surprise all viewers and readers of Jane Austen who consider her period pieces the very stuff of romance for all her witty balancing act between love and property. Then, too, it is from Austen's work that contemporary popular romance of the Harlequin *Mills & Boon, happy-ever-after variety derives its key storylines.

One of the problems which haunts both the critics and writers of romantic fiction is its enduring popularity as a genre: as the size of the reading public grew from the 18th cent. onwards and spread down the ladder of class, so too did the size of the public for romance, particularly the female public. Because of the gender and mass of its readers, critics are quick to lash out at the form and accuse it of corruption. 'He who burns a romance purifies the human mind', wrote Richard Carlisle, the radical 19th-cent. publisher, capturing the typical tone of puritan revulsion that the form elicits in the public sphere. 'Those damned romantic novels of romantically damned love!' echoes a *Guardian review of 1967, guarding our public morals against the possibility of female transgression. It is as if women readers—wives and daughters and servants—will be led forever astray once their imaginations have been fired by the likes of *Ouida's capricious heroine Cigarette in *Under Two Flags*, or, indeed, the passionate Anna Karenina (*Tolstoy), or the audacious Scarlett O'Hara (M. *Mitchell).

Women writers, who, like their male counterparts, are hardly averse to a little critical acclaim, have often been equally scathing about romantic fiction, much of it written by women. The didactic anti-*Jacobin writers of the late 18th cent.—for example Mary Ann Hanway and Jane West—in their attempt to consolidate ideals of bourgeois domesticity, inveighed against the passions and romance, only now and again to find themselves writing what everyone else called passionate romances. In *Northanger Abbey Jane Austen parodied the excesses of the *Gothic romance. George *Eliot—whose *Daniel Deronda, with its mysterious secrets and spirited, rather Gothic, heroine Gwendolen Harleth, borders on romance—in an exercise of distancing herself from lesser writers, wrote a scathing attack on 'Silly Novels by Lady Novelists', pointing out their absurdities, 'the particular quality of silliness that predominates in them—the frothy, the prosy, the pious or the pedantic'. Like the great mass of fiction, romance is not always well written, but unlike the great mass of what could be called male romance—stories of pistols and pirates and wild beasts, of criminal life, of spies in exotic locations and hard-boiled detectives—it has had more than its share of opprobrium. In part this is undoubtedly due to cultural fears about and for women, both as readers and writers.

Since an exploration of the life of the emotions is romantic fiction's predominant theme, any map of the genre must be a large one. Innumerable pseudonymous, anonymous, and forgotten novels as well as more famous ones find a place there. A quick historical charting of peaks and fertile valleys would have to begin with Richardson, who set out a psychological style plus the two storylines and two central characters which became archetypal. Through her sensitive, young, middle-class heroines with their sharp eye for the *mores* of the world in which they will meet their match, Fanny *Burney introduced a new note and combined romance with the novel of manners. Jane Austen perfected the form and made the story of the young woman's courtship, the misunderstandings during it, and the growth in self-knowledge which attends the process a model for English fiction.

All of Austen's fictions end with the desired goal of marriage. In one sense the Gothic romances, which were the great vogue of her day, provide the dark side of the post-marital coin. The strange, ghostly landscapes and frightening, claustrophobic castles of Ann *Radcliffe, or her even more sensational and lower-brow kin Charlotte Dacre (1782–c.1841), are settings where the innocent bride's fears and fantasies about terrifying husbands and fathers can be acted out. Amongst many other fictions, Daphne *du Maurier's famous *Rebecca* (1938) owes not a little to the Gothic romance: a pure young heroine, swept off her feet by a rake, is locked into the castle of marriage and made dependent on a man who turns out to have murdered his first wife because she was grand and promiscuous rather than docile and domestic. The more pedestrian side of post-marital relations is explored in an abundant list of domestic romances which sentimentalize the duties of the good wife and faithful daughter, but not without underlining problems and the occasional tug of a would-be seducer. The prolific Margaret *Oliphant, and E. D. E. N. Southworth are two in a long line which leads to the contemporary *Aga saga of Joanna Trollope.

Towering over the romantic fiction of the mid-19th cent. are the *Brontë sisters, in particular Emily and Charlotte, who with *Wuthering Heights* and *Jane Eyre* set a standard, the first for the novel of doomed love, the second for the novel of the young woman's climb towards moral independence and a passion underscored by equality. The much-read and much-castigated *sensation novelists of the end of the century, Wilkie *Collins and Mary *Braddon amongst them, are indebted to these, and not only for the secrets found in the attic or the family tree.

At the turn of the century, Henry *James hijacked romantic fiction and transformed it into the art of the novel of high consciousness. Meanwhile, scores of women wrote and read variations on the old themes. The romantic fiction of the 20th cent. may be pure exotic escapism, like Ethel M. Dell's *The Way of an Eagle* (1912), E. M. Hull's *The Sheik* (1919), or the many novels of Danielle Steel and Catherine *Cookson; or historical escapism, at its best in Georgette *Heyer's Regency romances; or the simplest but phenomenally successful Mills & Boon brand of romance, which sells 13 million books a year in the UK alone. Or it may—with more or less sensationalism or refinement, and marriages with the novel of manners, domestic life, or thriller—chart shifts in the place of women and the relations between the sexes. This is the terrain of the best-selling blockbusters of the 1980s and 1990s, written by Jackie Collins, Judith Krantz, Barbara Taylor Bradford, Jilly Cooper, Rosie Thomas, and Sally Beauman, or, in a more psychological vein, by Lisa Appignanesi and Susan Gee. One could say that it is also the terrain of Anita *Brookner, Mary *Wesley, and the Margaret *Drabble of *The Millstone* or *The Waterfall*. Whatever its critical reception or height of brow, whatever the recurrent accusations of corrupting women and imprisoning them in masochistic longing, it is clear that, by focusing on women and giving them the power to adventure or to tame the threatening male, romantic fiction is a form readers enjoy. In the hands of playful postmodernists, such as David *Lodge in *Small World: An Academic Romance* or A. S. *Byatt in *Possession*, it has even, once again, been turned into literary fiction.

A profound and irreversible transformation in artistic styles, in cultural attitudes, and in the relations between artist and society is evident in Western literature and other arts in the first half of the 19th cent. In Britain, a stark contrast appears between representative works of the preceding *Augustan age and those of leading figures in what became known as the Romantic movement or 'Romantic Revival' in the period from about 1780 to about 1848 (the 'Romantic period'): *Blake, *Burns, *Wordsworth, *Coleridge, *Southey, *Scott, *Byron, *Shelley, *Keats, *Hazlitt, *De Quincey, *Carlyle, Emily *Brontë and Charlotte *Brontë. To define the general character or basic principle of this momentous shift, which later historians have called Romanticism, though, is notoriously difficult, partly because the Romantic temperament itself resisted the very impulse of definition, favouring the indefinite and the boundless.

In the most abstract terms, Romanticism may be regarded as the triumph of the values of imaginative spontaneity, visionary originality, wonder, and emotional self-expression over the classical standards of balance, order, restraint, proportion, and objectivity. Its name derives from *romance, the literary form in which desires and dreams prevail over everyday realities.

Romanticism arose from a period of wider turbulence, euphoria, and uncertainty. Political and intellectual movements of the late 18th cent. encouraged the assertion of individual and national rights, denying legitimacy (forcibly in the American and French revolutions) to kings and courtiers. In Britain, the expansions of commerce, journalism, and literacy had loosened the dependency of artists and writers upon noble patrons, releasing them to discover their own audiences in an open cultural market place—as Scott and Byron did most successfully—or to toil in unrewarded obscurity, like Blake. Nourished by Protestant conceptions of intellectual liberty, the Romantic writers tended to cast themselves as prophetic voices crying in the wilderness, dislocated from the social hierarchy. The Romantic author, unlike the more socially integrated Augustan writers, was a sort of modern hermit or exile, who usually granted a special moral value to similar outcast figures in his or her own writing: the pedlars and vagrants in Wordsworth's poems, Coleridge's *Ancient Mariner, Mary *Shelley's man-made monster, and the many tormented pariahs in the works of Byron and P. B. Shelley—who were themselves wandering outcasts from respectable English society.

From this marginal position, the Romantic author wrote no longer to or on behalf of a special caste but, in Wordsworth's phrase, as 'a man speaking to men', his utterance grounded in the sincerity of his personal vision and experience. To most of the Romantics, the polished wit of the Augustans seemed shallow, heartless, and mechanically bound by artificial 'rules' of *neo-classical taste. Although some (notably Keats and Shelley) continued to employ elements of Greek mythology and to adapt the classical form of the *ode, they scorned the imitation of classical models as an affront to the autonomy of the all-important creative imagination. Well above *Horace or *Juvenal they revered Shakespeare and *Milton as their principal models of the *sublime embodied in the poet's boundless imaginative genius. In this, they took the partly nationalistic direction followed by Romantic poets and composers in other countries, who likewise rediscovered and revalued their local vernacular traditions.

Although inheriting much of the humane and politically liberal spirit of the *Enlightenment, the Romantics largely rejected its analytic rationalism, associating it with the coldly calculating mentality of contemporary commerce, politics, and moral philosophy (as for example in the work of *Bentham). Wordsworth warned against the destructive tendency of the 'meddling intellect' to intrude upon the sanctities of the human heart, and he argued that the opposite of poetry was not prose but science. The Romantic revolt against scientific empiricism is compatible with the prevailing trend of German philosophy, notably *Kant's 'transcendental' idealism, of which Coleridge and Carlyle were dedicated students. This new philosophical idealism endorsed the Romantics' view of the human mind as organically creative, and encouraged most of them to regard the natural world as a living mirror to the soul, not as dead matter for scientific dissection.

In reaction against the spiritual emptiness of the modern calculating age, Romanticism cultivated various forms of nostalgia and of *primitivism, following *Rousseau in contrasting the 'natural' man (or child) with the hypocrisies and corruptions of modern society. The imaginative sovereignty of the child, in the works of Blake and Wordsworth, implicitly shames the inauthenticity of adulthood, while the dignified simplicity of rural life is more generally invoked in condemnation of urban civilization. The superior nobility of the past tends also to be, as we now say, 'romanticized', although less for its actual social forms than for its imaginative conceptions of the ideal and the heroic, as reflected in Shakespeare, in chivalric romance, and in balladry. Antiquaries of the 18th cent., notably *Percy in his *Reliques and *Macpherson in his Ossianic poems, had won a new respect for the older forms of popular or 'folk' poetry and legend, upon which Southey, Scott, and several other Romantic writers drew for materials and forms, notably in the *Lyrical Ballads (1798) of Wordsworth and Coleridge.

These kinds of change manifest themselves in the literary productions of the Romantic writers in widely varied ways, as may be expected in a movement that unleashed individualism and that privileged the particular experience over the general rule. In general, though, Romantic writing exhibits a new emotional intensity taken to unprecedented extremes of joy or dejection, rapture or horror, and an extravagance of apparently egotistic self-projection. As a whole, it is usually taken to represent a second renaissance of literature in Britain, especially in lyric and narrative poetry, which displaced the Augustan cultivation of satiric and didactic modes. The prose styles of Hazlitt, De Quincey, Charles *Lamb, and Carlyle also show a marked renewal of vitality, flexibility, subjective tone, and what Hazlitt called 'gusto'. The arts of prose fiction were extended by Scott's historical novels, by the sensational effects of *Gothic fiction, and by the emergence of the short story form in the Edinburgh and London magazines. Although Byron, Shelley, and others wrote important dramatic poems, drama written for the theatres is generally agreed to be by far the weakest side of Romantic literature. On the other hand, despite the often vituperative and partisan conduct of reviewing in *Blackwood's Magazine and other periodicals, this was a great age of literary criticism and theory, most notably in the writings of Coleridge and Hazlitt, and in major essays by Wordsworth and Shelley.

Simplified accounts of Romanticism in Britain date its arrival from the appearance in 1798 of the Lyrical Ballads or in 1800 of Wordsworth's preface (effectively a manifesto) to that collection. Several important tendencies in the latter part of the 18th cent., however, have been recognized as 'pre-Romantic' currents, suggesting a more gradual evolution. Among these should be mentioned *'graveyard poetry', the novel of *sentiment, the cult of the sublime, and the *Sturm und Drang phase of German literature in the 1770s led by *Schiller and the young *Goethe; all of these influences encouraged a deeper emotional emphasis than Augustan or neo-classical convention allowed.

Romanticism flourished in the United States in the somewhat later period, between 1820 and 1860, with J. F. *Cooper's historical romances, *Emerson's essays, *Melville's novels, *Poe's tales, the poetry of Poe, *Longfellow, and *Whitman, and the nature writings of *Thoreau.

As for the point at which Romanticism ends, it would be safer to say, especially after the largely neo-Romantic cultural ferment of the 1960s, that this end still shows little sign of arriving. The convenient and conventional divisions of literary history into distinct 'periods' are particularly misleading if they obscure the extent to which the Romantic tradition remains unbroken in the later 19th cent. and through the 20th. The associated work of *Ruskin, the *Pre-Raphaelite Brotherhood, and the Victorian advocates of the *Gothic Revival, indeed displays a hardening of Romantic attitudes in its nostalgia and its opposition to an unpoetical modern civilization; and the same might be said of W. B. *Yeats and D. H. *Lawrence in the early 20th cent. Late 20th-cent. culture displays a spectrum of latter-day Romantic features, ranging from the rebelliousness of rock lyrics and other forms of songwriting, to the anti-Enlightenment themes of post-*structuralist literary theory.

Critical opposition to the Romantic inheritance, in the name of *'classical' ideals, was advanced by Matthew *Arnold in the 1850s, and by some later critics under his influence, including the American scholar Irving *Babbitt, whose book Rousseau and Romanticism (1919) condemned the Romantic movement as an irresponsible 'pilgrimage in the void' that had licensed self-indulgent escapism and nationalist aggression. His student T. S. *Eliot continued the anti-Romantic campaign, although Eliot's own poetry, like Arnold's, was nonetheless inescapably 'romantic' in its nostalgia and sense of alienation. Some damage was done by Eliot's disciples to the reputations of Shelley and other Romantic writers, from which they have since at least partially recovered.

See: M. H. Abrams, Natural Supernaturalism (1971); M. Butler, Romantics, Rebels, and Reactionaries (1981); J. McGann (ed.), The New Oxford Book of Romantic Period Verse (1993); A. Day, Romanticism (1996).

attributed to him. *Skeat (in *The Chaucer Canon*, 1900) argued that only Part A (1–1,705, corresponding to 1–1,672 in de Lorris's French) is by Chaucer, and that B (1,706–5,810, being the remainder of de Lorris, up to 4,432, and Jean de Meun as far as 5,154 of the French) and C (5,811–7,696, corresponding to de Meun 10,679–12,360) are not his. A. Brusendorff in *The Chaucer Tradition* (1925) argued against Skeat that all the parts were by Chaucer, but almost all modern authorities follow Skeat; his findings were strongly corroborated in 1967 by Ronald Sutherland who showed that A is descended from a different manuscript tradition from B and C.

In this dream poem the narrator enters the Garden of Mirth where he sees various allegorized figures and falls in love with a rosebud. Parts A and B describe the dreamer's instructions by the god of love, his being befriended by Bialacoil who is imprisoned, the opposition of Daunger and other adverse figures, and (in the Jean de Meun section) the discourse of Resoun; Part C is a fragment of Jean de Meun, satirizing the hypocrisy (represented by Fals-Semblant) of religion, women, and the social order. Part A is a closer translation than the other sections. See *The Romaunt of the Rose and Le Roman de la Rose: A Parallel-Text Edition*, ed. R. A. Sutherland (1967).

Romeo and Juliet, *Shakespeare's first romantic tragedy, based on Arthur Brooke's poem *The Tragicall Historye of Romeus and Juliet* (1562), a translation from the French of Boaistuau of one of *Bandello's *Novelle*. Shakespeare's play was probably written about 1595 and first printed in a 'bad' quarto in 1597; a good quarto published in 1599 and reprinted in 1609 served as the copy for the play's text in the First *Folio of 1623.

The Montagues and Capulets, the two chief families of Verona, are bitter enemies; Escalus, the prince, threatens anyone who disturbs the peace with death. Romeo, son of old Lord Montague, is in love with Lord Capulet's niece Rosaline. But at a feast given by Capulet, which Romeo attends disguised by a mask, he sees and falls in love with Juliet, Capulet's daughter, and she with him. After the feast he overhears, under her window, Juliet's confession of her love for him, and wins her consent to a secret marriage. With the help of Friar Laurence, they are wedded next day. Mercutio, a friend of Romeo, meets Tybalt, of the Capulet family, who is infuriated by his discovery of Romeo's presence at the feast, and they quarrel. Romeo comes on the scene, and attempts to reason with Tybalt, but Tybalt and Mercutio fight, and Mercutio falls. Then Romeo draws and Tybalt is killed. The prince, Montague, and Capulet come up, and Romeo is sentenced to banishment. Early next day, after spending the night with Juliet, he leaves Verona for Mantua, counselled by the friar, who intends to reveal Romeo's marriage at an opportune moment. Capulet proposes to marry Juliet to Count Paris, and when she seeks excuses to avoid this, peremptorily insists. Juliet consults the friar, who

bids her consent to the match, but on the night before the wedding drink a potion which will render her apparently lifeless for 42 hours. He will warn Romeo, who will rescue her from the vault on her awakening and carry her to Mantua. The friar's message to Romeo miscarries, and Romeo hears that Juliet is dead. Buying poison, he comes to the vault to have a last sight of Juliet. He chances upon Count Paris outside the vault; they fight and Paris is killed. Then Romeo, after a last kiss on Juliet's lips, drinks the poison and dies. Juliet awakes and finds Romeo dead by her side, and the cup still in his hand. Guessing what has happened, she stabs herself and dies. The story is unfolded by the friar and Count Paris's page, and Montague and Capulet, faced by the tragic results of their enmity, are reconciled. The play begins with a sonnet spoken by the chorus and in its poetry, language, and plot reflects the sonnet craze of the 1590s, from which period Shakespeare's own sequence dates.

ROMNEY, George (1734–1802), portrait painter, born in Dalton-in-Furness, the son of a builder. He spent two years in Italy (1773–5) and the poise and graceful rhythms of his most distinguished works suggest his love of *Raphael and the antique. Yet Romney (who was a friend of *Hayley, who later wrote Romney's life, and of *Flaxman) felt trapped by the demands of portraiture. His many drawings of literary and historical subjects develop from a neo-classical treatment towards a wilder, more violent style; and his increasing obsession with *sublime and horrific subject matter from *Aeschylus, *Milton, and Shakespeare links him to *Fuseli and J. H. Mortimer (c.1741–79). Romney, after 1781, became obsessed with Emma Hart, later Lady Hamilton, whom he painted many times.

Romola, a novel by G. *Eliot, published 1863.

The background of the novel is Florence at the end of the 15th cent., the troubled period, following the expulsion of the Medici, of the expedition of Charles VIII, distracted counsels in the city, the excitement caused by the preaching of *Savonarola, and acute division between the popular party and the supporters of the Medici. The various historical figures, including Charles VIII, Machiavelli, and Savonarola himself, are drawn with great care, as well as the whole picturesque complexion of the city, though the novel is generally held to be overloaded with detail, and has never been one of her most admired. The story is that of the purification by trials of the noble-natured Romola, devoted daughter of an old blind scholar. Into their lives comes a clever, adaptable young Greek, Tito Melema, whose self-indulgence develops into utter perfidy. He robs, and abandons in imprisonment, the benefactor of his childhood, Baldassare. He cruelly goes through a mock marriage ceremony with the innocent little contadina Tessa. After marrying Romola he wounds her deepest feelings by betraying her father's solemn trust. He plays a double game in the political intrigues of the day. Nemesis pursues and at last overtakes him in the person of old Baldassare, who escapes from imprisonment crazed with sorrow and suffering. Romola, with her love for her husband turned to contempt, and her trust in Savonarola destroyed by his falling away from his high prophetic mission, is left in isolation, from which she is rescued by the discovery of her duty in self-sacrifice. The novel was illustrated by *Leighton, much to George Eliot's satisfaction.

rondeau, a French verse form consisting of ten (or, in stricter sense, 13) lines, having only two rhymes throughout, and with the opening words used twice as a refrain. It became popular in England in the late 19th cent. and was much used by *Dobson, *Swinburne, and others. The rondel is a form of rondeau, again using two rhymes and a refrain, usually of three stanzas.

rondel, see RONDEAU.

RONSARD, Pierre de (1524–85), French poet, leader of the *Pléiade. He won early success with the publication of the *Odes* of 1550, and the first of a series of love sequences, *Les Amours* of 1552–3. The latter collection (the 'Cassandre' cycle) contains the famous 'Mignonne, allons voir si la rose'; there followed the *Continuation des Amours* of 1555 and the *Nouvelle Continuation des Amours* of 1556, forming the basis of the 'Marie' cycle. His last important love sequence, the *Sonets pour Hélène* of 1578, contains the sonnet 'Quand vous serez bien vieille, au soir à la chandelle'. Besides the collections of love poetry, Ronsard wrote on a wide variety of themes, political, philosophical, pastoral, and religious, his works including *Les Hymnes* (1555–6), the *Discours des misères de ce temps* (1562), written at the beginning of the religious wars, and the unfinished epic *La Franciade* (1572). He exercised considerable influence on the English sonnet writers of the 16th cent.

Room at the Top,, see BRAINE.

Room of One's Own, A, a feminist essay by V. *Woolf, published 1929 and based on two lectures on 'Women and Fiction' delivered in Oct. 1928 to Newnham College and Girton College, Cambridge.

The author describes the educational, social, and financial disadvantages and prejudices against which women have struggled throughout history (using the fate of a hypothetical talented sister of Shakespeare as an illustration; her literary aspirations end in suicide), arguing that women will not be able to write well and freely until they have the privacy and independence implied by 'a room of one's own' and 'five hundred a year'. She pays tribute to women writers of the past (including A. *Behn, D. *Osborne and J. *Austen, the *Brontës); to women's achievements in the form of the novel, which suited her because, unlike older forms of literature, it was 'young enough to be soft in her hands'; and projects a future in which increasing equality would enable women to become not only novelists but poets. In the last chapter she discusses the concept of 'androgyny', pleading for unity and harmony rather than a rigid separation into 'male' and 'female' qualities: 'Perhaps a mind that is purely masculine cannot create, any more than a mind that is purely feminine.'

Room with a View, A, a novel by E. M. *Forster, published 1908.

It opens in an English *pensione* in Florence with a confrontation between Lucy Honeychurch's chaperone Miss Bartlett and the upstart Mr Emerson and his son George; the two men offer to exchange rooms, in order to give the ladies the benefit of a room with a view, a favour which they reluctantly accept. The novel describes the inmates of the Pensione Bertolini, among them the clergyman Mr Beebe and the 'original' lady novelist Miss Lavish, and their reactions to Italy and to one another. Lucy, an artistic but immature girl, is disturbed first by witnessing a street murder, and then by an impulsive embrace from George Emerson during an excursion to Fiesole. Miss Bartlett removes her charge from these dangers, and the two return to Summer Street, in Surrey, where Lucy becomes engaged to a cultured dilettante, Cecil Vyse, whom Mr Beebe, who has reappeared as the local vicar, ominously describes as 'an ideal bachelor'. The Bertolini cast continues to reassemble as the Emersons take a villa in the neighbourhood. Lucy comes to realize that she loves George, not Cecil, but it takes her some time to extricate herself from what she describes as 'the muddle'. The second half of the drama is played against a sharply and intimately observed background of tennis and tea parties and amateur piano recitals; it ends in the Pensione Bertolini, with George and Lucy on their honeymoon.

Roots (1959) by A. *Wesker, a sequel to *Chicken Soup with Barley*. It portrays the effects of Ronnie Kahn's idealism on his fiancée Beatie Bryant, the daughter of a Norfolk agricultural labourer; she returns to her family for a visit full of his praises and his notions, but her mother and sister retaliate with talk of pop songs and gossip about operations. As she is trying to rouse them to share her interests, a letter arrives from Ronnie cancelling his impending visit and breaking off the engagement. Initially despairing, Beatie finds her own voice as she attacks her family for its acceptance of the third-rate. The third part of the trilogy, *I'm Talking about Jerusalem* (1960), shows the collapse of the Utopian dreams of Ronnie's sister Ada and her newly demobbed husband Dave. Beatie Bryant's story is continued in Wesker's first novel, *Honey* (2005).

ROPER, Margaret (1505–44), daughter of Sir T. *More. According to Stapleton (1535–98), she purchased the head of her dead father nearly a month after it had been exposed on London Bridge and preserved it in spices until her death. It is believed that it was buried with her. *Tennyson alludes to this:

her, who clasped in her last trance
Her murdered father's head.
('A Dream of Fair Women')

ROPER, William (1496–1578), of Lincoln's Inn. He married Sir T. *More's daughter Margaret (above) and wrote an early life of his father-in-law first published at Saint-Omer (1626).

RORTY, Richard (1931–   ), American philosopher, and the best-known contemporary advocate of pragmatism in the tradition of J. *Dewey. Influenced also by *Heidegger, *Derrida, and the later *Wittgenstein, his critique of the traditional philosophical project leads many to identify him as an exponent of *postmodernism. His major work *Philosophy and the Mirror of Nature* (1979) rejects conceptions of language and thought as representations mirroring an independent reality, while *Contingency, Irony and Solidarity* (1989) applies this anti-foundationalist perspective to ethics and politics, presenting an 'ironic' defence of liberalism.

ROS, Amanda McKittrick, née Anna Margaret McKittrick (1860–1939), Irish writer, known as 'the World's Worst Novelist', wrote *Irene Iddesleigh* (1897), *Delina Delaney* (1898), and other works, remarkable for their extraordinary and unselfconsciously colourful prose, to which A. *Huxley devoted an essay, 'Euphues Redivivus' (1923).

ROSA, Salvator (1615–73), Neapolitan painter, etcher, satirical poet, and actor. He painted genre scenes, battles, marines, and ambitious figure compositions, but has remained most famous for his macabre subjects (witches, monsters, meditations on death) and for his wild, craggy landscapes. In England his reputation rose steadily throughout the 18th cent. Horace *Walpole, crossing the Alps in 1739, exclaimed 'Precipices, mountains, torrents, wolves, rumblings—Salvator Rosa', and writers on the *picturesque frequently invoked his name. His stormy personality also fascinated artists, and with the publication of Lady *Morgan's biography in 1824 the legends associated with him—that he had lived with bandits and fought in a popular uprising in Naples—became more important than his pictures. He came to represent the archetypal Romantic artist, outlawed by a corrupt society, whose genius bore comparison with Shakespeare.

Rosa Bud, a character in Dickens's *Edwin Drood*.

Rosalind, (1) in Spenser's *Shepheardes Calender* and *Colin Clouts Come Home Againe*, an unknown lady celebrated by the poet as his love; (2) the heroine of Shakespeare's *As You Like It*, whose chief source was Lodge's *Rosalynde*.

Rosaline, (1) in Shakespeare's *Love's Labour's Lost*, a lady attendant on the princess of France, and loved by *Berowne; (2) in his *Romeo and Juliet*, Capulet's niece,

with whom Romeo is in love before he sees *Juliet. She is mentioned, but does not appear in the play. Both Rosalines are, like the lady of the *Sonnets, described as being dark.

Rosalynde, *Euphues Golden Legacie*, a pastoral romance in the style of Lyly's *Euphues, diversified with sonnets and eclogues, written by *Lodge during his voyage to the Canaries ('everie line was wet with a surge'), published 1590.

The story is borrowed in part from *The Tale of *Gamelyn* and was dramatized by Shakespeare in *As You Like It*. Lodge's Rosader is Shakespeare's Orlando; Saladyne is Oliver; Alinda, Celia; and Rosalind is common to both. Jaques and Touchstone have no equivalents. The ill-treatment of Rosader (Orlando) is more developed by Lodge, and the restoration of the rightful duke to his dukedom is effected by arms instead of persuasion. Lodge's romance, which includes such well-known lyrics as 'Love in my bosome like a Bee | Doth sucke his sweete', is also diversified by a variety of rhetorical speeches and descriptions.

ROSAMOND, Fair, Rosamond Clifford (d. ?1176), probably mistress of Henry II in 1174. She was buried in the choir of Godstow Abbey near Oxford, and her remains were removed to the chapter house there *c.*1191. A legend transmitted by *Stow following *Higden declares that Henry kept her in a maze-like house in Woodstock where only he could find her, but the queen, *Eleanor of Aquitaine, traced her whereabouts by following a thread and 'so dealt with her that she lived not long after'. The story is told in a ballad by *Deloney included in Percy's *Reliques; *Daniel published in 1592 'The Complaint of Rosamond', a poem in rhyme-royal; and *Addison wrote an opera, *Rosamond*, in 1707.

Rosciad, The (1761), a *mock-heroic satire by Charles *Churchill in heroic couplets, originally 730 lines, but expanded in later editions to 1,090.

It describes the attempt to find a worthy successor to Roscius, the celebrated Roman comic actor who died *c.*62 BC. It provides satiric sketches of many famous theatrical personalities of the day, both actors and critics (including *Quin, *Foote, and *Colman the elder). It caused a great sensation, and T. *Davies in his *Life of Garrick* wrote that 'the players . . . ran about like so many stricken deer.' But Churchill's criticism is not all negative, and his praise of *Garrick, chosen to succeed Roscius, is high.

ROSCOE, William (1753–1831), lawyer and banker, book-collector, writer, scholar, and botanist. He published his early verses in 1777, and from then until the end of his life, a considerable number of works of poetry, biography, jurisprudence, botany, and arguments against the slave trade. His principal work was his *Life of Lorenzo de' Medici* (1795). In 1805 (having now acquired Greek) he published the *Life of Leo the Tenth*, and in 1806 *The Butterfly's Ball and the Grass-*

hopper's Feast, which became a children's classic. His edition of *Pope appeared in 1824. He did much to stimulate an interest in Italy and Italian literature in England.

ROSCOMMON, earl of, see Dillon.

Rose and the Ring, The, a fairy story written and illustrated by *Thackeray, first published 1855.

The magic rose and ring have the property of making those who have possession of them seem irresistibly attractive, which introduces comic complications into the story of Prince Giglio and Princess Rosalba, who have been ousted from their proper positions as a result of the Fairy Blackstick's wish that they shall suffer 'a little misfortune'. Thackeray makes gentle fun both of *fairy-story conventions, and of 'improving' children's books in this 'Fireside Pantomime for Great and Small Children'.

'Rose Aylmer', a short poem by W. S. *Landor, published 1806, on the daughter of Lord Aylmer. She was an early love of Landor's, but on her mother's second marriage she was sent out to her aunt at Calcutta, where she died at the age of 20.

ROSENBERG, Isaac (1890–1918), war poet, born in Bristol. He moved with his family to Whitechapel in 1897; his parents were émigrés from western Russia, and his father, a scholarly Jew, worked as a pedlar and market-dealer. During his irregular East End schooling Isaac learned to paint, and began to experiment with poetry. He became an apprentice engraver at 14, but in 1911 another Jewish family paid for him to attend the Slade School of Art; in 1912 he published at his own expense a collection of poems, *Night and Day*, and was encouraged by *Bottomley, *Pound, and others. In 1915 he published another volume of verse, *Youth*, which passed largely unregarded. In the same year he defied his family's pacifist views and joined the army, arriving as a private in the trenches in 1916. He was killed in action. His poetry is forceful, rich in its vocabulary, and starkly realistic in its attitudes to war; Rosenberg greatly disliked *Brooke's 'begloried sonnets'. His poor Jewish urban background gives the poems a note not found in the work of his fellow war poets. His reputation was slow to grow with the public; Bottomley edited a selection of his poems and letters, introduced by *Binyon, in 1922, but it was not until his *Collected Works* appeared in 1937 that his importance became generally accepted. A biography by Jean Liddiard appeared in 1975 and there is an edition of his works, ed. V. M. Noakes (1998); see also J. M. Wilson, *Isaac Rosenberg: Poet and Painter* (1975).

ROSENCRANTZ and **Guildenstern,** courtiers who serve the king in Shakespeare's *Hamlet*; both of their names were current in Denmark at the time of the play's writing. In *Hamlet* the two men always appear together; their view of the play is interpreted in Stoppard's *Rosencrantz and Guildenstern Are Dead*.

Rosencrantz and Guildenstern Are Dead, a comedy by T. *Stoppard, performed and published 1966, which places the peripheral 'attendant lords' from *Hamlet at the centre of a drama in which they appear as bewildered witnesses and predestined victims. This device is used to serious as well as to comic effect, for underlying the verbal wit and Shakespearian parody there is a pervasive sense of man's solitude and lack of mastery over his own life reminiscent of *Beckett, whom Stoppard greatly admires.

ROSENTHAL, Jack Morris (1931–2004), dramatist, born in Manchester and educated at Colne Grammar School and Sheffield University. He is best known for an unusually wide-ranging television output. He honed his craft during the 1960s, writing 150 episodes of Granada Television's *Coronation Street*, and introduced (some thought, offensive) demotic speech into the sitcom (situation comedy) genre in *The Dustbin Men*. *The Evacuees* (1975) and *Bar Mitzvah Boy* (1976) were single plays drawing on his Jewish background, which through their wry and compassionate humour appealed to a wide audience. *The Knowledge* (1979) portrayed London cab-drivers facing a malevolent invigilator, *P'Tang Yang Kipperbang* (1982) portrayed schoolboy ritual, *London's Burning* (1986) dramatized the perils of the fire service, and *And a Nightingale Sang* (1989) evoked wartime nostalgia. *Eskimo Day* (1996) and its successor *Cold Enough for Snow* (1997) depicted the tragi-comic effects of social class upon parents as their children entered university. A posthumously published memoir, *By Jack Rosenthal: An Autobiography in Six Acts* (2005), has a postscript by his wife, actress Maureen Lipman.

Rose Tavern, the in Russell Street, Covent Garden, a favourite place of resort in the later part of the 17th and early 18th cents. It is frequently referred to in the literature of the period, e.g. by *Pepys (18 May 1668), and by Farquhar (*The Recruiting Officer*).

Rose Theatre, the on Bankside, Southwark, built in 1587, and altered and enlarged in 1592, closing in 1602. *Henslowe was its owner and Edward *Alleyn its leading actor. Shakespeare is thought to have acted there. Its foundations were discovered in 1989.

Rosicrucian, a member of a supposed society or order, 'the brethren of the Rosy Cross', reputedly founded by one Christian Rosenkreuz in 1484, but first mentioned in 1614. Its manifestos were the *Fama Fraternitatis* (1614) and the *Confessio Fraternitatis* (1615), which aroused intense interest on the Continent and in Britain. Its members were said to claim various forms of secret and magic knowledge, such as the transmutation of metals, the prolongation of life, and power over the elements and elemental spirits, and to derive much of their alchemy and mystical preoccupations from *Paracelsus. No Rosicrucian society appears to have actually existed, and the Rosicrucian movement seems to have been rooted in some kind of anti-Jesuit Protestant alliance, with deep religious interests, as well as interests in alchemy, medicine, and the Cabbala. F. *Yates, in her study *The Rosicrucian Enlightenment* (1972), describes the term as representing 'in the purely historical sense . . . a phase . . . intermediate between the Renaissance and the so-called scientific revolution of the 17th cent.', 'a historical label for a style of thinking', and names as major figures in the English Rosicrucian movement *Dee, *Fludd, and *Ashmole; she also discusses the Rosicrucian connections of F. *Bacon, *Comenius, I. *Newton, *Leibniz, and many others.

ROSS, Alan (1922–2001), poet, travel writer, and editor, born in Calcutta and educated at St John's College, Oxford. He published several volumes of poetry and prose, many evocatively describing sojourns and travels abroad, sometimes in pursuit of art and love, sometimes of cricket. *Open Sea* (1975) collects poems about the Second World War from earlier works, and includes his compressed epic 'J.W.51B', a grey, haunting, first-hand description of naval endurance on the Arctic convoy route. He edited the *London Magazine* from 1961 until his death.

ROSS, Alexander (1699–1784), a Forfarshire schoolmaster, and an early follower of *Ramsay, published a lengthy pastoral in *Scots entitled *The Fortunate Shepherdess* (1768); several editions are called *Helenore, or The Fortunate Shepherdess*. But he is best remembered as the author of various spirited songs, including 'Woo'd and Married and a''.

Ross, the Man of, see KYRLE.

Ross, Martin, see SOMERVILLE AND ROSS.

ROSS, Robert Baldwin (1869–1918), journalist, art dealer, and critic, and literary executor of O. *Wilde. He was born in Tours of Canadian parents but lived most of his life in England. Probably Wilde's first male lover, Ross was his loyal friend in life and death. He helped support him after his release from prison, and, entrusted with *De Profundis*, published a version in 1905 which, though omitting the more painful accusations against Lord A. *Douglas, led to the latter's undying enmity. A close friend of Wilde's sons, Ross cleared the estate of debt (1906), organized the *Collected Works* (completed 1908), encouraged performance of the plays, and commissioned the first biography from A. *Ransome (1912). This infuriated Douglas into a series of vicious legal actions, which continued until and may have contributed to Ross's early death. Ross commissioned the sphinx for Wilde's tomb from Jacob Epstein. His own ashes are interred in it.

ROSSETER, Philip (?1567–1623), court musician, composer, and lutenist, a friend of T. *Campion, who wrote half the songs in Campion's first *Book of Ayres* (1601). He was appointed a lutenist at the court of James I in 1603.

ROSSETTI, Christina Georgina (1830–94), sister of D. G. and W. M. *Rossetti. She was educated at home, shared her brothers' intellectual interests, and contributed to their childhood family journals. Ill health (possibly strategic when young, but later severe) ended her attempts to work as a governess, and confined her to a quiet life. Her engagement to the painter James Collinson, an original member of the *Pre-Raphaelite Brotherhood, was broken off in 1850 when he rejoined the Roman Catholic Church; Christina, like her mother and sister Maria, was a devout High Anglican, much influenced by the Tractarians (see OXFORD MOVEMENT). She contributed to the *Germ (1850), where five of her poems appeared under the pseudonym 'Ellen Alleyn'. In 1861 *Macmillan's Magazine* published 'Up-hill' and 'A Birthday', two of her best-known poems. *Goblin Market and Other Poems appeared in 1862, The Prince's Progress and Other Poems in 1866, Sing-Song, a Nursery Rhyme Book (with illustrations by Arthur Hughes) in 1872, and A Pageant and Other Poems in 1881. Time Flies: A Reading Diary (1885) consists of short passages and prose, one for each day of the year. She also published much prose and poetry in periodicals and anthologies, and many prose devotional works. Her *Poetical Works*, ed. W. M. Rossetti, with a memoir, was published in 1904. Her work ranges from poems of fantasy and verses for the young to ballads, love lyrics, sonnets, and religious poetry. Much of it is pervaded by a sense of melancholy, verging at times on the morbid. The recurrent themes of unhappy, delayed, or frustrated love and of premature resignation ('Grown old before my time') led her biographer L. M. Packer (1963) to suppose an unsatisfied passion for W. B. *Scott, who was already married when she met him in 1847; G. Battiscombe (*A Divided Life*, 1981) questions this, stressing the close connection in her work of the spiritual and the erotic. Her work has often been compared with that of E. *Brontë, but, while both share a sense of mystical yearning, Rossetti's is more subdued, more hopeless, less fulfilled. Her technical virtuosity was considerable, and her use of short, irregularly rhymed lines is distinctive.

ROSSETTI, Dante Gabriel (1828–82), whose full Christian names were Gabriel Charles Dante (but the form which he gave it has become inveterate), the son of Gabriele Rossetti (1783–1854), an Italian patriot who came to England in 1824. He was brought up in an atmosphere of keen cultural and political activity which contributed more to his artistic development than his formal education at King's College School, London. He studied painting with *Millais and H. *Hunt, and in 1848, with them and four others, founded the *Pre-Raphaelite Brotherhood. For many years he was known only as a painter, though he began to write poetry early. Several of his poems, including *'The Blessed Damozel' and 'My Sister's Sleep', and a prose piece, 'Hand and Soul', were published in the *Germ (1850), the year in which he met Elizabeth *Siddal (or Siddall), who modelled for him and many of his circle. In 1854 he met *Ruskin, who did much to establish the reputation of the Pre-Raphaelite painters, and in 1856 W. *Morris whom he greatly influenced; he was to paint Morris's wife Jane many times. In 1860 Rossetti and Lizzie married: she died in 1862, and Rossetti buried with her the manuscript of a number of his poems. Later that year he moved to 16 Cheyne Walk, Chelsea, where *Swinburne and *Meredith were briefly joint tenants; he filled the house with antiques, bric-à-brac, and a curious selection of animals, including a wombat. In 1868 he showed a renewed interest in poetry, possibly inspired by renewed contact with Jane Morris; sixteen sonnets, including the 'Willowwood' sequence, were published in March 1869 in the *Fortnightly Review. That summer he wrote many more, and also arranged the exhumation of the poems buried with his wife. Poems (1870) contained 'Sister Helen', 'Troy Town', 'Eden Bower', *'Jenny', and the first part of his sonnet sequence *'The House of Life'; it was well received, partly because Rossetti took care that his friends should review it. In 1871 Morris and Rossetti took a joint lease of Kelmscott Manor, where Rossetti continued his intimacy with Jane, with Morris's apparent consent, and continued to paint her; there also he wrote the ballad 'Rose Mary' and further sonnets for the 'House of Life' sequence. In Oct. 1871 appeared R. *Buchanan's notorious attack 'The Fleshly School of Poetry' (under the pseudonym Thomas Maitland) in the *Contemporary Review. This accused Rossetti and his associates of impurity and obscenity; the sonnet 'Nuptial Sleep' was singled out for particular criticism, and was not reprinted in the 1881 edition, though the prolonged and bitter controversy which Buchanan aroused ended with the Pre-Raphaelites on the whole victorious. Rossetti's reply, 'The Stealthy School of Criticism', appeared in the *Athenaeum, Dec. 1872. Rossetti's later years were overshadowed by ill health and chloral, though he continued to paint and to write and was recognized by a new generation of aesthetes, including *Pater and *Wilde, as a source of inspiration; the admiration was not wholly mutual. Poems and Ballads and Sonnets both appeared in 1881; the first was largely rearrangements of earlier works, and the second completed 'The House of Life' with 47 new sonnets, and also contained other new work, including 'The King's Tragedy' and 'The White Ship', both historical 'ballads'.

Rossetti's poetry is marred for many readers by its vast and cloudy generalities about Life, Love, and Death, though some of his work shows in contrast a Pre-Raphaelite sharpness of detail, and much of it has an undeniable emotional and erotic power. His letters (ed. O. Doughty and J. R. Wahl, 4 vols, 1965–7) reveal another side of his colourful and extravagant personality; they are witty, irreverent, at times coarse, and demonstrate the wide range of his artistic interests. Mention should also be made of his translations from the Italian (The Early Italian Poets Together with Dante's

Vita Nuova, 1861, known later as Dante and his Circle, 1874), and of *Villon. Many of his poems were written as commentaries on his own and other paintings.

The standard edition of his collected works, edited by W. M. *Rossetti, appeared in 1911. Oswald Doughty's life, A Victorian Romantic, was published in 1960.

ROSSETTI, William Michael (1829–1919), brother of D. G. *Rossetti, educated at King's College School, London; he worked as an official of the Inland Revenue, and is remembered as a man of letters and art critic. He was a member of the *Pre-Raphaelite Brotherhood, edited the *Germ, and wrote the sonnet that was printed on its cover. His reviews of art exhibitions for the *Spectator were published as Fine Art: Chiefly Contemporary (1867). He edited 15 volumes of *Moxon's Popular Poets, and was responsible for important editions of *Blake and *Shelley. He edited *Whitman in 1868, introducing him to a British public, and the two corresponded frequently. He translated *Dante, and was responsible for encouraging James *Thomson ('B. V.'). He also edited many of his family's papers, letters, and diaries, and wrote memoirs of his brother and his sister Christina (above). Ruskin: Rossetti: Preraphaelitism (1899); Preraphaelite Diaries and Letters (1900); Rossetti Papers, 1862–70 (1903); D. G. Rossetti, His Family Letters, with a Memoir (1895); Family Letters of Christina Rossetti (1908). His Some Reminiscences (1906) is a valuable biographical source. His diary for 1870–3 was edited with notes by O. Bornand (1977).

ROSSINI, Gioachino (1792–1868), Italian composer, and one of the greatest exponents of 19th-cent. opera. His early success was based on opera buffa, but he later devoted himself to serious drama, beginning with Otello. Unfortunately the text, adapted for him by a wealthy dilettante, Francesco di Salsa, has become a locus classicus of trivialization: 'They have been crucifying Othello into an opera', wrote *Byron: 'the music is good, but lugubrious; but as for the words, all the real scenes with Iago cut out, and the greatest nonsense inserted; the handkerchief turned into a billet-doux, and the singer would not black his face, for some exquisite reasons.' Nevertheless Otello is not without its qualities, particularly in the last act, of which it has been well said that Rossini here 'came of age as a musical dramatist'. But it was no match for *Boito and Verdi's version of 1887 and fell into relative oblivion. The only other British author on whom Rossini drew was W. *Scott, whose *The Lady of the Lake supplied the libretto of La donna del lago (1819). Two later works based on Scott, Ivanhoé (1826) and Robert Bruce (1846), are both pasticcios, and only very loosely connected with Scott. Also put together from pre-existing music was the Pianto delle muse in morte di Lord Byron which Rossini produced at the second of his London concerts in 1824, shortly after the news of Byron's death had reached London.

ROSTAND, Edmond (1868–1918), French playwright, author of *Les Romanesques* (1894), *La Princesse lointaine* (1895), *La Samaritaine* (1897), *L'Aiglon* (1900, based on the life of Napoleon's son), and *Chantecler* (1910). The poetic drama *Cyrano de Bergerac* (1897), his most popular and successful work, revives in romantic guise the 17th-cent. soldier and duellist *Cyrano. It has been translated into Glaswegian demotic by E. *Morgan (1992), and was successfully filmed (1990) with Gérard Depardieu in the title role, with English subtitles rendered into rhyming verse by A. *Burgess.

Rosy Cross, see ROSICRUCIAN.

ROTA, Bertram (1903–66), bookseller, who entered the book trade in 1918 in the bookshop conducted by his uncles Percy and Arthur Dobell. In 1923, at the age of 19, he began his own business with £100 borrowed from his mother's savings. The firm has continued its tradition of specializing in first editions of literature of the last 100 years.

ROTH, Joseph (1894–1939), Austrian-Jewish writer, who was born in Galicia and died in exile in Paris. Brilliantly successful as a journalist (on the *Frankfurter Zeitung*, among other papers) he also published 13 novels. In his books, he is a sardonic observer of post-war *mœurs*, an elegist for the Central European *shtetl*, and a belated apologist for the Dual Monarchy. He once wrote, 'My strongest experience was the War and the destruction of my fatherland, the only one I ever had, the Austro-Hungarian Dual Monarchy.' His characteristic locations are border garrison towns, his heroes decent men overtaken by events. *Radetskymarsch* (1932, *The Radetzky March*), his family epic, is commonly accounted his masterpiece, though unfortunately at the expense of other works. His later manner, in *Das falsche Gewicht* (1937, *Weights and Measures*), Die Kapuzinergruft (1938, *The Emperor's Tomb*), and *Die Legende vom heiligen Trinker* (1939, *The Legend of the Holy Drinker*), is supremely beautiful and desolate.

ROTH, Philip (1933–), novelist, born in New Jersey, of second-generation Jewish American parentage. His writing career has been combined with various teaching posts in America. His complex relationship with his Jewish background is reflected in most of his works, and his portrayal of contemporary Jewish life has aroused much controversy. His works include *Goodbye, Columbus* (1959, a novella with five short stories), *Letting Go* (1962), and a sequence of novels featuring Nathan Zuckerman, a Jewish novelist who has to learn to contend with success: *My Life as a Man* (1974), *The Ghost Writer* (1979), *Zuckerman Unbound* (1981), *The Anatomy Lesson* (1983), and *The Prague Orgy* (1985). He remains best known for *Portnoy's Complaint* (1969), which records its protagonist's confessions to his psychiatrist, and is remembered as a *succès de scandale*, but Roth's later novels have greatly increased his reputation: these include *The Counterlife* (1987), *Patrimony: A True Story* (1991), about his father

Herman Roth; *Operation Shylock: A Confession* (1993), and a trilogy, narrated by Nathan Zuckerman: *American Pastoral* (1997), *I Married A Communist* (1998), and *The Human Stain* (2000), which explore issues of race, politics, and persecution in public and private life.

ROUBILIAC, Louis François (1702 or 1705–62), French rococo sculptor, who settled in London *c.*1732. His first success was the statue of *Handel* (1738) commissioned for Vauxhall Gardens, which introduced a new informality into English sculpture. Roubiliac was successful as a tomb sculptor; the monuments to *General Hargrave* (1757) and to *Lady Elizabeth Nightingale* (1761; both Westminster Abbey), his most famous works, are strikingly original and sensationally baroque. As a portrait sculptor Roubiliac attracted a very wide circle of patrons; his image of *Pope (there are four marble busts dating from 1738, 1740, and 1741, all inscribed *ad vivum*; and one terracotta model) is unflinchingly realistic yet deeply poignant. Roubiliac also executed a series of vivid historical busts of famous scientists, writers, and men of letters for the library of Trinity College, Cambridge.

ROUGEMONT, Louis De, ssumed name of Swiss-born Louis Grin (1847–1921), an adventurer who decided at the age of 16 to see the world. He began as footman to Fanny *Kemble, touring through Europe and America, and eventually became butler to the governor of Australia. After spending many years there he contributed to *Wide World Magazine* in 1898 sensational articles relating to his extraordinary, mostly bogus, voyages and adventures in search of pearls and gold, where he encountered an octopus with tentacles 75 feet long and rode turtles in the water.

Round Table, the, in the Arthurian legend, the symbol of the common purpose of Arthur's court and knights. According to *Malory (in Vinaver's Tale 1) it was made for *Uther Pendragon who gave it to King Lodegrean (see LEODEGRANCE) of Camelerde (Cornwall). The latter gave it as a wedding gift, with 100 knights, to Arthur when he married Guinevere, his daughter. It would seat 150 knights, and all places round it were equal. The 'Siege Perilous' was reserved for the knight who should achieve the quest of the *Grail. In *Laȝamon's *Brut*, however, the table was made for Arthur by a crafty workman. It is first mentioned by *Wace.

Rousillon, countess of, *Bertram's mother and *Helena's guardian in Shakespeare's *All's Well that Ends Well*. Rousillon was a province in the south-west of France near Spain.

ROUSSEAU, Jean-Jacques (1712–78), born into a Protestant artisan family at Geneva. His mother having died soon after his birth, Jean-Jacques was cared for in childhood by an aunt, by his father, a watchmaker of unstable temperament, and (after the latter's departure for France) by a maternal uncle. He was apprenticed to an engraver when, at the age of 15, he decided to leave his master and Geneva. Thus began the movement of residence which was to become habitual and which took him to many parts of Switzerland, France, and Italy, and (in 1766–7) to England. During these peregrinations he owed much to the generosity of friends and patrons; otherwise he maintained himself by a succession of clerical, secretarial, and tutorial posts and by teaching and copying music. Rousseau's emotional nature, his often tempestuous personal relations, extreme sensitivity, and penchant for controversy fill his career with striking and dramatic episodes; while his critical and enquiring intellect, his lifelong interest in music and excursions into opera and drama, a voluminous correspondence, and important and influential contributions to social and political philosophy, the novel, autobiography, moral theology, and educational theory mark him out as one of the dominant writers and thinkers of the age.

Rousseau was 38 years old when his essay on a subject proposed by the Academy of Dijon, *Discours sur les sciences et les arts* (1750), was awarded first prize and published. In the *Discours*, the first of many works in which the natural man is preferred to his civilized counterpart, Rousseau argued that the development and spread of knowledge and culture, far from improving human behaviour, had corrupted it by promoting inequality, idleness, and luxury. The *Discours sur l'origine de l'inégalité* (1755) contrasts the innocence and contentment of primitive man in a 'state of nature'—his mode of existence determined by none but genuine needs—with the dissatisfaction and perpetual agitation of modern social man, the majority of whom are condemned to the legally sanctioned servitude necessary to preserve the institution of private property. The suggestion by d'Alembert that a theatre should be established at Geneva prompted the *Lettre sur les spectacles* (1758), in which the passive nature of playgoing, the preoccupation of modern plays with love, and the consequent unnatural bringing forward of women are seen as dangerous symptoms of the ills of society.

A return to primitive innocence being impossible, these ills were only to be remedied, Rousseau held, by reducing the gap separating modern man from his natural archetype and by modifying existing institutions in the interest of equality and happiness. *Émile* (1762) lays down the principles for a new scheme of education in which the child is to be allowed full scope for individual development in natural surroundings, shielded from the harmful influences of civilization, in order to form an independent judgement and a stable character. The 'Profession de foi du vicaire savoyard', contained in the fourth book of *Émile*, sets against institutional Christianity a form of Deism grounded in religious sentiment and guided by the divine instinct of conscience. The year 1762 also saw the publication of *Du contrat social*, his theory of politics, in which he advocated universal justice through equality before the law, a more equitable distribution of wealth, and defined government as fundamentally a matter of

contract providing for the exercise of power in accordance with the 'general will' and for the common good, by consent of the citizens as a whole, in whom sovereignty ultimately resides.

In the novel *Julie, ou la nouvelle Héloïse* (1761), Rousseau's greatest popular success, a critical account of contemporary manners and ideas is interwoven with the story of the passionate love of the tutor St Preux and his pupil Julie, their separation, Julie's marriage to the Baron Wolmar, and the dutiful, virtuous life shared by all three on the Baron's country estate.

The posthumously published autobiographical works *Les Confessions* (1781–8) and *Les Rêveries du promeneur solitaire* (1782) were written towards the end of Rousseau's life as exercises in self-justification and self-analysis. As expressions of the complex individuality of a personality and a sensibility, unexampled in their time for candour, detail, and subtlety, they remain landmarks of the literature of personal revelation and reminiscence.

ROUTH, Martin Joseph (1755–1854), president of Magdalen College, Oxford, for 63 years; he edited the *Gorgias* and *Eutheydemus* of *Plato, and *Reliquiae Sacrae* (1814–43), a collection of writings of ecclesiastical authors of the 2nd and 3rd cents. Routh was a man of immense learning, and a strong, old-fashioned 'High Churchman'. He was also, perhaps, the last man in England who always wore a wig. His long life (he died in his 100th year) and literary experience lend weight to his famous utterance: 'I think, Sir, you will find it a very good practice *always to verify your references.*' A life of Routh by R. D. Middleton was published in 1938.

ROWE, Nicholas (1674–1718), educated at Westminster School; he became a barrister of the Middle Temple, but abandoned the legal profession for that of a playwright, and made the acquaintance of *Pope and *Addison. He produced at Lincoln's Inn Fields his tragedies *The Ambitious Stepmother* (1700), *Tamerlane* (1701), and *The Fair Penitent* (1703). His *Ulysses* was staged in 1705, *The Royal Convert* in 1707, *Jane Shore* in 1714, and *Lady Jane Grey* in 1715. He also produced one unsuccessful comedy, *The Biter* (1704). He became *poet laureate in 1715, and was buried in Westminster Abbey. His poetical works include a famous translation of *Lucan (1718), 'one of the greatest productions of English poetry', according to Dr *Johnson. Rowe also did useful work as editor of Shakespeare's plays (1709), dividing them into acts and scenes, supplying stage directions, and generally making the text more intelligible. As a writer he is best remembered for his 'She-Tragedies' (his own phrase), which provided Mrs *Siddons, as Calista and Jane Shore, with two of her most famous roles: their tone is moral, their stress is on the suffering and penitence of victimized women, and their intention is to arouse 'pity; a sort of regret proceeding from good-nature'.

Rowe saw himself as the heir of *Otway, who had also been renowned for tenderness and pathos. See *Three Plays*, ed. J. R. Sutherland (1929), with a life and bibliography.

Rowland, Childe, see CHILDE ROLAND.

ROWLANDS, Samuel (?1565–1630), a writer of satirical tracts, epigrams, jests, etc., mainly in verse. His works include a satire on the manners of Londoners, *The Letting of Humors Blood in the Head-Vaine* (1600); *Tis Merrie when Gossips Meete* (1602), a vivid and dramatic character sketch of a widow, a wife, and a maid who meet in a tavern and converse; *Greene's Ghost* (1602), on the subject of 'coney-catchers' (see GREENE, R.); *Democritus, or Doctor Merry-man His Medicines against Melancholy Humors* (1607); and *The Melancholie Knight* (1615). His *Complete Works*, including *Martin Mark-all* (1610), now considered spurious, were edited with an essay by *Gosse and S. J. H. Herrtage in 1880.

ROWLANDSON, Thomas (1756–1827), painter, book illustrator, and caricaturist famous for his comic depiction of scenes from social life. Among his most important productions were *The Loyal Volunteers of London and Environs* (1799); *The Microcosm of London* (1808–10), with Augustus Pugin; *The Three Tours of Doctor Syntax*, for *Combe; *The English Dance of Death* (1815–16); and *The Dance of Life* (1816–17), also with Combe, all of which issued from R. *Ackermann. Rowlandson was equally adept at rendering the *picturesque landscape and the caricatured human figure. He is best remembered for his comic invention, for the spontaneity and fluid quality of his draughtsmanship, and for the often ribald jocularity of his social commentary. See Bernard Falk, *Thomas Rowlandson: His Life and Art* (1949), and John T. Hayes, *The Art of Thomas Rowlandson* (1990).

ROWLEY, Samuel (fl. 1597–1624), an actor in the Admiral's Company and a playwright employed by *Henslowe; he is believed to be responsible for the comic additions to Marlowe's *Dr Faustus*. His only extant play is a chronicle drama about Henry VIII, *When You See Me, You Know Me*, acted 1603.

ROWLEY, William (?1585–1626), dramatist and actor. Nothing is known about his birth and his early life, but he was probably Samuel *Rowley's brother. His first compositions were episodic adventure-plays for Queen Anne's Men, *The Travels of the Three English Brothers* (1607), written with *Day and Wilkins, *Fortune by Land and Sea* (1607–9, printed 1655), with *Heywood, and, unassisted, *A Shoemaker, a Gentleman* (1607–9, printed 1638). Collaborations, in which he usually contributed comic sub-plot, account for nearly all of his surviving dramatic work. His most notable partnership was with *Middleton with whom he wrote *Wit at Several Weapons* (1613, printed 1647), *A Fair Quarrel* (1615–16, printed 1617), *The Old Law* (c.1618, printed 1656), *The World Tossed at Tennis* (1619–20,

printed 1620), and *The Changeling* (1622, printed 1653). He also assisted in *The Witch of Edmonton* (1621, printed 1658), with *Dekker and *Ford; *The Maid in the Mill* (1623, printed 1647), with *Fletcher; *A Cure for a Cuckold* (1624–5, printed 1661), with *Webster; and *A New Wonder, a Woman Never Vexed* (1624–6, printed 1632), with an unknown collaborator. His non-dramatic work includes a satirical pamphlet, *A Search for Money* (1609), and elegies on Prince Henry and a fellow actor, Hugh Attwell. From 1609 he was a member of the Duke of York's (later Prince Charles's) Men, and by 1616 had become leader of the company. His speciality as an actor was the role of a fat clown, and he took the part of Jacques in his own *All's Lost by Lust* (c.1619). In 1625 he was cited in a legal action over *Keep the Widow Waking*, a sensational dramatization, now lost, of two contemporary scandals which he had written with Dekker, Ford, and Webster. He died before he could testify, and was buried at St James's, Clerkenwell.

Rowley Poems, see CHATTERTON.

ROWLING, J. K., See CHILDREN'S LITERATURE.

ROWSE, A(lfred) L(eslie) (1903–97), poet, biographer, and Tudor historian, born at St Austell, Cornwall, and educated at St Austell Grammar School and Christ Church, Oxford. Cornwall forms the setting for many of his poems and works of history and autobiography, including *A Cornish Childhood* (1942). He published several books on Shakespeare (1963, 1973, and 1977), and argued that Emilia *Lanier was the 'dark lady' of Shakespeare's *Sonnets.

Roxana, or *The Fortunate Mistress*, a novel by *Defoe, published 1724.

This purports to be the autobiography of Mlle Beleau, the beautiful daughter of French Protestant refugees, brought up in England and married to a London brewer, who, having squandered his property, deserts her and her five children. She enters upon a career of prosperous wickedness, passing from one protector to another in England, France, and Holland, amassing much wealth, and receiving the name Roxana by accident, in consequence of a dance that she performs. She is accompanied in her adventures by a faithful maid, Amy, a very human figure. She marries a respectable Dutch merchant in London and subsequently lives as a person of consequence in Holland. When one of her daughters appears on the scene in London, Roxana dares not acknowledge her, fearing that her past life will be revealed to her new spouse and her life of security will be ruined. When Amy says she will murder the girl, if necessary, to silence her inquiries about Roxana's identity, Roxana is filled with horror and relief. Both Amy and the girl disappear, and Roxana, miserable and apprehensive, is tormented by her conscience. Her husband discerns her iniquity and soon thereafter dies, leaving her only a small sum of money. In the company of her alter ego

Amy, Roxana descends into debt, poverty, and remorseful penitence.

ROXBURGHE, John Ker, third duke of (1740–1804), an ardent bibliophile, who secured an unrivalled collection of books from *Caxton's press. His splendid library, housed in St James's Square, was dispersed in 1812. Valdarfer's edition of *Boccaccio (1471), for which the second duke had paid 100 guineas, was then sold to the marquis of Blandford for £2,260. To celebrate this event the chief bibliophiles of the day dined together at St Alban's Tavern, St Alban's Street, under the presidency of Lord Spencer, and there inaugurated the Roxburghe Club, the first of the 'book-clubs', consisting of 25 members, with T. F. *Dibdin as its first secretary. The Club, at first rather convivial in character, began its valuable literary work with the printing of the metrical romance of *Havelok the Dane (1828). Each member is expected once in his career to present (and pay for a limited edition of) a volume of some rarity. See N. Barker, *The Publications of the Roxburghe Club 1814–1962* (1964).

ROY, Arundhati, see ANGLO-INDIAN LITERATURE.

Royal Academy of Arts, the, founded under the patronage of George III in 1768, for the annual exhibition of works of contemporary artists and for the establishment of a school of art. It was first housed in Pall Mall, moved in 1780 to Somerset House, then to the National Gallery, and finally to Burlington House, Piccadilly, in 1869. Sir Joshua *Reynolds was its first president. Since 1870 the Academy has also held important loan exhibitions and its Summer Exhibition remains a regular fixture. *Ruskin's *Notes on the Royal Academy* (1855–9 and 1875) were an important influence on public taste.

Royal Court Theatre, the, built in 1888; it has a historic association with new writing. Under the management of J. E. Vedrenne and Harley *Granville-Barker from 1904 to 1907, it staged premières by *Shaw, *Galsworthy, *Yeats, and *Masefield. But it was with the foundation of the *English Stage Company in 1956, under the direction of George Devine (1910–66), that it became a national centre of new writing. The initial intention was to encourage novelists to write for the stage but, although work by Angus *Wilson and Nigel *Dennis was presented, it was the production of *Look back in Anger* by Osborne (8 May 1956) that liberated other writers through its scalding rhetoric and social candour. The Court has subsequently championed many living dramatists including *Wesker, *Arden, *Bond, *Storey, *Friel, *Fugard, *Churchill, Mustapha Matura, and Timberlake *Wertenbaker as well as reviving, through the advocacy of Peter Gill, neglected masters such as D. H. *Lawrence. In the mid-1990s, under the direction of Stephen Daldry, it acquired fresh impetus through its encouragement of a new generation of socially angry, anti-materialist young writers, including Sarah *Kane and Mark Ravenhill, and its promotion of eloquent new Irish dramatists, notably Martin McDonagh and Conor McPherson.

Royal Historical Society, the, founded in 1868 and granted the title 'Royal' in 1887. Its aim is to promote the study of history by publishing documentary material and, from time to time, bibliographical and reference works; its papers are published annually as *Transactions*. In 1897 the *Camden Society was amalgamated with the Royal Historical Society, which now publishes the Camden Series.

Royal Literary Fund, the, a benevolent society to aid authors and their dependants in distress, founded in 1790 as the Literary Fund Society at the instigation of the Revd David Williams, a Dissenting minister. In 1818 it was granted a royal charter, and was permitted to add 'Royal' to its title in 1845. Beneficiaries have included *Coleridge, *Peacock, *Hogg, *Clare, D. H. *Lawrence, E. *Nesbit, *Joyce, and Dylan *Thomas. It has also made grants to literary refugees, including *Chateaubriand. The Fund receives no government subsidy and depends on gifts, subscriptions, and legacies—including authors' royalties.

Royal Society, the, more correctly the Royal Society of London for the Improving of Natural Knowledge; it obtained its royal charters in 1662 and 1663. The prehistory of the Society extends back to a variety of scientific meetings held in London and Oxford from 1645 onwards. Traditionally, the originator of these meetings is identified as Theodore Haak, known also as the first to translate *Milton into German. F. *Bacon provided the major philosophical inspiration for the Society; Solomon's House in *New Atlantis* has been taken as its model. No scientific society has made a more conspicuous debut—its founders and early members included *Boyle, Hooke, *Petty, *Ray, Wilkins, and *Wren. Among more literary figures, *Ashmole, *Aubrey, *Cowley, *Dryden, *Evelyn, and *Waller were members. The Society featured prominently in Dryden's *Annus Mirabilis*. Its *Philosophical Transactions* (1665–   ), first edited by Henry Oldenburg, is the first permanent scientific journal. Individual members of the Royal Society made an outstanding scientific contribution, but the Society itself was not entirely successful. It was attacked and ridiculed by a bizarre coalition of interests, including Henry Stubbe, S. *Butler, and *Shadwell; the latter's *The Virtuoso* threatened the stature of the latitudinarian 'Christian Virtuosi' of the Society. The Society was also drawn into the ancients versus moderns controversy (see BATTLE OF THE BOOKS). In replies to attacks by the ancients, the modernism of the Society was defended by J. *Glanvill and *Sprat. The latter's *History of the Royal Society* (1667) is known for its defence of the 'close, naked, natural way' of style. The Society risked degenerating into a squabbling London club. Its decline was temporarily arrested under I. *Newton. Its fortunes revived in the later 19th cent., but in the modern period the Royal Society has played a less active part in the nation's cultural life.

Royal Society of Edinburgh, the, established in 1783 for 'the cultivation of every branch of science, erudition, and taste'. The membership was originally divided into the Physical Class and a larger Literary Class, the latter including A. *Alison, *Beattie, H. *Blair, *Burke (elected 1784), A. *Carlyle, A. *Ferguson, A. *Gerard, J. *Home, *Jamieson (1803), H. *Mackenzie, T. *Reid, W. *Robertson (who was instrumental in the Society's creation), and Sir W. *Scott (elected 1800, president 1820–32). D. *Stewart was a member of the Physical Class. *Tennyson (1864) and T. *Carlyle (1866) had honorary membership. Scientific proceedings and publications have been predominant in the Society's work since the early 19th cent., but the Literary Class was revived in 1976. The Society is the successor of the Philosophical Society of Edinburgh (1737), of which *Hume was once joint secretary, and its library is the principal repository for Hume's correspondence and surviving manuscripts.

Royal Society of Literature, the, founded in 1820 at the suggestion of Thomas Burgess, bishop of St David's, and under the patronage of George IV, who assigned the sum of 1,100 guineas to be applied in pensions of 100 guineas to each of ten Royal Associates, and in a premium of 100 guineas for a prize dissertation. The Associates were elected by the council of the Society (*Malthus and S. T. *Coleridge were among the first ten). The Society published papers read to it under the title *Transactions*; publication was suspended during the First World War and was resumed in 1921 as a new series under the title *Essays by Divers Hands*. The Society has members, fellows, and, since 1961, companions; recipients of the title of companion have included * Betjeman, * Koestler, E. M. * Forster, Angus * Wilson, and many others. There is a history of the RSL by Isabel Quigly (2000).

Royns, see RYENCE.

RÓŻEWICZ, Tadeusz (1921–), Polish poet and playwright. With his compatriots Z. *Herbert and *Miłosz he is one of the most influential writers of post-war eastern Europe. His stark, powerful poems provide an often disturbingly realistic account of his country's recent history. *They Came to See a Poet* was published in 1991. Much of his controversial political drama, including *The Trap* (1981; English trans. 1984), has also been published in English.

Rubáiyát of Omar Khayyám, The, see OMAR KHAYYÁM.

RUBENS, Bernice Ruth (1923–2004), novelist, born in Cardiff into a musical Jewish family and educated at the University of Wales, Cardiff. Her first novel, *Set on Edge* (1960), was followed by *Madame Sousatzka* (1962), in which the piano teacher of the title, who lives in an eccentric household in Vauxhall, struggles to keep possession of child prodigy Marcus Crominski

from Stamford Hill. Her many other works include *The Elected Member* (1969, *Booker Prize 1970), which is the sombre story of an orthodox Jewish family: drug-addicted, mentally disturbed, and much-loved scapegoat son Norman Zweck brings sorrow to his widower father, Rabbi Zweck, to his unmarried sister Bella, and to his sister Esther, who has married out. *Spring Sonata* (1979) is the story of a musically gifted unborn child refusing to confront the prospect of its own birth. Later works include *A Solitary Grief* (1991), in which psychiatrist Alistair Crown finds himself literally unable to face his Down's syndrome daughter, and *The Waiting Game* (1997), a macabre tale of old age set in an old people's home.

RUBENS, Peter Paul (1577–1640), Flemish painter, the chief northern exponent of the baroque. Studying first under Flemish masters, he went to Italy in 1600 and became court painter to the duke of Mantua. He returned to Antwerp in 1608, became court painter to the Spanish ruler of Flanders, and set up a large and productive workshop with numerous assistants. In addition he served on various diplomatic missions, visiting Spain in 1628 and England in 1629, where he was knighted and commissioned to paint the ceiling of the Banqueting House. During his visit Rubens stayed with his friend the Zeeland-born painter and architect Sir Balthazar Gerbier (?1591–1667) whose children appear in his magnificent *Allegory of Peace and War* (1629, National Gallery, London). Rubens was a prolific and vital painter. His style was based on the great Italian masters, but in later life he painted for his own pleasure landscapes with a new feeling for the country. One of the few English writers to appreciate his full stature was G. *Eliot, who wrote from Munich (1858, in a letter), 'His are such real, breathing men and women . . . . What a grand, glowing, forceful thing life looks in his pictures.'

RUCK, Berta, see under ONIONS, G. O.

RUDKIN, David (1936–), playwright, born in London, the son of a Nonconformist minister, and educated at King Edward School, Birmingham, and Oxford; he then became a schoolteacher. He made his name with a powerful drama set in a rural district of the Black Country, *Afore Night Come* (1962; published in Penguin's *New English Dramatists 7*, 1963); subsequent works, informed by a dark and passionate surreal mysticism, include *Ashes* (1974, pub. 1977), *Penda's Fen* (TV 1974, pub. 1975), *Sons of Light* (1976), *The Triumph of Death* (1981), *Space Invaders* (1983), and *The Saxon Shore* (1986).

Ruggiero, see ROGERO.

RUGGLE, George, see IGNORAMUS.

'Ruin, The, a 45-line poem in Old English in the *Exeter Book*, one of the group known as 'elegies'. The poem describes the result of the devastation of a city, and it is thought likely that the reference is to the Roman city of

Bath which was a ruin in Anglo-Saxon times. There are two references to hot baths in the poem, the second of them extensive. Ed. R. F. Leslie, *Three Old English Elegies* (1961).

'Ruined Cottage, The', or 'The Story of Margaret', a poem by *Wordsworth, written in 1797, and subsequently embodied in Bk I of *The Excursion*.

It is a harrowing tale of misfortune befalling a cottager and his wife. The husband leaves his home and joins a troop of soldiers going to a distant land. The wife stays on, pining for his return in increasing wretchedness, until she dies and the cottage falls into ruin.

'Ruines of Time, The', a poem by *Spenser, included in the *Complaints* published in 1591. It is an allegorical elegy on the death of Sir P. *Sidney, which had also been the occasion of his earlier elegy *'Astrophel'. The poet passes to a lament on the decline of patronage and neglect of literature, with allusion to his own case. The poem is dedicated to the countess of *Pembroke, Sidney's sister.

Rule a Wife and Have a Wife, a comedy by J. *Fletcher, performed 1624.

Margarita, a rich heiress of Seville, plans to marry, but only in order to provide a cover for her own pleasures; she must therefore choose a husband 'of easy faith', who will allow her to dominate and deceive him, and serve as 'a shadow, an umbrella, | To keep the scorching world's opinion' from her good name. Altea, her companion, plots to win her for her brother Leon; he assumes the character of a fool, but, once married, abandons docility, asserts his authority, and finally wins her affection.

'Rule, Britannia'; for the words see THOMSON, J. The air was composed by *Arne for Thomson and *Mallet's masque *Alfred*.

rune, a letter or character of the earliest surviving Germanic script, most extensively used in inscriptions on wood or stone by the Scandinavians and Anglo-Saxons. The earliest runic alphabet seems to date from about the 3rd cent. AD, and is formed by modifying the letters of the Greek and Roman alphabets. Magical and mysterious powers were associated with runes from the Anglo-Saxon period, perhaps because of their employment in riddles, as in the *Rune Poem*, a 94-line piece illustrating the runes of the Anglo-Saxon runic alphabet, the *Futhorc (see ASPR 6, 28–30 for edition). The other important occurrence of runes in Old English literature is in the runic signature to the poems of *Cynewulf. See R. W. V. Elliott, *Runes: An Introduction* (1959).

Rupert of Hentzau, a novel by Anthony Hope (*Hawkins), a sequel to *The Prisoner of Zenda*.

Rural Rides, a collection of essays by W. *Cobbett, published 1830, which had originally appeared in the *Political Register*. A committee in 1821 had proposed certain remedies for the agricultural distress that followed the war. Cobbett disapproved of these and 'made up his mind to see for himself, and to enforce, by actual observation of rural conditions, the statements he had made in answer to the arguments of the landlords before the Agricultural Committee'. The result was this series of lively, opinionated accounts of his travels on horseback between Sept. 1822 and Oct. 1826, largely in the south and east of England. (Later journeys, in the Midlands and the north, were added in subsequent editions.) He rails against tax collectors, 'tax-eaters', landlords, gamekeepers, stockjobbers, and excisemen, and against the monstrous swelling of the 'Great Wen' of London; but the whole work is also informed with his own knowledge of and love of the land in all its minutely observed variety, and he breaks occasionally into rapturous praise for a landscape, a hedgerow, a hanging wood, or, less characteristically, the ruins of Malmesbury Abbey. The standard edition is by G. D. H. and M. *Cole (3 vols, 1930).

Ruritania, an imaginary kingdom in central Europe, the scene of *The Prisoner of Zenda* by Anthony Hope (*Hawkins). The name connotes more generally a world of make-believe romance, chivalry, and intrigue.

RUSHDIE, (Ahmed) Salman, (1947–), novelist and short story writer, born in Bombay to a Muslim family, educated at the Cathedral School, Rugby, and King's College, Cambridge. He worked for a time in television in Pakistan, as an actor in London, and as an advertising copywriter. Rushdie's bicultural upbringing informs all his work. He draws on the allegorical, fable-making traditions of both East and West and is often classed amongst the exponents of *magic realism—the narrative style in which the realistic mingles with the fantastic and the inexplicable. His first novel, *Grimus* (1975), was a fantasy based on a medieval Sufi poem and was followed by *Midnight's Children* (1981), the book that brought him to literary prominence and which won the *Booker Prize. It tells the story of Saleem Sinai, born on the stroke of midnight on the day that India was granted independence and whose life becomes emblematic of the political and social destiny of the new nation. In *Shame* (1983) the subject is Pakistan, the struggle between military and civilian rule, and the culture of shame and honour which oppresses women; the historical figures wear satirical and allegorical disguise, but the narrative is interrupted by direct autobiographical interventions from the author. *The Satanic Verses* (1988) is a jet-propelled panoramic novel which moves with dizzying speed from the streets and film studios of Bombay to multicultural Britain, from Argentina to Mount Everest, as Rushdie questions illusion, reality, and the power of faith and tradition in a world of hijackers, religious pilgrimages and warfare, and celluloid fantasy. Certain passages were interpreted by some Muslims as blasphemous and brought upon Rushdie the notorious sentence of death, or *fatwa*, invoked by the Ayatollah Khomeini in February 1989, which obliged him to seek police protection. *Haroun and the Sea of Stories*, a novel for children about a boy-hero who has to combat the enemy of storytelling, Prince Khattam-Shud, was published in 1990 (adapted for the stage at the *National Theatre, 1998), and *Imaginary Homelands*, a collection of critical journalism and interviews, in 1991. In 1994 Rushdie published his first collection of short stories, *East, West*, which, written on the cultural cusp between two traditions, also confronts the conflicting claims of the real and the imagined. *The Moor's Last Sigh* (1995) is a dense and exuberant study of cultural and personal inheritance narrated by the 'Moor' of the title, and *Shalimar the Clown* (2005) tackles the violent politics of Kashmir.

RUSKIN, John (1819–1900). The only child of John James and Margaret Ruskin, he grew up in Surrey. His father paid off family debts and built up the wine business of which he was a founding partner; he was able to pass on to his son a large fortune, of which Ruskin gave much away. To his parents Ruskin also owed a reliance on the Bible, a strong affection for romantic literature, stern political views, and an early attraction to contemporary landscape painting. Much of his schooling was given at home, and from 1836 to 1842 he was at Christ Church, Oxford, where he won the Newdigate Prize but did not find the curriculum profitable. Travel was a more important part of his education. The family took regular tours through the picturesque areas of Britain, and, from 1833, on the Continent. These helped fix Ruskin's lifelong preference for French cathedral towns, the Alps, and certain cities of northern Italy, and gave scope to what he spoke of as his main passion, the study of the facts of nature. Among his earliest publications were essays in Loudon's *Magazine of Natural History* (1834 and 1836). Others were 'The Poetry of Architecture' (*Architectural Magazine*, 1837–8) and numerous Byronesque poems and stories written for Christmas annuals. He contributed regularly from 1835 to 1846, mainly to *Friendship's Offering*, whose editor, W. H. Harrison, acted as his personal literary adviser. He also devoted time to drawing; he admired the work of Copley Fielding, J. D. Harding, Clarkson Stanfield, James Holland, David Roberts, Samuel Prout, and, above all, *Turner. He took lessons from two of these artists (Fielding and Harding), made friends of several, and bought the work of all. With the first of the five volumes of *Modern Painters* (1843) he became their public champion.

Seven months' work in Italy in preparation for *Modern Painters II* (1846) confirmed Ruskin in his 'function as interpreter'. They also compelled him to write of the medieval buildings of Europe before they should be destroyed by neglect, restoration, industrialization, and revolutions. He postponed further enquiry into natural beauty and its representation:

Modern Painters III and *IV* did not appear until 1856. The interval produced *The Seven Lamps of Architecture* (1849) and *The Stones of Venice* (1851–3), both written during the period of his marriage to Euphemia Chalmers Gray, for whom the lastingly popular *The King of the Golden River* had been a gift (written 1841, published 1851). In 1854, after seven years of marriage, she divorced him on grounds of impotence, and soon afterwards married *Millais. Ruskin had defended Millais and the *Pre-Raphaelites in letters to *The Times and the pamphlet *Pre-Raphaelitism* (1851). He continued to notice their work in *Notes on the Royal Academy* (1855–9 and 1875), guides intended to influence public taste and to intervene in the production and distribution of a national art.

Ruskin wrote for the Arundel Society (*Giotto and His Works in Padua*, 1853–4, 1860), taught at the Working Men's College in Red Lion Square, produced drawing manuals, helped with plans for the Oxford Museum of Natural History building, arranged for the National Gallery the drawings of the Turner bequest, tried to guide the work of individual artists (D. G. *Rossetti, J. Inchbold, J. W. Brett), gave evidence before parliamentary committees, and lectured extensively throughout the country. Some of these addresses appeared in *Lectures on Architecture and Painting* (1854) and *The Two Paths* (1859). But Ruskin's was a critical, not a collaborative intervention, and his judgements often offended. Speaking in Manchester on *The Political Economy of Art* (1857), Ruskin challenged economic laws affecting matters in which he had a standing. In the final volume of *Modern Painters* (1860) he denounced greed as the deadly principle guiding English life. In attacking the 'pseudo-science' of J. S. *Mill and *Ricardo in *Unto this Last* (1860) and *Essays on Political Economy* (1862–3; later *Munera Pulveris*, 1872), Ruskin entered new territory and declared open warfare against the spirit and science of his times.

This fight, against competition and self-interest, for the recovery of heroic, feudal, and Christian social ideals was to occupy Ruskin for the rest of his life. It is expressed in considerations of engraving or Greek myth (*The Cestus of Aglaia*, 1865–6; *The Queen of the Air*, 1869), geology lectures for children (*The Ethics of the Dust*, 1866), as essays on the respective duties of men and women (*Sesame and Lilies*, 1865, 1871), lectures on war, work, and trade (*The Crown of Wild Olives*, 1866, 1873), or letters to a workman (*Time and Tide*, by Weare and Tyne, 1867). The letter was a favourite mode with Ruskin. In *Fors Clavigera* (1871–8) he found a serial form well suited to his public teaching and to the diversity of his interests, which also expressed themselves during the 1870s and 1880s in a multitude of writings on natural history, travel, painting, etc., and in practical projects, many associated with the Guild of St George, a utopian society founded by Ruskin under his own mastership in 1871.

In 1870 Ruskin was elected first Slade professor of

art at Oxford. He started a drawing school, arranged art collections of his own gift, and drew crowds to his eleven courses of lectures. Seven volumes of them were published shortly after delivery: *Lectures on Art* (1870), *Aratra Pentelici*, *The Relation between Michael Angelo and Tintoret*, *The Eagle's Nest* (all 1872), *Love's Meinie* (1873, 1881), and *Ariadne Fiorentina* (1873–6). But, despite caution, Ruskin did not keep his 'own peculiar opinions' out of his lectures. Senior members of the university were alarmed, Ruskin offended: he resigned in 1878. Although Ruskin returned to Oxford in 1883 and gave two more courses of lectures, some of his statements were even more startling than before, and he resigned once more in 1885.

The isolation of his later years was barely mitigated by the loyalty of his disciples, who included J. W. Bunney and George Allen, both students of the Working Men's College, and W. G. Collingwood, who acted as Ruskin's secretary at Brantwood, the house in the Lake District which was his home after 1870. Older friends, such as Sir Henry Acland and *Carlyle, remained doubtful about the schemes, the vehemence and the frequent obscurity of his later pronouncements. They were also disturbed by Ruskin's private dreams of Rose La Touche. In middle and old age he made many young girls the objects of his affection. Rose, an Anglo-Irish girl, was 11 when Ruskin came across her in 1858, 18 when he proposed in 1866. But he could not share her evangelical religious views, her parents were also opposed, and she died, mad, in 1875. Four years later Ruskin himself went through the first of a series of delirious illnesses. He often wrote for her and, indirectly, of her, in later life, and in *Praeterita*, the autobiography on which he worked sporadically between 1885 and 1889, he would have spoken of her directly; but he did not complete it. After 1889 Ruskin wrote nothing and spoke rarely, but was cared for by his cousin, Joan Severn, at his house on Coniston Water.

RUSSELL, Bertrand Arthur William, third Earl Russell (1872–1970), educated privately and at Trinity College, Cambridge, of which he became a fellow. He wrote voluminously on philosophy, logic, education, economics, and politics, and throughout his life was the champion of advanced political and social causes. While much of his writing was relatively practical and ephemeral in intent, and successfully aimed at a wide audience, he also contributed work of lasting importance in some of the most technical fields of philosophy and logic. He was the inventor of the Theory of Descriptions. *The Principles of Mathematics* (1903) and *Principia Mathematica* (the latter in collaboration with A. N. *Whitehead, 1910) quickly became classics of mathematical logic. Other important philosophical works include *The Analysis of Mind* (1921), *An Inquiry into Meaning and Truth* (1940), and *Human Knowledge, Its Scope and Limits* (1948). Russell was awarded the *Nobel Prize for literature in 1950. For an account of his

relationships with Ottoline *Morrell, D. H. *Lawrence, G. *Murray, G. E. *Moore, *Wittgenstein, and many other figures in the literary and intellectual world, see a life by R. W. Clark (1975).

RUSSELL, George William (Æ) (1867–1935), born in Ireland. He became an art student in Dublin, and in 1894 published *Homeward*, his first volume of mystical verses, with the encouragement of *Yeats. His poetic drama *Deirdre* was performed in 1902 at the Irish National Theatre (later the *Abbey), which he helped to found. From 1905 to 1923 he edited *The Irish Homestead*, a journal which encouraged interest in Irish crafts, arts, writing, agriculture, and home economics, and achieved large sales in Ireland and the USA; meanwhile he continued to publish poetry, including *The Divine Vision* (1904), *Gods of War* (1915), *The Interpreters* (1922), and *Midsummer Eve* (1928). From 1923 until 1930 he edited the *Irish Statesman*, a literary and political journal supporting the Free State. *The Avatars*, a fantasy of the future, aroused much interest in 1933. In 1934 he published an ambitious poem of Celtic mythology, *The House of the Titans*, and in 1935 his *Selected Poems*. He published many political essays, and did much to support young Irish writers, such as *Colum and *Stephens. His pseudonym 'Æ' was a contraction of the word 'æon', which he had once used as a signature. See H. Summerfield, *That Myriad-Minded Man* (1975).

RUSSELL, Lord John, First Earl Russell: see REFORM BILLS.

Russell, Lady, a character in J. Austen's *Persuasion*.

Ruth, a novel by Mrs *Gaskell, published 1853.

Ruth Hilton, a 15-year-old orphan apprenticed to a dressmaker, is seduced and then deserted by the wealthy young Henry Bellingham. She is rescued from suicide by Thurston Benson, a Dissenting minister, who with the connivance of his sister and of his outspoken old servant Sally takes her into his own house under an assumed name as a widow. She bears Bellingham's son, and is redeemed by her love for her child and by the guidance of Benson. Later she is employed as a governess in the family of the tyrannical and pharisaical Mr Bradshaw, where she is discovered by Bellingham, whose offer of marriage she rejects. Bradshaw, learning the truth about her past, brutally dismisses her and quarrels with Benson. Ruth regains esteem by becoming a heroic hospital nurse during a cholera epidemic, and dies after nursing Bellingham to recovery. Mrs Gaskell's purpose in this novel was to arouse more sympathy for 'fallen women' who had been unprotected victims of seduction, but she shocked many contemporary readers.

RUTHERFORD, Mark, see WHITE, W. H.

Ruthwell Cross, a stone monument in the parish church at Ruthwell, Dumfriesshire, dating perhaps from the 8th cent., on which are inscribed in *runes some alliterating phrases closely corresponding to parts of the Old English poem *Dream of the Rood. It was thrown down by the Presbyterians in 1642 and the inscriptions partly effaced. See The Dream of the Rood, ed. B. Dickins and A. S. C. Ross (1934), 1–13; J. L. Dinwiddie, The Ruthwell Cross and Its Story (1927).

Ryence, Rion, Rience, or **Royns,** King, a British or Celtic king (usually of Ireland but of north Wales in *Malory) who sent an arrogant message to Arthur demanding his beard to make up a set of 12 taken from his vanquished enemies. He was overcome and taken prisoner by *Balyn and *Balan who delivered him to Arthur's court (in the first of Vinaver's eight Works of Malory). He is usually represented as a pagan giant, the same as the 'Ritho' mentioned by *Geoffrey of Monmouth and *Wace as a challenger of *Arthur.

RYLE, Gilbert (1900–76), educated at Brighton College and The Queen's College, Oxford; Waynflete professor of metaphysical philosophy in the University of Oxford (1945–68). The author of numerous articles on a wide variety of philosophical topics, he is best known for his attack on the traditional metaphysical dualism of mind and body, which he calls the 'dogma of the ghost in the machine'. His best-known book is The Concept of Mind (1949). A general account of his view of philosophical problems is contained in Dilemmas (1954).

RYMAN, Geoff (1951–   ), Canadian-born novelist, based in London since 1973. Having won awards for his science fiction, which includes The Unconquered Country (1986) and The Child Garden (1989), Ryman moved towards slightly more realistic territory with Was (1992), a novel about Dorothy from The Wizard of Oz. 253 (1996) was published initially on the Internet and later in a very successful 'print remix'. Set on London Underground's Bakerloo line between Embankment and Elephant & Castle on a particular day in 1995, 253 consists of character sketches (each 253 words long) of the 253 passengers there would be on a such a train if every seat were taken. See INTERACTIVE FICTION.

RYMER, Thomas (1641–1713), educated at Sidney Sussex College, Cambridge, chiefly remembered for his valuable collection of historical records, *Foedera (1704–35). He wrote a play in rhymed verse, Edgar, or The English Monarch (1678, unperformed), but is better known as a critic of considerable learning but dogmatic views, who supported the ancients in the battle between them and the moderns (see BATTLE OF THE BOOKS, THE) and upheld French *neo-classical principles. The Tragedies of the Last Age Considered (1678) was a critical attack on Elizabethan drama, continued in his A Short View of Tragedy (1692) which contains his famous condemnation of *Othello as 'a bloody farce'.

RYSBRACK, Michael (1694–1770), Flemish sculptor, trained in Antwerp, who settled in England; the classicism of his style made him popular with the virtuosi in the circle of Lord Burlington. Rysbrack's Roman reliefs in the chimney-pieces at Houghton (Norfolk) and Clandon Park (Surrey) satisfied the taste of an era formed by the writings of *Shaftesbury, and his bust of Daniel Finch, earl of Nottingham (1723), introduced the fashion for the portrait bust into English sculpture. *Pope (of whom he made an idealized bust, 1730) collaborated with him on some of his monuments in Westminster Abbey, where his most famous work is the monument to Sir I. *Newton; his contributions to *Poets' Corner include memorials to *Jonson (c.1737), *Gay (1736), *Prior, and N. *Rowe. The national pride that inspired Poets' Corner found striking expression in the cult of British Worthies; William Kent's Temple of British Worthies (1733) at Stowe is decorated with many busts by Rysbrack.

S

SABA, Umberto (1883–1957), Italian poet. Born Umberto Poli in Trieste of a Jewish mother, he adopted the name Saba from his nurse, his father having deserted him before his birth. He draws on different strands of Italian literary tradition, *Petrarch, *Pascoli, *d'Annunzio, and from Freudian ideas; but on the surface he remains a simple poet of nature and domestic affections. His main poems are in his *Canzoniere*, of which there are three different collections (1921, 1945, 1948). He has been translated by R. *Lowell.

Sabrina, a poetic name for the river Severn (see under ESTRILDIS). In Milton's *Comus*, Sabrina is the goddess of the Severn.

Miss Sabrina is the new schoolmistress in Galt's *Annals of the Parish*. 'Old Mr Hookie, her father, had, from the time he read his Virgil, maintained a sort of intromission with the Nine Muses, by which he was led to baptize her Sabrina, after a name mentioned by John Milton in one of his works.'

Sacharissa, see WALLER.

SACHS, Hans (1494–1576), shoemaker of Nuremberg, and author of a vast quantity of verse, including meistersongs and some 200 plays. He was raised to mythic status by *Wagner in his opera *Die Meistersinger von Nürnberg* (1868).

SACKS, Oliver (1933–), London-born neurologist and writer, educated at St Paul's School, the Queen's College, Oxford, and Middlesex Hospital; he has worked for many years as clinician and instructor in New York. *Awakenings* (1973, the source of *A Kind of Alaska* by *Pinter) is a description, with vividly written case histories, of the reactions of post-encephalitic 'sleeping-sickness' patients of the 1916–17 epidemic to the new drug L-DOPA. Other works include *Seeing Voices* (1989), *An Anthropologist on Mars* (1995), and *The Island of the Colour-Blind and Cycad Island* (1996). *The Man Who Mistook His Wife for a Hat* was adapted by Peter *Brook as *L'Homme qui* (Paris, 1993: UK, *The Man Who*, 1994).

SACKVILLE, Charles, Lord Buckhurst, and later sixth earl of Dorset (1638–1706), a favourite of Charles II and noted for dissipation, who later became a loyal supporter of William III. He was a friend and patron of poets, was praised as a poet by *Prior and *Dryden, and has been identified with the Eugenius of the latter's *Of Dramatick Poesy*. His poems, which appeared with those of *Sedley in 1701, include some biting satires and the ballad 'To all you Ladies now at Land'.

SACKVILLE, Thomas, first earl of Dorset and Baron Buckhurst (1536–1608), son of Sir Richard Sackville. He was probably educated at Oxford. He was a barrister of the Inner Temple. He entered Parliament in 1558, was raised to the peerage in 1567, and held a number of high official positions, including those of lord treasurer and chancellor of Oxford University. He wrote the induction and *The Complaint of Buckingham* for *A Mirror for Magistrates*, and collaborated (probably writing only the last two acts) with Thomas Norton in the tragedy of *Gorboduc*. He was an ancestor of V. *Sackville-West and is discussed in her *Knole and the Sackvilles* (1922).

SACKVILLE-WEST, Hon. Victoria Mary ('Vita'), CH (1892–1962), poet and novelist. She was born at Knole, Kent, about which she wrote *Knole and the Sackvilles* (1922) and which provided the setting for her novel *The Edwardians* (1930). In 1913 she married Harold *Nicolson, with whom she travelled widely during his diplomatic career before settling at Sissinghurst, Kent, where she devoted much time to gardening. In 1922 she met Virginia *Woolf, whose *Orlando* (1928) was inspired by their close friendship. Her other works include a pastoral poem, *The Land* (1926, Hawthornden Prize), *All Passion Spent* (1931, novel), *Collected Poems* (1933), and many works on travel, gardening, and literary topics. Her unorthodox marriage was described by her son Nigel Nicolson in *Portrait of a Marriage* (1973). A biography by Victoria *Glendinning was published in 1983.

Sacripant, (1) in *Orlando innamorato* and *Orlando furioso*, the king of Circassia and a lover of *Angelica. He catches *Rinaldo's horse *Bayard, and rides away on it, and Rinaldo calls him a horse-thief; (2) in Tassoni's *Seccia rapita* (*The Rape of the Bucket*), a hectoring braggart; (3) Sacrapant, a magician in Peele's *The Old Wives Tale*. In modern French *sacripant* is a rascal or blackguard.

SADE, Donatien Alphonse, comte, known as marquis de (1740–1814), French novelist and pornographer. His career as a cavalry officer was destroyed by the disorder of his life. During prolonged periods of imprisonment he wrote a number of pornographic novels, including *Justine ou les malheurs de la vertu* (1791), *La Philosophie dans le boudoir* (1795), and *Nouvelle Justine* (1797). Their obsession with the minutiae of sexual pathology and their extreme hedonistic nihilism have been seen to anticipate *Nietzsche, *Freud and *Foucault. Long censored in Britian, but now readily available, they have had a considerable influence on English literature, inspiring imitation and parody from writers as diverse as *Swinburne, Angus *Wilson, and A. *Carter. De Sade's period of imprisonment at the mental hospital of Charenton (where he died) was the basis of *Weiss's play, commonly known as the 'Marat/Sade' (1964), which, through Peter *Brook's production, had a powerful impact on British theatre. There is a life of de Sade by Maurice Lever (1991, trans. 1993).

SA'DĪ (d. ?1292), a celebrated Persian poet, whose principal works were the collections of verse known as the 'Gulistan' or Rose Garden, and the 'Bustan' or Tree Garden.

SADLEIR (formerly Sadler), Michael (1888–1957), bibliographer and novelist, educated at Rugby and Balliol College, Oxford. He joined the publishing house of Constable of which he became director in 1920. He amassed an outstanding collection of 19th-cent. books, often of less-known authors, and wrote important bibliographical works, including *Excursions in Victorian Bibliography* (1922) and *Nineteenth Century Fiction* (2 vols, 1951). His best-known novel, *Fanny by Gaslight* (1940), has been made into a film.

Sad Shepherd, The, *or A Tale of Robin Hood*, the last and unfinished play of *Jonson, a pastoral tragicomedy written c.1635, printed 1641.

Robin Hood invites the shepherds and shepherdesses of the Vale of Belvoir to a feast in Sherwood Forest, but the feast is marred by the arts of the witch Maudlin, aided by her familiar, Puck-Hairy. Aeglamour, the Sad Shepherd, relates the loss of his beloved Earine, whom he believes drowned in the Trent. In reality Maudlin has stripped her of her garments to adorn her daughter and shut her up in an oak as a prey for her son, the uncouth swineherd Lorel. The witch assumes the form of Maid Marian, sends away the venison prepared for the feast, abuses Robin Hood, and throws his guests into confusion. Lorel tries to win Earine but fails. The wiles of Maudlin are detected, and Robin's huntsmen pursue her. Only the first three acts of the play exist; there are continuations by Francis Waldron (1783) and Alan Porter (1935).

saga, an Old Norse word meaning 'story', applied to narrative compositions from Iceland and Norway in the Middle Ages. There are three main types of saga: family sagas, dealing with the first settlers of Iceland and their descendants; kings' sagas, historical works about the kings of Norway; and legendary or heroic sagas, fantastic adventure stories about legendary heroes. The family sagas and the kings' sagas share an elegant, laconic style, notable for its air of detached objectivity. This led early scholars to suppose that the family sagas were reliably historical, being based almost wholly on oral traditions from an earlier period; but modern critics see these works as literary fictions with some historical basis. The most celebrated of the family sagas is *Njáls saga*, a long but tightly structured narrative about Gunnarr, a brave and worthy man who marries the beautiful but morally flawed Hallgerr; she sets in motion a series of feuds which culminates first in her husband's heroic last stand and death, and then in the burning of Gunnarr's friend Njall, a wise and peaceable lawyer who accepts his fate with Christian resignation. The main concerns of the saga (the growth of social stability, legal and political, among the settlers of a new community, and the part played by human emotions, especially rivalry, loyalty, and sexual jealousy, in the course of this development) are characteristic of the other family sagas too, though *Njáls saga* stands out because of its scope and breadth of characterization. *Eyrbyggja saga* is especially concerned with the emergence of a politically stable community, though it also recounts some bizarre supernatural incidents. *Laxdaela saga* deals with the theme of a tragic love triangle and the fortunes of one of Iceland's most powerful families at that time. *Grettis saga* tells, with remarkable psychological depth and sublety, the story of a famous Icelandic outlaw; Grettir's fights with the monstrous walking corpse Glámr and with a troll woman are analogous to Beowulf's fight with Grendel and Grendel's mother (see BEOWULF). Snorri Sturluson's *Heimskringla* comprises a history of the kings of Norway; *Volsunga saga* recounts the legends of the Goths and Burgundians which underlie Wagner's *Ring des Nibelungen* cycle. *Sturlunga saga* is unique in being a compilation of sagas about figures almost contemporary with their 13th-cent. authors. W. *Morris did much to popularize Icelandic literature in England. (See SIGURD THE VOLSUNG.)

Njáls saga, trans. M. Magnusson and H. Pálsson (1960); *Eyrbyggja saga*, trans. H. Pálsson and P. Edwards (1973); *Laxdaela saga*, trans. M. Magnusson and H. Pálsson (1969); *The Saga of Grettir the Strong*, trans. G. A. Hight (1965).

SAID, Edward (1935–2003), Palestinian critic, born in Jerusalem, and educated at Victoria College, Cairo, then at Princeton and Harvard. He taught for many years at Columbia University, New York. His works of general literary theory, *Beginnings* (1975) and *The World*, the Text and the Critic (1983), show the influence of *Foucault. His most influential book, *Orientalism* (1978), shows how Western 'experts' have constructed a myth of the 'Orient'; it is a founding text of modern *post-colonial theory, complemented by the essays collected in *Culture and Imperialism* (1993). His other roles were as a music critic and a public defender of the Palestinian cause.

ST AUBIN DE TERÁN, Lisa (1953–), novelist, born in south London. Her father is Guyanese writer Jan Carew (1925–). She married a Venezuelan landowner when she was 16, and her travels and experiences are reflected in *Keepers of the House* (1982), a chronicle which tells the dramatic story of the decline of the Beltrán family, its feuds, its tragedies, its interbreeding, and its decaying elegance, from the days of Columbus through to the 1970s. This oral history is conveyed through the persona of English bride Lydia, married to Diego Beltrán. The vast plantation of sugar and avocado recurs again and again in St Aubin de Terán's works: the exiled Venezuelan husband Cesar in *The Slow Train to Milan* (1983) harks back to it in memory, though this novel is set in Europe (London, Oxford, Paris, Milan, Bologna) and evokes a life of a group of wandering exiles with a passion for 'the extravagance of clothes' and 'the comfort of travel'. The spirited first-person narration is by child-bride Lizaveta, herself the descendant of a highly eccentric family, and it brilliantly and wittily combines elements of the 'road' novels of the *Beat Generation with South American *magic realism and a tragi-comic sense of the heroic futility of political struggle. *The Tiger* (1984) returns to the history of a plantation in the Andes from Armistice Day, 1918, when it was dominated by a ferocious German-born tyrant from Tilsit: her grandson Lucien inherits, lives the high life for a short time in Caracas, and is condemned as a traitor to 25 years of brutal incarceration. Later works include *The Bay of Silence* (1986), *Black Idol* (1987), *Joanna* (1990), and short stories, *The Marble Mountain* (1988); *Off the Rails: Memoirs of a Train Addict* (1989) is ostensibly a memoir, returning to the erotic obsession with trains, but in her work fact, fantasy, and myth are deliberately entangled, and it is not always easy to tell where memoir ends and fiction begins. *The Hacienda: My Venezuelan Years* (1997) is a memoir.

ST AUBYN, Edward (1960–   ), novelist, author of a trilogy of short novels *Never Mind* (1992), *Bad News* (1992), and *Some Hope* (1994): the first describes with horrific conviction the indulged but appalling childhood of Patrick Melrose, sexually abused by his father on holiday in the south of France in the 1960s, and the two later volumes follow Patrick to New York (where his father lies dead in a funeral parlour) and back to London, as he struggles to cope with his drug addiction and his terrible paternal legacy. Sharp, understated, and stylish, they counteract the baroque nature of much *Chemical Generation writing. *On the Edge* (1998) is a journey through the *New Age cults of the 1990s, from Findhorn to California, and follows with some unease the spiritual and sexual quests of several pilgrims, including a drop-out English banker.

SAINTE-BEUVE, Charles-Augustin (1804–69), French critic. His famous articles in periodicals such as *La Revue de Paris* and *La *Revue des deux mondes* were collected as *Critiques et portraits littéraires* (1832, 1836–9). Between 1849 and 1869 he contributed weekly critical essays to Paris newspapers; these were the celebrated 'Causeries du lundi', appearing on Mondays and collected in book form as *Causeries du lundi* (15 vols, 1851–62) and *Nouveaux Lundis* (13 vols, 1863–70). His two long studies, each of which began life as a course of lectures, *Port-Royal* (6 bks, 1840–59), are classics of literary and biographical criticism. To

the care and method of the professional critic Sainte-Beuve joined a subtle and enquiring curiosity about books and authors, wide-ranging interests and a humane and tolerant spirit. He is generally regarded as one of the founders of modern criticism. Some of his early essays, and notably his *Tableau historique . . . de la poésie française . . . au XVIe siècle* (1828), helped to promote the poetry of the Romantic movement in France by tracing its affinities with 16th-cent. poetry. He later revised his opinion of the Romantics.

SAINT-EVRÉMOND, Charles de Saint-Denis (1613–1703), French critic. He spent the latter part of his life in exile in England, where he acted as arbiter of taste from the reign of Charles II to that of William III. In his sceptical epicureanism he was a representative freethinker who wrote with witty sobriety on a variety of subjects, including English comedy. His works were translated in 1714, some of his essays having previously appeared in English in 1693, with a preface by *Dryden.

SAINT-EXUPÉRY, Antoine de (1900–44), French novelist. He was actively involved in the early years of commercial aviation, and his novels are intimately linked with his flying experiences: *Courrier sud* (1928; *Southern Mail*, 1933), *Vol de nuit* (1931; *Night Flight*, 1932), *Terre des hommes* (1939; *Wind, Sand and Stars*, 1939), and *Pilote de guerre* (1942; *Flight to Arras*, 1942). He also wrote a book for children, *Le Petit Prince* (1943; *The Little Prince*, 1944). He failed to return from a reconnaissance mission in north Africa: his presumed death in the desert contributed to the success of an unfinished collection of desert meditations, *Citadelle* (1948; *Wisdom of the Sands*, 1952).

ST JOHN, Henry, see BOLINGBROKE, H. ST J.

SAINT-JOHN PERSE, pseudonym of Alexis Saint-Léger Léger (1887–1975), French poet and diplomat. His early poems, *Éloges* (1911), evoked his childhood in the French West Indies. He travelled widely for most of his life, his career in the French foreign service taking him as far afield as Peking. He first became known to the English-speaking world through T. S. *Eliot's translation of his epic poem *Anabase* (1924), a sumptuous chronicle of Asiatic tribal migrations. Exiled to the United States after 1940, he produced a succession of highly wrought prose poems of rare rhythmic subtlety: *Exil* (1942), *Pluies* (1943), *Neiges* (1944), and *Vents* (1946). His work as a whole displays an extraordinary command of the rhetorical possibilities of the French language. He was awarded the *Nobel Prize in 1960.

St Patrick's Day, a play in two acts by R. B. *Sheridan, produced 1785.

In this brief skit a wily lieutenant, in love with the daughter of a justice, impersonates a German quack and, when the justice is convinced he is poisoned, extracts the promise of the daughter's hand, as the price for a cure.

SAINT-PIERRE, Jacques-Henri Bernardin de, see BER-
NARDIN DE SAINT-PIERRE.

St Ronan's Well, a novel by Sir W. *Scott, published
1823.

The novel, one of only two set within Scott's lifetime,
is the only one in which he attempts contemporary
social satire. St Ronan's Well is a tawdry, third-rate spa,
inhabited by meretricious, pretentious characters.
Against this background, he sets the melodrama of
two half-brothers, sons of the late earl of Etherington,
both of whom are involved with Clara Mowbray,
daughter of the local laird. The younger son impersonates the elder, Francis, at a midnight marriage with
Clara, who is thus married to a man she detests, and the
novel ends in unrelieved tragedy.

SAINTSBURY, George Edward Bateman (1845–1933),
critic and journalist, educated at King's College School,
London, and Merton College, Oxford. He contributed
numerous articles to the *Fortnightly Review, *Pall Mall
Gazette,* and other journals. He was an industrious
journalist for the *Daily News* and the *Manchester
Guardian,* and was introduced by his friend *Lang to
the *Saturday Review,* of which he became assistant
editor (1883–94). His first book, *A Primer of French
Literature,* was published in 1880, and thereafter he
published voluminously. In 1895 he was appointed to
the chair of rhetoric and English literature at Edinburgh, which he held for 20 years, during which he
published some of his largest works, including *A
History of Nineteenth Century Literature* (1896), *The
History of Criticism and Literary Taste in Europe* (1900–
4), *A History of English Prosody* (1906–10), and books
on *Sir Walter Scott* (1897) and *Matthew Arnold* (1898).
Saintsbury was a connoisseur of wine and the success
of his *Notes on a Cellarbook* (1920) led to the founding
of the Saintsbury Club.

Saint's Everlasting Rest, The, see BAXTER, R.

SAINT-SIMON, Claude-Henri de Rouvroy, comte de
(1760–1825), French social philosopher and political
economist, whose father was a cousin of the duc de
*Saint-Simon. In his various writings Saint-Simon laid
down a set of principles for the reorganization of
European society after the French Revolution in
conformity with current scientific and economic notions. Conceiving of a nation as a vast productive
enterprise, he proposed that industrialists should hold
political power and that spiritual authority should be
vested in scientists and artists in order to secure the
physical and moral improvement of all classes. After
his death his followers formed a religious association
and elaborated his ideas along broadly socialist lines
into the doctrine known as *Saint-Simonisme.* They
advocated the abolition of the right of private inheritance and its transfer to the state, the institution of a
hierarchy of merit, and the enfranchisement of
women. The association was declared illegal in 1832.

SAINT-SIMON, Louis de Rouvroy, duc de (1675–1755),
French chronicler and memorialist. After a period of
reluctant army service, he sought advancement at
court until 1723, when the death of his patron, the duc
d'Orléans, put an end to his participation in public
affairs. His great work, the *Mémoires* (first authentic
edition in 21 vols, 1829–30), composed during the 20
years of his retirement, offers an incomparable record
of life at court in the latter part of Louis XIV's reign. The
verve of his writing, the liveliness of his observation,
and the penetration of his portraits have made this
work a classic of the genre. It was among *Proust's
favourite reading. A new translation in three volumes
by Lucy Norton was published 1967–72.

SAKI, pseudonym of Hector Hugh Munro (1870–
1916), known principally for his short stories; he
was born in Burma, the youngest of three children: his
mother died when he was an infant, and he was
brought up in north Devon by two aunts. In 1893 he
joined the military police in Burma, but was invalided
home and went to London to earn his living as a writer.
In 1899 he published *The Rise of the Russian Empire,* in
1900 wrote political satire for the *Westminster Gazette,*
and between 1902 and 1908 was correspondent for the
*Morning Post in Poland, Russia, and Paris. His first
characteristic volume of short stories, *Reginald,* was
published under the pseudonym Saki (of uncertain
origin) in 1904, followed by *Reginald in Russia* (1910),
The Chronicles of Clovis (1911), *Beasts and Super-
Beasts* (1914), *The Toys of Peace* (1919), and *The Square
Egg* (1924). *The Unbearable Bassington* (1912) and
When William Came (1913) are both novels. In 1914 he
enlisted as a trooper and he was killed in France, shot
through the head while resting in a shallow crater. His
stories include the satiric, the comic, the macabre, and
the supernatural, and show a marked interest in the use
of animals—wolves, tigers, bulls, ferrets, cats—as
agents of revenge upon mankind.

Sakúntalā, see SHAKÚNTALĀ.

SALA, George Augustus (1828–96), journalist and
illustrator. He began his literary career as editor of
Chat in 1848, and became a regular contributor to
Household Words (1851–6); he was sent by *Dickens
to Russia as correspondent at the end of the Crimean
War and subsequently wrote for the *Daily Telegraph.*
He published books of travel and novels.

SALADIN (Salah-ed-Din Yusuf ibn Ayub) (c.1138–93),
a Kurd who was the founder of the Ayyubid dynasty in
Egypt. He was established as caliph there in 1171, and
he took possession of southern Syria and Damascus on
the death of Nur-ed-Din in 1174. After defeat by the
Christians in 1177, he made further advances and he
defeated their forces led by Guy de Lusignan at the
battle of Tiberias on 4 July 1187. He then besieged and
captured Acre and Jerusalem (Oct. 1187). After several
defeats by the forces of the Third Crusade led by
*Richard I, Cœur de Lion, he made a truce with them in

1192 which allowed Henry of Champagne, titular king of Jerusalem, a strip of coastal land around Acre and access to Jerusalem itself. But the progress made by his conquests remained considerable at his death in 1193. Largely because of his clemency towards the defeated Christian forces after Tiberias, he is traditionally represented as chivalrous, loyal, and magnanimous: by Boccaccio who represents him thus in two stories in the *Decameron (Day 1, Tale 3; Day 10, Tale 9); by *Dante who places him in the limbo of heroes (Inferno, iv. 129); and by English writers such as Scott in *The Talisman. See H. A. R. Gibb, Studies on the Civilisation of Islam (1962), 91–107.

Salerio and **Solanio,** two (or possibly three, if 'Salarino' is distinct from Salerio) friends of *Antonio and *Bassanio in Shakespeare's *The Merchant of Venice.

SALINGER, J(erome) D(avid) (1919–   ), American novelist and short story writer, born in New York. He served with the 4th Infantry Division in the Second World War and was stationed at Tiverton, Devon, in Mar. 1944, an experience which inspired his story 'For Esme with Love and Squalor'. He is best known for his novel The Catcher in the Rye (1951), the story of adolescent Holden Caulfield who runs away from boarding school in Pennsylvania to New York, where he preserves his innocence despite various attempts to lose it. The colloquial, lively, first-person narration, with its attacks on the 'phoniness' of the adult world and its clinging to family sentiment in the form of Holden's affection for his sister Phoebe, made the novel accessible to and popular with a wide readership, particularly with the young. A sequence of works about the eccentric Glass family began with Nine Stories (1953, published in Britain as For Esmé—With Love and Squalor) and was followed by Franny and Zooey (1961), Raise High the Roof Beam, Carpenters, and Seymour: An Introduction (published together, 1963), containing stories reprinted from the *New Yorker. A notably reclusive character, he was the subject of a biographical exercise by Ian *Hamilton (1988).

SALKEY, Andrew (1928–95), Caribbean poet, short story writer, editor and broadcaster, born in Colón, Panama, of Jamaican parents, and educated in Jamaica and at London University. He was an active figure in the promotion of Caribbean culture in Britain and abroad: his later years were spent teaching at Amherst, Massachusetts. His novels include Escape to an Autumn Pavement (1960) and A Quality of Violence (1978). His many publications include stories and fables for younger readers, such as Anancy's Score (1973), which takes its name from the Jamaican folk-trickster hero spiderman Anancy. Havana Journal is a portrait of Cuba, and Georgetown Journal (1972) describes a visit to Guyana on the occasion of its independence celebrations in 1970.

SALLUST (Gaius Sallustius Crispus) (86–35 BC), Roman historian whose surviving works are two monographs

Bellum Catilinae (The Conspiracy of Catiline), a major source of Jonson's *Catiline, and Belum Iugurthinum (The War against Jugurtha). He was popular in the Middle Ages, and his practice of including speeches, gnomic sayings, and character sketches in his narrative was copied by William of Poitiers, the historian of the Norman Conquest, and by the 12th-cent. *William of Malmesbury. The Jugurtha was translated by A. *Barclay early in the 16th cent., and T. *Heywood translated both monographs (1608). Sallust's condemnations of corruption were much savoured in the 18th cent. by the architects of the American Revolution.

'Sally in Our Alley', a ballad by H. *Carey.

SALMASIUS, professional name of Claude de Saumaise (1588–1653), an eminent French scholar, professor at Leiden University in 1649 when Charles II was living at The Hague. At the age of 19 he discovered the Palatine library at Heidelberg and unearthed the 10th-cent. Palatine Anthology (The Greek *Anthology). He was commissioned by Charles to draw up a defence of his father and an indictment of the regicide government. This took the form of the Latin Defensio Regia which reached England by the end of 1649. *Milton was ordered by the Council in 1650 to prepare a reply to it, and in 1651 issued his Pro Populo Anglicano Defensio, also in Latin, a work which brought him an international reputation and attracted great attention, much of it hostile. It is a repetitious and tedious work, a mixture of scholarship and scurrilous invective, but Milton himself was well satisfied with it. Salmasius rejoined in his Responsio, which similarly contains much personal abuse, published posthumously in 1660. *Hobbes in his Behemoth said he found the two Defensiones 'very good Latin both . . . and both very ill reasoning'.

Salome, a play by O. *Wilde, which later formed the basis for the libretto of an opera by R. *Strauss.

SALTYKOV-SHCHEDRIN, N. (Mikhail Evgrafovich) (1826–89), Russian satirical writer and polemical journalist. Born in a merchant family near Tver, he was educated at Tsarskoe Selo, outside St Petersburg, and worked in government service while writing reviews for major journals and moving in circles interested in utopian socialism. After serving as vice-governor of provincial towns, he was retired in 1868 and devoted himself to literature, working first for the Contemporary and then for Notes of the Fatherland, eventually as editor. His novels often developed from journalistic sketches. With the passage of time he became increasingly radical and in 1884 Notes of the Fatherland was closed. *Turgenev (with uncharacteristic exaggeration) called him the Russian *Swift. Saltykov-Shchedrin's major works are The Story of a Town (1869–70; English trans. 1980), The Golovlev Family (1875–80; trans. 1931), and the semi-autobiographical Old Times in Poshekhonsk (1887–9). The first

English translation of his work, *Tchinovniks: Sketches of Provincial Life*, appeared in 1861.

SAMBER, Robert, see PERRAULT.

Samient, in Spenser's *Faerie Queene* (v. viii), the lady sent by Queen *Mercilla to Adicia, the wife of the *soldan, received by her with contumely, and rescued by Sir *Artegall.

Samson Agonistes, a tragedy by *Milton, published 1671, in the same volume as *Paradise Regained*. Its composition was traditionally assigned to 1666–70, but W. R. Parker in his biography (1968) argues that it was written much earlier, possibly as early as 1647. A closet drama never intended for the stage, it is modelled on Greek tragedy, and has been frequently compared to *Prometheus Bound* by *Aeschylus or *Oedipus at Colonus* by *Sophocles: other critics have claimed that its spirit is more Hebraic (or indeed Christian) than Hellenic. Predominantly in blank verse, it also contains passages of great metrical freedom and originality, and some rhyme. *Samson Agonistes* (i.e. Samson the Wrestler, or Champion) deals with the last phase of the life of the Samson of the Book of Judges when he is a prisoner of the Philistines and blind, a phase which many have compared to the assumed circumstances of the blind poet himself, after the collapse of the Commonwealth and his political hopes.

Samson, in prison at Gaza, is visited by friends of his tribe (the chorus) who comfort him; then by his old father Manoa, who holds out hopes of securing his release; then by his wife *Dalila, who seeks pardon and reconciliation, but being repudiated shows herself 'a manifest Serpent'; then by Harapha, a strong man of Gath, who taunts Samson. He is finally summoned to provide amusement by feats of strength for the Philistines, who are celebrating a feast to *Dagon. He goes, and presently a messenger brings news of his final feat of strength in which he pulled down the pillars of the place where the assembly was gathered, destroying himself as well as the entire throng. The tragedy, which has many passages questioning divine providence ('Just or unjust, alike seem miserable'), ends with the chorus's conclusion that despite human doubts, all is for the best in the 'unsearchable dispose | Of highest wisdom': its last words, 'calm of mind all passion spent', strike a note of Aristotelian *catharsis, and the whole piece conforms to the *neo-classical doctrine of *unities.

SANCHO, (Charles) Ignatius (?1729–80), Afro-British letter writer, born on a slave ship during the Middle Passage from Africa to the Americas. Brought to England as a child, he eventually became valet to the duke of Montague, who helped him to establish a Westminster grocery shop in 1774. Sancho published letters in newspapers on public affairs and was known as a correspondent and admirer of L. *Sterne. Sancho also composed music, wrote (lost) plays, and was the

first Afro-British patron of white writers and artists. He called Phillis *Wheatley a 'genius in bondage'. A former correspondent published *Letters of the Late Ignatius Sancho, an African* (1782), increasing Sancho's fame as writer, devoted husband and father, wit, man of feeling, critic, opponent of slavery and racial discrimination in England, Africa, and India, and friend of Sterne, *Garrick, and John Hamilton Mortimer. Sancho's letters have attracted many literary and social commentators, including Thomas Jefferson. See BLACK BRITISH LITERATURE.

Sancho Panza, the squire of *Don Quixote, who accompanies him in his adventures, shares many of their unpleasant consequences, and attempts to curb his master's enthusiasms by his shrewd common sense.

SAND, George, pseudonym of Aurore Dupin, Baronne Dudevant (1804–76), French novelist. After separating from her husband, the Baron Dudevant, a retired army officer, she went to Paris in 1831 to begin an independent life as a writer. Her fame now largely derives from two groups of novels, of the many that she wrote in a long career. The first, a series of romantic tales, portrayed the struggles of the individual woman against social constraints, especially those of marriage, e.g. *Indiana* (1832), *Lélia* (1833), *Jacques* (1834). The simple, artfully told idylls of rustic life that compose the second group are set in the region of Berry, where she had a country property at Nohant, and include *La Mare au diable* (1846), *La Petite Fadette* (1848), and *François le champi* (1850). *Elle et lui* (1859) fictionalizes her liaison with Alfred de *Musset; *Un hiver à Majorque* (1841) describes an episode in her long relationship with *Chopin. *Histoire de ma vie* (4 vols, 1854–5) is an autobiography.

SANDBURG, Carl August (1878–1967), American poet, born in Chicago of Swedish Lutheran immigrant stock. He challenged contemporary taste by his use of colloquialism and free verse, and became the principal among the authors writing in Chicago during and after the First World War. He published *Chicago Poems* (1916), *Cornhuskers* (1918), *Smoke and Steel* (1920), *Slabs of the Sunburnt West* (1922), *Good Morning America* (1928), and *Complete Poems* (1950). He also compiled a collection of folk songs, *The American Songbag* (1927), and wrote stories and poems for children. His major prose work is his monumental life of Abraham Lincoln (6 vols, 1926–39); his novel *Remembrance Rock* (1948) is on an epic scale and traces the growth of an American family from its English origins and its crossing on the *Mayflower* to the present day. *Always the Young Strangers* (1953) is a volume of autobiography.

SANDFORD, Jeremy (1930–2003), television playwright, born in London, remembered for his powerful BBC television drama *Cathy Come Home* (1966), directed by Ken Loach, which focused attention on the plight of a young family trapped in a downward spiral of poverty and homelessness. It was one of the landmarks of the socially committed drama documentary of the 1960s. This was followed by *Edna the Inebriate Woman* (1971, BBC), directed by Ted Kotcheff, a sympathetic portrayal of an elderly 'bag lady'.

Sandford and Merton, *The History of*, see DAY, T.

Sanditon, an unfinished novel by J. *Austen, written 1817.

Mr Parker is obsessed with the wish to create a large and fashionable resort out of the small village of Sanditon, on the south coast. His unquenchable enthusiasm sees crescents and terraces, a hotel and a library, and bathing machines. Charlotte Heywood, an attractive, alert young woman, is invited to stay with the Parkers, where she catches the fancy of Lady Denham, the local great lady. Lady Denham's nephew and niece, Sir Edward and Miss Denham, live nearby, and the second heroine of the novel, Clara Brereton, is staying with her. Edward plans (with a frankness of expression new to the author) to seduce Clara; but his aunt intends him to marry a West Indian heiress, under the care of a Mrs Griffiths and her entourage, whose visit to Sanditon is anticipated shortly. After a ludicrous series of complications, involving both Mrs Griffiths's party and a ladies' seminary from Camberwell, the excited inhabitants of Sanditon find the expected invasion of visitors consists merely of Mrs Griffiths and three young ladies.

This highly entertaining fragment was written in the first three months of 1817, when Jane Austen was already suffering from Addison's disease (of which she died on 18 July); one of its remarkable features is the spirit with which the author satirizes the hypochondria of the sisters and brother of Mr Parker (Diana, Susan, and Arthur) and the scorn she pours on their dependence on patent medicines and tonics for their imaginary illnesses.

SANDYS, George (1578–1644), educated at St Mary Hall, Oxford. He travelled in Italy and the Near East, and in 1621 went to America as treasurer of the Virginia Company, remaining there probably for ten years. His chief works were a verse translation of *Ovid's *Metamorphoses* (1621–6), a verse *Paraphrase upon the Psalmes* (1636), and *Christs Passion: A Tragedie*, a verse translation from the Latin of *Grotius (1640). He was a member of *Falkland's circle at Great Tew.

Sanglier, Sir, in Spenser's *Faerie Queene* (V. i), the wicked knight who has cut off his lady's head, and is forced by Sir *Artegall to bear the head before him, in token of his shame. He is thought to represent Shane O'Neill, second earl of Tyrone (?1530–67), a leader of the Irish, who invaded the Pale in 1566. Sanglier in French means 'wild boar'.

Sangreal, see GRAIL.

SANKEY, I. D., see MOODY AND SANKEY.

SANNAZAR (Jacopo Sannazzaro) (1457–1530), Neapolitan author and rediscoverer of the charms of nature and the rustic life. He was author of an influential pastoral, in prose and verse, the *Arcadia, and of Latin eclogues and other poems including five piscatorial eclogues, a genre of his own invention which was later adopted by *Walton.

Sansfoy, Sansjoy, and **Sansloy,** three brothers in Spenser's *Faerie Queene* (I. ii. 25 *et seq.*). Sansfoy ('faithless') is slain by the *Redcrosse Knight, who also defeats Sansjoy ('joyless'), but the latter is saved from death by *Duessa. Sansloy ('lawless') carries off *Una and kills her lion (I. iii). This incident is supposed to refer to the suppression of the Protestant religion in the reign of Queen Mary.

SANSOM, William (1912–76), short story writer, travel writer, and novelist, born in London and educated at Uppingham. He travelled widely as a young man, and worked at various jobs, including that of copy-writer for an advertising agency. His first stories were published in literary periodicals (*Horizon, *New Writing, the *Cornhill, and others) and his first volume, *Fireman Flower and Other Stories* (1944), reflects his experiences with the National Fire Service in wartime London. This was followed by many other collections of stories, some set in London, others making full use of backdrops from Germany, Scandinavia, and the Mediterranean. His most successful novel, *The Body* (1949), is set in London. A collection of stories, with an introduction by E. *Bowen, appeared in 1963.

SANTAYANA, George (1863–1952), a Spaniard brought up in Boston and educated at Harvard, where he taught philosophy from 1889 to 1912; he then came to Europe, living in France and England and later in Italy, where he died. He was a speculative philosopher, of a naturalist tendency and opposed to German idealism, whose views are embodied in his *The Life of Reason* (1905–6). He holds that the human mind is an effect of physical growth and organization; but that our ideas, though of bodily origin, stand on a higher and non-material plane; that the true function of reason is not in idealistic dreams but in a logical activity that takes account of facts. He analyses religious and other institutions, distinguishing the ideal element from its material embodiment. Thus the wisdom embodied in the ritual and dogmas of religion is not truth about existence, but about the ideals on which mental strength and serenity are founded. He later modified and supplemented his philosophy in a series of four books, *Realms of Being* (1927–40).

Santayana also published poetry, criticism, reviews, memoirs, etc.; his other works include *Soliloquies in England* (1922), essays on the English character; *Character and Opinion in the United States* (1920), one of several studies of American life; and *Persons and Places* (3 vols, 1944–53). His only novel, *The Last*

Puritan (1935), describes at length the antecedents and brief life of Boston-born Oliver Alden, 'the child of an elderly and weary man, and of a thin-spun race', whose European wanderings end in death by motor accident just after Armistice Day; few perhaps would endorse the comment made by a character to the supposed author, criticizing his fiction: 'Your women are too intelligent, and your men also.' Santayana's style has been variously praised for its richness and condemned for its 'purple passages'. He strongly influenced Wallace *Stevens, whose poem 'To an Old Philosopher in Rome' is a tribute to him.

SAPPER, the pseudonym of Herman Cyril McNeile (1888–1937), creator of Hugh 'Bulldog' Drummond, the hefty, ugly, charming, xenophobic, and apparently brainless British ex-army officer who foils the activities of Carl Peterson, the international crook. He appears in *Bull-dog Drummond* (1920), *The Female of the Species* (1928), and many other popular thrillers; after McNeile's death the series was continued under the same pseudonym by G. T. Fairlie. See R. Usborne, *Clubland Heroes* (1953, 1974).

SAPPHO (b. *c.* mid-7th cent. BC), a Greek lyric poet, born in Lesbos. Like her fellow countryman and contemporary Alcaeus, she appears to have left Lesbos in consequence of political troubles, gone to Sicily, and died there. The story of her throwing herself into the sea in despair at her unrequited love for Phaon the boatman is mere romance. Thanks to papyrus finds, we now have 12 poems in some form of preservation (see D. L. Page, *Sappho and Alcaeus*, 1955). Her principal subject is always love, which she expresses with great simplicity and a remarkable felicity of phrase.

Sapsea, Mr, in Dickens's *Edwin Drood*, an auctioneer and mayor of Cloisterham.

SARAMAGO, José (1922–   ), Portuguese novelist who was first brought to the attention of English readers with the translation (1988) of his novel *Memorial do convento* (1982; trans. as *Baltasar and Blimunda*). In his next novel, *Ano da morte de Ricardo Reis* (1984; *Year of the Death of Ricardo Reis*, 1991), Dr Ricardo Reis returns to Lisbon after a 16-year absence, and roams the city with, among others, the recently dead poet Fernando Pessoa. Set in 1936, this novel (generally considered Saramago's masterpiece) evokes a world where war is imminent, and where conventional boundaries between reality and illusion have lost their meaning. In *Ensaio sobre a cegueira* (1995; *Blindness*, 1997), in which the spread of an epidemic of white blindness brings about the collapse of a civilized society, Saramago uses allegory to illustrate the basic threat of latent human savagery. He was awarded the *Nobel Prize in 1998.

Sardanapalus, a poetic drama by Lord *Byron, published 1821.
    The subject was taken from the *Bibliotheca Historica*

of Siculus. Sardanapalus is represented as an effete but courageous monarch. When Beleses, a Chaldean soothsayer, and Arabaces, governor of Media, lead a revolt against him, he shakes off his slothful luxury and, urged on by Myrrha, his favourite Greek slave, fights bravely at the head of his troops. Defeated, he arranges for the safety of his queen, Zarina, and of his supporters, then prepares a funeral pyre round his throne and perishes in it with Myrrha.

Sarras, in the legend of the *Grail, the land to which *Joseph of Arimathea fled from Jerusalem. In the prose *La Queste del Saint Graal*, the three knights who are successful in the Quest, Galaad, Perceval, and Bohort (Bors), are borne there by Solomon's ship, and Galaad dies in ecstasy after seeing openly the ultimate mystery there.

SARRAUTE, Nathalie, see NOUVEAU ROMAN.

SARTORIS, Adelaide, née Kemble (?1814–79), singer and author, sister of Fanny *Kemble. After a distinguished operatic career she settled with her husband in Rome. She had many friends in the literary and artistic world, some of whom (notably *Leighton as Kioski) appear in *A Week in a French Country House* (1867), her *roman à clef*.

Sartor Resartus: *The Life and Opinions of Herr Teufelsdröckh*, by T. *Carlyle, originally published in *Fraser's Magazine* 1833–4, and as a separate volume, at Boston, Massachusetts, 1836 (partly through the intervention of *Emerson, who had visited Carlyle at Craigenputtock in 1833); first English edition 1838.
    This work was written under the influence of the German Romantic school and particularly of *Richter. It consists of two parts: a discourse on the philosophy of clothes (*sartor resartus* means 'the tailor re-patched') based on the speculations of an imaginary Professor Teufelsdröckh, and leading to the conclusion that all symbols, forms, and human institutions are properly clothes, and as such temporary; and a biography of Teufelsdröckh himself, which is in some measure the author's autobiography, particularly in the description of the village of Entepfuhl and of the German university (suggested by Ecclefechan and Edinburgh), and still more in the notable chapters on 'The Everlasting No', 'Centre of Indifference', and 'The Everlasting Yea', which depict a spiritual crisis such as Carlyle himself had experienced during his early Edinburgh days. The prose is highly characteristic, dotted with capital letters, exclamation marks, phrases in German, compound words of the author's own invention, wild apostrophes to the Reader, apocalyptic utterances, and outbursts of satire and bathos; an early example of what came to be known as 'Carlylese'.

SARTRE, Jean-Paul (1905–80), French philosopher, novelist, playwright, literary critic, and political activist. He was the principal exponent of *existentialism in France, and exercised a considerable influence on

French intellectual life in the decades following the Second World War. He was educated at the École Normale Supérieure, where he studied philosophy and psychology, and subsequently spent a period studying phenomenology at the French Institute in Berlin. He held various teaching posts in France until the outbreak of war. Mobilized in 1939, taken prisoner in 1940, he was released the following year and played a part in the resistance movement. After the war he devoted himself exclusively to writing and, with varying degrees of intensity, to the pursuit of socialist political objectives. Through the great range of his creative and critical energies, his personal involvement in many of the important issues of his time, and his unceasing concern with problems of freedom, commitment, and moral responsibility, he won a wide audience for his ideas. He made important contributions in many areas: existentialist and Marxist philosophy, L'Être et le néant (1943; Being and Nothingness, 1956) and Critique de la raison dialectique (1960; Critique of Dialectical Reason, 1976); the novel, La Nausée (1938; Nausea, 1949) and three volumes of a projected tetralogy Les Chemins de la liberté (1945–7; The Roads to Freedom, 1947–50), comprising L'Âge de raison, Le Sursis, and La Mort dans l'âme (The Age of Reason, The Reprieve, and Iron in the Soul); drama, Les Mouches (1943; The Flies, 1947), Huis clos (1945; In Camera, 1946; No Exit, 1947), Les Mains sales (1948; Dirty Hands, 1949, Crime Passionnel, 1949), and Les Séquestrés d'Altona (1960; Loser Wins, 1960; The Condemned of Altona, 1961); biography, with studies of *Baudelaire (1947), *Genet (1952), and *Flaubert (1971–2); literary criticism, Qu'est-ce que la littérature? (1948; What Is Literature? 1949). He was one of the founders of the influential literary and political review Les Temps modernes (1945). His autobiography, Les Mots (Words), appeared in 1964, in which year he was awarded the *Nobel Prize for literature. His friend and companion from her university days was Simone de *Beauvoir.

SASSOON, Siegfried Loraine (1886–1967), educated at Marlborough and Clare College, Cambridge. Destined by his mother to be a poet, he lived in Kent and Sussex, following country pursuits and publishing verse in private pamphlets. In the trenches in the First World War he began to write the poetry for which he is remembered; his bleak realism, his contempt for war leaders and patriotic cant, and his compassion for his comrades found expression in a body of verse which was not acceptable to a public revering R. *Brooke. During his first spell in the front line he was awarded the MC, which he later threw away. Dispatched as 'shell-shocked' to hospital, he encountered and encouraged W. *Owen, and organized a public protest against the war. In 1917 he published his war poems in The Old Huntsman and in 1918 further poems in Counter-Attack, both with scant success. Further volumes of poetry published in the 1920s finally estab-

lished a high reputation, and collections were published in 1947 and 1961. From the late 1920s Sassoon began to think of himself as a religious poet and was much influenced by G. *Herbert and *Vaughan. The spare, muted poems in Vigils (1935) and Sequences (1956) are much concerned with spiritual growth. In 1957 he became a Catholic.

Meanwhile he was also achieving success as a prose writer. His semi-autobiographical trilogy (Memoirs of a Fox-Hunting Man, 1928; Memoirs of an Infantry Officer, 1930; and Sherston's Progress, 1936) relates the life of George Sherston, a lonely boy whose loves are cricket and hunting, who grows into a thoughtless young gentleman and eventually finds himself a junior officer in the trenches, where he is brutally thrust into adulthood. The three books were published together as The Complete Memoirs of George Sherston in 1937. In 1938 Sassoon published The Old Century and Seven More Years, an autobiography of his childhood and youth, and his own favourite among his books. The Weald of Youth (1942) and Siegfried's Journey (1945) brought his story up to 1920. His attachment to the countryside emerges as a major theme in his post-1918 poetry and in most of his prose work. His diaries 1920–2 and 1915–18, ed. R. *Hart-Davis, were published 1981 and 1983.

Satanic school, the name under which R. *Southey attacks *Byron and the younger Romantics in the preface to his *A Vision of Judgement.

satire, from the Latin satira, a later form of satura, which means 'medley', being elliptical for lanx satura, 'a full dish, a hotch-potch'. The word has no connection with 'satyr', as was formerly often supposed. A 'satire' is a poem, or in modern use sometimes a prose composition, in which prevailing vices or follies are held up to ridicule [OED]. In English literature, satire may be held to have begun with *Chaucer, who was followed by many 15th-cent. writers, including *Dunbar. *Skelton used the octosyllabic metre, and a rough manner which was to be paralleled in later times by Butler in *Hudibras, and by *Swift. Elizabethan satirists include *Gascoigne, *Lodge, and *Marston, whereas J. *Hall claimed to be the first to introduce satires based on *Juvenal to England. The great age of English satire began with *Dryden, who perfected the epigrammatic and antithetical use of the *heroic couplet for this purpose. He was followed by *Pope, *Swift, *Gay, *Prior, and other satirists of the Augustan period (see MOCK-BIBLICAL and MOCK-HEROIC). The same tradition was followed by Charles *Churchill, and brilliantly revived by Byron in *English Bards and Scotch Reviewers. The Victorian age was not noted for pure satire, although the novel proved an excellent vehicle for social satire with *Dickens, *Thackeray, and others. In the early 20th cent. *Belloc, *Chesterton, and R. *Campbell (in his Georgiad) contributed to a moderate revival of the tradition, pursued in various verse forms by P. *Porter, J. *Fuller, Clive James

(1939–), and other young writers; and prose satire continued to flourish in the works of E. *Waugh, A. *Powell, Angus *Wilson, K. *Amis, and others. In theatre and television the 'satire boom' of the 1960s is generally held to have been pioneered by the satirical revue *Beyond the Fringe* (1960) by Alan *Bennett, Jonathan Miller, Peter Cook, and Dudley Moore.

Satiromastix, or *The Untrussing of the Humorous Poet*, a comedy by *Dekker, written 1601 (with John *Marston?), printed 1602.

Jonson in his *Poetaster* had satirized Dekker and Marston, under the names of Demetrius and Crispinus, while he himself figures as Horace. Dekker here retorts, bringing the same Horace, Crispinus, and Demetrius on the stage once more. Horace is discovered sitting in a study laboriously composing an epithalamium, and at a loss for a rhyme. Crispinus and Demetrius enter and reprove him gravely for his querulousness. Presently Captain Tucca (of the *Poetaster*) enters, and turns effectively on Horace the flow of his profanity. Horace's peculiarities of dress and appearance, his vanity and bitterness, are ridiculed; and he is finally untrussed and crowned with nettles.

The satirical part of the play uses a somewhat inappropriate romantic setting—the wedding of Sir Walter Terill at the court of William Rufus, and the drinking of poison (as she thinks) by his wife Caelestine, but really of a sleeping-potion, to escape the king's attentions.

Saturday Night and Sunday Morning, the first novel of A. *Sillitoe, published 1958.

Its protagonist, anarchic young Arthur Seaton, lathe operator in a Nottingham bicycle factory, provided a new prototype of the working-class *Angry Young Man; rebellious, contemptuous towards authority in the form of management, government, the army, and neighbourhood spies, he unleashes his energy on drink and women, with quieter interludes spent fishing in the canal. His affair with Brenda, married to his workmate Jack, overlaps with an affair with her sister Winnie, inaugurated in the night that Brenda attempts a gin-and-hot-bath abortion recommended by his Aunt Ada; both relationships falter when he is beaten up by soldiers, one of them Winnie's husband, and he diverts his attention to young Doreen, to whom he becomes engaged (after a fashion) in the penultimate chapter. Arthur's wary recklessness, at once aggressive and evasive, is summed up in his reaction to the sergeant-major who tells him, 'You're a soldier now, not a Teddy boy': 'I'm me, and nobody else; and whatever people think I am, that's what I'm not, because they don't know a bloody thing about me' (ch. 9). A landmark in the development of the post-war novel, with its naturalism relieved by wit, high spirits, and touches of lyricism, the novel provided the screenplay (also by Sillitoe) for Karel Reisz's 1960 film, a landmark in British cinema.

Saturday Review, an influential periodical founded in 1855, which ran until 1938. Among the many brilliant contributors of its early days were Sir Henry Maine (1822–88), Sir J. F. *Stephen, J. R. *Green, and *Freeman; it later became more literary in its interests (notably under the editorship of F. *Harris, 1894–8), publishing work by *Hardy, H. G. *Wells, *Beerbohm, Arthur *Symons, and others. G. B. *Shaw was dramatic critic from 1895 to 1898, and *Agate from 1921 to 1923.

Saturninus, the emperor in Shakespeare's *Titus Andronicus*, who marries *Tamora.

Satyrane, Sir, in Spenser's *Faerie Queene* (I. vi), a knight 'Plaine, faithfull, true, and enimy of shame', son of a satyr and the nymph Thyamis. He rescues *Una from the satyrs, perhaps symbolizing the liberation of the true religion by *Luther.

satyr drama, a humorous piece with a chorus of satyrs that authors in the 5th and 4th cents BC were expected to append to tragic trilogies offered for competition. This practice, which had the incidental virtue of providing light relief, may have been due to the fact recorded by *Aristotle (*Poetics*, ch. 4) that tragedy had its origin in performances by actors dressed as satyrs. The surviving fragments of *Aeschylus' *Diktyoulkoi* (The Net-Drawers) and *Sophocles' *Ichneutai* (The Trackers) reveal sympathy for the promptings of animal impulse and a lyrical feeling for nature. They were both probably superior to the one extant satyric drama, *Euripides' *Cyclops*. J. C. *Scaliger (*Poëtice*, 1561) sparked off a controversy when he claimed that Roman satire was descended from Greek satyric drama. The claim was contradicted by *Casaubon who demonstrated that the Latin 'satire' had no connection with satyrs (*De Satyrca Poesi*, 1605), a view that *Dryden was to accept.

Satyricon, see PETRONIUS.

SAUSSURE, Ferdinand de (1857–1913), born in Geneva; he entered the university there in 1875 but moved after a year to Leipzig to study Indo-European languages. After four years in the powerful language department there, he went to Paris in 1881 where he taught for ten years. In 1891 he became professor at Geneva where, between 1907 and 1911, he delivered the three courses of lectures which were reconstructed from students' notes into the *Cours de linguistique générale* (pub. 1915), a book which is the basis of 20th-cent. *linguistics and of much modern literary criticism. His most important and influential idea was the conception of language as a system of signs, arbitrarily assigned and only intelligible in terms of the particular system as a whole. (This idea was applied outside language in the new science called semiotics.) Language is a *structure* whose parts can only be understood in relation to each other; this *'structuralism' has been very influential in literary criticism and in other fields, such as sociology. Two other sets of distinctions made by Saussure might be noted, as axiomatic for the understanding of modern linguistics: the distinctions between *langage* (the human capacity of using language), *langue* (the particular language as a whole: e.g. English), and *parole* (a particular utterance or occurrence of language); and the division of language study into *synchronic* (the examination of a particular language as a system at one stage of its existence) and *diachronic* (the historical study of the development of a language). Saussure's emphasis was on the value of synchronic study (with which the term 'linguistics' is sometimes used synonymously, as distinct from 'philology' for historical study), rather than the diachronic philology with which he had previously been concerned. One of the compilers of the *Cours* was Charles Bally (1865–1947), who developed the ideas of Saussure and, with other followers, is sometimes assigned to the 'Geneva School'. Even if all Saussure's ideas were not entirely original with him, his originality and influence cannot easily be exaggerated. See *Course in General Linguistics*, trans. W. Baskin (1959); J. Culler, *Saussure* (1976).

SAVAGE, Richard (*c.*1697–1743). He claimed to be the illegitimate son of the fourth Earl Rivers and Lady Macclesfield, but the story of his birth and ill-treatment given by Dr *Johnson in his remarkable life (1744, repr. in *The Lives of the English Poets*) has been largely discredited (see *Notes and Queries*, 1858). Johnson describes with much sympathy Savage's career as a struggling writer, his pardon after conviction on a murder charge in 1727, and his poverty-stricken death in a Bristol jail. Savage wrote two plays (*Love in a Veil*, pub. 1719, and *The Tragedy of Sir Thomas Overbury*, pub. 1724), and various odes and satires, but is remembered as a poet for *The Wanderer* (1729) and 'The Bastard' (1728), a spirited attack on his 'Mother, yet no Mother', which contains the well-known line 'No tenth transmitter of a foolish face'. See Richard *Holmes, *Dr Johnson and Mr Savage* (1993).

Savage Club, a club with strong literary and artistic connections founded in 1857, with *Sala as one of the founder members; it was named after the poet (above). Members have included *Bridie, E. *Wallace, G. and W. *Grossmith, and Dylan *Thomas.

Saved, a play by E. *Bond, which caused much controversy when it was first seen (members only) at the *Royal Court in 1965, having been refused a licence for public performance. In short, minimalist-realist scenes, with dialogue of stark and stylized crudity, Bond evokes a bleak south London landscape of domestic and street violence and the somewhat caricatured impoverished pastimes of the working class—fishing, football pools, TV, pop music. In the central episode Pam's baby, which has been neglected by her and which cries loudly through much of the preceding action, is tormented and stoned to death in its pram by a gang of youths and its putative father,

Fred. The subsequent lack of response to the child's death adds to the sense of dramatic shock.

SAVILE, George, see HALIFAX.

SAVILE, Sir Henry (1549–1622), educated at Brasenose College, Oxford, and a fellow and subsequently warden of Merton College and provost of Eton. He was secretary of the Latin tongue to *Elizabeth I, perhaps also teaching her Greek, and one of the scholars commissioned to prepare the authorized translation of the Bible. He translated the *Histories* of *Tacitus (1591) and published a magnificent edition of St John *Chrysostom (1610–13) and of *Xenophon's *Cyropaedia* (1613) at Eton. Savile assisted *Bodley in founding his library and established the Savilian professorships of geometry and astronomy at Oxford. He left a collection of manuscripts and printed books, now in the Bodleian Library.

Savile Club, founded in 1868 as the Eclectic Club, renamed in 1869 the New Club, and from 1871, when it moved to independent premises in Savile Row, known as the Savile Club. It moved to its present home, 69 Brook Street, in 1927. The club has always had a strong literary tradition; members have included R. L. *Stevenson, *Hardy, *Yeats, L. *Strachey, H. *James, and S. *Potter. Sean Day-Lewis, in his biography of C. *Day-Lewis, describes the Savile as the home of Potter's invention of the concept of 'Gamesmanship'; and it was in the Savile billiards room that Stevenson is alleged to have said to H. *Spencer 'that to play billiards well was the sign of an ill-spent youth', though other clubs also claim this honour.

SAVONAROLA, Fra Girolamo (1452–98), Dominican monk, an eloquent preacher whose sermons at Florence gave expression to the religious reaction against the artistic licence and social corruption of the Renaissance. Savonarola was leader of the democratic party in Florence after the expulsion of the *Medici, and aroused the hostility of Pope Alexander VI (Rodrigo *Borgia) by his political attitude in favour of Charles VIII of France. His influence was gradually undermined, and he was tried, condemned, and executed as a heretic. There is a careful study of his character in G. Eliot's *Romola*.

Savoy, a short-lived but important periodical, edited by Arthur *Symons, of which eight issues appeared in 1896, with contributions by *Beardsley, *Conrad, *Dowson, and others.

Savoy operas, see GILBERT AND SULLIVAN OPERAS.

Sawles Warde, an allegorical work of alliterative prose, found in three manuscripts with the saints' lives called *'the Katherine Group', dating from the end of the 12th cent. and emanating from the west Midlands (probably Herefordshire). It is a loose translation of part of *De Anima* by Hugh of St Victor, and it presents a morality in which the body is the dwelling-place of the soul and comes under attack by the vices. It has connections then with the morality castle, found from *Grosseteste's *Chasteau d'Amour* to *The Castle of Perseverance.* Its prose has the same virtues—elegance and colloquialism—as *Ancrene Wisse* and the Katherine Group. Ed. J. A. W. Bennett, G. V. Smithers, and N. Davis, *Early Middle English Verse and Prose* (2nd edn, 1968).

Sawyer, Bob, a character in Dickens's *The Pickwick Papers.*

SAXO GRAMMATICUS, a 13th-cent. Danish historian, author of the *Gesta Danorum,* a partly mythical Latin history of the Danes (which contains the *Hamlet story). See *A History of the Danes,* vol. i, trans. P. Fisher (1970); vol. ii: *Commentary,* by H. Ellis-Davidson (1980).

SAYERS, Dorothy L(eigh) (1893–1957), daughter of a Fenland clergyman, and married in 1926 to a journalist, O. A. Fleming. She worked as a copy-writer in an advertising agency (where she considerably influenced the style of contemporary advertising) till the success of her detective novels gave her financial independence. Her detective fiction is among the classics of the genre, being outstanding for its well-researched backgrounds, distinguished style, observant characterization, and ingenious plotting, and for its amateur detective Lord Peter Wimsey; she reached her peak with *Murder Must Advertise* (1933) and *The Nine Tailors* (1934). She also wrote religious plays, mainly for broadcasting (see under BBC), and her learning, wit, and pugnacious personality made her a formidable theological polemicist. Her last years were devoted to a translation of Dante's *Divina commedia.* See James Brabazon, *Dorothy L. Sayers* (1981).

scald, scaldic verse, SEE SKALDIC VERSE.

SCALIGER, Joseph Justus (1540–1609), the son of J. C. *Scaliger, one of the greatest scholars of the Renaissance. His edition of Manilius (1579) and his *De Emendatione Temporum* (1583) revolutionized ancient chronology by insisting on the recognition of the historical material relating to the Jews, the Persians, the Babylonians, and the Egyptians. He also issued critical editions of many classical authors. He incurred the enmity of the Jesuits and retired from France to Lausanne in 1572, and subsequently to Leiden. He was attacked in his old age by Gaspar Scioppius on behalf of the Jesuits, who contested the claim of the Scaligers to belong to the Della Scala family. See Anthony Grafton, *Joseph Scaliger: A Study in the History of Classical Scholarship* (2 vols, 1983, 1993).

SCALIGER, Julius Caesar (1484–1558), classical scholar, born at Riva on Lake Garda. He settled at Agen in France as a physician. In the Renaissance debate about the purity of Latin, he was an advocate of *Cicero and so found himself in dispute with *Erasmus, against whom he wrote two tracts (1531, 1536).

He wrote an important treatise on poetics (1561) which contained the earliest expression of the conventions of classical tragedy.

SCANNELL, Vernon (1922–), poet and one-time boxer, born in Lincolnshire. His first volume of verse, *Graves and Resurrections* (1948), was followed by several others including *The Masks of Love* (1960), *A Sense of Danger* (1962), and *The Loving Game* (1975). *New and Collected Poems 1950–1980* appeared in 1980. Other collections include *Funeral Games* (1987), *Dangerous Ones* (1991), and *A Time for Fire* (1991). Many of the poems combine informal colloquial language and domestic subjects with a sense of underlying violence: poetry and human love 'build small barriers against confusion' in an essentially hostile world. He has also written several novels including *Ring of Truth* (1983), and two volumes of autobiography, *The Tiger and the Rose* (1971) and *Drums of Morning* (1992).

Scarlet, Scarlock, or **Scathelocke,** Will, one of the companions of *Robin Hood.

Scarlet Letter, The, a novel by N. *Hawthorne, published 1850.

The scene of the story is the Puritan New England of the 17th cent. An aged English scholar has sent his young wife, Hester Prynne, to Boston, intending to follow her, but has been captured by the Indians and delayed for two years. He arrives to find her in the pillory, with a baby in her arms. She has refused to name her lover, and has been sentenced to this ordeal and to wear for the remainder of her life the red letter A, adulteress, upon her bosom. The husband assumes the name of Roger Chillingworth and makes Hester swear that she will conceal his identity. Hester goes to live on the outskirts of the town, an object of contempt and insult, with her child, Pearl. Her ostracism opens for her a broader view of life, she devotes herself to works of mercy, and gradually wins the respect of the townsfolk. Chillingworth, in the character of a physician, sets out to discover her paramour. Hester's lover is, in fact, Arthur Dimmesdale, a young and highly revered minister whose lack of courage has prevented him from declaring his guilt and sharing Hester's punishment. The author traces the steps by which Chillingworth discovers him, the cruelty with which he fastens on and tortures him, and at the same time the moral degradation that this process involves for Chillingworth himself. When Dimmesdale at the end of seven years is on the verge of lunacy and death, Hester, emancipated by her experience, proposes to him that they shall flee to Europe, and for a moment he dallies with the idea. But he puts it from him as a temptation of the Evil One, makes public confession on the pillory which had been the scene of Hester's shame, and dies in her arms.

Scarlet Pimpernel, The, see ORCZY.

SCARRON, Paul (1610–60), French poet, dramatist, and writer of prose fiction. In 1652 he married Françoise d'Aubigné, who later became the secret wife of Louis XIV by whom she was created Mme de Maintenon. Besides a number of comedies, Scarron was the author of a collection of short fiction, *Nouvelles tragicomiques* (1661), and a burlesque novel of 17th-cent. provincial life, *Le Roman comique* (Pt I 1651, Pt II 1657), recounting the adventures of a touring company of actors in the town of Le Mans. His burlesque verse includes *Virgile travesti* (1648–52), a *mock-heroic parody of the *Aeneid* in which the ancient gods and heroes speak like ordinary mortals, and which inspired C. *Cotton's popular *Scarronides, or Virgile Travestie* (1664, 1665).

Scenes of Clerical Life, a series of three tales by G. *Eliot, published in two volumes 1858, having appeared in *Blackwood's Magazine* in the previous year.

'The Sad Fortunes of the Rev. Amos Barton' is the sketch of a commonplace clergyman, the curate of Shepperton, without learning, tact, or charm, underpaid, unpopular with his parishioners, who earns their affection by his misfortune—the death from overwork, childbearing, and general wretchedness of his beautiful, gentle wife Milly.

'Mr Gilfil's Love-Story' is the tale of a man whose nature has been warped by a tragic love experience. Maynard Gilfil was parson at Shepperton before the days of Amos Barton. He had been the ward of Sir Christopher Cheverel and his domestic chaplain, and had fallen deeply in love with Caterina Sastri (Tina), the daughter of an Italian singer, whom the Cheverels had adopted. But Capt. Anthony Wybrow, the heir of Sir Christopher, a shallow selfish fellow, had flirted with Tina and won her heart. At his uncle's bidding he had thrown her over for the rich Miss Assher. The strain of this brought Tina's passionate nature to the verge of lunacy. All this Gilfil had watched with sorrow and unabated love. Tina rallied for a time under his devoted care and finally married him, but died in a few months, leaving Gilfil like a tree lopped of its best branches.

'Janet's Repentance' is the story of a conflict between religion and irreligion, and of the influence of a sympathetic human soul. The Revd Edgar Tryan, an earnest evangelical clergyman, comes to the neighbourhood of Milby, an industrial town sunk in religious apathy, which the scanty ministration of the old curate, Mr Crewe, does nothing to stir. His endeavour to remedy this condition is opposed with the utmost vigour and bitterness by a group of inhabitants led by Dempster, a hectoring drunken brute of a lawyer, who beats and bullies his long-suffering wife Janet, until he drives her to drink. She shares her husband's prejudices against the methodistical innovator, until she discovers in him a sympathetic fellow sufferer. Her husband's ill-treatment, which culminates in an act of gross brutality, causes her to appeal to Tryan for help, and under his guidance her struggle against the craving for drink begins. Dempster dies after a fall

from his gig, and Janet gradually achieves self-conquest. The death of Tryan from consumption leaves her bereaved, but strengthened for a life of service.

scepticism, a philosophical stance which questions the possibility of attaining lasting knowledge about the reality, as distinct from the appearance, of things, and which rejects all dogmatism, fanaticism, and intolerance. As a historical movement, scepticism had its origin in the teaching of some of the Sophists in the 5th cent. BC. 'Pyrrhonian' scepticism, associated with Pyrrho in the following century, held that any argument supporting one side of a case could be balanced by a contrary argument of equal weight, so that the wise person suspends judgement and cultivates tranquillity and indifference to outward things. 'Academic' scepticism, associated with the Academy of Carneades, held that although the same evidence is always compatible with two contrary conclusions, some beliefs are more reasonable than others and we can act upon the balance of probabilities. *Montaigne and *Bayle in France and *Glanvill in England could combine scepticism with a devout theism, and sceptical techniques have frequently been practised by both supporters and opponents of religion to show that it rests on faith rather than reason. *Hume carried the study to new lengths in his *Treatise of Human Nature* in a detailed analysis of the rational factors which generate scepticism and the psychological factors which allay or moderate it. Since the time of *Descartes critics of scepticism, particularly in religion and morals, have tended to depict it as a form of negative dogmatism, i.e. as seeking actually to deny the existence of anything whose nature is in doubt.

SCÈVE, Maurice (*c*.1501–?64), French poet. Long neglected, he was rediscovered in the 20th cent. His current fame rests largely on his *Délie, object de plus haulte vertu*, a mysterious and emblematic sequence of 449 *dizains*, primarily concerned with the problems and conflicts of love, published in 1544. He also wrote a pastoral eclogue, *La Saulsaye* (1547), and *Le Microcosme* (1562), an epic poem dealing with the history of mankind since the fall of Adam.

Scheherazade, or **Shahrazad,** in the *Arabian Nights*, the daughter of the vizier of King Shahriyar, who married the king and escaped the death that was the usual fate of his wives by telling him the tales which compose that work, interrupting each one at an interesting point, and postponing the continuation till the next night. The Scheherazade framework of overlapping and interlinked stories has been adopted by many novelists and storytellers.

SCHELLING, Friedrich Wilhelm Joseph von (1775–1854), German philosopher, professor of philosophy at Jena, Würzburg, Munich, and Berlin. He was at first a disciple of *Fichte, but soon departed from his doctrine. Unlike Fichte, Schelling makes the universe rather than the ego the element of reality. Nature, obedient to the laws of human intelligence, is a single living organism working towards self-consciousness, a faculty dormant in inanimate objects and fully awake only in man, whose being consists in 'intellectual intuition' of the world he creates. Schelling's numerous works include *Ideen zu einer Philosophie der Natur* (*Ideas towards a Philosophy of Nature*, 1797) and *System des transcendentalen Idealismus* (*System of Transcendental Idealism*, 1800). The clarity of these earlier philosophical works gradually yielded to Schelling's growing pantheistic and eventually theistic enthusiasms. His doctrine of the interaction between subject and object, mind and nature, was fruitful for *Coleridge's formulation of the poetic Imagination as the reconciler of opposite qualities (see *Biographia Literaria*, 1817). His poems were collected and published posthumously in 1913.

SCHILLER, Johann Christoph Friedrich von (1759–1805), German dramatist and lyric poet, the son of an army surgeon, and, with his early play *Die Räuber* (*The Robbers*, 1781), the chief figure of the *Sturm und Drang* period of German literature. In this play Karl von Moor, the heroic robber, takes to the woods to redress the evils of his father's court, in contrast to his wicked brother Franz, who combines some of the characteristics of Shakespeare's *Richard III and Edmund in *King Lear*. The topicality of the theme of authoritarianism and liberty gave the play great popularity. In England *Hazlitt and *Coleridge read it with enthusiasm (see Coleridge's sonnet 'Schiller! That hour I would have wish'd to die', 1794). In his next important play, *Kabale und Liebe* (*Intrigue and Love*, 1784, the play on which *Verdi based his opera *Luisa Miller*), Schiller attacked contemporary society by showing the forces of a despotic state interfering tragically with the love of a patrician youth and a middle-class girl. There followed the blank verse drama *Don Carlos* (1787), and Schiller achieved his greatest dramatic success with the historical tragedy of *Wallenstein* (1799), composed of three parts, the second and third of which were translated into English verse by Coleridge in 1800. *Maria Stuart* (1800) also dramatizes history, as does *Die Jungfrau von Orleans* (*The Maid of Orleans*, 1801). Schiller then wrote a 'classical' drama with chorus, *Die Braut von Messina* (*The Bride of Messina*, 1803), and his last finished play was *Wilhelm Tell* (1804). All his plays are concerned with the problem of freedom and responsibility, either political, as in the early dramas, or personal and moral.

Schiller was also a fine poet, author of reflective and lyrical poems as well as ballads (he and *Goethe collaborated on a collection of ballads in 1797–8, as Wordsworth and Coleridge did in England at the same time). Some of the best-known poems are 'Die Künstler' ('The Artists'), a poem on the humanizing influence of art; 'Das Ideal und das Leben' ('The Ideal and Life'), a philosophical poem on the unbridgeable

gap between the real and the ideal; 'Die Glocke' ('The Bell'); and 'An die Freude' ('Ode to Joy'), which *Beethoven set to music in his Ninth Symphony.

Appointed professor of history at Jena in 1789, Schiller was also the author of historical works on the Revolt of the Netherlands (1788) and the Thirty Years War (the period of *Wallenstein*). He was also a serious student of *Kant's philosophy and the author of *Philosophische Briefe* (*Philosophical Letters*, 1786). Kant influenced his thinking about art, and of his many essays on aesthetics the most important were influential on German Romantic critics like the *Schlegels, and also possibly on Coleridge, who knew and admired his works. These are the *Briefe über die ästhetische Erziehung des Menschen* (*On the Aesthetic Education of Man*, 1795, trans. and introd. E. M. Wilkinson and L. A. Willoughby, 1967); *Über naive und sentimentalische Dichtung* (*On Naïve and Reflective Poetry*, 1795–6), in which Schiller contrasts his own 'modern', reflective mode of writing with Goethe's more 'antique', unselfconscious genius; and several essays on the liberating and moral influence of the theatre.

SCHLEGEL, August Wilhelm von (1767–1845), German Romanticist, critic, and philologist, chiefly known in England for his translation into German, with the assistance of his wife and others, of the plays of Shakespeare. He also became famous for his lectures *Über dramatische Kunst und Literatur* (1809–11), translated by John Black as *Lectures on Dramatic Art and Literature* (1815). *Wordsworth and *Hazlitt praised the lectures dealing with Shakespeare, and *Coleridge almost certainly borrowed from them for his own lectures on Shakespeare. Schlegel was also, with his younger brother Friedrich (below), the co-editor of *Das Athenäum* (1798–1800), a journal of German Romanticism.

SCHLEGEL, Friedrich von (1772–1829), younger brother of A. W. von Schlegel (above), notable for his studies of the history of literature, particularly *Geschichte der alten und neuen Literatur*, trans. *Lockhart as *Lectures on the History of Literature, Ancient and Modern* (1818); his recognition of the importance of ancient Hindu poetry, *Sprache und Weisheit der Inder* (*Language and Wisdom of the Indians*, 1808); and his critical fragments and essays, many of them published in the periodical he wrote with his brother, *Das Athenäum* (1798–1800). He contrasted classical and Romantic literature, and expounded his theory of 'romantic irony', or the consciousness on the part of the artist of the unbridgeable gap between the ideal artistic goal and the limited possibilities of achievement.

Schlemihl, Peter, in the story or allegory by *Chamisso, the impecunious young man who surrendered his shadow to the devil, a thin elderly gentleman in a grey coat, in exchange for a purse of Fortunatus (see OLD FORTUNATUS). The lack of a shadow exposes Peter to disagreeable notice, and in spite of his wealth he finds himself an outcast from human society.

SCHOENBAUM, Samuel (1927–96), American scholar. His *Shakespeare's Lives* (1970) is a history of accounts of Shakespeare's life; his *William Shakespeare: A Documentary Life* (1975) reproduces most of the relevant documents and this has been revised as *William Shakespeare: A Compact Documentary Life* (1977).

'Scholar-Gipsy, The', a poem by M. *Arnold, published 1853. The poem, pastoral in setting, is based on an old legend, narrated by *Glanvill in his *The Vanity of Dogmatizing*, of an 'Oxford scholar poor', who, tired of seeking preferment, joined the gypsies to learn their lore, roamed with them, and still haunts the Oxford countryside. With this is woven a vivid evocation of the places Arnold visited with his Oxford friends (Bagley Wood, Hinksey, the Cumnor moors, etc.) and reflections on the contrast between the single-minded faith of the scholar-gypsy and the modern world, 'the strange disease of modern life, | With its sick hurry, its divided aims'. The tone, as in many of Arnold's best works, is elegiac, but he wrote to *Clough condemning it for failing to 'animate': 'The Gipsy Scholar at best awakens a pleasing melancholy. But this is not what we want.'

Scholasticism, the doctrines of the *Schoolmen, and the predominant theological and philosophical teachings of the period 1100–1500, mainly an attempt to reconcile *Aristotle with the Scriptures, and Reason with Faith. It is characterized too by its dialectical method of argument, first associated with *Abelard. Its greatest monument is the *Summa Theologica* of *Aquinas. In the 14th cent., after *Ockham, Scholasticism had exhausted itself as an intellectual movement. See F. J. Copleston, SJ, *A History of Philosophy*, vol. ii (1950).

Scholemaster, The, see ASCHAM.

Schoole of Abuse, see GOSSON.

School for Scandal, The, a comedy by R. B. *Sheridan, produced 1777.

In this play, generally agreed to be one of the most masterly of English comedies, the author contrasts two brothers: Joseph Surface, the sanctimonious hypocrite, and Charles, the good-natured, reckless spendthrift. Charles is in love with Maria, the ward of Sir Peter Teazle, and his love is returned; Joseph is courting the same girl for her fortune, while at the same time dallying with Lady Teazle. Sir Peter, an old man who has married his young wife six months previously, is made wretched by her frivolity and the fashionable society she inhabits. Members of this society include Sir Benjamin Backbite, Crabtree, Lady Sneerwell, and Mrs Candour, who 'strike a character dead at every word' and chatter with malicious brilliance whenever they meet. Sir Oliver Surface, the rich uncle of Joseph and Charles, returns unexpectedly from India, and decides to test the characters of his nephews before revealing his identity. He visits Charles in the guise of a moneylender, Mr Premium, and Charles, always hard up, cheerfully sells him the family portraits—but refuses to sell the portrait of 'the ill-looking little fellow over the settee', who is Sir Oliver himself. Thus he unwittingly wins the old man's heart. Meanwhile Joseph receives a visit from Lady Teazle and attempts to seduce her. The sudden arrival of Sir Peter obliges Lady Teazle to hide behind a screen, where she is filled with shame and remorse as she listens to proof of Sir Peter's generosity to her, even though he suspects an attachment between her and Charles. The arrival of Charles sends Sir Peter in turn to hide. Sir Peter detects the presence of a woman behind the screen, but is told by Joseph that it is a little French milliner, so he takes refuge in a cupboard instead. The conversation between Charles and Joseph proves to Sir Peter that his suspicions of Charles were unfounded. On Joseph's leaving the room, Sir Peter emerges and together he and Charles agree to reveal the little French milliner. When Charles flings down the screen he reveals Lady Teazle. Lady Teazle begs Sir Peter's forgiveness and Joseph returns, to be upbraided by both. Sir Oliver then enters in the character of a needy relative, begging for assistance. Joseph refuses, giving as his reason the avarice of his uncle, Sir Oliver, and his character now stands fully revealed. Charles is united to Maria, and Sir Peter and Lady Teazle are happily reconciled.

Schoolmen, the succession of writers, from about the 11th to the 15th cent., who treat of logic, metaphysics, and theology, as taught in the 'schools' or universities of Italy, France, Germany, and England, that is to say on the basis of *Aristotle and the Christian Fathers, whom the schoolmen endeavoured to harmonize. Among the great Schoolmen were *Peter Lombard, *Abelard, *Albertus Magnus, *Aquinas, *Duns Scotus, and *Ockham. (See SCHOLASTICISM.)

Schoolmistress, The, see SHENSTONE.

School of Night, a name drawn from a satirical allusion in *Love's Labour's Lost* (IV. iii. 214), and first ascribed by Arthur Acheson in 1903 (*Shakespeare and the Rival Poet*) to a supposed circle of speculative thinkers, led by *Harriot and *Ralegh, and including *Marlowe, *Chapman, Lawrence Keymis, and the 'Wizard Earl' Northumberland. J. Dover *Wilson, G. B. *Harrison in his edition of *Willobie His Avisa* (1926), and M. C. *Bradbrook in *The School of Night* (1936) supported the theory that *Love's Labour's Lost* was an attack upon this coterie, which engaged in free-thinking philosophical debate (not necessarily atheistic) and dabbled in hermeticism, alchemy, and the occult. The existence of such a circle is now widely disbelieved.

SCHOPENHAUER, Arthur (1788–1860), the author of a pessimistic philosophy embodied in his *Die Welt als*

Wille und Vorstellung (*The World as Will and Idea*, 1818: title-page 1819). According to this, Will, of which we have direct intuition, is the 'thing-in-itself', the only reality. Will, which is self-consciousness in man, finds its equivalent in the unconscious forces of nature. Will, then, it is that creates the world; and the world is not only an illusion but a malignant thing, which inveigles us into reproducing and perpetuating life. Asceticism, and primarily chastity, are the duty of man, with a view to terminating the evil. Egoism, which manifests itself principally in the 'will to live', must be overcome. Its opposite is compassion, the moral law, based on the intuition of the essential identity of all beings. God, free will, and the immortality of the soul are illusions.

SCHREINER, Olive Emilie Albertina (1855–1920), born in Cape Colony, South Africa, the daughter of a missionary. She began to write while working as a governess, and when she came to England in 1881 had completed her best-known novel, *The Story of an African Farm*, published to much acclaim in 1883 under the pseudonym 'Ralph Iron'. Set in the vividly evoked landscape of her childhood, it recounts the lives of two orphaned cousins, stay-at-home Em and unconventional Lyndall, greeted by feminists as one of the first 'New Women', who breaks away from her Bible-belt origins, becomes pregnant by a lover whom she refuses to marry, and dies after the death of her baby; also of Waldo, son of the farm's German overseer, whose rebellious spirit is aroused (as was Schreiner's) by reading H. *Spencer's *First Principles*. This novel won her the friendship of Havelock *Ellis, and while in England she moved in progressive literary and political circles, returning in 1889 to South Africa, where she married the farmer and politician Samuel Cron Cronwright. In 1914 she came back to England, returning to the Cape to die. Her other novels, both with feminist themes, *From Man to Man* (1927) and *Undine* (1929), appeared posthumously, but during her lifetime she published various other works, including collections of allegories and stories, articles on South African politics, and *Woman and Labour* (1911). Courageous and unconventional as a woman and public figure, Schreiner as a writer has been acknowledged as a pioneer both in her treatment of women and in her fictional use of the African landscape. See Ruth First and Ann Scott, *Olive Schreiner* (1980); Joyce Avrech Berkman, *The Healing Imagination of Olive Schreiner* (1989); and Cherry Clayton, *Olive Schreiner* (1997).

SCHUBERT, Franz Peter (1797–1828), Austrian composer and successor to *Haydn, *Mozart, and *Beethoven in the Viennese classical school. It is as a writer of lieder that he has been most highly regarded, but out of more than 600 songs, only 14 are settings of texts of British origins (all in German translation). The most famous of these in his own lifetime were the W. *Scott songs, especially Ellen's three songs from *The Lady of the Lake* (1825) which include the 'Ave Maria'; from the same source are two part-songs, one of them the

beautiful 'Coronach'. Three more Scott songs, 'Lied der Anne Lyle', 'Gesang der Norna', and 'Romanze des Richard Löwenherz' (the king's song from *Ivanhoe*), were written at the same time, though not published till 1828. There are settings of C. *Cibber's 'The Blind Boy' and the Scottish ballad *Edward*. Most famous of all, however, are the Shakespeare settings of 1826: the clear freshness of 'Hark, hark, the lark' and the exquisite simplicity of 'Who is Sylvia?' remain undimmed in their appeal to listeners.

SCHUMANN, Robert (1810–56), German composer. Literary inspiration was very important to Schumann (who was also a writer and journalist) and although most of this was drawn from his own language there is a sprinkling of English associations in his work. The first of his major choral works, *Das Paradies und die Peri* (1843) is a setting of T. Moore's *Lalla Rookh*, treated as a kind of secular oratorio. More successful is the incidental music for Byron's *Manfred* (1849) for which (unlike Byron) he seems to have envisaged a stage presentation: it is not easy to bring off in performance, though the overture is the best of Schumann's late orchestral works. The late overture to *Julius Caesar* (1852) does not live up to its impressive opening. As a composer of songs, Schumann made nine settings of *Burns (eight included in the *Myrthen* cycle of 1840), several of which catch the simple lyricism of the words, and a later group of five *Gedichte der Königin Maria Stuart* (1852), written during the onset of his final illness and insanity, and on the whole less successful. Also in *Myrthen* are a single, very beautiful Byron song, 'Mein Herz ist schwer', and two *Venetianischer Lieder* of Moore. One Shakespeare setting, 'When that I was and a little tiny boy' in the new translation by Tieck and *Schlegel, appeared in 1840.

SCHWARTZ, Delmore (1913–68), poet and short story writer, born into a Jewish family in Brooklyn. He achieved early recognition with his family-dream story 'In Dreams Begin Responsibilities', published in 1937 in the *Partisan Review* (which he was later to edit, 1943–55): this became the title work of a celebrated volume of stories and poems (1938). *The World is a Wedding* (1948) also collects stories. *Shenandoah* (1941) is a verse drama. Volumes of verse include *Summer Knowledge* (1959) and *Last and Lost Poems* (1979). Schwartz's decline into drinking and loneliness and his death in a cheap hotel room created a 'doomed poet' legend, and inspired elegies from *Berryman: his exuberance is celebrated by *Bellow in a portrait of him as Von Humboldt Fleisher in *Humboldt's Gift*.

science fiction, see overleaf.

science, the literature of. Science writing in the 20th cent. built from the Victorian tradition that important ideas in science should be communicated to a wide audience. Charles Lyell (1797–1875) with his *Principles of Geology* (1830–3) and Charles *Darwin, with a stream of popular and successful books, are the obvious 19th-cent. pioneers, but John *Tyndall was a science popularizer (his American tours rivalled the success of those of *Dickens) whose books reached a wide audience. The periodical *Nature*, edited by Norman Lockyer, was founded in 1869 to bring scientific information to the general public, with the support of Darwin, T. H. *Huxley, and Tyndall. The archetypal figure of 20th-cent. science, Albert Einstein (1879–1955), wrote about his scientific work (notably in *The Theory of Relativity*, 1905) and also about wider issues (*Why War?*, 1933; *The World as I See It*, 1935). But, in the English-speaking world at least, the widest publicity for the theory of relativity came from the writings of astronomer Arthur Eddington (1882–1944), one of the pioneers of a great tradition of astronomers who have written accessible books. Eddington's contemporary James Jeans (1877–1946), also an astronomer, had no university post after 1912 but devoted himself to writing popular books and broadcasting, although still doing research.

In the biological sciences, Julian *Huxley summed up the theory of evolution by natural selection for both scientists and lay persons with his *Evolution: The Modern Synthesis* (1942) while a quantum physicist turned biologist, Erwin Schrödinger (1887–1961), pointed the way forward to an understanding of the genetic code with his enormously influential book *What is Life?* (1944). Among those who were influenced was Francis Crick (1916–), who, with James Watson (1928–), determined the structure of DNA. Watson himself went on to write the best-seller *The Double Helix* (1968), and other genetic researchers, notably Jacques Monod (1910–76) with *Chance and Necessity* (1970), presented their ideas to a wide public. Sir Peter Medawar (1915–87), zoologist and immunologist, also addressed a large readership with works such as *The Future of Man* (1960) and *The Limits of Science* (1984).

An important popularizer of science in the second half of the 20th cent. was George Gamow (1904–68), particularly with his 'Mr Tompkins' series. Other scientists who achieved success as writers include Fred Hoyle (1915–) and Nobel Prize-winning physicist Richard Feynman (1918–88). In the biological sciences, the superstars have been Richard Dawkins (1941–), Stephen Jay Gould (1941–2002), and the Pulitzer Prize-winning Edward O. Wilson (1929–), author of *On Human Nature* (1978) and *The Diversity of Life* (1992). But the phenomenal sales since 1988 of *A Brief History of Time* by Stephen Hawking (1942–) brought a flood of books by scientists onto the market, trying to emulate his success. Few of these are of any lasting value, and most are by scientists who will never write a book again; but the consistently good science writers of the 1990s include Paul Davies, Daniel Dennett, John Gribbin, and Ian Stewart.

Scientific progress in the 19th and 20th cents also led to the rise of *science fiction: although most of what is called science fiction today is actually *fantasy, there is a sub-genre, known as 'hard SF', which presents science and scientists in a realistic way. The great exponents of hard SF in its heyday of the 1950s were Isaac Asimov and Arthur C. *Clarke: the tradition is kept alive today by scientists such as Gregory Benford (*Against Infinity*, 1983; *Across the Sea of Suns*, 1984) and John Cramer (*Twistor*, 1989).

Scillaes Metamorphosis, a poem by T. *Lodge, later published (1610) under the title *Glaucus and Scilla*. It is the earliest of many Ovidian epyllia, or minor epics, in the Elizabethan period, and describes the sea-god Glaucus' courtship of the nymph Scilla, who is punished for her cruelty to him by being metamorphosed into a lonely rock in the sea. It bears both a generic and a specific relationship to Shakespeare's *Venus and Adonis*, including a brief account of the death of Adonis beginning:

> He that hath seene the sweete *Arcadian* boy
> Wiping the purple from his forced wound.

SCOGAN, Henry (?1361–1407), a poet whose only surviving literary work is the 'Moral Balade', dedicated to the four sons of Henry IV to whom he was tutor. It is generally agreed that he is the dedicatee of *Chaucer's 'Lenvoy de Chaucer a Scogan', written towards the end of 1393. *Leland says he was a man given to all sort of jocoseness and wit, and he is perhaps mentioned by Shakespeare (2 *Henry IV*, III. ii. 30—though the reference may be to John Scogan, below).

SCOGAN, John, a celebrated jester of Edward IV, whose exploits, real or imagined, are recorded in *The Jestes of Skogyn* (c.1570).

Scoop, a novel by E. *Waugh, published 1938.

Lord Copper, proprietor of the *Daily Beast* (which stands for 'strong mutually antagonistic governments everywhere'), is persuaded to send novelist John Boot to cover the war in Ishmaelia, but William Boot, writer of nature notes (torn reluctant and bewildered from his quiet life at Boot Magna), is dispatched by mistake. After many adventures he returns to find himself covered with glory, although in another case of mistaken identity John Boot has been knighted in his stead. Based on Waugh's own experiences in Abyssinia in 1936, where he was writing for the *Daily Mail*, the novel is a brilliantly comic satire of Fleet Street ethics and manners, and on the battle for readership between the *Beast* and the *Brute*.

SCOT, Michael, see SCOTT, M. (c.1175–c.1235).

SCOT, or **SCOTT,** Reginald (c.1537–99), educated at Hart Hall, Oxford, and MP for New Romney, 1588–9, author of *The Discoverie of Witchcraft* (1584). This was written with the aim of preventing the persecution of poor, aged, and simple persons who were popularly believed to be witches, by exposing the impostures on the one

(cont. on p.908)

The label 'science fiction' suggests a hybrid form, not quite ordinary fiction, not quite science, yet partaking of both. Beneath this label, we find a variety of wares, some of which trail off from a hypothetical central point into utopianism or dystopianism, heroic fantasy, horror, and books on UFOs and the paranormal. Yet its startlements are normally based either on a possible scientific advance, or on a natural or social change, or on a suspicion that the world is not as it is commonly represented. It follows that one of the unacknowledged pleasures of reading science fiction (or SF) is that it challenges readers to decide whether what they are reading is within the bounds of the possible. The altitude for a willing suspension of disbelief varies considerably from one novel to another. H. G. *Wells's The Time Machine (1895) is a case in point. The machine of the title is an impossibility, as far as we know; but the book (more properly a novella) has been taken seriously as both sociological and cosmological speculation ever since its publication in 1895.

Perhaps the safest broad definition of SF is to say that it is a series of mythologies of power, whether it be the power to travel through time or space, or to enter the thoughts of another, or to overcome death or the ineluctable process of evolutionary forces. The long-running TV series Star Trek utilizes all these elements at one time or another. Thus it is able, within a stereotyped format, to produce those surprises which are an inescapable element of the genre.

Of course, such elements, touching as they do on basic human fears, have a long ancestry. But it is really with Mary *Shelley's *Frankenstein: or, The Modern Prometheus (1818), that the fundamental lever of power and human control enters. Mary Shelley, as recent research has shown, was well versed in the science of her time. While human beings, golems, and so forth, had been brought back to life before Shelley wrote, some kind of supernatural agency was involved. Shelley rejects all that. Only when Victor Frankenstein has engaged in scientific research does he achieve the seemingly impossible, and bring forth life from death. The shade of Frankenstein and his monster has become a cultural reference and a standard part of our imaginings. As if she wished to be understood as the mother of science fiction, Shelley repeated her

futuristic experiment, publishing The Last Man in 1826. This disaster novel, set far into the future, features a plague which wipes out all humanity except for one man. It did not win the acclaim of its predecessor.

Jules *Verne's vigorous adventure writings, such as Journey to the Centre of the Earth (1864), proved to be the next great worldwide success. Then there is small beer until Wells emerges on the scene. Undoubtedly, Wells was the great innovator, originating many themes, such as the invasion of the earth by alien beings, which have since been extensively cultivated. A writer who acknowledges his debt to Wells, while pursuing his own concerns, is W. Olaf Stapledon. His two great books are Last and First Men (1930) and Star-Maker (1937). These quasi-novels transcend the SF genre. The brilliantly imaginative Star-Maker presents, in full icy grandeur, an atheist's vision of the cosmos, past, present, and to come. More continuously popular, because more accessible, is the C. S. *Lewis trilogy beginning with Out of the Silent Planet (1938), which presents—for once—a favourable view of the planet Mars.

British writers are less cut off from the main vein of literary culture than their American colleagues. So we find well-known authors turning occasionally to SF. *Bulwer-Lytton, Rudyard *Kipling, E. M. *Forster, Aldous *Huxley, C. S. Lewis, Kingsley *Amis, Anthony *Burgess, and, most considerably, Doris *Lessing, have all written in this mode. George *Orwell's fame rests partly on *Nineteen Eighty-Four (1949), an apotropaic novel much filmed and televised.

In the 1960s, the rather tame British SF magazine New Worlds was taken over and transformed by editor Michael *Moorcock. The future had arrived: among Moorcock's revolutionaries, the names of J. G. *Ballard and Brian *Aldiss stand out. These three writers seem to have followed the English pattern, and have written on other themes, without entirely forsaking SF. During this period, SF reached a level of popularity among intellectuals as well as the general public that it has since lost. Its involvement with the future and with technological advance has made it more enduringly popular with scientists than with the literary fraternity. What can be created must first be imagined. Moreover, events have made the USA the centre of a science-fictional industry which not only encroaches on movies and television, but also on such forward-looking institutions as NASA. Against such forces, Britain and other countries which produce SF writers (most notably Russia, Japan, and China) cannot compete.

The invention in the 1880s of linotype machines, which were cheaper and faster than their predecessors, led to a proliferation of newsprint and magazines of all kinds. The magazines had an unquenchable thirst for short stories. The segregation of types of story into separate magazines, while tending to produce ghetto mentalities, proved commercially viable. The first magazine to be devoted entirely to a kind of gadget SF was the New York-based *Amazing Stories*, beginning publication in 1926. It fostered a vigorous but conservatively minded fandom, which still flourishes and holds many conventions, large and small.

The so-called Paperback Revolution, in the 1950s, accounts for another advance in the output of popular SF, increasing the number of novels available, many of them prophetically looking towards the coming Space Age. Then, with the arrival of television, another channel for SF opened. SF is not the only genre to have close links with technology; but, significantly, both the movies (with Georges Méliès) and British television (with Nigel Kneale's Quatermass series and Orwell's *Nineteen Eighty-Four*) first acquired their mass audiences with science-fictional themes. The computer has again diversified and diluted the original strain of power-based ideas. SF's ability to generate strange and striking images has made it an ideal medium for filmic special effects.

Inevitably, the wider popularity of science fiction has led to a diminution of challenging ideas. Yet there are those who still succeed in making readers think while being entertained. Among these are authors of long standing, such as Arthur C. *Clarke, who commanded a worldwide audience with his novels of the 1950s, *The City and the Stars* (1950) and *Childhood's End* (1953), and who still continues to hold our attention.

Many authors suffer from writing too much (a habit easily acquired in the days when magazines paid writers 2 cents a word). Isaac Asimov is a case in point, although such early novels as *The Naked Sun* (1957) and his first *Foundation Trilogy* (1963), both essentially products of the 1950s, were de-

servedly popular, so much so that, by 1995, Asimov became the eighth most translated author in the world (to be overtaken by Lenin, whose popularity has subsequently dwindled).

If the USA dominates the market place, it does leave British writers free to go their own sweet way, at least to some extent. Noteworthy examples are Robert Holdstock with his Mythago series, Stephen Baxter, and the idiosyncratic Iain M. *Banks, who rose to prominence with his first novel, *The Wasp Factory* (1984). Nor should one forget that most successful lord of misrule and creator of Discworld, Terry Pratchett.

Some of the best-known names in the international language of SF have been American. A. E. Van Vogt, Robert Heinlein, Philip K. Dick, Frank Herbert, Harry Harrison, Ursula *Le Guin, William *Burroughs, William Gibson, the inventor of Cyberpunk, Gregory Benford, and Greg Bear. Bear's *Blood Music* (1985) is all that SF should be: its narrative changes the world and makes us see everything anew.

But the man whose example changed the direction of SF itself is J. R. R. *Tolkien, the learned Merton professor of English language and literature at the University of Oxford, whose *Lord of the Rings* was published in three volumes (1954–5). Tolkien's Secondary Universe became, in paperback, a campus favourite, inspiring many imitations and 'good long reads'. These imaginary worlds, the recounting of whose affairs often sprawls across several volumes, generally provide a platform for a pre-industrial struggle between Good and Evil. By removing the centre of science-fictional speculation to easier pastures, dream-pastures, they lower the intellectual temperature of a genre still struggling to attain some philosophical status.

A significant development in recent years has been the growth of SF scholarship. Institutions like the SFRA (Science Fiction Research Association) and the lively IAFA (International Association for the Fantastic in the Arts) publish learned papers and hold annual conferences. The SF Foundation in Liverpool is encouraging a research and teaching facility.

See: Brian W. Aldiss, with David Wingrove, *Trillion Year Spree: The History of Science Fiction* (1986); John Clute and Peter Nicholls (eds), *The Encyclopaedia of Science Fiction* (1993).

hand, and the credulity on the other, that supported the belief in sorcery. He also wrote *A Perfite Platforme of a Hoppe Garden* (1574).

Scotist, see DUNS SCOTUS.

Scots is a historical offshoot of the Northumbrian dialect of Anglo-Saxon, sharing with northern Middle English a strong Norse element in vocabulary and vowel and consonant developments which still mark off northern speech from Standard English. To this Gaelic, French (Norman and Parisian), and Dutch elements accrued and the political independence of Scotland gave this speech a national status. It became also the vehicle of a considerable literature in *Barbour, *Henryson, *Dunbar, *Douglas, Sir D. *Lindsay, and there was much prose translation as well, but the failure to produce a vernacular Bible at the Reformation, the Union of the Crowns in 1603, and that of the Parliaments in 1707 all helped to extend the bounds of English and prevent the evolution of an all-purpose Scots prose. The 18th-cent. literary revival of Scots under *Ramsay, *Fergusson, and *Burns, who gave it the name of 'Lallans' (Lowlands), was confined to poetry, with prose used merely to represent the colloquy of rustic characters, in Sir W. *Scott, *Hogg, *Galt, R. L. *Stevenson, and the *'Kailyard School'. With the renaissance of the period 1920–50, writers like *MacDiarmid, Robert Maclellan (1907–85), S. G. *Smith, Douglas Young (1913–73), Alexander Scott (1920–   ), Robert Kemp (1908–67), and others, attempted a re-creation of a full canon of Scots to cope with modern themes, which was also called Lallans, the name now connoting the new experimental speech rather than the old historical vernacular which had been losing ground in the previous 100 years.

Scots Musical Museum, The (1787–1803), edited by James Johnson, an important collection of songs with music, some genuinely antique, some fake antique, and some new. *Burns made many notable contributions to the later volumes.

'Scots wha hae', a battle song by *Burns published in *The Scots Musical Museum.*

SCOTT, C. P., see MANCHESTER GUARDIAN.

SCOTT, Geoffrey (1883–1929), poet and biographer, son of a Unitarian manufacturer and nephew of C. P. Scott, editor of the *Manchester Guardian*. He was educated at Rugby and New College, Oxford, where he won the Newdigate Prize in 1906 with a poem, 'The Death of Shelley'. His interest in architectural theory was confirmed by his friendship with *Berenson, and culminated in his study *The Architecture of Humanism* (1914). Scott had great conversational talents, which, combined with what the artist William Rothenstein described as his 'Botticellian' beauty, made him disastrously attractive to women, not least, it would appear, to Berenson's wife Mary. Scott's best-known book is *The Portrait of Zélide* (1925), an elegant and evocative life of Mme de Charrière (see ZÉLIDE) which his friend Edith *Wharton described as a 'wellnigh perfect' book; Scott wrote in a 'Note', 'I have sought to give her the reality of fiction; but my material is fact.' In the same year appeared *Four Tales* by Zélide, translated by Scott's wife Lady Sybil (*née* Cuffe). Scott was working on a biography of *Boswell and an edition of a collection of Boswell papers when he died in New York of pneumonia.

SCOTT, John (1783–1821), educated at the same Aberdeen school as *Byron. He was the first editor, 1820–1, of the remarkable *London Magazine*; he had by then edited the *Champion*, and published *A Visit to Paris* (1814) and *Paris Revisited* (1816), both books of high repute and admired by many, including *Wordsworth. He began his editorial career approving of *Blackwood's Magazine* for its 'spirit of life', and he based the *London* on roughly the same plan, but with a greater emphasis on books and original writing. He attracted a brilliant set of contributors; De Quincey's *Confessions of an English Opium Eater*, *Lamb's earlier 'Elia' essays, and much of *Hazlitt's *Table-Talk* first appeared in the *London Magazine*, as well as work by *Keats, *Clare, *Hood, *Darley, *Carlyle, *Cunningham, and others. His reviewers aimed to seek out excellence rather than to condemn, and they were permitted no political bias. Scott's own writing on Wordsworth, Sir W. *Scott, *Shelley, Keats, Byron, and other young writers, is of high quality. *Talfourd described him as 'a critic of remarkable candour, eloquence and discrimination'. Eventually he found conflict with *Blackwood's* impossible to avoid; he came to detest what he saw as its 'scurrility' and 'duplicity and treachery', and he felt obliged to defend his *'Cockney School'. His attacks on *Blackwood's*, in particular on *Lockhart, led to a series of confusions which culminated in a duel with J. H. Christie, a close friend of Lockhart, in which Scott was killed. There is a biography, *Regency Editor* (1983), by Patrick O'Leary.

SCOTT, or **SCOT,** Michael (*c.*1175–*c.*1235), a Scottish scholar, born at Balwearie, who studied at Oxford, Bologna, and Paris, and was attached to the court of Frederick II at Palermo, probably in the capacity of official astrologer. He translated works of *Aristotle from Arabic to Latin (including *De Anima*, pre-1220), and perhaps *Averroës' great Aristotelian Commentary, which he certainly began. Because the science he studied was astronomy, legends of his magical power grew up and served as a theme for many writers from *Dante (*Inferno*, xx. 116) to Sir W. Scott in *The Lay of the Last Minstrel*. Works of his on astronomy and alchemy, and various translations, still remain in manuscript. See Lynn Thorndike, *Michael Scot* (1965).

SCOTT, Michael (1789–1835). He was for some years an estate manager in Jamaica, which he left in 1822 to settle in his native Glasgow. Between 1829 and 1833 he published in *Blackwood's Magazine* the anonymous

Tom Cringle's Log, entertaining sketches of the life he had known in the Caribbean. It was very successful, and *Coleridge found it 'most excellent', yet Scott concealed his identity all his life. In 1834–5 he published *The Cruise of the Midge*, a work with a similar background, equally well received.

SCOTT, Paul Mark (1920–78), novelist, born in north London and educated at Winchmore Hill Collegiate School. He served in the Indian army during the Second World War, and worked in publishing and for a literary agency before becoming a full-time writer. His first novel, *Johnnie Sahib* (1952), was followed by 12 others, most of them dealing with Anglo-Indian relationships. He is best remembered for the novels known as the 'Raj Quartet': *The Jewel in the Crown* (1966), *The Day of the Scorpion* (1968), *The Towers of Silence* (1971), and *A Division of the Spoils* (1975). These interwoven narratives, set in India during and immediately after the Second World War, portray political, personal, racial, and religious conflicts in the period leading up to Independence and Partition, presenting events from various points of view in a complex chronological sequence that only gradually reveals a total picture. There are two key episodes in the first volume: the death of a missionary, Edwina Crane, who commits suicide by burning herself to death after a violent incident in which an Indian colleague is killed, and the alleged rape in the Bibighar Gardens of Mayapore of the symbolically named young Englishwoman Daphne Manners. A group of young Indians, including Daphne's friend, the English-reared and public-school-educated Hari Kumar, is accused, and all are brutally interrogated by ex-grammar-school and repressed homosexual Ronald Merrick, the district superintendent of police. The affair's repercussions include, in the fourth volume, Merrick's murder, Daphne having died in childbirth after refusing to implicate Kumar. Other characters in the large canvas include Barbara Batchelor, lonely spinster and retired missionary, who dies insane; Mildred Layton, hard-drinking wife of prisoner-of-war Colonel Layton, and their two daughters, sensible Sarah and vain Susan; Muslim leader and ex-minister Mohammed Ali Kasim, known as MAK, who is imprisoned by the British despite his pro-British sympathies, and his son Ahmed, one of the first victims of the massacres attending Partition; and Count Bronowsky, Russian émigré adviser to the nawab of Mirat. Scott's last novel, *Staying On* (1977, *Booker Prize), picks up the story of two minor characters from the Quartet, Colonel 'Tusker' Smalley and his wife Lucy, social misfits who decide to stay on after Independence, surviving on a small pension as they attempt to adjust to the new India. Although respectfully reviewed during Scott's lifetime, the novels won a high posthumous reputation and gained a popular readership, partly through the televising of the Raj Quartet in 1984 under the title of

The Jewel in the Crown. There is a life by Hilary Spurling (1990).

SCOTT, Reginald, see SCOT, R.

SCOTT, Robert Falcon (1868–1912), Antarctic explorer, who commanded the National Antarctic Expedition (1900–2), discovering King Edward VII Island, which he recorded in his *The Voyage of the Discovery* (1905). His notable journal, published as *Scott's Last Expedition* (1913), describes his second Antarctic expedition, the last entry of which was made as Scott lay dying, stormbound on his return from the South Pole. See also Apsley Cherry-Garrard's remarkable account, *The Worst Journey in the World* (1922), a work which owes much to the encouragement and editing of G. B. *Shaw, and Beryl *Bainbridge's novel *The Birthday Boys* (1991).

SCOTT, Sarah, née Robinson (1723–95), novelist and historian, from a Yorkshire gentry family, and sister to Elizabeth *Montagu. After a brief marriage ending in legal separation she lived in Bath with Lady Barbara Montagu, engaging in philanthropy on an income supplemented by the proceeds of writing. Between 1750 and 1772 she published five novels and three histories, including a life of Gustavus of Sweden. The hero of *Sir George Ellison* (1766) first appeared in her best-known novel, the utopian *Millenium Hall* (1762), in which gentlewomen tired of men create a sheltered community for elderly, disabled, female, or otherwise unfortunate persons.

SCOTT, Sir Walter (1771–1832), son of Walter Scott, a writer to the signet, born in College Wynd, Edinburgh, educated at Edinburgh High School and University, and apprenticed to his father. He was called to the bar in 1792. His interest in the old Border tales and ballads had early been awakened, and was stimulated by Percy's *Reliques and by the study of the old romantic poetry of France and Italy and of the modern German poets. He devoted much of his leisure to the exploration of the Border country. In 1797 he published anonymously *The Chase and William and Helen*, a translation of Bürger's 'Der wilde Jäger' (*'The Wild Huntsman') and *'Lenore', and in 1799 a translation of *Goethe's *Götz von Berlichingen*. In 1797 he married Margaret Charlotte Charpentier (or Carpenter), daughter of Jean Charpentier of Lyons in France, and was appointed sheriff-depute of Selkirkshire in 1799. In 1802–3 appeared the three volumes of Scott's *Minstrelsy of the Scottish Border*; and in 1805 his first considerable original work, the romantic poem *The Lay of the Last Minstrel*. He then became a partner in James *Ballantyne's printing business and published *Marmion in 1808. This was followed by *The Lady of the Lake* (1810), *Rokeby and *The Bridal of Triermain* (1813), *The Lord of the Isles* (1815), and *Harold the Dauntless* (1817), his last long poem. In 1809 he had entered into partnership with James's brother John *Ballantyne in the bookselling business known as

'John Ballantyne & Co.', and in 1811 he had purchased Abbotsford on the Tweed, where he built himself a residence. Scott promoted the foundation in 1809 of the Tory *Quarterly Review—he had been a contributor to the *Edinburgh Review, but seceded from it owing to its Whig attitude. In 1813 he refused the offer of the laureateship and recommended *Southey for the honour. Eclipsed in a measure by *Byron as a poet, in spite of the great popularity of his verse romances, he now turned his attention to the novel as a means of giving play to his wide erudition, his humour, and his sympathies. His novels appeared anonymously in the following order: *Waverley (1814); *Guy Mannering (1815); *The Antiquary (1816); *The Black Dwarf and *Old Mortality (1816), as the first series of *Tales of My Landlord; *Rob Roy (1817); *The Heart of Midlothian (1818), the second series of Tales of My Landlord; *The Bride of Lammermoor and *A Legend of Montrose (1819), the third series of Tales of My Landlord; *Ivanhoe (1819); *The Monastery (1820); *The Abbot (1820); *Kenilworth (1821); *The Pirate (1821); *The Fortunes of Nigel (1822); *Peveril of the Peak (1823); *Quentin Durward (1823); *St Ronan's Well (1823); *Redgauntlet (1824); *The Betrothed and *The Talisman (1825), together as Tales of the Crusaders; *Woodstock (1826); *Chronicles of the Canongate (1827, containing *'The Highland Widow', *'The Two Drovers', and *The Surgeon's Daughter); Chronicles of the Canongate (2nd series): Saint Valentine's Day, or *The Fair Maid of Perth (1828); *Anne of Geierstein (1829); Tales of My Landlord (4th series): *Count Robert of Paris and *Castle Dangerous (1831). Scott was created a baronet in 1820, and avowed the authorship of the novels in 1827. In 1826 James Ballantyne & Co. became involved in the bankruptcy of Constable & Co., and Scott, as partner of the former, found himself liable for a debt of about £114,000. He shouldered the whole burden himself and henceforth worked heroically, shortening his own life by his strenuous efforts to pay off the creditors, who received full payment after his death.

Scott's dramatic work, in which he did not excel, includes Halidon Hill (1822), Macduff's Cross (1823), The Doom of Devorgoil, a Melodrama and Auchindrane or The Ayrshire Tragedy (both 1830). Of these Auchindrane is the best. It is founded on the case of Mure of Auchindrane in Pitcairn's Ancient Criminal Trials. Mention must also be made of the important historical, literary, and antiquarian works written by Scott or issued under his editorship: The Works of Dryden with a life (1808); The Works of Swift with a life (1814); Provincial Antiquities of Scotland (1819–26); an abstract of the 'Eyrbiggia Saga' in Northern Antiquities (1814); Description of the Regalia of Scotland (1819); Lives of the Novelists prefixed to Ballantyne's Novelist's Library (1821–4); essays on Chivalry (1818), the Drama (1819), and Romance (1824) contributed to the *Encyclopaedia Britannica; The Life of Napoleon Buonaparte (1827); *The Tales of a Grandfather (1827–30); History of Scotland (1829–30); Letters on Demonology

and Witchcraft (1830); Original Memoirs Written during the Great Civil War of Sir H. Slingsby and Captain Hodgson (1806); the *Memoirs of Captain Carleton (1808); the State Papers of Sir Ralph Sadler (1809); the Secret History of James I (1811); and Memorie of the Somervilles (1815). *Paul's Letters to His Kinsfolk appeared in 1816. Scott founded the *Bannatyne Club in 1823. In 1826 he addressed to the Edinburgh Weekly Journal three letters 'from Malachi Malagrowther', 'Thoughts on the proposed Change of Currency', defending the rights of Scotland.

Scott's Life by J. G. *Lockhart, published in 1837–8, is one of the great biographies of the 19th cent. Scott's Journal was published in 1890 and again in 1939–46, in three volumes, edited by J. G. Tait; there is a modern edition by W. E. K. Anderson (1972). An edition of his letters in 12 volumes was published by H. J. C. Grierson (1932–7) with an index and notes by J. C. Corson (1979). Sir Walter Scott: The Great Unknown, a biography by Edgar Johnson, two volumes, was published in 1970.

Scott's influence as a novelist was incalculable; he established the form of the *historical novel, and, according to V. S. Pritchett, the form of the short story (with 'The Two Drovers' and 'The Highland Widow'). He was avidly read and imitated throughout the 19th cent., not only by historical novelists such as *Ainsworth and *Bulwer-Lytton, but also by writers like Mrs *Gaskell, G. *Eliot, the *Brontës, and many others, who treated rural themes, contemporary peasant life, regional speech, etc., in a manner that owed much to Scott. His reputation gradually declined (though his medieval and Tudor romances retained a popular readership) until there was a revival of interest from European *Marxist critics in the 1930s (see LUKÁCS), who interpreted his works in terms of historicism. In 1951 three seminal essays were published, David *Daiches's 'Scott's Achievement as a Novelist' (Nineteenth-Century Fiction), Arnold Kettle's chapter in his Introduction to the English Novel (vol. I), and S. Stewart Gordon's 'Waverley and the "Unified Design"' (English Literary History, 18); these heralded a considerable upsurge of scholarly activity and reappraisal, most of which concurs in regarding the Scottish 'Waverley' novels (including The Antiquary, Old Mortality, The Heart of Midlothian) as his masterpieces. For a survey of critical attitudes, see Walter Scott: Modern Judgements (ed. D. D. Devlin 1968), and Walter Scott (1982) by T. Crawford.

SCOTT, William Bell (1811–90), poet, artist, and art critic, who taught for many years in Newcastle upon Tyne; his mural Iron and Coal (1862) at Wallington Hall, Northumberland, is one of the earliest representations in art of heavy industry. Scott was a friend of D. G. *Rossetti (who made his acquaintance through an admiring letter) and later of *Swinburne; he was associated with the birth of the *Pre-Raphaelite movement, and contributed to the *Germ. His poems and verses (of which he published several volumes, some illustrated by himself) range from rambling Pindaric *odes to sonnets and medieval-style ballads. His *Autobiographical Notes* (1892), edited by W. Minto, gave much offence to the Rossetti family.

Scottish Chaucerians, see CHAUCERIANS, SCOTTISH.

Scottish Enlightenment, a phrase used to describe an intellectual movement originating in Glasgow in the early 18th cent. but reaching fruition mainly in Edinburgh between 1750 and 1800. Several threads are traceable in the attitudes of the scientists, philosophers, and *literati associated with the movement, although no single tenet was held by all: a deep concern for the practical implications and social benefits of their enquiries (proclaimed as leading to 'improvement'), an emphasis on the interconnection between separable human practices, and an interest in the philosophical principles underlying them. Several of the group developed an interest in history, and many were at least nominal *Deists.

The main philosophers were *Hutcheson, *Hume, Adam *Smith, A. *Ferguson; for his leadership of the so-called 'common-sense' opposition, *Reid should be mentioned, and later D. *Stewart. The political, economic, and social thought of Hume, Smith, and Ferguson was particularly influential in France and America, and the works of Reid and Stewart played a central role in the development of American college education, along with the lectures on rhetoric of H. *Blair. The scientists of the movement included William Cullen, who established chemistry as a discipline in its own right, Joseph Black, who propounded the theories of latent and specific heat, James Hutton, the founder of modern geology, and the Doctors Monro, who were instrumental in establishing the reputation of the Edinburgh Medical School. The names of James Watt and John Loudon McAdam should also be listed. The literary figures, like their French contemporaries, were often ambivalent towards the theories and practices of their scientific and speculative colleagues, and increasingly distanced themselves towards the end of the century. *Boswell and *Burns were never part of the movement, although Sir W. *Scott is associated with its closing decades. Numerous learned societies and journals flourished during the period, and the founding of the *Encyclopaedia Britannica was in part a product of the movement. (See also ROYAL SOCIETY OF EDINBURGH.)

Scottish Text Society, the, founded in 1882 for the purpose of printing and editing texts illustrative of the Scottish language and literature. It has issued editions of many works of general literary interest, such as *The Kingis Quair*, *Barbour's *Bruce*, Gawin *Douglas's *Eneados*, the *Basilikon Doron* (*James I and VI), and the poems of *Dunbar, *Henryson, *Drummond of Hawthornden, and Sir D. *Lindsay. Although the Society's primary concern has been with medieval and Renaissance works, it has also produced a few important editions of later writers, including A. *Ramsay and R. *Fergusson.

SCOTUS, John Duns, see DUNS SCOTUS.

SCOTUS ERIGENA, John (John the Scot) (c.810–77), of Irish origin. He was employed as teacher at the court of Charles the Bald, afterwards emperor, c.847. The leading principle of his philosophy, as expounded in his great work *De Divisione Naturae*, is that of the unity of nature; this proceeds from (1) God, the first and only real being (Nature which creates and is not created); through (2) the Creative Ideas (Nature which creates and is created); to (3) the sensible Universe (Nature which is created and does not create); everything is ultimately resolved into (4) its First Cause (immanent, unmoving God: Nature which is not created and does not create). He was one of the originators of the mystical thought of the Middle Ages, as well as a precursor of *Scholasticism (though with no Aristotelian elements). His originality lies in departing from the mainstream Latin tradition of theology to incorporate into it elements drawn from Pseudo-*Dionysius and others in the *Neoplatonic tradition. He translated the works of Pseudo-Dionysius in 858, as well as of other Neoplatonists, and he wrote a commentary on the *Celestial Hierarchy* of Pseudo-Dionysius. The presence of a Neoplatonic element in all medieval philosophers, including *Aquinas, owes much to his influence. See *Works*, ed. H. J. Floss in *Migne's *Patrologia Latina*, 122.

Scriblerus Club, an association of which *Swift, *Arbuthnot, T. *Parnell, *Pope, and *Gay were members, and the earl of Oxford (R. *Harley) a regularly invited associate member. The group appears to have met from January to July 1714, though various members later collaborated on joint projects. Its object was to ridicule 'all the false tastes in learning', but nothing was produced under the name of *Martinus Scriblerus for some years. See *Memoirs of the Extraordinary Life, Works and Discoveries of Martinus Scriblerus*, ed. C. Kerby-Miller (1950); *A Manner of Correspondence* (1997) by Patricia C. Brückmann.

Scrooge, a character in Dickens's *A Christmas Carol*.

Scrutiny, a Cambridge periodical which ran for 19 volumes, 1932–53, edited by L. C. *Knights, Donald Culver, Denys Thompson, D. W. Harding, and others, but dominated largely by F. R. *Leavis; a 20th issue, with a 'Retrospect' by Leavis, appeared in 1963. Its contributors included Q. D. *Leavis, H. A. Mason, E. *Rickword, D. A. Traversi. It published little creative work of importance, with the exception of the posthumous poems of *Rosenberg, but was an important vehicle for the views of the new Cambridge school of criticism, and published many seminal essays, particularly in the pre-war years, on J. *Austen, Shakespeare, *Marvell, etc. Its critical standards proved less illuminating when applied to contemporary writing; it ignored most of *Orwell, dismissed G. *Greene, Dylan *Thomas, and most of V. *Woolf (Leavis described *Between the Acts as a work of 'extraordinary vacancy and pointlessness'), and in later years attacked the reputations of *Spender and *Auden, both of whom had been originally greeted as heralds of a Poetic Renascence which, by 1940, Leavis declared not to have taken place. In a preface to A Selection from Scrutiny (2 vols, 1968) Leavis deplored the lack of support that this indisputably important periodical had received, which he claimed amounted to 'positively hostile non-recognition of our existence', and went on to blame the British Council, the BBC, the 'intellectuals of literary journalism', etc., for the climate of opinion that had allowed it to perish, while demanding reprints of its back numbers.

Scudamour, Sir, in Spenser's *Faerie Queene (Bk IV), the lover of *Amoret, who is reft from him on his wedding day by the enchanter *Busirane.

SCUDÉRY, Madeleine de (1607–1701), author of French heroic romances. Her Artamène, ou le Grand Cyrus (10 vols, 1649–53) and Clélie, histoire romaine (10 vols, 1654–60) consisted of an interweaving of improbable tales of love and war in an antique setting with ingenious systems and codes of contemporary allusions. They had an immense vogue that extended well beyond the frontiers of France, and influenced heroic plays of the court of Charles II.

Scythrop, a character in Peacock's *Nightmare Abbey, a satirical portrait of the style and literary opinions of *Shelley.

SEACOLE, Mary, see BLACK BRITISH LITERATURE.

Seafarer, The, an Old English poem of about 120 lines in the *Exeter Book, one of the group known as 'elegies'. The opening section of the poem ostensibly discusses the miseries and attractions of life at sea, before moving by an abrupt transition to moral reflections on the transience of life and ending in an explicitly Christian part (the text of which is uncertain), concluding with a prayer. *Pound made a loose but highly evocative translation of the first half of the poem.

The structure of the poem and the coherence of the relationship between its two halves have been much debated. Some critics regard the didactic second part as an appendage to an earlier secular poem; others see the whole as an allegorical representation of human exile from God on the sea of life. A comparable pattern (though not so sharply divided) can be seen in such poems as *The Wanderer and *The Husband's Message. Whichever view is taken of the coherence of the whole, nobody disputes that the powerful sea description of the opening section is much more appealing than the second half, at least to a post-Romantic readership. Ed. I. L. Gordon (1960).

Seagrim, Molly, a character in Fielding's *Tom Jones.

Seasons, The, a poem in blank verse, in four books and a final hymn, by J. *Thomson (1700–48), published 1726–30.

'Winter' was composed first, and its first version, of 405 lines, was written and published in 1726; it was gradually expanded to 1,069 lines by 1746 (the other books were also expanded over the years, but less extensively). It describes the rage of the elements and the sufferings of men and animals; two well-known episodes are the visit of the redbreast to a family who feed him crumbs from the table, and the death of a shepherd in a snowdrift while his family wait anxiously (the latter much illustrated). Many of the passages are notably *sublime.

Next came 'Summer' (1727), which sets forth the progress of a summer's day, with scenes of haymaking, sheep-shearing, and bathing, followed by a panegyric to Great Britain and its 'solid grandeur'. It also includes two narrative episodes, one of the lover Celadon whose Amelia is struck by lightning, the other of Damon who beholds Musidora bathing, the latter highly popular, according to *Wordsworth, because it was titillating.

'Spring' (1728) describes the influence of the season on all the natural world, and ends with a panegyric on nuptial love; its opening lines were particularly admired by *Clare.

'Autumn' (1730) gives a vivid picture of shooting and hunting, sports condemned for their barbarity, and of harvesting, wine-making, etc., and ends with a panegyric to the 'pure pleasures of the rural life'. It includes the episode of Palemon who falls in love with Lavinia, a gleaner in his fields, based on the story of Ruth and Boaz. The whole was completed by a Hymn (1730) and illustrations by William Kent.

The work contains many elegant compliments to Thomson's various patrons and their country seats (*Lyttelton, *Dodington, and others). It was immensely popular and went through many editions in the 18th and 19th cents. The text of *Haydn's oratorio Die Jahreszeiten (1801) was adapted from Thomson by Baron van Swieten, whose version did not please the composer; he objected to having to represent the croaking of frogs and unpoetic sentiments such as 'Fleiss, O edler Fleiss' ('Oh Industry, noble Industry!'). Ed. J. Sambrook (1981).

SEATON, Thomas (1684–1741), a fellow of Clare College, Cambridge, who founded by legacy the Seatonian Prize at Cambridge for sacred poetry. This is referred to in Byron's *English Bards and Scotch Reviewers.

Sebastian, (1) Viola's twin brother in Shakespeare's *Twelfth Night; (2) in his *The Tempest, brother to *Alonso whom he tries to murder.

Second Mrs Tanqueray, The, a play by Sir A. *Pinero, first performed 1893.

Tanqueray, knowing of Paula's past reputation, still determines to marry her, in the belief that his love and the generosity of his friends will prove strong enough to counter prejudice and hypocrisy. Ellean, his young convent-bred daughter from a previous marriage, comes to live with him and Paula; soon Tanqueray begins to realize that Ellean, his friends, and his own suspicions are proving too powerful an opposition to his once-loving marriage. When Paula also realizes that she has lost his love, she kills herself. Because of its daring theme Pinero had great difficulty in having the play accepted for production; but once produced it was an immediate and abiding success.

'Second Nun's Tale', see CANTERBURY TALES, 21.

Secret Agent, The, a novel by *Conrad, published 1907.

A seedy shop in Soho provides cover for Verloc, the secret agent, who is working as a spy for a foreign embassy and as informer for Chief Inspector Heat of Scotland Yard. His wife Winnie has married him chiefly to provide security for her simple-minded younger brother Stevie, and is ignorant of Verloc's spying activities. The shop is a meeting place for a bunch of ill-assorted political fanatics united only in their effort to arouse some extremism in the over-moderate British. We are introduced to the Russian *agent provocateur* Vladimir; the terrorist 'the Professor'; and Ossipon, Yundt, and Michaelis who easily accommodate their principles to their material needs. The foreign embassy is planning a series of outrages aimed at discrediting the revolutionary groups, which will be held responsible. The first target is the Greenwich Observatory and an unwilling Verloc is ordered to engineer the explosion. He uses the poor innocent Stevie as an accomplice and the boy is blown to pieces while carrying the bomb. Winnie, stricken by her brother's death and outraged by Verloc's lack of remorse, kills him with a knife. Fleeing, she encounters Ossipon who flirts with her and they plan to leave the country. But when he discovers Verloc's murder he steals her money and abandons her. Winnie, alone and in terror of the gallows, throws herself overboard from the Channel ferry. Treating this melodramatic theme with ironical humour, Conrad expresses his profound scepticism about the anarchist world.

Secreta Secretorum, a compendium of pronouncements on political and ethical matters, written in Syriac in the 8th cent. AD and claiming to be advice from Aristotle to Alexander. It reached Europe through Arabic and 12th-cent. Hispano-Arabic. The main version in Latin was translated in Spain *c.*1230 and was influential on poets from then until the 16th cent. It influenced in particular the tradition of writing works of advice to kings; it was translated in part by *Lydgate, and Egidio Collona's *De Regimine Principum* (an important source for *Hoccleve's *Regiment of Princes*) drew on it.

Secret Commonwealth of Elves, Fauns and Fairies, The, a tract on the fairy world, second sight, etc., by

Robert Kirk (?1641–92), minister of Aberfoyle, of which the first text, from a manuscript dating from 1691, dates from 1815; it was printed with a commentary by A. *Lang in 1893 and edited by R. B. *Cunninghame Graham in 1933.

SEDLEY, or **SIDLEY,** Sir Charles (?1639–1701), dramatist and poet, friend of *Rochester and *Dryden, famous for his wit and urbanity and notorious for his profligate escapades. His tragedy *Antony and Cleopatra* (1677) was followed by two comedies, **Bellamira* (1687) and *The Mulberry Garden* (1668), which was based partly on *Molière's *L'École des maris*. His poems and songs ('Phillis is my only joy', 'Love still has something of the sea', etc.) were published in 1702, with his *Miscellaneous Works*. *Malone identified him as the Lisideius of Dryden's *Of Dramatick Poesy*, who defends the imitation of French drama in English. He also had a hand in a translation of *Corneille's *Pompée* with *Waller, Godolphin, C. *Sackville, and *Filmer.

Sedley, Mr, Mrs, Joseph, and Amelia, characters in Thackeray's *Vanity Fair*.

SEFERIS, George (1900–71), Greek poet and diplomat, born in Smyrna and educated in Athens. He spent several periods in Britain, including some years as ambassador (1957–62), and in 1963 was awarded the *Nobel Prize. He published several volumes of poetry, from 1931 onwards, much of it strongly imbued with classical mythology: translations include *Poems* (1960), by R. *Warner, and *Collected Poems* (1981), by E. Keeley and P. Sherrard.

Sejanus His Fall, a Roman tragedy by *Jonson, performed by the King's Men 1603, with Shakespeare and *Burbage in the cast, printed 1605. At its first performance it was hissed from the stage.

Based mainly on *Tacitus, the play deals with the rise of Sejanus during the reign of Tiberius, his destruction of the family of Germanicus, and his poisoning of Tiberius' son Drusus. Suspecting the scope of his favourite's ambition, Tiberius leaves Rome, setting his agent Macro to spy on him. Tiberius denounces Sejanus in a letter to the Senate, which condemns him to death, and the mob, stirred up by Macro, tears him to pieces.

Selborne, Natural History and Antiquities of, see WHITE, G.

SELDEN, John (1584–1654), English jurist, orientalist, and legal historian, born near Worthing, Sussex, and educated at Hart Hall, Oxford. He then became an eminent lawyer and bencher of the Inner Temple. His *History of Tythes* (1618) gave offence to the clergy and was suppressed by public authority. In Parliament he took an active part against the Crown until 1649, when he withdrew from public affairs on the principle that 'The wisest way for men in these times is to say nothing.' He won fame as an orientalist with his treatise *De Diis Syriis* (1617), and subsequently made a valuable collection of oriental manuscripts, most of which passed at his death to the Bodleian Library. His *Table Talk*, containing reports of his utterances from time to time during the last 20 years of his life, composed by his secretary Richard Milward, appeared in 1689. His works include *Marmora Arundelliana* (1628), *Mare Clausum* (1635), translated by *Nedham, in which he maintained against the *Mare Liberum* of *Grotius that the sea is capable of sovereignty, and *Illustrations* to the first 18 'songs' of Drayton's *Poly-Olbion*. His works were collected by Dr David Wilkins (1726).

Select Society, the, an association of educated Scotsmen formed in 1754, whose members met in Edinburgh to discuss philosophical questions. *Hume and W. *Robertson were among its prominent members.

SELF, Will (1961–), novelist and journalist, born in London. Self is a former cartoonist whose first collection of stories, *The Quantity Theory of Insanity* (1991), commanded immediate attention, both for the fertility of its ideas and for its hectic, energetic prose, crammed with word-play and arcane vocabulary. *Cock and Bull* (1992) contained a pair of novellas, each a wry commentary on gender reversal. *My Idea of Fun* (1993), his first full-length novel, was a surreal and disturbing *Bildungsroman*. Subsequent story collections are *Grey Area* (1994) and *Tough Tough Toys for Tough Tough Boys* (1998); in between Self published a selection of journalism, *Junk Mail* (1995), which included some candid pieces about his drug addiction, and a novella of urban life, *The Sweet Smell of Psychosis* (1996). His most sustained and accomplished work is the novel *Great Apes* (1997), which (like 'Scale', a story of skewed perspectives from *Grey Area*) shows his ability to seize upon an absurd premiss and see it through to its logical conclusion. This long satiric parable of a society where human beings find themselves transformed into monkeys recalls *Swift in its ambition and scatological vigour. Later titles include *How the Dead Live* (2000), which violently addresses the problem of ageing, and another collection of journalism, *Feeding Frenzy* (2001).

SELKIRK, Alexander (1676–1721), born in Fife. He ran away to sea and joined the privateering expedition of *Dampier in 1703. Having quarrelled with his captain, Thomas Stradling, he was put ashore on one of the uninhabited Pacific islands of Juan Fernández in 1704, and remained there until 1709 when he was rescued by W. *Rogers. On his return he met *Steele, who published an account of his experiences in the *Englishman* (3 Dec. 1713). Defoe used the story in *Robinson Crusoe* and *Cowper in his poem 'I am monarch of all I survey'.

SELVON, Sam(uel Dickson) (1923–94), Trinidad-born novelist, playwright, and short story writer, educated at San Fernando in Trinidad. He began to write while serving as a wireless operator in the Royal Navy during the Second World War, and came to England in 1950, travelling on the same boat as G. *Lamming. His first novel, *A Brighter Sun* (1952), set in Trinidad during the war, was written in London: it describes the life and brightening prospects of Tiger, a young Indian peasant. Selvon became well known for his novels about London: these include *The Lonely Londoners* (1956), *Moses Ascending* (1975), and *Moses Migrating* (1983), which chart with comedy, sympathy, and a pioneering use of Caribbean idiom the experiences of black immigrants trying to find fame and fortune, or at least a bed, in the unknown terrain of Earls Court, Notting Hill, and Bayswater. Selvon also wrote many plays for *BBC radio before leaving to settle in Canada in 1978. See also BLACK BRITISH LITERATURE.

semiotics, see SAUSSURE and STRUCTURALISM.

SENANCOUR, Étienne Pivert de (1770–1846), French author, now chiefly remembered for his *Obermann* (1804), a lightly fictionalized series of letters to a friend supposed to have been written over a period of years, mostly from a remote Alpine valley. The author reflects on the society he has fled and on man, describing his own frustrated inactivity, melancholy, and ennui, his solitude and mystical attachment to Nature. The mental and emotional condition given voice in *Obermann* appealed to many first-generation Romantic writers in France. Senancour was much admired by *Sainte-Beuve and by M. *Arnold, who discerned in his sentimentalism a distinctive 'gravity and severity'. Two well-known poems by Arnold, 'Stanzas in Memory of the Author of Obermann' (1852) and 'Obermann Once More' (1867), take the form of meditations that develop from reflecting on Senancour's book in its Alpine setting. Arnold also wrote an essay 'Obermann' (*Academy*, 9 Oct. 1869).

SENECA, Lucius Annaeus (*c*.4 bc–ad 65), Roman Stoic philosopher, tragic poet, and, like his father the elder Seneca, a noted rhetorician; born in Córdoba, Spain. He was appointed tutor to the young Nero and, when the latter became emperor, acted as one of his chief advisers, checking his crimes for a period; but, finding this position untenable, he withdrew from the court in AD 62. Three years later he was accused of being implicated in a conspiracy and was forced to commit suicide. His writings consist of tragedies in verse, dialogues, treatises, and letters in prose, which in their different ways all aim to teach *Stoicism. Most of his nine plays are on subjects drawn from Greek mythology and treated in extant Greek dramas, but his manner is very different from that of Greek tragedy. He uses an exaggerated rhetoric, dwells habitually on bloodthirsty details, and introduces ghosts and magic; the plays were almost certainly not intended for performance but for reading aloud, probably by the author himself, to a select audience. Senecan drama was familiar in the 16th cent. at a time when Greek tragedies were scarcely known; all the nine plays were translated (1559–81) and imitated by dramatists from the time of *Gorboduc onwards. For an account of Seneca's influence, see T. S. *Eliot's important essay 'Seneca in Elizabethan Translation' (1927) and his 'Shakespeare and the Stoicism of Seneca' (1927). *Dryden's Troilus and Cressida (1679), more than a century later than the Elizabethan imitations, still shows traces of Senecan influence. Seneca's prose writings consist of treatises, some of which are clumsily disguised as dialogues (De Clementia, De Ira, etc.) and a collection of what purport to be letters addressed to one Lucilius after the author's retirement, constituting a sort of elementary course in Stoicism. These writings were widely read in the 17th and 18th cents. *L'Estrange's digest of them (1678) reached ten editions by 1711, so that there is an undercurrent of Stoicism in much of early 18th-cent. thinking, visible not only in Addison's *Cato but also in a wide range of writers from *Pope to *Duck. (For Senecan drama, see also LUCAN.)

SENIOR, Olive (1941–   ), poet and short story writer, born and brought up in Jamaica, and educated at Carleton University, Ottawa; she divides her time between Jamaica and Canada. Her collections of poetry, Talking of Trees (1985) and Gardening in the Tropics (1994), employ a wide range of voices, from the colloquial and the conversational to the prophetic, to explore the struggles and history of her land and its people. Her volumes of short stories are Summer Lightning (1986), Arrival of the Snake Woman (1989), and Discerner of Hearts (1995).

sensation, novel of, an enormously popular genre of fiction that flourished from c.1860 onwards. It relocated the terrors of the *Gothic novel to a recognizably modern, middle-class England. Its high-impact narrative style employed cliffhanging conclusions to chapters, which gave the genre a reputation for 'preaching to the nerves'. Its plots commonly involved guilty family secrets, bigamy, insanity, and murder (especially poisoning), often taking inspiration from real criminal cases. This accounts for an intense interest in legal papers, telegrams, diary entries, and written testimony. Indeed, many of Wilkie *Collins's sensation novels represent themselves as bundles of documents authored by witnesses in the case. The genre was also noted for its energetic—and frequently criminal—heroines, and for its enervated, hypersensitive heroes. The 'sensation' label, however, was a pejorative one, and its practitioners rarely declared themselves as such. The most influential works in the genre are Wilkie Collins's *The Woman in White (1860) and *The Moonstone (1868); Mrs H. *Wood's East Lynne (1861); M. E. *Braddon's Lady Audley's Secret (1862); and C. *Reade's *Hard Cash (1863). The novels of Rhoda *Broughton and *Ouida are usually considered to be on the margins of the genre. Modern *detective fiction can trace its roots back to sensation fiction.

Sense and Sensibility, a novel by J. Austen, which grew from a sketch entitled 'Elinor and Marianne'; revised 1797–8 and again 1809; published 1811.

Mrs Henry Dashwood and her daughters Elinor and Marianne, together with the younger Margaret, are left in straitened circumstances, because the estate of which Mrs Dashwood's husband had the life interest has passed to her stepson John Dashwood. Henry Dashwood, before his death, had urgently recommended to John that he look after his stepmother and sisters, but John's selfishness, encouraged by his grasping wife (the daughter of the arrogant Mrs Ferrers), defeats his father's wish. Mrs Henry Dashwood and her daughters accordingly retire to a cottage in Devon, but not before Elinor and Edward Ferrers, brother of Mrs John Dashwood, have become much attracted to each other. However, Edward shows a strange uneasiness in his relations with Elinor. In Devon Marianne is thrown into the company of John Willoughby, an attractive but impecunious and unprincipled young man, with whom she falls desperately—and very obviously—in love. Willoughby likewise shows signs of a strong affection for her, and their engagement is expected daily. Willoughby suddenly departs for London, leaving Marianne in acute distress. Eventually Elinor and Marianne also go to London, on the invitation of their tactless and garrulous old friend Mrs Jennings. Here Willoughby shows complete indifference to Marianne, and finally, in a cruel and insolent letter, informs her of his approaching marriage to a rich heiress. Marianne makes no effort to hide her great grief. Meanwhile Elinor has learned, under pledge of secrecy, from Lucy Steele (a sly, self-seeking young woman) that she and Edward Ferrers have been secretly engaged for four years. Elinor, whose self-control is in strong contrast to Marianne's demonstrative emotions, silently conceals her distress. Edward's engagement, which had been kept secret because of his financial dependence on his mother, now becomes known to her. In her fury at Edward's refusal to break his promise to Lucy, she dismisses him from her sight, and settles on his younger brother Robert the property that would otherwise have gone to Edward. At this juncture a small living is offered to Edward, and the way seems open for his marriage with Lucy. But Robert, a fashionable young fop, falls in love with Lucy, who, seeing her best interest in a marriage with the wealthier brother, throws over Edward and marries Robert. Edward, immensely relieved to be released from an engagement he has long and painfully regretted, proposes to Elinor and is accepted. Marianne, slowly recovering from the despair that followed her abandonment by Willoughby, eventually accepts the proposal of Colonel Brandon, an old family friend, whose considerable quiet attractions had been eclipsed by his brilliant rival.

sensibility, see SENTIMENT, NOVEL OF.

sentiment, or **sensibility, novel of.** The object of this type of novel was to illustrate the alliance of acute sensibility with true virtue. An adherence to strict morality and honour, combined with copious feeling and a sympathetic heart, were (with whatever consequences of failure or humiliation) the marks of the man or woman of sentiment. The cult may be traced particularly to the work of *Marivaux, *Richardson, and S. *Fielding; the most popular and influential novels to which they gave rise were probably H. Brooke's *The Fool of Quality*, Sterne's *A Sentimental Journey*, and Mackenzie's *The Man of Feeling*, together with the work of F. *Brooke, C. *Lennox, and F. *Sheridan. Late in the century *Lamb's *The Tale of Rosamund Gray* (1798) was in the mainstream of such novels, but the cult was then dying. The early chapters of J. Austen's *Northanger Abbey* mock the 'refined susceptibilities' of the novel of sentiment, and *Sense and Sensibility* was intended to demonstrate the serious consequences of following its standards. (See also NOVEL, RISE OF THE.)

sentimental comedy, a type of sentimental drama introduced by *Steele, a reaction from the comedy of the *Restoration. In France it evolved into *la comédie larmoyante* of La Chaussée (1692–1754). (See KELLY.)

Sentimental Journey, A, *through France and Italy*, by L. *Sterne, published 1768.

The narrator, Parson Yorick (borrowed from *Tristram Shandy*), is a man of great charm, sensibility, and gallantry, who sets out to travel through France and Italy. At the end of the book he has gone little further than Lyons, and it is not known whether Sterne intended any further volume. As it is, the work begins by breaking into the middle of a dialogue (with the famous words, 'They order, said I, these matters better in France') and ends ambiguously in mid-sentence: 'So that when I stretch'd out my hand, I caught hold of the Fille de Chambre's—' Sterne referred to the book as his 'Work of Redemption' and declared that its aim was 'to teach us to love the world and our fellow creatures'. The amiable Yorick, who reveres 'Dear sensibility!' and is frequently moved to tears, does indeed find much to commend and little to condemn in France and the French. In parodying fashionable works of travel, he contrasts his own appreciation with Smelfungus (a caricature of *Smollett) and with Mundungus (perhaps a Dr Sharp), both of whom had written disparaging travel books about Europe. Whether Sterne is serious or ironic in describing Yorick's displays of acute sensibility is a matter of conjecture. Certainly the parson is as full of gaiety and irony as of tender feeling. In his travels from Calais to Amiens, Paris, the Bourbonnais, and nearly to Modane, with his servant La Fleur, he enjoys many encounters with all manner of men, from marquis to potboy, and, more especially, with pretty women, who range from ladies of wealth and elegance to chambermaids and shop-girls, and

include the pathetic Maria from vol. ix of *Tristram Shandy*.

The book was no doubt based on Sterne's two journeys abroad in 1762–4 and 1765. It was well received by the public, and in 1769, after Sterne's death, was continued by a *'Eugenius', traditionally assumed to be Sterne's old friend *Hall-Stevenson. *A Sentimental Journey* is probably the first English novel to survive in the handwriting of its author. There is a scholarly edition, ed. G. D. Stout Jr (1967).

Serious Call, A, *to a Devout and Holy Life*, see LAW.

Serious Money, by Caryl *Churchill (perf. 1987). Inspired by the deregulation of the City in 1986, known as the Big Bang, the play, written largely in spirited rhyming verse, evokes the ruthless greed, buoyant materialism, changing culture, and cynicism of the financial world in the monetarist 1980s. The play opens with a short satirical extract on speculation from *Shadwell's comedy *The Volunteers, or The Stockjobbers* (pub. 1693), and then introduces a noisy gallery of contemporary traders, dealers, jobbers, bankers, and stockbrokers. The plot revolves round Scilla Todd's investigations into the suspicious death of her brother Jake, involved in insider dealing and an attempted takeover bid of the symbolically named company Albion: Churchill's ear for the new jargon of the media, PR, and the City itself is acute and the play, launched at the *Royal Court, was also a West End success, much enjoyed by those it mocked. The play ends with a chorus singing in praise and hope of 'Five more Glorious Years'—'pissed and promiscuous, the money's ridiculous—five more glorious years'.

SERVICE, Robert William (1874–1958), poet, born in Preston and brought up in Glasgow. He emigrated to Canada in 1895 where he observed the gold rush in the Yukon; this inspired his best-known ballads, which include 'The Shooting of Dan McGrew' and 'The Cremation of Sam McGee', published in *Songs of a Sourdough* (1907, Toronto; as *The Spell of the Yukon*, New York). Its sequel, *Ballads of a Cheechako*, followed in 1909. Other volumes include *Rhymes of a Rolling Stone* (1912) and *Rhymes of a Red Cross Man* (1916). *Ploughman of the Moon* (1945) and *Harper of Heaven* (1948) are both autobiographical. Collected volumes appeared in 1933, 1955, and 1960.

sestina, a poem of six six-line stanzas (with an envoy) in which the line-endings of the first stanza are repeated, but in different order, in the other five [*OED*].

Setebos, a god of the Patagonians, worshipped by Caliban's mother Sycorax (in Shakespeare's *The Tempest*). His purpose in creating the world is worked out by Caliban in R. *Browning's 'Caliban upon Setebos'.

SETH, Vikram (1952–), poet, novelist, short story and travel writer, born in India and educated at Corpus Christi, Oxford, Stanford University, and Nanjing University, China. Early works included collections of poems, *Mappings* (1981) and *The Humble Admin-istrator's Garden* (1985). A travel book, *From Heaven Lake: Travels through Sinkiang and Tibet*, appeared in 1983. *The Golden Gate* (1986) is a novel set in San Francisco written in 14-line rhyming stanzas, a vir-tuoso performance of Byronic verve with audacious rhymes and great metrical fluency, dealing with ultra-modern protagonists in what might have been thought an archaic medium. *A Suitable Boy* (1993) is a long and intricately structured novel about the Mehras' search for a suitable husband for a daughter, Lata. The novel is set in India some years after Independence and en-twines the domestic and the political. *An Equal Music* (1999), set largely in London, is a romance narrated by the second violinist in a string quartet, and *Two Lives* (2005) is a memoir of Seth's Indian great-uncle and German great-aunt. Other works include *Arion and the Dolphin* (1994), a children's book and opera libretto. See ANGLO-INDIAN LITERATURE.

SETTLE, Elkanah (1648–1724), educated at Trinity College, Oxford, the author of a series of bombastic Oriental melodramas which threatened *Dryden's popularity and aroused his hostility. He appears to have written *Cambyses* (1667) while still at Oxford, and his *The Empress of Morocco* (1673) had such a vogue that Dryden, with *Crowne and *Shadwell, wrote a pamphlet of criticism of it. Settle retorted with an attack on Dryden's *Almanzor and Almahide*, and Dryden vented his resentment by satirizing Settle as Doeg in the second part of *Absalom and Achitophel*. Settle published *Absalom Senior, or Achitophel Trans-pros'd* in 1682, and *Reflections on Several of Mr Dryden's Plays* in 1687. He was appointed city poet in 1691, took to writing *drolls for Bartholomew Fair (as he may have done before his success), and died in the Charterhouse. He also wrote two interesting rogue biographies (see ROGUE LITERATURE).

Seven Champions of Christendom, *The Famous History of the*, see JOHNSON, R.

Seven Deadly Sins, usually given as Pride, Envy, Anger, Sloth, Covetousness, Gluttony, and Lust; fre-quently personified in medieval literature (e.g. *Piers Plowman*, B, *Passus V*; *Dunbar's 'The Dance of the Sevin Deidly Synnis'), and used too in Chaucer's 'Parson's Tale' (see CANTERBURY TALES, 24) and in Spenser's *Faerie Queene* where they are personified again. They provide one of the organizing structures for *Dante's *Inferno* and *Purgatorio*; the most import-ant medieval source authority for these literary oc-currences is believed to be Guilielmus Peraldus' *Summa seu Tractatus de Viciis* which dates from the mid-13th cent. See M. W. Bloomfield, *The Seven Deadly Sins* (1952).

Seven Liberal Arts, see QUADRIVIUM and TRIVIUM.

Seven Pillars of Wisdom, The, see LAWRENCE, T. E.

Seven Sages of Rome, The, a metrical romance of the early 14th cent., varying in length in different versions from 2,500 to 4,300 lines. In form it is a framed collection of tales, derived through Latin and French from Eastern collections, the original of which is the Indian *Book of Sindibad* (see SYNTIPAS), of interest as one of the earliest English instances of the form of short verse story used by Chaucer in *The Canterbury Tales*.

The Emperor Diocletian has his son educated by seven sages. His stepmother is jealous of the boy and accuses him to the emperor of attempting to seduce her; the boy is silent for seven days, under the influence of the stepmother's magic, and he is ordered to execution. On each of the seven nights a tale is told by the queen to illustrate the dangers of supplantation of the emperor by his son, and on each of the following mornings a tale is told by one of the sages on the theme of the danger of trusting women. The emperor is alternately persuaded by the queen and the sages. When the seven days are passed, the boy speaks and exposes the stepmother, who is burnt. The most widely attested manuscript version ('A') in 3,974 lines of short couplets has been edited by K. Brunner (EETS os 191, 1933; repr. 1971).

Seven Sleepers of Ephesus, seven noble Christian youths of Ephesus who, fleeing from the persecution of Decius (AD 250), concealed themselves in a cavern in a neighbouring mountain. They were ordered by the emperor to be walled up therein, and fell into a deep slumber, which was miraculously prolonged for 187 years. At the end of that time the slaves of one Adolius, to whom the inheritance of the mountain had des-cended, removed the stones with which the cavern had been walled up, and the seven sleepers were permitted to awake. Under the impression that they had slept a few hours, one of them proceeded to the city for food, but was unable to recognize the place. His singular dress and obsolete speech (or, in some versions, the fact that he tried to buy food with obsolete money) caused him to be brought before a magistrate, and the miracle was brought to light. The people, headed by the bishop, hastened to visit the cavern of the sleepers, 'who bestowed their benediction, related their story, and at the same instant peaceably expired' (Gibbon, *Decline and Fall*, xxxiii). The legend was translated from the Syriac by *Gregory of Tours, and is also given by other authors. It is included in the *Koran (sura 18) among Muhammad's revelations.

Seven Types of Ambiguity, a critical work by W. *Empson, published 1930, rev. 1947, 1953; one of the most enjoyable and influential offshoots from I. A. *Richards's experiments with *practical criticism.

Empson uses the term ambiguity 'in an extended sense', to refer to 'any verbal nuance, however slight, which gives room for alternative reactions to the same piece of language'. The first, or simplest, type of ambiguity he defines as simple metaphor, 'a word or a grammatical construction effective in several ways at once'. The second occurs 'when two or more meanings are resolved into one' (as by 'Double Grammar' in Shakespeare); the third consists of two apparently disconnected meanings given simultaneously, as in a pun, or, by extension, in allegory or pastoral, where reference is made to more than one 'universe of discourse'; the fourth occurs when 'alternative meanings combine to make clear a complicated state of mind in the author' (with examples from Shakespeare, *Donne, and G. M. *Hopkins); the fifth consists of what Empson calls 'fortunate confusion', with examples from *Shelley and *Swinburne, suggesting the possibility that 19th-cent. technique is 'in part the metaphysical tradition dug up when rotten'; the sixth occurs when a statement in itself meaningless or contradictory forces the reader to supply interpretations; and an account of the seventh, which 'marks a division in the author's mind', is accompanied by quotations from *Freud and illustrations from *Crashaw, *Keats, Hopkins. In detail, the work is an interesting example of the rewards of close linguistic analysis, applied to a wide though well-established range of authors; more broadly, it indicates the tendency of the period to elevate intellectual and verbal complexity and richness above simplicity.

SEVERN, Joseph (1793–1879), painter, and devoted friend and correspondent of *Keats, of whom he made several drawings and portraits, and of whom he took a death-mask. He won the RA Gold Medal in 1818 but had little public success. He accompanied Keats to Italy in 1820 and attended him at his death. His care of Keats brought him to general notice and for a time he prospered as a painter, especially in English circles in Rome. He attempted fiction, without success, but published *The Vicissitudes of Keats's Fame* in 1863. He was eventually given the British consulship in Rome.

SÉVIGNÉ, Marie de Rabutin-Chantal, marquise de (1626–96), French letter writer. Orphaned at a very young age, she was brought up by an uncle as a person of wide culture. She frequented the Hôtel de Rambouillet, made a fashionable marriage in 1644, and was widowed seven years later. Her reputation rests on her lifelong correspondence with her daughter, published posthumously 1735–54: a small selection had appeared in 1725. It gives a portrait of Paris under Louis XIV unique for its charm, vivacity, and acute observation.

SEWARD, Anna (1742–1809), poet, essayist, and letter writer, born in Eyam, Derbyshire; known as the 'Swan of Lichfield', where she lived from the age of 10, and where her father was canon: he also edited the works of *Beaumont and Fletcher (10 vols, 1750). Her grandfather John Hunter had taught the young Dr *Johnson and she furnished *Boswell with many details of his early life, while admitting that she did not much care for him. Her poems included *Elegy on Captain Cook* (1780), *Llangollen Vale, with Other Poems* (1796, of

which the title poem records a visit to Eleanor Butler and Sarah Ponsonby: see under LLANGOLLEN, LADIES OF), and *Original Sonnets* (1799). Her literary friends included E. *Darwin (of whom she wrote a memoir, 1804), T. *Day, and *Hayley. In 1802 she wrote an admiring letter to Sir W. *Scott, who found some merit in her poetry and edited her works in three volumes, with a memoir, in 1810, at her suggestion. Her letters were published in 1811 (6 vols) and there is a selection in H. *Pearson's *The Swan of Lichfield* (1936).

SEWELL, Anna (1820–78). She wrote only one book, *Black Beauty* (1877), a story for children relating the life of a black horse, which suffers much but eventually finds a happy home. The book, for which she received £20, was published three months before her death; its immediate success and fame survived for many generations, and it became established as a children's classic. There is a life by S. Chitty (1971).

SEXTON, Anne (1928–1974), American poet, born into a privileged Massachusetts family. Following an early elopement, children, and a breakdown, she started to write poetry as therapy. She attended Robert *Lowell's classes with Sylvia *Plath, with whom she shares the use of a dramatic, apparently *confessional, 'I', and the thematic territory of family life, jealous passion, and mental illness. Her early work makes dynamic use of strict poetic form, but, from the Pulitzer Prize-winning *Live or Die* (1966), this is replaced by free verse which relies on dense, sometimes surreal, metaphors, wit, and rhythmic lists for impact. Her later work is increasingly haunted by a troubled relationship with God. Despite much success, especially with her adaptation of *Grimm, *Transformations* (1971), Sexton took her own life, an event which has overshadowed her considerable gift, range, and influence, notably on Sharon *Olds. *Collected Poems* was published in 1981, *Selected Poems* in 1988.

Shadow, Simon, in Shakespeare's 2 *Henry IV* (III. ii), one of Falstaff's recruits.

Shadow of a Gunman, The, see O'CASEY.

SHADWELL, Thomas (?1642–92), dramatist, whose first play *The Sullen Lovers* (1668) was based on *Molière's *Les Fâcheux*; in its preface he proclaimed himself a follower of *Jonson's comedy of humours. He wrote some 14 comedies, including *The Squire of Alsatia* (1688), *The Virtuoso* (1676, a satire on the *Royal Society), *Epsom Wells* (1672), and *Bury Fair* (1689); the last two give an interesting if scurrilous picture of contemporary manners, watering places, and amusements. He also wrote operas, adapting Shakespeare's *The Tempest* as *The Enchanted Island* (1674). A successful dramatist in his day, he has been perhaps unfairly remembered for his 1682 quarrel with *Dryden. He was probably the author of *The Medal of John Bayes* (1682) and other anonymous attacks on Dryden; Dryden's counter-attacks include

Mac Flecknoe and the second part of *Absalom and Achitophel*, where Shadwell appears as Og. Shadwell somewhat plaintively defends himself from the charge of dullness in his dedication to *Sedley of his translation of the *Tenth Satire of Juvenal* (1687). As a 'true-blue' Whig, he succeeded Dryden as *poet laureate and historiographer at the revolution in 1689; their quarrel had been partly political, for Shadwell had been virtually unable to get his plays performed during the last years of Charles II's reign, or in James II's.

SHAFFER, Peter Levin (1926–   ), playwright, born in Liverpool, and educated at Trinity College, Cambridge. His first play, *Five Finger Exercise* (1958), a drama of middle-class family life, was followed by many other successes, including *The Royal Hunt of the Sun* (1964, pub. 1965), an epic about the conquest of Peru; *Black Comedy* (1965, pub. 1967), a cleverly constructed *farce set in a London apartment which reverses dark and light, so that the cast, in full glare of the lights and view of the audience, stumbles around during the pitch darkness of a dramatic electricity failure; *Equus* (1973), a drama about an analyst's relationship with his horse-obsessed patient; *Amadeus* (1979, pub. 1980), which deals with the nature of creativity through a portrayal of the composers *Mozart and Salieri; *Lettice and Lovage* (1987); and *The Gift of the Gorgon* (1992).

His twin brother Anthony Shaffer (d. 2001), author of *Sleuth* (1970, pub. 1971), was also a successful playwright.

SHAFTESBURY, Anthony Ashley Cooper, first Baron Ashley and first earl of (1621–83), a statesman prominent on the king's side in the Civil War, as leader of the parliamentary opposition to *Cromwell, after the Restoration as a member of the *Cabal and chancellor. After his dismissal he was leader of the opposition, a promoter of the Exclusion Bill, and a supporter of Monmouth. He is closely associated with the foundation of the Whig party and was for a time its most prominent politician. He died in Holland. He was satirized as Achitophel in Dryden's *Absalom and Achitophel*, by Otway in *Venice Preserv'd*, and by many others.

SHAFTESBURY, Anthony Ashley Cooper, third earl of (1671–1713). Excluded by ill health from active politics after 1702, he devoted himself to intellectual pursuits, and in particular to moral and aesthetic philosophy. His principal writings are embodied in his *Characteristics of Men, Manners, Opinions, and Times*, published 1711 (rev. edn. 1714), which included various treatises previously published (notably his *Inquiry Concerning Virtue, or Merit*, 1699). Shaftesbury was influenced by *Deism; he was at once a Platonist and a churchman, an opponent of the selfish theory of conduct advocated by *Hobbes. Man has 'affections', Shaftesbury held, not only for himself but for the creatures about him. 'To have one's affections right and entire, not only in respect of oneself, but of society and

the public: this is rectitude, integrity, or virtue.' And there is no conflict between the self-regarding and social affections; for the individual's own good is included in the good of society. Moreover, man has a capacity for distinguishing right and wrong, the beauty or ugliness of actions and affections, and this he calls the 'moral sense'. To be truly virtuous, a man must have a *disinterested* affection for what he perceives to be right. Shaftesbury's aesthetic thought, by its attempt to explain nature by the analogy of art and its assertion of a close connection between art and morality, had some influence on later writers, such as *Arbuckle in *Hibernicus's Letters*, and *Akenside in *The Pleasures of Imagination*. His influence is also seen in the writing of *Fielding, and in the philosophy of *Hutcheson and *Turnbull. A master satirist, Shaftesbury employs an amalgam of irony, indirection, ambiguity, and juxtaposition to achieve a broad range of witty effects. His principle that ideas and arguments should be subject to 'the test of ridicule' influenced many 18th-cent. writers.

SHAFTESBURY, Anthony Ashley Cooper, seventh earl of (1801–85), philanthropist, active in many movements for the protection of the working classes and the benefit of the poor.

SHAH, Idries (1924–96), writer and teacher, born in the north of India, whose many works have done much to introduce Sufi thought to the West. They include *The Sufis* (1964), *The Tales of the Dervishes* (1967), *Caravan of Dreams* (1968), *The Way of the Sufi* (1968), and *Learning How to Live* (1978, with an introduction by D. *Lessing, 1981: Lessing has been much influenced by his work). He also collected stories from the *Nasrudin corpus and published other selections of Oriental tales. His works are unconventional mixtures of jokes, anecdotes, questions, precepts, and illuminations, inspired by Sufi wisdom and psychology.

Shahrazad, see SCHEHERAZADE.

SHAKESPEARE, William (1564–1616), dramatist, man of the theatre, and poet, baptized in Holy Trinity Church, Stratford-upon-Avon, on 26 Apr. 1564. His birth is traditionally celebrated on 23 Apr., which is also known to have been the date of his death. He was the eldest son of John Shakespeare, a glover and dealer in other commodities who played a prominent part in local affairs, becoming bailiff and justice of the peace in 1568, but whose fortunes later declined. John had married *c.*1557 Mary Arden, who came from a family of higher social standing. Of their eight children, four sons and one daughter survived childhood.

The standard and kind of education indicated by William's writings are such as he might have received at the local grammar school, whose records for the period are lost. On 28 Nov. 1582 a bond was issued permitting him to marry Anne Hathaway of Shottery, a village close to Stratford. She was eight years his senior. A daughter, Susanna, was baptized on 26 May 1583, and twins, Hamnet and Judith, on 2 Feb. 1585.

We do not know how Shakespeare was employed in early manhood; the best-authenticated tradition is *Aubrey's: 'he had been in his younger yeares a Schoolmaster in the Countrey.' This has fed speculation that he is the 'William Shakeshafte' named in the will of the recusant Alexander Houghton, of Lea Hall, Lancashire, in 1581, and in turn that he had Catholic sympathies.

Nothing is known of his beginnings as a writer, nor when or in what capacity he entered the theatre. In 1587 an actor of the Queen's Men died through manslaughter shortly before the company visited Stratford. That Shakespeare may have filled the vacancy is an intriguing speculation. The first printed allusion to him is from 1592, in the pamphlet *Greenes Groats-Worth of Witte, ostensibly by R. *Greene but possibly by *Chettle. Mention of 'an upstart Crow' who 'supposes he is as well able to bombast out a blanke verse as the best of you' and who 'is in his owne conceit the onely Shake-scene in a countrey' suggests rivalry, and parody of a line from 3 *Henry VI shows that Shakespeare was established on the London literary scene. He was a leading member of the Lord Chamberlain's Men soon after their refoundation in 1594. With them he worked and grew prosperous for the rest of his career as they developed into London's leading company, occupying the *Globe Theatre from 1599, becoming the King's Men on James I's accession in 1603, and taking over the Blackfriars as a winter house in 1608. He is the only prominent playwright of his time to have had so stable a relationship with a single company.

Theatrical life centred on London, which necessarily became Shakespeare's professional base, as various records testify. But his family remained in Stratford. In 1596 his father applied, successfully, for a grant of arms, and so became a gentleman; in August William's son Hamnet died, and was buried in Holy Trinity churchyard. In October Shakespeare was lodging in Bishopsgate, London, and in May of the next year he bought a substantial Stratford house, New Place. His father died in 1601, and in the following year William paid £320 for 127 acres of land in Old Stratford. In 1604 he lodged in London with a Huguenot family called Mountjoy. In the next year he paid £440 for an interest in the Stratford tithes, and there in June 1607 his daughter Susanna married a physician, John Hall. His only granddaughter, Elizabeth Hall, was christened the following February; in 1608 his mother died and was buried in Holy Trinity.

Evidence of Shakespeare's increasing involvement with Stratford at this time suggests that he was withdrawing to New Place, but his name continues to appear in London records; in Mar. 1613, for instance, he paid £140 for a gatehouse close to the Blackfriars Theatre, probably as an investment. In the same month he and the actor R. *Burbage received 44 shillings each for providing an *impresa* to be borne by the earl of Rutland at a court tourney. In Feb. 1616 his second daughter Judith married Thomas Quiney, causing her father to make alterations to the draft of his will, which he signed on 25 Mar. He died, according to the inscription on his monument, on 23 Apr., and was buried in Holy Trinity. His widow died in 1623 and his last surviving descendant, Elizabeth Hall, in 1670.

Shakespeare's only writings for the press (apart from the disputed 'Funeral Elegy' of 1613) are the narrative poems *Venus and Adonis and *The Rape of Lucrece, published 1593 and 1594 respectively, each with the author's dedication to Henry Wriothesley, earl of Southampton, and the short poem *'The Phoenix and the Turtle', published 1601 in Robert Chester's *Loves Martyr*, a collection of poems by various hands. His *Sonnets, dating probably from the mid-1590s, appeared in 1609, apparently not by his agency; they bear a dedication to the mysterious 'Mr W.H.' over the initials of the publisher, Thomas Thorpe. The volume also includes the poem *'A Lover's Complaint'.

Shakespeare's plays were published by being performed. Scripts of only half of them appeared in print in his lifetime, some in short, sometimes manifestly corrupt, texts, often known as 'bad quartos'. Records of performance are scanty and haphazard: as a result dates and order of composition, especially of the earlier plays, are often difficult to establish. The list that follows gives dates of first printing of all the plays other than those that first appeared in the 1623 *Folio.

Probably Shakespeare began to write for the stage in the late 1580s. The ambitious trilogy on the reign of Henry VI, now known as *Henry VI Parts 1, 2, and 3, and its sequel *Richard III, are among his early works. Parts 2 and 3 were printed in variant texts as *The First Part of the Contention betwixt the Two Famous Houses of York and Lancaster* (1594) and *The True Tragedy of Richard, Duke of York* (1595). *Henry VI Part 1* may have been written after these. A variant quarto of *Richard III* appeared in 1597. Shakespeare's first Roman tragedy is *Titus Andronicus, printed 1594, and his earliest comedies are *The Two Gentlemen of Verona, *The Taming of the Shrew (a derivative play, *The Taming of a Shrew*, was printed 1594), *The Comedy of Errors (acted 1594), and *Love's Labour's Lost (printed 1598). All these plays are thought to have been written by 1595.

Particularly difficult to date is *King John: scholars still dispute whether a two-part play, *The Troublesome Reign of John, King of England*, printed 1591, is its source or (as seems more probable) a derivative. *Richard II, printed 1597, is usually dated 1595. For some years after this, Shakespeare concentrated on comedy, in *A Midsummer Night's Dream and *The Merchant of Venice (both printed 1600), *The Merry Wives of Windsor (related to the later history plays, and printed in a variant text 1602), *Much Ado about Nothing (printed 1600), *As You Like It (mentioned in 1600), and *Twelfth Night, probably written in 1600 or soon afterwards. *Romeo and Juliet (ascribed to the mid-1590s) is a tragedy with strongly comic elements, and the tetralogy begun by *Richard II* is completed by three comical histories: *Henry IV Parts 1 and 2, each printed a year or two after composition (Part 1 1598, Part 2 1600), and *Henry V, almost certainly written 1599, printed, in a shortened, possibly corrupt, text, 1600.

In 1598 *Meres, a minor writer, published praise of Shakespeare in Palladis Tamia: Wit's Treasury, mentioning 12 of the plays so far listed (assuming that by Henry the 4 he means both Parts) along with another, Love's Labour's Won, apparently either a lost play or an alternative title for an extant one.

Late in the century Shakespeare turned again to tragedy. A Swiss traveller saw *Julius Caesar in London in September 1599. *Hamlet apparently dates from the following year, but was only entered in the register of the *Stationers' Company in July 1602; a short text probably reconstructed from memory by an actor appeared in 1603, and a good text printed from Shakespeare's manuscript in late 1604 (some copies bear the date 1605). A play that defies easy classification is *Troilus and Cressida, probably written 1602, printed 1609. The comedy *All's Well that Ends Well, too, is probably of this period, as is *Measure for Measure, played at court in December 1604. The tragedy *Othello, played at court the previous month, reached print abnormally late in 1622. *King Lear probably dates, in its first version, from 1605; the quarto printed in 1608 is now thought to have been badly printed from Shakespeare's original manuscript. The text printed in the Folio appears to represent a revision dating from a few years later. Much uncertainty surrounds *Timon of Athens, printed in the Folio from uncompleted papers, and probably written in collaboration with T. *Middleton. *Macbeth, probably adapted by Middleton, is generally dated 1606, *Antony and Cleopatra 1606–7, and *Coriolanus 1607–9.

Towards the end of his career, though while still in his early forties, Shakespeare turned to romantic tragicomedy. *Pericles, printed in a debased text 1609, certainly existed in the previous year; it is the only play generally believed to be mostly, if not entirely, by Shakespeare that was not included in the 1623 Folio. *Forman, the astrologer, records seeing both *Cymbeline and *The Winter's Tale in 1611. *The Tempest was given at court in Nov. 1611.

The last three plays associated with Shakespeare appear to have been written in collaboration with J. *Fletcher. They are *Henry VIII, known in its own time as All Is True, which 'had been acted not passing 2 or 3 times' before the performance at the Globe during which the theatre burnt down on 29 June 1613; a lost play, *Cardenio, acted by the King's Men in 1613 and attributed to the two dramatists in a Stationers' Register entry of 1653; and *The Two Noble Kinsmen, which appears to incorporate elements from a 1613 masque by F. *Beaumont, and was first printed 1634. No Shakespeare play survives in authorial manuscript, though three pages of revisions to a manuscript play, Sir Thomas *More, variously dated about 1593 or

1601, are often thought to be by Shakespeare and in his hand.

It may have been soon after Shakespeare died, in 1616, that his colleagues *Heminges and Condell began to prepare Mr William Shakespeare's Comedies, Histories, and Tragedies, better known as the First Folio, which appeared in 1623. Only once before, in the 1616 *Jonson folio, had an English dramatist's plays appeared in collected form. Heminges and Condell, or their agents, worked with care, assembling manuscripts, providing reliable printed copy when it was available, but also causing quartos to be brought wholly or partially into line with prompt-books. Their volume includes a dedicatory epistle to William and Philip Herbert, earls of Pembroke and Montgomery, an address 'To the great Variety of Readers' by themselves, and verse tributes, most notably the substantial poem by Jonson in which he declares that Shakespeare 'was not of an age, but for all time'. Above all, the Folio is important because it includes 16 plays which in all probability would not otherwise have survived. Its title-page engraving, by *Droeshout, is, along with the half-length figure bust by Gheerart Janssen erected in Holy Trinity, Stratford, by 1623, the only image of Shakespeare with strong claims to authenticity. The Folio was reprinted three times in the 17th cent.; the second issue (1664) of the third edition adds Pericles and six more plays. Other plays, too, have been ascribed to Shakespeare, but few scholars would add anything to the accepted canon except part (or even all) of *Edward III, printed anonymously 1596.

Over 200 years after Shakespeare died, doubts were raised about the authenticity of his works (see BACONIAN THEORY). The product largely of snobbery—reluctance to believe that a man of humble origins wrote many of the world's greatest dramatic masterpieces—and of the desire for self-advertisement, they are best answered by the facts that the monument to William Shakespeare of Stratford-upon-Avon compares him with *Socrates and *Virgil, and that Jonson's verses in the Folio identify the author of that volume as the 'Sweet Swan of Avon'.

The documents committed to print between 1593 and 1623 have generated an enormous amount of varied kinds of human activity. The first editor to try to bring them into order, reconcile their discrepancies, correct their errors, and present them for readers of his time was the dramatist *Rowe, in 1709. His 18th-cent. successors include *Pope (1723–5), *Theobald (1733), Dr *Johnson (1765), *Capell (1767–8), and *Malone (1790; third variorum 1821 by James Boswell the younger, out of Malone's edition). The most important 19th-cent. edition is the Cambridge Shakespeare (1863–6, rev. 1891–3), on which the Globe text (1864) was based. The American New Variorum edition, still in progress, began to appear in 1871. Early in the 20th cent. advances in textual studies transformed attitudes to the text. Subsequent editions include *Quiller-Couch's and J. Dover *Wilson's New

Shakespeare (Cambridge, 1921–66), G. L. Kittredge's (1936), Peter Alexander's (1951), and the Riverside (1974). The Arden edition appeared originally 1899–1924; it was revised and largely replaced 1951–81. A new series, Arden 3, started to appear in 1995. The Oxford multi-volume edition (paperbacked as World's Classics) started to appear in 1982, and the New Cambridge in 1983. The Oxford single-volume edition, edited by S. Wells and G. Taylor, was published in 1986.

Great critics who have written on Shakespeare include *Dryden, Samuel Johnson, S. T. *Coleridge, *Hazlitt, A. C. *Bradley, and (less reverently) G. B. *Shaw. The German *Shakespeare Jahrbuch* has been appearing since 1865; other major periodicals are *Shakespeare Survey* (annual from 1948), *Shakespeare Quarterly* (from 1950), and *Shakespeare Studies* (annual from 1965). The standard biographical studies are E. K. *Chambers, *William Shakespeare: A Study of Facts and Problems* (2 vols, 1930) and S. *Schoenbaum, *William Shakespeare: A Documentary Life* (1975). The play scripts have been translated into over 90 languages and have inspired poets, novelists, dramatists, painters, composers, choreographers, film-makers, and other artists at all levels of creative activity. They have formed the basis for the English theatrical tradition, and they continue to find realization in readers' imaginations and, in richly varied transmutations, on the world's stages.

Shakespearean Criticism, a two-volume collection of the lectures of S. T. *Coleridge given between 1808 and 1818, ed. T. M. Raysor (1930).

Coleridge himself never published these lectures. Vol. i consists of notes and fragments patched together from his papers; vol. ii of shorthand reports, and contemporary accounts made by members of his audience. Uneven in quality, at his best Coleridge combines acute insight into details of dramatic psychology, with his broad general theories about the 'organic' form of the Shakespearian play and the process of creating character from 'within'. Coleridge drew heavily on the aesthetics of *Schelling about the role of the unconscious in art, and on the dramatic criticism of A. W. *Schlegel (1811).

Shakespeare–Bacon controversy, see BACONIAN THEORY.

Shakespeare's Heroines, see JAMESON, A. B.

Shakúntalá, a celebrated Sanskrit drama by *Kālidāsa, translated by Sir W. *Jones. It tells the story of King Dushyanta's love for the maiden Shakúntalá, whom he sees while hunting in the forest; he contracts a summary marriage with her and departs, leaving her a royal ring as a pledge. She is then laid under a curse by the sage Durvasas, who thinks he has been treated with insufficient respect; he decrees that her husband the king shall forget her until he once more sees the ring. Unfortunately she loses the ring while bathing, and when she goes to the palace, she is rejected; she returns to the forest, where she gives birth to Bharata. The ring is shortly recovered by a fisherman from the belly of a fish, the king remembers his lost love, seeks her, and finds her, and they are reunited. Kālidāsa's play was greatly admired by *Goethe.

Shallow, in Shakespeare's 2 *Henry IV* a foolish country justice. He appears again in *The Merry Wives of Windsor*, upbraiding Falstaff for beating his men and killing his deer. This event has been taken as a reference to a poaching incident in Shakespeare's early days.

'Shalott, The Lady of', see LADY OF SHALOTT, THE, and LAUNCELOT OF THE LAKE.

Shamela Andrews, *An Apology for the Life of Mrs*, a parody by H. *Fielding, published pseudonymously 1741.

Richardson's *Pamela* was published in 1740, and in 1741 Fielding, irritated by what he regarded as the sententious hypocrisy of the book, replied with the lively travesty *Shamela*. The gullible Parson Tickletext, overcome by the beauty of the person and character of Pamela, writes to his friend, Parson Oliver, commending 'sweet, dear, pretty Pamela'. Oliver, however, has in his possession certain letters which reveal the true nature and history of the heroine. Events and characters remain as in *Pamela*, but all is now seen in a very different light, with Parson Williams appearing as a scheming rogue, Mr B as Mr Booby, Pamela as a calculating hussy, and morality equated with expediency throughout. Richardson was convinced the work was Fielding's and never forgave him. The novel's title satirically alludes to *An Apology for the Life of Colley* *Cibber (1740).

Shandean, derived from 'shandy', a word of obscure origin, meaning 'crack-brained, half-crazy', now used to describe anyone or anything reminiscent of Sterne's *Tristram Shandy*.

Shandy, Tristram, Walter, Mrs, and Captain Tobias (Toby), see TRISTRAM SHANDY.

SHAPCOTT, Jo (1953–   ), poet, born in London and educated at Trinity College, Dublin, Oxford, and Harvard. Her first collection was *Electroplating the Baby* (1988), of which the title poem explored a characteristic vein of scientific and medical fantasia: this was followed by *Phrase Book* (1992), with its invigorating sequence of 'Mad Cow' poems (1996), and *My Life Asleep* (1998). Her poetry combines contemporary references (to film, cartoon, news stories) with literary and historical allusions, and is distinguished by sharp word-play and a disturbing surreal animism. She edited *Emergency Kit* (1996), an eclectic anthology of contemporary verse, with Matthew *Sweeney.

SHARP, Cecil (1859–1924), English folk-music collector and editor. He began collecting folk songs in 1903, and soon became the most important of all the workers in this field, transcribing during the course of his life a total of 4,977 tunes of which he published 1,118. Apart from the intrinsic value of this achievement, his work and the enthusiasm he brought to it profoundly influenced a whole school of English composers, of whom *Vaughan Williams and *Holst were the leading figures.

SHARP, James (1618–79), appointed archbishop of St Andrews in 1661 as a reward for his assistance in restoring episcopacy in Scotland. His treachery to the Presbyterian cause made him obnoxious to the Covenanters, a party of whom murdered him on Magus Muir. Oliver *Cromwell had already nicknamed him 'Sharp of that ilk'. The murder figures in Scott's *Old Mortality.

Sharp, Rebecca ('Becky'), a leading character in Thackeray's *Vanity Fair.

SHARP, William ('Fiona Macleod') (1855–1905), born in Paisley, educated at Glasgow University. He wrote under his own name essays, verse, minor novels, and lives of D. G. *Rossetti (1882), *Shelley (1887), *Heine (1888), and R. *Browning (1890). He is chiefly remembered for his mystic Celtic tales and romances of peasant life by 'Fiona Macleod' written in the manner of the *'Celtic Twilight' movement. These include Pharais (1893), The Mountain Lovers (1895), The Sin Eater (1895), and plays, including The House of Usna (1903) and The Immortal Hour (1900). Sharp successfully concealed the identity of 'Fiona Macleod' (including writing a bogus entry in *Who's Who) until his death.

SHARPE, Tom (1928–), novelist, born in London and educated at Lancing and Pembroke College, Cambridge. He spent some years in South Africa (1951–61) and his first two novels, Riotous Assembly (1971) and Indecent Exposure (1973), are political satires set in that country. On his return to England he taught for a decade in Cambridge, and Porterhouse Blue (1974) is a farcical *campus novel set in a fictitious college. Other works, all in a vein of fierce and sometimes grotesque satiric comedy, include Blott on the Landscape (1975), Wilt (1976), and Ancestral Vices (1980).

SHAW, (George) Bernard (1856–1950), born in Dublin, the youngest child of unhappily married and inattentive parents. In 1876 he moved to London, joining his mother and sister, and began his literary career by ghosting music criticism and writing five unsuccessful novels (including Cashel Byron's Profession, 1886, and An Unsocial Socialist, 1887, both first published in Today, in 1885–6 and 1884 respectively). During his first nine years in London he calculated that he earned less than £10 by his pen. He wrote music, art, and book criticism for the Dramatic Review (1885–6), Our Corner (1885–6), the *Pall Mall Gazette (1885–8), the World (1886–94), and the Star (1888–90, as 'Corno di Bassetto'). His music criticism has been collected in three

volumes as Shaw's Music (1981, ed. Dan H. Laurence) (see also under MUSIC, LITERATURE OF) and his theatre criticism in four volumes as The Drama Observed (1993, ed. B. Dukore). He was a drama critic for the *Saturday Review (1895–8) and produced a series of remarkable and controversial weekly articles (published in book form as Our Theatres in the Nineties, 3 vols, 1932), voicing his impatience with the artificiality of the London theatre and pleading for the performance of plays dealing with contemporary social and moral problems. He campaigned for a theatre of ideas in Britain comparable to that of *Ibsen and *Strindberg in Scandinavia, and came nearest to achieving this with *Granville-Barker at the Court Theatre in London between 1904 and 1907. During this period he took up various causes and joined several literary and political societies, notably the *Fabian Society, serving on the executive committee from 1885 to 1911. Not naturally a good public speaker, he schooled himself to become a brilliant one and gave over 1,000 lectures. He edited and contributed to Fabian Essays in Socialism (1889) and wrote many tracts setting down his socialist and collectivist principles. He was a freethinker, a supporter of women's rights, and an advocate of equality of income, the abolition of private property, and a radical change in the voting system. He also campaigned for the simplification of spelling and punctuation and the reform of the English alphabet. He was well known as a journalist and public speaker when his first play, *Widowers' Houses (pub. 1893), was produced in 1892, but it met with little success. There followed Arms and the Man (1894, pub. 1898: partly used for Oscar Straus's musical The Chocolate Soldier), The Devil's Disciple (perf. NY 1897, pub. 1901), You Never Can Tell (1899, pub. 1898), Caesar and Cleopatra (pub. 1901, perf. Berlin 1906), Mrs Warren's Profession (pub. 1898, perf. 1902), and *John Bull's Other Island (1904, pub. NY 1907), a play which, thanks to its characteristic 'Shavian' wit, brought his first popular success in London. The critics also were gradually persuaded that the plays were not simply dry vehicles for his reformist zeal.

Shaw was an indefatigable worker, writing over 50 plays, including *Man and Superman (pub. 1903, perf. 1905), *Major Barbara (1905, pub. NY 1907), The Doctor's Dilemma (1906, pub. Berlin 1908), Getting Married (1908, pub. Berlin 1910), Misalliance (1910, pub. Berlin 1911), Fanny's First Play (1911, pub. Berlin 1911), Androcles and the Lion (pub. Berlin 1913, perf. Hamburg 1913), *Pygmalion (perf. Vienna 1913, pub. Berlin 1913, later turned into the popular musical My Fair Lady), *Heartbreak House (pub. 1919, perf. 1920, both NY), *Back to Methuselah (pub. and perf. NY 1921, 1922), Saint Joan (perf. NY 1923, pub. 1924), The Apple Cart (perf. Warsaw 1929, pub. Berlin 1929), *Too True to Be Good (perf. Boston 1932, pub. Berlin 1932), Village Wooing (pub. Berlin 1933, perf. Dallas 1934), The Simpleton of the Unexpected Isles (perf. NY 1935, pub. Berlin 1935), In Good King Charles's Golden Days (perf. and pub. 1939), and *Buoyant Billions* (perf. and pub. Zurich 1948).

These plays were published (some in collections: *Plays Pleasant and Unpleasant*, 1898; *Three Plays for Puritans*, 1901) with lengthy prefaces in which Shaw clearly expresses his views as a non-romantic and a champion of the thinking man. The dramatic conflict in his plays is the conflict of thought and belief, not that of neurosis or physical passion. Discussion is the basis of the plays, and his great wit and intelligence won audiences over to the idea that mental and moral passion could produce absorbing dramatic material. He believed that war, disease, and the present brevity of our lifespan frustrate the 'Life Force' (see under MAN AND SUPERMAN) and that functional adaptation, a current of creative evolution activated by the power of human will, was essential to any real progress, and indeed to the survival of the species. The plays continued to be performed regularly both during and after his lifetime (several were made into films) and his unorthodox views, his humour, and his love of paradox have become an institution. Amongst his other works should be mentioned *The Quintessence of Ibsenism* (1891, revised and expanded 1913), which reveals his debt to Ibsen as a playwright and presents an argument for Fabian socialism; *The Perfect Wagnerite* (1898); *Common Sense about the War* (1914); **The Intelligent Woman's Guide to Socialism and Capitalism* (1928); and *Everybody's Political What's What* (1944). Shaw was a prolific letter writer. His correspondence with the actresses Ellen *Terry and Mrs Patrick Campbell, with friends and colleagues such as H. G. *Wells and Gabriel Pascal, as well as several volumes of collected letters, are available in book form.

In 1898 Shaw married Charlotte Payne-Townshend. It seems to have been a marriage of companionship, and they lived together until her death in 1943. He was a strict vegetarian and never drank spirits, coffee, or tea. He died at the age of 94, as independent as ever and still writing for the theatre. He was awarded the *Nobel Prize in 1925. See *The Bodley Head Collected Plays with Their Prefaces* (7 vols, 1970–4).

SHEBBEARE, John (1709–88), an apothecary and surgeon who gave up his practice in about 1754 to devote himself to writing. He became a pungent and often scurrilous pamphleteer (twice imprisoned for libel), and was a bitter opponent of *Smollett, who satirized him as Ferret in *Sir Launcelot *Greaves*. He also wrote many political and medical works, and two novels, *The Marriage Act* (1754) and *Lydia* (1755), in which a wide-ranging miscellany of episodes, reflections, and pugnacious opinions is haphazardly held together by the character of a 'Noble Savage', the Native American Cannassetego. (See PRIMITIVISM.)

SHEFFIELD, John, third earl of Mulgrave and afterwards first duke of Buckingham and Normanby (1648–1721), a patron of *Dryden and a friend of *Pope, and a statesman who held high offices but was 'neither esteemed nor beloved'. He wrote an *Essay upon Satire* (published anonymously, ?1680), which cost Dryden a beating at the hands of *Rochester's bravoes, and an *Essay upon Poetry* (1682) of no great value. He erected the monument to Dryden in Westminster Abbey.

Sheik, The, a best-selling novel by E(dith) M(aude) Hull, the retiring wife of a Derbyshire pig-farmer. Published in 1919, it had an international success, and was to provide Rudolph Valentino with one of his most famous film roles. It is the erotic and sadomasochistic story of 'proud Diana Mayo', an English girl kidnapped by the sheik, whose brutal treatment of her finally wins her devotion; at this point it emerges he is not an Arab at all, but, in Claud Cockburn's words, 'son of a tip-top British peer and his beautiful Spanish wife . . . everything is race-wise and class-wise OK.' (*Bestseller: The Books that Everyone Read 1900–1939*, 1972). See ROMANTIC FICTION.

SHELDON, Gilbert (1598–1677), warden of All Souls College, Oxford, 1636–48, and archbishop of Canterbury from 1663 until his death. As chancellor of Oxford he built and endowed, at his own expense, in 1669, the Sheldonian Theatre, where much of the printing work of the university was conducted until the Clarendon Building was erected in 1713.

SHELLEY, Mary Wollstonecraft (1797–1851), only daughter of W. *Godwin and Mary *Wollstonecraft. Her mother died a few days after her birth. In 1814 she left England with P. B. *Shelley, and married him in 1816 on the death of his wife Harriet. Only one of their children, Percy, survived infancy. She returned to England in 1823, after Shelley's death. She is best remembered as the author of **Frankenstein, or The Modern Prometheus* (1818), but wrote several other works. *Valperga* (1823) is a romance set in 14th-cent. Italy. *The Last Man* (1826), a novel set in the future, describes England as a republic, and the gradual destruction of the human race by plague; its narrator, Lionel Verney, begins life as a shepherd boy and after many wanderings finds himself as the last survivor amidst the ruined grandeurs of Rome in the year 2100, an interesting variation of the 'Noble Savage' motif (see PRIMITIVISM). The same motif is seen in *Lodore* (1835); the heroine, Ethel, is taken as a child by her father, Lord Lodore, to the wilds of Illinois and reared amidst the grandest objects of nature, whence she returns to a life of romance and penury in London reminiscent of Mary Shelley's early years. She wrote other novels, several biographies, and many short stories, most of which were published in the *Keepsake*; some have *science fiction elements, others are *Gothic or *historical, and many are continental in setting. Her *Rambles in Germany and Italy, in 1840, 1842 and 1843* (1844) was well received. She also edited her husband's poems (1830) and his essays, letters, etc. (1840). Her children's story *Maurice*, written in 1820, about a kidnapped boy's chance meeting with his father, was rediscovered in 1997 and published in 1998 with an introduction by C. *Tomalin. See *The Journals of Mary Shelley*, ed. P. R. Feldman and D. Scott-Kilvert (2 vols, 1987) and *The Letters of Mary Wollstonecraft Shelley*, ed. Betty T. Bennett (3 vols, 1980–8).

Shelley, Memoirs of, by *Peacock, published 1858. Not a full-dress biography, it originated as a review of reminiscences by *Trelawny and T. J. *Hogg, which Peacock thought inaccurate, particularly in relation to Shelley's first wife Harriet Westbrook. Peacock's book is polished and reliable, but its reticence and its willingness to question Shelley's veracity have not endeared it to the poet's admirers.

SHELLEY, Percy Bysshe (1792–1822). The eldest son of the MP for Horsham (and later baronet), he was born at Field Place, Sussex, and destined for a parliamentary career. Active, mischievous, and highly imaginative as a child, he was conventionally educated at Syon House Academy, Eton, and University College, Oxford; an upbringing that made him deeply unhappy and rebellious. At school he was mocked and bullied as 'Mad Shelley' and the 'Eton Atheist'; at home he was worshipped by a tribe of younger sisters; a pattern that recurs throughout his life.

Early encouraged in his 'printing freaks', he privately published a series of *Gothic-horror novelettes and verses in his teens: *Zastrozzi* (1810); *Original Poetry by Victor and Cazire* (1810, with his beloved sister Elizabeth); and *St Irvyne or The Rosicrucian* (1811). At Oxford he read radical authors—*Godwin, *Paine, Condorcet—dressed and behaved with provoking eccentricity, and in Mar. 1811 was summarily expelled for circulating a pamphlet, *The Necessity of *Atheism*, written with his friend T. J. *Hogg. He quarrelled violently with his father, and eloped to Scotland with 16-year-old Harriet Westbrook, the daughter of a coffee-house proprietor. They married in Edinburgh in August 1811, though Shelley disapproved of matrimony, as well as royalty, meat-eating, and religion. Three years of nomadic existence followed. At York he tried sharing Harriet with Hogg; in the Lakes he argued with R. *Southey; in Dublin he spoke on public platforms, and published *An Address to the Irish People* (1812) and *Proposals* for reform associations. He corresponded with Godwin; circulated pamphlets on vegetarianism and on the free press (*A Letter to Lord Ellenborough*, 1812); and fly-posted a democratic broadsheet, *A Declaration of Rights* (for which his servant was democratically arrested). He tried setting up a radical commune of 'like spirits' first at Lynmouth, Devon, and later at Tremadoc, north Wales. Much of his early philosophy, both in poetry and politics, is expressed in *Queen Mab* (1813), with its remarkable *Notes*: they show Shelley as the direct heir to the French and British revolutionary intellectuals of the 1790s.

In 1814 his marriage with Harriet collapsed, despite the birth of two children and the kindly intervention of *Peacock. After suicidal scenes, Shelley eloped abroad with Mary Godwin (see SHELLEY, M.W. above), together with her 15-year-old stepsister Jane 'Claire' Clairmont: their triangular relationship endured for the next eight years. His unfinished novella *The Assassins* (1814) reflects their dreamy travels through post-war France, Switzerland, and Germany, as does their combined journal, *History of a Six Weeks Tour* (1817). He returned to London, an annuity of £1,000, and, after many upheavals, a house with Mary on the edge of Windsor Great Park. Here he wrote *Alastor* (1816), a non-political poem of haunting beauty, which first brought him general notice and reviews. His favourite son William was born. The summer of 1816 was spent on Lake Geneva with *Byron. Mary began *Frankenstein*, and Shelley composed two philosophic poems much influenced by *Wordsworth, the 'Hymn to Intellectual Beauty' (partly about his childhood) and 'Mont Blanc', a meditation on the nature of power in a Godless universe.

In the autumn of 1816 Harriet drowned herself in the Serpentine. Shelley immediately married Mary and began a Chancery case for the custody of his first two children, which he lost. The experience shook him deeply, and is recalled in many verse fragments, such as the 'Invocation to Misery', 'Lines: The cold earth slept below . . .', and the cursing 'To the Lord Chancellor' (1817—a so-called *'flyting'). However, friendships developed with Leigh *Hunt, *Keats, *Hazlitt, and others of the liberal *Examiner circle; while Peacock, now an intimate family confidant, drew a portrait of Shelley as Scythrop Glowry in *Nightmare Abbey*. In 1817 the family settled at Great Marlow, on the Thames, where Shelley wrote his polemical 'Hermit of Marlow' pamphlets, drafted a self-searching 'Essay on Christianity', and slowly composed 'Laon and Cythna', which was published, with alterations to avoid prosecution, as *The Revolt of Islam* in 1818.

Harried by creditors, ill health, and 'social hatred', Shelley took his household permanently abroad, to Italy in the spring of 1818, leaving behind his sonnet 'Ozymandias' and a mass of unpaid bills. He stayed at Lucca, where he translated Plato's *Symposium and wrote a daring essay 'On the Manners of the Ancient Greeks'; and then at Venice and Este, where he composed *'Julian and Maddalo', based on his friendship with Byron. He wintered in Naples, where he wrote the passionately unhappy 'Stanzas Written in Dejection'; he also registered a mysterious baby, Elena Adelaide Shelley, as his adopted—or probably illegitimate—child. In the spring of 1819 he was working on *Prometheus Unbound*.

His domestic situation was increasingly strained. His little daughter Clara had died at Venice; now his favourite 'Willmouse' died at Rome and Mary suffered a nervous breakdown. The shaken family settled in

Tuscany: first outside Livorno, then at Florence, and finally at Pisa, which became their more or less permanent home until 1822.

Yet the twelve months from the summer of 1819 saw Shelley's most extraordinary and varied burst of major poetry. He completed the fourth act of *Prometheus* (pub. 1820); wrote *The Mask of Anarchy* (Sept. 1819); *'Ode to the West Wind'* (Oct. 1819); the satirical *Peter Bell the Third* (Dec. 1819); his long political odes, 'To Liberty' and 'To Naples' (both spring 1820); the lively, intimate 'Letter to Maria Gisborne' (July 1820); and the *'Witch of Atlas'* (Aug. 1820). Much of this work was inspired by news of political events, which also produced a number of short, angry, propaganda poems: 'Young Parson Richards', 'Song to the Men of England', and 'Sonnet: England 1819'. At the same time he dashed off several pure lyric pieces, including 'To a Skylark' and 'The Cloud' (both spring 1820), of dazzling metrical virtuosity; and completed a verse melodrama, *The Cenci* (1819). Yet despite this period of creativity, he could get very little accepted for publication in England, and he felt increasingly isolated and despondent. The birth of his youngest son, Percy Florence, somewhat cheered his domestic life.

The quieter period at Pisa which followed (1820–1) saw him at work on a number of prose pieces: *A Philosophical View of Reform* (1820); the impish 'Essay on the Devil'; and his famous *Defence of Poetry* (1821). He also wrote some of his most delicate, low-keyed, and visually suggestive short poems: 'The Two Spirits', 'To the Moon', 'The Aziola', and 'Evening: Ponte Al Mare, Pisa'.

In the spring of 1821 news of the death of Keats in Rome produced *Adonais*. The absence of Claire and growing restlessness precipitated a platonic love affair with Emilia Viviani, a beautiful 17-year-old heiress 'tyrannized' in a convent at Pisa. Instead of a third elopement this resulted in *Epipsychidion* (1821).

In the winter of 1821 Byron also moved to Pisa, and a raffish circle formed round the two poets, including E. J. *Trelawny, Edward and Jane Williams, and eventually Leigh Hunt, who came from England to edit a monthly journal, the *Liberal* (1822–4). Shelley was roused again to public utterance: his last completed verse drama, *Hellas* (1822), though 'a mere improvise', was inspired by the Greek war of independence. He also began 'Charles I', a political drama of the English Civil War, with its touching song by Archy, the jester, 'A widow-bird sat mourning for her love'.

In April 1822 he moved his household to an isolated beach house on the bay of Lerici. Here Mary suffered a dangerous miscarriage; Claire reacted violently to news of the sudden death of Allegra, her daughter by Byron; and Shelley saw the ghost of a child in the sea. Here he began his last major poem, *The Triumph of Life*. At the same time he composed a number of short lyrics, some to Jane Williams, of striking melodic grace: 'When the lamp is shattered', 'With a Guitar, to Jane', and the melancholy 'Lines Written in the Bay of Lerici'.

His letters, still full of political hope and magically descriptive of the Italian seascape, are nonetheless shadowed with personal premonitions. Shelley was drowned in August 1822, in his small schooner the 'Ariel', together with Edward Williams and an English boatboy, on a return trip from visiting Byron and Hunt at Livorno. Overtaken by a violent summer squall, the boat went down without lowering its sails.

His lyric powers and romantic biography have until recently obscured Shelley's most enduring qualities as a writer: his intellectual courage and originality; his hatred of oppression and injustice; and his mischievous, sometimes macabre, sense of humour (especially evident in his light verse and letters). He was widely read in the classics, philosophy, and contemporary science; he translated from Greek (Plato and Homer), Latin (Spinoza), Spanish (Calderón), German (Goethe), Italian (Dante), and some Arabic fragments. His essays—very few published in his lifetime—are highly intelligent, his political pamphlets both angry and idealistic.

His weaknesses as a writer have always been evident: rhetorical abstraction; intellectual arrogance; and moments of intense self-pity. But in great poems like the 'West Wind', or in great prose like passages from the *Defence*, it is precisely these limitations that he transcends, and indeed explodes. Among the English Romantics, he has recovered his position as an undoubted major figure: the poet of volcanic hope for a better world, of fiery aspirations shot upwards through bitter gloom.

Shelley's *Letters* have been edited by F. L. Jones (2 vols, 1964); the standard life remains that by N. I. White (2 vols, 1947); see also R. *Holmes, *The Pursuit* (1974). The major political reinterpretation of his career is by K. N. Cameron, *Young Shelley: Genesis of a Radical* (1951) and *Shelley: The Golden Years* (1974). Excellent modern criticism has been produced by Harold Bloom (1959), Neville Rogers (1967), Judith Chernaik (1972), Timothy Webb (1976), and P. M. Dawson (1980). Among many *Selected Poems*, that edited by Timothy Webb (1977) best reflects the new appreciation of Shelley. Biographical memoirs by Trelawny, Peacock, and Hogg remain vivid and amusing: everyone under Shelley's influence wrote exceptionally well, including Mary Shelley in her *Notes* reprinted in the Oxford Standard edition of the *Collected Poems* (1904; new edn 1972–).

SHENSTONE, William (1714–63), poet, essayist, and landscape gardener of the Leasowes, Halesowen. Educated at Solihull and Pembroke College, Oxford, where he published his *Poems upon Various Occasions* (1737), he established his reputation with *The Judgement of Hercules* (1741) and *The Schoolmistress* (1742). His poetic works included elegies, odes, songs, ballads, and levities, the most famous being 'A Pastoral Ballad' and 'Lines Written at an Inn' (which Dr *Johnson once quoted by heart). From 1743 he transformed the

Leasowes, a grazing farm, into a *ferme ornée*, an early example of a natural landscape garden, beautified with cascades, pools, vistas, urns, and a grove to *Virgil, encircled by a winding walk. His friends included Lord *Lyttelton from nearby Hagley, *Somervile, Lady Luxborough, Richard *Graves, and *Jago. Later he was befriended by *Dodsley, whose *Collection of Poems* he helped to edit, and he worked with *Percy on editing the *Reliques of Ancient English Poetry*, as well as providing the Birmingham printer *Baskerville with advice. His poetry, mainly pastoral in treatment, was popular in the 18th cent.; his 'Essays on Men and Manners', in the style of *La Rochefoucauld, included his views on 'landskip gardening'; his essay on elegy contributed to the development of that form. Though his way of life was criticized by Johnson and Horace *Walpole, he was respected by friends for his good taste. His correspondence reveals a sensitive, educated man living a provincial semi-rural life.

SHEPARD, E(rnest) H(oward) (1879–1976), painter and illustrator, chiefly remembered for his popular and enduring illustrations of the works of A. A. *Milne, beginning with *When We Were Very Young* (1924) and continuing through the Winnie-the-Pooh stories. He also illustrated works by K. *Grahame, R. *Jefferies, and L. *Housman. His delicate, innocent drawings were finely attuned to the 'golden age' vision of childhood that haunted the early decades of the 20th cent.

SHEPARD, Sam (1943–), American playwright and actor, born in Illinois. Having staged his first plays in New York, Shepard spent four years (from 1971) living in London, where a number of his own plays were produced at the *National Theatre and the *Royal Court. His work deals with American mythologies, the death of the American Dream, and Americans' relationship to their land and history. His most famous work is *True West* (1980), in which two brothers in southern California argue over the nature of the 'true' American West—real or mythologized—where each character fights to maintain his own identity and destroy his brother's. Shepard's other plays include *Buried Child* (1978), which won the *Pulitzer Prize for drama in 1979, and which links *True West* in a trilogy with *Curse of the Starving Class* (1976); and *Fool for Love* (1983), which Shepard directed off-Broadway and acted in on screen. He is also the author of a number of screenplays, including *Paris, Texas* (1984).

Shepheardes Calender, The, the earliest important work of *Spenser, published 1579, dedicated to *Sidney. It was illustrated by woodcuts and had accompanying glosses by one 'E.K.' (see KIRKE).

It consists of 12 eclogues, one for each month of the year, written in different metres, and modelled on the eclogues of *Theocritus, *Virgil, and more modern writers, such as *Mantuan and *Marot. They take the form of dialogues among shepherds, except the first and last, which are complaints by 'Colin Clout', the author himself. Four of them deal with love, one is in praise of Elisa (Queen Elizabeth), one a lament for a 'mayden of greate bloud', four deal allegorically with matters of religion or conduct, one describes a singing-match, and one laments the contempt in which poetry is held.

SHEPHERD, Lord Clifford, the, (Henry de Clifford, 14th Baron Clifford) (?1455–1523), celebrated in *Wordsworth's 'Brougham Castle' and *The White Doe of Rylstone*. His father was attainted and his estates forfeited in 1461. Henry de Clifford was brought up as a shepherd, and restored to his estates and title on the accession of Henry VII.

Shepherd's Calendar, The, a volume of verse by J. *Clare.

Shepherd's Week, The, a series of six pastorals by J. *Gay, published 1714.

They are eclogues in mock-classical style, five of them based more or less closely on *Virgil, but presenting shepherds and milkmaids not of the golden age but of the poet's day, in their earthy simplicity. They were designed to parody those of A. *Philips, but they have a charm and freshness of their own; Gay portrays his rustic characters (Blouzelinda, Bowzybeus, Cloddipole, Grubbinol, etc.) at work as well as at play, paints (in his own words) a 'lively landscape', and includes many references to folklore, games, superstitions, etc. *Empson provides an interesting commentary on mock-pastoral in *Some Versions of Pastoral* (1935).

SHEPPARD, John, 'Jack Sheppard' (1702–24), a notorious thief and highwayman, who, after repeated escapes from prison, was hanged at Tyburn. He was the subject of tracts by *Defoe, of many plays and ballads, and of a novel by W. H. *Ainsworth. See NEWGATE CALENDAR.

SHERIDAN, Frances (1724–66), the wife of Thomas and the mother of R. B. Sheridan (below). She was greatly encouraged in her writing by *Richardson, who arranged for the publication of *The Memoirs of Miss Sydney Biddulph* ('after the manner of *Pamela*') in 1761, and in an expanded version in 1767. The novel, which ends not happily but in despair, describes with honesty and precision the terrible misfortunes and distress of conscience of Sydney, who feels she has not the first claim to her beloved Faulkland. The novel was warmly received and translated into French and German, but Dr *Johnson wondered whether Mrs Sheridan had the moral right to make her readers suffer so. *The Discovery*, a comedy in which *Garrick took part, was very successful in 1763. *The History of Nourjahad*, a much admired and highly moral *Oriental novel, appeared in 1767. An apparently indulgent sultan permits his friend to indulge all desires, and to enjoy life to eternity; but the liberty is a trick, and retribution falls.

SHERIDAN, Richard Brinsley (1751–1816), the son of Thomas Sheridan, an Irish actor-manager, and Mrs F. *Sheridan. Richard learned early that as a livelihood the theatre was both precarious and ungentlemanly. He was sent to Harrow School, where he was unhappy and regarded as a dunce. In Bath, however, where he joined his family in 1770, he was at once at home. His skit, written for the local paper, on the opening of the New Assembly Rooms was considered good enough to be published as a separate pamphlet. He fell in love with Eliza Linley, a beautiful and accomplished young singer, with whom he eloped to France and entered into an invalid form of marriage contract, and on whose behalf he fought two farcical duels with her overbearing admirer Captain Matthews. Sheridan's angry father sent him to London to study law, but eventually the fathers withdrew their opposition and in 1773 he was lawfully married to Eliza. Very short of money, he decided to try his hand at a play, and in a very few weeks wrote *The Rivals, which was produced at Covent Garden in 1775. It was highly successful and established Sheridan in the fashionable society he sought. The Rivals was followed in a few months by the farce *St Patrick's Day, again a success; and in the autumn by *The Duenna, an operatic play which delighted its audiences. In 1776 Sheridan, with partners, bought *Garrick's half-share in the *Drury Lane Theatre and became its manager. Early in 1777 appeared *A Trip to Scarborough, loosely based on Vanbrugh's *The Relapse, and this again was a success. In March of that year Sheridan was elected a member of the *Club, on the proposal of Dr *Johnson. Meanwhile he was working hard and long on *The School for Scandal, which was produced, with Garrick's help and with a brilliant cast, in May. The play was universally acclaimed, and all doors, from those of the duchess of Devonshire and Lady Melbourne downwards, were open to the dramatist—whose personal expenses rose accordingly. Although The School for Scandal had 73 performances between 1777 and 1789 and made a profit of £15,000, Sheridan's financial anxieties, which were to dog him to the end of his life, became even more acute. In 1779 he became the sole proprietor of Drury Lane, and began to live far beyond his means. Although he seems to have been a sympathetic and creative producer, he found the business side of management increasingly irksome. In 1779 he produced his new play *The Critic, based on *The Rehearsal by Buckingham; once again he enjoyed a huge success, and the world regarded him as the true heir of Garrick. But it was not what he wanted. He had grown up with a positive dislike of the theatre, and he declared he never saw a play if he could help it. He wished to shine only in politics, but he had neither the correct family connections nor the financial stability. He became the friend and ally of *Fox and in 1780

won the seat at Stafford. After only two years as an MP he became the under-secretary for foreign affairs, but he neglected his office work, both as a politician and as the manager of Drury Lane. Fortunately his father had secured both Mrs *Siddons and J. P. *Kemble, who brought the required audiences to the theatre. In 1783 he became secretary to the treasury and established his reputation as a brilliant orator in the House of Commons. In 1787 *Burke persuaded him into supporting the impeachment of *Hastings, and his eloquent speech of over five hours on the Begums of Oude ensured that he was made manager of the trial. He was by now confirmed an intimate friend of the prince regent and other royal figures. Eliza died in 1792, and in the same year the Drury Lane Theatre was declared unsafe and had to be demolished. Sheridan raised £150,000 for a new theatre with apparent ease, but he was plunging himself yet deeper into debt, and payments to his actors became more uncertain than ever. In 1795 he married Esther Ogle. All through these years he was speaking eloquently in the House and hoping for eventual political advancement. *Pizarro, adapted by Sheridan from *Kotzebue, was performed in 1799 and was successful enough to bring a brief reprieve, but in 1802 the theatre funds were impounded and the bankers put in charge. Enormous sums were owing to the landlord, the architect, the actors, and stage staff. Although he was still speaking daily at the Commons, Sheridan's friendship with Fox was fading, and when Grenville formed the 'ministry of all the talents' in 1806 Sheridan was offered only the treasurership to the navy, without cabinet rank. The money which came with his appointment to a post with the duchy of Cornwall was soon spent. In 1809 the new Drury Lane was destroyed by fire, the debts became crushing, and Sheridan was excluded from all aspects of management. In 1811 he lost his seat at Stafford, and in 1813 he was arrested for debt. Friends rallied, but he and his wife became ill. His house was discovered to be filthy and denuded of almost all furnishings. He died in July 1816 and was given a fine funeral, with four lords as pall-bearers. He wished to be remembered as a man of politics and to be buried next to Fox, but he was laid near Garrick instead. He is remembered chiefly as the author of two superb comedies, but his speeches and letters have also been published. The standard edition of the plays is The Plays and Poems of Sheridan, ed. R. C. Rhodes (3 vols, 1928): see also Harlequin Sheridan (1933), a life by R. C. Rhodes. The Letters were edited by C. Price (3 vols, 1966).

SHERLOCK, Thomas (1678–1761), son of W. *Sherlock, who succeeded his father as master of the Temple (1704–53), obtained a high reputation as a preacher, and was successively bishop of Bangor, Salisbury, and London. He strongly attacked *Hoadly in the Bangorian controversy. His best-known work was A Trial of the Witnesses of the Resurrection of Jesus (1729), a defence of the historical occurrence of miracles.

SHERLOCK, William (1641–1707). He became master of the Temple and dean of St Paul's. He was author of *A Practical Discourse Concerning Death* (1689), his most popular work, and various controversial treatises. In 1688 he sided with the nonjurors who refused to swear the oath of allegiance to William and Mary and was suspended, but took the oath in 1690, an act which made him the object of many attacks, vindications, and pasquinades.

SHERRIFF, R(obert) C(edric) (1896–1975), playwright, born in Kingston upon Thames, who worked in a local insurance office and began to write plays to raise money for his rowing club. His best-known play is *Journey's End* (1928, pub. 1929), based on his experiences in the trenches as a captain during the First World War. Realistic and low-key, it was praised by G. B. *Shaw as a 'useful corrective to the romantic conception of war', and has also proved lastingly popular on the stage. It portrays the relationships under stress of Captain Stanhope, new lieutenant Raleigh (with whose sister Stanhope is in love), the reliable second-in-command Osborne, the cowardly Hibbert, etc., and ends in mid-battle after the deaths of Osborne and Raleigh. Other plays include *Badger's Green* (1930), a comedy of village politics and cricket; *St Helena* (1934), about Napoleon's last years; *Home at Seven* (1950), in which a banker suffering from amnesia fears he may have committed a crime; and *The White Carnation* (1953), a ghost story about a conscience-stricken stockbroker. Sherriff also wrote several novels, including *The Fortnight in September* (1931).

SHERWOOD, Mrs Mary Martha (1775–1851). She published nearly 100 books of stories and tracts, many for children and young people. *Susan Gray*, a very successful pious work intended for the poor, appeared in 1802. *Little Henry and His Bearer*, a tale published in 1815 after a period spent in India, was translated into French, German, Hindustani, Chinese, and Sinhalese. The best known of all her works is *The History of the Fairchild Family*, which appeared in 1818, its tremendous success leading to a second part in 1842 and a third in 1847. (See CHILDREN'S LITERATURE.)

She Stoops to Conquer, or *The Mistakes of a Night*, a comedy by *Goldsmith, produced 1773.

The principal characters are Hardcastle, who loves 'everything that's old; old friends, old times, old manners, old books, old wine'; Mrs Hardcastle, and Miss Hardcastle their daughter; Mrs Hardcastle's son by a former marriage, Tony Lumpkin, a frequenter of the Three Jolly Pigeons, idle and ignorant, but cunning and mischievous, and doted on by his mother; and young Marlow, 'one of the most bashful and reserved young fellows in the world', except with barmaids and servant-girls. His father, Sir Charles Marlow, has proposed a match between young Marlow and Miss Hardcastle, and the young man and his friend Hastings accordingly travel down to pay the Hardcastles a visit. Losing their way they arrive at night at the Three Jolly Pigeons, where Tony Lumpkin directs them to a neighbouring inn, which is in reality the Hardcastles' house. The fun of the play arises largely from the resulting misunderstanding, Marlow treating Hardcastle as the landlord of the supposed inn, and attempting to seduce Miss Hardcastle, whom he takes for one of the servants. This contrasts with his bashful attitude when presented to her in her real character. The arrival of Sir Charles Marlow clears up the misconception and all ends well, including a subsidiary love affair between Hastings and Miss Hardcastle's cousin Miss Neville, whom Mrs Hardcastle destines for Tony Lumpkin.

The mistaking of a private residence for an inn was said by Goldsmith's sister Mrs Hodson to have been founded on an actual incident in his own youth.

The play was greeted from its opening with immense success, and was seen as a victory in the newly formulated battle against 'that monster called *Sentimental Comedy' (*London Magazine*, 1773).

She Wou'd if She Cou'd, the second of the comedies by *Etherege, produced 1668.

Sir Oliver Cockwood and his wife, Sir Joslin Jolley and his young kinswomen Ariana and Gatty, come up from the country to London to divert themselves, Sir Oliver and Sir Joslin with dissipation, Lady Cockwood, in spite of her virtuous professions, with an affair, and the two spirited young ladies with innocent flirtations. Lady Cockwood pursues Mr Courtal, a gentleman of the town, with her unwelcome attentions. Mr Courtal and his friend Mr Freeman strike up acquaintance with the young ladies, and take them and Lady Cockwood to the Bear in Drury Lane for a dance, where Sir Joslin and Sir Oliver arrive, bent on less innocent pleasures. Sir Oliver gets drunk, dances with his wife, supposing her to be someone quite different, and confusion ensues. The ladies go home. Freeman arrives to console Lady Cockwood. Courtal arrives and Freeman is concealed in a cupboard. Sir Oliver arrives and Courtal is hidden under the table. Sir Oliver drops a 'China orange', which rolls under the table. The two men are discovered, the young ladies are awarded to them, and Lady Cockwood resolves to 'give over the great business of the town' and confine herself hereafter to the affairs of her own family.

SHIELDS, Carol (1935–2003), novelist and poet, born in Oak Park, Illinois, lived in Canada from 1957. She studied at Hanover College and the University of Ottawa. None of her novels was published in the UK until 1990, when *Mary Swann* established her as a major writer. *Happenstance* followed in 1991 plus the epistolary novel *A Celibate Season*, co-authored with Blanche Howard. *The Republic of Love* (1992) was shortlisted for the Guardian fiction prize and is her only novel set in her home town of Winnipeg. In 1995 *The Box Garden* (first pub. 1977)

appeared in Britain; through the novel's correspondence between Charleen Forrest and a mysterious,
religious figure, the alluring Brother Adam, Shields's
talent for investing the small and insignificant with a
passionate reality appears at its most trenchant and
poignant. In 1998 *Larry's Party* was published and
shortlisted for the Guardian fiction prize. In Shields's
characteristically restrained and witty style, the novel
charts the journey of Larry Weller towards a dramatic
and powerfully observed dinner party. Shields's poetry, including *Coming to Canada* (1992), like her novels,
focuses on the 'small ceremonies' of life, valuing and
illuminating the normal and everyday. Her last novel,
Unless, appeared in 2002.

'Shipman's Tale, The', see CANTERBURY TALES, 15.

Ship of Fools, The, an adaptation of the famous
Narrenschiff of Sebastian Brant. The *Narrenschiff* was
written in the dialect of Swabia and first published in
1494. It became extremely popular and was translated
into many languages. Its theme is the shipping off of
fools of all kinds from their native land to the Land of
Fools. The fools are introduced by classes and reproved
for their folly. The popularity of the book was largely
due to the spirited illustrations, which show a sense of
humour that the text lacks.

It was translated into English 'out of Laten, Frenche,
and Doche' by A. *Barclay, and published in England in
1509; the translation is not literal but is an adaptation
to English conditions, and gives a picture of contemporary English life. It starts with the fool who has great
plenty of books, 'But fewe I rede, and fewer under-
stande', and the fool 'that newe garmentes loves, or
devyses', and passes to a condemnation of the various
evils of the time, notably the misdeeds of officials and
the corruption of the courts. The work is interesting as
an early collection of satirical types. Its influence is
seen in *Cocke Lorells Bote*.

Shipwreck, The, see FALCONER.

Shirburn Ballads, The, edited in 1907 by Andrew
Clark from a manuscript of 1600–16 (a few pieces are
later) at Shirburn Castle, Oxfordshire, belonging to the
earl of Macclesfield. The collection contains ballads not
found elsewhere, dealing with political events, with
legends and fairy tales, or with stories of domestic life.
Some of them are homilies.

Shirley, a novel by C. Brontë, published 1849.
The scene of the story is Yorkshire, and the period
the latter part of the Napoleonic wars, the time of the
*Luddite riots, when the wool industry was suffering
from the almost complete cessation of exports. In spite
of these conditions, Robert Gérard Moore, half English,
half Belgian by birth, a mill-owner of determined
character, persists in introducing the latest labour-
saving machinery, undeterred by the opposition of
the workers, which culminates in an attempt first to
destroy his mill, and finally to take his life. To overcome

his financial difficulties he proposes to Shirley Keeldar,
an heiress of independent spirit, while under the
mistaken impression that she is in love with him; he
himself loves not her but his gentle and retiring cousin
Caroline Helstone, who is pining away for love of him
and through enforced idleness in the oppressive
atmosphere of her uncle's rectory. Robert is indignantly rejected by Shirley, who is in fact in love with his
brother Louis, a tutor in her family, also of proud and
independent spirit. The misunderstandings are resolved, and the two couples united.

Despite touches of melodrama (such as the sub-plot,
which reveals that Shirley's companion and one-time
governess Mrs Pryor is in fact Caroline's long-lost
mother) this is Charlotte Brontë's most social novel,
intended in her own words to be 'unromantic as Monday
morning', and one of its recurrent themes is its plea for
more useful occupations for women, condemned by
society either to matrimony or, as old maids, to a life
of self-denial and acts of private charity. Caroline is
forbidden even the career of governess by her uncle,
and this career is itself painted by Mrs Pryor as 'seden-
tary, solitary, constrained, joyless, toilsome'. Shirley
herself is an attempt to portray a woman with freedom
and power to act; Charlotte told Mrs *Gaskell that she
was intended to be what Emily *Brontë might have been
'had she been placed in health and prosperity',
but despite certain recognizable characteristics (her
relationship with her dog Tartar, her physical courage,
her nickname of 'Captain'), the fictitious character for
most readers sheds little light on her enigmatic original.

SHIRLEY, James (1596–1666), born in London and
educated at Merchant Taylors' School, St John's College, Oxford, and St Catharine's Hall, Cambridge. His
first work appears to have been a poem on the Echo and
Narcissus story, published as 'Eccho' in a lost edition of
1618 and as 'Narcissus' in 1646.

Shirley took Anglican orders, and was a master at St
Albans Grammar School until 1624, when he moved to
London. The reason for his departure is said to have
been his conversion to Roman Catholicism. His first
recorded play, *Love Tricks, or The School of Compliment*
(1625), was produced at the Cockpit Theatre, and he
continued to write for it, probably under contract, until
1636. In the dedication to his play *The Bird in a Cage*
(1632–3), he sarcastically complimented *Prynne, who
was then in prison awaiting trial for writing *Histriomastix*. Perhaps because of this dedication, Shirley was
made a member of Gray's Inn and invited to supply the
literary part of the Inns of Court masque *The Triumph
of Peace* (1634).

During the plague closure of 1636–7 he went to
Ireland, where he wrote a number of plays for the
Dublin theatre, including *St Patrick for Ireland* (c.1639).
At his return in 1640 he succeeded *Massinger,
recently deceased, as principal dramatist for the
King's Men, but the outbreak of the Civil War put
an end to this career. He was in the Royalist army under

the earl of *Newcastle, who was both his patron and possibly a former collaborator on a play (*The Country Captain*, 1639–40). After the defeat of the Royalist cause he returned to London and was for a time patronized by T. *Stanley; he then returned to his career as a schoolmaster. Such works as he wrote during the rest of his life seem designed for school performance. His *Contention of Ajax and Ulysses* (pub. 1659) was also written during this period; it is largely a dramatic debate interspersed with songs, one of which, 'The glories of our blood and state', was a favourite with Charles II. Shirley and his wife are said to have died as a result of terror and exposure when they were driven from their home by the Great Fire of London.

Shirley wrote some 40 dramas, most of which are extant, including *The Traitor* (1631), *Hyde Park* (1632), *The Gamester* (1633), *The Lady of Pleasure* (1635), and *The Cardinal* (1641). He had a considerable reputation in his lifetime and died very well off; Dryden's bracketing of him with *Heywood and *Shadwell in *Mac Flecknoe* probably does not represent a considered judgement of his work.

SHIRLEY, John (?1366–1456), the scribe of many works of *Chaucer, *Lydgate, and others, whose attributions have been particularly important for the ascriptions to Chaucer of some of the shorter poems, including the Complaints 'To Pity', 'To His Lady', and 'Of Mars'; 'Adam Scriveyn'; 'Truth'; 'Lak of Stedfastnesse'; and 'The Complaint of Venus'. He is said to have been a traveller in various lands, and he translated a number of works from French and Latin, among the latter being 'A Full Lamentable Cronycle of the Dethe and False Murdure of James Stewarde, Late Kynge of Scotys' (see JAMES I OF SCOTLAND).

Shoemakers' Holiday, The, or, *The Gentle Craft*, a comedy by *Dekker, written 1599, published 1600.

Rowland Lacy, a kinsman of the earl of Lincoln, loves Rose, the daughter of the lord mayor of London. To prevent the match the earl sends him to France in command of a company of men. Lacy resigns his place to a friend and, disguised as a Dutch shoemaker, takes service with Simon Eyre, who supplies the family of the lord mayor with shoes. Here he successfully pursues his suit, is married in spite of the efforts of the earl and the lord mayor to prevent it, and is pardoned by the king. The most entertaining character in the play is that of Eyre, the cheery, eccentric master-shoemaker, who becomes lord mayor of London. See also DELONEY.

SHOLOKHOV, Mikhail Alexandrovich (1905–84), Russian novelist, of mixed Cossack, peasant, and lower-middle-class background, who became well known in the West for his lengthy regional epic novel about Cossack life in the early 20th cent., *And Quiet Flows the Don* (4 vols, 1928–40), which has been much admired (despite allegations of plagiarism: he was accused in some circles of having made use of the manuscript of a

dead White Army officer). His other works include a novel which has been described as a classic of *Socialist Realism, *Virgin Soil Upturned* (1931), which chronicles life under a five-year plan in south Russia. Sholokhov was awarded the *Nobel Prize in 1965.

SHORE, Jane (d. ?1527), mistress of Edward IV. She was the daughter of a Cheapside mercer and wife of a Lombard Street goldsmith, and exercised great influence over Edward IV by her beauty and wit. She was afterwards mistress of Thomas Grey, first marquess of Dorset. She was accused by Richard III of sorcery, imprisoned, and made to do public penance in 1483, and she died in poverty.

She is the subject of a ballad included in Percy's *Reliques, of *Churchyard's *Shore's Wife* in *Mirror for Magistrates*, of a remarkable passage in Sir T. *More's *History of Richard the Thirde*, and of a descriptive note by *Drayton (*Englands Heroicall Epistles*). The last two passages are quoted in Percy's *Reliques*. Her adversities are the subject of a tragedy by *Rowe.

Short, Codlin and, see CODLIN.

Shortest Way with the Dissenters, see DEFOE.

SHORTHOUSE, Joseph Henry (1834–1903), born into a Birmingham Quaker family. He became an Anglican convert, and the historical novel by which he is remembered, *John Inglesant* (1881, privately printed 1880), is an evocation of 17th-cent. religious intrigue and faith. Inglesant becomes a tool of the Jesuit faction, joins the court of Charles I, and after the king's death visits Italy to seek vengeance for his brother's murder; the most interesting part of the book is an account of N. *Ferrar's religious community at *Little Gidding. Inglesant falls in love with Mary Collet in a wholly fictitious episode, but the background is on the whole drawn in accurate detail. The novel had a considerable vogue in its day, and bears witness to the religious and historical interests revived by the *Oxford movement and the *Pre-Raphaelites.

Short View of the Immorality and Profaneness of the English Stage, see COLLIER, JEREMY.

SHOSTAKOVICH, Dmitri Dimitrievich (1906–75), one of the most distinguished Russian composers of the Soviet era. He was above all a symphonist, though he wrote in most other forms as well. The best known and most controversial of his early operas, *Lady Macbeth of the Mtsensk District* (1932), from a story by *Leskov, has no connection with Shakespeare except for a certain propensity to murder on the part of the heroine. Shakespearian in a more normal sense is the incidental music written for films of *Hamlet* (1964) and *King Lear* (1970), and there is a group of *Six Songs* with texts by *Ralegh, *Burns, and Shakespeare, dating from 1942.

Shropshire Lad, A, see HOUSMAN, A. E.

SHUTE, Nevil (1899–1960), the pen-name of Nevil

Shute Norway, popular novelist, born in England, who later (1950) settled in Australia. His many readable, fast-moving novels, several based on his involvement with the aircraft industry and his own wartime experiences, include *Pied Piper* (1942); *No Highway* (1948); *A Town Like Alice* (1950), in which an English girl is captured by the Japanese and survives the war to settle in Australia; and *On the Beach* (1957), which describes events after a nuclear holocaust.

SHUTTLE, Penelope (1947–), poet and novelist, born in Staines, Middlesex. Her first volume of poetry was *The Orchard Upstairs* (1980), which was followed by several others, including *Adventures with My Horse* (1988), *Taxing the Rain* (1992), and *Selected Poems 1980–1996* (1998). Her poetry is distinguished by a rich, sensuous awareness of sexuality and the natural and animal world: her use of female imagery (as in 'Home Birth', 1992, which combines knitting and childbirth) is arresting and celebratory. Her novels include *Wailing Monkey Embracing a Tree* (1973). She was married to Peter *Redgrove, with whom she collaborated in several works. She lives in Cornwall.

Shylock, the Jewish usurer in Shakespeare's *The Merchant of Venice*.

Sibylline Leaves, a volume of poems by S. T. *Coleridge.

SIDDAL, Elizabeth ('Lizzie') Eleanor (1829–62), poet, painter, and red-haired model to the Pre-Raphaelites. She was 'discovered' by the painter Walter Howard Deverell while she was working as a milliner in a shop near Leicester Square. She met D. G. *Rossetti in 1850, and in 1852 modelled as the drowned Ophelia for *Millais, who put her health at risk by demanding that she lie for hours in a bath of cold water. Rossetti appears to have encouraged her artistic talents, but their relationship was vexed and complicated: he married her belatedly in 1860 but she was by this time an invalid, and after a brief recovery of health and spirits she gave birth in 1861 to a stillborn child. She died in 1862, from an overdose of laudanum, and was buried in Highgate Cemetery, with the manuscript notebook of a number of Rossetti's poems, which he later exhumed. Her own poems were not circulated during her lifetime, but 15 of them were published by W. M. *Rossetti in his collections of letters and reminiscences: his essay on her appeared in the *Burlington Magazine*, May 1903.

SIDDONS, Mrs Sarah (1755–1831), the eldest child of a strolling actor-manager, Roger Kemble (1721–1802), and sister of C. *Kemble, J. P. *Kemble, Stephen Kemble, and other theatrical siblings. On her second attempt on London in 1782 she was heralded as a tragic actress without peer, and until her official retirement in 1812 she never fell from that position. Her great roles were in tragic and heroic parts, and she rarely attempted comedy. Jane *Shore, in *Rowe's play of that

name, Belvidera in Otway's *Venice Preserv'd*, Shakespearian heroines, and in particular Lady Macbeth, were her great roles. *Hazlitt wrote that 'Power was seated on her brow ... She was tragedy personified.' She returned briefly to the stage in 1819 but was no longer a success. She was a friend of Dr *Johnson, Horace *Walpole, Joshua *Reynolds, and many other eminent figures. Reynolds's portrait of her as 'The Tragic Muse' is at Dulwich, and *Gainsborough's portrait in the National Portrait Gallery.

SIDGWICK, Henry (1838–1900), educated at Rugby and Trinity College, Cambridge, where he became a fellow in 1859. He was from 1883 professor of moral philosophy at that university. A follower in economics and politics of J. S. *Mill, his attitude on the question of our knowledge of the external world resembles that of *Reid. But his most important work as a philosophical writer relates to ethics, and his reputation rests on *The Methods of Ethics* (1874). Here he considers three 'methods' of determining the right course of action: intuitionism, according to which we have direct apprehension of moral principles; egoism, according to which an agent's own interests determine what he should do; utilitarianism, according to which right and wrong are fixed by considerations of the interests of everyone affected by our actions. Intuitionism and utilitarianism, Sidgwick believes, combine to form a coherent system; but egoism will sometimes conflict with the other methods, producing practical contradictions which we cannot resolve.

In 1876 Sidgwick married Eleanor Mildred Balfour (1845–1936), who was from 1892 to 1910 principal of Newnham College, Cambridge; it was partly through their efforts on behalf of women's higher education that the college was founded. She and Sidgwick's brother Arthur wrote a memoir of Henry (1906).

SIDNEY, Algernon (1622–83), the grandnephew of Sir P. *Sidney and younger brother of *Waller's 'Sacharissa'. He took up arms against Charles I and was wounded at Marston Moor. He was employed on government service until the Restoration, but his firm republicanism aroused *Cromwell's hostility. At the Restoration he refused to give pledges to Charles II, and lived abroad in poverty and exile until 1677. He was imprisoned in the Tower after the discovery of the Rye House Plot, tried before *Jeffreys, and condemned to death without adequate evidence, though there was little doubt of his guilt. His *Discourses Concerning Government* were published in 1698, and a treatise on *Love* in 1884. *Burnet described him as 'a man of most extraordinary courage ... who had set up Marcus Brutus for his pattern'.

SIDNEY, Sir Philip (1554–86), born at *Penshurst Place, eldest son of Sir Henry Sidney (who was thrice lord deputy governor of Ireland), educated at Shrewsbury School (with his close friend Fulke *Greville), and Christ Church, Oxford, where his contemporaries included *Camden, *Hakluyt, and *Ralegh. He may have spent some time also at Cambridge. Between 1572 and 1575 he travelled in France, where he witnessed the massacre of St *Bartholomew's day in Paris, and in Germany, Austria, and Italy. During his year in Italy, most of it spent in Venice, he was painted by Veronese, but gave most of his time to serious study of history and ethics, and to correspondence with the elderly Protestant statesman Hubert Languet. After his return to England, in spite of a successful embassy to Vienna in 1577, Sidney did not achieve any official post which matched his ambitions until his appointment as governor of Flushing in 1585. His knighthood was awarded for reasons of court protocol in 1583.

Years of comparative idleness enabled him to write and revise the *Arcadia, and to complete the *Defence of Poetry, *The Lady of May, and *Astrophel and Stella. The first Arcadia, and probably other works, were composed while he was staying with his younger sister Mary, countess of *Pembroke, at Wilton. We do not know his exact relations with Penelope Devereux (later *Rich), whose father's dying wish had been that she should marry Philip Sidney. Though this did not happen (Penelope in 1581 marrying Lord Rich, and Philip in 1583 marrying Frances, daughter of Sir Francis Walsingham), verbal and heraldic references leave no room for doubt that she was the 'Stella' of Sidney's sonnet sequence. During these years Sidney also became a notable literary patron, receiving dedications from a variety of authors, the best known being that of Spenser's *The Shepheardes Calender in 1579. Sidney was interested in experimenting with classical metres in English on the lines prescribed by Thomas Drant, but it is unlikely that his discussion of this and other matters with Greville, *Dyer, and *Spenser (the 'Areopagus') amounted to anything so formal as an academy or learned society. The last year of his life was spent in the Netherlands, where his greatest military success was a surprise attack on the town of Axel, in alliance with Count Maurice. On 22 Sept. 1586 he led an attack on a Spanish convoy bringing supplies to the fortified city of Zutphen; he received a musket shot in his thigh and died of infection three weeks later. Greville, who was not present, subsequently told the story of Sidney's death with two famous embellishments, claiming that Sidney left off his thigh-armour deliberately, so as not to be better armed than the marshal of the camp, and that as he was being carried wounded from the field he saw a dying soldier gazing at his water bottle, and gave it to him with the words, 'Thy necessity is yet greater than mine.' Sidney was buried in St Paul's Cathedral, and the almost immediate appearance of volumes of Latin elegies from Oxford, Cambridge, and the Continent testified to the great political and literary promise he had shown. Among many English elegies on him the best known, Spenser's *'Astrophel', was not printed until 1595, among his Complaints. This included elegies by Lodowick Bryskett, Matthew Royden,

Ralegh, and Dyer. Royden's is unusual in evoking the hero's presence, his 'sweet attractive kind of grace'. Sidney's posthumous reputation, as the perfect Renaissance patron, soldier, lover, and courtier, far outstripped his documented achievements, and can be seen as having a life independent of them which has become proverbial, as when *Yeats paid tribute to Major Robert *Gregory as 'our Sidney and our perfect man'.

None of Sidney's works was published during his lifetime, but Greville and the countess of Pembroke seem to have taken pains to preserve the texts they thought best. The revised Arcadia was published in 1590, and again in 1593 with the last three books of the earlier version appended; Astrophel and Stella in 1591, first in a pirated and then in an authorized text; and A Defence of Poetry, also in two slightly varying texts, in 1595. Editions of the Arcadia from 1598 onwards included all the literary works except his version of the Psalms. These were completed posthumously by his sister, and not printed until 1823. *Ruskin admired them and published selections under the title Rock Honeycomb (1877). Sidney's complete Poems were edited by W. A. Ringler in 1962, the Old Arcadia (1973) by Jean Robertson, The New Arcadia by Victor Skretkowicz (1987), and the Miscellaneous Prose by K. Duncan-Jones and J. van Dorsten (1973); the standard life is by M. W. Wallace (1915). See also K. Duncan-Jones, Sir Philip Sidney: Courtier and Poet (1991).

SIDNEY, Sir Robert (1563–1626), the younger brother of Sir P. *Sidney. His early career closely followed that of his brother, whom he succeeded as governor of Flushing in 1589, a post he continued to hold for over 25 years. He was created Baron Sidney by James I in 1603, Viscount Lisle in 1605, and earl of Leicester in 1618; he held the post of lord chamberlain to Anne of Denmark. It has been claimed that he wrote lyrics for settings by Robert Dowland, who was his godson. An autograph manuscript of his poems, consisting of sonnets, pastorals, songs, and epigrams, apparently written in the mid-1590s, was identified by P. J. Croft in 1973; he edited them for the Clarendon Press (1984).

Siege of Corinth, The, a poem by Lord *Byron, published 1816.

The poem is founded on the story of the Turkish siege of Corinth, then held by the Venetians, and it was the last of Byron's Eastern tales. The Turks, guided by the fierce and daring renegade Alp, who loves the daughter of the Venetian governor Minotti, make their way into the fortress. Minotti, discovering the betrayal, fires the magazine and violently destroys both victors and defenders, including himself.

Siege of Rhodes, The, one of the earliest attempts at English opera, by *D'Avenant, performed 1656.

Dramatic performances having been suppressed by the Commonwealth government, D'Avenant obtained permission in 1656 to produce at Rutland House an

'Entertainment after the manner of the ancients', in which *Diogenes and *Aristophanes argue against and for public amusements, and a Londoner and Parisian compare the merits of their two cities; this was accompanied by vocal and instrumental music, composed by Henry *Lawes. Immediately after this prologue was given *The Siege of Rhodes* (at first in one, but in 1662 in two parts), a heroic play, the 'story sung in recitative music', which was composed by Dr Charles Coleman and George Hudson. The play deals with the siege of Rhodes by Solyman the Magnificent, and the devotion by which Ianthe, wife of the Sicilian Duke Alphonso, saves her husband and the defenders of the island.

Siege Perilous, see ROUND TABLE.

SIGAL, Clancy (1926–   ), American writer and journalist, born in Chicago and educated at the University of California. He came to England in the 1950s, where he wrote *Weekend in Dinlock* (1960), a fictionalized exploration of life in a mining community in south Yorkshire, to which the American narrator is introduced by a young miner who is also an artist. *Going Away* (1963) is a first-person 'road' novel: here the narrator leaves Hollywood and drives across the USA in search of his lost idealism, embarking in the last pages for Europe. *Zone of the Interior* (USA 1976, UK 2005) is set in the 1960s England of R. D.*Laing, Kingsley Hall, and LSD. Sigal lived for some 30 years in England, and contributed regularly to the *New Statesman*. He now lives and writes in California.

Sigismonda (Ghismonda), in Boccaccio's *Decameron* (Day 4, Tale 1), daughter of Tancred, prince of Salerno. Her father, having discovered her love for his squire Guiscardo, slew the latter and sent his heart in a golden cup to Sigismonda, who took poison and died. The father, repenting his cruelty, caused the pair to be buried in the same tomb. The story is the subject of *Dryden's 'Sigismunda and Guiscardo', and of Robert Wilmot's *Tancred and Gismund*. James Thomson's *Tancred and Sigismunda* (1745) deals with a different story.

Sigmund, in the *Volsunga saga* and in W. Morris's *Sigurd the Volsung*, the son of King Volsung and the father of Sigurd.

signifier, a linguistic or semiotic term for the concretely perceptible component of a sign, as distinct from its conceptual component (the 'signified'). A signifier may be a meaningful sound, a written alphabetic character, or a more complex unit such as a word or phrase. The distinction made by *Saussure between signifier and signified lies at the foundation both of modern linguistics and of the broader intellectual tradition of *structuralism.

Sigurd the Volsung and the Fall of the Niblungs, The Story of, an epic in anapaestic couplets by W. *Morris, founded on the *Volsunga saga, and published 1876.

Although a loose rendering, and at times slack in its versification, it did much to awaken popular interest in Icelandic literature. Morris described its subject as 'the Great Story of the North which should be to all our race what the Tale of Troy was to the Greeks'.

It is in four books; the first, 'Sigmund', is the story of Volsung's son Sigmund and of the fatal marriage of his sister Signy to the king of the Goths; the second and third, 'Regin' and 'Brynhild', deal with Sigmund's son Sigurd, his betrothal to Brynhild, his subsequent marriage (under the influence of a magic potion) to Gudrun, the Niblung king's daughter, and the deaths of Sigurd and Brynhild; the last, 'Gudrun', tells of Gudrun's own death and the fall of the Niblungs. (See also SAGA.)

Sikes, Bill, a character in Dickens's *Oliver Twist.

Silas Marner, a novel by G. *Eliot, published 1861.

Silas Marner, a linen-weaver, has been driven out of the small religious community to which he belongs by a false charge of theft, and has taken refuge in the agricultural village of Raveloe. His only consolation in his loneliness is his growing pile of gold. This is stolen from his cottage by the squire's reprobate son Dunstan Cass, who disappears. Dunstan's elder brother Godfrey is in love with Nancy Lammeter, but is secretly and unhappily married to a woman of low class in a neighbouring town. Meditating revenge for Godfrey's refusal to acknowledge her, this woman carries her child one New Year's Eve to Raveloe, intending to force her way into the Casses' house; but dies in the snow. Her child, Eppie, finds her way into Silas's cottage, is adopted by him, and restores to him the happiness which he has lost with his gold. After many years the draining of a pond near Silas's door reveals the body of Dunstan with the gold. Moved by this revelation, Godfrey, now married to Nancy, acknowledges himself the father of Eppie and claims her, but she refuses to leave Silas. The solemnity of the story is relieved by the humour of the rustic travellers at the Rainbow Inn, and the genial motherliness of Dolly Winthrop, who befriends Silas.

Silence, in Shakespeare's 2 *Henry IV*, a country justice and cousin to *Shallow.

Silent Woman, The, see EPICENE.

SILKIN, Jon (1930–97), poet, born in London, the son of a solicitor, and educated at Wycliffe and Dulwich colleges. He established himself as a poet while working as a manual labourer, then as a teacher, and subsequently lectured extensively. His first volume, *The Peaceable Kingdom* (1954), was followed by many others, including *Nature with Man* (1965, which contains many of his piercingly observed 'flower poems'), *Amana Grass* (1971, with work inspired by visits to Israel and America), and *The Principle of Water* (1974); his *Selected Poems* was published in 1980. Other volumes include *The Psalms with Their Spoils*

(1980), *Autobiographical Stanzas* (1984), and *The Lens-Breakers* (1992). His anthologies include *Out of Battle: Poetry of the Great War* (1972). He founded the literary quarterly *Stand* in 1952; his wife Lorna Tracy, short story writer, was his co-editor.

SILLITOE, Alan (1928–), writer, brought up in Nottingham, one of five children of an illiterate and often unemployed labourer. He started work aged 14 in a bicycle factory, became a cadet, then served in the RAF in Malaya. On demobilization he was found to have tuberculosis and spent 18 months in hospital, during which he began to read widely and to write. He met the American poet Ruth *Fainlight (whom he married in 1952), and together they travelled in Europe, spending some years in Majorca, where Robert *Graves encouraged him to write a novel set in Nottingham. His first volume of verse, *Without Beer or Bread* (1957), was followed by his much-praised first novel, *Saturday Night and Sunday Morning* (1958), which describes the life of Arthur Seaton, a dissatisfied young Nottingham factory worker. It differed from other provincial novels of the 1950s (see COOPER, W.; AMIS, K.; LARKIN; BRAINE; WAIN) in that its hero is a working man, not a rising member of the lower middle class. The title story of *The Loneliness of the Long Distance Runner* (1959) is a first-person portrait of a rebellious and anarchic Borstal boy who refuses both literally and metaphorically to play the games of the establishment. Many other novels and volumes of prose followed, including the novels *The Death of William Posters* (1965); *A Tree on Fire* (1967); *A Start in Life* (1970); *Lost Loves* (1990); the semi-autobiographical *Raw Material* (1972), a vivid evocation of his own family ancestry and working-class attitudes to the First World War and the Depression; *Men, Women and Children* (1973), a collection of short stories; *Mountains and Caverns* (1975), a collection of autobiographical and critical essays; *The Widower's Son* (1976, a novel). His many other volumes of poetry include *Storm and Other Poems* (1974) and *Barbarians and Other Poems* (1974), and written plays and screenplays from his own fiction. His *Collected Poems* appeared in 1993.

SILONE, Ignazio (Secondo Tranquilli) (1900–78), Italian novelist, critic, and founder member of the Italian Communist Party in 1921. To escape Fascist persecution he went into exile to Switzerland in 1930, where he remained until 1945. The peasant south, its deprivation, and the impact on it of Fascism, are the themes of his best-known novels: *Fontamara* (1930) and *Pane e vino* (published first in English, *Bread and Wine*, 1936; in Italian 1937, rev. 1955 as *Vino e pane*). His memoir in *The God that Failed* (1950) indicates his importance for Anglo-American culture as the type of the European ex-communist.

Silurist, the, see VAUGHAN, H.

SILVA, Feliciano de (16th cent.), a Spanish romance writer, who composed sequels to *Amadis of Gaul* and *Celestina*, and was ridiculed in *Don Quixote*.

silver-fork school, see FASHIONABLE NOVEL.

Silvia, in Shakespeare's *The Two Gentlemen of Verona*, the duke of Milan's daughter, who is loved by Valentine. The famous song 'Who is Silvia?' (iv. ii) is addressed to her.

SIMENON, Georges (1903–89), Belgian-French popular novelist. One of the most prolific of modern writers, he launched his celebrated detective Maigret in 1931. The sympathy and range of his observation of French life, his sensitivity to local atmosphere, his insight into human motives, and the naturalness and accuracy of his use of the French language have earned him a respect rarely accorded to writers in the genre of *detective fiction.

SIMIC, Charles (1938–), Serbian-born poet, who moved to America at the age of 15. His collection *White* (1972) returns to the foreign country he equates with his past, one which in recent history suffered the ravages of war. His poems in this collection typically combine this perspective on a historical 'elsewhere' with his characteristically original depictions of everyday objects. This portrayal of the familiar in startling, often unsettling ways runs through his later collections, most notably *Charon's Cosmology* (1977), *Classic Ballroom Dances* (1980), and *Austerities* (1982), and betrays the influence of the *surrealists, as well as of Serbian poetry, which he has done much to promote. He has translated widely, and edited *The Horse Has Six Legs* (1992), a collection of his own translations of Serbian poetry. Much of his work deals with this dual identity, as a Serbian writer who returns to his 'psychic roots', but 'with foreign words in my mouth'. A revised and expanded edition of his *Selected Poems 1963–1983* was published in 1990.

simile, an object, scene, or action introduced by way of comparison for explanatory, illustrative, or merely ornamental purpose, e.g. 'as strong as an ox', or more poetically, 'The moon, like a flower | In heaven's high bower | With silent delight | Sits and smiles on the night' (Blake, 'Night', *Songs of Innocence*); or, in more *Modernist vein, 'the evening is spread out against the sky | Like a patient etherised upon a table' (T. S. *Eliot, 'The Love Song of J. Alfred Prufrock'). See also EPIC SIMILE.

Simon Legree, the brutal slave-owner in H. B. *Stowe's *Uncle Tom's Cabin*, who beats Tom to death.

Simon Pure, a character in S. Centlivre's *A Bold Stroke for a Wife*.

Simple Story, A, a romance by Mrs *Inchbald, published in 1791.

The author's avowed purpose is to show the value of 'a proper education', but the interest of the work lies in its blend of melodramatic Gothic sexual intensity and realistic psychological observation. Miss Milner, a headstrong, clever, pleasure-loving orphaned heiress, falls in love with her attractive and sensitive guardian Dorriforth, a Roman Catholic priest: when he inherits a title to become Lord Elmwood he renounces his vows and marries her, but later undergoes a personality change, and becomes violently autocratic. During his prolonged absence overseas she is unfaithful to him, and dies estranged. Their daughter Matilda, forbidden her father's presence, and brought up under many restrictions, is finally reconciled with him, and marries her cousin and her father's favourite, Rushbrook. The expiation of jealousy and guilt over two generations has been compared to *The Winter's Tale, in which Mrs Inchbald probably appeared, and Dorriforth may be in part modelled on her friend J. P. *Kemble.

Simplicissimus, The Adventurous, the English title of *Der abenteuerliche Simplicissimus Teutsch* (1669), by J. J. C. von *Grimmelshausen: a description of the life of a strange vagabond named Melchior Sternfels von Fuchshaim. The work was first translated into English (with an account of the author) in 1912; its chief interest lies in the fact that it is one of the few existing contemporary records of the life of the people during the Thirty Years War.

SIMPSON, N(orman) F(rederick) (1919–), playwright, whose surreal comedies *A Resounding Tinkle* (perf. 1957) and *One-Way Pendulum* (perf. 1959) established him as a writer of the Theatre of the *Absurd. His work shows an affinity with that of Ionesco, which enjoyed a considerable vogue in Britain in the late 1950s. Other works include *The Cresta Run* (1965) and a novel, *Harry Bleachbaker* (1976).

SINCLAIR, Catherine (1800–64), philanthropist and prolific Scottish writer of travel, biography, children's books, novels, essays, and reflections. In *Holiday House* (1839) she produced a classic children's novel that made a conscious stand against the prevailing fashion for moralizing tales for the young and enjoyed success for many years.

SINCLAIR, Clive (1948–), novelist and short story writer, born in London and brought up in its northwestern suburbs, and educated at the universities of East Anglia and Santa Cruz. The title of his first novel, *Bibliosexuality* (1973), indicates a characteristic and idiosyncratic strain of verbal play and erotic bravura. This was followed by *Hearts of Gold* (1979, stories) and *Bedbugs* (1982, stories) and the novel *Blood Libels* (1985). *Cosmetic Effects* (1989) is a neo-Gothic self-reflexive thriller, in which the action is divided between Israel and St Albans: narrator Dr Jonah Isaacson, who teaches film studies, becomes unwittingly involved in a terrorist plot and loses an arm, an injury which does not preclude much sexual activity and a macabre and successful bid to prevent his wife Sophie from procuring an abortion. *Augustus Rex* (1992), a novel about the resurrection of *Strindberg, and *The*

Lady with the Laptop (1996, stories) were followed by *Kidneys in the Mind: A Lecture* (delivered at the British Library, May 1996; pub. 1996), which discusses the kidney as organ and metaphor, and describes his own experience of dialysis and transplant with stoic wit and scholarship. Sinclair has also written a study of the brothers *Singer (1983).

SINCLAIR, Iain (1943–), British novelist, short story writer, non-fiction author, poet, and film-maker, born in Cardiff, educated in Dublin, based in London. An influential poet with collections including *Lud Heat* (1975) and *Suicide Bridge* (1979), he published his first novel, *White Chapell, Scarlet Tracings*, in 1987. Its subject matter, the mythology of *Jack the Ripper, the 'psychogeography' of east London, would resurface frequently in his work. *Downriver* (1991) examines the changing face of London as seen from its evolving rail and waterways. It was followed by *Radon Daughters* (1994), east London's answer to William Hope Hodgson's *The House on the Borderland*. *Slow Chocolate Autopsy* (1997) is Sinclair's first collection of short stories and graphic tales (with artist Dave McKean). *Lights out for the Territory* (1997), ostensibly a book of London walks, is his most accessible document yet. In it he explores a number of enthusiasms including *Hawksmoor churches, the secret state, and the films of Patrick Keiller.

SINCLAIR, May (Mary Amelia St Clair Sinclair) (1863–1946), novelist, the youngest daughter of a shipowner who went bankrupt; he died in 1881, and May (who was educated at home, apart from one year at Cheltenham Ladies' College) lived with her mother in London lodgings until her mother's death in 1901. She never married, and supported herself by reviews, translations, etc., and by writing fiction. She was a supporter of *women's suffrage, and deeply interested in psychoanalysis; her reviews and novels show considerable knowledge of both *Jung and *Freud. Among the most notable of her 24 novels are *The Divine Fire* (1904), *The Three Sisters* (1914, a study in female frustration with echoes of the *Brontë story), *The Tree of Heaven* (1917), *Mary Olivier: A Life* (1919), and *Life and Death of Harriett Frean* (1922). The last two are *stream-of-consciousness novels, taking a woman from girlhood to unmarried middle age, and both show themselves keenly aware (though not necessarily wholly critical) of woman's tendencies towards self-denial; much of *Mary Olivier* (the alcoholic father, the loved but dominating mother, the deaths of several brothers from heart failure, the intellectual curiosity and thirst for unprovided knowledge) is clearly autobiographical. Her novels had a considerable influence on R. *West and R. *Lehmann, but were largely forgotten until their revival (by *Virago) in the 1980s. See T. E. M. Boll, *Miss May Sinclair: Novelist* (1973). (See CHILDREN'S LITERATURE.)

SINCLAIR, Upton Beall (1878–1968), American novelist and journalist, born in Baltimore, who paid his way through the College of the City of New York by writing novels, and continued to write prolifically in many genres. He is best known for his novel *The Jungle* (1906), an exposé of the Chicago meat-packing industry to which the public reacted so violently that an investigation of the yards was instituted by the US government; it also marks a conversion to socialism on the part of its author and of its protagonist, Slav immigrant Jurgis Rudkus. Sinclair's many other works include *The Metropolis* (1908), *King Coal* (1917), *Oil!* (1927), and *Boston* (1928); and a series with international settings featuring Lanny Budd, illegitimate son of a munitions manufacturer, who appears in *World's End* (1940), *Dragon's Teeth* (1942), *The Return of Lanny Budd* (1953), and other works.

SINGER, Isaac Bashevis (1904–91), Polish-born Yiddish author, the son and grandson of rabbis, educated at the Warsaw Rabbinical Seminary. In 1935 he emigrated to New York, in the footsteps of his brother, the novelist Israel Joshua Singer (1893–1944), and became a journalist, writing in Yiddish for the *Jewish Daily Forward*, which published most of his short stories. The first of his works to be translated into English was *The Family Moskat* (1950), which was followed by many other works, including *Satan in Goray* (Yiddish, 1935; English, 1955); *The Magician of Lublin* (1960); *The Slave* (1962); *The Manor* (1967) and its sequel *The Estate* (1969). His collections of stories include *Gimpel the Fool* (1957); *The Spinoza of Market Street* (1961); *Zlateh the Goat* (1966); and *A Friend of Kafka* (1970). Singer's work portrays with a colourful intensity and much realistic detail the lives of Polish Jews of many periods of Polish history, illumined by hints of the mystic and supernatural; many of his novels and stories describe the conflicts between traditional religion and rising scepticism, between varying forms of nationalism, and between the primitive, the exotic, and the intellectually progressive. He provides an extraordinarily vivid record to a vanished way of life which lives on in his art; in an interview in *Encounter* (Feb. 1979) he claimed that although the Jews of Poland had died 'something—call it spirit, or whatever—is still somewhere in the universe. This is a mystical kind of feeling, but I feel there is truth in it.' Singer's writings have been increasingly admired internationally, and he was awarded the *Nobel Prize for literature in 1978. There is a life by P. Kresh (1979), and see also *The Brothers Singer* (1983) by Clive *Sinclair, which includes an account of the life of the Singers' sister, novelist Esther Kreitman (1891–1954).

Singleton, Adventures of Captain, a romance of adventure by *Defoe, published 1720.

Singleton, the first-person narrator, having been kidnapped in his infancy is sent to sea. Having 'no sense of virtue or religion', he takes part in a mutiny and is put ashore in Madagascar with his comrades; he reaches the continent of Africa and crosses it from east to west, encountering many adventures and obtaining much gold, which he dissipates on his return to England. He takes once more to the sea, becomes a pirate, carrying on his depredations in the West Indies, Indian Ocean, and China Seas, acquires great wealth, which he brings home, and finally marries the sister of a shipmate.

Sinners, Beware, a 13th-cent. homiletic poem in 354 lines of six-line rhyming stanzas, concerned with the pains of hell and the *Seven Deadly Sins. Ed. in R. Morris (ed.), *An Old English Miscellany* (EETS 49, 1872: repr. 1973).

Sir Charles Grandison, see GRANDISON, SIR CHARLES.

Sir Courtly Nice, or *It Cannot Be*, a comedy by *Crowne, produced 1685.

This, the best of Crowne's plays, is founded on a comedy, *No puede ser el guardar una mujer*, by the Spanish dramatist Moreto. Leonora is in love with Farewel, a young man of quality, but her brother Lord Bellguard, owing to a feud between the families, is determined she shall not marry him. Bellguard keeps Leonora under watch by her aunt, 'an old amorous envious maid', and a pair of spies, Hothead and Fanatick, who hold violently opposed views on religious matters and quarrel amusingly. Thanks to the resourcefulness of Crack, who introduces himself in an assumed character into Lord Bellguard's house, Farewel is enabled to carry off and marry Leonora; while her rival suitor Sir Courtly Nice, favoured by Lord Bellguard, a fop whose 'linen is all made in Holland by neat women that dip their fingers in rosewater', is fobbed off with the aunt; and Surly, the rough ill-mannered cynic, gets no wife at all.

Sir Launcelot Greaves, *The Life and Adventures of*, see GREAVES, SIR LAUNCELOT.

Sir Launfal, by Thomas Chestre, a late 14th-cent. *Breton lay, in 1,044 lines in 12-line, tail-rhyme stanzas. It is one of the two English versions of *Marie de France's *Lanval* (given in an appendix to Bliss's edition: see below). Launfal is a knight of the Round Table who leaves the court, affronted by tales of *Guinevere's misconduct. He falls in love with a fairy lady, Tryamour. When he returns to Arthur's court Guinevere declares her love for him, but he rejects her, declaring that even his beloved's maids are more beautiful than the queen. The queen accuses him of trying to seduce her and at his trial he is asked to produce the beautiful lady he has boasted of. Tryamour appears and breathes on Guinevere's eyes, blinding her, and the lovers depart happily. The poem has the oversimplicity, but also the narrative liveliness, of its kind and it has been much edited in romance anthologies.

Ed. A. J. Bliss (1960); included in vol. i, *Medieval*

Literature, of *The New Pelican Guide to English Literature* (1982), 440–72.

Sir Patrick Spens, an early Scottish *ballad, included in Percy's *Reliques*. The subject is the dispatch of Sir Patrick to sea, on a mission for the king, in winter; his foreboding of disaster; and his destruction with his ship's company. Sir W. *Scott, in his version, makes the object of the expedition the bringing to Scotland of the Maid of Norway (1283–90), who died on her voyage to marry Edward, prince of Wales.

Sir Thomas More, see MORE, SIR THOMAS.

sirvente, a form of poem or lay, usually satirical, employed by the *troubadours.

SISMONDI, Léonard Simond de (1773–1842), Swiss historian who lived mainly in Geneva. His famous work was *L'Histoire des républiques italiennes du Moyen-Âge* (1809–18). He had many friends, including Mme de *Staël's circle and the duchess of Albany, widow of the Young Pretender, and he was an interesting letter writer.

SISSON, C(harles) H(ubert) (1914–2003), poet and translator, born in Bristol, and educated at Bristol University. He worked for many years in the civil service, of which he has been at times an outspoken critic. His volumes of poetry include *The London Zoo* (1961), *Numbers* (1965), *Metamorphoses* (1968), *Anchises* (1976), *In the Trojan Ditch: Collected Poems and Selected Translations* (1974), *God Bless Karl Marx!* (1988), and *Antidotes* (1991). Translations include works of *Heine, *Catullus, *Horace, and Dante's *Divina commedia* (1980). His poetry mingles biblical and classical themes and imagery with Arthurian references drawn from his native Somerset (as in one of his major poems, 'In Insula Avalonia'); many are satiric, but the satire is based on a religious preoccupation with man's fallen nature and a classical view of his limitations. A volume of autobiography, *On the Look Out*, was published in 1989. Prose works include a novel, *Christopher Homm* (1965), *The Avoidance of Literature: Collected Essays* (1978), *Anglican Essays* (1983), and *English Perspectives* (1991). He was made a CH in 1993. His *Collected Poems* were published in 1998.

Sister Peg, a political satire published in London in 1760, full title *The History of the Proceedings in the Case of Margaret, Commonly Called Peg, Only Lawful Sister to John Bull, Esq.* The work is modelled on *Arbuthnot's *History of John Bull*. It satirizes Anglo-Scottish relations after the Act of Union of 1707 and the cynicism of the politicians in the Scots militia controversy of 1760. *Hume laid claim to the authorship, but most historians follow A. *Carlyle in ascribing the work to A. *Ferguson.

SITWELL, Dame Edith Louisa (1887–1964), brought up at Renishaw Hall, where an unhappy childhood was made bearable by the company of her brothers Osbert and Sacheverell (below). She began to write poetry when young, and her first published poem, 'Drowned Suns', appeared in the *Daily Mirror* in 1913. With her brothers she actively encouraged *Modernist writers and artists; she despised much of the work published in *Georgian Poetry*, and from 1916 to 1921 edited *Wheels*, an anti-Georgian magazine, which first published W. *Owen. Her first volume of verse, *The Mother and Other Poems* (1915), was followed by many others, and she quickly acquired a reputation as an eccentric and controversial figure, confirmed by the first public performance, in 1923, of *Façade*, a highly original entertainment (with music by W. *Walton) with verses in syncopated rhythms. *Gold Coast Customs* (1929), a harsh and powerful work, compared modern Europe with ancient barbaric Africa. Her prose works (which she wrote reluctantly, for money) include a study of *Pope (1930), *English Eccentrics* (1933), and *Victoria of England* (1936). Her only novel, *I Live under a Black Sun* (1937), was poorly received, but it was followed by a period of great acclaim, aroused by her poems of the Blitz and the atom bomb (*Street Songs*, 1942; *Green Song*, 1944; *The Song of the Cold*, 1945; *The Shadow of Cain*, 1947); as J. *Lehmann said, 'The hour and the poet were matched.' Triumphal lecture tours in America followed the war, but in the 1950s her reputation began to fade, as the new austerity of the *Movement became fashionable. She remained, however, a considerable public figure, well known outside literary circles for her theatrical dress and manner (recorded by many artists and photographers) and by her indignant response to real or suspected criticism. F. R. *Leavis had claimed in 1932 that 'the Sitwells belong to the history of publicity, rather than that of poetry', but her status as a poet survived this dismissal, although it remains a matter of controversy. See V. *Glendinning, *Edith Sitwell* (1981).

SITWELL, Sir (Francis) Osbert (Sacheverell) (1892–1969), brother of Edith and Sacheverell *Sitwell. He grew up at Renishaw Hall, Derbyshire, which he later inherited. After Eton he reluctantly served in the First World War, and his early poetry (e.g. *The Winstonburg Line*, 1919) is sharply satirical and pacifist in tone. He produced many volumes of poetry, fiction, and autobiography, and was, with his brother and sister, an outspoken enemy of the *Georgian poets (whom he regarded as philistine) and an ardent supporter of *Pound, T. S. *Eliot, W. *Lewis, and W. *Walton (for whose *Belshazzar's Feast*, 1931, he wrote the words). His prose works include *Triple Fugue* (1924), a collection of satirical stories; *Before the Bombardment* (1926), a novel describing the shelling of Scarborough in 1914 and its effect on the lonely, genteel female society of the town; *Winters of Content* (1932), describing travels in Italy; and *Escape with Me!* (1939), describing travels in China and the Far East. His most sustained achievement was his autobiography, in five volumes (*Left Hand! Right Hand!*, 1945; *The Scarlet Tree*, 1946; *Great Morning!*, 1948; *Laughter in the Next Room*, 1949; *Noble Essences*, 1950: with a later addition, *Tales My Father Taught Me*, 1962). These are remarkable for the portrait of the eccentric, exasperating figure of his father Sir George, and their tone is romantic, acidic, nostalgic, and affectionate in turn. See John Pearson, *Façades* (1978), a biography of all three Sitwells. There is a life by P. Ziegler (1998).

SITWELL, Sir Sacheverell (1897–1988), brother of Osbert and Edith (above). His first volume of verse, *The People's Palace* (1918), was followed by several others; his *Collected Poems*, with an introduction by Edith, appeared in 1936, and a volume of poetry, *An Indian Summer*, in 1982. Many of his prose works combine an interest in art and travel; they include *Southern Baroque Art* (1924) and *German Baroque Art* (1927), both written when the baroque was little studied; *Conversation Pieces* (1936), again on a not yet fashionable subject; the monumental *British Architects and Craftsmen* (1945); and *Bridge of the Brocade Sash* (1959), on the arts of Japan. He also wrote biographies of *Mozart (1932) and *Liszt (1934). His imaginative prose includes *The Dance of the Quick and the Dead* (1936), a series of interlocked reflections on literature, art, travel, etc.; *Valse des fleurs* (1941), a re-creation of a day in St Petersburg in 1868; and *Journey to the Ends of Time* (1959), a macabre and despairing work about the condition of man.

skaldic, or **scaldic, verse,** a form of Old Norse poetry distinguished by its elaborate metre, alliteration, consonance, and riddling diction. The most usual skaldic metre is 'dróttkvaett', a strophe which consists of eight six-syllable lines, each ending in a trochee. In regular 'dróttkvaett' each odd line contains two alliterating syllables in stressed positions, and the alliteration is continued on one stressed syllable in each following even line. Odd lines also contain two internal half-rhymes; even lines two full rhymes. The first known skald was Bragi Boddason who probably wrote in the late 9th cent. Skaldic verse flourished in the 10th cent. and on into the 11th, and much of it was composed to commemorate the deeds of chieftains who ruled in Norway at this time. Such verses are preserved mainly in the kings' sagas; many 'lausavísur' or occasional verses, and some love poetry are included in the narratives of family sagas (see SAGA).

E. O. G. Turville-Petre, *Scaldic Poetry* (1976), gives parallel translation and discussion.

SKEAT, W(alter) W(illiam) (1835–1912), one of the greatest of the 19th-cent. editors of Old and Middle English literature. He was educated at Christ's College, Cambridge, where he became a mathematics lecturer in 1864. He devoted much of his time to the study of Early English and in 1878 he was appointed to the chair of Anglo-Saxon at Cambridge. His edition of *Lancelot of the Laik* was one of the first publications of the *Early

English Texts Society (no. 6, 1865). He edited *Ælfric, *Barbour's *Bruce*, *Chatterton, and the Anglo-Saxon Gospels; his greatest works were the editions of Langland's *Piers Plowman* (published 1886 after 20 years' work) setting out in parallel the three manuscript versions, the existence of which was Skeat's discovery, and of *Chaucer (7 vols, 1894–7), largely establishing the canon and publishing non-canonical works in vol. vii), both of which have been reprinted throughout the 20th cent. He founded the English Dialect Society in 1873, which led to the appearance of Joseph *Wright's *English Dialect Dictionary* (1896–1905), and his own *Etymological Dictionary* (1879–82, rev. and enl. 1910) was begun with the object of collecting material for the *New English Dictionary* (see MURRAY, J. A. H.). He also began the systematic study of place names in English. His autobiography (to that date) can be found in *A Student's Pastime* (1896).

SKEFFINGTON, Sir Lumley St George (1771–1850), fop, playwright, and devoted man of the theatre, who belonged to the Carlton House circle. His most successful works, *The Word of Honour*, *The High Road to Marriage*, and *The Sleeping Beauty*, were produced in the years 1802–5. He was caricatured by *Gillray, and his dramatic works were described by Byron in *English Bards and Scotch Reviewers* (1809) as 'skeletons of plays'.

SKELTON, John (?1460–1529), created 'poet-laureate' by the universities of Oxford, Louvain, and Cambridge, an academical distinction. He became tutor to Prince Henry (Henry VIII) and enjoyed court favour despite his outspokenness. He was admitted to holy orders in 1498 and became rector of Diss in Norfolk. From about 1511 until his death he seems to have lived in Westminster. His principal works include: *The Bowge of Courte* (a satire on the court of Henry VII), printed by Wynkyn de *Worde; *A Garlande of Laurell* (a self-laudatory allegorical poem, describing the crowning of the author among the great poets of the world); *Phyllyp Sparowe* (a lamentation put into the mouth of Jane Scroupe, a young lady whose sparrow has been killed by a cat, followed by a eulogy of her by Skelton, and a defence of himself and the poem); *Collyn Clout* (a complaint by a vagabond of the misdeeds of ecclesiastics), which influenced *Spenser. Not only this last poem, but also his satires 'Speke Parrot' and *Why come ye nat to Courte*, contained attacks on Cardinal Wolsey, setting forth the evil consequences of his dominating position. However, he seems to have repented of these, for *A Garlande of Laurell* and his poem on the duke of Albany, both of 1523, are dedicated to Wolsey. His most vigorous poem was *The Tunnyng of Elynour Rummyng*. His play *Magnyfycence* (1516) is an example of the *morality. Skelton's *Ballade of the Scottysshe Kynge* is a spirited celebration of the victory of *Flodden. A number of Skelton's poems were printed and reprinted in the 16th cent., most of the extant copies being, though undated, evidently later than the poet's death; in 1568 appeared a fairly full collected edition in one volume. There is a complete edition of the English poems by John Scattergood, 1983. Anecdotes of Skelton appeared in the popular *Merie Tales* (1567) and similar collections.

The verse form now known as 'Skeltonic verse' is derived from his favourite metre, 'a headlong voluble breathless doggrel, which rattling and clashing on through quick-recurring rhymes . . . has taken from the name of its author the title of Skeltonical verse' (J. C. *Collins). As he himself said (*Collyn Clout*, 53–8):

> For though my ryme be ragged,
> Tattered and jagged,
> Rudely rayne-beaten,
> Rusty and mothe-eaten,
> Yf ye take well therwith,
> It hath in it some pyth.

Skelton's modern admirers include Robert *Graves.

Skeltonic verse, see SKELTON.

Sketches by Boz, a collection of sketches of life and manners, by *Dickens, first published in various periodicals, and in book form in 1836–7 (in 1 vol., 1839). These are some of Dickens's earliest literary work.

Skewton, the Hon. Mrs, in Dickens's *Dombey and Son*, the mother of Edith, Dombey's second wife.

Skimpole, Harold, a character in Dickens's *Bleak House*.

SKINNER, Cyriack (1627–1700), a grandson of Sir E. *Coke, and a student, then a friend (and possibly also an early biographer), of *Milton. Milton addressed two sonnets to him, written c.1654: 'Cyriack, whose grandsire on the Royal Bench' and 'To Mr Cyriack Skinner upon His Blindness'.

SKINNER, John (1721–1807), an Aberdeenshire minister chiefly remembered as the author of *Tullochgorum* (1776), pronounced by *Burns 'the best Scotch song Scotland ever saw'. His poems and songs were published in vol. iii of his *Theological Works* (1809).

SKINNER, Martyn (1906–93), poet, educated at Clifton and Oxford ('no degree taken'), author of *Letters to Malaya* (1941, 1943) in the form of a verse letter to a friend in Changi Jail; *The Return of Arthur* (1966, but set in 1999); and *Old Rectory* (1970, 1977). He was deeply interested in rural life, and a celebrated letter writer, a friend of John Stewart *Collis, R. C. *Hutchinson, and Rupert *Hart-Davis.

ŠKVORECKY, Josef (1924–   ), Czech novelist, born in Náchod in north-east Bohemia, and educated at Charles University, Prague. He worked for a while in publishing, and emigrated to Canada in 1969 with his novelist wife Zdena Salivarová, where they founded a Czech-language publishing house. He is known internationally for his comic and frequently subversive novels of wartime and post-war life, many of them featuring his hero Danny, passionate about women and jazz, who graduates from small-town adolescence in Bohemia to become a professor in Canada. Titles include *Zbabělci* (*The Cowards*, 1958) and *The Engineer of Human Souls* (1977).

slavery, literature of. This refers to the literature written during or about the period between the 16th and 19th cents when Europeans colonized the Americas and the Caribbean using slave labour from Africa. Slavery played an important role in the development of European thought and literature especially in the 18th cent. The anti-slavery movement, at its peak in the 1780s and 1790s, attracted many poets to its cause, including *Wordsworth, *Blake, *Cowper, and *Southey, and 'The Dying Negro' (1773) by Thomas *Day became one of the best-known abolitionist poems of the day. Slavery became a fashionable literary topic. Two of the century's most popular plays in Britain, *Southerne's *Oroonoko* (1696) and Colman's *Inkle and Yarico* (1787: one of 45 different versions of the tale that circulated through Europe), were concerned with slavery. A critique of civilization and commerce links anti-slavery with *primitivism; stock images of the Noble Savage were used as a comparison with the greed and cruelty of Europeans. As an arena for the expression of pity and suffering, slavery was the perfect subject for *sentimental novels such as H. *Mackenzie's *Julia de Roubigné* (1777) and Sarah *Scott's *The History of Sir George Ellison* (1766). Despite its success in attracting a wide readership to the issue, the compassion displayed towards the slave's predicament is often directed towards indulging the sensibility and benevolence of the reader rather than as a challenge to the institution of slavery. Even sympathetic observers such as John Stedman, whose *Narrative* (1796) catalogued the horrors of slavery in Surinam, argued for amelioration of the slaves' conditions and not their freedom. Anti-slavery politics did not usually transcend the belief in the superiority of European culture of the age and rarely provided insights into the experiences of slaves with their own histories and cultures. Recent scholarship has focused on literature produced by ex-slaves such as I. *Sancho and Olaudah Equiano. Books such as Equiano's played an important role in the abolition movement because writing and art were given value as expressions of humanity and civilization; by writing his own narrative Equiano countered the argument that Africans could not be considered human. (*Hume's comment that 'I am apt to suspect the negroes to be naturally inferior to the whites . . . No ingenious manufactures amongst them, no arts, no sciences' was representative of attitudes that did not consider Africans worthy of such categories.) These 18th-cent. narratives may be seen as the precursors of the hundreds of slave narratives written in 19th-cent.

America, the most famous of which were written by Frederick Douglass (1817–95) and Harriet Jacobs (1813–97). Since the 1960s these narratives have been central to attempts to recover works by black writers previously excluded from literary history and have formed the basis of newly constructed *black British and African-American canons. Literature has continued to be produced which rewrites the experience of slavery, especially in recent decades. The most famous of these to come out of America was T. *Morrison's *Beloved (1987): she stated that her aim in writing was 'to fill in the blanks that the slave narratives left, to part the veil that was so frequently drawn'. In Britain, F. *D'Aguiar, D. *Dabydeen, C. *Phillips, and Beryl Gilroy have all written literature that reimagines the history of slavery, and novels by Phillipa Gregory, B. *Unsworth, and M. *Warner have explored the role slavery played in British society. In the Caribbean, the need to decolonize literature and develop a post-colonial identity has encouraged writers such as G. *Lamming, D. *Walcott, and Earl Lovelace to explore and reinterpret the slave past.

See Eva Dykes, *The Negro in Romantic Thought* (1942); Wylie Sypher, *Guinea's Captive Kings* (1942); Peter Hulme, *Colonial Encounters* (1986); Markman Ellis, *The Politics of Sensibility* (1996); A. Rampersad, *Slavery and the Literary Imagination* (1989); V. Carretta, *Unchained Voices* (1996).

Slay-good, in Pt. II of Bunyan's *Pilgrim's Progress*, a giant whom Mr *Great-heart killed, rescuing Mr Feeble-mind from his clutches.

Sleary, the circus proprietor in Dickens's *Hard Times*.

'Sleepy Hollow, The Legend of', a story by W. *Irving, included in *The Sketch Book*. Ichabod Crane is a schoolmaster and suitor for the hand of Katrina van Tassel. He meets his death, or, according to another report, leaves the neighbourhood, in consequence of being pursued at night by a headless horseman, an incident for which his rival Brom Bones is suspected of having been responsible.

Slender, Abraham, a cousin of *Shallow's and unsuccessful lover of Anne *Page in Shakespeare's *The Merry Wives of Windsor*.

Slipslop, Mrs, a character in Fielding's *Joseph Andrews*.

SLOANE, Sir Hans (1660–1753), a physician, secretary to the *Royal Society, 1693–1712, and president of the Royal College of Physicians, 1719–35. He purchased the manor of Chelsea in 1712 and endowed the Chelsea Physic Garden. He published (1696) a Latin catalogue of the plants of Jamaica (where he had been physician to the governor, 1687–9). His collection (including a large number of books and manuscripts) was purchased by the nation and placed in Montague House, afterwards the *British Museum; the geological and zoological specimens formed the basis of the Natural History Museum in South Kensington, opened in 1881. Sloane Square and Hans Place are named after him.

Slop, Dr, in Sterne's *Tristram Shandy*, a thoroughly incompetent and argumentative physician, now known to be a caricature of Dr John Burton, a male midwife and Tory politician of York, and an enemy of Sterne's. The name was later applied to Sir John Stoddart (1773–1856), who was editor of the *New Times* from 1817 until 1828.

Slope, the Revd Obadiah, a character in Trollope's *The Warden* and *Barchester Towers*.

Slough of Despond, in Bunyan's *Pilgrim's Progress*, a bog into which Christian and Pliable fall shortly after quitting the City of Destruction. Calvinist horror of sin accompanying conversion is symbolized as a rank fen which the king's surveyors have been attempting to drain 'for this sixteen hundred years') (i.e. since Christ's crucifixion). As fen drainage was a preoccupation of the age, the image had immediacy, and has since passed into the realm of the proverbial.

Sludge, Dicky, or 'Flibbertigibbet', a character in Scott's *Kenilworth*.

Slumkey, the Hon. Samuel, in Dickens's *Pickwick Papers*, the Blue candidate in the Eatanswill election.

Sly, Christopher, see TAMING OF THE SHREW, THE.

Small House at Allington, The, a novel by A. *Trollope, published 1864, the fifth in the *'Barsetshire' series.

Lily Dale becomes engaged to Adolphus Crosbie, an ambitious civil servant, but Crosbie is invited to a house party at Courcy Castle where he proposes to Lady Alexandrina de Courcy. When news comes back to Allington that Crosbie has jilted her, Lily behaves well, but Johnny Eames, her childhood sweetheart, tries to take some revenge on her behalf by assaulting Crosbie at Paddington station. Crosbie finds that he and his bride are incompatible; Lady Alexandrina returns to her family and travels to Baden, Crosbie taking refuge in wounded bachelordom. Meanwhile Eames's reputation continues to develop. He grows out of his juvenile dissipations, clears up an unfortunate entanglement with the daughter of his London boarding-house keeper, and begins to spend much of his free time at Allington. There he becomes the protégé of Lord de Guest, and at the intercession of Lady Julia renews his suit to Lily. Lily, however, considers herself bound to Crosbie for life.

Lily's sister Bell is expected to marry the heir of Squire Dale of the Great House at Allington, but she rejects him in favour of the worthy Dr Crofts.

SMART, Christopher (1722–71), born in Kent, but educated in Durham and at Pembroke Hall, Cambridge, where he distinguished himself as a classical scholar and as a poet, winning the Seatonian Prize for sacred poetry five times. In 1749 he came to London and began to write poems and reviews under various pseudonyms, including 'Mrs Midnight', for *Newbery, whose stepdaughter he married in 1752. Newbery published his first collection of verse, *Poems on Several Occasions* (1752), which included a blank-verse georgic in two books, 'The Hop-Garden', and lighter verse. *The Hilliad*, a *mock-heroic satire on the quack doctor John Hill, written with the help of A. *Murphy and modelled on *The Dunciad*, appeared in 1753. In 1756 Smart was dangerously ill, and a year later he was admitted to a hospital for the insane; he spent the years 1759–63 in a private home for the mentally ill in Bethnal Green. His derangement took the form of a compulsion to public prayer, which occasioned the famous comment of Dr *Johnson: 'I'd as lief pray with Kit Smart as anyone else.' After leaving the asylum he published his best-known poem, *A Song to David* (1763), a hymn of praise to David as author of the Psalms, and a celebration of the Creation and the Incarnation; the poem is built on a mathematical and mystical ordering of stanzas grouped in threes, fives, and sevens, and was compared by R. *Browning, one of Smart's few 19th-cent. admirers, to a great cathedral, in both its structure and imagery. Smart also published in these later years translations of the Psalms, of *Horace, two oratorios, and poems, and was supported by the friendship of W. *Mason, Dr *Burney, and others (though Mason, on reading *A Song to David*, declared him 'as mad as ever'); however he declined into poverty and debt and died within the 'Rules' of the King's Bench Prison. His work was little regarded until the 1920s, when there was a wave of biographical interest, and his reputation as a highly original poet was confirmed by the publication of his extraordinary work *Jubilate Agno* in 1939 (ed. W. F. Stead as *Rejoice in the Lamb: A Song from Bedlam*). This unfinished work had been composed between 1758/9 and 1763, largely at Bethnal Green; Smart described it as 'my Magnificat', and it celebrates the Creation in a verse form based on the antiphonal principles of Hebrew poetry. It was to consist of parallel sets of verses, one beginning 'Let . . .', with a response beginning 'For . . .' The arrangement of the lines intended by Smart himself was demonstrated in 1950 by W. H. Bond, from the autograph manuscript in the Houghton Library at Harvard. It contains an extremely wide range of references, biblical, botanical, zoological, scientific (Smart was opposed to I. *Newton's view of the universe), personal, and cabbalistic; the most celebrated passage is the one on Smart's cat, which begins 'For I will consider my cat Jeoffry . . .' There is a scholarly edition of the complete works, ed. K. Williamson and M. Walsh (5 vols, 1980–96). There is a biography by A. Sherbo (1967).

SMART, Elizabeth (1913–86), Canadian-born writer, born in Ottawa, who went to England in 1930 to study music and settled there after the Second World War.

She is remembered for her prose poem *By Grand Central Station I Sat Down and Wept* (1945), an account of her love for G. *Barker, whom she met in California in 1940, and by whom she was to have four children. It is passionate and lyrical, with biblical echoes from the Song of Songs, and was described by B. *Brophy as 'shelled, skinned, nerve-exposed'. She also published poetry (*A Bonus*, 1977; *In the Meantime*, 1984) and her journals have been edited (1986, 1994) by Alice Van Wart.

Smectymnuus, the name under which five Presbyterian divines, Stephen Marshall, Edmund Calamy, Thomas Young, Matthew Newcomen, and William Spurstow, published a pamphlet in 1641 attacking episcopacy and Bishop J. *Hall. It was answered by Hall, and defended by *Milton (who had been a pupil of Young, the eldest of the five) in his *Animadversions upon the Remonstrant's Defence against Smectymnuus* (1641) and his *An Apology against a Pamphlet Call'd A Modest Confutation of the Animadversions upon the Remonstrant against Smectymnuus* (1642). In the latter Milton also defends himself against the allegations of the anonymous *A Modest Confutation* (possibly by Hall's son or by the Revd Robert Duncan, ?1599–?1622), which include the charge that Milton had 'spent his youth in loitering, bezelling and harlotting', and that he had been 'vomited out' of the University: it contains an interesting account of his early studies. From 'Smectymnuus' is derived the 'Legion Smec' in *Hudibras* (II. ii), signifying the Presbyterians:

> New modell'd the army and cashier'd
> All that to Legion Smec adher'd.

SMEDLEY, Francis Edward (1818–64), a cripple from childhood, who was for three years editor of *Cruikshank's Magazine* and author of three high-spirited novels of sport, romance, and adventure, including the popular *Frank Fairleigh* (1850), illustrated by *Cruikshank, *Lewis Arundel* (1852), and *Harry Coverdale's Courtship* (1855).

Smelfungus, in Sterne's *A Sentimental Journey*, a caricature of *Smollett, who in 1766 had published his *Travels through France and Italy*.

SMETANA, Bedřich (1824–84), Czech composer, most of whose work depends on texts from his own country. He had however an admiration for Shakespeare and one of his earliest orchestral works is the symphonic poem based on *Richard III*, written when the composer was still unknown and living in Sweden: it contains a successful musical portrait of the hump-backed king with his uneven, halting walk. At about the same time Smetana wrote a long piano piece, *Macbeth and the Witches*, of considerable originality. There is also a late fragment (less than one act) of *Viola*, an opera based on *Twelfth Night*, which would probably have been more interesting than the Shakespearian March, a *pièce d'occasion* written for the culmination of the Shakespeare tercentenary concert organized by Smetana in Prague in 1864.

Smike, a character in Dickens's *Nicholas Nickleby.*

SMILES, Samuel (1812–1904), son of a Haddington shopkeeper. He had a mobile and varied career as surgeon, newspaper editor, secretary for a railway company, etc., and devoted his leisure to the advocacy of political and social reform, on the lines of the *Manchester school, and to the biography of industrial leaders and humble self-taught students. He published a *Life of George Stephenson* (1875), *Lives of the Engineers* (1861–2), *Josiah Wedgwood* (1894), and many similar works, but is now principally remembered for his immensely successful *Self-Help* (1859), which was translated into many languages. It preached industry, thrift, and self-improvement, and attacked 'over-government'; it has been much mocked as a work symbolizing the ethics and aspirations of mid-19th-cent. bourgeois individualism. The titles of other works on similar themes (*Character*, 1871; *Thrift*, 1875; *Duty*, 1880) are self-explanatory.

SMILEY, Jane (1951–   ), American novelist, born in Los Angeles, best known for her novel *A Thousand Acres* (1992), for which she was awarded the *Pulitzer Prize for fiction. In this grim retelling of the *King Lear story, set like much of Smiley's work in the American Midwest, Larry King decides to retire and pass his farm down to his three daughters, Ginny, Rose, and Caroline; Smiley describes the tragic consequences of this decision eloquently and with a remarkable sense of both morality on an epic scale and intimate details of character.

Her other novels include the thriller *Duplicate Keys* (1984) and *Moo* (1995), a wryly satirical look at university campus life in Midwestern America. She has also published a collection of short stories, *The Age of Grief* (1988).

SMITH, Adam (1723–90), born at Kirkcaldy. He studied at Glasgow University and as a Snell exhibitioner at Balliol College, Oxford. In 1748 he was appointed to lecture in rhetoric and belles-lettres in Edinburgh where he was associated with the publication of *Hamilton of Bangour's *Poems*. He was appointed professor of logic at Glasgow in 1751, and in 1752 professor of moral philosophy. He became the friend of *Hume. His contributions to the original *Edinburgh Review* (1755–6) included a critical review of *Johnson's *Dictionary*. In 1759 he published *The Theory of Moral Sentiments*, which brought him into prominence. In 1764 he resigned his professorship and accompanied the young duke of Buccleuch as tutor on a visit to France, where he saw *Voltaire and was admitted into the society of the *physiocrats. After his return he settled down at Kirkcaldy and devoted himself to the preparation of his great work *An Inquiry into the Nature and Causes of the *Wealth of Nations*, published in 1776. This revolutionized the economic

theories of the day. Its appearance on the actual date of the 'Declaration of Independence' of the American rebels was of importance if only for the prophecy in Bk IV, 'They will be one of the foremost nations of the world': to obviate the danger he proposed the representation of the colonies in the British Parliament. Smith's edition of the autobiography of Hume in 1777 occasioned some controversy. A projected work on the theatre was never completed, but an essay on the imitative arts was included in his posthumous *Essays on Philosophical Subjects* (1795). He was a member of Johnson's *Club. A critical edition of Smith's works in six volumes was published for the University of Glasgow in 1976–80, but the *Correspondence* volume is defective.

SMITH, Alexander (?1830–67), by occupation a lace-pattern designer in Glasgow. He published in 1853 *Poems* (including 'A life-drama'), which were received at first with enthusiasm, and satirized, along with other works of the *Spasmodic school, in *Aytoun's *Firmilian*. He published in 1855 sonnets on the Crimean War jointly with S. T. *Dobell; *City Poems* in 1857; and some prose essays, *Dreamthorp*, in 1863. His best prose is to be seen in *A Summer in Skye* (1865), a vivid evocation of the region, its history, and its inhabitants.

SMITH, Charlotte, née Turner (1749–1806), novelist and poet, who also wrote many stories and sketches, and enjoyed considerable success. She began her career with *Elegiac Sonnets* in 1784, followed by a second volume of sonnets (a form for which she was particularly admired) in 1797: the melancholy which informed much of her poetry was not merely fashionable, as some supposed, but sprang in part from intense marital, family, and financial difficulties. *Beachy Head; with Other Poems* was published posthumously in 1807. Her 11 novels appeared between 1788 and 1802, and include *Emmeline* (1788), which was admired by Sir W. *Scott, and *The Old Manor House* (1793), which Scott, and posterity, considered her best. Orlando, who is favoured by a rich widow, Mrs Rayland, is forced to leave his beloved Monimia, Mrs Rayland's ward, in order to seek a livelihood. He joins the army in America, and after many hardships among battles and Native Americans returns to find himself Mrs Rayland's heir and to marry Monimia. At her best the author's work is brisk, ironic, and confident.

SMITH, Clark Ashton, see FANTASY FICTION.

SMITH, Dodie (1896–1990), playwright and novelist, who wrote as C. L. Anthony until 1935. Trained for the stage, she later worked in Heal's furniture store in London. She wrote ten plays, among them *Dear Octopus* (1938), and six adult novels, including the romantic minor classic *I Capture the Castle* (1949). Her children's book *One Hundred and One Dalmatians* (1956) has been successfully filmed in cartoon and live action. See *Dear Dodie* (1996) by Valerie Grove.

SMITH, George (1824–1901). He joined in 1838 the firm of Smith & Elder, publishers and East India agents, of 65 Cornhill, London, which his father had founded in partnership with Alexander Elder in 1816, soon after coming in youth to London from his native town of Elgin. In 1843 Smith took charge of some of the firm's publishing operations, and on his father's death in 1846 became sole head of the firm. Under his control the business quickly grew in both the India agency and publishing directions. The chief authors whose works he published in his early career were *Ruskin, C. *Brontë, whose *Jane Eyre he issued in 1848, and W. M. *Thackeray, whose Esmond he brought out in 1852. Charlotte Brontë visited Smith and his mother in London on friendly terms, and Smith later acknowledged that 'In Villette my mother was the original of "Mrs Bretton", several of her expressions are given verbatim. I myself, I discovered, stood for "Dr John".' ('Recollections of Charlotte Brontë', Cornhill Magazine, Dec. 1900.)

In 1853 he took a partner, H. S. King, and after weathering the storm of the Indian Mutiny, founded in 1859 the *Cornhill Magazine, with Thackeray as editor and numerous leading authors and artists as contributors. In 1865 Smith (with Frederick Greenwood) founded the *Pall Mall Gazette, a London evening newspaper of independent character and literary quality, which remained his property till 1880. In 1868 he dissolved partnership with King, leaving him to carry on the India agency branch of the old firm's business, and himself taking over the publishing branch, which he thenceforth conducted at 15 Waterloo Place, London. His chief authors now included R. *Browning, M. *Arnold, (Sir) L. *Stephen, and Anne Thackeray *Ritchie, all of whom were intimate personal friends. He was founder (1882) and proprietor of the *Dictionary of National Biography.

SMITH, Goldwin (1823–1910), educated at Eton and Christ Church, Oxford, Regius professor of modern history at Oxford, 1858–66, and subsequently professor of history at Cornell University in America, finally settling at Toronto in 1871. He was an active journalist and vigorous controversialist, supporting the cause of the North in the American Civil War, and the sentiment of national independence in Canada.

SMITH, Horatio (Horace) (1779–1849), brother of James *Smith. He became famous overnight as the joint author, with his brother, of *Rejected Addresses in 1812, and of Horace in London (1813), imitations of certain odes of *Horace, chiefly written by his brother. He then turned to the writing of historical romance. In 1826 his Brambletye House, the story of a young Cavalier and a pale shadow of Scott's *Woodstock (published in the same year), went through many editions. The Tor Hill followed in the same year, and between then and 1846 he wrote nearly 20 further novels, as well as plays and poems and work for the *New Monthly Magazine.

SMITH, Iain Crichton (1928–98), poet, born into a Gaelic-speaking family on the Isle of Lewis, and educated at the University of Aberdeen. He taught for many years, first at Clydebank, then (1955–77) in Oban. His first volume of poetry, The Long River (1955), was followed by others, including The White Noon (1959), Thistles and Roses (1961), Deer on the High Hills (1962), The Law and the Grace (1965), Hamlet in Autumn (1972), The Emigrants (1983, translated from the author's own Gaelic), A Life (1986, an autobiography in verse), and The Village and Other Poems (1989): his Collected Poems was published in 1992. His work celebrates landscape and place (Aberdeen, Oban, Edinburgh, the Highlands, and 'bare Lewis without tree or branch'), writers and painters, and the often constrained and difficult lives of his fellow Scots: the tone is of a strange lyric stoic irony, at times elegiac:

> The herring girls,
> where did they go to
> with their necklaces of salt? (1983)

SMITH, James (1775–1839), elder brother of Horatio *Smith. He was solicitor to the board of ordnance, and produced with his brother *Rejected Addresses in 1812 and Horace in London (1813), imitations of certain odes of *Horace, largely written by James. He also wrote entertainments for the comic actor Charles Mathews.

SMITH, Captain John (1580–1631). He set out with the Virginia colonists in 1606 and is said to have been rescued by *Pocahontas when taken prisoner by the Native Americans. He became head of the colony and explored the coasts of the Chesapeake. He was author of The General History of Virginia, New England, and the Summer Isles (1624).

SMITH, John (1618–52), see CAMBRIDGE PLATONISTS.

SMITH, John Thomas (1776–1833), engraver and artist, and eventually keeper of prints and drawings at the *British Museum. He was particularly interested in the history and character of London. Among other writings he published Antiquities of London (1800) and Vagabondiana (1817), a description of London's beggars, illustrated by himself. He wrote a remarkably candid life of the sculptor *Nollekens, published in 1828, and in 1839 Cries of London: A Book for a Rainy Day, or Recollections of the Events of the Years 1766–1833 (1845), which provides a lively account of the literary and artistic life of the time.

SMITH, Ken (1938–2003), poet, born in east Yorkshire, educated at Leeds University. The Pity (1967) introduced Smith as a nature poet with a stronger human focus than Ted *Hughes. Smith's work then appeared fugitively until Bloodaxe Books published Burned Books (1981) and The Poet Reclining: Selected Poems 1962–1980 (1982), which showed Smith's kinship with American speech-based poetry (rather than the image-driven practice of English contemporaries) when he dealt, in fragmentary or overheard form, with themes of loss and exile. *Fox Running* (1980) applies these methods to a period of breakdown in London. *Terra* (1986) is Smith's reading of the Thatcher–Reagan years 'from below', while *Wormwood* (1987) draws on experience as writer in residence at HM Prison Wormwood Scrubs. After 1989 Smith travelled extensively in eastern Europe (see *The Heart, the Border*, 1990, and *Wild Root*, 1988). *A Book of Chinese Whispers* (1987) collects his short fiction.

SMITH, (Lloyd) Logan Pearsall (1865–1946), man of letters, born in Philadelphia of Quaker stock. He spent most of his life in England, devoting himself to the study of literature and the English language; he was (with *Bridges and others) a founder of the *Society for Pure English. One of his sisters became the first wife of Bertrand *Russell, another married *Berenson, and his own circle of literary friends included R. *Fry, H. *James, and C. *Connolly. His works include *Trivia* (1902), *More Trivia* (1921), and *Afterthoughts* (1931), collections of much-polished observations and aphorisms; one of his more memorable, 'People say that life is the thing, but I prefer reading', indicates the nature of his success and limitations as an author. See *Recollections of Pearsall Smith* (1949), an unsparing account by R. Gathorne-Hardy.

SMITH, Stevie (Florence Margaret) (1902–71), poet and novelist, who was born in Hull but brought up in Palmers Green, north London, where she spent most of her adult life with an aunt. She wrote three novels, *Novel on Yellow Paper* (1936), *Over the Frontier* (1938), and *The Holiday* (1949), but has been more widely recognized for her witty, caustic, and enigmatic verse, much of it illustrated by her own comic drawings. Her first volume, *A Good Time Was Had by All* (1937), was followed by seven others, including *Not Waving but Drowning* (1957), of which the title poem (originally published in the *Observer) is perhaps the best known. She was an accomplished reader of her own verse, and found a new young audience at the poetry readings which flourished in the 1960s. Her *Collected Poems* appeared in 1975; see also *Ivy & Stevie* (1971) by her friend, the novelist Kay Dick.

SMITH, Sydney (1771–1845), educated at Winchester and New College, Oxford. He lived for a time as a tutor in Edinburgh, where he became a friend of *Jeffrey and *Brougham with whom he founded the *Edinburgh Review* in 1802. He was himself the original 'projector' of the *Review*, the object of which was to provide a voice for liberal and Whig opinion to balance the Tory *Quarterly. Smith was a humane man, who campaigned vigorously, in the *Review* and elsewhere, against the Game Laws, transportation, prisons, slavery, and for Catholic emancipation, church reform, and many other matters. He tried for a time to restrain what he saw as Jeffrey's tendency, as editor of the *Review*, to 'analyse and destroy'; but his own contributions became less frequent, then ceased altogether, as he came to feel that Jeffrey was making it 'perilous' for a cleric to be connected with the *Review*. He came to London in 1803, lectured with great success on moral philosophy at the Royal Institution, and became the wittiest and one of the most beloved of the Whig circle at *Holland House. In 1807 he published *The Letters of Peter *Plymley* in defence of Catholic emancipation, and he published a considerable number of sermons, speeches, essays, and letters. He held the livings, first of Foston in Yorkshire, then of Combe Florey in Somerset, and in 1831 was made a canon of St Paul's. His superb wit was chiefly displayed in his conversation, but may also be found in his numerous letters, reviews, and essays. See biography by H. *Pearson, *The Smith of Smiths* (1934).

SMITH, Sydney Goodsir (1915–75), poet, critic, and journalist, born in New Zealand, who settled in Scotland as a young man and is remembered for his part in the 20th-cent. revival of poetry in the *Scots language. His first volume, *Skail Wind* (1941), was followed by several others, and he also edited various works on Scottish literature.

Smith, W. H., and Son, Ltd, a firm of stationers, newsagents, and booksellers, which originated in a small newsvendor's shop opened in London in Little Grosvenor Street in 1792 by Henry Walton Smith and his wife Anna. He died within a few months, leaving the shop to his widow, who on her death in 1816 left it to her sons; the younger, William Henry Smith (1792–1865), gave the firm its name of W. H. Smith in 1828. When his son, also William Henry (1825–91), became a partner in 1846, the words 'and Son' were added, and have remained ever since. The business prospered, profiting from the railway boom by opening station bookstalls throughout the country (of which the first was at Euston, 1848), and establishing a circulating *library which lasted until 1961; it was a joint owner (from 1966) of Book Club Associates. In the 20th cent. the wholesale and retail activities of the business expanded greatly, and the name of W. H. Smith is now associated with a wide range of products. The W. H. Smith Literary Award has been awarded annually since 1959, for a work of any genre that constitutes 'the most outstanding contribution to English literature' in the year under review.

SMITH, Sir William (1813–93), lexicographer, classical scholar, and editor of the *Quarterly Review* (1867–93). He is associated with the revival of classical teaching in England and among his many educational works are his *Dictionary of Greek and Roman Antiquities* (1842), a *Dictionary of Greek and Roman Biography and Mythology* (1844–9), and a *Dictionary of the Bible* (1860–3).

SMOLLETT, Tobias George (1721–71), the son of a Scots laird, born near Dunbarton. After attendance at Glasgow University he was apprenticed to a surgeon, but did not prosper and lived in some poverty. He wrote a play, *The Regicide*, which he brought to London in 1739, but he could not get it accepted, then or at any future time. He joined the navy, became surgeon's mate, and sailed in 1741 for the West Indies on an expedition against the Spaniards. He was present at the abortive attack on Cartagena, when the fleet retired, a fact which greatly disturbed Smollett, who later wrote about the failure in *Roderick Random* and (probably) in *A Compendium of . . . Voyages*. While in Jamaica he met Anne Lassells, a young woman of some property and means, whom he married, probably in 1743. In 1744 he set himself up as a surgeon in Downing Street, and began to entertain generously among a wide circle of friends, many of them his Scots compatriots.

Although never a Jacobite, Smollett's first publication, in 1746, was a much-admired poem, 'The Tears of Scotland', elicited by the duke of *Cumberland's cruel treatment of the Scots after 1745. Further poems followed, notably two satires on London life, *Advice* (1746) and *Reproof* (1747). In the course of eight months in 1747 he wrote *The Adventures of *Roderick Random* which was published in 1748 and was a lasting success. The Smolletts' only child, Elizabeth, was born in 1747 or 1748. Smollett toured France and the Low Countries in 1749, the first of various travels in Europe. Back in London he continued to practise as a surgeon, without any great success, and although he laboured hard at various tasks of editing and translation he was chronically short of money. In 1750 he moved to Chelsea, where he kept open board in his fine large house. In the same year he received his MD from Aberdeen, and travelled to Paris, a journey of which he made use in *The Adventures of *Peregrine Pickle* (1751). Long, ferocious, and often savagely libellous, the novel was only reasonably successful; Smollett considerably toned down the second edition of 1758. He may have been the author, in 1752, of the scurrilous pamphlet, *The Faithful Narrative of Habbakkuk Hilding*, attacking *Fielding for plagiarism and on many other counts. He and Fielding conducted intermittent warfare, chiefly in the *Critical Review* and the *Covent Garden Journal*, but Smollett eventually gave his rival handsome praise in his *Continuation of the Complete History* (see below).

In 1753 he published *The Adventures of *Ferdinand Count Fathom*, a story of cruelty and treachery which did not appeal to the public. Smollett was again in financial difficulties, and took on every medical or literary employment that he could find. In the same year he set out on an extended tour of his native Scotland, and began to exhibit symptoms of consumption. He had long been translating *Cervantes, and in 1755 his *History and Adventures of Don Quixote* appeared, but to his great disappointment received little attention. In 1756 he became co-founder and editor of the *Critical Review*; his stormy and brilliant editorship lasted till 1763, but the *Review* was not a commercial success. *A Compendium of Authentic and Entertaining Voyages*, an anthology of travel, appeared in 1756, and contained an account, probably by his pen, of the retreat at Cartagena. In 1757–8 he published his *Complete History of England* which engendered much angry controversy, but its sales were immense and at last Smollett could feel financially secure. Also in 1757 he had a success at Drury Lane with his naval farce *The Reprisal*, staged by *Garrick. The first volume of the *Continuation of the Complete History* appeared in 1760; and *The Life and Adventures of Sir Launcelot *Greaves*, the story of a quixotic 18th-cent. Englishman, began to appear in instalments in Smollett's new venture, the *British Magazine*, to which *Goldsmith was a major contributor and which ran until 1767. In the same eventful year of 1760 Smollett was fined £100 and sentenced to three months' imprisonment for a libel on Admiral Knowles in the *Critical Review*. His edition of a new translation of *The Works of . . . Voltaire* began to appear in 1761, and in 1762 *Sir Launcelot Greaves* was published in book form, but met with little interest. In 1762–3 Smollett wrote and edited the Tory journal the *Briton*, which was rapidly killed by Wilkes's the *North Briton*.

Smollett's health had long been deteriorating, and he attempted without success to obtain work abroad. In 1763 his daughter died. He gave up his house and all his literary work and left England with his wife and household for France and Italy. They returned in 1765 and in 1766 he published his *epistolary *Travels through France and Italy*, a caustic work which earned him from *Sterne the nickname of Smelfungus. In 1767 he tried again, and again without success, to obtain a consulship abroad. *The Present State of All Nations*, a complex work of geography, history, statistics, and other matters (a long labour in which he was probably assisted by other hands), was finally published in eight volumes in 1768–9.

In 1768 he and his wife left again for Italy, and in 1769 appeared *The Adventures of an *Atom*, a rancorous satire on public men and affairs. Meanwhile he had been completing *The Expedition of *Humphry Clinker*, an epistolary novel generally agreed to be Smollett's crowning achievement. It was published in London in 1771, some months before Smollett died at his home near Livorno.

Smollett's passion for controversy did not always endear him to the literary or fashionable world, but his major novels were admired and successful; his reputation sank considerably in the 19th and early 20th cents, but now stands high. His avowed purpose in writing was to arouse 'generous indignation' against cruelty and injustice, but his relish in the exploits of his 'heroes' sometimes distorts his professed moral purpose. He was greatly attracted by the 'anti-romance' of *Lesage and many of the episodes of his novels are set in scenes of squalor and violence 'where the . . . passions are undisguised by affectation': his works are often (if somewhat loosely) described as *picaresque. See Louis Martz, *The Later Career of Tobias Smollett* (1942); Paul-Gabriel Boucé, *The Novels of Tobias Smollett* (1976); and James G. Basker, *Tobias Smollett: Critic and Journalist* (1988).

Smorltork, Count, in Dickens's *Pickwick Papers*, 'the famous foreigner' at Mrs Leo Hunter's party, 'a well-whiskered individual in a foreign uniform', who is 'gathering materials for his great work on England'.

Snagsby, Mr and Mrs, characters in Dickens's *Bleak House*.

Snake, a character in Sheridan's *The School for Scandal*.

Sneerwell, Lady, one of the scandal-mongers in Sheridan's *The School for Scandal*.

Snevellicci, Mr, Mrs, and Miss, in Dickens's *Nicholas Nickleby*, actors in Crummles's company.

Snobs of England, The see THACKERAY.

Snodgrass, Augustus, in Dickens's *Pickwick Papers*, one of the members of the Corresponding Society of the Pickwick Club.

SNORRI STURLUSON (1178–1241), an Icelandic historian and literary antiquary, the author of *Heimskringla*, the Prose *Edda*, and perhaps *Egils saga*, the biography of a Viking poet. Snorri is the most important figure in Old Icelandic literature; our knowledge of Norse myth and understanding of Old Norse poetry is due largely to him. He was politically ambitious, involved in the chief political intrigues of his time, and at last ignominiously assassinated on the order of King Håkon of Norway.

Snout, Tom, in Shakespeare's *A Midsummer Night's Dream*, an Athenian tinker. He is cast for the part of Pyramus' father in the play of 'Pyramus and Thisbe', but appears as Wall.

SNOW, C(harles) P(ercy) (Baron Snow of Leicester) (1905–80), novelist, born and educated in Leicester, the son of a church organist. His early career was devoted to scientific research in Cambridge, but he turned increasingly to administration, and in later life held many important public posts. His first novel was a detective story, *Death under Sail* (1932), followed by *New Lives for Old* (1933) and *The Search* (1934), which deals with the frustrations of a scientist's life. His novel sequence (see ROMAN FLEUVE) *Strangers and Brothers* (the original title of the first volume, 1940, retitled subsequently *George Passant*) spanned 30 years of writing, and more years in the life of its narrator, Lewis Eliot, a barrister who, like Snow himself, rose from lower-middle-class provincial origins to enjoy worldly success and influence. The settings of the novels (*The Light and the Dark*, 1947; *Time of Hope*, 1949; *The Masters*, 1951; *The New Men*, 1954; *Homecomings*, 1956; *The Conscience of the Rich*, 1958; *The Affair*, 1959; *Corridors of Power*, 1963; *The Sleep of Reason*, 1968; *Last Things*, 1970) are largely academic or scientific; *The Masters*, a study of the internal politics of a Cambridge college, is perhaps his best known, but he was equally at home writing of crises in the life of a

small-town solicitor or a fashionable and wealthy Jewish family. His interest in public affairs is reflected in his work, and his novel on Westminster life, *The Corridors of Power*, added a phrase to the language of the day, as did his Rede Lecture on *The Two Cultures and the Scientific Revolution* (1959). He published several other novels and critical works, including a critical biography of *Trollope (1975), a novelist whose influence is evident in his own work. In 1950 he married Pamela Hansford *Johnson.

Snowe, Lucy, the narrator of *Villette*.

Snubbin, Mr Serjeant, in Dickens's *Pickwick Papers*, counsel for the defendant in *Bardell* v. *Pickwick*.

Snug, in Shakespeare's *A Midsummer Night's Dream*, a joiner, who takes the part of the lion in 'Pyramus and Thisbe'.

SOANE, Sir John (1753–1837), architect. He was architect to the Bank of England from 1788 to 1833 and founder of the museum in Lincoln's Inn Fields which bears his name and contains his library, antiquities, and works of art—perhaps most notably his collection of *Hogarth paintings. The library is famous for its hoard of architectural drawings by *Wren, the Adam brothers, Dance, and Soane. He published several volumes of his own designs and an extensive description of the museum. His Royal Academy lectures, his only major literary enterprise, were published in 1929.

Social Contract, The, the English title of *Du contrat social*, by J. J. *Rousseau.

social problem novel, a phrase used to describe mid-19th-cent. fiction which examined specific abuses and hardships which affected the working classes. These included many of the topics which were simultaneously being exposed by non-fictional writers on social issues, such as poor housing and sanitation; conditions in factories; child labour; the exploitation of seamstresses; and the exhausting nature of agricultural labour. Largely written from a middle-class perspective, it sometimes sought to stimulate legislation, and on other occasions (as in E. Gaskell's *Mary Barton*, 1848, and *North and South*, 1854–5) promoted understanding between masters and men on the basis of shared humanity, and shared material interests, as a way forward. Other notable examples include C. Kingsley's *Alton Locke* (1850) and *Yeast* (1848), B. Disraeli's *Sybil* (1845), F. *Trollope's *Michael Armstrong, the Factory Boy* (1840) and *Jessie Phillips* (1842–3), and C. E. Tonna's *Helen Fleetwood* (1841), and works by A. Mayhew, F. Paget, and E. Meteyard. Whilst *Dickens's fiction is usually regarded as more complex in its focus than many of these novels, much of his writing, especially *Oliver Twist* (1838), The *Chimes* (1845), *Bleak House* (1852), and *Hard Times* (1854), deals very directly with poverty, inequality, and their consequences. The term can be extended to include writing about 'fallen women' and prostitution (as in Gaskell's *Ruth*, 1853, Felicia Skene's *Hidden Depths*, 1866). In its search for resolution, whether practical or emotional, the social problem novel differs from later realist fiction by writers like G. *Gissing and A. *Morrison. See also CONDITION OF ENGLAND.

socialism, a theory or policy of social organization that aims at the control of the means of production, capital, land, property, etc., by the community as a whole, and their administration or distribution in the interests of all. The early history of the word is obscure, but it was claimed that it was first used in something like the modern sense in 1827 in the Owenite *Co-operative Magazine*, and it is found in the 1830s used in the sense of Owenism. (See OWEN, ROBERT.) William *Morris was active in the socialist movement, as was Bernard *Shaw, who published in 1928 *The Intelligent Woman's Guide to Socialism and Capitalism*.

Socialist Realism, the official artistic and literary doctrine of the Soviet Union, and consequently of its satellite Communist Parties, promulgated in 1934 at the First Congress of Soviet Writers with the encouragement of the dictator Josef Stalin (1879–1953) and of *Gorky, whose early novel *The Mother* (1906–7) was held up as a model. The doctrine condemned *Modernist works such as those of *Joyce or *Kafka as symptoms of decadent bourgeois pessimism, and required writers to affirm the struggle for socialism by portraying positive heroic actions. These principles were condemned by major Marxist critics and writers (*Brecht, *Lukács, Trotsky) for propagandist optimism and aesthetic conservatism, and many writers sympathetic to communism found them an embarrassment. Under Stalin's tyranny, the doctrine was employed as a pretext for the persecution and silencing of nonconformist writers (see *Akhmatova, *Mandelstam, *Pasternak). Hardly any work of significant value conformed to the official line, except by retrospective adoption, as with *Sholokov's *Virgin Soil Upturned* (1932). The principal legacy was in painting and statuary of the Soviet period, typified by the omnipresent image of the muscular and smiling tractor-driver.

Society for Psychical Research, the, a body founded in 1882 by F. W. H. *Myers, H. *Sidgwick, and others 'to examine without prejudice . . . those faculties of man, real or supposed, which appear to be inexplicable in terms of any recognised hypothesis'. The Society, in a period of intense interest in spiritualism and the supernatural, investigated with high standards of scientific detachment such matters as telepathy, apparitions, etc., and was instrumental in exposing the fraudulent claims of, for example, Mme *Blavatsky. Its presidents have included A. J. *Balfour, W. *James, and Sir Oliver Lodge (1851–1940, a physicist less sceptical than many of the SPR); members and associates have included *Ruskin, *Tennyson, *Gladstone, and A. R.

*Wallace. See R. Haynes, *The Society for Psychical Research 1882–1982* (1982).

Society for Pure English, the, an association of writers and academics, inspired by *Bridges, which included H. *Bradley, Sir W. *Raleigh, and L. P. *Smith in its original committee. The Society was formed in Oxford in 1913, but suspended its activities until the end of the First World War. Between 1919 and 1946 it issued a total of 66 tracts of which the last, by R. W. Chapman, was a retrospective account of its work. The name of the Society was somewhat misleading in that the founders had no objections to the entry of foreign words into English, and the writers of its tracts were not for the most part purists in the dogmatic sense. A typical tract would offer an urbane and well-researched enquiry into some question of grammar, pronunciation, etymology, or vocabulary, and there were occasional treatments of quite exotic subjects; for instance, the language of C. M. *Doughty or the pronunciation of *Gladstone.

Society of Antiquaries, the, founded about the year 1572 at the instance of Archbishop *Parker, but suppressed on the accession of James I. The present Society was founded in Jan. 1717/18, with Peter Le Neve as president and W. *Stukeley as secretary. Its *Archaeologia* was first printed in 1770. From 1921 it has also published the *Antiquaries' Journal*.

Society of Authors, the, an organization founded in 1884 by W. *Besant to promote the business interests of authors and fight for their rights, especially in copyright. Progress was slow, but by 1914 much had been achieved; Britain had joined the International Copyright Convention (Berne Union), the USA had offered limited protection to foreign authors, while domestic copyright had undergone a major reform under the Copyright Act of 1911. By then too the Society had succeeded in radically improving publishing contracts and in dealing with recalcitrant publishers in and out of the courts.

Besant's example was followed by G. B. *Shaw, who fought arduously for playwrights *vis-à-vis* theatre managers, and to liberalize stage censorship; the League of Dramatists was founded in 1931 as an autonomous section of the Society. Since then the Society has formed other specialized groups, and has also laboured effectively to improve the author's lot with regard to taxation, libel, social security, etc. It conducted a successful 28-year campaign for *Public Lending Right, and has helped to set up the Authors' Lending and Copyright Society, in order to secure income in respect of rights (e.g. photocopying) only possible on a collective basis. Its quarterly publication is the *Author*. See Victor Bonham-Carter, *Authors by Profession* (2 vols, 1978, 1984).

Society of Friends, the, see FRIENDS, SOCIETY OF.

Society of Jesus, the, see IGNATIUS LOYOLA and XAVIER.

Socinianism, the doctrine of Lelio Sozini (Socinus) (1525–62) and his nephew Fausto Sozzini (1539–1604) that Jesus was not God but a divine prophet of God's word, and that the sacraments had no supernatural quality. The doctrine was set forth in the Confession of Rakow (1605), and was an influence on early *Unitarianism.

SOCRATES (469–399 BC), Greek philosopher, born near Athens, the son of a sculptor or stonemason. He served in the army, saving the life of Alcibiades at Potidea (432 BC). Late in life he held public office, and showed moral courage in resisting illegalities. Legend allotted the role of shrew to his wife Xanthippe. He occupied his life with oral instruction, frequenting public places and engaging in discourse designed to reveal truth and expose error. He incurred much enmity, was caricatured by *Aristophanes in the *Clouds*, and was finally accused by Meletus, a leather-seller, of introducing strange gods and corrupting youth. He was sentenced to death, and 30 days later took hemlock. Socrates wrote nothing, but his teaching methods are preserved in the Dialogues of *Plato and a more homely account is to be found in *Xenophon's *Memorabilia*. The prominent features of his teaching appear to have been: the view that it is the duty of philosophy to investigate ethical questions; and the view that virtue is knowledge: no one is willingly wicked, for happiness lies in virtue; if a man is wicked, it is from ignorance. He inclined to belief in the immortality of the soul, and thought himself subject to divine promptings. (For Socratic method see PLATO.)

'Sofa, The', see TASK, THE.

Sofronia, or **Sophronia,** a character in Tasso's *Jerusalem Delivered*.

'Sohrab and Rustum', a poem by M. *Arnold, published 1853. The story is taken from *Firdusi's Persian epic, via a French translation by J. Mohl, *Le Livre des rois*. It recounts, in blank verse adorned by *epic similes, the fatal outcome of Sohrab's search for his father Rustum, the leader of the Persian forces. Rustum (who believes his own child to be a girl) accepts the challenge of Sohrab, now leader of the Tartars: the two meet in single combat, at first unaware of one another's identity, which is confirmed only when Sohrab has been mortally wounded.

soldan (from the Arabic *sultan*). The soldan or souldan, in Spenser's *Faerie Queene (V. viii) represents Philip II of Spain. He is encountered by Prince *Arthur and Sir *Artegall with a bold defiance from Queen *Mercilla (Elizabeth), and the combat is undecided until the prince unveils his shield and terrifies the soldan's horses, so that they overturn his chariot and the soldan is torn 'all to rags'. The unveiling of the shield signifies divine interposition.

Solinus, the duke of Ephesus in Shakespeare's *The Comedy of Errors*.

Solmes, a character in Richardson's *Clarissa*.

Solomon Daisy, in Dickens's *Barnaby Rudge*, the parish clerk and bell-ringer at Chigwell.

Solyman and Perseda, *The Tragedye of,* see KYD.

SOLZHENITSYN, Alexander Isayevich (1918–   ), Russian prose writer. Born in Kislovodsk in the Caucasus, the son of an army officer, he studied mathematics and physics at the University of Rostov-on-Don. He joined the Red Army in 1941. Arrested in 1945 for remarks critical of Stalin, he was sent to a labour camp where in 1952 he developed stomach cancer. In 1953 he was released into 'administrative exile'. In 1956 he returned to Ryazan, in central Russia, to work as a teacher. His first published story, *One Day in the Life of Ivan Denisovich* (1962), caused a sensation through its honest and pioneering description of camp life. This was followed by *Matrena's House* (1963) and other stories. His major novels, *Cancer Ward* (1968) and *The First Circle* (1969), which continue the basic Solzhenitsyn theme of men in extreme situations facing basic moral choices, could only be published abroad, and in late 1969 he was expelled from the Union of Soviet Writers. In 1970 he was awarded the *Nobel Prize for literature. The appearance abroad of the first volume of *The Gulag Archipelago* (1973–5), an epic 'history and geography' of the labour camps, caused the Soviet authorities to deport Solzhenitsyn to West Germany on 13 Feb. 1974; he later moved to the United States, where he continued a series of novels begun with *August 1914* (1971), offering an alternative picture of Soviet history. His memoirs were published in English as *The Oak and the Calf* in 1980. *Rebuilding Russia* appeared in English in 1990. A life by D. M. *Thomas was published in 1997.

Some Experiences of an Irish R.M., a collection of stories by *Somerville and Ross, published 1899.

This exuberant and skilful series of stories is narrated by Major Yeates, the resident magistrate, whose misfortune is to attract calamity. With his gallant wife Philippa, he lives at the centre of a vigorous and wily community as the tenant of a dilapidated demesne, Shreelane, which he rents from a well-to-do rogue, Flurry Knox, whose old grandmother lives in squalid splendour at neighbouring Aussolas, overrun with horses. Frequent rain, flowing drink, unruly hounds, and the eccentricities of the populace contribute to innumerable confusions involving collapsing carts, missed meals, sinking boats, shying horses, and outraged visitors. Yet few of the stories are merely farcical, and some have a sombre echo.

SOMERVILE, William (1675–1742), a country gentleman, remembered as the author of *The Chace* (1735), a poem in four books of Miltonic blank verse on the pleasures of hunting which had a considerable success. In 1740 he published *Hobbinol*, a *mock-heroic account of rural games in Gloucestershire (see COTSWOLD

OLIMPICK GAMES), and in 1742 his 'Field Sports', a short poem on hawking, appeared. Dr *Johnson commented in *The Lives of the English Poets* that 'he writes very well for a gentleman'.

SOMERVILLE (Edith) and **ROSS** (Martin), the pen-names of second cousins Edith Œnone Somerville (1858–1949, born in Corfu) and Violet Florence Martin (1862–1915, born in Co. Galway), who first met in 1886. Separately and together they wrote many books, mainly set in Ireland, as well as many articles, letters, diaries, and jottings. Their first collaboration, *An Irish Cousin* (1889), was well received. In their most sustained novel, *The Real Charlotte* (1894), Francie Fitzpatrick, a beautiful girl from Dublin, finds herself, on the estate of the wealthy Dysarts, becoming enmeshed with the malign Charlotte Mullen, who is jealous of the attention devoted to Francie by the flash estate manager Lambert. Francie, finding herself in love with a handsome English officer, discovers he is already engaged and marries Lambert, only to be killed riding her horse. In 1897 came *The Silver Fox*, their first book with hunting as a major theme, then *Some Experiences of an Irish R.M.* (1899). The international success of this book led in 1908 to *Further Experiences of an Irish R.M.* and in 1915 to the third of the series, *In Mr Knox's Country*. After Martin Ross's death Edith Somerville wrote another 13 books, including *The Big House at Inver* (1925), a historical romance, but continued to name Ross as co-author.

'Somnium Scipionis' (Dream of Scipio) is the fable with which *Cicero ends his *De Republica*. The only extant manuscript of Cicero's treatise breaks off early in the last book, and the survival of the *Somnium* is due to the accident of its being reproduced by a certain Macrobius, who in the 4th cent. AD furnished it with a *Neoplatonist commentary that interested medieval thinkers.

The fable relates how the younger Scipio saw his grandfather, the elder Scipio, in a dream and was shown the dwelling set aside in the Milky Way for those who follow virtue and especially for those who distinguish themselves in the service of their country. The *Somnium* may have inspired *Petrarch's choice of Scipio Africanus as the hero of his epic *Africa*. Since the fable expressed to perfection the humanist ideal of combining a quest for personal distinction with tranquillity of mind and patriotic effort, it attracted numerous editors during the Renaissance. Chaucer gives a poetical summary of it in *The Parliament of Fowls* and mentions it in other passages.

'Song of the Shirt, The', a poem by T. *Hood, originally published anonymously in *Punch* in 1843. One of Hood's best-known serious poems, it takes the form of a passionate protest by an overworked and underpaid seamstress—'It is not linen you're wearing out | But human creatures' lives.' The poem was a popular theme for illustration, and was treated by *Leech in *Punch* and by the painters Richard Redgrave (1844) and G. F. Watts (1850).

Songs of Experience, see SONGS OF INNOCENCE.

Songs of Innocence, a collection of poems written and etched by W. *Blake, published 1789. Most of the poems are about childhood, some of them written, with apparent simplicity, as if by children (e.g. 'Little lamb, who made thee?' and 'The Chimney Sweeper'); others commenting on the state of infancy ('The Ecchoing Green'); and yet others introducing the prophetic tone and personal imagery of Blake's later work ('The Little Girl Lost', 'The Little Girl Found').

In 1795 Blake issued a further volume, entitled *Songs of Innocence and of Experience: Shewing the Two Contrary States of the Human Soul*, to which he added the 'Songs of Experience', some of them (e.g. 'The Chimney Sweeper' and 'Nurse's Song') bearing identical titles to poems in the first collection, but replying to them in a tone that questions and offsets their simplicities, and manifests with great poetic economy Blake's profoundly original vision of the interdependence of good and evil, of energy and restraint, of desire and frustration. They range from fairly straightforward, if highly provocative, attacks on unnatural restraint ('The Garden of Love', 'London') to the extraordinary lyric intensity of 'Infant Sorrow', 'Ah! Sun-Flower', and 'Tyger! Tyger!'

sonnet, a poem consisting of 14 lines (of 11 syllables in Italian, generally 12 in French, and 10 in English), with rhymes arranged according to one or other of certain definite schemes, of which the Petrarchan and the Elizabethan are the principal, namely: (1) a b b a a b b a, followed by two, or three, other rhymes in the remaining six lines, with a pause in the thought after the octave (not always observed by English imitators, of whom *Milton and *Wordsworth are prominent examples); (2) a b a b c d c d e f e f g g. The *sonnets of Shakespeare are in the latter form.

The sonnet was introduced to England by *Wyatt and developed by *Surrey and was thereafter widely used, notably in the sonnet sequences of Shakespeare, *Sidney, *Daniel, *Spenser, and other poets of the *Golden period, most of which are amatory in nature, and contain a certain narrative development: later sonnet sequences on the theme of love include those of D. G. *Rossetti and E. B. *Browning. *Milton, *Donne, *Keats, *Hopkins, and *Yeats have all used the form to great and varied effect, and it continues to flourish.

Sonnets from the Portuguese, a sonnet sequence by E. B. *Browning first published 1850; the so-called 'Reading Edition' of 1847 was a forgery by T. J. *Wise. It describes the growth and development of her love for Robert *Browning, at first hesitating to involve him in her sorrowful invalid life, then yielding to gradual conviction of his love for her, and finally rapturous in late-born happiness. The title, chosen to disguise the personal nature of the poems by suggesting that they were a translation, was a secret reference for the Brownings to his nickname for her, 'the Portuguese', based on her poem 'Catarina to Camoens', which Browning particularly admired and which portrayed a Portuguese woman's devotion to her poet lover.

sonnets of Shakespeare, the, printed in 1609 and probably dating from the 1590s. In 1598 F. *Meres referred to Shakespeare's 'sugred Sonnets among his private friends', but these are not necessarily identical with the ones we now have. Most of them trace the course of the writer's affection for a young man of rank and beauty: the first 17 urge him to marry to reproduce his beauty, numbers 18 to 126 form a sequence of 108 sonnets, the same number as in Sidney's sequence *Astrophel and Stella*. The complete sequence of 154 sonnets was issued by the publisher Thomas Thorpe in 1609 with a dedication 'To the onlie begetter of these insuing sonnets Mr W.H. '. Mr W.H. has been identified as (among others) William, Lord Herbert, afterwards earl of Pembroke, or Henry Wriothesley, earl of Southampton, and further as the young man addressed in the sonnets. Another view argues that Mr W.H. was a friend of Thorpe, through whose good offices the manuscript had reached his hands—'begetter' being used in the sense of 'getter' or 'procurer'. Other characters are alluded to in the sequence, including a mistress stolen by a friend (40–2), a rival poet (78–80 and 80–6), and a dark beauty loved by the author (127–52). Numerous identifications for all the 'characters' involved in the sequence, as well as for Mr W.H., have been put forward: none of them is certain. Perhaps the most ingenious and amusing of these is *Wilde's The Portrait of Mr W.H.

For the form of these poems see SONNET.

Sons and Lovers, by D. H. *Lawrence, published 1913, a closely autobiographical novel set in the Nottinghamshire coalmining village of Bestwood.

Walter Morel has married a sensitive and high-minded woman better educated than himself. She begins to shrink from his lack of fine feeling and drunkenness; embittered, she turns their marriage into a battle. Morel, baffled and thwarted, is sometimes violent, while Mrs Morel rejects him and turns all her love towards her four children, particularly her two eldest sons, William and Paul. She struggles with the poverty and meanness of her surroundings to keep herself and her family 'respectable' and is determined that her boys will not become miners. William goes to London to work as a clerk, and Paul also gets a job as a clerk with Mr Jordon, manufacturer of surgical appliances; William develops pneumonia and dies. Mrs Morel, numbed by despair, is roused only when Paul also falls ill. She nurses him back to health, and subsequently their attachment deepens. Paul is friendly with the Leivers family of Willey Farm, and a tenderness grows between him and the daughter Miriam, a soulful, shy girl. They read poetry together, and Paul instructs her in French and even algebra and

shows her his sketches. Mrs Morel fears that Miriam will exclude her and tries to break up their relationship, while Paul, himself sickened at heart by Miriam's romantic love and fear of physical warmth, turns away and becomes involved with Clara Dawes, a married woman, separated from her husband Baxter, and a supporter of women's rights. Paul is made an overseer at the factory, times are easier, and he now begins to be noticed as a painter and designer. His affair with Clara peters out and she returns to her husband. Meanwhile Mrs Morel is ill with cancer and Paul is in misery at the thought of losing her. At last, unable to bear her suffering, he and his sister Annie put an overdose of morphia in her milk. Paul resists the urge to follow her 'into the darkness' and, with a great effort, turns towards life. *Sons and Lovers* was perhaps the first English novel with a truly working-class background, and certainly Lawrence's first major novel.

SONTAG, Susan (1933–2004), American cultural critic, essayist, and novelist. Born in New York, she studied at the universities of California, Chicago, Harvard, Oxford, and the Sorbonne. Settling in New York as a teacher and an essayist for *Partisan Review* and other journals, she wrote two experimental novels, *The Benefactor* (1963) and *Death Kit* (1967), and collected her essays in two volumes, *Against Interpretation* (1966) and *Styles of Radical Will* (1969), in which she surveys a range of topics, from the 'camp' sensibility and pornographic writing to avant-garde music and painting. The title essay of the first volume protests against the hunt for 'meanings' in art, calling for a sensuous appreciation of its surfaces. These early essays foreshadow many of the emphases of *postmodernism. While undergoing treatment for cancer in the 1970s, she wrote two provocative essays, *On Photography* (1977) and *Illness as Metaphor* (1978), and collected her short stories as *I, Etcetera* (1978). Later works include *AIDS and Its Metaphors* (1989) and a historical romance about Nelson and the Hamiltons, *The Volcano Lover* (1992). She also worked as a theatrical and cinematic director.

Sophia Western, the heroine of Fielding's *Tom Jones*.

SOPHOCLES (496–406 BC), Greek tragedian who wrote c.120 plays, of which seven survive, including *Ajax, The Women of Trachis, Electra*, and *Philoctetes*. The group known as the Theban plays, *Oedipus Rex, Oedipus at Colonus*, and *Antigone*, have long been influential in English literature, either directly or in versions by *Seneca. T. *Watson's translation of the *Antigone* into Latin (1581) was widely read, and both Milton's *Samson Agonistes* and *Dryden's *Oedipus* draw on Sophocles, though Dryden is chiefly indebted to *Seneca. It was in the 19th cent. that Sophocles really came into favour. *Shelley read him on his last and fatal sailing trip. *Bulwer-Lytton adapted his *Oedipus the King* (1846). M. *Arnold produced his Sophoclean play *Merope* (1858) and two Sophoclean fragments, an

Antigone (1849) and a *Dejaneira* (1867). *Swinburne introduced Sophoclean touches into his *Erechtheus* (1876); and during the first decade of the 20th cent. *Freud hit on the term 'Oedipus complex' to describe certain features of infantile sexuality. This caught the public imagination and led to numerous translations and adaptations of the Theban plays. *Yeats drew on Sophocles, *Pound produced a version of *Women of Trachis*, and *Heaney adapted *Philoctetes* as *Cure at Troy* (1990).

Sophonisba, the daughter of Hasdrubal, a Carthaginian general, who avoided captivity by taking poison at the instigation of her betrothed Masinissa, was the subject of several plays, notably by *Marston, N. *Lee, and James *Thomson. The notorious line 'Oh! Sophonisba, Sophonisba, Oh!' occurs in Thomson's version (1730), was altered to 'Oh Sophonisba, I am wholly thine' in later editions, and parodied by Fielding in *Tom Thumb* as 'O Huncamunca, Huncamunca O!'

Sophy Crewler, in Dickens's *David Copperfield*, 'the dearest girl in the world', whom Traddles marries.

SORDELLO (*c*.1200–?69), a poet born near Mantua but whose political connection with Charles of Anjou, lord of Provence, kept him in Provence for much of his later life. He accordingly wrote 'troubadour' poetry in *Provençal and so became an important link between the love poetry of Provence and that of Italy which was descended from it. *Dante places him in the ante-purgatory where he acts as guide to Virgil and Dante, pointing out to them the valley of the kings in *Purgatorio* vii, a role assigned to him perhaps because of his famous lament for the death of Blacatz. Ed. M. Boni (1954).

Sordello, a narrative poem in iambic pentameter couplets by R. *Browning, published 1840. The poem had taken seven years to complete, and was interrupted by the composition of *Paracelsus* and *Strafford*; Browning intended it to be more 'popular' than the former, but the poem was received with incomprehension and derision by the critics and the public, and its notorious 'obscurity' caused severe and prolonged damage to Browning's reputation. The *Pre-Raphaelites, for whom it became a cult text, were its first defenders, followed later by *Pound; it is now coming to be recognized as one of the finest long poems of the century, and of central importance in the interpretation of Browning's work, particularly its relation to the Romanticism on whose tenets it heavily relies and which, at the same time, it challenges and disputes. Its genuine difficulty springs from the swiftness and compression of the language, the convoluted time-scheme of the narrative, and the fusion of intense specificity (of historical detail, landscape, etc.) with the abstract ideas which form the core of the argument.

The narrative is set in Italy during the period of the Guelf–Ghibelline wars of the late 12th and 13th cents,

and traces the 'development of a soul', that of the troubadour Sordello (above), along a path of self-realization where political, aesthetic, and metaphysical ideas reflect each other; all this in the framework of a plot strongly influenced by the elements of fairy tale (lost heir, wicked stepmother, unattainable princess, etc.). The whole defies summary and demands rereading.

SORLEY, Charles Hamilton (1895–1915), poet, educated at Marlborough; he spent a year in Germany before returning on the outbreak of war in 1914, when he was commissioned and served in the trenches in France where he was killed. He left only 37 complete poems; his posthumous collection, *Marlborough and Other Poems* (1916), was a popular and critical success in the 1920s, but his verse was then long neglected, despite the efforts of Robert *Graves (who considered him, with W. *Owen and *Rosenberg, 'one of the three poets of importance killed during the War') and of *Blunden. The best known of his poems include 'The Song of the Ungirt Runners', 'Barbury Camp', and the last, bitter 'When you see millions of the mouthless dead'. See *The Letters of Sorley*, ed. W. R. Sorley (1919), and *The Ungirt Runner* (1965) by T. B. Swann.

Sorrel, Hetty, a character in G. Eliot's *Adam Bede*.

Soul's Tragedy, A, a play by R. *Browning, published 1846, together with *Luria*, as no. VIII of *Bells and Pomegranates*. Its subtitle—'Act First, being what was called the Poetry of Chiappino's life: and Act Second, its Prose'—indicates both the play's genre, tragi-comedy, and also its unusual form: the division (as opposed to mixture) of verse and prose represents Browning's idiosyncratic adaptation of Elizabethan and Jacobean models (see also PIPPA PASSES).

Chiappino, the 'hero', is a discontented liberal in 16th-cent. Faenza, who, at the climax of Act I, nobly (or egotistically?) takes on himself the punishment for the supposed assassination of the tyrannical provost by his friend Luitolfo. He expects to be lynched by the provost's guards, but is instead acclaimed by the people as their liberator, and is unable to resist the temptation of his new-found role. The provost turns out not to have been killed after all and, just as Chiappino is about to become the new provost himself, he is unmasked by the papal legate Ogniben, who has sardonically played up to his self-deceiving justification for seizing power. Ogniben, who had arrived in Faenza remarking that he had seen 'three-and-twenty leaders of revolts', utters the famous line 'I have seen *four*-and-twenty leaders of revolts!' as he watches Chiappino fleeing the town after his humiliation.

SOUTAR, William (1898–1943), Scottish poet, born in Perth, the son of a master-joiner, and educated at Perth Academy. He served in the navy during the First World War, and contracted an illness which, after his subsequent studies at Edinburgh University, left him paralysed for the last 14 years of his life. He published several volumes of poetry from 1923 onwards; he wrote in both *Scots and English, though his Scots work is generally considered more significant. All his poems are short; they include lyrics, epigrams, riddles, pieces for children which he described as 'bairn-rhymes', and other short works which he called 'whigmaleeries'. Several of his poems sing the praises and frustrations of the lost heritage of 'the lawland tongue'. His *Collected Poems* (1948) has an introduction by *MacDiarmid, and his *Diaries of a Dying Man*, ed. A. Scott, were published in 1954.

South, Marty, a character in Hardy's *The Woodlanders*.

SOUTHCOTT, Joanna (1750–1814), a religious fanatic and farmer's daughter who acquired a large following through her doggerel prophecies and supernatural claims.

SOUTHERNE, or **SOUTHERN,** Thomas (1659–1746), of Irish parentage. He was educated at Trinity College, Dublin, but came to London in 1680 and settled there. He was a friend of *Dryden, for several of whose plays he wrote prologues and epilogues. His first tragedy, *The Loyal Brother: or The Persian Prince* (1682), was, like Otway's *Venice Preserv'd*, its immediate contemporary, an attack on *Shaftesbury and the Whigs. He wrote several comedies, but is chiefly remembered for his two highly successful tragedies, *The Fatal Marriage* (1694) and *Oroonoko* (1695), both founded on novels by A. *Behn. Remarkably little is known of his long and, in later years, unproductive life, though there are many affectionate references to his good nature by Dryden, *Swift, *Dennis, *Cibber, and other friends. He became known as the Nestor of poets, and William Broome in a letter to *Pope (1725/6), on being asked to supply a preface to one of his late works, commented, 'His bays are withered with extreme age . . . It requires some skill to know when to leave off writing.' Southerne is regarded as a successor to *Otway in the art of pathos, and as a link between Restoration tragedy and the sentimental tragedies of the 18th cent. See J. W. Dodds, *Thomas Southerne, Dramatist* (1933).

SOUTHEY, Robert (1774–1843), the son of a Bristol linen draper, of a respectable Somerset family. Much of his lonely childhood was spent in the home of an eccentric aunt, Miss Tyler, where he acquired a precocious love of reading; he gives a vivid account of these years in letters written when he was 46 to his friend John May. He was expelled from Westminster School for originating a magazine, the *Flagellant*, and proceeded to Oxford with 'a heart full of poetry and feeling, a head full of Rousseau and Werther, and my religious principles shaken by Gibbon'. He became friendly with S. T. *Coleridge and together they planned their Pantisocratic society (see PANTISOCRACY). At Oxford he wrote a play, *Wat Tyler*, and another with Coleridge, *The Fall of Robespierre*. From this time on his literary output was prodigious. In 1795 he travelled to Portugal, married Edith Fricker (Coleridge married her sister Sara), and wrote *Joan of Arc* (1796). Between 1796 and 1798 he wrote many ballads, including *'The Inchcape Rock' and 'The Battle of *Blenheim', which had an influence in loosening the constrictions of 18th-cent. verse. In 1800 he went to Spain, and on his return settled in the Lake District, where he remained for the rest of his life as one of the *'Lake poets'. A narrative *Oriental verse romance, *Thalaba*, appeared in 1801, but sold poorly. In 1803 he published a translation of *Amadis of Gaul* (revised from an older version); in 1805, *Madoc*; and in 1807, the year in which he received a government pension, appeared a version of *Palmerin of England* and *Letters from England by Don Manuel Alvarez Espriella*, purporting to be from a young Spaniard and giving a lively account of life and manners in England. In 1808 he translated the *Chronicle of the Cid* and in 1809 began his long association with the *Quarterly Review*, which provided almost his only regular income for most of the rest of his life. A long Oriental poem, *The Curse of Kehama*, featuring much complex Hindu mythology, appeared in 1810 and *Omniana*, an original commonplace book, with contributions by Coleridge, in 1812. He was appointed in 1813 *poet laureate, a post which he came greatly to dislike, and in the same year published his short but admirable *Life of Nelson*. A narrative poem *Roderick: The Last of the Goths* appeared in 1814. In 1817 he produced an edition of *Malory and had to endure the publication, by his enemies, of his youthful and revolutionary *Wat Tyler*. The final volume of his *History of Brazil* (3 vols, 1810–19) appeared a year before his *Life of Wesley*. In 1821, to commemorate the death of George III, he wrote *A Vision of Judgement*, in the preface to which he vigorously attacked *Byron. Byron's parody in riposte, *The Vision of Judgement*, appeared in 1822, and Southey is frequently mocked in *Don Juan*. From 1823 to 1832 Southey was working on his *History of the Peninsular War*. In 1824 appeared *The Book of the Church* and in 1825 *A Tale of Paraguay*. His *Sir Thomas More*, in which he converses with the ghost of More, came out in 1829. In the same year appeared *All for Love; and The Pilgrim to Compostella*, and in 1832 *Essays Moral and Political* and the last volume of *History of the Peninsular War* (1823–32), which was overshadowed by *Napier's work on the same subject. Between 1832 and 1837 he worked on a life and an edition of *Cowper, and on his *Lives of the British Admirals* (1833). In 1835 he was granted a pension of £300 by Peel. His wife died in 1837, and in 1839 he married Caroline *Bowles. *The Doctor, etc.* was begun in 1834 (7 vols, 1834–47). Southey's last years were marked by an increasing mental decline.

His longer poems, now little read, were admired by men as diverse as *Fox, Sir W. *Scott, and *Macaulay. The scope of his reading and of his writing was vast, and his clear, firm prose style has been much esteemed; but in no sphere was his work of the highest distinction. Although an honest, generous man (who was particularly kind to Coleridge's abandoned family), he incurred the enmity of many of his contemporaries, in particular *Hazlitt and Byron, who felt that in accepting pensions and the laureateship, and in retracting his youthful Jacobinism, he was betraying principles. In *Melincourt T. L. Peacock caricatures him as Mr Feathernest.

See J. Simmons, *Robert Southey* (1945); *New Letters of Robert Southey*, ed. K. Curry (1965); *Robert Southey: The Critical Heritage*, ed. L. Madden (1972).

South Sea Company, the, formed in 1711 by *Harley (later earl of Oxford) to trade with Spanish America under the expected treaty with Spain. An exaggerated idea prevailed of the wealth to be acquired from the trading privileges granted by the Treaty of Utrecht and the Asiento Treaty, and money was readily invested in the Company. A bill was passed in 1720 by which persons to whom the nation owed money were enabled to convert their claims into shares in the Company, and the shares rose in value from £100 to £1,000. The Company shortly afterwards failed. But the scheme meanwhile had given rise to a fever of speculation, of which many unprincipled persons took advantage to obtain subscriptions from the public for the most impossible projects. The collapse of these and of the South Sea scheme caused widespread ruin. The whole affair was known as the South Sea Bubble and was the subject of satires by *Swift and *Hogarth. But the original idea of the South Sea Company was a sound one for perfectly honest trade. See John Carswell, *The South Sea Bubble* (rev. edn 1993).

The South-Sea House, where the Company had its offices, is the subject of one of Lamb's *Essays of Elia.

SOUTHWELL, St Robert (?1561–95), educated by the Jesuits at Douai and Rome. He took Roman orders and came to England in 1586 with Henry Garnett (who was subsequently executed for complicity in the Gunpowder Plot). He became in 1589 domestic chaplain to the countess of Arundel, was captured when going to celebrate mass in 1592, repeatedly tortured, and executed after three years' imprisonment. His poems were mainly written in prison. Of these it was his object to make spiritual love, instead of 'unworthy affections', the subject. His chief work was *St Peters Complaint*, published 1595, a long narrative of the closing events of the life of Christ in the mouth of the repentant Peter, in which the spiritual is contrasted with the material by numerous comparisons and antitheses. He also wrote many shorter devotional poems (some of them collected under the title *Moeoniae*, 1595) of a high order, notably 'The Burning Babe', praised by *Jonson. He was beatified in 1929 and canonized in 1970. His poems were edited by J. H. McDonald and N. P. Brown (1967).

SOUTHWORTH, E. D. E. N., see ROMANTIC FICTION.

Sowdone of Babylon, The, see FERUMBRAS, SIR.

Sowerberry, in Dickens's *Oliver Twist*, an undertaker, to whom Oliver is apprenticed when he leaves the workhouse.

SOYINKA, Wole (1934–), Nigerian dramatist and probably Africa's most versatile author, educated at the universities of Ibadan and Leeds. He was play reader at the *Royal Court Theatre, London, where his The Swamp Dwellers (1958), The Lion and the Jewel and The Invention (both 1959) were produced. These already demonstrated his development from simple Nigerian village comedies to a more complex and individual drama incorporating mime and dance. Back in Nigeria from 1960, a variety of university posts and the opportunity of producing and acting in his own plays gave him the self-confidence to undertake even more daring innovations, e.g. in A Dance of the Forests (1960), a half-satirical, half-fantastic celebration of Nigerian independence. Soyinka's first novel, The Interpreters (1965), captures the idealism of young Nigerians regarding the development of a new Africa—possibly anticipating a new Biafra. In prison for pro-Biafran activity during 1967–9, he produced increasingly bleak verse and prose, Madmen and Specialists (1970), and his second novel, Season of Anomy (1973). His translation of the Bacchae of *Euripides was commissioned by and performed at the *National Theatre in 1973. Death and the King's Horseman (1975) embodied his post-Biafran cultural philosophy, enunciated in Myth, Literature and the African World (1976), of the need for the distinct aesthetics of Africa and Europe to cross-fertilize each other. Another bleak period, coloured by the deteriorating political situation in Nigeria, followed this patch of optimism: later works include the drama A Play of Giants (1984), savagely portraying a group of African ex-dictators taking refuge in New York, and The Open Sore of a Continent (1996), denouncing the military regime in Nigeria, and the brutal execution in November 1995 of Nigerian writer and political activist Ken Saro-Wiwa. Soyinka himself had his Nigerian passport confiscated in 1994, and has since lived abroad, largely in the USA, while continuing actively to campaign for human rights. He was awarded the *Nobel Prize in 1986.

Spanish Bawd, The, see CELESTINA.

Spanish Curate, The, a comedy by J. *Fletcher, probably in collaboration with *Massinger, written and performed 1622, and based on *Gerardo, the Unfortunate Spaniard* (1622), translated from the Spanish of Céspedes by L. Digges. It was very popular after the Restoration.

The main plot deals with the intrigues of Don Henrique's mistress Violante, the failure of which leads to the reconciliation of Don Henrique with his divorced wife Jacinta and his brother Don Jamie; Violante is consigned to a nunnery. In the underplot, from which the play takes its name, Leandro, a rich young gentleman, plays on the cupidity of a priest and his sexton, and, with their help, on that of the lawyer Bartolus, the jealous husband of a beautiful wife, Amaranta, to facilitate his affair with her.

Spanish Fryar, The, a tragi-comedy by *Dryden, produced and published 1681.

The serious plot is characteristically about a usurpation. Torrismond, though he does not know it, is lawful heir to the throne, and secretly marries the reigning but unlawful queen, who has allowed Torrismond's father, the true king, to be murdered in prison. The sub-plot is dominated by Father Dominic, a monstrous corrupt friar, who uses the cant terms of Dissenters and who pimps for the libertine and whiggish Lorenzo. The latter is a highly dubious character, yet ironically it is through his agency that the lawful Torrismond is rescued. The woman Lorenzo is pursuing, however, turns out to be his sister. The play is like *Mr Limberham in breaching comic as well as tragic decorum and in its deeply sceptical treatment of religious and political orthodoxies.

Spanish Gipsy, The, (1) a romantic comedy by T. *Middleton and others (1625); (2) a dramatic poem by G. *Eliot (1868).

Spanish Tragedy, The, a tragedy, mostly in blank verse, by *Kyd, written c.1587, printed 11 times between 1592 and 1633.

The political background of the play is loosely related to the victory of Spain over Portugal in 1580. Lorenzo and Bel-imperia are the children of Don Cyprian, duke of Castile (brother of the king of Spain); Hieronimo is marshal of Spain and Horatio his son. Balthazar, son of the viceroy of Portugal, has been captured in the war. He courts Bel-imperia, and Lorenzo and the king of Spain favour his suit for political reasons. Lorenzo and Balthazar discover that Bel-imperia loves Horatio; they surprise the couple by night in Hieronimo's garden and hang Horatio on a tree. Hieronimo discovers his son's body and runs mad with grief. He succeeds nevertheless in discovering the identity of the murderers, and carries out revenge by means of a play, *Solyman and Perseda*, in which Lorenzo and Balthazar are killed, and Bel-imperia stabs herself. Hieronimo bites out his tongue before killing himself. The whole action is watched over by Revenge and the Ghost of Andrea who was previously killed in battle by Balthazar.

The play was the prototype of the English *revenge tragedy genre. It returned to the stage for decades and was seen by *Pepys as late as 1668.

*Jonson is known to have been paid for additions to the play, but the additional passages in the 1602 edition are probably not his. The play was one of Shakespeare's sources for *Hamlet and the alternative title given to it in 1615, *Hieronimo Is Mad Againe*, provided T. S. *Eliot with the penultimate line of *The Waste Land.

SPARK, Dame Muriel Sarah, née Camberg (1918–2006), author, of Scottish–Jewish descent, born and educated in Edinburgh. After spending some years in central Africa, which was to form the setting for several of her short stories, including the title story of *The Go-Away Bird* (1958) and one of its other tales, 'The Seraph and the Zambesi', she returned to Britain where she worked for the foreign office during the Second World War. She began her literary career as editor and biographer, working for the *Poetry Society and editing its *Poetry Review* from 1947 to 1949; the problems of biography and autobiography form the subject of *Loitering with Intent* (1981). She turned to fiction after winning the *Observer* short story competition in 1951, and in 1954 became a Roman Catholic. Her first novel, *The Comforters* (1957), was followed by many others, including *Memento Mori* (1959), a comic and macabre study of old age; *The Ballad of Peckham Rye* (1960), a bizarre tale of the underworld, mixing shrewd social observation with hints of necromancy; perhaps her best-known work, *The Prime of Miss Jean Brodie* (1961), a disturbing portrait of an Edinburgh schoolmistress and her group of favoured pupils, her 'crème de la crème'; *The Girls of Slender Means* (1963), a tragicomedy set in a Kensington hostel in 1945; *The Public Image* (1968); *The Driver's Seat* (1970), about a woman possessed by a death-wish; *The Abbess of Crewe* (1974), a satirical fantasy about ecclesiastical and other kinds of politics; and *The Take Over* (1976), set in Italy, where she settled. Her novels, with the exception of the lengthy and uncharacteristic *The Mandelbaum Gate* (1965), are short, elegant, eccentric, and sophisticated, with touches of the bizarre and the perverse; many have a quality of fable or parable, and her use of narrative omniscience is highly distinctive. She also wrote plays and poems; her *Collected Poems* and *Collected Plays* were both published in 1967. A collected edition of her stories appeared in 1986. Later novels include *A Far Cry from Kensington* (1988), and *Aiding and Abetting* (2000), which is based on the real story of Lord Lucan. A volume of autobiography, *Curriculum Vitae*, appeared in 1992. A volume of poems, *Going up to Sotheby's*, was published in 1982.

Sparkish, a character in Wycherley's *The Country Wife.

Sparkler, Edmund, a character in Dickens's *Little Dorrit*, who marries Fanny, Little Dorrit's sister.

Sparsit, Mrs, a character in Dickens's *Hard Times.

Spasmodic school, a term applied by *Aytoun to a group of poets which included P. J. *Bailey, J. W. *Marston, S. T. *Dobell, and Alexander *Smith. Their works for a brief while enjoyed great esteem; this was largely destroyed by Aytoun's attacks and by his parody *Firmilian* (1854), which also satirized their critical champion, *Gilfillan. Spasmodic poems tended to describe intense interior psychological drama, were violent and verbose, and were characterized by obscurity, *pathetic fallacy, and extravagant imagery;

their heroes (who owed much to *Byron and *Goethe) were lonely, aspiring, and disillusioned, and frequently poets themselves. See M. A. Weinstein, *W. E. Aytoun and the Spasmodic Controversy* (1968).

Specimens of English Dramatic Poets *Who Lived about the Time of Shakespeare*, by C. *Lamb, published 1808; an anthology, with brief but cogent and illuminating critical comments, of extracts of scenes and speeches from Elizabethan and Jacobean dramatists, many of them little known or regarded in Lamb's day. His selections include extracts from *Beaumont and *Fletcher, *Jonson, *Marlowe, *Webster, and some dozen others. The book did much to draw the attention of Lamb's contemporaries to this period of drama, which Lamb himself greatly enjoyed 'beyond the diocese of strict conscience'.

Spectator, (1) a periodical conducted by *Steele and *Addison, from 1 Mar. 1711 to 6 Dec. 1712. It was revived by Addison in 1714, when 80 numbers (556–635) were issued, but the first series has been generally considered superior, except by *Macaulay, who found the last volume to contain 'perhaps the finest Essays, both serious and playful, in the English language' (*Edinburgh Review*, July 1843). It appeared daily, and was immensely popular, particularly with the new growing middle-class readership. Addison and Steele were the principal contributors, in about equal proportions; other contributors included *Pope, *Tickell, *Budgell, A. *Philips, *Eusden, and Lady M. W. *Montagu.

It purported to be conducted (see the first two numbers) by a small club, including Sir Roger de *Coverley, who represents the country gentry, Sir Andrew Freeport, Captain Sentry, and Will Honeycomb, representing respectively commerce, the army, and the town. Mr Spectator himself, who writes the papers, is a man of travel and learning, who frequents London as an observer, but keeps clear of political strife. The papers are mainly concerned with manners, morals, and literature. Their object is 'to enliven morality with wit, and to temper wit with morality', and succeeding generations of readers endorsed *E. Young's view that the periodical (which succeeded the *Tatler) provided 'a wholesome and pleasant regimen'; both its style and its morals were considered exemplary by Dr *Johnson, H. *Blair, and other arbiters. There is a five-volume edition by Donald F. Bond, published 1965.

(2) A weekly periodical started in 1828 by Robert Stephen Rintoul, with funds provided by Joseph Hume and others, as an organ of 'educated radicalism'. It supported Lord John Russell's *Reform Bill of 1831 with a demand for 'the Bill, the whole Bill, and nothing but the Bill'. R. H. *Hutton was joint editor, 1861–97. John St Loe Strachey (1860–1927) was editor and proprietor from 1898 to 1925, and his cousin Lytton *Strachey was a frequent contributor. Other notable contributors in later years include P. *Fleming, G.

*Greene, E. *Waugh, P. *Quennell, K. *Amis, Clive James, Bernard Levin, Peregrine Worsthorne, Katharine Whitehorn, and Auberon *Waugh: a lively new wave of younger writers is represented by Simon Heffer, Andrew Roberts, and Boris Johnson (editor, 1999).

Speculum Meditantis (*Mirour de l'omme*), see GOWER, J.

Speculum Stultorum, see WIREKER.

SPEDDING, James (1808–81), educated at Trinity College, Cambridge. He edited *The Works of Francis Bacon* (7 vols, 1857–9). His *Evenings with a Reviewer* (1848) was a refutation of *Macaulay's 'Essay' on *Bacon which he subsequently developed in his *The Letters and Life of Francis Bacon* (1861–72).

Speed, Valentine's servant in Shakespeare's *The Two Gentlemen of Verona*.

SPEED, John (?1552–1629), historian and cartographer. He made various maps of English counties, and was encouraged by *Camden, *Cotton, and others to write his *History of Great Britaine* (1611). The maps were far more valuable than the history; they began about 1607, and an atlas of them appeared in 1611. There were several later editions of this (called *The Theatre of the Empire of Great Britaine*), and the maps are now constantly detached and sold separately.

Speed the Plough, see MORTON, T.

SPEGHT, Rachel (b. 1597, fl. 1621), daughter of a London Puritan minister, James Speght, who published at the age of 19 a spirited rebuttal of Joseph Sweetnam's misogynist *Arraignment of Lewd, Idle, Froward and Inconstant Women*. Her *A Mouzell for Melastomus* (1617) (A Muzzle for a Black Mouth) objected to the 'excrement of your raving cogitations' as a slander on woman, who, as Eve's daughter, was fashioned from Adam's side, not his head or foot, 'near his heart, to be his equal'. In 1621 she published *Mortalities Memorandum, with a Dreame Prefixed*, the latter being an allegorical narrative poem urging the education of women, under guidance of tutelary female personifications (Thought, Experience, Industrie, Desire, Truth). *A Mouzell* is reprinted in S. Shepherd (ed.), *The Women's Sharp Revenge* (1984).

SPEKE, John Hanning (1827–64), explorer, who discovered Lake Victoria Nyanza, Lake Tanganyika, and gave information to Sir S. *Baker which led to the discovery of Lake Albert Nyanza. He published in 1863 his *Journal of the Discovery of the Source of the Nile* and in 1864 *What Led to the Discovery of the Source of the Nile*.

SPENCE, Joseph (1699–1768), clergyman, anecdotist, scholar, who succeeded T. *Warton as professor of poetry at Oxford in 1728. A man of much generosity, he befriended *Dodsley in his early days, later helping him to edit his celebrated *Collection of Poems*, and also S. *Duck, whose life he wrote (1731, reprinted with Duck's poems, 1736). He also wrote a life of the blind poet *Blacklock (1754). He was a close friend of *Pope, whose version of the *Odyssey* he defended, and from 1726 collected anecdotes and recorded conversations with Pope and other literary figures. These, although not published until 1820, were well known and widely quoted during the 18th cent., and were made available to and used by *Warburton and Dr *Johnson. They are usually referred to under the title *Spence's Anecdotes*: an edition by J. M. Osborn appeared in 1966 under the title *Observations, Anecdotes, and Characters of Books and Men, Collected from Conversation*.

SPENCER, Herbert (1820–1903), the son of a school-master, who was largely self-taught and showed few intellectual interests until he was over 16. He worked as a civil engineer for the London and Birmingham Railway Company, and was discharged on its completion in 1841; he then turned his attention to philosophy and published *Social Statics* (1850) and *Principles of Psychology* (1855); in 1860, after reading C. *Darwin, he announced a systematic series of treatises, to the elaboration of which he devoted the remainder of his life: *First Principles* (1862), *Principles of Biology* (1864–7), *Principles of Sociology* (1876–96), and *Principles of Ethics* (1879–93). Among his other works were *Essays on Education* (1861), *The Classification of the Sciences* (1864), *The Study of Sociology* (1873), *Man versus the State* (1884), and *Factors of Organic Evolution* (1887). His *Autobiography* was published in 1904.

Spencer was the founder of evolutionary philosophy, pursuing the unification of all knowledge on the basis of a single all-pervading principle, that of evolution, which he defines as follows: 'an integration of matter and concomitant dissipation of emotion; during which matter passes from an indefinite incoherent homogeneity to a definite coherent heterogeneity; and during which the retained motion undergoes a parallel transformation'. The process continues until equilibrium is reached, after which the action of the environment will in time bring about disintegration. The law holds good of the visible universe as well as of smaller aggregates, suggesting the conception of past and future evolutions such as that which is now proceeding.

This theory of a physical system leads up to Spencer's ethical system, where he is less successful in producing a consistent whole. He was essentially an individualist, and his first ethical principle is the equal right of every individual to act as he likes, so long as he does not interfere with the liberty of others. His effort is to reconcile utilitarian with evolutionary ethics, but he had to confess that for the purpose of deducing ethical principles 'the Doctrine of Evolution has not furnished guidance to the extent that I had hoped'. Special reference should be made to *Education, Intellectual,*

Moral and Physical (1861), a collection of articles previously published in magazines in which he criticized standard methods of teaching Latin and Greek, which crushed the spirit of individual enquiry, and advocated the teaching of the sciences, including social sciences, because they were concerned with the problems of survival. Art, although it had no problem-solving power, was important because it yielded immediate good.

In a literary context Spencer is remembered for his friendship with G. *Eliot, whom he met in 1851; he found her 'the most admirable woman, mentally, I have ever met' and wrote to *Lewes praising *Middlemarch* highly, but after her death he was at pains to quell any rumour that they had ever been more than friends. She appears to have been much more strongly attached to him, but transferred her affections to Lewes (c.1852–3). Spencer died a bachelor.

SPENCER, Sir Stanley (1891–1959), a biblically inspired artist famous for resurrecting the natives of the village of Cookham-on-Thames in Berkshire where he lived. He was one of the models for Gully Jimson, the painter in Joyce *Cary's novel *The Horse's Mouth*, and the subject of a play, *Stanley*, by Pam Gems, performed at the *National Theatre in 1996.

Spence's Anecdotes, see SPENCE.

SPENDER, Sir Stephen Harold (1909–95), poet and critic. His father E. H. Spender was a distinguished liberal journalist, and on his mother's side he was partly of German–Jewish descent. He was brought up in Hampstead, and educated at University College School, London, and University College, Oxford, where he became friendly with *Auden and *MacNeice and met *Isherwood. After leaving Oxford he lived in Germany for a period, in Hamburg and near Isherwood in Berlin, an experience which sharpened his political consciousness. In 1930 a small collection of his verse, *Twenty Poems*, was published, and in 1932 some of his work appeared in *New Signatures*; his *Poems* (1933) contained both personal and political poems, including 'I think continually of those who are truly great', 'The Landscape near an Aerodrome', and the notorious 'The Pylons', which gave the nickname of *'Pylon poets' to himself and his friends. He also published a critical work, *The Destructive Element* (1935), largely on H. *James, T. S. *Eliot, and *Yeats and their differing responses to a civilization in decline, which ends with a section called 'In Defence of a Political Subject', in which he discusses the work of Auden and *Upward, and argues the importance of treating 'politico-moral' subjects in literature. During the Spanish Civil War he did propaganda work in Spain for the Republican side, a period reflected in his volume of poems *The Still Centre* (1939). During the Second World War he was a member of the National Fire Service. He was co-editor of *Horizon (1939–41) and of *Encounter (1953–67). A gradual shift in his political allegiances may be seen in his poetry, in his critical works (e.g. *The Creative Element*, 1953, which retracts some of his earlier suggestions, laying more stress on the creative power and resistance of the individual), and in his contribution to *The God that Failed*; he also gives an account of his relationship with the Communist Party in his autobiography *World within World* (1951). His interest in the public and social role and duty of the writer (a duty which he subsequently maintained in his work for the magazine *Index on Censorship*) has tended to obscure the essentially personal and private nature of much of his own poetry, including his elegies for his sister-in-law, in *Poems of Dedication* (1947), and many of the poems in such later volumes as *Collected Poems 1928–1953* (1955). His other works include *Trial of a Judge* (1938), many translations (of *García Lorca, *Rilke, *Schiller, *Toller, and others), *The Thirties and after* (1978, a volume of memoirs), *Collected Poems 1982–85* (1985), and his lively and often comically self-deprecating *Journals 1939–83* (1985). *The Temple* (1988) is a novel inspired by an abandoned manuscript written in 1929 about a young Englishman on vacation in Germany, it contains fictionalized portraits of Auden, Isherwood, and photographer Herbert List, and evokes a brief Golden Age in Germany before the imminent rise of National Socialism. See *Stephen Spender: A Literary Life* (2004) by John Sutherland.

Spenlow, Dora, in Dickens's *David Copperfield*, the hero's 'child-wife'.

Spenlow and Jorkins, in Dickens's *David Copperfield*, a firm of proctors in Doctors' Commons, to whom Copperfield is articled. Jorkins is a gentle, retiring man who seldom appears, but Spenlow makes his partner's supposed intractable character the ground for refusing any inconvenient request.

Spens, Sir Patrick, see SIR PATRICK SPENS.

SPENSER, Edmund (*c*.1552–99), the elder son of John Spenser, who was probably related to the Spencers of Althorp, and was described as a journeyman in the art of cloth-making. Edmund Spenser was probably born in East Smithfield, London, and was educated at Merchant Taylors' School, under *Mulcaster, and Pembroke Hall, Cambridge. In 1569, while still at Cambridge, he contributed a number of 'Visions' and sonnets, from *Petrarch and *du Bellay, to van der Noodt's *Theatre for Worldlings*. To the 'greener times' of his youth belong also the 'Hymne in Honour of Love' and that of 'Beautie' (not published until 1596), which reflect his study of *Neoplatonism. After possibly spending some time in the north, he became secretary to John Young, bishop of Rochester, in 1578, and in 1579, through his college friend G. *Harvey, obtained a place in Leicester's household. There he became acquainted with Sir P. *Sidney, to whom he dedicated his *Shepheardes Calender* (1579). He probably married Machabyas Chylde in the same year, and also began to write *The Faerie Queene*. In 1580 he was

appointed secretary to Lord Grey of Wilton, then going to Ireland as lord deputy. In 1588 or 1589 he became one of the 'undertakers' for the settlement of Munster, and acquired Kilcolman Castle in Co. Cork. Here he settled and occupied himself with literary work, writing his elegy *'Astrophel', on Sidney, and preparing *The Faerie Queene* for the press. The first three books of it were entrusted to the publisher during his visit to London in 1589. He returned reluctantly to Kilcolman, which he liked to regard as a place of exile, in 1591, recording his visit to London and return to Ireland in *Colin Clouts Come Home Againe* (printed 1595). The success of *The Faerie Queene* led the publisher, Ponsonby, to issue his minor verse and juvenilia, in part rewritten, as *Complaints, Containing Sundrie Small Poemes of the Worlds Vanitie* (1591). This volume included *'The Ruines of Time', which was a further elegy on Sidney, dedicated to Sidney's sister, the countess of *Pembroke, *'Mother Hubberds Tale', *Muiopotmos*, *'The Tears of the Muses', and *'Virgils Gnat'. Also in 1591 *Daphnaïda* was published, an elegy on Douglas Howard, the daughter of Lord Byndon and wife of Sir A. *Gorges. In 1594 he married Elizabeth Boyle, whom he had wooed in his *Amoretti*, and celebrated the marriage in his superb *Epithalamion*: the works were printed together in 1595. He published Books IV–VI of *The Faerie Queene* and his *Fowre Hymnes* in 1596, being in London for the purpose at the house of his friend the earl of Essex, where he wrote his *Prothalamion* and also his well-informed though propagandist *View of the Present State of Ireland*. He returned to Ireland, depressed both in mind and health, in 1596 or 1597. His castle of Kilcolman was burnt in October 1598, in a sudden insurrection of the natives, chiefly O'Neills, under the earl of Desmond; he was compelled to flee to Cork with his wife and three children. We do not know what works, if any, were lost at Kilcolman, but Ponsonby in 1591 had mentioned various other works by Spenser which are not now extant, and in *The Shepheardes Calender* reference is made to his discourse of the 'English Poet'. He died in London in distress, if not actual destitution, at a lodging in King Street, Westminster. His funeral expenses were borne by the earl of Essex, and he was buried near his favourite *Chaucer in Westminster Abbey. His monument, set up some 20 years later by Lady Anne Clifford, describes him as 'THE PRINCE OF POETS IN HIS TYME': there have been few later periods in which he has not been admired, and the poetry of both *Milton and *Keats had its origins in the reading of Spenser.

See the Variorum edition of his works, with a biography and full critical commentary, ed. E. Greenlaw, C. G. Osgood, F. M. Padelford, et al. (10 vols, 1932–57).

Spenserian stanza, the stanza invented by E. *Spenser, in which he wrote *The Faerie Queene*. It consists of eight five-foot iambic lines, followed by an iambic line of six feet, rhyming a b a b b c b c c.

SPINOZA, Benedict (Baruch) de (1632–77), a Jew of Portuguese origin, born at Amsterdam, who lived there and at The Hague. He was expelled from the Jewish community on account of his criticism of the Scriptures. The principal source of his philosophy was the doctrine of *Descartes, transformed by a mind steeped in the Jewish Scriptures. Spinoza rejected the Cartesian dualism of spirit and matter, and saw only 'one infinite substance, of which finite existences are modes or limitations'. The universe must be viewed 'sub specie aeternitatis', and the errors of sense and the illusions of the finite eliminated. God for him is the immanent cause of the universe, not a ruler outside it. 'By the government of God, I understand the fixed and unalterable order of nature and the interconnection of natural things.' His system is thus in a sense pantheistic. Among his conclusions are determinism, a denial of the transcendent distinction between good and evil, and a denial of personal immortality.

Spinoza's famous *Ethics*, finished about 1665, was not published until 1677, after his death. His morality is founded on the 'intellectual love' of God. Man is moved by his instinct to develop and perfect himself, and to seek this development in the knowledge and love of God. And the love of God involves the love of our fellow creatures. It is by goodness and piety that man reaches perfect happiness: virtue is its own reward.

Spinoza founds his political doctrine on man's natural rights. Man, in order to obtain security, has surrendered part of his rights to the state. But the state exists to give liberty, not to hold in slavery. The sovereign in his own interest must rule with justice and wisdom, nor must the state interfere with freedom of thought. Spinoza's *Tractatus Theologico-politicus* was published in 1670; his unfinished *Tractatus Politicus* in 1677.

Spirit of the Age, The, essays by W. *Hazlitt, published 1825, presented as a portrait gallery of the eminent writers of his time: *Bentham, W. *Godwin, *Coleridge, *Wordsworth, W. *Scott, *Byron, *Southey, *Malthus, C. *Lamb, and several others. The essays combine character-sketches with lively critical assessments of the subjects' works and summaries of their reputations, placed in the context of the political and intellectual ferment of their times. They are strongly animated by Hazlitt's political loyalties, especially in the sustained assault upon the Tory critic *Gifford for his 'ridiculous pedantry and vanity'.

Spiritual Exercises, see IGNATIUS LOYOLA.

Spiritual Quixote, The, see GRAVES, RICHARD.

Spleen, The, (1) a poem by Anne Finch, countess of *Winchilsea (1709); (2) a poem by M. *Green (1737).

spondee, see METRE.

Sponge, Mr Soapey, see SURTEES, R. S.

Spoonerism, see METATHESIS.

Sporus, the name under which *Pope satirizes Lord *Hervey in his *Epistle to Dr Arbuthnot* (ll. 305 ff.). The original Sporus was an effeminate favourite of the Emperor Nero.

SPRAT, Thomas (1635–1713), educated at Wadham College, Oxford, bishop of Rochester and dean of Westminster. Politically he was inclined to be a '*vicar of Bray'; he sat on James II's objectionable ecclesiastical commission in 1686 and allowed the Declaration of Indulgence to be read (amid deep murmurs of disapproval) in the abbey. As a writer he is chiefly remembered for his history of the *Royal Society (1667), of which he was one of the first members, but he was also known as a poet (*The Plague of Athens*, 1659, was his most popular poem) and for his life of his friend *Cowley, which was attached to Cowley's works from 1668 onwards.

SPRING, (Robert) Howard (1889–1965), journalist and novelist, born in Cardiff, where he began his literary career as a newspaper errand boy; he worked for years on the *Manchester Guardian and as book reviewer on the *Evening Standard*. Of his many novels, the best remembered are his first success *O Absalom!* (1938; published in the USA and later in Britain as *My Son, My Son!*) and *Fame Is the Spur* (1940), the latter being the story of a Labour politician's rise to power.

sprung, or **'abrupt', rhythm,** a term invented by G. M. *Hopkins to describe his own idiosyncratic poetic metre, as opposed to normal 'running' rhythm, the regular alternation of stressed and unstressed syllables. It was apparently based partly on Greek and Latin quantitative metre and influenced by the rhythms of Welsh poetry and Old and Middle English *alliterative verse. Hopkins maintained that sprung rhythm existed, unrecognized, in Old English poetry and in Shakespeare, *Dryden, and *Milton (notably in *Samson Agonistes*). It is distinguished by a metrical foot consisting of a varying number of syllables. The extra, 'slack' syllables added to the established patterns are called 'outrides' or 'hangers'. Hopkins demonstrated the natural occurrence of this rhythm in English by pointing out that many nursery rhymes employed it, e.g.

> Díng, Dóng, Béll,
> Pússy's in the wéll.

Conventional metres may be varied by the use of 'counterpoint', by which Hopkins meant the reversal of two successive feet in an otherwise regular line of poetry; but sprung rhythm itself cannot be counterpointed because it is not regular enough for the pattern to be recognized under the variations. Hopkins, an amateur composer, often described his theory in terms of musical notation, speaking of rests, crotchets, and quavers. He felt strongly that his poetry should be read aloud, but seems to have felt that the words themselves were not enough to suggest the intended rhythms, and frequently added various diacritical markings to indicate where a sound was to be drawn out, and where syllables were to be spoken quickly. Some critics have suggested that sprung rhythm is not a poetic metre at all, properly speaking, merely Hopkins's attempt to force his own personal rhythm into an existing pattern, or recognizable variation of one, and that his sprung rhythm is in fact closer to some kinds of free verse or polyphonic prose.

SPURGEON, Caroline (1886–1942), American critic, whose *Shakespeare's Imagery* (1935) was the first detailed study of its subject.

spy fiction, see overleaf.

Square, a character in Fielding's *Tom Jones*.

Squeers, Wackford, in Dickens's *Nicholas Nickleby*, the headmaster of Dotheboys Hall. He has a heartless wife, who joins him in bullying his miserable pupils, a spiteful daughter, Fanny, and a spoilt son, Wackford.

Squeezum, Justice, a character in *Fielding's Rape upon Rape*.

SQUIRE, J(ohn) C(ollings) (1884–1958), educated in Devon and at St John's College, Cambridge; he became a highly influential literary journalist and essayist, a skilful parodist, and a poet. He established the *London Mercury* in 1919, and as sometime literary editor of the *New Statesman* and chief literary critic of the *Observer* he exercised considerable power. In the 1920s and 1930s he and his friends formed a literary establishment which was violently opposed by the *Sitwells and the *Bloomsbury Group, and was irreverently known as 'the Squirearchy'. Squire edited a large number of successful anthologies, including *A Book of Women's Verse* (1921) and *The Comic Muse* (1925), and between 1921 and 1934 edited three widely popular volumes of *Selections from Modern Poets*. His own *Collected Parodies* appeared in 1921, he was knighted in 1933, and his *Collected Poems*, edited by *Betjeman, were published posthumously in 1959.

Squire of Dames, a humorous character in Spenser's *Faerie Queene* (III. vii). He had been ordered by his lady to 'do service unto gentle Dames' and at the end of 12 months to report progress. At the end of the year he was able to bring pledges of 300 conquests. Thereupon his lady ordered him not to return to her till he had found an equal number of dames who rejected his advances. After three years he had only found three, a courtesan because he would not pay her enough, a nun because she could not trust his discretion, and a 'Damzell' of low degree 'in a countrey cottage found by chaunce'.

Squire of Low Degree, The, a metrical romance, probably mid-15th cent., opening with the much-quoted distich:

> It was a squier of lowe degree
> That loved the Kings doughter of Hungré.

The squire declares his love to the princess, who consents to marry him when he has proved himself a distinguished knight. But he is seen in his tryst by a steward whom he kills after the steward reports to the king. The squire is imprisoned but finally released because the princess is inconsolable, whereupon he sets out on his quest, proves his worth, and marries the princess. There is no manuscript of the full-length, 1,131-line version, so the romance is known from a printing c.1560 by W. Copland and fragments of a 1520 printing by Wynkyn de *Worde; de Worde's edition is dramatically entitled 'Undo youre Dore' from one of its episodes. Ed. D. B. Sands, *Middle English Verse Romances* (1966), 249–78.

'Squire's Tale, The', see CANTERBURY TALES, 11.

Squyre Meldrum, The Historie of, see LINDSAY, SIR D.

STACPOOLE, H(enry) de Vere (1863–1951), novelist and ship's doctor, of Irish ancestry, whose first publication was a poem in *Belgravia*, but who is remembered for his best-selling romance *The Blue Lagoon* (1908), the story of two cousins, Dick and Emmeline, marooned at the age of 8 on a tropical island; they grow up, mature, produce a baby, and are eventually swept away by accident across their lagoon to the ocean and the oblivion of 'the never-wake berries' which they providentially carry with them in their dinghy.

STAËL, Anne-Louise-Germaine Necker, Mme de (1766–1817), French writer of Swiss parentage. Daughter of the finance minister Necker and mistress of *Constant, she occupied a central place in French intellectual life for over three decades. Her critical study *De la littérature considérée dans ses rapports avec les institutions sociales* (1800) was the first piece of criticism to treat literature as a product of social history and environment. Another study, *De l'Allemagne* (1810), banned on publication by Napoleon, opened French literature to the influence of the German writers and thinkers of the end of the 18th cent. Her two novels, *Delphine* (1802) and *Corinne* (1807), offer to her age a new image of woman as independent artist. She was a major precursor of French Romanticism.

STAINER, Pauline (1941–), poet, educated at St Anne's College, Oxford, and Southampton University. Her first collection, *The Honeycomb* (1989), introduced a characteristic mingling of sacred, archaeological, scientific, and wintry ice-haunted imagery, and a cool, spare lyric line. This was followed by *Sighting the Slave Ship* (1992), which contains poems in homage to Rembrandt, Satie, Henry Moore, and illustrator and war artist Eric Ravilious, who died in 1942 when the Coastal Command aeroplane from Iceland on which he was a passenger disappeared. Other volumes include *The Ice-Pilot Speaks* (1994) and *The Wound-Dresser's Dream* (1996).

Stalky & Co., tales of schoolboy life, by *Kipling.

STALLWORTHY, Jon (1935–), poet, critic, editor, translator, and biographer, born in London and educated at Rugby and Magdalen College, Oxford. He subsequently worked for the *Oxford University Press and taught in Oxford, where in 1992 he became professor of English literature. His first collection of poetry, *The Astronomy of Love* (1961), was followed by several others, including *A Familiar Tree* (1978), a sequence which mixes deep-rooted family and local history with a story of migration, and *The Guest from the Future* (1995), which celebrates female survival in the person of *Akhmatova and others. The title of *Rounding the Horn: Collected Poems* (1998) pays homage, as do many of his individual poems, to his New Zealand ancestry. He has published biographies of W. *Owen (1974), whose work he has also edited, and L. *MacNeice (1995), and has edited several anthologies, with a particular interest in war poetry.

Stand, a literary quarterly founded in 1952 by J. *Silkin, and published from 1965 in Newcastle upon Tyne. It publishes poetry, fiction, and criticism, and contributors have included G. *Hill, G. *MacBeth, Lorna Tracy (also a co-editor), D. *Abse, and many others; it has also published many works in translation by M. *Holub (Czechoslovakia), N. Hikmet (Turkey), *Brodsky and *Yevtushenko (USSR), etc. An anthology, *Poetry of the Committed Individual*, appeared in 1973.

STANFORD, Sir Charles Villiers (1852–1924), British composer and teacher. With *Parry, Stanford was a founder figure of the English musical renaissance in the last decades of the 19th cent., whose pupils included virtually all the most successful English composers of the following generation, from *Holst and *Vaughan Williams to *Lambert and *Bliss. His list of compositions includes many settings of English texts. Of the choral works the larger ones, like the oratorio *Eden* to words by *Bridges (1891), are now forgotten, but the less pretentious examples, the setting of *Tennyson's 'The Revenge' (1886) or the later *Newbolt cantatas, *Songs of the Sea* (1904) and *Songs of the Fleet* (1910), combine perfect craftsmanship with a racy vigour that has commended them to festivals and choral societies over the years. His nine operas have had little success, with the possible exception of *Shamus O'Brien* (1896, with a text after *Le Fanu); others that perhaps deserved a better fate are *Much Ado about Nothing* (1901), *The Critic* (based on *Sheridan's play, 1916), and, perhaps best, *The Travelling Companion* (1926), with a libretto by Newbolt after H. C. *Anderson.

STANHOPE, Lady Hester (1776–1839), the niece of the younger *Pitt, in whose house she gained a reputation as a brilliant political hostess. In 1810 she left Europe for good, and in 1814 established herself for the rest of her life in a remote ruined convent at Djoun in the Lebanon. Here she lived in great magnificence among a semi-oriental retinue; her high rank and imperious character gained her some political power in Syria and the desert. In later years her debts accumulated, her eccentricity increased, and she claimed to be an inspired prophetess and mistress of occult sciences. She became a legendary figure, and was visited by many distinguished European travellers, including *Lamartine and *Kinglake.

Stanhope press, an iron printing press invented by Charles, third Earl Stanhope (1753–1816), the father of Lady Hester (above). He also devised a stereotyping process, and a microscopic lens which bears his name.

STANLEY, Arthur Penrhyn (1815–81), educated at Rugby under T. *Arnold (by whom he was much influenced) and at Balliol College, Oxford. On Arnold's death he was commissioned to write a biography by his widow, which appeared in 1844 as *The Life and Correspondence of Thomas Arnold*. Stanley was an ecclesiastical historian, a leader of the *Broad Church movement, and a courageous champion of religious toleration.

STANLEY, Sir Henry Morton (1841–1904), explorer and journalist, born in Wales; he first bore the name John Rowlands. He went to New Orleans as a cabin boy in 1859 where he was adopted by a merchant named Stanley. He fought in the American Civil War and in 1867 joined the *New York Herald*. He went as its correspondent to Abyssinia and Spain, and in 1869 was instructed by his editor Gordon Bennett to find *Livingstone. He first travelled through Egypt for the opening of the Suez Canal, and to Palestine, Turkey, Persia, and India; he found Livingstone at Ujiji in 1871. *How I Found Livingstone* (1872) relates these adventures. His further explorations and discoveries in Africa are described in *Through the Dark Continent* (1878) and *In Darkest Africa* (1890). In 1890 he married Dorothy Tennant who edited his autobiography in 1909.

STANLEY, Thomas (1625–78), a descendant of Edward Stanley, third earl of Derby, educated at Pembroke Hall, Cambridge. He was author of *The History of Philosophy* (1655–62), an edition of *Aeschylus (1663), and translations from *Theocritus, *Bion, Ausonius, *Moschus, *Marino, and others, besides original poems.

Stanzaic Life of Christ, The, a 14th-cent. compilation surviving in three 15th-cent. manuscripts in 10,840 lines of English quatrains, drawn from the *Polychronicon* of *Higden and the *Legenda Aurea* of Jacobus de Voragine (see GOLDEN LEGEND, THE). It was written by a monk of St Werburgh's, Chester, and it was an influence on the Chester *mystery plays. Ed. F. A. Foster (EETS OS 166, 1926).

STAPLEDON, Olaf, see SCIENCE FICTION.

One of the most popular forms of fiction over the last 100 years, the British spy novel emerged during the international tensions of the years preceding the First World War. Scandals like the *Dreyfus affair in France highlighted the activities of spies and the intelligence services that employed them, while armaments rivalries such as the Anglo-German naval race fuelled a volatile mood of jingoism and xenophobia receptive to novels of espionage, intrigue, and violence, in which secret agent heroes battled against the evil machinations of villainous spies. The 20th cent.'s record of war, revolution, subversion, genocide, and the threat of nuclear war has sustained the appeal.

Erskine *Childers's *The Riddle of the Sands* (1903), a suspenseful tale of two amateur British agents foiling a German invasion plot, is often described as the first spy novel, and has become a classic. But the first spy writer to spring to public fame was William Tufnell Le Queux (1864–1927), whose highly successful invasion novel *The Great War in England in 1897* (1893), featuring an enemy spy, heralded a cascade of best-sellers over the next three decades, all of which employ a series of heroic male agents cut from sturdy patriotic cloth who save the nation from the plots of foreign spies. Setting an enduring trend in spy fiction, Le Queux—who fantasized about being a spy himself—deliberately blurred the line between fact and fiction to make spurious claims of authenticity and realism, and his fiction was often thinly disguised propaganda for strengthened national security. The lurid portrait of an army of German spies in Britain in his *Spies of the Kaiser* (1909) did much to create the mood of spy fever that prompted the creation in that year of the Secret Service Bureau, later to become MI5 and MI6. Le Queux's great Edwardian rival was E. Phillips Oppenheim (1866–1946), who wrote a succession of novels featuring glamorous seductresses and society high life that continued until the Second World War and which, unlike those of Le Queux, also sold well in North America; amongst the best known are *The Kingdom of the Blind* (1916) and *The Great Impersonation* (1920). The year 1920 also saw the creation by *Sapper of the unabashed xenophobe and anti-Semite Bulldog Drummond, a muscular agent who over the next two decades robustly thwarted the plots of the communist arch-villain Carl Peterson and assorted foreigners in such titles as *The Black Gang* (1922), *The Final Count* (1926), and *The Return of Bulldog Drummond* (1932).

Yet from this inaugural period the writer who has best endured is John *Buchan, whose secret agent hero Richard Hannay first appeared in *The Thirty-Nine Steps* (1915), a novel its author described as 'a romance where the incidents defy the probabilities, and march just inside the borders of the possible', which defines much other spy fiction as well. There followed such classics as *Greenmantle* (1916), *Mr Standfast* (1919), and *The Three Hostages* (1924). Hannay and his adventures set their stamp on the imagination of a generation and beyond. Recurrent criticism of the hearty clubland ethos of Buchan's fiction provides exasperated testimony of how popular his novels have remained to this day.

The First World War, the Great Depression, and the rise of Fascism created a sombre inter-war climate that saw the emergence of a new generation of spy writers who broke sharply with the patriotic orthodoxies of their predecessors. Some, such as Compton *Mackenzie and Somerset *Maugham, had worked for British wartime intelligence and painted a far less glamorized and more realistic picture of the secret agent's life, such as in Maugham's *Ashenden* (1928), his influential collection of short stories based closely on his personal experience. Mackenzie, prosecuted under the Official Secrets Act for indiscretions in his third volume of wartime memoirs, *Greek Memories* (1932), took his revenge in his classic parody of the bureaucratic absurdities of the secret service, *Water on the Brain* (1933).

Building on the foundations laid by Maugham and Mackenzie, Eric *Ambler crafted plots of considerable technical skill and authenticity, combined with a leftist outlook that featured innocent protagonists caught up in the machinations of 'merchants of death' and other capitalist villains. His best-known and most successful novel of this period was *The Mask of Dimitrios* (1939), but his post-war production retained its vigour in such masterpieces as *Passage of Arms* (1959), *Dr. Frigo* (1974), and *Send No More Roses* (1977). Ambler's ideological outlook was shared by Graham *Greene, whose *The Stamboul Train* (1932), *The Confidential Agent* (1939), and *The Ministry of Fear* (1943) presaged his even better-known spy novels that appeared after the Second World War when he worked as a British intelligence officer for the Secret

Intelligence Service (MI6): *The Quiet American* (1955), *Our Man in Havana* (1959), and *The Human Factor* (1978), which struck a typically Greene-ish theme in its reflections on betrayal, loyalty, and trust.

The dominating figure of the immediate post-war years was Ian *Fleming, whose *Casino Royale* (1953) introduced the iconic figure of James *Bond, undoubtedly the most famous fictional secret agent of all time. By the year of Fleming's premature death his eleven Bond spy novels, including such classics as *From Russia with Love* (1957) and *Goldfinger* (1959), had sold over 40 million copies and his hero was beginning to appear in blockbuster movies that continue to this day. The Bond adventures were updated versions of Le Queux and Buchan designed for the Cold War consumer boom and changed sexual *mores* of the 1950s and 1960s; the enemy is Moscow or, in later novels such as *Thunderball* (1961), megalomaniacs of international ambition such as the unforgettable Ernst Stavro Blofeld. Bond was a cultural phenomenon that spawned imitations, parodies, comic strips, and even a communist rival in the shape of Avakum Zakhov, penned by the Bulgarian novelist Andrei Gulyashki. Outraged critics deplored the novels as both cause and symptom of cultural decay, and for their sex, snobbery, and violence. Others praised their technical skill and robust good fun. They also provided intriguing texts for their times, for Fleming had wartime intelligence experience and was a practising journalist with an acute and perceptive eye for the cross-currents of tradition and change that revolutionized Britain and its place in the post-war world.

Such change had already cast its post-imperial shadow by the time of Fleming's death. The 1961 building of the Berlin Wall brought a serious chill to the Cold War climate and in *The Spy Who Came in from the Cold* (1963) John *Le Carré marked out the territory that was to dominate spy fiction until the end of the Cold War and the collapse of the Soviet Union. Making an explicit and conscious break with Bond, he created the anti-heroic figure of George Smiley, the protagonist of several of his novels that culminate in *Smiley's People* (1980), an eternally middle-aged and all too human intelligence officer who grapples with the ambiguities and moral maze of real-life Cold War espionage. However noble the end, Le Carré's spy fiction proclaims, those who

work in intelligence always risk their humanity. *The Looking-Glass War* (1965) is a particularly bleak dissection of a Cold War operation, while *Tinker, Tailor, Soldier, Spy* (1974), inspired by the infamous case of the KGB traitor Kim Philby, explores the theme of the Soviet 'mole' within the service. Here, Le Carré was firmly in tradition, for he, too, had worked for British intelligence and drew heavily (as he continued to do in the 1990s) from personal knowledge. Exploring similar terrain in this period were writers like Len Deighton (1929–) who made his name with *The Ipcress File* (1962) and *Funeral in Berlin* (1964), the former intelligence officer Ted Allbeury (1917–), and the highly productive William Haggard (pseudonym of Richard Henry Michael Clayton, 1907–93).

Yet even as Le Carré and others explored the moral ambiguities of Cold War espionage, Frederick Forsyth (1938–) was marking yet another shift in mood. In thrill-packed and highly successful blockbusters such as *The Day of the Jackal* (1971) and *The Odessa File* (1972), and continuing through *The Fourth Protocol* (1984) and *The Fist of God* (1994), he returned to adventure stories on a global scale in which tough male heroes save the world from a variety of disasters, a trend reflected too in the novels of Ken Follett (1949–) such as *Eye of the Needle* (1978) and *The Man from St. Petersburg* (1982).

The spy novel has always been a hybrid form, sliding over into the *detective, crime, or even romance novel. Yet in whatever shape, the jury is still out on whether the end of the Cold War and superpower confrontation will terminally affect its health. Real-world espionage has predictably survived, and the enduring conflicts of nation-states will continue to provide ample raw material for the spy writer. Yet spy fiction has flourished best in times of crisis or anticipated disaster, such as invasion or nuclear war. National security nightmares have now fragmented into wars against international crime, ethnic conflict, and drugs, threats that to many potential readers may seem distant or remote. Spy fiction can only reflect the results.

See: Ralph Harper, *The World of the Thriller* (1974); Michael Denning, *Cover Stories* (1987); David Stafford, *The Silent Game* (1988); Wesley Wark (ed.), *Spy Fiction, Spy Films, and Real Intelligence* (1991).

Staple of News, The, a comedy by *Jonson, performed 1626, printed 1631.

Pennyboy Junior learns from a beggar, whom he takes on as a servant, that his father has died. He begins to squander his inheritance, buying gaudy clothes, pursuing the rich Lady Pecunia, his miserly uncle's ward, and purchasing a clerkship for his barber at the Staple of News, an office for the collection, sorting, and dissemination of news and gossip, 'authentical and apocryphal'. The beggar reveals that he is Pennyboy's father, and, appalled by his extravagance, disinherits him, but Pennyboy redeems himself, and wins the hand of Lady Pecunia, when he thwarts a plot to ruin his father hatched by the scheming lawyer Picklock. The play is watched throughout by four gossips, Mirth, Tattle, Expectation, and Censure, who sit on the stage and offer an undiscerning commentary at the end of each act.

Stareleigh, Mr Justice, in Dickens's *Pickwick Papers,* the judge in the case of *Bardell* v. *Pickwick.*

STARK, Freya (1893–1993), daughter of a sculptor. She was born in Paris, spent her childhood between Devon and Italy, and was educated at Bedford College and the School of Oriental Studies, London. In 1927, having mastered Arabic, she began travelling in the Middle East, and in the next decade made adventurous solitary journeys in that region. During the Second World War she worked for the Ministry of Information in Aden, Cairo, Baghdad, the USA, and India. In 1947 she married the writer Stewart Perowne. Throughout her wanderings her home base was Italy, and she settled in Asolo. She was made a DBE in 1972.

Among her many books on her travels in Iran, Iraq, southern Arabia, and Turkey, the most notable are *The Valleys of the Assassins* (1934), *The Southern Gates of Arabia* (1936), *Iona: A Quest* (1954), *The Lycian Shore* (1956). Four volumes of autobiography, including *Traveller's Prelude* (1950), and six volumes of letters appeared in 1950–61 and 1974–81. Her books reveal her as a natural traveller, disregarding discomforts and dangers in spite of poor health, with an unassuming friendliness and curiosity which make her observant and humane descriptions of the life of remote communities memorably lifelike. Her knowledge of classical Arabic and Greek literature gives backbone to her accounts of Middle East travel. Her later works are sometimes diffuse and sententious, without the unaffected charm of her pre-war books. A brilliant photographer, she illustrated her books with portraits of human and architectural splendours and oddities.

STARKE, Mariana, see GRAND TOUR and MURRAY, JOHN.

STARKIE, Walter (1894–1976), Irish-born writer, translator, musicologist, and Hispanist, educated at Trinity College, Dublin, who lived for many years in Madrid, where he was founder and director of the British Institute (1940–54). He is best remembered for *Raggle-Taggle: Adventures with a Fiddle in Hungary and Romania* (1933), which describes his adventures with the gypsies: this was followed by *Spanish Raggle Taggle* (1934) and *Scholars and Gypsies* (1963), all of which joyfully celebrate in a vivid and colourful prose reminiscent of *Borrow the freedom and adventures of the open road and 'the music of the wind on the heath'. His sister Enid Starkie (1897–1970) was also a linguist, and taught for many years in Oxford, where she was well known as a colourful and eccentric figure. She wrote on *Baudelaire, *Flaubert, and others, and wrote a foreword to *Gide's contribution to *The God that Failed* (1950), which she edited from his published records.

Starveling, in Shakespeare's *A Midsummer Night's Dream,* a tailor, who is cast for the part of 'Thisby's mother' in the play of 'Pyramus and Thisbe', but appears as 'Moonshine'.

Stationers' Company, the, incorporated by royal charter in 1557. No one not a member of the Company might print anything for sale in the kingdom unless authorized by special privilege or patent. Moreover, by the rules of the Company, every member was required to enter in the register of the Company the name of any book that he desired to print, so that these registers furnish valuable information regarding printed matter during the latter part of the 16th cent. The Company's control of the printing trade waned during the 17th cent., to be revived in a modified form under the Copyright Act of 1709.

STATIUS, Publius Papinius (AD c.45–96), Roman epic poet and Silver Age imitator of *Virgil. The son of a Naples schoolmaster, he made a name for himself winning poetic competitions at an early age. Encouraged by success, he went to Rome, collected rich patrons, and with fulsome flattery won, but failed to keep, the favour of the tyrant Domitian. His surviving works consist of the five books of his *Silvae,* occasional verses which include a famous piece on sleep that inspired *Drummond of Hawthornden, an epic, *The-bais,* in 12 books, relating the bloody quarrel between the sons of Oedipus, and another unfinished epic, the *Achilleis.* Statius' style is mannered and over-ornamental, and his narratives abound in romantic features: magicians, dragons, parted lovers, enchanted woods. These qualities recommended him to medieval taste, and so did the legend of his conversion to Christianity which appears in *Dante. Chaucer based his 'Knight's Tale' (see *CANTERBURY TALES, 1) on *Boccaccio who had used the *Thebais,* but in the Renaissance Statius was studied rather than imitated. The *Thebais* was not translated till 1648 when Thomas Stephens produced a version of the first five books. The *Achilleis* was translated by Robert Howard (1660) and both *Pope and *Gray tried their hands briefly at translating the *Thebais.* *Dryden deplored his 'bladdered greatness: he never thought an expression bold enough if a bolder could be found.'

STEAD, C(hristian) K(arlson) (1932–   ), New Zealand poet, critic, and novelist, born and brought up in Auckland; he went to university there and taught in the English department 1959–86. Since then he has been a full-time writer. From the beginning, Stead's poems were seen as highly intelligent and sophisticated, influenced by such Modernists as Ezra *Pound. In 1964 he published both his own first volume of poems, *Whether the Will Is Free*, and a critical book, *The New Poetic: Yeats to Eliot*. The latter was particularly well received, going into many impressions. Stead covered something of the same ground but with renewed incisiveness and persuasiveness in *Pound, Yeats, Eliot and the Modernist Movement* (1986). He has published several novels, including *All Visitors Ashore* (1984), *The Death of the Body* (1986), and *The Singing Whakapapa* (1994), all of which show his characteristic mixing of New Zealand personal material with experimental techniques. As editor (for example of *The Faber Book of Contemporary South Pacific Stories*, 1994) and as reviewer, Stead has a reputation for provocation. His most recent selection of poems is *Straw into Gold* (1997).

STEAD, Christina Ellen (1902–83), Australian novelist, born in Sydney and educated at Sydney University Teachers' College. She came to London in 1928 and subsequently worked and travelled in Europe and America with her companion, then husband, the American political economist and ex-broker William J. Blake. In 1953 they settled near London; she returned to Australia on his death in 1968. Her wandering life and her left-wing views (which also raised difficulties for her in Hollywood during the McCarthy period) may have contributed to the neglect of her work, which towards the end of her life received renewed attention and admiration. Her first collection of stories, *The Salzburg Tales* (1934), was followed by several full-length novels, which include her best-known work, *The Man Who Loved Children* (1940), a bitterly ironic view of American family life and conflict; *For Love Alone* (1945), in which Teresa escapes to Australia to seek her own freedom; *Letty Fox: Her Luck* (1946), a first-person narration describing the adventurous, unconventional, and ambitious life of a New York office girl; and *Cotter's England* (1967; USA as *Dark Places of the Heart*, 1966) which presents a vivid portrait of post-war working-class Britain, centred on the extraordinary personality of chain-smoking, emotional, destructive Nellie Cook, née Cotter, a 'beaky, restless, gabby' and insatiably curious journalist, working on a left-wing London paper. Many of the novels manifest the author's admiration for *Zola, and her feminism and politics are deeply interwoven, independent, and personal.

STEAD, W(illiam) T(homas) (1849–1912). He was assistant editor of the *Pall Mall Gazette* in 1880 and during his editorship (1883–8) initiated new and influential political and social movements. He achieved wide notoriety for his 'Maiden Tribute of Modern Babylon' (1885) exposing sexual vice, which led to Parliament raising the age of consent to 16 years. He founded the *Review of Reviews* in 1890 and continued his work for peace, friendship with Russia, and spiritualism (for which he was much ridiculed). He was drowned in the *Titanic* disaster.

STEELE, Sir Richard (1672–1729), born in Dublin, in the same year as *Addison, and educated with him at Charterhouse. He was subsequently at Merton College, Oxford, whence he entered the army as a cadet in the Life Guards. As a result of a poem on Queen Mary's funeral dedicated to Lord Cutts, colonel of the Coldstream Guards, he became his secretary and obtained the rank of captain. He published *The Christian Hero* in 1701, in which he first displayed his missionary and reforming spirit. In the same year he produced his first comedy, *The Funeral. Neither this nor his two next comedies, *The Lying Lover* (1703) and *The Tender Husband* (1705), proved very successful. In 1706 he was appointed gentleman waiter to Prince George of Denmark, and in 1707 gazetteer; and in the same year was married to Mary Scurlock ('dear Prue'), his second wife. In 1709 he started the *Tatler, which he carried on with the help of Addison till Jan. 1711. He was made a commissioner of stamps in 1710, but lost the gazetteership after the accession of the Tories. In conjunction with Addison he carried on the *Spectator during 1711–12. This was followed by the *Guardian, to which Addison, *Berkeley, and *Pope contributed, and which was attacked by the Tory *Examiner. Steele next conducted the *Englishman* (1713–14), a more political paper. In 1713 he was elected MP for Stockbridge. In 1714 he published *The Crisis*, a pamphlet in favour of the Hanoverian succession, which was answered by *Swift, and led to Steele's expulsion from the House on 18 Mar. 1714. In October of that year he issued his *Apology for Himself and His Writings*, and during the same year conducted the *Lover*, a paper in the manner of the *Spectator*. The tide turned in his favour with the accession of George I. He was appointed supervisor of Drury Lane Theatre, and to other posts, and was knighted in 1715. In 1718 he denounced in *The Plebeian* Lord Sunderland's Peerage Bill, and was answered by Addison in *The Old Whig*. This incident led to the revocation of Steele's Drury Lane patent, and to an estrangement from Addison. He established the *Theatre*, a bi-weekly paper, which continued until 1720, in which year he issued pamphlets against the South Sea mania (see SOUTH SEA COMPANY). His last comedy, *The Conscious Lovers, was produced in 1722. Money difficulties forced him to leave London in 1724, and he died at Carmarthen. His letters to Mary Scurlock were printed in 1787. Less highly regarded as an essayist than Addison, his influence was nevertheless great; his attacks on *Restoration drama (*Spectator*, No. 65, on *Etherege, 'I allow it to be Nature, but it is Nature in its utmost Corruption and Degeneracy'); his approval of the 'sober and polite Mirth' of *Terence; his praise of tender and affectionate domestic and family life; and his own reformed and sentimental dramas (described by *Fielding's Parson Adams as 'almost solemn enough for a sermon') did much to create an image of polite behaviour for the new century. There is a life by George A. Aitken (2 vols, 1889).

Steele Glas, The, a satire in verse by *Gascoigne, published 1576.

The poet's 'steele glas' reveals abuses and how things should be, whereas the common looking-glass only 'shewes a seemely shew', i.e. shows the thing much better than it is. Looking into his 'steele glas' the author sees himself with his faults and then successively the faults of kings; covetous lords and knights; greedy, braggart, and drunken soldiers; false judges; merchants; and lastly priests. Finally the ploughman is held up as a model:

> Behold him (priests) & though he stink of sweat
> Disdaine him not: for shal I tel you what?
> Such clime to heaven, before the shaven crownes.

Steerforth, James, a character in Dickens's *David Copperfield.*

STEEVENS, George (1736–1800), Shakespearian commentator, who in 1766 issued in four volumes *Twenty of the Plays of Shakespeare, Being the Whole Number Printed in Quarto during His Lifetime, or before the Restoration,* and in 1773 a complete annotated edition (including notes by Dr *Johnson) in ten volumes, to which a supplementary volume of poems, together with seven plays ascribed to Shakespeare, was added in 1780. He constantly quarrelled with his literary associates and was called by *Gifford 'the Puck of commentators', but was befriended by Johnson and elected a member of the *Club in 1774. He was extremely widely read in Elizabethan literature, and supplied to his edition a vast range of illustrative quotations from other works, but was in other respects less scholarly, rejecting as inauthentic various scenes and plays which he appears merely to have disliked. He assisted *Tyrwhitt in his edition of the Rowley poems of *Chatterton, but declared his disbelief in them. He attacked W. H. *Ireland, and satirized literary crazes.

STEIN, Gertrude (1874–1946), American author, born in Pennsylvania into a progressive and intellectual family of German–Jewish origin. She studied psychology at Radcliffe College, where she was a student of W. *James, and then studied the anatomy of the brain at Johns Hopkins. In 1902 she went with her brother Leo to Paris, where she settled; her home in the rue de Fleurus became a literary salon and art gallery and a home of the avant-garde, attracting painters (including *Picasso, Matisse, and Juan Gris) and writers (including *Hemingway, F. M. *Ford, and S. *Anderson, but not *Joyce, with whom she was not acquainted). Her friend, secretary, and companion from 1907 was San Francisco-born Alice B. Toklas (1877–1967), whom she made the ostensible author of her own memoir, *The Autobiography of Alice B. Toklas* (1933). Her fiction includes *Three Lives* (1909), of which the second portrait, 'Melanctha', was described by R. *Wright as 'the first long serious literary treatment of Negro life in the United States' (but see also under CULTURAL APPROPRIATION); *The Making of Americans* (written 1906–8, pub. 1925), an enormously long work intended as a history of her family; and *A Long Gay Book* (1932). *Tender Buttons* (1914) is an example of her highly idiosyncratic poetry, of which she said in her *Lectures in America* (1935), 'I struggled with the ridding myself of nouns. I knew that nouns must go in poetry as they had gone in prose if anything that is everything was to go on meaning something.' Her characteristic repetitions and reprises, her flowing, unpunctuated prose, and her attempts to capture the 'living moment' owe much to William James and to *Bergson's concept of time, and represent a highly personal but nevertheless influential version of the *stream-of-consciousness technique. Her many varied published works include essays, sketches of life in France, works of literary theory, short stories, portraits of her friends, a lyric drama called *Four Saints in Three Acts* (first published in *transition*, 1929, and performed in the USA, 1934), and *Wars I Have Seen* (1945), a personal account of occupied Paris. For an influential early study of her work, see E. *Wilson, *Axel's Castle* (1931).

STEINBECK, John Ernst (1902–68), American novelist, born in California. He took his native state as the background for his early short stories and novels and described the lives of those working on the land with realism and understanding. *Tortilla Flat* (1935) was his first success, and he confirmed his growing reputation with two novels about landless rural workers, *In Dubious Battle* (1936) and *Of Mice and Men* (1937), the story of two itinerant farm labourers, one of huge strength and weak mind, exploited and protected by the other. His best-known work, *The Grapes of Wrath* (1939), is an epic account of the efforts of an emigrant farming family from the dust bowl of the West to reach the 'promised land' of California. Among his later novels are *East of Eden* (1952), a family saga, and *The Winter of Our Discontent* (1961). He was awarded the *Nobel Prize in 1962.

STEINER, (Francis) George (1929–), American critic and author, born in Paris, and educated at the Sorbonne, the University of Chicago, Harvard, and Oxford. His critical works include *Tolstoy or Dostoevsky: An Essay in the Old Criticism* (1959); *The Death of Tragedy* (1961); *Language and Silence* (1967); *In Bluebeard's Castle: Some Notes towards the Re-definition of Culture* (1971); and *After Babel: Aspects of Language and Translation* (1975). Steiner's criticism is wide-ranging and multicultural in its references and controversial in its content: one of his recurrent themes is the way in which the 20th-cent. experiences of totalitarianism and world war, and, more specifically, of the Holocaust, have destroyed the assumption (self-evident, he claims, to Dr *Johnson, *Coleridge, and M. *Arnold) that literature is a humanizing influence. Silence is the only appropriate response to 20th-cent. horrors. The Holocaust is also the subject of his novella *The Portage to San Cristobal of A.H.* (1979; dramatized by Christopher *Hampton, 1982), which puts in the mouth of Hitler (who is supposed to have survived the war and taken refuge in South America) the argument that the Jews (through monotheism, Christianity, and Marxism) had provoked their own destruction by offering 'the blackmail of transcendence . . . the virus of Utopia'. Other works: *Real Presences: Is There Anything in What We Say?* (1989), *Proofs and Three Parables* (fiction, 1992). *Errata: An Examined Life* (1997) is a memoir recalling his childhood, education, and intellectual development.

Stella, (1) the chaste lady loved by Astrophel in Sidney's sonnet sequence *Astrophel and Stella*, based on Penelope *Rich; (2) Swift's name for Esther Johnson; see SWIFT, and in particular the account there of the *Journal to Stella*.

STENDHAL, pseudonym of Henri Beyle (1783–1842), French novelist, who spent his early years in his native Grenoble and later lived for long periods in Italy. His two recognized masterpieces, *Le Rouge et le noir* (1830) and *La Chartreuse de Parme* (1839), the first following the rise and fall of the young provincial Julien Sorel in the France of the Restoration (1814–30), the second chronicling the fortunes of Fabrice del Dongo at a small Italian court during the same period, figure among the great French novels of the 19th cent. Each is remarkable for its political dimension, for the detail and variety of the experience portrayed, for the energy and passion of the principal characters, and for penetrating psychological analysis. Stendhal also wrote studies of music and musicians, and of Italian painting (*Histoire de la peinture en Italie*, 1817), travel books (*Rome, Naples et Florence en 1817*, 1817), and much occasional journalism. *De l'amour* (1822) considers the passion both psychologically and in relation to historical and social conditions. With the two pamphlets entitled *Racine* and *Shakespeare* (1823, 1825) he entered the classic–Romantic controversy on the side of the latter. Of his other novels, *Armance* (1822) and *L'Abbesse de Castro* (1839) appeared during his lifetime; the unfinished *Lucien Leuwen* (1894) and the fragmentary *Lamiel* (1889) were published posthumously. *La Vie de Henri Brulard* (1890), the *Journal* (1888) of, mainly, the years 1801 to 1815, and *Souvenirs d'égotisme* (1892), covering the years 1822–30, are all autobiographical.

Stephano, a drunken butler in Shakespeare's *The Tempest*.

STEPHEN, Sir James (1789–1859), father of Sir J. F. *Stephen and Sir L. *Stephen. He was under-secretary of state for the colonies (1836–47) and professor of modern history at Cambridge (1849–59), meanwhile contributing articles to the *Edinburgh Review* including an admirable essay on *Wilberforce. He is remembered as author of *Essays in Ecclesiastical Biography* (1849) and *Lectures on the History of France* (1851).

STEPHEN, Sir James Fitzjames (1829–94), son of Sir J. *Stephen and brother of Leslie *Stephen, a barrister, legal member of council in India (1869–72), and high court judge (1879–91). In 1861 he was counsel for Rowland Williams in the *Essays and Reviews* case. He was a member of the *Apostles and the *Metaphysical Society and vigorously contributed articles on social, moral, and controversial theological subjects to periodicals including *Fraser's Magazine* and the *Cornhill; he was chief writer for the *Pall Mall Gazette* for five years. Among his works were *A History of the Criminal Law in England* (1883), *Horae Sabbaticae* (1892, collected articles from the *Saturday Review*), and *Liberty, Equality, Fraternity* (1873, repub. 1967) in which he criticized J. S. *Mill's utilitarian position in his essay *On Liberty*. There is a life by Leslie Stephen.

STEPHEN, James Kenneth (1859–92), younger son of Sir J. F. *Stephen and cousin of V. *Woolf, educated at Eton and King's College, Cambridge. He was called to the bar but devoted most of his time to journalism and in 1888 began a weekly paper called the *Reflector*, chiefly written by himself. He was author (as 'J.K.S.') of highly successful parodies and light verse, collected as *Lapsus Calami* and *Quo Musa Tendis* (both 1891). His promising career ended as a result of an accident in 1886 which slowly drove him insane, and he has been suggested as a candidate for the role of *Jack the Ripper. See M. Harrison, *Clarence* (1972).

STEPHEN, Sir Leslie (1832–1904), son of Sir J. *Stephen and brother of Sir J. F. *Stephen, educated at Eton and Trinity Hall, Cambridge, where he became tutor, having taken orders. From his family he inherited a strong tradition of evangelicalism and muscular Christianity, and he became a noted mountaineer: he edited the *Alpine Journal*, 1868–72, and the best of his Alpine essays were collected in 1871 as *The Playground of Europe*.

Stephen's reading of J. S. *Mill, *Comte, and *Kant inclined him to scepticism, and by 1865 he had abandoned all belief in even the broadest of *Broad Church doctrine. In 1864 he came to London and embarked on a literary career of prodigious industry and output, contributing articles to many periodicals. In 1871 he became editor of the *Cornhill, a post he held until 1882 when he undertook the editorship of the *Dictionary of National Biography* (the *DNB*). During these years he published several volumes, some defining his position as an agnostic; his great work, *History of English Thought in the 18th Century* (1876), reviews the Deist controversy of that age, and the intuitional and utilitarian schools of philosophy. He also contributed several biographies to the English Men of Letters series, despite the amount of time consumed by the vast undertaking of the *DNB*, to which he himself contributed almost 400 entries, and from which strain and ill health forced him to resign in 1891. His last important volume was *English Literature and Society in the Eighteenth Century* (1904). Many of his literary judgements are now questioned, but he was one of the most prominent intellectuals of his day (portrayed by his friend *Meredith as Vernon Whitford, 'a Phoebus Apollo turned fasting friar', in *The Egoist*) and his influence was great and lasting.

Stephen's first wife was *Thackeray's daughter 'Minny', who died in 1875. His acute grief, and his second marriage to Julia Duckworth, are both recorded in his autobiographical papers, written for their children (one of whom was V. *Woolf) and his step-children. Woolf portrays some aspects of his character in her portrait of Mr Ramsay in *To the Lighthouse* (1927). See also Noël Annan, *Leslie Stephen: His Thought and Character in Relation to His Time* (1951, rev. 1984).

STEPHENS, James (1882–1950), Irish poet and story writer, born in poverty, whose best-known work, the prose fantasy *The Crock of Gold* (1912), has overshadowed much other less whimsical work. *Insurrections* (1909) was the first of many volumes of poetry; the *Collected Poems* appeared in 1926, revised 1954. His first novel, *The Charwoman's Daughter* (1912), was followed by *The Demi-Gods* (1914) and *Deirdre* (1923). Many volumes of stories include *Irish Fairy Tales* (1920, illustrated by A. *Rackham); and *Etched in Moonlight* (1928). Stephens became a widely known broadcaster, of stories and verses and conversation. A biography by A. Martin appeared in 1977.

STERLING, John (1806–44), educated at Trinity College and Trinity Hall, Cambridge, a leading member of the *Apostles and a disciple of *Coleridge. With *Maurice he was briefly proprietor of the *Athenaeum* (1828). He was offered in 1834 the curacy of Herstmonceux by his old tutor *Hare, who was vicar, but he resigned the following year. Sterling owes his fame to his close friendship with *Carlyle, whose vivid *Life of Sterling* (1851) reveals the tragic history of Sterling's short life, interrupted by persistent ill health necessitating numerous voyages abroad. His monthly meetings of literary friends, from 1838, became known as the Sterling Club; among its members were Carlyle, Hare, J. S. *Mill, and *Tennyson. He contributed to various periodicals and among his few published works were a novel, *Arthur Coningsby* (1833), *Poems* (1839), and *Essays and Tales* (1848) collected and edited with a memoir by J. Hare, to whom with Carlyle his papers were entrusted.

STERNE, Laurence (1713–68), the son of an impoverished infantry ensign (who was, however, the grandson of an archbishop of York). He spent his early childhood in various barracks in Ireland and England, where he developed an affection for military men evident in his adult writings. At the age of 10 he was sent to school in Yorkshire, under the care of an uncle, and from there proceeded, on a scholarship founded by Archbishop Sterne, to Jesus College, Cambridge, where he encountered and embraced the philosophy of *Locke, and where he made a lifelong friend of *Hall-Stevenson, who was probably the model for *Eugenius. Sterne had by this time already contracted tuberculosis. He took holy orders and obtained the living of the Yorkshire parish of Sutton-on-the-Forest in 1738. In 1741 he became a prebendary of York Cathedral, and married Elizabeth Lumley, a cousin of Elizabeth *Montagu, but his domestic and family life was not happy, and of their several children all were stillborn but a daughter, Lydia. He became a JP, earned a reputation as a good country pastor, and his sermons at York Minster were eagerly attended. In 1744 the living of Stillington was added to that of Sutton. For recreation he played the violin, read widely, painted, dined with the local gentry, and, it seems, indulged his considerable interest in women. In 1759, in the course of an ecclesiastical quarrel, he wrote *A Political Romance* (later entitled *The History of a Good Warm Watch Coat*), a satire on local ecclesiastical courts so barbed that the authorities had it burned. In the same year he passed his parish over to the care of a curate and began *Tristram Shandy*. The first version of vols i and ii was rejected by the London printer *Dodsley. At the same time Sterne had to face the deaths of his mother and uncle, and the mental breakdown of his wife. The next version of vols i and ii was 'written under the greatest heaviness of heart', and published in York in 1759, with Dodsley agreeing to take half the printing for sale in London. While waiting for the public's reception of his work, Sterne was enjoying a flirtation with Catherine Fourmantel, a singer then staying in York, who is traditionally (though uncertainly) supposed to be the 'dear Jenny' of *Tristram Shandy*. Early in 1760 Sterne found himself famous. He went to London and (although his book was not liked by Dr *Johnson, *Goldsmith, *Richardson, and others) he was fêted by society, had his portrait painted by *Reynolds, was invited to court, and saw published a second edition of vols i and ii. In the same year he was presented with a third Yorkshire living, that of Coxwold, where he happily settled himself into 'Shandy Hall'. He published *The Sermons of Mr Yorick*, a volume whose title caused some scandal, and continued with *Tristram Shandy*. In 1761 four more volumes appeared and *Tristram Shandy* continued its highly successful career. Meanwhile Sterne's health was deteriorating steadily. In 1762 his voice was much affected, and in the hope of improvement he and his wife and daughter left for France, where they lived at Toulouse and Montpelier until 1764, when Sterne returned alone to England, and in 1765 published vols vii and viii of *Tristram Shandy*. In 1765 he returned to France, visited his family (who were to remain there permanently), and undertook an eight-month tour of France and Italy, which clearly provided him with much of the material for *A Sentimental Journey through France and Italy*. In 1766 he published two further volumes of sermons. The ninth and last volume of *Tristram Shandy* appeared in 1767. In the same year Sterne met and fell in love with Elizabeth *Draper, the young wife of an official of the East India Company, and after her enforced departure for India began his *Journal to *Eliza*, which he did not publish. He finished and published *A Sentimental Journey* in the same year, but his health rapidly collapsed and he died in London in Mar. 1768. A Shandean fate overtook his body, which was taken by grave-robbers, recognized at an anatomy lecture in Cambridge, and secretly returned to its grave.

A spate of forgeries appeared after Sterne's death, including another volume of *Tristram Shandy*, *Posthumous Works*, and a continuation by 'Eugenius' (an author whose identity is not known, but who was not Hall-Stevenson) of *A Sentimental Journey*.

Sterne is generally acknowledged as an innovator of the highest originality, and has been seen as the chief begetter of a long line of writers interested in the *'stream of consciousness'. He acknowledges in *Tristram Shandy* his own debt in this respect to Locke, whose *Essay Concerning Human Understanding* seemed to Sterne 'a history-book . . . of what passes in man's own mind'. Throughout his work he parodies, with a virtuosity that has proved inimitable, the developing conventions of the still-new 'novel', and its problems in presenting reality, space, and time. His sharp wit, often sly and often salacious, is balanced by the affection and tolerance he displays towards the delights and absurdities of life. The standard life is by A. H. Cash, *Laurence Sterne: The Early and Middle Years* (1975) and *Laurence Sterne: The Later Years* (1986). There is a scholarly edition of *Tristram Shandy*, ed. Melvin New et al. (3 vols, 1978–84); see also *The Sermons of Laurence Sterne*, ed. Melvin New (2 vols, 1992).

STERNHOLD, Thomas (d. 1549), and **HOPKINS,** John (d. 1570), joint versifiers of the Psalms. A collection of 44 of these metrical Psalms appeared in 1549; music was first supplied in the Geneva edition of 1556, and by 1640 about 300 editions had been published. In 1562 *The Whole Book of Psalmes*, by Sternhold, Hopkins, Norton, and others, was added to the Prayer Book. This version was ridiculed by Dryden in *Absalom and Achitophel* (II. 403), and it provoked *Rochester's epigram 'Spoken Extempore to a Country Clerk after Having Heard Him Sing Psalms':

Sternhold and Hopkins had great qualms
When they translated David's psalms
To make the heart full glad;
But had it been poor David's fate
To hear thee sing, and them translate,
    By God! 'twould have made him mad.

STEVENS, Henry (1819–86), American book-dealer and bibliographical entrepreneur, who came to London in 1845 and became an agent for the *British Museum library, purchasing American books which did much to build up its collection, and also purchasing English books for American collectors. See his own *Recollections of James Lenox and the Formation of His Library* (1886) and W. W. Parker, *Henry Stevens of Vermont* (1963).

STEVENS, Wallace (1879–1955), American poet, born in Pennsylvania and educated at Harvard, where he met *Santayana. He became a lawyer, and from 1916 worked at Hartford, Connecticut, on the legal staff of the Hartford Accident and Indemnity Company, where he remained until his death, becoming vice-president in 1934. Meanwhile, he had begun to publish poems in *Poetry* and elsewhere, and his first volume, *Harmonium*, which contains 'Thirteen Ways of Looking at a Blackbird', was published in 1923. This was followed by other collections (including *Ideas of Order*, 1935; *The Man with the Blue Guitar and Other Poems*, 1937; *Notes towards a Supreme Fiction*, 1942; *The Auroras of Autumn*, 1950; *Collected Poems*, 1954) which slowly brought him recognition, but it was not until his last years that his enigmatic, elegant, intellectual, and occasionally startling meditations on order and the imagination, on reality, appearance, and art, gained the high reputation that they now enjoy. See *Letters*, ed. Holly Stevens (1996).

STEVENSON, Anne (1933–   ), poet and biographer, born in England of American parents and educated in America; she settled in Britain in the 1960s and now lives partly in Wales. Her collections include *Living in America* (1965), *Reversals* (1970), *Enough of Green* (1977), *The Fiction Makers* (1985), and *The Other House* (1990); *The Collected Poems 1955–1995* appeared in 1996. Many of her poems celebrate the landscapes and cultures of her two nations, and their interconnections: her tone is at times conversational, at times lyrical, at times wry. Her controversial biography of Sylvia *Plath, *Bitter Fame*, written with the approval of the poet's estate, appeared in 1989: her own work shows an affinity to Plath's, whom she also powerfully evokes in 'Three Poems for Sylvia Plath' (1990).

STEVENSON, John Hall-, see HALL-STEVENSON.

STEVENSON, Robert Louis (originally Lewis) Balfour (1850–94), son of Thomas Stevenson, joint engineer to the Board of Northern Lighthouses, born in Edinburgh. A sickly child, he was originally intended for his father's strenuous profession, but ill health encouraged him to abandon the study of engineering at Edinburgh University for the law. He was admitted advocate in 1875, but had already determined to be a writer, and had published in periodicals. He was fascinated by Edinburgh low life, and cultivated a bohemian style, despite the constraint of financial dependence on his father. In 1875 L. *Stephen introduced him to W. E. *Henley, who became a close friend, and with whom he was to collaborate on four undistinguished plays (Deacon Brodie, 1880; Beau Austin, 1884; Admiral Guinea, 1884; Macaire, 1885). From this time on much of his life was spent travelling in search of health; he suffered from a chronic bronchial condition (possibly tuberculosis) and frequent haemorrhages. In France in 1876 he met his future wife, Mrs Fanny Osbourne. An Inland Voyage, describing a canoe tour in Belgium and France, appeared in 1878. Travels with a Donkey in the Cevennes, the description of a tour taken with his donkey Modestine, appeared in 1879, the year in which he travelled to California by emigrant ship and train in pursuit of Fanny, whom he married shortly after her divorce in 1880; she was ten years his senior, and proved a spirited yet protective companion, caring for him through many bouts of serious illness. After a stay at Calistoga (recorded in The Silverado Squatters, 1883) he returned to Europe, settling at Bournemouth for three years in 1884, where he consolidated a friendship with H. *James. By this time he had published widely in periodicals, and many of his short stories, essays, and travel pieces were collected in volume form (Virginibus Puerisque, 1881; Familiar Studies of Men and Books, 1882; New Arabian Nights, 1882). His first full-length work of fiction, *Treasure Island, published in book form in 1883, brought him fame, which increased with the publication of The Strange Case of *Dr Jekyll and Mr Hyde (1886). This was followed by his popular Scottish romances, *Kidnapped (1886), its sequel Catriona (1893), and *The Master of Ballantrae (1889).

In 1888 Stevenson had set out with his family entourage for the South Seas, becoming a legend in his lifetime. He visited the leper colony at Molokai, which inspired his celebrated defence of Father Damien (1841–89), the Belgian priest who had devoted his life to caring for 700 neglected lepers, himself finally dying of the disease (Father Damien: An Open Letter to the Reverend Dr Hyde of Honolulu, 1890). He finally settled in Samoa at Vailima, where he temporarily regained his health, and gained a reputation as 'Tusitala' or 'The Story Teller'. He died there suddenly from a brain haemorrhage, while working on his unfinished masterpiece, *Weir of Hermiston (1896).

In addition to the titles mentioned above, Stevenson published many other volumes, including The Merry Men (1887, with 'Markheim' and his earliest Scottish story, 'Thrawn Janet'); many travel books; The Black Arrow (1888), a historical romance; Island Nights' Entertainments (1893), which includes 'The Beach of Falesá'; and St Ives (1897, unfinished, completed

by *Quiller-Couch). With his stepson Lloyd Osbourne he wrote The Wrong Box (1889), The Wrecker (1892), and The Ebb-Tide (1894). He also published volumes of poetry, including A Child's Garden of Verses (1885) and Underwoods (1887): his Collected Poems, ed. Janet Adam Smith, appeared in 1950. In them, as in many of his prose works, critics have detected beneath the lightness of touch a sense of apprehension, sin, and suffering, and biographers have attributed this darker side to the early influence of Calvinism, as well as to his ill health. The theme of dualism and the doppelgänger recurs in his work, as does an admiration for morally ambiguous heroes or anti-heroes. Although his more popular books have remained constantly in print, and have been frequently filmed, his critical reputation has been obscured by attention to his vivid personality and adventurous life; also by his apparent refusal to take his art seriously. 'Fiction is to grown men what play is to the child', he stated, and his delight in storytelling, swashbuckling romances, and historical 'tushery', as he called it, gave him an audience of readers rather than critics. His weightier admirers include James, G. *Greene, and *Borges. See Vailima Letters (to Sidney Colvin, 1895); Selected Letters, ed. Colvin (2 vols, 1899; 4 vols, 1911); lives by G. Balfour (1901); J. C. Furnas (1952); J. Calder (1980). Edinburgh edition of his collected works, ed. Colvin (28 vols, 1894–8); Pentland edition, ed. *Gosse (20 vols, 1906–7).

STEWART, Dugald (1753–1828), educated at Edinburgh High School and at Edinburgh and Glasgow universities. He was professor of mathematics at Edinburgh from 1775 to 1785, and then professor of moral philosophy from 1785 to 1810, in which post he exercised a powerful influence on Scottish thought, largely because of his brilliant pedagogy and his elegant prose. Although Stewart considered himself a disciple of T. *Reid, he was an eclectic thinker who borrowed from a wide range of sources. He was particularly indebted to the writings of Adam *Smith, and his lectures on political economy were eagerly attended by the coterie of young Whigs who founded the *Edinburgh Review. However, in both his lectures and his publications Stewart was primarily concerned with the inculcation of virtue rather than with abstract theorizing, and it cannot be said that he was either an original or a profound thinker. His works, collected by Sir W. *Hamilton (11 vols, 1854–60), include: Elements of the Human Mind (1792, 1814, 1827), Outlines of Moral Philosophy (1793), Philosophical Essays (1810), Biographical Memoirs (1810), consisting of lives of Adam Smith, W. *Robertson, and Reid, and his once influential Dissertation . . . Exhibiting a General View of the Progress of Metaphysical and Ethical Philosophy, Since the Revival of Letters in Europe (1815, 1821), written originally for the *Encyclopaedia Britannica.

STEWART, J(ohn) I(nnes) M(ackintosh) (1906–94), novelist and critic, born in Edinburgh and educated at the Edinburgh Academy and Oriel College, Oxford. In 1949 he became a Student (i.e. a fellow) of Christ Church, Oxford, where he remained for over 20 years. Under the pseudonym Michael Innes he wrote a highly successful series of novels and stories featuring Inspector John Appleby which contributed greatly to the vogue for donnish detective fiction, rich in literary allusions and quotations. They include *Death at the President's Lodging* (1936), *Hamlet, Revenge!* (1937), *The Secret Vanguard* (1940), *The Daffodil Affair* (1941), *Appleby on Ararat* (1941), *A Private View* (1952), *The Long Farewell* (1958), and *Appleby at Allington* (1968). Under his own name he wrote a quintet of novels (1974–8) about Oxford with the collective title *A Staircase in Surrey*.

Stewart of the Glens, James, a character in R. L. Stevenson's *Kidnapped* and *Catriona*, a real character, who was executed in 1752 for a murder which he did not commit, after trial by a jury of Campbells (the foes of his clan).

Steyne, marquis of, a character in Thackeray's *Vanity Fair*.

stichomythia, in classical Greek drama, dialogue in alternate lines of verse, employed in sharp disputation. The form is sometimes imitated in English drama, e.g. in the dialogue between Richard III and Elizabeth in Shakespeare's *Richard III* (IV. iv).

Stiggins, Mr, a character in Dickens's *Pickwick Papers*.

Stoicism a system of thought which originated in Athens during the 3rd cent. BC, flourished in Rome c.100 BC–c.AD 200, and enjoyed a vigorous revival at the time of the Renaissance. The Stoics' prime concern was ethics, but they held that right behaviour must be grounded on a general understanding of the universe, and their theories extended to cover the nature of the physical world, logic, rhetoric, epistemology, and politics. The founders held that to be virtuous consisted in following reason undeterred by pain, pleasure, desire, or fear, emotions which belonged to a lower level of existence: the pursuit of health, wealth, success, and pleasure had no real importance. Only fragments of these early founders have survived, and we know of their works through their followers, who include their disciple *Cicero. The Stoics whose writings survive are those who lived under the Roman Empire: *Seneca, *Epictetus, and *Marcus Aurelius.

Stoicism had much in common with Christianity, and a compilation of Stoic maxims, the *Distichs of Cato*, was the most popular of medieval schoolbooks. *Petrarch in the 14th cent. expounded a Christian Stoicism in his *De Remediis Fortunae*, and in the 16th cent. a life of Marcus Aurelius, supposedly ancient but actually by the Spaniard Antonio de Guevara, proved enormously popular. Translated into French and English in the 1530s, it may have served to promote the Stoic revival which came at the end of the century with *Mon-

taigne's *Essais* (1580) and *Lipsius' *De Constantia* (1585). In England the years 1595–1615 saw translations of Lipsius, Montaigne, his disciple Charron, Epictetus, and Seneca, and the influence of Stoicism can be traced in a great number of writers from *Chapman and Sir William Cornwallis (d. ?1631) to *Addison.

STOKER, Bram (Abraham) (1847–1912), born in Dublin. He gave up his career as a civil servant there in 1878 to become Sir H. *Irving's secretary and touring manager for the next 27 years, an experience that produced *Personal Reminiscences of Henry Irving* (1906). Stoker wrote a number of novels and short stories, as well as some dramatic criticism, but is chiefly remembered for *Dracula* (1897), a tale of vampirism influenced by 'Carmilla', one of the stories in Le Fanu's *In a Glass Darkly* (1872).

STONE, Lawrence (1919–99), historian, born in Surrey and educated at Charterhouse School and Christ Church, Oxford; he was long associated with Princeton University, where he became a professor in 1963. His works include *The Crisis of the Aristocracy 1588–1641* (1965) and *The Causes of the English Revolution* (1972). *The Family, Sex and Marriage in England 1500–1800* (1977) is a study of the origins of the modern family and shifting attitudes towards sexual and domestic relationships, illustrated with much literary evidence from sources such as *Boswell, Mrs *Thrale, and Jane *Austen; this was followed by *Road to Divorce: England 1930–1987* (1990) and other studies of marital breakdown.

Stones of Venice, The, by *Ruskin, was published in three volumes, the first in 1851, the second and third in 1853. It is an architectural study in which immense original scholarship is put to moralistic use.

Volume i sets out first principles for discrimination between good and bad architectural features; there follows, in this and volume ii, a criticism of the romantic, *Byronic vision of Venice that blinds the traveller to present misery and disorder. From the remnants of the past Ruskin creates a myth of Venice, where power is decommercialized and desecularized, and religion pre-Catholic. The famous chapter 'The Nature of Gothic' contrasts feudal relations between authority and workman with those resulting from the division of labour and mechanical mass production in English manufacturing: *Clark described it as 'one of the noblest things written in the 19th cent.; even now, when the ideas it expresses are accepted, and the causes it advocates are dead, we cannot read it without a thrill, without a sudden resolution to reform the world', a response which indicates the emotional force of Ruskin's passionate plea for the liberty of the workman. Volume iii describes phases in Renaissance architectural history as illustrations of the gradual degradation of Europe.

STOPES, Marie Charlotte Carmichael (1880–1958),

distinguished palaeobotanist and pioneer birth control campaigner, whose *Married Love* (1918) was published after the annulment of her first marriage, when, she alleged, she was still a virgin. With the help of her second husband she established the first birth control clinic in England in 1921, in Holloway, London, and she continued to write on such subjects as *Wise Parenthood* (1918, which appeared with a preface by Arnold *Bennett), *Radiant Motherhood* (1920), and sexual fulfilment within marriage. She also published several volumes of plays and of poetry, mostly of a semi-mystical character.

STOPPARD, Sir Tom (1937–   ), dramatist, born in Czechoslovakia; his family moved to Singapore in 1939, where his father, Dr Eugene Straussler, was killed, and he subsequently, on settling in England after the war, took his English stepfather's name. He left school at 17 and worked as a journalist before his first play, *A Walk on the Water*, was televised in 1963 (staged in London in 1968 as *Enter a Free Man*). He published a novel, *Lord Malquist and the Moon* (1965), and in 1966 his play *Rosencrantz and Guildenstern Are Dead* attracted much attention. This was followed by many witty and inventive plays, including *The Real Inspector Hound* (1968, a play-within-a-play which parodies the conventions of the stage thriller); *Jumpers* (1972); *Travesties* (1974); *Dirty Linen* (1976, a satire of political life and parliamentary misdemeanours); *Every Good Boy Deserves Favour* (1977, about a political dissident in a Soviet psychiatric hospital); *Night and Day* (1978), about the dangers of the 'closed shop' in journalism; *The Real Thing* (1982), a marital tragicomedy; *Arcadia* (1993), set in a country house in 1809; and *Indian Ink* (1995), an exploration of cultural identity. *The Invention of Love* (1997) presents, through the contrasted fates of A. E. *Housman and Oscar *Wilde, and the sexual complexities of the *Aesthetic movement. *The Coast of Utopia* (2002) is a political-philosophical trilogy set in mid-19th-cent. Russia. Stoppard has written many works for film, radio, and television: *Professional Foul* (TV, 1977), set in Prague, portrays the concurrent visits of an English philosopher and a football team, and dramatizes the inner conflicts of the philosopher, caught between the abstractions of his own discipline and the realities of a regime which stifles free intellectual exchange. Stoppard's work displays a metaphysical wit, a strong theatrical sense, and a talent for pastiche which enables him to move from mode to mode within the same scene with great flexibility and rapidity; yet the plays appear far from frivolous in intention, increasingly posing (though not always choosing to solve) considerable ethical problems.

STOREY, David Malcolm (1933–   ), novelist and playwright, born in Wakefield, the third son of a miner; he was educated at the Queen Elizabeth Grammar School, Wakefield, and at the Slade School of Fine Art. He worked as professional footballer, teacher, farm worker, and erector of show tents, acquiring a variety of experience which is evident in his works. His first novel, *This Sporting Life* (1960), describes the ambitions and passions of a young working man, Arthur Machin, a Rugby League player who becomes emotionally involved with his landlady. This was followed by *Flight into Camden* (1960), about the unhappy affair of a miner's daughter with a married teacher, and the highly ambitious *Radcliffe* (1963), a sombre, violent, Lawrentian novel about class conflict, the Puritan legacy, and destructive homosexual passion. Later novels include *Pasmore* (1972, an account of a young lecturer in a state of mental breakdown) and *Saville* (1976, *Booker Prize), an epic set in a south Yorkshire mining village. Meanwhile Storey had also established himself as a playwright, with such works as *In Celebration* (1969), a play in which three educated sons return north to visit their miner father; *The Contractor* (1970), which presents the audience with the construction, then the dismantling, of a wedding marquee, a spectacle which forms the background for the presentation of the relationship of the contractor Ewbank (who had appeared in *Radcliffe*) with his university-educated son; *Home* (1970), set in a mental home; *The Changing Room* (1971), again using Rugby League as a setting; *Life Class* (1974), set in an art college; and *Mother's Day* (1976), a violent black comedy set on a housing estate. Action, in Storey's plays, tends to be offstage, obliquely presented through low-key, episodic encounters in a realistic setting; both plays and novels show a preoccupation with social mobility and the disturbance it frequently appears to cause, and combine documentary naturalism with the symbolic and unspoken. Later works include the plays *Sister* (1978), *Early Days* (1980), and *The March on Russia* (1989) and the novels *A Prodigal Child* (1982) and *Present Times* (1984). A collection of poems, *Storey's Lives: Poems 1951–1991*, appeared in 1992.

Story of an African Farm, The, a novel by O. *Schreiner.

Story of My Heart, The, a discourse by R. *Jefferies, published 1883.

Tracing the course of his spiritual and imaginative growth from the age of 18, Jefferies describes his longing for harmony with 'the visible universe' and his sense of 'the great earth speaking through me'. He feels the trees, the grass, the stars 'like exterior nerves and veins', yet acknowledges a frustrating inadequacy in expressing his experience. Long reading in philosophy and many branches of knowledge has convinced him that learning is an encumbrance, that causality and purposive evolution do not exist, that there is a soul-life (represented for him by the ocean) higher than any conception of a god, and that the orthodox Christian deity has no existence. His atheism caused considerable scandal, but the book soon established itself as a significant autobiography and has passed through innumerable editions.

Story of Rimini, The, a poem by Leigh *Hunt published
1816. The work (with which Hunt had assistance from
*Byron) is based on *Dante's story of Paolo and
Francesca.

On a fine May morning Francesca leaves Ravenna as
a bride, and journeys in moonlight to Rimini. The
events which overtake her, and the feelings which
arise, lead to her adulterous love for Paolo. The lovers
are discovered, and their deaths conclude the poem.
Although of doubtful quality, the work, with its
flexibility of couplets, its use of common speech,
and the luxuriance of its southern imagery, suggested
new possibilities to the younger Romantic poets.
Blackwood's Magazine, in attacking 'the Cockney
School', derided Hunt's 'glittering and rancid obscenities'. (See ROMANTICISM.)

STOW, John (1525–1605), chronicler and antiquary. He
followed at first the trade of a tailor, and was admitted a
freeman of the Merchant Taylors' Company in 1547. At
first his interest was English poetry; then from about
1564 he began to collect and transcribe manuscripts
and to compose historical works, the first to be based
on systematic study of public records. He was suspected of recusancy, and in 1569 and 1570 was charged
with possessing popish and dangerous writings; he
was examined before the ecclesiastical commission,
but escaped without punishment. He is said to have
spent as much as £200 a year on books and manuscripts; he was patronized by the earl of *Leicester and
received a pension from the Merchant Taylors. A fine
effigy of Stow, based on one erected by his wife,
survives in the church of St Andrew Undershaft,
Leadenhall Street, London.

As well as assisting M. *Parker with editing historical texts, his chief publications were: *The Workes of
Geoffrey Chaucer* (1561)—his further notes on *Chaucer were subsequently printed by T. Speght (1598);
Summarie of Englyshe Chronicles (1565), an original
historical work; *The Chronicles of England* (1580), later
entitled *The Annales of England*; the second edition of
*Holinshed's *Chronicles* (1585–7); and lastly *A Survay
of London* (1598 and 1603), invaluable for the detailed
information it gives about the ancient city and its
customs. It was brought down to his day by J. *Strype
in 1720, and modernized and annotated editions have
since been published. The fullest edition of the original
work was C. L. Kingsford's of 1908.

STOWE, Mrs Harriet Elizabeth Beecher (1811–96),
born in Connecticut, sister of Henry Ward Beecher
(1813–87, divine, religious author, and journalist). She
was a schoolteacher in Cincinnati before marrying in
1836 C. E. Stowe, a professor at her father's theological
seminary. Her anti-slavery novel *Uncle Tom's Cabin*,
which was serialized in the *National Era* in 1851–2 and
published in book form in 1852, had a sensational
success and stirred up great public feeling. A powerful
if melodramatic tale, it describes the sufferings caused
by slavery; pious old Uncle Tom, sold by his well-

intentioned Kentucky owner Mr Shelby to meet his
debts, is bought first by the handsome, idealistic,
sensitive Augustine St Clair, in whose New Orleans
household he becomes the favourite of the daughter,
the saintly little Eva. But both Eva and St Clair die, and
Tom is sold again, this time to a brutal cotton plantation
owner, Simon Legree, who finally beats the unprotest-
ing Tom to death just before Shelby's son arrives to
redeem him. A parallel plot describes the escape to
freedom in Canada of Shelby's slave, the beautiful (and
almost white) quadroon Eliza, her child, and her
husband George. Mrs Stowe's stress on the anguish
of parted families was extremely telling, and her
contrast between Southern, New England, and Kentucky ways is well observed, but the sensational
religiosity of the story and its dubious conclusion
(in which most of the survivors, including the once-
irrepressible little slave *Topsy, disappear back to
Africa to become missionaries) contributed to a shift of
attitude which came to use the phrase 'Uncle Tom'
pejoratively, to indicate a supine collaboration with the
oppressor. The novel's success brought Mrs Stowe to
England in 1853, 1856, and 1859, where she was
rapturously received, and honoured by Queen *Victoria, although she later alienated British opinion by
her *Lady Byron Vindicated* (1870), in which she
charged *Byron with incestuous relations with his
half-sister. Her other works include *Dred: A Tale of the
Dismal Swamp* (1856), which also deals with slavery;
The Minister's Wooing (1859), a protest against the
doctrines of Calvinism; *Old Town Folks* (1869), set in
New England; and *Poganuc People* (1878), another tale
of New England family life with 'solidly remembered
scenes—of candlemakings, quiltings and apple bees,
chestnuttings and huckleberryings' praised by E.
*Wilson in *Patriotic Gore* (1962).

STRACHEY, John St Loe, see SPECTATOR.

STRACHEY, (Giles) Lytton (1880–1932), biographer
and essayist, born in London; he was the 11th child of
an eminent soldier and public administrator who had
served for more than 30 years in India, and he was
named after his godfather, the first earl of *Lytton,
viceroy of India. After an unhappy and sickly childhood and a miserable year at Liverpool University, he
found intellectual stimulus and liberation at Trinity
College, Cambridge; he became a member of the
*Apostles and a friend of G. E. *Moore, J. M. *Keynes
and L. *Woolf. He was thereafter a prominent member
of the *Bloomsbury Group, advocating both in words
and life its faith in tolerance in personal relationships:
he spent the last 16 years of his life in a *ménage à trois*
with Dora *Carrington and her husband Ralph Partridge. He was also, in the First World War, a conspicuous conscientious objector. After an abortive
attempt at an academic career, Strachey began to write
extensively for periodicals (including the *Spectator*,
the *Edinburgh Review*, the *Nation*, and the *Athenaeum*, and, later, *Life and Letters*). His flamboyant

Landmarks in French Literature appeared in 1912, but he did not achieve fame until 1918, with the publication of *Eminent Victorians*, itself a landmark in the history of *biography. This was a collection of four biographical essays, on Cardinal *Manning, F. Nightingale, T. *Arnold, and General Gordon; Strachey's wit, iconoclasm, satiric edge, and narrative powers captured a large (though at times hostile) readership, and *Connolly was later to describe the work as 'the first book of the twenties . . . the light at the end of the tunnel'. His irreverent but affectionate life of Queen *Victoria (1921), which combined careful construction, telling anecdote, and an elegant mandarin style, was also highly successful. His last full-length work, *Elizabeth and Essex: A Tragic History* (1928), is more lurid and pictorial; some critics found it erotic and salacious (E. *Wilson described it as 'slightly disgusting'), and its emphasis on Elizabeth's relationship with her father and its effect on her treatment of Essex shows a clear (and early) debt to *Freud. Various collections of Strachey's essays, on subjects ranging from *Voltaire to the *Muggletonians, appeared during his life and posthumously, and a two-volume critical biography by M. *Holroyd was published in 1967–8.

Strafford, a tragedy in blank verse by R. *Browning, published 1837. It was written at the instigation of *Macready, who produced it at Covent Garden on the day of publication, with himself in the title role. The play received mixed notices and had only a brief run; it has never been professionally revived. Browning drew some of his material from the biography of *Strafford which he helped J. *Forster to write.

The action deals with the events surrounding the impeachment of Strafford; Browning's interest lies in the interplay of love and loyalty between Strafford and the three other main characters: King Charles I, whose weakness causes Strafford's downfall; John Pym, his closest friend until Strafford joined the Royalist party and 'betrayed' the people; and Lady Carlisle, whose love for him Strafford, blinded by his devotion to the king, does not perceive. As with his other historical works, Browning's speculations about the characters' motives are idiosyncratic, and the action of the play is only loosely related to the actual course of events.

STRAFFORD, Sir Thomas Wentworth, first earl of (1593–1641), English statesman, and from 1639 chief adviser of Charles I. He was impeached by the Commons in 1640, but as it was manifestly impossible to convict him of high treason, a bill of attainder was substituted, and he was executed, after the king's assent, on Tower Hill. His death was the subject of many epitaphs, the best known of which (attributed to *Cleveland) contains the lines 'Strafford, who was hurried hence | Twixt Treason and Convenience'; also of a tragedy by R. *Browning (above).

STRAHAN, or **STRACHAN,** William (1715–85), born in Edinburgh. He was by 1738 apprenticed to a printer in London, and became established in the forefront of his trade, aided partly by the printing of *Johnson's *Dictionary*. He was a friend and correspondent of *Hume and of B. *Franklin, and printed work by the leading writers of the age, including *Gibbon, Adam *Smith, *Smollett, and *Warburton, with most of whom he maintained remarkably friendly personal relations. He became *king's printer in 1770. There is a life by J. A. Cochrane, *Dr Johnson's Printer* (1964).

Strand Magazine, a popular illustrated monthly founded in 1891 by G. *Newnes, which included amongst its contributions fiction by A. C. *Doyle (the third appearance of Sherlock Holmes), H. G. *Wells, *Morrison, and a vast number of the short stories of P. G. *Wodehouse. It closed in 1950. See R. Pound, *The Strand Magazine 1891–1950* (1966).

Strange Case of Dr Jekyll and Mr Hyde, The, see DR JEKYLL AND MR HYDE.

Strange Story, A, a novel by *Bulwer-Lytton.

STRANGFORD, Percy Clinton, sixth Viscount (1780–1855), born and educated in Dublin. He became a highly successful diplomat and public man. Profiting by his first posting to Lisbon, he published in 1803 *Poems from the Portuguese of Camoens*, which went into many editions. He was mocked as 'Hibernian' Strangford by Byron in *English Bards and Scotch Reviewers* (1809), but he was the friend of G. *Moore, *Croker, S. *Rogers, and other literary men, and a contributor to the *Gentleman's Magazine*.

STRAPAROLA, Gianfrancesco (c.1490–1557), Italian author of *novelle* entitled *Piacevoli Notti* (*Pleasant Nights*), published in two parts, 1550 and 1553. It enjoyed much popularity and introduced various folk tales to European literature, including the stories of Puss in Boots and *Beauty and the Beast. Painter, in his *Palace of Pleasure*, drew on Straparola among others.

STRAUSS, David Friedrich (1808–74), German biblical critic, who studied theology at Tübingen. He resigned his teaching post at Tübingen University in 1833, because of his unorthodox approach to biblical texts. His most famous work was *Das Leben Jesu, kritisch bearbeitet* (*The Life of Jesus, Critically Examined*, 1835–6), in which Strauss subjected the Gospel accounts of the life of Jesus to close historical criticism, finding them based on myth rather than historical fact. G. *Eliot translated the work into English in 1846 (her first published work), and her study of it helped to confirm her break with Christianity.

STRAUSS, Richard (1864–1949), German composer, whose early rise to fame was based largely on the orchestral tone poems that he wrote in the last decades of the 19th cent. The first was *Macbeth*, completed in 1888 and later revised (though not performed until after its more famous successor, *Don Juan*, in 1890).

Strauss once more returned to Shakespeare, with the three Ophelia songs in the *Sechs Lieder* (1918). The vast majority of Strauss's song texts are German. He first triumphed as an opera composer with a German version of *Wilde's Salome* (1905). There was an element of scandal in the success of this *fin-de-siècle* decadent piece but within two years *Salome* had been performed at 50 opera houses and has remained a staple of the repertoire. None of the operas Strauss wrote in collaboration with *Hofmannsthal had English sources, but after Hofmannsthal's death he accepted from S. *Zweig a libretto based on Jonson's *Epicene*, which became *Die schweigsame Frau*, one of the wittiest and most brilliant of his operas: it received four performances in 1935, but was then banned because of the Jewish origins of the librettist.

STRAVINSKY, Igor Fyodorovich (1882–1971), Russian composer who later adopted French and then American nationality. Not until he emigrated to the USA did he write his first and most important composition to English words, *The Rake's Progress* (1951). This opera had a fine libretto by *Auden assisted by Chester Kallman, and the result was a remarkable tour de force; both composer and librettist accepted the idea of a strongly marked operatic convention and the 18th-cent. environment imposed by the *Hogarth drawings on which the tale was based, yet the result is not pastiche but rather a work of classical precision. In the period immediately following *The Rake's Progress* Stravinsky's style underwent a profound change, absorbing aspects of the serial practice developed by Schoenberg; among the first works to adopt the new manner was the little *Cantata* (1952) made up of four late medieval English lyrics, and a year later the *Three Songs from William Shakespeare*. Auden offered Stravinsky another libretto (a masque entitled *Delia*) but Stravinsky turned to Dylan *Thomas, who proposed as a subject 'the rediscovery of our planet following an atomic misadventure'. The composer left a touching account of their one meeting in 1953, but the only music that resulted from it was *In Memoriam Dylan Thomas* (1954), a setting of 'Do not go gentle' for tenor, string quartet, and four trombones. Another 'in memoriam' piece is the miniature *Elegy for J.F.K.* (1964), for which he asked Auden to write 'a very quiet little lyric', which he set for baritone and three clarinets. The death of his friend T. S. *Eliot produced the short *Introitus*, first heard in Apr. 1965 together with the orchestral *Variations* dedicated to the memory of another close friend, A. *Huxley. His only setting of an Eliot text was the short polyphonic *Anthem* for unaccompanied chorus, 'The Dove descending breaks the air' (1962, 'Little Gidding', *Four Quartets*). Stravinsky's last work for the stage was the 'musical play' *The Flood*, a 24-minute version of part of the York miracle play. His actual last composition, at the age of 84, was a setting for soprano and piano of *Lear's 'The Owl and the Pussycat' which he dedicated to his wife.

Straw, Jack, see JACK STRAW.

Strawberry Hill, near Twickenham, about 10 miles west of the centre of London. Horace *Walpole settled there in 1747, and with advice from his friends *Chute and Richard *Bentley transformed it into 'a little Gothic castle', housing in it his collection of articles of virtu, and establishing in 1757 a private press; its first printing was of *Gray's *Odes*. Walpole also printed many of his own works. (See also GOTHIC REVIVAL.)

stream of consciousness, a term used variously to describe either the continuity of impressions and thoughts in the human mind, or a special literary method for representing this psychological principle in unpunctuated or fragmentary forms of *interior monologue. The term was coined in W. *James's *Principles of Psychology* (1890), in the first sense. The literary sense of the term was introduced in 1918 by May *Sinclair in a review of early volumes in D. *Richardson's novel sequence *Pilgrimage* (1915–38), which include the first notable English uses of the technique. As used by Richardson, and more famously by J. *Joyce in his novel *Ulysses* (1922), the stream-of-consciousness style represents the 'flow' of impressions, memories, and sense-impressions through the mind by abandoning accepted forms of syntax, punctuation, and logical connection. Joyce himself attributed the origin of the technique to the little-known French novel *Les Lauriers sont coupés* (1888) by Édouard Dujardin (1861–1949). After Joyce's virtuoso demonstration of its possibilities in the unpunctuated final chapter of *Ulysses*, the stream-of-consciousness method of rendering characters' thought processes became an accepted part of the modern novelist's repertoire, used by V. *Woolf, W. *Faulkner, and others.

Strephon, the shepherd whose lament for his lost Urania forms the opening of Sidney's *Arcadia*. 'Strephon' has been adopted as a conventional name for a rustic lover.

Strether, Lewis Lambert, a character in H. James's *The Ambassadors*.

STRETTON, Hesba, the *nom de plume* of Sarah Smith (1832–1911), a prolific writer of tracts, pamphlets, stories, and booklets, largely published by the Religious Tract Society. *Jessica's First Prayer* (1867) was reprinted innumerable times, brought tears to the eyes of *Kilvert, and remained popular for many years. She also wrote three long novels, which were well received: *Paul's Courtship* (1867), *The Clives of Burcot* (1868), and *Through a Needle's Eye* (1879). She contributed to *Dickens's *All the Year Round*, and to other periodicals. (See CHILDREN'S LITERATURE.)

STRINDBERG, (Johan) August (1849–1912), Swedish playwright and author, born in Stockholm, the son of a steamship agent who married his housekeeper after she had already borne him three sons: hence the title of his autobiography, *The Son of a Servant* (1886).

Strindberg achieved theatrical success only after much difficulty and attempts at other careers, and his works, dramatic and non-dramatic, are marked by a deeply neurotic response to religion, social class, and sexuality; he married three times, gained a reputation for anti-feminism and misogyny, and was tried for blasphemy, though acquitted. His first important play, *Master Olof* (written 1872–7, performed 1881), was followed by others, including *The Father* (1887), *Miss Julie* (1888), and *Creditors* (1889), works which combine a highly aggressive and original version of *naturalism with a sense of the extreme and pathological. His later works are tense, symbolic, psychic dramas, marked by a sense of suffering and a longing for salvation and absolution; they include *To Damascus* (1898–1901; 3 parts), *The Dance of Death* (1901), *A Dream Play* (1902), and *The Ghost Sonata* (1907), all distinctive and innovative works which influenced the psychological and symbolic dramas of *O'Neill and the writers of the Theatre of the *Absurd. G. B. *Shaw, who met Strindberg in Stockholm in 1908 and saw a specially arranged performance of *Miss Julie*, was a generous advocate of his work, but it was nevertheless some years before his plays were performed and accepted in England.

Strindberg's non-dramatic works include a novel, *The Red Room* (1879), *Getting Married* (1884, 1885; 2 vols of short stories), and *Inferno* (written and published in French, 1898), an extraordinary account of his life in Paris after the collapse of his second marriage, when, tormented by loneliness and driven to the verge of insanity by guilt and a sense of failure, he studied *Swedenborg, dabbled in alchemy, and suffered severe hallucinations. Many of Strindberg's plays have been translated into English by Michael Meyer, who also published a biography in 1985, and several of his works have been translated by Mary Sandbach.

STRODE, Ralph (fl. 1350–1400), minor Scholastic philosopher and logician, fellow of Merton College, Oxford, where he was the colleague of *Wyclif with whom he entered into controversy. As 'philosophical Strode' (V. 1857) he was the dedicatee of Chaucer's *Troilus and Criseyde*, along with *Gower.

STRODE, William (1600–45), poet and dramatist, educated at Oxford, where his tragi-comedy *The Floating Island* (pub. 1655) was performed before Charles I by the students of Christ Church in 1636, with songs set to music by H. *Lawes. His poems were collected by Bertram Dobell from manuscript and published with the play as *The Poetical Works of William Strode* (1907), with a memoir of the author. The poems include some fine love lyrics and epitaphs.

Strong, Dr, in Dickens's *David Copperfield*, an amiable old schoolmaster, who dotes on his young wife Annie and supports her worthless cousin Jack Maldon.

STRONG, L(eonard) A(lfred) G(eorge) (1896–1958), poet and novelist, born in Devon of half-Irish ancestry.

He was educated at Wadham College, Oxford, and later taught for some years in Oxford, before becoming a full-time writer; during this period he befriended the young *Day-Lewis. His many novels (which show a strain of the macabre and violent) include *Dewer Rides* (1929, set in Dartmoor) and *Sea Wall* (1933, set in Dublin). His autobiography of his early years, *Green Memory*, was published posthumously in 1961.

structuralism and **post-structuralism,** see p.978.

Struldbrugs, see GULLIVER'S TRAVELS.

STRUTT, Joseph (1749–1802), author, artist, engraver, and antiquary, author of many works valuable for their research and engravings, including a *Chronicle of England* (1777–8), *Dresses and Habits of the English People* (1796–9), and *Sports and Pastimes of the People of England* (1801). An unfinished novel by Strutt was completed by Sir W. *Scott (*Queenhoo Hall*, 1808), and suggested to him the publication of his own *Waverley.

Struwwelpeter, a book of comic illustrated morality rhymes published in 1845 by Dr Heinrich Hoffmann (1809–94), a German physician, who wrote the book for the amusement of his children: its anti-hero, with his grotesquely sprouting hair and nails, became an internationally recognizable figure, and has appeared in several English versions, sometimes as Slovenly Peter, more often as Shock-Headed Peter. The macabre humour of Belloc's *Cautionary Tales* (1907) owes much to him.

STRYPE, John (1643–1737), ecclesiastical historian, educated at St Paul's School, Jesus College and St Catharine's Hall, Cambridge. He formed a magnificent collection of original documents, mostly of the Tudor period, now in the *Harleian and Lansdowne manuscripts. He published lives of *Cranmer (1694), *Cheke (1705), Grindal (1710), M. *Parker (1711), and Whitgift (1718). He corrected and enlarged *Stow's *Survey of London* (1720).

STUART, Daniel (1766–1846), journalist, and an early press baron, who in 1795 bought the *Morning Post* and increased its circulation fourfold, later amalgamating with it the *Gazetteer* and the *Telegraph*. In 1796 he bought the *Courier* and when he sold the *Morning Post* in 1803 he proceeded to do for the *Courier* what he had done for his earlier paper. He employed excellent journalists and writers, including *Southey, *Lamb, *Wordsworth, and *Coleridge. Between 1799 and 1802 Coleridge wrote many articles, both political and literary, for the *Post*.

STUBBES, or **STUBBS,** Philip (fl. 1583–91), a Puritan pamphleteer, author of *The Anatomie of Abuses* (1583), a denunciation of evil customs of the time which, in the author's opinion, needed abolition. It contains a section on stage plays and is one of the principal sources of information on the social and economic conditions of the period. His account of his wife

Katherine, *A Christal Glasse for Christian Women* (1591), was very popular.

STUBBS, George (1724–1806), the greatest of the English 18th-cent. animal painters. Stubbs was also a brilliant anatomist. His paintings of sporting and country pursuits, in which grooms feature as prominently as their noble employers, are realistic and honest. His pictures of horses attacked by lions, a theme which recurred in his work from 1763 when his *Startled Horse* moved *Walpole to verse (*Public Advertiser*, 4 Nov. 1763), anticipated *Romanticism. *Reapers* and *Haymakers* (1783, 1785; London, Tate Gallery), possibly painted to appeal to the taste for pastoral scenes inspired by Thomson's **The Seasons*, proved too unsentimental to be widely popular.

STUBBS, John (c.1541–90), educated at Trinity College, Cambridge, and Lincoln's Inn. In August 1579 he published *The Discoverie of a Gaping Gulf whereinto England Is Like to Be Swallowed* when the queen's marriage to the French king's brother François, duc d'Alençon. For this he was imprisoned and had his right hand cut off, whereupon he 'put off his hat with his left and said with a loud voice "God save the Queen"'. The pamphlet has been edited by L. E. Berry (1968).

STUBBS, William (1825–1901), historian. Educated at Ripon Grammar School and Christ Church, Oxford, he was elected a fellow of Trinity College, Oxford, in 1848 but resigned in 1850 to take the living of Navestock, Essex; in 1866 he was appointed Regius professor of modern history at Oxford. He was the first substantial scholar to hold such a chair at either university, and may be said to have created the discipline of English medieval history single-handed. He showed his supreme professional skill, acquired by the study of contemporary German academic method, in the 18 volumes of medieval texts he edited for the *Rolls Series*, and this was the foundation for his great *Constitutional History of [Medieval] England* (3 vols, 1874–8), which has been described as 'one of the most astonishing achievements of the Victorian mind', fit to rank with *Darwin's *Origin of Species*. Together with his *Select Charters and Other Illustrations of English Constitutional History to 1307* (1870), it imposed a pattern and a method on the teaching of history in all British universities which survived until the mid-20th cent. (in Oxford longer), though he published nothing more after his elevation to the bishopric of Chester in 1884 and subsequently (1888) Oxford. The chief criticism of his work was that it partook of the attitudes of his time: he assumed that medieval England was a unified nation with common ideals, that its better kings had a formed and consistent plan of constitutional action, and that the development of Parliament was inevitable and evolutionary—ideas which might have had a shorter life had they been put forward by a lesser man.

His letters were published by W. H. Hutton (1904). See Helen Cam, 'Stubbs Seventy Years after', in *Cambridge Historical Journal*, 9 (1948); J. G. Edwards, *William Stubbs* (1952); J. W. Burrow, *A Liberal Descent* (1981).

Stukeley, a character in George Peele's **Battle of Alcazar*. The real Thomas Stukeley was said to be a natural son of *Henry VIII. He was an adventurer, who entered the service of the French king, was sent on a spying expedition to England, and betrayed his employer to Cecil. He next entered the service of Charles V; then embarked on a privateering expedition, for which Queen Elizabeth provided one of his ships, till the remonstrances of foreign powers led to his arrest. He proceeded to Ireland, where his ambitious schemes were distrusted and discountenanced by Elizabeth, then escaped to Spain, having been in treasonable correspondence with Philip II. He joined the king of Portugal's expedition against Morocco and was killed at the battle of Alcazar. Fuller in his **Worthies of England* gives an amusing account of a conversation between him and Queen Elizabeth.

STUKELEY, William (1687–1765), antiquary, who started life as a student of law, took a degree as doctor of medicine, and became secretary to the *Society of Antiquaries, which he shared in founding (1718). He wrote on many varied topics, ranging from flute music to earthquakes, but was particularly interested in Druidism, and his discussions of Stonehenge (*Stonehenge: A Temple Restor'd to the British Druids*, 1740) and Avebury (*Abury*, 1743) claimed (after *Aubrey) that they had been built by the Druids. He believed that the beliefs of the Druids were 'near akin to the Christian doctrine', that they believed in a Trinity, and that their alleged human sacrifices prefigured the Crucifixion; he defended them from the attacks of *Toland who had implied that they were superstitious, debauched, and corrupt. His views may have influenced *Blake's vision of *Albion, and *Wordsworth was also familiar with them. See A. L. Owen, *The Famous Druids* (1962) and Stuart Piggott, *William Stukeley: An Eighteenth Century Antiquary* (1985). (See PRIMITIVISM.)

STURGIS, Howard Overing (1855–1920), American-born novelist who lived for many years in England. He is remembered for *Belchamber* (1904), a novel called after the country house that dominates the plot. The elder son, nicknamed Sainty, is frail, high-minded, clever, and lame from a childhood riding accident: his younger brother Edward is sporting and extrovert, and marries an actress. Sainty inherits house and title, and is wooed for them under pressure from her mother by the determined young Cissy Ecclestone. She, as Lady Belchamber, refuses to consummate the marriage, and eventually gives birth to a bastard son, which Sainty agrees to recognize as his. The Jamesian undertones and Sturgis's love of the English aristocracy are marked.

Structuralism and post-structuralism are broad schools of thought that arose in Paris from the 1950s to the 1970s, asserting a powerful influence across a range of different kinds of cultural analysis, from anthropology and psycho-analysis to literary criticism and the study of cinema. Structuralism had the ambition of bringing these various realms under a single general 'science of signs' called semiotics or semiology and thus of uncovering the basic codes or systems of meaning that underlie all human cultural activity. Post-structuralism tends to abandon such grand scientific ambitions, although it still roves freely among widely different cultural forms. Both currents share the same founding principle, which is the primacy of 'Language', conceived as an abstract system of differences, in all human activities. An important consequence is that the autonomous human mind, hitherto assumed to be the maker of all meanings and cultural artefacts, is demoted to a subordinate position, as 'the subject' generated by Language. This agreed, structuralism and post-structuralism disagree only on the question of whether Language is knowably fixed as an object of science, or unstably indeterminate and slippery. Diametrically opposed conclusions about the relations between literature and science ensue: for structuralism, fictional texts are to be seen as instances of scientific laws, while post-structuralism often regards scientific laws as instances of textual fictions.

The origins of these movements lie in the foundation of modern linguistics by the Swiss scholar Ferdinand de *Saussure, who redirected the study of languages away from 'diachronic' questions of their historical development and towards 'synchronic' study of their workings at a given time. Structuralism and post-structuralism are inimical to historical enquiry into the origins of any phenomenon, and usually dismiss notions of evolution and progress as 19th-cent. superstitions. Saussure's second condition for the reconstruction of linguistics as a science was that its object of study should be, not individual utterances and their meanings (*parole*), but the system of rules and distinctions (the *langue*) that underlies them in a given language. Structuralism follows suit by showing less interest in what a cultural product (a poem, an advertisement, a culinary ritual) may mean than in the implicit rules that allow it to mean something. The key principle of Saussure's linguistic theory is that a word is an 'arbitrary sign': that is, its form and meaning derive not from any natural quality of its referent in the world outside language, but solely from its differences from other words. Saussure's general conclusion here is that 'in a language, there are only differences, without positive terms'. Meanings are, then, not to be found 'in' words but only through the differential relations between them, as conventionally established within a given language. Structuralism and post-structuralism alike are founded upon this principle of the 'relational' nature of signification and thus of all meanings. Abstracting from Saussure's work, which applies to the analysis of a given language such as English, they often invoke 'Language' as such, as a self-contained realm or general principle of differentiation. This permits the discovery of 'Language' at work in all kinds of activity not usually regarded as properly linguistic: cuisine, costume, dance, photography, and structures of kinship, for example, may all now be read as 'sign-systems'. Indeed, for the influential structuralist psychoanalyst Jacques Lacan (1901–81), it is Language that turns infants into human 'subjects', splitting their minds forever into conscious and unconscious levels as they enter its system of interchangeable pronouns.

After Saussure, the second founding father was the Russian linguist Roman Jakobson (1896–1982), whose career links his early work in the Russian *formalist school with full-blown structuralism in his later writings. Jakobson helped to shape the ideas of the leading French structuralists of the 1960s—*Lévi-Strauss, *Barthes, Lacan, and the Marxist philosopher Louis Althusser (1918–90)—with his claim that the basic principles by which all sign-systems combine their elements into meaningful compounds are those of *metaphor and *metonymy.

As applied to the analysis of particular literary works, the structuralist method is not concerned with critical evaluation, but with uncovering the basic 'binary oppositions' (nature/culture, male/female, active/passive, etc.) that govern the text. It rejects traditional conceptions in which literature is held to express an author's meaning or to reflect the real world; instead, it regards the 'text' as a self-contained structure in which conventional codes of meaning are activated. The most significant contribution it has made to literary study has been in the realm of *narratology, in the writings of A. J. Greimas, Gérard Genette, and Tzvetan Todorov. In the English-speaking world, some critics such as *Kermode, D. *Lodge in his *Modes of Modern Writing* (1977), and Jonathan Culler in his *Struc-

turalist Poetics (1975) have adopted elements of structuralist analysis, albeit cautiously. The anglophone tradition of literary criticism was already partly inoculated against these influences, having developed its own conceptions of literary language in the work of the *New Critics, and of generic structures in the work of *Frye.

Post-structuralism cannot be disentangled fully from structuralism: some of its leading figures, notably Barthes, show a transition from one to the other. In general, post-structuralism pursues structuralist arguments about the autonomy of Language from the world, to the point at which structuralism's own authority is undermined. The philosophical pioneer in this new phase is *Derrida, who began to unpick the logic of structuralism in 1966, pointing out certain basic instabilities in the founding concepts of 'structure' and 'binary opposition'. Under his corrosive re-examination, fixed structures appear to dissolve, binary opposites appear to contaminate one another, and determinate meanings become indeterminate. Post-structuralism thus challenges the 'scientific' pretensions, not only of structuralism but of other explanatory systems (notably Marxism), by appealing to the inherent uncertainty of Language. In particular, it discredits all 'metalanguages' (that is, uses of language that purport to explain other uses: linguistics, philosophy, criticism, etc.) by pointing out that they are just as unreliable as the kinds of language they claim to comprehend. Post-structuralism usually allows no appeal to a reality outside Language that could act as a foundation for linguistic meanings; instead, it sees every *discourse as circularly self-confirming. This is not quite the same as denying the existence of a real world outside Language, although Derrida's notorious declaration that 'il n'y a pas d'hors-texte' (rather misleadingly Englished as 'there is nothing outside the text') has given this impression. The radical scepticism of this movement reflected in part the libertarian politics of the 1960s and in part the influence of *Nietzsche, in its rejection of 'hierarchical' and 'totalitarian' systems of thought, its denial of objectivity, and its hostility to the 'grand narratives' of historical explanation associated with the *Enlightenment.

In terms of linguistic theory, the distinctive view of post-structuralism is that the *signifier (a written word, for example) is not fixed to a particular 'signified' (a concept), and so all meanings are provisional. Derrida's philosophical account of this idea found support in the psychoanalytic teachings of Lacan, which stress the instability of individual identity within Language. Lacan's writings created an intersection of psychological, linguistic, and political concerns in which much post-structuralist theory operates, notably the work of Julia Kristeva, Gilles Deleuze, and Jean-François Lyotard. A similar conjunction characterizes the work of *Foucault, which examines the power of Language as revealed in institutionalized 'discourses' and intellectual systems. In the social sciences and beyond, this body of post-structuralist theory encouraged cultural relativism and the associated view that our models of reality are 'constructed' in Language or discourse. It also shaped the concept of *postmodernism.

In academic literary criticism, post-structuralism has won a greater influence than the more narrowly scientific propositions of structuralism, partly because it respects such literary values as verbal complexity and paradox. In some versions, indeed, it threatens to treat history, philosophy, anthropology, and even natural science merely as branches of literature or 'text'. Many philosophers and social scientists regard Derrida and Lacan primarily as literary jesters, as both are noted for their elaborate punning and impenetrably dense style. Post-structuralist literary theory and criticism have assumed varied forms, from the kind of linguistic and rhetorical analysis inspired by Derrida and known as *deconstruction, to the *New Historicism inspired by Foucault. They include a version of *feminist criticism derived in part from Lacan and associated with the work of Kristeva. Another important figure is Barthes, whose writings of the 1970s present the process of reading less as a decoding of structures than as a kind of erotic sport. Both Barthes and Kristeva championed *Modernist literary experiment, in which they detected a politically liberating value opposed to the conservative implications of literary *realism. Post-structuralist criticism is in general more sympathetic to 'open', unstable, or self-referential writing than to what it regards as 'closed' literary forms; and it disparages realism in particular because it disguises the active power of Language in 'constructing' reality. See J. Sturrock (ed.), *Structuralism and since* (1979), and M. Sarup, *An Introductory Guide to Post-structuralism and Postmodernism* (1988).

STURLA THORDARSON (c.1214–84), nephew of *Snorri Sturluson, Icelandic historian, author of the *Sturlunga saga*, or contemporary history of the house of Sturla, a vivid picture of old Icelandic life.

Sturm und Drang (Storm and Stress), the name (taken from the title of a romantic drama of the American War of Independence by the German playwright Klinger, 1777) given to a period of literary ferment which prevailed in Germany during the latter part of the 18th cent. It was inspired by *Rousseau's fervent idealism and characterized by a revolt against literary conventions (particularly the *unities in drama), by the cult of genius, and by a return to 'nature'. The principal figures of the movement were the young *Goethe, *Herder, and *Schiller. Many of the plays were translated and adapted for the English stage during the 1790s.

STURT, George (1863–1927), born in Farnham, Surrey, where in 1884 he inherited the long-established family business described in *The Wheelwright's Shop* (1923), which records the traditions of and changes in local craftsmanship and relationships. Earlier works, published as 'George Bourne', include *The Bettesworth Book* (1901) and *Change in the Village* (1912). Selections from his journal were edited by G. *Grigson (1941) and E. D. Mackerness (1967).

STYRON, William (1925–   ), American novelist, born in Virginia, whose works include *Lie Down in Darkness* (1951), *The Long March* (1953), and *Set This House on Fire* (1960). He is best known internationally for two controversial novels, both of which raised issues of *cultural appropriation. *The Confessions of Nat Turner* (1967) is a work of *historical fiction, narrated by the leader of a slave revolt in Virginia in 1831, and *Sophie's Choice* (1979) deals with the *Holocaust.

sublime, the, an idea associated with religious awe, vastness, natural magnificence, and strong emotion which fascinated 18th-cent. literary critics and aestheticians. Its development marks the movement away from the clarity of *neo-classicism towards *Romanticism, with its emphasis on feeling and imagination; it was connected with the concept of original genius which soared fearlessly above the rules.

Sublimity in rhetoric and poetry was first analysed in an anonymous Greek work, *On the Sublime*, attributed to *Longinus, which was widely admired in England after *Boileau's French translation of 1674. The concept was elaborated by many writers, including *Addison, *Dennis, *Hume, *Burke, and H. *Blair and the discussion spread from literature to other areas. Longinus had described the immensity of objects in the natural world, of the stars, of mountains and volcanoes, and of the ocean, as a source of the sublime, and this idea was of profound importance to the growing feeling for the grandeur and violence of nature. The most widely read work, and most stimulating to writers and painters, was Burke's *Philosoph-* *ical Enquiry into the Origin of Our Ideas of the *Sublime and Beautiful* (1757). Burke put a new emphasis on terror: 'Whatever is fitted in any sort to excite the ideas of pain, and danger . . . or is conversant about terrible objects, or operates in a manner analogous to terror, is a source of the sublime; that is, it is productive of the strongest emotion which the mind is capable of feeling.' Burke saw the sublime as a category distinct from beauty. With the former he associated obscurity, power, darkness, solitude, and vastness and with the latter smoothness, delicacy, smallness, and light. These varied ideas were brought together, and discussed with greater philosophical rigour, by *Kant in the *Critique of Judgement* (1790). Burke's theory was popular, and stimulated a passion for terror that culminated in the Gothic tales of A. *Radcliffe and the macabre paintings, crowded with monsters and ghosts, of Barry, Mortimer, and *Fuseli. The cult drew strength from *Macpherson's Ossianic poems; Ossian took his place beside *Homer and *Milton as one of the great poets of the sublime, whose works were frequently illustrated by painters. The sublime of terror kindled the enthusiasm for wild scenery and cosmic grandeur already apparent in the writings of Addison and *Shaftesbury, and of E. *Young and James *Thomson. Many writers making the *Grand Tour dwelt on the sublimity of the Alps; they contrasted them with the pictures of *Rosa, whose stormy landscapes provided a pattern for 18th-cent. descriptions of savage nature. By the 1760s, when picturesque journeys in England became popular, travellers sought out the exhilarating perils of the rushing torrent, the remote mountain peak, and the gloomy forest. Many published their impressions in 'Tours', and sublimity became a fashion, pandered to by the dramatic storms shown by de Loutherbourg's Ediophusikon, a small theatre with lantern slides, and later by J. *Martin's vast panoramas of cosmic disaster.

The Romantic poets rejected the categories of 18th-cent. theorists and yet these writers on the sublime were moving, albeit clumsily, towards that sense of the mystery of natural forces that is so powerful in the poetry of *Byron, *Shelley, and *Wordsworth, and in the paintings of *Turner. See S. H. Monk, *The Sublime: A Study of Critical Theories in XVIII Century England* (1935).

Sublime, On the, see SUBLIME and LONGINUS.

Sublime and Beautiful, *A Philosophical Enquiry into the Origin of Our Ideas of the*, a treatise by E. *Burke, published anonymously 1757, with an 'Introduction on Taste' added 1759.

This is one of the earliest of Burke's publications, in which he discusses the distinctions between the *sublime, with its associations of infinity, darkness, solitude, terror, and vacuity, and the beautiful, which consists in relative smallness, smoothness, and brightness of colour. There are interesting sections on pleasure gained from distress (as in tragedy, or in the sight of a conflagration), and his descriptions of 'a sort of delightful horror, a sort of tranquillity tinged with terror' had much influence on the aesthetic theory of the later 18th cent. and in particular on G. E. *Lessing. Aphorisms like 'A clear idea is another name for a little idea' mark the transition from the lucidity admired by *Pope to the sublimity of writers like T. *Gray. Ed. J. T. Boulton (1958). See vol. i: *Early Writings* (1997) of *The Writings and Speeches of Edmund Burke*.

Subtle, the false alchemist and astrologer of Jonson's *The Alchemist*.

SUCKLING, Sir John (1609–42), of an old Norfolk family, educated at Trinity College, Cambridge. He inherited large estates, travelled on the Continent, and was knighted on his return in 1630. In 1631 he was in Germany, as a member of Sir Henry Vane's embassy to Gustavus Adolphus. He returned to London in 1632 and lived at court in great splendour. He became a leader of the Royalist party in the early troubles, then fled to France and is said by *Aubrey to have committed suicide in Paris. His chief works are included in *Fragmenta Aurea* (1646) and consist of poems, plays, letters, and tracts, among them the famous 'Ballad upon a Wedding'. His 'Sessions of the Poets', in which various writers of the day, including *Jonson, *Carew, and *D'Avenant, contend for the laurel, was written in 1637, and is interesting as an expression of contemporary opinion on these writers. Suckling's play *Aglaura* (with two fifth acts, one tragic, the other not) was lavishly staged and printed in 1638 at his own expense. *The Goblins* (1646), a romantic drama in which outlaws disguise themselves as devils, was said by *Dryden to illustrate Suckling's professed admiration for Shakespeare, 'his Reginella being an open imitation of Shakespeare's Miranda; his spirits, though counterfeit, yet are copied from Ariel.' *Brennoralt* (1646), an expansion of the *Discontented Colonell* (1640), a tragedy, is interesting for the light which the melancholy colonel throws on the author himself. The plays are, however, chiefly valuable for their lyrics, and Suckling has enjoyed a steady reputation as one of the most elegant and brilliant of the *Cavalier poets. D'Avenant speaks of his sparkling wit, describing him further as the greatest gallant and gamester of his day. According to Aubrey, he invented the game of cribbage. A two-volume edition of his works, ed. T. Clayton and L. A. Beaurline, appeared in 1971. (See also FALKLAND.)

SUE, Eugène (1804–57), French novelist, a prolific writer of novels of the Parisian underworld. The best known include *Les Mystères de Paris* (1842–3) and *Le Juif errant* (1844–5): see WANDERING JEW.

SUETONIUS (Gaius Suetonius Tranquillus) (AD c.70–c.140), Roman biographer whose major surviving work, the *Lives of the Caesars*, was composed in part while he was in charge of the imperial archives. Suetonius, writing about the Julio-Claudian and Fla-

vian emperors under a new dynasty, saw no reason to treat them as heroes. His aim was to bring out the moral character of his subjects, and for this purpose (and also because he was an inveterate gossip) he paid attention to their private habits as well as to their imperial policy. His method was adopted by later Roman biographers and may be said to have paved the way for the intimate biographies that began to appear in the second half of the 17th cent. But the flavour of his writing has been best caught by Robert *Graves in *I, Claudius* and *Claudius the God*.

Sullen, Squire and Mrs, characters in Farquhar's *The Beaux' Stratagem*.

SULLIVAN, Sir Arthur (1842–1900), English composer. Such is the popularity of the *Gilbert and Sullivan operas that it is often forgotten that Sullivan made a distinguished career as a composer in his own right, and was considered the leading musician in the period preceding *Parry and *Stanford.

Sullivan's Op. 1, written when he was a 19-year-old student at Leipzig, was a group of 12 pieces of incidental music for *The Tempest*: they seem never to have been used in the theatre, though their first performance in London made Sullivan famous and later, in Paris, he played them in a piano duet version with *Rossini, who apparently liked them very much. He subsequently wrote successful incidental music for other Shakespeare plays—*The Merchant of Venice* (1871), *Henry VIII* (1877), *Macbeth* (1888)—and there are a number of Shakespeare settings in the cantata *Kenilworth* (1865). His *Five Shakespeare Songs* (1866) include the famous setting of 'Orpheus with his lute', and were among the earliest of an enormous number of songs and ballads written for the Victorian drawing room, and he also collaborated with *Tennyson on a song cycle, *The Window, or The Songs of the Wrens* (1871).

The bigger choral works tend to be on sacred subjects, though *The Golden Legend*, which Sullivan himself regarded as his masterpiece, is based on *Longfellow. His one attempt at serious opera, *Ivanhoe* (after Sir W. *Scott, 1891), opened with much publicity but did not last, and certainly could not compare with the brilliance of the comic operas, for which (and perhaps, less happily, for the hymn tune 'Onward, Christian soldiers') he is remembered today.

'Sumer is icumen in', one of the earliest known English lyrics, found in BL MS Harley 978, a miscellany of Reading Abbey from the first half of the 13th cent. The music, and Latin instructions for singing it, are also in the manuscript.

SUMMERS, Montague (1880–1948), vampirologist and man of letters. He was born in Clifton, Bristol, and attended Clifton College and Trinity College, Oxford. An admirer of *Wilde and *Symons, he was unsuccessful both as a 'Decadent' poet and as an Anglican priest, and so turned to schoolteaching,

Roman Catholicism, collecting rare books, and exploring the less reputable byways of literature and superstition. An energetic champion of the Restoration dramatists, he edited the works of *Behn, *Congreve, *Wycherley, *Otway, *Shadwell, and *Dryden, but was condemned by better scholars for inaccuracy and plagiarism. Another literary hobby was *Gothic fiction: his projected history of this tradition began with the prolix *The Gothic Quest* (1938), but was never completed. His reputation as an authority on occult practices and legends rests upon his *History of Witchcraft and Demonology* (1926), *The Geography of Witchcraft* (1927), *The Vampire* (1928), and *The Werewolf* (1933). He also edited a number of ghost story anthologies.

Summers Last Will and Testament, a play by T. *Nashe, published 1600, but written in the autumn of 1592 or 1593. It is framed by the jocular comments of Will Summers, *Henry VIII's jester (who died *c.*1560), and is an allegorical pageant in which Summer, personified as a dying old man, decides to whom to leave his riches. The play reflects fear of the plague, of which there was a prolonged outbreak in 1592–3, in the famous lyric:

> Adieu, farewell earths blisse,
> This world uncertaine is,
> Fond are lifes lustfull joyes,
> Death proves them all but toyes,
> None from his darts can flye;
> I am sick, I must dye:
>> Lord, have mercy on us.

Summerson, Esther, a character in Dickens's *Bleak House*, and one of the narrators of the tale.

'Summoner's Tale, The', see CANTERBURY TALES, 8.

Sunday Times, a Sunday paper founded in 1822 by Henry White, and still in existence, despite several periods of obscurity. It grew greatly in circulation and influence from the 1930s onwards, earning a high reputation for its arts pages and, recently, for its investigative journalism; notable reviewers have included J. *Agate, D. *MacCarthy, C. *Connolly, Dilys Powell (film critic, 1939–76), and Sir Harold Hobson (drama critic, 1947–76). The gossip column 'Atticus', started by T. P. *O'Connor, has been written by (among others) J. *Buchan, S. *Sitwell, and I. *Fleming. See *The Pearl of Days* (1972), a memoir of the paper by H. Hobson, P. Knightley, and L. Russell.

Supposes, a comedy in prose, one of the earliest in English, by G. *Gascoigne, translated from *Ariosto's *I suppositi*, and performed at Gray's Inn in 1566. It concerns a series of disguises and confused identities; the scenes with servants are effectively comic, especially those with the old nurse Balia.

Surface, Joseph and Charles, the two brothers in Sheridan's *The School for Scandal*.

Surgeon's Daughter, The, a novel by Sir W. *Scott, published 1827 as one of the stories in *Chronicles of the Canongate*. In this story Scott goes to India (a country he never visited) for a melodramatic tale of treachery and betrayal. The best part is the opening description of the home of Dr Gideon Gray, where the orphaned Richard Middlemas is reared with the surgeon's daughter, Menie, whom he later lures out to India to be sold as a concubine to Tippoo Sahib. Menie is rescued but dies single; Richard is killed on the order of Hyder Ali by being trampled to death by an elephant.

'Surprised by Joy—Impatient as the Wind', a sonnet by *Wordsworth, first published in 1815, suggested by the death of his daughter Catherine in 1812, but written, by his own account, 'long after'.

Surrealism, a movement founded in Paris in 1924 with the publication of A. *Breton's first *Surrealist Manifesto*. It was conceived as a revolutionary mode of thought and action, concerned with politics, philosophy, and psychology as well as literature and art. The *Manifesto* attacked rationalism and narrow logical systems; drawing on *Freud's theories concerning the unconscious and its relation to dreams, it called for the exploration of hidden and neglected areas of the human psyche, not necessarily from the standpoint of psychoanalysis, and the resolution 'of the apparently contradictory states of dream and reality'. The group of writers and painters that gathered round Breton experimented with automatic processes, which were considered the best means of producing the surreal poetic image: the spontaneous coupling of unrelated objects. An extended conception of poetry, which was to be part of, not separate from, life, was central to Surrealism. A great variety of poetry was published by, for example, Breton, *Aragon, *Éluard, Robert Desnos, Benjamin Péret, René Crevel; but much surrealist writing falls outside conventional literary categories, e.g. Aragon's *Paris Peasant* (1926) or Breton's *Communicating Vessels* (1932). Breton's *Nadja* (1928), for instance, both records an intense personal relationship and challenges socially determined definitions of sanity and insanity. Surrealist artists in the 1920s sought equivalents to automatic writing, e.g. André Masson's free ink drawings, Max Ernst's *frottages*, or Joan Miró's field painting. In 1929 *Dali joined the movement, introducing a more illusionistic 'dream' imagery heavily indebted to Freud. In the 1930s writers and artists alike collected or fabricated surrealist objects (often relying on chance), and Breton mixed words and images in his poem-objects. Several surrealists joined the Communist Party and theoretical texts, including Breton's *Surrealist Manifesto* of 1930, try to reconcile Freud and *Marx.

Surrealism was a major intellectual force between the wars, although as it spread internationally in the 1930s interest tended to concentrate on surrealist art.

In England the movement attracted some attention among literary circles, but it was only after the International Surrealist Exhibition of 1936 that a surrealist group was established, its members including D. *Gascoyne, H. *Read, Roland Penrose (1900–84), the documentary film-maker Humphrey Jennings (1907–50), and Hugh Sykes Davies (1909–84).

SURREY, Henry Howard, (by courtesy) earl of (?1517–47), poet, the son of Thomas Howard (afterwards third duke of Norfolk). He married Frances Vere in 1532. He was with the army during the war with France (1544–6), being wounded before Montreuil, and was commander of Boulogne, 1545–6. He was accused of various minor offences, but tried and executed on the charge of treasonably quartering the royal arms. His works consist of sonnets and poems in various metres notable for their elegance of construction. Like *Wyatt he studied Italian models, especially *Petrarch, but his sonnets were predominantly in the 'English' form (a b a b c d c d e f e f g g), later to be used by Shakespeare, which appears to have been his invention. (See SONNET.) A still more durable innovation was his use of blank verse in his translation of the *Aeneid, Bks 2 and 4. Forty of his poems were printed by *Tottel in his Miscellany (1557). *Nashe and *Drayton built up a picture of Surrey as the languishing lover of 'Geraldine' (Elizabeth, daughter of the ninth earl of Kildare); but he seems to have done no more than address a single sonnet to this lady, possibly when she was as young as 9.

Surrey's poems were edited together with those of Wyatt by G. F. Nott, 1815–16; and, in selection, by Emrys Jones in 1964.

SURTEES, Robert (1779–1834), educated at Christ Church, Oxford, an antiquary and topographer. He spent his life in collecting materials for his History of Durham (1816–40). He is commemorated in the Surtees Society, which publishes original materials relating to the history of the region constituting the old kingdom of Northumbria. Sir W. Scott included in his *Minstrelsy of the Scottish Border a spurious and spirited ballad by him, 'The Death of Featherston-haugh'. 'Barthram's Dirge' in the same collection is suspected of being also by Surtees (J. H. Burton, The Book-Hunter, 1862).

SURTEES, Robert Smith (1805–64), born in Durham, the son of a country squire. After attending Durham Grammar School he became articled to a solicitor and practised as a lawyer. From 1830 he built up a reputation as a sporting journalist, contributing to the Sporting Magazine, and in 1831 founded, with R. Ackermann the younger, and edited the New Sporting Magazine to which he contributed his comic sketches of Mr Jorrocks, the sporting cockney grocer, later collected as Jorrocks's Jaunts and Jollities (1838, illustrated by 'Phiz', H. K. *Browne, and later by H. T. Alken). Jorrocks, whose adventures to some extent

suggested the original idea of *Pickwick Papers, reappears in Handley Cross (1843; expanded and illustrated by *Leech, 1854), one of Surtees's most successful novels, and in the less popular Hillingdon Hall (1845). His second great character, Mr Soapey Sponge, appears in Mr Sponge's Sporting Tour (1853, illustrated by Leech), which is probably his best work; another celebrated character was Mr Facey Romford, who appears in his last novel, Mr Facey Romford's Hounds (1865). Surtees had abandoned his legal practice in 1835, resigned his editorship in 1836, inherited his father's Hamsterley estate in 1838, and thereafter devoted his time to his favourite pursuits of hunting and shooting (he became high sheriff of Durham in 1856) while continuing his literary work. His eight long novels deal mainly with the characteristic aspects of English fox-hunting society, but his vivid caricatures, the absurd scenes he describes, the convincing dialect and often repeated catchphrases, and perceptive social observation distinguish him from other writers of this genre and won him praise from *Thackeray and others; the illustration of his novels by Leech, Alken, and Phiz also contributed to their success. Young Tom Hall, originally serialized in the New Monthly Magazine in 1853, remained unfinished and was first published in book form in 1926.

Survay of London, A, see STOW.

Suspicious Husband, The, a comedy by Dr B. *Hoadly and his brother John 'Chancellor' Hoadly, produced 1747 at Covent Garden, *Garrick taking the part of Ranger.

Strictland, the suspicious husband of a young wife, is guardian of the wealthy Jacintha. She and Bellamy are in love, but Strictland will not hear of the match. So Jacintha, a young lady of spirit, decides to run away with her lover, who provides a rope ladder for the purpose. Clarinda, a sprightly young friend of Mrs Strictland, is staying in her house. Frankly, a friend of Bellamy, who has fallen in love with her at Bath, pursues her to London. Frankly and Bellamy meet outside the house at night, just when Jacintha is about to escape and when Clarinda, after a late whist party, is coming home. A general imbroglio ensues. Bellamy suspects Frankly of an intrigue with Jacintha; Strictland, discovering the latter's attempted flight, goes off in pursuit. Meanwhile Ranger, an adventurous rake and friend of Bellamy and Frankly, happening to pass and seeing a rope ladder hanging from the window, climbs up in search of adventure, and makes his way to the bedroom of Mrs Strictland, whom he has never seen before. The return of Strictland with the captured Jacintha puts him to flight, but he drops his hat in Mrs Strictland's room where it is discovered by her husband, who is now convinced that his suspicions were well founded and sentences his wife to banishment to the country. Meanwhile Ranger, who has taken refuge in another room, discovers Jacintha, and enables her to escape, this time successfully. On the morrow there is a general confrontation and explanation, and all ends happily.

SUTCLIFF, Rosemary, see CHILDREN'S LITERATURE.

Svejk, the Good Soldier, see HAŠEK.

Svengali, see TRILBY.

SVEVO, Italo (Ettore Schmitz) (1861–1928), Italian novelist, who also wrote plays, short stories, and criticism, born in Trieste from a Jewish Italo-German background (indicated by his pen-name). His novels are: *Una vita* (*A Life*, 1893), *Senilità* (a title translated by *Joyce as *As a Man Grows Older*, 1898), *La coscienza del Zeno* (*Confessions of Zeno*, 1923), *La novella del buon vecchio e della bella fanciulla* (*The Tale of the Good Old Man and of the Lovely Young Girl*, 1929). He was working on a fifth novel, *Il vecchione* (*The Grand Old Man*, 1967), when he died in a car crash. Svevo's work was unknown until Joyce met him in Trieste and helped him to publish his masterpiece, *Confessions of Zeno*. Svevo's style stood out against prevailing trends based on *d'Annunzio and *Fogazzaro. *Zeno* is a complex and delicately balanced novel in which time and point of view are relative. Arguing with his psychoanalyst, Zeno struggles with chance, time, marriage, and tobacco, disclosing the source of his malady as the Oedipus complex.

Swan Theatre, built by Frances Langley on the Bankside in London in 1595, and closed down temporarily in 1597, following a performance by Lord Pembroke's Company of *Nashe's controversial play *The Isle of Dogs*. The Lady Elizabeth's Company is believed to have performed *A Chaste Mayd in Cheapside* there around 1613. Johannes de Witt's sketch (*c*.1596) of the theatre is believed to be the only surviving representation of the interior of an Elizabethan playhouse. The name was adopted by the Royal Shakespeare Company for its galleried playhouse, which opened in Stratford in 1986.

SWEDENBORG, Emanuel (1688–1772), born Swedberg, Swedish philosopher, scientist, and mystic, the son of a professor of theology at Uppsala. He studied at Uppsala, and travelled extensively in England, where he was influenced by Henry More, J. *Locke, and I. *Newton. He was appointed to a post on the Swedish board of mines in 1716, and in his capacity as scientist and engineer anticipated many subsequent hypotheses and inventions. He was gradually led to seek a comprehensive scientific explanation of the universe, attempting to demonstrate that it had, essentially, a spiritual structure, and in his later years he began to experience visions and to converse with angels, not only in his dreams, but, he claimed, in his waking life. According to his theosophic system, God, as Divine Man, is infinite love and infinite wisdom, from whom emanate the two worlds of nature and spirit, distinct but closely related. God is not a 'windy or ethereal spirit', but 'very Man. In all the Heavens, there is no other idea of God, than that of a Man' (*Divine Love and Wisdom*, 1763). The end of creation is the approximation of Man to God; this end having been endangered by evil spirits, Jehovah descended into nature, restored the connection between God and Man, and left the Scriptures as his testimony, with Swedenborg as his appointed interpreter. Swedenborg died in London, and his followers there organized themselves into the New Church, of which *Blake was for a while an active member. Blake was deeply influenced by Swedenborg's writings, which began to appear in English from 1750, a printing society being founded in Manchester in 1782 to propagate his works; Blake's pencilled annotations to Swedenborg's *Wisdom of Angels Concerning Divine Love and Divine Wisdom*, written *c*.1789, survive. See J. G. Davies, *The Theology of William Blake* (1948) and K. *Raine, *Blake and Tradition* (2 vols, 1969). Swedenborg also had a considerable influence on other writers, including *Strindberg and the French *symbolists.

Sweedlepipe, Paul or Poll, in Dickens's *Martin Chuzzlewit*, bird-fancier and barber, Mrs Gamp's landlord.

SWEENEY, Matthew (1952–   ), Irish poet, born in Co. Donegal. He moved to England in 1973, where he now lives. His six collections include *A Dream of Maps* (1981), *A Round House* (1983), *The Lame Waltzer* (1985), *Blue Shoes* (1989), and *Cacti* (1992). Early influences from *Kafka and *Simic are detectable in the development of Sweeney's strange, often sinister, territory. His storytelling gifts, however, are firmly rooted in the Irish tradition, and the narrative voice, at once disquieting and seductive, is highly original. *The Bridal Suite* (1997) is laced with an obsession with mortality, to which his work almost inevitably returns.

Sweeney Agonistes, a poetic drama by T. S. *Eliot.

SWEET, Henry (1845–1912), a great phonetician and (after A. J. Ellis) one of the founders of that study in England, educated at Heidelberg University and Balliol College, Oxford, where he got a fourth class in Lit. Hum. (1873). He lived in Oxford from 1895 until his death, but he never fully received the recognition there that his eminence warranted; the readership in phonetics he was accorded in 1901 was a poor compensation for his failure to gain a number of chairs, especially the chair of comparative philology on the death of *Max Müller in 1901. He is said to be the inspiration for Shaw's Henry Higgins in *Pygmalion*, though Higgins's hypersensitivity about judgements on him is lighter than the original's. His works are still a staple of the study of Old English and the philology of English; the most celebrated are *History of English Sounds* (1874, 1888); *Anglo-Saxon Reader* (1876); *Anglo-Saxon Primer* (1882); *A New English Grammar* (1892, 1898); *The History of Language* (1900); and *The Sounds of English: An Introduction to Phonetics* (1908).

SWIFT, Graham (1949–   ), English novelist, born in London. He studied at Queens' College, Cambridge, and worked as a part-time teacher in and around London for much of the 1970s. There is a didactic strain in many of Swift's novels, and their themes frequently pertain to history and its bearing upon the present lives of his troubled and questioning characters. His first novel, *The Sweet Shop Owner* (1980), was a low-key and melancholy portrait of an emotionally unfulfilled shopkeeper in the last few hours of his life. It was followed by *Shuttlecock* (1981), which features an archetypal Swift protagonist: a police archivist whose work leads him to dig up wartime secrets which cast doubt on the integrity of his father and also, by extension, himself. *Learning to Swim* (1982) was a versatile collection of short stories. With *Waterland* (1984), Swift produced what many consider to be his finest book: a dense, multi-layered narrative which is at once a history of domestic upheaval and of the English fen country. The novel attempted to integrate a meditation on the nature of history (its hero is a schoolteacher specializing in that subject) with touches of the whodunnit, but it was Swift's vivid and precise sense of landscape that drew comparisons with Thomas *Hardy. His next two novels allowed their main characters similar scope for excavating the past: Harry Beech in *Out of This World* (1988) is a photo-journalist estranged (like Willy Chapman in *The Sweet Shop Owner*) from his embittered daughter, while Bill Unwin in *Ever after* (1992) is a university professor burying himself in ancestral research while recovering from a suicide attempt. Death also hangs over *Last Orders* (1996, *Booker Prize) which tells the story of four south Londoners who make a pilgrimage to the coast to scatter the ashes of a lifelong friend. The working-class demotic in which the novel is narrated is a highly literary construct, like the Glaswegian dialect of James *Kelman, but this does not detract from the book's compassion and power. *The Light of Day* (2003) is narrated by a former policeman, and confined to the events of a single day.

SWIFT, Jonathan (1667–1745), born in Dublin after his father's death. He was son of Jonathan Swift by Abigail (Erick) of Leicester, and grandson of Thomas Swift, the well-known Royalist vicar of Goodrich, descended from a Yorkshire family. He was a cousin of *Dryden. He was educated with *Congreve, at Kilkenny Grammar School, then at Trinity College, Dublin, where he was censured for offences against discipline, obtaining his degree only by 'special grace'. He was admitted (1689) to the household of Sir W. *Temple, and there acted as secretary. He was sent by Temple to William III to convince him of the necessity of triennial parliaments, but his mission was not successful. He wrote Pindaric *odes, one of which, printed in the *Athenian Mercury* (1692), provoked, according to Dr *Johnson, Dryden's remark, 'Cousin Swift, you will never be a poet.' Chafing at his position of dependence, and indignant at Temple's delay in getting him preferment,

he returned to Ireland, was ordained (1694), and received the small prebend of Kilroot. He returned to Temple at Moor Park in 1696, where he edited Temple's correspondence, and in 1697 wrote *The Battle of the Books*, which was published in 1704 together with *A Tale of a Tub*, his celebrated satire on 'corruptions in religion and learning'. At Moor Park he first met Esther Johnson ('Stella'), the daughter of a servant or companion of Temple's sister. On the death of Temple in 1699, Swift went again to Ireland, where he was given a prebend in St Patrick's, Dublin, and the living of Laracor. He wrote his *Discourse of the Contests and Dissensions between the Nobles and the Commons in Athens and Rome*, with reference to the impeachment of the Whig lords, in 1701. In the course of numerous visits to London he became acquainted with *Addison, *Steele, Congreve, and Halifax. He was entrusted in 1707 with a mission to obtain the grant of Queen Anne's Bounty for Ireland, and in 1708 began a series of pamphlets on church questions with his ironical *Argument against Abolishing Christianity*, followed in the same year by his *Letter Concerning the Sacramental Test*, an attack on the Irish Presbyterians which injured him with the Whigs. Amid these serious occupations, he diverted himself with the series of squibs upon the astrologer John Partridge (1708–9, see under BICKERSTAFF), which have become famous, and his 'Description of a City Shower' and 'Description of the Morning', poems depicting scenes of London life, which were published in the *Tatler* (1709). Disgusted at the Whig alliance with Dissent, he went over to the Tories in 1710, joined the Brothers' Club, attacked the Whig ministers in the *Examiner*, which he edited, and in 1711 wrote *The Conduct of the Allies* and *Some Remarks on the Barrier Treaty*, pamphlets written to dispose the mind of the nation to peace. He became dean of St Patrick's in 1713. He had already begun his *Journal to Stella*, a series of intimate letters (1710–13) to Esther Johnson and her companion Rebecca Dingley, who had moved to Ireland in 1700/1; it is written partly in baby language, and gives a vivid account of Swift's daily life in London where he was in close touch with Tory ministers. Swift's relations with Stella remain obscure; they were intimate and affectionate, and some form of marriage may have taken place. Another woman, Esther Vanhomrigh (pron. 'Vanummery'), entered his life in 1708; his poem *Cadenus and Vanessa* suggests that she fell deeply in love with him ('She wished her Tutor were her Lover') and that he gave her some encouragement. She is said to have died of shock in 1723 after his final rupture with her, inspired by her jealousy of Stella. Stella died in 1728.

Swift wrote various political pamphlets, notably *The Importance of the Guardian Considered* (1713) and *The Public Spirit of the Whigs* (1714), in reply to Steele's *Crisis*; and about the time of the queen's death in 1714 and the fall of the Tory ministry, several papers (published much later) in defence of the latter. In the same year he joined *Pope, *Arbuthnot, *Gay, and others in the celebrated *Scriblerus Club. He returned to Ireland in Aug. 1714 and occupied himself with Irish affairs, being led by his resentment of the policy of the Whigs to acquire a sense of their unfair treatment of Ireland. By his famous *Drapier's Letters (1724) he prevented the introduction of 'Wood's Half-pence' into Ireland. He came to England in 1726, visited Pope and Gay, and dined with Sir R. *Walpole, to whom he addressed a letter of remonstrance on Irish affairs with no result. He published *Gulliver's Travels in the same year, and paid a last visit to England in 1727, when the death of George I created for a moment hopes of dislodging Walpole. He wrote some of his most famous tracts and characteristic poems during his last years in Ireland, The Grand Question Debated (1729); Verses on the Death of Dr Swift (1731, pub. 1739), in which with mingled pathos and humour he reviews his life and work; A Complete Collection of Polite and Ingenious *Conversation (1738); and the ironical Directions to Servants (written about 1731 and published after his death). He kept up his correspondence with *Bolingbroke, Pope, Gay, and Arbuthnot, attracted to himself a small circle of friends, and was adored by the people. He spent a third of his income on charities, and saved another third to found St Patrick's Hospital for Imbeciles (opened 1757). The symptoms of the illness from which he suffered for most of his life (now thought to have been Ménière's disease) became very marked in his last years, and his faculties decayed to such a degree that many considered him insane, though modern biographical opinion rejects this view. He was buried by the side of Stella, in St Patrick's, Dublin, his own famous epitaph 'ubi saeva indignatio ulterius cor lacerare nequit' (where fierce indignation cannot further tear apart the heart) being inscribed on his tomb. Nearly all his works were published anonymously, and for only one, Gulliver's Travels, did he receive any payment (£200). Dr Johnson, *Macaulay, and *Thackeray, among many other writers, were alienated by his ferocity and coarseness, and his works tended to be undervalued in the late 18th–19th cents. The 20th cent. has seen a revival of biographical and critical interest, stressing on the whole Swift's sanity, vigour, and satirical inventiveness rather than his alleged misanthropy.

Swift published a great number of works. Besides the more important, referred to above, mention may be made of the following:

Political writings: The Virtues of Sid Hamet the Magician's Rod (1710), an attack on Godolphin; The W—ds—r Prophecy (1711), attacking the duchess of Somerset; A Short Character of T[homas] E[arl] of W[harton] (1711); The Fable of Midas (1711); Some Advice Humbly Offered to the Members of the October Club, the extreme Tories (1712); Some Free Thoughts upon the Present State of Affairs (1714); Traulus (1730), attacking Lord Allen; and the History of the Four Last Years of the Queen [Anne] (1758), which contains his famous character of *Harley.

Pamphlets relating to Ireland: A Proposal for the Universal Use of Irish Manufacture (1720); The Swearer's-Bank (1720); The Story of the Injured Lady (?1746); A Short View of the State of Ireland (1728); *A Modest Proposal (1729); An Examination of Certain Abuses, Corruptions and Enormities in the City of Dublin (1732); The Legion Club (the Irish Parliament, 1736).

Pamphlets on church questions: The Sentiments of a Church of England Man with Respect to Religion and Government (1708); A Project for the Advancement of Religion and the Reformation of Manners (1709); A Preface to the B—p of S—r—m's Introduction (1713), an attack on Bishop *Burnet; Mr C—ns's Discourse on Free Thinking, a satire on Anthony *Collins (1713); A Letter to a Young Gentleman, Lately Entered into Holy Orders (1721). Swift's Sermons (of which four were published in 1744), are marked by the author's usual characteristics of vigour and common sense.

Miscellaneous verses and other writings: 'Mrs Frances Harris's Petition', a servant who has lost her purse, an amusing burlesque (1709); *Baucis and Philemon (1709); 'On Mrs Biddy Floyd' (1709); 'A Meditation upon a Broom-Stick' (1710); A Proposal for Correcting, Improving and Ascertaining the English Tongue (1712); imitations of the Seventh Epistle of the First Book of *Horace and the First Ode of the Second Book of Horace (1738); A Letter of Advice to a Young Poet (1721); a 'Letter to a Very Young Lady on Her Marriage' (1727); the 'Journal of a Dublin Lady' (1729); The Lady's Dressing-Room (1732); The Beasts Confession to the Priest (1732), a satire on 'the universal folly of mankind in mistaking their talents'; A Serious and Useful Scheme to Make an Hospital for Incurables—whether the incurable disease were knavery, folly, lying, or, infidelity (1733); On Poetry, a Rhapsody (1733), satirical advice to a poet; A Beautiful Young Nymph Going to Bed; and Strephon and Chloe (1734).

The Prose Works have been edited by Herbert Davis (16 vols, 1939–74); Journal to Stella by H. Williams (2 vols, 1948); Poems by H. Williams (1937); Correspondence by H. Williams (5 vols, 1963–5); Complete Poems ed. P. Rogers (Penguin, 1983), with an important commentary. See also Irvin Ehrenpreis, Swift: The Man, His Works and the Age (3 vols, 1962–83) and a useful short study by R. Quintana, Swift: An Introduction (1955).

SWINBURNE, Algernon Charles (1837–1909), of an old Northumbrian family. He spent much of his childhood in the Isle of Wight, where he acquired a lasting love of the sea, reflected in much of his work. He was educated at Eton, where he developed an equally lasting interest in flagellation, and at Balliol College, Oxford, where he was associated with *Rossetti and the *Pre-Raphaelite circle. His first published volume, The Queen-Mother; Rosamund (1860), shows the influence of Elizabethan dramatists, notably of *Chapman, and attracted little attention, but *Atalanta in Calydon (1865), a drama in classical Greek form, with choruses (e.g. 'When the hounds of spring are on winter's traces') that revealed his great metrical skills, brought him celebrity; *Tennyson wrote praising his 'wonderful rhythmic invention'. *Chastelard*, the first of three dramas on the subject of *Mary Queen of Scots, which appeared the same year, raised some doubts about the morality of Swinburne's verse, doubts reinforced by the first series of *Poems and Ballads* (1866), which brought down a torrent of abuse from R. *Buchanan, J. *Morley, and others. The volume contains many of his best as well as his most notorious poems (*'Dolores', 'Itylus', 'Hymn to Proserpine', 'The Triumph of Time', 'Faustine', 'Laus Veneris', etc.) which clearly demonstrate the preoccupation with de *Sade, masochism, and *femmes fatales* which he shared with a circle of friends which by now included M. *Milnes and Richard *Burton: also his outspoken repudiation of Christianity, which was to impress *Hardy and his heroine Sue Bridehead (in *Jude the Obscure*). *A Song of Italy* (1867) and *Songs before Sunrise* (1871) express his support for Mazzini in the struggle for Italian independence, and a hatred of authority which owes much to *Blake. *Bothwell* (1874) and a second Greek drama, *Erechtheus* (1876), were followed by the more subdued *Poems and Ballads: Second Series* (1878), which contains 'A Forsaken Garden'. By this time Swinburne's health, always delicate and subject to fits of intense nervous excitement, was seriously undermined by heavy drinking and other excesses. In 1879 he moved to Putney with his friend *Watts-Dunton, who gradually weaned him from drink and restored his health. He published many more volumes, including *Mary Stuart* (1881), *Tristram of Lyonesse and Other Poems* (1882), *Marino Faliero* (1885, a tragedy on the same subject as Byron's of the same title), and *Poems and Ballads: Third Series* (1889), but they lack the force of his earlier work, and often fall into a kind of self-parody which he himself referred to as 'a tendency to the dulcet and luscious form of verbosity which has to be guarded against'.

Swinburne commanded an impressive variety of verse forms, writing in classical metres, composing burlesques, modern and mock-antique ballads, roundels, etc.; he also translated the ballads of *Villon. His published prose works include two novels, *A Year's Letters* (serialized pseudonymously 1877, repub. 1905 as *Love's Cross Currents*) and *Lesbia Brandon* (ed. R. Hughes, 1952). His influence on fellow aesthetes like *Pater and a later generation of poets was considerable, and was deplored by T. S. *Eliot and *Leavis. Swinburne himself was a critic of perception and originality; his studies of Chapman (1875), *Marlowe (1883, *Encyclopaedia Britannica*), *Middleton (1887), *Tourneur (1889, *EB*), and others were the first important successors to *Lamb in the revival of interest in Elizabethan and Jacobean drama, and those of Blake (1868) and the *Brontës (1877, 1883, etc.) in many ways laid the foundation of modern appreciation.

His letters were edited in six volumes, 1959–62, by

C. Y. Lang, and the most recent of several biographies is by P. Henderson (1974). Many of his writings remain unpublished, presumably unpublishable.

SWINNERTON, Frank (1884–1982), critic and prolific novelist. He left school at 14 and worked as office boy, proof-reader, then editor at Chatto and Windus. His novels, often set in contemporary London, include *Nocturne* (1917, his greatest success) and *Harvest Comedy* (1937). He was literary critic of *Truth and Nation*, the *Evening News*, and the *Observer and a familiar figure in the literary life of the first half of the 20th cent., Arnold *Bennett and *Galsworthy being among his friends. His knowledge of the period provided material for his literary reminiscences, notably *The Georgian Literary Scene* (1935), and two autobiographical works, *Swinnerton: An Autobiography* (1937) and *Reflections from a Village* (1969). *Arnold Bennett: A Last Word* (1978) appeared in his 94th year. He was president of the *Royal Literary Fund (1962–6).

Swiss Family Robinson, The, the romance of a family wrecked on a desert island, written in German by Johann David Wyss (1743–1818), a Swiss pastor. It was published in two parts in Zurich in 1812–13 and the first English translation was a year later.

Swiveller, Dick, a character in Dickens's *The Old Curiosity Shop*.

sword-dance, a medieval folk custom, of ritual origin, probably symbolizing the death and resurrection of the year. The stock characters were the fool, dressed in the skin of an animal, and the 'Bessy', a man dressed in woman's clothes. In many of the extant dances one of the characters is surrounded with the swords of the other dancers or slain. The characters were introduced in rhymed speeches. The sword-dance is one of the origins of the *mummers' play and so of English drama. See also REVESBY PLAY.

Sword of Honour, a trilogy by E. *Waugh, published under this title in 1965.

Men at Arms (1952) introduces 35-year-old divorced Catholic Guy Crouchback, who after much effort succeeds in enlisting in the Royal Corps of Halberdiers just after the outbreak of the Second World War. Much of the plot revolves around his eccentric fellow officer Apthorpe, an old Africa hand who suffers repeatedly from 'Bechuana tummy', is deeply devoted to his 'thunder box' (or chemical closet), and dies in West Africa at the end of the novel of some unspecified tropical disease, aggravated by Guy's thoughtful gift of a bottle of whisky. Other characters include Guy's ex-wife, the beautiful socialite Virginia Troy, her second (but not her final) husband Tommy Blackhouse, and the ferocious one-eyed Brigadier Ritchie-Hook, who involves Guy in a near-disastrous escapade.

Officers and Gentlemen (1955) continues Waugh's semi-satiric, semi-emotional portrayal of civilian and military life with an account of Guy's training on the Hebridean island of Mugg with a commando unit, and of the exploits of ex-hairdresser Trimmer, now Captain McTavish, which include an affair with Virginia and the blowing up of a French railway; the action moves to Alexandria, then to the withdrawal from Crete, with all but four of 'Hookforce' taken prisoner.

Unconditional Surrender (1961) opens with a frustrated and disillusioned Captain Guy Crouchback in London, working at Hazardous Offensive Operations Headquarters: he then injures himself learning to parachute, and on his sickbed is wooed by Virginia, now pregnant by Trimmer, and conscious that Guy has inherited his father's fortune. He remarries her out of a sense of chivalry and compassion, is transferred to the chaos and conflicts of Yugoslavia as a liaison officer with the Partisans, and there learns that Virginia has given birth to a son, then that she has been killed in an air raid. The baby survives, and an epilogue informs us that Guy marries again, and has more children of his own. Waugh revised this ending for the 1965 recension of the three works, and decided that Guy and his new wife Domenica should be childless.

Sybil, *or The Two Nations,* a novel by B. *Disraeli, published 1845.

This is the second book of the trilogy *Coningsby—Sybil—*Tancred. It was written, like *Coningsby,* to celebrate the ideas of the 'Young England' Tories and was designed to describe 'the Condition of the People' and of the 'Two Nations of England, the Rich and the Poor'. An ambitious, crowded book, it points to reforms a generation before Disraeli's government was able to introduce them. Poverty and oppression are described with feeling, and the radical *Chartist spirit is sympathetically shown in Gerard, Morley, and others; aspects of the wealthy social and political world, particularly as seen in Mowbray Castle, are described with irony and contempt.

After a long historical introduction, setting the background in the prime ministership of *Wellington, the story of the Marneys begins. Charles Egremont, the younger brother of the pitiless landowner Lord Marney, master of splendid Marney Abbey, meets in the starlit ruins of the old abbey the beautiful young novice Sybil. She is the daughter of the Chartist Walter Gerard (who becomes Egremont's friend) and is beloved by Stephen Morley, a radical and atheist; all three live in the oppressed industrial town of Mowbray some miles away. Egremont falls in love with Sybil, and when she refuses him because of his rank, begins to live a life painfully divided between the poverty-stricken town of Mowbray, the glittering life of his brother's abbey, and his parliamentary life in London. His brother's plan to marry him into the Fitzwarene family, which owns Mowbray Castle and most of Mowbray, is indignantly resisted, as he sets himself earnestly to discover the true condition of the poor in Mowbray and to understand the feelings of the

Chartists and incendiaries. Events of the present are seen in a long historical perspective. The plight of the poor, whose land has been taken by the rich, is compared with that of the Saxons despoiled by the Normans, and Sybil's ancestry provides her with rights to the lands of Marney which had been confiscated from her family at the Reformation. Much of the narrative is concerned with the development of the Chartist rising, Gerard's imprisonment, the activities of Morley, the radical parson St Lys, the good employer Trafford, and many others less principled; and with Egremont's struggle in the House of Commons to secure reforms and his failure to win Sybil. Five years pass of increasing poverty and unrest. The riots in which they culminate are of great violence; Sybil and St Lys, in Mowbray Castle, fail to persuade the mob to disperse, while Morley searches for the Marney deeds which are rightfully Sybil's. The yeomanry arrive, Gerard is killed, Lord Marney stoned to death by rioters, Morley shot, and the castle burned down. Egremont rescues Sybil and the true heir marries the new earl of Marney.

Sycorax, in Shakespeare's *The Tempest* a witch, the mother of *Caliban; she does not appear in the play.

syllepsis, a figure of speech by which a word, or a particular form or inflection of a word, is made to refer to two or more words in the same sentence, while properly applying to them in different senses: e.g. 'Miss Bolo . . . went home in a flood of tears and a sedan chair' (Dickens, *Pickwick Papers,* ch. 35). Cf. *zeugma.

SYLVESTER, Josuah (c.1563–1618), a London merchant, whose translation into rhyming couplets of *The Divine Weeks and Works* of *Du Bartas was, according to John Davies of Hereford, 'admir'd of all'. The first instalment appeared in 1592, more in 1598, further parts in 1605–7, and a complete translation in 1608, which was reprinted for the fifth time in 1641. The edition of 1621 contained many of Sylvester's other works, including his poems in the important collection *Lachrymae Lachrymarum* (1613). This contained elegies by Joseph *Hall and *Donne, among others, on Prince Henry, to whom Sylvester had attached himself. His translation of Du Bartas has been edited by Susan Snyder (2 vols, 1973).

Sylvia's Lovers, a novel by Mrs *Gaskell, published 1863.

The scene is the whaling port of Monkshaven (based on Whitby in Yorkshire) during the Napoleonic wars, and the plot hinges on the activities of the press-gangs whose seizure of Monkshaven men to man naval warships provokes bitter resentment. Sylvia's father, the farmer Daniel Robson, leads a mob attack on the press-gang's headquarters, and he is tried and hanged for this. Her lover, the 'specksioneer' (harpooner) Charley Kinraid, is carried off by the press-gang, but sends her a message promising constancy and return by Sylvia's cousin, the pedantic, hard-working shopkeeper Philip Hepburn, who has long loved Sylvia. Philip yields to the temptation of concealing the message, and Sylvia, believing Charley dead, and left in poverty after her father's execution, agrees to marry Philip. Years later, Charley returns and Philip's treachery is revealed to Sylvia, who swears never to forgive him. He flees from Monkshaven and enlists, but eventually returns disfigured and beggared, and— recognized on his deathbed—dies in the arms of the now repentant Sylvia. The last few chapters of the book, full of heroic rescues, improbable encounters, and deathbed reunions, are notably inferior to the earlier part of the novel, which is remarkable for its vivid reconstruction of life in the little town dominated by the whaling industry (which Mrs Gaskell carefully researched) and at the farm where noisy, unreasonable Daniel Robson, his quiet, devoted wife, and their sturdy old servant Kester combine to cherish the much-loved and lovely but hapless Sylvia.

Symbolism, symbolists (*Symbolisme, les symbolistes*), a group of French writers of the 19th cent. The term is widely applied, but in its most useful and restricted sense refers to the period *c.*1880–95. The movement may be seen as a reaction against dominant *realist and *naturalist tendencies in literature generally and, in the case of poetry, against the descriptive precision and 'objectivity' of the *Parnassians. The symbolists stressed the priority of suggestion and evocation over direct description and explicit analogy (cf. *Mallarmé's dictum, 'Peindre, non la chose, mais l'effet qu'elle produit'), and to the symbol was ascribed a pre-eminent function in the effort to distil a private mood or to evoke the subtle affinities which were held to exist between the material and spiritual worlds. Symbolist writers were particularly concerned to explore the musical properties of language, through the interplay of connotative sound relationships, but were deeply interested in all the arts and much influenced by the synthesizing ideals of *Wagner's music dramas. Other influences on the movement were the mystical writings of *Swedenborg, and the poetry of *Nerval, *Baudelaire (see the sonnet 'Correspondances'), and *Poe.

Generally associated with the symbolist movement are: the poets Mallarmé, *Verlaine, *Rimbaud, and *Laforgue; the dramatists *Villiers de l'Isle-Adam (*Axël*, 1890) and *Maeterlinck, whose *Pelléas et Mélisande* (1892) was the source of *Debussy's opera of that name; and the novelists *Huysmans (*A rebours*, 1884) and Édouard Dujardin, whose *Les Lauriers sont coupés* (1888) influenced *Joyce. The movement exercised an influence on painting (Odilon Redon, Gustave Moreau) and on a wide range of 20th-cent. writers, including *Pound, T. S. *Eliot, W. *Stevens, *Yeats, Joyce, V. *Woolf, *Claudel, *Valéry, Stefan George, and *Rilke. It was the subject of A. W. *Symons's *The Symbolist Movement in Literature* (1899) and played a part in the development of the Russian symbolist movement and of the *modernista* movement in Latin America.

Symkyn, or **Symond,** the miller of Trumpington in *Chaucer's 'The Reeve's Tale' (see CANTERBURY TALES, 3).

SYMONDS, John Addington (1840–93), born in Bristol, the son of an eminent physician, educated at Harrow and Balliol College, Oxford, where he won the Newdigate Prize, and became a fellow of Magdalen. He suffered from tuberculosis, and spent much of his life in Italy and Switzerland. He was much attracted by the Hellenism of the Renaissance, and both his prose and poetry are coloured by his concept of *platonic love and his admiration for male beauty. His largest work, *Renaissance in Italy* (1875–86), is more picturesque than scholarly, and at times overburdened with detail and anecdote, but remains a valuable source of information. His works include volumes on *Jonson, *Sidney, *Shelley, *Whitman, and *Michelangelo; collections of travel sketches and impressions; several volumes of verse (including *Many Moods*, 1878; *New and Old*, 1880); a translation of the autobiography of *Cellini (1888); and translations of Greek and Italian poetry. He had a wide circle of literary friends (among them *Lear, *Swinburne, L. *Stephen, and R. L. *Stevenson), and his aesthetic prose had its admirers, but his life was marked by physical and mental stress. He married in 1864, but acknowledged increasingly his own homosexuality, and campaigned, albeit discreetly, for legal reform and more outspoken recognition of inversion, which he saw as a congenital condition. His privately printed pamphlets *A Problem in Greek Ethics* (1883) and *A Problem in Modern Ethics* (1891) were reproduced in part by H. *Ellis in *Sexual Inversion* (1897), a work originally planned as a collaboration. See Phyllis Grosskurth, *John Addington Symonds* (1964).

SYMONS, A(lphonse) J(ames) A(lbert) (1900–41), bibliographer, bibliophile, dandy, and epicure, who became an authority on the literature of the 1890s and published *An Anthology of 'Nineties' Verse* in 1928. He wrote several biographies, but is best remembered for *The *Quest for Corvo: An Experiment in Biography* (1934), a life of F. W. *Rolfe. *A. J. A. Symons: His Life and Speculations* (1950), by his brother Julian *Symons, is a vivid evocation of his paradoxical personality, diverse interests, and social ambitions.

SYMONS, Arthur William (1865–1945), son of a West Country Methodist minister. He moved to London when a young man and quickly abandoned his narrow upbringing for city life. He became a friend of *Yeats, G. A. *Moore, and H. *Ellis, and attended the *Rhymers Club; his early volumes of poetry (*Days and Nights*, 1889; *London Nights*, 1895) were very much of their time in their celebration of decadence and the *demimonde* of stage, street, and *Café Royal. He was editor of the *Savoy*, 1896, and published *Beardsley, *Conrad, *Dowson, L. P. *Johnson, etc. His *The Symbolist Movement in Literature* (1899) was an attempt to introduce French *Symbolism to England, and he wrote many other critical studies, of *Blake, *Baudelaire, *Pater, *Wilde, and others; but his fascination with the morbid and the extreme took its revenge when, in 1908–9, he suffered a complete nervous collapse, from which he largely recovered through the ministrations of his friends (including *Gosse and Augustus *John) and the help of the *Royal Literary Fund. He is largely remembered as a leading spirit in the Decadent movement, a defender of *'art for art's sake', although his biographer Roger Lhombreaud (*Arthur Symons: A Critical Biography*, 1963) argues for a more modest but wider role.

SYMONS, Julian Gustave (1921–94), crime writer, critic, biographer, and scholar of crime fiction, born in London, brother of A. J. A. *Symons. His many novels, which include *Bland Beginning* (1949) and *The Belting Inheritance* (1965), showed interests in anarchy, forgery, and bibliography. His survey of the genre, *Bloody Murder: From the Detective Story to the Crime Novel*, appeared in 1972.

Symposium, The, or 'The Banquet', the title of a dialogue in which *Plato describes a drinking party where *Socrates, *Aristophanes, and others propound their views of love and distinguish three forms of the emotion: the sensual, the altruistic, and the wisdom-oriented. Written soon after 371 BC, the dialogue appears to have had for its aim the rehabilitation of Socrates against the charge of corrupting the young, but its influence, once it had been translated into Latin by *Ficino (1482), had a far wider scope. It popularized the identification of love with a quest for the highest form of spiritual experience, and although the love discussed in Plato's dialogue was primarily a homosexual one, the exalted claims made on its behalf were easily transferred to heterosexual relationships and came to be linked with the conventions of *courtly love. Another idea in the *Symposium* that gained wide currency was the fanciful notion advanced by Aristophanes in his speech that each human being is a male or female half of a whole which was originally hermaphrodite, and that every person necessarily seeks his or her lost half. The belief that every person has a single predestined mate was to become a romantic commonplace. (See also PLATONIC LOVE.)

synecdoche (pron. 'sinekdoki'), a figure of speech by which a more comprehensive term is used for a less comprehensive or vice versa, as whole for part or part for whole, e.g. 'There were six guns out on the moor' where 'guns' stands for shooters; and 'Oxford won the match', where 'Oxford' stands for 'the Oxford eleven'.

synesthesia, or **synaesthesia,** a rhetorical figure in which one kind of sense impression is rendered by using words that normally describe another, as in 'loud perfume', 'warm colour', or 'delicious sight'.

SYNGE, (Edmund) John Millington (1871–1909), Irish playwright, born near Dublin; his father was a barrister, and died when Synge was an infant. He was educated at Trinity College, Dublin, and then spent some years in Paris, where he met W. B. *Yeats in 1896. Following a suggestion from Yeats, he went to the Aran Islands in order to write of Irish peasant life, and stayed there annually from 1898 to 1902; his description, *The Aran Islands*, was published in 1907. The first of his plays, *In the Shadow of the Glen*, was performed in 1903; it is a grim one-act peasant comedy, in which an elderly husband feigns death to test his wife's fidelity. *Riders to the Sea*, an elegiac tragedy in which an elderly mother, Maurya, stoically anticipates 'a great rest' after the death of the last of her six sons, followed in 1904; both were published, as was *The Well of the Saints*, in 1905. His best-known play, and in its time the most controversial, *The Playboy of the Western World*, was performed in 1907; the anticlerical *The Tinker's Wedding* was published in 1908. All except the last were performed at the *Abbey Theatre, of which Synge became a director in 1906. His *Poems and Translations* (many of which foreshadow his imminent death) appeared in 1909. From 1897 Synge had suffered from Hodgkin's disease, and he virtually completed his last play, *Deirdre of the Sorrows*, as he was dying; it was performed and published posthumously, in 1910. In this, as in his other work, Synge uses a spare, rhythmic, lyric prose to achieve effects of great power and resonance; both tragedies and comedies display the ironic wit and realism which many of his countrymen found offensive. Yeats commented in his preface to *Poems and Translations*, 'He was but the more hated because he gave his country what it needed, an unmoved mind', and described him in 'In Memory of Major Gregory' as one who had come 'Towards nightfall upon certain set apart | In a most desolate stony place, | Towards nightfall upon a race | Passionate and simple like his heart'. The authorized biography is *J. M. Synge 1871–1909* (1959) by D. H. Greene and E. M. Stephens, and the *Collected Works* (4 vols, 1962–8) were edited by Robin Skelton; his *Collected Letters*, edited by Ann Saddlemyer, appeared 1983–4.

Syntax, Dr, see COMBE.

Syntipas, the Greek form of the name Sindabar, Sandabar, or Sindibad, an Indian philosopher, said to have lived about 100 BC, the supposed author of a collection of tales generally known as *The Seven Wise Masters*. Their main outline is the same as that of *The Seven Sages of Rome*, though details of the several stories vary. 'Syntipas' was translated from Greek into Latin (under the title 'Dolopathos') in the 12th cent., and thence into French. The names Syntipas, Sindabar, etc., are probably corruptions of the original Sanskrit word from which *Bidpai and Pilpay are derived.

SZYMBORSKA, Wisława (1923–   ), Polish poet. After completing her studies at the University of Cracow, in 1953 she joined the staff of the literary journal *Życie Literackie*, where she was to work as poetry editor for almost 30 years. During this time she published six collections of poetry. *People on a Bridge* (1986) has been most widely translated: there is an English translation (1990) by Adam Czerniawski. She was awarded the *Nobel Prize in 1996.

T

TABUCCHI, Antonio (1943–), Italian novelist, translator (from the Portuguese), and critic, born in Pisa. His works include *Notturno indiano* (trans. 1988 by Tim Parks as *Indian Nocturne*), *Requiem* (1991; trans. 1994), a haunted evocation of Lisbon in July, and *Sostiene Pereira* (1994; *Declares Pereira*, 1995), a concentrated, deceptively simple, and resonant novel set in 1938 in Portugal, in which a middle-aged cultural journalist finds himself obliged to confront political repression and violence. *Piccoli equivoci senza importanza* (1987; *Little Misunderstandings of No Importance*, 1988) is a volume of short stories.

TACITUS, Cornelius (*c.* AD 55–after 115), the greatest historian of imperial Rome. His first work was a dialogue that discussed the shortcomings of contemporary oratory. He followed this by a biography of his father-in-law Julius Agricola (*c.*98) and by an ethnographical account of the German tribes. The former provides a useful description of Roman Britain, the latter contains one of the earliest representations of the Noble Savage (see PRIMITIVISM). His fame rests on his *Annals* and his *Histories* which related events from the death of Augustus to the Flavian period. Tacitus' avowed aim was to keep alive the memory of virtuous and vicious actions so that posterity could judge them, and his great achievement was to have drawn a picture of how men must live under tyranny. Little known in the Middle Ages, Tacitus was rediscovered by *Boccaccio in the 14th cent. The *Agricola* and the *Histories* were translated into English by Sir H. *Savile (1591), the *Germania* and *Annals* by R. Grenewey (1598); and after this Tacitus became in *Donne's phrase the 'Oracle of Statesmen' or at any rate the model for historians like F. *Bacon in his *History of *Henry VII* (1622) and Sir John *Hayward. He was also influential as a stylist in the 17th cent., when attempts were made to imitate his concision and trenchancy.

Tadpole and **Taper,** in Disraeli's *Coningsby* and *Sybil*, typical party wire-pullers. 'Tadpole worshipped registration; Taper adored a cry.'

TAGORE, Rabindranath (1861–1941), most eminent modern Bengali poet. He was also critic, essayist, composer, and author of short fiction innovative in Bengali literature. He is known outside India principally in English translation. *Gitanjali: Song Offering* (1912), his free verse re-creations of his Bengali poems modelled on medieval Indian devotional lyrics, won him the *Nobel Prize for literature in 1913, its first award to an Asian. Representative translations followed, of philosophical plays such as *Chitra* (1913) and *The King of the Dark Chamber* (1914), and of his novels *The Home and the World* (1919) and *Gora* (1924). His short fiction often comments powerfully and courageously on Indian national and social concerns, in the collections *Hungry Stones* (1916), *Broken Ties* (1925), and *The Housewarming* (1965), and in the novella *The Broken Nest* (1971). Tagore had an excellent command of English, but he wrote primarily in Bengali and tirelessly encouraged writers of the Indian vernaculars.

TAILLEFER (Incisor Ferri), a minstrel in the army of William the Conqueror who (according to the *Carmen de Hastingae Proelio* and to *Henry of Huntingdon and *Gaimar) marched in front of the army at Hastings, singing of the deeds of *Roland to encourage the Normans.

tail-rhyme, translated from the Latin *rhythmus caudatus*, the measure associated in particular with a group of Middle English romances in which a pair of rhyming lines is followed by a single line of different length and the three-line pattern is repeated to make up a six-line stanza. Chaucer's 'Sir Thopas' (see CANTERBURY TALES, 17) is an example; six are edited by M. Mills in *Six Middle English Romances* (1973).

Tain-Bo-Cuailgne, the chief epic of the Ulster cycle of Irish mythology, the story of the raid of Queen *Maeve of Connaught to secure the Brown Bull of Cuailgne (pron. 'Cooley'), and her defeat by *Cuchulain. There is a modern translation by T. Kinsella (1969).

TAINE, Hippolyte (1828–93), French philosopher, historian, and critic, the leading exponent in his age of the view that historical and artistic phenomena are susceptible of explanation by the application of the methods of natural science. Taine's determinist and mechanistic theory of mental activity is fully set out in *De l'intelligence* (1870). Its moral corollary was given a provocative formulation in the introduction to his *Histoire de la littérature anglaise* (3 vols, 1863; trans. H. Van Laun, 1871): 'vice and virtue are products like vitriol and sugar'. In the same introduction he laid down the principle that hereditary, environmental, and historical factors ('la race, le milieu, le moment') could sufficiently account for the entire range and character of a national literature. Taine wrote widely on art and aesthetics, e.g. *Philosophie de l'art* (1865), *De l'idéal dans l'art* (1867), as well as books on the art of Italy, Greece, and the Low Countries. *Les Origines de la France contemporaine* (6 vols, 1875–94) is a history of France in the late 18th and early 19th cents, centring on the revolutionary period and deploring the centralizing tendency of which, to his mind, the revolution was an expression. Taine's numerous travel books include *Notes sur l'Angleterre* (1872), impressions of the country and of life and manners gathered during his stays in England, together with reflections on the English mind, system of government, etc.

Tale of a Tub, A, a comedy by *Jonson, performed 1633, printed 1640.

It concerns the attempts, in the course of St Valentine's day, of various suitors to marry Audrey, the daughter of Toby Turf, high constable of Kentish Town. Her father wishes to marry her to John Clay, tile-maker, and he and the wedding-party set off for the church. But his intention is defeated by Squire Tub and Canon Hugh the vicar, by means of a bogus story of a highway robbery, of which John Clay is accused. Squire Tub's desire to marry Audrey is in turn frustrated by Justice Preamble, who conspires with Hugh to get her for himself. Tub warns Toby Turf, who recovers his daughter. But she is presently lured away from him again (together with £100) by the justice, is intercepted by Tub, and finally carried off and married out of hand by Pol Martin, usher to Tub's mother, 'a groom was never dreamt of'. This was Jonson's last completed play.

Tale of a Tub, A, a satire in prose by *Swift, written, according to his own statement, about 1696, but not published until 1704.

The author explains in a preface that it is the practice of seamen when they meet a whale to throw out an empty tub to divert it from attacking the ship. Hence the title of the satire, which is intended to divert Hobbes's *Leviathan* and the wits of the age from picking holes in the weak sides of religion and government. The author proceeds to tell the story of a father who leaves as a legacy to his three sons Peter, Martin, and Jack a coat apiece, with directions that on no account are the coats to be altered. Peter symbolizes the Roman Church, Martin (from Martin *Luther) the Anglican, Jack (from John *Calvin) the Dissenters. The sons gradually disobey the injunction, finding excuses for adding shoulder-knots or gold lace according to the prevailing fashion. Finally Martin and Jack quarrel with the arrogant Peter, then with each other, and separate. The satire is directed with especial vigour against Peter, his bulls and dispensations, and the doctrine of transubstantiation. But Jack is also treated with contempt. Martin, as representing the Church to which Swift himself belonged, is spared, though not very reverently dealt with. The narrative is freely interspersed with digressions, on critics, on the prevailing dispute as to ancient and modern learning, and on madness—this last an early example of Swift's love of paradox and of his misanthropy.

Tale of Genji, The, a classic Japanese novel written *c.* AD 1001–15 by Lady Murasaki (?978–?1031) and translated in a slightly abridged version by A.

*Waley in 6 vols (1925–33): i 'The Tale of Genji', ii 'The Sacred Tree', iii 'A Wreath of Cloud', iv 'Blue Trousers', v 'The Lady of the Boat', vi 'The Bridge of Dreams'.

Prince Genji is an illegitimate son of the emperor, living about the time of the author's childhood, and volumes i–iv are mainly concerned with the rivalry between the various women whom he loved. Between volumes iv and v there is a gap in the narrative of eight years, during which time Genji has died, and the last two volumes deal with the rivalry in love between Kaoru, Genji's supposed son, and Niou, Genji's grandson.

The author, who became lady-in-waiting to the empress *c.*1005 and spent a certain amount of her time at court, was nicknamed 'Murasaki' in allusion to the heroine of her book: her real name remains unknown. A fuller translation by E. G. Seidensticker appeared in 1976.

Tale of Two Cities, A, a novel by *Dickens, published 1859.

The 'two cities' are Paris, in the time of the French Revolution, and London. Dr Manette, a French physician, having been called in to attend a young peasant and his sister in circumstances that made him aware that the girl had been outrageously treated and the boy mortally wounded by the marquis de St Évremonde and his brother, has been confined for 18 years in the Bastille to secure his silence. He has just been released, demented, when the story opens; he is brought to England, where he gradually recovers his sanity. Charles Darnay, who conceals under the name the fact that he is a nephew of the marquis, has left France and renounced his heritage from detestation of the cruel practices of the old French nobility; he falls in love with Lucie, Dr Manette's daughter, and they are happily married. During the Terror he goes to Paris to try to save a faithful servant, who is accused of having served the emigrant nobility. He is himself arrested, condemned to death, and saved only at the last moment by Sydney Carton, a reckless wastrel of an English barrister, whose character is redeemed by his generous devotion to Lucie. Carton, who strikingly resembles Darnay in appearance, smuggles the latter out of prison, and takes his place on the scaffold.

The book gives a vivid picture (modelled on Carlyle's *The French Revolution*) of Paris at this period. Critics complained on publication of its lack of humour, but it later achieved wide popularity, partly through successful dramatizations and film adaptations.

Tales in Verse, a collection of poems by *Crabbe, published 1812.

There is humour and tenderness, as well as horror, in these 21 tales, whose object is largely to reveal the destruction of happiness by uncontrolled passions.

Tales of a Grandfather, The, a history of Scotland from the Roman occupation to the close of the 1745

Jacobite rebellion, by Sir W. *Scott, published in 1827–9. A later series (1831) deals with the history of France. They were written for Scott's first grandchild, John Hugh Lockhart, who died in 1831, aged 10.

Tales of My Landlord, four series of novels by Sir W. *Scott: *The Black Dwarf, *Old Mortality (1st series); *The Heart of Midlothian (2nd series); *The Bride of Lammermoor, *A Legend of Montrose (3rd series); *Count Robert of Paris, *Castle Dangerous (4th series). Jedediah Cleishbotham, schoolmaster and parish clerk of Gandercleugh, by a fiction of Scott, sold these tales to a publisher. They were supposed to be compiled by his assistant Peter Pattieson. The title of the series is a misnomer as Scott himself admitted, for the tales were not told by the landlord; nor did the landlord have any hand in them at all.

Tales of the Genii, see RIDLEY, J.

Tales of the Hall, a collection of poems by *Crabbe, published 1819.

The work shows a falling-off in care and skill, but is otherwise very similar in character to *Tales in Verse.

TALFOURD, Sir Thomas Noon (1795–1854), son of a Reading brewer, a judge and member of Parliament but also a literary critic and author of Ion (1836), The Athenian Captive (1838), and other lifeless tragedies in insipid blank verse, for which only *Macready's acting secured momentary celebrity. Talfourd is, however, remembered for his editing of the letters of his friend Charles *Lamb, and for having introduced an Act securing real legal protection for authors' copyright. The friendships of this warm-hearted though excessively loquacious man spanned the literary generation from Lamb and *Coleridge to M. R. *Mitford and *Dickens, who dedicated *Pickwick Papers to him. See J. A. Brain, An Evening with Thomas Noon Talfourd (1889).

TALIESIN (fl. 550), a British bard, perhaps a mythic personage, first mentioned in the Saxon Genealogies appended to the Historia Britonum (c.690). A mass of poetry, probably of later date, has been ascribed to him, and the Book of Taliesin (14th cent.) is a collection of poems by different authors and of different dates. The village of Tre-Taliesin in Cardiganshire sprang up near the supposed site of his grave. Taliesin figures prominently in Peacock's *The Misfortunes of Elphin, and he is mentioned in Tennyson's *Idylls of the King as one of the Round Table.

Talisman, The, a novel by Sir W. *Scott, published 1825, forming part of the Tales of the Crusaders. The novel is set in the army led to the Crusades by Richard I of England. It chronicles the adventures of a poor but valiant Scottish knight, Sir Kenneth, who is caught up in the intrigues between Richard, the king of France, the duke of Austria, and the Knights Templar and is eventually discovered to be Prince David of Scotland. The most striking portrait in the novel is that of *Saladin, whose wisdom and chivalry is contrasted throughout with the scheming and corruption of the Christian leaders.

TALLIS, Thomas (c.1505–85), composer and organist and colleague of W. *Byrd, largely known for his church music and for the tune known as 'Tallis's Canon' which he composed for M. *Parker's Whole Psalter (?1567).

Talus, a character in Spenser's *Faerie Queene. When Astraea left the world and returned to heaven, she

> left her groome
> An yron man, which did on her attend
> Always to execute her steadfast doome.
> (V. i. 12)

He thus represents the executive power of government. He attends on *Artegall, wielding an iron flail, with which he dispatches criminals.

TAMBIMUTTU, see POETRY LONDON.

Tamburlaine the Great, a drama in blank verse by *Marlowe, written not later than 1587, published 1590. It showed an immense advance on the blank verse of *Gorboduc and was received with much popular approval. The material for it was taken by the author from Pedro Mexia's Spanish Life of Timur, of which an English translation had appeared in 1571.

Pt I of the drama deals with the first rise to power of the Scythian shepherd-robber Tamburlaine; he allies himself with Cosroe in the latter's rebellion against his brother, the king of Persia, and then challenges him for the crown and defeats him. Tamburlaine's unbounded ambition and ruthless cruelty carry all before him. He conquers the Turkish emperor *Bajazet and leads him about, a prisoner in a cage, goading him and his empress Zabina with cruel taunts till they dash out their brains against the bars of the cage. His ferocity is softened only by his love for his captive Zenocrate, daughter of the soldan of Egypt whose life he spares in deference to the pleadings of Zenocrate when he captures Damascus.

Pt II deals with the continuation of his conquests, which extend to Babylon, whither he is drawn in a chariot dragged by the kings of Trebizond and Soria, with the kings of Anatolia and Jerusalem as relay, 'pampered Jades of Asia' (a phrase quoted by Pistol in Shakespeare, 2 *Henry IV, II. iv); it ends with the death of Tamburlaine himself.

Tamerlane, a tragedy by *Rowe, produced 1701, of some historical interest because under the name of Tamerlane the author intended to characterize William III, while under that of Bajazet he held up Louis XIV to detestation. The play was, for more than 100 years, annually revived on 5 Nov., the date of William III's landing in England.

Taming of the Shrew, The, a comedy by *Shakespeare, first printed in the *Folio of 1623, probably written c.1592 or earlier and based in part on the *Supposes adapted by G. Gascoigne from *Ariosto. In 1594 a quarto text called 'The Taming of a Shrew' was published; this was once thought to be Shakespeare's source, but its exact relationship with Shakespeare's play is uncertain: it may represent in part a reported version of it.

The play begins with an induction in which Christopher Sly, a drunken Warwickshire tinker, picked up by a lord and his huntsmen on a heath, is brought to the castle, sumptuously treated, and in spite of his protestations is assured that he is a lord who has been out of his mind. He is set down to watch the play that follows, performed solely for his benefit by strolling players. Sly appears again at the end of I. ii, but disappears after that in the Folio text; in the bad quarto he is given five more short scenes throughout the play.

Baptista Minola of Padua has two daughters, Katherina the Shrew, who is the elder of the two, and Bianca, who has many suitors, but who may not marry until a husband has been found for Katherina. Petruchio, a gentleman from Verona, undertakes to woo the shrew to gain her dowry and to help his friend Hortensio win Bianca. To tame her he pretends to find her rude behaviour courteous and gentle and humiliates her by being late for their wedding and appearing badly dressed. He takes her off to his country house and, under the pretext that nothing there is good enough for her, prevents her from eating or sleeping. By the time they return to Baptista's house, Katherina has been successfully tamed, and Lucentio, a Pisan, has won Bianca by disguising himself as her schoolmaster, while the disappointed Hortensio has to console himself with marriage to a rich widow. At the feast which follows the three bridegrooms wager on whose wife is the most docile and submissive. Katharina argues that 'Thy husband is thy lord, thy life, thy keeper, | Thy head, thy sovereign' and Petruchio wins the bet.

A play by J. Fletcher, *The Woman's Prize, shows Petruchio tamed in a second marriage after Kate's death. Petruchio's three times repeated request 'kiss me, Kate' supplied the title for Cole Porter's popular musical of 1948.

Tam Lin, the subject of an old *ballad. Janet wins back to mortal life her elfin lover, Tam Lin, from the queen of the fairies, who has captured him.

Tamora, queen of the Goths in Shakespeare's *Titus Andronicus.

'Tam o' Shanter', a narrative poem by *Burns, published 1791.

Tam, a farmer, spends the cold evening of Ayr's market-day in a snug alehouse, where he becomes tipsy and amorous ('Tam was glorious'). Eventually riding home, he passes the kirk of Alloway. Seeing it mysteriously lighted, he stops and looks in. Weird warlocks and witches are dancing to the sound of the bagpipes, played by Old Nick, the devil. Roused by the sight of one 'winsome wench' among the old beldams, Tam shouts to her. At once the lights go out and the horde of witches rush out in pursuit of Tam. Terrified, he wildly spurs his grey mare, Meg, and just reaches the middle of the bridge over the Doon before the girl catches him. Once over the middle of the bridge he is out of her power, but his mare's tail is still within the witches' jurisdiction, and this the girl pulls off. The narrative is swift, and both the humour and the horror are effectively conveyed.

Tanaquil, in Roman legend, the wife of Tarquinius Priscus, the first of the Tarquin (Etruscan) kings of Rome. Spenser uses the name to signify Queen Elizabeth in the introduction to Book I of *The Faerie Queene.

Tancred, one of the Norman heroes of the First Crusade, figures in Tasso's *Jerusalem Delivered as one of the principal knights serving under Godfroi de *Bouillon.

Tancred, or The New Crusade, a novel by B. *Disraeli, published 1847.

This is the last of the trilogy *Coningsby—*Sybil—Tancred. Much of the novel is devoted to an attempt to resolve the antagonism between Judaism and Christianity and to establish a role for a reforming faith and revitalized Church in a progressive society. Tancred, whose brilliant social and political future is assured, declares to his bewildered parents, Lord and Lady Montacute, that he must reject their plans for him and seek a faith and philosophy for himself in the Holy Land, where the secrets of the 'Asian mystery' may be revealed to him. He abandons the London of society hostesses and the young bloods of White's, travels to Jerusalem, and thence to Sinai, where he receives a revelation from the Angel of Arabia of 'a common Father'. But he soon becomes embroiled in war and intrigue between the Druses and the Maronites, and is used as a pawn to increase the power and prestige of the fiery Fakredeen, a dissembling and brilliant emir, who manœuvres Tancred into battle. Tancred, wounded and captured, is saved by a potion given him by the beautiful Jewess Eva, with whom he falls in love. This, and his conviction that Christianity owes everything to the Jews, leads him to beg her to marry him. But his parents, the duke and duchess, arrive at Jerusalem to claim him.

Tancred and Gismund, The Tragedie of, or Gismond of Salerne, a play by R. Wilmot (fl. c.1566–1608) and others, published 1591 but dating from 1566 or 1568. Act II is by Henry Noel, Act IV by *Hatton. The play is founded on a tale by *Boccaccio (see SIGISMONDA).

Tancred and Sigismunda, a tragedy by J. *Thomson, published 1745, produced (with *Garrick as Tancred) 1752.

It is based on the story inserted in *Lesage's Gil Blas, IV. iv, in which Tancred, the heir to the kingdom of

Sicily, is lured by the cunning Siffredi into accepting with the throne a bride, Constantia, whom he does not love, and abandoning Siffredi's daughter Sigismunda, whom he does. The latter, in despair at her desertion, consents to marry Osmond, her father's choice. But Tancred does not give up his lady-love so easily. He kills Osmond, but not before the latter has fatally stabbed Sigismunda.

Tanglewood Tales, see HAWTHORNE.

TANIZAKI, Junichiro (1886–1965), Japanese novelist, whose early work is marked by a conscious air of *fin-de-siècle* French decadence. After moving to Osaka in 1923, in the wake of the Tokyo earthquake, he explored the tensions between modern, Westernized life and classical Japanese culture. His most famous novels in the West are *Makioka Sisters* (1943–8), *The Key* (1956), and his masterpiece of erotic obsession, *Diary of a Mad Old Man* (1961–2).

TANNAHILL, Robert (1774–1810), born in Paisley. He became an apprenticed handloom weaver to his father at the age of 12 and showed signs of talent in poetic composition. At 17 he paid homage to *Burns in Ayrshire and was inspired to write his first song 'My Ain Kind Dearie O'. From 1805 his work began to appear in newspapers and journals and in 1807 he published by subscription a volume of *Poems and Songs*, some of which were harshly criticized. Bitterly grieved on having a revised edition declined by a publisher, he burnt his manuscripts and drowned himself in a culvert near Paisley.

TANNHÄUSER, a German *minnesinger of the 13th cent. and the subject of the legend embodied in the 16th-cent. ballad, the *Tannhäuserlied*, in which he becomes enamoured of a beautiful woman who beckons him into the grotto of Venus in the 'Venusberg' (located in Thuringia), where he spends seven years in revelry. When he emerges he goes to Rome to seek absolution from the pope, who replies that it is as impossible for Tannhäuser to be forgiven as for his dry staff to burgeon. Tannhäuser departs in despair. After three days the pope's staff breaks into blossom, and he urgently sends for Tannhäuser, but he is not to be found, having returned to Venus. The story is the subject of an opera by *Wagner (perf. 1845), and of *Swinburne's poem 'Laus Veneris' (1866), a characteristically overheated dramatic monologue of guilt, passion, and sensual abandon, which provided the basis for some of *Beardsley's best-known illustrations.

Tappertit, Simon, in Dickens's *Barnaby Rudge*, Gabriel Varden's apprentice.

TARKINGTON, (Newton) Booth (1869–1946), American novelist, whose works include *The Gentleman from Indiana* (1899), *Monsieur Beaucaire* (1900, a historical romance which first won him popularity), *The Magnificent Ambersons* (1918, a chronicle of the Midwest),

The Plutocrat (1927, a study of a self-made businessman abroad), and *The Heritage of Hatcher Ide* (1941), portraying the Depression in the Midwest. He also wrote for children; *Penrod* (1914) and its sequels describe the adventures of an American boy and his gang of friends in a small Midwestern city.

TARLTON, Richard (fl. 1570–88), actor, a man of humble origin and imperfect education, who attracted attention by his '*happy unhappy* answers' and was introduced to Queen Elizabeth through the earl of *Leicester. He became one of the queen's players in 1583, and attained an immense popularity by his jests, comic acting, and improvisations of doggerel verse. He led a dissipated life and died in poverty. He is perhaps to be identified with *Spenser's 'Pleasant Willy' (see 'Tears of the Muses') and Shakespeare's *Yorick. Many fictitious anecdotes connected with him were published, notably *Tarltons Jests*, in three parts (1613) and *Tarltons Newes out of Purgatorie* (1590). See also FOOL.

Tartar, Mr, a character in Dickens's *Edwin Drood*.

Tartuffe, Le, in Molière's comedy of that name, an odious hypocrite, who, under an assumption of piety, introduces himself into the household of the credulous Orgon, attempts to seduce his wife, and being repulsed, endeavours to ruin the family. The normal spelling of the word (= hypocrite) is *tartufe*.

TARZAN, see BURROUGHS, E. R.

Task, The, a poem in six books by *Cowper, published 1785.

When Cowper's friend Lady Austen (whom he met in 1781) suggested to him the sofa in his room as the subject of a poem in blank verse, the poet set about 'the task'. Its six books are entitled 'The Sofa', 'The Time-Piece', 'The Garden', 'The Winter Evening', 'The Winter Morning Walk', and 'The Winter Walk at Noon'. Cowper opens with a mock-heroic account of the evolution of the sofa ('I sing the sofa') and thence digresses to description, reflection, and opinion. The poem stresses the delights of a retired life ('God made the country, and man made the town', Bk I, 749); describes the poet's own search for peace ('I was a stricken deer, that left the herd', Bk III, 108); and evokes the pleasures of gardening, winter evenings by the fire, etc. The moral passages condemn blood sports, cards, and other diversions; the poet manifests tenderness not only for his pet hare, but even for worms and snails. The poem was extremely popular: *Burns found it 'a glorious poem' that expressed 'the Religion of God and Nature', and it helped to create and supply the growing demand for natural description and tender emotion that found a fuller expression in Wordsworth's *Prelude*, a poem which contains many echoes of Cowper.

TASSO, Torquato (1544–95), son of Bernardo Tasso (author of an epic on *Amadis of Gaul). He was born at Sorrento and spent many years at the court of Ferrara. He was from early life in constant terror of persecution and adverse criticism, and his conduct at Ferrara was such as to make it necessary for the duke, Alphonso II of Este, to lock him up as mad from 1579 to 1586. The legend of his passion for Leonora d'Este, the duke's discovery of it, and his consequent imprisonment was for long widely believed; *Milton refers to it (in a Latin poem), Byron's *The Lament of Tasso* is based on it, and *Goethe's play *Torquato Tasso* (1790) supports it, as does *Donizetti's opera (1833) of the same title. Tasso was released on condition that he would leave Ferrara, and he spent the rest of his life wandering from court to court, unhappy, poverty-stricken, and paranoid, though widely admired. He died in Rome.

His chief works were *Rinaldo*, a romantic epic (1562); a pastoral play, *Aminta* (1573), which had a great success; *Jerusalem Delivered* (1580–1); and a less successful tragedy, *Torrismondo* (1586). He also wrote Pindaric *odes, and Spenser used his sonnets in many of his *Amoretti*. Tasso's epics and his critical works (*Discorsi dell'arte poetica, Discorsi del poema eroico*) had a great influence on English literature, displayed in the works of *Daniel, Milton, Giles and Phineas *Fletcher, *Cowley, *Dryden, and others; Milton refers to his theory of the epic in *The Reason of Church Government* and *Of Education*. *Fairfax's translation of *Jerusalem Delivered* (1600) also had an influence in its own right; according to Dryden, *Waller said that he 'derived the harmony of his numbers' from it. In the following century, *Gray translated a passage (Bk XIV, 32–9), and *Collins recorded ('Ode on the Popular Superstitions of the Highlands') his great admiration for both Tasso and Fairfax: 'How have I trembled, when at Tancred's stroke | Its gushing blood, the gaping Cypress pour'd.'

TATE, (John Orley) Allen (1899–1979), American poet and critic, born in Kentucky, who began his literary career as editor of the little magazine the *Fugitive* (1922–5), published at Nashville, Tennessee, which published work by J. C. *Ransom, L. *Riding, R. P. *Warren, and others and supported a sense of regionalism as a defence against the 'all-destroying abstraction America'. He is best known for his poetry; his collections include *Mr Pope and Other Poems* (1928), *Poems 1928–1931* (1932), and *Collected Poems* (1977). As a critic he is associated with the *New Criticism.

TATE, Nahum (1652–1715), playwright, most of whose dramatic works were adaptations from earlier writers; his 1681 version of *King Lear* omits the Fool, makes Edgar and Cordelia fall in love, and ends happily. It was highly popular; Dr *Johnson defended it on the grounds that the original is too painful, and the full text was not restored until the 19th cent.: *Kean was the first actor to conclude with Lear's death. Tate also wrote, with *Dryden, the second part of *Absalom and Achitophel*; also the libretto of *Purcell's *Dido and Aeneas*. In 1696 he published with Nicholas Brady the well-known metrical version of the Psalms that bears

their name. He was appointed *poet laureate in 1692, and was pilloried by Pope in *The Dunciad*.

TATE and BRADY, see TATE, N.

Tatler, a periodical founded by R. *Steele, of which the first issue appeared on 12 Apr. 1709; it appeared thrice weekly until 2 Jan. 1711.

According to No. 1, it was to include 'Accounts of Gallantry, Pleasure and Entertainment . . . under the Article of White's Chocolate House'; poetry under that of Will's Coffee House; foreign and domestic news from St James's Coffee-house; learning from the Grecian; and so on. Gradually it adopted a loftier tone; the evils of duelling and gambling are denounced in some of the earlier numbers, and presently all questions of good manners are discussed from the standpoint of a more humane civilization, and a new standard of taste is established. The ideal of a gentleman is examined, and its essence is found to lie in forbearance. The author assumes the character of Swift's *Bickerstaff, the marriage of whose sister, Jenny Distaff, with Tranquillus gives occasion for treating of happy married life. The rake and the coquette are exposed, and virtue is held up to admiration in the person of Lady Elizabeth Hastings (1682–1739), somewhat inappropriately named Aspasia—'to love her is a liberal education.' Anecdotes, essays, and short stories illustrate the principles advanced.

From an early stage in the history of the *Tatler* Steele had the collaboration of *Addison, who contributed notes, suggestions, and a number of complete papers. It was succeeded by the *Spectator*, which they edited jointly. There is a scholarly edition ed. Donald F. Bond (3 vols, 1987).

Tattle, a character in Congreve's *Love for Love*.

Tattycoram, in Dickens's *Little Dorrit*, a foundling brought up in the Meagles household.

TAUCHNITZ, Christian Bernhard von (1816–95), the founder of a publishing house at Leipzig which in 1841 began to issue piratically, then from 1843 to 1943 by sanction or copyright, a series of 5,370 volumes eventually designated 'Collection of British and American Authors'. This and other textually significant English-language 'collections', though specified for sale only on the Continent, were distributed worldwide and reportedly exceeded 40 million copies. Post-war Tauchnitz editions have been issued from Hamburg (1946–9) and Stuttgart (1952–5).

TAWNEY, R(ichard) H(enry) (1880–1962), educated at Rugby and Balliol College, Oxford; historian, socialist (of the *Ruskin, *Morris, and Christian Socialist tradition), and teacher and activist in the *Workers' Educational Association. He joined the executive committee of the WEA in 1905, remained on it for 42 years, and was profoundly affected by the movement, as well as himself influencing its course. From 1917 he was attached to the London School of Economics, becoming professor of economic history in 1931. His works include *The Acquisitive Society* (1921), *Religion and the Rise of Capitalism* (1926), and *Land and Labour in China* (1932).

TAYLOR, A(lan) J(ohn) P(ercivale) (1906–90), historian, educated at Bootham School, York, and Oriel College, Oxford. His many publications include *The Habsburg Monarchy* (1941), *The Troublemakers* (1957, from his Ford lectures), *The Origins of the Second World War* (1961), and a life of *Beaverbrook (1972). He also became widely known as a journalist and television personality, and his autobiography, *A Personal History* (1983), gives a lively and frequently iconoclastic account of his colleagues and acquaintances (including a hostile portrait of Dylan *Thomas), and traces the evolution of his political sympathies from his support of the workers in the General Strike to his support of the Campaign for Nuclear Disarmament.

TAYLOR, Edgar, see CHILDREN'S LITERATURE.

TAYLOR, Edward (c.1644–1729), American poet and divine, born in England. He emigrated to Boston in 1668, and was educated at Harvard. His devotional poems remained in manuscript, at his own request, and were not published until 1937, when their importance to the history of early American letters, and their own considerable quality, were at once recognized. He belongs to the metaphysical tradition of G. *Herbert and *Quarles. A full edition of his works, ed. D. E. Stanford, was published in 1960.

TAYLOR, Elizabeth (1912–75), novelist and short story writer. She was educated in Reading, then worked locally as tutor and librarian until she married in 1936. Her first novel, *At Mrs Lippincote's* (1945), was followed by 11 more: shrewd observations of middle-class life in which self-deceit is always exposed, while compassion is afforded to loneliness and vulnerability. Unobtrusively crafted, underpinned by wit, her work is concerned with moments that detonate understanding. Among the best known of her novels are *A Wreath of Roses* (1950), in which Camilla Hill, a reserved school secretary on the brink of middle age, becomes involved with a handsome but suspect young man, and *Mrs Palfrey at the Claremont* (1971), a study of the pathos of impoverished but genteel old age. Her collections of short stories, *Hester Lilly* (1954), *The Blush* (1958), *A Dedicated Man* (1965), and *The Devastating Boys* (1972), are also much admired for what Angus *Wilson described as her 'warm heart and sharp claws'. *Dangerous Calm*, a selection of her stories (including two previously uncollected) ed. Lynn Knight, appeared in 1995.

TAYLOR, Sir Henry (1800–86). He held an appointment in the colonial office from 1824 to 1872, during which time he published a number of verse dramas which had a considerable vogue in their day, but are now largely forgotten. The most admired was *Philip van Artevelde*

(1834), a lengthy work set in Flanders in the 14th cent.; he describes its hero, a retiring citizen raised to prominence during the power struggles between Ghent and Bruges, as 'a statesman and a man of business'. His only work with any lasting reputation is *The Statesman* (1836), an ironical exposition of the arts of succeeding as a civil servant; its apparent cynicism shocked many of its readers, but 20th-cent. editors (H. J. Laski, 1927; L. Silberman, 1957) found it a shrewd and interesting commentary on the changing and expanding role of the civil service. Taylor was a friend of *Southey and his literary executor. His *Autobiography 1800–75* was published in 1885 (privately printed 1877) and his complete works in five volumes appeared in 1877–8.

TAYLOR, Jane (1783–1824) and Ann (1782–1866), authors of books for children. In 1804 they published *Original Poems for Infant Minds*, which was translated into German, Dutch, and Russian, and ran into 50 editions in England alone. In 1806 followed *Rhymes for the Nursery*, which included one of the most famous poems in the English language, 'Twinkle, twinkle little star'. Other nursery rhymes and stories followed, and in 1810 *Hymns for Infant Minds*. In 1816 Jane produced *Essays in Rhyme*, and until 1822 contributed regularly to *Youth's Magazine*. Both Sir W. *Scott and R. *Browning expressed admiration for the Taylors' work.

TAYLOR, Jeremy (1613–67), born at Cambridge, the son of a barber. He was educated at Gonville and Caius College, Cambridge. Having attracted *Laud's attention as a preacher, he was sent by him to Oxford and became a fellow of All Souls College. He was chaplain to Laud and Charles I, and was appointed rector of Uppingham in 1638. He was taken prisoner in the Royalist defeat before Cardigan Castle in 1645, and retired to Golden Grove, Carmarthenshire, where he wrote most of his greater works. After the Restoration he was made bishop of Down and Connor, and subsequently of Dromore. He died at Lisburn and was buried in his cathedral of Dromore. His fame rests on the combined simplicity and splendour of his style, of which *The Rule and Exercises of Holy Living* (1650) and *The Rule and Exercises of Holy Dying* (1651) are perhaps the best examples. Among his other works, *The Liberty of Prophesying*, an argument for toleration, appeared in 1647; his *Eniautos*, or series of sermons for the Christian Year, in 1653; *The Golden Grove*, a manual of daily prayers, in 1655; his *Ductor Dubitantium*, 'a general instrument of moral theology' for determining cases of conscience, in 1660; and *The Worthy Communicant* in the same year.

TAYLOR, John (1580–1653), the 'water poet', born of humble parentage in Gloucester. He was sent to Gloucester Grammar School, but becoming 'mired' in his Latin accidence was apprenticed to a waterman, pressed for the navy, and was present at the siege of

Cadiz. He then became a Thames waterman, and increased his earnings by writing rollicking verse and prose; he obtained the patronage of *Jonson and others, and diverted both court and city. He went on foot from London to Braemar, visited the Continent, started from London to Queenborough in a brown-paper boat and narrowly escaped drowning, and accomplished other journeys, each one resulting in a booklet with an odd title. He published in 1630 a collective edition of his works, *All the Workes of John Taylor, the Water-Poet* (reprinted, with other pieces, by the Spenser Society, 1868–78), but continued to write a good deal after this, notably royalist ballads and newssheets.

TAYLOR, John (1781–1864), publisher, who first distinguished himself, amid much controversy, by identifying *'Junius' as Sir P. *Francis in 1813. After the death of J. *Scott, he became the editor of the *London Magazine*, 1821–4, and he became a very perceptive partner in the publishing firm of Taylor and Hessey. He published the work of *De Quincey, *Lamb, *Hazlitt, *Keats, *Clare, *Carey, and others, many of whom had already appeared in the *London Magazine*. He greatly encouraged and assisted Clare, published his first volume of *Poems* in 1820, and raised a subscription, to which he contributed generously himself, for the joint benefit of the indigent Clare and Keats. But Clare felt that the comparative failure of *The Shepherd's Calendar* in 1827 was Taylor's fault, and although Taylor offered Clare all the remaining copies to sell for his own benefit, he advanced no more money to the poet and was not the publisher of *The Rural Muse* (1835). He caused some offence to Keats, and to other writers, by his occasional 'revisions' of their works. He held regular dinners for writers, lent money to Keats to travel to Italy, and seems generally to have happily combined the qualities of businessman and friend.

TAYLOR, Philip Meadows (1808–76), Anglo-Indian novelist and historian, born in Liverpool. He joined the Indian army and became a correspondent for *The Times* from 1840 to 1853. He was author of the successful *Confessions of a Thug* (1839), a result of his investigation into Thuggism, the secret terrorist movement in India. His reputation rests mainly on stories written after his retirement to England in 1860, notably the trilogy *Tara: A Mahratta Tale* (1843), *Ralph Darnell* (1865), and *Seeta* (1872), which delineate epochs of Indian history from the 17th cent. to his own time. His autobiography, edited by his daughter, appeared in 1877.

TAYLOR, Thomas (1758–1835), classical scholar, mathematician, and *Neoplatonist, the friend of T. L. *Peacock and other literary men and painters. He was the first to embark on a systematic translation and exposition of Orphic and Neoplatonic literature, and he also devoted himself to the metaphysical aspect of mathematics. He published a great many works covering these interests.

TAYLOR, Tom (1817–80), educated at Trinity College, Cambridge, of which he became a fellow, editor of *Punch*, 1874–80. He produced a number of successful plays (some in collaboration with C. *Reade), most of them adaptations. His comedy *Our American Cousin* (1858) contained the character of the brainless peer Lord Dundreary, who was played with great panache by E. A. Sothern. He edited *Haydon's autobiography in 1853.

TAYLOR, William (1765–1836), born in Norwich, author and translator, who did much to popularize German literature through his translations of Bürger's ballads (see LENORE), and of G. E. *Lessing's *Nathan der Weise* (1791) and *Goethe's *Iphigenia in Tauris* (1793): also through his *Historic Survey of German Poetry* (3 vols, 1828–30) and many contributions on the subject to the *Monthly Magazine*, for which he wrote over 800 reviews, essays, and translations. He was a friend of *Southey, his correspondence with whom is printed in a *Memoir* by J. W. Robberds (1843).

TCHAIKOVSKY, Peter Ilich (1840–93), Russian composer, whose fantasy overture *Romeo and Juliet* (1869) has reached out to a wide audience—perhaps wider than any other Shakespeare-inspired musical work—and yet retains its qualities as a serious work of art. It was his first masterpiece (rev. 1870, and again in 1880), brilliantly integrating the dramatic and passionate elements of the play into the requirements of a compact musical structure. In the last months of his life Tchaikovsky used the love theme (one of the most ravishing of his melodic ideas) as the basis for a duet version of the opening of Shakespeare's III. v, but there is no evidence that he considered making an opera out of the play. There are two other important Shakespearian orchestral works: the symphonic fantasia *The Tempest* (1873) and the fantasy overture *Hamlet* (1888).

The *Manfred Symphony* (1885), after *Byron, is usually regarded, with the Sixth Symphony, as his finest orchestral work: 'the symphony has turned out to be huge, serious and difficult,' he wrote, 'absorbing all my time, sometimes to my utter exhaustion', yet rarely did he realize so large a musical form with such success.

Tearsheet, Doll, *Falstaff's mistress in Shakespeare's 2 *Henry IV*.

'Tears of the Muses, The', a poem by *Spenser, included in the *Complaints*, published 1591. In this the poet deplores, through the mouth of several Muses, the decay of literature and learning.

Teazle, Sir Peter and Lady, characters in Sheridan's *The School for Scandal*.

TEILHARD DE CHARDIN, Pierre (1881–1955), French palaeontologist and Jesuit priest, author of a series of posthumously published works, notably *Le Phénomène humain* (1955), in which he elaborated a system of cosmic evolution. In Teilhard's conception, every physical being was endowed with an inner consciousness whose concentration varied in direct proportion to its material complexity. All matter and material systems were continually and irreversibly evolving along related and converging paths towards physical synthesis and spiritual perfection. The appearance of man in evolutionary history marks the emergence of self-consciousness and has added to the earth, superimposed as it were upon the biosphere, a new dimension, the noosphere, or domain of thought. The development of this specifically human sphere of activity initiates a critical phase in the process of simultaneous complexification and integration, which is to attain its natural term in the unification of cultures, together with a concomitant intensification of collective consciousness to a 'hyperpersonal' level. Evolutionary integration thus reaches its ultimate stage, the point of maximum differentiated unity, which is designated as Omega, and which is arrived at simultaneously with a full realization of the principle of love inherent in the universe.

TELFORD, Thomas (1757–1834), civil engineer and architect, who loved literature and versifying. He was interested in *Goethe and *Kotzebue and was a close friend of *Southey and *Campbell. He is said to have assisted Campbell in the composition of 'Hohenlinden', and he travelled in Scotland with Southey. He built over 1,000 miles of road, 1,200 bridges, churches, docks, aqueducts, and canals, notably the Caledonian. His *Life*, a long and detailed autobiography, was published in 1838.

Temora, see FINGAL.

Tempest, The, a romantic drama by *Shakespeare probably written in 1611, when it was performed before the king at Whitehall; in 1613 it was included in the wedding celebrations for the Princess Elizabeth and the elector palatine. It was not printed until 1623 when it appeared as the first play in the First *Folio. It is usually taken to be his last play written without a collaborator for the London stage before his retirement to Stratford. Although there are several analogues for the story of *The Tempest*, and contemporary accounts of the shipwreck of the *Sea-Venture* in 1609 on the Bermudas and passages from *Golding's Ovid and *Florio's Montaigne contribute details to the play, no single source for it is known. As Dr *Johnson observed, *The Tempest*'s 'plan is regular', that is, it conforms to the *unities.

Prospero, duke of Milan, ousted from his throne by his brother Antonio, and turned adrift on the sea with his child Miranda, has been cast upon a lonely island. This had been the place of banishment of the witch Sycorax. Prospero, by his knowledge of magic, has released various spirits (including Ariel) formerly imprisoned by the witch, and these now obey his orders. He also keeps in service the witch's son Caliban, a misshapen monster, formerly the sole inhabitant of the island. Prospero and Miranda have lived thus for 12 years. When the play begins a ship carrying the usurper, his confederate Alonso, king of Naples, his brother Sebastian and son Ferdinand, is by the art of Prospero wrecked on the island. The passengers are saved, but Ferdinand is thought by the rest to be drowned, and he thinks this is their fate. According to Prospero's plan Ferdinand and Miranda are thrown together, fall in love, and plight their troths. Prospero appears to distrust Ferdinand and sets him to carrying logs. On another part of the island Sebastian and Antonio plot to kill Alonso and Gonzalo, 'an honest old Councellor' who had helped Prospero in his banishment. Caliban offers his services to Stephano, a drunken butler, and Trinculo, a jester, and persuades them to try to murder Prospero. As their conspiracy nears him, Prospero breaks off the masque of Iris, Juno, and Ceres, which Ariel has presented to Ferdinand and Miranda. Caliban, Stephano, and Trinculo are driven off and Ariel brings the king and his courtiers to Prospero's cell. There he greets 'My true preserver' Gonzalo, forgives his brother Antonio, on the condition that he restores his dukedom to him, and reunites Alonso with his son Ferdinand, who is discovered playing chess with Miranda. While Alonso repents for what he has done, Antonio and Sebastian do not speak directly to Prospero, but exchange ironical and cynical comments with each other. The boatswain and master of the ship appear to say that it has been magically repaired and that the crew is safe. Before all embark for Italy Prospero frees Ariel from his service, renounces his magic, and leaves Caliban once more alone on the island.

The Tempest has inspired numerous other works of art, including Milton's *Comus*, an incomplete opera by *Mozart, *Shelley's 'Ariel to Miranda' (see also under ARIEL), *Browning's 'Caliban upon Setebos', music by *Berlioz and *Tchaikovsky, and more recently W. H. *Auden's series of poetic meditations *The Sea and the Mirror* and an excellent science fiction film, *Forbidden Planet* (1954).

Templars, Knights, an order founded about 1118, consisting originally of nine knights whose profession was to safeguard pilgrims to Jerusalem, and who were granted by Baldwin, king of Jerusalem, a dwelling-place in his palace near the temple. Many noblemen joined the order, and it acquired great wealth and influence in France, England, and other countries. Active always in the field, they were really a source of weakness to the Christian king of Jerusalem from their direct dependence on the pope and their constant violation of treaties with the Muslim powers. After the battle of 1187 *Saladin made an example of the Templars and the (much less guilty) Hospitallers who became his prisoners, and beheaded them all, about 200 in number, while sparing nearly all his other prisoners. From a state of poverty and humility they became so insolent that the order was suppressed by the kings of Europe in their various dominions with circumstances, especially in France, of great cruelty. It was also officially suppressed by the pope and the Council of Vienne (1312). *Browning's poem 'The Heretic's Tragedy' alludes to the burning of Jacques de Bourg-Molay, the grand master, in 1314.

Temple, Miss, a character in C. Brontë's *Jane Eyre*.

TEMPLE, Sir William (1628–99), educated at Emmanuel College, Cambridge. He was envoy at Brussels in 1666, and visited The Hague, where he effected the triple alliance between England, Holland, and Sweden, aiming at the protection of Spain from French ambition. He went again to The Hague in 1674, where he brought about the marriage between William of Orange and Mary. In 1654 he married Dorothy *Osborne, whose letters to him give a vivid picture of the times. He settled first at Sheen, then at Moor Park, near Farnham, where he was much occupied with gardening, and where *Swift was a member of his household. His principal works include *Observations upon . . . the Netherlands* (1672), an essay upon *The Advancement of Trade in Ireland* (1673), and three volumes of *Miscellanea* (1680, 1692, 1701). The second of these contains 'Of Ancient and Modern Learning', an essay which, by its uncritical praise of the spurious epistles of *Phalaris, exposed Temple to the censure of *Bentley and led to a vigorous controversy. The *Miscellanea* also include 'Upon the Gardens of Epicurus', 'Of Health and Long Life', 'Of Heroic Virtue', and 'Of Poetry'. Temple's letters were published by Swift, 1700–3, after Temple's death. His *Memoirs*, relating to the period 1672–9, published in 1692, are an interesting blend of public and private affairs.

Tenant of Wildfell Hall, The, a novel by A. *Brontë, published 1848.

Written in the first person with a male narrator, Gilbert Markham, it has an ambitious and complex epistolary and diary structure. Markham, a young farmer, falls in love with Helen Graham, a young widow and talented painter newly arrived in the neighbourhood with her son Arthur, and the tenant of the title. Her youth, beauty, and seclusion, and her mysterious relationship with her landlord Lawrence, give rise to local gossip, which Markham refuses to credit until he himself overhears Helen and Lawrence in intimate conversation. He violently assaults Lawrence, and Helen, distressed at the threatened rupture of their friendship, reveals the truth of her past to him through a lengthy document. Despite the warnings of her family, she had married Arthur Huntingdon, who, after a period of initial happiness, had relapsed, despite her efforts, into a life of drinking, debauchery, and infidelity. She had fled, to protect her child, to Wildfell Hall, provided for her by Lawrence, who is in fact her

brother. Shortly after the revelation of this secret, Helen returns to nurse her husband through a fatal illness, his death hastened by his intemperance, and the way is left clear for Markham successfully to renew his suit. In her 'Biographical Notice' (1850) Charlotte *Brontë suggested that the portrait of the dissolute Huntingdon was based on their brother Branwell, in whom Anne Brontë had had ample opportunity to observe 'the terrible effects of talents misused and faculties abused', and the novel was generally considered 'coarse', 'brutal', and excessively morbid. The author defended it in a preface to the second edition: 'I am at a loss to conceive how a man should permit himself to write anything that would be really disgraceful to a woman, or why a woman should be censured for writing anything that would be proper and becoming for a man.'

TENNANT, Emma (1938–   ), novelist, born in London but brought up largely in Scotland. She founded and edited the literary review *Bananas*, and her novels (which have been variously described as neo-*Gothic and *magic realist, and which are written in a powerful poetic prose) include *Hotel de Dream* (1976); *The Bad Sister* (1978); *Wild Nights* (1979); *Alice Fell* (1980); *Woman Beware Woman* (1983); *The House of Hospitalities* (1987); *A Wedding of Curiosity* (1988); *Sisters and Strangers: A Moral Tale* (1990); *Faustine* (1992); and *Tess* (1993). *Pemberley*, her sequel to Jane Austen's *Pride and Prejudice*, was published in 1993 and its continuation, *An Unequal Marriage*, in 1994. *Strangers* (1998) is an autobiographical novel, blending real characters from the author's ancestry and childhood with fictionalized incident.

TENNANT, William (1784–1848), educated at St Andrews University, a parish schoolmaster (at Anstruther in Fife) learned in oriental languages, of which he became professor at St Andrews. He is remembered in a literary connection for his poem in six cantos *Anster Fair* (1812), a mock-heroic description of the humours of the fair (in James V's reign) and of the courting, with fairy interposition, of Maggie Lauder by Rob the Ranter.

TENNIEL, Sir John (1820–1914), illustrator. He worked for *Punch from 1850, and from 1864 succeeded *Leech as its chief cartoonist; 'Dropping the Pilot' (1890), referring to Bismarck's resignation, is one of his best-known cartoons. His illustrations for *Alice's Adventures in Wonderland* (1865) and *Through the Looking-Glass* (1871) are perfect examples of the integration of illustration with text.

TENNYSON, Alfred, first Baron Tennyson (1809–92), born at Somersby, Lincolnshire, the third surviving son of the rector, George Tennyson. He was educated partly by his father, then at Trinity College, Cambridge, where he joined the *Apostles and became acquainted with A. H. *Hallam. In 1829 he won the chancellor's medal for English verse with 'Timbuctoo', the first poem in blank verse to win. *Poems by Two Brothers* (1827) contains some early work that he chose not to reprint even in his Juvenilia, as well as poems by his brothers Charles and Frederick (below). *Poems Chiefly Lyrical* (1830, including *'Mariana'*) was unfavourably reviewed by *Lockhart and John *Wilson. In 1832 he travelled with Hallam on the Continent, visiting among other places Cauteret, a landscape that was to be a lasting inspiration. Hallam died abroad in 1833, and in that year Tennyson began *In Memoriam*, expressive of his grief for his lost friend.

He became engaged to Emily Sellwood, to whom, however, he was not married until 1850; poverty caused by the disinheritance of the Somersby Tennysons in favour of his socially ambitious uncle Charles Tennyson (D'Eyncourt) was long accepted as the principal reason for this delay, but R. B. Martin suggested (*Tennyson: The Unquiet Heart*, 1980) that Alfred feared the 'black blood' of the Tennysons, a notoriously melancholic and unstable family, and suspected that he, like his father, suffered from epilepsy. (George Tennyson, a violent alcoholic, had died in 1831.) In Dec. 1832 he published a further volume of *Poems* (dated 1833), which included 'The Two Voices', 'Oenone', 'The Lotos-Eaters', and 'A Dream of Fair Women'; *'Tithonus', published 1860, was composed 1833–4. In 1842 appeared a selection from the previous two volumes, many of the poems much revised, with new poems, including *'Morte d'Arthur' (the germ of the *Idylls*), *Locksley Hall*, *'Ulysses', and 'St Simeon Stylites'. From 1845 until his death he received a civil list pension of £200 per annum. In 1847 he published *The Princess* and in 1850 *In Memoriam*, and in the latter year he was appointed *poet laureate in succession to *Wordsworth. He wrote his 'Ode' on the death of *Wellington in 1852 (see ODE) and *'The Charge of the Light Brigade' in 1854, having at this time settled in Farringford on the Isle of Wight.

Tennyson's fame was by now firmly established, and *Maud, and Other Poems* (1855, see MAUD) and the first four *Idylls of the King* (1859) sold extremely well. Among the many friends and admirers who visited Farringford were E. *FitzGerald, who had helped him financially in early years, *Lear, *Patmore, *Clough, F. T. *Palgrave, and *Allingham. Prince Albert called in 1856, but despite the high esteem with which she regarded him Queen *Victoria never visited him, preferring to summon him to Osborne or Windsor. Although suspicious of unknown admirers, Tennyson was a sociable man, with a fondness for declaiming his work to a respectful audience; his wife and his son Hallam protected him from hostile criticism, to which he was highly sensitive. In London he frequented the literary and artistic salon of Mrs Prinsep at Little Holland House; her sister, the photographer Julia Margaret *Cameron, moved to the Isle of Wight in 1860, where she frequently used Tennyson and his family as subjects. *Enoch Arden Etc.* (see ENOCH ARDEN)

appeared in 1864, *The Holy Grail and Other Poems* (including 'Lucretius') in 1869 (dated 1870), 'The Last Tournament' in the *Contemporary Review* in 1871, and *Gareth and Lynette, etc.* in 1872. Tennyson began building his second residence, Aldworth, near Haslemere in Surrey, in 1868. His dramas *Queen Mary* and *Harold* were published in 1875 and 1876, and *The Falcon, The Cup*, and *Becket* in 1884, in which year he was made a peer. H. *Irving and Ellen *Terry appeared in *The Cup* in 1881 and, with much success, in *Becket* in 1893. In 1880 appeared *Ballads and Other Poems*, including 'The Voyage of Maeldune', *'Rizpah', and 'The Revenge'. He published *Tiresias, and Other Poems* (see TIRESIAS) in 1885, and *The Foresters* appeared in 1892. He was buried in Westminster Abbey, and a life by his son Hallam appeared in 1897.

In his later years there were already signs that the admiration Tennyson had long enjoyed was beginning to wane; the *Idylls*, although admired by readers as various as *Longfellow, Clough, *Macaulay, *Thackeray, *Gladstone, and Queen Victoria, were found by *Carlyle, despite their 'finely elaborated execution' to express 'the inward perfectn. of *vacancy'*, and *Swinburne referred to them as 'Morte d'Albert, or Idylls of the Prince Consort'. *Bagehot found 'Enoch Arden' 'ornate' and G. M. *Hopkins found it 'Parnassian'. In 1870 A. *Austin described Tennyson's work as 'poetry of the drawing room'. Critical opinion has tended to endorse *Auden's view that 'his genius was lyrical', and that he had little talent for the narrative, epic, and dramatic forms to which he devoted such labour. T. S. *Eliot called him 'the great master of metric as well as of melancholia', who has 'the finest ear of any English poet since Milton', and *Leavis suggested that his influence, like *Milton's, was unfortunate. More recently there has been a revival of interest in some of the longer poems, e.g. 'Locksley Hall', *The Princess*, and 'Enoch Arden'. There is an excellent annotated edn by C. Ricks (1969); see also his *Tennyson* (1972). There is a life by Robert Martin, *Tennyson: The Unquiet Heart* (1980).

TENNYSON, Frederick (1807–98), elder brother of A. *Tennyson. He contributed to the *Poems by Two Brothers* (1827), and published *Days and Hours* (1854), *The Isles of Greece* (1890), and other volumes of verse.

TENNYSON TURNER, Charles (1808–79), elder brother of A. *Tennyson. He contributed to *Poems by Two Brothers* (1827) and published from time to time volumes of sonnets (1830–80), simple and restrained in manner, some of them depicting the rustic aspects of the Lincolnshire wolds.

TERENCE (Publius Terentius Afer) (*c.*190 or *c.*180–159 BC), Roman comic poet. He was born in North Africa and came as a slave to Rome, where he was eventually freed by his master, whose name he adopted. Four of his plays, *Andria, Adelphi, Eunuchus*, and *Heautonti-*

morumenos, are adaptations of *Menander; his other two plays, *Hecyra* and *Phormio*, are imitations of Greek plays by Menander's imitator Apollodorus of Carystus. Although he employs the same limited range of characters that is found in *Plautus, he gives them greater depth and presents a world of genuine relationships. He was famed already in antiquity for the elegance and colloquial character of his Latin. It was as a stylist that he was studied in the Middle Ages and figured in the curriculum of most Tudor schools: there is an early translation of the *Andria*, probably by *Rastell (*c*.1520), a later one specifically for schools by M. Kyffin (1588), and an English version of all the six comedies by R. Bernard (1598). But Terence was known more through imitations than through translations. Along with Plautus, he contributed plots, characters, and tone to the mainstream of Renaissance comedy in 16th-cent. Italy, then (with original features) in the France of *Corneille and *Molière, from where it spread to Restoration London.

TERESA, or **THERESA, St** (Teresa of Ávila) (1515–82), a Spanish saint and author, who entered the Carmelite sisterhood and became famous for her mystic visions. Her works include *El castillo interior* (*The Interior Castle*, written 1577, pub. 1588), an account of her visions, and *El camino de la perfección* (*The Way of Perfection*, written 1563–73, pub. 1583), a book of counsel for the ascetic life. Her *Libro de las fundaciones* (*Book of the Foundation*, 1610) narrates her ceaseless journeys as an energetic reformer of the Carmelite order and a foundress of new convents. She is the subject of *Crashaw's 'Hymne to Sainte Teresa', which relates her childish attempt to court martyrdom by preaching to the Moors (an incident taken from her own spiritual autobiography) and her progress towards a state of mystic ecstasy or spiritual 'marriage'. She is also the subject of Bernini's celebrated erotic masterpiece, the *Ecstasy of Saint Teresa* (1645) in S. Maria della Vittoria, Rome.

TERRY, Ellen Alice (1847–1928), celebrated actress, and member of a distinguished theatrical family. She married the painter G. F. Watts in 1864, when only 16, a union that soon ended, and had two children by E. W. Godwin (1833–86), the architect and theatrical designer, one of whom was Gordon *Craig. She was H. *Irving's leading lady during his brilliant management of the Lyceum Theatre.

TERSON, Peter, the pseudonym of Peter Patterson (1932–   ), playwright, born in Newcastle upon Tyne; he was associated with the Victoria Theatre, Stoke-on-Trent, with its tradition of social documentary and theatre-in-the-round, then with the National Youth Theatre, where he excelled in writing for large casts. His works include *Mooney and His Caravans* (TV 1966, pub. 1970), a poignant play about a young and inadequate couple victimized by the owner of a caravan site; *Zigger Zagger* (1967, pub. 1970), about

a football fan, which skilfully incorporates the drama of the football terraces; and *Good Lads at Heart* (1971), set in a Borstal. Later works include *Geordie's March* (1979) and *Strippers* (1984), about a group of working-class women forced to take up stripping to support themselves.

TERTULLIAN (b. *c*.150), one of the greatest of the early Christian writers in Latin, author of the *Apologeticus* (197), an eloquent appeal to Roman governors on behalf of the Christians, and of many treatises on the Christian life. He was opposed to the introduction of classical authors into Christian schools, and posed the famous question adapted by St *Jerome and *Alcuin: 'What has Athens to do with Jerusalem?' (*De Spectaculis*).

terza rima, the measure adopted by Dante in the *Divina commedia*, consisting of lines of five iambic feet with an extra syllable, in sets of three lines, the middle line of each rhyming with the first and third lines of the next set (a b a, b c b, c d c, etc.).

TESSIMOND, A(rthur) S(eymour) J(ohn) (1902–62), poet, born in Birkenhead and educated at Charterhouse and Liverpool University. He published three volumes of verse in his lifetime (*The Walls of Glass*, 1934; *Voices in a Giant City*, 1947; *Selection*, 1958): his *Collected Poems* (ed. Hubert Nicholson) appeared in 1985. He is remembered for his wry, low-key, urban pieces, some of them much anthologized, which include 'Cats', 'The Man in the Bowler Hat', and 'Not Love Perhaps. . .'

Tess of the D'Urbervilles: *A Pure Woman*, a novel by T. *Hardy, published 1891.

The subtitle was important to Hardy's purpose. Tess Durbeyfield is the daughter of a poor villager of Blackmoor Vale, whose head is turned by learning that he is descended from the ancient family of D'Urberville. Tess is cunningly seduced by Alec, a young man of means, whose parents, with doubtful right, bear the name of D'Urberville. Tess gives birth to a child, which dies after an improvised midnight baptism by its mother. Later, while working as a dairymaid on a prosperous farm, in a beautiful summer, she becomes blissfully engaged to Angel Clare, a clergyman's son. On their wedding night she confesses to him the seduction by Alec; and Angel, although himself no innocent, cruelly and hypocritically abandons her. Misfortunes and bitter hardships come upon her and her family, and accident throws her once more in the path of Alec D'Urberville. He has become an itinerant preacher, but his temporary religious conversion does not prevent him from persistently pursuing her. When her pathetic appeals to her husband, now in Brazil, remain unanswered, she is driven for the sake of her family to become the mistress of Alec. Clare, returning from Brazil and repenting of his harshness, finds her living with Alec in Sandbourne. Maddened by this second wrong that has been done her by Alec,

Tess stabs and kills him to liberate herself. After a brief halcyon period of concealment with Clare in the New Forest, Tess is arrested at Stonehenge, tried, and hanged. Hardy's closing summary reads: '"Justice" was done, and the President of the Immortals (in Aeschylean phrase) had ended his sport with Tess.'

The publication of the novel created a violent sensation (see also JUDE THE OBSCURE). Some reviewers were deeply impressed, but most considered the work immoral, pessimistic, extremely disagreeable, and, as H. *James wrote, 'chockful of faults and falsity'.

Testament of Cresseid, The, a poem in 616 lines of rhyme-royal by *Henryson. The poet describes in the prologue how he took up Chaucer's *Troilus and Criseyde and proceeded to tell of the retribution that came upon Cresseid. Diomede grows tired of Cresseid and leaves her; she takes refuge with her father Calchas and bitterly reproaches Venus and Cupid. A council of the gods discusses the punishment for her blasphemy; Saturn deprives her of joy and beauty, and the Moon strikes her with leprosy. As she sits by the roadside with her leper's cup and clapper, Troilus rides by with a party of victorious Trojans and, though the leper brings Cresseid to his mind, he does not recognize her. Neither does she recognize him, but she receives alms from him and then learns who he is. She dies after sending him a ring he had once given her.

Testament of Love, The, see USK.

Tetrachordon, the third of *Milton's pamphlets on divorce, published 1645, a substantial work of 110 pages. It deals with four sets of passages on marriage and nullities in marriage from Genesis, Deuteronomy, St Matthew, and the First Epistle to the Corinthians. Milton seeks to reconcile the passages and to prove their essential harmony. (A tetrachordon was a four-stringed Greek lyre.) Milton wrote two sonnets in defence of his views on divorce, attacking his detractors; one is specifically related to Tetrachordon, which, he says, 'walk'd the Town a while, | Numbring good intellects; now seldom por'd on'.

Teufelsdröckh, Herr Diogenes, the fictitious mystical German philosopher from the University of Weissnichtwo whose life and opinions are described in Carlyle's *Sartor Resartus.

TEY, Josephine (1896–1952), the pen-name of Elizabeth Mackintosh, detective story writer, born in the Highlands. Her best-known works include The Franchise Affair (1948), in which a mother and daughter are falsely accused of abduction, and Brat Farrar (1949), a mystery in which a young man presumed to have committed suicide as a child returns to claim an inheritance to which the reader knows he has no right. The Daughter of Time (1951) is an investigation of the murder of the Princes in the Tower. Under the name of Gordon Daviot she wrote Richard of

Bordeaux (1933), a historical drama based on the life of Richard II.

THACKERAY, Anne Isabella, see RITCHIE.

THACKERAY, William Makepeace (1811–63), born in Calcutta, the son of Richmond Thackeray, a collector in the East India Company's service. His father died when he was 3, and Thackeray was sent home to England in 1817, to be rejoined by his mother, who had married again, in 1820. Thackeray was educated at Charterhouse, where he was not happy, and at Trinity College, Cambridge, where he became a close friend of E. *Fitzgerald. He left Cambridge in June 1830 without taking a degree, having lost some of his inheritance through gambling. He visited Paris, and spent the winter of 1830–1 in Weimar, where he met *Goethe. He entered the Middle Temple, but he had little enthusiasm for the law, and never practised as a barrister. He began his career in journalism by becoming the proprietor of a struggling weekly paper, the National Standard, in 1833. It ceased publication a year later, but the experience had given Thackeray an entrée to the London literary world. He also pursued his other enthusiasm, for art, and studied in a London art school and a Paris atelier. By the end of 1833 virtually all his inherited money had been lost, probably in the collapse of the Indian agency-houses. Thackeray lived in Paris from 1834 until 1837, making a meagre living from journalism. For a short while he had a regular income as Paris correspondent of the Constitutional, a newspaper bought by his stepfather, and he married Isabella Shawe in 1836, the year in which his fiirst publication in volume form, Flore et Zephyr, a series of ballet caricatures, appeared. The Constitutional failed, and the Thackerays returned to London, where their fiirst child Anne (Anne Thackeray *Ritchie) was born in 1837. Thackeray began to contribute regularly to *Fraser's Magazine, and also wrote for many other periodicals, including the *Morning Chronicle, the *New Monthly Magazine, and *The Times. A second daughter born in 1839 did not live long, and after the birth of their third child, Harriet Marian (later the first wife of Leslie *Stephen), in 1840 Isabella Thackeray suffered a mental breakdown which proved permanent. Thackeray was forced to place her first in the care of a French doctor, later in a private home in England, and to send his children to live with his mother in Paris.

During the 1840s Thackeray began to make a name for himself as a writer. He first came to the attention of the public with The Yellowplush Papers, which appeared in Fraser's Magazine in 1837–8: these were a critique of what Carlyle called 'flunkeyism', delivered through the device of a footman-narrator. These were followed by *Catherine, narrated by 'Ikey Solomon' (1839) and 'A Shabby Genteel Story' (1840). His first full-length volume, The Paris Sketch Book, containing miscellaneous early journalism, appeared in the same year, and in 1841 appeared The Great Hoggarty

Diamond, a mock-heroic tale about a diamond which brings bad luck to Samuel Titmarsh, an amiable young clerk who inherits the gem: this is narrated by Sam's cousin, Michael Angelo Titmarsh, who provided Thackeray with his most familiar pseudonym. Other pseudonyms included 'George Savage FitzBoodle', a bachelor clubman, 'author' of *The FitzBoodle Papers* (1842–3), narrator of *Men's Wives* (1843) and 'editor' of *The Luck of Barry Lyndon* (1844): Jeames de la Pluche, and 'Our Fat Correspondent'. *The Irish Sketch Book* of 1843 (a personal, impressionistic and prejudiced account of an 1842 tour of Ireland) has a preface signed, for the first time, with Thackeray's own name.

Thackeray began his association with *Punch* in 1842, and contributed to it caricatures as well as articles and humorous sketches. *The Snobs of England, by One of Themselves* (later published as *The Book of Snobs*, 1848), appeared there 1846–7: this constitutes his great anatomy of the English vice of snobbery, a term he invented. *Mr Punch's Prize Novelists* (1847) parodies the leading writers of the day. His children returned to live with him in 1846. In 1847 his first major novel, *Vanity Fair*, began to appear in monthly numbers, with illustrations by the author. *Pendennis* followed in 1848–50. In 1841 Thackeray's increasing love for Jane Brookfield, the wife of an old Cambridge friend, led to a rupture in their friendship, and his next novel *The History of Henry Esmond* shows signs, as Thackeray confessed, of his melancholy at this time. It was published in three volumes in 1852, and was followed by *The Newcomes*, published in numbers in 1853–5.

As well as the major novels, Thackeray continued to produce lighter work; he wrote for *Punch* until 1854, and produced a series of 'Christmas Books' which he illustrated himself: *The Rose and the Ring* (by 'Mr M. A. Titmarsh'), a delightful children's story, was published in 1855. In 1851 he gave a series of lectures on *The English Humourists of the Eighteenth Century*, and in 1855–7 he lectured on *The Four Georges*. He twice visited the United States to deliver his lectures, in 1852–3 and 1855–6. *The Virginians*, set partly in America, appeared in numbers in 1857–9. In 1860 he became the first editor of the *Cornhill Magazine*, for which he wrote his delightfully casual improvisations, the *Roundabout Papers*. *Lovel the Widower*, *The Adventures of Philip*, and the unfinished *Denis Duval* all first appeared in the *Cornhill*. Thackeray died suddenly on Christmas Eve 1863.

There is an authoritative biography of Thackeray by Gordon Ray in two volumes: *Thackeray: The Uses of Adversity* (1955) and *Thackeray: The Age of Wisdom* (1958). Ray also edited Thackeray's *Letters and Private Papers* (1945–6), and his study of the relation between Thackeray's fiction and his life, *The Buried Life*, was published in 1952. Anne Thackeray Ritchie published *Chapters from Some Memoirs* in 1894, and her introductions to the *Biographical Edition* (1899) of her father's works contain many anecdotes about his life.

Thaisa, in Shakespeare's *Pericles*, the wife of Pericles.

theatre criticism, in the journalistic sense, began in Britain in the early 18th cent. Despite earlier attempts by *Dryden in his prefaces and Thomas *Rymer in *A Short View of Tragedy* to uphold French neo-classical principles, it was not governed by a continental adherence to aesthetic rules. Its emergence was determined by pragmatic factors: the rise of the opinionated essayist, the strength of Restoration acting, and the need to protect the stage from moral censure. All three converge in *Steele who, writing on the death of *Betterton in 1710, claims, 'There is no human invention so aptly calculated for the forming a free-born people as that of the theatre.' But while Steele and *Addison were occasional commentators, Aaron *Hill and William *Popple in *The Prompter* (1734–6) became the first professional theatre critics pursuing a campaign for realistic acting that paved the way for *Garrick.

The proliferation of late 18th-cent. journalism, the centrality of the stage in London life, and the presence of great actors all promoted a lively criticism based on personal observation. But it was Leigh *Hunt and *Hazlitt who transformed dramatic criticism from a transient record into a durable art. Both were writing, between 1805 and 1830, in the period William *Archer called 'the winter solstice of English drama': both, however, were witness to legendary performances. Hunt was often at his best writing about comic actors such as Charles James Mathews or Robert William Elliston: Hazlitt was inspired by the demonic genius of Edmund *Kean. His reviews of Kean's Shakespearian performances combine astute technical analysis with vivid impressionistic images: describing the battle scenes in *Richard III*, he writes that Kean 'fought like one drunk with wounds'.

Hazlitt argued that Shakespeare's best commentators were his actors; and actor-led criticism continued in the later 19th cent. with G. H. *Lewes and Joseph Knight. But, with the emergence of *Ibsen and the new drama, the rules changed. *Shaw used his coruscating columns in the *Saturday Review* in the 1890s to attack the reigning actor-manager Henry *Irving, and to endorse a drama that addressed social and moral issues: he was keenly supported by William Archer who was both an advocate of Shaw and translator of Ibsen. Shaw's successor, Max *Beerbohm, was more a whimsical essayist than an embattled campaigner and James *Agate, who wrote for the *Sunday Times* from 1923 to 1947, was a distinguished connoisseur of acting rather than a reliable analyst of plays. But the separate traditions of graphic reporter and militant enthusiast converged in Kenneth *Tynan, who both enshrined legendary performances, particularly those of Olivier, and used his *Observer* columns to champion *Brecht and *Osborne. Harold Hobson, his opposite number on the *Sunday Times*, was equally persuasive about the work of *Beckett, *Pinter, and

*Duras. American theatre criticism, with a shorter historical tradition, in the 20th cent. produced a pugnacious essayist in George Jean *Nathan, a gracious stylist in Stark Young, and a distinguished blend of academic, practitioner, and journalist in Eric Bentley, Robert Brustein, and Harold Clurman. The distinguishing feature of English-language theatre criticism remains, however, a suspicion of intellectual theory and a trust in subjective impressions.

Théâtre de Complicité, influential physical theatre group founded in 1983 by Annabel Arden, Simon McBurney, Marcello Magni, and Fiona Gordon. Their early work fed on European mime traditions and surreal British humour and later embraced a fascination with a wide range of textual sources. A production of Friedrich *Dürrenmatt's *The Visit* in 1988 was a powerful spectacle of post-war nightmare, revenge, and materialism. *The Street of Crocodiles* (1992) and *Out of a House Walked a Man* (1994), both co-produced with the Royal *National Theatre, gave stunning new articulation to the forgotten absurdists Bruno Schulz and Daniel Kharms. Complicité helped to redraw the map of British theatre in the 1980s, raising the ensemble performance stakes alongside the continuing wealth of new playwriting. Their version of John *Berger's *The Three Lives of Lucie Cabrol* (1994) combined the best of both worlds in a work of intellectual passion and physical distinction.

Theatre of the Absurd, see ABSURD, THEATRE OF THE.

Thel, The Book of, see BLAKE.

THELWALL, John (1764–1834), English radical, who in 1794 was arrested with *Tooke for his revolutionary views, and subsequently tried and acquitted. He published several volumes of verse, political essays, tracts on elocution, etc. He was an acquaintance of *Wordsworth and *Coleridge, whom he visited in Somerset in 1797, having walked on foot from London, a journey described in part (although anonymously) in the *Monthly Magazine, 1799.

Thenot, (1) a shepherd in Spenser's *The Shepheardes Calender; (2) a character in Fletcher's *The Faithful Shepherdess.

THEOBALD, Lewis (1688–1744), Shakespearian scholar and author of poems, essays, and dramatic works. His *Shakespeare Restored* (1726) exposed *Pope's incapacity as an editor of Shakespeare; Pope retaliated with his devastating portrait of Theobald as hero of his *Dunciad. Nevertheless Pope incorporated many of Theobald's corrections in his second edition, and Theobald's 1733–4 edition of Shakespeare surpassed that of his rival. Over 300 emendations made to the texts by Theobald are still accepted by most modern editors and he was a pioneer in the study of Shakespeare's sources. *Double Falsehood* (1728), a dramatization of *Cardenio, bears the inscription on the title-page: 'Written Originally by W.

Shakespeare; and now Revised and Adapted to the Stage By Mr. Theobald.' *Cardenio*, a lost play, had been entered in the Stationers' Register in 1653 as 'by Mr Fletcher & Shakespeare' and it is likely that *Double Falsehood* is Theobald's attempt at establishing a vital relationship between Shakespeare and *Cervantes. The fact that Theobald failed to publish the original or comment on it in any detail in his 1733–4 edition subjected him to further ridicule by, among others, *Fielding in his *A Journey from This World to the Next.

THEOCRITUS (c.308–c.240 BC), a native of Sicily who lived in Cos and Alexandria. He was the most important of the Greek bucolic poets and the one who established for the *pastoral the formal characteristics, setting, and tone which it was to retain for centuries. His most distinctive poems evoke the life and rustic arts of the shepherds on his native island, maintaining a successful balance between idealization and realism. Remembered primarily as a pastoral poet, he was in fact a most versatile writer, and a bridal hymn, a panegyric, and a mime describing two middle-class women at a showy religious ceremony are among his best pieces. Theocritus wrote in the Doric dialect, and the difficulties this produced for his readers led to his comparative neglect during the Renaissance. Editions of his text did not appear in substantial numbers until the end of the 18th cent., and modern writers of pastoral from *Petrarch to *Pope tended rather to take *Virgil for a model. There was however an excellent anonymous translation of six of Theocritus' idylls in 1588, and in 1684 Thomas Creech put all his works into English, a year before *Dryden (whose preface praised Theocritus' 'tenderness and naturalness') contributed some translations to *Tonson's *Miscellany*. Victorian imitators, such as *Tennyson in 'The Lotos-Eaters' (1833), delighted in the sensuality of Theocritus' world of pastoral delights.

THEODORE (602–90), archbishop of Canterbury, a native of Tarsus in Cilicia. He studied at Athens, and was well versed in Greek and Latin literature. He was consecrated archbishop of Canterbury by Pope Vitalius in 668. He imposed the Roman order and was the first archbishop to whom (according to *Bede) the whole English Church agreed in submitting after the divisions leading up to the Synod of Whitby (663/4). He founded a school of learning at Canterbury, and created many new bishoprics. Theodore was a great organizer, the effects of his work surviving to the present day; and was author, at least in part, of the *Poenitentiale*, of considerable ecclesiastical and historical interest. See *Councils and Ecclesiastical Documents Relating to Great Britain and Ireland*, ed. A. W. Haddan and W. Stubbs (1871), iii. 173–204.

THEODORIC, see DIETRICH OF BERN.

THEOPHRASTUS (c.372–287 BC), Greek philosopher, head of the Peripatetic school after *Aristotle. He is reputed to have written on style, and two of his works on plants survive. But his interest for English literature derives from his *Characters*, brief sketches of human types embodying particular faults: the toady, the overproud, the churlish. The popularity of Theophrastus in modern times dates from the edition of his *Characters* with Latin translations by I. *Casaubon in 1592. An English rendering by John Healey appeared in 1616, but before then J. *Hall enlarged Theophrastus' scope, adding good qualities to bad in his *Characters of Vertues and Vices* (1608), and Sir T. *Overbury produced, in collaboration with J. *Webster, *Dekker, and *Donne, a volume of *Characters* that, enlarged after his death, ran into a great number of editions (1614). The genre remained popular throughout the century. (See also CHARACTER-WRITING.)

Theophrastus Such, see IMPRESSIONS OF THEOPHRASTUS SUCH, THE.

Theory of Moral Sentiments, The, a philosophical work by Adam *Smith, published 1759, and originally delivered in the form of lectures at Glasgow.

The author advances the view that all moral sentiments arise from sympathy, the principle which gives rise to our notions of the merit or demerit of the agent. The basis of morality is pleasure in mutual sympathy, which moderates our natural egocentricity. The desire for such pleasure requires us to see ourselves 'in the light in which others see us', a thought quoted admiringly by *Burns ('To a Louse'):

> O wad some Pow'r the giftie gie us
> To see oursels as others see us.

Smith's account of the role of the imagination in the operation of sympathy influenced *Sterne, in *A Sentimental Journey*, and other contemporary writers.

Theosophical Society, see BLAVATSKY.

THERESA, St, see TERESA.

THEROUX, Paul Edward (1941–), travel writer, novelist, and short story writer, born in Medford, Massachusetts, and educated at Medford High School and the University of Massachusetts. He spent some time teaching in Africa, and then, through D. J. *Enright, secured an appointment to teach at the University of Singapore. His time there provided inspiration for a collection of stories, *Sinning with Annie* (1972), and a novel, *Saint Jack* (1973). His first novel *Waldo*, a surreal comedy, had been published in 1966. Then came *Fong and the Indians* (1968), a satire set in east Africa; *Girls at Play* (1969), set in Kenya; and *Jungle Lovers* (1971), set in Malawi (the former Nyasaland, where Theroux had served in the Peace Corps). His name was made, however, by a series of vivid travel books, written with all the instincts of a novelist, about epic railway journeys: *The Great Railway Bazaar* (1975), describing a journey across Europe and Russia to Japan; *The Old Patagonian Express* (1978), depicting travels in South America; and *Riding the Iron Rooster* (1988), an account of a journey through China. In *The Kingdom by the Sea* (1983) he turned his attention to the coastline of Britain, his adopted home for many years, while *The Happy Isles of Oceania* (1992) describes a voyage across the South Pacific. At the same time he continued to produce a steady stream of novels, including *The Black Horse* (1974), about an English anthropologist returning from Africa; *The Family Arsenal* (1976), a thriller set in the London underworld; *Doctor Slaughter* (1984); *The Mosquito Coast* (1982), one of his finest novels, subsequently filmed, in which an American engineer seeks a new life in Honduras; *My Secret History* (1989); *O-Zone* (1986), a dystopian fantasy; *Millroy the Magician* (1993); *The Pillars of Hercules* (1995); and *My Other Life* (1996), an 'imaginary memoir' which disconcertingly mixes fact and fiction. Both *The Consul's File* (1977) and *The London Embassy* (1982) are collections of episodic short stories dealing with expatriate communities. A volume of *Collected Stories* was also published in 1995. *Sir Vidia's Shadow: A Friendship across Five Continents* (1998) charts the decline of his personal relationship with V. S. *Naipaul, a writer he much admires.

Thersites, the most querulous and ill-favoured of the Greek host in the Trojan War. He was killed by Achilles for laughing at the latter's grief over the death of Penthesilea, the queen of the Amazons. He figures in Shakespeare's *Troilus and Cressida* as a scabrous cynic.

Theseus, a son of Poseidon, or, according to later legend, of Aegeus, king of Athens. His exploits (in association with Medea, the Minotaur, Ariadne, Phaedra, etc.) form the basis of many literary works, and he appears as the duke of Athens in Shakespeare's *A Midsummer Night's Dream*, with his newly won bride *Hippolyta, and also in Fletcher's *The Two Noble Kinsmen*.

THESIGER, Sir Wilfred (Patrick) (1910–2003), travel writer, explorer, soldier, and photographer, born in the British legation in Addis Ababa (Abyssinia, now Ethiopia) where his father was British minister. He was educated at Eton and Oxford. In 1933–4 he explored the little-known territories of the Danakil people (see his *Danakil Diary*, pub. 1998) and became increasingly taken with a desire to live among herdsmen, hunters, and swamp-dwellers, far from the Europeanized capitals of Addis Ababa and Khartoum. *Arabian Sands* (1959) is a solemn epitaph for traditional Arabia, based on the years he spent in the Empty Quarter with the Bedu, and *The Marsh Arabs* (1964) describes the years he spent in the marshes of southern Iraq. In 1960 he moved to the northern highlands of Kenya. His autobiographical works are *Desert, Marsh and Mountain* (1979, which includes accounts of travels in Persia and Iraqi Kurdistan as well as many photographs); *The Life of My Choice* (1987); and *My Kenya Days* (1994).

Thierry King of France, and His Brother Theodoret, The Tragedy of, a play by J. *Fletcher, with the collaboration probably of *Massinger and possibly of *Beaumont, published 1621.

Theodoret, king of Austrasia, reproves his mother Brunhalt for her licentiousness, and to revenge herself she attempts to sow enmity between him and his younger brother Thierry, but fails. With the assistance of her lover Protaldy, and a physician, specialist in poisons, she destroys the happiness of Thierry and his young bride Ordella, then has Theodoret assassinated, then attempts to procure the death of Ordella, and finally poisons Thierry. Vengeance then falls upon Brunhalt and her accomplices. There are incidents in the play which may be allusions to the queen regent of France, Marie de Médicis, and her favourite Concini (murdered in 1617).

THIONG'O, Ngugi Wa, formerly known as James T. Ngugi (1938–   ), Kenyan novelist, born at Limuru, Kenya, and educated at the University of Makerere and at Leeds University. *Weep Not, Child* (1964), a novel of childhood that draws largely from his own upbringing and mission-school education, ends by rejecting the romantic individualism of its protagonist. *The River between* (1965; the first written, though the second to be published, of his novels) also ends with a reversal, in which Waiyaki recognizes on his deathbed the need for political activity if clannish divisions and cultural fragmentation are to be overcome; education can bring individual but not national advancement. *A Grain of Wheat* (1967) blends the realism and compassion of his undergraduate short stories with the messianic political search of his first two novels. When Ngugi took to writing in his own language, Gikuyu, his government arrested him in 1977, and he wrote his first Gikuyu novel largely in prison; it was translated as *Devil on the Cross* (1982), after being published in Nairobi in 1980 in its original version. *Detained: A Prison Writer's Diary* (1981) was, however, written in English. Several extracts from works banned in Kenya have appeared in *Index on Censorship*. See also POST-COLONIAL LITERATURE.

THIRKELL, Angela Margaret, née Mackail (1890–1961), prolific writer who enjoyed great popularity in the 1930s with novels, many set in a rural Barsetshire borrowed from *Trollope (*Ankle Deep*, 1933, *August Folly*, 1936, *The Brandons*, 1939, *Peace Breaks Out*, 1945, etc.). She was a granddaughter of *Burne-Jones and her son (by her first marriage) was the writer Colin *MacInnes: her second husband George Thirkell was an Australian engineer, but the marriage failed, and having spent some ten years in Australia (which she disliked) she returned to England to earn her living, very successfully, as a writer of idealized English country life.

THIRLWALL, Connop (1797–1875), educated at Charterhouse and Trinity College, Cambridge, where he became a fellow in 1818. He was ordained priest in 1828. He translated Schleiermacher's *Essay on the*

Gospel of St Luke (1825) and his introduction to this work was remarkable for its acquaintance with German theology. This was followed by a translation with *Hare of *Niebuhr's *History of Rome* (1828–42) and their *Vindication of Niebuhr's History* (1829). Also with Hare he edited the *Philological Museum* (1832–3) which contained Thirlwall's important essay on 'The Irony of Sophocles'. In 1832 he was appointed assistant tutor at Trinity College but was forced to resign his university posts in 1834 owing to his denunciation of compulsory attendance in chapel in the controversy over the admission of Dissenters to the universities. He was immediately offered the living of Kirby Underdale where he wrote his chief work, the *History of Greece* (1835–44, for *Lardner's Cyclopaedia*, rev. 1847–52). In 1840 Lord Melbourne appointed him bishop of St David's. He supported the admission of Jews to Parliament, the disestablishment of the Irish Church, and allowed Bishop *Colenso to preach in his diocese. These subjects and the *Essays and Reviews* controversy are dealt with in his 'Charges' (published in *Remains, Literary and Theological*, 1877–8).

THOMAS, (Walter) Brandon, see CHARLEY'S AUNT and FARCE.

THOMAS, D(onald) M(ichael) (1935–   ), poet, novelist, and translator, was born in Cornwall and educated there, in Australia, and at New College, Oxford; he learned Russian while doing his National Service, and his work has been much influenced by his familiarity with Russian literature. His translations include two volumes of the poems of *Akhmatova (1976, 1979) and *Pushkin's *The Bronze Horseman and Other Poems* (1982); his own volumes of poetry include *Two Voices* (1968), *Logan Stone* (1971), *Love and Other Deaths* (1975), *The Honeymoon Voyage* (1978), *Dreaming in Bronze* (1981), and *Selected Poems* (1983). His first novel, *The Flute-Player* (1979), is a surreal fantasy set in a totalitarian state, in which flute-player Elena represents in part the persecuted creative spirit of the Russian poets (*Mandelstam, *Pasternak, *Tsvetayeva, and Akhmatova) to whom the book is dedicated. *Birthstone* (1980), set in Cornwall, is an idiosyncratic blend of fantasy, comedy, realism, eroticism, and magic. With *The White Hotel* (1981) he achieved international success. The novel combines an invented but carefully documented case history of one of *Freud's patients, Russian-Jewish Lisa Erdman, with her erotic and nightmare fantasies in prose and verse, a realistic account of her cure, her career as opera singer and subsequent marriage, and the steps that lead her and her stepson Kolya to her dreamforeseen death in the 1941 massacre at Babi Yar. *Ararat* (1983) shows a similar brooding on the theme of holocaust (this time of the Armenians) and on the relationship between sex and death, and a similar narrative complexity: Russian poet Sergei Rozahov, grandson of an Armenian storyteller, improvises one night in Gorky to a blind admirer a tale of improvisation within improvisation, with a central section inspired by Pushkin's unfinished *Egyptian Nights*, in which Cleopatra offers a night of love in exchange for death. This was followed by *Swallow* (1984); *Sphinx* (1986); *Summit* (1987); *Lying Together* (1990); and *Flying into Love* (1992), based on the assassination of John F. Kennedy; *Pictures at an Exhibition* (1993), and *Eating Pavlova* (1994). A frank volume of autobiography, *Memories and Hallucinations*, was published in 1988. *Alexander Solzhenitsyn: A Century in His Life* (1997) is a biography.

THOMAS, Dylan Marlais (1914–53), poet, born in Swansea, the son of the English master at Swansea Grammar School, where he himself was educated; he knew no Welsh. He began to write poetry while still at school, and worked in Swansea as a journalist before moving to London in 1934; his first volume of verse, *18 Poems*, appeared in the same year. He then embarked on a Grub Street career of journalism, broadcasting, and film-making, spending much time in the flourishing afternoon drinking clubs of the era, and rapidly acquiring a reputation for exuberance and flamboyance, as both poet and personality. In 1937 he married Caitlin Macnamara; they settled for a while at Laugharne in Wales, returning there permanently after many wanderings in 1949. Despite some allegations of deliberate obscurity, Thomas's romantic, affirmative, rhetorical style gradually won a large following; it was both new and influential (and much imitated by his contemporaries of the *New Apocalypse movement), and the publication of *Deaths and Entrances* (1946), which contains some of his best-known work (including 'Fern Hill' and 'A Refusal to Mourn the Death by Fire of a Child in London') established him with a wide public: his *Collected Poems 1934–1952* (1952) sold extremely well. His work sheets, minutely and continually laboured over, reveal him as an impassioned, even obsessional, craftsman; a great part of his mature work consists of the reworking of the early poetic outbursts of his youth, controlled by a strict discipline.

Thomas also wrote a considerable amount of prose. *The Map of Love* (1939) is a collection of prose and verse; *Portrait of the Artist as a Young Dog* (1940) is a collection of largely autobiographical short stories; *Adventures in the Skin Trade* (1955) is a collection of stories, including the unfinished title story (also edited separately by his friend V. *Watkins, 1955); *A Prospect of the Sea* (1955) is a collection of stories and essays. He was a popular entertainer on radio and with students; in 1950 he undertook the first of his lecture tours to the United States, and he died there on his fourth visit, as legend grew about his wild living and hard drinking. Shortly before his death he took part in a reading in New York of what was to be his most famous single work, *Under Milk Wood*. His *Notebooks* (ed. R. N. Maud) were published in 1968, and a new edition of *The Poems of Dylan Thomas* (1971) is enriched by authoritative critical notes and personal comments by his friend and early collaborator, the composer Daniel Jones (1912–   ). See also a life by C. Fitzgibbon (1965), who also edited his *Selected Letters* (1960).

THOMAS, (Philip) Edward (1878–1917), poet, born in Lambeth and educated at St Paul's and Lincoln College, Oxford. He married young and moved to Kent, supporting his family by producing many volumes of prose, much of it topographical and biographical, including a biography of R. *Jefferies (1909), who profoundly influenced him. In 1913 *Hodgson introduced him to *Frost, with whose encouragement he turned to poetry. In 1915 Frost returned to America and Thomas enlisted in the army. He was killed at Arras. Most of his poetry was published posthumously, though a few pieces appeared under the pseudonym 'Edward Eastaway' between 1915 and 1917. Various collections followed, the fullest, *Collected Poems*, edited by R. George Thomas, 1978. His work shows a loving and accurate observation of the English pastoral scene, combined with a bleak and scrupulous honesty and clarity. Both he and Frost advocated the use of natural diction, and of colloquial speech rhythms in metrical verse. *Leavis singled him out as 'an original poet of rare quality, who has been associated with the Georgians by mischance' and his work is now highly regarded. There are memoirs by his widow Helen Thomas, *As It Was* (1926) and *World without End* (1931), and by E. *Farjeon. See also A. *Motion, *The Poetry of Edward Thomas* (1980).

THOMAS, R(onald) S(tuart) (1913–2000), poet and clergyman, born in Cardiff, and educated at St Michael's College, Llandaff, and University College, Bangor; he was ordained as clergyman in the Church in Wales in 1936. From 1942 to 1954 he was rector of Manafon, Montgomeryshire, and subsequently was vicar of Eglwysfach, then of St Hywyn, Aberdaron, with Y Rhiw and Llanfaelrhys; he retired in 1978. His first volume of poems, *The Stones of the Field* (1946), was followed by many others, including *Song at the Year's Turning* (1955), *Tares* (1961), *Pietà* (1966), *Not that He Brought flowers* (1968), and *Laboratories of the Spirit* (1975); his *Selected Poems 1946–68* was published in 1973. His poetry is deeply coloured by his experience of working in remote rural communities, where some of the churches had tiny congregations and where life was harsh and the landscape bleak; he has created his own form of bleak Welsh pastoral, streaked with indignation over the history of Wales and the Welsh— 'an impotent people, | Sick with inbreeding | Worrying the carcase of an old song' ('Welsh Landscape', 1955). The poet's evocation of his peasant parishioners (who are frequently portrayed as vacant, sullen, miserly, mean-spirited) is unsparing: 'There is no love | For such, only a willed | gentleness' ('They'). Many of the poems unite religious and rural imagery (see the title poem of *Pietà*), but the religious affirmation is always hard won. Later volumes include *Experimenting with an Amen*

(1986), *The Echoes Return Slow* (1988), *Counterpoint* (1990), and *Mass for Hard Times* (1992). *Complete Poems 1945–90* was published in 1993 to coincide with his eightieth birthday. Thomas has also edited various anthologies, including *The Penguin Book of Religious Verse* (1963), and selections from E. *Thomas (1964), G. *Herbert (1967), and *Wordsworth (1971). See *Furious Interiors: Wales, R. S. Thomas and God* (1996) by Justin Wintle.

THOMAS À BECKET, or **THOMAS BECKET** see BECKET, ST THOMAS.

THOMAS À KEMPIS (Thomas Hämmerlein or Hämmerken) (1380–1471), born of humble parents at Kempen near Cologne. He became an Augustinian monk and wrote Christian mystical works, among which is probably to be included the famous *De Imitatione Christi*, which has been translated from the Latin into many languages (into English in the middle of the 15th cent.). This work was at one time attributed to Jean Charlier de Gerson, a French theologian. It traces in four books the gradual progress of the soul to Christian perfection, its detachment from the world, and its union with God; and obtained wide popularity by its simplicity and sincerity and the universal quality of its religious teaching.

Thomas the Rhymer, see ERCELDOUNE.

THOMASON, George (d. 1666), a London bookseller and publisher and friend of *Prynne and *Milton; Milton's sonnet 'When Faith and Love which parted from thee never' was written in 1646 on the death of Thomason's wife Katherine. Thomason's collection of political tracts and broadsides published between the outbreak of the Civil War and the Restoration was presented to the *British Museum in 1762; it includes four items donated by Milton personally. The tracts were catalogued in 1908 by George Fortescue.

Thomist (pron. 'Tomist'), a follower of the *Scholastic philosopher St Thomas *Aquinas.

THOMPSON, E(dward) P(almer) (1924–93), historian, educated at Corpus Christi College, Cambridge, and for many years (1948–65) an extramural lecturer at Leeds University. His works include a study of W. *Morris (1955) and *The Making of the English Working Class* (1963), a work in which he sought 'to rescue the poor stockinger, the Luddite cropper, the "obsolete" hand-loom weaver, the "utopian" artisan, and even the deluded follower of Joanna Southcott, from the enormous condescension of posterity'. He also wrote and lectured in support of the Campaign for Nuclear Disarmament. *Witness against the Beast*, a study of William *Blake, was published posthumously in 1993.

THOMPSON, Flora Jane, née Timms (1876–1947), the daughter of a builder's labourer, born at Juniper Hill, near Brackley, a hamlet on the borders of Oxfordshire and Northamptonshire. She left school at 14, and worked as a post-office clerk before marrying John Thompson, who became a postmaster. They lived from 1916 at Liphook in Hampshire, moving in 1928 to Dartmouth. In the early years she supplemented their meagre income with journalism, writing nature essays for the *Catholic Fireside*, the *Daily News, the *Lady*, and other papers, and in 1921 she published a volume of verse, *Bog-Myrtle and Peat*. She is remembered for her autobiographical trilogy *Lark Rise to Candleford* (1945), published originally as *Lark Rise* (1939), *Over to Candleford* (1941), and *Candleford Green* (1943), works which evoke through the childhood memories and youth of third-person 'Laura' a vanished world of agricultural customs and rural culture. There is a selection of works by Margaret Lane, *A Country Calendar and Other Writings* (1979), with a biographical introduction.

THOMPSON, Francis (1859–1907), son of a Roman Catholic doctor, born in Preston, Lancashire, and educated at Ushaw College. He was intended for the priesthood, but was judged not to have a vocation. He also failed to qualify as a doctor, and in 1885 left home to spend three years of homeless and opium-addicted destitution in London, till he was rescued by Wilfrid and Alice *Meynell, who secured him literary recognition and organized his life in London lodgings and monasteries in Sussex and Wales. He never married, and never for long freed himself from opium which, together with tuberculosis, caused his early death. His best-known poems are 'The Hound of Heaven' and 'The Kingdom of God'; he published three volumes of verse, in 1893, 1895, and 1897, and much literary criticism in Meynell's *Merry England*, the *Academy*, and the *Athenaeum*. His finest work conveys intense religious experience in imagery of great power, but some of his poetry sounds ornate, overheated, and derivative; he was influenced especially by *Shelley, *De Quincey, and *Crashaw. His poetry has been more popular with the general public (especially with Catholic readers) than with the critics.

The standard life is by Everard Meynell (1913): see also J. C. Reid, *Francis Thompson, Man and Poet* (1959), which gives a full and scholarly account of the poet's opium addiction, and John Walsh, *Strange Harp, Strange Symphony* (1968), which has the fullest account of his personal life.

THOMPSON, Hunter S(tockton) (1939–2005), American journalist and writer, born in Louisville, Kentucky. He spent many years writing for *Rolling Stone* magazine, in which the two works for which he is best known first appeared. *Fear and Loathing in Las Vegas* (1972), subtitled 'a savage journey to the heart of the American Dream', is an account of a heavily drugged visit to Las Vegas, offering a brutal, funny, and often horrifying dissection of American culture. No less provocative was *Fear and Loathing on the Campaign Trail '72* (1973), his coverage for *Rolling Stone* of the 1972 American presidential campaign. He spent a year riding with the

Hell's Angels, ran for sheriff of Aspen, Colorado, in 1970, and subsequently awarded himself a doctorate. With Tom *Wolfe and Joan *Didion a pioneer of New Journalism, his own irreverent political and cultural writing ('Gonzo Journalism') has been collected into four volumes. *Proud Highway*, the first volume of his *Letters*, was published in 1997, and a novel *The Rum Diary* (written in 1959) in 1998.

THOMS, William John (1803–85), antiquary, who became successively clerk and deputy librarian to the House of Lords. He was author of several works including *The Book of the Court* (1838), and edited a number of volumes including a collection of *Early Prose Romances* (1827–8) and *The History of Reynard the Fox* (1844) for the *Percy Society. He was secretary of the *Camden Society from 1838 to 1873. In 1846, in an article in the *Athenaeum* headed 'Folk Lore' he introduced this term into the English language. Encouraged by *Dilke he founded *Notes and Queries* in 1849.

THOMSON, James (1700–48), born at Ednam on the Scottish border, the son of a minister, and educated at Edinburgh University, where he already showed promise as a poet. Encouraged by his friend *Mallet, he came to London in 1725, and wrote 'Winter', the first of *The Seasons*, which appeared successively in 1726–30. He made the acquaintance of *Arbuthnot, *Gay, and *Pope, found patrons, and eventually, through the influence of Lord *Lyttelton, received a sinecure. He travelled in France and Italy as tutor to Charles Talbot, son of the solicitor-general, and in 1735–6 published his long patriotic poem *Liberty*, in which Liberty narrates her progress through the ages in Greece, Rome, and Britain. He produced a series of tragedies, *Sophonisba* (1730), *Agamemnon* (1738), *Edward and Eleanora* (1739); *Tancred and Sigismunda* (published 1745) and *Coriolanus* (1749) were produced after his death. In 1740 was performed the masque of *Alfred* by Thomson and Mallet, containing 'Rule, Britannia', probably written by Thomson. In 1748, a few weeks before his death, appeared *The Castle of Indolence*, which contains a portrait of himself ('A bard here dwelt, more fat than bard beseems') supposed to have been written by Lyttelton, the first line by J. *Armstrong, which affectionately mocks the poet's notorious love of idleness. He was buried in Richmond church; his friend William *Collins, also then living at Richmond, wrote an elegy, 'In yonder Grave a Druid lies' (1749). *The Seasons*, one of the most popular (and frequently reprinted and illustrated) of English poems, was immensely influential, offering both in style and subject a new departure from the urbanity of Pope and developing in a highly distinctive manner the range of *topographical poetry; *Wordsworth recognized Thomson as the first poet since *Milton to offer new images of 'external nature'. Yet most of the Romantics and, later, *Tennyson deplored his artificial diction. *Coleridge's summary was 'Thomson was a

great poet, rather than a good one; his style was as meretricious as his thoughts were natural.' He contributed greatly to the vogue for the *picturesque and his landscapes were influenced by those of *Claude, *Poussin, and *Rosa; he was himself greatly admired by J. M. W. *Turner, who drew inspiration from his works. See *Poetical Works*, ed. J. L. Robertson (1908, 1951).

THOMSON, James (1834–82), born in Scotland, the son of a poor merchant seaman. He attended the Royal Caledonian Asylum school when the family moved to London. He was trained as an army schoolmaster, in which capacity he was sent in 1851–2 to Ireland, where he met *Bradlaugh, who became his staunch friend, and also a young girl, Matilda Weller, who died in 1853 but who became an important symbolic figure in Thomson's later poetry. Between 1852 and 1862 he worked at army stations in England and Ireland and wrote much poetry, some of which was accepted by various journals, including Bradlaugh's *National Reformer*. For his early work he used the pseudonym 'B.V.', representing his admiration for *Shelley with 'Bysshe' and for the German poet *Hardenberg ('Novalis') with 'Vanolis'. Signs of growing alcoholism appeared in the late 1850s and in 1862 Thomson was discharged from the army, probably for drunkenness. He came to London, and until 1868 lodged with the Bradlaughs. He took various jobs and wrote poems, essays, and translations for several magazines, publishing among other work 'Vane's Story', 'Sunday up the River', and 'Sunday at Hampstead'. 'Weddah', a long poem relating a tragic Arabian love story, appeared in 1871, and led to friendship with W. M. *Rossetti. For part of 1872 Thomson was with a gold company in Colorado, and in 1873 in Spain as a war reporter; on his return he completed his best-known poem, 'The City of Dreadful Night', which appeared in the *National Reformer* in 1874, and received some favourable notice, including encouragement from G. *Eliot and later from *Meredith. This long poem, which much influenced the mood of *fin-de-siècle* poetic pessimism, is a powerful evocation of a half-ruined city, a 'Venice of the Black Sea', through which flows the River of the Suicides; the narrator, in vain search of 'dead Faith, dead Love, dead Hope', encounters tormented shades wandering in a Dantesque vision of a living hell, over which presides the sombre and sublime figure of Melancolia (based on *Dürer's engraving of 1514). In 1880 his first volume of verse, *The City of Dreadful Night and Other Poems*, and a second volume later in the same year, were well received. *Essays and Phantasies* appeared in 1881. But his alcoholism was by now out of control; *Satires and Profanities* was published posthumously in 1884. There is a life by H. S. Salt, 1889; see also *Poems and Some Letters of James Thomson* (1963) edited with a biographical introduction by Anne *Ridler. See also

Places of the Mind: The Life and Work of James Thomson (1993) by Tom *Leonard.

THOMSON, Rupert (1955–), novelist, born in Eastbourne. His first novel, *Dreams of Leaving* (1987), an ambitious mix of fantasy and realism, was followed by *The Five Gates of Hell* (1991), set in a surreal, Gothic landscape reminiscent of Miami, and *Air and Fire* (1993), a historical tale set in Mexico. Playful and sinister, *The Insult* (1996) took Thomson to another invented territory, a conflation of Edward Hopper's lonely cityscapes and the myth of Central Europe: Martin Blom may or may not have problems with his eyesight, but he can definitely see that something is going on. Is his doctor trying to pull the wool over his eyes or is Blom really blind? You decide. In *Soft* (1998), three main characters are linked by an innovative marketing strategy for a new soft drink. The title pertains as much to the novel's structure—the construction folding in on itself like one of Dali's soft clocks—as it does to 'Kwench!'.

THOMSON, Sir William, first Baron Kelvin (1824–1907), educated at Glasgow, where he later became professor of natural philosophy, and at Peterhouse, Cambridge. His formulation of the second law of thermodynamics, predicting that the world would sooner or later suffer a heat death as a result of entropy, contributed significantly to late 19th-cent. pessimism. The ignorance of this law displayed by most 20th-cent. literary intellectuals was used as an illustration of the gap between the *'Two Cultures' by C. P. *Snow.

'Thopas, The Tale of Sir', see CANTERBURY TALES, 17.

THOREAU, Henry David (1817–62), American author, born in Concord, Massachusetts, and educated at Harvard. He became a follower and friend of *Emerson, and was, in his own words, 'a mystic, a transcendentalist, and a natural philosopher to boot'. He supported himself by a variety of occupations, as lead pencil-maker (his father's trade), as schoolteacher, tutor, and surveyor; a few of his poems were published in the *Dial, but he made no money from literature, and published only two books in his lifetime. The first, *A Week on the Concord and Merrimack River* (1849), described a journey undertaken in 1839 with his brother; the second, *Walden, or Life in the Woods* (1854), attracted little attention, but has since been recognized as a literary masterpiece and as one of the seminal books of the century. It describes his two-year experiment in self-sufficiency (1845–7) when he built himself a wooden hut on the edge of Walden Pond, near Concord; he describes his domestic economy, his agricultural experiments, his visitors and neighbours, the plants and wildlife, and his sense of the Indian past, with a deeply challenging directness that questions the materialism and the prevailing work ethic of the age. Yet he is constantly aware of the surrounding world, to which he eventually returns; he can hear from his hut 'the rattle of railroad cars, now dying away and then

reviving like the beat of a partridge'. The work is studded with apparently casual illuminations ('The mass of men lead lives of quiet desperation') and with lines of poetic sensibility ('A field of water betrays the spirit that is in the air'). Equally influential in future years was his essay on 'Civil Disobedience' (1849; originally entitled 'Resistance to Civil Government'), in which he argues the right of the individual to refuse to pay taxes when conscience dictates, as he and Bronson Alcott had done in 1843, in protest against the Mexican War and slavery, for which he had in 1845 been briefly imprisoned. Thoreau's reputation as philosopher and political thinker, as well as naturalist, was strengthened by a biography (1890) by the British socialist Henry S. Salt, and by the admiration of E. *Carpenter and H. *Ellis in Britain; his technique of passive resistance, as described in 'Civil Disobedience', was adopted by Gandhi. He has also been hailed as a pioneer ecologist. His *Journal* (14 vols) was published in 1906, his collected *Writings* (20 vols) also in 1906, and a new scholarly edition of works began publication in 1971.

THORPE, Adam (1956–), novelist and poet, born in Paris and brought up in India, Cameroon, and England. Educated at Marlborough and Magdalen College, Oxford, he subsequently worked in drama, both performing and teaching, before leaving England in 1990 to live in France. His novels are *Ulverton* (1992), *Still* (1995), and *Pieces of Light* (1998) and he has published three books of poetry, most recently *From the Neanderthal* (1999). He rose to prominence with his first novel, a dense subversive tour de force which places Ulverton, a fictional Wessex village, at the still centre of three centuries of social, linguistic, and historical flux, with each chapter narrated in a different but appropriate style. All his work is in some way connected with the continuum of history and an exploration of Englishness.

Thorpe, John and Isabella, characters in J. Austen's *Northanger Abbey*.

Thousand and One Nights, The, see ARABIAN NIGHTS ENTERTAINMENTS.

THRALE, Hester Lynch, Mrs, née Salusbury (1741–1821), married against her inclinations in 1763 to Henry Thrale, the son of a wealthy brewer. The following year they met Dr *Johnson, who became very friendly with both. He wrote election addresses for Thrale, and spent much time in their company, at one period becoming almost domesticated at their house in Streatham Place. Mrs Thrale, a lively and intelligent woman, bore several children, of whom only four daughters survived to maturity. Three years after Thrale's death in 1781, and amid much opposition from family and friends (including F. *Burney), she married Gabriel Piozzi, an Italian musician; this drew from Johnson a letter of anguished protest, which he regretted, but their intimacy was at an end, and there is evidence that Mrs Thrale had already begun to find him a demanding guest. She published several works, including *Anecdotes of the Late Samuel Johnson* (1786); *Thraliana*, a mixture of diary, anecdotes, poems, and jests, covering the period 1776–1809, was edited in 1942, 2 vols, by K. C. Balderston.

Three Clerks, The, a novel by A. *Trollope, published 1858.

The three clerks are Harry Norman, Alaric Tudor, and Alaric's gauche cousin Charley. In the course of the novel each marries one of the daughters of Mrs Woodward, a widow living near Hampton Court. At first Harry and Alaric vie for the attentions of the eldest daughter Gertrude, and in this, as in every other matter where the two come into competition, Alaric gets his way. Alaric, clever and dynamic, profits from the new system of promotion by examination in the civil service; but with responsibility comes temptation, and Alaric falls. He is arrested for the abuse of a trust fund, is tried, and, despite the best efforts of his counsel, Chaffanbrass, imprisoned. His wife Gertrude, and the dependable Harry Norman, help him through the ordeal and into Australian exile.

Meanwhile Charley has built up a literary reputation, won promotion, and settled down to married life. Charley's experiences reflect Trollope's own in his early days as a clerk at the Post Office.

Three Hours after Marriage (1717), a comedy by *Arbuthnot, *Gay, and *Pope.

Three Men in a Boat, see JEROME, J. K.

Threepenny Opera, The (*Die Dreigroschenoper*), *Brecht's updated version of *The Beggar's Opera*.

Three Weeks after Marriage, a comedy by *Murphy, performed 1764. It satirizes the parvenu tastes of a rich retired tradesman, Mr Drugget, who has married his eldest daughter to Sir Charles Rackett, and proposes to marry his second daughter to another penniless man of fashion, Lovelace. But his experiences with the recently wedded couple resolve him to abjure all dealings with fashionable society.

Thrie Estaitis, Satyre of the, see PLEASANT SATYRE OF THE THRIE ESTAITIS, ANE.

Through the Looking-Glass and *What Alice Found There*, a book for children by Lewis Carroll (see DODGSON), published 1872.

Alice (see ALICE'S ADVENTURES IN WONDERLAND) walks in a dream through the looking-glass into Looking-Glass House, where she finds that the chessmen, particularly the red and white queens, are alive; meets with Tweedledum and Tweedledee and Humpty-Dumpty; and so forth. The story ends with Alice, who has the red queen in her arms, 'shaking her into a kitten' (for she had gone to sleep playing with the black and white kittens). The well-known verses about

the *Jabberwock and the Walrus and the Carpenter occur in the course of the story.

THUBRON, Colin (1939–   ), novelist and travel writer, born in London. His travel writings began in the eastern Mediterranean and include *Mirror to Damascus* (1967), *The Hills of Adonis* (1968), and *Journey into Cyprus* (1975), which provided the setting for his first novel, *The God in the Mountain* (1977). Later travel books took on increasingly difficult terrain, and include *Among the Russians* (1983, a journey to Moscow, the Caucasus, the Ukraine, and the Crimea), *Behind the Wall* (1987, a journey through China), and *The Lost Heart of Asia* (1994). His novels, which also tend to emphasize man's essentially solitary or estranged condition, include *Emperor* (1978), *A Cruel Madness* (1984, set in a mental institution), and *Falling* (1989). *Turning back the Sun* (1991) is set in an unnamed country where the doctor Rayner, a lonely idealist, tries to prevent the persecution of the 'savage' natives who are suspected of violence against the white population and of spreading a new plague. *Distance* (1996) is an exploration of time, love, and memory through the narration of an astrophysicist suffering from amnesia.

THUCYDIDES (*c*.460–*c*.395 BC), Athenian historian who left a brilliant account of the disastrous war Athens waged against Sparta. Outstanding talent as a writer enabled him to bestow on his subject the inevitable character of a tragedy. He was prepared to trace effects to rational causes; his handling of eyewitness accounts (all-important in a contemporary history) was securely scientific; and although his obvious desire to trace the psychological laws underlying political action has been held to have damaged his standing as a pure historian, some readers have found his political speculations of interest. Like other difficult Greek authors, Thucydides was little read before the 19th cent., although there was a translation by T. Niccols (1550) and one by *Hobbes (1629) which he said was intended to display the follies of democracy. Then in 1829 S. T. Bloomfield produced an annotated translation. In 1830–5 T. *Arnold published a commentary in which he tried to derive lessons for his own time from the text of Thucydides, and *Jowett's elegant translation followed in 1881.

Thunderer, The, a nickname given to *The Times* in the middle of the 19th cent., in allusion to the style of writing of Edward Sterling (1773–1847), a member of its staff, and father of John *Sterling. *Trollope similarly alludes in some of his novels to *The Times* as 'The Jupiter' (from Jupiter Tonans).

THURBER, James Grover (1894–1961), American humorist, many of whose essays, stories, and sketches appeared in the *New Yorker*, including one of his best-known short stories, 'The Secret Life of Walter Mitty' (1932), which describes the colourful escapist fantasies of a docile husband.

Thurio, 'a foolish rivall to Valentine' as *Silvia's suitor in Shakespeare's *The Two Gentlemen of Verona*.

THURLOW, Edward, second Baron Thurlow (1781–1829), public servant and minor writer, who contributed frequently to the *Gentleman's Magazine*. In 1810 he published an edition of Sidney's *A Defence of Poetry* and in 1813 his own *Poems*, followed by further volumes. In 1822 he published *Angelica*, an attempted continuation of Shakespeare's *The Tempest*.

Thwackum, a character in Fielding's *Tom Jones*.

THWAITE, Anthony Simon (1930–   ), poet and critic, born at Chester, and educated at Christ Church, Oxford. His varied literary career has included academic posts in Japan (1955–7), Libya (1965–7), and Kuwait (1974); some years as producer for the BBC, and as literary editor (1962–5) of the *Listener*; he was co-editor of *Encounter* from 1973 to 1985. His volumes of poetry include *Home Truths* (1957), *The Stones of Emptiness* (1967), and *A Portion for Foxes* (1977). An early allegiance to *Larkin has expanded into a wide variety of theme and subject matter, ranging from the domestic to the exotic: *Victorian Voices* (1980) is a collection of fourteen dramatic monologues which takes as subjects such lesser Victorian figures as P. H. Gosse (father of E. *Gosse), J. C. *Collins, and Alma-Tadema. His collected *Poems 1953–1983* was published in 1984, and enlarged in 1989 as *Poems 1953–1988*. His engagement with Japanese culture was again reflected in *Letter from Tokyo* (1987). His *Selected Poems 1956–1996* appeared in 1997 and *A Move in the Weather* in 2003. He edited the *Collected Poems* of Larkin in 1988 and Larkin's *Selected Letters* in 1992. He is married to the literary biographer Ann Thwaite.

'Thyrsis, A Monody, to commemorate the author's friend, Arthur Hugh Clough, who died at Florence, 1861', a poem by M. *Arnold, first published in *Macmillan's Magazine*, 1866. The poem is a pastoral elegy lamenting *Clough as Thyrsis, recalling his 'golden prime' in the days when he and Arnold wandered through the Oxfordshire countryside, their youthful rivalry as poets, and Clough's departure for a more troubled world, where his poetry took on 'a stormy note | Of men contention-tossed'. It invokes the *Scholar-Gipsy as an image of hope and perpetual quest: 'Roam on! The light we sought is shining-still.'

Tibert, the cat in *Reynard the Fox. The name is the same as Tybalt (see the exchange between Mercutio and Tybalt in *Romeo and Juliet*, III. i. 75 ff.: 'Tybalt, you rat-catcher ... Good King of Cats, nothing but one of your nine lives').

TIBULLUS, Albius (*c.*48–19 BC), Roman elegiac poet, noted for the refinement and simplicity of his plain style and his idealization of the countryside. Of the three books that bear his name, the first is a celebration of his love for a mistress (Delia) and a boy (Marathus),

the second a short account of his love for a woman whom he calls Nemesis, and the third a collection of poems by members of his literary circle. His influence has been discerned in T. *Campion and *Herrick, and *Dryden compared him to *Sedley.

TICKELL, Thomas (1685–1740), educated at The Queen's College, Oxford. He contributed verse to the *Guardian*, the *Spectator* and other publications, and was author of various poems, including *Oxford* (1707), *On the Prospect of Peace* (1713), and *Kensington Garden* (1722); his sentimental *ballad *Lucy and Colin* (1725) was much admired by *Gray and *Goldsmith. But he is chiefly remembered as a friend and supporter of *Addison; he may have occasioned the quarrel between *Pope and Addison by publishing in 1715 a translation of the first book of the *Iliad* at the same time as Pope, at Addison's instigation, as Pope supposed. He edited Addison's works (1721), publishing in the first volume an elegy on Addison's death.

Tigg, Montague, a character in Dickens's *Martin Chuzzlewit*.

Tilburina, the heroine of Mr Puff's tragedy 'The Spanish Armada' in Sheridan's *The Critic*. It is she who observes that even an oyster may be crossed in love.

Till Eulenspiegel, see EULENSPIEGEL.

TILLOTSON, John (1630–94), educated at Clare Hall, Cambridge, a latitudinarian who became archbishop of Canterbury. His sermons, which were very popular, show a marked difference from the earlier *metaphysical style of *Donne and *Andrewes; they were both plainer and shorter, and were extolled as models of lucidity and good sense through most of the 18th cent.

TILLYARD, E(ustace) M(andeville) W(etenhall) (1889–1962), scholar and critic. Among weightier publications such as *Milton* (1930), *Shakespeare's Last Plays* (1938), *Shakespeare's History Plays* (1944), and *Shakespeare's Problem Plays* (1950), probably his short essay *The Elizabethan World Picture* (1943) has been the most influential. *The Personal Heresy*, his debate with C. S. *Lewis about the value of searching for a writer's true state of mind through his works, was first published in 1939.

Tilney, General, his sons Henry and Frederick, and his daughter Eleanor, characters in J. Austen's *Northanger Abbey*.

Timber or *Discoveries Made upon Men and Matter*, by *Jonson, printed in the folio of 1640, a collection of notes, extracts, and reflections on miscellaneous subjects, made in the course of the author's wide reading, varying in length from a single sentence to short essays. They are, for the greater part, adapted from Latin writers.

Time and Tide: *An Independent Non-Party Weekly Review*, a periodical founded in 1920 by Viscountess Rhondda (Margaret Haig Thomas, 1883–1958), with the support of R. *West, Cicely Hamilton, and others. Originally a strongly left-wing and feminist publication, under the editorship of Helen Archdale, it went through many shades of political opinion before its disappearance in 1977. Its contributors included D. H. *Lawrence, V. *Woolf, S. *Jameson, G. B. *Shaw, and Robert *Graves; in 1929 it serialized E. M. *Delafield's *Diary of a Provincial Lady*; *Betjeman's poem 'Caprice' describes how he was sacked from his post as its literary adviser in 1953.

Times, The, founded under the name of 'The Daily Universal Register' on 1 Jan. 1785 by John Walter, the name being changed to *The Times* in 1788. The founder and his son, also John Walter, introduced great improvements both in the mechanism of newspaper printing and in the collection of intelligence. Among the famous editors of *The Times* have been Thomas Barnes (1817–41) and John Thaddeus Delane (1841–77). The latter was followed by Thomas Chenery, and in 1884 by G. E. Buckle. *The Times* was one of the first papers to employ special foreign correspondents (H. C. *Robinson was sent to north Germany in this capacity in 1807) and war correspondents (W. H. Russell in the Crimea). Among notable men of letters who contributed to *The Times* in early days were *Borrow (from Spain), Leigh *Hunt, and B. *Disraeli ('Runnymede Letters').

In the 20th cent. *The Times* has been edited by G. Robinson (1912–19); H. W. Steed (1919–22); G. Dawson (1922–41); R. M. Barrington Ward (1941–8); W. F. Casey (1948–52); W. Haley (1952–66); W. Rees-Mogg (1966–81); H. Evans (1981–2); C. Douglas-Home (1982–5); C. Wilson (1985–90); S. Jenkins (1990–2); P. Stothard (1992–). The most dramatic change in the appearance of the paper during this period was the removal, on 3 May 1966, of the column marked 'Personal' from the front page, and its replacement by news. Of the three weekly supplements published by *The Times* group, the *Times Literary Supplement* was founded in 1901, the *Times Educational Supplement* in 1910, and the *Times Higher Educational Supplement* in 1971. In 1967 both *The Times* and the *Sunday Times* came under the control of Times Newspapers Limited, a group set up by Lord Thomson of Fleet (1894–1976). Because of strike action both papers and the supplements closed down for some months in 1978–9; in 1981 they were all acquired by the News Corporation Limited, of which Rupert Murdoch is chief executive.

Times Literary Supplement (1902–), a weekly literary periodical of high international standing which first appeared with *The Times* in 1902, then in 1914 became a separate publication. The first editor, Bruce *Richmond (later knighted), supported and encouraged many writers of his time, including V.

*Woolf, T. S. *Eliot, J. M. *Murry, E. *Blunden, the historians *Namier and E. H. Carr, and many others, both by commissioning articles from them and by giving publicity to their own works. Reviews continued to be anonymous until 1974 when under the editorship of John Gross they began to be signed. The journal endeavours to cover most of the important works of literature and scholarship, and remains influential.

Timias, in Spenser's *Faerie Queene*, Prince *Arthur's squire, may represent *Ralegh. When wounded (III. v), he is healed by *Belphoebe. The incident of Timias and *Amoret, in IV. vii. 35 and 36, may allude to Ralegh's relations with Elizabeth Throckmorton.

Timon, a misanthropical citizen of Athens who lived about the time of the Peloponnesian War, the subject (1) of one of *Lucian's finest Dialogues; (2) of Shakespeare's *Timon of Athens.

Pope's Timon, in *Moral Essays* IV. 98, an example of ostentatious wealth without sense or taste, was said to be drawn from the duke of Chandos, but Pope repudiated this charge, apparently to the duke's satisfaction, and it is more likely to be a composite portrait.

Timon of Athens, a drama by *Shakespeare, probably in collaboration with *Middleton, written probably about 1607 and apparently left unfinished; it was not printed until the First *Folio of 1623. The material for the play is in *Plutarch's *Life of Antony*, Painter's *Palace of Pleasure*, *Lucian's *Timon, or the Misanthrope*, and possibly an anonymous play *Timon* among the Dyce MSS in the Victoria and Albert Museum.

Timon, a rich and noble Athenian of good and gracious nature, having ruined himself by his prodigal liberality to friends, flatterers, and parasites, turns to the richest of his friends for assistance in his difficulties, and is denied it and deserted by all who had previously frequented him. He surprises these by inviting them once more to a banquet; but when the covers are removed from the dishes (Timon crying, 'Uncover, dogs, and lap', III. vi), they are found to contain warm water, which with imprecations he throws in his guests' faces. Cursing the city, he betakes himself to a cave, where he lives solitary and misanthropical. While digging for roots he finds a hoard of gold, which has now no value for him. His embittered spirit is manifested in his talk with the exiled Alcibiades, the churlish philosopher Apemantus, the thieves and flatterers attracted by the gold, and his faithful steward Flavius. When the senators of Athens, hard pressed by the attack of Alcibiades, come to entreat him to return to the city and help them, he offers them his fig-tree, on which to hang themselves as a refuge from affliction. Soon his tomb is found by the seashore, with an epitaph expressing his hatred of mankind.

Tina Sastri, a character in G. Eliot's 'Mr Gilfil's Love-Story' (see SCENES OF CLERICAL LIFE).

TINDAL, Matthew, see DEISM.

TINDAL, William, see TYNDALE.

TINDALL, Gillian (1938–   ), novelist, short story writer, critic, and historian, born in London, and educated at Oxford. Her works, which show a keen and sensitive interest in contemporary social and moral issues, and frequently feature the dilemmas of the liberal conscience, include *The Youngest* (1967), in which a mother gives birth to a deformed child; *Fly away Home* (1971), an exploration in diary form of an early marriage and its consequences, set in Paris, London, and Israel; *Dances of Death* (1973, stories centred on a subject which, she suggests, had replaced sex as a 20th-cent. taboo); *The Traveller and His Child* (1975), a novel about parental responsibility, set in North London and France; *The Intruder* (1979, novel); *The China Egg* (1981, stories); and *Journey of a Lifetime* (1990), which collects stories connected by the themes of travel, death, memory, and age. *The Fields beneath* (1977) is a topographical study of Kentish Town, a North London neighbourhood; *City of Gold* (1981) is a 'biography' of Bombay; and *Célestine* (1995) is a study of a French village: all show her sense of the influence and importance of place.

Tintagel, a castle on the north coast of Cornwall, of which ruins remain. It figures in *Malory as the castle where *Uther Pendragon was wedded to Igraine, and subsequently as the home of King Mark of Cornwall.

'Tintern Abbey, Lines Composed a Few Miles above, on Revisiting the Banks of the Wye during a Tour', a poem by *Wordsworth published in the first edition of the *Lyrical Ballads* (1798).

Wordsworth had visited Tintern in 1793; the second visit recorded in this work was with his sister Dorothy, who is addressed in its closing passage, and the poem was composed as they walked towards Bristol. Written in blank verse, its style is far removed from the deliberately 'low' manner of the ballads, and Wordsworth himself referred to 'the impassioned music of the versification', which resembled the elevation of an ode. It is a central statement of Wordsworth's faith in the restorative and associative power of nature; he describes the development of his own love of nature from the 'coarser pleasures' of boyhood, through the 'aching joys' and 'dizzy raptures' of young manhood, to the more reflective, moral, philosophic pleasures of maturity, informed by 'the still, sad music of humanity'.

TIPPETT, Sir Michael (1905–98), English composer, and, with *Britten, one of the most important to reach maturity after the Second World War. He made his first substantial impression with the oratorio *A Child of Our Time* (1944). At an early stage in its creation he had interested T. S. *Eliot in writing the libretto, but Eliot finally declined, suggesting Tippett would do better to write the words himself. He followed this advice and adopted the same procedure in the four operas of his maturity, *The Midsummer Marriage* (1955), *King Priam* (1962), *The Knot Garden* (1970; influenced by R. D. *Laing), and *The Ice Break* (1977).

There are two important song settings from the earlier period, both for solo voice and piano: the cantata *Boyhood's End* (1943), to words by *Hudson, and the passionate song cycle *The Heart's Assurance* (1951), to poems by A. *Lewis and *Keyes. His choral works include settings of E. *Sitwell (the motet *The Weeping Babe*, 1944), C. *Fry (the cantata *Crown of the Year*, 1958), *Shelley and *Yeats (*Music for Words Perhaps*, 1960). But perhaps Tippett's most important work is *The Vision of St Augustine* (1965), a dense and complex setting of words from St *Augustine and the Bible, arranged by the composer himself as a mystical testament of his own beliefs.

'Tiresias', a dramatic monologue in blank verse by *Tennyson, published 1885, but composed in 1833. The prophet Tiresias, blinded and doomed to 'speak the truth that no man may believe' as a consequence of glimpsing Athene naked, urges Menoeceus, son of Creon, to sacrifice himself for Thebes.

TIRSO DE MOLINA, the pseudonym of Gabriel Téllez (1583–1648), a Spanish dramatist, famous outside Spain principally as the creator of the prototype of *Don Juan in his play *El burlador de Sevilla* (1630, *The Seville Deceiver* or *Jester*).

'Tis Pity She's a Whore, a tragedy by J. *Ford, printed 1633.

The play deals with the guilty passion of Giovanni and his sister Annabella for each other. Being with child, Annabella marries one of her suitors, Soranzo, who discovers her condition. She refuses to name her lover, though threatened with death by Soranzo. On the advice of Vasques, his faithful servant, Soranzo feigns forgiveness, Vasques undertaking to discover the truth, which he does. Soranzo invites Annabella's father and the magnificoes of the city, with Giovanni, to a sumptuous feast, intending to execute his vengeance. Although warned of Soranzo's intentions, Giovanni boldly comes. He has a last meeting with Annabella just before the feast and, to forestall Soranzo's vengeance, stabs her himself. He then enters the banqueting room with her heart on his dagger, defiantly tells what he has done, fights with and kills Soranzo, and is himself killed by Vasques.

'Tis Pity is an obsessive, passionate play, focusing on the sensationalist incest taboo, but treating it seriously and with penetrating honesty (see I. ii). It is portrayed, with rich symbolic imagery, as doomed but intensely beautiful, and this has made it Ford's most famous play, in the study and on the stage.

Titania, in Shakespeare's *A Midsummer Night's Dream*, the queen of the fairies, and wife of Oberon.

The name is given by *Ovid in the *Metamorphoses* to Latona, Pyrrha, Diana, and Circe, as descendants of the Titans.

Tit-Bits, a popular weekly magazine, founded in 1881 by G. *Newnes. It ceased publication in 1984. The original formula included jokes, quizzes, correspondence, short stories and serialized fiction, snippets of news, etc., 'from all the Most Interesting Books, Periodicals and Contributors in the World', and over the years such ingredients as comic strips, cartoons, and sports coverage were added. In its early years it attracted short stories by Arnold *Bennett, *Conrad, and other aspiring literary figures.

'Tithonus', a dramatic monologue in blank verse by *Tennyson, published in the *Cornhill* in 1860, then in 1864, but composed in 1833 and described by the poet as 'originally a pendent to the "Ulysses" in my former volume'. Tithonus is granted perpetual life but not perpetual youth by Aurora, and in a dramatic monologue he longs for death; like *In Memoriam*, the poem reflects Tennyson's anxiety about the nature of personal immortality.

TITIAN (*c.*1487–1576), Venetian painter, whose handling of oil paint is unrivalled. Titian's output was prodigious and he excelled in every kind of painting; in religious and history paintings, scenes from allegory and mythology; landscape and portraiture. He was a close friend of *Aretino, whose letters and poems describe his works. Titian's early pictures were influenced by *Giorgione and Bellini; his mature works are more dramatic and glow with rich colour. His pagan subjects, such as the *Bacchus and Ariadne* (1523, London, National Gallery), are radiantly sensuous and joyful. *The Death of St Peter Martyr* (completed 1530), once his most famous picture, was destroyed by fire in 1867. From 1532 the Emperor Charles V became a powerful patron; for him and for the Farnese family Titian created increasingly opulent portraits and, for Philip II of Spain, a series of erotic 'poesie'. His late style is characterized by its extraordinarily free and expressive handling and tragic mood. 'Titian's warmth divine' (*Pope: 'Epistle to Mr Jervas') has always been popular with the literary English; E. Panofsky suggested that Shakespeare's interpretation of Adonis as a reluctant lover (*Venus and Adonis*, ll. 811–16) may have been inspired by Titian's *Adonis Taking Leave of Venus* (Madrid, Prado). Travellers on the *Grand Tour invariably commented on the *Venus of Urbino* (1538, Uffizi, Florence) which then hung in the Tribuna with the *Medici Venus*. The Romantics—*Haydon, *Hazlitt, Sir T. *Lawrence—admired the *Bacchus and Ariadne*; this picture inspired *Keats's description of the 'swift bound of Bacchus' in *Sleep and Poetry*.

Titmarsh, (1) Michael Angelo, a pseudonym used by *Thackeray for much of his early journalism. 'Michael Angelo' is a comic reference to his broken nose and to his aspirations to be an artist. (2) Samuel, a character in his *The Great Hoggarty Diamond*.

Tito Melema, a character in G. Eliot's *Romola*.

Titurel, a German *Grail legend of the 13th cent., left incomplete by *Wolfram von Eschenbach. Titurel (the great-grandfather of Parsifal) is entrusted by heaven with the guardianship of the Grail, and he builds a chapel at Mount Selvagge (Montsalvatsch) where he reposes it and organizes a band of defenders for it.

Titus Andronicus, a tragedy by *Shakespeare. It is probably his earliest tragedy and may date from 1590; in 1594 it was published in a quarto which was reprinted twice before its appearance in the First *Folio of 1623, with an added scene (III. ii). Shakespeare's authorship has been questioned, but it is now generally agreed that he was responsible for the whole play. Various sources for *Titus Andronicus* have been put forward, including the *Hecuba* of *Euripides. *Seneca's *Thyestes* and *Troades* contributed to the plot, as did *Ovid's version of 'the tragic tale of Philomel', in *Metamorphoses* Book 13, and *Plutarch.

The first half of the play deals with the return of Titus Andronicus to Rome after his sixth victory over the Goths. He brings with him their Queen Tamora and her three sons, the eldest of whom, Alarbus, is sacrificed to avenge his own sons' deaths. Titus is offered the imperial mantle, but gives it instead to the late emperor's son Saturninus, to whose marriage with his daughter Lavinia Titus consents. Saturninus' brother Bassianus claims Lavinia as his own and, while taking her off, Titus kills his son Mutius, who had tried to block his way. Saturninus now changes his mind, renounces Lavinia, and marries Tamora, who engineers a false reconciliation between the emperor and Titus, whom she plans to destroy. She does this with the help of her lover Aaron, the Moor, who gets Tamora's sons Chiron and Demetrius to murder Bassianus, whose body is thrown into a pit, rape Lavinia, and cut off her tongue and hands. Titus' sons Quintus and Martius are then lured by Aaron to fall into the pit, where they are found and accused of Bassianus' murder. Aaron tells Titus that his sons will not be executed if he sacrifices his hand and sends it to the emperor. Titus does this, but gets it back again with the heads of his two sons.

In the second half of the play Titus discovers who raped and mutilated his daughter, and with his brother Marcus, and last remaining son Lucius, vows revenge. Lucius leaves Rome, but returns with an army of Goths, which captures Aaron and his child by Tamora. Tamora and her sons Demetrius and Chiron visit Titus disguised as Revenge, Rapine, and Murder and ask him to have Lucius' banquet at his house, where the emperor and the empress and her sons will be brought. Titus recognizes his enemies and with the help of Lavinia slits the throats of Chiron and Demetrius and uses their flesh in a pie, some of which Tamora eats at the banquet before Titus kills her. He also stabs Lavinia, but is killed by Saturninus, who is in turn killed by Lucius. He is elected emperor and sentences Aaron to be buried breast-deep in the ground and starved to death.

Critical judgement of the play has tended to be unfavourable. It was dismissed by its Restoration adapter Edward Ravenscroft, with the sentence: 'It seems rather a heap of Rubbish than a Structure.' More recent critics have related the play to *revenge tragedy, and praised it for its anticipation of Shakespeare's great tragedies, in particular *Othello and *King Lear. A drawing ascribed to Henry *Peacham depicting 'Tamora pleadinge for her sonnes going to execution' perhaps dated 1595 is at Longleat and is the first known surviving illustration of one of Shakespeare's plays.

(Andronicus in the play is accentuated thus, on the second syllable; in Latin it is Andronicus.)

TITUS LIVIUS FOROJULIENSES, an Italian in the service of Duke *Humphrey of Gloucester, who wrote, about 1440, a chronicle of the reign of Henry V.

Toad of Toad Hall, a dramatic adaptation by A. A. *Milne of K. *Grahame's The Wind in the Willows.

'To Autumn', a poem by *Keats, written Sept. 1819, published 1820. It was his last major poem, and although usually included in a discussion of the Odes (see under ODE), it was not so labelled by Keats himself.

The poem, in three stanzas, is at once a celebration of the fruitfulness of autumn (lightly personified as a figure in various autumnal landscapes) and an elegy for the passing of summer and the transience of life, and its mood has been generally taken to be one of acquiescence. The association of autumn and early death in the mind of Keats is poignantly revealed in a letter to Reynolds (21 Sept. 1819), written immediately after the composition of the poem, in which he says, 'I always somehow associate Chatterton with the autumn.'

Toby, Uncle, Captain Tobias Shandy, in Sterne's *Tristram Shandy.

TOCQUEVILLE, Alexis de (1805–59), French sociologist and historian. Until the coup d'état of 1851 he was active in the judicature and in politics, serving for a time as foreign minister. An official visit to the United States in 1851 produced the first of his two classic works, La Démocratie en Amérique (1835 and 1840), a subtle and prescient analysis of the strengths and weaknesses of a democratic society in evolution. The second, L'Ancien Régime (1856), is a profound social and political study of pre-revolutionary France, regarded as the source rather than the contradiction of the revolution that destroyed it. No 19th-cent. historian discerned with greater exactness the tensions hidden in large-scale contemporary communities. He corresponded extensively with J. S. *Mill.

Todgers, Mrs, in Dickens's *Martin Chuzzlewit, mistress of a boarding house.

TÓIBÍN, Colm (1955–   ), Irish novelist, journalist, and travel writer. His first novel The South (1990) told of an Irish Protestant living in Spain, who then returns to Dublin for a bitter-sweet reunion with her son; The Heather Blazing (1992), an account of a retired couple's strained marriage, was similarly lyrical and compassionate. The Story of the Night (1996), set in Argentina, describes a young man's gradual awakening to his homosexuality. The Master (2004) is based on the life of Henry *James. Like his fiction, Tóibín's travel writing (including Homage to Barcelona, 1990) is distinguished by its political awareness and refreshing lack of machismo.

TOKLAS, Alice B., see STEIN.

TOLAND, John (1670–1722), freethinker, born on Inishowen in Donegal (Ireland). 'Educated from the cradle in the grossest superstition', as he says in his Apology (1697), he threw off Roman Catholicism at the age of 15. After studying at universities in Scotland and Holland, he settled in Oxford where he completed Christianity not Mysterious (1696), which made him notorious. It also began the Deist controversy (see DEISM) and initiated the one great epoch of Irish philosophy.

In 1702 he travelled to Berlin, where he discussed theology with the queen of Prussia. To her he addressed his Letters of Serena (1704), whose materialistic pantheism—he coined the word 'pantheist' in 1705—he flamboyantly expressed in Pantheisticon (1720). He was a prolific controversialist. In 1698 he wrote a life of *Milton and edited his prose works. Toland's Tetradymus (1720) contains perhaps the first essay on the esoteric/exoteric distinction. *Pope ridiculed him; *Swift called him 'the great Oracle of the Anti-Christians'.

TOLKIEN, J(ohn) R(onald) R(euel) (1892–1973), Merton professor of English language and literature at Oxford, 1945–59. He published a number of philological and critical studies, such as 'Beowulf: The Monsters and the Critics' (in Proceedings of the British Academy, 1936), and became internationally known for two books based on a mythology of his own: The Hobbit (1937) and its sequel The Lord of the Rings (3 vols, 1954–5). The Silmarillion (1977), which has an earlier place in this sequence of stories, was published posthumously. A life by Humphrey Carpenter was published in 1977. See also FANTASY FICTION.

TOLLER, Ernst (1893–1939), German revolutionary poet and dramatist, associated with the short-lived Bavarian communist government of 1918. He was imprisoned for five years after the war, during which period he wrote *Expressionist plays such as Die Maschinenstürmer (1922; The Machine Wreckers).

After the rise of Hitler he moved to New York, where he committed suicide, an act commemorated in an elegy by *Auden ('In Memory of Ernst Toller'), who had met Toller in 1936 in Portugal and translated the lyrics for his satirical musical play *Nie wieder Friede!* (*No More Peace!*, 1937).

TOLSTOY, Count Lev Nikolaevich (1828–1910), Russian prose writer. He was born at Yasnaya Polyana, in central Russia, which he inherited in 1847. His first published work was *Childhood* (1852), the first part of a remarkably perceptive trilogy on his early years completed by *Boyhood* (1854) and *Youth* (1857). His Caucasian tale *The Raid* appeared in 1853. He served in the army and took part in the Crimean War: his *Sevastopol Sketches* (1855–6) are marked by an unromantic view of war indebted to *Stendhal. He then published *Family Happiness* (1859) and *The Cossacks* (1863), but much of the next decade (1863–9) was engaged in the creation of *War and Peace* (pub. 1865–9), an epic novel of the Napoleonic invasion and the lives of three aristocratic families. This was followed by *Anna Karenina*, begun in 1873 and published 1875–8, the story of a married woman's passion for a young officer and her tragic fate. From about 1880 Tolstoy's constant concern with moral questions developed into a spiritual crisis which led to radical changes in his life and to the writing of such works as *A Confession* (1879–82), *What Men Live by* (1882), *What I Believe* (1883), and *What is Art?* (1898). The major fictional works of this late period, bearing the imprint of changes in his thinking, are *The Death of Ivan Ilyich* (1886), *The Kreutzer Sonata* (pub. 1891), *Master and Man* (1895), *Resurrection* (1899–1900), and *Hadji Murad* (1904, published posthumously in 1912). Tolstoy's moral positions, involving non-resistance to evil, the renunciation of property, the abolition of governments and churches, but a belief in God and love of men, led to the banning of many of his works by the censors, and to his excommunication by the Orthodox Church in 1901. But they also brought him a unique moral authority and influence, and Yasnaya Polyana became a place of pilgrimage. He died at Astapovo railway station after having fled his home. *The Cossacks* appeared in English translation in 1878, and there were a large number of translations in the 1880s. His collected works were translated 1899–1902 and have been retranslated many times since. Among those who played a part in establishing his English reputation were M. *Arnold, G. B. *Shaw, *Galsworthy, E. M. *Forster, and D. H. *Lawrence.

TOMALIN, Claire (1933–   ), biographer, born in London, educated at Newnham College, Cambridge. Her biographies, which have been notable for their scholarly and sensitive reclamation of women's lives from historical neglect or misunderstanding, include *The Life and Death of Mary Wollstonecraft* (1974), *Katherine Mansfield: A Secret Life* (1987), *The Invisible Woman: The Story of Nelly Ternan and Charles Dickens* (1990), *Mrs Jordan's Profession* (1994, a study of the actress Mrs *Jordan, inspired by her research into the theatrical profession during her work on Ellen Ternan), and lives of Jane *Austen (1997) and Samuel *Pepys (2002).

Tom and Jerry, the two chief characters in *Egan's *Life in London*; hence used in various allusive senses, e.g. of riotous behaviour: they gave their names to the well-known cartoon characters.

Tom Brown's Schooldays, see HUGHES, T.

Tom Jones, The History of, a novel by H. *Fielding, published 1749.

Although very long, the novel is highly organized, and was thought by *Coleridge to have one of the three great plots of all literature. The kindly, prosperous Mr Allworthy, a widower, lives in Somerset with his ill-humoured unmarried sister Bridget. Late one evening Allworthy finds a baby boy lying on his bed. He is charmed with the mysterious baby, names it Tom, and adopts it, adding the surname Jones on the assumption that the mother is Jenny Jones, a maidservant to the wife of the schoolmaster Partridge, who is eventually accused of being the father and dismissed his post. Both Jenny and Partridge vanish from the neighbourhood. Meanwhile Bridget marries the obnoxious Captain Blifil and they have a son, Master Blifil, who is brought up with Tom. They are taught by the brutish chaplain Thwackum, and the philosopher Square, and have as family neighbours the bluff fox-hunting Squire Western, his sister, and his daughter Sophia, as well as Allworthy's gamekeeper Black George Seagrim and his wife and daughters.

The story moves on to the point when Tom is 19, and begins to find that his childhood affection for the beautiful and sweet-natured Sophia (whose portrait Fielding founded upon his own wife) has grown into adult love. However, Sophia is destined by her father for Master Blifil, and Tom allows himself to be distracted by the charms of Molly Seagrim. By clever misrepresentation the scheming young Blifil converts Allworthy's affection for Tom into anger, and with the help of Thwackum and Square he succeeds in having the harum-scarum Tom expelled from the house. Filled with despair that he has alienated his beloved foster-father and is leaving all he loves, Tom sets off for Bristol intending to go to sea. Meanwhile Sophia, disgusted by Blifil's courtship, runs away with her maid Honour, hoping to find her kinswoman Lady Bellaston in London. Amid numerous adventures on the road, during which he falls in with redcoats and is deflected from his plan of going to sea, Tom encounters Partridge, once supposed to be his father, who is now travelling the country as a barber-surgeon. Unknown to Tom, he and Sophia both find themselves in an inn at Upton, but because of Partridge's malicious stupidity Sophia believes that Tom (now in bed with Mrs Waters, of whom we are to hear more) no longer loves her, and flees on towards London. Tom follows, and in London is ensnared by the rich and amorous Lady Bellaston. She and her friend Lord Fellamar, who is in pursuit of Sophia, contrive together to keep Tom away from his love, but the abrupt eruption of Squire Western saves Sophia from Fellamar's snare. Partridge now reveals that Mrs Waters is none other than Jenny Jones, supposed to be Tom's mother, and for a brief period Tom believes he has committed incest. But Jenny reveals that Tom's mother was really Bridget Allworthy (later Blifil), who has confessed all to her brother on her deathbed, and that his father was a young man long since dead. Lady Bellaston and Lord Fellamar attempt to have Tom press-ganged, but instead he is arrested and imprisoned after a fight in which it first appears he has killed his assailant. Sophia cannot forgive his entanglement with Lady Bellaston and Tom's fortunes are at their lowest ebb. Blifil arranges that the gang shall give evidence against Tom, but, with the help of a long letter from Square to Allworthy, Blifil's envious machinations, dating from their earliest boyhood, are finally revealed, and Tom is reinstated in his repentant uncle's affection. He meets Sophia again at last, learns that she loves him, and receives the hearty blessing of her father. In the generosity of his heart, Tom forgives all who have wronged him, even including the detestable Blifil.

In chapter 1, 'Bill of Fare', Fielding informs the reader that 'The provision . . . we have here made is no other than Human Nature' and in his Dedication to *Lyttelton declares, 'that to recommend goodness and innocence hath been my sincere endeavour in this history'. The book was enthusiastically received by the general public of the day, although Fielding's robust distinctions between right and wrong (which, for instance, permit his high-spirited hero various sexual escapades before his final blissful marriage) were a severe irritant to many, including Dr *Johnson. The book is generally regarded as Fielding's greatest, and as one of the first and most influential of English novels.

TOMKINS, Thomas (1572–1656), Welsh composer and organist, who studied under *Byrd. He is chiefly remembered as a composer of *madrigals, but also wrote many sacred works, published posthumously as *Musica Deo Sacra* (1668).

TOMKIS, Thomas (?1580–?1634), fellow of Trinity College, Cambridge, and author of two university comedies, *Lingua: Or The Combat of the Tongue and the Five Senses for Superiority* (1607) and *Albumazar* (1615). The latter was acted before James I at Cambridge. Albumazar (historically an Arabian astronomer, 805–85) is a rascally wizard who transforms the rustic Trincalo into the person of his master, with absurd consequences. It was revived (1668) with a prologue by *Dryden, wrongly charging *Jonson with adopting it as a model for *The Alchemist*. It was again revived by *Garrick.

TOMLINSON, (Alfred) Charles (1927–   ), poet and artist, born in Stoke-on-Trent and educated locally and at Queens' College, Cambridge, where he was taught by D. *Davie. His aspirations as a painter are reflected in the visual qualities of his verse, which also shows the influence of W. *Stevens, W. C. *Williams, and M. *Moore. His first volume, *Relations and Contraries* (1951), was followed by several others including *Seeing is Believing* (USA 1958; London 1960), *The Way of the World* (1969), *Written on Water* (1972), *The Way in and Other Poems* (1974), and *The Flood* (1981). A volume of *Collected Poems* was published in 1985. Subsequent collections include *The Return* (1987), *The Door in the Wall* (1992), and *Jubilation* (1995). He edited *The Oxford Book of Verse in Translation* in 1980.

TOMLINSON, H(enry) M(ajor) (1873–1958), novelist and journalist, born in Poplar, the son of a foreman at the West India Dock; his early love of ships and the sea is reflected in his life and works, e.g. *The Sea and the Jungle* (1912, an account of a voyage to Brazil and up the Amazon), *London River* (1921, essays and reflections), and his first novel, *Gallions Reach* (1927). *All Our Yesterdays* (1930) is an anti-war novel about the First World War. As a journalist he contributed to the radical *Morning Leader* and the *English Review*, and was literary editor of the *Nation* from 1917 to 1923.

Tom o' Bedlam, a wandering beggar. After the dissolution of the religious houses, where the poor used to be relieved, there was for long no settled provision for them. In consequence they wandered over the country, many assuming disguises calculated to obtain them charity. Among other disguises some affected madness, and were called Bedlam beggars (so in *Gammer Gurtons Nedle* 'Diccon the Bedlam'). Edgar, in *King Lear*, II. iii, adopts this disguise:

> Of Bedlam beggars, who, with roaring voices,
> Strike in their numb'd and mortified bare arms
> Pins, wooden pricks, nails, sprigs of rosemary.

In *Dekker's *Belman of London* (1608) 'Tom of Bedlam's band of mad caps' are enumerated among the species of beggars. Some of these Bedlam beggars sang mad songs, examples of which are given in Percy's *Reliques. They were also called 'Abraham-men', from the name, it is said (Brewer), of one of the wards in Bedlam.

Tom Sawyer, The Adventures of, a novel by Mark *Twain, published 1876.

Tom, a lively and adventurous lad, lives with his priggish brother Sid and his good-hearted Aunt Polly in the quiet town of St Petersburg, Missouri. His companion is the irrepressible Huckleberry Finn, and together they embark on many exploits, during one of which they happen to observe Injun Joe stab the town doctor to death and attempt to incriminate the drunken Muff Potter; Tom is later able to absolve Potter at his trial. Tom and his sweetheart Becky Thatcher wander away from a school picnic and are lost for three days in a cave, where Tom spies Injun Joe; after the children are rescued Injun Joe is found dead and his treasure is divided between Tom and Huck. Huck's subsequent escapades become the subject of the classic sequel *The Adventures of *Huckleberry Finn.*

Tom Thumb, *a Tragedy*, a farce by H. *Fielding, performed and published 1730, and published in a different version 1731 under the title of *The Tragedy of Tragedies, or, The Life and Death of Tom Thumb the Great.*

The most successful of Fielding's many plays, this is an exuberant farce in the mock-heroic manner, ridiculing the 'Bombastic Greatness' of the fashionable grandiose tragedies of authors such as N. *Lee and J. *Thomson, and similar in form to Buckingham's *The Rehearsal.* It was published with a heavy apparatus of absurd scholarly notes, and a frontispiece by *Hogarth. *Swift declared that he had laughed only twice in his life, once at a Merry-Andrew and once at a performance of *Tom Thumb.*

TONSON, Jacob (1656–1737), publisher and bookseller, the son of a barber-surgeon; he established himself in 1678 with his brother Richard (d. 1689) and eventually took his nephew Jacob into the business, in whose favour he resigned in 1720; the firm was continued by a great-nephew of the same name. He published the foremost poets and playwrights of the age; his long association with *Dryden began in 1679, with the publication of his version of *Troilus and Cressida*, and his other writers included A. *Behn, *Otway, *Cowley, *Rowe, *Addison, and *Pope; he also acquired the profitable copyright of *Paradise Lost.* He was well known for his *Miscellanies*, in six parts, of which the earliest were edited and largely written by Dryden; they appeared between 1684 and 1709, and contained translations from *Horace, *Ovid, *Lucretius, *Virgil, etc., as well as original work by *Pope, A. *Philips, *Swift, and others. A conspicuous figure in literary society, he was secretary of the *Kit-Cat Club (which occasionally met at his home in Barnes) and the butt of satire from Dryden (who mocked his 'two left legs, and Judas-coloured hair') and Pope, who took up the theme of his ungainly legs in the *Dunciad.*

Tony Lumpkin, a character in Goldsmith's *She Stoops to Conquer.*

Toodle, Polly and Robin ('Rob the Grinder'), her son, characters in Dickens's *Dombey and Son.* Polly was Paul Dombey's foster-mother.

TOOKE, John Horne (1736–1812), radical politician, and the son of a poulterer named Horne; he added the name of his friend William Tooke of Purley to his own in 1782. He vigorously supported *Wilkes in connection with the Middlesex election, but later quarrelled with him. He was more than once in conflict with the authorities, and was tried for high treason and acquitted in 1794. His varied acquaintance included *Boswell, *Bentham, *Godwin, *Paine, and *Coleridge.

His principal work, "Επεα πτερόεντα, *or The Diversions of Purley* (1786–1805, two volumes of a planned three) established his reputation as a philologist and was extremely popular; it was much admired by James *Mill and the utilitarians, but its philosophical (rather than historical or philological) approach to language and grammar and its wildly speculative etymologies delayed for decades, it has been alleged, the introduction of the new and sounder philology from the Continent. See H. Aarsleff, *The Study of Language in England, 1780–1860* (1967).

Too True to Be Good (1931), a three-act political extravaganza by Bernard *Shaw which opens in one of the richest cities in England, in a patient's bedroom inhabited by a 'poor innocent microbe' apparently made of luminous jelly, and then moves to a sea beach in a mountainous country patrolled by the omnipresent Private Meek, Shaw's imaginative portrait of T. E. *Lawrence. The surreal plot, which progresses by means of a series of fantastical illusions and proliferating identities, contains echoes from *The Pilgrim's Progress* and *The Tempest*, and reaches its climax in a long peroration on the place of human beings in the evolution of the world.

Toots, Mr, a character in Dickens's *Dombey and Son.*

Top Girls, a play by Caryl *Churchill, first performed at the *Royal Court Theatre in 1982. The first act is set in a London restaurant as Marlene celebrates her promotion as managing director of the 'Top Girls' employment agency: her guests are five historical and quasi-historical characters, Isabella *Bird, the 13th-cent. Japanese courtesan Lady Nijo, Dull Gret (who is drawn from an image in a *Bruegel painting), Pope Joan, and *Patient Griselda. The second and third acts, which move between the agency office and the poor East Anglian home of Marlene's sister, reveal the hard choices Marlene has made to achieve her success, which include the loss of her illegitimate and slow-witted daughter Angie to her childless sister Joyce. Each member of the all-female cast (apart from Marlene) plays several parts. The play explores the changing social, sexual, and above all financial expectations of British women in the 1980s, and contrasts them both with historical attitudes and with contemporary American aspirations.

TOPLADY, Augustus Montague (1740–78), from 1768 vicar of Broad Hembury, remembered for his hymns, especially 'Rock of Ages', published in the *Gospel Magazine* in 1775. At first influenced by *Wesley, he later became his bitter opponent, and an extreme Calvinist.

topographical poetry, described by Dr *Johnson as 'local poetry, of which the fundamental object is some particular landscape . . . with the addition of . . . historical retrospection or incidental meditation'. *Cooper's Hill* (1642) by *Denham is an early example of a genre that flourished principally in the 18th cent.: see DYER; GARTH; JAGO; THOMSON, J. (1700–48), for example. Many topographical poems are also 'prospect poems', i.e. written from a high point, surveying a large view, and many were written in praise of particular parks, estates, and gardens, evidently in the hope of patronage. The genre had a renewed vogue in the late 20th cent., when the emphasis has been less on the country estate, more on the vanishing rural scene; distinguished examples include *Remains of Elmet* (1979) and the less precisely located *River* (1983), both by Ted *Hughes.

Topsy, the lively little slave girl in H. B. *Stowe's *Uncle Tom's Cabin*, who asserted that she had neither father nor mother, and being asked who made her, replied, 'I 'spect I grow'd'. One of Mrs Stowe's most original creations, she forms a contrast to the virtuous, ethereal *Little Eva, and is carried off to Vermont after Eva's death by Eva's aunt, the orderly Miss Ophelia.

TORQUEMADA, Tomás de (1420–98), a Spanish Dominican monk, appointed in 1483 the first inquisitor-general by Ferdinand and Isabella. He was famous for the untiring energy with which the work of the Inquisition in Spain was carried on under his direction. Hence his name became a synonym for a cruel persecutor. The *Instrucciones Antiguas*, a code of instructions for the application of torture, begun in 1481, which Torquemada himself expanded and developed over the next 15 years, set out in great detail the procedures for the torture, mutilation, and execution of heretics. In the course of his 18-year term of office some 2,000 heretics were burnt alive, and many more were mutilated.

Torre, Sir, in *Malory, the illegitimate son of a cowherd's wife and King *Pellinore; his knighting before Gawain by Arthur causes further rancour amongst the sons of King Lot whose father had been slain by Torre's father Pellinore, developing the long feud between their two houses.

To the Lighthouse, a novel by V. *Woolf published 1927, which draws powerfully on the author's recollections of family holidays at St Ives, Cornwall, although the setting is ostensibly the Hebrides; her parents, as she acknowledged, provided the inspiration for the maternal, managing, gracious, much-admired Mrs Ramsay, and the self-centred, self-pitying, poetry-reciting, absurd, and tragic figure of the philosopher, Mr Ramsay, who become the focus of one of her most profound explorations of the conflict between the male and female principles.

The novel is in three sections, of which the first and longest, 'The Window', describes a summer day, with the Ramsays on holiday with their eight children and assorted guests, who include the plump and lethargic elderly poet Augustus Carmichael; the painter Lily Briscoe (who represents in part the struggle and cost of female creativity); and the graceless lower-middle-class academic Charles Tansley. Family tension centres on the desire of the youngest child, James, to visit the lighthouse, and his father's apparent desire to thwart him: the frictions of the day are momentarily resolved around the dinner table, and a triumphant *bœuf en daube*, as Mrs Ramsay reflects that 'something . . . is immune from change, and shines out . . . in the face of the flowing, the fleeting, the spectral, like a ruby'. The second section, 'Time Passes', records with laconic brevity the death of Mrs Ramsay and of her son Andrew, killed in the war, and dwells with a desolate lyricism on the abandoning of the family home, and its gradual post-war reawakening; it ends with the arrival of Lily Briscoe and Mr Carmichael. The last section, 'The Lighthouse', describes the exhausting but finally successful efforts of Lily, through her painting, to recapture the revelation of shape-in-chaos which she owes to the vanished Mrs Ramsay, and the parallel efforts of Mr Ramsay, Camilla, and James to reach the lighthouse, which they also accomplish, despite the undercurrents of rivalry, loss, and rebellion that torment them. The novel represents a heroic exploration and re-creation of the bereavements and (real or imagined) tyrannies of the past; it also displays Woolf's technique of narrating through *stream of consciousness and imagery at its most assured, rich, and suggestive.

TOTTEL, Richard (*c*.1530–93), a publisher who carried on business at 'The Hand and Star' within Temple Bar from 1553 to 1594, is chiefly known as the compiler (with *Grimald) of *Songes and Sonettes*, known as *Tottel's Miscellany* (1557), comprising the chief works of *Wyatt and *Surrey. He also published, besides lawbooks, Sir T. *More's *Dialoge of Comfort* (1553) and Surrey's *Aeneid* (1557).

Slender, in Shakespeare's *The Merry Wives of Windsor*, had 'rather than forty shillings' he had Tottel's 'book of Songs and Sonnets' with him when courting Anne Page; and the grave-digger in *Hamlet* mumbles Lord *Vaux's song from the same collection.

Touchett, Mr, Mrs, and Ralph, characters in H. James's *The Portrait of a Lady*.

Touchstone, the jester to the exiled Duke Senior's court in Shakespeare's *As You Like It*.

TOURNEUR, Cyril (?1575–1626), dramatist. Practically nothing is known of his life. He appears to have worked for a time in the Netherlands, and died at Kinsale in Ireland after accompanying Sir Edward Cecil to Cadiz in 1625 on an unsuccessful raid of Spanish treasure ships. His small known output includes an allegorical poem, *The Transformed Metamorphosis* (1600), a lost play, *The Nobleman* (1612), *The Atheist's Tragedy* (1611), an elegy on the death of Prince Henry (1613), and several minor and disputed works. *The Revenger's Tragedy*, printed anonymously in 1607, was first ascribed to him in 1656 by Edward Archer in a play list, and was generally accepted as his until the end of the 19th cent., when *Middleton was proposed as the author. Since then there has been prolonged debate over attribution, with Middleton gradually emerging as the most likely candidate, a view confirmed by recent statistical analysis, though some critics and editors still favour Tourneur. G. Parfitt, after a brief summary of the arguments in his edition *The Plays of Cyril Tourneur* (1978), concludes that 'unless new evidence emerges . . . the play has to be regarded as anonymous.' The *Complete Works* were edited by Allardyce Nicoll (1930). (See also REVENGE TRAGEDY.)

TOUSSAINT L'OUVERTURE, François (1743–1803), to whom *Wordsworth addressed a sonnet, the leader of a slave revolt which began in 1791 in the French colony of Saint-Domingue: it has been acclaimed as the only successful slave uprising in history. For some years Toussaint administered the colony (which was eventually to achieve independence as Haiti) with great skill, but he was overcome by a military expedition sent out by Napoleon, and was transported to France, where he died in prison in the Jura mountains. He remained a hero to radical writers: H. *Martineau published a life in 1840, and C. L. R. *James described the Haitian revolution in *The Black Jacobins: Toussaint Louverture and the San Domingo Revolution* (1938).

Towneley plays, see under MYSTERY PLAYS.

TOWNLEY, Revd James (1714–78), educated at Merchant Taylors' School and St John's College, Oxford, and headmaster of Merchant Taylors' from 1760. He was a friend of *Garrick, and author of the successful farce *High Life below Stairs* (1759).

Townly, Lord, in Vanbrugh and Cibber's *The Provok'd Husband*, the title character.

Town Mouse and Country Mouse, a fable told by *Horace (Sat. 2. 6) and by *La Fontaine (though the latter substitutes rats for mice). The city mouse, contemptuous of the country mouse's cave and humble fare, invites it to a sumptuous supper in its palace. But the feast is disturbed by an alarm, and the mice scurry away. The country mouse concludes that it prefers its safe wood and cave and its homely fare.

M. *Prior was part-author of *The Hind and the Panther Transvers'd to the Story of the Country Mouse and the City Mouse*.

TOWNSHEND, Aurelian (?1583–?1643). He travelled in France and Italy, then appears in 1632 as a writer of court *masques. He seems to have collaborated with I. *Jones in *Albion's Triumph* and to have contributed verses for the queen's masque of *Tempe Restored*. He enjoyed favour at the court of Charles I, as his lyric 'On His Hearing Her Majesty Sing' records. His poems were not collected, but scattered through various miscellanies, until E. K. *Chambers's edition, *Poems and Masks* (1912).

TOWNSHEND, Charles, second Viscount Townshend (1674–1738), a distinguished statesman of the reign of George I. He carried on at Rainham agricultural experiments which earned him his nickname of 'Turnip' Townshend. *Pope (*Imitations of Horace*, Ep. 2. 2. 273) refers to Townshend's turnips, and in a footnote states that 'that kind of rural improvement which arises from turnips' was 'the favourite subject of Townshend's conversation'.

Tow-wouse, Mr and Mrs, characters in Fielding's *Joseph Andrews*.

Toxophilus, see ASCHAM.

TOYNBEE, Arnold Joseph (1889–1975), historian, educated at Winchester and Balliol College, Oxford. He was professor of Byzantine and modern Greek language, literature, and history at King's College, London, 1919–24, the director of studies at the Royal Institute of International Affairs, and research professor of international history until he retired in 1955. His great work *A Study of History*, published in ten volumes between 1934 and 1954, is a survey of the chief civilizations of the world, and an enquiry into cycles of creativity and decay. His view that the fragmentation and waning of Western civilization could already be detected, and that hope lay in a new universal religion which would recapture 'spiritual initiative', aroused much controversy. His other works include *Civilization on Trial* (1948) and *The World and the West* (1953). *Comparing Notes: A Dialogue across a Generation* (1963) was written with his son, novelist, critic, and journalist Philip Theodore Toynbee (1916–81). Polly Toynbee, daughter of Philip, is a distinguished journalist and writer on social policy.

T.P.'s Weekly, see O'CONNOR, T. P.

Tractarian movement, Tracts for the Times, see OXFORD MOVEMENT.

Traddles, a character in Dickens's *David Copperfield*.

TRADESCANT, John (d. 1638), traveller, naturalist, and gardener, probably author of *A Voiag of Ambasad* (1618), a manuscript account of a voyage under Sir Dudley Digges to Archangel, containing the earliest known account of Russian plants. From the expedition (1620) against the Algerian pirates he brought back the 'Algier apricot'. He established a physic (i.e. medicinal) garden at Lambeth. His son John Tradescant (1608–62) was likewise a traveller and gardener. He published *Musaeum Tradescantianum* in 1656, and gave his collection to *Ashmole, who presented it to the University of Oxford. Both Tradescants held the appointment of gardener to Charles I. See Mea Allan, *The Tradescants* (1964).

tragedy, a word of uncertain derivation, applied, broadly, to dramatic (or, by extension, other) works in which events move to a fatal or disastrous conclusion. Aristotle's *Poetics* was the first attempt to define the characteristics of tragedy and its effect upon the spectator, and it profoundly influenced the neo-classic concept of tragedy in France and England. Shakespeare and other English dramatists of the Elizabethan period evolved new tragic conventions (see REVENGE TRAGEDY), partly derived from *Seneca, and the genre continued to flourish in the *Jacobean period (see WEBSTER, J.; MIDDLETON, T.; BEAUMONT, F.; FLETCHER, J.). A period of predominantly dull and frigid *neo-classicism followed, and tragedy as a form, with odd exceptions, did not seriously revive until the 20th cent., when the works of *Ibsen, *Strindberg, *O'Neill, A. *Miller, T. *Williams, and S. *Beckett brought it a new seriousness, relevance, and urgency.

TRAHERNE, Thomas (1637–74), son of a shoemaker in Hereford. It seems possible that both his parents died while he and his brother Philip were infants, and the boys were brought up by a wealthy innkeeper, Philip Traherne, twice mayor of Hereford. They evidently had a good education, but no record exists of their attending Hereford Cathedral School. Thomas went up to Brasenose College, Oxford, as a commoner in Mar. 1653 and took his BA in Oct. 1656. In 1657 the parliamentary commissioners appointed him rector of Credenhill, Herefordshire, but he seems not to have resided there until 1661. He was ordained in 1660, and the following year took his Oxford MA. At Credenhill he joined the religious circle centring on Susanna Hopton at Kington, for whom he was to write the *Centuries*. During this period he evidently travelled to Oxford to work on *Roman Forgeries* in the Bodleian. Probably in recognition of this work he gained his BD in 1669, and also his appointment the same year as chaplain to Sir Orlando Bridgeman, lord keeper of the great seal, which necessitated his moving to London. He was buried at Teddington.

Traherne led a 'single and devout life', according to A. *Wood. He left five houses in Hereford in trust for the poor people of All Saints parish. He told *Aubrey that he had visions, seeing, on one occasion, the phantom of an apprentice who was asleep in the same house, and on another a basket of fruit sailing in the air over his bed. Traherne's *Centuries* and many of his poems were discovered in a notebook (now in the Bodleian) which was picked up for a few pence on a London bookstall in the winter of 1896–7 by W. T. Brooke. Bertram Dobell identified Traherne as the author, and edited the *Poetical Works* (1903) and the *Centuries of Meditations* (1908). More poems, prepared for publication by Traherne's brother Philip as 'Poems of Felicity', were discovered in a British Museum manuscript and published by H. I. Bell in 1910. A further manuscript of *Select Meditations* has since come to light, and is in the collection of the late J. M. Osborn. In his lifetime Traherne published *Roman Forgeries* (1673), which exposes the falsifying of ecclesiastical documents by the Church of Rome, concentrating in the mid-9th-cent. collection known

as the 'False Decretals' which had, in fact, already been decisively discredited by several 16th-cent. scholars. His *Christian Ethicks* (1675) was prepared for the press before he died. But his major achievement comprises the *Centuries*, the poems, and the Thanksgivings, written in exuberant, unconventional verse, and at times foreshadowing *Whitman, which appeared in 1699. He expresses a rapturous joy in creation unmatched by any other 17th-cent. writer, and his memories, in the *Centuries*, of his own early intuitions are the first convincing depiction of childhood experience in English literature. He is also among the first English writers to respond imaginatively to new ideas about infinite space, and at times virtually equates infinite space with God. The boundless potential of man's mind and spirit is his recurrent theme, as is the need for adult man to regain the wonder and simplicity of the child. In both, his thought is influenced by *Neoplatonism, especially by the Hermetic books.

Centuries, Poems and Thanksgivings, ed. H. M. Margoliouth (2 vols, 1958); *Christian Ethicks*, ed. C. L. Marks and G. R. Guffey (1968); G. Wade, *Thomas Traherne* (1944); K. W. Salter, *Thomas Traherne, Mystic and Poet* (1964).

Traitor, The, a tragedy by J. *Shirley, acted 1631, printed 1635.

This play was highly successful both before and after the Civil War; *Pepys saw it several times and praised it highly. It is based on the assassination of the Florentine Duke Alessandro de' Medici by his kinsman Lorenzo. Unlike the hero of the best-known play on this subject, de *Musset's *Lorenzaccio*, Shirley's Lorenzo is a scheming villain who talks of republicanism and liberty only to gain the support of others. The plot interweaves a number of devices already used by earlier dramatists. Lorenzo encourages the duke's lust for Amidea, sister of Sciarrha, while simultaneously urging Sciarrha to take revenge on the duke. The duke, though unmoved by a moral masque presented him by Sciarrha, is nearly converted by Amidea's courageous virtue. Later, however, Lorenzo persuades him to blackmail her into yielding to save her brother's life. Sciarrha, to test Amidea's virtue, threatens to kill her unless she accepts this proposal; she, to save him from the guilt of murder, pretends to accept, whereupon he stabs her for dishonouring him. Her final act of virtue is to pretend that her death was suicide. When the duke comes to her bed, he finds only a corpse. Lorenzo then seizes the opportunity to kill him, and he and Sciarrha kill each other in the ensuing scuffle.

Tranio, *Lucentio's servant in Shakespeare's *The Taming of the Shrew.

Transatlantic Review, a literary periodical edited from Paris by F. M. *Ford, from Jan. 1924 to Jan. 1925, in which he published *Joyce, E. E. *Cummings, and others. B. *Bunting worked for a while as sub-editor. The title was revived in 1959 by J. McCrindle: the new

Transatlantic Review (of which B. S. *Johnson was for a time poetry editor) published fiction, poetry, interviews, etc., and contributors have included W. *Trevor, I. *Murdoch, J. G. *Ballard, A. *Burgess, D. M. *Thomas, and J. *Arden. It ceased publication in 1977.

Transcendental Club, a group of American intellectuals who met informally for philosophical discussion at *Emerson's house and elsewhere during some years from 1836, the embodiment of a movement of thought, philosophical, religious, social, and economic, produced in New England between 1830 and 1850 by the spirit of revolutionary Europe, German philosophy, and *Wordsworth, *Coleridge, and *Carlyle. The philosophical views of this Transcendentalism may be gathered from Emerson's short treatise *Nature* (1836). Its literary organ was the *Dial.

Its social and economic aspects took form in the Brook Farm Institute (1841–7) of George Ripley, a self-supporting group of men and women, who shared in manual labour and intellectual pursuits.

transition: *an international quarterly for creative experiment*, a periodical founded in 1927 in Paris by Eugène and Maria Jolas, and edited for some ten years by Eugène Jolas and Elliot Paul. It proclaimed 'the revolution of the word', and published new and experimental work by *Joyce, G. *Stein, Dylan *Thomas, *Durrell, *Beckett, etc.; its distinguished art coverage included work by Duchamp, Miró, and Man Ray.

translation, theory and art of. Literary translation is almost as ancient as literature itself, but Roman renderings of Greek originals gave the art its foundations and first recorded theorists in the West. *Cicero proclaimed himself primarily a translator of ideas and styles; his objections to literalism were endorsed and extended by *Horace, *Quintilian, and St *Jerome, and echoed in the 20th cent. by theorists such as W. *Benjamin. Issues such as the impossibility of exact fidelity were raised especially sharply by the translation of the *Bible, first into Latin, then into the European vernaculars.

After some translation of Christian texts in the Old English period, the first major English literary practitioner is *Chaucer. But his versions of individual French and Latin works are of less aesthetic interest than his transformations of e.g. *Boccaccio, *Virgil and *Ovid, involving translation in a broader sense. Medieval English translations were predominantly of devotional works, fashionable French literature, and occasionally Latin classics. To the Renaissance period of extensive experiment, dedicated primarily to the enhancement of the vernacular languages and literatures, belong the names of *Chapman, *Marlowe, *Golding, and *Jonson. It saw the arrival of Greek literature in English; the rise of the specialist translator; the 'conquest' (as Philemon *Holland revealingly says) of almost the whole Latin canon; and greatly increased attention to European languages such as Italian and Spanish. The 'colonizing' English attitude was exaggerated and theorized by the 17th-cent. French 'Belles Infidèles' translators, who aimed to improve the classics by adapting them to current sensibilities.

Translation was central to the *Augustan programme to classicize English literary culture. As translators *Dryden and *Pope are best known for their complete Virgil (1697) and *Homer (1715–26) respectively. These are dialogues with, not copies of, the originals, and represent a full creative commitment. Questions about the boundaries between translation and imitation, also an increasingly popular form, are raised by Dryden, who in 1689 proposes a tripartite classification of translations as 'metaphrase' (literal), 'paraphrase' ('with latitude'), or 'imitation'. Such questions are differently answered at the end of this period in Alexander Tytler's *Essay on the Principles of Translation* (1791), a systematic discussion favouring close translation.

An expanding theoretical literature in the 19th cent. owes much to the German Romantics, including *Schlegel, who translated Shakespeare. They focus debate on the necessity of 'foreignizing', of retaining features specific to the foreign text even and especially when not assimilable to the norms of the target language and literature. In Britain such issues came to a head over M. *Arnold's *On Translating Homer* (1861). For Arnold, Homer was most faithfully represented by modern English hexameters and in contemporary language, but for his 'foreignizing' opponents only antiquated poetic forms and obsolete words gave the true flavour. A rash of Homeric translations on one principle or the other ensued.

Arnold's view of translation was strongly echoed in the 20th cent. by *Pound, the most influential and eclectic of modern translators. Like Arnold, Pound includes scholarship as a major component in translation. But for much of the 20th cent. translation became too exclusively the province of the scholar—purely functional work, often by academics, proliferated. However, translation is re-establishing itself as a normal part of the creative output of English poets and dramatists: T. *Hughes, S. *Heaney. D. *Mahon, T. *Harrison, and M. *Longley are examples. See Douglas Robinson (ed.), *Western Translation Theory from Herodotus to Nietzsche* (1997); George *Steiner, *After Babel* (1975, 1992); Rita Copeland, *Rhetoric, Hermeneutics, and Translation in the Middle Ages* (1991); T. R. Steiner, *English Translation Theory: 1650–1800* (1975); Lawrence Venuti, *The Translator's Invisibility* (1995); Douglas Robinson, *The Translator's Turn* (1991); William Radice and Barbara Reynolds (eds.), *The Translator's Art* (1987).

Transome, Harold, a character in G. Eliot's *Felix Holt.

TRAPIDO, Barbara (1941–), South African-born novelist, resident in England since 1963. Her first novel *Brother of the More Famous Jack* (1982) tells the story of Katherine, a timid student, and her sentimental education at the hands of the bohemian Goldman family. This and its successors *Noah's Ark* (1984) and *Temples of Delight* (1990) established her reputation as a writer of tart, witty, but endlessly surprising novels where the traditional distinction between comedy and tragedy is often transgressed. In *Juggling* (1994), where the story of identical twins purposely recalls *The Comedy of Errors*, Trapido began to push the boundaries of the realistic novel even further in her zeal for comic coincidence, and this trend continued with *The Travelling Hornplayer* (1998), which revisits the character of a sadder and wiser Katherine, and reunites the protagonists in a final scene of joyous implausibility. The semi-autobiographical *Frankie and Stankie* (2003) vividly evokes her South African childhood.

TRAPNEL, Anna (fl. 1642–60). Daughter of a Poplar shipwright, this vociferous rhyming prophetess of the Fifth Monarchist movement was associated with John Simpson's revolutionary church at All Hallows the Great in London. Her spiritual and political extemporizations flowed forth in trances and were transcribed in shorthand. She achieved notoriety by a 12-day ecstasy at Whitehall attacking *Cromwell's Protectorate, after which she travelled to Cornwall, was arrested on suspicion of sedition, and committed to Bridewell, a journey she vividly recorded in *Anna Trapnel's Report and Plea*. Trapnel published six inflammatory pamphlets 1654–8.

Traveller, The, or *A Prospect of Society*, a poem by *Goldsmith, published 1764, and the first production under his own name. It is dedicated and addressed to his brother, a country clergyman.

The poet as traveller, from a vantage point in the Alps, surveys and compares the social, political, and economic conditions of the various countries spread before his eyes and his imagination, and endeavours to illustrate that (in the words of his preface) 'there may be equal happiness in states, that are differently governed from our own'. The vividly drawn landscapes of Italy, the Loire valley, and the 'slow canals' of Holland are clearly based on Goldsmith's own continental tour in 1755. The poem ends with a lament for rural decay in the face of growing commerce that foreshadows the theme of *The Deserted Village*. Dr *Johnson, who greatly admired the poem, contributed nine lines to it, ll. 420, 429–34, 437–8.

Travels in Arabia Deserta, see DOUGHTY.

Travels in France, a record of travel in that country during the years 1787–90, by A. *Young, published 1792. The first journey takes him through the southwest (Berri, Poitou, Languedoc), the second through Brittany and Anjou, the third through Alsace-Lorraine, the Jura, Burgundy, and Provence. Visiting France shortly before and during the revolution, Young draws attention to the defective social and economic conditions of the *ancien régime*. The work was translated into various languages and has always been highly valued in France. It contains the famous phrase 'The magic of property turns sand into gold.' It was edited by M. Betham-Edwards (1892) and C. Maxwell (1929).

Travels through France and Italy, a work by *Smollett, published 1766.

The book covers the period of Smollett's main sojourn abroad, between mid-1763 and mid-1765. It is sharply observant, prejudiced and idiosyncratic, often highly entertaining, and almost universally derogatory about all levels of French and Italian society. Smollett's attitude induced *Sterne to describe him in *A Sentimental Journey* as 'the learned Smelfungus'. In search of better health, Smollett travelled with his wife and a party of three others, starting at Boulogne, proceeding to Paris, Lyons, Montpellier, and eventually to Nice. In that distance he asserts he met only one pleasant innkeeper. But although manners, arts, and religion are generally deprecated (sometimes with humour but more often with disgust), Smollett's enjoyment of food, drink, and the company of other travelling or expatriate Britons is conveyed with relish. His party was based in Nice, where the scenery, walking, bathing, riding, and the bounty of the countryside delighted him, and where his health intermittently improved. During this time he travelled for two months in Italy, visiting Pisa, Florence, and Rome, in all of which the art and architecture greatly impressed him. After many wearisome episodes on road and sea, they returned to Nice, and then with relief to England. The *Travels* were reviewed kindly, sold well, quickly reprinted, and translated into German; but not into French or Italian.

Travels with a Donkey, see STEVENSON, R. L.

travel writing. Early examples of travel writing widely popular in Britain included the fabulous 14th-cent. travel book ascribed to Sir John *Mandeville, and the supposedly factual accounts of Marco *Polo's journey to China. The great Elizabethan age of navigation, and the discovery of the Americas and the West Indies, produced the reports of *Hakluyt, Sir W.*Ralegh, Sir F. *Drake and others, which were widely read and continued to inspire novelists and poets, particularly during the Romantic period. In the 17th cent. Thomas *Coryate's accounts of his travels through Europe and on to India established his reputation as one of the first great British eccentrics of the genre. Travellers at home, whose works have been of lasting historical and social value, include Celia *Fiennes, *Defoe, and *Cobbett. The 18th cent. produced the literature and art of the *Grand Tour. The Victorian traveller ventured far afield, sometimes, like David *Livingstone, in the guise of a missionary-explorer. Several women writers and travellers of this period made lasting names for themselves; examples include Mary *Kingsley, with accounts of West Africa, and Isabella *Bird, with descriptions of the Far East.

Travel writing developed into a genre in its own right in the 19th and 20th cents: British writers have been particularly attracted to the Arab countries of the Middle East (see for example under KINGLAKE, STARK, and THESIGER). In recent decades the form has continued to flourish: distinguished practitioners include Norman *Lewis; Jan *Morris; Eric Newby (1919–   ), author of many works based round the Mediterranean; and Gavin Young (1928–2001), whose works include *Return to the Marshes* (1977), describing time spent with the Marsh Arabs of Iraq; *Iraq: Land of Two Rivers* (1980), and *Slow Boats to China* (1980). Paul *Theroux, Bruce *Chatwin, Colin *Thubron, and Jonathan *Raban in the 1970s and early 1980s found radically different approaches to new and old material as the age of mass tourism impinged on the terrain of the solitary travel writer. Since then, in notable additions to and variations on the canon, American author Bill Bryson (1951–   ) has explored England; Redmond O'Hanlon (1947–   ) has travelled up the Congo and the Amazon and visited Borneo with James *Fenton (*Into the Heart of Borneo*, 1984); the Australian Robyn Davidson (1951–   ) has crossed the Australian desert on a camel (*Tracks*, 1980); Duncan Fallowell has created the gay travelogue; B. *Bainbridge in *The Birthday Boys* (1991) has drawn on the polar narratives of R. F. *Scott and Apsley Cherry-Garrard, and poets Simon *Armitage and Glyn *Maxwell (*Moon Country*, 1996) have visited Iceland in the footsteps of *Auden and *MacNeice. See Ian Jack (ed.), *The Granta Book of Travel* (1991) and Lisa *St Aubin de Terán (ed.), *The Virago Book of Wanderlust and Dreams* (1998).

TRAVEN, B. (?1882–1969), novelist and short story writer, whose first stories appeared in German in Berlin in 1925 as *Die Baumwollpflücker* (*The Cottonpickers*) followed by his highly successful novel *The Death Ship* (1925). It recounts the wanderings of an American seaman after the First World War, bereft of passport and nationality. Traven, whose identity remained for many years shrouded in mystery, went to Mexico in the 1920s, whence appeared some 12 novels and collections of stories, including *The Treasure of Sierra Madre* (1934), filmed by John Huston in 1947. *The Man Who Was B. Traven* (1980) by W. Wyatt established that he was Albert Otto Max Feige, later known as Ret Marut, born in Swiebodzin, a Polish town then in Germany, of working-class origins, a radical pamphleteer and survivor of the German revolution of 1919. He eschewed publicity, appearing in later years to visitors under the guise of his own 'translator', Hal Croves.

TRAVERS, Ben, see under FARCE.

Travesties, a comedy by T. *Stoppard, performed 1974, published 1975.

The play is largely set, with various time shifts, in Zurich during the First World War, where Lenin, *Joyce, and Tristan Tzara happened to be residing; they appear as characters, as does the marginally historical figure of Henry Carr (1894–1962), through whose memories much of the action is portrayed. Stoppard takes a minor incident from *Ellmann's life of Joyce, describing a semi-amateur performance in Zurich in 1918 of *The Importance of Being Earnest*, in which both Joyce and Carr were involved, and builds from it an extravaganza which plays on *Wilde's original (in terms of stylistic parody and of the plot of assumed and mistaken identities) to produce a theatrical, informative, and witty commentary on the birth of *Dada, the writing of *Ulysses*, and the genesis of the doctrine of *Socialist Realism, and on the nature of the artist as revolutionary or conformist. Stoppard uses a dazzling range of literary and theatrical effects, from Wildean epigram to a scene written entirely in limericks, from a suggestion of strip-tease to a lecture on Marxist theory.

Treasure Island, a romance by R. L. *Stevenson, published in book form 1883. It had previously appeared in *Young Folks*, July 1881–June 1882, under the title 'The Sea Cook or Treasure Island', and the concept grew from a map that Stevenson and his stepson Lloyd Osbourne devised together on holiday in Scotland. The flamboyant one-legged anti-hero Long John Silver was suggested by Stevenson's friend *Henley.

The narrator is Jim Hawkins, whose mother keeps the Admiral Benbow inn somewhere on the coast in the west of England in the 18th cent. An old buccaneer takes up his quarters at the inn. He has in his chest information, in the shape of a manuscript map, as to the whereabouts of Captain Flint's treasure. Of this his former confederates are determined to obtain possession, and a body of them, led by the sinister blind pirate Pew, makes a descent on the inn. But Jim Hawkins outwits them, secures the map, and delivers it to Squire Trelawney. The squire and his friend Dr Livesey set off for Treasure Island in the schooner *Hispaniola* taking Jim with them. Some of the crew are the squire's faithful dependants, but the majority are old buccaneers recruited by Long John Silver. Their design to seize the ship and kill the squire's party is discovered by Jim, and after a series of thrilling fights and adventures is completely thwarted; and the squire, with the help of the marooned pirate Ben Gunn, secures the treasure.

Treatise of Human Nature, A, a philosophical work by *Hume, written in France 1734–7, published in three volumes in London 1739–40. The work was recast as three separate and simpler works published between 1748 and 1757: *An Enquiry* (originally *Philosophical Essays*) *Concerning Human Understanding, An Enquiry Concerning the Principles of Morals*, and *A Dissertation on the Passions*. Scholars differ as to whether these recastings involve any significant changes in Hume's philosophical position.

Hume's work has been traditionally depicted as the culmination of one of two philosophical traditions. His contemporary critic T. *Reid established the common view that Hume was heir to a tradition set by *Locke and *Berkeley, notwithstanding Berkeley's rejection of the central theses of Locke's philosophy. Equally influential in the 20th cent. has been the view of Kemp Smith (1941) that Hume sought to extend and redirect the philosophy of *Hutcheson. Hume indicates his familiarity with their writings, and with the writings of other (otherwise incompatible) British predecessors like B. de *Mandeville and J. *Butler, but cites them mostly for their pioneer work on the science of human nature. Current biographical research suggests that the main formative influences on Hume's thought were his reading of *Cicero (on *Stoicism and *scepticism), *Descartes, Nicolas Malebranch (1638–1715), and *Bayle.

Hume saw the disputes of philosophers as centred upon the conflicting roles of reason and instinct or sentiment, and tried to define these roles for metaphysics in Book I of the *Treatise* and for the passions and morals in Books II–III. He agreed with Locke, against Descartes, that there are no innate ideas, and that all the data of reason stem from experience, and derived from Descartes the thesis that whatever may be conceived distinctly may be distinct. He argued that reason has insufficient data in experience to form adequate ideas of the external world, distance, bodily identity, causality, the self, and other minds, and that any beliefs we form about these must fall short of knowledge. Reason can attain certainty only in abstract mathematics—from which, in the *Treatise*, he even excluded geometry, owing to the empirical basis of our idea of space. We also employ reason when we use the experience of acquired associations to identify causes and effects, past events and future contingencies; this does not warrant the name 'certainty' and the process cannot be independently justified. It ceases to be rational altogether, and is then due to the imaginative faculty, when, as in religion, it involves inferences beyond the bounds of familiar experience.

Compensating for the inadequate data of experience and the infirmity of unaided reason are certain 'natural instincts' by which the imagination forges its own links between distinct ideas according to certain principles of association and habituation. Through these acquired but unavoidable associations, which Hume assumed to be explainable in terms of the brain science of the day, we project onto the world a sense of the continuity and externality of bodies, or of the necessity which we feel when some particular sequence of cause and effect has become habitual with us. In calling these mental constructions 'fictions' Hume meant only that they are not directly given in experience. Taken on their own, they can indeed lead us into false judgements, e.g. in misidentifying our sense impressions as the external object. But 'philosophical decisions are nothing but the reflections of common life, methodized and corrected' by the balanced interplay of reason, sense, and natural instinct, a standpoint Hume

characterized in the first *Enquiry* as 'mitigated scepticism'. Hume was, however, dissatisfied with his account of the self as 'a bundle or collection of different perceptions' appropriately associated, because he thought this failed to explain the sense each person has of the unity of consciousness.

In regard to morals, Hume again argued for an accommodation between reason and experience on the one hand (in determining facts and consequences) and sentiment on the other (in so far as moral distinctions are felt, not judged). Hume shared Hutcheson's belief in a moral sense, but not the theological framework or the psychological simplicity of Hutcheson's theory. In so far as there is a common structure of human nature, which approves whatever quality or character gives happiness to the parties affected without giving unhappiness to others, and enables us by the mechanisms of association or sympathy to share the sentiments of others, there is general consensus as to the motives and acts that are accounted morally virtuous and vicious. Hume's distinction between natural and artificial virtues was widely misconstrued in his lifetime: artificial virtues, e.g. justice, involve the determination and application of appropriate conventions in circumstances of need, where merely spontaneous virtues like benevolence are inadequate.

TREE, Sir Herbert Beerbohm (1853–1917), one of the most successful actor-managers of his day, and half-brother to Max *Beerbohm. He was famed for his spectacular productions (embellished with waterfalls, horses, and other special effects) and his many roles included Svengali in *Trilby* (1895) and Higgins in Shaw's *Pygmalion*.

TREECE, Henry, see NEW APOCALYPSE.

TRELAWNY, Edward John (1792–1881), of Cornish descent, born in London. He is remembered principally for his connection with and records of *Shelley and *Byron. When he met Shelley in Pisa in Jan. 1822 Trelawny had survived unhappy years as a midshipman in the navy, followed by marriage and divorce: from this time he attached himself first to Shelley (he was present at Livorno when Shelley was drowned) and later to Byron, whom he accompanied to Greece in July 1823. Byron had remarked on first meeting that Trelawny was 'the personification of my Corsair', and he did his best to live up to that image. He was the author of the notable *Adventures of a Younger Son* (1831), an autobiographical novel published with the encouragement of Mary *Shelley (who provided its title); it tells the story of a handsome, romantic, buccaneering youth, a lawless daredevil, warped in youth by the harshness of his father, who deserts from the navy and takes to a life of wandering during which he becomes involved in many wild escapades and desperate ventures. It is highly unreliable as autobiography, but written with much verve. His other publication was *Recollections of the Last Days of Shelley* *and Byron* (1858), again unreliable, but again written with great poetry and panache; it was later expanded to *Records of Shelley, Byron,* and the Author (1878). See William St Clair, *Trelawny: The Incurable Romancer* (1977) and David Crane, *Lord Byron's Jackal* (1998).

TREMAIN, Rose (1943–   ), novelist, short story writer, and playwright, born in London, educated at the Sorbonne in Paris and at the University of East Anglia. Her first novel, *Sadler's Birthday,* was published in 1976 and was followed by *Letter to Sister Benedicta* (1979), *The Swimming Pool Season* (1985), and *The Cupboard* (1989). Her best-known work of fiction, *Restoration,* published in 1989, is a first-person historical novel in which the central character, Robert Merivel, the son of a glove-maker and a student of anatomy, is taken up by Charles II but suffers the king's disfavour after he marries Celia Clemence, Charles's former mistress. As a result, Merivel exiles himself with a Quaker friend in a hospital for the insane before being 'restored' to a state of spiritual and social acceptance. *Sacred Country,* a novel which moves from Suffolk farmland to Nashville, Tennessee, in its exploration of gender and identity, was published in 1992. Her short stories have been collected as *The Colonel's Daughter* (1984), *The Garden of the Villa Mollini* (1987), and *Evangelista's Fan* (1994). *The Way I Found Her* (1997), charged with adolescent eroticism, describes a hot summer day in Paris, seen through the eyes of a precocious 13-year-old boy. *Music and Silence* (1999) is set in the early 17th cent. and recounts the experiences of an English lute player at the Danish court. *The Colour* (2003) is an action-packed account of the Gold Rush in New Zealand in the 1860s. She has also written many radio plays.

TRENCH, Frederic Herbert (1865–1923), born in Co. Cork and educated at Keble College, Oxford. He travelled widely in southern Europe and the Near East, and was from 1909 to 1911 artistic director of the Haymarket Theatre. His own plays had little success. Of his various poetic works, the most interesting is 'Apollo and the Seaman' (1907), a haunting narrative poem with echoes of the *Ancient Mariner*, in which Apollo and the seaman debate the sinking of the great ship, Lost Immortality, and the future of the soul.

TRENCH, Richard Chenevix (1807–86), educated at Trinity College, Cambridge, and afterwards dean of Westminster and archbishop of Dublin. He was the author of works dealing with history and literature, poetry, divinity, and philology. As a philologist, and notably by his *On the Study of Words* (1851) and *English Past and Present* (1855), he popularized the scientific study of language. The scheme of the *Oxford English Dictionary* originated in a resolution passed at his suggestion in 1858 by the *Philological Society. He also published several volumes of poetry, and his anthology *Sacred Latin Poetry, Chiefly Lyrical* (1849) drew attention to the masterpieces of Latin hymnody.

Trent, Fred, a character in Dickens's *The Old Curiosity Shop.* His sister is 'Little Nell'.

TRESSELL, Robert, the pen-name of Robert Noonan (?1870–1911), a house painter of Irish extraction, remembered for his posthumously published novel *The Ragged Trousered Philanthropists,* which first appeared in 1914, edited from a manuscript left in the care of his daughter. It draws on his experiences while working for a builder in Hastings, where he settled in 1902 after various wanderings. He died of tuberculosis in Liverpool. An abridged edition of his novel appeared in 1918, but on the discovery of the original handwritten manuscript in 1946 it became clear that the author's intentions had been widely altered, and it reappeared, edited by F. C. Ball, in 1955.

The action takes place during one year in the lives of a group of working men in the town of Mugsborough, and the novel is a bitter but spirited attack on the greed, dishonesty, and gullibility of employers and workers alike, and on the social conditions that gave rise to these vices. Debates on socialism, competition, employment, and capitalism are skilfully interwoven with a realistic and knowledgeable portrayal of skilled and unskilled labour in the decorating and undertaking business, and with the human stories of the families of the workers. Principal characters include Frank Owen, socialist craftsman and atheist; Barrington, socialist son of a wealthy father, intent on first-hand experience of labour; the inadequate but well-intentioned Eastons with their unfortunate baby whom they feed on fried bacon; and Slyme, a canting and unprincipled teetotaller. Noonan's coining of names for local worthies—Sweater, Didlum, Grinder, Botchit, etc.—indicates his attitude towards the widespread corruption and hypocrisy that he exposes, and the book has become a classic text of the Labour movement. The ironically named 'philanthropists' of the title are the workers who for pitiful wages 'toil and sweat at their noble and unselfish task of making money' for their employers, while making no effort to understand or better their lot.

TREVELYAN, G(eorge) M(acaulay) (1876–1962), historian, son of Sir G. O. *Trevelyan, educated at Harrow and Trinity College, Cambridge, where he became a member of the *Apostles. He was appointed Regius professor of modern history at Cambridge in 1927, and master of Trinity in 1940. He was author of three remarkable works on Garibaldi, *Garibaldi's Defence of the Roman Republic* (1907), *Garibaldi and the Thousand* (1909), and *Garibaldi and the Making of Italy* (1911), which owe some of their vividness of narrative and description to the fact that Trevelyan himself, a tireless walker, retraced on foot every mile of the scenes of campaign. His many other works include lives of John Bright (1913), Lord Grey (1920), and Grey of Falloden (1937); a three-volume work on *England under Queen Anne* (1930–4); and his popular and nostalgic *English Social History* (1944). In *Layman's Love of Letters*

(1954), delivered in 1953 as the Clark Lectures, he speaks warmly of R. *Browning, Sir W. *Scott, *Meredith, *Housman, the poetry of mountaineering, etc., and mildly deplores the professional view of literature as 'a set of intellectual conundrums, to be solved by certain rules. It is joy, joy in our inmost heart.'

TREVELYAN, Sir George Otto (1838–1928), nephew of *Macaulay, educated at Harrow and Trinity College, Cambridge. He entered Parliament as a Liberal in 1865 and held several important offices. Some of his early humorous writings were collected in *The Ladies in Parliament* (1869), others mainly about India included *The Dawk Bungalow* (1863, a comedy), *The Competition Wallah* (1864), and *Cawnpore* (1865). The first of his great works, *The Life and Letters of Lord Macaulay*, appeared in 1876, and was followed by *The Early History of George the Third and Charles Fox* (1912–14).

TREVISA, John of (?1340–1402), born in Cornwall, a fellow of Exeter (1362–9) and the Queen's (1369–79) colleges, Oxford. He was expelled from Oxford for 'unworthiness' and became vicar of Berkeley. In 1387 he translated the *Polychronicon* of *Higden, adding a short continuation and an introduction; part of this has become famous as an account of the state of the English language in its time (see K. Sisam, *Fourteenth Century Verse and Prose*, 1921, no. XIII). The *Polychronicon* translation is written in a vigorous and colloquial style, though he also has claims to a more elaborate manner; his principles of translation are declared in two short essays prefixed to the *Polychronicon*. He also translated Egidio Colonna's *De Regimine Principum*, one of the sources of *Hoccleve's *Regiment of Princes*, and in 1398 the *De Proprietatibus Rerum* of *Bartholomaeus Anglicus. In the edition of his *Dialogus* by A. J. Perry (EETS OS 167, 1925—also containing works by other writers) there is a good account of his life.

TREVOR, William (William Trevor Cox) (1928–   ), Anglo-Irish novelist and short story writer, born in Co. Cork and educated at Trinity College, Dublin; he has spent much of his life in Ireland, which provides the setting for many of his works. His novels include *The Old Boys* (1964), *Mrs Eckdorf in O'Neill's Hotel* (1969), *Elizabeth Alone* (1973), and *Fools of Fortune* (1983); collections of short stories include *The Day We Got Drunk on Cake* (1969), *Angels at the Ritz* (1975), and *Beyond the Pale* (1981). A Penguin collection of his stories appeared in 1983. The title story of *The Ballroom of Romance* (1972), which like many of Trevor's works, has been successfully televised, is a characteristically low-key, poignant evocation of a rural Ireland where men drink and women wait whereas that of *Lovers of Their Time* (1978) deals with middle-aged romance in a hotel bathroom at Paddington, and the novel *The Children of Dynmouth* (1976) describes an English seaside resort terrorized by a delinquent teenager. Trevor writes with insight of the elderly, the lonely, and the unsuccessful, and his more recent works (e.g.

'Attracta', 1978, the story of an ageing schoolmistress) show an increasing preoccupation with the effects of terrorism in Northern Ireland. Other story collections include *The News from Ireland* (1986) and *Family Sins* (1989). Two novellas, *Two Lives*, appeared in 1991. Collected editions of his short stories were published in 1983 and 1992. Amongst later novels are *The Silence in the Garden* (1988) and *Felicia's Journey* (1994), which won the *Sunday Express* Book of the Year Award and the Whitbread Novel Award and is a powerful account of a young girl's journey from her home in rural Ireland to industrial Britain. *Excursions in the Real World* (1994) is a collection of personal essays on childhood, people, and places.

Triamond, in Spenser's *Faerie Queene* (IV. iii. iv), the Knight of Friendship. After an inconclusive fight with *Cambello in the contest to decide to which of her suitors *Canacee (Cambello's sister) is to be awarded, Triamond and Cambello swear eternal friendship. In the tournament arranged by *Satyrane, Triamond, though wounded, returns to rescue Cambello. He marries Canacee.

Tribulation Wholesome, the fanatical Puritan elder in Jonson's *The Alchemist*.

Trilby, a novel written and illustrated by George *du Maurier, published 1894.

The setting of the story reflects the writer's years as an art student in Paris, and the three student friends of Trilby O'Ferrall (the Laird, Little Billee, and Taffy) are portraits of friends. The charming Trilby, an artist's model, slowly falls under the mesmeric spell of Svengali, a German-Polish musician, who trains her voice and establishes her as a famous singer. His power over her is such that when he dies her voice collapses, she loses her eminence, languishes, and finally dies herself. The novel was immensely popular for many years, and in 1895 was dramatized with Beerbohm *Tree as Svengali. Trilby's hat, a soft felt with an indented crown, is the origin of the 'trilby'.

TRILLING, Lionel (1905–75), American critic, whose many works include *The Liberal Imagination* (1950), *The Opposing Self* (1955), and *Sincerity and Authenticity* (1972). His works are written from the standpoint of liberal humanism (increasingly conceived as being under threat) and manifest a marked admiration for *Freud, 'one of the few great Plutarchian characters of our time', without in any way committing themselves to doctrinaire *Freudian criticism. Trilling's wide range of subjects includes *Keats, H. *James, J. *Austen, *Wordsworth, F. S. *Fitzgerald, S. *Anderson, etc. His works appeared in a 12-volume edition, 1978–80. He also wrote one novel, *The Middle of the Journey* (1947).

trilogy, in Greek antiquity, a series of three tragedies (originally connected in subject) performed at Athens at the festival of Dionysus. Hence any series of three related dramatic or other literary works.

Trim, Corporal, the devoted servant of Toby in Sterne's *Tristram Shandy*.

trimeter, see METRE.

trimmer, originally applied to one who trims between opposing parties in politics; hence, one who inclines as his interest dictates. But *Halifax in his *Character of a Trimmer* (1682) accepted the nickname in the sense of 'one who keeps even the ship of state'.

Trimmer, Character of a, see HALIFAX.

TRIMMER, Mrs Sarah, née Kirby (1741–1810), known as 'Good Mrs Trimmer', the author of the popular children's book *The History of the Robins*, originally entitled *Fabulous Histories* (1786), and of many exemplary tales, educational works, and textbooks for charity schools. In her periodical *The Guardian of Education* (1802–6) she attacked traditional children's literature, and in particular fairy stories, describing *Cinderella* as a tale inculcating 'envy, jealousy, a dislike for mothers-in-law and half-sisters, vanity, a love of dress'.

Trinculo, companion to *Stephano in Shakespeare's *The Tempest*.

triolet, a poem of eight lines, with two rhymes, in which the first line is repeated as the fourth and seventh, and the second as the eighth.

triplet, three successive lines of verse rhyming together, occasionally introduced among heroic couplets, e.g. by *Dryden.

Trip to Scarborough, A, a musical play by R. B. *Sheridan, produced 1777. The play is based on Vanbrugh's *The Relapse*, but it was considerably rewritten, coarse language was carefully expunged, and music and songs were added. In Sheridan's version Berinthia is no longer altogether an unscrupulous coquette; she tempts Loveless in order to punish Towneley (the Worthy of the earlier play) for deserting her in favour of Amanda, Loveless's wife.

Eventually it is his sense of shame and honour, and not the threat of exposure, that restores Loveless to Amanda.

'Tristram and Iseult', a poem in three parts by M. *Arnold, published 1852. This is the first modern version of the story that was made familiar by *Wagner and *Tennyson; it deals with the death of Tristram (Tristan, in earlier editions of the same work), who lies dying, watched over by Iseult of Brittany, and dreaming in his fever of his love for Iseult of Ireland, the wife of Marc. She arrives, and after a brief passionate dialogue he dies. In Part III Iseult of Brittany tells her children the story of Merlin, entranced by Vivian.

Tristram and Isoud (*Tristan and Isolde*). The long story of Tristram de Lyones is the fifth of Vinaver's eight *Works* of *Malory. The love of Tristram and Isoud is much older than the corresponding Arthurian story of the love of Launcelot and Guinevere, and it was incorporated into the Arthurian legends only at a late stage. Denis de Rougemont (*Passion and Society*, 1940) declares Tristan to be the prototype of the courtly lover, a view corroborated by repeated references to him in courtly love lyrics and romances (see COURTLY LOVE). It is thought likely that there was a *Tristan* romance (since lost) by *Chrétien de Troyes in the 1170s, and it is possible, judging from repeated references in the poetry of the troubadours, that there was an early Provençal *Tristan*. There are three versions surviving from the 12th cent.: Béroul's fragment of 4,485 lines (c.?1190) in the Norman dialect; Thomas's French fragment (c.1170); and the version in literary Rhenish German by Eilhart (c.1170). The most authoritative medieval version is by Gottfried von Strassburg (c.?1200; nothing is known of his life) in German, of which the last sixth is missing and which is based to some extent on Thomas. The best English translation (by A. T. Hatto, 1960) supplies the last sixth from Thomas's version. The first English version is *Sir Tristrem*, a northern 3,344-line romance in 11-line stanzas, dating from c.1300 (unpersuasively attributed to Thomas of *Erceldoune). In Malory, Tristram is the child of Meliodas, king of *Lyonesse, and Elizabeth, the sister of King Mark of Cornwall, who dies soon after his sorrowful birth. The sad child is brought up at the court of King Mark whose attitude to the boy varies in different versions from great affection to jealousy. Tristram defeats and kills Sir Marhalt (Marhaus), the brother of Isoud, queen of Ireland. Tristram is sent to Ireland to be cured of his wounds by Isoud the queen, and he falls in love with her daughter Isoud; when the queen discovers that this knight (whom she too holds in special esteem) is the slayer of her brother, Tristram returns to Cornwall. Later King Mark sends Tristram as ambassador in seeking for him the hand of the younger Isoud. The princess and her maid Brangwayn return by ship to Cornwall; Brangwayn has been given a love potion by Queen Isoud to be given on their wedding-night to Isoud and King Mark, which will bind them in unending love. By mistake the love potion is drunk by Tristram and Isoud who are bound thereafter in endless passion, though Isoud has to marry Mark. The rest of the story is concerned with the fated love of Tristram and Isoud (in a manner broadly reminiscent of the Irish epic stories of *Deirdre and the sons of Usnach, and Diarmait and *Grainne), and the subterfuges (often ingenious and morally reprehensible) which the lovers have to adopt; as in Chrétien's *Lancelot*, love is represented as a value that transcends morality. Tristram leaves Mark's court and, while fighting for Howel of Brittany, falls in love with and marries a third Isoud (Isolde of the White Hands). But, on the invitation of Isoud of Ireland, he returns to Cornwall where he is killed by Mark while playing his harp before Isoud. In some versions his death is not mentioned at all; in the most celebrated (adopted by *Wagner) Tristram sends for Isoud while he lies dying in Brittany. If she is on the ship when it returns, a white flag is to be flown; if not, a black one. The flag is white, but Isoud of the White Hands tells Tristram it is black, whereupon he dies. When Isoud comes to his bedside, she dies too. The story is the classic of medieval romance (with its strong mythical overtones and themes which recur in the romance, such as Tristram's madness, his harping, and the blood from his betraying wound) and of medieval love poetry. See D. de Rougemont, *Passion and Society* (1940; trans. of French *L'Amour et l'occident*, 1939); W. T. H. Jackson, *The Anatomy of Love: The Tristan of Gottfried von Strassburg* (1971).

Tristram of Lyonesse, a poem in heroic couplets by *Swinburne, published 1882, which tells the story of Tristram's love for Queen Iseult, his marriage to Iseult of Brittany, and his death. W. *Morris, whose own medieval romances had much influenced Swinburne, was prompted by it to comment that his friend's work 'always seemed to me to be founded on literature, not on nature'.

Tristram Shandy, Gentleman, The Life and Opinions of, by L. *Sterne, published 1759–67.

This unique work, although itself the culmination of experiments by lesser authors, is generally regarded as the progenitor of the 20th-cent. *stream-of-consciousness novel. It owes much to *Rabelais, to Robert *Burton, and to Locke's *Essay Concerning Human Understanding*. The word 'shandy', of obscure origin, means 'crack-brained, half-crazy', and Tristram in volume vi of his book declares that he is writing a 'civil, nonsensical, good humoured *Shandean* book'.

Set in the Shandys' small parlour and garden, the book, erratically narrated by Tristram, consists of a slim line of narrative constantly and flagrantly interrupted by exuberant digressions, exploiting the relativity of time in human experience by deliberately disordering the sequence and emphasis of events. Parodying the new 'novel' form of his contemporaries, the narrator mocks the absurdity of development in narrative, insisting on beginning at the moment of his own conception, and deliberately providing no consistent plot or conclusion. Sterne's wayward typography, which includes rows of asterisks, dashes, diagrams, blank pages, various typefaces and other devices, paradoxically emphasizes his cheerful view of the unreality of the 'novel' form which he is himself using.

The chief character of the book is the narrator, Tristram, through whose thoughts, feelings, and observations we encounter the people and events about which he writes. He is shrewd and bawdy, delighting in the idiosyncrasy of the Shandy household, and filled with such vitality his words can scarcely keep up with his headlong thought. The main characters he introduces are his excitable and devoted father Walter, whose flamboyant eloquence flows on through philosophy, paradox, and hypothesis, filled with references to the classics, history, science, medicine, law, the arts, and all learning run wild; Uncle Toby, Walter's soldier brother, whose portrait *Hazlitt described as 'one of the finest compliments ever paid to human nature', a man benign and practical, whose most passionate interest is aroused only by the problems of military fortifications and, more fleetingly, by the widow Wadman; Corporal Trim, Toby's devoted and loquacious servant, who shares his master's passion for fortifications; the bewildered Mrs Shandy; the impulsive and argumentative parson Yorick; Dr *Slop, an incompetent physician; the Shandys' neighbour Mrs Wadman, who designs to marry Toby; and the irrepressible household servant Obadiah. Tristram's persistent interest and amusement in sexual matters (such as his own conception or Toby's wound in the groin) is demonstrated in frequent ironical parades of discretion, indiscretion, and innuendo.

A sketch of the 'story' may be attempted but cannot be very helpful. In volume i Tristram is noted as arriving in 'the scurvy and disastrous world', and with much learned digression and other distraction his family and friends are introduced and described. Volume ii concentrates chiefly on the past military experiences of Toby and Corporal Trim, and their present enthusiasms, and on a lengthy discussion of a controversial sermon read aloud by Trim. Tristram's birth is now fully described in volume iii, but only after many diversions and asides, including the mighty curse of Ernulphus of Rochester—at which time the author finds occasion to produce his overdue Preface. Volume iv contains Walter's exposition to his bewildered brother Toby of Slawkenbergius's Latin treatise on noses (for which the Shandys are famous), and an account of the misnaming of the infant 'Tristram' instead of 'Trismegistus'. Volume v covers the death of Tristram's brother Bobby and Walter's response, the reflections of Trim on death, and the devising of the *Tristapaedia* for Tristram's education. Volume vi relates the pathetic tale of Lieutenant Le Fever and his son, together with Toby's great kindness to them; includes the ludicrous bedtime discussion between Mr and Mrs Shandy on the putting of Tristram into breeches; describes the tremendous model of military earthworks constructed by Toby and Trim in the garden; and begins the story of Toby's amour with the widow Wadman. In volume vii the Shandy family narrative is broken by a description of Tristram's travels and adventures in France. Volume viii follows the complex emotions developing between Toby and Mrs Wadman, and Trim's attempt to tell his story of the king of Bohemia. Volume ix includes the pathetic tale of mad Maria (who appears again in *A Sentimental Journey*) and continues the story of Toby's love affair, until its sad collapse. The final brief episode of the book contains a confused conversation about Walter's bull. 'L—d! said my mother, what is all this story about?—A

COCK and a BULL, said Yorick—And one of the best of its kind, I ever heard.'

The first version of volumes i and ii was rejected by *Dodsley, and Sterne had a revised version of them published in York in 1759. The rest of the work was published in London between 1761 and 1767 and enjoyed great general success, although Dr *Johnson, *Richardson, *Goldsmith, and certain other literary figures expressed their reservations on both literary and moral grounds.

Triumph of Life, The, an unfinished visionary poem by P. B. *Shelley, written in the bay of Lerici in summer 1822, published from rough drafts 1824.

Composed in *terza rima, the poem is strongly influenced by *Dante's *Inferno*, *Petrarch's *Trionfi*, and the carvings of Roman triumphal processions Shelley had seen in the Forum. The 'triumph' or masquerade (as the *'Mask of Anarchy') belongs to the cruel Chariot of Life, here shown as one of Shelley's Tyrant-figures. Life appears to vanquish the hope and ideals of all men, dragging in its train even the greatest, like Plato, Alexander, or Napoleon. Only the 'sacred few', like Jesus and Socrates, who early 'Fled back like eagles to their native noon', escape compromise and captivity. The poetry has a bitter, lucid directness that is new to Shelley; it contains a grim and masterful passage about growing old and sexually disillusioned (ll. 137–69). But it is impossible to know how he would have concluded the vision, had he lived.

The poet is conducted by the spirit of *Rousseau (as Dante is led through Hell by Virgil); he observes that most men do not know themselves truly, and are destroyed by 'the mutiny within'. The atmosphere of the poem, full of images drawn from the sea, is darkly hypnotic.

Triumph of Peace, The, a masque by J. *Shirley, acted and printed 1634.

This was the best known of all 17th-cent. *masques, mainly because of the spectacular torchlight procession (or 'triumph') of the masquers, from Holborn to Whitehall, which preceded the masque proper. It was an expression of loyalty to the Crown on the part of the four Inns of Court, after *Prynne—a member of Lincoln's Inn—had published his *Histriomastix* (1633) with a dedication to his fellow benchers at the Inn. Shirley's plot is simple: the chief anti-masquer, Fancy, presents a series of interludes showing the benefit and abuses of Peace; these are finally driven away by the entry of Peace, Law, and Justice—qualities which, the lawyers were eager to point out, cannot flourish apart from one another. The masque was designed by I. *Jones, and its score (by W. *Lawes and Simon Ives) is among the few examples of masque music that have survived.

TRIVET, Nicholas (c.1258–?1334), of a family with connections in Norfolk and Somerset, a Dominican who studied at Oxford and Paris. He made early commentaries on a number of classical texts, including *Boethius, but he is most celebrated as the writer of three histories in the 1320s: his Anglo-Norman Chronicle, extending from the Creation to 1285, surviving in eight manuscripts and containing the tale of Constance, told by *Gower in *Confessio Amantis* and by Chaucer's Man of Law (see CANTERBURY TALES, 5); secondly, *Annals of Six Kings of England 1136–1307*, pro-Angevin and particularly useful for the reign of Edward I; and third, the *Historia ab Orbe Condito* (1327–9), an encyclopaedic history influenced by *Vincent of Beauvais.

Trivia, or *The Art of Walking the Streets of London*, a poem by J. *Gay in three books, published 1716. It is a town eclogue, owing 'some hints' to *Swift, whose 'City Shower' (1710) is in the same vein. Gay conducts the reader through the streets of London, by day and then by night, offering advice on coats and boots (Book I contains a mock-heroic derivation of the word 'patten'), on the hazards of pavement, gutters, and rubbish, and on the characters he will encounter—boot-boys, ballad-singers, footmen, bullies, fishwives, etc. It is a lively, affectionate, and entertaining piece, and a mine of information. 'Trivia' means 'streets', from the root meaning of 'road junction', and Gay, who invokes Trivia as a goddess of the highways, also refers to the murder of Laius by Oedipus at the crossroads in Book III, l. 217.

Trivium, the lower division of the Seven Liberal Arts, consisting of the methodological subjects Grammar, Rhetoric, and Logic, as distinct from the mathematically based sciences of the *Quadrivium. The Trivium had great importance throughout the period of the Roman Empire, and it was taught from the time of Aristotle in Greek. Its period of greatest importance was the 11th and 12th cents, at Chartres and in such writers as *John of Salisbury. Gradually logic became the all-important member, so that in the 12th cent. the Trivium was redefined as grammar, rhetoric, and dialectic, regarded as sub-sections of logic; in the 13th cent. concern for argumentative precision meant that the literary aspects of the Trivium disappeared almost entirely, and grammar and rhetoric as expressive skills ceased to be taught. The derogatory adjective 'trivial' (first found in English in the 16th cent.) reflects this progressive decline.

TROCCHI, Alexander (1925–84), novelist, poet, translator, and editor, born in Glasgow, and educated at Glasgow University. He lived in Paris during the 1950s, where he published several novels (as 'Frances Lengel') for the *Olympia Press, notably the haunting canal-drowning mystery *Young Adam* (1954) and edited, with C. *Logue, the short-lived but influential magazine *Merlin* (1952–5) which published work by *Beckett, *Genet, *Neruda, and others. He is best remembered for *Cain's Book* (USA 1961, UK 1963), a classic story of heroin addiction.

trochee, trochaic, see METRE.

Troilus and Cressida, a tragedy by *Shakespeare probably written 1602, perhaps with a performance at one of the Inns of Court in mind. It was first printed 1609, in a quarto of which there are two issues, with different title-pages, one of which has a prefatory epistle, 'A never writer, to an ever reader. News.' This was not included in the First *Folio, where *Troilus and Cressida* is the first play in the section of tragedies. As well as *Homer's and *Chaucer's handling of material concerning the lovers and the siege of Troy, Shakespeare knew of Henryson's *Testament of Cresseid*, *Caxton's *Recuyell of the Historyes of Troye*, and *Lydgate's *Troy Book*, and drew on *Ovid's *Metamorphoses* Books 11 and 12, R. *Greene's *Euphues His Censure to Philautus* (1587) and *Chapman's *Seven Books of the Iliads* (1598).

Shakespeare's treatment of the love of Troilus and Cressida and its betrayal, against the setting of the siege of Troy by the Greeks, is conventional. The play contains much formal debate, and takes the story up to the death of Hector at the hands of Achilles: Troilus fails to kill his rival Diomedes, and the cynically railing Thersites escapes death. Modern criticism has tended to agree with *Coleridge's view that 'there is none of Shakespeare's plays harder to characterize'.

Troilus and Criseyde, *Chaucer's longest complete poem, in 8,239 lines of rhyme-royal, probably written in the second half of the 1380s (J. D. North, *RES*, 1969, has shown that the events of the poem take place in calendar circumstances corresponding on astrological evidence to dates between 1385 and 1388). Chaucer takes his story from *Boccaccio's *Il filostrato*, adapting its eight books to five and changing the characters of Criseyde and *Pandarus. In Boccaccio Troilo falls in love with Criseida whose cousin, Troilo's friend Pandaro, persuades her, not unwillingly, to become Troilo's lover. In the end Criseida has to leave the Trojan camp to join her father who had defected to the Greeks; in the Greek camp she betrays Troilo by falling in love with Diomede. While following the same narrative pattern, Chaucer deepens the sense of seriousness in the story by making Pandaro Criseida's uncle and guardian, by showing her deliberating at more length (this series of exchanges between uncle and niece in Book II is one of the most admired and anthologized parts of the poem), and by introducing deliberative material, principally from *Boethius, calling into question the lovers' freedom of action. The poem ends with an adjuration to the young to repair home from worldly vanity and to place their trust, not in unstable fortune as Troilus did, but in God. Discussion of the poem has centred largely on the appropriateness of the epilogue to the preceding action, on the attitudes to love (*courtly love in particular) in the poem, and on the personality of the narrator and his effect on the narrative. The love story has no basis in classical antiquity but is the invention of *Benoît de Sainte-Maure in his *Roman de Troie*, which was based on the pretended histories of Troy by *Dares Phrygius and *Dictys Cretensis. Boccaccio's intermediate source was *Guido delle Colonne (see TROPHEE). After Chaucer, the story was treated by Henryson in *The Testament of Cresseid* and by Shakespeare in *Troilus and Cressida*.

Ed. B. A. Windeatt (1984). N. R. Havely, *Chaucer's Boccaccio* (1980); J. D. North, *Chaucer's Universe* (1988); B. A. Windeatt, *Troilus and Criseyde* (1992); S. A. Barney (ed.), *Chaucer's Troilus: Essays in Criticism* (1980); C. D. Benson (ed.), *Critical Essays on Chaucer's Troilus and Criseyde and His Major Early Poems* (1991).

TROLLOPE, Anthony (1815–82), born in London. His *Autobiography*, written 1875–6, published posthumously 1883, describes his life with a characteristic blend of candour and reticence. His father, a fellow of New College, Oxford, before his marriage, failed both as a lawyer and as a farmer. The family's poverty made Trollope miserable at school (he went to both Harrow and Winchester), and when financial difficulties became acute, the family moved to Belgium, where Trollope's father died. Mrs Frances *Trollope had already begun to support the family through her belated career as an author; she was already in her fifties when her successful *Domestic Manners of the Americans* was published in 1832. Trollope became a junior clerk in the General Post Office in London in 1834, but only began to make any professional progress when transferred to Ireland in 1841. He married Rose Heseltine of Rotherham in 1844; they had two sons, the younger of whom was to settle in Australia. Trollope did not return permanently to England until 1859, although he travelled extensively on Post Office business; he undertook important postal missions at various times to Egypt, the West Indies, and the United States. By the end of his professional career Trollope had become a successful and important if also highly individual civil servant. Among his achievements is the introduction in Great Britain of the pillar-box for letters. He resigned from the Post Office in 1867, and stood unsuccessfully for Parliament as a Liberal in 1868. Trollope thought that a seat in Parliament ought to be 'the highest object of ambition to every educated Englishman'. He edited the *St Paul's Magazine*, 1867–70.

His literary career began with the appearance of *The Macdermots of Ballycloran* in 1847, but not until his fourth novel, *The Warden* (1855), did he establish the manner and material by which he is best known. This, the first of the 'Barsetshire' series, was followed by *Barchester Towers* (1857), *Doctor Thorne* (1858), *Framley Parsonage* (1861), *The Small House at Allington* (1864), and *The Last Chronicle of Barset* (1867). The action of these novels is for the most part set in the imaginary West Country county of Barset and its chief town, Barchester, of which Trollope says in the *Autobiography*, 'I had it all in my mind,—its roads and railroads, its towns and parishes, its members of Parliament, and the different hunts which rode over it. I knew all the great lords and their castles, the squires and their parks, the rectors and their churches . . . Throughout these stories there has been no name given to a fictitious site which does not represent to me a spot of which I know all the accessories, as though I had lived and wandered there.' Trollope regarded *The Last Chronicle of Barset* as his best novel, taken as a whole. The Barset novels are also interconnected by characters who appear in more than one of them, and Trollope developed this technique in his second series, known as the 'Political' novels or—perhaps more appropriately—as the 'Palliser' novels, after Plantagenet Palliser, who appears in all of them. This series began with *Can You Forgive Her?* (1864) and continued with *Phineas Finn* (1869), *The Eustace Diamonds* (1873), *Phineas Redux* (1876), *The Prime Minister* (1876), and *The Duke's Children* (1880). The two series taken together thus span over 20 years of Trollope's writing life. Trollope established the novel sequence in English fiction. His use of reappearing characters had been anticipated by *Balzac (who uses them on an even grander scale), but there is no evidence that Trollope was in any way indebted to the French author. The characters of Palliser and his wife Lady Glencora, together with that of Mr Crawley from *The Last Chronicle of Barset*, seemed to Trollope to give his work its best chance of survival. The Palliser novels also allowed Trollope to express his views on political matters.

Although modest in claiming literary excellence, Trollope prided himself on his workmanlike attitude towards his art, as well as on its sheer quantity. He attributed his remarkable output, which included 47 novels, several travel books, biographies, as well as collections of short stories and sketches, to a disciplined regularity of composition. He trained himself to produce a given number of words an hour in the early morning before going off to his post office duties (which he also managed to combine with an almost fanatical devotion to hunting). He also wrote when travelling by rail and sea, and as soon as he finished one novel began another. He was always much more concerned with character than with plot, and made the degree to which an author really knows his characters a fundamental test of his or her merit. In the *Autobiography* Trollope writes eloquently of the novelist's need to live with his creatures 'in the full reality of established intimacy. They must be with him as he lies down to sleep, and as he wakes from dreams.' He also stresses the importance of recording change and the effects of time: 'On the last day of each month recorded, every person in his novel should be a month older than on the first.' Trollope attributed whatever success he had obtained to the intimacy with which he himself had lived with the characters in his lifelike imagination. His popularity was at its peak during the 1860s; readers admired his treatment of family and professional life, the variety and delicacy of his heroines, and the photographic accuracy of his pictures of social life.

Apart from the two series, Trollope's other principal novels include: *The Three Clerks* (1857), *The Bertrams* (1859), *Orley Farm* (1862), *The Belton Estate* (1866), *The Claverings* (1867), *He Knew He Was Right* (1869), *The Vicar of Bullhampton* (1870), *The Way We Live Now* (1875), *The American Senator* (1877), *Doctor Wortle's School* (1881), *Ayala's Angel* (1881), *Mr Scarborough's Family* (1883). The *Autobiography* records that, down to 1879, his publications had brought him some £70,000, which he thought 'comfortable, but not splendid'. Despite a sometimes overbearing public manner, Trollope became a popular figure in London and literary society in his later years. He was on good terms with the major novelists of his day: he greatly admired *Thackeray, of whom he nevertheless wrote a clear-sighted study (1879), and was a close friend of G. *Eliot and G. H. *Lewes. In an obituary essay on Trollope written in 1883, H. *James summed up his achievement by saying that 'His great, his inestimable merit was a complete appreciation of the usual . . . Trollope's great apprehension of the real, which was what made him so interesting, came to him through his desire to satisfy us on this point—to tell us what certain people were and what they did in consequence of being so.' See D. Smalley (ed.), *The Critical Heritage* (1969); *Letters*, ed. N. John Hall (2 vols, 1983).

TROLLOPE, Frances (1780–1863), a woman, and writer, of indefatigable energy, who made an unfortunate marriage, conducted several ventures into, for instance, farming, and when she was past 50 wrote the first of over 40 books, by which she proceeded to support her large family, and eventually achieved wealth and fame. After the failure of their farm at Harrow (later to appear in her son Anthony *Trollope's *Orley Farm*) she sailed to New Orleans in 1827 with Utopian aspirations and three of her children, and opened an exotic bazaar in Cincinnati. This venture failing, she travelled for 15 months in America, then in 1832, back in England, published her caustic *Domestic Manners of the Americans*. Its resounding success brought contracts to write on the Belgians, the French, the Austrians, and others, and she lived for the next few years on the Continent. *Paris and the Parisians* appeared with great success in 1835, *Vienna and the Austrians* in 1838, and in 1842 *A Visit to Italy* (where she became the friend of the *Brownings, *Dickens, and *Landor). Meanwhile, by working both early and late every day, she was writing a long sequence of popular novels, some of which, like *Michael Armstrong, the Factory Boy* (1840), dealt with social issues, and by the early 1840s was earning a considerable income. (See SOCIAL PROBLEM NOVEL.) She built a house at Penrith, and was invited to meet the elderly *Wordsworth (whom she disliked).

Trompart, in Spenser's *Faerie Queene (II. iii),

wylie witted, and growne old
In cunning sleights and practick knavery,

attends *Braggadochio as his squire, and with him is finally exposed and beaten out of court.

Trophee, an unknown writer mentioned by *Chaucer in 'The Monk's Tale' (see CANTERBURY TALES, 19):

At bothe the worldes endes, seith Trophee,
In stide of boundes he [i.e. Hercules] a pileer sette.
(CT VII. 2117–18)

A marginal note in the Ellesmere and Hengwrt manuscripts says 'Ille vates Chaldeorum Tropheus'. *Lydgate says that Chaucer in his youth made a translation of a book called in the Lombard tongue *Trophe*, and that he later named it 'Troilus and Cressida'. No such book, or author, is known; of the explanations offered, the most likely is either that the Latin word for the pillars (of Hercules), *trophea*, has been interpolated and interpreted as an author's name, or that *Trophea* represents *Guido delle *Colonne* ('Pillars') and that it is he that Chaucer is indicating.

Trotter, Job, in Dickens's *Pickwick Papers* Jingle's servant.

Trotwood, Betsey, a character in Dickens's *David Copperfield*.

troubadours, poets composing in *Provençal during the 12th and early 13th cents (and perhaps earlier). They were famous for the complexity of their verse forms in the lyric, and for the conception of *courtly love which is founded to an important degree in their poems. Guilhem IX (1071–1127), count of Poitiers and duke of Aquitaine, is the first known troubadour; Jaufre Rudel (d. before 1167) developed the theme of 'amor de lonh', love from afar. The most admired troubadour love poets are Bernart de Ventadorn (fl. 1140–75), Raimbaut d'Aurenga (c.1144–73), Guiraut de Borneil (c.1165–1212: the most admired in his own time, the 'maestre dels trobadors'), and Arnaut Daniel (fl. 1180–1200), whom *Dante and *Petrarch admired most, an admiration shared in the 20th cent. by *Pound, who composed excellent translations of Daniel. The troubadours flourished in the courts of Spain, Italy, and northern France, as well as in the south of France, and courtly poetry in Provençal was being written and cultivated in Italy in the later 13th cent. (see SORDELLO and DANTE) when it was disappearing in the Midi. Through their influence on the northern French poets (such as *Chrétien, and the writers of the *Roman de la rose) and on the German poets of the minnesang (see MINNESINGERS) they had a major effect on all the subsequent development of European lyric poetry. Though love was their major subject, it was not their only one; they also composed moralizing, satirical, and political poems called sirventes (of which Guiraut de Borneil was the recognized master), and military poems in which Bertran de Born (c.1140–c.1215) excelled. See A. R. Press (ed. and trans.), *Anthology of Troubadour Lyric Poetry* (1971: parallel text); L. T. Topsfield, *Troubadours and Love* (1975).

Troubles, literature of the. The term 'the Troubles' is used to refer both to the years of the war for Irish independence, which followed the Easter Rising of 1916 and ended with the ceasefire of 1923, and to the later (not unconnected) post-1968 period of the Northern Irish Troubles. In the first sense, the Troubles inspired work by *Yeats, *O'Casey, *O'Flaherty, and many other Irish patriots and critics of Irish nationalism, and gave a title to J. G. *Farrell's *historical novel *Troubles* (1970). The latter period has also produced an important body of work. 'The [Northern Irish] Troubles came in October 1968,' writes Seamus *Deane in *Reading in the Dark*, an enigmatic work of fiction about a family and a society scuppered by inherited blight which was published nearly 30 years later in 1996. The intervening years had thrown up a good deal of 'Troubles' writing, in prose as well as poetry, though little of the former to equal the extraordinary poetic efflorescence which coincided with the years of upheaval. 'Troubles' fiction tends to encompass the activities of IRA 'godfathers' and their adversaries, as in M. S. Power's 'Children of the North' trilogy, beginning in 1985 with *The Killing of Yesterday's Children*, or to consist of low-key accounts of life in fraught circumstances such as Mary Beckett's *Give Them Stones* (1986).

Silver's City (1981) by Maurice Leitch points up a ravaged Belfast while tackling Protestant terrorism, graft, and brutality; and Naomi May's *Troubles* (1976) has as one of its themes the defeat of liberalism among unionists during the 1960s, with the consequent cataclysm. John Morrow brings a blackly comic imagination to bear on the Troubles, particularly in *The Essex Factor* (1982), which has an unfortunate Englishman, an opposition backbencher on a fact-finding trip to Northern Ireland, trying and failing to make sense of the imbroglio. One of Anne Devlin's stories, 'Naming the Names', in *The Way-Paver* (1986), gets to the heart of republican disaffection in the mutilated streets of west Belfast. A 'Troubles' memoir which reads like a novel is Mary Costello's high-spirited *Titanic Town* (1992), which includes such details as the man who has to ring home every lunchtime to let his wife know he has not been shot, the school whose classrooms are a repository for explosives, and the jangle of bin-lids livening up the night. Violent lives, violent times; these conditions might suit the thriller-writer down to the ground, but no really high-grade thriller appeared before Brian *Moore's *Lies of Silence* (1990) about a hotel manager in the hands of gunmen. Eugene McEldowney's *A Kind of Homecoming* (1994) looked as though it might be the start of a 'police-procedural' series set in the north, but for its sequels McEldowney shifted the scene of action to Howth, near Dublin.

B. *MacLaverty's *Cal* (1983) dramatizes the ironies inherent in the situation through a doomed love affair. *Shadows on Our Skin* (1977), by J. *Johnston, deals with sectarian imperatives. Glenn Patterson's *Burning Your Own* (1988) goes back to 1969 and a Protestant housing estate in Belfast to show up sectarian posturing and rancour. Many other writers have been drawn to the topic, from the exuberant Robert McLiam Wilson (*Eureka Street*, 1996) to the downcast Deirdre Madden (*One by One in the Darkness*, 1996); but no one more compellingly than Benedict Kiely (*Proxopera*, 1977; *Nothing Happens in Cairncross*, 1985)—an ebullient author whose imagination is exercised by the degradation of republicanism. At some point along the line, as Kiely sees it, a break occurred between the integrity of the republican ideal and the enormities later sanctioned under this tag. Like W. *Trevor (who has treated the subject only peripherally—in, for example, the title story from *Beyond the Pale*, 1982), he is crucially aware of present-day adulterations, along with the deforming pressures of history. The great 'Troubles' novel may not yet have been written, but enough thought-provoking and illuminating work has appeared to constitute a distinctive genre.

trouvères, poets composing narrative, dramatic, satiric, comic, and especially lyric verse in the north of France during the late 12th and 13th cents. They were either professional entertainers (overlapping with *jongleurs*), *clercs*, or (when courtly society developed and the lyrics lost their energy) feudal lords composing fashionable verse. *Chrétien de Troyes was a *clerc*; other prominent trouvères were Conon de Béthune (d. *c*.1224), a Picard nobleman who composed crusading songs, Gâce Brulé (d. *c*.1220), *Blondel de Nesle (late 12th cent.), and Thibaut de Champagne, count of Champagne and king of Navarre. Their poetry was much influenced by that of the Provençal *troubadours (which however it never equalled) one of whom, Bernart de Ventadorn, came north to the court of *Eleanor of Aquitaine, who was herself the granddaughter of Guilhem IX of Aquitaine, the first known troubadour. The most successful poets are those around 1200, particularly Gâce Brulé; thereafter their poetry becomes feebler and less inspired.

Troy, Sergeant, a character in Hardy's *Far from the Madding Crowd*.

Troynovant, see BRUT.

True Law of Free Monarchies, The a political treatise attributed to James I, published 1598, and written to combat the Calvinist theory of government advocated by G. *Buchanan in his *De Jure Regni* (1579). It sets forth the doctrine of the divine right of kings and of the king's responsibility to God alone.

Truewit, the gallant and chief wit of Jonson's *Epicene*, a model for the wits of *Restoration comedy.

Trumpet Major, The, a novel by T. *Hardy, published

1880. The story is set during the Napoleonic wars, at a time in which there were busy preparations against the threat of invasion. It tells of the wooing of Anne Garland, whose mother is tenant of a part of Overcombe Mill, where the dragoons come down from the nearby camp to water their horses. One of these dragoons is John Loveday, the trumpet-major, the gentle, unassuming son of the miller. He loves Anne Garland, but has a rival in his brother Bob, a cheerful, light-hearted sailor. Her third suitor is the boorish yeoman Festus Derriman. In the course of events Anne meets King George III, on a military inspection, and later watches the departure of the *Victory* for Trafalgar. The story ends with the discomfiture of Festus and the success of Bob's courtship, while John marches off with his dragoons, to die on a battlefield in Spain.

Tryamour, see SIR LAUNFAL.

TSVETAYEVA, Marina Ivanovna (1892–1941), Russian poet and prose writer. Born in Moscow, the daughter of a professor of art and a gifted pianist, she spent much of her childhood in western Europe. She published her poetry of 1907–9 privately as *Evening Album* (1910) with great success. In 1912 she married Sergei Yakovlevich Efron, who became an officer in the tsarist army, and published a second book of poetry. She totally rejected the October Revolution and wrote a cycle of poems *The Encampment of the Whites* (Munich 1957; English trans. Robin Kemball, 1980), glorifying the White Army. At the end of the Civil War she got permission to join her husband (whom she had thought dead) in Prague, and in 1922 much of her poetry appeared in Moscow and Berlin, consolidating her reputation. In exile she engaged in an exalted correspondence with *Rilke and *Pasternak, two poets whom she greatly admired. In 1925 she moved to Paris, and in Mar. 1926 she spent two weeks in London. She became increasingly estranged from her fellow emigrants and, finding it difficult to publish, lived in great poverty, while continuing to write poetry and critical prose of lasting importance. Her husband became more and more pro-Soviet, and on the orders of the Soviet secret police he assassinated a Soviet official who had defected in the West, then fled to the USSR. Ostracized by the Emigration, Tsvetayeva decided, despite her better judgement, to return to Russia. She arrived in Moscow in June 1939 to be shunned by most of her former friends, and later that year her daughter Ariadna was arrested and her husband arrested and shot. During the war she was evacuated to the Tatar town of Yelabuga, near Kaza, where in despair she hanged herself. Much of her poetry was republished in the Soviet Union after 1961, and her passionate yet articulate and precise work, with its daring linguistic experimentation, brought her increasing recognition as a major poet. She has been much translated into English, notably in *Selected Poems* (trans. E. *Feinstein, 1971, 1981) and in *A Captive Spirit: Selected Prose* (trans. J. Marin King, 1980).

Tuatha Dé Danann, in Gaelic mythology, the gods, the 'Folk of the goddess Danu', the enemies of the *Fomors. They are represented as invaders of Ireland, subsequent to the Fomors and the *Fir Bolgs. They rout the Fomors at the battle of Moytura, and are ousted in their turn by the *Milesians. Conspicuous among the Tuatha Dé Danann are Lugh, the Gaelic sun-god, their leader; and *Lêr, the god of the sea.

Tucca, Captain Pantilius, the swaggering bully of Jonson's *Poetaster, who reappears in Dekker and Marston's *Satiromastix.

Tuck, Friar, see FRIAR TUCK.

TUCKER, Abraham (1705–74), a country gentleman and one of the first writers of the utilitarian school of philosophy. In his great work *The Light of Nature Pursued*, of which three volumes were published in 1768 and three after his death in 1778, he rejects the moral sense theory of *Shaftesbury and *Hutcheson and finds the criterion of moral conduct in general happiness, and the motive of the individual in his own happiness. The coincidence of these two is almost, but not quite, complete. There comes a point where virtue requires a self-sacrifice that prudential motives do not justify. Here Tucker finds the place for religion and its promise of a future life, where 'the accounts of all are to be set even', and the sacrifice of personal happiness required by virtue is to be made good.

Tucker's writings are diffuse and unmethodical, but marked by humour and quaint illustration and comment. His theories were systematized by *Paley.

Tuirenn, The Fate of the Sons of, one of the 'three sorrowful tales of Erin', a mythological tale in which the three sons of Tuirenn are punished for killing Cian, the father of the hero-god Lugh, by being required, by way of a fine, to achieve a number of quests, in the last of which they perish.

Tulkinghorn, a character in Dickens's *Bleak House.

Tulliver, Mr and Mrs, Tom and Maggie, the principal characters in G. Eliot's *The Mill on the Floss.

Tully, see CICERO.

Tunnyng of Elynour Rummyng, The, a poem by *Skelton, a vigorous description of contemporary low life. Elinour Rumming is an alewife who dwells beside Leatherhead and brews 'noppy ale' for 'travellars, to tynkers, | To sweters, to swynkers, | And all good ale drynkers', and the poem, coarse but full of humour and life, describes the mixed company who throng to drink it.

Tupman, Tracy, in Dickens's *Pickwick Papers, one of the members of the Corresponding Society of the Pickwick Club.

TUPPER, Martin Farquhar (1810–89), prolific writer of verse and prose, educated at Christ Church, Oxford. His *Proverbial Philosophy* (1838–76, 4 series), present-ing maxims and reflections couched in vaguely rhythmical form, became the favourite of millions who knew nothing about poetry, and remained a best-seller in Britain and America for more than a generation. His two novels, *The Crock of Gold* (1844) and *Stephan Langton* (1858), and his numerous other published works are now forgotten.

TURBERVILLE, George (c.1544–c.1597), scholar of Winchester and fellow of New College, Oxford. He published *Epitaphes, Epigrams, Songs and Sonets* (1567); and various translations from *Ovid and *Mantuan, including Mantuan's eclogues (1567); and an account of the state of 'Muscovia', later repr. by *Hakluyt. *The Booke of Faulconrie* (1575) is usually found bound with *The Noble Art of Venerie or Hunting* (1575, repr. 1908) which is actually an adaptation by *Gascoigne of a contemporary French work. His poems reflect the use of Italian models and show the influence of *Wyatt and *Surrey.

TURGENEV, Ivan Sergeyevich (1818–83), Russian novelist and playwright. He was born in Orel, in central Russia, and studied at Moscow and St Petersburg universities. He published some poetry in 1838 and studied in Berlin, 1838–41. On returning to Russia he served briefly in the civil service, but from 1845 he devoted himself to literature. He also fell in love with the singer Pauline Garcia Viardot, and partly for this reason was to live much of his life abroad, mainly in Baden-Baden and Paris, where he died. His first important prose work was *A Hunter's Notes* (1847–51), the limpid prose of which, in such masterpieces as 'Bezhin Meadow' and 'The Living Relic', is one of his greatest achievements. This was followed by a series of novels in which individual lives are examined to illuminate the social, political, and philosophical issues of the day: *Rudin* (1856), *A Nest of Gentlefolk* (1859), *On the Eve* (1860), *Fathers and Sons* (1862), in which, in Bazarov, he created a *nihilist hero, *Smoke* (1867), and *Virgin Soil* (1877). His greatest short stories are 'Asya' (1858), 'First Love' (1860), and 'Torrents of Spring' (1870). His best play is *A Month in the Country* (first version 1850; perf. 1872), a psychological comedy of frustrated love and inertia which anticipated the drama of *Chekhov. Turgenev was the first major Russian writer to find success in the rest of Europe. This resulted partly from his living largely in western Europe, where he was personally acquainted with *Flaubert, G. *Sand, *Mérimée, and others, but also from the fact that he was closer in both sensibility and literary practice to western Europe than his contemporaries *Tolstoy and *Dostoevsky. Turgenev first visited England in 1847 and returned many times up to 1881: *Fathers and Sons* was planned on the Isle of Wight. He received an honorary DCL at Oxford in 1879 for 'advancing the liberation of the Russian serfs'. He was extremely widely read in English literature; of his English contemporaries, he most valued *Dickens and G. *Eliot, both of whom he knew. He was acquainted with *Thackeray, *Trollope, *Carlyle, R. *Browning, *Tennyson, the *Rossettis, and *Swinburne, and in correspondence with *Gissing. He was one of the earliest admirers of H. *James, who first met him in Paris in 1875 and on whom he had a substantial influence. Perhaps the greatest English debt to him is owed by G. A. *Moore, whose mature career was given shape by the discovery of Turgenev's artistry, and who, in *The Lake* (1905), came as close as anyone to writing a Turgenev novel in English. *A Hunter's Notes* was translated into English by J. D. Meiklejohn in 1855, and by 1890 most of Turgenev's major work had appeared in English. The most complete early translation is C. *Garnett's *Turgenev—The Novels and Tales* (1894–9), the edition through which he exerted his influence on such writers as *Galsworthy, *Conrad, and V. *Woolf.

TURGOT, Anne-Robert-Jacques, see PHYSIOCRATS.

Turkish Spy, Letters Written by a, eight volumes, published ?1687–94. The first is a translation of 'L'Espion du Grand Seigneur' by Giovanni Paolo Marana, a Genoese residing in Paris, published in French in 1684–6, partly itself a translation from an Italian version. The work inaugurated a new genre in European literature, the pseudo-foreign letter, of which the *Lettres persanes* of *Montesquieu is the chief example.

A continuation to the *Letters*, probably by *Defoe, was published in England in 1718.

TURNBULL, George (1698–1748), educated at Edinburgh, regent at Marischal College, Aberdeen, 1721–7, and teacher of T. *Reid. He was an early member of the *Rankenian Club, and his published lectures (*Principles of Moral and Christian Philosophy*, 2 vols, 1740) and surviving correspondence show him as an ardent follower of *Shaftesbury in his advocacy of civic virtue and educational reform, and the prominence he attached to the sense of beauty. He sought to turn natural science to the service of religion, and to construct a moral science based on experimental laws of human nature, in which the association of ideas had a central role. His *Treatise on Ancient Painting* (1739), which figures in a caricature by *Hogarth, discusses the place of the fine arts in education. Turnbull stresses the links between the sense of beauty and the moral sense, and between beauty and truth, and sees a close parallel between the didactic moral function of good painting and good poetry.

TURNER, J(oseph) M(allord) W(illiam) (1775–1851), English landscape painter, whose mature works convey a Romantic vision of the violence of the elements. He travelled in England and in France, Switzerland, and Italy, and his subjects and styles are astonishingly varied. He moved from conventional topographical watercolours of *picturesque subjects to historical landscapes which vie with the grandeur of *Poussin and *Claude; in his late, increasingly violent, and

almost abstract works (*Snowstorm at Sea*, 1842; *Rain, Steam and Speed*, 1844, both London, National Gallery) forms are dissolved in the sweep of light and brilliant colour patterning the surface of the canvas. Turner was devoted to the 18th-cent. doctrine of *Ut Pictura Poesis* ('as is painting, so is poetry': *Horace, *Ars Poetica*, 361) and was often inspired by contemporary poetry. He was committed to the values of the *Royal Academy, where he was appointed professor of perspective in 1807 and lectured in 1811, and sought to ennoble the genre of landscape painting by suggesting that it could attain the imaginative power and complexity of poetry. From 1798 many of his pictures exhibited at the Royal Academy were accompanied by verses printed in the catalogue; from 1800 he added lines composed by himself. His quotations are frequently from James *Thomson (1700–48), who influenced his literary style, and in 1811 his picture *Thomson's Aeolian Harp* was accompanied by 32 lines honouring the poet. *Snowstorm; Hannibal and His Army Crossing the Alps* (1812, London, Tate Gallery) was exhibited with the first quotation taken from his gloomy 'M. S. P. Fallacies of Hope'. There is no trace of this projected epic poem beyond excerpts in Royal Academy catalogues; it was influenced by Akenside's *Pleasures of Imagination* and Campbell's *Pleasures of Hope*. Between 1806 and 1815 Turner frequently wrote poems beside the drawings in his sketchbooks; they have been transcribed by Jack Lindsay in *The Sunset Ship* (1968). In the 1830s Turner did many designs for book illustrations, amongst them charming vignettes for *Rogers's *Italy* (1830) and *Poems* (1834). He also illustrated works by *Milton, *Byron, Sir W. *Scott, and T. *Campbell. Turner endured much ridicule, including *Hazlitt's famous description of his work as 'pictures of nothing and very like', but *Ruskin became his passionate admirer and the first volume of *Modern Painters* (1843) was written in his defence.

TURNER, Sharon (1768–1847), a lawyer who became an enthusiastic student of Icelandic and Anglo-Saxon literature, and found much new material, especially among the unexplored Cottonian manuscripts (see COTTON, R. B.). His interest was, however, more historical than literary. Between 1799 and 1805 he published his *History of the Anglo-Saxons from the Earliest Period to the Norman Conquests*, which was greatly admired, by H. *Hallam, *Southey, and Sir W. *Scott, among others. He continued his histories up to the death of Queen Elizabeth I. His insistence on the use of original first sources was important to the future writing of history. He has a place in literary history as the legal adviser to J. *Murray and was much embroiled in the controversies surrounding the publication of Byron's *Don Juan*. He was also legal adviser to the *Quarterly Review*.

TURNER, Walter James Redfern (1884–1946), born in Melbourne. He came to London in 1907. He was music critic of the *New Statesman*, drama critic of the

London Mercury, and literary editor of the *Spectator*. He wrote novels, including *The Aesthetes* (1927, with a portrait of Ottoline *Morrell), *Blow for Balloons* (1935), and *The Duchess of Popocatapetl* (1939); an Expressionist drama, *The Man Who Ate the Popomack* (1922); and several volumes of verse. He was associated with *Yeats's enthusiasm for the chanting and singing of poetry, and his work is generously represented by Yeats in his *Oxford Book of Modern Verse* (1936). Turner's well-known poem 'Romance', with the lines 'Chimborazo, Cotopaxi, | They have stolen my heart away!' | was published in his first collection, *The Hunter and Other Poems* (1916). With Sheila Shannon he edited a book, *Exmoor Village* (1947), based on Mass-Observation (see MADGE) reports.

Turn of the Screw, The, a *ghost story by H. *James, published 1898.

The narrator is a young governess, sent off to a country house, Bly, to take charge of two orphaned children. She has been engaged by their uncle, a handsome man to whom she feels attracted, on the understanding that she takes all responsibility for the children and the entire household. She finds a pleasant house and a comfortable housekeeper, Mrs Grose, while the children, Miles and Flora, are unusually beautiful and charming. But she soon begins to feel the presence of intense evil, and sees the figure of the ex-valet Peter Quint and that of her own predecessor Miss Jessel. In fact they are both dead, and she learns of the guilty liaison that existed between them. For the young woman these apparitions emanate a fearful wickedness and she becomes convinced that, despite their denials, Miles and Flora are communicating with them. These terrible figures have returned to claim the children, to draw them into their web of sin and evil, and the governess is determined to exorcize them. After a dramatic scene by the pond, where the narrator believes that Flora is meeting Miss Jessel, the little girl is taken off to safety by the housekeeper, and Miles, left with the governess, dies in her arms as she battles for his soul with the apparition of Peter Quint. It is left to the reader to decide whether these ghosts and their designs exist for anyone else in the story, or whether they are simply the hysterical fantasies of the young governess. James himself described this story as 'a trap for the unwary'. B. *Britten wrote a chamber opera (1954) based on this tale.

Turveydrop, father and son, characters in Dickens's *Bleak House*.

TUSSER, Thomas (?1524–80), agricultural writer and poet, educated at St Paul's School, Eton, King's College and Trinity Hall, Cambridge. He farmed at Cattawade, Suffolk, and introduced the culture of barley to England. He published his *Hundreth Good Pointes of Husbandrie* in 1557 (amplified in later editions) in verse of quaint and pointed expression, many proverbs being traceable to this work. It is a collection of instructions on farming, gardening, and housekeeping, together with humorous and wise maxims on conduct in general.

TWAIN, Mark, pseudonym of Samuel Langhorne Clemens (1835–1910), American writer, born in Florida, Missouri, of a Virginian family, and brought up in Hannibal, Missouri. After his father's death in 1847 he was apprenticed to a printer, and wrote for his brother's newspaper; from 1857 to 1861 he was a pilot on the Mississippi, and from 1862 worked as a newspaper correspondent for various Nevada and Californian magazines, adopting the pseudonym 'Mark Twain', familiar to him as the leadsman's call on the Mississippi. Under this name he published his first successful story, 'Jim Smiley and his Jumping Frog', in 1865 in the New York *Saturday Press*. This comic version of an old folk tale became the title story of *The Celebrated Jumping Frog of Calaveras County, and Other Sketches* (1867), which established him as a leading humorist, a reputation consolidated by *The Innocents Abroad* (1869), an account of a voyage through the Mediterranean. *Roughing It* (1872), an account of his adventures as miner and journalist in Nevada, appeared in the year of his first English lecture tour; England provided the background for his democratic historical fantasy *The Prince and the Pauper* (1882), in which Edward VI as a boy changes places with Tom Canty, a beggar, and for *A Connecticut Yankee in King Arthur's Court* (1889), a disturbing and not wholly amiable fantasy that satirizes both past and present. Meanwhile appeared his most famous works, both deeply rooted in his own childhood, *The Adventures of *Tom Sawyer* (1876) and its sequel *The Adventures of *Huckleberry Finn* (1884), which paint an unforgettable picture of Mississippi frontier life, and combine picaresque adventure with challenging satire and great technical innovative power. *Life on the Mississippi* (1883), an autobiographical account of his life as a river pilot, contains a notable attack on the influence of Sir W. *Scott, whose romanticism ('silliness and emptinesses, sham grandeurs, sham gauds and sham chivalries') did 'measureless harm' to progressive ideas and progressive works, creating, Twain alleges, the myth of the southern gentleman that did much to precipitate the Civil War.

In the last two decades of his life Clemens was beset with financial anxieties and dissipated time and money on chimerical business enterprises, trying to recoup by lecture tours (in 1895–6 he toured New Zealand, Australia, India, and South Africa) and by writing potboilers; his pessimism and bitterness were increased by the death of his wife in 1904, of two of his three daughters, and by other family troubles. In these last years, however, he wrote some memorable if sombre works, including *The Man that Corrupted Hadleyburg* (1900), a fable about the venality of a smug small town, and *The Mysterious Stranger* (published posthumously in 1916, in a much-edited version), an extraordinary tale set in 16th-cent. Austria, in which Satan appears as a morally indifferent but life-enhancing visitor, to reveal the hypocrisies and stupidities of the village of Eseldorf. He dictated his autobiography during his last years to his secretary A. B. Paine, and various versions of it have appeared.

Twelfth Night, or *What You Will*, a comedy by *Shakespeare probably written 1601. John *Manningham saw a performance of it in the Middle Temple in February 1602; it was first printed in the *Folio of 1623. Shakespeare's immediate source for the main plot was 'The History of Apolonius and Silla' in B. *Rich's *Riche His Farewell to Militarie Profession* (1581). This is derived from Belleforest's version, which by way of *Bandello can be traced back to a Sienese comedy *Gl'ingannati* (*The Deceived*), written and performed 1531.

Sebastian and Viola, twin brother and sister and closely resembling one another, are separated in a shipwreck off the coast of Illyria. Viola, brought to shore in a boat, disguises herself as a youth, Cesario, and takes service as page with Duke Orsino, who is in love with the lady Olivia. She rejects the duke's suit and will not meet him. Orsino makes a confidant of Cesario and sends her to press his suit on Olivia, much to the distress of Cesario, who has fallen in love with Orsino. Olivia in turn falls in love with Cesario. Sebastian and Antonio, captain of the ship that had rescued Sebastian, now arrive in Illyria. Cesario, challenged to a duel by Sir Andrew Aguecheek, a rejected suitor of Olivia, is rescued from her predicament by Antonio, who takes her for Sebastian. Antonio, being arrested at that moment for an old offence, claims from Cesario a purse that he had entrusted to Sebastian, is denied it, and hauled off to prison. Olivia coming upon the true Sebastian, takes him for Cesario, invites him to her house, and marries him out of hand. Orsino comes to visit Olivia. Antonio, brought before him, claims Cesario as the youth he has rescued from the sea; while Olivia claims Cesario as her husband. The duke, deeply wounded, is bidding farewell to Olivia and the 'dissembling cub' Cesario, when the arrival of the true Sebastian clears up the confusion. The duke, having lost Olivia, and becoming conscious of the love that Viola has betrayed, turns his affection to her, and they are married.

Much of the play's comedy comes from the sub-plot dealing with the members of Olivia's household: Sir Toby Belch, her uncle, Sir Andrew Aguecheek, his friend, Malvolio, her pompous steward, Maria, her waiting-gentlewoman, and her clown Feste. Exasperated by Malvolio's officiousness, the other members of the household make him believe that Olivia is in love with him and that he must return her affection. In courting her he behaves so outrageously that he is imprisoned as a madman. Olivia has him released and the joke against him is explained, but he is not amused

by it, threatening, 'I'll be reveng'd on the whole pack of you.'

The play's gentle melancholy and lyrical atmosphere is captured in two of Feste's beautiful songs 'Come away, come away, death' and 'When that I was and a little tiny boy, | With hey, ho, the wind and the rain'.

Twentieth Century, see NINETEENTH CENTURY.

Twitcher, Jemmy, in Gay's *The Beggar's Opera*, one of Captain Macheath's associates, who betrays him. The nickname was given to the fourth earl of Sandwich (1718–92), who had been associated with *Wilkes in the *Medmenham 'brotherhood' and yet, when Wilkes's papers were seized, was active in collecting evidence against him. The allusion is to a line in the play: 'That Jemmy Twitcher should peach me, I own surprised me.'

Two Cultures and the Scientific Revolution, The. 'The Two Cultures' is a phrase coined by C. P. *Snow in the Rede Lecture delivered at Cambridge in 1959 and published the same year. In it, he contrasts the culture of 'literary intellectuals' and that of 'scientists, and as the most representative, physical scientists'. He describes the increasing gulf between them, claiming that 30 years earlier the two sides could at least manage 'a frozen smile' but are now incapable of communication. His analysis of the educational attitudes that produced this situation and his recommendations for change were strongly attacked by *Leavis in his Richmond Lecture *Two Cultures? The Significance of C. P. Snow* (1962). (See also THOMSON, SIR W., and second law of thermodynamics.)

'Two Drovers, The', a short story by Sir W. *Scott, one of the *Chronicles of the Canongate*, published 1827. One of the most perfect of Scott's shorter tales, the tragedy is constructed round an opposition of racial types, Highland and Lowland. A trivial quarrel occurs between Robin Oig M'Combich and Harry Wakefield, long-standing companions on the drove-roads. Wakefield wants to settle it with his fists, English fashion; Robin Oig rejects this as beneath the dignity of a Highland gentleman. He is knocked down by his friend and in revenge kills him with his dirk. 'I give a life for the life I took,' he says, when he is arrested, 'and what can I do more?'

Two Foscari, The, a poetic drama by *Byron, published 1821.

Jacopo, son of the doge of Venice, Francesco Foscari, has twice been exiled, once for venality and once for complicity in murder. He has been brought back from exile on a charge of treasonable correspondence, and the play opens with his examination on the rack. The doge, his father, broken-hearted at his disgrace, signs the sentence for his third perpetual exile. But Jacopo's love for Venice is so intense that he dies with horror at the prospect of yet another banishment. The Council of Ten meanwhile decide to require the abdication of the old doge. He at once leaves the palace, and as he descends the steps he falls and dies.

Two Gentlemen of Verona, The, a comedy by *Shakespeare, probably written about 1592–3. Some scholars, however, regard it as Shakespeare's first play, or at least his earliest comedy. There is no record of a performance before the Restoration. It was first printed in the *Folio of 1623, where it is the second play in the section of comedies. The play's main source is the story of Felix and Felismena in the *Diana* of *Montemayor.

The two gentlemen of Verona are the friends Valentine and Proteus. Proteus is in love with Julia, who returns his affection. Valentine leaves Verona for Milan 'to see the wonders of the world abroad', and there falls in love with Silvia, the duke of Milan's daughter. Presently Proteus is sent also on his travels, and exchanges vows of constancy with Julia before starting. But arriving at Milan, Proteus is at once captivated by Silvia, and, betraying both his friend and his former love, reveals to the duke the intention of Valentine to carry off Silvia. Valentine is banished and becomes a captain of outlaws and Proteus continues his courting of Silvia. Meanwhile Julia, pining for Proteus, comes to Milan dressed as a boy and takes service as Proteus' page, unrecognized by him. Silvia, to escape marriage with Thurio, her father's choice, leaves Milan to rejoin Valentine, is captured by outlaws and rescued from them by Proteus. Proteus is violently pressing his suit on Silvia when Valentine comes on the scene. Proteus is struck with remorse, and his contrition is such that Valentine is impelled to surrender Silvia to him, to the dismay of Proteus' page, the disguised Julia. She swoons, and is then recognized by Proteus, and the discovery of her constancy wins back his love. The duke and Thurio arrive. Thurio shows cowardice in face of Valentine's determined attitude, and the duke, approving Valentine's spirit, accords him Silvia and pardons the outlaws. Launce, the clownish servant of Proteus, and his dog Crab, 'the sourest-natured dog that lives', provide much humour.

Two Nations, The, see Disraeli's *Sybil.

Two Noble Kinsmen, The, a tragi-comedy attributed to J. *Fletcher and Shakespeare, published 1634. In spite of its absence from the First *Folio (1623), recent studies of the play suggest that it is probably a genuine work of collaboration between Fletcher and Shakespeare, taking more or less equal shares, written in about 1613.

The play is closely based on Chaucer's 'Knight's Tale' (see CANTERBURY TALES, 1), which Shakespeare had drawn on before in *A Midsummer Night's Dream*. The main addition to the plot is the jailer's daughter who falls in love with Palamon, runs melancholy mad, and is cured by a lower-class wooer pretending to be Palamon. The overall tone is considerably lighter than in Chaucer's poem, the play being diversified with

songs and lyrical passages such as Emilia's reminiscence of her friendship with Flavina (I. iii. 55–82); there is also a country festival with morris dancing, presided over by a pedantic schoolmaster (III. v). Theseus is a much less weighty and ominous figure than in Chaucer, and Arcite's death is rapid and dignified.

The play is not often performed.

Two on a Tower, a novel by T. *Hardy, published 1882.

Lady Constantine, whose disagreeable husband is away, falls in love with Swithin St Cleeve, an astronomer, younger than herself, who works at the top of a tower, where many of the scenes of the novel occur. Hearing her husband has died, Lady Constantine secretly marries Swithin, but later learns, first, that by so doing she had deprived him of a legacy; and, second, that her husband, though now dead, was alive when she married Swithin. Thus her marriage to Swithin is void, and she nobly insists on his leaving her, to take up employment abroad. She then finds she is pregnant by him; under pressure from her brother she accepts an offer of marriage from Bishop Helmsdale and a son is born. Swithin returns after the bishop's death, and is appalled that she is no longer a young woman. Eventually he offers to marry her, but the joy is too great and she falls dead in his arms.

Hardy's object was 'to set the history of two infinitesimal lives against the tremendous background of the stellar universe' and to show 'that of these contrasting magnitudes the smaller might be the greater to them as men'. But, as he acknowledged, the effect of the novel falls far short of his ambitions.

Two Years Ago, a novel by C. *Kingsley, published 1857.

In the last of his reforming novels, Kingsley describes the descent of cholera upon the little West Country fishing village of Aberalva, attacks the poor sanitary conditions and public apathy that allowed it to take hold, and praises the gallantry and dedication of various of the inhabitants. These include the much-travelled doctor, Tom Thurnall, rescued from shipwreck in the second chapter by the noble Nonconformist schoolmistress Grace Harvey, who converts him to Christianity and whose love he wins by the end of the novel, and Frank Headley, the High Church curate, also redeemed by the love of a good woman, who finally wins the confidence of his Dissenting flock. A secondary plot involves a denunciation of slavery in the United States, influenced by H. B. *Stowe's *Uncle Tom's Cabin*, and there are also many references to the Crimean War, which brings about a crisis in Thurnall's spiritual life. Contrasted with the practical Thurnall is Elsley Vavasour (once an apothecary's assistant under his real name, John Briggs), an opium-taking poet evidently of the *Spasmodic school, who is condemned for preferring Art to Action, and who demonstrates the dangers of unleashed emotion by running wild on Snowdon in the aptly titled chapter XXI, 'Nature's Melodrama', before a deathbed scene in which he desires that his poetry be burned and his children be prevented ever from writing verse. This portrait caused a temporary rift with *Tennyson, who wrongly took it to be aimed at him.

Tybalt, a Capulet in Shakespeare's *Romeo and Juliet* who is killed by Romeo. For the allusion in the play to cats in connection with his name, see TIBERT.

TYLER, Anne (1941–   ), American novelist, who grew up in North Carolina but has spent most of her adult life in Baltimore, Maryland. Her novels are people-centred, using anecdote and badinage, and she was early inspired by E. *Welty. Her presentations of a stratified Baltimore and of contemporary cultural shifts make her the first urban southern novelist. Her fiction reveals the necessity for individuals, however isolated, to receive recognition, however tenuous, if society is to be healthily pluralist. *A Slipping Down Life* (1970), a tender portrait of a fat young rock-music groupie, is in Tyler's view her first successful novel. *Searching for Caleb* (1976) has the generous canvas now associated with her. Outstanding novels, each offsetting a character in crisis against the demands of others, include *Dinner at the Homesick Restaurant* (1982), *The Accidental Tourist* (1985), *Breathing Lessons* (1989), *Saint Maybe* (1991, movingly charting guilt and awkward expiation), *Ladder of Years* (1995), and *Patchwork Planet* (1998), a fine example of Tyler's empathy with the late 20th-cent. male.

TYLER, Wat (d. 1381), the leader of the Peasants' Revolt of 1381, who with *Jack Straw led the peasants of Kent and Essex to London. He was killed by William Walworth, the lord mayor of London, in the course of a discussion with Richard II at Smithfield. He is the subject of a drama by *Southey.

TYNAN, Katharine (1859–1931), poet and novelist, born in Dublin, now remembered principally for her association with the *Irish Revival and as a friend of *Yeats. Her first volume of verse, *Louise de La Vallière and Other Poems* (1885), was followed by many volumes of poems, fiction, and autobiography; Yeats's *Letters to Katharine Tynan*, ed. R. McHugh, was published in 1953.

TYNAN, Kenneth Peacock (1927–80), dramatic critic, educated at Magdalen College, Oxford. He wrote for various papers, most influentially for the *Observer (1954–63), and championed the plays of *Osborne, *Wesker, S. *Delaney, N. F. *Simpson, *Beckett, and others, playing a leading role in the shift of taste from drawing-room comedy and the poetic drama of T. S. *Eliot and C. *Fry (which he disliked) to naturalism and 'working class drama'. (See KITCHEN SINK DRAMA.) He also vigorously attacked theatre censorship and the lord chamberlain ('The Royal Smut-Hound', 1965). His various collections of reviews and essays include *Curtains* (1967), *The Sound of Two Hands Clapping* (1975), and *A View of the English Stage* (1976), which

pay tribute to the role of the *English Stage Company in the development of British theatre. Tynan was also a moving force in the creation of the *National Theatre, and its literary manager from 1963 to 1969. There is a life by his widow Kathleen Tynan (1987) who also edited his *Letters* (1994). See also THEATRE CRITICISM.

TYNDALE, William (c.1495–1536), the translator of the *Bible. He studied at Oxford and Cambridge. About 1522 he formed the project of translating the Scriptures into the vernacular, but finding difficulties in England went to Hamburg for the purpose. He visited *Luther at Wittenberg, and commenced printing his translation of the New Testament at Cologne in 1525. He completed the work at Worms and introduced copies into England, which were denounced by the bishops and destroyed. He eventually settled at Antwerp, became a Zwinglian and an active pamphleteer, and engaged in controversy with Sir T. *More, writing *An Answere unto Sir Thomas Mores Dialoge* in 1531. He was betrayed to imperial officers and arrested for heresy, imprisoned at Vilvorde in 1535, and strangled and burnt at the stake there, in spite of Cromwell's intercession. Tyndale was one of the most remarkable of the *Reformation leaders; his original writings show sound scholarship, but his translation of the Bible—consisting of the New Testament (1525), Pentateuch (1530), and Jonah (?1531)—the accuracy of which has been endorsed by the translators of the Authorized Version, is his surest title to fame. See David Daniell, *William Tyndale: A Biography* (1994).

TYNDALL, John (1820–93), professor of natural history at the Royal Institution in 1853, and later superintendent there, who did much in his writings and lectures to popularize science. He had many friends in literary and scientific circles, including *Tennyson, C. *Darwin, H. *Spencer, and L. *Stephen. His famous address to the British Association in Belfast in 1874, on the relation between science and theology, gave rise to acute controversy.

Typee or *A Peep at Polynesian Life*, a novel by H. *Melville, published 1846, first in Britain by John *Murray, under the non-fiction title *Narrative of a Four Months Residence among the Natives of a Valley of the Marquesas Islands*, and shortly after by Harpers in New York, who censored some 'sea freedoms' and satirical attacks on imperialism and missionaries. It was Melville's first book, and his most popular during his lifetime.

Like Melville himself, *Typee*'s hero Tommo and his friend Toby jump ship in the Marquesas, but the *Defoe-like factual account masks a symbolic tale of the ambiguity of innocence. Hoping to find the Johnsonian 'Happy Valley' (see RASSELAS) of the peaceful Happars, Toby and the injured Tommo stumble instead upon the cannibalistic Typees, who live in an apparent Eden of sensuous plenty yet lack respect for life.

'Typhoon', a story by J. *Conrad, published 1903.

The unimaginative and imperturbable Captain MacWhirr pilots his steamer *Nan-Shan* through a typhoon of such violence that even he is moved to doubt the possibility of survival. Nevertheless, to avoid trouble between decks, he sends his appalled chief mate Mr Jukes down to confiscate the money of his 200 Chinese passengers. Later, the money redistributed and the ship safe in Fuchau harbour, Jukes is forced to conclude that MacWhirr 'got out of it very well for a stupid man'.

Tyranipocrit Discovered, one of the best written of the radical pamphlets of the Commonwealth, published anonymously in Rotterdam, 1649. The writer attacks the 'White Devil' of hypocrisy, which cloaks tyrannical power, idleness, and greed with Christian piety, finding it yet more pernicious than the 'Black Devil' of undisguised oppression, or the petty crimes of the poor. It is an eloquent plea for equality: 'O to give unto everyone with discretion, as near as may be, an equal portion of earthly goods, to maintain him in this life, that is the greatest actuall justice that man can doe.' Extracts are printed in Orwell and Reynolds, *British Pamphleteers* (1948).

Tyrannick Love, or *The Royal Martyr*, a heroic play by *Dryden, produced and published 1669.

Based on the legend of the martyrdom of St Catherine by the Roman emperor Maximin, it contains some of Dryden's most extravagant heroic verse. Possibly deliberately comic at times, it is also seriously concerned with contrasting Lucretian and Christian conceptions of God. It was ridiculed in *The Rehearsal*, and by *Shadwell. Dryden himself satirizes its excesses in *Mac Flecknoe*.

TYRWHITT, Thomas (1730–86), scholar and editor. He had an early career in politics (clerk of the House of Commons, 1762–8), but is remembered partly for his edition and exposure of *Chatterton's Rowley poems; he published them in 1777, then in an appendix in 1778 stated authoritatively that they were modern, not ancient, a view he elaborated in his *Vindication* (1782). His *Observations and Conjectures upon Some Passages of Shakespeare* (1765, dated 1766) insisted on the importance of careful collation, and criticized Dr *Johnson's edition for its lack of attention to the early texts. His greatest contribution was his edition of Chaucer's *Canterbury Tales* (4 vols, 1775, vol. v with Glossary, 1778), which expounded *Chaucer's versification and helped to establish the canon.

TYUTCHEV, Fedor Ivanovich (1803–73), Russian lyric poet, who served as a diplomat in Munich (1822–37), where he was a friend of *Heine. From 1858 until his death he worked as president of the committee of foreign censorship. His first poetry appeared in 1819 and throughout the 1820s and 1830s he was widely published; he was praised by *Nekrasov and *Turgenev in the 1850s, and his first volume of poetry appeared in 1854. His poetry is notable for the delicacy and profundity of its analysis of often paradoxical or overtly tragic human feeling, and for its analysis of man's position in nature. Tyutchev's reputation waned in the period 1860–90, only to rise again in the early 20th cent. when the Russian symbolists, including *Blok, acknowledged him as a significant influence.

U

Ubi sunt, derived from the opening words of a type of Medieval Latin poem ('Where are they?'), taken up in Old English poems such as *Beowulf and particularly *The Wanderer (ll. 92–3) and in many Middle English lyrics (especially the one beginning 'Where beth they, beforen us weren', c.1300). Many later medieval French poems use the theme, most famously *Villon's 'Ballade des dames du temps jadis' with its refrain, 'Mais où sont les neiges d'antan?'—'Where are the snows of yesteryear?'

UDALL, or **UVEDALE, Nicholas** (c.1505–56), dramatist and scholar, educated at Winchester and Corpus Christi College, Oxford, successively headmaster of Eton and Westminster. He was author of *Ralph Roister Doister, the earliest known English comedy. He translated selections from *Terence and other works, and wrote Latin plays on sacred subjects. *Tusser (*Five Hundreth Points) complains of having been severely flogged by Udall 'For fault but small, or none at all'. Udall got into grave trouble at Eton and was sent to the Marshalsea by the Privy Council. He figures in F. M. *Ford's novel *The Fifth Queen* (1906).

Udolpho, *The Mysteries of*, see MYSTERIES OF UDOLPHO, THE.

UGOLINO DELLA GHERARDESCA (d. 1289), an Italian Guelf leader who twice made himself master of Pisa by treachery, in 1284 and 1288, by forming an intrigue with the Ghibelline leader Ruggieri degli Ubaldini. But Ruggieri betrayed him in turn, and he was locked with his two sons and two of his grandsons in a tower and starved to death. The story is told by Ugolino himself in *Dante's *Inferno*, xxxiii, and it is told among the tragedies of Fortune in Chaucer's 'The Monk's Tale' (see CANTERBURY TALES, 19; VII. 2407–62); though he knew the source was Dante, Chaucer tells of three sons and says the youngest was 5 years old, although three of the four in Dante were grown men. The story was used again as the basis for a poem in *Heaney's *Field Work* (1981).

ULFILAS, or **WULFILA** (AD 311–81), a Christian of Cappadocian origin, was consecrated bishop of the Arian Visigoths in 341, and subsequently migrated with them to the neighbourhood of Nicopolis in Moesia. He translated the Bible into Gothic from the Greek, inventing, it is said, an alphabet for the purpose. Fragments of this translation, chiefly of the NT, survive (e.g. the Codex Argenteus at Uppsala), and are of great value to the philological science of the Germanic languages.

Ulysses, a Greek commander in Shakespeare's *Troilus and Cressida. His speech on order and 'degree' occurs in I. iii.

'Ulysses', a poem by *Tennyson, composed 1833, published 1842. In a dramatic monologue Ulysses describes how he plans to set forth again from Ithaca after his safe return from his wanderings after the Trojan War, 'to sail beyond the sunset'. The episode is based not on *Homer but on *Dante (*Inferno*, xxvi), which Tennyson probably read in the translation of *Cary, and expresses the poet's sense of 'the need of going forward and braving the struggle of life' after the death of A. H. *Hallam.

Ulysses, a novel by J. *Joyce, serialized in the *Little Review from 1918. The editors of the *Little Review* were prosecuted and found guilty of publishing obscenity, which led to the novel's publication in a non-English-speaking country: it was published in Paris by Sylvia *Beach in 1922. Copies of the first English edition were burned by the New York post office authorities, and the Folkestone customs authorities seized the second edition in 1923. Various later editions appeared abroad, and, after the United States District Court found the book not obscene in 1933, the first English edition appeared in 1936, and the first unlimited edition in America and England in 1937.

The novel deals with the events of one day in Dublin, 16 June 1904 (the anniversary of Joyce's first walk with Nora Barnacle, who became his wife), now known as 'Bloomsday'.

The principal characters are Stephen Dedalus (the hero of Joyce's earlier, largely autobiographical, *A Portrait of the Artist as a Young Man); Leopold Bloom, a Jewish advertisement canvasser; and his wife Molly. The plot follows the wanderings of Stephen and Bloom through Dublin, and their eventual meeting. The last chapter is a monologue by Molly Bloom. The various chapters roughly correspond to the episodes of Homer's *Odyssey, Stephen representing Telemachus, Bloom Odysseus, and Molly Penelope. In the course of the story a public bath, a funeral, a newspaper office, a library, public houses, a maternity hospital, and a brothel are visited. A number of other Dublin scenes and characters are introduced. The style is highly allusive and employs a variety of techniques, especially those of *interior monologue and of *parody, and ranges from extreme realism to fantasy.

Joyce described the theme of the *Odyssey* to one of his students in 1917 as 'the most beautiful, all-embracing theme . . . greater, more human, than that of *Hamlet*, Don Quixote, Dante, *Faust*', and refers to

Ulysses himself as pacifist, father, wanderer, musician, and artist: 'I am almost afraid to treat such a theme; it's overwhelming.'

Umbriel, 'a dusky melancholy sprite' in Pope's *The Rape of the Lock.*

Una, in Bk I of Spenser's *Faerie Queene*, typifies singleness of the true religion. She is separated from the *Redcrosse Knight of Holiness (the Anglican Church) by the wiles of *Archimago, but meets and is protected by a lion, until the latter is killed by *Sansloy, who carries Una off to a forest. She is rescued by fauns and satyrs, and is finally united to the Redcrosse Knight.

UNAMUNO Y JUGO, Miguel de (1864–1936), Spanish writer and philosopher, born into a Basque family at Bilbao, and educated at the University of Madrid. He became professor of Greek at the University of Salamanca in 1892 and later became rector. A fierce and often eccentric critic of Spanish intellectual, social, and political life, who was at one point exiled for his views, he nevertheless opposed thoughtless 'Euro-peanization'. He wrote plays, poems, novels, travel books, and short stories, but is perhaps best known in English-speaking countries for his philosophical essays, which show the influence of *Kierkegaard, W. *James, and *Bergson. *La vida de Don Quijote y Sancho* (1905) is, in his own words, 'a free and personal exegesis' which perceives *Don Quixote as the em-bodiment of the Spanish genius; *Del sentimiento trágico de la vida* (1912; *The Tragic Sense of Life*, 1921) is a deeply unorthodox meditation on man's religious aspirations, which suggests that 'God is not the cause, but the consequence of man's longing for immortality', and concludes that all dogma, religious or anti-religious, is false: the only tenable philosophical position is that of doubt and wonder.

Uncle Remus, see HARRIS, J. C.

Uncle Silas, a novel by J. S. *Le Fanu, published 1864.
  Maud Ruthyn, aged 17, is the only child of Austin Ruthyn, an elderly recluse of considerable wealth. Her mother, whom he married late in life, is dead. Austin has a younger brother Silas, suspected by many of the murder of a wealthy gambler who, years before, was found with his throat cut in mysterious circumstances at Bartram-Haugh, Silas's Derbyshire home. Believing in Silas's innocence, Austin at his death leaves a will designed to demonstrate his confidence in his brother: Silas is made Maud's guardian, and her entire fortune is to go to him if she dies under age. Uncle Silas, who has been involved in many scandals and is heavily in debt, loses no time in summoning Maud to Bartram-Haugh, where he attempts to marry her to his boorish son Dudley, who is in fact already secretly married. When she refuses, he pretends that he is sending her to school in France; but when, after two days' travel, she wakes up believing she is in Dover, she finds herself a

prisoner back at Bartram-Haugh, where Silas and Dudley, aided by a grotesque and sinister French governess, Mme de la Rougierre, attempt to murder her. The plot miscarries and the governess is horribly murdered by Dudley in mistake for Maud, who escapes. The tale is one of suspense, without any supernatural element; but Maud's mounting terror at these events, seen through her eyes, is conveyed to the reader in a masterly manner. Uncle Silas himself is a fearful figure, tall, marble-faced, with black eyebrows and long silver hair, a laudanum-taker prone to strange cataleptic trances.

Uncle Tom's Cabin, a novel by Mrs H. E. B. *Stowe.

UNDERDOWNE, Thomas (fl. 1566–87). He translated the *Aethiopica of Heliodorus under the title *An Aethiopian Historie* (?1569).

Underground, Poems on the, a scheme launched in Jan. 1986 to display poster-poems on the London Underground, on the initiative of American-born London-based novelist Judith Chernaik, and support-ed by London Transport, the *Arts Council, and other bodies. Short poems, including some newly commis-sioned translations, are selected by Chernaik and poets Cicely Herbert and Gerard Benson, and displayed for a limited period: they are sold to the public both in poster and volume form.

underground poetry, a phrase used to describe the work of a number of writer-performers active in Britain between the late 1950s and mid-1970s, includ-ing A. *Mitchell, Jeff Nuttall (1933–), Tom *Pickard, Alexander *Trocchi, Heathcote *Williams, Michael *Horovitz, and the *Liverpool poets.

UNDERHILL, Evelyn (1875–1941), writer on religious subjects, and notably on the mystics; she was much influenced by F. *von Hügel, whom she met after the publication of her study *Mysticism* (1911); she became a practising Anglican in 1921. She produced editions of *The Cloud of Unknowing* (1912) and W. *Hilton's *The Scale of Perfection* (1923), and wrote many books, meditations, and pamphlets on the spiritual life.

Under Milk Wood, a radio drama by Dylan *Thomas, first broadcast by the BBC on 25 Jan. 1954 and subsequently adapted for the stage; the published version was completed shortly before his death, although he was still at work on the text.
  Set in the small Welsh seaside town of Llaregyb, it evokes the lives of the inhabitants—Myfanwy Price the dressmaker, and her lover Mog Edwards the draper; twice-widowed Mrs Ogmore-Pritchard; Butcher Beynon and his daughter Gossamer; the Reverend Eli Jenkins; the romantic and prolific Polly Garter; nostalgic Captain Cat, dreaming of lost loves; and many others. The poetic, alliterative prose is interspersed with songs and ballads. An earlier version of the first part of this play appeared in *Botteghe oscure* in 1952 under the title 'Llaregyb'.

Under the Greenwood Tree, a novel by T. *Hardy, published 1872.

This is a gentle, humorous novel, skilfully interweaving the love story of Dick Dewy and Fancy Day with the fortunes and misfortunes of a group of villagers, many of whom are musicians and singers in Mellstock church. Dick Dewy, the son of the local 'tranter', or carrier, falls in love with the new schoolmistress, the pretty and capricious Fancy Day. Her other two suitors (Shiner, a rich local farmer, and Maybold, the vicar in charge of the school) are rejected, after a series of vicissitudes, and in spite of the opposition of Fancy's father, in favour of Dick. Dick and his father are among the small band of musicians who have always sung and played the music in the gallery of Mellstock church, and who find themselves ousted by the new-fangled organ. This story of the displaced musicians reflected the true story of the Hardys' own church at Stinsford, and Hardy originally wished to call his book 'The Mellstock Choir'. The novel marks the first appearance of Hardy's village rustics, who drew much critical comment, both favourable and unfavourable, and who were to reappear frequently in later novels.

Under the Volcano, a novel by M. *Lowry, published 1947, considered his masterpiece.

It opens in Quauhnahuac, Mexico, on the Day of the Dead, Nov. 1939, as film-maker Jacques Laruelle looks back on the dramatic events of the same day in the preceding year, which occupy with many flashbacks and shifts of time sequence the main action of the book. The characters are the British ex-consul Geoffrey Firmin, an alcoholic, his wife Yvonne, an ex-film star who has returned after a year's estrangement, Laruelle, with whom she has had an affair, and the consul's half-brother Hugh, an anti-Fascist journalist much preoccupied by the Spanish Civil War. The theme of self-destruction is linked with the menace to Western civilization, and the mood grows increasingly sombre, ending with the consul's death. The narrative technique is complex, showing debts to *Conrad, *Joyce, and *Faulkner, and the text is packed with allusions to classical, Elizabethan, and Jacobean tragedy and to 'poètes maudits' such as *Swinburne and *Baudelaire. The Mexican landscape, over which brood the two volcanoes Popocatapetl and Ixtaccihuatl, is described with much vividness. Half-way through the book the consul reflects that 'It was already the longest day in his entire experience, a lifetime', and Lowry's control over the consul's confused and alcoholic sense of time and memory is remarkable. Like most of his work, the novel is highly autobiographical.

Underwood, The, or **Underwoods,** a collection of poems by *Jonson, printed in the folio of 1640. It includes 'A Celebration of Charis', 'An Ode to Himself', 'An Execration upon Vulcan' (concerning the fire in Jonson's library in 1623), 'An Epigram on the Court Pucelle', and the ode to Sir Lucius Cary and Sir Henry Morison. Like Jonson's *The Forest and *Timber, the title was suggested by Latin silva, which meant both 'collection' and 'wood'.

Underwoods (1887) is also the name (confessedly adopted from Jonson) of a book of poems by R. L. *Stevenson.

Unfortunate Traveller, The, or The Life of Jacke Wilton, a prose tale of adventure by T. *Nashe, published 1594, the earliest *picaresque romance in English, and the most remarkable work of the kind before *Defoe. It is dedicated to the earl of Southampton.

Jack Wilton is 'a certain kind of an appendix or page' attending on the court of Henry VIII at the time of the siege of Tournay. He lives by his wits, playing tricks on a niggardly old victualler and other gullible occupants of the camp, and gets whipped for his pains. He goes to Münster, which the Anabaptists are holding against the emperor, and sees John of Leyden hanged. The earl of Surrey, the lover of the Fair Geraldine, takes him to Italy as his page. During their travels they meet Erasmus, Sir Thomas More, Cornelius Agrippa, and Aretino. They hear Luther disputing at Wittenberg. Wilton passes himself off as the earl of Surrey and runs away with an Italian courtesan. There is a pleasant scene where the true earl discovers them and treats the escapade with singular good humour. After a tourney at Florence, where the earl defeats all comers in honour of the Fair Geraldine, Wilton leaves him, and is at Rome during an outbreak of the plague. Here, turning from lighter themes, he depicts scenes of violence and tragedy, rapes, murders, tortures, and executions. Depressed by what he has seen, he is converted to a better way of life, marries his courtesan, and is last seen at the Field of the Cloth of Gold, in the king of England's camp. The book includes much literary parody and pastiche.

UNGARETTI, Giuseppe (1888–1970), Italian poet. He founded *hermeticism with his first two collections of poems L'allegria di naufragi (Gaiety of Shipwrecks, written 1914–15) and Il porto sepolto (The Buried Port, 1916), in which he used neither rhyme nor punctuation. His later poems, of which the best are in Il dolore (Sorrow, 1947) and Sentimento del tempo (1933: The Feeling of Time, 1950), depart from hermeticism by reviving the tradition of *Leopardi and *Petrarch. He translated *Blake's visionary poems (Visioni di William Blake, 1965) and has himself been translated by R. *Lowell.

Unitarianism, a Christian body which rejects the Trinity and the divinity of Christ in favour of the single personality of the Godhead. As an organized community it became established in Poland, Hungary, and England in the 16th–17th cents. In England John Biddle (1615–62) published Unitarian tracts in 1652–4 and from 1652 his followers (Biddelians, *Socinians, or 'Unitarians') began regular Sunday worship. More than 100 years later Joseph *Priestley in his Appeal to *the Serious and Candid Professors of Christianity* (1770) defended Unitarian principles, and in 1773 Theophilus Lindsey (1723–1808) formed the first Unitarian denomination, opening in 1774 Essex Chapel in London. Both Priestley and his friend R. *Price became original members of the Unitarian Society in 1791. In the 18th cent. Dissenting congregations, including the English Presbyterians, turned to Unitarian views. Later in the 19th cent. J. *Martineau influenced the organization of the Unitarian body in England and Ireland and led the advance from biblical to rational Unitarianism.

unities, the, principles of dramatic composition supposedly derived from Aristotle's *Poetics*. Recording the practice of the tragedians whose works he knew, Aristotle states that a play should have the unity of a living organism, and that the action it represents should last, if possible, no longer than a single revolution of the sun. It was from these hints that 16th-cent. critics developed the rule of the three unities: action, time, and place. The most influential of these critics, *Castelvetro, had a low opinion of the imaginative powers of the average audience and held that they would be upset by the time of the action lasting longer than the time of its performance and that they could not be made to accept changes of scene. Castelvetro's ideas left their mark on neo-classical drama, especially in France, but they did not go unchallenged. The exclusion of sub-plots became the rule in France only after the controversy over *Corneille's *Le Cid* (1637). The time allowed for the action of a tragedy was extended by common consent to 24 hours. The place the stage represented was allowed to shift from one point to another within a larger area: a palace or even a city. Moreover, dramatists learnt to circumvent the limitations of the unities by avoiding the mention of specific times and places. The impact of *neo-classicism on English tragedy was delayed by the disturbances connected with the Civil War and was weakened by the taste for exciting action that was a legacy from the Jacobean stage. Dryden's essay *Of Dramatick Poesy* (1668) offers the unities only half-hearted support, and in spite of the efforts of French-inspired critics like *Rymer and *Dennis, and the success of Addison's *Cato* (1713), neo-classical drama never took firm root in England.

University of East Anglia (UEA), noted in a literary context for its creative writing programme, founded in 1970 through the joint efforts of A. *Wilson and M. *Bradbury and in its early days supported financially by Joe McCrindle, editor of the *Transatlantic Review*. Its first student was Ian *McEwan, and later graduates include C. *Sinclair, R. *Tremain, and K. *Ishiguro. See *Class Work* (1995), a collection of short fiction by UEA graduates edited by M. Bradbury. UEA also houses the British Centre for Literary Translation.

university presses. The appointment of printers by European academies to produce learned books under some control and protection was common by the end of the 16th cent. As early as 1470 Jean Heynlin, prior of the Sorbonne, brought printers from Germany to work in the college; but his press had no sanction from the University of Paris and lasted only two years. A printer worked at Oxford from *c*.1478 until 1486, but his relation to the university is not known.

With the advent of the 'new learning' universities needed new texts and printers needed help and protection for issuing them. The University of Leipzig, devoted to humane studies since 1502, took the lead in attracting printers, directing them to Greek and elegant Latin, and defending their books from attack by conservative authorities. The advantages of printing in a university were exemplified in the polyglot Bible produced in 1502–22 at Alcalá de Henares.

The modern conception of a university press owes much to Leiden. The academy founded there in 1575 appointed an official printer from the first, and was served in that capacity by Christophe Plantin (in 1584–5), by the erudite Raphelengius (d. 1595), and three generations of Elzeviers. Their books, edited or approved by the resident professors and well corrected at the press, established the benefits of authority, continuity, and universality that a university can bestow in publishing.

In England the University of Cambridge had power by royal charter to appoint printers to work in its precinct and sell books anywhere from 1534, mainly, no doubt, with a view to propagating defence against heresy (see CAMBRIDGE UNIVERSITY PRESS). It exercised the power from 1583, and Oxford followed the year after (see OXFORD UNIVERSITY PRESS), apparently with only oral warrant from the queen. Costly conflicts with vested interests contesting the universities' right to override private monopolies in such lucrative works as the *Bible in English, the Book of *Common Prayer, and the Metrical Psalms induced both universities to forgo this privilege in return for money during most of two centuries and to sponsor only works of scholarship.

The press owned, financed, and conducted by a university, as distinct from one censored and protected by it but privately financed and managed, had its origin in England and is still confined to English-speaking countries. Oxford acquired such a press in 1690, when the printing equipment and rights in copy of *Fell came to it by bequest from him. Cambridge took immediate control of its printing in 1698 and exercises it through a board of syndics.

The style of 'university press' is used by many publishing firms, particularly in Great Britain, the USA, and Canada, some of which also print. They are variously related to the academies from which they take their names. In the USA Cornell opened a small press in 1869, which lasted until 1894, and Johns Hopkins established an agency for publishing in 1875.

The University of Chicago has owned its printing and publishing office since 1894. Harvard, Yale, Princeton, Columbia, California, Toronto, among other North American universities, are equipped to print at least some of their publications.

University Wits, name given by *Saintsbury to a group of Elizabethan playwrights and pamphleteers, of whom *Nashe, R. *Greene, *Lyly, and T. *Lodge were the chief.

Unquiet Grave, The, (1) a ballad included in *Child's collection, in which a lover laments his dead love for a twelvemonth and a day, at the end of which time she speaks to him from the grave, telling him to content himself and let her sleep; (2) see CONNOLLY.

Unreason, Abbot of, see MISRULE.

UNSWORTH, Barry (1930–   ), novelist, son of a mining family, born and brought up in Durham, and educated at the University of Manchester. The wide range of his subsequent travels and his interest in history are reflected in his work: his novels include *The Partnership* (1966), *Mooncranker's Gift* (1973), *Pascali's Island* (1980), and *Stone Virgin* (1985). *Sacred Hunger* (*Booker Prize, 1992) is a powerful and carefully researched narrative set in the mid-17th cent. describing the voyage (and appalling conditions on board) of a slave ship, the *Liverpool Merchant*, from England to Africa to America, where, after the death of Captain Thurso, some of the crew and the surviving slaves set up a commune under the influence of the principles of *Rousseau. The ship's doctor, freethinking Matthew Paris, becomes a leader in this new world, but is pursued by his cousin Erasmus Kemp, son of the doomed ship's bankrupt owner, motivated by vengeance and the 'sacred hunger' for profit. *Morality Play* (1995) is a detective story set amidst a troupe of medieval travelling players, and *After Hannibal* (1996) a fable of greed and exploitation set in modern summer-home Umbria which incidentally foresees the earthquake that devastated Assisi in 1997.

UPDIKE, John Hoyer (1932–   ), American novelist, short story writer, and poet, born in Pennsylvania (where his early works are set) and educated at Harvard. His novels include the tetralogy *Rabbit, Run* (1960), *Rabbit Redux* (1971), *Rabbit is Rich* (1981), and *Rabbit at Rest* (1990), a small-town domestic tragi-comedy which traces the career of ex-basketball champion Harry Angstrom from the early days of his precarious (but, as it turns out, lasting) marriage to alcoholic Janice, through the social and sexual upheavals of the 1960s, to the compromises of middle age. *The Centaur* (1963) uses a mythological framework to explore the relationship of a schoolmaster father and his teenage son and *Couples* (1968) is a portrait of sexual passion and realignment amongst a group of young suburban married couples in Tarbox, Massachusetts, a town which in this and succeeding works takes on an archetypal quality. Updike's characteristic preoccupations are with the erotic, with the pain and striving implicit in human relationships, and with the sacred (at times explicitly religious) in daily life; these are conveyed in an ornate, highly charged prose which reaches its most flamboyant in an atypical work, *The Coup* (1979), an exotic first-person narration by the ex-dictator of a fictitious African state. Other novels include *The Witches of Eastwick* (1984, subsequently filmed), *Memoirs of the Ford Administration* (1993), and *Brazil* (1994). *A Month of Sundays* (1975), *Roger's Version* (1986), and *S* (1988) form a linked sequence based on reworkings of *Hawthorne's *The Scarlet Letter*. His volumes of short stories (many of which were first published in the *New Yorker*, and several of which feature the representative and recurring marital crises of a couple called the Maples) include *Pigeon Feathers and Other Stories* (1962), *Museums and Women* (1972), *Problems and Other Stories* (1979), *Trust Me* (1987), and *The Afterlife and Other Stories* (1995). His reviews and essays have been collected in *Assorted Prose* (1965), *Picked-up Pieces* (1978), *Hugging the Shore* (1983), *Just Looking: Essays on Art* (1990), and *Odd Jobs: Essays and Criticism* (1991). His *Collected Poems 1953–1992* were published in 1993.

UPWARD, Edward Falaise (1903–   ), novelist, born in Essex, and educated at Repton and Corpus Christi College, Cambridge, with *Isherwood, whose lifelong friend he became; at Cambridge they both wrote *Barbellion-inspired diaries, and invented the surreal imaginary world of 'Mortmere'. A long Mortmere fragment appeared in Upward's *The Railway Accident and Other Stories* (1969) and its fantasies are described in Isherwood's *Lions and Shadows* (1938), in which Upward appears as Allen Chalmers. Upward's *Journey to the Border* (1938) describes the progress of a neurotic tutor in an upper-middle-class household towards commitment to the workers' movement (Upward was for some years a member of the Communist Party); his trilogy *In the Thirties* (1962), *The Rotten Elements* (1969), and *No Home but the Struggle* (1977), published together in 1977 as *The Spiral Ascent*, describes the alternating political and artistic conflicts, over some decades, in the life of Marxist poet and schoolmaster Alan Sebrill. The last, and most introspective, volume affirms the narrator's need for a union of personal and political commitment in his work.

URBAN, Sylvanus, the pseudonym of E. *Cave and, by succession, of the later editors of the *Gentleman's Magazine*.

URFÉ, Honoré d', see D'URFÉ.

Urizen, a principal character in the symbolic books of *Blake, represented as god of reason and law-maker, to some extent to be identified with the Hebrew Jehovah; Dorothy Plowman (facsimile edn, *The Book of Urizen*,

1929) suggests his name is taken from the Greek οὐρίζειν to limit. *The Book of Urizen* (1794) is Blake's version of the myth of Genesis, describing the creation of the material world by Urizen from the 'abominable void', from which is engendered Urizen's opponent, *Los, and Pity, the first female form, who is named *Enitharmon. The spirit of the book is of anguish, revolt, and suffering, and Urizen, after long struggles with Los, surveys his creation in a sorrow that engenders a web, 'The Net of Religion'. In the first plate of *Europe*, Urizen is portrayed majestically as an aged, Newtonian figure leaning down from the sun with a great pair of compasses to create the world.

Urn Burial, see HYDRIOTAPHIA.

URQUHART, Sir Thomas (1611–60), of Cromarty, educated at King's College, Aberdeen. He fought at Turriff against the Covenanters, withdrew to London, and was knighted in 1641. He followed Prince Charles to Worcester, where many of his manuscripts were lost, was imprisoned 1651–2, and died abroad. His best-known work is a translation of the first three books of *Rabelais, the first two 1653, the third 1693 (completed by *Motteux). He wrote a number of curious treatises on mathematics, linguistics, etc., with strange Greek titles, collected in 1774 and 1834; among them is *Ekskubalauron* (1651, known as 'The Jewel'), which contains in his 'Vindication of the Honour of Scotland' the story of the 'Admirable' *Crichton. A modern edition, *The Jewel*, ed. R. D. S. Jack and R. J. Lyall, was published in 1984.

Ursula, (1) Hero's maidservant in Shakespeare's *Much Ado about Nothing*; (2) the pig-woman in Jonson's *Bartholomew Fair*; (3) one of the Brangwen sisters in D. H. Lawrence's *The Rainbow* and *Women in Love*.

USK, Thomas (d. 1388), the author of *The Testament of Love*, formerly ascribed to *Chaucer and included in Skeat's *Chaucerian and Other Pieces* appended to his edition of Chaucer as vol. vii. He was under-sheriff of London in 1387, by the mandate of Richard II, and he was proceeded against and executed by the 'Merciless Parliament' in 1388. *The Testament of Love* is an allegorical prose work perhaps written by Usk in prison to elicit sympathy; it is sometimes dated in 1385, though this seems too early for the borrowings from *Troilus and Criseyde* which it contains (as well as from *Piers Plowman*). Skeat noticed that the first letters of the sections formed an acrostic reading 'Margaret of virtu have merci on TSKNVI', and Henry Bradley rearranged the text so that the last letters read THINUSK, i.e. 'thine Usk'. This cryptogram is typical of the allusiveness of the poem, part of which is now impenetrable. C. S. *Lewis (*The Allegory of Love*, 1936, 222–31) regards the way Margarete is at once real and symbolic as the great interest of the work, while attributing its flaws in style to the excessive influence of Chaucer's *Boece* from which the work borrows its form as instructive debate.

Usnach, the Sons of, see DEIRDRE.

USSHER, James (1581–1656), educated at the newly founded Trinity College, Dublin. He became archbishop of Armagh in 1625 and came to London in 1640. He wrote much on theological subjects, and was learned in patristic literature and ancient Irish history. His chief work is the *Annales Veteris et Novi Testamenti*, a chronological summary in Latin of the history of the world from the Creation to the dispersion of the Jews under Vespasian, said to be the source of the dates later inserted in the margins of the Authorized Version of the Bible, which fix the Creation at 23 Oct. 4004 BC. He bequeathed his collection of books and manuscripts to Trinity College, Dublin.

Uther Pendragon, in the Arthurian legend, king of the Britons and father of *Arthur. Pendragon means 'chief dragon', and Uther has been variously explained; it may be a misreading as a proper name of the Welsh word *uthr*, 'terrible' (an interpretation that squares with *Geoffrey of Monmouth's calling him 'Utherpendragon', undivided). After he became king of the Britons, he lusted after *Igraine, wife of Gorlois, duke of Cornwall. He picked a quarrel with Gorlois and was transformed by Merlin's magic into his shape, whereupon he slept with Igraine. After the death of Gorlois he married Igraine who bore him two children, Arthur and Anna. See Geoffrey of Monmouth, *The History of the Kings of Britain*, trans. L. Thorpe (1966), 151–211 (summary 368–9).

Utilitarianism, an essay by J. S. *Mill, first published in a series of articles in *Fraser's Magazine* in 1861, in book form 1863. The term 'utilitarian' was first adopted by Mill in 1823, from Galt's *Annals of the Parish*. In this work, Mill, while accepting the Benthamite principle (see BENTHAM) that Utility, or the greatest happiness of the greatest number, is the foundation of morals, departs from it by maintaining that pleasures differ in kind or quality as well as in quantity, 'that some *kinds* of pleasure are more desirable and more valuable than others'; also by recognizing in 'the conscientious feelings of mankind' an 'internal sanction' to be added to Bentham's 'external sanctions'. 'The social feelings of mankind, the desire to be in unity with our fellow creatures' constitute 'the ultimate sanction of the greatest happiness, morality'.

Utopia, the principal literary work of Sir T. *More, is a speculative political essay written in Latin. The work was published in 1516 at Louvain, *Erasmus supervising the printing. The form was probably suggested by the narrative of the voyages of Vespucci, printed 1507. The subject is the search for the best possible form of government. More meets at Antwerp a traveller, one Raphael *Hythloday, who has discovered 'Utopia', 'Nowhere land'. Communism is there the general law, a national system of education is extended to men and women alike, and the freest toleration of religion is recognized. The work at once became popular, and was translated by Ralph Robinson into English in 1551, and into French (in 1550), German, Italian, and Spanish. The rapid fame of the book is shown by the reference to Utopians by *Rabelais (III. i, pub. 1546).

The name 'Utopia' ('no place'), coined by More, passed into general usage, and has been used to describe, retrospectively, Plato's *Republic, and many subsequent fictions, fantasies, and blueprints for the future, including Bacon's *New Atlantis, Harrington's *The Commonwealth of Oceana, Morris's *News from Nowhere, and *Bellamy's Looking Backward. Satirical utopias include Swift's *Gulliver's Travels and Samuel Butler's *Erewhon, and the

word 'dystopia' ('bad place') has been coined to describe nightmare visions of the future, such as Huxley's *Brave New World, *Zamyatin's We, and Orwell's *Nineteen Eighty-Four, in which present-day social, political, and technological tendencies are projected in an extreme and unpleasant form. Many works of *science fiction use the utopian and dystopian forms.

UTTLEY, Alison (1884–1976), born on a farm in rural Derbyshire. She published many popular children's books, and is best remembered for her 'Little Grey Rabbit' series (of which the first was published in 1929) and for her 'Sam Pig' series (1940 onwards). The Country Child (1931) is a vivid and largely autobiographical account of a country childhood. (See also CHILDREN'S LITERATURE.)

V

VACHELL, H(orace) A(nnesley) (1861–1955), prolific novelist and playwright, educated at Harrow and Sandhurst. He is best remembered for *The Hill: A Romance of Friendship* (1905), a story of an intense schoolboy relationship between young Harrovian John Verney and Henry Desmond, who is later to die in the Boer War. Other titles include *Her Son* (1907), *The Fourth Dimension* (1920), and *The Fifth Commandment* (1932); *Distant Fields* (1937) is a memoir.

Vainlove, a character in Congreve's *The Old Bachelor*.

Vala, see FOUR ZOAS, THE.

Valentine, (1) one of *The Two Gentlemen of Verona* in Shakespeare's play; (2) one of *Orsino's court in his *Twelfth Night*.

Valentine and Orson, the subject of an early French romance. Bellisant, sister of King Pepin, is married to Alexander, emperor of Constantinople. The archpriest treacherously accuses Bellisant to her husband and she is banished. A bear carries away one of her children (Orson), who is reared as a wild man. The other (Valentine) is found by Pepin and brought up as a knight. Valentine meets Orson, conquers him, brings him to the court, and tames him. Numerous adventures follow, the principal of which is the imprisonment of Valentine and Orson and their mother Bellisant in the castle of Clerimond, sister of the giant Ferragus, and their rescue by Pacolet, the dwarf messenger of Ferragus, who has a little magic horse of wood which conveys him instantly wherever he wishes.

The story appeared in English about 1510 translated by Henry Watson as the 'History of two Valyannte Brethren, Valentyne and Orson'. A ballad in Percy's *Reliques* deals with it.

Valentinian, The Tragedy of, a play by J. *Fletcher, performed between 1610 and 1614, published 1647.

A sensational drama with elements of *revenge tragedy, it deals with the vengeance of Maximus, a general under Valentinian III, for the dishonour of his wife by the emperor, and her suicide. A dense web of intrigue and treachery results in the slow death of Valentinian by poisoning (to the accompaniment of the well-known lyric 'Care charming sleep'), and the subsequent death of Maximus, poisoned, again to musical accompaniment, by the widowed empress Eudoxa, as he is inaugurated as Valentinian's successor.

Vale Press, see PRIVATE PRESSES.

Valerian, the husband of St Cecilia, whose story is told in Chaucer's 'The Second Nun's Tale' (see CANTERBURY TALES, 21).

VALÉRY, Paul (1871–1945), French poet, essayist, and critic. As a young man he was deeply influenced by the *symbolists and, in particular, by the work of *Mallarmé. He became widely known for the poetry of *La Jeune Parque* (1917) and the collection *Charmes* (1922). The latter contains 'Le Cimetière marin' (English trans., 'The Graveyard by the Sea', 1932, and, by *Day-Lewis, 1946). He wrote little poetry after 1922, but published essays on a variety of literary, philosophical, and aesthetic subjects (*Variété*, 1924–44) and two Socratic dialogues, *Eupalinos ou l'architecte* and *L'Âme et la danse* (1923). His notebooks (*Cahiers*), covering the years 1894 to 1945, were published posthumously.

Valley of Humiliation, in Bunyan's *Pilgrim's Progress*, the place where *Christian encounters *Apollyon. There is a beautiful description of it in Pt II, where Mr *Great-heart explains its true character.

Valley of the Shadow of Death, see Psalm 23: 4. Christian, in Bunyan's *Pilgrim's Progress*, passes through it, 'a very solitary place', with a dangerous quag on one side and a deep ditch on the other, and the mouth of hell is close by one side of it, from which issue flames and fiends.

VANBRUGH, Sir John (1664–1726), dramatist and architect, son of a London tradesman, whose father, a merchant of Ghent, had fled to England from Alva's persecutions. He was imprisoned in France between 1688 and 1692 for spying. In 1696 he produced *The Relapse, or Virtue in Danger*, with immense success, and *The Provok'd Wife* in 1697. His other principal comedies are *The Confederacy* (1705) and *The Provok'd Husband*, which he left unfinished and C. *Cibber completed and brought out in 1728. His collected dramatic works appeared in 1730. He, together with *Congreve, was specially attacked by Jeremy *Collier in his *Short View*.

Vanbrugh's first building was Castle Howard, 1699–1726. This already shows the grandeur and dramatic quality of his style, which reaches its climax in *Blenheim Palace. *Hawksmoor assisted him in many of his projects. Vanbrugh was Clarenceux king-of-arms and in 1714 was the first man knighted by George I. (See RESTORATION.)

van der POST, Sir Laurens Jan (1906–96), writer, soldier, farmer, and explorer, born in South Africa, whose many works of travel, anthropology, and adventure (much influenced by *Jung) include *The Lost World of the Kalahari* (1958), *The Heart of the Hunter* (1961), *A Story Like the Wind* (1972), *A Far-Off Place* (1974), *A Mantis Carol* (1975), *Jung and the Story of Our Time* (1976), *Yet Being Someone Other* (1982), and *A Walk with a White Bushman* (1986). He was knighted in 1981.

Van DYCK, Sir Anthony (1599–1641), Flemish painter, born in Antwerp, who worked in *Rubens's studio in his youth. In 1623 he came to England as court painter to Charles I. He was knighted and enjoyed great success, painting many portraits of the royal family and the court. He married a lady of the Scottish house of Ruthven in 1640. He died in England and was buried in Old St Paul's. Van Dyck's success lay in his ability to portray the poetic ideals that sustained the Caroline court. He painted the king both as warrior monarch and as perfect gentleman; his mythological portraits (Venetia, Lady Digby, as Prudence) and those which convey an Arcadian mood suggest the atmosphere of the *masque. Van Dyck was the friend of men of letters and of the most cultivated patrons of his day; among others, he painted the earl of Arundel, *Laud, E. *Porter, and T. *Killigrew the elder. *Waller praised his portraits for showing 'Not the form alone, and grace | But art and power of a face'.

VANE, Frances Anne, Viscountess, née Hawes (1713–88), was the source of the notorious chapter 81 of *Peregrine Pickle*, 'Memoirs of a Lady of Quality', in which the said lady relates her scandalous adventures to Peregrine. It is probable that *Smollett compiled the memoirs for her, though whether from a written or verbal account remains uncertain. Horace *Walpole referred to Lady Vane as 'that living academy of love-life'.

Vanessa, *Swift's name for Esther Vanhomrigh.

VANHOMRIGH, Esther, see SWIFT, J.

Vanity Fair, in Bunyan's *Pilgrim's Progress*, a fair in the town of Vanity, on the way to the Celestial City: the 'Vanity' tradition begins in Eccles. 1: 2 ('Vanity of vanities, saith the preacher . . .'). Here Bunyan satirizes Restoration society in which all 'merchandise' is for sale, including houses, wives, souls, and precious stones, and which penalizes dissidents who only 'buy the truth'. The episode culminates in the trial and martyrdom of Faithful, who is burnt to death after being abused by Judge Hategood, a compound personification of Puritan-hounding judges such as Kellynge and Jeffreys.

Vanity Fair, a novel by *Thackeray, published in numbers 1847–8, illustrated by the author.

The story is set at the time of the Napoleonic wars, and gives a satirical picture of a worldly society, which Thackeray intended to be applied also to his own times. It follows the fortunes of two sharply contrasted characters, Rebecca (Becky) Sharp, the penniless orphaned daughter of an artist and a French opera dancer, and Amelia Sedley, the sheltered child of a rich City merchant. The two girls, as unlike in character as they are in fortune, have been educated at Miss Pinkerton's Academy for young ladies. Becky, having failed to force a proposal of marriage from Amelia's elephantine brother Jos, 'the Collector of Boggley Wallah', becomes governess to the children of Sir Pitt Crawley, a coarse, brutal old man who bullies his fading second wife. Becky manages to charm the Crawley family, and becomes a favourite of Miss Crawley, Sir Pitt's rich and capricious sister. When his wife dies Sir Pitt proposes to Becky, but she has to confess that she is already married, to his younger son Rawdon. The young couple abruptly fall from favour with Miss Crawley, and have to live on Becky's wits.

Meanwhile Amelia's apparently secure life has been disrupted. Her father has lost all his money, and her engagement to George Osborne, the handsome but vain and shallow son of another City magnate, has been broken off in consequence. William Dobbin, George's awkward, loyal friend, who is secretly in love with Amelia, persuades George to defy his father and go on with the marriage, and Mr Osborne disinherits his son.

George, Rawdon, and Dobbin are all in the army, and Amelia and Becky accompany their husbands to Belgium, where Becky carries on an intrigue with George Osborne. George is killed at Waterloo, and Amelia, with her baby son Georgy, goes to live in poverty with her parents, while Becky and Rawdon manage to make a brilliant display in London society on 'nothing a year'. Amelia's devotion to her son is contrasted with Becky's neglect of hers, but she is finally forced by poverty to part with Georgy, who is growing up to be much like his father, to his grandfather. Dobbin, despairing of ever winning Amelia's love, for she is dedicated to the memory of her husband, has spent ten years in India. Becky and Rawdon part, after Rawdon has discovered his wife in a compromising situation with Lord Steyne, who has, it turns out, been paying for Becky's extravagances. Becky leads an increasingly disreputable life on the Continent, and it is hinted that she may be responsible for the death of Jos Sedley, who has insured his life in her favour. Rawdon, who has become governor of Coventry Island, dies of fever. Amelia steadfastly refuses to marry Dobbin, until a chance meeting with Becky, who tells her of George Osborne's infidelity. Disillusioned, she marries Dobbin, but by then his love for her has lost much of its intensity.

Vanity of Human Wishes, The, a poem by Dr *Johnson, published 1749, in imitation of the Tenth Satire of *Juvenal. Less topical than his other long poem, *London*, it owes its success to its moral seriousness and to its weighty but well-illustrated generalizations. Johnson comments on the vanities of various ambitions—for power, learning, military glory, and beauty—and cites the examples of Wolsey, *Clarendon, *Laud, and others: the passage on Charles XII of Sweden is perhaps the finest in the poem, 'quite perfect in form', according to T. S. *Eliot. Johnson's deep religious faith transforms the *Stoicism of the original's conclusion: 'Still raise for good the supplicating voice, | But leave to heav'n the measure and the choice.' This was the first complete work to which he put his name.

VANSITTART, Peter (1920–), educated at Haileybury and Worcester College, Oxford. He was a schoolteacher for 25 years before becoming a full-time writer for both adults and children. His many novels range from experimental historical narratives (*Pastimes of a Red Summer*, 1969; *Lancelot*, 1978) to portraits of contemporary life, such as *Landlord* (1970) and *Quintet* (1976). Other novels include *Aspects of Feeling* (1986) and *Parsifal* (1988). *A Safe Conduct* (1996), set in late 15thcent. Germany, interweaves historical and late 20thcent.millennial issues through the story of a Children's Revolt. An autobiography, *Paths from the White Horse*, was published in 1985.

Van VOGT, A. E., see SCIENCE FICTION.

Varden, Gabriel, a character in Dickens's *Barnaby Rudge*, father of *Dolly Varden.

VARGAS LLOSA, Mario (1936–), novelist and playwright, who was born in Arequipa, Peru, and lives in London. His novel exposing a military academy, *La ciudad y los perros* (1962; *The Time of the Hero*, 1966), caused a scandal. Astute realist manipulations focus on Peru in *La casa verde* (1965; *The Green House*, 1968), *Conversación en la catedral* (1970; *Conversation in the Cathedral*, 1975), *Pantaleón y las visitadoras* (1973; *Captain Pantoja and the Special Service*, 1978), *La tia Julia y el escribidor* (1977; *Aunt Julia and the Script Writer*, 1982), *La historia de Mayta* (1984, *The Real Life of Alejandro Mayta*, 1986), and other titles. *La guerra del fin del mundo* (1981) is a study of fanaticism in Brazil. He has published a memoir (*A Fish in the Water*, 1994), plays, and criticism (*Making Waves*, 1996). He stood for the presidency of Peru in 1990.

VASARI, Giorgio (1511–74), Italian painter, architect, and author of *The Lives of the Most Excellent Italian Architects, Painters and Sculptors* (1550 and 1568), for generations the main source for the history of Italian art. Selections translated by G. Bull appeared in 1965 and 1987.

Vathek, *an Arabian Tale*, by W. *Beckford, published in English 1786. The book was written in French and translated into English, with the author's assistance, by Samuel Henley. It was one of the most successful of the *Oriental tales then in fashion.

The cruel and sensual Caliph Vathek, whose eye can kill with a glance, is compelled, by the influence of his sorceress mother and by the unbridled pride of his own nature, to become a servant of Eblis, the Devil. He makes a sacrifice of 50 children, and sets off from his capital, Samarah, to the ruined city of Istakar, where he is promised the sight of the treasures of the pre-Adamite sultans. On the way he falls in love with Nouronihar, the exquisite daughter of one of his emirs, who accompanies him on his journey. After various exotic and terrifying incidents, he obtains admission to the great subterranean halls of Eblis, only to discover the sickening worthlessness of the riches that he sees there, and to receive the penalty of his sin, when his own heart and the hearts of all the damned burst into flame in their living bodies. The febrile excitement of the story is sustained by the use of rapid action, exotic locales, and exaggerated passions, often cruel or prurient. *Hazlitt objected to 'the diabolical levity of its contempt for mankind', but critics disagree as to whether the tale is related with a sly irony. Beckford wrote three further 'Episodes' (the last unfinished) for insertion in the story, and included them in his French version of 1815.

Vatican II (1962–5), the Council of the Roman Catholic Church which had an incalculable effect on world literature by reinvigorating local vernaculars through the medium of the mass, which no longer had to be celebrated in Latin.

vaudeville, a light popular song or a stage performance of a light and amusing character interspersed with songs, from *vau de vire*, in full *chanson du Vau de Vire*, a song of the Valley of the Vire (in Calvados, Normandy). The name is said to have been first given to songs composed by Olivier Basselin, a fuller of Vire (15th cent.).

'Vaudracour and Julia', see WORDSWORTH, W.

VAUGHAN, Henry (1621–95), born at Newton-upon-Usk, Breconshire, the eldest son of a Welsh gentleman, Thomas Vaughan of Tretower, and his wife Denise. Henry's twin brother Thomas (below) became a controversial 'natural magician'. Probably in 1628 a third brother William was born. Henry and Thomas were brought up bilingual in Welsh and English, tutored by Matthew Herbert, a noted schoolmaster at Llangattock. By May 1638 Thomas was at Jesus College, Oxford, and Henry almost certainly accompanied him, though his residence is not recorded. Around 1640 Henry probably went to London to study law, though it is not known which Inn admitted him. He may have come within the orbit of the literary set of which *Jonson had been the leader. He returned to Breconshire, probably at the outbreak of the Civil War, and after a spell as clerk to Sir Marmaduke Lloyd, chief justice of the sessions, he saw military service on the Royalist side. About 1646 he married Catherine Wise. They had a son, Thomas, and three daughters. His wooing of Catherine is apparently recalled in the poem 'Upon the Priory Grove' printed in *Poems with the Tenth Satire of Juvenal Englished* (1646), his first collection. His second, *Olor Iscanus* (The Swan of Usk), has a dedication

1055

bearing the date 1647, but was not published till 1651. The poems in these two volumes are almost wholly secular, including fashionable love verses and translations from *Ovid, Ausonius, *Boethius, and the Polish Jesuit Latin poet Casimir Sarbiewski (1595–1640). There is little in them that anticipates the great religious poetry of Vaughan's next volume, *Silex Scintillans* (Flashing Flint, 1650). The poems suggest that a profound spiritual experience, connected with the death of his brother William in 1648 and the defeat of the Royalist cause, accounted for the despair and renewal which inspired the composition of *Silex*. Further devotional works followed: *The Mount of Olives, or Solitary Devotions* (1652) and *Flores Solitudinis* (1654), which consists of three pious prose translations and a life of St Paulinus of Nola. In 1655 appeared the second edition of *Silex Scintillans*, with a second part added, and also a translation of the *Hermetical Physick* of Henry Nollius. A translation of *The Chymists Key* by the same author followed in 1657. Vaughan's first wife having died, he married her younger sister Elizabeth, probably in 1655. They had a son, Henry, and three daughters. According to a letter he sent to *Aubrey in 1673 he had by that date been practising physic 'for many years with good success'. There is no record of a medical degree. His brother Thomas died in 1666, and in 1678 *Thalia Rediviva*, containing poems by both twins, was published. His later life was marred by litigious feuds between his first and second families.

Vaughan's religious poetry is uneven, but its best moments, like the start of 'The World' ('I saw Eternity the other night'), have a quality which is wholly distinctive, and which has prevailed with critics to class him as a 'mystic'; his lyrics ('The Bird', 'The Water-Fall', 'The Timber') show a sense of man's unity with and God's love of creaturely life, and he believed (with his brother) that nature would be resurrected at the end of time, and that even stones had feeling. He was seized with the idea of childish innocence, and the child's recollections of prenatal glory. He writes, in 'The Retreat', of his own 'Angel-infancy', when he would muse on clouds and flowers and see in them 'Some shadows of eternity'. He acknowledged, in the preface to the second part of *Silex Scintillans*, his great debt to G. *Herbert, 'whose holy life and verse gained many pious Converts, (of whom I am the least)'. Vaughan's fascination with hermeticism, and particularly with the idea of sympathetic bonds uniting microcosm and macrocosm, is clear in his poems, many of which share ideas and even phrases with his brother Thomas's treatises. On the title-pages of *Olor Iscanus* and *Silex Scintillans* Vaughan calls himself a 'Silurist', presumably because his native Brecon was anciently inhabited by the British tribe of Silures.

Works, ed. L. C. Martin (2nd edn, 1957); *Complete Poems*, ed. Alan Rudrum (1976); F. E. Hutchinson, *Henry Vaughan: A Life and Interpretation* (1947; corrected repr. 1971); S. Davies, *Henry Vaughan* (1995).

The Vaughan Society was founded in 1995 and its journal, *Scintilla*, is edited by Anne *Cluysenaar.

VAUGHAN, Thomas (1621–66), twin brother of Henry *Vaughan, whose entry gives details of his background. Thomas, an ordained Anglican minister, was evicted from his living at Llansantffraed in 1650 for misconduct ('for being a common drunkard, a common swearer ... a whoremaster'). He was a disciple of Cornelius *Agrippa, published various treatises on alchemy, magic, and mysticism, including *Anima Magia Abscondita; or A Discourse on the Universall Spirit of Nature* (1650) and *Magia Adamica; or The Antiquity of Magic* (1650); *Aula Lucis, or The House of Light* (1652); and a preface to a *Rosicrucian work, *The Fame and Confession of the Fraternity of R.C., Commonly, of the Rosie Cross* (1652). Most of his works were published under the pseudonym of 'Eugenius Philalethes' ('Good Truth-Loving Man'). He engaged in furious controversy with the Platonist Henry *More who had attacked his *Anthroposophia* (1650) as nonsense. After the Restoration, Thomas enjoyed the patronage of Sir Robert Moray, first president of the *Royal Society. Moran and Vaughan accompanied the court to Oxford to flee the plague in 1665, and Vaughan died at Albury, according to A. *Wood, of mercury poisoning. He was satirized by S. *Butler in his 'Character of a Hermetic Philosopher' (published posthumously) and is said to have suggested some aspects of Ralpho in *Hudibras: Swift in *A Tale of a Tub described him as a writer of the greatest gibberish 'ever published in any language'. *Works*, ed. A. Rudrum with J. Drake-Brockman (1984).

VAUGHAN WILLIAMS, Ralph (1872–1958), one of the central figures in the English musical renascence of the first half of the 20th cent. His interest in folk song, amateur music-making, and the works of *Byrd and *Purcell enabled him to escape from the European Romantic inheritance of his predecessors and create a new and personal style. He made many English language settings, and his first published work, the song 'Linden Lea' (W. *Barnes), achieved early popularity, as did 'Silent Noon' (D. G. Rossetti's *'The House of Life') and *Songs of Travel* (R. L. *Stevenson). His *Housman cycle *On Wenlock Edge* (1909) proved a landmark, and two years later his *Five Mystical Songs* (poems by G. *Herbert) brought out the visionary quality characteristic of his later work. In the 1920s came settings of *Chaucer, Shakespeare, *Whitman, and another Housman cycle: then, after a long gap, *Ten Blake Songs* (1957) and *Four Last Songs* (1954–8), settings of words by his second wife Ursula Wood. On a larger scale, *Towards the Unknown Region* (choral, 1907) and *A Sea Symphony* (1909) are both from Whitman, as is the cantata *Dona Nobis Pacem* (1936). The *Five Tudor Portraits* (1935) are made up of extracts from *Skelton, racy, boisterous, and delicate by turns. *Serenade to Music* (1938) is a setting of Lorenzo's speech from the last act of *The Merchant of Venice. An

Oxford Elegy (1949, from M. Arnold's *'The Scholar Gipsy' and *'Thyrsis') is an effective experiment with speaker, chorus, and orchestra. Vaughan Williams also contributed to the liberation of English opera. *Hugh the Drover* (1924) was a pioneering work, leaning heavily on folk song, and *Sir John in Love* (1929) counterposed an English *Falstaff to *Verdi's. *Riders to the Sea* (1937) is a highly successful, intense, and economical setting of *Synge's tragedy. Vaughan Williams's last opera, *The Pilgrim's Progress* (1951), was based on *Bunyan.

VAUVENARGUES, Luc de Clapiers, marquis de (1715–47), French moralist. After serving as an army officer in the War of the Austrian Succession, he was forced by broken health into premature retirement. His *Introduction à la connaissance de l'esprit humain, suivie de réflexions et de maximes* (1746) put him in the literary tradition of *Pascal and *La Rochefoucauld. Less sceptical than the first and less cynical than the second, he sought in the natural feelings of men and women the source of their best thought and the springs of their moral energy.

VAUX, Thomas, second Baron Vaux of Harrowden (1509–56), educated at Cambridge and employed by Wolsey and Henry VIII until 1536, when he fell out of favour until Mary's accession. He was a contributor to *Tottel's *Miscellany* and *The Paradise of Dainty Devises*. He is chiefly remembered now as the author of 'The Aged Lover Renounceth Love', the song mumbled by the grave-digger in *Hamlet*, V. i. His poems were edited by L. P. Vonalt (1960).

Vauxhall, or **Fox Hall** (originally 'Falkes Hall', said to be from Falkes de Breauté, captain of King John's mercenaries, and lord of the manor in the early 13th cent.), famous for the gardens laid out there in the middle of the 17th cent., and at first called 'the New Spring Gardens', because they replaced the old Spring Gardens adjoining St James's Park. Vauxhall Gardens are frequently referred to from that time by dramatists and other writers, including *Pepys. Sir Roger de Coverley visited them with Mr Spectator (he commented on the scarcity of nightingales in the gardens as compared with less desirable visitors—*Spectator*, No. 383). Thackeray in chapter vi of *Vanity Fair* and Fanny Burney in *Evelina* describe the visits to them of certain of their characters. The gardens were finally closed in 1859.

Veal, (1) Captain, the ship's captain in Fielding's *Journal of a Voyage to Lisbon*; (2) Mrs, see DEFOE.

VEGA, Garcilaso, see GARCILASO DE LA VEGA.

VEGA CARPIO, Lope Felix de (1562–1635), Spanish poet and playwright, born in Madrid. He took part in the expedition to the Azores in 1582, and later sailed with the Armada in 1598, an experience which inspired one of his less-regarded works, an epic in ten cantos, *La Dragontea* (1598), which violently attacks England and *Drake. His personal life was passionate and turbulent; his many love poems are addressed to several mistresses. He was immensely prolific and versatile in many genres, and is regarded as the founder of Spanish drama; he claimed to have written 1,500 plays, of which several hundred survive. These include dramas of intrigue and chivalry, historical dramas, sacred dramas, plays of peasant life, and plays on biblical subjects. His other works include pastoral romances, imitations of *Tasso, and a novel in dialogue called *La Dorotea* (1632). The immense energy and fecundity of his imagination made a profound impact not only in Spain, but on European literature in general, particularly that of France.

Vendice, or **Vindice,** see REVENGER'S TRAGEDY, THE.

Veneering, Mr and Mrs, in Dickens's *Our Mutual Friend*, types of flashy social parvenus.

Venice Preserv'd, or *A Plot Discovered*, a tragedy in blank verse by *Otway, produced 1682.

Jaffeir, a noble Venetian youth, has secretly married Belvidera, daughter of a proud senator, Priuli, who has repudiated her. Jaffeir, reduced to poverty, begs Priuli for assistance, but is met with insults. Pierre, a foreign soldier with a grievance against the Venetian republic, stimulates Jaffeir's desire for revenge, confides to him a plot that is hatching against the state, and introduces him to the conspirators. As a pledge of his loyalty to them Jaffeir places Belvidera in the charge of their leader, Renault, but without explaining the reason. Renault tries to rape her in the night. She escapes to her husband, who, in spite of his pledge to the contrary, makes known to her the conspiracy. To save her father, who as one of the senators is to be killed, she persuades Jaffeir to reveal the plot to the Senate, but to claim as reward the lives of the conspirators. These are arrested. Jaffeir, loaded by them with insults, is overwhelmed with remorse. The senators, in spite of their promise, condemn the conspirators to death. Jaffeir threatens to kill Belvidera unless she secures their pardon from her father. She succeeds, but Priuli's intervention is too late. Belvidera goes mad. Jaffeir stabs his friend Pierre on the scaffold and then himself, and Belvidera dies broken-hearted.

The play, with *Betterton as Jaffeir and Mrs *Barry as Belvidera, was very well received and frequently revived. It was popular throughout the 18th and early 19th cents, and is still occasionally performed. The bawdy comic scenes in which the masochistic senator Antonio is kicked and abused by his whore Aquilina ('Nicky-Nacky') are strikingly different in tone from the rest of the play, and were at first popular, though by 1750 it was customary to cut them. Antonio is a caricature of *Shaftesbury.

Venn, Diggory, a character in Hardy's *The Return of the Native*.

Ventidius, (1) in Shakespeare's *Timon of Athens*, one of the faithless friends of Timon; (2) in his *Antony and*

Cleopatra and in Dryden's **All for Love*, one of Antony's generals.

Venus, Mr, in Dickens's **Our Mutual Friend*, a preparer of anatomical specimens and for a time an ally of Silas Wegg.

Venus and Adonis, an Ovidian poem by *Shakespeare, published 1593, the same year in which Marlowe's **Hero and Leander* was registered, and dedicated to Henry Wriothesley, earl of Southampton, who has been connected with the *Sonnets. The poem is written in *sesta rima*, a quatrain followed by a couplet, which Spenser used in **Astrophel* (1595) and Lodge in **Scillaes Metamorphosis* (1589). Shakespeare's poem was probably his first publication, and was first printed by Richard Field, another Stratford man, in 1593: it was extremely popular, being reprinted at least 15 times before 1640.

Venus, in love with the youth Adonis, detains him from the chase and woos him, but cannot win his love. She begs him to meet her the next day, but he is then to hunt the boar. She tries in vain to dissuade him. When the morning comes she hears his hounds at bay; filled with terror she goes to look for him and finds him killed by the boar.

Vercelli Book, The, an Old English manuscript, made in England before the year 1000, now in the possession of the chapter of Vercelli in north Italy. It contains prose sermons and about 3,500 lines of Old English poetry; its most distinguished contents are the poems **Dream of the Rood* and **Andreas*, and two of the four signed poems of *Cynewulf: *Elene* and *The Fates of the Apostles*.

ASPR 2. *The Vercelli Book Poems*, ed. F. P. Magoun (1960).

Verdant Green, The Adventures of, see BRADLEY, E.

VERDI, Giuseppe (1813–1901), Italian composer, mainly of operas, three of which are based on Shakespeare and two on *Byron. *I due foscari* (1844) and *Il corsaro* (*The Corsair*, 1848) are relatively early works. *Macbeth* (1847), the most remarkable of the operas before *Rigoletto*, is in a different class. Verdi gave his librettist (Francesco Piave) a more than usually rough passage in his determination to get the text as he wanted it; he took immense pains over the first production, and subjected the opera to a thorough revision for Paris in 1865. The Paris version, in which the opera is now heard, betrays its dual origin, yet remains a work of nobility, and Verdi was stung by Parisian criticism that he did not know his Shakespeare: 'Maybe I haven't done *Macbeth* justice', he wrote, 'but that I don't know, don't feel, don't understand Shakespeare—no, for God's sake no. I have had him in my hands from earliest youth, and I read and re-read him continually.'

This preoccupation continued throughout his life, although his next project, for a **King Lear*, proved abortive, probably because of dissatisfaction with the text. It was the problem of the libretto that made Verdi hesitate to set Shakespeare. But at the end of his life, after he had apparently concluded his career with *Aida* and the *Requiem Mass*, he found in *Boito a librettist who could give him what he needed. The story of their collaboration is touching, and its outcome the two greatest of all Shakespeare operas. *Otello* (1887) is perhaps the more remarkable achievement, particularly from a man in his seventies, yet the fleeting, boisterous tender wisdom of *Falstaff* (1893) and the technical perfection of its musical realization make this work Verdi's most personal expression of love for the English writer.

VERGA, Giovanni (1840–1922), Italian novelist, dramatist, and writer of short stories, born at Catania. His finest works portray life at the lower levels of society in his native Sicily. The novels *I malavoglia* (1881) and *Mastro-don Gesualdo* (1889) deal respectively with a family of poor Sicilian fisherfolk and an ambitious master stonemason in economic competition with the local gentry. The story 'Cavalleria rusticana' ('Rustic Chivalry', 1880), after being dramatized by the author, was adapted as a libretto for Mascagni's opera. True to the principles of **verismo*, Verga sought to eliminate from his works all trace of his own personality and outlook, and perfected a unique narrative style, which combined the literary language with idioms and constructions from popular and dialect speech. His English translators include D. H. *Lawrence, whose *Little Novels of Sicily* (1925) and *Cavalleria rusticana and Other Stories* (1928) contain the best of Verga's tales. Lawrence also translated the second of the great Sicilian novels under the title *Master don Gesualdo* (1923).

Verges, head borough or petty constable to *Dogberry's constable in Shakespeare's **Much Ado about Nothing*; his name suggests a possible spelling of 'verjuice' and so his sourness.

VERGIL, the Roman poet, see VIRGIL.

VERGIL, Polydore (?1470–?1555), a native of Urbino, who came to England in 1502 as sub-collector of Peter's pence, and held various ecclesiastical preferments; he was archdeacon of Wells 1508–54. He was a friend of Sir T. *More and other English humanists. He published his *Anglicae Historiae Libri XXVI* in 1534–55, a chronicle of special value for the reign of *Henry VII. He was also author of a *Proverbiorum Libellus* (Venice, 1498) anticipating the *Adagia* of *Erasmus.

verismo, a movement in 19th-cent. Italian literature akin to *Naturalism, whose greatest writer was the Sicilian *Verga. The affirmation of dialects, after the Unity of Italy (1870), ran counter both to state policies for linguistic unification and to *Manzoni's literary programme for a standard language. Literature was to document social conditions—particularly the 'southern question' which arose in the unified country because of exploitation of southern resources by the industrializing north. *Verismo* influenced the early works of the southern writers *d'Annunzio and *Pirandello, and it relates to post-war *neo-realism.

Verisopht, Lord Frederick, a character in Dickens's *Nicholas Nickleby.*

VERLAINE, Paul (1844–96), French poet. Some of his poems appeared in *Le Parnasse contemporain* of 1866; his *Poèmes saturniens* were published in the same year, and his *Fêtes galantes* in 1869. From the end of 1871 he came under the influence of *Rimbaud and their violently emotional homosexual relationship culminated in Verlaine's arrest and imprisonment, in 1873, for wounding Rimbaud with a revolver. His most interesting work, characterized by an intense musicality and metrical inventiveness, appeared in *Romances sans paroles* in 1874. His influential 'Art poétique' ('De la musique avant toute chose') dates from the same time, but remained unpublished for ten years. *Sagesse* (a religious work, written after his conversion to Catholicism) appeared in 1881, *Jadis et naguère* in 1884, and in the same year he published a number of short studies of contemporary poets (including *Mallarmé, and Rimbaud) under the title *Les Poètes maudits.* Verlaine's relationship with Rimbaud is the subject of a play by Christopher *Hampton, *Total Eclipse* (perf. 1968, pub. 1969).

Verloc, a character in Conrad's *The Secret Agent.*

VERNE, Jules (1828–1905), French novelist, who achieved great popularity with a long series of books combining adventure and popular science. Among his most successful stories are: *Voyage au centre de la terre* (1864; *Journey to the Centre of the Earth,* 1871); *Vingt mille lieues sous les mers* (1870; *20,000 Leagues under the Sea,* 1872), the adventures of Captain Nemo and his crew aboard the submarine *Nautilus;* and *Le Tour du monde en quatre-vingts jours* (1873; *Around the World in Eighty Days*), recounting the travels of the Englishman Phileas Fogg and his valet Passepartout.

vers de société, a term applied to a form of light verse dealing with events in polite society, usually in a satiric or playful tone, sometimes conversational, sometimes employing intricate forms such as the *villanelle or the *rondeau. English writers noted for their *vers de société* include *Prior, *Goldsmith, *Praed, *Calverley, *Dobson, and *Locker-Lampson.

vers libre, a term used to describe many forms of irregular, syllabic, or unrhymed verse, in which the ordinary rules of prosody are disregarded: *Whitman pioneered a form of *vers libre* in America, and its independent evolution in France and Belgium (in the works of *Laforgue, *Maeterlinck, and others in the 1890s) had a great influence on the early *Modernists such as T. S. *Eliot and *Pound.

VERTUE, George (1684–1756), engraver and antiquary, whose notes for a history of the arts in Britain are a major source of information. His notebooks were sold to Horace *Walpole, who used them as a basis for his *Anecdotes of Painting in England:* they were published separately by the Walpole Society (6 vols, 1930–55).

Verver, Adam and his daughter Maggie, characters in *The Golden Bowl* by H. James.

Very Woman, A, see MASSINGER.

VESEY, Mrs Elizabeth (?1715–91), an Irishwoman, the first, and perhaps the most loved and successful, of the *Blue Stocking hostesses. In the early 1750s she determined, with the support of her husband, who was an Irish MP, to open her doors to literary and fashionable society for an entirely new kind of evening party. Vivacious, intelligent, but always modest, she liked to break her parties into small, ever-changing groups; Horace *Walpole, a devoted attender at all Blue Stocking functions, described her gatherings as 'Babels'. She set the pattern of Blue Stocking evenings for the next 50 years and, according to Hannah *More in her poem *Bas Bleu,* shared with Mrs *Montague and Mrs *Boscawen 'the triple crown' among Blue Stocking hostesses.

Vestiges of Creation, see CHAMBERS, ROBERT.

Vholes, a lawyer in Dickens's *Bleak House.*

VIAN, Boris, see ABSURD, THEATRE OF THE.

'Vicar of Bray, The', a well-known song of unknown authorship, dating from the 18th cent. The subject is a time-serving parson, who boasts that he has accommodated himself to the religious views of the reigns of Charles, James, William, Anne, and George, and that 'whatsoever king may reign' he will remain vicar of Bray.

Various suggestions have been made as to who this vicar was. Haydn (*Dictionary of Dates*) quotes *Fuller as stating that Symon Symonds, vicar of Bray, Berkshire, in the reigns of Henry VIII, Edward VI, Mary, and Elizabeth, was twice a papist and twice a Protestant. When charged with being a time-server he is said to have replied, 'Not so, neither, for if I changed my religion, I am sure I kept true to my principle, which is to live and die the vicar of Bray' (see D'ISRAELI, *Curiosities of Literature,* s.v. 'Vicar of Bray').

Vicar of Bullhampton, The, a novel by A. *Trollope, published 1870.

Carry Brattle is a 'fallen woman', and her brother Sam is accused of the murder of a local farmer. A feud ensues between the arbitrary old marquis of Trowbridge and the vicar, Frank Fenwick, one of the best of Trollope's worldly and energetic clergymen, who takes the side of the Brattles. Sam's name is cleared and Carry is restored to her family at the mill. A sub-plot concerns the love of Fenwick's friend Harry Gilmore for Mary Lowther. Against her own better judgement and over-persuaded by the Fenwicks, she accepts him, but breaks her engagement when her previous suitor Walter Marrable unexpectedly comes into the family estate.

Vicar of Wakefield, The, a novel by *Goldsmith, published 1766.

This minor classic was sold for £60 by Dr *Johnson on Goldsmith's behalf, to prevent the author's arrest for debt. Dr Primrose and his wife Deborah live an idyllic life in a country parish with their six children, the most important of whom are George and Moses, Olivia and Sophia. On the eve of their son George's wedding to Arabella Wilmot, the vicar loses all his money through the bankruptcy of a merchant, and the young people cannot marry. George is sent away to town, and the family move to a meagre living on the land of a Squire Thornhill. Many references are made to the reputed worthiness of the squire's uncle, Sir William Thornhill. A poor, eccentric friend, Mr Burchell, rescues Sophia from drowning, but her attraction to him is not encouraged by her ambitious mother. Another period of frugal happy family life is disrupted by the attentions of the dashing squire, who captivates Olivia and encourages the social pretensions of Mrs Primrose and her daughters to a ludicrous degree. Two fashionable ladies from London offer 'places' to Olivia and Sophia, and the girls angrily dismiss Burchell's warnings. Then the girls hear, to their indignation, that because of a letter of Burchell's the London offer has been withdrawn.

Shortly, Olivia is reported as having fled, and Burchell is suspected. The vicar's anguished pursuit ends in three weeks of fever, after which he encounters Arabella, and falls in with a travelling theatre company. One of the players turns out to be his long-lost son George, who has been travelling abroad seeking a livelihood, and has recently returned. Thornhill reappears, now seriously courting Arabella, and obtains a commission in the army for his rival, George. Further along the road home Dr Primrose observes a young woman being ejected from an inn, and discovers she is his daughter Olivia. Thornhill had pretended to marry her, seduced her, and later cast her off, intending to add her to his other abandoned 'wives', now all prostitutes, but she had escaped. She exonerates Burchell, who had warned her against Thornhill. The vicar receives her with joy, and they proceed home, only to find a terrible fire destroying their house.

A period of grim poverty follows: Thornhill reappears, unrepentant, and offers to find a husband for the ailing Olivia. When he is rejected he demands his rent, which the vicar cannot pay, so he takes all the family's cattle instead. He then has the vicar removed to the debtors' prison where Primrose encounters every degradation: he hears of Olivia's death, is told that Sophia has been abducted, and finds that George has been brought bleeding and half-dead into the prison, having been set upon by Thornhill's servants.

At this point Sophia appears with Burchell. She explains how he rescued her from abduction by Thornhill, and in his gratitude the vicar offers her to Burchell as his wife. Meanwhile George has recognized Burchell as none other than the good Sir William Thornhill. The nephew is denounced as a scheming villain, and Arabella, disabused, is united with George. Olivia, who is not after all dead, was apparently legally wed to Thornhill after all, and he thus loses Arabella's fortune. All proceed home, where Sophia and Sir William, Arabella and George, are married at a double ceremony.

The well-known poems 'The Hermit', the 'Elegy on the Death of a Mad Dog', and 'When lovely woman stoops to folly' are placed at three turning points of the story.

Vice, the, a *fool or buffoon introduced into some of the *interludes and later moralities as a figure of evil. The descent of the figure from characters in *mystery cycles and *morality plays (such as 'The Vices', the *Seven Deadly Sins) is likely, though they are related too to the mischievous devil figure. See L. W. Cushman, *The Devil and the Vice in the English Dramatic Literature before Shakespeare* (1900; 1970); B. Spivack, *Shakespeare and the Allegory of Evil* (1958).

VICO, Giambattista (1668–1744), Italian philosopher and classical scholar. The son of a poor Neapolitan bookseller, he suffered penury until his appointment in 1734 as royal historian. His most important work is *Principii di una scienza nuova intorno alla natura delle nazioni* (*Principles of a New Science of Nations*, 1725, rev. 1729–30, 1744), in which he developed his theory of historical change as a redemptive design based on 'corsi' and 'ricorsi'—recurring cycles of barbarism, heroism, and reason. To each of these phases correspond cultural, linguistic, and political modes, and at the end of each cycle of phases there is a fall into disorder from which the next cycle is born. The language of poetry, being metaphoric and sensuous, flourishes in the heroic age. It is typified by the Homeric epics, for which Vico was first to postulate collective authorship. Prose enters with the age of reason. This scheme of cycles was put to artistic use by *Joyce.

VICTORIA (1819–1901), queen of England from 1837. She wrote innumerable letters and accumulated over 100 volumes of diaries and journals, kept from the age of 13 until shortly before her death. Much was excised by her family, at her wish, but many selections have been published. They are factual and practical, but observant and often vivid in detail. Her only writings published in her lifetime were *Leaves from a Journal of Our Life in the Highlands 1848–61*, which appeared in 1868. In spite of a limited vocabulary, the queen's love of Scotland comes clearly through her observations on the views, the weather, and the domestic events of her holidays. Expeditions, such as that up Lochnagar, are undertaken in all weathers, by pony and on foot, with lengthy pauses for spartan picnics and to watch Prince Albert shoot. *More Leaves* covered the years 1862–3 and appeared in 1883. Apart from her huge official correspondence, the queen's lively and heavily underlined letters to her eldest daughter Vicky have been published, and also a selection of her daughter's replies.

In her diaries the queen notes her reading, which included many sermons; some Shakespeare; some *Macaulay; F. *Burney and J. *Austen. She took an interest in the novelists of her own reign, including Sir W. *Scott, *Dickens, the *Brontës, Mrs *Gaskell, G. *Eliot, and *Disraeli. But she preferred poetry ('in all shapes'), a preference which led to her friendship with *Tennyson, whom she regarded as the perfect poet of 'love and loss'. Their correspondence has been published. Among many biographical studies, mention may be made of L. *Strachey's highly unauthorized life (1921) and E. Longford's authorized version (1964).

VIDAL, Gore (Eugene Luther Jr) (1925–   ), American novelist and essayist, born at West Point, New York, where his father was an instructor at the US Military Academy. He saw army service during the Second World War, the experience of which was drawn on for his first novel, *Williwaw* (1946). *In a Yellow Wood* (1947) was the story of a Nonconformist army veteran, and this was followed by *The City and the Pillar* (1948), a study of homosexuality, and *The Season of Comfort* (1949), about the conflict between a boy and his mother. In *A Search for the King* (1950), concerning the affection of a troubadour for Richard the Lionheart, he signalled his interest in the utilization of history, often as a means of analysing the present. Novels in this vein include *Julian* (1964), about the Roman emperor Julian the Apostate; *Two Sisters* (1970), which juxtaposes the Roman world of the 4th cent. with contemporary life; and *Creation* (1981), set in the 5th-cent. world of Darius, Xerxes, and Confucius. A sequence of 'Narratives of a Golden Age', chronicling the history of America from the mid-19th cent., includes *Washington, D.C.* (1967), *1876* (1976), *Lincoln* (1984), *Empire* (1987), *Burr* (1973), and *Hollywood* (1990). His most celebrated novel, *Myra Breckenridge* (1968), wittily chronicled the adventures of a transsexual; its sequel, *Myron*, was published in 1974. Other works include *Dark Green, Bright Red* (1950), about an American army officer caught up in a Latin American revolution; *The Judgement of Paris* (1952), a contemporary version of the classic tale; *Kalki* (1978), a satire on feminism; and *Duluth* (1983), set in the late 20th cent. *Live from Golgotha* (1992) was a satirical fantasy on television culture. A collection of stories, *A Thirsty Evil*, was published in 1956. His essays—elegant and pungent in equal measure—on history, literature, culture, and politics have been collected in *Rocking the Boat* (1962), *Reflections upon a Sinking Ship* (1969), *Homage to Daniel Shays* (1973), *Matters of Fact and of*

Fiction (1977), *The Second American Revolution* (1982), *Armageddon* (1987), and *A View from the Diner's Club* (1991). He has also written plays for television and the stage, including *Visit to a Small Planet* (1956), and detective stories under the pseudonym Edgar Box. A candid memoir of Vidal's life up to the age of 40, *Palimpsest*, was published in 1995.

vignette, an ornamental design on a blank space in a book, especially at the beginning or end of a chapter, of small size, and unenclosed in a border. The word is a diminutive of the French *vigne*, a vine; originally meaning an ornament of leaves and tendrils. It is now, by extension, used for any miniature work, visual, verbal, or musical.

VIGNY, Alfred de (1797–1863), French poet. His ten-year career as an army officer was undistinguished, and he was discharged in 1827. His career as a poet, however, consistently upheld a basic romantic value: stoic pride as the only valid response to the inflexibility of Divine Justice. His historical novel *Cinq-Mars* (1826), based on a conspiracy against Cardinal *Richelieu, his three tales *Servitude et grandeur militaires* (1835), illustrating the self-sacrifice of Napoleon's armies, and his play *Chatterton* (1835), on the fate of the solitary poet in the world, form part of what he called his 'epic of disillusionment' which argued in favour of a reasoned pessimism as a condition for survival. A number of powerful individual poems, such as 'La Mort du loup', 'Le Mont des oliviers', and 'La Bouteille à la mer' (collected posthumously in 1863), proclaim a more positive, though equally romantic, faith in 'man's unconquerable mind'.

Village, The, a poem by *Crabbe, published 1783.

The poet contrasts the cruel realities of country life with the Arcadian pastoral favoured by poets. He was assisted in the writing of the work (which Dr *Johnson found 'original, vigorous, and elegant') both by his patron *Burke and by Johnson. The poem established Crabbe's reputation as a writer.

villanelle, a poem, usually of a pastoral or lyrical nature, consisting normally of five three-lined stanzas and a final quatrain, with only two rhymes throughout. The first and third lines of the first stanza are repeated alternately in the succeeding stanzas as a refrain, and form a final couplet in the quatrain [OED]. The form has been much employed in light verse and *vers de société by *Lang, *Dobson, and others, and in the 20th cent. was used to more serious purpose by *Auden, *Empson ('Slowly the poison the whole blood stream fills'), Dylan *Thomas ('Do not go gentle into that good night'), and others.

VILLEHARDOUIN, Geoffroi de (*c.*1152–1212), a member of a powerful French crusading family which ruled over a great court at Achaea, marshal of Champagne. He was an eyewitness of the events described in his *Conquête de Constantinople*, an account of the so-called

Fourth Crusade, the first great literary work in French prose. Villehardouin relates with vigour and picturesqueness the negotiations with the doge of Venice, the departure of the crusading host, its diversion from its proper purpose to various more secular undertakings, including the capture of Constantinople, the subsequent dissensions and intrigues, culminating in the crowning of Baldwin of Flanders as emperor of the East, and the grant of the kingdom of Macedonia to Boniface of Montferrat. See M. R. B. Shaw, *Chronicles of the Crusades: Joinville and Villehardouin* (1963).

Villette, a novel by C. *Brontë, published 1853.

The novel, like its predecessor *The Professor* (then unpublished), is based on the author's experiences in Brussels, here renamed Villette, and also has as its centre a pupil–teacher relationship. The narrator, Lucy Snowe, poor, plain, and friendless, finds herself a post as teacher in a girls' school in Villette, where she wins the respect of the capable, if unscrupulous, headmistress, Mme Beck, and gains authority over the boisterous girls. She becomes deeply attached to the handsome John Bretton, the school's English doctor, in whom she recognizes an acquaintance from her childhood, the son of her own godmother; she watches his infatuation with the shallow and flirtatious Ginevra Fanshawe, followed by a happier love for his childhood friend Paulina Home, and represses her own strong feelings for him. These feelings gradually attach themselves to the waspish, despotic, but good-hearted little professor, M. Paul Emanuel, Mme Beck's cousin, whose own response to her changes from asperity to esteem and affection, despite Mme Beck's attempts to discourage the friendship. His generosity leaves her mistress of her own school when he is called away on business to the West Indies; the ending is ambiguous, and the reader is left to decide whether he returns to marry her or is drowned on his way home. The novel combines a masterly portrayal of Belgian daily life with a highly personal use of the elements of *Gothic fiction; Charlotte Brontë uses hints of the supernatural (the story of a ghostly nun, a visit to the mysterious and deformed Mme Walravens) to heighten the impression of her heroine's nervous isolation and heroic fortitude; but all the apparitions are found to have realistic explanations, and in Paul Emanuel she successfully creates an unromantic hero very far removed from the *Byronic Rochester of *Jane Eyre*.

VILLIERS DE L'ISLE-ADAM, Philippe-Auguste (1838–89), French novelist, dramatist, and aesthete. His best-known work, the visionary drama *Axël* (1890, English trans. Fineberg, 1925), which first appeared in symbolist reviews, is a Wagnerian narrative of love and death set in an isolated German castle, which enshrines *Rosicrucian mysteries. Its symbolic subtleties have exerted an influence on English writing which has only recently begun to be recognized; it provided a title for E. *Wilson's study of symbolist writers, *Axel's Castle* (1931).

VILLON, François (1431–after 1463), French poet. He studied at the University of Paris, gaining a master's degree in 1452. The little that is known of his life suggests nearly constant turmoil: he was imprisoned several times for violent crime and theft, and narrowly escaped death by hanging in 1463. His surviving work consists mainly of *Le Lais* (or *Petit Testament*) and *Le Testament* (or *Grand Testament*); the latter contains the famous 'Ballade des dames du temps jadis', with its refrain, 'Mais où sont les neiges d'antan?' In addition to these two works a number of short poems survive, including Villon's own epitaph, 'Frères humains qui après nous vivez', written under sentence of death. He is now recognized as pre-eminent among the poets of medieval France. He has been frequently translated into English since the 19th cent.; there are versions of individual poems by *Rossetti, *Swinburne, and R. *Lowell, among others.

VINCENT OF BEAUVAIS, the Dominican author of *Speculum Naturale, Historiale, Doctrinale* (c.1250), an enormous compilation of all the knowledge known at the time. He is mentioned by Chaucer in one version of the prologue to *The Legend of Good Women* (G 307).

Vincentio, (1) Lucentio's father in Shakespeare's *The Taming of the Shrew*; (2) the duke in his *Measure for Measure*.

Vincy, Fred and Rosamond, characters in G. Eliot's *Middlemarch*.

Vindication of a Natural Society, A, a treatise by E. *Burke, published anonymously 1756, his first substantial work. It is an ironical answer to *Bolingbroke's indictment of revealed religion, in imitation of his style and in the form of a *reductio ad absurdum*; it was so successful a parody that even *Warburton was deceived by it, and in 1765 Burke published another edition with a preface explaining his ironical stance. Bolingbroke had exalted the claims of natural religion by pointing to the unfortunate results of religious creeds; Burke points to the evil results of artificial society and the artificial division of rich and poor, but expects his exposition to reinforce 'the necessity of political institutions, weak and wicked as they are'.

Vindication of the Rights of Woman, A, by M. *Wollstonecraft, published 1792.

In this work the author attacks the educational restrictions and 'mistaken notions of female excellence' that keep women in a state of 'ignorance and slavish dependence'. She argues that girls are forced into passivity, vanity, and credulity by lack of physical and mental stimulus, and by a constant insistence on the need to please; she attacks the educational theories of the 'unmanly, immoral' *Chesterfield, of *Rousseau (who in her view made false and discriminatory distinctions in his approach to the sexes in *Émile*), and of other writers, concluding that 'From the tyranny of man . . . the greater number of female follies proceed.' The work was much acclaimed, but also inevitably attracted hostility; Horace *Walpole referred to its author as 'a hyena in petticoats'.

Vindice, see REVENGER'S TRAGEDY, THE.

VINE, Barbara, see RENDELL.

Violenta, one of the dramatis personae of Shakespeare's *All's Well that Ends Well* who appears only once (III. v) in the play and does not speak; sometimes referred to as a typical nonentity.

Virago Press, see CALLIL.

virelay, a song or short lyric piece, of a type originating in France in the 14th cent., usually consisting of short lines arranged in stanzas with only two rhymes, the end-rhyme of one stanza being the chief one of the next [*OED*].

Virgidemiarum, Sex Libri, by J. *Hall, two volumes of English satires, 1597 and 1598. The first volume, called 'Toothless', satirizes certain literary conventions in the spirit of *Martial and *Horace; the second volume, Juvenalian in character, 'bites' fiercely into such ills as sexual promiscuity, ostentatious piety, impostures in astrology and genealogy, economic injustices, etc. The title means 'a sheaf of rods', with which the satirist delivers his blows. The books were condemned by the high commission in 1599, along with satires by *Marston, *Nashe, and others; but Hall's books were reprieved.

VIRGIL (Publius Vergilius Maro) (70–19 BC), the greatest of Roman poets, valued particularly for his craftsmanship, love of nature, and sense of pathos. Maturing at a time when the Romans were struggling to produce a literature that would match the Greek, he imitated successively the pastorals of *Theocritus, the didactic poems of *Hesiod and Aratus, and the epics of *Homer, making original contributions to all three genres. In his *Eclogues* he added a new level of meaning to the pastoral's idealization of country life by alluding to topics of contemporary interest; in the *Georgics* he transformed the bald didacticism of his models into a panegyric of Italy and the traditional ways of rural life; and in the *Aeneid* he committed the epic to the presentation of a major patriotic theme. He began like most poets of his generation by working within the conventions of *Hellenistic poetry, but later, when he came to enjoy the patronage of Augustus, he widened his stylistic range and, drawing also on earlier and more naïve authors, created a diction and a manner of presentation that were all his own.

Everyone who could read Latin (and until the latter half of the 19th cent. that covered all educated persons) read Virgil; and although it is easy to trace borrowings from his works, these fall far short of representing the totality of his influence, which was pervasive rather than specific. Many generations found in him their main gateway to the *sublime. In the Middle Ages he

was regarded as a seer and a magician, and the 'Messianic Eclogue' (below) led *Dante to choose him as a guide through hell and purgatory. His *Aeneid* served as a model for all the Latin epics of the medieval period and then for the new classical epic of the Renaissance. There are Virgilian similes in *Spenser, Virgilian motifs in Shakespeare's *Rape of Lucrece* and Milton's *Paradise Lost*. The *Georgics*, comparatively neglected earlier, came into their own in the 18th cent., when they provided a model for descriptive poets like J. *Thomson and were seriously discussed by writers on agriculture. In the 19th cent. came *Wordsworth's 'Laodamia' and *Tennyson's avowal in 'To Virgil' of an indebtedness beyond the obvious.

A legion of translators was attracted to Virgil. *Dryden's version of his works (1697) remains probably the finest in spite of its occasional defects. Gavin *Douglas, writing in Scots, produced a vivid *Aeneid* (1513) and W. *Morris a ponderously medieval one (1885). There have been interesting translations by C. *Day-Lewis of the *Georgics* (1940) and the *Aeneid* (1952).

Virgilia, in Shakespeare's *Coriolanus*, the wife of Coriolanus.

'Virgil's Fourth or Messianic Eclogue', written 40 BC, celebrated the coming birth of a child who would bring back the Golden Age and preside over a world at peace. Christian scholars from *Augustine to the present have read the poem as a prophecy of the birth of Christ, an interpretation that appeared the more plausible because of similarities to passages in Isaiah believed by Christians to be Messianic prophecies. It is possible that Virgil was familiar with the Septuagint text of Isaiah 7: 14 which predicts that a virgin will conceive, but it is more likely that he was drawing on Sibylline writings originating in a south Italian culture that had come under Phoenician influence.

'Virgils Gnat', a poem by *Spenser, published 1591, and adapted from the *Culex* attributed to *Virgil. A shepherd sleeping in the shade is about to be attacked by a serpent, when a gnat, to warn him, stings him on the eyelid. The shepherd crushes the gnat, and sees and kills the serpent. The next night the ghost of the gnat reproaches him for his cruelty. The shepherd, filled with remorse, raises a monument to the gnat. In what way the poem reflects Spenser's relations with the earl of Leicester, to whom it was dedicated 'Long since', will probably never be known.

Virginia, a daughter of the centurion Lucius Virginius. Appius Claudius, the decemvir, became enamoured of her and sought to get possession of her. For this purpose she was claimed by one of his favourites as daughter of a slave, and Appius in the capacity of a judge gave sentence in his favour and delivered her into the hands of his friend. Virginius, informed of these proceedings, arrived from the camp, and plunged a dagger into his daughter's breast to save her from the tyrant. He then rushed to the camp with the bloody knife in his hand. The soldiers, incensed against Appius Claudius, marched to Rome and seized him. But he destroyed himself in prison and averted the execution of the law. This story (which is in *Livy, 3. 44 *et seq.*) is the basis of two plays called *Appius and Virginia*, one by *Webster and/or *Heywood, one by *Dennis; of *Knowles's tragedy *Virginius*; and one of Macaulay's *Lays of Ancient Rome*.

Virginians, The, a *historical novel of the American Revolution by *Thackeray, published in numbers, Nov. 1857–Oct. 1859, and illustrated by the author. George Washington plays a prominent part in the narrative, a fact which offended some American readers. The novel takes up the story of the Esmond family a generation after the events of *The History of Henry Esmond*, and mainly concerns the fortunes of Esmond's twin grandsons, George and Harry Warrington, in America and England. Their mother, Esmond's only daughter Rachel, favours her younger son Harry, and is capricious and autocratic in her treatment of George. The boys are alike in appearance, but totally different in character, George being serious and scholarly, Harry cheerful, volatile, and attractive. However, they always remain close friends. When George disappears in a military expedition against the French and is presumed dead, Harry, now the heir, visits England, and meets his Castlewood relations, whose corrupt behaviour is in marked contrast to Harry's New World innocence. Under their influence Harry plunges into gambling and dissipation, and is inveigled into an engagement to his much older cousin Maria. He is arrested for debt and imprisoned in a sponging-house. He is rescued by the sudden reappearance of George, who has escaped from the French and come to England. Maria releases Harry from his engagement, since he is no longer heir to a fortune. But when George falls in love with and marries Theo, the daughter of a poor soldier, General Lambert, rather than an American heiress, his mother cuts off his allowance, and he is only saved from penury by becoming the heir of Sir Miles Warrington, of the English branch of the family. Harry has become a favourite of the rakish old Baroness Bernstein, the former Beatrix Esmond, and she leaves money to him in her will. Harry joins the army, and is with Wolfe at the capture of Quebec. He falls in love with Fanny Mountain, the daughter of his mother's housekeeper, and marries her rather than Hetty Lambert, Theo's sister, who is in love with him. When the War of Independence breaks out, Harry joins Washington, and George, who is in the British army, resigns his commission rather than run the risk of fighting against his brother. He settles on the Warrington estates in England, and gives up the Virginian property to Harry. George Warrington in *Pendennis* is a descendant of the Warrington family of this novel.

Virgin Martyr, The, a tragedy by *Massinger and *Dekker, printed 1622.

The Emperor Diocletian bids his daughter Artemia choose whom she will marry. She chooses Antoninus, a brave soldier, son of Sapritius, governor of Caesarea. He declines the dangerous honour, being moreover devoted to Dorothea, a maid of the Christian sect, which is at the time subject to persecution. Theophilus, a zealous persecutor, and his secretary Harpax, 'an evil spirit', betray Antoninus and Dorothea to Artemia, who finds them together, and at once orders them to execution, but presently allows Theophilus to send his daughters to Dorothea to convert her to the pagan religion. The daughters, instead, are converted by Dorothea to Christianity, and on their boldly professing it are killed by their own father. Dorothea, attended by her 'good spirit' Angelo, is subjected to extremes of torture and indignity and finally executed, Antoninus dying by her side. In the last act, Angelo and Harpax, the good and evil spirits, contend for the soul of Theophilus. Theophilus, summoned before Diocletian, proclaims his conversion to Christianity, courageously suffers torture, and dies. The same story has been treated in poems by *Swinburne and G. M. *Hopkins.

virtuosi, see LITERATI.

Vision of Judgement, A, a poem in hexameters by R. *Southey, published 1821, at the time when he was *poet laureate.

The preface, written in defence of this metrical innovation, contains, in a digression, a violent attack on the works of *Byron, 'those monstrous combinations of horrors and mockery, lewdness and impiety'. Byron retorted with his parody *The Vision of Judgement* (below).

The poet in a trance sees George III (who had died in 1820) rise from the tomb and, after receiving from the shade of Perceval news of affairs in England, proceed to the gates of heaven. The devil, accompanied by *Wilkes, comes forward to arraign him, but retires discomfited, and the king, after receiving a eulogy from Washington, is admitted to Paradise, where he is greeted by previous English sovereigns, the worthies of England, and finally by his family.

'Vision of Judgment, The', a satirical poem in *ottava rima* by *Byron, published in the *Liberal*, 1822.

In 1821 appeared *A Vision of Judgement* by *Southey (see above), which in its preface described Byron as the leader of the 'Satanic school' of poetry. Byron replied with an exuberant travesty of Southey's poem. George III, at the celestial gate, is claimed by Satan, who catalogues his crimes against freedom and the national and individual woes that he condoned: Satan then calls a crowd of witnesses, including the 'merry, cock-eyed', and forgiving sprite of *Wilkes and the unforgiving *Junius, to testify to the king's disastrous reign. Southey is swept up from the Lake District by a devil, and is mocked by Byron for his 'spavin'd dactyls' and derided as a political renegade, a time-server, and a hack—Southey demonstrates his venality by offering to add Satan's biography to his life of Wesley. The poem ends as Southey attempts to read from his own manuscript; this causes such distress to the assembled spirits that he is knocked back down to his own lake by St Peter, and in the confusion King George is allowed to slip into heaven. The work is a tour de force of mock-heroic wit, savage in its attack, yet buoyant with its own inventiveness, and the indictment of the king himself is lightened by references to his dull domestic virtues—

> A better farmer ne'er brushed dew from lawn,
> A worse king never left a realm undone!

'Vision of Mirzah, The', an allegory by *Addison, published in the *Spectator* (No. 159). Mirzah has a vision of human life as a bridge over which multitudes are passing, some dropping through concealed trap-doors into the flood beneath; he also sees the happy islands of the virtuous dead.

Vita nuova, see DANTE.

VITRUVIUS POLLIO (fl. 40 BC), Roman architect and author of *De Architectura*, the only surviving classical treatise on architecture. It was much studied by Renaissance and later architects; the first printed edition was published in 1486.

Vittoria Corombona, see WHITE DEVIL, THE.

Vivian Grey, a novel by B. *Disraeli, published 1826, with a continuation in 1827.

This was the first of Disraeli's novels, published anonymously when he was 22 and written, as he later observed, 'with imagination acting upon knowledge not acquired by experience'. The first of a group of three novels (the others were *Alroy* and *Contarini Fleming*), it represented, in its author's words, 'my active and real ambition'. Vivian, a brilliant and difficult boy, is expelled from school, and discovers that by clever manipulation of his charm and social skills he can advance himself in the world of politics. He becomes the protégé of the marquis of Carabas, a powerful but disappointed politician, and by cynically playing on the follies of various discontented peers and MPs builds a faction round the marquis. His secret efforts to create a new party are exposed by the tempestuous Mrs Lorraine (a reminiscence of Lady Caroline *Lamb). Vivian is challenged to a duel by the outraged Cleveland, leader-designate of the party, whom Vivian kills. All hopes destroyed, the young man leaves England and begins a desultory life of intrigue, adventure, and lost love among German princelings and principalities. The last four books were added by popular demand in 1827.

Disraeli came to dislike the novel, and the character of the unprincipled Vivian dogged him for many years: he tried to suppress the book, but pirated editions abroad forced him to reprint, and in 1853 he drastically revised the work. Among various identifications, the kindly, scholarly Mr Grey represents Disraeli's father, Isaac *D'Israeli, the dashing Lord Alhambra has something of *Byron, the marquis of Carabas of John *Murray (who was extremely angry), and Cleveland of *Lockhart.

Vivieni, Emilia, see EPIPSYCHIDION.

Vivien, see LADY OF THE LAKE.

VIZETELLY, Henry (1820–94), son of a publisher and engraver, of a family Italian in origin, but long settled in England; he became an engraver, publisher, journalist, and editor, whose defiance of censorship and policy of issuing cheap reprints had a considerable impact on the literary scene. In 1885 he joined forces with G. A. *Moore to publish a cheap one-volume edition of *A Mummer's Wife*, an act which did much to break the power of the circulating *libraries and the three-decker novel; in 1886 with H. *Ellis he founded the *Mermaid Series of unexpurgated reprints of 'Best Plays of the Old Dramatists'. He also published translations of *Flaubert, *Gogol, *Tolstoy, the *Goncourts, etc., and 17 novels by *Zola; it was his publication of Zola's *La Terre* that led to his three-month imprisonment in 1888 on an obscenity charge, despite the protests of *Bradlaugh, *Gosse, Ellis, and others. This bankrupted his publishing company. Vizetelly had many friends in the artistic and literary world, including *Thackeray, *Doré, and *Sala, and his memoirs, *Glances back through Seventy Years* (1893), give a lively portrait of bohemian society.

VOLNEY, Constantin François de Chassebœuf, comte de (1757–1820), French historian, travel writer, and *philosophe*, author of *Les Ruines, ou méditation sur les révolutions des empires* (1791), in which contemplation of the ruins of Palmyra becomes the occasion for reflections on the rise, progress, and decline of ancient civilizations and the prospect for modern ones. The soul of the narrator, enlightened by a spirit, the Genius of Tombs and Ruins, comprehends through a conspectus of human history that man's miseries have at all times been the result of his ignorance, greed, and neglect of natural law; but that, guided by Nature and Reason, he will at last come to know his own best interest. Putting aside the dual tyranny of religious superstition and political despotism, he will perfect his nature and establish freedom, equality, and justice. *Les Ruines* was translated into English in 1795 and (generally known as *Ruins of Empire*) had a certain currency in England through the early 19th cent., especially among rationalists and freethinkers. It was a favourite book of *Shelley's, providing the plan for his *Queen Mab*; in Mary Shelley's *Frankenstein* it is one of four books by means of which the monster receives his education.

Volpone, or *The Fox*, a comedy by *Jonson, performed by the King's Men in 1605–6, printed 1607.

Volpone, a rich Venetian without children, feigns that he is dying, in order to draw gifts from his would-be heirs. Mosca, his parasite and confederate, persuades each of these in turn that he is to be the heir, and thus extracts costly presents from them. One of them, Corvino, even attempts to sacrifice his wife to Volpone in hope of the inheritance. Finally Volpone over-reaches himself. To enjoy the discomfiture of the vultures who are awaiting his death, he makes over his property by will to Mosca and pretends to be dead. Mosca takes advantage of the situation to blackmail Volpone, but rather than be thus defeated Volpone chooses to reveal all to the authorities. They direct that Volpone shall be cast in irons until he is as infirm as he pretended to be, Mosca whipped and confined to the galleys, Corvino made to parade in ass's ears, and his wife be returned to her family with a trebled dowry. A secondary plot involves Sir Politic Would-be, an English traveller who has absurd schemes for improving trade and curing diseases, and his Lady, a loquacious, hectoring pedant. Sir Politic is chastened when Peregrine, a wiser English traveller, pretends to have him arrested for treason. The names of the principal characters, Volpone (the fox), Mosca (the fly), Voltore (the vulture), Corbaccio (the crow), Corvino (the raven), indicate their roles and natures.

Volscius, Prince, a character in Buckingham's *The Rehearsal.* He is torn between love and honour, and comes on the stage with one boot on and one off, his legs illustrating his distraction.

Volsunga saga, a prose version of a lost cycle of heroic songs of which fragments survive in the poetic *Edda, dealing with the families of the Volsungs and the Niblungs. It has been translated by W. *Morris and E. Magnusson (1888). For the treatment in it of the story of Sigurd and Brunhild, see SIGURD THE VOLSUNG.

VOLTAIRE, pseudonym of François-Marie Arouet (1694–1778), French satirist, novelist, historian, poet, dramatist, polemicist, moralist, critic, and correspondent. Voltaire was the universal genius of the *Enlightenment. Welcomed in the free-thinking circles of Parisian society, he was committed to the Bastille for his satires in 1717–18, and again exiled to England in 1726–9. The remainder of his life was divided between long periods of retreat in the provinces (first in Champagne with Mme du Châtelet, finally at Ferney near Geneva) and brief returns to metropolitan centres (Paris, Versailles, Berlin). His literary principles were fundamentally neo-classical: his epic poem *La Henriade* (1723 and 1728), on the career of Henry of Navarre, and his heroic tragedies, notably *Zaïre* (1732), a Turkish tale of fated love, exhibit all the formality, decorum, artificiality, and lucidity of the mode. His political principles were essentially liberal. The *Lettres philosophiques* (1734, English version 1733), inspired by his residence in England, which mention *Congreve and *Addison, attack the abuses of the *ancien régime* in

the name of tolerance and liberty, while his history *Le Siècle de Louis XIV* (1751) disregards providence as an explanatory principle, seeking instead evidence of social and moral progress. His most characteristic works, however, were his philosophical tales, notably *Zadig* (1747) and *Candide* (1759) in which the rapidity, cleverness, and precision of his mind are put to the service of elaborating a rational protection against the basic evils of life. His relentless mockery of the cruelty and obscurantism of the civil and ecclesiastical establishments was the source of both his persecution and his immense prestige.

Volumnia, in Shakespeare's *Coriolanus,* the mother of Coriolanus. A proud, imperious Roman matron, she rejoices in her son's exploits; but it is her eloquence that saves Rome from the Volscians, at her son's expense.

von ARNIM, Elizabeth (1866–1941), novelist and cousin of K. *Mansfield, born Mary Annette Beauchamp in Sydney, Australia. In 1890 she married Count Henning August von Arnim-Schlagenthin, who appears as 'the Man of Wrath' in her best-known work, *Elizabeth and Her German Garden,* published anonymously in 1898; it describes her family life and the garden she created at Nassenheide in Pomerania. E. M. *Forster and Hugh *Walpole were tutors to her children there. After von Arnim's death she was married in 1916 to Bertrand *Russell's brother, the second Earl Russell. She published many novels, including *Pastor's Wife* (1914), *Vera* (1921), and *The Enchanted April* (1922, adapted for film in 1992), and a quirky autobiography, *All the Dogs of My Life* (1936). Noted for its descriptive power and irreverent wit, her work reveals a keen sense of women's struggle for autonomy within marriage.

von HÜGEL, Friedrich, baron of the Holy Roman Empire (1852–1925), Roman Catholic theologian and philosopher. He was born in Florence and after a cosmopolitan education settled in England in 1867. He studied natural science, philosophy, and religious history, adopting the critical views of the Old Testament. In 1905 he founded the London Society for the Study of Religion, which brought him into touch with thinkers and scholars of the most diverse views. His works include *The Mystical Element of Religion* (1908), *Eternal Life* (1912), and *The Reality of God* (published posthumously, 1931).

VONNEGUT, Kurt (1922–), American novelist and short story writer who attended Cornell before serving in the air force in the Second World War. Captured by the Germans, he survived the bombing of Dresden in 1945, an experience that he would later use in his most famous novel, *Slaughterhouse-Five; or The Children's Crusade* (1969). His earlier works drew on *science fiction and fantasy to satirize the increasing mechanization and dehumanization of the post-war world. His first novel, *Player Piano* (1952), envisages a New York factory town whose automated structure turns its workers and scientists into virtual robots. In *The Sirens of Titan* (1959) the human race is stumbled upon by aliens searching for a new spaceship; whilst *Cat's Cradle* (1963) imagines how a scientific discovery threatens to destroy the planet. He has also written plays, of which *Happy Birthday Wanda June* (1970) is the best known, and collections of stories, chief among which is *Welcome to the Monkey House* (1968). Other novels include *Breakfast of Champions* (1973), *Slapstick* (1976), *Jailbird* (1979), and *Deadeye Dick* (1983).

VORAGINE, Jacobus de, see GOLDEN LEGEND.

Vorticism, an aggressive literary and artistic movement that flourished 1912–15; it attacked the sentimentality of 19th-cent. art and celebrated violence, energy, and the machine. The Vorticists, dominated by W. *Lewis, included *Pound, *Gaudier-Brzeska, the painters C. R. Nevinson and Edward Wadsworth; they were associated with T. E. *Hulme, F. M. *Ford, and the sculptor Jacob Epstein (*Rock Drill*, 1913, Tate Gallery, London). In the visual arts this revolutionary fervour was expressed in abstract compositions of bold lines, sharp angles, and planes; the Vorticist style was indebted to Cubism and *Futurism, although Lewis mocked the Futurist obsession with speed (E. Wadsworth, *Abstract Composition*, 1915, Tate Gallery, London; Wyndham Lewis, *Composition*, 1913, Tate Gallery, London). *Blast: The Review of the Great English Vortex*, published in June 1914 and edited by Lewis, was an ambitious attempt to establish in England a magazine dedicated to the modern movement and to draw together artists and writers of the avant-garde. Its long lists of the blasted and blessed, its mixture of flippancy and rhetoric, and its provocative title and typography were designed to jolt the English out of their complacent insularity. Several artists adapted the Vorticist style to First World War subjects, but the real impetus petered out after the Vorticist Exhibition held at the Doré Gallery in 1915.

Vortigern, a legendary 5th-cent. king of Britain who is reputed to have enlisted Hengist and Horsa against his former allies the Picts, thus causing the transfer of Britain to the Anglo-Saxons. He marries Renwein (Rowena), the daughter of Hengist. After a lifetime of feuds and alliances with the Germanic invaders, in the course of which he meets Merlin and is astonished by his prophecies, he is burnt alive in the tower in Wales to which he had retired. The story is told in *Geoffrey of Monmouth's *History* (vi. 6–viii. 2) and *Laȝamon's *Brut*, 14,255–396.

Vortigern and Rowena, see IRELAND, W. H.

VOSSIUS, Gerhard Jan (1577–1649), and Isaac (1618–89), his son, eminent Dutch scholars. The father, who was invited to England and made a canon of Canterbury, was professor of history at Amsterdam and author of *Historia Pelagiana*. The son came to England and was a canon of Windsor 1673–89. He published editions of *Catullus and *Juvenal and *Observations* on classical subjects.

Vox Clamantis, see GOWER, J.

VOYNICH, Ethel Lillian, née Boole (1864–1960), novelist, born in Cork, remembered for her revolutionary novel *The Gadfly* (1897), set in pre-1848 Italy, which sold in vast quantities in translation in the Soviet Union. She married a Polish revolutionary, and worked in London for the periodical *Free Russia*.

VOZNESENSKY, Andrey (1933–), Russian poet, born in Moscow and trained as an architect at the Moscow Institute of Architecture. His first successful volume, *Mosaika* (1960), was followed by others including *Antimiri* (trans. as *Antiworlds* 1963, by Max Hayward, R. *Wilbur, *Auden, and others) and *On the Edge: Poems and Essays from Russia* (trans. R. McKane, 1991). His poems are lyrics of contemporary life: he is a defender of *Modernism, with a strong visual sense and an interest in the visual arts, culminating in his development of the genre of the 'video-poem' in the 1990s.

Vulgar Errors, see PSEUDODOXIA EPIDEMICA.

Vulgate, the, from the Latin *vulgatus*, 'made public or common', a term applied more particularly to St *Jerome's Latin version of the Bible completed in *c*.404. The Clementine text of this, a recension made by order of Clement VIII (1592–1605), is the authorized Latin text of the Roman Catholic Church. See BIBLE.

Vulgate Cycle, the, a very important group of Arthurian romances in French prose, dating from 1215–30. It comprises the three romances which make up the Prose *Lancelot* (*Lancelot* itself, the *Queste del Saint Graal*, and *Mort Artu*) and two others: the *Estoire del Saint Graal*, and a version of Robert de *Boron's partially surviving *Merlin*. The group is the most influential version of the Arthurian legends between *Geoffrey of Monmouth and *Malory. Ed. H. O. Sommer (7 vols, 1908–13); see chs. 22–3 by J. Frappier and H. Micha in *Arthurian Literature in the Middle Ages* (1959).

VYAZEMSKY, Prince Pyotr Andreevich (1792–1878), Russian poet and intimate friend of *Pushkin. His poetry is elegant, polished, and witty; as a critic he is one of the main theorists of Russian Romanticism. His use of the term in an article of 1817 is considered to be the first mention of it in Russia. He was a great admirer of *Byron and Sir W. *Scott, and did much to advance their reputation in Russia. In 1838 Vyazemsky visited England, taking a cure of sea-bathing at Brighton, spending time in the circle of Lady *Morgan, and meeting Horace *Smith. He visited the Royal Pavilion, discussed the woman question with Lady Morgan in the light of her book *The Woman and Her Master*, listened to the Chartist O'Connor, visited the duke of Norfolk's estate at Arundel and the Isle of Wight, read the *Spectator*, and discussed the Irish question (Vyazemsky's mother was an Irishwoman by the name of O'Reilly, and he made vague attempts to trace his ancestors). He then spent some time in London, visiting Westminster, Newgate Prison, and Drury Lane. His impressions of England are contained in the thirteenth of his 'Notebooks'. His conclusion is uncannily like that of *Zamyatin 80 years later: 'In English life there is nothing unexpected, *imprévu*, and therefore the general result must be boredom.'

Vye, Eustacia, a character in Hardy's *The Return of the Native*.

W

WACE (c.1100–after 1171) wrote in French verse of 15,000 short couplets the *Roman de Brut* (or *Geste des Bretons*), completed 1155 and dedicated to *Eleanor of Aquitaine, which is based on *Geoffrey of Monmouth's *Historia Regum Britanniae*. This work was the principal source of *Laȝamon's *Brut*. He also wrote a *Roman de Rou* (i.e. Rollo) (or *Geste des Normands*), a history of the dukes of Normandy in the course of which he provided some apparently autobiographical information. He was made a canon of Bayeux by Henry II. The *Roman de Brut* is circumstantial, commonsensical, and well written, adding substantially to Geoffrey's version. It survives in 22 manuscripts, including the four manuscripts of *Gaimar in which Wace's poem has been substituted for Gaimar's account of the *Historia*. It retained considerable influence up to the 14th cent.

Ed. I. Arnold (2 vols, 1938–40); trans. in E. Mason, *Arthurian Chronicles* (1912).

Wackles, Mrs and the Misses Melissa, Sophy, and Jane, in Dickens's *The Old Curiosity Shop*, kept a 'Ladies' Seminary' at Chelsea.

WADDELL, Helen Jane (1889–1965), medieval scholar and translator, born in Tokyo, and educated at Queen's University, Belfast. She is best remembered for her popular study of the 'vagantes' of the Middle Ages, *The Wandering Scholars* (1927), for her anthology of imaginative but sometimes misleading translations from their works in her *Medieval Latin Lyrics* (1929), and for her novel *Peter Abelard* (1933), based on the life of *Abelard.

Wade, Miss, a character in Dickens's *Little Dorrit*, a suspicious, venomous woman who entices away Tattycoram from the Meagles family.

Wade's boat in *Chaucer's 'The Merchant's Tale' (see CANTERBURY TALES, 10):

> And eek thise olde wydwes, God it woot,
> They konne so muchel craft on Wades boot,
> So muchel broken harm, whan that hem leste
> (IV. 1423–5)

According to *Skeat's note, Wade was a famous hero of antiquity who is mentioned in various poems and in *Malory (Caxton VII. ix; interestingly, it appears to be Caxton's addition, not being in Vinaver's *Sir Gareth* from the Winchester manuscript: *Works*, 188). The 'tale of Wade' is also mentioned in *Troilus and Criseyde*, III. 614. Speght in his 1598 edition of the *Tales* forbears from telling the story of Wade on the ground that it is too familiar. Wade (mentioned in the Old English

Widsith, 22) was the father of Wayland, who in Norse legend built a famous boat to escape his pursuers.

Wadman, Widow, or Mrs, in Sterne's *Tristram Shandy*.

Wagg, Mr, in Thackeray's *Vanity Fair* and *Pendennis*, a parasitical journalist and diner-out, based on T. *Hook.

Waggoner, The, a poem by *Wordsworth, composed 1805, published 1819 with a dedication to Charles *Lamb.

It tells how Benjamin the Waggoner, driving home his team of eight horses through the night among the Lakeland hills, escapes the temptation of the Swan Inn, but falls victim to that of the Cherry-Tree, and loses his place in consequence. But no one else can drive the team, and Lakeland loses both waggoner and wain.

Wagner, the attendant of Faust in Marlowe's *Dr Faustus* and in *Goethe's *Faust*.

WAGNER, Richard (1813–83), German composer, dramatist, and writer, whose theories and works were the subject of vigorous controversy throughout the second half of the 19th cent. He set himself to create a new synthesis of music and drama for which he wrote both words and music. His ideas, like his personality, were on the grandest scale; Der *Ring des Nibelungen (based on the *Nibelungenlied), planned as a single drama, developed backwards (each episode requiring previous explanation for its proper understanding) until the finished work required four separate evenings and eventually the construction of a new type of theatre. His theoretical writings reached beyond the musical field: a revolutionary in 1848–9, he later came under the influence of *Schopenhauer, and his writings contain much that has social, political, and cultural implications. His first champion in this country was G. B. *Shaw; later Ernest Newman became 'the perfect Wagnerite'. (See MUSIC, LITERATURE OF.) His complete prose works were translated into English by W. Ashton Ellis (8 vols, 1892–9). Among the English musical public early resistance gave way to passionate involvement: *Swinburne wrote poems on the preludes to *Lohengrin* and *Tristan* and an elegy, 'The Death of Richard Wagner' (all in *A Century of Roundels*, 1883) and D. H. *Lawrence's *The Trespasser* (originally entitled *The Saga of Siegmund*) is deeply Wagnerian in its symbolism, as is much of Lawrence's later work. G. A. *Moore and C. *Morgan also make substantial reference to Wagner, as do three of the most influential works of the 20th cent., *The Waste Land*, *Ulysses*, and

Finnegans Wake, all of which quote directly from Wagner's operas.

The music of Wagner's mature operas is indissolubly linked with the German texts: of his early works, however, *Das Liebersbot* (1836) is an adaptation of *Measure for Measure*: its successor, *Rienzi*, modelled more on French grand opera, is based on *Bulwer-Lytton and, to some extent, M. R. *Mitford. The later masterpieces, *Tristan und Isolde* and *Parsifal*, are drawn entirely from German sources and can claim only a generic connection with British legend.

WAIN, John Barrington (1925–94), poet, critic, and novelist, born in Stoke-on-Trent and educated at Newcastle under Lyme and St John's College, Oxford. He lectured at Reading, 1947–55, and was professor of poetry at Oxford 1973–8. His first novel, *Hurry on down* (1953), is an episodic and *picaresque account of the career of Charles Lumley, who, on leaving university, rejects his lower-middle-class origins by working as window-cleaner, crook, hospital orderly, chauffeur, and bouncer. It has been linked with the novels of W. *Cooper, K. *Amis, and J. *Braine as a manifestation of the spirit of the *'Angry Young Men' of the 1950s. Other novels include *The Contenders* (1958), *A Travelling Woman* (1959), and *Strike the Father Dead* (1962), again a novel about a rebellious young man, who runs away from school and the expectations of his 'redbrick' professor father to become a jazz pianist. As a poet Wain was associated with the *Movement and contributed to *New Lines. He published several volumes of verse, collected in *Poems 1949–79* (1981), a volume of autobiography, *Sprightly Running* (1962), and a biography of Dr *Johnson (1974). Later fiction includes *The Young Visitors* (1965), *The Pardoner's Tale* (1978), *Young Shoulders* (1982), *Where the Rivers Meet* (1988), *Comedies* (1990), and *Hungry Generations* (1994), his last novel which, with the two previous, make up his Oxford Trilogy.

WAINEWRIGHT, Thomas Griffiths (1794–1852), apprentice painter, soldier, then art journalist. He wrote as an art critic for the *London Magazine*, 1820–3, and became the friend of *Hazlitt, *Lamb, *De Quincey, and others. He exhibited at the *Royal Academy, 1821–5, began to live far beyond his means, and forged an order on the bank. In 1827 he published *The Life of Egomet Bonmot Esq.*, largely consisting of sneers at writers. After insurance frauds, a poisoning, and prison in Paris, he was tried and transported to Tasmania, where he died. He is the original of Varney in *Bulwer-Lytton's *Lucretia* and the victim in *Dickens's story 'Hunted Down'.

Waiting for Godot, the first stage play of S. *Beckett, published in French as *En attendant Godot*, 1952, staged in French in Paris, 1953, first staged in English at the Arts Theatre, London, 1955.

One of the most influential plays of the post-war period, it portrays two tramps, Estragon and Vladimir, trapped in an endless waiting for the arrival of a mysterious personage named Godot, while disputing the appointed place and hour of his coming. They amuse themselves meanwhile with various bouts of repartee and word-play, and are for a while diverted by the arrival of whip-cracking Pozzo, driving the oppressed and burdened Lucky on the end of a rope. Towards the end of each of the two acts, a boy arrives, heralding Godot's imminent appearance, but he does not come; each act ends with the interchange between the two tramps, 'Well, shall we go?' 'Yes, let's go', and the stage direction, 'They do not move.' There are strong biblical references throughout, but Beckett's powerful and symbolic portrayal of the human condition as one of ignorance, delusion, paralysis, and intermittent flashes of human sympathy, hope, and wit has been subjected to many varying interpretations. The theatrical vitality and versatility of the play have been demonstrated by performances throughout the world. (See also ABSURD, THEATRE OF THE.)

WAKEFIELD, H. Russell, see GHOST STORIES.

Wakefield Master, Wakefield (or Towneley) **plays,** see MYSTERY PLAYS.

Wakem, Mr and Philip, characters in G. Eliot's *The Mill on the Floss*.

WALCOTT, Derek Alton (1930–), poet and playwright, born in St Lucia, in the West Indies, and educated at the University College of the West Indies. He founded the Trinidad Theatre Workshop in 1959, and many of his own plays had their first performances there. These include *Dream on Monkey Mountain* (1967, pub. 1971), *The Joker of Seville* (1974, pub. 1978; based on *Tirso da Molina's *El burlador de Sevilla*), *O Babylon!* (1976, pub. 1978; set amongst a Rastafarian community in Kingston, Jamaica), and *Viva Detroit* (1992). His collections of poetry include *In a Green Night: Poems 1948–60* (1962), *The Castaway and Other Poems* (1965), *Sea Grapes* (1976), *The Fortunate Traveller* (1982), *Midsummer* (1983), *Collected Poems* (1986), *The Arkansas Testament* (1987), and his epic Caribbean Odyssey *Omeros* (1989). Both plays and poetry show a preoccupation with the national identity of the West Indies and their literature, and with the conflict between the heritage of European and West Indian culture ('the choice of home or exile, self-realization or spiritual betrayal of one's country', in his own words). Walcott's plays mingle verse and prose, Creole vocabulary and the rhythms of calypso, and his poems, many of which are confessional and self-questioning, are rich in classical allusion and evoke with equal vividness both Caribbean and European landscapes. He was awarded the *Nobel Prize for literature in 1992. See also POST-COLONIAL LITERATURE.

Walden, or *Life in the Woods*, see THOREAU.

Waldenses, or **Waldensians** (in French, *Vaudois*), the adherents of a religious sect which originated in the south of France about 1170 through the preaching of Peter Waldo, a rich merchant of Lyons. They rejected the authority of the pope and various rites, and were excommunicated in 1184 and subjected to persecution. But they survived and eventually became a separately organized church, which associated itself with the Protestant Reformation of the 16th cent. and still exists, chiefly in northern Italy and the adjacent regions. Their persecution by the duke of Savoy in 1655 led to *Milton's sonnet, 'Avenge, O Lord, thy slaughtered saints', and caused *Cromwell to insist on his new ally, France, putting an instant stop to the massacre.

'Waldhere', the name given to two short fragments of an Old English poem in a manuscript of the late 10th cent., totalling 63 lines. It is thought that the poem they come from is an epic of considerable length, perhaps 1,000 lines. The manuscript is in the Royal Library at Copenhagen. We know from other sources that Waldhere was the son of a king of Aquitaine, who was given up to Attila the Hun and became one of his generals. He escapes with Hiltgund, a Burgundian princess to whom he has been betrothed as a child. In the course of their flight they are attacked, and Waldhere, after slaying his assailants in a fist fight, is ambushed and wounded the next day. But they are able to continue the journey and are finally married. It is paralleled by the 10th-cent. Latin poem *Waltharius*. Ed. F. Norman (1933; rev. 1949).

WALEY, Arthur David (1889–1966), poet and authority on Chinese and Japanese literature, which he introduced to a wide public through his well-known translations. He taught himself the languages while working in the Print Room at the *British Museum, and in 1918 published *A Hundred and Seventy Chinese Poems*, which went into several editions, appealing (in his own words) 'to people who do not ordinarily read poetry', largely through their emphasis on the concrete and particular. His translations are unrhymed, elegant, and lucid; his use of stressed and unstressed syllables had, he believed, something in common with G. M. Hopkins's *sprung rhythm. His other translations in prose and verse include *The Tale of Genji* (1925–33), *The Pillow-Book of Sei Shonagon* (1928, from the diary of a 10th-cent. Japanese court lady), and *Monkey* (1942, translation of a 16th-cent. Chinese novel). He also published many works on oriental art, history, and culture, but, despite frequent invitations, never visited the Far East. He spent most of his life in Bloomsbury, where he was on friendly terms with many of the *Bloomsbury Group and the *Vorticists. See Alison Waley, *A Half of Two Lives: A Personal Memoir* (1982).

WALKER, Alice (1944–   ), black American novelist, poet and short story writer, best known as the writer of *The Color Purple* (1982), which won the *Pulitzer Prize for fiction in 1983. This epistolary novel tells the harrowing story of Celie, a young black woman in the segregated Deep South, raped by the man she believes to be her father and then forced to marry an older man she despises. Told through letters from Celie to God, and to and from her missionary sister Nettie, this story, like much of Walker's work, celebrates the strength of women engaged in struggles against the twin oppressions of sexism and racism.

She has published four collections of poetry, including *Once: Poems* (1968) and *Revolutionary Petunias and Other Poems* (1973). Her other work includes two volumes of short stories and a collection of essays, *In Search of My Mother's Garden: Womanist Prose* (1983).

Most recently she has published two novels, *Possessing the Secret of Joy* (1992), a harsh examination of female circumcision, and *By the Light of My Father's Smile* (1998); and a memoir, *The Same River Twice* (1996).

WALKER, Thomas (1784–1836), of Trinity College, Cambridge; called to the bar 1812; magistrate of Lambeth Police Court 1829. He is noted as the author of a weekly periodical, the *Original*, of which 29 numbers appeared (20 May to 2 Dec. 1835). Each number contains short articles on a variety of subjects; its purpose was to raise 'the national tone in whatever concerns us socially or individually', and it is especially remembered for Walker's admirable papers on health and gastronomy.

WALLACE, Alfred Russel (1823–1913). He left school at 14, was apprenticed to a schoolmaster in Leicester, then accompanied the naturalist Henry Walter Bates on a trip to the Amazon in 1848, an expedition described in Wallace's *Travels on the Amazon and Rio Negro* (1853). A further voyage to the Malay archipelago is described in *The Malay Archipelago* (1869). In 1858, during an attack of fever at Ternate in the Moluccas, the idea of natural selection as the solution to the problem of evolution flashed upon him, and he at once communicated it to C. *Darwin. The outcome, a testimony to the generosity of both, was the famous joint communication to the *Linnean Society on the theory of evolution. He published numerous other works and scientific papers and in 1905 his autobiography, *My Life*.

WALLACE, (Richard Horatio) Edgar (1875–1932), a very successful and prolific writer of thrillers, which include *The Four Just Men* (1905), *The Crimson Circle* (1922), and *The Green Archer* (1923). He also wrote successful plays, and died in Hollywood, where he had been working on the screenplay of *King Kong*, which was produced after his death.

WALLACE, Sir William (?1272–1305), Scottish patriot of the time of Edward I, who devoted his life to resistance to the English and was finally captured by treachery and executed in London. He is the subject of a long poem by *Henry the Minstrel.

WALLENSTEIN, Albrecht Eusebius von (1583–1634), a general celebrated for his campaigns in the Thirty Years War. After many victories he was defeated by Gustavus Adolphus at Lützen in 1632. He now prepared to abandon the imperial cause; but Ferdinand II, suspecting his intention, removed him from his command. Wallenstein was murdered by some of his officers when he was believed to be on the point of going over to the Swedes. His career is the subject of a great historical trilogy by *Schiller, of which the two last parts were translated by *Coleridge.

WALLER, Edmund (1606–87), educated at Eton and King's College, Cambridge. He entered Parliament early and was at first an active member of the opposition. In 1631 he married a London heiress who died in 1634. Later he became a Royalist, and in 1643 was leader in a plot to seize London for Charles I. For this he was imprisoned, fined, and banished. He made his peace with *Cromwell in 1651, returned to England, and was restored to favour at the Restoration. After the death of his first wife he unsuccessfully courted Lady Dorothy Sidney, the 'Sacharissa' of his poems; he married Mary Bracey as his second wife in 1644. Waller was a precocious poet; he wrote, probably as early as 1625, a complimentary piece on *His Majesty's Escape at St Andere* (Prince Charles's escape from shipwreck at Santander) in heroic couplets, one of the first examples of a form that prevailed in English poetry for some two centuries. His verse, much of it occupied with praise of Sacharissa, Lady Carlisle, and others, is of a polished simplicity; *Dryden repeatedly praised his 'sweetness', describing him as 'the father of our English numbers', and linking his name with *Denham's as poets who brought in the *Augustan age. His early poems include 'On a Girdle' and 'Go, lovely rose'; his later *Instructions to a Painter* (1666, on the battle of Sole Bay) and 'Of the Last Verses in the Book', containing the famous lines, 'The Soul's dark cottage, battered and decayed, | Lets in new light through chinks that time hath made.' His *Poems* first appeared in 1645, *Divine Poems* in 1685, and *Poems*, ed. G. Thorn-Drury (2 vols, 1893).

WALMSLEY, Leo, see REGIONAL NOVEL.

WALPOLE, Horace, fourth earl of Orford (1717–97), fourth son of Sir Robert *Walpole, educated at Eton, where he formed a happy 'Quadruple Alliance' with friends of like tastes, T. *Gray, R. *West, and Thomas Ashton; then at King's College, Cambridge. In 1737 his mother, to whom he was deeply attached, died, and six months later his father married his long-term mistress Maria Skerrett. In 1739–41 Walpole travelled in France and Italy with Gray, and met in Florence H. *Mann, who became one of his most valued correspondents. At Reggio he and Gray quarrelled and parted company, for reasons which have given rise to much inconclusive discussion, and were probably connected with Walpole's more sociable and less studious notions of

entertainment. Walpole was MP successively for Callington, Castle Rising, and Lynn, 1741–67. From 1741 he spent some time at his father's new home at Houghton, where the dullness of country life was alleviated by the excellent collection of paintings, which he catalogued and described in *Aedes Walpolianae* (1747). His father died in 1745, and in 1747 Walpole, supported by various sinecures, settled in Twickenham in the house he made known as *Strawberry Hill: he made it into 'a little Gothic castle', aided by his fellow enthusiasts *Chute and R. *Bentley (the younger), and in it collected articles of virtu. In 1748 he had three poems published in *Dodsley's *Collection*, and in 1757 he established his own printing press at Strawberry Hill. His first publication was Gray's Pindaric *odes; he and Gray had been lastingly reconciled in 1745. In 1758 he printed his own *A Catalogue of the Royal and Noble Authors of England*, a light-hearted work which later attracted much censure when it reached a wider public through a London bookseller. In the same year he printed several minor poems, essays, etc., as *Fugitive Pieces in Verse and Prose*, and in 1762 his *Anecdotes of Painting in England*. His Gothic novel *The Castle of Otranto* (1764) appeared at first pseudonymously, purporting to be a translation from an Italian work of 1529. In 1765 he paid the first of several visits to Paris, where he received a warm welcome, and met Mme du *Deffand, with whom he formed a lasting friendship; he was less enchanted (though not himself religious) with the prevailing atmosphere of rationalism and freethinking. In 1768 he published *Historic Doubts on the Life and Reign of King Richard the Third*, in which he attempted to acquit Richard of the crimes imputed to him by history, and in the same year appeared his tragedy *The Mysterious Mother*. In 1787/8 he met the sisters Agnes and Mary Berry, who became intimate friends of his last years; in 1791 they settled at Little Strawberry Hill, where Mrs *Clive had been his neighbour until her death six years earlier. In the same year he succeeded his nephew to the earldom, and inherited an estate loaded with debt. Although he had been plagued by severe gout for many years, and was increasingly dependent on Mary Berry's company for his good spirits, he seems to have remained cheerful and mentally active until the end of his life.

Walpole left his Memoirs ready for publication in a sealed chest, which was opened in 1818. *Memoires of the Last Ten Years of the Reign of George II* was edited by Lord Holland (2 vols 1822), and *Memoirs of the Reign of King George the Third* by D. Le Marchant (4 vols, 1845). His literary reputation rests largely on his letters, which are remarkable for their charm, their wit, and their autobiographical, political, and social interest. His model was Mme de *Sévigné, whose letters he greatly admired, and he clearly wrote for posterity as well as for his correspondents, who included Mann, his cousin Henry Seymour Conway, the countess of Upper Ossory, George Montagu, Mary Berry, and others to whom he could express his many varied interests. His letters to Mme du Deffand were destroyed at his own wish, possibly because he was ashamed of his imperfect French; hers to him were edited by Mrs Paget Toynbee in 1912. Some of his correspondence appeared with his works in 1798, edited by Mary Berry in her father's name: Mrs P. Toynbee's edition (16 vols, 1903–5, plus various later volumes) has been followed by the monumental Yale edition, ed. W. S. Lewis et al. (42 vols, 1937–81, with one vol. additions and corrections and 5 vols index to follow). These later editions, with 20th-cent. biographies (e.g. R. W. Ketton-Cremer, *Horace Walpole*, 1946), have done much to dispel the 19th-cent. image of Walpole, inspired by *Macaulay's famous attack in the *Edinburgh Review*, 1833, as a malicious and affected gossip, though even Macaulay had allowed that he possessed 'irresistible charm'. His name has now also been cleared of the accusation that he hastened *Chatterton's suicide by his neglect: initially deceived by a fake manuscript sent to him by Chatterton in 1769, he later suspected a hoax and withdrew his active support, for which Chatterton bitterly reviled him, although Walpole was in no way to blame for the incident and indeed throughout treated Chatterton with consideration, and spoke of him after his death with much respect.

WALPOLE, Sir Hugh Seymour (1884–1941), novelist. He was born in New Zealand, the son of a bishop, and came to England aged 5. He was educated at King's School, Canterbury, and Emmanuel College, Cambridge; his short experience of teaching is reflected in his third novel, *Mr Perrin and Mr Traill* (1911), which set a vogue for novels and plays about schoolmasters. *The Dark Forest* (1916) is based on his wartime service with the Russian Red Cross. Other works include *Jeremy* (1919), the first of three stories about a young boy, and the *Herries Chronicle*, a historical sequence set in Cumberland (where Walpole lived from 1924), consisting of *Rogue Herries* (1930), *Judith Paris* (1931), *The Fortress* (1932), and *Vanessa* (1933). Although proud of his popularity, he worried that his work was 'old-fashioned' and expressed envy of the *Modernism of his friend and correspondent V. *Woolf; he was deeply offended by *Maugham's portrait of him as Alroy Kear, a hypocritical literary careerist, in *Cakes and Ale* (1930). There is a life by R. Hart-Davis (1952).

WALPOLE, Sir Robert, first earl of Orford (1676–1745), father of Horace *Walpole, and the leader of the Whig party, prime minister and chancellor of the exchequer 1715–17, and again 1721–42. His long-standing relationship with his mistress Maria Skerrett (whom he married on his wife's death in 1737) is satirized in Gay's *The Beggar's Opera* ('How happy could I be with either'), as are his quarrels with *Townshend in the quarrel between Peachum and Lockit. In 1737, provoked by this and other satirical attacks in the theatre (by *Fielding in particular), he introduced the Licensing Act, which was bitterly attacked by writers of the time and has been blamed for the decline of English drama in the 18th cent.

WALSH, Jill Paton (1937–   ), novelist and children's writer, educated at St Anne's College, Oxford. Her novels include *Lapsing* (1986), set in Oxford of the 1950s; *A School for Lovers* (1989), a country-house romance, and *Goldengrove Unleaving* (1997), set in Cornwall. *Knowledge of Angels* (1994) is a medieval romance which opens dramatically on a Mediterranean island with the discovery of a wild child reared by wolves and the arrival of a shipwrecked stranger who claims to be an atheist and to come from a pluralist society. Through the fates of these contrasted figures the novel discusses the nature and grounds of belief, and the question of whether or not we have innate knowledge of the existence of God. Walsh's detective stories featuring Imogen Quy include *The Wyndham Case* (1993) and *A Piece of Justice* (1995). *Thrones, Dominations* (1998) is a continuation of an unfinished work by D. L. *Sayers.

WALSH, William (1663–1708), poet, was author of various pastorals, elegies, and songs, but is chiefly remembered for his encouragement of and influence on the young *Pope, whose 'Pastorals' he praised; according to *Spence, he imparted to Pope the desire to make correctness his 'study and aim'. Pope praised him in his *Essay on Criticism* as 'the Muse's judge and friend'.

WALTON, Izaak (1593–1683), born at Stafford. He was apprenticed in London to a kinsman who was a draper and a member of the Ironmongers' Company, and later carried on trade there on his own account. He was a friend of *Donne and *Wotton and of Bishops Morley, Sanderson, and *King. He was twice married, and spent the latter part of his life at Winchester, where his son-in-law was prebendary. His biographies of Donne (1640), Wotton (1651), *Hooker (1665), G. *Herbert (1670), and Sanderson (1678) are gentle and admiring in tone. He is chiefly known for *The Compleat Angler, first published 1653, and largely rewritten for the second edition (1655), which is half as long again. Often reprinted, this work combines practical information about angling with folklore, quotations from writers as diverse as *Pliny, *Du Bartas and Herbert, pastoral interludes of songs and ballads, and glimpses of an idyllic rural life of well-kept inns and tuneful milkmaids. (See also COTTON, C.)

WALTON, Sir William Turner (1902–83), English composer, whose early association with the Sitwell family was the background to the work by which he first became known, the brilliant entertainment *Façade* (1922) for voice with six instrumental soloists. Twenty-one poems by Edith *Sitwell (recited at early performances by the poet herself) were accompanied by a score derived from the rhythms, sounds, and allusions of the words: the first public performance provoked a scandal ('Drivel They Paid to Hear' ran one headline) but the piece is now regarded as a minor classic. (Walton later arranged two orchestral suites from *Façade*, though without reference to the texts that gave them birth.) Three poems for E. Sitwell were also set as independent songs, but the other main Sitwell contribution to Walton's musical output was the text of the dramatic cantata *Belshazzar's Feast* (1931), skilfully arranged by Osbert Sitwell from biblical sources. A later choral work, *In Honour of the City of London* (1937), is a setting of *Dunbar. Walton came late to opera with *Troilus and Cressida* (1954), from *Chaucer. He wrote excellent incidental music for Laurence Olivier's three Shakespeare films of *Henry V* (1944), *Hamlet* (1947), and *Richard III* (1955). Of these, only three pieces from *Henry V* have been published, because the composer believed that his film music should be heard in its original context. The same restriction applies to the score which he wrote for a stage production of *Macbeth* (1941).

WALWYN, William (fl. 1649), pamphleteer and a leader of the Leveller movement. He came from an upper-middle-class background in Worcestershire and prospered as a cloth merchant. He was imprisoned in 1649 with *Lilburne, *Overton, and T. Prince as one of the authors of *England's New Chains Discovered*, and was accused of communism and atheism. He was released later that year, after the publication of *Walwyn's Just Defence*. A well-read man, he advocated in his many tracts liberty of conscience and voluntary community of property, quoting *Montaigne in support of his own humane rationalism.

Wanderer, The, an Old English poem of 115 lines in the *Exeter Book, one of the group known as 'elegies', telling of the hardships of a man who has lost his lord. It is a plangent lament for the transience of life, culminating towards its end in a powerful *ubi sunt* passage. It begins and ends with a brief and bald statement of Christian consolation, but that is not the prevailing sentiment of the poem. It is paralleled in spirit and structure by the *Seafarer, particularly in the latter's first half, and similar arguments have been advanced for and against the coherence of organization in both poems. The poem was admired by *Auden, among other modern poets, and he translated it loosely. Ed. R. F. Leslie (1966), A. J. Bliss and T. P. Dunning (1969).

Wanderer, The, a poem in five cantos by R. *Savage (1729); some of it has been attributed to his friend A. *Hill. Its design is obscure; its message, conveyed to the Wanderer by a Hermit, appears to be that 'affliction purifies the mind', but its most noteworthy passages are descriptive, and it contains some fresh observations of nature and landscape. Dr *Johnson observed that it was 'a heap of shining materials thrown together by accident, which strikes . . . with the solemn magnificence of a stupendous ruin'.

Wanderer, The, or *Female Difficulties*, the last novel of F. *Burney, published in 1814. Less successful than her earlier works, it was criticized for improbabilities of plot (*Hazlitt in the *Edinburgh Review*, Feb. 1815, commented that the female difficulties were 'created out of nothing') and for its convoluted style—according to *Macaulay 'a sort of broken Johnsonese, a barbarous *patois*'. It describes the adventures of its mysterious and, for much of the novel, nameless heroine, Juliet, escaped from revolutionary France and hard pressed by poverty, unwanted male attention, and the social conventions which prevent her from earning her own living. Her friend and foil, the passionate Elinor Joddrel, who is in love with Juliet's admirer Harleigh, provides an interesting portrait of the emancipated woman of the period, possibly based in part on Mme de *Staël, whom Burney had met in 1793 at Juniper Hall in Surrey, as one of a circle of French émigrés which included her own future husband. The novel, though full of implausibilities, has some lively passages and acute observations of social and rural life.

Wandering Jew, the, a Jew condemned to wander about the world until Christ's second coming because, according to the legend, as Christ bore the cross to Calvary the Jew chid him, and urged him to go faster.

A pamphlet was published in Leiden in 1602, relating that Paulus von Eizen, bishop of Schleswig, had in 1542 met a man named Ahasuerus, who declared that he was the Jew in question. The story, which had previously flourished in Spain and Italy, became popular, and many instances of the Wandering Jew are recorded from the 16th to the 19th cents.

But a somewhat similar story is told much earlier by *Roger of Wendover, in his *Flores Historiarum*. An Armenian archbishop visited England in 1228, and, while being entertained at St Albans, was asked if he had ever seen or heard of Joseph, who was present at the Crucifixion, and was said to be still alive, as a testimony to the Christian faith. The prelate replied that the man had recently dined at his own table. He had been Pontius Pilate's porter, by name Cartaphilus, who, when they were dragging Jesus from the Judgement Hall, had struck him on the back, saying, 'Go faster, Jesus, why dost thou linger?', to which Jesus replied, 'I indeed am going, but thou shalt tarry till I come.' This man had been converted soon after and named Joseph. He lived for ever, and was now a very grave and holy person.

The legend of the Wandering Jew has been the subject of many German works; *Goethe contemplated (but did not write) a poem on the subject of a meeting of Ahasuerus and *Spinoza, and C. F. D. Schubart (1739–91) wrote a romantic version identifying the Jew with the turmoil of wild nature. There are elements of the story in Lewis's *The Monk* and Maturin's *Melmoth the Wanderer*, a ballad on the subject is in Percy's *Reliques*, and *Croly wrote a version called *Salathiel: A Story of the Past, the Present and the Future* (1828), in which the Wanderer takes on a tragic nationalist grandeur: he is also treated with sympathy in Caroline *Norton's Byronic poem (1830). Other treatments include *Sue's *Le Juif errant* (1844–5) and *Kingsmill's 'W.J.' (*The Dawn's Delay*, 1924). See *The Haunted Castle* (1927) by Eino Railo, and 'The Changing Myth of the Jew', in *Speaking of Literature and Society* (1982) by L. *Trilling.

Wandering Willie, (1) Willie Steenson, the blind fiddler in Scott's *Redgauntlet*. 'Wandering Willie's Tale' is an episode in the novel, an example of the author's successful use of the supernatural. (2) The name of a song by *Burns.

WANLEY, Humfrey (1672–1726). He began life as a draper's assistant at Coventry, but read widely and went to Oxford in 1695, and became an assistant in the Bodleian Library in 1696. He displayed remarkable skill in palaeography and assisted Edward Bernard in the preparation of the *Catalogi Librorum Manuscriptorum Angliae et Hiberniae* (1697). He produced in 1705 a catalogue of Anglo-Saxon manuscripts, which is still a standard work. He was librarian to the first and second earls of Oxford, and began the catalogue of the *Harleian manuscripts, a work on which he was engaged when he died.

WANLEY, Nathaniel (1634–80), divine and compiler, and father of Humfrey *Wanley. He published *The Wonders of the Little World* (1678), a collection of tales and superstitions in which R. *Browning found the story of the 'Pied Piper of Hamelin' and other oddities. His poems, some in the vein of H. *Vaughan, were edited by L. C. Martin (1928).

war poetry, 20th-cent. It is generally agreed that the First World War inspired poetry of the highest order, some of it ground-breaking in both treatment of subject and technique: combatants included W. *Owen, *Sassoon, *Rosenberg, R. *Graves, E. *Thomas, and R. *Brooke (the last of whom died before seeing active service), and memorable poems and elegies on the theme were contributed by *Hardy, *Binyon, *Housman, and others. *Kipling's poetry struck a different and more patriotic note from that of most of his contemporaries, but the anguish of losing his son to the conflict left a deep mark on him and his work. The Spanish Civil War, very much a writers' war, attracted some important British poets, including John *Cornford, *Spender, *Auden, and *MacNeice, as well as less well-remembered names like those of Clive Branson, Miles Tomalin, Bernard Gutteridge, and H. B. Mallalieu. (See Valentine Cunningham, *The Penguin Book of Spanish Civil War Verse*, 1980.) The Second World War produced a more disparate response: the poets most commonly associated with it are Keith *Douglas, Alun *Owen, and Sidney *Keyes, all of whom died in the conflict. However, F. T. *Prince, John *Pudney, and Henry *Reed are widely remembered for single, much-anthologized war poems, as well as other

work, and later anthologies have revealed a considerable wealth and diversity of responses, some by writers like Alan *Ross and Charles *Causley who moved on to other subjects, some by writers who moved on to other careers. See Brian Gardner (ed.), *The Terrible Rain: The War Poets 1939–1945* (1966, rev. 1987) and Desmond Graham (ed.), *Poetry of the Second World War: An International Anthology* (1995). British writing on the *Holocaust was largely a post-war phenomenon.

WARBURTON, Eliot (Bartholomew Eliott George) (1810–52), an Irish barrister who gave up his profession for travel and the literary life. He is remembered for his account of an eastern tour, *The Crescent and the Cross; or Romance and Realities of Eastern Travel* (1845), a highly successful work which covered much the same ground as his friend *Kinglake's *Eothen*. He also wrote two historical novels, *Reginald Hastings* (1850) and *Darien* (1852). He died at sea, when the ship on which he had embarked for the West Indies caught fire off Land's End.

WARBURTON, John (1682–1759), herald and antiquary. He was an indefatigable collector and owned many rare manuscripts. Most of the rare Elizabethan and Jacobean plays in his possession were through his own 'carelessness and the ignorance' of Betsy Baker, his servant, 'unluckily burned or put under pye bottoms'. A list in his handwriting of the 55 destroyed and those saved, three and a fragment, has been preserved. Some of the burnt manuscripts were unique.

WARBURTON, William (1698–1779). He rose to be bishop of Gloucester in 1759. He was much engaged in theological controversy, writing with vigour and arrogance. His most famous work was *The Divine Legation of Moses* (1738–41), a paradoxical argument that the very absence in the Mosaic law of any reference to a future life, a necessary element in a scheme of morality, is a proof of the divine mission of the lawgiver. *A View of Lord Bolingbroke's Philosophy* (1754) attacked *Bolingbroke's views on natural religion and *The Doctrine of Grace* (1762) the 'enthusiasm' of *Wesley. He brought out in 1747 an edition of Shakespeare in eight volumes which was sharply criticized as unscholarly, and in 1751 an edition of *Pope's works. He was Pope's literary executor, and is said to have encouraged him in the composition of *The New Dunciad*. A quarrelsome man who made many enemies, he was nevertheless admired by Dr *Johnson, who remained grateful for his early praise of his essay on *Macbeth (1747): 'He praised me at a time when praise was of value to me.'

WARD, Artemus, see Browne, C. F.

WARD, Edward ('Ned') (1667–1731), tavern keeper and writer (under various pseudonyms) of *Hudibrastic sketches of London life. Some of the best of these are contained in *The London-Spy* (1698–1709), a simply told tale of a country resident who visits London, meets a cockney acquaintance, and with him ranges about the town noting sights, sounds, smells, and odd characters. His *Hudibras Redivivus*, a burlesque poem, was published in 1705–7.

WARD, John (1571–1638), English composer, remembered chiefly as a composer of *madrigals, including 'Come, sable night' and 'If the deep sighs'.

WARD, Mary Augusta, better known as Mrs Humphry Ward (1851–1920), granddaughter of T. *Arnold of Rugby, and daughter of Thomas Arnold, inspector of schools, whose conversion to Roman Catholicism, return to the Anglican faith, and subsequent reconversion to Catholicism caused his family much distress. In 1872 she married Thomas Humphry Ward, then an Oxford don and later on the staff of *The Times* in London. Her most famous novel, *Robert Elsmere* (1888), is in part a vivid evocation of the Oxford of *Pater, *Pattison, and T. H. *Green, and of the many varieties of religious faith and doubt which succeeded the ferment of the *Oxford movement. Its protagonist, an earnest but questioning clergyman, resigns his orders for a life of social service in the East End, to the distress of his devout wife Catherine. The novel sold extremely well, was reviewed by *Gladstone, and initiated much debate; the author herself compared it to *Froude's *The Nemesis of Faith* and *Newman's *Loss and Gain*, novels which also dealt with the crisis of mid-Victorian faith. Most of her other novels deal with social and religious themes, frequently contrasting traditional belief with the values of progress and intellectual freedom; they include *The History of David Grieve* (1892), *Marcella* (1894), *Helbeck of Bannisdale* (1898), *Lady Rose's Daughter* (1903), and *The Marriage of William Ashe* (1905). She inherited the Arnold sense of high moral purpose, was an active philanthropist and a leading figure in the intellectual life of her day; she supported the movement for higher education for women, but opposed women's suffrage, on the grounds that women's influence was stronger in the home than in public life. Her *A Writer's Recollections* (1918) draws a striking picture of Oxford life and of the domestic influence of W. *Morris, *Burne-Jones, and Liberty prints; it also contains portraits of *Jowett, Pater, H. *James, and other friends. There is a life by John Sutherland (1990).

WARD, Plumer (formerly Robert) (1765–1846), a lawyer and MP who held minor government posts and wrote much on legal and political matters. When he was 60 he became, somewhat eccentrically, an exponent of the *fashionable novel with the publication of his first novel, *Tremaine, or A Man of Refinement* (1825). He hoped that his works of fiction (which he did not care to call 'novels') would display 'Philosophy teaching by examples', and demonstrate how the standards of public and private morality could be upheld amid the luxury and dissipation of the times. In 1827 appeared *De Vere, or The Man of Independence* and in 1841 *De Clifford, or The Constant Man*. All are lengthy, ponderous works, in which (to use the author's own words of *Tremaine*) 'variety and incident are equally wanting'.

WARD, William George (1812–82), theologian, fellow of Balliol College, Oxford, and a follower of *Newman. In 1844 he published *The Ideal of a Christian Church* in praise of the Roman Catholic Church from which he gained the title 'Ideal' Ward. He was subsequently deprived of his degrees for heresy, and in 1845 joined the Roman Catholic Church. In later life he became increasingly controversial in his writings and joined the Ultramontane party, which upheld anti-liberal views and papal infallibility.

Warden, The, a novel by A. *Trollope, published in 1855, and the first in the *'Barsetshire' series.

The income of Hiram's Hospital, a charitable institution, has grown in real terms down the centuries, but the 12 old bedesmen have not benefited. The surplus has created a pleasant sinecure for the mild-mannered old warden, the Revd Septimus Harding, a fact which John Bold, a local surgeon with a passion for causes, makes known to the national press. Harding finds himself the object of unpleasant publicity, and his son-in-law, the combative Archdeacon Grantly, bullies him to dispute the case along party lines. But Harding is not the man for the fight, sees the anomaly in his position, and with considerable personal courage resigns. The novel ends in an atmosphere of quiet goodwill, with Bold withdrawing his accusations and marrying the warden's daughter Eleanor, and Harding receiving a new preferment in the cathedral close.

Wardle, Mr, a character in Dickens's *Pickwick Papers*.

Wardour Street English, a term used to describe the pseudo-archaic diction frequently affected by historical novelists (otherwise referred to in R. L. *Stevenson's coinage as 'tushery'); it derives from the days when Wardour Street was a centre not as now of the film industry but of the antique and mock-antique furniture trade.

WARLOCK, Peter, pseudonym of Philip Heseltine (1894–1930), English composer, almost entirely of songs. Under his own name he made a distinguished contribution to musical scholarship, particularly in the Elizabethan and Jacobean periods: some of his songs, like the lovely setting of 'Sleep' (1922, poem by *Fletcher), reflect this interest but in many others the influence of his friend *Delius produced a richer harmonic idiom, while in others again the extrovert, even bawdy, side of Warlock's character finds expression. His choice of texts was varied: many of them come from the earlier periods of English literature, though some of the best of his later songs are settings of Arthur *Symons, *Belloc, and Bruce Blunt. The intense and haunting setting of 'The Curlew' (1922), with words by *Yeats, is considered by many his masterpiece, and reveals a desolation of spirit perhaps not unconnected with his eventual suicide.

WARNER, Alan (1964–), Scottish novelist and short story writer, born in Oban, Argyll. His acclaimed first novel, *Morvern Callar* (1995), is written in the voice of a semi-literate young woman living in the West Highlands of Scotland in the early 1990s. When her mysterious older boyfriend dies, he leaves her money and an unpublished manuscript: she seizes both with gusto and runs away to live a life of hedonism in Spain. The novel's style combines spoken Scots with sophisticated poetic ideas in an intensely metaphorical way. Warner's second novel, *These Demented Lands* (1997), returned to the Morvern story in what was widely seen as a more experimental but less successful sequel, evoking a *New Age nightmare of shipwreck on an offshore island, with echoes of W. *Golding and *Conrad. His third, *The Sopranos* (1998), a more traditionally structured story about a group of drunken Highland schoolgirls on a day trip to Edinburgh, was viewed with scepticism. Warner has sometimes been seen as a leader of the so-called 'Chemical Generation', along with Irvine *Welsh. The term refers loosely to a group of younger writers, predominantly Scottish, whose work displays a comfortable familiarity with 1990s youth culture: music, fashion, nightclubs, and drugs.

WARNER, Marina Sarah (1946–), novelist, critic, and cultural historian, born in London of an Italian mother and English father, and educated at Lady Margaret Hall, Oxford. Her novels, which cover a wide cultural and geographical range, both in Europe and beyond, are *In a Dark Wood* (1977); *The Skating Party* (1983), which recounts a single day's events as a group of friends skate down a frozen river; *The Lost Father* (1988); and *Indigo; or, Mapping the Waters* (1992), an exploration of colonialism and displacement, set on an imaginary Caribbean island and inspired in part by Shakespeare's *The Tempest. She has also published a volume of short stories, *The Mermaids in the Basement* (1993), which rework traditional folk tales and legends, and several books for children. Her scholarly works include *Alone of All Her Sex* (1976), a study of the myth and cult of the Virgin Mary; *Joan of Arc: The Image of Female Heroism* (1981); *Monuments and Maidens* (1985), which traces the often paradoxical uses of the female form in iconography and public art; and *From the Beast to the Blonde* (1994), a study of *fairy tales. In 1994 she became the first woman to deliver the *BBC's Reith Lectures, which were published in the same year as *Making Monsters: Six Myths of Our Time*: these offered a feminist analysis of various aspects of popular culture, and explored the adaptation of myth and folklore to modern usage. *No Go the Bogeyman* (1998) is a study of ghouls and ogres.

WARNER, Rex (1905–86), poet, novelist, and translator, educated at Wadham College, Oxford, where he was a close friend of *Auden and *Day-Lewis. His first volume of poetry, *Poems* (1937), shares their Messianic revolutionary fervour, and the fourth of Auden's six 'Odes' in *The Orators* (1932) is a buoyant address to Warner's infant son John. Warner's early novels, which include *The Wild Goose Chase* (1937), *The Professor* (1938), and *The Aerodrome* (1941; ironically subtitled 'A Love Story'), are more sombre, Kafkaesque political parables, which reflect the gathering gloom of the 1930s, and in which the matter-of-fact and the uncanny mingle with disturbing effect. His later fiction is based largely on Greek or Roman historical subjects, and he also translated the *Medea* (1944), *Hippolytus* (1950), and *Helen* (1951) of *Euripides, and the *Prometheus Bound* (1947) of *Aeschylus.

WARNER, Sylvia Townsend (1893–1978), novelist and poet, born in Harrow, the daughter of a housemaster at Harrow School. She worked as one of the editors of *Tudor Church Music* (10 vols, 1922–9) and her love of early music is reflected in her later fiction. Her first volume of verse, *The Espalier* (1925), was followed by several others, including *Whether a Dove or a Seagull* (1933), written in collaboration with her friend and companion Valentine Ackland, and the posthumous *Twelve Poems* (1980); her *Collected Poems* appeared in 1982. Her poetry shows her admiration for *Hardy, *Crabbe, and E. *Thomas. Her original voice is heard more strongly in her novels, which include *Lolly Willowes* (1926), a tale of the supernatural in which a maiden aunt realizes her vocation as a witch; *Mr Fortune's Maggot* (1927), which describes the visit of ex-clerk missionary Timothy Fortune to the remote South Sea island of Fanua, where he makes only one doubtful convert and in the process loses his own faith through his love of the islanders; and *The True Heart* (1929), set in the Essex marshes, which retells the story of Cupid and Psyche through the medium of a Victorian orphan, Sukey Bond. Her later works include a biography of T. H. *White (1967), and various collections of short stories, many previously first published in the *New Yorker. Her *Letters* (1982, ed. W. Maxwell) describe her brief friendships, notably with T. F. *Powys, and her love for Valentine Ackland, with whom she lived for many years. Her diaries, ed. C. Harman, were published in 1994.

WARNER, William (c.1558–1609), an attorney in London. He published *Pan His Syrinx*, seven prose tales (1584), and a translation of the *Menaechmi* of *Plautus (1595) may be his. His chief work was *Albions England*, a metrical British history, with mythical and fictitious episodes, extending in the first edition (1586) from Noah to the Norman Conquest. It was brought up to *Elizabeth's reign in 1592; and a continuation, reaching James I, was published in 1606. *Meres, in his *Palladis Tamia* (1598), claimed to have heard Warner called 'our English *Homer', and *Drayton praised him in his elegy *To Henery Reynolds*; the assessment of C. S. *Lewis, in more modern times, was that 'The good things in *Albion's England* are as far divided as the suns in space.'

War of the Worlds, The, a *science fiction fantasy by H. G. *Wells, published 1898, and written while he was living in Woking; it describes the arrival of the Martians in Woking, driven from their own planet by its progressive cooling to take refuge in a warmer world. In a letter Wells described his plan for the work, in which: 'I completely wreck and sack Woking— killing my neighbours in painful and eccentric ways— then proceed via Kingston and Richmond to London, selecting South Kensington for feats of peculiar atrocity'; much of the novel's power depends on the contrast between the familiar stupid bourgeois complacent reactions of the humans and the terrifying destructive intelligence of the Martians, which consist of round bodies, each about 4 feet in diameter, each body containing a huge brain. They live by the injection into themselves of the fresh living blood of other creatures, mostly of human beings, and they devastate the country before eventually falling victims to terrestrial bacteria. A radio broadcast by Orson *Welles of a dramatization of the novel in the USA on 30 Oct. 1938 caused a furore, many of its millions of listeners taking it for a factual report of the invasion by Martians of New Jersey.

WARREN, John Byrne Leicester, Baron de Tabley (1835–95), educated at Christ Church, Oxford. He published some volumes of verse under the pseudonyms 'George F. Preston' (1859–62) and 'William Lancaster' (1863–8), and two tragedies, also under pseudonyms, *Philoctetes* (1866) and *Orestes* (1867). In 1893–5 he published under his own name two series of *Poems, Dramatic and Lyrical*; also *A Guide to the Study of Book Plates* (1880). He was a botanist, and his best poems manifest his close observation of nature.

WARREN, Robert Penn (1905–89), American poet, novelist, and critic, born in Kentucky and educated at the universities of California, Yale, and Harvard. His novels include *All the King's Men* (1946), a study of a power-crazed, corrupt Southern politician, Willie Stark, *Band of Angels* (1955), *The Cave* (1959), and *Meet Me in the Green Glen* (1971); his volumes of poetry include *Selected Poems 1923–43* (1944), *Promises* (1957), *Selected Poems 1923–1966* (1966), *Now and Then: Poems 1976–1978* (1978), *Being Here: Poetry 1977–1980* (1980), *New and Selected Poems 1923–1985* (1985), and *Portrait of a Father* (1988). His critical works are associated with the *New Criticism, and include two anthologies-with-commentaries, compiled in collaboration with Cleanth *Brooks, *Understanding Poetry* (1938) and *Understanding Fiction* (1943).

WARREN, Samuel (1807–77). After studying medicine at Edinburgh, he became successively barrister, re-

corder of Hull, MP for Midhurst, and master of lunacy. From early youth he aimed for literary fame. His first publication, the morbid, melodramatic *Passages from the Diary of a Late Physician* (1832–8, first published in *Blackwood's*), provoked criticism from the *Lancet* for revealing professional secrets. Warren also wrote the sensationally popular *Ten Thousand a Year* (1840–1), a story of greed and imposture concerning Mr Titlebat Titmouse, a draper's assistant who inherits a vast fortune by way of documents forged by the lawyers Quirk, Gammon, and Snap, and whose unexpected elevation to wealth leads to absurd consequences.

Warrington, George, a character in Thackeray's *Pendennis*, and *The Newcomes*. He is a descendant of the Warringtons in *The Virginians*.

Wars of the Roses, The, the collective title given to director John Barton's adaptation of Shakespeare's history cycle of *Henry VI*, Parts 1, 2, and 3, and *Richard III*, first performed at Stratford in 1963, directed by Peter *Hall.

Wart, Thomas, in Shakespeare's 2 *Henry IV*, one of the recruits for Falstaff's force.

WARTON, Joseph (1722–1800), son of Thomas *Warton and brother of Thomas *Warton the younger. He held various livings and was a conspicuously unsuccessful headmaster of Winchester (1766–93), forced into retirement by the protests of his pupils. He published various poems and odes (including *The Enthusiast; or The Lover of Nature*, 1744; *An Ode to Evening*, 1749), but is better remembered as a critic of wide knowledge and independent judgement. His *An Essay on the Writings and Genius of Pope* (1756, 1782) distinguishes between the poets of 'the sublime and pathetic' (see SUBLIME) and the 'men of wit and sense', Shakespeare, *Spenser, and *Milton belonging to the first and higher category, and *Pope to the second: 'wit and satire are transitory and perishable, but nature and passion are eternal.' He contributed to the *Adventurer* at Dr *Johnson's request (1752–4), and was elected member of the *Club in 1777.

WARTON, Thomas (c.1688–1745), father of Joseph and Thomas *Warton, from 1718 to 1728 professor of poetry at Oxford; his poems, including some 'runic odes', were published posthumously in 1748, edited by his son Thomas.

WARTON, Thomas (1728–90), son of Thomas *Warton the elder and brother of Joseph *Warton. He was professor of poetry at Oxford (1757–67), and became *poet laureate in 1785, an appointment celebrated in the *Probationary Odes* (see ROLLIAD). His many poetic works included odes, sonnets (a form then unfashionable, which he did much to revive), and light verse; he edited the early poems of *Milton (1785), and his own work shows the marked influence of *'Il Penseroso'. He also edited *The Oxford Sausage* (1764), a celebrated miscellany of university verse. He was a friend of Dr *Johnson, contributed three numbers to the *Idler (Nos. 33, 93, 96), and was elected to the *Club in 1782. He is, however, best remembered for his valuable work The History of English Poetry (3 vols, 1774–81), the first literary history of any real scope, which combines a respect for classicism with a warm admiration for *Chaucer, the Scottish *Chaucerians, *Dante, *Spenser, and other early poets. It lacks method, but throws much light on the taste of the time and the interest in *primitivism, and has been seen as an important stage in the transition towards *Romanticism.

WASHINGTON, Booker T(aliaferro) (1856–1915), son of a black slave and a white man. He was born into slavery on a Virginia plantation. Freed, he taught himself to read, studied at the Hampton Institute in Virginia, and became the founder and head of the Tuskegee Institute, Alabama, a school for blacks. He was an eloquent speaker and a voluminous writer, and became a spokesman for his people. His works include an autobiography, Up from Slavery (1901), and Working with the Hands (1904).

Washington Square, a novel by H. *James, published 1881.

Catherine Sloper lives in Washington Square with her widowed father, a rich physician. She is plain, shy, without social graces or conversation. Dr Sloper cannot conceal his disappointment that she has nothing of her dead mother's beauty and wit. When the handsome, but penniless and indolent, Morris Townsend begins to court her, he casts him, correctly, as a fortune-hunter. Both Catherine's romantic hopes and Morris's pecuniary ones are encouraged and abetted by the girl's silly aunt, Lavinia Penniman. Dr Sloper will disinherit Catherine if she marries Morris, and although she has a certain fortune in her own right it is not enough for the greedy Morris and he jilts her. Even the dull Catherine is not deceived by his assertion that he is renouncing her to preserve her inheritance. Life in Washington Square continues soberly. Catherine, despised by her father, pitied by her aunt, refuses later chances of a suitable match and withdraws into a lonely humdrum life. After her father's death (cautiously, he has largely disinherited her in any case) Morris reappears to try his luck again. His continued lack of success has made him less ambitious. But Catherine finds no charm in this balding middle-aged stranger. With some bitter reminders of his past cruelty, she turns him away.

Waste Land, The, a poem by T. S. *Eliot, first published 1922 in the *Criterion.

It consists of five sections, 'The Burial of the Dead', 'A Game of Chess', 'The Fire Sermon', 'Death by Water', and 'What the Thunder Said', together with Eliot's own 'Notes' which explain his many varied and multicultural allusions, quotations, and half-quotations (from *Webster, *Dante, *Verlaine, *Kyd, etc.), and express a general indebtedness to the Grail legend (see in this connection GRAIL, and BALYN) and to the vegetation ceremonies in *Frazer's The Golden Bough. (Eliot himself was later to describe these 'Notes' as 'a remarkable exposition of bogus scholarship', written to pad out the text of the poem when it first appeared as a little book; he admits that they were a temptation to critics, and had achieved 'almost greater popularity than the poem itself': 'The Frontiers of Criticism', 1956.) The poem was rapidly acclaimed as a statement of the post-war sense of depression and futility; it was seriously praised by I. A. *Richards as 'a perfect emotive description of a state of mind which is probably inevitable for a while to all meditative people' (Science and Poetry, 1926), and less seriously but significantly chanted as a kind of protest against the older generation by the undergraduates of the day. Complex, erudite, cryptic, satiric, spiritually earnest, and occasionally lyrical, it became one of the most recognizable landmarks of *Modernism, an original voice speaking through many echoes and parodies of echoes. The Waste Land: A Facsimile and Transcript of the Original Drafts (1971), edited by Valerie Eliot, sheds much light on the circumstances of the poem's composition, and particularly on the well-heeded and detailed textual advice offered by *Pound (through which the poem's length was very considerably reduced); it also quotes a remark by Eliot himself, that the poem could be seen not so much as 'an important bit of social criticism', but as 'the relief of a personal and wholly insignificant grouse against life; it is just a piece of rhythmical grumbling.'

Watchman (1796), a political and literary journal, of ten issues only, produced by *Coleridge. The journal was pacifist and anti-*Pitt, and included literary contributions from, among others, *Beddoes and *Poole.

Water-Babies, The: A Fairy Tale for a Land-Baby, by C. *Kingsley, serialized in *Macmillan's Magazine 1862–3, published in book form 1863, with illustrations by (Sir) Noel Paton.

Kingsley wrote this, his best-loved work, for his youngest son Grenville. Despite considerable didactic and satiric content, Kingsley's imagination works with unusual ease and freedom, and the tale displays at its most attractive his knowledgeable love of the underwater world of river and sea, his sense of landscape, his open-minded interest in evolutionary theory, and his philanthropic concern. The story tells of the adventures of Tom, the chimney-sweep, employed by the bully Mr Grimes. Tom stumbles down a chimney into the bedroom of a little girl, Ellie, and for the first time he becomes aware of his own grimy body; he runs away, hounded by the household, falls into a river, and is transformed into a water-baby. In his underwater life he makes the acquaintance of many vividly realized creatures, from caddis flies to salmon, and also of Mrs Doasyouwouldbedoneby and Mrs Bedonebyasyoudid, who play a large part in the moral re-education which finally unites him with Ellie. The story was a favourite with Queen *Victoria, who read it to her children, and it remains popular with children today, though it also provides rich opportunities for psychoanalytic interpretation, much of it based on Kingsley's obsession with water, washing, and the public-school cold bath.

WATERHOUSE, Keith Spencer (1929–   ), journalist, novelist, and dramatist, born and educated in Leeds. He had a considerable success with his second novel, *Billy Liar*, a regional comedy about a youth who attempts to escape his dull family life through fantasy, which he adapted for the stage in collaboration with W. *Hall (1960). Other novels include *Billy Liar on the Moon* (1976), *Office Life* (1978), *Maggie Muggins* (1981), and *Unsweet Charity* (1992). Waterhouse and Hall subsequently worked together on many stage, screen, and television plays, adaptations, and musicals, including the film *Whistle down the Wind* (1961). Waterhouse also wrote the screenplay of S. *Barstow's *A Kind of Loving* (1960). *Jeffrey Bernard Is Unwell* (1989) was Waterhouse's successful adaptation for the stage of Bernard's *Spectator* columns. *City Lights* (1994) is the first part of his autobiography.

Waterloo, see WELLINGTON.

water poet, the, see TAYLOR, JOHN (1580–1653).

Waterstone's, a chain of bookshops founded by Tim Waterstone, who, while working for W. H. *Smith, perceived the need for a store with late-hour trading and well-informed staff. He raised the money for his first shop, which opened on 1 Sept. 1982, at 99 Old Brompton Road, London. It prospered, and other branches were opened in London and the regions. The firm was sold to W. H. Smith in 1993, but bought back in 1998, at which point it became the biggest bookseller in Britain, with a successful promotional programme of poetry and prose readings.

WATKINS, Vernon Phillips (1906–67), poet, born in Wales of Welsh-speaking parents, and educated at Magdalene College, Cambridge. He lived most of his life in and near Swansea, working as a bank clerk before taking various teaching posts, and was for many years a friend of Dylan *Thomas. Their relationship is recorded in *Dylan Thomas: Letters to Vernon Watkins* (1957). Although in his early years he was associated with the poets of the *New Apocalypse, his poetry was, as *Larkin was to record, 'much more controlled than theirs and reached further back to the symbolist poets of Europe' ('An Encounter and a Re-encounter', a memorial essay in *Vernon Watkins*, 1970, ed. Leslie Norris). His first volume demonstrated his range; the title poem of *Ballad of the Mari Lwyd* (1941) is a long, rhetorical piece rooted in Welsh folklore and mythology, whereas 'The Collier' and other poems in the collection are marked by simplicity and a restrained compassion. Watkins's lyric gift was developed in many subsequent volumes, including *The Lamp and the Veil* (1945), *Cypress and Acacia* (1959), and

Fidelities (1968), and his *Selected Poems 1930–60* appeared in 1967. His work shows an awareness of, and was influenced by, German and French poetry, and he translated two cycles of poems of *Heine (*The North Sea*, 1955), and paid tributes in his own verse to *Hölderlin, *Rilke, *Baudelaire, and others, some of whose work he also translated.

Watson, Dr (John), companion of Sherlock *Holmes, a character created by A. C. *Doyle.

WATSON, John, see KAILYARD SCHOOL.

WATSON, Richard (1737–1816), from 1782 bishop of Llandaff. He wrote a notable *Apology for Christianity* (1776), in reply to *Gibbon (who responded with respect), and an *Apology for the Bible* (1796), in reply to *Paine. *Wordsworth's long *Letter to the Bishop of Llandaff*, in which he supports the French republicans and attacks *Burke and the British constitution, was written in 1793 but not published until 1876; it was a reply to Watson's sermon on 'The Wisdom and Goodness of God in having made both Rich and Poor'.

WATSON, Thomas (*c*.1556–92). He was possibly educated at Oxford, and was a law student in London. He published a Latin version of the *Antigone* of *Sophocles, with an appendix of Latin allegorical poems and experiments in classical metres (1581). His most important work was *The Ἑκατομπαθια or Passionate Centurie of Love* (1582), 18-line poems, called sonnets, often based on classical, French, and Italian sources, and accompanied by learned explanatory notes. He published Latin versions of *Tasso's *Aminta* (1585), which was translated without authority by Abraham *Fraunce (1587), and *Helenae Raptus* from the Greek of Coluthus (1586). He also published *The First Sett of Italian Madrigalls Englished* (1590), which were set to music by W. *Byrd and an *Eglogue*, in Latin and English versions, on the death of Sir Francis Walsingham (1590). His Latin pastoral *Amintae Gaudia* appeared posthumously (1592), and a few previously unpublished poems by him were included in *The Phoenix Nest and *Englands Helicon. He was a close friend of *Marlowe, and was mentioned as 'Amyntas' in Spenser's *Colin Clouts Come Home Againe. His 'sonnets', among the earliest in English, were an influence on Shakespeare and others.

WATSON, Sir William (1858–1935), poet, born in Yorkshire. He gained a certain reputation with *Wordsworth's Grave and Other Poems* (1890) and *Lachrymae Musarum* (1892, verses on the death of *Tennyson), but his many subsequent volumes of verse are now forgotten, and his memory lingers largely in his anthology piece 'April, April, | Laugh thy girlish laughter'.

Watsons, The, an unfinished novel by J. *Austen, written some time between 1804 and 1807.

This story is regarded by some, with little justification, as an early version of *Emma. Although it is only a fragment, probably never revised, the characters are fully realized. The story is set at a social level below that of the other novels, and largely concerns the unremitting efforts of Emma's three sisters to get themselves married. Emma Watson, who has been brought up by a well-to-do aunt, returns to her family, who live unfashionably in genteel poverty in a Surrey village. A pretty, sensible girl, Emma is here surrounded by people in every way inferior to herself. Even her good-natured sister Elizabeth is as intent on a good match as her unpleasant sisters Margaret and Penelope. The other principal characters are Lady Osborne, handsome and dignified; her son, Lord Osborne, a fine but cold young man; Mr Howard, a gentlemanly clergyman; and Tom Musgrave, a cruel and hardened flirt. The intention appears to have been that the heroine should marry Mr Howard, but the author left no hint as to the future course of events, or why she abandoned the novel.

WATT, A. P., see AGENTS, LITERARY.

WATT, Robert (1774–1819), Scottish bibliographer, who began life as a farm and road labourer, and in his boyhood met *Burns—'an extraordinary character'. He learned Greek and Latin, and proceeded to Glasgow and then Edinburgh University, where he studied classics, anatomy, and divinity. He became a very successful doctor, but the work for which he is remembered, and on which he spent over 30 years, is his remarkable *Bibliotheca Britannica, or A General Index to British and Foreign Literature*, published in 1824.

WATTEAU, Jean-Antoine (1684–1721), French rococo painter who invented the 'fête-galante'—small pictures where elegant men and women, among them players from the *commedia dell'arte*, play music, and make love in a soft and dreamy parkland; the most famous of them is *The Embarkation for* [or *from*] *Cythera* (1717). Watteau died young, of consumption, and was notorious for his discontent and restlessness; his popularity declined in the late 18th cent., but Romantic writers, among them *Gautier and *Nerval, created around him an aura of mystery; they saw him as the tragic artist whose work is touched with melancholy and the transience of human pleasure. A vision of the enchanted, aristocratic 18th cent. in contrast to the bourgeois 19th cent. (expressed, notably, in an evocative essay by the *Goncourt brothers in *L'Art du dix-huitième siècle*), inspired many *fin-de-siècle* poets and artists, including *Dobson, *Beardsley, *Ricketts, and Michael *Field; *Pater's story 'A Prince of Court Painters' (in *Imaginary Portraits*, 1877), a study of ill-fated genius, is based on Watteau's life.

WATTS, Isaac (1674–1748), the son of a Nonconformist Southampton tradesman and keeper of a boarding school, educated at the Stoke Newington Academy 1690–4. He became a minister, but was forced into early retirement by ill health. He published four collections of verse, *Horae Lyricae* (1706), *Hymns and Spiritual Songs* (1707), *Divine Songs for the Use of Children* (1715), and *The Psalms of David Imitated* (1719). He also wrote a number of theological and educational works. He is chiefly remembered for his hymns, which include 'O God, our help in ages past' and 'When I survey the wondrous Cross', and for his songs for children ('How doth the little busy bee'), some of which foreshadow those of *Blake; they became widely enough known to be parodied in the 'Alice' books of Lewis Carroll (C. L. *Dodgson). But he was also the author of Pindaric *odes, blank verse, and of daring technical experiments such as his alarming 'The Day of Judgement' (1706), in English Sapphics. He was included in *The Lives of the English Poets* at Johnson's own suggestion. (See CHILDREN'S LITERATURE.)

WATTS-DUNTON, (Walter) Theodore (1832–1914), born Watts, from 1896 by deed poll Watts-Dunton. He gave up his profession as solicitor to devote himself to literature. He reviewed for the *Examiner*, and then from 1876 to 1902 without a break was one of the most influential writers for the *Athenaeum*, and its chief poetry reviewer, in which capacity he supported the work of his friends in the *Pre-Raphaelite movement. Like *Borrow, whom he met in 1872, he was much interested in the gypsies, and republished in *The Coming of Love* (1898) scenes in verse previously printed in the *Athenaeum*, in which the gypsy girls Rhona Boswell and Sinfi Lovell feature prominently. These characters reappear in his novel *Aylwin* (1898), a curious work which he was many years writing; it recounts the love of Henry Aylwin for a Welsh girl, Winifred, his separation from her through a Gnostic curse, and his pursuit of her until their final reunion (with Sinfi Lovell's aid) on Snowdon. Its romantic mysticism and sensational plot brought it much success.

His other works include introductions to Borrow's *Lavengro* (1893) and *The Romany Rye* (1900), reminiscent sketches of *Rossetti, *Tennyson, etc., collected as *Old Familiar Faces* (1916), an article on 'Poetry' in the *EB* (9th edn, 1885) and an essay, 'The Renascence of Wonder in English Poetry' (in Chambers's *Cyclopaedia of English Literature*, vol. iii, 1901), in which he strongly defends the Romantic movement. He is probably best remembered, however, for his loyal support of *Swinburne, whom he rescued from declining health, and who lived with him from 1879 until his death in 1909, at the Pines, Putney, in an intimacy little interrupted by Watts-Dunton's late marriage, in 1905, to a woman much younger than himself.

WAUGH, Alec (Alexander Raban) (1898–1981), novelist and travel writer, brother of Evelyn *Waugh. His first novel, *The Loom of Youth* (1917), became a *succès de scandale* through its colourful suggestions of public-school homosexuality. It was followed by many others, including the late success *Island in the Sun* (1956), and several autobiographical volumes, including *My Brother Evelyn and Other Profiles* (1967).

WAUGH, Auberon (1939–2001), novelist, provocative and iconoclastic journalist, diarist, political satirist, and editor from 1986 of the *Literary Review*. Son of E. Waugh (below), he was educated at Downside School and Oxford University. His first novel, *The Foxglove Saga* (1960), was written after recovering from a serious accident with a machine gun in an army training exercise, and is based on his experiences of illness and of school and military life. His other novels are *The Path of Dalliance* (1963), *Who Are the Violets Now?* (1965), *Consider the Lilies* (1968), and *A Bed of Flowers* (1972). He published several works of non-fiction, including collected articles from his columns in the *Spectator and the *Daily Telegraph*, an autobiography (*Will This Do?*, 1991), and two volumes of diaries (1976, 1985).

WAUGH, Evelyn Arthur St John (1903–66), novelist, born in Hampstead, the son of a publisher, Arthur Waugh. He was educated at Lancing and Hertford College, Oxford, where he devoted himself more to social than to academic life; his literary and artistic interests were strengthened by new friendships, notably with H. *Acton. He took a third-class degree, then worked for some years (unhappily) as assistant schoolmaster in various posts which provided material for *Decline and Fall* (1928), his first and immensely successful novel, which followed the publication of an essay on the *Pre-Raphaelites (1926). In 1928 he married Evelyn Gardner; in 1930 he was divorced, and received into the Roman Catholic Church. His career as a novelist prospered, with *Vile Bodies* (1930, set in Mayfair), *Black Mischief* (1932, set in Africa), *A Handful of Dust* (1934), and *Scoop* (1938), works of high comedy and social satire which capture the brittle, cynical, determined frivolity of the inter-war generation. He also established himself as journalist and travel writer with accounts of a journey through Africa (*Remote People*, 1931), a journey through South America (*Ninety-Two Days*, 1934), and Mussolini's invasion of Abyssinia (*Waugh in Abyssinia*, 1936). In 1937 he married Laura Herbert, a cousin of his first wife, and from this time made his home in the West Country, first at Piers Court in Gloucestershire, then at Combe Florey in Somerset, where he cultivated the image of the country squire, with, eventually, a family of six children.

The war, however, intervened; *Put out More Flags* (1942) was written while he was serving in the Royal Marines, and his wartime experiences in Crete and Yugoslavia appear in his trilogy *Sword of Honour* (1965), originally published as *Men at Arms* (1952), *Officers and Gentlemen* (1955), and *Unconditional Surrender* (1961). In the interim appeared one of his most popular works, *Brideshead Revisited* (1945), which struck a more serious note, and a macabre comedy about Californian funeral practices, *The Loved One* (1948). *The Ordeal of Gilbert Pinfold* (1957) is a bizarre novel about a famous 50-year-old Roman Catholic novelist, corpulent, heavy-drinking, insomniac, out of tune with modern life, plagued by disgust and boredom, who sets off on a cruise to Ceylon to escape growing hallucinations, but becomes increasingly paranoid, imagining himself accused of being homosexual, Jewish, Fascist, alcoholic, a social climber, etc.; it is a self-caricature which ends in salvation. He casts an equally cold eye on himself in his revealing *Diaries* (1976, ed. M. Davie); see also *Evelyn Waugh* (1975) by Christopher Sykes. Waugh's other works include biographies of E. *Campion (1935) and R. *Knox (1959), and a volume of autobiography, *A Little Learning* (1964); his *Letters*, edited by M. Amory, appeared in 1980.

Waverley, the first of the novels of Sir W. *Scott, published 1814. Much of it had been written, and thrown aside, some years before.

Edward Waverley, a romantic young man, has been brought up partly by a Hanoverian father, partly by his uncle Sir Everard Waverley, a rich landowner of *Jacobite leanings. Thus ambivalent in politics, he is commissioned in the army in 1745 and joins his regiment in Scotland. He visits his uncle's friend the Baron Bradwardine, a kind-hearted but pedantic old Jacobite, and attracts the interest of his daughter Rose. Impelled by curiosity, he visits Donald Bean Lean, a Highland freebooter, and Fergus MacIvor (Vich Ian Vohr) of Glennaquoich, a young Highland chieftain, active in the Jacobite cause. At Glennaquoich, he falls in love with Fergus's sister Flora, whose beauty and ardent loyalty to the Stuarts appeal to his romantic disposition. These visits, unwise in a British officer at a time of acute political tension, compromise Edward with his colonel. Through the intrigues of Donald Bean Lean, he is accused of fomenting mutiny in his regiment and is cashiered and arrested. He is rescued by the action of Rose Bradwardine and, influenced by a sense of unjust treatment, by Flora's enthusiasm, and by a kind reception by Prince Charles Edward, he joins the Jacobite forces. At the battle of Prestonpans he saves from death Colonel Talbot, a distinguished English officer and friend of his family, and Talbot's influence, after the eventual defeat and rout of the pretender's army, secures his pardon and the rehabilitation of Baron Bradwardine. Meanwhile Edward, decisively rejected by the spirited Flora, has turned his affections to the more amenable Rose whom he marries. Fergus, convicted of treason, meets his end bravely; Flora retires to a convent.

Scott claimed to have written *Waverley* in haste and 'without much skill'; in fact, it is one of the best plotted of his novels, every strand well knitted into the story, and the pace graduated carefully from the slow beginning to the tumultuous end. Equally skilful is the progress of Waverley ('a sneaking piece of imbecility' in Scott's own words) from his woolly-minded ignorance at the opening to the knowledge of the world he acquires from experience. In his first novel, Scott sounded the theme of the opposition of romance and realism which was to reappear in many of his later works, though the irony with which romantic pretensions are undercut is rarely better deployed. Among the minor characters, the faithful Evan Dhu Maccombich and the 'innocent', Davie Gellatley, mouthpiece of some of Scott's most beautiful lyrics, stand out.

Waves, The, a novel by V. *Woolf, published 1931, and regarded by many as her masterpiece.

It traces the lives of a group of friends (Bernard, Susan, Rhoda, Neville, Jinny, and Louis) from childhood to late middle age, evoking their personalities through their reflections on themselves and on one another: the effect is not so much of *stream of consciousness as of what *Daiches has called 'recitative', in that each character speaks formally his or her own thoughts, within inverted commas. There is no attempt to differentiate the speech patterns of the six friends; their individuality is presented through a highly patterned sequence of recurring phrases and images, and what we learn of their daily lives (that Susan marries a farmer, that Bernard's ambitions as a writer are disappointed, that Louis becomes a man of power and wealth) we learn obliquely. The organization of the novel is highly formal: the main text is introduced and divided by sections of lyrical prose describing the rising and sinking of the sun over a seascape of waves and shore. There is one additional character, Percival, whose thoughts are never directly presented: his death in India in his mid-twenties, halfway through the novel, becomes the focus for fears and defiance of death and mortality. One of the dominant images of the novel, used by phrase-maker Bernard, is that of a fin breaking from the water; this was, as Woolf's diary reveals, her starting point for the work ('One sees a fin passing far out', 30 Sept. 1926) and on 7 Feb. 1931, having just written the last words, she recorded in her diary, 'I have netted that fin . . .' It is the most intense and poetic of all her works, and after it, significantly, she turned to a much less concentrated form in *The Years.

Way of All Flesh, The, a novel by S. *Butler (1835–1902), published posthumously 1903.

In this study of four generations, dissecting the stultifying effects of inherited family traits and attitudes, many experiences of Butler's life are clearly visible. He completed the book some 17 years before his death, but he never revised the second half. The story (narrated by a family friend, Overton) was originally called *Ernest Pontifex*; Ernest is the awkward and unhappy great-grandson of John Pontifex, a village carpenter, whose natural instinctive character he comes to revere. His own father, Theo, is a tyrannical, canting parent, repeating the attitudes of Ernest's grandfather George. After his ordination the inept Ernest, taking a respectable woman for a prostitute, is

sentenced to prison, where he begins to try to free himself from his immediate forebears and return to the simplicity of Old Pontifex. On his release he plunges into a disastrous union with Ellen, a drunken maidservant, and with her engages in tailoring and running a shop. Fortunately she turns out to be already married, and Ernest's beloved aunt Alethea leaves him sufficient money to devote himself to literature.

Aunt Alethea was based on Butler's friend Miss Savage, who gave him much help with the first half of the book before her death. The book received much praise, led by G. B. *Shaw, and reached the height of its success in the 1920s.

Way of the World, The, a comedy by *Congreve, produced 1700.

Mirabell is in love with Millamant, a niece of Lady Wishfort, and has pretended to court the aunt in order to conceal his suit of the niece. The deceit has been revealed to Lady Wishfort by Mrs Marwood to revenge herself on Mirabell, who has rejected her advances. Lady Wishfort, who now hates Mirabell 'more than a quaker hates a parrot', will deprive her niece of the half of the inheritance which is in her keeping if Millamant marries Mirabell. The latter accordingly contrives that his servant Waitwell shall impersonate an uncle of his, Sir Rowland, make love to Lady Wishfort, and pretend to marry her, having, however, first married Lady Wishfort's woman Foible. He hopes by this deception to force Lady Wishfort to consent to his marriage to her niece. The plot is discovered by Mrs Marwood, and also the fact that Mirabell has in the past had an intrigue with Mrs Fainall, daughter of Lady Wishfort. She conspires with Fainall, her lover and the pretended friend of Mirabell, to reveal these facts to Lady Wishfort, while Fainall is to threaten to divorce his wife and discredit Lady Wishfort, unless he is given full control of Mrs Fainall's property and Millamant's portion is also handed over to him. The scheme, however, fails. Mrs Fainall denies the charge against her and brings proof of Fainall's affair with Mrs Marwood, while Mirabell produces a deed by which Mrs Fainall, before her last marriage, made him trustee of her property. Lady Wishfort, in gratitude for her release from Fainall's threats, forgives Mirabell and consents to his marriage to Millamant.

Congreve enlivens the action with a fine gallery of fools, including Sir Wilfull Witwoud, Lady Wishfort's boisterous and good-natured country nephew; they serve to highlight the central contrast between the passionate and grasping relationship of Fainall and Mrs Marwood and the delicate process by which Mirabell persuades Millamant that even in such a mercenary society, love can survive into marriage. The dialogue is exceptionally brilliant, and many critics also consider the play a study of the battle between good and evil, rather than of the characteristically *Restoration conflict between the witty and the foolish.

Way We Live Now, The, a novel by A. *Trollope, published 1875.

Augustus Melmotte has the reputation of a great financier, and huge quantities of money pass through his hands. He entertains the emperor of China, and is offered a seat in Parliament. Yet no one thinks to examine the nature of the Melmotte millions until Melmotte is caught forging the title deeds to one of the estates he is buying up. Subsequent enquiries into Melmotte's prize speculation, a Central American railway, prove it to be a gigantic confidence trick, and when it becomes clear that the 'great financier' has tampered with his daughter's trust fund, his disgrace is absolute. After a drunken appearance in the House of Commons he commits suicide. The sordidness of Melmotte's career is matched by his daughter Marie's experiences in the marriage-mart. She is treated as a commodity by the cautious Lord Nidderdale, and as a diversion by the shamelessly dissipated Sir Felix Carbury. When Carbury entices Marie to elope with him she steals the money necessary for the elopement, only to find that Carbury does not keep his appointment, having gambled the money away. At the end of the novel she marries the stockjobber Hamilton K. Fisker, a leading promoter of the American railway scheme.

Trollope conceived the novel as an attack on 'the commercial profligacy of the age', and his perspective is shared by the upright Roger Carbury, head of the dissolute Carbury family. Lady Carbury's shifts as a glib authoress lead to an exposition of the lower levels of contemporary literary life.

weak ending, the occurrence of an unstressed or proclitic monosyllable (such as a preposition, conjunction, or auxiliary verb) in the normally stressed place at the end of an iambic line.

Wealth of Nations, An Inquiry into the Nature and Causes of the, a treatise on political economy by Adam *Smith, published 1776, originally delivered in the form of lectures at Glasgow.

Smith's work is the first comprehensive treatment of the whole subject of political economy, and is remarkable for its breadth of view. Smith shared the objection of the French *physiocrats to the mercantile system, but he did not share their view that land is the sole source of wealth. The *Wealth of Nations* sets out with the doctrine that the labour of the nation is the source of its means of life. It insists on the value of the division of labour. Labour is the standard of value, and originally was the sole determinant of price; but in a more advanced state of society three elements enter into price—wages, profit, and rent—and these elements are discussed separately.

The second book deals with capital, its nature, accumulation, and employment. With the increase of capital there is an increase of productive labour and a decrease in the rate of interest.

After this exposition the author proceeds to an elaborate attack on the mercantile system, and an advocacy of freedom of commerce and industry. His political economy is essentially individualistic; self-interest is the proper criterion of economic action. But the universal pursuit of one's own advantage contributes, in his view, to the public interest.

WEAVER, Harriet Shaw (1876–1961), editor, publisher, and benefactor, born in Cheshire. Business manager and later (1914) editor of the *Egoist, she saw *Joyce's *A Portrait of the Artist as a Young Man* through serial publication (1914–15), though the printer's objections to certain passages caused her to remove the journal to others. When Joyce could find no British publisher for the book, Weaver brought it out under the imprint of the Egoist Press (with sheets from B. W. Huebsch's US publication, 1916), which also published work by T. S. *Eliot, R. *Aldington, *H.D., Marianne *Moore, and others. In 1917 she anonymously provided the first of what would be many benefactions to Joyce; in this year Eliot became assistant editor of the *Egoist.* Under their editorship the journal published work by *Pound, Eliot, W. *Lewis, W. C. *Williams, and others, as well as early instalments of *Ulysses.* It ceased publication in Dec. 1919 and the press closed in 1923. Weaver continued her financial support of Joyce and became literary executor of his estate.

WEBB, Beatrice, née Potter (1858–1943), born into a wealthy and well-connected family. She was from an early age deeply interested in both the theoretical and practical aspects of social reform, political economy, and sociology, concerns that were shared by her husband Sidney Webb (1859–1947), the son of a London shopkeeper, whom she married in 1892. Both were leading spirits in the *Fabian Society, and they produced jointly numerous works on social history, served on many royal commissions, and helped to found the London School of Economics. Beatrice also wrote two autobiographical works (*My Apprenticeship,* 1926; *Our Partnership,* 1948), and kept a remarkable diary, of which selections were published in 1952 and 1956, edited by M. Cole; a fuller four-volume edition, edited by N. and J. Mackenzie, appeared 1982–5. These show the width of her human and intellectual interests and considerable literary skill, and are a valuable record of social life and progressive thought of the period. Sidney and Beatrice Webb appear in H. G. *Wells's novel *The New Machiavelli* (1911) as the Baileys, 'two active self-centred people, excessively devoted to the public service . . . the most formidable and distinguished couple conceivable' (Bk II, ch. 2, 'Margaret in London').

WEBB, (Gladys) Mary, née Meredith (1881–1927), novelist, born in Shropshire, the daughter of a schoolmaster. In 1912 she married Henry Bertram Law Webb, also a schoolmaster; they lived for some years in Shropshire, working as market gardeners and selling their produce at Shrewsbury market, before moving to

London in 1921. She had contracted Graves' disease while still young, an affliction which found its fictional counterpart in the harelip of Prudence Sarn, the narrator of her most famous novel, *Precious Bane* (1924). Her other works include *The Golden Arrow* (1916), *Gone to Earth* (1917), and *The House in Dormer Forest* (1920). They are tales of rustic life, romantic, passionate, morbid, and frequently naïve, written in a fervid prose easily ridiculed by Stella Gibbons in *Cold Comfort Farm*, but they nevertheless retain a certain emotional power. They had little success in her lifetime; her great posthumous success was due largely to the championship of Stanley Baldwin, who spoke warmly of her at a *Royal Literary Fund dinner after her death, and wrote an introduction to a reprint of *Precious Bane* in 1928 in which he praised her lyrical intensity, her evocation of the Shropshire landscape, and her 'blending of human passion with the fields and skies'.

WEBB, Sidney, see WEBB, B.

WEBER, Carl Maria von (1786–1826), German composer, and one of the founders of the Romantic movement in Germany. After the success of *Der Freischütz* in 1821, Weber's reputation was assured. In 1824 he was asked by Charles *Kemble to write and conduct an opera for the 1825 season at Covent Garden; he accepted, at once beginning a crash course of English lessons. He acquired reasonable proficiency in the language, which stood him in good stead when he temporarily took over a task previously done by *Haydn and *Beethoven and provided instrumental accompaniments for 12 Scottish folk songs early in 1825. Meanwhile, he had received the first instalment of *Oberon; or The Elf King's Oath* from *Planché: based on an 18th-cent. English translation of the German poet Wieland's *Oberon* (itself a reworking of the medieval French epic *Huon de Bordeaux*), the libretto's only link with Shakespeare is the quarrel between Oberon and Titania (already incorporated by Wieland from *A Midsummer Night's Dream*), and the names of Oberon and Puck among the dramatis personae. For this unpromising jumble Weber succeeded in producing music which includes much that is among the most poetic, and indeed prophetic, that he ever wrote. *Oberon* (1826) remains one of the great 'sports' in the history of opera.

WEBSTER, Augusta, née Davies (1837–94), poet and local government activist, born in Poole, Dorset, the daughter of a vice-admiral. She had a varied and mobile education and in 1867 married Thomas Webster, a lawyer. Her earliest works were published under the pseudonym 'Cecil Home': under her own name appeared *Dramatic Studies* (1866), *A Woman Sold and Other Poems* (1867), and *Portraits* (1870). These volumes show her skilled use of the *dramatic monologue, particularly in the forceful presentation of female character and predicament: 'The Castaway'

(1870) is a notable variant on the popular Victorian theme of the 'Fallen Woman'. Her last volume, a sonnet sequence called *Mother and Daughter*, appeared in 1895 with a preface by W. M. *Rossetti.

WEBSTER, Daniel (1782–1852), born in New Hampshire. He rose to great eminence as an orator, in the law courts, in the American House of Representatives and Senate, and in public speeches, when he urged the union of the American states. He was twice secretary of state. His speeches, even in ordinary criminal trials, show a rare literary quality comparable to that of speeches by *Burke. Among the best known are the discourse on the 200th anniversary of the landing of the Pilgrims (1825), the Bunker Hill oration (1825), and the Adams and Jefferson speech (1826).

WEBSTER, John (c.1578–c.1626), the son of a prosperous London coachmaker of Smithfield. He was himself admitted by patrimony to the Merchant Taylors' Company, and combined the careers of coachmaker and playwright. He wrote several plays in collaboration with other dramatists; these include *Westward Hoe* and *Northward Hoe*, with *Dekker, written 1604 and 1605, both printed 1607; *A Cure for a Cuckold* (printed 1661, written ?1625), probably with *Rowley (and possibly *Heywood); and a lost play with *Ford, Dekker, and Rowley, *Keep the Widow Waking* (1624). It has also been suggested that he had a hand in *Middleton's *Anything for a Quiet Life* (1661, written ?1621) and *Fletcher's *The Fair Maid of the Inn* (1625). He expanded Marston's *The Malcontent* for the King's Men in 1604, and published elegies on Prince Henry in 1613 with Heywood and *Tourneur. In 1615 he contributed several sketches to the sixth impression of *Overbury's *Characters*. *The Devil's Law Case*, a tragi-comedy, published 1623, written 1617–21, mentions in its dedication a lost play, *Guise*, which would have brought Webster's total of single-handed plays up to four; as it is, his great reputation rests on his two major works, *The White Devil* (which dates from between 1609 and 1612, when it was published) and *The Duchess of Malfi* (pub. 1623, written 1612/13). With these two tragedies Webster has achieved a reputation second only to Shakespeare's; they have been revived in this century more frequently than those of any other of Shakespeare's contemporaries. However, critics have by no means agreed on his virtues. Attempts by N. *Tate and *Theobald to accommodate the plays to 18th-cent. taste were followed in 1808 by *Lamb's influential *Specimens*, which singled out the 'beauties', in terms of poetic passages, and many 19th-cent. critics continued to complain about Webster's poor sense of structure, his inconsistencies, his excessive use of horror. (*Saintsbury, 1887, on *The Duchess*: 'the fifth act is a kind of gratuitous appendix of horrors stuck on without art or reason.') The 20th cent. saw a strong revival of interest in the plays as drama, and in Webster as satirist and moralist. The works were edited by F. L. *Lucas (4 vols, 1927).

WEBSTER, Noah (1758–1843), American lexicographer and philologist, born in Connecticut. He was educated at Yale University, and worked subsequently as teacher, lawyer, and journalist. The chief work for which he is remembered is his great and scholarly *An American Dictionary of the English Language* (2 vols, 1828), in which he challenged the parochialism of British dictionaries and, with a strong national pride and spirit, established Americanisms and American usages. He revised and expanded it himself in 1840, and it has been through several subsequent revisions. (See also DICTIONARY.)

WEDDERBURN, John (?1500–56). With his brothers James (?1495–1553) and Robert (?1510–?57) he produced a metrical translation from German Protestant sources of 22 Psalms. The earliest known edition is of 1565 and the collection became known as the 'Dundee Psalms'.

WEDGWOOD, Josiah (1730–95), the first English potter with an international reputation, founder of the pottery at Etruria, Staffordshire, where he produced both useful and ornamental ware, maintaining high standards of quality despite large-scale production. He contributed much to the taste for *neo-classicism in design, and was a generous patron; *Flaxman worked for him from 1775 to 1787.

Thomas Wedgwood (1771–1805), son of Josiah, was the first to produce (unfixed) photographs, and was a patron of S. T. *Coleridge.

WEDGWOOD, Dame (Cicely) Veronica, OM, DBE (1910–97), historian, educated privately and at Lady Margaret Hall, Oxford. Her publications include *Strafford* (1935), *The Thirty Years' War* (1938), *Oliver Cromwell* (1939, rev. 1973), *The King's Peace* (1955), *The King's War* (1958), and *The Great Rebellion* (1966).

WEELKES, Thomas (?1576–1623), English composer. With *Wilbye, he was the most important of the English madrigalists who followed the lead given by T.*Morley in 1593 and 1594. Little is known of his life before the publication of his *Madrigals to 3. 4. 5. & 6. Voyces* in 1597; in the next year he became organist at Winchester College and later held the same post at Chichester Cathedral. *The Balletts and Madrigals to Five Voyces* came out in 1598, and the best of his works, the *Madrigals of 5. and 6. Parts, Apt for the Viols and Voices*, in 1600. He contributed one of the finest *madrigals to *The Triumphes of Oriana* in 1601, but his last collection, *Ayeres or Phantasticke Spirites for Three Voices* (1608), is less interesting.

In the best of Weelkes's madrigals the Italianate manner of Morley is developed into a more characteristically English style, often more serious in content and laid out for larger forces with great contrapuntal brilliance and richness of harmony. As with most of the madrigalists, the authors of the texts are generally not known, though Weelkes is one of the composers whose imagination is most evidently fired by the bold and vivid imagery of the age of *Donne.

'Wee Willie Winkie', a short story by Rudyard *Kipling; see also NIGHT AND DAY.

Wegg, Silas, in Dickens's *Our Mutual Friend*, a one-legged impudent old rascal, with a smattering of education, who becomes reader to Mr Boffin and attempts to blackmail him.

WEIL, Simone (1909–43), French essayist and thinker. Equally independent in her life and her work, she devoted herself to resisting the oppression inherent in organized institutions and to achieving identification with the sufferings of its victims. Although an *agrégée de philosophie*, she worked for a year on the shop floor of the Renault factory, joined the International Brigade in 1936, and after the outbreak of war found employment as a farm servant. Broken by her voluntary privations, and suffering from tuberculosis, she died in England where she had been engaged by the provisional French government. Her moral intellectual authority became generally apparent only posthumously. *Le Pesanteur et la grâce* (1947), *L'Attente de Dieu* (1950; *Waiting on God*, 1951), and *Cahiers* (1951–6) have earned her a unique respect for their intensity of thought, their moral commitment, and their religious inwardness.

WEILL, Kurt (1900–50), German composer, most famous for the music he wrote for *Brecht's *Threepenny Opera* (1928) and *Mahagonny* (1930), in which, in keeping with Brecht's break with dramatic tradition and attack on the bourgeoisie, Weill mingled popular songs and jazz of the 1920s with ironic echoes of Wagnerian opera. Weill settled in New York in 1935.

Weir of Hermiston, an unfinished novel by R. L. *Stevenson, published 1896, which contains some of Stevenson's finest work.

Archie Weir is the only child of Adam Weir, Lord Hermiston, the lord justice clerk, a formidable 'hanging judge', based on the character of Robert Macqueen, Lord Braxfield (1722–99), known as 'the Jeffrey of Scotland'. His mother, a pale, ineffectual, religious woman, dies young, leaving Archie to the care of a father he dreads and dislikes. The conflict between the two comes to a head when Archie witnesses his father hounding a wretched criminal to death at a trial with sadistic glee; he publicly confronts his father, speaking out against capital punishment, and is banished to Hermiston, a remote Lowland village. There he lives as a recluse with Kirstie, his devoted housekeeper and distant relative, who is aunt to four notable brothers, the 'Black Elliotts', famed for hunting down their father's murderer. Archie falls in love with their sister, and Kirstie's niece, Christina. The novel ends as Archie, warned by the jealous Kirstie, tells Christina that their *secret meetings must end. We know from Stevenson's notes that the novel was to end with another confrontation between father and son, in which Archie is on trial for his life for the alleged murder of Christina's seducer Frank Innes. Archie and Christina escape to America, but the old man dies of shock. In this novel, Stevenson returns to the Edinburgh and Lowland landscapes of his youth, which he evokes with a grim but poetic power, and many have seen in Archie's rebellion Stevenson's rejection of his own Calvinist ancestry, though in real life he was able to achieve a reconciliation and understanding with his parents, and their approval of his career as a writer. Critics agree that it promised to be the most ambitious and profound of his works.

WEISS, Peter (1916–82), German playwright, born in Berlin, and best known in England for his *Marat/Sade* (*The Persecution and Assassination of Marat as Performed by the Inmates of the Asylum of Charenton under the Direction of the Marquis de Sade*) which was first performed in London in 1964 in an adaptation by Geoffrey Skelton and Adrian *Mitchell, directed by Peter *Brook. This was a landmark in the theatre of the 1960s, uniting elements of the Theatre of the *Absurd, the Theatre of *Cruelty, and the revolutionary Marxism of the period, and illustrating interest in attitudes to mental illness and imprisonment expressed in the writings of *Laing and *Foucault.

WELCH, (Maurice) Denton (1915–48), born in Shanghai. He spent part of his childhood in China, and was educated at Repton and Goldsmith's School of Art. He intended to be a painter, but in 1935 was severely injured in a bicycle accident; he spent months in hospital and a sanatorium, and was an invalid for the rest of his life. A volume of autobiography, *Maiden Voyage* (1943), was followed by a novel about adolescence, *In Youth is Pleasure* (1944), and a volume of short stories, *Brave and Cruel, and Other Stories* (1949). His most distinctive work is the unfinished, autobiographical, posthumously published *A Voice through a Cloud* (1950), a vivid, heightened, and at times painfully sensitive account of accident and illness.

WELDON, Fay, née Birkinshaw (1933–), novelist, dramatist, and television screenwriter, born in Worcester and educated at the University of St Andrews; she worked for some time in advertising before becoming a full-time writer. She is perhaps best known for her novels, which express the rising feminist consciousness of the 1970s, and which deal, frequently in tragi-comic vein, with women's troubled relationships with parents, men, and children and with one another; these include *The Fat Woman's Joke* (1967), *Down among the Women* (1971), *Female Friends* (1975), *Praxis* (1978), *Puffball* (1980), *The President's Child* (1982), *The Life and Loves of a She-Devil* (1983), subsequently adapted for television and film), *The Hearts and Lives of Men* (1987), *The Cloning of Joanna*

May (1989), *Darcy's Utopia* (1990), *Growing Rich* (1992), *Life Force* (1992), *Natural Love* (1993), and *Affliction* (1994). *Big Women* (1998) is a sharply observed account, loosely based on real events, of a group of women who found a feminist publishing company. Her gift for realistic dialogue is manifested both in her fiction and in her many plays and free adaptions (notably of Jane *Austen) for television, and she has also been a pioneer in her bold address of many contemporary issues, such as cloning, genetic engineering, and what she sees as the questionable value of the 'therapy culture'.

Well-Beloved, The, a novel by T. *Hardy, published serially 1892, revised and reissued 1897.

The scene is the Isle of Slingers (i.e. Portland). The central figure is Jocelyn Pierston, a sculptor of the Isle, who falls in love successively with three generations of island women: Avice Caro, her daughter, and her granddaughter, all of the same name. He is seeking in each the perfect form in woman, as he seeks it in stone. Perversity of circumstances, and the varying natures of the women, prevent him from marrying any of them. Despairing of the pursuit of art and beauty, he eventually marries an elderly widow, Marcia, when both he and she have been, like the rock of Portland, subjected to the raspings and chisellings of time.

Weller, Samuel, in Dickens's *Pickwick Papers*, Mr Pickwick's devoted servant, formerly boots at the White Hart in the Borough, a cheerful, facetious, and resourceful character, with an endless store of humorous illustrations apposite to the various incidents of life; and his father Tony, a coach-driver.

WELLES, Orson (1915–84), American actor and director, best remembered for his work in the cinema, e.g. *Citizen Kane* (1941); and *The Magnificent Ambersons* (1942), which he directed, and *The Third Man* (1949), script by G. *Greene, directed by Carol Reed, in which he starred. His radio version of H. G. Wells's *The War of the Worlds* (1938) was a sensational success. He also directed himself in film versions of Shakespeare, notably as Macbeth (1948), Othello (1952), and as *Falstaff in his own adaptation called *Chimes at Midnight* (1966).

WELLESLEY, Dorothy Violet, duchess of Wellington, née Ashton (1889–1956), remembered as a poet chiefly through the admiration of *Yeats, who included a disproportionate number of her poems in his *Oxford Book of Modern Verse* (1936). His *Letters on Poetry*, originally written to her, were published in 1940. She herself published several volumes of poetry, collected in 1955 as *Early Light*. She was a friend of V. *Sackville-West, and sponsored and edited the Hogarth Living Poets series for the *Hogarth Press.

WELLINGTON, Arthur Wellesley, first duke of (1769–1852), soldier and statesman, who fought in the Indian Campaign (1799–1803), the Peninsular Campaign

(1808–14), and was the hero of the battle of Waterloo (18 June 1815) at which Napoleon was decisively defeated. He first became a national figure with the victory of Talavera in 1809, and was created marquess of Douro and duke of Wellington in 1814. He was prime minister 1828–30, and secretary of state for foreign affairs 1834–5. Known as the 'Iron Duke', or, more familiarly, as 'Old Nosey', he was much portrayed by caricaturists, notably John Doyle (father of R. *Doyle) and William Heath ('Paul Pry', 1795–1840). Although a less romantic figure than Napoleon, his exploits and his phlegmatic utterances (e.g. 'Publish and be damned', attributed to him) caught the imagination of contemporary and later writers: the battle of Waterloo is depicted in Byron's *Childe Harold's Pilgrimage (III. xxi, 'There was a sound of revelry by night') and in *Vanity Fair; he inspired much of the Juvenilia of C. *Brontë; and he appears in historical novels by A. C. *Doyle, *Henty, and others. By the queen's wishes he was given the most magnificent state funeral ever accorded to a subject, a pageant commemorated in *Tennyson's 'Ode on the Death of the Duke of Wellington' (1852). There is a biography (2 vols, 1969, 1973) by Elizabeth Longford.

Well of Loneliness, The, see HALL, R.

WELLS, Charles Jeremiah (1800–79), author (under the pseudonym of H. L. Howard) of *Joseph and His Brethren: A Scriptural Drama* (1824), a verse play much admired by *Rossetti, republished in 1876 with an essay by *Swinburne, and again in 1908 by the *World's Classics.

WELLS, H(erbert) G(eorge) (1866–1946), born in Bromley, Kent, the son of an unsuccessful small tradesman and professional cricketer. He was apprenticed to a draper in early life, a period reflected in several of his novels. He then became assistant teacher at Midhurst Grammar School, studying by night and winning a scholarship in 1884 to the Normal School of Science in South Kensington, where he came under the lasting influence of T. H. *Huxley. For some years, in poor health, he struggled as a teacher, studying and writing articles in his spare time; his marriage in 1891 to his cousin Isabel proved unhappy, and he eloped with his student Amy Catherine ('Jane') Robbins, whom he married in 1895 (though this did not prevent him from embarking on further liaisons, and continuing to criticize conventional marriage). In 1903 he joined the *Fabian Society, but was soon at odds with it, his sponsor G. B. *Shaw, and Sidney and Beatrice *Webb; impatient and turbulent, his career as writer and thinker was marked by a provocative independence.

His literary output was vast and extremely varied. As a novelist he is perhaps best remembered for his scientific romances, among the earliest products of the new genre of *science fiction. The first, *The Time Machine* (1895), is a social allegory set in the year

802701, describing a society divided into two classes, the subterranean workers, called Morlocks, and the decadent Eloi. This was followed by *The Wonderful Visit* (1895), *The Island of Doctor Moreau* (1896), *The Invisible Man* (1897), *The War of the Worlds* (1898, a powerful and apocalyptic vision of the world invaded by Martians), *When the Sleeper Wakes* (1899), *The First Men in the Moon* (1901), *Men Like Gods* (1923), and others. These combine, in varying degrees, political satire, warnings about the dangerous new powers of science, and a desire to foresee a possible future (see also *A Modern Utopia*, 1905); Wells's preoccupation with social as well as scientific progress distinguishes them from the fantasies of *Verne.

Another group of novels evokes in comic and realistic style the lower-middle-class world of his youth. *Love and Mr Lewisham* (1900) tells the story of a struggling teacher; *Kipps* (1905) that of an aspiring draper's assistant, undone by an unexpected inheritance and its consequences; *The History of Mr Polly* (1910) recounts the adventures of Alfred Polly, an inefficient shopkeeper who liberates himself by burning down his own shop and bolting for freedom, which he discovers as man-of-all-work at the Potwell Inn.

Among his other novels, *Ann Veronica* (1909) is a feminist tract about a girl who, fortified by the concept of the *'New Woman', defies her father and conventional morality by running off with the man she loves. *Tono-Bungay* (1909), one of his most successful works (described by himself as 'a social panorama in the vein of Balzac'), is a picture of English society in dissolution, and of the advent of a new class of rich, embodied in Uncle Ponderevo, an entrepreneur intent on peddling a worthless patent medicine. *The Country of the Blind, and Other Stories* (1911), his fifth collection of short stories, contains, as well as the well-known title story, originally published in 1904, the memorable 'The Door in the Wall' (originally published 1906). *The New Machiavelli* (1911), about a politician involved in sexual scandal, was seen to mark a decline in his creative power, evident in later novels, which include *Mr Britling Sees It Through* (1916) and *The World of William Clissold* (1926). He continued to reach a huge audience, however, notably with his massive *The Outline of History* (1920) and its shorter offspring *A Short History of the World* (1922), and with many works of scientific and political speculation (including *The Shape of Things to Come*, 1933) which confirmed his position as one of the great popularizers and one of the most influential voices of his age; the dark pessimism of his last prediction, *Mind at the End of Its Tether* (1945), may be seen in the context of his own ill health and the course of the Second World War. One of his last statements (made after Hiroshima) was an exhortation to man to confront his 'grave and tragic' destiny with dignity and without hysteria.

His *Experiment in Autobiography* (1934) is a striking portrait of himself, his contemporaries (including Arnold *Bennett, *Gissing, and the Fabians) and their times. See also a life by N. and J. MacKenzie, *The Time Traveller* (1973), and a memoir by his son by Rebecca *West, *Anthony West* (1914–87), *Aspects of a Life* (1984).

WELSH, Irvine (1957–   ), Scottish writer, born in Edinburgh, generally seen as the first and most important member of the so-called 'Chemical Generation' of younger British writers, politically disaffected, culturally sophisticated, and centrally engaged with the music, drugs, and *mores* of 1990s club culture. Welsh grew up in Muirhouse, one of Edinburgh's peripheral housing estates. After leaving school at 16, he did many jobs in Edinburgh and London, among them TV repair work, property development, and working for local government for the City of Edinburgh District Council. He took an MBA at Heriot-Watt University, Edinburgh, in 1990. His first novel, *Trainspotting* (1993), about a group of young heroin addicts in 1980s Edinburgh, was sexually and scatologically explicit, written in a pungent Edinburgh vernacular, and distinguished by great comic verve. It quickly became a best-seller and cultural byword; a stage version was followed in 1996 by a film adaptation. Its characters reappear in *Porno* (2002). Other works of fiction include short story collections *The Acid House* (1994) and *Ecstasy: Three Tales of Chemical Romance* (1996), and novels *Marabou Stork Nightmares* (1995), *Filth* (1998), and *Glue* (2001). The language is progressively explicit but also rather repetitive in its use of obscenity and extreme violence: the poorly received *Filth*, the story of a corrupt Edinburgh policeman, includes the narrative 'voice' of the protagonist's own excrement, and a first stage play, *You'll Have Had Your Hole* (West Yorkshire Playhouse, 1998), centres around episodes of torture and sexual cruelty. He has claimed to be as interested in music as he is in writing, and in the mid-1990s worked as a DJ (disc jockey) in London and Amsterdam.

WELSH, Jane, see CARLYLE, J. B. W.

WELTY, Eudora (1909–2001), American short story writer and novelist, born in Jackson, Mississippi, her lifelong home. The stories of *A Curtain of Green* (1941) derive from her experiences with the New Deal's Works Progress Administration, for which she travelled through her native state photographing inhabitants both black and white and learning 'a story-teller's truth ... the moment in which people reveal themselves'. Her first novel, *The Robber Bridegroom* (1942), is an elaborately worked fairy tale set in the Natchez Trace country *c.*1798. Also historical are the two most remarkable stories in her second collection, *The Wide Net* (1943), 'First Love' and 'A Still Moment': both exhibit intense rapport with place and concern with angles of vision. These also distinguish *The Golden Apples* (1949), a series of linked stories that followed her humorous, poetic, but restricted novel *Delta Wedding* (1946). *The Ponder Heart* (1954) is a tragi-comic

first-person narrative. *Losing Battles* (1970), propelled largely through dialogue, returns to the Depression to assemble three generations for a 90th birthday. *The Optimist's Daughter* (1972) centres on the antagonism after a judge's death between his middle-aged daughter and insensitive young widow. *The Eye of the Story* (1978) collects essays, *A Writer's Eye* (ed. P. A. McHatlaney) book reviews. *Collected Stories* (1980) brought Welty belated wide recognition; in *One Writer's Beginnings* (1984) she traces her imaginative development. See *The Still Moment: Eudora Welty; Portrait of a Writer* (1994) by Paul Binding.

Wemmick, in Dickens's **Great Expectations*, clerk to Mr Jaggers the lawyer, and Pip's good friend.

Wentworth, Captain, a character in J. Austen's **Persuasion.*

WENTWORTH, Sir Thomas, see STRAFFORD.

WERTENBAKER, Timberlake (1951–   ), American dramatist, long resident in Britain, best known for *Our Country's Good* (1987), based on *Keneally's novel *The Playmaker*, which dealt with the first play (Farquhar's **Recruiting Officer*) performed by penal settlers in Australia: it has been much revived around the world. Her other plays include *The Grace of Mary Travers* (1985), which dealt with a woman coming to personal and political awareness during the Gordon riots of the 1780s, and *Three Birds Alighting on a Field* (1992), which dealt with the commercial art market at the height of the Thatcher economic boom. *After Darwin* (1998) uses the historical figure of *Darwin and mixes past and present in an examination of evolution and extinction. She has also written frequent stage, radio, and TV adaptations, including E. *Wharton's *The Children*; *Marivaux's *False Admissions* and *Successful Strategies* (both for Shared Experience touring players) and his *La Dispute*; *Anouilh's *Leocadia*; *Maeterlinck's *Pelléas et Mélisande*; Mnouchkine's *Mephisto*; *Sophocles' *Theban Plays* (for the RSC); and *Euripides' *Hecuba*. Her work, frequently directed by Max Stafford-Clark, has never been altogether final on the written page: 'I like to work my plays in rehearsal', she has said, 'and even well into their run as I watch them performed in front of an audience. It's part of the travelling you do.'

Wertherism, a cultural phenomenon resulting from the fame throughout Europe of *Goethe's early novel *Die Leiden des jungen Werthers* (*The Sorrows of Young Werther*, 1774). This was a semi-autobiographical work about a sensitive artist, melancholy, at odds with society, and hopelessly in love with a girl, Charlotte (Lotte), who was engaged to someone else. Its combination of the hero's 'Weltschmerz' (sense of ill-ease with the world) and 'Ichschmerz' (dissatisfaction with self), together with the scandalous suicide of Werther, made the work a huge success throughout Europe. Young men wore blue coats and yellow breeches in imitation of Werther, china tea-sets were produced with scenes from the novel depicted on them, and perfumes named after Werther were sold. Goethe was later much embarrassed by this early work and by the assumption that it was autobiographical. *Thackeray wrote a well-known sardonic poem about Werther and Charlotte, and the term 'Wertherism' became current in English to describe a man's early self-indulgent moods of melancholy (for example, C. *Kingsley accused his brother-in-law J. A. *Froude of catching the disease of Wertherism in his youthful novel *The Nemesis of Faith*, 1849).

WESKER, Sir Arnold (1932–   ), playwright, born in Stepney of Jewish immigrant parents, and educated in Hackney. He left school at 16 and worked at various jobs (including furniture-maker's apprentice and pastrycook) before making his name as a playwright. His early work was closely associated with the *English Stage Company, although his first play to be performed, *Chicken Soup with Barley* (1958), transferred there from the Belgrade Theatre, Coventry, which also put on the first productions of *Roots* (1959) and *I'm Talking about Jerusalem* (1960), three plays now grouped together as the Wesker Trilogy. *The Kitchen* (1959), which first appeared at the *Royal Court, shows the stresses and conflicts of life behind the scenes in a restaurant, which culminate in tragedy; its use of the rhythms of working life was highly innovative and did much to stimulate the growth of what was to be known (though in a slightly different sense) as *kitchen sink drama. Wesker's political commitments were also manifested in 1960–1 in his efforts to establish Centre 42, a movement which aimed to popularize the arts through trade union support. His subsequent plays include *Chips with Everything* (1962), a study of class attitudes in the RAF during National Service; *The Four Seasons* (1965), about a love affair; *Their Very Own and Golden City* (1966) and *The Friends* (1970), both of which deal in different ways with the disappointment of political and social hope; *The Merchant* (1977; subsequently retitled *Shylock*), which treats the story of *Shylock in a manner that constitutes an attack on anti-Semitism; *Caritas* (1981), which shows the spiritual anguish of a 14th-cent. anchoress who realizes she has mistaken her vocation; and *Annie Wobbler* (1984), one of several one-woman plays. He has also published essays, screenplays, and volumes of short stories; the title story of *Love Letters on Blue Paper* (1974), about the relationship of a dying trade unionist and his wife, was televised and adapted (1978) for the stage. *As Much as I Dare*, a volume of autobiography, was published in 1994. *The Birth of Shylock and the Death of Zero Mostel* is a gripping account of the disastrous New York production of *Shylock*. *Honey* (2005) is his first novel (see ROOTS).

WESLEY, Charles (1707–88), brother of John *Wesley, and also an active member of the Oxford Methodists. He accompanied John to Georgia in 1735, and like him was influenced by the Moravians, though he remained faithful to the Anglican Church and regretted his brother's departure from it. He composed many thousands of hymns, including such favourites as 'Jesu, lover of my soul'. He left a *Journal*, published in 1849.

WESLEY, John (1703–91), the fifteenth child and second surviving son of the Revd Samuel Wesley, educated at Oxford. He became a fellow of Lincoln College in 1726. In Oxford he was the centre of a group of devout Christians (including his brother Charles, above, and *Whitefield); they practised severe self-discipline and self-examination, and were nicknamed the 'Holy Club' or 'Methodists'. On his father's death in 1735 he went to Georgia on an (unsuccessful) mission; he became a member of the Moravian society at Fetter Lane. He visited the Moravian colony at Herrnhut in 1738, and appointed his first lay preacher in the same year. He then began field preaching and opened a Methodist chapel at Bristol, and for the rest of his life conducted his ministry with extraordinary energy, preaching 40,000 sermons, and travelling thousands of miles a year, mainly on horseback. His literary output was also prodigious. He published from 1737 many collections of hymns; the singing of hymns to familiar tunes by the whole congregation was a new practice and contributed greatly to the fervent Methodist spirit. He wrote educational works, practical treatises, edited *Thomas à Kempis (1735), published selections from W. *Law, by whom he was deeply influenced, and kept a *Journal* (standard edn ed. N. Curnock, 1909–11) remarkable not only as a record of his spiritual life and tireless organizational activities, but also for its pathos and humour. Dr *Johnson found him a good conversationalist, but 'never at leisure'. Wesley's impact on public and private life, notably in his concern for the illiterate industrial poor, was enormous, and has even been credited (or discredited) with preventing a proletarian revolution. An edition of his complete works (ed. F. Baker, 34 vols), containing some unpublished material, began to appear in 1975.

WESLEY, Mary (Mary Aline Siepmann) (1912–2002), novelist and children's writer. Her first novel, *Jumping the Queue* (1983), a tragi-comedy whose 'happy ending' is successful suicide, was published when she was 71. Since then she published many novels, often with recurring characters, of which perhaps the best known is *The Camomile Lawn* (1984).

WESLEY, Mehitabel (Hetty) (1697–1750), the seventh surviving child of Samuel Wesley and sister of John and Charles *Wesley. Her life was erratic: in 1725 she was unhappily married to William Wright, and attacked the institution of marriage in 'Wedlock. A Satire', written *c*.1730 and published posthumously in 1862. Some verse was published and circulated during her life: 'To an Infant Expiring the Second Day of its Birth' appeared in the *Gentleman's Magazine*, 1733.

Wessex, the name used by *Hardy to designate the south-west counties, principally Dorset, which form the setting of many of his works.

WEST, Benjamin (1738–1820), an American painter who studied in Rome and settled in London in 1763. He was a founder member of the Royal Academy in 1768 and succeeded *Reynolds as president in 1792. A mediocre painter, his importance derives from his invention of the modern history painting with *The Death of Wolfe* (1770; Ottawa, National Gallery), with characters wearing contemporary dress, contrary to the dictates of the grand manner. His innovation was an important turning point in taste. Later, with *Death on a Pale Horse* (1802), he anticipated *Romanticism, and with his paintings of the life of Edward III (1787–9: Windsor, Royal Collection) pioneered a medieval subject.

WEST, Jane, see ROMANTIC FICTION.

WEST, Nathanael, the pseudonym of Nathan Wallenstein Weinstein (1903–40), American novelist, born in New York. He is known principally for two macabre and tragic novels, *Miss Lonelyhearts* (1933), the story of a heavy-drinking agony columnist who becomes involved in the life of one of his correspondents, and *The Day of the Locust* (1939), a satire of Hollywood life based on West's own experiences as a scriptwriter. He was killed in a car crash.

WEST, Dame Rebecca, the adopted name of Cecily Isabel Fairfield (1892–1983), daughter of Charles Fairfield, of Anglo-Irish descent, who became known in London for his witty defence of extreme individualism in debates with H. *Spencer and G. B. *Shaw. He moved his family to Edinburgh, where he died, leaving his widow and four daughters in straitened circumstances. Rebecca (who adopted this name, after *Ibsen's heroine in *Rosmersholm*, at 19) was educated in Edinburgh, trained briefly for the stage in London, then became a feminist and journalist, much influenced at this stage by the Pankhursts (see WOMEN'S SUFFRAGE); from 1911 she wrote for the *Freewoman*, the *New Freewoman*, and the *Clarion*. Many of her shrewd, witty, and combative pieces have been collected and reprinted as *The Young Rebecca* (1982, ed. Jane Marcus); this includes her outspoken review of H. G. *Wells's *Marriage* (1912), which led to a ten-year love affair and the birth of a son, Anthony West. Her first novel, *The Return of the Soldier* (1918), which describes the return home of a shell-shocked soldier, was followed by *The Judge* (1922), *The Strange Necessity* (1928), *Harriet Hume* (1929), and *The Thinking Reed* (1936); then, after a long gap, *The Fountain Overflows* (1956) and *The Birds Fall down* (1966). Meanwhile, in 1930, she had married a banker, Henry Maxwell Andrews, who accompanied her on the journey which produced her two-volume study of the Yugoslav nation, *Black Lamb and Grey Falcon* (1941). She was present at the Nuremberg trials, and

The Meaning of Treason (1949) grew out of articles originally commissioned by the *New Yorker*; an updated version in 1965 added accounts of more recent spy scandals (e.g. Vassall and Ward) to her study of 'Lord Haw Haw' (William Joyce) and others. She continued to write and to review with exceptional vigour almost until her death, at 90. The reputation of her novels tends to have been eclipsed somewhat by the aggressive panache of her reportage and journalism, and they have frequently been described as 'too intellectual', but feminist reassessments in the 1980s have admired her strong and unconventional heroines, and her fine craftsmanship.

WEST, Richard (1716–42), son of a lawyer. He became at Eton a close friend of T. *Gray and Horace *Walpole. Gray wrote a moving sonnet on his early death, 'In vain to me the smileing Mornings shine', first printed in 1775, which *Wordsworth used to illustrate his views on poetic diction in the *Preface* of 1800 to the *Lyrical Ballads*.

Western, Squire, and Sophia, characters in Fielding's *Tom Jones*.

West Indian, The, a comedy by R. *Cumberland, produced 1771.

Stockwell, having secretly married in Jamaica the daughter of his rich employer, old Belcour, has had a son by her, who has been passed off on old Belcour as a foundling, been brought up by him, and has inherited his property. Young Belcour, as he is called, comes home, but Stockwell postpones recognizing him as his son until he has made trial of his character. Young Belcour, a Rousseauesque child of nature, falls in love with Louisa, daughter of the impecunious Captain Dudley, but is misled into thinking her the mistress of Charles, who is actually her brother. Charles is in love with his rich cousin Charlotte, but because of his poverty will not confess his love, although it is returned. Belcour generously comes to the financial assistance of Captain Dudley, but his impetuous gift to Louisa of some jewels entrusted to him for Charlotte leads to grave complications. The imbroglio is eventually cleared up; Belcour discovers his mistake, is pardoned by Louisa and obtains her hand, and is acknowledged by his father, Stockwell. Charles is discovered to be the real heir of his grandfather's property, and marries Charlotte. Belcour's generosity and simplicity are favourably contrasted with the civilized decadence of London. (See PRIMITIVISM.) The play was produced by *Garrick, and enjoyed great success.

Westlock, John, a character in Dickens's *Martin Chuzzlewit*, at one time pupil of Mr Pecksniff.

Westminster Review (1824–1914), established by J. *Mill, an ardent supporter of *Bentham, as the journal of the 'philosophical radicals', in opposition to the *Edinburgh Review* and the *Quarterly Review*. The conservatism of the *Quarterly* and the quality of the *Edinburgh* reviewers both came under attack. *Byron, *Coleridge, *Tennyson, and *Carlyle were among the literary figures it supported, but political and philosophical attitudes were always put first. The journal survived several changes of name and ownership, and under the editorship of John *Chapman from 1851 (when G. *Eliot became the assistant editor) published *Froude, *Pattison, *Pater, George Eliot herself, and other important writers. It became a monthly in 1887, and in the 20th cent. dropped its literary interests.

Westward for Smelts, a collection of tales borrowed from *The Decameron* and similar sources, recounted by seven fishwives who embark after selling their fish in London; by 'Kinde Kit of Kingstone' (1620).

Westward Ho!, see KINGSLEY, C.

Westward Hoe, a comedy by *Webster and *Dekker, printed 1607.

The main plot deals with an escapade of three merry wives and their gallants to Brentford, where their husbands find them at an inn, but their innocence is established. In the sub-plot Justiniano, an Italian merchant, convinced of his wife's infidelity, abandons her and lives disguised, enjoying the comedy of London life. Mistress Justiniano is involved in an intrigue with a profligate earl, but conscience intervenes and repentance and reconciliation follow.

WEYMAN, Stanley John (1855–1928). He established his reputation as a historical novelist with *A Gentleman of France* (1893, dealing with the period of Henry of Navarre) followed by a number of other romances of a similar character, including *The Red Cockade* (1895), *Under the Red Robe* (1896, afterwards successfully dramatized at the Haymarket), *Count Hannibal* (1901, based on the massacre of St *Bartholomew), and *Chippinge* (1906, in an English setting, at the time of the *Reform Bill).

WHARTON, Edith, née Newbold Jones (1862–1937), American novelist and short story writer, born in New York of a distinguished and wealthy New York family. She was educated privately at home and in Europe, where she travelled widely; she married Edward Robbins Wharton in 1885 and they settled in France in 1907. The marriage was not happy; she suffered from nervous illnesses, and her husband's mental health declined in later years. They were divorced in 1913. She devoted her considerable energy to a cosmopolitan social life, which included a close friendship with H. *James, and to a literary career, which began with the publication of poems and stories in *Scribner's Magazine*. Her first volume of short stories, *The Greater Inclination* (1899), was followed by a novella, *The Touchstone* (1900), but it was *The House of Mirth* (1905), the tragedy of failed social climber Lily Bart, which established her as a leading novelist. Many

other works followed, including the less characteristic but much admired *Ethan Frome* (1911), a grim and ironic tale of passion and vengeance on a poor New England farm; *Madame de Treymes* (1907), which describes the American-born marquise de Malrive's adjustments to aristocratic Parisian society; *The Reef* (1912), also set in France, at the château of Givré, where widowed Anna Leath's expectations of a happy second marriage are frustrated when she learns of her fiancé's fleeting past dalliance with her daughter's governess; and *The Custom of the Country* (1913). *The Age of Innocence* (1920) describes the frustrated love of a New York lawyer, Newland Archer, for Ellen Olenska, the separated wife of a dissolute Polish count; her unconventional and artistic nature is contrasted with the timid but determined calculations of Archer's fiancée May, who, backed by all the authority of society, keeps him within her grasp and marries him. *The Mother's Recompense* (1925) concerns the struggle between runaway mother Kate Clephane and her daughter Anne for the hand of the same young man, and *Hudson River Bracketed* (1929) contrasts Midwest with New York society. She also published many volumes of short stories, various travel books, and an autobiography, *A Backward Glance* (1934). Edith Wharton's chief preoccupation is with the conflict between social and individual fulfilment which frequently leads to tragedy. Her observant, satiric, witty portrayal of social nuance, both in America and Europe, shows her keen interest in anthropology and in what she called the 'tribal behaviour' of various groups. There is a biography by R. W. B. Lewis, published in 1975.

WHATELY, Richard (1787–1863), educated at Oriel College, Oxford, of which he became fellow and tutor. He contributed to the *Quarterly Review* 1820–1. From 1829 to 1831 he was professor of political economy at Oxford, and was then appointed archbishop of Dublin. He was active in Irish cultural and political life, founding a professorship of political economy at Dublin in 1832 and 15 years later a Statistical Society, and involving himself in educational reform at all levels. He published a great number of works on philosophy and religion, supporting *Broad Church views, but his reputation rested largely on his *Logic* (1826) and *Rhetoric* (1828).

What Maisie Knew, a novel by H. *James, published 1897.

With insight and humour James takes us into the world of Maisie, the child of divorced parents who use her, neglect her, and expose her to their own world of emotional chaos.

Her father, Beale Farrange, marries Maisie's governess, Miss Overmore, while her mother marries a handsome, weak, and younger man, Sir Claude, to whom Maisie becomes devoted. These new marriages collapse, the step-parents become lovers, and her parents enter into new amorous entanglements. A new governess, Mrs Wix, appears to offer support, but also becomes infatuated with Sir Claude. Maisie is used as a pawn in the power games of the adults who surround her; her perception of their corrupt lives leads her to an odd and disconcerting maturity, yet she is not of their world and retains a fundamental honesty and innocence.

What You Will, the subtitle of Shakespeare's *Twelfth Night*; it is his only play (with the possible exception of *King *Henry VIII*) with an alternative title—its meaning is 'whatever you want to call it'. It is clearly connected, in some way, with *Marston's *What You Will* which probably appeared in 1601.

WHEATLEY, Phillis (?1735–84), a black poet born in Africa and shipped as a child to the slave-market of Boston, where she was purchased by John Wheatley, who encouraged her literary talent. Her *Poems on Various Subjects, Religious and Moral* were first published in London in 1773.

WHELAN, Peter (1931–), dramatist, born in Staffordshire, the area that provides the setting for two of his plays, *Clay* (1983) and *The Bright and Bold Design* (1991), which specifically concerns the Stoke-on-Trent pottery industry in the 1930s. Like many of his plays, these display a humane interest in working-class history and political change and were presented by the Royal Shakespeare Company. The RSC also staged *Captain Swing* (1978), about peasant uprisings in the 19th cent., *The Accrington Pals* (1981) about a First World War battalion, and two well-received plays respectively concerning *Marlowe and Shakespeare's daughter Susanna, *The School of Night* (1992) and *The Herbal Bed* (1996). Whelan has also collaborated with Don Kinkaid on a documentary musical about the Sioux massacres, *Lakota* (1990), and himself written a futuristic play, *Divine Right* (1996), in which a character clearly based on Prince William disguises himself in order to discover the realities of a sometimes grim Britain.

Where Angels Fear to Tread, E. M. *Forster's first novel, published 1905.

It is a tragi-comedy describing the consequences of the marriage of Lilia Herriton, an impulsive young widow, to the son of an Italian dentist, Gino Carella, whom she meets while touring in Tuscany, ineffectively chaperoned by well-meaning and romantic spinster Caroline Abbott. Lilia's brother Philip is dispatched by his mother, too late, to break off the match. Lilia dies shortly afterwards in childbirth and Philip is dispatched once more to rescue the baby. He himself falls in love with Italy and with Miss Abbott, but she falls in love with Gino, the baby is accidentally killed, and all ends in inconclusive loss.

WHETSTONE, George (1550–87), author of miscellaneous verse, especially elegies, and prose tales, principally remembered for his *Promos and Cassandra* (1578), a play in rhymed verse (based on a tale in

*Cinthio's *Hecatommithi*), which provided the plot for Shakespeare's *Measure for Measure* and is an early example of English romantic comedy. There is a life by T. C. Izard (1942).

WHEWELL, William (1794–1866), the son of a carpenter, educated at Lancaster Grammar School and Trinity College, Cambridge. A philosopher and scientist of wide range and copious output, he was professor of moral philosophy at Cambridge from 1838 to 1855 and master of Trinity College from 1841 till his death. His principal works were *The History* (1837) and *The Philosophy* (1840) *of the Inductive Sciences* and *Astronomy and Physics in Reference to Natural Philosophy* (1833). He published and edited many other works in natural and mathematical science, philosophy, and theology, including *Lectures on Systematic Morality* (1846) and *Lectures on the History of Moral Philosophy in England* (1852).

WHICHCOTE, Benjamin, see CAMBRIDGE PLATONISTS.

Whig Examiner, a literary and political periodical published by *Addison. Five numbers appeared, Sept.–Oct. 1710.

Whiskerandos, Don Ferolo, a character in Sheridan's *The Critic.

WHISTLER, James Abbott McNeill (1834–1903), an American painter, who moved between Paris and London. He was first influenced by Courbet's realism, but later emphasized that a painting is 'an arrangement of line, form and colour first'. His most famous works are the *Nocturnes*, paintings of the Thames at dusk. G. du Maurier's *Trilby* describes his bohemian life as a student in Paris (1855–9). Whistler moved to London in 1859; he mixed in *Pre-Raphaelite circles, and discussed his ideas on art with *Swinburne; Swinburne dedicated a poem to the *Little White Girl* (1864, London, Tate Gallery). Whistler, notorious as a dandy and wit, was at the centre of the Aesthetic movement. In 1877 *Ruskin attacked him for 'flinging a pot of paint into the public's face'; Whistler sued him, won, and was awarded a farthing damages. The trial stimulated Whistler's gifts as a polemicist; he wrote a series of pamphlets and vituperative letters to the press, later published together in *The Gentle Art of Making Enemies* (1890). His most serious and elegant attack on Ruskin's belief in the moral purpose of art was his *Ten O'Clock Lecture*. He had discussed many of his ideas with *Wilde, whom he later accused of plagiarism; Whistler's influence is evident in Wilde's lectures in America (1882) and in 'The Decay of Lying' and 'The Critic as Artist'. After 1891 Whistler again lived in Paris, where both his writing and the shadowy beauty of his pictures were deeply admired by symbolist writers. *Mallarmé, a close friend, translated his *Ten O'Clock Lecture* (1888). *Proust's Elstir is generally considered to be drawn from the characters of Whistler and Monet.

WHITAKER, Joseph (1820–95), publisher and at one time editor of the *Gentleman's Magazine* (1856–9). He founded the *Educational Register* (1850), *Whitaker's Clergyman's Diary* (1850), the *Artist* (1855), the *Bookseller* (1858), and *Whitaker's Almanack* (1868), a compendium of general information regarding the government, finances, population, and commerce of the world, with special reference to the British Commonwealth and the United States. (See ALMANACS.)

WHITE, Antonia (1899–1979), novelist and translator, the daughter of C. G. Botting, a classics master at St Paul's School. She was educated at the Convent of the Sacred Heart, Roehampton, and at St Paul's School for Girls. In 1930 she married H. T. Hopkinson, later editor of *Picture Post*. Her convent childhood is described in her first autobiographical novel, *Frost in May* (1933), which she began to draft when she was 16. The heroine of this work, Nanda Grey, becomes Clara Batchelor in her three subsequent novels, also largely autobiographical, *The Lost Traveller* (1950), *The Sugar House* (1952), and *Beyond the Glass* (1954), which give a vivid account of her experiences as an actress in provincial repertory, her struggles as a freelance copy-writer attempting to write seriously at the same time, her complex relationship with her possessive father, and her descent into mental illness and confinement in an asylum. Clara is named after Clara Middleton of Meredith's *The Egoist*, a novel much admired by her father. Antonia White also translated many of the novels of *Colette (whose love of the sensuous, the eccentric, and the bohemian is reflected in her own work), and published an account of her reconversion to Catholicism, *The Hound and the Falcon* (1966). There is a life by Jane Dunn (1998).

WHITE, Edmund (1940–   ), American novelist and essayist, born in Cincinnati, Ohio. *Nocturnes for the King of Naples* (1978) is a non-realistic novel dealing with homosexual themes which were pursued more realistically in *A Boy's Own Story* (1982), a poignant, poetic, frank, yet restrained first-person narration describing the gay adolescence of a child of divorced parents, both of whom are vividly evoked. This work brought him much acclaim, and was followed by the sequels *The Beautiful Room Is Empty* (1988) and *The Farewell Symphony* (1997), the last of which moves into the AIDS era. His other works include *States of Desire: Travels in Gay America* (1980); *Caracole* (1985), a Venetian fairy story; *The Darker Proof: Stories from a Crisis* (1987, with A. *Mars-Jones), and a biography of *Genet (1993).

WHITE, Gilbert (1720–93), born at Selborne in Hampshire. He became fellow of Oriel College, Oxford, but spent most of his life as curate of Selborne, refusing various livings in order to remain in his beloved birthplace. He began in 1751 to keep a 'Garden Kalendar' and later a 'Naturalist's Journal'. He made the acquaintance of two distinguished naturalists,

Thomas *Pennant and Daines *Barrington, with whom he carried on a correspondence from 1767 which formed the basis of his *Natural History and Antiquities of Selborne* (published Dec. 1788, title-page 1789), a work which displays his affectionate and detailed observations of wildlife and nature, and his love of the *picturesque in landscape. It slowly gathered a wide reputation, with both scientists (C. *Darwin read it with enthusiasm as a boy) and general readers, went through many editions, and remains a classic. *A Naturalist's Calendar*, ed. Dr John Aikin, appeared in 1795, and his *Journals*, ed. W. Johnson, in 1931.

WHITE, Henry Kirke (1785–1806), son of a butcher, articled to a lawyer in Nottingham. His volume of verses in 1803 attracted the attention of *Southey, who encouraged and assisted him. He obtained a sizarship at Cambridge, where overwork helped to bring about his early death. Southey collected his works, with a memoir, and published them in 1807. Little is remembered of his work except a few hymns, such as 'Oft in danger, oft in woe'.

WHITE, Joseph Blanco (1775–1841), born in Seville. He became a Catholic priest, soon abandoned the priesthood, and came to England in 1810. With the help of Lord Holland (see HOLLAND HOUSE) he started a journal, *El español*, which ran from 1810 to 1814. He wrote for the *New Monthly Magazine* and later for J. S. Mill's *London Review*. He went to study at Oxford and became an Anglican cleric, and the friend of *Whately, *Newman, *Pusey, and R. H. *Froude. His *Evidences against Catholicism* appeared in 1825. His other publications include *Observations on Heresy and Orthodoxy* (1835), translations into Spanish of *Paley's *Evidences*, and other ecclesiastical works. In 1828 the *Bijou* published his sonnet 'Night and Death', which *Coleridge declared 'the finest . . . sonnet in our language'.

WHITE, Patrick Victor Martindale (1912–90), Australian novelist, born in England; he was taken to Australia (where his father owned a sheep farm) when he was six months old, but educated in England, at Cheltenham College and King's College, Cambridge. He settled in London, where he wrote several unpublished novels, then served in the RAF during the war; he returned after the war to Australia with Manoly Lascaris, who was to be his lifelong companion. His first published novel, *Happy Valley* (1939), set in New South Wales, was followed by *The Living and the Dead* (1941), set in pre-war London, and *The Aunt's Story* (1948), a comic and sympathetic account of the travels of an independent Australian spinster, Theodora Goodman. *The Tree of Man* (1955) is an epic account of a young farmer, Stan Parker, at the beginning of the 20th cent., and his struggles to build himself a life and a family in the Australian wilderness; the epic theme was continued in *Voss* (1957), which returns to the heroic Australian past in its description of the doomed attempt of a Nietzschean German visionary and aspiring hero, Johann Voss, to lead an expedition across the continent in 1845. He is bound in a form of mystic communion with Laura Trevelyan, who, at home in Sydney, suffers with him and is released from fever at the moment when, already *in extremis*, he is decapitated by the Aboriginal boy Jackie. Voss lives on as an increasingly legendary, martyred figure. The story was suggested by the true record of Ludwig Leichardt, who died in the desert in 1848. These two novels gave White an international reputation, which he strengthened with several subsequent works, including *Riders in the Chariot* (1961); *The Solid Mandala* (1966); *The Vivisector* (1970, about a painter, Hurtle Duffield, and 'wet, boiling, superficial, brash, beautiful, ugly Sydney'); *The Eye of the Storm* (1973); *A Fringe of Leaves* (1976, a tale of shipwreck on the Australian coast in 1836); and *The Twyborn Affair* (1979), a baroque novel with an international canvas, which ends apocalyptically in the London Blitz; he also published *Four Plays* (1965), volumes of short stories, and a frank self-portrait, *Flaws in the Glass* (1981), which contains a brief and revealing account of his allegedly 'ungracious' reception of the *Nobel Prize for literature in 1973, which he persuaded his friend, the artist Sidney Nolan, to accept in Stockholm on his behalf. A selection of letters, edited by D. Marr, was published in 1995.

WHITE, T(erence) H(anbury) (1906–64), best known for his novels on the Arthurian legend, published under the title *The Once and Future King* (1958). The first book in this sequence, *The Sword in the Stone*, originally published separately in 1938, is a classic children's novel, as is *Mistress Masham's Repose* (1947). He also wrote several adult novels. *The Goshawk* (1951) is an account of how he trained a hawk. *The Book of Beasts* (1954) is a translation from a 12th-cent. Latin *bestiary. There is a life by S. T. *Warner, published in 1967. See also FANTASY FICTION.

WHITE, William Hale (1831–1913), known as a writer under the pseudonym of 'Mark Rutherford', born in Bedford, the son of William White, Dissenter, bookseller, and later a well-known doorkeeper in the House of Commons and author of *The Inner Life of the House of Commons* (1897). Hale White was educated with a view to becoming an independent minister, but disillusion with his teachers and growing religious doubts led him to abandon this course, and in 1854 he entered the civil service, rising to a responsible post as assistant director of contracts at the admiralty. He supplemented his income by parliamentary and literary journalism, and in 1881 published *The Autobiography of Mark Rutherford, Dissenting Minister*. This relates the spiritual development of a young Dissenter, supposedly edited after his death by his friend Reuben Shapcott; Rutherford, born in a small Midlands town, attends a Dissenting college and then becomes a minister, but is beset both by theological doubts and by distress at the narrowness and hypocrisy of his colleagues and congregations. Loneliness makes him an easy prey to melancholy, and he gradually loses his faith, becoming as disillusioned by the Unitarians as he was by his own Church. It is a compact and powerful account of the progress of 19th-cent. doubt; Rutherford cannot believe in personal immortality (though he is somewhat reassured by Wordsworthian pantheism), and finally sees himself as one born 100 years too late, for whom it would be 'a mockery to think about love for the only God whom I knew, the forces that maintained the universe'. The book was well received, and was followed by other imaginative works, all under the same pseudonym: these were *Mark Rutherford's Deliverance* (1885), *The Revolution in Tanner's Lane* (1887, a novel which draws an intimate and sympathetic portrait of Dissenting circles, radical politics, and working men's lives earlier in the century), *Miriam's Schooling and Other Papers* (1893), *Catherine Furze* (1893), and *Clara Hopgood* (1896). His other pseudonymous works include *Pages from a Journal* (1900), a collection of essays and stories, *More Pages from a Journal* (1910), and *Last Pages from a Journal* (1915); works published under his own name include a life of *Bunyan (1905), a writer who profoundly influenced him. His own life was overshadowed by the prolonged illness of his wife, who died in 1891, and whose patient suffering he saw as 'salvation through Crucifixion'. See a biography by C. D. Maclean, published in 1955.

White Devil, The (*The White Divel; or, The Tragedy of . . . Brachiano, with the Life and Death of Vittoria Corombona*), a tragedy by *Webster, written between 1609 and 1612, when it was published.

The duke of Brachiano, husband of Isabella, the sister of Francisco, duke of Florence, is weary of her and in love with Vittoria, wife of Camillo. The *Machiavellian Flamineo, Vittoria's brother, helps Brachiano to seduce her, and contrives (at her suggestion, delivered indirectly in a dream) the death of Camillo:- Brachiano causes Isabella to be poisoned. Vittoria is tried for adultery and murder in the celebrated central arraignment scene (III. ii), and defends herself with great spirit; *Lamb's phrase for her manner was 'innocence-resembling boldness', and *Hazlitt found in her 'that forced and practised presence of mind' of the hardened offender, pointing out that she arouses sympathy partly through the hypocrisy of her accusers. She is sentenced to confinement in 'a house of penitent whores', whence she is carried off by Brachiano, who marries her. Flamineo quarrels with his younger brother, the virtuous Marcello, and kills him; he dies in the arms of their mother Cornelia, who later, driven out of her wits by grief, sings the dirge 'Call for the robin redbreast, and the wren', a scene which elicits from Flamineo a speech of remorse. ('I have a strange thing in me to the which I I cannot give a name, without it be I Compassion.') Meanwhile

Francisco, at the prompting of Isabella's ghost (see REVENGE TRAGEDY), avenges her death by poisoning Brachiano, and Vittoria and Flamineo, both of whom die Stoic deaths, are murdered by his dependants.

WHITEFIELD, George (1714–70), a popular evangelical preacher. He came under the influence of John and Charles *Wesley while at Oxford, and followed them on a mission to Georgia, where he founded an orphanage. On his return he attracted much attention at large open-air meetings by his fervent and emotional sermons. His views diverged from those of the Wesleys, as he became increasingly Calvinistic. He became domestic chaplain to Lady *Huntingdon and through her patronage opened a Tabernacle in Tottenham Court Road; she was the founder of the body of Calvinistic Methodists known as 'Lady Huntingdon's Connexion', and she warmly supported Whitefield in his disputes with Wesley. Whitefield died near Boston on the last of several evangelical visits to America. His Journals were published in 7 parts, 1738–41, and Hymns for Social Worship in 1753. He was ridiculed by *Foote in his play The Minor and satirized by *Graves in The Spiritual Quixote. *Garrick was said to have greatly admired his preaching, but Dr *Johnson, while respecting his ministry, found he had more 'familiarity and noise' than 'knowledge, art and elegance'.

WHITEHEAD, A(lfred) N(orth) (1861–1947), educated at Sherborne and Trinity College, Cambridge, professor of applied mathematics in the Imperial College of Science and Technology (1911–24), professor of philosophy at Harvard University (1924–36). He was the author of many important philosophical and mathematical works, including Principia Mathematica (with B. *Russell, 1910), Science and the Modern World (1925), Religion in the Making (1926), Symbolism (1927), Process and Reality (1929), Adventures of Ideas (1933).

WHITEHEAD, Charles (1804–62), poet, novelist, and dramatist. He published in 1831 The Solitary, a poem which met with warm approval. His quasi-historical romances, The Autobiography of Jack Ketch (1834) and Richard Savage (1842), and his play The Cavalier (1836), were also successful. His career was ruined by intemperance and he died miserably in Australia.

WHITEHEAD, William (1715–85), educated at Winchester and Clare Hall, Cambridge. He published in 1741 a verse epistle, The Danger of Writing Verse, in which he describes the temerity of those embarking on a literary career, and the hazards of neglect, notoriety, and the whims of patrons. In his day he was best known for his successful *neo-classical tragedy The Roman Father (1750), a version of *Corneille's Horace; this was followed by another tragedy, Creusa (1754), and a comedy, The School for Lovers (1762). A contributor to *Dodsley's Collection of Poems (1748–59), in 1757 he was appointed *poet laureate, an elevation which caused much satiric comment, notably from Charles

*Churchill; he replied both to his detractors and to his own first publication in another verse epistle, A Charge to the Poets (1762), in which he recommends his fellow poets to remain calm in the face of hostile and favourable criticism alike, and to see themselves as 'the firm spectators of a bustling world'. His Plays and Poems were collected in 1774, and a complete edition of his poems appeared in 1788.

WHITING, John (1917–63), playwright, whose plays, at first ill-received, marked a historic break from the prevailing vogue for drawing-room comedy. A Penny for a Song (1956, pub. 1969), Saint's Day (perf. and pub. 1951), Marching Song (perf. and pub. 1954), and The Gates of Summer (1956, pub. 1969) show a powerful and individual talent, but he did not achieve popular success until The Devils, adapted from The Devils of Loudun by A. *Huxley, was performed by the Royal Shakespeare Company in 1961. A highly theatrical piece, influenced by *Brecht, it deals with a case of hysterical demonic possession in a French nunnery. His Collected Plays (1969, ed. R. Hayman) includes several performed posthumously.

WHITMAN, Walt (1819–92), born on Long Island, New York, and brought up partly in Brooklyn. He had little formal education, and started work as an office boy; he subsequently worked as printer, wandering school-teacher, and contributor to and editor of various magazines and newspapers, entering politics as a Democrat, and travelling in 1848 to New Orleans, where he wrote for the Crescent. He returned to New York and the Brooklyn Times via St Louis and Chicago, and the experience of the frontier merged with his admiration for *Emerson to produce the first edition of Leaves of Grass, 12 poems saturated, as he describes it, 'with the vehemence of pride and audacity of freedom necessary to loosen the mind of still-to-be-form'd America from the folds, the superstitions, and all the long, tenacious and stifling anti-democratic authorities of Asiatic and European past'. When Emerson was sent a copy he replied hailing the work, with good reason, as 'the most extraordinary piece of wit and wisdom that America has yet contributed'. The second edition (1856) added 21 poems, and the third edition (1860) 122, including the group entitled 'Calamus', which has been taken as a reflection of the poet's homosexuality, although in his own words they celebrate the 'beautiful and sane affection of man for man'. The six further editions that appeared in Whitman's lifetime were revised or added to, the work enlarging as the poet developed. During the Civil War Whitman worked as a clerk in Washington, but his real business was as a volunteer hospital visitor among the wounded, an experience which affected him deeply, as can be seen in his prose Memoranda during the War (1875) and in the poems published under the title of Drum-Taps in 1865. In the Sequel to these poems (1865–6) appeared the great elegy on Abraham Lincoln, 'When Lilacs Last in the Dooryard Bloom'd'. In spite of his achievement, and his efforts at self-publicity, Whitman was disregarded by the public at large, some of whom were offended by his outspokenness on sexual matters, some by his pose as rough working man; his reputation began to rise after recognition in England by W. M. *Rossetti, *Swinburne (who compared him to *Blake), Mrs *Gilchrist, and E. *Carpenter. After a paralytic stroke in 1873 he left Washington and lived quietly in Camden, New Jersey, still writing, though without the originality of his early years. The free, vigorous sweep of his verse conveys subjects at once national ('Pioneers! O Pioneers!', 1865), mystically sexual ('I sing the body electric', 1855), and deeply personal ('Out of the Cradle Endlessly Rocking', 1860), and his work proved a liberating force for many of his successors, including H. *Miller, D. H. *Lawrence, H. *Crane, and the poets of the *Beat Generation.

WHITNEY, Geoffrey, see EMBLEM BOOKS.

WHITTIER, John Greenleaf (1807–92), American poet, born of Quaker parents at Haverhill, Massachusetts, where Thomas Whittier, his Puritan ancestor, had built the oak farmhouse described in *Snow-Bound*. He began life as a farmer's boy, and supported himself while at Haverhill Academy by shoemaking and teaching. He became an ardent Abolitionist, and wrote tracts and edited various periodicals for the cause as well as writing poems on the subject of slavery, collected as *Voices of Freedom* (1846). He was a regular contributor to the *Atlantic Monthly*, which he helped to found. A prolific and popular poet, he wrote in many genres; his first book, *Legends of New-England in Prose and Verse* (1831), which demonstrates his lifelong interest in local history, was followed by many volumes of verse on political and rural themes, by verse narratives, sonnets, and ballads. Among his best-known works are 'The Barefoot Boy' (1856), a celebration of rural boyhood which manifests his admiration for *Burns, and *Snow-Bound* (1866), a recollection of winter evenings with his family in the old homestead.

WHITTINGTON, Richard (d. 1423), son of Sir William Whittington, a mercer in London. He rose to be lord mayor of London, 1397–8, 1406–7 (a year of plague), and 1419–20. He was a liberal benefactor of the city, leaving legacies for rebuilding Newgate Prison and other purposes (including a city library). The popular legend of Dick Whittington and his cat, the germ of which is probably of very remote origin, is not known to have been narrated before 1605, when a dramatic version and a ballad were licensed for the press. The story of a cat helping its owner to fortune has been traced in many countries of Europe. It is also suggested that it is based on a confusion between 'a cat' and the French *achat*, in the sense of 'trade'. According to the story, Whittington, when in the service of Mr Fitzwarren, a London merchant, sent his cat, the only thing he possessed, as part of one of his master's trading

ventures; the king of Barbary, who was plagued with rats and mice, purchased the cat for an enormous sum. Meanwhile Whittington, ill-treated by the cook under whom he served as scullion, ran away. He rested at Holloway, and hearing Bow Bells ringing, as he fancied, the words,

Turn again, Whittington, Lord Mayor of London,

returned to Fitzwarren's house.

Whole Duty of Man, The, a devotional work published 1658, in which man's duties in respect of God and his fellow men are analysed and discussed in detail. The book was at one time attributed to Lady Dorothy Pakington (d. 1679). She was, however, probably only the copyist. The book, by internal evidence, is the work of a practised divine, acquainted with Hebrew, Syriac, and Arabic, probably Richard Allestree (1619–81), chaplain in ordinary to the king, Regius professor of divinity, and provost of Eton. It had enormous popularity, lasting for over a century; it is comparable in this respect to *Thomas à Kempis's *De Imitatio Christi* and *Law's *Serious Call*.

Who's Who, an annual biographical dictionary of contemporary men and women. It was first issued in 1849 but took its present form in 1897, when it incorporated material from another biographical work, *Men and Women of the Time*; earlier editions of *Who's Who* had consisted merely of professional lists, etc. The entries are compiled with the assistance of the subjects themselves, and contain some agreeable eccentricities particularly in the section labelled 'Recreations'.

The first *Who Was Who 1897–1916* appeared in 1920, and the eighth (1981–1990) in 1991. These decennial volumes contain the biographies removed from *Who's Who* on account of death, with final details and date of death added.

WHYTE-MELVILLE, George John (1821–78), born in Fife, educated at Eton. He joined the 93rd Highlanders, then the Coldstream Guards, and served in the Crimean War. He then returned to England and devoted his time to field sports on which he was an authority. Most of his literary works were novels, sometimes historical, and hunting figures largely in many of them. His first, *Digby Grand*, was published in 1853; *Galsworthy, at Oxford, fell under the spell of the 'Bright Things' in Whyte-Melville's novels and Digby Grand was Jolyon's (in *The Forsyte Saga*) first idol. He achieved fame with *Holmby House* (1859), a historical romance describing the Civil War. *Market Harborough* (1861) and *The Gladiators* (1863), also very popular, were followed by several others. *Riding Recollections* (1879) was a notable book on horsemanship. He was killed in a hunting accident.

WHYTHORNE, Thomas (1528–96), educated at Magdalen College, Oxford. After three years as 'servant and scholar' in the household of J. *Heywood he became a teacher of music and composer of madrigals. His autobiography, *A Book of Songs and Sonetts*, discovered in manuscript in 1955, was edited by James M. Osborn and published in 1961. It is not only an interesting document of Tudor life, poetry, and music, but also, because Whythorne wrote in his own phonetic system, a key to the pronunciation of his day.

Wickfield, Mr and Agnes, characters in Dickens's *David Copperfield*.

WICKHAM, Anna, pseudonym of Edith Alice Mary Harper (1884–1947), poet, born in Wimbledon, and educated in Queensland and New South Wales, Australia. She returned to London in 1905 to study singing, went to Paris to be coached for opera by de Reszke, but married in 1906 Patrick Hepburn, solicitor and astronomer, by whom she had four sons. More popular in the USA and France than at home, she was an original and copious poet; in imagery and subject matter in advance of her time, she charted the struggle of a woman artist to achieve freedom to work as well as to fulfil herself as wife and mother. Her friends included D. H. *Lawrence, M. *Lowry, Dylan *Thomas, and Kate *O'Brien. Her publications include *The Contemplative Quarry* (1915), *The Little Old House* (1921), and *Thirty-Six New Poems* (1936); a collection, *The Writings of Anna Wickham* (1984), was edited by R. D. Smith.

'Widdicombe Fair', the title of a popular song. 'For some reason or other, not exactly known,' writes S. *Baring-Gould in *English Minstrelsie*, 'this has become the accepted Devonshire song . . . The date of words and tune is probably the end of the last [18th] century.'

Tom Pearse lends his grey mare to carry a party (including Old Uncle Tom Cobbleigh) to Widdicombe Fair, but the mare takes sick and dies, and is still to be seen haunting the moor at night. Widdicombe, or Widecombe-in-the-Moor, is near Ashburton.

Widmerpool, a character in A. *Powell's *A Dance to the Music of Time*.

Widowers' Houses, a play by Bernard *Shaw, first performed 1892, published 1893, and published (with *The Philanderer* and *Mrs Warren's Profession*) in *Plays Unpleasant* (1898). It is designed to show the manner in which the capitalist system perverts and corrupts human behaviour and relationships, through a demonstration, in Shaw's words, of 'middle-class respectability and younger son gentility fattening on the poverty of the slum as flies fatten on filth'.

Dr Harry Trench, on a Rhine holiday, meets Blanche Sartorius, travelling with her wealthy father, and proposes marriage to her: Sartorius is willing to permit the match if Trench's family (including his aunt Lady Roxdale) agrees to accept her as an equal. All seems well, until it is revealed in Act II that Sartorius is a slum landlord. Trench is horrified, refuses to accept Sartorius' money, suggests that he and Blanche should live on

his £700 a year, and is even more horrified when Sartorius points out that this income is derived from a mortgage of Sartorius' property, and that he himself and his miserable rent collector Lickcheese are merely intermediaries: 'You are the principal.' Blanche, revealing a passionate and violent nature, rejects Trench for his hesitations. In the third act Lickcheese, himself now rich through dubious dealings in the property market, approaches Sartorius with an apparently philanthropic but in fact remunerative proposition, which involves Lady Roxdale as ground landlord and Trench as mortgagee. Trench, now considerably more cynical, accepts the deal, and he and Blanche are reunited.

Widsith, a poem of 143 lines in Old English, named from its opening word, in the *Exeter Book. It is constructed around three 'thulas' (i.e. mnemonic name-lists), connected by the ostensible experience of the eponymous minstrel: the first names great rulers; the second lists the tribes among whom the minstrel claims to have travelled; and the third speaks of people that the minstrel sought out. The poem, although it contains some later interpolations, is thought to date substantially from the 7th cent. and thus to be the earliest poem in the language. Both the editions are important, and Malone's contains a very full bibliography. Ed. R. W. Chambers (1912); K. Malone (1962).

Wife of Bath, (1) see CANTERBURY TALES, 6; (2) the title of an unsuccessful comedy by J. *Gay (1713).

Wife of Usher's Well, The, a ballad of the Scottish Border. The wife sends her three sons to sea, and soon gets tidings of their death. Their ghosts come back on one of the long nights of Martinmas, and the mother, deceived by the apparitions, orders a feast; but at cock-crow they disappear.

Wife's Lament, The, an Old English poem of 53 lines in the *Exeter Book, one of the group usually called 'Elegies'. That the speaker is female is established by feminine grammatical endings in the first two lines, making it (like 'Wulf and Eadwacer') a rare early English example of a *Frauenlied*. It is a poem about the pain of separation, apparently visited on the speaker by the absent husband/lover and his family. The precise situation is impossible to determine; the speaker has been made to live in an earth-barrow so the poem can plausibly be interpreted as a revenant voice from the grave. Like the other Elegies, the situation seems primarily to be an image of the separation of the soul from God; but, as in *The Seafarer* (the opening of which this poem echoes closely), the obscure literal location is hauntingly evoked. By the 20th cent. it had become one of the most admired Old English short poems.

Ed. and trans. R. Hamer, *A Choice of Anglo-Saxon Verse* (1970); ed. B. J. Muir, *The Exeter Anthology of Old English Poetry* (1994), 331–3.

WIGGLESWORTH, Michael (1631–1705), colonial American poet and divine, born in Yorkshire, who emigrated in 1638. He is known chiefly for his long Calvinistic poem in ballad metre, *The Day of Doom: A Poetical Description of the Great and Last Judgement* (1662), a work of little literary merit which had a great success both in America and England. See R. Crowder's life, *No Feather Bed to Heaven* (1962).

WILBERFORCE, William (1759–1833), educated at St John's College, Cambridge, and an MP for Yorkshire. He devoted himself to the abolition of the slave trade and to other philanthropic projects. He published in 1797 *A Practical View of the Prevailing Religious System of Professed Christians*, a work which was influential and widely read. He was the leading layman of the evangelical *'Clapham Sect', and he lived just long enough to see carried the second reading of the Bill abolishing slavery.

WILBUR, Richard Purdy (1921–), American poet, born in New York City, and educated at Amherst College and Harvard. His elegant, urbane, and witty poetry appears in several collections, from *Ceremony* (1950) to *Seven Poems* (1981), and he has also translated several plays by *Molière into English verse.

WILBYE, John (1574–1638), English composer, with *Weelkes, the most important of the English madrigalists who followed the lead given by *Morley in 1593 and 1594. Born in Norfolk, Wilbye spent most of his life in the service of the Kytson family at Hengrave Hall, in Suffolk; he published only two sets of *madrigals, the first in 1598, the second in 1609, and contributed one madrigal to *The Triumphes of Oriana* in 1601.

As a madrigalist Wilbye stays closer than Weelkes to the Italianate manner pioneered by Morley: 'Adieu, sweet Amaryllis' is a famous example of the delicate balance he achieved in this style. In the second set, generally regarded as the finest of all the English madrigal collections, he brought together a poetic understanding, purity of style, musical expressiveness, subtlety and variety of texture, and structural power that make madrigals like the six-part 'Draw on sweet night' outstanding.

WILCOX, Ella Wheeler (1850–1919), American poet, born in Wisconsin, whose many volumes of romantic, sentimental, and mildly erotic verse (with titles such as *Poems of Passion* and *Poems of Cheer*) brought her a vast readership. She also wrote short stories and novels, and two volumes of autobiography.

WILD, Jonathan (?1682–1725). He worked as a buckle-maker in London, became head of a large corporation of thieves, and opened offices in London for the recovery and restoration of property stolen by his dependants. He gained notoriety as a thief-taker, and was ultimately hanged at Tyburn. His 'Life and Actions' were related by *Defoe (1725). For Fielding's satire, see JONATHAN WILD THE GREAT. There is a life by G. Howson, *Thief-Taker General* (1970).

Wildair, Sir Harry, a character in Farquhar's *The Constant Couple* and in its sequel, *Sir Harry Wildair*.

WILDE, Oscar Fingal O'Flahertie Wills (1854–1900), born in Dublin, the son of Sir William Wilde, Irish surgeon, and Jane Francesca Elgee, well known as writer and literary hostess under the pen-name 'Speranza'. A brilliant classical scholar, Wilde studied at Trinity College, Dublin, then at Magdalen College, Oxford, where in 1878 he won the Newdigate Prize for his poem 'Ravenna'. His flamboyant aestheticism attracted attention, much of it hostile; he scorned sport, collected blue china and peacock's feathers, and proclaimed himself a disciple of *Pater and the cult of *'art for art's sake' mocked in *Gilbert and Sullivan's *Patience* (1881). Wilde successfully lived up to the image of the satire, and its impetus took him on a lecture tour of the United States in 1882, after the publication of his first volume of *Poems* (1881). In 1883 he attended the first night of his play *Vera* in New York but it was not a success. In 1884 he married, and in 1888 published a volume of fairy stories, *The Happy Prince and Other Tales*. In 1891 followed *Lord Arthur Savile's Crime, and Other Stories* and his only novel, *The Picture of Dorian Gray*, a Gothic melodrama which had aroused scandalized protest when it appeared in *Lippincott's Magazine* (1890). Wilde claimed in his preface, 'There is no such thing as a moral or an immoral book. Books are well written or badly written. That is all.' In 1891 he published more fairy stories, *A House of Pomegranates*. His second play, *The Duchess of Padua* (1891), is a dull verse tragedy, but epigrammatic brilliance and shrewd social observation brought theatrical success with *Lady Windermere's Fan* (1892), *A Woman of No Importance* (1893), and *An Ideal Husband* (1895). His masterpiece was *The Importance of Being Earnest* (1895). *Salomé* (now known chiefly by R. *Strauss's opera), written in French, was refused a licence, but performed in Paris in 1896 and published in 1894 in an English translation by Lord Alfred *Douglas with illustrations by *Beardsley. Lord Alfred's father, the marquess of Queensberry, disapproved of his son's friendship with Wilde and publicly insulted the playwright. This started a chain of events which led to Wilde's imprisonment for homosexual offences in 1895. He was declared bankrupt while in prison and wrote a letter of bitter reproach to Lord Alfred, published in part in 1905 as *De Profundis*: in it he provided an apologia for his own conduct, claiming to have stood 'in symbolic relations to the art and culture' of his age. He was released in 1897 and went to France where he wrote *The Ballad of Reading Gaol* (1898), inspired by his prison experience. In exile he adopted the name Sebastian Melmoth, after the romance by *Maturin. He died in Paris. His other writings include critical dialogues ('The Decay of Lying' and 'The Critic as Artist', in *Intentions*, 1891) and *The Soul of Man* *under Socialism*, a plea for individualism and artistic freedom, which Wilde wrote after hearing G. B. *Shaw speak, and which was first published in the *Fortnightly Review* in 1891. The publication of his *Collected Works* (1908) was organized by his loyal friend Robert *Ross.

A volume of letters, ed. R. *Hart-Davis, appeared in 1962 and there are biographies by H. *Pearson (1946) and R. *Ellmann (1987).

Wilde-Goose Chase, The, a comedy by J. *Fletcher, acted with great success in 1621, printed 1652; it was very popular on the *Restoration stage.

Mirabell, the 'wild goose', a boastful Don Juan with an aversion to marriage, is 'chased' by Oriana, his betrothed, who tries various wiles to bring him to the altar. She feigns madness for love of him, but he sees through the pretence, and she finally traps him in the disguise of a rich Italian lady. His two companions, Pinac and Belleur, with less assurance and more at the mercy of their high-spirited mistresses, alternately pursue and are pursued by Rosalura and Lillia-Bianca. *Farquhar's comedy *The Inconstant* is based on this play.

WILDER, Thornton Niven (1897–1975), American novelist and dramatist, born in Wisconsin. *The Bridge of San Luis Rey* (1927) is the best known of his novels, but *The Ides of March* (1948), among others, is also notable. He scored considerable success in the theatre with *Our Town* (1938), *The Skin of Our Teeth* (1942), and *The Merchant of Yonkers* (1938), a comedy which was revised as *The Matchmaker* (1954) and adapted as the musical comedy *Hello, Dolly!* (1963).

Wildeve, Damon, a character in Hardy's *The Return of the Native*.

Wildfell Hall, see TENANT OF WILDFELL HALL, THE.

Wild Huntsman, the, a spectral huntsman of German folklore, the subject of a ballad ('Der wilde Jäger') by Gottfried August Bürger (1747–94), imitated by Sir W. *Scott. Scott's version was included in *The Chase and William and Helen: Two Ballads from the German*, published anonymously in 1797. The legend is that a wildgrave (keeper of a royal forest), named Falkenburg, not only hunted on the Sabbath but also tyrannized over the peasants under his authority. After his death he continued to haunt the forest, and he and his hound might be heard, though rarely seen. (See also LENORE.)

Wild Oats, a play by J. *O'Keeffe.

Wilfer family, characters in Dickens's *Our Mutual Friend*.

WILKES, John (1727–97), the son of a Clerkenwell distiller. He studied at Leiden, and after marrying an heiress ten years older than himself (who bore him his much-loved daughter Polly) led a life of dissipation and became a member of the *Medmenham Abbey fra-

ternity. He was elected MP for Aylesbury in 1757 and in 1762 founded the *North Briton* in which, aided by his friend Charles *Churchill, he attacked Bute's government. In the notorious No. 45 he denounced the King's Speech, and was arrested for libel on a general warrant, but released; he was then expelled from Parliament for publishing an obscene libel, the *Essay on Woman* (a parody of *Pope), and retired to Paris. (For Lord Sandwich's role in this affair, see TWITCHER.) He returned in 1768, and after various setbacks (see PRESENT DISCONTENTS) took his seat unopposed as MP for Middlesex in 1774, in which year he was also lord mayor of London.

A man of wit, learning, and ability, and a popular hero in the cause of liberty, he secured important legal rights, including the illegality of general warrants, the freedom of choice of the electorate, and the freedom of the press. His friendly meeting over dinner with his old political adversary Dr *Johnson, on 15 May 1776, provides one of the finest moments of *Boswell's *Life*.

WILKIE, William (1721–72), author of *The Epigoniad*, an epic poem in heroic couplets, in nine books, on the theme of the siege of Thebes: it was modelled on *Homer and inspired by the 'heroic Tragedy' of *Sophocles, and went into two editions (1757, 1759). It was highly regarded by *Hume and by Adam *Smith. Wilkie was raised on a Scottish farm, and claimed to have 'shaken hands with poverty up to the very elbow'; he became a skilled classicist and mathematician and was appointed professor of natural philosophy at St Andrews. He was a member of the *Select Society.

Wilkins, Peter, see PETER WILKINS.

Willet, John, in Dickens's *Barnaby Rudge*, the host of the Maypole Inn, and Joe his son, finally the successful wooer of *Dolly Varden.

William of Cloudesley, see ADAM BELL.

WILLIAM OF MALMESBURY (*c.*1095–1143), the first full-scale writer of history in England after *Bede. He was educated at Malmesbury Abbey in Wiltshire of which he became librarian. He was a polymath who may have been influenced by the historiographical traditions of Worcester and Evesham. His major works were the *Gesta Regum Anglorum*, a history of England from 449 to 1120; the *Gesta Pontificum Anglorum*, an ecclesiastical history of England from 597 to 1125; the *Historia Novella*, the sequel to the *Gesta Regum*, dealing with 1128 to 1142 and left unfinished at his death in 1143; *De Antiquitate Glastoniensis Ecclesiae* (a work which has led to the speculation that he may have lived at Glastonbury, written between 1129 and 1139); and the *Life of St Dunstan*, a hagiographical work. As well as being an authoritative and serious historian, William was a picturesque and circumstantial writer who enlivened his narrative with topographical observation, anecdote, reminiscence, and comment. The *Gesta*

Regum has two stories about *Arthur whom William regards as a great warrior while discrediting many of the stories about him. See A. Gransden, *Historical Writing in England, c.550–c.1307* (1974), 166–85; H. Farmer, 'William of Malmesbury's Life and Work' in *Journal of Ecclesiastical History*, 13 (1962), 39–54.

WILLIAM OF NEWBURGH (1135/6–?98), a canon of the priory of Newburgh (near Richmond) in Yorkshire who began in 1196 his *Historia Rerum Anglicarum*, suddenly abandoned in 1198, presumably at his death. The work was commissioned by Ernald, abbot of the Cistercian abbey of Rievaulx. The *Historia* deals with events from 1066 to 1198, especially the reigns of Stephen (with its hardships) and Henry II. It is a well-written, critical, and personal work with regard for historicity; it exposes the *Historia*, of *Geoffrey of Monmouth, for instance, as legend rather than fact.

WILLIAM OF WYKEHAM (1324–1404), bishop of Winchester and chancellor of England, founder of New College, Oxford (1379), and Winchester College (1382). He was first employed as clerk of the king's works at Windsor, and he administered the rebuilding of Windsor Castle for Edward III. He became chancellor in 1367 but was dismissed, as a symbol of the clerical establishment, in 1371. He was one of the leaders of the bishops who opposed *John of Gaunt, and he was a lifelong opponent of Wyclifitism. His political power waned with the ascendance of Gaunt, who seized Wykeham's lands, after the death of Edward III in 1377.

'William and Helen', see LENORE.

'William and Margaret', a ballad by *Mallet in the 18th-cent. mock-antique style, written 1723, and published in A. *Hill's *Plain Dealer*, 36, July 1724. It is included in Percy's *Reliques* under the title 'Margaret's Ghost'.

Margaret's 'grimly ghost' visits her faithless lover William just before dawn and summons him to visit her grave; he lays his cheek upon her grave 'and word spake never more'.

William of Palerne, one of the earliest of the 14th-cent. English romances of the *Alliterative Revival, of 5,540 lines in a west Midland dialect. It was written for Humphrey de Bohun, based on the late 12th-cent. French *Roman de Guillaume de Palerne*.

William is a prince of Apulia who is saved from his uncle's attempts to poison him by a werewolf who is really a prince of Spain turned into that shape by his wicked stepmother. William falls in love with and wins the daughter of the Roman emperor and finally defeats the king of Spain, forcing the queen to undo her dastardly magic and restore the prince to his rightful form. While William and his love, Melior, are fleeing, they disguise themselves as bears and deer. Within this improbable framework, the poet has incorporated a discussion of courtliness and love which is not without sophistication.

Ed. W. W. Skeat, EETS ES 1 (1867; repr. Kraus, 1973).

WILLIAMS, Charles Walter Stansby (1886–1945), poet, novelist, and theological writer who worked for many years at the *Oxford University Press. His novels, which have been described as supernatural thrillers, include *War in Heaven* (1930), *Descent into Hell* (1937), and *All Hallows Eve* (1944). Of his theological writings the most important was *The Descent of the Dove* (1939). His literary criticism included a study of *Dante, *The Figure of Beatrice* (1943). In verse he wrote a number of plays on religious themes, including *Thomas Cranmer* (1936) and *Seed of Adam* (1948), but his most original poetic achievement is perhaps his cycle on the Arthurian legend, *Taliessin through Logres* (1938) and *The Region of the Summer Stars* (1944), afterwards reissued in one volume (1974) together with *Arthurian Torso*, a study of Williams's poetry by his friend C. S. *Lewis. He was a member of Lewis's group 'the *Inklings'.

WILLIAMS, Heathcote (1941–   ), poet, actor, performance poet, and playwright, born in Cheshire. He is perhaps best known for his stage play *AC/DC* (1970), a powerful innovative piece about the effects of the new technology and the media (what the author has described as 'psychic capitalism'), and for his three 'ecological epics' of poems with pictures, *Whale Nation* (1988), *Falling for a Dolphin* (1989), and *Sacred Elephant* (1989). Other plays include *The Speakers* (1964), *Hancock's Last Half Hour* (1977), and *The Immortalist* (1978).

WILLIAMS, Helen Maria (1761?–1827). She published her first poem, a ballad, *Edwin and Eltruda*, in 1782, and travelled in 1788 to Paris, where she was chiefly to reside. She became friendly with the leading Girondists, and made the acquaintance of M. *Wollstonecraft; her *Letters* (1790–5) contain interesting information on the state of Paris and France just before and during the revolution. She was a friend of *Bernardin de Saint-Pierre, whose *Paul et Virginie* she translated (1796); she also translated A. von *Humboldt's travels (1814–29). *Wordsworth's first printed poem was 'Sonnet on Seeing Miss Helen Maria Williams Weep at a Tale of Distress' (1787, under the pseudonym 'Axiologus'), but despite its title he appears not to have met her until 1820 in Paris.

WILLIAMS, Hugo (1942–   ), poet, born in Windsor, the son of the actor Hugh Williams, who is portrayed in *Writing Home* (1985). Educated at Eton, he worked as an editorial assistant on the *London Magazine* for two years before leaving to travel round the world, which provided material for *All the Time in the World* (1966). His first collection of poems, *Symptoms of Loss*, was published in 1965, the year of his marriage. He returned to work on the *London Magazine* until 1970, the year in which his second volume of poems, *Sugar Daddy*, was published. His other volumes include *Some Sweet Day* (1975), *Love-Life* (1979), *No Particular Place to Go* (1981), *Writing Home*, and *Self-Portrait with a Slide* (both 1990).

WILLIAMS, Isaac (1802–65), poet and theologian, educated at Trinity College, Oxford, where he was influenced by *Keble and participated in the *Oxford movement. He was author of poems in *Lyra Apostolica* and other poetical works including *The Cathedral* (1838) and *The Baptistery* (1842). His contribution to *Tracts for the Times* on 'Reserve in communicating Religious Knowledge' lost him the election to the chair of poetry (1842). His autobiography (edited by Sir G. Prevost, 1892) is an interesting record of the days of the Oxford movement.

WILLIAMS, John, known as Anthony Pasquin (1761–1818), a voluminous satirist and miscellaneous writer, often threatened with prosecution for libel. *The Children of Thespis* (1786–8) was his most successful poem, but he produced various volumes of poetry, biography, politics, satire, and plays.

WILLIAMS, Nigel (1948–   ), novelist, and playwright, born in Cheshire, and educated at Oriel College, Oxford. His novels include the ambitious *Witchcraft* (1987), which evokes the horrors of the Civil War through the medium of a contemporary screenwriter. He is best known for his suburban comedies, *The Wimbledon Poisoner* (1990), which describes Henry Farr's abortive attempt to murder his wife, and its derivative, *Scenes from a Poisoner's Life* (1994). *They Came from SW19* (1992, the first-person adolescent tale of the son of a spiritualist mother) and *East of Wimbledon* (1993) are also set in south London.

WILLIAMS, Raymond (1921–88), critic and novelist. The son of a railway signalman, he was born in Pandy, near Abergavenny, where he attended the grammar school. His studies at Trinity College, Cambridge, were interrupted by wartime service in an anti-tank regiment. He taught first as an adult education tutor in Sussex from 1946 to 1961, then at Cambridge as fellow of Jesus College and later as professor of drama. His best-known book, *Culture and Society, 1780–1950* (1958), surveys the history of the idea of 'culture' in British thought; and his later works, beginning with *The Long Revolution* (1961), attempt to extend this concept in more democratic directions than those envisaged by T. S. *Eliot and others. His scope of critical investigation included television and other modern forms of communication, as well as the history and sociology of drama and fiction. More traditional literary studies include *The English Novel from Dickens to Lawrence* (1970) and *The Country and the City* (1974). A leading figure of the British 'New Left', he tried to move beyond the limits of previous *Marxist literary criticism into a more dynamic materialist view of cultural changes, explored in *Marxism and Literature* (1977) and other books. His early novels, including

Border Country (1960) and *Second Generation* (1964), are semi-autobiographical works in the realist tradition which, as a critic, he defended against the new orthodoxy of *Modernism.

WILLIAMS, Tennessee (Thomas Lanier Williams) (1911–83), American dramatist, born in Mississippi, the son of a travelling salesman, and brought up there and in St Louis; he studied at Washington, St Louis, and Iowa, and in New York, while embarking on a career as a playwright with *American Blues* (1939, pub. 1945) and *Battle of Angels* (1940, pub. 1945; revised 1957 as *Orpheus Descending*). He achieved success with the semi-autobiographical *The Glass Menagerie* (1944, pub. 1945), a poignant and painful family drama set in St Louis, in which a frigid and frustrated mother's dreams of her glamorous past as a Southern belle conflict with the grimness of her reduced circumstances, as she persuades her rebellious son Tom to provide a 'gentleman caller' for her crippled daughter Laura. His next big success was *A Streetcar Named Desire* (1947), a study of sexual frustration, violence, and aberration, set in New Orleans, in which Blanche Dubois's fantasies of refinement and grandeur are brutally destroyed by her brother-in-law Stanley Kowalski, whose animal nature fascinates and repels her. Williams continued to write prolifically, largely in a Gothic and macabre vein, but with insight into human passion and its perversions, and a considerable warmth and compassion; his other works include *The Rose Tattoo* (1950), a comedy about a Sicilian woman and her quest for love; the symbolic and anti-naturalistic *Camino Real* (1953); *Cat on a Hot Tin Roof* (1955), a Freudian family drama which takes place at wealthy cotton planter Big Daddy's 65th birthday celebration, while his daughter-in-law Maggie fights to save her marriage to the alcoholic and despairing Brick; *Suddenly Last Summer* (1958); *Sweet Bird of Youth* (1959); *The Night of the Iguana* (1962); and a novella, *The Roman Spring of Mrs Stone* (1950), about an ageing actress's affair with a gigolo. He also published collections of poems, and his *Memoirs* appeared in 1975.

WILLIAMS, William Carlos (1883–1963), American poet, novelist, short story writer, and, for many years, a paediatrician in his home town of Rutherford, New Jersey; his profession as doctor deeply affected his literary life, giving him, in his own words, an entry into 'the secret gardens of the self . . . a badge to follow the poor, defeated body into those gulfs and grottos' (*Autobiography*, 1951). In his student days he was a friend of *Pound and H. *Doolittle, and some early poems (*Poems*, 1909; *The Tempers*, 1913) are Imagist, although he was to move from *Imagism to what he called Objectivism. (See also under ZUKOFSKY.) His poems range from the minimal, eight-line, 16-word 'The Red Wheelbarrow' (1923) to his most ambitious production, *Paterson* (1946–58), a long, five-part, free-verse, collage-mixed evocation of a characteristic industrial city, with the mystic motif, 'man is himself a city'. The title of his last collection, *Pictures from Brueghel* (1963), suggests the plain, poverty-stricken subjects of some of his verse and prose; and his skill at painting the ordinary with freshness and compassion is manifested in his short stories, collected as *The Farmers' Daughters* (1961). Other prose works include *In the American Grain* (1925), an important series of essays exploring the nature of American literature and the influence of Puritanism in American culture, and urging his own faith that 'all art begins in the local.' Despite his growing reputation at home, Williams's work was more or less disregarded in Britain until the 1950s; *Leavis in 1933 somewhat prematurely dismissed it as already outdated, and only a handful of writers, such as D. H. *Lawrence and B. *Bunting, took him seriously. Recently interest has increased considerably, and he is now established as one of the masters of *Modernism.

WILLIAMSON, David (1942–   ), Australian playwright, born in Melbourne. While he began his career in the counter-cultural 'New Wave' drama of the late 1960s and 1970s in Melbourne, Williamson has charted the lives of his own generation of well-educated middle-class Australians with unerring satiric wit and comic flair. Each play captures a current social predicament or preoccupation, particularly power plays in groups or institutions. *The Club* (1978) and *The Department* (1975) are concerned with a football club and an academic department, while corruption in business, government, the law, and the press is criticized in *Sons of Cain* (1985), *Emerald City* (1987), and *Top Silk* (1989). *After the Ball* (1998) employs autobiography to reflect on Australia's social changes over the past 30 years. The satire and social criticism often seem blunted by the plays' many brilliant one-liners and sheer comic verve, which may earn critical censure but delight audiences.

WILLIAMSON, Henry (1895–1977), born in south London, the son of a bank clerk, educated at Colfe's Grammar School, Lewisham. He joined the army in the First World War and was commissioned in 1915; his experience of warfare permanently affected him, convincing him of the futility of war and the need for understanding between nations. After the war he worked briefly in Fleet Street while writing his first novel, *The Beautiful Years* (1921: vol. i of *The Flax of Dream* quartet). In 1921 he moved to north Devon, and embarked on a modest country life (much influenced by R. *Jefferies) which produced his most widely known work, *Tarka the Otter* (1927), a remarkably observed, unsentimental tale which was much admired and remains a popular classic. This was followed by other tales of wildlife and the countryside, including *Salar the Salmon* (1935). In the 1930s Williamson became an admirer of Hitler and Sir Oswald Mosley, addressing Hitler in a notorious foreword to *The Flax of Dream* (1936) as 'the great man across the Rhine, whose life symbol is the happy child'. This led, in the short

term, to a brief internment at the outbreak of the Second World War, and in the long run, to the neglect of his most ambitious work, a series of 15 novels known under the collective title *A Chronicle of Ancient Sunlight*, a panoramic survey which opens in the mid-1890s with *The Dark Lantern* (1951) and closes with *The Gale of the World* (1969). This traces the career of Philip Maddison, writer, from birth to the aftermath of the Second World War and the point at which he resolves to write a series of novels 'to reveal the past' of his own generation to the next, and to explain the true meaning of his Mosley–*Birkin character's philosophy. Less politically tendentious is Williamson's short, devastating account of trench warfare, *The Patriot's Progress* (1930), seen through the eyes of a naïve, suffering Everyman, City clerk John Bullock, which was one of the most telling of the anti-war novels of the 1930s, and admired by T. E. *Lawrence. Williamson wrote about his friendship and correspondence with Lawrence in *Genius of Friendship* (1941).

Willobie His Avisa, one of the books which, with G. *Harvey's and T. *Nashe's satirical works, was called in by the high commission in 1599. The poem, first published in 1594, consists of 74 serviceable but uninspired songs and a few other poems by Henry Willoby (?1574–?96). They narrate the unsuccessful courting of Avisa, a country innkeeper's wife, by a nobleman before her marriage, and by four foreign suitors after it. The last of these has a 'familiar friend W.S.' as a companion; he has been identified with Shakespeare, who is also mentioned as author of *The Rape of Lucrece* in prefatory verses.

Willoughby, (1) Sir Clement, a character in F. Burney's *Evelina*; (2) John, a character in J. Austen's *Sense and Sensibility*.

WILLS, W(illiam) G(orman) (1828–91), a highly successful but unremembered Irish verse dramatist, whose first play, *A Man and His Shadow*, was produced in London in 1865. A long succession of popular plays led to his appointment as 'Dramatist to the Lyceum', for which he wrote many historical dramas, including *Charles I* (1872, with H. *Irving). He produced a version of *Faust* in 1885, and a long poem, *Melchior*, dedicated to R. *Browning, in the same year. He was also a successful portrait painter.

WILMOT, John, see ROCHESTER, EARL OF.

WILMOT, Robert, see TANCRED AND GISMUND.

WILSON, A(ndrew) N(orman) (1950–   ), novelist, biographer, and reviewer, born in Stone, Staffordshire, and educated at Rugby and New College, Oxford. From 1981 to 1983 he was literary editor of the *Spectator*. His novel writing began in a vein of slightly acid social comedy with *The Sweets of Pimlico* (1977) and *Unguarded Hours* (1978), both written somewhat in the shadow of Evelyn *Waugh. Satire was blended with more complex explorations of individual character in two of his best works: *The Healing Art* (1980), about a mistaken diagnosis of cancer, and *Wise Virgin* (1982), a study of a father–daughter relationship. These were followed by *Scandal* (1983) and *Gentlemen in England* (1985). *Incline Our Hearts* (1989), *A Bottle in the Smoke* (1990), *Daughters of Albion* (1991), *Hearing Voices* (1995), and *Watch in the Night* (1996) form the Lampitt Papers quintet. *The Vicar of Sorrows*, the story of a disillusioned clergyman's infatuation with a New Age traveller, was published in 1993. He has also published a number of accomplished biographical studies of Sir Walter *Scott (1980), *Milton (1983), Hilaire *Belloc (1994), *Tolstoy (1988), and C. S. *Lewis (1990). His controversial study of Jesus appeared in 1992. *Penfriends from Porlock* (1988) is a collection of his literary criticism.

WILSON, Sir Angus Frank Johnstone (1913–91), born in Bexhill, educated at Westminster and Merton College, Oxford. During the war he worked on decoding at Bletchley Park, returning in 1946 to the *British Museum where he became deputy superintendent of the Reading Room, a post he resigned in 1955 to become a freelance writer. His first two volumes, *The Wrong Set* (1949) and *Such Darling Dodos* (1950), were of short stories, followed by *Hemlock and After* (1952), a novel about the doomed attempts of a middle-aged novelist, Bernard Sands, to establish a writer's centre in a country house. *Anglo-Saxon Attitudes* (1956, novel) also has a middle-aged protagonist, historian Gerald Middleton, separated from his grotesque Danish wife and his ex-mistress Dolly, and involved in an attempt to reconstruct and understand the past, including the mystery of a possible archaeological forgery, reminiscent of the Piltdown case. *A Bit off the Map* (1957, short stories) was followed by *The Middle Age of Mrs Eliot* (1958), a novel about the reversed fortunes of Meg Eliot, the sociable, handsome, and contented wife of an apparently wealthy barrister, who finds herself suddenly widowed in reduced circumstances. *The Old Men at the Zoo* (1961), about a doomed attempt to set up a large natural reservation for wild animals, reflects Wilson's concern with conflicts between the wild and the tame, the disciplined and the free, and ends with a portrayal of Europe at war. *Late Call* (1964), set with telling accuracy in a New Town, tells of the search for purpose and understanding of the retired hotel manageress Sylvia Calvert, obliged to live with her widowed headmaster son Harold and his family. *No Laughing Matter* (1967), his most ambitious novel, is a family saga covering some 50 years in the history of the Matthews family, but despite its subject it marks a departure from the realism of earlier works, mingling parody and dramatization with direct narration in a rich and complex evocation of family politics and neuroses. *As if by Magic* (1973) follows through various parts of the world the adventures of Hamo Langmuir, breeder of 'magic' rice, and his god-daughter Alexandra Grant, ex-student, involved in a sexual triangle and a search for purpose. *Setting the World on Fire* (1980) is a more tightly constructed novel, contrasting the characters and destinies of two brothers, one a theatre director in love with artistic daring, the other a lawyer dismayed by disorder and encroaching chaos. Wilson also wrote on *Zola (1952), *Dickens (1970), and *Kipling (1977), and a pioneering account of his own creative process, *The Wild Garden* (1963). His works display satiric wit, acute social observation, and a love of the macabre and the farcical, combined with a lively interest in human affairs. A biography by M. *Drabble was published in 1995.

WILSON, Colin Henry (1931–), born and brought up in Leicester. He left school at 16, and after working at a variety of jobs and reading widely in his spare time, published *The Outsider* (1956), a work which enjoyed a considerable vogue. It describes the sense of alienation of the man of genius, using a mixture of texts, from Barbusse, *Camus, *Sartre, T. E. *Lawrence, *Hesse, etc. and did much to popularize a version of *existentialism in Britain; it appeared in the same week as *Osborne's *Look Back in Anger*, and Wilson was promptly labelled an *Angry Young Man, though he had little in common with others allocated to the same group. Wilson has since written many works on mysticism, existentialism, the occult, etc., and published many novels in various genres (*Ritual in the Dark*, 1960; *The Philosopher's Stone*, 1969; *The Space Vampires*, 1976, etc.).

WILSON, Edmund (1895–1972), American author, born in New Jersey, and educated at Princeton (where A. *Noyes, whom he did not admire, was at the time professor of poetry). He served abroad during the First World War, an experience which inspired verse and short stories published in a lively and eccentric little anthology about death, *The Undertaker's Garland* (1922, with his friend J. P. *Bishop). He then worked for various magazines, including *Vanity Fair* (1920–1), the *New Republic* (1926–31) and the *New Yorker* (1944–8). His novel *I Thought of Daisy* (1929, rev. 1967) is set in bohemian literary New York, and his short stories, *Memoirs of Hecate Country* (1946), are also set largely in New York. He is principally known for his influential, wide-ranging, and independent works of literary and social criticism, which include *Axel's Castle* (1931), a study of *symbolist literature (*Yeats, *Valèry, *Stein, and others, including *Villiers de l'Isle-Adam, whose play *Axël* gave the volume its title); *The Triple Thinkers* (1938); *To the Finland Station* (1940), which traces socialist and revolutionary theory from *Michelet and R. *Owen through *Marx to *Lenin; *The Wound and the Bow* (1941), a series of studies with a *Freudian angle, taking its title from an essay on the *Philoctetes* of *Sophocles; and *Patriotic Gore: Studies in the Literature of the American Civil War* (1962), a comprehensive survey of major and minor writers of the period, and the war's roots in the national psyche. His other works include experimental plays, collections of articles and reviews, and memoirs of early and later life (*A Prelude*, 1967; *Upstate*, 1971). His third wife was the novelist Mary *McCarthy, and he was a friend from college days of F. S. *Fitzgerald, whose posthumously published works he edited.

WILSON, Frank Percy (1889–1963), scholar and Merton professor of English literature at Oxford University (1947–57). Apart from his general editorship from 1935 of the *Oxford History of English Literature* and revision of *The Oxford Dictionary of English Proverbs* (1970), almost all his work was concerned with Elizabethan and Jacobean literature. His most important works were *The Plague in Shakespeare's London* (1927, rev. 1963), *Shakespeare and the New Bibliography* (1945, rev. 1970), and his revision of *McKerrow's edition of *Nashe's works (1958).

WILSON, Harriette, née Dubochet (1786–1846), courtesan, daughter of a Swiss-born London shopkeeper, who left a spirited account of her adventures and amours in the fashionable Regency world in *Memoirs of Harriette Wilson, Written by Herself* (1825), which went through many editions. It opens with panache, with the sentence 'I shall not say why and how I became at the age of fifteen, the mistress of the earl of Craven', and proceeds to describe with much frankness and some art her impressions of and friendships with *Brummell, Prince Esterhazy, the dukes of *Wellington, Argyle, Beaufort, Leinster, etc. She also wrote two slight novels, *Paris Lions and London Tigers* (1825) and *Clara Gazul* (1830), both *romans à clef.

WILSON, John (?1627–96), educated at Oxford. He became recorder of Londonderry. His two principal plays, of which the first was popular, are *The Cheats* (1663) and *The Projectors* (printed 1665, no recorded performance); they are Jonsonian satires in which sharks, gulls, usurers, and astrologers are vigorously and effectively displayed.

WILSON, John (1785–1854). He enjoyed a brilliant university career at Glasgow and Oxford, and was in youth a friend of *Wordsworth and *Coleridge (to whose *Friend* he contributed). He joined the editorial staff of *Blackwood's* shortly after its foundation and became its most copious single contributor. For the 'Maga' he provided more than half the series *Noctes Ambrosianae*, in which he appears as 'Christopher North'; he was part-author of the notorious *'Chaldee MS'; he wrote a ferocious attack on Coleridge's *Biographia Literaria*; and joined in *Lockhart's prolonged onslaught on the *Cockney School. He supported *Shelley, and dubbed Wordsworth, Sir W. *Scott, and *Byron, as poets, 'the three great master-spirits of our day'. But his praise alternated bewilderingly with derision and he declared, 'I like to abuse my friends.' He wrote some poetry and three sentimental novels of Scottish life, *Lights and Shadows of Scottish Life* (1822); *The Trials of Margaret Lyndsay* (1823); and *The Foresters* (1825), which Wordsworth described as 'mawkish stuff'. In 1820 he was appointed, for political reasons, to the chair of moral philosophy at Edinburgh, but his inadequacy was such that for many years a friend wrote his lectures for him.

WILSON, John Dover (1881–1969), Shakespearian scholar and editor. Using the methods of the new bibliography, he was responsible for editing most of the plays in the New Cambridge Shakespeare series which was begun in 1921. As well as this and many other scholarly works he produced several popular and influential books about Shakespeare, notably the 'biographical adventure' *The Essential Shakespeare* (1932), *What Happens in Hamlet* (1935), and *The Fortunes of Falstaff* (1943).

WILSON, Snoo (1948–), playwright and novelist, born in Reading and educated at the University of East Anglia. His play *The Beast*, which explores the life of Aleister *Crowley, was first performed by the Royal Shakespeare Company in 1974, and in an updated version as *The Number of the Beast* at the *Bush in 1982. Other plays include *Blow Job* (1971), *The Pleasure Principle* (1973), *England, England* (1977), and *More Light* (1990), based on the life of G. *Bruno. His novel *Spaceache* (1984) is a dystopian fantasy of a grim and ruthless high-technology low-competence future.

WILSON, Thomas (c.1523–81), educated at Eton and King's College, Cambridge. He was privy counsellor and secretary of state in 1577. He published *The Rule of Reason*, a work on logic (1551); and the *Arte of Rhetorique* (1553; revised and improved, 1560). The *Arte* is a notable landmark in the history of English prose. Wilson provides interesting examples of epistles and orations in a variety of English styles. Most of them are for emulation, but some of the more amusing, such as the famous *'inkhorn' letter from a Lincolnshire clergyman seeking preferment, exhibit the worst excesses of Latinism and affectation:

> There is a Sacerdotall dignitie in my native Countrey contiguate to me, where I now contemplate: which your worshipfull benignitie could sone impetrate for mee, if it would like you to extend your sedules, and collaude me in them to the right honourable lord Chaunceller, or rather Archgrammacian of Englande.

The *Arte of Rhetorique* was edited by G. H. Mair (1909).

Wilton, Jacke, see UNFORTUNATE TRAVELLER, THE.

Wilton House, in Wiltshire, seat of the earls of Pembroke, is associated with Sir P. *Sidney, who is said to have written much of the first version of the *Arcadia there while staying with his sister Mary, countess of *Pembroke. According to *Aubrey, 'In her time Wilton house was like a College, there were so many learned and ingeniose persons.' She was undoubtedly a literary patroness, but the claim made to W. J. *Cory in 1865 that Shakespeare was her guest and that *As You Like It* was performed there before James I has never been confirmed.

Wimble, Will, in the *Spectator*, a friend of Sir Roger de *Coverley, introduced in No. 108 as a good-natured fellow 'who hunts a pack of dogs better than any man in the country' and is generally esteemed for the obliging services he renders to all.

WINCHILSEA, Anne Finch, countess of, née Kingsmill (1661–1720), poet, born near Newbury, the daughter of Sir William Kingsmill, and orphaned when young: she was probably brought up by her mother's brother. She was a maid of honour to Mary of Modena, wife of the duke of York, and in 1684 married Colonel Heneage Finch who succeeded his nephew to the title in 1712. She was a friend of *Pope, *Swift, *Gay, and *Rowe. Her *Miscellany Poems on Several Occasions* appeared in 1713, at first anonymously; they were admired by *Wordsworth, who found affinities in them, and chose a selection for an album (1819). Her best-known poem is her *ode 'The Spleen: A Pindaric Poem' (pub. 1701 in Charles Gildon's *New Collection of Poems*): her couplet about the jonquil and 'aromatic pain' was echoed by Pope in his *Essay on Man*, and J. M. *Murry, in his preface to his 1928 selection, singles out from the same poem the lines 'Nor will in fading silks compose | Faintly the inimitable rose.' V. Woolf in *A Room of One's Own* (1928) concluded that she 'suffered terribly from melancholy'. Many of the poems which remained in manuscript at her death have since appeared in various anthologies and selections.

WINCKELMANN, Johann Joachim (1717–68), the son of a German shoemaker, who became the founder of the modern study of Greek sculptures and antiquities. By his understanding of the ideal of Greek art, its spiritual quality, its sense of proportion, and its 'noble simplicity and quiet grandeur', he exerted an immense influence on subsequent thought and literature (e.g. on *Goethe and *Schiller). *Nietzsche later rebelled against Winckelmann's 'Apollonian' view of Greek culture in his first work, *The Birth of Tragedy*. Winckelmann was the subject of an essay by *Pater and of *The Conversion of Winckelmann* by A. *Austin.

Wind in the Willows, The, see GRAHAME.

Windsor Forest, a *topographical poem by *Pope in the genre of *Cooper's Hill* by *Denham. Begun in 1704, it was published in 1713 to celebrate the Peace of Utrecht; it combines description of landscape with historical, literary, and political reflections.

WING, Donald Goddard (1904–72), American scholar, librarian, and bibliographer, who was responsible for compiling the *Short-Title Catalogue of Books Printed in England, Scotland, Ireland, Wales and British America, and of English Books Printed in Other Countries 1641–1700*, published by the Index Society in 1945. A second edition, revised and enlarged, appeared in 1972.

Wings of the Dove, The, a novel by H. *James published 1902.

In this novel James, for the first time, takes passionate human love as his central theme. The handsome and clever Kate Croy allows herself to be taken up by her rich aunt Maud Lowder. Fearful of the poverty surrounding her disgraced father and widowed sister, she is as determined to feather her nest as she is genuinely in love with Merton Densher, a journalist without bright financial prospects. While on a visit to New York Densher meets Milly Theale, an orphaned, gentle girl who is immensely rich. Her wings are weighted with gold. Milly travels to Europe with her friend Susan Stringham, and in London she is gathered into Mrs Lowder's circle. She is anxious to meet Densher again and is disturbed to learn, from a disapproving Mrs Lowder, of his interest in Kate. While in London she learns that she is doomed and is advised by the sympathetic doctor Sir Luke Strett to seize what joy she can from life. She installs herself in a palazzo in Venice, and with their varying motives her friends gather round her: Kate and Mrs Lowder, Densher, the fortune-hunting Sir Mark, the faithful Susan Stringham, and even the London doctor. Kate and Densher become lovers while Milly is deliberately misled into believing that Kate does not return Densher's interest. The predatory Kate persuades a reluctant Densher to make a show of love for Milly in the hope that, dying, she will provide for him—and for them. After Milly's death Densher does indeed discover that she has done so. But Kate has reckoned without his growing unease and distaste for the role he has been forced to play; Densher finds himself unable to accept the money, and Kate. Their very success in this dreadful game has brought about the death of their relationship.

Winkle, Nathaniel, in Dickens's *Pickwick Papers*, one of the members of the Corresponding Society of the Pickwick Club.

'Winkle, Rip Van', see RIP VAN WINKLE.

Winner and Waster, see WYNNERE AND WASTOUR.

Winnie-the-Pooh, the bear of very little brain, and friend of Piglet, Eeyore, and others, in the popular stories of A. A. *Milne.

WINSTANLEY, Gerrard (c.1609–76), radical pamphleteer and leader of the Diggers, or True Levellers. He was born in Wigan, the son of a mercer, went to London as a clothing apprentice in 1630, and set up for himself in 1637, unsuccessfully; by 1643 he described himself as 'beaten out of both trade and estate', and he worked subsequently as a hired labourer. He published several religious pamphlets in 1648, and in 1649 with a group of comrades started digging and planting crops on St George's Hill, in Surrey, in a bold but short-lived attempt to claim the common land for 'the common people of England'. His first Digger manifesto, *The True*

Levellers' Standard Advanced, is dated 20 April 1649, and it was followed by others putting forward his political and collectivist programme, e.g. *A Watchword to the City of London, and the Army* (1649), *Fire in the Bush* (1650), ending with his last and most systematic work, *The Law of Freedom, in a Platform* (1652), which also expresses his disillusion at the collapse of his agrarian experiment. He believed that the sin of covetousness had brought mankind into bondage, and his work expresses a deep compassion for the poor, while remaining remarkably fair-minded and free of sectarian virulence. His prose is powerful and lucid, addressed to plain readers, and avoiding 'the traditional, parrot-like speaking' of the universities, which in his view drew a veil over truth with 'dark interpretation and glosses': many of his metaphors are drawn from daily life, but he can also express himself with poetic and passionate intensity, and with a personal and inventive use of biblical imagery that prefigures *Blake. Nothing is known of his later years, and his contribution to literature and political thought was neglected until the 20th cent., no doubt because of the apparent failure of his ideas, but there has been a considerable revival of interest, and he is now acclaimed by many as one of the most original and prophetic writers of his time. See *The Works of Gerrard Winstanley*, ed. G. H. Sabine (1941); Winstanley, *The Law of Freedom and Other Writings*, ed. C. *Hill (Penguin, 1973).

Winterborne, Giles, a character in Hardy's *The Woodlanders*.

WINTERS, (Arthur) Yvor (1900–68), American poet and critic, whose own poems exemplify his critical doctrine of classicism, restraint, moral judgement, and 'cold certitude'. (See NEW CRITICISM.) His *In Defense of Reason* (1947) contains three earlier works, *Primitivism and Decadence* (1937), *Maule's Curse* (1938), and *The Anatomy of Nonsense* (1943), all of which attack obscurantism and *Romanticism, and an essay on his friend, the highly dissimilar Hart *Crane, for whom he also wrote an elegy, 'Orpheus'.

WINTERSON, Jeanette (1959–   ), novelist, born in Manchester. She became the adopted daughter of Pentecostal evangelist parents. Her upbringing and training for evangelistic service, as well as the realization of her lesbian identity, were drawn on heavily, and to brilliant effect, for her first novel, *Oranges Are Not the Only Fruit* (1985), which won the Whitbread Award for a first novel and was successfully adapted for television in 1990. She was educated at Accrington Girls' Grammar School and, after a period of miscellaneous employment, read English at St Catherine's College, Oxford. *Boating for Beginners* (1985), a comic fable based on the story of Noah, was followed by *The Passion* (1987), a bawdy historical fantasy in which a French peasant, Henri, who worships Napoleon, be-

comes his hero's chicken chef and falls in love with a bisexual Venetian girl with webbed feet. Her fourth novel, *Sexing the Cherry* (1989), transforms the fairy tale of the 12 dancing princesses, juxtaposing 17th-cent. characters with their counterparts in the 20th cent. Its main character, the Dog Woman, and her foster-son Jordan, fished from the Thames as a baby, are notable creations. *Written on the Body* (1992) is an exploration of gender within a triangular relationship. The controversial *Art and Lies* (1994) develops Winterson's unconventional narrative style even further through the deployment of three separate voices named Handel, Picasso, and Sappho.

Winter's Tale, The, a play by *Shakespeare written 1610 or 1611, in which year it was performed at the Globe (recorded by *Forman). It was one of the plays put on to celebrate the marriage of Princess Elizabeth and the elector palatine in 1612–13 and was first printed in the *Folio of 1623 where it is the last play in the section of comedies. Its main source is Greene's *Pandosto*.

Leontes, king of Sicily, and Hermione, his virtuous wife, are visited by Leontes's childhood friend Polixenes, king of Bohemia. Leontes presently convinces himself that Hermione and Polixenes are lovers, attempts to procure the death of the latter by poison, and on his escape imprisons Hermione, who in prison gives birth to a daughter. Paulina, wife of Antigonus, a Sicilian lord, tries to move the king's compassion by bringing the baby to him, but in vain. He orders Antigonus to leave the child on a desert shore to perish. He disregards a Delphian oracle declaring Hermione innocent. He soon learns that his son Mamillius has died of sorrow for Hermione's treatment, and shortly after that Hermione herself is dead, and is filled with remorse. Meanwhile Antigonus leaves the baby girl, Perdita, on the shore of Bohemia, and is himself killed by a bear. Perdita is found and brought up by a shepherd. Sixteen years pass. When she grows up, Florizel, son of King Polixenes, falls in love with her, and his love is returned. This is discovered by Polixenes, to avoid whose anger Florizel, Perdita, and the old shepherd flee from Bohemia to the court of Leontes, where the identity of Perdita is discovered, to Leontes's great joy, and the revival of his grief for the loss of Hermione. Paulina offers to show him a statue that perfectly resembles Hermione, and when the king's grief is intensified by the sight of this, the statue comes to life and reveals itself as the living Hermione, whose death Paulina had falsely reported in order to save her life. Polixenes is reconciled to the marriage of his son with Perdita, on finding that the shepherd-girl is really the daughter of his former friend Leontes. The rogueries of Autolycus, the pedlar and 'snapper-up of unconsidered trifles', add amusement to the later scenes of the play; and his songs 'When daffodils begin to peer' and 'Jog on, jog on, the footpath way' are famous.

WIREKER, Nigel (fl. 1190), precentor of Christ Church, Canterbury, author of *Burnellus* or *Speculum Stultorum*, a satire on monks recounting the adventures of *Burnell the ass. It is found in T. Wright (ed.) *Anglo-Latin Satirical Poets of the Twelfth Century* (Rolls Series, 1872, i). (See also ANGLO-LATIN LITERATURE.)

Wisden: *A Cricketer's Almanac*, first published under this title by John Wisden and Co. in 1870 (previously known, 1864–9, as *The Cricketer's Almanac*). The first number contains the laws of cricket, scores of 100 and upwards from 1850 to 1863, records of extraordinary matches, etc. The publication continues, and it remains the cricket enthusiast's vade-mecum.

Wisdom (also *Mind, Will and Understanding* or *Wisdom, Who Is Christ*), a *morality play from *c.*1460, one of the group called *Macro plays, describing the seduction by Lucifer of Mind, Will, and Understanding in a series of dances. Ed. Mark Eccles in *The Macro Plays* (EETS 262, 1969).

WISE, Thomas James (1859–1937), bibliographer, collector, and editor, who formed the great Ashley Library (see LIBRARIES). In 1934 his credit as a bibliographer was gravely damaged by the publication of a book (*An Enquiry into the Nature of Certain 19th-Century Pamphlets* by J. Carter and G. Pollard) which proved that a large number of rare pamphlets whose authenticity depended upon Wise's statements were in fact forgeries—in particular an edition of E. B. Browning's *Sonnets from the Portuguese* said to have been published in Reading in 1847.

WISHART, William (*c.*1692–1753), Scots cleric and controversialist, and co-founder of the *Rankenian Club. An early collaborator with *Arbuckle, *Turnbull, and *Hutcheson, he was an energetic exponent of the moral sense philosophy of *Shaftesbury and Hutcheson. In addition to sermons, he published anonymous satires on *Berkeley's *Alciphron* in 1734 and *Doddridge's *Life of Col. Gardiner* in 1747. As principal of Edinburgh University, he led the successful opposition to *Hume's appointment as a professor in 1744–5.

Wishfort, Lady, a character in Congreve's *The Way of the World*.

Witch, The, a play by T. *Middleton, written before 1616, not printed until 1778.

The principal part of the plot is based on the story of the revenge exacted by Rosamond in 572 on her husband Alboin, ruler of Lombardy. In Middleton's play the duchess is obliged by her husband to drink a health at a banquet out of a cup made from her father's skull and, to avenge herself, purchases by her pretended favours the help of a courtier Almachides, to kill her husband. (The same subject is treated in *D'Avenant's *Albovine*, and in *Swinburne's *Rosamund, Queen of the Lombards*.) In this and the subordinate intrigue, the assistance of the witch Hecate is called in, and part of the interest of the play lies in the comparison between Middleton's Hecate and the witches in Shakespeare's *Macbeth*. *Lamb in his *Specimens* indicated the difference between them.

'Witch of Atlas, The', a fantasy poem by P. B. *Shelley, written in the summer of 1820, on his return from a solitary pilgrimage to Monte San Peligrino, Lucca, in Italy, published 1824.

Shelley composed this playful work of 78 stanzas in *ottava rima* within the space of three days. The beautiful Witch (whom he had presumably met on his pilgrimage) is the daughter of Apollo, and the spirit of mischief and poetry. She besports herself amid pyrotechnic imagery of magic boats, airships, storms, and fireballs. Her mysterious companion is the Hermaphrodite, and together they circle the globe, weaving spells over recalcitrant kings, priests, soldiers, and young lovers (whose inhibitions are blissfully dissolved). Mary *Shelley disliked the poem; Shelley replied in verse, asking if she were 'critic-bitten'.

Witch of Edmonton, The, a tragi-comedy by *Dekker, *Ford, *Rowley, 'etc.' (possibly *Webster?), first performed probably 1621, not published until 1658. It is partly based on the story of Elizabeth Sawyer, who was hanged as a witch in April 1621.

Frank Thorney marries his fellow servant Winifred, without his father's knowledge and against his will. To save himself from being disinherited, at his father's bidding he also marries Susan Carter, and presently, to extract himself from his embarrassment, murders her and attempts to throw the guilt on her two rejected suitors, but is discovered and in due course executed.

In a second distinct plot, the old woman of Edmonton is persecuted by her neighbours because she is, in her own words, 'poor, deform'd and ignorant', and to revenge herself she sells her soul to the devil, who appears to her in the form of a dog. 'Some call me witch;|And being ignorant of my self, they go|About to teach me how to be one.' Her character is notable for the characteristic sympathy shown by Dekker for the poor outcast, and the tone of the play is markedly humane. Both plots reflect the theme of revenge, but are otherwise little connected.

WITHER, George (1588–1667), poet and pamphleteer, born at Bentworth in Hampshire, educated at Magdalen College, Oxford. His satires *Abuses Stript and Whipt*, published 1613, in spite of the innocuous character of their denunciations of Avarice, Gluttony, and so on, earned him imprisonment in the Marshalsea. There he wrote five pastorals under the title of *The Shepherds Hunting*, a continuation of *The Shepheards Pipe*, which he had written in conjunction with William *Browne, the 'Willie' of these verses. In the second of these, Wither (in the character of Philarete) describes the 'hunting of foxes, wolves and beasts of prey' (the abuses) which got him into trouble with the government. His *Fidelia*, a poetical epistle from a faithful nymph to her inconstant lover, appeared in 1617 (privately printed 1615) and again, with the famous song 'Shall I, wasting in despair', in 1619; it was this song, printed by Percy in his *Reliques*, that was to rescue Wither's reputation from a century of neglect.

Wither's self-aggrandizing *Motto: Nec Habeo, nec Careo, nec Curo* (1621) led to another, but not his last, spell of imprisonment. In 1622 appeared *Faire-Virtue, the Mistresse of Phil'Arete*, a long sequence of poems in various verse forms (octosyllabics, sonnets, diamond-shaped verses, etc.) in praise of his semi-allegorical mistress. From this time Wither's poetry became increasingly religious and satirical in tone, which led to accusations that he was a Puritan, and his portrayal as 'Chronomastix' in *Jonson's masque *Time Vindicated* (1623). He published *The Hymnes and Songs of the Church* in 1623, a poem on the plague in 1628, a book of *emblems in 1634–5, and *Heleluiah* in 1641. During the Civil War he raised a troop of horse and wrote many pamphlets for Parliament, and in 1642 was captain and commander of Farnham Castle, but after the war devoted much energy to petitions and litigation on behalf of his own lost property.

No complete edition of Wither's work has been published, but several collections were printed by the Spenser Society from 1871, and there is a two-volume edition with a biographical introduction by F. Sidgwick (1902).

Wititterly, Mr and Mrs, in Dickens's *Nicholas Nickleby*, typical snobs.

Wits, The, a comedy by *D'Avenant, published 1636, revised by him after the Restoration, and generally considered his best comedy.

Young Pallatine, a wit, who lives in London on an allowance, but finds it unequal to his wants, is in love with Lucy, who sells her jewels to provide him with money and is in consequence turned out by her cruel aunt, who suspects her of misconduct. She takes refuge with Lady Ample, the rich ward of Sir Tyrant Thrift, who proposes to force an unwelcome marriage on his ward before he loses control over her. Meanwhile Pallatine's wealthy elder brother comes to town, with old Sir Morglay Thwack, for a spell of dissipation. He tells young Pallatine that he will never more give him money, but that he must live by his wits, as he himself and Thwack propose to do. In pursuit of this purpose they become involved in a series of adventures, are thoroughly fooled, and the elder Pallatine is released from his troubles only on making liberal provision for his brother and Lucy. Thrift is likewise fooled and held to ransom.

WITTGENSTEIN, Ludwig Josef Johann (1889–1951), born in Vienna, and educated at Linz and Berlin. He came to England in 1908; he lived most of his adult life in Cambridge, where he was professor of philosophy (1939–47). Trained as an engineer, he came to philosophy through the study of the philosophy of math-

ematics with B. *Russell. He himself published only the *Tractatus Logico-Philosophicus* (1922); in this aphoristic and difficult book he presents the view that the only meaningful use of language is as a picture of empirical, scientific fact; otherwise language will be tautological, as in logic and mathematics, or nonsensical, as in metaphysics and judgements of value. About 1930 he began to doubt the correctness of this approach; he gradually developed the view that language had a vast multiplicity of uses, which he likened to the multiplicity of tools in a carpenter's tool-bag, and that the traditional problems of philosophy arose from a misunderstanding of the use of those concepts in terms of which the problems arose; this misunderstanding he likened to mental cramp or bewilderment, and held that the problems could be dissolved by carefully bringing out the true character of the language in which they were framed. Thus there were no philosophical results, in the form of answers to questions, but only the growth and dissolution of philosophical puzzlement. Among other posthumously published writings, the *Philosophical Investigations* (1953) contain a full account of this later position.

Wives and Daughters, the last and unfinished novel of E. *Gaskell, published in the *Cornhill Magazine*, 1864–6, and in volume form 1866.

This novel, Mrs Gaskell's masterpiece, centres on two families, the Gibsons and the Hamleys. Mr Gibson, surgeon in the little country town of Hollingford, is a widower with one daughter, Molly, who is a child when the story starts, but as she grows up her father feels he ought to marry again for her sake, and proposes to a widow, Mrs Kirkpatrick, formerly governess in the family of Lord Cumnor, the local magnate. Molly passionately resents her father's marriage, and is made unhappy by her graceful stepmother's shallow selfishness, but she loyally tries to accept the new situation, and her lot is improved when her stepmother's daughter by her previous marriage, Cynthia, who has been brought up in France, joins the household. Cynthia is a fascinating beauty, more sincere than her mother, but with few moral principles.

The Hamleys are an ancient county family—the proud and hot-tempered squire, his invalid wife, their elder son Osborne who is handsome and clever and his parents' favourite, and a younger son, Roger, sturdy, honest, and a late developer. Molly Gibson often stays with the Hamleys, and discovers by accident that Osborne is secretly married to a French nursery-maid. Molly, who at first found Roger unattractive, has begun to love and admire him, but he becomes engaged to Cynthia, and, being by now a successful scientist, goes off on an expedition to Africa. Cynthia is in fact already secretly engaged to Preston, Lord Cumnor's clever but ill-bred agent, and she enlists Molly's help in extricating herself from this entanglement, by a series of secret meetings which compromise Molly's reputation. Osborne Hamley is bitterly estranged from his father, but when Osborne dies and the secret of his marriage is revealed, Squire Hamley, repenting his harshness, adopts Osborne's baby son. Cynthia throws over Roger Hamley and marries a man more suited to her, and when Roger returns he has realized that it is Molly whom he really loves. Like the plants and insects that Roger shows Molly through his microscope, the habits, loyalties, prejudices, petty snobberies, rumours, adjustments of a whole countryside hierarchy are displayed by Mrs Gaskell with minute and loving observation, equally acute for the aristocratic Lady Cumnor and her satirical and kind-hearted daughter Lady Harriet, who befriends Molly, and for old Silas, Squire Hamley's dying gamekeeper. Unlike some of Mrs Gaskell's earlier novels, *Wives and Daughters* is expertly constructed, convincing in all its incidents and dialogues, and peopled by fully realized characters.

WODEHOUSE, Sir P(elham) G(renville) (1881–1975), born in Guildford, the son of a civil servant who became a judge in Hong Kong. He spent much of his childhood in England in the care of various aunts, and was educated at Dulwich College, which he always remembered with affection. He soon abandoned a career with the Hong Kong Bank for literature; he began by writing short stories for boys' magazines, and later published extensively in the *Strand Magazine, *Punch, etc., establishing himself as one of the most widely read humorists of his day. His first novel was published in 1902, and his prolific output, of over 120 volumes, included *The Man with Two Left Feet* (1917), the collection of stories which first introduced *Jeeves and Bertie *Wooster; a series of Jeeves volumes (*My Man Jeeves*, 1919; *The Inimitable Jeeves*, 1923; *Carry On, Jeeves*, 1925, etc.); and other works featuring such favourite characters as Lord Emsworth (and his prize sow, the Empress of Blandings), Mr Mulliner, Psmith, several redoubtable aunts, and many patrons of the Drones Club. Wodehouse's amiable career, which also embraced successes in musical comedy, the theatre, and Hollywood, was interrupted by the Second World War, when he was captured by the Germans at Le Touquet in 1940. He was interned and then released, but not allowed to leave Germany, and unwisely accepted an invitation to broadcast to America. Despite the innocuous nature of the broadcasts, this caused a scandal in England, and after the war he settled in America (where he had previously lived for some years), taking American citizenship in 1955. He continued to write prolifically until the end of his life, and to retain the warm admiration of his many readers. See Frances Donaldson, *P. G. Wodehouse* (1982).

WODROW, Robert (1679–1734), minister of Eastwood, near Glasgow, and university librarian of Glasgow. His works include a *History of the Sufferings of the Church of Scotland from the Restoration to the Revolution* (1721–2). He also kept private notebooks (partly in cipher) published by the Maitland Club in 1842–3 as *Analecta, or Materials for a History of Remarkable Providences*. He was a great book-collector, and left a valuable collection of broadsides and pasquinades (see J. H. Burton, *The Book-Hunter*, 1862). He is commemorated in the Wodrow Society, devoted to the history of Presbyterianism and the works of eminent Presbyterians.

WOFFINGTON, Peg (Margaret) (*c.*1714–60), celebrated actress, daughter of a Dublin bricklayer. She was engaged by J. *Rich for Covent Garden in 1740, and was immediately successful, acting in a great number of leading comic roles. She had many lovers, and lived for some time with *Garrick. She is the subject of *Masks and Faces* (1852), a play by C. *Reade and Tom *Taylor, on which Reade based his novel *Peg Woffington* (1853).

WOLCOT, John (1738–1819), satirist, who wrote under the pseudonym 'Peter Pindar'. He began his career as a physician, took holy orders, then returned to the practice of medicine until 1778, when he came to London and began the writing of vigorous and witty satirical verses. Among these were *Lyric Odes to the Royal Academicians* (1782–5), mocking their painting; a *mock-heroic poem, *The Lousiad*, published in five cantos between 1785 and 1795, and various other satires on George III. *Bozzy and Piozzi*, in which *Boswell and Mrs *Thrale set forth their reminiscences of Dr *Johnson, appeared in 1786, as did his *Poetical and Congratulatory Epistle to James Boswell*. In 1787 appeared *Instructions to a Celebrated Laureate*, which professes to teach *Warton how he should celebrate the visit of George III to Whitbread's brewery.

WOLFE, Charles (1791–1823), educated at Trinity College, Dublin, curate of Donoughmore, Co. Down, from 1818 to 1821. He was the author of the well-known lines on 'The Burial of Sir John Moore', his only poem of note, apparently based on *Southey's narrative in the *Annual Register*, and first published in the *Newry Telegraph* in 1817. His *Poems*, with a memoir by C. L. Falkiner, were published in 1903.

WOLFE, Humbert (1886–1940), poet and civil servant, born in Milan and educated at Bradford Grammar School and Wadham College, Oxford. He was a prolific essayist and published several volumes of poetry: *London Sonnets* (1920) was followed by other volumes including the successful *Requiem* (1927) and the posthumously published *Kensington Gardens in Wartime* (1940). He is remembered as a writer of serious light verse, more urbane than Georgian in tone.

WOLFE, Reyner or Reginald (*c.*1530–73), bookseller and printer, who came from Strasbourg and established himself in London at St Paul's Churchyard. He was the first printer in England to possess a large stock of Greek type of good quality, and he printed in 1543, with Greek and Latin text, the *Homilies* of *Chrysostom, edited by *Cheke, the first Greek book printed in this country. In 1547 he was appointed king's printer in Latin, Greek, and Hebrew. He also came under the patronage of Archbishop *Parker. His son John Wolfe (d. 1601) inherited the business.

WOLFE, Thomas Clayton (1900–38), American novelist, born in North Carolina, the son of a stonecutter, and educated at the university there and at Harvard, where he studied playwriting. He made his name with his autobiographical novel *Look Homeward, Angel* (1929), which describes at length and with much intensity the adolescence of Eugene Gant; this was followed by a sequel, *Of Time and the River* (1935), and various posthumous works, which include *The Web and the Rock* (1939) and its sequel *You Can't Go Home Again* (1940). Passionate, prolix, rhetorical, and shapeless, Wolfe's novels lacked discipline; he was unable or unwilling to prune his own work, which owed much in its published form to editorial assistance, but its emotional power won many readers, particularly among the young. He died of an infection following pneumonia.

WOLFE, Tom (1931–), American novelist and journalist; born Thomas Kennerly Wolfe Jr in Richmond, Virginia, he began his career as a journalist reporting for the *Washington Post* (1959–62). With his contemporaries Joan *Didion and Hunter S. *Thompson he was a pioneer of New Journalism (he co-edited the anthology *The New Journalism* in 1973), bringing to journalism techniques of writing usually employed by fiction writers. He published a number of volumes of non-fiction in the 1960s and 1970s (much of which had first appeared in periodicals such as *Rolling Stone* magazine), including *The Electric Kool-Aid Acid Test* (1968) and *The Right Stuff* (1979), about the early stages of the American space programme. His other works of non-fiction include *From Bauhaus to Our House* (1981), a succinct overview of 20th-cent. architecture.

He is now best known for his satirical first novel *The Bonfire of the Vanities* (1987), a sharply critical look at Reagan's America, which traces the downfall of ambitious Wall Street dealer Sherman McCoy. Wolfe published his second novel, *A Man in Full*, in 1998.

WOLFF, Tobias (1945–), American writer of short stories and memoirs, educated at Oxford and Stanford. His first collection of stories, *Hunters in the Snow*, was published in 1982. In this collection he introduces his recurring preoccupation with ordinary characters who are somehow alienated from society, whether because their dreams do not coincide with the reality of life in small-town America, because they have critical moral dilemmas they need to solve, or because they have painful confessions to make and difficult memories to placate. This was followed in 1984 by *The Barracks Thief*, a short novel set during the Vietnam War, *Back in the World* (1986, stories), and *The Night in Question* (1996, stories). He is perhaps most widely known for two volumes of autobiography; *This Boy's Life* (1989) describes his early adolescence and his difficult relationships with his unstable mother and violent step-

father. This was followed by an account, often comic as well as moving, of his experiences of service in Vietnam, *In Pharaoh's Army* (1994).

WOLFRAM VON ESCHENBACH (fl. *c.*1200–20), a Bavarian knight and a great German epic poet, whose principal works were the epics *Parzifal* and *Willehalm*. He also composed fragments of *Titurel* and several *Tagelieder* (dawn pieces) the most famous of which begins 'Sîne klâwen'. Wolfram appears as a character in *Wagner's *Tannhäuser*. (See MINNE-SINGERS.)

WOLLSTONECRAFT, Mary (1759–97). After an unsettled childhood, she opened a school at Newington Green in 1784 with her sister Eliza and a friend; there she made the acquaintance of R. *Price and other eminent Dissenters. In 1786, after writing *Thoughts on the Education of Daughters* (1787) (see EDUCATION, LITERATURE OF), she went to Ireland as governess to Lord Kingsborough's children; she returned in 1788 and spent some years writing reviews and translations for the radical publisher J. *Johnson, who published her novel *Mary* (1788), her *A Vindication of the Rights of Men* (1790, a reply to *Burke), and her most famous work, *A Vindication of the Rights of Woman* (1792). During these years she met the members of Johnson's circle, which included W. *Godwin, *Holcroft, and *Fuseli. In 1792 she went to Paris, where she met Gilbert Imlay, an American writer, by whom she had a daughter, Fanny, in 1794; in the same year she published her 'View' of the French Revolution. In 1795 she travelled through Scandinavia, accompanied by her maid and her daughter, a journey which produced her remarkable and observant travel book *Letters Written during a Short Residence in Sweden, Norway and Denmark*, published by Johnson in Jan. 1796. She returned to London later in 1795, where Imlay's neglect drove her to two suicide attempts; she reintroduced herself in 1796 to Godwin, and in 1797 she married him. She died from septicaemia shortly after the birth of her daughter, the future Mary *Shelley. Godwin published a memoir in 1798, edited her *Posthumous Works* (which included her unfinished novel *Maria*) in the same year, and portrayed her in his novel *St Leon* (1799). See C. *Tomalin, *The Life and Death of Mary Wollstonecraft* (1974); *A Short Residence*, published with Godwin's *Memoirs*, ed. R. *Holmes (1987); *The Works*, ed. Janet Todd and Marilyn Butler (1989).

Wolsey, The Life and Death of Cardinal, see CAVENDISH, G.

Woman in the Moone, The, a prose play by *Lyly, published 1597. The shepherds of Utopia ask Nature to provide a woman to comfort their 'sole estate'. Nature creates Pandora, endowing her with the qualities of the Seven Planets. Pandora's moods and actions vary as the planets in turn assume the ascendant, with consequent complications among the shepherds.

Woman in White, The, a novel by Wilkie *Collins, published 1860.

The narrative, related in succession by Walter Hartright and other characters in the story, starts with his midnight encounter on a lonely road with a mysterious and agitated woman dressed entirely in white, whom he helps to escape from pursuers. When working as a drawing master in the family of Mr Fairlie, a selfish valetudinarian, he falls in love with his niece Laura, who strikingly resembles the woman in white. She returns his love, but is engaged to Sir Percival Glyde, whom she marries. It comes to light that Sir Percival, whose affairs are embarrassed, has married Laura to get possession of her wealth, that he was responsible for the confinement of the woman in white, Anne Catherick, in an asylum, and that Anne Catherick and her mother know a secret concerning Sir Percival, the revelation of which he is determined to prevent. Unable to obtain Laura's signature to the surrender of her money, Sir Percival and his friend Count Fosco (a fat, smooth villain, admirably conceived) contrive to get Laura confined in an asylum as Anne Catherick, while Anne Catherick, who dies, is buried as Laura Glyde. The device is discovered by the courage and resource of Marian Halcombe, Laura's half-sister, and Laura is rescued. Hartright, who has been abroad, returns and takes Laura and Marian under his care, and discovers Sir Percival's secret (that he was born out of wedlock and has no right to the title). Sir Percival is burnt to death while tampering with a parish register in a last effort to save his position. Fosco is forced to supply the information which restores Laura to her identity, and is killed by a member of an Italian secret society which he has betrayed.

Woman Killed with Kindness, A, a domestic tragedy by T. *Heywood, acted about 1603, printed 1607.

Frankford, a country gentleman, is the husband of Anne, a 'perfect' wife. But his happiness is ruined by the treachery of Wendoll, a guest to whom Frankford has shown every kindness and hospitality. Frankford discovers the adultery of Anne and Wendoll, but instead of taking immediate vengeance on her, he determines to 'kill her even with kindness'. He sends her to live in comfort in a lonely manor-house, only prohibiting her from seeing him or her children again. She dies from remorse, after having sent for Frankford to ask forgiveness on her deathbed and received it.

The sub-plot, in which Susan Mountford is used as a pawn to redeem her bankrupt brother from prison, but finds herself loved by her new husband, offers interesting perspectives on the main plot. The play is one of the most successful examples of English domestic tragedy.

Woman's Prize, The, or *The Tamer Tamed*, a comedy by J. *Fletcher, written 1604–?17, printed 1647. It shows the second marriage of Petruchio, from Shakespeare's *The Taming of the Shrew*; Katharine is dead, and he marries Maria, who locks him out of his house on his wedding night, and further humiliates him until he is thoroughly subdued.

Woman Who Did, The, see ALLEN, G.

Women Beware Women, a tragedy by T. *Middleton, published 1657, 30 years after his death; a composition date has not been established.

Set in Florence, the action involves two interwoven plots. The sub-plot is concerned with the guilty love of Hippolito for his niece Isabella. Hippolito's sister Livia acts as go-between, persuading Isabella she is no blood relation of her uncle: Isabella then consents to marry a foolish young heir as a screen for her own passion for Hippolito.

The main plot is loosely based on the life of the historical Bianca Cappello, who became the mistress, and then the consort, of Francesco de' Medici (1541–87), second grand duke of Tuscany. In Middleton's version, she is at the opening of the play innocently but secretly married to the poor but honest young Leantio, a merchant's clerk. The duke sees her at a window and falls in love with her: in II. ii, while Livia outwits Leantio's mother at chess (a scene invoked by T. S. *Eliot in *The Waste Land*), the duke gains access to Bianca and seduces her. Thereafter both she and Leantio are plunged into the corruption of the court, and consumed by it. Bianca becomes the duke's mistress: the duke, reproved by the cardinal, his brother, for his sin, contrives the death of Leantio, who has sworn everlasting enmity to Bianca, and accepted both financial and amorous compensation for her loss. These various crimes, in the last act, meet with retribution in a wholesale massacre of the characters, through the theatrical medium of a masque accompanied by poisoned incense: Bianca destroys herself by drinking deliberately from a poisoned cup.

Women in Love, a novel by D. H. *Lawrence, published in London 1921.

The sisters Ursula and Gudrun Brangwen (who first appeared in *The Rainbow*) live in Beldover, a Midlands colliery town. Ursula has been teaching for some years at the grammar school and Gudrun has just returned from art school in London. Ursula is in love with Rupert Birkin (a self-portrait of Lawrence), a school inspector involved in an unsatisfactory affair with Hermione Roddice, an eccentric and dominating literary hostess. Gudrun meets Gerald Crich, friend of Birkin and son of the local colliery owner. As a boy Gerald has accidentally killed his brother and now he feels responsible when his sister Diana is drowned. His father Walter is dying and he takes over management of the mine, his ruthless efficiency being both feared and respected by the miners; but with Gudrun he becomes increasingly helpless. Birkin breaks free from Hermione and her demanding love and hopes to find with Ursula the complete union between man and woman in which he believes. Gerald suffers in his relationship with Gudrun, his mixture of violence and weakness arousing a destructive demon in her. Birkin recognizes an emptiness in Gerald, and offers him love and friendship to be based on a new intimacy between men, but Gerald is unable to accept. Ursula and Birkin are married and together with Gudrun and Gerald they take a trip to the Alps where they meet the corrupt sculptor Loerke, the 'wizard rat', with whom Gudrun flirts. While Ursula and Birkin move towards a real tenderness and fulfilment the relationship between Gudrun and Gerald becomes purely destructive until finally, in blankness and despair, Gerald wanders off into the snow and dies. Lawrence completed *Women in Love* in 1916 but was unable to find a publisher until 1920 in the USA and the following year in London where it was described by a reviewer as an 'analytical study of sexual depravity' and an 'epic of vice'. Lawrence himself thought it his best book.

Women's Press, the, see FEMINIST CRITICISM.

women's suffrage. The campaign for women's suffrage began in 1866 when a group of women presented a petition to J. S. *Mill requesting female enfranchisement. Mill moved an amendment to the *Reform Act of 1867 to include women, which was defeated. Thereafter organizations sprang up all over the country and joined forces to form the National Union of Women's Suffrage Societies (NUWSS). Owing to their agitation and to that of the female textile workers, by the end of the century a majority of MPs had pledged themselves to vote for women's suffrage bills, which passed their second readings three times only to be blocked by governments.

To invigorate the campaign Mrs Emmeline Pankhurst (1858–1928) founded in 1903 the Women's Social and Political Union (WSPU), and her daughter Christabel (1880–1958) in 1905 initiated mildly militant tactics, designed to make the incoming Liberals take the women's demand seriously. Because of their youthfulness militants were known as suffragettes, and members of the NUWSS, led by Millicent Garrett Fawcett (1847–1929), as suffragists.

In 1912, when it became evident that other means were failing to break Asquith's resistance, the Pankhursts resorted to destruction of empty property on a massive scale, which antagonized the public. The war brought the campaign virtually to an end; women's patriotism (coupled with a fear of renewed militancy) induced Parliament in 1918 to enfranchise women over 30, provided they occupied or were the wives of occupiers of premises of not less than £5 annual value.

The campaign was supported by many writers; in 1908 the Women Writers Suffrage League was founded by Cicely Hamilton (1872–1952), journalist, playwright, and novelist, and journalist Bessie Hatton. Its president was Elizabeth Robins (1862–1952), who under the pseudonym 'C. E. Raimond' had written several novels; her play *Votes for Women* (1907) was highly influential. Other supporters included O. *Schreiner, M. *Sinclair, A. *Meynell, S. *Grand,

R. *West, and V. *Hunt. Suffragists and suffragettes were widely portrayed in the literature of the period: see V. *Woolf's *Night and Day*, H. G. *Wells's *Ann Veronica*, G. B. *Shaw's *Press Cuttings*, and many other works. Accounts of the movement were also written by leading feminists, including the Pankhursts and E. Pethick-Lawrence (1867–1954). It produced many periodicals, including *Women's Suffrage Journal*, the *Common Cause*, *Votes for Women*, and *Women's Dreadnought*.

WOOD, Anthony, or, as he latterly called himself, Anthony à Wood (1632–95), historian and antiquary, educated at New College School, Oxford, Thame School, and Merton College, Oxford. He prepared a treatise on the history of the University of Oxford, which was translated into Latin and edited (with alterations) by *Fell and published as *Historia et Antiquitates Univ. Oxon.* (1674). Of this an English version by Wood, issued by John Gutch, is the standard edition. He received much ill-acknowledged help from *Aubrey. Wood published *Athenae Oxonienses* (1691–2), a biographical dictionary of Oxford writers and bishops, containing severe judgements on some of these, and was expelled from the university in 1693 at the instance of Henry Hyde, for a libel which the work contained on his father, the first earl of *Clarendon. Several antiquarian manuscripts left by Wood were published posthumously. His *Life and Times*, ed. A. Clark, occupy five volumes of the Oxford Historical Society's publications (1891–1900) in which series, also edited by Clark, appeared his *History of the City of Oxford* (3 vols, 1889–99).

WOOD, Ellen, née Price, better known as Mrs Henry Wood (1814–87), daughter of a glove manufacturer. She lived till her marriage at Worcester, whose neighbourhood she used as the background for her *Johnny Ludlow* short story series (1868–89). In 1836 she married Henry Wood, a banker, and lived in the Dauphiné till she returned in 1856 to spend the rest of her life in London. She had an immense success with her first novel *East Lynne* (1861), a celebrated example of the novel of *sensation. She subsequently owned and edited the magazine the *Argosy*, and wrote nearly 40 novels, among the best of which are *Mrs Halliburton's Troubles* (1862), *The Channings* (1862), and *The Shadow of Ashlydyat* (1863). Her ingenious plots about murders, thefts, and forgeries, her numerous court scenes and well-planted clues, make her in such novels as *Lord Oakburn's Daughters* (1864), *Elster's Folly* (1866), and *Roland Yorke* (1869) one of the forerunners of the modern *detective story. The sensational, and occasionally supernatural, events in her novels are presented in solidly detailed settings of middle-class country-town communities of doctors and lawyers, bankers and manufacturers. She often used industrial and trade union problems—slumps, unemployment, strikes—in her novels; her hostile description of a strike in *A Life's Secret* (1867) caused her publisher's office to be besieged by an angry mob. In spite of a commonplace style and a strong element of moralizing, many of her novels were world best-sellers, outstripping even *Dickens in Australian sales. *East Lynne* was repeatedly dramatized and filmed, and translated into many languages, from Welsh to Hindustani. See C. W. Wood, *Memorials of Mrs Henry Wood* (1894).

Woodcourt, Allan, a character in Dickens's *Bleak House.*

WOODFORDE, the Revd James (1740–1803), fellow of New College, Oxford. He held curacies in Somerset, then was rector of Weston Longeville, Norfolk, from 1774 (in residence from 1776) until his death. His diary, known as *The Diary of a Country Parson* (5 vols, ed. J. Beresford, 1924–31), was published in extracts, and covers the period of the American War of Independence and the French Revolution, but in the main the life he describes is matter-of-fact, concerned with local friends, minor travels, and daily events. His love of food and drink is recorded in frequent descriptions of meals ('Fowls boiled, Rabbitts smothered in onions', etc.). He is uninterested in literary matters, or in landscape and the natural world (though he writes of agricultural matters). The prose is not distinguished, and the abiding popularity of the work is due more to its social interest and period charm than to its literary qualities.

Woodhouse, Mr, the heroine's father in J. Austen's *Emma.*

Woodlanders, The, a novel by T. *Hardy, published 1887.

The scene is set in Little Hintock, a village deep in the woods of Dorset. In this luxuriant woodland country, lovingly described, live a group of native woodlanders, whose living depends upon trees, and certain outsiders with whom their lives become entwined. Giles Winterbourne, who tends trees and travels in the autumn with his cider-press, loves and is betrothed to Grace Melbury, daughter of a well-to-do Hintock timber merchant. But when she returns from her finishing school she appears as the social superior of Giles. At about the same time Giles suffers financial misfortune, and these facts together induce Grace's father to bring the engagement to an end and to press his daughter into marriage with Edred Fitzpiers, a handsome and attractive young doctor who has settled nearby. Meanwhile Marty South, a village girl who had always loved Giles, has to sell her splendid hair to help herself and her sick father to live. Fitzpiers is soon lured away from Grace by a wealthy widow, Felice Charmond, who has come to live in the great house. The hope of divorce brings Grace and the faithful Giles together again. But the hope is illusory, and when Fitzpiers returns from his travels with Mrs Charmond Grace flies for refuge to Giles's cottage in the woods. Not wishing to offend her by remaining in the cottage, Giles, although ill, makes

for himself a shelter of hurdles: Grace discovers his condition, drags him back into his hut, and fetches Fitzpiers to assist her, but despite their efforts Giles dies. The loving, faithful Marty meets Grace by Giles's deathbed, and together they regularly visit his burial-place. With Mrs Charmond's death Grace and Fitzpiers are reconciled, and Marty is left alone to tend Giles's grave.

Writing to a friend in 1912, Hardy said of *The Woodlanders,* 'I think I like it, *as a story,* the best of all.'

Woodstock; or, *The Cavalier. A Tale of the Year 1651,* a novel by Sir W. *Scott, published 1826. The work was written when misfortunes were heaping themselves upon the author: his financial ruin, the death of his wife, and the serious illness of his beloved grandson; and there are clear parallels between the situation of Sir Henry Lee and himself. Incredibly, thus situated, he has produced an outstanding novel. Set in the Civil War, the novel centres on the escape from England of Charles II after the battle of Worcester. The scene is laid in the royal lodge and park of Woodstock, of which the old Cavalier, Sir Henry Lee, is ranger. His nephew Everard Markham, who, to his uncle's displeasure, has taken the Parliamentarian side, is in love with Lee's daughter Alice. Charles arrives, disguised as the page of Lee's son Colonel Albert Lee. The climax, when Cromwell arrives to capture the king, and discovers that he has escaped, results first in Cromwell's ordering the execution of all his prisoners, down to Sir Henry's wolfhound, and then, more generously, in his pardoning them.

WOOLF, Leonard Sidney (1880–1969), author, Fabian, and social reformer, the second son of a Jewish barrister who died in 1892. He was educated at St Paul's, then at Trinity College, Cambridge, where he became a member of the *Apostles and was much influenced by G. E. *Moore. He entered the colonial service and in 1904 went to Ceylon, which was to form the background for his first novel, *The Village in the Jungle* (1913), a sympathetic study of the difficulties and dangers of rural life, threatened by superstition, drought, disease, and the encroaching jungle: the effect of imperial government is shown as minimal. Woolf returned to England on leave in 1911, and in 1912 left the colonial service to marry Virginia Stephen (see below). After the publication of his second and last novel, *The Wise Virgins* (1914), he devoted himself to social studies, journalism, and political writing, although he and his wife continued to share a close intellectual comradeship and a commitment to the *Hogarth Press; her delicate mental health exacted constant care and attention, but despite this his energy and output remained impressive. He wrote on the Co-operative movement, socialism, imperialism, the League of Nations, and international affairs, was literary editor of the *Nation* (1923–30), and co-founder and joint editor of the *Political Quarterly* (1931–59). *After the Deluge* (2 vols, 1931 and 1939) and *Principia*

Politica (1953) were his most sustained attempt to formulate a political philosophy, but the five volumes of his autobiography, written after his wife's death, reached a wider audience: *Sowing* (1960), *Growing* (1961), *Beginning Again* (1964), *Downhill All the Way* (1967), and *The Journey Not the Arrival Matters* (1969) together constitute a clear-sighted view of a life devoted to social progress and international understanding, and rich in intellectual and literary friendships. See D. Wilson, *Leonard Woolf: A Political Biography* (1978) for an account of Woolf's political thought and writings.

WOOLF, (Adeline) Virginia (1882–1941), daughter of Leslie *Stephen and Julia Duckworth (1847–95), born at Hyde Park Gate, where she lived with her sister Vanessa (later Vanessa *Bell) and her brothers until her father's death in 1904. The Stephen children then moved to Bloomsbury, where they formed the nucleus of the *Bloomsbury Group. In 1905 she began to write for the *Times Literary Supplement*, a connection which lasted almost until her death. In 1912 she married Leonard *Woolf; she was already working on her first novel, *The Voyage Out*, published in 1915. Realistic in form but already foreshadowing the lyric intensity of her later work, it describes the voyage to South America of a young Englishwoman, Rachel Vinrace; her engagement there to Terence Hewet; and her subsequent fever and rapid death. Virginia herself had meanwhile experienced one of the bouts of acute mental disturbance from which she had suffered since her mother's death, and it was partly as therapy for her that she and Leonard founded, in 1917, the *Hogarth Press; its first production was *Two Stories*, one by each of them. Her second novel, also realistic, *Night and Day* (1919), set in London, centres on Katherine Hilbery, daughter of a famous literary family (modelled on Vanessa), whose pursuits are contrasted with her friend Mary's involvement with *women's suffrage. *Jacob's Room* (1922), a novel evoking the life and death (in the First World War) of Jacob Flanders (clearly related to the death of her brother Thoby in 1906), was recognized as a new development in the art of fiction, in its indirect narration and poetic impressionism; it was hailed by friends such as T. S. *Eliot ('you have freed yourself from any compromise between the traditional novel and your original gift') and attacked by, e.g., J. M. *Murry for its lack of plot. Shortly afterwards she published one of her important statements on modern fiction, 'Mr Bennett and Mrs Brown', in the *Nation and Athenaeum*, 1 Dec. 1923 (afterwards revised and reprinted in various forms), which attacked the realism of Arnold *Bennett and advocated a more fluid, internal approach to the problem of characterization, etc. From this time onwards she was regarded as one of the principal exponents of *Modernism, and her subsequent major novels, *Mrs Dalloway* (1925), *To the Lighthouse* (1927), and *The Waves* (1931), established her reputation securely. The

intensity of her creative work was accompanied by mental suffering and ill health, but she was able to intersperse her more serious works with more playful productions, such as *Orlando* (1928), a fantastic biography inspired by her friend V. *Sackville-West, which traces the history of the youthful, beautiful, and aristocratic Orlando through four centuries and both male and female manifestations; *Flush* (1933), a slighter work, is the 'biography' of E. B. *Browning's spaniel. *The Years* (1937) is in form a more conventional novel, whereas her last work, *Between the Acts* (1941), is again highly experimental. It was shortly after finishing it, and before its publication, that the last of her attacks of mental illness led to her drowning herself in the Ouse, near her home at Rodmell, Sussex.

Virginia Woolf is now acclaimed as one of the great innovative novelists of the 20th cent., many of whose experimental techniques (such as the use of the *stream of consciousness, or interior monologue) have been absorbed into the mainstream of fiction; her novels have been particularly highly regarded from the 1970s onwards by the new school of *feminist criticism. She was also a literary critic and journalist of distinction. *A Room of One's Own* (1929) is a classic of the feminist movement; a sequel, *Three Guineas* (1938), articulates Woolf's view that tyranny at home, within patriarchy, is connected to tyranny abroad. Her critical essays were published in several collections, including *The Common Reader* (1925; 2nd series, 1932), and the posthumous *The Death of the Moth* (1942), *The Captain's Death Bed* (1950), and *Granite and Rainbow* (1958). A volume of short stories, *A Haunted House* (1943), collects earlier stories and some not previously published. She was also a tireless letter writer and diarist. Her letters (ed. Nigel Nicolson and J. Trautmann, 6 vols, 1975–80) are a dazzling, at times malicious evocation of a world of literary and social friendships and intrigues, with a cast list that includes *Strachey, the *Sitwells, Ottoline *Morrell, R. *Fry, and many others; her diaries (5 vols, ed. Anne Olivier Bell and A. McNeillie, 1977–84) are a unique record of the joys and pains of the creative process. See also *Virginia Woolf* (2 vols, 1972), a biography by her nephew Quentin Bell; *Deceived with Kindness* (1984), a poignant memoir by her niece Angelica Bell; and *Virginia Woolf* (1996) by Hermione Lee.

WOOLMAN, John (1720–72), American Quaker, who travelled during many years preaching the faith, and both wrote and spoke against slavery. He is best remembered for his *Journal* (1774), notable for its purity and simplicity of style. *Lamb wrote, 'Get the writings of John Woolman by heart, and love the early Quakers.'

WOOLNER, Thomas (1825–92), poet and sculptor, one of the original *Pre-Raphaelite brethren, who contributed to the *Germ* two cantos of what was to become *My Beautiful Lady* (1863). At first he met with small success as a sculptor, and in 1852 sailed for the Australian gold fields (his departure inspiring Ford Madox Brown's picture *The Last of England*), but returned in 1854 and became a prosperous portrait sculptor, doing busts and statues of (among many others) *Tennyson, *Newman, C. *Kingsley, and J. S. *Mill. His other poems include the blank verse *Pygmalion* (1881). 'The Piping Shepherd', which appears as a frontispiece to *Palgrave's *Golden Treasury*, is by him.

Wooster, Bertram (familiarly known as 'Bertie'), an amiable, vacuous young man-about-town in the stories of P. G. *Wodehouse; the employer of *Jeeves.

Wopsle, Mr, in Dickens's *Great Expectations*, a parish clerk who turns actor and plays Hamlet with indifferent success.

WORDE, Wynkyn de (d. 1535), printer from Wörth in Alsace, probably met *Caxton in Cologne and was brought by him to London in 1476. He was Caxton's principal assistant until his death in 1491/2 whereupon de Worde succeeded to the printing business which he managed until his death, moving it to Fleet Street. He printed many important literary works in the 1490s, and the catalogue of his works is evidence of bibliographical demand between 1490 and 1535: for instance he sometimes printed several editions of the same grammar in a single year. See H. R. Plomer, *Wynkyn de Worde and His Contemporaries* (1925); J. Moran, *Wynkyn de Worde* (Wynkyn de Worde Society, 1960).

WORDSWORTH, Dorothy (1771–1855), the sister of William *Wordsworth and his treasured companion throughout their adult lives. After an unsettled and partly orphaned childhood, away from her three brothers, Dorothy settled with William in 1795, and from that time they lived together, through William's marriage until his death. After a short time in Dorset they moved to Alfoxden in Somerset, to be near *Coleridge at Nether Stowey. Here in 1798, when she, William, and Coleridge walked and talked, as Coleridge wrote, 'as three persons with one soul', she began her first journal. This was the *Alfoxden Journal*, but the manuscript has disappeared and only the months Jan.–Apr. 1798 remain. It is, however, valuable, not only for its close description of the Quantocks and the sea, but for the revelation of the companionship of the three friends in the heady year of the *Lyrical Ballads*. In 1799 William and Dorothy moved to Dove Cottage at Grasmere in the Lake District. The *Grasmere Journal* covers the years 1800–3 and was begun 'because I shall give William pleasure by it'. The entries are again filled with her love of landscape, season, walking, and weather; her skill with words is evident in the precise descriptions both of the world about them and of the daily events of life in Dove Cottage.

Dorothy kept several other journals of travels and expeditions, which also were not published until after her death. She wrote a brief Journal of a *Visit to Hamburgh and a Journey . . . to Goslar 1798–99*. In 1805 she finished *Recollections of a Tour Made in Scotland 1803*, which exists in five manuscripts; the earlier, less formal, versions vividly describe the wild countryside and weather, the tremulous horse, the uneatable oatcake, and the wet sheets. (Coleridge, overwhelmed, abandoned the expedition at Loch Long.) Her spirited accounts of *An Excursion on the Banks of Ullswater 1805* and *An Excursion up Scawfell Pike 1818* were both used by Wordsworth in his *Guide to the Lakes* (1823). A long *Journal of a Tour on the Continent 1820* conveys her intoxication with, especially, Switzerland, and the rubs of life on the road with William. A sprightly *Journal of a Second Tour in Scotland* followed in 1822, and a *Journal of a Tour in the Isle of Man* in 1828.

It is clear from passages in his notes and from certain of his poems (for instance, the untitled 'Daffodils') that Wordsworth made use of his sister's journals. Coleridge seems also to have used the Alfoxden journal for certain passages in *'Christabel'. Several of Wordsworth's poems, as well as the famous closing lines of *'Tintern Abbey', are addressed to Dorothy, including 'The Glow Worm', 'Ode to Lycoris', and 'To the Same'. Dorothy died, after many years of illness and senility, from arteriosclerosis. In his life (1933) her editor Ernest de Selincourt finds her 'probably . . . the most distinguished of English writers who never wrote a line for the general public'.

WORDSWORTH, William (1770–1850), born at Cockermouth, Cumbria, the son of an attorney; he attended (with Mary Hutchinson, his future wife) the infants' school in Penrith and, from 1779 to 1787, Hawkshead Grammar School. His mother died in 1778, his father in 1783, losses recorded in *The Prelude*, which describes the mixed joys and terrors of his country boyhood with a peculiar intensity. He attended St John's College, Cambridge, but disliked the academic course. In 1790 he went on a walking tour of France, the Alps, and Italy, and returned to France late in 1791, to spend a year there; during this period he was fired by a passionate belief in the French Revolution and republican ideals, and also fell in love with the daughter of a surgeon at Blois, Annette Vallon, who bore him a daughter (see E. Legouis, *William Wordsworth and Annette Vallon*, 1922). (This love affair is reflected in 'Vaudracour and Julia', composed ?1804, published 1820, and incorporated somewhat anomalously in Book IX of *The Prelude*.) After his return to England he published in 1793 two poems in heroic couplets, *An Evening Walk* and *Descriptive Sketches*, both conventional attempts at the *picturesque and the *sublime, the latter describing the Alps. In this year he also wrote (but did not publish) a *Letter to the Bishop of Llandaff* (see WATSON, R.) in support of the French Republic. England's declaration of war against France shocked him deeply, but the institution of the Terror marked the beginning of his disillusion with the French Revolution, a period of depression reflected in his verse drama *The

Borderers (composed 1796–7, pub. 1842) and in 'Guilt and Sorrow' (composed 1791–4, pub. in part in 1798 as 'The Female Vagrant'). In 1795 he received a legacy of £900 from his friend Raisley Calvert, intended to enable him to pursue his vocation as a poet, which also allowed him to be reunited with his sister Dorothy (above); they settled first at Racedown in Dorset, then at Alfoxden in Somerset, where they had charge of the son of their friend Basil *Montagu. The latter move (aided by T. *Poole) was influenced by a desire to be near *Coleridge, then living at Nether Stowey, whom Wordsworth had met in 1795. This was a period of intense creativity for both poets, which produced the *Lyrical Ballads* (1798), a landmark in the history of English *Romanticism. (See ANCIENT MARINER; IDIOT BOY, THE; TINTERN ABBEY.) The winter of 1798–9 was spent in Goslar in Germany, where Wordsworth wrote sections of what was to be *The Prelude* and the enigmatic *'Lucy' poems. In 1799 he and Dorothy settled in Dove Cottage, Grasmere; to the next year belong 'The Recluse', Book I (later *The Excursion*), 'The Brothers', *'Michael', and many of the poems included in the 1800 edition of the *Lyrical Ballads* (which, with its provocative preface on *poetic diction, aroused much criticism). In 1802 Wordsworth and Dorothy visited Annette Vallon in France, and later that year William married Mary Hutchinson, his financial position having been improved by the repayment of a debt on the death of Lord Lonsdale. In the same year he composed *'Resolution and Independence', and began his ode on *'Intimations of Immortality from Recollections of Early Childhood', both of which appeared in *Poems in Two Volumes* (1807), along with many of his most celebrated lyrics. To the same period belong the birth of five children (of whom the eldest, John, was born in 1803), travels with Dorothy and Coleridge, and new friendships, notably with Sir W. *Scott, Sir G. *Beaumont, and *De Quincey. Wordsworth's domestic happiness was overcast by the death of his sailor brother John in 1805 (which inspired several poems, including 'Elegiac Stanzas Suggested by a Picture of Peele Castle', 1807), the early deaths of two of his children (one of which inspired his sonnet 'Surprised by joy', 1815), and the physical deterioration of Coleridge, from whom he was for some time estranged, and with whom he was never entirely reconciled. But his productivity continued, and his popularity gradually increased. *The Excursion* was published in 1814, *The White Doe of Rylstone* and two volumes of *Miscellaneous Poems* in 1815, and *Peter Bell* and *The Waggoner* in 1819. In 1813 he had been appointed stamp distributor for Westmorland, a post which brought him some £400 a year, and in the same year moved from Allan Bank (where he had lived from 1808) to Rydal Mount, Ambleside, where he lived the rest of his life. The great work of his early and middle years was now over, and Wordsworth slowly settled into the role of patriotic, conservative public man, abandoning the radical politics and idealism of his

youth. Much of the best of his later work was mildly topographical, inspired by his love of travel; it records journeys to Scotland, along the river Duddon, to the Continent, etc. He was left a legacy by Sir George Beaumont in 1827, and in 1842 received a Civil List pension of £300 a year; in 1843 he succeeded *Southey as *poet laureate. He died at Rydal Mount, after the publication of a finally revised text of his works (6 vols, 1849–50), and *The Prelude* was published posthumously in 1850. His prose works include an essay, *Concerning the Relations of Great Britain, Spain and Portugal . . . as Affected by the Convention of Cintra* (1809), castigating the supine English policy, and *A Description of the Scenery of the Lakes in the North of England*, written in 1810 as an introduction to Wilkinson's *Select Views of Cumberland*.

De Quincey wrote of Wordsworth in 1835, 'Up to 1820 the name of Wordsworth was trampled underfoot; from 1820 to 1830 it was militant; from 1830 to 1835 it has been triumphant.' Early attacks in the *Edinburgh Review* and by the anonymous author of a parody, *The Simpliciad* (1808), were followed by criticism and satire by the second generation of Romantics; *Byron and *Shelley mocked him as 'simple' and 'dull', *Keats distrusted what he called the *'egotistical sublime', and *Hazlitt, and later *Browning, deplored him as *'The Lost Leader', who had abandoned his early radical faith. But these doubts were counterbalanced by the enormous and lasting popularity of much of his work, which was regarded by writers such as M. *Arnold and J. S. *Mill with almost religious veneration, as an expression in an age of doubt of the transcendent in nature and the good in man. A great innovator, he permanently enlarged the range of English poetry, both in subject matter and in treatment (a distinction he would not himself have accepted).

Wordsworth's *Poetical and Prose Works*, together with Dorothy Wordsworth's *Journals*, ed. W. Knight, appeared in 1896, and his *Poetical Works* (ed. E. de Selincourt and H. Darbishire, 5 vols) in 1940–9 and 1952–4. *Letters of the Wordsworth Family 1787–1855* were edited by W. Knight in 1907, and *Letters of William and Dorothy Wordsworth* (ed. de Selincourt) appeared in 1935–9. His biography by M. Moorman was published in 1968 (2 vols), and a long-lost collection of letters between Mary and William appeared as *The Love Letters of William and Mary Wordsworth*, ed. B. Darlington (1982). See also Stephen Gill, *William Wordsworth* (1989).

Workers' Educational Association, a movement founded in 1903 by Albert Mansbridge (1876–1952) to promote 'the Higher Education of Working Men', which soon received recognition from most universities. It provided tutorial classes (one of the pioneer tutors being R. H. *Tawney), and continues its work today, providing day and evening classes for democratically organized voluntary groups, with courses worked out in partnership between tutor and students.

World, by 'Adam Fitz-Adam', a weekly 'paper of entertainment', owned by R. *Dodsley, and edited by E. *Moore. It ran from 1753 to 1756, and its contributors included *Chesterfield, Horace *Walpole, and *Jenyns.

Worldly Wiseman, Mr, in Bunyan's *Pilgrim's Progress*, an inhabitant of the town of Carnal Policy, who tries to dissuade *Christian from going on his pilgrimage.

World's Classics, the, a series of cheap reprints of standard works of English literature, launched in 1901 by G. *Richards; its first titles included *Jane Eyre*, *The Vicar of Wakefield*, and *Barham's *The Ingoldsby Legends*, and the spine decoration of the series was designed by L. *Housman. In 1905 the series was bought by Henry Frowde for the *Oxford University Press; he introduced pocket editions on thin paper and by 1907 the ordinary edition was available in eight different styles, at prices ranging from 1s. to 5s. 6d. The series (which includes some translations, e.g. of *Tolstoy, *Montaigne, and others) was relaunched in paperback in 1980 and rebranded as Oxford World's Classics in 1998.

World Wide Web (www), a global *hypertext medium based on the Internet, invented in 1990 by Tim Berners-Lee. Viewed on a computer screen, Web pages range in appearance from plain text to complex colour graphics. Links may be followed from page to page. Search engines will locate pages containing specified words or phrases. Information can be found rapidly by a combination of these methods. A fast, cheap publishing medium less permanent than print, the Web carries a mixture of scholarly, personal, and social traffic.

Worthies of England, *The History of the*, by T. *Fuller, published 1662, after his death.

The work is a kind of gazetteer of England, in which the author takes the counties one by one, describes their physical characteristics, natural commodities, and manufactures, with comments on each, some his own aphorisms ('Knives . . . are the teeth of old men'), some proverbial ('Bean-belly Leicestershire, so called from the great plenty of that grain growing therein'). After these come short biographies of the local saints, Protestant martyrs, prelates, statesmen, writers, etc., and lists of the gentry and sheriffs. This work (which was used without acknowledgement by A. *Wood) is the source of many well-known anecdotes, such as that of *Ralegh laying his cloak for the queen in 'a plashy place'.

Worthies of the World, the Nine, 'three Paynims, three Jews, and three Christian men', namely Hector of Troy, Alexander the Great, and Julius Caesar; Joshua, David, and Judas Maccabaeus; Arthur, Charlemagne, and

Godefroi de *Bouillon (Caxton, preface to *Le *Morte D'Arthur*.) The list of worthies in Shakespeare's *Love's Labour's Lost*, v. ii, is not quite the same, for it includes Pompey and Hercules.

WOTTON, Sir Henry (1568–1639), educated at Winchester and New and Queen's colleges, Oxford, where he became a close friend of *Donne. He entered the Middle Temple, then became agent and secretary to the earl of Essex, 1595, and was employed by him in collecting foreign intelligence. He was ambassador at the court of Venice and employed on various other diplomatic missions from 1604 to 1624. While on a visit to Augsburg he wrote in his host's album his famous definition of an ambassador, 'vir bonus peregre missus ad mentiendum Reipublicae causa', 'which he would have been content should have been thus englished "An Ambassador is an honest man, sent to lie abroad for the good of his country" ' (I. *Walton); Scioppius mentioned this in his printed diatribe against James I (1611). Wotton was provost of Eton, 1624–39. He published *Elements of Architecture* (1624). A collection of his poetical and other writings appeared under the title *Reliquiae Wottonianae*, containing his famous 'Character of a Happy Life' and 'On His Mistress, the Queen of Bohemia' ('You meaner beauties of the night') in 1651 (enlarged edns, 1672, 1685). His life was written by his friend Izaak Walton (1651). His poems appeared in J. Hannah's edition *The Courtly Poets from Raleigh to Montrose* (1870) and *Life and Letters*, by L. Pearsall *Smith, appeared in 1907.

Would-be, Sir Politic and Lady, the foolish traveller and his garrulous wife in Jonson's *Volpone*.

Wrayburn, Eugene, a character in Dickens's *Our Mutual Friend*.

'Wreck of the Deutschland, The', a poem by G. M. *Hopkins occasioned by the shipwreck in Dec. 1875 of a German transatlantic steamer off the Kentish coast. Among the dead were five Franciscan sisters from Westphalia; the poem identifies them as victims of Bismarck's anti-Catholic 'Falk' laws, which forced many into exile. The complex, two-part poem juxtaposes the extraordinary bravery and Christian witness of the 'tall nun' ('a prophetess towered in the tumult, a virginal tongue told') with the situation of the speaker, 'way in the loveable west, | On a pastoral forehead of Wales', who has also experienced his master's 'lightning and lashed rod'. Ultimately the speaker reconciles the terrible deaths in the 'widow-making unchilding unfathering deeps' with Christ's sacrifice and God's providence. When Hopkins joined the Society of Jesus in 1868, his scruples precluded writing poetry; in 1875, when his rector suggested that 'someone should write a poem on the subject' of the *Deutschland* catastrophe, Hopkins seized the opportunity. The text experiments with a new metric he 'long had haunting [his] ear', *sprung rhythm. The *Month*, a Jesuit journal, would not publish the poem in 1876; R. *Bridges included it in the 1918 edition of Hopkins's poetry, but cautioned readers about 'the dragon at the gate'. Some critics consider 'The Wreck' an *ode.

WREN, Sir Christopher (1632–1723), son of Christopher Wren, dean of Windsor, 1635–58, educated at Westminster School and Wadham College, Oxford. He was a prominent member of the circle of scholars who later were founder members of the *Royal Society. With them he studied anatomy, mathematics, and astronomy, being appointed professor of anatomy at Gresham College, London, in 1657 and Savilian professor of astronomy at Oxford in 1661. His first architectural works were the chapel of Pembroke College, Cambridge (1663–5), and the Sheldonian Theatre, Oxford (1664–9). A few days after the Fire of London in 1666, he presented a plan for rebuilding the City, but it was not adopted. He was, however, made surveyor in charge of the City churches, and designed 52 of them. He had prepared a scheme for repairing St Paul's before the fire, and when it became clear in 1668 that it must be rebuilt he prepared designs: work began on the new building in 1675 and it was finished in 1710. Wren also designed many other buildings, including the library of Trinity College, Cambridge, and Tom Tower, Christ Church, Oxford. *Parentalia, or Memories of the Family of the Wrens* (1750) is a collection of family documents made by Wren's son Christopher.

Wren, Jenny, the business name of the doll's dressmaker in Dickens's *Our Mutual Friend.* Her real name was Fanny Cleaver.

WREN, P(ercival) C(hristopher) (1885–1941), born in Devon and educated at Oxford. He had a varied and much-travelled life, working at one time as a member of the French Foreign Legion, and later for some years in India as assistant director of education. His first book of stories, *Dew and Mildew* (1912), was set in India, but he did not achieve popular success until the publication of *Beau Geste* (1924), the first of his Foreign Legion novels, a romantic adventure story which became a best-seller, and which was followed by *Beau Sabreur* (1926), *Beau Ideal* (1928), etc.

WRIGHT, David (1920–94), poet, born in Johannesburg, who lost his hearing at the age of 7. He was educated at Oriel College, Oxford, and subsequently lived in London, Cornwall, and the Lake District. His volumes of poetry include *Poems* (1949), which appeared in Tambimuttu's *Poetry London* imprint: he himself was a founder editor of the quarterly review *X*, 1959–62. He also published translations of *Beowulf* (1957) and *The Canterbury Tales* (1964). *Deafness: A Personal Account* was published in 1969.

WRIGHT, Joseph, of Derby (1734–97), English painter, who worked mainly in Derby. Wright's subjects are novel—scientific experiments, industrial activity—and he was celebrated for effects of light—candlelight, moonlight, the flames of a forge, the windows of a mill

at night. Wright was patronized by J. *Wedgwood and Arkwright, and his works reflect the scientific curiosity that dominated intellectual life in the industrial Midlands. He was a friend of E. *Darwin, whose poem *The Botanic Garden* is close in subject and feeling to Wright's pictures; painter and poet move easily from modern engineering to classical allegory. In the 1770s and 1780s Wright, a friend of W. *Hayley, began to choose his subjects from literature; he was attracted by the macabre and by the Romantic melancholy of contemporary literature. He painted scenes from Shakespeare, *Milton, and from contemporary writers, including *Beattie, *Sterne, and *Langhorne. *The Dead Soldier*, from Langhorne, became a highly popular engraving.

WRIGHT, Joseph (1855–1930), lexicographer and philologist, of working-class Yorkshire origins and largely self-educated; editor (1891–1905) of the *English Dialect Dictionary* (published at his own expense) and author of the *English Dialect Grammar* (1905) and several primers and grammars of Old and Middle English, Old and Middle High German, and Gothic; his wife Elizabeth Mary Wright was his collaborator in several of his works.

WRIGHT, Judith (1915–2000), Australian poet, brought up in New South Wales. Her first book, *The Moving Image* (1946), made her reputation, which has been enhanced through more than a dozen later volumes, most recently the *Collected Poems* of 1994. From the beginning, her poems have been shapely in form, lyrical and meditative, concerned with love (as in her classic 'Woman to Man'), and with the rural and wild landscapes of Australia. Since the 1960s she was much involved with the conservation movement and its political implications: this resulted in a sharper, more combative tone, angry with what she saw as white Australia's betrayal of the Aborigines in matters of landownership and spiritual inheritance.

WRIGHT, Kit (1944–   ), poet, born in Kent, educated at Oxford; he now lives in London. Wright has been much praised as a master of light verse for his comic observations of human behaviour and his characteristic offbeat wit. His poems reveal a fascination with English eccentricity, and, as in *The Bear Looked over the Mountain* (1977), compassionate portraits of characters who are often lost, failed, or doubting their sanity. *Bump-Starting the Hearse* (1983) includes 'The Day Room', a moving sequence on life in a psychiatric ward, and both books are collected in *Poems 1974–1983* (1988). His third collection is *Short Afternoons* (1989). Wright is also a successful children's author.

WRIGHT, Richard (1908–60), black American writer, brought up in Memphis, and largely self-educated; he joined the Communist Party in the 1930s, but left in the 1940s, as he records in *The God that Failed* (1950). His best-known novels are the powerful and violent *Native*

Son (1940) and *The Outsider* (1953), both of which deal with tragedy in the lives of black victims of poverty and politics.

WRIGHT, Thomas (1810–77), educated at Trinity College, Cambridge. He was instrumental in founding the *Camden, *Percy, and Shakespeare societies. His published works, mainly on historical, literary, and antiquarian subjects, included *Biographia Literaria* (1842–6) and *A History of Domestic Manners and Sentiments in England during the Middle Ages* (1862). Among the many volumes he edited are *Queen Elizabeth and Her Times* (1838), *The Vision and the Creed of Piers Plowman* (1842), and *Anecdota Literaria* (1844).

'Wulf and Eadwacer', an Old English poem in 19 lines of varying length, one of the group called 'Elegies' from the *Exeter Book. Its theme seems to be the separation of lovers, but it is very unclear, despite its powerfully suggestive atmosphere. It is often translated by modern poets, including Craig Raine in *Rich* (1984). See also *The Old English Elegies*, ed. M. Green (1983).

WULFILA, see ULFILAS.

WULFSTAN (d. 1023), archbishop of York, author of homilies in English including the famous 'Address to the English', *Sermo Lupi ad Anglos*, in which he describes the desolation of the country brought about by the Danish raids and castigates the vices and demoralization of the people. Like his predecessor Oswald he held the sees of Worcester and York simultaneously from 1002 to his death (whereupon he was buried at Ely); this pluralism is possibly the reason why he is called *reprobus* and *impius* by some contemporary commentators. He was bishop of London in 996 and he reformed the monastery of St Peter's, Gloucester, in 1022. He had contacts with *Ælfric, with whom he shares a distinction as a writer of sermons in rhythmical, alliterative prose; only four sermons and one Pastoral Letter can be ascribed to him with any probability, on stylistic grounds. He drafted codes of laws for Ethelred from 1008 to 1015, and for Cnut (*Canute), despite his earlier deploring of the Danish raids, from his accession in 1016 to Wulfstan's death in 1023.

Ed. D. Whitelock, *Sermo Lupi ad Anglos* (1939; rev. 1963); ed. D. Bethurum, *Homilies* (1957).

Wuthering Heights, a novel by E. *Brontë, published 1847.

The story is narrated by Lockwood, temporary tenant of Thrushcross Grange, who at the opening of the novel stumbles unsuspecting into the violent world of Wuthering Heights, the home of his landlord Heathcliff. The narration is taken up by the housekeeper, Nelly Dean, who had been witness of the interlocked destinies of the original owners of the Heights, the Earnshaw family, and of the Grange, the Linton family. In a series of brilliantly handled flash-

backs and time-shifts, Emily Brontë unfolds a tale of exceptional emotional and imaginative force. Events are set in motion by the arrival at the Heights of Heathcliff, picked up as a waif of unknown parentage in the streets of Liverpool by the elder Earnshaw, who brings him home to rear as one of his own children. Bullied and humiliated after Earnshaw's death by his son Hindley, Heathcliff's passionate and ferocious nature finds its complement in Earnshaw's daughter Catherine. Their childhood collusions develop into an increasingly intense though vexed attachment, but Heathcliff, overhearing Catherine tell Nelly that she cannot marry him because it would degrade her, and failing to stay to hear her declare her passion for him, leaves the house. He returns three years later, mysteriously enriched, to find Catherine married to the insignificant Edgar Linton. Heathcliff is welcomed by Hindley, by now widowed with a son, Hareton, and a hardened gambler. Heathcliff's destructive force is now unleashed; he marries Edgar's sister Isabella and cruelly ill-treats her, hastens Catherine's death by his passion as she is about to give birth to a daughter, Cathy, and brings Hareton and Hindley under his power, brutalizing the latter in revenge for Hindley's treatment of himself as a child. Edgar Linton dies, after doing his best to prevent a friendship between Cathy and Heathcliff's son Linton; Heathcliff has lured Cathy to his house, and forces a marriage between her and young Linton in order to secure the Linton property. Young Linton, always sickly, also dies, and an affection springs up between her, an unwilling prisoner at the Heights, and the ignorant Hareton, whom she does her best to educate. Heathcliff's desire for revenge has now worn itself out, and he longs for the death that will reunite him with Catherine; at his death there is a promise that the two contrasting worlds and moral orders represented by the Heights and the Grange will be united in the next generation, in the union of Cathy and Hareton.

Early reviewers tended to dwell on the novel's morbid and painful aspects, but their neglect has been overtaken by what is now a general recognition of the mastery of an extremely complex structure, acute evocation of place, poetic grandeur of vision, and a highly original handling of *Gothic and Romantic elements inherited from lesser works.

WYATT, Sir Thomas (1503–42). He came from a Yorkshire family, and was educated at St John's College, Cambridge. He held various diplomatic posts in the service of *Henry VIII in France, Italy, Spain, and the Netherlands. His first visit to Italy in 1527 probably stimulated him to translate and imitate the poems of *Petrarch. In the same year he made a version of a *Plutarch essay, based on Budé's French translation, *The Quyete of Mynde*, which he dedicated to the queen (Catherine of Aragon) whom the king was in process of divorcing. Wyatt's relationship with Henry VIII's next bride, Anne Boleyn, was more problematic. He was certainly closely acquainted with her before her marriage and, according to three 16th-cent. accounts, confessed to the king that she had been his mistress and was not fit to be a royal consort. Possibly this frankness explains why Wyatt was not executed, along with Anne's other lovers, in 1536, suffering only a period of imprisonment in the Tower. After his release his career soon recovered; he became a sheriff of Kent, and in 1537–9 held the important post of ambassador to Charles V's court in Spain. He celebrated his departure from Spain, June 1539, in the epigram 'Tagus fare well'. In 1540 the tide of Wyatt's fortunes turned, with the execution of his friend and patron Thomas *Cromwell, which is probably referred to in the sonnet (based on Petrarch) 'The piller pearisht is whearto I Lent'. Wyatt himself was arrested, on charges of treason, in July 1541; though released two months later he never fully regained favour. He died in Oct. 1542, of a fever contracted by hard riding on a last diplomatic errand for the king.

Wyatt's poetry is beset by problems in three main areas; authorship, biographical relevance, and artistic aims. Though the canon of Wyatt's poems is generally taken to include all the poems in the Egerton manuscript, even this cannot be proved with certainty, and there are many other poems whose attribution to him depends mainly upon association. The authenticated poems and translations include sonnets, rondeaux, epigrams, satires, lute songs, and a version (based on *Aretino) of the seven Penitential Psalms, whose framing poems depict David repenting of his adulterous love for Bathsheba. Much controversy surrounds Wyatt's artistic purpose in making translations from Italian poems. His metre must have been perceived as irregular even 20 years later, since *Tottel in his Songes and Sonettes (1557) adapted many of Wyatt's poems to conventional iambic stress, including 'They fle from me that sometyme did me seke'. Critical estimates of Wyatt's poetry in the 20th cent. varied widely. C. S. *Lewis called him 'the father of the Drab Age', but others have viewed him as a complex and original writer whose love poems anticipate those of *Donne. The poems have been frequently edited, for instance by K. Muir and P. Thomson (1969), by Joost Daalder (1975), and by R. A. Rebholz (Penguin, 1978). Muir and Thomson's Life and Letters (1962) assembles most of the biographical material; Thomson's Critical Heritage collection (1974) assembles critical views through the ages.

WYCHERLEY, William (1641–1715), of a Shropshire family. He was educated first in France, then at The Queen's College, Oxford, but he never matriculated, afterwards enrolling as a student in the Inner Temple. His first play, Love in a Wood, or, St James's Park, a comedy of intrigue set in St James's Park, was probably acted in 1671, and published in 1672, and brought him the favour of the duchess of Cleveland, the king's mistress. In 1679 he secretly married the widowed countess of Drogheda, daughter of the first earl of Radnor, and incurred thereby the displeasure of Charles II, who had offered him the tutorship of his son, the duke of Richmond. His second play, *The Gentleman Dancing-Master, was probably acted 1671, published 1673; *The Country Wife was published and probably first acted 1675; his last play, *The Plain-Dealer, was probably acted 1676, published 1677. His Miscellany Poems (1704) led to a friendship with *Pope, who revised many of his writings. His Posthumous Works appeared in 1728.

Wycherley's plays, admired by *Lamb but condemned by *Macaulay as licentious and indecent, are highly regarded for their acute social criticism, particularly of sexual morality and the marriage conventions; his characterization and thematic organization are also strong, and his last two plays have been successfully revived many times. The standard edition is by A. Friedman (1979). (See also RESTORATION.)

WYCLIF, John (c.1330–84), probably born at Hipswell (near Wycliffe), a village near Richmond in north Yorkshire. He came to Oxford in 1354 and was connected with Merton, Balliol, and the Queen's colleges during his period there, from 1354 to 1381. He was a protégé of *John of Gaunt, and it was probably at his instance that he preached against *William of Wykeham and the Good Parliament in 1376. He was a trained scholastic who lectured and wrote on logic, 1361–72, and modern accounts of him often stress the philosophical (in which area he could be called an extreme exponent of *Realism) rather than the radically reforming side of him. His attacks on the authority and abuses in the Church, and ultimately his denial of Transubstantiation, led to repeated attempts to condemn him from at least 1378 onwards; he was finally condemned in 1380, and in 1381 he retired to Lutterworth, the living of which he had held since 1374, where he remained until his death on 31 Dec. 1384. His followers were known as *Lollards, and many of them were executed in the first quarter of the 15th cent. (such as *Oldcastle in 1417 and John Badby in 1410: for the latter, see *Hoccleve's Regiment of Princes, 285–7). He was also an influence on John Huss and his followers in Bohemia, and through them perhaps ultimately on *Luther. His great significance lies in the Bible translations which he instigated and in the importance he and his followers have in the writings of such poets as *Chaucer and *Langland. Modern authorities, such as Anne Hudson, are reluctant to attribute particular English works, at least in the versions in which they survive, to Wyclif himself rather than to the Wyclifites in general. The earliest versions of Bible translations come from the 1380s and are traditionally associated with Purvey and Nicholas of Hereford. Recently such works as the 294-item Wyclifite sermon cycle have come under scholarly scrutiny, but Hudson says their literary merit is slight.

H. B. Workman, *John Wyclif* (2 vols, 1926); K. B. McFarlane, *John Wycliffe and the Beginning of English Nonconformity* (1952); G. Leff, *Heresy in the Later Middle Ages* (1967), ii. 494–605; A. M. Hudson (ed.), *Selections from English Wycliffite Writings* (1978).

WYKEHAM, William of, see WILLIAM OF WYKEHAM.

WYLIE, Elinor Morton Hoyt (1885–1928), American poet and novelist, who left her first husband to elope with Horace Wylie, and left Wylie to marry the poet William Rose Benét (1886–1950), brother of S. V. *Benét. Her works include *Nets to Catch the Wind* (1921, poems); *The Venetian Glass Nephew* (1925, novel); and *The Orphan Angel* (1926; in England as *Mortal Image*, 1927), a novel based on *Shelley's life after his supposed rescue from drowning, infused by her 'patent adoration' of Shelley, which E. *Garnett tried to dissuade her from publishing. Her *Collected Poems* appeared in 1932. Beautiful, vain, and histrionic, she aroused both passionate admiration and passionate hostility; the latter, notably, from V. *Woolf, whom she met in London in 1926. See S. Olson, *Elinor Wylie; A Life Apart* (1979).

WYNDHAM, Francis (1924–   ), short story writer, editor and novelist, the author of two volumes of interlinked short stories, *Out of the War* (1974) and *Mrs Henderson and Other Stories* (1985); his milieu is that of the slightly fraying nostalgic upper middle class and its bohemian fringes: and the sexuality of the Older Woman is a recurrent theme. *The Other Garden* (1987) is a novella set during the Second World War and narrated by a young man who observes the misery and difficulties of the domestic front, particularly those of the repressed but compelling Kay Demarest, living a tragic and second-hand life through movie stars and novels. See *The Collected Fiction* (1992) with an introduction by A. *Hollinghurst. Wyndham co-edited (with Diana Melly) the *Letters* of Jean *Rhys (1984).

WYNDHAM, John, the best-known pseudonym of John Wyndham Parkes Lucas Beynon Harris (1903–69), son of a barrister, who pursued several different careers before settling to a successful life as a writer, principally of *science fiction, a genre to which he was attracted partly through his early admiration of H. G. *Wells and *Verne. He preferred the description 'logical fantasy' for his own works, which included *The Day of the Triffids* (1951), *The Kraken Wakes* (1953), *The Chrysalids* (1955), and *The Midwich Cuckoos* (1957). Several of his works were filmed; most are distinguished by the contrast between a comfortable English background and the sudden invasion of catastrophe, usually of a fantastic or metaphysical rather than a technologically suggestive nature.

The word 'triffid' has passed into the language to describe almost any kind of imaginary hostile and dangerous plant: Wyndham's species, lethal and mobile monsters on average 7 feet high, were so called because of their three-pronged roots, on which they propelled themselves.

WYNKYN DE WORDE, see WORDE.

Wynnere and Wastour, an alliterative dream-poem of about 500 lines in a north-west Midland dialect, based on events of 1352–3 and thought to have been written shortly after that, discussing the economic problems of the day. The poet says that he saw in his dream two opposing armies drawn up against each other on the plain, with Edward III encamped above them. The king sends his son, the *Black Prince, to intervene and prevent the battle. The leaders of the two armies explain their causes: with Winner (the gainer of wealth in society) are the pope and the traditionally avaricious friars; with Waster (the prodigal spender) are the nobility and the soldiery. In the king's judgement speech (which is unfinished), he sends Waster to the markets of London to stimulate the economy and Winner to the rich courts of the pope and the cardinals. In its concerns and methods, the poem has often been compared to, and said to be an influence on, *Piers Plowman*. Ed. F. Berry in B. Ford (ed.), *The Age of Chaucer* (1959).

WYNTOUN, Andrew of (c.1350–c.1425), a canon regular of St Andrews and author of *The Orygynale Cronykil* (c.1420), a metrical history of Scotland in octosyllabics, from the beginning of the world to the accession of James I. He becomes a valuable authority later in the work; among his stories is that of Macbeth and the witches, and of Macduff and Malcolm. The chronicle was first published in 1795. (See HUCHOWN.) Ed. F. J. Amours (Scottish Text Society, 6 vols, 1902–5, 1914).

X

Xanadu, in Coleridge's *'Kubla Khan', the place where the Khan decreed 'a stately pleasure-dome'.

XAVIER, St Francis (1506–52), a Spaniard, one of the founders of the Society of Jesus, and a famous missionary in the Far East. He died on his way to China and is buried in Goa. *Dryden's life of St Francis Xavier (1688), a translation of a French work, *La Vie de Saint François Xavier* (1682), by D. Bouhours, is dedicated to Mary of Modena, the queen of James II.

XENOPHON (*c.*430–352 BC), Athenian historian who left an account of a military expedition in which he participated (*Anabasis*), a history of his own times (*Hellenica*), a panegyric on a contemporary monarch (*Agesilaus*), chatty memoirs about *Socrates (*Memorabilia, Symposium*), and treatises on domestic economy, horsemanship, and hunting. His most popular work was however the *Cyropedia*, a fictionalized biography of the Persian king Cyrus. This created a vogue for such biographies in which the fictional element became progressively greater until the world saw the emergence of a new genre—the novel. The *Cyropedia* was translated into English by William Barker (?1552), contributed a story to Painter's **Palace of Pleasure* (1566), and was described by *Sidney as an 'absolute heroical poem'. *Milton, on the other hand, spoke highly of the *Memorabilia*, whose account of Socrates he placed on a level with *Plato's.

Ximena (in French Chimène), the wife of the *Cid. C. *Cibber wrote an adaptation of *Corneille's *Le Cid*, called *Ximena, or The Heroick Daughter* (1712).

XIMÉNEZ DE CISNEROS, Cardinal Francisco (1436–1517), a Spanish statesman and Grand Inquisitor, who founded the University of Alcalá in 1506 and recruited the team of scholars who produced the *Complutensian Polyglot Bible.

Y

Yahoo, the name of the beasts in human form described by Swift in the fourth part of *Gulliver's Travels*: the word has become widely known as the trade name of an Internet search engine.

'Yardley-Oak', a poem by *Cowper.

Yarico, see INKLE AND YARICO.

YATES, Dornford, the pseudonym of Cecil William Mercer (1885–1960), whose sequence of stories about 'Berry' Pleydell and his family includes *The Brother of Daphne* (1914), *Berry and Co.* (1920), and *The House that Berry Built* (1945). Both this group and Yates's 'Chandos' thrillers (*Blind Corner*, 1927, etc.) were much influenced by Anthony Hope (*Hawkins); both reflect a world of wealth and idleness and were immensely popular between the wars. See R. Usborne, *Clubland Heroes* (1963, 1974) and a life by A. J. Smithers (1982).

YATES, Dame Frances Amelia (1899–1981), Renaissance scholar, educated at University College London. Some of her most important work was on *Neoplatonism and the *Rosicrucian tradition in Renaissance thought, and their connections with literature and the drama; her publications include studies of *Florio (1934), *The French Academies of the Sixteenth Century* (1947), *Bruno (1964), *The Valois Tapestries* (1959, rev. 1975), *The Art of Memory* (1966), and *Astraea: The Imperial Theme in the Sixteenth Century* (1975).

year books, reports of English common law cases for the period 1292–1534, of great interest from a historical as well as a legal standpoint. They were succeeded by the law 'Reports'. F. W. *Maitland began editing them, and the work is still going on.

Years, The, a novel by V. *Woolf, published 1937.

Her longest novel, and the most traditional of her later works, it traces the history of a family, opening in 1880 as the children of Colonel and Mrs Pargiter, living together in a large Victorian London house (later described by one of them as 'Hell'), wait for their mother's death and the freedom it will bring; it takes them through several carefully dated and documented sections to the 'Present Day' of 1936, and a large family reunion, where two generations gather. Its composition caused the author much difficulty, and she was even more than usually apprehensive about its reception, fearing that her return to the 'novel of fact' would be seen as a false step in her career; many of her friends were critical, but it was on the whole well reviewed, and sold well.

YEARSLEY, Ann, née Cromartie (1752–1806). She was born at Clifton, Bristol, the daughter of a dairywoman, and pursued her mother's trade. She married in 1774 and had several children. She published three collections of poems (*Poems, on Several Occasions*, 1785; *Poems on Various Subjects*, 1787; *The Rural Lyre*, 1796). She was initially patronized by Hannah *More, whom she addressed as 'Stella' in the persona of 'Lactilla', but the friendship ended in some bitterness. She also wrote a play, *Earl Goodwin* (1791), and a *Gothic historical novel, *The Royal Captives* (1795), based on the story of the Man in the Iron Mask. See R. *Southey, *Lives of the Uneducated Poets* (1836; ed. J. S. Childers, 1925); *The Polite Marriage* ('The Bristol Milkwoman') (1938) by J. M. S. Tompkins; *Lactilla: Milkwoman of Clifton* (1996) by Mary Waldron. See also PRIMITIVISM.

Yeast, a novel by C. *Kingsley, published in *Fraser's Magazine* 1848, in volume form 1851.

This was the first of Kingsley's novels and is crude as a literary work. It deals with some of the social and religious problems of the day (the miserable conditions of the rustic labourer, the Game Laws, and Tractarianism: see OXFORD MOVEMENT), largely by means of dialogues between the hero and various other characters. The story is that of the reactions of the generous but undisciplined nature of Lancelot Smith to the influences exercised on him by the philosophical Cornish gamekeeper Tregarva, the worldly Colonel Bracebridge, the Romanizing curate Luke, Lancelot's orthodox love Argemone Lavington, and the philanthropic banker Barnakill; he is seen suffering the loss, first of his fortune, and then of Argemone. The story ends in a vague and semi-mystical indication that Lancelot is to seek his salvation in contribution to the regeneration of England.

YEATS, Jack Butler (1871–1957), painter and illustrator, brother of W. B. *Yeats, who contributed for many years to *Punch (1910–41) under the pseudonym 'W. Bird', and also did many illustrations for the *Cuala Press, although he remains better known for his oil paintings of Irish life and landscape.

YEATS, John Butler (1839–1922), Irish portrait painter, father of W. B. and J. B. *Yeats; his *Letters to His Son W. B. Yeats and Others, 1869–1922* (ed. J. Hone, 1946) give a vivid portrait of cultural life in Ireland, in London (where he lived for some years from 1887 in Bedford Park), and in New York, where he spent his last 14 years, renowned, in Hone's words, less as a painter than as 'a critic, philosopher and conversationalist'.

YEATS, William Butler (1865–1939), eldest son of J. B. *Yeats and brother of Jack *Yeats, both celebrated painters. He was born in Dublin and educated at the Godolphin School, Hammersmith, and the High School, Dublin. For three years he studied at the School of Art in Dublin, where with a fellow student, G. *Russell (Æ), he developed an interest in mystic religion and the supernatural. At 21 he abandoned art as a profession in favour of literature, writing *John Sherman and Dhoya* (1891) and editing *The Poems of William Blake* (1893), *The Works of William Blake* (with F. J. Ellis, 3 vols, 1893), and *Poems of Spenser* (1906). A nationalist, he helped to found an Irish Literary Society in London in 1891 and another in Dublin in 1892; and he subsequently applied himself to the creation of an Irish national theatre, an achievement which, with the help of Lady *Gregory and others, was partly realized in 1899 when his play **The Countess Cathleen* (1892) was acted in Dublin. The English actors engaged by the *Irish Literary Theatre gave place in 1902 to an Irish amateur company, which produced Yeats's *Cathleen ni Houlihan* in that year. The Irish National Theatre Company was thereafter created, and, with the help of Miss A. E. *Horniman, acquired the *Abbey Theatre in Dublin. Yeats's early study of Irish lore and legends resulted in *Fairy and Folk Tales of the Irish Peasantry* (1888), **The Celtic Twilight* (1893), and *The Secret Rose* (1897). Irish traditional and nationalist themes and the poet's unrequited love for Maude Gonne, a beautiful and ardent revolutionary, provided much of the subject matter for *The Wanderings of Oisin and Other Poems* (1889), *The Land of Heart's Desire* (1894), *The Wind among the Reeds* (1899), *The Shadowy Waters* (1900), and such of his later plays as *On Baile's Strand* (1904) and *Deirdre* (1907).

With each succeeding collection of poems Yeats moved further from the elaborate, *Pre-Raphaelite style of the 1890s. *In the Seven Woods* (1903) was followed by *The Green Helmet and Other Poems* (1910), *Poems Written in Discouragement* (1913), *Responsibilities: Poems and a Play* (1914), and *The Wild Swans at Coole* (1917). His mounting disillusionment with Irish politics came to a head in 1912 and 1913 with the controversy over the Lane Bequest of French Impressionist paintings. The Easter Rising of 1916, however, restored his faith in the heroic character of his country. The following year he married Georgie Hyde-Lees, who on their honeymoon attempted automatic writing, an event that exercised a profound effect on his life and work. His wife's 'communicators' ultimately provided him with the system of symbolism described in *A Vision* (1925) and underlying many of the poems in *Michael Robartes and the Dancer* (1921), *Seven Poems and a Fragment* (1922), *The Cat and the Moon and Certain Poems* (1924), *October Blast* (1927), *The Tower* (1928), *The Winding Stair* (1929), *Words for Music Perhaps and Other Poems* (1932), *Wheels and Butterflies* (1934), *The King of the Great Clock Tower* (1934), *A Full Moon in March* (1935), *New Poems* (1938), and *Last Poems and Two Plays* (1939). In the poems and plays written after his marriage he achieved a spare, colloquial lyricism wholly unlike his earlier manner, although many themes of his early manhood reach their full flowering in the later period.

Yeats served as a senator of the Irish Free State from 1922 to 1928; was chairman of the commission on coinage; and in 1923 received the *Nobel Prize for literature. He died in the south of France, but in 1948 his body was brought back to Ireland and interred at Drumcliff in Sligo, where much of his childhood had been spent.

Yeats's other publications include such collections of essays as *Ideas of Good and Evil* (1903), *Discoveries* (1907), *Per Amica Silentia Lunae* (1918), *The Cutting of an Agate* (1919), and *On the Boiler* (1939). Most important of the many books he edited and introduced was *The Oxford Book of Modern Verse* (1936), a somewhat eccentric and personal selection. He wrote good letters, and five major collections have been made: *Letters on Poetry from W. B. Yeats to Dorothy Wellesley* (1940), *Florence Farr, Bernard Shaw and W. B. Yeats* (1941), *W. B. Yeats and T. Sturge Moore: Their Correspondence 1901–37* (1953), *W. B. Yeats: Letters to Katharine Tynan* (1953), and Allan Wade's notable edition of *The Letters of W. B. Yeats* (1954). Also posthumously published were his *Collected Poems* (1950), *Collected Plays* (1952), *Autobiographies* (1955), *The Variorum Edition of the Poems* (1957), *Mythologies* (1959), *Essays and Introductions* (1961), *The Senate Speeches of W. B. Yeats* (1961), and *Explorations* (1962). There are biographies by Joseph Hone, *W. B. Yeats 1865–1939* (1942), and A. N. Jeffares, *W. B. Yeats, Man and Poet* (1949, rev. 1962). See also *Yeats: The Man and the Masks* (1948, rev. 1979) by R. *Ellmann. A third edition, revised by R. K. Alspach, of Allan Wade's *A Bibliography of the Writings of W. B. Yeats* was published in 1968. R. J. Finneran's controversial edition, *The Poems: A New Edition*, appeared in 1984. There is a two-volume biography by Roy Foster: *W. B. Yeats: The Apprentice Poet* (1997) and *The Arch-Poet* (2003).

'Ye Banks and Braes', a lyric by *Burns.

yellow-backs, cheap editions of novels, so called from being bound in yellow boards. They were the ordinary 'railway novels' of the 1870s and 1880s.

Yellow Book (1894–7), a handsome, short-lived publication, startling in its time and immediately notorious, devoted to literature and art. Published by J. *Lane and edited by H. *Harland, with the initial assistance of *Beardsley as art editor, its first issue (which included *Beerbohm's essay 'A Defence of Cosmetics') provoked a public storm which did not subside during the three years of the *Book*'s life. Writers published included H. *James, *Gosse, *Le Gallienne, Arnold *Bennett, and *Dowson; among artists represented were Beardsley, Walter Sickert, and Wilson Steer.

Yeobright, Clym, Thomasin, and Mrs, characters in Hardy's *The Return of the Native*.

YEVTUSHENKO, Yevgeny (1933–), Russian poet, born in Zima in southern Siberia and educated in Moscow. He travelled extensively and became widely known internationally as a writer who attempted to represent a new generation of Russian writers, who defended *Modernism and protested against censorship in the post-Stalin era. His first volume of verse appeared in 1952, and he achieved recognition with the long poem *Zima Railway Station* (*Winter Station*, 1956); this was followed by *Babii Yar* (literally, 'the women's cliff', 1961), a poem evoking the notorious wartime massacre of women and children near Kiev and tackling the dangerous theme of Russian anti-Semitism. Other works include his *Letter to Esenin* (1965), hailing *Esenin as a free spirit. *A Precious Autobiography* (1963) aroused much controversy when it was published in Paris.

Yiddish, derived, either directly, or through the German-Jewish *jiddisch*, from the German *jüdisch*, Jewish; the language used by Jews in Europe and America, consisting mainly of German, with Balto-Slavic or Hebrew words, and printed in Hebrew characters. One of the few Yiddish writers to achieve an international reputation is I. B. *Singer.

YONGE, Bartholomew (1560–1612). He travelled in Spain in 1578–80, and subsequently translated the Spanish romance *Diana* by *Montemayor; his version was published in 1598, with a dedication to Lady *Rich. It has been edited by J. M. Kennedy (1968).

YONGE, Charlotte M(ary) (1823–1901), daughter of an army officer. She was born and lived all her life in the Hampshire village of Otterbourne, and was educated at home by her parents. In 1838 she came under the influence of *Keble, then rector of the neighbouring parish of Hursley, and absorbed the Tractarian religious views which thereafter coloured all her writings. Her best-known novel is *The Heir of Redclyffe* (1853); her other novels of contemporary life include *Heartsease* (1854), *The Daisy Chain* (1856), *Dynevor Terrace* (1857), *Hopes and Fears* (1860), *The Trial* (1864), *The Clever Woman of the Family* (1865), *The Pillars of the House* (1873), and *Magnum Bonum* (1879). She also wrote many historical romances for children (including *The Little Duke*, 1854; *The Dove in the Eagle's Nest*, 1866; and *The Chaplet of Pearls*, 1868) and numerous historical textbooks, short stories of village life, and a biography of Bishop Patteson (1874). For 40 years she edited a girls' magazine, the *Monthly Packet*.

Her chief excellence as a novelist was her loving depiction of life in large families, particularly sibling relationships, presented with convincing dialogue and unstinted incident. Her novels of her own times are incidentally a mine of information about social mobility, ecclesiastical change, and developments in education and housing. She wrote mainly for young women readers, of whom she had a world-wide following, but her books were also admired by *Tennyson, *Kingsley, *Rossetti, and W. *Morris, and were said to have been the favourite reading of young officers in the Crimean War. See G. Battiscombe, *Charlotte Mary Yonge* (1943); M. Mare and A. C. Percival, *Victorian Best-Seller: The World of Charlotte M. Yonge* (1947). (See CHILDREN'S LITERATURE.)

Yorick, (1) in Shakespeare's *Hamlet* (v. i), the king's jester, whose skull the grave-diggers throw up when digging Ophelia's grave; (2) in Sterne's *Tristram Shandy*, 'the lively, witty, sensible, and heedless parson', of Danish extraction, and probably a descendant of Hamlet's Yorick. Sterne adopted 'Yorick' as a pseudonym in his *Sentimental Journey and entitled his own homilies *The Sermons of Mr Yorick*, first published in 1760.

Yorick to Eliza, Letters from, by *Sterne, published 1773.

A collection of ten brief letters from Sterne to Mrs E. *Draper, written in 1767, and following the course of his growing passion for her.

Yorkshire Tragedy, A, a play published 1608, stated in the title to be by Shakespeare; but internal evidence and the late date make it extremely improbable that he had any part in its authorship. It is probably by *Middleton.

The play is based on certain murders actually committed in 1605. The husband, a brutal and depraved gamester, suddenly filled with remorse when he realizes his shame, murders his two children and stabs his docile and devoted wife. It is extremely brief and probably formed part of a composite programme of *Four Plays in One*.

YOUNG, Andrew John (1885–1971), born in Scotland, educated at school and university in Edinburgh, ordained a minister of the Free Church in 1912. In 1910 his father paid for the publication of his *Songs of Night*, the first of many slim volumes of poetry which were greatly admired by an ever-widening circle. The first *Collected Poems* appeared in 1936 and the verse play *Nicodemus* in 1937. In 1939 Young was ordained in the Church of England. *The Green Man* (1947) is sometimes considered his best collection. In 1952 he published a long, disturbing poem, 'Into Hades', which was later combined with the visionary 'A Traveller in Time' to create *Out of the World and Back* (1958), his most ambitious work. His lifelong interest in botany was reflected in a prose account of his travels and searches, *A Prospect of Flowers* (1945), but also in many lyrics, whose subjects also included many aspects of the natural world. His spare line, sharp specific imagery, quiet concision, and skill with conceit brought him much admiration. The influence of literary fashions barely touched him, but he acknowledged a particular debt to *Hardy, and to *Crabbe and G. *Herbert. *The Complete Poems* were revised in 1974.

YOUNG, Arthur (1741–1820), the son of a Suffolk clergyman, who became well known as an agricultural theorist, though unsuccessful as a practical farmer. He wrote a large number of works on agricultural subjects and edited the periodical *Annals of Agriculture* (1784–1809), which extended to 47 volumes (parts of another volume were published in 1812 and 1813). His power of political and social observation is shown by his *Political Arithmetic* (1774) and his *Tour in Ireland* (1780), the latter highly praised as a true account of the country by M. *Edgeworth, but his fame rests chiefly on *Travels in France* (1792). Young was connected with the *Burneys, and his country house, Bradfield Hall, Suffolk, is described in Fanny Burney's *Camilla*. He took her to hear *Hastings's trial in Westminster Hall and she was charmed with him. The death of a much-loved daughter in 1797, and a growing religious melancholia (influenced by his friend W. *Wilberforce), darkened his later years, and he went blind about 1811. His autobiography, edited by M. Betham-Edwards, appeared in 1898, and there is a life by J. G. Gazley (1973).

YOUNG, Edward (1683–1765), born near Winchester and educated there and at Oxford. His early works include the tragedies *Busiris*, successfully produced at Drury Lane in 1719, and *The Revenge*, produced at the same theatre in 1721. In 1725–8 he published a series of satires under the title *The Universal Passion* (the love of fame), which were much admired until eclipsed by those of *Pope, who was a few years younger. Disappointed in more worldly ambitions, he took orders and became rector of Welwyn in 1730, where he spent the remainder of his long life; in 1731 he married Elizabeth Lee, daughter of the second earl of Lichfield, who died in 1740. Young's most celebrated poem, *The Complaint, or Night Thoughts on Life, Death and Immortality* (1742–5, see NIGHT THOUGHTS), is thought to commemorate her, her daughter by a previous marriage, and her son-in-law. A noted example of the *graveyard genre, it was extremely popular in both England and Europe. *The Brothers*, a tragedy written decades earlier, was performed and published in 1753, and *Resignation*, his last considerable poem, with a preface to Mrs *Boscawen, appeared in 1762. He was a friend of *Richardson, with whom he corresponded for many years. Dr *Johnson concludes his life with the words, 'But, with all his defects, he was a man of genius and a poet.'

YOUNG, Francis Brett (1884–1954), novelist, short story writer, poet, and doctor. He was educated at the University of Birmingham, practised for some years in Devon, and served during the First World War in East Africa. He is remembered largely for his solid, traditional novels of the west Midlands, which include *Portrait of Clare* (1927) and *My Brother Jonathan* (1928), but he also wrote novels based on his African experiences, including *Jim Redlake* (1930) and *They Seek a Country* (1937). *Poems 1916–1918* (1919) was written in Africa while he was convalescing from what proved permanent damage to his health, and *The Island* (1944) is a verse history of England, employing the verse forms of succeeding periods in strict chronological sequence.

YOURCENAR, Marguerite (1903–88), French classical scholar and historical novelist, born Marguerite de Crayencour in Brussels. Her first novel, *Alexis* (1929), was followed by many others, notably *Mémoires d'Hadrien* (1951, translated by her friend and companion Grace Frick, 1954, as *Memoirs of Hadrian*).

Ywain and Gawain, a northern romance from the first half of the 14th cent. of 4,032 lines in short couplets, surviving in a single manuscript. In spite of its title, the poem is principally concerned with Ywain, being a translation (with variations) from the 6,818 lines of *Yvain* by *Chrétien de Troyes. As well as being briefer, the English translation (which is about 150 years later than the original) has some elements in common with other versions of the Ywain story (such as the Welsh *Owein*), and there has been much discussion of the relation it bears to the original. The English romance is much admired for its narrative life and clarity of diction.

Ywain kills the knight of a castle who seems to have magical connections with the weather, and, aided by her serving-lady Lunet, marries his widow Alundyne (Lunete and Laudine in Chrétien). Gawain persuades him to go, assisted by a lion, in search of adventure, abandoning his lady. The two knights have many adventures, ending by fighting each other incognito; but they recognize each other and are reconciled. At the end, Ywain is reconciled to Alundyne, again by the skills of Lunet. Many of the incidental themes in Chrétien (such as his commenting on *courtly love by cross-reference to Lancelot, his explanation of the name of Lunete by reference to the moon, and his general interest in the characters' motivation) are played down or entirely suppressed in the English version.

Ed. A. B. Friedman and N. T. Harrington, EETS os 254 (1964); extracts in A. V. C. Schmidt and N. Jacobs, *Medieval English Romances*, ii (1980).

Z

ZAMYATIN, Evgeny Ivanovich (1884–1937), Russian writer born in central Russia, the son of a teacher. From 1902 he studied in St Petersburg and joined the Bolshevik Party (which he later left). He was arrested and exiled in 1905. From 1911 he lectured in naval architecture at the St Petersburg Polytechnic Institute: he spent 18 months in Newcastle upon Tyne, 1916–17, supervising the construction of Russian ice-breakers, and the two stories that sprang from this experience, 'Islanders' (1917) and 'The Fisher of Men' (1918), are devastating assessments of English life. After the revolution Zamyatin produced a steady flow of stories and edited collections by H. G. *Wells, G. B. *Shaw, Jack *London, and O. *Henry. His novel *We* (1920–1) was published abroad in the late 1920s, leading to a vicious campaign against him; he wrote to Stalin in June 1931 asking permission to emigrate and left Russia in November, eventually settling in Paris. Among Zamyatin's best stories are 'The North' (1918), 'The Cave' (1920), 'Mamai' (1920), 'The Yawl' (1928), and 'The Flood' (1929), in which his major theme, the cult of obsession and the primitive, is apparent, but he is best known for the dystopian satire *We*. (See UTOPIA.) Indebted to Wells, in particular *The Time Machine*, it was in turn acknowledged by *Orwell as an influence on *Nineteen Eighty-Four*, though its widely suggested influence on *Brave New World* was denied by A. *Huxley.

ZANGWILL, Israel (1864–1926), a noted Jewish spokesman, writer, and translator. The popular novel *Children of the Ghetto* (1892) established his reputation by its realistic and sympathetically critical portrayal of London's poor Jews, when alien immigration was a burning issue. *Ghetto Tragedies* (1899), *Ghetto Comedies* (1907), and *The King of Schnorrers* (1894), a *jeu d'esprit*, contain vignettes of Jewish life. The historical *Dreamers of the Ghetto* (1898) testifies both to Judaism's inner strength and to its role in civilization. *The War for the World* (1916) and *The Voice of Jerusalem* (1920) combine apologia with polemic. His plays are vehicles for ideas, notably *The Melting Pot* (1909), which coined the phrase.

Zanzis (or possibly 'Zauzis'), a wise writer referred to by Chaucer in *Troilus and Criseyde* (IV. 414), referring to Zeuxis who is a sage in the Alexander story. The form may come from a misreading of the text of *Boccaccio that Chaucer is following; but this is unlikely, since the Athenian painter Zeuxis is called 'Zanzis' in 'The Physician's Tale' (see CANTERBURY TALES, 13; VI. 16).

Zapolya, a 'dramatic poem . . . in humble imitation of "The Winter's Tale" of Shakespeare', by S. T. *Coleridge, published 1817. Zapolya is a dowager queen of Illyria driven from the throne by the usurper Emerick. After an interval of 20 years she returns to power with her son Bethlen.

Zarathustra, see ZOROASTER.

Zarathustra, *Thus Spake*, see NIETZSCHE.

Zastrozzi, see SHELLEY, P. B.

Zeal-of-the-land Busy, in Jonson's *Bartholomew Fair*, a canting, gluttonous Puritan, 'a Banbury man'. Banbury was a town dominated by Puritans, who in 1610 had destroyed the ancient cross celebrated in the nursery rhyme.

Zeitgeist (German), the spirit of genius which marks the thought or feeling of a period.

ZÉLIDE, the name given to herself in a self-portrait by Isabella van Tuyll van Serooskerken, also known as Mme de Charrière (1740–1805), a Dutchwoman of good family, great intelligence and originality, and considerable beauty. She numbered among her many suitors *Boswell, who quickly reconciled himself to her rejection of his hand. Declining more brilliant matches, she married her brother's Swiss tutor, the dull but worthy M. de Charrière. Her unhappy married life was brightened by friendship with *Constant, until she was ousted by Mme de *Staël. She wrote in French a number of novels, of which the best known are *Lettres neuchâteloises* (1784), *Mistress Henley* (1784), and *Lettres écrites de Lausanne* (1787). There is an interesting account of her life in G. *Scott's *Portrait of Zélide*.

Zelmane, in Sidney's *Arcadia*, the name assumed by Pyrocles when disguised as a woman.

Zeluco, a novel by Dr J. *Moore, published 1786.

In the author's words, this novel 'traces the windings of vice' through the life of a wholly wicked man. Zeluco, a Sicilian noble, exhibits from childhood a character of cruelty, treachery, lust, and violence. He tyrannizes, maims, and murders, even killing his own child and driving its mother mad. In the end he is himself killed. The savagery is curiously interspersed with humorous episodes, several of which involve two comic Scotsmen, Buchanan and Targe.

ZENO of Elia (early 5th cent. BC), a monistic philosopher famous for his paradoxes which, revealing the inconsistencies in man's picture of the universe, were intended to discredit belief in the multiplicity of entities. Sir T. Browne was to attack his paradoxes in the *Pseudodoxia Epidemica* (1646).

Zenobia, a character in Hawthorne's *The Blithedale Romance.*

Zenocrate, the wife of Tamburlaine, in *Marlowe's play of that name.

ZEPHANIAH, Benjamin Obadiah Iqbal (1958–   ), poet and playwright who left school aged 13, and spent most of his teenage years in youth institutions and the criminal underworld of Birmingham. He came to public attention as a performance poet with the anti-racist demonstrations of the late 1970s and early 1980s. *Job Rocking* (pub. 1989) is recognized as Britain's first rap play. In 1991 he co-wrote *Dread Poets Society*, a BBC-TV play, in which he played himself in a fictional encounter with *Shelley, Mary *Shelley, and *Byron. After *Streetwise* (1990), he stopped writing for the stage on the grounds that most theatre did not reach ethnic minorities or the most disadvantaged communities. Collections of poetry include *City Psalms* (1992) and *Propa Propaganda* (1996). *Talking Turkeys* (1994) and *Funky Chickens* (1996) collect verse for children.

Zerbino, in *Orlando furioso*, a Scottish prince and perfect knight, of whom it was said that Nature broke the mould in which he had been fashioned. He was the lover of *Isabella. He was rescued by Orlando when about to be executed on a false charge, but was killed by *Mandricardo when attempting to defend the arms that Orlando in his madness had thrown away.

zeugma, a figure of speech by which a single word is made to refer to two or more words in a sentence, when properly applying literally to only one of them; e.g. 'See Pan with flocks, with fruits Pomona crowned'. Cf. SYLLEPSIS.

ZHUKOVSKY, Vasily Andreyevich (1783–1852), Russian poet, regarded as the father of Russian Romanticism. His 1802 translation of Gray's *Elegy*, his first publication, is seen as ushering in the new age. His first ballads, 'Lyudmila' and 'Svetlana' (1808, his most famous work), both based on Bürger's *'Lenore', gave rise to a fashion for the ballad. Zhukovsky served in the army, and later was tutor to the future Alexander II. He met and befriended both *Pushkin and *Gogol. He wrote a small number of elegies, ballads, lyrics, and humorous epistles, and his lasting influence on Russian poetry depends on his metrical and linguistic innovations and his moves towards the direct expression of feeling in poetry. But perhaps his most important achievement in the history of Russian literature lies in his translations of the *Odyssey* (from a German translation), German poets including Uhland and *Schiller, and, from the English, *Dryden ('Alexander's Feast'), James *Thomson (1700–48), *Gray, *Southey, Sir W. *Scott, T. *Moore (*Lalla

Rookh), T. *Campbell, and *Byron (*The Prisoner of Chillon*). The first translations of Zhukovsky's works into English, by John Bowring, appeared in 1821 and 1823.

Zimri, name for the duke of *Buckingham in Dryden's *Absalom and Achitophel.*

ZOLA, Émile (1840–1902), the leading figure in the French school of *naturalistic fiction, of which *Thérèse Raquin* (1867) is his earliest example. The first volume (*La Fortune des Rougon*) of his principal work, *Les Rougon-Macquart*, which he termed the 'natural and social history of a family under the Second Empire', appeared in 1871; 19 more volumes followed, the last (*Le Docteur Pascal*) in 1893. In this series of novels, which was influenced by contemporary theories of heredity and experimental science, Zola chronicles the activities of the two branches (the Rougons and the Macquarts) of a family, whose conduct is seen as conditioned through several generations by environment and inherited characteristics, chiefly drunkenness and mental instability. The result is a panorama of mid-19th-cent. French life, especially in the middle and working classes, carefully documented and focusing attention on vice, misery, and the powerful claims of human appetites and instincts. *Germinal* (1885) depicts the life of a mining community, *La Terre* (1887) the life of the agricultural peasant, *Le Ventre de Paris* (1873) the markets of the metropolis, *L'Assommoir* (1877) its taverns, *Au bonheur des dames* (1883) the world of the great department store, *La Débâcle* (1892) the catastrophe of the war of 1870. The prevailing pessimism of the cycle is relieved by passages of lyrical beauty (e.g. in *La Faute de l'abbé Mouret*, 1875) and by faith in scientific and social meliorism. The essays of *Le Roman expérimental* (1880) establish an analogy between the novelist's aims and practices and those of the scientist. In the later trilogy *Les Trois Villes* (*Lourdes*, 1894; *Rome*, 1896; *Paris*, 1898) Zola examines, in a mode of heightened symbolism, the claims of the religious and social organizations of the day to minister to human needs. The novels of his final, unfinished, work, *Les Quatre Évangiles* (*Fécondité*, 1899; *Travail*, 1901; *Vérité*, 1903) are optimistic presentations of social ideals. The last of these refers to the *Dreyfus case in which Zola intervened with trenchant vigour, notably in his letter to the newspaper *L'Aurore*, 'J'Accuse'. To foil the sentence of imprisonment for libel that followed the publication of the letter, he spent 11 months in exile in England (1898–9). Zola's works were themselves the cause of the imprisonment in 1888 of his English publisher *Vizetelly. (See ROMAN FLEUVE.)

Zoroaster, the Greek form of Zarathustra, the founder of the Magian system of religion, probably a historical personage who has become the subject of legends; a Persian who is believed to have lived in the 6th cent. BC during the reigns of Cyrus, Cambyses, and Darius.

The Zoroastrian religion was founded on the old Aryan folk religion, but the polytheistic character of the latter was completely changed. The essential feature of Zoroastrianism is the existence of two predominant spirits: Ahura-Mazda (Ormazd) the wise one, the spirit of light and good; and Ahriman, the spirit of evil and darkness. The conflict between these two is waged in this world, and centres in man, created a free agent by Ormazd. (See also NIETZSCHE.)

ZUKOFSKY, Louis (1904–78), American poet, born in the Yiddish melting pot of New York. In 1931 with *Pound's sponsorship he edited the 'Objectivists' issue of *Poetry*, Chicago, followed in 1932 by *An 'Objectivists' Anthology*, featuring among others Carl Rakosi, George Oppen, and B. *Bunting. Zukofksy's lyrics, collected in the *Complete Short Poetry* (1991), are vividly textual, often witty, always stylish and lapidary. They are challenging and opaque or else clear as crystal. Like many of his contemporaries a deep philosophical puzzlement also attaches to his work, finally making it some of the most intellectually inimitable in the US canon. The hermeneutic drive within Objectivism, differentiating it from *Imagism's lyric base, is fully explored in Zukofsky's long poem *A*, a paean to his nuclear family. Written over 45 years in 24 categorical parts, *A* shows itself as a compendium of forms and forces: translation, music, drama, and reiteration hustle and contend. A *Modernist and postmodernist epic, in places it performs the play of sestina or sonnet in an absurd or unusual light; it recasts regular and irregular histories, offering speaking parts alongside dumbshow. It is moving, political, and tragi-comic, covering the Second World War and its aftermath. Its range of practices and influences dictates ultra-modern readings.

Zuleika, (1) according to Muslim tradition the name of Potiphar's wife; (2) the heroine of Byron's *The Bride of Abydos*.

Zuleika Dobson, the eponymous heroine of *Beerbohm's novel, a great beauty who pays a fatal visit to her grandfather, the warden of Judas College, Oxford, in Eights Week. All the young men fall madly in love with her and, when rejected, they rush 'like lemmings' and drown themselves in the Isis. The only survivor is the less agile Noaks, who trips on the way.

ZWEIG, Stefan (1881–1942), novelist and biographer. Born in Vienna to Jewish parents, he studied in Vienna, where he published his first collection of poetry (1901) and a biography of *Verlaine (1902). After the First World War he and his wife Frederike moved to Salzburg, where he published several collections of shorter fiction including *Amok* (1922) and *The Invisible Collection* (1927). These were followed by biographies of *Erasmus, Magellan, and *Balzac. His only novel, *Ungeduld des Herzens* (*Beware of Pity*, 1938), is a powerful psychological study of the destructive nature of pity and its implications. His autobiography, *The World of Yesterday* (1942), records his meetings and friendship with, among others, *Gorky, *Yeats, *Joyce, *Rilke, *Pirandello, and *Freud. His books were banned under the Nazis and Zweig eventually fled to Europe; he finally settled in Brazil where he committed suicide.

ZWINGLI, Ulrich (1484–1531), a famous Swiss leader of the Reformation. He first found his inspiration in *Erasmus and *Luther, but soon drew away from the latter, and by 1525 had rejected the mass altogether; this split Switzerland into Catholic and Protestant cantons. To Zwingli the Eucharist was purely symbolic; there was no 'real presence' at all, not even in the (later) Calvinistic sense, still less in the Lutheran sense of 'consubstantiation'.

APPENDIX 1 · CHRONOLOGY

THE Chronology has two related lines of information, allowing readers to review key works of English literature in relation to their time. In the left-hand column are listed the significant literary works published in a given year. In the right-hand column a parallel range of information is provided on ruling monarchs; historical and literary events; birth and death dates of important authors, thinkers, musicians, and painters; and a selection of significant works of European literature, musical works, etc.

Date	Principal literary works	Other events
c.1000	Four surviving MSS of Anglo-Saxon poetry: Vercelli, Exeter, Cædmon, and *Beowulf* (latter written ?second half 8th cent.)	
1042		**Edward the Confessor** (−1066)
1066		Battle of Hastings; **William I** (−1087)
1086		Domesday survey
1087		**William II** (−1100)
1100		**Henry I** (−1135)
1135		**Stephen** (−1154)
c.1136	Geoffrey of Monmouth, *Historia Regum Britanniae*	
1139–53		Civil war between Stephen and Matilda
1154		**Henry II** (−1189)
1155		Geoffrey of Monmouth d.
c.1155	Wace, *Roman de Brut*	
1170		Thomas Becket murdered
1175	*Poema Morale*	
1187		Jerusalem captured by Saladin
1189		**Richard I** (−1199)
c.1190–1225	Katherine Group of devotional prose works	
1199		**John** (−1216)
c.1200	*The Owl and the Nightingale*	
c.1205?	Laȝamon, *Brut*	
1215		Magna Carta signed
1216		**Henry III** (−1272)
1221		Dominicans arrive in England
1224		Franciscans arrive in England
c.1225	*King Horn*	
c.1230	*Ancrene Wisse* (*Ancrene Riwle*)	Guillaume de Lorris, *Roman de la Rose*
c.1235–59	Matthew Paris, *Chronica Majora*	
1237		Guillaume de Lorris d.
1249		University College, Oxford, founded
1259		Matthew Paris d.
1265		Simon de Montfort's Parliament
1272		**Edward I** (−1307)
1282–4		**Edward I**'s conquest of Wales
1284		Peterhouse, Cambridge, founded
1290		Jews expelled from England
c.1290–4		Dante, *Vita nuova*

Date	Principal literary works	Other events
1295		**Edward I**'s Model Parliament
1296		**Edward I** invades Scotland
c.1300	*Cursor Mundi*	Richard Rolle b.
1305		Execution of William Wallace
1306		Robert Bruce crowned
c.1307–21		Dante, *Divina Commedia*
1307		**Edward II** (–1327)
1314	*King Alisaunder; Sir Orfeo*	Battle of Bannockburn
c.1320		
1321		Dante d.
1327		**Edward III** (–1377)
c.1330		John Gower b.; John Wyclif b.; William Langland b.
1337		Hundred Years War begins
c.1340	Harley Lyrics	
c.1342		Julian of Norwich b.
c.1343		Geoffrey Chaucer b.
1346		Battle of Crécy
1348		First outbreak of plague in Britain
1349		Richard Rolle d.
c.1350	Thomas Chestre, *Sir Launfal*	
c.1350–2		Boccaccio, *Decameron*
c.1350–1400	*The Cloud of Unknowing*	
1356		English victory at Poitiers
c.1367–70	Langland, *Piers Plowman* (A-Text)	
c.1369	Chaucer, *Book of the Duchess*	Thomas Hoccleve b.
c.1370		John Lydgate b.
1372–86	Chaucer, *The Legend of Good Women*	
c.1373		Margery Kempe b.
c.1374–85	Chaucer, *The House of Fame*	
1377		**Richard II** (–1399); First Poll Tax
c.1377–9	Langland, *Piers Plowman* (B-Text)	
1378		The Great Schism (–1417)
c.1380	Bible tr. into vernacular by Wyclif and others	
c.1380–6	Chaucer, *The Parliament of Fowls*	
1381		Peasants' Revolt
1384		John Wyclif d.
c.1385	Chaucer, *Troilus and Criseyde*	
c.1385–6	Langland, *Piers Plowman* (C-Text)	
1386		Treaty of Windsor
c.1386		William Langland d.
c.1387–1400	Chaucer, *The Canterbury Tales*	
c.1390	Gower, *Confessio Amantis*	
1396		Walter Hilton d.1397
1397		R. Whittington Lord Mayor of London
1399		**Henry IV** (–1413)
1400		Chaucer d.
c.1400	Sole surviving MS (Cotton Nero A x) of *Sir Gawain and the Green Knight, Pearl, Cleanness,* and *Patience*	Fra Angelico b.
1408		John Gower d.
1411	Hoccleve, *The Regiment of Princes*	
1412–20	Lydgate, *Troy Book*	

Date	Principal literary works	Other events
1413		**Henry V**
1415		Battle of Agincourt
c.1420 (–1504)	The Paston Letters	
1420–2	Lydgate, *The Siege of Thebes*	
1421	Hoccleve; The 'Series' Poems (–1422)	
1422		**Henry VI** (–1461)
c.1422		William Caxton b.
c.1424		Robert Henryson b.
1426		Thomas Hoccleve d.
1429		Slege of Orleans
1431		Joan of Arc burned
1431–8	Lydgate, *The Fall of Princes*	
c.1432–8	Margery Kempe, *The Book of Margery Kempe*	
1439		Margery Kempe d.
1441		King's College, Cambridge, founded; Jan van Eyck d.
1444		Sandro Botticelli b.
1449		John Lydgate d.
c.1450	*The Floure and the Leaf*	Hieronymus Bosch b.
1452		Leonardo da Vinci b.
1455		Battle of St Albans; Wars of the Roses begin; Fra Angelico d.
c.1456		William Dunbar b.
c.1460		John Skelton b.
1461		**Henry VI** deposed **Edward IV** (–1470)
1466		Donatello d.
c.1467		Desiderius Erasmus b.
1469		Niccolò Machiavelli b.
1470		**Henry VI** restored (–1471)
1471		**Henry VI** deposed and murdered; **Edward IV** restored (–1483); Sir Thomas Malory d.; Albrecht Dürer b.
1473–4	Caxton, *Recuyell of the Historyes of Troye*	
1474		Gavin Douglas b.; Ludovico Ariosto b.
1475		Michelangelo b.
c.1475	Caxton, *The Game and Playe of the Chesse*	Alexander Barclay b.
c.1476	Caxton, *The Canterbury Tales*	
c.1476–8		Giorgione b.
c.1477		Thomas More b.
1483	Caxton, *The Golden Legend*; Caxton, *Confessio Amantis*	**Edward V** (reigns two months); **Richard III** (–1485); Raphael b.
1484	Caxton, *Troilus and Criseyde*	
1485	Caxton, *Le Morte d'Arthur*	Battle of Bosworth; **Henry VII** (–1509)
c.1487		Titian b.
c.1490		Thomas Elyot b.
1491		William Caxton d.
1492		Columbus lands in W. Indies; Piero della Francesca d.
c.1494		François Rabelais b.
c.1497–8		Hans Holbein b.
c.1498	Skelton, *The Bowge of Courte*	
1500		Wynkyn de Worde establishes new press

Date	Principal literary works	Other events
c.1500–6		Leonardo, *Mona Lisa*
1503	Atkinson, [Aquinas] *Imitation of Christ* (first English tr.); Erasmus, *Enchiridion Militis Christiani*	Thomas Wyatt b.
1504		Nicholas Udall b.; Colet made Dean of St Paul's
c.1505		Thomas Tallis b.
1506		Columbus d.
c.1506		Robert Henryson d.
1509	Barclay, *The Ship of Fools*	**Henry VIII** (–1547); Jean Calvin b.
c.1509–19	(Anon.), *Everyman*	
1510		Giorgione d.; Botticelli d.
1511	Erasmus, *Encomium Moriae* (The Praise of Folly)	Erasmus at Cambridge
1513	Skelton, *Ballade of the Scottysshe Kynge*	Battle of Flodden Field; Machiavelli, *Il Principe* (The Prince) written
c.1513		William Dunbar d.
c.1515		Roger Ascham b.
1516	More, *Utopia*; Skelton, *Magnyfycence*	John Foxe b.; Ariosto, *Orlando Furioso* (see 1532); Hieronymus Bosch d.
1517		Henry Howard, Earl of Surrey, b.; Magellan's first voyage; Luther's Wittenberg theses
1518		Tintoretto b.
1519		Leonardo da Vinci d.
1520	Murdoch Nisbet (tr.), Scots New Testament	Field of the Cloth of Gold; Raphael d.
1521		Luther condemned at Diet of Worms; Magellan killed in Philippines
1522		Gavin Douglas d.
1523	Skelton, *The Garlande of Laurell*	
1525	Tyndale (tr.), New Testament (printed at Worms)	
1527		Machiavelli d.; Castiglione, *Il Cortegiano*; Sack of Rome
1528		Dürer d.
1529		John Skelton d.; Fall of Cardinal Wolsey
1530	Tyndale (tr.), the Pentateuch (pub. Antwerp)	Wolsey d.; Andrea del Sarto d.
1531	Elyot, *The Boke named the Governour*	**Henry VIII** separates from Catherine of Aragon
1532	Chaucer (d. 1400), *Works*, ed. W. Thynne	Ariosto, *Orlando Furioso* (final form); Rabelais, *Pantagruel*, i
1533	J. Heywood, *The Play of the Wether*; *A Play of Love*; More, *The Apology of Syr Thomas More*	Michel de Montaigne b.; **Henry VIII** marries Anne Boleyn
c.1533	Elyot, *The Doctrinall of Princis*	
1534		Rabelais, *Pantagruel (Gargantua)*, ii.; Act of Supremacy
1535	Coverdale's Bible (first pub. probably Zürich)	Sir Thomas More executed; St John Fisher executed; Ariosto d.
1536		William Tyndale burned; Anne Boleyn executed; Erasmus d.; Dissolution of the monasteries (–1539); Calvin, *Institution de la religion chrétienne* (Latin edn)
c.1536	Elyot, *The Castel of Helth*	

Date	Principal literary works	Other events
1537	Coverdale's Bible (modified version): first Bible printed in England; Cranmer, *Institution of a Christian Man*	
1538	Elyot, *Dictionary* (Latin/English)	
1539	The Great Bible	Act of Six Articles
1540	Elyot, *The Image of Governance*	Thomas Cromwell executed
1541	Udall (tr.), *Apophthegms of Erasmus*	Paracelsus d.; Calvin, *Institution de la religion chrétienne* (French edn)
1542		Sir Thomas Wyatt d.
1543	More, *History of Richard III* (in Grafton's *Chronicle*)	Copernicus (d. 1543), *De Revolutionibus*; Holbein d.
c.1543		William Byrd b.
1544		Torquato Tasso b.
1545	Ascham, *Toxophilus*	Mary Rose sinks in Solent; Council of Trent (–1563)
1546		Martin Luther d.; Sir Thomas Elyot d.
1547		**Edward VI** (–1553); Henry Howard executed; Miguel de Cervantes (Saavedra) b.; Nicholas Hilliard b.
1548	Bale, *King John*	
1549	Cranmer, Book of Common Prayer	
1550		Vasari, *Lives of the Artists* (completed 1568)
1551		William Camden b.
1552		Alexander Barclay d.; Christ's Hospital founded
c.1552		Edmund Spenser b.
1553		**Lady Jane Grey** (reigns nine days); **Mary I** (–1558); Rabelais d.
1554		Philip Sidney b.; Walter Ralegh b.?
1555		**Mary I**; marries Philip of Spain; Hugh Latimer and Nicholas Ridley burned
1556	Foxe, *Christus Triumphans*; The Geneva Psalter; J. Heywood, *The Spider and the Flie*	Thomas Cranmer burned; Nicholas Udall d.; Agricola, *De Re Metallica*
1557	North, *The Diall of Princes*; Surrey (tr.), *Aeneid* (bks. II, IV); Tottel and Grimald, *Songs and Sonnets (Tottel's Miscellany)*	Stationers obtain Charter of Incorporation
1558	Knox, *First Blast of the Trumpet Against the Monstrous Regiment of Women*	English lose Calais; **Elizabeth I** (–1603); Robert Greene b.; Thomas Kyd b.
c.1558		Thomas Lodge b.
1559	*The Mirror of Magistrates*	Act of Uniformity
1560	The Geneva ('Breeches') Bible	Westminster School founded
1561	Hoby, *The Courtyer* (tr. of Castiglione's *Il libro del cortegiano*, 1528); Norton (tr.), [Calvin] *The Institution of Christian Religion*	Francis Bacon b.; Merchant Taylors' School founded
1562		Samuel Daniel b.; Lope de Vega b.
1563	Foxe, *Actes and Monuments* ('Book of Martyrs'); The Thirty-Nine Articles	Michael Drayton b.; John Dowland b.
1564		William Shakespeare b.; Christopher Marlowe b.; Galileo b.; Michelangelo d.; Calvin d.; Hawkins' first voyage opens slave trade
1565	Norton and Sackville, *Gorboduc* (perf. 1561)	

Date	Principal literary works	Other events
c.1566	Udall (d. 1556), *Ralph Roister Doister* pub. (perf. c.1552)	
1566	Gascoigne, *Supposes*	
1567		Thomas Nashe b.; Thomas Campion b.
1568	The Bishops' Bible	
1569		Pieter Bruegel (the Elder) d.
1570	Ascham (d. 1568), *The Scholemaster*	**Elizabeth I** excommunicated by Pius V
c.1570		Thomas Dekker b.; Thomas Middleton b.
1571		Kepler b.; Battle of Lepanto; Caravaggio b.
1572		St Bartholomew's Day Massacre; John Donne b.; John Knox d.
1572–4	Matthew Parker, *De Antiquitate Britannicae*	
1573	Gascoigne, *A Hundreth Sundrie Flowres*	
c.1573		Ben Jonson b.
1575	*Gammer Gurton's Needle*	Titian d.
c.1575		John Marston b.; Cyril Tourneur b.
1576		Burbage's Theatre built in London
1577	Holinshed, *Chronicles*	Robert Burton b.; Drake's circumnavigation of the globe (–1580); Rubens b.
1578	Lyly, *Euphues. The Anatomy of Wit*	Master of the Revels becomes censor of plays
1579	North (tr.), Plutarch's *Lives*; Spenser, *The Shepheardes Calendar*; P. Sidney, *A Defence of Poetry* (–1580)	John Fletcher b.
1580	Stow, *Chronicles of England*	Camoëns d.
c.1580		John Webster b.
1581	Sidney, *Old Arcadia* (completed by)	
1582	Hakluyt, *Diverse voyages touching the discoverie of America*	Shakespeare marries Anne Hathaway
1583	Stubbes, *Anatomy of Abuses*	
1583–4	Sidney, *New Arcadia* (completed by)	
1584	Peele, *Arraignment of Paris*; Scot, *Discoverie of Witchcraft*	
1585		Thomas Tallis d.; Virginia colonized by W. Ralegh
1586	Camden, *Britannia*	Sir Philip Sidney d.
1587	Hakluyt, *Voyages Made into Florida*; Knox, *History of the Reformation in Scotland*	Mary Queen of Scots executed
c.1587	Kyd, *The Spanish Tragedy*	
1588		Defeat of Spanish Armada; Thomas Hobbes b.; Martin Marprelate controversy (–1590); Byrd, *Psalmes, Sonets and Songs*
1589	Greene, *Menaphon*; Hakluyt, *Principal Navigations, Voiages, and Discoveries . . .*; Lodge, *Scillaes Metamorphosis*; Nashe, *The Anatomie of Absurditie*; Puttenham, *The Arte of English Poesie*	Byrd, *Songs of Sundrie Natures*
1590	Greene, *Greenes Mourning Garment*; Lodge, *Rosalynde*; Marlowe, *Tamburlaine*; Sidney (d. 1586), *Arcadia* (revised version); Spenser, *Faerie Queene*, i–iii	

Date	Principal literary works	Other events
c.1590	Shakespeare, *The Comedy of Errors* written (pub. 1623); *Titus Andronicus* written (pub. 1594)	
1590–2	Shakespeare, *1 Henry VI* written (pub. 1623); *2 Henry VI* written (pub. 1594, anon. and retitled); *3 Henry VI* written (pub. 1595, anon. and retitled)	
1591	Harrington (tr.), *Orlando Furioso*; Lyly, *Endimion*; Sidney, *Astrophel and Stella*	Robert Herrick b.
c.1591	Shakespeare, *Richard III* written (pub. 1597)	
1592	*Arden of Faversham*; Daniel, *Delia*; Greene, *Greenes Groats-worth of Witte*; Lyly, *Midas*; Nashe, *Pierce Pennilesse his Supplication to the Divell*	Montaigne d.; Plague closes theatres for two years
c.1592	Shakespeare, *The Taming of the Shrew* written (pub. 1623)	
1593	Drayton, *Idea*; Hooker, *Of the Laws of Ecclesiastical Politie*, i–iv; Nashe, *Christs Teares over Jerusalem*; Shakespeare, *Venus and Adonis*; Sidney, *Arcadia* (revised version plus three books of early version)	Izaak Walton b.; George Herbert b.; Christopher Marlowe d.
1594	Drayton, *Ideas Mirrour*; Greene, *Orlando Furioso*; Marlowe (d. 1593), *Edward the Second*; Nashe, *The Terrors of the Night*; *The Unfortunate Traveller*; Shakespeare, *The Rape of Lucrece*	Lord Chamberlain's Men established; Tintoretto d.; T. Kyd d.
1595	Sidney, *Apologie for Poetry*	Robert Southwell executed; Tasso d.
c.1595	Shakespeare, *Love's Labour's Lost* written (pub. 1598); *Romeo and Juliet* written (pub. 1597, 1599); *Richard II* written (pub. 1597)	
1595–6	Shakespeare, *A Midsummer Night's Dream* written (pub. 1600)	
1596	Davies, *Orchestra*; Nashe, *Have with you to Saffron-walden*; Spenser, *Faerie Queene*, iv–vi	René Descartes b.; Essex storms Cadiz
c.1596–8	Shakespeare, *The Merchant of Venice* written (pub. 1600)	
1597	Bacon, *Essays* (other edns. 1612, 1625); Gerard, *Herball*; Hooker, *Laws of Ecclesiastical Politie*, v	Dowland, *The First Book of Songes*
c.1597	Shakespeare, *1 Henry IV* written (pub. 1598); *2 Henry IV* written (pub. 1600); *The Merry Wives of Windsor* written (pub. 1602, 1623)	
1598	Marlowe (d. 1593), *Hero and Leander*; Stow, *A Survey of London* (and 1603)	Edict of Nantes
c.1598–9	Shakespeare, *Much Ado About Nothing* written (pub. 1600)	
1599	Nashe, *Nashes Lenten Stuffe*; Shakespeare, *Henry V* written (pub. 1600)	Edmund Spenser d.; First Globe Theatre opened; Anthony Van Dyck b.
c.1599	Shakespeare, *Julius Caesar* written (pub. 1623); *As You Like It* registered (pub. 1623)	
1599–1601	Shakespeare, *Hamlet* written (pub. 1603; short text)	
1600	Dekker, *The Shoemaker's Holiday*; Jonson, *Every Man out of his Humour* (perf. 1599); Nashe, *Summers Last Will and Testament* (perf. 1599)	East India Company founded; Dowland, *Second Booke of Songes*; Pedro Calderón de la Barca b.; Claude Lorraine (Gellée) b.

Date	Principal literary works	Other events
1601	Holland (tr.), Pliny's *Natural History*; Jonson, *Every Man in his Humour* (perf. 1598); Shakespeare, *Twelfth Night* written (pub. 1623); 'The Phoenix and the Turtle' (in Chester's *Loves Martyr*)	Earl of Essex executed; Thomas Nashe d.; Poor Law Act
1602	Campion, *Art of English Poesie*; Dekker, *Satiromastix*; Marston, *Antonio and Mellida*; *Antonio's Revenge*	Bodleian Library opened
c.1602	Shakespeare, *Troilus and Cressida* written (pub. 1609)	
c.1602–4	Shakespeare, *Othello* written (pub. 1622)	
1603	Daniel, *Defence of Ryme*; Dekker, *The Wonderfull Yeare*; Florio (tr.), Montaigne's *Essays*	**James I** (–1625); Dowland, *Third and Last Booke of Songes*
1603–4	Shakespeare, *All's Well that Ends Well* written (pub. 1623)	
1604	Dekker, *The Honest Whore* (Parts 1 and 11)(1604–5), *Westward Hoe*; Marlowe (d. 1593), *Dr Faustus*; Marston, *The Malcontent*	Hampton Court Conference; Book of Common Prayer Authorized
c.1604	Shakespeare, *Measure for Measure* written (pub. 1623)	
1604–5	Shakespeare, *King Lear* written (pub. 1608)	
1605	Bacon, *Advancement of Learning*; Jonson, *Sejanus his Fall* (perf. 1603)	Gunpowder Plot; Sir Thomas Browne b.; Byrd, *Ave verum corpus*; Cervantes, *Don Quixote*, i
1606	Dekker, *Newes from Hell*	Edmund Waller b.; John Lyly d.; Pierre Corneille b.; Rembrandt b.
c.1606	Shakespeare, *Macbeth* written (pub. 1623)	
c.1606–7	Shakespeare, *Antony and Cleopatra* written (pub. 1623)	
1607	Chapman, *Bussy D'Ambois*; T. Heywood, *A Woman Killed With Kindness*; Jonson, *Volpone* (perf. 1605–6); Marston, *What You Will*; *The Revenger's Tragedy* (Tourneur? Middleton?)	Monteverdi, *Orfeo*; Settlement of Virginia
c.1607	Beaumont, *The Knight of the Burning Pestle* perf.; Shakespeare (with Middleton?), *Timon of Athens* written (pub. 1623)	
1608	Middleton, *A Mad World, My Masters*	John Milton b.
c.1608	Shakespeare, *Coriolanus* written (pub. 1623)	
1609	Dekker, *The Gul's Hornebooke*; Shakespeare, *Sonnets*	Edward Hyde, Earl of Clarendon, b.
1609–10	Shakespeare, *Cymbeline* written (pub. 1623)	
1610	Donne, *Pseudo-Martyr*	Monteverdi, *Vespers*; Caravaggio d.
1610–11	Shakespeare, *The Winter's Tale* written (pub. 1623)	
1611	Authorized Version of the Bible; Jonson, *Catiline* perf.; Tourneur, *The Atheist's Tragedy*	Bermuda settled
c.1611	Shakespeare, *The Tempest* written (pub. 1623)	
1612	Bacon, *Essays* (2nd edn.); Drayton, *Poly-Olbion*, i (completed 1622); Jonson, *The Alchemist* (perf. 1610); Webster, *The White Devil*	Henry, Prince of Wales d.
1613	Samuel Purchas, *Purchas his Pilgrimage*	Samuel Butler b.; Jeremy Taylor b.; Sir Thomas Bodley d.; Globe Theatre burns down

Date	Principal literary works	Other events
1614	Ralegh, *History of the World*	Addled Parliament
1615	Beaumont and Fletcher, *Cupid's Revenge*	Cervantes, *Don Quixote*, ii
1616	Chapman, *The Whole Works of Homer*; Jonson, *Mercury Vindicated*; *Epicene* (perf. 1609–10)	William Shakespeare d.; Francis Beaumont d.; Cervantes d.; Harvey expounds circulation of the blood
1618		Sir Walter Ralegh executed; Thirty Years War
1619	Beaumont (d. 1616) and Fletcher, *The Maid's Tragedy*	Samuel Daniel d.; Nicholas Hilliard d.
1619–22		Inigo Jones designs the Banqueting House, Whitehall
1620	Bacon, *Novum Organum*	Pilgrim Fathers emigrate to New World; John Evelyn b.; Thomas Campion d.
1621	Burton, *The Anatomy of Melancholy*; Dekker *et al.*, *The Witch of Edmonton*	Andrew Marvell b.; Henry Vaughan b.; Thomas Vaughan b.; Jean de La Fontaine b.
1622	Drayton, *Poly-Olbion*, ii	Virginia settlers massacred
c.1622	Middleton and Rowley, *The Changeling*	
1623	Webster, *The Duchess of Malfi*; Shakespeare (d. 1616), 'First Folio', ed. Heminge and Condell	William Byrd d.; Blaise Pascal b.
1624	Donne, *Devotions Upon Emergent Occasions*	War against Spain
1625	Bacon, *Essays* (3rd edn.)	Charles I (–1649); John Fletcher d.
1626		Francis Bacon d.; Cyril Tourneur d.; John Dowland d.
1627		Robert Boyle b.; War against France; Thomas Middleton d.
1628	Earle, *Microcosmographie*; W. Harvey, *De motu cordis*	John Bunyan b.; Buckingham assassinated; Fulke Greville d.
1629	Lancelot Andrewes, *XCVI Sermons*	
1630	Middleton (d. 1627), *A Chaste Mayd in Cheap-side*	
1631	Jonson, *Bartholomew Fair* (perf. 1614); Stow, *Annals of England* (final form)	John Dryden b.; John Donne d.; Michael Drayton d.; Peace with Spain
1632	Donne (d. 1631), *Death's Duell*	John Locke b.; Benedict de Spinoza b.; Thomas Dekker d.; Jan Vermeer b.; Jean-Baptiste Lully b. John Webster d.
c.1632		
1633	Donne (d. 1631), *Poems*; Ford, *The Broken Heart*; *'Tis Pity She's a Whore*; Herbert (d. 1633), *The Temple*; Marlowe (d. 1593), *The Jew of Malta*; Massinger, *A New Way to Pay Old Debts*	Samuel Pepys b.; George Herbert d.; Laud appointed Archbishop of Canterbury
1634		John Marston d.
1635	Francis Quarles, *Emblems*	
1636		Nicholas Boileau b.
1637	Milton, *Comus* (perf. 1634)	Ben Jonson d.
c.1637		Thomas Traherne b.
1638	Milton, *Lycidas*	Monteverdi, *Madrigals of Love and War*
1639		First Bishops' War
1640	Donne (d. 1631), *LXXX Sermons* (with life by I. Walton); Carew, *Poems*	The Long Parliament; Aphra Behn b.; Philip Massinger d.; Rubens d.
c.1640		John Ford d.
1641		Strafford executed Irish rebellion; Thomas Heywood d.

Date	Principal literary works	Other events
1642	Denham, *Cooper's Hill* (final version 1655); Milton, *Reason of Church Government*; *Apology for Smectymnuus*	Civil War begins (–1649); Public theatres closed (–1660); Galileo d.
1643	Browne, *Religio Medici*; D'Avenant, *The Unfortunate Lovers*	Solemn League and Covenant
1644	Milton, *Areopagitica*	Battle of Marston Moor
1645	Milton, *Tetrachordon*; *Poems*; Waller, *Poems*	William Laud executed; Battle of Naseby
1646	Browne, *Pseudodoxia Epidemica*; Crashaw, *Steps to the Temple*; H. Vaughan, *Poems*	
1647		John Wilmot, Earl of Rochester, b.
1648	Beaumont, *Psyche*; Herrick, *Hesperides*	
1649	Lovelace, *Lucasta*; Milton, *Tenure of Kings and Magistrates*; *Eikonoklastes*	Execution of **Charles I**; **The Commonwealth** (–1660); William Drummond d.
1650	Baxter, *The Saints' Everlasting Rest*; Taylor, *Rule and Exercise of Holy Living*; H. Vaughan, *Silex Scintillans*; T. Vaughan, *Anthroposophia Theomagica*	Descartes d.; Massacres of Drogheda and Wexford
1651	D'Avenant, *Gondibert*; Donne (d. 1631), *Essays in Divinity*; Hobbes, *Leviathan* (definitive Latin text 1668); Taylor, *Rules and Exercises of Holy Dying*	Battle of Worcester
1652	Ashmole, *Theatrum Chemicum*; H. Vaughan, *Mount of Olives*	Act of Settlement (Ireland)
1652–4		First Dutch War
1653	Walton, *The Compleat Angler* (2nd edn., 1655)	Oliver Cromwell becomes Protector
1656	Bunyan, *Some Gospel Truths Opened*; Cowley, *Poems*	War against Spain (–1659)
1657		Richard Lovelace d.
1658	Browne, *Hydrotaphia, or Urn Burial*; Massinger (d. 1640), *The City Madam* (perf. 1632)	Oliver Cromwell dies; succeeded by his son Richard
1659	Lovelace (d. 1657), *Posthume Poems*	
1660		The Restoration; **Charles II** (–1685); Samuel Pepys begins his diary (–1669); Bunyan imprisoned; Velázquez d.; Anne Marshall first woman on English stage
1661		Anne Finch, Countess of Winchilsea, b.
c.1661		Daniel Defoe b.
1662	Prayer Book (final version); Butler, *Hudibras*; Fuller (d. 1661), *Worthies of England*	Act of Uniformity; Dunkirk sold to France; Royal Society's first charter
1663	Butler, *Hudibras*, ii	
1664	Dryden, *The Rival Ladies*	Sir John Vanbrugh b.; Matthew Prior b.
1665	Bunyan, *The Holy City*; Lord Herbert of Cherbury, *Poems*; Marvell, *The Character of Holland*	The Great Plague; Second Dutch War (–1667)
1666	Bunyan, *Grace Abounding*; Glanvill, *Philosophical Considerations Concerning Witches and Witchcraft*	James Shirley d.; Thomas Vaughan d.; Great Fire of London; Molière, *Le Misanthrope*; *Le Médecin malgré lui*
1667	Dryden, *Annus Mirabilis*; Milton, *Paradise Lost* (10 books); Sprat, *History of the Royal Society*	Jonathan Swift b.; Jeremy Taylor d.; Abraham Cowley d.; Racine, *Andromaque*; Molière, *Tartuffe*

Date	Principal literary works	Other events
1668	Dryden, *Essay of Dramatick Poesie*; Etherege, *She wou'd if she cou'd*	William D'Avenant d.; Dryden Poet Laureate; Racine, *Les Plaideurs*; La Fontaine, *Fables*, i; François Couperin b.
1669	Dryden, *The Wild Gallant*	Rembrandt d.
1670		William Congreve b.; Pascal (d. 1662), *Pensées*; Molière, *Le Bourgeois gentilhomme*
1671	Milton, *Paradise Regained*; *Samson Agonistes*	
1672	Buckingham *et al.*, *The Rehearsal*	Joseph Addison b.; Richard Steele b.; Molière, *Les Femmes savantes*
1672–4		Third Dutch War
1673	Aphra Behn, *The Dutch Lover*; D'Avenant (d. 1668), *Collected Works*; Dryden, *Marriage à la Mode*	Test Act passed
1674	Milton (d. 1674), *Paradise Lost* (2nd edn., 12 books)	Robert Herrick d.; John Milton d.; Thomas Traherne d.; Edward Hyde d.
1675	Traherne (d. 1674), *Christian Ethics*; Wycherley, *The Country Wife*	Jan Vermeer d.
1676	Etherege, *The Man of Mode*	
1677	Aphra Behn, *The Rover*, i; Wycherley, *The Plain Dealer*	Spinoza (d. 1677), *Ethics*; Racine, *Phèdre*
1678	Bunyan, *Pilgrim's Progress*, i (ii pub. 1684); Butler, *Hudibras*, iii	Popish Plot; Andrew Marvell d.; La Fontaine, *Fables*, ii; Mme de Lafayette, *La Princesse de Clèves*
1679		Thomas Hobbes d.
1680	Bunyan, *The Life and Times of Mr Badman*	Samuel Butler d.; Joseph Glanvill d.; John Wilmot, Earl of Rochester, d.; La Rochefoucauld d.
1681	Aphra Behn, *The Rover*, ii; Dryden, *Absalom and Achitophel*, i; Hobbes (d. 1679), *Behemoth*; Marvell (d. 1678), *Miscellaneous Poems*	
1682	Bunyan, *The Holy War*; Dryden, *Religio Laici*; *Mac Flecknoe*, i; *Absalom and Achitophel*, ii; Otway, *Venice Preserv'd*	Sir Thomas Browne d.; Claude Lorraine d.
1683		Rye House Plot; Izaak Walton d.; Turks besiege Vienna
1684	Bunyan, *Pilgrim's Progress*, ii	Corneille d.; Jean-Antoine Watteau b.
1685		**James II** (–1688); John Gay b.; Thomas Otway d.; Monmouth's rebellion; J. S. Bach b.; G. F. Handel b.
1687	Dryden, *Song for St Cecilia's Day*; *The Hind and the Panther*	Jean-Baptiste Lully d.
1688	Dryden, *Britannia Rediviva*	**James II** abdicates; Glorious Revolution; Alexander Pope b.; John Bunyan d.
*c.*1688	A. Behn, *Oroonoko*	
1689	Marvell (d. 1678), *Poems on Affairs of State* (–1697)	**Mary II** (–1694) and **William III** (–1702); Siege of Londonderry; Samuel Richardson b.; Aphra Behn d.; Thomas Shadwell Poet Laureate
1690	Locke, *Essay Concerning Human Understanding*	Battle of the Boyne

Date	Principal literary works	Other events
1691	Wood, *Athenae Oxoniensis*	Sir George Etherege d.; Richard Baxter d.; Robert Boyle d.; George Fox d.; Purcell, *Dido and Aeneas*
1692		Purcell, *The Fairy Queen*
1693	Congreve, *The Old Bachelor*; Cotton Mather, *Wonders of the Invisible World*	La Fontaine, *Fables*, iii; Mme de Lafayette d.
1694	Congreve, *The Double Dealer*; Dryden, *Love Triumphant*	**Mary II** d.; **William III** reigns alone; Bank of England founded; Voltaire (François-Marie Arouet) b.
1695	Congreve, *Love for Love*	Henry Vaughan d.; Jean de La Fontaine d.; Purcell, *The Indian Queen*; Purcell d.
1696	Aubrey, *Miscellanies*	
1697	Dryden, *Alexander's Feast*; Vanbrugh, *The Relapse*; *The Provok'd Wife*	William Hogarth b.
1698		J. Collier attacks stage profanity
1699		Jean Racine d.; Fénelon, *Télémaque*
1700	Congreve, *The Way of the World*	James Thomson b.; John Dryden d.
1701	Dryden (d. 1700), *Collected Plays*	Act of Settlement; War of Spanish Succession begins
1702	Clarendon, *History of the Rebellion* (completed 1704); Defoe, *Shortest Way With Dissenters*	**Anne** (–1714)
1703		Defoe pilloried and imprisoned; Samuel Pepys d.; Perrault d.
1704	Swift, *A Tale of a Tub*; *The Battle of the Books*	Battle of Blenheim; John Locke d.; Bossuet d.
1705	Addison, *The Campaign*	
1706	Defoe, *Apparition of Mrs Veal*; Farquhar, *The Recruiting Officer*	Act of Succession; Benjamin Franklin b.; John Evelyn d.
1707	Farquhar, *The Beaux' Stratagem*; Watts, *Hymns*	Henry Fielding b.; George Farquhar d.; Union of England and Scotland
1709	Berkeley, *New Theory of Vision*; Defoe, *History of the Union of Great Britain*; Swift, *Baucis and Philemon*	Steele starts *The Tatler* (–1711); First Copyright Act; Samuel Johnson b.
1710	Berkeley, *Principles of Human Knowledge*; Swift, *Meditations upon a Broomstick*	
1711	Pope, *Essay on Criticism*; Shaftesbury, *Characteristics of Men and Manners*	*The Spectator* started (–1712); David Hume b.; Boileau d.
1712	Pope, *The Rape of the Lock* (in Lintot's *Miscellanies*); Swift, *Proposal for Correcting the English Language*	Jean-Jacques Rousseau b.; Stamp Act
1713	Addison, *Cato*; Pope, *Windsor Forest*	Laurence Sterne b.; Swift becomes Dean of St Paul's; Denis Diderot b.
1714		**George I** (–1727); Leibniz, *Monadologie*
1715	Pope (tr.), *Iliad*, i (ii: 1716; iii: 1717; iv: 1718; v–vi: 1720); Watts, *Divine Songs for Children*	First Jacobite Rebellion; Nicholas Rowe Poet Laureate; Louis XIV d.
1716		Thomas Gray b.; William Wycherley d.; Leibniz d.
1717	Pope, *Collected Works* (inc. 'Verses to the Memory of an Unfortunate Lady' and 'Eloisa to Abelard')	Horace Walpole b.; David Garrick b.; Handel, *Water Music*
1718		Laurence Eusden Poet Laureate; Handel, *Acis and Galatea*
1719	Defoe, *Robinson Crusoe*; Watts, *Psalms of David*	Joseph Addison d.
1720	Defoe, *Memoirs of a Cavalier*; *Captain Singleton*; Gay, *Collected Poems*	South Sea Bubble; Giovanni Battista Piranesi b.

Date	Principal literary works	Other events
1721	Swift, *Letter to a Young Gentleman*; *Letter of Advice to a Young Poet*	William Collins b.; Tobias Smollett b.; Mark Akenside b.; Matthew Prior d.; Bach, *Brandenburg Concertos 1–6*; Watteau d.
1722	Defoe, *Journal of the Plague Year*; *Moll Flanders*; *Colonel Jack*	Christopher Smart b.; Joseph Wharton b.
1723		Adam Smith b.; Sir Joshua Reynolds b.
1724	Defoe, *Roxana*; *Tour through [. . .] Great Britain* (completed 1726); Oldmixon, *Critical History of England* (completed 1726); Swift, *Drapier's Letters*	Immanuel Kant b.; Bach, *St John Passion*
1725	Pope (ed.), Shakespeare's Works (2nd edn, 1728); (tr., with William Broome and Elijah Fenton) *Odyssey*, i–iii (iv–v: 1726); Swift, *Jonathan Wild*	
1726	Swift, *Gulliver's Travels*; Theobald, *Shakespeare Restored* (criticism of Pope's edn. of Shakespeare); Thomson, *Winter*	Charles Burney b.; Sir John Vanbrugh d.; Voltaire in England (three years)
1727	Defoe, *History and Reality of Apparitions*; Dyer, *Grongar Hill*; Gay, *Fables*, i (ii: 1738; completed 1750); Thomson, *Summer*	**George II** (–1760); John Wilkes b.; Sir Isaac Newton d.; Bach, *St Matthew Passion*; Thomas Gainsborough b.
1728	Gay, *The Beggar's Opera*; Law, *A Serious Call to a Devout and Holy Life*; Pope, *The Dunciad*, i–iii; iv (the *New Dunciad*): 1742; complete 1743; Swift, *Short View of the State of Ireland*; Thomson, *Spring*	Robert Bage b.; Gay's *Polly* banned by Lord Chamberlain
1729	Swift, *A Modest Proposal*	Edmund Burke b.; Richard Steele d.; William Congreve d.; G. E. Lessing b.
1730	Fielding, *Tom Jones*; Thomson, *The Seasons* (inc. 'Autumn')	Oliver Goldsmith b.; Colley Cibber Poet Laureate
1731	Pope, *Of Taste*	William Cowper b.; Daniel Defoe d.; Prévost, *L'Histoire du chevalier des Grieux et de Manon Lescaut*
1732	Gay, libretto for *Acis and Galatea* (Handel); Pope, *Of the Use of Riches*; Swift, *The Lady's Dressing-Room*; *The Beast's Confession to the Priest*	John Gay d.; Voltaire, *Zaïre*; Franz Joseph Haydn b.
1733	Pope, *An Essay on Man* (1733–4); *Imitations of Horace*, i; Swift, *A Serious and Useful Scheme . . .*	Joseph Priestley b.; François Couperin d.
1734	Fielding, *Don Quixote in England*; Gay, *The Distressed Wife*; Pope, *Imitations of Horace*, ii; George Sale (tr.), the Koran; Swift, *A Beautiful Young Nymph Going to Bed*	Bach, *Christmas Oratorio*; Joseph Wright (of Derby) b.
1735	Pope, *Epistle to Dr Arbuthnot*; Thomson, 'Italy'; 'Greece'; 'Rome' (pts. i–iii of *Liberty*)	
1736	Thomson, 'Britain'; 'The Prospect' (pts. iv and v of *Liberty*)	
1737	Shenstone, *Poems Upon Various Occasions*	Edward Gibbon b.; Thomas Paine b.; Robert Walpole's Licensing Act
1738	Gay, *Fables*, ii; Johnson, *London*; Swift, *A Complete Collection of Polite and Ingenious Conversation*	
1739	Hume, *Treatise of Human Nature* (completed 1740); Swift, *Verses on the Death of Dr Swift*	Wesley, John and Charles, *Hymns and Sacred Poems*; War of Jenkins's Ear

Date	Principal literary works	Other events
1740	Cibber, *An Apology for the Life of Mr Colley Cibber*; Dyer, *The Ruins of Rome*; Thomson, *Alfred* (containing 'Ode in Honour of Great Britain', i.e. 'Rule Britannia'); Richardson, *Pamela*	James Boswell b.; War of the Austrian Succession
1741	Fielding, *Shamela*; Hume, *Essays Moral and Political* (completed 1742); Shenstone, *The Judgement of Hercules*; Watts, *Improvement of the Mind*	Edmond Malone b.; Choderlos de Laclos b.; Vivaldi d.
1742	Collins, *Persian Eclogues*; Fielding, *Joseph Andrews*; Pope, *New Dunciad*; Shenstone, *The Schoolmistress*; Young, *The Complaint, or Night Thoughts . . .* (–1745)	Richard Bentley d.; Voltaire, *Mahomet*; Handel, *Messiah*
1743	Blair, *The Grave*	
1744	Akenside, *Pleasures of Imagination*; Thomson, *The Seasons* (revised version); J. Warton, *The Enthusiast*	Alexander Pope d.; Wesley, John and Charles, *A Collection of Psalms and Hymns*
1745	Akenside, *Odes on Several Subjects*	Second Jacobite Rebellion; Jonathan Swift d.
1746	Collins, *Odes on Several Descriptive and Allegorical Subjects*; J. Warton, *Odes on Various Subjects*	Robert Blair d.; Battle of Culloden; Francisco de Goya b.
1747	Gray, *Ode on a Distant Prospect of Eton College*; Johnson, *Plan of a Dictionary of the English Language*; Richardson, *Clarissa* (8 vols., 1747–9); J. Warton, *The Pleasures of Melancholy*; Warburton's edition of Shakespeare; Wortley Montagu, *Town Eclogues*	Voltaire, *Zadig*
1748	Hume, *Enquiry Concerning Human Understanding*; Smollett, *The Adventures of Roderick Random*; Thomson (d. 1748), *The Castle of Indolence*	Jeremy Bentham b.; James Thomson d.; Isaac Watts d.
1749	Cleland, *Memoirs of a Woman of Pleasure* (*Fanny Hill*; see 1750); Fielding, *The History of Tom Jones*; Johnson, *The Vanity of Human Wishes*; *Irene*; Smollett (tr.), *Gil Blas*; J. Warton, *The Triumph of Isis*	Bach, Mass in B minor
1750	Cleland, *Memoirs of Fanny Hill* (abridged version of Cleland, 1749); Thomson (d. 1748), *Poems on Several Occasions*	J. S. Bach d.
1751	Fielding, *Amelia*; Gray, *Elegy Written in a Country Church-Yard*; Hume, *Enquiry Concerning Principles of Morals*; Smollett, *The Adventures of Peregrine Pickle*	Richard Brinsley Sheridan b.
1752	Law, *The Way to Divine Knowledge*; Lennox, *The Female Quixote*; Smart, *Poems on Several Occasions*	Thomas Chatterton b.; Fanny Burney b.; Gregorian Calendar adopted: eleven days 'lost'
1753	Richardson, *The History of Sir Charles Grandison* (7 vols, 1753–4); Smollett, *The Adventures of Ferdinand, Count Fathom*	Wesley, John and Charles, *Hymns and Spiritual Songs*; Charter of the British Museum
1754	Hume, *History of England*, i (ii: 1757; final version 1762)	George Crabbe b.; Henry Fielding d.
1755	Fielding (d. 1754), *Journal of a Voyage to Lisbon*; Johnson, *A Dictionary of the English Language*	Lisbon Earthquake

Date	Principal literary works	Other events
1756	J. Warton, *Essay on the Writings and Genius of Pope*	William Godwin b.; Thomas Rowlandson b.; Mozart b.; Seven Years War
1757	Burke, *Philosophical Enquiry into . . . the Sublime and the Beautiful*; Dyer (d. 1757), *The Fleece*; Gray, *Odes by Mr Gray* (inc. 'The Progress of Poesy', 'The Bard'); Smollett, *A Complete History of England* (completed 1758)	William Blake b.; Colley Cibber d.; John Dyer d.; William Whitehead Poet Laureate
1758	Akenside, *Ode to the Country Gentlemen of England*; Johnson, *The Idler* (in the *Universal Chronicle*, collected 1758)	
1759	Goldsmith, *An Enquiry into the Present State of Polite Learning*; Johnson, *Rasselas, Prince of Abyssinia*; Sterne, *A Political Romance*	Robert Burns b.; Mary Wollstonecraft b.; William Beckford b.; William Collins d.; Handel d.; Schiller b.; Voltaire, *Candide*; British Museum opens; Capture of Quebec
1760	Macpherson, *Fragments of Ancient Poetry, Collected in the Highlands*; Sterne, *The Life and Opinions of Tristram Shandy*, i–ii (iii–vi: 1761–2; vii and viii: 1765; ix: 1767); *Sermons of Yorick* (completed 1769)	**George III** (–1811)
1761	Churchill, *The Rosciad*; *The Apology*	Samuel Richardson d.; William Law d.; Kotzebue d.; Rousseau, *Julie, ou la Nouvelle Héloïse*
1762	Churchill, *The Ghost*, i–iii (iv: 1763); Goldsmith, *The Citizen of the World*; Macpherson, *Fingal, an Ancient Epic Poem*; Smollett, *The Adventures of Sir Launcelot Greaves*; Walpole, *Anecdotes of Painting* (completed 1780); E. Young, *Resignation*	William Cobbett b.; Lady Mary Wortley Montagu d.; Rousseau, *Du contrat social*; *Émile*; Wilkes starts *North Briton*
1763	Hugh Blair, *A Critical Dissertation on the Poems of Ossian*; Macpherson, *Temora*; C. Smart, *A Song to David*	Samuel Rogers b.; William Shenstone d.; John Wilkes prosecuted; Johnson meets Boswell; Jean-Paul Richter b.; Peace of Paris
1764	Goldsmith, *The History of England in a Series of Letters*; *The Traveller*; T. Warton, the younger (ed.), *The Oxford Sausage*	Ann Radcliffe b.; Charles Churchill d.; William Hogarth d.; Voltaire, *Dictionnaire philosophique portatif*; Jean-Philippe Rameau d.
1765	Blackstone, *Commentaries on the Laws of England* (completed 1769); Johnson (ed.), *The Works of Shakespeare*; Macpherson, *Works of Ossian*; Percy, *Reliques of Ancient English Poetry*; Smart (tr.), *The Psalms of David*; Walpole, *The Castle of Otranto*	Edward Young d.
1766	Anstey, *The New Bath Guide*; Goldsmith, *The Vicar of Wakefield*; Smollett, *Travels Through France and Italy*	Thomas Malthus b.; Robert Bloomfield b.; Mme de Staël b.; Lessing, *Laokoon*
1767		Maria Edgeworth b.; Wesley, John and Charles, *Hymns for the Use of Families*
1768	Boswell, *An Account of Corsica*; Gray, *Poems by Mr Gray* (inc. 'The Fatal Sisters', 'The Descent of Odin'); Sterne (d. 1768), *A Sentimental Journey through France and Italy*; Walpole, *The Mysterious Mother*	Laurence Sterne d.; Royal Academy of Arts founded; Chateaubriand b.; Canaletto d.

Date	Principal literary works	Other events
1769	Smollett, *The Adventures of an Atom*	Amelia Opie b.; Garrick's Shakespeare Jubilee; Napoleon b.; James Watt's steam engine patented
1770	Goldsmith, *The Deserted Village*; Percy, *Northern Antiquities*	William Wordsworth b.; James Hogg b.; Mark Akenside d.; Thomas Chatterton d.; Holbach, *Le Système de la nature*; Hölderlin b.; Beethoven b.
1771	Beattie, *The Minstrel* i (ii: 1774); Smollett, *The Expedition of Humphrey Clinker*	Sir Walter Scott b.; Thomas Gray d.; Tobias Smollett d.
1772	'Junius', *Letters*	S. T. Coleridge b.; Emanuel Swedenborg d.
1773	Barbauld, *Poems*; Goldsmith, *She Stoops to Conquer*; Richard Graves, *The Spiritual Quixote*; Sterne (d. 1768), *Letters from Yorick to Eliza*	James Mill b.; Boston Tea Party
1774	Burke, *Speech on American Taxation*; Chesterfield, *Letters to His Natural Son*; T. Warton the younger, *History of English Poetry* (3 vols, 1774–81)	Robert Southey b.; Oliver Goldsmith d.; Goethe, *Die Leiden des jungen Werthers* (The Sorrows of Young Werther); Bürger, *Lenore*
1775	Johnson, *A Journey to the Western Islands of Scotland*; Sheridan, *The Rivals*	Jane Austen b; Charles Lamb b.; Walter Savage Landor b.; M. G. Lewis b.; War of American Independence; J. M. W. Turner b.; John Constable b.; Beaumarchais, *Le Barbier de Seville*
1776	Gibbon, *Decline and Fall of the Roman Empire*, i (ii and iii: 1781; iv–vi: 1788); Smith, *The Wealth of Nations*	David Hume d.; American Declaration of Independence
1777	Chatterton (d. 1770), *Poems, Supposed to Have Been Written by Thomas Rowley*; Sheridan, *The School for Scandal* perf.	
1778	Burney, *Evelina* (pub. anonymously)	Rousseau d.; Piranesi d.
1779	Richard Graves, *Columella*; Johnson, *The Works of the English Poets*; Sheridan, *The Critic* perf.	
1780	Crabbe, *The Candidate*	Gordon Riots; Wieland, *Oberon*
1781	Bage, *Mount Henneth*; Crabbe, *The Library*; Gibbon, *Decline and Fall of the Roman Empire*, ii and iii	Rousseau (d. 1778), *Les Confessions*, i–vi (vii–xii: 1788); G. E. Lessing d.; British surrender at Yorktown
1782	Burney, *Cecilia*; Cowper, *Poems*; 'The Diverting History of John Gilpin' (in *Public Advertiser*; repr. 1785); I. Sancho, *Letters*	C. R. Maturin b.; Laclos, *Les Liaisons dangereuses*
1783	Beckford, *Dreams, Waking Thoughts and Incidents*; Blake, *Poetical Sketches*; Crabbe, *The Village*; Thomas Day, *The History of Sandford and Merton*	Peace of Versailles; Washington Irving b.; Stendhal b.
1784	Bage, *Barham Downs*	Leigh Hunt b.; Samuel Johnson d.; Diderot d.; Beaumarchais, *Le Mariage de Figaro*
1785	Boswell, *Journal of Tour of the Hebrides with Johnson*; Cowper, *The Task* (also inc. 'John Gilpin'); Richard Graves, *Eugenius*; Paley, *The Principles of Moral and Political Philosophy*; Rudolf Raspe, *Baron Munchausen's Travels*	Thomas De Quincey b.; Thomas Love Peacock b.; Thomas Warton Poet Laureate
1786	Beckford, *Vathek* (first English tr.); Burns, *Poems Chiefly in the Scottish Dialect*; Hester Lynch Piozzi, *Anecdotes of Samuel Johnson*	Frederick the Great d.; Mozart, *Le nozze di Figaro* (The Marriage of Figaro)

Date	Principal literary works	Other events
1787	Bage, *The Fair Syrian*; Wollstonecraft, *Thoughts on the Education of Daughters*	Mary Russell Mitford b.; American Constitution signed; Mozart, *Don Giovanni*
1788	Bage, *James Wallace*; Gibbon, *Decline and Fall of the Roman Empire*, iv–vi; 'Peter Pindar', *The Poetical Works of Peter Pindar*	Byron b.; Charles Wesley d.; Thomas Gainsborough d.; Trial of Warren Hastings; *The Times* started
1789	Blake, *Songs of Innocence*; *The Book of Thel*; E. Darwin, *Loves of the Plants*; Equiano, *Interesting Narrative*; G.White, *The Natural History of Selborne*	French Revolution
1790	Blake, *The Marriage of Heaven and Hell*; Burke, *Reflections on the Revolution in France*; Radcliffe, *A Sicilian Romance*	Adam Smith d.; Henry James Pye Poet Laureate; Benjamin Franklin d.; Lamartine b.; Mozart, *Così fan tutte*
1791	Blake, *The French Revolution*; Boswell, *The Life of Samuel Johnson*; Burns, *Tam o'Shanter*; Isaac D'Israeli, *Curiosities of Literature*, i (ii: 1793; iii: 1817; iv and v: 1823; vi: 1834); Benjamin Franklin (d. 1790), *Autobiography*; Paine, *The Rights of Man*, i (ii: 1792); Radcliffe, *Romance of the Forest*	Michael Faraday b.; *The Observer* started; Mozart, *Die Zauberflöte* (The Magic Flute); Mozart d.; Louis XVI's flight to Varennes (June)
1792	Aiken and Barbauld, *Evenings at Home*; Bage, *Man as He Is*; Blake, *Song of Liberty*; Holcroft, *Anna St Ives*; Rogers, *The Pleasures of Memory*; Mary Wollstonecraft, *A Vindication of the Rights of Woman*	Percy Bysshe Shelley b.; John Keble b.; Frederick Marryat b.; Sir Joshua Reynolds d.; Paine flees to France; Monarchy abolished in France
1793	Blake, *Visions of the Daughters of Albion*; *America*; Burns, *Poems*; Godwin, *An Enquiry Concerning Political Justice*; Wordsworth, *An Evening Walk*; *Descriptive Sketches*	John Clare b.; Gilbert White d.; Execution of Louis XVI (Jan.); War with France
1794	Blake, *Songs of Experience*; *Europe*; *The Book of Urizen*; Godwin, *Caleb Williams*; Paine, *The Age of Reason*, i (ii: 1795; iii: 1811); Paley, *View of the Evidences of Christianity*; Radcliffe, *The Mysteries of Udolpho*	Edward Gibbon d.; Execution of Robespierre
1795	Blake, *The Book of Los*; *The Book of Ahania*; *The Song of Los*; *Songs of Innocence and Experience*; Chatterton (d. 1770), *Poetical Works*; Landor, *Poems*	John Keats b.; Thomas Carlyle b.; Thomas Arnold b.; James Boswell d.; Goethe, *Wilhelm Meisters Lehrjahre* (Wilhelm Meister's Apprenticeship, 1795–6)
1796	Bage, *Hermsprong*; Burney, *Camilla*; Lewis, *The Monk*	Robert Burns d.
1797	Bewick, *A History of British Birds*; Radcliffe, *The Italian*; Southey, *Poems*; *Letters Written in Spain and Portugal*	Mary Wollstonecraft Godwin d.; Edmund Burke d.; Horace Walpole d.; Franz Schubert b.; Alfred de Vigny b.; Joseph Wright (of Derby) d.; Haydn, *Die Schöpfung* (The Creation, 1797–8)
1798	Coleridge, 'Fears in Solitude', 'France: an ode', 'Frost at Midnight'; Landor, *Gebir*; Malthus, *An Essay on the Principles of Population*; Wordsworth and Coleridge, *Lyrical Ballads* (1st edn; see 1800, 1802)	
1799	T. Campbell, *The Pleasures of Hope*; Godwin, *St Leon*; M. G. Lewis, *Tales of Terror*; Mungo Park, *Travels in the Interior of Africa*	Thomas Hood b.; Religious Tract Society founded; Napoleon First Consul; Balzac b.

Date	Principal literary works	Other events
1800	Bloomfield, *The Farmer's Boy*; Burns (d. 1796), *Works* (with life); Coleridge, tr. of Schiller's *Wallenstein*; Dibdin, *History of the English Stage*; Edgeworth, *Castle Rackrent*; Wordsworth and Coleridge, *Lyrical Ballads* (2 vols: Preface, 1798 poems, and new poems)	Thomas Babington Macaulay b.; Edward Pusey b.; William Cowper d.; Beethoven, Symphony No. 1
1801	Edgeworth, *Moral Tales for Young People*; *Belinda*; M. G. Lewis, *Tales of Wonder*; T. Moore, *Poems by Thomas Little*; Southey, *Thalaba the Destroyer*	J. H. Newman b.; Robert Bage d.; Union with Ireland; Chateaubriand, *Atala*; Haydn, *Die Jahreszeiten* (The Seasons)
1802	Lamb, *John Woodvil*; Landor, *Poetry by the Author of Gebir*; Paley, *Natural Theology*; W. Scott, *Minstrelsy of the Scottish Border*; Wordsworth and Coleridge, *Lyrical Ballads* (3rd edn., with new Preface)	Harriet Martineau b.; Erasmus Darwin d.; Peace of Amiens; Alexandre Dumas (Dumas *père*) b.; Victor Hugo b.; Mme de Staël, *Delphine*
1803	E. Darwin (d. 1802), *The Temple of Nature*; Repton, *Theory and Practice of Landscape Gardening*; Southey (tr.), *Amadis of Gaul*	T. L. Beddoes b.; George Borrow b.; Ralph Waldo Emerson b.; Edward Bulwer (Lytton) b.; Prosper Merimée b.; Hector Berlioz b.; Beethoven, Symphony No. 3 ('Eroica');
1804	Blake, *Jerusalem* (1804–20); *Milton* (1804–8); Edgeworth, *Popular Tales*; *A Modern Griselda*	Benjamin Disraeli b.; Nathaniel Hawthorne b.; John Wilkes d.; Napoleon crowned Emperor; Kant d.; George Sand (Lucile-Aurore Dupin) b.
1805	Cary (tr.), Dante's *Inferno*; W. Scott, *The Lay of the Last Minstrel*; Southey, *Madoc*	W. H. Ainsworth b.; Robert Surtees b.; Battle of Trafalgar; Battle of Austerlitz; Schiller d.; Samuel Palmer b.; Beethoven, *Fidelio*
1806	Byron, *Fugitive Pieces*; Landor, *Simonidea*; Lingard, *Antiquities of the Anglo-Saxon Church*; W. Scott, *Ballads and Lyrical Pieces*	Elizabeth Barrett b.; J. S. Mill b.; Charles James Fox d.
1807	Byron, *Hours of Idleness*; *Poems on Various Occasions*; Crabbe, *Poems* (inc. 'The Parish Register'); Charles and Mary Lamb, *Tales from Shakespeare*; T. Moore, *Irish Melodies*; Southey, *Letters from England*; Wordsworth, *Poems in Two Volumes*	Henry Wadsworth Longfellow b.; Mme de Staël, *Corinne*
1808	M. G. Lewis, *Romantic Tales*; W. Scott, *Marmion*; S. Smith, *The Letters of Peter Plymley*	Peninsular War begins; Convention of Cintra; Goethe, *Faust*, i; Beethoven, Symphony No. 6 ('Pastoral')
1809	Byron, *English Bards and Scotch Reviewers*; Coleridge, *The Friend* (–1810); Wordsworth, *Concerning the Relations of Great Britain, Spain and Portugal as Affected by the Convention of Cintra*	Charles Darwin b.; Alfred Tennyson b.; W. E. Gladstone b.; Thomas Paine d.; Edgar Allan Poe b.; Haydn d.
1810	Crabbe, *The Borough*; W. Scott, *The Lady of the Lake*; P. B. Shelley, *Original Poetry by Victor and Cazire*; *Zastrozzi*; Southey, *The Curse of Kehama*	Elizabeth Gaskell b.; Robert Schumann b.; Frédéric Chopin b.
1811	Austen, *Sense and Sensibility* (pub. anonymously); W. Scott, *The Vision of Don Roderick*; P. B. Shelley, *The Necessity of Atheism*	W. M. Thackeray b.; **Regency declared**; Shelley expelled from Oxford; Gautier b.; Liszt b.

Date	Principal literary works	Other events
1812	Byron, *Childe Harold*, i and ii; *The Curse of Minerva*; Cary (tr.), Dante's *Purgatorio* and *Paradiso*; Combe, *Tour of Dr Syntax in Search of the Picturesque*; Edgeworth, *Tales of Fashionable Life*, 2nd ser.; Southey and Coleridge, *Omniana*	Robert Browning b.; Charles Dickens b.; Edward Lear b.; Edmond Malone d.; French retreat from Moscow
1813	Austen, *Pride and Prejudice* (pub. anonymously); Byron, *The Bride of Abydos*; *The Giaour*; Coleridge, *Remorse*; W. Scott, *Rokeby*; P. B. Shelley, *Queen Mab*; Southey, *Life of Nelson*	Southey Poet Laureate; Richard Wagner b.; Giuseppe Verdi b.
1814	Austen, *Mansfield Park* (pub. anonymously); Byron, *The Corsair*; *Lara*; *Ode to Napoleon*; Hunt, *Feast of the Poets* (book form); W. Scott, *Waverley* (pub. anonymously); Southey, *Roderick, the Last of the Goths*; Wordsworth, *The Excursion*	Charles Reade b.; Abdication of Napoleon
1815	Byron, *Hebrew Melodies*; Hunt, *The Descent of Liberty*; W. Scott, *Guy Mannering*; *The Lord of the Isles*; *The Field of Waterloo*	Anthony Trollope b.; Byron married; Wellington and Blücher defeat Napoleon at Waterloo, 18 June
1816	Austen, *Emma* (pub. anonymously); Byron, *The Prisoner of Chillon and other Poems*; *Childe Harold*, iii; *The Siege of Corinth*; Coleridge, *Christabel and Other Poems* (inc. 'Kubla Khan', 'The Pains of Sleep'); Hunt, *The Story of Rimini*; Lady Caroline Lamb, *Glenarvon*; Peacock, *Headlong Hall*; W. Scott, *The Antiquary* (*Tales of My Landlord*, 1st ser.); P. B. Shelley, *Alastor and Other Poems*	Charlotte Brontë b.; Richard Brinsley Sheridan d.; Shelley's marriage to Mary Godwin; Leigh Hunt's essay on Shelley and Keats in *The Examiner*; Rossini, *Il barbiere di Siviglia*; Benjamin Constant, *Adolphe*
1817	Byron, *Manfred*; *The Lament of Tasso*; Coleridge, *Sybilline Leaves*; Hazlitt, *Characters of Shakespeare's Plays*; Keats, *Poems* (inc. 'Sleep and Poetry'); T. Moore, *Lalla Rookh*; Peacock, *Melincourt*; W. Scott, *Rob Roy*; P. B. Shelley, *Laon and Cythna* (see 1818); Southey, *Wat Tyler*	G. H. Lewes b.; Jane Austen d.; Henry David Thoreau b.; *Blackwood's Magazine* started; Mme de Staël d.
1818	Austen (d. 1817), *Northanger Abbey* and *Persuasion* (with Memoir); Bowdler, *The Family Shakespeare*; Byron, *Childe Harold*, iv; *Beppo*; Hazlitt, *Lectures on the English Poets*; Keats, *Endymion*; T. Moore, *The Fudge Family in Paris*; Peacock, *Nightmare Abbey*; *Rhododaphne*; W. Scott, *The Heart of Midlothian* (*Tales of My Landlord*, 2nd ser.); M. Shelley, *Frankenstein*; P. B. Shelley, *The Revolt of Islam* (orig. *Laon and Cythna*, 1817)	Emily Brontë b.; M. G. Lewis d.; Shelley's final departure from England; Attack on Keats in *Quarterly Review*; Karl Marx b.
1819	Byron, *Mazeppa*; *Don Juan*, i and ii; Hazlitt, *Lectures on the English Comic Writers*; Lockhart, *Peter's Letters to His Kinfolk*; Macaulay, *Pompeii*; Mitford, *Our Village* (in *Lady's Magazine*; pub. in book form 1824–32); J. H. Reynolds, *Peter Bell*; W. Scott, *The Bride of Lammermoor* (in *Tales of My Landlord*, 3rd ser.); *Ivanhoe*; P. B. Shelley, *The Cenci*; *Rosalind and Helen*; Wordsworth, *Peter Bell*; *The Waggoner*	Charles Kingsley b.; John Ruskin b.; A. H. Clough b.; George Eliot (Mary Ann Evans) b.; Walt Whitman b.; Peterloo Massacre

Date	Principal literary works	Other events
1820	Elizabeth Barrett, *The Battle of Marathon*; Clare, *Poems, Descriptive of Rural Life*; Galt, *The Ayrshire Legatees*; Irving, *The Sketch-book of Geoffrey Crayon*; Keats, *Lamia, The Eve of St Agnes, Hyperion, and Other Poems*; C. Lamb, *Essays of Elia* (in *London Magazine* 1820–3, collected 1823); Maturin, *Melmoth the Wanderer*; Peacock, *The Four Ages of Poetry*; W. Scott, *The Abbot*; *The Monastery*; P. B. Shelley, *Prometheus Unbound and Other Poems*; Southey, *Life of John Wesley*; Wordsworth, *The River Duddon*; *Vaudracour and Julia*	**George IV** (–1830); Anne Brontë b.; Herbert Spencer b.; Jean Ingelow b.; Trial of Queen Caroline
1821	Beddoes, *The Improvisatore*; Byron, *Cain*; *Don Juan*, iii–v; *Marino Faliero*; Clare, *The Village Minstrel and Other Poems*; J. F. Cooper, *The Spy*; De Quincey, *Confessions of an English Opium Eater* (in *London Magazine*; pub. separately 1822); Egan, *Life in London* (vol. pub.); Galt, *Annals of the Parish*; Hazlitt, *Table Talk* (completed 1822); W. Scott, *Kenilworth*; Shelley, *Epipsychidion*; *Adonais*; Southey, *A Vision of Judgement*	Keats d.; Greek War of Liberation; Famine in Ireland (1821–3); Baudelaire b.; Flaubert b.; Dostoevsky b.; Napoleon d.
1822	Beddoes, *The Bride's Tragedy*; Byron, *Werner*; 'The Vision of Judgment' (in *The Liberal*: see 1821, Southey); Galt, *The Provost*; Irving, *Bracebridge Hall*; Peacock, *Maid Marian*; S. Rogers, *Italy*, i (ii: 1828; completed 1830); W. Scott, *The Fortunes of Nigel*; *The Pirate*; *Peveril of the Peak*; Shelley, *Hellas*; Wordsworth, *Ecclesiastical Sketches*	Matthew Arnold b.; Shelley d.; *Sunday Times* started
1823	Byron, *Don Juan*, vi–viii (July); ix–xi (Aug.); xii–xiv (Dec.); Carlyle, *Life of Schiller* (in *London Magazine*, pub. separately 1825); J. F. Cooper, *The Pioneers*; Galt, *The Entail*; Hazlitt, *Liber Amoris*; C. Lamb, *Essays of Elia* (see 1820); T. Moore, *The Loves of the Angels*; W. Scott, *Quentin Durward*; Southey, *History of the Peninsular War* (completed 1832)	Charlotte Yonge b.; Coventry Patmore b.; Ann Radcliffe d.; Beethoven, *Missa Solemnis* (completed)
1824	Byron, *Don Juan*, xv and xvi; *The Deformed Transformed*; Hogg, *Confessions of a Justified Sinner*; Landor, *Imaginary Conversations of Literary Men and Statesmen*, i; M. R. Mitford, *Our Village* (completed 1832); W. Scott, *Redgauntlet*; *St Ronan's Well*	Wilkie Collins b.; Byron d.; National Gallery, London, founded; Beethoven, Symphony No. 9 ('Choral')
1825	Coleridge, *Aids to Reflection*; Hazlitt, *The Spirit of the Age*; W. Scott, *The Talisman*; *The Betrothed*; Southey, *A Tale of Paraguay*	T. H. Huxley b.; R. D. Blackmore b.; Stockton and Darlington railway opened
1826	J. F. Cooper, *The Last of the Mohicans*; Landor, *Imaginary Conversations*, ii; M. Shelley, *The Last Man*	
1827	Clare, *The Shepherd's Calendar*; De Quincey, 'Murder as One of the Fine Arts' (in *Blackwood's Magazine*); Keble, *The Christian Year*; W. Scott, *Chronicles of the Canongate*, 1st ser.	William Blake d.; Thomas Rowlandson d.; Thomas Arnold becomes Headmaster of Rugby School; Beethoven d.

Date	Principal literary works	Other events
1828	Landor, *Imaginary Conversations*, iii; Lockhart, *Life of Robert Burns*; Napier, *History of the Peninsular War* (completed 1840); W. Scott, *Tales of a Grandfather*, 1st ser.; *Chronicles of the Canongate*, 2nd ser.	D. G. Rossetti b.; George Meredith b.; Taine b.; Tolstoy b.; Ibsen b.; Schubert d.; Goya d.
1829	Hood, *The Dream of Eugene Aram* (in *The Gem*, pub. separately 1831); Landor, *Imaginary Conversations*, iv and v; Lytton, *Devereux*; Peacock, *The Misfortunes of Elfin*; W. Scott, *Anne of Geierstein*; *Tales of a Grandfather*, 2nd ser.	J. E. Millais b.; Catholic Emancipation; Rossini, *Guillaume Tell*
1830	Cobbett, *Rural Rides*; Lytton, *Paul Clifford*; W. Scott, *Tales of a Grandfather*, 3rd and 4th ser.; Tennyson, *Poems, Chiefly Lyrical* (inc. 'Mariana')	**William IV** (–1837); Christina Rossetti b.; William Hazlitt d.; Camille Pisarro b.; Mendelssohn, Hebrides Overture (rev. 1832); Berlioz, *Symphonie fantastique*
1831	Peacock, *Crotchet Castle*; Poe, *Poems*; Trelawny, *Adventures of a Younger Son*	Hegel d.; Stendhal, *Le Rouge et le Noir*
1832	Disraeli, *Contarini Fleming*; Lytton, *Eugene Aram*; W. Scott, *Tales of My Landlord*, 4th ser.; Tennyson, *Poems* (dated 1833, inc. 'The Lady of Shalott'); F. Trollope, *Domestic Manners of the Americans*	Lewis Carroll (Charles Lutwidge Dodgson) b.; Leslie Stephen b.; Sir Walter Scott d.; Jeremy Bentham d.; George Crabbe d.; First Reform Bill; Goethe, *Faust*, ii; Balzac, *Le Peau de chagrin*; *Le Curé de Tours*; Goethe d.
1833	R. Browning, *Pauline*; Carlyle, *Sartor Resartus* (in *Fraser's Magazine* 1833–4; first English edn. 1838); Lamb, *Last Essays of Elia*; Lytton, *Godolphin*; *England and the English*; Newman, Pusey, *et al.*, *Tracts for the Times* (90 numbers, 1833–41)	William Wilberforce d.; A. H. Hallam d.; Keble's sermon on 'national apostasy'; Balzac, *Eugénie Grandet*; Johannes Brahms b.
1834	Ainsworth, *Rookwood*; Lady Blessington, *Conversations with Lord Byron*; Lytton, *The Last Days of Pompeii*; Southey, *The Doctor*	William Morris b.; George du Maurier b.; S. T. Coleridge d.; Thomas Malthus d.; Slavery abolished in British Empire; Edgar Degas b.; James Abbott McNeill Whistler b.
1835	R. Browning, *Paracelsus*; Dickens, *Sketches by Boz*, 1st ser.; Lytton, *Rienzi*; T. Moore, *The Fudges in England*; Mary Shelley, *Lodore*; Wordsworth, *Yarrow Revisited and Other Poems*	Samuel Butler b.; William Cobbett d.; Mark Twain (Samuel Langhorne Clemens) b.; Balzac, *Le Père Goriot*
1836	Dickens, *Sketches by Boz*, 2nd ser.; *The Posthumous Papers of the Pickwick Club* (monthly Apr. 1836–Nov. 1837); Marryat, *Mr Midshipman Easy*; Newman, Keble, *et al.*, *Lyra Apostolica*	W. S. Gilbert b.; William Godwin d.; Francis Bret Harte b.
1837	Carlyle, *The French Revolution*; Dickens, *The Pickwick Papers* (vol. pub.); *Oliver Twist* (monthly, Feb. 1837–Apr. 1839); Disraeli, *Henrietta Temple*; *Venetia*; Hawthorne, *Twice-told Tales* (2nd ser., 1842); Lockhart, *Life of Scott* (completed 1838); Lytton, *Ernest Maltravers*; Thackeray, *The Yellowplush Papers* (in *Fraser's Magazine*, 1837–8)	**Victoria** (–1901); Algernon Charles Swinburne b.; John Constable d.; Berlioz, *Grande Messe des morts*
1838	Elizabeth Barrett, *The Seraphim*; Dickens, *Nicholas Nickleby* (monthly, Apr. 1838–Oct. 1839); Lady Charlotte Guest (tr.), *The Mabinogion*; Surtees, *Jorrocks's Jaunts and Jollities* (orig. serialized 1831–4); Wordsworth, *Sonnets*	English Historical Society founded; Anti-Corn Law League established; Sir Charles Lyell, *Elements of Geology*

Date	Principal literary works	Other events
1839	Ainsworth, *Jack Sheppard*; C. Darwin, *Journal of Researches into the Geology and Natural History of the Various Countries Visited by H.M.S. Beagle*; Dickens, *Nicholas Nickleby* (vol. pub.); Thackeray, *Catherine* (serialized pseudonymously 1839–40; vol. pub. 1869)	Walter Pater b.; John Galt d.; Chartist Riots; Paul Cézanne b.
1840	Ainsworth, *The Tower of London*; Barham, *The Ingoldsby Legends*, 1st ser.; R. Browning, *Sordello*; J. F. Cooper, *The Pathfinder*; Dickens, *The Old Curiosity Shop* (weekly, 25 Apr. 1840–6 Feb. 1841)	Thomas Hardy b.; **Queen Victoria** marries Prince Albert; Penny post introduced; Zola b.; Claude Monet b.; Auguste Rodin b.; Tchaikovsky b.
1841	Ainsworth, *Old Saint Paul's*; Boucicault, *London Assurance*; R. Browning, *Pippa Passes*; Carlyle, *On Heroes, Hero-worship and the Heroic in History*; Dickens, *The Old Curiosity Shop* (vol. pub.); *Barnaby Rudge* (weekly, 13 Feb.–27 Nov. 1841); Lever, *Charles O'Malley*; Marryat, *Masterman Ready*	*Punch* started; Pierre-Auguste Renoir b.; Antonin Dvořák b.
1842	Dickens, *American Notes*; Lytton, *Zanoni*; Macaulay, *Lays of Ancient Rome*; Tennyson, *Poems* (inc. 'Locksley Hall', 'Morte d'Arthur'); Wordsworth, *Poems Chiefly of Early and Late Years*	Thomas Arnold d.; Mallarmé b.; Stendhal d.
1843	Ainsworth, *Windsor Castle*; Borrow, *The Bible in Spain*; Carlyle, *Past and Present*; Dickens, *A Christmas Carol*; *Martin Chuzzlewit* (monthly, Jan. 1843–July 1844); Horne, *Orion*; Lytton, *The Last of the Barons*; Macaulay, *Critical and Historical Essays*; J. S. Mill, *System of Logic*; Ruskin, *Modern Painters*, i (ii: 1846; iii and iv 1856; v: 1860); Surtees, *Handley Cross* (expanded 1854)	Henry James b.; Robert Southey d.; Wordsworth Poet Laureate
1844	Barnes, *Poems of Rural Life in the Dorset Dialect*; Elizabeth Barrett, *Poems*; Dickens, *Martin Chuzzlewit* (vol. pub.); Disraeli, *Coningsby*; Horne, *The New Spirit of the Age*; Kinglake, *Eothen*; Thackeray, *The Luck of Barry Lyndon* (serialized Jan.–Dec. 1846, rev. and repr. 1856)	Robert Bridges b.; Gerard Manley Hopkins b.; William Beckford d.; Railway mania (–1845); Verlaine b.; Nietzsche b.; Dumas, *Les Trois Mousquetaires*
1845	Dickens, *The Cricket on the Hearth*; Poe, *Tales of Mystery and Imagination*	Thomas Hood d.; Sydney Smith d.; Mérimée, *Carmen*
1846	C. Brontë, E. Brontë, and A. Brontë, *Poems by Currer, Ellis and Acton Bell*; Dickens, *Pictures from Italy*; *Dombey and Son* (monthly, Oct. 1846–Apr. 1848); G. Eliot, tr. Strauss's *The Life of Jesus Critically Examined*; Hawthorne, *Mosses from an Old Manse*; Lear, *A Book of Nonsense* (enlarged edns. 1861, 1863); Melville, *Typee*; Ruskin, *Modern Painters*, ii	Marriage of Robert Browning and Elizabeth Barrett; Corn Law abolished; Balzac, *La Cousine Bette*; Berlioz, *La Damnation de Faust*
1847	A. Brontë, *Agnes Grey* (by 'Acton Bell'); C. Brontë, *Jane Eyre* (by 'Currer Bell'); E. Brontë, *Wuthering Heights* (by 'Ellis Bell'); Disraeli, *Tancred*; Marryat, *Children of the New Forest*; Tennyson, *The Princess*; Thackeray, *Vanity Fair* (monthly,	Balzac, *Le Cousin Pons*

Date	Principal literary works	Other events
1847	Jan. 1847–July 1848); Trollope, *The Macdermots of Ballycloran*	
1848	Ainsworth, *The Lancashire Witches*; A. Brontë, *The Tenant of Wildfell Hall*; Catherine Crowe, *The Night-side of Nature*; Dickens, *Dombey and Son* (vol. pub.); Gaskell, *Mary Barton*; Lytton, *Harold*; J. S. Mill, *Principles of Political Economy*; Thackeray, *Vanity Fair* (vol. pub.); *The History of Pendennis* (monthly, Nov. 1848–Dec. 1850)	Emily Brontë d.; Branwell Brontë d.; Frederick Marryat d.; Pre-Raphaelite Brotherhood formed; Revolution in France; Chateaubriand d.; Marx and Engels, *Communist Manifesto*
1849	M. Arnold, *The Strayed Reveller and Other Poems*; C. Brontë, *Shirley*; Dickens, *David Copperfield* (monthly, May 1849–Nov. 1850); Macaulay, *History of England*, i and ii (iii and iv: 1855); Ruskin, *The Seven Lamps of Architecture*	Edmund Gosse b.; Anne Brontë d.; Maria Edgeworth d.; T. L. Beddoes d.; Edgar Allan Poe d.; *Notes and Queries* started; Sir Austin Layard, *Nineveh and its Remains*; Frédéric Chopin d.;
1850	Beddoes (d. 1849), *Death's Jest Book*; E. B. Browning, *Poems* (inc. 'Sonnets from the Portuguese'); R. Browning, *Christmas Eve and Easter Day*; W. Collins, *After Dark*; Dickens, *David Copperfield* (vol. pub.); Hawthorne, *The Scarlet Letter*; Hunt, *Autobiography*; Kingsley, *Alton Locke*; Lytton, *The Caxtons*; Tennyson, *In Memoriam*; Wordsworth (d. 1850), *The Prelude*	R. L. Stevenson b.; Wordsworth d.; Tennyson Poet Laureate; Guy de Maupassant b.; Balzac d.; Wagner, *Lohengrin*
1851	Borrow, *Lavengro*; Hawthorne, *The House of the Seven Gables*; Kingsley, *Yeast*; Melville, *Moby Dick*; Meredith, *Poems*; Ruskin, *The King of the Golden River*; *The Stones of Venice*, i (ii and iii: 1853)	The Great Exhibition; Turner d.; Verdi, *Rigoletto*
1852	M. Arnold, *Empedocles on Etna and Other Poems*; Dickens, *Bleak House* (monthly, Mar. 1852–Sept. 1853); Stowe, *Uncle Tom's Cabin*; Thackeray, *The History of Henry Esmond*	George Moore b.; Thomas Moore d.
1853	M. Arnold, *Poems* (inc. 'Sohrab and Rustum', 'The Scholar-Gipsy'); C. Brontë, *Villette*; Dickens, *Bleak House* (vol. pub.); Gaskell, *Ruth*; *Cranford* (vol. pub.); Hawthorne, *Tanglewood Tales*; Kingsley, *Hypatia*; Surtees, *Mr Sponge's Sporting Tour*; Thackeray, *The Newcomes* (monthly, Oct. 1853–Aug. 1855)	Vincent van Gogh b.; Verdi, *Il trovatore*; *La traviata*
1854	W. Collins, *Hide and Seek*; Dickens, *Hard Times* (weekly, 1 Apr.–12 Aug. 1854, and vol. pub.); Patmore, *The Betrothal* (*The Angel in the House*, i); Tennyson, 'The Charge of the Light Brigade' (*Examiner*, 9 Dec.); Thoreau, *Walden*; Yonge, *The Little Duke*	Oscar Wilde b.; Crimean War (–1856); Rimbaud b.
1855	R. Browning, *Men and Women*; Dickens, *Little Dorrit* (monthly, Dec. 1855–June 1859); Gaskell, *Lizzie Leigh and Other Tales*; *North and South* (vol. pub.; serialized Sept. 1854–Jan. 1855); Kingsley, *Westward Ho!*; G. H. Lewes, *Life of Goethe*; Longfellow, *Hiawatha*; Tennyson, *Maud and Other Poems*; Trollope, *The Warden*; Whitman, *Leaves of Grass*	Charlotte Brontë d.; Mary Russell Mitford d.; *Daily Telegraph* started; Stamp Duty abolished

Date	Principal literary works	Other events
1856	Kingsley, *The Heroes*; Melville, *The Piazza Tales*; Patmore, *The Espousals* (*The Angel in the House*, ii); Ruskin, *Modern Painters*, iii and iv	George Bernard Shaw b.; National Portrait Gallery founded; Freud b.; Heine d.; Flaubert, *Madame Bovary*; Robert Schumann d.
1857	Borrow, *The Romany Rye*; C. Brontë (d. 1855), *The Professor*; E. B. Browning, *Aurora Leigh*; Gaskell, *Life of Charlotte Brontë*; T. Hughes, *Tom Brown's Schooldays*; Trollope, *Barchester Towers*	Joseph Conrad b.; George Gissing b.; Museum of Ornamental Art (Victoria and Albert Museum) founded; Edward Elgar b.; Baudelaire, *Les Fleurs du mal*
1858	Clough, *Amours de voyage*; G. Eliot, *Scenes of Clerical Life*; Farrar, *Eric, or Little by Little*; Holmes, *The Autocrat of the Breakfast Table*; MacDonald, *Phantastes*; Trelawny, *Recollections of the Last Days of Shelley and Byron*; Trollope, *Doctor Thorne*; *The Three Clerks*	Indian Mutiny; Giacomo Puccini b.
1859	C. Darwin, *On the Origin of Species by means of Natural Selection*; Dickens, *A Tale of Two Cities* (monthly, Apr.–Nov., and vol. pub.); G. Eliot, *Adam Bede*; E. Fitzgerald, *The Rubáiyát of Omar Khayyám*; Meredith, *The Ordeal of Richard Feverel*; J. S. Mill, *On Liberty*; Tennyson, *Idylls of the King* ('Enid', 'Vivien', 'Elaine', 'Guinevere'); Trollope, *The Bertrams*	Arthur Conan Doyle b.; Kenneth Grahame b.; A. E. Housman b.; Thomas de Quincey d.; Leigh Hunt d.; Lord Macaulay d.; War of Italian Liberation; Georges Seurat b.
1860	E. B. Browning, *Poems Before Congress*; Collins, *The Woman in White* (vol. pub.; serialized 26 Nov. 1859–25 Aug. 1860); Dickens, *Great Expectations* (weekly, 1 Dec. 1860–3 Aug. 1861); G. Eliot, *The Mill on the Floss*; Patmore, *Faithful for Ever* (*The Angel in the House*, iii); Ruskin, *Modern Painters*, v	J. M. Barrie b.; Chekhov b.; Gustav Mahler b.; Walter Sickert b.; Schopenhauer d.
1861	Beeton, *Book of Household Management* (serialized 1859–61); Dickens, *Great Expectations* (vol. pub.); G. Eliot, *Silas Marner*; T. Hughes, *Tom Brown at Oxford*; Palgrave, *The Golden Treasury* (2nd ser. 1897); Peacock, *Gryll Grange* (serialized 1860); Reade, *The Cloister and the Hearth*; Thackeray, *Lovel the Widower* (serialized Jan.–June 1860); Trollope, *Framley Parsonage* (serialized Jan. 1860–Apr. 1861)	Elizabeth Barrett Browning d.; A. H. Clough d.; Prince Albert d.; American Civil War (–1865)
1862	Borrow, *Wild Wales*; Braddon, *Lady Audley's Secret*; E. B. Browning (d. 1861), *Last Poems* (ed. R. Browning); W. Collins, *No Name* (serialized Mar. 1862–Jan. 1863); Lytton, *A Strange Story*; Meredith, *Modern Love*; Patmore, *Victories of Love* (*The Angel in the House*, iv); C. Rossetti, *Goblin Market and Other Poems*; Trollope, *Orley Farm* (serialized Mar. 1861–Oct. 1862)	M. R. James b.; Edith Wharton b.; Hugo, *Les Misérables*; Claude Debussy b.
1863	G. Eliot, *Romola*; Gaskell, *Sylvia's Lovers*; Kingsley, *The Water Babies*; Kinglake, *The Invasion of the Crimea*, i and ii (iii–iv: 1868; v: 1875; vi: 1880; vii and viii: 1887); Le Fanu, *The House by the Churchyard*; M. Oliphant, *Salem Chapel* (first of the Chronicles of Carlingford series); Reade, *Hard Cash* (serialized Mar.–Dec. 1863); Thackeray	Arthur Quiller-Couch b.; W. M. Thackeray d.; Tolstoy, *War and Peace* (1863–9); Edvard Munch b.

Date	Principal literary works	Other events
1863	(d. 1863), *Roundabout Papers* (serialized Jan. 1860–Feb. 1863)	
1864	Dickens, *Our Mutual Friend* (monthly, May 1864–Nov. 1865); Gaskell, *Cousin Phillis*; Le Fanu, *Uncle Silas*; *Wylder's Hand*; Newman, *Apologia pro vita sua*; Trollope, *The Small House at Allington* (serialized Sept. 1862–Apr. 1864); *Can You Forgive Her?* (serialized Jan. 1864–Aug. 1865)	W. S. Landor d.; John Clare d.; R. S. Surtees d.; Nathaniel Hawthorne d.; Henri de Toulouse-Lautrec b.; Richard Strauss b.
1865	M. Arnold, *Essays in Criticism*, 1st ser.; Carroll, *Alice in Wonderland*; Dickens, *Our Mutual Friend* (vol. pub.); Meredith, *Rhoda Fleming*; Swinburne, *Atalanta in Calydon*; Trollope, *The Belton Estate* (serialized May 1865–Jan. 1866)	Rudyard Kipling b.; W. B. Yeats b.; A. E. W. Mason b.; Elizabeth Gaskell d.; Palmerston d.; Abraham Lincoln assassinated; Jean Sibelius b.; Wagner, *Tristan und Isolde*
1866	W. Collins, *Armadale* (serialized Nov. 1864–June 1866); Gaskell (d. 1865), *Wives and Daughters*; Kingsley, *Hereward the Wake*; Reade, *Griffith Gaunt*; Ruskin, *The Ethics of the Dust*; *The Crown of Wild Olives*; Swinburne, *Poems and Ballads*, 1st ser.	H. G. Wells b.; Thomas Love Peacock d.; John Keble d.; Jane Welsh Carlyle d.; Dostoevsky, *Crime and Punishment*
1867	M. Arnold, *New Poems* (inc. 'Thyrsis'); Bagehot, *The English Constitution*; Swinburne, *Song of Italy*; Trollope, *The Last Chronicle of Barset* (serialized Dec. 1866–July 1867); *The Claverings* (serialized Feb. 1866–May 1867)	Arnold Bennett b.; John Galsworthy b.; Arthur Rackham b.; Baudelaire d.; Second Reform Bill
1868	Alcott, *Little Women*; R. Browning, *The Ring and the Book*; W. Collins, *The Moonstone* (serialized Jan.–Aug. 1868); Morris, *The Earthly Paradise*, i (completed 1870); Queen Victoria, *Leaves from a Journal of Our Life in the Highlands*	Gioachino Rossini d.; Dostoevsky, *The Idiot*
1869	M. Arnold, *Culture and Anarchy*; Blackmore, *Lorna Doone*; Gilbert, *Bab Ballads*; J. S. Mill, *On the Subjection of Women*; Tennyson, *The Holy Grail and Other Poems*; Trollope, *Phineas Finn: The Irish Member* (serialized Oct. 1867–May 1869); *He Knew He Was Right* (serialized Oct. 1868–May 1869)	Suez Canal opened; André Gide b.; Gandhi b.; Berlioz d.; Henri Matisse b.
1870	Dickens, *The Mystery of Edwin Drood* (6 of 12 monthly parts completed, Apr.–Sept.); Disraeli, *Lothair*; Trollope, *The Vicar of Bullhampton* (serialized July 1869–May 1870)	Hilaire Belloc b.; Charles Dickens d.; Franco-Prussian War (–1871); Dumas d.; Mérimée d.; Lenin b.; First Married Women's Property Act
1871	Carroll, *Through the Looking-Glass*; G. Eliot, *Middlemarch* (8 parts, Dec. 1871–Dec. 1872); Hardy, *Desperate Remedies*; Lear, *Nonsense Songs, Stories, Botany and Alphabets*; Lytton, *The Coming Race*; MacDonald, *At the Back of the North Wind*; Meredith, *The Adventures of Harry Richmond*; Ruskin, *Fors Clavigera* (8 vols, 1871–84); Swinburne, *Songs Before Sunrise*	Marcel Proust b.; Paul Valéry b.; Verdi, *Aida*
1872	S. Butler, *Erewhon*; G. Eliot, *Middlemarch* (vol. pub.); Forster, *Life of Dickens*, i (ii: 1873; iii: 1874); Hardy, *Under the Greenwood Tree*; Lear, *More Nonsense, Pictures, Rhymes, Botany etc.*; MacDonald, *The Princess and the Goblin*; Tennyson, *Gareth and Lynette*	Max Beerbohm b.; Bertrand Russell b.; Aubrey Beardsley b.; Ralph Vaughan Williams b.; Gautier d.; Voting by ballot introduced

Date	Principal literary works	Other events
1873	M. Arnold, *Literature and Dogma*; Hardy, *A Pair of Blue Eyes*; J. S. Mill (d. 1873), *Autobiography*; Pater, *Studies in the Renaissance*; Trollope, *The Eustace Diamonds* (serialized July 1871–Feb. 1873)	Walter de la Mare b.; J. S. Mill d.; Edward Bulwer-Lytton d.; Tolstoy, *Anna Karenina* (–1877); Sergei Rachmaninov b.
1874	Hardy, *Far From the Madding Crowd*; J. Thomson, *City of Dreadful Night* (in *National Reformer*, pub. separately 1880); Trollope, *Phineas Redux* (serialized July 1873–Jan. 1874)	G. K. Chesterton b.; Winston Churchill b.; Somerset Maugham b.; Gertrude Stein b.; Arnold Schoenberg b.; Verdi, *Requiem*; Wagner, *Ring* cycle completed
1875	Keble, *Sermons for the Christian Year* (1875–80); Trollope, *The Way We Live Now* (serialized Feb. 1874–Sept. 1875)	Charles Kingsley d.; Maurice Ravel b.
1876	Carroll, *The Hunting of the Snark*; G. Eliot, *Daniel Deronda*; Hardy, *The Hand of Ethelberta*; H. James, *Roderick Hudson*; Meredith, *Beauchamp's Career*; Morris, *The Story of Sigurd the Volsung, and the Fall of the Niblungs*; Trollope, *The Prime Minister* (serialized May 1876–July 1877); Twain, *Adventures of Tom Sawyer*	George Sand d.; Brahms, First Symphony (completed)
1877	H. James, *The American*; Lear, *Laughable Lyrics*; Trollope, *The American Senator*	Ibsen, *Pillars of Society*; Tchaikovsky, *Swan Lake*
1878	Hardy, *The Return of the Native*; H. James, *The Europeans*; Swinburne, *Poems and Ballads*, 2nd ser.; Trollope, *Is He Popinjoy?* (serialized Oct. 1877–July 1878)	John Masefield b.; G. H. Lewes d.; Augustus John b.
1879	H. James, *Daisy Miller*; Meredith, *The Egoist*	E. M. Forster b.; Ibsen, *A Doll's House*; Tchaikovsky, *Eugene Onegin*; Stalin b.
1880	Disraeli, *Endymion*; Hardy, *The Trumpet-Major*; Joel Chandler Harris, *Uncle Remus*; Shorthouse, *John Inglesant*; Trollope, *The Duke's Children* (serialized Oct. 1879–July 1880)	Lytton Strachey b.; George Eliot d.; First Anglo-Boer War (–1881); Flaubert d.; Dostoevsky, *The Brothers Karamazov*
1881	Revised Version of the New Testament; Hardy, *A Laodicean*; H. James, *Portrait of a Lady*; *Washington Square*; D. G. Rossetti, *Ballads and Sonnets*; Stevenson, *Virginibus Puerisque*; Wilde, *Poems*	P. G. Wodehouse b.; Thomas Carlyle d.; Benjamin Disraeli d.; George Borrow d.; Samuel Palmer d.; Ibsen, *Ghosts*; Dostoevsky d.; Pablo Picasso b.; Béla Bartók b.
1882	Anstey, *Vice Versa*; Hardy, *Two on a Tower*; Jefferies, *Bevis*; Stevenson, *The New Arabian Nights*	James Joyce b.; Virginia Woolf b.; W. H. Ainsworth d.; Charles Darwin d.; Ralph Waldo Emerson d.; D. G. Rossetti d.; Anthony Trollope d.; Second Married Women's Property Act; Wagner, *Parsifal*
1883	MacDonald, *The Princess and Curdie*; Schreiner, *The Story of an African Farm*; Stevenson, *Treasure Island* (serialized Oct. 1881–Jan. 1882); Trollope (d. 1882), *Mr Scarborough's Family* (serialized May 1882–June 1883); *An Autobiography*	William Carlos Williams b.; Nietzsche, *Also sprach Zarathustra*; Wagner d.; Marx d.; Mussolini b.
1884	Gissing, *The Unclassed*; Twain, *The Adventures of Huckleberry Finn*	Sean O'Casey b.; Hugh Walpole b.; Ivy Compton Burnett b.; Charles Reade d.; first *OED* begins to appear (–1928); Society of Authors founded; Huysmans, *A Rebours*.

Date	Principal literary works	Other events
1885	Revised Version of the Old Testament; H. Rider Haggard, *King Solomon's Mines*; Meredith, *Diana of the Crossways*; Pater, *Marius the Epicurean*; Ruskin, *Praeterita* (completed 1889); Stevenson, *A Child's Garden of Verses*; *More New Arabian Nights*; Swinburne, *Marino Faliero*; Tennyson, *Tiresias and Other Poems*	D. H. Lawrence b.; Ezra Pound b.; Fall of Khartoum; Victor Hugo d.; Zola, *Germinal*; Brahms, Fourth Symphony
1886	Alcott, *Jo's Boys*; Burnett, *Little Lord Fauntleroy*; Hardy, *The Mayor of Casterbridge*; H. James, *The Bostonians*; *The Princess Casamassima*; Kipling, *Departmental Ditties*; Stevenson, *The Strange Case of Dr Jekyll and Mr Hyde*; *Kidnapped*; Tennyson, *Locksley Hall Sixty Years After*	Charles Williams b.; Ronald Firbank b.; Franz Liszt d.
1887	Conan Doyle, *A Study in Scarlet*; Haggard, *She*; *Allan Quartermain*; Hardy, *The Woodlanders*; Pater, *Imaginary Portraits*	Rupert Brooke b.; Edith Sitwell b.; Richard Jefferies d.; Verdi, *Otello*
1888	M. Arnold (d. 1888), *Essays in Criticism*, 2nd ser.; Barrie, *Auld Licht Idylls*; Hardy, *Wessex Tales*; H. James, *The Aspern Papers*; Kipling, *Plain Tales from the Hills*; Stevenson, *The Black Arrow*	T. S. Eliot b.; T. E. Lawrence b.; Raymond Chandler b.; Eugene O'Neill b.; Matthew Arnold d.; Edward Lear d.
1889	Carroll, *Sylvie and Bruno*; Conan Doyle, *The Sign of Four*; Jerome, *Three Men in a Boat*; Stevenson, *The Master of Ballantrae*; *The Wrong Box* (with Lloyd Osbourne); Swinburne, *Poems and Ballads*, 3rd ser.; Tennyson, *Demeter and Other Poems*; Twain, *A Connecticut Yankee in King Arthur's Court*	Robert Browning d.; Gerard Manley Hopkins d.; Wilkie Collins d.; Tolstoy, *The Kreutzer Sonata*; Adolf Hitler b.; Ibsen's *The Doll's House* perf. in England
1890	Kipling, *The Light that Failed*	Agatha Christie b.; J. H. Newman d.; Ibsen, *Hedda Gabler*; Tchaikovsky, *The Sleeping Beauty*; Vincent van Gogh d.
1891	Bierce, *Tales of Soldiers and Civilians*; Conan Doyle, *The Adventures of Sherlock Holmes*; Gissing, *New Grub Street*; Hardy, *Tess of the d'Urbervilles*; *A Group of Noble Dames*; Kipling, *Life's Handicap*; Wilde, *Lord Arthur Savile's Crime and Other Stories*; *The Picture of Dorian Gray*	Herman Melville d.; Rimbaud d.; Huysmans, *Là-bas*; Sergei Prokofiev b.; Stanley Spencer b.
1892	Gissing, *Born in Exile*; Kipling, *Barrack-Room Ballads*; Shaw, *Widowers' Houses*	J. R. R. Tolkien b.; H. MacDiarmid b.; Rebecca West (Cecily Fairfield) b.; Lord Tennyson d.; Ibsen, *The Master Builder*; Tchaikovsky, *Nutcracker*
1893	Conan Doyle, *The Memoirs of Sherlock Holmes*; Stevenson, *Catriona*; Weyman, *A Gentleman of France*; Wilde, *Lady Windermere's Fan* (perf. 1892); Yeats, *The Celtic Twilight*	Guy de Maupassant d.; Taine d.; Joan Miró b.; Tchaikovsky, Sixth Symphony ('Pathétique'); Tchaikovsky d.; Dvořák, Symphony No. 9 ('From the New World')
1894	du Maurier, *Trilby*; G. and W. Grossmith, *The Diary of a Nobody*; Hardy, *Life's Little Ironies*; Hope, *The Prisoner of Zenda*; Kipling, *The Jungle Book*; Moore, *Esther Waters*; Swinburne, *Astrophel and Other Poems*; Wilde, *A Woman of No Importance* (perf. 1893); *Salomé* (English tr. Lord Alfred Douglas, illus. Aubrey Beardsley; perf. Paris 1896); Yeats, *The Land of Heart's Desire*	Aldous Huxley b.; J. B. Priestley b.; Robert Louis Stevenson d.; Walter Pater d.; Christina Rossetti d.; Beardsley *et al.*, *The Yellow Book* (–1897); Debussy, *Prélude à 'L'après-midi d'un faune'*

Date	Principal literary works	Other events
1895	Grant Allen, *The Woman Who Did*; Conrad, *Almayer's Folly*; Crane, *The Red Badge of Courage*; Hardy, *Jude the Obscure*; Kipling, *The Second Jungle Book*; Wells, *The Time Machine*	Robert Graves b.; L. P. Hartley b.; F. R. Leavis b.; Chekhov, *The Seagull*; Jameson's raid into the Transvaal
1896	Belloc, *A Bad Child's Book of Beasts*; Conrad, *An Outcast of the Islands*; Housman, *A Shropshire Lad*; Stevenson (d. 1894), *Weir of Hermiston*; Wells, *The Island of Dr Moreau*	F. Scott Fitzgerald b.; William Morris d.; Coventry Patmore d.; George du Maurier d.; Alfred Austin Poet Laureate; J. E. Millais d.; Verlaine d.; Strauss, *Also sprach Zarathustra*; Puccini, *La Bohème*
1897	Conrad, *The Nigger of the 'Narcissus'*; Hardy, *The Well-Beloved*; H. James, *What Maisie Knew*; *The Spoils of Poynton*; Maugham, *Liza of Lambeth*; Meredith, *Essay on Comedy*; Wells, *The Invisible Man*; Yeats, *Adoration of the Magi*	Tate Gallery opened; Rostand, *Cyrano de Bergerac*; Brahms d.
1898	Hardy, *Wessex Poems*; H. James, *The Two Magics* (inc. 'The Turn of the Screw'); Wells, *The War of the Worlds*; Wilde, *The Ballad of Reading Gaol*	C. S. Lewis b.; Ernest Hemingway b.; Lewis Carroll d.; Mallarmé d.; Aubrey Beardsley d.; Zola, 'J'accuse'
1899	Hornung, *The Amateur Cracksman*; H. James, *The Awkward Age*; Kipling, *Stalky & Co.*; Somerville and Ross, *Some Experiences of an Irish R. M.*; Wilde, *The Importance of Being Earnest* (perf. 1895); *An Ideal Husband* (perf. 1895)	Noël Coward b.; Second Anglo-Boer War (–1902); Vladimir Nabokov b.; Tolstoy, *Resurrection*; Elgar, *Enigma Variations*; Sibelius, *Finlandia*
1900	Conrad, *Lord Jim*; Dreiser, *Sister Carrie*; Wells, *Love and Mr Lewisham*	John Ruskin d.; Oscar Wilde d.; Nietzsche d.; Boxer Rising(–1901); S. Freud, *The Interpretation of Dreams*; Elgar, *The Dream of Gerontius*; Mahler, Fourth Symphony; Puccini, *Tosca*; Kurt Weill b.
1901	Bennett, *Anna of the Five Towns*; Butler, *Erewhon Revisited*; Hardy, *Poems of the Past and Present*; Jacobs, *Light Freights*; Kipling, *Kim*; Wells, *The First Men in the Moon*	Edward VII (–1910); Roy Campbell b.; C. M. Yonge d.; Chekhov, *Three Sisters*; Walt Disney b.; Giuseppe Verdi d.; Toulouse-Lautrec d.
1902	Barrie, *The Admirable Crichton* (perf.; pub. 1914); *Quality Street* (perf.; pub. 1913); Conrad, *Youth*; *Typhoon*; De la Mare, *Songs of Childhood* (as 'Walter Ramal'); Conan Doyle, *The Hound of the Baskervilles*; H. James, *The Wings of the Dove*; W. James, *The Varieties of Religious Experience*; Kipling, *Just So Stories*; Mason, *The Four Feathers*; Potter, *Peter Rabbit*; Yeats, *Cathleen Ni Houlihan*	Samuel Butler d.; *Times Literary Supplement* started; Zola d.; C. Rhodes d.; William Walton b.; Debussy, *Pelléas et Mélisande*; Anglo-Japanese Treaty
1903	Butler (d. 1902), *The Way of all Flesh*; Childers, *The Riddle of the Sands*; Gissing (d. 1903), *The Private Papers of Henry Ryecroft*; H. James, *The Ambassadors*; London, *The Call of the Wild*; Yeats, *Ideas of Good and Evil*	George Orwell (Eric Blair) b.; Evelyn Waugh b.; George Gissing d.; Herbert Spencer d.; *Daily Mirror* started; J. A. M. Whistler d.; Paul Gauguin d.
1904	Barrie, *Peter Pan* (stage version); Chesterton, *The Napoleon of Notting Hill*; Conrad, *Nostromo*; Hardy, *The Dynasts*, i; Hudson, *Green Mansions*; H. James, *The Golden Bowl*; M. R. James, *Ghost Stories of an Antiquary*; Rolfe, *Hadrian the Seventh*	Graham Greene b.; Christopher Isherwood b.; C. Day-Lewis b.; Sir Leslie Stephen d.; Abbey Theatre, Dublin, founded; Chekhov, *The Cherry Orchard*; Chekhov d.; Salvador Dali b.; Dvořák d.; Puccini, *Madame Butterfly*

Date	Principal literary works	Other events
1905	Forster, *Where Angels Fear to Tread*; Orczy, *The Scarlet Pimpernel*; Shaw, *Major Barbara* (perf., pub. 1907); Wells, *A Modern Utopia*; *Kipps*; Wharton, *The House of Mirth*; Wilde (d. 1900), *De Profundis*	C. P. Snow b.; Arthur Koestler b.; Jean-Paul Sartre b.; Debussy, *La Mer*; Mutiny on *Battleship Potemkin*; Sinn Fein founded in Dublin
1906	Barrie, *Peter Pan in Kensington Gardens*; Conrad, *The Mirror of the Sea*; Galsworthy, *A Man of Property*; Hardy, *The Dynasts*, ii; Kipling, *Puck of Pook's Hill*; London, *White Fang*; Nesbit, *The Railway Children*	Samuel Beckett b.; Ibsen d.; Cézanne d.; Elgar, *The Kingdom*
1907	Belloc, *Cautionary Tales for Children*; Conrad, *The Secret Agent*; Forster, *The Longest Journey*; Gosse, *Father and Son*; Joyce, *Chamber Music*; Synge, *The Playboy of the Western World*; Yeats, *Deirdre*	W. H. Auden b.; Louis MacNeice b.; Daphne du Maurier b.; J. K. Huysmans d.; H. Bergson, *L'Evolution Créatrice*
1908	Barrie, *What Every Woman Knows*; Bennett, *The Old Wives' Tale*; Chesterton, *The Man Who Was Thursday*; W. H. Davies, *The Autobiography of a Super-Tramp*; Forster, *A Room With a View*; Grahame, *The Wind in the Willows*; Hardy, *The Dynasts*, iii; Pound, *A Lume Spento*; Wells, *The War in the Air*	Ian Fleming b.; Simone de Beauvoir b.
1909	Hardy, *Time's Laughingstocks*; Pound, *Personae*; Wells, *Tono-Bungay*	George Meredith d.; A. C. Swinburne d.; J. M. Synge d.; S. Spender b.
1910	Bennett, *Clayhanger*; Buchan, *Prester John*; Forster, *Howards End*; Kipling, *Rewards and Fairies*; Wells, *The History of Mr Polly*	**George V** (–1936); William James d.; Mark Twain d.; Tolstoy d.; Elgar, Violin Concerto; Vaughan Williams, *Fantasia on a Theme by Tallis*; Stravinsky, *The Firebird*; Henri ('Douanier') Rousseau d.
1911	Beerbohm, *Zuleika Dobson*; Bennett, *Hilda Lessways*; R. Brooke, *Poems 1911*; Burnett, *The Secret Garden*; Chesterton, *The Innocence of Father Brown*; Conrad, *Under Western Eyes*; Munro ('Saki'), *Chronicles of Clovis*; Pound, *Canzoni*; Hugh Walpole, *Mr Perrin and Mr Traill*; Wells, *The Country of the Blind*; Wharton, *Ethan Frome*	William Golding b.; Mervyn Peake b.; Terence Rattigan b.; Tennessee Williams b.; W. S. Gilbert d.; Gustave Mahler d.; Strauss, *Der Rosenkavalier*; Agadir crisis; Copyright Act extends posthumous copyright
1912	E. C. Bentley, *Trent's Last Case*; De la Mare, *The Listeners and Other Poems*; Munro ('Saki'), *The Unbearable Bassington*; Pound, *Ripostes*; Shaw, *Pygmalion*	Lawrence Durrell b.; Roy Fuller b.; Patrick White b.; Thomas Mann, *Der Tod in Venedig* (Death in Venice); Jackson Pollock b.; John Cage b.; Ravel, *Daphnis et Chloé*
1913	Conrad, *Chance*; De la Mare, *Peacock Pie*; Flecker, *The Golden Journey to Samarkand*; D. H. Lawrence, *Sons and Lovers*; Mackenzie, *Sinister Street*, i	Angus Wilson b.; S. Freud, *Totem and Taboo*; Proust, *Du côté de chez Swann* (Swann's Way, vol. i of *A la recherche du temps perdu*, completed 1927); Alain-Fournier, *Le Grand Meaulnes*; Benjamin Britten b.; Stravinsky, *The Rite of Spring*
1914	Hardy, *Satires of Circumstance*; Joyce, *Dubliners*; Mackenzie, *Sinister Street*, ii; Yeats, *Responsibilities*	Dylan Thomas b.; Britain declares war on Germany (4 Aug.); Alain-Fournier d.; Vaughan Williams, *The Lark Ascending*

Date	Principal literary works	Other events
1915	R. Brooke (d. 1915), *1914 and Other Poems*; Buchan, *The Thirty-Nine Steps*; Conrad, *Victory*; F. M. Ford, *The Good Soldier*; D. H. Lawrence, *The Rainbow*; Maugham, *Of Human Bondage*; Pound, *Cathay*; D. Richardson, *Pointed Roofs* (*Pilgrimage*, I); V. Woolf, *The Voyage Out*; Yeats, *Reveries Over Childhood and Youth*	Rupert Brooke d.; Mary Elizabeth Braddon d.; James Elroy Flecker d.; First Zeppelin attack on London
1916	Bennett, *These Twain*; Buchan, *Greenmantle*; Graves, Over *the Brazier*; Joyce, *A Portrait of the Artist as a Young Man*; G. Moore, *The Brook Kerith*; Pound, *Lustra*	Henry James d.; H. H. Munro ('Saki') d.; Battle of Verdun 21 Feb.–16 Dec.; Battle of the Somme 1 July–8 Nov.; Easter Rising, Dublin; Execution of Roger Casement, 3 August.
1917	Conrad, *The Shadow-Line*; T. S. Eliot, *Prufrock and Other Observations*; A. Waugh, *The Loom of Youth*; Mary Webb, *Gone to Earth*; Yeats, *The Wild Swans at Coole*	Anthony Burgess b.; Edward Thomas d.; Battle of Paschendaele 31 July–6 Nov.; Russian Revolution; Auguste Rodin d.; Edgar Degas d.
1918	R. Brooke (d. 1915), *Collected Poems* (memoir by E. Marsh); Hopkins (d. 1889), *Poems* (ed. R. Bridges); Joyce, *Exiles*; W. Lewis, *Tarr*; Strachey, *Eminent Victorians*; R. West, *The Return of the Soldier*	Wilfred Owen d.; 'Spanish flu' pandemic; Armistice (11 Nov.); Women over 30 gain vote; Guillaume Apollinaire d.; Claude Debussy d.
1919	Ashford, *The Young Visiters*; Beerbohm, *Seven Men*; Buchan, *Mr Standfast*; T. S. Eliot, *Poems*; Hardy, *Collected Poems*; M. Keynes, *The Economic Consequences of the Peace*; Pound, *Quia Pauper Amavi*; Sassoon, *War Poems*; Shaw, *Heartbreak House*; May Sinclair, *Mary Olivier: a Life*; V. Woolf, *Night and Day*	Elgar, Cello Concerto; Renoir d.; Treaty of Versailles; Lady Astor first woman MP
1920	T. S. Eliot, *The Sacred Wood*; F. Scott Fitzgerald, *This Side of Paradise*; Galsworthy, *In Chancery*; D. H. Lawrence, *Women in Love*; O'Neill, *Beyond the Horizon*; Pound, *Hugh Selwyn Mauberley*; Wells, *The Outline of History*; Wharton, *The Age of Innocence*; Yeats, *Michael Robartes and the Dancer*	Paul Scott b.; Amedeo Modigliani d.; League of Nations established
1921	De la Mare, *Memoirs of a Midget*; Galsworthy, *To Let*; A. Huxley, *Crome Yellow*; Shaw, *Back to Methuselah*; Svevo, *Confessions of Zeno*; Yeats, *Four Plays for Dancers*	Irish Free State established; Vaughan Williams, Pastoral Symphony; Prokofiev, *The Love of Three Oranges*
1922	Crompton, *Just William*; T. S. Eliot, *The Waste Land*; F. Scott Fitzgerald, *Tales of the Jazz Age*; *The Beautiful and the Damned*; Galsworthy, *The Forsyte Saga* (in one vol.); D. Garnett, *Lady into Fox*; Hardy, *Late Lyrics and Earlier*; Joyce, *Ulysses*; D. H. Lawrence, *Aaron's Rod*; May Sinclair, *The Life and Death of Harriet Frean*; V. Woolf, *Jacob's Room*; Yeats, *Later Poems*	Philip Larkin b.; Wilfrid Scawen Blunt d.; T. S. Eliot founds *The Criterion*; Marcel Proust d.; Michael Collins assassinated; Gandhi imprisoned for civil disobedience; Mussolini's march on Rome; Wittgenstein, *Tractatus Logico-Philosophicus*
1923	Bennett, *Riceyman Steps*; Conrad, *The Rover*; A. Huxley, *Antic Hay*; D. H. Lawrence, *Kangaroo*; Masefield, *Collected Poems*; E. Sitwell, *Façade*; W. Stevens, *Harmonium*	Katherine Mansfield d.

Date	Principal literary works	Other events
1924	Arlen, *The Green Hat*; R.Firbank, *Prancing Nigger*; Forster, *A Passage to India*; Milne, *When We Were Very Young*; I. A. Richards, *Principles of Literary Criticism*; Shaw, *Saint Joan*; Webb, *Precious Bane*; Wodehouse, *The Inimitable Jeeves*	James Baldwin b.; Joseph Conrad d.; Franz Kafka d.; First Labour government; Lenin d.; Puccini d.
1925	Compton-Burnett, *Pastors and Masters*; Coward, *Hay Fever*; Dreiser, *An American Tragedy*; T. S. Eliot, *Poems 1905–25*; F. Scott Fitzgerald, *The Great Gatsby*; A. Huxley, *Those Barren Leaves*; Loos, *Gentlemen Prefer Blondes*; O'Casey, *Juno and the Paycock*; Pound, *A Draft of XVI Cantos*; Wodehouse, *Carry On, Jeeves*; V. Woolf, *Mrs Dalloway*; *The Common Reader*, 1st ser.; Yeats, *A Vision*	Sir Henry Rider Haggard d.; A. C. Benson d.; *New Yorker* started; Hitler, *Mein Kampf*, Vol. 1; S. Eisenstein, *Battleship Potemkin*
1926	Christie, *The Murder of Roger Ackroyd*; Hemingway, *Fiesta (The Sun Also Rises)*; D. H. Lawrence, *The Plumed Serpent*; T. E. Lawrence, *The Seven Pillars of Wisdom*; Milne, *Winnie-the-Pooh*; O'Casey, *The Plough and the Stars*; Warner, *Lolly Willowes*	Ronald Firbank d.; General Strike 3–12 May; Rainer Maria Rilke d.; Claude Monet d.; Alban Berg, *Wozzeck*; Hitler, *Mein Kampf*, Vol. 2; Fritz Lang, *Metropolis*; Rudolf Valentino d.
1927	Forster, *Aspects of the Novel*; Hemingway, *Men Without Women*; R. Lehmann, *Dusty Answer*; S. Lewis, *Elmer Gantry*; Milne, *Now We Are Six*; T. F. Powys, *Mr Weston's Good Wine*; Wilder, *The Bridge of San Luis Rey*; V. Woolf, *To the Lighthouse*	Jerome K. Jerome d.; *The Jazz Singer*, with Al Jolson; Rex Whistler's frescoes for Tate Gallery
1928	T. S. Eliot, *For Lancelot Andrewes*; R. Hall, *The Well of Loneliness*; A. Huxley, *Point Counter Point*; Joyce, *Anna Livia Plurabelle*; D. H. Lawrence, *Lady Chatterley's Lover* (privately printed, Florence); Milne, *The House at Pooh Corner*; J. Rhys, *Quartet*; Sassoon, *Memoirs of a Fox-hunting Man*; E. Waugh, *Decline and Fall*; V. Woolf, *Orlando*; Yeats, *The Tower*	Thomas Hardy d.; Edmund Gosse d.; Ravel, *Boléro*; Women's Suffrage extended to women over 21
1929	Bridges, *The Testament of Beauty*; Compton-Burnett, *Brothers and Sisters*; Faulkner, *The Sound and the Fury*; Graves, *Goodbye to All That*; H. Green, *Living*; Hemingway, *A Farewell to Arms*; R. Hughes, *A High Wind in Jamaica*; Priestley, *The Good Companions*; Wolfe, *Look Homeward, Angel*; V. Woolf, *A Room of One's Own*; Yeats, *The Winding Stair*	John Osborne b.
1930	Auden, *Poems*; Coward, *Private Lives*; Delafield, *The Diary of a Provincial Lady*; Empson, *Seven Types of Ambiguity*; Faulkner, *As I Lay Dying*; Hammett, *The Maltese Falcon*; A. W. Lewis, *The Apes of God*; Maugham, *Cakes and Ale*; Priestley, *Angel Pavement*; H. Walpole, *The Herries Chronicle* (completed 1933); E. Waugh, *Vile Bodies*	D. H. Lawrence d.; Sir Arthur Conan Doyle d.; Robert Bridges d.; Ted Hughes b.; *The Blue Angel* with Marlene Dietrich; France begins building Maginot line
1931	Coward, *Cavalcade*; Hanley, *Boy*; O'Neill, *Mourning Becomes Electra*; Powell, *Afternoon Men*; E. Wilson, *Axel's Castle*; V. Woolf, *The Waves*	Arnold Bennett d.; Oswald Mosley forms new party; Britain abandons gold standard; *Frankenstein,* with Boris Karloff

Date	Principal literary works	Other events
1932	Auden, *The Orators*; T. S. Eliot, *Sweeney Agonistes*; *Selected Essays*; Gibbons, *Cold Comfort Farm*; Hardy (d. 1928), *Collected Poems*; Hemingway, *Death in the Afternoon*; A. Huxley, *Brave New World*; Isherwood, *The Memorial* D. H. Lawrence, *Lady Chatterley's Lover* (expurgated); F. R. Leavis, *New Bearings in English Poetry*; Powell, *Venusberg*; E. Waugh, *Black Mischief*; Yeats, *Words for Music Perhaps*	Lytton Strachey d.; Kenneth Grahame d.; *Scrutiny* started
1933	Auden, *The Dance of Death*; Day-Lewis, *The Magnetic Mountain*; T. S. Eliot, *The Use of Poetry and the Use of Criticism*; Orwell, *Down and Out in Paris and London*; J. C. Powys, *A Glastonbury Romance*; Sayers, *Murder Must Advertise*; Spender, *Poems*; Stein, *The Autobiography of Alice B. Toklas*; Wells, *The Shape of Things to Come*; A. White, *Frost in May*; Yeats, *Collected Poems*	Joe Orton b.; John Galsworthy d.; George Moore d.; Mario Praz, *The Romantic Agony*; Hitler becomes German Chancellor
1934	Christie, *Murder on the Orient Express*; F. Scott Fitzgerald, *Tender is the Night*; Graves, *I, Claudius*; *Claudius the God*; J. Hilton, *Goobye Mr Chips*; H. Miller, *Tropic of Cancer*; Sayers, *The Nine Tailors*; E. Waugh, *A Handful of Dust*; W. Carlos Williams, *Collected Poems*	Sir Edward Elgar d.; Gustav Holst d.; Frederick Delius d.
1935	Bagnold, *National Velvet*; E. F. Benson, *Mapp and Lucia*; Day-Lewis, *A Time to Dance*; T. S. Eliot, *Murder in the Cathedral*; Empson, *Some Versions of Pastoral*; *Poems*; Isherwood, *Mr Norris Changes Trains*; MacNeice, *Poems*; Wodehouse, *Blandings Castle*; Yeats, *A Full Moon in March*	T. E. Lawrence d.; A. Hitchcock, *The Thirty-Nine Steps*
1936	Auden, *Look, Stranger!*; Auden and Isherwood, *The Ascent of F6* (perf. 1937); T. S. Eliot, *Collected Poems 1909–35* (inc. 'Burnt Norton'); Faulkner, *Absalom, Absalom!*; Forster, *Abinger Harvest*; A. Huxley, *Eyeless in Gaza*; C. S. Lewis, *The Allegory of Love*; Mitchell, *Gone With the Wind*; Orwell, *Keep the Aspidistra Flying*; Sassoon, *Sherston's Progress*; Dylan Thomas, *Twenty-five Poems*	**Edward VIII** (Jan.–Dec.); **Edward VIII** abdicates (11 Dec.); **George VI** (–1952); G. K. Chesterton d.; Rudyard Kipling d.; A. E. Housman d.; M. R. James d.; Penguin Books founded by Allen Lane; BBC Television Service begins (Nov.); Spanish Civil War; Maxim Gorky d.; Luigi Pirandello d.
1937	Auden and MacNeice, *Letters from Iceland*; Hemingway, *To Have and Have Not*; D. Jones, *In Parenthesis*; Kipling (d. 1936), *Something of Myself*; Orwell, *The Road to Wigan Pier*; Priestley, *Time and the Conways*; Steinbeck, *Of Mice and Men*; Tolkien, *The Hobbit*; V. Woolf, *The Years*	J. M. Barrie d.; Edith Wharton d.; Ravel d.; Picasso, *Guernica*; W. Disney, *Snow White and the Seven Dwarfs*
1938	Beckett, *Murphy*; E. Bowen, *The Death of the Heart*; Connolly, *Enemies of Promise*; Dos Passos, *U.S.A.*; Du Maurier, *Rebecca*; Orwell, *Homage to Catalonia*; E. Waugh, *Scoop*; Wodehouse, *The Code of the Woosters*; Yeats, *New Poems*	Munich agreement (September 30); Prokofiev, *Romeo and Juliet*; A. Hitchcock, *The Lady Vanishes*; S. Eisenstein, *Alexander Nevsky*

Date	Principal literary works	Other events
1939	Ambler, *The Mask of Dimitrios*; Compton-Burnett, *A Family and a Fortune*; T. S. Eliot, *The Family Reunion*; *Old Possum's Book of Practical Cats*; Forester, *Captain Hornblower, RN*; Greene, *The Confidential Agent*; Household, *Rogue Male*; A. Huxley, *After Many a Summer*; Isherwood, *Goodbye to Berlin*; Joyce, *Finnegan's Wake*; MacNeice, *Autumn Journal*; H. Miller, *Tropic of Capricorn*; F. O'Brien, *At Swim Two-Birds*; Orwell, *Coming Up for Air*; Steinbeck, *The Grapes of Wrath*; Flora Thompson, *Lark Rise*; T. H. White, *The Sword in the Stone*; Yeats (d. 1939), *Last Poems and Two Plays*	W. B. Yeats d.; Ford Madox Ford d.; Second World War begins (3 Sept.); Film of *Gone With the Wind*; Arthur Rackham d.; Sigmund Freud d.; *The Wizard of Oz*, with Judy Garland
1940	Auden, *Another Time*; Betjeman, *Old Lights for New Chancels*; Chandler, *Farewell, my Lovely*; Day-Lewis, *Poems in Wartime*; T. S. Eliot, 'East Coker' (in *New English Weekly*); Greene, *The Power and the Glory*; Hemingway, *For Whom the Bell Tolls*; Koestler, *Darkness at Noon*; Dylan Thomas, *Portrait of the Artist as a Young Dog*	F. Scott Fitzgerald d.; W. H. Davies d.; Fall of France; Battle of Britain; Leon Trotsky d.; *The Great Dictator*, with C. Chaplin
1941	Auden, *New Year Letters* (*The Double Man*); Compton-Burnett, *Parents and Children*; Coward, *Blithe Spirit*; T. S. Eliot, 'The Dry Salvages' (in *New English Weekly*); F. Scott Fitzgerald (d. 1940), *The Last Tycoon*; P. Hamilton, *Hangover Square*; E. Wilson, *The Wound and the Bow*; V. Woolf (d. 1941), *Between the Acts*	James Joyce d.; Virginia Woolf d.; J. G. Frazer d.; Rabindranath Tagore d.; Sherwood Anderson d.; Japanese attack Pearl Harbour; USA and Soviet Union enter war; Brecht, *Mutter Courage*; Orson Welles, *Citizen Kane*
1942	De la Mare, *Collected Poems*; T. S. Eliot, 'Little Gidding' (in *New English Weekly*); C. S. Lewis, *The Screwtape Letters*; E. Waugh, *Put Out More Flags*; V. Woolf (d. 1941), *The Death of the Moth*	Walter Sickert d.; Anouilh, *Antigone*; Fall of Singapore; *Casablanca*, with Humphrey Bogart
1943	Graves, *Wife to Mr Milton*	Allied invasion of Italy; Rachmaninov d.; M. Powell and E. Pressburger, *Life and Death of Colonel Blimp*
1944	Auden, *For the Time Being*; Betjeman, *New Bats in Old Belfries*; J. Cary, *The Horse's Mouth*; Compton-Burnett, *Elders and Betters*; T. S. Eliot, *Four Quartets*; L. P. Hartley, *The Shrimp and the Anemone*	Normandy landings, (6 June); Laurence Olivier's film of *Henry V*; Saint-Exupéry d.; Sartre, *Huis Clos* (In Camera); Edvard Munch d.
1945	Connolly, *The Unquiet Grave*; T. S. Eliot, *What is a Classic?*; H. Green, *Loving*; N. Mitford, *The Pursuit of Love*; Orwell, *Animal Farm*; E. Waugh, *Brideshead Revisited*; Wells, *Mind at the End of its Tether*	Charles Williams d.; Theodor Dreiser d.; Second World War ends (VE Day 8 May; VJ Day 15 Aug./2 Sept. (US)); Hitler d.; F. D. Roosevelt d.; Mussolini d.; Paul Valéry d.; Britten, *Peter Grimes*; Béla Bartók d.; David Lean, *Brief Encounter*
1946	R. Campbell, *Talking Bronco*; De la Mare, *The Traveller*; L. P. Hartley, *The Sixth Heaven*; O'Neill, *The Iceman Cometh*; Peake, *Titus Groan*; Priestley, *An Inspector Calls*; Rattigan, *The Winslow Boy*	M. Sinclair d.; H. G. Wells d.; Damon Runyon d.; Nuremberg trials; Nationalization of major industries begins; Bertrand Russell, *History of Western Philosophy*; Prokofiev, *Betrothal in a Monastery* (*The Duenna*)

Date	Principal literary works	Other events
1947	Graves, *The White Goddess*; L. P. Hartley, *Eustace and Hilda*; Larkin, *A Girl in Winter*; Lowry, *Under the Volcano*; MacNeice, *The Dark Tower*; Snow, *The Light and the Dark*; T. Williams, *A Streetcar Named Desire*	Flora Thompson d.; Partition of India, Pakistan established; Camus, *La Peste* (The Plague)
1948	Auden, *The Age of Anxiety*; Betjeman, *Selected Poems*; T. S. Eliot, *Notes Towards the Definition of Culture*; Greene, *The Heart of the Matter*; F. R. Leavis, *The Great Tradition*; Mailer, *The Naked and the Dead*; Paton, *Cry, the Beloved Country*; Pound, *Pisan Cantos*; Rattigan, *The Browning Version*; E. Waugh, *The Loved One*	Gandhi assassinated; Strauss, *Four Last Songs*; *Hamlet*, with L. Olivier
1949	C. Fry, *The Lady's Not for Burning*; Orwell, *Nineteen Eighty-four*; A. Miller, *Death of a Salesman*; N. Mitford, *Love in a Cold Climate*; Snow, *Time of Hope*	NATO founded; Richard Strauss d.; Film of *The Third Man* (see Greene 1950)
1950	Auden, *Collected Shorter Poems 1930–1944*; T. S. Eliot, *The Cocktail Party*; Greene, *The Third Man*; C. S. Lewis, *The Lion, the Witch, and the Wardrobe*; D. Lessing, *The Grass is Singing*; Peake, *Gormenghast*; Pound, *Seventy Cantos*; A. Wilson, *Such Darling Dodos*	Bernard Shaw d.; George Orwell d.; Kurt Weill d.; Korean war begins
1951	Auden, *Nones*; W. Robertson Davies, *Tempest-Tost* (*The Salterton Trilogy*, i); Forster, *Two Cheers for Democracy*; Greene, *The End of the Affair*; Powell, *A Question of Upbringing* (first vol. in *A Dance to the Music of Time*); Salinger, *The Catcher in the Rye*; Snow, *The Masters*; Wyndham, *The Day of the Triffids*	André Gide d.; Schoenberg d.; Britten, *Billy Budd*; Defection of Burgess and Maclean; *The Archers* begins on BBC Light Programme
1952	Christie, *The Mousetrap*; R. Ellison, *Invisible Man*; Hemingway, *The Old Man and the Sea*; F. R. Leavis, *The Common Pursuit*; D. Lessing, *Martha Quest*; Powell, *A Buyer's Market*; Dylan Thomas, *Collected Poems 1934–52*; E. Waugh, *Men at Arms*; A. Wilson, *Hemlock and After*	**Elizabeth II**; Britain produces atomic bomb; Mau Mau active in Kenya
1953	Baldwin, *Go Tell It on the Mountain*; Beckett *Watt* (written 1944); R. Bradbury, *Fahrenheit 451*; Brophy, *Hackenfeller's Ape*; I. Fleming, *Casino Royale*; L. P. Hartley, *The Go-Between*; R. Lehmann, *The Echoing Grove*; A. Miller, *The Crucible*; Wain, *Hurry On Down*	Dylan Thomas d.; Hilaire Belloc d.; Eugene O'Neill d.; Stalin d.; Prokofiev d.; Conquest of Everest; Coronation (2 June); Execution of Rosenbergs in US
1954	K. Amis, *Lucky Jim*; Betjeman, *A Few Late Chrysanthemums*; W. Robertson Davies, *Leaven of Malice* (*The Salterton Trilogy*, ii); T. S. Eliot, *The Confidential Clerk*; Golding, *Lord of the Flies*; T. Gunn, *Fighting Terms*; A. Huxley, *The Doors of Perception*; D. Lessing, *A Proper Marriage*; MacNeice, *Autumn Sequel*; Murdoch, *Under the Net*; Rattigan, *Separate Tables*; W. Stevens, *Collected Poems*; Dylan Thomas (d. 1953), *Under Milk Wood* (broadcast); Tolkien, *The Fellowship of the Ring*; *The Two Towers* (pts. i and ii of *The Lord of the Rings*)	Henri Matisse d.; Nasser seizes power in Egypt; E. Kazan, *On the Waterfront*

Date	Principal literary works	Other events
1955	K. Amis, *That Uncertain Feeling*; Auden, *The Shield of Achilles*; Beckett, *Waiting for Godot* (pub. in French 1952); Donleavy, *The Ginger Man*; Greene, *The Quiet American*; Larkin, *The Less Deceived*; C. S. Lewis, *Surprised by Joy*; Nabokov, *Lolita*; Powell, *The Acceptance World*; Tolkien, *The Return of the King* (pt. iii of *The Lord of the Rings*); E. Waugh, *Officers and Gentlemen*; T. Williams, *Cat on a Hot Tin Roof*	Thomas Mann d.; Albert Einstein d.; *Rebel Without a Cause*, with James Dean; L. Olivier's film of *Richard III*
1956	Baldwin, *Giovanni's Room*; Beckett, *Malone Dies* (French, 1951); Bedford, *A Legacy*; Highsmith, *The Talented Mr Ripley*; R. Macaulay, *The Towers of Trebizond*; O'Neill (d. 1953), *Long Day's Journey into Night* (written 1940–1); J. Osborne, *Look Back in Anger*; A. Wilson, *Anglo-Saxon Attitudes*; C. Wilson, *The Outsider*	Walter de la Mare d.; Sir Max Beerbohm d.; Jackson Pollock d.; Suez crisis; Copyright Act; First Aldermaston march; Hungarian uprising; *My Fair Lady*
1957	Braine, *Room at the Top*; L. Durrell, *Justine* (*Alexandria Quartet*, i); T. S. Eliot, *On Poetry and Poets*; Ted Hughes, *The Hawk in the Rain*; Kerouac, *On the Road*; J. Osborne, *The Entertainer*; Powell, *At Lady Molly's*; E. Waugh, *The Ordeal of Gilbert Pinfold*; P. White, *Voss*	Malcolm Lowry d.; D. Richardson d.; Dorothy L. Sayers d.; Sibelius d.; Bernstein, *West Side Story*; I. Bergman, *The Seventh Seal*
1958	Achebe, *Things Fall Apart*; Bates, *The Darling Buds of May*; Beckett, *Krapp's Last Tape*; W. Robertson Davies, *A Mixture of Frailties* (*The Salterton Trilogy*, iii); Delaney, *A Taste of Honey*; L. Durrell, *Balthazar*, *Mountolive* (*Alexandria Quartet*, ii and iii); Galbraith, *The Affluent Society*; Greene, *Our Man in Havana*; Murdoch, *The Bell*; Pinter, *The Birthday Party*; Sillitoe, *Saturday Night, Sunday Morning*; A. Wilson, *The Middle Age of Mrs Eliot*	Roy Campbell d.; Ralph Vaughan Williams d.; European Common Market
1959	M. Bradbury, *Eating People is Wrong*; Burroughs, *The Naked Lunch*; R. Ellmann, *James Joyce*; L. Lee, *Cider With Rosie*; R. Lowell, *Life Studies*; G. Painter, *Proust* (vol. 1); Peake, *Titus Alone*; Sillitoe, *The Loneliness of the Long Distance Runner*; Spark, *Memento Mori*; Waterhouse, *Billy Liar*	Raymond Chandler d.; Stanley Spencer d.; Jacob Epstein d.; Leavis and Snow Two Cultures debate
1960	K. Amis, *Take a Girl Like You*; Auden, *Homage to Clio*; L. Banks, *The L-Shaped Room*; Barstow, *A Kind of Loving*; Betjeman, *Summoned by Bells*; Bolt, *A Man for all Seasons*; L. Durrell, *Clea* (*Alexandria Quartet*, iv); Ted Hughes, *Lupercal*; D. H. Lawrence (d. 1930), *Lady Chatterley's Lover* (full text); O. Manning, *The Great Fortune* (*The Balkan Trilogy*, i); Harper Lee, *To Kill a Mockingbird*; E. O'Brien, *The Country Girls*; Pinter, *The Caretaker*; Powell, *Casanova's Chinese Restaurant*; Storey, *This Sporting Life*; Updike, *Rabbit, Run*	Boris Pasternak d.; A. Eichmann captured; J. F. Kennedy wins election

Date	Principal literary works	Other events
1961	New English Bible (New Testament); Heller, *Catch–22*; Murdoch, *A Severed Head*; Naipaul, *A House for Mr Biswas*; Spark, *The Prime of Miss Jean Brodie*; E. Waugh, *Unconditional Surrender*; A. Wilson, *The Old Men at the Zoo*	Ernest Hemingway d.; Augustus John d.; C. G. Jung d.; Berlin Wall built
1962	Albee, *Who's Afraid of Virginia Woolf?*; Baldwin, *Another Country*; Burgess, *A Clockwork Orange*; M. Duffy, *That's How It Was*; Gunn, *My Sad Captains*; D. Lessing, *The Golden Notebook*; O. Manning, *The Spoilt City* (*The Balkan Trilogy*, ii); P. Mortimer, *The Pumpkin Eater*; Powell, *The Kindly Ones*; A.Wesker, *Chips with Everything*	Britten, *War Requiem*; Faulkner d.
1963	Burgess, *Inside Mr Enderby*; le Carré, *The Spy Who Came in from the Cold*; M. McCarthy, *The Group*; Plath, *The Bell Jar*; Pynchon, *V*; S. Selvon, *Lonely Londoners*; Spark, *The Girls of Slender Means*	C. S. Lewis d.; Aldous Huxley d.; William Carlos Williams d.; Robert Frost d.; Plath d.; Beatles' first LP; J. F. Kennedy assassinated
1964	Bellow, *Herzog*; Brophy, *The Snow Ball*; Golding, *The Spire*; B. S. Johnson, *Albert Angelo*; Orton, *Entertaining Mr Sloane*; J. Osborne, *Inadmissible Evidence*; Powell, *The Valley of Bones*; Snow, *Corridors of Power*; Trevor, *The Old Boys*; A. Wilson, *Late Call*	Sean O'Casey d.; Edith Sitwell d.; Ian Fleming d.; Brendan Behan d.; Vietnam War (–1975); Nelson Mandela imprisoned
1965	Larkin, *The Whitsun Weddings*; O. Manning, *Friends and Heroes* (*The Balkan Trilogy*, iii); G. Painter, *Proust* (vol. 2); Pinter, *The Homecoming*; Plath, *Ariel*	T. S. Eliot d.; Somerset Maugham d.; Sir Winston Churchill d.; Albert Schweitzer d.; Malcolm X assassinated
1966	Bunting, *Briggflatts*; Drabble *The Millstone*; Fowles, *The Magus*; Greene, *The Comedians*; Heaney, *Death of a Naturalist*; Orton, *Loot*; Powell, *The Soldier's Art*; J. Rhys, *Wide Sargasso Sea*; P. Scott, *The Jewel in the Crown* (*The Raj Quartet*, i)	Evelyn Waugh d.; F. O'Brien d.
1967	Ayckbourn, *Relatively Speaking*; A. Carter, *The Magic Toyshop*; Holroyd, *Lytton Strachey* (vol. 1); F. O'Brien (d.; 1966), *The Third Policeman*; Stoppard, *Rosencrantz and Guildenstern Are Dead*; A. Wilson, *No Laughing Matter*	P. Kavanagh d.; John Masefield d.; C. Day-Lewis Poet Laureate; Joe Orton d.; S. Sassoon d.; Six-Day War (Israel); Nigerian Civil War
1968	Ackerley, *My Father and Myself*; G. Hill, *King Log*; Mailer, *The Armies of the Night*; Powell, *The Military Philosophers*; P. Scott, *The Day of the Scorpion* (*The Raj Quartet*, ii); Stoppard, *The Real Inspector Hound*; Vidal, *Myra Breckenridge*	Mervyn Peake d.; John Steinbeck d.; Martin Luther King assassinated; Theatres Act abolishes power of Lord Chamberlain; Civil Rights march in Derry
1969	K. Amis, *The Green Man*; Atwood, *The Edible Woman*; Blythe, *Akenfield*; D. Dunn, *Terry Street*; Fowles, *The French Lieutenant's Woman*; Greene, *Travels With My Aunt*; B. S. Johnson, *The Unfortunates*; D. Lessing, *The Four-gated City*; Roth, *Portnoy's Complaint*	Dame Ivy Compton-Burnett d.; John Wyndham d.; Jack Kerouac d.; Manned landing on the moon; First Booker-McConnell Prize for Fiction (P. H. Newby, *Something to Answer For*)
1970	W. Robertson Davies, *Fifth Business* (*The Deptford Trilogy*, i); Hampton, *The Philanthropist*; Hare, *Slag*; Ted Hughes, *Crow*; J. Mortimer, *A Voyage Round my Father*; Pound, *Drafts and Fragments of Cantos CX to CXVII*	E. M. Forster d.; John Dos Passos d.; Bertrand Russell d.

Date	Principal literary works	Other events
1971	Forster (d. 1970), *Maurice* (written 1913–14); G. Hill, *Mercian Hymns*; Murdoch, *An Accidental Man*; Naipaul, *In a Free State*; Powell, *Books Do Furnish a Room*; P. Scott, *The Towers of Silence* (*The Raj Quartet*, iii); Storey, *The Changing Room*; Updike, *Rabbit Redux*	Igor Stravinsky d.
1972	Ayckbourn, *Absurd Person Singular*; Berger, *G*; W. Robertson Davies, *The Manticore* (*The Deptford Trilogy*, ii); Heaney, *Wintering Out*; Stoppard, *Jumpers*	Ezra Pound d.; C. Day-Lewis d.; Sir John Betjeman Poet Laureate; L. P. Hartley d.; Sir Compton Mackenzie d.; Berryman d.; 'Bloody Sunday' (Belfast) 30 October
1973	M. Amis, *The Rachel Papers*; Ayckbourn, *The Norman Conquests*; J. G. Farrell, *The Siege of Krishnapur*; Greene, *The Honorary Consul*; B. S. Johnson, *Christy Malry's Own Double-Entry*; Murdoch, *The Black Prince*; Powell, *Temporary Kings*; Pynchon, *Gravity's Rainbow*; Shaffer, *Equus*	W. H. Auden d.; J. R. R. Tolkien d.; Noël Coward d.; B. S. Johnson d.; Britain enters Common Market; Watergate hearings; Picasso d.; American troops withdraw from Vietnam
1974	K. Amis, *Ending Up*; Bainbridge, *The Bottle Factory Outing*; S. Hill, *In the Springtime of the Year*; Larkin, *High Windows*; le Carré, *Tinker, Tailor, Soldier, Spy*; D. Lessing, *The Memoirs of a Survivor*	H. E. Bates d.; David Jones d.
1975	M. Amis, *Dead Babies*; Bellow, *Humboldt's Gift*; M. Bradbury, *The History Man*; W. Robertson Davies, *World of Wonders* (*The Deptford Trilogy*, iii); Drabble, *The Realms of Gold*; S. Heaney, *North*; Jhabvala, *Heat and Dust*; D. Lodge, *Changing Places*; Pinter, *No Man's Land*; Powell, *Hearing Secret Harmonies* (last vol. in *Dance to the Music of Time*); P. Scott, *A Division of the Spoils* (*The Raj Quartet*, iv); Theroux, *The Great Railway Bazaar*	P. G. Wodehouse d.
1976	Bawden, *Afternoon of a Good Woman*; Banville, *Doctor Copernicus*; Gunn, *Jack Straw's Castle*	Agatha Christie d.; Benjamin Britten d.
1977	Chatwin, *In Patagonia*; Fowles, *Daniel Martin*; P. Scott, *Staying On*; Ted Hughes, *Gaudete*	Sir Terence Rattigan d.; Robert Lowell d.; Vladimir Nabokov d.; *Gay News* trial
1978	K. Amis, *Jake's Thing*; M. Amis, *Success*; Bainbridge, *Young Adolf*; Byatt, *The Virgin in the Garden*; Greene, *The Human Factor*; Hare, *Plenty*; Irving, *The World According to Garp*; McEwan, *The Cement Garden*; Murdoch, *The Sea, The Sea*; Pinter, *Betrayal*; Potter, *Brimstone and Treacle*	Paul Scott d.; F. R. Leavis d.
1979	A. Carter, *The Bloody Chamber and Other Stories*; P. Fitzgerald, *Offshore*; Golding, *Darkness Visible*; Gordimer, *Burger's Daughter*; Heaney, *Field Work*; Mailer, *The Executioner's Song*; Naipaul, *A Bend in the River*; Raine, *A Martian Sends a Postcard Home*	Jean Rhys d.; J. G. Farrell d.; Public Lending Right established
1980	Burgess, *Earthly Powers*; Friel, *Translations*; Golding, *Rites of Passage*; Hoban, *Riddley Walker*; le Carré, *Smiley's People*; Muldoon, *Why Brownlee Left*; A. N. Wilson, *The Healing Art*	C. P. Snow d.; Olivia Manning d.; Jean-Paul Sartre d.

Date	Principal literary works	Other events
1981	Banville *Kepler*; Boyd, *A Good Man in Africa*; Brookner, *A Start in Life*; Coetzee, *Waiting for the Barbarians*; W. Robertson Davies, *The Rebel Angels* (*The Cornish Trilogy*, i); M. Duffy, *Gor Saga*; A. Gray, *Lanark*; Rushdie, *Midnight's Children*; Spark, *Loitering with Intent*; D. M. Thomas, *The White Hotel*	Pamela Hansford Johnson d.; Samuel Barber d.
1982	P. Barker, *Union Street*; Boyd, *An Ice-Cream War*; Keneally, *Schindler's Ark*; Theroux, *The Mosquito Coast*	Falklands campaign
1983	Ackroyd, *The Last Testament of Oscar Wilde*; Coetzee, *The Life and Times of Michael K.*; Edgar, *Maydays*; S. Hill, *The Woman in Black*; Kelman, *Not Not While the Giro*; G. Swift, *Waterland*; Trevor, *Fools of Fortune*; Weldon, *The Life and Loves of a She-Devil*	Rebecca West d.; Tennessee Williams d.; Arthur Koestler d.; Sir William Walton d.; Joan Miró d.
1984	M. Amis, *Money*; Ballard, *Empire of the Sun*; Bainbridge *Watson's Apology*; I. Banks, *The Wasp Factory*; J. Barnes, *Flaubert's Parrot*; Brookner, *Hotel du Lac*; A. Carter, *Nights at the Circus*; A. Gray, *Janine*; R. Holmes, *Footsteps*; Lodge, *Small World*; Raine, *Rich*	Sir John Betjeman d.; Ted Hughes Poet Laureate; J. B. Priestley d.
1985	Ackroyd, *Hawksmoor*; Atwood, *The Handmaid's Tale*; Carey, *Illywhacker*; W. Robertson Davies, *What's Bred in the Bone* (*The Cornish Trilogy*, ii); Dunn, *Elegies*; Ishiguro, *An Artist of the Floating World*; Winterson, *Oranges Are Not the Only Fruit*	Philip Larkin d.; Robert Graves d.; Marc Chagall d.
1986	K. Amis, *The Old Devils*; Banville, *Mefisto*; Cope, *Making Cocoa for Kingsley Amis*; Seth, *The Golden Gate*	Christopher Isherwood d.; Simone de Beauvoir d.; Henry Moore d.; Chernobyl nuclear accident
1987	Ackroyd, *Chatterton*; Alan Bennett, *Talking Heads* (televised; pub. 1988); Boyd, *The New Confessions*; C. Churchill, *Serious Money*; Drabble, *The Radiant Way*; Golding, *Close Quarters*; Lively, *Moon Tiger*; McEwan, *The Child in Time*; T. Morrison, *Beloved*; Naipaul, *The Enigma of Arrival*	James Baldwin d.; Jean Anouilh d.
1988	Atwood, *Cat's Eye*; Carey, *Oscar and Lucinda*; W. Robertson Davies, *The Lyre of Orpheus* (*The Cornish Trilogy*, iii); Larkin (d. 1985), *Collected Poems*; Hollinghurst, *The Swimming Pool Library*; D. Lessing, *The Fifth Child*; Lodge, *Nice Work*; Rushdie, *The Satanic Verses*; T. Wolfe, *The Bonfire of the Vanities*	Alan Paton d.
1989	M. Amis, *London Fields*; Bainbridge, *An Awfully Big Adventure*; Banville, *The Book of Evidence*; J. Barnes, *A History of the World in 10 1/2 Chapters*; Bedford, *Jigsaw*; Fenton, *Manila Envelope*; Golding, *Fire Down Below*; Ishiguro, *The Remains of the Day*; Tremain, *Restoration*	Samuel Beckett d.; Bruce Chatwin d.; Daphne du Maurier d.; Robert Penn Warren d.; *Fatwa* issued against Salman Rushdie; Salvador Dali d.
1990	Boyd, *Brazzaville Beach*; Byatt, *Possession*; Coetzee, *Age of Iron*; Mosley, *Hopeful Monsters*; Walcott, *Omeros*	Patrick White d.; Lawrence Durrell d.; Reunification of Germany; Iraq invades Kuwait; Resignation of Margaret Thatcher; R. Lehmann d.; Nelson Mandela Released

Date	Principal literary works	Other events
1991	M. Amis, *Time's Arrow*; P. Barker, *Regeneration*; A. Carter, *Wise Children*; Longley, *Gorse Fires*; J. Osborne, *Déjavu*; C. Phillips, *Cambridge*	Graham Greene d.; Angus Wilson d.; Roy Fuller d.; John Cage d.
1992	McEwan, *Black Dogs*; Ondaatje, *The English Patient*	Angela Carter d.
1993	P. Barker, *The Eye in the Door*; R. Doyle, *Paddy Clarke Ha Ha Ha*; Fenton, *Out of Danger*; Malouf, *Remembering Babylon*; Seth, *A Suitable Boy*; Stoppard, *Arcadia*; Welsh, *Trainspotting*	Anthony Burgess d.; William Golding d.; Dame Freya Stark d.; Mandela and de Klerk Share Nobel Peace Prize
1994	Atwood, *The Robber Bride*; Edgar, *Pentecost*; Kelman, *How Late It Was, How Late*; A. Miller, *Broken Glass*; Muldoon, *The Annals of Chile*; Raine, *History: The Home Movie*	Opening of Channel Tunnel; John Osborne d.; Dennis Potter d.; J. I. M. Stewart d.; John Wain d.; Mandela becomes president of South Africa
1995	M. Amis, *The Information*; Barker, *The Ghost Road*; Boyd, *The Destiny of Nathalie 'X'*; P. Fitzgerald, *The Blue Flower*; Hornby, *High Fidelity*; Rushdie, *The Moor's Last Sigh*	Kingsley Amis d.; Robert Bolt d.; Gerald Durrell d.; Julian Symons d.; Ken Saro-Wiwa hanged in Nigeria
1996	Byatt, *Babel Tower*; Deane, *Reading in the Dark*; Heaney, *The Spirit Level*; G. Swift, *Last Orders*	George Mackay Brown d.; Norman MacCaig d.; Charles Madge d.
1997	Crace, *Quarantine*; D'Aguiar, *Feeding the Ghosts*; Kennedy, *Original Bliss*; McEwan, *Enduring Love*; Michéle Roberts, *Impossible Saints*; Self, *Great Apes*	Laurie Lee d.; S. MacLean d.; A. L. Rowse d.; Jon Silkin d.; Labour government elected in Britain; Diana, Princess of Wales d.; Mother Teresa of Calcutta d.
1998	Ted Hughes, *Birthday Letters* Michael Cunningham, *The Hours*; W. Boyd, *Armadillo*; A. Hollinghurst, *The Spell*; N. Hornby, *About a Boy*; T. Hughes, *Birthday Letters*; I. McEwan, *Amsterdam*	Ted Hughes d.; Dame Iris Murdoch d.; British Library opens at St Pancras
1999	J. Crace, *Being Dead*; J. M. Coetzee, *Disgrace*; M. Holroyd, *Basil Street Blues*; D. Lessing, *Mara and Dann*; V. Seth, *An Equal Music*; R. Tremain, *Music and Silence*	J. Heller d.; Sarah Kane d.; Andrew Motion Poet Laureate; War in Kosovo; Introduction of the Euro
2000	M. Bradbury, *To the Hermitage*; Zadie Smith, *White Teeth*; M. Atwood, *The Blind Assassin*; Lorna Sage, *Bad Blood*	M. Bradbury d.; A. Powell d.; R. S. Thomas d.; Tate Modern opens
2001	B. Bainbridge, *According to Queeney*; J. Coe, *The Rotters' Club*; Ali Smith, *Hotel World*	Lorna Sage d.; R. K. Narayan d.; 9/11 terrorist attack in New York; US invades Afghanistan
2002	A. S. Byatt, *A Whistling Woman*; C. Hampton, *The Talking Cure*; T. Stoppard, *The Coast of Utopia*	W. Cooper d.; D. J. Enright d.; M. Wesley d.; Terrorists bomb Bali
2003	Monica Ali, *Brick Lane*; M. Frayn, *Democracy*; C. Phillips, *A Distant Shore*	C. Causley d.; K. Raine d.; P. Redgrove d.; E. Said d.; Second Gulf War in Iraq
2004	Maggie Gee, *The Flood*; Alan Hollingurst, *The Line of Beauty*; Andrea Levy, *Small Island*; V. Brittain and G. Slovo, *Guantanamo*	J. Derrida d.; T. Gunn d.; S. Sontag d.; George W. Bush re-elected US President; Boxing Day tsunami in Indian Ocean
2005	J. Barnes, *Arthur and George*; K. Ishiguro, *Never Let Me Go*; I. McEwan, *Saturday*; S. Rushdie, *Shalimar the Clown*; D. Hare, *Stuff Happens*	S. Bellow d.; C. Fry d.; A. Miller d.; British detainees released from Guantanamo; Hurricane floods New Orleans

Appendix 2 · Poets Laureate

1619–37	Ben *Jonson	1785–90	Thomas *Warton
1638–?	Sir William *D'Avenant	1790–1813	Henry James *Pye
		1813–43	Robert *Southey

OFFICIAL HOLDERS

		1843–50	William *Wordsworth
1668–89	John *Dryden	1850–92	Alfred *Tennyson
1689–92	Thomas *Shadwell	1896–1913	Alfred *Austin
1692–1715	Nahum *Tate	1913–30	Robert *Bridges
1715–18	Nicholas *Rowe	1930–67	John *Masefield
1718–30	Laurence *Eusden	1968–72	Cecil *Day-Lewis
1730–57	Colley *Cibber	1972–84	Sir John *Betjeman
1757–85	William *Whitehead	1984–98	Ted *Hughes
		1999–	Andrew *Motion

Appendix 3 · Literary Awards

(A) NOBEL PRIZE FOR LITERATURE

1901	René-François-Armand-Sully Prudhomme	1933	Ivan *Bunin	1972	Heinrich *Böll
1902	Theodor Mommsen	1934	Luigi *Pirandello	1973	Patrick *White
1903	Björnstjerne Björnson	1935	No award	1974	Eyvind Johnson/Harry Martinson
1904	José Echegaray/Frédéric Mistral	1936	Eugene *O'Neill	1975	Eugenio *Montale
		1937	Roger Martin du Gard	1976	Saul *Bellow
1905	Henryk Sienkiewicz	1938	Pearl S. Buck	1977	Vicente Aleixandre
1906	Giosuè *Carducci	1939	F. E. Sillanpää	1978	Isaac Bashevis *Singer
1907	Rudyard *Kipling	1940–3	No awards	1979	Odysseus *Elytis
1908	Rudolf Eucken	1944	Johannes V. Jensen	1980	Czesław *Milosz
1909	Selma Lagerlöf	1945	Gabriela Mistral	1981	Elias *Canetti
1910	Paul Heyse	1946	Hermann *Hesse	1982	Gabriel *García Márquez
1911	Maurice *Maeterlinck	1947	André *Gide	1983	William *Golding
1912	Gerhart *Hauptmann	1948	T. S. *Eliot	1984	Jaroslav Seifert
1913	Rabindranath *Tagore	1949	William *Faulkner	1985	Claude Simon
1914	No award	1950	Bertrand *Russell	1986	Wole *Soyinka
1915	Romain *Rolland	1951	Pär Lagerkvist	1987	Joseph *Brodsky
1916	Verner von Heidenstam	1952	François *Mauriac	1988	Naguib *Mahfouz
1917	Karl Gjellerup/Henrik Pontoppidan	1953	Winston S. *Churchill	1989	Camilo José *Cela
		1954	Ernest *Hemingway	1990	Octavio *Paz
		1955	Halldór Laxness	1991	Nadine *Gordimer
1918	No award	1956	Juan Ramón Jiménez	1992	Derek *Walcott
1919	Carl Spitteler	1957	Albert *Camus	1993	Toni *Morrison
1920	Knut *Hamsun	1958	Boris *Pasternak	1994	Kenzaburo *Oë
1921	Anatole *France	1959	Salvatore *Quasimodo	1995	Seamus *Heaney
1922	Jacinto *Benavente y Martínez	1960	*Saint-John Perse	1996	Wisława *Szymborska
		1961	Ivo Andrić	1997	Dario *Fo
1923	W. B. *Yeats	1962	John *Steinbeck	1998	José *Saramago
1924	Władysław Reymont	1963	George *Seferis	1999	Günter *Grass
1925	G. B. *Shaw	1964	Jean-Paul *Sartre	2000	Gao Xingjian
1926	Grazia *Deledda	1965	Mikhail *Sholokhov	2001	V. S. *Naipaul
1927	Henri *Bergson	1966	S. Y. Agnon/Nelly Sachs	2002	Imre Kertesz
1928	Sigrid Undset	1967	Miguel Angel Asturias	2003	J. M. *Coetzee
1929	Thomas *Mann	1968	Yasunari *Kawabata	2004	Elfriede Jelinek
1930	Sinclair *Lewis	1969	Samuel *Beckett	2005	Harold *Pinter
1931	Erik Axel Karlfeldt	1970	Alexander *Solzhenitsyn		
1932	John *Galsworthy	1971	Pablo *Neruda		

(B) PULITZER PRIZE FOR FICTION

1918 Ernest Poole, *His Family*
1919 Booth *Tarkington, *The Magnificent Ambersons*
1920 No award
1921 Edith *Wharton, *The Age of Innocence*
1922 Booth *Tarkington, *Alice Adams*
1923 Willa *Cather, *One of Ours*
1924 Margaret Wilson, *The Able McLaughlins*
1925 Edna Ferber, *So Big*
1926 Sinclair *Lewis, *Arrowsmith*
1927 Louis Bromfield, *Early Autumn*
1928 Thornton *Wilder, *The Bridge of San Luis Rey*
1929 Julia Peterkin, *Scarlet Sister Mary*
1930 Oliver LaFarge, *Laughing Boy*
1931 Margaret Ayer Barnes, *Years of Grace*
1932 Pearl S. Buck, *The Good Earth*
1933 T. S. Stribling, *The Store*
1934 Caroline Miller, *Lamb in His Bosom*
1935 Josephine Winslow Johnson, *Now in November*
1936 Harold L. Davis, *Honey in the Horn*
1937 Margaret *Mitchell, *Gone With the Wind*
1938 John Phillips Marquand, *The Late George Apley*
1939 Marjorie Kinnan Rawlings, *The Yearling*
1940 John *Steinbeck, *The Grapes of Wrath*
1941 No award
1942 Ellen *Glasgow, *In this Our Life*
1943 Upton *Sinclair, *Dragon's Teeth*
1944 Martin Flavin, *Journey in the Dark*
1945 John Hersey, *A Bell for Adamo*
1946 No award
1947 Robert Penn *Warren, *All the King's Men*
1948 James A. Michener, *Tales of the South Pacific*
1949 James Gould Cozzens, *Guard of Honour*
1950 A. B. Guthrie Jr., *The Way West*
1951 Conrad Richter, *The Town*
1952 Herman Wouk, *The Caine Mutiny*
1953 Ernest *Hemingway, *The Old Man and the Sea*
1954 No award
1955 William *Faulkner, *A Fable*
1956 Mackinley Kanter, *Andersonville*
1957 No award
1958 James *Agee, *A Death in the Family*
1959 Robert Lewis Taylor, *The Travels of Jamie McPheeters*
1960 Allen Drury, *Advise and Consent*
1961 Harper Lee, *To Kill a Mockingbird*
1962 Edwin O'Connor, *The Edge of Sadness*
1963 William *Faulkner, *The Reivers*
1964 No award
1965 Shirley Ann Grau, *The Keepers of the House*
1966 Katherine Anne *Porter, *The Collected Stories of Katherine Anne Porter*
1967 Bernard *Malamud, *The Fixer*
1968 William *Styron, *The Confessions of Nat Turner*
1969 N. Scott Momaday, *House Made of Dawn*
1970 Jean Stafford, *Collected Stories*
1971 No award
1972 Wallace Stegner, *Angle of Repose*
1973 Eudora *Welty, *The Optimist's Daughter*
1974 No award
1975 Michael Shaara, *The Killer Angels*
1976 Saul *Bellow, *Humboldt's Gift*
1977 No award
1978 James Alan McPherson, *Elbow Room*
1979 John *Cheever, *The Stories of John Cheever*
1980 Norman *Mailer, *The Executioner's Song*
1981 John Kennedy Toole, *A Confederacy of Dunces*
1982 John *Updike, *Rabbit is Rich*
1983 Alice *Walker, *The Color Purple*
1984 William Kennedy, *Ironweed*
1985 Alison *Lurie, *Foreign Affairs*
1986 Larry McMurtry, *Lonesome Dove*
1987 Peter Taylor, *A Summons to Memphis*
1988 Toni *Morrison, *Beloved*
1989 Anne *Tyler, *Breathing Lessons*
1990 Oscar Hijuelos, *The Mambo Kings Play Songs of Love*
1991 John *Updike, *Rabbit at Rest*
1992 Jane *Smiley, *A Thousand Acres*
1993 Robert Olen Butler, *A Good Scent From a Strange Mountain*
1994 E. Anne *Proulx, *The Shipping News*
1995 Carol *Shields, *The Stone Diaries*
1996 Richard *Ford, *Independence Day*
1997 Steven Millhauser, *Martin Dressler: The Tale of an American Dreamer*
1998 Philip *Roth, *American Pastoral*
1999 Michael Cunningham, *The Hours*
2000 Jhumpa Lahiri, *Interpreter of Maladies*
2001 Michael Chabon, *The Amazing Adventures of Kavalier & Clay*
2002 Richard Russo, *Empire Falls*
2003 Jeffrey Eugenides, *Middlesex*
2004 Edward P. Jones, *The Known World*
2005 Marilynne Robinson, *Gilead*

(C) LIBRARY ASSOCIATION CARNEGIE MEDALLISTS

Instituted in 1936 to mark the centenary of the birth of Andrew Carnegie, philanthropist and benefactor of libraries, the Library Association Carnegie Medal is awarded annually for an outstanding book for children written in English and receiving its first publication in the United Kingdom during the preceding year.

1936 Arthur *Ransome, *Pigeon Post*
1937 Eve Garnett, *The Family From One End Street*
1938 Noel Streatfeild, *The Circus is Coming*
1939 Eleanor Doorly, *The Radium Woman* (children's biography of Marie Curie)
1940 Kitty Barne, *Visitors From London*
1941 Mary Treadgold, *We Couldn't Leave Dinah*
1942 'B. B.' (D. J. Watkins-Pitchford), *The Little Grey Men*
1943 No award

1944	Eric *Linklater, *The Wind on the Moon*	1973	Penelope *Lively, *The Ghost of Thomas Kempe*
1945	No award	1974	Mollie Hunter, *The Stronghold*
1946	Elizabeth Goudge, *The Little White Horse*	1975	Robert Westall, *The Machine-Gunners*
1947	Walter *de la Mare, *Collected Stories for Children*	1976	Jan Mark, *Thunder and Lightnings*
1948	Richard Armstrong, *Sea Change*	1977	Gene Kemp, *The Turbulent Term of Tyke Tyler*
1949	Agnes Allen, *The Story of Your Home* (nonfiction)	1978	David Rees, *The Exeter Blitz*

1944   Eric *Linklater, *The Wind on the Moon*
1945   No award
1946   Elizabeth Goudge, *The Little White Horse*
1947   Walter *de la Mare,
            Collected Stories for Children
1948   Richard Armstrong, *Sea Change*
1949   Agnes Allen, *The Story of Your Home*
            (nonfiction)
1950   Elfrida Vipont, *The Lark on the Wing*
1951   Cynthia Harnett, *The Wool-Pack*
1952   Mary Norton, *The Borrowers*
1953   Edward Osmond, *A Valley Grows Up*
            (nonfiction)
1954   Ronald Welch, *Knight Crusaders*
1955   Eleanor *Farjeon, *The Little Bookroom*
1956   C. S. *Lewis, *The Last Battle*
1957   William Mayne, *A Grass Rope*
1958   Philippa *Pearce, *Tom's Midnight Garden*
1959   Rosemary *Sutcliff, *The Lantern Bearers*
1960   Ian W. Cornwall and Howard M. Maitland,
            The Making of Man (non-fiction)
1961   Lucy M. Boston, *A Stranger at Green Knowe*
1962   Pauline Clarke, *The Twelve and the Genii*
1963   Hester Burton, *Time of Trial*
1964   Sheena Porter, *Nordy Bank*
1965   Philip Turner, *The Grange at High Force*
1966   No award
1967   Alan Garner, *The Owl Service*
1968   Rosemary Harris, *The Moon in the Cloud*
1969   K. M. Peyton, *The Edge of the Cloud*
1970   Edward Blishen and Leon Garfield, *The God
            Beneath the Sea*
1971   Ivan Southall, *Josh*
1972   Richard *Adams, *Watership Down*

1973   Penelope *Lively, *The Ghost of Thomas Kempe*
1974   Mollie Hunter, *The Stronghold*
1975   Robert Westall, *The Machine-Gunners*
1976   Jan Mark, *Thunder and Lightnings*
1977   Gene Kemp, *The Turbulent Term of Tyke Tyler*
1978   David Rees, *The Exeter Blitz*
1979   Peter Dickinson, *Tulku*
1980   Peter Dickinson, *City of Gold*
1981   Robert Westall, *The Scarecrows*
1982   Margaret Mahy, *The Haunting*
1983   Jan Mark, *Handles*
1984   Margaret Mahy, *The Changeover*
1985   Kevin *Crossley-Holland, *Storm*
1986   Berlie Doherty, *Granny Was a Buffer Girl*
1987   Susan Price, *The Ghost Drum*
1988   Geraldine McCaughrean, *A Pack of Lies*
1989   Anne Fine, *Goggle-Eyes*
1990   Gillian Cross, *Wolf*
1991   Berlie Doherty, *Dear Nobody*
1992   Anne Fine, *Flour Babies*
1993   Robert Swindells, *Stone Cold*
1994   Theresa Breslin, *Whispers in the Graveyard*
1995   Philip Pullman, *Northern Lights*
1996   Melvin Burgess, *Junk*
1997   Tim Bowler, *River Boy*
1998   David Almond, *Skelling*
1999   Aidan Chambers, *Postcards from No Man's
            Land*
2000   Beverley Naidoo, *The Other Side of Truth*
2001   Terry Pratchett, *The Amazing Maurice and his
            Educated Rodents*
2002   Sharon Creech, *Ruby Holler*
2003   Jennifer Donnelly, *A Gathering Light*
2004   Frank Cottrell Boyce, *Millions*

(D) BOOKER PRIZE FOR FICTION

1969   P. H. *Newby, *Something to Answer For*
1970   Bernice *Rubens, *The Elected Member*
1971   V. S. *Naipaul, *In a Free State*
1972   John *Berger, *G*
1973   J. G. *Farrell, *The Siege of Krishnapur*
1974   Nadine *Gordimer, *The Conservationist*
            Stanley *Middleton, *Holiday*
1975   Ruth Prawer *Jhabvala, *Heat and Dust*
1976   David *Storey, *Saville*
1977   Paul *Scott, *Staying On*
1978   Iris *Murdoch, *The Sea, The Sea*
1979   Penelope *Fitzgerald, *Offshore*
1980   William *Golding, *Rites of Passage*
1981   Salman *Rushdie, *Midnight's Children*
1982   Thomas *Keneally, *Schindler's Ark*
1983   J. M. *Coetzee, *Life and Times of Michael K*
1984   Anita *Brookner, *Hotel du Lac*
1985   Keri *Hulme, *The Bone People*
1986   Kingsley *Amis, *The Old Devils*
1987   Penelope *Lively, *Moon Tiger*

1988   Peter *Carey, *Oscar and Lucinda*
1989   Kazuo *Ishiguro, *The Remains of the Day*
1990   A. S. *Byatt, *Possession*
1991   Ben *Okri, *The Famished Road*
1992   Michael *Ondaatje, *The English Patient*
            Barry *Unsworth, *Sacred Hunger*
1993   Roddy *Doyle, *Paddy Clarke Ha Ha Ha*
1994   James *Kelman, *How Late It Was, How Late*
1995   Pat *Barker, *The Ghost Road*
1996   Graham *Swift, *Last Orders*
1997   Arundhati Roy, *The God of Small Things*
1998   Ian *McEwan, *Amsterdam*
1999   J. M. *Coetzee, *Disgrace*
2000   Margaret *Atwood, *The Blind Assassin*
2001   Peter *Carey, *True History of the Kelly Gang*
2002   Yann Martel, *Life of Pi*
2003   D. C. B. Pierre, *Vernon God Little*
2004   Alan *Hollinghurst, *The Line of Beauty*
2005   John *Banville, *The Sea*